PRAISE FOR
THE BANTAM NEW COLLEGE
ITALIAN AND ENGLISH DICTIONARY

". . . thorough, accurate, well-organized, clear, and up to date . . . Relevant to the student's contemporary life . . . It is bound to become a mainstay in the field."
—Albert N. Mancini, Professor of Romance Languages,
The Ohio State University

"Both the method and the execution seem to me excellent . . . It would be impossible to find elsewhere as good a dictionary of this size."
—Beatrice Corrigan, Professor Emeritus, Editor,
University of Toronto Press

"Apart from its accurate philological approach, its most useful grammatical apparatus, and other singular features, this concise dictionary is the first which is based primarily on *American* English usage . . . It contains numerous up-to-date colloquial and technical terms which cannot be found in any other similar dictionary."
—M. Ricciardelli, Professor of Italian and Comparative
Literatures, Editor of *Forum Italicum*

Comprehensive, authoritative, and completely modern, **THE BANTAM NEW COLLEGE ITALIAN AND ENGLISH DICTIONARY** is a landmark in foreign language reference works.

THE BANTAM NEW
COLLEGE DICTIONARY SERIES

Robert C. Melzi, Author

ROBERT C. MELZI, D. in L., A.M., Ph.D., was trained in Italy, at the University of Padua, and in the United States, at the University of Pennsylvania. He has done extensive linguistic research, traveling frequently to his native country. Now Professor of Romance Languages at Widener College, he has contributed articles and reviews to many learned journals and is the author of *Castelvetro's Annotations to the Inferno,* The Hague and Paris, 1966. (Castelvetro was one of Italy's foremost philologists.) Professor Melzi is a Cavaliere in the Order of Solidarity of the Republic of Italy.

Edwin B. Williams (1891–1975), General Editor

EDWIN B. WILLIAMS, A.B., A.M., Ph.D., Doct. d'Univ., LL.D., L.H.D., was Chairman of the Department of Romance Languages, Dean of the Graduate School, and Provost of the University of Pennsylvania. He was a member of the American Philosophical Society and the Hispanic Society of America. Among his many works on the Spanish, Portuguese, and French languages are *The Williams Spanish and English Dictionary* (Scribner's, formerly Holt) and *The Bantam New College Spanish and English Dictionary*. He created and coordinated the Bantam series of original dictionaries—English, Spanish, French, Italian, Latin, and (forthcoming) German.

THE BANTAM NEW COLLEGE
ITALIAN & ENGLISH
DICTIONARY

DIZIONARIO
INGLESE ed ITALIANO
BY ROBERT C. MELZI
Widener College

THE BANTAM NEW COLLEGE
ITALIAN & ENGLISH DICTIONARY
A Bantam Book / April 1976
2nd printing ...... *January 1978*   3rd printing .... *February 1979*
4th printing .... *April 1980*

ISBN 0-553-14210-0

Published simultaneously in the United States and Canada

Bantam Books are published by Bantam Books, Inc. Its trade-
mark, consisting of the words "Bantam Books" and the por-
trayal of a bantam, is Registered in U.S. Patent and Trademark
Office and in other countries. Marca Registrada. Bantam
Books, Inc., 666 Fifth Avenue, New York, New York 10019.

PRINTED IN THE UNITED STATES OF AMERICA

13 12 11 10 9 8 7 6 5 4

CONTENTS

PREFACE

Inasmuch as the basic function of a bilingual dictionary is to provide semantic equivalences, syntactical constructions are shown in both the source and the target languages on both sides of the Dictionary. In performing this function, a bilingual dictionary must fulfill six purposes. That is, an Italian and English dictionary must provide (1) Italian words which an English-speaking person wishes to use in speaking and writing (by means of the English-Italian part), (2) English meanings of Italian words which an English-speaking person encounters in listening and reading (by means of the Italian-English part), (3) the spelling, pronunciation, and inflection of Italian words and the gender of Italian nouns which an English-speaking person needs in order to use Italian words correctly (by means of the Italian-English part), (4) English words which an Italian-speaking person wishes to use in speaking and writing (by means of the Italian-English part), (5) Italian meanings of English words which an Italian-speaking person encounters in listening and reading (by means of the English-Italian part), and (6) the spelling, pronunciation, and inflection of English words which an Italian-speaking person needs in order to use English words correctly (by means of the English-Italian part).

It may seem logical to provide the pronunciation and inflection of English words and the pronunciation and inflection of Italian words and the gender of Italian nouns where these words appear as target words inasmuch as target words, according to (1) and (4) above, are sought for the purpose of speaking and writing. Thus the user would find not only the words he seeks but all the information he needs about them in one and the same place. But this technique is impractical because target words are not alphabetized and could, therefore, be found only by the roundabout and uncertain way of seeking them through their translations in

PREFAZIONE

Dato che la funzione principale di un dizionario bilingue è quella di fornire all'utente equivalenze semantiche, le costruzioni sintattiche sono indicate in entrambe le lingue, quella di partenza e quella di arrivo, in entrambe le parti del Dizionario. Per compiere questa funzione, un dizionario bilingue deve raggiungere sei scopi differenti. Cioè, un dizionario italiano e inglese deve fornire (1) nella parte inglese-italiana, le parole italiane che la persona anglofona vuole adoperare parlando e scrivendo l'italiano; (2) nella parte italiano-inglese, il significato in inglese delle parole italiane che tale persona oda nella lingua parlata o legga in libri o giornali; (3) nella parte italiano-inglese, l'ortografia, la pronunzia, la flessione delle parole italiane e il genere dei nomi italiani che la persona anglofona deve conoscere per servirsi correttamente della lingua italiana; (4) nella parte italiano-inglese, le parole inglesi che la persona italofona vuole adoperare parlando o scrivendo l'inglese; (5) nella parte inglese-italiano, il significato in italiano delle parole inglesi che tale persona oda nella lingua parlata o legga in libri o giornali; (6) nella parte inglese-italiano, l'ortografia, la pronunzia figurata e la flessione delle parole inglesi che la persona italofona deve conoscere per servirsi correttamente della lingua inglese.

A prima vista potrebbe sembrare logico che la pronunzia e la flessione delle parole inglesi e la pronunzia e la flessione delle parole italiane e il genere dei nomi italiani fossero indicati dove queste parole si trovano nella lingua d'arrivo, dato che le parole della lingua d'arrivo, secondo i punti (1) e (4) enunciati più sopra, sono consultate da coloro che vogliono parlare e scrivere in lingua straniera. In questa maniera l'utente troverebbe non solo le parole che cerca, ma tutte le informazioni che gli sono necessarie, nello stesso luogo. Questa tecnica, peraltro, non è pratica poiché le parole della lingua d'arrivo non si trovano in ordine

the other part of the dictionary. And this would be particularly inconvenient for persons using the dictionary for purposes (2) and (5) above. It is much more convenient to provide immediate alphabetized access to pronunciation and inflection where the words appear as source words.

alfabetico e potrebbero quindi essere trovate solo in maniera complicata nella parte opposta del dizionario. E ciò sarebbe specialmente scomodo per coloro che usano il dizionario per gli scopi (2) e (5) menzionati più sopra. È molto più semplice aggiungere la pronunzia e la flessione nella serie alfabetica in cui le parole si trovano nella loro lingua di partenza.

Since Italian is an almost perfectly phonetic language, IPA transcription of Italian words has been omitted. The only elements of pronunciation not shown by standard spelling are the values of tonic e and o (§1; pp. 3, 4) the stress of words stressed on the third syllable from the end (§3,3; p. 5), the value of intervocalic s when unvoiced, and the values of z and zz when voiced (§1; p. 4); these are shown in the entry words themselves.

Dato che l'italiano è una lingua quasi perfettamente fonetica, non si è data la trascrizione delle parole italiane nell'alfabeto dell'Associazione Fonetica Internazionale. Considerando che l'ortografia comune non mostra il vario timbro della e (§1, p. 3) e della o (§1, p. 4) quando esse sono toniche, l'accento delle parole sdrucciole (§3,3, p. 5), la pronunzia della s sorda (§1, p. 4) e la pronunzia delle z e zz sonore (§1, p. 4), si è data tale informazione nell'esponente stesso.

All words are treated in a fixed order according to the parts of speech and the functions of verbs, as follows: adjective, article, substantive, pronoun, adverb, preposition, conjunction, transitive verb, intransitive verb, reflexive verb, auxiliary verb, impersonal verb, interjection.

Ogni singola voce è trattata secondo uno schema fisso che si riferisce alle parti del discorso o alle funzioni del verbo, nel seguente ordine: aggettivo, articolo, sostantivo, pronome, avverbio, preposizione, congiunzione, verbo transitivo, verbo intransitivo, verbo riflessivo, verbo ausiliare, verbo impersonale e interiezione.

Meanings with labels come after more general meanings. Labels (printed in roman and in parentheses) refer to the preceding entry or phrase (printed in boldface).

I significati accompagnati da sigle si trovano dopo quelli di accezione più generale. Tali sigle (che sono sempre stampate in carattere romano e in parentesi) si riferiscono all'esponente precedente, stampato in grassetto, o alla frase precedente, ugualmente stampata in grassetto.

In view of the fact that the users of this Italian and English bilingual dictionary are for the most part English-speaking people, definitions and discriminations are provided in English. They are printed in italics and in parentheses and refer to the English word which they particularize:

Dato che gli utenti di questo dizionario bilingue italiano e inglese sono per lo più anglofoni, definizioni e locuzioni esplicative sono apportate in inglese. Sono stampate in corsivo e in parentesi e si riferiscono sempre alla parola inglese il cui significato cercano di spiegare:

porter ['porter] s (doorman) portiere m; (man who carries luggage) facchino; . . .
órdine m order; . . . series (e.g., of years); college (e.g., of surgeons); . . .

English adjectives are always translated by the Italian masculine form

Gli aggettivi inglesi sono sempre tradotti in maschile italiano, anche se il

regardless of whether the translation of the exemplary noun modified would be masculine or feminine:

tough [tʌf] *adj* duro; ...; (*luck*) cattivo; ...

In order to facilitate the finding of the meaning and use sought for, changes within a vocabulary entry in part of speech and function of verb, in irregular inflection, in the use of an initial capital, in the gender of Italian nouns, and in the pronunciation of English words are marked with parallels: ||, instead of the usual semicolons.

Per facilitare l'uso del Dizionario, i raggruppamenti sono stati fatti secondo le parti del discorso, la funzione del verbo, la flessione irregolare, l'uso della maiuscola iniziale, il genere dei nomi italiani e la pronunzia delle parole inglesi e sono separati da sbarrette verticali: ||, invece del punto e virgola che è stato generalmente usato.

Since vocabulary entries are not determined on the basis of etymology, homographs are included in a single entry. When the pronunciation of an English homograph changes, this is shown in the proper place after parallels:

Dato che gli esponenti in questo Dizionario non sono stati selezionati su base etimologica, tutti gli omografi sono inclusi sotto il medesimo esponente. Il cambio di pronunzia di un omografo inglese è indicato al posto adatto dopo sbarrette verticali:

frequent ['frikwənt] *adj* frequente || [fri'kwent]
or ['frikwənt] *tr* ...

However, when the pronunciation of an Italian homograph changes, the words are entered separately:

Però, quando la pronunzia di un omografo italiano cambia, si hanno esponenti separati:

retina *f* small net
rètina *f* (anat) retina
tóc·co -ca (-chi -che) *adj* ... || *m* touch; ...
tòc·co *m* (-chi) chunk, piece; ...

Periods are omitted after labels and grammatical abbreviations and at the end of vocabulary entries.

Il punto è stato omesso dopo sigle, abbreviazioni grammaticali, ed alla fine di ogni articolo.

Proper nouns are listed in their alphabetical position in the main body of the Dictionary. Thus **Svezia** and **svedese** do not have to be looked up in two different sections of the book. And all subentries are listed in strictly alphabetical order.

Tutti i nomi propri sono posti nella loro posizione alfabetica nel corpo del Dizionario: quindi **Svezia** e **svedese** non si trovano in sezioni separate di questo libro. Per la medesima ragione di semplicità d'uso, le parole e frasi contenute sotto ogni esponente sono poste in ordine alfabetico.

The gender of Italian nouns is shown on both sides of the Dictionary, except that the gender of masculine nouns ending in -o, feminine nouns ending in -a and -ione, masculine nouns modified by an adjective ending in -o, and feminine nouns modified by an adjective

nome che qualificano sia un femminile italiano:

Il genere dei nomi italiani è indicato in entrambe le parti del Dizionario, eccezion fatta nella parte inglese-italiano, per le parole maschili che terminano in -o, per le parole femminili che terminano in -a e in -ione, per i nomi maschili accompagnati da un

ending in -a is not shown on the English-Italian side.

The feminine form of an Italian adjective used as a noun (or an Italian feminine noun having identical spelling with the feminine form of an adjective) which falls alphabetically in a separate position from the adjective is treated in that position and is listed again as a cross reference under the adjective:

nòta f mark, score, ...
nò·to -ta adj ... ‖ m ... ‖ f see nota

The centered period is used in vocabulary entries of inflected words to mark off, according to standard orthographic principles in the two languages, the final syllable that has to be detached before the syllable showing the inflection is added:

vèc·chio -chia (-chi -chie) adj ...
put·ty ['pʌti] s (-ties) ... ‖ v (pret & pp -tied) ...
hap·py ['hæpi] adj (-pier; -piest) ...

If the entry word cannot be divided by a centered period the full form is given in parentheses:

mouse [maʊs] s (mice [maɪs]) ...
mouth [maʊθ] s (mouths [maʊðz]) ...
die [daɪ] s (dice [daɪs]) ... ‖ s (dies) ... ‖ v (pret & pp died; ger dying) intr ...

Many Italian verbs which take an indirect object have, as their equivalent, English verbs which take a direct object. This is shown on both sides of this Dictionary by the insertion of (with dat) after the Italian verb, e.g.,

ubbidire §176 intr ... ; (with dat) to obey
obey [o'be] tr ubbidire (with dat)

On the Italian-English side inflection is shown by: a) numbers that refer to the grammatical tables of articles, pronouns, etc., and to the tables of model verbs; they are placed before the abbreviation indicating the part of speech:

mì·o -a §6 adj & pron poss
lui §5 pron pers
congiùngere §183 tr & ref

aggettivo che termina in -o e per i nomi femminili accompagnati da un aggettivo che termina in -a.

Quando un nome femminile italiano ha la medesima grafia della forma femminile di un aggettivo o quando tale forma femminile di aggettivo è usata come nome, lo si trova elencato nella sua posizione alfabetica come nome e poi di nuovo come rinvio interno sotto l'aggettivo:

Qualora l'esponente italiano o inglese sia un vocabolo a flessione, un punto leggermente elevato sopra il rigo è stato usato per separare, secondo le regole ortografiche di ciascuna delle due lingue, la sillaba finale che dev'essere rimossa prima che la sua desinenza di flessione possa essere attaccata al corpo dell'esponente, per es.:

Se l'esponente non può essere scisso a mezzo del suddetto punto, la forma completa è indicata in parentesi:

Molti verbi italiani che reggono un oggetto indiretto hanno come equivalenti inglesi verbi che reggono un oggetto diretto. Questa equivalenza è indicata in entrambe le parti del Dizionario con l'aggiunta di (with dat) dopo il verbo italiano, per es.:

Nella parte italiano-inglese la flessione si indica: a) con numeri che si riferiscono alle tavole grammaticali degli articoli, dei pronomi, ecc., e alle tavole dei verbi modello; questi numeri sono posti innanzi all'abbreviazione indicante la parte del discorso:

b) the first person singular of the present indicative of verbs in which the stress falls on either an **e** or an **o** not stressed in the infinitive or on the third syllable from the end, whatever the vowel may be:

b) con la prima persona singolare del presente dell'indicativo dei verbi non sdruccioli all'infinito in cui l'accento tonico cade o su una **e** o su una **o**, o su qualsiasi vocale di una parola sdrucciola:

> ritornare (ritórno) *tr* ...
> visitare (vìsito) *tr* ...

c) the feminine endings of all adjectives which end in **-o**:

c) con la desinenza femminile di tutti gli aggettivi che terminano in **-o** nel maschile:

> laborió•so -sa [s] *adj* ...

d) the plural endings of nouns and adjectives which are formed irregularly:

d) con la desinenza plurale dei nomi e aggettivi che si formano in maniera irregolare:

> bràc•cio *m* (-cia *fpl*) ... ‖ *m* (-ci) ...
> cit•tà *f* (-tà) ..
> dià•rio -ria (-ri -rie) *adj* ... ‖ *m* ... ‖ *f* ...
> fotogram•ma *m* (-mi) ...
> fràn•gia *f* (-ge) ...
> laburi•sta (-sti -ste) *adj* ... ‖ *mf* ...
> la•go *m* (-ghi) ...
> òr•co *m* (-chi) ...
> òtti•co -ca (-ci -che) *adj* ... ‖ *m* ... ‖ *f* ...

e) the full plural forms of all nouns that cannot be divided by a center period or whose plural cannot be shown by such division:

e) con la completa forma plurale di quei nomi che non possono essere scissi col suddetto punto o che hanno mutamenti interni:

> re *m* (re) ...
> caporeparto *m* (capireparto) ...

I wish to express my gratitude to many persons who helped me in the production of this book and particularly to Dr. Edwin B. Williams who, ever since graduate school, has been a constant inspiration and who has established the principles upon which this book was compiled, to my wife and children, who patiently aided and abetted me through ten years of research and compilation, to Richard J Wiezell, Sebastiano DiBlasi, Walter D. Glanze, and to Giacomo De Voto, Miro Dogliotti, and Michele Ricciardelli.

Labels and abbreviations

Sigle ed abbreviazioni

abbr abbreviation—abbreviazione
(acronym) word formed from the initial letters or syllables of a series of words—parola costituita dalle lettere o sillabe iniziali di una serie di parole
adj adjective—aggettivo
adv adverb—avverbio
(aer) aeronautics—aeronautica
(agr) agriculture—agricoltura
(alg) algebra—algebra
(anat) anatomy—anatomia
(archaic) arcaico
(archeol) archeology—archeologia
(archit) architecture—architettura
(arith) arithmetic—aritmetica
art article—articolo
(astr) astronomy—astronomia
(astrol) astrology—astrologia
(aut) automobile—automobile
aux auxiliary verb—verbo ausiliare
(bact) bacteriology—batteriologia
(baseball) baseball
(basketball) pallacanestro
(bb) bookbinding—legatoria
(Bib) Biblical—biblico
(billiards) biliardo
(biochem) biochemistry—biochimica
(biol) biology—biologia
(bot) botany—botanica
(bowling) bowling
(boxing) pugilato
(bridge) bridge
(Brit) British—britannico
(cards) carte da gioco
(carp) carpentry—falegnameria
(checkers) gioco della dama
(chem) chemistry—chimica
(chess) scacchi
(coll) colloquial—familiare
(com) commercial—commerciale
comb form elemento di parola composta
comp comparative—comparativo
cond conditional—condizionale
conj conjunction—congiunzione
(cricket) cricket
(culin) cooking—cucina
dat dative—dativo
def definite—determinativo, definito
dem demonstrative—dimostrativo
(dentistry) medicina dentaria
(dial) dialectal—dialettale
(dipl) diplomacy—diplomazia

(disparaging) sprezzante
(eccl) ecclesiastical—ecclesiastico
(econ) economics—economia
(educ) education—istruzione
e.g., or *e.g.*, per esempio
(elec) electricity—elettricità
(electron) electronics—elettronica
(ent) entomology—entomologia
(equit) horseback riding—equitazione
f feminine noun—nome femminile
(fa) fine arts—belle arti
fem feminine—femminile
(fencing) scherma
(fig) figurative—figurato
(fin) financial—finanziario
(football) football americano
fpl feminine noun plural—nome femminile plurale
fut future—futuro
(geog) geography—geografia
(geol) geology—geologia
(geom) geometry—geometria
ger gerund—gerundio
(golf) golf
(gram) grammar—grammatica
(herald) heraldry—araldica
(hist) history—storia
(hort) horticulture—orticoltura
(hunt) hunting—caccia
(ichth) ichthyology—ittiologia
i.e., cioè
imperf imperfect—imperfetto
impers impersonal verb—verbo impersonale
impv imperative—imperativo
ind indicative—indicativo
indef indefinite—indefinito, indeterminativo
inf infinitive—infinito
(ins) insurance—assicurazione
interj interjection—interiezione
interr interrogative—interrogativo
intr intransitive verb—verbo intransitivo
invar invariable—invariabile
(Italian cards) carte italiane
(jewelry) gioielleria
(joc) jocular—faceto
(journ) journalism—giornalismo
(law) diritto, legge
(letterword) word in the form of an abbreviation which is pronounced by sounding the names of its letters in

succession and which functions as a part of speech—parola in forma di abbreviazione che si ottiene pronunziando consecutivamente la denominazione di ciascuna lettera e che funziona come parte del discorso

(lexicography) lessicografia
(ling) linguistics—linguistica
(lit) literary—letterario
(log) logic—logica
m masculine noun—nome maschile
(mach) machinery—macchinario
masc masculine—maschile
(math) mathematics—matematica
(mech) mechanics—meccanica
(med) medicine—medicina
(metallurgy) metallurgia
(meteor) meteorology—meteorologia
mf masculine or feminine noun according to sex—nome maschile o nome femminile secondo il sesso
m & f see below between (mythol) and (naut)
(mil) military—militare
(min) mining—lavorazione delle miniere
(mov) moving pictures—cinematografo
mpl masculine noun plural—nome maschile plurale
(mus) music—musica
(mythol) mythology—mitologia
m & f masculine and feminine noun without regard to sex—nome maschile e femminile senza distinzione di sesso
(naut) nautical—nautico
(nav) naval—navale
neut neuter—neutro
num number—numero
(obs) obsolete—in disuso
(obstet) obstetrics—ostetricia
(opt) optics—ottica
(orn) ornithology—ornitologia
(painting) pittura
(pathol) pathology—patologia
(pej) pejorative—peggiorativo
perf perfect—perfetto, passato
pers personal—personale; person—persona
(pharm) pharmacy—farmacia
(philately) filatelia
(philol) philology—filologia
(philos) philosophy—filosofia
(phonet) phonetics—fonetica
(phot) photography—fotografia
(phys) physics—fisica
(physiol) physiology—fisiologia
pl plural—plurale
(poet) poetical—poetico
(poker) poker
(pol) politics—politica
pp past participle—participio passato
poss possessive—possessivo
pref prefix—prefisso
prep preposition—preposizione

prep phrase prepositional phrase—**frase** preposizionale
pres present—presente
pret preterit—passato remoto
pron pronoun—pronome
(pros) prosody—prosodia
(psychoanal) psychoanalysis—psicanalisi
(psychol) psychology—psicologia
(psychopath) psychopathology—psicopatologia
qlco or *qlco* qualcosa—something
qlcu or *qlcu* qualcuno—someone
(racing) corse
(rad) radio—radio
ref reflexive verb—verbo riflessivo o pronominale
rel relative—relativo
(rel) religion—religione
(rhet) rhetoric—retorica
(rok) rocketry—studio dei razzi
(rowing) canottaggio
(rr) railroad—ferrovia
(rugby) rugby
s substantive—sostantivo
(scornful) sprezzante
(Scot) Scottish—scozzese
(sculp) sculpture—scultura
(sew) sewing—cucito
sg singular—singolare
(slang) gergo
s.o. or *s.o.* someone—qualcuno
(soccer) calcio
spl substantive plural—sostantivo plurale
(sports) sport
ssg substantive singular—sostantivo singolare
s.th or *s.th* something—qualcosa
subj subjunctive—congiuntivo
suf suffix—suffisso
super superlative—superlativo
(surg) surgery—chirurgia
(surv) surveying—agrimensura, topografia
(taur) bullfighting—tauromachia
(telg) telegraphy—telegrafia
(telp) telephone—telefonia
(telv) television—televisione
(tennis) tennis
(tex) textile—tessile
(theat) theater—teatro
(theol) theology—teologia
tr transitive verb—verbo transitivo
(trademark) marchio di fabbrica
(typ) printing—tipografia
(U.S.A.) S.U.A.
v verb—verbo
var variant—variante
(vet) veterinary medicine—medicina veterinaria
(vulg) vulgar—volgare, ordinario
(wrestling) lotta
(zool) zoology—zoologia

PART ONE

Italian-English

Italian Spelling and Pronunciation

§1. The Italian Alphabet. 1. The twenty-one letters of the Italian alphabet are listed below with their names and their sounds in terms of approximate equivalent English sounds. Their gender is masculine or feminine.

LETTER	NAME	APPROXIMATE SOUND
a	a	Like *a* in English *father*, e.g., **facile, padre.**
b	bi	Like *b* in English *boat*, e.g., **bello, abate.**
c	ci	When followed by **e** or **i**, like *ch* in English *cherry*, e.g., **cento, cinque;** if the **i** is unstressed and followed by another vowel, its sound is not heard, e.g., **ciarla, cieco.** When followed by **a, o, u,** or a consonant, like *c* in English *cook*, e.g., **casa, come, cura, credere.** The digraph **ch**, which is used before **e** and **i**, has likewise the sound of *c* in English *cook*, e.g., **chiesa, perché.**
d	di	Like *d* in English *dance*, e.g., **dare, madre.**
e	e	Has two sounds. One like *a* in English *make*, shown on stressed syllables in this DICTIONARY by the acute accent, e.g., **séra, trénta;** and one like *e* in English *met*, shown on stressed syllables in this DICTIONARY by the grave accent, e.g., **fèrro, fèsta.**
f	effe	Like *f* in English *fool*, e.g., **farina, efelide.**
g	gi	When followed by **e** or **i**, like *g* in English *general*, e.g., **gelato, ginnasta;** if the **i** is unstressed and followed by another vowel, its sound is not heard, e.g., **giallo, giorno.** When followed by **a, o, u,** or a consonant, like *g* in English *go*, e.g., **gamba, goccia, gusto, grado.** The digraph **gh**, which is used before **e** and **i**, has likewise the sound of *g* in English *go*, e.g., **gherone, ghisa.** When the combination **gli** (a) is a form of the definite article or the personal pronoun, (b) is final in a word, or (c) is intervocalic, it has the sound of Castilian *ll*, which is somewhat like *lli* in English *million*, e.g., (a) **gli uomini, gli ho parlato ieri,** (b) **battagli,** (c) **figlio, migliore.** When it is (a) initial (except in the word **gli**, above), (b) preceded by a consonant, or (c) followed by a consonant, it is pronounced like *gli* in English *negligence*, e.g., (a) **glioma,** (b) **ganglio,** (c) **negligenza.** The combination **gl** followed by **a, e, o,** or **u** is pronounced like *gl* in English *globe*, e.g., **glabro, gleba, globo, gluteo, inglese, poliglotto.** The digraph **gn** has the sound of Castilian *ñ*, which is somewhat like *ni* in English *onion*, e.g., **signore, gnocco.**
h	acca	Always silent, e.g., **ah, hanno.** See **ch** under **c** above and **gh** under **g** above.
i	i	Like *i* in English *machine*, e.g., **piccolo, sigla.** When unstressed and followed by another vowel, like *y* in English *yes*, e.g., **piatto, piede, fiore, fiume.** For **i** in **ci**, see **c** above, in **gi**, see **g** above, and in **sci**, see **s** below.

3

LETTER	NAME	APPROXIMATE SOUND
l	elle	Like *l* in English *lamb*, e.g., **labbro, lacrima.**
m	emme	Like *m* in English *money*, e.g., **mano, come.**
n	enne	Like *n* in English *net*, e.g., **nome, cane.**
o	o	Has two sounds. One like *o* in English *note*, shown on stressed syllables in this DICTIONARY by the acute accent, e.g., **dópo, sóle;** and one like *ou* in English *ought*, shown on stressed syllables in this DICTIONARY by the grave accent, e.g., **còsa, dònna.**
p	pi	Like *p* in English *pot*, e.g., **passo, carpa.**
q	cu	This letter is always followed by the letter **u** and the combination has the sound of *qu* in English *quart*, e.g., **quanto, questo.**
r	erre	Like *r* in English *rubber*, with a slight trill, e.g., **roba, carta.**
s	esse	Has two sounds. When initial and followed by a vowel, when preceded by a consonant and followed by a vowel, and when followed by **c** [k] **f, p, q,** or **t,** like *s* in English *see*, e.g., **sale, falso, scappare, spazio, stoffa;** and when standing between two vowels and when followed by **b, d, g** [g]**, l, m, n, r** or **v,** like *z* in English *zero*, e.g., **paese, sbaglio, svenire.** However, **s** standing between two vowels and initial **s** followed by **b, d, g** [g]**, l, m, n, r,** or **v** in some foreign borrowings are pronounced like *s* in *see*, e.g., **casa*, tesa, smoking, slam** In this DICTIONARY this is indicated by the insertion of [s] immediately after the entry word. However, when initial **s** stands between two vowels in a compound, its pronunciation remains that of initial **s,** e.g., **autoservizio** and this is not indicated. The digraph **sc,** when followed by **e** or **i** has the sound of *sh* in English *shall*, e.g., **scelta, scimmia;** if the **i** is unstressed and followed by another vowel, its sound is not heard, e.g., **sciame, sciopero.** The trigraph **sch** has the sound of *sc* in English *scope*, e.g., **scherzo, schiavo.**
t	ti	Like *t* in English *table*, e.g., **terra, pasto.**
u	u	Like *u* in English *rule*, e.g., **luna, mulo.** When followed by a vowel, like *w* in English *was*, e.g., **quanto, guerra, nuovo.**
v	vu	Like *v* in English *vain*, e.g., **vita, uva.**
z	zeta	Has two sounds. One like *ts* in English *nuts*, e.g., **grazia, zucchero;** and one like *dz* in English *adze*, e.g., **zero, mezzo.** In this DICTIONARY the sound of *dz* in *adze* is indicated by the insertion of [dz] immediately after the entry word. If the sound is long, [ddzz] is inserted

* Intervocalic **s** is generally voiced in the north of Italy.

2. The following five letters are found in borrowings from other languages.

LETTER	NAME	EXAMPLES
j	i lunga	**jazz, jingo**
k	cappa	**kiosco, kodak**
w	doppia vu	**water-polo, whisky**
x	ics	**xenofobo, xilofono**
y	ìpsilon	**yacht, yoghurt**

3. Consonants written double are longer than consonants written single, that is, it takes a longer time to pronounce them, e.g., **camino** *chimney* and **cam-**

4

mino *road*, capello *hair* and cappello *hat*. Special attention is called to the following double consonants: **cc** followed by **e** or **i** has the sound of *ch ch* in English *beach chair*, that is, a lengthened *ch* (not the sound of *ks*), e.g., **accento; cch** has the sound of *kk* in English *bookkeeper*, e.g., **becchino; cq** has the sound of *kk* in English *bookkeeper*, e.g., **acqua; gg** followed by **e** or **i** has the sound of *ge j* in English *carriage joiner*, e.g., **peggio; ggh** has the sound of *g g* in English *tag game*, e.g., **agghindare.**

§2. Division of Syllables. In the application of the following rules for the syllabic division of words, the digraphs **ch, gh, gl, gn,** and **sc** count as single consonants.

(a) When a single consonant stands between two vowels it belongs to the following syllable, e.g., **ca·sa, fu·mo, aml·che, la·ghi, fi·glio, biso·gno, la·sciare.**

(b) When a consonant group consisting of two consonants of which the second is **l** or **r** stands between two vowels, the group belongs to the following syllable, e.g., **nu·cleo, so·brio, qua·dro.**

(c) When a consonant group consisting of two or more consonants of which the first or the second is **s** stands between two vowels, that part of the group beginning with **s** belongs to the following syllable, e.g., **ta·sca, bo·schi, fine·stra, super·sti·zione, sub·strato.**

(d) When a consonant group consisting of two or three consonants of which the first is **l, m, n,** or **r** stands between two vowels, the **l, m, n,** or **r** belongs to the preceding syllable, the other consonant or consonants to the following syllable, e.g., **al·bero, am·pio, prin·cipe, mor·te, in·flazione, com·pleto.**

(e) When a double consonant stands between two vowels or between a vowel and **l** or **r**, the first belongs to the preceding syllable, the second to the following syllable, e.g., **bab·bo, caval·lo, an·no, car·ro, mez·zo, sup·plica, lab·bro, quat·tro.**

§3. Stress and Accent Marks. 1. Whenever stress is shown as part of regular spelling, it is shown on **a, i,** and **u** by the grave accent mark, e.g., **libertà, giovedì, gioventù,** on close **e** and **o** by the acute accent mark, e.g., **perché,** and on open **e** and **o** by the grave accent mark, e.g., **caffè, parlò.** This occurs (a) in words ending in a stressed vowel, as in the above examples, (b) in stressed monosyllables in which the vocalic element is a diphthong of which the first letter is unstressed **i** or **u**, e.g., **già, più, può,** and (c) on the stressed monosyllable of any pair of monosyllables of which one is stressed and the other unstressed, in order to distinguish one from the other, e.g., **dà** *he gives* and **da** *from*, **è** *is* and **e** *and*, **sé** *himself* and **se** *if*, **sì** *yes* and **si** *himself*.

2. Whenever stress is not shown as part of regular spelling, it is often difficult to determine where it falls.

(a) In words of two syllables, the stress falls on the syllable next to the last, e.g., **ca'sa, mu'ro, ter'ra.** If the syllable next to the last contains a diphthong, that is, a combination of a strong vowel (**a, e,** or **o**) and a weak vowel (**i** or **u**), the strong vowel is stressed, regardless of which vowel comes first, e.g., **da'ino, ero'ico, ne'utro, fia'to, dua'le, sie'pe, fio're, buo'no.**

(b) In words of more than two syllables, the stress may fall on the syllable next to the last, e.g., **anda'ta, canzo'ne, pasto're** or on a preceding syllable, e.g., **fis'sile, gon'dola, man'dorla.** In these positions also the stressed syllable may contain a diphthong, e.g., **inca'uto, idra'ulico, fio'cina.**

(c) If a weak vowel in juxtaposition with a strong vowel is stressed, the two vowels constitute two separate syllables, e.g., **abba·i'no, ero·i'na, pa·u'ra, miri'ade, vi'a.**

(d) Two strong vowels in juxtaposition constitute two separate syllables, e.g., **pa·e'se, aure'ola, ide'a, oce'ano.**

(e) Two weak vowels in juxtaposition generally constitute a diphthong in which the first vowel is stressed in some words, e.g., **flu'ido** and the second vowel in others, e.g., **piu'ma.**

(f) If a word ends in a diphthong, the diphthong is stressed, e.g., **marina'i, parla'i, ero'i.**

3. In this DICTIONARY, stress is understood or shown on all words that do not bear an accent mark as part of regular spelling according to the following principles. In the application of these principles, individual vowels and not diphthongs are counted as units. In some words in which it is not necessary to show stress, an accent mark is used to show the quality of the stressed vowels **e** and **o**.

As in regular Italian spelling, stress is shown on **a, i,** and **u** by the grave accent mark, on close **e** and **o** by the acute accent mark, and on open **e** and **o** by the grave accent mark.

(a) It is understood that in words of more than one syllable in which no accent mark is shown, the stress falls on the vowel next to the last, e.g., **casa,** fiato, duale, abbaino, paura. In such words as sièpe, fióre, buòno, paése, fluènte, eròe, nói, pòi, the accent mark is used to show the quality of the vowel.

(b) An accent mark is placed on the stressed vowel if the word is stressed on the third vowel from the end, e.g., mùsica, sìmbolo, dàino, incàuto, marinàio, contìnuo, infànzia. If this vowel is e or o, the acute or grave accent mark must correspond to the quality of the vowel, e.g., fiòcina, ròmpere, nèutro, eròico, assèdio, filatóio.

(c) Contrary to the above-mentioned principle of counting vowels, an accent mark is placed on the strong vowel of a final diphthong, e.g., marinài, assài.

(d) Contrary to the above-mentioned principle of counting vowels, an accent mark is placed on the i of final ia, ie, ii, and io, e.g., farmacìa, scìa, farmacìe, mormorìi, gorgoglìo, fìo.

(e) An accent mark is placed on some borrowings ending in a consonant, e.g., hàrem, revòlver.

(f) The loss of the last vowel or last syllable of a word does not alter the position of the stress of the word, e.g., la maggior parte, in alcun modo, fan bene.

84. The Definite Article and Combinations with Prepositions.

		MASC BEFORE CONSONANT	MASC BEFORE S IMPURE OR Z[1]	MASC BEFORE VOWEL	FEM BEFORE CONSONANT	FEM BEFORE VOWEL
	SG	il	lo	l'[2]	la	l'
	PL	i	gli	gli[2]	le	le[3]
WITH a	SG	al	allo	all'[2]	alla	all'
	PL	ai	agli	agli[2]	alle	alle[3]
WITH di	SG	del	dello	dell'	della	dell'
	PL	dei	degli	degli[2]	delle	delle[3]
WITH con	SG	col	collo	coll'	colla	coll'
	PL	coi	cogli	cogli[2]	colle	colle[3]
WITH da	SG	dal	dallo	dall'	dalla	dall'
	PL	dai	dagli	dagli[2]	dalle	dalle[3]
WITH in	SG	nel	nello	nell'	nella	nell'
	PL	nei	negli	negli[2]	nelle	nelle[3]
WITH su	SG	sul	sullo	sull'	sulla	sull'
	PL	sui	sugli	sugli[2]	sulle	sulle[3]

[1] Other letters and groups of letters, which occur in a few words, are gn, pn, ps, sc, x, and i before a vowel, sometimes spelled j or y.

[2] These forms may drop the i before words beginning with i, e.g., gl'inglesi.

[3] The e of these forms is not elided, e.g. le erbe.

7

85. Personal and Reflexive Pronouns.

PERSONS	SUBJECT	PERSONAL DIRECT OBJECT	PERSONAL INDIRECT OBJECT	REFLEX. & RECIPROCAL DIRECT & INDIRECT OBJECT	PERSONAL PREPOSITIONAL OBJECT	REFLEX. & RECIPROCAL PREPOSITIONAL OBJECT
SG						
1	io *I*	mi *me*	mi *to me*	mi *myself; to myself*	me *me*	me *myself*
2	tu *you*	ti *you*	ti *to you*	ti *yourself; to yourself*	te *you*	te *yourself*
3 MASC	egli, lui *he*	lo *him or it*	gli *to him*	si *himself; to himself*	lui *him*	sé *himself*
3 FEM	lei, essa *she*	la *her or it*	le *to her*	si *herself; to herself*	lei, essa *her*	sé *herself*
2 FORMAL	Lei *you*	La *you*	Le *to you*	si *yourself; to yourself*	Lei *you*	sé *yourself*
PL						
1	noi *we*	ci *us*	ci *to us*	ci *ourselves; to ourselves; each other; to each other*	noi *us*	noi *ourselves; each other*
2	voi *you*	vi *you*	vi *to you*	vi *yourselves; to yourselves; each other; to each other*	voi *you*	voi *yourself; yourselves; each other*
3 MASC	loro, essi *they*	li *them*	loro *to them*	si *themselves; to themselves; each other; to each other*	loro, essi *them*	sé *themselves; each other*
3 FEM	loro, esse *they*	le *them*	loro *to them*	si *themselves; to themselves; each other; to each other*	loro, esse *them*	sé *themselves; each other*
2 FORMAL	Loro *you*	Li } *you* Le }	Loro *to you*	si *yourselves; to yourselves; each other; to each other*	Loro *you*	sé *yourselves; each other*

ci and **vi** both mean also *here, there, to it, in it, to them, in them, about it.*
ne means *of, from, or with him, her, it, them; some, any; from here, from there, thence, about it.*

meco *with me,* **teco** *with you,* and **seco** *with him, with himself; with her, with herself; with you, with yourself, with yourselves; with them, with themselves; with each other* may be used instead of **con me, con te,** and **con sé** respectively.

8

COMBINATION OF DIRECT AND INDIRECT OBJECT

PERSONS		
1 SG & 3 SG	me lo / me la }	him, her, it to me
1 SG & 3 PL	me li / me le }	them to me
2 SG & 3 SG	te lo / te la }	him, her, it to you
2 SG & 3 PL	te li / te le }	them to you
3 SG & 3 SG	glielo / gliela }	him, her, it to him / him, her, it to her
3 SG & 3 PL	glieli / gliele }	them to him / them to her
2 SG FORMAL & 3 SG	Glielo / Gliela }	him, her, it to you
2 SG FORMAL & 3 PL	Glieli / Gliele }	them to you

PERSONS		
1 PL & 3 SG	ce lo / ce la }	him, her, it to us
1 PL & 3 PL	ce li / ce le }	them to us
2 PL & 3 SG	ve lo / ve la }	him, her, it to you
2 PL & 3 PL	ve li / ve le }	them to you
3 SG & 3 SG	lo / la } VERB loro	him, her, it to them
3 SG & 3 PL	li / le } VERB loro	them to them
3 SG & 2 PL FORMAL	lo / la } VERB Loro	him, her, it to you
3 PL & 2 PL FORMAL	li / le } VERB Loro	them to you

The form **si** (third singular and plural reflexive and reciprocal indirect object) changes to **se** before one of the direct objects **lo, la, li, le,** and before **ne,** e.g., **se lo mette** he puts it on; **se n'è andato** he went away.

In combinations, **ne** occupies the same position as **lo, la, li,** and **le,** e.g., **me ne,** and forms one word with **gli,** namely, **gliene,**

9

§6 Possessive Adjectives and Pronouns

PERSON, NUMBER & SEX OF POSSESSOR	GENDER & NUMBER OF POSSESSIVE ADJECTIVE OR PRONOUN ACCORDING TO THE GENDER & NUMBER OF THE PERSON OR THING POSSESSED				MEANING OF ADJECTIVE	MEANING OF PRONOUN
	MSG	MPL	FSG	FPL		
SG						
1	il mio	i miei	la mia	le mie	*my*	*mine*
2	il tuo	i tuoi	la tua	le tue	*your*	*yours*
3 MASC	il suo	i suoi	la sua	le sue	*his*	*his*
3 FEM	il suo	i suoi	la sua	le sue	*her*	*hers*
3 NEUT	il suo	i suoi	la sua	le sue	*its*	*its*
2 FORMAL	il Suo	i Suoi	la Sua	le Sue	*your*	*yours*
PL						
1	il nostro	i nostri	la nostra	le nostre	*our*	*ours*
2	il vostro	i vostri	la vostra	le vostre	*your*	*yours*
3	il loro	i loro	la loro	le loro	*their*	*theirs*
2 FORMAL	il Loro	i Loro	la Loro	le Loro	*your*	*yours*

The definite article, shown here, is not generally used (a) in direct address, e.g., **mio caro amico** *my dear friend*, (b) after the verb **essere**, e.g., **la casa è nostra** *the house is ours*, and (c) when a singular form modifies the name of a relative, e.g., **sua sorella** *his sister*. With forms of the indefinite article, the possessive adjective, whether standing before or after the noun, is translated by *of*

plus the possessive pronoun, e.g., **un amico mio** *a friend of mine*; **una sua zia** *an aunt of his* (or *of hers*). The forms of the possessive pronouns also have the force of nouns, e.g., **il mio** *my property, my belongings*; **i suoi** *his people, relatives, followers, troops, retinue*, etc.; **la mia** *my letter*; **la sua** *his opinion*.

87. The Demonstrative Adjective.

	MASC BEFORE CONSONANT	MASC BEFORE s IMPURE OR z (see note 1, p. 7)	MASC BEFORE VOWEL	FEM BEFORE CONSONANT	FEM BEFORE VOWEL
SG PL	quel *that* quel *those*	quello quegli	quell' quegli	quella quelle	quell' quelle
SG PL	questo *this* questi *these*	questo questi	questo or quest' questi	questa queste	questa or quest' queste

11

§8. The Demonstrative Pronoun.

	MASC	FEM	MASC
SG	**quello** *that one*	**quella**	**quegli** *that one; the former*
PL	**quelli** *those*	**quelle**	
SG	**questo** *this one*	**questa**	**questi** *this one; the latter*
PL	**questi** *these*	**queste**	

The demonstrative pronoun **quello** is often followed by **che**, **di**, or **da** and the masculine singular form may be shortened to **quel** before these words.

SG	**colui** *that one*	**colei**
PL	**coloro** *those*	**coloro**
SG	**costui** *this one*	**costei**
PL	**costoro** *these*	**costoro**

code·sto -sta -sti -ste and **cote·sto -sta -sti -ste** are demonstrative adjectives and demonstrative pronouns and mean *that (of yours)*.

89. Indefinite Article and Numeral Adjective.

MASC	MASC	MASC	FEM	FEM
BEFORE CONSONANT	BEFORE S IMPURE OR z (see note 1, p. 7)	BEFORE VOWEL	BEFORE CONSONANT	BEFORE VOWEL
un *a, an; one*	uno	un	una	un'

§10. Indefinite Pronoun uno.

MASC	FEM
uno *one*	una

§11. Correlative Indefinite Pronoun.

	MASC	FEM
SG	l'uno . . . l'altro *one . . . the other*	l'una . . . l'altra
PL	gli uni . . . gli altri *some . . . the others*	le une . . . le altre

§12. Reciprocal Indefinite Pronoun.

	MASC	FEM
SG	l'un l'altro *each other, one another*	l'una l'altra
PL	gli uni gli altri	le une le altre

Table of Regular Endings of Italian Verbs

The stem to which the endings of the gerund, past participle, present participle, imperative, present indicative, present subjunctive, imperfect indicative, preterit indicative, and imperfect subjunctive are attached is obtained by dropping the ending of the infinitive, viz., **-are, -ere, -ire.**

The stem to which the endings of the future indicative and present conditional are attached is obtained by dropping the **-e** of the ending of the infinitive of all conjugations and changing the **a** of the ending of the infinitive of the first conjugation to **e.**

The letters before the names of some of the tenses of this table correspond to the designation of the tenses shown on the following page.

Letters printed in italics have a written accent that is not part of the regular spelling.

TENSE	FIRST CONJUGATION	SECOND CONJUGATION	THIRD CONJUGATION
inf	-are	-*é*re (or *'*ere)	-ire
ger	-ando	-*è*ndo	-*è*ndo
pp	-ato	-uto	-ito
pres part	-ante	-*è*nte	-*è*nte
(a) *impv*	-a -ate	-i -*é*te	-i -ite
(b) *pres ind*	-o -i -a -iamo -ate -ano	-o -i -e -iamo -*é*te -ono	-o -i -e -iamo -ite -ono
(c) *pres subj*	-i -i -i -iamo -iate -ino	-a -a -a -iamo -iate -ano	-a -a -a -iamo -iate -ano
(d) *imperf ind*	-avo -avi -ava -avamo -avate -*à*vano	-*é*vo -*é*vi -*é*va -evamo -evate -*é*vano	-ivo -ivi -iva -ivamo -ivate -*í*vano
(e) *pret ind*	-*à*i -asti -*ò* -ammo -aste -*à*rono	-*é*i -*é*sti -*è* -*é*mmo -*é*ste -*é*rono	-*í*i -isti -*í* -immo -iste -*í*rono
imperf subj	-assi -assi -asse -*à*ssimo -aste -*à*ssero	-*é*ssi -*é*ssi -*é*sse -*é*ssimo -*é*ste -*é*ssero	-issi -issi -isse -*í*ssimo -iste -*í*ssero
(f) *fut ind*	-er-*ò* -er-*à*i -er-à -er-*é*mo -er-*é*te -er-anno	-*ò* -*à*i -à -*é*mo -*é*te -anno	-*ò* -*à*i -à -*é*mo -*é*te -anno

TENSE	FIRST CONJUGATION	SECOND CONJUGATION	THIRD CONJUGATION
pres cond	-er-èi	-èi	-èi
	-er-ésti	-ésti	-ésti
	-er-èbbe	-èbbe	-èbbe
	-er-émmo	-émmo	-émmo
	-er-éste	-éste	-éste
	-er-èbbero	-èbbero	-èbbero

MODEL VERBS
ORDER OF TENSES

(a) imperative   (d) imperfect indicative
(b) present indicative   (e) preterit indicative
(c) present subjunctive   (f) future indicative

In addition to the infinitive, gerund, and past participle, which are shown in line one of these tables, all simple tenses are shown if they contain at least one irregular form, except (1) the present conditional, which is always formed on the stem of the future indicative, (2) the imperfect subjunctive, which is always formed on the stem of the *2nd sg* of the preterit indicative, and (3) the present participle, which is generally formed by changing the final -**do** of the gerund to -**te** (exceptions being shown in parentheses after the gerund).

Letters printed in italics have a written accent that is not part of the regular spelling.

§100 **ACCÈDERE**—accedèndo—acceduto
    (e) accedètti *or* accedéi *or* accèssi; accedésti; accedètte *or* accedé *or* accèsse; accedémmo; accedéste; accedèttero *or* accedérono *or* accèssero

§101 **ACCÈNDERE**—accendèndo—accéso
    (e) accési, accendésti, accése, accendémmo, accendéste, accésero

§102 **ADDURRE**—adducèndo—addótto
    (b) adduco, adduci, adduce, adduciamo, adducéte, addùcono
    (c) adduca, adduca, adduca, adduciamo, adduciate, addùcano
    (d) adducévo, adducévi, adducéva, adducevamo, adducevate, adducévano
    (e) addussi, adducésti, addusse, adducémmo, adducéste, addùssero

§103 **AFFÌGGERE**—affiggèndo—affisso
    (e) affissi, affiggésti, affisse, affiggémmo, affiggéste, affìssero

§104 AFFLÌGGERE—affliggèndo—afflitto
(e) afflissi, affliggésti, afflisse, affliggémmo, affliggéste, afflìssero

§105 ALLÙDERE—alludèndo—alluso
(e) allusi, alludésti, alluse, alludémmo, alludéste, allùsero

§106 ANDARE—andando—andato
(a) va *or* va' *or* vai, andate
(b) vò *or* vado, vai, va, andiamo, andate, vanno
(c) vada, vada, vada, andiamo, andiate, vàdano
(f) andrò, andrài, andrà, andrémo, andréte, andranno

§107 ANNÈTTERE—annettèndo—annèsso or **annéttere**, annetténdo, annésso
(e) annettéi *or* annèssi *or* annéssi; annettésti; annetté *or* annèsse *or* annésse; annettémmo; annettéste; annettérono *or* annèssero *or* annéssero

§108 APPARIRE—apparèndo—apparso
(a) apparisci *or* appari; apparite
(b) apparisco *or* appàio; apparisci *or* appari; apparisce *or* appare; appariamo; apparite; appariscono *or* appàiono
(c) apparisca *or* appàia; apparisca *or* appàia; apparisca *or* appàia; appariamo; appariate; appariscano *or* appàiano
(e) apparvi *or* apparìi *or* apparsi; apparisti; apparve *or* apparì *or* apparse; apparimmo; appariste; appàrvero *or* apparìrono *or* appàrsero

§109 APPÈNDERE—appendèndo—appéso
(e) appési, appendésti, appése, appendémmo, appendéste, appésero

§110 APRIRE—aprèndo—apèrto
(e) aprìi *or* apèrsi; apristi; aprì *or* apèrse; aprimmo; apriste; aprìrono *or* apèrsero

§111 ÀRDERE—ardèndo—arso
(e) arsi, ardésti, arse, ardémmo, ardéste, àrsero

§112 ASPÈRGERE—aspergèndo—aspèrso
(e) aspèrsi, aspergésti, aspèrse, aspergémmo, aspergéste, aspèrsero

§113 ASSÌDERE—assidèndo—assiso
(e) assisi, assidésti, assise, assidémmo, assidéste, assìsero

§114 ASSÌSTERE—assistèndo—assistito
(e) assistéi *or* assistètti; assistésti; assisté *or* assistètte; assistémmo; assistéste; assistérono *or* assistèttero

18

§115 ASSÒLVERE—assolvèndo—assòlto *or* assoluto
    (e) assolvéi *or* assolvètti *or* assòlsi; assolvésti; assolvé *or*
        assolvètte *or* assòlse; assolvémmo; assolvéste; as-
        solvérono *or* assolvèttero *or* assòlsero

§116 ASSÙMERE—assumèndo—assunto
    (e) assunsi, assumésti, assunse, assumémmo, assuméste,
        assùnsero

§117 ASSÙRGERE—assurgèndo—assurto
    (e) assursi, assurgésti, assurse, assurgémmo, assurgéste,
        assùrsero

§118 AVÈRE—avèndo—avuto
    (a) abbi, abbiate
    (b) ho, hai, ha, abbiamo, avete, hanno
    (c) *a*bbia, *a*bbia, *a*bbia, abbiamo, abbiate, *a*bbiano
    (e) èbbi, avésti, èbbe, avémmo, avéste, èbbero
    (f) avrò, avr*a*i, avrà, avrémo, avréte, avranno

§119 AVVIARE—avviando—avviato
    (b) avvìo, avvìi, avvìa, avviamo, avviate, avvìano
    (c) avvìi, avvìi, avvìi, avviamo, avviate, avvìino

§120 BÉRE—bevèndo—bevuto
    (a) bévi, bevéte
    (b) bévo, bévi, béve, beviamo, bevéte, bévono
    (c) béva, béva, béva, beviamo, beviate, bévano
    (d) bevévo, bevévi, bevéva, bevevamo, bevevate, bevévano
    (e) bévvi *or* bevéi *or* bevètti; bevésti, bévve *or* bevé *or*
        bevètte; bevémmo; bevéste; bévvero *or* bevérono *or*
        bevèttero
    (f) berrò, berr*a*i, berrà, berrémo, berréte, berranno

§121 CADÉRE—cadèndo—caduto
    (e) caddi, cadésti, cadde, cadémmo, cadéste, c*a*ddero
    (f) cadrò, cadr*a*i, cadrà, cadrémo, cadréte, cadranno

§122 CECARE—cecando—cecato
    (a) cièca *or* cèca; cecate
    (b) cièco *or* cèco; cièchi *or* cèchi; cièca *or* cèca; cechiamo;
        cecate; ciècano *or* cècano
    (c) cièchi *or* cèchi; cièchi *or* cèchi; cièchi *or* cèchi;
        cechiamo; cechiate; cièchino *or* cèchino
    (f) cecherò, cecher*a*i, cecherà, cecherémo, cecheréte,
        cecheranno

§123 CÈDERE—cedèndo—ceduto
    (e) cedéi *or* cedètti; cedésti; cedé *or* cedètte; cedémmo;
        cedéste; cedérono *or* cedèttero

§124 CHIÈDERE—chiedèndo—chièsto
    (e) chièsi, chiedésti, chièse, chiedémmo, chiedéste, chièsero

§125 CHIÙDERE—chiudèndo—chiuso
    (e) chiusi, chiudésti, chiuse, chiudémmo, chiudéste, chiùsero

§126 CÌNGERE—cingèndo—cinto
    (e) cinsi, cingésti, cinse, cingémmo, cingéste, cìnsero

§127 CÒGLIERE—coglièndo—còlto
    (a) còigli, cogliéte
    (b) còlgo, còigli, còiglie, cogliamo, cogliéte, còlgono
    (c) còlga, còlga, còlga, cogliamo, cogliate, còlgano
    (e) còlsi, cogliésti, còlse, cogliémmo, cogliéste, còlsero

§128 COMINCIARE—cominciando—cominciato
    (b) comìncio, cominci, comìncia, cominciamo, cominciate, comìnciano
    (c) cominci, cominci, cominci, cominciamo, cominciate, comìncino
    (f) comincerò, comincerài, comincerà, comincerémo, cominceréte, cominceranno

§129 COMPÈTERE—competèndo—*pp* missing

§130 CÒMPIERE—compièndo—compiuto
    (a) cómpi, compite
    (b) cómpio, cómpi, cómpie, compiamo, compite, cómpiono
    (c) cómpia, cómpia, cómpia, compiamo, compiate, cómpiano
    (d) compivo, compivi, compiva, compivamo, compivate, compìvano
    (e) compiéi *or* compìi; compiésti *or* compisti; compié *or* compì; compiémmo *or* compimmo; compiéste *or* compiste; compiérono *or* compìrono

§131 COMPRÌMERE—comprimèndo—comprèsso
    (e) comprèssi, comprimésti, comprèsse, comprimémmo, compriméste, comprèssero

§132 CONCÈDERE—concedèndo—concèsso
    (e) concedéi *or* concèssi *or* concedètti; concedésti; concedé *or* concèsse *or* concedètte; concedémmo; concedéste; concedérono *or* concèssero *or* concedèttero

§133 CONCÈRNERE—concernèndo—*pp* missing
    (e) concernéi *or* concernètti; concernésti; concerné *or* concernètte; concernémmo; concernéste; concernérono *or* concernèttero

20

§134 **CONÓSCERE**—conoscèndo—conosciuto
    (e) conóbbi, conoscésti, conóbbe, conoscémmo, conoscéste, conóbbero

§135 **CONQUÌDERE**—conquidèndo—conquiso
    (e) conquisi, conquidésti, conquise, conquidémmo, conquidéste, conquìsero

§136 **CONSÙMERE**—*ger* missing—consunto
    (a) missing
    (b) missing
    (c) missing
    (d) missing
    (e) consunsi, consunse, consùnsero
    (f) missing

§137 **CONVÈRGERE**—convergèndo—convèrso
    (e) convèrsi *or* convergéi; convergésti; convèrse *or* convergé; convergémmo; convergéste; convèrsero *or* convergérono

§138 **CONVERTIRE**—convertèndo—convertito
    (e) convertìi *or* convèrsi; convertisti; convertì or convèrse; convertimmo; convertiste; convertìrono *or* convèrsero

§139 **CÓRRERE**—corrèndo—córso
    (e) córsi, corrésti, córse, corrémmo, corréste, córsero

§140 **COSTRUIRE**—costruèndo—costruito
    (a) costruisci, costruite
    (b) costruisco, costruisci, costruisce, costruiamo, costruite, costruìscono
    (c) costruisca, costruisca, costruisca, costruiamo, costruiate, costruìscano
    (e) costruìi *or* costrussi; costruisti; costruì *or* costrusse; costruimmo; costruiste; costruìrono *or* costrùssero

§141 **CRÉDERE**—credèndo—creduto
    (e) credéi *or* credètti; credésti; credé *or* credètte; credémmo; credéste; credérono *or* credèttero

§142 **CRÉSCERE**—crescèndo—cresciuto
    (e) crébbi, crescésti, crébbe, crescémmo, crescéste, crébbero

§143 **CUCIRE**—cucèndo—cucito
    (b) cùcio, cuci, cuce, cuciamo, cucite, cùciono
    (c) cùcia, cùcia, cùcia, cuciamo, cuciate, cùciano

§144a **CUÒCERE**—cuocèndo *or* cocèndo (cocènte)—còtto *or* cociuto

    (a) cuòci, cocéte
    (b) cuòcio, cuòci, cuòce, cociamo, cocéte, cuòciono
    (c) cuòcia, cuòcia, cuòcia, cociamo, cociate, cuòciano
    (d) cocévo, cocévi, cocéva, cocevamo, cocevate, cocévano
    (e) còssi, cocésti, còsse, cocémmo, cocéste, còssero
    (f) cocerò, cocerài, cocerà, cocerémo, coceréte, coceranno

§144b **DARE**—dando—dato
    (a) dà *or* dài *or* da'; date
    (b) dò *or* dò; dài; dà; diamo; date; danno
    (c) dìa, dìa, dìa, diamo, diate, dìano
    (e) dièdi *or* dètti; désti; dиède *or* dètte *or* diè; démmo;
        déste; dièdero *or* dèttero
    (f) darò, darài, darà, darémo, daréte, daranno

§145 **DECÌDERE**—decidèndo—deciso
    (e) decisi, decidésti, decise, decidémmo, decidéste, decìsero

§146 **DELÌNQUERE**—delinquèndo—*pp* missing
    (a) missing
    (c) missing
    (e) missing

§147 **DEVÒLVERE**—devolvèndo—devoluto
    (e) devolvéi *or* devolvètti; devolvésti; devolvé *or* devolvètte;
        devolvémmo; devolvéste; devolvérono *or* devolvèttero

§148 **DIFÈNDERE**—difendèndo—diféso
    (e) difési, difendésti, difése, difendémmo, difendéste,
        difésero

§149 **DILÌGERE**—diligèndo—dilètto
    (a) missing
    (b) missing
    (c) missing
    (d) missing
    (e) dilèssi, diligésti, dilèsse, diligémmo, diligéste, dilèssero
    (f) missing

§150 **DIPÈNDERE**—dipendèndo—dipéso
    (e) dipési, dipendésti, dipése, dipendémmo, dipendéste,
        dipésero

§151 **DIRE**—dicèndo—détto
    (a) di' *or* dì; dite
    (b) dico, dici, dice, diciamo, dite, dìcono
    (c) dica, dica, dica, diciamo, diciate, dìcano
    (d) dicévo, dicévi, dicéva, dicevamo, dicevate, dicévano
    (e) dissi, dicésti, disse, dicémmo, dicéste, dìssero
    (f) dirò, dirài, dirà, dirémo, diréte, diranno

§152 DIRÌGERE—dirigèndo—dirètto
   (e) dirèssi, dirigésti, dirèsse, dirigémmo, dirigéste, dirèssero

§153 DISCÈRNERE—discernèndo—*pp* missing
   (e) discernéi; discernésti; discerné *or* discernètte; discernémmo; discernéste; discernérono *or* discernèttero

§154 DISCÙTERE—discutèndo—discusso
   (e) discussi, discutésti, discusse, discutémmo, discutéste, discùssero

§155 DISSÒLVERE—dissolvèndo—dissòlto
   (e) dissòlsi *or* dissolvéi *or* dissolvètti; dissolvésti; dissòlse *or* dissolvé *or* dissolvètte; dissolvémmo; dissolvéste; dissòlsero *or* dissolvérono *or* dissolvèttero

§156 DISTÌNGUERE—distinguèndo—distinto
   (e) distinsi, distinguésti, distinse, distinguémmo, distinguéste, distìnsero

§157 DIVÈRGERE—divergèndo—*pp* missing
   (e) obsolete

§158 DIVÌDERE—dividèndo—diviso
   (e) divisi, dividésti, divise, dividémmo, dividéste, divìsero

§159 DOLÉRE—dolèndo—doluto
   (a) duòli, doléte
   (b) dòlgo, duòli, duòle, doliamo, doléte, dòlgono
   (c) dòlga, dòlga, dòlga, doliamo, doliate, dòlgano
   (e) dòlsi, dolésti, dòlse, dolémmo, doléste, dòlsero
   (f) dorrò, dorrài, dorrà, dorrémo, dorréte, dorranno

§160 DOVÉRE—dovèndo—dovuto
   (b) dèbbo *or* dèvo; dèvi; dève; dobbiamo; dovéte; dèbbono *or* dèvono
   (c) dèva *or* dèbba; dèva *or* dèbba; dèva *or* dèbba; dobbiamo; dobbiate; dèvano *or* dèbbano
   (e) dovéi *or* dovètti; dovésti; dové *or* dovètte; dovémmo; dovéste; dovérono *or* dovèttero

§161 ELÌDERE—elidèndo—eliso
   (e) elisi, elidésti, elise, elidémmo, elidéste, elìsero

§162 EMÈRGERE—emergèndo—emèrso
   (e) emèrsi, emergésti, emèrse, emergémmo, emergéste, emèrsero

§163 ÉMPIERE & EMPÌRE—empièndo—empito *or* empiuto
   (a) émpi, empite

23

    (b) émpio, émpi, émpie, empìamo, empite, émpiono
    (c) émpia, émpia, émpia, empiamo, empiate, émpiano
    (d) empivo, empivi, empiva, empivamo, empivate, em-
        pìvano
    (e) empiéi *or* empìi; empiésti; *or* empisti; empié *or* empì;
        empiémmo *or* empimmo; empiéste *or* empiste;
        empiérono *or* empìrono
    (f) empirò, empirài, empirà, empirémo, empiréte, em-
        piranno

§164 ÈRGERE—ergèndo—èrto
    (e) èrsi, ergésti, èrse, ergémmo, ergéste, èrsero

§165 ESÌGERE—esigèndo—esatto
    (e) esigéi *or* esigètti; esigésti; esigé *or* esigètte; esigémmo;
        esigéste; esigérono *or* esigèttero

§166 ESÌMERE—esimèndo—*pp* missing
    (e) esiméi *or* esimètti; esimésti; esimé *or* esimètte;
        esimémmo; esiméste; esimérono *or* esimèttero

§167 ESPÀNDERE—espandèndo—espanso
    (e) espandéi *or* espandètti *or* espansi; espandésti; espandé
        or espandètte *or* espanse; espandémmo; espandéste;
        espandérono *or* espandèttero *or* espànsero

§168 ESPÈLLERE—espellèndo—espulso
    (e) espulsi, espellésti, espulse, espellémmo, espelléste,
        espùlsero

§169 ESPLÒDERE—esplodèndo—esplòso
    (e) esplòsi, esplodésti, esplòse, esplodémmo, esplodéste,
        esplòsero

§170 ÈSSERE—essèndo—stato
    (a) sii, siate
    (b) sóno, sèi, è, siamo, sièto, sóno
    (c) sìa, sìa, sìa, siamo, siate, sìano
    (d) èro, èri, èra, eravamo, eravate, èrano
    (e) fui, fósti, fu, fummo, fóste, fùrono
    (f) sarò, sarài, sarà, sarémo, saréte, saranno

§171 ESTÒLLERE—estollèndo—*pp* missing
    (e) missing

§172 EVÀDERE—evadèndo—evaso
    (e) evasi, evadésti, evase, evadémmo, evadéste, evàsero

§173 FARE—facèndo—fatto
    (a) fa *or* fài *or* fa'; fate

(b) fàccio *or* fò; fài; fa; facciamo; fate; fanno
(c) fàccia, fàccia, fàccia, facciamo, facciate; fàcciano
(d) facévo, facévi, facéva, facevamo, facevate, facévano
(e) féci, facésti, féce, facémmo, facéste, fécero
(f) farò, faràì, farà, farémo, faréte, faranno

§174 **FÈNDERE**—fendèndo—fenduto *or* fésso
(e) fendéi *or* fendètti; fendésti; fendé *or* fendètte; fendémmo; fendéste; fendérono *or* fendèttero

§175 **FÈRVERE**—fervèndo—*pp* missing
(e) fervéi *or* fervètti; fervésti; fervé *or* fervètte; fervémmo; fervéste; fervérono *or* fervèttero

§176 **FINIRE**—finèndo—finito
(a) finisci, finite
(b) finisco, finisci, finisce, finiamo, finite, finìscono
(c) finisca, finisca, finisca, finiamo, finiate, finìscano

§177 **FLÈTTERE**—flettèndo—flèsso
(e) flettéi *or* flèssi; flettésti; fletté *or* flèsse; flettémmo; flettéste; flettérono *or* flèssero

§178 **FÓNDERE**—fondèndo—fuso
(e) fusi, fondésti, fuse, fondémmo, fondéste, fùsero

§179 **FRÀNGERE**—frangèndo—franto
(e) fransi, frangésti, franse, frangémmo, frangéste, frànsero

§180 **FRÌGGERE**—friggèndo—fritto
(e) frissi, friggésti, frisse, friggémmo, friggéste, frìssero

§181 **GIACÉRE**—giacèndo—giaciuto
(b) giàccio; giaci; giace; giacciamo *or* giaciamo; giacete; giàcciono
(c) giàccia, giàccia, giàccia, giacciamo, giacciate, giàcciano
(e) giàcqui, giacésti, giàcque, giacémmo, giacéste, giàcquero

§182 **GIOCARE**—giocando—giocato
(a) giuòca *or* giòca; giocate
(b) giuòco *or* giòco; giuòchi *or* giòchi; giuòca *or* giòca; giochiamo; giocate; giuòcano *or* giòcano
(c) giuòchi *or* giòchi; giuòchi *or* giòchi; giuòchi *or* giòchi; giochiamo; giochiate; giuòchino *or* giòchino
(f) giocherò, giocheràì, giocherà, giocherémo, giocheréte, giocheranno

§183 **GIÙNGERE**—giungèndo—giunto
(e) giunsi, giungésti, giunse, giungémmo, giungéste, giùnsero

25

§184 GODÉRE—godèndo—goduto
(e) godéi *or* godètti; godésti; godé *or* godètte; godémmo; godéste; godérono *or* godèttero
(f) godrò, godrài, godrà, godrémo, godréte, godranno

§185 IMBÉVERE—imbevèndo—imbevuto
(e) imbévvi, imbevésti, imbévve, imbevémmo, imbevéste, imbévvero

§186 INCÓMBERE—incombèndo—*pp* missing
(e) incombéi *or* incombètti; incombésti; incombé *or* incombètte; incombémmo; incombéste; incombérono *or* incombèttero

§187 INDÙLGERE—indulgèndo—indulto
(e) indulsi, indulgésti, indulse, indulgémmo, indulgéste, indùlsero

§188a INFERIRE—inferèndo—inferito *or* infèrto
(a) inferisci, inferite
(b) inferisco, inferisci, inferisce, inferiamo, inferite, inferìscono
(c) inferisca, inferisca, inferisca, inferiamo, inferiate, inferìscano
(e) inferìi *or* infèrsi; inferisti; inferì *or* infèrse; inferimmo; inferiste; inferìrono *or* infèrsero

§188b INSTARE—instando—*pp* missing

§189 INTRÌDERE—intridèndo—intriso
(e) intrisi, intridésti, intrise, intridémmo, intridéste, intrìsero

§190 INTRÙDERE—intrudèndo—intruso
(e) intrusi, intrudésti, intruse, intrudémmo, intrudéste, intrùsero

§191 IRE—*ger* missing—ito
(a) *sg* missing, ite
(b) missing
(c) missing
(d) ivo, ivi, iva, ìvamo, ìvate, ìvano
(e) *1st sg* missing, isti, *3rd sg* missing, *1st pl* missing, iste, ìrono

§192 LÈDERE—ledèndo—léso *or* lèso
(e) lési, ledésti, lése, ledémmo, ledéste, lésero

§193 LÈGGERE—leggèndo—lètto
(e) lèssi, leggésti, lèsse, leggémmo, leggéste, lèssero

§194 LIQUEFARE—liquefacèndo—liquefatto
 (a) liquefà, liquefate
 (b) liquefò or liquefàccio; liquefài; liquefà liquefacciamo;
     liquefate; liquefanno
 (c) liquefàccia, liquefàccia, liquefàccia, liquefacciamo,
     liquefacciate, liquefàcciano
 (d) liquefacévo, liquefacévi, liquefacéva, liquefacevamo,
     liquefacevate, liquefacévano
 (e) liqueféci, liquefacésti, liqueféce, liquefacémmo, lique-
     facéste, liquefécero
 (f) liquefarò, liquefarài, liquefarà, liquefarémo, liquefaréte,
     liquefaranno

§195 MALEDIRE—maledicèndo—maledétto
 (a) maledici, maledite
 (b) maledico, maledici, maledice, malediciamo, maledite,
     maledìcono
 (c) maledica, maledica, maledica, malediciamo, malediciate,
     maledìcano
 (d) maledicévo or maledivo; maledicévi or maledivi;
     maledicéva or malediva; maledicevamo or male-
     divamo; maledicevate or maledivate; maledicévano
     or maledìvano
 (e) maledìi or maledissi; maledisti or maledicésti; maledì
     or maledisse; maledimmo or maledicémmo; male-
     diste or maledicéste; maledìrono or maledìssero
 (f) maledirò, maledirài, maledirà, maledirémo, malediréte,
     malediranno

§196 MALVOLÉRE—*ger* missing—malvoluto
 (a) missing
 (b) missing
 (c) missing
 (d) missing
 (e) missing
 (f) missing

§197 MANCARE—mancando—mancato
 (b) manco, manchi, manca, manchiamo, mancate, màncano
 (c) manchi, manchi, manchi, manchiamo, manchiate,
     mànchino
 (f) mancherò, mancherài, mancherà, mancherémo, manche-
     réte, mancheranno

§198 MÉTTERE—mettèndo—mésso
 (e) misi, mettésti, mise, mettémmo, mettéste, mìsero

§199 MÌNGERE—mingèndo—minto
 (e) minsi, mingésti, minse, mingémmo, mingéste, mìnsero

§200 MÒRDERE—mordèndo—mòrso
    (e) mòrsi, mordésti, mòrse, mordémmo, mordéste, mòrsero

§201 MORIRE—morèndo—mòrto
    (a) muòri, morite
    (b) muòio, muòri, muòre, moriamo, morite, muòiono
    (c) muòia. muòia, muòia, moriamo, moriate, muòiano
    (f) morrò or morirò; morràì or moriràì; morrà or morirà;
        morrémo or morirémo; morréte or moriréte; mor-
        ranno or moriranno

§202 MUÒVERE—muovèndo or movèndo (movènte)—mòsso
    (a) muòvi, movéte
    (b) muòvo, muòvi, muòve, moviamo, movéte, muòvono
    (c) muòva, muòva, muòva, moviamo, moviate, muòvano
    (d) movévo, movévi, movéva, movevamo, movevate,
        movévano
    (e) mòssi, movésti, mòsse, movémmo, movéste, mòssero
    (f) moverò, moveràì, moverà, moverémo, moveréte, move-
        ranno

§203 NÀSCERE—nascèndo—nato
    (e) nàcqui, nascésti, nàcque, nascémmo, nascéste, nàcquero

§204 NASCÓNDERE—nascondèndo—nascósto
    (e) nascósi, nascondésti, nascóse, nascondémmo, nas-
        condéste, nascósero

§205 NEGLÌGERE—negligèndo—neglètto
    (a) missing
    (b) missing
    (c) missing
    (e) neglèssi, negligésti, neglèsse, negligémmo, negligéste,
        neglèssero

§206 NUÒCERE—nuocèndo—nociuto
    (a) nuòci, nocéte
    (b) nuòccio or nòccio; nuòci; nuòce; nociamo; nocéte;
        nuòcciono or nòcciono
    (c) nòccia, nòccia, nòccia, nociamo, nociate, nòcciano
    (d) nocévo, nocévi, nocéva, nocevamo, nocevate, nocévano
    (e) nòcqui, nocésti, nòcque, nocémmo, nocéste, nòcquero
    (f) nocerò, noceràì, nocerà, nocerémo, noceréte, noceranno

§207 OFFRIRE—offrèndo (offerènte)—offèrto
    (e) offrìì or offèrsi; offristi; offrì or offèrse; offrimmo;
        offriste; offrìrono or offèrsero

§208 OTTÙNDERE—ottundèndo—ottuso
    (e) ottusi, ottundésti, ottuse, ottundémmo, ottundéste,
        ottùsero

§209 PAGARE—pagando—pagato
(b) pago, paghi, paga, paghiamo, pagate, pàgano
(c) paghi, paghi, paghi, paghiamo, paghiate, pàghino
(f) pagherò, pagheràI, pagherà, pagherémo, pagheréte, pagheranno

§210 PARÉRE—parèndo (parvènte)—parso
(a) missing
(b) pàio; pari; pare; pariamo *or* paiamo; paréte; pàiono
(c) pàia; pàia; pàia; pariamo *or* paiamo; pariate *or* paiate; pàiano
(e) parvi, parésti, parve, parémmo, paréste, pàrvero
(f) parrò, parràI, parrà, parrémo, parréte, parranno

§211 PÀSCERE—pascèndo—pasciuto
(a) pascéi *or* pascètti; pascésti; pascé *or* pascètte; pascémmo; pascéste; pascérono *or* pascèttero

§212 PÈRDERE—perdèndo—pèrso *or* perduto
(e) perdéi *or* pèrsi *or* perdètti; perdésti; perdé, *or* pèrse *or* perdètte; perdémmo; perdéste; perdérono *or* pèrsero *or* perdèttero

§213 PERSUADÉRE—persuadèndo—persuaso
(e) persuasi, persuadésti, persuase, persuadémmo, persuadéste, persuàsero

§214 PIACÉRE—piacèndo—piaciuto
(b) piàccio, piaci, piace, piacciamo, piacéte, piàcciono
(c) piàccia, piàccia, piàccia, piacciamo, piacciate, piàcciano
(e) piàcqui, piacésti, piàcque, piacémmo, piacéste, piàcquero

§215 PIÀNGERE—piangèndo—pianto
(e) piansi, piangésti, pianse, piangémmo, piangéste, piànsero

§216 PIÒVERE—piovèndo—piovuto
(e) piòvvi, piovésti, piòvve, piovémmo, piovéste, piòvvero

§217 PÒRGERE—porgèndo—pòrto
(e) pòrsi, porgésti, pòrse, porgémmo, porgéste, pòrsero

§218 PÓRRE—ponèndo—pósto
(a) póni, ponéte
(b) póngo, póni, póne, poniamo, ponéte, póngono
(c) pónga, pónga, pónga, poniamo, poniate, póngano
(d) ponévo, ponévi, ponéva, ponevamo, ponevate, ponévano
(e) pósi, ponésti, póse, ponémmo, ponéste, pósero

§219 POTÉRE—potèndo (potènte *or* possènte)—potuto
(a) missing
(b) pòsso, puòi, può, possiamo, potéte, pòssono

(c) pòssa, pòssa, pòssa, possiamo, possiate, pòssano
(e) potéi or potètti; potésti, poté or potètte; potémmo; potéste; potérono or potèttero
(f) potrò, potrài, potrà, potrémo, potréte, potranno

§220 **PRÈNDERE**—prendèndo—préso
(e) prési, prendésti, prése, prendémmo, prendéste, présero

§221 **PROVVEDÉRE**—provvedèndo—provveduto or provvisto
(e) provvidi, provvedésti, provvide, provvedémmo, provvedéste, provvìdero

§222 **PRÙDERE**—prudèndo—*pp* missing
(e) *1st sg* missing; *2nd sg* missing; prudé or prudètte; *1st pl* missing; *2nd pl* missing; prudérono or prudèttero

§223 **RÀDERE**—radèndo—raso
(e) rasi, radésti, rase, radémmo, radéste, ràsero

§224 **REDÌGERE**—redigèndo—redatto
(e) redassi, redigésti, redasse, redigémmo, redigéste, redàssero

§225 **REDÌMERE**—redimèndo—redènto
(e) redènsi, redimésti, redènse, redimémmo, rediméste, redènsero

§226 **RÈGGERE**—reggèndo—rètto
(e) rèssi, reggésti, rèsse, reggémmo, reggéste, rèssero

§227 **RÈNDERE**—rendèndo—réso
(e) rési or rendéi or rendètti; rendésti; rése or rendé or rendètte; rendémmo; rendéste; résero or rendérono or rendèttero

§228 **RETROCÈDERE**—retrocedèndo—retrocèsso or retroceduto
(e) retrocèssi or retrocedéi or retrocedètti; retrocedésti; retrocèsse or retrocedé or retrocedètte; retrocedémmo; retrocedéste; retrocèssero or retrocedérono or retrocedèttero

§229 **RIAVÉRE**—riavèndo—riavuto
(a) riabbi, riabbiate
(b) riò, riài, rià, riabbiamo, riavéte, rianno
(c) riàbbia, riàbbia, riàbbia, riabbiamo, riabbiate, riàbbiano
(e) rièbbi, riavésti, rièbbe, riavémmo, riavéste, rièbbero
(f) riavrò, riavrài, riavrà, riavrémo, riavréte, riavranno

§230 **RIDARE**—ridando—ridato
(a) ridài or ridà; ridate
(b) ridò, ridài, ridà, ridiamo, ridate, ridanno
(c) ridìa, ridìa, ridìa, ridiamo, ridiate, ridìano

30

(e) ridièdi *or* ridètti; ridésti; ridiède *or* ridètte; ridémmo; ridéste; ridièdero *or* ridèttero

(f) ridarò, ridarài, ridarà, ridarémo, ridaréte, ridaranno

§231 RÌDERE—ridèndo—riso
(e) risi, ridésti, rise, ridémmo, ridéste, rìsero

§232 RIFLÈTTERE—riflettèndo—riflèsso *or* riflettuto

§233 RIFÙLGERE—rifulgèndo—rifulso
(e) rifulsi, rifulgésti, rifulse rifulgémmo, rifulgéste, rifùlsero

§234 RILÙCERE—rilucèndo—*pp* missing

§235 RIMANÉRE—rimanèndo—rimasto
(b) rimango, rimani, rimane, rimaniamo, rimanéte, rimàngono

(c) rimanga, rimanga, rimanga, rimaniamo, rimaniate, rimàngano

(e) rimasi, rimanésti, rimase, rimanémmo, rimanéste, rimàsero

(f) rimarrò, rimarrài, rimarrà, rimarrémo, rimarréte, rimarranno

§236 RINCORARE—rincorando—rincorato
(a) rincuòra, rincorate

(b) rincuòro, rincuòri, rincuòra, rincoriamo, rincorate, rincuòrano

(c) rincuòri, rincuòri, rincuòri, rincoriamo, rincoriate, rincuòrino

§237 RISOLARE—risolando—risolato
(a) risuòla, risolate

(b) risuòlo, risuòli, risuòla, risoliamo, risolate, risuòlano

(c) risuòli, risuòli, risuòli, risoliamo, risoliate, risuòlino

§238 RISPÓNDERE—rispondèndo—rispósto
(e) rispósi, rispondésti, rispóse, rispondémmo, rispondéste, rispósero

§239 RÓDERE—rodèndo—róso
(e) rósi, rodésti, róse, rodémmo, rodéste, rósero

§240 RÓMPERE—rompèndo—rótto
(e) ruppi, rompésti, ruppe, rompémmo, rompéste, rùppero

§241 ROTARE—rotando—rotato
(a) ruòta, rotate

(b) ruòto, ruòti, ruòta, rotiamo, rotate, ruòtano

(c) ruòti, ruòti, ruòti, rotiamo, rotiate, ruòtino

\

§242 SALIRE—salèndo—salito
  (b) salgo, sali, sale, saliamo, salite, sàlgono
  (c) salga, salga, salga, saliamo, saliate, sàlgano

§243 SAPÉRE—sapèndo (sapiènte)—saputo
  (a) sappi, sappiate
  (b) sò, sai, sa, sappiamo, sapéte, sanno
  (c) sàppia, sàppia, sàppia, sappiamo, sappiate, sàppiano
  (e) sèppi, sapésti, sèppe, sapémmo, sapéste, sèppero
  (f) saprò, saprài, saprà, saprémo, sapréte, sapranno

§244 SCÉGLIERE—sceglièndo—scélto
  (a) scégli, scegliéte
  (b) scélgo, scégli, scéglie, scegliamo, scegliéte, scélgono
  (c) scélga, scélga, scélga, scegliamo, scegliate, scélgano
  (e) scélsi, scegliésti, scélse, scegliémmo, scegliéste, scélsero

§245 SCÉNDERE—scendèndo—scéso
  (e) scési, scendésti, scése, scendémmo, scendéste, scésero

§246 SCÈRNERE—scernèndo—*pp* missing
  (e) scernéi *or* scernètti; scernésti; scerné *or* scernètte; scer-
      némmo; scernéste; scernérono *or* scernèttero

§247 SCÌNDERE—scindèndo—scisso
  (e) scissi, scindésti, scisse, scindémmo, scindéste, scìssero

§248 SCOIARE—scoiando—scoiato
  (a) scuòia, scoiate
  (b) scuòio, scuòi, scuòia, scoiamo, scoiate, scuòiano
  (c) scuòi, scuòi, scuòi, scoiamo, scoiate, scuòino

§249 SCÒRGERE—scorgèndo—scòrto
  (e) scòrsi, scorgésti, scòrse, scorgémmo, scorgéste, scòrsero

§250 SCRÌVERE—scrivèndo—scritto
  (e) scrissi, scrivésti, scrisse, scrivémmo, scrivéste, scrìssero

§251 SCUÒTERE—scotèndo—scòsso
  (a) scuòti, scotéte
  (b) scuòto, scuòti, scuòte, scotiamo, scotéte, scuòtono
  (c) scuòta, scuòta, scuòta, scotiamo, scotiate, scuòtano
  (d) scotévo, scotévi, scotéva, scotevamo, scotevate, scoté-
      vano
  (e) scòssi, scotésti, scòsse, scotémmo, scotéste, scòssero

§252 SEDÉRE—sedèndo—seduto
  (a) sièdi, sedéte
  (b) sièdo *or* sèggo; sièdi; sìede; sediamo; sedéte; sièdono
      or sèggono
  (c) sièda *or* sègga; sièda *or* sègga; sièda *or* sègga; sediamo;
      sediate; sièdano *or* sèggano
  (e) sedéi *or* sedètti; sedésti; sedé *or* sedètte; sedémmo;
      sedéste; sedérono *or* sedèttero

§253 SEPPELLIRE—seppellèndo—sepólto *or* seppellito
- (a) seppellisci, seppellite
- (b) seppellisco, seppellisci, seppellisce, seppelliamo, seppellite, seppellìscono
- (c) seppellisca, seppellisca, seppellisca, seppelliamo, seppelliate, seppellìscano

§254 SODDISFARE—soddisfacèndo—soddisfatto
- (a) soddisfa *or* soddisfài *or* soddisfa'
- (b) soddisfàccio *or* soddisfò *or* soddisfo; soddisfài *or* soddisfi; soddisfà *or* soddisfa; soddisfacciamo; soddisfate; soddisfanno *or* soddìsfano
- (c) soddisfàccia *or* soddisfi; soddisfàccia *or* soddisfi; soddisfàccia *or* soddisfi; soddisfacciamo; soddisfacciate; soddisfàcciano *or* soddìsfino
- (d) soddisfacévo, soddisfacévi, soddisfacéva, soddisfacevamo, soddisfacevate, soddisfacévano
- (e) soddisféci, soddisfacésti, soddisféce, soddisfacémmo, soddisfacéste, soddisfécero
- (f) soddisfarò, soddisfarài, soddisfarà, soddisfarémo, soddisfaréte, soddisfaranno

§255 SOLÉRE—solèndo—sòlito
- (a) missing
- (b) sòglio, suòli, suòle, sogliamo, soléte, sògliono
- (c) sòglia, sòglia, sòglia, sogliamo, sogliate, sògliano
- (e) missing
- (f) missing

§256 SÒLVERE—solvèndo—soluto
- (e) solvéi *or* solvètti; solvésti; solvé *or* solvètte; solvémmo; solvéste; solvérono *or* solvèttero

§257 SONARE—sonando—sonato
- (a) suòna, sonate
- (b) suòno, suòni, suòna, soniamo, sonate, suònano
- (c) suòni, suòni, suòni, soniamo, soniate, suònino

§258 SÓRGERE—sorgèndo—sórto
- (e) sórsi, sorgésti, sórse, sorgémmo, sorgéste, sórsero

§259 SOSPÈNDERE—sospendèndo—sospéso
- (e) sospési, sospendésti, sospése, sospendémmo, sospendéste, sospésero

§260 SPÀNDERE—spandèndo—spanto
- (e) spandéi *or* spandètti *or* spansi; spandésti; spandé *or* spandètte *or* spanse; spandémmo; spandéste; spandérono *or* spandèttero *or* spànsero

§261 SPÀRGERE—spargèndo—sparso
- (e) sparsi, spargésti, sparse, spargémmo, spargéste, spàrsero

§262 SPÈGNERE—spegnèndo—spènto
- (b) spéngo *or* spèngo; spégni *or* spègni; spégne *or* spègne; spegniamo; spegnéte; spéngono *or* spèngono
- (c) spénga *or* spènga; spénga *or* spènga; spénga *or* spènga; spegniamo; spegniate; spéngano *or* spèngano
- (e) spènsi, spegnésti, spènse, spegnémmo, spegnéste, spènsero

§263 STARE—stando—stato
- (a) sta *or* stai *or* sta'; state
- (b) stò, stài, sta, stiamo, state, stanno
- (c) stìa, stìa, stìa, stiamo, stiate, stìano
- (e) stètti, stésti, stètte, stémmo, stéste, stèttero
- (f) starò, starài, starà, starémo, staréte, staranno

§264 STRÌDERE—stridèndo—*pp* missing
- (e) stridéi *or* stridètti; stridésti; stridé *or* stridètte; stridémmo; stridéste; stridérono *or* stridèttero

§265 STRÌNGERE—stringèndo—strétto
- (e) strinsi, stringésti, strinse, stringémmo, stringéste, strìnsero

§266 STRÙGGERE—struggèndo—strutto
- (e) strussi, struggésti, strusse, struggémmo, struggéste, strùssero

§267 SVÈLLERE—svellèndo—svèlto
- (b) svèllo *or* svèlgo; svèlli; svèlle; svelliamo; svelléte; svèllono *or* svèlgono
- (c) svèlla *or* svèlga; svèlla *or* svèlga; svèlla *or* svèlga; svelliamo; svelliate; svèllano *or* svèlgano
- (e) svèlsi, svellésti, svèlse, svellémmo, svelléste, svèlsero

§268 TACÉRE—tacèndo—taciuto
- (b) tàccio, taci, tace, taciamo, tacéte, tàcciono
- (c) tàccia, tàccia, tàccia, taciamo, taciate, tàcciano
- (e) tàcqui, tacésti, tàcque, tacémmo, tacéste, tàcquero

§269 TÀNGERE—tangèndo—*pp* missing
- (a) missing
- (b) *1st sg* missing; *2nd sg* missing; tange; *1st pl* missing; *2nd pl* missing; tàngono
- (c) *1st sg* missing; *2nd sg* missing; tanga; *1st pl* missing; *2nd pl* missing; tàngano
- (d) *1st sg* missing; *2nd sg* missing; tangéva; *1st pl* missing; *2nd pl* missing; tangévano
- (e) missing
- (f) *1st sg* missing; *2nd sg* missing; tangerà; *1st pl* missing; *2nd pl* missing; tangeranno

§270 TÈNDERE—tendèndo—téso
(e) tési, tendésti, tése, tendémmo, tendéste, tésero

§271 TENÉRE—tenèndo—tenuto
(a) tièni, tenéte
(b) tèngo, tièni, tiène, teniamo, tenéte, tèngono
(c) tènga, tènga, tènga, teniamo, teniate, tèngano
(e) ténni, tenésti, ténne, tenémmo, tenéste, ténnero
(f) terrò, terrài, terrà, terrémo, terréte, terranno

§272 TÒRCERE—torcèndo—tòrto
(e) tòrsi, torcésti, tòrse, torcémmo, torcéste, tòrsero

§273 TRARRE—traèndo—tratto
(a) trài, traéte
(b) traggo, trài, trae, traiamo, traéte, tràggono
(c) tragga, tragga, tragga, traiamo, traiate, tràggano
(d) traévo, traévi, traéva, traevamo, traevate, traévano
(e) trassi, traésti, trasse, traémmo, traéste, tràssero

§274 UCCÌDERE—uccidèndo—ucciso
(e) uccisi, uccidésti, uccise, uccidémmo, uccidéste, uccìsero

§275 UDIRE—udèndo *or* udièndo—udito
(a) òdi, udite
(b) òdo, òdi, òde, udiamo, udite, òdono
(c) òda, òda, òda, udiamo, udiate, òdano
(f) udirò *or* udrò; udirài *or* udrài; udirà *or* udrà; udirémo *or* udrémo; udiréte *or* udréte; udiranno *or* udranno

§276 ÙRGERE—urgèndo—*pp* missing
(a) missing
(e) missing

§277 USCIRE—uscèndo—uscito
(a) èsci, uscite
(b) èsco, èsci, èsce, usciamo, uscite, èscono
(c) èsca, èsca, èsca, usciamo, usciate, èscano

§278 VALÉRE—valèndo—valso
(b) valgo, vali, vale, valiamo, valéte, vàlgono
(c) valga, valga, valga, valiamo, valiate, vàlgano
(e) valsi, valésti, valse, valémmo, valéste, vàlsero
(f) varrò, varrài, varrà, varrémo, varréte, varranno

§279 VEDÉRE—vedèndo—veduto *or* visto
(e) vidi, vedésti, vide, vedémmo, vedéste, vìdero
(f) vedrò, vedrài, vedrà, vedrémo, vedréte, vedranno

§280 VEGLIARE—vegliando—vegliato
(b) véglio, végli, véglia, vegliamo, vegliate, végliano
(c) végli, végli, végli, vegliamo, vegliate, véglino

§281 VÉNDERE—vendèndo—venduto
  (e) vendéi *or* vendètti; vendésti; vendé *or* vendètte; ven-
      démmo; vendéste; vendérono *or* vendèttero

§282 VENIRE—venèndo (veniènte)—venuto
  (a) vièni, venite
  (b) vèngo, vièni, vième, veniamo, venite, vèngono
  (c) vènga, vènga, vènga, veniamo, veniate, vèngano
  (e) vénni, venisti, vénne, venimmo, veniste, vénnero
  (f) verrò, verrài, verrà, verrémo, verréte, verranno

§283 VÈRTERE—vertèndo—*pp* missing

§284 VÌGERE—vigèndo—*pp* missing
  (a) missing
  (b) *1st sg* missing; *2nd sg* missing; vige; *1st pl* missing;
      2d pl missing; vìgono
  (c) *1st sg* missing; *2d sg* missing; viga; *1st pl* missing;
      2d pl missing; vìgano
  (d) *1st sg* missing; *2d sg* missing; vigéva; *1st pl* missing;
      2d pl missing; vigévano
  (e) missing

§285 VÌNCERE—vincèndo—vinto
  (e) vinsi, vincésti, vinse, vincémmo, vincéste, vìnsero

§286 VÌVERE—vivèndo—vissuto
  (e) vissi, vivésti, visse, vivémmo, vivéste, vìssero
  (f) vivrò, vivrài, vivrà, vivrémo, vivréte, vivranno

§287 VIZIARE—viziando—viziato
  (b) vìzio, vizi, vìzia, viziamo, viziate, vìziano
  (c) vizi, vizi, vizi, viziamo, viziate, vìzino

§288 VOLÉRE—volèndo—voluto
  (a) vògli, vogliate
  (b) vòglio, vuòi, vuòle, vogliamo, voléte, vògliono
  (c) vòglia, vòglia, vòglia, vogliamo, vogliate, vògliano
  (e) vòlli, volésti, vòlle, volémmo, voléste, vòllero
  (f) vorrò, vorrài, vorrà, vorrémo, vorréte, vorranno

§289 VÒLGERE—volgèndo—vòlto
  (e) vòlsi, volgésti, vòlse, volgémmo, volgéste, vòlsero

§290 VOLTEGGIARE—volteggiando—volteggiato
  (b) voltéggio, voltéggi, voltéggia, volteggiamo, volteggiate,
      voltéggiano
  (c) voltéggi, voltéggi, voltéggi, volteggiamo, volteggiate,
      voltéggino
  (f) volteggerò, volteggerài, volteggerà, volteggerémo, vol-
      teggeréte, volteggeranno

A

A, a [α] *m & f* first letter of the Italian alphabet

a *prep* (**ad** in front of a vowel) to, e.g., **diede il libro a Giovanni** he gave the book to John; in, e.g., **a Milano** in Milan; at, e.g., **a casa** at home; within, e.g., **a tre miglia da qui** within three miles from here; on, e.g., **portare una catena al collo** to wear a chain on one's neck; e.g., **al sabato** on Saturdays; for, e.g., **a vita** for life; by, e.g., **fatto a mano** made by hand; with, e.g., **una gonna a pieghe** a skirt with pleats; as, e.g., **eleggere a presidente** to elect as chairman; into, e.g., **fu gettato a mare** he was thrown into the sea; of, e.g., **un quarto alle due** fifteen minutes of two

àba·co *m* (**-chi**) (archit) abacus

abate *m* abbot

abbacchiare §287 *tr* to knock down (*e.g., olives*); to sell too cheap ‖ *ref* to lose courage; to be dejected

abbacchia·to -ta *adj* (coll) dejected

abbàc·chio *m* (**-chi**) baby lamb (*slaughtered*)

abbacinare (**abbàcino**) *tr* to dazzle; to deceive

abbadéssa *f* var of **badessa**

abbagliante *adj* dazzling ‖ *m* (aut) bright light, high beam

abbagliare §280 *tr* to dazzle; to deceive; to blind (*with the lights of a car*)

abbà·glio *m* (**-gli**) error; **prendere abbaglio** to make a mistake

abbaiaménto *m* bark (*of dog*)

abbaiare §287 *intr* to bark; to yelp

abbaino *m* dormer window; skylight; attic

abbambinare *tr* to walk (*a heavy piece of furniture*)

abbandonare (**abbandóno**) *tr* to abandon; to give up; to let go (*e.g., the reins*); to let fall; (sports) to withdraw from ‖ *ref* to yield; to lose courage

abbandóno *m* abandon, abandonment; desertion; neglect; relaxation; renunciation (*of a right*); cession (*of property*); withdrawal (*from a fight*)

abbarbicare §197 (**abbàrbico**) *intr & ref* to cling; to hold on

abbassalin·gua *m* (**-gua**) tongue depressor

abbassaménto *m* lowering; reduction; drop, fall

abbassare *tr* to lower; to dim (*lights*); to turn (*the radio*) lower; **abbassare le armi** to surrender; **abbassare la cresta** to yield ‖ *ref* to lower oneself; to drop

abbas·so *m* (**-so**) angry shout (*of a crowd*) ‖ *adv* down, below; downstairs ‖ *interj* down with!

abbastanza *adj invar* enough ‖ *adv* enough; rather, fairly

abbàttere *tr* to demolish; to fell; to shoot down; to refute (*an argument*); to depress ‖ *ref* to be depressed, be downcast

abbattiménto *m* demolition; felling; shooting down; chill; (fig) depression; **abbattimento alla base** (econ) basic exemption (*from taxes*)

abbattu·to -ta *adj* dejected, downcast ‖ *f* clearing (*of trees*)

abbazìa *f* abbey; abbacy

abbecedà·rio *m* (**-ri**) speller, primer

abbelliménto *m* embellishment, ornamentation

abbellire §176 *tr* to embellish, adorn; to landscape

abbeverare (**abbévero**) *tr* to water (*animals*) ‖ *ref* to quench one's thirst

abbevera·tóio *m* (**-tói**) watering trough

abbic·cì *m* (**-cì**) alphabet; speller; primer; ABC's, rudiments

abbiènte *adj* well-to-do ‖ *m*—**gli abbienti** the haves; **gli abbienti e nullatenenti** the haves and the have-nots

abbiettézza or **abiettézza** *f* abjectness, baseness

abbièt·to -ta or **abièt·to -ta** *adj* abject, base, low

abbiezióne or **abiezióne** *f* wretchedness, baseness

abbigliaménto *m* attire, wear

abbigliare §280 *tr & ref* to dress; to dress up

abbinaménto *m* coupling; merger

abbinare *tr* to couple; to join, merge

abbindolare (**abbìndolo**) *tr* to dupe, deceive

abbiosciare §128 *ref* to fall down; to lose heart, be downcast

abbisognare (**abbisógno**) *intr* to be in need

abboccaménto *m* interview, conversation

abboccare §197 (**abbócco**) *tr* to swallow (*the hook*); to fit (*pipes*) ‖ *intr* to bite (*said of fish*); to fall; to fit (*said of pipes*) ‖ *ref* to confer

abbocca·to -ta *adj* palatable; slightly sweet (*wine*)

abbonacciare §128 *ref* to calm down, abate (*said of weather*)

abbonaménto *m* subscription; **abbonamento postale** mailing permit

abbonare (**abbòno**) *tr* to take out a subscription for (*s.o.*) ‖ *ref* to subscribe ‖ §257 *tr* to remit (*a debt*); to forgive

abbona·to -ta *mf* subscriber; commuter

abbondante *adj* abundant, plentiful; heavy (*rain*)

abbondanza *f* abundance, plenty

abbondare (**abbóndo**) *intr* (ESSERE & AVERE) to abound; to exceed; **abbondare di** or **in** to abound in

abbonire §176 *tr* to calm; to placate ‖ *ref* to calm down

abbordàbile *adj* accessible, approachable; negotiable (*curve*)

abbordàg·gio *m* (**-gi**) boarding (*of an enemy ship*); **andare all'abbordaggio di** to board

abbordare (**abbórdo**) *tr* to board (*an enemy ship*); to negotiate (*a curve*); to face (*a problem*); (fig) to button-hole

abborracciare §128 *tr* to botch, bungle

abborracciatura *f* botch, bungle

abbottonare (**abbottóno**) *tr* to button || *ref* (coll) to keep to oneself

abbottonatura *f* buttoning; row of buttons

abbozzare (**abbòzzo**) *tr* to sketch; to hew (*e.g., a statue*); (naut) to tie up || *intr* (coll) to take it

abbòzzo *m* sketch, draft

abbracciabò·sco *m* (**-schi**) (bot) woodbine

abbracciare *m* embrace, embracing || §128 *tr* to embrace, hug; to seize (*an opportunity*); to become converted to (*e.g., Christianity*); to enter (*a profession*); to span, encompass || *ref* to cling; to embrace one another

abbràc·cio *m* (**-ci**) embrace, hug

abbrancare §197 *tr* to grab; to herd || *ref* to cling; to join a herd

abbreviaménto *m* abbreviation, shortening

abbreviare §287 (**abbrèvio**) *tr* to abbreviate, shorten, abridge

abbreviatura *f* shortening, abridgment

abbreviazióne *f* abbreviation

abbrivo or **abbrivio** *m* headway (*of a ship*); **prendere l'abbrivio** to gather momentum

abbronzante [dz] *adj* suntanning || *m* suntan lotion

abbronzare [dz] (**abbrónzo**) *tr & ref* to bronze; to tan

abbronza·to -ta [dz] *adj* tanned, suntanned

abbronzatura [dz] *f* tan, suntan

abbruciacchiare §287 *tr* to singe

abbrunare *tr* to brown; to hang crepe on || *ref* to wear mourning

abbrunire §176 *tr* to turn brown; to tan; to burnish

abbrustolire §176 *tr* to toast; to singe || *ref* to tan; to become sunburned

abbrutiménto *m* degradation, brutishness

abbrutire §176 *tr* to degrade; to brutalize || *intr & ref* to become brutalized

abbuiare §287 *tr* to darken; to hush up, hide || *ref* to grow dark; to become gloomy || *impers*—**abbuia** it's growing dark

abbuòno *m* allowance, discount; handicap (*in racing*)

abburattaménto *m* sifting

abburattare *tr* to sift, bolt

abdicare §197 (**àbdico**) *tr & intr* to abdicate; **abdicare a** to give up, renounce; to abdicate (*e.g., the throne*)

abdicazióne *f* abdication

aberrare (**abèrro**) *intr* to deviate

aberrazióne *f* aberration

abéte *m* fir

abetina *f* forest of fir trees

abiàti·co *m* (**-ci**) (coll) grandson

abièt·to -ta *adj* abject, base, low

abigeato *m* (law) cattle rustling

àbile *adj* able, clever, capable; (mil) fit

abili·tà *f* (**tà**) ability, skill

abilitare (**abìlito**) *tr* to certify (*e.g., a teacher*); to qualify, license

abilita·to -ta *adj* certified (*teacher*)

abilitazióne *f* qualification; certification (*of teachers*)

abissale *adj* abysmal

Abissinia, l' *f* Abyssinia

abissi·no -na *adj & mf* Abyssinian

abisso *m* abyss; fountain (*of knowledge*); slough (*of degradation*)

abitàbile *adj* inhabitable

abitàcolo *m* (aer) cockpit; (aut) cab, interior; (naut) compass bowl; **abitacolo eiettabile** (aer) ejection capsule

abitante *mf* inhabitant; resident

abitare (**àbito**) *tr* to inhabit; to occupy || *intr* to dwell, live, reside

abitati·vo -va *adj* living, e.g., **condizioni abitative** living conditions

abita·to -ta *adj* inhabited, populated || *m* built-up area

abita·tóre -trice *mf* dweller

abitazióne *f* dwelling; housing

àbito *m* suit (*for men*); dress (*for women*); garb, attire; habit; **abiti clothes**; **abito da ballo** evening gown; **abito da cerimonia** formal dress; **abito da inverno** winter suit; winter clothes; **levarsi l'abito** to doff the cassock; **prender l'abito** to enter the Church

abituale *adj* habitual

abituare (**abìtuo**) *tr* to accustom || *ref* to grow accustomed

abitudinà·rio -ria *adj* (**-ri -rie**) set in his ways

abitùdine *f* habit, custom

abituro *m* (poet) shanty, hut

abiura *f* abjuration

abiurare *tr* to abjure

ablati·vo -va *adj & m* ablative

ablazióne *f* (med) removal; (geol) erosion

abluzióne *f* ablution

abnegare §209 (**abnégo & abnègo**) *tr* to renounce, abnegate

abnegazióne *f* abnegation, self-denial

abnòrme *adj* abnormal

abolire §176 *tr* to abolish

abolizióne *f* abolition

abominàbile *adj* abominable

abominare (**abòmino**) *tr* to abominate, detest

abominazióne *f* abomination

abominévole *adj* abominable

aborìge·no -na *adj* aboriginal || *m* aborigine; **aborigeni** aborigines

aborrire §176 & (**abòrro**) *tr* to abhor, loathe || *intr*—**aborrire da** to shun, shrink from

abortire §176 *intr* to abort

abòrto *m* abortion, miscarriage; **aborto di natura** monstrosity

abrasióne *f* abrasion; erosion

abrasi·vo -va *adj & m* abrasive

abrogare §209 (**àbrogo**) *tr* to abrogate

abrogazióne *f* abrogation

abruzzése *adj* of the Abruzzi ‖ *mf* person of the Abruzzi ‖ *m* dialect of the Abruzzi

àbside *f* (archit) apse

abusare *intr*—**abusare di** to go to excesses in (*e.g., smoking*); to take advantage of; to impose on

abusi·vo -va *adj* illegal, abusive; unwarranted

abuso *m* abuse, excess

acà·cia *f* (-**cie**) acacia

acanto *m* acanthus

àcaro *m* (ent) acarus, mite, tick; **acaro della scabbia** itch mite

ac·ca *m & f* (-**ca** or -**che**) h (*letter*); **non valere un'acca** (coll) to not be worth a fig

accadèmia *f* academy

accadèmi·co -ca (-**ci** -**che**) *adj* academic ‖ *mf* academician

accadére §121 *intr* (ESSERE) to happen, occur

accadu·to -ta *adj* happened, occurred ‖ *m* fact, event; what has taken place

accagliare §280 *tr*, *intr* (ESSERE) & *ref* to curdle, coagulate

accalappiaca·ni *m* (-**ni**) dogcatcher

accalappiare §287 *tr* to catch (*a dog*); to snare; (fig) to fool

accalcare §197 *tr* to crowd ‖ *ref* to throng

accaldare *ref* to get hot; to become flushed

accalda·to -ta *adj* hot; perspired

accalorare (**accalóro**) *tr* to excite ‖ *ref* to get excited

accalora·to -ta *adj* excited, animated

accampaménto *m* encampment, camp; camping

accampare *tr* to encamp; to advance, lay (*a claim*) ‖ *ref* to camp, encamp

accaniménto *m* animosity, bitterness; obstinacy, stubbornness

accanire §176 *ref* to persist; to work doggedly; **accanirsi contro** to harass

accani·to -ta *adj* obstinate, persistent; furious; fierce, ruthless, bitter (*fight*)

accanto *adv* near, nearby; **accanto a** near

accantonaménto *m* tabling (*e.g., of a discussion*); reserve (*of money*); (mil) billeting; (sports) camping

accantonare (**accantóno**) *tr* to set aside (*money*); (mil) to billet

accaparraménto *m* cornering (*of market*)

accaparrare *tr* to corner (*merchandise*); to hoard; to put a down payment on (*e.g., a house*); (coll) to gain (*somebody's affection*)

accaparra·tóre -trice *mf* monopolizer, hoarder

accapigliare §280 *ref* to pull each other's hair; to scuffle; to come to blows

accapo or **a capo** *m* paragraph

accappa·tóio *m* (-**tói**) bathrobe

accapponare (**accappóno**) *tr* to castrate (*a rooster*) ‖ *ref* to wrinkle; **mi si accappona la pelle** I get gooseflesh

accarezzare (**accarézzo**) *tr* to caress, fondle; to pet; to nurture (*e.g., a*

hope); **accarezzare le spalle di** to strike; to club

accartocciare §128 (**accartòccio**) *tr* to wrap up in a cone ‖ *ref* to curl up

accartoccia·to -ta *adj* curled up

accasare [s] *tr & ref* to marry

accasciaménto *m* dejection

accasciare §128 *tr* to weaken, enfeeble; to depress ‖ *ref* to weaken; to lose heart

accasermare [s] (**accasèrmo**) *tr* to quarter, billet

accatastare *tr* to register (*real estate*); to pile, heap up

accattabri·ghe *mf* (-**ghe**) quarrelsome person, scrapper

accattare *tr* to beg for; to borrow (*e.g., ideas*) ‖ *intr* to beg

accattonàg·gio *m* (-**gi**) begging, mendicancy

accattó·ne -na *mf* mendicant, beggar

accavalcare §197 *tr* to straddle; to go over

accavalciare §128 *tr* to bestride

accavallare *tr* to superimpose; to cross (*one's legs*) ‖ *ref* to pour forward, run high (*said of waves*)

accecaménto *m* blinding

accecare §122 *tr* to blind; to countersink ‖ *intr* (ESSERE) to become blind ‖ *ref* to blind oneself

acceca·tóio *m* (-**tói**) countersink

accèdere §100 *intr* (ESSERE) to enter, approach; to accede

acceleraménto *m* acceleration

accelerare (**accèlero**) *tr & intr* to accelerate

accelera·to -ta *adj* accelerated; intensive (*course*); local (*train*) ‖ *m* local train

acceleratóre *m* accelerator

accelerazióne *f* acceleration

accèndere §101 *tr* to kindle; to turn on (*e.g., the light*); to light (*e.g., a match, a cigar*) ‖ *ref* to catch fire; to become lit; **accendersi in viso** to become flushed

accendisìgaro *m* lighter

accendi·tóio *m* (-**tói**) candle lighter

accenditóre *m* lighter

accennare (**accénno**) *tr* to nod; to point at; to sketch ‖ *intr* to refer; to hint

accénno *m* nod; sign; allusion

accensióne *f* lighting, kindling; (aut) ignition; (law) contraction (*of a debt*); **accensione improvvisa** spontaneous combustion

accentare (**accènto**) *tr* to accent

accènto *m* accent; stress; (poet) accent (*word*); **accento tonico** stress accent

accentraménto *m* centralization

accentrare (**accèntro**) *tr* to concentrate, centralize

accentuare (**accèntuo**) *tr* to accentuate ‖ *ref* to become aggravated

accentuazióne *f* accentuation

accerchiaménto *m* encirclement

accerchiare §287 (**accérchio**) *tr* to encircle, surround

accertàbile *adj* verifiable

accertaménto *m* ascertainment, verification; determination (*e.g., of taxes*)

accertare (accèrto) *tr* to assure; to ascertain, verify; to determine (*the tax due*) || *ref* to make sure

accé·so -sa [s] *adj* lit; turned on; on (*e.g., radio*); excited, aroused; bright (*color*)

accessìbile *adj* accessible; moderate (*price*)

accessióne *f* accession

accèsso *m* access, approach; admittance, entry; fit (*of anger, of coughing*)

accessò·rio -ria (-ri -rie) *adj* accessory || *m* accessory; (mach) accessory, attachment

accétta *f* hatchet, axe, cleaver; **tagliato con l'accetta** rough-hewn

accettàbile *adj* acceptable

accettare (accètto) *tr* to accept

accettazióne *f* acceptance; receiving room; (econ) acceptance

accèt·to -ta *adj* agreeable; welcome; **male accetto** unwelcome

accezióne *f* meaning, acceptation

acchiappafarfal·le *m* (-le) butterfly net

acchiappamó·sche *m* (-sche) fly catcher

acchiappare *tr* to grab, seize; (coll) to catch in the act

acchito *m* (billiards) break; **di primo acchito** at first

acciaccare §197 *tr* to crush; to trample upon; (coll) to lay low (*e.g., by illness*)

acciac·co *m* (-chi) illness, infirmity, ailment

acciaiare §287 *tr* to convert into steel; to strengthen with steel

acciaierìa *f* steel mill, steelworks

ac·ciàio *m* (-ciài) steel; **acciaio inossidabile** stainless steel

acciaiòlo *m* whetstone

acciambellare (acciambèllo) *tr* to shape in the form of a doughnut || *ref* to curl up

acciarino *m* flintlock; linchpin; (nav) war nose (*of a torpedo*)

accidèmpoli *interj* (slang) darn it!

accidentale *adj* accidental

accidenta·to -ta *adj* paralyzed; uneven, rough (*road*); broken (*ground*)

accidènte *m* accident; crack-up; (coll) paralytic stroke; (coll) hoot, fig; (coll) pest, menace (*child*); (mus) accidental; **accidenti!** (coll) darn!, damn!; **correre come un accidente** to run like the devil; **mandare un accidente a** to wish ill luck to; **per accidente** perchance

accidia *f* sloth

accidió·so -sa [s] *adj* slothful

accigliare §280 *ref* to frown, knit one's brow

accìngere §126 *ref*—**accingersi a** to get ready to

-àccio -àccia *suf adj & mf* (-acci -acce) no good, e.g., **gentaccia** no good people; good-for-nothing, e.g., **ragazzaccio** good-for-nothing boy

acciò or **acciocché** *conj* (poet) so that

acciottolare (acciòttolo) *tr* to pave with cobblestones

acciottola·to -ta *adj* cobblestone || *m* cobblestone pavement

acciottolì·o *m* (-ì) clatter (*e.g., of dishes*)

accipìcchia *interj* (coll) darn it!

acciuffare *tr* to seize, grab, pinch (*a thief*)

acciu·ga *f* (-ghe) anchovy

acclamare *tr* to acclaim || *intr* to voice one's approval

acclamazióne *f* acclamation

acclimatare (acclìmato) *tr & ref* to acclimate

acclimatazióne *f* acclimatation

acclive *adj* (poet) steep

acclivi·tà *f* (-tà) acclivity

acclùdere §105 *tr* to enclose

acclu·so -sa *adj* enclosed

accoccare §197 (accòcco & accócco) *tr* (poet) to nock (*the arrow*)

accoccolare (accòccolo) *ref* to squat down

accodare (accódo) *tr* to line up || *ref* to line up, queue

accogliènte *adj* cozy, hospitable, inviting

accogliènza *f* reception, welcome

accògliere §127 *tr* to receive; to welcome; to grant (*a request*) || *ref* (poet) to gather

accoglitrice *f* receptionist

accòlito *m* acolyte, altar boy; follower

accollare (accòllo) *tr* to overload (*a cart*); **accollare qlco a qlcu** to charge s.o. with s.th || *intr* to go up to the neck (*said of a dress*) || *ref* to assume, take upon oneself

accolla·to -ta *adj* high-necked (*dress*); high-cut (*shoes*) || *f* accolade

accollatura *f* neck, neckhole

accòlta *f* (poet) gathering

accoltellare (accoltèllo) *tr* to knife

accomandante *m* limited partner

accomandatà·rio *m* (-ri) (law) general partner

accomàndita *f* (law) limited partnership

accomiatare *tr* to dismiss || *ref* to take leave

accomodaménto *m* arrangement; compromise; settlement

accomodante *adj* accommodating, obliging

accomodare (accòmodo) *tr* to arrange; to fix; to settle || *intr* to be convenient || *ref* to adapt oneself; to agree; to sit down; **si accomodi** have a seat, make yourself comfortable

accomodatura *f* arrangement; repair

accompagnaménto *m* retinue; cortege; (mus) accompaniment; (law) writ of mandamus; (mil) softening-up (*by gunfire*)

accompagnare *tr* to accompany; to escort; to follow; to match || *ref*—**accompagnarsi a** or **con** to join

accompagna·tóre -trice *mf* escort; guide; (mus) accompanist

accomunare *tr* to mingle, mix; to unite, associate; to share

acconciaménto *m* arrangement

acconciare §128 (accóncio) *tr* to prepare for use; to arrange; to set (*e.g., the hair*) || *ref* to adorn oneself; to dress one's hair; to adapt oneself

acconcia·tóre -trice *mf* hairdresser

acconciatura *f* hairdo; headdress
accón·cio -cia *adj* (**-ci -ce**) proper, fitting
accondiscendènte *adj* acquiescing, acquiescent
accondiscendènza *f* acquiescence
accondiscéndere §245 *intr* to acquiesce, consent; to yield
acconsentire (**acconsènto**) *intr* to consent, acquiesce
acconsenziènte *adj* consenting, acquiescing
accontentare (**accontènto**) *tr* to satisfy, please ‖ *ref* to be satisfied, be pleased
accónto *m* installment
accoppare (**accòppo**) *tr* (coll) to kill; (coll) to beat to death ‖ *ref* (coll) to get killed
accoppiaménto *m* pairing; mating; (mach) parallel operation
accoppiare §287 (**accòppio**) *tr* to couple, pair, cross (*e.g., animals*) ‖ *ref* to mate, copulate
accoppiata *f* daily double (*in races*)
accoraménto *m* sadness, sorrow
accorare (**accòro**) *tr* to stab to death; to sadden ‖ *ref* to sadden, grieve
accora·to -ta *adj* saddened, grieving
accorciare §128 (**accórcio**) *tr & ref* to shorten; to shrink
accorciatura *f* shortening; shrinking
accordare (**accòrdo**) *tr* to harmonize (*colors*); to reconcile (*people*); to tune up; to grant; (gram) to make agree ‖ *ref* to agree; to match
accorda·to -ta *adj* tuned up ‖ *m* (econ) credit limit
accorda·tóre -trice *mf* (mus) tuner
accordatura *f* tuning
accòrdo *m* agreement, accordance; (law) mutual consent; (mus) harmony; **d'accordo** O.K., agreed; **d'accordo con** in accord with; **di comune accordo** with one accord; **essere d'accordo** to agree; **mettersi d'accordo** to come to an agreement
accòrgere §249 *ref* to perceive, notice; **accorgersi di** to become aware of, realize; **senza accorgersi** inadvertently
accorgiménto *m* smartness; device, trick
accórrere §139 *intr* (ESSERE) to run up, rush up
accortézza *f* alertness; shrewdness, perspicacity
accòr·to -ta *adj* alert; shrewd, perspicacious
accosciare §128 (**accòscio**) *ref* to squat
accostàbile *adj* approachable
accostaménto *m* approach; combination (*e.g., of colors*)
accostare (**accòsto**) *tr* to approach; to bring near; to leave (*a door*) ajar ‖ *intr* to be near; to cling, adhere; (naut) to come alongside; (naut) to maneuver alongside a pier; (naut) to change direction, haul ‖ *ref* to approach, come near; to cling (*e.g., to a faith*)
accosta·to -ta *adj* ajar
accò·sto -sta *adj* (coll) near ‖ *m* approach; help ‖ **accosto** *adv* near; **accosto a** near, close to
accovacciare §128 *ref* to crouch
accovonare (**accovóno**) *tr* to sheave
accozzàglia *f* hodgepodge; motley crowd
accozzare (**accòzzo**) *tr* to jumble up; to collect, gather (*people*) together ‖ *ref* to collect, congregate
accòzzo *m* jumble, medley
accreditàbile *adj* chargeable (*e.g., account*); creditable
accreditaménto *m* crediting
accreditare (**accrédito**) *tr* to credit, believe; to accredit (*an ambassador*); to credit (*one's account*)
accredita·to -ta *adj* confirmed (*news*); accredited
accréscere §142 *tr & ref* to increase
accresciménto *m* increase
accucciare §128 *ref* to curl up (*said of dogs*)
accudire §176 *tr* (coll) to attend (*a sick person*) ‖ *intr*—**accudire a** to take care of
acculturazióne *f* acculturation
accumulare (**accùmulo**) *tr, intr & ref* to accumulate; to gather
accumulatóre *m* storage battery
accumulazióne *f* accumulation
accuratézza *f* care, carefulness
accura·to -ta *adj* careful, painstaking
accusa *f* accusation, charge; **pubblica accusa** (law) public prosecutor
accusare *tr* to accuse, charge; to betray; to acknowledge (*receipt*); (cards) to declare, bid
accusati·vo -va *adj & m* accusative
accusa·to -ta *adj* accused ‖ *mf* defendant
accusató·re -trice *mf* accuser; **pubblico accusatore** (law) public prosecutor, district attorney
accusatò·rio -ria *adj* (**-ri -rie**) accusatory, accusing
acèfa·lo -la *adj* headless; without the first page (*said of a manuscript*)
acèr·bo -ba *adj* unripe, green, sour
àcero *m* maple tree, sugar maple
acèrri·mo -ma *adj* bitter, fierce
acetato *m* acetate
acèti·co -ca *adj* (**-ci -che**) acetic
acetificare §197 (**acetifico**) *tr* to acetify
acetilène *m* acetylene
acéto *m* vinegar; **aceto aromatico** aromatic spirits; **sotto aceto** pickled
acetóne *m* acetone
acetósa [s] *f* (bot) sorrel
acetosèlla [s] *f* wood sorrel
acetó·so -sa [s] *adj* vinegarish ‖ *f* see acetosa
Acherónte *m* Acheron
Achille *m* Achilles
acidificare §197 (**acidífico**) *tr* to acidify
acidi·tà *f* (**-tà**) acidity; **acidità di stomaco** heartburn
àci·do -da *adj* acid, sour ‖ *m* acid; **sapere d'acido** to taste sour
acidu·lo -la *adj* acidulous
àcino *m* berry (*of grapes*); bead (*of rosary*)
acme *f* acme; crisis
acne *f* acne

acònito m (bot) monkshood
àcqua f water; rain; purity (e.g., of a diamond); **acqua a catinelle** pouring rain; **acqua alta** high water; **acqua corrente** running water; **acqua dolce** fresh water; drinking water; **acqua in bocca!** mum's the word!; **acqua morta** stagnant water; **acqua ossigenata** hydrogen peroxide; **acqua potabile** drinking water; **acqua salata** salt water; **acqua viva** spring; **all'acqua di rose** very mild; **avere l'acqua alla gola** to be in dire straits; **della più bell'acqua** of the first water; **fare acqua** to leak (said of a boat); **fare un buco nell'acqua** to waste one's efforts; **portare acqua al mare** to carry coals to Newcastle; **prendere l'acqua** to get wet; **sott'acqua** (fig) underhand; **tirare l'acqua al proprio mulino** to be grist to one's mill; **versare acqua in un cesto** to waste one's efforts
acquafòrte f (acquefòrti) etching
acquaforti·sta mf (-sti -ste) etcher
ac·quàio -quàia (-quài -quàie) adj watering (trough) || m sink
acquaiò·lo -la adj water || m water carrier; (sports) water boy
acquamarina f (acquemarine) aquamarine
acquaplano m aquaplane
acquaràgia f turpentine
acquarèllo m var of acquerello
acquà·rio m (-ri) aquarium || **Acquario** m (astr) Aquarius
acquartierare (acquartièro) tr (mil) to quarter || ref to be quartered
acquasanta f holy water
acquasantièra f (eccl) stoup
acquàti·co -ca adj (-ci -che) aquatic, water
acquattare ref to crouch, squat
acquavite f brandy; liquor, rum
acquazzóne m downpour, heavy shower
acquedótto m aqueduct
àcque·o -a adj aqueous, watery
acquerelli·sta mf (-sti -ste) watercolorist
acquerèllo m watercolor; watered-down wine
acquerùgiola f fine drizzle
acquiescènte adj acquiescent
acquietare (acquièto) tr to pacify, placate || ref to quiet down
acquirènte mf buyer, purchaser; **il miglior acquirente** the highest bidder
acquisire §176 tr to acquire
acquisi·tóre -trice mf salesperson, agent || m salesman || f saleswoman
acquistare tr to purchase, buy; to acquire; to gain (e.g., ground) || intr to improve
acquisto m buy, purchase; acquisition
acquitrino m marsh
acquitrinó·so -sa [s] adj marshy
acquolina f—far venire l'acquolina in bocca a to make one's mouth water
acquó·so -sa [s] adj watery
acre adj sour; pungent; acrid; bitter (words)
acrèdine f acrimony, sourness
acrimònia f acrimony

acro m acre
acròba·ta mf (-tì -te) acrobat
acrobàti·co -ca (-ci -che) adj acrobatic || f acrobatics
acrobatismo m acrobatics
acrobazìa f acrobatics; stunt, feat
acrocòro m plateau
acrònimo m acronym
acròpo·li f (-li) acropolis
acròsti·co m (-ci) acrostic
acuire §176 tr to sharpen, whet
acuità f acuity
acùle·o m (-i) quill; prickle; thorn; stinger (of an insect)
acume m acumen
acuminare (acùmino) tr to sharpen, whet
acumina·to -ta adj pointed, sharp
acùsti·co -ca (-ci -che) adj acoustic(al) || f acoustics
acutézza f acuteness, sharpness
acutizzare [ddzz] tr & ref to sharpen
acu·to -ta adj acute, sharp || m high note
ad prep var of a before words beginning with a vowel
adagiare §290 tr to lay down gently; to lower gently || ref to lie down; to stretch out
adà·gio m (-gi) adage; (mus) adagio || adv slowly; gently; (mus) adagio
Adamo m Adam
adattàbile adj adaptable
adattaménto m adaptation; adaptability
adattare tr to adapt, fit || ref to adapt oneself; to become adapted; **adattarsi a** to go with; to match; to be becoming to
adat·to -ta adj suitable, adequate
addebitaménto m debiting
addebitare (addébito) tr to debit; **addebitare una spesa a qlcu** to debit s.o. with an expense
addébito m charge; (com) debit; **elevare l'addebito di qlco a qlcu** (law) to charge s.o. with s.th
addènda mpl addenda
addèndo m (math) addend
addensare (addènso) tr to thicken || ref to thicken; to gather, throng
addentare (addènto) tr to bite || ref (mach) to mesh
addentatura f bite; (carp) tongue (of tongue and groove)
addentella·to -ta adj toothed, notched || m chance, occasion; (archit) toothing
addentrare (addèntro) tr to penetrate || ref to penetrate; to proceed
addèntro adv inside; **addentro in** into; inside of
addestraménto m traïning
addestrare (addèstro) tr & ref to train
addestra·tóre -trice mf trainer
addét·to -ta adj assigned; attached; pertaining || m attaché; **addetto stampa** press secretary
addì adv the (+ a certain date), e.g., **addì 27 gennaio** the 27th of January
addiàc·cio m (-ci) sheepfold; bivouac
addiètro m (naut) stern; **per l'addietro** in the past || adv behind; ago; **dare**

addietro to back up; **lasciarsi addietro** to delay; **tempo addietro** some time ago; **tirarsi addietro** to back away

addì·o m (-i) farewell; **dare l'addio** to say good-bye; **dare l'estremo addio** to pay one's last respects; **fare gli addii** to say good-bye || *interj* farewell!, good-bye!

addire §151 tr (poet) to consecrate || ref to be suitable, be becoming; **addirsi a** to be becoming to

addirittura adv directly; even, without hesitation; absolutely, positively

addirizzare tr to straighten up; **addirizzare le gambe ai cani** to try the impossible

additare tr to point out

additi·vo -va adj & m additive

addivenire §282 intr (ESSERE)—**addivenire a** to come to, reach (*e.g., an agreement*)

addizionale adj additional || f supplementary tax

addizionare (**addizióno**) tr & intr to add

addizionatrice f adding machine

addizióne f addition

addobbaménto m adornment, decoration

addobbare (**addòbbo**) tr to adorn, bedeck, decorate

addobba·tóre -trice mf decorator

addòbbo m adornment, decoration; hangings (*in a church*)

addocilire §176 tr to soften up

addolcire §176 tr to sweeten; to calm down || ref to mellow, soften

addolorare (**addolóro**) tr & ref to grieve; **addolorarsi per** to grieve over, lament

addolora·to -ta adj sorrowful || **l'Addolorata** f (eccl) Our Lady of Sorrows

addòme m abdomen

addomesticàbile adj tamable

addomesticaménto m taming

addomesticare §197 (**addomèstico**) tr to tame; to accustom || ref to become accustomed

addomestica·to -ta adj tame, domesticated

addominale adj abdominal

addormentare (**addorménto**) tr to put to sleep; to numb || ref to fall asleep; to be asleep (*of a limb*)

addormenta·to -ta adj asleep; numbed

addossare (**addòsso**) tr to put on; **addossare qlco a qlco** to lean s.th against s.th; **addossare qlco a qlcu** to put s.th on s.o.; (fig) to entrust s.o. with s.th || ref to take upon oneself; to crowd together; **addossarsi a** to lean against; to crowd

addossa·to -ta adj leaning

addòsso adv on; on oneself, on one's back; about oneself; **addosso a** on, upon; against; **avere la sfortuna addosso** to be always unlucky; **dare addosso a qlcu** to assail s.o.; **levarsi d'addosso** to get rid of; **levarsi i panni d'addosso** to take the shirt off one's back

addót·to -ta adj adduced, alleged

addottorare (**addottóro**) tr to confer the doctor's degree on || ref to receive the doctor's degree

addurre §102 tr to adduce; to allege; (poet) to bring

Ade m Hades

adeguare (**adéguo**) tr to equalize; to bring in line || ref to conform, adapt oneself

adegua·to -ta adj adequate

adeguazióne f equalization

adémpiere §163 tr to fulfill, accomplish || ref to come true

adempiménto m fulfillment, discharge (*of one's duty*)

adempire §176 tr to fulfill, accomplish || ref to come true

adenòide adj adenoid || **adenoidi** fpl adenoids

adèpto m follower; initiate

aderènte adj adherent || mf adherent, supporter

aderènza f adherence; (mach) friction; (pathol) adhesion; **aderenze** connections

aderire §176 intr to adhere; to stick; **aderire a** to grant (*e.g., a request*); to concur with; to subscribe to

adescare §197 (**adésco**) tr to lure, bait, entice; (mach) to prime (*a pump*)

adesióne f adhesion; support; (phys) adherence

adesi·vo -va adj & m adhesive

adèsso adv now, just now; **da adesso in poi** from now on; **per adesso** for the time being

adiacènte adj adjacent

adiacènza f adjacency; **adiacenze** vicinity

adianto m (bot) maidenhair

adibire §176 tr to assign; to use

àdipe m fat

adipó·so -sa [s] adj adipose

adirare ref to get angry

adira·to -ta adj angry, mad

adire §176 tr to apply to (*the court*); to enter into possession of (*an inheritance*)

adocchiare §287 (**adòcchio**) tr to eye; to ogle; to spot

adolescènte adj & mf adolescent

adolescènza f adolescence

adombrare (**adómbro**) tr to shade; to hide, veil || ref to shy (*said of a horse*); (fig) to take umbrage

Adóne m Adonis

adontare (**adónto**) tr (obs) to offend || ref to take offense

adoperare (**adòpero** & **adópero**) tr to use, employ || ref to exert oneself; to do one's best

adoràbile adj adorable

adorare (**adóro**) tr to adore; to worship || intr (archaic) to pray

adora·tóre -trice mf worshiper || m (joc) admirer, suitor

adorazióne f adoration, worship

adornare (**adórno**) tr to adorn || ref to bedeck oneself

adór·no -na adj adorned, bedecked; (poet) fine, beautiful

adottante mf (law) adopter

adottare (adòtto) *tr* to adopt
adotti·vo -va *adj* adoptive; foster (*child*)
adozióne *f* adoption
Adriàti·co -ca *adj* (**-ci -che**) Adriatic || **Adriatico** *m* Adriatic
adulare (àdulo) *tr* to flatter; to fawn on
adula·tóre -trice *mf* flatterer
adulató·rio -ria *adj* (**-ri -rie**) flattering; fawning
adulazióne *f* adulation; fawning
adulterante *adj & m* adulterant
adulteri·no -na *adj* bastard; adulterated
adultè·rio *m* (**-ri**) adultery
adùlte·ro -ra *adj* adulterous || *m* adulterer || *f* adulteress
adul·to -ta *adj & mf* adult
adunanza *f* assembly
adunare *tr & ref* to assemble, gather
adunata *f* reunion, meeting; (mil) muster
adun·co -ca *adj* (**-chi -che**) hooked, crooked
adunghiare §287 *tr* (poet) to claw
adu·sto -sta *adj* skinny; (poet) burnt
aerare (àero) *tr* to air, ventilate
aerazióne *f* aeration; airing
aère·o -a *adj* aerial; air; overhead; high, lofty; airy, fanciful || *m* airplane; (rad & telv) aerial
aerobrigata *f* (mil) wing
aerocistèrna *f* (aer) tanker
aerodinàmi·co -ca (**-ci -che**) *adj* aerodynamic(al); streamlined || *f* aerodynamics
aeròdromo *m* airfield, airdrome
aerofaro *m* airport beacon
aerofotogram·ma *m* (**-mi**) aerial photograph
aerogiro *m* helicopter
aerògrafo *m* spray gun (*for painting*)
aerolìnea *f* airline; **aerolinea principale** trunkline
aeròlito *m* aerolite, meteorite
aeromaritti·mo -ma *adj* air-sea
aeròmetro *m* aerometer
aeromòbile *m* aircraft; **aeromobile senza pilota** drone, pilotless aircraft
aeromodellismo *m* model-airplane building
aeromodelli·sta *mf* (**-sti -ste**) model-airplane builder
aeromodèllo *m* model airplane
aeromotóre *m* windmill; aircraft motor
aeronàu·ta *m* (**-ti**) aeronaut
aeronàuti·co -ca (**-ci -che**) *adj* aeronautic(al) || *f* aeronautics
aeronave *f* airship, aircraft
aeroplano *m* airplane
aeropòrto *m* airport, airfield
aeroportuale *adj* airport
aerorazzo [ddzz] *m* rocket spaceship
aerorimessa *f* hangar
aerosbar·co *m* (**-chi**) landing of airborne troops
aeroservi·zio [s] *m* (**-zi**) air service
aerosilurante [s] *f* torpedo plane
aerosiluro [s] *m* aerial torpedo
aerosòl [s] *m* aerosol
aerosostenta·to -ta [s] *adj* airborne
aerospaziale *adj* aerospace
aerospà·zio *m* (**-zi**) aerospace

aerostàti·co -ca (**-ci -che**) *adj* aerostatic(al) || *f* aerostatics
aeròstato *m* aerostat
aerostazióne *f* air terminal
aerotas·sì *m* (**-sì**) taxiplane
aerotrasportare (aerotraspòrto) *tr* to airlift
aerotrasporta·to -ta *adj* airlifted; airborne
aerovìa *f* (aer) beam (*course indicated by a radio beam*); (aer) air lane
afa *f* sultriness; **fare afa a** (coll) to be a pain in the neck to
aferesi *f* apheresis
affàbile *adj* affable, agreeable
affaccendare (affaccèndo) *tr* to busy || *ref* to busy oneself, bustle
affaccenda·to -ta *adj* busy, bustling; occupied with busywork
affacciare §128 *tr* to show or display at the window; to bring forward (*e.g., an objection*); to raise (*a doubt*) || *ref* to show oneself (*at the door or window*); to present itself (*said of a doubt*)
affaccia·to -ta *adj* facing
affagottare (affagòtto) *tr* to bundle || *ref* to bundle up; to dress sloppily
affamare *tr* to starve
affama·to -ta *adj* starved, ravenous || *mf* starveling; hungry person; wretch
affannare *tr* to worry, to afflict || *intr* to pant; to be out of breath || *ref* to worry; to bustle around
affanna·to -ta *adj* panting; out of breath; worried
affanno *m* shortness of breath; grief, sorrow
affannó·so -sa [s] *adj* panting; wearisome
affardellare (affardèllo) *tr* to bundle together; (mil) to pack
affare *m* affair, matter; business; condition, quality; deal; **affari** business; **affari esteri** foreign affairs; **un buon affare** a good deal; a bargain
affarismo *m* sharp business practice
affari·sta *mf* (**-sti -ste**) unscrupulous operator
affaristi·co -ca *adj* (**-ci -che**) sharp
affascinante *adj* fascinating, charming
affascinare (affàscino) *tr* to fascinate, charm; to seduce; to spellbind || (affàscino) *tr* to bundle, to sheave
affascina·tóre -trice *adj* fascinating, charming || *mf* charmer, spellbinder
affastellare (affastèllo) *tr* to fagot (*twigs*): to sheave, bundle (*e.g., hay*); to pile, heap (*wood, crops, etc*); (fig) to jumble up
affaticare §197 *tr* to fatigue, tire, weary || *ref* to get tired; to weary; to toil
affatica·to -ta *adj* weary, tired
affatto *adv* quite, entirely; **niente affatto** not at all; **non . . . affatto** not at all
affatturare *tr* to bewitch; to adulterate (*e.g., food*)
affermare (afférmo) *tr* to affirm, assert || *intr* to nod assent || *ref* to take hold (*said, e.g., of a new product*)
affermati·vo -va *adj & f* affirmative
affermazióne *f* affirmation; assertion,

statement; success (e.g., of a new product); (sports) victory

afferrare (**afferro**) tr to grab, grasp; to catch, nab || ref to cling

affettare (**affetto**) tr to slice; to cut up || (**affetto**) tr to affect

affetta·to -ta adj affected || m cold cuts

affettatrice f slicing machine

affettazione f affectation

affetti·vo -va adj emotional

affèt·to -ta adj afflicted, burdened || m affection, love; feeling

affettuosi·tà [s] f (**-tà**) love, affection

affettuó·so -sa [s] adj affectionate, loving, tender

affezionare (**affezióno**) tr to inspire affection in || ref—**affezionarsi a** to become fond of

affeziona·to -ta adj affectionate, loving; **Suo affezionatissimo** best regards; **tuo affezionatissimo** love, as ever

affezióne f affection

affiancare §197 tr to place next; to favor, help; (mil) to flank

affiatamento m harmony; teamwork

affiatare tr to harmonize

affibbiare §287 tr to buckle, fasten; to deliver (a blow); to play (a trick); to slap (a fine)

affidamento m consignment, delivery; trust, confidence; **dare affidamento** to be trustworthy; **fare affidamento su** to rely upon

affidare tr to entrust; to commit (to memory); **affidare qlco a qlcu** to entrust s.o with s.th || ref to trust; **affidarsi a** to trust in

affievoliménto m weakening

affievolire §176 tr to weaken || ref to grow weaker

affiggere §103 tr to post; to fix (one's eyes or glance) || ref to gaze, stare

affigliare §280 tr & ref var of **affiliare**

affilacoltèl·li m (**-li**) steel (for sharpening knives)

affilara·sóio m (**-sói**) strop

affilare tr to sharpen, hone, whet; to make thin || ref to become thin

affila·to -ta adj sharp, sharpened; thin || f sharpening

affila·tóio m (**-tói**) sharpener

affilatrice f grindstone

affiliare §287 tr to affiliate || ref to become affiliated; **affiliarsi a** to become a member of

affilia·to -ta adj affiliated || mf affiliate; foster child; member of a secret society

affiliazióne f affiliation

affinare tr to sharpen; to refine, purify; to improve (e.g., one's style) || ref to improve

affinché conj so that, in order that; **affinché non** lest

affine adj akin, related; similar || mf in-law || m kinsman || f kinswoman || adv—**affine di** in order to

affini·tà f (**-tà**) affinity

affiochire §176 tr to make hoarse; to weaken || ref to become hoarse; to grow dim (said of a candle)

affioraménto m surfacing; (min) outcrop

affiorare (**affióro**) intr to surface, emerge; to appear, to show

affissare tr (poet) to fix || ref to concentrate; (poet) to gaze

affissióne f posting, bill posting

affis·so -sa adj fixed; posted || m bill, poster; door or window; (gram) affix

affittacàme·re m (**-re**) landlord || f landlady

affittanza f rent

affittare tr to rent || ref—**si affitta** for rent

affitto m rent, rental; **dare in affitto** to rent (to grant by lease); **prendere in affitto** to rent (to take by lease)

affittuà·rio -ria mf (**-ri -rie**) renter; tenant

affliggènte adj tormenting, distressing

affliggere §104 tr to afflict, distress || ref to grieve

afflit·to -ta adj afflicted, grieving || mf afflicted person, wretch

afflizióne f affliction, distress

afflosciare §128 (**afflòscio**) tr to cause to sag; to weaken || ref to droop; to sag; to be deflated; to faint

affloscire §176 tr & ref var of **afflosciare**

affluènte adj & m confluent

affluènza f confluence; abundance; crowd

affluire §176 intr (ESSERE) to flow (said of river); to flock (said of people); to pour in (said of earnings)

afflusso m flow

affogaménto m drowning

affogare §209 (**affógo**) tr to drown; to smother || intr (ESSERE) to drown

affoga·to -ta adj drowned; poached (egg)

affollaménto m crowd, throng

affollare (**affòllo & affòllo**) tr to crowd; to overcome || ref to crowd

affolla·to -ta adj crowded

affondaménto m sinking

affondami·ne m (**-ne**) mine layer

affondare (**affóndo**) tr to sink; to stick || ref to sink

affondata f (aer) nosedive

affóndo m (fencing) lunge || adv deeply

afforestare (**afforèsto**) tr to reforest

affossare (**affòsso**) tr to ditch; (fig) to table (e.g., a proposal); to hollow out || ref to become sunken or hollow (said, e.g., of cheeks)

affossatóre m ditchdigger; gravedigger

affrancare §197 tr to set free; to free; to redeem (a property); to stamp || ref to free oneself; to take heart

affrancatrice f postage meter

affrancatura f stamp, stamping

affràngere §179 tr to weary; (obs) to break down (the spirit)

affran·to -ta adj weary; broken down, broken-hearted

affratellaménto m fraternization

affratellare (**affratèllo**) tr to bind in brotherly love || ref to fraternize

affrescare §197 (**affrésco**) tr to fresco; to paint in fresco

affré·sco *m* (**-schi**) fresco

affrettare (**affrétto**) *tr & ref* to hurry, hasten

affretta· to -ta *adj* hurried

affrontare (**affrónto**) *tr* to face, confront ‖ *ref* to meet in combat; to come to blows

affronta·to -ta *adj*—**affrontati** (herald) combattant

affrónto *m* affront, offense

affumicare §197 (**affùmico**) *tr* to smoke; to blacken; to smoke out; to smoke (*meat or fish*)

affumica·to -ta *adj* smoked; dark (*glasses*)

affusolare [s] (**affùsolo**) *tr & ref* to taper

affusola·to -ta [s] *adj* tapered; slender

affusto *m* gun carriage

afga·no -na *adj & mf* Afghan

àfo·no -na *adj* voiceless

afori·sma *m* (**-smi**) aphorism

afó·so -sa [s] *adj* sultry

Africa, l' *f* Africa

africa·no -na *adj & mf* African

afrodisìa·co -ca *adj & m* (**-ci -che**) aphrodisiac

afta *m* mouth ulcer; **afta epizootica** (vet) foot-and-mouth disease

àgata *f* agate ‖ **Agata** *f* Agatha

agènda *f* notebook; agenda

agènte *adj* active ‖ *m* agent; broker; merchant; officer; **agente delle tasse** tax collector; **agente di cambio** stockbroker; money changer; **agente di commercio** broker, commission merchant; **agente di custodia** jailer; **agente di polizia** police officer, policeman; **agente di spionaggio** informer; **agente provocatore** agent provocateur

agenzìa *f* agency; office, branch; **agenzia immobiliare** real-estate office

agevolare (**agévolo**) *tr* to facilitate, help

agevolazióne *f* facility; **agevolazione di pagamento** easy terms

agévole *adj* easy

agevolézza *f* facility

agallare *intr* to come to the surface

agganciaménto *m* docking (*in space*); (rr) coupling

agganciare §128 *tr* to hook; (rr) to couple; (mil) to engage (*the enemy*)

aggàn·cio *m* (**-ci**) docking (*in space*); (rr) coupling

aggég·gio *m* (**-gi**) gadget

aggettivale *adj* adjectival

aggettivo *m* adjective

agghiacciaménto *m* freezing

agghiacciante *adj* hair-raising, frightful

agghiacciare §128 *tr* to freeze ‖ *ref* to freeze; to be horrified

agghiaccia·to -ta *adj* frozen, icy

agghindare *tr & ref* to preen, primp

àg·gio *m* (**-gi**) agio; **fare aggio** to be at a premium

aggiogare §209 (**aggiógo**) *tr* to yoke

aggiornaménto *m* adjournment (*e.g., of a meeting*); bringing up to date

aggiornare (**aggiórno**) *tr* to bring up to date; to adjourn ‖ *ref* to keep up with the times

aggiraménto *m* surrounding, outflanking

aggirare *tr* to surround, outflank; to swindle ‖ *ref* to roam, wander; **aggirarsi su** to approximate; to be almost

aggiudicare §197 (**aggiùdico**) *tr* to adjudicate, award ‖ *ref* to win

aggiudicazióne *f* adjudication, award

aggiùngere §183 *tr* to add; to join, connect ‖ *ref* to be added; to join

aggiunta *f* addition

aggiuntare *tr* to attach, join

aggiun·to -ta *adj & m* associate, assistant, deputy ‖ *f* see **aggiunta**

aggiustàbile *adj* repairable

aggiustaménto *m* settlement; adjustment; (mil) correction (*of fire*)

aggiustare *tr* to fix, repair; to adjust; (mil) to correct (*cannon fire*); **aggiustare per le feste** (coll) to fix; (coll) to give a good beating to ‖ *ref* (archaic) to come closer; (coll) to manage; (coll) to come to an agreement

aggiusta·tóre -trice *mf* repairer, fixer ‖ *m* repairman

aggiustatura *f* fixing, repairing, repair

agglomerare (**agglòmero**) *tr & ref* to pile up; to crowd together

agglomerato *m* built-up area; **agglomerato urbano** urban center

agglutinare (**agglùtino**) *tr & ref* to agglutinate

agglutinazióne *f* agglutination

aggobbire §176 *tr* to bend, bend over ‖ *intr* (ESSERE) *& ref* to hunch over

aggomitolare (**aggomìtolo**) *tr* to coil ‖ *ref* to curl up

aggradare *intr* (with *dat*) (poet) to please; **come Le aggrada** as you please

aggradire §176 *tr* to appreciate ‖ *intr* (poet) (with *dat*) to please

aggraffare *tr* to hook; to grab; to join (*metal sheets*) with a double seam; to stitch, staple

aggraffatrice *f* folding machine; (mach) can sealer

aggranchire §176 *tr* to benumb; to deaden, stupefy ‖ *intr* to become numb

aggrappare *tr* to grab; to clamp ‖ *ref* to cling

aggravaménto *m* aggravation

aggravante *adj* (law) aggravating (*circumstances*)

aggravare *tr* to aggravate; to overload (*e.g., one's stomach*) ‖ *ref* to get worse

aggrà·vio *m* (**-vi**) burden (*e.g., of taxes*); **fare aggravio a qlcu di qlco** to impute s.th to s.o.

aggraziare §287 *tr* to embellish; to render graceful ‖ *ref* to win, gain; to ingratiate oneself

aggrazia·to -ta *adj* graceful; polite

aggredire §176 *tr* to assail, attack, assault

aggregare §209 (**aggrègo**) *tr & ref* to join, unite

aggrega·to -ta *adj* adjunct ‖ *m* aggregation

aggressióne *f* aggression

aggressi·vo -va adj aggressive ‖ m (mil) poison gas

aggressóre m aggressor

aggricciare §128 tr to wrinkle; (slang) to knit (e.g., the brow) ‖ ref (poet) to shiver

aggrinzare tr & ref to wrinkle

aggrinzire §176 tr & ref var of **aggrinzare**

aggrondare (aggróndo) tr to knit (the brow)

aggrottare (aggròtto) tr to knit (the brow)

aggrovigliare §280 tr to tangle, entangle ‖ ref to become entangled

aggrumare tr & ref to clot; to coagulate

aggruppare tr to group

agguagliare §280 tr to level; to equalize; to compare

agguantare tr to grab; to nab; (coll) to hit; **agguantare per il collo** to grab by the neck ‖ ref—**agguantarsi a** to get hold of

agguato m ambush; **cadere in un agguato** to fall into a trap; **stare in agguato** to wait in ambush

agguerrire §176 tr to train for war; to inure to war; to inure

aghétto m shoestring; (mil) lanyard

agiatézza f comfort, wealth; **vivere nell'agiatezza** to live in comfort

agia·to -ta adj well-to-do, comfortable

àgile adj agile, nimble; prompt

agili·tà f (-tà) agility, nimbleness; promptness

à·gio m (-gi) comfort; opportunity; ease; **agi** conveniences, comforts; **a Suo agio** at your convenience; **aver agio** to have time; **stare a proprio agio** to feel at ease; **to be comfortable; vivere negli agi** to live comfortably

agiografia f hagiography

agiògrafo m hagiographer

agire §176 intr to act; to work; (theat) to act, perform

agitare (àgito) tr to agitate, shake; to stir; to stir up; to discuss (e.g., a problem) ‖ ref to toss; to shake; to stir; to get excited

agita·to -ta adj rough, choppy (sea); troubled, upset ‖ mf violently insane person

agita·tóre -trice mf agitator ‖ m shaker

agitazióne f agitation

agli §4

agliàce·o -a adj garlicky

à·glio m (-gli) garlic

agnellino m little lamb, lambkin

agnèllo m lamb

agnizióne f recognition

agnòsti·co -ca adj & mf (-ci -che) agnostic

a·go m (-ghi) needle; pointer (of scales); stem (of valve)

agognare (agógno) tr to covet

agóne m contest; arena

agonìa f agony, death struggle; anguish

agonìsti·co -ca adj (-ci -che) competitive, aggressive (spirit); athletic (competition) ‖ f athletics

agonizzare [ddzz] intr to agonize, be in agony; (fig) to die out

agopuntura f acupuncture

ago·ràio m (-rài) needle case

agosta·no -na adj August, e.g., **pomeriggio agostano** August afternoon

agostinia·no -na adj & m Augustinian

agósto m August

agrà·rio -ria (-ri -rie) adj & m agrarian ‖ m landlord ‖ f agriculture

agrèste adj country

agrìco·lo -la adj agricultural

agricoltóre m farmer; agriculturist

agricoltura f agriculture

agrifò·glio m (-gli) holly

agrimensóre m surveyor

agrimensura f surveying

a·gro -gra adj sour, bitter ‖ m citrus juice; sourness, bitterness; surrounding country

agrodólce adj sweet and sour; (fig) acidulous (tone)

agronomìa f agronomy

agrònomo m agronomist

agrume m citrus (tree and fruit); **agrumi** citrus fruit

agucchiare §287 intr to knit or sew idly

agùglia f spire; top; (ichth) gar; (poet) eagle; (obs) needle

aguzzare tr to sharpen; to whet (the appetite)

aguzzino [ddzz] m slave driver; jailer

aguz·zo -za adj sharp, pointed

ah interj ah!, aha!; ha!

ahi interj ouch!

ahimè interj alas!

àia f yard, barnyard; threshing floor; governess ‖ **L'Aia** f the Hague

Aiace m Ajax

àio m (ài) tutor

aiòla f lawn; flower bed

àire m push; short run (preparing for a jump); **dare l'aire a** to start off; **prendere l'aire** to take off

airóne m heron

aitante adj robust, stalwart

aiuòla f (poet) var of **aiola**

aiutante adj helping ‖ mf assistant ‖ m (mil) adjutant; **aiutante di campo** aide-de-camp; **aiutante di sanità** orderly

aiutare tr to help ‖ ref to strive; to help oneself; to help one another

aiutato m first assistant (e.g., of a surgeon)

aiuto m aid, help; assistant; first assistant (of a surgeon)

aizzare (aìzzo) tr to incite, to incite to riot; to sic (a dog)

al §4

a·la f (-li & -le) wing; sail, vane (of windmill); blade (e.g., of fan); brim (of hat); (football) wing; **ala a freccia** backswept wing; **ala di popolo** throng; **fare ala a** to line up along

alabarda f halberd

alabardière m halberdier

alabastri·no -na adj alabaster; white as alabaster

alabastro m alabaster

àlacre adj eager, lively

alacrità f alacrity

alàg·gio m (-gi) hauling, towing
alamaro m braid, gimp
alambic·co m (-chi) still
alano m Great Dane
alare adj wing (e.g., span) ‖ m andiron ‖ tr to haul
Alasca, l' f Alaska
ala·to -ta adj winged, sublime
alba f dawn, daybreak
albagìa f haughtiness
albanése [s] adj & mf Albanian
Albania, l' f Albania
àlbatro m (orn) albatross
albeggiaménto m dawning
albeggiare §290 (albéggio) intr (ESSERE) to dawn; (poet) to sparkle (said, e.g., of ice) ‖ impers (ESSERE)—**albeggia** the day dawns
alberare (àlbero) tr to plant (trees); to reforest; to hoist (a mast); to mast (a ship)
albera·to -ta adj tree-lined; (naut) masted
alberèllo m small tree; apothecary's jar
albergare §209 (albèrgo) tr to lodge; to put up at a hotel; (fig) to harbor ‖ intr to lodge; to put up
alberga·tóre -trice mf hotelkeeper
alberghiè·ro -ra adj hotel
albèr·go m (-ghi) hotel; refuge; hospitality; **albergo diurno** day hostel; **albergo per la gioventù** youth hostel
àlbero m tree; poplar; (mach) shaft; (naut) mast; **albero a camme** (aut) camshaft; **albero a gomito** (aut) crankshaft; **albero di distribuzione** (aut) camshaft; **albero di Natale** Christmas tree; **albero di trasmissione** (aut) transmission; **albero genealogico** family tree
albicòc·ca f (-che) apricot
albicòc·co m (-chi) apricot tree
al·bo -ba adj (poet) white ‖ m album; bulletin board; (law) roll; comic book; **albo d'onore** honor roll ‖ f see **alba**
albóre m (poet) whiteness; (poet) dawn
album m (album) album, scrapbook
albume m albumen
albumina f albumin
àlca·li m (-li) alkali
alcali·no -na adj alkaline
alce m moose; elk
alchìmia f alchemy
alchimi·sta m (-sti) alchemist
alcióne m halcyon
alciò·nio -nia adj (-ni -nie) halcyon
àlco·le m alcohol
alcolici·tà f (-tà) alcoholic content
alcòli·co -ca adj (-ci -che) alcoholic ‖ m alcoholic beverage
alcolismo m alcoholism
alcolizzare [ddzz] tr to intoxicate ‖ ref to become intoxicated
alcolizza·to -ta [ddzz] adj intoxicated ‖ mf alcoholic
alcool m (alcool) var of **alcole**
alcoolici·tà f (-tà) var of **alcolicità**
alcoòli·co -ca (-ci -che) adj & m var of **alcolico**
alcoolismo m var of **alcolismo**
alcoolizzare [ddzz] tr var of **alcolizzare**

alcoolizza·to -ta [ddzz] adj & mf var of **alcolizzato**
alcòva f bedroom; bed; alcove
alcunché pron something, anything
alcu·no -na adj & pron some; **alcu·ni -ne** some; quite a few, several, a good many
aldilà m life beyond, afterlife
àlea f chance, hazard; **correre l'alea** to try one's luck
aleggiare §290 (aléggio) intr to flutter; to flap the wings; to hover
aleróne m var of **alettone**
alesàg·gio m (-gi) (mach) bore
alesare (alèso) tr (mach) to bore
alesatóre m reamer
alesatrice s boring machine
Alessandria d'Egitto f Alexandria
alessandri·no -na adj & mf Alexandrian ‖ m Alexandrine (verse)
Alessandro m Alexander; **Alessandro Magno** Alexander the Great
alétta f small wing; fin (of fish); (aer) tab; **aletta di compensazione** trim tab; **aletta parasole** (aut) sun visor
alettóne m (aer) aileron, flap
Aleuti·no -na adj—**Isole Aleutine** Aleutian Islands
al·fa m (-fa) alpha ‖ f esparto
alfabèti·co -ca adj (-ci -che) alphabetical
alfabetizzazióne [ddzz] f teaching to read; learning to read
alfabèto m alphabet; code (e.g., Morse)
alfière m flagbearer, standardbearer; (chess) bishop
alfine adv finally, at last
al·ga f (-ghe) alga; **alga marina** seaweed
àlgebra f algebra
algèbri·co -ca adj (-ci -che) algebraic
Algèri f Algiers
Algeria, l' f Algeria
algeri·no -na adj & mf Algerian
aliante m (aer) glider
alianti·sta mf (-sti -ste) glider pilot
àli·bi m (-bi) alibi
alice f anchovy
alienàbile adj alienable
alienare (alièno) tr to alienate; to transfer, convey ‖ ref—**alienarsi dalla ragione** to go out of one's mind
aliena·to -ta adj alienated ‖ mf insane person; dispossessed person
alienazióne f alienation
alieni·sta mf (-sti -ste) alienist
alièno -na adj disinclined; (poet) foreign, alien
alimentare adj alimentary ‖ **alimentari** mpl food, foodstuff ‖ v (aliménto) tr to feed; to fuel
alimentari·sta m (-sti) food merchant; food-industry worker
alimenta·tóre -trice mf stoker ‖ m (mach) stoker, feeder
alimentazióne f nourishment; feeding; (mil) loading; **alimentazione artificiale** intravenous feeding
aliménto m food, nourishment; feed; **alimenti** alimony (maintenance)
alimònia f alimony
alinea f (law) paragraph, section

alìquota *f* share; parcel, quota

aliscafo *m* hydrofoil

alisè·o -a *adj* trade (*wind*) || *m* trade wind

alitare (àlito) *intr* to breathe; to blow gently; **non alitare** to not breathe a word

àlito *m* breath; (fig) breeze

alìvo·lo -la *adj* (poet) winged; (fig) swift

alla §4

allacciaménto *m* binding; connection, linking

allacciare §128 *tr* to bind, tie; to connect; to buckle; (fig) to deceive

allacciatura *f* lacing; buckling

allagare §209 *tr* to flood, overflow

allampana·to -ta *adj* tall and lean, lanky

allargare §209 *tr* to broaden, widen; **allargare la mano** to be lenient; to be liberal; **allargare il freno** to give free rein || *ref* to widen, spread out; **mi si allarga il cuore** I feel relieved

allargatura *f* widening

allarmante *adj* alarming

allarmare *tr* to alarm || *ref* to worry, become alarmed

allarme *m* alarm; **allarme aereo** air-raid warning; **cessato allarme** all clear; **falso allarme** false alarm; **stare in allarme** to be alarmed

allascare §197 *tr* (naut) to ease, slacken (*a rope*)

allato *adv* (poet) near; **allato a** near; beside; in comparison with

allattaménto *m* nursing, feeding; **allattamento artificiale** bottle feeding

allattare *tr* to nurse (*at the breast*); to feed (*with a bottle*)

alle §4

alleanza *f* alliance

alleare (allèo) *tr* to ally || *ref* to become allied; to be connected

allea·to -ta *adj* allied || *mf* ally

allegare §209 (allégo) *tr* to enclose; to adduce; to allege; **allegare i denti** to set the teeth on edge || *intr* (hort) to ripen

allega·to -ta *adj* enclosed || *m* enclosure

alleggeriménto *m* lightening, easing

alleggerire §176 *tr* to lighten; to alleviate || *ref* to put on lighter clothes; **alleggerirsi di** (naut) to jettison

allegoria *f* allegory

allegòri·co -ca *adj* (-ci -che) allegorical

allegraménte *adv* cheerfully, merrily; thoughtlessly

allegrézza *f* joy, cheerfulness

allegria *f* cheer, gaiety; **stare in allegria** to be merry || *interj* good cheer!

allé·gro -gra *adj* cheerful, merry, gay || *m* (mus) allegro

allelùia *m* hallelujah

allenaménto *m* training

allenare (allèno) *tr* & *ref* to train

allena·tóre -trice *adj* training || *mf* trainer, coach

allentare (allènto) *tr* to loosen, slacken; to mitigate; (coll) to deliver (*a blow*); **essere allentato** to have a hernia || *ref* to slow up; to loosen up; to diminish

allergìa *f* allergy

allèrgi·co -ca *adj* (-ci -che) allergic

allérta *f* alert || *adv* alert, on the alert

alessare (allésso) *tr* to boil

allés·so -sa *adj* boiled || *m* boiled meat, boiled beef

allestire §176 *tr* to prepare, make ready; to rig (*e.g., a ship*); to produce (*e.g., a play*)

allettaménto *m* allure, fascination

allettante *adj* alluring, enticing

allettare (allètto) *tr* to allure, entice; to confine to bed; to bend (*plants*) to the ground || *ref* to be confined to bed

allevaménto *m* raising, breeding; flock

allevare (allèvo) *tr* to raise, breed; to rear

alleva·tóre -trice *mf* raiser, breeder

alleviare §287 (allèvio) *tr* to alleviate, lighten

allibire §176 *intr* (ESSERE) to turn pale; to be astonished, be dismayed

allibraménto *m* registration, entry; booking (*of bets*)

allibrare *tr* to register, enter; to book (*a bet*) on a horse

allibratóre *m* bookmaker (*at races*)

allietare (alliéto) *tr* to cheer, enliven

alliè·vo -va *mf* pupil, student; follower, disciple || *m* trainee; **allievo ufficiale** cadet

alligatóre *m* alligator

allignare *intr* to take root; to do well, prosper

allineaménto *m* alignment; falling in line

allineare (allìneo) *tr* to align; (typ) to justify || *ref* to align oneself, be aligned

allinea·to -ta *adj* aligned; **non allineato** nonaligned, uncommitted

allitterazióne *f* alliteration

allo §4

allòc·co *m* (-chi) horned owl; (fig) dolt, nincompoop

allocu·tóre -trice *mf* (poet) speaker

allocuzióne *f* (poet) speech, address

allòdola *f* lark, skylark

allogare §209 (allògo) *tr* to place; to let, lease; to find employment for; to invest (*money*); to marry off (*a daughter*)

allòge·no -na *adj* minority || *mf* member of an ethnic minority

alloggiaménto *m* (mil) lodging, quarters; (carp, mach) housing

alloggiare §290 (allòggio) *tr* to lodge, put up || *intr* to lodge, stay

allòg·gio *m* (-gi) lodging, living quarters; accommodations

allontanaménto *m* removal; estrangement

allontanare *tr* to remove; to send away; to exonerate; to dismiss; to alienate || *ref* to go away; to withdraw; to become estranged

allóra *m* (adv) then || *adv* then; at that time; in that case; **da allora** ever since; **da allora in poi** from that time on; **fino allora** until then; **per allora** at that time

allorché *conj* when

allòro *m* laurel; **riposare sugli allori** to rest on one's laurels

allorquando *conj* (poet) when

àlluce *m* big toe

allucinante *adj* hallucinating; dazzling; deceptive

allucinare (allùcino) *tr* to hallucinate; to dazzle; to deceive

allucinazióne *f* hallucination

allùdere §105 *intr* to allude

allume *m* alum

alluminare (allùmino) *tr* to illuminate (*a manuscript*); (poet) to light

alluminio *m* aluminum

allunàg·gio *m* (-gi) lunar landing; **allunaggio morbido** soft lunar landing

allunare *intr* to land on the moon

allunga *f* (mach) adapter

allungàbile *adj* extensible; extension (*table*)

allungaménto *m* lengthening

allungare §209 *tr* to lengthen; to stretch out (*e.g., the hand*); to dilute (*e.g., wine*); (coll) to deliver (*e.g., a slap*); (sports) to pass (*the ball*); **allungare il collo** to crane the neck; **allungare il passo** to walk faster || *ref* to grow longer; to stretch; to grow taller

allun·go *m* (-ghi) (sports) sprint; (sports) forward pass

allusióne *f* allusion

alluvióne *f* flood

almanaccare §197 *tr* to dream of || *intr* to dream, muse

almanac·co *m* (-chi) almanac

alméno *adv* at least; if only

alno *m* (bot) alder

àloe *m* & *f* aloe

alògeno *m* halogen

alogenuro *m* halide

alóne *m* halo

alòsa *f* (ichth) shad

alpacca *f* German silver

alpe *f* high mountain, alp || **le Alpi** the Alps

alpèstre *adj* mountainous; (fig) uncouth

alpigia·no -na *adj* mountain, mountainous; (fig) uncouth || *mf* mountaineer

alpinismo *m* mountain climbing

alpini·sta *mf* (-sti -ste) mountain climber

alpinìsti·co -ca *adj* (-ci -che) mountainclimbing

alpi·no -na *adj* alpine; Alpine || *m* alpine soldier

alquan·to -ta *adj* & *pron* some; **alquanti -te** some; quite a few, several, a good many || **alquanto** *adv* somewhat, rather

Alsàzia, l' *f* Alsace

alsazia·no -na *adj* & *mf* Alsacian

alt *m* (alt) halt, stop || *interj* halt!, stop!

altaléna *f* seesaw; swing; (fig) ups and downs; **altalena a bilico** seesaw; **altalena sospesa** swing

altalenare (altaléno) *intr* to seesaw; to swing

altana *f* roof terrace

altare *m* altar

altarìno *m* small altar; **svelare gli alta**-

rini (joc) to expose the skeleton in the closet

altèa *f* marsh mallow

alterare (àltero) *tr* to alter; to falsify; to adulterate; to anger || *ref* to alter; to become adulterated; to get angry

altera·to -ta *adj* altered; adulterated; feverish; angry

alterazióne *f* change, alteration; adulteration; slight fever

altèr·co *m* (-chi) altercation; **venire a un alterco** to get into a quarrel

alterìgia *f* haughtiness

alternare (altèrno) *tr* & *ref* to alternate

alternati·vo -va *adj* alternating || *f* alternative; choice

alterna·to -ta *adj* alternate; alternating (*current*)

alternatóre *m* (elec) alternator

altèr·no -na *adj* alternate

altè·ro -ra *adj* proud, haughty

altézza *f* height; width (*of cloth*); depth (*of water*); pitch (*of sound*); (astr, geom) altitude; (fig) loftiness, nobility; (naut) latitude; (typ) size; **essere all'altezza di** to be up to, be equal to; (naut) to be off || **Altezza** *f* Highness

altezzó·so -sa [s] *adj* haughty

altìc·cio -cia *adj* (-ci -ce) tipsy

altìmetro *m* altimeter

altipiano *m* var of **altopiano**

altisonante [s] *adj* high-sounding

altìssi·mo -ma *adj* very high, highest || **l'Altissimo** *m* the Most High

altitùdine *f* altitude

al·to -ta *adj* high; tall; wide (*cloth*); deep (*water*); upper; full (*day*); late (*e.g., Easter*); deep (*sleep*); early (*Middle Ages*); loud (*voice*); lofty (*peak*) || *m* top; upper part; high quarters; **alti e bassi** ups and downs; **fare alto e basso** to be the undisputed boss; **guardare qlcu dall'alto in basso** to look down one's nose at s.o.; **in alto up** || **alto** *adv* up

altofórno *m* (altifórni) blast furnace

altoloca·to -ta *adj* high-placed, highranking

altoparlante *m* loudspeaker

altopiano *m* (altipiani) plateau

altrettan·to -ta *adj* & *pron* as much; the same; **altrettan·ti -te** as many || **altrettanto** *adv* as much; the same

altri *indef pron invar* someone; someone else; **non altri che** no one else but

altrièri *m* & *adv* day before yesterday

altriménti *adv* otherwise

al·tro -tra *adj* other; next (*world*); **altro ieri** day before yesterday; **chi altro?** who else?; **domani l'altro** the day after tomorrow; **fra l'altro** among other things; **ieri l'altro** the day before yesterday; **l'altro anno** last year; **l'altro giorno** the other day; **noi altri** we; **qualcun altro** somebody else; anybody else; **quest'altro** (**giorno, mese, anno**) next (day, month, year) || *pron* other; anything else; **altro che!** why yes! ‖ **l'altro** §11 correlative indef pron ‖ **l'altro** §12 reciprocal pron

altrónde adv (poet) somewhere else; **d'altronde** besides; on the other hand

altróve adv elsewhere, somewhere else

altrui adj invar somebody else's, other people's ‖ pron invar somebody else ‖ m—**l'altrui** what belongs to someone else

altrui·sta (-sti -ste) adj altruistic ‖ mf altruist

altura f height; (naut) high seas

alun·no -na mf pupil, student

alveare m beehive

àlveo m bed (of a river)

alvèolo m alveolus; socket (of tooth); cell (of honeycomb)

alzabandiè·ra m (-ra) raising of the flag

alzacristal·li m (-li) (aut) crank (to raise a window)

alzàia f tow line; towpath

alzare tr to lift, raise; to cut (cards); to shrug (one's shoulders); to set (sail); **alzare al cielo** to praise to the sky; **alzare i tacchi** to show a clean pair of heels; **alzare la cresta** to get cocky ‖ ref to rise; to get up; **alzarsi in piedi** to stand up

alzata f raising, lifting; shrugging (of shoulders); standing up; riser (of step); three-tier candy tray; **alzata di scudi** rebellion; **alzata di testa** whim, caprice

alzavàlvo·le m (-le) (aut) valve lifter

alzo m gunsight

amàbile adj amiable; sweetish (wine)

amabili·tà f (-tà) amiability, kindness

ama·ca f (-che) hammock

amàlga·ma m (-mi) amalgam

amalgamare (amàlgamo) tr to amalgamate ‖ ref to amalgamate; to blend

amalgamazióne f amalgamation

amante adj loving, fond ‖ m lover ‖ f mistress

amanuènse m amanuensis, scribe

amare tr to love; to like ‖ ref to love one another

amareggiare §290 (amaréggio) tr to make bitter; to sadden ‖ ref to become bitter; to sadden

amarèna f sour cherry

amarétto m macaroon

amarézza f bitterness

ama·ro -ra adj bitter ‖ m bitters; bitterness

amarógno·lo -la adj bitterish

amarra f (naut) hawser

amarrare tr & intr var of **ammarrare**

ama·tóre -trice mf lover; amateur

amató·rio -ria adj (-ri -rie) amatory, of love

amàzzone [ddzz] f horsewoman; female jockey; (obs) riding habit; **cavalcare all'amazzone** to ride sidesaddle ‖ **Amazzone** f (myth) Amazon

ambage f winding path; **ambagi** circumlocutions; **senz'ambagi** without beating about the bush

ambascerìa f embassy

ambà·scia f (-sce) shortness of breath; grief, sorrow

ambasciata f embassy; ambassadorship; errand, mission

ambasciatóre m ambassador

ambasciatrice f ambassadress

ambedùe adj invar—**ambedue i** or **le** both ‖ pron invar both

ambiare §287 intr to amble, pace (said of a horse)

ambiatura f pacing (said of a horse)

ambidè·stro -stra adj ambidextrous

ambidùe adj & pron invar var of **ambedue**

ambientare (ambiènto) tr to accustom; to place (a story in a certain period) ‖ ref to get accustomed to one's surroundings; to orient oneself

ambienta·tóre -trice mf interior decorator; (theat) decorator

ambiènte adj room, e.g., **temperatura ambiente** room temperature ‖ m environment; habitat; milieu; room; **trovarsi fuori del proprio ambiente** to be out of one's element

ambigui·tà f (-tà) ambiguity

ambì·guo -gua adj ambiguous

àm·bio m (-bi) amble, pacing

ambire §176 tr to be eager for ‖ intr to be ambitious; **ambire a** to be ambitious for

àmbito m range, circle; (mus) range; **nell'ambito di** within

ambizióne f ambition

ambizióso -sa [s] adj ambitious ‖ mf ambitious person

ambo or **am·bi -be** adj pl—**ambo i, ambo le, ambi i, ambe le** both

ambosèssi adj invar of both sexes, e.g., **giovani ambosessi** young people of both sexes

ambra f amber; **ambra grigia** ambergris

ambròsia f ambrosia; (bot) ragweed

ambulante adj itinerant; circulating; ambulant ‖ m mail car

ambulanza f ambulance

ambulare (àmbulo) intr (coll) to ambulate

ambulatò·rio -ria (-ri -rie) adj ambulatory ‖ m clinic, first-aid department

Amburgo m Hamburg

amèba f amoeba

a·men m (-men) amen ‖ interj amen!

ameni·tà f (-tà) f amenity; pleasantry

amèno -na adj pleasant, agreeable; amusing (fellow)

Amèrica, l' f America; **l'America del Nord** North America; **l'America del Sud** South America

americana f bicycle race between pairs

americanismo m Americanism

americanizzare [ddzz] tr to Americanize ‖ ref to become Americanized

america·no -na adj & mf American ‖ m vermouth with bitters ‖ f see **americana**

ametista f amethyst

amianto m asbestos

amicale adj (poet) friendly

amichévole adj friendly; (sports) noncompetitive

amicìzia f friendship; **stringere amicizia con** to make friends with

ami·co -ca (-ci -che) *adj* friendly || *mf* friend; beloved || *m* boy friend; lover, paramour; **amico del cuore** bosom friend || *f* girl friend; mistress

amidàce·o -a *adj* starchy

amidatura *f* starching

àmido *m* starch

Amlèto *m* Hamlet

ammaccare §197 *tr* to crush; to pound; to bruise; to dent

ammaccatura *f* bruise; dent

ammaestraménto *m* instruction, teaching; training

ammaestrare (ammaèstro & ammaéstro) *tr* to teach, to educate; to train (*animals*)

ammainare (ammàino) *tr* to lower (*e.g., a flag*)

ammalare *intr* (ESSERE) to fall ill || *ref* to fall ill; **ammalarsi di** to come down with

ammala·to -ta *adj* ill, sick || *mf* patient

ammaliare §287 *tr* to cast a spell on; to charm, enchant, fascinate; to bewitch

ammalia·tóre -trice *adj* charming, enchanting || *mf* charmer || *m* enchanter, sorcerer || *f* enchantress, sorceress

amman·co *m* (-chi) shortage

ammanettare (ammanétto) *tr* to handcuff

ammaniglia·to -ta *adj* shackled; (fig) closely bound, closely tied

ammannare *tr* to sheave (*grain*)

ammannire §176 *tr* to prepare (*a dish*); to dish up (*a meal*)

ammansare *tr & ref* var of **ammansire**

ammansa·tóre -trice *mf* (poet) tamer

ammansire §176 *tr* to tame; to calm || *ref* to become tamed; to calm down

ammantare *tr* to mantle, clothe; to cover; to hide (*the truth*)

ammanto *m* mantle, cloak; (fig) authority

ammaràg·gio *m* (-gi) landing on water; splashdown (*of a space vehicle*)

ammaraménto *m* var of **ammaraggio**

ammarare *intr* (aer) to land on water; (rok) to splash down

ammarrare *tr* (naut) to moor

ammassare *tr* to amass || *ref* to crowd, throng

ammasso *m* heap, pile; cluster (*of stars*); government stockpile

ammattiménto *m* worry, nuisance

ammattire §176 *intr* (ESSERE) to go crazy; **fare ammattire** to drive crazy

ammattonare (ammattóno) *tr* to floor with bricks

ammattona·to -ta *adj* floored with bricks || *m* brick floor; bricklaying

ammazzare *tr* to kill || *ref* to kill oneself; to get killed

ammazzasèt·te *m* (-te) braggart

ammazza·tóio *m* (-tói) slaughterhouse

ammènda *f* fine; satisfaction (*for injury*); **fare ammenda** to make amends

ammendaménto *m* emendation: improvement (*of land*)

ammendare (ammèndo) *tr* to emendate; to improve (*land*)

ammennìcolo *m* excuse; trifle; **ammennìcoli** extras

ammés·so -sa *adj* admitted; **ammesso che** supposing that; **ammesso e non concesso** for the sake of argument

amméttere §198 *tr* to admit; to accept, suppose

ammezzare [ddzz] (ammèzzo) *tr* to leave half-finished (*a piece of work*); to fill halfway; to empty halfway

ammezzato [ddzz] *m* mezzanine

ammiccare §197 *intr* to wink; to cock one's eye

amministrare *tr* to administer, manage

amministra·tóre -trice *mf* administrator, manager; **amministratore delegato** chairman of the board

amministrazióne *f* administration, management: **ordinaria amministrazione** run-of-the-mill business

ammiràbile *adj* admirable

ammiràglia *f* (nav) flagship

ammiragliato *m* admiralty

ammirà·glio *m* (-gli) admiral; **ammiraglio d'armata** admiral; **ammiraglio di divisione** rear admiral; **ammiraglio di squadra** vice admiral; **grande ammiraglio** admiral of the fleet

ammirare *tr* to admire || *intr* to wonder

ammirati·vo -va *adj* admiring; exclamation (*mark*)

ammira·tóre -trice *mf* admirer || *m* suitor

ammirazióne *f* admiration

ammirévole *adj* admirable

ammissibile *adj* admissible; permissible

ammissióne *f* admission; (mach) intake; **ammissione comune** consensus

ammobiliaménto *m* furnishing; furniture

ammobiliare §287 *tr* to furnish

ammodernare (ammodèrno) *tr* to modernize

ammòdo *adj invar* well-mannered, polite || *adv* properly

ammogliare §280 (ammóglio) *tr* to marry, give in marriage || *ref* to marry, get married

ammoglia·to *adj* married || *m* married man

ammollare (ammòllo) *tr* to soften; to soak; to slacken (*e.g., a hawser*); to deliver (*a slap*) || *ref* to get soaked

ammollire §176 *tr* to soften; to weaken || *ref* to soften; to mellow

ammonìaca *f* ammonia

ammoniménto *m* warning

ammonire §176 *tr* to admonish, reprimand

ammoni·tóre -trice *adj* warning

ammonizióne *f* admonition, warning

ammontare *m* amount, total || *v* (ammónto) *tr* to pile up || *intr* (ESSERE) to amount

ammonticchiare §287 *tr* to pile up, heap up

ammorbare (ammòrbo) *tr* to infect, contaminate

ammorbidènte *m* softener

ammorbidire §176 *tr* to soften; to mitigate || *ref* to soften

ammortaménto *m* amortization; payment, redemption (*of a loan*)

ammortare (ammòrto) *tr* to amortize
ammortire §176 *tr* to deaden; to weaken, soften
ammortizzaménto [ddzz] *m* amortization, amortizement
ammortizzare [ddzz] *tr* to amortize; (aut) to absorb (*shocks*)
ammortizzatóre [ddzz] *m* (aut) shock absorber
ammosciare §128 (**ammóscio**) *tr*, *intr* & *ref* var of **ammoscire**
ammoscia·to -ta *adj* (coll) downcast
ammoscire §176 *tr* to make sag; to make flabby ǁ *intr* & *ref* to sag; to become flabby; to droop
ammucchiare §287 *tr* to heap up, pile up ǁ *ref* to crowd together
ammuffire §176 *intr* (ESSERE) to become moldy
ammusare *tr* & *intr* to nuzzle
ammutinaménto *m* mutiny, riot
ammutinare (**ammùtino** & **ammutino**) *tr* to incite to riot ǁ *ref* to mutiny
ammutinato *m* mutineer
ammutolire §176 *intr* (ESSERE) to become silent; to be dumfounded
amnesìa *f* amnesia
amnistìa *f* amnesty
amnistiare §287 or §119 *tr* to amnesty
amo *m* hook; **abboccare all'amo** to bite, to swallow the hook
amorale *adj* immoral; amoral
amorali·tà *f* (-**tà**) immorality; amorality
amóre *m* love; eagerness; **amor proprio** amour-propre, self-esteem; **con amore** with pleasure; **d'amore e d'accordo** in perfect agreement; **fare all'amore** to make love; **fare l'amore** to flirt; **per amor del cielo** for heaven's sake; **per amore di** for the sake of; **un amore di bambino** a charming child; **un amore di cappello** a darling hat
amoreggiare §290 (**amoréggio**) *intr* to flirt; to play around
amorévole *adj* loving; kindly
amòr·fo -fa *adj* amorphous; safety (*match*)
amorino *m* cupid; cute child; love seat; (bot) mignonette
amoró·so -sa [s] *adj* loving; kindly; amorous; love (*e.g., life*) ǁ *mf* lover ǁ *m* fiancé ǁ *f* fiancée
amovibile *adj* removable
amperàg·gio *m* (-**gi**) amperage
ampère *m* ampere
amperòmetro *m* ammeter
amperóra *m* ampere-hour
ampiézza *f* width, breadth; trajectory (*of a missile*); amplitude; **ampiezza di vedute** open-mindedness
àm·pio -pia *adj* (-**pi -pie**) ample; wide; roomy
amplèsso *m* (poet) embrace
ampliaménto *m* amplification, extension
ampliare §287 *tr* to enlarge, widen ǁ *ref* to widen
amplificare §197 (**amplìfico**) *tr* to amplify; to widen; to exaggerate
amplifica·tóre *m* (rad & telv) amplifier
amplificazióne *f* amplification
amplitùdine *f* amplitude
ampólla *f* cruet; (eccl) ampulla
ampollièra *f* cruet stand

ampollosi·tà [s] *f* (-**tà**) grandiloquence, turgidity
ampolló·so -sa [s] *adj* grandiloquent, turgid
amputare (**àmputo**) *tr* to amputate
amputazióne *f* amputation
amulèto *m* amulet, charm
anabbagliante *m* (aut) low beam; **anabbaglianti** (aut) dimmers
anacàr·dio *m* (-**di**) cashew
ànace *m* var of **anice**
anacorè·ta *m* (-**ti**) anchorite, hermit
anacronismo *m* anachronism
anacronìsti·co -ca *adj* (-**ci -che**) anachronistic(al)
anàgrafe *m* bureau of vital statistics; registry of births, deaths, and marriages
anagram·ma *m* (-**mi**) anagram
analcòli·co -ca *adj* (-**ci -che**) nonalcoholic; soft (*drink*) ǁ *m* soft drink
analfabè·ta *mf* (-**ti -te**) illiterate
analfabèti·co -ca *adj* (-**ci -che**) unalphabetized, unalphabetic
analfabetismo *m* illiteracy
analgèsi·co -ca *adj* & *m* (-**ci -che**) analgesic
anàli·si *f* (-**si**) analysis; breakdown; **analisi grammaticale** parsing; **analisi dell'urina** urinalysis
anali·sta *mf* (-**sti -ste**) analyst; **analista finanziario** financial analyst; **analista tempi e metodi** efficiency expert, efficiency engineer
analìti·co -ca *adj* (-**ci -che**) analytic(al)
analizzare [ddzz] *tr* to analyze; to assay (*ores*); (telv) to scan
analogìa *f* analogy
anàlo·go -ga *adj* (-**ghi -ghe**) analogous; similar
anamnè·si *f* (-**si**) (med) case history
ananasso *m* pineapple
anarchìa *f* anarchy
anàrchi·co -ca (-**ci -che**) *adj* anarchical ǁ *m* anarchist
anatè·ma or **anàte·ma** *m* (-**mi**) anathema
anatomìa *f* anatomy
anatòmi·co -ca *adj* (-**ci -che**) anatomic(al)
ànatra *f* duck; drake
anatròccolo *m* duckling
an·ca *f* (-**che**) hip; (coll) thigh (*e.g., of a chicken*); **dare d'anche** to run away; **menare anca** to walk
ancèlla *f* maidservant
ancestrale *adj* ancestral
anche *adv* also, too; even; (poet) yet; **anche a** + *inf* even if + *ind*
anchilosare (**anchilòso**) *tr* to paralyze ǁ *ref* to become paralyzed
anchilòsto·ma *m* (-**mi**) hookworm
àn·cia *f* (-**ce**) (mus) reed
ancillare *adj* servant
ancòra *adv* still, yet; again; more e.g., **ancora cinque minuti** five minutes more
àncora *f* anchor; keeper (*of magnet*); armature (*of buzzer or electric bell*); **ancora di salvezza** last hope; **gettar l'ancora** to cast anchor; **salpare** or **levar l'ancora** to weigh anchor
ancoràg·gio *m* (-**gi**) anchorage, berth

ancorare (àncoro) *tr* to anchor; to tie (*e.g.*, *a currency to gold*) ‖ *ref* to anchor; to hold fast

ancorché *conj* although

andalu·so -sa *adj & mf* Andalusian

andaménto *m* course, progress

andante *adj* ordinary, common; continuous

andare *m* going; gait; **a lungo andare** in the long run; §106 *intr* (ESSERE) to go; to spread (*said of news*); to be (*e.g.*, *proud*); to work (*said of machinery*); (with *dat*) to fit, e.g., **quel vestito non gli va** that suit does not fit him; (with *dat*) to please, e.g. **quel vestito non le va** that dress does not please her; **andare a cavallo** to go horseback riding; **andare a finire** to wind up; **andare a male** to spoil; **andare a picco** to sink; **andare d'accordo** to agree; **andare in cerca di** to seek; **andare in macchina** to be in press; **andare in onda** (rad & telv) to go on the air; **andare per i vent'anni** to be bordering on twenty years; **andare pazzo per** to be crazy about; **andare soldato** to be drafted; **andare via** to go away; **come va?** how are things?; **mi va il vino dolce** I like sweet wine; **ne va della vita** life is at stake; **va da sé** it goes without saying ‖ *ref*—**andarsene** to go away, leave

anda·to -ta *adj* gone, past; finished; (coll) spoiled (*e.g.*, *meat*) ‖ *f* going; journey, trip; **a lunga andata** in the long run; **andata e ritorno** round trip; **dare l'andata a** to give the go-ahead to

andatura *f* gait; pace; **fare l'andatura** to set the pace

andazzo *m* bad practice, bad habit; fad

Ande, le the Andes

andicappare *tr* to handicap

andi·no -na *adj* Andean

andiriviè·ni *m* (-ni) coming and going; maze; ado

àndito *m* corridor, hallway

andróne *m* hall, lobby

aneddòti·co -ca *adj* (-ci -che) anecdotal

anèddoto *m* anecdote

anelante *adj* panting

anelare (anèlo) *tr* to long for ‖ *intr* to yearn; (poet) to pant

anèlito *m* last breath; yearning; (poet) panting; **mandare l'ultimo anelito** to breathe one's last

anellino *m* ringlet

anèllo *m* ring; link (*of a chain*); traffic circle; segment (*of a worm*); (sports) track; **ad anello** ring-shaped; **anello di congiunzione** (fig) link; **anello di fidanzamento** engagement ring ‖ **anella** *fpl* (poet) ringlets; (archaic) rings

anemia *f* anemia

anèmi·co -ca *adj* (-ci -che) anemic

anestesia *f* anesthesia

anestesi·sta *mf* (-sti -ste) anesthetist

anestèti·co -ca *adj & m* (-ci -che) anesthetic

anestetizzare [ddzz] *tr* to anesthetize

aneuri·sma *m* (-smi) aneurysm

anfi·bio -bia (-bi -bie) *adj* amphibian; (fig) ambiguous ‖ *m* amphibian

anfiteatro *m* amphitheater

anfitrióne *m* (lit) generous host

anfratto *m* ravine; narrow, winding, rugged spot

anfrattuosi·tà [s] *f* (-tà) rough broken ground; winding, rough spot

anfrattuó·so -sa [s] *adj* winding, rough, craggy

angariare §287 *tr* to pester, oppress

angèli·co -ca *adj* (-ci -che) angelic(al)

àngelo *m* angel; **angelo custode** guardian angel

angheria *f* vexation; outrage; imposition

angina *f* quinsy; **angina pectoris** angina pectoris

angipòrto *m* blind alley; narrow lane

anglica·no -na *adj & mf* Anglican

anglicismo *m* Anglicism

anglicizzare [ddzz] *tr* to Anglicize ‖ *ref* to become Anglicized

anglòfo·no -na *adj* English-speaking ‖ *m* English-speaking person

anglosàssone *adj & mf* Anglo-Saxon

angolare *adj* angular; corner (*stone*) ‖ *m* angle iron ‖ *v* (àngolo) *tr* to take an angle shot of; (sports) to kick (*the ball*) into the corner of the goal

angolazióne *f* (mov) angle shot

angolièra *f* corner shelving; corner cupboard

àngolo *m* angle; corner

angoló·so -sa [s] *adj* angular

àngora *f* Angora cat; Angora goat

angò·scia *f* (-sce) anxiety, distress, anguish

angosciare §128 (angòscio) *tr* to distress

angoscia·to -ta *adj* tormented, distressed

angoscló·so -sa [s] *adj* agonizing

anguilla *f* eel

anguillé·sco -sca *adj* (-schi -sche) as slippery as an eel

angùria *f* watermelon

angùstia *f* narrowness; scarcity; **stare in angustia** to be worried

angustiare §287 *tr* to distress, grieve ‖ *ref* to worry

angu·sto -sta *adj* narrow

ànice *m* anise

anicino *m* anise cookie

anidride *f* anhydride

àni·dro -dra *adj* anhydrous

anilina *f* aniline

ànima *f* soul; life (*e.g.*, *of the party*); core; kernel; bore (*of gun*); mold (*of button*); mind; enthusiasm; pith (*of fruit*); sounding post (*of violin*); web (*of rail*); **anima dannata** evil counselor; **anima mia!** darling!; **anima nera** villain; **anima viva** living soul; **buon'anima** late, e.g., **mio padre, buon'anima** my late father; **dannare l'anima** to lose patience; **la buon'anima di** the late; **rompere l'anima a** to annoy

animale *adj* animal; (poet) of the soul; (poet) animate ‖ *m* animal; (fig) boor, lout

animalé·sco -sca *adj* (-schi -sche) animal, bestial

animare (**ànimo**) *tr* to animate, to enliven; to promote ‖ *ref* to become lively or heated

anima·to -ta *adj* animated (*cartoon*); animated, lively; animal

anima·tóre -trice *adj* animating ‖ *m* moving spirit; (*mov*) animator

animazióne *f* animation

animèlla *f* sweetbread

ànimo *m* mind; heart, affection; courage; **aprire l'animo** to open one's heart; **avere in animo di** to have a mind to; **mal animo** ill will; **mettersi l'animo in pace** to resign oneself; **perdersi d'animo** to lose heart; **serbare nell'animo** to keep in mind

animosi·tà [s] *f* (-tà) animosity, ill will

animó·so -sa [s] *adj* bold; spirited (*animal*); hostile

anióne *m* anion

anisétta *f* anisette

ànitra *f* var of **anatra**

anitròccolo *m* var of **anatroccolo**

annacquare (**annàcquo**) *tr* to water; to water down

annaffiare §287 *tr* to sprinkle; to water (*wine*)

annaffia·tóio *m* (-tói) sprinkling can

annaffia·tóre -trice *adj* watering, sprinkling

annali *mpl* annals *spl*

annaspare *tr* to reel ‖ *intr* to gesticulate; to grope; to flounder

annata *f* year; year's activity; year's rent; year's issues (*of a magazine*)

annebbiare §287 (**annébbio**) *tr* to befog; to dim ‖ *ref* to become foggy; to become dim

annegaménto *m* drowning

annegare §209 (**annégo**) *tr & intr* (ESSERE) to drown

anneriménto *m* blackening

annerire §176 *tr* to blacken ‖ *ref* to turn black

annessióne *f* annexation

annès·so -sa *adj* united, attached ‖ *m* annex; **con tutti gli annessi e connessi** everything included

annèttere §107 *tr* to annex; to attach, enclose; to unite; to ascribe (*importance*)

annichilante *adj* annihilating; devastating (*e.g., reply*)

annichilare (**annichilo**) *tr* to annihilate ‖ *ref* to destroy oneself; (fig) to humble oneself

annichilire §176 *tr & ref* var of **annichilare**

annidare *tr* to nest; (fig) to nourish, cherish ‖ *ref* to nest; to hide; (fig) to settle

annientaménto *m* annihilation

annientare (**anniènto**) *tr* to annihilate; to knock down, demolish; (fig) to crush ‖ *ref* to humble oneself

annivèrsa·rio -ria *adj & m* (-ri -rie) anniversary

anno *m* year; **anno bisestile** leap year; **anno luce** light-year; **anno nuovo** New Year; **anno scolastico** school

year; **avere ... anni** to be ... years old; **l'anno che viene** next year; **l'anno corrente** this year; **quest'altr'anno** next year; **un anno dopo l'altro** year in, year out

annobilire §176 *tr* to ennoble

annodare (**annòdo**) *tr* to knot, tie; (fig) to tie up ‖ *ref* to get entangled

annoiare §287 (**annòio**) *tr* to bore ‖ *ref* to become bored

annòna *f* food; food-control agency

annonà·rio -ria *adj* (-ri -rie) food; rationing (*card*)

annó·so -sa [s] *adj* old, aged

annotare (**annòto**) *tr* to jot down; to chalk up; to annotate; to comment

annotazióne *f* note; notation, annotation

annottare (**annòtta**) *impers* (ESSERE) & *ref* to grow dark; e.g., **si annotta** it's growing dark; **è annottato** it grew dark

annoverare (**annòvero**) *tr* to count, number

annuale *adj* annual ‖ *m* anniversary

annuà·rio *m* (-ri) annual, yearbook

annuire §176 *intr* to nod assent; to consent

annullaménto *m* nullification, annulment

annullare *tr* to annul, nullify, cancel; to call off ‖ *ref* to cancel one another

annunciare §128 *tr* var of **annunziare**

Annunciazióne *f* Annunciation

annunziare §287 *tr* to announce; (fig) to forecast, foreshadow

annunzia·tóre -trice *mf* announcer, newscaster

annùn·zio *m* (-zi) announcement, notice; **annunzio economico** classified ad; **annunzio pubblicitario** advertisement; **annunzio pubblicitario radiofonico** (rad) commercial

ànnu·o -a *adj* yearly, annual

annusare [s] *tr* to smell; to snuff (*tobacco*)

annuvolaménto *m* cloudiness

annuvolare (**annùvolo**) *tr* to cloud, becloud ‖ *ref* to become cloudy; to turn somber

anòdi·no -na *adj* pain-relieving; ineffective; weak, colorless (*person*)

ànodo *m* anode

anomalìa *f* anomaly

anòma·lo -la *adj* anomalous

anonimìa *f* anonymity

anòni·mo -ma *adj* anonymous ‖ *m* anonymous author; **serbare l'anonimo** to preserve one's anonymity

anormale *adj* abnormal ‖ *m* queer fellow

anormali·tà *f* (-tà) abnormality

ansa *f* handle (*of vase*); pretext; bend (*of a river*)

ansante *adj* panting

ansare *intr* to pant

ànsia *f* anxiety; **essere in ansia** to be worried

ansie·tà *f* (-tà) anxiety

ansimare (**ànsimo**) *intr* to pant

ansió·so -sa [s] *adj* anxious

antagonismo *m* antagonism

antagoni•sta (-sti -ste) *adj* antagonistic || *mf* antagonist, opponent
antagonìsti•co -ca *adj* (-ci -che) antagonistic
antàrti•co -ca *adj* (-ci -che) antarctic || **Antartico** *m* Antarctic
antecedènte *adj* preceding || *m* antecedent
antecedènza *f* antecedence
antecessóre *m* predecessor
antefatto *m* background, antecedents
anteguèr•ra (-ra) *adj* prewar || *m* prewar period
anteluca•no -na *adj* (poet) predawn
antenato *m* ancestor
antènna *f* lance; (naut) yard; (rad & telv) aerial, antenna; (zool) antenna
antepórre §218 *tr* to prefer; to place before
anteprìma *f* (mov & theat) preview
anterióre *adj* fore, front; previous; earlier
antesignano [s] *m* forerunner
anti- *pref adj* anti-, e.g., **anticomunìstico** anticommunist; un-, e.g., **antieconomico** uneconomical || *pref mf* anti-, e.g., **anticomunìsta** anticommunist
antiabbagliante *adj* antiglare || *m* low beam
antiàci•do -da *adj & m* antacid
antiaère•o -a *adj* antiaircraft || *f* antiaircraft defense
antibattèri•co -ca *adj* (-ci -che) antibacterial || *m* bactericide
antibiòti•co -ca *adj & m* (-ci -che) antibiotic
anticà•glia *f* (-glie) antique, curio; rubbish, junk
anticàmera *f* waiting room, anteroom; **fare anticamera** to cool one's heels
anticarro *adj invar* antitank
antichi•tà *f* (-tà) antiquity; **antichità** *fpl* antiques
anticipare (antìcipo) *tr* to advance; to speed up; to pay in advance; to leak (*news*); to expect, anticipate || *intr* to be early
anticipa•to -ta *adj* in advance (e.g., *payment*)
anticipazióne *f* advance; collateral loan; expectation, anticipation
antìcipo *m* advance; loan (*on accounts receivable*); **in anticipo** in advance
anti•co -ca *adj* (-chi -che) antique, ancient, old; **all'antica** in the old-fashioned manner; **gli antichi** the ancients; the forefathers; **in antico** in olden times
anticoncezionale *adj & f* contraceptive
anticonformi•sta *mf* (-sti -ste) nonconformist
anticonformìsti•co -ca *adj* (-ci -che) unconventional
anticongelante *adj & m* antifreeze
anticongiunturale *adj* crisis, emergency
anticòrpo *m* antibody
anticristo *m* Antichrist
antidatare *tr* to predate
antiderapante *adj* nonskid
antidetonante *adj* antiknock || *m* antiknock compound

antidiluvia•no -na *adj* antediluvian
antìdoto *m* antidote
antievanescènza *f* (rad) antifading device
antifecondati•vo -va *adj & m* contraceptive
antìfona *f* antiphon; **capire l'antifona** (fig) to get the message
antifurto *adj invar* antitheft || *m* antitheft device
antigàs *adj invar* gas (e.g., *mask*)
antigièni•co -ca *adj* (-ci -che) unsanitary
antìlope *f* antelope
antimeridia•no -na *adj* antemeridian, A.M.
antimìssile *adj invar* antimissile
antimònio *m* antimony
antincèndio *adj invar* fire-fighting; fire, e.g., **scala antincendio** fire escape
antinéb•bia *adj invar* fog || *m* (-bia) fog light
antinéve *adj invar* snow, e.g., **catena antineve** snow chain
antiorà•rio -ria *adj* (-ri -rie) counterclockwise
antipatìa *f* antipathy, dislike
antipàti•co -ca *adj* (-ci -che) antipathetic; disagreeable; uncongenial
antipièga *adj invar* crease-resistant, wrinkle-proof
antìpodi *mpl* antipodes
antipòlio *adj invar* polio (e.g., *vaccine*)
antipòrta *f* stormdoor; corridor
antiquà•rio -ria *adj* (-ri -rie) antiquarian || *m* antiquary, antiquarian
antiqua•to -ta *adj* obsolete; antiquated
antireligió•so -sa [s] *adj* antireligious, irreligious
antirùggine *adj invar* antirust
antirumóre *adj invar* antinoise
antisala [s] *f* anteroom, waiting room
antisassi [s] *adj invar* protecting against falling stones
antischiavi•sta *adj & mf* (-sti -ste) abolitionist
antisemi•ta [s] (-ti -te) *adj* anti-Semitic || *mf* anti-Semite
antisemìti•co -ca [s] *adj* (-ci -che) anti-Semitic
antisemitismo [s] *m* anti-Semitism
antisètti•co -ca [s] *adj & m* (-ci -che) antiseptic
antisociale [s] *adj* antisocial
antisóle [s] *adj invar* sun (*glasses*); suntan (*lotion*)
antisommergìbile [s] *adj* antisubmarine
antistatale *adj* antigovernment
antitàrmi•co -ca *adj* (-ci -che) mothproof
antitèmpo *adv* early, prematurely
antìte•si *f* (-si) antithesis
antitèti•co -ca *adj* (-ci -che) antithetic(al)
antitossìna *f* antitoxin
antiuòmo *adj invar* (mil) antipersonnel
antivigìlia *f*—**l'antivigilia di** two days before
antologìa *f* anthology
antònimo *m* antonym
antrace *m* anthrax
antracite *f* anthracite

antro *m* cave; den, hovel
antròpi·co -ca *adj* (-ci -che) human
antropofagìa *f* cannibalism
antropòfa·go -ga (-gi -ghe) *adj* cannibalistic ‖ *m* cannibal
antropòlde *adj* anthropoid
antropologìa *f* anthropology
antropomòrfi·co -ca *adj* (-ci -che) anthropomorphic
antropomòr·fo -fa *adj* see **scimmia**
anulare *adj* ring-shaped, annular ‖ *m* ring finger
Anvèrsa *f* Antwerp
anzi *adv* on the contrary, rather; **anzi che no** rather ‖ *prep* (poet) before
anziani·tà *f* (-tà) seniority
anzia·no -na *adj* old, elderly; senior ‖ *m* senior
anziché *conj* rather than
anzidét·to -ta *adj* aforesaid
anzitutto *adv* above all, first of all
apatìa *f* apathy
apàti·co -ca *adj* (-ci -che) apathetic
ape *f* bee; **ape operaia** worker; **ape regina** queen bee
aperitivo *m* apéritif
apèr·to -ta *adj* open; frank, candid ‖ *m* open space; **all'aperto** in the open
apertura *f* opening; aperture; approach; **ad apertura di libro** at sight; **apertura alare** (*of a bird*) wingspread; (aer) wingspan
apià·rio *m* (-ri) apiary
àpice *m* apex, top; climax
apicol·tóre -trice *mf* beekeeper, apiarist
apicoltura *f* beekeeping, apiculture
Apocalisse *f* Apocalypse, Revelation
apocalìtti·co -ca *adj* (-ci -che) apocalyptic(al)
apòcri·fo -fa *adj* apocryphal
apofonìa *f* ablaut
apogèo *m* apogee
apòlide *adj* stateless ‖ *m* man without a country
apolìti·co -ca *adj* (-ci -che) nonpolitical, nonpartisan
apologè·ta *m* (-ti) apologist
apologèti·co -ca *adj* (-ci -che) apologetic
apologìa *f* apology
apòlo·go *m* (-ghi) apologue
apoplessìa *f* apoplexy
apoplètti·co -ca *adj & m* (-ci -che) apoplectic
apostasìa *f* apostasy
apòsta·ta *mf* (-ti -te) apostate
apostolato *m* apostolate
apostòli·co -ca *adj* (-ci -che) apostolic(al)
apòstolo *m* apostle
apostrofare (**apòstrofo**) *tr* to write with an apostrophe; to apostrophize
apòstrofe *f* apostrophe (*to a person*)
apòstrofo *m* (gram) apostrophe
apoteò·si *f* (-si) apotheosis
appagare §209 *tr* to satisfy, gratify ‖ *ref*—**appagarsi di** to be content with
appaiare §287 *tr* to pair, couple; to match ‖ *ref* to match (*said, e.g., of colors*)
appallottolare (**appallòttolo**) *tr* to

crumple into a ball ‖ *ref* to become lumpy
appaltare *tr* to contract for
appalta·tóre -trice *mf* contractor
appalto *m* contract; state monopoly; **appalto di sali e tabacchi** tobacco shop
appannàg·gio *m* (-gi) appanage; (fig) prerogative
appannare *tr* to tarnish; to befog, becloud ‖ *ref* to become clouded (*said, e.g., of one's eyesight*)
apparato *m* decoration; display; appliance; leadership (*of political party*); (rad, telv) set
apparecchiare §287 (**apparécchio**) *tr* to prepare; to set (*the table*) ‖ *ref* to get ready
apparecchiatura *f* sizing (*of paper; of a wall*); preparation (*of a canvas*); apparatus
apparéc·chio *m* (-chi) apparatus; sizing; preparation; gadget; (rad, telv) set; airplane; **apparecchio da caccia** fighter plane; **apparecchio telefonico** telephone
apparentare (**apparènto**) *tr* to tie, unite (*through marriage*) ‖ *ref* to become related; to become intimate; (pol) to form a coalition
apparènte *adj* apparent, seeming
apparènza *f* appearance; **in apparenza** seemingly
apparigliare §280 *tr* to pair, team (*horses*)
apparire §108 *intr* (ESSERE) to appear, seem; to look
appariscènte *adj* showy, flashy, gaudy
apparizióne *f* apparition; appearance
appartaménto *m* apartment
appartare *tr* to set aside ‖ *ref* to withdraw, retire
apparta·to -ta *adj* secluded, solitary
appartenènza *f* belonging, membership; **appartenenze** accessories; annexes
appartenére §271 *intr* (ESSERE & AVERE) to belong; to pertain ‖ *impers* (ESSERE & AVERE)—**appartiene a** it behooves, it is up to
appassionaménto *m* excitement, interest, enthusiasm
appassionare (**appassióno**) *tr* to move; to interest; to excite ‖ *ref* to be deeply interested
appassiona·to -ta *adj* impassioned; deep, ardent ‖ *m* fan, amateur
appassire §176 *intr* (ESSERE) to wilt, wither; to decay; to dry up (*said, e.g., of grapes*)
appellare (**appèllo**) *tr* (law) to appeal; (poet) to call ‖ *ref* to appeal; **appellarsi da** or **contro** (law) to appeal
appèllo *m* call, roll call; **fare appello a** to summon (*e.g., one's strength*); **fare l'appello** to call the roll; **mancare all'appello** to be absent
appéna *adv* hardly, scarcely; only; just ‖ *conj* as soon as; **non appena** as soon as, no sooner
appèndere §109 *tr* to hang
appendice *f* appendix; feuilleton
appendicectomìa *f* appendectomy

appendicite *f* appendicitis
Appennino, l' *m* the Appennines
appesantire [s] §176 *tr* to make heavy; to burden, overwhelm || *ref* to get heavy; to get fat
appestare (appèsto) *tr* to infect; to stink up
appesta·to -ta *adj* plague-ridden || *m* plague victim
appetire §176 *tr* to crave, long for || *intr* (ESSERE & AVERE) to be appetizing
appetito *m* appetite
appetitó·so -sa [s] *adj* appetizing, tempting
appètto *adv* opposite; appetto a opposite; in comparison with
appezzaménto *m* plot, parcel (*of land*)
appianare *tr* to smooth, level; to settle (*a dispute*); to get around (*a difficulty*)
appiana·tóio *m* (-tói) road grader
appiattare *tr & ref* to hide
appiattiménto *m* leveling; equalization
appiattire §176 *tr & ref* to flatten, to level
appiccare §197 *tr* to hang; appiccare il fuoco a to set on fire; appiccare una lite to pick a fight
appicciare §128 *tr* (coll) to string together; (coll) to kindle, light
appiccicare §197 (appìccico) *tr* to stick, glue; appiccicare uno schiaffo a to slap || *ref* to stick, adhere
appiccicati·cio -cia *adj* (-ci -ce) sticky
appic·co *m* (-chi) grip; steep wall (*of mountain*); (fig) pretext
appiè *adv*—appiè di at the foot of; at the bottom of
appiedare (appièdo) *tr* to order (*a cavalryman*) off a horse; to order (*e.g., troops*) off a vehicle; to force out of a car (*said, e.g., of motor trouble*)
appièno *adv* (poet) fully
appigionare (appigióno) *tr* to rent || *ref*—appigionasi for rent
appigiónasi [s] *m* for-rent sign
appigliare §280 *ref* to cling, adhere; appigliarsi a un pretesto to seize a pretext
appì·glio *m* (-gli) grip; (fig) pretext
appiómbo *m* perpendicular || *adv* plumb, perpendicularly
appioppare (appiòppo) *tr* to plant with poplar trees; to tie (*a vine*) to a poplar tree; (coll) to deliver (*a blow*); (coll) to pass off (*e.g., inferior goods*)
appisolare (appisolo) *ref* to snooze, doze
applaudire §176 & (applàudo) *tr* to applaud || *intr* to applaud, clap the hands; (with *dat*) to applaud
appláuso *m* applause; applausi applause
applicàbile *adj* applicable
applicare §197 (àpplico) *tr* to apply; to attach; to give (*e.g., a slap*); to put into effect (*a law*); to assign || *ref* to apply oneself
applica·to -ta *adj* applied; appliqué || *m* clerk
applicazióne *f* application; appliqué

applique *m* (elec) wall fixture
appoggiaca·po *m* (-po) headrest; tidy (*on back of chair*)
appoggiagómi·ti *m* (-ti) elbowrest
appoggiama·no *m* (-no) mahlstick
appoggiare §290 (appòggio) *tr* to lean; to rest; to prop, support; to raise (*the tone of voice*); to give (*a slap*); to second (*a motion*); (fig) to back, support || *intr* to lean; to rest || *ref*—appoggiarsi a or su to lean on
appoggia·tóio *m* (-tói) support, rest; banister
appoggiatura *f* (mus) grace note
appòg·gio *m* (-gi) support, prop; backer; backing, support; grip; (mach) bearing
appollaiare §287 *ref* to roost
appórre §218 *tr* to affix, append
apportare (appòrto) *tr* to cause; to presage; (poet) to carry
appòrto *m* carrying; contribution; (law) share
appositaménte *adv* expressly, on purpose
appòsi·to -ta *adj* proper, fitting
apposizióne *f* apposition
appòsta *adj invar* suitable || *adv* on purpose, expressly, intentionally
appostaménto *m* ambush
appostare (appòsto) *tr* to ambush || *ref* to lie in ambush
apprèndere §220 *tr* to learn || *ref* (poet) to take hold
apprendi·sta *mf* (-sti -ste) apprentice
apprendistato *m* apprenticeship
apprensióne *f* apprehension, fear
apprensí·vo -va *adj* apprehensive
appressare (apprèsso) *tr* (poet) to approach || *ref* to come near
appresso *adj invar* next, following || *adv* near; later on; appresso a near; after
apprestare (apprèsto) *tr* to prepare; to supply, provide (*e.g., help*) || *ref* to prepare, get ready
apprettare (apprètto) *tr* to dress (*leather*); to size (*cloth*)
apprètto *m* tan (*for leather*); sizing (*for cloth*)
apprezzàbile *adj* appreciable
apprezzaménto *m* appreciation; estimation
apprezzare (apprèzzo) *tr* to appreciate
apprezza·to -ta *adj* esteemed
appròc·cio *m* (-ci) approach; approcci advances
approdare (appròdo) *intr* (ESSERE & AVERE) to land; (with *dat*) (poet) to benefit; approdare a to come to
appròdo *m* landing
approfittare *intr*—approfittare di to capitalize on || *ref*—approfittarsi di to take advantage of
approfondire §176 *tr* to make deep; to study thoroughly || *ref*—approfondirsi in to go deep into
approntare (apprónto) *tr* to prepare, make ready
appropriare §287 (appròprio) *tr* to adapt; to bestow || *ref*—appropriarsi a to befit; appropriarsi di to appropriate; to embezzle

appropria·to -ta *adj* appropriate

appropriazióne *f* appropriation; **appropriazione indebita** fraudulent conversion, embezzlement

approssimare (appròssimo) *tr* to bring near || *ref* to approach, come near

approssimati·vo -va *adj* approximate

approssimazióne *f* approximation

approvàbile *adj* laudable

approvare (appròvo) *tr* to approve, countenance; to subscribe to (*an opinion*); to pass (*a student; a law*); to confirm

approvazióne *f* approval; confirmation; passage (*of a law*)

approvvigionaménto *m* supply

approvvigionare (approvvigióno) *tr* to supply || *ref* to be supplied

appuntaménto *m* appointment; date; **appuntamento amoroso** assignation

appuntare *tr* to sharpen; to fasten, pin; to stick (*a pin*) in; to point; to jot down, take note of; to prick up (*one's ears*); (fig) to reproach || *ref* to be turned; to aim

appunta·to -ta *adj* sharpened || *m* corporal (*of Italian police*)

appuntellare (appuntèllo) *tr* to shore up, prop up

appuntellatura *f* shoring up, propping up

appuntino *adv* precisely, meticulously

appuntíre §176 *tr* to sharpen

appunti·to -ta *adj* sharp, pointed

appunto *m* note; blame, charge; **muovere un appunto a** to blame; **per l'appunto** just, precisely || *adv* exactly, precisely

appurare *tr* to ascertain

appuzzare *tr* to befoul, pollute

apribottí·glie *m* (**-glie**) bottle opener

apri·co -ca *adj* (**-chi -che**) (poet) sunny, bright

aprile *m* April

apripí·sta *m* (**-sta**) blade (*of bulldozer*); bulldozer

apríre §110 *tr* to open; to turn on; to dig (*e.g., a grave*) || *ref* to open; to clear up (*said of the weather*); **aprirsi con** to open one's heart to; **aprirsi il varco** tra to press through

apriscàto·le *m* (**-le**) can opener

aquà·rio *m* (**-ri**) aquarium || **Aquario** *m* (astr) Aquarius

aquàti·co -ca *adj* (**-ci -che**) aquatic

àquila *f* eagle; genius

aquili·no -na *adj* aquiline

aquilóne *m* north wind; kite

aquilòtto *m* eaglet; cadet (*in Italian Air Force Academy*)

Aquinate, l' *m* Saint Thomas Aquinas

ara *f* (poet) altar; are (*100 square meters*)

arabé·sca *f* (**-sche**) (mus) arabesque

arabesca·to -ta *adj* arabesque

arabé·sco -sca (**-schi -sche**) *adj* arabesque || *m* arabesque; doodle || *f* see **arabesca**

Aràbia, l' *f* Arabia

aràbi·co -ca *adj* (**-ci -che**) Arabic

aràbile *adj* tillable

àra·bo -ba *adj* Arabic, Arabian || *mf* Arab (*person*) || *m* Arabic (*language*)

aràchide *f* peanut (*vine*)

aragonése [s] *adj* & *mf* Aragonese

aragósta *f* (*Palinurus vulgaris*) lobster

aràldi·co -ca (**-ci -che**) *adj* heraldic || *f* heraldry

araldo *m* herald

arancéto *m* orange grove

aràn·cia *f* (**-ce**) orange

aranciata *f* orangeade

aràn·cio *adj invar* orange (*in color*) || *m* (**-ci**) orange tree

arancióne *adj* & *m* orange (*color*)

arare *tr* to plow; (naut) to drag (*the anchor*)

aratro *m* plow

arazzo *m* tapestry, arras

arbitràg·gio *m* (**-gi**) (sports) umpiring; (com) arbitrage

arbitrale *adj* judge's, umpire's

arbitrare (àrbitro) *tr* to umpire, referee || *intr* to arbitrate || *ref*—**arbitrarsi di** to take the liberty to

arbitrà·rio -ria *adj* (**-ri -rie**) arbitrary; wanton

arbitrato *m* arbitration

arbí·trio *m* (**-tri**) will; abuse, violation; **libero arbitrio** free will

àrbitro *m* arbiter; judge, referee, umpire

arboscèllo *m* small tree

arbusto *m* shrub, bush

ar·ca *f* (**-che**) sarcophagus; ark; chest; **arca di Noè** Noah's Ark; **arca di scienza** (fig) fountain of knowledge

àrcade *adj* & *m* Arcadian

Arcàdia *f* Arcadia, Arcady

arcài·co -ca *adj* (**-ci -che**) archaic

arcaísmo *m* archaism

arcàngelo *m* archangel

arca·no -na *adj* mysterious, arcane || *m* mystery

arcata *f* arch; arcade

archeologìa *f* archaeology

archeològi·co -ca *adj* (**-ci -che**) archaeological

archeòlo·go -ga *mf* (**-gi -ghe**) archaeologist

archètipo *m* archetype

archétto *m* (archit) small arch; (elec) trolley pole; (mus) bow

archi- *pref adj* archi-, e.g., **architettonico** architectonic || *pref m* & *f* archi-, e.g., **architettura** architecture

archibù·gio *m* (**-gi**) harquebus

Archimède *m* Archimedes

architettare (architétto) *tr* to plan (*a building*); (fig) to contrive, plot

architétto *m* architect

architettòni·co -ca *adj* (**-ci -che**) architectural

architettura *f* architecture

architetturale *adj* architectural

architrave *m* architrave; doorhead, lintel

archiviare §287 *tr* to file; to lay aside, shelve; (law) to throw out

archì·vio *m* (**-vi**) archives; record office; chancery, public records

archivi·sta *mf* (**-sti -ste**) archivist, file clerk

arci- *pref adj* archi-, e.g., **arcivescovile** archiepiscopal ‖ *pref m & f* arch-, e.g., **arciprete** archpriest

arcicontèn·to -ta *adj* (coll) very glad

arcidiàcono *m* archdeacon

arcidu·ca *m* (**-chi**) archduke

arciduchéssa *f* archduchess

arcière *m* archer, bowman

arci·gno -gna *adj* gruff, surly

arcióne *m* saddlebow; **montare in arcioni** to mount, to mount a horse

arcipèla·go *m* (**-ghi**) archipelago

arciprète *m* archpriest; dean

arcivescovado *m* archbishopric

arcivéscovo *m* archbishop

ar·co *m* (**-chi**) bow; (archaic) arch; (geom, elec) arc; **arco rampante** flying buttress

arcobaléno *m* rainbow

arco·làio *m* (**-lài**) reel; **girare come un arcolaio** to spin like a top

arcuare (**àrcuo**) *tr* to arch; to bend; to camber

arcua·to -ta *adj* bent, curved; bow (*e.g., legs*); **avere le gambe arcuate** to be bowlegged

ardènte *adj* burning; hot; ardent, impassioned

àrdere §111 *tr* to burn ‖ *intr* to burn; to be in full swing (*said, e.g., of a war*)

ardèsia *f* slate

ardiménto *m* boldness, daring

ardire *m* boldness; presumption, impudence ‖ §176 *intr*—**ardire** + *inf* or **ardire di** + *inf* to dare to + *inf*

arditézza *f* daring; temerity

ardi·to -ta *adj* daring; rash ‖ *m* (hist) shock trooper

ardóre *m* intense heat; ardor

àr·duo -dua *adj* arduous

àrea *f* area, surface; group, camp; **area arretrata** backward area

àrem *m* (**àrem**) harem

arèna *f* arena; **scendere nell'arena** to throw one's hat in the ring

aréna *f* sand

arenare (**aréno**) *intr* (ESSERE) & *ref* to run aground

arenària *f* sandstone

arén·go *m* (**-ghi**) (hist) town meeting

arenile *m* sandy beach

arenó·so -sa [*s*] *adj* sandy

areòmetro *m* hydrometer

aeronàuti·co -ca *adj & f* (**-ci -che**) var of aeronautico

areoplano *m* var of aeroplano

areopòrto *m* var of aeroporto

areòstato *m* var of aerostato

àrgano *m* winch; (naut) capstan

argentare (**argènto**) *tr* to silver; to silver-plate; to back (*a mirror*) with foil

argenta·to -ta *adj* silver; silvery; silver-plated

argentatura *f* silver plating; silver plate; foil (*of mirror*)

argènte·o -a *adj* silver, silvery

argentería *f* silverware

argentière *m* silversmith; jeweler

argenti·no -na *adj* silver, silvery; Argentine ‖ *mf* Argentine ‖ *f* high-necked sweater ‖ **l'Argentina** *f* Argentina

argènto *m* silver; (archaic) money; **argenti** silverware; **argento vivo** quicksilver

argentóne *m* German silver

argilla *f* clay

argilló·so -sa [*s*] *adj* clayey

arginare (**àrgino**) *tr* to dam, dike; to hold back, check

àrgine *m* embankment, dam; (fig) defense

ar·go *m* (**-ghi**) (chem) argon; (orn) grouse ‖ **Àrgo** *m* Argus

argomentare (**argoménto**) *tr & intr* to argue

argomentazióne *f* argumentation, discussion

argoménto *m* argument; pretext; subject; **fuori dell'argomento** beside the point

argonàu·ta *m* (**-ti**) Argonaut

arguire §176 *tr* to deduce, infer; (archaic) to denote

argutézza *f* wit; witty remark

argu·to -ta *adj* keen, acute; witty

argùzia *f* keenness; wit

ària *f* air; climate; look; mien; aria, tune; opera; **all'aria aperta** in the open air; **a mezz'aria** in midair; halfway; **andare all'aria** to fail; **aria condizionata** air conditioning; **avere l'aria di** to seem to; to look like; **dare aria a** to air; **in aria** in the air; **tira un'aria pericolosa** a mean wind is blowing

aria·no -na *adj & mf* Aryan

aridi·tà *f* (**-tà**) dryness, aridity; dearth

àri·do -da *adj* arid, dry, barren; (fig) dry

arieggiare §290 (**arièggio**) *tr* to air; to imitate ‖ *ref*—**arieggiarsi a** to give oneself the airs of

ariète *m* ram; (mil) battering ram ‖ **Ariete** *m* (astr) Aries

ariétta *s* breeze; (mus) short aria

arin·ga *f* (**-ghe**) herring; **aringa affumicata** kippered herring, kipper

arin·go *m* (**-ghi**) assembly; field; joust; **scendere nell'aringo** to throw one's hat in the ring

arió·so -sa [*s*] *adj* airy, breezy; (fig) of wide scope

àrista *f* loin of pork

arista *f* (bot) awn

aristocràti·co -ca (**-ci -che**) *adj* aristocratic ‖ *mf* aristocrat

aristocrazìa *f* aristocracy

Aristòtele *m* Aristotle

aristotèli·co -ca *adj & m* (**-ci -che**) Aristotelian

aritmèti·co -ca (**-ci -che**) *adj* arithmetical ‖ *m* arithmetician ‖ *f* arithmetic

arlecchino *adj invar* harlequin; fiesta (*e.g., dishes*) ‖ **Arlecchino** *m* Harlequin

ar·ma *f* (**-mi**) arm, weapon; (fig) army; (mil) corps, service; **alle prime armi** at the beginning; **arma bianca** steel blade; **arma da taglio** cutting weapon; **arma delle trasmissioni** signal corps

armacòllo *m*—**ad armacollo** slung across the shoulders (*said of a rifle*)

armà·dio *m* (**-di**) cabinet; closet; **armadio a muro** built-in closet; **armadio**

d'angolo corner cupboard; **armadio farmaceutico** medicine cabinet; **armadio guardaroba** armoire

armaiòlo m gunsmith

armamentà·rio m (-**ri**) outfit, set (of tools)

armaménto m armament; crew; gun crew; crew (of rowboat); outfit, equipment

armare tr to arm; to dub (s.o. a knight); to outfit, commission (a ship); to cock (a gun); to brace, shore up (a building); (rr) to furnish with track || ref to arm oneself; to outfit oneself

arma·to -ta adj armed; reinforced (concrete) || m soldier || f army; navy; fleet; (nav) task force

arma·tóre -trice adj outfitting || m shipowner; (min) carpenter; (rr) trackwalker

armatura f armor; scaffold; framework, support; reinforcement (for concrete); (elec) plate (of condenser)

armeggiare §290 (**arméggio**) intr to fumble, fool around; to scheme; (archaic) to handle arms; (archaic) to joust

armeggi·o m (-**i**) fooling around; scheming, intriguing

armè·no -na adj & mf Armenian

arménto m herd

armerìa f armory

armière m (aer) gunner

armìge·ro -ra adj warlike, bellicose || m warrior; bodyguard

armistiziale adj armistice

armistì·zio m (-**zi**) m armistice

armonìa f harmony; **in armonìa con** according to

armòni·co -ca (-**ci -che**) adj harmonic; resonant; harmonious || f harmonica; **armonica a bocca** mouth organ

armonió·so -sa [s] adj harmonious

armonizzare [ddzz] tr & intr to harmonize

arnése [s] m tool, implement; garb, dress; (coll) gadget; **bene in arnese** well-heeled; **male in arnese** down at the heels

àrnia f beehive

arò·ma m (-**mi**) aroma, odor; zest

aromàti·co -ca adj (-**ci -che**) aromatic

aromatizzare [ddzz] tr to flavor; to spice

arpa f harp

arpeggiare §290 (**arpéggio**) intr to play arpeggios; to play a harp; to strum

arpég·gio m (-**gi**) arpeggio

arpìa f Harpy; (coll) harpy

arpionare (**arpióno**) tr to harpoon

arpióne m hinge (of door); hook; harpoon; spike (for mountain climbing)

arpionismo m ratchet

arpi·sta mf (-**sti -ste**) harpist

arrabattare ref to exert oneself, to strive, to endeavor

arrabbiare §287 intr (ESSERE) to go mad (said of dogs) || ref to become angry (said of people)

arrabbia·to -ta adj mad (dog); angry; obstinate; confirmed

arrabbiatura f rage; **prendersi un'arrabbiatura** to burn up (with rage)

arraffare tr to snatch

arrampicare §197 (**arràmpico**) ref to climb, climb up

arrampicata f climbing

arrampica·tóre -trice mf climber; mountain climber; **arrampicatore sociale** social climber

arrancare §197 intr to hobble, limp; to struggle, work hard; to row hard

arrangiaménto m agreement; (mus) arrangement

arrangiare §290 tr to arrange; to fix; (coll) to steal || ref to manage, get along

arrecare §197 (**arrèco**) tr to cause; to carry, deliver

arredaménto m furnishing; furnishings; equipment

arredare (**arrèdo**) tr to furnish; to equip

arreda·tóre -trice mf interior decorator; upholsterer; (mov) property man

arrèdo m furnishings, furniture; piece of furniture; **arredi sacri** church supplies

arrembàg·gio m (-**gi**) boarding (of a ship)

arrenare (**arréno**) tr to sand

arrèndere §227 tr (archaic) to surrender || ref to surrender; **arrendersi a discrezione** to surrender unconditionally

arrendévole adj yielding, compliant, flexible

arrendevolézza f suppleness; compliance

arrestare (**arrèsto**) tr to stop; to arrest || ref to stop, stay

arrèsto m arrest; stop; pause; (mach) stop, catch; **arresti** (mil) house arrest; **in stato d'arresto** under arrest

arretrare (**arrètro**) tr to withdraw || intr (ESSERE & AVERE) & ref to withdraw

arretra·to -ta adj withdrawn; backward; back (issue); overdue || **arretrati** mpl arrears

arricchiménto m enrichment

arricchire §176 tr to enrich || intr (ESSERE) & ref to get rich

arricchi·to -ta mf nouveau riche

arricciacapél·li m (-**li**) curler

arricciare §128 tr to curl; to wrinkle; to screw up (one's nose); **arricciare il pelo** to bristle (said of a person); to bristle up (said of an animal) || ref to curl up

arriccia·to -ta adj curled up || m first coat (of cement)

arricciatura f curling (of hair); pleating (of a skirt); kink (in a rope)

arrìdere §231 tr (poet) to grant || intr to smile

arrìn·ga f (-**ghe**) harangue; (law) lawyer's plea

arringare §209 tr to harangue; (law) to plead

arrischiare §287 tr to endanger; to risk || ref to dare, venture

arrischia·to -ta adj risky; daring

arrivare tr to reach || intr (ESSERE) to arrive; to happen; to get along, be

successful; **arrivare a** to reach; to
succeed in

arriva•to -ta *adj* arrived; successful;
ben arrivato welcome

arrivedér•ci *m* (**-ci**) good-bye ‖ *interj*
good-bye!, so long!

arrivedéria *interj* good-bye!

arrivismo *m* social climbing, ruthless
ambition

arrivi•sta *mf* (**-sti -ste**) social climber

arrivo *m* arrival; (sports) goal line;
(sports) finishing line

arroccare §197 (**arròcco**) *tr* to put (*e.g.*,
flax) on the distaff ‖ §197 (**arròcco**)
tr to shelter; (chess) to castle ‖ *ref*
to seek shelter; (chess) to castle

arròc•co *m* (**-chi**) castling

arrochire §176 *tr* to make hoarse ‖ *intr*
(ESSERE) to become hoarse

arrogante *adj* arrogant, insolent

arroganza *f* arrogance, insolence

arrogare §209 (**arrògo**) *tr*—**arrogare a
sé** to arrogate to oneself ‖ *ref* to
arrogate to oneself

arrolare §237 *tr* var of **arruolare**

arrossare (**arrósso**) *tr* to redden

arrossire §176 *intr* (ESSERE) to blush; to
change color

arrostire §176 *tr* to roast; to toast; **arrostire allo spiedo** to barbecue on the
spit ‖ *intr* (ESSERE) & *ref* to roast

arrò•sto *m* (**-sto** & **-sti**) roast

arrotare (**arròto**) *tr* to grind, hone; to
smooth; to strike, run over; to grit
(*one's teeth*) ‖ *ref* to grind (*to work
hard*); to sideswipe

arrotatrice *f* floor sander

arrotatura *f* sharpening

arrotino *m* grinder

arrotolare (**arròtolo**) *tr* to roll

arrotondaménto *m* rounding; rounding
out; increase (*in salary*)

arrotondare (**arrotóndo**) *tr* to make
round; to round out; to supplement
(*a salary*) ‖ *ref* to round out, become
plump

arrovellare (**arrovèllo**) *tr* to vex ‖ *ref*
to become angry; to strive, endeavor;
arrovellarsi il cervello to rack one's
brains

arroventare (**arrovènto**) *tr* to make red-
hot ‖ *ref* to become red-hot

arroventire §176 *tr* & *ref* var of **arroventare**

arruffapòpo•li *m* (**-li**) rabble-rouser

arruffare *tr* to tangle; to muss, rumple;
to confuse

arruf•fio *m* (**-fii**) tangle; confusion,
mess

arruffó•ne -na *mf* blunderer; swindler

arrugginire §176 *tr*, *intr* (ESSERE) & *ref*
to rust

arruolaménto *m* enlistment; draft

arruolare (**arruòlo**) *tr* to recruit; to
draft ‖ *ref* to enlist

arruvidire §176 *tr* to make rough,
roughen ‖ *intr* (ESSERE) to become
rough

arsenale *m* arsenal; navy yard

arsèni•co -ca (**-ci -che**) *adj* arsenic, ar-
senical ‖ *m* arsenic

ar•so -sa *adj* burnt; dry, parched; **arso
di** consumed with

arsura *f* sultriness; dryness

arte *f* art; ability; guile; **ad arte** on purpose; **arti e mestieri** arts and crafts

artefare §173 *tr* to adulterate

artefat•to -ta *adj* adulterated; artificial

artéfice *m* craftsman; creator

artèria *f* artery

arterioscleròsi *m* arteriosclerosis

arterió•so -sa [s] *adj* arterial

artesia•no -na *adj* artesian

àrti•co -ca *adj* (**-ci -che**) arctic ‖ **Artico**
m Arctic

articolare *adj* articular ‖ *v* (**artìcolo**)
tr & *ref* to articulate

articola•to -ta *adj* articulated; articulate; (gram) combined; jagged (*coast-
line*)

articolazióne *f* articulation

articoli•sta *mf* (**-sti -ste**) columnist; feature writer

artìcolo *m* article; item; paragraph;
articolo di fondo editorial; **articolo
di spalla** comment

artificiale *adj* artificial

artifi•cio *m* (**-ci**) artifice; sophistication,
affectation; **artificio d'illuminazione**
(mil) flare

artificiosi•tà [s] *f* (**-tà**) artfulness, craftiness; artificiality

artifició•so -sa [s] *adj* artful, crafty;
artificial, affected

artigianato *m* craftsmanship

artigia•no -na *adj* of craftsmen ‖ *m*
craftsman

artigliare §280 *tr* (poet) to claw

artiglière *m* artilleryman

artiglieria *f* artillery; **artiglieria a cavallo** mounted artillery

artù•glio *m* (**-gli**) claw; **cadere negli
artigli di** to fall into the clutches of

arti•sta *mf* (**-sti -ste**) artist; actor

artìsti•co -ca *adj* (**-ci -che**) artistic

ar•to -ta *adj* (poet) narrow ‖ *m* limb

artrite *f* arthritis

artrìti•co -ca *adj* & *mf* (**-ci -che**) arthritic

arturia•no -na *adj* Arthurian

arzigogolare [dz] (**arzigògolo**) *intr* to
muse; to cavil

arzigogolo [dz] *m* fantasy; cavil

arzil•lo -la [dz] *adj* lively, sprightly;
(coll) sparkling (*wine*)

arzin•ga *f* (**-ghe**) tong (*of a blacksmith*)

asbèsto *m* asbestos

ascèlla *f* armpit

ascendènte *adj* ascendant ‖ *m* upper
hand, ascendancy; **ascendenti** forefathers

ascendènza *f* ancestry, lineage

ascéndere §245 *tr* to climb ‖ *intr*
(ESSERE & AVERE) to ascend, climb

ascensionale *adj* rising; lifting

ascensióne *f* ascent, climb ‖ **Ascensióne**
f Ascension, Ascension Day

ascensóre *m* elevator

ascésa [s] *f* ascent

ascèsso *m* abscess

ascè•ta *mf* (**-ti -te**) ascetic

ascèti•co -ca *adj* (**-ci -che**) ascetic

ascetismo *m* asceticism

à•scia *f* (**-sce**) adze

asciugacapél·li *m* (-li) hair drier

asciugamano *m* towel; **asciugamano spugna** Turkish towel

asciugante *adj* drying; blotting; soaking ‖ *m* dryer

asciugare §209 *tr* to dry, dry up; to wipe; to drain (*e.g., a glass of wine*) ‖ *ref* to dry oneself; to dry, dry up

asciuga-tóio *m* (-tói) towel; bath towel

asciugatrice *f* dryer

àsciut·to -ta *adj* dry; skinny; blunt (*in speech*) ‖ *m* dry land; dry climate; **all'asciutto** pennyless

ascoltare (ascólto) *tr* to listen to ‖ *intr* to listen

ascolta·tóre -trice *mf* listener

ascólto *m* listening; **stare in ascolto** to listen

ascòrbi·co -ca *adj* (-ci -che) ascorbic

ascrit·to -ta *adj* ascribed; belonging ‖ *m* member

ascrivere §250 *tr* to inscribe, register; to ascribe, attribute

ascultare *tr* to sound (*s.o.'s chest*)

asèpsi [s] *f* asepsis

asètti·co -ca [s] *adj* (-ci -che) aseptic

asfaltare *tr* to tar, pave

asfalto *m* asphalt

asfissìa *f* asphyxia

asfissiante *adj* asphyxiating; poison (*gas*); boring

asfissiare §287 *tr* to asphyxiate; to bore ‖ *intr* (ESSERE) to be asphyxiated

asfodèlo *m* asphodel

Àsia, l' *f* Asia; **l'Asia Minore** Asia Minor

asiàti·co -ca *adj & mf* (-ci -che) Asian, Asiatic

asilo *m* shelter; asylum; home; **asilo di mendicità** poorhouse; **asilo infantile** kindergarten; **asilo per i vecchi** old-age home, nursing home

asimmetrìa [s] *f* asymmetry

asimmètri·co -ca [s] *adj* (-ci -che) asymmetric(al)

asinàggine [s] *f* stupidity, asininity

asi-nàio [s] *m* (-nài) donkey driver

asinata [s] *f* stupidity, folly

asinerìa [s] *f* asininity

asiné-sco -sca [s] *adj* (-schi -sche) asinine

asini·no -na [s] *adj* asinine

àsino [s] *m* ass, donkey; **fare l'asino a** (a slang) to play up to; **qui casca l'asino** here is the rub

asma *f* asthma

asmàti·co -ca [s] *adj & mf* (-ci -che) asthmatic

àsola *f* buttonhole; buttonhole hem

aspàra·go *m* (-gi) asparagus; piece of asparagus; **asparagi** asparagus (*as food*)

aspèrgere §112 *tr* to sprinkle

aspersióne *f* aspersing, sprinkling

aspettare (aspètto) *tr* to wait for, await; to expect; **aspettare al varco** to be on the lookout for ‖ *intr* to wait; **fare aspettare** to keep waiting ‖ *ref* to expect

aspettativa *f* expectancy, expectation; leave of absence without pay

aspètto *m* waiting; aspect, look; **al primo aspetto** at first sight

àspide *m* asp

aspirante *adj* suction (*pump*) ‖ *m* aspirant; applicant, candidate; suitor; upperclassman (*in naval academy*)

aspirapólve·re *m* (-re) vacuum cleaner

aspirare *tr* to inhale, breathe in; to suck (*e.g., air*); (phonet) to aspirate ‖ *intr* to aspire

aspiratóre *m* exhaust fan

aspirazióne *f* aspiration; (aut) intake

aspirina *f* aspirin

aspo *m* reel

asportàbile *adj* removable

asportare (aspòrto) *tr* to remove, take away

asportazióne *f* removal

asprézza *f* sourness; roughness, harshness

a·spro -spra *adj* sour; rough, harsh

assaggiare §290 *tr* to taste; to sample, test; **assaggiare il terreno** (fig) to see how the land lies

assaggia·tóre -trice *mf* taster

assàg·gio *m* (-gi) taste, sample; tasting; test, trial

assài *adj invar* a lot of ‖ *m* much ‖ *adv* enough; fairly; very

assale *m* axle

assalire §242 *tr* to attack, assail; (fig) to seize

assali·tóre -trice *mf* assailant

assaltare *tr* to assault; **assaltare a mano armata** to stick up

assalto *m* assault, attack; (law) battery; **cogliere d'assalto** to catch unawares; **prendere d'assalto** to assault

assaporare (assapóro) *tr* to taste; to relish, enjoy

assassinare *tr* to assassinate; (fig) to murder

assassì·nio *m* (-ni) assassination, murder

assassì·no -na *adj* murderous ‖ *mf* assassin, murderer

asse *m* axle; shaft, spindle; (geom, phys) axis; **asse ereditario** estate; **asse stradale** median strip ‖ *f* plank; **asse da stiro** ironing board

assecondare (assecóndo) *tr* to help; to second; to uphold

assediante *adj* besieging ‖ *m* besieger

assediare §287 (assèdio) *tr* to lay siege to, besiege

assè·dio *m* (-di) siege; **assedio economico** economic sanctions; **cingere d'assedio** to besiege

assegnaménto *m* awarding; allowance; faith, reliance; **fare assegnamento su** to rely upon

assegnare (asségno) *tr* to assign; to prescribe; to distribute; to award

assegnatà·rio -ria *mf* (-ri -rie) assignee

assegnazióne *f* assignment; awarding

asségno *m* allowance; check; **assegni** fringe benefits; **assegni familiari** family allowance; **assegno a copertura garantita** certified check; **assegno a vuoto** worthless check; **assegno di studio** (educ) stipend; **assegno turistico** traveler's check; **assegno vademecum** certified check; **contro assegno** C.O.D.

assemblàg·gio m (-gi) (mach) assembling, assembly

assemblèa f asembly

assembraménto m gathering

assembrare (assémbro) tr & ref to gather

assennatézza f good judgment, discretion

assenna·to -ta adj sensible, prudent

assènso m approval, consent

assentare (assènto) ref to be absent, to absent oneself

assènte adj absent || mf absentee

assenteìsmo m absenteeism

assentire (assènto) tr (poet) to grant || intr to assent, acquiesce; **assentire con un cenno** to nod assent

assènza f absence

assenziènte adj consenting, approving

assèn·zio m (-zi) absinthe; (bot) wormwood

asserire §176 tr to affirm, assert

asserragliare §280 tr to barricade || ref to barricade oneself

assèrto m (poet) assertion

asser·tóre -trice mf advocate, supporter

asserviménto m enslavement

asservire §176 tr to enslave; to subjugate

asserzióne f assertion

assessóre m councilman; alderman

assestaménto m arrangement; settling (of a building)

assestare (assèsto) tr to arrange; to adapt, regulate; to deliver, deal (a blow) || ref to become organized; to settle (said of a building)

assesta·to -ta adj sensible, prudent

assetare (asséto) tr to make thirsty; (fig) to inflame

asseta·to -ta adj thirsty; parched; eager || mf thirsty person

assettare (assètto) tr to tidy, straighten up || ref to straighten oneself up

assetta·to -ta adj tidy

assètto m arrangement; order; (naut) trim; **assetto longitudinale** (aer) pitch, attitude; **in assetto di guerra** ready for war; **male in assetto** in poor shape

asseverare (assèvero) tr to asseverate, assert

assicèlla f roofing board, lath; batten

assicuràbile adj insurable

assicurare tr to assure; to insure; to protect; to fasten; to deliver (e.g., a thief) || ref to make sure; to take out insurance

assicura·to -ta adj & mf insured || f insured letter

assicura·tóre -trice mf insurer

assicurazióne f assurance; insurance; **assicurazione contro gli infortuni sul lavoro** workman's compensation insurance; **assicurazione contro i danni** casualty insurance; **assicurazione incendio** fire insurance; **assicurazione infortuni** accident insurance; **assicurazione per la vecchiaia** old age insurance; **assicurazione sociale** social security; **assicurazione sulla vita** life insurance

assideraménto m freezing; frostbite

assiderare (assìdero) ref to freeze; to become frostbitten

assìdere §113 ref (poet) to take one's seat (e.g., on the throne)

assì·duo -dua adj assiduous, diligent

assième m ensemble || adv together; **assieme a** together with

assiepare (assièpo) tr & ref to crowd

assillante adj disturbing, troublesome

assillare tr to beset, trouble

assillo m gadfly; (fig) stimulus, goad

assimilare (assìmilo) tr to assimilate; to compare

assimilazióne f assimilation

assiòlo m horned owl

assiò·ma m (-mi) axiom

assiomàti·co -ca adj (-ci -che) axiomatic

assì·ro -ra adj & mf Assyrian

assisa f (poet) uniform, livery; (geol) layer; (archaic) duty, tax; **assise** criminal court; assembly, session; (hist) assises

assistènte mf assistant; **assistente sanitario** practical nurse; **assistente sociale** social worker || m—**assistente ai lavoro** foreman || f—**assistente di volo** (aer) hostess

assistènza f assistance, help; intervention; **assistenza pubblica** relief

assistenziale adj welfare, charity

assistere §114 tr to assist, help || intr—**assistere a** to attend, be present at

assito m flooring, boarding

assiuòlo m var of assiolo

asso m ace; **asso del volante** speed king; **piantare in asso** to walk out on

associare §128 (assòcio) tr to associate; **associare alle carceri** to take to prison || ref to associate; to become a member; to subscribe; to participate

associa·to -ta adj associate || mf associate, partner

associazióne f association; union; subscription; membership

assodare (assòdo) tr to solidify; to strengthen; to ascertain || ref to solidify; to strengthen

assoggettare (assoggètto) tr to subject, subdue || ref to submit

assola·to -ta adj sunny, exposed to the sun

assolcare §197 (assólco) tr to furrow

assoldare (assòldo) tr to hire, recruit

assólo m (mus) solo

assolutismo m absolutism

assolutìsti·co -ca adj (-ci -che) absolutist, despotic

assolu·to -ta adj & m absolute

assoluzióne f absolution

assòlvere §115 tr to absolve; to fulfill

assomigliare §280 tr to compare; to make similar, make equal || intr (ESSERE & AVERE) (with dat) to resemble, to look like; to be like || ref to resemble each other, look alike; **assomigliarsi a** to resemble

assommare (assómmo) tr to add; to be the epitome of; (archaic) to complete || intr to amount

assonna·to -ta adj sleepy

assopire §176 tr to lull to sleep; to

soothe || *ref* to drowse, to nod; to calm down

assorbènte *adj* absorbent || *m* sanitary napkin

assorbiménto *m* absorption

assorbire §176 & (**assòrbo**) *tr* to absorb

assorbi‧to -ta *adj* absorbed; **assorbito da** consumed with

assordare (**assórdo**) *tr* to deafen || *ref* to become deaf; to dim; to lessen

assortiménto *m* assortment; **avere in assortimento** (com) to carry, stock

assortire §176 *tr* to assort, sort out; to stock

assorti‧to -ta *adj* assorted; **bene assortito** well matched

assòr‧to -ta *adj* engrossed, absorbed

assottigliare §280 *tr* to thin; to sharpen; to reduce || *ref* to grow thinner

assuefare §173 *tr* to accustom || *ref* to become accustomed

assuefazióne *f* habit, custom

assùmere §116 *tr* to assume; to hire; to raise, elevate; (law) to accept in evidence

Assunta *f* Assumption

assunto *m* thesis, argument; (poet) task

assun‧tóre -trice *mf* contractor

assunzióne *f* assumption; hiring; (law) examination || **Assunzione** *f* Assumption

assurdi‧tà *f* (-tà) absurdity

assur‧do -da *adj* absurd || *m* absurdity

assùrgere §117 *intr* (ESSERE) (poet) to rise

asta *f* staff; rod; arm (*e.g., of scale*); lance; leg (*of compass*); stroke (*in handwriting*); shaft (*of arrow*); auction; (naut) boom; (naut) mast; (elec) trolley pole; **a mezz'asta** half-mast; **vendere all'asta** to auction, auction off

astante *mf* bystander || *m* physician on duty (*in a hospital*)

astanterìa *f* receiving ward

astato *m* (chem) astatine

astè‧mio -mia *adj* abstemious, temperate || *mf* teetotaler

astenére §271 *ref* to abstain

astensióne *f* abstension

astenuto *m* person who abstains from voting; abstention (*vote withheld*)

astèrgere §164 (*pp* **astèrso**) *tr* to wipe

asteri‧sco *m* (-schi) asterisk

asticcìola *f* penholder; rib (*of umbrella*); temple (*of eyeglasses*)

àstice *m* (*Hommarus vulgaris*) lobster

asticèlla *f* (sports) bar

astinènte *adj* abstinent

astinènza *f* abstinence

à‧stio *m* (-stii) grudge, rancor

astió‧so -sa [s] *adj* full of malice, spiteful

astóre *m* goshawk

astràgalo *m* astragalus, anklebone

astrakàn *m* Persian lamb

astrarre §273 *tr* to abstract || *intr—* **astrarre da** to leave aside, overlook

astrat‧to -ta *adj* abstract || *m* abstract

astrazióne *f* abstraction

astringènte *adj* & *m* astringent

-astro -astra *suf adj* -ish, e.g., **verdastro**

greenish || *suf mf* -aster, e.g., **poetastro** poetaster

astro *m* star, heavenly body; (bot) aster; (fig) star

astrologìa *f* astrology

astrològi‧co -ca *adj* (-ci -che) astrological

astròlo‧go *m* (-gi or -ghi) astrologer

astronàu‧ta *mf* (-ti -te) astronaut

astronàuti‧co -ca *adj* (-ci -che) astronautic(al) || *f* astronautics

astronautizzare [ddzz] *intr* (ESSERE) to be an astronaut

astronave *f* spaceship, spacecraft

astronomìa *f* astronomy

astrònomo *m* astronomer

astronòmi‧co -ca *adj* (-ci -che) astronomic(al)

astruserìa *f* abstruseness

astrusi‧tà *f* (-tà) abstruseness

astru‧so -sa *adj* abstruse

astùc‧cio *m* (-ci) case, box

astu‧to -ta *adj* astute, crafty

astùzia *f* astuteness, craftiness

àta‧vo -va *mf* ancestor

ateìsmo *m* atheism

atei‧sta *mf* (-sti -ste) atheist

Atène *f* Athens

atenèo *m* athenaeum; university

ateniése [s] *adj* & *mf* Athenian

àte‧o -a *adj* atheistic || *mf* atheist

atlante *m* atlas || **Atlante** *m* Atlas

atlànti‧co -ca *adj* (-ci -che) Atlantic || **Atlantico** *m* Atlantic

atlè‧ta *mf* (-ti -te) athlete

atletéssa *f* female athlete

atlèti‧co -ca (-ci -che) *adj* athletic || *f* athletics; **atletica leggera** track and field

atmosfèra *f* atmosphere

atmosfèri‧co -ca *adj* (-ci -che) atmospheric

atòllo *m* atoll

atòmi‧co -ca *adj* (-ci -che) atomic; (coll) stunning

atomizzare [ddzz] *tr* to atomize

atomizzatóre [ddzz] *m* atomizer

àtomo *m* atom

atòni‧co -ca *adj* (-ci -che) (pathol) weak

àto‧no -na *adj* (gram) atonic

atout *m* (atouts) trump

à‧trio *m* (-tri) entrance hall, lobby

atróce *adj* atrocious

atroci‧tà *f* (-tà) atrocity

atrofìa *f* atrophy

atròfi‧co -ca *adj* (-ci -che) atrophied

atrofizzare [ddzz] *tr* & *ref* to atrophy

attaccabottó‧ni *mf* (-ni) bore, pest, buttonholer

attaccabri‧ghe *mf* (-ghe) (coll) quarrelsome person, scrapper

attaccaménto *m* attachment, affection

attaccapan‧ni *m* (-ni) coathanger

attaccare §197 *tr* to attach; to bind, unite; to sew on; to stick; to hitch (*a horse*); to hang; to attack; to strike up (*a conversation*); to begin; to communicate (*a disease*); **attaccare un bottone a** (fig) to buttonhole || *intr* to stick; to gain a foothold, take root; to begin || *ref* to stick; to cling; to spread (*said of a disease*); (fig) to become attached

attaccatìc·cio -cia *adj* (**-ci -ce**) sticky

attacchino *m* billposter

attac·co *m* (**-chi**) attachment; onslaught; fastening; beginning; seizure (*e.g., of epilepsy*); spell (*e.g., of coughing*); (elec) plug; (rad) jack; (sports) forward line; **attacco cardìaco** heart attack

attagliare §280 *ref*—**attagliarsi a** to fit, become

attanagliare §280 *tr* to grip; to seize; to hold (*e.g., with tongs*)

attardare *ref* to tarry, delay

attecchire §176 *intr* to take root; to take hold

atteggiaménto *m* attitude

atteggiare §290 (**attéggio**) *tr* to compose (*e.g., one's face*); to place || *ref* to pose; to strike an attitude

attempa·to -ta *adj* elderly

attendaménto *m* camping; jamboree (*of Boy Scouts*)

attendare (**attèndo**) *ref* to encamp; to pitch one's tent

attendènte *m* (mil) orderly

attèndere §270 *tr* to await; (archaic) to keep; **attendere l'ora propizia** to bide one's time || *intr*—**attendere a** to attend to

attendìbile *adj* reliable

attendismo *m* wait-and-see attitude

attendì·sta (**-sti -ste**) *adj* wait-and-see || *mf* fence-sitter

attenére §271 *tr* (poet) to keep (*a promise*) || *intr*—**attenere** (with *dat*) to concern, e.g., **ciò non gli attiene** this does not concern him || *ref*—**attenersi a** to conform to

attentare (**attènto**) *intr*—**attentare a** to attempt (*s.o.'s life*) || *ref* to make an attempt, dare

attentato *m* attempt

attenta·tóre -trìce *mf* would-be murderer; attacker

attèn·ti *m* (**-ti**) attention || *interj* (mil) attention!

attèn·to -ta *adj* attentive; careful

attenuare (**attènuo**) *tr* to extenuate, play down; to attenuate; to mitigate

attenzióne *f* attention; **fare attenzione** to take care; **prestare attenzione** to pay attention

atterràg·gio *m* (**-gi**) landing; **atterraggio di fortuna** emergency landing; **atterraggio senza carrello** crash-landing

atterraménto *m* landing; pinning, pin (*in wrestling*); (boxing) knocking down; **atterramento frenato** (aer) arrested landing

atterrare (**attèrro**) *tr* to fell; to knock down; to pin (*in wrestling*); (fig) to humiliate || *intr* to land; **atterrare scassando** or **atterrare senza carrello** to crash-land

atterrire §176 *tr* to frighten, terrify || *ref* to become frightened

attè·so -sa [s] *adj* awaited; expected; **atteso che** considering that || *f* waiting; expectation; **in attesa (di)** waiting (for)

attestare (**attèsto**) *tr* to certify, attest; to prove; to join; (mil) to deploy || *ref* (mil) to take a stand

attestato *m* certificate

attestazióne *f* testimony; affidavit; attestation, proof

àtti·co -ca (**-ci -che**) *adj* & *mf* Attic || *m* attic

attì·guo -gua *adj* adjacent, contiguous

attillare *tr* & *ref* to preen

attilla·to -ta *adj* tight, close-fitting; tidy, all dressed up

àttimo *m* moment, split second; **di attimo in attimo** any moment

attinènte *adj* related, pertinent

attinènza *f* relation; **attinenze** appurtenances; annexes

attìngere §126 *tr* to draw (*water*); to get; (poet) to attain (*e.g., glory*)

attingi·tóio *m* (**-tói**) ladle

attirare *tr* to draw, attract

attitùdine *f* aptitude; attitude

attivare *tr* to activate; to expedite

attivazióne *f* activation; reassessment

attivi·tà *f* (**-tà**) activity; **attività** *fpl* assets

attì·vo -va *adj* active; profit-making || *m* assets

attizzare *tr* to stir, poke (*a fire*); (fig) to stir up

attizza·tóio *m* (**-tói**) poker

at·to -ta *adj* apt, fit || *m* act, action; gesture; (law) instrument; **all'atto pràtico** in reality; **atti** proceedings (*of a learned society*); **atti notarili** legal proceedings; **atto di nàscita** birth certificate; **fare atto di presenza** to put in a brief formal appearance; **atto di vèndita** bill of sale; **nell'atto** o **sull'atto** in the act

attòni·to -ta *adj* astonished

attorcigliare §280 *tr* to twist || *ref* to wind; to coil up

attóre *m* actor; (law) plaintiff; **attore giòvane** (theat) juvenile; **primo attore** (theat) lead

attorniare §287 (**attórnio**) *tr* to surround; (fig) to dupe

attórno *adv* around; **andare attorno** to walk around; **attorno a** around, near; **darsi d'attorno** to busy oneself; **levarsi qlcu d'attorno** to get rid of s.o.

attortigliare §280 *tr* to twist || *ref* to wind; to coil up

attraccare §197 *tr* & *intr* to moor, dock

attràc·co *m* (**-chi**) mooring, docking

attraènte *adj* attractive

attrarre §273 *tr* to attract, draw

attrattì·vo -va *adj* attractive; alluring || *f* attraction, charm

attraversaménto *m* crossing; **attraversamento pedonale** pedestrian crossing

attraversare (**attravèrso**) *tr* to cross; to go through; to thwart; **attraversare il passo a** to stand in the way of

attravèrso *adv* across; crosswise; **andare attraverso** to go down the wrong way (*said of food or drink*); (fig) to go wrong; **attraverso a** through, across || *prep* through, across

attrazióne *f* attraction

attrezzare (**attrézzo**) *tr* to outfit, equip

attrezzatura *f* outfit; gear, equipment; **attrezzatura di una nave** rigging; **attrezzatura** facilities

attrezzi·sta (**-sti -ste**) *mf* gymnast ‖ *m* toolmaker; (theat) property man

attrézzo *m* tool, utensil; **attrezzi** gymnastic equipment

attribuire §176 *tr* to award; to attribute; **attribuire qlco a qlcu** to credit s.o. with s.th ‖ *ref* to ascribe to oneself, claim for oneself

attributo *m* attribute

attribuzióne *f* attribution

attrice *f* actress; (law) plaintiff; **prima attrice** (theat) lead

attristare *tr* (poet) to sadden ‖ *ref* to become sad

attri·to -ta *adj* worn, worn-out ‖ *m* attrition; disagreement

attruppare *tr* to band, group ‖ *ref* to mill about, throng

attuàbile *adj* feasible

attuale *adj* present; present-day, current

attuali·tà *f* (**-tà**) timeliness; reality; **attualità** *fpl* current events; **di viva attualità** newsworthy; timely; in the news

attualizzare [ddzz] *tr* to bring up to date ‖ *ref* to become a reality

attuare (**àttuo**) *tr* to carry out, make come true ‖ *ref* to come true

attuà·rio -ria (**-ri -rie**) *adj* (hist) transport (*e.g., ship*) ‖ *m* actuary

attuazióne *f* realization

attutire §176 *tr* to mitigate; to deaden (*a sound, a blow*) ‖ *ref* to diminish (*said of a sound*)

audace *adj* audacious

audàcia *f* audacity

audiofrequènza *f* audio frequency

audiovisi·vo -va *adj* audio-visual

auditi·vo -va *adj* var of **uditivo**

auditóre *m* var of **uditore**

auditò·rio *m* (**-ri**) auditorium

audizióne *f* program; audition; (law) hearing

àuge *f* acme; **essere in auge** to enjoy a great reputation; to be in vogue; to be on top of the world

augurale *adj* well-wishing; salutatory

augurare (**àuguro**) *tr* to wish; to bid (*good day*) ‖ *intr* to augur ‖ *ref* to hope; to expect

àugure *m* augur

augù·rio *m* (**-ri**) wish; augury, omen

augustè·o -a *adj* Augustan

augu·sto -sta *adj* august, venerable

àula *f* hall; classroom; (poet) chamber (*of a palace*)

àuli·co -ca *adj* (**-ci -che**) courtly; noble, elevated

aumentare (**auménto**) *tr* to augment, increase ‖ *intr* (ESSERE) to increase, rise

aumént o *m* increase

àura *f* (poet) breeze; (poet) breath

àure·o -a *adj* golden, gold

aurèola *f* halo

auricolare *adj* ear; first-hand ‖ *m* (telp) receiver; (rad) earphone

auròra *f* dawn; (fig) aurora

ausiliare *adj* auxiliary ‖ *m* collaborator, helper

ausilià·rio -ria (**-ri -rie**) *adj* auxiliary; (mil) supply ‖ *m* helper; (mil) reserve officer ‖ *f* female member of the armed forces

ausì·lio *m* (**-li**) (poet) help

auspicare §197 (**àuspico**) *tr* to wish, augur

àuspice *m* sponsor; (hist) augur

auspì·cio *m* (**-ci**) sponsorship; (hist, poet) augury, omen; **sotto gli auspici di** under the auspices of

austeri·tà *f* (**-tà**) austerity

austè·ro -ra *adj* austere

australe *adj* austral, southern

Austràlia, l' *f* Australia

australia·no -na *adj & mf* Australian

Austria, l' *f* Austria

austrì·aco -ca *adj & mf* (**-ci -che**) Austrian

autarchìa *f* autarky; autonomy (*of an administration*)

autàrchi·co -ca *adj* (**-ci -che**) autonomous, independent

autènti·ca *f* (**-che**) authentication of a signature or a document

autenticare §197 (**autèntico**) *tr* to authenticate

autentici·tà *f* (**-tà**) authenticity

autènti·co -ca *adj* (**-ci -che**) authentic, genuine ‖ *f* see **autentica**

autière *m* (mil) driver

auti·sta *mf* (**-sti -ste**) (aut) driver

au·to *f* (**-to**) auto

autoabbronzante [dz] *adj* tanning ‖ *m* tanning lotion

autoaffondaménto *m* scuttling

autoambulanza *f* ambulance

autobiografìa *f* autobiography

autobiogràfi·co -ca *adj* (**-ci -che**) autobiographical

autoblinda·to -ta *adj* armored

autoblin·do *m* (**-do**) armored car

autobótte *f* tank truck

àuto·bus *m* (**-bus**) bus

autocarro *m* truck, motor truck

autocèntro *m* (mil) motor pool

autocistèrna *f* tank truck

autocivétta *f* unmarked police car

autocolónna *f* row of cars

autocombustióne *f* spontaneous combustion

autocontròllo *m* self-control

autocorrièra *f* intercity bus, highway bus

autocrazìa *f* autocracy

autocriti·ca *f* (**-che**) self-criticism

autòcto·no -na *adj* autochthonous, independent

autodecisióne *m* free will

autodeterminazióne *f* self-determination

autodidat·ta *mf* (**-ti -te**) self-taught person

autodidàtti·co -ca *adj* (**-ci -che**) self-instructional

autodifésa [s] *f* self-defense

autodisciplìna *f* self-discipline

autòdromo *m* automobile race track

autoemotè·ca *f* (**-che**) bloodmobile

autofilettante *adj* self-threading

autofurgóne *m* van; **autofurgone cellu-**

lare police van; **autofurgone funebre** hearse

autogiro *m* autogyro

autogovèrno *m* self-government

autògra·fo -fa *adj* autographic(al) || *m* autograph

auto·grù *f* (-**grù**) tow truck

autolesioni·sta *mf* (-**sti** -**ste**) person who wounds himself to avoid the draft or collect insurance

autoletti·ga *f* (-**ghe**) ambulance

autolibro *m* bookmobile

autolínea *f* bus line

autò·ma *m* (-**mi**) automaton, robot

automàti·co -ca (-**ci** -**che**) *adj* automatic || *m* snap

automatizzare [ddzz] *tr* to automate

automazióne *f* automation

automèzzo [ddzz] *m* motor vehicle

automòbile *f* automobile, car; **automobile da corsa** racing car; **automobile di serie** stock car; **automobile fuori serie** custom-made car

automobilismo *m* motoring

automobili·sta *mf* (-**sti** -**ste**) motorist

automobilìsti·co -ca *adj* (-**ci** -**che**) car, automobile

automo·tóre -trice *adj* self-propelled || *f* (rr) automotive rail car

autonolég·gio *m* (-**gi**) car rental agency

autonomìa *f* autonomy; (aer, naut) cruising radius

autonomi·sta *adj* (-**sti** -**ste**) autonomous

autòno·mo -ma *adj* autonomous, independent

autoparchég·gio *m* (-**gi**) parking; parking lot

autopar·co *m* (-**chi**) parking; parking lot

autopiano *m* player piano

autopilò·ta *m* (-**ti**) (aer) automatic pilot

autopómpa *f* fire engine

autopsìa *f* autopsy

autorà·dio *f* (-**dio**) car radio

autóre *m* author; perpetrator; creator, maker

autoreattóre *m* ramjet engine

autorespiratóre *m* aqualung

autorévole *adj* authoritative

autoriméssa *f* garage

autori·tà *f* (-**tà**) authority

autorità·rio -ria *adj* (-**ri** -**rie**) authoritarian

autoritratto *m* self-portrait

autorizzare [ddzz] *tr* to authorize

autorizzazióne [ddzz] *f* authorization

autoscala *f* hook and ladder; ladder (*of hook and ladder*)

autoscuòla *f* driving school

autoservì·zio *m* (-**zi**) bus service, bus line; self-service

autosilo *m* parking garage

autostazióne *f* bus station

autostèllo *m* roadside motel

auto·stòp *m* (-**stòp**) hitchhiking; **fare l'autostop** to hitchhike

autostoppi·sta *mf* (-**sti** -**ste**) hitchhiker

autostrada *f* highway, turnpike

autosufficiènte *adj* self-sufficient

autote·làio *m* (-**lài**) (aut) frame

autotrasportare (**autotraspòrto**) *tr* to truck

autotrasportatóre *m* trucker

autotreni·sta *m* (-**sti**) truck driver, teamster

autotrèno *m* tractor trailer

autoveicolo *m* motor vehicle

autovettura *f* car, automobile

autrice *f* authoress

autunnale *adj* autumnal, fall

autunno *m* autumn, fall

avallare *tr* to endorse (*a promissory note*); to guarantee

avallo *m* endorsement (*of a promissory note*)

avambràc·cio *m* (-**ci**) forearm

avampósto *m* outpost

avancàrica *f*—**ad avancarica** muzzle-loading

avanguàrdia *f* vanguard; avant-garde

avanguardismo *m* avant-garde

avanguardi·sta *m* (-**sti**) avant-gardist; (hist) member of Fascist youth organization

avannòtto *m* small fry (*young freshwater fish*)

avanti *adj* preceding || *m* forward || *adv* forward, ahead; **andare avanti** to proceed, to go ahead; **andare avanti negli anni** to be up in years; **avanti** in front of; **avanti che** rather than; **avanti di** before; **essere avanti** to be advanced (*in work or study*); **in avanti** ahead || *prep*—**avanti Cristo** before Christ; **avanti giorno** before daybreak || *interj* come in!

avantièri *adv* day before yesterday

avantrèno *m* (aut) front-axle assembly; (mil) limber

avanzaménto *m* advancement

avanzare *tr* to advance; to overcome; to be creditor for, e.g., **avanza cento dollari da suo fratello** he is his brother's creditor for one hundred dollars; to save || *intr* (mil) to advance || *intr* (ESSERE) to advance; to stick out; to be abundant; to be left over, e.g., **avanzano due polpette** two meatballs are left over; **avanzare negli anni** to grow older || *ref* to advance, come forward

avanza·to -ta *adj* advanced; progressive || *f* (mil) advance

avanzo *m* remainder; **avanzi** remains

avarìa *f* damage, breakdown; (naut) average

avariare §287 *tr* to damage, spoil || *intr* to spoil

avarìa·to -ta *adj* damaged, spoiled

avarìzia *f* avarice, greed

ava·ro -ra *adj* avaricious, stingy || *mf* miser

avellana *f* filbert

avellano *m* filbert tree

avèllo *m* (poet) tomb

avéna *f* oats

avére *m* belongings, property; assets, credit; amount due || §118 *tr* to have; to hold; to wear; to receive, get; to stand (*a chance*); to be, e.g., **avere . . . anni** to be . . . years old; **avere caldo** to be hot; to be warm; **avere fame** to be hungry; **avere freddo** to be cold; **avere fretta** to be in a hurry;

avere paura to be afraid; avere ragione to be right; avere sete to be thirsty; avere sonno to be sleepy; avere torto to be wrong; avere vergogna to be ashamed; avere voglia di to be anxious to; avere qlco da + inf to have s.th or to + inf, e.g., ho molto lavoro da fare I have a lot of work to do; averla con to be angry at; non avere niente a che fare con to have nothing to do with || impers—v'ha there is || to have, e.g., ha letto il giornale he has read the newspaper; avere da + inf to have to + inf, e.g., avevo da lavorare I had to work; to be to + inf, e.g., ha da venire alle cinque he is to arrive at five o'clock

avià•rio -ria (-ri -rie) adj bird || m aviary

avia•tóre -trice mf aviator || f aviatrix

aviazióne f aviation

avicoltóre m bird raiser; poultry farmer

avidi•tà f (-tà) avidity, greediness

àvi•do -da adj avid, greedy

avière m airman

aviogètto m jet plane

aviolìnea f airline

aviopista f (aer) airstrip

avioriméssa f (aer) hangar

aviotrasporta•to -ta adj airborne

avi•to -ta adj ancestral

a•vo -va mf grandparent; ancestor || m grandfather || f grandmother

avocare §197 (àvoco) tr to demand (jurisdiction); to expropriate

avò•rio m (-ri) ivory

avul•so -sa adj (poet) torn, uprooted; (poet) separated

avalére §278 ref—avvalersi di to avail oneself of

avallaménto m sinking, settling

avallare tr (poet) to lower (e.g., one's eyes) || ref to sink; (lit) to humiliate oneself

avalorare (avvalóro) tr to strengthen, confirm || ref to gain strength

avampare tr (poet) to inflame || intr (ESSERE) to burn

avantaggiare §290 tr to be profitable to; to benefit || ref to profit; avvantaggiarsi su to overcome; to beat

avedére §279 ref—avvedersi di to notice, become aware of

avedutézza f discernment; shrewdness

avedu•to -ta adj prudent; shrewd; fare qlcu avveduto di to inform s.o. of

avelenaménto m poisoning

avelenare (avveléno) tr to poison || ref to take poison; to be poisoned

aveniménto m happening, event

avenire adj invar future, to come || m future; in avvenire in the future || §282 intr (ESSERE) to happen, occur; avvenga quel che vuole come what may

aventare (avvènto) tr to hurl; to deliver (a blow); to venture (an opinion) || ref to throw oneself

aventatézza f thoughtlessness, heedlessness

aventa•to -ta adj thoughtless, heedless; all'avventata heedlessly

aventì•zio -zia adj (-zi -zie) outside, exterior; temporary, occasional

avvènto m advent; elevation, rise

aven•tóre -tóra mf customer, consumer

aventura f adventure

aventuriè•ro -ra adj adventurous || m adventurer || f adventuress

aventuró•so -sa [s] adj adventurous, adventuresome

averare (avvéro) tr to make true || ref to come true

avèr•bio m (-bi) adverb

aversà•rio -ria (-ri -rie) adj opposing, contrary || mf adversary, opponent

aversióne f aversion

aversi•tà f (-tà) adversity

avèr•so -sa adj adverse; (obs) opposite || avverso prep (law) against

avertènza f prudence, caution; advice; avvertenze instructions, directions

avertiménto m caution, warning; advice

avertire (avvèrto) tr to caution, warn; to notice

avezzare (avvézzo) tr to accustom; to inure; to train; avvezzar male to spoil || ref to get accustomed

avvéz•zo -za adj accustomed

aviaménto m starting; introduction; trade school; good shape (of a business); (mach) starting; (typ) adjustment (of printing press)

aviare §119 tr to start, set in motion; to introduce; to initiate; to begin || ref to set out

avvia•to -ta adj going, thriving (concern)

avicendaménto m alteration, rotation (of crops)

avicendare (avvicèndo) tr & ref to alternate

avicinaménto m approach; rapprochement

avicinare tr to bring near or closer; to approach, go or come near to || ref to approach, come near; avvicinarsi a to come closer, approach

avviliménto m discouragement, dejection

avilire §176 tr to degrade; to deject || ref to become dejected, become discouraged

aviluppare tr to entangle, snarl; to wrap

avinazza•to -ta adj & mf drunk

avincènte adj fascinating

avincere §285 tr to fascinate, charm; (poet) to twine

avinghiare §287 tr to claw; to clasp, clutch || ref to grip one another

avvì•o m (-i) beginning

avisàglia f skirmish; prime avvisaglie onset; first signs

avisare tr to inform, advise; (archaic) to observe, notice

avvisa•tóre -trice mf announcer, messenger || m alarm; (theat) callboy; avvisatore acustico (aut) horn; avvisatore d'incendio fire alarm

aviso m advise; notice; poster; opinion; avviso di chiamata alle armi notice of induction; **sull'avviso** on one's guard

avvistare *tr* to sight

avvitaménto *m* (aer) tailspin

avvitare *tr* to screw; to fasten || *ref* (aer) to go into a tailspin

avviticchiare §287 *tr* to entwine || *ref* to cling

avvivare *tr* to revive; to stir up

avvizzire §176 *tr* & *intr* (ESSERE) to wither

avvocatéssa *f* woman lawyer

avvocato *m* lawyer, attorney

avvocatura *f* law, legal profession

avvòlgere §289 *tr* to wind; to wrap up; to spread over, surround || *ref* to wind around; to wrap oneself up

avvolgiménto *m* winding; wrapping; (elec) coil; (mil) envelopment

avvol·tóio *m* (-tói) vulture

avvoltolare (avvòltolo) *tr* to roll up || *ref* to roll around, wallow

azièenda [dz] *f* business, firm

azionare (azióno) *tr* to start; to drive, propel

aziona·rio -ria *adj* (-ri -rie) (com) stock

azióne *f* action, act; (law) suit; (com) share (*of stock*); **azione legale** prosecution; **azione privilegiata** preferred stock

azioni·sta *mf* (-sti -ste) stockholder, shareholder

azòto [dz] *m* nitrogen

azoturo [dz] *m* nitride

aztè·co -ca *adj* & *mf* (-chi -che) Aztec

azzannare *tr* to seize with the fangs

azzardare [ddzz] *tr* to risk; to advance || *ref* to dare

azzarda·to -ta [ddzz] *adj* daring

azzardo [ddzz] *m* chance, hazard

azzardó·so -sa [ddzz] [s] *adj* hazardous, risky

azzeccagarbu·gli *m* (-gli) shyster

azzeccare §197 (azzécco) *tr* to hit; to deliver; to pass off (*counterfeit money*); **azzeccarla** (coll) to hit the mark

azzimare [ddzz] (àzzimo) *tr* & *ref* to spruce up

àzzi·mo -ma [ddzz] *adj* unleavened (*bread*)

azzittare & azzittire §176 *tr* to hush || *ref* to keep quiet

azzoppare (azzòppo) *tr* to cripple || *ref* to become lame or crippled

Azzòrre [ddzz] *fpl* Azores

azzuffare *ref* to come to blows; to scuffle

azzur·ro -ra [ddzz] *adj* blue || *m* blue; Italian athlete (*in international competition*)

azzurrógno·lo -la [ddzz] *adj* bluish

B

B, b [bi] *m* & *f* second letter of the Italian alphabet

ba·bàu *m* (-bàu) bogey, bugbear

babbè·o -a *adj* foolish || *mf* fool

babbo *m* (coll) daddy, father

babbù·cia *f* (-ce) babouche; bedroom slipper

babbuino *m* baboon

babèle *f* babel || **Babele** *f* Babel

babilònia *f* confusion || **Babilònia** *f* Babylon

babórdo *m* (naut) port

bacare §197 *ref* to become worm-eaten

baca·to -ta *adj* worm-eaten; rotten

bac·ca *f* (-che) berry

bacca·là *m* (-là) dried codfish; (coll) skinny person; (coll) lummox

baccalaureato *m* baccalaureate, bachelor's degree

baccanale *m* bacchanal

baccano *m* noise, hubbub; **fare baccano** to carry on

baccante *f* bacchant

baccellière *m* (hist) bachelor

baccèllo *m* pod

baccellóne *m* simpleton, fool

bacchétta *f* rod, wand, baton; **bacchetta magica** magic wand; **bacchette del tamburo** drumsticks

bacchétto *m* stick; handle (*of a whip*)

bacchettó·ne -na *mf* bigot

bàcchi·co -ca *adj* (-ci -che) Bacchic

Bacco *m* Baccus

bachè·ca *f* (-che) showcase

bachelite *f* bakelite

bacheròzzo *m* worm; earthworm; (coll) cockroach

bachicoltura *f* silkworm raising

baciama·no *m* (-ni) kissing of the hand

baciapi·le *mf* (-le) bigot

baciare §128 *tr* to kiss; **baciare la pólvere** to bite the dust || *ref* to kiss one another

bacia·to -ta *adj* kissed; rhymed (*couplet*)

bacile *m* basin

bacillo *m* bacillus

bacinèlla *f* small basin; (phot) tray

bacino *m* basin; reservoir; cove; (anat) pelvis; **bacino carbonifero** coal field; **bacino di carenaggio** drydock; **bacino fluviale** river basin

bà·cio *m* (-ci) kiss; **a bacio** with a northern exposure

baciucchiare §287 *tr* to keep on kissing || *ref* to pet

ba·co *m* (-chi) worm; **baco da seta** silkworm

bacuc·co -ca *adj* (-chi -che)—**vecchio bacucco** dotard

bada *f*—**tenere a bada** to stave off; to delay

badare *tr* to tend, take care of || *intr* to attend; to take care; to pay attention; **badare a** to mind; to watch over; to attend to; **badare alla salute** to take care of one's health

badéssa f abbess

badìa f abbey

badilata f shovelful

badile m shovel

baffo m whiskers; whisker; **baffi** mustache; whiskers; **baffo di gatto** (rad) cat's whiskers; **leccarsi i baffi** to lick one's chops; **sotto i baffi** up one's sleeve

baga·glìalo m (-gliài) (rr) baggage car; (rr) baggage room; (aut) baggage rack

bagaglièra f baggage room

bagaglière m baggage master

bagà·glio m (-gli) baggage, luggage; (of knowledge) fund

bagagli·sta m (-sti) porter (in a hotel)

bagarinàg·gio m (-gi) profiteering; (theat) scalping

bagarino m profiteer; scalper

bagà·scia f (-sce) harlot, prostitute

bagattèlla f trifle, bauble

baggiano m nitwit, simpleton

bà·glio m (-gli) (naut) beam

baglióre m shine, gleam

bagnante mf bather, swimmer; vacationer at the seashore

bagnare tr to bathe; to wet; to soak; to water, sprinkle; to moisten; (fig) to celebrate || ref to bathe; to wet one another

bagnaròla f (coll) bathtub

bagnasciu·ga f (-ghe) (naut) waterline

bagnino m lifeguard

bagno m bath; bathroom; bathtub; **bagno di luce** diathermy; **bagno di schiuma** bubble bath; **bagno di sole** sun bath; **bagno di vapore** steam bath; **bagno turco** Turkish bath; **essere in un bagno di sudore** to be soaked with perspiration; **fare il bagno** to take a bath

bagnomaria m (**bagnimarìa**) double boiler; bain-marie; **a bagnomaria** in a double boiler

bagórdo m carousal, revelry; **far bagordi** to carouse, revel

bàio bàia (bài bàie) adj & m bay || f bay; jest; trifle; **dare la baia a** to make fun of, tease

baionétta f bayonet; **baionetta in canna** with fixed bayonet

bàita f mountain hut

balaustrata f balustrade

balaùstro m baluster

balbettaménto m stammering

balbettare (**balbétto**) tr to stammer; to speak poorly (a foreign language) || intr to stammer; to babble (said of a baby)

balbettì·o m (-i) babble (of a baby); stammering

balbùzie f stammering

balbuziènte adj stammering || mf stammerer

Balcani, i the Balkans

balcàni·co -ca adj (-ci -che) Balkan

balconata f balcony; (theat) upper gallery

balcóne m balcony

baldacchino m canopy, baldachin

baldanza f boldness; aplomb, assurance

baldanzó·so -sa [s] adj bold; self-assured

bal·do -da adj bold; self-assured

baldòria f carousal, revelry; **fare baldoria** to carouse, revel

baldrac·ca f (-che) harlot, prostitute

baléna f whale

balenare (**baléno**) intr to stagger || intr (ESSERE) to flash, e.g., **gli balena un pensiero** a thought flashes through his mind || impers (ESSERE)—**balena,** it is lightning

balenièra f whaler, whaleboat

baléno m flash; flash of lightning; **in un baleno** in a flash

balenòttera f rorqual

balèstra f crossbow; (aut) spring, leaf spring

balestrière m crossbowman

bàlia f wet nurse; **balia asciutta** dry nurse; **prendere a balia** to wet-nurse

balìa f power; **in balìa di** at the mercy of

balìsti·co -ca (-ci -che) adj ballistic || f ballistics

balla f bale; (vulg) lie

ballàbile adj dance || m dance tune

ballare tr to dance || intr to dance; to shake; to be loose; to wobble (said, e.g., of a chair)

ballata f ballad; (mus) ballade

balla·tóio m (-tói) gallery; perch (in birdcage)

balleri·no -na adj dancing || m ballet dancer; dancer; dancing partner || f dancing girl; ballerina; chorus girl; ballet slipper; (orn) wagtail

ballétto m ballet; chorus

ballo m dance; chorus; ball; stake; **ballo di San Vito** Saint Vitus's dance; **ballo in maschera** masked ball; **in ballo** at stake; in question; **tirare in ballo** to drag in

ballonzolare (**ballónzolo**) intr to hop around

ballottàg·gio m (-gi) runoff

ballottare (**ballòtto**) tr to ballot (e.g., a candidate)

balneare adj bathing; water, watering

baloccare §197 (**balòcco**) tr to amuse with toys || ref to play; to trifle, to fool around

balòc·co m (-chi) toy; hobby

balordàggine f silliness

balór·do -da adj silly, foolish

balsàmi·co -ca adj (-ci -che) balmy; antiseptic

balsamina f balsam

bàlsamo m balm, balsam

bàlti·co -ca adj (-ci -che) Baltic

baluardo m bastion, bulwark

baluginare (**balùgino**) intr (ESSERE) to flicker; to flash (through one's mind)

balza f crag, cliff; flounce (on dress); fringe (on curtains, bedspreads, etc.)

balza·no -na adj white-footed (horse); odd, funny || f flounce; fringe; white mark (on horse's foot)

balzare tr to throw (a rider; said of a horse) || intr (ESSERE) to jump, leap;

to bounce; **balzare in mente a** to suddenly dawn on

balzellare (balzèllo) *intr* to hop

balzèllo *m* hop; tribute; tax; toll; **stare a balzello** to lie in wait

balzellóni *adv*—a **balzelloni** leaping, skipping

balzo *m* leap; bounce; **pigliare la palla al balzo** to take time by the forelock

bambàgia *f* cotton wool

bambinàggine *f* childishness

bambinàia *f* nursemaid; **bambinaia ad ore** baby sitter

bambiné·sco -sca *adj* (**-schi -sche**) childish

bambi·no -na *adj* childish || *mf* child

bambòc·cio *m* (**-ci**) fat baby; doll; rag doll

bàmbola *f* doll; **bambola di pezza** rag-doll

bam·bù *m* (**-bù**) bamboo

banale *adj* banal, commonplace

banali·tà *f* (**-tà**) banality, commonplaceness, triviality

banana *f* banana; hair with curls shaped as rolls

bananièra *f* banana boat

banano *m* banana plant

ban·ca *f* (**-che**) bank; embankment

bancàbile *adj* negotiable

bancarèlla *f* cart, pushcart; stall

bancà·rio -ria (**-ri -rie**) *adj* bank, banking || *m* bank clerk

bancarótta *f* bankruptcy; **fare bancarotta** to go bankrupt

banchettare (banchétto) *intr* to feast, banquet

banchétto *m* banquet

banchière *m* banker

banchina *f* garden bench; bicycle path; sidewalk; shoulder (*of highway*); dock, pier; (rr) platform; (mil) banquette

ban·co *m* (**-chi**) bench; seat; bank; witness stand; school (*of fish*); **banco di coralli** coral reef; **banco di ghiaccio** ice pack; **banco di nebbia** fog bank; **banco di prova** (mach) bench; **banco di sabbia** sandbar; **banco d'ostriche** oyster bed; **banco lotto** lottery office

bancogiro *m* (com) transfer of funds

bancóne *m* counter; bench

banconòta *f* banknote

banda *f* band; **andare alla banda** (naut) to list; **da ogni banda** from every side; **mettere da banda** to put aside

bandèlla *f* hinge (*of door or window*); hinged leaf (*of table*)

banderuòla *f* banderole; weather vane

bandièra *f* flag; banner; **battere la bandiera** (*e.g.*, **italiana**) to fly the (*e.g* *Italian*) flag; **mutar bandiera** to change sides

bandierare (bandièro) *tr* (aer) to feather

bandire §176 *tr* to announce (*e.g.*, *a competitive examination*); to banish

bandìsti·co -ca *adj* (**-ci -che**) (mus) band

bandi·to -ta *adj* announced; open (*house*) || *m* bandit | *f* preserve (*for hunting or fishing*)

bandi·tóre -trice *mf* town crier; auctioneer; barker

bando *m* announcement; banishment; **bandi matrimoniali** (eccl) banns; **mandare in bando** to exile, banish

bandolièra *f* bandoleer; **a bandoliera** slung across the shoulders

bàndolo *m* end of a skein; **perdere il bandolo** to lose the thread (*e.g.*, *of a story*)

bara *f* bier, coffin

barac·ca *f* (**-che**) hut, cabin; (fig) household; **fare baracca** to carouse around

baracca·to -ta *adj* lodged in a hut or a cabin; slum (*e.g.*, *section*) || *m* dweller in a hut or a cabin; slum dweller

baraccóne *m* big circus tent

baraónda *f* hubbub; mess

barare *intr* to cheat (*e.g.*, *at cards*)

bàratro *m* abyss, chasm

barattare *tr* to barter; **barattare le carte in mano a uno** to distort someone's words; **barattar parole** to chat, talk || *intr* to barter

barattière *m* grafter

baratto *m* barter

baràttolo *m* can, canister, jar

barba *f* beard; whiskers; barb, vane (*of feather*); (naut) line; **barba a punta** imperial, goatee; **fare la barba (a)** to shave; **farla in barba a qlcu** to act in spite of s.o.; to dupe s.o.; **mettere barbe** to take root; **radersi la barba** to shave

barbabiètola *f* beet; sugar beet

barbafòrte *m* horseradish

barbagian·ni *m* (**-ni**) owl; (fig) jackass

barbà·glio *m* (**-gli**) glitter, dazzle

barbaré·sco -sca (**-schi -sche**) *adj* Barbary || *m* inhabitant of the Barbary States

barbàri·co -ca *adj* (**-ci -che**) barbaric

barbà·rie *f* (**-rie**) barbarism, barbarity

barbarismo *m* barbarism

bàrba·ro -ra *adj* barbarous, barbaric || *m* barbarian

barbazzale *m* curb (*of bit*)

Barberìa, la Barbary States

barbétta *f* fetlock (*tuft of hair on horse*); goatee; (mil) barbette; (naut) painter

barbière *m* barber

barbierìa *f* barbershop

barbì·glio *m* (**-gli**) barb (*of arrow*)

barbi·no -na *adj* shoddy; botched; stingy

bàr·bio *m* (**-bi**) (ichth) barbel

barbiturato *m* barbiturate

barbitùri·co -ca (**-ci -che**) *adj* barbituric || *m* barbiturate

barbo *m* var of **barbio**

barbó·gio -gia *adj* (**-gi -gie**) senile

barbóne *m* long beard, thick beard; poodle; (coll) bum, hobo

barbó·so -sa [s] *adj* boring

barbugliare §280 *tr* to stutter (*e.g.*, *a word*) || *intr* to stutter; to bubble, gurgle

barbu·to -ta *adj* bearded

bar·ca *f* (**-che**) boat; heap; (fig) family

affairs; **barca a motore** motorboat; **barca da pesca** fishing boat; **barca a remi** rowboat

barcàc·cia f (-ce) (theat) stage box

barcaiòlo m boatman

barcamenare (**barcaméno**) ref to manage, get along

barcarizzo m (naut) gangway

barcaròla f barcarole

barcata f boatful

barchéssa f tool shed

barchétta f small boat; (naut) log chip

barcollare (**barcòllo**) intr to totter, stagger

barcollóni adv staggering, tottering

barcóne m barge

bardare tr to harness || ref to get dressed

bardatura f harnessing; harness

bardo m bard

bardòsso m—**a bardosso** (archaic) bareback

barèlla f stretcher

barellare (**barèllo**) tr to carry on a stretcher || intr to totter, stagger

barenatura f (mach) boring

bargèllo m (hist) chief of police; (hist) police headquarters

bargì·glio m (-gli) wattle

baricèntro m center of gravity; (fig) essence, gist

barile m barrel, cask

barilòtto m keg

bàrio m barium

bari·sta mf (-sti -ste) bartender, barkeeper || m barman || f barmaid

baritonale adj baritone

baritò·no -na adj barytone || m baritone

barlume m glimmer, gleam

baro m cheat, cardsharp

baròc·co -ca adj & m (-chi -che) baroque

baròmetro m barometer

baróne m baron

baronéssa f baroness

barra f bar; link; rod; sandbar; **andare alla barra** to plead a case; **barra del timone** (naut) tiller; **barra di torsione** (aut) torsion bar; **barra spaziatrice** space bar (of typewriter)

barrare tr to cross, draw lines across (a check)

barrétta f bar (e.g., of chocolate)

barricare §197 (**bàrrico**) tr to barricade || ref to barricade oneself

barricata f barricade

barrièra f barrier; bar; **barriera corallina** barrier reef

barrire §176 intr to trumpet (said of elephant)

barrito m trumpeting, cry of an elephant

barroc·ciàio m (-ciài) cart driver

barròc·cio m (-ci) cart

baruffa f fight, quarrel

barzellétta [dz] f joke

basale adj basal

basalto m basalt

basaménto m foundation (of building); baseboard; base (of column)

basare tr to base || ref—**basarsi su** to be based on; to rest on

ba·sco -sca adj & mf (-schi -sche) Basque

basculla f balance, scale

base f base, foundation; (fig) basis; **a base di** composed of, made of; **base navale** naval base, naval station; **in base a** according to

basétta f sideburns

bàsi·co -ca adj (-ci -che) (chem) basic

basilare adj basic, fundamental

Basilèa f Basel

basìli·ca f (-che) basilica

basìli·co m (-ci) basil

basilissa f (fig) queen bee

bàsolo m large paving stone

bassacórte f barnyard

bassézza f baseness

bas·so -sa adj low; shallow; late (e.g., date); (fig) base, vile; **basso di statura** short || m bottom; hovel (in Naples); (mus) basso || **basso** adv low; down; **a basso, da basso** or **in basso** downstairs

bassofóndo m (**bassifóndi**) (naut) shallows, shallow water; **bassifondi** underworld, slums

bassopiano m lowland

bassorilièvo m bas-relief

bassòt·to -ta adj stocky || m basset hound

bassotuba m bass horn

bassura f lowland; (fig) baseness

basta f hem; basting (with long stitches) || interj enough!

bastante adj sufficient, adequate; comfortable (income)

bastar·do -da adj bastard; irregular || m bastard

bastare intr to suffice, be enough; **basta!** enough!; **basta che** + subj as long as + ind; **bastare a sé stesso** to be self-sufficient; **non basta che** + subj not only + ind

bastévole adj sufficient

bastiménto m ship; shipload

bastióne m bastion; (fig) defense, rampart

basto m packsaddle; (fig) burden

bastonare (**bastóno**) tr to club, cudgel; **bastonare di santa ragione** to give a good thrashing to

bastonata f clubbing, cudgeling; **darsi bastonate da orbi** to thrash one another soundly

bastoncino m small stick; roll; (anat) rod

bastóne m stick, cane; pole; club; baton; staff; French bread; **bastone a leva** crowbar; **bastone animato** sword cane; **bastone da golf** club; **bastone da montagna** alpenstock; **bastone da passeggio** walking stick; **bastone da sci** ski pole; **bastoni** suit in Neapolitan cards corresponding to clubs; **mettere il bastone tra le ruote** to throw a monkey wrench into the machinery

batàc·chio m (-chi) clapper (of bell); cudgel

batata f sweet potato

batisfèra f bathysphere
batista f batiste, cambric
batòsta f blow; (fig) blow
bàtrace or **batrace** m batrachian
battà·glia f (-glie) battle; campaign
battagliare §280 intr to fight
battagliè·ro -ra adj fighting, warlike
battà·glio m (-gli) clapper (of bell); knocker
battaglióne m battalion
battèllo m boat; **battello di salvataggio** lifeboat; **battello pneumatico** rubber raft
battènte m leaf (e.g., of door); knocker; tapper (of alarm clock)
bàttere m—**in un batter d'occhio** in the twinkling of an eye || tr to beat; to hit; to strike; to strike (the hour; said of a clock); to click (teeth, heels); to clap (hands); to stamp (one's foot); to mint (coins); to fly (a flag); to beat (time); to scour (the countryside); to flap (the wings); (sports) to bat; (sports) to kick (a penalty); **battere a macchina** to type; **battere il naso in** to chance upon; **battere la fiacca** to goof off; **battere la grancassa per** to ballyhoo; **battere la strada** to be a streetwalker; **senza batter ciglio** without batting an eye || intr (ESSERE) to beat down (said, e.g., of rain); to chatter (said of teeth); to knock (at the door); **battere in ritirata** to beat a retreat; **battere in testa** (aut) to knock
batterìa f battery; set (of utensils); (sports) heat
batterici·da (-di -de) adj bactericidal || m bactericide
battèri·co -ca adj (-ci -che) bacterial
battè·rio m (-ri) bacterium
batteriologìa f bacteriology
batterìòlo·go -ga mf (-gi -ghe) bacteriologist
batteri·sta mf (-sti -ste) jazz drummer
battesimale adj baptismal
battésimo m baptism; **tenere a battesimo** to christen
battezzare (**battézzo**) [ddzz] tr to christen || ref to receive baptism; to assume the name of
battibaléno m—**in un battibaleno** in the twinkling of an eye
battibéc·co m (-chi) squabble
batticuòre m palpitation; (fig) trepidation
battilò·ro m (-ro) goldsmith; silversmith
battimano m applause
battimuro m—**giocare a battimuro** to pitch pennies (against a wall)
battipalo m pile driver
battipan·ni m (-ni) clothes beater
battira·me m (-me) coppersmith
battiscó·pa m (-pa) washboard, baseboard
batti·sta adj & mf (-sti -ste) Baptist
battistèro m baptistry
battistra·da m (-da) outrider; (sports) leader; (aut) tread
battitappéto m carpet sweeper
bàttito m beating; palpitation; ticking;

wink; pitter-patter (of rain)
batti·tóio m (-tói) leaf (e.g., of door); casement; cotton beater
battitóre m (hunt) beater; (baseball) batter
battitrice f threshing machine
battitura f thrashing, whipping; threshing (e.g., of wheat)
battu·to -ta adj beaten; hammered || m pavement || f beat; stroke, keystroke; meter (in poetry); witticism, quip; (hunt) battue; (mus) bar; (tennis) service; (theat) line; (theat) cue; **battuta d'aspetto** (mus) pause; **dare la battuta** to give the cue
batùffolo m wad; (fig) bundle
baule m trunk; **baule armadio** wardrobe trunk; **fare i bauli** to be on one's way; **fare il baule** to pack one's trunk
baulétto m small trunk; handbag; jewel case
bava f slobber; foam, froth; burr (on metal edge); **avere la bava alla bocca** to be frothing at the mouth; **bava di vento** breath of air, soft breeze
bavaglino m bib
bavà·glio m (-gli) gag
bavaróse [s] adj & mf Bavarian || f Bavarian cream; chocolate cream
bàvero m collar
bavièra f beaver (of helmet) || **la Baviera** Bavaria
bavó·so -sa [s] adj slobbering, slobbery
bazza [ddzz] f protruding chin; windfall
bazzana [ddzz] f sheepskin
bazzècola [ddzz] f trifle, bauble
bazzicare §197 (**bàzzico**) tr to frequent
bazzòt·to -ta [ddzz] adj soft-boiled; uncertain (weather)
beare (**bèo**) tr to delight || ref to be delighted, be enraptured
beatificare §197 (**beatìfico**) tr to beatify
beatitùdine f beatitude, bliss
bea·to -ta adj blissful, happy; blessed || mf blessed
be·bè m (-bè) baby
beccàc·cia f (-ce) woodcock
beccaccino m snipe
beccafi·co m (-chi) figpecker, beccafico
bec·càio m (-cài) butcher
beccamòr·ti m (-ti) gravedigger
beccare §197 (**bécco**) tr to peck; to pick; (coll) to catch || ref to peck one another; to quarrel
beccata f peck
beccheggiare §290 (**becchéggio**) intr (naut) to pitch
becchég·gio m (-gi) (naut) pitching
beccherìa f butcher shop
becchime m food for poultry
becchino m gravedigger
béc·co m (-chi) beak, bill; tip, point; nozzle (e.g., of teapot); billy goat; (vulg) cuckold; **bagnarsi il becco** (joc) to wet one's whistle; **mettere il becco in** (coll; joc) to stick one's nose into; **non avere il becco di un quattrino** to not have a red cent
beccùc·cio m (-ci) small bill; lip, spout
beccuzzare tr to peck || ref to bill (said of doves)

béce·ro -ra adj (coll) boorish || m (coll) boor

beduí·no -na adj & m Bedouin

befana f (coll) Epiphany; old hag

bèffa f jest, mockery; **farsi beffa di** to make fun of

beffar·do -da adj mocking

beffare (**bèffo**) tr to mock, deride || ref —**beffarsi di** to make fun of

beffeggiare §290 (**befféggio**) tr to scoff at, deride

bè·ga f (-ghe) quarrel; trouble

beghina f Beguine; bigoted woman

begònia f begonia

bèl adj apocopated form of **bello**, used only before masculine singular nouns beginning with a consonant except impure s, z, gn, ps, and x, e.g., **bel ragazzo**

belare (**bèlo**) tr to croon || intr to bleat, baa; to moan

belato m bleat, baa

bèl·ga adj & mf (-gi -ghe) Belgian

Bèlgio, il Belgium

bèll' adj apocopated form of **bello**, used only before singular nouns of both genders beginning with a vowel, e.g., **bell'amico; bell'epoca**

bèlla adj fem of **bello** || f belle; girl-friend; final draft; (sports) final game; (sports) rubber match; **alla bell'e meglio** the best one could; **bella di notte** (bot) four-o'clock

belladònna f belladonna

bellétto m rouge, makeup

bellézza f beauty; **che bellezza!** how lovely!; **la bellezza di** as much as

bellici·sta adj (-sti -ste) bellicose

bèlli·co -ca adj (-ci -che) war, warlike

bellicó·so -sa [s] adj bellicose

belligerante adj & m belligerent

belligeranza f belligerence

bellimbusto m fop, dandy, beau

bèl·lo -la (declined like **quello** §7) adj beautiful; lovely; handsome; good-looking; pleasing; fine; quite a, e.g., **una bella cifra** quite a sum; fair; pretty; **bell'e fatto** ready-made; taken care of; **farla bella** to start trouble; (coll) to do it, e.g., **l'hai fatta bella** you've done it; **farsi bello** to dress up; **farsi bello di** to appropriate || m beauty; beautiful; climax; fine weather; beau; **il bello è** the funny thing is; **sul più bello** just then; **sul più bello che** just when || f see **bella** || **bello** adv—**bel bello** slowly

bellospírito m (**begli spiriti**) wit, bel-esprit

belluí·no -na adj wild, fierce

bellumóre m (**begli umori**) jolly fellow

bel·tà f (-tà) beauty (woman); (lit) beauty

bélva f wild beast

belvedére adj (rr) observation (car) || m belvedere; (naut) topgallant

Belzebù m Beelzebub

bemòlle m (mus) flat

benama·to -ta adj beloved

benarriva·to -ta adj welcome

benché conj although, albeit

bènda f bandage; band; blindfold; **benda gessata** cast, surgical dressing

bendàg·gio m (-gi) bandage

bendare (**bèndo**) tr to bandage; **bendare gli occhi a** to blindfold

bendispó·sto -sta adj well-disposed

bène adj well; well-born || m goal, aim; good; love; sake; **bene dell'anima** profound affection; **beni** (econ) assets, goods; **beni di consumo** consumer goods; **beni immobili** real estate; **beni mobili** personal property, chattels; **beni rifugio** hedge (e.g., against inflation); **è un bene** it is a blessing; **fare del bene** to do good; **per il Suo bene** for your sake; **voler bene a** to love, like; to care for || adv well; all right; properly; **ben bene** quite carefully; **star bene** to be well; **va bene** O.K., all right

benedetti·no -na adj & m Benedictine

benedét·to -ta adj blessed; holy

benedire §195 tr to bless; to praise; **andare a farsi benedire** (coll) to go to wrack and ruin; **mandare a farsi benedire** (coll) to get rid of, dump

benedizióne f benediction; boon

beneduca·to -ta adj well-behaved

benefattóre m benefactor

benefattrice f benefactress

beneficare §197 (**benèfico**) tr to benefit, help

beneficènza f welfare; charity, benefi-cence

beneficiale adj beneficial

beneficiare §128 intr to benefit

beneficià·rio -ria adj & mf (-ri -rie) beneficiary

beneficiata f benefit performance; streak of good luck; streak of bad luck

benefi·cio m (-ci) benefice; profit; favor; benefit

benèfi·co -ca adj (-ci -che) beneficial; beneficent

benemerènte adj deserving, well-deserving

benemèri·to -ta adj worthy, deserving || m—**benemerito della patria** national hero || f—**la Benemerita** the Carabinieri

beneplàcito m approval, consent; **a beneplacito di** at the pleasure of

benèssere m well-being, comfort; prosperity

benestante adj well-to-do || mf well-to-do person

benestare m approval; prosperity; **dare il benestare a** to approve

benevolènte adj benevolent

benevolènza f benevolence

benèvo·lo -la adj well-meaning; benev-olent

benfat·to -ta adj well-done; well-favored; shapely

benga·la m (-li & -la) fireworks

benga·la adj m & (-li) Bengalese

beniami·no -na mf favorite child; favo-rite

benigni·tà f (-tà) benignity; gracious-ness; mildness (of climate)

beni-gno -gna *adj* benign; gracious; mild (*climate*)

benintenziona•to -ta *adj* well-meaning

benintéso [s] *adv* of course, naturally

bènna *f* bucket, scoop (*e.g., of dredge*)

benna•to -ta *adj* (lit) well-born

benpensante *m* sensible person; conformist

benportante *adj* well-preserved

benservito *m* testimonial, recommendation; **dare il benservito a** to dismiss, fire

bensì *adv* indeed || *conj* but

bentorna•to -ta *adj & m* welcome || *interj* welcome back!

benvenu•to -ta *adj & m* welcome; **dare il benvenuto a** to welcome

benvi-sto -sta *adj* well-thought-of

benvolére *tr*—**farsi benvolere da qlcu** to enter the good graces of s.o.; **prendere a benvolere qlcu** to be well-disposed toward s.o.

benvolu•to -ta *adj* liked, loved

benzina *f* gasoline, gas; benzine; **far benzina** (coll) to get gas

benzi-nàio *m* (**-nài**) gasoline dealer; gas-station attendant

benzòlo *m* benzene

beóne *m* drunkard, toper

bequadro *m* (mus) natural

berciare §128 (**bèrcio**) *intr* (coll) to yell

bére *m* drink, drinking || §120 *tr* to drink; (fig) to swallow; **bere come una spugna** to drink like a fish; **darla a bere** to make believe

bergamòt•to -ta *adj* bergamot || *m* bergamot orange || *f* bergamot pear

berìllio *m* beryllium

berlina *f* pillory; berlin, coach; (aut) sedan; **mettere alla berlina** to pillory

berlinése [s] *adj* Berlin || *mf* Berliner

Berlino *m* Berlin

bermuda *mpl* Bermuda shorts || **le Bermude** Bermuda

bernòccolo *m* bump, protuberance; (fig) knack

berrétta *f* biretta

berrétto *m* cap; **berretto a sonagli** cap and bells; **berretto da notte** nightcap; **berretto gogliardico** student cap

bersagliare §280 *tr* to harass, pursue; to bomb, bombard

bersà-glio *m* (**-gli**) target; butt (*of a joke*); target (*of criticism*)

bèrta *f* pile driver; **dar la berta a** to ridicule

bertùc-cia *f* (**-ce**) Barbary ape; **fare la bertuccia di** to ape

bestémmia *f* blasphemy

bestemmiare §287 (**bestémmio**) *tr* to blaspheme, curse

bestemmia•tóre -trice *adj* blasphemous || *mf* blasphemer

béstia *f* beast, animal; **andare in bestia** to fly into a rage; **bestia da soma** beast of burden; **bestia nera** pet aversion, bête noire; **bestie grosse** cattle

bestiale *adj* beastly, bestial

bestiali•tà [*f*] (**-tà**) beastliness; blunder

bestiame *m* livestock; **bestiame da cortile** barnyard animals; **bestiame grosso** cattle

bestino *m* gamy odor; stench of perspiration

bestiòla *f* tiny animal; pet

bestsèl•ler *m* (**-ler**) best seller

Betlèmme *f* Bethlehem

betonièra *f* cement mixer

béttola *f* tavern

bettolière *m* tavern keeper

bettònica *f* betony; **conosciuto più della bettonica** very well-known

betulla *f* birch

bèuta *f* flask

bevanda *f* drink, beverage

beveràg•gio *m* (**-gi**) beverage, potion

bevìbile *adj* drinkable

bevi-tóre -trice *mf* drinker

bevuta *f* drink, drinking

bezzicare §197 (**bézzico**) *tr* to peck; **to bezzicarsi** || *ref* to fight one another

biacca *f* white lead

biada *f* feed; **biade** harvest

bianca-stro -stra *adj* whitish

biancheria *f* laundry; linen; underwear; **biancheria da letto** bed linen; **biancheria da tavola** table linen; **biancheria di bucato** freshly laundered clothes; **biancheria intima** underclothes

bianchézza *f* whiteness

bianchire §176 *tr* to blanch; to bleach; to polish

bian-co -ca (**-chi -che**) *adj* white; clean; **bianco come un cencio lavato** as white as a ghost || *m* white; **dare il bianco a** to whitewash; **in bianco** blank (*paper*); **mangiare in bianco** to eat a bland or non-spicy diet; **ricamare in bianco** to embroider

biancóre *m* whiteness

biancospino *m* hawthorn

biascicare §197 (**biàscico**) *tr* to chew with difficulty; to peck at (*one's food*); to mumble

biasimare (**biàsimo**) *tr* to blame

biasimévole *adj* blamable, censurable

biàsimo *m* blame, censure; **dare una nota di biasimo a** to censure

biauricolare *adj* binaural

Bibbia *f* Bible

bibe-rón *m* (**-rón**) nursing bottle

bìbita *f* soft drink

bìbli-co -ca *adj* (**-ci -che**) Biblical

bìblio-bus *m* (**-bus**) bookmobile

bibliòfi-lo -la *mf* bibliophile

bibliografìa *f* bibliography

bibliotè-ca *f* (**-che**) library; bookshelf, stack; collection (*of books*); **biblioteca ambulante** walking encyclopedia

bibliotecà-rio -ria *mf* (**-ri -rie**) librarian

bìbu-lo -la *adj* absorbent (*e.g., paper*)

bi-ca *f* (**-che**) pile of sheaves

bicarbonato *m* bicarbonate; **bicarbonato di soda** bicarbonate of soda, baking soda

bicchierata *f* glassful; wine party

bicchière *m* glass

bicchierino *m* small glass, liquor glass; **bicchierino da rosolio** whiskey glass, jigger

biciclétta *f* bicycle

bicilìndri-co -ca *adj* (**-ci -che**) two-cylinder

bicìpite adj two-headed || m biceps

bicòc·ca f (-che) castle built on a hill; shanty, hut

bicolóre adj two-color

bicòrno m two-cornered hat

bidèllo m school janitor, caretaker

bidènte m two-pronged pitchfork

bidimensionale adj two-dimensional

bidóne m can (for milk); drum (for gasoline or oil); jalopy; (slang) fraud

bidon·vìlle f (-ville) shantytown

biè·co -ca adj (-chi -che) awry; sullen; cross; fierce; **guardar bieco** to look askance (at)

bièlla f connecting rod

biennale adj biennial || f biennial show

biènne adj biennial

bièn·nio m (-ni) biennium

biètola f Swiss chard

biétta f wedge, chock; (naut) batten

bifase adj diphase

biffa f (surv) rod

biffare tr to cross out; (surv) to level

bìfi·do -da adj bifurcate

bifocale adj bifocal

bifól·co m (-chi) ox driver; clodhopper, boor

biforcaménto m bifurcation

biforcare §197 (bifórco) tr to bifurcate

biforcazióne f bifurcation, branching off; fork (of a road)

biforcu·to -ta adj forked; cloven (e.g., hoof)

bifrónte adj two-faced

bì·ga f (-ghe) chariot

bigamìa f bigamy

bìga·mo -ma adj bigamous || mf bigamist

bighellonare (**bighellóno**) intr to idle, dawdle, dally

bighell-ó·ne -na mf idler, dawdler

bigìno m (slang) pony (used to cheat)

bì·gio -gia adj (-gi -gie) gray, grayish; (fig) undecided

bigiotterìa f costume jewelry; costume jewelry store

bigliardo m billiards

bigliet·tàio m (-tài) ticket agent; (rr) conductor

biglietterìa f ticket office; (theat) box office

bigliétto m note; card; ticket; **biglietto d'abbonamento** commutation ticket; season ticket; **biglietto d'andata e ritorno** round-trip ticket; **biglietto di banca** banknote; **biglietto di lotteria** lottery ticket, chance; **biglietto d'invito** invitation; **biglietto di visita** calling card; business card; **biglietto di Stato** banknote; **mezzo biglietto** half fare

bigné m (bigné) puff, creampuff

bigodino m curler; roller

bigón·cia f (-ce) vat; bucket; **a bigonce** abundantly

bigón·cio m (-ci) vat; tub; (theat) ticket box (for stubs)

bigottismo m bigotry

bigòt·to -ta adj bigoted || mf bigot

bilàn·cia f (-ce) balance, scale; **bilancia commerciale** balance of trade; **bilan**-cia **dei pagamenti** balance of payments || **Bilancia** f (astr) Libra

bilanciare §128 tr & ref to balance

bilancière m balance; balance wheel; rope-walker's balancing rod

bilàn·cio m (-ci) balance; **bilancio consuntivo** balance sheet; **bilancio preventivo** budget; **fare il bilancio** to balance; to strike a balance

bile f bile; **rodersi dalla bile** to burn with anger

bìlia f billiard ball; marble; (billiards) pocket

biliardino m pocket billiards; pinball machine

biliardo m billiards

biliare adj bile; gall (stone)

bilì·co m (-chi) balance, equipoise; **in bilico** in balance; **tenere in bilico** to balance

bilìngue adj bilingual

biliónee m billion; trillion (Brit)

bilió·so -sa [s] adj bilious

bìm·bo -ba mf child

bimensile adj bimonthly

bimèstre m period of two months

bimotóre adj twin-engine || m twin-engine plane

binà·rio -ria (-ri -rie) adj binary || m (rr) track; **binario morto** (rr) siding; **uscire dai binari** (rr) to run off the track; (fig) to go astray

binà·to -ta adj binary; twin (e.g., guns)

binda f (aut) jack

binòcolo m binoculars; **binocolo da teatro** opera glasses

binò·mio -mia (-mi -mie) adj binomial || m binomial; couple, pair

biòccolo m wad (of cotton); flake (of snow); flock (of wool)

biochìmi·co -ca (-ci -che) adj biochemical || m biochemist || f biochemistry

biodegradàbile adj biodegradable

biofisica f biophysics

biografìa f biography

biogràfi·co -ca adj (-ci -che) biographic(al)

biògra·fo -fa mf biographer

biologìa f biology

biòlo·go·m (-gi) biologist

biondeggiare §290 (biondéggio) intr to be or become blond; to ripen (said of grain)

bión·do -da adj blond, fair || m blond; blondness || f blonde

biopsìa f biopsy

biòssido m dioxide

bipartìti·co -ca adj (-ci -che) two-party, bipartisan

bipartì·to -ta adj bipartite || m two-party government

bìpede adj & m biped

bipènne f double-bitted ax

biplano m biplane

bipòsto adj invar having seats for two || m two-seater

birba f rascal, rogue

birbante m scoundrel, rascal; (joc) madcap, wild young fellow

birbanterìa f knavery; trick

birbonata f trick

birbó·ne -na *adj* wicked ‖ *mf* rascal, rogue, scoundrel

bireattóre *m* twin jet

birichinata *f* prank

birichi·no -na *adj* prankish; spirited ‖ *mf* rogue; urchin

birillo *m* pin; **birilli** ninepins; tenpins

Birmània, la Burma

birra *f* beer; **birra chiara** light beer; **birra scura** dark beer

bir·ràio *m* (**-rài**) brewer; beer distributor

birrería *f* brewery; tavern; beer saloon

bis *adj invar*—**treno bis** (rr) second section ‖ *m* (**bis**) encore ‖ *interj* encore!

bisàc·cia *f* (**-ce**) knapsack; saddlebag; bag (*of mendicant friar*)

Bisànzio *m* Byzantium

bisa·vo -va *mf* great-grandparent; ancestor ‖ *m* great-grandfather ‖ *f* great-grandmother

bisbèti·co -ca (**-ci -che**) *adj* shrewish; crotchety; cantankerous ‖ *f* (fig) shrew

bisbigliare §280 *tr & intr* to whisper

bisbì·glio *m* (**-gli**) whisper

bisbòccia *f*—**fare bisboccia** to revel

bisboccióne *m* reveler

bis·ca *f* (**-che**) gambling house

Biscàglia *f* Biscay, e.g., **Baia di Biscàglia** Bay of Biscay; **la Biscaglia** Biscay Bay

biscaglína *f* (naut) Jacob's ladder

biscazzière *m* gaming-house operator; habitué of a gaming house; marker (*at billiards*)

bìschero *m* (mus) peg

bi·scia *f* (**-sce**) snake; **biscia d'acqua** water snake

biscottare (**biscòtto**) *tr* to toast

biscotterìa *f* cookie factory; cookie store

biscottièra *f* cookie jar

biscottifi·cio *m* (**-ci**) cookie factory

biscòt·to -ta *adj* twice-baked ‖ *m* cookie

biscròma *f* (mus) demisemiquaver

bisdòsso *m*—**a bisdosso** bareback

bisecare [s] §197 (**biseco**) *tr* to bisect

bisènso [s] *m* double meaning

bisessuale [s] *adj* bisexual

bisestile *adj* leap (*year*)

bisettimanale [s] *adj* biweekly

bisettrice *f* bisector

bisezióne [s] *f* bisection

bisìlla·bo -ba [s] *adj* disyllabic

bislac·co -ca *adj* (**-chi -che**) queer, extravagant

bislun·go -ga *adj* (**-ghi -ghe**) oblong

bismuto *m* bismuth

bisnòn·no -na *mf* great-grandparent; **bisnonni** ancestors ‖ *m* great-grandfather ‖ *f* great-grandmother

bisógna *f* (lit) task, job

bisognare (**bisógna**) *intr* (with *dat*) to need, e.g., **gli bisognavano tre litri di benzina** he needed three liters of gasoline ‖ *impers*—**bisogna** + *inf* it is necessary to, e.g., **bisogna partire** it is necessary to leave; **bisogna che** + *subj* must, to have to, e.g., **bisogna che me ne vada** I must go,

I have to go; **bisognando** if need be; **non bisogna** one should not; **più che non bisogna** more than necessary

bisognévole *adj* needy

bisógno *m* need; want, lack; **aver bisogno di** to need; **c'è bisogno di** there is need of; **se ci fosse bisogno** if need be

bisognó·so -sa *adj* needy ‖ **i bisognosi** the needy

bisolfato [s] *m* bisulfate

bisolfito [s] *m* bisulfite

bisolfuro [s] *m* bisulfide

bisónte *m* bison

bistec·ca *f* (**-che**) beefsteak, steak; **bistecca al sangue** rare steak

bisticciare §128 *intr & ref* to quarrel, bicker

bistic·cio *m* (**-ci**) quarrel, bickering; play on words, pun

bistrattare *tr* to mistreat

bìstu·ri *m* (**-ri**) bistouri, surgical knife

bisul·co -ca [s] *adj* (**-chi -che**) cloven

bisun·to -ta *adj* greasy

bitagliènte *adj* double-edged

bitórzolo *m* wart (*on humans, plants, or animals*); pimple (*on human face*)

bitta *f* (naut) bollard

bitume *m* bitumen, asphalt

bituminó·so -sa [s] *adj* bituminous

bivaccare §197 *intr* to bivouac; to spend the night

bivac·co *m* (**-chi**) bivouac

bì·vio *m* (**-vi**) fork (*of road*); **essere al bivio** (fig) to be at the crossroads

bizanti·no -na [dz] *adj* Byzantine

bizza [ddzz] *f* tantrum; **fare le bizze** to go into a tantrum

bizzarrìa [ddzz] *f* extravagance, oddity

bizzar·ro -ra [ddzz] *adj* bizarre, odd; skittish (*e.g., horse*)

bizzèffe [ddzz] *adv*—**a bizzeffe** plenty, in abundance

bizzó·so -sa [ddzz] [s] *adj* irritable

blandire §176 *tr* to blandish, coax; to soothe, mitigate

blandìzie *fpl* blandishment

blan·do -da *adj* bland

blasfemare (**blasfèmo**) *tr & intr* to blaspheme

blasfè·mo -ma *adj* blasphemous

blasona·to -ta *adj* emblazoned

blasóne *m* coat of arms, blazon

blaterare (**blàtero**) *intr* to babble

blatta *f* water bug, cockroach

blenorraggìa *f* gonorrhea

blè·so -sa *adj* lisping

blindàg·gio *m* (**-gi**) armor

blindare *tr* to armor

bloccare §197 (**blòcco**) *tr* to block; to blockade; to stop; to jam; to close up; to freeze (*e.g., prices*); (sports) to block ‖ *intr*—**bloccare su** to vote as a block for ‖ *ref* to stop

blòc·co *m* (**-chi**) block; blockade; notebook, pad; freezing (*e.g., of wages*); **in blocco** in bulk

bloc-notes *m* (**-notes**) notebook

blu *adj invar & m* blue

blua·stro -stra *adj* bluish

bluffare *intr* to bluff

blusa *f* blouse; smock

bò·a *m* (-a) boa ‖ *f* buoy
boà·rio -ria *adj* (-ri -rie) cattle
boa·ro -ra *adj* ox ‖ *m* stable boy
boato *m* roar; **boato sonico** sonic boom
bobina *f* spool (*of thread*); coil (*of wire*); reel (*of movie film; of magnetic tape*); roll (*of film*); cylinder, bobbin; (elec) coil; **bobina d'accensione** spark coil
bóc·ca *f* (-che) mouth; nozzle; muzzle (*of gun*); pit (*of the stomach*); opening; straits; pass; **a bocca aperta** agape; **bocca da fuoco** cannon; **di buona bocca** easily pleased; **in bocca al lupo!** good luck!; **per bocca** orally; **rimanere a bocca asciutta** to be foiled; to be left high and dry; **tieni la bocca chiusa!** shut up!
boccaccé·sco -sca *adj* (-schi -sche) written by or in the style of Boccaccio; bawdy, licentious
boccàc·cia *f* (-ce) ugly mouth; grimace; **fare le boccacce** to make faces
boccà·glio *m* (-gli) nozzle (*of hose or pipe*); mouthpiece (*of megaphone*)
boccale *adj* oral ‖ *m* jug, tankard
boccapòrto *m* hatch; port; mouth (*of oven or furnace*); **chiudere i boccaporti** to batten the hatches
boccascè·na *m* (-na) proscenium, front (*of stage*)
boccata *f* mouthful; **andare a prendere una boccata d'aria** to go out for a breath of fresh air
boccétta *f* small bottle, vial; small billiard ball
boccheggiante *adj* gasping; moribund
boccheggiare §290 (bocchéggio) *intr* to gasp
bocchétta *f* nozzle (*of sprinkling can*); mouthpiece (*of wind instrument*); opening (*of drainage or ventilation system*); **bocchetta stradale** manhole
bocchino *m* cigarette holder; mouthpiece (*of cigarette or of musical instrument*)
bòc·cia *f* (-ce) decanter; ball (*for bowling*); **bocce** bowls
bocciare §128 (bòccio) *tr* to score (*at bowling*); to reject (*a proposal*); to flunk (*a student*)
bocciatura *f* failure
boccino *m* jack (*at bowls*)
bocciòlo *m* bud
bóccola *f* buckle; earring; (mach) bushing
boccone *m* mouthful; piece; morsel; **buttar giù un boccone amaro** to swallow a bitter pill; **levarsi il boccone di bocca** to take the bread out of one's mouth (to help someone); **mangiare un boccone** to have a bite ‖ **bocconi** *adv* flat on one's face
boè·mo -ma *adj* & *mf* Bohemian
boè·ro -ra *adj* & *m* Boer
bofonchiare §287 (bofónchio) *intr* to snort, grumble
bò·ia *m* (-ia) hangman, executioner
boiata *f* (slang) infamy; (slang) trash
boicottàg·gio *m* (-gi) boycott
boicottare (boicòtto) *tr* to boycott

bòl·gia *f* (-ge) pit (*in hell*)
bólide *m* (astr) bolide, fireball; (aut) racer; (joc) lummox; **andare come un bolide** to go like a flash
bolina *f* (naut) bowline; **di bolina** (naut) close-hauled
bolivià·no -na *adj* & *mf* Bolivian
bólla *f* bubble; blister; ticket; **bolla di consegna** receipt; **bolla di spedizione** delivery ticket; **bolla di sapone** soap bubble; **bolla papale** papal bull
bollare (bóllo) *tr* to stamp; to brand
bolla·to -ta *adj* stamped; sealed
bollatura *f* stamp; brand; postage
bollènte *adj* boiling, scalding hot
bollétta *f* ticket; receipt; bill; **essere in bolletta** (coll) to be broke
bollettà·rio *m* (-ri) receipt book
bollettino *m* bulletin; receipt; **bollettino dei prezzi correnti** price list; **bollettino di versamento** (com) deposit ticket; **bollettino meteorologico** weather forecast
bollire (bóllo) *tr* & *intr* to boil
bolli·to -ta *adj* boiled ‖ *m* boiled beef
bollitura *f* boiling
bóllo *m* mark, cancellation; revenue stamp; postmark; seal; **bollo a freddo** seal (*embossed*); **bollo postale** cancellation, postmark
bollóre *m* boiling; sultriness; (fig) passion, excitement; **alzare il bollore** to begin to boil
bolló·so -sa [s] *adj* blistery
bolscevì·co -ca *adj* & *mf* (-chi -che) Bolshevik
bolscevismo *m* Bolshevism
ból·so -sa *adj* broken-winded (*horse*); asthmatic
bòma *f* (naut) boom
bómba *f* bomb; bubble gum; fireworks; (aer) double loop; (journ) scandal; **bomba a idrogeno** hydrogen bomb; **bomba a mano** hand grenade; **bomba antisommergibile** depth charge; **bomba a orologeria** time bomb; **bomba atomica** atom bomb; **bomba H** (acca) H bomb; **tornare a bomba** (fig) to get back to the point
bombàggio *m* swelling (*of a spoiled can of food*)
bombardaménto *m* bombing, bombardment
bombardare *tr* to bomb, bombard; to besiege (*with questions*)
bombardière *m* (aer) bomber; (mil) artilleryman
bombétta *f* derby (*hat*)
bómbola *f* bottle, cylinder; **bombola d'ossigeno** oxygen tank
bombonièra *f* candy box
bomprèsso *m* (naut) bowsprit
bonàc·cia *f* (-ce) calm; calm sea; (fig) normalcy; (com) stagnation
bonacció·ne -na *adj* good-hearted, good-natured
bonarie·tà *f* (-tà) kindheartedness, good nature
bonà·rio -ria *adj* (-ri -rie) kindhearted, good-natured
boncinèllo *m* hasp
bonì·fica *f* (-che) reclamation; re-

claimed land; improvement (e.g., of morals); clearing of mines; (metallurgy) hardening and tempering

bonificare §197 (bonífico) tr to reclaim; to discount, make a reduction of; to clear of mines

bonifi·co m (-ci) discount

bonomìa f good nature; simple-heartedness

bon·tà f (-tà) goodness; kindness; **avere la bontà di** to be kind enough to; **bontà mia (sua, etc.)** through my (his, her, etc.) kindness; **per mia (sua, etc.) bontà** through my (his, her, etc.) efforts

bòra f northeast wind

borace m borax

borbogliare §280 (borbóglio) intr to gurgle; to rumble

borbòni·co -ca (-ci -che) adj Bourbon || m Bourbonist

borbottare (borbòtto) tr to mutter || intr to mutter; to gurgle; to rumble (said, e.g., of thunder)

borbottì·o m (-ì) mutter; gurgle; rumble

bòrchia f upholsterer's nail; boss, stud

bordare (bórdo) tr to border, hem

bordata f (naut) tack; (nav) broadside

bordatura f border, hem

bordeggiare §290 (bordéggio) intr (naut) to tack

bordèllo m brothel

borde·rò m (-rò) list; note; (theat) box office; receipts

bórdo m side (of ship); border, hem; edge, rim; (naut) tack; (naut) board; **a bordo** on board; **a bordo di** on board; on, in; **bordo d'entrata** (aer) leading edge; **bordo d'uscita** (aer) trailing edge; **d'alto bordo** (naut) big, sea-going; (fig) high-toned; **virare di bordo** (naut) to change course

bordóne m staff; bass stop (of organ); drone (of insect); **tener bordone a** (mus) to accompany; (fig) to hold the bag for

bordura f hem, edge; rim

boreale adj northern, boreal

borgata f hamlet, village

borghése [s] adj middle-class || mf bourgeois, person of the middle class; civilian; **in borghese** in civilian clothes; in plainclothes

borghesìa f bourgeosie, middle class; **alta borghesìa** upper middle class

bór·go m (-ghi) borough; small town; suburb

borgógna m Burgundy (wine) || **la Borgógna** Burgundy

borgognóne m iceberg

borgomastro m burgomaster

bòria f haughtiness, vainglory

bòri·co -ca adj (-ci -che) boric

borió·so -sa [s] adj haughty, puffed-up; blustery

bòro m boron

borotal·co m (-chi) talcum powder

bórra f flock (for pillows); (fig) rubbish, filler

borràc·cia f (-ce) canteen (e.g., for carrying water)

bórro m gully

bórsa f bag; pouch; bourse, exchange; (sports) purse; **borsa da viaggio** traveling bag; **borsa dell'acqua** hot-water bag; **borsa della spesa** shopping bag; **borsa di ghiaccio** ice bag; **borsa di studio** scholarship; **borsa merci** commodity exchange; **borsa nera** black market; **borsa valori** stock exchange; **essere di borsa larga** to be generous; **o la borsa o la vita!** your money or your life!; **pagare di borsa propria** to pay out of one's own pocket

borsaiòlo m pickpocket

borsanéra f black market

borsaneri·sta mf (-sti -ste) black marketeer

borseggiare §290 (borséggio) tr to pick the pocket of; to rob

borseggia·tóre -trice mf pickpocket

borség·gio m (-gi) theft

borsellino m purse

borsétta f handbag, pocketbook

borsétto m man's purse

borsi·sta mf (-sti -ste) recipient of a scholarship; stockbroker

borsìsti·co -ca adj (-ci -che) stock-exchange

borsite f bursitis

boscàglia f thicket, underbrush

boscaiòlo m woodcutter

boscheréc·cio -cia adj (-ci -ce) wood, woodland; rustic; pastoral

boschétto m coppice, copse

boschì·vo -va adj wooded, wood

bò·sco m (-schi) woods, forest; **bosco ceduo** or **da taglio** tree farm

boscó·so -sa [s] adj wooded, woody

bòsforo m (lit) straits || **Bosforo** m Bosphorus

bòsso m boxwood

bòssolo m box; cartridge case

botàni·co -ca (-ci -che) adj botanic(al) || m botanist || f botany

bòtola f trap door

bòtolo m small snarling dog

bòtta f hit; bump; rumble (e.g., of an explosion); thrust, lunging (in fencing); (fig) disaster; **botta dritta** (fencing) lunge; **botta e risposta** give-and-take; **botte da orbi** severe beating

bot·tàio m (-tài) cooper

bótte f barrel, cask, casket

botté·ga f (-ghe) store, shop; **chiudere bottega** to close up shop

botte·gàio -gàia (-gài -gàie) adj store, shop || mf storekeeper, shopkeeper

botteghino m box office; lottery agency

bottìglia f bottle; **bottìglia Molotov** Molotov cocktail

bottiglierìa f wine store, liquor store

bottino m booty, spoil; capture; cesspool; sewage

bòtto m hit, bump; explosion; noise; toll (of bell); **di botto** all of a sudden

bottoncino m small button; cuff button; **bottoncino di rosa** rosebud

bottóne m button; bud; bud; **attaccare un bottone a** (fig) to buttonhole; **botton d'oro** (bot) buttercup; **bottone automatico** snap; **bottone della**

luce (elec) pushbutton; **bottoni gemelli** cuff links; **bottoni gustativi** taste buds

bottonièra f row of buttons; buttonhole; (elec) panel (*with buttons*)

bova·ro -ra adj & m var of **boaro**

bovile m ox stable

bovi·no -na adj cattle, cow; bovine || m bovine

box m (**box**) locker (*e.g., in a station*); box stall (*for a horse*); pit (*in auto racing*); garage (*on the ground floor of a split-level*); play pen

boxare (**bòxo**) intr to box

boxe f boxing

bòzza f stud, boss; bump (*caused by blow*); rough copy, draft; **bozze** (typ) galleys, galley proof

bozzèllo m (mach) block and tackle

bozzétto m sketch

bòzzolo m cocoon; lump (*of flour*)

bra·ca f (**-che**) safety belt; (naut) sling; **brache** (archaic) breeches; (joc) trousers

braccare §197 tr to stalk; to hunt out

braccétto—**a braccetto** arm in arm

bracciale m armlet, armband; arm rest

braccialétto m bracelet

bracciante m laborer

bracciata f armful; stroke (*in swimming*); **bracciata a rana** breaststroke; **bracciata sul dorso** backstroke

bràc·cio m (**-cia** fpl) arm (*of body*); unit of length (*about 60 centimeters*); **a braccia aperte** with open arms; **avere le braccia legate** to have one's hands tied; **braccia** laborers; **braccio destro** right-hand man; **braccio di ferro** Indian wrestling; **fare a braccio di ferro** to play at Indian wrestling; **sentirsi cascare le braccia** to lose courage || m (**-ci**) arm (*e.g., of sea, chair, lamp, etc.*); beam (*of balance*); **braccio diretto** cutoff (*of river*)

bracciòlo m arm; arm rest; banister

brac·co m (**-chi**) hound, beagle

bracconàg·gio m (**-gi**) poaching

bracconière m poacher

brace f embers; (coll) charcoal; **farsi di brace** to blush

brachétta f flap (*of trousers*); (bb) joint; **brachette** shorts

brachière m truss (*for hernia*)

bracière m brazier

braciòla f chop, cutlet

bra·do -da adj wild, untamed

bra·go·m (**-ghi**) (lit) mud, slime

brama f ardent desire; covetousness; longing

bramare tr to desire intensely; to covet; to long for

bramino m Brahmin

bramire §176 intr to roar; to bell (*said of a deer*)

bramito m bell (*of deer*)

bramosìa [s] f covetousness; greed

bramó·so -sa [s] adj (lit) covetous, greedy

bran·ca f (**-che**) branch (*of tree*); flight (*of stairs*); **branche** (poet) clutches

brànchia f gill

brancicare §197 (**bràncico**) tr to finger, handle || intr to grope

bran·co m (**-chi**) flock, herd; (pej) crowd

brancolare (**bràncolo**) intr to grope

branda f cot

brandèllo m tatter, shred

brandire §176 tr to brandish

brando m (lit) sword

brano m shred, bit; excerpt; **cadere a brani** to fall apart; **fare a brani** to tear apart

brasare tr to braze (*to solder with brass*); (culin) to braise

brasile m brazil (*nut*) || **il Brasile** Brazil

brasilià·no -na adj & mf Brazilian

bravàc·cio m (**-ci**) braggart, swaggerer

bravare tr to challenge; to threaten || intr to brag

bravata f swagger, bluster; boast; stunt

bra·vo -va adj good, able; honest; goodhearted; brave; **alla brava** rapidly; **bravo ragazzo** good boy; **fare il bravo** to boast, be a braggart || m mercenary soldier; bravo, hired assassin || **bravo!** interj well done!, bravo!

bravura f ability; bravery; bravura

brèc·cia f (**-ce**) breach, gap; crushed stone

brefotrò·fio m (**-fi**) foundling hospital

Bretagna, la Britanny

bretèlla f suspenders; strap, shoulder strap

brètone adj Breton; Arthurian

brève adj brief, short; **in breve** in a nutshell; **per farla breve** in short || m (eccl) brief || adv (lit) in short

brevettare (**brevétto**) tr to patent

brevétto m patent; (aer) license; (obs) commission

brevià·rio m (**-ri**) compendium; handbook, vade mecum; (eccl) breviary

brevi·tà f (**-tà**) brevity

brézza [ddzz] f breeze

brezzare (**brézzo**) [ddzz] tr to winnow || intr to blow gently

bricchétta f briquet

bric·co m (**-chi**) kettle, pot

bricconata f rascality

briccó·ne -na mf rascal

bricconerìa f rascality

briciola f crumb; **ridurre in briciole** to crumb, crumble

briciolo m bit, fragment; (fig) least bit; **andare in briciòli** to crumble; **mandare in briciòli** to crumble

bri·ga f (**-ghe**) worry, trouble, **attaccar briga** to pick a fight; **darsi la briga di** to worry about; **trovarsi in una briga** to be in trouble

brigadière m noncommissioned officer (*in carabinieri*); (hist) brigadier

brigantàg·gio m (**-gi**) brigandage

brigante m brigand

brigantino m (naut) brig, brigantine; **brigantino goletta** (naut) brigantine

brigare §209 tr to plot; to scheme to get || intr to plot, scheme

brigata f company; (mil) brigade

bri·glia f (**-glie**) bridle; harness (*for holding baby*); (naut) bobstay; **a briglia sciolta** at full speed; **tirare le briglie a** to bridle

brillante adj brilliant || m cut diamond

brillare *tr* to husk, hull (*rice*); to explode (*e.g., a mine*) ‖ *intr* to shine, sparkle; **far brillare** to explode, blow up

brill·o *m* (**-i**) shine, sparkle

bril·lo -la *adj* tipsy

brina *f* frost

brinare *tr* to frost; to turn (*e.g., hair*) gray ‖ *impers* (ESSERE)—**è brinato** there was frost; **brina** there is frost

brinata *f* frost

brindare *intr* to toast; **brindare alla salute di** to toast

brìndisi *m* (**-si**) toast; pledge; **fare un brindisi a** to toast

brì·o *m* (**-i**) sprightliness, liveliness, verve, spirit

briò·scia *f* (**-sce**) brioche

briò·so -sa [s] *adj* sprightly, lively

briscola *f* briscola (*game*); trump (*card*)

britànni·co -ca *adj* (**-ci -che**) British, Britannic

britan·no -na *adj* British ‖ *mf* Briton

brìvido *m* shake, shiver; thrill; **brivido di freddo** chill, shiver

brizzola·to -ta *adj* grizzled

bròc·ca *f* (**-che**) pitcher; pitcherful; shoot, bud; hobnail

broccatèllo *m* brocatel

broccato *m* brocade

bròc·co *m* (**-chi**) twig; shoot; center pin (*of shield or target*); (coll) nag; **dar nel brocco** to hit the bull's eye

bròccolo *m* (bot) broccoli; **broccoli** broccoli (*as food*)

bròda *f* slop, thin or tasteless soup; mud

brodàglia *f* slop

brodétto *m* fish soup

bròdo *m* broth; **andar in brodo di giuggiole** (fig) to swoon with joy; **brodo in dadi** cube bouillon; **brodo ristretto** consommé

brodó·so -sa [s] *adj* thin, watery (*soup*)

brogliàc·cio *m* (**-ci**) (com) daybook, first draft; (naut) first draft of logbook

bròglio *m* (**-gli**) plot, intrigue; maneuver; **broglio elettorale** political maneuver

bròlo *m* (archaic) garden; (lit) garland

bromìdri·co -ca *adj* (**-ci -che**) hydrobromic

bròmo *m* bromine

bromuro *m* bromide

bronchite *f* bronchitis

brón·cio *m* (**-ci**) pout, pouting; **fare il broncio** to sulk; **tenere il broncio a** to harbor a grudge against

brón·co *m* (**-chi**) bronchial tube; thorny branch; ramification (*of antlers*)

brontolare (**bróntolo**) *tr* to grumble (*to express with a grumble*); to grumble at ‖ *intr* to grumble, mutter; to rumble; to gurgle (*said of water*)

brontolì·o *m* (**-i**) grumble, mutter; rumble; gurgle

brontoló·ne -na *mf* grumbler; curmudgeon

bronzare [dz] (**brónzo**) *tr* to bronze

brónze·o -a [dz] *adj* bronze; tanned

bronzina [dz] *f* little bell; (mach) bearing; (mach) bushing

brónzo [dz] *m* bronze

brossura *f* brochure; **in brossura** paperback

brucare §197 *tr* to browse, graze

bruciacchiare §287 *tr* to singe

bruciante *adj* burning

bruciapélo *m*—**a bruciapelo** point-blank

bruciare §128 *tr* to burn; to burn down; to singe; to scorch; to cauterize (*a wound*); (sports) to overcome with a burst of speed; **bruciare le tappe** to go straight ahead; to press on ‖ *intr* (ESSERE) to burn; to smart, sting ‖ *ref* to burn (*e.g., one's fingers*); to get burnt; to blow (*one's brains*) out; to burn out (*said of an electric light or fuse*); **bruciarsi i vascelli alle spalle** to burn one's bridges behind one

bruciatìc·cio *m* (**-ci**) burnt material; **sapere di bruciaticcio** to taste burnt

brucia·to -ta *adj* burnt; burnt out ‖ *m* burnt taste or smell ‖ *f* roast chestnut

bruciatóre *m* burner; heater; **bruciatore a gas** gas burner; **bruciatore a nafta** oil burner

bruciatori·sta *m* (**-sti**) oil burner mechanic

bruciatura *f* burn

brucióre *m* burning; burn; inflammation; **bruciore agli occhi** eye inflammation; **bruciore di stomaco** heartburn

bru·co *m* (**-chi**) caterpillar; worm

brùffolo *m* (coll) small boil

brughièra *f* waste land; heath

brulicare §197 (**brùlico**) *intr* to crawl; to swarm (*e.g., with bees*); to teem (*with people*)

brulichì·o *m* (**-i**) crawling; swarming; teeming

brul·lo -la *adj* barren, bare

bruma *f* shipworm; (lit) fog; (lit) winter

bruna·stro -stra *adj* brownish

brunire §176 *tr* to burnish

bru·no -na *adj* brown; dark (*bread; complexion*) ‖ *m* brown; dark; brunet; **vestire a bruno** to dress in black ‖ *f* brunette

bru·sca *f* (**-sche**) horse brush; **con le brusche** curtly

bruschézza *f* brusqueness

bruschino *m* scrub brush

bru·sco -sca *adj* (**-schi -sche**) sour; curt, gruff; sharp (*weather*); dangerous; sudden ‖ *m* twig ‖ *f* see **brusca**

brùscolo *m* speck, mote; **fare di un bruscolo una trave** to make a mountain out of a molehill

brusì·o *m* (**-i**) buzz, buzzing; (fig) whispering (*gossip*)

brutale *adj* brutal

brutali·tà *f* (**-tà**) brutality

brutalizzare [ddzz] *tr* to brutalize

bru·to -ta *adj* & *m* brute

brutta *f* rough copy

bruttare *tr* (lit) to soil

bruttézza *f* ugliness; (fig) lowliness

brut·to -ta *adj* ugly, homely; foul (*weather*); bad (*news*); **alle brutte** at the worst; **con le brutte** harshly; **farla brutta a** to play a mean trick on;

guardare brutto to look irritated; **vedersela brutta** to foresee trouble ‖ *m* worst; bad weather ‖ *f* see **brutta**

bruttura *f* ugliness

bùbbola *f* lie; trifle

bùbbolo *m* jingle bell (*on horse*)

bubbòni·co -ca *adj* (**-ci -che**) bubonic

bu·ca *f* (**-che**) hole; pit; hollow; **buca cieca** trap (*for hunting*); **buca del biliardo** pocket; **buca delle lettere** mailbox; **buca del suggeritore** prompter's box; **buca sepolcrale** grave

bucané·ve *m* (**-ve**) snowdrop

bucanière *m* buccaneer

bucare §197 *tr* to pierce; to prick; to puncture (*a tire*)

bucato *m* wash; laundry; **di bucato** freshly laundered; **fare il bucato in famiglia** (fig) to not air one's family affairs, to not wash one's dirty linen in public

bucatura *f* piercing; puncturing; puncture; **bucatura di una gomma** flat tire

bùc·cia *f* (**-ce**) rind, peel; skin (*of a person; of fruit and vegetables*); tender bark; **fare le bucce a** (coll) to thwart, frustrate

bucherellare (**bucherèllo**) *tr* to riddle

bu·co *m* (**-chi**) hole; **fare un buco nell'acqua** to fail miserably

bucòli·co -ca *adj* (**-ci -che**) bucolic, pastoral

Budda *m* Buddha

buddismo *m* Buddhism

buddi·sta *mf* (**-sti -ste**) Buddhist

budèl·lo *m* (**-la** *fpl*) bowel; **budella** bowels; guts ‖ *m* (**-li**) casing (*for salami*); pipe; blind alley

budino *m* pudding

bùe *m* (**buòi**) ox (*for draft*); steer (*for meat*); **bue muschiato** musk ox

bùfalo *m* buffalo

bufèra *f* storm; **bufera di neve** snowstorm; **bufera di pioggia** rainstorm; **bufera di vento** windstorm

buffa *f* cowl; gust of wind; (archaic) trick, jest

buffare *tr* to huff (*at checkers*) ‖ *intr* to joke; (archaic) to blow

buffetteria *f* (mil) accouterments

buffétto *m* tap, slight blow

buf·fo -fa *adj* funny, comical ‖ *m* gust of wind; comic ‖ *f* see **buffa**

buffonata *f* buffoonery; antics

buffóne *m* buffoon, clown; (hist) jester; **buffone di corte** court jester

buffoneria *f* buffoonery

buffoné·sco -sca *adj* (**-schi -sche**) clownish

bugìa *f* lie; candlestick; **bugia ufficiosa** white lie

bugiar·do -da *adj* lying, false ‖ *mf* liar

bugigàttolo *m* cubbyhole

bugna *f* ashlar; (naut) clew

bugnato *m* ashlar; (archit) boss

bù·io -ia (*pl* **-i -ie**) *adj* dark ‖ *m* darkness; **buio pesto** pitch dark

bulbo *m* bulb

bùlga·ro -ra *adj* & *mf* Bulgarian ‖ *m* Russian leather

bulinare *tr* to engrave

bulino *m* burin

bullétta *f* tack

bullonare (**bullóno**) *tr* to bolt

bullóne *m* bolt

buon *adj* apocopated form of **buono**, used before masculine singular nouns except those beginning with impure s, z, gn, ps, and x

buon' *adj* apocopated form of **buona** used before feminine singular nouns beginning with a vowel, e.g., **buon'ora**

buonagràzia *f* (**buonegràzie**) courtesy, good manners; **con Sua buonagrazia** with your permission

buonamano *f* (**buonemani**) tip, gratuity

buonànima *f* departed; **la buonanima di** the late lamented

buonavò·glia *m* (**-glia**) intern (*in a hospital*); (coll) lazybones ‖ *f* good will

buoncostume *m* morals

buongu·stàio *m* (**-stài**) gourmet; connoisseur

buò·no -na *adj* good; kind; high (*society*); cheap (*price*); **alla buona** plainly; without ceremony; **buono a nulla** good-for-nothing; **con le buone** kindly, gently; **che Dio la mandi buona** a may God be kind with; **essere in buona con** to be on good terms with ‖ *m* good person; bond; ticket; **buono a nulla** ne'er-do-well; **buono del tesoro** government bond; **buono di consegna** delivery order; **buono premio** trading stamp

buonsènso *m* common sense

buontempó·ne -na *adj* jolly ‖ *m* playboy ‖ *f* fun-loving girl; playgirl

buonumóre *m* good humor, good cheer

buonuscita *f* indemnity, bonus; severance pay

burattare *tr* to sift

buratti·nàio *m* (**-nài**) puppeteer; puppet maker

burattinata *f* clowning

burattino *m* puppet

buratto *m* sifter, sifting machine

burbanza *f* haughtiness, arrogance

burbanzó·so -sa [s] *adj* haughty, arrogant

bùrbe·ro -ra *adj* gruff, surly

bùr·chio *m* (**-chi**) (naut) lighter

burgùn·do -da *adj* & *mf* Burgundian

burla *f* joke, jest; prank; **mettere in burla** to ridicule; **fuori di burla** joking aside

burlare *tr* to ridicule ‖ *intr* to be joking ‖ *ref*—**burlarsi di** to make fun of

burlé·sco -sca (**-schi -sche**) *adj* funny; mocking; burlesque; jocose ‖ *m* burlesque; mock-heroic

burlétta *f* joke, jest; **mettere in burletta** to ridicule

burló·ne -na *mf* joker, jester

burócrate *m* bureaucrat

burocràti·co -ca *adj* (**-ci -che**) bureaucratic; clerical (*error*)

burocrazìa *f* bureaucracy; red tape

burra·sca *f* (**-sche**) storm

burrascó·so -sa [s] *adj* stormy

burrièra *f* butter dish

burrifi·cio *m* (**-ci**) butter factory, dairy

burro *m* butter

burróne *m* canyon, ravine

burró·so -sa [s] *adj* buttery

buscare §197 *tr* to get; to catch ‖ *intr* to be damaged ‖ *ref*—**buscarsi un malanno** to catch a cold

busécchia *f* casing (*for sausage*)

busillis *m*—**qui sta il busillis** here's the rub, that's the trouble

bussa *f* hit, blow; **venire alle busse** to come to blows

bussare *intr* to knock; **bussare a quattrini** (fig) to hit somebody for a loan

bussata *f* knock (*at the door*)

bussa·tòio *m* (**-tòi**) knocker

bùssola *f* sedan chair; door; revolving door; swinging door; ballot box; (mach) bushing; (aer & naut) compass; **perdere la bussola** to lose one's bearings

bussolòtto *m* dice box

busta *f* envelope; briefcase; **busta a finestrella** window envelope; **busta primo giorno** first-day cover; **in busta a parte** under separate cover

bustapa·ga *f* (**-ga**) pay envelope

bustarèlla *f* bribery; kickback

bustina *f* powder, dose; small envelope; (mil) cap, fatigue cap

busto *m* chest, trunk; bust; corset

butirró·so -sa [s] *adj* buttery

buttafuò·ri *m* (**-ri**) bouncer (*in a night club*); (theat) callboy; (naut) outrigger

buttare *tr* to throw; to waste (*e.g., time*); to give off (*e.g., smoke*); **buttar giù** to demolish; to swallow; (fig) to discredit; to jot down; **buttar via** to throw away; to cast aside ‖ *intr* to secrete, ooze ‖ *ref* to throw oneself; to let oneself fall; **buttarsi giù** (fig) to become downcast

butterare (**bùttero**) *tr* to pock, pit

bùttero *m* pockmark; cowboy

buzzo [ddzz] *m* (vulg) belly; **di buzzo buono** with energy; willingly

C

C, c [t∫i] *m & f* third letter of the Italian alphabet

càbala *f* cabala; cabal, intrigue

cabina *f* cabin, stateroom; car, cage (*of elevator*); cockpit (*of airplane*); booth (*of telephone*); cab (*of locomotive*)

cablàg·gio *m* (**-gi**) (elec) cable (*in auto or radio*)

cablare *tr* to cable

cablografare (**cablògrafo**) *tr* to cable

cablogram·ma *m* (**-mi**) cablegram, cable

cabotàg·gio *m* (**-gi**) coasting trade, coastal traffic

cabrare *intr* to zoom

cabrata *f* zoom

cacào *m* cocoa

cacasènno *m* (slang) wiseacre

cacatò·a *m* (**-a**) cockatoo

càc·cia *m* (**-cia**) pursuit plane, fighter; (nav) destroyer ‖ *f* chase, hunt; pursuit; **caccia alle streghe** witch hunt

cacciagióne *f* small game; venison; kill (*e.g., of game birds*)

cacciapiè·tre *m* (**-tre**) (rr) cowcatcher

cacciare §128 *tr* to hunt; to chase; to rout; to send out; to stick, thrust; to utter (*e.g., a cry*); **cacciar fuori** to pull out; **cacciar via** to chase away ‖ *ref* to hide; to intrude; to get; to wind up; to thrust oneself; **cacciarsi negli affari di** to butt into the affairs of

cacciasommergìbi·li *m* (**-li**) subchaser, submarine chaser

cacciata *f* hunting party; expulsion

cacciatóra *f* hunting jacket; **alla cacciatora** (culin) stewed with herbs

cacciatóre *m* hunter; (aer) fighter pilot; **cacciatore di frodo** poacher; **cacciatore di teste** headhunter

cacciatorpediniè·re *m* (**-re**) destroyer

cacciatrice *f* huntress

cacciavi·te *m* (**-te**) screwdriver

càccola *f* gum (*on edge of eyelid*); (slang) snot

caccoló·so -sa [s] *adj* gummy (*eyelid*); (slang) snotty

ca·chi (**-chi**) *adj* khaki ‖ *m* Japanese persimmon; khaki

cacìc·co *m* (**-chi**) Indian chief; boss (*in Latin America*)

cà·cio *m* (**-ci**) cheese; **come il cacio sui maccheroni** (coll) at the right moment

cacofóni·co -ca *adj* (**-ci -che**) cacophonous

cac·tus *m* (**-tus**) cactus

cadau·no -na *adj* each ‖ *pron* each one

cadàvere *m* corpse, cadaver

cadavèri·co -ca *adj* (**-ci -che**) cadaverous

cadènte *adj* falling (*star*); rickety (*house*); run-down, decrepit (*person*)

cadènza *f* cadence, rhythm; accent (*peculiar to a region*)

cadére §121 *intr* (ESSERE) to fall; to sink; to slough (*said, e.g., of crust*); to fail; (gram) to end; **cadere a proposito** to come in handy; to come at the right moment; **cadere dalle nuvole** to be dumfounded

cadétto *m* cadet

càdmio *m* cadmium

caducità *f* transiency, brevity

cadu·co -ca *adj* (**-ci -che**) fleeting; deciduous

cadu·no -na *adj & pron* var of **cadauno**

cadu·to -ta *adj* fallen; lost, gone astray; **i caduti** the fallen, the dead ‖ *f* fall; crash (*of stock market*); slump (*of prices*)

caf·fè *m* (**-fè**) coffee; café

caffeina *f* caffeine

caffetteria *f* cafeteria

caffettièra *f* coffeepot

cafó·ne -na *adj* loud, gaudy ‖ *m* boor, lout

cagionare (cagióno) *tr* to cause, produce

cagióne *f* cause, reason; **a cagione di** because of

cagionévole *adj* sickly, delicate

cagliare §280 *tr, intr* (ESSERE) & *ref* to curdle, curd

cagliata *f* curd

cà·glio *m* (-gli) rennet

cagna *f* bitch

cagnara *f* barking (*of dogs*); uproar, confusion

cagné·sco -sca (-schi -sche) *adj* dog-like, doggish ‖ *m*—**guardare in cagnesco** to look askance at; **stare in cagnesco con** to be angry with

Caino *m* Cain

Càiro, il Cairo

cala *f* cove; (naut) hold

calabrése [s] *adj* & *mf* Calabrian

calabróne *m* hornet

calafatare *tr* (naut) to caulk

cala·màio *m* (-mài) inkwell

calamaro *m* squid

calamita *f* magnet; (*mineral*) loadstone; (fig) magnet, attraction

calami·tà *f* (-tà) calamity, disaster

calamitare *tr* to magnetize

calamitó·so -sa [s] *adj* calamitous

càlamo *m* reed, quill

calandra *f* calender; (aut) grille

calandrare *tr* to calender

calante *adj* waning (*moon*)

calàp·pio *m* (-pi) snare; noose

calapran·zi *m* (-zi) dumbwaiter

calare *tr* to lower; to strike (*sails*) ‖ *intr* (ESSERE) to fall, sag (said, e.g., of prices); to grow shorter (said of days); to come down; to shrink (said, e.g., of meat); to lose weight; to set (said, e.g., of the sun); to wane (said of the moon); (mus) to drop in pitch ‖ *ref* to let oneself down; to dive

calata *f* lowering; descent; invasion; fall; wharf; (coll) intonation; **calata del sole** sunset

cal·ca *f* (-che) crowd, throng

calca·gno *m* (-gni) heel ‖ *m* (-gna *fpl*) (fig) heel; **alle calcagna di** at the heels of

calcare *m* limestone ‖ §197 *tr* to trample; to trace (*on paper*); to tread (*the boards*); to emphasize; **calcare la mano** to exaggerate; **calcare le orme di** to follow in the footsteps of

calce *m*—**in calce** at the foot of the page; **in calce a** at the foot of ‖ *f* lime; **calce viva** quicklime

calcedònio *m* chalcedony

calcestruzzo *m* concrete

calciare §128 *tr* & *intr* to kick

calciatóre *m* soccer player; football player

calcificare §197 (calcìfico) *tr* & *ref* to calcify

calcificazióne *f* calcification

calcina *f* mortar; lime

calcinàc·cio *m* (-ci) flake of plaster; **calcinacci** ruins, rubble

calci·nàio *m* (-nài) lime pit

calcinare *tr* to calcine; to lime (e.g., a field)

càl·cio *m* (-ci) kick; soccer; calcium; (e.g., of rifle) butt; **calcio d'inizio** (sports) kickoff

calciocianamide *m* calcium cyanamide

cal·co *m* (-chi) tracing; cast; imprint

calcografia *f* copper engraving

calcolare (càlcolo) *tr* to calculate; to estimate, reckon; to compute; to consider

calcola·tóre -trice *adj* calculating ‖ *m* calculator; computer; schemer ‖ *f* calculating machine, adding machine

càlcolo *m* calculation; estimate; planning; calculus; (pathol) calculus, stone; **calcolo biliare** gallstone; **calcolo errato** miscalculation; **fare calcolo su** to count upon

calcolò·si *f* (-si) (pathol) stones

calcomania *f* decalcomania

caldàia *f* boiler

cal·dàio *m* (-dài) cauldron, boiler

caldalléssa *f* boiled chestnut

caldana *f* flush

caldano *m* brazier

caldarròsta *f* roast chestnut

caldeggiare §290 (caldéggio) *tr* to favor, support; to recommend

calde·ràio *m* (-rài) coppersmith; boilermaker

calderóne *m* cauldron

cal·do -da *adj* warm; hot; rich (*voice*); **caldo, caldo** quite recent ‖ *m* heat; warmth; **aver caldo** to be warm (said of people); to be hot (said of people); **fa caldo** it is warm; it is hot; **non mi fa nè caldo nè freddo** it leaves me cold, it does not move me

calefazióne *f* heating

caleidoscò·pio *m* (-pi) kaleidoscope

calendà·rio *m* (-ri) calendar

calènde *fpl*—**calende greche** Greek calends

calendimàggio *m* May Day

calèsse *m* buggy, gig

calére *impers*—**non mi cale** (lit) I don't care

calettare (calétto) *tr* to dovetail, mortise ‖ *intr* to fit

calibrare (càlibro) *tr* to gauge, calibrate

càlibro *m* caliber; (mach) calipers; (fig) quality, importance

càlice *m* wine cup; (bot) calyx; (eccl) chalice

cali·cò *m* (-cò) calico

califfo *m* caliph

calìgine *f* fog, mist; (fig) darkness

caliginó·so -sa [s] *adj* foggy, misty; (fig) dark, gloomy

calla *f*—**calla dei fioristi** calla lily

calle *f* lane, alley

callifu·go *m* (-ghi) corn remedy

calligrafia *f* penmanship; handwriting

calli·sta *mf* (-sti -ste) chiropodist

callo *m* corn; callus; **fare il callo a** to get used to; **pestare i calli a qlcu** to step on s.o.'s feet

callosi·tà [s] *f* (-tà) callosity; callus

calló·so -sa [s] *adj* corny; callous; hard

calma *f* calm, tranquillity

calmante *adj* sedative, calming, soothing ‖ *m* sedative

calmare *tr* to calm, soothe, appease ‖ *ref* to calm down; to subside, abate

calmierare (calmièro) *tr* to fix the price of

calmière *m* ceiling price; price control

cal·mo -ma *adj* calm, quiet, still ‖ *f* see **calma**

calo *m* decrease; shrinkage

calomelano *m* calomel

calóre *m* heat; warmth; fervor, ardor; (pathol) rash, inflammation; (vet) rut, mating season

caloria *f* calorie

calòri·co -ca *adj* (**-ci -che**) caloric

calorìfero *m* heater, radiator

caloró·so -sa [s] *adj* warm; hot; cordial; heated

calò·scia *f* (**-sce**) var of **galoscia**

calòtta *f* skullcap; case (*e.g., of watch*); (aut) hubcap; (mach) cap; **calotta cranica** skull

calpestare (calpésto) *tr* to trample

calpestì·o *m* (**-ì**) trampling

calùgine *f* down (*of bird*)

calùnnia *f* calumny, slander

calunniare §287 *tr* to calumniate, slander

calunnia·tóre -trice *mf* slanderer

calunnió·so -sa [s] *adj* slanderous

Calvàrio *m* (Bib) Calvary

calvìzie *f* baldness

cal·vo -va *adj* bald

calza *f* sock; stocking; wick; **calza da donna** stocking; **calze** hose, hosiery; **fare la calza** to knit

calzamàglia *f* tights

calzare *m* footwear ‖ *tr* to wear, put on (*shoes, gloves, or socks*) ‖ *intr* to fit (*said of any garment*); to suit

calzascar·pe *m* (**-pe**) shoehorn

calza·tóio *m* (**-tói**) shoehorn

calzatura *f* footwear; **calzature** footwear

calzaturière *m* shoe manufacturer

calzaturiè·ro -ra *adj* shoe (*e.g., industry*) ‖ *m* shoe worker

calzaturifì·cio *m* (**-ci**) shoe factory

calzeròtto *m* woolen sock

calzet·tàio *m* (**-tài**) hosier

calzettóne *m* knee-high woolen sock (*for mountain boots*)

calzifì·cio *m* (**-ci**) hosiery mill

calzino *m* sock; **calzini corti** socks; half hose; **calzini lunghi** knee-high socks

calzo·làio *m* (**-lài**) shoemaker; cobbler

calzolerìa *f* shoemaker's shop; shoe store

calzoncini *mpl* shorts

calzóne *m* trouser leg; **calzoni** trousers, pants; slacks; **calzoni a zampe d'elefante** bell-bottom trousers, flares

camaleònte *m* chameleon

camarilla *f* cabal, clique

cambiadì·schi *m* (**-schi**) record changer

cambiale *f* promissory note, IOU

cambiaménto *m* change, modification

cambiare §287 *tr* to change, exchange; to shift (*gears*) ‖ *intr* to change, switch ‖ *ref* to change (*clothing*); **cambiarsi in** to turn into

cambiavalu·te *m* (**-te**) moneychanger

càm·bio *m* (**-bi**) change; switch; rate of exchange; (mil) relief; **cambio a cloche** shift lever, stick; **cambio di velocità** gearshift; **in cambio di in** exchange for, in place of

cambrètta *f* staple (*to hold a wire*)

cam·brì *m* (**-brì**) cambric

cambusa *f* (naut) galley

cambusière *m* steward

càmera *f* room; bedroom; chamber; **camera ardente** funeral parlor; **Camera dei comuni** House of Commons; **Camera dei deputati** House of Representatives; **camera d'aria** inner tube; **camera di sicurezza** detention cell; vault (*of bank*)

camera·ta *m* (**-ti**) friend, comrade ‖ *f* dormitory; barracks; roomful (*of students or soldiers*)

cameratismo *m* comradeship

camerièra *f* waitress; maid; chambermaid

camerière *m* waiter; steward; valet

camerino *m* small room; toilet, lavatory; (nav) noncommissioned officer's quarters; (theat) dressing room

càmice *m* gown (*of physician*); smock (*of painter*); (eccl) alb

camicerìa *f* shirt store; shirt factory

camicétta *f* blouse

camìcia *f* shirt; casing; jacket (*e.g., of boiler*); lining (*e.g., of furnace*); vest (*of sailor*); folder; **camicia da giorno** chemise; **camicia da notte** nightgown; **camicia di forza** strait jacket; **camicia di maglia** coat of mail; **camicia nera** black shirt (*Fascist*); **camicia rossa** red shirt (*Garibaldine*); **dare la camicia** to give the shirt off one's back; **essere nato con la camicia** to be born with a silver spoon in one's mouth; **perdere la camicia** to lose one's shirt

cami·ciàio -ciàia *mf* (**-ciài -ciàie**) shirtmaker, haberdasher

camiciòla *f* sport shirt; undershirt; T-shirt; (obs) vest

camiciòtto *m* smock (*of mechanic*); jumper; sport shirt

caminétto *m* small fireplace; fireplace

camino *m* fireplace; chimney, smokestack; shaft (*in mountain*); mouth (*of volcano*); (naut) funnel

cà·mion *m* (**-mion**) truck

camionale *f* highway

camioncino *m* small truck; panel truck, pickup truck

camionétta *f* small truck; van (*e.g., of police*)

camioni·sta *m* (**-sti**) truckdriver, teamster

camma *f* (mach) cam; (mach) wiper

cammellière *m* camel driver

cammèllo *m* camel

cammèo *m* cameo

camminaménto *m* (mil) communication trench

camminare *intr* to walk; to go, run

camminata *f* walk; gait; (obs) hall with fireplace

cammina·tóre -trice *mf* walker; runner

cammino *m* road, way, route; path (*e.g., of the moon*); course; journey; **cammin facendo** on the way; **cammino battuto** beaten path; **cammino coperto** (mil) covered way; **mettersi in cammino** to set out, start out

camomilla *f* camomile

camòrra *f* underworld

camò·scio *m* (-**sci**) chamois

campagna *f* country; countryside; country property; season (*for harvesting*); campaign; **andare in campagna** to go on vacation (in the country)

campagnò·lo -la *adj* country, rural ‖ *mf* peasant

campale *adj* field (*artillery*); pitched, decisive (*battle*)

campana *f* bell; bell glass, bell jar; lamp shade; (archit) bell; **a campana** bell-bottomed; **campana a martello** alarm bell, tocsin; **campana di vetro** bell glass; **campana pneumatica** caisson

campanàc·cio *m* (-**ci**) cowbell

campanaro *m* bell ringer; (archaic) bell founder

campanèlla *f* small bell; door knocker; curtain ring; (bot) bluebell

campanèllo *m* bell; small bell; doorbell, chimes; **campanello d'allarme** alarm bell

campanile *m* steeple, belfry; native city or town

campanilismo *m* parochialism

campano *m* cowbell

campare *tr* to keep alive; to save; to bring out the details of ‖ *intr* (ESSERE) to live; to survive; **si campa** one ekes out a living

campa·to -ta *adj*—**campato in aria** without any foundation ‖ *f* span

campeggiare §290 (**campéggio**) *intr* to camp, encamp; to stand out

campeggia·tóre -trice *mf* camper

campég·gio *m* (-**gi**) camping, outing; campground; (bot) logwood

campeggi·sta *mf* (-**sti** -**ste**) camper

campèstre *adj* field, country; (sports) cross-country

campidò·glio *m* (-**gli**) capitol ‖ **Campidoglio** *m* Capitoline (*hill*); Capitol (*temple*)

campionare (**campióno**) *tr* to sample

campionà·rio -ria (-**ri** -**rie**) *adj* of samples; trade (*exposition*) ‖ *m* sample book, catalogue, pattern book

campionato *m* championship, title

campióne *m* champion; sample; specimen; standard; **campione senza valore** uninsured parcel, sample post

campionéssa *f* championess

campionissimo *m* world champion, ace

campo *m* field; camp; ground; tennis court; golf course; center (*e.g., for refugees*); **campo addestramento** training camp; **campo d'aviazione** airfield, airport; **campo di battaglia** battlefield; **campo petrolifero** oil field; **lasciare il campo** to retreat; **mettere in campo** to bring up, adduce; **piantare il campo** to pitch camp

camposanto *m* cemetery, churchyard

camuffare *tr* to disguise, mask; to camouflage ‖ *ref* to disguise oneself

camu·so -sa *adj* snub-nosed

Canadà, il Canada

canadése [s] *adj & mf* Canadian

canàglia *f* scoundrel; rabble

canagliata *f* knavery, mean trick

canale *m* canal; irrigation ditch; network (*of communications*); pipe, drain; (anat) duct, tract; (rad, telv) channel; (theat) aisle; **Canale della Manica** English Channel; **Canale di Panama** Panama Canal; **Canale di Suez** Suez Canal

canalizzare [ddzz] *tr* to channel; to install pipes in; (elec) to wire

canalizzazióne [ddzz] *f* channeling; piping; ductwork; (elec) wiring

canalóne *m* ravine

cànapa *f* hemp

cana·pè *m* (-**pè**) sofa, couch; (culin) canapé

cànapo *m* rope, cable

Canàrie, le the Canaries

canarino *m* canary

cancàn *m* noise, racket

cancellare (**cancèllo**) *tr* to cancel, erase; to obliterate; to write off (*a debt*); to scratch (*a horse*) ‖ *ref* to vanish, fade

cancellata *f* railing

cancellatura *f* erasure

cancellazióne *f* cancellation; erasure (*of a tape*)

cancelleria *f* chancellery; stationery

cancellière *m* chancellor; court clerk; registrar, recorder

cancèllo *m* gate, railing, grating

canceró·so -sa [s] *adj* cancerous ‖ *mf* cancer victim

cànchero *m* trouble; troublesome person; (coll) cancer

cancrèna *f* gangrene; **andare in cancrena** to become gangrenous

cancrenó·so -sa [s] *adj* gangrenous

cancro *m* cancer; (bot) canker ‖ **Cancro** *m* (astr) Cancer

candeggiante *adj* bleaching ‖ *m* bleaching agent, bleach

candeggiare §290 (**candéggio**) *tr* to bleach

candeggina *f* bleach

candég·gio *m* (-**gi**) bleaching

candéla *f* candle; candlestick; candlepower; (aut) spark plug; **studiare a lume di candela** to burn the midnight oil; **tenere la candela a** to favor the love affair of

candelabro *m* candelabrum

candelière *m* candlestick

candelòra *f* Candlemas

candelòtto *m* big wax candle; **candelotto lacrimogeno** tear-gas canister

candida·to -ta *mf* candidate

candidatura *f* candidature, candidacy

càndi·do -da *adj* white; candid

candire §176 *tr* to candy

candi·to -ta *adj* candied ‖ *m* candied fruit

candóre *m* whiteness; candor

cane *m* dog; hound; hammer, cock (*of gun*); ham actor; **cane barbone**

poodle; **cane bastardo** mongrel; **cane da ferma** setter; **cane da guardia** watchdog; **cane da presa** retriever; **cane da punta** pointer; **cane grosso** big shot; **cane guida per ciechi** seeing eye dog; **cane sciolto** (pol) lone wolf; **come un cane** all alone; **come un cane in chiesa** as an unwelcome guest; **da cani** poorly; **menare il can per l'aia** to beat around the bush; **non c'è un cane** there is nobody there; **raddrizzare le gambe ai cani** to perform an impossible task

canèstro *m* basket

cànfora *f* camphor

cangiante *adj* changeable (*color*); changing, iridescent

canguro *m* kangaroo

canìcola *f* dog days

canile *m* doghouse, kennel

canino *adj* canine || *m* canine tooth

canìzie [*dzz*] *f* gray hair; head of gray hair; old age

canna *f* cane, reed; rod (*for fishing or measuring*); pipe (*of organ*); barrel (*of gun*); **canna da zucchero** sugar cane; **canna di caduta** disposal chute; **canna fumaria** chimney; **canna della gola** (coll) windpipe

cannèlla *f* small tube; tap (*of barrel*); cinnamon

cannèllo *m* pipe, tube; stick (*e.g., of licorice*); (chem) pipette; **cannello ossiacetilenico** acetylene torch; **cannello ossidrico** oxyhydrogen blowpipe

cannellóni *mpl* cannelloni

cannéto *m* cane field

cannìbale *m* cannibal

cannìc·cio *m* (**-ci**) wicker frame; shade made out of rushes

cannocchiale *m* spyglass; **cannocchiale astronomico** telescope

cannonata *f* cannonade, cannon shot; (slang) hit

cannoncino *m* small gun; **cannoncino antiaereo** antiaircraft gun

cannóne *m* gun, cannon; pipe, stovepipe; box pleat; shin (*of cattle*); **è un cannone** (coll) he's the tops

cannoneggiare §290 (**cannonéggio**) *tr* to cannonade, shell

cannonièra *f* gunboat

cannonière *m* gunner, artilleryman; kicker (*in soccer*)

cannùc·cia *f* (**-ce**) reed; thin tube; stem (*e.g., of pipe*); straw (*for drinking*); (chem) pipette

canòa *f* canoe; launch

canòcchia *f* mantis shrimp

cànone *m* canon; rule; rent; fee, charge (*for use of radio*)

canonicato *m* canonry

canòni·co -**ca** (**-ci** -**che**) *adj* canonical, canon (*law*) || *m* canon; priest || *f* parsonage, rectory

canonizzare [*ddzz*] *tr* to canonize

canò·ro -**ra** *adj* song (*bird*); melodious

canottàg·gio *m* (**-gi**) boating, rowing

canottièra *f* undershirt, T-shirt; skimmer, boater

canottière *m* oarsman

canòtto *m* skiff, scull, shell

canovàc·cio *m* (**-ci**) dishcloth; embroidery cloth; plot (*of novel or play*)

cantàbile *adj* singable; songlike; cantabile || *m* song

cantamban·co *m* (**-chi**) jongleur, wandering minstrel; mountebank

cantante *adj* singing, song || *mf* singer

cantare *m* song; chant; laisse, epic strophe || *tr* to sing; to chant || *intr* to sing; to chant; (coll) to squeal

cantàride *f* Spanish fly

càntaro *m* urn

cantastò·rie *mf* (**-rie**) minstrel

canta·tóre -**trice** *adj* singing || *mf* singer

cantau·tóre -**trice** *mf* singer composer

canterano *m* chest of drawers

canterellare (**canterèllo**) *tr* & *intr* to sing in a low voice, hum

canteri·no -**na** *adj* singing, warbling; decoy (*bird*) || *mf* songster, singer

càntero *m* urinal

canticchiare §287 *tr* & *intr* to hum

cànti·co *m* (**-ci**) canticle

cantière *m* shipyard, dockyard; navy yard; undertaking, work in progress; **avere in cantiere** to have in hand, be working at; **cantiere edile** building site; builder's yard

cantilèna *f* singsong; **la stessa cantilena** the same old tune

cantimban·co *m* (**-chi**) var of **cantambanco**

cantina *f* cellar; wine cellar; wine shop, canteen

cantinière *m* cellarman; butler; wineshop keeper; sommelier

canto *m* song, singing; chant; canto; crow (*of rooster*); chirping (*of grasshopper*); corner, edge; (mus) voice part; **canto del cigno** swan song; **dal canto mio** for my part; **d'altro canto** on the other hand; **da un canto** on the one hand

cantonata *f* corner (*of street*); **prendere una cantonata** to make a blunder

cantóne *m* corner (*of room or building*); canton

cantonièra *f* corner cupboard; (rr) section worker's house

cantonière *m* road laborer; (rr) section hand

cantóre *m* choir singer; cantor; (poet) singer

cantùc·cio *m* (**-ci**) nook, niche

canutézza *f* hoariness

canutìglia *f* gold thread

canu·to -**ta** *adj* gray-haired; white-haired; (poet) white

canzonare (**canzóno**) *tr* to mock, ridicule

canzonatò·rio -**ria** *adj* (**-ri** -**rie**) mocking

canzonatura *f* mockery, gibe

canzóne *f* song; canzone

canzonétta *f* canzonet; popular song

canzonetti·sta *mf* (**-sti** -**ste**) singer (*e.g., in a nightclub*) || *m* songster || *f* songstress

canzonière *m* songbook; collection of poems; song writer

caolino *m* kaolin

caos *m* chaos

caòti·co -ca *adj* (-ci -che) caotic

capace *adj* capacious; capable, intelligent; legally qualified; **capace di** with a capacity of (*e.g., fifty people*); **essere capace di** to be able to; **fare capace di** to convince of

capaci·tà *f* (-tà) capacity; capability

capacitare (capàcito) *tr* to persuade || *ref* to become convinced

capanna *f* hut, cabin; thatched cottage; bathhouse

capannèllo *m* group, crowd

capanno *m* hunting box; cabana, bathhouse

capannóne *m* large shed; hangar

caparbiàggine *f* var of **caparbietà**

caparbie·tà *f* (-tà) obstinacy, stubborness

capàr·bio -bia *adj* (-bi -bie) stubborn, hard-headed

caparra *f* down payment, deposit; performance bond

capatina *f* short visit

capeggiare §290 (capéggio) *tr* to lead

capeggia·tóre -trice *mf* leader

capellini *mpl* small vermicelli

capéllo *m* hair; averne fin sopra i capelli to have one's fill; capelli hair; capelli a spazzola crew cut; c'è mancato un capello che + *subj* he came close to + *ger*; far rizzare i capelli a qlcu to make s.o.'s hair stand on end

capellóne *m* hippie, beatnik

capellu·to -ta *adj* hairy; long-haired

capelvènere *m* maidenhair

capèstro *m* halter; gallows

capezzale *m* bolster; (fig) bedside

capézzolo *m* nipple, teat; udder

capidò·glio *m* (-gli) var of **capodoglio**

capiènza *f* capacity (*e.g., of bus*)

capigliatura *f* head of hair

capillare *adj* capillary; (fig) far-reaching

capinéra *f* (orn) blackcap

capintè·sta *m* (-sta) boss; (sports) head, leader

capire §176 *tr* to understand; **capire a volo** to grasp immediately || *intr* — **non capire dalla contentezza** to be bursting with joy || *ref* to understand each other; to agree

capitale *adj* capital; mortal (*sin*) || *m* capital; principal; **capitale sociale** capital stock || *f* capital (*of country*)

capitalismo *m* capitalism

capitali·sta *mf* (-sti -ste) capitalist

capitalisti·co -ca *adj* (-ci -che) capitalistic

capitalizzare [ddzz] *tr* to capitalize; to compound (*interest*)

capitana *f* flagship

capitanare *tr* to lead, captain

capitaneria *f* (hist) captaincy; **capitaneria di porto** harbor-master's office; coast guard office; port authority's office

capitano *m* captain; skipper, master (*of ship*); commander (*in air force*); **capitano di corvetta** or **capitano di fregata** (nav) lieutenant commander;

capitano di gran cabotaggio master; capitano di lungo corso master; capitano di porto harbor master; **capitano di vascello** (nav) commander

capitare (càpito) *intr* (ESSERE) to arrive; to happen, occur; to happen to get, e.g., **capitò a casa mia alle tre** he happened to get to my house at three; **capitare bene** to be lucky; **dove capita** at random

capitazióne *f* poll tax

capitèllo *m* (archit) capital; (bb) headband

capitolare *adj & m* capitular || *v* (capìtolo) *intr* to capitulate, surrender

capitolato *m* (com) specifications

capitolazióne *f* capitulation

capitolo *m* chapter; article, paragraph (*of contract*)

capitombolare (capitómbolo) *intr* to tumble

capitómbolo *m* tumble; **fare un capitombolo** (fig) to collapse

capitóne *m* big eel

capitozzare (capitòzzo) *tr* to poll (*a tree*)

capo *m* head; chief; boss, leader; top; (geog) cape; (nav) chief petty officer; **a capo scoperto** bareheaded; **capo d'accusa** (law) charge; **capo del governo** prime minister; **capo dello stato** president, chief of state; **capo di vestiario** garment; **capo scarico** scatterbrain; **col capo nel sacco** (fig) heedlessly; **da capo** all over (again); **fare capo a** to flow into; **in capo a** at the end of (*e.g., one month*); **in capo al mondo** at the end of the world; **per sommi capi** briefly; **rompersi il capo** to rack one's brain; **scoprirsi il capo** to take one's hat off; **senza capo né coda** without rhyme or reason; **venire a capo di** to come to the end of

capobanda *m* (capibanda) bandmaster; ringleader

capocameriere *m* headwaiter

capocannonière *m* (capicannonièri) petty gunnery officer; (soccer) leader in number of goals

capòcchia *f* head (*e.g., of a match*)

capòc·cia *m* (-ci & -cia) head of household; foreman, boss (*e.g., of roadworkers or farmers*)

capocòmi·co *m* (-ci) head of dramatic company

capocòr·da *m* (capicòrda) (elec) binding post, terminal

capocrònaca *m* (capicrònaca) leading article

capocronista *m* (capicronisti) city editor

capocuòco *m* (capocuòchi & capicuòchi) chef

capodanno *m* (capodanni & capi d'anno) New Year's Day

capodò·glio *m* (-gli) sperm whale

capofàbbrica *m* (capifàbbrica) foreman, superintendent

capofabbricato *m* (capifabbricato) air-raid warden

capofamìglia *m* (**capifamìglia**) head of the family

capofila *m* (**capifila**) head of a line ‖ *f* (**capofila**) head of a line

capofitto *adj invar*—**a capofitto** headlong

capogiro *m* vertigo, dizziness; **da capogiro** dizzying, e.g., **prezzi da capogiro** dizzying prices

capolavó·ro *m* (**-ri**) masterpiece

capolèttera *m* (**capilèttera**) letterhead; (typ) first large bold letter of a paragraph

capolìnea *m* (**capilìnea**) terminal, terminus

capolino *m*—**fare capolino** to peep

capolista *m* (**capilista**) first (*of a list*); (sports) leader ‖ *f* (**capolista**) first (*of a list*)

capoluò·go *m* (**-ghi**) capital (*of province*); county seat

capomacchini·sta *m* (**-sti**) chief engineer

capomastro *m* (**capomastri** & **capimastri**) foreman; building contractor

capomùsica *m* (**capimùsica**) bandmaster

capoofficina *m* (**capiofficina**) superintendent (*of shop*)

capopàgina *m* (**capipàgina**) heading (*of newspaper*)

capopèzzo *m* (**capipèzzo**) gunnery sergeant

capopòpolo *m* (**capipòpolo**) demagogue

caporale *m* corporal

caporeparto *m* (**capireparto**) department manager, floor walker; shop foreman

caporióne *m* ringleader

caposaldo *m* (**capisaldi**) (fig) main point, basis; (mil) stronghold; (surv) datum

caposezióne *m* (**capisezióne**) department head

caposquadra *m* (**capisquadra**) group leader; (sports) team captain

capostazióne *m* (**capistazióne**) station master

capostìpite *m* founder (*of family*); prototype, archetype

capotaménto *m* var of **cappottamento**

capotare (**capòto**) *intr* var of **cappottare**

capotasto *m* nut (*of violin*)

capotàvola *m* (**capitàvola**) head of the table, honored guest

capòte *f* (aut) top

capotrèno *m* (**capitrèno** & **capotrèni**) (rr) conductor

capottaménto *m* var of **cappottamento**

capottare (**capòtto**) *intr* var of **cappottare**

capoufficio *m* (**capiufficio**) office manager

capovèrso *m* paragraph; (typ) indentation

capovòlgere §289 *tr* to overturn; (fig) to upset ‖ *ref* to overturn; (fig) to be or become reversed

capovolgiménto *m* upset; (fig) reversal

capovòlta *f* overturn; turn (*in swimming*)

cappa *f* cape, cloak; mantle; letter K; shroud (*of clouds*); (naut) trysail;

cappa del cielo vault of heaven; **navigare alla cappa** (naut) to lay to

cappèlla *f* chapel; **cappella mortuaria** undertaker's parlor ‖ **Cappella Sistina** Sistine Chapel

cappel·làio *m* (**-lài**) hatter, hat maker or dealer

cappellano *m* chaplain

cappellata *f* hatful

cappellerìa *f* hat store

cappellièra *f* hatbox

cappèllo *m* hat; bonnet; cap (*of mushroom*); head (*of nail*); cowl (*of chimney*); preamble (*of newspaper article*); **cappello a cencio** slouch hat; **cappello a cilindro** top hat; **cappello a cono** dunce cap; **cappello a due punte** cocked hat; **cappello a tre punte** three-cornered hat; **cappello del lume** lampshade; **cappello di feltro** felt hat; **cappello di paglia** straw hat; **cappello floscio** fedora; **fare di cappello** to take one's hat off; **prendere cappello** to take offense

cappellóne *adj invar* Western (*movie*) ‖ *m* big hat; (coll) recruit; (mov) Western character

càppero *m* (bot) caper; **capperi!** (coll) wow!

càp·pio *m* (**-pi**) bow; noose; loop

capponàia *f* chicken coop

cappóne *m* capon

cappòtta *f* cape; navy coat; hood (*of car*)

cappottaménto *m* upset, rolling over

cappottare (**cappòtto**) *intr* to upset, roll over

cappottatura *f* (aer) cowl

cappòtto *m* overcoat; lurch (*at the close of game*); (cards) slam; **cappotto da mezza stagione** lightweight coat

cappuccino *m* espresso with cream; Capuchin (*friar*)

Cappuccétto *m*—**Cappuccetto Rosso** Little Red Ridinghood

cappùc·cio *m* (**-ci**) hood, cowl; cabbage; cap (*of fountain pen*)

capra *f* goat; nanny goat; tripod

ca·pràio -pràia *mf* (**-prài -pràie**) goatherd

caprét·to -ta *mf* kid

capriata *f* truss (*to support roof*)

capríc·cio *m* (**-ci**) whim, fancy, caprice; tantrum; flirting; (mus) capriccio

capricció·so -sa [s] *adj* whimsical, capricious; naughty; fanciful, bizarre

Capricòrno *m* (astr) Capricorn

caprifò·glio *m* (**-gli**) honeysuckle

caprimul·go *m* (**-gi**) (orn) goatsucker

capri·no -na *adj* goatlike, goatish ‖ *m* smell of goat

capriòla *f* female roe deer; caper, somersault; **fare capriole** to cut capers, to caper

capriòlo *m* roe deer; roebuck

capro *m* he-goat, billy goat; **capro espiatorio** scapegoat

capróne *m* he-goat, billy goat

càpsula *f* capsule; percussion cap; cap (*of bottle*); (rok) capsule

captare *tr* to captivate; to catch, intercept; to harness (a waterfall); (rad, telv) to pick up (a signal)

captazióne f undue influence (to secure an inheritance)

capzió·so -sa [s] adj insidious, treacherous

carabàttola f (coll) trifle

carabina f carbine

carabinière m carabineer; Italian military policeman, carabiniere; (hist) cavalryman

caracollare (caracòllo) intr to caracole, caper; (coll) to trot along

caracòllo m caracole, caper

caraffa f carafe, decanter

caràmbola f carom

carambolare (caràmbolo) intr to carom

caramèlla f piece of hard candy; taffy; (coll) monocle; **caramelle** hard candy

carameliare (caramèllo) tr to caramel; to candy

caramèllo m caramel (burnt sugar)

caraménte adv affectionately

caráti·sta m (-sti) shareholder (in ship or business)

carato m carat; share (of ship)

caràttere m character; type; handwriting; characteristic; disposition; **carattere corsivo** (typ) italic; **carattere maiuscolo** capital; **carattere minuscolo** small letter, lower case; **carattere neretto** or **grassetto** (typ) boldface

caratteri·sta m (-sti) character actor || f (-ste) character actress

caratteristi·co -ca (-ci -che) adj & f characteristic

caratterizzare [ddzz] tr to characterize

caratura f share (in business or ship)

cara·vàn f (-vàn) trailer, mobile home

caravanserrà·glio m (-gli) caravansary

caravèlla f caravel; carpenter's glue

carbo·nàio -nàia (-nài -nàie) adj coal || m coal man, coal dealer || f charcoal pit; coalbin, bunker; coal yard

carbonato m carbonate

carbón·chio m (-chi) (agr) smut (on wheat); (jewelry) carbuncle

carboncino m charcoal (pencil and drawing)

carbóne m coal; charcoal; carbon (of arc light or primary battery); **carbone bianco** hydroelectric power; **carbone dolce** charcoal; **carbone fossile** coal; **fare carbone** to coal

carbòni·co -ca adj (-ci -che) carbonic

carbonièra f coal yard; (naut) collier; (rr) tender

carbonile m (naut) bunker

carbònio m (chem) carbon

carbonizzare [ddzz] tr to carbonize; to char

carbùncolo m boil, carbuncle; (archaic) ruby

carburante m fuel

carburatóre m carburetor

carburazióne f (aut) mixture

carburo m carbide

carcassa f carcass; framework; (aut) jalopy; (fig) wreck

carcerare (càrcero) tr to jail

carcerà·rio -ria adj (-ri -rie) jail, prison

carcera·to -ta adj imprisoned || mf prisoner

càrce·re m (-ri fpl) jail, prison

carcerière m jailer, prison guard

carciòfo m artichoke

cardàni·co -ca adj (-ci -che) universal (e.g., joint)

cardano m universal joint

cardatrice f carding machine

cardellino m goldfinch

cardìa·co -ca (-ci -che) adj heart, cardiac || m heart patient

cardinale adj cardinal || m (eccl, orn) cardinal

cardinalì·zio -zia adj (-zi -zie) cardinal, cardinal's

càrdine m hinge; (fig) pivot, mainstay (e.g., of theory)

càr·dio m (-di) cockle (mollusk)

cardiochirurgia f heart surgery

cardiogram·ma m (-mi) cardiogram

cardiòlo·go m (-gi) cardiologist

cardiopalmo m tachycardia

cardiopatìa f heart disease

cardo m (bot) thistle; (bot) cardoon

carèna f ship's bottom; (aer) outer cover (of airship); (bot) rib

carenàg·gio m (-gi) careening a ship; careen

carenare (carèno) tr to careen (a ship)

carenatura f streamlining; **carenatura di fusoliera** (aer) turtleback

carènza f lack, want

carestìa f famine; scarcity (e.g., of manpower)

carézza f caress; **fare una carezza a** to caress

carezzare (carézzo) tr to caress

carezzévole adj caressing, fondling; sweet, suave; blandishing

cariare §287 tr to cause (a tooth) to decay; to corrode || ref to decay; to rot

cariàtide f caryatid

caria·to -ta adj decayed

càri·ca f (-che) office, appointment; charge; (fig) insistence

caricaménto m loading

caricare §197 (càrico) tr to load; to burden; to wind (a watch); to fill (a pipe); to charge (a battery); to deepen (a color); **caricare la mano** to exceed; **caricare le dosi** to exaggerate || ref to burden oneself

carica·to -ta adj exaggerated, affected

carica·tóre -trice adj loading || m clip, magazine (for rifle); loader (of gun); cassette (of tape recorder); charger (of battery); longshoreman; (phot) cartridge, cassette

caricatura f caricature, cartoon; **mettere in caricatura** to ridicule

caricaturi·sta mf (-sti -ste) cartoonist, caricaturist

càrice m (bot) sedge

càri·co -ca (-chi -che) adj loaded; burdened; vivid (color); strong (tea); charged (battery) || m loading; load, burden; charge; cargo || f see **carica**

càrie f caries, decay

cari·no -na adj nice, pretty, cute; **questa è carina!** this is funny!

cari·tà f (-tà) charity; alms; (poet) love; **per carità** please

caritatévole adj charitable

caritati·vo -va adj (obs) charitable

carlin·ga f (-ghe) fuselage

Carlo m Charles

Carlomagno m Charlemagne

carlóna f—**alla carlona** carelessly, haphazardly

carlòtta f charlotte ‖ **Carlòtta** Charlotte

carme m poem, lyric poem

carmi·nio m (-ni) carmine

carnagióne f complexion

car·nàio m. (-nài) carnage; slaughter house; mass of humanity

carnale adj carnal, sensual; full (e.g., brother, cousin)

carname m carrion

carne f flesh; meat; **bene in carne** plump; **carne da macello** cannon fodder; **carne suina** pork; **carne viva** open wound; **essere solo carne ed ossa** to be nothing but skin and bones; **in carne ed ossa** in person, in the flesh; **troppa carne al fuoco** too many irons in the fire

carnéfice m executioner

carneficina f slaughter, carnage

càrne·o -a adj fleshy, meaty; flesh-colored

carnet m (**carnet**) notebook; checkbook; backlog

carnevale m carnival

carnièra f hunting jacket; gamebag

carnière m gamebag

carnìvo·ro -ra adj carnivorous ‖ mpl carnivores; Carnivora

carnó·so -sa [s] adj fleshy

ca·ro -ra adj dear (beloved; high in price) ‖ **caro** adv dear ‖ m high price; beloved; **i miei cari** my parents; my relatives; my friends

carógna f carcass; cad, rotter; **carogne** carrion

carosèllo m tournament; carousel, merry-go-round

caròta f carrot; (fig) lie

caròtide f carotid artery

carovana f caravan; group, crowd; union of longshoremen; apprenticeship; (naut, nav) convoy; **far carovana** to join a tour; **fare la carovana** to be an apprentice

carovaniè·ro -ra adj caravan ‖ f desert trail

carovi·ta m (-ta) high cost of living; cost-of-living increase

carovive·ri m (-ri) high cost of living; cost-of-living increase

carpa f (ichth) carp

carpentière m carpenter

carpire §176 tr to snatch, seize; to extract, worm (a secret)

carpóni adv on all fours; **avanzare carponi** to crawl

carradóre m cart maker, wheelwright

car·ràio -ràia (-rài -ràie) adj passable for vehicles ‖ f cart road

carrarèc·cia f (-ce) country road; rut

carreggiata f paved road; track (of vehicles); (fig) right path

carrellare (**carrèllo**) intr (mov, telv) to dolly

carrellata f (mov) dolly shot, tracking shot

carrèllo m car (for narrow-gauge track); carriage (of typewriter); cart (for shopping); (aer) landing gear; (mach, rr) truck; (mov, telv) dolly; **carrello d'atterraggio** (aer) undercarriage, landing gear; **carrello elevatore** fork-lift truck

carrétta f cart; tramp steamer

carrettata f cartful; **a carrettate** abundantly

carrettière m cart driver, drayman; teamster

carrétto m small cart; **carretto a mano** pushcart

carriàg·gio m (-gi) wagon; **carriaggi** (mil) baggage train

carrièra f career; **di gran carriera** at top speed

carrieri·sta mf (-sti -ste) unscrupulous go-getter

carriòla f wheelbarrow

carro m wagon; cart; wagonload; cartload; carload; (rr) car; (astr) Plough; (poet) chariot; **carri armati** (mil) armor; **carro allegorico** float (in a pageant); **carro armato** (mil) tank; **carro attrezzi** (aut) tow truck, wrecker; **carro bestiame** (rr) cattle car; **carro botte** or **carro cisterna** (aut) tank truck; (rr) tank car; **carro di Tespi** traveling show; **carro funebre** hearse; **carro gru** (rr) wrecking crane; **carro marsupio** (rr) double decker (used to transport automobiles); **carro merci** (rr) freight car; **Gran Carro** (astr) Big Dipper; **mettere il carro innanzi ai buoi** to put the cart before the horse; **Piccolo Carro** (astr) Little Dipper ‖ m (**carra** fpl) carload; wagonload; cartload

carròzza f wagon carriage; **carrozza letti** (rr) sleeping car; **carrozza ristorante** (rr) dining car; **carrozza salone** (rr) club car; **con la carrozza di S. Francesco** on shank's mare; **signori, in carrozza!** (rr) all aboard!

carrozzàbile adj open to vehicular traffic ‖ f road open to vehicular traffic

carrozzèlla f small wagon; baby carriage; wheelchair; hackney

carrozzino m baby carriage; sidecar

carrozzóne m wagon; hearse; caravan (e.g., of gypsies); (rr) car

carruba f carob

carrubo m carob tree

carrùcola f pulley

carta f paper; document (e.g., of identification); **alla carta** à la carte; **carta assorbente** blotter; **carta astronomica** astronomical map; **carta bianca** carte blanche; **carta bollata** stamped paper (for official documents); **carta carbone** carbon paper; **carta catramata** tar paper; **carta da disegno** drawing paper; **carta da gioco** playing card; **carta da giornale** newsprint; **carta da imballaggio** or **da impacco** wrapping paper; **carta da lettera** or **da lettere** writing paper; **carta geografica** map, chart; **carta igienica** toilet paper; **carta oleata** wax paper; **carta torna-**

sole litmus paper; **carta velina** India paper; tissue paper; **carta vetrata** sandpaper; **carte papers**, writings; **carte francesi** cards in the four suits spades, hearts, diamonds, and clubs; **carte napoletane** cards in the four suits gold coins, cups, swords, and clubs; **fare le carte** to shuffle the cards; **fare le carte a qlcu** to tell s.o.'s fortune with cards

cartacarbóne f (**cartecarbóne**) carbon paper

cartàc·cia f (**-ce**) waste paper

cartàce·o -a adj (**-i -e**) paper

Cartàgine f Carthage

car·tàio m (**-tài**) papermaker; paper dealer; (cards) dealer

cartamonéta f paper money

cartapècora f parchment

cartapésta f papier-mâché

carta·rio -ria adj (**-ri -rie**) paper

cartastràccia f (**cartestracce**) wrapping paper; wastepaper

cartég·gio m (**-gi**) correspondence; (aer, naut) reckoning

cartèlla f lottery ticket; card (*e.g., of bingo*); page of manuscript; Manila folder; schoolbag; briefcase; binding (*of book*); **cartella clinica** clinical chart; **cartella di rendita** government bond; **cartella esattoriale** tax bill; **cartella fondiaria** bond certificate

cartellino m label; nameplate (*on door*); file; (sports) contract; **cartellino di presenza** timecard; **cartellino signaletico** criminal record

cartèllo m poster; sign (*on store*); (com) cartel, trust; **cartello di sfida** challenge; **cartello stradale** traffic sign

cartellóne m show bill, theater poster; bill (*for advertising*); **tenere il cartellone** to find public favor, make a hit, be the rage

car·ter m (**-ter**) chain guard (*of bicycle*); (aut) crankcase

cartièra f papermill

cartilàgine f cartilage, gristle

cartina f dose; cigarette paper; small map

cartòc·cio m (**-ci**) paper cone; charge (*of gun*); cornhusk; (archit) scroll

cartògrafo m cartographer

carto·làio m (**-lài**) stationer

cartoleria f stationery store

cartolina f card, post card; **cartolina precetto** induction notice

cartomante mf fortuneteller

cartoncino m light cardboard, calling card; **cartoncino natalizio** Christmas card

cartóne m cardboard, carton; **cartone animato** (mov) animated cartoon

cartùc·cia f (**-ce**) cartridge; shot, shell; **mezza cartuccia** (fig) half pint

cartuccièra f cartridge belt

casa [s] f house; dwelling; home; household; **andare a casa** to go home; **casa base** (baseball) home base; **casa colonica** farm house; **casa da gioco** gambling house; **casa del diavolo** faraway place; **casa di bambole** playhouse, doll's house; **casa di correzione** reform school; **casa di cura**

sanatorium, private clinic; **casa di riposo** convalescent home, nursing home; **casa di spedizione** shipping agency; **casa di tolleranza** bawdyhouse; **casa madre** home office, headquarters; **esser di casa** to be intimate; **fuori casa** (sports) away; **in casa** (sports) home; **metter su casa** to set up housekeeping; **sentirsi a casa** to feel at home; **stare a casa** to stay at home; **star di casa** to dwell, live

casac·ca f (**-che**) coat; **voltar casacca** to be a turncoat

casàccio m—**a casaccio** at random; heedlessly

casalin·go -ga (**-ghi -ghe**) [s] adj home, domestic; stay-at-home; homey; home-made ‖ **casalinghi** mpl household articles ‖ f housewife

casamatta [s] f casemate, bunker

casaménto [s] m apartment house, tenement; tenants

casata [s] f house, lineage

casato [s] m birth, family; (obs) family name

cascame m waste; remnants (*e.g., of silk*)

cascante adj flabby, loose; (poet) languid, dull

cascare §197 intr (ESSERE) to fall, droop; to fit (*said of clothes*); **cascare dalla noia** to be bored to death; **cascare dal sonno** to be overwhelmed with sleep; **cascare diritto** to escape unscathed; **non casca il mondo** the world is not coming to an end

cascata f fall, waterfall; necklace (*e.g., of pearls*); **a cascata** flood of, e.g., **telefonate a cascata** flood of telephone calls ‖ **le Cascate del Niagara** Niagara Falls

cascina f farm house; dairy barn

ca·sco m (**-schi**) helmet, crash helmet; electric hairdrier; cluster (*e.g., of bananas*)

caseggiato [s] m built-up zone; block, row of houses; apartment house

caseifi·cio m (**-ci**) dairy, creamery, cheese factory

casèlla [s] f pigeonhole; square (*of paper*); **casella postale** post-office box

casellante [s] mf gatekeeper ‖ m (rr) trackwalker

casellà·rio [s] m (**-ri**) filing cabinet; row of post-office boxes; **casellario giudiziale** criminal file

casèllo [s] m tollgate (*on turnpike*); (rr) trackwalker's house

casèrma f barracks; fire station

casino [s] m country house; clubhouse; (slang) whorehouse; (slang) noise, racket

casìsti·ca f (**-che**) case study; (eccl) casuistry

caso m case; chance; fate; vicissitude; opportunity; **a caso** inadvertently; **al caso** eventually; **caso fortuito** (law) act of God; **caso mai** assuming that, in the event that; **è il caso** it is the moment; **far caso a qlco** to notice s.th; **in ogni caso** in any event; **mettere il caso che** suppose; **mi fa caso** I am surprised; **non fare caso a** to make nothing of, pay no attention to; **per caso** perchance

casolare [s] *m* hut, hovel; isolated farmhouse

casòtto [s] *m* cabana, bathhouse; sentry box

Càspio *adj* Caspian

càspita *interj* you don't say!

cassa *f* box; chest; case; stock (*of rifle*); cash; cash register; desk (*e.g., in hotel*); check-out (*in a supermarket*); **a pronta cassa** by cash; **cassa acustica** loudspeaker; **cassa di risparmio** savings bank; **cassa malattia** health insurance; **cassa rurale** farmers' credit cooperative; **in cassa** in hand (*said of money*)

cassafórma *f* (**casseforme**) (archit) form (*for cement*)

cassafòrte *f* (**casseforti**) safe

cassapanca *f* (**cassapanche** & **cassepanche**) wooden chest

cassare *tr* to erase, cancel; to cross off; (law) to annul

cassata *f* Neapolitan ice cream with soft core; Sicilian cake

cassazióne *f* annulment, abolition; cancellation

casserétto *m* (naut) poop

càssero *m* (naut) quarterdeck; **cassero di poppa** (naut) cockpit

casseruòla *f* saucepan

cassétta *f* small box; coach box; (theat) box office; **cassetta dei ferri** workbox; **cassetta delle lettere** mail box; **cassetta di cottura** dish warmer; **cassetta di sicurezza** safe-deposit box; **cassetta per ugnature** miter box

cassettièra *f* chest of drawers

cassétto *m* drawer; **cassetto di distribuzione** (mach) slide valve

cassettóne *m* chest of drawers; (archit) coffer, caisson

cassiè·re -ra *mf* cashier; teller

cassóne *m* large case, large box; chest; caisson (*for underwater construction*); body (*of truck*); (mil) caisson

cassonétto *m* cornice

cast *m* cast (*of actors*)

casta *f* caste

castagna *f* chestnut; **castagna d'India** horse chestnut

castagnéto *m* chestnut grove

castagno *m* chestnut tree; chestnut (*lumber*); **castagno d'India** horse chestnut tree

casta·no -na *adj* chestnut (*color*)

castellana *f* chatelaine

castellano *m* lord of the castle, squire

castellétto *m* scaffold; (min) gallows, headframe

castèl·lo *m* castle; works (*e.g., of watch*); scaffold; jungle gym; hydraulic boom, bucket lift (*on truck*); (naut) forecastle; **castello di menzogne** pack of lies; **castello in aria** castle in Spain ‖ *m* (**-la** *fpl*) (archaic) castle

castigare §209 *tr* to punish; (poet) to correct, castigate

castigatéz·za *f* purity (*e.g., of style*)

castiga·to -ta *adj* decent, modest; pure (*language*)

Castiglia, la Castile

castiglia·no -na *adj* & *mf* Castilian

casti·go *m* (**-ghi**) punishment; (fig) scourge; **mettere in castigo** (coll) to punish

casti·tà *f* (**-tà**) chastity; (fig) purity

ca·sto -sta *adj* chaste; pure, elegant (*language or style*)

castóne *m* setting (*of stone*)

castòro *m* beaver

castrare *tr* to castrate; to spay; (fig) to expurgate

castra·to -ta *adj* castrated; spayed; (fig) effeminate ‖ *m* mutton (*of castrated sheep*); eunuch

castróne *m* wether (*sheep*); gelding (*horse*); (fig) nincompoop

castroneria *f* (vulg) stupidity

casuale *adj* fortuitous, casual; sundry (*e.g., expenses*)

casuali·tà *f* (**-tà**) chance, accident

casùpola [s] *f* hut, hovel

cataclì·sma *m* (**-smi**) cataclysm

catacómba *f* catacomb

catafal·co *m* (**-chi**) catafalque

catafàscio *adv*—**a catafascio** topsy-turvy

catalès·si *f* (**-si**) catalepsy

catàli·si *f* (**-si**) catalysis

catalizza·tóre -trice [dzdz] *adj* catalytic ‖ *m* catalyst

catalogare §209 (**catàlogo**) *tr* to catalogue

catàlo·go *m* (**-ghi**) catalogue

catapècchia *f* hovel

catapla·sma *m* (**-smi**) poultice, plaster; (fig) bore

catapulta *f* catapult

catapultare *tr* to catapult

cataratta *f* cataract; sluice (*of canal*)

catarro *m* catarrh

catar·si *f* (**-si**) catharsis

catàrti·co -ca *adj* (**-ci -che**) cathartic

catasta *f* pile, heap

catastale *adj* land (*office*)

catasto *m* real-estate register; land office

catàstrofe *f* catastrophe; wreck

catastròfi·co -ca *adj* (**-ci -che**) catastrophic

catechismo *m* catechism

catechizzare [dzdz] *tr* to catechize

categoria *f* category; weight (*in boxing*); (sports) class

categòri·co -ca *adj* (**-ci -che**) categorical; classified (*telephone directory*)

caténa *f* chain; range (*of mountains*); (archit) tie beam; **catene da neve** tire chains; **mordere la catena** to champ the bit

catenàc·cio *m* (**-ci**) bolt; (fig) jalopy; (journ) giant-size headline

catenèlla *f* chain

cateratta *f* var of **cataratta**

catèrva *f* great quantity, large number

catetère *m* catheter

cateterizzare [dzdz] *tr* to catheterize

catinèlla *f* water basin; **piovere a catinelle** (coll) to rain cats and dogs

catino *m* basin

càtodo *m* cathode

Catóne *m* Cato; **Catone il Maggiore** Cato the Elder

catòr·cio *m* (**-ci**) (coll) piece of junk

catramare *tr* to tar

catramatrice *f* asphalt-paving machine

catrame *m* tar, coal tar

càttedra *f* desk (*of teacher*); chair, professorship

cattedrale *adj* & *f* cathedral

cattedràti·co **-ca** (**-ci** **-che**) *adj* pedantic ‖ *m* professor

catte·gù *m* (**-gù**) catgut

cattivare *tr* to captivate

cattivèria *f* wickedness; piece of wickedness

cattivi·tà *f* (**-tà**) captivity

catti·vo **-va** *adj* bad; wicked; vicious (*animal*); worthless; poor (*reputation; condition*); nasty; naughty; (archaic) unwell ‖ *mf* wicked person ‖ *m* bad taste; **sapere di cattivo** to taste bad

cattolicità *f* catholicity

cattòli·co **-ca** (**-ci** **-che**) *adj* catholic ‖ *adj* & *mf* Catholic

cattura *f* capture, seizure; arrest

catturare *tr* to capture, seize; to arrest

caucàsi·co **-ca** *adj* & *mf* (**-ci** **-che**) Caucasian

caucciù *m* (**caucciù**) rubber

càusa *f* cause, motive; fault; lawsuit, action; **a causa di** on account of; **causa civile** civil suit; **causa penale** criminal suit; **fare causa** to take legal action; **intentare causa a** to bring suit against

causale *adj* causal ‖ *f* cause

causare (**càuso**) *tr* to cause

causìdi·co *m* (**-ci**) amicus curiae; (joc) pettifogger

càusti·co **-ca** *adj* (**-ci** **-che**) caustic

cautèla *f* caution; precaution, care

cautelare *adj* guaranteeing, protecting ‖ *v* (**cautèlo**) *tr* to guarantee, protect ‖ *ref* to take precautions

cauterizzare [ddzz] *tr* to cauterize

càu·to **-ta** *adj* cautious, prudent; cagey

cauzióne *f* security, bail; **dare cauzione** to give bail

cava *f* quarry; cave; (fig) mine

cavadènti *m* (**-ti**) (coll) tooth puller, poor dentist

cavagno *m* (coll) basket

cavalcare §197 *tr* to ride; to cross over (*e.g., a river*) ‖ *intr* to ride; **cavalcare a bisdosso** to ride bareback; **cavalcare all'amazzone** to ride sidesaddle

cavalcata *f* ride; cavalcade

cavalcatura *f* mount

cavalca·via *m* (**-via**) bridge (*between two buildings*); overpass

cavalcióni *adj—a* **cavalcioni** (**di**) astride

cavalierato *m* knighthood

cavalière *m* rider (*on horseback*); knight; cavalier; chevalier; **a cavaliere** astride; **cavaliere d'industria** adventurer; **cavaliere errante** knight errant; **essere a cavaliere di** to overlook (*e.g., a valley*); to stretch over (*e.g., two centuries*)

cavalla *f* mare

cavalleggièro *m* cavalryman

cavalleré·sco **-sca** *adj* (**-schi** **-sche**) chivalrous, knightly

cavallerìa *f* cavalry; chivalry, knighthood; (fig) chivalry

cavallerizza *f* manège, riding school; horsemanship; horsewoman

cavallerizzo *m* horseman; riding master

cavallétta *f* grasshopper

cavallétto *m* tripod; easel; trestle (*of ski lift*); scaffold (*e.g., of stonemason*); sawhorse, sawbuck

cavalli·no **-na** *adj* horse, horse-like ‖ *m* foal, colt ‖ *f* foal, filly; **correre la cavallina** to be on the loose; to sow one's wild oats

cavallo *m* horse; knight (*in chess*); crotch (*of pants*); **a cavallo** on horseback; **a cavallo di** astride; **andare col cavallo di San Francesco** to ride shank's mare; **cavallo a dondolo** hobbyhorse; **cavallo di battaglia** battle horse; (fig) specialty, forte; **cavallo da corsa** race horse; **cavallo da tiro** draft horse; **cavallo di Frisia** cheval-de-frise; **cavallo di ritorno** confirmed news; **cavallo vapore** metric horsepower; **essere a cavallo** (fig) to have turned the corner

cavallóne *m* big horse; billow

cavallùc·cio *m* (**-ci**) little horse; **a cavalluccio** on one's shoulders; **cavalluccio marino** (ichth) sea horse

cavare *tr* to dig; to extract (*e.g., a tooth*); to pull out (*e.g., money*); to draw; **cavare il cuore a qlcu** to move s.o. to compassion; **cavare una spina dal cuore a qlcu** to ease s.o.'s mind ‖ *ref* to take off (*e.g., one's hat*); **cavarsela** to overcome an obstacle; to get out of trouble; **cavarsi la camicia di dosso** to give the shirt off one's back; **cavarsi la fame** to eat one's fill; **cavarsi la voglia** to satisfy one's wishes

cavastiva·li *m* (**-li**) bootjack

cavatap·pi *m* (**-pi**) corkscrew

cavaturàccio·li *m* (**-li**) corkscrew

cavèrna *f* cave, cavern

cavernó·so **-sa** [*s*] *adj* cavernous; deep (*voice*)

cavézza *f* halter; (fig) check

càvia *f* guinea pig; **cavia umana** (fig) guinea pig

caviale *m* caviar

cavìc·chio *m* (**-chi**) peg

cavì·glia *f* (**-glie**) ankle; bolt; pin, dowel, peg

caviglièra *f* ankle support

cavillare *intr* to cavil, quibble

cavillo *m* quibble

cavilló·so **-sa** [*s*] *adj* quibbling, captious

cavi·tà *f* (**-tà**) cavity

ca·vo **-va** *adj* hollow ‖ *m* hollow; cable; trough (*between two waves*); (naut) hawser; **cavo di rimorchio** towline; **cavo telefonico** telephone cable ‖ *f* see **cava**

cavolfióre *m* cauliflower

càvolo *m* cabbage; **cavolo di Bruxelles** Brussels sprouts (*food*); (bot) Brussels sprout; **non capire un cavolo** (vulg) to not understand a blessed thing

cazzòtto *m* (vulg) punch, sock

cazzuòla *f* trowel

ce §5
cecare §122 *tr* to blind
cèc·ca *f* (-che) magpie; **fare cecca** to misfire
cecchino *m* sniper
céce *m* chickpea
ceci·tà *f* (-tà) blindness
cè·co -ca *adj* & *mf* (-chi -che) Czech
Cecoslovàcchia, la Czechoslovakia
cecoslovac·co -ca *adj* & *mf* (-chi -che) Czechoslovak
cèdere §123 *tr* to cede; to give up; to sell at cost; **cedere il passo** to let s.o. through; **cedere la strada** to yield the right of way; **non cederla** to be second to none ‖ *intr* to give in, yield; to give way, succumb; to sag
cedévole *adj* yielding; soft; pliable
cedìglia *f* cedilla
cediménto *m* cave-in; (fig) yielding
cèdola *f* slip; coupon
cedri·no -na *adj* citron; citron-like; cedar, cedar-like
cédro *m* (*Citrus medica*) citron; (*Cedrus*) cedar; **cedro del Libano** cedar of Lebanon
CEE *m* (letterword) (**Comunità Economica Europea**) EEC (*European Economic Community - Common Market*)
cefalèa *f* slight headache; headache
cèfalo *m* (ichth) mullet
cèffo *m* snout; (pej) face; **brutto ceffo** ugly mug
ceffóne *m* slap in the face
celare (cèlo) *tr* to hide, conceal
cela·to -ta *adj* hidden ‖ *f* sallet
celebèrri·mo -ma *adj* very famous, renowned
celebrare (cèlebro) *tr* & *intr* to celebrate
celebrazióne *f* celebration
cèlebre *adj* famous, renowned, celebrated
celebri·tà *f* (-tà) celebrity
cèlere *adj* swift, rapid; express (*train*); short, quick; prompt ‖ **Celere** *f* special police
celeri·tà *f* (-tà) swiftness, rapidity; speed (*e.g., of a machine gun*)
celèste *adj* heavenly, celestial; blue, sky-blue ‖ *m* blue, sky blue; **celesti** heavenly spirits; (mythol) gods
celestiale *adj* celestial, heavenly
cèlia *f* jest; **mettere in celia** to deride; **per celia** in jest
celiare §287 (cèlio) *intr* to jest, joke
celibatà·rio -ria (-ri -rie) *adj* single ‖ *m* old bachelor
cèlibato *m* celibacy; bachelorhood
cèlibe *adj* single, unmarried ‖ *m* bachelor
cèlla *f* cell; **cella frigorifera** walk-in refrigerator; **cella campanaria** belfry
cèllofan *or* cèllofàn *m* cellophane
cèllula *f* cell; **cellula fotoelettrica** photoelectric cell
cellulare *adj* cellular; ventilated (*fabric*); solitary (*confinement*)
cellulòide *f* celluloid
celluló·so -sa [*s*] *adj* cell-like, cellular ‖ *f* cellulose
cèl·ta *mf* (-ti -te) Celt

cèlti·co -ca *adj* (-ci -che) Celtic; venereal (*disease*)
cementare (ceménto) *tr* to cement
ceménto *m* cement, concrete; **cemento armato** reinforced concrete
céna *f* supper; **Ultima Cena** Last Supper
cenàcolo *m* cenacle
cenare (céno) *intr* to sup, have supper
cenciaiò·lo -la *mf* ragpicker
cén·cio *m* (-ci) rag, duster (*for cleaning*)
cenció·so -sa [*s*] *adj* tattered, ragged
cénere *adj* ashen ‖ *f* ash; cinder; **andare in cenere** to go up in smoke; **ceneri** ashes (*of a person*); **ridurre in cenere** to burn to ashes ‖ **le Ceneri** Ash Wednesday
cenerèntola *f* (fig) Cinderella ‖ **Cenerèntola** *f* Cinderella (*of the fable*)
cén·gia *f* (-ge) ledge (*of a mountain*)
cénno *m* sign; wave (*with hand*); nod; wag; wink; gesture; hint; notice; **ai cenni di** at the orders of; **fare cenno a** *or* **di** to mention; **fare cenno di no** to shake one's head; **fare cenno di sì** to nod assent
cenò·bio *m* (-bi) monastery
cenobì·ta *m* (-ti) monk, cenobite
censiménto *m* census
censire §176 *tr* to take the census of
cènso *m* wealth, income; census (*in ancient Rome*)
censóre *m* censor; faultfinder; (educ) proctor
censuà·rio -ria (-ri -rie) *adj* income; tax (*register*) ‖ *m* taxpayer
censura *f* censure; censorship; fault-finding
censurare *tr* to censure; to criticize, find fault with
centàuro *m* centaur
centellinare *tr* to sip; to take a nip of
centellino *m* sip, nip
centenà·rio -ria (-ri -rie) *adj* & *mf* centenary, centennial ‖ *m* centenary, centennial (*anniversary*)
centèsi·mo -ma *adj* hundredth ‖ *m* hundredth; centime; cent; penny
cenfigrado *m* centigrade
centigrammo *m* centigram
centimetro *m* centimeter; tape measure
cèntina *f* (archit) centering; (aer) rib
centi·nàio *m* hundred; **un centinaio di** about a hundred ‖ *m* (-nàia *fpl*)—a hundred; **centinaia** by the hundreds
cènto *adj*, *m* & *pron* a hundred, one hundred; **per cento** per cent
centomila *adj*, *m* & *pron* a hundred thousand, one hundred thousand
centóne *m* cento
centopiè·di *m* (-di) centipede
centrale *adj* central ‖ *f* headquarters, home office; powerhouse, generating station; telephone exchange; **centrale di conversione** (elec) transformer station; **centrale telefonica** central
centralini·sta *mf* (-sti -ste) telephone operator
centralino *m* telephone exchange
centralizzare [*ddzz*] *tr* to centralize
centrare (cèntro) *tr* to center; to hit the center of

centrattac·co m (-chi) (sports) center forward

centrìfu·go -ga adj (-ghi -ghe) centrifugal ‖ f centrifuge

centrìno m centerpiece

centrìpe·to -ta adj centripetal

centri·sta mf (-sti -ste) (pol) centrist

cèntro m center; **al centro** downtown; **far centro** to hit the mark

centrocampo m (soccer) midfield

centuplicare §197 (**centùplico**) tr to multiply a hundredfold

cèntu·plo -pla adj & m hundredfold

céppo m trunk, stump; log; block (for beheading); brake shoe; stock (of anchor); ceppi stocks, fetters ‖ il Ceppo (coll) Christmas

céra f wax; face, aspect, air, look; **di cera** waxen; pale; **cera da scarpe** shoe polish; **avere buona cera** to look well; **fare buona cera a** to welcome

ceralac·ca f (-che) sealing wax

ceràmi·co -ca (-ci -che) adj ceramic ‖ f ceramics

cerare (**céro**) tr to wax

Cèrbero m Cerberus

cerbiatto m fawn

cerbottana f blowgun, peashooter

cer·ca f (-che) search, quest; **in cerca di** in search of

cercare §197 (**cérco**) tr to seek, look for; to desire, yearn for; **cercare il pelo nell'uovo** to be a faultfinder, to nitpick ‖ intr to try

cerca·tóre -trice adj seeking ‖ mf seeker; mendicant ‖ m prospector

cérchia f coterie; compass, limits (of a wall); circle (of friends)

cerchiare §287 (**cérchio**) tr to hoop (a barrel); to circle, encircle

cér·chio m (-chi) circle; hoop; loop; **fare il cerchio della morte** (aer) to loop the loop; **in cerchio** in a circle ‖ m (-chia fpl) (archaic) circle

cerchióne m rim; tire (of metal)

cereale adj & m cereal

cerebrale adj cerebral

cère·o -a adj waxen; wax-colored, pale

cerfò·glio m (-gli) chervil

cerimònia f ceremony; **fare cerimonie** to stand on ceremony; to make a fuss

cerimoniale adj & m ceremonial

cerimonière m master of ceremonies (at court)

cerimonió·so -sa [s] adj ceremonious

cerino m wax match; taper

cernéc·chio m (-chi) tuft (of hair)

cernièra f hinge; clasp (of handbag); **a cerniera** hinged; **cerniera lampo** zipper

cèrnita f sorting, selection, grading

céro m church candle; **offrire un cero** to light a candle

ceróne m make-up (of actor)

ceròtto m adhesive tape; (fig) bore; **cerotto per i calli** corn plaster

certame m (poet) combat; competition, contest (of poets)

certézza f certitude, assurance, conviction, certainty

certificare §197 (**certìfico**) tr to certify, certificate

certificato m certificate

cèr·to -ta adj such, some; convinced; certain; real, positive ‖ m certainty; **di certo** or **per certo** for certain ‖ **certi** pron some ‖ **certo** adv undoubtedly

certósa f Carthusian monastery, charterhouse

certosi·no m Carthusian monk; chartreuse (liquor); **da certosino** with great patience

certu·no -na adj (obs) some ‖ **certuni** pron some

cerùle·o -a adj cerulean

cerume m ear wax

cervellétto m cerebellum

cervelli·no -na adj & mf scatterbrain

cervèllo m (**cervèlli** & **cervèlla** fpl) brain; head; mind; **dare al cervello** to go to one's head

cervellòti·co -ca adj (-ci -che) queer, extravagant

cervice f (anat) cervix; (poet) nape of the neck

cerviè·ro -ra adj lynx-like; ‖ m lynx

cervi·no -na adj deer-like ‖ **Cervino** m Matterhorn

cèrvo m deer; (ent) stag beetle; **cervo volante** kite

Cèsare m Caesar

cesàre·o -a adj Caesarean; (poet) courtly

cesellare (**cesèllo**) tr to chase, chisel; to carve, engrave; to polish (e.g., a poem)

cesella·tóre -trice mf chaser, engraver, chiseler

cesellatura f chasing, engraving; polished writing

cesèllo m burin, graver

cesóia f shears, metal shears; **cesoie** shears (for gardening)

cesoiatrice f shearing machine

cèspite m source (of income); (poet) tuft

cèspo m tuft

cespù·glio m (-gli) bush, shrub, thicket

cèssa f—**senza cessa** without letup

cessare (**cèsso**) tr to stop, interrupt ‖ intr to cease, stop; **cessare di** + inf to stop + ger

cessazióne f cessation, discontinuance; **cessazione d'esercizio** going out of business

cessionà·rio m (-ri) assignee

cèsso m (vulg) privy, outhouse

césta f basket, hamper

cestinare tr to throw into the wastebasket; to reject (a book, article, etc.)

césto m basket; tuft; head (e.g., of lettuce)

cesura f caesura

cetàceo m cetacean

cèto m class; **ceto medio** middle class

cétra f lyre; cither; inspiration

cetriolino m gherkin

cetrìolo m cucumber; (fig) dolt

che adj what; which; what a, e.g., **che bella giornata!** what a beautiful day! ‖ pron interr what ‖ pron rel who; whom; that; which; (coll) in which ‖ m—**essere un gran che** to be a big shot, to be somebody || *adv* how, e.g., **che bello!** how nice!; **non . . . che** only, e.g., **non venne che Luigi** only Luigi came; no one but, e.g., **non restò che mio cugino** no one but my cousin stayed || *conj* that; (*after comparatives*) than, as

ché *adv* (coll) why || *conj* (coll) because; (coll) so that

checché *pron* (lit) whatever, no matter what

checchessìa *pron* (lit) anything, everything

chèla *f* claw

che·pì *m* (**-pì**) kepi

cherubino *m* cherub

chetare (**chéto**) *tr* to quiet; to placate || *ref* to quiet down, become quiet

chetichèlla *f*—**alla chetichella** surreptitiously, stealthily

ché·to -ta *adj* quiet, still

chi *pron interr* who; whom || *pron rel* who; whom; **chi . . . chi** some . . . some

chiàcchiera *f* chatter, idle talk; gossip; glibness; **fare quattro chiacchiere** to have a chat

chiacchierare (**chiàcchiero**) *intr* to chat; to gossip

chiacchierata *f* talk, chat; **fare una chiacchierata** to visit

chiacchieri·no -na *adj* talkative, loquacious

chiacchierì·o *m* (**-i**) chattering, jabbering (*of a crowd*)

chiacchieró·ne -na *adj* talkative, loquacious || *mf* chatterbox

chiama *f* roll call; **fare la chiama** to call the roll; **mancare alla chiama** to be absent at the roll call

chiamare *tr* to call; to hail (*a cab*); to invoke, call upon; **chiamare al telefono** to call up; **esser chiamato a** to have the vocation for || *ref* to be named; **si chiama Giovanni** his name is John

chiamata *f* call; (law) designation (*of an heir*); (telp) ring; (theat) curtain call; (typ) catchword

chiappa *f* (vulg) buttock; (slang) catch (*e.g., of fish*)

chiarét·to -ta *adj* & *m* claret

chiarézza *f* clarity, clearness

chiarificare §197 (**chiarìfico**) *tr* to clarify

chiariménto *m* explanation

chiarire §176 *tr* to clear up, explain; to unravel || *intr* (ESSERE) to clear, become clear || *ref* to make oneself clear; to assure oneself

chia·ro -ra *adj* clear; bright; light (*color*); honest; clear-cut; plain (*language*); illustrious, famous || *m* light; bright color; brightness; **chiaro di luna** moonlight; **con questi chiari di luna** in these troubled times; **mettere in chiaro** to clarify, explain || **chiaro** *adv* plainly; **chiaro e tondo** bluntly, frankly

chiaróre *m* light, glimmer

chiaroveggènte *adj* & *mf* clairvoyant

chiaroveggènza *f* clairvoyance

chiassata *f* uproar, disturbance, racket; noisy scene

chiasso *m* noise; uproar; alley; **fare chiasso** to cause a sensation

chiassó·so -sa [s] *adj* noisy; gaudy

chiatta *f* barge; pontoon

chiavarda *f* bolt

chiave *f* key; wrench; (archit) keystone; (mus) clef; **avere le chiavi di** to own; **chiave a rollino** adjustable wrench; **chiave a tubo** socket wrench; **chiave di volta** keystone; **chiave inglese** monkey wrench; **fuori chiave** off key; **sotto chiave** under lock and key

chiavétta *f* key; cock; cotter pin

chiàvi·ca *f* (**-che**) sewer

chiavistèllo *m* bolt

chiazza *f* spot, blotch

chiazzare *tr* to spot, blotch; to mottle

chiazza·to -ta *adj* spotted, mottled

chic·ca *f* (**-che**) sweet, candy

chìcchera *f* cup

chicchessìa *pron indef* anyone, anybody

chicchirichì *m* cock-a-doodle-doo

chic·co *m* (**-chi**) grain, seed; bead (*of rosary*); bean (*of coffee*); **chicco di grandine** hailstone; **chicco d'uva** grape

chièdere §124 *tr* to ask; to ask for; to beg (*pardon*); to require; to sue (*for damages or peace*); **chiedere a qlcu di** + *inf* to ask s.o. to + *inf*; **chiedere in prestito** to borrow; **chiedere qlco a qlcu** to ask s.o. for s.th || *ref* to wonder

chiéri·ca *f* (**-che**) tonsure; priesthood

chiéri·co *m* (**-ci**) clergyman; altar boy; (archaic) clerk

chièsa *f* church

chiesuòla *f* small church; clique, set (*e.g., of artists*); (naut) binnacle

chi·glia *f* (**-glie**) keel; **chiglia mobile** (naut) centerboard

chilo *m* kilo, kilogram; **fare il chilo** to take a siesta

chilociclo *m* kilocycle

chilogrammo *m* kilogram

chilohèrtz *m* kilohertz

chilometràg·gio *m* (**-gi**) distance in kilometers

chilomètri·co -ca *adj* (**-ci -che**) kilometric; interminable (*e.g., speech*)

chilòmetro *m* kilometer

chilo·watt *m* (**-watt**) kilowatt

chimèra *f* chimera; daydream, utopia

chimèri·co -ca *adj* (**-ci -che**) chimerical

chìmi·co -ca *adj* (**-ci -che**) chemical || *m* chemist || *f* chemistry

chimòno *m* kimono

china *f* slope, decline; India ink; cinchona

chinare *tr* to bend; to lower (*one's eyes*); **chinare il capo** to nod assent; **chinare la fronte** to yield, give in || *ref* to bend, stoop

china·to -ta *adj* bent, lowered; bitter; with quinine, e.g., **vino chinato** wine with quinine

chincàglie *fpl* notions, knicknacks, sundries

chincaglière *m* notions or knicknack dealer

chincaglierìa *f* knicknack; **chincaglierie** knicknacks, notions

chinina *f* quinine (*alkaloid*)

chinino *m* quinine (*salt of the alkaloid*)

chi·no -na *adj* bent, lowered ‖ *f* see **china**

chiòc·cia *f* (-ce) brooding hen

chiocciare §128 (**chiòccio**) *intr* to cluck; to sit, brood; to crouch

chiocciata *f* brood

chiòc·cio -cia (-ci -ce) *adj* hoarse ‖ *f* see **chioccia**

chiòcciola *f* snail; (anat) cochlea; (mach) nut

chioccolì·o *m* (-ì) cackle (*of hen*); gurgle (*of water*)

chiodare (**chiòdo**) *tr* to nail

chioda·to -ta *adj* nailed shut; hobnailed

chiòdo *m* nail; spike; obsession; craze; (coll) debt; **chiodi** climbing irons; **chiodo a espansione** expansion bolt; **chiodo da cavallo** horseshoe nail; **chiodo di garofano** clove; **chiodo ribattino** rivet

chiòma *f* hair; mane; foliage; (astr) coma

chioma·to -ta *adj* hairy, long-haired; leafy

chiòsa *f* gloss

chiosare (**chiòso**) *tr* to gloss, comment on

chiò·sco *m* (-schi) kiosk, stand, newsstand; pavilion, bandstand

chiòstra *f* circular range (*of mountains*); (poet) enclosure; (poet) set (*of teeth*); (poet) zone, region

chiòstro *m* cloister

chiòt·to -ta *adj* quiet, still; **chiotto chiotto** still as a mouse

chiromante *mf* palmist

chiromanzìa *f* palmistry

chiropràtica *f* chiropractice

chirurgìa *f* surgery

chirùrgi·co -ca *adj* (-ci -che) surgical

chirùr·go *m* (-ghi & -gi) surgeon

chissà *adv* maybe

chitarra *f* guitar; **chitarra hawaiana** ukulele

chitarri·sta *mf* (-sti -ste) guitar player

chiùdere §125 *tr* to shut, close; to lock; to turn off; to fasten; to block (*a road*); to fence in; to nail shut (*a box*); to strike (*a balance*); to conclude, wind up; **chiudere a chiave** to lock; **chiudere bottega** to go out of business; **chiudere il becco** (slang) to shut up ‖ *intr* to shut, close; to lock ‖ *ref* to shut, close; to lock; to withdraw; to cloud over

chiùnque *pron indef invar* anybody, anyone ‖ *pron rel invar* whoever, whomever; anyone who, anyone whom

chiurlo *m* (orn) curlew

chiusa [s] *f* fence; lock (*of canal*); end, conclusion (*e.g., of letter*)

chiusino [s] *m* manhole

chiu·so -sa [s] *adj* shut, closed, locked; stuffy (*air*); high-bodiced (*dress*);

close (*vowel*) ‖ *m* enclosure, corral; close ‖ *f* see **chiusa**

chiusura [s] *f* closing, end; fastener; lock; **chiusura lampo** zipper, slide fastener

ci §5

ciabatta *f* slipper; old shoe

ciabat·tàio *m* (-tài) cobbler

ciabattare *intr* to shuffle along

ciabattino *m* cobbler, shoemaker

ciàc·f (mov) clappers

cialda *f* wafer; thin waffle

cialdóne *m* cone (*for ice cream*)

cialtró·ne -na *mf* rogue, scoundrel; slovenly person

ciambèlla *f* doughnut; **ciambella di salvataggio** life saver

ciambellano *m* chamberlain

ciampicare §197 (**ciàmpico**) *intr* to stumble along

ciana *f* (slang) fishwife

cianamide *f* cyanamide

ciàn·cia *f* (-ce) chatter, prattle, idle gossip

cianciare §128 (**ciàncio**) *intr* to chatter, prattle

cianciafrùscola *f* trifle, bagatelle

cianfrusà·glia *f* (-glie) trifle, trinket; rubbish, trash, junk

cianìdri·co -ca *adj* (-ci -che) hydrocyanic

cianògeno *m* cyanogen

cianuro *m* cyanide

ciao *interj* (coll) hi!, hello!; (coll) goodbye!, so long!

ciarla *f* chatter, prattle, idle talk; gossip

ciarlare *intr* to chatter, prattle

ciarlatanata *f* charlatanism, quackery

ciarlatanerìa *f* charlatanism

ciarlatané·sco -sca *adj* (-schi -sche) charlatan

ciarlatano *m* charlatan, quack

ciarliè·ro -ra *adj* talkative, garrulous

ciarpame *m* rubbish, junk

ciaschedu·no -na *adj indef* each ‖ *pron indef* each one, everyone

ciascu·no -na *adj indef* each ‖ *pron indef* each one, everyone

cibare *tr & ref* to feed

cibà·rio -ria (-ri -ria) *adj* alimentary ‖ **cibarie** *fpl* foodstuffs, victuals

cibo *m* food; meal; (fig) dish

cicala *f* cicada; grasshopper; locust; (fig) chatterbox; (naut) anchor ring

cicalare *intr* to prattle, babble; to chatter

cicaléc·cio *m* (-ci) prattle, babble; chatter

cicatrice *f* scar

cicatrizzare [ddzz] *tr* to heal (*a wound*) ‖ *intr* (ESSERE) & *ref* to heal, scar

cicatrizzazióne [ddzz] *f* closing, healing (*of a wound*)

cic·ca *f* (-che) butt (*of cigar or cigarette*); (slang) chewing gum

ciccare §197 *intr* to chew tobacco; (coll) to boil with anger

cicchettare (**cicchétto**) *tr* (slang) to prime (*a carburetor*); (slang) to dress down, reprimand ‖ *intr* to tipple

cicchétto *m* nip (*of liquor*); (slang) dressing down

cìc·cia f (-ce) (joc) flesh; (joc) fat

cicció·ne -na mf fatty

ciceróne m guide || **Cicerone** m Cicero

ciclàbile adj open to bicycles; bicycle, e.g., **pista ciclabile** bicycle trail

cìcli·co -ca adj (-ci -che) cyclic(al)

cicli·sta mf (-sti -ste) cyclist, bicyclist

ciclo m cycle; (coll) bicycle; **ciclo operativo** (econ) turnover

ciclomotóre m motorbike

ciclomotori·sta mf (-sti -ste) driver of motorbike

ciclóne m cyclone

ciclòpe m cyclops

ciclòpi·co -ca adj (-ci -che) cyclopean, gigantic

ciclopista f bicycle trail

ciclostilare tr to mimeograph

ciclostile or **ciclostilo** m mimeograph

ciclotróne m cyclotron

cicógna f stork

cicòria f chicory; endive

cicuta f hemlock

ciè·co -ca (-chi -che) adj blind; **alla cieca** blindly || mf blind person || m blind man; **i ciechi** the blind

cièlo m sky; heaven; weather, climate; roof (e.g., of wagon); **a ciel sereno** in the open air; **cielo a pecorelle** mackerel or fleecy sky; **dal cielo** from above; **non stare né in cielo né in terra** to be utterly absurd; **per amor del cielo** for heaven's sake; **portare al cielo** to praise to the skies; **santo cielo!** good heavens!; **volesse il cielo che . . . !** would that . . . !

cifra f number, figure; Arabic numeral; sum, total; digit; initial, monogram; cipher, code; **cifra d'affari** amount of business, turnover; **cifra tonda** round number

cifrare tr to cipher, code; to embroider (a monogram)

cifrà·rio m (-ri) code, cipher

cì·glio m (-glia fpl) eyelash; eyebrow; **a ciglio asciutto** with dry eyes; **ciglia** (zool) cilia; **senza batter ciglio** without batting an eye || m (-gli) (fig) edge, brow

ciglióne m bank, embankment

cigno m swan; cob

cigolante adj creaky, squeaky

cigolare (**cigolo**) intr to squeak, creak

cigolì·o m (-i) squeak, creak

Cile, il Chile

cilécca f—**fare cilecca** to misfire

cileccare §197 (**cilécco**) intr to goof, blunder; to fail

cilè·no -na adj & mf Chilean

cilè·stro -stra adj (poet) azure, blue

cilì·cio m (-ci) sackcloth

ciliè·gia f (-gie & -ge) cherry

ciliè·gio m (-gi) cherry tree

cilindrare tr to calender (e.g., paper); to roll (a road)

cilindrata f (aut) cylinder capacity, piston displacement

cilìndri·co -ca adj (-ci -che) cylindric(al)

cilindro m cylinder; top hat; roll, roller

cima f top, summit; tip (e.g., of a pole); peak (of mountain); edge, end; rope, cable; head (e.g., of let-

tuce); (coll) genius; **da cima a fondo** from top to bottom

cimare tr to cut the tip off; to shear; (agr) to prune

cimasa f (archit) coping

cìmbalo m gong; (obs) cymbal; **in cimbali** tipsy; in a tizzy

cimè·lio m (-li) relic, souvenir, memento

cimentare (**ciménto**) tr to risk (e.g., one's life); to provoke; (archaic) to assay || ref to expose oneself; to venture

ciménto m risk, danger; (archaic) assay

cìmice f bug; bedbug; (coll) thumbtack

cimièro m crest; (poet) helmet

ciminièra f chimney (of factory); smokestack (of locomotive); funnel (of steamship)

cimitèro m cemetery, graveyard; (fig) ghosttown

cimósa [s] or **cimóssa** f selvage; blackboard eraser

cimurro m distemper; (joc) cold

Cina, la China

cinabro m cinnabar; crimson; red ink

cìn·cia f (-ce) titmouse

cinciallégra f great titmouse

cincilla f chinchilla

cincischiare §287 tr to shred; to wrinkle, crease; to waste (time); to mumble (words) || intr to wrinkle, crease

cine m (coll) cinema

cineamatóre m amateur movie maker

cine·asta m (-sti) motion-picture producer; movie fan; movie actor || f movie actress

cinecàmera f movie camera

cinedilettante mf amateur movie maker

cinegiornale m newsreel

cinelàndia f movieland

cìne·ma m (-ma) movies; movie house

cinematografare (**cinematògrafo**) tr to film, shoot

cinematografìa f cinema, motion pictures, movie industry

cinematogràfi·co -ca adj (-ci -che) movie, motion-picture; movie-like

cinematògrafo m motion picture; movie theater; (fig) hubbub; (fig) funny sight

cineparchég·gio m (-gi) drive-in movie

cinepar·co m (-chi) drive-in movie

cineprésa [s] f movie camera

cinère·o -a adj ashen

cinescò·pio m (-pi) kinescope, TV tube

cinése [s] adj & mf Chinese

cineteatro m movie house; **cineteatro all'aperto** outdoor movie

cinetè·ca f (-che) film library

cinèti·co -ca (-ci -che) adj kinetic || f kinetics

cingallégra f var of **cinciallegra**

cìngere §126 tr to surround; to gird (e.g., the head); to gird on (e.g., the sword); **cingere cavaliere** to dub a knight; **cingere d'assedio** to besiege

cìnghia f belt, strap; **tirare la cinghia** to tighten one's belt

cinghiale m wild boar

cinghiata f lash

cingola·to -ta adj track-driven, caterpillar

cìngolo m endless metal belt, track; girdle, belt (of a priest)

cinguettare (**cinguétto**) intr to chirp, twitter; to babble

cinguettì·o m (-ì) chirp, twitter; (fig) babble

cìni·co -ca (-ci -che) adj cynical || m cynic

cinìglia f chenille

cinismo m cynicism

cinòfilo m dog lover

cinquanta adj, m & pron fifty

cinquantenà·rio -ria (-ri -rie) adj fifty-year-old; occurring every fifty years || m fiftieth anniversary

cinquantènne adj fifty-year-old || mf fifty-year-old person

cinquantèn·nio m (-ni) period of fifty years, half century

cinquantèsi·mo -ma adj, m & pron fiftieth

cinquantìna f about fifty; **sulla cinquantina** about fifty years old

cìnque adj & pron five; **le cinque** five o'clock || m five; fifth (in dates)

cinquecenté·sco -sca adj (-schi -sche) sixteenth-century

cinquecènto adj, m & pron five hundred || f small car || **il Cinquecento** the sixteenth century

cinquìna f set of five; five numbers (drawn at Italian lotto); (mil) pay

cìnta f fence, wall; circuit, enclosure; circumference (of a city)

cintare tr to surround; to fence in; to hold (in wrestling)

cìn·to -ta adj surrounded, girded || m belt; girdle; **cinto erniario** truss || f see **cinta**

cìntola f waist; belt; **con le mani alla cintola** idling, loafing

cintura f belt; waist; waistband; lock (in wrestling); **cintura di salvataggio** life preserver; **cintura di sicurezza** safety belt

cinturare tr to surround

cinturino m strap (of watch or shoes); hem (e.g., of cuffs)

cinturóne m belt; Sam Browne belt

ciò pron this; that; **a ciò** for that purpose; **a ciò che** so that; **ciò nondimeno** or **ciò nonostante** though, nevertheless; **con tutto ciò** in spite of everything; **per ciò** therefore

ciòc·ca f (-che) lock (of hair); cluster (e.g., of cherries)

ciòc·co m (-chi) log; **dormire come un ciocco** to sleep like a log

cioccolata adj invar chocolate || f chocolate (beverage)

cioccolatino m chocolate candy

cioccolato m chocolate; **cioccolato al latte** milk chocolate

cioè adv that is to say, namely; to wit; rather

ciondolare (**cióndolo**) tr to dangle || intr to dawdle; to stroll, saunter

cióndolo m pendant, charm

ciondolóne m idler || adv dangling

ciòtola f bowl

ciòttolo m pebble, small stone; cobblestone

ciottoló·so -sa [s] adj pebbly

cip m (**cip**) chip (in gambling)

cipì·glio m (-gli) frown

cipólla f onion; bulb (e.g., of a lamp); nozzle (of sprinkling can)

cippo m column; bench mark

ciprèsso m cypress

cìpria f face powder; **cipria compatta** compact

cipriò·ta adj & mf (-ti -te) Cypriot

Cipro m Cyprus

circa adv about, nearly || prep concerning, regarding, as to

cìr·co m (-chi) circus; **circo equestre** circus; **circo glaciale** cirque; **circo lunare** walled plain

circolante adj circulating; lending (library) || m available cash (of a corporation)

circolare adj circular; cashier's (check) || f circular (letter); (rr) beltline || v (**cìrcolo**) intr to circulate

circolazióne f circulation; traffic; currency; **circolazione sanguigna** bloodstream; circulation of blood

cìrcolo m circle; circulation (of blood); reception (e.g., at court); club, set, group

circoncidere §145 tr to circumcise

circoncisióne f circumcision

circonci·so -sa adj circumcised

circondare (**circóndo**) tr to surround, encircle; to overwhelm (e.g., with kindness) || ref to surround oneself; to be surrounded

circondà·rio m (-ri) district; surrounding territory

circonduzióne f rotation (e.g., of the body in calisthenics)

circonferènza f circumference

circonflès·so -sa adj circumflex

circonlocuzióne f circumlocution

circonvallazióne f city-line road; (rr) beltline

circonvenire §282 tr to circumvent; to outwit

circonvenzióne f circumvention

circonvici·no -na adj neighboring, nearby

circoscrit·to -ta adj circumscribed

circoscrìvere §250 tr to circumscribe

circoscrizióne f district; circuit

circospèt·to -ta adj circumspect, cautious

circospezióne f circumspection

circostante adj neighboring, surrounding, nearby || m circostanti mpl neighbors; bystanders, onlookers

circostanza f circumstance

circostanziale adj circumstantial

circostanziare §287 tr to describe in detail; to circumstanciate

circostanzia·to -ta adj detailed, circumstantial

circuire §176 tr to circumvent

circùito m circuit; race (of automobiles or bicycles); **circuito stampato** (rad, telv) printed circuit

circumnavigare §209 (**circumnàvigo**) tr to circumnavigate

circumnavigazióne f circumnavigation

cirìlli·co -ca adj (-ci -che) Cyrillic

Ciro m Cyrus
cirro m cirrus
cirrò·si f (-si) cirrhosis
cispa f gum (on edge of eyelids)
cisposità [s] f gum; gumminess
cispó·so -sa [s] adj gummy
ciste f cyst
cistèrna f cistern; tank
cisti f cyst
cistifèllea f gall bladder
citante mf (law) plaintiff
citare tr to cite, quote; to mention; (law) to summon, subpoena
citazióne f citation, quotation; mention; (law) summons, subpoena; (mil) commendation
citillo m (zool) gopher
citòfono m intercom
citostàti·co -ca adj (-ci -che) (biochem) cancer-inhibiting
citrato m citrate
cìtri·co -ca adj (-ci -che) citric
citrul·lo -la adj simple, foolish ‖ mf simpleton, fool
cit·tà f (-tà) city, town ‖ Città del Capo Cape Town; Città del Messico Mexico City; Città del Vaticano Vatican City; città fungo boom town
cittadèlla f citadel
cittadinanza f citizenship
cittadi·no -na adj city, town, civic ‖ mf citizen; city dweller, urbanite ‖ m townsman
ciù·co m (-chi) (coll) donkey, ass
ciuffo m lock, forelock; tuft; (bot) tassel
ciuffolòtto m (orn) bullfinch
ciurlare intr—ciurlare nel manico to play fast and loose
ciurma f crew, gang, mob
ciurmare tr (archaic) to charm; (archaic) to trick, inveigle
ciurmatóre m swindler, charlatan
civètta f barn owl, little owl; unmarked police car; ship used as decoy; (fig) coquette, flirt
civettare (civétto) intr to flirt
civetteria f coquettishness, coquetry
civettuò·lo -la adj coquettish; attractive
civi·co -ca adj (-ci -che) civic; town, city
civile adj civil; civilian ‖ mf civilian
civili·sta mf (-sti -ste) attorney, solicitor
civilizzare [ddzz] tr to civilize ‖ ref to become civilized
civilizzazióne [ddzz] f civilizing (e.g., of barbarians); civilization
civil·tà f (-tà) civilization; civility
civismo m good citizenship
clac·son m (-son) horn (of a car)
claire f (claire) grating (in front of a store window)
clamóre m clamor, uproar
clamoró·so -sa [s] adj noisy; clamorous
clan m (clan) clan; clique
clandesti·no -na adj clandestine
clangóre m clangor, clang
clarinetti·sta mf (-sti -ste) clarinet player
clarinétto m clarinet
clarino m clarion
classe f class

classicheggiante adj classicistic
classicismo m classicism
classici·sta mf (-sti -ste) classicist
classici·tà f (-tà) classical spirit; classical antiquity
clàssi·co -ca (-ci -che) adj classic(al) ‖ m classic
classifi·ca f (-che) rank, rating (in competitive testing); classification; (sports) rating
classificare §197 (classìfico) tr to classify; to rate, rank ‖ ref to score
classificazióne f classification
claudicante adj lame, limping
claudicare §197 (clàudico) intr to limp
clauné·sco -sca adj (-schi -sche) clownish
ciàusola f provision, proviso; clause; close, conclusion (e.g., of a speech); clausola rossa instructions for payment (in bank-credit documents); clausola verde shipping instructions (in bank-credit documents)
clausura f (eccl) seclusion; (fig) secluded place
clava f club, bludgeon
clavicémbalo m harpsichord
clavìcola f clavicle, collarbone
clemàtide f clematis
clemènte adj clement, indulgent; mild (climate)
clemènza f clemency; mildness
cleptòmane adj & mf kleptomaniac
clericale adj clerical ‖ m clericalist
clericalismo m clericalism
clèro m clergy
clessidra f water clock; sandglass
clicchetti·o m (-i) clicking, click-clack (e.g., of a typewriter)
cli·ché m (-ché) cliché; stereotype (plate)
cliènte m client, customer, patron
clientèla f clientele, customers; practice (of a professional man)
cli·ma m (-mi) climate
climatèri·co -ca adj (-ci -che) climacteric; crucial
climatè·rio m (-ri) climacteric; crucial period
climàti·co -ca adj (-ci -che) climatic
climatizzazióne [ddzz] f air conditioning
clìni·co -ca (-ci -che) adj clinic ‖ m clinician; highly skilled physician ‖ f clinic; private hospital
cli·sma m (-smi) enema
clistère m enema; clistere a pera fountain syringe
cloa·ca f (-che) sewer
cloche f (cloche) woman's wide-brimmed hat; (aer) stick; (aut) floor gearshift
clorare (clòro) tr to chlorinate
clorato m chlorate
clorìdri·co -ca adj (-ci -che) hydrochloric
clòro m chlorine
clorofilla f chlorophyll
clorofòr·mio m (-mi) chloroform
cloroformizzare [ddzz] tr to chloroform
cloruro m chloride

coabitare (coàbito) *intr* to live together; to cohabit

coabitazióne *f* sharing (*of an apartment*)

coaccusà·to -ta *adj* jointly accused ‖ *m* codefendant

coacèrvo *m* accumulation (*e.g., of interest*)

coadiutóre *m* coadjutor

coadiuvante *adj* helping ‖ *m* helper

coadiuvare (coàdiuvo) *tr* to assist, advise

coagulare (coàgulo) *tr & ref* to coagulate, clot

coagulazióne *f* coagulation, clotting

coàgulo *m* clot

coalescènza *f* coalescence

coalizióne *f* coalition

coalizzare [ddzz] *tr & ref* to unite, rally

coartare *tr* to coerce, force

coartazióne *f* coercion, forcing

coatti·vo -va *adj* forceful, compelling

coat·to -ta *adj* coercive

coautóre *m* coauthor

coazióne *f* coercion

cobalto *m* cobalt

cocaina *f* cocaine

cocainòmane *mf* cocaine addict

coc·ca *f* (-che) notch (*of arrow*); corner, edge (*e.g., of a handkerchief*); three-mast galley

coccarda *f* cockade

cocchière *m* coachman, cab driver

cocchiume *m* bung

còc·cia *f* (-ce) sword guard; (coll) head, noggin

còccige *m* coccyx

coccinèlla *f* ladybug

cocciniglia *f* cochineal

còc·cio *m* (-ci) earthenware; broken piece of pottery

cocciutàggine *m* stubborness

cocciu·to -ta *adj* stubborn

còc·co *m* (-chi) coconut (*tree and nut*); (bact) coccus; (coll) egg; (coll) darling, favorite

cocco·dè *m* (-dè) cackle

coccodrillo *m* crocodile

còccola *f* berry (*of cypress*); darling girl

coccolare (còccolo) *tr* to fondle, cuddle ‖ *ref* to nestle, cuddle up; to bask

còcco·lo -la *adj* (coll) nice, darling ‖ *m* darling boy ‖ *f* see **coccola**

coccolóne or **coccolóni** *adv* squatting

cocènte *adj* burning

cocktail *m* (cocktail) cocktail; cocktail party

còclea *f* dredge; (anat) cochlea

cocómero *m* watermelon; (coll) simpleton

cocorita *f* parakeet

cocuzza *f* (coll) pumpkin; (coll) head, noggin

cocùzzolo *m* crown (*of hat*); peak (*of mountain*)

códa *f* tail; train (*of skirt*); pigtail (*of hair*); **coda di paglia** (coll) uneasy conscience; **con la coda dell'occhio** out of the corner of the eye; **con la coda tra le gambe** with its tail between its legs; (fig) crestfallen; **di**

coda last; **fare la coda** to stand in line; **in coda** in a row; at the tail end

codardìa *f* (lit) cowardice

codar·do -da *adj* cowardly ‖ *mf* coward

codazzo *m* (pej) trail (*of people*)

codeina *f* codein

codé·sto -sta §7 *adj* ‖ §8 *pron*

còdice *m* code; codex; **codice della strada** traffic laws; **codice di avviamento postale** zip code

codicillo *m* codicil

codificare §197 **(codìfico)** *tr* to codify

codi·no -na *adj* reactionary; conformist ‖ *m* pigtail (*of a man*); (fig) reactionary; conformist ‖ *f* small tail

códolo *m* tang, shank (*e.g., of knife*); handle (*of spoon or knife*); head (*of violin*)

coeducazióne *f* coeducation

coefficiènte *m* coefficient

coerciti·vo -va *adj* coercive

coercizióne *f* coercion

coerède *mf* coheir

coerènte *adj* coherent; consistent

coerènza *f* coherence; consistency

coesióne *f* cohesion

coesistènza *f* coexistence

coesistere §114 *intr* to coexist

coesi·vo -va *adj* cohesive

coetàne·o -a *adj & m* contemporary

coè·vo -va *adj* contemporaneous, coeval

cofanétto *m* small chest, small coffer

còfano *m* chest, coffer; box, case (*for ammunition*); (aut) hood

còffa *f* masthead, crow's-nest

cofirmatà·rio -ria *adj & mf* (-ri -rie) cosigner

cogitabón·do -da *adj* (poet & joc) thoughtful, meditative

cogitare (cògito) *tr & intr* (poet & joc) to cogitate

cógli §4

cògliere §127 *tr* to gather; to hit (*the target*); to pluck (*flowers*); to grab, seize; (fig) to guess; **cogliere in flagrante** to catch in the act; **cogliere la palla al balzo** to seize time by the forelock; **cogliere nel giusto** to hit the nail on the head; **cogliere qlcu alla sprovvista** to catch s.o. napping; **cogliere sul fatto** to catch in the act

coglióne *m* (vulg) testicle; (vulg) simpleton, fool

coglioneria *f* (vulg) great stupidity

cognata *f* sister-in-law

cognato *m* brother-in-law

cògni·to -ta *adj* (poet & law) well-known

cognizióne *f* cognition, knowledge

cognóme *m* surname, family name

coguaro *m* cougar

cói §4

coibènte *adj* nonconducting ‖ *m* nonconductor

coincidènza *f* coincidence; harmony, identity; transfer (*from one streetcar or bus to another*); (rr) connection

coincìdere §145 *intr* to coincide

coinquilino *m* fellow tenant

cointeressare (cointerèsso) *tr* to give a share (*of profit*) to

cointeressa·to -ta *adj* jointly interested || *mf* party having a joint interest

cointeressènza *f* interest, share

coinvòlgere §289 *tr* to involve

còito *m* coitus, intercourse

cól §4

colà *adv* over there

colabròdo *m* colander, strainer

colàg·gio *m* (-gi) loss, leak

colapa·sta *m* (-sta) colander

colare (cólo) *tr* to filter, strain; to sift (*wheat*); to cast (*metals*); **colare a picco** to sink || *intr* to leak, drip; to flow (*said of blood*); **colare a picco** to sink

colata *f* casting (*of metal*); stream of lava; slide (*of snow or rocks*)

colatic·cio *m* (-ci) drip, dripping

cola·tólo *m* (-tól) colander, strainer

colazióne *f* breakfast; lunch; **colazione al sacco** picnic; **prima colazione** breakfast; **seconda colazione** lunch

colbac·co *m* (-chi) busby

colèi §8 *pron dem*

colèn·do -da *adj* (archaic) honorable

colè·ra *m* (-ra) cholera

colesterìna *f* cholesterol

coli·brì *m* (-brì) hummingbird

còli·co -ca & *f* (-ci -che) colic

colino *m* strainer

cólla §4

còlla *f* glue; paste; **colla di pesce** isinglass

collaborare (collàboro) *intr* to collaborate; to contribute (*to newspaper or magazine*)

collaboratóre *m* collaborator; contributor (*to newspaper or magazine*)

collaborazióne *f* collaboration

collaborazioni·sta *mf* (-sti -ste) collaborationist

collana *f* necklace; series, collection (*of literary works*)

collante *adj* & *m* adhesive

collare *m* collar || *v* (còllo) *tr* to lift or lower (*with a rope*)

collasso *m* collapse

collaterale *adj* & *m* collateral

collaudare (collàudo) *tr* to test; to approve; to pass

collauda·tóre -trice *mf* tester

collàudo *m* test

collazionare (collazióno) *tr* to collate

cólle §4

còlle *m* hill; low peak; mountain pass

collè·ga *mf* (-ghi -ghe) colleague, associate

collegaménto *m* connection, telephone connection; contact; (mil) liaison

collegare §209 (collégo) *tr* to join, connect || *intr* to agree, be in harmony || *ref* to become allied; to make contact, make connection (*e.g., by phone*)

collegiale *adj* collegiate || *mf* boarding-school student

collegiata *f* collegiate church

collè·gio *m* (-gi) college (*e.g., of surgeons*); boarding school, academy

còllera *f* anger, wrath; **montare in collera** to become angry

collèri·co -ca *adj* (-ci -che) hot-tempered, choleric

collètta *f* collection; collect (*in church*)

collettivismo *m* collectivism

collettivi·tà *f* (-tà) collectivity, community

colletti·vo -va *adj* collective || *m* party worker (*of leftist party*)

collétto *m* collar; flank (*of a tooth*)

collet·tóre -trice *adj* connecting; collecting (*pipe*) || *m* collector; tax collector; manifold; (elec) commutator (*of D.C. device*); (elec) collector (*of A.C. device*); **collettore d'ammissione** intake manifold; **collettore di scarico** exhaust manifold

collettorìa *f* tax office; small post office

collezionare (collezióno) *tr* to collect (*e.g., stamps*)

collezióne *f* collection; collection, series (*of literary works*)

collezioni·sta *mf* (-sti -ste) collector

collìdere §135 *intr* to collide

collimare *tr* to point (*a telescope*) || *intr* to coincide; match; to dovetail

collina *f* hill; **in collina** in the hill country

collinó·so -sa [*s*] *adj* hilly

colli·rio *m* (-ri) eyewash

collisióne *f* collision; (fig) conflict; **entrare in collisione** to collide

cóllo §4

còllo *m* neck; piece (*of baggage*); package, parcel; **al collo** in a sling; (fig) downhill; **collo del piede** instep; **collo d'oca** crankshaft; **in collo** in one's arms (*said of a baby*)

collocaménto *m* placement, employment; **collocamento a riposo** retirement; **collocamento in aspettativa** leave of absence without pay; **collocamento in malattia** sick leave

collocare §197 (còlloco) *tr* to place; to find employment for; to sell; **collocare a riposo** to retire; **collocare in aspettativa** to give a leave of absence without pay to; **collocare in malattia** to grant sick leave to

collocazióne *f* location (*of a book in a library*); catalogue card

colloidale *adj* colloidal

collòide *m* colloid

colloquiale *adj* colloquial

collò·quio *m* (-qui) talk, conference; colloquy; colloquium, symposium

colló·so -sa [*s*] *adj* gluey, sticky

collotòrto *m* (collitòrti) bigot, hypocrite

collòttola *f* nape or scruff of the neck

collùdere §105 *intr* to be in collusion

collusióne *f* collusion

collutó·rio *m* (-ri) mouthwash

colluttare *intr* to scuffle, fight

colluttazióne *f* scuffle, fight

cólma *f* high-water level (*during high tide*)

colmare (cólmo) *tr* to fill, fill up; to fill in (*with dirt*); to overwhelm; **colmare una lacuna** to bridge a gap

colmata *f* silting; reclaimed land; sand bank

cól·mo -ma *adj* full, filled up || *m* top, peak, summit; (archit) ridgepole; (fig) acme; **al colmo di** at the height of; **è il colmo** that's the limit || *f* see **colma**

colofóne *m* colophon

colofònia *f* rosin

colombàia *f* dovecot

colombèlla *f* ingenue; **a colombella** vertically

colóm·bo -ba *mf* pigeon, dove || **Colombo** *m* Columbus

colònia *f* colony; cologne; settlement; summer camp; **colonia penale** penal colony; penitentiary || **Colonia** *f* Cologne

coloniale *adj* colonial || *m* colonial; colonist; **coloniali** imported foods

colòni·co -ca *adj* (**-ci -che**) farm (*e.g., house*)

colonizzare [ddzz] *tr* to colonize; to settle

colonizzazióne [ddzz] *f* colonization

colonna *f* column; row; **colonna sonora** sound track; **Colonne d'Ercole** Pillars of Hercules

colonnato *m* colonnade

colonnèllo *m* colonel

colonnétta *f* small column; gasoline pump

colò·no -na *mf* sharecropper; colonist; settler; (*poet*) farmer

colorante *adj* coloring || *m* dye; stain

colorare (colóro) *tr & ref* to color; to stain

colora·to -ta *adj* colored; stained (*glass*)

colorazióne *f* coloring

colóre *m* color; paint; suit (*of cards*); flush (*at poker*); shade; character (*of a deal*); **di colore** colored (*man*); **farne di tutti i colori** to be up to all kinds of deviltry; **farsi di tutti i colori** to change countenance

colorifi·cio *m* (**-ci**) paint factory; dye factory

colorire §176 *tr* to color

colori·to -ta *adj* colored, flushed; expressive || *m* color, complexion; (*fig*) expression

coloritura *f* coloring; characteristic; political complexion

colóro §8

colossale *adj* colossal

Colossèo *m* Coliseum

colòsso *m* colossus

cólpa *f* fault; sin; guilt; (*law*) injury; **avere la colpa** to be guilty; to be wrong; **essere in colpa** to be guilty

colpévole *adj* guilty || *mf* guilty person, culprit

colpevoli·sta *m* (**-sti -ste**) person who prejudges s.o. guilty

colpire §176 *tr* to hit, strike; to harm; to impress; **colpire nel segno** to hit the mark

cólpo *m* hit, blow; strike; tip, rap; knock; shot; round (*of gun*); cut, slash (*of knife*); thrust (*e.g., of spear*); lash (*of animal's tail*); toot (*of car's horn*); **andare a colpo sicuro** to know where to hit; **colpo apoplettico** stroke; **colpo da maestro** master stroke; **colpo d'aria** draft; **colpo d'ariete** water hammer; **colpo di fortuna** stroke of luck; **colpo di fulmine** love at first sight; **colpo di grazia** coup de grâce; **colpo di mano** surprise attack; **colpo di scena** dramatic turn of events; **colpo di sole** sunstroke; **colpo di spugna** wiping the slate clean; **colpo di stato** coup d'état; **colpo di telefono** telephone call; **colpo di testa** sudden decision, inconsiderate action; **colpo di vento** gust of wind; **colpo d'occhio** view; glance, look; **di colpo** at once; **fallire il colpo** to miss the mark; **fare colpo** to make a hit; **sul colpo** then and there; **tutto in un colpo** all at once

colpó·so -sa [s] *adj* unpremeditated; involuntary (*e.g., manslaughter*)

coltèlla *f* butcher knife; (*elec*) knife switch

coltellàc·cio *m* (**-ci**) hunting knife; butcher knife; (*naut*) studding sail

coltellata *f* stab, gash, slash; **fare a coltellate** to fight with knives

coltelleria *f* cutlery

coltelli·nàio *m* (**-nài**) cutler

coltèllo *m* knife; **a coltello** edgewise (*said of bricks*); **avere il coltello per il manico** to have the upper hand; **coltello a serramanico** switchblade knife; pocketknife

coltivare *tr* to cultivate

coltiva·to -ta *adj* cultivated

coltivatóre *m* farmer

coltivazióne *f* cultivation

cól·to -ta *adj* cultivated; learned (*word*) || *m* garden; (*archaic*) worship

cóltre *f* blanket; comforter; (*fig*) pall; **coltri** bedclothes

coltróne *m* quilt

coltura *f* cultivation; crop; culture (*e.g., of silkworms, bacteria*)

colubrina *f* culverin

colùi §8 *pron dem*

comandaménto *m* commandment

comandante *m* commanding officer; commandant; (*nav*) captain; **comandante del porto** harbor master; **comandante in seconda** (*naut*) first mate

comandare *tr* to command, order; to direct (*employees*); to register (*a letter*); (*mach*) to regulate; (*mach*) to control; (*poet*) to overlook, command the view of (*e.g., a valley*); **comandare a bacchetta** to command in a dictatorial manner || *intr* to command; **comandi!** (*mil*) at your orders!

comando *m* command, order

comare *f* godmother; (*coll*) friend, neighbor; (*coll*) gossip

combaciare §128 *tr* (*archaic*) to gather || *intr* to fit closely together; to tally, dovetail; to coincide

combattènte *adj* fighting || *m* combatant

combàttere *tr & intr* to combat || *ref* to fight one another

combattiménto *m* combat; fight; battle; **fuori combattimento** knockout, K.O.; **fuori combattimento tecnico** technical knockout, T.K.O.; **mettere fuori combattimento** to knock out; (*fig*) to weaken

combatti·vo -va *adj* pugnacious, combative

combattu·to -ta *adj* heated (*discussion*); overcome (*by doubt*); torn (*between two opposing feelings*)

combinare *tr* to combine; to match (*e.g., colors*); to organize || *intr* to agree; **combinare a** to succeed in || *ref* to agree; to chance, happen; to combine

combinazióne *f* combination; chance; coverall (*for mechanics or flyers*)

combrìccola *f* gang

combustìbile *adj* combustible || *m* fuel, combustible

combustióne *f* combustion; (poet) upheaval

combutta *f* gang, band; **essere in combutta** to be in cahoots

cóme *m* manner, way; **il come e il perchè** the why and the wherefore || *adv* as; like; as for; how; **come mai?** why?; **e come!** and how!; **ma come?** what?, how is it? || *conj* as; as soon as; while; how; because; since; **come se as if**

comecché *conj* (lit) although; (poet) wherever

comedóne *m* blackhead

cométa *f* comet

comici·tà *f* (-tà) comicalness

còmi·co -ca (-ci -che) *adj* comic(al) || *m* comic; author of comedies; comic actor

comìgnolo *m* chimney pot; ridge (*of roof*)

cominciare §128 *tr & intr* to begin, start, commence

comitato *m* committee

comitiva *f* group, party; (poet) retinue

comì·zio *m* (-zi) (pol) meeting, rally; (hist) comitia

còm·ma *m* (-mi) paragraph, article (*of law or decree*)

commèdia *f* comedy; play, drama; (fig) farce; **commedia di carattere** comedy of character; **commedia d'intreccio** comedy of intrigue; **far la commedia** to pretend, feign; **finire in commedia** to end ludicrously; **finire la commedia** to stop faking

commediante *mf* actor; comedian (*amusing person*); (fig) hypocrite

commediògra·fo -fa *mf* playwright, comedian

commemorare (commèmoro) *tr* to commemorate

commemorati·vo -va *adj* commemorative, memorial

commemorazióne *f* commemoration

commènda *f* commandership (*of an order*); (eccl) commendam

commendàbile *adj* commendable

commendare (commèndo) *tr* (lit) to commend, praise; (obs) to entrust

commendati·zio -zia (-zi -zie) *adj* introductory || *f* letter of introduction; recommendation

commendatóre *m* commander (*of an order*)

commendévole *adj* commendable

commensale *mf* guest; table companion

commensurare (commènsuro & commensuro) *tr* to compare; to proportion, prorate

commentare (comménto) *tr* to comment, comment on

commentà·rio *m* (-ri) commentary; diary, journal

commenta·tóre -trice *mf* commentator

comménto *m* comment; **fare commenti** to criticize; **non far commenti!** don't waste your time talking!

commerciàbile *adj* marketable

commerciale *adj* commercial; common, ordinary

commerciali·sta *mf* (-sti -ste) business-administration major; attorney specializing in commercial law

commerciante *mf* merchant, dealer

commerciare §128 (commèrcio) *tr* to deal in; to buy and sell || *intr* to deal

commèr·cio *m* (-ci) commerce, trade; illegal traffic; (poet) intercourse; **commercio all'ingrosso** wholesale (trade); **commercio al minuto** retail (trade); **fuori commercio** not for sale; **in commercio** for sale

commés·so -sa *adj* committed || *mf* clerk (*in a store*) || *m* salesman; clerk (*in a court*); janitor (*in a school*); **commesso viaggiatore** traveling salesman || *f* saleslady; order (*of merchandise*)

commestìbile *adj* edible || **commestibili** *mpl* staples, groceries; foodstuffs

commèttere §198 *tr* to join, connect; to commit; to charge, commission; to peg; (poet) to entrust || *intr* to join, fit

committitura *f* joint, seam

commiato *m* leave; **dare commiato a** to dismiss; **prender commiato** to take one's leave

commilitóne *m* comrade, comrade in arms

comminare *tr* (law) to determine, fix (*a penalty*)

comminatò·rio -ria *adj* threatening

commiserare (commìsero) *tr* to pity, feel sorry for

commiserazióne *f* commiseration

commissariale *adj* commissioner's, e.g., **funzioni commissariali** commissioner's functions; commissar's functions

commissariato *m* commissary; inspector's office

commissà·rio *m* (-ri) commissary; inspector; commissioner; **commissario del popolo** commissar; **commissario di bordo** purser; **commissario di pubblica sicurezza** police inspector; **commissario tecnico** (sports) soccer commissioner

commissionare (commissióno) *tr* to commission, order

commissionà·rio -ria (-ri -rie) *adj* commission || *m* commission merchant

commissióne *f* commission, agency; order (*of merchandise*); committee; errand; commitment (*of an act*)

commisurare *tr* to proportion (*e.g., crime to punishment*)

committènte *mf* buyer, customer

commodòro *m* commodore

commòs·so -sa *adj* moved; moving

commovènte *adj* moving, touching

commozióne *f* commotion; emotion; **commozione cerebrale** (pathol) concussion

commuòvere §202 *tr* to move; to touch; to stir ‖ *ref* to be moved; to be touched

commutare *tr* to commute; to switch ‖ *ref* to turn

commuta·tóre -trice *adj* commutative ‖ *m* (elec) change-over switch; (elec) commutator (*switch*); (telp) plugboard ‖ *f* converter

commutatori·sta *mf* (**-sti -ste**) (telp) operator

commutazióne *f* commutation; (telp) selection; (elec) switchover

co·mò *m* (**-mò**) chest; chest of drawers

còmoda *f* commode

comodare (**còmodo**) *tr* to lend ‖ *intr* (with *dat*) to please, e.g., **non le comoda** it doesn't please her

comodino *m* night table; (theat) bit player; **fare il comodino a** (coll) to follow sheepishly

comodi·tà *f* (**-tà**) comfort; convenience; opportunity

còmo·do -da *adj* comfortable; convenient; easy; loose-fitting; calm ‖ *m* convenience; ease; advantage; comfort; opportunity; **a Suo comodo** at your convenience; **comodo di cassa** credit (*at the bank*); **con comodo** without hurrying; **fare comodo** to come in handy; (with *dat*) to please, e.g., **non gli fa comodo** it doesn't please him; **fare il proprio comodo** to think only of oneself; **stia comodo!** make yourself at home! ‖ *f see* **comoda**

compaesa·no -na *mf* fellow citizen ‖ *m* fellow countryman ‖ *f* fellow countrywoman

compàgine *f* strict union; connection; assemblage; (fig) cohesion

compagna *f* companion, mate; (archaic) company

compagnia *f* company; **Compagnia di Gesù** Society of Jesus; **compagnia stabile** (theat) stock company

compa·gno -gna *adj* like, similar ‖ *m* fellow; companion, comrade; mate; partner; **compagno d'armi** comrade in arms; **compagno di viaggio** fellow traveler ‖ *f see* **compagna**

companàti·co *m* (**-ci**) food to eat with bread

comparàbile *adj* comparable

comparati·vo -va *adj & m* comparative

compara·to -ta *adj* comparative

comparazióne *f* comparison

compare *m* godfather; best man (*at wedding*); fellow; confederate

comparíre §108 *intr* to appear; to be known; to cut a figure

comparizióne *f* appearance (*in court*)

comparsa *f* appearance; (theat) extra, supernumerary; (law) petition, brief; **far comparsa** to cut a figure

compartecipare (**compartécipo**) *intr* to share

compartecipazióne *f* sharing; **compartecipazione agli utili** profit sharing

compartécipe *adj* sharing

compartiménto *m* circle, clique; district; (naut, rr) compartment

compartíre §176 & (**comparto**) *tr* to divide up, distribute

compassa·to -ta *adj* measured; stiff, formal; reserved; self-controlled

compassionare (**compassióno**) *tr* to pity

compassióne *f* compassion, pity

compassionévole *adj* compassionate; pitiful

compasso *m* compass; **compasso a grossezza** calipers

compatíbile *adj* excusable; compatible

compatiménto *m* compassion; condescension

compatíre §176 *tr* to pity; to forgive, overlook; to bear with; **farsi compatire** to become an object of ridicule ‖ *intr* to pity

compatriò·ta *mf* (**-ti -te**) compatriot

compattézza *f* compactness

compat·to -ta *adj* compact, tight

compendiare §287 (**compèndio**) *tr* to epitomize, summarize

compèn·dio *m* (**-di**) compendium, summary; **fare un compendio di** to abstract

compendió·so -sa [s] *adj* compendious, brief, succinct

compenetràbile *adj* penetrable

compenetrabilità *f* penetrability

compenetrare (**compènetro**) *tr* to penetrate; to permeate; to pervade ‖ *ref* to be overcome; **compenetrarsi di** to be conscious of

compensare (**compènso**) *tr* to compensate, pay; to balance, offset; to clear (*checks*)

compensa·to -ta *adj* compensated; laminated ‖ *m* laminate; plywood

compensazióne *f* compensation; offset; (com) clearing (*of checks*)

compènso *m* reward; retribution, pay; **in compenso** on the other hand

cómpera *f var of* **compra**

comperare (**cómpero**) *tr & intr var of* **comprare**

competènte *adj* competent

competènza *f* competence; jurisdiction; **competenze honoraria**

compètere §129 *intr* to compete; to concern; to have jurisdiction

competiti·vo -va *adj* competitive

competi·tóre -trice *mf* competitor, contender

competizióne *f* competition, contest

compiacènte *adj* complaisant, obliging

compiacènza *f* complaisance, kindness; pleasure

compiacére §214 *tr* to gratify ‖ *intr* (with *dat*) to please, e.g., **non posso compiacere a tutti** I cannot please everybody ‖ *ref* to be pleased; **compiacersi con** to congratulate; **compiacersi di** to be kind enough to

compiaciménto *m* pleasure; congratulation; approval

compiaciu·to -ta *adj* pleased, satisfied

compiàngere §215 *tr* to pity || *ref* to feel sorry

compian·to -ta *adj* lamented (*departed person*) || *m* sympathy; (poet) sorrow; (poet) lament

compiegare §209 (**compiègo**) *tr* to enclose (*in a letter*)

cómpiere §130 *tr* to complete, finish; to fulfill, accomplish; **compiere . . . anni** to be . . . years old; **compiere gli anni** to have a birthday || *ref* to happen; to come true

compilare *tr* to compile

compila·tóre -**trice** *mf* compiler

compilazióne *f* compilation

compiménto *m* fulfillment, accomplishment

compire §176 *tr* to complete, finish; to fulfill, accomplish; **per compir l'opera** as if it weren't enough || *ref* to happen; to come true

compitare (**cómpito**) *tr* to syllabify; to read poorly; to spell, spell letter by letter

compitazióne *f* spelling letter by letter

compitézza *f* courtesy, politeness

cómpito *m* task; exercise; homework

compi·to -ta *adj* courteous, polite; (poet) adequate

compiu·to -ta *adj* accomplished

compleanno *m* birthday; **buon compleanno** happy birthday

complementare *adj* complementary; additional (*tax*) || *f* graduated income tax

compleménto *m* complement; (mil, nav) reserve

complessióne *f* build, physique

complessi·tà *f* (-**tà**) complexity

complessi·vo -va *adj* total, aggregate

complès·so -sa *adj* complex, complicated; compound (*fracture*) || *m* whole; complex; **in complesso** in general

completare (**complèto**) *tr* to complete, carry through; to supplement, round off

complè·to -ta *adj* complete, full; overall, thoroughgoing; **al completo** full (*e.g., bus*) || *m* set (*of matching items*); suit of clothes; **completo femminile** lady's tailor-made suit; **completo maschile** suit

complicare §197 (**còmplico**) *tr* to complicate || *ref* to become complicated

complica·to -ta *adj* complicated, complex

complicazióne *f* complication

còmplice *mf* accomplice, accessory

complici·tà *f* (-**tà**) complicity

complimentare (**compliménto**) *tr* to compliment || *ref*—**complimentarsi con** to congratulate

compliménto *m* compliment; congratulation; favor; **complimenti** regards; **complimenti!** congratulations!; **fare complimenti** to stand on ceremony; **senza complimenti** without ceremony, without any further ado

complimento·so -sa [s] *adj* ceremonious; complimentary

complottare (**complòtto**) *intr* to plot

complòtto *m* plot, machination

complù·vio *m* (-**vi**) valley (*of roof*)

componènte *adj* component || *mf* member || *m* component (*component part*) || *f* component (*force*)

componibile *adj* sectional (*e.g., bookcase*)

componiménto *m* composition, settlement (*of a dispute*)

compórre §218 *tr* to compose; to arrange; to settle (*a quarrel*); to lay out (*a corpse*); (typ) to set

comportaménto *m* behavior

comportare (**compòrto**) *tr* to allow, tolerate; to entail || *ref* to behave; to handle (*said, e.g., of a motor*); **comportarsi male** to misbehave

compòrto *m* (com) delay

compòsi·to -ta *adj* composite || **composite** *fpl* (bot) Compositae

composi·tóio *m* (-**tói**) (typ) composing stick

composi·tóre -**trice** *mf* compositor, typesetter; composer || *f* typesetting machine

composizióne *f* composition; settlement

compósta *f* compote; **composta di frutta** stewed fruit

compostézza *f* neatness, tidiness; good behavior; orderliness

compostièra *f* compote, compotier

compó·sto -sta *adj* compound; neat, tidy; well-behaved || *m* compound || *f* see **composta**

cómpra *f* purchase; shopping; **compre** shopping

comprare (**cómpro**) *tr* to buy; purchase; to buy off || *intr* to buy, shop; to trade

compra·tóre -**trice** *mf* buyer, purchaser

compravéndere §281 *tr* to make a deal in, to transfer (*e.g., a house*)

compravéndita *f* transaction; transfer (*e.g., of real estate*)

comprèndere §220 *tr* to comprehend, include, comprise; to overwhelm; to understand; to forgive

comprendò·nio *m* (-**ni**) (joc) understanding

comprensibile *adj* understandable, comprehensible

comprensióne *f* comprehension, understanding

comprensi·vo -va *adj* comprehensive; understanding

comprenso·rio *m* (-**ri**) land to be reclaimed; area, zone, e.g., **comprensorio turistico** tourist area

comprè·so -sa [s] *adj* comprised, included; understood; deeply touched; immersed

compréssa *f* compress

compressióne *f* compression

comprès·so -sa *adj* compressed; (fig) repressed; (aut) supercharged || *f* see **compressa**

compressóre *m* compressor; **compressore stradale** road roller

comprimà·rio *m* (-**ri**) (med) associate chief of staff; (theat) second lead comprìmere §131 *tr* to compress; to repress, restrain; to tamp

compromés·so -sa *adj* jeopardized, in danger || *m* compromise; referral (*to arbitration*)

compromettènte *adj* compromising

comprométtere §198 *tr* to compromise; to endanger; to involve, commit; (law) to refer (*to arbitration*)

comproprie·tà *f* (-tà) joint ownership

comproprietà·rio -ria *mf* (-ri -rie) joint owner

compròva *f* confirmation

comprovare (compròvo) *tr* to confirm; to circumstantiate

compulsare *tr* to consult, peruse; to summon (*to appear in court*)

compulsi·vo -va *adj* compulsive

compun·to -ta *adj* contrite, repentant

compunzióne *f* compunction

computàbile *adj* computable

computare (còmputo) *tr* to compute

computi·sta *mf* (-sti -ste) bookkeeper

computisterìa *f* bookkeeping

còmputo *m* computation, reckoning

comunale *adj* municipal, town (*e.g., hall*); community-owned; (poet) common

comunanza *f* community; in comunanza in common

comune *adj* common || *m* normalcy; commune, municipality, town; town hall; (hist) guild; (nav) common seaman; in comune in common || *f* commune (*in communist countries*); (theat) main stage entrance; andare per la comune to follow the crowd; per la comune commonly

comunèlla *f* cabal, clique; passkey (*in a hotel*); (law) mutual insurance (*of cattlemen*); fare comunella con to consort with

comunicàbile *adj* communicable

comunicante *adj* communicant; communicating || *m* priest who gives communion

comunicare §197 (comùnico) *tr* to communicate; to administer communion to || *intr* to communicate || *ref* to spread; to receive communion, to commune

comunicati·vo -va *adj* communicable, spreading; communicative

comunicato *m* communiqué; comunicato commerciale advertisement, ad; comunicato stampa press release

comunicazióne *f* communication; statement; (telp) connection; comunicazioni communications

comunióne *f* community; (law) community property || Comunione *f* Communion

comunismo *m* communism

comuni·sta (-sti -ste) *adj* communist || *mf* communist; (law) joint tenant

comunìsti·co -ca *adj* (-ci -che) communistic

comuni·tà *f* (-tà) community

comunità·rio -ria *adj* (-ri -rie) community, e.g., interessi comunitari community interests

comùnque *adv* however, nevertheless || *conj* however, no matter how

cón §4 *prep* with; by (*e.g., boat*); con + art + inf by + ger, e.g., col leggere by reading

conato *m* effort, attempt

cón·ca *f* (-che) washbowl, washbasin; copper water jug; valley, hollow; (poet) shell; conca idraulica drydock

concatenaménto *m* (poet) concatenation

concatenare (concaténo) *tr* to link || *ref* to unfold, ensue

concatenazióne *f* concatenation

concàusa *f* joint cause; (law) aggravation

cònca·vo -va *adj* concave; hollow || *m* hollow

concèdere §132 *tr* to grant, concede; to stretch (*a point*) || *ref* to let oneself go, give oneself over

concènto *m* harmony; (fig) agreement

concentraménto *m* concentration

concentrare (concèntro) *tr* to concentrate; to center || *ref* to concentrate, focus; to center

concentra·to -ta *adj* concentrated; condensed (*e.g., milk*) || *m* purée (*e.g., of tomatoes*)

concentrazióne *f* concentration; (chem) condensation

concèntri·co -ca *adj* (-ci -che) concentric

concepìbile *adj* conceivable

concepiménto *m* conception; (fig) formulation

concepire §176 *tr* to conceive; (fig) to nurture

concerìa *f* tannery

concèrnere §133 *tr* to concern

concertare (concèrto) *tr* to scheme, concert; (mus) to orchestrate, arrange || *ref* to agree

concerta·to -ta *adj* agreed upon; (mus) with accompaniment || *m* ensemble (*of orchestra, soloists, and chorus*)

concerta·tóre -trice *mf* arranger || *m* plotter, schemer

concertazióne *f* (mus) arrangement

concerti·sta *mf* (-sti -ste) concert performer, soloist

concèrto *m* concert; concerto; (fig) choir

concessionà·rio *m* (-ri) sole agent, concessionaire; dealer; lessee (*of business establishment*)

concessióne *f* concession; dealership; admission

concessi·vo -va *adj* concessive

concès·so -sa *adj* granted, admitting

concètto *m* concept; opinion

concettó·so -sa [s] *adj* concise; full of ideas; full of conceits

concettuale *adj* conceptual

concezióne *f* conception; formulation

conchìglia *f* shell, conch; (sports) jock guard, protective cup

conchiùdere §125 *tr, intr & ref* var of concludere

cón·cia *f* (-ce) tanning

conciapèl·li *m* (-li) tanner

conciare §128 (cóncio) *tr* to tan; to cure (*e.g., tobacco*); to arrange; to straighten up; to reduce; to cut (*a precious stone*); **conciare per le feste** (coll) to give a good beating to ‖ *ref* to get messed up, get dirty

conciatét·ti *m* (**-ti**) roofer

conciató·re -trice *mf* tanner

conciliàbile *adj* reconcilable

conciliàbolo *m* conventicle, secret meeting

conciliante *adj* conciliatory

conciliare *adj* council ‖ *m* member of an ecclesiastical council ‖ §287 *tr* to conciliate, reconcile; to settle (*a fine*); to promote (*e.g., sleep*); to obtain (*a favor*) ‖ *ref* to become reconciled

concilia·tóre -trice *adj* conciliatory ‖ *mf* conciliator, peacemaker ‖ *m* justice of the peace

conciliazióne *f* conciliation ‖ **la Conciliazione** the Concordat (*of 1929 between Italy and the Vatican*)

concì·lio *m* (**-li**) council; church council

concimàia *f* manure pit

concimare *tr* to manure

concimazióne *f* spreading of manure; chemical fertilization

concime *m* manure; fertilizer

cón·cio -cia (**-ci -ce**) *adj* tanned ‖ *m* ashlar; dung, manure; (archaic) agreement; **concio di scoria** cinder block ‖ *f* see **concia**

conciofossecosaché *conj* (archaic) since

concionare (**concióno**) *intr* (archaic) to harangue

concióne *f* (archaic) harangue; (archaic) assembly

conciossiacosaché *conj* (archaic) since

concisióne *f* concision, brevity

concì·so -sa *adj* concise, brief

concistòro *m* consistory; (fig) assembly

concitare (**còncito**) *tr* to excite, stir up

concita·to -ta *adj* excited; (poet) decisive

concitazióne *f* impetus; excitement

concittadi·no -na *mf* fellow citizen

conclave *m* conclave

conclùdere §105 *tr* to conclude ‖ *intr* to conclude; to be convincing ‖ *ref* to conclude, end; **concludersi con** to end with; to result in

conclusionale *adj* (law) summary

conclusióne *f* conclusion; **conclusioni** (law) summation

conclusi·vo -va *adj* conclusive

conclu·so -sa *adj* concluded; terminated; (poet) closed

concomitante *adj* concomitant

concordanza *f* concordance, agreement; (gram) concord; **concordanze** concordance (*e.g., to the Bible*)

concordare (**concòrdo**) *tr* to agree on; to make agree ‖ *intr & ref* to come to an agreement

concordato *m* agreement; concordat; settlement (*with creditors*)

concòrde *adj* in agreement

concòrdia *f* concord, harmony

concorrènte *adj* competitive ‖ *m* (com) competitor; (sports) contestant

concorrènza *f* competition

concorrenziale *adj* competitive (*e.g., price*)

concórrere §139 *intr* to converge; to concur; to compete

concórso *m* attendance; concurrence; combination (*of circumstances*); competition; competitive examination; contest; **concorso di bellezza** beauty contest; **concorso di pubblico** turnout; **fuori concorso** not entering the competition; in a class by itself

concretare (**concrèto**) *tr* to realize (*e.g., a dréam*); to conclude, accomplish ‖ *ref* to come true

concretézza *f* concreteness, consistency

concrè·to -ta *adj* concrete, real; practical (*e.g., matter*); **in concreto** really, in reality

concubina *f* concubine

concubinàg·gio *m* (**-gi**) concubinage

concubinato *m* var of **concubinaggio**

conculcare §197 *tr* (lit) to trample under foot; (lit) to violate

concupire §176 *tr* (poet) to lust for

concupiscènza *f* concupiscence, lust

concussióne *f* extortion, shakedown; **concussione cerebrale** (pathol) concussion

condanna *f* conviction; sentence; (fig) blame, condemnation

condannare *tr* to condemn; to find guilty, convict; to sentence; to damn (*to eternal punishment*); to declare incurable; to wall up

condanna·to -ta *adj* condemned ‖ *m* convict

condensare (**condènso**) *tr & ref* to condense

condensa·to -ta *adj* condensed (*e.g., milk*)

condensatóre *m* condenser

condensazióne *f* condensation

condiménto *m* condiment, seasoning

condire §176 *tr* to season

condiret·tóre -trice *mf* associate manager

condiscendènte *adj* condescending

condiscendènza *f* condescension

condiscéndere §245 *intr* to condescend

condiscépo·lo -la *mf* schoolmate, school companion

condivìdere §158 *tr* to share

condizionale *adj & m* conditional ‖ *f* (law) suspended sentence

condizionare (**condizióno**) *tr* to condition; to treat (*to prevent spoilage*)

condizionatóre *m* air conditioner

condizióne *f* condition; term (*of sale*); **a condizione che** provided that; **condizioni** condition, shape (*e.g., of a shipment*); **essere in condizione di** to be in a position to

condoglianza *f* condolence; **fare le condoglianze a** to extend one's sympathy to

condolére §159 *ref* to condole

condomì·nio *m* (**-ni**) condominium

condòmi·no -na *mf* joint owner (*of real estate*)

condonare (**condóno**) *tr* to condone; to remit

condóno *m* pardon, parole

condót·to -ta *adj* country (*doctor*) ‖ *m* duct, canal; conduit ‖ *f* behavior, conduct; district (of country doctor); transportation; pipeline; (theat) baggage; **condotta forzata** flume

conducènte m driver; bus driver; motorman

condù·plex mf (-plex) (telp) party-line user

condurre §102 tr to lead; to drive (a car); to round up (cattle); to pipe (e.g., gas); to conduct; to trace (a line); to take; to bring; to manage; **condurre a termine** to bring to fruition, realize || intr to lead || ref to behave; to betake oneself, go; **condursi a** (poet) to be reduced to (e.g., poverty)

conduttivi·tà f (-tà) conductivity

condutti·vo -va adj conductive

condut·tóre -trice adj guiding, leading || m operator (of a bus); driver (of a car); (rr) engineer; (rr) ticket collector; (phys) conductor

conduttura f conduit, pipeline

conduzióne f conduction; leasing

conestàbile m constable (keeper of a castle)

confabulare (confàbulo) intr to confabulate, commune; to connive, scheme

confacènte adj suitable, appropriate; helpful

confare §173 ref—**confarsi a** to agree with, e.g., **le uova non gli si confanno** eggs do not agree with him

confedera·to -ta adj & m confederate

confederare (confèdero) tr & ref to confederate

confederazióne f confederation

conferènza f conference; lecture; **conferenza illustrata** chalk talk; **conferenza stampa** press conference

conferenziè·re -ra mf speaker, lecturer

conferiménto m conferring, bestowal

conferire §176 tr to confer, bestow; to add; to contribute || intr to confer; to contribute; **conferire alla salute** to be healthful

confèrma f confirmation; **a conferma di** (com) in reply to, confirming

confermare (confèrmo) tr to confirm; to verify; to retain (in office) || ref to become more sure of oneself; to prove to be; to remain (in the conclusion of a letter)

confessare (confèsso) tr & ref to confess

confessionale adj confessional; church; church-related, parochial (e.g., school) || m confessional

confessióne f confession

confès·so -sa adj acknowledged, self-admitted; **confesso e comunicato** having made one's confession and taken communion

confessóre m confessor

confetteria f candy store, confectioner's shop

confettièra f candy box

confettière m candy maker; candy dealer, confectioner

confètto m sugar-covered nut, sweetmeat; losenge, drop

confettura f candy; preserves, jam; **confetture** confectionery

confezionare (confezióno) tr to make; to tailor (a suit)

confezióne f preparation, manufacturing; packaging; **confezioni** ready-made clothes

confezioni·sta mf (-sti -ste) ready-made clothier

conficcare §197 tr to drive (a nail); to thrust (a knife) || ref to become embedded

confidare tr to trust (a secret) || intr to trust || ref to confide

confidènte adj confident || mf confident; informer

confidènza f confidence; secret; familiarity

confidenziale adj confidential; friendly

configgere §104 tr to plunge, thrust

configurazióne f configuration

confinante adj bordering || mf neighbor

confinare tr to exile; to confine || intr to border

confinà·rio -ria adj (-ri -rie) border (e.g., zone)

Confindùstria f (acronym) **Confederazione Nazionale degli Industriali** National Confederation of Industrialists

confine m border, boundary line; boundary mark, landmark

confino m exile (in a different town)

confi·sca f (-sche) confiscation

confiscare §197 tr to confiscate

confit·to -ta adj nailed; bound; tied; **confitto in croce** nailed to the cross

conflagrazióne f conflagration

conflitto m conflict

conflittualità f confrontation; belligerent attitude

confluènte m confluent

confluènza f confluence

confluire §176 intr to flow together, join; to converge

confóndere §178 tr to confuse; to overwhelm (with kindness); to humiliate; **confondere con** to mistake for || ref to mix; to become confused

conformare (confórmo) tr to shape; to conform || ref to conform

conformazióne f conformation

confórme adj faithful, exact; in agreement; true (copy)

conformeménte adv in conformity

conformi·sta mf (-sti -ste) conformist

conformi·tà f (-tà) conformity; **in conformità di** in conformity with, in accord with

confortante adj comforting

confortare (confòrto) tr to comfort

confortévole adj comforting, consoling; comfortable

confòrto m comfort, solace; convenience; corroboration; **conforti religiosi** last rites

confratèllo m brother, confrere

confratèrnita f brotherhood

confricare §197 tr to rub

confrontare (confrónto) tr to compare, confront; to consult || intr to correspond

confrónto *m* comparison; (law) cross examination; **a confronto di** or **in confronto a** in comparison with; **with regard to**

confusaménte *adv* vaguely, hazily

confusionale *adj* confusing; confused

confusionà·rio -ria (-ri -rie) *adj* blundering; scatterbrain || *mf* blunderer; scatterbrain

confusióne *f* confusion, disorder; noise; error; embarrassment; shambles

confu·so -sa *adj* confused, mixed; vague, hazy; **in confuso** indistinctly

confutare (cònfuto) *tr* to confute

confutazióne *f* confutation

congedare (congèdo) *tr* to dismiss; to let (*a tenant*) go; (mil) to discharge || *ref* to take leave

congedá·to -ta *adj* discharged || *m* discharged soldier

congèdo *m* dismissal; leave; permission to leave; (mil) to discharge; envoi; **congedo per motivi di salute** sick leave; **dare il congedo a** to discharge; **prènder congedo** to take leave

congegnare (congégno) *tr* to assemble (*machinery*); to contrive, cook up

congégno *m* contrivance, gadget; mechanism; design (*of a play*)

congelaménto *m* freezing; frostbite

congelare (congèlo) *tr* & *ref* to freeze, congeal

congela·tóre -trice *adj* freezing || *m* freezer; freezer unit; freezing compartment (*of a refrigerator*)

congènere *adj* similar, alike

congeniale *adj* congenial

congèni·to -ta *adj* congenital

congèrie *f* congeries

congestionare (congestióno) *tr* to congest

congestióne *f* congestion

congettura *f* conjecture

congetturare *tr* to conjecture

congiùngere §183 *tr* & *ref* to unite, join

congiuntiva *f* (anat) conjunctiva

congiuntivite *f* (pathol) conjunctivitis

congiunti·vo -va *adj* conjunctive; subjunctive || *m* subjunctive || *f* see **congiuntiva**

congiun·to -ta *adj* joined; joint || *m* relative

congiuntura *f* juncture; joint; circumstance, situation; **bassa congiuntura** (econ) unfavorable circumstance; (econ) crisis

congiunzióne *f* conjunction

congiura *f* conspiracy, plot

congiurare *intr* to conspire, plot

congiura·to -ta *adj* & *m* conspirator

conglobare (conglòbo) *tr* to lump together

conglomerare (conglòmero) *tr* & *ref* to pile up, conglomerate

conglomera·to -ta *adj* & *m* conglomerate

congratulare (congràtulo) *intr* to rejoice || *ref*—**congratularsi con** to congratulate

congratulazióne *f* congratulation

congrèga *f* gang; cabal; religious brotherhood

congregare §209 (congrègo) *tr* & *ref* to congregate

congregazióne *f* congregation

congressi·sta *mf* (-sti -ste) delegate || *m* congressman || *f* congresswoman

congrèsso *m* congress, assembly; conference; convention

congruènte *adj* congruous

congruènza *f* congruence

còn·gruo -grua *adj* congruous; congruent

conguagliare §280 *tr* to adjust; to make up (*what is owed*)

conguà·glio *m* (-gli) balance; adjustment (*of wages*)

coniare §287 (cònio) *tr* to mint, coin

coniatura *f* mintage, coinage

còni·co -ca (-ci -che) *adj* conic(al) || *f* conic section

conìfera *f* conifer

coniglièra *f* warren, rabbit hutch

coni·glio *m* (-gli) rabbit

cò·nio *m* (-ni) die (*to mint coins*); mintage; wedge; **dello stesso conio** (fig) of the same feather; **di nuovo conio** newly-minted; new-fangled

coniugale *adj* conjugal

coniugare §209 (còniugo) *tr* to conjugate || *ref* to marry, get married

coniuga·to -ta *adj* coupled, paired || *mf* spouse, consort

coniugazióne *f* conjugation

còniuge *mf* spouse; **coniugi** *mpl* husband and wife

connaturale *adj* inborn, innate

connatura·to -ta *adj* deep-seated, deep-rooted; congenital

connazionale *mf* fellow countryman

connessióne *f* connection

connès·so -sa & **connès·so -sa** *adj* connected, tied

connèttere & **connèttere §107** *tr* to connect, link || *ref* to refer

connetti·vo -va *adj* connective

connivènte *adj* conniving

connivènza *f* connivance

connotare (connòto) *tr* to connote

connotato *m* personal characteristic

connù·bio *m* (-bi) wedding, union

còno *m* cone

conòcchia *f* distaff

conoscènte *mf* acquaintance

conoscènza *f* knowledge; acquaintance; understanding; consciousness; **conoscenza di causa** full knowledge; **essere a conoscenza di** to be acquainted with; **prèndere conoscenza di** to take cognizance of

conóscere §134 *tr* to know; to recognize; **conoscere i propri polli** to know one's onions; **conoscere per filo e per segno** to know thoroughly; **conoscere ragioni** to listen to reason; **darsi a conoscere** to make oneself known; to reveal oneself || *intr* to reason || *ref* to acknowledge oneself to be; to know one another

conoscìbile *adj* knowable

conosci·tóre -trice *mf* connoisseur, expert

conosciu·to -ta *adj* known, well-known; proven

conquìdere §135 *tr* (poet) to conquer

conquista f conquest
conquistare tr to conquer, win
conquista·tóre -trice adj conquering ‖ m conqueror; lady killer
consacrare tr to consecrate ‖ ref to dedicate oneself
consacrazióne f consecration
consanguineità f consanguinity
consanguìne·o -a adj consanguineous; **fratello consanguineo** half brother on the father's side ‖ m kin
consapévole adj aware, conscious
consapevolézza f awareness, consciousness
còn·scio -scia adj (-sci -sce) conscious
consecuti·vo -va adj consecutive
conségna f delivery; (mil) order; (mil) confinement (to barracks); **in consegna** (com) on consignment
consegnare (conségno) tr to deliver; to entrust; (mil) to confine (to barracks)
consegnatà·rio m (-ri) consignee
conseguènte adj consequent; consistent; **conseguente a** resulting from; consistent with
conseguènza f consequence; consistency; **in conseguenza di** as a result of
conseguìbile adj attainable
conseguiménto m attainment
conseguire (conséguo) tr to attain; to obtain ‖ intr to ensue, result
consènso m consent, approval; consensus
consensuale adj mutual-consent (e.g., agreement)
consentiménto m consent
consentire (consènto) tr to allow, permit ‖ intr to agree, consent; to yield; to admit
consenziènte adj consenting
consèr·to -ta adj intertwined; folded (arms); **di conserto** in agreement
consèrva f preserve; purée (e.g., of tomatoes); tank (for water); sauce (e.g., of cranberries); **conserve alimentari** canned goods; **di conserva** together, in a group; **far conserva di** to preserve
conservare (consèrvo) tr to preserve; to keep; to cure (e.g., meat); to cherish (a memory) ‖ ref to keep; to remain; to keep in good health
conservati·vo -va adj preserving; conservative ‖ m conservative
conserva·tóre -trice adj preserving; conservative ‖ mf keeper, curator; conservative
conservatorìa f registrar's office (in a court house)
conservatò·rio m (-ri) conservatory; girl's boarding school (run by nuns)
conservatorismo m conservatism
conservazióne f conservation; preservation; self-preservation; canning
consèsso m assembly
consideràbile adj considerable; large, important
considerare (consìdero) tr to consider; to rate; (law) to provide for
considera·to -ta adj considered; **considerato che** considering that, since;

tutto considerato all in all, considering
considerazióne f consideration
considerévole adj considerable
consigliare adj council, councilmanic ‖ §280 tr to advise, counsel ‖ ref to consult
consiglè·re -ra mf counselor, advisor ‖ m chancellor (of embassy); councilman; **consigliere delegato** chairman of the board
consì·glio m (-gli) advice, counsel; will (of God); decision, idea; council; **consiglio d'amministrazione** (com) board of directors; **consiglio dei ministri** cabinet; **consiglio municipale** city council; **l'eterno consiglio** the will of God; **venire a più miti consigli** to become more reasonable
consìmile adj similar
consistènte adj consistent, solid; trustworthy
consistènza f consistency, resistance; foundation, grounds
consistere §114 intr to consist; **consistere in** to consist of
consociare §128 (consòcio) tr to syndicate, unite
consocia·to -ta adj syndicated, united
consociazióne f syndicate, association, group
consò·cio -cia mf (-ci -cie) fellow shareholder; associate, partner
consolare (consòlo) adj consular ‖ v (consòlo) tr to console, cheer, comfort ‖ ref to rejoice; to take comfort
consolato m consulate
consola·tóre -trice adj comforting ‖ mf comforter
consolazióne f consolation
cònsole m consul
consò·le f (-le) console
consòlida f—**consolida maggiore** comfrey; **consolida reale** field larkspur
consolidaménto m consolidation
consolidare (consòlido) tr to consolidate ‖ ref to consolidate; to harden
consolida·to -ta adj consolidated; joint (e.g., balance sheet); hardened ‖ m funded public debt; **government bonds**
consonante adj & f consonant
consonànti·co -ca adj (-ci -che) consonant
consonanza f consonance; agreement; (mus) harmony
cònso·no -na adj consonant
consorèlla adj sister (e.g., company) ‖ f sister of charity; sister branch; sister firm
consòrte adj (poet) equally fortunate; (poet) united ‖ mf consort, mate, spouse
consorterìa f political clique
consòr·zio m (-zi) syndicate, consortium; (poet) society
constare (cònsto) intr to consist ‖ impers to be known; to be proved; to understand, e.g., **gli consta che Lei ha torto** he understands that you are wrong
constatare (constato & cònstato) tr to verify, ascertain, establish

constatazióne *f* ascertainment, verification

consuè·to -ta *adj* usual, customary; **consueto a** accustomed to, used to || *m* manner, custom; **di consueto** generally

consuetudinà·rio -ria *adj* (**-ri -rie**) customary; common (*law*)

consuetùdine *f* custom; common law; (*poet*) familiarity

consulènte *adj* advising, consulting || *mf* adviser, expert

consulènza *f* expert advice

consulta *f* council

consultare *tr* to consult || *ref* to take counsel; to counsel with one another; **consultarsi con** to take counsel with

consultazióne *f* consultation; reference; **consultazione popolare** referendum

consulti·vo -va *adj* advisory

consulto *m* consultation (*of physicians*); legal conference

consul·tóre -trice *mf* adviser, expert || *m* councilman

consultò·rio *m* (**-ri**) clinic, dispensary

consumare *tr* to consume; to perform, to consummate || *ref* to be consumed, to waste away

consuma·to -ta *adj* consummate, accomplished; consummated (*marriage*); consumed, worn out

consuma·tóre -trice *adj* consuming || *mf* consumer; customer (*of a restaurant*)

consumazióne *f* consummation (*e.g., of a crime*); consumption (*of food*); food or drink

consumismo *m* consumerism

consumo *m* consumption; wear

consunti·vo -va *adj* end-of-year (*e.g., report*); (econ) consumption || *m* balance sheet

consun·to -ta *adj* worn-out

consunzióne *f* consumption

contàbile *adj* bookkeeping || *mf* accountant; bookkeeper, clerk; **esperto contabile** certified public accountant

contabili·tà *f* (**-tà**) accounting, bookkeeping; accounts

contachilòme·tri *m* (**-tri**) odometer; (coll) speedometer

contadiné·sco -sca *adj* (**-schi -sche**) farm, farmer; rustic

contadi·no -na *adj* rustic || *mf* peasant, farmer

contado *m* country, countryside

contagiare §290 *tr* to infect

contà·gio *m* (**-gi**) contagion

contagió·so -sa [s] *adj* contagious

contagi·ri *m* (**-ri**) tachometer

contagóc·ce *m* (**-ce**) dropper, eye-dropper

contaminare (**contàmino**) *tr* to contaminate; to pollute

contaminazióne *f* contamination; pollution

contante *adj* & *m* cash; **in contanti** cash

contare (**cónto**) *tr* to count; to limit; to regard, value; to propose; **contarle grosse** (coll) to tell tall tales || *intr* to count; **contare su** to count on

contasecón·di *m* (**-di**) watch with second hand

conta·to -ta *adj* limited; numbered (*e.g., days*)

conta·tóre -trice *adj* counting || *mf* counter || *m* meter; **contatore dell'acqua** water meter; **contatore della luce** electric meter

contattare *tr* to contact

contatto *m* contact

cónte *m* count

contèa *f* county

conteggiare §290 (**contéggio**) *tr* to charge (*e.g., a bill*) || *intr* to count

contég·gio *m* (**-gi**) reckoning, calculation; (sports) count; **conteggio alla rovescia** countdown

contégno *m* behavior; reserve, reserved attitude; air

contegnó·so -sa [s] *adj* reserved, dignified

contemperare (**contèmpero**) *tr* to adapt; to mitigate, moderate

contemplare (**contèmplo**) *tr* to contemplate

contemplati·vo -va *adj* contemplative

contemplazióne *f* contemplation

contèmpo *m*—**nel contempo** meanwhile

contemporaneaménte *adv* at the same time

contemporàne·o -a *adj* contemporaneous || *mf* contemporary

contendènte *adj* fighting || *m* contender, fighter; (law) contestant

contèndere §270 *tr* to contest, oppose || *intr* to contend, fight || *ref* to fight

contenére §271 *tr* to contain || *ref* to restrain oneself; to behave

conteniménto *m* containment

contenitóre *m* container

contentare (**contènto**) *tr* to satisfy, content || *ref* to be satisfied

contentézza *f* gladness, contentedness, contentment

contentino *m* gratuity, makeweight, gift to a customer

contèn·to -ta *adj* contented, glad, happy; satisfied || *m* (poet) happiness, contentedness

contenuto *m* content; contents

contenzióne *f* contention

contenzióso [s] *m* legal matter; legal department (*of a corporation*)

conterìe *fpl* beads, sequins

conterrà·neo -nea *adj* from the same country || *m* fellow countryman || *f* fellow countrywoman

conté·so -sa [s] *adj* coveted || *f* contest; dispute; **venire a contesa** to dispute

contéssa *f* countess

contestare (**contèsto**) *tr* to serve (*e.g., a summons*); to deny; to challenge, contest; **contestare qlco a qlcu** to charge s.o. with s.th

contestazióne *f* notification, summons; dispute, confrontation; challenge

contè·sto -sta *adj* (poet) intertwined || *m* context

contì·guo -gua *adj* contiguous

continentale *adj* continental

continènte *adj* & *m* continent

continènza *f* continence

contingentaménto *m* import quota

contingentare (**contingènto**) *tr* to assign a quota to (*imports*)

contingènte *adj* possible, contingent; (obs) due || *m* contingent; import quota; **contingente di leva** draft quota

contingènza *f* contingency

continuare (**continuo**) *tr* to continue || *intr* to last, continue; **continuare a +** *inf* to keep on + *ger*

continuazióne *f* continuation

continuità *f* (-**tà**) continuity

contì·nuo **-nua** *adj* continuous; direct (*current*); **di continuo** continuously

cón·to **-ta** *adj* (archaic) well-known; (poet) gentle; (poet) narrated || *m* figuring; account; bill, invoice; check (*in a restaurant*); opinion; worth, value; **a conti fatti** everything considered; **chiedere conto di** to call to account; **conto all'indietro** countdown; **di conto** valuable; **estratto conto** (com) statement; **fare conto di +** *inf* to intend to + *inf*; **fare conto su** to count on; **fare di conto** to count; **fare i conti senza l'oste** to reckon without one's host; **il conto non torna** the sums do not jibe; **in conto** on account; **in conto di** in one's position as; **per conto di** in the name of; **per conto mio** as far as I am concerned; **render conto di** to give an account of; **rendersi conto di** to realize, be aware of; **tener conto di** to reckon with; **tener di conto** to treat with care; **torna conto** it is worthwhile

contòrcere §272 *tr* to twist || *ref* to writhe

contorciménto *m* contortion, writhing

contornare (**contórno**) *tr* to surround

contórno *m* outline; contour; circle (*of people*); side dish (*of vegetables*)

contorsióne *f* contorsion; gyration (*e.g., of a dancer*); squirm

contòr·to **-ta** *adj* twisted (*e.g., face*)

contrabbandare *tr* to smuggle

contrabbandiè·re **-ra** *adj* smuggling || *mf* smuggler; bootlegger

contrabbando *m* contraband; smuggling; **di contrabbando** by smuggling; (fig) without paying

contrabbasso *m* contrabass, bass viol

contraccambiare §287 *tr* to reciprocate, return || *intr* to reciprocate

contraccàm·bio *m* (-**bi**) exchange; **in contraccambio di** in exchange for, in return for

contraccólpo *m* shock, rebound; recoil (*of a rifle*); backlash (*of a machine*)

contrada *f* road; (poet) region

contraddire §151 (*impv sg* **contraddici**) *tr* to contradict || *ref* to contradict oneself; to contradict one another

contraddistinguere §156 *tr* to earmark || *ref* to stand out

contraddittò·rio **-ria** (-**ri** -**rie**) *adj* contradictory; incoherent || *m* open discussion, debate

contraddizióne *f* contradiction

contraènte *adj* contracting; acting || *mf* contractor (*person who makes a contract*); (law) party

contraère·o **-a** *adj* antiaircraft

contraffare §173 *tr* to counterfeit; to fake, sham || *intr* (archaic) to disobey || *ref* to camouflage oneself, disguise oneself

contraffat·to **-ta** *adj* counterfeit; adulterated; apocryphal

contraffat·tóre **-trice** *mf* counterfeiter; falsifier

contraffazióne *f* forgery; fake; imitation; piracy (*of book*); mockery (*of justice*)

contrafförte *m* spur (*of mountain*); crossbar (*to secure door*); (archit) buttress

contraggènio *m*—**a contraggenio** against one's will

contral·to (-**to**) *adj* alto || *m* contralto (*voice*) || *f* contralto (*singer*)

contrammirà·glio *m* (-**gli**) rear admiral

contrappasso *m* retributive justice

contrappesare [s] (**contrappéso**) *tr* to counterweight, counterbalance

contrappéso [s] *m* counterweight, counterpoise

contrappórre §218 *tr* to oppose; to compare || *ref*—**contrapporsi a** to oppose

contrappó·sto **-sta** *adj* opposing || *m* opposite, antithesis

contrappunto *m* counterpoint

contrare (**cóntro**) *tr* (boxing) to counter; (bridge) to double

contrariare §287 *tr* to oppose; counter; to thwart; to contradict; to bother, vex

contrarie·tà *f* (-**tà**) contrariety, vexation; setback

contrà·rio **-ria** (-**ri** -**rie**) *adj* contrary, opposite || *m* opposite; **al contrario** on the contrary; **al contrario di** unlike; **avere qlco in contrario** to have some objection, object

contrarre §273 *tr & ref* to contract

contrassegnare (**contrasségno**) *tr* to earmark, mark

contrasségno *m* earmark; proof

contrastare *tr* to oppose; to obstruct; to prevent || *intr* to contrast; to disagree; (poet) to quarrel || *ref* to contend

contrasto *m* contrast; fight, dispute; (telv) contrast knob

contrattàbile *adj* negotiable

contrattaccare §197 *tr* to counterattack

contrattac·co *m* (-**chi**) counterattack

contrattare *tr* to contract for, negotiate a deal for || *intr* to bargain

contrattèmpo *m* mishap

contrat·to **-ta** *adj* contracted || *m* contract

contrattuale *adj* contractual

contravveléno *m* antidote

contravvenire §282 *intr* (with *dat*) to contravene; **contravvenire a** to infringe upon

contravvenzióne *f* violation; ticket, fine; **in contravvenzione** in the wrong; **intimare una contravvenzione a** to give a ticket to

contrazióne *f* contraction

contribuènte *mf* taxpayer

contribuire §176 *intr* to contribute

contributo *m* contribution

contribu·tóre **-trice** *mf* contributor

contribuzióne *f* contribution
contristare *tr* & *ref* to sadden
contri·to -ta *adj* contrite
contrizióne *f* contrition
cóntro *m* con, contrary opinion || *adv* —**contro** *di* against, versus; **dar contro a** to oppose; **di contro** opposite, facing; **per contro** on the other hand || *prep* against, versus; at; **contro pagamento** upon payment; **contro vento** into the wind; **contro voglia** unwillingly
controbàttere *tr* (mil) to counterattack; (fig) to contest
controbilanciare §128 *tr* to counterpoise, counterbalance
controcanto *m* (mus) counterpoint
controcarro *adj invar* antitank
controchiglia *f* keelson
controcorrènte *f* countercurrent; undertow; (fig) undercurrent || *adv* upstream
controdado *m* lock nut
controffensiva *f* counteroffensive
controfigura *f* (mov) stand-in; (mov) stuntman
controfilo *m*—**a controfilo** against the grain
controfinèstra *f* storm window
controfirma *f* countersign
controfirmare *tr* to countersign
controfòdera *f* inner facing (*of a suit, between lining and cloth*)
controfuò·co *m* (-chi) backfire (*to check the advance of a forest fire*)
controindicare §197 (**controìndico**) *tr* to contraindicate
controllare (**contròllo**) *tr* to control, check || *ref* to control oneself
contròllo *m* control, check; restraint; (rad, telv) knob
controllóre *m* (com) comptroller; (rr) ticket collector, conductor
controluce *f* picture taken against the light || *adv* against the light
contromano *adv* against traffic
contromar·ca *f* (-che) check, stub (*e.g., of ticket*)
contromàr·cia *f* (-ce) countermarch; (aut) reverse, reverse gear
contromezzana [ddzz] *f* (naut) topsail
contronòta *f* countermanding note
contropalo *m* strut
controparte *f* (law) opponent
contropedale *m* foot brake (*of a bicycle*)
contropélo *m* close shave (*in the opposite direction of hair's growth*) || *adv* against the grain, the wrong way (*said of the hair*); against the nap; **accarezzare contropelo** to stroke the wrong way
contropiède *m* counterattack; **cogliere in contropiede** to catch off balance
contropòrta *f* storm door
controproducènte *adj* counterproductive, self-defeating
contropropósta *f* counterproposition
contropròva *f* proof; second balloting
contrórdine *m* countermand
controrèplica *f* retort; (law) rejoinder
controrifórma *f* Counter Reformation

controrivoluzióne *f* counterrevolution
controsènso *m* nonsense; mistranslation
controspallina *f* (mil) epaulet
controspionàg·gio *m* (-gi) counterespionage
controvalóre *m* equivalent
controvènto *m* (archit) strut; (archit) crossbrace || *adv* windward
controvèrsia *f* controversy
controvèr·so -sa *adj* controversial, moot
controvòglia *adv* unwillingly
contumace *adj* (archaic) contumacious; (law) absent from court; (law) guilty of nonappearance
contumàcia *f* quarantine; (archaic) contumacy; (law) nonappearance; **in contumacia** (law) in absentia
contumèlia *f* contumely
contundènte *adj* blunt
conturbante *adj* disturbing, upsetting
conturbare *tr* to disturb, upset || *ref* to become perturbed
contusióne *f* bruise, contusion
contu·so -sa *adj* bruised
contuttoché *conj* although
contuttociò *conj* although
convalescènte *adj* convalescent
convalescènza *f* convalescence
convalescenzià·rio *m* (-ri) convalescent home
convàlida *f* validation; confirmation
convalidare (**convàlido**) *tr* to validate; to confirm; to strengthen (*e.g., a suspicion*)
convégno *m* meeting, convention
conveniènte *adj* convenient; adequate; useful; profitable (*business*); cheap, reasonable
conveniènza *f* convenience; suitability, fitness; propriety; profit; **convenienze** conventions
convenire §282 *tr* to fix (*e.g., a price*); (law) to summon || *intr* (ESSERE) to convene; to agree; to fit, be appropriate; (poet) to flow together || *ref* to be proper; (with *dat*) to behoove, befit, *e.g.*, **gli si conviene** it behooves him || *impers*—**conviene** it is necessary
convènto *m* convent; monastery
convenu·to -ta *adj* agreed upon || *m* agreement; (law) defendant; **convenuti** conventioners, delegates
convenzionale *adj* conventional
convenzióne *f* convention
convergènte *adj* converging, convergent
convergènza *f* convergence
convèrgere §137 *intr* to converge
convèrsa *f* lay sister; flashing (*on a roof*)
conversare (**convèrso**) *intr* to converse
conversazióne *f* conversation
conversióne *f* conversion; change of heart; (mil) wheeling
convèrso *m* lay brother
convertìbile *adj* convertible || *m* (aer) fighter-bomber || *f* (aut) convertible
convertibili·tà *f* (-tà) convertibility
convertìre §138 *tr* to convert, change; to translate || *ref* to convert, change; (poet) to address oneself

converti·to -ta *adj* converted ‖ *mf* convert
convertitóre *m* converter
convès·so -sa *adj* convex
convincènte *adj* convincing
convincere §285 *tr* to convince; to convict ‖ *ref* to become convinced
convincimènto *m* conviction
convin·to -ta *adj* convinced, confirmed; convicted
convinzióne *f* conviction
convita·to -ta *adj* invited ‖ *mf* guest (*at a banquet*)
convito *m* banquet
convitto *m* boarding school
convit·tóre -trice *mf* boarding-school student
convivènte *adj* living together
convivènza *f* living together; **convivenza illecita** cohabitation; **convivenza umana** human society
convìvere §286 *intr* to live together; to cohabit
conviviale *adj* convivial
convì·vio *m* (**-vi**) banquet
convocare §197 (**cònvoco**) *tr* to summon, convoke; to convene
convocazióne *f* convocation
convogliare §280 (**convòglio**) *tr* to convoy, escort; to convey, carry
convò·glio *m* (**-gli**) convoy; cortege; (**rr**) train
convolare (**convólo**) *intr*—**convolare a nozze** to get married
convòlvolo *m* (bot) morning-glory
convulsióne *f* convulsion
convul·so -sa *adj* convulsive; convulsed; choppy (*style*)
coonestare (**coonèsto**) *tr* to justify, palliate
cooperare (**coòpero**) *intr* to cooperate
cooperati·vo -va *adj* & *f* cooperative
coopera·tóre -trice *adj* coadjutant, cooperating ‖ *m* coadjutor
cooperazióne *f* cooperation
coordinaménto *m* coordination
coordinare (**coórdino**) *tr* to coordinate; to collect (*ideas*)
coordinati·vo -va *adj* (gram) coordinate
coordina·to -ta *adj* & *f* coordinate
coordinazióne *f* coordination
coòrte *f* cohort
copèr·chio *m* (**-chi**) lid, cover; top (*of box*)
copertina *f* small blanket, child's blanket; cover (*of book*)
copèr·to -ta *adj* covered; protected; cloudy; obscure ‖ *m* cover; shelter; **al coperto** under cover; indoors; secure ‖ *f* blanket, cover; seat cover; case, sheath; (naut) deck; **coperta da viaggio** steamer rug, lap robe; **far coperta a** to cover up for
copertóne *m* canvas; casing, shoe (*of tire*); **copertone cinturato** belted tire
copertura *f* covering; cover; coverage; whitewash; (boxing) defensive stance; (archit) roof
còpia *f* copy; (poet) abundance; (archaic) opportunity; **brutta copia** first draft; **copia a carbone** carbon copy; **copia dattiloscritta** typescript; **per**

copia conforme certified copy (*formula appearing on a document*)
copialètte·re *m* (**-re**) letter file; copying press
copiare §287 (**còpio**) *tr* to copy
copiati·vo -va *adj* indelible; copying
copiatura *f* copying; copy; plagiarism
copiglia *f* cotterpin
copilò·ta *mf* (**-ti -te**) copilot
copióne *m* (theat) script
copiosi·tà [s] *f* (**-tà**) copiousness
copió·so -sa [s] *adj* copious
copi·sta *mf* (**-sti -ste**) scribe; copyist
copisterìa *f* copying office; public typing office
còppa *f* cup, goblet; bowl; pan (*of balance*); trophy; (aut) crankcase; (aut) housing; **coppe** suit of Neapolitan cards corresponding to hearts
coppàia *f* chuck (*of lathe*)
còppia *f* couple; pair; **a coppie** two by two; **far coppia fissa** to go steady
coppière *m* cupbearer
coppìglia *f* var of **copiglia**
cóppo *m* earthenware jar (*for oil*); roof tile
copribu·sto *m* (**-sto**) bodice
copricapo *m* headgear
copricatè·na *m* (**-na**) chain guard (*on bicycle or motorcycle*)
coprifuò·co *m* (**-chi**) curfew
coprinu·ca *m* (**-ca**) havelock
coprire §110 *tr* to cover; to occupy (*a position*); to coat (*e.g., a wall*); to drown (*a noise*) ‖ *ref* to cover oneself; (econ) to hedge
copriteiè·ra *m* (**-ra**) cozy
coprivivan·de *m* (**-de**) dish cover
cò·pto -pta *adj* Coptic ‖ *mf* Copt
còpula *f* copulation; (gram) copula
coque *f* see **uovo**
coràg·gio *m* (**-gi**) courage; effrontery; (obs) heart; **fare coraggio a** to hearten, encourage; **prendere il coraggio a quattro mani** to screw up one's courage
coraggió·so -sa [s] *adj* courageous
corale *adj* choral; (archaic) cordial; (fig) unanimous ‖ *m* chorale
coralli·no -na *adj* coral
corallo *m* coral
corame *m* engraved leather
coramèlla *f* razor strop
Corano *m* Koran
corata *f* haslet
coratèlla *f* giblets
corazza *f* breastplate, cuirass; shoulder pad (*in football*); armor plate; carapace, shell
corazzare *tr* to armor ‖ *ref* to armor, protect oneself
corazza·to -ta *adj* armor-plated, armored; plated; protected ‖ *f* battleship, dreadnought
corazzière *m* cuirassier; mounted carabineer
còrba *f* basket
corbellerìa *f* (coll) blunder
corbèllo *m* basket; basketful
corbézzolo *m* (bot) arbutus; **corbezzoli!** gosh!
còrda *f* rope; tightrope; string (*of an*

instrument); chord; woof; cord; plumbline; **dare la corda** to a wind (*a clock*); **essere con la corda al collo** to have a rope around one's neck; **mostrare la corda** to be threadbare; **tagliare la corda** to take off, leave; **tenere sulla corda** to keep in suspense

cordame *m* cordage

cordata *f* group of climbers tied together

cordellina *f* (mil) braided cord, braid; (mil) lanyard

cordiale *adj & m* cordial

cordiali·tà *f* (-**tà**) cordiality

cordièra *f* (mus) tailpiece

cordò·glio *m* (-**gli**) sorrow, grief

cordonata *f* gradient

cordóne *m* cordon; (anat, elec) cord; curbstone; **cordone litorale** sandbar; **cordone sanitario** sanitary cordon

corèa *f* St. Vitus's dance ‖ **Corèa** *f* Korea

corea·no -na *adj & mf* Korean

coréggia *f* leather strap

coreografìa *f* choreography

coreògrafo *m* choreographer

coriàce·o -a *adj* tough, leathery

coriàndolo *m* (bot) coriander; **coriandoli** confetti

coricare §197 (còrico) *tr* to put to bed ‖ *ref* to lie down, go to bed

corindóne *m* corundum

corìn·zio -zia *adj & mf* (-**zi** -**zie**) Corinthian

cori·sta *mf* (-**sti** -**ste**) choir singer, choirmaster ‖ *m* chorus man; (mus) tuning fork; (mus) pitch pipe

coriza [dz] *or* **corìzza** [ddzz] *f* coryza

cormorano *m* cormorant

cornàcchia *f* rook, crow

cornamusa *f* bagpipe

cornata *f* butt; hook, goring (*by bull*)

còrne·o -a *adj* horn, horn-like ‖ *f* cornea

cornétta *f* (mus) cornet; (mus) cornet player; (telp) receiver; (hist) pennon (*of cavalry*)

cornétto *m* little horn; amulet (*in shape of horn*); crescent (*bread*); ear trumpet

cornice *f* cornice; frame; (typ) box; (archit) pediment

cornicióne *m* (archit) ledge; (archit) cornice

cornificare §197 (**cornìfico**) *tr* (joc) to cuckold

corniòla *f* carnelian

còrniola *f* (bot) dogberry

còrniolo *m* (bot) dogwood

còrno *m* horn; wing (*of army*); edge, end; (mus) horn; **corno da caccia** hunting horn; **corno da scarpe** shoe horn; **corno dell'abbondanza** horn of plenty; **corno dogale** (hist) Doge's hat; **corno inglese** (mus) English horn; **non capire un corno** to not understand a blessed thing; **non valere un corno** to not be worth a fig; **un corno!** (slang) heck no! ‖ *m* (**còrna** *fpl*) horn (*of animal*); **alzare le corna** to raise one's head; to become rambunctious; **dire corna di** to speak evil of; **fare le corna** to make horns, to touch wood (*to ward off the evil eye*); **mettere le corna a** to cuckold (*one's husband*); **portare le corna** to be cuckolded; **rompersi le corna** to get the worst of it

cornu·to -ta *adj* horny; horn-shaped; (vulg) cuckolded

còro *m* choir; chorus; chancel

corollà·rio *m* (-**ri**) corollary

coróna *f* crown; coronet; wreath, garland; range (*of mountains*); collection (*e.g., of sonnets*); stem (*of watch*); felloe (*of wheel*); (astr) corona; (rel) string (*of beads*); (mus) pause; **fare corona a** to surround

coronaménto *m* crowning; (archit) capstone; (naut) taffrail

coronare (coróno) *tr* to crown; to top, surmount

coronà·rio -ria *adj* (-**ri** -**rie**) coronary; (hist) rewarded with a garland

corpétto *m* baby's shirt; waistcoat, vest

corpino *m* bodice; vest

còrpo *m* body; substance; staff (*of teachers*); (mil) corps; (typ) em quad; **a corpo a corpo** hand-to-hand (*fight*); (sports) in a clinch; **a corpo morto** heavily; doggedly; **andare di corpo** to have a bowel movement; **avere in corpo** (fig) to have inside; **corpo del reato** corpus delicti; **corpo di Bacco!** good Heavens!; **corpo di ballo** ballet; **corpo di commissariato** (mil) supply corps; **corpo di guardia** guard, guardhouse; **corpo semplice** (chem) simple substance; **prendere corpo** to materialize

corporale *adj* bodily, body ‖ *m* (eccl) corporal, Communion cloth

corporativismo *m* corporatism (*e.g., of Fascist Italy*)

corporati·vo -va *adj* corporative, corporate

corpora·to -ta *adj* corporate

corporatura *f* size, build

corporazióne *f* corporation

corpòre·o -a *adj* corporeal

corpó·so -sa [s] *adj* heavy-bodied

corpulèn·to -ta *adj* corpulent

corpùscolo *m* particle; (phys) corpuscle

Corpus Dòmini *m* (eccl) Corpus Christi

corredare (corrèdo) *tr* to provide, furnish; to annotate, accompany

corredino *m* layette

corrèdo *m* trousseau; outfit, garb; actor's kit; furniture; equipment; apparatus (*e.g., footnotes*)

corrèggere §226 *tr* to correct; to straighten (*e.g., a road*); to rewrite, revise (*news*); to touch up the flavor of ‖ *ref* to reform

corrég·gia *f* (-**ge**) leather strap

corregionale *adj* fellow ‖ *mf* person of the same section of the country

correità *f* complicity

correlare (corrèlo) *tr* to correlate

correlati·vo -va *adj* correlative

correla·tóre -trice *mf* second reader (*of a doctoral dissertation*)

correlazióne *f* correlation; (gram) sequence

corrènte *adj* current; running; fluent; recurring; run-of-the-mill ‖ *m*—**essere al corrente di** to be acquainted with; to be abreast of; **mettere al corrente di** to acquaint with ‖ *f* current; draft (*of air*); stream (*of water*); mass (*of lava*); (elec) current; (fig) tide; **contro corrente** upstream; **corrente alternata** (elec) alternating current; **corrente continua** (elec) direct current; **corrente di rete** (elec) house current

córrere §139 *tr* to travel; to run (*a risk; a race*); **correre la cavallina** to sow one's wild oats ‖ *intr* (ESSERE & AVERE) to run; to speed; to race; to flow; to fly (*said of time*); to elapse; to be (*e.g., the year 1820*); to be current (*said of coins*); to spread (*said of gossip*); to mature (*said of interest*); to intervene (*said of distance*); to have dealings; **ci corre!** there is quite a difference!; **ci corse poco che cadesse** he narrowly escaped falling; **correre a gambe levate** to run at breakneck speed; **corre l'uso** it is the fashion; **corrono parole grosse** they are having words; **non corre buon sangue fra loro** there is bad blood between them

corresponsàbile *adj* jointly responsible

corresponsióne *f* payment; (fig) gratitude

correttézza *f* correctness

correttì·vo -va *adj* corrective ‖ *m* flavoring

corrèt·to -ta *adj* correct; flavored; spiked

corret·tóre -trice *mf* corrector; **correttore di bozze** proofreader

correzionale *adj* correctional

correzióne *f* correction

còrri còrri *m* rush

corri·dóio *m* (-**dói**) corridor; hallway; (tennis) alley; (theat) aisle

corridóre *adj* running ‖ *m* racer; runner (*in baseball*)

corrièra *f* mail coach; bus

corrière *m* courier; mail; carrier (*of merchandise*)

corrispettì·vo -va *adj* equivalent, proportionate ‖ *m* requital, compensation

corrispondènte *adj* corresponding, equivalent ‖ *mf* correspondent

corrispondènza *f* correspondence

corrispóndere §238 *tr* to pay, compensate ‖ *intr* to correspond

corrì·vo -va *adj* rash; indulgent

corroborante *adj* corroborating ‖ *m* tonic

corroborare (corròboro) *tr* to corroborate; to invigorate

corroborazióne *f* corroboration

corródere §239 *tr* to corrode; to erode

corrómpere §240 *tr* to spoil; to corrupt; to suborn ‖ *ref* to putrefy, rot

corrosióne *f* corrosion

corrosì·vo -va *adj & m* corrosive

corró·so -sa *adj* corroded; eroded

corrót·to -ta *adj* corrupted, corrupt; putrefied, rotten ‖ *m* (archaic) lament

corrucciare §128 *tr* to anger, vex ‖ *ref* to get angry

corrùc·cio *m* (-**ci**) anger, vexation

corrugaménto *m* wrinkling; (geol) fold

corrugare §209 *tr* to wrinkle, knit (*one's brow*) ‖ *ref* to frown

corruscare §197 *intr* (poet) to shine

corruttèla *f* corruption

corruttìbile *adj* corruptible

corrut·tóre -trice *adj* corrupting, depraving ‖ *m* seducer; briber

corruzióne *f* corruption; putrefaction, decomposition

córsa *f* race; run; trip; fare; (mach) stroke; (hist) privateering; **a tutta corsa** at full speed; **corsa al galoppo** flat race; **corsa al trotto** harness racing; **corsa semplice** one-way ticket; **corse** horse racing; **da corsa** race, for racing, e.g., **cavallo da corsa** race horse; **di corsa** running, in a hurry; **fare una corsa** to run an errand; **prendere la corsa** to begin to run

corsalétto *m* corselet

corsa·ro -ra *adj* privateering ‖ *m* privateer, corsair, pirate

corsétto *m* corset

corsìa *f* aisle; ward (*in hospital*); runner (*of carpet*); lane (*of highway*); **corsia d'accesso** entrance lane; **corsia d'uscita** exit lane

Còrsica, la Corsica

corsi·vìsta *mf* (-**sti -ste**) (journ) political writer

corsì·vo -va *adj* cursive; (poet) running; (poet) current ‖ *m* cursive handwriting; (typ) italics

córso *m* course; navigation (*by sea*); path (*of stars*); parade; large street; boulevard; tender (*of currency*); current rate, current price (*of stock at the exchange*); **corso d'acqua** watercourse; **fuori corso** (coin) no longer in circulation; **in corso** in circulation; in progress; **in corso di** in the course of; **in corso di stampa** in press

cor·sólo -sóia (-**sól -sóia**) *adj* running (*knot*); (mach) on rollers ‖ *m* slide (*of slide rule*); (mach) slide

córte *f* court; **corte bandita** open house; **Corte d'appello** appellate court; **Corte di cassazione** Supreme Court; **fare la corte a** to pay court to, woo

cortéc·cia *f* (-**ce**) bark; crust (*of bread*); (fig) appearance; (anat) cortex

corteggiaménto *m* courtship

corteggiatóre *m* wooer, suitor

cortég·gio *m* (-**gi**) retinue; cortege

cortèo *m* procession; parade; funeral train; wedding party

cortése *adj* courteous, polite; (lit) liberal; (poet & hist) courtly

cortesìa *f* courtesy, politeness; (lit) liberality; (poet & hist) courtliness; **per cortesia** please

còrtice *f* cortex

cortigia·no -na *adj* flattering; courtly ‖ *mf* courtier; flatterer ‖ *f* courtesan

cortile *m* courtyard; barnyard

cortìna *f* curtain; **cortìna di ferro** iron curtain; **cortìna di fumo** smoke screen; **oltre cortìna** behind the iron curtain

cortisóne *m* cortisone

cór·to -ta *adj* short; close (*haircut*); **alle corte** in short; **essere a corto di** to be short of; **per farla corta** in short

cortocircùito *m* short circuit

cortometràg·gio *m* (-gi) (mov) short

cor·vè *f* (-vè) tiresome task, drudgery; **corvè di cucina** kitchen police

corvétta *f* corvette

corvi·no -na *adj* raven-black

córvo *m* raven; crow

cò·sa [s] *f* thing; **belle cose!** or **buone cose!** regards!; **che cosa** what; **cosa da nulla** a mere trifle, nothing at all; **cos'ha?** what's the matter with you (him, her)?; **cosa pùbblica** commonweal; **cosa strana** no wonder; **cose belongings; **per la qual cosa** wherefore; **per prima cosa** first of all; **sopra ogni cosa** above all; **tante belle cose!** best regards!; **una cosa** something; **una cosa nuova** a piece of news

cosac·co -ca (-chi -che) *adj* Cossack's || *mf* Cossack

cò·scia *f* (-sce) thigh; haunch; leg (*of gun*); (archit) abutment; **coscia di montone** leg of lamb

cosciènte *adj* conscious; sensible; aware

cosciènza *f* conscience; consciousness; consciousness; awareness

coscienzió·so -sa [s] *adj* conscientious

cosciòtto *m* leg; leg of lamb

coscrit·to -ta *adj* conscript || *m* conscript, recruit, draftee

coscrìvere §250 *tr* to conscript

coscrizióne *f* conscription, draft

così [s] *adj invar*—**un così... or un...** **così** such a || *adv* thus; like this; so; **così ... come as ... a; così così** so so; **e così via** and so on, and so forth; **per così dire** so to speak

cosicché [s] *conj* so that

cosiddét·to -ta [s] *adj* so-called

cosiffat·to -ta [s] *adj* such, similar

cosìno [s] *m* (coll) little fellow

cosmèti·co -ca *adj* & *m* (-ci -che) cosmetic

còsmi·co -ca *adj* (-ci -che) cosmic; outer (*space*)

còsmo *m* cosmos; outer space

cosmòdromo *m* space center

cosmologìa *f* cosmology

cosmonàu·ta *mf* (-ti -te) cosmonaut, astronaut

cosmopolì·ta *adj* & *mf* (-ti -te) cosmopolitan

còso [s] *m* (coll) thing, what-d'you-call-it

cospàrgere §261 *tr* to spread; to sprinkle

cospèrgere §112 *tr* (poet) to wet, sprinkle

cospètto *m* presence; **al cospetto di** in the presence of

cospì·cuo -cua *adj* distinguished, outstanding; huge, immense; (poet) conspicuous

cospirare *intr* to conspire, plot

cospira·tóre -trice *mf* conspirator

cospirazióne *f* conspiracy, plot

còsta *f* side; rib; coast, seashore; slope; welt (*along seam*); wale (*in fabric*); (naut) frame

costà *adv* there; over there

costaggiù *adv* down there

costante *adj* & *f* constant

Costantinòpoli *f* Constantinople

costanza *f* constancy || **Costanza** *f* Constance

costare (cósto) *intr* (ESSERE) to cost; to be expensive; **costare caro** to cost dear; **costare un occhio della testa** to cost a fortune

costarica·no -na or **costaricènse** *adj* & *mf* Costa Rican

costassù *adv* up there

costata *f* rib roast; side

costeggiare §290 (costéggio) *tr* to sail along; to run along; to border on || *intr* to coast

costèi §8 *pron dem*

costellare (costèllo) *tr* to stud, star

costellazióne *f* constellation

costernare (costèrno) *tr* to dismay, cause consternation to

costernazióne *f* consternation

costì *adv* there

costiè·ro -ra *adj* coast, coastal; offshore || *f* coastline; gentle slope

costipare *tr* to constipate; to heap, pile || *ref* to become constipated

costipazióne *f* constipation

costituènte *adj* constituent; constituting || *m* member of constituent assembly; (chem) constituent

costituire §176 *tr* to constitute; to form || *ref* to form; to become; to appoint oneself; to give oneself up (*to justice*); **costituirsi in giudizio** (law) to sue (*in civil court*); **costituirsi parte civile** (law) to appear as a plaintiff (*in civil court*)

costituto *m* (law) pact, agreement; (naut) master's declaration (*to health authorities*)

costituzionale *adj* constitutional

costituzióne *f* constitution; charter; composition; (law) appearance; surrender (*to justice*)

còsto *m* cost; **a costo di** at the price of; **ad ogni costo** at any cost; **a nessun costo** by no means; **a tutti i costi** at any cost, in any event; **costo della vita** cost of living; **sotto costo** below cost

còstola *f* rib; spine (*of book*); back (*of knife*); **avere qlcu alle costole** to have s.o. at one's heels; **rompere le costole a** (fig) to break the bones of; **stare alle costole di** to be at the back of

costolétta *f* chop, cutlet

costolóne *m* (archit) groin

costóro §8 *pron dem*

costó·so -sa [s] *adj* costly

costrìngere §265 *tr* to force, constrain; (poet) to compress

costrittì·vo -va *adj* constrictive

costrizióne *f* constriction

costruire §140 *tr* to construct, build

costrut·to -ta *adj* constructed ‖ *m* profit; sense; (gram) construction; **dov'è il costrutto?** what's the point?

costruttóre *m* builder

costruzióne *f* construction; building

costùi §8 *pron dem*

costumanza *f* custom

costumare *intr* (+ *inf*) to be in the habit of (+ *ger*) ‖ *intr* (ESSERE) to be the custom; to be in use

costumatézza *f* good manners

costumà·to -ta *adj* polite, well-bred

costume *m* custom, manner; costume, dress; bathing suit

costumi·sta *mf* (**-sti -ste**) (theat) costumer

costura *f* seam

cotale *adj & pron* such ‖ *adv* (archaic) thus

cotan·to -ta *adj & pron* (poet) so much ‖ **cotanto** *adv* (poet) such a long time

còte *f* flint

coténna *f* pigskin; rind; (coll) hide, skin

coté·sto -sta §7 *adj dem* ‖ §8 *pron dem*

còti·ca *f* (**-che**) (coll) hide, skin (of *porker*)

cotógna *f* quince (*fruit*)

cotognata *f* quince jam

cotógno *m* quince (*tree*)

cotolétta *f* chop, cutlet

cotóne *m* cotton; thread; **cotone fulminante** guncotton; **cotone idrofilo** absorbent cotton; **cotone silicato** mineral wool

cotonière *m* cotton manufacturer

cotoniè·ro -ra *adj* cotton ‖ *mf* cotton worker

cotonifi·cio *m adj* (**-ci**) cotton mill

cotonó·so -sa [s] *adj* cotton; cottony

còtta *f* cooking, baking; drying (of *bricks*); (sports) exhaustion; (coll) drunkenness; (joc) infatuation, love; (eccl) surplice; **cotta d'armi** coat of mail

cottimi·sta *mf* (**-sti -ste**) pieceworker

còttimo *m* piecework

còt·to -ta *adj* cooked; baked; burnt; suntanned; (joc) half-baked; (joc) in love; (sports) exhausted ‖ *m* brick ‖ *f see* **cotta**

cottura *f* cooking; **a punto di cottura** (culin) done just right

coutènte *mf* (law) joint user; (telp) party-line user

cóva *f* brooding; nest

covare (**cóvo**) *tr* to brood, to hatch; to harbor or nurse (*an enmity*); to nurture (*a disease*); **covare con gli occhi** to look fondly at; **covare le lenzuola** to loll around ‖ *intr* to smolder (*said of fire or passion*)

covata *f* brood, covey

covile *m* doghouse; den

cóvo *m* shelter; den, lair; **farsi il covo** (fig) to gather a nestegg; **uscire dal covo** to stick one's nose out of the house

covóne *m* sheaf; cock (of *hay*)

còzza *f* cockle

cozzare (**còzzo**) *tr* to hit; to butt (*one's head*) ‖ *intr* to butt; (fig) to clash;

cozzare contro to bump into ‖ *ref* to hit one another; to fight

còzzo *m* butt; clash, conflict

crac *m* crash

crampo *m* cramp

crà·ni·co -ca *adj* (**-ci -che**) cranial

crà·nio *m* (**-ni**) cranium, skull

cràpula *f* excess (*in eating and drinking*)

cras·so -sa *adj* crass, gross; large (*intestine*)

cratère *m* crater; bomb crater

cràuti *mpl* sauerkraut

cravatta *f* tie, necktie; **cravatta a farfalla** bow tie; **fare cravatte** to be a usurer

creanza *f* politeness; **buona creanza** good manners

creare (**crèo**) *tr* to create; to name, elect

creati·vo -va *adj* creative

crea·to -ta *adj* created ‖ *m* creation, universe

crea·tóre -trice *adj* creative ‖ *mf* creator

creatura *f* creature; baby; **povera creatura!** poor thing!

creazióne *f* creation; (poet) election

credènte *adj* believing ‖ *mf* believer

credènza *f* credence, faith, belief; sideboard, buffet; (coll) credit

credenziale *f* letter of credit; **credenziali** credentials

credenzière *m* butler

crédere §141 *tr* to believe; to think; **lo credo bene!** I should say so! ‖ *intr* to believe; to trust; **credere a** to believe in; **credere in Dio** to believe in God ‖ *ref* to believe oneself to be

credìbile *adj* credible

credibilità *f* credibility

crédito *m* credit

credi·tóre -trice *mf* creditor

crèdo *m* credo, creed

credulità *f* credulity

crèdu·lo -la *adj* credulous

crèma *f* cream; custard; **crema da scarpe** shoe polish; **crema di bellezza** beauty cream; **crema di pomodoro** cream of tomato soup; **crema evanescente** vanishing cream; **crema per barba** shaving cream

cremaglièra *f* rack; cogway, cograil

cremare (**crèmo**) *tr* to cremate

crema·tóio *m* (**-tói**) crematory

crematò·rio *m* (**-ri**) crematory

cremazióne *f* cremation

cremería *f* creamery

crèmisi *adj & m* crimson

Cremlino *m* Kremlin

cremlinología *f* Kremlinology

cremortàrtaro *m* cream of tartar

cremó·so -sa [s] *adj* creamy

crèn *m* horseradish

creolina *f* creolin

crè·o·lo -la *adj & mf* Creole

creosòto *m* creosote

crèpa *f* crack, crevice; rift

crepàc·cio *m* (**-ci**) crevasse; fissure

crepacuòre *m* heartbreak

crepapància *m*—**mangiare a crepapancia** to burst from eating too much

crepapèlle *m*—**ridere a crepapelle** to split one's sides laughing

crepare (**crèpo**) *intr* to burst; to crack; to chip; (slang) to croak; **crepare dalla sete** to die of thirst; **crepare dalle risa** to die laughing; **crepare d'invidia** to be green with envy

crepitare (**crèpito**) *intr* to crackle (*said of fire or weapons*); to rustle (*said of leaves*)

crepiti-o *m* (**-i**) crackle; rustle; pitter-patter (*of rain*)

crepuscolare *adj* twilight; (fig) dim

crepùscolo *m* twilight

crescènte *adj* rising, growing; crescent (*moon*) || *m* (astr & heral) crescent

crescènza *f* growth

créscere §142 *tr* to grow, raise; to increase || *intr* (ESSERE) to grow; to increase; to rise (*said, e.g., of prices*); to wax (*said of the moon*); **farsi crescere** to grow (*a beard*)

crescióne *m* watercress

créscita *f* growth; outgrowth; rise (*of water*)

crèsima *f* confirmation

cresimare (**crèsimo**) *tr* to confirm

Crèso *m* (mythol) Croesus

cré-spo -spa *adj* crispy, kinky; (archaic) wrinkled || *m* crepe || *f* wrinkle; ruffle

crèsta *f* comb (*of chicken*); crest; **abbassare la cresta** to come down a peg or two; **alzare la cresta** to become insolent

crestàia *f* (coll) milliner

créta *f* clay

cretése [s] *adj & mf* Cretan

cretinerìa *f* idiocy

creti-no -na *adj & mf* idiot, cretin

cribro *m* (poet) sieve

cric-ca *f* (**-che**) clique, gang; group; crevice

cric-co *m* (**-chi**) (aut) jack

cricéto *m* hamster

cri cri *m* chirping (*of crickets*)

criminale *adj* criminal; (law) penal || *mf* criminal

criminali-sta *mf* (**-sti -ste**) penal lawyer, criminal lawyer

criminalità *f* criminality

crìmine *m* crime

criminologìa *f* criminology

criminòlo-go *m* (**-gi**) criminologist

criminó-so -sa [s] *adj* criminal

crinale *adj* (poet) hair || *m* ridge (*of mountains*)

crine *m* horsehair; (poet) hair; (poet) sunbeam

crinièra *f* mane

crinolina *f* crinoline

cripta *f* crypt

criptocomuni-sta *mf* (**-sti -ste**) fellow traveler

crisàlide *f* chrysalis

crisantèmo *m* chrysanthemum

cri-si *f* (**-si**) crisis; shortage (*of houses*); attack (*e.g., of fever*); outburst (*of tears*); (econ) slump; **crisi ancillare** or **domestica** servant problem; **in crisi** in difficulties

cristallerìa *f* glassware; crystal service; glassware shop; glassworks

cristallièra *f* china closet

cristalli-no -na *adj* crystalline || *m* crystalline lens

cristallizzare [ddzz] *tr & ref* to crystallize

cristallo *m* crystal; glass; pane (*of glass*); windshield; **cristallo di rocca** rock crystal; **cristallo di sicurezza** (aut) safety glass

cristianaménte *adv* in a Christian manner, like a Christian; (coll) decently; **morire cristianamente** to die in the faith

cristianésimo *m* Christianity

cristianità *f* Christendom

cristia-no -na *adj & mf* Christian

Cristo *m* Christ; **avanti Cristo** before Christ (B.C.); **dopo Cristo** after Christ (A.D.); **un povero cristo** (slang) a poor guy

critè-rio *m* (**-ri**) criterion; judgment

crìti-ca *f* (**-che**) criticism; critique; slur

criticare §197 (**crìtico**) *tr* to criticize, censure; to find fault with

crìti-co -ca (**-ci -che**) *adj* critical || *mf* critic; (coll) faultfinder || *f* see **critica**

crittografìa *f* cryptography

crittogram-ma *m* (**-mi**) cryptogram

crivellare (**crivèllo**) *tr* to riddle

crivèllo *m* sieve, riddle

croa-to -ta *adj & mf* Croatian

Croàzia, la Croatia

croccante *adj* crisp, crunchy || *m* almond brittle, peanut brittle

crocchétta *f* croquette

cròcchia *f* chignon, topknot

crocchiare §287 (**cròcchio**) *intr* to crackle; to sound cracked or broken; to cluck (*said of a hen*); to crack (*said of joints*)

cròc-chio *m* (**-chi**) group (*of people*); **far crocchio** to gather around

cróce *f* cross; x (*mark made by illiterate person*); tail (*of coin*); (fig) trial; **Croce del Sud** Southern Cross; **croce di Malta** Maltese cross; **Croce Rossa** Red Cross; **croce uncinata** swastika; **fare una croce sopra** to forget about; **gettare la croce addosso** (fig) to put the blame on; **mettere in croce** to crucify

crocefisso *m* crucifix

crocerossina *f* Red Cross worker

croceségno *m* cross, x (*mark made instead of signature*)

crocétta *f* (naut) crosstree

croce-vìa *m* (**-vìa**) crossroads, intersection

crocia-to -ta *adj* crossed; crusading; see **parola** || *m* crusader || *f* crusade

crocièra *f* cruise; (archit) cross (*vault*); (mach) cross (*of universal joint*)

crocière *m* (orn) crossbill

crocifìggere §104 *tr* to crucify

crocifissióne *f* crucifixion

crocifis-so -sa *adj* crucified || *m* crucifix

cròco *m* (**-chi**) crocus

crogiolare (**crògiolo**) *tr* to cook on a low fire; to simmer; to temper (*glass*) || *ref* to bask; to snuggle (*e.g., in bed*)

crògiolo *m* cooking on a low fire; simmering; tempering (*of glass*)

crogiòlo *m* crucible; (fig) melting pot

crollare (**cròllo**) *tr* to shake (*e.g., one's head*) || *intr* (ESSERE) to fall down, collapse || *ref* to shake

cròllo m shake; fall, collapse

cròma f (mus) quaver

cromare (cròmo) tr to plate with chromium

croma·to -ta adj chromium-plated; chrome || m chrome yellow

cromatura f chromium plating

cròmo m chrome, chromium

cromosfèra f chromosphere

cromosò·ma [s] m (-mi) chromosome

cròna·ca f (-che) chronicle; report, news; **cronaca bianca** news of the day; **cronaca giudiziaria** court news; **cronaca mondana** social column; **cronaca nera** police and accident report; **cronaca rosa** wedding column; stork news

cròni·co -ca (-ci -che) adj chronic || mf incurable

croni·sta mf (-sti -ste) reporter; chronicler

cronistòria f chronicle

cronologia f chronology

cronològi·co -ca adj (-ci -che) chronologic(al)

cronometrare (cronòmetro) tr to time

cronomètri·co -ca adj (-ci -che) chronometric(al); split-second

cronometri·sta m (-sti) (sports) timekeeper

cronòmetro m stopwatch; chronometer

crosciare §128 (cròscio) tr (archaic) to heave, throw || intr to rustle (said of dry leaves); to pitter-patter (said of rain)

cròsta f crust; bark (of tree); scab; slough; shell (of crustacean); poor painting

crostàceo m crustacean

crostata f pie

crostino m toast

crostó·so -sa [s] adj crusty

croupier m (croupier) croupier

crucciare §128 tr to worry, vex; to chagrin || ref to worry; to become angry

cruccia·to -ta adj afflicted; worried; angry; chagrined

cràc·cio m (-ci) sorrow; (obs) anger; **darsi cruccio** to fret

cruciale adj crucial

crucivèr·ba m (-ba) crossword puzzle

crudèle adj cruel

crudel·tà f (-tà) cruelty

crudézza f crudity; harshness

cru·do -da adj raw; rare (meat); (poet) cruel

cruèn·to -ta adj (lit) bloody

crumiro m scab (in strikes)

cruna f eye (of a needle)

cru·sca f (-sche) bran; (coll) freckles

cruscante adj Della-Cruscan; affected || m member of the Accademia della Crusca

cruschèllo m middlings

cruscòtto m (aut) dashboard; (aer) instrument panel

cuba·no -na adj & mf Cuban

cubatura f volume

cùbi·co -ca adj (-ci -che) cubic; cube (root)

cubitale adj very large (handwriting or type)

cùbito m cubit; (poet) elbow

cubo m cube

cuccagna f plenty; windfall; Cockaigne

cuccétta f berth

cucchiàia f large spoon; ladle; trowel; bucket (of power shovel); **cucchiaia bucata** skimmer

cucchiaiàta f spoonful; tablespoonful

cucchiaino m teaspoon; teaspoonful; spoon (lure)

cuc·chiàio m (-chiài) spoon; spoonful; tablespoon; **cucchiaio da minestra** soupspoon

cucchiaióne m ladle

cùc·cia f (-ce) dog's bed; **a cuccia!** lie down!

cucciare §128 intr (ESSERE) & ref to lie down (said of a dog)

cucciolata f litter (e.g., of puppies)

càcciolo m puppy; cub; (fig) greenhorn

cuc·co m (-chi) cuckoo; simpleton; darling (child)

cuccuru·cù m (-cù) cock-a-doodle-doo

cucina f kitchen; cuisine; kitchen range; **cucina componibile** kitchen with sectional cabinets; **cucina economica** kitchen range; **fare da cucina** to prepare a meal

cucinare tr to cook; (fig) to fix

cucinétta f kitchenette

cuciniè·re -ra mf cook

cucire §143 tr to sew; to stitch || ref—**cucirsi la bocca** to keep one's mouth shut

cucirino m sewing thread

cuci·tóre -trice adj sewing || mf sewing machine operator || f seamstress; sewing machine (for bookbinding); **cucitrice a grappe** stapler

cuci·to -ta adj sewn || m sewing; needle work

cucitura f seam; sewing; stitches

cu·cù m (-cù) cuckoo

cuculo m or **cùculo** m cuckoo

cùffia f bonnet (for baby); coif; (rad) headset; (telp) headpiece; (theat) prompter's box

cugi·no -na mf cousin

cui pron invar whose; to which; whom; which; of whom; of which; **per cui** (coll) therefore

culatta f breech (of a gun)

culinà·rio -ria (-ri -rie) adj culinary || f gastronomy

culla f cradle

cullare tr to rock (a baby); (fig) to delude || ref to have delusions

culminante adj highest; culminating

culminare (cùlmino) intr to culminate

cùlmine m top, summit

culo m (vulg) behind; (slang) bottom (of glass or bottle); **culi di bicchiere** (coll) fake diamonds

cul·to -ta adj cultivated; learned (e.g., word) || m cult, worship

cul·tóre -trice mf devotee

cultura f culture; **cultura fisica** physical culture

culturale adj cultural

cumino m (bot) caraway seed; (bot) cumin

cumulati·vo -va adj cumulative

cùmulo *m* heap, pile; concurrence (*of penal sentences*); cumulus

cuna *f* cradle

cùneo *m* wedge; chock; (archit) voussoir

cunétta *f* ditch; gutter

cunicolo *m* small tunnel; burrow

cuòcere §144a *tr* to cook; to bake (*bricks*); to burn, dry up; (fig) to stew ‖ *intr* to cook; to burn; to dry up; (with *dat*) to grieve, to pain

cuò·co -ca *mf* (**-chi -che**) cook

cuòio *m* (**cuòi**) leather; **avere il cuoio duro** to have a tough hide; **cuoio capelluto** scalp ‖ *m* (**cuoia** *fpl*) (archaic) leather; **tirare le cuoia** (slang) to croak, to kick the bucket

cuòre *m* heart; **avere il cuore da coniglio** to be chicken-hearted; **avere il cuore da leone** to be lion-hearted; **cuori** (cards) hearts; **di cuore** gladly; heartily; **fare cuore a** to encourage; **stare a cuore** to be important

cupidìgia *f* cupidity, greed, covetousness

Cupìdo *m* Cupid

cùpi·do -da *adj* greedy, covetous

cu·po -pa *adj* dark; deep (*color, voice*); sad, gloomy

cùpola *f* dome, cupola; crown (*of hat*)

cura *f* care; interest; cure; ministry; (poet) anxiety; **a cura di** edited by (*e.g., text*)

curare *tr* to take care of; to heed ‖ *intr* to see to it ‖ *ref* to take care of oneself; to care; to deign; **curarsi di** to care for

curatèla *f* (law) guardianship

curati·vo -va *adj* curative

cura·to -ta *adj* cured; healed ‖ *m* curate

cura·tóre -trice *mf* curator; trustee; editor (*of critical edition*); receiver (*in bankruptcy*)

curculióne *m* (ent) weevil

cur·do -da *adj* & *mf* Kurd

cùria *f* curia; bar

curiale *adj* curia; legal

curialé·sco -sca *adj* (**-schi -sche**) hairsplitting, legalistic

curiosare [s] (**curióso**) *intr* to pry around, snoop; to browse around

curiosi·tà [s] *f* (**-tà**) curiosity; whim; curio

curió·so -sa [s] *adj* curious; bizarre, quaint

curro *m* roller

cursóre *m* process server; court messenger; slide (*of slide ruler*)

curva *f* curve, bend; sweep; **curva di livello** contour line

curvare *tr* to curve, bend; **curvare la fronte** to bow down, yield ‖ *intr* to curve (*said of a road*); to take a curve, negotiate a curve ‖ *ref* to curve, bend; to bow; to become bent; to warp

curvatura *f* curving, bending; warp; stoop, curvature; camber

cur·vo -va *adj* bent, curved ‖ *f* see **curva**

cuscinétto *m* small pillow; pad (*for ink*); buffer (*zone*); (mach) bearing; **cuscinetto a rulli** roller bearing; **cuscinetto a sfere** ball bearing

cuscino *m* pillow; cushion

cùspide *f* point (*e.g., of arrow*); (archit) steeple

custòde *adj* guardian (*angel*) ‖ *m* custodian; janitor; warden; guard; (coll) policeman, cop

custòdia *f* safekeeping, custody; case (*e.g., of violin*); trust; (mach) housing

custodìre §176 *tr* to keep; to protect, guard; to be in charge of (*prisoners*); to take care of; to cherish (*a memory*)

cutàne·o -a *adj* cutaneous

cute *f* (anat) skin

cuticagna *f* (joc) nape of the neck

cutìcola *f* epidermis; cuticle; dentine

cutireazióne *f* skin test (*for allergic reactions*)

cutréttola *f* (orn) wagtail

D

D, d [di] *m* & *f* fourth letter of the Italian alphabet

da *prep* from; to; at; on; through; between; since; with; by, e.g., **è stato arrestato dalla polizia** he was arrested by the police; worth, e.g., **un libro da mille lire** a book worth a thousand lire; worthy of, e.g., **azione da gentiluomo** action worthy of a gentleman; at the house, office, shop, etc., of, e.g., **dal pittore** at the house of the painter; **da Giovanni** at John's; **dall'avvocato** at the lawyer's office; **d'altro lato** on the other hand; **d'ora in poi** from now on

dabbasso *adv* downstairs; down below

dabbenàggine *f* simplicity, foolishness

dabbène *adj invar* honest, upright, e.g., **un uomo dabbene** an honest man; simple, foolish, e.g., **un dabben uomo** a Simple Simon

daccanto *adv* near, nearby

daccapo *adv* again, all over again; **andar daccapo** to begin a new paragraph; **daccapo a piedi** from top to bottom

dacché *conj* since

dado *m* cube; pedestal (*of column*); (mach) nut; (mach) die (*to cut threads*); **dadi** dice; **giocare ai dadi** to shoot craps; **il dado è tratto** the die is cast

daffare *m* things to do; bustle; **darsi daffare** to bustle, bustle about

da·ga *f* (**-ghe**) dagger

dagli §4 ‖ *interj*—**dagli al ladro!** stop thief!; **e dagli!** cut it out!

dài §4

dài·no -na *mf* fallow deer ‖ *m* fallow deer; buckskin

dal §4

dàlia *f* dahlia

dalla §4

dallato *adv* aside; sideways

dalle §4

dalli *interj*—**dalli al ladro!** stop thief!; **e dalli!** cut it out!

dallo §4

dàlma·ta *adj & mf* (**-ti -te**) Dalmatian

Dalmàzia, la Dalmatia

daltòni·co -ca *adj* (**-ci -che**) color-blind

daltonismo *m* color blindness

dama *f* lady; dancing partner; checkers; **andare a dama** (checkers) to be crowned; **dama di compagnia** companion; **dama di corte** lady-in-waiting

damare *tr* (checkers) to crown

damascare §197 *tr* to damask

damaschinare *tr* to damascene

dama·sco *m* (**-schi**) damask ‖ **Damasco** *f* Damascus

damerino *m* fop, dandy

damigèlla *f* (lit) damsel; (orn) demoiselle; **damigella d'onore** bridesmaid

damigiana *f* demijohn

danaro *m* var of **denaro**

danaró·so -sa [s] *adj* wealthy, rich

dande *fpl* leading strings

danése [s] *adj* Danish ‖ *mf* Dane ‖ *m* Danish (*language*); Great Dane

Danimarca, la Denmark

dannare, tr to damn; to bedevil ‖ *ref* to be damned; to fret

danna·to -ta *adj* damned; wicked; terrible (*e.g., fear*) ‖ *m* damned soul

dannazione *f* damnation

danneggiare §290 (**dannéggio**) *tr* to damage; to injure, impair

danneggia·to -ta *adj* damaged; injured, impaired ‖ *mf* victim

danno *m* damage; injury; (ins) loss; **chiedere i danni** to ask for indemnification; **far danni a** to damage; **rifare i danni a** to indemnify; **tuo danno** so much the worse for you

dannó·so -sa [s] *adj* damaging, harmful

dante *m*—**pelle di dante** buckskin

danté·sco -sca *adj* (**-schi -sche**) Dantean, Dantesque

danti·sta *mf* (**-sti -ste**) Dante scholar

Danùbio *m* Danube

danza *f* dance; dancing

danzare *tr & intr* to dance

danza·tóre -trice *mf* dancer

dappertutto *adv* everywhere

dappiè *adv*—**dappiè di** at the foot of

dappiù *adv*—**dappiù di** more than

dappòco *adj invar* worthless

dappòi *adv* (obs) afterwards, after

dapprèsso *adv* near, nearby, close

dapprima *adv* first, in the first place

dapprincìpio *adv* first, in the beginning; over again

dardeggiare §290 (**dardéggio**) *tr* to hurl darts at; to beat down on; to look daggers at ‖ *intr* to hurl darts; to beat down

dardo *m* dart, arrow; tip (*of blowtorch*)

da·re *m* (**-re**) (com) debit; **dare e avere** debit and credit ‖ §144b *tr* to give; to set (*fire*); to hand over; to lay down (*one's life*); to render (*e.g., unto Caesar*); to give away (*a bride*); to take (*an examination*); to tender (*one's resignation*); to say (*good night*); to shed (*tears*); **dare acqua a** to water; **dare alla luce** to give birth to; to bring out (*e.g., a book*); **dare aria a** to air; **dare . . . anni a qlcu** to think that s.o. is . . . years old; **dare a ridire** to give rise to complaint; **dare a intendere** to lead to believe; **dare da intendere** to lead to believe; **dare fastidio a** to bother, annoy; **dare fondo a** to use up; **dare gli otto giorni a** to dismiss, fire; **dare il benvenuto a** to welcome; **dare il via a** to start (*e.g., a race*); **dare la colpa a** to declare guilty; to put the blame on; **dare la mano a** to shake hands with; **dare l'assalto a** to assault; **dare luogo a** to give rise to; **dare noia a** to bother; **dare per certo a** to assure; **dare ragione a** to agree with; **dare torto a** to disagree with; **dare via** to give away ‖ *intr* to burst; to begin; to beat down (*said of the sun*); **dare a** to verge on; to face, overlook; **dare addosso a** to attack, persecute; **dare ai** or **sui nervi di** to irritate, irk; **dare alla testa a** to go to one's head, e.g., **il vino gli dà alla testa** wine goes to his head; **dare contro a** to disagree with; **dare del ladro a** to call (s.o.) a thief; **dare del Lei a** to address formally; **dare del tu a** to address familiarly; **dare di volta il cervello a** to go raving mad, e.g., **gli ha dato di volta il cervello** he went raving mad; **dare giù** to abate; **dare in** to hit; **dare in affitto** to rent, lease; **dare nell'occhio** to attract attention; to hit the eye; **dare nel segno** to hit the target ‖ *ref* to put on, e.g., **darsi la cipria** to put powder on; **darsela a gambe** to take to one's heels; **darsela per intesa** to become convinced; to take for granted; **darsele** to strike one another; **darsi a** to give oneself over to; **darsi delle arie** to put on airs; **darsi il vanto di** to boast of; **darsi un bacio** to kiss one another; **darsi la mano** to shake hands; **darsi la morte** to commit suicide; **darsi pace** to resign oneself; **darsi pensiero** to worry; **darsi per malato** to declare oneself ill; to fall ill; **darsi per vinto** to give in, submit; **può darsi** it's possible, maybe; **si dà il caso** it happens

dàrsena *f* dock; basin

data *f* date; deal (*of cards*); **a . . . data** (com) . . . days hence, on or before . . . days; **di fresca data** new (*e.g., friend*); **di vecchia data** old (*e.g., friend*)

datare *tr* to date ‖ *intr*—**a datare da** beginning with

datà·rio *m* (**-ri**) date stamp

dati·vo -va *adj & m* dative

da·to -ta *adj* inclined, bent; addicted; given; appointed (*date*); **dato e non concesso** assumed for the sake of argument; **dato che** since || *m* datum || *f* see **data**

da·tóre -trice *mf* giver, donor; **datore di lavoro** employer; **datore di sangue** blood donor; **datori di lavoro** management

dàttero *m* date; (zool) date shell

dattilografare (dattilògrafo) *tr* to typewrite, type

dattilografia *f* typewriting

dattilògra·fo -fa *mf* typist

dattiloscopia *f* examination of fingerprints

dattiloscrit·to -ta *adj* typewritten || *m* typescript

dattórno *adv* near, nearby; **darsi dattorno** to strive; **stare dattorno a** to cling to; **togliersi dattorno qlcu** to get rid of s.o.

davanti *adj invar* fore, front || **davan·ti** *m* (-ti) front, face || *adv* ahead, in front; **davanti a** in front of; **levarsi davanti a qlcu** to get out of someone's way; **passare davanti a** to pass, outstrip

davanzale *m* window sill

davanzo *adv* more than enough

davvéro *adv* indeed; **dire davvero** to speak in earnest

daziare §287 *tr* to levy a duty on

dà·zio *m* (-zi) duty, custom; custom office

dèa *f* goddess

debellare (debèllo) *tr* (lit) to crush

debilitare (debìlito) *tr* to debilitate

debilitazióne *f* debilitation

débi·to -ta *adj* due || *m* debit; debt; **debito pubblico** national debt

debi·tóre -trice *mf* debtor

débole *adj* weak; faint; gentle (*sex*); **debole di mente** feeble-minded || *m* weakness, weak point; weakness, foible; weakling

debolézza *f* weakness, debility

debordare (debórdo) *intr* (ESSERE & AVERE) to overflow

debòscia *f* debauchery

deboscia·to -ta *adj* debauched || *mf* debauchee

debuttante *adj* beginning || *mf* beginner || *f* debutante

debuttare *intr* to come out, make one's debut; (theat) to perform for the first time; (theat) to open

debutto *m* debut; (theat) opening night, opening

dècade *f* ten; period of ten days; (mil) ten days' pay

decadènte *adj* & *m* decadent

decadènza *f* decadence; lapse (*of insurance policy*); (law) forfeiture

decadére §121 *intr* (ESSERE) to decline; to lose one's standing; (ins) to lapse; **decadere da** (law) to forfeit

decadiménto *m* decadence; (law) forfeiture

decadu·to -ta *adj* fallen upon hard times

decaffeinizzare [ddzz] *tr* to decaffeinate

decalcificatóre *m* water softener

decalcomania *f* decalcomania

decàlo·go *m* (-ghi) decalogue

decampare *intr* to decamp; **decampare da** to abandon (*a plan*)

decano *m* dean

decantare *tr* to praise, extol; to decant; (lit) to purify || *intr* to undergo decantation

decapàggio *m* (metallurgy) pickling

decapitare (decàpito) *tr* to behead, decapitate

decapitazióne *f* beheading

decappottàbile *adj* & *f* (aut) convertible

decèdere §123 *intr* (ESSERE) to die; to decease

decelerare (decèlero) *tr* & *intr* to decelerate

decennale *adj* & *m* decennial

decènne *adj* & *mf* ten-year-old

decèn·nio *m* (-ni) decade

decènte *adj* decent; proper

decentralizzare [ddzz] *tr* to decentralize

decentrare (decèntro) *tr* to decentralize

decènza *f* decency; propriety

decèsso *m* decease, demise

decidere §145 *tr* to decide; to persuade || *intr* & *ref* to decide; **deciditi!** make up your mind!

decifràbile *adj* decipherable

decifrare *tr* to decipher, decode; (fig) to puzzle out (*e.g., somebody's intentions*); (mus) to sight-read

dècima *f* tithe

decimale *adj* & *m* decimal

decimare (dècimo) *tr* to decimate

dècimetro *m* decimeter; **doppio decimetro** ruler

dèci·mo -ma *adj, m* & *pron* tenth || *f* see **decima**

decisionale *adj* decision-making

decisióne *f* decision

decisi·vo -va *adj* decisive, conclusive

deci·so -sa *adj* determined, resolute; appointed (*time*)

declamare *tr* to declaim || *intr* to declaim; to inveigh

declamazióne *f* declamation

declaratò·rio -ria *adj* (-ri -rie) declarative

declinare *tr* to decline; to declare, show; (gram) to decline; (lit) to bend || *intr* to set (*said, e.g., of a star*); to slope; to diminish

declinazióne *f* declination; (gram) declension

declino *m* decline

decli·vio *m* (-vi) declivity, slope

decollàg·gio *m* (-gi) take-off; lift-off

decollare (decòllo) *tr* to decapitate || *intr* (aer) to take off; (rok) to lift off

decòllo *m* take-off; lift-off

decolorante *adj* bleaching || *m* bleach

decompórre §218 *tr, intr* & *ref* to decompose

decomposizióne *f* decomposition

decompressióne *f* decompression

decongelare (decongèlo) *tr* to thaw; (com) to unfreeze

decontaminare (decontàmino) *tr* to decontaminate

decorare (decòro) *tr* to decorate

decorati·vo -va *adj* decorative

decora·tóre -trice *mf* decorator

decorazióne *f* decoration

decòro *m* decorum, propriety; decor; dignity; decoration

decoró·so -sa [s] *adj* fitting, decorous, proper; dignified

decorrènza *f* beginning, effective date; lapse

decórrere §139 *intr* (ESSERE) to elapse; to begin; (lit) to run; **a decorrere da** effective, beginning with

decór·so -sa *adj* past ‖ *m* period, span; course; development; **nel decorso di** in the course of

decòt·to -ta *adj* (com) insolvent ‖ *m* decoction

decozióne *f* (com) insolvency

decrèpi·to -ta *adj* decrepit

decréscere §142 *intr* (ESSERE) to decrease

decretare (**decréto**) *tr* to decree

decréto *m* decree; **decreto legge** decree law

decùbito *m* recumbency

decuplicare §197 (**decùplico**) *tr* to multiply tenfold

dècu·plo -pla *adj* tenfold ‖ *m* tenfold part

decurtare *tr* to diminish, decrease

decurtazióne *f* decrease

dèda·lo -la *adj* (lit) ingenious ‖ *m* maze, labyrinth

dèdi·ca *f* (-che) dedication; inscription (*in a book*)

dedicare §197 (**dèdico**) *tr* to dedicate; to inscribe (*a book*) ‖ *ref* to devote oneself

dèdi·to -ta *adj* devoted; addicted

dedizióne *f* devotion; (obs) surrender

dedurre §102 *tr* to deduce; to deduct; to derive; (hist) to found (*a colony*)

deduzióne *f* deduction

defalcàbile *adj* deductible

defalcare §197 *tr* to deduct, withhold

defal·co *m* (-chi) deduction, withholding

defecare §197 (**defèco**) *tr* (chem) to purify ‖ *intr* to defecate

defenestrare (**defenèstro**) *tr* to throw out of the window; (fig) to fire; (pol) to unseat

defenestrazióne *f* defenestration; (fig) firing, dismissal

deferènte *adj* deferential; (anat) deferent

deferènza *f* deference

deferire §176 *tr* to submit; (law) to commit; **deferire il giuramento a qlcu** to put s.o. under oath ‖ *intr* to defer

defezionare (**defezióno**) *intr* to desert, defect

defezióne *f* defection

deficiènte *adj* deficient, lacking ‖ *mf* idiot

deficiènza *f* deficiency; idiocy

dèfi·cit *m* (-cit) deficit

deficità·rio -ria *adj* (-ri -rie) lacking; deficit (*e.g., budget*)

defilare *tr* to defilade ‖ *ref* to protect oneself

denfinìbile *adj* definable

definire §176 *tr* to define; to settle (*an argument*)

definiti·vo -va *adj* definitive; **in definitiva** after all

definì·to -ta *adj* definite

definizióne *f* definition; settlement (*of an argument*)

deflagrare *intr* to burst into flame; (fig) to burst out

deflazionare (**deflazióno**) *tr* (com) to deflate

deflazióne *f* deflation

deflèttere §177 *intr* to deflect

deflettóre *m* (aut) vent window; (mach) baffle

deflorare (**deflòro**) *tr* to deflower

defluire §176 *intr* (ESSERE) to flow down; (fig) to pour out

deflusso *m* flow; outflow, outpour; ebbtide

deformare (**defórmo**) *tr* to deform; to cripple; to alter (*a word*)

defórme *adj* deformed, crippled

deformi·tà *f* (-tà) deformity

defraudare (**defràudo**) *tr* to defraud, bilk

defun·to -ta *adj* dead; deceased; defunct; late ‖ *mf* dead person, deceased ‖ *m* deceased; **i defunti** the deceased

degenerare (**degènero**) *intr* (ESSERE & AVERE) to degenerate; to worsen

degenera·to -ta *adj* degenerate, perverted ‖ *mf* degenerate, pervert

degenerazióne *f* degeneracy, degeneration

degènere *adj* degenerate

degènte *adj* bedridden; hospitalized ‖ *mf* patient; inpatient

degènza *f* confinement; hospitalization

dégli §4

deglutire §176 *tr* to swallow

degnare (**dégno**) *tr* to honor ‖ *ref* to deign, condescend

degnazióne *f* condescension

dé·gno -gna *adj* worthy; **degno di nota** noteworthy

degradante *adj* degrading

degradare *tr* to degrade; to downgrade; (mil) to break ‖ *ref* to become degraded

degradazióne *f* degradation

degustare *tr* to taste

degustazióne *f* tasting

dèh *interj* oh!

déi §4

deiezióne *f* excrement; (geol) detritus

deificare §197 (**deìfico**) *tr* to deify

dei·tà *f* (-tà) deity

dél §4

dela·tóre -trice *mf* informer

delazióne *f* informing; (law) administration of an oath

dèle·ga *f* (-ghe) proxy, power of attorney

delegare §209 (**dèlego**) *tr* to delegate

delega·to -ta *adj* delegated ‖ *m* delegate; (eccl) legate

delegazióne *f* delegation

deletè·rio -ria *adj* (-ri -rie) deleterious

delfino *m* dolphin; (hist) dauphin

delibare *tr* to relish; to touch on; to ratify (*a foreign decree*)

delibazióne *f* ratification (*of a foreign decree*)

deliberare (delìbero) *tr* to deliberate; to decide; to award (*at auction*) || *intr* to deliberate

delìbera·to -ta *adj* deliberate; resolved

deliberazióne *f* deliberation; decision

delicatézza *f* delicacy; gentleness; tactfulness; luxury

delica·to -ta *adj* delicate; gentle; tactful

delimitare (delìmito) *tr* to delimit

delineare (delìneo) *tr* to outline, sketch || *ref* to take shape; to appear

delinquènte *m* criminal

delinquènza *f* delinquency; **delinquenza minorile** juvenile delinquency

delìnquere §146 *intr* to commit a crime

delì·quio *m* (-qui) fainting spell, swoon; **cadere in deliquio** to faint

delirare *intr* to be delirious; to rave; (*lit*) to stray

delì·rio *m* (-ri) delirium; frenzy; **andare in delirio** to go wild; **cadere in delirio** to become delirious

delitto *m* crime

delittuó·so -sa [s] *adj* criminal

delìzia *f* delight; (*hort*) Delicious (*variety of apple*)

deliziare §287 *tr & ref* to delight

delizió·so -sa [s] *adj* delicious; delightful

délla §4

délle §4

déllo §4

dèl·ta *m* (-ta) delta

delucidare (delùcido) *tr* to elucidate; to remove the sheen from

delucidazióne *f* elucidation; removal of sheen

delùdere §105 *tr* to disappoint; to deceive; to foil

delusióne *f* disappointment; deception

delu·so -sa *adj* disappointed; deceived

demagnetizzare [ddzz] *tr* to demagnetize

demagogìa *f* demagogy

demagò·go *m* (-ghi) demagogue

demandare *tr* (law) to commit

demà·nio *m* (-ni) state land, state property

demarcare §197 *tr* to demarcate

demarcazióne *f* demarcation

demènte *adj* demented, crazy; idiotic || *mf* insane person; idiot

demènza *f* insanity, madness; idiocy

demèrito *m* demerit

demilitarizzare [ddzz] *tr* to demilitarize

democràti·co -ca (-ci -che) *adj* democratic || *mf* democrat

democrazìa *f* democracy || **Democrazia Cristiana** Christian Democratic Party

democristia·no -na *adj* Christian Democratic || *mf* Christian Democrat

demogràfi·co -ca *adj* (-ci -che) demographic

demolire §176 *tr* to demolish

demoli·tóre -trice *adj* wrecking; destructive || *mf* wrecker

demolizióne *f* demolition

dèmone *m* demon

demonìa·co -ca *adj* (-ci -che) fiendish; demoniacal

demò·nio *m* (-ni) demon; **avere il demonio addosso** to be full of the devil

demoralizzare [ddzz] *tr* to demoralize || *ref* to become demoralized

demoralizza·to -ta [ddzz] *adj* demoralized, dejected

denaro *m* money; denier (*of nylon thread*); **avere il denaro contato** to be short of money; **denari** suit of Neapolitan cards corresponding to diamonds

denatura·to -ta *adj* denatured

denegare §209 (**dènego** or **denégo**) *tr* to deny

denigrare *tr* to denigrate; to backbite

denominare (denòmino) *tr* to call, designate

denomina·tóre -trice *adj* designating || *m* denominator

denominazióne *f* denomination; designation

denotare (denòto) *tr* to denote

densi·tà *f* (-tà) density

dèn·so -sa *adj* dense, thick

dentale *adj & f* dental

dentare (dènto) *tr* to notch, scallop || *intr* to teethe

dentaruòlo *m* teething ring

denta·to -ta *adj* toothed

dentatura *f* set of teeth; teeth (*of gear*)

dènte *m* tooth; peak (*of mountain*); pang (*of jealousy*); fluke (*of anchor*); prong (*of fork*); **battere i denti** to shiver; **dente canino** canine tooth; **dente del giudizio** wisdom tooth; **dente di latte** baby tooth; **dente di leone** (bot) dandelion; **mettere i denti** to teethe

dentellare (dentèllo) *tr* to notch, scallop; to perforate (*stamps*)

dentellatura *f* notch; perforation (*of postage stamps*); (archit) denticulation

dentèllo *m* notch, scallop; lace; (archit) dentil

dentièra *f* denture, plate; cog

dentifrì·cio -cia (-ci -cie) *adj* tooth || *m* dentifrice

denti·sta *mf* (-sti -ste) dentist

dentizióne *f* teething

déntro *adv* inside, in; **dentro di** inside of; within; **essere dentro** (coll) to be behind bars; **in dentro** inward || *prep* inside of

denuclearizzare [ddzz] *tr* to denuclearize

denudare *tr* to denude; to strip; (lit) to unveil

denunciare §128 *tr* var of **denunziare**

denùnzia *f* denunciation; announcement; report

denunziare §287 *tr* to denounce; to accuse; to announce; to report

denutrì·to -ta *adj* undernourished

denutrizióne *f* undernourishment

deodorante *adj & m* deodorant

deodorare (deodóro) *tr* to deodorize

depauperare (depàupero) *tr* to impoverish

depennare (depénno) *tr* to strike out, expunge

deperìbile *adj* perishable

deperiménto *m* deterioration; decline

deperire §176 *intr* (ESSERE) to deteriorate; to perish; to decay

depilató·rio -ria *adj & m* (**-ri -rie**) depilatory

deplorare (**deplòro**) *tr* to deplore; to reproach

deploré·vole *adj* deplorable; reproachable

depolarizzare [ddzz] *tr* to depolarize

depórre §218 *tr* to lay; to lay down (*crown, arms*); to depose (*e.g., a king*); to take off (*clothes*); to give up (*hope*); to renounce; **deporre l'abito talare** to doff the cassock

deportare (**depòrto**) *tr* to deport

deporta·to -ta *adj* deported ‖ *mf* deportee

deportazióne *f* deportation

depositare (**depòsito**) *tr* to deposit; to register, check ‖ *intr* to settle (*said, e.g., of sand*)

depositá·rio -ria (**-ri -rie**) *adj* deposit ‖ *mf* depositary

depòsito *m* deposit; checking (*e.g., of a suitcase*); registration; heap (*e.g., of refuse*); warehouse; morgue; receiving ward; (mil) depot; **deposito bagagli** baggage room

deposizióne *f* deposition; Descent from the Cross

deprava·to -ta *adj* depraved

depravazióne *f* depravation

deprecare §197 (**dprèco**) *tr* to deprecate

depredare (**deprèdo**) *tr* to plunder

depredazióne *f* depredation

depressióne *f* depression

deprès·so -sa *adj* depressed

deprezzaménto *m* depreciation

deprezzare (**deprèzzo**) *tr* to depreciate; to underestimate ‖ *intr* (ESSERE) to depreciate

deprimènte *adj* depressing

deprimere §131 *tr* to humble, discourage; to depress

depurare *tr* to purify

deputare (**dèputo**) *tr* to deputize, delegate

deputa·to -ta *mf* deputy, delegate; representative

deputazióne *f* deputation, delegation

deragliaménto *m* derailment

deragliare §280 *intr* to be derailed, to run off the track

derapàg·gio *m* (**-gi**) skidding

derapare *intr* to skid

derelit·to -ta *adj & mf* derelict

derelizióne *f* dereliction

dereta·no -na *adj & m* posterior

deridere §231 *tr* to deride, mock

derisióne *f* derision, ridicule

derisò·rio -ria *adj* (**-ri -rie**) derisory, derisive

deriva *f* (aer) vertical stabilizer; (aer, naut) leeway; (naut) drift; **alla deriva** adrift

derivare *tr* to derive; to branch off (*e.g., a canal*) ‖ *intr* (ESSERE) to be derived, arise; to drift

deriva·to -ta *adj* derivative ‖ *m* derivative (*word*) ‖ *f* (math) derivative

derivazióne *f* derivation; (elec) shunt; (telp) extension

dermatòlo·go *m* (**-gi**) dermatologist

dermòlde *f* imitation leather

dèro·ga *f* (**-ghe**) exception; **in deroga a** deviating from

derogare §209 (**dèrogo**) *intr* to transgress; **derogare a** to deviate from

derrata *f* foodstuff; **derrate** foodstuff, produce

derubare *tr* to rob

dèr·vis *m* (**-vis**) or **dervì·scio** *m* (**-sci**) dervish

desalazióne [s] *f* desalinization

desalificare [s] §197 (**desalífico**) *tr* to desalt

dé·sco *m* (**-schi**) dinner table; meal

descritti·vo -va *adj* descriptive

descrìvere §250 *tr* to describe

descrizióne *f* description

desegregazióne [s] *f* desegregation

desensibilizzare [s] [ddzz] *tr* to desensitize

desèrti·co -ca *adj* (**-ci -che**) desert, wild

desèr·to -ta *adj* deserted; **andare deserto** to be unattended ‖ *m* desert

desideràbile [s] *adj* desirable

desiderare (**desìdero**) [s] *tr* to desire; **farsi desiderare** to make oneself scarce; to be dilatory

desidè·rio [s] *m* (**-ri**) desire; craving; lust; **lasciar desiderio di sé** to be greatly missed

desideró·so -sa [s] *adj* desirous

designare [s] *tr* to designate

designazióne [s] *f* designation

desinare *m* dinner ‖ *intr* to dine

desinènza *f* (gram) ending

desì·o *m* (**-ì**) (lit) desire

desìstere §114 *intr* to desist

desolante *adj* distressing

desolare (**dèsolo**) *tr* to distress; (lit) to devastate

desola·to -ta *adj* desolate; distressed

desolazióne *f* desolation; distress

dèspo·ta *m* (**-ti**) despot

despòti·co -ca *adj* (**-ci -che**) var of **dispotico**

despotismo *m* var of **dispotismo**

des·sèrt *m* (**-sèrt**) dessert

destare (**désto**) *tr* to awaken; to stir up ‖ *ref* to wake up

destinare *tr* to destine; to assign; to address

destinatà·rio -ria *mf* (**-ri -rie**) consignee; addressee

destinazióne *f* destination; assignment

destino *m* destiny; (com) destination

destituire §176 *tr* to demote; to dismiss; to deprive

destituzióne *f* demotion; dismissal

dé·sto -sta *adj* awake; (fig) wide-awake

dèstra *f* right, right hand

destreggiare §290 (**destréggio**) *intr* to maneuver ‖ *ref* to manage shrewdly

destrézza *f* skill, dexterity

destrière or **destrièro** *m* (lit) steed

dè·stro -stra *adj* right; skillful ‖ *f* see **destra**

destròr·so -sa *adj* clockwise; right-hand; (bot) dextrorse

destròsio *m* dextrose

desùmere [s] §116 *tr* to obtain; to infer

detecti·ve *m* (-ve) detective

detèc·tor *m* (-tor) (rad) detector

detenére §271 *tr* to hold; to detain

deten·tóre -trice *mf* holder; receiver (*of stolen goods*)

detenu·to -ta *mf* prisoner

detenzióne *f* illegal possession; detention

detergènte *adj & m* detergent

detèrgere §164 (*pp* detèrso) *tr* to cleanse; to wipe

deterioràbile *adj* perishable

deteriorare (deterióro) *tr* to spoil || *intr* (ESSERE) & *ref* to deteriorate, spoil

determinare (detèrmino) *tr* to determine; to fix; to decide; to cause || *ref* to decide; to happen

determinatézza *f* determination; precision

determinati·vo -va *adj* (gram) definite

determina·to -ta *adj* given; resolved, determined

determinazióne *f* determination

deterrènte *adj & m* deterrent

detersi·vo -va *adj* cleansing || *m* cleanser; detergent

detestàbile *adj* detestable

detestare (detèsto) *tr* to detest

detettóre *m* detector; **detettore di bugie** lie detector

detonare (detòno) *intr* to explode, detonate

detonatóre *m* blasting cap, detonator

detonazióne *f* detonation; report

detrarre §273 *tr* to take away; (lit) to detract

detrat·tóre -trice *mf* detractor

detrazióne *f* detraction; deduction

detriménto *m* detriment

detrito *m* debris; detritus; (fig) outcast, outlaw

detronizzare [ddzz] *tr* to dethrone

détta *f*—**a detta di** according to

dettagliante *m* retailer

dettagliare §280 *tr* to tell in detail; to itemize; to retail || *intr*—**pregasi dettagliare** please send detailed information

dettà·glio *m* (-gli) detail; retail

dettame *m* (lit) law, norm

dettare (détto) *tr* to dictate; (lit) to compose, write; **dettar legge** to impose one's will

dettato *m* dictation; (lit) style

dettatura *f* dictation

dét·to -ta *adj* called, named; **detto (e) fatto** no sooner said than done || *m* saying || *f* see **detta**

deturpare *tr* to disfigure, mar

deturpazióne *f* disfigurement, disfiguration

devalutazióne *f* devaluation

devastare *tr* to devastate, lay waste; (fig) to disfigure

devasta·tóre -trice *adj* devastating || *m* devastator

devastazióne *f* devastation

deviaménto *m* switching; derailment; (fig) straying

deviare §119 *tr* to turn aside; to lead astray; (rr) to switch; (rr) to derail

|| *intr* to deviate; to wander; to go astray; (rr) to run off the track

deviatóre *m* (rr) switchman; (elec) two-way switch

deviazióne *f* deviation; detour; curvature (*of the spine*); (phys) declination; (phys) deflection; (rr) switching

deviazionismo *m* deviationism

deviazioni·sta *mf* (-sti -ste) deviationist

devoluzióne *f* transfer

devòlvere §147 *tr* to transfer || *intr & ref* (lit) to roll down

devò·to -ta *adj* devoted; devout, pious || *m* devout person; worshiper

devozióne *f* devotion

di §4 *prep* of; in, e.g., **la più bella della famiglia** the prettiest one in the family; (*with definite article*) some, e.g., **mi occorrono dei fiammiferi** I need some matches; than, e.g., **più veloce del baleno** faster than lightning; from, e.g., **è di Milano** he is from Milan; off, e.g., **smontare di sella** to get off the saddle; about, e.g., **discutere di politica** to talk about politics; with, e.g., **ornare di fiori** to adorn with flowers; made of, e.g., **una casa di mattoni** a house made of bricks; by, e.g., **di notte** by night; for, e.g., **amor di patria** love for one's country; worth, e.g., **casa di dieci milioni** house worth ten million; in the amount of, e.g., **multa di mille lire** fine in the amount of one thousand lire; son of, e.g., **Carlo Giovannini di Filippo** Carlo Giovannini son of Philip; daughter of, e.g., **Anna Ponti di Antonio** Anna Ponti daughter of Anthony; **di corsa** running; **di gran lunga** greatly; by far; **di . . . in** from . . . to; **di là da** beyond; **di nascosto** stealthily; **di qua da** on this side of; **di quando in quando** from time to time; **di tre metri** three meters long or wide or high

dì *m* (dì) day; **a dì** (e.g., **ventisei**) this (e.g., twenty-sixth) day; **conciare per il dì delle feste** (coll) to beat up

diabète *m* diabetes

diabèti·co -ca *adj & mf* (-ci -che) diabetic

diabòli·co -ca *adj* (-ci -che) diabolic(al)

diàcono *m* deacon

diadè·ma *m* (-mi) diadem (*of king*); tiara (*of lady*)

diàfa·no -na *adj* diaphanous

diafonìa *f* (telp) cross talk

diafram·ma *m* (-mi) diaphragm; (fig) partition

diàgno·si *f* (-si) diagnosis

diagnosticare §197 (diagnòstico) *tr* to diagnose

diagonale *adj & f* diagonal

diagram·ma *m* (-mi) diagram; chart

diagrammare *tr* to diagram

dialettale *adj* dialectal

dialètti·co -ca (-ci -che) *adj* dialectic(al) || *m* dialectician || *f* dialectic; (philos) dialectics

dialètto *m* dialect

dialettòfo·no -na *adj* dialect-speaking || *m* dialect-speaking person

dialogare §209 (diàlogo) *intr* to carry on a dialogue

dialoga·to -ta *adj* written in the form of a dialogue ‖ *m* dialogue

diàlo·go *m* (-ghi) dialogue

diamante *m* diamond; **diamante tagliavetro** glass cutter

diametrale *adj* diametric(al)

diàmetro *m* diameter

diàmine *interj* good heavens!; the devil!; sure!

diana *f* (mil) reveille ‖ **Diana** *f* Diana

dianzi *adv* (lit) a short while ago

diàpa·son *m* (-son) (mus) pitch; (mus) tuning fork

diapositiva *f* (phot) slide, transparency

dià·rio -ria (-ri -rie) *adj* daily ‖ *m* diary; journal; **diario scolastico** homework book ‖ *f* per diem

diarrèa *f* diarrhea

diascò·pio *m* (-pi) slide projector

diaspro *m* jasper

diàstole *f* diastole

diatermìa *f* diathermy

diatriba *f* diatribe

diavolàc·cio *m* (-ci) devil; **buon diavolaccio** good fellow

diavolerìa *f* deviltry; devilment; evil plot

diavolè·rio *m* (-ri) hubbub, uproar

diavoléto *m* hubbub, uproar

diavolétto *m* little devil, imp

diàvolo *m* devil; **avere il diavolo in corpo** to be nervous; **avere un diavolo per capello** to be in a horrible mood; **buon diavolo** good fellow; **essere come il diavolo e l'acqua santa** to be at opposite poles; **fare il diavolo a quattro** to make a racket; to try very hard

dibàttere *tr* to debate ‖ *ref* to struggle; to writhe

dibattiménto *m* debate; (law) pleading, trial

dibàttito *m* debate

dicastèro *m* department, ministry

dicèmbre *m* December

dicerìa *f* rumor, gossip

dichiarare *tr* to declare, state; to find (*guilty*); to proclaim; to nominate, name ‖ *ref* to declare oneself to be; to declare one's love; to plead (*e.g., guilty*)

dichiarazióne *f* declaration; avowal (*of love*); return (*of income tax*); **dichiarazioni** representations

diciannòve *adj & pron* nineteen; **le diciannove** seven P.M. ‖ *m* nineteen; nineteenth (*in dates*)

diciannovèsi·mo -ma *adj, m & pron* nineteenth

diciassètte *adj & pron* seventeen; **le diciassette** five P.M. ‖ *m* seventeen; seventeenth (*in dates*)

diciassettèsi·mo -ma *adj, m & pron* seventeenth

diciottèsi·mo -ma *adj, m & pron* eighteenth

diciòtto *adj & pron* eighteen; **le diciotto** six P.M. ‖ *m* eighteen; eighteenth (*in dates*)

dici·tóre -trice *mf* reciter

dicitura *f* caption, legend; (lit) wording, language

dicotomìa *f* dichotomy

didascalìa *f* note, notice; caption; legend (*e.g., on coin*); (mov) subtitle

didascàli·co -ca *adj* (-ci -che) didactic

didàtti·co -ca *adj* (-ci -che) *adj* didactic; elementary school (*director, principal*) ‖ *f* didactics

didéntro *m* (coll) inside

didiètro *m* behind; back (*of house*) ‖ *adv* behind

dièci *adj & pron* ten; **le dieci** ten o'clock ‖ *m* ten; tenth (*in dates*)

diecimila *adj, m & pron* ten thousand

diecina *f* about ten

dière·si *f* (-si) dieresis

diè·sis *m* (-sis) (mus) sharp

dièta *f* diet; **dieta idrica** fluid diet

dietèti·co -ca (-ci -che) *adj* dietetic ‖ *f* dietetics

dieti·sta *mf* (-sti -ste) dietitian

diètro *adj invar* back, rear ‖ *m* back, rear ‖ *adv* back, behind; **dal di dietro** from behind; **di dietro** hind (*legs*); back (*side*); behind, back (*e.g., of cupboard*) ‖ *prep* behind; beyond; after; upon; **dietro a** behind; beyond; after; according to; **dietro consegna** on delivery; **dietro domanda** upon application; **dietro versamento** upon payment; **essere dietro a** to be in the process of

dietrofrónt *m* (mil) about face

difatti *adv* indeed

difèndere §148 *tr* to defend, protect ‖ *ref* to protect oneself; (coll) to get along

difensi·vo -va *adj & f* defensive

difen·sóre -sóra *or* **difenditrice** *adj* defense ‖ *mf* defender

difésa [s] *f* defense; bulwark; protection; **legittima difesa** self-defense; **pigliare le difese di** to defend, back up; **venire in difesa di** to go to the defense of

difettare (difètto) *intr* to be lacking; to be defective; **difettare di** to lack

difetti·vo -va *adj* defective

difètto *m* lack; blemish; fault; defect; **essere in difetto** to be at fault; **far difetto a** to lack, e.g., **gli fa difetto il denaro** he lacks money

difettó·so -sa [s] *adj* defective

diffamare *tr* to defame, slander

diffama·tóre -trice *mf* defamer, slanderer

diffamazióne *f* defamation, slander

differènte *adj* different

differènza *f* difference; spread; variance; **a differenza di** unlike; **c'è una bella differenza** it's a horse of another color

differenziale *adj & m* differential

differenziare §287 (differènzio) *tr* to differentiate

differiménto *m* deferment

differire §176 *tr* to postpone, defer ‖ *intr* to be different; to differ

difficile *adj* hard, difficult; awkward (*situation*); hard-to-please; unlikely

|| *mf* hard-to-please person || *m—fare il difficile* to be hard to please; *qui sta il difficile!* here's the trouble!

difficol·tà *f* (*-tà*) difficulty; defect; obstacle; objection

difficoltó·so -sa [*s*] *adj* difficult, troublesome; fastidious

diffida *f* notice; warning

diffidare *tr* to give notice to; to warn || *intr* to mistrust

diffidènte *adj* distrustful

diffidènza *f* mistrust

diffóndere §178 *tr* to spread; to circulate; to broadcast || *ref* to spread; to dwell at length

diffórme *adj* unlike; (*obs*) deformed

diffrazióne *f* diffraction

diffusióne *f* spreading; circulation (*of a newspaper*); diffusion; (*rad*) broadcast

diffu·so -sa *adj* diffuse; widespread

diffusóre *m* diffuser (*to soften light*); baffle (*of loudspeaker*); (*mach*) choke

difilato *adv* forthwith, right away

difrónte *adj invar* in front

difterite *f* diphtheria

di·ga *f* (*-ghe*) dike; dam

digerènte *adj* alimentary (*canal*), digestive (*tube*)

digeribile *adj* digestible

digerire §176 *tr* to digest; to tolerate, stand

digestióne *f* digestion

digesti·vo -va *adj* digestive

digèsto *m* digest

digitale *adj* digital || *f* (*bot*) digitalis

digitalina *f* (*pharm*) digitalin

digiunare *intr* to fast

digiu·no -na *adj* without food; deprived; *digiuno di cognizioni* ignorant; *tenere digiuno* to keep in ignorance || *m* fast; *a digiuno* on an empty stomach; *fare digiuno* to fast

digni·tà *f* (*-tà*) dignity; *dignità fpl* dignitaries

dignità·rio *m* (*-ri*) dignitary

dignitó·so -sa [*s*] *adj* dignified

digradare *tr* to shade (*colors*) || *intr* to slope; to fade

digredire §176 *intr* to digress

digressióne *f* digression

digrignare *tr* to show (*one's or its teeth*); to grit (*one's teeth*)

digrossare (*digròsso*) *tr* to rough-hew; to whittle down; (*fig*) to refine || *ref* to become refined

diguazzare *tr* to beat (*a liquid*) || *intr* to wallow; to splash

dilagare §209 *intr* to flood, to overflow; to spread abroad

dilaniare §287 *tr* to tear to pieces || *ref* to slander one another

dilapidare (*dilàpido*) *tr* to squander

dilatare *tr* to expand; to dilate || *ref* to expand; to spread

dilatazióne *f* expansion; dilation

dilatò·rio -ria *adj* (*-ri -rie*) delaying; dilatory

dilavare *tr* to wash away, erode

dilava·to -ta *adj* dull, flat; wan

dilazionare (*dilazióno*) *tr* to delay, put off; (*com*) to extend

dilazióne *f* delay; (*com*) extension

dileggiare §290 (*diléggio*) *tr* to mock

dilég·gio *m* (*-gi*) mockery, scoffing; *mettere in dileggio* to scoff at

dileguare (*diléguo*) *tr* to scatter || *intr* (ESSERE) to disappear, vanish; to melt

dilèm·ma *m* (*-mi*) dilemma

dilettante *mf* amateur; dilettante

dilettanté·sco -sca *adj* (*-schi -sche*) amateurish

dilettare (*dilètto*) *tr* to delight || *ref* to delight; *dilettarsi a + inf* to delight *in + ger*; *dilettarsi di* to pursue as a hobby, e.g., *si diletta di pittura* he pursues painting as a hobby

dilettévole *adj* delectable, delightful

dilèt·to -ta *adj* beloved || *m* loved one; pleasure; hobby

diligènte *adj* diligent

diligènza *f* diligence; stagecoach

dilucidare (*dilùcido*) *tr* to elucidate

diluire §176 *tr* to dilute

dilungare §209 *tr* (*archaic*) to stretch || *ref* to expatiate; to be ahead by several lengths (*said of a race horse*)

dilungo *m—a un dilungo* more or less

diluviare §287 *tr* to devour || *intr* (ESSERE & AVERE) to rain (*said, e.g., of bullets*) || *impers* (ESSERE)—*diluvia* it is pouring

dilù·vio *m* (*-vi*) deluge, flood; *diluvio universale* Flood

dimagrante *adj* reducing

dimagrare *tr* to thin down || *intr* (ESSERE) to become thin; to lose weight; to become exhausted (*said of land*); (*fig*) to become meager

dimagrire §176 *intr* (ESSERE) to become thin; to lose weight, reduce

dimanda *f* var of **domanda**

dimane *adv* (*coll*) tomorrow

dimani *m* & *adv* var of **domani**

dimenare (*diméno*) *tr* to wag (*the tail*); to beat (*eggs*); to wave (*one's arms*); to stir up (*a question*) || *ref* to toss; to busy oneself

dimensióne *f* dimension; (*fig*) nature

dimenticanza *f* oversight; neglect; *andare in dimenticanza* to be forgotten

dimenticare §197 (*diméntico*) *tr* to forget; to forgive || *ref* to forget; *dimenticarsi di* to forget; to neglect

dimenticatóio *m—mettere nel dimenticatoio* (*coll*) to forget

diménti·co -ca *adj* (*-chi -che*) forgetful; neglectful

dimés·so -sa *adj* humble, modest (*demeanor*); low (*voice*); shabby (*clothes*)

dimestichézza *f* familiarity

dimèttere §198 *tr* to dismiss; to release || *ref* to resign

dimezzare [*ddzz*] (*dimèzzo*) *tr* to halve

diminuire §176 *tr* to lessen, reduce; to lower (*prices*) || *intr* (ESSERE) to diminish

diminuti·vo -va *adj* & *m* diminutive

diminuzióne *f* diminution

dimissionare (*dimissióno*) *tr* to dismiss, discharge || *ref* to resign

dimissionà·rio -ria *adj* (*-ri -rie*) resigning, outgoing

dimissióne f resignation; **dare le dimissioni** to resign

dimól·to -ta adj & m (coll) much || **dimolto** adv (coll) much

dimòra f stay; residence; (lit) delay; **mettere a dimora** to install; to plant (trees); **senza dimora** (lit) without delay; **senza fissa dimora** vagrant

dimorare (dimòro) intr to stay; to reside; (lit) to delay

dimostràbile adj demonstrable

dimostrante m demonstrator

dimostrare (dimóstro) tr to demonstrate; to register (e.g., anger); **dimostrare trent'anni** to look thirty || ref to demonstrate || ref to prove oneself to be

dimostrati·vo -va adj demonstrative; (mil) diverting

dimostra·tóre -trice mf demonstrator

dimostrazióne f demonstration

dinàmi·co -ca (-ci -che) adj dynamic || f dynamics

dinamismo m dynamism

dinamite f dynamite

dìna·mo f (-mo) generator, dynamo

dinanzi adj invar front, e.g., **la porta dinanzi** the front door; preceding, e.g., **il mese dinanzi** the preceding month || adv ahead; beforehand; (lit) before; **dinanzi a** before, in front of

dina·sta m (-sti) dynast

dinastìa f dynasty

dinàsti·co -ca adj (-ci -che) dynastic

dindo m (coll) turkey

dindòn m ding-dong || interj ding-dong! (gait)

diniè·go m (-ghi) denial

dinoccola·to -ta adj gangling; clumsy (gait)

dinosàuro [s] m dinosaur

dintórno m—**dintorni** surroundings, neighborhood || adv around; **dintorno a** around

dì·o -a adj (-i -e) (poet) godly || m (dèi) god; **gli dei the gods** || **Dio** m God; **che Dio la manda** cats and dogs (said of rain); **come Dio volle** at long last; **come Dio vuole** botched (piece of work); **Dio ci scampi!** God forbid!; **Dio santo!** good heavens!; **grazie a Dio** God willing; thank God; **voglia Dio** God grant

dioce·si f (-si) diocese

diòdo m (electron) diode

diomedèa f (orn) albatross

diottrìa f (opt) diopter

dipanare tr to unravel, unwind

dipartiménto m department

dipartire §176 tr (archaic) to divide || intr (diparto) (ESSERE) & ref (lit) to depart

dipartita f (lit) departure; (lit) demise

dipendènte adj dependent || mf employee

dipendènza f dependence; employment; annex; (com) branch; **in dipendenza di** as a consequence of

dipèndere §150 intr (ESSERE) to depend; **dipendere da** to depend on

dipingere §126 tr to paint; **dipingere a olio** to paint in oils; **dipingere a tempera** to distemper || ref to paint one-

self; to put make-up on; to appear, e.g., **gli si dipinse in volto la paura** fear appeared on his face

dipin·to -ta adj painted || m painting, picture

diplò·ma m (-mi) diploma, certificate

diplomare (diplòmo) tr to grant a degree to; to graduate || ref to receive a degree; to graduate

diplomàti·co -ca (-ci -che) adj diplomatic; true, faithful (copy) || m diplomat || f diplomatics

diploma·to -ta adj graduated || mf graduate || m alumnus || f alumna

diplomazìa f diplomacy

dipòi adv after, thereafter

diportare (dipòrto) ref (lit) to behave; (obs) to have a good time

dipòrto m recreation; (obs) sport; **andare a diporto** to go on an outing; to go for a walk

diprèsso adv—**a un dipresso** about, approximately

diradare tr to thin out (vegetation); to disperse; to space out (one's visits) || intr (ESSERE) & ref to diminish; to disperse

diramare tr to prune; to circulate (notices); to issue (a communiqué) || ref to branch out; to spread

diramazióne f branch; ramification; issuance

dire m talk; hearsay; **per sentito dire** by hearsay; **stando al dire** according to his words || §151 tr & intr to say; to tell; to call (e.g., s.o. a genius); to talk; **detto (e) fatto** no sooner said than done; **dica pure!** go ahead!; speak up!; **dire bene di** to speak well of; **dire di no** to say no; **dire di sì** to say yes; **direi quasi** I dare say; **dire la sua** to have one's say; **dire male di** to speak ill of; **dirla grossa** to make a blunder; to tell a tall tale; **dirlo chiaro e tondo** to speak bluntly; **dirne un sacco e una sporta a** to pour insults upon; **è tutto dire** that's all; **non c'è che dire** it's a fact; **non fo per dire** I do not want to boast; **per così dire** so to speak; **per meglio dire** rather; **trovarci a dire** to find fault with; **trovare da dire con** to have words with; **voler ben dire** to be sure; **voler dire** to mean || ref—**dirsela con** to connive with; **si dice** it is said

dirètro m & adv (archaic) behind, back

direttìssima f (rr) high-speed line; **per direttìssima** straight up (in mountain climbing)

direttìssimo m express train

diretti·vo -va adj managerial || m board of directors || f directive; direction; guideline

dirèt·to -ta adj direct; **diretto a** addressed to; directed at; bound for || m through train

diret·tóre -trice mf manager; principal || m director; **direttore di macchina** (naut, nav) chief engineer; **direttore di tiro** (nav) gunnery officer; **direttore di un giornale** editor; **direttore d'or-**

chestra orchestra leader; **direttore responsabile** publisher; **direttore tecnico** (sports) manager ‖ *f* see **direttrice**

direttò·rio -ria (**-ri -rie**) *adj* directorial ‖ *m* directory

direttrice *adj fem* directing; guiding; front (*wheels*) ‖ *f* directress; line of action

direzionale *adj* directional; managerial

direzione *f* direction; management; run (*of events*)

dirigènte *adj* leading; managerial ‖ *m* employer; boss; leader; executive

dirigere §152 *tr* to direct; to turn; to lead ‖ *ref* to address oneself; **dirigersi verso** to head for

dirigìbile *adj & m* dirigible

dirimpètto *adj invar & adv* opposite; **dirimpetto a** opposite to; in comparison with

dirit·to -ta *adj* straight; right; unswerving; (coll) smart ‖ *m* law; obverse, face (*of coin*); fee, dues; (fin) right; **a buon diritto** rightly so; **di diritto** by law; **diritti d'autore** copyright; **diritti di segreteria** registration fee; **diritti doganali** customs duty; **diritti speciali di prelievo** (econ) special drawing rights; **diritto canonico** canon law; **diritto consuetudinario** common law; **diritto internazionale** international law; **in diritto** according to law ‖ *f* right, right hand ‖ **diritto** *adv* straight; **tirare diritto** to go straight ahead

dirittura *f* direction; uprightness; (sports) straightaway, home stretch

dirizzóne *m* blunder

diroccare §197 (**diròcco**) *tr* to knock down ‖ *intr* (ESSERE) (archaic) to fall down

dirocca·to -ta *adj* dilapidated, rickety

dirompènte *adj* fragmentation (*bomb*)

dirottaménto *m* hijacking; skyjacking (*of an airplane*)

dirottare (**diròtto**) *tr* to detour (*traffic*); to hijack (*e.g., a ship*); to skyjack (*an airplane*) ‖ *intr* to change course

dirottatóre *m* hijacker; skyjacker (*of a plane*)

diròt·to -ta *adj* copious, heavy (*rain, tears*); (lit) craggy; **a dirotto** cats and dogs (*said of rain*)

dirozzare [ddzz] (**diròzzo**) *tr* to roughhew; to refine ‖ *ref* to become polished

dirugginire §176 *tr* to take the rust off; to limber up; to gnash (*one's teeth*); to clear (*one's mind*)

dirupa·to -ta *adj* rocky, craggy

dirupo *m* rock; crag, cliff

disabbigliare §280 *tr & ref* to undress, disrobe

disabita·to -ta *adj* uninhabited

disabituare (**disabìtuo**) *tr* to disaccustom ‖ *ref* to become unaccustomed

disaccenta·to -ta *adj* unaccented

disaccòrdo *m* disagreement

disadat·to -ta *adj* unfit

disadór·no -na *adj* unadorned, bare

disaffezionare (**disaffezióno**) *tr* to alien-

ate the affection of; to estrange ‖ *ref* to become estranged

disaffezióne *f* dislike

disagévole *adj* troublesome, uncomfortable

disagiare §290 *tr* to trouble, inconvenience

disagia·to -ta *adj* uncomfortable; needy

disà·gio *m* (**-gi**) discomfort; need

disalberare (**disàlbero**) *tr* to dismast

disambienta·to -ta *adj* bewildered, strange

disàmina *f* examination, scrutiny

disaminare (**disàmino**) *tr* to scrutinize; to weigh

disamorare (**disamóro**) *tr* to alienate the affection of; to estrange ‖ *ref* to become estranged

disancorare (**disàncoro**) *intr* to weigh anchor; to leave port ‖ *ref* to weigh anchor; (fig) to free oneself

disanimare (**disànimo**) *tr* to dishearten

disappetènza *f* loss of appetite

disapprovare (**disappròvo**) *tr* to disapprove

disapprovazióne *f* disapproval

disappunto *m* disappointment

disarcionare (**disarcióno**) *tr* to unsaddle, unhorse; to kick out

disarmare *tr* to disarm; to dismantle (*a scaffold*); to ship (*oars*); (naut) to unrig ‖ *ref* to disarm; (fig) to give up

disarma·to -ta *adj* unarmed, defenseless

disarmo *m* disarmament; dismantling; unrigging

disarmonìa *f* discord; contrast

disarmòni·co -ca *adj* (**-ci -che**) discordant

disarticolare (**disartìcolo**) *tr* to limber up; to disjoint ‖ *ref* to become dislocated

disassociare §128 (**disassòcio**) *tr* to disassociate

disastra·to -ta *adj* damaged ‖ *mf* victim

disastro *m* disaster, calamity; wreck

disastró·so -sa [s] *adj* disastrous

disattèn·to -ta *adj* inattentive; careless

disattenzióne *f* inattention; carelessness

disattivare *tr* to deactivate (*e.g., a mine*)

disavanzo *m* (com) deficit

disavvedu·to -ta *adj* heedless

disavventura *f* misfortune

disavvertènza *f* inadvertence

disavvezzare (**disavvézzo**) *tr* to break (*s.o.*) of a habit ‖ *ref*—**disavvezzarsi da** to give up or lose the habit of

disavvéz·zo -za *adj* unaccustomed

disbórso *m* disbursement, outlay

disboscare §197 (**disbòsco**) *tr* to deforest

disbrigare §209 *tr* to dispatch ‖ *ref* to extricate oneself

disbri·go *m* (**-ghi**) prompt execution, dispatch

discacciare §128 *tr* (lit) to chase away

discanto *m* (mus) harmonizing

discàpito *m* damage; **tornare a discapito di** to be detrimental to

discàri·ca *f* (**-che**) discharge (*e.g., of pollutants*); dumping (*of refuse*); unloading (*of a ship*)

discàri·co *m* (**-chi**) exculpation; **a discarico di** in defense of

discatóre *m* hockey player; discus thrower

discendènte *adj* descending; sloping; down (*train*) ‖ *mf* descendant

discendènza *f* descent; pedigree

discéndere §245 *tr* to go down ‖ *intr* (ESSERE & AVERE) to descend, go down; to slope; to fall (*said, e.g., of thermometer*); to get off; **discendere in picchiata** (aer) to nose-dive

discènte *mf* student, pupil

discépo·lo -la *mf* disciple

discèrnere §153 *tr* to discern

discernìbile *adj* discernible

discerniménto *m* discernment

discésa [s] *f* descent; slope; drop

discettare (**discètto**) *tr* (lit) to discuss

dischiodare (**dischiòdo**) *tr* to take the nails out of

dischiùdere §125 *tr* to open; to reveal

discìn·to -ta *adj* scantily dressed; untidy; **in disarray**

disciògliere §127 *tr* to dissolve, melt; (lit) to untie ‖ *ref* to dissolve, melt

disciplina *f* discipline; whip; scourge

disciplinare *adj* disciplinary ‖ *m* regulation ‖ *tr* to discipline

disciplina·to -ta *adj* obedient

di·sco *m* (**-schi**) disk; (phonograph) record; bob (*of pendulum*); (ice hockey) puck; (sports) discus; (rr) signal; (pharm) tablet; **disco combinatore** (telp) dial; **disco microsolco** microgroove record; **disco volante** flying saucer

discòfilo *m* record lover

discòide *m* (pharm) tablet, pill

dìsco·lo -la *adj* undisciplined, wild ‖ *m* rogue, rascal

discolorare (**discolóro**) *tr* to discolor ‖ *ref* to pale

discolorazióne *f* discoloration; paleness

discólpa *f* defense

discolpare (**discólpo**) *tr* to defend

disconnèttere §107 *tr* to disconnect

disconóscere §134 *tr* to ignore, to disregard; to be ungrateful for

discontinuare (**discontìnuo**) *tr* to perform sporadically ‖ *intr* to lose continuity

discontì·nuo -nua *adj* uneven

disconvenire §282 *intr* (ESSERE) (lit) to disagree ‖ *impers* (ESSERE) (lit) to be improper

discoprire §110 (**discòpro**) *tr* to discover

discordante *adj* discordant

discordare (**discòrdo**) *intr* (ESSERE) to disagree, differ

discòrde *adj* discordant; opposing

discòrdia *f* discord, dissension

discórrere §139 *intr* to talk, chat; (coll) to keep company; **discorrere del più e del meno** to make small talk; **e via discorrendo** and so forth

discórso *m* discourse; conversation; speech; **pochi discorsi!** (coll) cut it out!

discostare (**discòsto**) *tr* to remove ‖ *ref* to withdraw; to differ

discò·sto -sta *adj* distant ‖ **discosto** *adv* far

discotè·ca *f* (**-che**) record library; discotheque

discreditare (**discrédito**) *tr* to discredit

discrédito *m* discredit

discrepanza *f* discrepancy

discretaménte *adv* rather; fairly well

discré·to -ta *adj* discreet; fairly large; fair

discrezióne *f* discretion

discriminante *adj* discriminatory; extenuating ‖ *m* (math) discriminant

discriminare (**discrìmino**) *tr* to discriminate; to extenuate

discriminazióne *f* discrimination

discussióne *f* discussion; argument

discus·so -sa *adj* controversial

discùtere §154 *tr* to discuss ‖ *intr* to discuss; to argue

discutìbile *adj* moot, debatable

disdegnare (**disdégno**) *tr* to disdain, scorn ‖ *ref* (obs) to be angry

disdégno *m* disdain, scorn

disdegnó·so -sa [s] *adj* disdainful

disdétta *f* ill luck; (law) notice

disdicévole *adj* unbecoming, unseemly

disdire §151 *tr* to retract; to belie; to cancel; to countermand; to terminate the contract of ‖ *ref* to retract; **disdire a** to be unbecoming to

disdòro *m* shame; **tornare a disdoro di** to bring shame on

disegnare [s] (**diségno**) *tr* to draw; to sketch; to design; (obs) to elect

disegna·tóre -trice [s] *mf* cartoonist; designer ‖ *m* draftsman

diségno [s] *m* drawing; sketch; outline; plan; design; **disegno animato** (mov) cartoon; **disegno di legge** (law) bill

disellare [s] (**disèllo**) *tr* var of **dissellare**

diserbante *adj* weed-killing ‖ *m* weed-killer

diseredare (**disèredo**) *tr* to disinherit

diséreda·to -ta *adj* disinherited ‖ **i diseredati** the underprivileged

disertare (**disèrto**) *tr* to desert; (lit) to lay waste ‖ *intr* to desert

disertóre *m* deserter

diserzióne *f* desertion

disfaciménto *m* disintegration

disfare §173 *tr* to undo; to defeat; to melt; to unknit; to break up (*housekeeping*); **disfare il letto** to remove the bedclothes ‖ *ref* to spoil (*said, e.g., of meat*); **disfarsi di** to get rid of

disfatta *f* defeat

disfattismo *m* defeatism

disfattì·sta *mf* (**-sti -ste**) defeatist

disfat·to -ta *adj* undone; defeated; melted; broken up; ravaged ‖ *f* see **disfatta**

disfida *f* (lit) challenge

disfunzióne *f* malfunction

disgelare (**disgèlo**) *tr* & *intr* to thaw

disgèlo *m* thaw

disgiùngere §183 *tr* & *ref* to separate

disgiuntì·vo -va *adj* disjunctive

disgràzia *f* disfavor; bad luck, misfortune; accident; **per disgrazia** unfortunately

disgrazia·to -ta *adj* unlucky; wretched
disgregaménto *m* disintegration
disgregare §209 **(disgrègo)** *tr* & *ref* to disintegrate
disgregazióne *f* disintegration
disguido *m* miscarriage, missending (*of a letter*)
disgustare *tr* to disgust, sicken ‖ *ref* to become disgusted, sicken; to have a falling-out, to part company
disgusto *m* disgust, repugnance
disgustó·so -sa [s] *adj* disgusting
disidratare *tr* to dehydrate
disilla·bo -ba *adj* disyllabic ‖ *m* disyllable
disillùdere §105 *tr* to delude, deceive ‖ *ref* to become disillusioned
disillusióne *f* disillusion
disimboscare §197 **(disimbòsco)** *tr* to put back in circulation
disimparare *tr* to unlearn, forget
disimpegnare (disimpégno) *tr* to release; to free, to open; to loosen; to redeem (*a pledge*); to clear; to perform ‖ *ref* to succeed
disimpégno *m* release; redemption; performance; disengagement; **di disimpegno** for every day (*e.g., a suit*); main (*e.g., hallway*)
disimpiè·go *m* **(-ghi)** unemployment; (mil) withdrawal
disincagliare §280 *tr* to set afloat; (fig) to disentangle
disincantare *tr* disenchant
disinfestare (disinfèsto) *tr* to exterminate
disinfestazióne *f* extermination
disinfettante *adj* & *m* disinfectant
disinfettare (disinfètto) *tr* to disinfect
disingannare *tr* to disillusion ‖ *ref* to become disillusioned
disinganno *m* disillusion
disinnescare §197 **(disinnésco)** *tr* to defuse
disinnestare (disinnèsto) *tr* to disconnect; to throw out, disengage
disinserire §176 *tr* (elec) to disconnect; (aut) to disengage
disintasare [s] *tr* to unclog
disintegrare (disìntegro) *tr* & *ref* to disintegrate
disintegrazióne *f* disintegration
disinteressare (disinterèsso) *tr* to make (*s.o.*) lose interest ‖ *ref* to lose interest; to take no interest
disinteressa·to -ta *adj* selfless, unselfish
disinterèsse *m* disinterest; unselfishness
disintossicare §197 **(disintòssico)** *tr* to free of poison; (fig) to clean the air in ‖ *ref* to shake the drug habit
disinvòl·to -ta *adj* free and easy; fresh, forward
disinvoltura *f* naturalness, ease of manners, offhandedness; freshness; impudence
disì·o *m* (-i) (poet) desire
disistima *f* scorn, low regard, disesteem
disistimare *tr* to scorn, hold in low regard
dislivèllo *m* difference of level; disparity
dislocaménto *m* transfer of troops; (naut) displacement

dislocare §197 **(dislòco)** *tr* to transfer (*troops*); to post (*sentries*); (naut) to displace
dislocazióne *f* (mil) transfer; (geog, naut, psychol) displacement
dismisura *f* excess; **a dismisura** excessively
disobbedire §176 *intr* var of **disubbidire**
disobbligare §209 **(disòbbligo)** *tr* to free from an obligation ‖ *ref* to repay a favor
disoccupa·to -ta *adj* unemployed, jobless; idle; unoccupied ‖ *m* unemployed person; **i disoccupati** the jobless
disoccupazióne *f* unemployment
disone·stà *f* (-stà) dishonesty; shamelessness
disonè·sto -sta *adj* dishonest; shameless; immoral
disonorante *adj* disgraceful
disonorare (disonóro) *tr* to dishonor, disgrace; to seduce
disonóre *m* dishonor, shame
disonorévole *adj* dishonorable; shameful
disoppilare (disòppilo) *tr* to clear of obstructions
disópra *adj invar* upper ‖ *m* **(disópra)** upper part, top; **prendere il disopra** to have the upper hand ‖ *adv* above; **al disopra di** above
disordinare (disórdino) *tr* to cancel, countermand; to confuse; to mess up ‖ *intr* to indulge ‖ *ref* to become disorganized
disordina·to -ta *adj* confused; messy; untidy; intemperate
disórdine *m* confusion; mess; disarray; disorder; intemperance
disorganizzare [ddzz] *tr* to disorganize; to disrupt
disorganizzazióne [ddzz] *f* disorganization, disorder; disruption
disorientaménto *m* disorientation; confusion, bewilderment
disorientare (disoriènto) *tr* to cause (*s.o.*) to lose his way; to confuse; to disorient ‖ *ref* to be bewildered; to lose one's bearings
disorienta·to -ta *adj* disoriented; confused, bewildered; lost, astray
disormeggiare §290 **(disorméggio)** *tr* to unmoor
disossare (disòsso) *tr* to bone ‖ *ref* (lit) to lose weight
disòtto [s] *adj invar* below ‖ *m* **(disótto)** lower part, bottom ‖ *adv* below; **al disotto di** below, underneath
disotturare *tr* to unclog
dispà·cio *m* **(-ci)** dispatch; urgent letter; **dispaccio telegrafico** telegram
dispara·to -ta *adj* disparate
disparére *m* disagreement
dìspari *adj invar* odd, uneven
dispari·tà *f* (-tà) disparity
dispàrte *adv* — **in disparte** apart, aside; **starsene in disparte** to keep aloof
dispèn·dio *m* **(-di)** expenditure; waste
dispendió·so -sa [s] *adj* expensive; wasteful

dispènsa *f* cupboard; pantry; distribution; number (*of magazine*); installment (*of book*); dispensation; (naut) storeroom; (coll) store

dispensare (**dispènso**) *tr* to exempt, free; to distribute ‖ *ref*—**dispensarsi da** to get out of

dispensà·rio *m* (**-ri**) dispensary

dispensa·tóre -trice *mf* dispenser

dispensiè·re -ra *mf* dispenser ‖ *m* steward

dispepsìa *f* dyspepsia

dispèpti·co -ca *adj* & *mf* (**-ci -che**) dyspeptic

disperare (**dispèro**) *intr* to despair; **fare disperare** to drive crazy ‖ *ref* to despair

dispera·to -ta *adj* hopeless ‖ *m* poor wretch; **come un disperato** desperately ‖ *f*—**alla disperata** with all one's might

disperazióne *f* desperation, despair

disperdere §212 *tr* to scatter; to waste ‖ *ref* to disperse; (fig) to waste one's energies

dispersióne *f* dispersion; loss; (elec) leakage

dispersività *f* tendency toward disorganization

dispersì·vo -va *adj* dispersive; disorganized

dispèr·so -sa *adj* scattered; lost; dispersed; missing in action

dispersóre *m* (elec) leakage conductor

dispètto *m* spite; (lit) haughtiness; **a dispetto di** in spite of; **far dispetto a** to provoke

dispettó·so -sa [s] *adj* pestiferous; spiteful, resentful

dispiacènte *adj* sorry; distressing

dispiacére *m* sorrow, displeasure ‖ §214 *intr* (ESSERE) to be displeasing; to be sorry, e.g., **mi dispiace** I am sorry; (with *dat*) to displease; (with *dat*) to dislike, e.g., **le mie parole gli dispiacciono** he dislikes my words; **Le dispiace?** would you please?; **se non Le dispiace** if you don't mind

dispiegare §209 (**dispiègo**) *tr* to manifest; (lit) to unfurl ‖ *ref* to spread out; to flow out

displù·vio *m* (**-vi**) divide, watershed; ridge (*of roof*)

disponibile *adj* available; open-minded

disponibili·tà *f* (**-tà**) availability; inactive status; **disponibilità** *fpl* available funds

dispórre §218 *tr* to dispose; to prepare ‖ *intr* to provide; to dispose; **disporre di** to have (*available*) ‖ *ref* to get ready

dispositivo *m* gadget; device; (mil) deployment

disposizióne *f* arrangement; inclination; disposition; disposal; instruction; (law) provision

dispó·sto -sta *adj* arranged; disposed; provided; willing; **ben disposto** disposed ‖ *m* (law) proviso

dispòti·co -ca *adj* (**-ci -che**) despotic

dispotismo *m* despotism

dispregiatì·vo -va *adj* disparaging; (gram) pejorative

disprè·gio *m* (**-gi**) contempt; disrepute

disprezzàbile *adj* contemptible; negligible

disprezzare (**disprèzzo**) *tr* to despise

disprèzzo *m* contempt, scorn

dìsputa *f* dispute; debate

disputàbile *adj* debatable

disputare (**disputo**) *tr* to contest; to discuss; to vie for (*victory*) ‖ *intr* to dispute, debate; to vie ‖ *ref* to vie for

disqualificare §197 (**disqualìfico**) *tr* to disqualify

disquisizióne *f* disquisition

dissacrare *tr* to desecrate

dissacrazióne *f* desecration

dissaldare *tr* to unsolder

dissanguare (**dissànguo**) *tr* to bleed ‖ *ref* to bleed; to ruin oneself

dissangua·to -ta *adj* bled white; **morire dissanguato** to bleed to death

dissapóre *m* disagreement

disseccare §197 (**dissécco**) *tr* to dry ‖ *ref* to dry; to dry up

disselciare §128 (**dissélcio**) *tr* to remove the cobblestones from

dissellare (**dissèllo**) *tr* to unsaddle

disseminare (**dissèmino**) *tr* to disseminate; to scatter

dissenna·to -ta *adj* foolish, unwise; crazy, mad

dissensióne *f* dissension

dissènso *m* dissent; disagreement

dissenterìa *f* dysentery

dissentire (**dissènto**) *intr* to dissent

dissenziènte *adj* dissenting ‖ *mf* dissenter

disseppellire §176 *tr* to exhume

dissertare (**dissèrto**) *intr* to discourse

dissertazióne *f* dissertation

disservì·zio *m* (**-zi**) poor service

dissestare (**dissèsto**) *tr* to unsettle; to disarrange

dissesta·to -ta *adj* financially embarrassed; mentally deranged

dissèsto *m* financial embarrassment; mental derangement

dissetante *adj* thirst-quenching

dissetare (**dissèto**) *tr* to quench the thirst of ‖ *ref* to quench one's thirst

dissezióne *f* dissection

dissidènte *adj* & *m* dissident

dissidènza *f* dissent

dissì·dio *m* (**-di**) dissent; disagreement

dissigillare *tr* to unseal ‖ *ref* (lit) to melt

dissìmile *adj* unlike

dissimulare (**dissìmulo**) *tr* to dissimulate, disguise ‖ *intr* to dissimulate

dissimulazióne *f* dissimulation

dissipare (**dissìpo**) *tr* to dissipate; to squander; to clear up (*a doubt*) ‖ *ref* to dissipate

dissipa·to -ta *adj* & *mf* profligate

dissipa·tóre -trice *mf* squanderer

dissipazióne *f* dissipation

dissociare §128 (**dissòcio**) *tr* to dissociate, disassociate ‖ *ref* to dissociate or disassociate oneself

dissociazióne *f* dissociation

dissodare (dissòdo) *tr* to cultivate

dissolutézza *f* profligacy

dissolu·to -ta *adj & mf* profligate

dissoluzióne *f* dissolution

dissolvènza *f* (mov) fade-out; **dissolvenza incrociata** (mov) lap dissolve

dissòlvere §155 *tr* to dissolve; to clear up (*a doubt*); (obs) to untie ‖ *ref* to dissolve

dissomiglianza *f* dissimilarity

dissonanza *f* dissonance

dissotterrare (dissottèrro) *tr* to exhume; to unearth

dissuadére §213 *tr* to dissuade

dissuè·to -ta *adj* (lit) unaccustomed

dissuggellare (dissuggèllo) *tr* to unseal

distaccaménto *m* (mil) detachment

distaccare §197 *tr* to detach; to remove; to transfer; to outdistance ‖ *ref* to stand out; to withdraw, become separated

distacca·to -ta *adj* detached; branch (*office*)

distac·co *m* (-chi) detachment; separation; (sports) spread (*in points*)

distante *adj* distant; aloof; different ‖ *adv* far away

distanza *f* distance; **mantenere le distanze** to keep one's distance; **tenere a distanza** to keep at arm's length

distanziare §287 *tr* to outdistance

distare *intr* to be distant

distèndere §270 *tr* to stretch; to spread; to unfurl; to relax; to knock down; to write ‖ *ref* to stretch; to spread out; to relax

distensióne *f* relaxation; relaxation of tension

disté·so -sa [s] *adj* stretched out; full (*voice*); lank (*hair*) ‖ *m*—**per disteso** in full ‖ *f* expanse; row; **a distesa** with full voice; at full peal

distillare *tr* to distill; to exude; to pour; to trickle ‖ *intr* (ESSERE) to trickle ‖ *ref*—**distillarsi il cervello** to rack one's brain

distilla·to -ta *adj* distilled ‖ *m* distillate

distilla·tóre -trice *mf* distiller ‖ *m* still

distillería *f* distillery

distinguíbile *adj* distinguishable

distínguere §156 *tr* to distinguish; to make out; to tell (*one thing from another*); to divide

distínta *f* note, list; **distinta di versamento** deposit slip

distintaménte *adv* distinctly; sincerely yours

distintí·vo -va *adj* distinctive ‖ *m* emblem, insignia, badge

distín·to -ta *adj* distinct; distinguished; sincere (*greetings*); reserved (*seat*); **Distinto Signor . . .** (*on an envelope*) Mr. . . . ‖ *f* see **distinta**

distinzióne *f* distinction

distògliere §127 *tr* to dissuade; to deter; to distract; to turn (*one's eyes*) away

distòrcere §272 *tr* to distort; to twist ‖ *ref* to become distorted; to sprain (*e.g., one's ankle*)

distorsióne *f* distortion; sprain; **distorsione acustica** wow

distrarre §273 *tr* to distract; to divert;

to amuse; to pull (*a muscle*) ‖ *ref* to become distracted; to relax

distrat·to -ta *adj* absent-minded

distrazióne *f* absent-mindedness; distraction; diversion (*of money*); pull (*of muscle*)

distrét·to -ta *adj* (obs) close; (obs) hard-pressed ‖ *m* district; precinct (*e.g., of police*); circuit (*of court*); ward (*in city*); **distretto militare** draft board; **distretto postale** postal zone ‖ *f* stricture; necessity

distrettuale *adj* district

distribuire §176 *tr* to distribute; to pass out; to allot; to deploy (*troops*); (theat) to cast (*roles*); (mov) to release; (mil) to issue (*e.g., clothing*)

distribu·tóre -trice *adj* distributing, dispensing ‖ *mf* distributor, dispenser ‖ *m* distributor; **distributore automatico** vending machine; **distributore di benzina** gasoline pump

distribuzióne *f* distribution; issue; delivery; (aut) timing gears; (mov) release; (fig) dispensation

districare §197 *tr* to unravel ‖ *ref* to extricate oneself

distrofia *f* dystrophy

distrúggere §266 *tr* to destroy; to ruin

distrutti·vo -va *adj* destructive

distruzióne *f* destruction

disturbare *tr* to disturb, bother; **disturbo?** may I come in? ‖ *ref* to bother; to go out of one's way

disturba·tóre -trice *mf* disturber; **disturbatore della quiete pubblica** disturber of the peace

disturbo *m* trouble, bother; disturbance; (rad) interference; **disturbi atmosferici** static, atmospherics; **togliere il disturbo a** to take leave of

disubbidiènte *adj* disobedient

disubbidiènza *f* disobedience

disubbidire §176 *intr* to disobey; (with *dat*) to disobey

disuguaglianza *f* inequality; disparity

disuguale *adj* uneven; unequal

disuma·no -na *adj* inhumane; unbearable

disunióne *f* disunion

disunire §176 *tr* to disunite

disusa·to -ta *adj* obsolete, out of use

disuso *m* disuse; **in disuso** obsolete

disùtile *adj* useless; burdensome ‖ *m* worthless fellow; (com) loss

disvì·o *m* (-i) miscarriage, missending (*of a letter*)

ditale *m* thimble; fingerstall

ditata *f* poke with a finger; finger mark; dab (*with a finger*)

dito *m* (dita *fpl*) finger; toe; **avere le dita d'oro** to have a magic touch; **dita della mano** fingers; **dita del piede** toes; **legarsela al dito** to never forget ‖ *m* (diti) finger, e.g., **dito indice** index finger; **dito anulare** ring finger; **dito medio** middle finger; **dito mignolo** little finger; **dito pollice** thumb

ditta *f* firm, house; office

dittàfono *m* intercom; dictaphone

dittatóre *m* dictator

dittatura f dictatorship
dittongare §209 (**dittòngo**) tr to diphthongize
dittòn·go m (**-ghi**) diphthong
diurèti·co -ca adj & m (**-ci -che**) diuretic
diur·no -na adj daily; daytime ‖ f (theat) matinée
diutur·no -na adj long-lasting
diva f diva; (mov) star; (lit) goddess
divagare §209 tr to amuse; to distract ‖ intr to digress ‖ ref to relax
divagazióne f distraction; digression; relaxation
divampare intr (ESSERE & AVERE) to blaze, flare
divano m divan; couch, sofa
divaricare §197 (**divàrico**) tr to spread (one's legs); to open up (an incision)
divà·rio m (**-ri**) difference
divèllere §267 tr to eradicate, uproot
diveni·re m (**-re**) (philos) becoming ‖ §282 intr (ESSERE) (lit) to become; (archaic) to come
diventare (**divènto**) intr (ESSERE) to become; **diventare di tutti i colori** to blush; to be embarrassed; **diventare grande** to grow up; **diventare matto** to go mad; **diventare pallido** to turn pale; **diventare piccolo** to grow smaller; **diventare rosso** to blush
divèr·bio m (**-bi**) argument; **venire a diverbio** to have an altercation
divergènza f divergency
divèrgere §157 intr to diverge
diversificare §197 (**diversìfico**) tr to diversify ‖ ref to be diversified; to differ
diversióne f diversion
diversi·tà f (**-tà**) diversity
diversi·vo -va adj diverting ‖ m diversion
divèr·so -sa adj different; **diver·si -se** several, e.g., **diverse ragazze** several girls ‖ **diver·si -se** pron several
divertènte adj diverting, amusing
divertiménto m amusement, pastime; fun; (mus) divertimento
divertire (**divèrto**) tr to amuse, entertain; (lit) to turn aside ‖ ref to have fun, enjoy oneself; (lit) to go away
diverti·to -ta adj amused; amusing
divétta f starlet
divezzare (**divézzo**) tr to wean ‖ ref—**divezzarsi da** to get out of the habit of
dividèndo m dividend
dividere §158 tr to divide; to partition; to split; to share in (e.g., s.o.'s grief) ‖ ref to be divided; to become separated; **dividersi fra** to divide one's time between
divièto m prohibition; **divieto d'affissione** post no bills; **divieto di parcheggio** no parking; **divieto di sosta** no stopping; **divieto di svolta** no turns; **divieto di transito** no thoroughfare
divinare tr (lit) to divine
divina·tóre -trice adj divining ‖ m diviner

divinazióne f divination
divincolare (**divìncolo**) tr & ref to wriggle
divini·tà f (**-tà**) divinity
divinizzare [ddzz] tr to deify
divi·no -na adj divine
divisa f uniform; motto; part (in hair); **divise foreign exchange**
divisare tr (lit) to intend
divisibile adj divisible
divisióne f division; partition; (sports) league
divisionismo m (painting) divisionism; (pol) separatism
divismo m (mov) star system; (mov) adulation of stars
divisóre m (math) divisor
divisò·rio -ria (**-ri -rie**) adj dividing ‖ m partition; (math) divisor
di·vo -va adj (lit) divine ‖ m (theat, mov) star; (lit) god ‖ f see **diva**
divolgare §209 (**divólgo**) tr & ref var of **divulgare**
divorare (**divóro**) tr to devour; to gulp down; to consume; **divorare la via** to burn up the road
divora·tóre -trice adj consuming ‖ mf consumer (e.g., of food, books)
divorziare §287 (**divòrzio**) intr to become divorced; **divorziare da** to divorce
divorzia·to -ta adj divorced ‖ m divorcé ‖ f divorcée
divòr·zio m (**-zi**) divorce
divulgare §209 tr to divulge; to publicize; to popularize ‖ ref to spread; to become popular
divulga·tóre -trice adj popularizing ‖ mf popularizer; **divulgatore di calunnie** scandalmonger; **divulgatore di notizie** telltale
divulgazióne f publicizing; popularization
divulsióne f (surg) dilation
dizionà·rio -ria m (**-ri**) dictionary; **dizionario geografico** gazetteer
dizióne f diction; reading (of poetry)
do [dɔ] m (**do**) (mus) do; (mus) C
dóc·cia f (**-ce**) shower; gutter (on roof); spout; (fig) dash of cold water; **fare la doccia** to take a shower
docciare §128 (**dóccio**) tr, intr (ESSERE) & ref to shower
doccióne m trough, gutter; gargoyle
docènte adj teaching ‖ m teacher; **libero docente** certified university teacher
docènza f teaching post; **libera docenza** lectureship
dòcile adj docile; tame; amenable (person); workable (material)
documentare (**documénto**) tr to document ‖ ref to gather information
documentà·rio -ria adj & m (**-ri -rie**) documentary
documènto m document; paper; **documenti di bordo** ship's papers
dodecafonìa f twelve-tone system
dodecasilla·bo -ba adj twelve-syllable, dodecasyllable
dodicèsi·mo -ma adj, m & pron twelfth
dódici adj & pron twelve; **le dodici**

twelve o'clock || *m* twelve; twelfth (*in dates*)

dó·ga *f* (**-ghe**) stave

dogale *adj* (hist) of the doge

dogana *f* duty; customs; custom house

doganière *m* customs officer

dòge *m* (hist) doge

dò·glia *f* (**-glie**) (lit) pain, pang; **doglie** labor pains

dò·glio *m* (**-gli**) barrel; (lit) large jar

doglió·so -sa [s] *adj* (lit) sorrowful

dòg·ma *m* (**-mi**) dogma

dogmàti·co -ca (**-ci -che**) *adj* dogmatic || *mf* dogmatist

dogmatismo *m* dogmatism

dólce *adj* sweet; soft; gentle; fresh (*water*); mild (*climate*); delicate (*feet*); **dolce far niente** sweet idleness || *m* sweet; sweet dish; **dolci** candy

dolceama·ro -ra *adj* bittersweet

dolcézza *f* sweetness; mildness; gentleness

dolcia·stro -stra *adj* sweetish

dolcière *m* candy maker; pastry baker

dolcificare §197 (**dolcìfico**) *tr* to sweeten

dolciume *m* sweet; **dolciumi** candy

dolènte *adj* aching; sorrowful; sorry

dolére §159 *intr* (ESSERE & AVERE) to ache, e.g., **gli dolgono i denti** his teeth ache || *ref* to grieve || *impers* (ESSERE) to be sorry, e.g., **mi duole che Lei non possa venire** I am sorry that you won't be able to come

dolicònice *m* bobolink

dòllaro *m* dollar

dòlo *m* fraud, malice, guile

dolomite *f* dolomite || **Dolomiti** *fpl* Dolomites

dolorante *adj* aching

dolorare (**doló·ro**) *intr* (lit) to ache

dolóre *m* ache; sorrow; contrition

doloró·so -sa [s] *adj* painful; sorrowful

doló·so -sa [s] *adj* intentional, fraudulent; (law) felonious

domàbile *adj* tamable

domanda *f* question; application; appeal; (econ) demand; **domanda suggestiva** (com) leading question; **fare una domanda** to ask a question

domandare *tr* to ask; to ask for; **domandare la parola** to ask for the floor || *intr* to inquire || *ref* to wonder; (lit) to be called

doma·ni *m* (**-ni**) tomorrow || *adv* tomorrow; **a domani** until tomorrow; **domani a otto** a week from tomorrow; **domani l'altro** the day after tomorrow

domare (**dómo**) *tr* to tame; to extinguish; to quell

doma·tóre -trice *mf* tamer

domattina *adv* tomorrow morning

doméni·ca *f* (**-che**) Sunday

domenicale *adj* Sunday (*e.g., rest*)

domenica·no -na *adj* & *m* Dominican (*e.g., order*)

domesticare §197 (**domèstico**) *tr* to domesticate

domèsti·co -ca (**-ci -che**) *adj* family; household; familiar; domestic || *mf* domestic, servant || *f* maid; **alla**

domestica family style; **domestica a mezzo servizio** part-time domestic

domiciliare §287 *tr* (com) to draw || *ref* to dwell; to settle

domicilia·to -ta *adj* residing

domicì·lio *m* (**-li**) domicile, residence; principal office; **domicilio coatto** imprisonment; **franco domicilio** free delivery

dominare (**dòmino**) *tr* to dominate, rule; to master; to overlook || *intr* to prevail; to reign || *ref* to control oneself

domina·tóre -trice *mf* ruler

dominazióne *f* domination; rule

domineddìo *m invar* (coll) the Lord God

dominica·no -na *adj* & *mf* Dominican (*e.g., Republic*)

domì·nio *m* (**-ni**) dominion; domain

dòmi·no *m* (**-no**) domino (*cloak*); dominoes (*game*)

dòn *m* (used only before singular Christian name) don (*Spanish title*); Don (*priest*); uncle (*familiar title of elderly man*)

donare (**dóno**) *tr* to donate; to give as a present || *intr*—**donare a** to be becoming to

dona·tóre -trice *mf* donor; **donatore di sangue** blood donor

donazióne *f* gift, donation

donchisciotté·sco -sca *adj* (**-schi -sche**) quixotic

dónde *adv* wherefrom, whence

dondolare (**dóndolo**) *tr* to swing, rock || *ref* to swing, rock; to loaf around

dondolì·o *m* (**-ìi**) swinging, rocking

dóndolo *m*—**a dondolo** rocking (*chair, horse*); **andare a dondolo** to loaf around

dondoló·ne -na *mf* idler, loafer

dongiovan·ni *m* (**-ni**) Don Juan

dònna *f* woman; ladyship; (lit) lady; (coll) Mrs.; (coll) maid; (cards) queen; **da donna** woman's, e.g., **scarpe da donna** woman's shoes; **donna cannone** fat lady (*of circus*); **donna di casa** housewife; **Nostra Donna** Our Lady

donnaiòlo *m* ladies' man, philanderer

donné·sco -sca *adj* (**-schi -sche**) womanly, feminine

dònnola *f* weasel

dóno *m* gift; **in dono** as a gift

donzèlla [dz] *f* (lit) damsel

donzèllo [dz] *m* (coll) doorman; (lit) page

dópo *adv* afterwards, later; **dopo che** after; **dopo di** after || *prep* after; **dopo** + *pp* after having + *pp*

dopobar·ba *adj invar* after-shaving || *m* (**-ba**) after-shaving lotion

dopodomani *m* & *adv* the day after tomorrow

dopoguèr·ra *m* (**-ra**) postwar era

dopolavóro *m* government office designed to organize workers' leisure time

dopopranzo *m* afternoon || *adv* in the afternoon

doppiàg·gio *m* (**-gi**) (mov) dubbing

doppiare §287 (**dóppio**) *tr* to double; (mov) to dub

doppière *m* candelabrum

doppiétta *f* double-barreled shotgun; (aut) double shift

doppiézza *f* duplicity

dóp·pio **-pia** (**-pi** **-pie**) *adj* double; coupled; double-dealing ‖ *adv* twice, twofold ‖ *m* double; twice as much; (tennis) doubles; (theat) understudy

doppióne *m* duplicate; (philol) doublet

doppiopèt·to *adj invar* double-breasted ‖ *m* (**-to**) double-breasted suit

dorare (**dòro**) *tr* to gild; (culin) to brown; **dorare la pillola** to sugar-coat the pill

dora·to **-ta** *adj* gilt, golden

doratura *f* gilding

dormicchiare §287 *intr* to doze

dormiènte *adj* sleeping ‖ *mf* sleeper

dormiglió·ne **-na** *mf* sleepyhead

dormire (**dòrmo**) *tr & intr* to sleep; **dormire a occhi aperti** to be overcome with sleep; **dormire della grossa** to sleep profoundly; **dormire tra due guanciali** to be safe and secure

dormita *f* long sleep; **fare una bella dormita** to have a long sleep

dormitò·rio *m* (**-ri**) dormitory

dormivé·glia *m* (**-glia**) drowsiness

dorsale *adj* dorsal; back (*bone*) ‖ *m* head (*of bed*); back (*of chair*) ‖ *f* (geog) ridge

dòrso *m* back; (sports) backstroke

dosàg·gio *m* (**-gi**) dosage

dosare (**dòso**) *tr* to dose

dosatura *f* dosage

dòse *f* dose

dòsso *m* back; (lit) summit; **levarsi di dosso** to take off; **mettersi in dosso** to put on

dotare (**dòto**) *tr* to provide with a dowry; to endow; to bless

dotazióne *f* dowry; endowment; supply

dòte *f* dowry; gift; endowment

dòt·to **-ta** *adj* learned, erudite ‖ *m* scholar; (anat) duct

dottorale *adj* doctoral

dottó·re **-réssa** *mf* doctor

dottrina *f* doctrine; Christian doctrine

dóve *m* where; **per ogni dove** everywhere ‖ *adv* where; **da dove** or **di dove** from where; which way; **fin dove** up to what point; **per dove** which way ‖ *conj* where; whereas

dovére *m* duty, obligation; homework; **a dovere** properly; **doveri** regards; **farsi un dovere di** to feel duty-bound to; **mettere qlcu a dovere** to put s.o. in his place; **più del dovere** more than one should; **sentirsi in dovere di** to feel duty-bound to ‖ §160 *tr & intr* to owe ‖ *aux* (ESSERE & AVERE) must, e.g., **deve farlo** you must do it; to have to, e.g., **dovei partire** I had to leave; ought to, e.g., **dovrebbe lucidare la macchina** he ought to polish the car; should, e.g., **dovresti immaginarti** you should imagine; to be to, e.g., **il treno doveva arrivare alle sei** the train was to arrive at six; to be supposed to, e.g., **deve aver**

fatto un lungo viaggio he is supposed to have taken a long journey

doveró·so **-sa** [s] *adj* proper, right

dovizia *f* (lit) abundance, wealth

dovunque *adv* wherever, anywhere; everywhere

dovu·to **-ta** *adj & m* due

dozzina [ddzz] *f* dozen; room and board; **da** or **di dozzina** common, ordinary; **tenere a dozzina** to board

dozzinale [ddzz] *adj* common, ordinary

dozzinante [ddzz] *mf* boarder

dra·ga *f* (**-ghe**) dredge

dragàg·gio *m* (**-gi**) dredging

dragami·ne *m* (**-ne**) minesweeper

dragare §209 *tr* to dredge

dràglia *f* (naut) stay

dra·go *m* (**-ghi**) dragon; **drago volante** kite

dragóna *f* sword strap

dragoncèllo *m* (bot) tarragon

dragóne *m* dragon; dragoon

dram·ma *m* (**-mi**) drama, play; **dramma musicale** (hist) melodrama ‖ *f* drachma; dram

drammàti·co **-ca** (**-ci** **-che**) *adj* dramatic ‖ *f* drama, dramatic art

drammatizzare [ddzz] *tr* to dramatize

drammatur·go *m* (**-ghi**) playwright, dramatist

drappég·gio *m* (**-gi**) drape; pleats

drappeggiare §290 (**drappéggio**) *tr* to drape ‖ *ref* to be draped

drappèlla *f* pennon (*on bugler's trumpet*)

drappèllo *m* squad, platoon

drapperia *f* dry goods; dry-goods store

drappo *m* cloth, silk cloth; (billiards) green cloth, baize

dràsti·co **-ca** *adj* (**-ci** **-che**) drastic

drenàg·gio *m* (**-gi**) drainage

drenare (**drèno**) *tr* to drain

dressàg·gio *m* (**-gi**) *m* training (*of animals*)

dribblare *tr & intr* (sports) to dribble

drit·to **-ta** *adj* straight; (lit) correct; **dritto come un fuso** straight as a ramrod ‖ *m* (fig) old fox ‖ *f* right; (naut) starboard

drizza *f* (naut) halyard

drizzare *tr* to straighten; to address; to erect; to cock (*the head*); to direct (*a blow*); **drizzare le gambe ai cani** to do the impossible; **drizzare le orecchie** to prick up one's ears ‖ *intr* (naut) to hoist the halyard ‖ *ref* to stand erect

drò·ga *f* (**-ghe**) drug; spice; seasoning

drogare §209 (**drògo**) *tr* to drug; to spice, season

drogheria *f* grocery (store)

droghière *m* grocer

dromedà·rio *m* (**-ri**) dromedary

dru·do **-da** *adj* (archaic) faithful; (lit) strong ‖ *m* (obs) vassal; (lit) lover

drùi·da *m* (**-di**) druid

drupa *f* (bot) drupe, stone fruit

duale *adj & m* dual

dualismo *m* dualism

duali·tà *f* duality

dùb·bio **-bia** (**-bi** **-bie**) *adj* doubtful ‖ *m* doubt; misgiving; **mettere in dub-**

bio to question; to risk; **senza dubbio** no doubt

dubbió·so -sa [s] *adj* dubious; doubtful; (lit) dangerous

dubitare (**dùbito**) *intr* to doubt; to suspect; **dubitare di** to mistrust; to doubt; **non dubitare!** don't worry!

du·ca *m* (**-chi**) duke; (lit) leader

ducato *m* duchy; ducat

duce *m* leader; duce

duchéssa *f* duchess

duchessina *f* young duchess

duchino *m* young duke

due *adj & pron* two; **le due** two o'clock || *m* two; second (*in dates*) || *f—fra* **le due** between two alternatives

duecenté·sco -sca *adj* (**-schi -sche**) thirteenth-century

duecentèsi·mo -ma *adj, m & pron* two hundredth

duecènto *adj, m & pron* two hundred || **il Duecento** the thirteenth century

duellante *adj* dueling || *m* duelist

duellare (**duèllo**) *intr* to duel

duèllo *m* duel; contest; debate; **sfidare a duello** to challenge to a duel

duemila *adj, m & pron* two thousand || **Duemila** *m* twenty-first century

duepèz·zi *m* (**-zi**) two-piece bathing suit

duétto *m* (mus) duet

dulcamara *f* (bot) bittersweet

dulcina *f* artificial sweetening

duna *f* dune

dunque *m*—**venire al dunque** to come

to the point || *adv* then || *conj* therefore, hence || *interj* well!

duodèno *m* (anat) duodenum

duòlo *m* (lit) grief

duòmo *m* cathedral; dome (*e.g., of a boiler*)

du·plex *m* (**-plex**) (telp) party line

duplicare §197 (**dùplico**) *tr* to duplicate

duplica·to -ta *adj & m* duplicate

duplicatóre *m* duplicator

dùplice *adj* twofold, double || *f* (racing) daily double

duplici·tà *f* (**-tà**) duplicity

duràbile *adj* durable, lasting

duràci·no -na *adj* clingstone || *f* clingstone peach

duralluminio *m* duralumin

durare *tr* to endure, bear || *intr* to last; **durare a** + *inf* to keep on + *ger*; **durare in carica** to remain in office

durata *f* duration; lasting quality; **di lunga durata** long-lasting

durante *prep* during; throughout

duratu·ro -ra *adj* enduring, lasting

durévole *adj* lasting, durable

durézza *f* hardness; toughness; rigidity

du·ro -ra *adj* hard; hard-boiled (*egg*); durum (*wheat*); tough (*skin*); harsh; (phonet) voiceless || *m* hard part; hard floor; hard soil; **il duro sta che . . .** the trouble is that . . . ; **tener duro** to hold out

duróne *m* callousness, callosity

dùttile *adj* ductile; tractable

E

E, e [e] *m & f* fifth letter of the Italian alphabet

e *conj* and

ebani·sta *m* (**-sti**) cabinetmaker

ebanisterìa *f* cabinetmaking; cabinetmaker's shop

ebanite *f* ebonite, vulcanite

èbano *m* ebony

ebbène *interj* well!

ebbrézza *f* intoxication, drunkenness

èb·bro -bra *adj* intoxicated || *mf* drunk

ebdomadà·rio -ria *adj & m* (**-ri -rie**) weekly

èbete *adj* stupid, dull, dumb

ebollizióne *f* boil, boiling

ebrài·co -ca (**-ci -che**) *adj* Hebrew, Hebraic || *m* Hebrew (*language*)

ebrè·o -a *adj & mf* Hebrew || *m* Hebrew (*language*); Jew; **ebreo errante** Wandering Jew

è·bro -bra *adj & mf* var of **ebbro**

ebùrne·o -a *adj* (lit) ivory

ecatòmbe *f* hecatomb, slaughter

eccedènte *adj* exceeding || *m* excess

eccedènza *f* excess, surplus

eccèdere §123 *tr* to exceed || *intr* to go too far

eccellènte *adj* excellent

eccellènza *f* excellence || **Eccellenza** *f* Excellency

eccèllere §162 *intr* (ESSERE) to excel

eccèl·so -sa *adj* unexcelled; very high || **—l'Eccelso** *m* the Most High

eccentrici·tà *f* (**-tà**) eccentricity

eccèntri·co -ca (**-ci -che**) *adj* eccentric; suburban || *mf* vaudeville performer || *m* (mach) eccentric

eccepibile *adj* objectionable

eccepire §176 *tr* (law) to take exception to || *intr* (law) to object

eccessi·vo -va *adj* excessive; overweening (*opinion*)

eccèsso *m* excess; **all'eccesso** excessively; **andare agli eccessi** to go to extremes; **dare in eccessi** to fly into a rage; **eccesso di peso** excess weight

eccètera *adv* and so forth, et cetera

eccètto *prep* except, but; **eccetto che** except that; unless

eccettuare (**eccèttuo**) *tr* to except

eccettua·to -ta *adj* excepted || **eccettuato** *prep* except

eccezionale *adj* exceptional

eccezióne *f* exception; objection; **ad eccezione di** with the exception of; **d'eccezione** extraordinary; **sollevare un'eccezione** (law) to take exception

ecchimò·si *f* (**-si**) bruise

eccì·dio *m* (**-di**) massacre

eccitàbile *adj* excitable

eccitaménto *m* instigation; excitement
eccitante *adj* stimulating || *m* stimulant
eccitare (**èccito**) *tr* to excite || *ref* to become excited or aroused; (sports) to warm up
eccitazióne *f* excitement; (elec) excitation
ecclesiàsti·co -ca (**-ci -che**) *adj* ecclesiastical || *m* clergyman
ècco *tr invar* here is (are), there is (are); **ecco che** here, e.g., **ecco che viene** here he comes; **eccoci** here we are; **ecco fatto** that's it; **eccola** here she is; here it is; **eccomi** here I am; **eccone** here are some || *intr invar* here I am; here it is; **quand'ecco** suddenly || *interj* look!
eccóme *interj* and how!, indeed!
echeggiare §290 (**echéggio**) *intr* (ESSERE & AVERE) to echo
eclètti·co -ca *adj* & *mf* (**-ci -che**) eclectic
eclissare *tr* to eclipse || *ref* to be eclipsed; (coll) to vanish, sneak away
eclis·si *f* (**-si**) eclipse
eclìtti·ca *f* (**-che**) ecliptic
èclo·ga *f* (**-ghe**) var of **egloga**
è·co *m* & *f* (**-chi** *mpl*) echo; **far eco a** to echo
ecogoniòmetro *m* sonar
ecologìa *f* ecology
economato *m* comptroller's or administrator's office
economìa *f* administration; management; economy; economics; **economìa aziendale** business management; **economìa di mercato** free enterprise; **economìa domestica** home economics; **economìa polìtica** political economy; economics; **economìe** savings; **fare economìa** to save
econòmi·co -ca *adj* (**-ci -che**) economic(al); cheap
economi·sta *mf* (**-sti -ste**) economist
economizzare [ddzz] *tr* & *intr* to economize, save
ecòno·mo -ma *adj* thrifty || *m* comptroller; administrator
ecosistè·ma [s] *m* (**-mi**) ecosystem
ecumèni·co -ca *adj* (**-ci -che**) ecumenical
eczè·ma [dz] *m* (**-mi**) eczema
édera *f* ivy
edìcola *f* shrine; newsstand
edificante *adj* edifying
edificare §197 (**edìfico**) *tr* to build; to edify || *intr* to build
edifica·tóre -trice *adj* building || *mf* builder
edificazióne *f* building; edification
edifì·cio *m* (**-ci**) building, edifice; pack (*e.g., of lies*); structure
edile *adj* building, construction || *m* builder, construction worker
edilì·zio -zia (**-zi -zie**) *adj* building, construction || *f* building trade
edipi·co -ca *adj* (**-ci -che**) Oedipus (*e.g., complex*)
Edipo *m* Oedipus
èdi·to -ta *adj* published
edi·tóre -trice *adj* publishing || *mf* publisher; editor (*e.g., of a text*)
editorìa *f* publishing; publishers

editoriale *adj* editorial; publishing || *m* editorial
editoriali·sta *mf* (**-sti -ste**) editorial writer
editto *m* edict
edizióne *f* edition; performance; (fig) vintage
edonismo *m* hedonism
edoni·sta *mf* (**-sti -ste**) hedonist
edòt·to -ta *adj* (lit) informed, acquainted; **rendere qlcu edotto su qlco** (lit) to inform s.o. of s.th
edredóne *m* eider, eider duck
educanda *f* boarding-school girl; convent-school girl
educandato *m* (convent) boarding school for girls
educare §197 (**èduco**) *tr* to educate; to rear, bring up; to train; to accustom, inure; (lit) to grow
educati·vo -va *adj* educational
educa·to -ta *adj* educated; polite, well-bred
educa·tóre -trice *mf* educator
educazióne *f* education; breeding, manners; **educazione civica** civics
edule *adj* edible
efèbo *m* (coll) sissy
efèlide *f* freckle
effeminatézza *f* effeminacy
effemina·to -ta *adj* effeminate; frivolous
efferatézza *f* savagery
effervescènte *adj* effervescent
effervescènza *f* effervescence
effettivaménte *adv* really
effetti·vo -va *adj* real, true; effective; full (*e.g., member*); regular (*e.g., army officer*) || *m* effective; total amount; (mil) manpower
effètto *m* effect, result; (com) promissory note; (billiards) English; (sports) spin; **a questo effetto** for this purpose; **effetti** effects, belongings; **effetto di luce** play of light; **effetto ottico** optical illusion; **fare effetto** to make a sensation; **fare l'effetto di** to give the impression of; **in effetto** in fact; **mandare a effetto** to carry out; **porre in effetto** to put into effect
effettuàbile *adj* feasible
effettuare (**effèttuo**) *tr* to bring about; to contrive; to actuate; **effettuare** (**una corsa, un servizio**) to run, e.g., **l'autobus effettua una corsa ogni mezz'ora** the bus runs every half hour
efficace *adj* effective; forceful (*writer*)
efficà·cia *f* (**-cie**) effectiveness, efficacy; (law) validity
efficiente *adj* efficient
efficiènza *f* efficiency; **in piena efficienza** in full working order; in top condition
effigiare §290 *tr* to portray, represent
effì·gie *f* (**-gie** or **-gi**) effigy; image
effìme·ro -ra *adj* ephemeral
efflusso *m* flow, outflow
efflù·vio *m* (**-vi**) effluvium; emanation (*e.g., of light*)
effrazióne *f* (law) burglary
effusióne *f* effusion; outflow; shedding (*of blood*); effusiveness
egemonìa *f* hegemony

egè·o -a *adj* Aegean
ègida *f* aegis
Egitto, l' *m* Egypt
egizia·no -na *adj & mf* Egyptian
eglantina *f* sweetbrier
eglefino *m* haddock
égli §5 *pron pers* he
èglo·ga *f* (-ghe) eclogue
egocèntri·co -ca *adj & mf* (-ci -che) egocentric
egoismo *m* egoism, selfishness
egoi·sta (-sti -ste) *adj* selfish || *mf* egoist
egoìsti·co -ca *adj* (-ci -che) egoistic(al)
egotismo *m* egotism
egoti·sta (-sti -ste) *adj* egotistic || *mf* egotist
egrè·gio -gia *adj* (-gi -gie) (*lit*) outstanding; Egregio Signore Mr. (*before a man's name in an address on a letter*); Dear Sir
eguaglianza *f* equality
eguale *adj* var of uguale
egualità·rio -ria *adj & m* (-ri -rie) equalitarian
éhi *interj* hey!
éi *pron* (*lit*) he; (*archaic*) they
eiaculazióne *f* ejaculation
eiettàbile *adj* ejection (*seat*)
eiezióne *f* ejection
él *pron* (*archaic*) he
elaborare (elàboro) *tr* to elaborate; to digest; to secrete
elabora·to -ta *adj* elaborate || *m* written exercise
elaboratóre *m* computer
elaborazióne *f* elaboration; data processing
elargire §176 *tr* to donate
elargizióne *f* donation
elastici·tà *f* (-tà) elasticity; agility; (com) oscillation; (com) range
elàsti·co -ca *adj* (-ci -che) elastic || *m* rubber band; bedspring
élce *m & f* holm oak
elefante *m* elephant; elefante marino sea elephant
elefantéssa *f* female elephant
elegante *adj* elegant, fashionable
elegantó·ne -na *mf* fashion plate || *m* dandy, dude
eleganza *f* elegance, stylishness
elèggere §193 *tr* to elect
eleggìbile *adj* eligible
elegia *f* elegy
elegìa·co -ca *adj* elegiac
elementare *adj* elementary || elementari *fpl* elementary schools
eleménto *m* element; rudiment; member; cell (*of battery*); elementi personnel, e.g., elementi femminili female personnel
elemòsina *f* alms; (eccl) collection; chiedere l'elemosina to beg; vivere d'elemosina to live on charity
elemosinare (elemòsino) *intr* to beg
Èlena *f* Helen
elencare §197 (elènco) *tr* to list; to enumerate
elèn·co *m* (-chi) list; elenco telefonico telephone directory
eletti·vo -va *adj* elective
elèt·to -ta *adj* elect; distinguished

(*audience*); precious (*metal*); chosen (*people*) || *mf* elect
elettorato *m* electorate, constituency
elet·tóre -trice *mf* voter; elector
elettràuto *m* automobile electrician; automotive electric shop
elettrici·sta *mf* (-sti -ste) electrician
elettrici·tà *f* (-tà) electricity
elèttri·co -ca *adj* (-ci -che) electrical || *m* electrical worker
elettrificare §197 (elettrìfico) *tr* to electrify
elettrizzare [ddzz] *tr* to electrify (*e.g., a person*) || *ref* to become electrified
ellètro *m* amber
elettrocalamita *f* electromagnet
elettrocardiògrafo *m* electrocardiograph
elettrocardiogram·ma *m* (-mi) electrocardiogram
elettrodinàmi·co -ca *adj* (-ci -che) electrodynamic || *f* electrodynamics
elèttrodo *m* electrode
elettrodomèsti·co -ca *adj* (-ci -che) electric household || *m* electric household appliance
elettroesecuzióne *f* electrocution
elettròge·no -na *adj* generating (*unit*)
elettròli·si *f* (-si) electrolysis
elettrolìti·co -ca *adj* (-ci -che) electrolytic
elettròlito *m* electrolyte
elettromagnèti·co -ca *adj* (-ci -che) electromagnetic
elettromo·tóre -trice *adj* electromotive || *m* electric motor || *f* electric train; electric railcar
elettróne *m* electron
elettróni·co -ca *adj* (-ci -che) electronic || *f* electronics
elettropómpa *f* electric pump
elettrosquasso *m* electroshock
elettrostàti·co -ca *adj* (-ci -che) electrostatic || *f* electrostatics
elettrotècni·co -ca *adj* (-ci -che) electrotechnical || *m* electrician; electrical engineer || *f* electrical engineering
elettrotrèno *m* electric train
elevaménto *m* elevation
elevare (èlevo & élevo) *tr* to lift, elevate; (math) to raise || *ref* to rise
elevatézza *f* loftiness, dignity
eleva·to -ta *adj* high, lofty
eleva·tóre -trice *adj* elevating || *m* elevator
elevazióne *f* elevation; (sports) jump; (math) raising
elezióne *f* election; choice
èlfo *m* elf
èli·ca *f* (-che) propeller; (geom) helix
elicoidale *adj* helicoidal
elicòttero *m* helicopter
elìdere §161 *tr* to annul; to elide || *ref* to neutralize one another
eliminare (elìmino) *tr* to eliminate
eliminatò·rio -ria *adj* eliminating || *f* (sports) heat
eliminazióne *f* elimination; extermination
èlio- *comb form adj* helio-, e.g., eliocentrico heliocentric || *comb form*

m & f helio-, e.g., **elioterapìa** helio-therapy

èlio *m* helium

eliocèntri·co -ca *adj* (**-ci -che**) helio-centric

eliògrafo *m* heliograph

elioteràpi·co -ca *adj* (**-ci -che**) sunshine (*treatment*); sunbathing (*establishment*)

eliotròpio *m* (**-pi**) heliotrope; blood-stone

elipòrto *m* heliport

elisabettia·no -na *adj* Elizabethan

eli·sio -sia *adj* (**-si -sie**) Elysian

elisióne *f* elision

eli·sir *m* (**-sir**) elixir

èlitra *f* elytron, shard

élla *pron* (lit) she ‖ **Ella** *pron* (lit) you

ellèboro *m* hellebore

ellèni·co -ca *adj* (**-ci -che**) Hellenic

ellisse *f* ellipse

ellis·si *f* (**-si**) (gram) ellipsis

ellìtti·co -ca *adj* (**-ci -che**) elliptical

-èllo -èlla *suf adj* little, e.g., **poverello** poor little

elmétto *m* helmet; tin hat

élmo *m* helmet

elogiare §290 (**elògio**) *tr* to praise

elò·gio *m* (**-gi**) praise, encomium; write-up; **elogio funebre** eulogy

eloquènte *adj* eloquent

eloquènza *f* eloquence

elò·quio *m* (**-qui**) (lit) speech, diction

élsa *f* hilt

elucidare (**elùcido**) *tr* to elucidate

elùdere §105 *tr* to elude, evade

elusi·vo -va *adj* elusive

elvèti·co -ca *adj & mf* (**-ci -che**) Helvetian

elzevi·ro -ra [dz] *adj* Elzevir ‖ *m* Elzevir book; (journ) literary article

emacia·to -ta *adj* emaciated, lean

emanare *tr* to send forth; to issue ‖ *intr* (ESSERE) to emanate; to come forth

emanazióne *f* emanation; issuance

emancipare (**emàncipo**) *tr* to emancipate ‖ *ref* to become emancipated

emancipazióne *f* emancipation

emarginare (**emàrgino**) *tr* to note in the margin; (fig) to put aside, neglect

emarginato *m* marginal note

emàti·co -ca *adj* (**-ci -che**) blood, hematic

ematite *f* hematite

embar·go *m* (**-ghi**) embargo

emblè·ma *m* (**-mi**) emblem

emblemàti·co -ca *adj* (**-ci -che**) emblematic

embolìa *f* embolism

èmbrice *m* flat roof tile; shingle

embriologìa *f* embryology

embrionale *adj* embryonic

embrióne *m* embryo

emendaménto *m* emendation (*of a text*); amendment (*to a law*)

emendare (**emèndo**) *tr* to correct; to emend; to amend (*a law*) ‖ *ref* to reform

emergènza *f* emergence; emergency

emèrgere §162 *intr* (ESSERE) to emerge;

to surface (*said of a submarine*); to loom; to stand out

emèri·to -ta *adj* emeritus (*professor*); famous

emerotè·ca *f* (**-che**) periodical library

emersióne *f* emersion; surfacing

emèr·so -sa *adj* emergent

emèti·co -ca *adj & m* (**-ci -che**) emetic

eméttere §198 *tr* to emit, send forth; to utter (*a statement*); (com) to issue

emicìclo *m* hemicycle; floor (*of legislative body*)

emicrània *f* migraine, headache

emigrante *adj & mf* emigrant

emigrare *intr* (ESSERE & AVERE) to emigrate

emigra·to -ta *adj & m* emigrant

emigrazióne *f* emigration; migration (*e.g., of birds*)

eminènte *adj* eminent

eminènza *f* eminence; (eccl) Eminence

emisfèro *m* hemisphere

emissà·rio *m* (**-ri**) emissary; outlet (*river or lake*); drain

emissióne *f* emission; issuance; (rad) broadcast

emistì·chio *m* (**-chi**) hemistich

emittènte *adj* emitting; issuing; (rad) broadcasting ‖ *f* (rad) transmitting set; broadcasting station

emofilìa *f* hemophilia

emoglobina *f* hemoglobin

emolliènte *adj & m* emollient

emoluménto *m* fee, emolument

emorragìa *f* hemorrhage

emorròidi *fpl* hemorrhoids, piles

emostàti·co -ca (**-ci -che**) *adj* hemostatic ‖ *m* hemostat

emotè·ca *f* (**-che**) blood bank

emotività *f* (**-tà**) emotionalism

emoti·vo -va *adj* emotional ‖ *mf* emotional person

emottisi *f* (pathol) hemoptysis

emozionante *adj* emotional, moving

emozionare (**emozióno**) *tr* to move, stir; to thrill

emozióne *f* emotion

empiastro *m* var of **impiastro**

émpiere §163 *tr & ref* var of **empire**

empie·tà *f* (**-tà**) impiety; cruelty

ém·pio -pia *adj* (**-pi -pie**) impious; pitiless, wicked

empire §163 *tr* to fill; (lit) to fulfill; **empire qlcu di insulti** to heap insults on s.o. ‖ *ref* to get full

empire·o -a *adj* heavenly, sublime ‖ *m* empyrean

empìri·co -ca (**-ci -che**) *adj* empirical ‖ *mf* empiricist

empirìsmo *m* empiricism

empiri·sta *mf* (**-sti -ste**) empiricist

émpito *m* (lit) rush; fury

empò·rio *m* (**-ri**) emporium, mart

emulare (**èmulo**) *tr* to emulate

emulazióne *f* emulation, rivalry; (law) evil intent

èmu·lo -la *adj* emulous ‖ *mf* emulator

emulsionare (**emulsióno**) *tr* to emulsify

emulsióne *f* emulsion

encefalite *f* encephalitis

encìcli·ca *f* (**-che**) encyclical

enciclopedìa *f* encyclopedia

enciclopèdi·co -ca *adj* (-ci -che) encyclopedic
enclave *f* enclave
enclìti·co -ca *adj & f* (-ci -che) enclitic
encomiàbile *adj* praiseworthy
encomiare §287 (encòmio) *tr* to praise
encò·mio *m* (-mi) encomium, praise
endecasìlla·bo -ba *adj* hendecasyllabic
‖ *m* hendecasyllable
endemìa *f* endemic
endèmi·co -ca *adj* (-ci -che) endemic
èndice *m* nest egg; (obs) souvenir
endocàr·dio *m* (-di) (anat) endocardium
endocarpo *m* (bot) endocarp
endòcri·no -na *adj* endocrine
endourba·no -na *adj* inner-city
endovéno·so -sa [s] *adj* intravenous
energèti·co -ca *adj* (-ci -che) *adj* energy
(*e.g., crisis*); (med) tonic ‖ *m* (med)
tonic
energìa *f* energy, power
enèrgi·co -ca *adj* (-ci -che) energetic
energùme·no -na *mf* wild or mad person
ènfa·si *f* (-si) emphasis; forcefulness
enfàti·co -ca *adj* (-ci -che) emphatic
enfise·ma *m* (-mi) emphysema
enfitèu·si *f* (-si) lease (*of land*)
enìg·ma *m* (-mi) enigma, riddle, puzzle
enigmàti·co -ca *adj* (-ci -che) enigmatic,
puzzling
-ènne *suf adj* -year-old, e.g., *ragazzo
diciassettenne* seventeen-year-old boy
‖ *suf mf* -year-old person, e.g., *diciassettenne* seventeen-year-old person
ennèsi·mo -ma *adj* nth
-èn·nio *suf m* (-ni) period of . . . years,
e.g., *ventennio* period of twenty years
enòlo·go -ga *mf* (-gi -ghe) oenologist
enórme *adj* enormous
enormeménte *adv* enormously
enormi·tà *f* (-tà) enormity; outrage;
absurdity
Enrico *m* Henry
ènte *m* being; entity; corporation;
agency, body
enterocli·sma *m* (-smi) enema
enti·tà *f* (-tà) entity; value, importance
entomologìa *f* entomology
entram·bi -be *adj*—entrambi i both ‖
pron both
entrante *adj* next (*e.g., week*)
entrare (éntro) *intr* (ESSERE) to enter;
to go (*said of numbers*); to get (*into
one's head*); **entrarci** to make it, e.g.,
con questi soldi non c'entro I can't
make it with this money; **entrarci
come i cavoli a merenda** to be completely out of line; **entrare a** to begin
to; **entrare in** to enter (*e.g., a room*);
to fit in; to go in (*said of a number*);
to get into (*one's head*); **entrare in
amore** to be in heat (*said of animals*);
entrare in ballo to come into play;
entrare in carica to take up one's
duties; **entrare in collera** to get angry;
entrare in collisione to collide;
entrare in contatto to establish contact; **entrare in gioco** to come into
play; **entrare in guerra** to go to war;
entrare in società to make one's
debut; **entrare nella parte di** (theat)

to play the role of; **entrare in vigore**
to become effective; **Lei non c'entra**
this is none of your business; **questo
non c'entra** this is beside the point
entrata *f* entry; entrance; **entrata di
favore** (theat) complimentary ticket;
entrate income
entratura *f* entry; entrance; assumption
(*of a position*); familiarity
éntro *adv* inside ‖ *prep* within; **entro di**
within, inside of
entrobórdo *m* inboard motorboat
entrotèrra *f* inland, hinterland
entusiasmare *tr* to carry away, enthuse
‖ *ref* to be carried away, to become
enthused
entusiasmo *m* enthusiasm
entusia·sta -sta (-sti -ste) *adj* enthusiastic ‖
mf enthusiast, devotee
entusiàsti·co -ca *adj* (-ci -che) enthusiastic
enucleare (enùcleo) *tr* to elucidate;
(surg) to remove
enumerare (enùmero) *tr* to enumerate
enumerazióne *f* enumeration
enunciare §128 *tr* to enunciate, state
enunciati·vo -va *adj* (gram) declarative
enunciazióne *f* enunciation, statement
enzi·ma [dz] *m* (-mi) enzyme
èpa *f* (lit) belly, paunch
epàti·co -ca *adj* (-ci -che) hepatic, liver
epatite *f* (pathol) hepatitis
epènte·si *f* (-si) epenthesis
eperlano *m* (ichth) smelt
èpi·co -ca *adj & f* (-ci -che) epic
epicurè·o -a *adj & m* epicurean
epidemìa *f* epidemic
epidèmi·co -ca *adj* (-ci -che) epidemic
(al)
epidèrmi·co -ca *adj* (-ci -che) epider-
mal; (fig) superficial, skin-deep
epidèrmide *f* epidermis
Epifanìa *f* Epiphany
epiglòttide *f* (anat) epiglottis
epìgono *m* follower; descendant
epìgrafe *f* epigraph
epigram·ma *m* (-mi) epigram
epigrammàti·co -ca *adj* (-ci -che) epi-
grammatic
epilessìa *f* (pathol) epilepsy
epilètti·co -ca *adj & m* (-ci -che) epileptic
epìlo·go *m* (-ghi) epilogue; conclusion
episcopale *adj* episcopal
episcopalia·no -na *adj & mf* Episcopalian
episcopato *m* episcopate, bishopric
episòdi·co -ca *adj* (-ci -che) episodic
episò·dio *m* (-di) episode
epìstola *f* epistle
epistolà·rio *m* (-ri) letters, correspondence
epitàf·fio *m* (-fi) epitaph
epitè·lio *m* (-li) epithelium
epìteto *m* epithet; insult
epitomare (epìtomo) *tr* to epitomize
epìtome *f* epitome
èpo·ca *f* (-che) epoch; period; moment;
fare epoca to be epoch-making
epopèa *f* epic
eppure *conj* yet, and yet
epsomite *f* Epsom salt

epurare *tr* to cleanse; to purge

epurazióne *f* purification; purge

equànime *adj* calm, composed; impartial

equanimità *f* equanimity; impartiality

equatóre *m* equator

equatoriale *adj* & *m* equatorial

equazióne *f* equation

equèstre *adj* equestrian

equilàte·ro -ra *adj* equilateral

equilibrare *tr* to balance; (aer) to trim || *ref* to balance one another

equilibra·to -ta *adj* level-headed

equilibra·tóre -trice *adj* stabilizing || *m* (aer) horizontal stabilizer

equili·brio *m* (-bri) equilibrium, balance; (fig) proportion; equilibrio politico balance of power

equilibri·sta *mf* (-sti -ste) acrobat, equilibrist

equi·no -na *adj* & *m* equine

equinoziale *adj* equinoctial

equinò·zio *m* (-zi) equinox

equipaggiaménto *m* equipment, outfit

equipaggiare §290 *tr* to equip, outfit; (naut) to fit out; (naut) to man

equipàg·gio *m* (-gi) equipage; (naut) crew, complement; (sports) team; (rowing) crew

equiparare *tr* to equalize (*e.g., salaries*)

équipe *f* team

equipollènte *adj* equivalent

equi·tà *f* (-tà) equity, fair-mindedness

equitazióne *f* horsemanship

equivalènte *adj* & *m* equivalent

equivalére §278 *intr* (ESSERE & AVERE) —equivalere a to be equivalent to || *ref* to be equal

equivocare §197 (equìvoco) *intr*—equivocare su to mistake, misunderstand

equìvo·co -ca (-ci -che) *adj* equivocal; ambiguous || *m* misunderstanding

è·quo -qua *adj* equitable, fair

èra *f* era, age; era spaziale space age

erà·rio *m* (-ri) treasury

èrba *f* grass; erba limoncina lemon verbena; erba medica alfalfa; erbe vegetables; erbe aromatiche herbs; far l'erba to cut the grass; in erba (fig) budding; metter a erba to put to pasture

erbàc·cia *f* (-ce) weed

erbaggi *mpl* vegetables

erbaiò·lo -la *mf* fresh vegetable retailer

erbici·da *m* (-di) weed-killer

erbivéndo·lo -la *mf* fresh fruit and vegetable retailer

erbìvo·ro -ra *adj* herbivorous

erbori·sta *mf* (-sti -ste) herbalist

erbó·so -sa [s] *adj* grassy

Èrcole *m* Hercules

ercùle·o -a *adj* Herculean

erède *m* heir || *f* heiress

eredi·tà *f* (-tà) inheritance; heredity

ereditare (erèdito) *tr* to inherit

eredità·rio -ria *adj* (-ri -rie) hereditary; crown (*prince*)

ereditièra *f* heiress

eremi·ta *m* (-ti) hermit

eremitàg·gio *m* (-gi) hermitage

èremo *m* hermitage

eresìa *f* heresy

ereslar·ca *m* (-chi) heretic

erèti·co -ca (-ci -che) *adj* heretical || *mf* heretic

erèt·to -ta *adj* erect, straight

erezióne *f* erection

ergastola·no -na *mf* lifer

ergàstolo *m* life imprisonment; prison for persons sentenced to life imprisonment

èrgere §164 *tr* (lit) to erect; (lit) to lift || *ref* to rise (*said, e.g., of a mountain*)

èrgo *m invar*—venire all'ergo to come to a conclusion || *adv* thus, hence

èri·ca *f* (-che) heather

erìgere §152 *tr* to erect, build || *ref* to rise; erigersi a to set oneself up as

eritrè·o -a *adj* & *mf* Eritrean

ermafrodi·to -ta *adj* & *m* hermafrodite

ermellino *m* ermine

ermèti·co -ca *adj* (-ci -che) airtight; watertight; hermetic

èrnia *f* hernia; ernia del disco (pathol) herniated disk

eródere §239 *tr* to erode

eròe *m* hero

erogare §209 (èrogo) *tr* to distribute; to bestow

erogazióne *f* distribution; bestowal

eròi·co -ca *adj* (-ci -che) heroic

eroicòmi·co -ca *adj* (-ci -che) mock-heroic

eroìna *f* heroine; (pharm) heroin

eroismo *m* heroism

erómpere §240 *intr* to erupt, burst out

erosióne *f* erosion

eròti·co -ca *adj* (-ci -che) erotic

erotismo *m* eroticism

èrpete *m* (pathol) herpes, shingles

erpicare §197 (èrpico) *tr* to harrow

érpice *m* harrow

errabón·do -da *adj* (lit) wandering

errante *adj* errant; wandering

errare (èrro) *intr* to wander; to err; (lit) to stray

erra·to -ta *adj* mistaken, wrong

erròne·o -a *adj* erroneous

erróre *m* error, mistake; fault; (lit) wandering; errore di lingua slip of the tongue; errore di scrittura slip of the pen; errore di stampa misprint; errore giudiziario miscarriage of justice; salvo errore od omissione barring error or omission

ér·to -ta *adj* arduous, steep; erect || *f* arduous ascent; all'erta on the alert

erudire §176 *tr* to educate, instruct

erudi·to -ta *adj* erudite, learned || *m* scholar, savant

erudizióne *f* erudition, learning

eruttare *tr* to belch forth (*e.g., lava*); to utter (*obscenities*) || *intr* to belch

erutti·vo -va *adj* eruptive

eruzióne *f* eruption

esacerbare (esacèrbo) *tr* to embitter; to exacerbate || *ref* to become embittered

esagerare (esàgero) *tr* & *intr* to exaggerate

esagera·to -ta *adj* exaggerated, excessive || *mf* exaggerator

esagerazióne *f* exaggeration

esagitare (esàgito) *tr* to perturb

esàgono *m* hexagon

esalare *tr* to exhale; esalare l'ultimo respiro to breathe one's last || *intr* to spread (*said of odors*)

esalazióne *f* exhalation; fume, vapor

esaltare *tr* to exalt; to excite || *ref* to glorify oneself; to become excited

esalta·to -ta *adj* frenzied, excited || *mf* hothead

esame *m* examination; checkup, test; dare gli esami to take an examination; esame attitudinale aptitude test; esame del sangue blood test; esame di riparazione make-up test; fare gli esami to prepare a test (*for a student*); prendere in esame to take in consideration

esàmetro *m* hexameter

esaminan·do -da *mf* candidate; examinee

esaminare (esàmino) *tr* to examine; to test

esamina·tóre -trice *mf* examiner

esàngue *adj* bloodless; (fig) pale

esànime *adj* lifeless

esasperante *adj* exasperating

esasperare (esàspero) *tr* to exasperate || *ref* to become exasperated

esasperazióne *f* exasperation

esattézza *f* exactness; punctuality

esat·to -ta *adj* exact; punctual

esattóre *m* tax collector; bill collector

esattorìa *f* tax collector's office; bill collector's office

esaudire §176 *tr* to grant

esauriènte *adj* exhaustive; convincing

esauriménto *m* depletion (*e.g., of merchandise*); (pathol) exhaustion; (naut) drainage

esaurire §176 *tr* to exhaust; to play out (*e.g., a hooked fish*); to use up || *ref* to be exhausted; to be depleted; to be sold out

esauri·to -ta *adj* exhausted; depleted; sold out; out of print

esau·sto -sta *adj* exhausted; empty

esautorare (esàutoro) *tr* to deprive of authority; to discredit (*a theory*)

esazióne *f* exaction; collection

é·sca *f* (-sche) bait; punk (*for lighting fireworks*); tinder (*for lighting powder*); dare esca a to foment

escandescénza *f*—dare in escandescenze to fly off the handle

escava·tóre -trice *mf* excavator, digger || *m* excavator; escavatore a vapore steam shovel || *f* (mach) excavator

escavazióne *f* excavation

eschimése [s] *adj & mf* Eskimo

esclamare *tr & intr* to exclaim

esclamati·vo -va *adj* exclamatory; exclamation (*mark*)

esclùdere §105 *tr* to exclude; to keep or shut out

esclusióne *f* exclusion; a esclusione di with the exception of

esclusìva *f* sole right, monopoly; (journ) scoop

esclusivi·sta (-sti -ste) *adj* clannish; bigoted || *mf* bigot; (com) sole agent

esclusi·vo -va *adj* exclusive; intolerant, bigoted || *f* see esclusiva

esclu·so -sa *adj* excluded, excepted

escogitare (escògito) *tr* to think up, invent; to think out

escoriare §287 (escòrio) *tr & ref* to skin

escoriazióne *f* abrasion

escreménto *m* excrement

escrescènza *f* excrescence

escrè·to -ta *adj* excreted || *m* excreta

escursióne *f* excursion; (mach) sweep; (mil) transfer; escursione termica (meteor) temperature range

escursioni·sta *mf* (-sti -ste) excursionist, sightseer

escussióne *f* (law) examination, cross-examination

esecrare (esècro) *tr* to execrate

esecrazióne *f* execration

esecuti·vo -va *adj & m* executive

esecu·tóre -trice *mf* (mus) performer || *m* executor; esecutore di giustizia executioner || *f* executrix

esecuzióne *f* accomplishment, completion; performance; execution; esecuzione capitale capital punishment

esegè·si *f* (-si) exegesis

eseguire (eséguo) & §176 *tr* to execute, carry out; to perform

esèm·pio *m* (-pi) example; a mo' d'esempio as an illustration; dare il buon esempio to set a good example; per esempio for instance

esemplare *adj* exemplary || *m* copy; specimen || *v* (esèmplo) *tr* (lit) to copy

esemplificare §197 (esemplìfico) *tr* to exemplify

esentare (esènto) *tr* to exempt

esènte *adj* exempt, free

esenzióne *f* exemption

esèquie *fpl* obsequies, funeral rites

esercènte *adj* practicing || *mf* dealer, merchant

esercire §176 *tr* to practice; to run (*a store*)

esercitare (esèrcito) *tr* to exercise; to tax (*e.g., s.o.'s patience*); to practice, ply (*a trade*); to wield (*e.g., power*) || *ref* to practice

esercitazióne *f* exercise, training; esercitazioni militari drilling

esèrcito *m* army; (fig) flock; Esercito della Salvezza Salvation Army

esercì·zio *m* (-zi) exercise; practice; training; homework; occupation; drill; d'esercizio (com) administrative (*expenses*); esercizio finanziario fiscal year; esercizio provvisorio (law) emergency appropriation; esercizio pubblico establishment open to the public; esercizio spirituale (eccl) retreat

esibire §176 *tr* to exhibit || *ref* to show oneself, appear; esibirsi di to offer to

esibizióne *f* exhibition

esigènte *adj* demanding, exigent

esigènza *f* demand, requirement, exigency

esìgere §165 *tr* to demand; to require; to exact; to collect

esigìbile *adj* due; collectable

esigui·tà *f* (-tà) meagerness, scantiness

esì·guo -gua *adj* meager, scanty

esilarante *adj* exhilarating; laughing (*gas*)

esilarare (**esìlaro**) *tr* to amuse ‖ *ref* to be amused

èsile *adj* slender, thin; weak

esiliare §287 *tr* to exile ‖ *ref* to go into exile; to withdraw

esìlia·to -ta *adj* exiled ‖ *m* exile (*person*)

esì·lio *m* (**-li**) exile, banishment

esìmere §166 *tr* to exempt ‖ *ref—esìmersi da* to avoid (*an obligation*)

esì·mio -mia *adj* (**-mi -mie**) distinguished, eminent

-èsi·mo -ma *suf adj & pron* -eth, e.g., **ventesimo** twentieth; -th, e.g., **diciannovesimo** nineteenth

esistènte *adj* existent; extant

esistènza *f* existence

esistenzialismo *m* existentialism

esìstere §114 *intr* (ESSERE) to exist

esitante *adj* hesitant

esitare (**èsito**) *tr* to retail ‖ *intr* to hesitate; (med) to resolve itself

esitazióne *f* hesitation; haw (*in speech*)

èsito *m* result, outcome; sale; outlet; (philol) late form; **dare esito a** (com) to reply

esiziale *adj* ruinous, fatal

èsodo *m* exodus, flight

esòfa·go *m* (**-gi**) esophagus

esonerare (**esònero**) *tr* to exempt, release

esònero *m* exemption, release

Esòpo *m* Aesop

esorbitante *adj* exorbitant

esorbitare (**esòrbito**) *intr—esorbitare da* to go beyond

esorcismo *m* exorcism

esorcizzare [ddzz] *tr* to exorcise

esordiènte *adj* beginning, budding ‖ *mf* beginner ‖ *f* debutante

esòr·dio *m* (**-di**) beginning

esordire §176 *intr* to make a start; (theat) to debut; (theat) to open

esortare (**esòrto**) *tr* to exhort

esortazióne *f* exhortation

esò·so -sa *adj* greedy, avaricious; hateful; exorbitant (*price*)

esòti·co -ca *adj* (**-ci -che**) exotic

esotismo *m* exoticism; borrowing (*from a foreign language*)

espàndere §167 *tr* to expand ‖ *ref* to spread out; to confide

espansióne *f* expansion; effusiveness

espansionismo *m* expansionism

espansivi·tà *f* (**-tà**) effusiveness

espansi·vo -va *adj* expansive; effusive

espan·so -sa *adj* flared; expanded, dilated

espatriare §287 *intr* to emigrate

espà·trio *m* (**-tri**) emigration

espediènte *m* expedient, makeshift; ruse; **vivere di espedienti** to live by one's wits

espedire §176 *tr* to expedite ‖ *ref—espedirsi di* to get rid of

espèllere §168 *tr* to expel, eject

esperiènza *f* experience; experiment

esperimento *m* experiment; test

espèr·to -ta *adj & m* expert

espettorare (**espèttoro**) *tr & intr* to expectorate

espiare §119 *tr* to expiate; to placate (*the gods*); **espiare una pena** to serve a sentence

espiató·rio -ria *adj* (**-ri -rie**) expiatory

espiazióne *f* expiation

espirare *tr & intr* to breath out, to exhale

espletare (**esplèto**) *tr* to dispatch, complete

esplicare §197 (**èsplico**) *tr* to carry out; (lit) to explain

esplicati·vo -va *adj* explanatory

esplìci·to -ta *adj* explicit

esplòdere §169 *tr* to shoot; to fire (*a shot*) ‖ *intr* (ESSERE & AVERE) to explode; to burst forth

esploditóre *m* blasting machine

esplorare (**esplòro**) *tr* to explore; to search, probe; (telv) to scan

esplora·tóre -trice *mf* explorer ‖ *m* (nav) gunboat; **giovane esploratore** boy scout

esplorazióne *f* exploration; (telv) scanning

esplosióne *f* explosion, blast; (fig) outburst

esplosi·vo -va *adj & m* explosive

esponènte *adj* (typ) superior ‖ *m* spokesman; dictionary entry; catchword (*of dictionary*); (math) exponent; (naut) net weight

espórre §218 *tr* to expose, show; to expound; to abandon (*a baby*); to lay out (*a corpse*); to lay open (*to danger*) ‖ *intr* to show, exhibit ‖ *ref* to expose oneself

esportare (**espòrto**) *tr* to export

esporta·tóre -trice *mf* exporter

esportazióne *f* export, exportation

esposìmetro *m* exposure meter

esposi·tóre -trice *mf* commentator; exhibitor

esposizióne *f* exposition; abandonment (*of a baby*); exhibit, fair; line (*of credit*); exposure (*of a house*); (phot) exposure

espó·sto -sta *adj* exposed; aforementioned ‖ *m* petition, brief; foundling

espressióne *f* expression; feeling

espressi·vo -va *adj* expressive

esprès·so -sa *adj* manifest; express; prepared on the spot ‖ *m* espresso; messenger; special-delivery letter; special-delivery stamp

esprìmere §131 *tr* to express; to convey (*an opinion*); (lit) to squeeze ‖ *ref* to express oneself

espropriare §287 (**espròprio**) *tr* to expropriate ‖ *ref* to deprive oneself; **espropriarsi di** to divest oneself of

esprò·prio *m* (**-pri**) expropriation

espugnare *tr* to take by storm

espulsióne *f* expulsion; (mach) ejection

espulsóre *m* ejector

espurgare §209 *tr* to expurgate

éssa §5 *pron pers* she; it

ésse §5 *pron pers* they

essènza *f* essence

essenziale *adj* essential ‖ *m* main point

èssere *m* being; existence; condition; (coll) character; **in essere** in good shape ‖ §170 *intr* (ESSERE) to be;

c'è there is; **ci sono** there are; **ci sono!** I get it!; **come sarebbe a dire?** what do you mean?; **come se nulla fosse** as if nothing had happened; **esserci** to have arrived, to be there; **essere di** to belong to; **essere per** to be about to; **può essere** maybe; **sarà** maybe; **sia . . . sia** both . . . and; whether . . . or || *aux* (ESSERE) (to form passive) to be, e.g., **fu investito da un tassametro** he was run over by a taxi; (to form the compound tenses of certain intransitive verbs and all reflexive verbs) to have, e.g., **sono arrivati** they have arrived; **mi sono appena alzato** I have just got up || *impers* (ESSERE) to be, e.g., **è giusto** it is fair

éssi §5 *pron pers* they

essiccare §197 *tr* to dry || *ref* to dry up

essicca·tóio *m* (**-tói**) drier

essiccazióne *f* drying

èsso §5 *pron pers* he; it; **chi per esso** his representative

essudare *intr* to exude

èst *m* east

èsta·si *f* (**-si**) ecstasy; **andare in estasi** to become enraptured

estasiare §287 *tr* to enrapture, delight || *ref* to become enraptured

estate *f* summer

estàti·co -ca *adj* (**-ci -che**) ecstatic, enraptured

estemporàne·o -a *adj* extemporaneous

estèndere §270 *tr* to extend; to broaden (*e.g.*, one's knowledge); to draw up (*a document*) || *ref* to extend

estensìbile *adj* applicable; **inviare saluti estensibili a** to send greetings to be extended to (*e.g.*, another person)

estensióne *f* extension; extent; expanse (*e.g.*, of water); (mus) compass, range

estensi·vo -va *adj* extensive

estèn·so -sa *adj—***per esteso** fully

estensóre *adj* extensible || *m* compiler (*e.g.*, of a dictionary); (sports) exerciser, chest expander

estenuante *adj* exhausting

estenuare (**estènuo**) *tr* to exhaust || *ref* to become exhausted

esterióre *adj* exterior || *m* outside appearance

esteriori·tà *f* (**-tà**) appearance

esternare (**estèrno**) *tr* to reveal, manifest || *ref* to confide

estèr·no -na *adj* external; outside; day (*student*) || *m* exterior, outside; (baseball) outfielder; **all'esterno** outside; **in esterno** (mov) on location

èste·ro -ra *adj* foreign || *m* foreign countries; **all'estero** abroad

esterrefat·to -ta *adj* terrified

esté·so -sa [*s*] *adj* extended, wide; **per esteso** in full

estè·ta *mf* (**-ti -te**) aesthete

estèti·co -ca (**-ci -che**) *adj* aesthetic || *f* aesthetics

esteti·sta *mf* (**-sti -ste**) beautician

estima·tóre -trice *mf* appraiser; admirer

èstimo *m* appraisal; assessment

estìnguere §156 *tr* to extinguish; to quench (*thirst*); to pay off (*a debt*) || *ref* to die out

estinguìbile *adj* extinguishable; payable

estìn·to -ta *adj* extinguished; extinct || *m* deceased, dead person

estintóre *m* fire extinguisher

estirpare *tr* to uproot; to eradicate; to pull (*a tooth*)

estirpa·tóre -trice *mf* eradicator || *m* (agr) weeder

estivare *tr & intr* to summer

esti·vo -va *adj* summer; summery

estòllere §171 *tr* to extol

èstone *adj & mf* Estonian

estòrcere §272 *tr* to extort; **estorcere qlco a qlcu** to extort s.th from s.o.

estorsióne *f* extortion

estradare *tr* (law) to extradite

estradizióne *f* extradition

estràne·o -a *adj* extraneous, foreign; aloof || *mf* outsider

estrapolare (**estràpolo**) *tr* to extrapolate

estrarre §273 *tr* to extract, draw; to pull (*a tooth*)

estrat·to -ta *adj* extracted || *m* extract; abstract; certified copy; (typ) offprint; **estratto conto** bank statement; **estratto dell'atto di nascita** copy of one's birth certificate

estrazióne *f* extraction; drawing (*of lottery*)

estrèma *f* (sports) wing, end

estremi·sta *adj & mf* (**-sti -ste**) extremist

estremi·tà *f* (**-tà**) end; tip, top; extremity; **le estremità** the extremities

estrè·mo -ma *adj* extreme; **esalare l'estremo respiro** to breath one's last || *m* extremity; end, extreme; **essere agli estremi** to be near the end; **estremi** essentials || *f* see estrema

estrìnse·co -ca *adj* (**-ci -che**) extrinsic

èstro *m* horsefly; whim, fancy; inspiration; **estro venereo** heat (*of female animal*)

estrométtere §198 *tr* to oust, expel

estró·so -sa [*s*] *adj* fanciful, whimsical; inspired

estrovèr·so -sa or **estroverti·to -ta** *adj & mf* extrovert

estrùdere §190 *tr* to extrude

estuà·rio *m* (**-ri**) estuary

esuberante *adj* exuberant; buoyant

esuberanza *f* exuberance; buoyancy; **a esuberanza** abundantly

esulare (**èsulo**) *intr* (ESSERE & AVERE) to go into exile; **esulare da** to be alien to

esulcerare (**esùlcero**) *tr* to ulcerate on the surface; (fig) to exacerbate

esulcerazióne *f* superficial ulceration; (fig) exasperation, exacerbation

èsule *mf* exile (*person*)

esultante *adj* exultant, jubilant

esultare *intr* to exult

esumare *tr* to exhume; to revive (*e.g.*, a custom)

esumazióne *f* exhumation; revival

e·tà *f* (**-tà**) age; **che età ha?** how old is he (or she)?; **ha la sua età** he (or she) is no longer a youngster; **l'età di mezzo** Middle Ages; **maggiore età** majority; **mezza età** middle age; **minore età** minority

etamine *f* cheesecloth

ètere *m* ether

etère·o -a *adj* ethereal

eternare (etèrno) *tr* to immortalize ‖ *ref* to become immortal

eterni·tà *f* (-tà) eternity

etèr·no -na *adj* eternal, everlasting ‖ *m* eternity; **in eterno** forever

eterodòs·so -sa *adj* heterodox

eterogène·o -a *adj* heterogeneous

èti·ca *f* (-che) ethics

etichétta *f* label; card (*e.g., of a library*); etiquette; **etichetta gommata** sticker

etichettare (etichétto) *tr* to label

èti·co -ca (-ci -che) *adj* ethical; consumptive ‖ *m* consumptive ‖ *f* see **etica**

etile *m* ethyl

etilène *m* ethylene

etìli·co -ca *adj* (-ci -che) ethyl

ètimo *m* etymon

etimologìa *f* etymology

etìope *adj* & *mf* Ethiopian

Etiòpia, l' *f* Ethiopia

etiòpi·co -ca *adj* (-ci -che) Ethiopian

etisìa *f* tuberculosis

ètni·co -ca *adj* (-ci -che) ethnic(al)

etnografìa *f* ethnography

etnologìa *f* ethnology

etru·sco -sca *adj* & *mf* (-schi -sche) Etruscan

ettàgono *m* heptagon

èttaro *m* hectare

ètte *m* (coll) particle, jot, whit, tittle

ètto or **ettogrammo** *m* hectogram

-étto -étta *suf adj* rather, e.g., **piccoletto** rather small; -ish, e.g., **rotondetto** roundish

ettòlitro *m* hectoliter

eucalipto *m* eucalyptus

eucaristìa *f* Eucharist

eufemìsmo *m* euphemism

eufonìa *f* euphony

eufòni·co -ca *adj* (-ci -che) euphonic

euforìa *f* euphoria

eufòri·co -ca *adj* (-ci -che) euphoric

eufuìsmo *m* euphuism

eugenèti·co -ca (-ci -che) *adj* eugenic ‖ *f* eugenics

eunu·co *m* (-chi) eunuch

europè·o -a *adj* & *mf* European

Euròpa, l' *f* Europe

eurovisióne *f* European television chain

eutanasìa *f* euthanasia

Èva *f* Eve

evacuaménto *m* evacuation

evacuare (evàcuo) *tr* to evacuate ‖ *intr* to evacuate; to have a bowel movement

evacuazióne *f* evacuation; bowel movement

evàdere §172 *tr* to evade; to complete (*a deal*); to answer (*a letter*); to execute (*orders*) ‖ *intr* (ESSERE) to flee, escape

evanescènza *f* evanescence; (rad) fading

evanescènte *adj* evanescent; vanishing

evangèli·co -ca *adj* (-ci -che) evangelic (al)

evangelì·sta *m* (-sti) evangelist

evangelizzare [ddzz] *tr* to evangelize; to campaign for; to subject to political propaganda

evaporare (evapóro) *tr* & *intr* to evaporate

evaporatóre *m* evaporator; humidifier

evaporazióne *f* evaporation

evasióne *f* evasion, escape; (com) reply; **dare evasione a** to complete (*an administrative matter*)

evasì·vo -va *adj* evasive

evasóre *m* tax dodger

eva·so -sa *adj* escaped ‖ *m* escapee

evenìenza *f* eventuality, contingency; **nell'evenienza che** in the event (that); **per ogni evenienza** just in case

evènto *m* event; **eventi correnti** current events; **fausto** or **lieto evento** happy event

eventuale *adj* contingent

eventuali·tà *f* (-tà) eventuality

eversì·vo -va *adj* upsetting; destructive

evidènte *adj* evident; clear

evidènza *f* evidence; clearness; **mettersi in evidenza** to make oneself conspicuous; **tenere in evidenza** (com) to keep active

evirare *tr* to emasculate

evitare (èvito) *tr* to avoid, shun; **evitare qlco a qlcu** to spare s.o. s.th, to save s.o. from s.th

èvo *m* age, era; **evo antico** ancient times; **evo moderno** modern times; **medio evo** Middle Ages

evocare §197 **(èvoco)** *tr* to evoke

evoluìre §176 *intr* (aer, nav) to maneuver

evolu·to -ta *adj* developed; progressive; modern

evoluzióne *f* evolution

evòlvere §115 *tr* to develop ‖ *ref* to evolve

evvi·va *m* (-va) cheer ‖ *interj* long live!, hurrah for!

èx *adj invar* ex-, e.g., **la sua ex moglie** his ex-wife; ex, e.g., **ex dividendo** ex dividend

ex li·bris *m* (-bris) bookplate

extraconiugale *adj* extramarital

extraeuropè·o -a *adj* non-European

ex vó·to *m* (-to) votive offering

eziologìa *f* etiology

F

F, f ['ɛffe] *m* & *f* sixth letter of the Italian alphabet

fa *m* (fa) (mus) F, fa

fabbisógno *m invar* need; requirement

fàbbri·ca *f* (-che) building, construction; factory, plant

fabbricante *mf* builder, manufacturer

fabbricare §197 **(fàbbrico)** *tr* to manufacture; to fabricate

fabbrica·to -ta *adj* built ‖ *m* building

fabbricazióne *f* building; erection; manufacturing; fabrication (*invention*)

fabbro *m* blacksmith; locksmith; (fig) master; **fabbro ferraio** blacksmith

faccènda *f* business, matter; **faccende domestiche** household chores

faccendiè·re -ra *mf* operator, schemer

faccétta *f* small face; face, facet

facchinàg·gio *m* (-gi) porterage; (fig) drudgery

facchino *m* porter; **lavorare come un facchino** to work like a slave

fàc·cia *f* (-ce) face; countenance; **avere la faccia di** to have the gall to; **di faccia a** opposite; **faccia da galeotto** (coll) gallows bird; **faccia tosta** cheek, gall; **in faccia a** in front of

facciale *adj* facial

facciata *f* façade; page; (fig) surface appearance

face *f* (lit) torch

facè·to -ta *adj* facetious

facèzia *f* pleasantry, banter; **scambiar facezie** to banter with each other

fachiro *m* fakir

fàcile *adj* easy; inclined; loose (*morals*); glib (*tongue*); **è facile** it is probable ‖ *m* something easy

facili·tà *f* (-tà) facility, ease; inclination; **facilità di pagamento** easy payments, easy terms; **facilità di parola** glibness

facilitare (**facìlito**) *tr* to facilitate; to grant (*credit*); to give (*easy terms*)

facilitazióne *f* facilitation; easy terms; cut rate

facinoró·so -sa [s] *adj* criminal ‖ *m* hoodlum, thug

facoltà *f* (-tà) faculty; power; school (*of a university*); **facoltà** *fpl* means, wealth

facoltati·vo -va *adj* optional

facoltó·so -sa [s] *adj* wealthy, affluent

facóndia *f* loquacity, gift of gab

facón·do -da *adj* loquacious

facsìmi·le *m* (-le) facsimile

faènza *f* faïence ‖ **Faenza** *f* Faenza

fàg·gio *m* (-gi) (bot) beech

fagia·no -na *mf* pheasant

fagiolino *m* string bean

fagiòlo *m* bean; (coll) sophomore; **andare a fagiolo a** (coll) to fit perfectly; **fagiolo bianco** lima bean

fà·glia *f* (-glie) (geol) fault

fagòtto *m* bundle; (mus) bassoon; **far fagotto** (coll) to pack up

fàida *f* vengeance, vendetta

faìna *f* stone marten

falange *f* phalanx

fal·bo -ba *adj* tawny

falcata *f* step, stride; bucking

falce *f* scythe; crescent (*of moon*); **falce messoria** sickle

falcétto *m* sickle

falciare §128 *tr* to mow

falcia·tóre -trice *mf* mower ‖ *f* mowing machine

falcidiare §287 *tr* to reduce; to cut down

fal·co *m* (-chi) hawk; **falco pescatore** osprey

falcóne *m* falcon

falconerìa *f* falconry

falconière *m* falconer

falda *f* band, strip; flake (*of snow*); gable (*of roof*); brim (*of hat*); foot (*of mountain*); slab (*of stone*); waist plate (*of armor*); hem (*of suit*); flounce (*of dress*); layer (*of rock*); flap, coattail; **falda della camicia** shirttail; **falde straps** (*to hold a baby*); **mettersi in falde** to wear tails

falegname *m* carpenter; cabinetmaker

falegnamerìa *f* carpentry; cabinetmaking; carpenter shop; woodworker shop

falèna *f* moth

falla *f* hole, leak; (archaic) fault

fallace *adj* fallacious, deceptive

fallà·cia *f* (-cie) fallacy

fallare *intr & ref* (lit) to be mistaken

fallìbile *adj* fallible

fallimentare *adj* bankrupt; ruinous

falliménto *m* bankruptcy; (fig) collapse, failure

fallire §176 *tr* to miss (*the target*) ‖ *intr* (ESSERE) to go bankrupt; to fail ‖ *intr* (AVERE) to be mistaken

falli·to -ta *adj & mf* bankrupt

fallo *m* error, fault; sin; flaw; phallus; (sports) penalty; (sports) foul; **cadere in fallo** to make the wrong move; to be mistaken; **cogliere in fallo** to catch in the act; **far fallo a** to fail, e.g., **gli faccio fallo** I fail him; **senza fallo** without fail

fa·lò *m* (-lò) bonfire

falpa·là *f* (-là) flounce, furbelow

falsare *tr* to falsify, alter; (lit) to forge

falsari·ga *f* (-ghe) guideline (*for writing*); model, pattern; **seguire la falsariga di** to follow in the footsteps of

falsà·rio *m* (-ri) forger; counterfeiter

falsétto *m* falsetto

falsificare §197 (**falsìfico**) *tr* to falsify; to forge, fake

falsificazióne *f* falsification; forgery; misrepresentation

falsi·tà *f* (-tà) falsehood; falsity

fal·so -sa *adj* false; wrong (*step*); assumed (*name*); bogus, counterfeit, fake (*money*); phony ‖ *m* falsehood; perjury; forgery; **commettere un falso** to perjure oneself; to commit forgery; **giurare il falso** to bear false witness; to perjure oneself

fama *f* fame; reputation; **cattiva fama** notoriety

fame *f* hunger; dearth; **aver fame** to be hungry; **avere una fame da lupo** to be as hungry as a wolf, to be as hungry as a bear; **morire di fame** to starve to death; to be ravenous

famèli·co -ca *adj* (-ci -che) starving, famished

famigera·to -ta *adj* notorious

famiglia *f* family; community; **di famiglia** intimate; **in famiglia** at home

fami·glio *m* (-gli) beadle, usher; hired man

familiare *adj* family; familiar, intimate; homelike ‖ *m* member of the family

familiari·tà *f* (-tà) familiarity; **avere familiarità con** to be familiar with

familiarizzare [ddzz] *tr* to familiarize
famó·so -sa [s] *adj* famous, illustrious
fanale *m* lamp, lantern; (rr) headlight;
fanale di coda taillight
fanalino *m* small light; (aut) parking
light; (aut) tail light
fanàti·co -ca (-ci -che) *adj* fanatic,
fanatical ‖ *mf* fanatic
fanatismo *m* fanaticism
fanatizzare [ddzz] *tr* to make a fanatic
of
fanciulla *f* girl; spinster; bride
fanciullé·sco -sca *adj* (-schi -sche)
childish; children's
fanciullézza *f* childhood; (fig) infancy
fanciulo·lo -la *adj* childish; childlike
‖ *mf* child ‖ *m* boy ‖ *f* see **fanciulla**
fandònia *f* fib, tale, yarn
fanèllo *m* (orn) linnet; (orn) finch
fanfara *f* military band; fanfare
fanfaróne *m* braggart
fangatura *f* mud bath
fanghìglia *f* mud, slush
fan·go *m* (-ghi) mud; **fare i fanghi** to
take mud baths
fangó·so -sa [s] *adj* muddy
fannullo·ne -na *mf* idler, loafer
fanóne *m* whalebone
fantaccino *m* infantryman, foot soldier
fantascientìfi·co -ca *adj* (-ci -che)
science-fiction
fantasciènza *f* science fiction
fantasia *f* fantasy, fancy, whim; (mus)
fantasia; **di fantasia** fancy
fantasió·so -sa [s] *adj* fanciful; imaginative
fanta·sma *m* (-smi) ghost, spirit; phantom; **fantasma poetico** poetic fancy
fantasticare §197 (**fantàstico**) *tr* to
imagine, dream up ‖ *intr* to daydream
fantasticheria *f* imagination, daydreaming
fantàsti·co -ca *adj* (-ci -che) fantastic ‖
fantastico *interj* unbelievable!
fante *m* infantryman, foot soldier;
(cards) jack; (obs) youth
fanteria *f* infantry
fanté·sca *f* (-sche) (joc, lit) housemaid
fantino *m* jockey
fantòc·cio *m* (-ci) puppet
fantomàti·co -ca *adj* (-ci -che) ghostly;
mysterious
farabutto *m* scoundrel, heel
faraóna *f* guinea fowl
faraóne *m* Pharaoh; (cards) faro
farcire §176 *tr* to stuff
fardèllo *m* bundle; burden; **far fardello**
to pack one's bags
fare *m* doing; break (*of day*); way (*of
acting*); **sul far della sera** at nightfall
‖ §173 *tr* to do; to make; to work;
to take (*e.g., a walk, a step*); to give
(*a sigh*); to deal (*cards*); to suffer
(*hunger*); to lead (*a good or bad life*);
to render (*service*); to log (*e.g., 15
m.p.h.*); to be, e.g., **tre volte tre fa
nove** three times three is nine; to
build (*e.g., a house*); to put together
(*a collection*); to prepare (*dinner*);
to say, utter (*a word*); to have (*a
dream*); to give (*fruit*); to pay (*atten-

tion*); to play (*a role*); to stir up
(*pity*); to mention (*a name*); **fare
il** (or **la**) to be a (*e.g., carpenter*);
fare + *inf* to have + *inf*, e.g., **gli
ho fatto . . .** I had him . . . ; to
make + *inf*, e.g., **il medico mi
fece . . .** the doctor made me . . .; to
have + *pp*, e.g., **farò fare . . .** I shall
have . . . done; **fare acqua** to leak,
to take in water; to get a supply of
water; (coll) to urinate; **fare a metà**
to divide in half; **fare a pugni** to come
to blows; **fare a tempo** to be on time;
fare benzina to buy gasoline; **fare
caldo** a to keep warm, e.g., **questa
coperta gli fa caldo** this blanket keeps
him warm; **fare carbone** to coal; **fare
. . . che** to have been . . . since, e.g.,
**fanno tre mesi che siamo in questa
città** it has been three months since
we have been in this city; **fare che** +
subj to see to it that + *ind*, e.g.,
**faccia che comincino a lavorare su-
bito** see to it that they begin to work
at once; **fare colpo** to make an impression; **fare corona** a to crown;
fare cuore a to encourage; **fare del
male** a to harm; **fare di** + *inf* to see
to it that + *ind*; **fare di tutto** to do
one's best; **fare festa** a to cheer; **fare
fiasco** to fail; **fare finta di** to pretend
to; **fare fronte** a to face, meet; **fare
fuoco su** to fire upon; **fare il gioco di**
to play into the hands of; **fare il
pappagallo** to parrot, ape; **fare il
pieno** to fill up (*with gasoline*); **fare
la bocca** a to get used to; **fare la
calza** to knit; **fare la coda** to queue
up, line up; **fare la festa** a to kill;
fare la guardia to stand guard; **fare
la mano** a to get used to; **fare le cose
in famiglia** to wash one's dirty linen
at home; **fare le cose in grande stile**
to splurge; **fare legna** to gather firewood; **fare l'occhio** to become accustomed; **fare mente** a to pay attention;
fare onore a to do honor to; **fare
paura** a to frighten; **fare sangue** to
bleed; **fare sapere** a qlcu to let s.o.
know; **fare scalo** (aer, naut) to make
a call; **fare sì che** to act in such a
way that; to see to it that; **fare silenzio** to keep silent; **fare specie** a to
amaze, e.g., **il tuo comportamento
gli fa specie** your behavior amazes
him; **fare tesoro di** to prize; **fare una
bella figura** to look good; to make a
fine appearance; **fare una mala figura**
to look bad; to make a bad showing;
fare una malattia (coll) to get sick;
fare vela to set sail; **fare venire** to
send for; **fare vigilia** to fast; **farla
corta** to cut it short; **farla franca**
to get off scot-free; **farla grossa** to
commit a blunder; **farla in barba a**
to outwit; **farne di cotte e di crude,
farne di tutti i colori,** or **farne più
di Carlo in Francia** to engage in all
sorts of mischief; to paint the town
red; **non fare che** + *ind* to do nothing
but + *inf* ‖ *intr*—**averla a che fare
con** to have words with; to have to

deal with; **fare a coltellate** to have a fight with knives; **fare a girotondo** to play ring-around-the-rosy; **fare al caso di** to fit; to suit; **fare a meno di** to do without; **fare da** to serve as, e.g., **fare da cuscino** to serve as a pillow; **fare da cena** to fix dinner; **fare di cappello** to take one's hat off; **fare presto** to hurry; **fare per** to be just the thing for; **fare tardi** to be late || *ref* to become; to cut (*e.g.*, *one's hair*); to move, e.g., **farsi in là** to move farther; **farsi avanti** to come forward; **farsi beffe di** to make fun of; **farsi bello** to bedeck oneself; to dress up; **farsi bello di** to make fun about; to appropriate; **farsi gioco di** to make fun of; **farsi le labbra** to put lipstick on; **farsi strada** to make one's way; **farsi una ragione di** to rationalize, explain to oneself; **farsi un baffo** to not give a hoot; **si fa giorno** it is getting light; **si fa tardi** it is getting late || *impers—***che tempo fa?** what's the weather like?; **fa** ago, e.g., **alcune settimane fa** a few weeks ago; **fa estate** it is like summer; **fa fino** it is smart; **fa freddo** it is cold; **fa luna** there is moonlight, the moon is out; **fa nebbia** it is foggy; **fa notte** it is nighttime; it is dark; it is getting dark; **fa sole** it is sunny, the sun is out; **fa tipo** or **fa tono!** that's classy!; **non fa nulla** it doesn't matter, never mind

farètra *f* quiver

farfalla *f* butterfly; bow tie; (mach) butterfly valve; (coll) promissory note

farfallóne *m* large butterfly; blunder; Don Juan

farfugliare §280 *intr* to mumble, mutter

farina *f* flour; **farina d'avena** oatmeal; **farina di legno** sawdust; **farina di ossa** bone meal; **farina gialla** yellow corn meal

farinàce·o -a *adj* farinaceous || **farinacei** *mpl* flour-yielding cereals

farinata *f* porridge

faringe *f* pharynx

faringite *f* pharingitis

farinó·so -sa [s] *adj* floury; powdery (*snow*); crumbly, friable

farisèo *m* Pharisee; (fig) pharisee

farmacèuti·co -ca *adj* (-ci -che) pharmaceutical, drug

farmacìa *f* pharmacy; drugstore; medicine cabinet; **farmacia di guardia** or **di turno** drugstore open all night and Sunday

farmaci·sta *mf* (-sti -ste) pharmacist, druggist

fàrma·co *m* (-ci or -chi) remedy, medicine

farneticare §197 (farnètico) *intr* to rave

farnèti·co -ca *adj* (-chi -che) raving || *m* delirium; craze

faro *m* lighthouse, beacon; (aut) headlight; **faro retromarcia** (aut) back-up light

farràgine *f* hodgepodge

farraginó·so -sa [s] *adj* confused, mixed

farsa *f* farce; burlesque

farsé·sco -sca *adj* (-schi -sche) farcical, ludicrous

farsétto *m* sweater; (hist) doublet

fascétta *f* girdle; band; wrapper; clamp; **fascetta editoriale** advertising band (*of book*)

fà·scia *f* (-sce) band; belt; bandage; newspaper wrapper; **fascia del cappello** hatband; **fascia di garza** gauze bandage; **fascia elastica** abdominal supporter; (aut) piston ring; **fasce del neonato** swaddling clothes; **in fasce** newborn; **sotto fascia** in a wrapper

fasciame *m* (naut) planking; (naut) plating

fasciare §128 to bind; to bandage; to wrap; to surround

fasciatura *f* bandaging, dressing

fascicolo *m* number, issue; pamphlet; file, dossier; (bb) fasciculus

fascina *f* fagot

fascina·tóre -trice *mf* charmer

fàscino *m* fascination, charm

fà·scio *m* (-sci) bundle; sheaf; bunch (*of flowers*); pencil or beam (*of rays*); fascist party

fascismo *m* fascism

fasci·sta *adj* & *mf* (-sti -ste) fascist

fase *f* phase, stage; (aut) cycle; (astr, elec, mach) phase

fastèllo *m* bundle, fagot

fasti *mpl* records, annals; notable events; (hist) Roman calendar

fasti·dio *m* (-di) annoyance; (coll) loathing, nausea; **avere in fastidio** to loathe; **dar fastidio a** to annoy; **fastidi** troubles, worries

fastidió·so -sa [s] *adj* annoying, irksome; irritable; (obs) disgusting

fasti·gio *m* (-gi) top, summit

fa·sto -sta *adj* (lit) propitious || *m invar* pomp, display || *mpl* see **fasti**

fastó·so -sa [s] *adj* pompous, ostentatious

fata *f* fairy; **buona fata** fairy godmother; **Fata Morgana** Fata Morgana (*mirage; Morgan le Fay*)

fatale *adj* fatal; inevitable; irresistible (*woman*)

fatalismo *m* fatalism

fatali·sta *mf* (-sti -ste) fatalist

fatali·tà *f* (-tà) fatality, fate

fatalóna *f* vamp

fata·to -ta *adj* fairy, enchanted; (lit) predestined

fati·ca *f* (-che) fatigue, weariness; labor; **a fatica** with difficulty; **da fatica** draft (*e.g.*, *horse*); of burden (*beast*); **durar fatica a** + *inf* to have trouble in + *ger*

faticare §197 *intr* to toil; **faticare a** to be hardly able to

faticó·so -sa [s] *adj* burdensome, heavy; (lit) weary

fatìdi·co -ca *adj* (-ci -che) fatal

fato *m* fate, destiny

fatta *f* kind, sort; **essere sulla fatta di** to be on the trail of

fattàc·cio *m* (-ci) (coll) crime

fattézze *fpl* features

fattìbile adj feasible, possible

fattispècie f—**nella fattispecie** in this particular case

fat·to -ta adj made, e.g., **fatto a mano** handmade; broad (daylight); deep (night); ready-made (e.g., suit); **ben fatto** well-done; shapely; **esser fatto per** to be cut out for; **fatto di** made of; **venir fatto** a to happen, chance, e.g., **gli venne fatto d'incontrarmi** he happened to meet me ‖ m fact; act, deed; feat; action; business, affair; **badare ai fatti propri** to mind one's own business; **cogliere sul fatto** to catch in the act; **dire a qlcu il fatto suo** to give s.o. a piece of one's mind; **fatto compiuto** fait accompli; **fatto d'arme** feat of arms; **fatto si è** the fact remains that; **in fatto di** concerning; as of; **sapere il fatto proprio** to know one's business; **venire al fatto** to come to the point ‖ f see **fatta**

fat·tóre -tóra or **-toréssa** mf farm manager ‖ m maker; factor; steward ‖ f stewardess; manager's wife

fattoria f farm; stewardship

fattorino m delivery boy, messenger boy; conductor (of streetcar)

fattrice f (zool) dam

fattucchiè·re -ra mf magician ‖ m sorcerer ‖ f sorceress, witch

fattura f preparation; workmanship; bill, invoice; (coll) witchcraft; (lit) creature

fatturare tr to adulterate; to invoice, bill

fattura·to -ta adj adulterated ‖ m (com) turnover

fatturi·sta mf (-sti -ste) billing clerk

fà·tuo -tua adj fatuous

fàuci fpl jaws; (fig) mouth

fàuna f fauna

fàuno m faun

fàu·sto -sta adj propitious, lucky

fau·tóre -trice mf supporter, promoter

fava f broad bean; **pigliare due piccioni con una fava** to catch two birds with one stone

favèlla f speech; (lit) tongue

favilla f spark; **far** or **mandare faville** to sparkle

favo m honeycomb

fàvola f fable; tale; **favola del paese** talk of the town

favoló·so -sa [s] adj fabulous; mythical

favóre m favor; help; cover (e.g., of night); **a favore di** for the benefit of; **di favore** special (price); complimentary (ticket); **favore politico** patronage; **per favore** please; **per favore di** courtesy of

favoreggiaménto m abetting, support

favoreggiare §290 (**favoréggio**) tr to abet, support

favoreggia·tóre -trice mf abettor, supporter, backer

favorévole adj favorable; propitious

favorire §176 tr to favor; to accept; to oblige, accommodate; **favorire qlcu di qlco** to oblige s.o. with s.th; **favorisca** + inf please + inf, be kind

enough to + inf; **favorisca alla cassa** please pay the cashier; **favorisca uscire!** please leave!; **tanto per favorire?** won't you please join us (at a meal)?; please help yourself!

favorita f royal mistress

favoritismo m favoritism

favori·to -ta adj & mf favorite ‖ m protegé; **favoriti** sideburns ‖ f see **favorita**

fazióne f faction; **essere di fazione** to be on guard duty

fazió·so -sa [s] adj factious ‖ m partisan

fazzolétto m handkerchief; **fazzoletto da collo** neckerchief

fé f var of **fede**

feb·bràio m (-brài) February

fèbbre f fever; fever blister; **febbre da cavallo** (coll) very high fever; **febbre da fieno** hay fever; **febbre dell'oro** gold fever

febbricitante adj feverish

febbrile adj feverish

Fèbo m Phoebus

féc·cia f (-ce) dregs; (fig) dregs (of society); **fino alla feccia** to the bitter end

fèci fpl feces

fècola f starch

fecondare (**fecóndo**) tr to fecundate

fecondazióne f fecundation; **fecondazione artificiale** artificial insemination

fecondi·tà f (-tà) fecundity

fecón·do -da adj fecund, prolific

féde f faith; certificate; wedding ring; faithfulness; **far fede** to bear witness; **in fede di che** in testimony whereof; **in fede mia!** upon my word! **prestar fede** a to put one's faith in; **tener fede alla parola data** to keep one's word

fedecomrnésso m fideicommissum; trusteeship

fedéle adj faithful, devoted ‖ mf faithful person; **i fedeli** the faithful

fedel·tà f (-tà) faithfulness, allegiance; fidelity; **ad alta fedeltà** hi-fi

fèdera f pillowcase

federale adj federal

federali·sta mf (-sti -ste) federalist

federati·vo -va adj federative

federa·to -ta adj federate, federated

federazióne f federation; (sports) league

Federico m Frederick

fedifra·go -ga adj (-ghi -ghe) unfaithful, treacherous

fedina f police record; **avere la fedina sporca** to have a bad record; **fedine** sideburns

fégato m liver; courage; **fegato d'oca** pâté de foie gras; **rodersi il fegato** to be consumed with rage

félce f fern

feldspato m feldspar

felice adj happy; blissful; glad; felicitous

felici·tà f (-tà) happiness; bliss

felicitare (**felìcito**) tr to make happy; **che Dio vi feliciti!** God bless you! ‖

ref to rejoice; **felicitarsi con qlcu per qlco** to congratulate s.o. for or on s.th

felicitazióne *f* congratulation

feli·no -na *adj & m* feline

fellóne *m* (lit) traitor

félpa *f* plush

felpa·to -ta *adj* covered with plush; soft (*e.g., step*)

féltro *m* felt; felt hat

felu·ca *f* (-**che**) two-cornered hat; (naut) felucca

fémmina *adj & f* female

femminile *adj* feminine, female || *m* feminine gender

femminili·tà *f* (-**tà**) femininity, womanliness

femminismo *m* feminism

fèmore *m* femur; thighbone

fendènte *m* slash with a sword

fèndere §174 *tr* to split, cleave; to plow (*water*); to rend (*air*); to make one's way through (*a crowd*) || *ref* to split; to come apart

fenditura *f* split, breach, fissure

fenice *f* phoenix

feni·cio -cia (-**ci -cie**) *adj & mf* Phoenician || **la Fenicia** Phoenicia

fèni·co -ca *adj* (-**ci -che**) carbolic

fenicòttero *m* flamingo

fenòlo *m* phenol

fenomenale *adj* phenomenal

fenòmeno *m* phenomenon; freak, monster; **essere un fenomeno** to be unbelievable

ferace *adj* (lit) fertile

ferale *adj* (lit) mortal, deadly

fèretro *m* bier, coffin

feriale *adj* working (*day*); weekday

fèrie *fpl* vacation; **ferie retribuite** vacation with pay

ferire §176 *tr* to wound; to strike; **senza colpo ferire** without striking a blow || *ref* to wound oneself

feri·to -ta *adj* wounded, injured || *m* wounded person; injured person; **i feriti** the wounded; the injured || *f* wound, injury

feritóia *f* loophole; embrasure

feri·tóre -trice *mf* assailant

férma *f* setting (*of setter or pointer*); (mil) service; (mil) enlistment

fermacarro *m* (rr) buffer

fermacar·te *m* (-**te**) paperweight; large paper clip

fermacravat·ta *m* (-**ta**) tiepin

fermà·glio *m* (-**gli**) clasp; buckle; clip; brooch

fermare (**férmo**) *tr* to stop; to pay (*attention*); to fasten; to close, shut; to detain (*in police station*); to set (*game*); to reserve (*seats*) || *ref* to stop; to stay

fermata *f* stop; **fermata a richiesta** or **facoltativa** stop on signal

fermentare (**ferménto**) *tr & intr* to ferment

fermentazióne *f* fermentation

ferménto *m* ferment

fermézza *f* firmness; steadfastness

fér·mo -ma *adj* firm; stopped; quiet (*water*); (fig) steadfast; **fermo in**

posta general delivery; **fermo restando che** seeing that; **stare fermo** to be quiet || *m* stop; detention; **mettere il fermo a** to stop (*a check*)

fermopòsta *m* general delivery || *adv* care of general delivery

feróce *adj* fierce; wild

ferò·cia *f* (-**cie**) ferocity, ferociousness, fierceness

feròdo *m* (aut) brake lining

ferragósto *m* Assumption; mid-August holiday

ferrame *m* ironware

ferramén·to *m* (-**ti**) iron or metal bracket; iron or metal trimming || *m* (-**ta** *fpl*)—**ferramenta** hardware

ferrare (**fèrro**) *tr* to shoe (*a horse*); to hoop (*a barrel*)

ferra·to -ta *adj* iron; ironclad; shod (*horse*); spiked (*shoe*); well-versed || *f* pressing, ironing; mark or burn (*caused by ironing*); (coll) iron grate

ferravèc·chio *m* (-**chi**) scrap-iron dealer, junkman

fèrre·o -a *adj* iron; ironclad

ferrièra *f* ironworks; (obs) iron mine

fèrro *m* iron; tool; anchor; sword; **ai ferri** on the grill, broiled (*e.g., steak*); **essere sotto i ferri del chirurgo** to go under the knife; **ferri** shackles; **ferri del mestiere** tools of the trade; **ferro battuto** wrought iron; **ferro da arricciare** curling iron; **ferro da calza** knitting needle; **ferro da cavallo** horseshoe; **ferro da stiro** iron, flatiron; **ferro fuso** cast iron; **ferro grezzo** pig iron; **mettere a ferro e fuoco** to put to fire and sword; **venire ai ferri corti** to get into close quarters

ferromodellismo *m* hobby of model railroads

ferrotranvièri *mpl* transport workers

ferrovìa *f* railroad; **ferrovia a dentiera** rack railway; **ferrovia sopraelevata** elevated railroad

ferrovià·rio -ria *adj* (-**ri -rie**) railroad

ferrovière *m* railroader

fèrtile *adj* fertile

fertilizzante [ddzz] *adj* fertilizing || *m* fertilizer

fertilizzare [ddzz] *tr* to fertilize

fervènte *adj* fervent

fervère §175 *intr* to be fervent; to rage (*said, e.g., of a battle*); to go full blast

fèrvi·do -da *adj* fervent

fervóre *m* fervor; (fig) heat

fervorino *m* lecture, sermon

fesserìa *f* (slang) stupidity, nonsense; (slang) trifle

fés·so -sa *adj* cracked; cleft; (slang) dumb || *m* (lit) cranny; **fare fesso qlcu** (slang) to play s.o. for a sucker

fessura *f* crack; cranny

fèsta *f* feast; holiday; birthday; saint's day; **a festa** festively; **buone feste!** happy holiday!; **conciare per le feste** to drub the daylights out of; **fare festa a** to welcome; **fare le feste** to spend the holidays; **far festa** to celebrate; to take the day off; **far la festa**

a to do in, kill; **festa del ceppo** Christmas; **festa da ballo** or **danzante** dancing party; **festa della mamma** Mother's Day; **festa del papà** Father's Day; **festa di precetto** (eccl) day of obligation; **festa nazionale** national holiday; **mezza festa** half holiday

festante *adj* cheerful

festeggiaménto *m* celebration

festeggiare §290 (**festéggio**) *tr* to celebrate, fete; to cheer

festi·no -na *adj* (lit) rapid ‖ *m* party

festivi·tà *f* (-**tà**) festivity

festi·vo -va *adj* festive, holiday

festóne *m* festoon

festó·so -sa [s] *adj* cheerful, merry

festu·ca *f* (-**che**) straw; (fig) mote

fetènte *adj* stinking; stink (*bomb*) ‖ *mf* (fig) stinker, louse

fetìc·cio *m* (-**ci**) fetish

feticismo *m* fetishism

fèti·do -da *adj* stinking, fetid

fèto *m* fetus

fetóre *m* stench

fétta *f* slice; **tagliare a fette** to slice

fettina *f* thin slice; twist (*of lemon*); **fettina di vitello** veal cutlet

fettùc·cia *f* (-**ce**) tape, ribbon

fettuccine *fpl* noodles

feudale *adj* feudal

feudalismo *m* feudalism

feudatà·rio -ria (-**ri -rie**) *adj* feudatory ‖ *m* feudal vassal

fèudo *m* fief

fiaba *f* fairy tale; tale, yarn

fiacca *f* tiredness; sluggishness; **batter la fiacca** to loaf, to goof off

fiaccare §197 *tr* to weary; to break ‖ *ref* to weaken; to break (*e.g., one's neck*)

fiacche·ràio *m* (-**rài**) (coll) hackman, cabman

fiacchézza *f* weakness; sluggishness

fiac·co -ca *adj* (-**chi -che**) weak; sluggish; slack ‖ *f* see **fiacca**

fiàccola *f* torch; **fiaccola della discordia** firebrand

fiaccolata *f* torchlight procession

fiala *f* vial, phial

fiamma *f* flame; blaze; (mil) insignia; (nav) pennant; **alla fiamma** (culin) flaming; **dare alle fiamme** to set on fire; **diventare di fiamma** to blush; **in fiamme** afire

fiammante *adj* blazing; **nuovo fiammante** brand-new

fiammata *f* blaze; flare-up

fiammeggiante *adj* flaming, blazing; (archit) flamboyant

fiammeggiare §290 (**fiamméggio**) *tr* to singe ‖ *intr* to flame, blaze

fiammifero *m* match

fiammin·go -ga (-**ghi -ghe**) *adj* Flemish; Dutch (*e.g., master*) ‖ *mf* Fleming ‖ *m* Flemish (*language*); (orn) flamingo

fiancata *f* blow with one's hip; dig, sarcastic remark; side, flank; (nav) broadside

fiancheggiare §290 (**fiancéggio**) *tr* to flank; to border (*a road*); to support

fiancheggia·tóre -trice *mf* supporter, backer

fian·co *m* (-**chi**) flank, side; hip; **di fianco** sideways; **fianco a fianco** side by side; **fianco destr'!** (mil) right face!; **fianco destro** (naut) starboard; **fianco sinistr'!** (mil) left face!; **fianco sinistro** (naut) port; **prestare il fianco a** to leave oneself wide open to; **tenersi i fianchi dal ridere** to split one's sides laughing

Fiandre, le *fpl* Flanders

fia·sca *f* (-**sche**) flask

fiaschetterìa *f* tavern, wine shop

fia·sco *m* (-**schi**) straw-covered wine bottle; flask; fiasco

fiata *f* (archaic) time

fiatare *intr* to breathe; **senza fiatare** without breathing a word

fiato *m* breath; (archaic) stench; **avere il fiato grosso** to be out of breath; **bere d'un fiato** to gulp down; **col fiato sospeso** holding one's breath; **dare fiato a** to blow, sound (*a trumpet*); **d'un fiato** or **in un fiato** without interruption; in one gulp; **fiati** (mus) winds; **senza fiato** out of breath

fiatóne *m*—**avere il fiatone** to be out of breath

fibbia *f* clasp, buckle

fibra *f* fiber

fibró·so -sa [s] *adj* fibrous

ficcana·so [s] *mf* (-**si** *mpl* -**so** *fpl*) (coll) busybody, meddler; nosy person

ficcare §197 *tr* to stick; to drive (*e.g., a nail*); to push; **ficcare gli occhi addosso a** to gaze at, stare at; **ficcare il naso negli affari degli altri** to poke one's nose in other people's business ‖ *ref* to hide; to butt in; to get involved

fi·co *m* (-**chi**) fig; fig tree

ficodìndia *m* (*pl* **fichidindia**) prickly pear

fidanzaménto *m* engagement, betrothal

fidanzare *tr* to betroth ‖ *ref* to become engaged

fidanza·to -ta *adj* engaged ‖ *m* fiancé ‖ *f* fiancée

fidare *tr* to entrust ‖ *intr* to trust ‖ *ref* to have confidence; **fidarsi a** (coll) to dare to; **fidarsi di** to trust, rely on

fida·to -ta *adj* trustworthy, reliable

fi·do -da *adj* (lit) faithful, trusted ‖ *m* loyal follower; credit; **far fido to** extend credit

fidùcia *f* faith, confidence; (com) credit; **di fiducia** trustworthy

fiducià·rio -ria (-**ri -rie**) *adj* fiduciary ‖ *mf* fiduciary, trustee

fiducó·so -sa [s] *adj* confident, hopeful

fièle *m* invar gall, bile; acrimony

fienile *m* hayloft

fièno *m* hay

fierìsti·co -ca *adj* (-**ci -che**) of a fair, e.g., **attività fieristica** activity of a fair

fiè·ro -ra *adj* fierce; dignified; proud ‖ *f* exhibit; wild beast

fièvole adj feeble, weak

fifa f (coll) scare; **avere la fifa** (coll) to be chicken; **avere una fifa blu** (coll) to be scared stiff

fifó·ne -na mf (coll) scaredy-cat

figgere §104 tr (lit) to drive, thrust || ref—**figgersi in capo** to get into one's head

figlia f daughter; (com) stub; **figlia consanguinea** stepdaughter on the father's side

figliare §280 tr & intr to whelp (said of animals)

figlia·stro -stra mf stepchild || m stepson || f stepdaughter

figliata f litter (e.g., of pigs)

fi·glio -glia mf child, offspring || m son; **figli** children; **figlio consanguineo** stepson on the father's side || f see **figlia**

figliòc·cio -cia (-ci -ce) mf godchild || m godson || f goddaughter

figliolanza f children, offspring

figliò·lo -la mf child || m. son, boy || f daughter, girl

figura f figure; illustration; figurehead; face card; **far bella figura** to make a good showing; **far cattiva figura** to make a poor showing; **far figura** to look good; **figura retorica** figure of speech

figurante mf (theat) extra, super

figurare tr to feign; to represent || intr to figure; to appear; to make a good showing || ref to imagine; **si figuri!** imagine!

figurati·vo -va adj (fa) figurative

figura·to -ta adj figurative (speech); transcribed (pronunciation); illustrated (book)

figurina f figurine; card, picture (of a series of athletes or entertainment celebrities)

figurini·sta mf (-sti -ste) dress designer; costume designer

figurino m fashion plate; fashion magazine

figuro m scoundrel; gangster

figuróne m—**fare un figurone** to make a very good showing

fila f row; file, line; series; **di fila in a** row; **fare la fila** to wait in line; **file ranks**

filàc·cia f (-ce) lint

filacció·so -sa [s] or **filaccio·so -sa** [s] adj thready, stringy

filaménto m filament

filamentó·so -sa [s] adj thready, stringy; thread-like

filanda f spinning mill; silk spinning mill

filante adj spinning; shooting (star); thready; flowing (e.g., line)

filantropia f philanthropy

filantròpi·co -ca adj (-ci -che) philanthropic

filàntro·po -pa mf philanthropist

filare m row, line || tr to spin; to drip, ooze; to rest on (one's oars); to make (e.g., ten knots); (naut) to pay out; (mus) to hold (a note); **filare l'amore** to be in love || intr to spin (said of a spider); to rope, thread (said of wine

or syrup); to make sense; to drip; **fare filare dritto** qlcu to keep s.o. in line; **filare a** to do (e.g., twenty miles an hour); **filare all'inglese** to take French leave; **fila via!** (coll) get out!

filarmòni·co -ca (-ci -che) adj philharmonic || f philharmonic society

filastròc·ca f (-che) rigmarole; nursery rhyme

filatelia f philately

filatèli·co -ca (-ci -che) adj philatelic(al) || mf philatelist

fila·to -ta adj spun; well-constructed (speech) || m yarn

fila·tóio m (-tói) spinning wheel

filatura f spinning; spinning mill

filettare (filétto) tr to fillet; (mach) to thread

filettatura f stripe (on a cap); (mach) thread

filétto m fillet; stripe; snaffle (on a horse's bit); fine stroke (in handwriting); (mach) thread; (typ) ornamental line, headband; (typ) rule

filiale adj filial || f branch office

filiazióne f filiation

filibustière m filibuster, buccaneer; adventurer

filièra f (mach) drawplate; (mach) die (to cut threads)

filigrana f filigree; watermark (in paper)

filippi·no -na adj Philippine || m Filipino || **le Filippine** the Philippines

Filippo m Philip

filistè·o -a adj & m philistine; Philistine

Fillide f Phyllis

film m (film) film; movie, motion picture; **film parlato** or **sonoro** talking picture

filmare tr to film

filmina f filmstrip

filmisti·co -ca adj (-ci -che) movie, motion-picture

filmotè·ca f (-che) film library

fi·lo m (-li) thread; wire; yarn; blade (of grass); breath (of air); string (of pearls); edge (of razor); **dare del filo da torcere** to cause trouble; **essere ridotto a un filo** to be only skin and bones; **fil di voce** thin voice; **filo a piombo** plumb line; **filo d'acqua** thin stream; **filo della schiena** or **delle reni** spine; **filo spinato** barbed wire; **passare a fil di spada** to put to the sword; **per filo e per segno** in detail; from beginning to end; **senza fili** wireless; **stare a filo** to stand upright; **tenere i fili** (fig) to pull wires; **tenere in filo** to keep in line; **un filo di** a bit of || m (-la fpl) string (e.g., of cooked cheese); (archaic) file, row

filo·bus m (-bus) trolley bus

filodiffusióne f wired wireless; cable TV

filodrammàti·co -ca adj & mf (-ci -che) (theat) amateur

filogovernati·vo -va adj on the government side

filologia f philology

filòlo·go -ga (-gi -ghe) adj philologic(al) || m philologist

filóne m vein (of ore); ripple (of a cur-

rent); stream; loaf (*of bread*); (lit) mainstream; **filone d'oro** gold lode

filó·so -sa [s] *adj* stringy

filosofìa *f* philosophy

filosòfi·co -ca *adj* (**-ci -che**) philosophic(al)

filòso·fo -fa *mf* philosopher

filovìa *f* trolley bus line

filtrare *tr* to filter; to percolate (*coffee*) || *intr* to filter, permeate

filtrazióne *f* filtering, filtration

filtro *m* filter; philter

filugèllo *m* silkworm

filza *f* string (*of pearls*); series (*of errors*); row; dossier, file; basting (*of dress*)

finale *adj* final, last; consumer (*goods*) || *m* end, ending; (mus) finale; (sports) finish || *f* end, ending; (sports) finals

finali·sta *mf* (**-sti -ste**) finalist

finali·tà *f* (**-tà**) end, purpose

finanche *adv* even

finanza *f* finance

finanziaménto *m* financing

finanziare §287 *tr* to finance

finanzià·rio -ria (**-ri -rie**) *adj* finance, financial || *f* (com) holding company

finanzia·tóre -trice *mf* financial backer

finanzièra *f* frock coat; **alla finanziera** with giblet gravy

finanzière *m* financier; (coll) customs officer

fin·ca *f* (**-che**) column, row (*of ledger*)

finché *conj* until, as long as; **finché non** until

fine *adj* fine, thin; choice, nice || *m* end, purpose; conclusion; (lit) limit, border; **a fin di bene** to good purpose, for the best; **secondo fine** ulterior motive || *f* end, conclusion; **condurre a fine** to bring to fruition; **fine di settimana** weekend; **in fin dei conti** after all; **senza fine** endless

fine-settimà·na *m* or *f* (**-na**) weekend

finèstra *f* window; (lit) gash, wound; **finestra a gangheri** casement window; **finestra a ghigliottina** sash window; **finestra panoramica** picture window; **finestre** (lit) eyes

finestrino *m* (aut, rr) window

finézza *f* thinness; delicacy; finesse; kindness

fingere §126 *tr* to feign, pretend; (lit) to invent || *intr* to feign, pretend || *ref* to pretend to be

finiménto *m* finishing touch; **finimenti** harness

finimóndo *m* fracas, uproar

finire §176 *tr* to end; to put an end to; **finiscila!** cut it out! || *intr* (ESSERE) to end, to be over; to abut; to wind up; **finire con** + *inf* to wind up + *ger*; **finire di** + *inf* to finish + *ger*, e.g., **ho finito di farmi la barba** I have finished shaving

fini·to -ta *adj* finished; accomplished; finite; exhausted; **aver finito** to be through; **falla finita!** cut it out!; **farla finita con** to be through with; **farla finita con la vita** to end one's life

finitura *f* finish, finishing touch

finlandése [s] *adj* Finnish || *mf* Finlander, Finn || *m* Finnish (*language*)

Finlàndia, la Finland

finni·co -ca *adj* & *mf* (**-ci -che**) Finnic

fi·no -na *adj* fine, thin; refined; pure; sheer; **fare fino** (coll) to be refined || *adv* even; **fin a quando?** till when?; **fin da domani** beginning tomorrow; **fin da ora** beginning right now; **fin dove?** how far?; **fino a** until; down to; up to; as far as; **fin in cima** up to the top; **fino qui** up to now; up to this point

finòc·chio *m* (**-chi**) fennel; (vulg) fairy, queer

finóra *adv* up to now, heretofore

finta *f* pretense; fly (*of trousers*); (sports) feint; **far finta di** + *inf* to pretend to + *inf*, to feign + *ger*

fintantoché *conj* until

fin·to -ta *adj* false (*teeth*); fake; fictitious; sham (*battle*) || *mf* hypocrite || *f* see **finta**

finzióne *f* pretense; fiction; figment

fio *m*—**pagare il fio** to pay the piper; **pagare il fio di** to pay the penalty for

fioccare §197 (**flòcco**) *intr* (ESSERE) to fall (*said of snow*); to flow (*said, e.g., of complaints*) || *impers* (ESSERE) —**fiocca** it is snowing

fiòc·co *m* (**-chi**) bow, knot; flake (*of snow*); flock, tuft (*of wool*); (naut) jib; **coi fiocchi** excellent; made to perfection; **fiocco pallone** (naut) spinnaker

fioccó·so -sa [s] *adj* flaky

fiòcina *f* harpoon

fiò·co -ca *adj* (**-chi -che**) feeble, faint

fiónda *f* sling; slingshot

fio·ràio -ràia (**-rài -ràie**) *mf* florist || *f* flower girl

fiorami *mpl*—**a fiorami** with flower design

fiordalìso *m* fleur-de-lis; (bot) iris; (lit) lily

fiòrdo *m* fjord

fióre *m* flower; prime (*of life*); best, pick; bloom; **a fior d'acqua** on the surface; skimming the water; **a fior di labbra** in a low tone, sottovoce; **a fior di pelle** skin-deep, superficial; **fior di** (coll) a lot of; **fiore di latte** cream; **fiori** (cards) clubs; **primo fiore** down (*soft hairy growth*)

fiorènte *adj* flourishing, thriving

fiorentì·no -na *adj* & *mf* Florentine

fiorettare (fiorétto) *tr* (fig) to overembellish

fiorétto *m* little flower; choice, pick; overembellishment; choice passage (*from life of saint*); foil; button of foil

fioricoltóre *m* var of **floricoltore**

fioricoltura *f* var of **floricoltura**

fiorino *m* florin

fiorire §176 *tr* to cause to flower; to adorn with flowers || *intr* (ESSERE) to flower, bloom; to flourish; to break out (*said of skin eruption*); to get moldy

fiorì·sta *mf* (**-sti -ste**) florist

fiorì·to -ta *adj* flowering; flowery;

mottled; moldy; studded (*e.g., with errors*)

fioritura *f* flowering; flourish; mold; (pathol) eruption

fiorrancino *m* (orn) kinglet, firecrest

fiorràn·cio *m* (-ci) marigold

fiòtto *m* gush, surge; (obs) wave

Firènze *f* Florence

firma *f* signature; power of attorney; good reputation; (mil) enlisted man; **buona firma** famous writer; **farci la firma** (coll) to accept quite willingly; **firma di favore** guarantor's signature

firmaiòlo *m* (mil) enlisted man

firmaménto *m* firmament

firmare *tr* to sign

firmatà·rio -ria (-ri -rie) *adj* signatory ‖ *mf* signer, signatory

fisarmòni·ca *f* (-che) accordion

fiscale *adj* fiscal, tax

fischiare §287 *tr* to whistle; to boo ‖ *intr* to whistle; to ring (*said of ears*); to blow (*said, e.g., of a factory whistle*)

fischiettare (**fischiétto**) *tr* & *intr* to whistle

fischiétto *m* whistle (*instrument*)

fi·schio *m* (-schi) whistle; hiss; boo; blow (*of whistle*); ringing (*in the ears*)

fi·sciù *m* (-sciù) kerchief, fichu

fisco *m invar* treasury; internal revenue service

fisi·co -ca (-ci -che) *adj* physical; bodily ‖ *m* physicist; physique; (obs) physician ‖ *f* physics

fisima *f* whim, fancy, caprice

fisiologìa *f* physiology

fisiològi·co -ca (-ci -che) *adj* physiological

fisionomìa or **fisonomìa** *f* physiognomy; countenance, face; appearance

fisionomi·sta *mf* (-sti -ste) person good at faces; physiognomist

fi·so -sa *adj* (lit) fixed

fissàg·gio *m* (-gi) (phot) fixing

fissare *tr* to fix; to fasten; to gaze at; to reserve; to hire; **fissare lo sguardo** to gaze ‖ *ref* to gaze, stare; to become obsessed; to settle down

fissati·vo -va *adj* fixing

fissa·to -ta *adj* fixed; (coll) cracked ‖ *mf* (coll) crackpot

fissa·tóre -trice *adj* (phot) fixing ‖ *m* fixer; **fissatore per capelli** hair spray; hair dressing

fissazióne *f* fixation; fixed idea

fissile *adj* fissionable

fissionàbile *adj* fissionable

fissióne *f* fission

fis·so -sa *adj* fixed; regular ‖ *m* pay

fistola *f* (pathol) fistula; (lit) pipe

fitta *f* pang, stitch; crowd; great amount; (coll) blow; (obs) quagmire

fittàvolo *m* tenant farmer

fittì·zio -zia (-zi -zie) fictitious

fit·to -ta *adj* fixed, dug in; thick, dense; pitch (*dark*) ‖ *m* thick; rent; tenancy ‖ *f* see **fitta**

fittóne *m* (bot) taproot

fiuma·no -na *adj* river; from Fiume ‖ *m* person from Fiume ‖ *f* flood, stream

fiumara *f* torrent

fiume *m* river; **a fiumi** like a river

fiutare *tr* to snuff, sniff; to smell

fiutata *f* snuff, sniff

fiuto *m* sense of smell; snuff; flair

flàcci·do -da *adj* flabby

flacóne *m* flacon

flagellare (**flagèllo**) *tr* to scourge, lash, flagellate

flagèllo *m* whip, scourge; pest, plague; (coll) mess

flagrante *adj* flagrant; **in flagrante** (**delitto**) in the act

flan *m* (flan) pudding; (typ) mat

flanèlla *f* flannel

flàn·gia *f* (-ge) flange

flato *m* gas, flatus

flatulènza *f* flatulence

flautino *m* flageolet

flauti·sta *mf* (-sti -ste) flutist

flàuto *m* flute; **flauto diritto** or **dolce** (mus) recorder

fla·vo -va *adj* (lit) blond, golden

flèbile *adj* mournful

flebite *f* phlebitis

flèmma *f* apathy; coolness; phlegm

flemmàti·co -ca *adj* (-ci -che) phlegmatic(al)

flessìbile *adj* flexible, pliable

flessióne *f* bending; (com) fall, drop; (gram) inflection

flessuó·so -sa [s] *adj* lithe, willowy; winding; flowing (*style*)

flèttere §177 *tr* to flex; (gram) to inflect

flirtare *intr* to flirt

flòra *f* flora

floreale *adj* floral

floricoltóre *m* floriculturist

floricoltura *f* floriculture

flòri·do -da *adj* florid; flourishing

flò·scio -scia *adj* (-sci -sce) flabby; soft (*hat*)

flòtta *f* fleet

flottante *adj* floating ‖ *m* (com) floating stock

flottare (**flòtto**) *tr* & *intr* to float

flottìglia *f* flottilla

fluènte *adj* flowing

fluidità *f* fluidity

flùi·do -da *adj* & *m* fluid; fluent (*style*)

fluire §176 *intr* (ESSERE) to flow; to pour

fluitazióne *f* log driving

fluorescènte *adj* fluorescent

fluorescènza *f* fluorescence

fluorìdri·co -ca *adj* (-ci -che) hydrofluoric

fluorite *f* fluor, fluorite

fluorizzazióne [ddzz] *f* fluoridation

fluòro *m* fluorine

fluoruro *m* fluoride

flusso *m* flow; flood (*of tide*); high tide; (pathol) flow (*e.g., of blood*); (phys) flux

flutto *m* (lit) wave

fluttuare (**flùttuo**) *intr* to fluctuate; to bob, toss; to waver; to surge, stream

fluviale *adj* fluvial, river

fobìa *f* phobia

fò·ca *f* (-che) seal; sealskin

focàc·cia *f* (-ce) flat, rounded loaf; cake

focaccina *f* bun

fo·càia _adj fem_ (-càie) flint

focale _adj_ focal

fóce _f_ mouth (_of river_)

focèna _f_ porpoise

fochi·sta _m_ (-sti) fireman, stoker; fireworks manufacturer

foco·làio _m_ (-lài) (pathol) focus; (fig) hotbed

focolare _m_ hearth; firebox; fireside, home

focó·so -sa [s] _adj_ fiery, high-spirited

fòdera _f_ lining (_of suit_); cover, case

foderare (fòdero) _tr_ to line; to cover

fòdero _m_ sheath, scabbard; raft

fó·ga _f_ (-ghe) ardor, impetus

fòg·gia _f_ (-ge) fashion, shape; **a foggia di** shaped like

foggiare §290 (fòggio) _tr_ to shape, fashion

fòglia _f_ leaf; petal; foil (_of gold_); **mangiare la foglia** (fig) to get wise, catch on

fogliame _m_ foliage

fò·glio _m_ (-gli) sheet; bill, banknote; folio; newspaper; permit; **foglio d'avviso** notice; **foglio di congedo** (mil) discharge; **foglio d'iscrizione** application; **foglio di via** (mil) travel orders; **foglio modello** blank form; **foglio rosa** (aut) permit; **foglio volante** flier, handbill

fógna _f_ sewer, drain

fognatura _f_ sewerage

fòla _f_ tale, fable

fola·ga _f_ (-ghe) (zool) coot

folata _f_ gust; (lit) flight (_of birds_)

folclóre _m_ folklore

folgorante _adj_ striking; flashing; meteoric (_career_)

folgorare (fólgoro) _tr_ to strike (with lightning) || _intr_ to flash by || _impers_ —**folgora** it is thundering

fólgore _m_ (lit) thunderbolt || _f_ flash of lightning; thunderbolt

fólla _f_ crowd; (fig) flock

follare (fóllo) _tr_ to full

fòlle _adj_ mad, crazy; (aut) neutral; (mach) loose (_pulley_)

folleggiare §290 (folléggio) _intr_ to act foolishly; to frolic

follemènte _adv_ desperately, madly

follétto _m_ elf; little imp

follìa _f_ madness, lunacy; folly; **alla follia** madly; **far follie per** to be crazy about

follicolo _m_ follicle

fól·to -ta _adj_ thick; beetle (_brow_); deep (_night_) || _m_ depth (_e.g., of the night_); thick (_e.g., of the battle_)

fomentare (foménto) _tr_ to foment

fòmite _m_ (lit) instigation; impetus

fónda _f_ anchorage; lowland; saddlebag; **alla fonda** at anchor

fónda·co _m_ (-chi) (hist) warehouse

fondale _m_ depth (_of river, sea_); (theat) backdrop

fondamentale _adj_ fundamental, basic

fondamén·to _m_ (-ti) ground, foundation; basis; **fare fondamento su** to count on; **fondamenti** elements; **senza fondamento** baseless; without getting anywhere || _m_ (-ta _fpl_)—**fondamenta** foundations (_of a building_)

fondare (fóndo) _tr_ to found; to build; to charter || _ref_—**fondarsi su** to rely on; to be based upon

fondatézza _f_ basis, ground, foundation

fonda·to -ta _adj_ well-founded

fonda·tóre -trice _mf_ founder

fondazióne _f_ foundation

fondèllo _m_ bottom, base

fondènte _m_ flux

fóndere §178 _tr_ to smelt; to melt; **to blow** (_a fuse_); to cast (_a statue_); to blend (_colors_) || _intr_ to melt; to blend || _ref_ to melt; to blend; to burn out

fonderìa _f_ foundry

fondià·rio -ria (-ri -rie) _adj_ real-estate, land || _f_ real-estate tax

fondina _f_ holster; (coll) soup dish

fondi·sta _mf_ (-sti -ste) editorialist; (sports) long-distance runner

fóndita _f_ (typ) font

fonditóre _m_ smelter, founder

fón·do -da _adj_ deep || _m_ bottom; fund; innermost nature; seat; end; background; land, property; **a doppio fondo** with a false bottom; **a fondo** thoroughly; **a fondo perduto** as an outright grant; **dar fondo** (naut) to cast anchor; **dar fondo a** to exhaust; **di fondo** (journ) editorial; (sports) long-distance; **fondi** funds; lees; **fondi di bottega** remnants; **fondi di caffè** coffee grounds; **fondo comune d'investimento** mutual fund; **fondo d'ammortamento** sinking fund; **fondo di beneficenza** community chest; **fondo tinta** foundation (_in make-up_); **in fondo** in the end; at the bottom; after all

fonè·ma _m_ (-mi) phoneme

fonèti·co -ca (-ci -che) _adj_ phonetic || _f_ phonetics

fonògeno _m_ pickup (_of record player_)

fonògrafo _m_ phonograph, Gramophone

fonogram·ma _m_ (-mi) telegram delivered by telephone

fonologìa _f_ phonology

fonorivelatóre _m_ pickup (_of record player_)

fonovalìgia _f_ portable phonograph

fontana _f_ fountain; spring; source

fónte _m_ (lit) spring, source; **fonte battesimale** font || _f_ spring; fountain; source; **da fonte autorevole** on good authority

foraggiare §290 _tr_ to subsidize || _intr_ to forage

foràg·gio _m_ (-gi) forage, provender, fodder

forà·neo -a _adj_ rural; outer; (naut) outer (_dock_)

forare (fóro) _tr_ to pierce; to bore; to puncture || _intr_ to have a flat tire || _ref_ to be punctured

foratura _f_ puncture

fòrbice _f_—**a forbice** (sports) scissors (_e.g., kick_); **forbici** scissors; clippers; **forbici per le unghie** nail clippers

forbire §176 _tr_ to wipe; to polish; to shine

fór·ca _f_ (-che) fork; pitchfork; gallows; mountain pass; **fare la forca a qlcu** (slang) to betray s.o.; (slang) to do s.o. dirt; **fatto a forca** V-shaped forcèlla *f* fork (*of bicycle or motor-cycle*); mountain pass; fork-shaped pole; hairpin; cradle (*of handset*); (coll) wishbone (*of chicken*)

forchétta *f* fork; (coll) wishbone (*of chicken*); alla forchetta (culin) cold (*e.g., lunch*)

forchettata *f* forkful; blow with a fork

forchettóne *m* carving fork

forcìna *f* hairpin

fòrcipe *m* forceps

forcóne *m* pitchfork

forellino *m* pinhole

forèsta *f* forest

forestale *adj* forest, park

foresterìa *f* guest quarters (*in college or monastery*)

forestierismo *m* borrowing (*from another language*)

forestiè·ro -ra *adj* foreign || *mf* foreigner; stranger; outsider

forfetta·rio -ria *adj* (-ri -rie) job, e.g., contratto forfettario job contract; all-inclusive, e.g., combinazione forfettaria all-inclusive price agreement

fórfora *f* dandruff

fòr·gia *f* (-ge) forge; smithy

forgiare §290 (fòrgio) *tr* to forge

forie·ro -ra *adj* forerunning || *mf* forerunner, harbinger

fórma *f* shape; form; mold (*e.g., for cakes*); wheel (*of cheese*); (typ) form; forma da cappelli hat block; forma da scarpe shoe tree; shoe last (*used by shoemaker*); forme shape, body; good manners; salvare le forme to save face

formaggièra *f* dish for grated cheese

formàg·gio *m* (-gi) cheese

formaldèide *f* formaldehyde

formale *adj* formal; prim

formalismo *m* formality

formali·tà *f* (-tà) formality

formalizzare [ddzz] *tr* to scandalize || *ref* to be shocked

formare (fórmo) *tr & ref* to form

forma·to -ta *adj* formed || *m* format

formazióne *f* formation

fòrmica *f* (trademark) Formica

formì·ca *f* (-che) ant

formi·càio *m* (-cài) anthill; (fig) swarm

formichière *m* anteater

formicolare (formìcolo) *intr* to swarm; to crawl || *intr* (ESSERE) to creep (*said, e.g., of a leg*)

formicolì·o *m* (-i) swarm; creeping sensation, numbness

formidàbile *adj* formidable

formó·so -sa [s] *adj* shapely, buxom

fòrmula *f* formula; (aut) category, class; formula dubitativa (law) lack of evidence; formula piena (law) acquittal

formulare (fòrmulo) *tr* to formulate

formulà·rio *m* (-ri) formulary; form

fornace *f* furnace, kiln

for·nàio -nàia *mf* (-nài -nàie) baker

fornèllo *m* stove, range; (*of boiler*) firebox; bowl (*of pipe*); (min) shaft; fornello a gas gas range; fornello a spirito kerosene stove; chafing dish

fornire §176 *tr* to furnish, supply

forni·tóre -trice *mf* supplier, purveyor

fornitura *f* supply; order; delivery

fórno *m* oven; furnace; kiln; bakery; (theat) empty house; al forno or in forno baked; alto forno blast furnace; forno crematorio crematorium; far forno (theat) to play before an empty house

fóro *m* hole

fòro *m* forum; (law) bar

forosétta [s] *f* (lit) peasant girl

fórse *m* doubt; mettere in forse to endanger; to put in doubt || *adv* perhaps, maybe

forsenna·to -ta *adj* mad, insane || *mf* lunatic

fòrte *adj* strong; firm; bad (*cold*); fat, hefty; fast (*color*); offensive (*joke*); hard (*smoker*); main (*dish*); (lit) thick || *m* strong person; fortress; bulk, main body; forte; (lit) thick; sapere di forte to have a strong flavor; farsi forte to bear up; farsi forte di to appropriate, use; to be cocksure of || *adv* hard, strong; much; loud; openly; a lot; fast; swiftly

fortézza *f* fortress; strength; fortitude

fortificare §197 (fortìfico) *tr* to fortify || *ref* to be strengthened; to dig in

fortificazióne *f* fortification

fortino *m* blockhouse, redoubt

fortùi·to -ta *adj* fortuitous

fortuna *f* fortune; luck; good luck; fate, destiny; (lit) storm; avere fortuna to be lucky; to be a hit; buona fortuna! good luck!; di fortuna makeshift, emergency; non aver la fortuna di to not be fortunate enough to; per fortuna luckily

fortunale *m* storm, tempest

fortuna·to -ta *adj* fortunate, lucky

fortunó·so -sa [s] *adj* eventful

forùncolo *m* boil; pimple

forviare §119 *tr* to mislead, lead astray || *intr* to go astray

fòrza *f* strength; force; power; police; (phys) force; a forza di by dint of; a tutta forza at full speed; bassa forza (mil) enlisted personnel; di forza by force; di prima forza first-rate; far forza a to encourage; to force; fare forza a sé stesso to restrain oneself; forza! courage!; forza di corpo (typ) height-to-paper; forza maggiore force majeure, act of God; forza muscolare brawn; forza pubblica police; forza viva kinetic energy; per forza of course; under duress

forzare (fòrzo) *tr* to force; to strain; to rape; to tamper with (*a lock*); forzare il passo to hasten one's step; forzare la consegna (mil) to violate orders

forza·to -ta *adj* forced; force (*e.g., feed*) || *m* convict

forzière *m* chest, coffer

forzó·so -sa [s] *adj* compulsory; imposed by law

forzu·to -ta *adj* husky, robust

foschìa *f* smog; mist; haze

fó·sco -sca *adj* (**-schi -sche**) dark; gloomy; misty
fosfato *m* phosphate
fosforeggiare §290 (**fosforéggio**) *intr* to phosphoresce; to glow
fosforescènte *adj* phosphorescent
fòsforo *m* phosphorus
fòssa *f* grave; hollow; hole, ditch; moat; pit; den (*of lions*); **fossa biologica** sewage-treatment plant; **fossa di riparazione** (aut) pit; **fossa settica** septic tank
fossato *m* ditch; moat
fossétta *f* dimple
fòssile *adj* & *m* fossil
fossilizzare [ddzz] *tr* to fossilize || *ref* to become fossilized
fòsso *m* ditch; moat
fò·to *f* (**-to**) photo
fotocòpia *f* photocopy
fotocopiare §287 (**fotocòpio**) *tr* to photocopy
fotoelèttri·co -ca (**-ci -che**) *adj* photo-electric || *f* (mil) searchlight
fotogèni·co -ca *adj* (**-ci -che**) photogenic
fotogiornale *m* pictorial magazine
fotografare (**fotògrafo**) *tr* to photograph
fotografìa *f* photography; photograph
fotogràfi·co -ca *adj* (**-ci -che**) photographic
fotògrafo *m* photographer
fotogram·ma *m* (**-mi**) (phot) frame
fotoincisióne *f* photoengraving
fotolampo *m* flashlight
fotòmetro *m* exposure meter
fotomontàg·gio *m* (**-gi**) photomontage
fototubo *m* phototube
fra *m invar* brother, e.g., **fra Cristoforo** Brother Christopher || *prep* among; between; in, within
frac *m* (**frac**) swallow-tailed coat
fracassare *tr* to crash, smash || *ref* to crash
fracasso *m* crash; uproar; (coll) slew
fràdi·cio -cia (**-ci -cie**) *adj* rotten; soaked || *m* rotten part; decay; wet ground
fràgile *adj* fragile; brittle; frail
fragilità *f* fragility, frailty
fràgola *f* strawberry
fragóre *m* din; peal; roar
fragoró·so -sa [s] *adj* noisy
fragrante *adj* fragrant
fraintèndere §270 *tr* to misunderstand
frammassóne *m* Freemason
frammassonerìa *f* Freemasonry
frammentare (**framménto**) *tr* to fragment
frammentà·rio -ria *adj* (**-ri -rie**) fragmentary
framménto *m* fragment
framméttere §198 *tr* to interpose || *ref* to meddle; **frammettersi in** to intrude in, to butt into
frammèzzo [ddzz] *adv* in the middle || *prep* in the midst of
frammischiare §287 *tr* to mix || *ref* to concern oneself
frana *f* landslide; (fig) collapse
franare *intr* to slide; to collapse

francesca·no -na *adj* & *mf* Franciscan
francé·sco -sca (**-schi -sche**) *adj* (archaic) French || **Francesco** *m* Francis || **Francesca** *f* Frances
francése *adj* French || *m* French (*language*); Frenchman (*person*); **i francesi** the French || *f* Frenchwoman
francesismo *m* gallicism
francesizzare [ddzz] *tr* to Frenchify
franchézza *f* frankness
franchi·gìa *f* (**-gie**) franchise; exemption; deductible insurance; (naut) shore leave; **franchigia postale** franking privilege
Frància, la France
fran·co -ca (**-chi -che**) *adj* free; frank; Frankish; **farla franca** to get off scot free; **franco di porto** prepaid, postpaid; **franco domicilio** home delivery, free delivery || *m* franc || **Franco** *m* Frank
francobóllo *m* postage stamp, stamp
frangènte *m* breaker, surf; **essere nei frangenti** to be in bad straits
fràngere §179 *tr* to crush; (lit) to break || *ref* to break, comb (*said of waves*)
frangétta *f* bangs
fràn·gia *f* (**-ge**) fringe; embellishment; shoreline; bangs; **frangia di corallo** coral reef
frangìbile *adj* breakable
frangiflut·ti *m* (**-ti**) breakwater
frangi·vènto *m* (**-vènto**) windbreak
frangizòl·le *m* (**-le**) disc harrow
Frankfur·ter *m* (**-ter**) hot dog
fran·tóio *m* (**-tói**) crusher; **frantoio a mascelle** jawbreaker
frantumare *tr* to crush; to break to pieces || *ref* to be crushed; to go to pieces
frantume *m* fragment; **andare in frantumi** to go to pieces
frappé *m* (**frappé**) shake; frappé; **frappé alla menta** mint julep; **frappé di latte** milk shake
frappórre §218 *tr* to interpose || *ref* to interfere; to intervene
frasà·rio *m* (**-ri**) language, speech
fra·sca *f* (**-sche**) branch; bush; ornament; whim; frivolous woman, flirt
frase *f* sentence; (mus) phrase; **frase fatta** cliché; **frase idiomatica** idiom; **frasi words**; **frasi di commiserazione** condolences
fraseggiare §290 (**fraséggio**) *intr* to use phrasing; to use big words; (mus) to phrase
fraseologìa *f* phraseology
fràssino *m* ash tree
frastagliare §280 *tr* to cut out (*e.g., paper*)
frastaglia·to -ta *adj* indented, jagged; ornamented
frastornare (**frastórno**) *tr* to disturb; (lit) to prevent
frastuòno *m* din, roar
frate *m* friar, monk, brother
fratellanza *f* brotherhood
fratellastro *m* stepbrother; half brother
fratèllo *m* brother; **fratelli** brothers and sisters; **fratello consanguineo** half brother on the father's side; **fratello**

di latte foster brother; **fratello ge-mello** twin

fraterni•tà f (-tà) fraternity

fraternizzare [ddzz] intr to fraternize

fratèr•no -na adj fraternal, brotherly

fratrici•da (-di -de) adj fratricidal ‖ mf fratricide

fratrici•dio m (-di) fratricide

fratta f brushwood; (coll) hedge

frattàglie fpl giblets, chitterlings, offal

frattanto adv meantime, meanwhile

frattèmpo m—**nel frattempo** meanwhile

frattura f fracture; break; breach

fratturare tr & ref to fracture, break

fraudolènte adj fraudulent

frazionare (frazióno) tr to fractionate; to break up

frazionà•rio -ria adj (-ri -rie) fractional

frazióne f fraction; hamlet; (eccl) breaking of the host

fréc•cia f (-ce) arrow, bolt; steeple, spire; clock (on hosiery); (archit) rise; (fig) aspersion; **freccia consensiva** arrow (on traffic light); **freccia direzionale** (aut) turn signal

frecciata f arrow shot; taunt, gibe; **dare una frecciata** to a hit for a loan

freddare (fréddo) tr to chill; to kill

freddézza f chill; cold, coldness; coolness, cold shoulder; sang-froid

fréd•do -da adj cold; cool, chilly; frigid ‖ m cold, cold weather; chill; **a freddo** cold; cooly; **avere freddo** to be cold (said of people); **fare freddo** to be cold (said of weather); **freddo cane** biting cold; **sentire freddo** to feel cold; **sudare freddo** to be in a cold sweat

freddoló•so -sa [s] adj chilly (person)

freddura f joke, pun; cold weather

fredduri•sta mf (-sti -ste) punster

fregagióne f rubbing, rubdown, massage

fregare §209 (frégo) tr to rub; to strike (a match); (slang) to steal; (slang) to cheat, dupe; (vulg) to make love with ‖ ref to rub (e.g., one's hands); **fregarsene di** (vulg) to not give a hoot about

fregata f rubbing; (nav) frigate; (orn) frigate bird; (slang) cheating

fregatura f (slang) cheating; (slang) hitch, halt

fregiare §290 (frégio) tr to decorate; to fret

fré•gio m (-gi) decoration; insignia (on cap of officer); (archit) frieze

fré•go m (-ghi) line, stroke

frégola f rut, heat; (slang) mania, craze

fremènte adj throbbing; thrilling

frèmere §123 (lit) to beg insistently ‖ intr to throb; to be thrilled; to shake, tremble, rustle; to shudder (with horror); (fig) to boil; (fig) to fret

frèmito m throb; thrill; shudder; roar; quiver

frenare (fréno) tr to brake, stop; to bridle (a horse); to curb (passions); to restrain (e.g., laughter); **frenare la corsa** to slow down ‖ intr to put the brakes on ‖ ref to control oneself

frenatóre m (rr) brakeman

frenesìa f frenzy; (fig) craze, fever; (lit) thought

frenèti•co -ca adj (-ci -che) frenzied; frantic; crazy, enthusiastic

fréno m bit, bridle; brake; (fig) check; (mach) lock; **freno ad aria compressa** air brake; **mordere il freno** to champ the bit; **senza freno** wild, unbridled; **tenere a freno** to keep in check

frenologìa f phrenology

frequentare (frequènto) tr to frequent; to attend ‖ intr to associate

frequenta•tóre -trice mf patron, customer; frequenter, habitué

frequènte adj frequent; rapid (pulse); (lit) crowded

frequènza f frequency; attendance; **frequenza ultraelevata** ultrahigh frequency

frèsa f milling cutter; burr (of dentist's drill)

fresatrice f milling machine

fresatura f (mach) milling

freschézza f freshness; coolness

fré•sco -sca (-schi -sche) adj fresh; cool; **fresco di malattia** just recovered; **fresco di stampa** fresh off the press; **fresco di studi** fresh out of school; **star fresco** to be in a fix; to be all wrong ‖ m cool weather; tropical fabric; **di fresco** recently; **fare fresco** to be cool (said of weather); **mettere al fresco** (coll) to put in the clink; **per il fresco** in cool weather

frescó•ne -na mf (slang) dumbell

frescura f coolness, freshness

frétta f hurry, haste; **avere fretta** to be in a hurry; **in fretta** in a hurry; **in fretta e furia** in a rush

frettazzo m plasterer's wooden trowel; steel brush

frettoló•so -sa [s] adj hurried, hasty

freudismo m Freudianism

friàbile adj friable, crumbly

friabilità f friableness

fricassèa f fricassee

friggere §180 tr to fry; **mandare qlcu a farsi friggere** to tell s.o. to go to the devil ‖ intr to fry; to sizzle; to fret

friggitorìa f fried-food shop

frigidézza f frigidity

frigidi•tà f (-tà) coldness; frigidity

frìgi•do -da adj cold; frigid

frì•gio -gia adj (-gi -gie) Phrygian

frignare intr to whimper

frigorìfe•ro -ra adj refrigerating ‖ m refrigerator; (journ) morgue

fringuèl•lo -la mf chaffinch, finch

frinire §176 intr to chirp

frisata f gunnel

frittata f omelet; **fare la frittata** (coll) to make a mess of it

frittèlla f fritter; pancake; (coll) grease spot

frit•to -ta adj fried; cooked, ruined ‖ m fry, fried platter

frittura f frying; fry, fried platter

frivolézza f frivolity

frìvo•lo -la adj frivolous; flighty

frizionare (frizióno) tr to massage

frizióne *f* friction; massage; (aut) clutch

frizzante [ddzz] *adj* crisp, brisk (*weather*); sparkling (*wine*)

frizzare [ddzz] *intr* to tingle; to sparkle, fizz (*said of wine*); (fig) to sting

frizzo [ddzz] *m* jest, witticism; gibe, dig

frodare (fròdo) *tr* to cheat, swindle

fròde *f* fraud; **frode fiscale** tax evasion or fraud

fròdo *m invar* customs evasion; **di frodo** smuggled

frò·gia *f* (-ge or -gie) nostril (*of horse*)

fròl·lo -la *adj* high (*meat*); soft, tender; (fig) weak

frónda *f* branch, bough; political opposition; **fronde** foliage; ornaments

frondó·so -sa [s] *adj* leafy

frontale *adj* front; frontal

frónte *m* (mil, pol) front; **far fronte a** to face; to face up to; to meet (*expenses*); **tenere fronte a** to face, resist || *f* forehead, brow; countenance; title page; headline; (fig) face; **a fronte** opposite, facing; **a fronte di** (com) in reference to; **dietro front!** (mil) about face!; **di fronte a** in the face of; facing; **di fronte a tutti** in plain view; **fronte destr'!** (mil) right face!; **mettere a fronte** to compare; **tenere a fronte** to have in front of one's eyes

fronteggiare §290 (frontéggio) *tr* to face, front || *ref* to face one another

frontespì·zio *m* (-zi) title page

frontièra *f* border, frontier

frontóne *m* (archit) pediment; (archit) gable

frónzolo *m* bauble, gewgaw; **fronzoli** finery, frippery

fròtta *f* crowd; swarm; flock

fròttola *f* fib; popular poem; **frottole** humbug

frugale *adj* frugal (*meal; life*); temperate (*in eating or drinking*)

frugare §209 *tr* to rummage through; to search (*a person*) || *intr* to rummage, poke around

frùgo·lo -la *mf* restless child, imp

fruire §176 *tr* to enjoy || *intr*—**fruire di** to enjoy

fruitóre *m* user

frullare *tr* to beat, whip || *intr* to flutter; to spin; **frullare per il capo a** to get into the head of, e.g., **cosa gli è frullato per il capo?** what got into his head?

frulla·to -ta *adj* whipped || *m* shake (*drink*)

frullatóre *m* electric beater

frullino *m* egg beater

fruménto *m* wheat

frumentóne *m* corn

frusciare §128 *intr* to rustle

frusci·o *m* (-i) rustle, rustling

frusta *f* whip; egg beater

frustare *tr* to whip, lash; (fig) to censure; (coll) to wear out (*clothes*)

frustata *f* lash; (fig) censure

frustino *m* whip, crop

fru·sto -sta *adj* worn out, threadbare || *f* see **frusta**

frustrare *tr* to frustrate, baffle; to discomfit

frut·ta *f* (-ta & -te) fruit; **essere alle frutta** to be at the end of the meal, to be having one's dessert

fruttare *tr & intr* to yield

fruttéto *m* orchard

frutticoltóre *m* fruit grower

fruttièra *f* fruit dish

fruttìfe·ro -ra *adj* fruit-bearing; fruitful, profitable; (lit) fecund

fruttificare §197 (fruttìfico) *intr* to fructify; to yield

fruttivéndo·lo -la *mf* fruit dealer

frutto *m* fruit; **frutti di mare** shellfish; **mettere a frutto** to make yield

fruttuó·so -sa [s] *adj* fruitful, profitable

fu *adj invar* late (*deceased*); **son of the late . . . ;** daughter of the late . . .

fucilare *tr* to shoot

fucilata *f* rifle shot

fucilazióne *f* execution by a firing squad

fucile *m* rifle, gun; **fucile ad aria compressa** air gun; **fucile da caccia** shotgun; **un buon fucile** a good shot

fucileria *f* fusillade

fucilière *m* rifleman

fucina *f* forge, smithy

fu·co *m* (-chi) (bot) rockweed; (zool) drone

fùcsia *f* fuchsia

fu·ga *f* (-ghe) flight; leak; row (*e.g., of rooms*); spurt (*in bicycle race*); (mus) fugue; **di fuga** hastily; **prendere la fuga** to take flight; **volgere in fuga** to put to flight; to take flight

fugace *adj* passing, fleeting

fugare §209 *tr* (lit) to avoid; (lit) to put to flight; (lit) to dispel

fuggènte *adj* passing, fleeting

fuggévole *adj* fleeting

fuggia·sco -sca (-schi -sche) *adj* fleeing, fugitive || *mf* fugitive; refugee

fuggi fug·gi *m* (-gi) stampede

fuggire *tr* to flee; to avoid || *intr* (ESSERE) to flee, run away; (sports) to take the lead; **fuggire a** to flee from

fuggiti·vo -va *adj & mf* fugitive

fulcro *m* fulcrum; (fig) pivot

fulgènte *adj* (lit) resplendent

fùlgi·do -da *adj* resplendent

fulgóre *m* resplendency, radiance

fulìggine *f* soot

fuligginó·so -sa [s] *adj* sooty

fulmicotóne *m* guncotton

fulminante *adj* crushing (*illness*); withering (*look*); explosive || *m* exploding cap; (coll) match

fulminare (fùlmino) *tr* to strike by lightning; to strike down; to confound, dumfound || *ref* (elec) to burn out, to blow out || *impers* (ESSERE)—**fulmina** it is lightning

fùlmine *m* lightning, thunderbolt; **fulmine a ciel sereno** bolt out of the blue

fulmìne·o -a *adj* swift, instant

ful·vo -va *adj* tawny

fumaiòlo *m* chimney; smokestack; (naut) funnel

fumante *adj* smoking; steaming; dusty
fumare *tr* to smoke; (lit) to exhale ‖ *intr* to smoke; to steam; to fume; **fumare come un turco** to smoke like a chimney
fumata *f* smoking; smoke signal; **fare una fumata** to have a smoke
fuma-tóre -trice *mf* smoker
fumetti·sta *mf* (**-sti -ste**) cartoonist
fumétto *m* cartoon; **fumetti** comics
fumigare §209 (**fùmigo**) *tr* (obs) to fumigate ‖ *intr* to steam, smoke
fumigazióne *f* fumigation
fumi·sta *m* (**-sti**) heater man; joker, hoaxer
fumisteria *f* fondness for practical jokes; bamboozling
fumo *m* smoke; vapor, steam; smoking; (coll) hot air; **andare in fumo** to go up in smoke; **fumi** vapors, fumes; **mandare in fumo** to squander; to thwart; **sapere di fumo** to taste smoky; **vedere qlcu come il fumo negli occhi** to not be able to stand s.o.; **vender fumo** to peddle influence
fumòge·no -na *adj* smoke, e.g., **cortina fumogena** smoke curtain
fumó·so -sa [s] *adj* smoky; obscure
funambolismo *m* tightrope walking; (fig) acrobatics
funàmbo·lo -la *mf* tightrope walker; (fig) acrobat
fune *f* rope, cable; **fune portante** suspension cable
fùnebre *adj* funeral; funereal, gloomy
funerale *adj* & *m* funeral
funerà·rio -ria *adj* (**-ri -rie**) funeral
funère·o -a *adj* funereal; funeral
funestare (**funèsto**) *tr* to afflict
funè·sto -sta *adj* baleful; mournful
fungàia *f* mushroom farm; mushroom bed; flock, swarm
fùngere §183 *intr*—**fungere da** to act as
fun·go *m* (**-ghi**) mushroom; fungus; **fungo atomico** mushroom cloud; **venir su come i funghi** to mushroom
fungó·so -sa [s] *adj* fungous
funicolare *adj* cable, cable-driven ‖ *f* funicular railway
funivìa *f* cableway
funzionale *adj* functional
funzionalità *f* functionalism
funzionaménto *m* working order; functioning
funzionare (**funzióno**) *intr* to work; to function; **funzionare da** to act as
funziona·rio -ria *adj* (**-ri -rie**) functionary, official; public official
funzióne *f* function; office; duty; (eccl) service; **facente funzione** acting; **mettere in funzione** to make (*s.th*) work
fuò·co *m* (**-chi**) fire; burner (*of gas range*); focus; (fig) home; (lit) thunderbolt; **al fuoco!** fire! (*warning*); **andare per il fuoco** (culin) to boil over; **cuocere a fuoco lento** (culin) to simmer; **dar fuoco a** to set fire to; **di fuoco** fiery; blushing; **far fuoco** to fire; **fuochi artificiali** fireworks; **fuoco di fila** enfilade; **fuoco!** (mil) fire!; **fuoco di paglia** (fig) flash in the pan; **fuoco di segnalazione** flare; **fuoco fatuo** will-o'-the-wisp; **fuoco**

incrociato cross fire; **fuoco nutrito** drumfire; **mettere a fuoco** to focus; **mettere una mano sul fuoco** to be absolutely sure, to swear by it
fuorché *prep* except; **fuorché di** except to
fuòri *adv* outside, out; aside; e.g., **lasciar fuori** to leave aside; **andar di fuori** (culin) to boil over; **dar fuori** to do away with; to squander; **di fuori** outside; **far fuori** to publish; **fuori di** out of; outside of; beyond (*a doubt*); off (*the road*); beside (*oneself*); **fuori d'uso** out of style; obsolete; **il di fuori** the outside; **in fuori** protruding; forward; **mettere fuori** to throw out; to spread; to exhibit ‖ *prep* beyond; out of; outside; **fuori commercio** not for sale; **fuori concorso** in a class by itself (*himself*, etc.); **fuori luogo** untimely, out of place; **fuori (di) mano** far away; solitary; **fuori testo** inserted, tipped in
fuoribór·do *m* (**-do**) outboard; outboard motor
fuoricombattimén·to (**-to**) *adj* knocked out ‖ *m* knockout
fuorigio·co *m* (**-co**) (sports) offside
fuorilég·ge *mf* (**-ge**) outlaw
fuorisè·rie (**-rie**) *adj* custom-built ‖ *m* & *f* custom model ‖ *f* custom-built car
fuoristra·da *m* (**-da**) land rover
fuoriusci·to -ta *adj* exiled ‖ *mf* political exile ‖ *f* leak; flow; protrusion
fuorvia·to -ta *adj* mislead, misguided
furbacchió·ne -na *mf* slippery person
furberìa *f* slyness, cunning
fur·bo -ba *adj* sly, cunning ‖ *mf* knave; **furbo di tre cotte** slicker
furènte *adj* furious
fureria *f* (mil) company headquarters
furétto *m* ferret
furfante *m* sharper, scoundrel
furfanterìa *f* rascality
furgoncino *m* small delivery van
furgóne *m* truck; patrol wagon; hearse; **furgone cellulare** prison van
furgoni·sta *mf* (**-sti -ste**) truck driver, teamster
fùria *f* fury; strength, violence; hurry; **a furia di** by dint of; **con furia** in a hurry; **far furia a** to urge; **montare in furia** to go berserk; to fly off the handle
furibón·do -da *adj* furious, wild
furière *m* soldier attached to company headquarters
furió·so -sa [s] *adj* furious; fierce; mad
furóre *m* furor, frenzy; violence; longing; **far furore** to be a hit, to be all the rage
furoreggiare §290 (**furoréggio**) *intr* to be a hit, be all the rage
furti·vo -va *adj* stealthy; furtive; stolen (*e.g., goods*)
furto *m* theft; stolen goods; **di furto** stealthily; **furto con scasso** burglary
fusa [s] *fpl*—**fare le fusa** to purr
fuscèllo *m* twig
fusciac·ca *f* (**-che**) sash (*around the waist*)

fusèllo [s] *m* spindle; axle, shaft
fusìbile *adj* fusible || *m* (elec) fuse
fusióne *f* fusion; melting; merger; blending (*of colors*)
fu·so -sa *adj* melted; molten
fuso [s] *m* spindle; shank (*of anchor*); shaft (*of column*); (aut) axle; **fuso orario** time zone
fusolièra *f* (aer) fuselage
fustagno *m* fustian
fustàia *f* adult forest, full-grown forest
fustèlla *f* (perforating) punch; (pharm) price stub

fustigare §209 (**fùstigo**) *tr* to whip
fusto *m* trunk (*of tree*); stalk; stem (*of key*); beam (*of balance*); butt (*of gun*); trunk, body; frame (*of armchair*); tank (*for holding liquids*); drum (*metal receptacle*); holding stick (*of umbrella*); shaft (*of column*); **d'alto fusto** full-grown (*tree*)
fùtile *adj* futile, trifling
futilità *f* futility
futurismo *m* futurism
futuri·sta *mf* (**-sti -ste**) futurist
futu·ro -ra *adj* & *m* future

G

G, g [dʒi] *m* & *f* seventh letter of the Italian alphabet
gabardi·ne *f* (**-ne**) gabardine; gabardine raincoat or topcoat
gabamón·do *m* (**-do**) cheat, sharper
gabbanèlla *f* gown (*of physician or patient*); robe
gabbano *m* cloak; frock; **mutare gabbano** to be a turncoat
gabbare *tr* to dupe, cheat || *ref*—**gabbarsi di** to make fun of
gàbbia *f* cage; ox muzzle; dock (*in courtroom*); (mach) housing; (naut) top; (naut) topsail; **gabbia d'imballaggio** crate; **gabbia toracica** rib cage
gabbiano *m* sea gull
gabbo *m*—**farsi gabbo di** to make fun of; **prendere a gabbo** to make light of
gabèlla *f* (obs) customs, duty
gabellare (**gabèllo**) *tr* to palm off; to swallow (*e.g., a tall story*); (obs) to tax
gabinétto *m* office (*of doctor, dentist, lawyer*); cabinet; chamber (*of judge*); toilet; closet; laboratory; **gabinetto da bagno** bathroom; **gabinetto di decenza** toilet, bathroom
ga·gà *m* (**gà**) fop, dandy; lounge lizard
gaggia *f* acacia
gagliardétto *m* pennon; pennant
gagliardìa *f* (lit) vigor; (lit) prowess
gagliar·do -da *adj* vigorous; stalwart; hearty (*e.g., voice*)
gagliòf·fo -fa *adj* loutish; rascal || *mf* lout; rascal
gaiézza *f* gaiety, vivacity
gàio gàia *adj* (**gài gàie**) gay, vivacious
gala *m* & *f* gala; gala affair; **di gala** formal; **mettersi in gala** to dress up || *f* frill; bow tie (*for formal attire*); (naut) bunting
galalite *f* casein plastic, galalith
galante *adj* gallant, courtly; amorous; pretty, graceful
galanterìa *f* gallantry, courtliness
galantuò·mo *m* (**-mini**) honest man; (coll) my good fellow
galàssia *f* galaxy
galatèo *m* good manners
galèna *f* (min) galena
galeóne *m* galleon
galeòt·to -ta *adj* (archaic) intermediary

(*in love affairs*) || *m* galley slave; convict; (archaic) procurer
galèra *f* galley; forced labor
gali·lèo -lèa (**-lèi -lèe**) *adj* & *m* Galilean
galla *f* (bot) gall; (pathol) blister; **a galla** afloat; **tenersi a galla** (fig) to keep alive; to manage; **venire a galla** to come to the surface
galleggiante *adj* floating || *m* float
galleggiare §290 (**galléggio**) *intr* to float
galleria *f* tunnel; gallery; balcony; mall, arcade; wind tunnel
Galles, il Wales
gallése [s] *adj* Welsh || *m* Welshman; Welsh (*language*) || *f* Welsh woman
gallétta *f* cracker; hardtack; (naut) ball on top of flagpole
gallétto *m* cockerel; (fig) gallant; (fig) whippersnapper; (mach) wing nut; **fare il galletto** to swagger
gàlli·co -ca *adj* & *m* (**-ci -che**) Gallic
gallina *f* hen; **gallina faraona** guinea fowl
gal·lo -la *adj* Gallic; (sports) Bantam (*weight*) || *m* rooster, cock; weathercock; Gaul; Gallic (*language*); **fare il gallo** to strut; **gallo cedrone** wood grouse; **gallo d'India** turkey
gallòc·cia *f* (**-ce**) (naut) cleat
gallóne *m* braid; stripe; chevron; gallon
galoppare (**galòppo**) *intr* to gallop; (fig) to rush around
galoppata *f* gallop
galoppa·tóio *m* (**-tói**) bridle path
galoppino *m* errand boy; **galoppino elettorale** ward heeler
galòppo *m* gallop; **andare al piccolo galoppo** to canter; **di gran galoppo** at full speed; **piccolo galoppo** canter
galò·scia *f* (**-sce**) overshoe, rubber
galvanizzare [ddzz] *tr* to electroplate; (fig) to galvanize
galvanoplàsti·ca *f* (**-che**) electroplating
gamba *f* leg; stem; (aer) shock strut; **a gambe all'aria** upside down; **a gambe levate** at top speed; upside down; **darsela a gambe** to take to one's heels; **essere in gamba** to be in good shape; to be on the ball; **essere male in gamba** to be in bad shape; **gamba di legno** peg leg; **gambe a ciambella** bowlegs; **le gambe mi fanno giacomo** my knees shake;

prendere qlcu sotto gamba to make light of s.o.; **raddrizzare le gambe ai cani** to try the impossible

gambale *m* legging, gaiter; boot last; leg (*of boot*)

gamberétto *m* shrimp

gàmbero *m* (*Astacus, Cambarus*) crawfish

gambétto *m* stumble; trip; (chess) gambit

gambo *m* stem

gamèlla *f* (mil) mess kit, mess tin

gamma *f* gamut; range; **gamma d'onda** (rad) wave band

ganà·scia *f* (-sce) jaw; (aut) brake shoe; **mangiare a quattro ganasce** to eat like a horse

gàn·cio *m* (-ci) hook; clasp; hanger

gan·ga *f* (-ghe) gang; (min) gangue

gànghero *m* hinge; clasp; **uscire dai gangheri** to fly off the handle

gàn·glio *m* (-gli) ganglion

ganzo [dz] *m* (slang) lover; (coll) slicker

gara *f* competition, match; **fare a gara** to compete; **gara d'appalto** competitive bidding

garagi·sta *m* (-sti) garage man

garante *adj* responsible ‖ *m* guarantor; **farsi garante per** to vouch for

garantire §176 *tr* to guarantee; to secure (*a mortgage*)

garanti·to -ta *adj* guaranteed, warranted; downright, absolute (*liar*)

garanzia *f* guarantee, warranty; insurance, assurance

garbare *tr* (naut) to shape (*a hull*) ‖ *intr* (ESSERE) (with *dat*) to like, e.g., **non gli garbano le Sue parole** he does not like your words

garbatézza *f* politeness, courtesy

garba·to -ta *adj* polite, courteous

garbo *m* politeness, good manners; gesture; act; shape (*of a hull*); good cut (*of clothes*); elegance (*in painting or writing*); **a garbo** correctly

garbù·glio *m* (-gli) tangle, confusion; mess

gardènia *f* gardenia

gareggiare §290 (garéggio) *intr* to compete, vie

garétta *f* var of **garitta**

garétto *m* var of **garretto**

garganèlla *f*—**bere a garganella** to gulp down

gargarismo *m* gargling; gargle

gargarizzare [ddzz] *intr & ref* to gargle

gargaròzzo *m* throat, gullet

garitta *f* railroad-crossing box; (mil) sentry box; (rr) brakeman's box

garòfano *m* carnation, pink

garrése [s] *m* withers

garrétto *m* ankle (*of man*); hock (*of horse*)

garrire §176 *intr* to chirp, twitter; to flap; (archaic) to quarrel

garrito *m* chirp, twitter

garròtta *f* garrote

gàrru·lo -la *adj* garrulous

garza [dz] *f* gauze

garzonato [dz] *m* apprenticeship

garzó·ne -na [dz] *mf* helper ‖ *m*

helper, boy; apprentice; (archaic) bachelor; **garzone di stalla** stableboy

gas *m* (**gas**) gas; gasoline; **gas asfissiante** poison gas; **gas delle miniere** firedamp; **gas esilarante** laughing gas; **gas illuminante** illuminating gas; **gas lacrimogeno** tear gas

gasdótto *m* gas pipeline

gasificare §197 (**gasìfico**) *tr* var of **gassificare**

gasòlio *m* Diesel oil

gasòmetro *m* var of **gassometro**

gassificare §197 (gassìfico) *tr* to gasify

gassi·sta *m* (-sti) gasworker; gas fitter; gas-meter reader

gassòmetro *m* gasholder, gas tank

gassó·so -sa [s] *adj* gaseous, gassy ‖ *f* soda, pop

gastronomìa *f* gastronomy

gatta *f* she-cat, tabby; **comprare la gatta nel sacco** to buy a pig in a poke; **gatta ci cova** something is rotten in Denmark; **pigliare una gatta da pelare** to take on a heavy burden, to get a tiger by the tail

gattabùia *f* (coll) clink, lockup

gattamòrta *f* (gattemòrte) hypocrite

gattino *m* kitten; (bot) catkin

gat·to -ta *mf* cat ‖ *m* tomcat; tamper, pile driver; **gatto a nove code** cat-o'-nine-tails; **gatto soriano** tortoiseshell cat; **quattro gatti** a handful of people ‖ *f* see **gatta**

gattóni *adv* on all fours

gattopardo *m* (zool) serval; **gattopardo americano** ocelot

gattùc·cio *m* (-ci) compass saw; (ichth) small dotted dogfish

gaudènte *adj* jovial ‖ *m* bon vivant

gàu·dio *m* (-di) joy, happiness

gavazzare *intr* (lit) to revel

gavétta *f* mess kit, mess gear; **venire dalla gavetta** to come up through the ranks

gavitèllo *m* buoy

gazza [ddzz] *f* magpie

gazzarra [ddzz] *f* racket, uproar

gazzèlla [ddzz] *f* gazelle

gazzétta [ddzz] *f* newspaper; gazette; newsmonger, gossip; **Gazzetta Ufficiale** Official Gazette (*in Italy*); Congressional Record (*U.S.A.*)

gazzettino [ddzz] *m* small newspaper; column, e.g., **gazzettino rosa** social column; newsmonger, gossip

gazzósa [ddzz] *f* var of **gassosa**

gèl *m* gel

gelare (**gèlo**) *tr* to freeze; to nip ‖ *intr* (ESSERE) & *ref* to freeze ‖ *impers* (ESSERE & AVERE)—**gela** it is freezing

gelata *f* frost

gela·tàio -tàia *mf* (-tài -tàie) ice-cream dealer

gelaterìa *f* ice-cream parlor

gelatièra *f* ice-cream freezer

gelatière *m* ice-cream dealer

gelatina *f* gelatin; jelly; **gelatina di frutta** fruit jelly; gum drop

gelatinizzare [ddzz] *tr & ref* to gelatinize; to jell

gela·to -ta *adj* frozen ‖ *m* ice cream;

gelato da passeggio ice cream on a stick, popsicle

gèli·do -da adj icy, ice-cold

gèlo m frost; ice; cold; diventare di gelo to remain dumfounded; farsi di gelo to be cold or aloof; sentirsi il gelo addosso to get a chill

gelóne m chilblain

gelosìa [s] f jealousy; great care; shutter

geló·so -sa [s] adj jealous; solicitous

gèlso m mulberry

gelsomino m jasmine

gemebón·do -da adj (lit) moaning

gemellàggio m sisterhood (of two cities)

gemèl·lo -la adj twin; sister (ship) || mf twin || gemelli mpl cufflinks || Gemelli mpl (astr) Gemini

gèmere §123 tr (lit) to lament || intr (ESSERE & AVERE) to moan, groan; to suffer; to squeak (said of a wheel); to ooze; to coo (said of a dove)

gèmito m moan; howl (of wind)

gèmma f gem; (bot) bud

gemma·to -ta adj gemmate; jeweled

gendarme m gendarme, policeman

genealogìa f genealogy

generalato m generalship

generale adj general || m general; generale d'armata (mil) general; generale di brigata brigadier general; generale di corpo d'armata lieutenant general; generale di divisione major general || f (mil) assembly; stare sulle generali to speak in vague generalities

generali·tà f (-tà) generality; majority; generalità fpl personal data

generalizzare [ddzz] tr to generalize; to bring into general use || intr to generalize, deal in generalities

generare (gènero) tr to beget; to generate || ref to occur

genera·tóre -trice adj generating || m generator || f generatrix

generazióne f generation

gènere m genus; kind, type; genre; (gram) gender; del genere similar, alike; farne di ogni genere to commit all sorts of mischief; genere umano mankind; generi alimentari foodstuffs; generi diversi sundries, assorted articles; in genere generally

genèri·co -ca (-ci -che) adj generic; vague; all-round; general (e.g., practitioner) || mf (theat) actor playing bit parts || m vagueness, imprecision

gènero m son-in-law

generosi·tà [s] f (-tà) generosity

generó·so -sa [s] adj generous; rich (wine)

gène·si f (-si) genesis || il Genesi Genesis

genèti·co -ca (-ci -che) adj genetic(al) || f genetics

genetlìa·co -ca (-ci -che) adj birth || m birthday

gengiva f (anat) gum

genìa f set, gang; (lit) breed

geniale adj clever; genial; inspired, genius-like

geniali·tà f (-tà) cleverness, ingeniousness; genius; (lit) geniality

genière m (mil) engineer

gè·nio m (-ni) genius; (mil) corps of engineers; andare a genio (with dat) to like, e.g., la musica moderna non gli va a genio he does not like modern music; fare qlco di genio to do s.th willingly

genitale adj genital || genitali mpl genitals

geniti·vo -va adj & m genitive

geni·tóre -trice mf parent

gen·nàio m (-nài) January

genocidio m genocide

Gènova f Genoa

genovése [s] adj f & mf Genoese

gentàglia f riffraff, rabble, scum

gènte adj (archaic) gentle || f people; nation; family; (nav) crew; gente d'arme soldiers; gente di mal affare riffraff; gente di mare sailors

gentildònna f gentlewoman

gentile adj gentle; nice; genteel || Gentili mpl heathen

gentilézza f gentleness; kindness; per gentilezza kindly, please

gentilì·zio -zia adj (-zi -zie) of noble family; (lit) ancestral

gentiluò·mo m (-mini) gentleman, nobleman

genuflèttere §177 ref to kneel down

genuì·no -na adj genuine

genziana f gentian

geofìsi·co -ca (-ci -che) adj geophysical || f geophysics

geografìa f geography

geogràfi·co -ca adj (-ci -che) geographic(al)

geògra·fo -fa mf geographer

geologìa f geology

geòlo·go -ga mf (-gi -ghe) geologist

geòme·tra m (-tri) geometrician; land surveyor

geometrìa f geometry

gerà·nio m (-ni) geranium

gerar·ca m (-chi) leader

gerarchìa f hierarchy

geràrchi·co -ca adj (-ci -che) hierarchical; per via gerarchica through proper channels

Geremìa f Jeremiah

geremìade f jeremiad

gerènte m manager, director; gerente responsabile (journ) managing editor

gèr·go m (-ghi) jargon

geriatrìa f geriatrics

Gèrico f Jericho

gèrla f pannier (carried on the back)

Germània, la Germany

germàni·co -ca adj (-ci -che) Germanic

germànio m germanium

germanizzare [ddzz] tr to Germanize

germa·no -na adj German, e.g., fratello germano brother-german; Germanic || m (lit) brother-german; germano nero (orn) coot; germano reale (orn) mallard

gèrme m germ; (lit) offspring

germici·da (-di) adj germicidal || m germicide

germinare (gèrmino) *intr* (ESSERE & AVERE) to germinate

germogliare §280 (germóglio) *tr* to put forth || *intr* (ESSERE & AVERE) to bud, sprout

germó·glio *m* (-gli) bud, sprout

geroglìfi·co -ca *adj & m* (-ci -che) hieroglyphic

Geròlamo *m* Jerome

gerontocò·mio *m* (-mi) or **gerotrò·fio** *m* (-fi) old people's home, nursing home

geràn·dio *m* (-di) gerund

Gerusalèmme *f* Jerusalem

gessare (gèsso) *tr* to plaster; to lime (*a field*)

gèsso *m* gypsum; plaster; chalk; (sculp) plaster cast

gessó·so -sa [s] *adj* plastery, chalky; chalklike

gèsta *f* (archaic) army; **gesta** *fpl* deeds, exploits

gestante *f* pregnant woman

gestazióne *f* gestation

gesticolare (gestìcolo) *intr* to gesticulate

gestióne *f* management, operation; data processing

gestire §176 *tr* to manage, operate || *intr* to gesticulate; (theat) to make gestures

gèsto *m* gesture; attitude; act, deed

ge·stóre -strìce *mf* manager, operator; **gestore di stazione** (rr) station agent

gestualità *f* bodily movements (*e.g., of an actor*)

Gesù *m* Jesus; **Gesù Cristo** Jesus Christ

gesuì·ta *m* (-ti) Jesuit

gesuìti·co -ca *adj* (-ci -che) Jesuitic(al)

gettare (gètto) *tr* to throw; to cast; to pour; to lay (*e.g., a floor*); to send forth; to yield; to broadcast (*seed*); to risk (*one's life*); **gettare la colpa addosso a qlcu** to lay the blame on s.o.; **gettare le armi** to lay down one's arms; **gettar giù** to fell, knock down; **gettar sangue** to bleed || *ref* to throw oneself; to plunge; to flow, empty (*said of a river*)

gettata *f* pour, pouring; jetty; shoot, sprout; cast; range (*of a gun*); **gettata cardìaca** (med) rate of flow of blood

gèttito *m* yield; waste; **far gettito di** to waste

gètto *m* throw; gush; shoot, sprout; cast; precast concrete slab; (aer) jet; **a getto** (aer) jet; **a getto continuo** continuously; **di getto** spontaneously; **far getto di** to waste; **primo getto** first draft

gettonare (gettóno) *tr* (coll) to call up from a pay station; (coll) to make the selection of (*a record in a juke-box*)

gettóne *m* counter, token; attendance fee; (cards) chip

gettopropulsióne *f* jet propulsion

ghepardo *m* cheetah

ghép·pio *m* (-pi) kestrel

gheri·glio *m* (-gli) kernel, meat (*of nut*)

gherlino *m* (naut) warp, line

gherminèlla *f* trick, sleight of hand; trickery

ghermire §176 *tr* to claw; to seize

gheróne *m* gusset

ghétta *f* gaiter; **ghette** spats

ghétto *m* ghetto

ghiacciàia *f* icebox, cooler

ghiac·ciàio *m* (-ciai) glacier; **ghiacciaio continentale** polar cap

ghiacciare §128 *tr* to freeze || *intr* (ESSERE) to freeze || *impers* (ESSERE) —**ghiaccia** it is freezing

ghiaccia·to -ta *adj* iced; ice-cold; frozen || *f* flavored crushed ice

ghiàc·cio -cia (-ci -ce) *adj* icy, ice-cold || *m* ice; **ghiaccio secco** dry ice

ghiacciò·lo -la *adj* crumbly, breakable || *m* icicle; popsicle

ghiàia *f* gravel, crushed stone

ghianda *f* fringe (*on a curtain*); (bot) acorn; **ghiande** mast (*for swine*)

ghiandàia *f* (orn) jay

ghiàndola *f* gland

ghibelli·no -na *adj & m* Ghibelline

ghièra *f* ferrule; ring

ghigliottìna *f* guillotine; **a ghigliottìna** sash (*window*)

ghigliottinare *tr* to guillotine

ghigna *f* (coll) grimace

ghignare *intr* to grimace; to sneer

ghigno *m* sneer, smirk; grin

ghinèa *f* guinea

ghìngheri *m invar*—**in ghìngheri** dressed up

ghiót·to -ta *adj* fond; gluttonous; eager; dainty (*food*) || *f* (culin) dripping pan

ghiottó·ne -na *mf* glutton; (zool) glutton, wolverine

ghiottonerìa *f* gluttony; tidbit; (fig) rarity

ghiòzzo [ddzz] *m* dolt; (ichth) gudgeon

ghirba *f* jar; (coll) skin, life

ghiribìzzo [ddzz] *m* (coll) whim, caprice

ghirigòro *m* doodle, curlicue

ghirlanda *f* garland, wreath

ghiro *m* dormouse; **dormire come un ghiro** to sleep like a log

ghisa *f* cast iron

già *adv* already; once upon a time; formerly || *interj* indeed!

giac·ca *f* (-che) jacket, coat; **giacca a due petti** double-breasted coat; **giacca a vento** windbreaker

giacché *conj* since

giacente *adj* lying; idle (*capital*); unclaimed (*letter*); in abeyance

giacènza *f* lying; stay, abeyance; **giacenze di capitali** idle capital; **giacenze di magazzino** unsold stock of merchandise

giacére §181 *intr* (ESSERE) to lie; to be in abeyance; (lit) to be prostrate

giaci·glio *m* (-gli) pallet, cot

giacimento *m* field, bed; **giacimento petrolìfero** oil field

giacinto *m* hyacinth

Giàcomo *m* James

giaculatòria *f* ejaculation (*prayer*); litany (*monotonous account*); curse

giada *f* jade

giaggiòlo *m* (bot) iris

giaguaro m jaguar

gialétto m jet (black coal)

gialappa f (pharm) jalap

gialla·stro -stra adj yellowish

gial·lo -la adj yellow; detective (book or picture); white (with fear) ‖ m yellow; detective story, whodunit; suspense movie; **giallo dell'uovo** egg yolk

giamaica·no -na adj & mf Jamaican

giàmbi·co -ca adj (-ci -che) iambic

giambo m iamb

giammài adv never

giansenismo m Jansenism

Giappóne, il Japan

giapponése [s] adj & mf Japanese

giara f crock, jar

giardinàg·gio m (-gi) gardening

giardinétta f station wagon

giardiniè·re -ra mf gardener ‖ f jardiniere; mixed pickles; mixed salad; wagonette; station wagon

giardino m garden; **giardino d'infanzia** kindergarten; **giardino pensile** roof garden; **giardino zoologico** zoological garden

giarrettièra f garter

Giasóne m Jason

giavanése [s] adj & mf Javanese

giavellòtto m javelin

gibbó·so -sa [s] adj gibbous, humped; humpbacked; rough (ground)

gibèrna f cartridge box; cartridge belt

gi·bus m (-bus) opera hat

gi·ga f (-ghe) gigue, jig

gigante adj & m giant

gigante·sco -sca adj (-schi -sche) gigantic

gigantéssa f giantess

gigióne m ham actor

gi·glio m (-gli) Madonna lily; fleur-de-lys

gilda f guild

gi·lè f (-lè) vest, waistcoat

gimnòto m electric eel

ginecología f gynecology

ginecòlo·go -ga m (-gi -ghe) gynecologist

gine·pràio m (-prài) juniper thicket; (fig) mess

ginépro m juniper

ginèstra f (bot) Spanish broom

Ginèvra f Geneva

ginevri·no -na adj & mf Genevan

gingillare ref to trifle; to idle

gingillo m trifle, bauble

ginnà·sio m (-si) secondary school; gymnasium

ginna·sta mf (-sti -ste) gymnast

ginnàsti·co -ca adj (-ci -che) gymnastic ‖ f gymnastics; **ginnastica a corpo libero** or **ginnastica da camera** calisthenics

ginni·co -ca adj (-ci -che) gymnastic

ginocchiata f blow with the knee; blow on the knee

ginocchièra f kneepad; elastic bandage (for knee); kneepiece (of armor)

ginòc·chio m (-chi) knee; **avere il ginocchio valgo** to be bowlegged; **avere il ginocchio varo** to be knock-kneed; **in ginocchio** on one's knees

‖ m (-chia fpl) knee; **fino alle ginocchia** knee-deep; **gettarsi alle ginocchia di** to go down on one's knees to; **mettere qlcu in ginocchio** to bring s.o. to his knees

ginocchióni adv on one's knees

giocare §182 tr to play; to stake, bet, risk, gamble; to make a fool of ‖ intr to play; to gamble; to circulate (said of air); (fig) to play a role; **giocare a** to play; to wager; **giocare a mosca cieca** to play blindman's buff; **giocare con** to risk; **giocare d'armi** to fence; **giocare d'azzardo** to gamble; **giocare di** to use (e.g., one's wits); **giocare di gomiti** to elbow one's way; **giocare di mano** to steal; **giocare sulle parole** to play on words; to pun ‖ ref to risk (e.g., one's life); to gamble away

giocata f wager, stake; game, play

gioca·tóre -trice mf player; gambler; speculator

giocàttolo m toy, plaything

giocherellare (giocherèllo) intr to play, trifle

giochétto m children's game; child's play; dirty trick

giò·co m (-chi) game; gambling; play; wager, stake; set; joke; (cards) hand; **entrare in gioco** to come into play; **fare gioco** to play into the hands of; **fare il doppio gioco** to be guilty of duplicity; **fare il gioco di** to play into the hands of; **giochi di equilibrio** balancing act; **gioco da ragazzi** child's play; **gioco d'azzardo** gambling; game of chance; **gioco dei bussolotti** (fig) jugglery; **gioco di destrezza** game of skill; **gioco di parole** play on words, pun; **gioco di prestigio** sleight of hand; **gioco di società** parlor game; **metter in gioco** to risk; to stake; **per gioco** for fun; **prendersi gioco di** to make fun of

giocofòrza m—**è giocoforza** + inf it is necessary + inf

giocolière m juggler

giocón·do -da adj merry, joyful

giocó·so -sa [s] adj jocose, jolly

giogàia f dewlap; chain of mountains

gió·go m (-ghi) yoke; beam (of balance); rounded peak; pass

giòia f joy, happiness; darling; jewel; **darsi alla pazza gioia** to have a wild time

gioielleria f jewelry; jewelry store

gioiellière m jeweler

gioièllo m jewel

gioió·so -sa [s] adj joyful

gioire §176 (pres part missing) intr to rejoice

Giòna m Jonas

Giordània, la Jordan (country)

giorda·no -na adj & mf Jordanian ‖ **Giordano** m Jordan (river)

Giórgio m George

giorna·làio -làia mf (-lài -làie) newsdealer

giornale m newspaper; magazine; (com) journal; **giornale di bordo** log, logbook; **giornale murale** poster; **giornale radio** newscast

giornaliè·ro -ra *adj* daily || *mf* day laborer

giornalismo *m* journalism

giornali·sta *mf* (**-sti -ste**) journalist; **giornalista pubblicista** free-lance writer || *m* newspaperman || *f* newspaperwoman

giornalménte *adv* daily

giornata *f* day; day's work; birthday; pay, salary; battle; day's march; **giornata campale** pitched battle; **giornata della mamma** Mother's Day; **giornata lavorativa** workday; **vivere alla giornata** to live from hand to mouth

giórno *m* day; **a giorni** within the next few days; **a giorni . . . a giorni** some days . . . others; **a giorno** open, openwork (*needlework*); full (*light*); **ai giorni nostri** nowadays; **al giorno d'oggi** nowadays; **buon giorno** good day; good morning; good-bye; **dare gli otto giorni** to dismiss, fire; **di ogni giorno** everyday (*e.g., clothes*); **essere a giorno** to be up to date; **giorno dei morti** All Souls' Day; **giorno di lavoro** workday; **giorno di paga** payday; **giorno fatto** broad daylight; **giorno feriale** weekday; **giorno festivo** holiday; **mettere a giorno** to bring up to date; **otto giorni oggi** one week from today; **passare un brutto giorno** to have a bad time; **un giorno o l'altro** one of these days

giòstra *f* joust; merry-go-round

giostrare (**giòstro**) *intr* to joust; to get along, manage; to idle, loiter

Glosuè *m* Joshua

Giottè·sco -sca *adj* (**-schi -sche**) of the school of Giotto

giovaménto *m* benefit, advantage

gió·vane *adj* young; youthful; fresh (*e.g., cheese*); Younger, Jr., **Plinio il Giovane** Pliny the Younger || *m* young man; boy, apprentice; **i giovani** the young || *f* young woman

giovanile *adj* youthful

Giovanni *m* John; **Giovanni Battista** John the Baptist

giovanòtta *f* young woman

giovanòtto *m* young man; (coll) bachelor

giovare (**gióvo**) *tr* (lit) to help || *intr* (with *dat*) to help, to be of use to || *ref* to avail oneself || *impers* (ESSERE) —**non giova** it's no use

Glòve *m* Jupiter

giove·dì *m* (**-dì**) Thursday; **giovedì santo** Maundy Thursday

giovèn·ca *f* (**-che**) heifer

gioventù *f* youth

giovévole *adj* helpful, beneficial

gioviale *adj* jovial

giovinézza *f* youth

gip *f* (**gip**) jeep

gippóne *m* large jeep, panel truck

giràbile *adj* endorsable

giradi·schi *m* (**-schi**) record player

giradito *m* (pathol) felon

giraffa *f* giraffe; (mov, telv) boom, crane

girafilièra *f* diestock

giramà·schio *m* (**-schi**) tap wrench

giraménto *m*—**giramento di testa** vertigo, dizziness

giramón·do *m* (**-do**) globetrotter

giràndola *f* girandole; pinwheel; (fig) weathercock

girandolare (**giràndolo**) *intr* to stroll, saunter

girante *mf* endorser || *f* blade (*e.g., of fan*)

girare *tr* to turn; to tour; to go around, travel over; to switch (*the conversation*); to film, shoot; to transfer (*a phone call*); to endorse; (mil) to surround || *intr* to turn; to circulate; to spin (*said of one's head*) || *ref* to turn; to toss and turn

girarrósto *m* turnspit; **girarrosto a motore** rotisserie

girasóle *m* sunflower

girata *f* turn; walk, ramble; (com) endorsement; (cards) deal; (coll) tongue-lashing

giratà·rio -ria *mf* (**-ri -rie**) endorsee

giravòlta *f* turn, pirouette; bend; sudden change of mind

girellare (**girèllo**) *intr* to stroll, wander around

girèllo *m* rump; go-cart, walker

girévole *adj* revolving

girino *m* tadpole; bicycle rider competing on the Tour of Italy

giro *m* periphery; turn, revolution; ride; size (*of hat*); edge (*of glass*); round (*of a doctor*); (sports) tour; (sports) lap; (com) transfer; (cards) hand; (theat) tour; **a giro di posta** by return mail; **andare in giro** to poke along; **giro collo** neckline; **giro d'affari** volume of business, turnover; **giro di parole** circumlocution; **fare il giro di** to tour; **mettere in giro** to spread (*news, gossip*); **nel giro di** within (*a period*); **prendere in giro** to poke fun at

girobùssola *f* gyrocompass

girondolare (**giróndolo**) *intr* var of girandolare

giróne *m* (sports) conference; (sports) division; (sports) league; (archaic) circle

gironzolare [dz] (**girónzolo**) *intr* to stroll, saunter

giropilò·ta *m* (**-ti**) gyropilot

giroscò·pio *m* (**-pi**) gyroscope

girotóndo *m* ring-around-a-rosy

giròtta *f* weather vane

girovagare §209 (**giròvago**) *intr* to roam, wander

giròva·go -ga (**-ghi -ghe**) *adj* wandering; strolling (*player*) || *m* vagrant, hobo

gita *f* trip, excursion, outing

gita·no -na *adj* & *mf* Gypsy

gitante *mf* excursionist, vacationist

gittata *f* range (*of gun*)

giù *adv* down; **andar giù** to go down; to deteriorate; to get worse; **buttar giù** to throw down; (culin) to start to cook, e.g., **buttar giù gli spaghetti** to start to cook the spaghetti; (fig) to jot down; **da . . . in giù** for the past . . . ; **dar giù** to look worse (*said* *of a sick person*); **esser giù** to be downcast; **giù di lì** thereabouts; **in giù** down; downstream; **mandar giù** to swallow; **non andar giù** to not be able to stomach or swallow, e.g., **non gli vanno giù i bugiardi** he cannot stomach liars; **venire giù** to come down; to crumble; to collapse

giubba *f* coat, jacket; mane

giubbétto *m* small coat; bodice; jerkin

giubbòtto *m* jacket (*e.g., of a motorcyclist*); **giubbotto salvagente** (aer, naut) life jacket

giubilare (**giùbilo**) *tr* to retire, to pension || *intr* to rejoice

giubilèo *m* jubilee

giùbilo *m* jubilation, exultation

giuda *m* Judas || **Giuda** *m* Judas

giudài·co -ca *adj* (**-ci -che**) Judaic

giudaismo *m* Judaism

giudè·o -a *adj* Judean; Jewish || *mf* Judean; Jew

giudicare §197 (**giùdico**) *tr* to judge; to find (*e.g., s.o. innocent*); to try (*a case*) || *intr* to judge, deem

giudicato *m* (hist) Sardinian region; **passare in giudicato** (law) to become final

giùdice *m* judge; magistrate, justice; **giudice conciliatore** justice of the peace; **giudice popolare** member of the jury

giudizià·rio -ria *adj* (**-ri -rie**) judicial, judiciary

giudi·zio *m* (**-zi**) judgment; wisdom; trial; sentence; **giudizio di Dio** (hist) ordeal; **giudizio finale** Last Judgment; **metter giudizio** to mend one's ways

giùggiola *f* jujube; (joc) trifle; **andare in brodo di giuggiole** to swoon, to become ecstatic

giugno *m* June

giugulare *adj* jugular || *v* (**giùgolo**) *tr* to cut the throat of

giulèbbe *m* julep

giuliana *f* (culin) julienne || **Giuliana** *f* Juliana

giuli·vo -va *adj* gay

giullare *m* jongleur; (pej) mountebank

giumén·to -ta *mf* beast of burden || *f* female saddle horse

giun·ca *f* (**-che**) (naut) junk

giunchìglia *f* (bot) jonquil

giun·co *m* (**-chi**) (bot) rush

giùngere §183 *tr* to join (e.g., *one's hands*) || *intr* (ESSERE) to arrive; **giungere a** or **in** to arrive at, reach; **giungere a + *inf*** to succeed in + *ger*; **mi giunge nuovo** it's news to me

giungla *f* jungle

Giunóne *f* Juno

giunòni·co -ca *adj* (**-ci -che**) Junoesque

giunta *f* addition; makeweight; strip (*of cloth*); junta; committee; **di prima giunta** at the very beginning; **per giunta** in addition

giuntare *tr* to join

giuntatrice *f* (mov) splicer

giunto *m* (mach) joint, coupling;

giunto a sfere ball-and-socket joint; **giunto cardanico** universal joint

giuntura or **giunzióne** *f* joint; juncture, seam

giuò·co *m* (**-chi**) var of **gioco**

giuraménto *m* oath; **deferire il giuramento a** to put under oath

giurare *tr* to swear, pledge || *intr* to swear

giura·to -ta *adj* sworn || *m* juror

giurìa *f* committee; jury

giurìdi·co -ca *adj* (**-ci -che**) juridical

giurisdizióne *f* jurisdiction

giurisprudènza *f* jurisprudence

giurì·sta *mf* (**-sti -ste**) jurist

Giusèppe *m* Joseph

Giuseppina *f* Josephine

giusta *prep* according to; in accordance with

giustappórre §218 *tr* to juxtapose

giustézza *f* correctness, justness; (typ) measure

giustificàbile *adj* justifiable

giustificare §197 (**giustìfico**) *tr* to justify || *ref* to excuse oneself

giustificazióne *f* justification

giustìzia *f* justice; **far giustizia a** to execute; **farsi giustizia da sé** to take the law into one's own hands; **render giustizia a** to do justice to

giustiziare §287 *tr* to execute

giustizière *m* executioner; (obs) judge

giu·sto -sta *adj* just; opportune || *m* just man; just price; rights, due || **giusto** *adv* just, justly

gla·bro -bra *adj* smooth (*face*)

glaciale *adj* glacial; (fig) icy

gladiatóre *m* gladiator

gladiòlo *m* gladiolus

glàndola *f* var of **ghiandola**

glassa *f* glaze, icing

glassare *tr* to glaze, ice

glèba *f* clod, lump of earth

gli §4 *art* || §5 *pers pron*

glicerina *f* glycerin

glìcine *m* wistaria

gliéla; gliéle; gliéli; gliélo; gliéne §5

globale *adj* total, aggregate

glòbo *m* globe; **globo oculare** eyeball

globulare *adj* globular, global

glòbulo *m* globule; (physiol) corpuscle

gloglottare (**gloglòtto**) *intr* to gobble; to gurgle

gloglottì·o *m* (**-i**) gobble, gobbling; gurgle

glòria *f* glory

gloriare §287 (**glòrio**) *tr* (lit) to exalt || *ref* to boast; to glory

glorificare §197 (**glorìfico**) *tr* to glorify

glorió·so -sa [s] *adj* glorious; proud

glòssa *f* gloss

glossà·rio *m* (**-ri**) glossary

glòttide *f* glottis

glottòlo·go -ga *mf* (**-gi -ghe**) linguist

glucòsio *m* glucose

glùtine *m* gluten

gnòc·co *m* (**-chi**) potato dumpling

gnòmo *m* gnome

gnòrri *m invar*—**fare lo gnorri** to feign ignorance

gòb·bo -ba *adj* hunchbacked || *mf*

hunchback || f hump; hunch; hump (of gibbous moon); hook (of nose)

góc•cia f (-ce) drop; bead; **avere la goccia al naso** to have a runny nose; **goccia d'acqua** raindrop

góc•cio m (-ci) drop, swallow

gócciola f drop; bead

gocciolare (gócciolo) tr & intr to drip

gocciola•tóio m (-tói) dripstone

goccioli•o m (-i) drip, trickle

godére §184 tr to enjoy || intr to take pleasure; to revel; to profit || ref to enjoy; **godersela** to have a good time

godìbile adj enjoyable

godiménto m enjoyment, pleasure

goffàggine f clumsiness

gòf•fo -fa adj awkward; ill-fitting

gógna f pillory; **mettere alla gogna** to pillory

góla f throat; neck; gluttony; gorge (of mountain); mouth (of cannon); flue (of chimney); (archit) ogee; **far gola a** to tempt; **mentire per la gola** to lie shamelessly; **tornare a gola** to repeat (said of food)

golétta f neck (of shirt); (naut) schooner

gòlf m (gòlf) sweater, cardigan; (sports) golf

gólfo m gulf; **golfo mistico** orchestra pit || **Golfo Persico** Persian Gulf

Gòlgota, il Golgotha

goliardo m goliard; university student

golosi•tà [s] f (-tà) gluttony; tidbit

goló•so -sa [s] adj gluttonous; appetizing

gómena f hawser

gomitata f blow with the elbow; nudge

gómito m elbow; bend; **alzare il gomito** to crook the elbow; **dare di gomito a** to nudge

gomìtolo m skein, clew

gómma f gum; rubber; eraser; tire; **bucare una gomma** to have a flat tire; **gomma arabica** gum arabic; **gomma a terra** flat tire; **gomma da masticare** chewing gum; **gomma lacca** shellac

gommapiuma f foam rubber

gomma•to -ta adj gummed; with tires

gommatura f gumming; (aut) tires

gommi•sta m (-sti) tire dealer; tire repairman

gommó•so -sa [s] adj gummy

góndola f gondola; (aer) pod

gonfalóne m gonfalon

gonfiare §287 (gónfio) tr to inflate, blow up; to bloat; to swell; to exaggerate; to puff up || intr (ESSERE) to swell || ref to swell; to puff up; to bulge, balloon

gonfiatura f inflation; exaggeration

gonfiézza f swelling; grandiloquence

gón•fio -fia (-fi -fie) adj inflated, swollen; conceited || m swelling, bulge

gonfiòre m swelling

gongolare (góngolo) intr to rejoice; to be elated

goniòmetro m goniometer; protractor

gònna f skirt; **gonna pantaloni** culottes

gonnèlla f skirt; (fig) petticoat

gonnellino m kilt; ballerina skirt

gón•zo -za [dz] mf simpleton, fool

góra f millpond; marsh; (coll) spot

górbia f tip (of umbrella)

gorgheggiare §290 (gorghéggio) tr & intr to warble; to trill

gorghég•gio m (-gi) warbling; trill

gór•go m (-ghi) whirlpool; (lit) river

gorgogliare §280 (gorgóglio) intr to gurgle

gorgó•glio m (-gli) gurgle

gorgogli•o m (-i) gurgling

goril•la m (-la) gorilla

gòta f cheek; (lit) side

gòti•co -ca adj & m (-ci -che) Gothic

Gòto m Goth

gótta f (pathol) gout

gottazza f (naut) scoop

gottó•so -sa [s] adj gouty

governale m fin (of bomb); (obs) rudder

governante adj governing || m ruler || f governess; housekeeper

governare (govèrno) tr to rule, govern; to steer (a ship); to tend (animals); to wash and dry (dishes); to run (e.g., a bank) || intr to steer

governati•vo -va adj government

govèrno m government; tending (e.g., of animals); running (of household); cleaning (of house); blending (of wine); (archaic) steering

gózzo m crop, craw (of bird); (pathol) goiter

gozzovigliare §280 intr to go on a spree

gracchiare §287 intr to caw

gràc•chio m (-chi) caw; (orn) chough

gracidare (gràcido) intr to croak; to honk (said, e.g., of a goose)

gràcile adj weak, frail; thin, delicate

gradasso m swaggerer, braggadocio

grada•to -ta adj graded; gradual

gradazióne f gradation; alcoholic proof; **gradazione vocalica** (phonet) ablaut

gradévole adj pleasant

gradiménto m pleasure; acceptance (of a product); liking

gradinata f steps; tier (of seats)

gradino m step; (fig) stepping stone

gradire §176 tr to like; to welcome

gradi•to -ta adj agreeable; welcome (guest); kind (letter)

grado m degree; rank; (nav) rating; (archaic) step; **a buon grado o a mal grado** willy-nilly; **a grado a grado** little by little; **a Suo grado** according to your wishes; **di buon grado** willingly; **di secondo grado** secondary (school); **essere in grado di** to be in a position to; **saper grado a** (lit) to be grateful to

graduale adj & m gradual

graduare (gràduo) tr to graduate

gradua•to -ta adj graduated || m noncommissioned officer

graduatòria f ranking; rank

graffa f clamp; brace; bracket

graffiare §287 tr to scratch; (coll) to swipe

graffiétto m tiny scratch; marking gage

gràf•fio m (-fi) scratch

grafìa f writing, spelling; (gram) graph

gràfi•co -ca (-ci -che) *adj* graphic ‖ *m* graph, diagram; designer (*for printing industry*); member of printers' union ‖ *f* graphic arts

grafite *f* graphite

grafologìa *f* graphology

gragnòla *f* hail

gramàglia *f* crepe; widow's weeds; **in gramaglie** in mourning

gramigna *f* couch grass; weed

grammàti•co -ca (-ci -che) *adj* grammatical ‖ *m* grammarian ‖ *f* grammar

grammo *m* gram

grammofòni•co -ca adj (-ci -che) phonograph, recording

grammòfono *m* phonograph, record player

gra•mo -ma *adj* poor, sad; wretched, miserable; frail, sickly

gran *adj* apocopated form of **grande**, used before singular and plural nouns beginning with a consonant sound other than *gn, pn, ps,* impure *s, x,* and *z*

gra•na *f* **(-na)** Parmesan cheese ‖ *f* **(-ne)** cochineal; grain (*of wood, metal, etc*); (slang) dough; (coll) trouble

granàglie *fpl* grain, cereals

gra•nàio *m* **(-nài)** granary, barn

granata *adj invar & m* garnet (*color*) ‖ *f* pomegranate (*fruit*); garnet; broom; grenade

granatière *m* grenadier

granatina *f* grenadine

Gran Bretagna, la Great Britain

grancassa *f* bass drum

grancèvola *f* spider crab

gràn•chio *m* **(-chi)** crab; claw (*of hammer*); (coll) cramp; **prendere un granchio** to make a blunder

grandangolare *adj* wide-angle

grande *adj* big, large; great; tall; high (*mass; voice*); long (*time*); capital (*letter*); full (*speed*); grown-up ‖ *m* grownup; grandeur; grandee; **fare il grande** to show off; **i grandi** the great; **in grande** on a large scale; lavishly

grandézza *f* size; enormity; greatness; quantity; **in grandezza naturale** lifesize; **grandezze** ostentatiousness

grandezzó•so -sa [s] *adj* ostentatious

grandiloquènza *f* grandiloquence

grandinare (gràndino) *tr* (obs) to hail ‖ *intr* to hail ‖ *impers* (ESSERE & AVERE)—**grandina** it is hailing

grandinata *f* hailstorm

gràndine *f* hail

grandiosi•tà [s] *f* **(-tà)** grandeur, magnificence

grandió•so -sa [s] *adj* grandiose, grand

grandu•ca *m* **(-chi)** grand duke

granduchéssa *f* grand duchess

granèllo *m* grain, seed; speck

grànfia *f* clutch

granico•lo -la *adj* grain, wheat

granire §176 *tr* to grain; to stipple; (mus) to make (*the notes*) clear-cut ‖ *intr* to teethe

granita *f* sherbet, water ice

granito *m* granite

granitura *f* knurl, milled edge

grano *m* wheat; grain of wheat; grain; speck; **grano duro** durum wheat; **grano saraceno** buckwheat; **grano turco** corn

granturco *m* corn

granulare *adj* granular ‖ *v* **(grànulo)** *tr* to granulate

granulatóre *m* crusher

grànulo *m* granule, pellet, bud

granuló•so -sa [s] *adj* granular; lumpy; gritty; friable, crumbly

grappa *f* eau de vie; clamp, brace

grappétta *f* staple; crampon

grappino *m* (naut) grapnel

gràppolo *m* bunch, cluster

grassàg•gio *m* **(-gi)** (aut) lubrication

grassatóre *m* highwayman

grassazióne *f* holdup

grassétto *m* boldface

grassézza *f* fatness; richness

gras•so -sa *adj* fat; rich; greasy; risqué ‖ *m* fat, suet; grease; shortening

grassòc•cio -cia *adj* **(-ci -ce)** pudgy, plump

grata *f* grate, grating

gratèlla *f* strainer; sieve; broiler

gratic•cia *f* **(-ce)** (theat) gridiron

gratic•cio *m* **(-ci)** lattice, trellis

graticola *f* gridiron; grating; graticule

gratìfi•ca *f* **(-che)** bonus

gratificare §197 (gratìfico) *tr* to give a bonus to; (fig) to pelt (*with insults*)

gratificazióne *f* bonus

gratis *adv* gratis, free, for nothing

gratitùdine *f* gratitude

gra•to -ta *adj* grateful, appreciative ‖ *f* see **grata**

grattacapo *m* trouble, worry

grattacièlo *m* skyscraper

grattare *tr* to scratch; to scrape; to grate; (slang) to snitch ‖ *intr* to scratch; to grate

grattùgia *f* grater

grattugiare §290 *tr* to grate

gratùi•to -ta *adj* gratuitous, free

gravame *m* burden; tax; (law) appeal; **fare gravame a qlcu di qlco** to impute s.th to s.o.

gravare *tr* to burden, oppress; (obs) to seize ‖ *intr* (ESSERE & AVERE) to weigh; to lie; to be sorry, e.g., **gli grava d'avermi disturbato** he is sorry to have bothered me ‖ *ref*—**gravarsi di** to take upon oneself

grave *adj* heavy; burdensome; grave, serious ‖ *m* (phys) body; **stare sul grave** to put on airs

graveolènte *adj* stinking

gravézza *f* heaviness; burden; oppression; (obs) taxation

gravidanza *f* pregnancy

gràvi•do -da *adj* pregnant; fraught

gravi•tà *f* **(-tà)** gravity

gravitare (gràvito) *intr* to gravitate; to weigh, lie

gravitazióne *f* gravitation

gravó•so -sa [s] *adj* heavy; hard, burdensome; oppressive

gràzia *f* grace; pardon, mercy; delicacy; kindness; **di grazia!** please!;

essere nelle grazie di qlcu to be in s.o.'s good graces; fare grazia di qlco a qlcu to spare s.o. s.th; grazia di Dio abundance, bounty; grazie! thank you!; grazie tante! thanks a lot!; in grazia di thanks to; male grazie bad manners; per grazie as a favor; render grazia a to thank; saper grazia a to be thankful to

graziare §287 tr to pardon; graziare qlcu di qlco to grant s.th to s.o.

grazió·so ·sa [s] adj graceful, pretty; gracious; (lit) free, gratuitous

Grècia, la Greece

grè·co ·ca (-ci -che) adj & mf Greek || f fret, fretwork; bullion (on Italian general's hat); tunic

gregà·rio ·ria (-ri -rie) adj gregarious || m private; follower

grég·ge m (-gi or -ge fpl) flock, herd

grég·gio ·gia (-gi -ge) adj coarse; raw, unrefined || m crude oil

gregoria·no ·na adj Gregorian

grembiale m var of grembiule

grembiule m apron; frock; smock

grembiulino m pinafore

grèmbo m lap; womb; bosom

gremire §176 tr to crowd || ref to become crowded

gremi·to ·ta adj overcrowded

gréppia f manger, crib

gréto m dry gravel bed of a river

grettézza f stinginess; narrow-mindedness

grét·to ·ta adj stingy; narrow-minded

grève adj heavy; uncouth; (lit) grievous

gréz·zo ·za [ddzz] adj raw, crude; coarse

gridare tr to cry out; to cry for (help); (coll) to scold || intr to cry out, shout

grido m cry (of animal) || m (grida fpl) cry; scream; shout; yell; fame; di grido famous; grido di guerra war cry; ultimo grido latest fashion

grifa·gno ·gna adj rapacious, fierce

griffa f hobnail; (mov, phot) sprocket

grifo m snout (of pig); (pej) snoot; (lit) griffin

grifóne m vulture; (mythol) griffin

grigia·stro ·stra adj grayish

gri·gio ·gia adj & m (-gi -gie) grey

grigiovérde adj invar olive-drab || m olive-drab uniform

griglia f gridiron, broiler; grate, grille; (elec) grid (of vacuum tube)

grillare tr to grill, broil || intr to sizzle; to bubble (said of fermenting wine); to have a sudden whim

grillétto m trigger

grillo m cricket; whim, fancy

grimaldèllo m picklock

grinfia f claw, clutch; grinfie clutches

grinta f grim or forbidding face

grinza f wrinkle; crease; non fare una grinza to be perfect

grinzó·so ·sa [s] adj wrinkled; creased

grippare intr & ref to bind, jam

grisèlla f (naut) ratline

gri·sou m (-sou) firedamp

grissino m breadstick

Groenlàndia, la Greenland

grómma f incrustation, deposit

grónda f eaves; slope (of ground)

grondàia f gutter (of roof)

grondare (gróndo) tr to drip || intr (ESSERE) to ooze (said, e.g., of perspiration); to drip; grondare di sangue to stream with blood

gròppa f back (of animal); top (of mountain); restare sulla groppa a to be stuck with, e.g., gli sono restati sulla groppa cento esemplari he is stuck with one hundred copies

groppata f bucking (of horse)

gróppo m knot; tangle; lump (in throat); squall

groppóne m back, rump

gròssa f gross; dormire della grossa to sleep like a log

grossézza f bigness; thickness; density; swelling (of river); (fig) coarseness; grossezza d'udito hardness of hearing

grossi·sta mf (-sti -ste) wholesaler

gròs·so ·sa adj big, large; thick; heavy (seas); swollen (river); hard (breathing); offensive (words); coarse (e.g., salt); pregnant; deep (voice); (coll) important; alla grossa approximately; di grosso a lot, very much; dirla grossa to talk nonsense; farla grossa to make a blunder; grosso d'udito hard of hearing; in grosso wholesale; sparare grosse to tell tall tales || m bulk; main body (e.g., of an army) || f see grossa

grossola·no ·na adj coarse; boorish, uncouth; big (blunder)

gròtta f grotto; (coll) inn

grotté·sco ·ca (-schi -sche) adj & m grotesque || f (hist) grotesque painting

grovièra f Gruyère cheese

grovì·glio m (-gli) tangle, snarl

gru f (gru) (orn, mach) crane

grùc·cia f (-ce) crutch; clothes hanger; (obs) wooden leg

grufolare (grùfolo) intr to nuzzle || ref to wallow (in mud)

grugnire §176 tr & intr to grunt

grugnito m grunt

grugno m snout; (pej) snoot; fare il grugno to sulk

grui·sta m (-sti) crane operator

grulleria f foolishness

grul·lo ·la adj silly, simple

gruma f deposit, incrustation

grumo m lump; clot

grùmolo m heart (e.g., of lettuce); small lump

grumó·so ·sa [s] adj lumpy; incrusted, scaly

gruppo m group; main body (e.g., of runners); club; gruppo elettrogeno generating unit; gruppo motore (aut) power plant

grùzzolo m hoard, pile; farsi il gruzzolo to feather one's nest

guadagnare tr to earn; to win; to gain; to pick up (speed); to reach (port) || intr to win; to look better || ref to win; to win over; guadagnarsi il pane or la vita to earn one's living

guadagno m earnings; profit; a basso

guadagno (rad, telv) low-gain; **ad alto guadagno** (rad, telv) high-gain
guadare *tr* to wade, ford
guado *m* ford; (bot) woad; **passare a guado** to ford
guài *interj* woe!
guaina *f* case; scabbard, sheath; corset; (aut) seat cover
guàio *m* (**guài**) trouble || *interj* see **guài**
guaire §176 *intr* to yelp; to whine
guaito *m* yelp, whine
gualcire §176 *tr* to crumple
gualdrappa *f* saddlecloth
Gualtièro *m* Walter
guàn·cia *f* (**-ce**) cheek; moldboard; cheek side (*of gunstock*)
guanciale *m* pillow; **dormire tra due guanciali** to sleep safe and sound
guan·tàio **-tàia** *mf* (**-tài -tàie**) glove maker; glove merchant
guanterìa *f* glove factory
guantièra *f* glove case; tray
guanto *m* glove; **gettare il guanto** to fling down the gauntlet; **raccogliere il guanto** to take up the gauntlet; **trattare con i guanti gialli** to handle with kid gloves
guantóne *m* big glove; **guantoni da pugilato** boxing gloves
guardabarriè·re *m* (**-re**) (rr) gatekeeper, crossing watchman
guardabò·schi *m* (**-schi**) forester
guardacàc·cia *m* (**-cia**) gamekeeper
guardacò·ste *m* (**-ste**) coast guard; coast-guard cutter
guardafi·li *m* (**-li**) (elec) lineman
guardalì·nee *m* (**-nee**) (rr) trackwalker; (sports) linesman
guardama·no *m* (**-no**) guard (*of sabre or rifle*); work glove; (naut) handrail
guardaportó·ne *m* (**-ne**) doorman
guardare *tr* to look at; to protect, watch; to pay attention to; to face, overlook; (obs) to keep to (*one's bed*); (obs) to keep (*a holiday*); **guardare a vista** to keep under close watch; **guardare dall'alto in basso** to look down one's nose at; **guardare di sotto in su** to leer at || *intr* to look; to pay attention; **Dio guardi!** God forbid!; **guardare a** to face (*said, e.g., of a room*); **guardare di non + inf** to be careful not to + *inf*; **guardare in faccia** to face (*e.g., danger*); **stare a guardare** to keep on the sidelines || *ref* to look at one another; to look at oneself; **guardarsi da** to keep from; to guard against
guardarò·ba *m* (**-ba**) wardrobe; linen closet; checkroom, cloakroom
guardarobiè·re -ra *mf* checkroom attendant || *f* hatcheck girl
guardasigil·li *m* (**-li**) minister of justice (*in Italy*); (Brit) Lord Privy Seal; (U.S.A.) attorney general; (hist) keeper of the seals
guardaspal·le *m* (**-le**) bodyguard
guardata *f* quick look, glance
guarda·vìa *m* (**-vìa**) guardrail; median strip
guàrdia *f* watch; guard; top water level; flyleaf; **di guardia** on duty;

fare la guardia a to watch; **guardia campestre** forester; **guardia carceraria** prison guard; **guardia del corpo** guard, body guard; **guardia di finanza** customs officer; **guardia d'onore** honor guard; **guardia forestale** forester; park guard; **guardia giurata** private policeman; **guardia medica** emergency clinic; **guardia municipale** police officer; **guardia notturna** night watch; **mettere qlcu in guardia** to warn s.o.; **montare la guardia** to be on guard duty, keep guard; **stare in guardia** to be on one's guard
guardiamari·na *m* (**-na**) (nav) ensign
guardiano *m* keeper; warden; watchdog; (eccl) superior; **guardiano notturno** night watchman
guardina *f* lockup; **in guardina** in jail
guardinfante *m* bustle (*worn under the back of a woman's skirt*)
guardin·go -ga *adj* (**-ghi -ghe**) wary
guàrdolo *m* welt (*in shoe*)
guardóne *m* peeping tom
guarenti·gìa *f* (**-gìe**) guarantee
guaribile *adj* curable
guarigióne *f* cure, recovery
guarire §176 *tr* to cure; to heal || *intr* (ESSERE) to recover; to heal
guaritóre *m* healer; quack
guarnigióne *f* (mil) garrison
guarnire §176 *tr* to equip; to rig; to trim; (naut) to rig; (culin) to garnish || *intr* to add beauty
guarnizióne *f* decoration; trimming; lining; (culin) garniture; (mach) gasket; (mach) washer
Guascógna, la Gascony
guascó·ne -na *adj & mf* Gascon
guastafè·ste *mf* (**-ste**) kill-joy
guastare *tr* to ruin, spoil; to undo; to wreck; (obs) to lay waste; **guastare le uova nel paniere a** to spoil the plans of || *ref* to spoil; to worsen (*said, e.g., of the weather*); (mach) to break down; **guastarsi con qlcu** to quarrel with s.o.; **guastarsi il sangue** to blow one's top
guastatóre *m* commando
gua·sto -sta *adj* ruined, spoiled; wrecked || *m* breakdown; corruption; discord
guatare *tr* (lit) to look askance or with fear at
Guayana, la Guyana
guazza *f* dew
guazzabù·glio *m* (**-gli**) muddle, mess
guazzare *tr* to make (*an animal*) wade in a river || *intr* to wallow
guazzétto *m* stew, ragout
guazzo *m* puddle, pool; gouache
guèl·fo -fa *adj & mf* Guelph
guèr·cio -cia *adj* (**-ci -ce**) cross-eyed; one-eyed; almost blind || *mf* cross-eyed person; one-eyed person
guèrra *f* war; warfare; **guerra a coltello** internecine feud; **guerra di Troia** Trojan war; **guerra fredda** cold war; **guerra lampo** blitzkrieg; **guerra mondiale** world war

guerrafon·dàio -dàia (-dài -dàie) *adj*
warmongering ‖ *mf* warmonger
guerreggiare §290 (guerréggio) *tr* to
fight, war against ‖ *intr* to fight ‖
ref to make war on one another
guerré·sco -sca *adj* (-schi -sche) warlike
guerriè·ro -ra *adj* war, warlike ‖ *mf*
fighter ‖ *m* warrior
guerriglia *f* guerrilla
guerriglièro *m* guerrilla (*soldier*)
gufo *m* misanthrope; (orn) horned owl
gùglia *f* spire; peak
gugliata *f* needleful
Guglièlmo *m* William
guida *f* guide; guidance; driving; runner (*rug*); guidebook; manual (*of instruction*); (aut) steering; **guida a
destra** right-hand drive; **guide reins**
(*of horse*); (mach) slide
guidaiòlo *m* leader (*among animals*)
guidare *tr* to guide, lead; to steer; to
drive ‖ *intr* to drive ‖ *ref* to restrain
oneself
guida·tóre -trice *mf* driver
guiderdóne *m* (lit) premium, prize
guidóne *m* pennant, pennon
guidoslitta *f* bobsled
guidovìa *f* ski lift

Guinèa, la Guinea
guinzà·glio *m* (-gli) leash; (fig) fetter,
shackle
guisa *f* way, manner; **in guisa che** so
that; **in guisa di** under the guise of
guit·to -ta *adj* miserly, niggardly ‖ *m*
strolling player
guizzare *intr* to dart; to wriggle; to
flash (*said of lightning*); (naut) to
yaw ‖ *intr* (ESSERE) to slip away
guizzo *m* dart; wriggle; flash
gù·scio *m* (-sci) shell; pod (*of pea*); tick
(*of mattress*); **guscio di noce** nutshell; **guscio d'uovo** eggshell
gustare *tr* to taste; to relish ‖ *intr*
(ESSERE & AVERE) to please; to like,
e.g., **gli gustano le gite in barca** he
likes boat rides
gusto *m* taste; pleasure, fun; whim;
style; **di cattivo gusto** tasteless; **di
gusto** gladly, with gusto; **prendere
gusto per** to take a liking for; **prendersi il gusto di** to relish; **provar
gusto** to have fun
gustó·so -sa [s] *adj* tasty
guttapèrca *f* gutta-percha
gutturale *adj & f* guttural

H

H, h ['akka] *m & f* eighth letter of the
Italian alphabet
handicappare *tr* var of **andicappare**
hangar *m* (hangar) hangar
havaia·no -na *adj & mf* Hawaiian
henné *m* henna
hertz *m* hertz

hertzia·no -na *adj* Hertzian
hi-fi *f* (coll) hi-fi
hockei·sta *m* (-sti) hockey player
hollywoodia·no -na *adj* Hollywood,
Hollywood-like
hurrà *interj* hurrah!

I

I, i, [i] *m & f* ninth letter of the Italian
alphabet
i §4 *def art* the
iarda *f* yard
iato *m* hiatus
iattanza *f* boasting, bragging
iattura *f* misfortune, calamity
ibèri·co -ca *adj* (-ci -che) Iberian
ibernare (ibèrno) *intr* to hibernate
ibi·sco *m* (-schi) hibiscus
ibridare (ìbrido) *tr & intr* to hybridize
ibri·do -da *adj & m* hybrid
icàsti·co -ca *adj* (-ci -che) figurative;
realistic
-ìccio -ìccia *suf adj* -ish, e.g., **gialliccio**
yellowish
iconocla·sta *mf* (-sti -ste) iconoclast
iconografìa *f* iconography
iconoscò·pio *m* (-pi) iconoscope
iddì·o *m* (-i) god ‖ **Iddio** *m* God
idèa *f* idea; goal, purpose; bit; touch;
avere idea di to have a mind to; **dare
l'idea di** to seem; **farsi un'idea di** to

grasp the notion of; **idea fissa** fixed
idea; **neanche per idea** not in the
least
ideale *adj & m* ideal
idealismo *m* idealism
ideali·sta *mf* (-sti -ste) idealist
idealisti·co -ca *adj* (-ci -che) idealistic
idealizzare [ddzz] *tr* to idealize
ideare (idèo) *tr* to conceive
idea·tóre -trice *mf* inventor
idem *adv* ditto
idènti·co -ca *adj* (-ci -che) identical
identificare §197 (identìfico) *tr* to identify ‖ *ref* to resemble each other;
identificarsi con to identify with
identificazióne *f* identification
identi·tà *f* (-tà) identity
ideologìa *f* ideology
idi *mpl & fpl* ides
idillìa·co -ca *adj* (-ci -che) idyllic
idìl·lio *m* (-li) idyll; romance
idiò·ma *m* (-mi) language, idiom
idiomàti·co -ca *adj* (-ci -che) idiomatic

idiosincrasìa *f* aversion; (med) idiosyncrasy

idiò·ta (-ti -te) *adj* idiotic || *mf* idiot

idiotismo *m* idiom; idiocy

idiozìa *f* idiocy

idolatrare *tr & intr* to idolize

idolatrìa *f* idolatry

ìdolo *m* idol

idonei·tà *f* (-tà) fitness, aptitude; qualification

idòne·o -a *adj* fit; qualified; opportune

idra *f* hydra

idrante *m* hydrant, fireplug

idratante *adj* moisturizing

idratare *tr & ref* to hydrate

idrato *m* hydrate

idràuli·co -ca (-ci -che) *adj* hydraulic || *m* plumber || *f* hydraulics

ìdri·co -ca *adj* (-ci -che) water, e.g., **forza idrica** water power

idrocarburo *m* hydrocarbon

idroelèttri·co -ca *adj* (-ci -che) hydroelectric

idròfi·lo -la *adj* absorbent

idrofobìa *f* hydrophobia, rabies

idròfo·bo -ba *adj* hydrophobic, rabid

idròfu·go -ga *adj* (-ghi -ghe) waterproof

idrogenare (**idrògeno**) *tr* to hydrogenate

idrògeno *m* hydrogen

idròpi·co -ca (-ci -che) *adj* dropsical || *mf* patient suffering from dropsy

idropisìa *f* dropsy

idroplano *m* hydroplane (*boat*)

idropòrto *m* seaplane airport

idrorepellènte *adj* water-repellent

idroscalo *m* seaplane airport

idro·scì *m* (-scì) water ski

idroscivolante *m* (naut) hydroplane

idrosilurante *m* torpedo plane

idròssido *m* hydroxide

idroterapìa *f* hydrotherapy

idrovìa *f* inland waterway

idrovolante *m* seaplane, hydroplane

idròvo·ro -ra *adj* suction (*pump*) || *f* suction pump

ièna *f* hyena

ièri *m & adv* yesterday; **ieri l'altro** the day before yesterday; **ieri notte** last night; **ieri sera** last evening, last night, yesterday evening

iettatóre -trice *mf* hoodoo

iettatura *f* evil eye; bad luck, jinx

igiène *f* hygiene; sanitation

igièni·co -ca *adj* (-ci -che) hygienic, sanitary

ìgname *m* yam

igna·ro -ra *adj* unaware; inexperienced

igna·vo -va *adj* (lit) slothful

ignizióne *f* ignition

ignòbile *adj* (lit) ignoble

ignomìnia *f* ignominy; outrage

ignominió·so -sa [s] *adj* ignominious

ignorante *adj* ignorant; illiterate || *mf* ignoramus

ignoranza *f* ignorance

ignorare (**ignòro**) *tr* to not know; to ignore

ignò·to -ta *adj & m* unknown

ignu·do -da *adj* (lit) naked || *m* (lit) naked person

il §4 *def art* the

ìlare *adj* cheerful

ilari·tà *f* (-tà) cheerfulness; laughter

ìlice *f* (lit) ilex, holm oak

ìlio *m* (anat) ilium

illanguidire §176 *tr* to weaken || *intr* (ESSERE) to get weak

illazióne *f* inference

illéci·to -ta *adj* illicit, unlawful || *m* unlawful act

illegale *adj* illegal

illeggiadrire §176 *tr* to embellish

illeggìbile *adj* illegible

illegìtti·mo -ma *adj* illegitimate

illé·so -sa *adj* unhurt, unharmed

illettera·to -ta *adj & mf* illiterate

illiba·to -ta *adj* spotless, pure

illimita·to -ta *adj* unlimited

illìri·co -ca *adj* (-ci -che) Illyrian

illògi·co -ca *adj* (-ci -che) illogical

illùdere §105 *tr* to delude

illuminare (**illùmino**) *tr* to illuminate; to brighten; to enlighten || *ref* to grow bright

illumina·to -ta *adj* illuminated; enlightened; educated

illuminazióne *f* illumination; enlightenment

illuminismo *m* Age of Enlightenment

illusióne *f* illusion; delusion; **farsi illusioni** to indulge in wishful thinking

illusionismo *m* sleight of hand; magic

illusioni·sta *mf* (-sti -ste) magician

illu·so -sa *adj* deluded || *mf* deluded person

illusò·rio -ria *adj* (-ri -rie) illusory, illusive

illustrare *tr* to illustrate; to explain, elucidate || *ref* to become famous

illustra·to -ta *adj* illustrated, pictorial

illustra·tóre -trice *mf* illustrator

illustrazióne *f* illustration; illustrious person

illustre *adj* illustrious, famous

illustrìssi·mo -ma *adj* distinguished; honorable; **Illustrissimo Signore** Dear Sir; Mr. (*addressing a letter*)

imbacuccare §197 *tr & ref* to muffle up; to wrap up

imbaldanzire §176 *tr* to embolden || *intr* (ESSERE) & *ref* to grow bold

imballàg·gio *m* (-gi) wrapping, packaging

imballare *tr* to wrap up, package; to bale; to race (*the motor*); **imballare in una gabbia** to crate || *ref* to race (*said of a motor*)

imballa·tóre -trice *mf* packer

imballo *m* packing; packaging, wrapping; racing (*of motor*)

imbalsamare (**imbàlsamo**) *tr* to embalm; to stuff (*animals*)

imbambola·to -ta *adj* gazing, staring; stunned, dumfounded; sleepy-eyed; sluggish

imbandierare (**imbandièro**) *tr* to bedeck with flags

imbandire §176 *tr* to prepare (*food, a meal, a table*) lavishly

imbarazzante *adj* embarrassing, awkward

imbarazzare *tr* to embarrass; to encumber, hamper; to upset (*the stomach*)

imbarazza·to -ta adj embarrassed, perplexed; upset (stomach); ill-at-ease

imbarazzo m embarrassment; annoyance; **imbarazzo di stomaco** upset stomach

imbarbarire §176 tr & ref to make barbarous; to corrupt (a language)

imbarcadèro m landing pier

imbarcare §197 tr to ship; to load, embark; to ship (water) || ref to sail; to embark; to curve (said of furniture)

imbarca·tóio m (-tói) landing pier

imbarcazióne f boat; **imbarcazione di salvataggio** lifeboat

imbar·co m (-chi) embarkation; port of embarkation

imbardare intr & ref (aer) to yaw; (aut) to swerve, lurch

imbardata f (aer) yaw; (aut) swerve, lurch

imbarilare tr to barrel

imbastardire §176 tr to corrupt || ref to become corrupt

imbastire §176 tr (sew) to baste; (fig) to sketch out

imbastitura f (sew) basting

imbàttere ref—**imbattersi bene** to be lucky; **imbattersi in** to come across; **imbattersi male** to have bad luck

imbattibile adj unbeatable

imbavagliare §280 tr to gag

imbeccare §197 (imbécco) tr to feed (a fledgling); (fig) to prompt

imbeccata f beakful; (fig) prompting

imbecillàggine f imbecility

imbecille adj & mf imbecile

imbecilli·tà f (-tà) imbecility

imbèlle adj unwarlike; cowardly

imbellettare (imbellétto) tr to apply rouge to, apply make-up on || ref to put on make-up

imbellire §176 tr to embellish

imbèrbe adj beardless; callow

imbestialire §176 tr to enrage || intr (ESSERE) & ref to become enraged

imbévere §185 tr to soak; to soak up; to imbue || ref to become soaked; to become imbued

imbiancare §197 tr to whiten; to bleach; to whitewash || intr (ESSERE) & ref to turn white (said, e.g., of hair); to clear up (said of weather)

imbiancatura f bleaching (of laundry); whitening; whitewashing

imbianchimènto m bleaching

imbianchino m whitewasher; house painter; (pej) dauber

imbianchire §176 tr to whiten; to bleach || ref to turn white

imbiondire §176 tr to bleach (hair) || intr to become blond; to ripen (said of wheat)

imbizzarrire [ddzz] intr (ESSERE) & ref to become skittish (said of a horse); to become infuriated

imbizzire [ddzz] §176 intr (ESSERE) to get angry

imboccare §197 (imbócco) tr to feed by mouth; to put (an instrument) in one's mouth; to take, enter (a road); to prompt || intr (ESSERE) to

flow; to open (said of a road); (mach) to fit

imboccatura f entrance (of street); inlet; opening, top (e.g., of bottle); bit (of bridle); (mus) mouthpiece; **avere l'imboccatura a** to be experienced in

imbóc·co m (-chi) entrance; inlet; opening

imbonimènto m claptrap

imbonire §176 tr to lure, entice (s.o. to buy or enter)

imbonitóre m barker

imborghesire §176 tr to render middle-class || intr (ESSERE) to become middle-class

imboscare §197 (imbòsco) tr to hide; to hide (s.o.) underground || ref to shirk; to be a slacker

imbosca·to -ta adj (mil) shirking, draft-dodging || m (mil) slacker; (mil) goldbrick || f ambush; **tendere un'imboscata** to set an ambush

imboscatóre m accomplice of a draft dodger; hoarder (of scarce items)

imboschire §176 tr to forest

imbottare (imbótto) tr to barrel

imbottigliare §280 tr to bottle; to bottle up || ref to get bottled up (said of traffic)

imbottire §176 tr to pad, fill; to stuff; to pad (a speech)

imbottita f bedspread, quilt

imbottitura f padding

imbra·ca f (-che) breeching strap (of harness); safety belt; (naut) sling

imbracare §197 tr to sling

imbracciare §128 tr to fasten (shield); to level (gun)

imbrancare §197 tr & ref to herd

imbrattacar·te mf (-te) scribbler

imbrattamu·ri mf (-ri) dauber

imbrattare tr to soil, dirty; to smudge, smear

imbrattatè·le mf (-le) dauber

imbratto m dirt; smudge, smear; daub; scribble; swill

imbrigliare §280 tr to bridle

imbroccare §197 (imbròcco) tr to hit (the target); to guess right

imbrodare (imbròdo) tr to soil

imbrogliare §280 (imbròglio) tr to cheat; to mix up; to tangle; to confuse; **imbrogliare le vele** (naut) to take in the reef || ref to get tangled up; to get confused; to turn bad (said of weather)

imbrò·glio m (-gli) cheat; tangle; (naut) reef; **cacciarsi in un imbroglio** to get involved in a mess

imbroglió·ne -na mf swindler

imbronciare §128 (imbróncio) intr (ESSERE) & ref to pout, sulk || ref to lower (said of the weather)

imbroncia·to -ta adj sulky, surly; cloudy, overcast

imbrunire m—**sull'imbrunire** at nightfall || §176 intr (ESSERE) to turn brown || impers (ESSERE)—**imbrunisce** it is growing dark

imbruttire §176 tr to mar; to make ugly || intr (ESSERE) to grow ugly

imbucare §197 tr to mail; to put in a hole || ref to hide imburrare *tr* to butter

imbuto *m* funnel

imène *m* (anat) hymen, maidenhead

imitare (ìmito) *tr* to imitate

imita·tóre -trice *mf* imitator; (theat) mimic

imitazióne *f* imitation

immacola·to -ta *adj* immaculate

immagazzinare [ddzz] *tr* to store, store up

immaginare (immàgino) *tr* to imagine; to guess; to invent || *ref*—si immagini! of course!; not at all!

immaginà·rio -ria *adj* (-ri -rie) imaginary

immaginativa *f* imagination

immaginazióne *f* imagination

immàgine *f* image; picture

immagino·so -sa [s] *adj* imaginative

immalinconire §176 *tr* to sadden || *intr* (ESSERE) & *ref* to become melancholy

immancàbile *adj* unfailing; certain

immane *adj* monstrous; gigantic

immangiàbile *adj* uneatable, inedible

immantinènte *adv* (lit) immediately

immarcescìbile *adj* incorruptible

immateriale *adj* immaterial

immatricolare (immatrìcolo) *tr* to matriculate

immatricolazióne *f* matriculation

immatu·ro -ra *adj* immature; premature

immedesimare (immedésimo) *tr* to identify; to blend || *ref* to identify oneself

immediataménte *adv* immediately

immediatézza *f* immediacy

immedia·to -ta *adj* immediate

immemoràbile *adj* immemorial

immèmore *adj* forgetful

immèn·so -sa *adj* immense, huge

immèrgere §162 *tr* to immerse; to plunge || *ref* to plunge; to become absorbed

immerita·to -ta *adj* undeserved

immeritévole *adj* undeserving

immersióne *f* immersion; submersion (*of a submarine*); (naut) draft

immèttere §198 *tr* to let in; immettere qlcu nel possesso di (law) to grant s.o. possession of

immigrante *adj* & *mf* immigrant

immigrare *intr* (ESSERE) to immigrate

immigrazióne *f* immigration; (biol) migration

imminènte *adj* imminent

imminènza *f* imminence

immischiare §287 *tr* to involve || *ref* to meddle; to become involved

immiserire §176 *tr* to impoverish || *intr* (ESSERE) & *ref* to become impoverished; to become debased

immissà·rio -ria *m* (-ri) tributary

immissióne *f* letting in, introduction; intake; insertion (*in lunar orbit*)

immòbile *adj* motionless, immobile; real (*property*) || immobili *mpl* real estate

immobiliare *adj* real, e.g., proprietà immobiliare real estate; real-estate, e.g., imposta immobiliare real-estate tax

immobilizzare [ddzz] *tr* to immobilize; to pin down; to tie up (*capital*)

immodè·sto -sta *adj* indecent; immodest

immolare (immòlo) *tr* to immolate

immondézza *f* filth; impurity

immondez·zàio *m* (-zài) rubbish heap, dump; garbage can

immondìzia *f* trash; garbage; filth

immón·do -da *adj* filthy, dirty; unclean

immorale *adj* immoral

immorali·tà *f* (-tà) immorality

immortalare *tr* to immortalize

immortale *adj* immortal

immortalità *f* immortality

immò·to -ta *adj* (lit) motionless

immune *adj* immune

immunizzare [ddzz] *tr* to immunize

immutàbile *adj* immutable

immuta·to -ta *adj* unchanged

i·mo -ma *adj* (lit) bottom, lowest || *m* (lit) bottom; (lit) depth

impaccare §197 *tr* to pack, wrap up

impacchettare (impacchétto) *tr* to pack, bundle

impacciare §128 *tr* to hamper; to embarrass || *ref* to meddle

impaccia·to -ta *adj* hampered; clumsy

impàc·cio *m* (-ci) embarrassment; hindrance; trouble; essere d'impaccio to be in the way

impac·co *m* (-chi) wrapping; (med) compress

impadronire §176 *ref*—impadronirsi di to seize; to take possession of; to master (*a language*)

impagàbile *adj* invaluable, priceless

impaginare (impàgino) *tr* (typ) to make up (*in pages*), paginate

impaginato *m* (typ) page proof

impagliare §280 *tr* to cane (*a chair*); to stuff (*an animal; a doll*); to pack in straw

impalare *tr* to impale; to tie to a pole or stake || *ref* to stiffen up

impala·to -ta *adj* stiff, rigid

impalcatura *f* scaffold; frame, framework

impallidire §176 *intr* to turn pale; to blanch; to grow dim (*said of a star*); (fig) to wane

impalmare *tr* (lit) to wed

impalpàbile *adj* impalpable

impaludare *tr* to make swampy or marshy || *intr* to become marshy

impanare *tr* to bread; to thread (*a screw*) || *intr* to screw in

impaniare §287 *tr* to trap, ensnare || *ref* to fall into the trap

impantanare *tr* to turn into a swamp || *ref* to get stuck, to sink (*in vice*)

impaperare (impàpero) *ref* to fluff, make a slip

impappinare *tr* to confuse || *ref* to blunder; to stammer

imparare *tr* to learn; imparare a memoria to learn by heart || *intr* imparare a to learn to, to learn how to

impareggiàbile *adj* peerless, unmatched

imparentare (imparènto) *tr* to bring into the family || *ref*—imparentarsi con to marry into

ìmpari *adj* odd, uneven

imparrucca·to -ta *adj* bewigged

impartire §176 *tr* to impart

imparziale *adj* impartial

impasse f blind alley; deadlock; (cards) finesse
impassìbile adj impassible, impassive
impastare tr to knead; to mix; to smear with paste
impasta·to -ta adj kneaded; smeared; **impastato di** tainted with; overwhelmed with (sleep)
impasto m paste; pastiche
impastoiare §287 (impastóio) tr to fetter, hamstring
impataccare §197 tr to besmear, soil
impattare tr to even up; to tie (a game); **impattarla con** to tie (a person)
impatto m impact
impaurire §176 tr to scare || ref to get scared
impàvi·do -da adj fearless
impaziènte adj impatient
impazientire §176 intr (ESSERE) & ref to get impatient
impaziènza f impatience
impazzare intr (ESSERE) to be wild with excitement; to go mad; (culin) to curdle
impazzata f—**all'impazzata** at top speed; berserk
impazzire §176 intr (ESSERE) to go crazy; **fare impazzire** to drive crazy
impeccàbile adj impeccable
impeciare §128 (impécio) tr to tar
impedènza f impedance
impediménto m hindrance, obstacle, impediment
impedire §176 tr to impede, hinder; to obstruct || intr to prevent; **impedire** (with dat) **di** + inf or **che** + subj to prevent from + ger
impegnare (impégno) tr to pawn; to reserve (a room); to engage (the enemy); to keep occupied; to pledge || ref to obligate oneself; to go all out; to become entangled
impegnati·vo -va adj demanding (activity); binding (promise)
impegna·to -ta adj pawned; pledged; occupied; committed
impégno m commitment; obligation; task; zeal; **senza impegno** without promising
impegolare (impégolo) tr to tar || ref to become entangled
impelagare §209 (impèlago) ref to bog down; to become entangled
impellicciare §128 tr to fur; to veneer
impenetràbile adj impenetrable
impenitènte adj impenitent; confirmed
impennàg·gio m (-gi) (aer) empennage
impennare (impénno) tr to feather; (fig) to give wings to || ref to rear (said of a horse); to take umbrage; (aer) to zoom
impennata f rearing (of horse); (aer) zoom
impensàbile adj unthinkable
impensa·to -ta adj unexpected
impensierire §176 tr & ref to worry
imperante adj prevailing
imperare (impèro) tr to rule, reign; to prevail; **imperare su** to rule over
imperati·vo -va adj & m imperative

imperatóre m emperor
imperatrice f empress
impercettìbile adj imperceptible
imperdonàbile adj unforgivable
imperfèt·to -ta adj & m imperfect
imperfezióne f imperfection
imperiale adj imperial || m upper deck (of bus or coach); **imperiali** imperial troops
imperiali·sta adj & mf (-sti -ste) imperialist
impè·rio m (-ri) empire; rule
imperió·so -sa [s] adj imperious; imperative
imperi·to -ta adj (lit) inexperienced
imperitu·ro -ra adj immortal; everlasting, imperishable
imperìzia f inexperience
imperlare (impèrlo) tr to bead; to cover with beads (of perspiration)
impermalire §176 tr to provoke || ref to become provoked
impermeàbile adj waterproof || m raincoat
imperniare §287 (impèrnio) tr to pivot; (fig) to base
impèro adj invar Empire || m empire; control, sway
imperscrutàbile adj inscrutable
impersonale adj impersonal
impersonare (impersóno) tr to impersonate || ref—**impersonarsi in** to be the embodiment of; (theat) to impersonate
impertèrri·to -ta adj undaunted
impertinènte adj impertinent, pert
impertinènza f impertinence
imperturbàbile adj imperturbable
imperturba·to -ta adj unperturbed
imperversare (impervèrso) intr to storm, rage; to be the rage
impèr·vio -via adj (-vi -vie) impassable
ìmpeto m impetus; onslaught; violence; outburst; **d'impeto** rashly
impetrare (impètro) tr to beg for; to obtain by entreaty || intr (ESSERE) (lit) to turn to stone
impetti·to -ta adj puffed up with pride
impetuó·so -sa [s] adj impetuous
impiallacciare §128 tr to veneer
impiallacciatura f veneer, veneering
impiantare tr to install (a machine); to set up (a business); to open (an account)
impiantito m floor, flooring
impianto m installation; plant; system
impiastrare tr to plaster; to dirty
impiastricciare §128 tr to plaster; to daub; to soil
impiastro m (med) plaster; (fig) bore
impiccagióne f hanging
impiccare §197 tr to hang
impicciare §128 tr to hinder; to bother || ref to meddle, butt in; **impicciarsi degli affari propri** to mind one's own business
impìc·cio m (-ci) hindrance; trouble; **essere d'impiccio** to be in the way
impicció·ne -na mf meddler
impiccolire §176 tr to reduce in size || ref to shrink in size
impiegare §209 (impiègo) tr to employ;

to use; to devote (*one's energies*); to spend (*time*); to invest (*capital*); to take (*time*) || *ref* to have a job

impiegatì·zio -zia *adj* (**-zi -zie**) employee, white-collar

impiega·to -ta *mf* employee; clerk

impiè·go *m* (**-ghi**) employment; use; job; place of business; investment

impietosire [s] §176 *tr* to move to pity || *ref* to be moved to pity

impietrire §176 *tr, intr* (ESSERE) & *ref* to turn to stone

impigliare §280 *tr* to entangle || *ref* to become entangled

impigrire §176 *tr* to make lazy || *intr* (ESSERE) & *ref* to get lazy

impinguare (impìnguo) *tr* & *ref* to fatten

impinzare *tr* to stuff || *ref* to stuff oneself; **impinzarsi il cervello** to stuff one's brain (*with knowledge*)

impiombare (impiómbo) *tr* to lead; to plumb, seal with lead; to fill (*a tooth*); (naut) to splice (*a cable*)

impiombatura *f* seal; filling (*of tooth*); (naut) splicing

impipare *ref*—**impiparsi di** (slang) to not give a hoot about

implacàbile *adj* implacable

implicare §197 (**ìmplico**) *tr* to implicate; to imply

implìci·to -ta *adj* implicit, implied

implorare (implòro) *tr* to implore

implume *adj* unfledged, featherless

impolìti·co -ca *adj* (**-ci -che**) unpolitical; impolitic, injudicious

impollinare (impòllino) *tr* to pollinate

impoltronire §176 *tr* to make lazy || *ref* to get lazy

impolverare (impólvero) *tr* to cover with dust || *ref* to get covered with dust

impomatare *tr* to pomade; to smear with pomade

imponderàbile *adj* imponderable; weightless

imponderabilità *f* imponderability; weightlessness

imponente *adj* imposing; stately

imponìbile *adj* taxable || *m* taxable income

impopolare *adj* unpopular

impopolarità *f* unpopularity

imporre §218 *tr* to place, put; to impose; to order; to compel; to give (*a name*) || *intr* (ESSERE) to be imposing; (with *dat*) to order, command || *ref* to command respect; to win favor; to be necessary

importante *adj* important; sizable || *m* important thing

importanza *f* importance; size; **darsi importanza** to assume an air of importance

importare (impòrto) *tr* to import; to imply; to involve || *intr* (ESSERE) to be of consequence || *impers* (ESSERE) —**importa** it matters; **non importa** never mind

importa·tóre -trice *mf* importer

importazióne *f* importation; import

impòrto *m* amount

importunare *tr* to bother, importune

importu·no -na *adj* importunate, bothersome || *mf* bore

imposizióne *f* imposition; giving (*of a name*); order, command; taxation

impossessare (impossèsso) *ref*—**impossessarsi di** to seize; to master (*a language*)

impossìbile *adj* & *m* impossible

impossibili·tà *f* (**-tà**) impossibility

impossibilitare (impossibilito) *tr* to make impossible; to make unable or incapable

impossibilita·to -ta *adj* unable

impòsta *f* tax; shutter; (archit) impost; **imposta complementare** surtax; **imposta sul valore aggiunto** value-added tax

impostare (impòsto) *tr* to start, begin; to state (*a problem*); to mail; to lay (*a stone*); to open (*an account*); to attune (*one's voice*); to lay the keel of (*a ship*) || *ref* to take one's position, get ready

impostazióne *f* beginning, starting; laying; mail, mailing; (com) posting

impo·stóre -stóra *mf* impostor

impostura *f* imposture

impotènte *adj* weak; impotent

impotènza *f* impotence

impoverimento *m* impoverishment

impoverire §176 *tr* to impoverish || *intr* (ESSERE) & *ref* to become impoverished

impraticàbile *adj* impracticable; impassable

impratichire §176 *tr* to train, familiarize || *ref* to become familiar (*e.g., with a task*)

imprecare §197 (**imprèco**) *tr* to wish (*e.g., s.o.'s death*) || *intr* to curse

imprecazióne *f* imprecation, curse

imprecisàbile *adj* undefinable

imprecisióne *f* inexactness, inaccuracy

imprecì·so -sa *adj* vague, inexact

impregnare (imprégno) *tr* to impregnate

impremedita·to -ta *adj* unpremeditated

imprendìbile *adj* impregnable

imprendi·tóre -trice *mf* contractor || *m*—**imprenditore di pompe funebri** undertaker

imprenditoriale *adj* managerial

imprepara·to -ta *adj* unprepared

impreparazióne *f* unpreparedness

imprésa [s] *f* enterprise; undertaking; achievement; firm, concern; (theat) management; **impresa (di) pompe funebri** undertaking establishment

impresà·rio [s] *m* (**-ri**) manager; (theat) impresario

imprescindìbile *adj* essential, indispensable; unavoidable

impresentàbile *adj* unpresentable

impressionàbile *adj* impressionable

impressionante *adj* striking, impressive; frightening

impressionare (impressióno) *tr* to impress; (phot) to expose || *ref* to become frightened; (phot) to be exposed

impressióne *f* impression

imprestare (imprèsto) *tr* (coll) to lend

imprèstito m (philol) borrowing
imprevedibile adj unforeseeable
imprevedu·to -ta adj unforeseen
imprevidènte adj improvident
imprevi·sto -sta adj unforeseen, unexpected || imprevisti mpl unforeseen events
imprigionare (imprigióno) tr to imprison
imprìmere §131 tr to impress; to imprint; to impart (e.g., motion)
improbàbile adj improbable, unlikely
impro·bo -ba adj dishonest; laborious
improdutti·vo -va adj unproductive
imprónta f print, imprint; mark; impronta digitale fingerprint
improntare (imprónto) tr to impress, imprint; to mark
improntitùdine f audacity, impudence
impronunziàbile adj unpronounceable
impropè·rio m (-ri) insult
improprie·tà f (-tà) impropriety; error
impro·prio -pria adj (-pri -prie) improper, inappropriate; (math) improper
improrogàbile adj unextendible
improvvi·do -da adj improvident
improvvisare tr to improvise || ref to suddenly decide to become
improvvisa·to -ta adj improvised; impromptu || f surprise; surprise party
improvvisazióne f improvisation
improvvi·so -sa adj sudden || m (mus) impromptu; all'improvviso or d'improvviso suddenly
imprudènte adj imprudent; rash
imprudènza f imprudence; rashness
impudènte adj shameless; brazen; impudent
impudènza f shamelessness; impudence
impudicìzia f immodesty
impudi·co -ca adj (-chi -che) immodest, indecent
impugnare tr to grip, seize; to take up (arms); to impugn, contest
impugnatura f handle; grip, hold; hilt, haft
impulsi·vo -va adj impulsive
impulso m impulse; dare impulso a to promote, foment
impunemènte adv with impunity
impunità f impunity
impuni·to -ta adj unpunished
impuntare intr to stumble, trip; to stutter || ref to stutter; to balk; to be stubborn; impuntarsi a or di + inf to stubbornly insist on + ger
impuntigliare §280 ref to persist, insist
impuntire §176 tr to tuft (e.g., a pillow)
impuntura f backstitch
impuri·tà f (-tà) impurity; unchastity
impu·ro -ra adj impure; unchaste
imputàbile adj attributable
imputare (ìmputo) tr to impute; to charge, accuse; (com) to post
imputa·to -ta mf accused, defendant
imputazióne f imputation; charge, accusation; (com) posting
imputridire §176 tr & intr (ESSERE) to rot
in prep in; at; into; to; on, upon; through; during; married to, e.g.,

Maria Roberti in Bianchi Marie Roberti married to Bianchi; as, e.g., in premio as a prize; by, e.g., in automobile by car; of, e.g., studente in legge student of law; essere in quattro to be four; in alto up; in breve soon; in a word; in giù down; in là there; in qua here; in realtà really; in seguito a because of
-ina suf fem about, e.g., cinquantina about fifty
inabbordàbile adj unapproachable
inàbile adj unfit; ineligible; awkward
inabili·tà f (-tà) unfitness; awkwardness; inability
inabilitare (inabilito) tr to incapacitate; to render unfit; to disqualify
inabilitazióne f disqualification
inabissare tr to plunge || ref to sink
inabitàbile adj uninhabitable
inabita·to -ta adj uninhabited
inaccessìbile adj inaccessible; unfathomable
inaccettàbile adj unacceptable
inacerbire §176 tr to exacerbate || ref to grow bitter
inacidire §176 tr & ref to sour
inadattàbile adj unadaptable; maladjusted
inadat·to -ta adj inadequate
inadegua·to -ta adj inadequate
inadempiènte adj not fulfilling; inadempiente agli obblighi di leva draftdodging
inafferràbile adj that cannot be caught or captured; incomprehensible; elusive
inalare tr to inhale
inalatóre m inhaler
inalberare (inàlbero) tr to hoist || ref to rear; to fly into a rage
inalteràbile adj unalterable
inamidare (inàmido) tr to starch
inamida·to -ta adj starched; pompous, starchy
inammissìbile adj inadmissible
inamovìbile adj irremovable
inamovibili·tà f (-tà) irremovability; tenure
inane adj inane; futile
inanella·to -ta adj curly; beringed
inanima·to -ta adj inanimate; lifeless
inanizióne f starvation
inappagàbile adj unquenchable
inappaga·to -ta adj unsatisfied
inappellàbile adj definitive, final
inappetènza f lack of appetite
inapprezzàbile adj inappreciable, imperceptible; inestimable
inappuntàbile adj faultless, impeccable
inarcare §197 tr to arch; to raise (one's eyebrows)
inargentare (inargènto) tr to silver
inaridire §176 tr to dry; to parch || ref to dry up
inarrestàbile adj irresistible
inarrivàbile adj unattainable; inimitable
inarticola·to -ta adj indistinct, inarticulate
inascolta·to -ta adj unheeded
inaspetta·to -ta adj unexpected
inasprimènto m exacerbation

inasprire §176 *tr* to aggravate ‖ *ref* to sour; to become embittered; to become sharper; to become fierce or furious

inastare *tr* to hoist (*flag*); to fix (*bayonets*)

inattaccàbile *adj* unattackable; unassailable; **inattacabile da** resistant to

inattendìbile *adj* unreliable

inatté·so -sa [s] *adj* unexpected

inatti·vo -ta *adj* inactive

inaudi·to -ta *adj* unheard-of

inaugurale *adj* inaugural; maiden (*voyage*)

inaugurare (**inàuguro**) *tr* to inaugurate; to usher in (*the New Year*); to open (*e.g., an exhibit*); to unveil (*a statue*); to sport for the first time

inaugurazióne *f* inauguration

inauspica·to -ta *adj* (lit) inauspicious

inavvedu·to -ta *adj* careless, rash

inavvertènza *f* inadvertence, oversight

inavverti·to -ta *adj* unnoticed; inadvertent, thoughtless

inazióne *f* inaction

incagliare §280 *tr* to hamper; to run aground ‖ *intr* (ESSERE) & *ref* to run aground; (fig) to get stuck

incà·glio *m* (**-gli**) running aground; hindrance, obstacle

incalcinare *tr* to whitewash; to lime (*a field*)

incalcolàbile *adj* incalculable

incallire §176 *tr* to make callous ‖ *intr* (ESSERE) to become callous; to become inured

incalli·to -ta *adj* callous; inveterate

incalzante *adj* pressing

incalzare *tr* to press, pursue ‖ *intr* to be imminent; to be pressing ‖ *ref* to follow one another in rapid succession

incamerare (**incàmero**) *tr* to confiscate

incamminare *tr* to launch; to guide, direct ‖ *ref* to set out; to be on one's way

incanagli·to -ta *adj* vile, despicable

incanalare *tr* to channel ‖ *ref* to flow

incancrenire §176 *tr* to affect with gangrene ‖ *ref* to become gangrenous; (fig) to become callous

incandescènte *adj* incandescent; (fig) red-hot

incandescènza *f* incandescence

incannare *tr* to reel, wind

incantare *tr* to bewitch; to auction off ‖ *ref* to become enraptured; to be spellbound; to jam, get stuck (*said of machinery*)

incanta·tóre -trice *adj* enchanting ‖ *m* enchanter ‖ *f* enchantress

incantésimo *m* enchantment, spell

incantévole *adj* enchanting, charming

incanto *m* enchantment; bewitchery; auction; **d'incanto** marvelously well

incanutire §176 *tr, intr* (ESSERE) & *ref* to turn gray-headed, to turn gray (*said of a person*)

incanuti·to -ta *adj* hoary

incapace *adj* incapable; (law) incompetent ‖ *mf* oaf; (law) incompetent

incapaci·tà *f* (**-tà**) incapacity; (law) incompetence

incaparbire §176 *intr* (ESSERE) & *ref* to be obstinate; to be determined

incaponire §176 *ref* to get stubborn; to be determined

incappare *intr* (ESSERE) to stumble

incappottare (**incappòtto**) *tr* to cover with a coat ‖ *ref* to wrap oneself in a coat

incappucciare §128 *tr* to cover with a hood

incapricciare §128 *ref*—**incapricciarsi di** to take a fancy to; to become infatuated with

incapsulare (**incàpsulo**) *tr* to encapsulate; to cap

incarcerare (**incàrcero**) *tr* to jail, incarcerate; (fig) to confine

incaricare §197 (**incàrico**) *tr* to charge ‖ *ref*—**incaricarsi di** to take charge of; to take care of

incarica·to -ta *adj* in charge; visiting (*professor*) ‖ *mf* deputy; **incaricato d'affari** chargé d'affaires

incàri·co *m* (**-chi**) task; appointment; position; **per incarico di** on behalf of

incarnare *tr* to incarnate, embody

incarna·to -ta *adj* incarnate ‖ *m* pink complexion

incarnazióne *f* incarnation

incarnire §176 *intr* (ESSERE) & *ref* to grow in (*said of a toenail*)

incarni·to -ta *adj* ingrown (*toenail*)

incartaménto *m* file, dossier

incartapecori·to -ta *adj* shriveled up

incartare *tr* to wrap up (*in paper*)

incasellare [s] (**incasèllo**) *tr* to file; to sort out

incasellatóre [s] *m* post-office file clerk

incassare *tr* to box up; to put (*a watch*) in a case; to mortise (*a lock*); to channel (*a river*); to cash (*a check*); (fig) to take (*e.g., blows*) ‖ *intr* to fit; to take it

incasso *m* receipts

incastellatura *f* scaffolding

incastonare (**incastóno**) *tr* to set, mount (*a gem*); **incastonare citazioni in un discorso** to stud a speech with quotations

incastrare *tr* to insert; to mortise; (fig) to corner ‖ *intr* to fit ‖ *ref* to fit; to become imbedded; to telescope (*said, e.g., of a train in a collision*)

incastro *m* joint; insertion; (carp) tenon; (carp) mortise

incatenare (**incaténo**) *tr* to chain, put in chains; to tie down, restrain

incatramare *tr* to tar

incàu·to -ta *adj* unwary, careless

incavallatura *f* truss (*to support roof*)

incavare *tr* to hollow out; to groove

incava·to -ta *adj* hollow

incavatura *f* hollow

incavicchiare §287 *tr* to peg

incavigliare §280 *tr* to peg

incavo *m* hollow; cavity; **incavo dell'ascella** armpit

incazzottare (**incazzòtto**) *tr* (naut) to furl

incèdere *m* stately walk ‖ §123 *intr* to walk stately

incendiare §287 (**incèndio**) *tr* to set on fire; (fig) to inflame ‖ *ref* to catch fire

incendià·rio -ria *adj & mf* (**-ri -rie**) incendiary

incèn·dio *m* (**-di**) fire; **incendio doloso** arson

incenerire §176 *tr* to reduce to ashes; to wither (*e.g., with a look*) ‖ *ref* to turn to ashes

inceneritóre *m* incinerator

incensare (**incènso**) *tr* (eccl) to incense; (fig) to flatter

incensa·tóre -trice *mf* incense burner; (fig) flatterer

incensière *m* incense burner

incènso *m* incense

incensura·to -ta *adj* uncensured; (law) having no previous record

incentivo *m* incentive

inceppare (**incèppo**) *tr* to hinder; to shackle ‖ *ref* to jam (*said of firearm*)

incerare (**incéro**) *tr* to wax

incerata *f* oilcloth; (naut) raincoat

incernierare (**incernièro**) *tr* to hinge

incertézza *f* uncertainty, incertitude

incèr·to -ta *adj* uncertain; irresolute ‖ *m* uncertainty; **incerti** extras; **incerti del mestiere** cares of office, occupational annoyances, occupational hazards

incespicare §197 (**incéspico**) *intr* to stumble

incessàbile *adj* (lit) ceaseless

incessante *adj* unceasing, incessant

incèsto *m* incest

incestuó·so -sa [s] *adj* incestuous

incètta *f* cornering (*of market*)

incettare (**incètto**) *tr* to corner (*market*)

incetta·tóre -trice *mf* monopolizer

inchiavardare *tr* to key, bolt

inchièsta *f* probe, inquest; (journ) inquiry

inchinare *tr* to bend; to bow (*the head*) ‖ *intr* (lit) to go down (*said of stars*) ‖ *ref* to bow; to yield

inchi·no -na *adj* bent; bowing ‖ *m* bow; curtsy

inchiodare (**inchiòdo**) *tr* to nail; to spike; to rivet; to tie, bind; to stop (*a car*) suddenly; to transfix ‖ *ref* to freeze (*said, e.g., of brakes*); (fig) to be tied down; (fig) to go into debt

inchiostrare (**inchiòstro**) *tr* (typ) to ink

inchiòstro *m* ink; **inchiostro di china** India ink, Chinese ink

inciampare *intr* to trip, stumble

inciampo *m* stumbling block, obstacle; **essere d'inciampo a** to be in the way of

incidentale *adj* incidental

incidènte *adj* incidental ‖ *m* incident; accident; argument, question

incidènza *f* incidence

incidere §145 *tr* to engrave; to cut; to record (*a record, a tape; a song*); **incidere all'acqua forte** to etch ‖ *intr*—**incidere su** to weigh heavily on (*expenses, a budget*); to leave a mark on

incinerazióne *f* incineration; cremation

incinta *adj fem* pregnant

incipiènte *adj* incipient

incipriare §287 *tr* to powder ‖ *ref* to powder oneself

incirca *adv* about; **all'incirca** more or less

incisióne *f* engraving; cutting (*of a record*); recording (*of a tape; of a song*); incision; **incisione all'acquaforte** etching

incisi·vo -va *adj* incisive; sharp (*photograph*) ‖ *m* incisor

inciso *m* (gram) parenthetical clause; (mus) theme; **per inciso** incidentally

incisóre *m* engraver, etcher

incitare *tr* to incite, provoke

incivile *adj* uncivilized; uncouth

incivilire §176 *tr* to civilize ‖ *ref* to become civilized

inclemènte *adj* inclement, harsh

inclemènza *f* inclemency, harshness

inclinare *tr* to tilt; to bow, bend; to incline ‖ *intr* (fig) to lean ‖ *ref* to bend

inclinazióne *f* inclination; slope; **inclinazione laterale** (aer) bank; **inclinazione magnetica** magnetic dip

incline *adj* inclined

incli·to -ta *adj* famous; noble

inclùdere §105 *tr* to enclose, include

inclusi·vo -va *adj* including; **inclusivo di** including

inclu·so -sa *adj* enclosed; included; inclusive ‖ *f* enclosed letter

incoerènte *adj* incoherent

incògliere §127 *tr* (lit) to catch in the act ‖ *intr*—**incogliere a** to happen to

incògni·to -ta *adj* unknown ‖ *m* incognito; unknown; **in incognito** incognito ‖ *f* (math) unknown quantity; (fig) puzzle

incollare (**incòllo**) *tr* to glue, paste; to size (*paper*) ‖ *intr* to stick ‖ *ref* to stick; to take on one's shoulders

incollatura *f* neck (*of horse*); glueing, sticking

incollerire §176 *intr & ref* to get angry

incolloca·to -ta *adj* unemployed

incolonnare (**incolónno**) *tr* to set up in columns

incolonnatóre *m* tabulator

incolóre *adj* colorless

incolpàbile *adj* blamable; (lit) guiltless

incolpare (**incólpo**) *tr*—**incolpare di** to charge with

incól·to -ta *adj* uncultivated; unkempt

incòlume *adj* unharmed, unhurt

incolumità *f* safety, security

incombènte *adj* (danger) impending; (*duty*) incumbent

incombènza *f* task, charge, incumbency

incómbere §186 *intr* (ESSERE) to be impending; to be incumbent

incombustibile *adj* incombustible

incominciare §128 *tr & intr* (ESSERE) to begin

incommensuràbile *adj* immeasurable; (math) incommensurable

incomodare (**incòmodo**) *tr* to bother, disturb ‖ *ref* to bother; **non s'incomodi!** don't bother!

incòmo·do -da *adj* bothersome, inconvenient ‖ *m* inconvenience; ailment;

levare l'incomodo a to get out of the way of

incomparàbile *adj* incomparable

incompatìbile *adj* incompatible; unforgivable

incompetènte *adj & mf* incompetent

incompiu·to -ta *adj* unfinished

incomplè·to -ta *adj* incomplete

incompó·sto -sta *adj* untidy; unkempt; unbecoming (*behavior*)

incomprensìbile *adj* incomprehensible

incomprensióne *f* lack of understanding

incompré·so -sa [s] *adj* misunderstood

incomprimìbile *adj* irrepressible; incompressible

inconcepìbile *adj* inconceivable

inconciliàbile *adj* irreconcilable

inconcludènte *adj* inconclusive; insignificant

inconcus·so -sa *adj* (lit) unshaken

incondiziona·to -ta *adj* unconditional

inconfessàbile *adj* unspeakable, vile

inconfessa·to -ta *adj* unavowed

inconfondìbile *adj* unmistakable

inconfutàbile *adj* irrefutable

incongruènte *adj* inconsistent

incòn·gruo -grua *adj* incongruous

inconoscìbile *adj* unknowable

inconsapèvole *adj* unaware, unconscious

incòn·scio -scia *adj & m* (-sci -sce) unconscious

inconseguènte *adj* inconsistent, inconsequential

inconsidera·to -ta *adj* inconsiderate

inconsistènte *adj* flimsy; inconsistent

inconsistènza *f* flimsiness; inconsistency

inconsolàbile *adj* inconsolable

inconsuè·to -ta *adj* unusual

inconsul·to -ta *adj* ill-advised, rash

incontamina·to -ta *adj* uncontaminated

incontenìbile *adj* irrepressible

incontentàbile *adj* insatiable; hard to please; exacting

incontinènza *f* incontinence

incontrare (incóntro) *tr* to meet; to encounter, meet with ‖ *intr* (ESSERE) to catch on (*said, e.g., of fashions*) ‖ *ref* to meet; to agree ‖ *impers* (ESSERE) to happen

incontrastàbile *adj* indisputable

incontrasta·to -ta *adj* undisputed

incóntro *m* meeting; encounter; success; meet; game, fight, match; occasion, opportunity; **all'incontro** on the other hand; opposite; **andare incontro a** to go towards; to go to meet; to face; to meet (*expenses*); to accommodate; **farsi incontro a** to advance toward

incontrollàbile *adj* uncontrollable

incontrolla·to -ta *adj* unchecked

incontrovertìbile *adj* incontrovertible

inconveniènte *adj* inconvenient ‖ *m* inconvenience, disadvantage

incoraggiante *adj* encouraging

incoraggiare §290 *tr* to encourage

incorare §257 (**incuòro**) *tr* to hearten

incordare (incòrdo) *tr* to string (*e.g., a racket*); to tie up (*with a cord*) ‖ *ref* to stiffen (*said of a muscle*)

incornare (incòrno) *tr* (taur) to gore

incorniciare §128 *tr* to frame; (journ) to border; (slang) to cuckold

incoronare (incoróno) *tr* to crown

incoronazióne *f* coronation

incorporàbile *adj* absorbable; adaptable

incorporare (incòrporo) *tr* to incorporate; to absorb ‖ *ref* to incorporate

incorpòre·o -a *adj* incorporeal

incorreggìbile *adj* incorrigible

incórrere §139 *intr* (ESSERE)—**incorrere in** to incur

incorrót·to -ta *adj* uncorrupt

incosciènte *adj* unconscious; unaware; irresponsible ‖ *mf* irresponsible person

incosciènza *f* unconsciousness; irresponsibility; madness

incostante *adj* inconstant, fickle

incredìbile *adj* incredible, unbelievable

incrèdu·lo -la *adj* incredulous ‖ *mf* disbeliever; doubter

incrementare (increménto) *tr* to increase; boost

increménto *m* increase, increment, boost

incresció·so -sa [s] *adj* disagreeable, unpleasant

increspare (incréspo) *tr* to ripple; to wrinkle; to knit (*the brow*); to pleat ‖ *ref* to ripple

incretinire §176 *tr* to make stupid; (fig) to deafen ‖ *intr* (ESSERE) to become stupid; to lose one's mind

incriminare (incrìmino) *tr* to incriminate

incrinare *tr* to flaw; to ruin

incrinatura *f* crack, flaw

incrociare §128 (**incrócio**) *tr* to cross ‖ *intr* (naut) to cruise ‖ *ref* to cross one another; to interbreed

incrociatóre *m* (nav) cruiser

incró·cio *m* (-ci) crossing; cross; crossroads; crossbreed

incrollàbile *adj* unshakable

incrostare (incròsto) *tr* to incrust; to inlay (*e.g., with mosaic*) ‖ *ref* to become incrusted

incrostazióne *f* incrustation

incrudelire §176 *tr* to enrage ‖ *intr* to commit cruelties ‖ *intr* (ESSERE) to become cruel; **incrudelire su** to commit cruelties upon

incruèn·to -ta *adj* bloodless

incubare (ìncubo & incùbo) *tr* to incubate

incubatrice *f* incubator; brooder

incubazióne *f* incubation; **in incubazione** brewing (*said of an infectious disease*)

ìncubo *m* nightmare

incùdine *f* anvil; **essere tra l'incudine e il martello** to be between the devil and the deep blue sea

inculcare §197 *tr* to inculcate

incunàbolo *m* incunabulum

incuneare (incùneo) *tr & ref* to wedge

incuràbile *adj & mf* incurable

incurante *adj* careless, indifferent

incùria *f* malpractice; neglect

incuriosire [s] §176 *tr* to intrigue ‖ *ref* to be intrigued

incursióne *f* incursion; **incursione aerea** air raid

incurvare *tr* to bend; (lit) to lower || *intr* (ESSERE) & *ref* to bend; to warp

incurvatura *f* bend, curve

incustodi·to -ta *adj* unguarded, unwatched

incùtere §154 *tr* to inspire; **incutere terrore a** to strike with terror

ìndaco *adj* & *m* indigo

indaffara·to -ta *adj* busy

indagare §209 *tr* & *intr* to investigate; **indagare su** to investigate

indagatóre -trice *adj* probing, searching || *mf* investigator

indàgine *f* investigation, inquiry

indarno *adv* (lit) in vain

indebitare (**indébito**) *tr* to burden with debts || *ref* to run into debt

indebita·to -ta *adj* indebted

indébi·to -ta *adj* undue; unjust; fraudulent (*conversion*) || *m* what one does not owe; excess payment

indebolimènto *m* weakening

indebolire §176 *tr*, *intr* (ESSERE) & *ref* to weaken

indecènte *adj* indecent

indecènza *f* indecency; outrage

indecifràbile *adj* indecipherable

indecisióne *f* indecision

indeci·so -sa *adj* uncertain; undecided; indecisive

indecoró·so -sa [s] *adj* indecorous, unseemly

indefès·so -sa *adj* indefatigable

indefinìbile *adj* indefinable

indefini·to -ta *adj* indefinite; undefined

indegni·tà *f* (**-tà**) indignity

indé·gno -gna *adj* unworthy; disgraceful

indelèbile *adj* indelible

indelica·to -ta *adj* indelicate

indemagliàbile *adj* runproof

indemonia·to -ta *adj* possessed by the devil; restless

indènne *adj* undamaged, unscathed; **tener indenne** to guarantee against harm or damage

indenni·tà *f* (**-tà**) indemnity; indemnification; **indennità di carica** special emolument; bonus; **indennità di carovita** cost-of-living allowance; **indennità di preavviso** severance pay; **indennità di trasferta** per diem

indennizzare [ddzz] *tr* to indemnify

indennizzo [ddzz] *m* indemnification; indemnity

inderogàbile *adj* inescapable

indescrivìbile *adj* indescribable

indesideràbile *adj* undesirable

indesidera·to -ta *adj* unwished-for; undesirable

indeterminati·vo -va *adj* indefinite

indetermina·to -ta *adj* indeterminate; (gram) indefinite

indi *adv* (lit) then; (lit) thence; **da indi innanzi** (lit) from that moment on

India, l' *f* India; **le Indie Occidentali** the West Indies; **le Indie Orientali** the East Indies

india·no -na *adj* & *mf* Indian; **fare l'indiano** to feign ignorance || *f* printed calico

indiavola·to -ta *adj* devilish, fierce; impish (*child*)

indicare §197 (**ìndico**) *tr* to indicate; to show

indicati·vo -va *adj* & *m* indicative

indica·to -ta *adj* appropriate, fitting; recommended, advisable

indica·tóre -trice *adj* indicating, pointing || *m* indicator; **indicatore di direzione** (aut) turn signal; **indicatore di livello** gauge; **indicatore di pressione** pressure gauge; **indicatore di velocità** (aut) speedometer; **indicatore stradale** road sign; **indicatore telefonico** telephone directory

indicazióne *f* indication; direction; **indicazioni per l'uso** instructions

ìndice *m* index finger; pointer, gauge; indicator; sign, indication; index; (typ) fist; **indice delle materie** table of contents || **Indice** *m* Index; **mettere all'Indice** to put on the Index; to ban, index

indicìbile *adj* inexpressible, unspeakable

indietreggiare §290 (**indietréggio**) *intr* (ESSERE & AVERE) to withdraw

indiètro *adv* back; behind; **all'indietro** backwards; **dare indietro** to return, give back; **domandare indietro** to ask back; **essere indietro** to be slow (*said of a watch*); to be behind; to be backward, be slow; **tirarsi indietro** to withdraw; to step back

indifendìbile *adj* indefensible

indifé·so -sa [s] *adj* defenseless

indifferènte *adj* indifferent; **essere indifferente a** to be the same to; **lasciare indifferente** to leave cold

indifferènza *f* indifference

indìge·no -na *adj* indigenous || *m* native

indigènte *adj* indigent, poor

indigestìbile *adj* indigestible

indigestióne *f* indigestion

indigè·sto -sta *adj* indigestible; (fig) dull, boring

indignare *tr* to anger, shock || *ref* to be aroused, be indignant

indigna·to -ta *adj* indignant, outraged

indignazióne *f* indignation

indigni·tà *f* (**-tà**) indignity

indimenticàbile *adj* unforgettable

indipendènte *adj* & *m* independent

indipendènza *f* independence

indire §151 *tr* to announce publicly; (lit) to declare (*war*)

indirèt·to -ta *adj* indirect

indirizzare *tr* to direct; to address

indirizzà·rio *m* (**-ri**) mailing list

indirizzo *m* address; direction

indiscernìbile *adj* indiscernible

indisciplina *f* lack of discipline

indisciplina·to -ta *adj* undisciplined

indiscré·to -ta *adj* indiscreet; tactless

indiscrezióne *f* indiscretion; gossip; news leak

indiscus·so -sa *adj* unquestioned

indiscutìbile *adj* indisputable

indispensàbile *adj* indispensable || *m* essential

indispettire §176 *tr* to annoy || *ref* to get annoyed

indisponènte *adj* vexing, irritating

indispórre §218 *tr* to indispose; to disgust

indisposizióne *f* indisposition

indispó·sto -sta *adj* indisposed

indissolùbile *adj* indissoluble

indistìn·to -ta *adj* indistinct

indistruttìbile *adj* indestructible

indisturbà·to -ta *adj* undisturbed

indìvia *f* endive

individuàbile *adj* distinguishable

individuale *adj* individual

individuali·tà *f* (-tà) individuality

individuare (**indìviduo**) *tr* to individuate; to outline; to single out

indìviduo *m* individual; fellow

indivisìbile *adj* indivisible

indivì·so -sa *adj* undivided

indiziare §287 *tr* to cast suspicion on

indizià·rio -ria *adj* (-ri -rie) circumstancial

indì·zio *m* (-zi) clue; token; symptom

indòcile *adj* indocile, unteachable

Indocìna, l' *f* Indochina

indocinése [s] *adj & mf* Indochinese

indoeuropè·o -a *adj & m* Indo-European

indolcire §176 *tr* to sweeten || *ref* to become sweet

ìndole *f* temper, disposition; nature

indolènte *adj* indolent

indolenzimento *m* soreness, stiffness; numbness

indolenzire §176 *tr* to make sore or stiff; to benumb || *ref* to become sore or stiff

indolenzì·to -ta *adj* sore, stiff; numb

indolóre *adj* painless

indomàbile *adj* indomitable

indomà·ni *m* (-ni) morrow, next day; **l'indomani di . . .** the day after . . .

indomà·to -ta *adj* (lit) indomitable, untamed

indòmi·to -ta *adj* (lit) indomitable, untamed

Indonèsia l' *f* Indonesia

indonesia·no -na *adj & mf* Indonesian

indorare (**indòro**) *tr* to gild; (culin) to brown; (fig) to sugar-coat

indoratura *f* gilding

indossare (**indòsso**) *tr* to wear; to put on

indossatrìce *f* mannequin, model

indòsso *adv* on, on one's back; **avere indosso** to have on, wear

Indostàn, l' *m* Hindustan

indosta·no -na *adj & mf* Hindustani

indòtto *m* (elec) armature (*of motor*)

indottrinare *tr* to indoctrinate

indovinare *tr* to guess; **indovinarla** to guess right; **non indovinarne una** to never hit the mark

indovina·to -ta *adj* felicitous

indovinèllo *m* puzzle, riddle

indovì·no -na *mf* soothsayer, fortune-teller

indù *adj invar & mf* Hindu

indùb·bio -bia *adj* (-bi -bie) undoubted, undisputed

indubita·to -ta *adj* undeniable

indugiare §290 *tr* to delay || *intr* to linger; to hesitate || *ref* to linger

indù·gio *m* (-gi) delay; **rompere gli indugi** to come to a decision; **senza ulteriore indugio** without further delay

indulgènte *adj* indulgent

indulgènza *f* indulgence

indùlgere §187 *tr* to grant; to forgive || *intr* to be indulgent; **indulgere a** to indulge; to yield to

indulto *m* (law) pardon

induménto *m* garment; **indumenti intimi** undergarments, unmentionables

indurire §176 *tr* to harden || *intr* (ESSERE) to harden; to get stiff

indurre §102 *tr* to induce

indùstria *f* industry; **grande industria** heavy industry

industriale *adj* industrial || *m* industrialist

industrializzare [ddzz] *tr* to industrialize

industriare §287 *ref* to try, try hard; **industriarsi a** or **per** + *inf* to try to + *inf*, to do one's best to + *inf*

industrió·so -sa [s] *adj* industrious

indut·tóre -trice *adj* inducing, provoking || *m* (elec) field (*of motor*)

induzióne *f* induction

inebetire §176 *tr* to dull; to stun || *intr* (ESSERE) & *ref* to become dull; to be stunned

inebriare §287 (**inèbrio**) *tr* to intoxicate || *ref* to get drunk

inebriante *adj* intoxicating

ineccepìbile *adj* unexceptionable

inèdia *f* starvation, inanition; boredom

inèdi·to -ta *adj* unpublished; new, novel

ineduca·to -ta *adj* uneducated; ill-mannered

ineffàbile *adj* ineffable

inefficace *adj* ineffectual, ineffective

inefficàcia *f* inefficacy

inefficiènte *adj* inefficient

ineguale *adj* unequal; uneven

inelegante *adj* inelegant; shabby

ineleggìbile *adj* ineligible

ineluttàbile *adj* inevitable, inescapable

inenarràbile *adj* unspeakable

inerènte *adj* inherent

inèrme *adj* unarmed, defenseless

inerpicare §197 (**inérpico**) *ref* to clamber

inèrte *adj* inert

inèrzia *f* inertia; inactivity

inesattézza *f* inaccuracy

inesat·to -ta *adj* inaccurate, inexact; uncollected

inesaurìbile *adj* inexhaustible

inescusàbile *adj* inexcusable

inesigìbile *adj* uncollectable

inesistènte *adj* inexistent

inesoràbile *adj* inexorable

inesperiènza *f* inexperience

inespèr·to -ta *adj* inexperienced; unskilled

inesplicàbile *adj* inexplicable

inesplica·to -ta *adj* unexplained

inesplora·to -ta *adj* unexplored

inesplò·so -sa *adj* unexploded

inespressì·vo -va *adj* inexpressive

inesprimìbile *adj* inexpressible

inespugnàbile *adj* impregnable; incorruptible

inespugna·to -ta *adj* unconquered

inestimàbile *adj* priceless, invaluable

inestinguìbile *adj* inextinguishable

inestirpàbile *adj* ineradicable

inestricàbile *adj* inextricable

inèt·to -ta *adj* inept

ineva·so -sa *adj* unfinished (*business*); unanswered (*mail*)

inevitàbile *adj* unavoidable, inevitable

inèzia *f* trifle, bagatelle

infagottare (infagòtto) *tr & ref* to bundle up

infallìbile *adj* infallible

infamante *adj* shameful, disgraceful

infamare *tr* to disgrace; to slander

infame *adj* infamous; villainous; (coll) horrible ‖ *mf* villain

infàmia *f* infamy; (coll) botch, bungle

infangare §209 *tr* to splash with mud; (fig) to stain, spot

infante *adj & mf* infant, baby ‖ *m* infante ‖ *f* infanta

infantile *adj* infantile, childish

infànzia *f* infancy, childhood

infarcire §176 *tr* to cram; (culin) to stuff

infarinare *tr* to sprinkle with flour; to powder; (fig) to cram ‖ *ref* to be covered with flour

infarinatura *f* sprinkling with flour; (fig) smattering

infastidire §176 *tr* to annoy ‖ *ref* to be annoyed, lose one's patience

infaticàbile *adj* indefatigable, tireless

infatti *adv* indeed; really

infatuare (infàtuo) *tr* to infatuate ‖ *ref* to become infatuated

infatua·to -ta *adj* infatuated

infàu·sto -sta *adj* unlucky, fatal

infecón·do -da *adj* barren

infedéle *adj* unfaithful; inaccurate ‖ *mf* infidel

infedel·tà *f* (-**tà**) unfaithfulness; inaccuracy; infidelity

infelice *adj* unhappy, unfortunate; unfavorable ‖ *mf* wretch

infelici·tà *f* (-**tà**) unhappiness

inferióre *adj* inferior; lower; **inferiore a** a lower than; less than; smaller than

inferiorità *f* inferiority

inferire §188a *tr* to inflict; to infer; (naut) to bend (*a sail*)

infermare (infèrmo) *tr* (lit) to weaken ‖ *intr* (ESSERE) to get sick

infermería *f* infirmary

infermiè·re -ra *adj* nursing ‖ *m* male nurse ‖ *f* nurse; **infermiera diplomata** trained nurse

infermierìsti·co -ca *adj* (-**ci** -**che**) nursing

infermi·tà *f* (-**tà**) infirmity

infér·mo -ma *adj* infirm; sick ‖ *m* patient

infernale *adj* infernal

infèr·no -na *adj* (lit) lower (*region*) ‖ *m* hell; inferno

inferocire §176 *tr* to infuriate ‖ *intr*—**inferocire su** to be pitiless to ‖ *intr* (ESSERE) to become infuriated

inferriata *f* grating, grill

infervorare (infèrvoro & infervóro) *tr* to excite, stir up ‖ *ref* to get excited; to become absorbed

infestare (infèsto) *tr* to infest

infettare (infètto) *tr* to infect

infetti·vo -va *adj* infectious

infèt·to -ta *adj* infected; corrupted

infezióne *f* infection

infiacchire §176 *tr* to weaken ‖ *intr* (ESSERE) & *ref* to grow weak

infiammàbile *adj* inflammable

infiammare *tr* to inflame; to ignite ‖ *ref* to catch fire, ignite

infiamma·to -ta *adj* burning; aflame; inflamed, excited

infiammazióne *f* inflammation

infi·do -da *adj* untrustworthy

infierire §176 *intr* to become cruel; to be merciless to; to rage (*said, e.g., of a disease*)

infievolire §176 *tr* to weaken

infìggere §103 *tr* to thrust, stick, sink ‖ *ref*—**infìggersi in** to creep in; to work in

infilare *tr* to thread (*a needle*); to insert (*a key*); to transfix (*with a sword*); to put on (*e.g., a coat*); to pull on (*one's pants*); to slip on (*a dress*); to slip (*e.g., one's arm into a sleeve*); to string (*beads*); to hit (*the target*); to take (*a road*); to enter through (*a door*); **infilare l'uscio** to slip away; **infilarle tutte** to succeed all the time; **non infilarne mai una** to never succeed ‖ *ref* to slip; to sink; to slide (*e.g., through a crowd*)

infilata *f* row; string (*e.g., of insults*); (mil) enfilade; **d'infilata** lengthwise

infiltrare *ref* to infiltrate; to seep; (fig) to creep

infilzare *tr* to pierce; to string; (sew) to baste

infilzata *f* string (*of pearls, of lies, etc.*)

ìnfi·mo -ma *adj* lowest, bottom

infine *adv* finally

infingar·do -da *adj* lazy, slothful

infini·tà *f* (-**tà**) infinity

infinitèsi·mo -ma *adj & m* infinitesimal

infiniti·vo -va *adj* (gram) infinitive

infini·to -ta *adj* infinite ‖ *m* infinite; infinity; (gram) infinitive; (math) infinity; **all'infinito** ad infinitum

infino *adv* (lit)—**infino a** until; as far as; **infino a che** as long as

infinocchiare §287 (infinòcchio) *tr* (coll) to fool, bamboozle

infioccare §197 (infiòcco) *tr* to adorn with tassels

infiorare (infióro) *tr* to adorn with flowers; (fig) to sprinkle; (fig) to embellish ‖ *ref* to be covered with flowers

infiorescènza *f* inflorescence

infirmare *tr* to weaken; to invalidate

infischiare §287 *ref*—**infischiarsi di** to not care a hoot about

infisso *m* frame (*e.g., of door*); fixture

infittire §176 *tr*, *intr* (ESSERE) & *ref* to thicken

inflazionare (inflazióno) *tr* to inflate

inflazióne *f* inflation

inflessìbile *adj* inflexible

inflessióne *f* inflection
inflèttere §177 *tr* (lit) to inflect
infliggere §104 *tr* to inflict
influènte *adj* influential
influènza *f* influence; (pathol) influenza
influenzare (influènzo) *tr* to influence, sway
influire §176 *intr* to have an influence; **influire su** to influence || *intr* (ESSERE) —**influire** in to flow into
influsso *m* influence; (lit) plague
infocare §182 *tr* to make glow with heat || *ref* to catch fire; to get excited
infoca·to -ta *adj* red-hot; sultry
infognare (infógno) *ref* (coll) to sink (*e.g., in vice*); (coll) to get stuck (*e.g., in debt*)
infoltire §176 *tr & intr* (ESSERE) to thicken
infonda·to -ta *adj* unfounded, groundless
infóndere §178 *tr* to infuse, instill
inforcare §197 (**infórco**) *tr* to pitch (*hay*); to bestride; to mount (*a horse or bicycle*); to put on (*one's eyeglasses*)
inforcatura *f* pitching with a fork; crotch
informare (infórmo) *tr* to inform; (fig) to mold || *ref* to conform; to inquire; **informarsi da** to seek or get information from; **informarsi di** or **su** to inquire about; to find out about
informati·vo -va *adj* informative, informational
informa·tóre -trice *adj* underlying || *mf* informer; (journ) reporter || *m* informant (*of a foreign language*)
informazióne *f* piece of information; **chiedere informazioni** or **sul conto di** to inquire about; **informazioni** information
infórme *adj* shapeless
informicolire §176 *ref* to tingle; **informicolirsi a** to go to sleep, *e.g.,* **gli si è informicolita la gamba** his leg went to sleep
infornare (infórno) *tr* to put in the oven; to bake
infornata *f* batch (*of bread*); (coll) flock
infortunare *ref* to get hurt
infortuna·to -ta *adj* injured || *mf* casualty, victim
infortù·nio *m* (-**ni**) accident, mishap; **infortunio sul lavoro** job-connected injury
infossare (infòsso) *tr* to bury || *ref* to cave in, settle; to become sunken (*said of eyes or cheeks*)
infracidare (infràcido) *tr* var of **infradiciare**
infracidire §176 *intr* to rot
infradiciare §128 (**infràdicio**) *tr* to drench || *ref* to get drenched; to rot (*said of fruit*)
inframmettènza *f* interference, meddling
inframméttere §198 *tr* to interpose || *ref* to meddle, interfere
inframmezzare [ddzz] (**inframmèzzo**) *tr* to intersperse

infràngere §179 *tr & ref* to break
infrangibile *adj* unbreakable
infran·to -ta *adj* broken, shattered
infrarós·so -sa *adj & m* infrared
infrascrit·to -ta *adj* mentioned below
infrastruttura *f* underpinning; infrastructure; (rr) roadbed
infrazióne *f* infraction, breach
infreddatura *f* mild cold
infreddolire §176 *ref* to feel cold, to be chilled
infrenàbile *adj* irrepressible
infrequènte *adj* infrequent
infrollire §176 *tr* to make (*meat*) high || *intr* (ESSERE) & *ref* to get high (*said of meat*); (fig) to soften
infruttuó·so -sa [s] *adj* unprofitable
infuòri *adv* out; **all'infuori** outward; **all'infuori di** except
infuriare §287 *tr* to infuriate, enrage || *intr* to get blustery; to rage || *intr* (ESSERE) to lose one's temper
infusióne *f* infusion; sprinkling (*of holy water*)
infuso *m* infusion
ingabbiare §287 *tr* to cage; to jail; to corner; to build the framework of
ingabbiatura *f* frame, framework
ingaggiare §290 *tr* to hire; to engage || *ref* to sign up; to get tangled up
ingàg·gio *m* (-**gi**) engagement; (sports) bonus (*for signing up*)
ingagliardire §176 *tr* to strengthen || *ref* to become strong
ingannare *tr* to deceive; to cheat; to elude; to beguile || *ref* to be mistaken
inganna·tóre -trice *adj* deceptive || *mf* impostor
ingannévole *adj* deceitful; deceptive
inganno *m* deception; illusion
ingarbugliare §280 *tr* to entangle; to jumble || *ref* to get mixed up; to become embroiled
ingegnare (ingégno) *ref* to manage; to scheme
ingegnère *m* engineer
ingegneria *f* engineering; **ingegneria civile** civil engineering; **ingegneria meccanica** mechanical engineering
ingégno *m* brain, intelligence; talent; genius; expediency; (lit) machinery
ingegnosità [s] *f* ingeniousness
ingegnó·so -sa [s] *adj* ingenious; euphuistic
ingelosire [s] §176 *tr* to make jealous || *intr* (ESSERE) & *ref* to become jealous
ingemmare (ingèmmo) *tr* to adorn or stud with gems
ingenerare (ingènero) *tr* to engender
ingèni·to -ta *adj* inborn
ingènte *adj* huge, vast
ingentilire §176 *tr* to refine
ingenui·tà *f* (-**tà**) ingenuousness; ingenuous act
ingè·nuo -nua *adj* ingenuous, artless || *m* (theat) artless character || *f* (theat) ingénue
ingerènza *f* interference
ingerire §176 *tr* to ingest, swallow || *ref* to meddle

ingessare (ingèsso) *tr* to put in a plaster cast; to plaster up

ingessatura *f* (surg) plaster cast

inghiaiare §287 *tr* to gravel, cover with gravel

Inghilterra, l' *f* England; **la Nuova Inghilterra** New England

inghiottire (inghiótto) & §176 *tr* to swallow; to swallow up; to pocket (*one's pride*)

inghirlandare *tr* to bedeck with garlands; (lit) to encircle

ingiallire §176 *tr* & *intr* (ESSERE) to turn yellow

ingiù *adv* down; **all'ingiù** downwards

ingigantire §176 *tr* to exaggerate ‖ *intr* (ESSERE) to grow larger, increase

inginocchiare §287 (inginòcchio) *ref* to kneel down

inginocchia∙tóio *m* (-tói) prie-dieu

ingioiellare (ingioièllo) *tr* to bejewel; (fig) to stud

ingiùngere §183 *tr* to order, command ‖ *intr* (with *dat*) to order, command, e.g., **il giudice ingiunse all'imputato di rispondere** the judge ordered the accused to answer

ingiunzióne *f* order; (law) injunction

ingiùria *f* insult, abuse; damage, wear

ingiuriare §287 *tr* to insult

ingiurió∙so -sa [s] *adj* insulting

ingiustificàbile *adj* unjustifiable

ingiustifica∙to -ta *adj* unjustified

ingiustizia *f* injustice

ingiu∙sto -sta *adj* unjust, unfair ‖ *m* unjust person

inglése [s] *adj* English; **all'inglese** in the English fashion; **andarsene all'inglese** to take French leave ‖ *m* Englishman; English (*language*) ‖ *f* Englishwoman

ingoiare §287 (ingóio) *tr* to swallow; to gulp down; **ingoiare un rospo** (fig) to swallow one's pride

ingolfare (ingólfo) *tr* (aut) to flood ‖ *ref* to form a gulf; to get involved; (aut) to flood

ingollare (ingóllo) *tr* to swallow, gulp down

ingolosire [s] §176 *tr* to make the mouth of (*s.o.*) water ‖ *intr* (ESSERE) & *ref* to have a craving

ingombrante *adj* cumbersome

ingombrare (ingómbro) *tr* to clutter

ingóm∙bro -bra *adj* encumbered, cluttered ‖ *m* encumbrance; **essere d'ingombro** to be in the way

ingommare (ingómmo) *tr* to glue

ingordìgia *f* greed

ingór∙do -da *adj* greedy, covetous

ingorgare §209 (ingórgo) *ref* to get clogged up

ingór∙go *m* (-ghi) blocking, congestion; **ingorgo stradale** traffic jam

ingovernàbile *adj* uncontrollable

ingozzare (ingózzo) *tr* to gobble, gulp down; to swallow; to cram (*e.g., a goose for fattening*)

ingranàg∙gio *m* (-gi) gear, gearwheel; (fig) meshes; **ingranaggio di distribuzione** (aut) timing gear; **ingranaggio elicoidale** worm gear

ingranare *tr* to engage (*a gear*); **ingranare la marcia** to throw into gear ‖ *intr* to be in gear; to succeed

ingrandiménto *m* enlargement; increase

ingrandire §176 *tr* to enlarge; to increase; ‖ *intr* (ESSERE) & *ref* to increase, get larger

ingrassare *tr* to fatten; to lubricate ‖ *intr* (ESSERE) & *ref* to get fat; to get rich

ingrassa∙tóre -trice *mf* greaser, lubricator ‖ *f* grease gun; lubricating machine

ingratitùdine *f* ingratitude

ingra∙to -ta *adj* ungrateful; thankless ‖ *mf* ingrate

ingraziare §287 *ref* to ingratiate oneself with

ingrediènte *m* ingredient

ingrèsso *m* entrance; admittance, entry; **ingressi** hallway furniture; **primo ingresso** debut

ingrossaménto *m* enlargement; swelling

ingrossare (ingròsso) *tr* to enlarge; to swell; to make bigger; to dull (*the mind*); to raise (*one's voice*) ‖ *intr* (ESSERE) & *ref* to swell; to thicken; to become fat; to become pregnant; to become important

ingròsso *m*—**all'ingrosso** wholesale; approximately, more or less

ingrullire §176 *tr* to drive crazy ‖ *intr* (ESSERE) & *ref* to become silly; **fare ingrullire** to drive crazy

inguadàbile *adj* not fordable

inguainare (inguaìno) *tr* to sheathe

ingualcìbile *adj* wrinkle-free, wrinkleproof

inguanta∙to -ta *adj* with gloves on; **con le mani inguantate** with gloves on

inguaribile *adj* incurable

inguine *f* (anat) groin

ingurgitare (ingùrgito) *tr* to swallow, gulp down

inibire §176 *tr* to inhibit

inibi∙tóre -trice *adj* inhibiting ‖ *m* inhibitor

inidòne∙o -a *adj* unfit, unqualified

iniettare (iniètto) *tr* to inject ‖ *ref* to become bloodshot; **iniettarsi di sangue** to become bloodshot

iniezióne *f* injection

inimicare §197 *tr* to make an enemy of; to alienate ‖ *ref*—**inimicarsi con** to fall out with

inimicìzia *f* enmity

inimitàbile *adj* inimitable, matchless

ininterrót∙to -ta *adj* uninterrupted

iniqui∙tà *f* (-tà) injustice; iniquity

ini∙quo -qua *adj* unjust; wicked

iniziale *adj* & *f* initial

iniziare §287 *tr* to initiate ‖ *ref* to begin

iniziativa *f* initiative; sponsorship; **iniziativa privata** private enterprise

inizia∙tóre -trice *adj* initiating ‖ *mf* initiator, promoter

iniziazióne *f* initiation

ini∙zio *m* (-zi) beginning, start

innaffiare §287 *tr* var of **annaffiare**

innaffia∙tóio *m* (-tói) var of **annaffiatoio**

innalzaménto *m* elevation

innalzare *tr* to raise; to elevate; **innalzare al cielo** to praise to the sky || *ref* to rise; to tower

innamorare (**innamóro**) *tr* to charm, fascinate; to inspire with love || *ref* to fall in love

innamora·to -ta *adj* in love, enamored; fond || *mf* sweetheart || *m* boyfriend || *f* girl friend

innanzi *adj invar* previous, prior (*e.g., day*) || *adv* ahead, before; **innanzi a** in front of; **innanzi di** + *inf* before + *ger*; **mettere innanzi** to prefer; to place before; to advance (*an excuse*); **per l'innanzi** before, in the past; **tirare innanzi** to get along || *prep* before; above; **innanzi tempo** ahead of time; **innanzi tutto** above all

innà·rio *m* (**-ri**) hymnal

inna·to -ta *adj* inborn, innate

innegàbile *adj* undeniable

inneggiare §290 (**innéggio**) *intr*—**inneggiare a** to sing the praises of

innervosire [s] §176 *tr* to make nervous

innescare §197 (**innésco**) *tr* to bait (*a hook*); to prime (*a bomb*)

innésco m (**-schi**) primer; detonator

innestare (**innèsto**) *tr* (hort & surg) to graft; (surg) to implant; (med) to inoculate (*a vaccine*); (mach) to engage; (elec) to plug in (*e.g., a plug*); **innestare la marcia** (aut) to throw into gear || *ref* to be grafted; **innestarsi in** to merge with; **innestarsi su** to connect with

innèsto *m* (hort & surg) graft; (surg) implant; (med) inoculation; (mach) engagement; (mach) coupling; (elec) plug

inno *m* hymn; **inno nazionale** national anthem

innocènte *adj* innocent || *m* innocent; **innocenti** foundlings

innocènza *f* innocence

innò·cuo -cua *adj* innocuous, harmless

innominàbile *adj* unmentionable

innomina·to -ta *adj* unnamed

innovare (**innòvo**) *tr* to innovate

innovazióne *f* innovation

innumerévole *adj* countless, innumerable

-ino -ina *suf adj* little, e.g., **poverino** poor little; hailing from, e.g., **fiorentino** hailing from Florence, Florentine || *suf f see* **-ina**

insa·no -na *adj* insane

inoccupa·to -ta *adj* unoccupied || *m* person looking for his first job

inoculare (**inòculo**) *tr* to inoculate

inoculazióne *f* inoculation

inodó·ro -ra *adj* odorless

inoffensi·vo -va *adj* inoffensive

inoltrare (**inóltro**) *tr* (com) to forward (*e.g., a request*) || *ref* to advance

inóltre *adv* besides, in addition

inóltro *m* (com) forwarding

inondare (**inóndo**) *tr* to inundate, flood; to swamp

inondazióne *f* flood, inundation

inoperosità [s] *f* idleness

inoperó·so -sa [s] *adj* idle

inopina·to -ta *adj* (lit) unexpected

inopportu·no -na *adj* inopportune, untimely

inoppugnàbile *adj* incontestable; indisputable

inorgàni·co -ca *adj* (**-ci -che**) inorganic

inorgoglire §176 *tr* to make proud || *intr* (ESSERE) & *ref* to grow proud

inorridire §176 *tr* to horrify || *intr* (ESSERE) to be horrified

inospitale *adj* inhospitable

inosservante *adj* unobservant

inosserva·to -ta *adj* unnoticed; unperceived

inossidàbile *adj* stainless

inquadrare *tr* to frame; to arrange

inquadratura *f* framing; (mov, phot) frame

inqualificàbile *adj* unspeakable

inquietante *adj* disquieting

inquietare (**inquièto**) *tr* to worry || *ref* to worry; to get angry

inquiè·to -ta *adj* worried; restless; angry; (lit) stormy

inquietùdine *f* worry; restlessness; preoccupation

inquili·no -na *mf* tenant

inquinaménto *m* pollution

inquinare *tr* to pollute

inquirènte *adj* investigating

inquisi·tóre -trice *adj* inquiring || *m* inquisitor

inquisizióne *f* inquisition

insabbiare §287 *tr* to cover with sand; to pigeonhole; to shelve || *ref* to get covered with sand; to bury oneself in sand; to get stuck

insaccare §197 *tr* to bag; to stuff (*e.g., salami*); (mil) to hem in; (fig) to bundle up; (coll) to gulp down || *ref* to be packed in; to crumple up; to disappear behind a thick bank of clouds (*said, e.g., of the sun*)

insaccato *m* participant in a sack race; **insaccati** cold cuts, lunch meat

insalata *f* salad; (fig) mess

insalatièra *f* salad bowl

insalubre *adj* unhealthy

insaluta·to -ta *adj* unsaluted; **andarsene insalutato ospite** to take French leave

insanàbile *adj* incurable; implacable

insanguinare (**insànguino**) *tr* to bloody; to cover with blood; to bathe in blood

insa·no -na *adj* insane

insaponare (**insapóno**) *tr* to soap; to lather; (fig) to soft-soap

insaporire §176 *tr* to flavor || *intr* (ESSERE) to become tasty

insaputa *f*—**all'insaputa di** without the knowledge of, unbeknown to

insaziàbile *adj* insatiable

insazia·to -ta *adj* insatiate, unsatisfied

inscatolare (**inscàtolo**) *tr* to can

inscenare (**inscèno**) *tr* to stage

inscindìbile *adj* inseparable

inscrìvere §250 *tr* (geom) to inscribe

inscrutàbile *adj* inscrutable

inscurire §176 *tr, intr* (ESSERE) & *ref* to darken

insecchire §176 *tr* to dry || *intr* (ESSERE) & *ref* to dry up

insediaménto *m* installation (*into an office*); assumption (*of an office*)

insediare §287 (insèdio) *tr* to install || *ref* to be installed; to take one's seat; to settle

inségna *f* badge, insignia, emblem; ensign, flag; coat of arms; motto; sign (*e.g., on a restaurant*); traffic sign

insegnaménto *m* education, instruction

insegnante *adj* teaching || *mf* teacher

insegnare (inségno) *tr* to teach; to show || *intr* to teach

inseguiménto *m* pursuit

inseguire (inséguo) *tr* to pursue, chase; to chase after

insellare (insèllo) *tr* to saddle; to put on (*e.g., one's glasses*); to bend

insellatura *f* saddling; bending

insenatura *f* inlet, cove

insensatézza *f* nonsense, folly

insensa·to -ta *adj* nonsensical, foolish || *mf* scatterbrain

insensibile *adj* insensible; unresponsive; insensitive

inseparàbile *adj* inseparable || *m* (orn) lovebird

insepól·to -ta *adj* unburied

inserire §176 *tr* to insert; to plug in || *ref* to slip in; to butt in

inseri·tóre -trice *adj* (elec) connecting || *m* (elec) connector, plug || *f* sorter (*of punch cards*)

insèrto *m* file, folder; insert; spliced film

inservìbile *adj* useless, worthless

inserviènte *m* attendant, porter; (eccl) server

inserzionare (inserzióno) *intr* to advertise

inserzióne *f* insertion; advertisement

inserzioni·sta (-sti -ste) *adj* advertising || *mf* advertiser

insettici·da *adj* & *m* (-di -de) insecticide

insettìfu·go *m* (-ghi) insect repellent

insètto *m* insect; insetti vermin

insìdia *f* trap, ambush; insìdie lure

insidiare §287 *tr* to ensnare; to try to trap; to try to seduce; to attempt (*someone's life*)

insidió·so -sa [s] *adj* insidious

insième *m* whole, entirety; harmony; ensemble; set; d'insième general, comprehensive; nell'insième as a whole || *adv* together

insigne *adj* famous; notable; arrant (*knave*)

insignificante *adj* insignificant; petty

insignire §176 *tr* to decorate; insignire qlcu di un titolo to bestow a title upon s.o.

insignorire §176 *tr* (lit) to invest with a fief || *intr* (ESSERE) to enrich oneself || *ref* to enrich oneself; insignorirsi di to seize; to take possession of

insilare *tr* to silo, ensile

insilato *m* ensilage

insincè·ro -ra *adj* insincere

insindacàbile *adj* final, indisputable

insino *adv* (lit)—insino a until; as far as; insino a che as long as

insinuante *adj* insinuating

insinuare (insìnuo) *tr* to stick, thrust;

to insinuate; (law) to register || *ref* to creep, filter; to ingratiate oneself; insinuarsi in to worm one's way into

insinuazióne *f* insinuation, hint

insipi·do -da *adj* insipid, vapid

insistènte *adj* insistent

insìstere §114 *intr* to insist

ìnsi·to -ta *adj* inborn, inherent

insociévole *adj* unsociable

insoddisfat·to -ta *adj* dissatisfied

insofferènte *adj* intolerant

insoffrìbile *adj* unbearable, insufferable

insolazióne *f* sunning; sun bath; sunstroke; sunny exposure

insolènte *adj* insolent

insolentire §176 *tr* to insult, abuse || *intr* to be insolent

insolènza *f* insolence; insult

insòli·to -ta *adj* unusual

insolùbile *adj* insoluble

insolu·to -ta *adj* unsolved; not dissolved; unpaid

insolvènza *f* insolvency

insolvìbile *adj* insolvent; bad (*debt*)

insómma *adv* in conclusion || *interj* well!

insommergìbile *adj* unsinkable

insondàbile *adj* unfathomable

insònne *adj* sleepless

insònnia *f* insomnia

insonnoli·to -ta *adj* sleepy, drowsy

insonorizzazióne [ddzz] *f* soundproofing

insopportàbile *adj* unbearable

insorgènte *adj* appearing || *mf* insurgent

insorgènza *f* appearance (*of illness*)

insórgere §258 *intr* (ESSERE) to rise up, revolt; to appear

insormontàbile *adj* unsurmountable, insurmountable

insór·to -ta *adj* & *m* insurgent

insospettàbile *adj* above suspicion; unexpected

insospetta·to -ta *adj* not suspect; unexpected

insospettire §176 *tr* to make suspicious || *intr* (ESSERE) & *ref* to become suspicious

insostenibile *adj* indefensible; unbearable

insostituibile *adj* irreplaceable

insozzare (insózzo) *tr* to soil, sully

inspera·to -ta *adj* unexpected; unhoped-for

inspiegàbile *adj* unexplainable

inspirare *tr* to inhale, breathe in

inspirazióne *f* inhalation

instàbile *adj* unstable

installare *tr* to install; to set up, settle; to induct (*in an office*) || *ref* to settle

installatóre *m* plumber; erector

installazióne *f* installation; plumbing

instancàbile *adj* untiring

instante *adj* insistent; impending || *m* petitioner

instare (*pp* missing) *intr* to insist; to threaten, be imminent

instaurare (instàuro) *tr* to establish

instaurazióne *f* establishment

instigare §209 *tr* var of istigare

instillare *tr* var of istillare

instituire §176 *tr* var of istituire

instruire §176 *tr* var of **istruire**
instrumento *m* var of **istrumento**
instupidire §176 *tr* var of **istupidire**
insù *adv* up; **all'insù** up
insubordina·to -ta *adj* insubordinate
insuccèsso *m* failure
insudiciare §128 (**insùdicio**) *tr* to soil, dirty; to sully || *ref* to get dirty
insufficiènte *adj* insufficient; failing (*in school*)
insufficiènza *f* insufficiency; failure (*in school*)
insulare *adj* insular
insulina *f* insulin
insulsàggine *f* silliness, nonsense
insul·so -sa *adj* insipid; simple, silly
insultante *adj* insulting
insultare *tr* to insult || *intr* (with *dat*) to insult
insulto *m* insult; (*pathol*) attack
insuperàbile *adj* insuperable; unparalleled
insupera·to -ta *adj* unsurpassed
insuperbire §176 *tr, intr* (ESSERE) & *ref* to swell with pride
insurrezióne *f* insurrection
insussistènte *adj* nonexistent, unfounded
intabarrare *tr* to wrap up
intaccare §197 *tr* to notch; to corrode; to scratch; to attack (*said of a disease*); to damage (*e.g., a reputation*); to cut into (*capital*) || *intr* to stutter
intaccatura *f* notch; (*carp*) mortise
intagliare §280 *tr* to carve; to engrave
intà·glio *m* (**-gli**) carving; intaglio
intanare *ref* to hide
intangìbile *adj* intangible; inviolable
intanto *adv* meanwhile; (coll) yet; (coll) finally; **intanto che** while; **per intanto** at present; in the meantime
intarsiare §287 *tr* to inlay; (fig) to stud
intarsia·to -ta *adj* inlaid
intàr·sio *m* (**-si**) inlay; inlaid work
intasare [s] *tr* to clog; to tie up (*traffic*); to stop up || *ref* to be clogged up; to be tied up; to be stopped up (*said of nose*)
intascare §197 *tr* to pocket
intat·to -ta *adj* intact, untouched
intavolare (**intàvolo**) *tr* to start (*a conversation*); to broach (*a subject*); to launch (*negotiations*)
intavolato *m* boarding, planking
integèrri·mo -ma *adj* of the utmost honesty
integrale *adj* integral; whole; wholewheat (*bread*); built-in || *m* integral
integralismo *m* policy of the complete absorption of the body politic by an ideology
integrante *adj* constituent, integral
integrare (**ìntegro**) *tr* to integrate || *ref* to complement each other
integrazióne *f* integration
integrità *f* integrity
ìnte·gro -gra *adj* whole, complete; honest, upright; intact
intelaiatura *f* frame; framework
intellètto *m* intellect, mind; understanding
intellettuale *adj* & *mf* intellectual

intellettuali·tà *f* (**-tà**) intellectuality; intelligentsia
intellettualòide *mf* highbrow
intelligènte *adj* intelligent; clever
intelligènza *f* intelligence; understanding; **essere d'intelligenza con** to be in collusion with
intellighènzia *f* intelligentsia
intelligìbile *adj* intelligible
intemera·to -ta *adj* pure, spotless || *f* reprimand, scolding; long, boring speech
intemperante *adj* intemperate
intemperanza *f* intemperance
intempèrie *fpl* inclement weather
intempesti·vo -va *adj* untimely
intendènte *m* district director; **intendente di finanza** director of customs office; **intendente militare** commissary, quartermaster
intendènza *f* office of the district director; intendance; **intendenza militare** quartermaster corps
intèndere §270 *tr* to understand; to hear; to intend; to turn (*e.g., one's eyes*); to mean; **dare ad intendere a** to lead (*s.o.*) to believe (*s.th*); **far intendere** to give to understand; **farsi intendere** to force obedience; to make oneself understood; **intender dire che** to hear that; **intendere a rovescio** to misunderstand; **intendere a volo** to catch on quickly (to); **intendere ragione** to listen to reason; **lasciare intendere** to give to understand || *intr* to aim (*toward a goal*) || *ref* to come to an agreement; **intendersela con** to be in collusion with; to have an affair with; **intendersi di** to be a good judge of; to be an expert in
intendiménto *m* understanding, comprehension; aim, goal
intendi·tóre -trice *mf* connoisseur, expert; **a buon intenditore poche parole** a word to the wise is sufficient
intenerire §176 *tr* to soften; (fig) to move || *ref* to soften; (fig) to be moved
intensificare §197 (**intensìfico**) *tr & ref* to intensify
intensi·tà *f* (**-tà**) intensity
intensi·vo -va *adj* intensive
intèn·so -sa *adj* intense
intentare (**intènto**) *tr* (law) to bring (*action*)
intenta·to -ta *adj* unattempted
intèn·to -ta *adj* intent || *m* intent, goal; **coll'intento di** with the purpose of
intenzionale *adj* intentional
intenziona·to -ta *adj*—**bene intenzionato** well-meaning; **essere intenzionato di** to intend to
intenzióne *f* intention; purpose; **con intenzione** on purpose
intepidire §176 *tr & ref* var of **intiepidire**
interbase *f* (baseball) shortstop
intercalare *m* refrain; pet word or phrase || *tr* to intercalate; to inset
intercalazióne *f* intercalation; inset
intercapèdine *f* air space
intercèdere §123 *tr* to seek, get (*a par-*

don for s.o.) || *intr* to intercede || *intr* (ESSERE)—**intercedere tra** to intervene or elapse between; to extend between; to exist between

intercettare (intercètto) *tr* to intercept; to tap (*a phone*)

intercetta·tóre -trice *mf* interceptor

intercettóre *m* (aer) interceptor

intercomunale *adj* long-distance (*call*)

intercórrere §139 *intr* (ESSERE) to elapse; to happen; to be, to stand

interdét·to -ta *adj* dumfounded; forbidden || *m* interdict; (coll) dumbell

interdire §151 *tr* to prohibit; (eccl) to interdict; (law) to disqualify

interessaménto *m* interest, concern

interessante *adj* interesting; **in stato interessante** in the family way

interessare (interèsso) *tr* to interest; to concern || *intr* to be of interest || *ref*—**interessarsi a** to take an interest in; **interessarsi di** to concern oneself with

interessa·to -ta *adj* interested; selfish || *m* interested party

interèsse *m* interest; self-interest

interessènza *f* (com) share, interest

interferènza *f* interference

interferire §176 *intr* to interfere

interfogliare §280 **(interfòglio)** *tr* to interleave

interiezióne *f* interjection

interinato *m* temporary office or tenure

interi·no -na *adj* acting || *m* temporary appointee

interióra *fpl* entrails

interióre *adj* interior || **interiori** *mpl* entrails

interlìnea *f* interlining; (typ) leading

interlineare *adj* interlinear || *v* **(interlìneo)** *tr* (typ) to lead

interlocu·tóre -trice *mf* participant (*in a discussion*); person speaking

interloquire §176 *intr* to take part in a discussion; to chime in

interlù·dio *m* (-di) interlude

intermedià·rio -ria (-ri -rie) *adj* & *mf* intermediary || *m* middleman

intermè·dio -dia (-di -die) *adj* intermediate || *mf* supervisor

intermèzzo [ddzz] *m* intermezzo; entr'acte; interval

interminàbile *adj* interminable, endless

intermissióne *f* intermission

intermittènte *adj* intermittent

internaménto *m* internment

internare (intèrno) *tr* to intern; to confine; to commit (*an insane person*) || *ref* to go deep (*into a problem*)

interna·to -ta *adj* interned || *m* internee; inmate; boarder; boarding school

internazionale *adj* international

internazionalizzare [ddzz] *tr* to internationalize

interni·sta *mf* (-sti -ste) internist

intèr·no -na *adj* inside, internal; inland; interior; boarding (*student*) || *m* inside; interior; (med) intern; lining (*of coat*); **all'interno** inside; **interni** (mov) indoor shots || **gli Interni** the Italian Ministry of Internal Affairs

intè·ro -ra *adj* entire, whole; full (*price*); (lit) upright, honest || *m* whole; **per intero** completely

interpellare (interpèllo) *tr* to interpellate; to question; to consult

interpetrare (intèrpetro) *tr* var of interpretare

interplanetà·rio -ria *adj* (-ri -rie) interplanetary

interpolare (intèrpolo) *tr* to interpolate

interpolazióne *f* interpolation

interpónte *m* (naut) between-deck

interpórre §218 *tr* to interpose || *ref* to intervene

interpretare (intèrpreto) *tr* to interpret

interpretazióne *f* interpretation

intèrprete *mf* interpreter

interpunzióne *f* punctuation

interrare (intèrro) *tr* to bury, inter; to fill in (*e.g., a marsh*) || *ref* to become silted

interra·to -ta *adj* underground; **piano interrato** basement

interrogare §209 **(intèrrogo)** *tr* to question; to interrogate

interrogati·vo -va *adj* interrogative || *m* why; question

interrogatò·rio -ria (-ri -rie) *adj* questioning || *m* (law) interrogatory; **interrogatorio di terzo grado** third degree

interrogazióne *f* interrogation; quiz, examination; **interrogazione retorica** rhetorical question

interrómpere §240 *tr* to interrupt

interruttóre *m* (elec) switch; **interruttore di linea** (elec) controller

interruzióne *f* interruption

interscàm·bio *m* (-bi) interchange

interscolàsti·co -ca *adj* (-ci -che) interscholastic; intercollegiate

intersecare §197 **(intèrseco)** *tr* & *adj* intersect

intersezióne *f* intersection

interstellare *adj* interstellar

interstì·zio *m* (-zi) interstice

interurba·no -na *adj* interurban, intercity; (telp) long-distance || *f* (telp) long-distance call

intervallo *m* interval; pause; (educ) recess; (theat) intermission

intervenire §282 *intr* (ESSERE) to intervene; (surg) to operate; **intervenire a** to take part in

interventi·sta *mf* (-sti -ste) interventionist

intervènto *m* intervention; attendance; (surg) operation

intervenzióne *f* intervention

intervista *f* interview; **fare un'intervista a** to interview

intervistare *tr* to interview

inté·so -sa [s] *adj* understood; intended, designed; **bene inteso** of course; **non darsene per inteso** to not pay attention; **rimanere inteso** to agree || *f* understanding, agreement; entente

intèssere (intèsso) *tr* to interweave; to wreathe (*a garland*)

intestardire §176 *ref* to get obstinate; to be determined

intestare (intèsto) *tr* to caption; to label; (typ) to head (*a page*); **intestare qlco a qlcu** to register s.th in the name of s.o.; **intestare una fattura a** to issue a bill in the name of || *ref* to become obstinate; to take it into one's head

intesta·to -ta *adj* headed; registered (*stock*); obstinate; (law) intestate

intestazióne *f* heading; registration (*of stock*)

intestinale *adj* intestinal

intesti·no -na *adj & m* intestine; **intestino crasso** large intestine; **intestino tenue** small intestine

intiepidire §176 *tr & ref* to warm up; to cool off

intiè·ro -ra *adj & m* var of **intero**

intimare (íntimo & íntimo) *tr* to intimate; to order, command; to declare (*war*); to impose (*a fine*); (law) to enjoin

intimazióne *f* intimation; order; (law) injunction

intimidazióne *f* intimidation

intimidire §176 *tr* to intimidate; to threaten || *ref* to become bashful

intimi·tà *f* (-tà) intimacy; privacy

ínti·mo -ma *adj* intimate; inmost; **biancheria intima** underwear, lingerie || *m* intimate friend; depth (*of one's heart*)

intimorire §176 *tr* to frighten

intíngere §126 *tr* to dip || *intr*—**intíngere in** to dip in || *ref*—**intíngersi in un affare** to have a finger in the pie

intíngolo *m* sauce, gravy; fancy dish

intirizzire [ddzz] §176 *tr* to benumb || *intr* (ESSERE) & *ref* to become numb or stiff; to become stiff and frostbitten

intirízzi·to -ta [ddzz] *adj* numb

intisichire §176 *tr* to make tubercular; (fig) to weaken || *intr* (ESSERE) to become tubercular; to wither

intitolare (intitolo) *tr* to title; to dedicate || *ref* to be named; to assume the title of

intoccàbile *adj & m* untouchable

intolleràbile *adj* intolerable

intollerante *adj* intolerant

intonacare §197 (intònaco) *tr* to plaster; to whitewash; to cover (*e.g., with tar*) || *ref*—**intonacarsi la faccia** (joc) to put on one's warpaint

intòna·co -co -chi (-chi) plaster; roughcast

intonare (intòno) *tr* to intone; to harmonize; (mus) to tune || *ref* to harmonize, go

intonazióne *f* intonation; harmony

intòn·so -sa *adj* uncut; (lit) unsheared

intontire §176 *tr* to stun || *intr* (ESSERE) & *ref* to become stunned

intoppare (intòppo) *tr* to stumble upon || *intr* (ESSERE) & *ref* to stumble

intòppo *m* obstacle, hindrance

intorbidare (intórbido) *tr* to cloud; to muddy; to obfuscate; to upset (*friendship*); to stir up (*passions*) || *ref* to become cloudy or muddy; to become obfuscated

intorbidire §176 *tr & ref* to cloud; to muddy

intormentire §176 *tr* to benumb || *intr* (ESSERE) to become numb

intórno *adv* around, about; **all'intorno** all around; **intorno a** around; about; **levarsi qlcu d'intorno** to get rid of s.o.

intorpidire §176 *tr* to benumb || *ref* to become numb

intossicare §197 (intòssico) *tr* to poison, intoxicate

intossicazióne *f* poisoning, intoxication

intraducíbile *adj* untranslatable; inexpressible

intraférro *m* spark gap; air gap

intralciare §128 *tr* to hamper; to intertwine || *ref* to become hampered

intràl·cio -cio (-ci) hindrance; **essere d'intralcio** to be in the way; **intralcio del traffico** traffic congestion

intralicciatura *f* lattice truss (*of high-tension tower*)

intrallazzare *intr* to deal in the black market

intrallazza·tóre -trice *mf* black marketeer

intrallazzo *m* black-market dealing; kickback

intramezzare [ddzz] (intramèzzo) *tr* to alternate

intramontàbile *adj* undying, immortal

intransigènte *adj & mf* intransigent, die-hard

intransitàbile *adj* impassable

intransiti·vo -va *adj* intransitive

intrappolare (intràppolo) *tr* to entrap

intraprendènte *adj* enterprising

intraprendènza *f* enterprise, initiative

intraprèndere §220 *tr* to undertake

intrattàbile *adj* unmanageable, intractable

intrattenére §271 *tr* to entertain || *ref* to linger; **intrattenersi su** to dwell upon

intratteniménto *m* entertainment

intravedére §279 *tr* to glimpse, catch a glimpse of; to foresee

intravenó·so -sa [s] *adj* intravenous

intrecciare §128 (intréccio) *tr* to braid; to twine; to cross (*one's fingers*); (fig) to weave; to begin (*a dance*) || *ref* to become embroiled; to become intertwined; to crisscross

intréc·cio *m* (-ci) knitting; intertwining; plot (*of novel*); (theat) intrigue

intrepidézza *f* intrepidness, intrepidity

intrèpi·do -da *adj* intrepid

intricare §197 *tr* (lit) to entangle

intrica·to -ta *adj* tangled; intricate

intri·co *m* (-chi) tangle, jumble

intridere §189 *tr* to soak; to knead

intrigante *adj* intriguing || *mf* schemer

intrigare §209 *tr* to tangle || *intr* to intrigue || *ref* (coll) to meddle

intri·go *m* (-ghi) intrigue; trouble

intrínse·co -ca (-ci -ca) *adj* intrinsic; intimate || *m* intimate nature, core

intri·so -sa *adj* soaked || *m* mash

intristire §176 *intr* (ESSERE) to wither; to waste away

introdót·to -ta *adj* introduced; well-known; knowledgeable, expert

introdurre §102 *tr* to introduce; to insert; to open (*a speech*); to show in ‖ *ref* to slip in

introdutti·vo -va *adj* introductory

introduzióne *f* introduction

introitare (intròito) *tr* to collect, take in

intròito *m* receipts, collection; (eccl) introit

intromèttere §198 *tr* to insert; to introduce; to involve ‖ *ref* to meddle; to pry

intromissióne *f* meddling; intrusion; intervention

intronare (intròno) *tr* to deafen; to stun

intronizzare [dddzz] *tr* to enthrone

introspetti·vo -va *adj* introspective

introspezióne *f* introspection

introvàbile *adj* unobtainable; inaccessible

introvèr·so -sa *adj & mf* introvert

intrùdere §190 *tr* (lit) to slip in ‖ *ref* to intrude; to trespass

intrufolare (intrùfolo) *tr* (coll) to slip (*e.g., one's hand into somebody's pocket*) ‖ *ref* to slip in, intrude

intrù·glio *m* (-**gli**) concoction, brew; hodgepodge; imbroglio; mess

intrusióne *f* intrusion

intru·so -sa *adj* intrusive ‖ *mf* intruder

intuire §176 *tr* to know by intuition; to guess; to sense

intuiti·vo -va *adj* intuitive; obvious

intùito *m* intuition; insight

intuizióne *f* intuition

inturgidire §176 *intr* (ESSERE) & *ref* to swell

inuma·no -na *adj* inhuman; inhumane

inumare *tr* to bury, inhume

inumazióne *f* burial, inhumation

inumidire §176 *tr* to moisten ‖ *ref* to get wet

inurbaménto *m* migration to the city

inurba·no -na *adj* uncouth, unmannerly

inurbare *ref* to move into the city; to become citified

inusa·to -ta *adj* unused; unusual

inusita·to -ta *adj* unusual; out-of-the-way

inùtile *adj* useless; worthless

inutilizzàbile [dddzz] *adj* unusable

inutilizzare [dddzz] *tr* to waste (*e.g., time*)

inutilizza·to -ta [dddzz] *adj* unused

inutilmente *adv* needlessly, to no purpose ‖ *interj* no use!

invadènte *adj* meddlesome, intrusive

invàdere §172 *tr* to invade; to encroach on; to spread over; to overcome

invaghire §176 *tr* to charm ‖ *ref* to fall in love

invalére §278 *intr* (ESSERE) to become established; to prevail

invalicàbile *adj* impassable, unsurmountable

invalidàbile *adj* voidable

invalidaménto *m* invalidity; invalidation

invalidare (invàlido) *tr* to void, invalidate; to negate (*e.g., evidence*)

invalidi·tà *f* (-**tà**) invalidity; invalidation; sickness, disability

invàli·do -da *adj* void, invalid; sick, disabled ‖ *m* disabled person; invalid

inval·so -sa *adj* prevailing

invano *adv* in vain, vainly

invariàbile *adj* invariable

invaria·to -ta *adj* unchanging; unchanged

invasare *tr* to pot (*a plant*); to fill up (*a reservoir*); to possess, obsess

invasa·to -ta *adj* possessed, obsessed

invasióne *f* invasion

inva·so -sa *adj* invaded ‖ *m* potting (*of plant*); capacity (*of reservoir*)

inva·sóre -ditrice *adj* invading ‖ *m* invader

invecchiaménto *m* aging

invecchiare §287 **(invècchio)** *tr & intr* (ESSERE) to age

invéce *adv* on the contrary, instead; **invece di** instead of

inveire §176 *intr* to inveigh, rail

invelenire §176 *tr* to envenom; to embitter ‖ *intr* (ESSERE) & *ref* to grow bitter

invendìbile *adj* unsalable

invendica·to -ta *adj* unavenged

invendu·to -ta *adj* unsold

inventare (invènto) *tr* to invent

inventariare §287 *tr* to inventory

inventà·rio *m* (-**ri**) inventory

inventi·vo -va *adj* inventive ‖ *f* inventiveness

inven·tóre -trice *adj* inventive ‖ *mf* inventor

invenzióne *f* invention; (lit) find

inverdire §176 *intr* (ESSERE) to turn green

inverecóndia *f* immodesty

inverecón·do -da *adj* immodest

invernale *adj* winter; wintry

inverniciare §128 *tr* to paint; to varnish

invèrno *m* winter

invéro *adv* (lit) truly, indeed

inverosimiglianza [s] *f* unlikelihood

inverosìmile [s] *adj* unlikely

inversióne *f* inversion

invèr·so -sa *adj* inverse, opposite; (coll) cross ‖ *m* inverse

inversóre *m* inverter; **inversore di spinta** (aer) thrust reverser

invertebra·to -ta *adj & m* invertebrate

invertire §176 & **(invèrto)** *tr* to invert; to reverse

inverti·to -ta *adj* inverted ‖ *m* invert

investigare §209 **(invèstigo)** *tr* to investigate

investiga·tóre -trice *adj* investigating ‖ *mf* investigator; detective

investigazióne *f* investigation

investiménto *m* investment; collision

investire (invèsto) *tr* to invest; to collide with; **investire di insulti** to cover with insults ‖ *ref*—**investirsi di** to become conscious of (*e.g., one's authority*); (theat) to become identified with (*a character*)

investi·tóre -trice *mf* investor

investitura *f* investiture

invetera·to -ta *adj* inveterate, confirmed

invetria·to -ta *adj* glazed || *f* window; window pane

invettiva *f* invective

inviare §119 *tr* to send

invia·to -ta *mf* envoy; correspondent

invìdia *f* envy

invidiàbile *adj* enviable

invidiare §287 *tr* to envy; to begrudge; **non aver niente da invidiare a** to be just as good as

invidió·so -sa [s] *adj* envious

invigorire §176 *tr* to strengthen, invigorate || *intr* (ESSERE) & *ref* to grow stronger

invilire §176 *tr* to dishearten; to vilify; to lower (*prices*) || *intr* (ESSERE) & *ref* to lose heart; to lose one's reputation

inviluppare *tr* to envelop; to wrap up

invincibile *adj* invincible

invì·o *m* (-i) dispatch; shipment; remittance; envoy (*of a poem*)

inviolàbile *adj* inviolable

inviperire §176 *ref* to become enraged

invischiare §287 *tr* to smear with bird-lime; to ensnare || *ref* to become ensnared

invisibile *adj* invisible

invi·so -sa *adj* disliked, hated

invitante *adj* attractive, inviting

invitare *tr* to invite; to summon; (*cards*) to bid; (*cards*) to open; (*mach*) to screw (*e.g., a light bulb*) in; to screw (*e.g., a lid*) on

invita·to -ta *adj* invited || *m* guest

invito *m* invitation; inducement; bottom of stairway; (*cards*) opening

invit·to -ta *adj* unvanquished

invocare §197 (invòco) *tr* to invoke

invocazióne *f* invocation

invogliare §280 (invòglio) *tr* to induce, entice || *ref* to yearn, long

involare (invòlo) *tr* to steal; to abduct || *intr* (ESSERE) (aer) to take off || *ref* to disappear; to fly away

invòlgere §289 *tr* to wrap, envelop; to involve || *ref* to become entangled

invòlo *m* (aer) take-off

involontà·rio -ria *adj* (-ri -rie) involuntary

invòlto *m* bundle; wrapper

invòlucro *m* wrapping; shell (*of boiler*); (aer) envelope

involu·to -ta *adj* (fig) involved; (lit) enveloped

invòlvere §147 (*pret* missing; *pp* also invòlto) *tr* (lit) to envelop

invulneràbile *adj* invulnerable

inzaccherare (inzàcchero) *tr* to bespatter

inzeppare (inzéppo) *tr* to cram, stuff

inzuccherare (inzùcchero) *tr* to sweeten

inzuppare *tr* to soak || *ref* to get drenched

lo *m* ego; self || §5 *pron pers*

iòdio *m* iodine

iodìdri·co -ca *adj* (-ci -che) hydriodic

ioduro *m* iodide

iògurt *m* yogurt

iò·le *f* (-le) (naut) yawl; (sports) shell

ióne *m* ion

iòni·co -ca *adj* & *m* (-ci -che) Ionic

ionizzare [ddzz] *tr* to ionize

iòsa [s] *f*—**a iosa** in abundance

iperacidità *f* hyperacidity

ipèrbole *f* (geom) hyperbola; (rhet) hyperbole

iperbòli·co -ca *adj* (-ci -che) hyperbolic(al)

ipereccita·to -ta *adj* overexcited

ipermercato *m* shopping center

ipersensìbile *adj* hypersensitive; supersensitive

ipersostentatóre *m* landing flap

ipertensióne *f* hypertension

ipnò·si *f* (-si) hypnosis

ipnòti·co -ca *adj* & *m* (-ci -che) hypnotic

ipnotismo *m* hypnotism

ipnotizzare [ddzz] *tr* to hypnotize

ipnotizza·tóre -trice [ddzz] *adj* hypnotizing || *m* hypnotizer

ipocondrìa·co -ca *adj* & *mf* (-ci -che) hypochondriac

ipocrisìa *f* hypocrisy

ipòcri·ta (-ti -te) *adj* hypocritical || *mf* hypocrite

ipodèrmi·co -ca *adj* (-ci -che) hypodermic

iposolfito [s] *m* hyposulfite

ipotè·ca *f* (-che) mortgage

ipotecare §197 (ipotèco) *tr* to mortgage

ipotecà·rio -ria *adj* (-ri -rie) mortgage

ipotenusa *f* hypotenuse

ipòte·si *f* (-si) hypothesis; **nella miglior delle ipotesi** at best; **nell'ipotesi che** in the event; **per ipotesi** by supposition

ipotèti·co -ca *adj* (-ci -che) hypothetic(al)

ipotizzare [ddzz] *tr* to hypothesize

ìppi·co -ca *adj* (-ci -che) horse, horseracing || *f* horse racing

ippocampo *m* sea horse

ippocastano *m* horse chestnut tree

ippòdromo *m* race track

ippoglòsso *m* (ichth) halibut

ippopòtamo *m* hippopotamus

iprite *f* mustard gas

ira *f* wrath, anger, ire

irachè·no -na *adj* & *mf* Iraqi

iracóndia *f* wrath, anger

iracón·do -da *adj* wrathful

irania·no -na *adj* & *mf* Iranian

irascìbile *adj* irascible

ira·to -ta *adj* irate, angry

ire §191 *intr* (ESSERE) (lit) to go

ìrida·to -ta *adj* rainbow-hued || *m* world bicycle champion

ìride *f* rainbow; (anat, bot) iris

Irlanda, l' *f* Ireland

irlandése [s] *adj* Irish || *m* Irishman; Irish (*language*) || *f* Irishwoman

ironìa *f* irony

iròni·co -ca *adj* (-ci -che) ironic(al)

iró·so -sa [s] *adj* angry, wrathful

irradiare §287 *tr* to illuminate; to irradiate, radiate; to brighten; (rad) to broadcast || *intr* to radiate || *ref* to radiate; to spread

irraggiare §290 *tr* to illuminate; to irradiate, radiate, beam; to brighten; (rad) to broadcast || *intr* to radiate || *ref* to radiate; to spread

irraggiungìbile *adj* unattainable
irragionévole *adj* unreasonable
irrancidire §176 *intr* (ESSERE) & *ref* to get rancid
irrazionale *adj* irrational
irreale *adj* unreal
irreconciliàbile *adj* irreconcilable
irrecuperàbile *adj* irretrievable, irrecoverable
irredentismo *m* irredentism
irredenti·sta *mf* (-sti -ste) irredentist
irredèn·to -ta *adj* not yet redeemed
irredimìbile *adj* irredeemable
irrefrenàbile *adj* unrestrainable
irrefutàbile *adj* irrefutable
irregimentare (irregimènto) *tr* to regiment
irregolare *adj* irregular
irregolari·tà *f* (-tà) irregularity
irregòio·so -sa [s] *adj* irreligious
irremovìbile *adj* irremovable; obstinate
irreparàbile *adj* irreparable; unavoidable
irreperìbile *adj* not to be found; unaccounted for (*e.g.*, *soldier*)
irreprensìbile *adj* irreproachable
irreprimìbile *adj* irrepressible
irrequiè·to -ta *adj* restless, restive
irresistìbile [s] *adj* irresistible
irresolùbile [s] *adj* unbreakable (*bond*; *contract*); insoluble; unsolvable
irresolu·to -ta [s] *adj* irresolute
irrespiràbile *adj* unbreathable
irresponsàbile *adj* irresponsible
irrestringìbile *adj* unshrinkable
irretire §176 *tr* to ensnare, entrap
irrevocàbile *adj* irrevocable
irriconoscìbile *adj* unrecognizable
irriducìbile *adj* irreducible; stubborn
irriflessi·vo -va *adj* thoughtless, rash
irrigare §209 *tr* to irrigate
irrigazióne *f* irrigation
irrigidire §176 *tr* to chill || *intr* & *ref* to stiffen, harden; to get cool
irri·guo -gua *adj* well-watered; irrigating
irrilevante *adj* irrelevant
irrilevanza *f* irrelevance
irrimediàbile *adj* irremediable
irripetìbile *adj* unrepeatable
irrisióne *f* (lit) derision, mockery
irrisò·rio -ria *adj* (-ri -rie) mocking; paltry
irritàbile *adj* peevish; irritable
irritante *adj* irritating || *m* irritant
irritare (ìrrito) *tr* to irritate; to anger; to chafe || *ref* to become irritated
irritazióne *f* irritation
irriverènte *adj* irreverent
irrobustire §176 *tr* & *ref* to strengthen
irrómpere §240 (*pp* missing) *intr* to burst
irrorare (irròro) *tr* to sprinkle; to bathe, wet; to spray
irroratrice *f* sprayer; **irroratrice a zaino** portable sprayer
irruènte *adj* impetuous, rash
irruzióne *f* foray, raid; irruption
irsu·to -ta *adj* hairy, bristling
ir·to -ta *adj* prickly; shaggy (*hair*); **irto di** bristling with
iscrìvere §250 *tr* to inscribe; to register || *ref* to register; to sign up

iscrizióne *f* inscription; registration
Islam, l' *m* Islam
Islanda, l' *f* Iceland
islandése [s] *adj* Icelandic || *mf* Icelander || *m* Icelandic (*language*)
ìsola *f* island; block; **isola spartitraffico** traffic island
isolaménto *m* isolation; (elec) insulation
isola·no -na *adj* island || *mf* islander
isolante *adj* insulating || *m* (elec) insulation
isolare (ìsolo) *tr* to isolate; (elec) to insulate || *ref* to keep apart
isola·to -ta *adj* isolated; (elec) insulated || *m* city block; (sports) independent
isolatóre *m* (elec) insulator
isolazionismo *m* isolationism
isolazioni·sta *mf* (-sti -ste) isolationist
isolétta *f* isle
isòscele *adj* isosceles
isòto·po -pa *adj* isotopic || *m* isotope
ispani·sta *mf* (-sti -ste) Hispanist
ispa·no -na *adj* Hispanic
ispanoamerica·no -na *adj* & *mf* Spanish-American
ispessire §176 *tr* & *ref* to thicken
ispettorato *m* inspectorship
ispet·tóre -trice *mf* inspector; **ispettore di produzione** (mov) production manager
ispezionare (ispezióno) *tr* to inspect
ispezióne *f* inspection
ìspi·do -da *adj* bristly
ispirare *tr* to inspire || *ref* to be inspired
ispirazióne *f* inspiration
Israèle *m* Israel
israelia·no -na *adj* & *mf* Israeli
israeli·ta *adj* & *mf* (-ti -te) Israelite
issare *tr* to hoist
issòpo *m* hyssop
istallare *tr* & *ref* var of **installare**
istantàne·o -a *adj* instantaneous || *f* snapshot
istante *m* instant, moment; petitioner
istanza *f* petition; request, application; (law) instance; **in ultima istanza** as a final decision
istèri·co -ca (-ci -che) *adj* hysteric(al) || *mf* hysteric
isterilire §176 *tr* to make barren || *ref* to become barren
isterismo *m* hysteria, hysterics
istigare §209 *tr* to instigate, prompt
istiga·tóre -trice *mf* instigator
istillare *tr* to instill, implant; **istillare il collirio negli occhi** to put drops in the eyes
istinti·vo -va *adj* instinctive
istinto *m* instinct
istituire §176 *tr* to institute, found; (lit) to decide
istituto *m* institute; institution; bank; **istituto di bellezza** beauty parlor
istitu·tóre -trice *mf* founder; teacher, instructor || *m* tutor || *f* governess; nurse
istituzionalizzare [ddzz] *tr* to institutionalize
istituzióne *f* institution
istmo *m* isthmus
istologìa *f* histology

istoriare §287 **(istòrio)** *tr* to adorn with historical figures

istradare *tr* to direct || *ref* to wend one's way

istrice *m & f* (European) porcupine

istrióne *m* ham actor; buffoon

istrióni·co -ca *adj* **(-ci -che)** histrionic

istrionismo *m* histrionics

istruire §176 *tr* to instruct; to train; (law) to draw up, prepare (*a case*) || *ref* to learn

istruí·to -ta *adj* learned, educated

istruménto *m* (law) instrument

istrutti·vo -va *adj* instructive

istrut·tóre -trice *mf* instructor; (sports) coach

istruttò·rio -ria (-ri -rie) *adj* investigating, preliminary || *f* (law) preliminary investigation

istruzióne *f* instruction; (law) prelimi-

nary investigation; **istruzioni** instructions; directions

istupidire §176 *tr* to make dull; to stupefy

Itàlia, l' *f* Italy

italia·no -na *adj & mf* Italian

itàli·co -ca *adj* **(-ci -che)** italic; Italic; (lit) Italian || *m* italics

italòfo·no -na *adj* Italian-speaking || *m* Italian-speaking person

itinerante *adj* itinerant

itinerà·rio *m* **(-ri)** itinerary

ittèri·co -ca *adj* **(-ci -che)** jaundiced

itterizia *f* jaundice

ittiologìa *f* ichthiology

Iugoslàvia, la Yugoslavia

iugosla·vo -va *adj & mf* Yugoslav

iugulare *adj & tr* var of **giugulare**

iuta *f* jute

ivi *adv* (lit) there

J
K
L

L, l ['ɛlle] *m & f* tenth letter of the Italian alphabet

la §4 *def art* the || *m* (mus) la, A; **dare il la** to set the tone || §5 *pers pron*

là *adv* there; **al di là da venire** to come, future; **al di là (di)** beyond; **andare di là** to go in the next room; **andare troppo in là** to go too far; **farsi in là** to move aside; **in là con gli anni** advanced in years; **l'al di là** the life beyond; **più in là** further; **più in là di** beyond; **va' là!** come on!

lab·bro *m* **(-bri)** edge (*of wound*); (lit) lip || *m* **(-bra** *fpl*) lip; **labbro leporino** harelip

labiale *adj & f* labial

làbile *adj* (coll) weak; (lit) fleeting

labiolettura *f* lip reading

labirinto *m* labyrinth, maze

laboratò·rio *m* **(-ri)** laboratory; workshop; **laboratorio linguistico** language laboratory

laborió·so -sa [*s*] *adj* hard-working, laborious; labored (*e.g., digestion*)

laburi·sta (-sti -ste) *adj* Labour || *mf* Labourite

lac·ca *f* (-che) lacquer

laccare §197 *tr* to lacquer; to japan; to polish (*nails*)

lac·chè *m* (-chè) lackey

lac·cio *m* (-ci) lasso; snare; noose; string; (fig) bond; **laccio delle scarpe** shoelace; **laccio emostatico** tourniquet

lacciòlo *m* snare

lacerare (làcero) *tr* to lacerate; to tear || *ref* to tear

làce·ro -ra *adj* torn; tattered

lacèrto *m* (lit) shred of flesh; (lit) biceps

lacòni·co -ca *adj* **(-ci -che)** laconic

làcrima *f* tear; drop

lacrimare (làcrimo) *tr* (lit) to weep

over || *intr* to water (*said of the eyes*); (lit) to weep

lacrima·to -ta *adj* (lit) lamented

lacrimévole *adj* pitiful

lacrimòge·no -na *adj* tear (*e.g., gas*)

lacrimó·so -sa [*s*] *adj* teary, watery (*eyes*); tearful; lachrymose

lacuna *f* gap, lacuna; blank (*in one's mind*); **colmare una lacuna** to bridge a gap

lacustre *adj* lake

laddóve *conj* while, whereas

ladré·sco -sca *adj* **(-schi -sche)** thievish

la·dro -dra *adj* thieving; foul (*weather*); bewitching (*eyes*) || *mf* thief; **ladro di strada** highwayman || *f* inside pocket (*of suit*)

ladróne *m* thief; highwayman; **ladrone di mare** pirate

ladrùncolo *m* petty thief, pilferer

laggiù *adv* down there

lagnanza *f* complaint

lagnare *ref* to complain; to moan

lagno *m* complaint, lament

la·go *m* (-ghi) lake; pool (*of blood*)

làgrima *f* var of **lacrima**

laguna *f* lagoon

lai *m* (lai) lay; **lai** *mpl* (lit) lamentations

laicato *m* laity

lài·co -ca *adj* **(-ci -che)** *adj* lay || *m* layman

làido -da *adj* foul; obscene

la·ma *m* (-ma) llama; lama || *f* (-me) blade (*of knife*); marsh; (lit) lowland

lambiccare §197 *tr* to distill || *ref* to strive; **lambiccarsi il cervello** to rack one's brains

lambi·co *m* (-chi) still

lambire §176 *tr* to lap; to graze, to touch lightly

lamèlla *f* thin sheet

lamentare (laménto) *tr* to bemoan, lament || *ref* to moan; to complain

lamentazióne *f* lamentation

lamentévole adj plaintive; lamentable

laménto m complaint, lament; moan

lamentó·so -sa [s] adj plaintive, doleful

lamétta f razor blade

lamièra f plate; armor plate

lamierino m sheet metal, lamina

làmina f sheet, lamina

laminare (làmino) tr to laminate; **to roll** (steel)

lamina·tóio m (-tói) rolling mill

làmpada f lamp, light; **lampada al neon** neon lamp; **lampada a petrolio** oil lamp; **lampada a stelo** pole lamp; **lampada di sicurezza** (min) safety lamp; **lampada fluorescente** fluorescent lamp; **lampada lampo** (phot) flash bulb

lampadà·rio m (-ri) chandelier

lampadina f bulb; **lampadina tascabile** flashlight

lampante adj shiny; clear; lamp (oil)

lampeggiare §290 (lampéggio) tr (lit) to flash (a smile) || intr to flash; (aut) to blink; (coll) to flash the turn signals || impers (ESSERE & AVERE)— **lampeggia** it lightens, it is lightning

lampeggiatóre m (aut) turn signal; (phot) flashlight

lampio·nàio m (-nài) lamplighter

lampióne m street lamp

lampìride f glowworm

lampo m lightning; flash of lightning; (fig) flash

lampóne m raspberry

lana f wool; **buona lana** (coll) rogue, rascal; **lana d'acciaio** steel wool; **lana di vetro** fiberglass, glass wool

lancétta f lancet; hand (of watch); pointer (of instrument)

làn·cia f (-ce) lance, spear; nozzle (of fire hose); launch; **lancia di salvataggio** lifeboat

lanciabóm·be m (-be) trench mortar

lanciafiam·me m (-me) flamethrower

lanciamìssi·li (-li) adj missile-launching || m missile launcher

lanciaraz·zi [ddzz] m (-zi) rocket launcher

lanciare §128 tr to throw, hurl; to drop (from an airplane); to launch (e.g., an advertising campaign) || ref to hurl oneself; (rok) to blast off; **lanciarsi col paracadute** to parachute, bail out

lanciasilu·ri m (-ri) torpedo tube

lancia·to -ta adj hurled, flung; flying, e.g., **partenza lanciata** flying start

lancia·tóre -trice mf hurler, thrower; (baseball) pitcher

lancière m lancer

lancinante adj piercing

làn·cio m (-ci) throw; publicity campaign; (aer) drop; (aer) release (of bombs); (baseball) pitch; (rok) launch; **lancio del peso** shot put

landa f moor; wasteland

lanerìe fpl woolens

languidézza f languidness, languor

làngui·do -da adj languid; sad (eyes)

languire (lànguo) & §176 intr to languish

languóre m languor; languishing; weakness; tenderness

laniè·ro -ra adj wool (industry)

lanifì·cio m (-ci) woolen mill

lanó·so -sa [s] adj woolly; **kinky** (hair); bushy (face)

lantèrna f lantern

lanùgine f down

lanzichenéc·co m (-chi) landsknecht

laónde conj (lit) wherefore

laotia·no -na adj & mf Laotian

lapalissia·no -na adj self-evident

lapidare (làpido) tr to stone (to death); (fig) to pick to pieces

làpide f stone tablet; tombstone

lapillo m lapillus

là·pis m (-pis) pencil

lappare intr to lap

làppola f (bot) burdock; (bot) bur

lappóne adj Lappish || mf Lapp || m Lapp (language)

Lappónia, la Lapland

lardellare (lardèllo) tr to lard; to stuff with bacon

lardo m lard; **nuotare nel lardo** to live on easy street

largheggiare §290 (larghéggio) intr to be liberal; to be lavish

larghézza f width; liberality; abundance; **larghezza di vedute** broadmindedness

largire §176 tr (lit) to bestow liberally

largizióne f bestowal; donation

lar·go -ga (-ghi -ghe) adj broad, wide; ample; liberal; abundant; (phonet) open; **prenderla larga** to keep away || m width; open sea; square; (mus) largo; **al largo di** (naut) off; **fare largo a** to open the way to; **farsi largo** to elbow one's way; **prendere il largo** to run away; (naut) to put to sea; **tenersi al largo** to keep at a distance || f—**alla larga!** keep away! || **largo** adv—**girare largo** to keep away

làrice m larch

laringe f larynx

laringite f laryngitis

laringoia·tra mf (-tri -tre) laryngologist

laringoscò·pio m (-pi) laryngoscope

larva f (ent) larva; (lit) ghost; (lit) skeleton; (lit) sham

lasagne fpl lasagne

lasciapassa·re m (-re) safe-conduct; permit

lasciare §128 tr to leave; to let; to let go of; **lasciar cadere** to drop; **lasciarci le penne** (coll) to die; (coll) to be skinned alive; **lasciar correre** to let go; **lasciar detto** to leave word; **lasciar fare** to leave alone; **lasciare in pace** to leave alone; **lasciare libero** to let go; **lasciare scritto** to leave in writing || ref to abandon oneself; to abandon one another

làscito m (law) bequest

lascivia f lasciviousness

lascì·vo -va adj lascivious

lassatì·vo -va adj mildly laxative || m mild laxative

lassismo m laxity

las·so -sa adj lax || m lasso; **lasso di tempo** period of time

lassù adv up there, up above

lastra f slab; paving stone; (phot)

plate; exposed X-ray film; **farsi le lastre** (coll) to be X-rayed

lastricare §197 (làstrico) *tr* to pave

lastricato *m* paving, pavement

làstri·co *m* (**-ci** or **-chi**) pavement; roadway; **ridursi sul lastrico** to fall into abject poverty

lastróne *m* slab; plate glass

latènte *adj* latent

laterale *adj* lateral || *m* (soccer) halfback

lateri·zio -zia (**-zì -zie**) *adj* brick || **laterizi** *mpl* bricks, tiles

làtice *m* latex

latifondi·sta *mf* (**-sti -ste**) rich landowner

latifóndo *m* large landed estate

lati·no -na *adj* Latin; lateen (*sail*) || *m* Latin

latitante *adj* hiding || *mf* fugitive

latitanza *f* flight from justice

latitùdine *f* latitude

la·to -ta *adj* wide; broad (*meaning*) || *m* side; **d'altro lato** on the other hand

la·tóre -trice *mf* bearer

latrare *intr* to bark

latrato *m* bark

latrina *f* toilet, lavatory, washroom

latta *f* tin; can

lattàia *f* milkmaid

lat·tàio *m* (**-tài**) milkman, dairyman

lattante *adj* & *m* suckling

latte *m* milk; **latte detergente** cleansing cream; **latte di gallina** flip; (bot) star-of-Bethlehem; **latte in polvere** powdered milk; **latte magro** or **scremato** skim milk

lattemièle *m* whipped cream

làtte·o -a *adj* milky

latterìa *f* dairy; creamery

làttice *m* var of **latice**

latticèllo *m* buttermilk

lattìci·nio *m* (**-ni**) dairy product

lattiginó·so -sa [*s*] *adj* milky

lattonière *m* tinsmith

lattu·ga *f* (**-ghe**) lettuce; head of lettuce; frill

làudano *m* paregoric, laudanum

laudati·vo -va *adj* laudatory

làurea *f* wreath; doctorate; doctoral examination

laureàn·do -da *mf* candidate for the doctorate

laureare (làureo) *tr* to confer the doctorate on; to award (*s.o.*) the title of; (lit) to wreathe || *ref* to receive the doctorate; (sports) to get the tile of

laurea·to -ta *adj* laureate || *m* alumnus, graduate

làuro *m* laurel

làu·to -ta *adj* sumptuous, rich

lava *f* lava

lavabianche·rìa *f* (**-rìa**) washing machine

lavàbile *adj* washable

lavabo *m* washstand; lavatory

lavacristallo *m* windshield washer

lavacro *m* washing; font; purification; **santo lavacro** baptism

lavàg·gio *m* (**-gi**) washing; **lavaggio a secco** dry cleaning; **lavaggio del cervello** brainwashing

lavagna *f* slate; blackboard; **lavagna di panno** felt board; **lavagna luminosa** overhead projector

lavama·no *m* (**-no**) washstand

lavanda *f* washing; pumping (*of stomach*); lavender

lavandàia *f* laundrywoman; **lavandaia stiratrice** laundress (*woman who washes and irons*)

lavan·dàio *m* (**-dài**) laundryman; **lavandaio stiratore** launderer

lavanderìa *f* laundry; **lavanderia a gettone** laundromat; **lavanderia a secco** dry-cleaning establishment

lavandino *m* sink

lavapiat·ti *mf* (**-ti**) dishwasher (*person*)

lavare *tr* to wash; to cleanse; **lavare a secco** to dry-clean; **lavare il capo a** to scold || *ref* to wash oneself; **lavarsi le mani** to wash one's hands

lavastovì·glie *mf* (**-glie**) dishwasher || *m & f* dishwasher (*machine*)

lavata *f* washing; **lavata di capo** scolding

lavativo *m* (coll) enema; (coll) bore; (coll) goldbricker

lava·tóio *m* (**-tói**) laundry room; washtub

lava·tóre -trice *mf* washer || *m* washerman; (mach) purifier || *f* washerwoman; washing machine

lavatura *f* washing; **lavatura a secco** dry cleaning; **lavatura di piatti** dishwater; washing of dishes; (fig) watery soup

lavèllo *m* wash basin; sink

lavoràbile *adj* workable

lavorante *mf* helper, apprentice

lavorare (lavóro) *tr* to work; to till || *intr* to work; to perform; to be busy; to trade; **lavorare ai ferri** to knit; **lavorare di fantasia** to daydream; **lavorare di ganasce** to eat voraciously; **lavorare di gomiti** to elbow one's way; **lavorare di mano** to pilfer; **lavorare di traforo** to work with a jig saw

lavorati·vo -va *adj* working; workable

lavora·to -ta *adj* wrought; tilled

lavora·tóre -trice *mf* worker || *m* workman; workingman || *f* workingwoman

lavorazióne *f* working; manufacturing; tilling

lavorì·o *m* (**-ì**) bustle; steady work; scheming

lavóro *m* work; labor; steady work; homework; piece of work; (coll) trouble; **a lavori ultimati** when the work is finished; **lavori forzati** hard labor; **lavori in economia** time and material contract work; **lavori teatrali** theatrical productions; **lavoro a cottimo** piecework; **lavoro a maglia** knitting; **lavoro di cucito** needlework; **mettere al lavoro** to press into service

lazzarétto [*ddzz*] *m* lazaretto

lazzaróne [*ddzz*] *m* cad; (coll) goldbricker

le §4 *def art* the || **§5** *pers pron*

leale *adj* loyal; sincere

leali·sta *mf* (**-sti -ste**) loyalist

leal·tà *f* (**-tà**) loyalty; sincerity

lébbra *f* leprosy

lebbró·so -sa [s] *adj* leprous || *mf* leper

lécca-léc·ca *m* (**-ca**) (coll) lollypop

leccapiat·ti *m* (**-ti**) glutton; sponger

leccapiè·di *mf* (**-di**) bootlicker

leccarda *f* dripping pan

leccare §197 (**lécco**) *tr* to lick; to fawn on; (fig) to polish || *ref* to make oneself up

lecca·to -ta *adj* affected; polished || *f* licking

léc·cio *m* (**-ci**) holm oak

leccornìa *f* dainty morsel, delicacy

léci·to -ta *adj* licit, permissible; **mi sia lecito** may I || *m* right

lèdere §192 *tr* to damage, injure

lé·ga *f* (**-ghe**) league; alloy; **di bassa lega** poor, in poor taste; **fare lega** to unite

legale *adj* legal; lawyer's; official || *m* lawyer

legali·tà *f* (**-tà**) legality, lawfulness

legalità·rio -ria *adj* (**-ri -rie**) (pol) observing the rule of law

legalizzare [ddzz] *tr* to legalize; to authenticate

legame *m* bond; connection; relationship

legaménto *m* tie, bond; ligament; (phonet) liaison

legare §209 (**légo**) *tr* to tie; to bind; to unite; to set (*a stone*); to bequeath; to alloy; (bb) to bind || *intr* to bond; to mix (*said of metals*); to go together || *ref* to unite; **legàrsela al dito** to never forget

legatà·rio -ria *mf* (**-ri -rie**) legatee

lega·to -ta *adj* muscle-bound || *m* legate; bequest; (mus) legato

lega·tóre -trice *mf* bookbinder

legatorìa *f* bookbindery

legatura *f* typing; binding; ligature; bookbinding; (mus) tie

legazióne *f* legation

légge *f* law; act; **dettar legge** to lay down the law; **è fuori della legge** he is an outlaw; **legge stralcio** emergency law

leggènda *f* legend; story, tall tale; (journ) caption

leggendà·rio -ria *adj* (**-ri -rie**) legendary

lèggere §193 *tr, intr & ref* to read

leggerézza *f* lightness; nimbleness; thoughtlessness; fickleness

leggè·ro -ra *adj* light; nimble; thoughtless; slight; fickle; **alla leggera** lightly || **leggero** *adv* lightly

leggia·dro -dra *adj* graceful, lovely

leggìbile *adj* legible, readable

leggì·o *m* (**-i**) lectern; music stand

legiferare (**legìfero**) *intr* to legislate

legionà·rio -ria *adj & m* (**-ri -rie**) legionary

legióne *f* legion

legislati·vo -va *adj* legislative

legisla·tóre -trice *mf* legislator

legislatura *f* legislature

legittimare (**legìttimo**) *tr* to legitimize

legittimi·tà *f* (**-tà**) legitimacy

legìtti·mo -ma *adj* legitimate; pure; just, right || *f* (law) legitim

lé·gna *f* (**-gna & -gne**) firewood; (fig) fuel

legnàia *f* woodpile; woodshed

legname *m* timber, lumber

legnata *f* clubbing, thrashing

légno *m* wood; stick; ship; coach; timber; **legno compensato** plywood; **legno dolce** softwood; **legno forte** hardwood

legnòlo *m* ply (*e.g., of a cable*)

legnó·so -sa [s] *adj* wooden; tough (*meat*); dry (*style*)

legu·lèio *m* (**-lèi**) pettifogger

legume *m* legume; **legumi** vegetables; legumes

leguminósa [s] *f* leguminous plant; **leguminose** legumes

lèi §5 *pron pers;* **dare del Lei a** to address formally

lémbo *m* edge, border; patch (*of land*)

lèm·ma *m* (**-mi**) entry (*in a dictionary*)

lèmme lèmme *adv* (coll) slowly

léna *f* energy; enthusiasm; (lit) breath

lèndine *m* nit

lène *adj* (lit) light, soft, gentle; (phonet) voiced

lenire §176 *tr* to soothe, assuage

lenóne *m* panderer, procurer

lenóna *f* procuress

lènte *f* lens; bob, pendulum bob; **lente d'ingrandimento** magnifying glass; **lenti** glasses

lentézza *f* slowness

lentìcchia *f* lentil

lentìggine *f* freckle

lentiginó·so -sa [s] *adj* freckly

lèn·to -ta *adj* slow; slack; (lit) loose (*hair*); (lit) loose-fitting (*garment*) || **lento** *adv* slowly

lènza *f* fishline

lenzuò·lo *m* (**-li**) sheet; (fig) blanket; **lenzuolo a due piazze** double sheet; **lenzuolo funebre** winding sheet, shroud || *m* (**-la** *fpl*) sheet; **lenzuola** pair of sheets (*in a bed*)

leoncino *m* lion cub

leóne *m* lion; **leone d'America** cougar; **leone marino** sea lion || **Leone** *m* (astr) Leo

leonéssa *f* lioness

leopardo *m* leopard

lepidézza *f* wit; witticism

lèpi·do -da *adj* witty, facetious

lepisma *f* (ent) silverfish

lèpre *adj invar* rendezvous, e.g., **razzo lepre** rendezvous rocket || *f* hare

lepròtto *m* leveret, young hare

lèr·cio -cia *adj* (**-ci -ce**) filthy

lerciume *m* filth, dirt

lèsbi·co -ca (**-ci -che**) *adj & mf* Lesbian || *f* Lesbian (*female homosexual*)

lésina *f* awl; stinginess; miser

lesinare (**lésino & lèsino**) *tr* to begrudge || *intr* to be miserly

lesionare (**lesióno**) *tr* to damage; to crack open

lesióne *f* damage; injury; lesion

lé·so -sa *adj* damaged; injured

lessare (**lésso**) *tr* to boil

lessicale *adj* lexical

lèssi·co *m* (**-ci**) lexicon

lessicografìa *f* lexicography

lessicogràfi·co -ca *adj* (**-ci -che**) lexicographic(al)

lessicògrafo *m* lexicographer

lessicologìa f lexicology
lés·so -sa adj boiled ‖ m boiled meat; soup meat
lè·sto -sta adj swift; nimble; quick; **alla lesta** hastily; **lesto di lingua** ready-tongued; **lesto di mano** light-fingered
lestofante m swindler
letale adj lethal, deadly
leta·màio m (**-mài**) dunghill
letame m manure, dung
letàrgi·co -ca adj (**-ci -che**) lethargic
letar·go m (**-ghi**) lethargy; hibernation
letìzia f happiness, joy
lèttera f letter; **alla lettera** literally; **lettera morta** unheeded, e.g., **le sue parole rimasero lettera morta** his words remained unheeded; **lettere credenziali** credentials; **scrivere in tutte lettere** to spell out
letterale adj literal
letterà·rio -ria adj (**-ri -rie**) literary; learned (word)
lettera·to -ta adj literary; literate ‖ m man of letters; (coll) literate, learned person
letteratura f literature
lettièra f litter, bedding
letti·ga f (**-ghe**) sedan chair; stretcher
lètto m bed; bedding; **di primo letto** born of the first marriage; **letti gemelli** twin beds; **letto a castello** bunk bed; **letto a due piazze** double bed; **letto a scomparsa** Murphy bed; **letto a una piazza** single bed; **letto bastardo** oversize bed; **letto caldo** hotbed; **letto di morte** deathbed; **letto operatorio** operating table
lèttone or **lettóne** adj Lettish ‖ mf Lett ‖ m Lett, Lettish (language)
Lettónia, La Latvia
let·tóre -trice mf reader; lecturer; meter reader ‖ m reader (e.g., for microfilm); **lettore perforatore** reader (of punch cards)
lettura f reading; lecture; **lettura del pensiero** mind reading
letturi·sta m (**-sti**) meter reader
leucemìa f leukemia
leucorrèa f leucorrhea
lèva f lever; (mil) draft; (mil) class; **essere di leva** to be of draft age; **fare leva su** to use (s.o.'s emotions)
levachio·di m (**-di**) claw hammer
levante adj rising ‖ m east; Levant
levanti·no -na adj & mf Levantine
levare (**lèvo**) tr to lift, raise; to weigh (anchor); to pull (a tooth); to break (camp); to collect (mail); to remove, take away; to subtract; **levare alle stelle** to praise to the sky; **levare il disturbo a** to take leave of ‖ ref to arise; to get up; to take off; to satisfy (e.g., one's hunger); to rise (said of wind); **levarsi dai piedi** to get out of the way; **levarsi dai piedi** or **di mezzo qlcu** to get rid of s.o.
levata f rise; reveille; collection (of mail); withdrawal (of merchandise from warehouse); **levata di scudi** uprising
levatàc·cia f (**-ce**) getting up at an im-

possible hour; **ho dovuto fare una levataccia** I had to get up way too early
leva·tóio -tóia adj (**-tói -tóie**)—**ponte levatoio** drawbridge
levatrice f midwife
levatura f intellectual breadth
leviatano m leviathan
levigare §209 (**lèvigo**) tr to polish
levigatrice f sander; buffer
levi·tà f (**-tà**) (lit) levity
levitazióne f levitation
levrière m greyhound
lezióne f lesson; lecture; reading
lezió·so -sa [s] adj affected, mincing
lézzo [ddzz] m stench; filth
lì def art masc plur (obs) the; **lì tre novembre** the third of November (in official documents) ‖ §5 pers pron
lì adv there; **di lì** that way; **di lì a un anno** a year hence; **essere lì lì per** to be about to; **fin lì** up to that point; **giù di lì** more or less; **lì per lì** on the spot
libanése [s] adj & mf Lebanese
Lìbano, il Lebanon
libare tr to toast; to taste ‖ intr to toast
libazióne f libation
lìbbra f pound
libéc·cio m (**-ci**) southwest wind
libèllo m libel; (law) brief
libèllula f dragonfly
liberale adj & m liberal
liberali·tà f (**-tà**) liberality
liberare (**lìbero**) tr to free; to pay in full for; to open into (said, e.g., of a hall opening into a room); to clear, empty (a room) ‖ ref—**liberarsi da** or **di** to get rid of
libera·tóre -trice adj liberating ‖ mf liberator
liberismo m free trade
lìbe·ro -ra adj free; vacant; without a revenue stamp (document); open (syllable; heart); outspoken
liber·tà f (**-tà**) freedom; release (e.g., from mortgage); **libertà provvisoria** bail, parole; **libertà vigilata** probation; **mettersi in libertà** to put comfortable house clothes on; **rimettere in libertà** to set free
liberti·no -na adj & mf libertine
Lìbia, la Libya
lìbi·co -ca adj & mf (**-ci -che**) Libyan
libìdine f lust; desire
libidinó·so -sa [s] adj lustful
libido f libido
li·bràio m (**-brài**) bookseller
librare ref to balance; to soar; (aer) to glide
libratóre m (aer) glider
librerìa f bookstore; library (room); bookshelf; book collection
libré·sco -sca adj (**-schi -sche**) bookish
librétto m booklet; card; (mus) libretto; **libretto di banca** passbook; **libretto degli assegni** checkbook; **libretto di circolazione** car registration; **libretto ferroviario** railroad pass; **libretto di risparmio** passbook (of savings bank)
libro m book; ledger; register (e.g., of births); **a libro** folding; **libro di**

bordo log; **libro in brossura** paperback; **libro mastro** ledger; **libro paga** (com) payroll

liceale adj high-school || mf high-school student

licènza f permit; license; diploma; (mil) leave; **con licenza parlando!** excuse my language!; **dar licenza a** to dismiss; **prender licenza da** to take leave of

licenziaménto m dismissal; **licenziamento in tronco** firing on the spot

licenziare §287 (licènzio) tr to dismiss; to O.K. (a book to be published); to graduate || ref to take leave; to give notice, resign; to graduate

licenzió·so -sa [s] adj licentious

licèo m high school; lycée

lichène m lichen

licitazióne f auction; (bridge) bidding

lido m shore; sand bar

liè·to -ta adj glad; blessed (event)

lième adj light; slight

lievitare (lièvito) tr to leaven || intr (ESSERE & AVERE) to rise; to ferment

lièvito m yeast; leaven; **lievito in polvere** baking powder

li·gio -gia adj (-gi -gie) devoted

lignàg·gio m (-gi) ancestry, lineage

ligustro m privet

lil·la (-la) adj invar & m lilac

lillipuzià·no -na adj & mf Lilliputian

lima f file; **lima per le unghie** nail file

limacció·so -sa [s] adj miry, muddy

limare tr to file; to polish (e.g., a speech); to gnaw, plague

limatura f filing; filings

limbo m (lit) edge; (fig) limbo || **Limbo** m (theol) Limbo

limétta f nail file; (bot) lime

limitare m threshold || v (lìmito) tr to limit; to bound

limitazióne f limitation

limite m limit; boundary; check; (soccer) penalty line; **limite di carico massimo** maximum weight; **limite di età retirement** age; **limite di velocità** speed limit; **senza limiti** limitless

limìtro·fo -fa adj neighboring (country)

limo m mud, mire

limonare (limóno) intr (coll) to spoon

limonata f lemonade; (med) citrate of magnesia

limóne m lemon tree; lemon

limó·so -sa [s] adj slimy

límpi·do -da adj limpid, clear

lince f lynx, wildcat

linciàg·gio m (-gi) lynching

linciare §128 tr to lynch

lin·do -da adj neat; clean

lìnea f line; degree (of temperature); **conservare la linea** to keep one's figure; **in linea** abreast; (telp) connected; **in linea d'aria** as the crow flies; **linea del fuoco** firing line; **linea del cambiamento di data** international date line; **linea di circonvallazione** (rr) beltline; **linea di condotta** policy; **linea di partenza** starting line; **linea laterale** (sports) side line

lineaménti mpl lineaments; elements

lineare adj linear || v (lìneo) tr to delineate

lineétta f dash; hyphen

linfa f (anat) lymph; (bot) sap; **dar linfa** (bot) to bleed

lingòtto m (metallurgy) pig, ingot; **lingotto d'oro** bullion

lingua f tongue; language; strip (of land); **essere di due lingue** to speak with a forked tongue; **in lingua** in the correct language; **lingua di gatto** ladyfinger; **lingua lunga** backbiter; **lingua sciolta** glib tongue; **mala lingua** wicked tongue

linguacciu·to -ta adj talkative; sharp-tongued

linguàg·gio m (-gi) language

linguèlla f (philately) gummed strip

linguétta f tongue (of shoe); (mach) pin; (mus) reed

linguìsti·co -ca (-ci -che) adj linguistic || f linguistics

linifì·cio m (-ci) flax-spinning mill

liniménto m liniment

lino m flax; linen

linósa [s] f flaxseed, linseed

linotipì·sta mf (-sti -ste) linotypist

liocòrno m unicorn

liofilizzare [ddzz] tr to freeze-dry

liquefare §194 tr & ref to liquefy

liquefazióne f liquefaction

liquidare (lìquido) tr to liquidate; to close out; to dismiss; to settle

liquidazióne f liquidation; clearance; **liquidazione del danno** (ins) adjustment

liquidità f liquidity

lìqui·do -da adj liquid; (com) due || m liquid; cash || f liquid

liqui·gàs m (-gàs) liquid gas

liquirìzia f licorice

liquóre m liqueur; (pharm) liquor

liquorì·sta mf (-sti -ste) liqueur manufacturer or dealer

lira f lira; pound; (mus) lyre || **Lira** f (astr) Lyra

lìri·co -ca (-ci -che) adj lyric; (mus) operatic || m lyric poet || f lyric; lyric poetry; opera

lirismo m lyricism

Lisbóna f Lisbon

li·sca f (-sche) fishbone; lisp

lisciare §128 tr to smooth; **lisciare il pelo a** to butter up, flatter; to beat up || ref to preen

li·scio -scia adj (-sci -sce) smooth; straight (drink); black (coffee); **passarla liscia** to get away scot-free

liscìvia f lye; bleach

lisciviatrice f washing machine

lì·so -sa adj worn-out, threadbare

lista f list; strip, band; stripe; **lista delle spese** shopping list; **lista delle vivande** bill of fare; **lista elettorale** slate (of candidates)

listare tr to border; to stripe

listèllo m lath; (archit) listel

listino m price list; market quotation

litanìa f litany

lite f quarrel; lawsuit

litigante adj quarreling || mf quarreler; (law) litigant

litigare §209 (lìtigo) *tr*—**litigare qlco a qlcu** to fight with s.o. for s.th || *intr* to quarrel; to litigate || *ref*—**litigarsi qlco** to strive for s.th
litì·gio *m* (-gi) quarrel, litigation
litigió·so -sa [s] *adj* quarrelsome
litio *m* lithium
litografia *f* lithography
litògrafo *m* lithographer
litorale *adj* littoral || *m* seashore, coastline
litro *m* liter
Lituània, la Lithuania
litua·no -na *adj & mf* Lithuanian || *m* Lithuanian (*language*)
liturgìa *f* liturgy
litùrgi·co -ca *adj* (-ci -che) liturgical
liu·tàio *m* (-tài) lute maker
liuto *m* lute
livèlla *f* level; **livella a bolla d'aria** spirit level
livellaménto *m* leveling; equalization
livellare (livèllo) *tr* to level; to equalize; to survey || *intr* (ESSERE) & *ref* to become level
livella·tóre -trice *adj* leveling || *mf* surveyor || *f* bulldozer
livellazióne *f* leveling
livèllo *m* level; **livello delle acque** sea level
lìvi·do -da *adj* livid, black-and-blue || *m* bruise
lividóre *m* bruise
livóre *m* grudge; hatred
Livórno *f* Leghorn
livrèa *f* livery
lizza *f* tilting ground; **entrare in lizza** to enter the lists
lo §4 *def art* the || §5 *pers pron*
lòb·bia *m & f* (-bia *mpl & fpl*) homburg
lòbo *m* lobe
locale *adj* local || *m* room; place (*of business*); (naut) compartment; **locale notturno** night spot
locali·tà *f* (-tà) locality, spot
localizzare [ddzz] *tr* to localize; to locate || *ref* to become localized
localizzazióne [ddzz] *f* localization; **localizzazione dei guasti** troubleshooting
locanda *f* inn
locandiè·re -ra *mf* innkeeper
locandina *f* playbill; flyer; small poster
locare §197 (lòco) *tr* to rent, lease
locatà·rio -ria *mf* (-ri -rie) lessee, renter
loca·tóre -trice *mf* lessor
locazióne *f* rent; lease; **dare in locazione** to rent
locomotiva *f* locomotive, engine
locomo·tóre -trice *adj* locomotive || *m & f* (rr) electric locomotive
locomotori·sta *m* (-sti) (rr) engineer
locomozióne *f* locomotion; transportation
lòculo *m* burial niche
locusta *f* locust
locuzióne *f* locution, expression; phrase; idiom
lodàbile *adj* praiseworthy
lodare (lòdo) *tr* to praise || *ref* to praise oneself, brag; **lodarsi di** (poet) to be pleased with

lodatì·vo -va *adj* laudatory
lòde *f* praise; **con la lode** cum laude; **con lode** plus (*on a report card*)
lodévole *adj* praiseworthy, commendable
lòdo *m* arbitration
logaritmo *m* logarithm
lòg·gia *f* (-ge) lodge; (archit) loggia
loggióne *m* (theat) upper gallery
lògi·co -ca (-ci -che) *adj* logical; **esser logico** to think logically || *m* logician || *f* logic
logìsti·co -ca (-ci -che) *adj* logistic || *f* logistics
lò·glio *m* (-gli) cockle
logoraménto *m* wear; attrition
logorare (lógoro) *tr* to wear out; to fray || *ref* to wear away; to become threadbare
logorì·o *m* (-i) wear and tear
lógo·ro -ra *adj* worn out; threadbare
lòlla *f* chaff
lombàggine *f* lumbago
lombar·do -da *adj & mf* Lombard
lombata *f* loin, sirloin
lómbo *m* loin; hip; (lit) ancestry
lombrì·co *m* (-chi) earthworm
londinése [s] *adj* London || *mf* Londoner
Londra *f* London
longànime *adj* patient, forbearing
longanimi·tà *f* (-tà) patience, forbearance
longevità *f* longevity
longè·vo -va *adj* long-lived
longherina *f* beam, girder
longheróne *m* (aer) longeron; (aer) spar; (aut) main frame member
longitùdine *f* longitude
longobar·do -da *adj & mf* Lombard
lontananza *f* distance
lonta·no -na *adj* distant, remote; vague; indirect || *m* (lit) far-away place || *f*—**alla lontana** from a distance; vaguely; distant (*e.g., relative*) || **lontano** *adv* far; **da lontano** from afar; **lontano da** away from; far from; **rifarsi da lontano** to start from the very beginning
lóntra *f* otter
lónza *f* pork loin; (poet) leopard
lòppa *f* chaff; skin (*of plant*); slag, dross
loquace *adj* loquacious; (fig) eloquent
loquèla *f* (lit) tongue; (lit) style
lordare (lórdo) *tr* to soil, dirty
lór·do -da *adj* soiled, dirty; gross (*weight*)
lordume *m* dirt, filth
lordura *f* dirt, filth; soil
lóro §5 *pron pers* || §6 *adj poss & pron*
losan·ga *f* (-ghe) rhombus; (herald) lozenge
lò·sco -sca *adj* (-schi -sche) squint-eyed; cross-eyed; (fig) shady
lóto *m* mud
lòto *m* lotus
lòtta *f* fight; struggle; wrestling; **essere in lotta** to be at war; **lotta libera** catch-as-catch-can
lottare (lòtto) *intr* to fight; to quarrel; to struggle; to wrestle

lotta·tóre -trice *mf* fighter; wrestler
lotterìa *f* lottery
lottizzare [ddzz] *tr* to divide into lots
lòtto *m* lotto; parcel, lot
lozióne *f* lotion
lùbri·co -ca *adj* (**-ci -che**) lewd; (lit) slippery
lubrificante *adj* & *m* lubricant
lubrificare §197 (**lubrìfico**) *tr* to lubricate
lucchétto *m* padlock
luccicare §197 (**lùccico**) *intr* to sparkle; to shine
luccichì·o *m* (**-i**) glittering; shining; sparkle
luccicóne *m* big tear
lùc·cio *m* (**-ci**) pike
lùcciola *f* firefly; usherette (*in movie*); **prendere lucciole per lanterne** to make a blunder; to be seeing things
luce *f* light; sunlight; opening; glass (*of mirror*); leaf (*e.g., of door*); (archit) span; (coll) electricity; **alla luce del sole** in plain view; **fare luce** to shed light; **luce degli occhi** eyesight; **luce del giorno** daylight; **luce della luna** moonlight; **luce di arresto** (aut) stoplight; **luce di incrocio** (aut) dimmer, low beam; **luce di posizione** (aut) parking light; **luce di profondità** (aut) high beam; **luci** (poet) eyes; **luci della ribalta** (fig) stage, boards; **mettere alla luce** to give birth to; **mettere in luce** to reveal; to publish; **venire alla luce** to be born; to come to light
lucènte *adj* shiny, shining
lucentézza *f* brightness; sheen
lucèrna *f* lamp; light; **lucerne** (lit) eyes ‖ **Lucerna** *f* Lucerne
lucernà·rio *m* (**-ri**) skylight
lucèrtola *f* lizard
lucherino *m* (orn) siskin
Lucìa *f* Lucy
lucidare (**lùcido**) *tr* to shine, polish; to trace (*a figure*)
lucida·tóre -trice *mf* polisher (*person*) ‖ *f* (mach) floor polisher
lucidatura *f* polish; tracing (*on paper*)
lucidi·tà *f* (**-tà**) polish; lucidity
lùci·do -da *adj* bright; lucid ‖ *m* shine; tracing; **lucido per le scarpe** shoe polish
lucìfe·ro -ra *adj* (poet) light-bringing ‖ **Lucifero** *m* Lucifer, morning star
lucìgnolo *m* wick
lucrare *tr* to win, acquire
lucrati·vo -va *adj* lucrative
lucro *m* gain, earnings, lucre; **lucro cessante** (law) loss of earnings
lucró·so -sa [s] *adj* lucrative
ludì·brio *m* (**-bri**) mockery; laughingstock
lù·glio *m* (**-gli**) July
lùgubre *adj* gloomy, dismal
lui §5 *pron pers*
luigi *m* louis ‖ **Luigi** *m* Louis
luma·ca *f* (**-che**) snail
lume *m* light; lamp; **lume degli occhi** eyesight; **lume delle stelle** starlight; **lumi** eyesight; **lumi di luna** hard times; **perdere il lume degli occhi**

to lose one's self-control; **reggere il lume a** to close one's eyes to; **studiare al lume di candela** to burn the midnight oil
lumeggiare §290 (**luméggio**) *tr* to illuminate, to shed light on
lumicino *m* faint light; **essere al lumicino** to be on one's last legs
luminare *m* star; luminary
luminària *f* illumination
lumino *m* night light; votive light; rush light
luminó·so -sa [s] *adj* luminous; bright (*idea*)
luna *f* moon; **andare a lune** to be fickle; **avere la luna di traverso** to be in a bad mood; **luna calante** waning moon; **luna crescente** crescent moon; **luna di miele** honeymoon
lunare *adj* lunar, moon
lunària *f* (min) moonstone; (bot) honesty
lunà·rio *m* (**-ri**) almanac; **sbarcare il lunario** to live from hand to mouth
lunàti·co -ca *adj* (**-ci -che**) moody; whimsical
lune·dì *m* (**-dì**) Monday
lunétta *f* lunette; fanlight
lunga *f*—**alla lunga** in the long run; **alla più lunga** at the latest; **andare per le lunghe** to last a long time, drag on; **di gran lunga** by far; **farla lunga** to dillydally
lungàggine *f* delay, procrastination
lunghézza *f* length; **lunghezza d'onda** wave length; **prendere la lunghezza di** to measure
lungi *adv* (lit) far
lungimirante *adj* (fig) far-sighted
lun·go -ga (**-ghi -ghe**) *adj* long; sharp (*tongue*); nimble (*fingers*); tall; thin (*soup*); (coll) slow; **a lungo** for a long time; at length; **a lungo andare** in the long run; **lungo disteso** sprawling ‖ *m* length; **in lungo e in largo** far and wide; **per il lungo** lengthwise ‖ *f* see **lunga** ‖ **lungo** *prep* along; during
lungofiume *m* river road
lungola·go *m* (**-ghi**) lakeshore road
lungomare *m* seashore road
lungometràg·gio *m* (**-gi**) full-length movie, feature film
lunòtto *m* (aut) rear window
luò·go *m* (**-ghi**) place; passage; site; (geom) locus; **aver luogo** to take place; **aver luogo in** to be laid in (*e.g., a certain place*); **dar luogo a** to give rise to; **del luogo** local; **far luogo** to make room; **fuori luogo** inopportune(ly); **in alto luogo** highplaced; **in luogo di** instead of; **luogo comune** commonplace; **luogo di decenza** toilet; **luogo di nascita** birthplace; **luogo di pena** penitentiary; **non luogo a procedere** (law) no ground for prosecution; (law) **nolle prosequi**; **sul luogo** on the spot; on the premises
luogotenènte *m* lieutenant
lupa *f* she-wolf
lupanare *m* (lit) brothel

lupé·sco -sca *adj* (**-schi -sche**) wolfish
lupétto *m* young wolf; cub (*in Boy Scouts*)
lupinèlla *f* sainfoin
lupi·no -na *adj* wolfish
lu·po -pa *mf* wolf; **lupo cerviero** lynx; **lupo di mare** seadog; **lupo mannaro** werewolf || *f* see **lupa**
lùppolo *m* hops
lùri·do -da *adj* filthy, dirty
lusco *m*—**tra il lusco e il brusco** at twilight
lusin·ga *f* (**-ghe**) flattery; illusion
lusingare §209 *tr* to flatter || *ref* to be flattered; to hope
lusinghiè·ro -ra *adj* flattering; promising
lussare *tr* to dislocate
lussazióne *f* dislocation

lusso *m* luxury; **di lusso** de luxe; **lusso di** abundance of
lussuó·so -sa [s] *adj* luxurious, sumptuous
lussureggiante *adj* luxuriant
lussùria *f* lust
lussurió·so -sa [s] *adj* lustful, lecherous
lustrare *tr* to polish, shine; to lick (*s.o.'s boots*) || *intr* to shine, be shiny
lustrascar·pe *m* (**-pe**) bootblack
lustrino *m* sequin; tinsel
lu·stro -stra *adj* shiny, polished || *m* shine, polish; period of five years; **dare il lustro a** to shine, polish
lutto *m* mourning; bereavement; **a lutto** black-edged (*e.g.*, *stationery*); **lutto stretto** deep mourning
luttuó·so -sa [s] *adj* mournful

M

M, m ['emme] *m & f* eleventh letter of the Italian alphabet
ma *m* but; **ma e se** ifs and buts || *conj* but; yet || *interj* who knows?; too bad!
màca·bro -bra *adj* macabre
maca·co *m* (**-chi**) macaque; (*fig*) dumbbell
macadàm *m* macadam
macadamizzare [ddzz] *tr* to macadamize
mac·ca *f* (**-che**) abundance; **a macca** (coll) abundantly; (coll) without paying
maccarèllo *m* mackerel
maccheróni *mpl* macaroni
màcchia *f* spot, stain; brushwood; thicket; (fig) blot; **alla macchia** clandestinely; (painting) done in pointillism; **darsi alla macchia** to join the underground; to escape the law; **macchia solare** sunspot; **senza macchia** spotless
macchiare §287 *tr* to stain, soil || *ref* to become stained; **macchiarsi d'infamia** to soil one's reputation
macchiétta *f* caricature; comedian; fare la **macchietta di** to impersonate, to parody
macchiettare (**macchiétto**) *tr* to speckle
macchietti·sta *mf* (**-sti -ste**) cartoonist; comedian; impersonator
màcchina *f* machine; engine; car, automobile; machination; **andare in macchina** to go to press; **fatto a macchina** machine-made; **macchina da presa** (mov) camera; **macchina da proiezione** projector; **macchina fotografica** camera; **macchina per** or **da cucire** sewing machine; **macchina per** or **da scrivere** typewriter; **scrivere a macchina** to typewrite
macchinale *adj* mechanical
macchinare (**màcchino**) *tr* to plot
macchinà·rio *m* (**-ri**) machinery
macchinazióne *f* machination

macchinétta *f* gadget; **macchinetta del caffè** coffee maker
macchini·sta *m* (**-sti**) engineer; (theat) stagehand
macchinó·so -sa [s] *adj* heavy, ponderous; complicated
macedònia *f* fruit salad, fruit cup
macel·làio *m* (**-lài**) butcher
macellare (**macèllo**) *tr* to butcher
macelleria *f* butcher shop
macèllo *m* slaughterhouse; butchering; carnage; disaster
macerare (**màcero**) *tr* to soak; to mortify (*the flesh*) || *ref* to waste away
macèria *f* low wall; **macerie** ruins
màce·ro -ra *adj* emaciated; skinny || *m* soaking vat (*for papermaking*)
machiavèlli·co -ca *adj* (**-ci -che**) Machiavellian
macigno *m* boulder
macilèn·to -ta *adj* emaciated, pale, wan
màcina *f* millstone; (coll) grind
macinacaf·fè *m* (**-fè**) coffee grinder
macinapé·pe *m* (**-pe**) pepper mill
macinare (**màcino**) *tr* to grind, mill; to burn up (*e.g.*, *the road*)
macina·to -ta *adj* ground || *m* grindings; ground meat || *f* grinding
macinino *m* grinder; (coll) jalopy
mà·cis *m & f* (**-cis**) mace (*spice*)
maciste *m* strong man (*in circus*)
maciullare *tr* to brake (*flax or hemp*); to crush
macrocòsmo *m* macrocosm
màdia *f* bread bin; kneading trough
màdi·do -da *adj* wet, perspiring
madònna *f* lady || **Madonna** *f* Madonna
madornale *adj* huge; gross (*error*)
madre *f* mother; stub; mold; **madre nubile** unwed mother
madreggiare §290 (**madréggio**) *intr* to take after one's mother
madrelìngua *f* mother tongue
madrepàtria *f* mother country
madrepèrla *f* mother-of-pearl
madresélva *f* (coll) honeysuckle

madrevite *f* (mach) nut; die; **madrevite ad alette** wing nut

madrigna *f* stepmother

madrina *f* godmother; **madrina di guerra** war mother

mae·stà *f* (-stà) majesty; **lesa maestà** lese majesty

maestó·so -sa [s] *adj* majestic, stately

maèstra *f* teacher; (fig) master; **maestra giardiniera** kindergarten teacher

maestrale *m* northwest wind (*in Mediterranean*)

maestranze *fpl* workmen

maestrìa *f* skill, mastery

maè·stro -stra *adj* masterly; main ‖ *m* teacher; master; instructor; northwester (*in Mediterranean*); **maestro di cappella** choirmaster ‖ *f see* maestra

mafió·so -sa [s] *adj* Mafia ‖ *mf* member of the Mafia; gaudy dresser

ma·ga *f* (-ghe) sorceress

magagna *f* fault, weak spot

magagna·to -ta *adj* spoiled (*fruit*)

magari *adv* even, maybe ‖ *conj* even if ‖ *interj* would that . . . !

magazzinàg·gio [ddzz] *m* (-gi) storage

magazziniè·re -ra [ddzz] *mf* stockroom attendant ‖ *m* warehouseman

magazzino [ddzz] *m* warehouse; store; inventory; (phot, journ) magazine; **grandi magazzini** department store

maggése [s] *adj* May ‖ *m* (agr) fallow

màg·gio *m* (-gi) May; May Day

maggiolino *m* cockchafer

maggiorana *f* sweet marjoram

maggioranza *f* majority

maggiorare (maggióro) *tr* to increase

maggiorazióne *f* increase, appreciation

maggiordòmo *m* butler; majordomo

maggióre *adj* bigger, greater; major; main; higher (*bidder*); older, elder; (mil) master (*e.g., sergeant*); biggest, greatest; highest; oldest, eldest; **andare per la maggiore** to be all the rage; **maggiore età** majority ‖ *m* (mil) major; oldest one; **maggiori** ancestors

maggiorènne *adj* of age ‖ *mf* grown-up, adult

maggiorènte *mf* notable

maggiori·tà *f* (-tà) (mil) C.O.'s office

maggiorità·rio -ria *adj* (-ri -rie) majority

magìa *f* magic

màgi·co -ca *adj* (-ci -che) magic

Magi *mpl* Magi, Wise Men

magióne *f* (lit) home, dwelling

magistèro *m* education, teaching, mastery; (chem) precipitation

magistrale *adj* teacher's; masterly ‖ *f* teacher's college

magistrato *m* magistrate

magistratura *f* judiciary

màglia *f* knitting; stitch; link; undershirt; sports shirt; (hist) mail; (fig) web; **lavorare a maglia** to knit

maglierìa *f* knitting mill; yarn shop; knitwear store

magliétta *f* polo shirt, T-shirt; buckle (*to secure rifle strap*); picture hook; buttonhole

maglifì·cio *m* (-ci) knitwear factory

mà·glio *m* (-gli) sledge hammer; mallet; drop hammer

maglióne *m* heavy sweater, jersey

magnàni·mo -ma *adj* magnanimous

magnano *m* (coll) locksmith

magnate *m* (lit) magnate, tycoon

magnèsio *m* magnesium

magnète *m* magnet; magneto

magnèti·co -ca *adj* (-ci -che) magnetic

magnetismo *m* magnetism

magnetite *f* loadstone

magnetizzare [ddzz] *tr* to magnetize

magnetòfono *m* tape recorder

magnificare §197 (magnìfico) *tr* to extol, praise; to magnify (*to exaggerate*)

magnificènza *f* magnificence

magnìfi·co -ca *adj* (-ci -che) magnificent; munificent; wonderful, splendid

ma·gno -gna *adj* (lit) great; the Great, e.g., **Alessandro Magno** Alexander the Great

magnòlia *f* magnolia

ma·go *m* (-ghi) magician; wizard

magóne *m* (coll) gizzard; (coll) grief; **avere il magone** (coll) to be in the dumps

magra *f* low water; (fig) dearth, want

magrézza *f* leanness; scarcity

ma·gro -gra *adj* lean, thin; meager ‖ *m* lean meat; meatless day ‖ *f see* magra

mài *adv* never; ever; **non . . . mai** never, not ever; **come mai?** how come?

maia·le -la *mf* pig; hog ‖ *m* pork ‖ *f* sow

maialé·sco -sca *adj* (-schi -sche) piggish

maiòli·ca *f* (-che) majolica

maionése [s] *f* mayonnaise

mà·is *m* (-is) corn, maize

maiuscolétto *m* (typ) small capital

maiùsco·lo -la *adj* capital ‖ *m*—**scrivere in maiuscolo** to capitalize ‖ *f* capital letter

Malacca, la Malay Peninsula

malaccèt·to -ta *adj* unwelcome

malaccòr·to -ta *adj* imprudent; awkward

malacreanza *f* (malecreanze) instance of bad manners; **malecreanze** bad manners

malafatta *f* (malefatte) defect; **malefatte** evildoings

malaféde *f* (malefédi) bad faith

malaffare *m*—**donna di malaffare** prostitute; **gente di malaffare** underworld

malagévole *adj* rough (*road*); hard (*work*)

malagràzia *f* (malegràzie) rudeness, uncouthness

malalìngua *f* (malelìngue) slanderer, backbiter

malanda·to -ta *adj* run-down; shabby

malandri·no -na *adj* dishonest; bewitching (*eyes*) ‖ *m* highwayman

malànimo *m* ill will; **di malanimo** reluctantly

malanno *m* misfortune; illness; (joc) menace

malaparata *f* (coll) danger, dangerous situation

malapéna *f*—**a malapena** hardly

malària f malaria

malàtic·cio -cia adj (-ci -ce) sickly

mala·to -ta adj sick, ill; essere malato agli occhi to have sore eyes; fare il malato to play sick || mf patient; i malati the sick

malattìa f sickness; illness; disease; malattie del lavoro occupational diseases

malaugura·to -ta adj unfortunate; ill-omened

malaugù·rio m (-ri) ill omen

malavita f underworld

malavòglia f (malevòglie) unwillingness; di malavoglia reluctantly

malcapita·to -ta adj unlucky || m unlucky person

malcàu·to -ta adj rash, heedless

malcón·cio -cia adj (-ci -ce) battered

malcontèn·to -ta adj dissatisfied, malcontent || mf malcontent || m dissatisfaction

malcostume m immorality; bad practice

malcrea·to -ta adj ill-bred

maldè·stro -stra adj clumsy, awkward

maldicènte adj gossipy, slanderous || mf gossip, slanderer, backbiter

maldicènza f gossip, slander

male m evil; ill; trouble; andare a male to go to pot; aversela a male to take offense; di male in peggio from bad to worse, worse and worse; fare del male to do ill; fare male to be in error; fare male a to hurt; farsi male to get hurt; to hurt oneself; far venire il mal di mare a to make seasick; (fig) to nauseate; Lei fa male you should not; mal d'aereo airsickness; mal di capo headache; mal di cuore heart disease; mal di denti toothache; mal di gola sore throat; mal di mare sea-sickness; mal di montagna mountain sickness; mal di pancia bellyache; mal di schiena backache; mandare a male to spoil; mettere male to sow discord; prendere a male to take amiss; voler male a to bear a grudge against || adv badly, poorly; male educato ill-bred; meno male! fortunately!; restar male to be disappointed; sentirsi male to feel sick; stare male to be ill; star male a to not fit, e.g., questo vestito gli sta male this suit does not fit him; veder male qlco to disapprove of s.th; veder male qlcu to dislike s.o.

maledettaménte adv (coll) damned

maledét·to -ta adj cursed, damned

maledire §195 tr to curse

maledizióne f malediction, curse || interj damn it!, confound it!

maleduca·to -ta adj ill-bred || mf boor

malefatta f var of malafatta

malefì·cio m (-ci) curse, spell; witchcraft; wickedness

malèfi·co -ca adj (-ci -che) maleficent

maleolènte adj (lit) malodorous

malèrba f weed, weeds

malése adj & mf Malay

Malèsia, la Malaysia

malèssere m malaise; uneasiness; worry

malevolènza f malevolence; malice

malèvo·lo -la adj malevolent; malicious

malfama·to -ta adj ill-famed; notorious

malfat·to -ta adj botched; misshapen || m misdeed

malfat·tóre -trice mf malefactor

malfér·mo -ma adj wobbly, unsteady

malfì·do -da adj untrustworthy

malgarbo m bad manners, rudeness

malgovèrno m misrule; mismanagement; neglect

malgrado prep in spite of; mio malgrado in spite of me || conj although

malìa f spell, charm

maliar·do -da adj enchanting, charming || mf magician || f enchantress, witch

malignare intr to gossip

maligni·tà f (-tà) maliciousness; malevolence; malignancy

mali·gno -gna adj malicious, evil; unhealthy; malignant || il Maligno the Evil One

malinconìa f melancholy; melancholia

malincòni·co -ca adj (-ci -che) melancholy, wistful

malincuòre m—a malincuore unwillingly, against one's will

malintenziona·to -ta adj evil-minded || mf evildoer

malinté·so -sa [s] adj misunderstood; misapplied || m misunderstanding

maliò·so -sa [s] adj malicious; cunning; mischievous; bewitching

malizia f malice; trick; mischief

maliziò·so -sa [s] adj malicious; clever, artful; mischievous

malleàbile adj malleable; manageable

malleva·dóre -drice mf guarantor

malleverìa f surety

mallo m hull, husk

mallòppo m bundle; (aer) trail cable; (coll) lump (in one's throat); (slang) swag, booty

malmenare (malméno) tr to manhandle

malmés·so -sa adj shabby, seedy; tasteless

malna·to -ta adj uncouth; unfortunate; harmful

malnutri·to -ta adj undernourished

malnutrizióne f malnutrition

ma·lo -la adj (lit) bad

malòc·chio m (-chi) evil eye

malóra f ruin; mandare in malora to ruin; va in malora! go to the devil!

malóre m malaise; fainting spell

malprài·co -ca adj (-ci -che) inexperienced

malsa·no -na adj unhealthy; unsound

malsicù·ro -ra adj unsafe; insecure

malta f mortar; plaster; (obs) mud

maltèmpo m bad weather

malto m malt

maltòlto m ill-gotten gains

maltrattaménto m mistreatment

maltrattare tr to mistreat, maltreat

malumóre m bad humor; di malumore in a bad mood

malva f mallow

malvà·gio -gia (-gi -gie) adj wicked || mf wicked person || il Malvagio the Evil One

malversare (malvèrso) *tr* to embezzle; to misappropriate

malversazióne *f* embezzlement; misappropriation

malvestì·to -ta *adj* shabby, seedy

malvi·sto -sta *adj* disliked; unpopular

malvivènte *mf* criminal; (*lit*) profligate

malvolentièri *adv* unwillingly

malvolére *m* malevolence; indolence || §196 *tr* to dislike

mamma *f* mother, mom; (*lit*) breast; **mamma mia** dear me!

mammaluc·co *m* (**-chi**) simpleton

mammèlla *f* breast; udder

mammìfe·ro -ra *adj* mammalian || *m* mammal

màmmola *f* violet; (*fig*) shrinking violet

mam·mùt *m* (**-mut**) mammoth

manata *f* slap; handful; **dare una manata a** to slap

man·ca *f* (**-che**) left hand, left

mancante *adj* missing, lacking; unaccounted for

mancanza *f* lack; absence; defect; mistake; **in mancanza di** for lack of

mancare §197 *tr* to miss || *intr* (AVERE) to be at fault; **mancare a** to break (*e.g.*, *one's word*); **mancare di** to be wanting; to lack; **mancare di parola** to break one's word || *intr* (ESSERE) to fail (*said, e.g., of electric power*); to be lacking, *e.g.*, **manca il sale nell'arrosto** salt is lacking in the roast; to be missing; to be absent, *e.g.*, **mancano tre soci** three members are absent; to be, *e.g.*, **mancano dieci minuti alle quattro** it is ten minutes to four; (*with dat*) to lack, *e.g.*, **gli mancano le forze** he lacks the strength; to miss, *e.g.*, **mi manca la sua compagnia** I miss his company; **mancare a** to be absent from (*e.g.*, *the roll call*); to be . . . from, *e.g.*, **mancano dieci chilometri all'arrivo** we are ten kilometers from the journey's end; **mancare ai vivi** (*lit*) to pass away; **sentirsi mancare** to feel faint || *impers*—**mancare poco che** + *subj* to narrowly miss + *ger*, *e.g.*, **ci mancò poco che fosse investito da un'automobile** he narrowly missed being hit by a car; **non ci mancherebbe altro!** that would be the last straw!, I should say not!

manca·to -ta *adj* unsuccessful; missed (*opportunity*); abortive (*attempt*), *e.g.*, **omicidio mancato** abortive attempt to murder; manqué, *e.g.*, **un poeta mancato** a poet manqué

manchévole *adj* faulty

manchevolézza *f* fault, shortcoming

màn·cia *f* (**-ce**) tip, gratuity; **mancia competente** reward

manciata *f* handful

manci·no -na *adj* left-handed; underhanded || *mf* left-handed person || *f* left hand, left; (*mach*) floating crane

man·co -ca (**-chi -che**) *adj* left; (*lit*) sinister, ill-omened; (*lit*) lacking || *m* (*lit*) lack; **senza manco** (*coll*) without fail || **manco** *adv*—**manco male!**

(*coll*) at least!; **manco per idea!** (*coll*) not at all! || *f* see **manca**

mandaménto *m* jurisdiction

mandante *m* (*law*) principal

mandare *tr* to send; to condemn (*to death*); to commit (*to memory*); to send forth (*e.g.*, *smoke, buds*); to operate (*a machine*); **che Dio ce la mandi buona!** may God help us!; **mandare ad effetto** to carry out; **mandare all'altro mondo** to dispatch, kill; **mandare a monte** to ruin; **mandare a picco** to sink; **mandare a quel paese** to send to the devil; **mandare a spasso** to fire, dismiss; to get rid of; **mandar giù** to swallow; **mandare in malora** to ruin; **mandare in pezzi** to break to pieces; **mandare per le lunghe** to delay || *intr*—**mandare a chiamare** to send for; **mandare a dire** to send word

mandarino *m* mandarin; (*Citrus nobilis*) tangerine; (*Citrus reticulata*) mandarin orange

mandata *f* sending; delivery (*of merchandise*); group; gang (*e.g.*, *of thieves*); turn (*of key*); **chiudere a doppia mandata** to double-lock

mandatà·rio *m* (**-ri**) mandatary, trustee

mandato *m* mandate; order; **mandato di cattura** arrest warrant; **mandato di comparizione** subpoena; **mandato di perquisizione** search warrant

mandìbola *f* jaw

mandolino *m* mandolin

màndorla *f* almond; kernel (*of fruit*)

mandorla·to -ta *adj* almond || *m* nougat

màndorlo *m* almond tree

mandràgola *f* mandrake

màndria *f* herd

mandriano *m* herdsman

mandrillo *m* mandrill

mandrino *m* (*mach*) mandrel; (*mach*) driftpin

mandritta *f*—**a mandritta** to the right

mane *f*—**da mane a sera** from morning till night

maneggévole *adj* usable; manageable; accessible to small craft (*sea*)

maneggiare §290 (**manéggio**) *tr* to work (*e.g.*, *clay*); to handle; to wield (*a sword*); to knead (*dough*); to manage; (*equit*) to train

manég·gio *m* (**-gi**) handling; intrigue; horsemanship; management; riding school; manege

mané·sco -sca *adj* (**-schi -sche**) ready-fisted; hand (*e.g.*, *weapons*)

manétta *f* throttle (*on a motorcycle*); **manette** handcuffs, manacles

manfòrte *f*—**dar manforte a** to help

manganèllo *m* bludgeon, cudgel

manganése [s] *m* manganese

màngano *m* calender; mangle

mangeréc·cio -cia *adj* (**-ci -ce**) edible

mangerìa *f* graft, peculation

mangiàbile *adj* edible

mangiana·stri *m* (**-stri**) tape recorder

mangia-pane *m* (**-pane**) idler

mangia·prèti *m* (**-prèti**) priest hater

mangiare *m* eating; food || *v* §290 *tr*

to eat; to bite, gnaw; to erode; to embezzle, graft; (cards, chess) to take; **mangiar la foglia** to get wise || *intr* to eat; **mangiare alle spalle di qlcu** to eat at the expense of s.o. || *ref* to eat up; **mangiarsi il fegato** to be green with envy; **mangiarsi la parola** to break one's promise; **mangiarsi le unghie** to bite one's nails; **mangiarsi una promessa** to break one's promise

mangiasòldi *adj invar* money-eating, e.g., **macchina mangiasoldi** money-eating contraption

mangiata *f* (coll) fill, hearty meal, bellyful

mangiatóia *f* manger, crib

mangia·tóre -trice *mf* eater

mangime *m* fodder; feed; poultry feed

mangimìsti·co -ca *adj* (-ci -che) feed, e.g., **attrezzature mangimìstiche** feed machinery

mangió·ne -na *mf* great eater, glutton

mangiucchiare §287 **(mangiùcchio)** *tr* to nibble

mangusta *f* mongoose

mania *f* mania, craze; complex; whim; **mania di grandezza** delusions of grandeur

mania·co -ca (-ci -che) *adj* maniacal; enthusiastic || *m* maniac; fan, enthusiast

màni·ca *f* (-che) sleeve; hose; (coll) crowd, bunch; **essere di manica larga** to be broad-minded; **essere nelle maniche di qlcu** to be in the favor of s.o.; **è un altro paio di maniche** this is a horse of another color; **in maniche di camicia** in shirt sleeves; **manica a vento** air sleeve, windsock; **manica per l'acqua** hose || **la Manica** the English Channel

manicarétto *m* dainty, delicacy

manichino *m* mannequin; cuff; (obs) handcuff; **fare il manichino** to model

màni·co *m* (-chi & -ci) handle; stock (*of rifle*); shaft (*of golf club*); stem (*of spoon*); (mus) neck; **manico di scopa** broomstick

manicò·mio *m* (-mi) insane asylum, madhouse

manicòtto *m* muff; (mach) collar; (mach) nipple; (mach) sleeve

manicu·re *mf* (-re) manicure, manicurist (*person*) || *f* (-re) manicure (*treatment*)

manicuri·sta *mf* (-sti -ste) manicurist

manièra *f* manner, fashion, way; **belle maniere** good manners; **di maniera** (lit, painting) Manneristic; **di maniera che** so that; **in nessuna maniera** by no means; **maniere bad manners**

maniera·to -ta *adj* mannered, affected; genteel

maniè·ro -ra *adj* tame, gentle || *m* manor house, mansion || *f* see **maniera**

manieró·so -sa *adj* genteel; mannered

manifattura *f* manufacture; factory; product; ready-made wear

manifestare (manifèsto) *tr* to manifest

|| *intr* to demonstrate || *ref* to turn out to be

manifestazióne *f* manifestation; demonstration

manifestino *m* leaflet, handbill

manifè·sto -sta *adj* manifest, clear || *m* poster, placard; manifest; (pol) manifesto; **manifesto di carico** (naut) manifest

maniglia *f* handle; knob; (naut) link (*of chain*)

manigóldo *m* criminal; scoundrel

manipolare (manìpolo) *tr* to concoct; to adulterate; (telg) to transmit

manipola·tóre -trice *mf* schemer || *m* telegraph key

manìpolo *m* sheaf; (eccl; hist) maniple; (fig) handful

maniscal·co *m* (-chi) blacksmith

manna *f* manna; godsend

mannàia *f* axe; knife (*of guillotine*)

mano *f* hand; way (*in traffic*); coat (*of paint*); (lit) handful; (fig) finger; fingertip; **alla mano** plain, affable; **a mani nude** barehanded; **a mano** by hand; **a mano a mano** little by little; **a mano armata** armed (*e.g., robbery*); at gunpoint; **andare contro mano** to buck traffic; **a quattro mani** four-handed; **avere le mani bucate** to be a spendthrift; **avere le mani in pasta** to have one's fingers in the pie; **avere le mani lunghe** to be light-fingered; **battere le mani** to clap; **con le mani in mano** idle; **dare la mano a** to shake hands with; **dare man forte a** to help; **dare una mano** to pitch in; **dare una mano a** to lend a hand to; **di lunga mano** beforehand; **essere colto con le mani nel sacco** to be caught red-handed; **essere svelto di mano** to be light-fingered; **far man bassa (su)** to plunder; **fuori mano** out of the way; **mani di burro** butterfingers; **mani in alto!** hands up!; **man mano (che)** as; **mettere mano a** to begin; **mettere le mani sul fuoco** to guarantee; to swear; **per mano di** at the hands of; **prendere la mano** to balk; to get out of hand; **tenere la mano a** to abet; **venire alle mani** to come to blows

manodòpera *f* labor, manpower; **manodopera qualificata** skilled labor

manòmetro *m* manometer

manomèttere §198 *tr* to tamper with

manomissióne *f* tampering

manomòrta *f* (law) mortmain

manòpola *f* mitten; handgrip; strap (*to hold on to*); (rad, telv) knob; (hist) gauntlet

manoscrìt·to -ta *adj* & *m* manuscript

manoscrìvere §250 *intr* to write in one's own handwriting

manovale *m* laborer, helper; hod carrier

manovèlla *f* handle, crank; lever

manòvra *f* maneuver; (rr) shifting; **fare manovra** to maneuver; (rr) to shift

manovrare (manòvro) *tr* to maneuver; to handle, drive; (rr) to shift || *intr* to maneuver; (rr) to shunt, shift; (fig) to plot

manovratóre *m* motorman; driver; (rr) brakeman; (rr) flagman

manrovè·scio *m* (-sci) backhanded slap

mansalva *f*—**rubare a mansalva** to help oneself freely (*e.g., to the till*)

mansarda *f* mansard

mansióne *f* duty, function

mansuè·to *-ta adj* tame; meek

mansuetùdine *f* tameness; meekness

mantèlla *f* coat; (mil) cape

mantellina *f* (mil) cape

mantèllo *m* woman's coat; coat (*of animal*); (fig) cloak; (mil) cape; (mach) casing

mantenére §271 *tr* to keep; to maintain; to hold (*e.g., a position*) || *ref* to stay alive; to last; to remain, stay, continue

mantenimento *m* keeping; maintenance

mantenu·to *-ta adj* kept || *m* gigolo || *f* kept woman

màntice *m* bellows; folding top (*of carriage*); (aut) convertible top

manto *m* mantle; coat; cloak

Màntova *f* Mantua

mantovana *f* valance

manuale *adj* & *m* manual

manualizzare [ddzz] *tr* to make (*e.g., a machine*) hand-operated; to include in a manual; to prepare a manual of

manù·brio *m* (-bri) handlebar; handle; dumbbell

manufat·to *-ta adj* manufactured || *m* manufactured product; manufacture

manutèngolo *m* accomplice

manutenzióne *f* maintenance, upkeep

manza [dz] *f* heifer

manzo [dz] *m* steer; beef

maomettaꞏno *-na adj* & *mf* Mahometan, Mohammedan

maomettismo *m* Mahometanism, Mohammedanism

Maométto *m* Mahomet

maóna *f* barge

mappa *f* map; bit (*of key*)

mappamóndo *m* globe; map of the world

marachèlla *f* mischief

maramèo *m*—**fare maramèo** to thumb one's nose

mara·sma *m* (-smi) utter confusion; (pathol) decrepitude, feebleness

maratóna *f* marathon

maratonè·ta *m* (-ti) Marathon runner

mar·ca *f* (-che) mark, label; make, brand; token; ticket; (hist, geog) march; **di marca** of quality; **marca da bollo** revenue stamp; **marca di fabbrica** trademark

marcare §197 *tr* to mark; to label; to brand; to keep the score of; to score (*e.g., a goal*); to accentuate

marcatèm·po *m* (-po) timekeeper

marca·to *-ta adj* marked, pronounced

marchésa *f* marchioness, marquise

marchése *m* marquess, marquis

marchia·no *-na adj* gross (*error*)

marchiare §287 *tr* to brand

màr·chio *m* (-chi) brand; initials; characteristic; trademark

màr·cia *f* (-ce) march; operation; pus; (aut) gear, speed; (mil) hike; (sports) walk; **far marcia indietro** to back up; (naut) to back water; **marcia indietro** (aut) reverse; **marcia nuziale** wedding march

marciapiède *m* sidewalk; (rr) platform

marciare §128 *intr* to march; (mil) to advance; (sports) to walk; (coll) to function; **far marciare qlcu** to keep s.o. in line

màr·cio *-cia* (-ci -ce) *adj* rotten; infected; corrupt || *m* rotten part; decayed part; corruption || *f* see **marcia**

marcire §176 *intr* (ESSERE) to rot

marciume *m* rot; pus; decay

marꞏco *m* (-chi) mark

marconigram·ma *m* (-mi) radiogram

marconi·sta *m/f* (-sti -ste) radio operator

mare *m* sea; bunch, heap; **al mare** at the seashore; **alto mare** high sea; **fa mare** the sea is rough; **gettare a mare** to throw overboard; **mare grosso** rough sea; **mare territoriale** territorial waters; **promettere mari e monti** to promise the moon; **tenere il mare** to be seaworthy

marèa *f* tide; sea (*e.g., of mud*); **alta marea** high tide; **bassa marea** low tide; **marea di quadratura** neap tide; **marea di sizigia** spring tide

mareggiata *f* coastal storm

maremòto *m* seaquake

mareògrafo *m* tide-level gauge

maresciallo *m* marshall; warrant officer

marétta *f* choppy sea; instability

margarina *f* margarine

margherita *f* daisy; **margherite** beads

marginale *adj* marginal

marginatóre *m* margin stop (*of typewriter*); (typ) try square

màrgine *m* margin; edge; **margine a scaletta** thumb index

marijuana *f* marijuana, marihuana

marina *f* seashore; seascape; navy; **marina mercantile** merchant marine

mari·nàio *m* (-nài) seaman, sailor

marinara *f* middy blouse

marinare *tr* to marinate; **marinare la scuola** to cut school, play truant

marinaré·sco *-sca adj* (-schi -sche) sailor, seamanlike

marina·ro *-ra adj* sea, sailor; seamanlike; nautical || *m* (coll) sailor || *f* see **marinara**

mari·no *-na adj* marine, nautical || *f* see **marina**

mariòlo *m* rascal

marionétta *f* puppet, marionette

maritale *adj* marital

maritare *tr* to marry || *ref* to get married

marito *m* husband

maritti·mo *-ma adj* maritime, sea || *m* merchant seaman

marmàglia *f* riffraff, rabble

marmellata *f* jam, preserves; **marmellata di arancia** orange marmalade

marmi·sta *m* (-sti) marble worker; marble cutter

marmitta *f* pot, kettle; (aut) muffler

marmittóne *m* (coll) sad sack

marmo *m* marble

marmòc·chio *m* (-chi) brat

marmòre·o -a *adj* marble
marmorizzare [ddzz] *tr* to marble
marmòtta *f* marmot; woodchuck; (fig) sluggard; (rr) switch signal
marmottina *f* salesman's sample case
marna *f* marl
marnare *tr* to marl
marocchi·no -na *adj & mf* Moroccan || *m* morocco leather
Maròcco, il Morocco
maróso [s] *m* billow, surge
marra *f* hoe; fluke (*of anchor*)
marrano *m* Marrano; (fig) scoundrel; (lit) traitor
marronata *f* (coll) blunder, boner
marróne *adj invar* maroon, tan || *m* chestnut; (coll) blunder
Marsíglia *f* Marseille
marsigliése [s] *adj* Marseilles || *m* native or inhabitant of Marseilles || *f* Marseillaise
marsina *f* swallow-tailed coat
Marte *m* Mars
marte·dì *m* (-**dì**) Tuesday; **martedì grasso** Shrove Tuesday
martellare (**martèllo**) *tr* to hammer; to pester (*with questions*) || *intr* to throb; (fig) to insist
martellata *f* hammer blow
martellétto *m* hammer (*of piano or bell*); lever (*of typewriter*)
martèllo *m* hammer; **martello dell'uscio** knocker; **martello perforatore** jack-hammer
martinétto *m* jack; **martinetto a vite** screw jack
martingala *f* half belt (*sewn in back of sports jacket*); martingale (*of harness*)
martini·ca *f* (-**che**) wagon brake
martin pescatóre *m* kingfisher
màrtire *m* martyr
martì·rio *m* (-**ri**) martyrdom
martirizzare [ddzz] *tr* to martyrize
màrtora *f* marten
martoriare §287 (**martòrio**) *tr* to torment
marxi·sta *adj & mf* (-**sti -ste**) Marxist
marzapane *m* marzipan
marziale *adj* martial
marzia·no -na *adj & mf* Martian
marzo *m* March
mas *m* (**mas**) torpedo boat
mascalzóne *m* cad, rascal
mascèlla *f* jaw; jawbone
màschera *mf* usher || *f* mask; masque; **maschera antigas** gas mask; **maschera di bellezza** beauty pack; **maschera respiratoria** oxygen mask; **maschera subacquea** diving helmet
mascheraménto *m* camouflage
mascherare (**màschero**) *tr*, *intr & ref* to mask; to camouflage
mascherata *f* masquerade
mascherina *f* little mask, loup; tip (*of shoe*); (aut) grille; (phot) mask
maschiare §287 *tr* (mach) to tap
maschiétta *f* tomboy; **alla maschietta** bobbed (*hair*); **tagliare i capelli alla maschietta** to bob the hair
maschiétto *m* baby boy; pintle
maschile *adj* masculine; manly; men's;

male (*sex*); boys' (*school*) || *m* masculine
mà·schio -schia *adj* manly, virile; male || *m* male; keep, donjon; tenon; (mach) tap; (carp) tongue
mascolinizzare [ddzz] *tr* to make masculine or mannish || *ref* to act like a man
mascoli·no -na *adj* masculine; mannish (*woman*)
masnada *f* mob, gang; (obs) group
masnadière *m* highwayman
massa *f* mass; body (*of water*); (elec) ground; **mettere a massa** (elec) to ground; **in massa** in a body; **massa ereditaria** (law) estate
massacrante *adj* killing, fatiguing
massacrare *tr* to massacre; to ruin; to wear out, fatigue
massacro *m* massacre
massaggiare §290 *tr* to massage
massaggiatóre *m* masseur
massaggiatrice *f* masseuse
massàg·gio *m* (-**gi**) massage
massàia *f* housewife
massèllo *m* block (*of stone*); (metallurgy) pig, ingot
masserìa *f* farm
masserìzie *fpl* household goods
massicciata *f* roadbed; (rr) ballast
massìc·cio -cia (-**ci -ce**) *adj* massive; bulky; heavy; (fig) gross || *m* massif
màssi·mo -ma *adj* maximum; top || *m* maximum; limit; **al massimo** at the most || *f* maxim; maximum temperature
massi·vo -va *adj* massive
masso *m* rock, boulder
Massóne *m* Mason
Massonerìa *f* Masonry
mastèllo *m* washtub
masticare §197 (**màstico**) *tr* to chew, masticate; to mumble (*words*); to speak (*a language*) poorly; **masticare amaro** to grumble
masticazióne *f* mastication
màstice *m* mastic; glue; putty
mastino *m* mastiff
mastodònti·co -ca *adj* (-**ci -che**) mammoth
ma·stro -stra *adj* master || *m* ledger; master, e.g., **mastro meccanico** master mechanic
masturbare *tr & ref* to masturbate
matassa *f* skein; trouble
matemàti·co -ca (-**ci -che**) *adj* mathematical || *m* mathematician || *f* mathematics
materassino *m* (sports) mat; **materassino pneumatico** air mattress
materasso *m* mattress; (boxing) sparring partner
matèria *f* matter; substance; subject; (coll) pus; **dare materia a** to give ground for; **materia grigia** gray matter; **materie coloranti** dyestuffs; **materie prime** raw materials
materiale *adj* material; rough, bulky || *m* material; equipment; supplies; (fig) makings, stuff; **materiale ferroviario** (rr) rolling stock; **materiale stabile** (rr) permanent way

materni·tà _f_ (-tà) maternity; maternity hospital; maternity ward

matèr·no -na _adj_ maternal; mother (_tongue, country_)

matita _f_ pencil; **matita per gli occhi** eye-shadow pencil; **matita per le labbra** lipstick; cosmetic pencil

matrice _f_ matrix; stub

matrici·da _mf_ (-di -de) matricide

matrici·dio _m_ (-di) matricide

matrìcola _f_ register, roll; registration (_number_); registry; beginner, novice; freshman (_in university_); **far la matricola a** to haze

matrìcola·to -ta _adj_ notorious, arrant

matrigna _f_ stepmother

matrimoniale _adj_ matrimonial; double (_bed_); married (_life_)

matrimonialménte _adv_ as husband and wife

matrimò·nio _m_ (-ni) matrimony, marriage; wedding

matròna _f_ matron

matronale _adj_ matronly

matta _f_ joker, wild card

mattacchió·ne -na _mf_ jester, prankster

mattana _f_ tantrum; fit of laughter

matta·tóio _m_ (-tói) slaughterhouse

matterèllo _m_ rolling pin

mattina _f_ morning; **di prima mattina** early in the morning; **la mattina** in the morning

mattinale _adj_ morning ‖ _m_ morning report

mattinata _f_ morning; (_theat_) matinée

mattiniè·ro -ra _adj_ early-rising

mattino _m_ morning; **di buon mattino** early in the morning

mat·to -ta _adj_ crazy; whimsical; dull; false (_jewelry_); wild (_desire_); **andare matto per** to be crazy about; **da matti** unbelievable; **fare il matto** to cut a caper; **matto da legare** raving mad ‖ _f_ see **matta**

mattòide _adj_ & _mf_ madcap

mattonare (**mattóno**) _tr_ to pave with bricks

mattonato _m_ brick floor; **restare sul mattonato** to be utterly destitute

mattóne _m_ brick; (fig) bore

mattonèlla _f_ tile; cushion (_of billiard table_)

mattuti·no -na _adj_ morning ‖ _m_ matins

maturan·do -da _mf_ lycée student who has to take the baccalaureate examination

maturare _tr_ to ripen; to ponder; to pass (_a lycée pupil_) ‖ _intr_ (ESSERE) to ripen, mature; to fall due

maturazióne _f_ ripening

maturi·tà _f_ (-tà) maturity; ripening; lycée final

matu·ro -ra _adj_ ripe; mature; due

Matusalèmme _m_ Methuselah

mausolèo _m_ mausoleum

mazza _f_ club; mallet; sledge hammer; cane; mace; golf club; (baseball) bat

mazzacavallo _m_ well sweep

mazzapìc·chio _m_ (-chi) mallet; sledge

mazzata _f_ heavy blow, wallop (_with club_)

mazzeran·ga _f_ (-ghe) (mach) tamper

mazzière _m_ macer; (cards) dealer

mazzo _m_ bunch; bouquet; deck (_of cards_); **fare il mazzo** to shuffle the cards

mazzuòla _f_ sledge hammer

mazzuòlo _m_ sledge; mallet; wedge (_of golf club_); drumstick (_for bass drum_)

me §5 _pron pers_

meandro _m_ meander; labyrinth

MEC _m_ (letterword) (**Mercato Europeo Comune**) European Economic Community, Common Market

Mècca, la Mecca; (fig) the Mecca

meccàni·co -ca (-ci -che) _adj_ mechanical ‖ _m_ mechanic ‖ _f_ mechanics; process (_e.g., of digestion_); machinery

meccanismo _m_ machinery; mechanism; movement (_of watch_)

meccanizzare [ddzz] _tr_ to mechanize ‖ _ref_ to become mechanized

mecenate _m_ patron (_of the arts_)

méco §5 _prep phrase_ (lit) with me

medàglia _f_ medal

medaglióne _m_ medallion; locket; biographical sketch

medési·mo -ma _adj_ & _pron_ same; -self, e.g., **egli medésimo** he himself; very e.g., **la verità medesima** the very truth

mèdia _f_ average; secondary school, middle school; (math) mean; **media oraria** average speed ‖ **mèdia** _mpl_ media (_of communication_)

mediana _f_ median; (soccer) middle line

mediàni·co -ca _adj_ (-ci -che) medium

media·no -na _adj_ median ‖ _m_ (sports) halfback ‖ _f_ see **mediana**

mediante _prep_ by means of

mediare §287 (**mèdio**) _tr_ & _intr_ (ESSERE) to mediate

media·to -ta _adj_ indirect

media·tóre -trice _adj_ mediating ‖ _mf_ mediator; broker; commission merchant

mediazióne _f_ mediation; brokerage; broker's fee, commission

medicaménto _m_ medicine

medicamentó·so -sa [s] _adj_ medicinal

medicare §197 (**mèdico**) _tr_ to medicate; to treat

medicastro _m_ quack

medicazióne _f_ medication; dressing

medichéssa _f_ (pej) lady doctor

medicina _f_ medicine

medicinale _adj_ medicinal ‖ _m_ medicine

mèdi·co -ca (-ci -che) _adj_ medical ‖ _m_ doctor, physician; healer; **fare il medico** to practice medicine; **medico chirurgo** surgeon; **medico condotto** board-of-health doctor; country doctor; **medico curante** family physician

medievale _adj_ medieval

medievali·sta _mf_ (-sti -ste) medievalist

mè·dio -dia (-di -die) _adj_ average; median; middle; secondary (_school_); medium ‖ _m_ middle finger ‖ _f_ see **media**

mediòcre _adj_ mediocre

mediocri·tà _f_ (-tà) mediocrity

medioèvo _m_ Middle Ages

medioleggèro _m_ welterweight

mediomàssimo *m* light heavyweight
meditabón•do -da *adj* meditative
meditare (mèdito) *tr & intr* to meditate
medita•to -ta *adj* considered
meditazióne *f* meditation
mediterrà•neo -nea *adj* inland (*sea*) || **Mediterraneo** *adj & m* Mediterranean
mè•dium *mf* (**-dium**) medium
medusa *f* jellyfish
mefistofèli•co -ca *adj* (**-ci -che**) Mephistophelian
mefíti•co -ca *adj* (**-ci -che**) mephitic
megaciclo *m* megacycle
megàfono *m* megaphone
megalomanìa *f* megalomania
megalòpo•li *f* (**-li**) megalopolis
mega•òhm *m* (**-òhm**) megohm
megèra *f* hag, termagant, vixen
mèglio *adj invar* better; (coll) best || *m*—**il meglio** the best; **nel meglio di** (coll) in the middle of || *f*—**avere la meglio** to get the upper hand; **avere la meglio di** to get the better of || *adv* better; best; rather; **stare meglio** to feel better; to be becoming; to fit better; **stare meglio a** to be becoming to; to fit; **tanto meglio!** so much the better!
méla *f* apple; nozzle (*of sprinkling can*); **mela cotogna** quince (*fruit*); **mela renetta** pippin
melagrana *f* pomegranate
melanzana [dz] *f* eggplant
melassa *f* molasses, treacle
mela•to -ta *adj* honey, honeyed
melèn•so -sa *adj* dull, silly
melissa *f* (bot) balm
mellìflu•o -a *adj* mellifluous
mélma *f* mud, slime
melmó•so -sa [s] *adj* muddy, slimy
mélo *m* apple tree
melodìa *f* melody
melòdi•co -ca *adj* (**-ci -che**) melodic
melodió•so -sa [s] *adj* melodious
melodram•ma *m* (**-mi**) melodrama; lyric opera; (fig) melodrama
melodrammàti•co -ca *adj* (**-ci -che**) melodramatic
melograno *m* pomegranate tree
melóne *m* melon; cantaloupe; **melone d'acqua** watermelon
membrana *f* membrane; parchment; diaphragm (*of telephone*); (zool) web
membratura *f* frame
mèm•bro *m* (**-bri**, *considered individually*) limb; member; penis || *m* (**-bra** *fpl*, *considered collectively*) limb (*of human body*)
membru•to -ta *adj* burly, husky
memoràbile *adj* memorable
memoràn•dum *m* (**-dum**) memorandum; agenda, calendar; note; note paper
mèmore *adj* (lit) mindful, grateful
memòria *f* memory; souvenir; memoir; dissertation; (law) brief
memoriale *m* memoir; memorial
memorizzare [ddzz] *tr* to memorize
ména *f* intrigue
mena•bò m -bò (typ) layout, dummy
menadíto *m*—**a menadito** at one's fingertips; perfectly
menare (méno) *tr* to lead; to bring

(*luck*); to wag (*the tail*); to deliver (*a blow*); (coll) to hit; **menare a effetto** to carry out; **menare buono di** to approve of; **menare il can per l'aia** to beat around the bush; **menare per le lunghe** to delay; **menare vanto to** boast
mènda *f* (lit) fault, flaw
mendace *adj* lying, false, mendacious
mendà•cio *m* (**-ci**) (law) falsehood
mendicante *adj & m* mendicant
mendicare §197 (**méndico**) *tr & intr* to beg
mendici•tà *f* (**-tà**) indigence, poverty
mendì•co -ca *adj & mf* (**-chi -che**) mendicant
menefreghismo *m* I-don't-care attitude
menestrèllo *m* minstrel
méno *adj invar* less || *m* less; least; minus (*sign*); **i meno** the few; **per lo meno** at least || *adv* less; least; minus; **a meno che** unless; **da meno** inferior; **fare a meno di** to do without; to spare; **meno . . . di** less . . . than; **meno male** fortunately; **meno . . . meno** the less . . . the less; **non poter fare a meno di** + *inf* to not be able to help + *ger*, e.g., **la conferenza non poteva fare a meno di essere un successo** the conference could not help being a success; **quanto meno** at least; **senza meno** without fail; **venir meno** to swoon, pass out; to fail; to lose, e.g., **gli venne meno il cuore** he lost his courage; **venir meno di** to break (*one's word*) || *prep* except; less, minus; of, e.g., **le sette meno dieci** ten minutes of seven
menomare (mènomo) *tr* to lessen, diminish; (fig) to hurt, damage
mèno•mo -ma *adj* least
menopàusa *f* menopause
mènsa *f* (prepared) table; mess, mess hall; (eccl) altar; communion table; (poet) mass; (poet) altar; **mensa aziendale** company cafeteria
mensile *adj* monthly || *m* monthly salary or allowance
mensili•tà *f* (**-tà**) monthly installment
mènsola *f* bracket; corner shelf; neck (*of harp*); mantel (*of chimney*); console
ménta *f* mint
mentale *adj* mental; (anat) chin
mentali•tà *f* (**-tà**) mentality, mind
ménte *f* mind; **a mente di** according to; **avere in mente** to mean; to intend; **di mente** mental; **mente direttiva** mastermind; **scappare di mente a qlcu** to escape s.o.'s mind, e.g., **gli è scappato di mente** it escaped his mind; **uscire di mente** to go out of one's mind; **venire in mente a qlcu** to remember, e.g., **non gli è venuto in mente di spedire la lettera** he did not remember to mail the letter
mentecat•to -ta *adj & mf* lunatic
mentína *f* mint; **mentina digestiva** after-dinner mint
mentire §176 & (**mènto**) *intr* to lie;

mentire per la gola to lie through one's teeth

menti·to -ta *adj* false; disguised

menti·tóre -trice *adj* lying || *mf* liar

ménto *m* chin

mentòlo *m* menthol

méntre *m*—**in quel mentre** at that very moment; **nel mentre che** at the time when || *conj* while; whereas

me·nù *m* (**-nù**) menu

menzionare (menzióno) *tr* to mention

menzióne *f* mention

menzógna *f* lie

menzognè·ro -ra *adj* false, deceptive; lying, untruthful

meravíglia *f* marvel, wonder; **a meraviglia** wonderfully; **destare le meraviglie di** to amaze; **dire meraviglie di** to praise to the skies; **fare meraviglia** (with *dat*) to amaze; **far meraviglie** to work wonders

meravigliare §280 (**meraviglio**) *tr* to amaze; to astonish || *ref* to be astonished

meraviglió·so -sa [*s*] *adj* marvelous, wonderful || *m* (lit) supernatural

mercan·te -téssa *mf* merchant, dealer

mercanteggiare §290 (**mercantéggio**) *tr* to sell || *intr* to deal; to haggle

mercantile *adj* mercantile; merchant (*marine*) || *m* cargo boat, freighter

mercanzìa *f* merchandise; (coll) junk

mercato *m* market; trafficking; **a buon mercato** cheap; **far mercato di** to traffic in; **sopra mercato** besides; into the bargain

mèrce *f* merchandise, goods; commodity

mercé *f* favor, grace; mercy; **alla mercé di** at the mercy of; **mercé a** thanks to; **mercé sua** thanks to him (her, etc.)

mercéde *f* pay; (lit) reward

mercenà·rio -ria *adj & m* (**-ri -rie**) mercenary

mercerìa *f* notions store; **mercerie** notions

mercerizzare [ddzz] *tr* to mercerize

mèr·ci *adj invar* freight (*train, car, etc.*) || *m* (**-ci**) freight train

mer·ciàio -ciàia *mf* (**-ciài -ciàie**) notions store owner

merciaiòlo *m* small businessman; **merciaiolo ambulante** peddler

mercole·dì *m* (**-dì**) Wednesday

mercuriale *f* market report; price ceiling

mercùrio *m* mercury || **Mercurio** *m* Mercury

merènda *f* afternoon snack, bite

meretrice *f* harlot

meridia·no -na *adj & m* meridian || *f* sundial

meridionale *adj* meridional, southern || *mf* southerner

meridióne *m* south; South

merìg·gio *m* (**-gi**) noon

merin·ga *f* (**-ghe**) meringue

meritare (mèrito) *tr* to deserve; to win || *intr* (eccl) to merit; **bene meritare di** to deserve the gratitude of || *impers*—**merita** it is worth while to

meritévole *adj* deserving, worthy

mèrito *m* merit; **in merito a** concerning; **per merito di** thanks to; **render merito a** to reward

meritò·rio -ria *adj* (**-ri -rie**) meritorious

merlan·go *m* (**-ghi**) whiting

merlatura *f* battlement

merlétto *m* lace, needlepoint

mèrlo *m* blackbird; merlon; (fig) simpleton

merluzzo *m* cod

mè·ro -ra *adj* bare, mere; (poet) pure

merovìngi·co -ca (**-ci -che**) *adj* Merovingian || *f* Merovingian script

mesata [*s*] *f* month's wages

méscere (*pp* **mesciuto**) *tr* to pour (*e.g., wine*); (poet) to mix

meschini·tà *f* (**-tà**) pettiness; narrowmindedness; meanness, stinginess

meschi·no -na *adj* petty; narrowminded; wretched; puny || *mf* wretch

méscita *f* pouring; counter; bar

mescolanza *f* mixture, blend

mescolare (méscolo) *tr* to mix, blend; to shuffle (*cards*); to stir (*e.g., coffee*) || *ref* to mix, blend; to mingle; to consort; **mescolarsi in** to mind (*somebody else's business*)

mescolatrice *f* mixer, blender

mése [*s*] *m* month; month's pay

mesétto [*s*] *m* short month

mesóne *m* (phys) meson

méssa *f* (eccl & mus) Mass; **messa a fuoco** (phot) focusing; **messa a punto** adjustment; clear statement, outline of a problem; (aut) tune-up; **messa a terra** (elec) grounding; **messa cantata** high mass; **messa in marcia** or **in moto** (mach) starting; **messa in orbita** (rok) orbiting; **messa in piega** waving (*of hair*); **messa in scena** staging; **messa in vendita** putting up for sale

messaggerìe *fpl* delivery service

messaggè·ro -ra *mf* messenger; postal clerk

messàg·gio *m* (**-gi**) message

messale *m* missal

mèsse *f* harvest; crop

Messìa *m* Messiah

messiàni·co -ca *adj* (**-ci -che**) Messianic

messica·no -na *adj & mf* Mexican

Mèssico, il Mexico

messinscèna *f* staging; faking

mèsso *m* clerk; (poet) messenger

mestare (mésto) *tr* to stir || *intr* to intrigue

mesta·tóre -trice *mf* ringleader; schemer

mèstica *f* (painting) filler

mesticare §197 (**mèstico**) *tr* to prime (*a canvas*); to mix (*colors*)

mestierante *mf* potboiler (*person*); tradesman, craftsman

mestière *m* trade, craft; (archaic) task; **di mestiere** by trade; habitual; **essere del mestiere** to be up in one's line

mestièri *m*—**essere di** or **far mestièri** to be necessary

mestìzia *f* sadness

mè·sto -sta *adj* sad

méstola *f* ladle; trowel

méstolo *m* kitchen spoon; **avere il mestolo in mano** to be the boss

mèstruo *m* menses, menstruation

mèta *f* goal, aim; (rugby) goal line

méta *f* heap, stack (*e.g., of hay*)

me·tà *f* (*-tà*) half; middle; halfway; better half; **a metà** halfway, in the middle; **aver qlco a metà con qlcu** to go half and half with s.o.

metabolismo *m* metabolism

metafisi·co -ca (*-ci -che*) *adj* metaphysical || *m* metaphysician || *f* metaphysics

metafonèsi *f* umlaut, metaphony

metafonìa *f* umlaut, metaphony

metàfora *f* metaphor

metafòri·co -ca *adj* (*-ci -che*) metaphoric(al)

metàlli·co -ca *adj* (*-ci -che*) metallic

metallizzare [*ddzz*] *tr* to cover with metal

metallo *m* metal; timbre (*of voice*); (poet) metal object; **il vile metallo** filthy lucre

metallòide *m* nonmetal

metallurgia *f* metallurgy

metallùrgi·co -ca (*-ci -che*) *adj* metallurgic(al) || *m* metalworker

metalmeccàni·co -ca (*-ci -che*) *adj* metallurgic(al) and mechanical || *m* metalworker

metamòrfo·si *f* (*-si*) metamorphosis

metanizzare [*ddzz*] *tr* to provide with methane

metano *m* methane

metanodótto *m* natural gas pipeline

metàte·si *f* (*-si*) metathesis

metèora *f* meteor; atmospheric phenomenon

meteorite *m & f* meteorite

meteorologia *f* meteorology

meteorològi·co -ca *adj* (*-ci -che*) meteorologic(al); weather (*forecast*)

meteoròlo·go -ga *mf* (*-gi -ghe*) meteorologist

metic·cio -cia *adj & mf* (*-ci -ce*) half-breed

meticoló·so -sa [*s*] *adj* meticulous

metìli·co -ca *adj* (*-ci -che*) methyl

metòdi·co -ca *adj* (*-ci -che*) methodical; subject (*e.g., index*) || *mf* methodical person || *f* methodology

metodi·sta *adj & mf* (*-sti -ste*) Methodist

mètodo *m* method

metràg·gio *m* (*-gi*) length in meters; **corto metraggio** short; **lungo metraggio** full-length movie, feature film

metratura *f* length in meters

mètri·co -ca (*-ci -che*) *adj* metric(al) || *f* metrics, prosody

mètro *m* meter; (fig) yardstick; (lit) words

métro *m* (coll) subway

metrònomo *m* (mus) metronome

metronòt·te *m* (*-te*) night watchman

metròpo·li *f* (*-li*) metropolis

metropolità·no -na *adj* metropolitan || *m* policeman, traffic cop || *f* subway

metrovìa *f* subway

méttere §198 *tr* to put, place; to set (*e.g., foot*); to run (*e.g., a nail into a board*); to cause (*fear; fever*); to employ; to admit; to put forth; to give out; (coll) to charge; (coll) to install; (aut) to engage (*a gear*); **metterci** to take (*e.g., an hour*); **mettere a confronto** to compare; **mettere a freno** to check; **mettere a fuoco** (phot) to focus; **mettere al bando** to banish; **mettere all'asta** to auction off; **mettere al mondo** to give birth to; **mettere a nudo** to lay bare; **mettere fuori** to pull out; to give out (*news*); to throw (*s.o.*) out; **mettere giù** to lower; **mettere in onda** to broadcast; **mettere in pericolo** to endanger; **mettere la pulce nell'orecchio a** to put a bug in the ear of; **mettere qlcu alla porta** to show s.o. the door; **mettere su** to set up; (coll) to put (*e.g., a coat*) on; **mettere su qlcu contro qlcu** to excite s.o. against s.o. || *intr* to sprout; to lead (*said, e.g., of a road*) || *ref* to put on, to don; to place oneself, put oneself; to take shape; **mettersi a** to begin to; **mettersi al bello** to clear up (*said of weather*); **mettersi a letto** to go to bed; **mettersi a sedere** to sit down; **mettersi con** to start to work with; **mettersi in ferie** to take one's vacation; **mettersi in malattia** to fall ill; **mettersi in mare** to put to sea; **mettersi in maschera** to wear a masked costume; **mettersi in salvo** to get out of danger; to save oneself; **mettersi in viaggio** to set out on a journey; **mettersi in vista** to make oneself conspicuous || *impers*—**mette conto** it is worth while

mettima·le *mf* (*-le*) troublemaker

mezzadrìa [*ddzz*] *f* sharecropping

mezza·dro -dra [*ddzz*] *mf* sharecropper

mezzaluna [*ddzz*] *f* (**mezzelune**) half-moon; crescent (*symbol of Turkey and Islam*); curved chopping knife; lunette (*of fortification*)

mezzana [*ddzz*] *f* procuress; (naut) mizzen

mezzanave [*ddzz*] *f*—**a mezzanave** amidships

mezzanino [*ddzz*] *m* mezzanine

mezza·no -na [*ddzz*] *adj* median; medium; middle || *m* procurer || *f* see **mezzana**

mezzanòtte [*ddzz*] *f* (**mezzenòtti**) midnight

mezzatìnta [*ddzz*] *f* (**mezzetinte**) halftone

méz·zo -za *adj* overripe, rotten

mèz·zo -za [*ddzz*] *adj* half; middle || *m* half; middle; medium; means; vehicle; **a mezzo (di)** by (*e.g., messenger*); **andar di mezzo** to suffer the consequences; to be the loser; **entrare di mezzo** to interpose oneself; **esserci di mezzo** to be present; to be at stake; **giusto mezzo** happy medium; **in mezzo a** among; in the lap of, e.g., **in mezzo alle delicatezze** in the lap of luxury; **in quel mezzo** meanwhile; **levar di mezzo** to get rid of; **mezzi** means; facilities; **mezzi di comunicazione di massa** mass media; **per mezzo di** by means of

mezzobusto [*ddzz*] *m* (**mezzibusti**) (sculp) bust; **a mezzobusto** half-length (*e.g., portrait*)

mezzo·dì [ddzz] *m* (**-dì**) noon; south; South

mezzogiórno [ddzz] *m* noon; south; South

mezzùc·cio [ddzz] *m* (**-ci**) expedient

mi §5 *pron*

miagolare (**miàgolo**) *intr* to meow

miagolì·o *m* (**-i**) meow, mew

mi·ca *f* (**-che**) mica; (obs) crumb ‖ *adv*—**mica male** (coll) not too bad!; **non . . . mica** not . . . ever; not at all

mìc·cia *f* (**-ce**) fuse

michelàc·cio *m* (**-ci**) (coll) lazy bum

micidiale *adj* deadly; (fig) unbearable

mì·cio -cia *mf* (**-ci -cie**) (coll) pussy cat

micrò·bio *m* (**-bi**) microbe

microbiologìa *f* microbiology

microbo *m* microbe

microfà·rad *m* (**-rad**) microfarad

microferrovìa *f* model railroad

micro·film *m* (**-film**) microfilm

microfilmare *tr* to microfilm

micròfono *m* microphone

microlettóre *m* microfilm reader

micromotóre *m* small motor; motorcycle

microónda *f* microwave

microschèda *f* microcard

microscòpi·co -ca *adj* (**-ci -che**) microscopic(al)

microscò·pio *m* (**-pi**) microscope

microsól·co *adj invar* microgroove ‖ *m* (**-chi**) microgroove; microgroove, long-playing record

microtelèfono *m* French telephone, handset

midólla *f* crumb; (coll) marrow

midól·lo *m* (**-la** *fpl*) marrow; (bot & fig) pith; **midollo spinale** (anat) spinal cord

mièle *m* honey

miètere (**mièto**) *tr* to reap; (lit) to kill

mietitrebbiatrice *f* combine

mieti·tóre -trice *mf* reaper, harvester

mietitura *f* harvesting

mi·gliàio *m* (**-gliàia** *fpl*) thousand

mi·glio *m* (**-glia** *fpl*) mile; milestone; **miglio marino** nautical mile; **miglio terrestre** mile ‖ *m* (**-gli**) millet

miglioraménto *m* improvement

migliorare (**miglióro**) *tr*, *intr* (ESSERE & AVERE) & *ref* to improve

miglióre *adj* better; best

migliorìa *f* improvement (*e.g., of real estate*)

mignatta *f* leech

mignolo *adj masc* little (*finger or toe*) ‖ *m* little finger; little toe

migrare *intr* to migrate

migra·tóre -trice *adj* & *m* migrant

migrazióne *f* migration

Milano *f* Milan

miliardà·rio -ria *adj* & *mf* (**-ri -rie**) billionaire

miliardo *m* billion

milionà·rio -ria *adj* & *mf* (**-ri -rie**) millionaire

milióne *m* million

milionèsi·mo -ma *adj* & *m* millionth

militante *adj* & *m* militant

militare *adj* military ‖ *m* soldier ‖ *v* (**milito**) *intr* to be a member; to mili-

tate; to be in the armed forces; **militare in** to be a member of (*e.g., a party*)

militaré·sco -sca *adj* (**-schi -sche**) military, soldierly

militarismo *m* militarism

militari·sta (**-sti -ste**) *adj* militaristic ‖ *mf* militarist

militarizzare [ddzz] *tr* to militarize; to fortify

milite *m* militiaman; soldier; **milite del fuoco** fireman; **Milite Ignoto** Unknown Soldier

militesènte *adj* exempt from military service ‖ *m* man exempt from military service

milìzia *f* militia; (mil) service; struggle; **milizie celesti** heavenly host

miliziano *m* militiaman

millantare *tr* to boast of ‖ *ref* to brag, boast

millanta·tóre -trice *mf* braggart

millanterìa *f* bragging

mille *adj*, *m* & *pron* (**mila**) thousand, a thousand, one thousand ‖ **il Mille** the eleventh century; the year one thousand

millecènto *m* eleven hundred ‖ *f* car with a 1100 cc. motor

millefò·glie *m* (**-glie**) puff-paste cake

millenà·rio -ria (**-ri -rie**) *adj* millennial ‖ *m* millennium

millèn·nio *m* (**-ni**) millennium

millepiè·di *m* (**-di**) millipede

millèsi·mo -ma *adj* & *m* thousandth

milliam·père *m* (**-père**) milliampere

milligrammo *m* milligram

millimetra·to -ta *adj* divided into squares of one millimeter square

millimetro *m* millimeter

milli·vòlt *m* (**-vòlt**) millivolt

milza *f* spleen

mimare *tr* & *intr* to mime

mimetizzare [ddzz] *tr* (mil) to camouflage

mimetizzazióne [ddzz] *f* (mil) camouflage

mìmi·co -ca (**-ci -che**) *adj* mimic; sign (*language*) ‖ *f* mimicry; (theat) gestures; (theat) miming

mì·mo -ma *mf* mime ‖ *m* (orn) mockingbird

mina *f* lead (*of pencil*); (mil) mine; **mina anticarro** antitank mine; **mina antiuomo** antipersonnel mine

minaccévole *adj* (lit) threatening

minàc·cia *f* (**-ce**) threat, menace

minacciare §128 *tr* to threaten, menace

minacció·so -sa [s] *adj* threatening

minare *tr* to mine; to undermine

minaréto *m* minaret

minatóre *m* miner

minatò·rio -ria *adj* (**-ri -rie**) threatening

minchionare (**minchióno**) *tr* (slang) to make a sucker of

minchióne *m* (slang) sucker

minerale *adj* mineral ‖ *m* mineral; ore

mineralogìa *f* mineralogy

minerà·rio -ria *adj* (**-ri -rie**) mining

minèr·va *m* (**-va**) safety match

minèstra *f* vegetable soup

minestróne *m* minestrone; hodgepodge

mìngere §199 *intr* to urinate

mingherli·no -na *adj* frail, thin

miniare §287 *tr* to paint in miniature; to illuminate

miniatura *f* miniature

miniaturizzare [ddzz] *tr* to miniaturize

miniaturizzazióne [ddzz] *f* miniaturization

minièra *f* mine

mini·gòlf *m* (-gòlf) miniature golf

minigònna *f* miniskirt

mìnima *f* lowest temperature; (mus) minim

minimizzare [ddzz] *tr* to minimize

mìni·mo -ma *adj* smallest, least; minimum || *m* minimum; **al minimo** at the least; **girare al minimo** or **tenere il minimo** (aut) to idle || *f* see **minima**

mìnio *m* red lead; rouge

ministeriale *adj* ministerial

ministèro *m* ministry; cabinet; department; **pubblico ministero** public prosecutor

ministra *f* (joc) wife of minister; (joc) female minister; (poet) minister

ministro *m* minister; secretary; administrator; **ministro degli Esteri** foreign minister; (U.S.A.) Secretary of State

minoranza *f* minority

minorare (minóro) *tr* to lessen; to disable

minora·to -ta *adj* disabled || *mf* disabled person

minorazióne *f* reduction; disability

minóre *adj* smaller, lesser; minor; smallest, least; younger; youngest || *m* minor

minorènne *adj* underage || *mf* minor

minorile *adj* juvenile (*e.g., court*)

minori·tà *f* (-tà) minority

minuétto *m* minuet

minù·gia *f* (-gia & -gie) (mus) catgut

minùsco·lo -la *adj* small (*letter*); diminutive || *m* & *f* small letter

minuta *f* first draft, rough copy

minutàglia *f* trifles; small fry

minutante *m* secretary; retailer

minuterìa *f* trinkets, notions

minu·to -ta *adj* minute; small (*change*); common (*people*) || *m* minute; **al minuto** retail; **di minuto in minuto** at any moment; **minuto secondo** second; **nel minuto** in detail; **per minuto** minutely || *f* see **minuta**

minùzia *f* trifle; **minuzie** minutiae

minuzió·so -sa [s] *adj* meticulous

minùzzolo *m* scrap, crumb; small boy

mìo mìa §6 *adj* & *pron poss* (mièi mìe)

mìope *adj* nearsighted || *mf* nearsighted person

miopìa *f* nearsightedness

mira *f* aim; sight; target, goal; **prendere di mira** to aim at; to torment

miràbile *adj* admirable || *m* wonder

mirabìlia *fpl* wonders; **far mirabilia** to perform wonders; **dir mirabilia di** to speak highly of

mirabolante *adj* amazing, astonishing

miracola·to -ta *adj* miraculously cured || *mf* miraculously cured person

miràcolo *m* miracle; wonder; **dir mira-**

coli di to praise to the skies; **per miracolo** by mere chance

miracoló·so -sa [s] *adj* miraculous; wonderful

miràg·gio *m* (-gi) mirage

mirare *tr* (lit) to look at; (lit) to aim at || *intr* to aim; **mirare a** to aim at; **mirare a** + *inf* to aim to + *inf;* to intend to + *inf*

mirìade *f* myriad

mirino *m* sight (*of gun*); (phot) finder

mirra *f* myrrh

mirtillo *m* blueberry; whortleberry, huckleberry

mirto *m* myrtle

misantropìa *f* misanthropy

misàntro·po -pa *adj* misanthropic || *mf* misanthrope

miscèla *f* mixture, blend

miscelare (**miscèlo**) *tr* to mix, blend

miscellàne·o -a *adj* miscellaneous || *f* miscellany

mischia *f* fight; (sports) scrimmage

mischiare §287 *tr* to mix, blend; to shuffle (*cards*) || *ref* to mix

misconóscere §134 *tr* to not appreciate, undervalue

miscredènte *adj* misbelieving || *mf* misbeliever

miscù·glio *m* (-gli) mixture, blend

miseràbile *adj* pitiful, miserable; poor, wretched

miseran·do -da *adj* pitiable

miserère *m* Miserere; **essere al miserere** to be in one's last hours

miserévole *adj* pitiful; pitiable

misèria *f* destitution, misery; wretchedness; lack, want; trifle; **piangere miseria** to cry poverty

misericòrdia *f* mercy

misericordió·so -sa [s] *adj* merciful

mìse·ro -ra *adj* unhappy, wretched; poor; meager; mean; too small, too short

misfatto *m* misdeed, misdoing

misiriz·zi [s] *m* (-zi) tumbler (*toy*); (fig) chameleon

misògi·no -na *adj* misogynous || *m* misogynist

missile *adj* & *m* missile; **missile antimissile** antimissile missile; **missile intercontinentale** I.C.B.M.; **missile teleguidato** guided missile

missilìsti·co -ca *adj* (-ci -che) missile

missionà·rio -ria *adj* & *m* (-ri -rie) missionary

missióne *f* mission

missiva *f* missive

misterió·so -sa [s] *adj* mysterious

mistèro *m* mystery

mìstica *f* mysticism; mystical literature

misticismo *m* mysticism

mìsti·co -ca (-ci -che) *adj* & *mf* mystic || *f* see **mistica**

mistificare §197 (**mistìfico**) *tr* to hoax

mistificazióne *f* hoax

mi·sto -sta *adj* mixed || *m* mixture; mixed train

mistura *f* mixture

misura *f* measure; size; bounds; fitting; **a misura che** in proportion as; **di**

misura (sports) with a narrow margin; **su misura** made-to-order
misuràbile *adj* measurable
misurare *tr* to measure; to deliver (*e.g., a slap*); to budget (*expenses*); to try on (*clothes*); to weigh (*the outcome*) || *intr* to measure || *ref* to compete; to limit oneself; **misurarsi con** to try conclusions with
misura·to -ta *adj* moderate; scanty
misurino *m* measuring spoon or cup
mite *adj* mild; tame; low (*price*)
miti·co -ca *adj* (*-ci -che*) mythical
mitigare §209 (**mìtigo**) *tr* to mitigate; to assuage, allay || *ref* to abate
mitilo *m* mussel
mito *m* myth
mitologìa *f* mythology
mitològi·co -ca *adj* (*-ci -che*) mythologic(al)
mitòmane *mf* compulsive liar
mi·tra *m* (*-tra*) submachine gun || *f* miter
mitràglia *f* grapeshot; scrap iron; (coll) machine gun
mitragliare §280 (**mitràglio**) *tr* to machine-gun
mitragliatrice *f* machine gun
mitraglièra *f* heavy machine gun
mitraglière *m* machine gunner
mittènte *mf* sender; shipper
mo' *m*—apocopated form of **modo** by way of; **a mo' d'esempio** as an illustration
mòbile *adj* movable; personal (*property*); (fig) fickle; (rr) rolling (*stock*) || *m* piece of furniture; cabinet; (phys) body; **mobili** furniture
mobilia *f* furniture
mobiliare *adj* (fin) security; (law) movable || §287 (**mobìlio**) *tr* to furnish
mobilière *m* furniture maker; furniture dealer
mobilità *f* mobility
mobilitare (**mobìlito**) *tr* & *intr* to mobilize
mobilitazióne *f* mobilization
mò·ca *m* (*-ca*) mocha; **caffè moca** Mocha coffee
mocassino *m* mocassin
moccicare §197 (**móccico**) *intr* (slang) to snivel; (slang) to run (*said of the nose*); (slang) to whimper
moccicó·so -sa [*s*] *adj* (slang) snotty
móc·cio *m* (*-ci*) snot, snivel
mocció·so -sa [*s*] *adj* snotty || *m* brat
mòccolo *m* end of candle, snuff; (joc) snot; (slang) curse word; **reggere il moccolo a qlcu** to be a third party to a couple's necking
mòda *f* fashion, vogue; **andar di moda** to be fashionable; to be all the rage; **fuori moda** outdated
modali·tà *f* (*-tà*) modality; method
modanatura *f* molding
mòdano *m* mold
modèlla *f* model
modellare (**modèllo**) *tr* to model; to mold || *ref* to pattern oneself
modella·tóre -trice *mf* pattern maker; molder

modellino *m* (archit) model, maquette
modèllo *adj invar* model || *m* model; fashion; style; pattern
moderare (**mòdero**) *tr* to moderate, control
moderatézza *f* moderation
modera·to -ta *adj* moderate; (mus) moderato || *m* middle-of-the-roader
modera·tóre -trice *adj* moderating || *m* moderator
modernizzare [*ddzz*] *tr* & *ref* to modernize
modèr·no -na *adj* & *m* modern
modèstia *f* modesty; scantiness, meagerness
modè·sto -sta *adj* modest; humble
mòdi·co -ca *adj* (*-ci -che*) reasonable
modìfi·ca *f* (*-che*) modification; alteration
modificare §197 (**modìfico**) *tr* to modify; to change; to alter
modiglióne *m* (archit) modillion
modista *f* milliner
modisterìa *f* millinery; millinery shop
mòdo *m* manner, mode, way; custom; idiom; (gram) mood; (mus) mode; **ad ogni modo** anyhow; nevertheless; **ad un modo** equally; **a modo** proper; properly; **a suo modo** in his own way; **bei modi** good manners; **di modo che** so that; **in malo modo** poorly; **in modo da** so as to; **in nessun modo** by no means; **in ogni modo** anyhow; **in qualche modo** somehow; **modo di dire** idiom; turn of phrase; **modo di fare** behavior; **modo di vedere** opinion; **per modo di dire** so to speak
modulare (**mòdulo**) *tr* to modulate
modulazióne *f* modulation; **modulazione d'ampiezza** amplitude modulation; **modulazione di frequenza** frequency modulation
mòdulo *m* module; blank, form
moffétta *f* skunk
mògano *m* mahogany
mòg·gio *m* (*-gi*) bushel
mò·gio -gia *adj* (*-gi -gie*) downcast, crestfallen
mó·glie *f* (*-gli*) wife
moìne *fpl* blandishments
mòla *f* grindstone; (coll) millstone
molare *adj* grinding; molar || *m* molar || *v* (**mòlo**) *tr* to grind
molassa *f* molasse, sandstone
molatóre *m* grinder (*person*); sander (*person*)
molatrice *f* grinder (*machine*); sander (*machine*); **molatrice di pavimenti** floor sander
mòle *f* size; pile; bulk, mass; huge structure
molècola *f* molecule
molestare (**molèsto**) *tr* to bother, annoy
molèstia *f* bother, trouble, annoyance
molè·sto -sta *adj* bothersome, troublesome
molibdèno *m* molybdenum
molinétto *m* (naut) winch
mòlla *f* spring; (fig) mainspring; **molla a balestra** leaf spring; **molle** tongs; **molle del letto** bedspring; **prendere**

qlco con le molle to keep at a reasonable distance from s.th

mollare (mòllo) *tr* to let go; to slacken; to drop (*anchor*); (coll) to soak ‖ *intr* to give up; (coll) to soak; molla! (coll) cut it out!

mòlle *adj* wet, soaked; soft; mild; easy (*life*); weak (*character*); flexible ‖ *m* softness; soft ground; tenere a molle to soak

mollécca *f* soft-shell crab

molleggiaménto *m* suspension; springiness

molleggiare §290 (molléggio) *tr* to provide with springs, to make elastic; (aut) to provide with suspension ‖ *intr* to be springy, to have bounce ‖ *ref* to bounce along

mollég·gio *m* (-gi) springs; (aut) suspension; springiness

mollétta *f* hairpin; clothespin; mollette sugar tongs

mollettièra *f* puttee

mollettóne *m* swansdown

mollézza *f* softness

molli·ca *f* (-che) crumb (*soft inner portion of bread*); molliche crumbs

mollificare §197 (mollìfico) *tr* & *ref* to mollify; to soften

mòl·lo -la *adj* soft ‖ *m*—mettere a mollo to soak ‖ *f* see molla

mollu·sco *m* (-schi) mollusk

mòlo *m* pier, wharf

moltéplice *adj* multiple, manifold

moltilaterale *adj* multilateral, many-sided

moltìpli·ca *f* (-che) front sprocket (*of bicycle*)

moltiplicare §197 (moltìplico) *tr* & *ref* to multiply

moltitùdine *f* multitude, crowd

mól·to -ta *adj* much, a lot of; very; e.g., ho molta sete I am very thirsty ‖ *pron* much; a lot; a dir molto mostly; ci corre molto there is a great difference ‖ mol·ti -te *adj* & *pron* many ‖ molto *adv* very; quite; much; a lot; widely; long; fra non molto before long; non . . . molto (coll) not . . . at all

momentàne·o -a *adj* momentary

moménto *m* moment; opportune time; (slang) trifle; (phys) momentum; dal momento che since; per il momento for the time being; sul momento this very moment

mòna·ca *f* (-che) nun

monacale *adj* monachal, conventual

monacato *m* monkhood

monachésimo *m* monachism, monasticism

monachina *f* little nun; monachine sparks

mòna·co *m* (-ci) monk; (archit) king post ‖ Monaco *m* Monaco ‖ *f* Munich

monar·ca *m* (-chi) monarch

monarchìa *f* monarchy

monàrchi·co -ca *adj* (-ci -che) monarchical; monarchist(ic) (*advocating a monarch*) ‖ *mf* monarchist

monastèro *m* monastery

monàsti·co -ca *adj* (-ci -che) monastic(al)

moncherino *m* stump (*without hand*)

món·co -ca (-chi -che) *adj* one-handed; one-armed; incomplete ‖ *mf* cripple

moncóne *m* stump

mondana *f* prostitute

mondani·tà *f* (-tà) worldliness

monda·no -na *adj* mundane; worldly; society; fashionable ‖ *m* playboy ‖ *f* see mondana

mondare (móndo) *tr* to peel, pare; to thresh; to weed; to prune; (fig) to cleanse

mondari·so *mf* (-so) rice weeder

mondez·zàio *m* (-zài) dump

mondiale *adj* world, world-wide; (coll) stupendous

mondìglia *f* chaff; trash; refuse

mondina *f* rice weeder

món·do da *adj* clean-peeled; (lit) pure ‖ *m* world; hopscotch; (coll) heap, bunch; bel mondo smart set; cascasse il mondo! (coll) come what may!; da che mondo è mondo since the world began; essere nel mondo della luna to be absent-minded; mandare all'altro mondo (coll) to send packing; mettere al mondo to give birth to; mondo della luna world of fancy; un mondo a lot; venire al mondo to be born ‖ Mondo *m*—Terzo Mondo Third World

monega·sco -sca *adj* & *mf* (-schi -sche) Monacan

monellerìa *f* prank

monèl·lo -la *mf* urchin, brat ‖ *f* romp

monéta *f* money; coin; piece of money; purse (*in horse races*); change; batter moneta to mint money; moneta sonante cash

monetà·rio -ria (-ri -rie) *adj* monetary ‖ *m*—falso monetario counterfeiter

monetizzare [ddzz] *tr* to express in money; to transform into cash

mòngo·lo -la *adj* & *mf* Mongolian

monile *m* necklace; jewel

mònito *m* admonition, warning

monitóre *m* monitor

mònna *f* (obs) lady; (coll) monkey

monoàlbero *adj invar* (aut) single-camshaft, valve-in-head (*distribution*)

monoaurale *adj* monaural

monoblòc·co (-co) *adj* single-block ‖ *m* (aut) cylinder block

monocilìndri·co -ca *adj* (-ci -che) (mach) single-cylinder

monòco·lo -la *adj* one-eyed ‖ *m* monocle

monocolóre *adj invar* one-color; one-party

monofa·se *adj* (-si & -se) single-phase

monogamìa *f* monogamy

monòga·mo -ma *adj* monogamous ‖ *m* monogamist

monografìa *f* monograph

monogram·ma *m* (-mi) monogram

monolìti·co -ca *adj* (-ci -che) monolithic

monolìto *m* monolith

monòlo·go *m* (-ghi) monologue

monomanìa *f* monomania

monò·mio *m* (-**mi**) monomial

monopàttino *m* scooter

monopèt·to (-**to**) *adj* single-breasted ‖ *m* single-breasted suit

monoplano *m* (aer) monoplane

monopò·lio *m* (-**li**) monopoly

monopolizzare [ddzz] *tr* to monopolize

monopósto *adj invar* one-man ‖ *m* single-seater

monorotàia *adj invar* single-track ‖ *f* monorail

monoscò·pio *m* (-**pi**) (telv) test pattern

monosìlla·bo -ba *adj* monosyllabic ‖ *m* monosyllable

monòssido *m* monoxide

monoteìsti·co -ca *adj* (-**ci -che**) monotheistic

monotipìa *f* monotype

monotipo *m* monotype

monotonìa *f* monotony

monòto·no -na *adj* monotonous

monsignóre *m* monsignor

monsóne *m* monsoon

mónta *f* horseback riding; stud; jockey

montacàri·chi *m* (-**chi**) freight elevator

montàg·gio *m* (-**gi**) (mach) assembly; (mov) editing; (mov) montage

montagna *f* mountain; **montagna di ghiaccio** iceberg; **montagne russe** roller coaster

montagnó·so -sa [s] *adj* mountainous

montana·ro -ra *adj* mountain ‖ *mf* mountaineer

monta·no -na *adj* mountain

montante *adj* rising ‖ *m* riser, upright; (football) goal post; (aer) strut; (boxing) uppercut; (com) aggregate amount

montare (**mónto**) *tr* to mount; to go up (*the stairs*); to set (*jewels*); to frame (*a painting*); to whip (*e.g., eggs*); to excite; to exaggerate (*news*); to decorate (*a house*); to cover (*said of a male animal*); (mach) to assemble; (mov) to edit; **montare la testa a** to excite; to give a swell head to ‖ *intr* (ESSERE) to jump; to climb; to go up; to rise; to swell; **montare alla testa a** to go to the head of; **montare in collera** to get angry ‖ *impers*—**non monta** it doesn't matter, never mind

monta·tóre -trìce *mf* (mach) assembler; (mov) editor

montatura *f* assembly; frame (*of glasses*); appliqué; setting (*of gem*); (journ) ballyhoo; (mov) editing; **montatura pubblicitaria** publicity stunt

montavivàn·de *m* (-**de**) dumbwaiter

mónte *m* mountain; bank; mount (*in palmistry*); (cards) discard; **a monte** uphill; upstream; **andare a monte** to fail; **mandare a monte** to cause to fail; **monte di pietà** pawnbroker's; **monte di premi** pot (*in a lottery*)

montenegrì·no -na *adj & mf* Montenegrin

montessoria·no -na *adj* Montessori

montóne *m* ram; mutton; rounded stone

montuó·so -sa [s] *adj* mountainous

montura *f* uniform

monumentale *adj* monumental

monuménto *m* monument

moquètte *f* (**moquète**) wall-to-wall carpeting

mòra *f* mulberry; blackberry; brunette; Moorish woman; arrears; penalty (*for arrears*); (archaic) heap of stones

morale *adj* moral ‖ *m* morale; **giù di morale** downcast; **su di morale** in high spirits ‖ *f* morals, ethics; moral (*of a fable*)

moraleggiare §290 (**moraléggio**) *intr* to moralize

moralismo *m* moralism

morali·tà *f* (-**tà**) morality; morals

moralizzare [ddzz] *tr & intr* to moralize

moratòria *f* moratorium

morbidézza *f* softness

mòrbi·do -da *adj* soft; sleek; pliable ‖ *m* soft ground

morbillo *m* measles

mòrbo *m* disease; plague

morbó·so -sa [s] *adj* morbid

mòrchia *f* sediment; dregs of oil

mordace *adj* biting, mordacious

mordènte *adj* biting; (chem) mordant; (mach) interlocking ‖ *s* strength; (chem) mordant

mòrdere §200 *tr* to bite; to grab; to corrode; **mordere il freno** to champ the bit

mordicchiare §287 (**mordìcchio**) *tr* to nibble

morèl·lo -la *adj* blackish; black (*horse*) ‖ *m* black horse

morènte *adj* dying ‖ *mf* dying person

moré·sco -sca (-**schi -sche**) *adj* Moresque, Moorish ‖ *f* Moorish dance

morét·to -ta *adj* brunet ‖ *m* Negro boy; dark-skinned boy; chocolate-covered ice-cream bar ‖ *f* Negro girl; dark-skinned girl; mask; (orn) scaup duck

morfè·ma *m* (-**mi**) morpheme

morfina *f* morphine

morfinòmane *mf* morphine addict

morfologìa *f* morphology

morìa *f* pestilence; high mortality

moribón·do -da *adj* moribund

morigera·to -ta *adj* temperate, moderate

morire §201 *intr* (ESSERE) to die; to die out; to end (*said of a street*); **morire di noia** to be bored to death

moritu·ro -ra *adj* about to die, doomed

mormóne *mf* Mormon

mormorare (**mórmoro**) *tr* to murmur; to whisper ‖ *intr* to murmur; to whisper; to babble (*said of a brook*); to rustle; to gossip

mormorì·o *m* (-**i**) whisper; murmur

mò·ro -ra *adj* Moorish; dark-skinned; dark-brown ‖ *m* Moor ‖ *m* mulberry tree ‖ *f see* **mora**

morosi·tà *f* (-**tà**) delinquency (*in paying one's bills*)

moró·so -sa [s] *adj* delinquent (*in paying one's bills*) ‖ *m* (coll) boyfriend; **i morosi** (coll) the lovers ‖ *f* (coll) girl friend

mòrsa *f* vise; (archit) toothing

morsétto *m* clamp; (elec) binding post

morsicare §197 (mòrsico) *tr* to bite

morsicatura *f* bite

morsicchiare §287 (morsìcchio) *tr* to nibble

mòrso *m* bite; bit

mor·tàio *m* (-tài) mortar

mortale *adj* mortal; deadly ‖ *m* mortal

mortali·tà *f* (-tà) mortality

mortarétto *m* firecracker

mòrte *f* death; end; **averla a morte con** to harbor hatred for; **morte civile** (law) attainder, loss of civil rights

mortèlla *f* myrtle

mortificare §197 (mortìfico) *tr* to mortify ‖ *ref* to feel ashamed

mòr·to -ta *adj* dead; still (*life*); **morto di fame** dying of hunger; **morto di paura** scared to death ‖ *mf* dead person, deceased ‖ *m* hidden treasure; (cards) dummy, widow; **fare il morto** to float on one's back; to play possum; **morto di fame** ne'er-do-well, good-for-nothing; **suonare a morto** to toll

mortò·rio *m* (-ri) funeral

mortuà·rio -ria *adj* (-ri -rie) mortuary

mosài·co -ca (-ci -che) *adj* Mosaic ‖ *m* mosaic

mó·sca *f* (-sche) fly; imperial (*beard*); **mosca bianca** one in a million; **mosca cieca** blindman's buff; **fare venire la mosca al naso a** to make angry ‖ **Mosca** *f* Moscow

moscaiòla *f* fly netting; flytrap

moscardino *m* dandy; (zool) dormouse

moscatèl·lo -la *adj* muscat ‖ *m* muscatel

moscato *m* muscat grape; muscat wine

moscerino *m* gnat

moschèa *f* mosque

moschettière *m* musketeer; Italian National soccer player

moschétto *m* musket

moschettóne *m* snap hook

moschici·da *adj* (-di -de) fly-killing

mó·scio -scia *adj* (-sci -sce) flabby, soft

moscóne *m* big fly; pesky suitor

moscovi·ta *adj & mf* (-ti -te) Muscovite

Mosè *m* Moses

mòssa *f* gesture; movement; move; fake; post; **fare la mossa** to sprout (*said of plants*); **mossa di corpo** bowel movement; **prendere le mosse** to begin; **stare sulle mosse** to be about to begin; to be eager to take off (*said of a horse*)

mossière *m* starter (*in a race*)

mòs·so -sa *adj* moved; in motion; plowed; rough (*sea*); blurred (*picture*); wavy (*hair; ground*) ‖ *f see* **mossa**

mostarda *f* mustard; candied fruit

mósto *m* must

móstra *f* show; pretense, simulation; exhibit; display window; lapel; face (*of watch*); sample; (mil) insignia; (obs) military parade; **far mostra di sé** to show off; **mettersi in mostra** to show off

mostrare (móstro) *tr* to show; to put on; **mostrare a dito** to point to;

mostrare la corda to be threadbare ‖ *ref* to show up; to show oneself

mostreggiatura *f* lapel; cuff

mostrina *f* (mil) insignia

móstro *m* monster

mostruó·so -sa [s] *adj* monstrous

mòta *f* mud, mire

mo·tèl *m* (-tèl) motel

motivare *tr* to cause; to justify

motivazióne *f* justification, reason

motivo *m* motive, reason; motif; theme; (coll) tune; **a motivo di** because of; **motivo per cui** wherefore

mò·to *m* (-ti) motion; movement; emotion; riot; **mettere in moto** to start ‖ *f* (-to) (coll) motorcycle

motobar·ca *f* (-che) motorboat

motocannonièra *f* gunboat

motocarro *m* three-wheeler (*truck*)

motocarrozzétta *f* three-wheeler (*vehicle with sidecar*)

motociclétta *f* motorcycle

motocicli·sta *mf* (-sti -ste) motorcyclist

motocorazza·to -ta *adj* armored, panzer

motofalciatrice *f* power mower

motofurgóne *m* delivery truck

motolàn·cia *f* (-ce) motorboat, speedboat

motonàuti·co -ca *adj* (-ci -che) motorboat ‖ *f* motorboating

motonave *f* motor ship

motopescheréc·cio *m* (-ci) motor fishing boat

mo·tóre -trice *adj* motive (*power*); (mach) drive ‖ *m* motor; engine; car; **a motore** motorized; motor; **motore rotativo** (aut) rotary engine; **primo motore** prime mover ‖ *f see* **motrice**

motorétta *f* motor scooter

motorino *m* small motor; motor bicycle; **motorino d'avviamento** (aut) starter

motori·sta *m* (-sti) mechanic

motorìsti·co -ca *adj* (-ci -che) motor

motorizzare [ddzz] *tr* to motorize

motoscafo *m* motorboat; **motoscafo da corsa** speedboat

motosé·ga *f* (-ghe) chain saw

motosilurante *f* torpedo boat

motoveìcolo *m* motor vehicle

motovelièro *m* motor sailer

motrice *f* (rr) engine, motor; (aut) tractor; **motrice a vapore** steam engine

motteggiare §290 (mottéggio) *tr* to mock, jeer at ‖ *intr* to jest

mottég·gio *m* (-gi) mockery, jest

mòtto *m* witticism; motto; (lit) word

movènte *m* stimulus, motive

movènza *f* bearing, carriage; flow (*of a sentence*); cadence

movìbile *adj* movable

movimenta·to -ta *adj* lively; eventful

moviménto *m* motion, movement; traffic; **movimento di cassa** cash turnover

moviòla *f* (mov) viewer and splicer

mozióne *f* motion; (lit) movement

mozzare (mózzo) *tr* to lop off; to sever; **mozzare la testa a** to cut off the head of

mozzicóne *m* stump; butt (*e.g., of cigar*)

móz·zo -za *adj* cut off; truncated; cropped (*ears*); docked (*tail*); hard (*breathing*) ‖ *m* cabin boy; **mozzo di stalla** stable boy

mòzzo [ddzz] *m* hub

muc·ca *f* (*-che*) milch cow

mùc·chio *m* (*-chi*) pile, heap; bunch

mucillàgine *f* mucilage

mu·co *m* (*-chi*) mucus, phlegm

mucó·so -sa [s] *adj* mucous ‖ *f* mucous membrane

muda *f* molt

muffa *f* mold; mildew; **fare la muffa** to be musty

muffire §176 *intr* (ESSERE) to be musty

mùffola *f* mitten; muffle (*of furnace*)

muflóne *m* mouflon

mugghiare §287 (**mùgghio**) *intr* to bellow; to roar

màggine *m* (ichth) mullet

muggire §176 & (**muggo**) *intr* to moo, low; to roar; to howl

muggito *m* bellow; moo, low; roar

mughétto *m* lily of the valley

mu·gnàio -gnàia *mf* (**-gnài -gnàie**) miller

mugolare (**mùgolo**) *intr* to yelp; to moan

mugolì·o *m* (*-i*) yelp; moan

mugò·lio *m* (*-li*) pine tar

mugugnare *intr* (coll) to mumble; (coll) to grumble

mugugno *m* (coll) grumble

mulattière *m* mule driver, muleteer

mulattiè·ro -ra *adj* mule ‖ *f* mule track

mulat·to -ta *adj* & *mf* mulatto

muliebre *adj* womanly, feminine

mulinare *tr* to twirl; to scheme ‖ *intr* to whirl; to muse; to buzz (*in the mind*)

mulinèllo *m* twirl; whirlpool; whirlwind; fishing reel; whirligig; **fare mulinello con** to twirl

mulino *m* mill; **mulino ad acqua** water mill; **mulino a vento** windmill

mu·lo -la *mf* mule; (slang) bastard

multa *f* penalty, fine

multare *tr* to fine

multilaterale *adj* multilateral, many-sided

mùlti·plo -pla *adj* & *m* multiple

mùmmia *f* mummy

mummificare §197 (**mummìfico**) *tr* to mummify

mùngere §183 *tr* to milk

mungi·tóre -trice *mf* milker ‖ *f* milking machine; milk maid

mungitura *f* milking

municipale *adj* municipal, city

municipalizzazióne [ddzz] *f* municipalization; city management

munici·pio *m* (*-pi*) municipality; city council; city hall

munificènza *f* munificence

munifi·co -ca *adj* (*-ci -che*) munificent

munire §176 *tr* to fortify; to provide; **munire di** to equip with ‖ *ref* to provide oneself

munizióne *f* (obs) fortification; **munizioni** ammunition; building supplies

muòvere §202 *tr* to move; to wag; to propel, run; to lift (*one's finger*); to take (*a step*); to pose (*a question*); to stir up (*laughter*); to institute (*a lawsuit*); **muovere accusa a** to reproach ‖ *intr* (ESSERE) to begin; to move, start ‖ *ref* to move; to travel; to stir; to set out; to be moved; **muoviti!** hurry up!

mura *fpl* see **muro**

muràglia *f* wall; (fig) obstacle; **muraglia cinese** Chinese Wall

muraglióne *m* high wall, rampart

murale *adj* & *m* mural

murare *tr* to wall; to wall in ‖ *intr* to build a wall; **murare a secco** to build a dry wall ‖ *ref* to close oneself in

murata *f* (naut) bulwark

muratóre *m* bricklayer, mason

muratura *f* bricklaying, stonework

muriàti·co -ca *adj* (*-ci -che*) muriatic

mu·ro *m* (*-ri*) wall; **muro del pianto** Wailing Wall; **muro del suono** sound barrier ‖ *m* (**-ra** *fpl*)—**mura** walls (*of a city*)

musa *f* muse

muschia·to -ta *adj* musk (*e.g., ox*)

mù·schio *m* (*-schi*) musk; (coll) moss

mu·sco *m* (*-schi*) moss

mùscolo *m* muscle; (fig) sinew; (coll) mussel

muscoló·so -sa [s] *adj* muscular

muscó·so -sa [s] *adj* (lit) mossy

musèo *m* museum

museruòla *f* muzzle

musétta *f* nose bag

mùsi·ca *f* (*-che*) music; band; **cambiare musica** to change one's tune

musicale *adj* musical

musicante *adj* music-playing (*angels*) ‖ *mf* band player; second-rate musician

musicare §197 (**mùsico**) *tr* to set to music

musicassétta *f* cassette, tape cartridge

music-hall *m* (**-hall**) *m* vaudeville, burlesque

musici·sta *mf* (*-sti -ste*) musician

musicologia *f* musicology

musicòlo·go *m* (*-gi*) musicologist

muso *m* muzzle, snout; (coll) mug; (fig) nose; **avere il muso lungo** to make a long face; **mettere il muso** to pout

musó·ne -na *mf* pouter, sulker

mussare *tr* to publish with great fanfare (*a piece of news*) ‖ *intr* to foam (*said of wine*)

mùssola or **mussolina** *f* muslin

mussolinia·no -na *adj* of Mussolini

mùssolo *m* mussel

mustàc·chio *m* (*-chi*) shroud (*of bowsprit*); **mustacchi** moustache

musulma·no -na [s] *adj* & *mf* Moslem

muta *f* change; shift; molt; set (*of sails*); pack (*of hounds*); (mil) watch

mutàbile *adj* changeable

mutande *fpl* shorts, briefs, drawers

mutandine *fpl* panties; **mutandine da bagno** trunks

mutare *tr, intr* (ESSERE) & *ref* to change

mutazióne *f* mutation; (biol) mutation, sport

mutévole *adj* changeable; fickle

mutilare (mùtilo) *tr* to mutilate, maim

mutila·to -ta *adj* mutilated || *mf* cripple; amputee; **mutilato di guerra** disabled veteran

mutismo *m* silence, willful silence; (pathol) dumbness

mu·to -ta *adj* mute; dumb; silent (*movie*); unexpressed || *mf* mute || *f* see **muta**

mùtria *f* sulking attitude; proud demeanor

mùtua *f* mutual benefit society; medical insurance; **mettersi in mutua** to go on sick leave

mutuali·tà *f* (**-tà**) mutuality; mutual benefit institutions

mutuare (mùtuo) *tr* to borrow; to lend

mutua·to -ta *mf* person insured by mutual benefit society; person insured by medical insurance

mù·tuo -tua *adj* mutual; borrowing || *m* loan || *f* see **mutua**

N

N, n ['enne] *m & f* twelfth letter of the Italian alphabet

nababbo *m* nabob

Nabucodònosor *m* Nebuchadnezzar

nàcchera *f* castanet

nafta *f* crude oil; naphta; Diesel oil

naftalina *f* naphthalene

nàia *f* cobra; (slang) army discipline; (slang) military service

nàiade *f* naiad

nàilon *m* nylon

nanna *f* sleep (*of child*); **fare la nanna** to sleep (*said of child*)

na·no -na *adj & mf* dwarf

nàpalm *m* napalm

napoleòne *m* napoleon (*gold coin*) || **Napoleone** *m* Napoleon

napoleòni·co -ca *adj* (**-ci -che**) Napoleonic

napoleta·no -na *adj & mf* Neapolitan || *f* espresso coffee machine

Nàpoli *f* Naples

nappa *f* tassel; tuft; kid (*leather*)

narciso *m* narcissus

narcòti·co -ca *adj & m* (**-ci -che**) narcotic

narcotizzare [ddzz] *tr* to drug, dope; to anesthetize

narghi·lè *m* (**-lè**) hookah

narice *f* nostril

narrare *tr* to narrate, tell, recount

narrati·vo -va *adj* narrative; fictional || *f* narrative; fiction

narra·tóre -trice *mf* narrator, storyteller

narrazióne *f* narration; tale, story; narrative

nasàle [s] *adj & f* nasal

nascènte *adj* nascent; budding; rising (*sun*); dawning (*day*)

nàscere *m* beginning, origin || §203 *intr* (ESSERE) to be born; to bud; to shoot; to dawn; to rise; to spring up; **nàscere con la camicia** to be born with a silver spoon in one's mouth

nàscita *f* birth; birthday; origin

nascitu·ro -ra *adj* unborn, future || *mf* unborn child

nascóndere §204 *tr* to hide; **nascondere a** to hide from || *ref* to hide; to lurk

nascondì·glio *m* (**-gli**) hiding place; hideout; cache

nascondino *m* hide-and-seek; **giocare a nascondino** to play hide-and-seek

nascó·sto -sta *adj* hidden, concealed; secret; **di nascosto** secretly

nasèllo [s] *m* catch (*of latch*); (ichth) hake

nasièra [s] *f* nose ring

naso [s] *m* nose; (fig) face; **aver buon naso** to have a keen sense of smell; **ficcare il naso negli affari degli altri** to pry into the affairs of others; **menare per il naso** to lead by the nose; **naso adunco** hooknose; **restare con un palmo di naso** to be duped

nassa *f* pot (*for fishing*); **nassa per aragoste** lobster pot

nastrino *m* ribbon; badge

nastro *m* ribbon; band; tape; streamer; tape measure; **nastro del cappello** hatband; **nastro isolante** friction tape; **nastro per capelli** hair ribbon

nastùr·zio *m* (**-zi**) nasturtium

natale *adj* native, natal || **natali** *mpl* birth; birthday; **dare i natali a** to be the birthplace of || **Natale** *m* Christmas

natali·tà *f* (**-tà**) birth rate

natali·zio -zia (**-zi -zie**) *adj* natal; Christmas || *m* birthday

natante *adj* swimming; floating || *m* craft

natatóia *f* fin

natató·rio -ria *adj* (**-ri -rie**) swimming

nàti·ca *f* (**-che**) buttock

nati·o -a *adj* (**-i -e**) (poet) native

nativi·tà *f* (**-tà**) birth, nativity || **Natività** *f* Nativity

nati·vo -va *adj* native; natural, inborn || *mf* native

N.A.T.O. *f* (acronym) (**North Atlantic Treaty Organization**)—**la N.A.T.O.** NATO

na·to -ta *adj* born; **nata** née; **nato e sputato** the spit and image of; **nato morto** stillborn || *mf* child

natura *f* nature; **natura morta** still life; **in natura** in kind

naturale *adj* natural || *m* nature, disposition; **al naturale** life-size

naturalézza *f* naturalness; spontaneity

naturalismo *m* naturalism

naturali·sta *mf* (**-sti -ste**) naturalist

naturali·tà *f* (**-tà**) naturalization

naturalizzare [ddzz] *tr* to naturalize || *ref* to become naturalized

naturalizzazióne [ddzz] *f* naturalization

naturalménte *adv* naturally; of course

naufragare §209 (**nàufrago**) *intr* (ESSERE

& AVERE) to be shipwrecked; to sink, to fail

naufrà·gio *m* (**-gi**) shipwreck; failure

nàufra·go **-ga** (**-ghi** **-ghe**) *adj* shipwrecked || *mf* shipwrecked person; (fig) outcast

nàusea *f* nausea; disgust; **avere la nausea** to be sick at one's stomach

nauseabón·do **-da** *adj* sickening, nauseating; (fig) unsavory

nauseante *adj* sickening, nauseous

nauseare (**nàuseo**) *tr* to nauseate, sicken

nausea·to **-ta** *adj* sickened, disgusted

nàuti·co **-ca** (**-ci** **-che**) *adj* nautical || *f* sailing, navigation

navale *adj* naval, navy, sea

navata *f* nave; **navata centrale** nave; **navata laterale** aisle

nave *f* ship, vessel, boat; craft; **nave ammiraglia** flagship; **nave a motore** motorboat; **nave appoggio** tender; **nave a vela** sailboat; **nave da carico** freighter; **nave da guerra** warship; **nave portaerei** tanker; **nave portaerei** aircraft carrier; **nave rompighiaccio** icebreaker; **nave traghetto** ferryboat

navétta *f* shuttle; **fare la navetta** to shuttle

navicèlla *f* nacelle, cabin (*of airship*); car (*of balloon*)

navigàbile *adj* navigable

navigabili·tà *f* (**-tà**) navigability; seaworthiness

navigante *adj* sailing || *m* sailor

navigare §209 (**nàvigo**) *tr & intr* to navigate, to sail

naviga·to **-ta** *adj* seawise; wordly-wise

naviga·tóre **-trice** *mf* navigator

navigazióne *f* navigation

navi·glio *m* (**-gli**) ship, craft, boat; fleet; navy; canal; **naviglio mercantile** merchant marine

nazionale *adj* national || *f* national team

nazionalismo *m* nationalism

nazionali·sta *mf* (**-sti** **-ste**) nationalist

nazionalisti·co **-ca** *adj* (**-ci** **-che**) nationalistic

nazionali·tà *f* (**-tà**) nationality

nazionalizzare [**ddzz**] *tr* to nationalize

nazionalizzazióne [**ddzz**] *f* nationalization

nazióne *f* nation

nazi·sta *adj & mf* (**-sti** **-ste**) Nazi

nazzarè·no **-na** [**ddzz**] *adj & mf* Nazarene || **il Nazzareno** the Nazarene

ne §5 *pron & adv*

né *conj* neither, nor; **né . . . né** neither . . . nor

neanche *adv* not even; nor; not . . . either

nébbia *f* fog, haze, mist; **fa nebbia** it is foggy; **nebbia artificiale** smoke screen

nebbióne *m* thick fog, pea soup

nebbió·so **-sa** [**s**] *adj* foggy, hazy, misty

nebulare *adj* nebular

nebulizzare [**ddzz**] *tr* to atomize

nebulizzatóre [**ddzz**] *m* atomizer

nebulósa [**s**] *f* nebula

nebulosi·tà [**s**] *f* (**-tà**) fogginess, haziness, mistiness

nebuló·so **-sa** [**s**] *adj* foggy, hazy, misty || *f* see **nebulosa**

néces·saire *m* (**-saire**) vanity case; sewing kit

necessariaménte *adv* necessarily

necessà·rio **-ria** (**-ri** **-rie**) *adj* necessary, needed; essential || *m* necessity; necessities (*of life*)

necessi·tà *f* (**-tà**) necessity; need, want; **di necessità** necessarily

necessitare (**necèssito**) *tr* to require; to force || *intr* to be in want; to be necessary; **necessitare di** to need

necrologia *f* necrology, obituary

necrològi·co **-ca** *adj* (**-ci** **-che**) obituary

necromanzìa *f* necromancy

necròsi *f* necrosis, gangrene

nefan·do **-da** *adj* heinous, nefarious

nefa·sto **-sta** *adj* ill-fated; ominous

nefrite *f* nephritis

negare §209 (**négo & nègo**) *tr* to deny, negate; to refuse

negati·vo **-va** *adj & f* negative

nega·to **-ta** *adj* unfit, unsuited

negazióne *f* negation, denial; (gram) negative

neghittó·so **-sa** [**s**] *adj* lazy, slothful

neglèt·to **-ta** *adj* neglected; untidy

négli §4

negligènte *adj* negligent, careless

negligènza *f* negligence, carelessness; dereliction (*of duty*)

neglìgere §205 *tr* to neglect

negoziàbile *adj* negotiable

negoziante *mf* merchant, shopkeeper; dealer; **negoziante all'ingrosso** wholesaler; **negoziante al minuto** retailer; shopkeeper, storekeeper

negoziare §287 (**negòzio**) *tr* to negotiate, transact || *intr* to negotiate, deal

negoziati *mpl* negotiations

negozia·tóre **-trice** *mf* negotiator

negò·zio *m* (**-zi**) business; transaction; store, shop; **negozio di cancelleria** stationery store

negrière *m* slave trader; slave driver

negriè·ro **-ra** *adj* slave || *m* slave trader; slave driver

né·gro **-gra** *adj & mf* Negro

negromante *m* sorcerer

néi §4

nél §4

nélla §4

nélle §4

néllo §4

némbo *m* rain cloud; cloud (*e.g., of dust*)

Nembròd *m* Nimrod

nèmesi *f invar* nemesis || **Nemesi** *f* Nemesis

nemi·co **-ca** (**-ci** **-che**) *adj* inimical, hostile, unfriendly, enemy; (fig) adverse || *mf* enemy, foe; **Il Nemico** the Evil One

nemméno *adv* not even; nor; not . . . either

nènia *f* funeral dirge; lamentation

nenùfaro *m* water lily

nèo *m* mole (*on the skin*); flaw, blemish; neon; beauty spot

neoclassicheggiante *adj* in the direction of the neoclassical

neòfi·ta *mf* (**-ti -te**) neophite

neolati·no -na *adj* Neo-Latin, Romance

neologismo *m* neologism

neomicina *f* neomycin

nèon *m* neon

neona·to -ta *adj* newborn ‖ *mf* infant, baby; newborn child

neozelandése [dz][s] *adj* New Zealand ‖ *mf* New Zealander

nepènte *f* nepenthe

Nepóte *m* Nepos

neppure *adv* not even; nor; not . . . either

nequìzia *f* iniquity, wickedness

nera·stro -stra *adj* blackish

nerbata *f* heavy blow

nèrbo *m* whip; sinew; bulk; strength (*of an opposing force*)

nerboru·to -ta *adj* muscular, sinewy

nereggiare §290 (**neréggio**) *intr* to look black; to be blackish

nerétto *m* (*typ*) boldface

né·ro -ra *adj* black; dark; gloomy; dark-red (*wine*) ‖ *mf* black; Negro ‖ *m* black

nerofumo *m* lampblack

Neróne *m* Nero

nervatura *f* ribbing

nervi·no -na *adj* nerve (*gas*); nervine (*medicine*)

nèrvo *m* nerve; sinew; **avere i nervi** to be in a bad mood

nervosismo [s] *m* nervousness, irritability

nervó·so -sa [s] *adj* nervous, irritable; sinewy, vigorous (*style*) ‖ *m* bad mood; **avere il nervoso** to be in a bad mood

nèsci *m*—**fare il nesci** to feign ignorance

nèspola *f* medlar; **nespole** (*coll*) blows

nèspolo *m* medlar tree

nèsso *m* connection, link; **avere nesso** to cohere

nessu·no -na *adj* no, not any ‖ **nessuno** *pron* nobody, no one; none; not anybody; not anyone; **nessuno dei due** neither one

nettapén·ne *m* (**-ne**) penwiper

nettare (**nétto**) *tr* to clean, to cleanse

nèttare *m* nectar

nettézza *f* cleanness, cleanliness; neatness; **nettezza urbana** department of sanitation; garbage collection

nét·to -ta *adj* clean; clear; sharp; net ‖ **netto** *adv* clearly, distinctly

nettùnio *m* neptunium

Nettuno *m* Neptune

netturbino *m* street cleaner

neurologìa *f* neurology

neurò·si *f* (**-si**) neurosis

neuròti·co -ca *adj* (**-ci -che**) neurotic

neutrale *adj & mf* neutral

neutrali·sta *adj & mf* (**-sti -ste**) neutralist

neutralità *f* (**-tà**) neutrality

neutralizzare [ddzz] *tr* to neutralize

nèu·tro -tra *adj* neuter; neutral

neutróne *m* neutron

ne·vàio *m* (**-vài**) snowfield; snowdrift

néve *f* snow; **neve carbonica** dry ice

nevicare §197 (**névica**) *impers* (ESSERE) —**nevica** it is snowing

nevicata *f* snowfall

nevìschio *m* sleet

nevó·so -sa [s] *adj* snowy

nevralgìa *f* neuralgia

nevrastèni·co -ca *adj & mf* (**-ci -che**) neurasthenic

nevvéro (i.e., **n'è vero** for **non è vero**) see **non**

niacina *f* niacin

nìb·bio *m* (**-bi**) (orn) kite

nìcchia *f* niche; nook, recess

nicchiare §287 (**nìcchio**) *intr* to waver

nìc·chio *m* (**-chi**) shell; nook

nichel *m* nickel

nichelare (**nìchelo**) *tr* to nickel, to nickel-plate

nichelatura *f* nickel-plating

nichelino *m* nickel (*coin*)

nichèlio *m* var of **nichel**

Nicòla *m* Nicholas

nicotina *f* nicotine

nidiata *f* nestful; brood

nidificare §197 (**nidìfico**) *intr* to build a nest, to nest

nido *m* nest; home; nursery; den (*of thieves*)

niènte *m* nothing; nothingness; **dal niente** from scratch; **di niente** you're welcome ‖ *pron* nothing; not . . . anything; **quasi niente** next to nothing

nientediméno *adv* no less, nothing less

Nilo *m* Nile

ninfa *f* nymph

ninfèa *f* white water lily

ninnananna *f* lullaby, cradlesong

nìnnolo *m* toy; trinket

nipóte *mf* grandchild ‖ *m* grandson; nephew; **nipoti** descendants ‖ *f* granddaughter; niece

nippòni·co -ca *adj* (**-ci -che**) Nipponese

nirvana, il nirvana

nìti·do -da *adj* clear, distinct

nitóre *m* brightness; elegance

nitrato *m* nitrate

nitrire §176 *intr* to neigh

nitrito *m* neigh; (chem) nitrite

nitro *m* niter; **nitro del Cile** Chile saltpeter

nitroglicerina *f* nitroglycerin

nitruro *m* nitride

niu·no -na *adj* (poet) var of **nessuno**

nìve·o -a *adj* snow-white

Nizza *f* Nice

no *adv* no; not; **come no?** why not; certainly; **dire di no** to say no; **no?** is it not so?; **non dir di no** to consent; **proprio no** certainly not

nòbile *adj* noble; second (*floor*) ‖ *m* nobleman ‖ *f* noblewoman

nobiliare *adj* noble, of nobility

nobilitare (**nobìlito**) *tr* to ennoble

nobil·tà *f* (**-tà**) nobility

nòc·ca *f* (**-che**) knuckle

nocchière *m* or **nocchièro** *m* petty officer; (poet) pilot, helmsman

nocchieru·to -ta *adj* knotty

nòc·chio *m* (**-chi**) knot (*in wood*)

nocciòla *adj invar* hazel (*in color*) ‖ *f* hazelnut; filbert

nocciolina *f* little nut; **nocciolina americana** peanut; roasted peanut

nòcciolo *m* stone, pit, kernel; **il noc-**

ciolo della questione the crux of the matter

nocciòlo *m* hazel (*tree*); filbert (*tree*)

nóce *m* walnut tree || *f* walnut (*fruit*); **noce del collo** Adam's apple; **noce di cocco** coconut; **noce di vitello** filet of veal; **noce moscata** nutmeg

nocévole *adj* harmful

noci·vo **-va** *adj* harmful, detrimental

nòdo *m* knot; crux, gist (*of a question*); junction; lump (*in one's throat*); (naut) knot; (phys) node; **lì è il nodo** there's the knot; **nodo d'amore** true-love knot; **nodo ferroviario** rail center, junction; **nodo scorsoio** noose; **nodo stradale** highway center, crossroads

nodó·so **-sa** [s] *adj* knotty

Noè *m* Noah

noi §5 *pron pers* we; us; **noi altri** we, e.g., **noi altri italiani** we Italians

nòia *f* boredom; bother, trouble; bug (*in a motor*); **venire a noia** (with *dat*) to weary; **dar noia** (with *dat*) to bother

noiàl·tri **-tre** *pron* we; us; **noiàltri italiani** we Italians

noió·so **-sa** [s] *adj* boring, annoying

noleggiare §290 (**noléggio**) *tr* to rent; to hire, to charter || *ref*—**si noleggia, si noleggiano** for rent

noleggiatóre *m* hirer; lessor (*e.g., of a car*)

nolég·gio *m* (**-gi**) rent, lease; car rental; chartering; freightage

nolènte *adj* unwilling

nòlo *m* rent, hire; **a nolo** for hire

nòmade *adj* nomad, nomadic || *mf* nomad

nóme *m* name; fame; reputation; (gram) noun; **a nome di** on behalf of; **in nome di** in the name of; **nome commerciale** firm name; **nome depositato** registered name; **nome di battesimo** Christian name; **nome e cognome** full name

nomèa *f* name, reputation; notoriety

nomignolo *m* nickname; **affibbiare un nomignolo a** to nickname

nòmina *f* appointment; **di prima nomina** newly appointed

nominale *adj* nominal; noun

nominare (**nòmino**) *tr* to name, call; to mention; to elect; to appoint

nominati·vo **-va** *adj* nominative; with names in alphabetical order; (fin) registered || *m* nominative; name; model number

non *adv* no, not; none, e.g., **non troppo presto** none too soon; **non appena** as soon as; **non c'è di che** you are welcome; **non . . . che** but, only; **non è vero?** is it not so?, isn't it so? La traduzione in inglese di questa domanda dipende generalmente dalla proposizione che la precede. Se la proposizione è affermativa, l'interrogazione sarà negativa, p.es. **Lei mi scriverà, non è vero?** You will write me. Won't you? Se la proposizione è negativa, l'interrogazione sarà positiva, p.es. **Lei non beve birra, non è**

vero? You do not drink beer. Do you? Se il soggetto della proposizione è un nome sostantivo, sarà rappresentato nell'interrogazione da un pronome personale, p.es. **Giovanni ha finito, non è vero?** John has finished. Hasn't he?

nonagenà·rio **-ria** *adj* & *mf* (**-ri** **-rie**) nonagenarian

nonagèsi·mo **-ma** *adj, pron* & *m* ninetieth

nonconformi·sta *mf* (**-sti** **-ste**) nonconformist

noncurante *adj* careless, indifferent

noncuranza *f* carelessness, indifference

nondiméno *conj* yet, nevertheless

nòn·no **-na** *mf* grandparent || *m* grandfather || *f* grandmother

nonnulla *m invar* nothing, trifle

nò·no **-na** *adj, m* & *pron* ninth

nonostante *prep* in spite of, notwithstanding; **nonostante che** although, even though

nonpertanto *adv* nevertheless, still, yet

non plus ultra *m* ne plus ultra, acme

nonsènso *m* nonsense

non so ché *adj invar* indefinable || *m invar* something indefinable

nontiscordardi·mé *m* (**-mé**) forget-me-not

nòrd *m* north

nòrdi·co **-ca** (**-ci** **-che**) *adj* Nordic; northern, north || *mf* northerner

nòrma *f* rule, regulation; **a norma di legge** according to law; **per Sua norma** for your guidance

normale *adj* normal; normative; perpendicular || *f* perpendicular line

normali·tà *f* (**-tà**) normality, normalcy

normalizzare [ddzz] *tr* to normalize, to standardize

Normandia, la Normandy

norman·no **-na** *adj* & *mf* Norman || *m* Norseman

normati·vo **-va** *adj* normative || *f* normativeness

normògrafo *m* stencil

norvegése [s] *adj* & *mf* Norwegian

Norvègia, la Norway

nosocò·mio *m* (**-mi**) hospital

nossignóra (*i.e.,* **no signora**) *adv* no, Madam

nossignóre (*i.e.,* **no signore**) *adv* no, Sir

nostalgìa *f* nostalgia, longing; homesickness

nostàlgi·co **-ca** (**-ci** **-che**) *adj* nostalgic; homesick || *m* worshiper of the good old days (*esp. of Fascism*)

nostra·no **-na** *adj* domestic, national; home-grown; regional

nò·stro **-stra** §6 *adj* & *pron poss*

nostròmo *m* boatswain

nòta *f* mark; score; memorandum; list; bill, invoice; report (*on a subordinate*); (mus) note; **note caratteristiche** personal folder, efficiency report (*of an employee*); **prender nota di** to take down

notàbile *adj* notable, noteworthy || *m* notable

no·tàio *m* (**-tài**) notary (public); lawyer

notare (nòto) *tr* to mark, check; to note, to jot down; to observe; to bring out; **farsi notare** to attract attention, make oneself conspicuous; **nota bene** note well, take notice

notariale or **notarile** *adj* notarial

notazióne *f* notation; annotation; observation

nò·tes *m* (-tes) notebook

notévole *adj* noteworthy, remarkable

notìfi·ca *f* (-che) notification, notice; service (*e.g., of a summons*)

notificare §197 (**notìfico**) *tr* to report; to serve (*a summons*); to declare ..(*e.g., one's income*)

notificazióne *f* notification, notice; service (*e.g., of a summons*)

notìzia *f* knowledge; report; piece of news; **aver notizie di** to hear from; **notizie news; una notizia** a news item

notizià·rio *m* (-ri) news; news report, news bulletin; (rad) newscast; **notiziario sportivo** sports page; (rad, telv) sports news

nò·to -ta *adj* known, well-known ‖ *m* south wind; (coll) swimming ‖ *f* see **nota**

notorie·tà *f* (-tà) general knowledge; affidavit; notoriety

notò·rio -ria *adj* (-ri -rie) well-known

nottàmbu·lo -la *adj* nighttime; night-wandering ‖ *mf* nightwalker; night owl

nottata *f* night; **far nottata bianca** to spend a sleepless night

nòtte *f* night; **buona notte** good night; **di notte** at night, by night, in the nighttime; **la notte di lunedì** Sunday night; Monday night; **lunedì notte** Monday night; **notte bianca** sleepless night; **notte di San Silvestro** New Year's Eve; watch night

nottetèmpo *adv*—**di nottetempo** at night, in the nighttime

nòttola *f* wooden latch; (zool) bat

nottolino *m* small wooden latch; ratchet, catch

nottur·no -na *adj* nocturnal, night ‖ *m* nocturne

novanta *adj, m & pron* ninety

novantènne *adj* ninety-year-old ‖ *mf* ninety-year-old person

novantèsi·mo -ma *adj, m & pron* ninetieth

novantina *f* about ninety; **sulla novantina** about ninety years old

nòve *adj & pron* nine; **le nove** nine o'clock ‖ *m* nine; ninth (*in dates*)

novecentismo *m* twentieth-century arts and letters

novecenti·sta (-sti -ste) *adj* twentieth-century ‖ *mf* artist of the twentieth century

novecènto *adj, m & pron* nine hundred ‖ **il Novecento** the twentieth century

novèlla *f* short story; (poet) news

novelliè·re -ra *mf* storyteller; short-story writer

novelli·no -na *adj* early, tender; inexperienced, green

novellìstica *f* storytelling; fiction

novèl·lo -la *adj* fresh, young, tender; new ‖ *f* see **novella**

novèmbre *m* November

novenà·rio -ria *adj* (-ri -rie) nine-syllable

noverare (nòvero) *tr* to count; to enumerate; (poet) to remember

nòvero *m* number; class

novilù·nio *m* (-ni) new moon

novìssi·mo -ma *adj* (lit) last, newest

novi·tà *f* (-tà) newness, originality; novelty, innovation; latest idea; late news

noviziato *m* novitiate; apprenticeship

novì·zio -zia (-zi -zie) *mf* novice; apprentice ‖ *f* novice (*in a convent*)

novocaina *f* novocaine

nozióne *f* notion, conception

nòzze *fpl* wedding, marriage; **nozze d'argento** silver wedding; **nozze d'oro** golden wedding

nube *f* cloud

nubifrà·gio *m* (-gi) cloudburst

nùbile *adj* unmarried, single (*woman*); marriageable ‖ *f* unmarried girl

nu·ca *f* (-che) nape of the neck, scruff

nucleare *adj* nuclear

nùcleo *m* nucleus; group; (elec) core

nudismo *m* nudism

nudi·sta *adj & mf* (-sti -ste) nudist

nudi·tà *f* (-tà) nudity, nakedness

nu·do -da *adj* naked, bare; barren; simple; **mettere a nudo** to lay bare; **nudo e crudo** stark-naked; destitute ‖ *m* nude

nùgolo *m* cloud; throng, swarm

nulla *pron* nothing ‖ *m invar* nothing; nothingness

nulla òsta *m* permission; visa

nullatenènte *adj* poor ‖ *mf* have-not

nullificare §197 (**nullìfico**) *tr* to nullify

nulli·tà *f* (-tà) nothingness; nonentity; invalidity (*of a document*)

nul·lo -la *adj* void, worthless ‖ *nullo pron* (poet) none, no one ‖ **nulla** *m & pron* see **nulla**

nume *m* divinity, deity

numerare (nùmero) *tr* to number

numeratóre *m* numerator; numbering machine

numèri·co -ca *adj* (-ci -che) numerical

nùmero *m* number; lottery ticket; size (*of shoes*); **numero dispari** odd number; **numero legale** quorum; **numero pari** even number

numeró·so -sa [s] *adj* numerous, large; harmonious

nùn·zio *m* (-zi) nuncio; (poet) news

nuòcere §206 *intr* to be harmful; (with *dat*) to harm

nuòra *f* daughter-in-law

nuotare (nuòto) *intr* to swim; to float; to wallow (*in wealth*)

nuotata *f* swim, dip, plunge

nuota·tóre -trice *mf* swimmer

nuòto *m* swimming; **gettarsi a nuoto** to jump into the water; **traversare a nuoto** to swim across

nuòva *f* news; late news

Nuòva York *f* New York
Nuòva Zelanda, la [dz] New Zealand
nuòvo -va *adj* new; **di nuovo** again; **nuovo di zecca** brand-new; **nuovo fiammante** brand-new; **nuovo venuto** new arrival || *m*—**il nuovo** the new || *f* see **nuova**
nùtria *f* coypu
nutrice *f* wet nurse; (lit) provider
nutriènte *adj* nourishing
nutriménto *m* nourishment
nutrire §176 & (**nutro**) *tr* to nourish;

to nurture; to harbor (*e.g.*, *hatred*) || *ref*—**nutrirsi di** to feed on or upon
nutri·vo -va *adj* nutritious, nutritive
nutri·to -ta *adj* well-fed; strong; rich (*food*); brisk, heavy (*gunfire*)
nutrizióne *f* nutrition; food
nùvo·lo -la *adj* cloudy || *m* cloudy weather; (lit) cloud; (fig) swarm || *f* cloud
nuvoló·so -sa [s] *adj* cloudy
nuziale *adj* wedding, nuptial
nuzialità *f* marriage rate

O

O, o [o] *m* & *f* thirteenth letter of the Italian alphabet
o *conj* or; now; **o . . . o** either . . . or; whether . . . or || *interj* oh!
òa·si *f* (-**si**) oasis
obbediènte *adj* var of **ubbidiente**
obbediènza *f* obedience
obbedire §176 *tr* & *intr* var of **ubbidire**
obbiettare (**obbiètto**) *tr* & *intr* var of **obiettare**
obbligare §209 (**òbbligo**) *tr* to oblige; to compel, to force || *ref* to obligate oneself
obbligatissi·mo -ma *adj* much obliged
obbligatò·rio -ria *adj* (-**ri -rie**) compulsory, obligatory
obbligazióne *f* obligation; burden; (com) debenture, bond
obbligazioni·sta *mf* (-**sti -ste**) bondholder
òbbli·go *m* (-**ghi**) obligation; duty; **d'obbligo** obligatory, mandatory; **fare d'obbligo a qlcu** + *inf* to be necessary for s.o. to + *inf*, *e.g.*, **gli fa d'obbligo lavorare** it is necessary for him to work
obbrò·brio *m* (-**bri**) opprobrium, disgrace; **obbrobri** insults
obbrobrió·so -sa [s] *adj* opprobrious, disgraceful
obeli·sco *m* (-**schi**) obelisk
obera·to -ta *adj* overburdened
obesità *f* obesity
obè·so -sa *adj* obese, stout
òbice *m* howitzer
obiettare (**obiètto**) *tr* & *intr* to argue; to object
obietti·vo -va *adj* & *m* objective
obiettóre *m* objector; **obiettore di coscienza** conscientious objector
obiezióne *f* objection
obitò·rio *m* (-**ri**) morgue
oblare (**òblo**) *tr* to willingly pay (*a fine*)
obla·tóre -trice *mf* donor
oblazióne *f* donation; (eccl) oblation; (law) payment of a fine
obliare §119 *tr* (lit) to forget
oblì·o *m* (-**i**) (lit) oblivion
oblì·quo -qua *adj* oblique
obliterare (**oblìtero**) *tr* to obliterate, cancel
o·blò *m* (-**blò**) (naut) porthole; **oblò di accesso** door (*of space capsule*)

to nurture; to harbor (*e.g.*, *hatred*)

oblun·go -ga *adj* (-**ghi -ghe**) oblong
òbo·e *m* (-**e**) oboe
oboi·sta *mf* (-**sti -ste**) oboist
òbolo *m* mite
ò·ca *f* (-**che**) goose; gander
ocarina *f* ocarina, sweet potato
occasionale *adj* chance; immediate (*cause*)
occasionare (**occasióno**) *tr* to occasion
occasióne *f* occasion; opportunity; ground, pretext; bargain; **all'occasione** on occasion; **d'occasione** second-hand; occasional (*verses*)
occhiàia *f* eye socket; **occhiaie** rings under the eyes
occhia·làio *m* (-**lài**) optician
occhiale *adj* eye, ocular || **occhiali** *mpl* glasses; goggles; **occhiali antisole** sunglasses; **occhiali a stringinaso** nose glasses
occhialétto *m* lorgnon; monocle
occhiata *f* glance
occhieggiare §290 (**occhièggio**) *tr* to eye || *intr* to peep
occhièllo *m* buttonhole; boutonniere; eyelet; half title; subhead
occhièra *f* eyecup
òc·chio *m* (-**chi**) eye; speck of grease (*in soup*); handle (*of scissors*); ring (*of stirrup*); (typ) face; (fig) bit; **a occhio e croce** at a rough guess; **a quattr'occhi** in private; **battere gli occhi** to blink; **cavarsi gli occhi** to strain one's eyes; **dar nell'occhio** to attract attention; **di buon occhio** favorably; **fare l'occhio a** to get used to; **fare tanto d'occhi** to be amazed, to open one's eyes wide; **lasciare gli occhi su** to covet; **non chiudere un occhio** not to sleep a wink; **occhio!** watch out!; **occhio della testa** outrageous price; **occhio di bue** (naut) porthole; **occhio di cubia** (naut) hawsehole; **occhio di pavone** (zool) peacock butterfly; **occhio di triglia** sheep's eyes; **occhio pesto** black eye; **occhio pollino** corn (*on toes*); **tenere d'occhio** to keep an eye on
occhiolino *m* small eye; **far l'occhiolino** to wink
occidentale *adj* western, occidental
occidènte *adj* (poet) setting (*sun*) || *m* west, occident

occìpite *m* occipital bone
occlusióne *f* occlusion
occlusì•vo -va *adj & f* occlusive
occlu•so -sa *adj* occluded
occorrènte *adj* necessary ‖ *m* necessary; (lit) occurrence
occorrènza *f* necessity; **all'occorrenza** if need be
occórrere §139 *intr* (ESSERE) to happen; (with *dat*) to need, e.g., **gli occorre dell'olio** he needs oil ‖ *impers* (ESSERE)—**occorre** it is necessary
occultaménto *m* concealment
occultare *tr & ref* to hide
occul•to -ta *adj* occult; (lit) hidden
occupante *adj* occupying ‖ *m* occupant
occupare (òccupo) *tr* to occupy; to employ ‖ *ref* to take employment;
occuparsi di to busy oneself with, to mind; to attend to
occupa•to -ta *adj* occupied; busy
occupazionale *adj* occupational
occupazióne *f* occupation
oceàni•co -ca *adj* (**-ci -che**) oceanic
ocèano *m* ocean
òcra *f* ocher
oculare *adj* ocular; see **testimone** ‖ *m* eyepiece
oculatézza *f* circumspection, prudence
ocula•to -ta *adj* circumspect, prudent
oculi•sta *mf* (**-sti -ste**) oculist
od *conj* or
odalì•sca *f* (**-sche**) odalisque
òde *f* ode
odepòri•co -ca (**-ci -che**) *adj* (lit) travel ‖ *m* (lit) travelogue
odiare §287 (òdio) *tr* to hate
odièr•no -na *adj* today's, current
ò•dio *m* (**-di**) hatred; **avere in odio** to hate; **essere in odio a** to be hated by
odió•so -sa [s] *adj* hateful, odious
odissèa *f* odyssey ‖ **Odissea** *f* Odyssey
Odissèo *m* Odysseus
odontoià•tra *mf* (**-tri -tre**) doctor of dental surgery, dentist
odontoiatrìa *f* odontology, dentistry
odorare (odóro) *tr & intr* to smell
odora•to -ta *adj* (poet) fragrant ‖ *m* smell
odóre *m* smell, odor, scent; **cattivo odore** bad odor; **odori** herbs, spice
odoró•so -sa [s] *adj* odorous, fragrant
offèndere §148 *tr & intr* to offend ‖ *ref* to take offense
offensì•vo -va *adj & f* offensive
offensóre *m* offender
offerènte *mf* bidder; **miglior offerente** highest bidder
offèrta *f* offer; offering, donation; (*at an auction*) bid; (com) supply
offésa [s] *f* offense; wrongdoing; ravage (*of time*); **da offesa** (mil) offensive; **recarsi a offesa** qlco to regard s.th as offensive
officina *f* shop, workshop; **officina meccanica** machine shop
offició•so -sa [s] *adj* helpful, obliging
offrire §207 *tr* to offer; to sponsor (*a radio or TV program*); to dedicate (*a book*); to bid (*at an auction*); (com) to tender ‖ *ref* to offer oneself, to volunteer

offuscare §197 *tr* to darken, obscure; to obfuscate; to dim (*mind; eyes*) ‖ *ref* to grow dark; to grow dim
oftàlmi•co -ca *adj* (**-ci -che**) opthalmic
oftalmòlo•go -ga *mf* (**-gi -ghe**) ophthalmologist
oggettività *f* objectivity
oggettì•vo -va *adj & m* objective
oggètto *m* object; subject, argument; article; **oggetti preziosi** valuables
òggi *m* today; **dall'oggi al domani** suddenly; overnight ‖ *adv* today; **d'oggi in poi** henceforth; **oggi a otto** a week hence; **oggi come oggi** at present; **oggi è un anno** one year ago
oggidì *m invar & adv* nowadays
oggigiórno *m invar & adv* nowadays
ogiva *f* ogive, pointed arch; nose cone
ógni *adj indef invar* each; every, e.g., **ogni due giorni** every two days; **ogni cosa** everything; **ogni tanto** every now and then; **per ogni dove** (lit) everywhere
ogniqualvòlta *conj* whenever
Ognissan•ti *m* (**-ti**) All Saints' Day
ognitèmpo *adj invar* all-weather
-ógno•lo -la *suf adj* -ish, e.g., **giallognolo** yellowish
ognóra *adv* (lit) always
ognu•no -na *adj* (obs) each ‖ *pron* each one, everyone
oh *interj* oh!
òhi *interj* ouch!
ohibò *interj* fie!
ohimè *interj* alas!
ohm *m* (**ohm**) ohm
olanda *f* Dutch linen ‖ **l'Olanda** *f* Holland
olandése [s] *adj* Dutch ‖ *m* Dutch (*language*); Dutchman; Dutch cheese ‖ *f* Dutch woman
oleandro *m* oleander
oleà•rio -ria *adj* (**-ri -rie**) oil
olea•to -ta *adj* oiled
oleifi•cio *m* (**-ci**) oil mill
oleodótto *m* pipeline
oleó•so -sa [s] *adj* oily
olezzare [ddzz] (olézzo) *intr* (lit) to smell sweet
olézzo [ddzz] *m* perfume, fragrance
olfatto *m* smell
oliare §287 (òlio) *tr* to oil
oliatóre *m* oiler, oil can
olìbano *m* frankincense
olièra *f* cruet
oligarchìa *f* oligarchy
olimpìade *f* Olympiad
olìmpi•co -ca *adj* (**-ci -che**) Olympic; Olympian
olimpiòni•co -ca *adj* (**-ci -che**) Olympic ‖ *mf* Olympic athlete
ò•lio *m* (**-li**) oil; **ad olio** oil, e.g., **quadro ad olio** oil painting; **olio di fegato di merluzzo** cod-liver oil; **olio di lino** linseed oil; **olio di ricino** castor oil; **olio solare** sun-tan lotion
oliva *f* olive
oliva•stro -stra *adj* livid; swarthy ‖ *m* wild olive (*tree*)
olivéto *m* olive grove
Olivièro *m* Oliver
olivo *m* olive tree

ólmo *m* elm tree

olocàu·sto -sta *adj* (lit) burnt; (lit) sacrificed || *m* holocaust; sacrifice

ològra·fo -fa *adj* holographic

olóna *f* sailcloth, canvas

oltracciò *adv* besides

oltraggiare §290 *tr* to outrage; to insult

oltràg·gio *m* (-gi) outrage; offense; ravages (*of time*); **oltraggio al pudore** offense to public morals; **oltraggio al tribunale** contempt of court

oltraggió·so -sa [s] *adj* outrageous

oltranza *f*—**a oltranza** to the bitter end

oltranzi·sta *mf* (-sti -ste) (pol) extremist

óltre *adv* beyond; ahead; further; **oltre a** apart from; in addition to; **troppo oltre** too far || *prep* beyond; past; more than

oltrecortina *adj invar* beyond-the-iron-curtain || *m* country beyond the iron curtain

oltremare *m invar* country overseas || *adv* overseas

oltremisura *adv* (lit) beyond measure

oltremòdo *adv* (lit) exceedingly

oltrepassare *tr* to overstep; to cross (*a river*); to be beyond (. . . *years old*); (sports) to overtake

oltretómba *m*—**l'oltretomba** the life beyond

omàg·gio *m* (-gi) homage; compliment; **in omaggio** complimentary; **rendere omaggio a** to pay tribute to

òmaro *m* Norway lobster

ombelì·co *m* (-chi) navel

ómbra *f* shade; shadow; umbrage; form; mass; **nemmeno per ombra** not in the least

ombreggiare §290 (ombréggio) *tr* to shade

ombrèlla *f* shade (*of trees*); (bot) umbel; (coll) umbrella

ombrel·làio *m* (-lài) umbrella maker

ombrellino *m* parasol

ombrèllo *m* umbrella

ombrellóne *m* beach umbrella

ombró·so -sa [s] *adj* shady; touchy; skittish (*horse*)

omelette *f* (omelette) omelet

omelìa *f* homily

omeopàti·co -ca (-ci -che) *adj* homeopathic || *m* homeopathist

omèri·co -ca *adj* (-ci -che) Homeric

òmero *m* (anat) humerus; (lit) shoulder

omertà *f* code of silence of underworld

ométtere §198 *tr* to omit

ométto *m* little man; (coll) clothes hanger; (billiards) pin; (archit) king post

omici·da (-di -de) *adj* homicidal, murderous || *mf* homicide, murderer

omicì·dio *m* (-di) homicide; murder; **omicidio colposo** (law) manslaughter; **omicidio doloso** (law) first-degree murder

ominó·so -sa [s] *adj* (lit) ominous

omissióne *f* omission

òmni·bus *m* (-bus) omnibus; way train

omnisciènte *adj* all-knowing, omniscient

omogène·o -a *adj* homogeneous

omologare §209 (omòlogo) *tr* to con-firm, ratify; to probate (*a will*); (sports) to validate

omòni·mo -ma *adj* of the same name || *m* namesake; homonym

omosessuale [s] *adj* & *mf* homosexual

ón·cia *f* (-ce) ounce; **oncia a oncia** little by little

ónda *f* wave; **a onde** wavy; wavily; **essere in onda** (rad, telv) to be on the air; **farsi le onde** to have one's hair waved; **mettere in onda** (rad, telv) to put on the air; **onda crespa** whitecap; **onda portante** (rad, telv) carrier wave

ondata *f* wave, billow; gust (*e.g., of smoke*); rush (*of blood*); wave (*of cold weather*)

ondatra *f* muskrat

ónde *pron* from which; of which || *adv* whereof; hence; (poet) wherefrom || *prep* **onde** + *inf* in order to || *conj* **onde** + *subj* so that

ondeggiante *adj* waving, swaying

ondeggiare §290 (ondéggio) *intr* to wave, sway; to waver

ondina *f* mermaid; (mythol) undine; (mythol) mermaid

ondó·so -sa [s] *adj* wavy

ondulare (óndulo & òndulo) *tr* to wave; to corrugate (*e.g., metal*) || *intr* to sway

ondula·to -ta *adj* wavy (*hair*); corrugated (*e.g., metal*); bumpy (*road*)

ondulazióne *f* undulation; **ondulazione permanente** permanent wave

-óne -óna *suf mf* big, *e.g.,* **librone** big book; **dormigliona** big sleeper || **-óne** *suf m* (applies to both sexes) big, *e.g.,* **donnone** *m* big woman

ònere *m* (lit) onus, burden

oneró·so -sa [s] *adj* onerous, burdensome

onestà *f* honesty; (poet) modesty

onè·sto -sta *adj* honest; fair; (poet) modest || *m* moderate amount; honest gain; honest person

ònice *m* onyx

onnipossènte & onnipotènte *adj* almighty, omnipotent

onnisciènte *adj* omniscient

onniveggènte *adj* all-seeing

onnìvo·ro -ra *adj* omnivorous

onomàsti·co -ca (-ci -che) *adj* onomastic || *m* name day || *f* study of proper names

onomatopèi·co -ca *adj* (-ci -che) onomatopeic

onoràbile *adj* honorable

onoranza *f* honor; **onoranze** homage; **onoranze funebri** obsequies

onorare (onóro) *tr* to honor || *ref* to deem it an honor

onorà·rio -ria (-ri -rie) *adj* honorary || *m* fee, honorarium

onora·to -ta *adj* honored; honest; honorable

onóre *m* honor; **d'onore** honest, *e.g.,* **uomo d'onore** honest man; **estremi onori** last rites; **fare gli onori di casa** to receive guests; **fare onore a** to honor; **onore al merito** credit where credit is due; **onor del mento** (lit) beard

onorévole *adj* honorable ‖ *m* honorable member (*of parliament*)

onorificènza *f* dignity; decoration

onorìfi·co -ca *adj* (**-ci -che**) honorific; honorary (*e.g., title*)

ónta *f* dishonor, shame; **a onta di in** spite of; **avere onta** to be ashamed; **fare onta a** to bring shame upon; **in onta a** against

ontano *m* alder

O.N.U. (acronym) *f* (**Organizzazione delle Nazioni Unite**) United Nations, U.N.

onu·sto -sta *adj* (poet) laden

opa·co -ca *adj* (**-chi -che**) opaque

opale *m* opal

opali·no -na *adj* opaline ‖ *f* shiny cardboard; luster (*fabric*)

òpera *f* work; organization, foundation; day's work; (mus) opera; **mettere in opera** to install; to start work on; to make ready; to begin using; **opera di consultazione** reference work; **opera morta** (naut) upper works; **opera viva** (naut) quickwork; **per opera di** thanks to

ope·ràio -ràia (**-rài -ràie**) *adj* workman's, worker's; working ‖ *m* workman, worker; **operaio a cottimo** pieceworker; **operaio a giornata** day laborer; **operaio specializzato** craftsman, skilled workman ‖ *f* workwoman

operante *adj* actively engaged; operative

operare (**òpero**) *tr* to operate; to work (*a miracle*); (surg) to operate on ‖ *intr* to operate; to be actively engaged ‖ *ref* to be operated on; to occur, take place

operati·vo -va *adj* operative; operations, e.g., **ricerca operativa** operations research

opera·to -ta *adj* operated; embossed ‖ *m* behavior; patient operated on

opera·tóre -trice *mf* operator ‖ *m* (mov) cameraman

operatò·rio -ria *adj* (**-ri -rie**) surgical (*operation*); operating (*room*); (math) operational

operazióne *f* operation; transaction

operétta *f* short work; (mus) operetta

operìsti·co -ca *adj* (**-ci -che**) operatic

operosi·tà [*s*] *f* (**-tà**) industry

operó·so -sa [*s*] *adj* industrious; active

opi·mo -ma *adj* (lit) fat; rich, fertile

opinare *intr* to opine, deem

opinióne *f* opinion

opòs·sum *m* (**-sum**) opossum

oppia·to -ta *adj* opiate (*mixed with opium*); dulled by drugs ‖ *m* opiate (*medicine containing opium*)

òppio *m* opium

oppiòmane *adj* opium-eating; opium-smoking ‖ *mf* opium addict

oppórre §218 *tr* to oppose; to offer, put up (*resistance*) ‖ *ref* to be opposite; **opporsi a** to oppose, to be against

opportuni·sta *mf* (**-sti -ste**) opportunist

opportuni·tà *f* (**-tà**) opportunity; opportuneness

opportu·no -na *adj* opportune

opposi·tóre -trice *mf* opponent

opposizióne *f* opposition; (law) appeal; **fare opposizione a** to object to

oppó·sto -sta *adj* opposite; contrary ‖ *m* opposite; **all'opposto** on the contrary

oppressióne *f* oppression

oppressi·vo -va *adj* oppressive

opprès·so -sa *adj* oppressed; overcome, overwhelmed ‖ **oppressi** *mpl* oppressed people

oppressóre *m* oppressor

opprimènte *adj* oppressive

opprìmere §131 *tr* to oppress; to overcome, overwhelm; to weigh down

oppugnare *tr* to refute, contradict

oppure *adv* otherwise ‖ *conj* or else; or rather

optare (**òpto**) *intr* to choose; (com) to exercise an option

optometri·sta *mf* (**-sti -ste**) optometrist

opulèn·to -ta *adj* opulent

opùscolo *m* booklet, brochure, pamphlet; **opuscolo d'informazioni** instruction manual

opzióne *f* option

ór *adv* now; **or ora** right now; **or sono** ago

óra *f* hour; time; period (*in school*); **alla buon'ora!** finally!; **a ore by the** hour; **a tarda ora** late; **che ora è?** or **che ore sono?** what time is it?; **da un'ora all'altra** from one moment to the next; **dell'ultima ora** up-to-date (*news*); **di buon'ora** early; early in the morning; **di ora in ora** at any moment; **d'ora in avanti** from this moment on; **d'ora in poi** from now on; **far l'ora** to kill time; **fin ora** until now; **non vedere l'ora di** + *inf* to be hardly able to wait until + *ind*; **ora di cena** suppertime; **ora di punta** rush hour, peak hour; **ora legale** daylight-saving time; **ore piccole** late hours; **un'ora di orologio** one full hour ‖ *adv* now

oràcolo *m* oracle

òra·fo -fa *adj* goldsmith's ‖ *m* goldsmith

orale *adj* & *m* oral

oralmente *adv* orally; by word of mouth

oramài *adv* now; already

oran·go *m* (**-ghi**) orangutan

orà·rio -ria *adj* (**-ri -rie**) hourly; per hour; clockwise ‖ *m* timetable; schedule; roster; **essere in orario** to be on time; **orario di lavoro** working hours; **orario d'ufficio** office hours

ora·tóre -trice *mf* orator

oratò·rio -ria *adj* (**-ri -rie**) oratorical ‖ *m* (eccl) oratory; (mus) oratorio ‖ *f* oratory, public speaking

orazióne *f* oration; prayer; **orazione domenicale** Lord's Prayer

orbare (**òrbo**) *tr* (lit) to bereave; (lit) to deprive

òrbe *f* (lit) orb; (lit) world

orbène *adv* well

òrbita *f* orbit; (fig) sphere
orbitare (**òrbito**) *intr* to orbit
orbitazióne *f* orbiting
òr·bo -ba *adj* bereaved; deprived; blind ‖ *m* blind man
òrca *f* killer whale
Òrcadi *fpl* Orkney Islands
orchèstra *f* orchestra; band; orchestra pit
orchestrale *adj* orchestral ‖ *mf* orchestra player, orchestra performer
orchestrare (**orchèstro**) *tr* to orchestrate; (fig) to organize
orchestrina *f* dance band; dance-band music
orchidèa *f* orchid
ór·cio -ci (**-ci**) jar, jug, crock
orciòlo *m*—a orciolo puckered up (*lips*)
òr·co -co *m* (**-chi**) ogre
òrda *f* horde
ordàlia *f* (hist) ordeal
ordigno *m* gadget, contrivance; tool; **ordigno esplosivo** infernal machine
ordinale *adj* & *m* ordinal
ordinaménto *m* disposition; regulation
ordinanza *f* ordinance; (mil) orderly; **d'ordinanza** regulation (*e.g., uniform*); **in ordinanza** (mil) in formation
ordinare (**órdino**) *tr* to order; to straighten up; to range; to regulate; to ordain; to trim
ordinà·rio -ria (**-ri -rie**) *adj* ordinary; plain; inferior; workday (*suit*) ‖ *m* ordinary; full professor; **d'ordinario** ordinarily, usually
ordina·to -ta *adj* orderly, tidy, ordained ‖ *f* ordinate; straightening up; (aer) frame; (naut) bulkhead
ordinazióne *f* order; ordination
órdine *m* order; row; tier; series (*e.g., of years*); college (*e.g., of surgeons*); nature (*of things*); (law) warrant, writ; **in ordine a** concerning; **ordine del giorno** order of the day; **ordine d'idee** train of thought
ordire §176 *tr* to warp (*cloth*); to hatch (*a plot*)
ordi·to -ta *adj* plotted ‖ *m* warp (*of fabric*)
orécchia *f* ear; dog-ear; **con le orecchie tese** all ears
orecchiale *m* earphone (*of sonar equipment*)
orecchiétta *f* (anat) auricle
orecchino *m* earring
oréc·chio -chi *m* (**-chi**) ear; hearing; dog-ear; moldboard; **fare orecchio da mercante** to turn a deaf ear ‖ *m* (**orécchia** *fpl*) (archaic) ear
orecchióne *m* long-eared bat; (mil) trunnion; **orecchioni** (pathol) mumps
oréfice *m* goldsmith; jeweler
oreficeria *f* goldsmith shop; jewelry shop
orfanézza *f* orphanage (*condition*)
òrfa·no -na *adj* orphaned ‖ *mf* orphan
orfanotrò·fio *m* (**-fi**) orphanage (*institution*)
Orfèo *m* Orpheus
organdi *m* organdy
organétto *m* hand organ; mouth organ; **organetto di Barberia** hand organ

organi·co -ca (**-ci -che**) *adj* organic ‖ *m* personnel, staff ‖ *f* (mil) organization
organigram·ma *m* (**-mi**) organization chart
organino *m* hand organ, barrel organ
organismo *m* organism
organi·sta *mf* (**-sti -ste**) organist
organizzare [ddzz] *tr* to organize
organizza·tóre -trice [ddzz] *mf* organizer
organizzazióne [ddzz] *f* organization; **Organizzazione delle Nazioni Unite** United Nations
òrgano *m* organ; part (*of a machine*); **organo di stampa** mouthpiece
orgasmo *m* orgasm; agitation, excitement
òr·gia *f* (**-ge**) orgy
orgó·glio *m* (**-gli**) pride
orgoglió·so -sa [s] *adj* proud
orientale *adj* & *mf* oriental; Oriental
orientaménto *m* orientation; bearing; trend; trim (*of sail*); **orientamento scolastico e professionale** aptitude test; vocational guidance
orientare (**oriènto**) *tr* to orient; to guide; to trim (*a sail*) ‖ *ref* to find one's bearings
oriènte *m* orient; **grand'oriente** grand lodge ‖ **Oriente** *m* Orient, East; **Estremo Oriente** Far East; **Medio Oriente** Middle East; **Vicino Oriente** Near East
orifí·zio *m* (**-zi**) orifice, opening
orìgano *m* wild marjoram
originale *adj* original; odd ‖ *mf* queer character, odd person ‖ *m* original; copy (*for printer*)
originare (**orìgino**) *tr* to originate ‖ *intr* (ESSERE) & *ref* to originate
originà·rio -ria *adj* (**-ri -rie**) originating; native; original
origine *f* origin; source; extraction
origliare §280 *intr* to eavesdrop
origlière *m* (lit) pillow
orina *f* var of **urina**
orinale *m* chamber pot, urinal
orinare *tr* & *intr* to urinate
orina·tóio *m* (**-tói**) urinal, comfort station
oriòlo *m* (orn) oriole
oriun·do -da *adj* native ‖ *m* (sports) native son
orizzontale [ddzz] *adj* horizontal ‖ **orizzontali** *fpl* horizontal words (*in crossword puzzle*)
orizzontare [ddzz] (**orizzónto**) *tr* to orient ‖ *ref* to get one's bearings
orizzónte [ddzz] *m* horizon
Orlando *m* Roland
orlare (**órlo**) *tr* to hem, border; **orlare a zigzag** to pink
órlo *m* edge; brim; hem, border; (fig) brink; **orlo a giorno** hemstitch
órma *f* footprint; **orme** remains, vestiges; **calcare le orme di** to follow the footsteps of
ormeggiare §290 (**orméggio**) *tr* & *ref* (naut) to moor
ormég·gio *m* (**-gi**) mooring; **mollare gli ormeggi** (naut) to cast off
ormóne *m* hormone

ornamentale *adj* ornamental
ornaménto *m* ornament
ornare (órno) *tr* to adorn
orna·to -ta *adj* adorned; ornate ‖ *m* ornament; ornamental design
ornitòlo·go -ga *mf* (-gi -ghe) ornithologist
òro *m* gold; (fig) money; d'oro gold, golden; ori gold objects; jewels; suit of Neapolitan cards corresponding to diamonds; oro zecchino pure gold; per tutto l'oro del mondo for all the world
orologeria *f* watchmaking; clockmaking; watchmaker's shop
orolo·giàio *m* (-giài) watchmaker; clockmaker
orolò·gio *m* (-gi) watch; clock; orologio a pendolo clock; orologio a polvere sandglass; orologio a scatto digital clock; orologio da polso wristwatch; orologio della morte deathwatch; orologio solare sundial
oròscopo *m* horoscope
orpèllo *m* Dutch gold; (fig) tinsel
orrèndo *m* horrible
orribile *adj* horrible
òrri·do -da *adj* horrid ‖ *m* horridness; gorge, ravine
orripilante *adj* bloodcurdling, hair-raising
orróre *m* horror; awe; aver in or per orrore to loath; fare orrore a to horrify
órsa *f* she-bear ‖ Orsa *f*—Orsa maggiore Great Bear; Orsa minore Little Bear
orsacchiòtto *m* bear cub; Teddy bear
ór·so -sa *mf* bear; orso bianco polar bear; orso grigio grizzly bear ‖ *f* see orsa
orsù *interj* come on!
ortàg·gio *m* (-gi) vegetable
ortàglia *f* vegetable garden; vegetable
ortènsia *f* hydrangea
orti·ca *f* (-che) nettle; hives
orticària *f* hives, nettle rash
orticoltóre *m* truck gardener; horticulturist
òrto *m* garden, vegetable garden; (lit) sunrise; orto botanico botanical garden; orto di guerra Victory garden
ortodòs·so -sa *adj* orthodox ‖ *m* Greek Catholic
ortografia *f* orthography; spelling
ortola·no -na *adj* garden ‖ *m* truck farmer, gardener
ortopèdi·co -ca (-ci -che) *adj* orthopedic ‖ *m* orthopedist
òrza *f* bowline; windward; andare all'orza to sail close to the wind
orzaiòlo [dz] *m* (pathol) sty
orzare (òrzo) *intr* to sail close to the wind; to luff
orzata [dz] *f* orgeat
orzata *f* (naut) luff
òrzo [dz] *m* barley
osannare *intr* to cry or sing hosanna; osannare a to acclaim, applaud
osare (òso) *intr* to dare
osceni·tà *f* (-tà) obscenity
oscè·no -na *adj* obscene; (coll) horrible
oscillante *adj* oscillating

oscillare *intr* to oscillate; to swing; to wobble; to waver, hesitate
oscillazióne *f* oscillation; fluctuation
oscuraménto *m* darkening, dimming; blackout
oscurare *tr* to darken; to blot out; to dim ‖ *ref* to get dark; oscurarsi in volto to frown
oscuri·tà *f* (-tà) obscurity; darkness; ignorance
oscu·ro -ra *adj* obscure, dark; opaque (style) ‖ *m* obscurity, darkness; essere all'oscuro di to be in the dark about
osmòsi *f* osmosis
ospedale *m* hospital
ospedalière *m* hospital worker
ospedaliè·ro -ra *adj* hospital ‖ *m* hospitaler
ospedalizzare [ddzz] *tr* to hospitalize
ospitale *adj* hospitable ‖ *m* hospital
ospitali·tà *f* (-tà) hospitality
ospitare (òspito) *tr* to lodge, shelter, accommodate; to entertain; (sports) to play (an opposing team) at home
òspite *mf* host; guest; andarsene insalutato ospite to take French leave; ospiti company (guests at home)
ospì·zio *m* (-zi) hospice; hostel; (lit) hospitality; ospizio dei vecchi nursing home; ospizio di mendicità poorhouse
ossatura *f* frame, framework; skeleton
òsse·o -a *adj* bony
ossequènte *adj* (lit) respectful; (lit) reverent
ossequiare §287 (ossèquio) *tr* to pay one's respects to; to honor
ossè·quio *m* (-qui) respect; reverence; i miei ossequi my best regards; in ossequio a in conformity with; porgere i propri ossequi a to pay one's respects to
ossequió·so -sa [s] *adj* obsequious; respectful
osservante *adj* & *m* observant
osservanza *f* observance; deference
osservare (ossèrvo) *tr* to observe
osserva·tóre -trice *adj* observing, observant ‖ *mf* observer
osservatò·rio *m* (-ri) observatory
osservazióne *f* observation; rebuke
ossessionare (ossessióno) *tr* to obsess; to harass, bedevil
ossessióne *f* obsession
ossès·so -sa *adj* possessed ‖ *mf* person possessed
ossìa *conj* or; to wit
ossidante *adj* oxidizing ‖ *m* oxidizer
ossidare (òssido) *tr* & *ref* to oxidize
òssido *m* oxide; ossido di carbonio carbon monoxide
ossìdulo *m* protoxide; ossidulo di azoto nitrous oxide
ossificare §197 (ossìfico) *tr* & *ref* to ossify
ossigenare (ossìgeno) *tr* to oxygenate; to bleach (the hair); to infuse strength into ‖ *ref* to bleach (the hair)
ossìgeno *m* oxygen; (fig) transfusion, shot in the arm
ossìto·no -na *adj* & *m* oxytone

òs·so *m* (-**si**) bone (*of animal*); stone (*of fruit*); **osso di balena** whalebone; **osso di seppia** cuttlebone; **osso duro da rodere** hard nut to crack; **osso sacro** sacrum; **rimetterci l'osso del collo** to be thoroughly ruined; **rompersi l'osso del collo** to break one's neck || *m* (-**sa** *fpl*) bone (*of a person*); **avere le ossa rotte** to be dead-tired

ossu·to -ta *adj* bony; scrawny

ostacolare (**ostàcolo**) *tr* to hinder; to obstruct; **ostacolare l'azione** (*sports*) to interfere

ostàcolo *m* obstacle; obstruction; (*golf*) hazard; (*sports*) hurdle

ostàg·gio *m* (-**gi**) hostage

ostare (**òsto**) *intr* (lit) to be in the way; (*with* *dat*) to hinder; **nulla osta** no objection, permission granted

òste ostéssa *mf* innkeeper || **oste** *m & f* (lit) army in the field || *m* (poet) enemy

ostèllo *m* hostel; (poet) abode

ostentare (**ostènto**) *tr* to show, display; to affect, feign

ostenta·to -ta *adj* affected, ostentatious

ostentazióne *f* show, ostentation

osteopatìa *f* osteopathy

osterìa *f* tavern, inn, taproom

ostéssa *f* see **oste**

ostètri·ca *f* (-**che**) midwife

ostetrìcia *f* obstetrics

ostètri·co -ca (-**ci -che**) *adj* obstetrical || *m* obstetrician || *f* see **ostetrica**

òstia *f* wafer; Host; sacrificial victim

òsti·co -ca *adj* (-**ci -che**) hard; (lit) repugnant, distasteful

ostile *adj* hostile

ostili·tà *f* (-**tà**) hostility

ostinare *ref* to be stubborn; to persist

ostina·to -ta *adj* obstinate; persistent

ostinazióne *f* obstinacy

ostracismo *m* ostracism; **dare l'ostracismo a** to ostracize

ostracizzare [ddzz] *tr* (poet) to ostracize

òstri·ca *f* (-**che**) oyster; **ostrica perlifera** pearl oyster

ostri·càio *m* (-**cài**) oyster bed; oyster-man

ostruire §176 *tr* to obstruct; to stop up

ostruzióne *f* obstruction

Otèllo *m* Othello

otorinolaringoia·tra *mf* (-**tri -tre**) ear, nose, and throat specialist, otorhinolaryngologist

ótre *f* wineskin; **otre di vento** windbag (*person*)

ottàni·co -ca *adj* (-**ci -che**) octane

ottano *m* octane

ottanta *adj, m & pron* eighty

ottantènne *adj* eighty-year-old || *mf* eighty-year-old person

ottantèsi·mo -ma *adj, m & pron* eightieth

ottantina *f* about eighty; **essere sull'ottantina** to be about eighty years old

ottava *f* octave

Ottaviano *m* Octavian

ottavino *m* (mus) piccolo; (com) commission of ⅛ of 1%

otta·vo -va *adj & pron* eighth || *m* eighth; octavo || *f* see **ottava**

ottemperare (**ottèmpero**) *intr* (with *dat*) to obey; **ottemperare a** to comply with

ottenebrare (**ottènebro**) *tr* to becloud

ottenére §271 *tr* to obtain, get

ottétto *m* octet

òtti·co -ca (-**ci -che**) *adj* optic(al) || *m* optician || *f* optics

ottimismo *m* optimism

ottimi·sta *mf* (-**sti -ste**) optimist

ottimìsti·co -ca *adj* (-**ci -che**) optimistic

òtti·mo -ma *adj* very good, excellent || *m* best; highest rating

òtto *adj & pron* eight; **le otto** eight o'clock || *m* eight; eighth (*in dates*); (*sports*) racing shell with eight oarsmen; **otto giorni** a week; **otto volante** roller coaster

ottóbre *m* October

ottocenté·sco -sca *adj* (-**schi -sche**) nineteenth-century

ottocènto *adj, m & pron* eight hundred || **l'Ottocento** the nineteenth century

ottoma·no -na *adj & m* Ottoman || *m* ottoman (*fabric*) || *f* ottoman (*sofa*)

ottomila *adj, m & pron* eight thousand

ottoname *m* brassware

ottonare (**ottóno**) *tr* to coat with brass

ottóne *m* brass; **ottoni** (mus) brasses || **Ottone** *m* Otto

ottuagenà·rio -ria *adj & mf* (-**ri -rie**) octogenerian

ottùndere §208 *tr* (fig) to deaden; (lit) to blunt

otturare *tr* to fill; to plug; to stop; to obstruct, stop up (*e.g., a channel*) || *ref* to clog up

otturatóre *m* breechblock; (phot, mov) shutter; (mach) cutoff (*of cylinder*)

otturazióne *f* filling (*of tooth*)

ottu·so -sa *adj* obtuse; blunt

ovàia *f* ovary

ovale *adj* oval || *m* oval; oval face

ovatta *f* wadding; absorbent cotton

ovattare *tr* to pad, wad; to muffle

ovazióne *f* ovation

óve *adv* (lit) where || *conj* (lit) if; (poet) while

òvest *m* west

Ovìdio *m* Ovid

ovile *m* sheepcote, fold

ovi·no -na *adj* ovine || **ovini** *mpl* sheep

òvo *m* var of **uovo**

ovoidale *adj* egg-shaped

òvulo *m* pill shaped like an egg; (biol) ovum; (bot) ovule

ovùnque *adv* (lit) wherever; (lit) everywhere

ovvéro *conj* or; to wit

ovvìa *interj* come on!

ovviare §119 *intr*—(with *dat*) to obviate

òv·vio -via *adj* (-**vi -vie**) obvious

oziare §287 (**òzio**) *intr* to idle, loiter

ò·zio *m* (-**zi**) idleness; leisure

oziosi·tà [s] *f* (-**tà**) idleness

ozió·so -sa [s] *adj* idle; useless, vain

ozòno [dz] *m* ozone

P

P, p [pi] *m & f* fourteenth letter of the Italian alphabet

pacare §197 *tr* (poet) to placate

pacatézza *f* tranquillity, serenity

paca·to ·ta *adj* serene, tranquil

pac·ca *f* (-che) slap

pacchétto *m* parcel, package; book (*of matches*); pack (*of cigarettes*)

pàcchia *f* (coll) hearty meal; (coll) godsend, windfall

pacchia·no ·na *adj* boorish, uncouth ‖ *mf* boor

pacciamantura *f* mulching

pacciame *m* mulch

pac·co *m* (-chi) package; **pacchi postali** parcel post (*service*); **pacco dono** gift package; **pacco postale** parcel by mail

paccottiglia *f* shoddy goods, junk; trinkets

pace *f* peace; **lasciare in pace** to leave alone; **mettersi il cuore in pace** to resign oneself

pachidèr·ma *m* (-mi) pachyderm

pachista·no ·na *adj & mf* Pakistani

paciè·re ·ra *mf* peacemaker

pacificare §197 (**pacìfico**) *tr* to pacify; to appease; to mediate ‖ *ref* to make one's peace

pacifica·tóre ·trice *adj* pacifying ‖ *mf* peacemaker

pacificazióne *f* pacification; appeasement

pacìfi·co ·ca (-ci -che) *adj* peaceful, pacific; **è pacifico che** it goes without saying that ‖ *m* peaceable person ‖ **Pacifico** *adj & m* Pacific

pacifismo *m* pacifism

pacifi·sta *mf* (-sti -ste) pacifist

pacioc·có·ne ·na *mf* chubby, easygoing person

padèlla *f* frying pan; bedpan; **cadere dalla padella nella brace** to jump from the frying pan into the fire

padiglióne *m* pavilion; hunting lodge; roof (*of car*); ward (*of a hospital*); (naut) rigging, tackle; **padiglione auricolare** (anat) auricle of the ear

Pàdova *f* Padua

padre *m* father; sire; **padre di famiglia** provider; (law) head of household; **Padre Eterno** Heavenly Father

padreggiare §290 (**padréggio**) *intr* to resemble one's father

padrino *m* godfather; second (*in duel*)

padrona *f* owner, boss, mistress; **padrona di casa** lady of the house

padronale *adj* proprietary; private (*e.g., car*)

padronanza *f* command; **padronanza di sé stesso** self-control

padróne *m* owner, boss, master; essere **padrone di** + *inf* to have the right to + *inf*; **padrone di casa** landlord; **padrone di sé** cool and collected

padroneggiare §290 (**padronéggio**) *tr* to master, control

paesàg·gio *m* (-gi) landscape

paesaggi·sta *mf* (-sti -ste) landscapist

paesa·no ·na *adj* country ‖ *mf* villager ‖ *m* countryman ‖ *f* countrywoman; **alla paesana** according to local tradition

paése *m* country; village; **i Paesi Bassi** the Netherlands; (hist) the Low Countries; **mandare a quel paese** to send to blazes

paesi·sta *mf* (-sti -ste) landscapist

paffu·to ·ta *adj* chubby, plump

pa·ga *f* (-ghe) salary; wages; repayment; **mala paga** poor pay (*person*)

pagàbile *adj* payable

pagàia *f* paddle

pagaménto *m* payment; **pagamento alla consegna** c.o.d.

paganésimo *m* paganism

paga·no ·na *adj & mf* pagan, heathen

pagare §209 *tr* to pay; to pay for; **far pagare** to charge; **pagare di egual moneta** to repay in kind; **pagare il fio per** to pay (the penalty) for; **pagare in natura** to pay in kind; **pagare salato** to pay dearly; **pagare un occhio della testa** to pay through the nose ‖ *intr* to pay

paga·tóre ·trice *mf* payer

pagèlla *f* report card

pàg·gio *m* (-gi) page (*boy attendant*)

paghe·rò *m* (-rò) promissory note, I.O.U.

pàgina *f* page (*e.g., of book*)

paginatura *f* pagination

pàglia *f* straw; thatch (*for roof*); **paglia di ferro** steel wool; **paglia di legno** excelsior

pagliac·cé·sco ·sca *adj* (-schi -sche) clownish

pagliaccétto *m* rompers

pagliacciata *f* buffoonery, antics

pagliàc·cio *m* (-ci) clown, buffoon; **fare il pagliaccio** to clown

pa·gliàio *m* (-gliài) heap of straw; haystack

paglieric·cio *m* (-ci) straw mattress

paglieri·no ·na *adj* straw-colored

pagliétta *f* skimmer, boater; steel wool; (coll) pettifogger

pagnòtta *f* loaf of bread; (coll) bread

pa·go ·ga *adj* (-ghi -ghe) satisfied ‖ *f* see **paga**

paguro *m* (zool) hermit crab

pà·io *m* (-ia *fpl*) pair, couple; **è un altro paio di maniche** this is a horse of another color; **fare il paio** to match perfectly

paiòlo *m* caldron, kettle; (mil) platform

Pakistan, il Pakistan

pala *f* shovel; blade (*e.g., of turbine*); paddle (*of waterwheel*); peel (*of baker*); **pala d'altare** altarpiece

paladi·no ·na *mf* champion ‖ *m* paladin; **farsi paladino di** to champion

palafitta *f* pile dwelling; piles (*to support a structure*)

palafrenière *m* groom

palafréno *m* palfrey

palan·ca *f* (-che) beam, board; (naut)

gangplank; copper coin; **palanche** (coll) money

palanchino m palanquin; (naut) pulley

palandrana f (joc) long, full coat

palata f shovelful; stroke (of oar); **a palate** by the bucketful

palatale adj & f palatal

palati·no -na adj palatine; (anat) palatal

palato m palate

palazzina f villa

palazzo m palace; large office or government building; mansion; **palazzo dello sport** sports arena; **palazzo di città** city hall; **palazzo di giustizia** courthouse

palchetti·sta (-sti -ste) mf (theat) box-holder ‖ m person who lays floors

palchétto m shelf; (theat) small box; (journ) box

pal·co m (-chi) flooring; scaffold; stand, platform; (theat) box; (theat) stage

palcoscèni·co m (-ci) (theat) stage

palesare (paléso) tr to reveal, manifest ‖ ref to show oneself

palése adj plain, manifest; **fare palese** to manifest, reveal

palèstra f gymnasium; palestra

palétta f small shovel, scoop; blade (of turbine)

palettata f shovelful

palétto m stake; bolt (of door)

palificazióne f pile work (in the ground for foundation); line of telephone poles

pà·lio m (-lii) embroidered cloth (given as prize); **metter in palio** to offer as a prize; **palio di Siena** colorful horse-race at Siena

palissandro m Brazilian rosewood

palizzata f palisade; picket fence

palla f ball; bullet; sphere; **dar palla nera a** to blackball; **palla da cannone** cannon ball; **palla di neve** snowball; **prendere la palla al balzo** to seize the opportunity

pallabase f baseball

pallacanè·stro f (-stro) basketball

pallamuro m handball

pallanuòto f water polo

pallavó·lo f (-lo) volleyball

palleggiare §290 (palléggio) tr to toss (e.g., a javelin); to shift from one hand to another ‖ intr (tennis) to knock a few balls; (soccer) to dribble ‖ ref—**palleggiarsi la responsabilità** to shift the responsibility

pallég·gio m (-gi) (tennis) knocking back and forth; (soccer) dribbling

palliati·vo -va adj & m palliative

pallidézza f paleness

pàlli·do -da adj pale; faint

pallina f marble; small ball; **pallina antitarmica** mothball

pallino m little ball; (bowling) jack; bullet; **a pallini** polka-dot; **avere il pallino di** to be crazy about; **pallini** buckshot; polka dots

palloncino m child's balloon; Chinese lantern

pallóne m (soccer) ball; (aer) balloon;

pallone di sbarramento barrage balloon; **pallone gonfiato** (fig) stuffed shirt; **pallone sonda** trial balloon

pallonétto m (tennis) lob

pallóre m pallor, paleness

pallòttola f pellet; ball; bullet

pallottolière m abacus

pallovale f rugby

palma f palm; **tenere in palma di mano** to hold in the highest esteem

palmare adj evident, plain

palménto m millstone; **mangiare a quattro palmenti** (coll) to stuff oneself eating

palméto m palm grove

palmìpede adj palmate, web-footed

palmì·zio m (-zi) palm tree

palmo m span; palm; palm (of hand); foot (measure); **a palmo a palmo** little by little; **restare con un palmo di naso** to be disappointed

palo m pole (of wood or metal); beam; pile; (soccer, football) goal post; **fare il palo** to be on the lookout (said of thieves); **palo indicatore** signpost; **saltare di palo in frasca** to digress

palombaro m diver

palómbo m dogfish

palpàbile adj palpable

palpare tr to touch; to palpate

pàlpebra f eyelid; **battere le palpebre** to blink

palpeggiare §290 (palpéggio) tr to finger, touch repeatedly

palpitante adj throbbing; burning (question); fluttering (e.g., with love)

palpitare (pàlpito) intr to palpitate, pulsate; (fig) to pine

palpitazióne f palpitation

pàlpito m heartbeat; (fig) throb

pal·tò m (-tò) overcoat

paltoncino m child's winter coat; lady's topcoat

paludaménto m (joc) array, attire

palude f marsh, bog

paludó·so -sa [s] adj marshy

palustre adj marshy

pàmpino m grape leaf

panacèa f panacea, cure-all

pàna·ma m (-ma) Panama hat

panamé·gno -gna adj & mf Panamenian

panamènse adj & mf Panamenian

panare tr (culin) to bread

pan·ca f (-che) bench; **scaldare le panche** (coll) to loaf around; (coll) to waste one's time at school

pancétta f potbelly; bacon

panchétto m footstool

panchina f bench

pàn·cia f (-ce) belly; **a pancia all'aria** on one's back; **mangiare a crepa pancia** to stuff oneself like a pig; **mettere su pancia** to grow a potbelly; **salvar la pancia per i fichi** to not take any chances; **tenersi la pancia dalle risate** to split one's side laughing

panciata f belly flop

pancièra f bellypiece; body girth

panciòlle m—**in panciolle** frittering one's time away

panciòtto *m* waistcoat; vest; **panciotto a maglia** cardigan

panciu·to -ta *adj* potbellied

pàncre·as *m* (-as) pancreas

pandemò·nio *m* (-ni) pandemonium

pane *m* bread; thread (*of screw*); cake (*e.g., of butter*); loaf (*of sugar*); (metallurgy) pig; **a pane di zucchero** conic(al); **dire pane al pane e vino al vino** to call a spade a spade; **essere come pane e cacio** to be hand and glove; **essere pane per i propri denti** to be a match for s.o.; **guadagnarsi il pane** to earn one's living; **pane a cassetta** sandwich bread; **pane azzimo** unleavened bread, matzoth; **pan di Spagna** angel food cake, sponge cake; **pane integrale** graham bread; **render pan per focaccia** to give tit for tat

panegìri·co *m* (-ci) panegyric

panetteria *f* bakery

panettière *m* baker

panétto *m* pat (*e.g., of butter*)

pànfilo *m* yacht

panfrutto *m* plum cake

pangrattato *m* bread crumbs

pània *f* birdlime; **cadere nella pania** to fall into the trap

pàni·co -ca (-ci -che) *adj* panicky ‖ *m* panic

pani·co *m* (-chi) (bot) Italian millet

panièra *f* basket; basketful

panière *m* basket; basketful

panificazióne *f* breadmaking

panifi·cio *m* (-ci) bakery

panino *m* roll, bun; **panino imbottito** sandwich

panna *f* cream, heavy cream; **essere in panna** (naut) to lie to; (aut) to have a breakdown; **mettere in panna** (naut) to heave to; **panna montata** whipped cream

panne *f* (aut) breakdown; **essere in panne** (aut) to have a breakdown

pannèllo *m* linen cloth; pane; panel (*of machine*); (archit; elec) panel

pannìcolo *m* (anat) membrane, tissue

panno *m* cloth; woolen cloth; film, membrane; **bianco come un panno** as white as a ghost; **mettersi nei panni di** to put oneself in the boots of; **non stare più nei propri panni** to be beside oneself with joy; **panni** clothes; **panno verde** baize

pannòcchia *f* ear (*of corn*)

pannolino *m* linen cloth; diaper; sanitary napkin

panòplia *f* panoply

panora·ma *m* (-mi) panorama

panoràmi·co -ca *adj* (-ci -che) panoramic ‖ *f* panoramic view; (mov) panoramic scene

pantaloncini *mpl* trunks

pantalóni *mpl* trousers; **pantaloni da donna** slacks

pantano *m* bog, quagmire

panteismo *m* pantheism

pànteon *m* pantheon

pantèra *f* panther; (slang) police car

pantòfola *f* slipper

pantomima *f* pantomine, mimicry

panzana *f* (lit) fib, lie

Pàolo *m* Paul

paonaz·zo -za *adj* & *m* purple

pa·pa *m* (-pi) pope; **ad ogni morte di papa** once in a blue moon; **morto un papa se ne fa un altro** nobody is indispensable

pa·pà *m* (-pà) daddy, papa

papàbile *adj* likely to be elected ‖ *mf* front runner ‖ *m* cardinal likely to be elected to the papacy

papale *adj* papal (*e.g., benediction*); Papal (*States*)

papalì·no -na *adj* papal ‖ *m* advocate of papal temporal power ‖ *f* skullcap

paparazzo *m* freelance photographer

papato *m* papacy

papàvero *m* poppy; **alto papavero** (fig) big shot

pàpera *f* young goose; slip of the tongue; spoonerism; **fare una papera** to make a boner

pàpero *m* gander

papiro *m* papyrus

pappa *f* bread soup, farina, pap; **pappa molla** (fig) jellyfish

pappafi·co *m* (-chi) (naut) topgallant; (slang) goatee

pappagallo *m* parrot; bedpan; (slang) masher

pappagòr·gia *f* (-ge) double chin, jowl

pappare *tr* (coll) to gulp; (fig) to gobble up fraudulently

pappata·ci *m* (-ci) gnat

pappina *f* light pap; poultice

pàpri·ca *f* (-che) paprika

para *f* crepe rubber

paràbola *f* parable; (geom) parabola

parabórdo *m* (naut) fender

parabréz·za [ddzz] *m* (-za) windshield

paracadutare *tr* to parachute, airdrop ‖ *ref* to parachute

paracadu·te *m* (-te) parachute

paracadutismo *m* parachute jumping; (sports) sky diving

paracaduti·sta *mf* (-sti -ste) parachutist; skydiver ‖ *m* paratrooper

paracarro *m* spur stone

paracól·pi *m* (-pi) doorstop

paràcqua *m* (paràcqua) umbrella

paradèn·ti *m* (-ti) (sports) mouthpiece

paradisìa·co -ca *adj* (-ci -che) heavenly

paradiso *m* paradise

paradossale *adj* paradoxical

paradòsso *m* paradox

parafa *f* initials

parafan·go *m* (-ghi) fender, mudguard

parafare *tr* to initial

paraffina *f* paraffin

parafiam·ma *m* (-ma) fire-proof partition

parafrasare (paràfraso) *tr* to paraphrase

paràfra·si *f* (-si) paraphrase

parafùlmine *m* lightning rod

parafuò·co *m* (-co) screen, fender (*in front of fireplace*)

paràg·gio *m* (-gi) lineage; **paraggi** neighborhood, vicinity

paragonàbile *adj* comparable

paragonare (paragóno) *tr* to compare

paragóne *m* comparison; **a paragone di**

in comparison with; **mettere a para-gone** to compare; **senza paragone** beyond compare

paragrafare (paràgrafo) tr to paragraph

paràgrafo m paragraph

paraguaia·no -na adj & mf Paraguayan

paràli·si f (-si) paralysis

paralìti·co -ca adj & mf (-ci -che) paralytic

paralizzare [ddzz] tr to paralyze

parallè·lo -la adj & m parallel || f (geom) parallel line; **parallele** (sports) parallel bars

paralume m lamp shade

paramano m cuff, wristband; (archit) facing brick

paramento s facing (of a wall); (eccl) vestment

parami·ne m (-ne) (nav) paravane

paramó·sche m (-sche) fly net

paran·co m (-chi) tackle

paranin·fo -fa mf matchmaker

paranòi·co -ca adj & mf (-ci -che) paranoiac

paraòc·chi m (-chi) blinker (on horse)

parapètto m parapet

parapì·glia m (-glia) hubbub

parapiòg·gia m (-gia) umbrella

parare tr to adorn; to hang; to protect; to parry (a thrust); to offer; to drive (e.g., cattle) || intr—**dove va a pa-rare?** what are you driving at? || ref to protect oneself; (eccl) to don the vestments; **pararsi dinanzi a** to loom up in front of

parasóle m parasol; (aut) sun visor

paraspal·le m (-le) (sports) shoulder pad

parassi·ta (-ti -te) adj parasitic || m parasite

parassità·rio -ria adj (-ri -rie) para-sitic(al)

parassìti·co -ca adj (-ci -che) para-sitic(al)

parastatale adj government-controlled || mf employee of government-con-trolled agency

parastin·chi m (-chi) (sports) shin guard

parata f fence, bar; (fencing) parry; (soccer) catch; (mil) parade; **mala parata** dangerous situation

paratìa f bulkhead

parato m hangings; **parati** hangings; (naut) bilgeways

paratóia f sluice gate

paraur·ti m (-ti) (aut) bumper; (rr) buffer

paravènto m screen

Par·ca f (-che) Fate

parcare §197 tr & intr to park

parcèlla f bill, fee, honorarium; parcel, lot (of land)

parcheggiare §290 (**parchéggio**) tr & intr to park

parchég·gio m (-gi) parking; parking lot

parchìmetro m parking meter

par·co -ca (-chi -che) adj frugal; parsi-monious || m park; parking; parking lot; **parco dei divertimenti** amuse-ment park

paréc·chio -chia (-chi -chie) adj indef

a good deal of, a lot of; **parecchi** several || pron a good deal, a lot; **parecchi** several || **parecchio** adv a lot; rather

pareggiare §290 (**paréggio**) tr to level; to equal; to match; to balance; to recognize || intr (sports) to tie

pareggia·to -ta adj accredited (school)

parég·gio m (-gi) leveling; matching; (sports) tie; **pareggio del bilancio** balancing of the budget

parentado m kinsfolk, kindred; rela-tionship; **concludere il parentado di** to arrange for the wedding of

parènte mf relative; (lit) parent; **pa-renti** kin

parentèla f relationship; relations

parènte·si f (-si) parenthesis; break, interval; **fra parentesi** parentheti-cally; in parentheses; **parentesi qua-dra** bracket

parére m opinion, mind; advice; **a mio parere** in my opinion || §210 intr (ESSERE) to seem; **che Le pare?** what is your opinion?; **ma Le pare!** not at all!; **mi pare che** + subj it seems to me that + ind; I guess that + ind; **non Le pare?** don't you think so?; **non mi pare vero** I can't believe it

paréte f wall; **tra le pareti domestiche** within the four walls of the home

pargolét·to -ta adj (poet) infantile || m (poet) child

pàrgo·lo -la adj (poet) infantile || mf (poet) child

pari adj invar equal, even; **camminare di pari passo** to walk at the same rate; **essere pari** to be quits; **essere pari al proprio compito** to be equal to the task; **fare un salto a piè pari** to jump with feet together; **pari pari** verbatim; **rimanere pari con** (sports) to be tied with; **saltare a piè pari** to skip (e.g., a page); to dodge (a difficulty); **trattare da pari a pari** to treat as an equal || m peer; **al pari di** as, like; **del pari** also; **in pari** even, leveled; **senza pari** matchless, peer-less || f—**stare alla pari con** to be an even match for

parìa f peerage

pà·ria m (-ria) pariah

parificare §197 (**parifico**) tr to level; to match; to accredit (a school); to balance

Parigi f Paris

parigi·no -na adj & mf Parisian || f slow-burning stove; Parisian woman; (rr) switching spur

parìglia f pair, couple; team (of horses); (cards) two of a kind; **ren-dere la pariglia** to give tit for tat

pariménti adv likewise

pari·tà f (-tà) parity

paritèti·co -ca adj (-ci -che) joint (e.g., committee)

parlamentare adj parliamentary || mf member of parliament || m (mil) envoy || v (parlaménto) intr to parley

parlaménto m parliament

parlante adj talking; life-like || mf speaker

parlantìna f glibness

parlare *m* talk, speech; dialect ‖ *tr* to speak (*a language*) ‖ *intr* to speak, talk; to discuss; **chi parla?** (*telp*) hello!; **far parlare di sé** to be talked about; **parlare chiaro** to speak bluntly; **parlare del più e del meno** to make small talk; **parlare tra sé e sé** to talk to oneself ‖ *ref* to talk to one another

parla·to -ta *adj* spoken; current (*speech*); talking (*movie*) ‖ *m* talkie; (*mov*) sound track; (*theat*) dialogue ‖ *f* speech, talk; dialect

parla·tóre -trice *mf* speaker

parlatò·rio *m* (**-ri**) visting room (*e.g., in jail*)

parlottare (parlòtto) *intr* to whisper in secret

parmigia·no -na *adj & mf* Parmesan ‖ *m* Parmesan cheese

parnaso *m* Parnassus (*poetry, poets*) ‖ **il Parnaso** Mount Parnassus

paro *m*—**in un par d'ore** in a couple of hours ‖ *adv*—**andare a paro** to keep abreast; **mettere a paro** to compare

parodia *f* parody; **fare la parodia di** to parody

parodiare §287 (**parò·dio**) *tr* to parody

paròla *f* word; speech; **avere parole con** to have words with; **buttare la mezza parola** to make an allusion; **dare la parola a** to give the floor to; **di poche parole** of few words; **domandare la parola a** to ask for the floor; **essere di parola** to keep one's word; **essere in parola con** to have dealings with; **mangiarsi la parola** to break one's word; **mangiarsi le parole** to slur one's words; **non far parola** to not breathe a word; **parola crociata** crossword puzzle; **parola d'ordine** password; **parola macedonia** acronym **parola sdrucciola** proparoxytone; **parole** lyrics; **parole di circostanza** occasional words; **prendere la parola** to take the floor; **rivolgere la parola a** to address; **venire a parole** to begin to quarrel

parolàc·cia *f* (**-ce**) dirty word; swearword

paro·làio -làia (**-lài -làie**) *adj* wordy, verbose ‖ *mf* windbag

parolière *m* lyricist

parossismo *m* paroxysm; climax

parossìto·no -na *adj* paroxytone

parotite *f* (*pathol*) parotitis; **parotite epidemica** (*pathol*) mumps

parrici·da *mf* (**-di -de**) patricide

parrocchétto *m* parakeet; (*naut*) fore-topsail; (*naut*) fore-topmast

parrocchia *f* parish

parrocchia·no -na *mf* parishioner

pàrro·co *m* (**-ci**) rector, parson

parruc·ca *f* (**-che**) wig; (*fig*) old fogey

parsimònia *f* parsimony

parsimonió·so -sa [s] *adj* parsimonious

partàc·cia *f*—**fare una partaccia** to break one's word; **fare una partaccia a** to make a scene in front of; to rebuke loudly

parte *f* part; share; section; side; party; partiality; (*theat*) role; **a parte** sepa-

---

rately; (*theat*) aside; **d'altra parte** on the other hand; **da parte** aside; **da parte mia** as for me; **fare le parti** to divide in shares; **gran parte di** a great deal of; **in parte** partially; **la maggior parte di** most of; **parte civile** (*law*) plaintiff; **parte . . . parte** some . . . some; **part . . . part**; **prendere in mala parte** to take amiss

partecipante *adj* participating ‖ *mf* participant; (*sports*) contestant

partecipare (partécipo) *tr* to announce; (*lit*) to share in ‖ *intr*—**partecipare a** to share in; to participate in; **partecipare di** to partake of (*e.g., the nature of an animal*)

partecipazióne *f* announcement; card; announcement (*of a wedding*); share in a business); participation (*in some action*)

partécipe *adj* sharing, partaking

parteggiare §290 (**partéggio**) *intr* to side; **parteggiare per** to side with

Partenóne *m* Parthenon

partènte *adj* departing ‖ *mf* person departing, traveler; (*sports*) starter

partènza *f* departure; sailing; (*sports*) start; **di partenza** or **in partenza** about to leave; **partenza lanciata** (*sports*) running start

particèlla *f* particle

partici·pio *m* (**-pi**) participle

particolare *adj* particular; private; **in particolare** especially ‖ *m* detail

particolareggiare §290 (**particolaréggio**) *tr* to detail

particolarismo *m* regionalism, particularism

particolarìsti·co -ca *adj* (**-ci -che**) particularistic; individualistic

particolari·tà *f* (**-tà**) peculiarity; detail

partigianerìa *f* partisanship, factionalism

partigia·no -na *adj & mf* partisan

partire §176 *tr* (*lit*) to divide ‖ *v* (**parto**) *intr* to depart; (*fig*) to arise; **a partire da** beginning with; **far partire** to start (*e.g., a car*) ‖ *ref* to depart, leave

parti·to -ta *adj* parted ‖ *m* match (*in marriage*); (*pol*) party; **ridotto a mal partito** in bad shape; **mettere la testa a partito** to reform; **partito preso** parti pris; **prendere partito** to take sides; to make up one's mind; **trarre il miglior partito da** to make the best of ‖ *f* panel (*e.g., of door*); lot (*of goods*); game; match; party; round (*of golf*); (*com*) entry; **partita di caccia** hunting party; **partita doppia** (*com*) double entry; **partita semplice** (*com*) single entry

partitura *f* (*mus*) score

partizióne *f* partition, division

parto *m* birth, childbirth

partorire §176 *tr* to bear, bring forth

parvènza *f* (*lit*) appearance

parziale *adj* partial, one-sided

parziali·tà *f* (**-tà**) partiality

pàscere §211 *tr, intr & ref* to pasture, graze

pa·scià *m* (**-scià**) pasha

pasciu·to -ta *adj* well-fed

pascolare (pàscolo) *tr & intr* to pasture
pàscolo *m* pasture
Pàsqua *f* Easter; **contento come una Pasqua** as happy as a lark; **Pasqua fiorita** Palm Sunday
pasquale *adj* paschal (*e.g., lamb*)
passàbile *adj* passable, tolerable
passàg·gio *m* (-**gi**) passage; transfer; crossing; traffic; passageway; ride; promotion; (sports) pass; **aprirsi il passaggio** to make one's way; **di passaggio** in passing; transient (*visitor*); **essere di passaggio** to be passing by; **passaggio a livello** railroad crossing; **passaggio zebrato** zebra crossing; **vietato il passaggio** no thoroughfare
passamano *m* passing from hand to hand; ribbon; (coll) railing, handrail
passante *adj* passing (*shot*) || *mf* passer-by || *m* strap
passapòrto *m* passport
passare *tr* to cross; to pass; to undergo (*a medical examination*); to move; to hand; to pay; to send (*word*); to pierce; to spend (*time*); to strain; to go over; to let have (*e.g., a slap*); to overstep (*the bounds*); **passare in rassegna** to pass in review; **passare per le armi** to execute; **passare un brutto quarto d'ora** to have a bad ten minutes; **passare un guaio** to have a hard time; **passarla a qlcu** (coll) to forgive s.o.; **passarla liscia** (coll) to get off unscathed; **passarsela bene** (coll) to have a good time || *intr* (ESSERE) to pass; to go; to filter (*said of air, light*); to move; to spoil (*said of food*); to be overcooked; to be promoted; to become; to enter; (lit) to be over; **fare passare qlcu** to let s.o. come in; **passare a nozze** to get married; **passare a seconde nozze** to remarry; **passare avanti a** to overcome; **passare di mente a** to forget, e.g., **gli è passata di mente la riunione** he forgot the meeting; **passare di moda** to go out of style; **passare in giudicato** (law) to be no longer appealable; **passare per** to pass as; **passare per il rotto della cuffia** to barely make it; **passare sopra qlco** to overlook s.th; **passi!** come in!; **passo!** (rad) over!; **passo** (cards) pass
passata *f* purée; **dare una passata a** to glance at; **dare una passata di straccio a** to rub lightly with a rag; to give a lick and a promise to; **di passata** hurriedly
passatèmpo *m* pastime; hobby
passati·sta *mf* (-**sti** -**ste**) traditionalist
passa·to -**ta** *adj* last; overcooked; **essere passato** (coll) to be no longer in one's prime; **passato di moda** out of fashion || *m* past; purée; **passato prossimo** present perfect; **passato remoto** preterit || *f* see **passata**
passatóia *f* runner (*rug*)
passa·tóio *m* (-**tói**) stepping stone
passeggè·ro -**ra** *adj* passing || *mf* passenger; **passeggero clandestino** stowaway

passeggiare §290 (passéggio) *tr* to walk (*e.g., a horse*) || *intr* to walk, promenade
passeggiata *f* promenade; walk; drive, ride; drive, road; **fare una passeggiata** to take a walk; to take a ride
passeggiatrice *f* streetwalker
passég·gio *m* (-**gi**) walk; promenade; **andare a passeggio** to take a walk
passerèlla *f* gangway; catwalk; footbridge
pàsse·ro -**ra** *mf* sparrow || *f*—**passera di mare** (ichth) flounder
passìbile *adj*—**passibile di** subject to, liable to
passiflòra *f* passionflower
passino *m* colander, strainer
passióne *f* passion
passivi·tà *f* (-**tà**) passivity; (com) deficit
passi·vo -**va** *adj* passive || *m* (com) liabilities; (com) debit side; (gram) passive
pas·so -**sa** *adj*—see **uva** || *m* step; passage; pass (*in mountain*); pace; footstep; pitch (*of screw, helix, etc.*); (aut) wheelbase; (phot) tread; (phot) size (*of roll*); **a grandi passi** with great strides; **andare al passo** to march in step; to walk (*said of a horse*); **a passi di gigante** by leaps and bounds; **a passo di corsa** running; **a passo d'uomo** walking, at a walk; **aprire il passo** to open the way; **di buon passo** at a good clip; **di pari passo** at the same rate; **fare quattro passi** to take a stroll; **passo doppio** paso doble; **passo d'uomo** manhole; step; **passo falso** misstep; (fig) stumble; **sbarrare il passo** to block the way; **seguire i passi di** to walk in the footsteps of || *interj* (cards) pass!; over!
pasta *f* paste; dough; **di pasta grossa** uncouth, coarse; **pasta alimentare** pasta, macaroni products; **pasta all'uovo** egg noodles; **pasta asciutta** pasta with sauce and cheese; **pasta dentifricia** toothpaste; **una pasta d'uomo** a good-natured man
pastasciutta *f* pasta with sauce and cheese
pasteggiare §290 (pastéggio) *intr* to dine
pastèllo *adj invar & m* pastel || *m* crayon
pastétta *f* batter; (coll) trickery
pastic·ca *f* (-**che**) lozenge, tablet; **pasticche per la tosse** cough drops
pasticceria *f* pastrymaking; pastry; pastry shop
pasticciare §128 (pastìccio) *tr & intr* to bungle; to scribble
pasticciè·re -**ra** *mf* pastry cook; confectioner
pasticcino *m* cookie; patty
pastìc·cio *m* (-**ci**) pie (*of meat, macaroni, etc*); bungle; mess; **cacciarsi nei pasticci** to wind up in the soup
pasticció·ne -**na** *mf* bungler
pastifì·cio *m* (-**ci**) spaghetti and macaroni factory
pastìglia *f* lozenge, tablet; **pastiglia per la tosse** cough drop

pastina·ca *f* (**-che**) parsnip
pa·sto -sta *adj* (archaic) fed || *m* meal;
pasto a prezzo fisso table d'hôte ||
f see **pasta**
pastóia *f* hobble; (fig) shackle
pastóne *m* mash
pastóra *f* shepherdess
pastorale *adj* pastoral
pastóre *m* shepherd; pastor
pastorì·zio -zia (**-zi -zie**) *adj* shepherd
|| *f* sheep raising
pastorizzare [ddzz] *tr* to pasteurize
pastó·so -sa [s] *adj* pasty; mellow
pastrano *m* overcoat
pastura *f* pasture; hay; fodder
patac·ca *f* (**-che**) large, worthless coin;
fake; (coll) medal; (coll) spot
patata *f* potato
patatràc *m* (**patatràc**) crash
patèlla *f* kneecap; (zool) limpet
patè·ma *m* (**-mi**) affliction; **patema
d'animo** anxiety
patenta·to -ta *adj* licensed; (coll) well-
known
patènte *adj* patent || *f* license; driver's
license; **patente sanitaria** (naut) bill
of health
patentino *m* (aut) permit
paterèc·cio *m* (**-ci**) whitlow
paternale *adj* (obs) paternal || *f* repri-
mand
paterni·tà *f* (**-tà**) paternity; authorship
patèr·no -na *adj* paternal; fatherly
paternòstro *m* Lord's Prayer; **è vero
come il paternostro** it is the gospel
truth
patèti·co -ca (**-ci -che**) *adj* pathetic;
mawkish || *m* pathos; mawkishness
pathos *m* pathos
patibile *adj* endurable
patibolare *adj* gallows
patibolo *m* executioner's instrument;
scaffold
patiménto *m* suffering
pàtina *f* patina; coating (*on paper*);
varnish; fur (*on tongue*)
patinare (**pàtino**) *tr* to gloss, glaze (*e.g.,
paper*)
patire §176 *tr* to suffer; (gram) to be
the recipient of (*an action*) || *intr* to
suffer
pati·to -ta *adj* suffering, sickly || *mf* fan
|| *m* boyfriend || *f* girlfriend
patòge·no -na *adj* pathogenic
patologia *f* pathology
patològi·co -ca *adj* (**-ci -che**) patho-
logic(al)
patos *m* var of **pathos**
patrasso *m*—**andare a patrasso** to die;
to go to ruin; **mandare a patrasso**
to kill; to ruin
pàtria *f* fatherland, native land
patriar·ca *m* (**-chi**) patriarch
patriarcale *adj* patriarchal
patrigno *m* stepfather
patrimoniale *adj* patrimonial; property
(*tax*); capital (*e.g., transaction*)
patrimò·nio *m* (**-ni**) patrimony; estate;
fortune; (fig) heritage
pà·trio -tria (**-tri -trie**) *adj* paternal; of
one's country (*e.g., love*) || *f* see
patria

patriò·ta *mf* (**-ti -te**) patriot; (coll) fellow citizen
patriòtti·co -ca *adj* (**-ci -che**) patriotic
patriottismo *m* patriotism
patrì·zio -zia (**-zi -zie**) *adj* & *m* patri-
cian || **Patrizio** *m* Patrick
patrocinante *adj* pleading (*lawyer*)
patrocinare *tr* to favor, sponsor; to
plead
patrocina·tóre -trice *mf* defender;
pleader
patroci·nio *m* (**-ni**) support; sponsorship; (law) defense; **patrocinio gratuito** public defense
patronato *m* patronage; charitable institution, foundation; **patronato scolastico** state aid fund
patronéssa *f* sponsor; trustee (*of charitable institution*)
patròno *m* patron saint; patron; sponsor; trustee (*of charitable institution*); (law) counsel
patta *f* flap (*of garment*); bill (*of
anchor*); (coll) potholder; **essere or
far patta** to be even, tie
patteggiaménto *m* negotiation
patteggiare §290 (**pattéggio**) *tr* & *intr*
to negotiate
pattinàggio *m* skating
pattinare (**pàttino**) *intr* to skate; to
skid (*said of a car*)
pattina·tóio *m* (**-tói**) skating rink
pattina·tóre -trice *mf* skater
pàttino *m* skate; guide block (*of an
elevator*); (aer) skid, runner; **pattino
a rotelle** roller skate
pattino *m* racing shell with outrigger
floats
patto *m* pact; **a nessun patto** by no
means; **a patto che** provided (that);
patto sociale social contract; **venire a
patti** to come to terms
pattùglia *f* patrol
pattugliare §280 *tr* & *intr* to patrol
pattuire §176 *tr* & *intr* to negotiate
pattui·to -ta *adj* agreed || *m* agreement
pattume *m* litter, garbage
pattumièra *f* dustpan; trash bin
patùrnie *fpl*—**avere le paturnie** (coll)
to be in the dumps
paura *f* fear; **aver paura di** to be afraid
of; **da far paura** frightful; **dar or
metter paura a** to frighten; **per paura
che** for fear that, lest
pauró·so -sa [s] *adj* fearful
pàusa *f* pause
pausare (**pàuso**) *tr* (lit) to interrupt ||
intr (lit) to pause
paventare (**pavènto**) *tr* & *intr* to fear
pavesare (**pavéso**) *tr* to deck with flags;
to dress (*a ship*)
pavése [s] *adj*—see **zuppa** || *m* pavis
(*shield*); (naut) bunting
pàvi·do -da *adj* cowardly, timid
pavimentare (**paviménto**) *tr* to pave
pavimentazióne *f* paving, pavement
paviménto *m* floor; bottom (*of sea*);
paving (*of street*)
pavoncèlla *f* lapwing
pavó·ne -na or **-néssa** *mf* peacock
pavoneggiare §290 (**pavonéggio**) *ref* to
swagger, strut
pazientare (**paziènto**) *intr* to be patient

paziènte adj & mf patient
paziènza f patience; **fare scappare la pazienza a** to drive mad; **pazienza!** too bad!
pazzé·sco -sca adj (-**schi** -**sche**) crazy, wild
pazzìa f madness, insanity; folly; **fare pazzie** to act like a fool
paz·zo -za adj crazy, insane; **andar pazzo per** to be crazy about ‖ mf crazy person
pèc·ca f (-**che**) imperfection
peccaminó·so -sa [s] adj sinful
peccare §197 (**pècco**) intr to sin; to be lacking; to be at fault
peccato m sin; **che peccato!** what a pity!; **è un peccato** it's a shame
pecca·tóre -trice mf sinner
pécchia f bee
pecchióne m drone
péce f pitch; **pece greca** rosin
pechinése [s] adj & mf Pekingese
Pechino f Peking
pècora f sheep
peco·ràio m (-**rài**) shepherd
pecorèlla f small sheep, lamb
pecorì·no -na adj sheep; sheepish ‖ m sheep-milk cheese ‖ f sheep manure
peculato m embezzlement, peculation
peculiare adj peculiar
peculiari·tà f (-**tà**) peculiarity
pecù·lio m (-**li**) nest egg, savings; (obs) cattle
pecùnia f (lit) money
pecuniâ·rio -ria adj (-**ri** -**rie**) pecuniary
pedàg·gio m (-**gi**) toll
pedagogìa f pedagogy, pedagogics
pedagògi·co -ca adj (-**ci** -**che**) pedagogic(al)
pedagò·go -ga mf (-**ghi** -**ghe**) pedagogue
pedalare intr to pedal
pedale m trunk (of tree); pedal; treadle (e.g., of sewing machine)
pedalièra f pedals, pedal keyboard; (aer) rudder bar
pedalino m (coll) sock, short stocking
pedana f footrest; platform; bedside rug; hem (of skirt); (aut) running board; (sports) springboard
pedante adj pedantic ‖ m pedant
pedanterìa f pedantry
pedanté·sco -sca adj (-**schi** -**sche**) pedantic
pedata f kick; footprint; tread (of step)
pedèstre adj pedestrian
pedia·tra mf (-**tri** -**tre**) pediatrician
pediatrìa f pediatrics
pedicu·re mf (-**re**) pedicure
pedicu·ro -ra mf var of **pedicure**
pedilù·vio m (-**vi**) foot bath
pedina f (checkers) checker, man; (chess) pawn
pedinare tr to shadow, follow about
pedìsse·quo -qua adj servile
pedivèlla f pedal crank
pedóne m pedestrian; (chess) pawn
pedule m stocking foot ‖ fpl climbing shoes, sneakers
pedùncolo m (anat, bot, zool) peduncle
pegamòide f imitation leather
pèggio adj invar worse; **il peggio** the worst, e.g., **il peggio ragazzo** the

worst boy; ‖ m worst; **andare per il peggio** to be getting worse ‖ f worst; **alla peggio** if worst comes to worst; **averne la peggio** to get the worst of it ‖ adv worse; worst; at worst; **peggio + pp** less + pp; least + pp; **tanto peggio** so much the worse
peggioraménto m deterioration, worsening
peggiorare (**peggióro**) tr & intr to worsen
peggió·re (-**ri**) adj worse; worst ‖ m worst
pégli §4
pégno m pledge, pawn
pégola f pitch; (coll) bad luck
péi §4
pél §4
pèla·go m (-**ghi**) (poet) open sea; (coll) mess; **pelago di guai** sea of trouble
pelame m hair, coat
pelandróne m (coll) shirker, do-nothing
pelapata·te m (-**te**) potato peeler
pelare (**pélo**) tr to fleece; to pluck; to pare, peel; to clear (land); (fig) to strip; to scald, burn ‖ ref (coll) to shed; to become bald
pela·to -ta adj peeled; hairless; bald; barren ‖ m (coll) baldy; **pelati** peeled tomatoes ‖ f fleecing, plucking; (joc) baldness, bald spot
pélla §4
pellàc·cia f (-**ce**) tough hide
pellame m skins, hides
pèlle f skin, hide; **a fior di pelle** slightly, superficially; **essere nella pelle di** to be in the boots of; **fare la pelle a** to bump off; **non stare più nella pelle** to be beside oneself with joy; **pelle di dante** buckskin; **pelle d'oca** goose skin, goose flesh; **pelle d'uovo** mull; **pelle pelle** skin-deep, superficial
pélle §4
pellegrinàg·gio m (-**gi**) pilgrimage
pellegrinare intr (lit) to go on a pilgrimage
pellegrì·no -na adj wandering; (lit) foreign; (lit) strange, quixotic ‖ mf pilgrim, traveler
pelleróssa mf (**pellirosse**) redskin
pelletterìa f leather goods; leather goods store
pélli §4
pellicano m pelican
pelliccerìa f furrier's store; furrier's trade, fur industry
pellìc·cia f (-**ce**) fur
pellic·ciàio -ciàia mf (-**ciài** -**ciàie**) furrier
pelliccióne m fur jacket
pellìcola f film; **pellicola in rotolo** roll film; **pellicola piana** film pack; **pellicola sonora** sound film; **pellicola vergine** unexposed film
pellirós·sa mf (-**se**) var of **pellerossa**
pélo m hair (of beard); pile (of carpet); fur; **avere pelo sul cuore** not to be easily moved; **cercare il pelo nell'uovo** to split hairs; **di primo pelo** green, inexperienced; **non avere peli sulla lingua** to not mince one's words; **pelo dell'acqua** water surface; **per un pelo** by a hair's breadth

peloponnesìa·co -ca *adj* (-ci -che) Peloponnesian

peló·so -sa [s] *adj* hairy; self-serving (*e.g., charity*)

péltro *m* pewter

pelùria *f* down, soft hair

péna *f* penalty; concern; compassion; pain, suffering; grief; **a mala pena** barely; **essere in pena per** to worry about; **fare pena** to arouse compassion; **pena infamante** degrading punishment; loss of civil rights; **sotto pena di** under penalty of; **valere la pena** to be worthwhile

penale *adj* penal || *f* penalty

penali·sta *mf* (-sti -ste) criminal lawyer

penali·tà *f* (-tà) penalty

penalizzare [ddzz] *tr* (sports) to penalize

penare (péno) *intr* to suffer; to find it difficult

pencolare (pèncolo) *intr* to totter; to waver

pendà·glio *m* (-gli) pendant; **pendaglio da forca** gallows bird

pendènte *adj* leaning; hanging; pending || *m* pendant

pendènza *f* inclination, pitch; controversy; balance; **in pendenza** pending

pèndere §123 *intr* to hang; to lean; to slope; to pitch

pendìce *f* slope, declivity

pen·dìo *m* (-dìi) slant; slope

pèndola *f* clock

pendolare *adj* pendulum-like; commuting; transient (*tourist*) || *mf* commuter || *v* (pèndolo) *intr* to sway back and forth; to waver; (nav) to cruise back and forth

pèndolo *m* pendulum; clock

pèndu·lo -la *adj* (lit) hanging

penetrante *adj* penetrating, piercing

penetrare (pènetro) *tr* to penetrate, pierce || *intr* to penetrate || *ref*—**penetrarsi di** to be convinced of; to become aware of

penicillina *f* penicillin

peninsulare *adj* peninsular

penìsola *f* peninsula

penitènte *adj & mf* penitent

penitènza *f* penitence; punishment

penitenzià·rio -ria *adj & mf* (-ri -rie) penitentiary

pénna *f* feather; pen; peen (*of hammer*); (mus) plectrum; **penna a sfera** ball-point pen; **penna d'oca** quill; **penna stilografica** fountain pen

pennàc·chio *m* (-chi) panache, plume, tuft; cloud (*of smoke*)

pennaiòlo *m* hack writer

pennarèllo *m* felt-tip pen

pennellare (pennèllo) *intr* to brush; (med) to pencil

pennellata *f* brush stroke

pennèllo *m* brush; (naut) signal flag; (naut) kedge; **pennello per la barba** shaving brush; **stare a pennello** to fit to a T

pennino *m* pen; penpoint, nib

pennóne *m* flagpole; (naut) yard; (mil) pennant

pennu·to -ta *adj* feathered || **pennuti** *mpl* birds

penómbra *f* penumbra; semidarkness; faint light; **vivere in penombra** to live in obscurity

penó·so -sa [s] *adj* painful

pensàbile *adj* thinkable

pensante *adj* thinking

pensare (pènso) *tr* to think; to think of || *intr* to think; to worry; **dar da pensare a** to cause worry to, e.g., **suo figlio gli dà da pensare** his son causes him worry; **pensa ai fatti tuoi** (coll) mind your own business; **pensa alla salute** (coll) don't worry!; **pensare a** to think of; **pensare di** to plan, intend to

pensata *f* bright idea, brainstorm

pensa·tóre -trice *mf* thinker

pensièro *m* thought; **dare pensiero a** to cause worry to; **darsi pensiero per** to worry about; **essere sopra pensiero** to be absorbed in thought

pensieró·so -sa [s] *adj* thoughtful, pensive

pènsile *adj* hanging, overhead

pensilina *f* marquee

pensionaménto *m* retirement

pensionante *mf* boarder, paying guest

pensionare (pensióno) *tr* to pension

pensiona·to -ta *adj* pensioned || *mf* pensioner || *m* boarding school

pensióne *f* pension; boarding house; **in pensione** retired; **tenere a pensione** to board (*a lodger*); **vivere a pensione** to board (*said of a lodger*)

pensó·so -sa [s] *adj* thoughtful, pensive

pentàgono *m* pentagon

pentagram·ma *m* (-mi) (mus) staff, stave

pentàmetro *m* pentameter

Pentecòste, la Pentecost, Whitsunday

pentiménto *m* repentance; correction (*e.g., in a manuscript*); change of heart

pentire (pènto) *ref* to repent; to change one's mind; **pentirsi di** to repent

penti·to -ta *adj* repentant, repenting; **pentito e contrito** in sackcloth and ashes

péntola *f* pot, kettle; potful; **pentola a pressione** pressure cooker

penùlti·mo -ma *adj* next to the last || *f* penult

penùria *f* shortage, scarcity

penzolare (pènzolo) [dz] *intr* to dangle, hang down

penzolóni [dz] *adv* dangling

peònia *f* peony

pepaiòla *f* pepper shaker; pepper mill

pepare (pépo) *tr* to pepper

pepa·to -ta *adj* peppered; peppery

pépe *m* pepper; **pepe della Giamaica** allspice; **pepe di Caienna** red pepper, cayenne pepper

peperóne *m* (bot) pepper

pepita *f* nugget

per *prep* by; through; throughout; for; because of; to, in order to; in favor of; considering; **essere per** to be about to; **per + adj or adv + che + subj** however + *adj or adv* + *ind*, e.g., **per intelligente che sia** however intelligent he is; **per caso** perchance; **per che cosa?** what for?; **per l'appunto** exactly, just; **per lungo** lengthwise; **per me** as for me; **per ora** now; **per parte mia** as for me; **per poco** hardly, scarcely, **per quanto** + *adj* or *adv* + *subj* however + *adj* or *adv* + *pres ind*, e.g., **per quanto disperatamente provi** however desperately he attempts; **per tempo** early; **per traverso** diagonally; **per via che** (coll) because; **stare per** to be about to

péra *f* pear (*fruit*); bulb, light bulb; (joc) head

peraltro *adv* besides, moreover

peranco *adv* yet

perbacco *interj* by Jove!

perbène *adj invar* nice, well brought up

percalle *m* percale

percènto *m* percent; percentage

percentuale *adj* percentage || *f* percent; commission, bonus

percepìbile *adj* collectable

percepire §176 *tr* to perceive; to receive (*a salary*)

percettìbile *adj* perceptible

percetti·vo -va *adj* perceptive

percezióne *f* perception

perché *m* why, reason; **il perché e il percome** the why and the wherefore || *pron rel* for which || *adv* why || *conj* because; so that

perciò *conj* therefore, accordingly

percóme *m & conj* wherefore

percorrènza *f* stretch, distance

percórrere §139 *tr* to cross; to cover, go through

percórso *m* crossing, distance

percòssa *f* hit, blow; contusion

percuòtere §251 *tr* to hit, beat; (fig) to shake || *intr* to strike

percussióne *f* percussion

percussóre *m* firing pin

perdènte *adj* losing || *mf* loser

pèrdere §212 *tr* to lose; to waste; to miss (*e.g., a train*); to ruin; to leak || *intr* to lose; to leak; to be inferior || *ref* to get lost; to waste one's time; **perdersi d'animo** to lose heart; **perdersi in un bicchier d'acqua** to become discouraged for nothing

perdifiato *m*—**a perdifiato** at the top of one's lungs

perdigiór·no *mf* (-**no**) idler

perdinci *interj* good Heavens!

pèrdita *f* loss; leak; **a perdita d'occhio** as far as the eye can see; **perdite** (mil) casualties

perditèm·po *mf* (-**po**) idler || *m* waste of time

perdizióne *f* perdition

perdonàbile *adj* pardonable

perdonare (**perdóno**) *tr* to forgive; to spare; **perdonare a qlcu qlco** or **perdonare qlcu di qlco** to forgive s.o. for s.th || *intr* (with *dat*) to pardon

perdóno *m* forgiveness, pardon

perdurare *intr* (ESSERE & AVERE) to last; to persevere

perdu·to -ta *adj* lost; **andar perduto** to be desperately in love; to get lost

peregrinare *intr* to wander

peregrinazióne *f* wandering

peregri·no -na *adj* far-fetched, outlandish

perènne *adj* everlasting; perennial

perentò·rio -ria *adj* (-**ri** -**rie**) peremptory

perequare (**perèquo**) *tr* to equalize

perequazióne *f* equalization

perfèt·to -ta *adj & m* perfect

perfezionaménto *m* improvement; (educ) specialization

perfezionare (**perfezióno**) *tr* to improve, polish up; to perfect || *ref* to improve; (educ) to specialize

perfezióne *f* perfection; **a** or **alla perfezione** to perfection

perfìdia *f* perfidy

pèrfi·do -da *adj* perfidious, treacherous; (coll) foul, nasty

perfini·re *m* (-**re**) punch line

perfino *adv* even

perforante *adj* piercing, perforating

perforare (**perfóro**) *tr* to pierce; to perforate; to punch; to bore

perfora·tóre -trice *mf* key-punch operator || *m* drill || *f* punch; drill; pneumatic drill, rock drill

perforazióne *f* perforation

pergamèna *f* parchment, vellum

pèrgamo *m* (lit) pulpit

pèrgola *f* bower, pergola

pergolato *m* arbor, pergola; grape arbor

pericolante *adj* tottering, unsafe

perìcolo *m* danger; **non c'è pericolo** don't worry

pericoló·so -sa [*s*] *adj* dangerous

periferìa *f* periphery; suburbs

perifèri·co -ca (*adj* (-**ci** -**che**) peripheral

perìfra·si *f* (-**si**) periphrasis

perìmetro *m* perimeter

periodare *m* writing style || *v* (**perìodo**) *intr* to turn a phrase

periòdi·co -ca (-**ci** -**che**) *adj* periodic(al) || *m* periodical

perìodo *m* period; age; (gram) sentence; (phys) cycle; **il periodo delle feste** holiday time

peripezìa *f* vicissitude

pèriplo *m* circumnavigation

perire §176 *intr* (ESSERE) to perish

periscò·pio *m* (-**pi**) periscope

perìtale *adj* expert

peritare (**pèrito**) *ref* (lit) to hesitate

perì·to -ta *adj* expert, skilled || *mf* expert; **perito agrario** land surveyor; **perito calligrafo** handwriting expert; **perito chimico** chemist; **perito industriale** industrial engineer

peritonèo *m* peritoneum

perìzia *f* skill; survey; appraisal

periziare §287 (**perizio**) *tr* to estimate, appraise

pèrla *f* pearl; (med) capsule

perlàce·o -a *adj* pearly

perla·to -ta *adj* pearly, smooth

perlìfe·ro -ra *adj* pearl-producing

perlina *f* bead

perloméno *adv* at least

perlopiù *adv* mostly, generally

perlustrare *tr* to patrol

perlustrazióne *f* patrol, patrolling

permaló·so -sa [s] *adj* touchy, grouchy
permanènte *adj* permanente ‖ *f* permanent wave
permanènza *f* permanence; stay; continuance (*in office*); duration (*of a disease*); **in permanenza** permanent (*employee*); **buona permanenza!** may your stay be happy!
permanére §235 (*pp* **permaso**) *intr* (ESSERE) to remain, stay
permeàbile *adj* permeable
permeare (**pèrmeo**) *tr* to permeate
permés·so -sa *adj* permitted, allowed; **è permesso?** may I come in? ‖ *m* permit; (mil) pass, leave
perméttere §198 *tr* to permit, allow, let; **permette?** do you mind? ‖ *ref* to take the liberty; to afford
permissìbile *adj* permissible
pèrmuta *f* barter; exchange
permutàbile *adj* tradable, exchangeable
permutare (**pèrmuto**) *tr* to barter; (math) to permute
pernàcchia *f* (vulg) raspberry
pernice *f* partridge
pernició·so -sa [s] *adj* pernicious ‖ *f* pernicious malaria
pèr·nio *m* (-ni) var of **perno**
pèrno *m* pivot; pin; kingbolt; swivel; heart (*of the matter*); kernel (*of the story*); support (*of the family*); (mach) journal; **fare perno** to pivot
pernottare (**pernòtto**) *intr* to spend the night, stay overnight
péro *m* pear tree
però *conj* but, yet; however, nevertheless; **e però** (lit) therefore
peróne *m* fibula
peronòspora *f* downy mildew
perorare (**pèroro**) *tr & intr* to perorate; (law) to plead
perorazióne *f* peroration; (law) pleading
peròssido *m* peroxide; **perossido d'idrogeno** hydrogen peroxide
perpendicolare *adj & f* perpendicular
perpendìcolo *m* plumb line; **a perpendicolo** perpendicularly
perpetrare (**pèrpetro & perpètro**) *tr* (lit) to perpetrate
perpètua *f* priest's housekeeper
perpetuare (**perpètuo**) *tr* to perpetuate
perpè·tuo -tua *adj* perpetual, life ‖ *f* see **perpetua**
perplessi·tà *f* (**-tà**) perplexity
perplès·so -sa *adj* perplexed; (lit) ambiguous
perquisire §176 *tr* to search
perquisizióne *f* search
persecu·tóre -trice *mf* persecutor, oppressor
persecuzióne *f* persecution
perseguire (**perséguo**) *tr* to pursue; to persecute; to pester
perseguitare (**perséguito**) *tr* to persecute; to pursue; to pester
perseveranza *f* perseverance
perseverare (**persèvero**) *intr* to persevere
persia·no -na *adj* Persian ‖ *m* Persian; Persian lamb ‖ *f* slatted shutter; **persiana avvolgibile** Venetian blind

pèrsi·co -ca (-ci -che) *adj* Persian ‖ *m* (ichth) perch; (obs) peach ‖ *f* (coll) peach
persino *adv* var of **perfino**
persistènte *adj* persistent
persistènza *f* persistence
persìstere §114 *intr* to persist
pèr·so -sa *adj* lost, wasted; (archaic) reddish-brown; **a tempo perso** in one's spare time
persóna *f* person; **per persona** apiece; per capita; **persona di servizio** servant; **persone** people
personàg·gio *m* (-gi) personage; character
personale *adj* personal ‖ *m* figure, body; personnel, staff; crew ‖ *f* one-man show
personali·tà *f* (**-tà**) personality; personage
personificare §197 (**personìfico**) *tr* to personify
perspicace *adj* perspicacious; far-sighted
perspicàcia *f* perspicacity
perspì·cuo -cua *adj* perspicuous
persuadére §213 *tr* to persuade ‖ *ref* to become convinced
persuasióne *f* persuasion
persuasì·vo -va *adj* persuasive; pleasing ‖ *f* persuasiveness
persua·so -sa *adj* convinced; resigned
pertanto *conj* therefore; **non pertanto** nevertheless
pèrti·ca *f* (-che) perch; pole
pertinace *adj* pertinacious, persistent
pertinà·cia *f* (-cie) pertinacity, obstinacy
pertinènte *adj* pertinent, relevant
pertinènza *f* pertinence; competence
pertósse *f* whooping cough
pertù·gio *m* (-gi) hole
perturbare *tr* to perturb ‖ *ref* to be perturbed
perturbazióne *f* perturbation; disturbance
Perù, il Peru; **valere un Perù** to be worth a king's ransom
peruvia·no -na *adj & mf* Peruvian
pervàdere §172 *tr* (lit) to pervade
pervenire §282 *intr* (ESSERE) to arrive; to come; **pervenire a** to reach
perversióne *f* perversion
perversi·tà *f* (**-tà**) perversity
pervèr·so -sa *adj* perverse; wicked
pervertiménto *m* perversion
pervertire (**pervèrto**) *tr* to pervert ‖ *ref* to become perverted
perverti·to -ta *adj* perverted ‖ *mf* pervert
pervicace *adj* (lit) obstinate
pervìn·ca *f* (-che) periwinkle
pésa [s] *f* weighing; scale
pesage *m* (pesage) weigh-in; place for weighing in jockeys
pesalètte·re [s] *m* (-re) postal scale
pesante [s] *adj* heavy
pesantézza [s] *f* heaviness; weight
pesare (**péso**) [s] *tr* to weigh ‖ *intr* to weigh; **pesare a qlcu** to weigh upon s.o.
pesa·tóre -trice [s] *mf* scale or weigh-

bridge operator; **pesatore pubblico** inspector for the department of weights and measures

pesatura [s] *f* weighing

pé·sca *f* (**-sche**) fishing; catch (*of fish*) **pesca alla traina** trawling; **pesca d'altura** deep-sea fishing; **pesca di beneficenza** benefit lottery

pè·sca *f* (**-sche**) peach

pescàg·gio *m* (**-gi**) (naut) draft

pescàia *f* dam, weir

pescare §197 (**pésco**) *tr* to fish; to draw (*a card*); to dig up (*a piece of news*); to dive for (*pearls*); **pescare con la lenza** to angle for (*fish*) || *intr* to fish; (naut) to displace; **pescare con la lenza** to angle; **pescare di frodo** to poach; **pescare nel torbido** to fish in troubled waters

pesca·tóre -trice *mf* fisher; **pescatore di canna** angler; **pescatore di frodo** poacher

pésce *m* fish; (typ) omission; (coll) biceps; **a pesce** headlong; **non sapere che pesci pigliare** to not know which way to turn; **pesce d'aprile** April fool; **pesce gatto** catfish; **pesce martello** hammerhead || **Pesci** *mpl* (astr) Pisces

pescecane *m* (**pescecani & pescicani**) shark; (fig) war profiteer

pescheréc·cio -cia (**-ci -ce**) *adj* fishing || *m* fishing boat

pescherìa *f* fish market

peschièra *f* fishpond; fishpound (*net*)

pescivéndo·lo -la *mf* fishmonger, fish dealer || *f* fishwife, fishwoman

pè·sco *m* (**-schi**) peach tree

pesi·sta [s] *m* (**-sti**) (sports) weight lifter

péso -sa [s] *adj* (coll) heavy || *m* weight; burden; bob (*of clock*); (racing) weigh-in; (sports) shot; **di peso** bodily; **peso lordo** gross weight; **peso massimo** (sports) heavyweight; **peso specifico** specific gravity; **rubare sul peso** to give short weight; **usare due pesi e due misure** to have a double standard || *f* see pesa

pessimismo *m* pessimism

pessimi·sta *mf* (**-sti -ste**) pessimist

pessimìsti·co -ca *adj* (**-ci -che**) pessimistic

pèssi·mo -ma *adj* very bad, very poor

pésta *f* track, footprint; **lasciar nelle peste** to leave in the lurch; **seguir le peste di** to follow in the footsteps of

pestàggio *m* beating, clubbing

pestare (**pésto**) *tr* to pound; to trample; to step on; **pestare le orme di** to follow in the footsteps of; **pestare i piedi** to stamp the feet; **pestare sodo** to beat up

pèste *f* plague, pest

pestèllo *m* pestle

pestife·ro -ra *adj* pestiferous

pestilènza *f* pestilence; stench

pestilenziale *adj* pestilential; pernicious

pé·sto -sta *adj* crushed; thick (*darkness*) || *m* Genoese sauce || *f* see pesta

pètalo *m* petal

petardo *m* petard, firecracker

petènte *mf* petitioner

petizióne *f* petition; **petizione di principio** begging the question

péto *m* wind, gas

Petrarca *m* Petrarch

petrarché·sco -sca *adj* (**-schi -sche**) Petrarchan

petrolièra *f* (naut) tanker

petrolière *adj* incendiary || *m* petroleum-industry worker; incendiary; oilman (*producer*)

petrolìfe·ro -ra *adj* oil-yielding

petrò·lio *m* (**-li**) petroleum; coal oil, kerosene

petró·so -sa [s] *adj* (lit) stony

pettegolare (**pettégolo**) *intr* to gossip

pettegolézzo [ddzz] *m* gossip, rumor

pettégo·lo -la *adj* gossipy || *mf* gossip

pettinare (**pèttino**) *tr* to comb; to card; (coll) to scold

pettinatóre *m* carder

pettinatrice *f* hairdresser; carding machine

pettinatura *f* coiffure, hairstyling

pèttine *m* comb; (zool) scallop; **a pettine** perpendicular (*parking*)

pettino *m* dickey; bib (*of an apron*); plastron

pettiròsso *m* robin redbreast

pètto *m* breast, chest; bust; bosom; **a un petto** single-breasted; **avere al petto** to feed at the breast; **a due petti** or **a doppio petto** double-breasted; **stare a petto** to be equal

pettorale *adj* pectoral || *m* pectoral; breast collar (*of horse*)

pettorina *f* var of pettino

pettoru·to -ta *adj* strutting, haughty

petulante *adj* importunate; impertinent

petulanza *f* importunity; impertinence

petùnia *f* petunia

pèzza *f* piece (*of cloth*); diaper; patch (*in suit or tire*); bolt (*of paper or cloth*); **pezza d'appoggio** supporting document, voucher; **trattare come una pezza da piedi** to wipe one's boots on

pezza·to -ta *adj* spotted, dappled

pezzatura *f* dapple (*on a horse*); size (*e.g., of a loaf of bread*)

pezzènte *mf* beggar

pezzétto *m* little bit; scrap, snip

pèzzo *m* piece; cut (*of meat*); coin; (journ) article; **andare** or **cadere a pezzi** to fall apart; **a pezzi e bocconi** by fits and starts; **fare a pezzi** to break to pieces; to blow to bits; **pezzo di ricambio** spare part; **pezzo d'uomo** hunk of a man; **pezzo duro** brick ice cream; **pezzo forte** forte; **pezzo fuso** cast, casting; **un bel pezzo** a good while; **un pezzo grosso** a big shot

pezzuòla *f* small piece of cloth; (coll) handkerchief

phy·lum *m* (**-lum**) phylum

piacènte *adj* attractive, pleasant

piacére *m* pleasure; **a piacere** at will; **a Suo piacere** as you please; **fare piacere a** to do a favor for; to please; **per piacere** please; **piacere!**

pleased to meet you! || §214 *intr* (ESSERE) to please; to be pleasing; (with *dat*) to please, e.g., **come piace a Dio** as it pleases God; to like, e.g., **gli piace il ballo** he likes dancing

piacévole *adj* pleasant, pleasing

piacevolézza *f* pleasantness; off-color joke

pia·ga *f* (-ghe) sore; ulcer; wound; plague; (joc) bore; **piaga di decubito** bedsore

piagare §209 *tr* to make sore, injure

piàg·gia *f* (-ge) (archaic) declivity; (lit) clime, country

piaggiare §290 *tr* (lit) to flatter, blandish || *intr* (archaic) to coast

piagnistèo *m* whining

piagnó·ne -na *mf* (coll) weeper, crybaby

piagnucolare (**piagnùcolo**) *intr* to whimper, whine

piagnucoló·ne -na *mf* whimperer, crybaby

piagnucoló·so -sa [s] *adj* whimpering, whining

pialla *f* (carp) plane

piallàc·cio *m* (-ci) veneer

piallare *tr* (carp) to plane

piallatrice *f* (carp) planer

piallatura *f* (carp) planing

piana *f* plain; wide table

pianale *m* plain; platform; (rr) flatcar, platform car

pianeggiante *adj* plane, level

pianèlla *f* mule (*slipper*); tile

pianeròttolo *m* landing (*of stairs*); ledge

piané·ta *m* (-ti) planet; horoscope || *f* (eccl) chasuble

piàngere §215 *tr* to shed (*tears*); to mourn, lament; **piangere miseria** to cry poverty || *intr* to cry, weep

piangimisè·ria *mf* (-ria) poverty-crying penny pincher

piangiucchiare §287 *intr* to whimper

pianificare §197 (**pianìfico**) *tr* to level; (econ) to plan

pianifica·tóre -trice *mf* planner

pianino *m* (coll) barrel organ

piani·sta *mf* (-sti -ste) pianist

pia·no -na *adj* plane; plain, flat || *m* plain; plane; floor; plateau; plan; map; (mus) piano; **di primo piano** first-class; **in piano** horizontal; **piano di coda** (aer) tail assembly; **piano di studio** curriculum; **piano regolatore** building plan; **piano terra** ground floor; **primo piano** (phot) close-up; (theat) foreground || *f* see **piana** || **piano** *adv* slowly; softly

pianofòrte *m* piano; **pianoforte a coda** grand piano

pianòla *f* player piano

pianòro *m* plateau

pianotèr·ra *m* (-ra) ground floor

pianta *f* plant; sole (*of foot*); plan, map; floor plan; **di sana pianta** wholly; **in pianta stabile** permanent (*employee*); **pianta rampicante** (bot) climber

piantagióne *f* plantation

piantana *f* scaffolding

piantare *tr* to plant; to set up (*e.g., a gun emplacement*); to pitch (*a tent*); **piantala!** (slang) cut it out!; **piantare baracca e burattini** (coll) to clear out; **piantar chiodi** (coll) to go into debt; **piantare gli occhi addosso a** to stare at; **piantare in asso** to leave in the lurch || *ref* to place oneself; to abandon one another

pianta·to -ta *adj* planted; stuck; driven; **bien piantato** well-built (*person*)

pianta·tóre -trice *mf* planter

pianterréno *m* ground floor

piantito *m* (coll) floor

pianto *m* weeping; tears; sadness; (bot) sap; (coll) sight, mess

piantonare (**piantóno**) *tr* to watch, guard

piantóne *m* watchman; (mil) orderly; (mil) sentry; (bot) cutting, shoot; **piantone di guida** (aut) steering wheel column

pianura *f* plain

piastra *f* plate; piaster (*coin*)

piastrèlla *f* tile; small flat stone; bounce (*of an airplane on landing*)

piastrellaménto *m* bump, bounce (*of motorboat or airplane*)

piastrèl·sta *m* (-sti) tiler, tile layer

piastrina *f* or **piastrino** *m* small plate; (mil) dog tag; (biol) platelet

piatire §176 *intr* (lit) to argue; (coll) to beg insistently

piattafórma *f* platform; roadbed (*of highway*); (rr) turntable; (pol) plank; **piattaforma di lancio** launching pad

piattèllo *m* small dish; bobèche; clay pigeon

piattina *f* electric cord; metal band; (min) wagon

piattino *m* saucer

piat·to -ta *adj* flat || *m* dish, plate; pan (*of scale*); pot (*in gambling*); course (*of meal*); cover (*of book*); flat (*e.g., of blade*); **piatti** (mus) cymbals; **piatto del grammofono** turntable; **piatto del giorno** plat du jour; **piatto di lenticchie** (Bib & fig) mess of pottage; **piatto fondo** soup dish; **piatto forte** pièce de résistance

piàttola *f* (zool) crab louse; (coll) cockroach; (vulg) bore

piazza *f* square; plaza; crowd; market; fortress; **andare in piazza** (coll) to become bald; **da piazza** common, ordinary; **di piazza** for hire (*e.g., cab*); **fare la piazza** (com) to canvass for customers; **far piazza pulita di** to get rid of; to clean out; **mettere in piazza** to noise abroad; **piazza d'armi** parade ground; **scendere in piazza** to take to the streets

piazzafòrte *f* (**piazzefòrti**) stronghold, fortress

piazzale *m* large square, esplanade, plaza

piazzaménto *m* placement; (sports) position (*of a team*)

piazzare *tr* to place; to sell || *ref* to place; to show (*said of a racing horse*)

piazza·to -ta *adj* placed; arrived (*at a high position*) || *f* row, brawl

piazzi·sta *m* (**-sti**) salesman; traveling salesman

piazzòla *f* court, place; rest area (*off a highway*); (*mil*) emplacement; **piazzola di partenza** (*golf*) tee

pi·ca *f* (**-che**) (*orn*) magpie

picaré·sco -sca *adj* (**-schi -sche**) picaresque

pic·ca *f* (**-che**) pike; pique; **per picca** out of spite; **picche** (*cards*) spades; **rispondere picche** (*fig*) to answer no

piccante *adj* piquant, racy

piccare §197 *tr* (*obs*) to prick || *ref* to become angry; **piccarsi di** to pride oneself on

pic·chè *f* (**-chè**) piqué

picchettaménto *m* picketing

picchettare (**picchétto**) *tr* to stake out; to picket

picchétto *m* stake; picket; (*mil*) detail

picchiare §287 *tr* to hit, strike || *intr* to knock; to strike; to tap (*said, e.g., of rain*); *intr* to nose-dive; **picchiare in testa** (*aut*) to knock || *ref* to hit one another

picchiata *f* hit, blow; (*aer*) nose dive

picchia·tóre -trice *mf* hitter || *m* (boxing) puncher

picchierellare (**picchierèllo**) *tr & intr* to tap

picchiettare (**picchiétto**) *tr* to tap; to scrape; to speckle || *intr* to tap

picchiet·tìo *m* (**-tìi**) patter (*e.g., of rain*)

pìc·chio *m* (**-chi**) knock; (*orn*) woodpecker; **di picchio** all of a sudden

picchiòtto *m* knocker (*on door*)

piccinerìa *f* pettiness

picci·no -na *adj* little, tiny; petty || *mf* child; baby

picciòlo *m* stem (*e.g., of cherry*); leafstalk, petiole

piccionàia *f* dovecote; loft; attic; (*theat*) upper gallery

piccióne -na *mf* pigeon; **pigliare due piccioni con una fava** to hit two birds with one stone

pic·co *m* (**-chi**) peak; (*naut*) gaff; **andare a picco** to sink; to go to ruin; **a picco** vertically; **picco di carico** (*naut*) derrick

piccolézza *f* smallness; trifle

picco·lo -la *adj* small; low (*speed*); short (*distance*); young; petty; **da piccolo** when young; **in piccolo** on a small scale; **nel mio piccolo** with my modest abilities || *mf* child

piccóne *m* pick

piccòzza *f* mattock (*for mountain climbing*)

pidocchierìa *f* stinginess; meanness

pidòc·chio *m* (**-chi**) louse; **pidocchio rifatto** (*slang*) parvenu

pidocchió·so -sa [*s*] *adj* lousy; stingy

piè *m* (**piè**) (*lit*) foot; **ad ogni piè sospinto** on every occasion; **saltare a piè pari** to skip with the feet together; (*fig*) I see **piena**

piède *m* foot; leg (*of table*); stalk (*of salad*); bottom (*of column*); trunk (*of tree*); footing; **alzarsi in piedi** to stand up; **a piede libero** free; **a piedi**

on foot; **a piedi nudi** barefooted; **con i piedi di piombo** cautiously; **essere in piedi** to be up and around; **fare con i piedi** to botch; **mettere un piede in fallo** to stumble; **piede di porco** crowbar; **prendere piede** to take hold; **puntare i piedi** to balk; **su due piedi** offhand; **tenere il piede in due staffe** to carry water on both shoulders

piedestallo or **piedistallo** *m* pedestal

piedritto *m* buttress

piè·ga *f* (**-ghe**) bend; crease; pleat; crimp; wrinkle; (*fig*) turn; **prendere una cattiva piega** to take a turn for the worse

piegare §209 (**piègo**) *tr* to bend; to wave (*hair*); to fold; to pleat; to bow (*head*) || *intr* to turn || *ref* to bow; to bend; to buckle; to yield

piega·tóre -trice *mf* folder || *f* folding machine

piegatura *f* fold, crease

pieghettare (**pieghétto**) *tr* to pleat

pieghévole *adj* folding; pliant; (*fig*) versatile || *m* folder

pieghevolézza *f* flexibility

piè·go *m* (**-ghi**) folder; bundle of papers

pièna *f* flood; rise (*of river*); crowd; (*fig*) overflow; **in piena** overflowing

pienézza *f* plenitude, fullness

piè·no -na *adj* full; solid; broad (*daylight*); full (*honors*); **a pieno** or **in pieno** to the full; **colpire nel pieno** to hit the bull's eye; **pieno di** alive with; **pieno di sé** conceited; **pieno zeppo** replete, chock-full || *m* fullness; height (*e.g., of winter*); **fare il pieno** (*aut*) to fill up || *f* see **piena**

pie·tà *f* (**-tà**) mercy; pity; (*lit*) piety

pietanza *f* main course

pietó·so -sa [*s*] *adj* pitiful, piteous; merciful

piètra *f* stone; rock; **pietra angolare** cornerstone; **pietra da affilare** whetstone; **pietra da sarto** French chalk; **pietra dello scandalo** source of scandal; **pietra di paragone** touchstone; **pietra focaia** flint; **pietra miliare** milestone; **pietra tombale** tombstone; **posare la prima pietra** to lay the cornerstone

pietrificare §197 (**pietrìfico**) *tr & ref* to petrify

pietrina *f* flint (*for lighter*)

pietri·sco *m* (**-schi**) rubble; (*rr*) ballast

Piètro *m* Peter

pietró·so -sa [*s*] *adj* (*lit*) stony

pievano *m* parish priest

piffero *m* pipe, fife

pìgia *m*—**pigia pigia** crowd, throng

pigia·ma *m* (**-ma & -mi**) pajamas

pigiare §290 *tr* to squeeze, press || *intr* to insist || *ref* to squeeze

pigia·tóre -trice *mf* presser (*of grapes*) || *f* wine press

pigiatura *f* pressing, squeezing

pigionante *mf* tenant

pigióne *f* rent, rental; **dare a pigione** to rent; to grant the possession of; **prendere a pigione** to rent; to hold for payment

pigliamó·sche *m* (-sche) flypaper; flytrap; (orn) flycatcher
pigliare §280 *tr* to take, catch; to mistake; **che Le piglia?** what's the matter with you? || *ref*—**pigliarsela** (con) to get angry (at)
pì·glio *m* (-gli) hold; countenance; **dar di piglio a** to grab
pigménto *m* pigment
pigmè·o -a *adj & mf* pygmy; Pygmy
pigna *f* strainer (*at the end of a suction pipe*); bunch (*of grapes*); (bot) pine cone
pignatta *f* pot
pignò·lo -la *adj* finicky, fussy || *m* pine nut
pignóne *m* pinion; embankment
pignoraménto *m* (law) seizure
pignorare (**pignoro**) *tr* (law) to seize
pigolare (**pigolo**) *intr* to peep (*said, e.g., of young birds*)
pigolì·o *m* (-ì) peep (*e.g., of a young bird*)
pigrizia *f* laziness
pì·gro -gra *adj* lazy; (lit) sluggish
pila *f* pier; buttress (*of bridge*); heap; sink; font; (elec) cell; (elec) battery; **pila atomica** atomic pile
pilastro *m* pier, pillar
pillàcchera *f* mud splash; (fig) fault
pillola *f* pill; (slang) bullet; **addolcire la pillola** to sugar-coat the pill
pilóne *m* pier; pylon
pilò·ta (**-ti -te**) *adj* pilot || *mf* pilot; (aut) driver
pilotàg·gio *m* (-gi) piloting; steering
pilotare (**pilòto**) *tr* to pilot; to drive
pilotina *f* (naut) pilot boat
piluccare §197 *tr* to pluck (*e.g., grapes one by one*); to nibble, pick at; to scrounge; (lit) to consume
piménto *m* allspice
pinacotè·ca *f* (-che) picture gallery
pinéta *f* pine grove
pìngue *adj* fat; rich
pinguèdine *f* fatness, corpulence
pinguino *m* penguin
pinna *f* fin (*of fish*); flipper; (zool) pen shell (*mussel*)
pinnàcolo *m* pinnacle
pino *m* pine tree; **pino marittimo** pinaster; **pino silvestre** Scotch fir
pinòlo *m* pine nut
pinta *f* pint
pinza *f* claw (*of lobster*); **pinza emostatica** hemostat; **pinza tagliafili** wire cutter; **pinze clippers**; pliers; pincers
pinzatrice *f* stapler
pinzétte *fpl* tweezers, pliers
pinzòche·ro -ra *mf* bigot
pì·o -a *adj* (-ì -e) pious; charitable || **Pio** *m* Pius
piòg·gia *f* (-ge) rain
piòlo *m* peg; rung (*of ladder*); picket, stake
piombàggine *f* graphite
piombare (**piómbo**) *tr* to lead; to seal; to knock down; to fill (*a tooth*) || *intr* to fall; to swoop down
piombatura *f* leading; filling (*of tooth*)
piombino *m* weight; seal; plumb; plumb bob

piómbo *m* lead; **a piombo** perpendicularly; **di piombo** suddenly
pioneristi·co -ca *adj* (-ci -che) pioneering
pionière *m* pioneer
piòppo *m* poplar; **pioppo tremolo** aspen
piorrèa *f* pyorrhea
piotare (**piòto**) *tr* to sod
piova·no -na *adj* rain (*water*)
piova·sco *m* (-schi) rain squall
piovènte *m* pitch, slope
piòvere §216 *intr* (ESSERE) to rain; to pour; to flock (*said of people*); **piovere addosso a** to rain down on; **piovere su** to flow down over || *impers* (ESSERE & AVERE)—**piove** it is raining; it is leaking (*from rain*); **piove a catinelle** or **a dirotto** it is raining cats and dogs
piovigginare (**piovìggina**) *impers* (ESSERE & AVERE)—**pioviggina** it is drizzling
piovigginó·so -sa [s] *adj* drizzling, drizzly
piovór·no -na *adj* (lit) var of **piovoso**
piovosi·tà [s] *f* (-tà) raininess; rainfall
piovó·so -sa [s] *adj* rainy
piòvra *f* octopus; (fig) leech
pipa *f* pipe; **non valere una pipa di tabacco** to not be worth a tinker's dam
pipare *intr* to smoke a pipe
pipata *f* pipe, pipeful
pipistrèllo *m* (zool) bat
pipita *f* hangnail; (vet) pip
pira *f* (lit) pyre
piràmide *f* pyramid
pira·ta *adj invar* pirate || *m* (-ti) pirate; **pirata dell'aria** skyjacker; **pirata della strada** hit-and-run driver
pirateggiare §290 (**piratéggio**) *intr* to pirate
pirateria *f* piracy; **pirateria letteraria** piracy of literary works
Pirenèi *mpl* Pyrenees
pìri·co -ca *adj* (-ci -che) fireworks; **polvere pirica** gunpowder
pirite *f* pyrite
piroétta *f* pirouette
pirò·ga *f* (-ghe) pirogue
pirolisi *f* (chem) cracking
piróne *m* (mus) tuning pin
piròscafo *m* steamship; **piroscafo da carico** (naut) freighter; **piroscafo da passeggeri** passenger ship
piroscissióne *f* (chem) cracking
pirotècni·co -ca (-ci -che) *adj* pyrotecnic || *m* pyrotecnist || *f* fireworks, pyrotechnics
pisciare §128 *intr* (vulg) to urinate
piscia·tóio *m* (-tói) (vulg) street urinal
piscina *f* swimming pool
pisèllo [s] *m* pea; **pisello odoroso** sweet pea
pisolare (**pìsolo**) *intr* (coll) to doze
pìsolo *m* (coll) nap; **schiacciare un pisolo** (coll) to take a nap
pisside *f* (eccl) pyx; (bot) pyxidium
pista *f* track; ring (*of circus*); race track, speedway (*for car races*); ski run; (aer) runway; **pista ciclabile** bicycle trail; **pista da ballo** dance

floor; **seguire una pista** to follow a clue

pistàc·chio m (-chi) pistachio
pistillo m (bot) pistil
pistòla f pistol
pistolettata f pistol shot
pistolòtto m lecture, talking-to; theatrical peroration
pistóne m piston; plunger
pitagòri·co -ca adj & m (-ci -che) Pythagorean
pitale m (coll) chamber pot
pitoccare §197 (pitòcco) intr to beg
pitòc·co m (-chi) beggar; miser
pitóne m python
pìttima f plaster; (fig) bore
pit·tóre -trice mf painter
pittoré·sco -sca adj (-schi -sche) picturesque
pittòri·co -ca adj (-ci -che) pictorial
pittura f painting; picture; (coll) paint
pitturare tr to paint; to varnish || ref to put on make-up
più adj invar more; several || m (più) plus; most; **credersi da più** to believe oneself superior; **dal più al meno** about, more or less; **i più** most, the majority; **parlare del più e del meno** (coll) to make small talk || adv more; again; **a più non posso** to the very utmost; **in più** besides; **mai più** never again; **non poterne più** to be exhausted; **per di più** besides; **per lo più** for the most part; **più o meno** more or less; **tanto più** moreover; **tutt'al più** mostly
piuma f feather, plume; **piume** (fig) bed
piumàc·cio m (-ci) feather pillow
piumàg·gio m (-gi) plumage
piumino m down; comforter; puff, powder puff; feather duster
piuttòsto adv rather; somewhat
piva f bagpipe; **tornare con le pive nel sacco** to return bitterly disappointed
pivèllo m greenhorn; whippersnapper
pivière m (orn) plover
pizza f pizza; (mov) canister; (coll) bore
pizzaiò·lo -la mf owner of pizzeria || m pizza baker || f—**alla pizzaiola** prepared with tomato and garlic sauce
pizzardóne m (coll) cop, officer
pizzicàgno·lo -la mf grocer; sausage dealer
pizzicare §197 (pìzzico) tr to pinch; to pluck; to bite, burn; (mus) to pick, twang
pizzicherìa f delicatessen, grocery
pìzzi·co m (-chi) pinch
pizzicóre m itch
pizzicòtto m pinch; **dar pizzicotti a** to pinch
pizzo m peak (of mountain); goatee; lace
placare §197 tr to placate || ref to calm down
plac·ca f (-che) plate; plaque; tag, badge; (elec, rad) plate; (pathol) blotch, spot
placcare §197 tr to plate; (sports) to tackle
plàci·do -da adj placid

plafond m (plafond) ceiling; (aer) ceiling; (com) top credit
pla·ga f (-ghe) (lit) clime, region
plagiare §290 tr to plagiarize
plagià·rio -ria (-ri -rie) adj plagiaristic || mf plagiarist
plà·gio m (-gi) plagiarism
planare intr (aer) to glide
planata f (aer) gliding
plàn·cia f (-ce) (naut) gangplank; (naut) bridge
planetà·rio -ria (-ri -rie) adj planetary || m planetarium; (aut) planetary gear
plantare m arch support
pla·sma m (-smi) plasma
plasmare tr to mold, shape
plàsti·ca f (-che) plastic art; plastics; plastic surgery; plastic
plasticare §197 (plàstico) tr to mold, shape; to cover with plastic
plàsti·co -ca (-ci -che) adj plastic || m relief map; maquette; plastic bomb || f see **plastica**
plastilina f modeling clay
plastron m (plastron) ascot
plàtano m plane tree; **platano americano** buttonwood tree
platèa f audience; (theat) orchestra; (archit) foundation
plateale adj obvious; plebeian
plàtina f (typ) platen
platinare (plàtino) tr to platinize; to bleach (hair)
plàtino m platinum
Platóne m Plato
plaudènte adj enthusiastic
plàudere (plàudo) & **plaudire** (plàudo) intr to applaud; (with dat) to applaud, e.g., **plaudere alla generosità** to applaud the generosity
plausìbile adj plausible
plàuso m (lit) applause, praise
plebàglia f rabble
plèbe f populace; (lit) crowd
plebè·o -a adj & mf plebeian
plebiscito m plebiscite
plenà·rio -ria adj (-ri -rie) plenary
plenilù·nio m (-ni) full moon
plenipotenzià·rio -ria adj & m (-ri -rie) plenipotentiary
plètora f plethora
plèttro m (mus) pick, plectrum
pleurite f (pathol) pleurisy
pli·co m (-chi) sealed document; bundle of papers; **in plico a parte** or **in plico separato** under separate cover
plotóne m platoon; **plotone d'esecuzione** firing squad
plùmbe·o -a adj lead, leaden
plurale adj & m plural; **al plurale** in the plural
plurilìngue adj multilingual
plurimotóre adj multimotored || m multimotor
pluristàdio adj invar (rok) multistage
plusvalènza f unearned increment
plusvalóre m; surplus value (in Marxist economics)
Plutarco m Plutarch
plutocrazìa f plutocracy
Plutóne m Pluto

plutònio *m* plutonium
pluviale *adj* rain ‖ *m* waterspout
pneumàti·co -ca (-ci -che) *adj* pneumatic, air ‖ *m* tire; **pneumatico da neve** snow tire
po' *m* see **poco**
pochézza *f* lack, scarcity
pò·co -ca (-chi -che) *adj* little; short (*distance*); poor (*health*; *memory*); (*with collective nouns*) few, e.g., **poca gente** few people; (*with plural nouns*) a few, e.g., **fra pochi mesi** in a few months; (*with plural nouns having singular meaning in English*) little, e.g., **pochi quattrini** little money ‖ *m invar* little; short distance; short time; **a ogni poco** often; **da poco** a little while ago; of no account; **da un bel po'** quite a while; quite a while ago; **fra poco** in a little while; **manca poco a** it won't be long till; **manca poco che** (*e.g., il ragazzo*) **non +** *subj* (*e.g., the boy*) almost **+** *ind*; **per poco non** almost; **poco di buono** good-for-nothing; **poco fa** a little while ago; **saper di poco** to taste flat; **un poco di** or **un po' di** a little ‖ *f*—**poca di buono** hussy ‖ **poco** *adv* little; **poco bene** poorly; **poco dopo** shortly after; **poco male** not too poorly
podagra *f* gout
podére *m* farm, country property
poderó·so -sa [s] *adj* powerful
pode·stà *m* (-**stà**) (hist) mayor; (hist) podesta
podia·tra *mf* (-**tri** -**tre**) chiropodist
pò·dio *m* (-**di**) podium; platform; (archit) base
podismo *m* foot racing
podi·sta *mf* (-**sti** -**ste**) foot racer
poè·ma *m* (-**mi**) long poem
poesìa *f* poetry; poem
poè·ta *m* (-**ti**) poet
poetéssa *f* poetess
poèti·co -ca (-ci -che) *adj* poetic(al) ‖ *f* poetics
pòg·gia *f* (-**ge**) leeward
poggiare §290 (**pòggio**) *tr* to lean ‖ *intr* to be based; (mil) to move; (naut) to sail before the wind; (archaic) to rise
poggiatè·sta *m* (-**sta**) headrest; (aut) head restrainer
pòg·gio *m* (-**gi**) hillock, knoll
poggiòlo *m* balcony
pòi *m* future ‖ *adv* then; later; **a poi** until later; **poi dopo** later on
poiana *f* buzzard
poiché *conj* since, as; (lit) after
pòker *m* poker (*game*); four of a kind; **poker di re** four kings
polac·co -ca -chi -che) *adj* Polish ‖ *mf* Pole ‖ *f* (mus) polonaise
polare *adj* pole, polar
polarizzare [ddzz] *tr* to polarize
pòl·ca *f* (-**che**) polka
polèmi·co -ca (-ci -che) *adj* polemical ‖ *f* polemics
polemizzare [ddzz] *intr* to engage in polemics
polèna *f* (naut) figurehead
polènta *f* corn mush

polentina *f* poultice
poliambulanza *f* clinic, emergency ward
policlìni·co *m* (-**ci**) polyclinic
polifonìa *f* polyphony
poliga·mo -ma *adj* polygamous ‖ *m* polygamist
poliglòt·ta *adj* & *mf* (-**ti** -**te**) polyglot
poliglòt·to -ta *adj* & *mf* polyglot
poligono *m* polygon; **poligono di tiro** shooting range
polìgrafo *m* author skilled in many subjects; multigraph
polinesìa·no -na *adj* & *mf* Polynesian
polinò·mio *m* (-**mi**) polynomial
pòlio *f* (coll) polio
poliomielite *f* poliomielitis, infantile paralysis
pòlipo *m* (pathol, zool) polyp
polisìlla·bo -ba *adj* polysyllabic ‖ *m* polysyllable
poli·sta *m* (-**sti**) polo player
politea·ma *m* (-**mi**) theater
politècni·co -ca (-ci -che) *adj* polytechnic ‖ *m* polytechnic institute
politei·sta (-sti -ste) *adj* polytheistic ‖ *mf* polytheist
politeisti·co -ca *adj* (-**ci** -**che**) polytheistic
politézza *f* smoothness
polìti·ca *f* (-**che**) politics; policy
politicante *mf* petty politician
polìti·co -ca (-ci -che) *adj* political ‖ *m* politician ‖ *f* see **politica**
polìtti·co *m* (-**ci**) polyptych
polizìa *f* police; **polizia sanitaria** health department; **polizia stradale** highway patrol; **polizia tributaria** income-tax investigation department
polizié·sco -sca *adj* (-**schi** -**sche**) police (*car*); detective (*story*)
poliziòtto *adj* *masc* police (*dog*) ‖ *m* policeman; detective; **poliziotto in borghese** plain-clothes man
pòlizza *f* policy; ticket (*e.g., of pawn-broker*); **polizza di carico** bill of lading
pólla *f* spring (*of water*)
pol·làio *m* (-**lài**) chicken coop
pollaiò·lo -la *mf* chicken dealer
pollame *m* poultry
pollastra *f* pullet; (coll) chick
pollerìa *f* poultry shop
pòllice *m* thumb; big toe; inch
pollicoltura *f* poultry raising
pòlline *m* pollen
pollivéndo·lo -la *mf* poultry dealer
póllo *m* chicken; (fig) sucker; **conoscere i propri polli** (fig) to know one's onions; **pollo d'India** turkey
pollóne *m* (bot) shoot; (fig) offspring
polmóne *m* lung; **a pieni polmoni** at the top of one lungs; **polmone d'acciaio** iron lung
polmonite *f* pneumonia
pòlo *m* pole; polo shirt; (sports) polo
Polònia, la Poland
pólpa *f* meat; pulp; flesh (*of fruit*); (fig) gist; **in polpe** (hist) in knee breeches
polpàc·cio *m* (-**ci**) calf (*of leg*); cut of meat; ball of thumb

polpastrèllo *m* finger tip

polpétta *f* meat ball; meat patty, cutlet

polpettóne *m* meat loaf; (fig) hash

pólpo *m* (zool) octopus

polpó·so -sa [s] *adj* pulpy, fleshy

polpu·to -ta *adj* meaty

polsino *m* cuff

pólso *m* pulse; wrist; cuff, wristband; strong hand, energy; **di polso** energetic

poltìglia *f* mash; slush

poltrire §176 *intr* to idle; to loll in bed

poltróna *f* armchair; (theat) orchestra seat; **poltrona a orecchioni** wing chair; **poltrona a sdraio** chaise longue; **poltrona letto** day bed

poltroncina *f* parquet-circle seat

poltró·ne -na *mf* lazybones, sluggard || *f* see **poltrona**

poltronerìa *f* laziness

poltronìssima *f* (theat) first-row seat

pólvere *f* dust; powder; **in polvere** powdered; **polvere da sparo** gunpowder; **polvere di stelle** stardust; **polvere nera** or **pirica** gunpowder; **polveri** gunpowder

polverièra *f* powder magazine; (fig) tinderbox, trouble spot

polverifì·cio *m* (-ci) powder works

polverina *f* (pharm) powder

polverino *m* pounce, sand

polverizzare [ddzz] *tr* to crush, powder; to atomize; to pulverize

polverizza·to -ta [ddzz] *adj* powdered (*sugar*)

polverizzatóre [ddzz] *m* atomizer

polveróne *m* dust cloud

polveró·so -sa [s] *adj* dusty; powdery (*snow*)

pomata *f* ointment; pomade

pomèlla·to -ta *adj* dapple-grey

pomèllo *m* cheek; cheekbone; pommel, knob

pomeridia·no -na *adj* afternoon, P.M.

pomerìg·gio *m* (-gi) afternoon

pomiciare §128 (pómicio) *tr* to pumice || *intr* (slang) to spoon

pomicióne *m* (slang) spooner

pomidòro *m* var of **pomodoro**

pómo *m* apple; knob; pommel (*of saddle*); **pomo della discordia** apple of discord; **pomo di Adamo** Adam's apple; **pomo di terra** potato

pomodòro *m* tomato; **pomodoro di mare** (zool) sea anemone

pómolo *m* (coll) knob, handle

pómpa *f* pump; pomp; state; **in pompa magna** all dressed up; **pompa aspirante** suction pump; **pompa premente** force pump; see **imprenditore** and **impresa**

pompare (pómpo) *tr* to pump; to pump up

pompèlmo *m* grapefruit

pompière *m* fireman

pompó·so -sa [s] *adj* pompous

pòn·ce *m* (-ci) punch

ponderare (pòndero) *tr* to weigh, ponder; to weigh || *intr* to think it over

pondera·to -ta *adj* considerate, careful

ponderó·so -sa [s] *adj* ponderous

ponènte *m* west; west wind; West; West Wind

pónte *m* bridge; metal scaffolding; (aut) axle; (naut) deck; **fare il ponte** to take the day off between two holidays; **fare ponti d'oro a** to offer a good way out to; **ponte aereo** airlift; **ponte delle segnalazioni** (rr) gantry; **ponte di chiatte** pontoon bridge; **ponte di comando** (naut) bridge; **ponte di volo** flight deck; **ponte levatoio** drawbridge; **ponte radio** radio communication; **ponte sospeso** suspension bridge

pontéfice *m* pontiff; (hist) pontifex

pontéggio *m* scaffolding

ponticèllo *m* small bridge; nosepiece (*of eyeglasses*); (mus) bridge

pontière *m* (mil) engineer

pontificale *adj* pontifical || *m* pontifical mass

pontifì·cio -cia *adj* (-ci -cie) papal

pontile *m* pier

pontóne *m* pontoon, barge

ponzare (pónzo) *tr* (coll) to strain to accomplish || *intr* (coll) to rack one's brains

popeli·ne *f* (-ne) broadcloth

popola·no -na *adj* popular || *mf* commoner

popolare *adj* popular || *v* (pòpolo) *tr* to people, populate || *ref* to be inhabited

popolarità *f* popularity

popola·to -ta *adj* peopled; crowded

popolazióne *f* population

pòpolo *m* people; crowd; **popolo grasso** (hist) rich bourgeoisie; **popolo minuto** (hist) artisans, common people

popoló·so -sa [s] *adj* populous

popóne *m* (coll) melon

póppa *f* breast; (naut) stern; (lit) ship; **a poppa** astern, aft

poppante *adj* & *mf* suckling

poppare (póppo) *tr* to suckle

poppa·tóio *m* (-tói) nursing bottle

poppavìa *f*—**a poppavìa** astern, aft

pòr·ca *f* (-che) ridge (*between furrows*); sow

porcacció·ne -na *m* cad, rake || *f* slut

por·càio *m* (-cài) swineherd; pigsty

porcellana *f* porcelain, china; (bot) purslane

porcellino *m* piggy; **porcellino d'India** guinea pig

porcherìa *f* dirt; (coll) dirty trick; (coll) botch

porchétta *f* roast suckling pig

porcile *m* pigsty

porci·no -na *adj* pig || *m* (bot) boletus

pòr·co -ca *mf* (-ci -che) pig, hog, swine; pork; **porco mondo!** (slang) heck! || *f* see **porca**

porcospino *m* porcupine

pòrfido *m* porphyry

pòrgere §217 *tr* to hand, offer; to relate; **porgere l'orecchio** to lend an ear || *intr* to declaim || *ref* to appear, show up

pornografìa *f* pornography

pòro *m* pore

poró·so -sa [s] *adj* porous

pórpora *f* purple

porpora·to -ta *adj* purple || *m* purple; cardinal

porpori·no -na *adj* purple

pórre §218 *tr* to put; to repose (*trust*); to set (*a limit; one's foot*); to lay (*a stone*); to pose (*a question*); to pay (*attention*); to suppose; to advance (*the candidacy*); **porre gli occhi addosso a** to lay one's eyes on; **porre in dubbio** to cast doubt on; **porre mano a** to set to work at; **porre termine a** to put an end to; **posto che** since, provided || *ref* to place oneself; **porsi in cammino** to set out or forth; **porsi in salvo** to reach safety

pòrro *m* wart; (bot) leek

pòrta *f* door; gate; (cricket) wicket; (sports) goal; **di porta in porta** door-to-door; **fuori porta** outside the city limits; **mettere alla porta** to dismiss, fire; **porta di servizio** delivery entrance; **porta scorrevole** sliding door; **porta stagna** (naut; theat) safety door

portabagà·gli *m* (**-gli**) porter; baggage rack

portabandiè·ra *m* (**-ra**) standard-bearer

portàbile *adj* portable

portàbi·ti *m* (**-ti**) coat hanger

portabottì·glie *m* (**-glie**) bottle rack

portacar·te *adj invar* & *m* (**-te**) folder

portacati·no *adj invar* washstand-supporting || *m* (**-no**) washstand

portacéne·re *m* (**-re**) ashtray

portachia·vi *m* (**-vi**) key ring

portaci·pria *m* (**-pria**) compact

portadi·schi *m* (**-schi**) record cabinet, record rack; turntable

portadól·ci *m* (**-ci**) candy dish

portaère·i *f* (**-i**) aircraft carrier

portaferi·ti *m* (**-ti**) (mil) stretcher bearer

portafinèstra *f* (**portefinèstre**) French window

portafió·ri *m* (**-ri**) flower vase

portafò·gli *m* (**-gli**) or **portafò·glio** *m* (**-gli**) billfold, wallet; pocketbook; portfolio

portafortu·na *m* (**-na**) charm, amulet

portafrut·ta *m* (**-ta**) fruit dish

portafusìbi·li *m* (**-li**) fuse box

portagiò·ie *m* (**-ie**) jewel box

portaimmondì·zie *m* (**-zie**) trash can, garbage can

portainsé·gna *m* (**-gna**) standard-bearer

portalàmpa·da *m* (**-da**) (elec) socket

portale *m* portal

portalètte·re *m* (**-re**) *mf* letter carrier || *m* postman, mailman

portamaz·ze *m* (**-ze**) caddie

portaménto *m* posture; gait; (fig) behavior

portami·na *m* (**-na**) mechanical pencil

portamìssi·li *m* (**-li**) *adj invar* missile-carrying || *m* missile carrier

portamoné·te *m* (**-te**) purse

portamùsi·ca *m* (**-ca**) music stand

portante *adj* carrying; (archit) weight-bearing; (aer) lifting; (rad) carrier || *m* amble

portantina *f* sedan chair; stretcher

portantino *m* bearer (*of sedan chair*); stretcher bearer

portanza *f* (archit) capacity; (aer) lift

portaombrèl·li *m* (**-li**) umbrella stand

portaórdi·ni *m* (**-ni**) (mil) messenger

portapac·chi *m* (**-chi**) parcel delivery man; basket (*on bicycle*)

portapén·ne *m* (**-ne**) penholder

portapiat·ti *m* (**-ti**) dish rack

portaposa·te [s] *m* (**-te**) silverware chest

portapran·zi [dz] *m* (**-zi**) dinner pail

portaraz·zi (**-zi**) [ddzz] *adj invar* missile-carrying || *m* missile carrier

portare (**pòrto**) *tr* to carry; to bring; to take; to carry along; to lead; to herald; to praise; to wear; to drive (*car*); to run (*a candidate*); to adduce; to nurture (*hatred*); (aut) to hold (*e.g., five people*); **portare a conoscenza di** to let know; **portare avanti** to carry forward; **portare in alto** to lift; **portare via** to steal; to take away || *intr* to carry (*said of a gun*) || *ref* to move; to behave; to be (*a candidate*)

portaritrat·ti *m* (**-ti**) picture frame

portasapó·ne *m* (**-ne**) soap dish

portasigarét·te *m* (**-te**) cigarette case

portasìga·ri *m* (**-ri**) cigar case; humidor

portaspil·li *m* (**-li**) pincushion

portata *f* course (*of a meal*); capacity; flow (*of river*); compass (*of voice*); range (*of voice or gun*); importance; (naut) burden; (naut) tonnage; **a portata di mano** within reach; **a portata di voce** within call, within earshot

portatèsse·re *m* (**-re**) card case

portàtile *adj* portable

porta·to -ta *adj* worn; **portato a** leaning toward || *m* result, effect || *f* see **portata**

porta·tóre -trice *mf* bearer

portatovagliòlo *m* napkin ring

portauò·vo *m* (**-vo**) eggcup

portavó·ce *m* (**-ce**) megaphone; (fig) mouthpiece

porte-enfant *m* (**porte-enfant**) baby bunting

portèllo *m* wicket; leaf (*of cabinet door*); (naut) porthole

portènto *m* portent

portica·to -ta *adj* arcaded || *m* arcade

pòrti·co *m* (**-ci**) portico, arcade, colonnade; shed

portiè·re -ra *mf* concierge || *m* janitor, doorman; (sports) goalkeeper || *f* **portiere** (*in church door*); (aut) door

porti·nàio -nàia (**-nài -nàie**) *adj* door, door-keeping || *mf* doorkeeper, concierge

portineria *f* janitor's quarters

pòrto *m* port, harbor; transportation charge; port wine; goal; **condurre a buon porto** to carry to fruition; **franco di porto** prepaid, postpaid; **porto a carico del mittente** postage prepaid; **porto assegnato** charges to be paid by addressee; **porto d'armi** permit to carry arms; **porto franco** free port

Portogallo, il Portugal

portoghése [s] *adj* & *mf* Portuguese;

fare il portoghese (theat) to crash the gate

portóne m portal

portorica·no -na adj & mf Puerto Rican

Portorico m Puerto Rico

portuale adj port, harbor || m dock worker, longshoreman

porzióne f portion

pòsa [s] f laying (e.g., of cornerstone); posing (for portrait); posture, affectation, pose; dregs; (phot) exposure; (lit) rest; **senza posa** relentless; relentlessly

posami·ne (-ne) [s] adj invar minelaying || f minelayer

posare [s] (pòso) tr to lay, put down || intr to lie; to settle; to pose; **posare a** to pose as || ref to settle; to alight; (lit) to rest

posata [s] f cover, place (at table); table utensil (knife, fork or spoon); **posate** knife, fork and spoon

posateria [s] f service (of knives, forks, and spoons)

posa·to -ta [s] adj sedate, quiet; placed || f see **posata**

posa·tóre -trice [s] mf poseur || m layer, installer (of cables or pipes)

pòscia adv then, afterwards; **poscia che** after

poscritto m postscript

posdatare tr var of **postdatare**

posdomani adv (lit) day after tomorrow

positivaménte adv for sure

positi·vo -va adj positive || f (phot) positive, print

posizióne f position; status; (fig) stand

pospórre §218 tr to put off, postpone; to put last; **posporre qlco a qlco** to put or place s.th after s.th

pòssa f (lit) strength, vigor

possanza f (lit) power

possedére §252 tr to possess; to own; to master (a language); **essere posseduto da** to be enthralled with; to be possessed by

possediménto m possession, property

posseditrice f owner, possessor

possènte adj (lit) powerful

possessióne f possession

possessi·vo -va adj possessive

possèsso m possession

possessóre m owner, possessor

possìbile adj possible || m—**fare il possibile** to do one's best

possibili·sta (-sti -ste) adj pragmatically flexible || mf pragmatically flexible person, possibilist

possibili·tà f (-tà) possibility; opportunity; **possibilità** fpl means

possidènte mf proprietor, owner; **possidente terriero** landowner

pòsta f post; mail; post office; box (in stable); ambush; bet; **a giro di posta** by return mail; **a posta** on purpose; **darsi la posta** to set up an appointment; **fare la posta a** to have under surveillance; **fermo in posta** general delivery; **levare la posta** to pick up the mail; **posta aerea** air mail; **posta dei lettori** (journ) letters to the editor; **poste** postal department

pósta f (archaic) planting; (archaic) footprint

postagi·ro m (-ro & -ri) postal transfer of funds

postale adj postal, mail || m mail; mail train (boat, bus, or plane)

postare (pòsto) tr (mil) to post || ref (mil) to take a position

postazióne f (mil) emplacement

postbèlli·co -ca adj (-ci -che) postwar

postbruciatóre m (aer) afterburner

postdatare tr to postdate

posteggiare §290 (postéggio) tr & intr to park

posteggia·tóre -trice mf parking-lot attendant; customer (in a parking lot); (coll) outdoor merchant; **posteggiatore abusivo** parking violator

postég·gio m (-gi) parking lot; stand (in outdoor market); **posteggio di tassì** cabstand

posterióre adj back; subsequent, later

posteri·tà f (-tà) posterity

pòste·ro -ra adj later, subsequent || **posteri** mpl posterity, descendants

postic·cio -cia (-ci -ce) adj artificial; false (e.g., tooth); temporary || m wiglet, ponytail || f row of trees

posticipare (posticìpo) tr to postpone

posticipa·to -ta adj deferred

postièria f postern

postiglióne m postilion

postilla f marginal note

postillare tr to annotate

posti·no -na mf letter carrier || m mailman, postman

pósto m place; room; seat; job, position; spot; (mil) post; **a posto** in order; orderly; **al posto di** instead of; **essere a posto** to have a good job; **mettere a posto** to find a good job for; (coll) to keep quiet; **quel posto** (coll) seat of the pants; (coll) toilet; **posto a sedere** seat; **posto di blocco** road block; (rr) signal tower; **posto di guardia** (mil) guardhouse; **posto di medicazione** or **di pronto soccorso** first-aid station; **posto in piedi** standing room; **posto letto** bed (e.g., in hospital); **posto telefonico pubblico** public telephone, pay station; **rimettere a posto** to fix, repair; **saper stare al proprio posto** to know one's place; **sul posto** on the spot

postrè·mo -ma adj (lit) last

postrìbolo m (lit) brothel

postulante adj petitioning || mf petitioner, applicant; (eccl) postulant

postulare (postùlo) tr to postulate

pòstu·mo -ma adj posthumous || **postumi** mpl sequel; (pathol) sequelae

potàbile adj drinkable

potare (póto) tr to trim, prune

potassa f potash

potàssio m potassium

potatura f pruning, polling

potentato m (lit) potentate

potènte adj powerful; influential || **i potenti** the powers that be

potènza f power, might; (math) power; **all'ennesima potenza** (math) to the nth power; (fig) to the nth degree; **in potenza** potential; potentially

potenziale adj & m potential

potére m ability; authority; power; **in potere di** in the hands of; **potere d'acquisto** purchasing power; **potere esecutivo** executive; **potere giudiziario** judiciary; **quarto potere** fourth estate ‖ §219 intr to be powerful; **non ne posso più** I am at the end of my rope; **si può?** may I come in? ‖ aux (ESSERE & AVERE) to be able; **non posso fare a meno di** + inf I can't help + ger; **non potere fare a meno di** to not be able to do without; **posso,** etc. I can; I may, etc.; **potrei,** etc. I could; I might, etc.

pote·stà f (-stà) power, authority

poveràc·cio -cia mf (-ci -ce) poor guy, poor soul

pòve·ro -ra adj poor; needy, wretched; lean (gasoline mixture); **povero in canna** as poor as a church mouse ‖ mf pauper; beggar; poor devil ‖ **i poveri** the poor

pover·tà f (-tà) poverty; paucity, scantiness

poveruòmo m (used only in sg) poor devil

poziòne f potion, brew

pózza f pool, puddle

pozzànghera f puddle

pozzétto m small well; manhole; forecastle (in small boat)

pózzo m well; shaft; **pozzo artesiano** artesian well; **pozzo delle catene** (naut) chain locker; **pozzo di scienza** fountain of knowledge; **pozzo di ventilazione** (min) air shaft; **pozzo nero** cesspool; **pozzo petrolifero** oil well; **pozzo trivellato** deep well; **un pozzo di** (fig) a barrel of

Praga f Prague

prammàti·co -ca (-ci -che) adj pragmatic ‖ f social custom; **di prammatica** obligatory, de rigueur

pranzare [dz] intr to dine

pranzo [dz] m dinner; **dopo pranzo** afternoon

pras·si f (-si) practice, praxis

prateria f prairie

pràti·ca f (-che) practice; knowledge; matter; file, dossier; business; experience; (naut) pratique; **aver pratica con** to be familiar with (people); **aver pratica di** to be familiar with (things); **far pratica** to be an apprentice; **fare le pratiche** to make an application; **in pratica** practically; **insabbiare una pratica** to pigeonhole a matter

praticàbile adj practicable; passable ‖ m (theat) raised platform

praticante adj practicing ‖ mf apprentice; novice; churchgoer

praticare §197 (pràtico) tr to practice; to frequent; to be familiar with; to make (e.g., a hole); to grant (a discount) ‖ intr to practice; **praticare in** to frequent

pratici·tà f (-tà) utility; practicality

pràti·co -ca (-ci -che) adj practical; experienced ‖ f see pratica

praticó·ne -na mf (pej) old hand

prato m meadow

pratolina f daisy

pra·vo -va adj (lit) wicked

preaccennare (preaccénno) tr to mention in advance

preaccenna·to -ta adj aforementioned

preallarme m early warning

Prealpi fpl foothills of the Alps

preàmbolo m preamble

preannunziare §287 **(preannùnzio)** tr to foretell, forebode

preannùn·zio m (-zi) advance information; foreboding

preautunnale adj pre-fall

preavvertire (preavvèrto) tr to forewarn

preavvisare tr to give advance notice to; to forewarn

preavviso m forewarning; notification of dismissal

prebèlli·co -ca adj (-ci -che) prewar

prebènda f prebend; (fig) easy money, sinecure

precà·rio -ria adj (-ri -rie) precarious

precauzióne f precaution

precedènte adj preceding ‖ m precedent; **precedenti** background; **precedenti penali** previous offenses, record

precedènza f precedence; (aut) right of way; (fig) priority

precèdere §123 tr & intr to precede

precettare (precètto) tr (mil) to call back from furlough

precètto m precept; (eccl) obligation

precettóre m tutor

precipitare (precìpito) tr to precipitate; to hasten; (chem) to precipitate ‖ intr (ESSERE) to fall; to fail; to rush (said of events); (chem) to precipitate ‖ ref to rush

precipitó·so -sa [s] adj hasty, headlong

precipì·zio m (-zi) precipice, cliff; ruin; **a precipizio** headlong

preci·puo -pua adj chief, principal, primary

precisare tr to say exactly, specify, clarify; to fix (a date)

precisazióne f clarification

precisióne f precision

preci·so -sa adj precise, exact; punctilious; identical, same; sharp, e.g., **alle sette precise** at seven o'clock sharp

precla·ro -ra adj (lit) illustrious

preclùdere §105 tr to preclude

precòce adj precocious, premature

preconcèt·to -ta adj preconceived ‖ m preconception; prejudice, bias

preconizzare [ddzz] tr to foretell, forecast; (eccl) to preconize

precórrere §139 tr (lit) to precede ‖ intr (lit) to occur before

precursóre m precursor

prèda f booty, prize; prey

predace adj (lit) preying, predatory

predare (prèdo) tr to pillage; to prey upon

preda·tóre -trice adj predacious, rapacious ‖ mf plunderer

predecessóre m predecessor

predèlla f dais; altar step; platform

predellino m footboard

predestinare (predestino & predèstino) tr to predestine

predét·to -ta adj aforementioned
prediale adj field, rural || f land tax
prèdi·ca f (-che) sermon
predicare §197 (**prèdico**) tr & intr to preach
predicato m predicate; **essere in predicato di** + inf to be rumored to + inf; **essere predicato per** to be considered for
predica·tóre -trice mf preacher
predicazióne f preaching; sermon
predicòzzo m (coll) lecture, scolding
predilèt·to -ta adj & m favorite
predilezióne f predilection
prediligere §149 (pres part missing) tr to prefer; to like best
predire §151 tr to foretell
predispórre §218 tr to predispose, prearrange || ref to prepare oneself
predisposizióne f predisposition
predizióne f prediction
predominare (**predòmino**) tr to overcome || intr to predominate; to prevail
predomì·nio m (-ni) predominance
predóne m marauder; **predone del mare** pirate
preesìstere §114 intr (ESSERE) to preexist
prefabbricare §197 (**prefàbbrico**) tr to prefabricate
prefazióne f preface
preferènza f preference; **a preferenza** rather; **usar preferenze a** to favor
preferìbile adj preferable
preferire §176 tr to prefer
preferi·to -ta adj preferred, favored || mf favorite; pet
prefètto m prefect
prefettura f prefecture
prèfi·ca f (-che) professional mourner, paid mourner; (coll) crybaby
prefiggere §103 tr to set, fix; (gram) to prefix || ref to plan
prefis·so -sa adj appointed; prefixed || m (gram) prefix; (telp) area code
prefissòide m prefixed combining form
pregare §209 (**prègo**) tr to beg, pray; to ask, request; **farsi pregare** to take a lot of asking; **La prego** please; **prego!** please!; beg your pardon!; you are welcome!
pregévole adj valuable
preghièra f entreaty; prayer
pregiare §290 (**prègio**) tr (lit) to praise, esteem || ref to be honored, to have the pleasure
pregia·to -ta adj precious; esteemed; **la Sua pregiata (lettera)** your favor, your kind letter; **pregiatissimo Signore** (com) dear Sir; **pregiato Signore** (com) dear Sir
prè·gio m (-gi) value, worth; esteem; **avere in pregio** to value
pregiudicare §197 (**pregiùdico**) tr to damage, harm, jeopardize
pregiudica·to -ta adj prejudged; prejudiced; compromised; bound to fail || m previous offender
pregiudiziale adj (law) pretrial; (pol) essential || f (law) pretrial
pregiudiziévole adj prejudicial, detrimental

pregiudì·zio m (-zi) prejudice, bias; harm, damage
pregnante adj pregnant
pré·gno -gna adj pregnant; saturated
prè·go m (-ghi) (lit) prayer || interj please!; beg your pardon!; you are welcome!
pregustare tr to foretaste, anticipate with pleasure
preistòri·co -ca adj (-ci -che) prehistoric(al)
prelato m prelate
prelazióne f (law) preemption; (obs) privilege
prelevaménto m (com) withdrawal
prelevare (**prelèvo**) tr to withdraw (money); to capture
preliba·to -ta adj excellent, delicious
prelièvo m withdrawal; (med) specimen
preliminare adj preliminary || **preliminari** mpl preliminary negotiations
prelùdere §105 intr to make an introductory statement; (with dat) to precede, usher in
prelù·dio m (-di) prelude; (of an opera) overture
prematu·ro -ra adj premature
premeditare (**premédito**) tr to premeditate
premeditazióne f premeditation; **con premeditazione** (law) with malice prepense
prèmere §123 tr to press; to push; to squeeze || intr (ESSERE & AVERE) to press; to be urgent; **premere a** to matter to, e.g., **gli preme** it matters to him; **premere su** to press, put pressure on
preméssa f premise; introduction (to a book)
preméttere §198 tr to state at the onset; to place at the beginning
premiare §287 (**prèmio**) tr to award a prize to, reward
premiazióne f awarding of prizes
preminènte adj prominent, preeminent
prè·mio m (-mi) prize; premium; bonus; award
prèmito m straining (to defecate)
premolare adj & m premolar
premonire §176 tr (lit) to foretell
premonizióne f premonition
premorire §201 intr (ESSERE) (with dat) to predecease
premunire §176 tr to fortify || ref—**premunirsi contro** to provide against; **premunirsi di** to provide oneself with
premura f haste; attention, care; **aver premura (di)** to be in a hurry (to); **di premura** hastily; **far premura** (with dat) to urge
premuró·so -sa [s] adj attentive, careful
prèndere §220 tr to take; to catch; to lift; to pick up; to fetch; to get; to receive; **prendere a calci** to kick; **prendere a pugni** to punch; **prendere a servizio** to employ, hire; **prendere commiato** to take leave; **prendere con le buone** to treat with kid gloves; **prendere in castagna** to catch in the act; **prendere il sole** to sun oneself; **prendere la fuga** to take flight;

prendere la mano to run away (*said of a horse*); prendere le mosse to begin (*said, e.g., of a story*); prendere lucciole per lanterne to commit a gross error; prender paura to get scared; prendere per to take for; prendere per il naso to lead by the nose; prendere quota (aer) to gain altitude; prendere sonno to fall asleep; prendere un granchio to make a blunder || *intr* to take root; to set (*said of cement*); to catch (*said of fire*); to turn (*left or right*); prendere a + *inf* to begin to + *inf* || *ref* to grab one another; to get along together; prendersela con to become angry with; to lay the blame on; prendersi a to take hold of

prendi•tóre -trice *mf* receiver; payee (*of a note*); margin buyer || *m* (baseball) catcher

prenóme *m* first name, given name

prenotare (prenòto) *tr* to reserve, book || *ref* to register

prenotazióne *f* reservation, booking

preoccupante *adj* worrisome

preoccupare (preòccupo) *tr* to preoccupy; preoccupare la mente di to win the favor of || *ref* to worry

preoccupazióne *f* preoccupation, worry

preordinare (preòrdino) *tr* to foreordain; to prearrange

preparare *tr* to prepare; to prime; to steep, brew || *ref* to be prepared; to brew (*said, e.g., of a storm*)

peparati•vo -va *adj* preparatory || preparativi *mpl* preparations

prepara•to -ta *adj* prepared; well-equipped || *m* patent medicine; (med) preparation; preparato anatomico dissection, anatomical specimen

preparatò•rio -ria *adj* (-ri -rie) preparatory

preparazióne *f* preparation

preponderante *adj* preponderant, prevailing

preponderanza *f* preponderance

prepórre §218 *tr* to prefix; to place before; to prefer; preporre (qlcu) a to place (*s.o.*) at the head of

preposizióne *f* preposition

prepósto *m* chief; (eccl) provost

prepotènte *adj* arrogant, overbearing; urgent (*desire*) || *m* bully

prepotènza *f* arrogance; outrage; di prepotenza by force

prerogativa *f* prerogative

présa [s] *f* hold, grip; handle; potholder; capture; pinch (*e.g., of salt*); setting (*of cement*); intake; (cards) trick; (elec) jack; (mov) take; a pronta presa quick-setting (*cement*); dar presa a to give rise to; essere alle prese to come to grips; far presa to stick (*said of glue*); to set (*said of cement*); to take root; far presa su to impress; mettere alle prese to pit (*e.g., animals*); presa d'acqua spigot, faucet; presa d'aria outlet (*of air hose*); air shaft; presa di corrente (elec) wall socket, outlet, receptacle; presa di terra (elec) ground; presa

in giro kidding, joke; venire alle prese to come to grips

presà•gio *m* (-gi) forecast; portent

presagire §176 *tr* to forecast; to portend

presalà•rio [s] *m* (-ri) (educ) stipend

prèsbite *adj* far-sighted || *mf* far-sighted person

presbiteria•no -na *adj* & *mf* Presbyterian

prescégliere §244 *tr* to choose, select

prescìndere §247 (*pret* prescindéi & prescissi) *intr*—a prescindere da except for; prescindere da to leave out

prescolàsti•co -ca *adj* (-ci -che) preschool

prescrit•to -ta *adj* prescribed

prescrìvere §250 *tr* to prescribe || *intr* (ESSERE) (law) to prescribe, to lapse

prescrizióne *f* prescription; (law) extinctive prescription

presegnale [s] *m* warning sign

presentàbile *adj* presentable

presentare (presènto) *tr* to present; to introduce; presentare la candidatura di to nominate; presentat'arm! present arms! || *ref* to show up, appear; to come, arise (*said, e.g., of an opportunity*)

presenta•tóre -trice *mf* presenter; (rad, telv) announcer || *m* master of ceremonies

presentazióne *f* presentation; introduction

presènte *adj* present; avere presente to have in mind; fare presente qlco a qlcu to bring s.th to s.o.'s attention; tenere presente to keep in mind || *m* present; bystander, onlooker; al presente at present; di presente immediately || *interj* here!

presentiménto [s] *m* presentiment, foreboding

presentire [s] (presènto) *tr* to have a presentiment of

presènza *f* presence; attendance; di presenza in person; presenza di spirito presence of mind

presenziare §287 (presènzio) *tr* to attend; to witness || *intr*—presenziare a to be present at; to witness

prese•pio *m* (-pi) Nativity, crèche

preservare [s] (presèrvo) *tr* to preserve, protect

preservati•vo -va [s] *adj* & *m* prophylactic

prèside [s] *m* principal (*of secondary school*); preside di facoltà dean

presidènte [s] *m* president; chairman; presidente del Consiglio premier

presidentéssa [s] *f* president; chairwoman

presidènza [s] *f* presidency; chairmanship

presì•dio [s] *m* (-di) garrison; (fig) defense, help; presidi medical aids

presièdere [s] §141 (presièdo) *tr* to preside over || *intr* to preside; presiedere a to preside over

prèssa *f* crowd; haste; (mach) press; far pressa (poet) to urge

pressacar•te [s] *m* (-te) paperweight

pressaforàg•gio *m* (-gio) baler, hay baler

pressante *adj* pressing, urgent

pressappòco *adv* more or less

pressare (**prèsso**) *tr* to press; to urge

pressióne *f* pressure; **far pressione su** to put pressure on; **pressione sanguigna** blood pressure; **sotto pressione** under steam

prèsso *m*—**nei pressi di** in the neighborhood of ‖ *adv* near, nearby; **a un di presso** approximately; **da presso** close; **press'a poco** more or less ‖ *prep* near; about; at; according to; at the house of; at the office of; care of; with, e.g., **godere fama presso to** enjoy popularity with

pressoché *adv* almost, about, nearly

pressurizzare [ddzz] *tr* to pressurize

prestabilire §176 *tr* to preestablish

prestabili·to -ta *adj* appointed

prestanó·me *m* (**-me**) straw man, figurehead

prestante *adj* strong, vigorous; comely

prestanza *f* vigor; (lit) comeliness

prestare (**prèsto**) *tr* to lend; to loan; to give (*ear; help*); to pay (*attention*); to render (*obedience*); to take (*oath*); to keep (*faith*); **prestar man forte** to give aid; **prestar servizio** to work ‖ *ref* to lend oneself; to be suitable; to be willing; to volunteer

presta·tóre -trice *mf* lender; **prestatore d'opera** worker; **prestatori d'opera** labor

prestazióne *f* service; performance

prestigia·tóre -trice *mf* magician, juggler

prestì·gio *m* (**-gi**) prestige; spell, influence; ledgerdemain

prestigió·so -sa [s] *adj* captivating, spellbinding; illusory

prèstito *m* loan; (philol) borrowing; **dare a prestito** to lend; **prendere a prestito** to borrow

prè·sto -sta *adj* (archaic) quick ‖ *m* (mus) presto ‖ **presto** *adv* soon; fast; quick, quickly; early; **al più presto** at the earliest possible time; **ben presto** soon; **far presto** to hurry; **più presto che può** as soon as you can; **presto detto** easy to say

presùmere §116 *tr & intr* to presume

presunti·vo -va *adj* presumptive; budgeted, estimated (*expenditure*)

presun·to -ta *adj* alleged, supposed; estimated (*expenditure*)

presuntuó·so -sa [s] *adj* presumptuous; bumptious

presunzióne *f* presumption; conceit

presuppórre [s] §218 *tr* to presuppose

presuppósto [s] *m* assumption

prète *m* priest; minister; wooden frame (*to hold bed warmer*)

pretendènte *m* suitor; pretender

pretèndere §270 *tr* to demand, claim; **pretenderla a** to pretend to be ‖ *intr*—**pretendere a** to be a suitor for; to claim (*e.g., a throne*)

pretensióne *f* demand; pretention; pretense

pretensió·so -sa [s] or **pretenzió·so -sa** [s] *adj* pretentious

preterintenzionale *adj* (law) unintentional; (law) justifiable

pretèri·to -ta *adj & m* preterit

preté·so -sa [s] *adj* alleged, ostensible; assumed (*name*) ‖ *f* pretense; pretension

pretèsto *m* pretext, excuse; **sotto il pretesto di** under pretense of

pretòni·co -ca *adj* (**-ci -che**) pretonic

pretóre *m* judge, magistrate (*of lower court*)

prèt·to -ta *adj* pure, genuine

pretura *f* lower court

prevalènte *adj* prevalent, prevailing

prevalènza *f* prevalence; **essere in prevalenza** to be in the majority; **in prevalenza** for the most part

prevalére §278 *intr* (ESSERE & AVERE) to prevail ‖ *ref* to take advantage

prevaricare §197 (**prevàrico**) *intr* to transgress; to graft

prevarica·tóre -trice *mf* grafter

prevedére §279 *tr* to foresee; to provide for (*said of a statute*)

prevedìbile *adj* foreseeable

prevenire §282 *tr* to precede; to anticipate; to forewarn; to prejudice

preventi·vo -va *adj* preventive; prior, estimated (*budget*) ‖ *m* estimate

prevenu·to -ta *adj* forewarned; biased, prejudiced ‖ *m* defendant

prevenzióne *f* prevention; prejudice, bias

previdènte *adj* provident, prudent

previdènza *f* providence; foresight; **previdenza sociale** social security

previdenziale *adj* social (*e.g., responsibility*); social-security (*e.g., contribution*)

prè·vio -via *adj* (**-vi -vie**) with previous, e.g., **previo accordo** with previous agreement

previsióne *f* foresightedness; **in previsione di** anticipating; **previsioni del tempo** weather forecast

previ·sto -sta *adj* foreseen, expected ‖ *m* expected time; estimated amount

prezió·so -sa [s] *adj* precious, valuable; affected; **fare il prezioso** (coll) to play hard to get ‖ **preziosi** *mpl* valuables, jewels

prezzare (**prèzzo**) *tr* to care about; to price

prezzèmolo *m* parsley

prèzzo *m* price; cost; **mettere a prezzo** (fig) to sell; **prezzo di favore** special price; **prezzo d'ingresso** admission; **tenere in gran prezzo** to value highly, to esteem highly; **ultimo prezzo** rock-bottom price

prezzolare (**prèzzolo**) *tr* to hire (*e.g., a gunman*); to bribe

prigióne *f* prison, jail; (naut) brig

prigionìa *f* imprisonment; bondage

prigioniè·ro -ra *adj* imprisoned ‖ *mf* prisoner ‖ *m* stud bolt

prillare *intr* to spin, whirl

prima *f* first grade (*in school*); (rr) first class; (theat) first night; (aut) first (gear); **alla prima** or **sulle prime** at the outset ‖ *adv* before; first; prior; ahead; **di prima** previous; **prima che** before; **prima di** ahead of; before;

prima o poi sooner or later; **quanto prima** as soon as possible

primàrio -ria (-ri -rie) *adj* primary || *m* (elec) primary; (med) chief of staff

primati·sta *mf* (**-sti -ste**) (sports) record holder

primato *m* primacy; (sports) record

primavèra *f* spring; springtime; (bot) primrose

primaverile *adj* spring; spring-like

primeggiare §290 (**priméggio**) *intr* to excel

primiè·ro -ra *adj* (lit) prior; (lit) pristine || *f* (cards) meld

primiti·vo -va *adj & m* primitive

primìzia *f* first fruits; scoop, beat

pri·mo -ma *adj* first; early (*dawn*); prime (*cost*); raw (*material*); **sulle prime** at first || *m* first; minute; **primo arrivato** first comer || *f* see **prima**

primogèni·to -ta *adj* first-born; (fig) beloved || *mf* first-born child

primòrdi *mpl* beginning, origin

primordiale *adj* primordial, primeval

prìmula *f* primrose || **Prìmula** *f*—**la Prìmula Rossa** the Scarlet Pimpernel

principale *adj* principal, main || *m* (coll) boss, chief

principalménte *adv* chiefly, mainly

principato *m* principality

prìncipe *adj* princeps || *m* prince; **il principe di Galles** the Prince of Wales; **principe ereditario** crown prince

principé·sco -sca *adj* (**-schi -sche**) princely

principéssa *f* princess

principiante *adj* beginning || *mf* beginner

principiare §287 *tr & intr* (ESSERE & AVERE) to begin; **a principiare da** beginning with

princì·pio *m* (**-pi**) beginning; principle; **in principio** at the beginning, at first

princisbécco *m* pinchbeck; **restare o rimanere di princisbecco** to be dumfounded

prióre *m* prior

priori·tà *f* (**-tà**) priority

priorità·rio -ria *adj* (**-ri -rie**) priority, e.g., **progetto prioritario** priority project

pri·sma *m* (**-smi**) prism

privare *tr* to deprive; to remove

privativa *f* government monopoly; salt and tobacco store; patent

priva·to -ta *adj* private || *m* private individual

privazióne *f* privation, loss

privilegiare §290 (**privilègio**) *tr* to privilege; (fig) to endow

privilegia·to -ta *adj* privileged; preferred (*stock*) || *m* privileged person

privilè·gio *m* (**-gi**) privilege

pri·vo -va *adj* deprived; **privo di** lacking

prò *m* (**pro**) profit, advantage; **a che pro?** what's the use?; **buon pro!** good appetite!; **far pro** to be good for the health; **il pro e il contro** the pros and the cons || *prep* pro, in favor of

probàbile *adj* probable

probabili·tà *f* (**-tà**) probability; chance; odds

probante *adj* proving; evidential

probatò·rio -ria *adj* (**-ri -rie**) probative, evidential

problè·ma *m* (**-mi**) problem

prò·bo -ba *adj* (lit) honest

procàc·cia *mf* (**-cia**) messenger; mail carrier

procacciare §128 *tr* to get, procure || *ref* to eke out (*a living*); to get into (*trouble*)

procace *adj* buxom, sexy; saucy, petulant

procèdere §123 (**procèdo**) *intr* to proceed, take action || *intr* (ESSERE) to proceed, go ahead

procediménto *m* procedure; behavior

procedura *f* procedure

procèlla *f* (lit) storm, tempest

procellària *f* (orn) petrel

processare (**procèsso**) *tr* to try, prosecute

processióne *f* procession

procèsso *m* process; trial; **processo verbale** minutes

processuale *adj* trial

procinto *m*—**in procinto di** on the point of

procióne *m* raccoon

procla·ma *m* (**-mi**) proclamation

proclamare *tr* to proclaim

proclamazióne *f* proclamation

proclìti·co -ca *adj & f* (**-ci -che**) proclitic

proclive *adj* inclined, disposed

proclivi·tà *f* (**-tà**) proclivity

procrastinare (**procràstino**) *tr* to procrastinate, put off || *intr* to procrastinate

procreare (**procrèo**) *tr* to procreate

procura *f* agency; power of attorney; **Procura della Repubblica** attorney general's office; district attorney's office

procurare *tr* to procure, to get; to cause; **procurare che** to see to it that; **procurare di** to try to || *ref* to get, acquire

procura·tóre -trice *mf* proxy; agent; attorney-at-law; (sports) manager; **Procuratore della Repubblica** district attorney

pròda *f* shore, bank; (archaic) prow

pròde *adj* brave || *m* brave person, hero

prodézza *f* prowess; accomplishment

prodiè·ro -ra *adj* prow, e.g., **cannone prodiero** prow gun; preceding (*in a row of ships*)

prodigare §209 (**pròdigo**) *tr* to squander, lavish || *ref* to do one's best

prodì·gio *m* (**-gi**) prodigy; wonder

prodigió·so -sa [s] *adj* prodigious; wonderful

pròdi·go -ga *adj* (**-ghi -ghe**) lavish, prodigal; **prodigo di** profuse in

proditò·rio -ria *adj* (**-ri -rie**) traitorous

prodótto *m* product; result; **prodotti in scatola** canned goods; **prodotti** (ortofrutticoli) produce

produrre §102 *tr* to produce; to turn out; to yield; to breed; to cause; (lit) to prolong; (law) to exhibit || *ref* (theat) to perform, appear

produtti·vo -va *adj* productive

produttivísti·co -ca *adj* (**-ci -che**) productivity, e.g., **fine produttivistico** productivity policy

produt·tóre -trice *adj* producing || *mf* producer; agent; manufacturer's representative || *m* salesman || *f* saleswoman

produzióne *f* production; output; **produzione in massa** or **in serie** mass production

proè·mio *m* (**-mi**) preamble, proem

profanare *tr* to profane, desecrate

profanazióne *f* profanation, desecration

profa·no -na *adj* profane; lay, uninformed || *m* layman; **il profano** the profane

proferire §176 *tr* (lit) to utter; (lit) to proffer

professare (profèsso) *tr* to profess; to practice (*e.g., law*) || *intr* to practice || *ref* to profess oneself to be

professionale *adj* professional; occupational (*disease*); trade (*school*)

professióne *f* profession; **fare il ladro di professione** to be a confirmed thief; **fare qlco di professione** to pursue the trade of s.th, e.g., **fa il falegname di professione** he pursues the trade of carpenter

professioni·sta *mf* (**-sti -ste**) professional

professorale *adj* professorial; pedantic

profes·sóre -soréssa *mf* professor; teacher; **professore d'orchestra** orchestra member

profè·ta *m* (**-ti**) prophet

profetéssa *f* prophetess

profèti·co -ca *adj* (**-ci -che**) prophetic

profetizzare [ddzz] *tr* to prophesy

profezía *f* prophecy

profferire §176 (*pp* **profferto**) *pret* **profferii** & **proffèrsi**) *tr* to offer; (lit) to utter

profí·cuo -cua *adj* profitable

profilare *tr* to outline; to sketch; to hem; (mach) to shape || *ref* to be outlined; to loom

profilas·si *f* (**-si**) prophylaxis

profila·to -ta *adj* outlined; hemmed; (mach) shaped || *m* structural piece

profilàtti·co -ca *adj* (**-ci -che**) prophylactic

profilatura *f* hemming; (mach) shaping

profilo *m* profile; sketch; outline

profittare *intr* to profit, benefit

profitta·tóre -trice *mf* profiteer

profittévole *adj* (lit) profitable

profitto *m* profit; progress; **profitti e perdite** profit and loss

proflù·vio *m* (**-vi**) overflow; (pathol) discharge

profondare (profóndo) *tr* & *intr* to sink

profóndere §178 *tr* to squander, lavish || *ref* to be profuse

profondi·tà *f* (**-tà**) depth

profón·do -da *adj* deep; profound; searching (*e.g., investigation*) || *m* bottom; depth; subconscious

pro fórma *adj invar* pro forma; perfunctory || *m* (coll) formality

pròfu·go -ga (**-ghi -ghe**) *adj* fugitive || *mf* refugee

profumare *tr* to perfume || *intr* to smell

profumataménte *adv* lavishly

profuma·to -ta *adj* perfumed, fragrant

profumería *f* perfumery; perfume shop

profumo *m* perfume; bouquet (*of wine*)

profusióne *f* profusion; **a profusione** in profusion

profu·so -sa *adj* profuse

progè·nie *f* (**-nie**) progeny, offspring; (pej) breed

progeni·tóre -trice *mf* ancestor

progettare (progètto) *tr* to plan; to design

progetti·sta *mf* (**-sti -ste**) planner; designer; wild dreamer

progètto *m* project; plan; draft (*of law*); **far progetti** to plan; **progetto di scala reale** (cards) possible straight flush

prògno·si *f* (**-si**) prognosis

program·ma *m* (**-mi**) program; plan; curriculum; cycle (*of washing machine*); (mov) feature; (theat) playbill; **programma politico** platform

programmare *tr* to program; to plan

programma·tóre -trice *mf* programmer

programmazióne *f* programming

progredire §176 *intr* (ESSERE & AVERE) to progress, advance

progredi·to -ta *adj* advanced

progressióne *f* progression

progressi·sta *adj* & *mf* (**-sti -ste**) progressive

progressi·vo -va *adj* progressive

progrèsso *m* progress; progression, advance; **fare progressi** to progress

proibire §176 *tr* to prohibit; to prevent

proibi·to -ta *adj* forbidden; **è proibito entrare** no admission; **è proibito fumare** no smoking

proibizióne *f* prohibition

proibizionismo *m* prohibition

proiettare (proiètto) *tr* to project; to cast (*a shadow*) || *intr* to project || *ref* to be projected, project

proièttile *m* projectile, missile

proiettóre *m* projector, projection machine; searchlight; (aut) headlight; **proiettore acustico** sonar projector

proiezióne *f* projection; **proiezione rallentata** slow motion

pròle *f invar* offspring, progeny

proletariato *m* proletariat

proletà·rio -ria *adj* & *mf* (**-ri -rie**) proletarian

proliferare (prolífero) *intr* to proliferate

prolificare §197 (**prolífico**) *intr* to proliferate

prolífi·co -ca *adj* (**-ci -che**) prolific

prolis·so -sa *adj* prolix, long-winded; long (*e.g., beard*)

prò·logo *m* (**-ghi**) prologue; preface

prolun·ga *f* (**-ghe**) extension

prolungaménto *m* prolongation, extension

prolungare §209 *tr* to prolong, extend || *ref* to extend; to speak at great length

prolunga·to -ta *adj* extended, protracted

prolusióne *f* inaugural lecture

promemò·ria or **pro memò·ria** m (-ria) reminder

promés·so -sa adj promised ‖ mf betrothed ‖ f promise; promising individual

promettènte adj promising

prométtere §198 tr to promise; to threaten (e.g., a storm) ‖ intr to promise; **promettere bene** to be very promising ‖ ref—**promettersi a Dio** to make a vow to God; **promettersi in matrimonio** to become engaged

prominènte adj prominent

promì·scuo -scua adj promiscuous; coeducational; mixed (marriage; races); (gram) epicene

promontò·rio m (-ri) promontory, cliff

promo·tóre -trice adj promoting ‖ mf promoter

promozióne f promotion

promulgare §209 tr to promulgate

promuòvere §202 tr to promote; to pass (a student); to initiate (legal suit); to induce (e.g., perspiration)

pronipóte mf great-grandchild ‖ m great-grandson; grandnephew; **pronipoti** descendants ‖ f great-granddaughter; grandniece

prò·no -na adj (lit) prone

pronóme m pronoun

pronominale adj (gram) pronominal; (gram) reflexive (verb)

pronosticare §197 (pronòstico) tr to prognosticate, forecast

pronòsti·co m (-ci) prognostication, forecast; sign, omen

prontézza f readiness; quickness, promptness

prón·to -ta adj ready; first (aid); quick; prompt; ready (cash) ‖ **pronto** interj (telp) hello!

prontuà·rio m (-ri) handbook

pronùn·cia f (-cie) or **pronunzia** f pronunciaton; (law) judgment

pronunziare §287 tr to pronounce; to utter; to pass (sentence); to make (a speech) ‖ ref to pass judgment

pronunzia·to -ta adj pronounced, marked; prominent (nose, chin, beard) ‖ m (law) sentence

propaganda f propaganda; advertisement; advertising

propagandi·sta mf (-sti -ste) propagandist; advertiser; agent; detail man

propagandìsti·co -ca adj (-ci -che) advertising

propagare §209 tr to propagate; to spread ‖ ref to spread

propàggine f offspring; (geog) spur, counterfort; (hort) layer

propalare tr (lit) to spread, divulge

propellènte adj & m propellent

propèllere §168 tr to propel

propèndere §123 (pp propènso) intr to incline, tend

propensióne f propensity, inclination

propèn·so -sa adj inclined, bent

propinare tr to administer (e.g., poison); **propinare qlco a qlcu** to put s.th over on s.o.

propìn·quo -qua adj (lit) near; (lit) related

propiziare §287 tr to propitiate, appease

propì·zio -zia adj (-zi -zie) propitious, favorable

proponiménto m intention, plan

propórre §218 tr to propose, present; to propound; **proporre come candidato** to nominate ‖ ref—**proporsi di** to propose to, resolve to

proporzionare (proporzióno) tr to proportion, prorate

proporzióne f proportion

propòsito m purpose; **a proposito** opportune; opportunely; proper; by the way; **a proposito di** on the subject of; **di proposito** deliberately; **fuor di proposito** out of place; **parlare a proposito** to speak to the point

proposizióne f proposition; (gram) clause; **proposizione subordinata** dependent clause

propósta f proposal; **proposta di legge** bill

propriaménte adv exactly; properly

proprie·tà f (-tà) propriety; ownership; property; **la proprietà** property owners; **proprietà immobiliare** real estate; **proprietà letteraria** copyright; **sulla proprietà** on the premises

proprietà·rio -ria mf (-ri -rie) owner, proprietor

prò·prio -pria (-pri -prie) adj peculiar, characteristic; proper (e.g., name); own, e.g., **il mio proprio libro** my own book ‖ m one's own; **i propri** one's folks; **lavorare in proprio** to work for oneself ‖ **proprio** adv just, really, exactly; **non . . . proprio** not . . . at all; **proprio adesso** just, just now

propugnare tr to advocate; (lit) to fight for

propugna·tóre -trice mf (lit) advocate

propulsare tr to propel; (lit) to repulse

propulsióne f propulsion

propulsóre m propeller, motor

pròra f prow, bow

proravia f—**a proravia** (naut) fore

pròro·ga f (-ghe) delay, extension

prorogare §209 (pròrogo) tr to extend; to put off, delay

prorómpere §240 intr to overflow; to burst (into tears)

prosa f prose

prosài·co -ca adj (-ci -che) prose; prosaic

prosàpia f (lit) ancestry

prosa·tóre -trice mf prose writer

proscè·nio m (-ni) forestage

prosciògliere §127 tr to free; to exonerate

prosciugare §209 tr to drain, reclaim ‖ ref to dry up

prosciutto m ham; **prosciutto cotto** boiled ham; **prosciutto crudo** prosciutto

proscrìvere §250 tr to proscribe, outlaw

prosecuzióne [s] f prosecution, pursuit

proseguiménto [s] m prosecution, pursuit

proseguire [s] (proséguo) tr to follow, pursue ‖ intr (ESSERE & AVERE) to continue

prosèlito *m* proselyte
prosodia *f* prosody
prosopopèa *f* conceit
prosperare (**pròspero**) *intr* to prosper, thrive
prosperi·tà *f* (**-tà**) prosperity || *interj* gesundheit!
pròspe·ro -ra *adj* prosperous, thriving; flourishing; successful || *m* (coll) match
prosperó·so -sa [s] *adj* flourishing; healthy; buxom
prospettare (**prospètto**) *tr* to face, overlook; to outline || *intr*—**prospettare su** to face || *ref* to look; to appear; to loom up
prospetti·vo -va *adj* prospective || *f* perspective; prospect; view
prospètto *m* prospect, view; front (*of building*); diagram; outline; prospectus
prospettóre *m* prospector
prospiciènte *adj* facing
prossimaménte *adv* shortly
prossimi·tà *f* **-tà** proximity, nearness; **in prossimità di** near
pròssi·mo -ma *adj* near, close; next; immediate (*cause*) || *m* neighbor, fellow man
pròstata *f* prostate
prosternare (**prostèrno**) *ref* to prostrate oneself
prostituire §176 *tr* to prostitute
prostituta *f* prostitute
prostituzióne *f* prostitution
prostrare (**pròstro**) *ref* to prostrate oneself
prostrazióne *f* prostration
protagoni·sta *mf* (**-sti -ste**) protagonist
protèggere §193 *tr* to protect; to help, defend; to favor, promote
proteina *f* protein
protèndere §270 *tr & ref* to stretch
pròte·si *f* (**-si**) (philol) prothesis; (surg) prosthesis
protèsta *f* protest, protestation
protestante *adj & mf* protestant; Protestant
protestare (**protèsto**) *tr* to protest; to reject (*faulty merchandise*) || *intr & ref* to protest
protestatà·rio -ria (**-ri -rie**) *adj* protesting || *m* protester
protèsto *m* (com) protest
protèt·to -ta *adj* protected || *m* protegé || *f* protegée
protettorato *m* protectorate
protet·tóre -trice *adj* patron || *mf* protector, guardian || *m* patron || *f* patroness
protezióne *f* protection; patronage
pròto *m* (typ) foreman
protocòllo *adj invar* commercial (*size*) || *m* protocol; **mettere a protocollo** to register, record
protopla·sma *m* (**-smi**) protoplasm
protòtipo *m* prototype; (fig) epitome
protozòi [dz] *mpl* protozoa
protrarre §273 *tr* to protract, extend || *ref* to continue
protrùdere §190 *intr* to protrude (said, *e.g., of a broken bone*)

protuberante *adj* protruding, bulging
pròva *f* test, examination; proof; try, attempt; probationary period (*of employment*); trial; token (*e.g., of friendship*); (sports) competition, event; (theat) rehearsal; **a prova di bomba** bombproof; foolproof; **a tutta prova** thoroughly tested; **in prova** on approval; **mettere a dura prova** to test (*e.g., one's patience*); **mettere alla prova** to test (*e.g., one's ability*); **mettere in prova** to fit (*a suit*); **prova del fuoco** trial by fire; **prova dell'acido** acid test; **prova generale** dress rehearsal; **prova indiziaria** circumstantial evidence
provare (**pròvo**) *tr* to test; to try; to try on; to try out; to taste; to prove; to feel (*e.g., anger*); (theat) to rehearse || *intr* to try || *ref* to compete
proveniènza *f* origin
provenire §282 *intr* (ESSERE) to stem, originate
provènto *m* income, proceeds
provenzale *adj & mf* Provençal
p_ver·bio *m* (**-bi**) proverb; byword
provétta *f* test tube
provèt·to -ta *adj* (lit) masterful
provìn·cia *f* (**-ce**) province; **in provincia** outside of the big cities
provinciale *adj* provincial || *mf* smalltown person || *f* provincial highway, state highway
provino *m* gauge; (mov) screen test
provocare §197 (**pròvoco**) *tr* to provoke; to bring about, cause; to arouse; to entice
provoca·tóre -trice *adj* provoking || *mf* provoker
provocatò·rio -ria *adj* (**-ri -rie**) provoking, provocative
provocazióne *f* provocation; challenge
provvedére §221 *tr* to prepare; to supply; **provvedere che** to see to it that || *intr* to take the necessary steps; **provvedere a** to provide for; **provvedere a** + *inf* to provide for + *ger*; **provvedere nei confronti di** to take steps against
provvediménto *m* measure, step
provvedi·tóre -trice *mf* provider || *m* superintendent; **provveditore agli studi** superintendent of schools
provvedu·to -ta *adj* supplied; careful
provvidènza *f* providence; windfall; **provvidenze** provisions, help
provvidenziale *adj* providential
provvidènza *f* (com) commission
pròvvi·do -da *adj* (lit) provident
provvigióne *f* (com) commission
provvisò·rio -ria *adj* (**-ri -rie**) provisional, temporary
provvi·sto -sta *adj* supplied || *f* supply, provision; **fare le provviste** to shop
prozia *f* grandaunt
prozi·o *m* (**-i**) granduncle
prua *f* bow, prow
prudènte *adj* prudent, cautious
prudènza *f* prudence, discretion
prùdere §222 *intr* to itch; **sentirsi prudere le mani** to feel like giving s.o. a beating
prugna *f* plum; **prugna secca** prune

prugno *m* plum tree
prùgnola *f* sloe
prùgnolo *m* sloe, blackthorn
pruno *m* thorn
prurito *m* itch
pseudònimo *m* pseudonym; alias; pen name
psicanàlisi *f* psychoanalysis
psicanali·sta *mf* (-sti -ste) psychoanalyst
psicanalizzare [ddzz] *tr* to psychoanalyze
psiche *f* psyche; cheval glass
psichia·tra *mf* (-tri -tre) psychiatrist
psichiatria *f* psychiatry
psìchi·co -ca *adj* (-ci -che) psychic
psicologìa *f* psychology
psicològi·co -ca *adj* (-ci -che) psychological
psicòlo·go -ga *mf* (-gi -ghe) psychologist
psicopàti·co -ca (-ci -che) *adj* psychopathic || *mf* psychopath
psicò·si *f* (-si) psychosis
psicosomàti·co -ca *adj* (-ci -che) psychosomatic
psicotècni·co -ca (-ci -che) *adj* psychotechnical || *m* industrial psychologist || *f* industrial psychology
psicòti·co -ca *adj* (-ci -che) psychotic
pubblicare §197 (pùbblico) *tr* to publish
pubblicazióne *f* publication; **pubblicazioni di matrimonio** marriage banns
pubblicismo *m* communications; advertising
pubblici·sta *mf* (-sti -ste) free-lance newspaper writer; publicist
pubblicìsti·co -ca (-ci -che) *adj* advertising; political-science || *f* newspaper business
pubblicità *f* publicity; advertising
pubblicità·rio -ria (-ri -rie) *adj* advertising || *m* advertising agent
publicizzare [ddzz] *tr* to publicize
publicizzazióne [ddzz] *f* publicizing
pùbbli·co -ca *adj* & *m* (-ci -che) public; **mettere in pubblico** to publish
pubertà *f* puberty
pudibón·do -da *adj* (lit) modest, bashful; (lit) prudish
pudicizia *f* modesty; prudery
pudi·co -ca *adj* (-chi -che) modest, chaste; bashful; (lit) reserved
pudóre *m* modesty; decency; shame
puericoltóre *m* pediatrician
puerile *adj* puerile, childish
puerili·tà *f* (-tà) puerility, childishness
puèrpera *f* lying-in patient
pugilato *m* boxing
pugilatóre *m* boxer, prize fighter
pùgile *m* boxer, prize fighter
pugili·sta *m* (-sti) boxer, prize fighter
pù·glia *f* (-glie) stake (*in gambling*)
pugnace *adj* (lit) pugnacious
pugnalare *tr* to stab
pugnalata *f* stab
pugnale *m* dagger
pugno *m* fist; fistful; punch; **avere in pugno** to have in one's grasp; **di proprio pugno** in one's own hand; **fare a pugni** to fight; to clash

pula *f* chaff
pulce *f* flea; **mettere una pulce nell'orecchio di** to put a bug in the ear of; **pulce tropicale** jigger, chigger
pulcèlla *f* maid, maiden
pulcinèlla *f*—**pulcinella di mare** (orn) Atlantic puffin || **Pulcinel·la** *m* (-la) buffoon; Punch, Punchinello
pulcino *m* chick
pulédra *f* filly
pulédro *m* colt, foal
pulég·gia *f* (-ge) pulley
pulire §176 *tr* to clean; to shine (*shoes*); to wipe; to polish
puliscipiè·di *m* (-di) doormat
puli·to -ta *adj* clean; polished; clear (*conscience*) || *f*—**dare una pulita a** to give a lick and a promise to
pulitura *f* cleaning; **pulitura a secco** dry cleaning
pulizia *f* cleaning; cleanliness; **fare le pulizie** to clean house
pullulare (pùllulo) *intr* to swarm
pùlpito *m* pulpit
pulsante *m* knob; push button
pulsare *intr* to throb; to pulsate
pulviscolo *m* fine dust; haze
pulzèlla *f* var of pulcella
pu·ma *m* (-ma) cougar
pungènte *adj* pungent; bitter (*cold*)
pùngere §183 *tr* to sting; (fig) to goad
pungiglióne *m* stinger (*of bee*); (fig) sting; (obs) goad
pungitòpo *m* (bot) butcher's broom
pungolare (pùngolo) *tr* to goad, prod
punire §176 *tr* to punish
punizióne *f* punishment; penalty
punta *f* point, tip; prong; brad; bit, trifle; needle (*of phonograph*); avantgarde; point (*of dog*); (lit) wound; (fig) peak; (mach) broach; **averne fino alla punta dei capelli** to be sick and tired; **fare la punta a** to sharpen; **in punta di penna** elegantly; **prendere di punta** to treat roughly; to face up to; **punta delle dita** fingertip; **punta di piedi** tiptoe
puntale *m* tip, ferrule
puntaménto *m* aiming
puntare *tr* to aim; to aim at; to point; to thrust; to dot; to bet; to stare at; to fix (*one's eyes*); **puntare i piedi** to stiffen up; (fig) to balk || *intr* to aim; to point; to pin; to bet; **puntare su** to count on; **puntare verso** march on; to sail toward
puntaspil·li *m* (-li) pincushion
puntata *f* jab (*with weapon*); excursion; bet; issue, number (*of magazine*); installment (*of story*); (mil) incursion
punteggiare §290 (puntéggio) *tr* to dot; (gram) to punctuate
punteggiatura *f* dotting; punctuation
puntég·gio *m* (-gi) score
puntellare (puntèllo) *tr* to prop, brace; to support
puntèllo *m* prop, brace; support
puntería *f* aiming; aiming gear; (aut) tappet
punteruòlo *m* punch; awl
puntì·glio *m* (-gli) obstinacy, stubbornness; punctilio

puntiglió·so -sa [s] *adj* punctilious, scrupulous; obstinate, stubborn

puntina *f* brad; needle; thumbtack

puntino *m* small dot; G-string; **a puntino** to a T

punto *m* point; period; dot; place, spot; extent; stitch; **dare dei punti a** to be superior to; **di punto in bianco** all of a sudden; **di tutto punto** thoroughly; **due punti** colon; **essere a buon punto** to be well advanced; **essere sul punto di + *inf*** to be about to + *inf*; **fare il punto** (fig; naut) to take one's bearings; **in punto** on the dot; **in punto franco** in bond; **in un punto** together; **mettere a punto** to get in working order; (aut) to tune up; **mettere i punti sulle i** to dot one's i's; **punto assistenza** service agency; **punto di partenza** starting point; **punto di vista** viewpoint; **punto esclamativo** exclamation point; **punto e virgola** semicolon; **punto fermo** full stop; **punto interrogativo** question mark; **punto morto** (mach) dead center; **punto stimato** (naut) dead reckoning; **qui sta il punto!** here's the rub!; **vincere ai punti** (boxing) to win by points, win by decision || *adv—né* **punto né poco** not at all; **non . . . punto** not at all

puntóne *m* rafter

puntuale *adj* punctual, prompt

puntuali·tà *f* (-**tà**) punctuality, promptness

puntura *f* sting; stitch (*sharp pain*); (coll) injection; **puntura lombare** spinal anesthesia

punzecchiare §287 (**punzécchio**) *tr* to keep on stinging; to tease, torment

punzecchiatura *f* sting, bite

punzonare (**punzóno**) *tr* to mark or stamp with a punch

punzonatrice *f* punch press

punzóne *m* punch; nailset

pupa *f* doll; (zool) pupa

pupazzetti·sta *mf* (-**sti** -**ste**) cartoonist

pupazzétto *m* caricature; cartoon; **pupazzetto di carta** paper doll

pupazzo *m* puppet; **pupazzo di stoffa** rag doll

pupil·lo -la *mf* pupil; ward, protégé || *f* pupil (*of eye*); protégée

pupo *m* (coll) baby

purché *conj* provided, providing

pure *adv* too, also; indeed; (lit) only; **pur di** only in order to; **quando pure** even if; **se pure** even if || *conj* though, although; but, yet

pu·rè *m* (-**rè**) purée; **purè di patate** mashed potatoes

purézza *f* purity

pur·ga *f* (-**ghe**) laxative; purification; purge

purgante *adj* purging || *m* laxative

purgare §209 *tr* to purge; to purify; to expurgate || *ref* to take a laxative

purgati·vo -va *adj* laxative

purgatò·rio *m* (-**ri**) purgatory

purificare §197 (**purifico**) *tr* to purify

purismo *m* purism

purità *f* purity

purita·no -na *adj & m* puritan; Puritan

pu·ro -ra *adj* pure; clear; simple, mere

purosàn·gue *adj invar & m* (-**gue**) thoroughbred

purpùre·o -a *adj* (lit) purple

purtròppo *adv* unfortunately

purulèn·to -ta *adj* purulent

pus *m* pus

pusillànime *adj* pusillanimous

pùstola *f* pustule; pimple

puta caso *adv* possibly, maybe

putifè·rio *m* (-**ri**) hubbub

putrefare §173 *intr* (ESSERE) & *ref* to putrefy, rot

putrefazióne *f* putrefaction

putrèlla *f* I beam

pùtri·do -da *adj* putrid || *m* corruption

putta *f* (coll) girl; (lit) prostitute

puttana *f* (vulg) whore

put·to -ta *adj* (archaic) meretricious || *m* figure of a child || *f* see **putta**

puzza *f* var of **puzzo**

puzzare *intr* to stink, smell

puzzo *m* stench, smell, bad odor

pùzzola *f* polecat, skunk

puzzolènte *adj* stinking, smelly

puzzonata *f* (coll) contemptible action; (coll) botch, bungle

puzzóne *m* (coll) skunk (*person*)

Q

Q, q [ku] *m & f* fifteenth letter of the Italian alphabet

qua *adv* here; **da un (giorno, mese, anno) in qua** for the past (day, month, year); **di qua da** on this side of; **in qua** on this side; here

quàcche·ro -ra or **quàcque·ro -ra** *adj & mf* Quaker; **alla quacquera** in a plain fashion

quadèrno *m* copybook; **quaderno di cassa** cash book

quadràngo·lo -la *adj* quadrangular || *m* quadrangle

quadrante *m* quadrant; dial; face (*of watch*); **quadrante solare** sundial

quadrare *tr* to square || *intr* (ESSERE & AVERE) to square; **quadrare a** to be satisfactory to; **quadrare con** to fit

quadra·to -ta *adj* square; sound (*mind*) || *m* square; diaper; (boxing) ring; (nav) wardroom

quadratura *f* squaring; concreteness; (astr) quadrature

quadrèl·lo *m* (-**li**) square ruler; square tile || *m* (-**la** *fpl*) (lit) bolt, arrow

quadreria *f* picture gallery; collection

quadretta·to -ta *adj* checkered

quadrétto *m* small painting; checker, small square; (fig) picture

quadriennale adj four-year || f quadrennial

quadrifò·glio m (-gli) four-leaf clover; **a quadrifoglio** cloverleaf

quadrì·glia m (-gli) (cards) quadrille

quadrimensionale adj four-dimensional

quadrimestrale adj four-month

quadrimèstre m four-month period; four-month payment

quadrimotóre adj four-motor || m four-motor plane

quadrireattóre m four-motor jet

qua·dro -dra adj square; (fig) solid || m picture; painting; sight; square; table, summary; panel, switchboard; (theat) scene; **quadri** bulletin board; (mil) cadres; (cards) diamonds

quadrùmane adj quadrumanous || m monkey; ape

quadruplicare §197 (quadrùplico) tr & ref to quadruple

quadrùplice adj quadruple; **in quadruplice copia** in four copies

quàdru·plo -pla adj & m quadruple

quaggiù adv down here

quàglia f quail

quagliare §280 tr, intr (ESSERE) & ref var of **cagliare**

qualche adj invar some, e.g., **qualche giorno** some day; some, e.g., **qualche elefante è bianco** some elephants are white; any, e.g., **ha qualche libro da vendere?** do you have any books to sell?; a few, e.g., **qualche giorno** a few days

qualchedu·no -na pron indef var of **qualcuno**

qualcòsa [s] m (fig) something; (fig) somebody || pron indef something; anything; **qualcosa di buono** something good

qualcu·no -na pron indef some; any; somebody; anybody || m somebody

quale adj which, what; what a, e.g., **quale onore!** what an honor!; as, e.g., **il pane, quale vedi, è fresco** the bread, as you can see, is fresh; **quale che sia** regardless of || pron which; what; (archaic) who; **il quale** who, whom; **per la quale** o.k.; well-bred; commendable; terrific; **quale . . . quale** some . . . some || prep as, e.g., **quale ministro** as a minister

qualìfi·ca f (-che) rating; position; quality, qualification

qualificare §197 (qualìfico) tr to qualify; to classify; to rate, give a rating to || ref to introduce oneself; to qualify

qualifica·to -ta adj aggravated (assault); qualified (personnel); specialized (worker)

qualì·tà f (-tà) quality; capacity

qualóra conj if; (lit) whenever

qualsìasi [s] adj invar any; whatever; ordinary

qualunque adj invar any; whatever; common, ordinary; **in qualunque modo** anyway, anyhow; **qualunque altro** anybody else; **qualunque cosa** anything; no matter what

qualvòlta conj (lit) whenever

quando m when || adv when; **di quando**

in quando from time to time; **quando . . . quando** sometimes . . . sometimes || conj when; whenever; while; **da quando** since

quantìsti·co -ca adj (-ci -che) quantum

quanti·tà f (-tà) quantity; number

quantitativo m quantity

quan·to -ta adj how much; as much; how great; how great a; what a; **quan·ti -te** how many; as many || m quantum || pron how much; as much; how great; how long; that which; what; whatever; **a quanto si dice** according to what is rumored; **da quanto** from what; for how long; **fra quanto** how soon; **per quanto io ne sappia** as far as I know; **quanto più** (or **meno**) . . . **tanto più** (or **meno**) the more (or the less) . . . the more (or the less); **quan·ti -te** how many; all those; as many as; **quanti ne abbiamo?** what's the date? || **quanto** adv how much; as much as; **in quanto** as; **in quanto che** inasmuch as; **per quanto** although; no matter; nevertheless; **quanto a** as to, as for; **quanto mai** as never before; **quanto meno** at least; **quanto prima** as soon as possible

quantunque conj although, though

quaranta adj, m & pron forty; **gli anni quaranta** the forties; **i quaranta** the forties (in age)

quarantèna f quarantine

quarantènne adj forty-year-old || mf forty-year-old person

quarantèsi·mo -ma adj, m & pron fortieth

quarantina f about forty; **essere sulla quarantina** to be about forty years old

quarantòtto adj forty-eight || m forty-eight; (coll) hubbub, uproar

quarésima f Lent

quartabuòno m triangle (in drafting); **tagliare a quartabuono** to miter

quartétto m quartet; **quartetto d'archi** string quartet

quartière m quarter, district; (mil) quarters; (coll) apartment; **quartier generale** headquarters; **senza quartiere** (fight) without quarter

quar·to -ta adj & pron fourth || m fourth; quarter; quarter of a kilo; quarter of a liter; (naut) watch; **l'una e un quarto** a quarter after one; **l'una meno un quarto** a quarter to one

quarzo m quartz

quasi adv almost, nearly; **quasi che** as if; **quasi mai** hardly ever; **senza quasi** without any ifs and buts

quassù adv up here

quat·to -ta adj crouching; squatting; **quatto quatto** stealthy, silent; **starsene quatto quatto** to not make a sound

quattordicènne adj fourteen-year-old || mf fourteen-year-old person

quattordicèsi·mo -ma adj, m & pron fourteenth

quattórdici adj & pron fourteen; **le**

quattordici two P.M. ‖ *m* fourteen; fourteenth (*in dates*)
quattrino *m* penny; (fig) bit; **quattrini** money
quattro *adj* four; a few, e.g., **quattro gatti** a few people; **a quattro mani** (mus) for four hands ‖ *pron* four; **dirne quattro** a to upbraid; **farsi in quattro** to go all out; **in quattro e quattr'otto** in a few minutes; **le quattro** four o'clock ‖ *m* four; fourth (*in dates*); racing shell with four oarsmen
quattrocènto *adj, m & pron* four hundred ‖ **il Quattrocento** the fifteenth century
quattromila *adj, m & pron* four thousand
quégli §7 *adj* ‖ §8 *pron*
quéi §7 *adj*
quél §7 *adj* ‖ §8 *pron*
quéll' §7 *adj*
quél·lo -la §7 *adj* ‖ §8 *pron*—**per quello che so io** as far as I know
quèr·cia *f* (-ce) oak tree
querci·no -na *adj* oaken
querèla *f* complaint
querelante *adj* complaining ‖ *mf* plaintiff
querelare (**querèlo**) *tr* to sue ‖ *ref* (law) to sue; (lit) to complain
querela·to -ta *adj* accused ‖ *mf* defendant
quèru·lo -la *adj* (lit) plaintive
quesito *m* question; problem; (lit) request
quésti §7 *pron*
questionare (**questióno**) *intr* to quarrel
questionà·rio *m* (-ri) questionnaire
questióne *f* question; (coll) quarrel; **questione di gabinetto** call for a vote of confidence; **venire a questione** to quarrel
qué·sto -sta §7 *adj* ‖ §8 *pron*—**e con questo?** so what?; **per questo** therefore; **questa** this matter; **questo . . . quello** the former . . . the latter
questóre *m* police commissioner; sergeant at arms (*of congress*)
quèstua *f* begging; collection of alms; **andare alla questua** to go begging; **vietata la questua** no begging
questura *f* police department; police headquarters

questurino *m* (coll) policeman
què·to -ta *adj* var of **quieto**
qui *adv* here; **di qui** hence, from here; this way; **di qui a un anno** one year hence; **di qui in avanti** from now on; **qui vicino** nearby
quiescènza *f* quiescence; retirement
quietanza *f* receipt
quietanzare *tr* to receipt
quietare (**quièto**) *tr* to quiet, calm; to satisfy (*e.g., thirst*) ‖ *ref* to quiet down
quiète *f* quiet, calmness
quiè·to -ta *adj* quiet, calm; still; **stia quieto!** don't worry! ‖ *m* quiet life
quindi *adv* then; therefore; (archaic) thence, from there
quindicènne *adj* fifteen-year-old ‖ *mf* fifteen-year-old person
quindicèsi·mo -ma *adj, m & pron* fifteenth
quindici *adj & pron* fifteen; **le quindici** three P.M. ‖ *m* fifteen; fifteenth (*in dates*)
quindicina *f* about fifteen; two weeks, fortnight; semimonthly pay
quindicinale *adj* fortnightly
quinquennale *adj* five-year
quinta *f* (theat) wing; (mus) fifth; **dietro le quinte** behind the scenes
quintale *m* quintal (*100 kilos*)
quintèrno *m* signature of five sheets; (bb) quire
quintessènza *f* quintessence
quintétto *m* quintet
quin·to -ta *adj, m & pron* fifth ‖ *f* see **quinta**
quisquìlia *f* trifle
quivi *adv* (lit) over there; (lit) then
quòrum *m* quorum
quòta *f* quota; share; altitude; elevation; level (*of stock market*); market average; odds (*in betting*); subscription (*to club*); **quota zero** (fig) point of departure
quotare (**quòto**) *tr* to quote (*a price*); to value, esteem ‖ *ref* to sign up for, e.g., **si quotò duemila lire** he signed up for two thousand lire
quotazióne *f* quotation
quotidia·no -na *adj & m* daily
quoziènte *m* quotient; (sports) percentage; **quoziente d'intelligenza** I.Q.

R

R, r ['ɛrre] *m & f* sixteenth letter of the Italian alphabet
rabàrbaro *m* rhubarb
rabberciare §128 (**rabbèrcio**) *tr* (coll) to patch up
ràbbia *f* rage, anger; rabies
rabbino *m* rabbi
rabbió·so -sa [s] *adj* furious; rabid
rabbonire §176 *tr* to pacify ‖ *ref* to calm down
rabbrividire §176 *intr* (ESSERE) to shiver, shudder

rabbuffare *tr* to rebuke; to dishevel
rabbuffo *m* rebuke; **fare un rabbuffo a** to rebuke
rabbuiare §287 *ref* to darken, turn dark
rabdomante *m* dowser, diviner
rabé·sco *m* (-schi) arabesque; scrawl, scribble
ràbi·do -da *adj* rabid
raccapezzare (**raccapézzo**) *tr* to put together; to gather (*news*); to find (*one's way*); to make out (*what is*

meant) ‖ *ref*—non raccapezzarsi to not be able to get one's bearings

raccapricciante *adj* bloodcurdling

raccapric·cio *m* (-ci) horror

raccartocciare §128 (**raccartòccio**) *tr* & *ref* to shrivel

raccattare *tr* to pick up; to gather

racchétta *f* racket; **racchetta da neve** snowshoe; **racchetta da sci** ski pole

ràc·chio -chia *adj* (-chi -chie) (coll) ugly, homely

racchiùdere §125 *tr* to contain, hold

raccògliere §127 *tr* to pick up; to gather; to collect (*e.g., stamps*); to take up (*the gauntlet*); to receive; to reap; to furl (*sail*); to draw in (*a net*); to fold (*the wings*); to shelter (*e.g., foundlings*); **raccogliere i passi** to stop walking ‖ *ref* to gather; to concentrate

raccoglimento *m* concentration; meditation

raccogli·tóre -trice *mf* collector, compiler ‖ *m* folder

raccòl·to -ta *adj* crouched; collected; engrossed; snug, intimate ‖ *m* harvest ‖ *f* harvest; collection; **chiamare a raccolta** to rally

raccomandàbile *adj* recommendable; **poco raccomandabile** unreliable

raccomandare *tr* to recommend; to secure (*e.g., a boat*); to register (*mail*); to exhort ‖ *ref* to recommend oneself; to entreat; **mi raccomando** please; **raccomandarsi a** to beg, implore; **raccomandarsi alle gambe** to take to one's heels

raccomanda·to -ta *adj* recommended; registered ‖ *m* protégé ‖ *f* protégée; **registered letter**

raccomandazióne *f* recommendation; registration (*of mail*); exhortation

raccomodare (**raccòmodo**) *tr* to fix; to mend

racconciare §128 (**raccóncio**) *tr* to fix; to mend ‖ *ref* to clear up (*said of the weather*); to tidy oneself up

raccontare (**raccónto**) *tr* to tell; **raccontarla bene** to be good at telling lies

raccónto *m* tale; story; narrative

raccorciaménto *m* shortening

raccorciare §128 (**raccòrcio**) *tr* to shorten

raccordare (**raccòrdo**) *tr* to link, connect

raccòrdo *m* link, connection; **raccordo a circolazione rotatoria** traffic circle; **raccordo anulare** (rr) belt line; **raccordo ferroviario** junction; spur; siding; **raccordo stradale** connecting road

raccostare (**raccòsto**) *tr* & *ref* to draw near

raccozzare (**raccòzzo**) *tr* to scrape together

ràchide *m* & *f* backbone; midrib (*of leaf*); shaft (*of feather*)

rachíti·co -ca *adj* (-ci -che) stunted; weak; (pathol) rickety

rachitismo *m* rickets

racimolare (**racìmolo**) *tr* to glean; to scrape together

rada *f* roadstead; cove

ràdar *m* radar

addobbare (**raddòbbo**) *tr* (naut) to refit

raddolcire §176 *tr* & *ref* to sweeten; to mellow

raddoppiare §287 (**raddóppio**) *tr, intr* (ESSERE) & *ref* to double, redouble

raddrizzare *tr* to straighten; (elec) to rectify ‖ *ref* to straighten up

raddrizzatóre *m* (elec) rectifier

ràdere §223 *tr* to shave; to raze; to graze, skim ‖ *ref* to shave

radézza *f* rarity, rareness; thinness; sparsity (*of vegetation*); space, distance (*e.g., between trees*)

radiante *adj* radiating

radiare §287 *tr* to strike off; to expel; to condemn (*a ship*); **radiare dall'albo degli avvocati** to disbar

radiatóre *m* radiator

radiazióne *f* radiation; expulsion

ràdi·ca *f* (-che) brier; (coll) root

radicale *adj* & *mf* radical ‖ *m* & *f* (philol) radical, root ‖ *m* (chem, math) radical

radicare §197 (**ràdico**) *tr* & *intr* to root

radice *f* root; base or foot (*e.g., of a mountain or tower*); **mettere radice** to take root; **svellere dalle radici** to pull up by the roots; to eradicate

rà·dio *adj invar* radio ‖ *m* (-di) (anat) radius; (chem) radium ‖ *f* (-dio) radio; **radio fante** (mil) grapevine

radioabbonato *m* (rad) subscriber (*to radio broadcasting*)

radioama·tóre -trice *mf* radio fan; radio ham

radioannunciatóre *m* radio announcer

radioascolta·tóre -trice *mf* radio-listener

radioatti·vo -va *adj* radioactive

radiobùssola *f* radio compass

radiocanale *m* radio channel

radiocomanda·to -ta *adj* radio-controlled

radiocrònaca *f* (-che) newscast

radiocroni·sta *mf* (-sti -ste) newscaster

radiodiffóndere §178 *tr* to broadcast

radiodiffusióne *f* broadcasting

radiofaro *m* radio beacon

radiofòni·co -ca *adj* (-ci -che) radio

radiofonògrafo *m* radiophonograph

radiofò·to *f* (-to) radiophoto

radiofrequènza *f* radiofrequency

radiologia *f* radiology

radiomontatóre *m* radio assembler

radioónda *f* radio wave; **radioonde airwaves**

radioricevènte *adj* radio ‖ *f* radio set; radio station

radioriparatóre *m* radio repairman

radiosegnale *m* radio signal

radiosentièro *m* range of a radio beacon

radió·so -sa [s] *adj* radiant

radiosorgènte *f* quasar

radiostazióne *f* radio station

radiostélla *f* quasar

radiotas·sì *m* (-sì) radio-dispatched taxi

radiotelescò·pio *m* (-pi) radiotelescope

radiotrasméttere §198 *tr* & *intr* to broadcast, radio

radiotrasmissióne *f* broadcast

radiotrasmittènte adj broadcasting ‖ f broadcasting station

ra·do -da adj rare; thin; sheer; sparse, scattered; **di rado** seldom, rarely

radunare tr & ref to assemble, gather

radunata f gathering; (mil) assembly; **radunata sediziosa** unlawful assembly

raduno m assembly, gathering

radura f clearing, glade

ràfano m (bot) radish

raffazzonare (raffazzóno) tr to mend, patch up

raffazzonatura f patchwork, hodge-podge

rafférma f confirmation; stay (in office); return to office; (mil) reenlistment

raffermare (raffèrmo) tr to reaffirm; to secure; (coll) to reconfirm; to reappoint, reelect; to return (e.g., a mayor) to office ‖ intr (ESSERE) & ref to reenlist; (coll) to harden

raffèr·mo -ma adj stale (bread) ‖ f see **rafferma**

ràffi·ca f (-che) gust; blast; burst (e.g., of machine gun); **a raffiche** gusty

raffigurare tr to represent; to symbolize

raffinare tr to refine; to polish ‖ intr (ESSERE) to become refined

raffinatézza f refinement, polish

raffinatura f refinement (of oil)

raffinazióne f refining

raffinerìa f refinery

ràf·fio m (-fi) hook; grappling iron

rafforzare (raffòrzo) tr to strengthen

raffreddaménto m cooling

raffreddare (raffréddo) tr to make cold; to cool; **raffreddare gli spiriti di qlcu** to dampen s.o.'s enthusiasm ‖ intr (ESSERE) & ref to get cold; to cool

raffreddóre m cold

raffrontare (raffrónto) tr to compare; (law) to bring face to face

raffrónto m comparison; confrontation

ràfia f raffia

raganèlla f rattle; (zool) tree frog

ragazza f girl; spinster; (coll) girl friend; **ragazza copertina** cover girl; **ragazza squillo** call girl

ragazzata f boyish prank

ragaz·zo -za mf youth, young person ‖ m boy; (coll) boyfriend ‖ f see **ragazza**

raggelare (raggèlo) intr (ESSERE) to freeze

raggiante adj radiant; beaming

raggiare §290 tr & intr to radiate

raggièra f rayed halo; **a raggiera** radially

ràg·gio m (-gi) ray; beam; spoke; (geom) radius; **raggio d'azione** radius, range of action; **raggio di sole** sunbeam

raggiornare (raggiórno) tr (coll) to bring up to date ‖ intr (ESSERE) to dawn ‖ impers (ESSERE)—**raggiorna** it is dawning

raggirare tr to trick, swindle ‖ ref to roam, wander; **raggirarsi su** to turn on (e.g., a certain subject)

raggiro m trickery, swindle

raggiungere §183 tr to reach; to catch up with, rejoin

raggiungìbile adj attainable

raggomitolare (raggomìtolo) tr to roll up ‖ ref to curl up; to cuddle

raggranellare (raggranèllo) tr to gather; to scrape together

raggrinzire §176 tr & ref to crease, wrinkle

raggrumare tr & ref to clot, coagulate

raggruppaménto m grouping; group

raggruppare tr & ref to group, assemble

ragguagliare §280 tr to compare; to balance; to inform in detail; to level

ragguà·glio m (-gli) comparison; detailed report

ragguardévole adj considerable, notable

ragionaménto m reasoning; discussion

ragionare (ragióno) intr to reason; to discuss ‖ impers ref—**si ragiona** it is rumored

ragióne f reason; account; rate; justice; (math) ratio; **a maggior ragione** with all the more reason; **a ragione** within reason; **aver ragione** to be right; **aver ragione di** to get the best of; **dar ragione a qlcu** to admit that s.o. is right; **di santa ragione** hard, a great deal; **farsi ragione** to be resigned; **in ragione di** at the rate of; **ragion per cui** and therefore; **ragione sociale** (com) trade name; **rendere di pubblica ragione** to publicize

ragionerìa f accounting; bookkeeping

ragionévole adj reasonable

ragioniè·re -ra mf accountant; bookkeeper

ragliare §280 intr to bray

rà·glio m (-gli) bray

ragnatéla f spider web

ragno m spider

ra·gù m (-gù) meat gravy; stew

ràion m rayon

rallegraménto m congratulation, act of congratulating; **rallegramenti** congratulations

rallegrare (rallégro) tr to cheer up; to rejoice, gladden ‖ ref to cheer up; to rejoice; **rallegrarsi con** to congratulate

rallentare (rallènto) tr, intr & ref to slow down; to lessen

rallentatóre m slow-motion projector; **al rallentatore** slow-motion

ra·màio m (-mài) tinker, coppersmith

ramaiòlo m ladle

ramanzina [dz] f reprimand

ramare tr to copperplate; (agr) to spray with copper sulfate

ramarro m green lizard

ramazza f broom; (mil) cleaning detail; (mil) soldier on cleaning detail

rame m copper; etching

ramerino m (coll) rosemary

ramificare §197 (ramìfico) intr & ref to branch; to branch off; to branch out, ramify

ramin·go -ga adj (-ghi -ghe) wandering

ramino m copper pot; rummy (card game)

rammagliare §280 tr to reknit; to mend a run in (a stocking)

rammaricare §197 (rammàrico) tr to afflict ‖ ref to be sorry, regret; **rammaricarsi di** to be sorry for

rammàri·co *m* (**-chi**) regret

rammendare (**rammèndo**) *tr* to darn

rammèndo *m* darn

rammentare (**rammènto**) *tr* to remember; to remind ‖ *ref*—**rammentarsi di** to remember

rammenta·tóre -trice *mf* prompter

rammollire §176 *tr·& ref* to soften

rammolli·to -ta *adj* soft; soft-headed ‖ *m* dodo, jellyfish

ramo *m* branch; bough; point (*of antler*); **ramo di pazzia** streak of madness

ramoscèllo *m* twig; **ramoscello d'olivo** olive branch

rampa *f* ramp; flight (*of stairs*); launching platform

rampicante *adj* climbing ‖ *m* (ichth) perch; (orn) climber

rampino *m* hook; tine, prong; pretext

rampógna *f* (lit) reprimand

rampóllo *m* spring (*of water*); scion; shoot (*of a plant*); (joc) offspring

rampóne *m* harpoon; crampon

rana *f* frog

ràncido -da *adj* rancid

ràn·cio -cia (**-ci -ce**) *adj* (poet) orange ‖ *m* (mil) mess

rancóre *m* rancor; grudge; **serbar rancore** to bear malice

randa *f* (naut) spanker; (obs) edge

randà·gio -gia *adj* (**-gi -gie**) wandering; stray

randellare (**randèllo**) *tr* to cudgel; to bludgeon; to blackjack

randèllo *m* cudgel; bludgeon

ran·go *m* (**-ghi**) rank; station

rannicchiare §287 *tr* to cause to curl up ‖ *ref* to crouch; to cower; to cuddle up

ranno *m* lye; **buttar via il ranno e il sapone** to waste one's time and effort

rannuvolare (**rannùvolo**) *tr & ref* to cloud; to darken

ranòcchia *f* frog

ranòc·chio *m* (**-chi**) frog

rantolare (**ràntolo**) *intr* to wheeze

ràntolo *m* wheezing; death rattle

ranùncolo *m* buttercup

rapa *f* turnip; **valere una rapa** to be not worth a fig

rapace *adj* rapacious ‖ **rapaci** *mpl* birds of prey

rapare *tr* to shave (*s.o.'s head*) ‖ *ref* to shave one's head; to have one's head shaved

rapidi·tà *f* (**-tà**) rapidity, swiftness

ràpi·do -da *adj* rapid, swift ‖ *m* (rr) express ‖ **rapide** *fpl* rapids

rapiménto *m* rape, abduction; rapture

rapina *f* pillage, plunder; misappropriation; prey; (lit) fury; **rapina a mano armata** armed robbery

rapinare *tr* to rob, plunder; to hold up; **rapinare qlco a qlcu** to rob s.o. of s.th

rapina·tóre -trice *mf* robber, plunderer

rapire §176 *tr* to rape, abduct; to kidnap; to enrapture

rapi·tóre -trice *mf* kidnaper

rappacificare §197 (**rappacìfico**) *tr* to reconcile ‖ *ref* to become reconciled

rappezzare (**rappèzzo**) *tr* to patch; to

piece; **rappezzarla** to get out of trouble

rappèzzo *m* patch; patchwork

rapportare (**rappòrto**) *tr* to report; to transfer (*a design*) ‖ *ref* to refer

rapporta·tóre -trice *mf* reporter ‖ *m* protractor

rappòrto *m* report; relation; relationship; (math) ratio; **chiamare a rapporto** to summon; **chiedere di mettersi a rapporto** to ask for a hearing; **fare rapporto** to report; **in rapporto a** concerning; **mettersi a rapporto** to report; **sotto ogni rapporto** in every respect

rapprèndere §220 *tr & ref* to coagulate

rappresàglia [s] *f* reprisal; retaliation

rappresentante *adj* representing; representative ‖ *mf* representative; agent; **rappresentante di commercio** agent

rappresentanza *f* delegation; proxy; agency; representation

rappresentare (**rappresènto**) *tr* to represent; to play; to portray

rappresentati·vo -va *adj* representative

rappresentazióne *f* representation; description; (theat) performance; **rappresentazione teatrale diurna** matinée; **sacra rappresentazione** (theat) mystery, miracle play

rapsodìa *f* rhapsody

raraménte *adv* seldom, rarely

rarefare §173 *tr* to rarefy ‖ *ref* to become rarefied

rari·tà *f* (**-tà**) rarity

ra·ro -ra *adj* rare; **di raro** seldom

rasare [s] *tr* to shave; to mow; to trim; to smooth ‖ *ref* to shave

raschiare §287 (**ràschio**) *tr* to scrape; to scratch ‖ *intr* to clear one's throat

raschiétto *m* scraper; erasing knife; footscraper

rà·schio *m* (**-schi**) clearing one's throat; hoarseness; frog in the throat

rasentare (**rasènto**) *tr* to graze; to scrape; to border on; to come close to

rasènte *adv* close; **rasente a** close to ‖ *prep* close to

ra·so -sa [s] *adj* shaved; trimmed; brimful; disreputable (*clothes*); flush ‖ *m* satin ‖ *adv*—**raso terra** down-to-earth; **volare raso terra** to skim the ground; to hedgehop

ra·sóio [s] *m* (**-sói**) razor; **rasoio a mano libera** straight razor; **rasoio di sicurezza** safety razor

raspa *f* rasp

raspare *tr* to rasp; to irritate; to stamp, paw; (coll) to steal ‖ *intr* to rasp; to scratch (*said of a chicken*); to scrawl

raspo *m* grape stalk; scraper; (vet) mange

rasségna *f* review; exposition

rassegnare (**rasségno**) *tr* to resign; **rassegnare le dimissioni** to resign ‖ *ref* to resign oneself; to submit

rassegnazióne *f* resignation

rasserenare (**rasseréno**) *tr & ref* to brighten; to cheer up

rassettare (**rassètto**) *tr & ref* to tidy up

rassicurare *tr* to reassure ‖ *ref* to be reassured

rassodare (rassòdo) *tr* to harden; to strengthen ‖ *intr* (ESSERE) & *ref* to harden

rassomigliare §280 (rassomìglio) *tr* to compare ‖ *intr* (ESSERE) (with *dat*) to resemble ‖ *ref* to resemble each other

rastrellaménto *m* roundup; mop-up operation

rastrellare (rastrèllo) *tr* to rake; to round up; to mop up; to drag (*e.g., the bottom*)

rastrellièra *f* rack; crib

rastrèllo *m* rake

rastremare (rastrèmo) *tr* to taper

rata *f* installment; quota; **a rate on** time; by installments

rateale *adj* installment

rateizzare [ddzz] *tr* to prorate; to divide (*a payment*) into installments

ratifi·ca *f* (**-che**) ratification

ratificare §197 (ratìfico) *tr* to ratify

rat·to -ta *adj* (lit) swift ‖ *m* rat; (lit) rape ‖ **ratto** *adv* (lit) swiftly

rattoppare (rattòppo) *tr* to patch, patch up

rattrappire §176 *tr* to cramp; to make numb, benumb ‖ *ref* to become cramped; to become numb

rattristare *tr* & *ref* to sadden

raucèdine *f* hoarseness

ràu·co -ca *adj* (**-chi -che**) hoarse, raucous

ravanèllo *m* radish

ravizzóne *m* (bot) rape

ravvedére §279 (*fut* **ravvedrò &** **ravvederò;** *pp* **ravveduto**) *ref* to repent; to mend one's ways

ravvedu·to -ta *adj* repentant; reformed

ravviare §119 *tr* to arrange, adjust; to poke (*fire*) ‖ *ref* to tidy up; (lit) to reform

ravvicinaménto *m* approach; reconciliation; rapprochement

ravvicinare *tr* to bring up; to reconcile ‖ *ref* to approach; to become reconciled; **ravvicinarsi a** to approach

ravviluppare *tr* to wrap up; to wind up; to bamboozle ‖ *ref* to become tangled

ravvisare ‖ to recognize

ravvivare *tr* to revive; to enliven; to brighten; to stir (*fire*) ‖ *ref* to revive

ravvòlgere §289 *tr* to wrap up

razioci·nio *m* (**-ni**) reasoning; reason; common sense

razionale *adj* rational

razionalizzare [ddzz] *tr* (com, math) to rationalize

razionaménto *m* rationing

razionare (razióno) *tr* to ration

razióne *f* ration; portion

razza *f* race; breed; kind; **di razza** purebred; **far razza** to reproduce; **passare a razza** to go to stud

razza [ddzz] *f* (ichth) ray; **razza cornuta** manta ray

razzìa *f* raid; foray; insect powder

razziale *adj* racial

razziare §119 *tr* & *intr* to foray

razzismo *m* racism

razzi·sta *mf* (**-sti -ste**) racist

razzo [ddzz] *m* rocket; (coll) spoke; (mil) flare

razzolare (ràzzolo) *intr* to scratch (*said of chickens*); (coll) to rummage

re [e] *m* (**re**) king

re [e] *m* (**re**) (mus) re

reagènte *m* reagent

reagire §176 *intr* to react

reale *adj* real, actual; royal, regal

realismo *m* realism; royalism

reali·sta *mf* (**-sti -ste**) realist; royalist

realìsti·co -ca *adj* (**-ci -che**) realistic

realizzare [ddzz] *tr* to carry out; to realize; to build ‖ *ref* to come true

realizzazióne [ddzz] *f* realization; **realizzazione scenica** production

realizzo [ddzz] *m* conversion into cash; profit taking; forced sale

realménte *adv* really, indeed

real·tà *f* (**-tà**) reality; actuality; **realtà romanzesca** truth stranger than fiction

reato *m* crime

reatti·vo -va *adj* reactive

reattóre *m* reactor; jet plane; jet engine

reazionà·rio -ria (**-ri -rie**) *adj* & *mf* reactionary

reazióne *f* reaction; (mach) backlash; **a reazione** jet-propelled

réb·bio *m* (**-bi**) prong

recalcitrante *adj* balky, restive; **essere recalcitrante a** to be opposed to, to resist

recalcitrare (recàlcitro) *intr* to be balky; to kick; (with *dat*) to buck, resist

recapitare (recàpito) *tr* to deliver

recàpito *m* address; delivery; **far recapito in** to be domiciled in; **recapiti** (com) notes

recare §197 (rèco) *tr* to bring; to cause; **recare ad effetto** to carry out; **recare qlco alla memoria di qlcu** to remind s.o. of s.th; **recare qlco a lode di qlcu** to praise s.o. for s.th ‖ *ref* to go, betake oneself

recèdere §123 *intr* (ESSERE & AVERE) to recede

recensióne *f* book review; collation

recensire §176 *tr* to review; to collate

recensóre *m* reviewer

recènte *adj* recent; **di recente** recently

recessióne *f* recession

recèsso *m* recess; subsiding (*of fever*); ebb tide

recìdere §145 *tr* to cut off; to chop off

recidiva *f* relapse; second offense

recìngere §126 *tr* to enclose, pen in

recinto *m* enclosure; pen, yard; compound; playpen; paddock; **recinto delle grida** floor of the exchange

recipiènte *m* container

reciprocità *f* reciprocity

recìpro·co -ca *adj* (**-ci -che**) reciprocal

reci·so -sa *adj* cut off; abrupt

rècita *f* show, performance

recitare (rècito) *tr* to recite; to portray, play; **recitare la commedia** to put on an act ‖ *intr* to perform, play; **recitare a soggetto** (theat) to improvise

recitazióne *f* recitation; diction; acting

reclamare *tr* to claim, demand ‖ *intr* to complain

récla·me *f* (-me) advertising; advertisement; **fare réclame a** to advertise; to boost

reclami·sta *mf* (-sti -ste) advertising agent; show-off ‖ *m* advertising man

reclamisti·co -ca *adj* (-ci -che) advertising

reclamo *m* complaint; **fare reclamo a** complain

reclinare *tr* to bow ‖ *intr* to recline

reclusióne *f* seclusion; imprisonment

reclu·so -sa *adj* recluse ‖ *mf* recluse; prisoner

reclusò·rio *m* (-ri) penitentiary

rècluta *f* recruit; rookie

reclutaménto *m* recruitment

reclutare (**rècluto**) *tr* to recruit

recòndi·to -ta *adj* concealed; inmost; recondite

recriminare (**recrìmino**) *intr* to recriminate

recuperare (**recùpero**) *tr* see **ricuperare**

redarguire §176 *tr* to berate

redat·tóre -trice *mf* compiler; newspaper editor; **redattore capo** managing editor; **redattore pubblicitario** copywriter; **redattore responsabile** publisher; **redattore viaggiante** correspondent

redazionale *adj* editorial, editor's (*e.g., policy*)

redazióne *f* writing; draft; version; (journ) city room

redazza *f* mop; (naut) swab

redditì·zio -zia (-zi -zie) lucrative

rèddito *m* income, revenue; yield; **reddito nazionale** gross national product

redèn·to -ta *adj* redeemed, set free

reden·tóre -trice *mf* redeemer ‖ **Redentore** *m*—**il Redentore** the Redeemer

redenzióne *f* redemption

redigere §224 *tr* to compile; to write up, compose

redimere §225 *tr* to redeem; to ransom; to save

rèdine *f* rein

redivì·vo -va *adj* come back to life

rèduce *adj* back (*from war*) ‖ *mf* veteran

réfe *m* thread

referèn·dum *m* (-dum) referendum; **referendum postale** mail questionnaire

referènza *f* reference

referenziare (**referènzio**) *tr* to give references to; to write references for ‖ *intr* to have good references

referenzia·to -ta *adj* with good references, e.g., **impiegato referenziato** employee with good references

refèrto *m* report (*of a physician*)

refettò·rio *m* (-ri) refectory

refezióne *f* lunch, light meal; **refezione scolastica** school lunch

refrattà·rio -ria *adj* (-ri -rie) refractory

refrigerante *adj* cooling ‖ *m* refrigerator; (chem) condenser

refrigerare (**refrìgero**) *tr* to refrigerate; to cool ‖ *ref* to cool off

refrigè·rio *m* (-ri) relief, comfort

refurtiva *f* stolen goods

refuso *m* misprint

regalare *tr* to present; to deliver (*a slap*); to throw away (*money*); **è regalato** it's a steal

regale *adj* regal; royal; imposing

regalìa *f* gratuity; bonus

regalità *f* regality, royalty

regalo *m* present, gift

regata *f* regatta

reggènte *adj & m* regent

reggènza *f* regency

règgere §226 *tr* to hold, hold up; to stand, withstand; to guide; (gram) to govern; **reggere il sacco a** to connive with; **reggere l'animo di** + *inf* to bear or stand + *ger*, e.g., **non gli regge l'animo di vederla piangere** he cannot stand seeing her cry ‖ *intr* to hold; to be valid; to last, hold out (*said of weather*); **reggere** (with *dat*) to withstand (*e.g., the cold*); **reggere al paragone** to bear comparison ‖ *ref* to stand up; to hold; to be ruled; **reggersi a** to hold on to; to be governed as (*e.g., a republic*); **reggersi a galla** to float

règ·gia *f* (-ge) royal palace

reggical·ze *m* (-ze) girdle

reggilibro *m* book end

reggimentale *adj* regimental

reggiménto *m* regiment

reggipètto *m* brassiere

reggisè·no *m* (-ni & -no) brassiere

regìa *f* monopoly; (mov) direction; (theat) production

regicì·da *mf* (-di -de) regicide

regicì·dio *m* (-di) regicide

regime *m* regime; diet; flow (*e.g., of river*); government; authoritarian government; (mach) rate; **regime secco** total abstinence

regina *f* queen; **regina claudia** greengage; **regina madre** queen mother

reginétta *f* young queen; queen (*of a beauty contest*)

rè·gio -gia *adj* (-gi -gie) royal ‖ **i regi** the king's soldiers

regióne *f* region

regi·sta *mf* (-sti -ste) coordinator; (theat) producer; (mov) director

registrare *tr* to register, record; to enter; to tally, log; to adjust; to tune up (*a musical instrument*) ‖ *ref* to register

registra·tóre -trice *mf* registrar ‖ *m* recorder; **registratore di cassa** cash register

registrazióne *f* registration; record, entry; adjustment; (aut) tune-up; (telv) videotaping; (telv) video-taping studio; (telv) video-taped program

registro *m* register; registration; classbook; regulator (*of watch*); stop (*of organ*); **cambiar registro** to change one's tune; **dar registro a** to regulate (*a watch*)

regnante *adj* reigning; prevailing ‖ **i regnanti** the rulers

regnare (**régno**) *intr* to reign, rule; to prevail; to take hold (*said of a root*)

régno *m* kingdom; reign

règola *f* rule; regulation; moderation; **a regola d'arte** to a T; **di regola** as a rule; **in regola** in good order; **mettere in regola** to put in order; **regole** menstruation; **secondo le regole** by the book

regolamentare *adj* regulation ‖ *v* (**regolaménto**) *tr* to regulate

regolaménto *m* regulation; settlement; **regolamento edilizio** building code

regolare *adj* regular; steady (*employment*); stock (*material*) ‖ *v* (**règolo**) *tr* to regulate; to adjust; to set (*a watch*); to focus (*a lens*); to settle (*an account*) ‖ *ref* to behave; to control oneself

regolari·tà *f* (**-tà**) regularity

regolarizzare [ddzz] *tr* to regularize

regolatézza *f* regularity; moderation

regola·to -ta *adj* regular, orderly

regola·tóre -trice *adj* regulating; see **piano** ‖ *m* ruler; regulator (*of watch*); (mach) governor; **regolatore dell'aria** register; **regolatore di volume** (rad, telv) volume control

regolazióne *f* regulation

regolizia *f* (coll) licorice

règolo *m* ruler; slat; (orn, hist) kinglet; **regolo calcolatore** slide rule

regredire §176 (*pres participle* **regrediènte**; *pp* **regredito** & **regrèsso**) *intr* (ESSERE & AVERE) to retrogress

regrèsso *m* regression; abatement (*of fever*); (com) recourse

reiè·t·to -ta *adj* rejected ‖ *mf* outcast

reimbarcare §197 *tr* & *ref* to reship; to transship

reimbar·co *m* (**-chi**) reshipment; transshipment

reincarnare *tr* to reincarnate ‖ *ref* to become reincarnated

reincarnazióne *f* reincarnation

reinseriménto *m* integration

reintegrare (**reìntegro**) *tr* to restore; to reinstate; to indemnify

reità *f* guilt

reiterare (**reìtero**) *tr* to reiterate

relativi·tà *f* (**-tà**) relativity

relati·vo -va *adj* relative

rela·tóre -trice *adj* reporting ‖ *mf* relator (*of proceedings*); presenter (*of a bill*); dissertation supervisor

relazióne *f* relation; relationship; report; **relazione amorosa** affair; **relazioni** relations; connections

re·lè *m* (**-lè**) (elec) relay

relegare §209 (**rèlego**) *tr* to banish; to store away

religióne *f* religion

religió·so -sa [s] *adj* religious ‖ *m* clergyman ‖ *f* nun

relìquia *f* relic

relit·to -ta *adj* residual ‖ *m* shipwreck; air crash; derelict; shoal, bar

remare (**rèmo** & **rémo**) *intr* to row

rema·tóre -trice *mf* rower ‖ *m* oarsman

reminiscènza *f* reminiscence

remissióne *f* submissiveness; remission

remissi·vo -va *adj* submissive

rèmo *m* oar; **remo alla battana** paddle

rèmora *f* hindrance; (lit) delay

remò·to -ta *adj* remote; **passato remoto** (gram) preterit

réna *f* sand

Renània, la the Rhineland

Renata *f* Renée

rèndere §227 *tr* to return, give back; to give (*thanks*); to render (*justice*); to yield; to translate; to make (*known*); **render conto di** to give an account of; **rendere di pubblica ragione** to publicize; **rendere l'anima a Dio** to give up the ghost; **rendere pan per focaccia** to give tit for tat ‖ *intr* to pay, yield ‖ *ref* to make oneself; to betake oneself; to become; (lit) to surrender; **rendersi conto di** to realize

rendicónto *m* account; report; **rendiconti** proceedings

rendiménto *m* rendering; yield; output; (mech) efficiency

rèndita *f* private income; yield; Italian Government bond

rène *m* kidney

renèlla *f* (pathol) gravel

renètta *f* pippin

réni *fpl* loins; **spezzare le reni a** to break the back of

renitènte *adj* opposed ‖ *m*—**renitente alla leva** draft dodger

rènna *f* reindeer; reindeer skin

Rèno *m* Rhine

rè·o -a *adj* guilty; (lit) wicked ‖ *m* guilty person; accused

reòstato *m* (elec) rheostat

reparto *m* department; (mil) unit; **reparto d'assalto** shock troops

repèllere §168 *tr* to repel

repentàglio *m* jeopardy; **mettere a repentaglio** to jeopardize

repènte *adj*—**di repente** suddenly

repenti·no -na *adj* sudden

reperibile *adj* available

reperiménto *m* finding

reperire §176 *tr* to find

repèrto *m* (archeol) find; (law) evidence; (law) exhibit; (med) report

repertò·rio *m* (**-ri**) repertory; catalogue

rèpli·ca *f* (**-che**) repetition; replica; (law) rebuttal; (theat) repeat performance; **in replica** in reply

replicare §197 (**rèplico**) *tr* to repeat; to reply, answer; (theat) to repeat (*a performance*)

reportàg·gio *m* (**-gi**) news coverage; reporting

repòr·ter *m* (**-ter**) reporter

repressióne *f* repression; constraint

repressi·vo -va *adj* repressive; controlling, checking (*e.g., a disease*)

reprìmere §131 *tr* to repress; to hold back (*tears*) ‖ *ref* to restrain oneself

rèpro·bo -ba *adj* & *m* reprobate

repùbbli·ca *f* (**-che**) republic

repubblica·no -na *adj* & *mf* republican

repulisti *m*—**fare repulisti** (coll) to make a clean sweep

repulsióne *f* repulsion

repulsi·vo -va *adj* var of **ripulsivo**

reputare (**rèputo**) *tr* to think, esteem, repute

reputazióne *f* reputation

rèquie *m* & *f* (eccl) requiem ‖ *f* rest, respite

Rèquiem *m* & *f* Requiem

requisire §176 *tr* to requisition, commandeer

requisito *m* requisite, requirement

requisitòria *f* scolding, reproach; (law) summation

requisizióne *f* requisition

résa [s] *f* surrender; rendering (*of an account*); delivery (*of merchandise*); return (*e.g., of newspapers*); yield; **resa a discrezione** unconditional surrender

rescìndere §247 *tr* to rescind

resezióne [s] *f* (surg) resection

residènte [s] *adj & mf* resident

residènza [s] *f* residence

residenziale [s] *adj* residential

residua·to -ta [s] *adj* residual

resì·duo -dua [s] *adj* residual ‖ *m* residue; remainder; balance

rèsina *f* resin

resipiscènza [s] *f* (lit) repentance

resistènte [s] *adj* resistant; strong; fast (*color*) ‖ *mf* member of the Resistance

resistènza [s] *f* resistance ‖ **Resistenza** *f* Resistance

resìstere [s] §114 *intr* to resist; (with *dat*) to withstand; (with *dat*) to endure; (with *dat*) to resist

rèso [s] *m* rhesus

resocónto [s] *m* report, relation

respingènte *m* (rr) bumper, buffer

respìngere §126 *tr* to drive back, beat off; to reject; to fail (*a student*); to vote down

respìn·to -ta *adj* rejected ‖ *mf* failure (*pupil*)

respirare *tr & intr* to breathe, respire

respiratò·rio -ria *adj* (-ri -rie) respiratory

respirazióne *f* breathing

respiro *m* breath; breathing; respite

responsàbile *adj* responsible; responsabile di responsible for

responsabili·tà *f* (-tà) responsibility

respònso *m* decision (*of an oracle*); report (*of a physician*); return (*of an election*); (lit) response

rèssa *f* crowd; **far ressa** to crowd

rèsta *f* string (*of garlic or onions*); awn (*e.g., of wheat*); (coll) fishbone; (for *a lance*) (hist) rest

restante *adj* remaining ‖ *m* remainder

restare (**rèsto**) *intr* (ESSERE) to remain; to stay; to be located; (lit) to stop; **non restare a...che** to have no alternative but to, e.g., **non gli resta che andarsene** he has no alternative but to go; **non restare a qlcu qlco da** + *inf* to not have s.th + to + *inf*, e.g., **non gli resta molto da finire** he does not have much to finish; **resta a vedere** it remains to be seen; **restare qlco a qlcu** to have s.th left, e.g., **gli restano tre dollari** he has three dollars left; **restare sul colpo** to die on the spot; **resti comodo** please don't get up!

restaurare (**restàuro**) *tr* to restore, renovate

restaurazióne *f* restoration

restàuro *m* restoration (*of a building*)

restì·o -a (-ì -e) *adj* balky, restive ‖ *m* balkiness

restituire §176 *tr* to give back, return; (lit) to restore ‖ *ref* (lit) to return

restituzióne *f* restitution, return

rèsto *m* remainder; change; balance; **del resto** besides, after all; **resti** remains

restrìngere §265 (*pp* **ristrétto**) *tr* to narrow down; to shrink; to take in (*a suit*); to limit (*expenses*); to tighten (*a knot*); to bind (*the bowels*); to restrict ‖ *ref* to contract; to narrow

restrizióne *f* restriction

retàg·gio *m* (-gi) (lit) heritage

retata *f* haul; (fig) roundup

réte [s] *f* net; network; (soccer) goal; **rete a strascico** trawl; **rete da pesca** fishing net; **rete del letto** bedspring; **rete metallica** wire mesh; window screen; **rete per i capelli** hair net; **rete viaria** highway network

reticèlla *f* small net; hair net; mantle (*of gas jet*)

reticènte *adj* secretive, dissembling; evasive, noncommittal

reticènza *f* secretiveness; evasiveness

reticolato *m* grid (*on map*); wire entanglement

reticolo *m* grid

retina *f* small net

rètina *f* (anat) retina

retino *m* small net; (typ) screen

retòri·co -ca (-ci -che) *adj* rhetorical ‖ *m* rhetorician ‖ *f* rhetoric

retràttile *adj* retractile

retribuire §176 *tr* to remunerate

retributì·vo -va *adj* retributive; **salary** (*e.g., conditions*)

retrì·vo -va *adj* backward

rètro *m* back; verso; back of store ‖ *adv* (lit) behind; **retro a** (lit) behind

retroattì·vo -va *adj* retroactive

retrobotté·ga *m & f* (-ga *mpl* -ghe *fpl*) back of store

retrocàmera *f* back room

retrocàrica *f*—**a retrocarica** breech-loading

retrocèdere §228 *tr* to demote; (com) to return; (com) to give a discount to ‖ *intr* (ESSERE & AVERE) to retreat

retrocessióne *f* demotion; (sports) assignment to a lower division

retrodatare *tr* to antedate, predate

retrògra·do -da *adj* backward; retrograde

retroguàrdia *f* rearguard

retromàr·cia *f* (-ce) (aut) reverse

retrorazzo [ddzz] *m* retrorocket

retrosapóre *m* aftertaste

retroscè·na *m* (-na) intrigue, maneuver ‖ *f* backstage

retrospettì·vo -va *adj* retrospective

retrotèr·ra *m* (-ra) hinterland; (fig) background

retrotrèno *m* rear end (*of vehicle*); (aut) rear assembly

retroversióne *f* retroversion; retranslation

retrovìe *fpl* zone behind the front

retrovisì·vo -va *adj* rear-view, e.g., **specchietto retrovisivo** rear-view mirror

retrovisóre m rear-view mirror

rètta f board and lodging; straight line; **dar retta a** to pay attention to

rettangolare adj rectangular

rettàngolo m rectangle

rettifi·ca f (-che) straightening; rectification; (mach) grinding; (mach) reboring

rettificare §197 (rettifico) tr to straighten; to rectify; (mach) to grind; (mach) to rebore

rettifica·tó·re -tríce adj rectifying || mf rectifier (person) || m rectifier (apparatus)

rettifilo m straightaway

rèttile m reptile

rettilì·neo -nea adj rectilinear || m straightaway || f straight line

rettitùdine f straightness; uprightness, rectitude

rèt·to -ta adj straight; correct; upright; (geom) right || m right; recto; (anat) rectum || f see retta

rettóre m rector; president (of university)

reumàti·co -ca adj (-ci -che) rheumatic

reumatismo m rheumatism

reverèn·do -da adj & m reverend

reverènte adj var of riverente

reverènza f var of riverenza

revisióne f revision; (mach) overhaul

revisionismo m revisionism

revisóre m inspector; **revisore dei conti** auditor; **revisore di bozze** proofreader

riviscènza f rebirth

rèvo·ca f (-che) revocation; recall; repeal

revocare §197 (rèvoco) tr to revoke; to recall; to repeal

revòl·ver m (-ver) revolver

revolverata f gun shot

revulsióne f (med) revulsion

ri- pref re-, e.g., **rivivere** to relive; again, e.g., **rifare** to do again; back, e.g., **riandare** to go back

riabbonare (riabbòno) tr to renew the subscription of || ref to renew one's subscription

riabbracciare §128 (riabbràccio) tr to embrace again; to greet again

riabilitare (riabilito) tr to rehabilitate || ref to reestablish one's good name

riaccèndere §101 tr to rekindle || ref to become rekindled

riaccompagnare tr to take home

riaccostare (riaccòsto) tr to bring near; to bring together || ref to draw near

riacquistare tr to buy back; to recover

riaddormentare (riaddorménto) tr to put back to sleep || ref to go back to sleep

riaffacciare §128 (riaffàccio) tr to present again || ref to reappear

riaffermare (riaffèrmo) tr to reaffirm

riaggravare tr to make worse || ref to get worse again

rialesare (rialèso) tr to rebore

riallacciare §128 (riallàccio) tr to tie again || ref to be tied or connected

rialto m knoll, height; **fare rialto** (coll) to eat better than usual

rialzare tr to lift, raise; to increase || ref to rise

rialzi·sta mf (-sti -ste) bull (in stock market)

rialzo m rise; raise; knoll, height; **giocare al rialzo** to bull the market

riammobiliare §287 tr to refurnish

rianimare (rianimo) tr to revive; to encourage || ref to revive; to recover one's spirits, to rally

riapertura f reopening

riapparire §108 intr (ESSERE) to reappear

riapparizióne f reappearance

riaprire §110 tr & ref to reopen

riarmare tr to rearm; to reinforce; to refit || intr & ref to rearm

riarmo m rearmament

riar·so -sa adj dry, parched

riassaporare (riassapóro) tr to relish again

riassettare (riassètto) tr to tidy up

riassicurare tr to reinsure; to fasten again; to reassure

riassorbire §176 & (riassòrbo) tr to reabsorb

riassùmere §116 tr to hire again; to summarize, sum up

riassunto m précis, abstract; résumé

riassunzióne f rehiring; resumption

riattaccare §197 tr to attach again; (coll) to begin again; (telp) to hang up

riattare tr to repair, fix

riattivare tr to reactivate

riavére §229 tr to get again; to recover; to get back || ref to recover

riavvicinaménto m var of ravvicinamento

riavvicinare tr & ref var of ravvicinare

ribadire §176 tr to clinch (a nail); to rivet; to drive home (an idea); to back up (a statement)

ribaldo m scoundrel, rogue

ribalta f lid with hinge; trap door; (theat) footlights; (theat) forestage; (fig) limelight; **a ribalta** hinged

ribaltàbile adj collapsable (e.g., seat) || m dump-truck lift; dump truck

ribaltare tr & ref to upset, turn over

ribassare tr & intr (ESSERE) to lower

ribassi·sta mf (-sti -ste) bear (in stock market)

ribasso m fall, decline; discount, rebate; **giocare al ribasso** to be a bear

ribàttere tr to clinch (a nail); to return (a ball); to iron smooth; to belabor (a point) || intr to answer back

ribattezzare [ddzz] (ribattézzo) tr to rebaptize

ribattino m rivet

ribellare (ribèllo) tr to rouse to rebellion || ref to rebel; **ribellarsi a** to rebel against

ribèlle adj rebellious || mf rebel

ribellióne f rebellion

ri·bes m (-bes) currant; gooseberry

ribobinazióne f rewind (of a tape)

riboccare §197 (ribócco) intr (ESSERE & AVERE) to overflow

ribollire (ribóllo) tr to boil again ||

intr to boil over; to simmer; to ferment

ribrézzo [ddzz] *m* repugnance, disgust

ributtare *tr* to return (*a ball*); to throw up; to reject; to push back ‖ *intr* to sprout; (with *dat*) to disgust, nauseate

ricacciare §128 *tr* to drive back ‖ *intr* to sprout ‖ *ref* to sneak away, disappear

ricadére §121 *intr* (ESSERE) to fall back; to fall down; to relapse; **ricadere su** to devolve upon

ricaduta *f* relapse

ricalcare §197 *tr* to transfer (*a design*); to imitate; **ricalcare le orme di** follow in the footsteps of

rical·co *m* (**-chi**) copy, copying; **a ricalco** multiple-copy

ricamare *tr* to embroider

ricambiare §287 *tr* to return; to repay ‖ *ref* to change clothes

ricàm·bio *m* (**-bi**) exchange; spare part; refill; metabolism; **di ricambio** spare (*part*)

ricamo *m* embroidery; needlework; **ricami** (*fig*) embellishments

ricapitolare (**ricapitolo**) *tr* to recapitulate

ricaricare §197 (**ricàrico**) *tr* to reload; to wind (*a watch*); to charge (*a battery*)

ricattare *tr* to blackmail

ricatta·tóre -trice *mf* blackmailer

ricatto *m* blackmail

ricavare *tr* to draw, extract; to obtain, derive

ricavato *m* proceeds; (fig) fruit, yield

ricavo *m* proceeds

ricchézza *f* wealth; **ricchezza mobile** income from personal property; **ricchezze** riches

ric·cio -cia (**-ci -ce**) *adj* curly ‖ *m* curl; shaving; burr; scroll (*of violin*); crook (*of crozier*); (zool) hedgehog; **riccio di mare** (zool) sea urchin

rìcciolo *m* curl

ricciolu·to -ta *adj* curly

ricciu·to -ta *adj* curly

ric·co -ca *adj* (**-chi -che**) rich ‖ **i ricchi** the rich

ricér·ca *f* (**-che**) search; research; **ricerca operativa** operations research

ricercare §197 (**ricérco**) *tr* to search for again; to seek; to investigate; (poet) to pluck (*a musical instrument*)

ricercatézza *f* affectation; sophistication

ricerca·to -ta *adj* sought after, wanted; affected; sophisticated

ricetrasmettitóre *m* two-way radio

ricètta *f* prescription; recipe

ricettàcolo *m* receptacle; depository

ricettare (**ricètto**) *tr* to receive (*stolen goods*); to prescribe

ricettà·rio *m* (**-ri**) recipe book; prescription pad

ricetta·tóre -trice *mf* fence, receiver of stolen goods

ricetti·vo -va *adj* receptive

ricètto *m* (poet) refuge

ricévere §141 *tr* to receive; to get; to contain; to withstand

riceviménto *m* reception; receipt

ricevi·tóre -trice *mf* addressee ‖ *m* receiver; collector; registrar of deeds; **ricevitore postale** postmaster

ricevitorìa *f* collection office; **ricevitoria postale** post office

ricevuta *f* receipt; **accusare ricevuta di** to acknowledge receipt of

ricezióne *f* (rad, telv) reception; **accusare ricezione** to acknowledge receipt

richiamare *tr* to call back; to recall; to call (*e.g., attention*); to quote; to chide ‖ *ref* to refer

richiamato *m* soldier recalled to active duty

richiamo *m* call; recall; admonition; cross reference; advertisement

richièdere §124 *tr* to ask again; to demand; to require; to apply for ‖ *ref* to be required

richiè·sto -sta *adj*—**essere richiesto** to be in demand ‖ *f* request; demand; petition, application

richiùdere §125 *tr* & *ref* to shut again

riciclare *tr* to recycle (*e.g., in the chemical industry*)

ricino *m* castor-oil plant

ricognitóre *m* scout; reconnaissance plane; (law) recognition

ricognizióne *f* recognition; (mil) reconnaissance

ricollegare §209 (**ricollégo**) *tr* to connect ‖ *ref* to be connected; to refer

ricolmare (**ricólmo**) *tr* to fill to the brim; to overwhelm

ricominciare §128 *tr* & *intr* (ESSERE) to begin again, resume

ricomparire §108 *intr* (ESSERE) to reappear

ricomparsa *f* reappearance

ricompènsa *f* compensation, recompense; reward; (mil) award

ricompensare (**ricompènso**) *tr* to compensate, recompense; to reward

ricomperare (**ricómpero**) *tr* var of ricomprare

ricompórre §218 *tr* to recompose; to plan again ‖ *ref* to regain one's composure

ricomprare (**ricómpro**) *tr* to buy again; to buy back

riconcentrare (**riconcèntro**) *tr* to concentrate again; to gather (*one's thoughts*) ‖ *ref* to be withdrawn

riconciliare §287 (**riconcìlio**) *tr* to reconcile ‖ *ref* to become reconciled

ricondurre §102 *tr* to bring back; to take back ‖ *ref* to go back

riconfermare (**riconférmo**) *tr* to reconfirm

riconfortare (**riconfòrto**) *tr* to comfort

ricongiùngere §183 *tr* & *ref* to reunite

riconoscènte *adj* grateful

riconoscènza *f* gratitude

riconóscere §134 *tr* to recognize; (mil) to reconnoiter

riconosciménto *m* recognition; **in riconoscimento di** in recognition of

riconquistare *tr* to reconquer

riconsegnare (**riconségno**) *tr* to give back, to return

riconsiderare (riconsìdero) *tr* to reconsider

ricontare (ricónto) *tr* to recount, count again

riconversióne *f* reconversion

riconvertire §138 *tr* to reconvert; to recycle

ricopèr·to -ta *adj* covered; coated

ricopertura *f* covering; seat cover

ricopiare §287 **(ricòpio)** *tr* to make a fair copy of; to recopy; to copy

ricoprire §110 *tr* to cover; to coat; to hide || *ref* to become covered

ricordanza *f* (poet) memory

ricordare (ricòrdo) *tr* to remember; to remind; to mention || *ref* to remember; **ricordarsi di** to remember

ricòrdo *m* memory; souvenir; **ricordo marmoreo** marble statue

ricorrènte *adj* recurrent, recurring

ricorrènza *f* recurrence; anniversary

ricórrere §139 *intr* (ESSERE & AVERE) to run again; to run back; to resort; to recur; (law) to appeal; **ricorrere a** to have recourse to

ricórso *m* recurrence; recourse; appeal

ricostituènte *adj* invigorating || *m* tonic

ricostituire §176 *tr* to reconstitute, to reform; to reinvigorate

ricostruire §140 *tr* to rebuild; to reconstruct

ricostruzióne *f* rebuilding; reconstruction

ricòtta *f* Italian cottage cheese; **di ricotta** weak

ricoverare (ricòvero) *tr* to shelter || *ref* to take shelter

ricòvero *m* shelter; nursing home; (med) admission; **ricovero antiaereo** air-raid shelter

ricreare (ricrèo) *tr* to recreate; to refresh || *ref* to relax

ricreati·vo -va *adj* refreshing; recreational

ricreatò·rio -ria (-ri -rie) *adj* recreation, recreational || *m* recreation room; playground

ricreazióne *f* recreation; recess

ricrédere §141 *intr*—**far ricredere qlcu** to make s.o. change his mind || *ref* to change one's mind

ricréscere §142 *intr* (ESSERE) to grow again; to swell

ricucire §143 *tr* to sew up

ricuòcere §144a *tr* to cook again; to anneal

ricuperare (ricùpero) *tr* to recover; (naut) to salvage; (sports) to make up for (*rained-out game*)

ricùpero *m* recovery; salvage; rally; making up (*for lost time or postponed game*)

ricur·vo -va *adj* bent; bent over

ricusare *tr* to refuse

ridacchiare §287 *intr* to titter, giggle

ridancia·no -na *adj* prone to laughter; amusing

ridare §230 (*1st sg pres ind* **ridò**) *tr* to give back; to give again; **ridare fuori** to vomit || *intr* (coll) to reappear, e.g., **gli ha ridato il foruncolo** his boil has reappeared || *intr*

(ESSERE)—**ridare giù** to have a relapse

ridda *f* round; confusion; throng

ridènte *adj* laughing; bright, pleasant

rìdere §231 *tr* (poet) to laugh at || *intr* to laugh; (poet) to shine; **far ridere i polli** to be utterly ridiculous; **ridere sotto i baffi** to laugh up one's sleeve || *ref*—**ridersi di** to laugh at

ridestare (ridèsto) *tr* & *ref* to reawaken

ridicolizzare [ddzz] *tr* to ridicule; to twit

ridìco·lo -la *adj* ridiculous || *m* ridicule; ridiculousness

ridipìngere §126 *tr* to paint again

ridire §151 *tr* to tell again; to repeat; to tell (*to express*); **avere** or **trovare a** or **da ridire (su)** to find fault (with)

ridistribuzióne *f* redistribution

ridivenire §282 or **ridiventare (ridivènto)** *intr* (ESSERE) to become again

ridonare (ridóno) *tr* to give back

ridondante *adj* redundant

ridondare (ridóndo) *intr* (ESSERE & AVERE) (fig) to overflow; **ridondare a** or **in** to redound to

ridòsso *m* back; shelter; **a ridosso** sheltered; as a shelter; behind, close behind

ridót·to -ta *adj* reduced; **mal ridotto** down at the heel || *m* lounge; (theat) foyer || *f* (mil) redoubt

ridurre §102 *tr* to reduce; to adapt; to translate; to lead; to curtail; (mus) to arrange || *ref* to be reduced; to retire

riduttóre *m* (mach) reduction gear

riduzióne *f* reduction; (mus) arrangement

riecheggiare §290 **(riechéggio)** *tr* & *intr* to echo

riedificare §197 **(riedìfico)** *tr* to rebuild

rieducare §197 **(rièduco)** *tr* to reeducate

rielèggere §193 *tr* to reelect

rielezióne *f* reelection

riemèrgere §162 *intr* to resurface

riempiménto *m* fill

riempire §163 *tr* to fill; to stuff

riempiti·vo -va *adj* expletive || *m* expletive; fill-in

rientrante *adj* hollow (*cheeks*); (mil) reentrant

rientranza *f* recess

rientrare (rièntro) *intr* (ESSERE) to reenter; to come back; to recede; (coll) to shrink; **rientrare in** to recover (*one's expenses*); **rientrare in sé** to come to one's senses

rièntro *m* reentry

riepilogare §209 **(riepìlogo)** *tr* to sum up, recapitulate

riepìlo·go *m* (-ghi) recapitulation

riesame *m* reexamination

riesaminare (riesàmino) *tr* to reexamine

riesumare *tr* to exhume; (fig) to dig up; (fig) to bring back

rievocare §197 **(rièvoco)** *tr* to recall

rifaciménto *m* adaptation; recasting

rifare §173 (*3d sg* **rifà**) *tr* to do again, redo; to remake; to imitate; to indemnify; to prepare again; to repeat;

to make (*a bed*) || *ref* to recover; to become again; to recoup one's losses; to begin; **rifarsi con** to get even with; **rifarsi da** to begin with

rifasciare §128 *tr* to rebind

riferiménto *m* reference

riferire §176 *tr* to wound again; to refer; to relate || *ref*—**riferirsi a** to refer to; to concern

riffa *f* raffle; lottery; (coll) violence; **di riffa o di raffa** by hook or crook

rifilare *tr* to trim; (coll) to reel off (*a list of names*); (coll) to deal (*a blow*); (coll) to palm off

rifinire §176 *tr* to give the finishing touch to; to wear out || *intr* to stop || *ref* to wear oneself out

rifiorire §176 *tr* (lit) to revive || *intr* to bloom again || *intr* (ESSERE) to flourish; to grow better; to reappear

rifischiare §287 *tr* to whistle again; (coll) to report || *intr* to talk, gossip

rifiutare *tr* to refuse; (lit) to reject || *intr* (cards) to renege, renounce || *ref* to refuse, deny

rifiuto *m* refusal; refuse, rubbish; rejection; rebuff, spurn; (fig) wreck; (cards) renege; **di rifiuto** waste, e.g., **materiale di rifiuto** waste material

riflessióne *f* reflexion

riflessi·vo -va *adj* thoughtful; (gram) reflexive

riflès·so -sa *adj* reflex, e.g., **azione riflessa** reflex action || *m* reflection; (physiol) reflex; **di riflesso** vicarious

riflèttere §177 (*pp* **riflettuto & riflèsso**) *tr & intr* to reflect || *ref* to be reflected

riflettóre *m* searchlight; reflector

rifluire §176 *intr* (ESSERE & AVERE) to flow; to flow back

riflusso *m* flow; ebb, ebb tide

rifocillare *tr* to refresh (*with food*) || *ref* to take refreshment

rifóndere §178 *tr* to melt again; to recast; to refund; to reedit

rifórma *f* reform; (mil) rejection || **Riforma** *f*—**la Riforma** the Reformation

riformare (**rifórmo**) *tr* to reform; to amend; (mil) to reject

riformati·vo -va *adj* reformatory

riforma·tóre -trice *adj* reforming || *mf* reformer

riformatò·rio *m* (**-ri**) reform school, reformatory

riforniménto *m* supply; refueling; **fare rifornimento di** to fill up with; **rifornimenti** supplies

rifornire §176 *tr* to supply; to restock; **rifornire di benzina** to refuel

rifràngere §179 *tr* to crush || *ref* to break (*said of waves*); §179 (*pp* **rifratto**) *tr* to refract || *ref* to be refracted

rifrat·tóre -trice *adj* refracting || *m* refractor

rifrazióne *f* refraction

rifriggere §180 *tr* to fry again; to rehash || *intr* to fry too long or in too much oil

rifrit·to -ta *adj* fried again; (fig) hack-

neyed || *m* taste of stale fat; (fig) rehash

rifuggire *tr* to avoid || *intr*—**rifuggire da** to abhor || *intr* (ESSERE) to take refuge

rifugiare §290 *ref* to take refuge, take shelter

rifugiato *m* refugee

rifù·gio *m* (**-gi**) refuge; **rifugio alpino** mountain hut; **rifugio antiaereo** air-raid shelter; **rifugio antiatomico** fall-out shelter

rifùlgere §233 *intr* (ESSERE & AVERE) to shine

rifusióne *f* recast; refund, reimbursement

ri·ga *f* (**-ghe**) line; row; rank; ruler; part (*in hair*); stripe; (fig) quality

rigàglie *fpl* giblets

rigàgnolo *m* rivulet; gutter (*at the side of a road*)

rigare §209 *tr* to rule, line; to stripe; to mark; to rifle (*gun*) || *intr*—**rigare diritto** to toe the line

rigatino *m* gingham

rigattière *m* second-hand dealer

rigatura *f* ruling; rifling (*of gun*)

rigenerare (**rigènero**) *tr* to regenerate; to reclaim; to recycle || *ref* to become regenerate

rigenera·tóre *m*—**rigeneratore per i capelli** hair restorer

rigettare (**rigètto**) *tr* to throw back; to reject; to recast; (slang) to throw up || *intr* to sprout

rigetto *m* rejection

righèllo *m* ruler

rigidi·tà *f* (**-tà**) rigidity; rigor; stiffness; **rigidità cadaverica** rigor mortis

rìgi·do -da *adj* rigid, stiff; severe

rigirare *tr* to keep turning; to dupe; to invest; to encircle || *intr* to ramble || *ref* to turn around; to tumble

ri·go *m* (**-ghi**) line; **rigo musicale** (mus) staff

rigò·glio *m* (**-gli**) luxuriance; bloom; gurgling

rigonfiare §287 (**rigónfio**) *tr* to inflate || *intr* (ESSERE) & *ref* to swell up

rigóre *m* rigor; severity; precision; **a rigor di termini** strictly speaking; **di rigore** de rigueur; (sports) penalty (*e.g., kick*)

rigorismo *m* rigorism, strictness, severity

rigori·sta *mf* (**-sti -ste**) rigorist || *m* (soccer) kicker of penalty goal

rigoró·so -sa [s] *adj* rigorous, strict

rigovernare (**rigovèrno**) *tr* to clean, wash (*dishes*); to groom, tend (*animals*)

riguadagnare *tr* to regain

riguardare *tr* to look again; to look back; to examine; to consider; to take care of; to concern || *intr*—**riguardare a** to look out for; to face (*said of a window*) || *ref* to take care of oneself; **riguardarsi da** to keep away from

riguardo *m* care; esteem; regard; **a questo riguardo** in this regard; **ri-**

guardo a as far as . . . is concerned; **senza riguardo a** irrespective of

riguardó·so -sa [s] *adj* considerate

rigurgitare (rigùrgito) *tr & intr* to regurgitate

rilanciare §128 *tr* to toss back; to re-establish (*e.g., fashions*); (poker) to raise

rilasciare §128 *tr* to free, let go; to relax; to grant || *ref* to relax

rilà·scio *m* (**-sci**) release; delivery; granting, issue (*of a document*)

rilassante *adj* relaxing

rilassare *tr & ref* to relax

rilassatézza *f* laxity

rilegare §209 **(rilégo)** *tr* to tie again; to bind, rebind (*a book*); to set (*a stone*)

rilega·tóre -trice *mf* binder

rilegatura *f* binding

rilèggere §193 *tr* to reread

rilènto *m*—**a rilento** slowly

rilevaménto *m* survey; (naut) bearing

rilevare (rilèvo) *tr* to lift again; to observe; to draw; to bring out; to survey; to take over; to pick up; (mil) to relieve || *intr* to be delineated; to be of import || *ref* to rise again; to recover

rilevatà·rio *m* (**-ri**) successor; (law) assignee

rilièvo *m* relief; survey; remark; assumption (*of debts*); taking over (*of business*); **mettere in rilievo** to bring out; to set off

rilò·ga *f* (**-ghe**) traverse rod

rilucènte *adj* shiny, shining

rilùcere §234 *intr* to shine

riluttante *adj* reluctant

riluttanza *f* reluctance

rima *f* rhyme; slit; crevice; **rispondere per le rime** to answer in kind, to retort

rimandare *tr* to send back; to refer; to dismiss; to put off, postpone; to refer; **rimandare a ottobre** to condition (*a student*)

rimando *m* delay; reference; footnote; repartee; postponement; (sports) return

rimaneggiare §290 **(rimanéggio)** *tr* to rearrange; to reshuffle; to shake up (*personnel*); to rewrite (*news*)

rimanènte *adj* remaining || *m* remainder; remnant; **i rimanenti** the rest

rimanènza *f* remainder

rimanére §235 *intr* (ESSERE) to remain, stay; to be in agreement; to have left, e.g., **mi sono rimasti solo tre dollari** I only have three dollars left; to be located; (poet) to stop; **rimanerci** (coll) to be killed; (coll) to be duped; **rimanere da** to depend on, e.g., **questo rimane da Lei** this depends on you

rimangiare §290 *tr* to eat again || *ref*—**rimangiarsi la parola** to go back on one's word

rimarcare §197 *tr* to mark again; to point out

rimar·co *m* (**-chi**) remark, notice

rimare *tr & intr* to rhyme

rimarginare (rimàrgino) *tr, intr & ref* to heal

rimaritare *tr & ref* to marry again

rimasù·glio *m* (**-gli**) leftover

rima·tóre -trice *mf* poet; rhymster

rimbalzare *intr* (ESSERE & AVERE) to bounce back, rebound

rimbalzo *m* rebound

rimbambire §176 *intr* (ESSERE) & *ref* to become feeble-minded (*from old age*)

rimbambi·to -ta *adj* feeble-minded || *mf* dotard

rimbeccare §197 **(rimbécco)** *tr* to peck; to retort

rimbecilli·to -ta *adj* feeble-minded

rimboccare §197 **(rimbócco)** *tr* to tuck up; to tuck in; to fill to the brim

rimbombare (rimbómbo) *intr* (ESSERE & AVERE) to thunder, boom

rimbómbo *m* thunder, boom

rimborsare (rimbórso) *tr* to reimburse, pay back

rimbórso *m* repayment

rimboscare §197 **(rimbòsco)** *tr* to reforest || *ref* to take to the woods

rimboschiménto *m* reforestation

rimboschire §176 *tr* to reforest || *intr* (ESSERE) to become wooded

rimbrottare (rimbròtto) *tr* to scold

rimbròtto *m* scolding

rimediare §287 **(rimèdio)** *tr* (coll) to scrape together; (coll) to patch up || *intr* (with *dat*) to remedy; to make up (*lost time*)

rimè·dio *m* (**-di**) remedy

rimembranza *f* remembrance

rimeritare (rimèrito) *tr* to reward

rimescolare (riméscolo) *tr* to stir; to shuffle (*cards*)

riméssa *f* remittance; shipment; harvest; store; loss; sprout; carriage house; garage; (sports) return; (sports) putting in play; **rimessa del tram** carbarn

rimestare (rimésto) *tr* to stir

rimèttere §198 *tr* to remit; to put back; to set back; to sprout; to postpone, defer; to ship; to vomit; to recover; to deliver; to straighten up; (sports) to return; **rimetterci** to lose; **rimettere a nuovo** to renovate; **rimettere in ordine** to tidy up; **rimettere in piedi** to rebuild, restore || *intr* (coll) to sprout; (coll) to grow; (lit) to abate || *ref* to recover; to quiet down; to defer; to be clearing (*said of weather*); **rimettersi a** to go back to (*e.g., bed*); **rimettersi a** + *inf* to start + *ger* + again; **rimettersi in cammino** to start off again

rimirare *tr* to stare at

rimmel *m* mascara

rimodellare (rimodèllo) *tr* to remodel

rimodernare (rimodèrno) *tr* to modernize; to remodel; to bring up to date || *ref* to become modern

rimónta *f* reassembly; return (*of migratory birds*); revamping (*of shoes*); (mil) remount

rimontare (rimónto) *tr* to rewind; to go up (*a stream*); to vamp (*shoes*); to renovate; to regain; to reassemble (a machine); (mil) to remount ‖ intr (ESSERE & AVERE) to climb again; to go back (in time)

rimorchiare §287 (rimòrchio) tr to tow; to drag along

rimorchiatóre m tugboat; tow car

rimòr·chio m (-chi) tow; trailer; prendere a rimorchio to take in tow

rimòrdere §200 tr to bite again; to prick (said, e.g., of conscience)

rimòrso m remorse

rimostranza f remonstrance

rimostrare (rimóstro) tr to show again ‖ intr to remonstrate; rimostrare a to remonstrate with

rimozióne f removal; demotion

rimpannucciare §128 tr to outfit better ‖ ref to be better dressed; to be better off

rimpastare tr to knead again; to reshuffle, remake

rimpasto m reshuffling, rearrangement

rimpatriare §287 tr to repatriate ‖ intr to be repatriated

rimpà·trio m (-tri) repatriation

rimpètto adv opposite; di rimpetto a opposite to; in comparison with

rimpiàngere §215 tr to regret; to mourn

rimpianto m regret

rimpiattare a ref to hide; giocare a rimpiattarsi to play hide-and-seek

rimpiattino m hide-and-seek

rimpiazzare tr to replace

rimpiazzo m replacement, substitute

rimpiccolire §176 tr to make smaller ‖ intr (ESSERE) to get smaller

rimpinzare tr to stuff, cram

rimproverare (rimpròvero) tr to chide, reproach; rimproverare qlcu di qlco or rimproverare qlco a qlcu to reproach s.o. for s.th

rimpròvero m reproach, rebuke

rimuginare (rimùgino) tr & intr to rummage; to stir; to ruminate

rimunerare (rimùnero) tr to reward ‖ intr to pay

rimunerati·vo -va adj remunerative; rewarding

rimunerazióne f remuneration

rimuòvere §202 tr to remove; to demote; to move

rinàscere §203 intr (ESSERE) to be born again; to grow again; to revive; far rinascere to revive

rinascimén to m rebirth ‖ Rinascimento m Renaissance

rinàscita f rebirth

rincagna·to -ta adj snub (nose)

rincalzare tr to hill (plants); to underpin; to tuck in

rincalzo m reinforcement; support

rincantucciare §128 tr & ref to hide in a corner

rincarare tr to raise the price of; to raise; rincarare la dose to add insult to injury ‖ intr (ESSERE) to rise, go up (said of prices)

rincasare [s] intr (ESSERE) to return home

rinchiùdere §125 tr to enclose, shut in

rinchiu·so -sa [s] adj shut in; musty ‖ m—saper di rinchiuso to smell musty

rincitrullire §176 intr (ESSERE) to grow stupid

rincóntro m—a rincontro opposite

rincorare §236 tr to encourage ‖ ref to take heart

rincórrere §139 tr to pursue, chase

rincórsa f—prendere la rincorsa to take off (for a jump); to get a running start

rincréscere §142 intr (ESSERE) (with dat) to displease; to be sorry, e.g., gli rincresce he is sorry; to mind, Le rincresce? do you mind?

rincresciménto m regret

rincrudire §176 tr to sharpen; to embitter ‖ intr (ESSERE) to become bitter; to get worse

rinculare intr (ESSERE & AVERE) to back up; to recoil

rinculo m recoil

rinfacciare §128 tr to throw in one's face

rinfarcire §176 tr to stuff

rinfiancare §197 tr to support

rinfocolare (rinfòcolo) tr to rekindle; to revive

rinfoderare (rinfòdero) tr sheathe

rinforzare (rinfòrzo) tr to reinforce; strengthen ‖ intr (ESSERE) & ref to become stronger

rinfòrzo m reinforcement

rinfrancare §197 tr to reassure ‖ ref to buck up

rinfrescante adj refreshing ‖ m mild laxative

rinfrescare §197 (rinfrésco) tr to refresh; to restore; to renew ‖ intr (ESSERE & AVERE) to cool off (said of the weather) ‖ ref to have some refreshments; to cool off

rinfré·sco m (-schi) refreshment

rinfusa f—alla rinfusa at random; pell-mell; in bulk

ringalluzzire §176 tr & ref to perk up

ringhiare §287 intr to growl, to snarl

ringhièra f railing

rin·ghio m (-ghi) growl, snarl

ringiovaniménto m rejuvenation

ringiovanire §176 tr to rejuvenate ‖ intr (ESSERE) to grow or look younger

ringraziaménto m thanks

ringraziare §287 tr to thank; to dismiss

ringuainare (ringuaìno) tr to sheathe

rinnegare §209 (rinnègo & rinnégo) tr to forswear; to repudiate

rinnega·to -ta adj & m renegade

rinnovaménto m renewal; reawakening

rinnovare (rinnòvo) tr to renew; to renovate; to restore; to replace ‖ ref to occur again; to renew

rinnovellare (rinnovèllo) tr to repeat; (poet) to renew ‖ intr (ESSERE) & ref to change; to renew

rinnòvo m renewal

rinocerónte m rhinoceros

rinomanza f renown

rinoma·to -ta adj renowned, famous

rinsaldare tr to starch; (fig) to strengthen ‖ ref to become confirmed (in one's opinion)

rinsanguare (rinsànguo) *tr* to give new strength to ‖ *ref* to regain strength; to recover

rinsavire §176 *intr* (ESSERE) to return to reason

rintanare *ref* to burrow; to hide

rintóc·co *m* (**-chi**) toll (*of bell*)

rintontire §176 *tr* to stun, to daze

rintracciare §128 *tr* to track down

rintronare (rintròno) *tr* to deafen; to make rumble ‖ *intr* (ESSERE & AVERE) to thunder; to rumble

rintuzzare *tr* to dull, blunt; to repel; to repress

rinùn·cia *f* (**-ce**) or **rinùnzia** *f* renunciation

rinunziare §287 *tr* to renounce ‖ *intr* (with *dat*) to give up, renounce, e.g., **rinunziò al trono** he renounced the throne

rinvangare §209 *tr* & *intr* var of **rivangare**

rinvenire §282 *tr* to find ‖ *intr* (ESSERE) to come to; far **rinvenire** to bring to, revive

rinviare §119 *tr* to send back; to postpone; to refer; to adjourn; to remit (*to a lower court*)

rinvigorire §176 *tr* to strengthen ‖ *intr* (ESSERE) & *ref* to regain strength

rinví·o *m* (**-i**) return; postponement; adjournment; reference; (law) continuance

rì·o *m* (**-i**) (lit) sin; (lit) brook; (coll) canal

rioccupare (riòccupo) *tr* to reoccupy

rioccupazióne *f* reoccupation

rionale *adj* neighborhood

rióne *m* district; neighborhood

riordinare (riórdino) *tr* to rearrange; to reorganize; to order again

riorganizzare [ddzz] *tr* to reorganize

riottó·so -sa [s] *adj* (lit) quarrelsome; (lit) unruly, rebellious

ripa *f* (lit) bank (*of river*); (lit) escarpment

ripagare §209 *tr* to repay; to pay again

riparare *tr* to protect; to mend, fix, repair; to make up (*an exam*) ‖ *intr* —**riparare a** to make up for ‖ *intr* (ESSERE) & *ref* to take refuge; to betake oneself

riparazióne *f* repair; reparation; redress; (educ) make-up

riparlare *intr* to speak again; **ne riparleremo!** you will see!

riparo *m* repair; shelter

ripartire §176 *tr* to divide; to distribute; to share ‖ (**riparto**) *intr* (ESSERE) to leave again; to start again ‖ §176 *ref* to split up

ripartizióne *f* division; distribution

riparto *m* division; distribution; allotment

ripassare *tr* to cross again; to brush up, review; to repass; to sift again; to check; to read over; (mach) to overhaul ‖ *intr* (ESSERE) to go by; to come by

ripassata *f* checkup; review; (coll) rebuke

ripassa·tóre -trice *mf* checker

ripasso *m* return (*of birds*); (coll) review

ripensare (ripènso) *intr* to keep thinking; **ripensare a** to think of again; to think over again

ripentire (ripènto) *ref* to repent; **ripentirsi di** to repent

ripercórrere §139 *tr* to retrace

ripercuòtere §251 *tr* to reflect; to strike again ‖ *ref* to reverberate

ripescare §197 (**ripésco**) *tr* to fish again; (fig) to dig up

ripètere *tr* & *intr* to repeat ‖ *ref* to be repeated

ripeti·tóre -trice *mf* repeater; coach; tutor ‖ *m* (rad, telv) rebroadcasting station; (rad) relay

ripetizióne *f* repetition; review; tutoring; **a ripetizione** repeating (*firearm*)

ripiano *m* terrace; ledge; shelf; landing; (com) balancing

ripic·co *m* (**-chi**) pique; spite

ripi·do -da *adj* steep

ripiegaménto *m* bend; (mil) withdrawal, retreat

ripiegare §209 (**ripiègo**) *tr* to fold, fold over ‖ *intr* to do better; (mil) to fall back ‖ *ref* to bend over; to withdraw into oneself

ripiè·go *m* (**-ghi**) expedient

ripiè·no -na *adj* full; stuffed ‖ *m* stuffing; (culin) filling

ripigliare §280 *tr* to reacquire; to catch again; to begin again ‖ *intr* to recover ‖ *ref* to renew a quarrel

ripiombare (ripiómbo) *tr* to make plumb; (fig) to plunge back ‖ *intr* (ESSERE) (fig) to plunge back

ripopolare (ripòpolo) *tr* to repopulate; to restock (*e.g., a pond*)

ripórre §218 *tr* to put back; to place (*one's hope*); to repose (*one's trust*) ‖ *ref* to back down; **riporsi a** + *inf* to start + *ger* again

riportare (ripòrto) *tr* to bring back; to report; to get; to transfer (*a design*); (com) to carry forward; (hunt) to retrieve; (math) to carry ‖ *ref* to go back

ripòrto *m* filler; retrieving; (com) balance carried forward; (math) number carried

riposante [s] *adj* restful

riposare [s] (**ripòso**) *tr*, *intr* & *ref* to rest

ripòso [s] *m* rest; repose; Requiem; retirement; **buon riposo!** sleep well!; **mettere a riposo** to retire; **riposo!** (mil) at ease

ripostì·glio *m* (**-gli**) closet

ripó·sto -sta *adj* innermost ‖ *m* (coll) pantry

riprèndere §220 *tr* to take back; to take up again; to get back; to take in (*a garment*); to catch (*s.th thrown in the air*); to take up (*arms*); to get; to reconquer; to start again, resume; to reprehend; to recover; (mov, telv) to shoot; **riprendere moglie** to remarry ‖ *intr* to start again; to recover, improve; to pick up (*said of a* *motor*) || *ref* to recover; to catch oneself up

riprésa [s] *f* resumption; (aut) pickup; (theat) revival; (mov) shooting, take; (boxing) round; (soccer) second half; (mus, pros) refrain; **a più riprese** several times

ripresentàre (ripresènto) *tr* to present again

ripristinàre (riprìstino) *tr* to restore; to reestablish

ripristino *m* revival, restoration

riprodurre §102 *tr* to reproduce; to express || *ref* to reproduce; to occur

riprodut·tóre -trice *adj* reproducing || *mf* reproducer || *m* reproducer (*e.g.*, *of sound*)

riproduzióne *f* reproduction; playback (*e.g.*, *of tape*)

ripromèttere §198 *tr* to promise again || *ref* to hope; to propose; to hope for

ripròva *f* new proof; confirmation

riprovàre (ripròvo) *tr* to try again; to try on again; to feel, experience again; to flunk; to censure || *ref* to try again

riprovazióne *f* disapproval

ripudiàre §287 *tr* to repudiate

ripugnànte *adj* repugnant, repulsive

ripugnànza *f* repugnance; aversion

ripugnàre *intr* (with *dat*) to disgust, revolt, be repugnant to

ripulìre §176 *tr* to clean again; to tidy up; to clean up; to polish || *ref* to be dressed up; to become polished

ripulìta *f*—**dare una ripulìta a** to give a lick and a promise to; **fare una ripulìta** (fig) to clean house

ripulsì·vo -va *adj* repulsive

riquadràre *tr* to square; to decorate (*a room*) || *intr* to measure; to square

riquadro *m* square

risac·ca [s] *f* (-che) undertow; backwash

risàia [s] *f* rice field

risalìre [s] §242 *tr* to go up again; to stem (*the tide*); **risalìre la corrente** to go upstream || *intr* (ESSERE) to climb again; to reascend; (com) to appreciate; to date back

risaltàre [s] *tr* to jump again || *intr* (ESSERE & AVERE) to rebound || *intr* to stand out; **far risaltàre** to emphasize

risàlto [s] *m* emphasis; prominence; relief; foil

risanàre [s] *tr* to heal; to reclaim (*land*); to redevelop (*urban areas*); to reorganize || *intr* (ESSERE) to heal; to improve

risapére [s] §243 *tr* to find out

risapù·to -ta [s] *adj* well-known

risarciménto [s] *m* indemnification, redress

risarcìre [s] §176 *tr* to indemnify; to compensate

risàta [s] *f* outburst of laughter

risatìna [s] *f* chuckle

riscaldaménto *m* heating; inflammation

riscaldàre *tr* to heat; to warm up; to inflame || *ref* to warm up; to go in heat; to perspire; to get excited

riscàldo *m* inflammation; prickly heat; padding (*for clothes*)

riscattàre *tr* to ransom; to redeem || *intr* (ESSERE) to click again (*said, e.g., of a ratchet*)

riscàtto *m* ransom; redemption

rischiaràre *tr*, *intr* (ESSERE) & *ref* to clear, clear up

rischiàre §287 *tr* to risk || *intr* to run a risk

rì·schio *m* (-schi) risk

rischió·so -sa [s] *adj* risky

risciacquàre (risciàcquo) *tr* to rinse

risciacquatùra *f* rinse; swill

risciàcquo *m* rinsing (*of mouth*); mouthwash

riscónto *m* (com) discount

riscontràre (riscóntro) *tr* to compare, collate; to check; to reply to || *intr* to reply; to tally || *ref* to tally

riscóntro *m* comparison; check, control; draft; correspondence; reply; **far riscóntro** to correspond; **far riscóntro con** to correspond to; **far riscóntro di** to check; **mettere a riscóntro** to compare; **riscóntri** drafts (*of air*); parts (*that fit together*)

riscoprìre §110 *tr* to rediscover

riscòssa *f* insurrection; recovery, reconquest; (mil) counterattack

riscossióne *f* collection

riscrìvere §250 *tr* to rewrite; to write back

riscuòtere §251 *tr* to shake; to wake up; to collect; to get; to redeem || *ref* to wake up; to come to one's senses

riseccàre [s] §197 **(risécco)** *tr*, *intr* (ESSERE) & *ref* to dry up

risecchìre [s] §176 *intr* (ESSERE) & *ref* to dry up

risentiménto [s] *m* resentment, pique

risentìre [s] **(risènto)** *tr* to hear again; to feel || *intr*—**risentìre di** to feel the effects of || *ref* to take offense; to wake up; to come to one's senses; (telp) to talk again; **a risentìrci!** (telp) until we talk again!; **risentìrsi con** to resent (*a person*); **risentìrsi di** to feel the effects of; **risentìrsi per** to resent (*an act*)

risentì·to -ta [s] *adj* heard again; resentful; strong; swift; incisive

riserbàre [s] **(risèrbo)** *tr* var of **riservàre**

risèrbo [s] *m* var of **risèrvo**

risèrva [s] *f* preservation; exclusive rights; preserve; reserve; supply; backlog; reservation; circumspection; vintage

riservàre [s] **(risèrvo)** *tr* to reserve

riservatézza [s] *f* reservedness

riservà·to -ta [s] *adj* reserved; private; classified

riservìsta [s] *m* (-sti) reservist

risèrvo [s] *m* discretion

risguardo *m* end paper

risièdere [s] *intr* to reside

rìsma *f* ream; (fig) type

rìso [s] *m* rice || *m* (**rìsa** *fpl*) laugh; laughter; jest; cheer; (lit) smile

risolàre [s] §257 *tr* to resole

risolìno [s] *m* smile; giggle

risollevare [s] **(risollèvo)** tr to raise again; to lift ‖ ref to rise

risolutézza [s] f resoluteness

risolu·to -ta [s] adj resolved, determined

risoluzióne [s] f resolution; resolve; dissolution

risòlvere [s] §256 *(pret ind* **risolvéi** *or* **risolvètti** *or* **risòlsi;** *pp* **risòlto)** tr to resolve; to solve; to dissolve; to persuade ‖ ref to dissolve; to resolve

risolvìbile [s] adj solvable

risonante [s] adj resounding

risonanza [s] f resonance; (fig) sensation

risonare [s] §257 tr to ring again; (lit) to repeat ‖ intr (ESSERE & AVERE) to resonate; to resound; to ring again; to echo

risórgere [s] §258 intr (ESSERE) to rise again; to revive, to come back to life; to recover

risorgiménto [s] m renaissance; resurgence ‖ **Risorgimento** m Risorgimento

risórsa [s] f resource

risór·to -ta [s] adj arisen; reborn

risòtto [s] m risotto, rice cooked with broth

risparmiare §287 tr to save; to spare

rispàr·mio m (-mi) saving; sparing; savings; **risparmi** savings; **senza risparmio** lavishly

rispecchiare §287 **(rispècchio)** tr to reflect

rispedire §176 tr to send back; to forward; to reship

rispedizióne f reshipment

rispettàbile adj respectable

rispettare (rispètto) tr to respect; **farsi rispettare** to command respect; **rispettare sé stesso** to have self-respect

rispettì·vo -va adj respective

rispètto m respect; observance; restriction (e.g., in building); comparison; regard; **con rispetto parlando** excuse the word; **di rispetto** (naut) spare (e.g., parts); **rispetti** regards; **rispetto di sé medesimo** self-respect; **rispetto umano** fear of what people will say

rispettó·so -sa [s] adj respectful; respectable (distance)

risplendènte adj resplendent

risplèndere §281 intr (ESSERE & AVERE) to shine

rispóndere §238 tr to answer; **risponder picche** (coll) to say no ‖ intr to answer; **rispondere a** to answer (e.g., a letter); **rispondere con un cenno del capo** to nod assent; **rispondere di** to be responsible for; **rispondere in** to face, overlook

risposare (rispòso) tr & ref to marry again, remarry

rispósta f answer, reply, response

rissa f scuffle, brawl

rissó·so -sa [s] adj quarrelsome

ristabilire §176 tr to reestablish ‖ ref to recover

ristagnare tr to tin; to solder ‖ intr to stagnate

ristampa f reprint

ristampare tr to reprint

ristorante m restaurant

ristorare (ristòro) tr & ref to refresh

ristora·tóre -trice adj refreshing ‖ m restaurant

ristòro m refreshment; compensation

ristrettézza f narrowness; scarcity; **ristrettezza d'idee** narrow-mindedness

ristrét·to -ta adj narrow; limited; in straitened circumstances; concentrated, condensed (e.g., broth)

ristrutturazióne f restructuring

risùc·chio [s] m (-chi) whirlpool

risultante [s] adj resulting ‖ m & f resultant; (phys) resultant

risultare [s] intr (ESSERE) to result; to prove to be, turn out to be; to appear

risultato [s] m result

risurrezióne [s] f resurrection

risuscitare [s] **(risùscito)** tr to resurrect; to revive ‖ intr to be resurrected; to be revived

risvegliare §280 **(risvéglio)** tr & ref to awaken; to reawaken

risvé·glio m (-gli) awakening, reawakening

risvòlto m cuff; lapel; inside flap (of book); minor aspect (of a question)

ritagliare §280 tr to cut again; to clip; to trim

rità·glio m (-gli) clipping (of paper); scrap (of meat); cutting (of fabric); bit (of time); **al ritaglio** retail

ritappezzare (ritappézzo) tr to repaper

ritardare tr to delay; to slow down, retard; ‖ intr to tarry; to be late; to be slow (said of a watch)

ritardatà·rio -ria mf (-ri -rie) latecomer; (com) delinquent

ritardo m delay; retard; lateness; **essere in ritardo** to be late

ritégno m reservation; discretion; **senza ritegno** shamelessly

ritemprare (ritèmpro) tr to temper again; to invigorate ‖ ref to harden

ritenére §271 tr to retain; to hold; to withhold; to believe, think ‖ ref to restrain oneself; to consider oneself; to be considered

ritentare (ritènto) tr to try again; (law) to retry

ritirare tr to withdraw; to pay (a note); to throw back; to shoot again; to accept delivery of; to take back (a promise) ‖ intr to shrink ‖ ref to shrink; to withdraw; to fall back, retreat; to retire

ritirata f toilet; (mil) retreat

ritiro m withdrawal; retreat; retirement; shrinkage; (metallurgy) shrinking

ritma·to -ta adj measured (step)

ritmi·co -ca adj (-ci -che) rhythmic(al)

ritmo m rhythm; **a ritmo serrato** at a quick pace

rito m rite; (fig) ritual, ceremony; **di rito** customary

ritoccare §197 **(ritócco)** tr to retouch; to brush up

ritóc·co m (-chi) retouch; improvement; change

ritòrcere §272 *tr* to twist, twine; to wring; to retort

ritornare (ritórno) *tr* to return, give back || *intr* (ESSERE) to return, go back, come back; **ritornare in sé** to come back to one's senses

ritornèllo *m* refrain; chorus (*of song*)

ritórno *m* return; reoccurrence; **di ritorno** reoccurring; **essere di ritorno** to be back; **far ritorno** to return; **ritorno di fiamma** backfire

ritòr·to -ta *adj* twisted || *m* twist

ritrarre §273 *tr* to retract; to draw; to portray || *intr*—**ritrarre da** to look like || *ref* to retreat; to portray oneself

ritrasméttere §198 *tr* (rad, telv) to retransmit, rebroadcast

ritrattare *tr* to treat again; to retract; (coll) to portray || *ref* to recant

ritrattazióne *f* retraction

ritratti·sta *mf* (-sti -ste) portrait painter

ritratto *m* portrait, picture; photograph; **ritratto parlante** spit and image

ritri·to -ta *adj* (fig) stale, trite

ritrósa [s] *f* (coll) cowlick

ritrosia [s] *f* coyness, shyness

ritró·so -sa *adj* coy, shy; **a ritroso** backwards || *f see* **ritrosa**

ritrovare (ritròvo) *tr* to discover; to find; to regain; to meet again || *ref* to meet again; to find oneself; to find one's bearings; **non ritrovarcisi** to be out of sorts

ritrovato *m* discovery, find

ritròvo *m* meeting; nightspot; **ritrovo estivo** summer resort; **ritrovo notturno** night club

rit·to -ta *adj* upright; straight; right || *m* face (*of medal*); prop; (sports) post || *f* (lit) right hand

rituale *adj* & *m* ritual

riunióne *f* reunion; meeting; assembly; **riunione alla sommità** summit conference

riunire §176 *tr* to assemble; to reunite; to reconcile || *ref* to gather together; to meet; to be reunited; to rally

riuscire §277 *intr* (ESSERE) to go out again; to turn out, turn out to be; to lead (*said, e.g., of a door*); to succeed; **riuscire a** + *inf* to succeed in + *ger* || *impers*—**riesce** (with *dat*) **di** + *inf* to succeed in + *ger*, e.g., **non gli è riuscito di farsi ricevere** he did not succeed in being received

riuscita *f* success; result; outlet

riva *f* shore; bank; (naut) board

rivale *adj* & *mf* rival

rivaleggiare §290 (**rivaléggio**) *intr* to compete; **rivaleggiare con** to rival

rivalére §278 *ref*—**rivalersi di** to use; **rivalersi su qlcu** to resort to s.o. for compensation; to fall back on s.o., to have recourse to s.o.

rivali·tà *f* (-tà) rivalry

rivalsa *f* compensation; revenge; (com) recourse

rivalutare (rivàluto & **rivaluto)** *tr* to revalue

rivalutazióne *f* reassessment

rivangare §209 *tr* to rake up; to mull over || *intr* to reminisce

rivedére §279 *tr* to see again; to review; to check; to reread; to revise; to read (*proof*) || *ref* to see one another; **a rivederci! good-bye!, au revoir!**

rivedìbile *adj* deferred (*for draft*)

rivelare (rivélo) *tr* to reveal; to detect; (phot) to develop

rivela·tóre -trice *adj* revealing || *m* (phot) developer; (rad) detector; **rivelatore di mine** mine detector

rivelazióne *f* revelation

rivéndere §281 *tr* to resell; (fig) to surpass

rivendicare §197 (**rivéndico**) *tr* to demand; to claim

rivendicazióne *f* demand; claim

rivéndita *f* resale; shop; **rivendita sali e tabacchi** cigar store

rivendi·tóre -trice *mf* seller, dealer, retailer

rivendùgliolo *m* peddler; huckster

rivèrbero *m* reverberation; reflection; glare; echo

riverènte *adj* reverent

riverènza *f* reverence; curtsy, bow

riverire §176 *tr* to revere; to pay one's respects to

riversare (rivèrso) *tr* to pour again; to transfer || *ref* to overflow

rivèr·so -sa *adj* on one's back

rivestiménto *m* coating; covering; lining

rivestire (rivèsto) *tr* to dress again; to coat; to line; to cover; to wear; to have (*importance*); to hold (*a rank*) || *ref* to get dressed again; to wear; to be covered

rivièra *f* coast || **Riviera** *f* Riviera

riviera·sco -sca *adj* (**-schi -sche**) coastal; riverside

rivincere §285 *tr* to win back

rivincita *f* revenge; return match; **prendersi la rivincita** to get even

rivista *f* review; parade; magazine, journal, revue; proofreading

rivivere §286 *tr* to relive || *intr* (ESSERE) to live again; to revive

rivo *m* (lit) rivulet, brook

rivolare (rivólo) *intr* (ESSERE & AVERE) to fly again

rivolére §288 *tr* to want back

rivòlgere §289 *tr* to turn again; to revolve; to overturn; to train (*a weapon*); to address; to deter || *ref* to turn; to turn around; **rivolgersi a** to apply to

rivolgiménto *m* turn; revolution; upheaval

rivòlta *f* revolt; cuff

rivoltante *adj* revolting

rivoltare (rivòlto) *tr* to overturn; to turn inside out; to toss (*salad*); to upset || *ref* to turn around; to revolt; to toss

rivoltèlla *f* revolver; spray gun

rivoltellata *f* revolver shot

rivoltó·so -sa [s] *adj* rebellious || *m* rioter; rebel

rivoluzionare (rivoluzióno) *tr* to revolutionize

rivoluzionà·rio -ria *adj & mf* (**-ri -rie**) revolutionary

rivoluzióne *f* revolution

rizza *f* (naut) rigging

rizzare *tr* to raise; to hoist; to pay (*attention*); to build; (naut) to lash || *ref* to rise; to bristle (*said of hair*); to rear up (*said of a horse*)

ròba *f* things, stuff; property

robìnia *f* locust tree

robivèc·chi *m* (**-chi**) junk dealer

robu·sto -sta *adj* robust; burly

róc·ca *f* (**-che**) distaff

ròc·ca *f* (**-che**) fortress

roccafòrte *f* (**rocchefòrti**) stronghold

rocchétto *m* spool; reel; coil; roll (*of film*); pinion, rear sprocket wheel; (eccl) rochet; **rocchetto d'accensione** ignition coil; **rocchetto d'induzione** induction coil

ròc·cia *f* (**-ce**) rock; crag; cliff

rocció·so -sa [s] *adj* rocky

ròc·co -ca *adj* (**-chi -che**) hoarse; (poet) faint

rodàg·gio *m* (**-gi**) breaking in, running in; adjustment period (*to a new situation*); **in rodaggio** (aut) being run in

Ròdano *m* Rhone

rodare (**ròde**) *tr* to break in; (aut) to run in

ródere §239 *tr* to gnaw; to bite; to corrode || *ref* to worry, to fret

Ròdi *f* Rhodes

rodì·o *m* (**-i**) gnawing

rodi·tóre -trice *adj* gnawing || *mf* rodent

rodomónte *m* braggart

rogare §209 (**rògo**) *tr* to draw up (*a contract*); (law) to request

rògito *m* (law) instrument, deed

rógna *f* mange; itch

rognóne *m* (culin) kidney

rognó·so -sa [s] *adj* scabby, mangy

rò·go *m* (**-ghi**) pyre; stake

rollì·o *m* (**-i**) roll (*of ship*)

Róma *f* Rome

romané·sco -sca *adj* (**-schi -sche**) Roman (*dialect*)

Romania, la Rumania

romàni·co -ca *adj & m* (**-ci -che**) Romanesque

roma·no -na *adj & mf* Roman; **pagare alla romana** to go Dutch

romanticismo *m* romanticism

romànti·co -ca (**-ci -che**) *adj* romantic || *mf* romanticist

romanza *f* romance; ballad

romanzare *tr* to fictionalize

romanzé·sco -sca *adj* (**-schi -sche**) romantic; of chivalry; novelistic

romanzière *m* novelist

roman·zo -za *adj* Romance (*language*) || *m* novel; story; romance; fiction; **romanzi** fiction; **romanzo a fumetti** comic strip; comic book; **romanzo d'appendice** serial story, feuilleton; **romanzo giallo** whodunit; **romanzo rosa** love story

rombare (**rómbo**) *intr* to thunder

rómbo *m* thunder, roar

romè·no -na *adj & mf* Rumanian

romi·to -ta *adj* (lit) lonely || *m* (coll) hermit

rómpere §240 *tr* to break; to bust; **rompere la testa a** to annoy, pester || *intr* to overflow; to be wrecked; to break; **rompere in pianto** to burst out crying || *ref* to fly to pieces; **rompersi la testa** to rack one's brains

rompicapo *m* annoyance; puzzle; jigsaw puzzle

rompicòllo *m* madcap; **a rompicollo** headlong, rashly; at breakneck speed

rompighiàc·cio *m* (**-cio**) icebreaker; ice pick

rompiscàto·le *m* (**-le**) bore, pest

ronci·glio *m* (**-gli**) (poet) hook

róncola *f* pruning hook

rónda *f* patrol; beat (*of policeman*)

rondèlla *f* (mach) washer

róndine *f* swallow

rondóne *m* European swift

ronfare (**rónfo**) *intr* (coll) to snore; (coll) to purr

ronzare [dz] (**rónzo**) *intr* to buzz; to hum

ronzino [dz] *m* jade, nag

ronzì·o [dz] *m* (**-i**) buzzing; humming

ròsa *adj invar & m* pink || *f* rose; group; rosette; **rosa dei venti** compass card; **rosa del Giappone** (bot) camelia; **rosa delle Alpi** (bot) rhododendron; **rosa di tiro** (mil) dispersion

ro·sàio *m* (**-sài**) rosebush

rosà·rio *m* (**-ri**) rosary; **recitare il rosario** to count one's beads

rosa·to -ta *adj* rosy

ròse·o -a *adj* rosy

roséto *m* rose garden

rosétta *f* rosette; hard roll; (mach) washer

rosicanti [s] *mpl* rodents

rosicchiare [s] §287 *tr* to gnaw; to pick (*a bone*); to bite (*one's fingernails*)

rosmarino *m* (bot) rosemary

rosolare (**ròsolo**) *tr* (culin) to brown

rosolìa *f* German measles

rosóne *m* (archit) rosette; (archit) rose window

ròspo *m* toad; ugly person; unsociable person; **ingoiare un rospo** to swallow a bitter pill

rossa·stro -stra *adj* reddish

rossétto *m* rouge; **rossetto per le labbra** lipstick

rós·so -sa *adj* red; red-headed; Red; **diventare rosso** to blush || *mf* red-head; Red (*Communist*) || *m* red

rossóre *m* redness; blush

rosticcerìa *f* grill; rotisserie

rotàbile *adj* open to vehicular traffic (*road*); (rr) rolling (*stock*) || *f* road open to vehicular traffic

rotàia *f* rail; rut; **uscire dalle rotaie** to jump the track; (fig) to go astray

rotare §257 *tr & intr* to rotate; to circle

rotativa *f* (typ) rotary press

rotazióne *f* rotation

roteare (**ròteo**) *tr* to roll (*the eyes*); to flourish (*a sword*) || *intr* to circle

rotèlla *f* small wheel; caster; roller; kneecap; disk (*of ski pole*); **gli**

manca una rotella he has a screw loose

rotocàl•co m (-chi) rotogravure

rotolare (ròtolo) tr & intr (ESSERE) to roll ‖ ref to turn over; to wallow

ròtolo m roll; bolt; coil; **a rotoli** to rack and ruin

rotolóne m tumble; **a rotoloni** falling down; to rack and ruin

rotón•do -da adj round; rotund ‖ f rotunda; terrace

rótta f break; rout; (aer, naut) course; **a rotta di collo** at breakneck speed; **mettere in rotta** to rout

rottame m fragment; wreck; **rottami** scraps, debris; wreckage; **rottami di ferro** scrap iron

rót•to -ta adj broken; shattered; inured ‖ m break, tear; **e rotti** odd, e.g., **duecento e rotti** two hundred odd; **per il rotto della cuffia** hardly; just about ‖ f see **rotta**

rottura f break; breakage; rupture; breakdown (of relations); crack

ròtula f kneecap

rovèllo m (lit) anger

rovènte adj red-hot

róvere m & f oak tree ‖ m oak (lumber)

rovè•scia f (-sce) cuff; **alla rovescia** inside out; upside down; the wrong way

rovesciaménto m upset; overturn

rovesciare §128 (rovèscio) tr to overturn; to upset; to throw back (one's head); to spill (liquid); to pour; to hurl (insults); to turn inside out ‖ intr to throw up ‖ ref to spill; to pour; to upset

rovè•scio -scia (-sci -sce) adj reverse; inverse; inside out; upside down; backwards ‖ m reverse; wrong side; downpour; upset; (com) crash; (tennis) backhand; **a rovescio** upside down; backwards ‖ f see **rovescia**

rovéto m bramble; brier patch

rovina f ruin; blight; **andare in rovina** to go to ruin; **mandare in rovina** to ruin; **rovine** ruins

rovinare tr to ruin ‖ intr (ESSERE) to collapse ‖ ref to go to ruin

rovinì•o m (-i) clatter; crash

rovinó•so -sa [s] adj ruinous

rovistare tr to rummage through

róvo m bramble

ròzza [ddzz] f nag

róz•zo -za [ddzz] adj rough; coarse

ruba f—**andare a ruba** to sell like hotcakes; **mettere a ruba** to plunder

rubacchiare §287 tr to pilfer

rubacuò•ri (-ri) adj ravishing ‖ m ladykiller ‖ f vamp

rubare tr to steal; **rubare a man salva** to pillage, loot ‖ intr to steal; **rubare sul peso** to give short measure

ruberìa f thieving, stealing

rubicón•do -da adj rubicund

rubinétto m faucet; cock

rubino m ruby; jewel (of watch)

rubiz•zo -za adj well-preserved (person)

rubrì•ca f (-che) title, heading; directory; (journ) section

rude adj (lit) rough; (lit) rude

rùdere m ruin

rudimentale adj rudimentary

rudiménto m rudiment

ruffia•no -na mf go-between ‖ m pimp, panderer ‖ f bawd, procuress

ru•ga f (-ghe) wrinkle; (bot) rocket

rùggine f rust; ill-will; (bot) blight

rugginó•so -sa [s] adj rusty

ruggire §176 tr & intr to roar

ruggito m roar

rugiada f dew

rugó•so -sa [s] adj wrinkled, wrinkly

rullàg•gio m (-gi) (aer) taxiing

rullare tr to roll ‖ intr to roll; to taxi

rullì•o m (-i) roll; rub-a-dub

rullo m roll; platen (of typewriter); pin (in tenpins); **rullo compressore** road roller

rumè•no -na adj & mf var of **romeno**

ruminare (rùmino) tr & intr to ruminate

rumóre m noise; rumor; ado; **far molto rumore** to create a stir

rumoreggiare §290 (rumoréggio) intr to rumble

rumoró•so -sa [s] adj noisy; rumbling; controversial

ruolino m roster

ruòlo m roll; role; list; **di ruolo** regular, full-time; **fuori ruolo** temporary, part-time

ruòta f wheel; paddle wheel; revolving server (in convent); **a quattro ruote** four-wheel; **dar la ruota** to sharpen; **esser l'ultima ruota del carro** to be the fifth wheel to a wagon; **fare la ruota** to spread its tail, strut (said, e.g., of a peacock); to turn cartwheels (said, e.g., of an acrobat); **ruota dentata** cog, cogwheel; **ruota idraulica** water wheel; **seguire a ruota** to follow closely

rupe f cliff

rurale adj rural, farm, farmer

ruscèllo m brook

ruspa f road grader

ruspante m barnyard chicken

russare intr to snore

Rùssia, la Russia

rus•so -sa adj & mf Russian

rustica•no -na adj rustic, boorish

rùsti•co -ca (-ci -che) adj rustic; coarse ‖ m tool shed; cottage; (lit) peasant

rutilante adj (lit) shiny

ruttare tr (lit) to belch ‖ intr (vulg) to belch

rutto m (vulg) belch

ruttóre m (elec) contact breaker

ruvidézza f or **ruvidi•tà** f (-tà) coarseness; roughness

rùvi•do -da adj coarse; rough

ruzzare [ddzz] intr to romp

ruzzolare (rùzzolo) tr to roll ‖ intr (ESSERE) to tumble down; to roll

ruzzolóne m tumble; **a ruzzoloni** tumbling down

S

S, s ['ɛsse] *m & f* seventeenth letter of the Italian alphabet

s- *pref* dis-, e.g., **sleale** disloyal; e.g., **sconto** discount; un-, e.g., **scatenare** to unchain, unleash

sàbato *m* Saturday; (*of Jews*) Sabbath; **sabato inglese** Saturday afternoon off

sabbàti·co -ca *adj* (**-ci -che**) sabbatical

sàbbia *f* sand; **sabbia mobile** quicksand

sabbiatura *f* sand bath; sandblast

sabbièra *f* (rr) sandbox

sabbió·so -sa [s] *adj* sandy

sabotàg·gio *m* (**-gi**) sabotage

sabotare (sabòto) *tr* to sabotage

sac·ca *f* (**-che**) bag; satchel; (mil) pocket; **sacca d'aria** (aer) air pocket; **sacca da viaggio** traveling bag; duffel bag

saccarina *f* saccharine

saccènte *mf* wiseacre, know-it-all

saccheggiare §290 (**sacchéggio**) *tr* to pillage, plunder

sacchég·gio *m* (**-gi**) pillage, plunder

sacchétto *m* little bag, pouch

sac·co *m* (**-chi**) bag; sack; sackcloth; pouch; (boxing) punching bag; (fig) heap, lot; **fare sacco** to sag; **mettere a sacco** to sack; **mettere nel sacco** to outwit; **sacco alpino** knapsack; **sacco a pelo** or **a piuma** sleeping bag; **sacco postale** mailbag

saccòc·cia *f* (**-ce**) (coll) pocket

sacerdòte *m* priest; (fig) devotee

sacerdotéssa *f* priestess

sacerdòzio *m* priesthood; ministry

sacramentale *adj* sacramental; (joc) habitual, ritual

sacraménto *m* sacrament

sacrà·rio *m* (**-ri**) memorial; sanctuary; shrine

sacrestìa *f* var of **sagrestia**

sacrificare §197 (**sacrifico**) *tr* to sacrifice; to waste; to force ‖ *ref* to sacrifice oneself

sacrifi·cio *m* (**-ci**) sacrifice

sacrilè·gio *m* (**-gi**) sacrilege

sacrile·go -ga *adj* (**-ghi -ghe**) sacrilegious

sacri·sta *m* (**-sti**) sexton

sacristìa *f* var of **sagrestia**

sa·cro -cra *adj* sacred

sacrosan·to -ta *adj* sacrosanct; sacred (*truth*)

sàdi·co -ca (**-ci -che**) *adj* sadistic ‖ *mf* sadist

sadismo *m* sadism

saétta *f* stroke of lightning; hand (*of watch*); (mach) bit; (lit) arrow

saettare (saétto) *tr* to shoot; **saettare sguardi a** to look daggers at

saettóne *m* (archit) strut

sagace *adj* sagacious, shrewd

sagà·cia *f* (**-cie**) sagacity

saggézza *f* wisdom

saggiare §290 *tr* to assay; to test; (dial) to taste

saggia·tóre -trice *mf* assayer ‖ *m* assay balance

saggina *f* sorghum

sàg·gio -gia (**-gi -ge**) *adj* wise ‖ *m* sage; assay; sample; proof; theme; test; rate (*of interest*); display; **di saggio** examination (*copy*)

saggi·sta *mf* (**-sti -ste**) essayist

sagittària *f* (bot) arrowhead

sagittà·rio *m* (**-ri**) (obs) archer ‖ **Sagittario** *m* Sagittarius

sàgola *f* (naut) halyard

sàgoma *f* outline; target; model, pattern; (joc) character

sagomare (sàgomo) *tr* to outline; to mold; to shape

sagomato *m* billboard

sagra *f* anniversary consecration (*of church*); festival

sagrato *m* elevated square in front of a church; churchyard; (coll) curse

sagrestano *m* sexton, sacristan

sagrestìa *f* sacristy, vestry

sàia *f* serge

sàio *m* (**sài**) habit (*of monk or nun*); doublet; frock coat

sala *f* axletree; hall, room; (bot) cattail, reed mace; **sala da ballo** dance hall; **sala da pranzo** dining room; **sala d'aspetto** waiting room; anteroom; **sala operatoria** operating room

salac·ca *f* (**-che**) (coll) sardine; (coll) shad

salace *adj* salacious; pungent

salamandra *f* salamander

salame *m* salami

salamelèc·co *m* (**-chi**) salaam

salamòia *f* brine

salare *tr* to salt; (coll) to cut (*school*)

salaria·to -ta *adj* wage-earning ‖ *m* wage earner

salà·rio *m* (**-ri**) pay, wages

salassare *tr* to bleed

salasso *m* bloodletting

sala·to -ta *adj* salted; salty; dear, expensive; (fig) sharp ‖ *m* salt pork; cold cuts ‖ *f* salting

salda *f* starch solution (*used in laundering*)

saldacón·ti *m* (**-ti**) bookkeeping department; credit department; ledger; bookkeeping machine

saldare *tr* to solder; to set (*a bone*); to weld; to pay, settle ‖ *ref* to knit (*said of a bone*); (lit) to heal

saldatóre *m* solderer; welder; soldering iron

saldatura *f* soldering; setting (*of bones*); joint; continuity; **saldatura autogena** welding

saldézza *f* firmness

sal·do -da *adj* firm; valid (*reason*); flawless ‖ *m* balance; clearance sale; job lot; payment; **saldi** remnants ‖ *f* see **salda**

saldobrasatura *f* soldering

sale *m* salt; wit; (lit) sea; **restare di sale** to be dumbfounded; **sale inglese** Epsom salts; **sali aromatici** smelling salts; **sali da bagno** bath salts

salgèmma *f* rock salt

sàlice m willow tree; **salice piangente** weeping willow

salicilato m salicylate

saliènte adj projecting; (fig) salient || m projection

salièra f saltcellar, salt shaker

salini·tà f (-tà) salinity

sali·no -na adj saline; salty || f salt bed

salire §242 tr to climb || intr (ESSERE) to climb; to go up; to rise; **salire in** or **su** to get on (e.g., a train)

saliscén·di m (-di) latch; **saliscendi** mpl ups and downs

salita f climbing; ascent, rise; slope; **in salita** uphill

saliva f saliva

salma f corpse, body

salma·stro -stra adj briny; saltish || m— **sapere di salmastro** to smell or taste salty

salmerìe fpl wagon train; (mil) supplies

salmì m—**in salmì** (culin) in a stew

salmo m psalm

salmodiare §287 (salmòdio) intr to chant, sing hymns, intone

salmóne m salmon

salnitro m saltpeter

Salomóne m Solomon

salóne m hall; salon, drawing room; (naut) saloon; **salone da barbiere** barber shop; **salone dell'automobile** auto show

salòtto m drawing room; living room, parlor; reception room

salpare tr to weigh (anchor) || intr (ESSERE) to weigh anchor

salsa f sauce

salsapariglia f sarsaparilla

salsèdine f saltiness

salsìc·cia f (-ce) sausage

salsièra f gravy boat

sal·so -sa adj salty; saline || m saltiness || f see **salsa**

saltabeccare §197 (saltabécco) intr to hop

saltaleóne m coil spring

saltare tr to jump; to skip; to sauté; (sports) to vault; hurdle; **far saltare** to kick out; to blow up (e.g., a mine); **saltare la sbarra** (coll) to go A.W.O.L. || intr (ESSERE & AVERE) to jump; to pop off, e.g., **mi è saltato un bottone** one of my buttons has popped off; to blow out (said of a fuse); **saltare agli occhi** to be self-evident; **saltare a piè pari** to skip with both feet; **saltar fuori** to pop out (said of the eyes); to appear suddenly; **saltare in mente a** to come to the mind of; **saltare il ticchio a (qlcu) di** to feel like + ger, e.g., **gli è saltato il ticchio di cantare** he felt like singing; **saltare la mosca al naso a (qlcu)** to blow one's top, e.g., **le è saltata la mosca al naso** she blew her top; **saltare per aria** to blow up; **saltare su** to start (to make a sudden jerk); **saltare su a** + inf to begin suddenly to + inf

salta·tóre -trice mf jumper, hurdler

saltellare (saltèllo) intr to skip, hop

saltellóni adv—**a saltelloni** skipping, hopping

saltimban·co m (-chi) acrobat, tumbler; mountebank

salto m jump; leap; fall; skip; (of animals) mating; (fig) step; **a salti** skipping, jumping; **al salto** sauté; **fare quattro salti** to dance; **fare un salto** to hop, hurry; **salto a pesce** jackknife (dive); **salto coll'asta** pole vaulting; **salto in altezza** high jump; **salto in lunghezza** broad jump; **salto mortale** somersault; **salto nel vuoto** leap in the dark

saltuà·rio -ria adj (-ri -rie) desultory, occasional

salubre adj salubrious, healthy, healthful

salume m pork product

salumerìa f pork butcher shop

salumiè·re -ra mf pork butcher

salutare adj healthful || tr to greet; to salute; (lit) to proclaim

salute f health; salvation; safety || interj good luck!; to your health!; gesundheit!

saluto m salute; greeting; salutation; **distinti saluti** sincerely yours

salva f salvo; outburst; **a salve** with blank cartridges, with blanks

salvacondótto m safe-conduct

salvada·nàio m (-nài) piggy bank

salvagèn·te m (-te & -ti) life preserver; fender (of trolley car) || m (-te) safety island

salvaguardare tr to safeguard

salvaguàrdia f safeguard

salvaménto m safety

salvamotóre m circuit breaker; fuse box

salvapun·te m (-te) pencil cap; tap (on sole of shoe)

salvare tr to save; to spare (a life); to rescue || ref to save oneself; to be rescued; **si salvi chi può!** every man for himself!

salvatàg·gio m (-gi) rescue

salvatóre m savior, rescuer || **il Salvatore** the Saviour

salvazióne f salvation

salve interj hello!, hail!

salvézza f salvation; safety

sàlvia f (bot) sage

salviétta f napkin; paper napkin; paper towel

sal·vo -va adj safe; saved; secure || m —**mettere in salvo** to put in a safe place; **mettersi in salvo** to reach safety || f see **salva** || **salvo** prep except; **salvo che** unless; **salvo il vero** unless I am mistaken

samarita·no -na adj & mf Samaritan

sambu·co m (-chi) elder tree

san adj apocopated and unstressed form of **santo**

sanàbile adj curable

sanare tr to heal; to remedy; to reclaim (land); to normalize

sanatò·rio m (-ri) sanatorium

sancire §176 tr to ratify, sanction; to establish

sàndalo m sandal; sandalwood; flat-bottom boat

sandolino *m* canoe, skiff, kayak

sangue *m* blood; **agitarsi il sangue** to fret; **all'ultimo sangue** (*duel*) to the death; **al sangue rare** (*meat*); **a sangue freddo** in cold blood; **cold-blooded**; **cavar sangue da una rapa** to draw blood from a stone; **farsi cattivo sangue** to get angry; **il sangue non è acqua** blood is thicker than water; **puro sangue** thoroughbred; **sangue dal naso** nosebleed; **sangue freddo** calmness, composure

sangui·gno -gna *adj* blood (*circulation*); bloody; sanguine, ruddy || *m* (lit) color of blood

sanguinante *adj* bloody, bleeding

sanguinare (**sànguino**) *intr* to bleed; to be rare (*said of meat*)

sanguinà·rio -ria *adj* (**-ri -rie**) sanguinary

sanguinó·so -sa [s] *adj* bloody; bleeding; (fig) stinging

sanguisu·ga [s] *f* (**-ghe**) leech

sani·tà *f* (**-tà**) health; healthfulness; soundness (*of body*); sanity; health department

sanità·rio -ria (**-ri -rie**) *adj* health; sanitary || *m* physician

sa·no -na *adj* healthy; sound; **sano e salvo** safe and sound

sant' *apocopated form of* **santo** *and* **santa**

santa *f* saint

santabàrbara *f* (**santebàrbare**) (nav) powder magazine

santarellina *f* goody-goody girl

santificare §197 (**santifico**) *tr* to sanctify

santissi·mo -ma *adj* most holy || *m* Eucharist

santi·tà *f* (**-tà**) sanctity, holiness; sainthood, saintliness

san·to -ta *adj* saintly, holy; sacred; blessed, livelong, e.g., **tutto il santo giorno** all the livelong day || *m* saint; name day; (fig) someone || *f* see **santa**

santorég·gia *f* (**-ge**) (bot) savory

santuà·rio *m* (**-ri**) sanctuary

sanzionare (**sanzióno**) *tr* to sanction; to ratify

sanzióne *f* sanction

sapére *m* knowledge; **sapere fare savoir-faire** || §243 *tr* to know; to find out; to know how to; **far sapere** to let know; **saperla lunga** to know a thing or two; **un certo non so che** a certain something, something vague || *intr*— **sapere di** to know; to taste; to smell; to smack of; **mi sa che** I think that; **non voler più saperne di** to not want to have anything to do with; **sapere male** (with *dat*) to feel sorry, e.g., **gli sa male** he feels sorry || *rej*— **che io mi sappia** as far as I know

sàpido -da *adj* savory; witty

sapiènte *adj* wise; talented; trained (*dog*) || *m* wise man

sapientó·ne -na *mf* wiseacre, know-it-all

sapiènza *f* wisdom; knowledge

saponària *f* (bot) soapwort

saponata *f* soapsuds; lather; (fig) soft soap

sapóne *m* soap; **sapone da toletta** toilet soap; **sapone per la barba** shaving soap

saponétta *f* cake of soap

saponière *m* soap maker

saponifi·cio *m* (**-ci**) soap factory

saponó·so -sa [s] *adj* soapy

sapóre *m* taste; savor; flavor

saporire §176 *tr* to savor

saporitaménte *adv* heartily; soundly

sapori·to -ta *adj* tasty; flavorful; salty; expensive

saporó·so -sa [s] *adj* savory; witty

saputèl·lo -la *adj* cocksure || *m* smart aleck

sarac·co *m* (**-chi**) hand saw

saracè·no -na *adj* Saracen, Saracenic || *m* Saracen; quintain

saraciné·sca *f* (**-sche**) metal shutter (*of store*); sluice gate; (hist) portculis

sarcasmo *m* sarcasm

sarcàsti·co -ca *adj* (**-ci -che**) sarcastic

sarchiare §287 *tr* to weed

sarchia·tóre -trice *mf* weeder || *f* (agr) cultivator

sarchièllo *m* weeding hoe

sàr·chio *m* (**-chi**) hoe

sarcòfa·go *m* (**-gi** & **-ghi**) sarcophagus

sacràuti *mpl* sauerkraut

Sardégna, la Sardinia

sardèlla *f* pilchard; sardine

sardina *f* pilchard; sardine

sar·do -da *adj* & *mf* Sardinian

sardòni·co -ca *adj* (**-ci -che**) sardonic

sarménto *m* vine shoot, running stem

sarta *f* dressmaker

sàrtie *fpl* (naut) shrouds

sarto *m* tailor

sartorìa *f* dressmaker's shop; tailor shop; dressmaking; tailoring

sassaiòla *f* shower of stones

sassata *f* blow with a stone

sasso *m* stone, rock; pebble; (poet) tombstone; **di sasso** stony; **restare di sasso** to be taken aback; **tirare sassi in colombaia** to cut one's nose to spite one's face

sassòfono *m* saxophone

sàssone *adj* & *mf* Saxon

sassó·so -sa [s] *adj* stony

Sàtana *m* Satan

satanasso *m* Satan; devil

satèllite *m* satellite

sa·tin *m* (**-tin**) sateen

satinare *tr* to gloss

sàtira *f* satire

satireggiare §290 (**satiréggio**) *tr* to satirize, lampoon || *intr* to compose satires

satiri·co -ca *adj* (**-ci -che**) satiric(al) || *m* satirist

sàtiro *m* satyr

satól·lo -la *adj* sated, full

saturare *tr* (**sàturo**) *tr* to saturate; to steep; (fig) to fill; (com) to glut (*a market*)

saturni·no -na *adj* Saturnian; saturnine

Saturno *m* (astr) Saturn

sàtu·ro -ra *adj* saturated; (fig) full; (lit) sated

sàu·ro -ra *adj & m* sorrel (*horse*)

Savèrio *m* Xavier

sà·vio -via (-vi -vie) *adj* wise ‖ *m* wise man, sage

savoiar·do -da *adj & mf* Savoyard ‖ *m* ladyfinger

saxòfono *m* saxophone

saziare §287 *tr* to satisfy; to cloy, satiate

sazietà *f* satiety, surfeit; **mangiare a sazietà** to eat one's fill

sà·zio -zia *adj* (**-zi -zie**) sated; full; satisfied

sbaciucchiare §287 (**sbaciùcchio**) *tr* to kiss again and again ‖ *ref* to neck

sbadatàggine *f* carelessness; oversight

sbada·to -ta *adj* careless; heedless

sbadigliare §280 *intr* to yawn

sbadì·glio *m* (**-gli**) yawn

sbafa·tóre -trice *mf* sponger

sbafo *m*—**a sbafo** sponging; **mangiare a sbafo** to sponge

sbagliare §280 *tr* to miss; to mistake; **sbagliarla** to be sadly mistaken ‖ *intr & ref* to be mistaken; to make a mistake

sbaglia·to -ta *adj* wrong; mistaken

sbà·glio *m* (**-gli**) error, mistake

sbalestrare (**sbalèstro**) *tr* to fling with the crossbow; to send (*an employee*) far away ‖ *intr* to speak amiss; to ramble; to blunder

sbalestra·to -ta *adj* unbalanced; ill-at-ease

sballare *tr* to unpack; **sballarle grosse** to tell tall tales ‖ *intr* to overbid

sballa·to -ta *adj* unpacked; absurd, wild

sballottare (**sballòtto**) *tr* to toss

sbalordire §176 *tr* to stun; to amaze; to bewilder ‖ *intr* to lose consciousness; to be dumfounded

sbalorditi·vo -va *adj* amazing

sbalzare *tr* to upset; to send far away; to overthrow; to emboss ‖ *intr* (ESSERE) to bounce

sbalzo *m* leap, jump; climb; embossment, relief; **a sbalzi** by leaps and bounds; **di sbalzo** all of a sudden

sbancare §197 *tr* to clear (*ground*) of rocks; to ruin; (*cards*) to break (*the bank*)

sbandaménto *m* skid; swerve; disbandment; breaking up; (naut) list

sbandare *tr* to disband; (naut) to cause to list ‖ *intr* to list; to skid; to swerve; to deviate ‖ *ref* to disband; to break up

sbanda·to -ta *adj* disbanded; stray; alienated ‖ *mf* alienated person ‖ *m* straggler ‖ *f* listing (*of ship*); skidding (*of vehicle*); **prendere una sbandata per** to get a crush on

sbandierare (**sbandièro**) *tr* to wave (*a flag*); to display

sbaragliare §280 *tr* to rout; to crush

sbaràglio *m*—**mettere allo sbaraglio** to endanger

sbarazzare *tr* to clear out; to free ‖ *ref* —**sbarazzarsi di** to get rid of

sbarazzi·no -na *adj* mischievous ‖ *mf* scamp; **alla sbarazzina** cocked, at an angle (*said of a hat*)

sbarbare *tr* to shave; to uproot ‖ *ref* to shave

sbarbatèllo *m* greenhorn, fledgling

sbarcare §197 *tr* to unload; to discharge; to disembark; to pass; to strew (*fodder*); **sbarcare il lunario** to make ends meet ‖ *intr* (ESSERE) to come ashore, land

sbarca·tóio *m* (**-tói**) landing pier

sbar·co *m* (**-chi**) unloading; landing

sbarra *f* bar; (typ) dash

sbarraménto *m* barrage; obstacle

sbarrare *tr* to bar; to block (*the way*); to open (*one's eyes*) wide, e.g., **sbarrò gli occhi** he opened his eyes wide

sbarrétta *f* bar; **sbarrette verticali** (typ) parallels

sbatacchiare §287 *tr* to slam; to flap ‖ *intr* to slam

sbatàc·chio *m* (**-chi**) shore, prop

sbàttere *tr* to flap; to fling; to slam; to beat; to toss; to send away; to make pale; **sbatter fuori** to throw out ‖ *intr* to flap; to slam

sbattighiàc·cio *m* (**-cio**) cocktail shaker

sbattitóre *m* electric mixer

sbattiuò·va *m* (**-va**) egg beater

sbattu·to -ta *adj* haggard, downcast

sbavare *tr* to slobber over; (mach) to trim ‖ *intr* to drivel, slobber; to run (*said of colors*)

sbavatura *f* drivel; run (*of colors*); burr (*of metal*); deckle edge; verbosity

sbeccare §197 *tr & ref* to chip

sbeffeggiare §290 (**sbefféggio**) *tr* to make fun of

sbellicare §197 *ref*—**sbellicarsi dalle risa** to burst with laughter

sbèrla *f* (coll) slap

sberlèffo *m* scar; grimace; **fare gli sberleffi a** to make faces at

sbevazzare *intr* to guzzle

sbevucchiare §287 *intr* to tipple

sbiadire §176 *tr & intr* (ESSERE) to fade

sbiadi·to -ta *adj* faded; dull

sbiancare §197 *tr* to whiten ‖ *ref* to become white; to pale

sbianchire §176 *tr* (culin) to blanch

sbiè·co -ca (**-chi -che**) *adj* oblique; **di sbieco** on the bias; **guardare di sbieco** to look askance at ‖ *m* cloth cut diagonally

sbigottire §176 *tr* to terrify, dismay ‖ *intr* (ESSERE) & *ref* to be dismayed

sbilanciare §128 *tr* to unbalance; to upset ‖ *intr* to lose one's balance ‖ *ref* to commit oneself

sbilàn·cio *m* (**-ci**) disequilibrium; (com) deficit

sbilèn·co -ca *adj* (**-chi -che**) twisted, crooked

sbirciare §128 *tr* to leer at, ogle; to eye closely

sbir·ro -ra *adj* (coll) smart ‖ *m* (pej) cop

sbizzarrire [ddzz] §176 *tr* to cure the whims of ‖ *ref* to indulge one's whims

sbloccare §197 (**sblòcco**) *tr* to unblock; to raise the blockade of; to free

sbòbba *f* slop, dishwater

sboccare §197 (**sbócco**) *tr* to break the

mouth of (*a bottle*); to remove a few drops from (*a bottle*) || *intr* (ESSERE) to flow; to open (*said of a street*); **sboccare in** to turn out to be

sbocca·to -ta *adj* foulmouthed; foul (*language*); chipped at the mouth (*said of a bottle*)

sbocciare §128 (**sbòccio**) *intr* (ESSERE) to bud, burgeon, bloom

sbòc·co *m* (**-chi**) outlet; avere uno sbocco di sangue to spit blood

sboccancellare (**sboccancèllo**) *tr* to nibble at; to chip, nick

sbollentare (**sbollènte**) *tr* to blanch

sbollire §176 *intr* to stop boiling; to calm down

sbolognare (**sbológno**) *tr* (coll) to palm off; (coll) to get rid of

sbòrnia *f* (coll) drunk, jag; **smaltire la sbornia** to sober up

sborsare (**sbórso**) *tr* to pay out, disburse

sbórso *m* disbursement, outlay

sbottare (**sbòtto**) *intr*—**sbottare a** + *inf* to burst out + *ger*

sbottonare (**sbottóno**) *tr* to unbutton || *ref* (fig) to unbosom oneself

sbozzare (**sbòzzo**) *tr* to rough-hew; to sketch, outline

sbraca·to -ta *adj* without pants; slovenly; vulgar

sbracciare §128 *intr* to gesticulate || *ref* to roll up one's sleeves; to wear sleeveless clothes; to gesticulate; to do one's best

sbraccia·to -ta *adj* bare-armed

sbraitare (**sbràito**) *intr* to scream

sbraitó·ne -na *mf* bigmouth

sbranare *tr* to tear to pieces

sbrano *m* tear, rent

sbrattare *tr* to clean; to clear

sbreccare §197 (**sbrécco**) *tr* to chip, nick

sbrecciare §128 (**sbréccio**) *tr* to open a gap in

sbréndolo *m* tatter, rag

sbriciolare (**sbrìciolo**) *tr* to crumb || *ref* to crumble

sbrigare §209 *tr* to transact; to take care of || *ref* to hasten, hurry; **sbrigarsela** to get out of trouble; **sbrigarsi di** to get rid of; **sbrigati!** make it snappy!, hurry up!

sbrigativ·o -va *adj* quick, brisk; businesslike

sbrigliare §280 *tr* to unbridle; to reduce (*a hernia*); to lance (*an infected wound*) || *ref* to cut loose

sbrinare *tr* to defrost

sbrindella·to -ta *adj* tattered

sbrodolare (**sbròdolo**) *tr* to soil; (fig) to drag out || *ref* to slobber

sbrogliare §280 (**sbròglio**) *tr* to untangle; to clean up || *ref* to extricate oneself; **sbrogliarsela** to get out of a tight spot

sbronzare (**sbrónzo**) *ref* (coll) to get drunk

sbruffare *tr* to squirt out of the mouth; to spatter; to bribe || *intr* to tell tall tales

sbruffo *m* sprinkle, squirt; bribe

sbruffó·ne -na *mf* braggart

sbucare §197 *intr* (ESSERE) to pop out, come out

sbucciare §128 *tr* to peel; to skin || *ref* to slough (*said of snakes*); **sbucciarsela** (coll) to goldbrick

sbucciatura *f* slight abrasion

sbudellare (**sbudèllo**) *tr* to disembowel || *ref*—**sbudellarsi dalle risa** to burst with laughter, split one's sides laughing

sbuffare *tr* & *intr* to puff

sbuffo *m* puff; gust (*of wind*); **a sbuffo** puffed (*sleeve*)

sbullonare (**sbullóno**) *tr* to unbolt

sc- *pref* dis-, e.g., **sconto** discount; **es-**, e.g., **scalare** to escalate; **ex-**, e.g., **scusare** to excuse

scàbbia *f* scabies

sca·bro -bra *adj* rough; stony; tight (*style*)

scabró·so -sa [s] *adj* scabrous

scacchièra *f* checkerboard; chessboard

scacchière *m* (mil) sector; (obs) checkerboard; exchequer

scacciacà·ni *m* & *f* (-ni) toy gun; gun shooting only blanks

scacciamó·sche *m* (-sche) fly swatter

scacciapensiè·ri *m* (-ri) jew's-harp

scacciare §128 *tr* to chase away, drive away; to expel

scaccino *m* sexton, sacristan

scac·co *m* (-chi) chessman; checker; check; square; **a scacchi** checkered; **dare scacco matto a** to checkmate; **in scacco** or **sotto scacco** in check; **scacchi** chess; **scacco matto** checkmate

scàccoli *mpl* cement piles

scaccomatto *m* checkmate

scadènte *adj* inferior, poor, shoddy

scadènza *f* term, maturity; obligation; **a breve scadenza** short-term; **a lunga scadenza** long-term

scadére §121 *intr* (ESSERE) to decay, to decline; to fall due; to expire; (naut) to drift

scafandro *m* diving suit; **scafandro astronautico** space suit

scaffale *m* bookcase; shelf

scafo *m* hull

scagionare (**scagióno**) *tr* to exonerate, exculpate

scàglia *f* scale (*of fish*); chip; plate (*of medieval armor*); flake (*of soap*); tile (*of slate roof*)

scagliare §280 *tr* to hurl, fling, throw; to scale (*fish*) || *ref* to dash, to rush; to flake

scaglionare (**scaglióno**) *tr* to echelon; to stagger (*e.g., payments*)

scaglióne *m* terrace (*of mountain*); echelon; scale; **a scaglioni** graded (*e.g., income tax*)

scala *f* stairs; ladder; scale; (cards) straight; (rad) dial; **a scale** scaled, graded; **fare la scale** to climb the stairs; **scala a chiocciola** spiral stairway; **scala a gradini** or **a libretto** stepladder; **scala mobile** escalator; (econ) sliding scale; **scala porta** aerial ladder; **scala reale** (poker) straight flush; **su larga scala** large-scale; **su scala nazionale** on a national scale

scalandróne *m* (naut) gangway

scalare *adj* graded, scaled; gradual || *m* (com) running balance || *tr* to climb, ascend; to scale, grade; to reduce

scalata *f* climb, ascent; **dar la scalata a** to climb; to climb up to

scalcagna·to -ta *adj* down-at-the-heel

scalcare §197 *tr* to slice, carve

scalciare §128 *intr* to kick

scalcina·to -ta *adj* (*wall or plaster*) that is peeling off; worn-out; down-at-the-heels

scalda-acqua *m* (-acqua) hot-water heater

scaldaba·gno *m* (-gno) hot-water heater; **scaldabagno a gas** gas heater

scaldalèt·to *m* (-ti & -to) bedwarmer

scaldare *tr* to warm, warm up; to heat, heat up || *intr* (mach) to become hot || *ref* to warm up; to heat up; **scaldarsi la testa** to get excited

scaldavivan·de *m* (-de) hot plate

scaldino *m* hand warmer

scalèa *f* flight of stairs, stairway

scalèo *m* stepladder

scalétta *f* small ladder; small stairs; (mov) rough draft

scalfire §176 *tr* to graze, scratch; to cut (*e.g., glass*)

scalfittura *f* graze, scratch

scalinata *f* stairway, perron

scalino *m* step (*of a stair*); (fig) ladder

scalmana *f* chill; flush; **prendere una scalmana per** to take a fancy to

scalmanare *ref* to hustle, bustle; to fuss

scalmana·to -ta *adj* panting; hotheaded

scalmo *m* (naut) oarlock

scalo *m* pier, dock; (naut) ways; (naut) port of call; **fare scalo** (naut) to call, stop; (aer) to land; **scalo di alaggio** (naut) slip; **scalo merci** (rr) freight yard; **senza scalo** (aer, naut) nonstop

scalógna *f* (coll) bad luck

scalógno *m* (bot) scallion

scalòppa *f* veal chop

scaloppina *f* veal cutlet, scallop

scalpellare (**scalpèllo**) *tr* to chisel

scalpellino *m* stone cutter

scalpèllo *m* chisel; (surg) scalpel; **scalpello a taglio obliquo** skew chisel

scalpicciare §128 *tr* & *intr* to shuffle

scalpitare (**scàlpito**) *intr* to paw the ground

scalpóre *m* scene; **fare scalpore** to raise a fuss

scaltrézza *f* shrewdness, cunning

scaltrire §176 *tr* to polish, refine; to sharpen the wits of || *ref* to catch on; to improve

scal·tro -tra *adj* shrewd, smart

scalzare *tr* to take the shoes or stockings off of; to undermine || *ref* to take off one's shoes or stockings

scal·zo -za *adj* barefoot

scambiare §287 *tr* to exchange; to mistake || *ref* to exchange (*presents*)

scambiévole *adj* mutual

scàm·bio *m* (-bi) exchange; (rr) switch;

---

libero scambio free trade; **scambio di persona** mistaken identity

scamicia·to -ta *adj* in shirt sleeves; extremist || *m* extremist; tunic, waist

scamoscia·to -ta *adj* chamois, suede

scampagnata *f* excursion, outing

scampanare *intr* to peal, chime; to flare (*said of a garment*)

scampanellare (**scampanèllo**) *intr* to ring loud and clear

scampanì·o *m* (-ì) toll, peal

scampare *tr* to save, rescue; **scamparla bella** to have a narrow escape || *intr* (ESSERE)—**scampare a** to escape from; to take refuge in

scampo *m* escape; safety; (zool) Norway lobster; **non c'è scampo** there is no way out

scàmpolo *m* remnant; **scampoli di tempo** free moments

scanalare *tr* to channel, groove, rabbet || *intr* to overflow

scanalatura *f* channel, groove, rabbet

scandagliare §280 *tr* to sound

scandà·glio *m* (-gli) sounding lead; **fare uno scandaglio** to make a sounding or survey

scandalismo *m* scandalmongering, yellow journalism

scandalizzare [ddzz] *tr* to scandalize, shock || *ref* to be scandalized

scàndalo *m* scandal

scandaló·so -sa [s] *adj* scandalous

scandìna·vo -va *adj* & *mf* Scandinavian

scandire §176 *tr* to scan; to syllabize; (telv) to scan

scàndola *f* wood shingle

scannare *tr* to slaughter, butcher

scanna·tóio *m* (-tói) slaughterhouse; gyp joint

scanno *m* bench; seat; sand bar

scansafati·che *mf* (-che) loafer

scansare *tr* to move; to avoid || *ref* to get out of the way

scansìa *f* shelf; bookcase

scansióne *f* scansion; (telv) scanning

scanso *m*—**a scanso di** in order to avoid

scantinare *intr* to make a blunder; (mus) to be out of tune

scantinato *m* basement

scantonare (**scantóno**) *tr* to round (*a corner*) || *intr* to duck around the corner

scanzona·to -ta *adj* flippant; unconventional

scapaccióne *m* clout; **dare uno scapaccione a** to clout, slap

scapa·to -ta *adj* scatterbrained || *m* scatterbrain

scapestra·to -ta *adj* & *m* libertine

scapigliare §280 *tr* to dishevel || *ref* to be disheveled

scapiglia·to -ta *adj* disheveled; libertine; unconventional; free and easy

scapitare (**scàpito**) *intr* to lose

scàpito *m* damage; loss; **a scapito di** to the detriment of

scàpola *f* shoulder blade

scapolare *m* scapular || *v* (**scàpolo**) *tr* (coll) to escape, avoid || *intr*—**scapolare da** to get out of (*danger*)

scàpo·lo -la *adj* unmarried || *m* bachelor || *f* see **scapola**

scappaménto *m* escapement (*of watch, of piano*); (aut) exhaust

scappare *tr*—**scapparla bella** to have a narrow escape || *intr* (ESSERE) to flee; to abscond; to run; to get away; to escape; to stick out; to burst out (*said, e.g., of sun*); **far scappare la pazienza a qlcu** to make s.o. lose his patience, to tax s.o.'s patience; **scappare a gambe levate** to run away, beat it; **scappare da** to burst out, e.g., **gli è scappato da ridere** he burst out laughing; **scappar detto di** to blurt out that, e.g., **gli scappò detto di non poterne più** he blurted out that he could not hold out; **scappare di mente** to escape one's mind; **scappar fuori con** to come out with **scappare fuori con** to come out with influence

scappata *f* excursion; sally; escapade; bolt (*of horse*); **fare una scappata** to take a run; **scappata spiritosa** witticism

scappatóia *f* subterfuge; loophole

scappellare (**scappèllo**) *ref* to tip one's hat

scappellòtto *m* smack, slap (on the head); **entrare a scappellotto** (coll) to squeeze in; **passare a scappellotto** (coll) to squeeze through with influence

scapricciare §128 *tr* to satisfy the whims of

scarabèo *m* beetle; scarab (*stone*); **scarabeo sacro** scarab; **scarabeo stercorario** dung beetle

scarabocchiare §287 (**scarabòcchio**) *tr* to scribble; to blot (*with ink*)

scarabòc·chio *m* (**-chi**) ink blot; scribble; scrawl

scarafàg·gio *m* (**-gi**) cockroach

scaramanzìa *f* exorcism; **per scaramanzia** to ward off the evil eye, for good luck

scaramazza *adj fem* irregular (*pearl*)

scaramùc·cia *f* (**-ce**) skirmish

scaraventare (**scaravènto**) *tr* to hurl, chuck; to transfer suddenly

scarcerare (**scàrcero**) *tr* to release from jail

scardinare (**scàrdino**) *tr* to unhinge

scàri·ca *f* (**-che**) discharge; volley; evacuation; (elec) discharge; (fig) shower

scaricabarili *m*—**giocare a scaricabarili** (fig) to pass the buck

scaricare §197 (**scàrico**) *tr* to unload; to discharge; to hurl (*insults*); to wreak (*anger*); to free (*from responsibility*) || *ref* to unburden oneself; to flow (*said of a river*); to discharge; to run down (*said of a battery or a watch*)

scaricatóre *m* longshoreman; (elec) lightning arrester

scàri·co -ca (**-chi -che**) *adj* empty, unloaded; discharged; clear (*sky*); free; run-down (*e.g., clock*) || *m* unloading; discharge; exhaust; waste, refuse; **a mio (tuo, etc.) scarico** in my (your, etc.) defense || *f* see **scarica**

scarlattina *f* scarlet fever

scarlat·to -ta *adj & m* scarlet

scarmigliare §280 *tr* to dishevel

scarnificare §197 (**scarnifico**) or **scarnire** §176 *tr* to bone, take the flesh off; to make thin; to wear down to the bone

scarni·to -ta or **scar·no -na** *adj* boned; meager; skinny

scaròla *f* escarole, endive

scarpa *f* shoe; wedge, skid; scarp; **fare le scarpe a** to undercut; **scarpe al sole** violent death; **scarpe da sci** ski boots

scarpata *f* escarp, escarpment; slope (*of embankment*); blow with a shoe; **scarpata continentale** continental slope

scarpétta *f* small shoe; low shoe; **scarpette chiodate** spikes; **scarpette da ginnastica** gym shoes

scarpinare *intr* to trudge

scarpóne *m* heavy boot; clodhopper

scarròc·cio *m* (**-ci**) (aer, naut) leeway

scarrozzare (**scarròzzo**) *tr* to take for a ride || *intr* to go for a ride; to go for a walk

scarrozzata *f* ride, drive

scarseggiare §290 (**scarséggio**) *intr* (ESSERE) to be scarce, be in short supply; **scarseggiare di** to be short of

scarsèlla *f* pocket; (obs) purse

scarsézza *f* or **scarsi·tà** *f* (**-tà**) scarcity, dearth, lack

scar·so -sa *adj* short; scarce; scanty, scant; weak (*wind*); **scarso a** short of

scartabellare (**scartabèllo**) *tr* to leaf through (*a book*)

scartafàc·cio *m* (**-ci**) note pad, notebook; poorly-bound copybook

scartaménto *m* (rr) gauge; **a scartamento ridotto** narrow-gauge; small-size; small-scale

scartare *tr* to unpack, unwrap; to discard (*cards*); to remove; to scrap (*e.g., a machine*); (mil) to reject || *intr* to swerve; to side-step

scartata *f* unwrapping; side step; swerving; (fig) scolding

scartina *f* discard

scarto *m* discard; reject; swerve; (mil) rejected soldier; (sports) difference; **di scarto** inferior

scartocciare §128 (**scartòccio**) *tr* to unwrap; to unfold; to husk (*corn*)

scartòffie *fpl* old papers, trash

scassare *tr* to uncrate; to plow up; (coll) to ruin, bust || *ref* (coll) to break down

scassinare *tr* to pick (*a lock*); to burglarize; to break open

scassina·tóre -trice *mf* burglar; **scassinatore di casseforti** safe-cracker

scasso *m* plowing, tilling; burglary

scatenare (**scaténo**) *tr* to unchain; to trigger; to excite, stir up || *ref* to break loose

scàtola *f* box; can; **a scatola chiusa** sight unseen; **in scatola** canned; **rompere le scatole a** (vulg) to bug, pester; **scatola armonica** music box; **scatola a sorpresa** jack-in-the-box;

scàtola cranica cranium, skull; **scatola del cambio** (aut) transmission, gear box

scatolame m boxes; canned food

scatolifi·cio m (-ci) box factory

scattare tr to take (a picture) ‖ intr (ESSERE & AVERE) to jump, spring; to go off (said of a trap); to go up (said of the cost of living); to go into action, begin

scatto m click (of camera, gun); outburst; sprint; automatic increase (in salary); shutter release; **a scatti** in jerks; **di scatto** suddenly

scaturire §176 intr (ESSERE) to spring; to pour, gush; to stem

scavalcare §197 tr to jump over; to pass over; to unsaddle; to skip (a stitch) ‖ intr (ESSERE) to dismount ‖ ref (coll) to rush

scavallare intr to caper, cavort

scavare tr to dig; to dig up, unearth

scava·tóre -trice adj excavating ‖ m digger ‖ f digger, excavator

scavezzacòllo m scamp; daredevil; **a scavezzacollo** headlong, at breakneck speed

scavezzare (scavézzo) tr to lop; to burst; to break; to take the halter off (a horse)

scavo m digging, excavation

scazzottare (scazzòtto) tr to beat up

scégliere §244 tr to choose; to pick out

sceic·co m (-chi) sheik

scelleratàggine f or **scelleratézza** f wickedness, villainy

scellera·to -ta adj wicked ‖ m villain

scellino m shilling

scél·to -ta adj choice; selected; (mil) first-class ‖ f choice; pick; selection; **di prima scelta** choice

scemare (scémo) tr to diminish, reduce; to lower the level of ‖ intr (ESSERE) & ref to lessen, diminish

scemènza f foolishness, stupidity

scé·mo -ma adj silly, foolish ‖ mf simpleton, fool

scempiàggine f silliness, foolishness

scém·pio -pia (-pi -pie) adj simple; single; (lit) wicked ‖ m ruination; (lit) slaughter; **fare scempio di** to ruin; (lit) to slaughter

scèna f scene; stage; acting; scenery; **esser di scena** (theat) to be on; **mettere in scena** (theat) to stage; **scene di prossima programmazione** (mov) coming attractions

scenà·rio m (-ri) scenery; scenario, setting

scenari·sta mf (-sti -ste) scenarist; script writer

scenata f scene (outbreak of anger)

scéndere §245 tr to descend, go down; to bring down ‖ intr (ESSERE) to descend, go down; to get off; to come (to an agreement); to step (into the ring); to put up (at a hotel); to check in (at a hotel)

scendilèt·to m (-to) scatter rug; bathrobe

sceneggiare §290 (scenéggio) tr to write a scenario for; to adapt for the stage

sceneggia·tóre -trice mf scenarist

sceneggiatura f (mov) screenplay; (rad, telv) continuity

scenètta f (theat) sketch

scenògrafo m scene designer

scenotècni·ca f (-che) stagecraft

sceriffo m sheriff

scèrnere §246 tr to discern; to distinguish; to select

scervellare (scervèllo) ref to rack one's brains

scervella·to -ta adj scatterbrained

scésa [s] f discent; slope

scespiria·no -na adj Shakesperean

scetticismo m skepticism

scètti·co -ca (-ci -che) adj skeptic(al) ‖ m skeptic

scèttro m scepter

sceverare (scévero) tr (lit) to distinguish

scé·vro -vra adj (lit) free, exempt

schèda f card; slip, form; **scheda elettorale** ballot; **scheda perforata** punch card

schedare (schèdo) tr to file

schedà·rio m (-ri) card index, card catalogue; file cabinet

schég·gia f (-ge) splinter; chip

scheggiare §290 (schéggio) tr & ref to splinter

schelètri·co -ca adj (-ci -che) skeleton, skeletal; succint

schèletro m skeleton

schè·ma m (-mi) diagram; draft; model; scheme; **schema di montaggio** (electron) hookup

schèrma f fencing

schermàglia f argument

schermare (schèrmo) tr to screen; (elec) to shield

schermire §176 tr to protect; (obs) to fence with ‖ ref—**schermirsi da** to ward off, parry; to protect oneself from

schermi·tóre -trice mf fencer

schérmo m screen; protection; (elec) shield; **farsi schermo di** to use as protection; **farsi schermo delle mani** to ward off a blow with one's hands

schernire §176 tr to deride

schèrno m derision, ridicule, mockery

scherzare (schèrzo) tr (coll) to mock ‖ intr to play; to joke, trifle

schèrzo m play; joke, jest; freak (of nature); child's play; trick; **neppure per scherzo** under no circumstances; **per scherzo** in jest; **stare allo scherzo** to take a joke

scherzó·so -sa [s] adj joking; playful

schiacciaménto m crushing; flattening

schiaccianó·ci m (-ci) nutcracker

schiacciante adj crushing

schiacciapata·te m (-te) ricer

schiacciare §128 tr to crush; to take (a nap); to squelch (a rumor); to subdue (the details of a painting); to mash (potatoes); to tread on, step on (s.o.'s foot); to flatten; to run (s.o.) over; to make (s.o.'s figure) look squatty; to crack (nuts); to flunk; (tennis) to smash

schiacciata f hot cake; (tennis) smash

schiaffare *tr* (coll) to fling, clap
schiaffeggiare §290 (schiafféggio) *tr* to slap; to buffet
schiaffo *m* slap, box
schiamazzare *intr* to squawk, cackle; to honk; to make a racket
schiamazzo *m* squawking, cackle; honk; hubbub
schiantare *tr* to crush, burst ‖ *intr* (ESSERE) (coll) to burst; (coll) to croak ‖ *ref* to break, crack, split
schianto *m* break, crack; crash; bang; knockout (*extraordinary, attractive person or thing*); **di schianto** all of a sudden; **schianto al cuore** heartache
schiappa *f* splinter; (coll) good-for-nothing
schiarimento *m* elucidation
schiarire §176 *tr* to make clearer; to make (*the hair*) light; to clear; to explain; to elucidate ‖ *intr* (ESSERE) to become light ‖ *ref* to clear up (*said of the weather*); to clear (*one's throat*); to fade ‖ *impers* (ESSERE) —schiarisce it is getting light
schiarita *f* clearing (*of weather*); improvement (*in relations*)
schiatta *f* race, stock
schiattare *intr* (ESSERE) to burst
schiavi·sta (-sti -ste) *adj* slave (*e.g., state*) ‖ *mf* antiabolitionist
schiavi·tù *f* (-tù) slavery; bondage
schia·vo -va *adj* enslaved ‖ *mf* slave
schiccherare (schìcchero) *tr* to scribble; to soil; to sketch; to dash off; to blurt out; (coll) to clean out
schidionare (schidióno) *tr* to put on the spit
schidióne *m* spit
schièna *f* back; divide; crown (*of road*); **giocare di schiena** to buck
schienale *m* back (*of chair; cut of meat*)
schièra *f* crowd; flock; herd; (mil) rank
schieraménto *m* alignment
schierare (schièro) *tr* to line up ‖ *ref* to line up; **schierarsi dalla parte di** to side with
schiètt·o -ta *adj* pure; frank, honest
schifare *tr* to loathe; to disgust ‖ *ref*—schifarsi di to feel disgusted with
schifa·to -ta *adj* disgusted
schifiltó·so -sa [s] *adj* fastidious; squeamish
schifo *m* disgust, loathing; skiff; shell; **fare schifo a** to disgust; to make sick
schifó·so -sa [s] *adj* disgusting; sickening; (slang) tremendous
schioccare §197 (schiocco) *tr* to snap (*the fingers*); to click (*the tongue*); to smack (*the lips*); to crack (*a whip*) ‖ *intr* to crack
schiòc·co *m* (-chi) crack, snap; click; smack
schiodare (schiòdo) *tr* to take the nails out of
schioppettata *f* gunshot; earshot
schiòppo *m* gun, shotgun; **a un tiro di schioppo** within earshot
schiùdere §125 *tr* & *ref* to open
schiuma *f* foam, froth; lather; head (*of beer*); dregs, scum; meerschaum;

avere la schiuma alla bocca to froth at the mouth
schiumaiòla *f* skimmer
schiumare *tr* to scum; to skim ‖ *intr* to foam, froth; to lather
schiumó·so -sa [s] *adj* foamy
schivare *tr* to avoid; to avert ‖ *ref* to shy
schi·vo -va *adj* averse; bashful, shy
schizzare *tr* to spray; to sprinkle; to ooze (*venom*); to sketch; **schizzare fuoco dagli occhi** to have fire in one's eyes ‖ *intr* (ESSERE) to gush; to squirt; to dart; **gli occhi gli schìzzano dall'orbita** his eyes are popping out of his head
schizzétto *m* sprayer; syringe; water pistol
schizzinó·so -sa [s] *adj* finicky, fastidious
schizzo *m* spray; splash; sketch; survey (*e.g., of literature*)
sci *m* (sci) ski
scia *f* wake; track; trail; **scia di condensazione** contrail
sciàbola *f* saber
sciabordare (sciabórdo) *tr* to shake, agitate ‖ *intr* to break (*said of waves*)
sciacallo *m* jackal
sciacquadi·ta *m* (-ta) finger bowl
sciacquare (sciàcquo) *tr* to rinse
sciacquatura *f* rinse
sciacqui·o *m* (-i) splash, dash
sciàcquo *m* rinsing (*of the mouth*); mouthwash
sciagura *f* calamity, misfortune
sciagura·to -ta *adj* unfortunate; wretched
scialacquare (scialàcquo) *tr* to squander
scialare *tr* to squander ‖ *intr* to be well off; to live it up
scial·bo -ba *adj* pale, faded; wan
scialle *m* shawl; **scialle da viaggio** traveling blanket
scialo *m* squandering; opulence; **a scialo** lavishly
scialuppa *f* launch; lifeboat
sciamanna·to -ta *adj* slovenly
sciamannó·ne -na *mf* slovenly person ‖ *f* slattern
sciamare *intr* (ESSERE & AVERE) to swarm
sciame *m* swarm; flock
sciampagna *f* champagne
scianca·to -ta *adj* cripple, lame; wobbly (*table*)
sciangài *m* pick-up-sticks ‖ **Sciangài** *f* Shanghai
sciarada *f* charade
sciare §119 *intr* to ski; to back water
sciarpa *f* scarf; sash (*e.g., of an officer or of a mayor*)
scias·sì *m* (-sì) chassis
sciàtica *f* (pathol) sciatica
scia·tóre -trice *mf* skier
sciatterìa *f* or sciattézza *f* slovenliness
sciat·to -ta *adj* slovenly, sloppy
scìbile *m* knowledge
sciènte *adj* conscious; knowing
scientìfi·co -ca *adj* (-ci -che) scientific
scìenza *f* science; knowledge

scienzia·to -ta *mf* scientist
scilinguàgnolo *m* frenum (*of tongue*); **avere lo scilinguagnolo sciolto** to have a loose tongue
Scilla *f* Scylla; **fra Scilla e Cariddi** between Scylla and Charibdis
scimitarra *f* scimitar
scìmmia *f* monkey; (coll) drunk; **fare la scimmia a** to ape; **scimmia antropomorfa** anthropoid ape
scimmié·sco -sca *adj* (**-schi -sche**) monkeyish; apish
scimmiottare (scimmiòtto) *tr* to ape
scimpan·zé *m* (**-zé**) chimpanzee
scimuni·to -ta *adj* idiotic ‖ *mf* idiot
scìndere §247 *tr* (lit) to split; to separate
scintìlla *f* spark; sparkle; (fig) scintilla; **scintilla elettrica** jump spark
scintillare *intr* to spark; to sparkle
scintillì·o *m* (**-i**) sparkle, brilliance
scioccare §197 *tr* to shock
sciocchézza *f* silliness; trifle
sciòc·co -ca (**-chi -che**) *adj* silly, foolish ‖ *mf* fool, blockhead
sciògliere §127 *tr* to loosen; to release; to unfasten, untie; to solve; to disperse; to dissolve; to limber; to fulfill (*a promise*); to unfurl (*sails*) ‖ *ref* to loosen up; to get loose; to dissolve; to melt (*into tears*)
scioglilìn·gua *m* (**-gue**) tongue twister
sciogliménto *m* melting; dissolution; fulfillment; denouement
sciolìna *f* ski wax
scioltézza *f* nimbleness, agility; freedom (*of movement*); ease
sciòl·to -ta *adj* loose; glib; free; blank (*verse*)
scioperante *adj* striking ‖ *mf* striker
scioperare (sciòpero) *intr* to strike
sciopera·to -ta *adj* loafing; lazy ‖ *m* loafer
sciòpero *m* strike; walkout; **sciopero a singhiozzo** slowdown strike; **sciopero bianco** sit-down strike; **sciopero della fame** hunger strike; **sciopero di solidarietà** sympathy strike; **sciopero pignolo** slowdown
sciorinare *tr* to display; to tell (*lies*); to air (*laundry*)
sciovìa *f* ski lift
sciovinismo *m* chauvinism, jingoism
scipi·to -ta *adj* insipid
scippo *m* snatching (*e.g., of a bag*)
sciròc·co *m* (**-chi**) sirocco; southeast
sciròppo *m* syrup
sci·sma *m* (**-smi**) schism
scismàti·co -ca *adj* (**-ci -che**) schismatic
scissióne *f* split; (biol, phys) fission
scis·so -sa *adj* split, rent
scisto *m* schist
sciupare *tr* to spoil; to wear out; to waste; to rumple ‖ *ref* to wear; to run down (*said of health*); to get rumpled
sciupa·to -ta *adj* ruined; worn out; wasted; run down
sciupì·o *m* (**-i**) waste
sciupó·ne -na *mf* waster, squanderer
sciu·scià *m* (**-scià**) bootblack; urchin
scìvola *f* chute

scivolare (scìvolo) *intr* (ESSERE & AVERE) to slide, glide; to steal; **scivolare d'ala** (aer) to sideslip
scivolata *f* slide, glide; **scivolata d'ala** (aer) sideslip
scìvolo *m* chute; (aer) slip (*for seaplanes*)
scivolóne *m* slip, slide
scivoló·so -sa [s] *adj* slippery
scoccare §197 (**scòcco**) *tr* to shoot (*an arrow*); to give (*a buss*); to strike (*the hour*) ‖ *intr* (ESSERE) to dart; to spring; to strike (*said of a clock*); to shoot
scocciare §128 (**scòccio**) *tr* (coll) to break; (coll) to bother; (naut) to unhook ‖ *ref* to be bored
scoccia·tóre -trice *mf* (coll) nuisance
scocciatura *f* (coll) bother, annoyance
scòc·co *m* (**-chi**) darting; stroke (*e.g., of three*); (naut) hook; **scocco di baci** bussing, kissing
scodèlla *f* bowl; soup plate
scodellare (scodèllo) *tr* to dish out
scodellino *m* small bowl; (mil) pan (*of musket lock*)
scodinzolare (scodìnzolo) *intr* to wag its tail; to waddle (*said of a woman*)
scoglièra *f* reef (*of rocks*); **scogliera corallina** coral reef
scò·glio *m* (**-gli**) rock; reef; cliff; stumbling block
scoiare §248 *tr* to skin
scoiàttolo *m* squirrel
scolabrò·do *m* (**-do**) colander, strainer
scolafrit·to *m* (**-to**) strainer
scolapa·sta *m* (**-sta**) (coll) colander
scolare (scólo) *tr* to drain; (fig) to polish off ‖ *intr* (ESSERE) to drip ‖ *ref* to melt
scolaré·sco -sca (**-schi -sche**) *adj* school ‖ *f* schoolchildren; student body
scola·ro -ra *mf* pupil; student
scolàsti·co -ca (**-ci -che**) *adj* school; scholastic ‖ *m* scholastic, schoolman ‖ *f* scholasticism
scola·tóio *m* (**-tói**) drain; strainer
scolatura *f* drip, drippings; dregs
scollacciar·to -ta *adj* low-necked; wearing a low-cut dress; dirty, obscene
scollare (scòllo) *tr* to cut off at the neck; to unglue ‖ *ref* to wear a low-necked dress; to come unglued
scollatura *f* neckline; ungluing; **scollatura a barchetta** low neck; **scollatura a punta** V neck
scòllo *m* neck, neckline
scólo *m* drain; drainage; (slang) clap
scolopèndra *f* centipede
scolorare (scolóro) *tr*, *intr* (ESSERE), & *ref* to fade, discolor; to pale
scolorire §176 *tr*, *intr* (ESSERE), & *ref* to fade, discolor
scolpare (scólpo) *tr* to excuse
scolpire §176 *tr* to sculpture; to engrave; to emphasize
scòlta *f* (lit) sentry; **fare la scolta** to stand guard
scombaciare §128 *tr* to pull apart, separate
scombinare *tr* to disarrange; to upset
scómbro *m* mackerel

scombù·glio *m* (-gli) (coll) disorder

scombussolare (scombùssolo) *tr* to upset

scomméssa *f* bet, wager

scomméttere §198 *tr* to bet; to separate

scommetti·tóre -trice *mf* bettor

scomodare (scòmodo) *tr* to trouble, disturb || *ref* to take the trouble

scomodi·tà *f* (-tà) trouble, inconvenience

scòmo·do -da *adj* awkward, unwieldy; uncomfortable || *m* inconvenience

scompaginare (scompàgino) *tr* to upset; (typ) to pi

scompagna·to -ta *adj* odd

scomparire §108 *intr* (ESSERE) to disappear; to make a bad showing

scompar·so -sa *adj* disappeared; extinct || *mf* deceased || *f* disappearance; death

scompartiménto *m* compartment; partition

scompènso *m* lack of compensation; imbalance

scompigliare §280 *tr* to disarray; to trouble, upset

scompì·glio *m* (-gli) disarray; upset

scompisciare §128 *tr* (vulg) to piss on || *ref* (vulg) to wet oneself; scompisciarsi dalle risa (coll) to split one's sides laughing

scomplè·to -ta *adj* incomplete

scompórre §218 *tr* to decompose, disintegrate; to rumple; to dishevel; to upset; to dismantle, take apart; (typ) to pi || *ref* to lose one's composure

scompó·sto -sta *adj* unseemly

scomùni·ca *f* (-che) excommunication

scomunicare §197 (scomùnico) *tr* to excommunicate; (joc) to ostracize

sconcertare (sconcèrto) *tr* to upset; to disconcert || *ref* to become disconcerted

sconcézza *f* obscenity, indecency

scón·cio -cia (-ci -ce) *adj* dirty, filthy, obscene || *m* obscenity; shame

sconclusiona·to -ta *adj* inconsequential; incoherent; rambling

sconcordanza *f* disagreement; (gram) lack of agreement

scondi·to -ta *adj* unseasoned

sconfessare (sconfèsso) *tr* to disavow; to retract

sconfessióne *f* disavowal

sconfiggere §104 *tr* to defeat, rout; to pull (*a nail*); to unfasten

sconfinare *intr* to cross the border; sconfinare da to stray from

sconfina·to -ta *adj* boundless, unlimited

sconfitta *f* defeat, rout

sconfortante *adj* discouraging

sconfortare (sconfòrto) *tr* to discourage; to distress || *ref* to become discouraged

sconfòrto *m* depression; distress

scongelare (scongèlo) *tr* to thaw

scongiurare *tr* to conjure; to implore

scongiuro *m* conjuration; entreaty

sconnès·so -sa *adj* disconnected; incoherent

sconnèttere §107 *tr* to disconnect; to take apart || *intr* to be incoherent

sconoscènte *adj* unappreciative

sconosciu·to -ta *adj* unknown || *mf* stranger

sconquassare *tr* to smash, shatter

sconquassa·to -ta *adj* broken-down; upset

sconquasso *m* destruction; confusion; smash-up

sconsacrare *tr* to desecrate

sconsideratézza *f* thoughtlessness

sconsidera·to -ta *adj* inconsiderate

sconsigliare §280 *tr* to dissuade, discourage

sconsiglia·to -ta *adj* thoughtless

sconsola·to -ta *adj* disconsolate

scontare (scónto) *tr* to expiate; to discount; to serve (*time in jail*)

scontentare (scontènto) *tr* to dissatisfy

scontèn·to -ta *adj* & *m* discontent

scónto *m* discount; part payment; (fig) partial remission

scontrare (scóntro) *tr* to meet; (naut) to turn (*the wheel*) sharply || *ref* to clash; to collide; to come to blows

scontrino *m* check, ticket

scóntro *m* collision; battle, encounter; clash; ward (*of key*)

scontró·so -sa [s] *adj* peevish, cross

sconveniènte *adj* unfavorable; unseemly, unbecoming; indecent

sconvenire §282 *intr* (ESSERE) to be unseemly or unbecoming

sconvòlgere §289 *tr* to upset; to disconcert

sconvolgiménto *m* upsetting; sconvolgimento di stomaco stomach upset; sconvolgimento tellurico upheaval

sconvòl·to -ta *adj* upset; disconcerted; distracted

scópa *f* broom; scopa per lavaggio mop

scopare (scópo) *tr* to sweep

scopata *f* sweep

scoperchiare §287 (scopèrchio) *tr* to uncover; to take the lid off

scopèr·to -ta *adj* uncovered; open; bare; exposed; unpaid || *m* open ground; open air; overdraft; (econ) short sale; (com) balance; allo scoperto in the open; overdrawn (*check*); short (*sale*) || *f* discovery; alla scoperta openly

scòpo *m* purpose, goal, aim

scoppiare §287 (scòppio) *tr* to uncouple || *intr* (ESSERE) to burst; to blow; to explode; to break (*said, e.g., of news*); (fig) to die (*e.g., of overeating*); scoppiare a to burst out (*laughing or crying*)

scoppiettare (scoppiétto) *intr* to crackle

scoppietti·o *m* (-i) crackle

scòp·pio *m* (-pi) burst; explosion; outbreak; outburst; blowout (*of tire*); a scoppio internal-combustion (*engine*); scoppio di tuono clap of thunder

scòppola *f* drop (*of plane in air pocket*); (coll) rabbit punch

scopriménto *m* uncovering; unveiling

scoprire §110 *tr* to uncover; to unveil; to discover; to expose || *ref* to take off one's clothes; to take one's hat off; to reveal oneself

scopri·tóre **-trìce** *mf* discoverer

scoraggiaménto *m* discouragement

scoraggiante *adj* discouraging

scoraggiare §290 *tr* to discourage, dishearten || *ref* to be or become discouraged

scoraménto *m* (lit) discouragement

scorbuto *m* scurvy

scorciare §128 (**scórcio**) *tr* to shorten; to foreshorten || *intr* (ESSERE) to shorten, grow shorter; to look foreshortened || *ref* to shorten, grow shorter

scorciatóia *f* shortcut, cutoff

scór·cio *m* (-ci) foreshortening; end, close (*of a period*); **di scorcio** foreshortened

scordare (**scòrdo**) *tr* to forget; to put out of tune || *ref* to forget; to get out of tune

scorég·gia *f* (-ge) (vulg) fart

scoreggiare §290 (**scoréggio**) *intr* (vulg) to fart

scòrgere §249 *tr* to perceive, to discern

scòria *f* slag, dross; (fig) scum, dregs; **scorie atomiche** atomic waste

scorna·to **-ta** *adj* humiliated, ridiculed; hornless

scòrno *m* humiliation, ridicule

scorpacciata *f* bellyful; **fare una scorpacciata di** to stuff oneself with

scorpióne *m* scorpion || **Scorpione** *m* (astrol) Scorpio

scorrazzare *tr* to wander over || *intr* to run around; to move about; (fig) to ramble; (mil) to raid

scórrere §139 *tr* to raid; to glance over || *intr* (ESSERE) to flow; to run; to glide

scorreria *f* raid, foray, incursion

scorrettézza *f* imprecision; impropriety

scorrèt·to **-ta** *adj* incorrect; improper

scorrévole *adj* sliding; flowing, fluent || *m* slide (*of slide rule*)

scorribanda *f* raid, foray, incursion

scór·so **-sa** *adj* past, last || *m* error, slip || *f* glance; short stay

scor·sóio **-sóia** *adj* (-sói -sóie) slip (*knot*)

scòrta *f* escort; provision, stock; **di scorta** spare (*tire*); **fare di scorta a** to escort; **scorta d'onore** (mil) honor guard; **scorte** (com) stockpile; (com) supplies; **scorte morte** agricultural supplies; **scorte vive** livestock

scortare (**scòrto**) *tr* to escort; to foreshorten

scortecciare §128 (**scortéccio**) *tr* to strip the bark from; to peel off; to scrape || *ref* to peel off

scortése *adj* discourteous, impolite

scortesìa *f* discourtesy, impoliteness

scorticare §197 (**scórtico**) *tr* to skin; to be overdemanding with (*students*); to fleece || *ref* to skin (*e.g., one's arm*)

scòrza *f* bark; skin, hide; (fig) appearance; **scorza di limone** lemon peel

scoscendiménto *m* landslide; cliff

scoscé·so **-sa** [s] *adj* sloping, steep

scòssa *f* shake; jerk; **scossa di pioggia** downpour; **scossa di terremoto** earth tremor; **scossa elettrica** electric shock; **scossa tellurica** earthquake

scossóne *m* jolt, jerk

scostaménto *m* removal; separation

scostare (**scòsto**) *tr* to move away; to try to avoid || *intr* (ESSERE) to stand away || *ref* to step aside; to stray

scostuma·to **-ta** *adj* dissolute, debauched

scotennare (**scoténno**) *tr* to scalp; to skin (*an animal*)

scòtta *f* whey; (naut) sheet

scottante *adj* burning (*question*); outrageous (*offense*)

scottare (**scòtto**) *tr* to burn; to scald; to sear; to boil (*eggs*); (fig) to sting || *intr* to burn; to be hot (*said of stolen goods*) || *ref* to get burnt

scottatura *f* burn; (fig) blow, jolt

scòt·to **-ta** *adj* overcooked, overdone || *m*—**pagare lo scotto** to foot the bill; **pagare lo scotto di** to expiate || *f* see **scotta**

scoutismo *m* scouting

scovare (**scóvo**) *tr* to rouse (*game*); to find, discover

scovolino *m* pipe cleaner; (mil) small swab

scóvolo *m* (mil) swab

scòzia *f* (archit) scotia || **la Scozia** Scotland

scozzése [s] *adj* Scotch, Scottish || *m* Scotch, Scottish (*language*); Scotchman || *f* Scotchwoman

scozzonare (**scozzóno**) *tr* to break in (*a horse*); to train

scranna *f* (hist) seat

screanza·to **-ta** *adj* ill-mannered, rude

screditare (**scrédito**) *tr* to discredit

scremare (**scrèmo**) *tr* to cream

scrematrice *f* cream separator

screpolare (**scrèpolo**) *tr*, *intr* (ESSERE), & *ref* to crack; to chap

screpolatura *f* crack; chap (*of skin*)

screziare §287 (**scrèzio**) *tr* to mottle, variegate

serè·zio *m* (-zi) tiff

scrì·ba *m* (-bi) scribe (*Jewish scholar*)

scribacchiare §287 *tr* to scribble, scrawl

scribacchino *m* scribbler; hack

scricchiolare (**scrìcchiolo**) *intr* to crack, creak

scricchiolì·o *m* (-i) crack, creak

scricciolo *m* wren

scrigno *m* jewel box

scriminatura *f* part (*in hair*)

scrìt·to **-ta** *adj* written || *m* writing || *f* sign; inscription; contract; **scritta luminosa** electric sign

scrit·tóio *m* (-tói) writing desk

scrit·tóre **-trìce** *mf* writer

scrittura *f* handwriting; penmanship; writing; contract; entry; (theat) booking; **Sacra Scrittura** Holy Scripture; **scrittura privata** contract; **scrittura pubblica** deed, indenture; **scrittura a macchina** typing

scritturale *adj* scriptural || *m* clerk; copyist; fundamentalist

scritturare *tr* (theat) to book, engage

scrivanìa *f* desk

scrivano m clerk, copyist, typist
scrìvere §250 tr & intr to write; **scrivere a macchina** to type
scroccare §197 (scròcco) tr to sponge (a meal); to manage to get (a prize) || intr to sponge
scrocca·tóre -trice mf sponger
scròc·co m (-chi) sponging; creaking; **a scrocco** sponging; spring (lock); switchblade (knife)
scroccó·ne -na mf sponger
scròfa f sow; slut
scrollare (scròllo) tr to shake; to shrug (one's shoulders) || ref to get into action; to pull oneself together
scrollata f shake; **scrollata di spalle** shrug
scrosciare §128 (scròscio) intr (ESSERE & AVERE) to pelt down; (fig) to thunder
scrò·scio m (-sci) thunder, roar; **scroscio di pioggia** downpour; **scroscio di tuono** thunderclap
scrostare (scròsto) tr to pick (a scab); to scrape; to peel off || ref to peel off
scrosta·to -ta adj peeling; scaly
scròto m scrotum
scrùpolo m scruple; scrupulousness
scrupoló·so -sa [s] adj scrupulous
scrutare tr to scan, scrutinize
scruta·tóre -trice adj inquisitive || mf teller (of votes)
scrutina·tóre -trice mf teller (of votes)
scruti·nio m (-ni) poll, vote; evaluation (of an examination); count (of votes); **scrutinio segreto** secret ballot
scucire §143 tr to unstitch; (coll) to cough up || ref to come unstitched
scucitura f unstitching; rip
scuderìa f stable
scudétto m badge; escutcheon; (sports) badge of victory
scudièro m esquire
scudisciare §128 tr to whip
scudì·scio m (-sci) whip
scudo m shield; escutcheon; **far scudo a** to shield
scùffia f (coll) load (intoxication); **fare scuffia** to capsize; **prendersi una scuffia per** to fall for, to fall in love with
scugnizzo m Neapolitan urchin
sculacciare §128 tr to spank
sculacciata f spank, spanking
sculacció·ne m spank, spanking
sculettare (sculétto) intr to waddle
scul·tóre -trice mf sculptor || f sculptress
scultura f sculpture
scuòla f school; **scuola allievi ufficiali** military academy; officers' candidate school; **scuola dell'obbligo** mandatory education; **scuola di danza** dancing school; **scuola di dressaggio** obedience school (for dogs); **scuola di guerra** war college; **scuola di guida** driving school; **scuola di perfezionamento per laureati** postgraduate school; **scuola di taglio** sewing school; **scuola materna** kindergarten; **scuola mista** coeducational school

scuòla·bus m (-bus) school bus
scuòtere §251 tr to shake; to shake up; **scuotere di dosso** to shake off
scure f ax; cleaver
scurire §176 tr, intr (ESSERE), & ref to darken
scu·ro -ra adj dark || m darkness; dark; shutter; **essere allo scuro** to be in the dark
scurrile adj scurrilous
scusa f excuse; apology; pretext; **chiedere scusa** to apologize
scusare tr to excuse; to pardon; to apologize for; **scusi!** pardon me! || ref to apologize; to beg off
sdaziare §287 tr to clear through customs
sdebitare (sdébito) tr to free from debt || ref to become free of debt; **sdebitarsi con** to repay a favor to
sdegnare (sdégno) tr to scorn; to arouse, enrage || ref to get mad
sdégno m indignation, anger; (lit) scorn
sdegnó·so -sa [s] adj indignant; haughty
sdenta·to -ta adj toothless
sdilinquire §176 tr to weaken || intr (ESSERE) & ref to swoon; to become mawkish
sdoganare tr to clear through customs
sdolcina·to -ta adj mawkish
sdolcinatura f mush, slobber
sdoppiare §287 (sdóppio) tr & ref to split
sdoppiaménto m splitting
sdottoreggiare §290 (sdottoréggio) intr to pontificate
sdràia f chaise longue; deck chair
sdraiare §287 tr to lay down || ref to stretch out (e.g., on the ground)
sdràio m (sdrài) stretching out; **mettersi a sdraio** to lie down
sdrucciolare (sdrùcciolo) intr (ESSERE & AVERE) to slip, slide
sdrucciolévole adj slippery
sdrùccio·lo -la adj proparoxytone || m slip; slope; proparoxytone
sdruccioló·ni adv slipping, sliding
sdrucire (sdrùcio) & §176 tr to tear, rend, rip
sdrucitura f tear, rend, rip
se m (se) if || §5 pron || conj if; whether; **se mai** in the event; **se no** otherwise; **se non tu** (lui, lei, etc.) nobody else but you (him, her, etc.), e.g., **non puoi essere stato se non tu** it could not have been anyone else but you; **se non altro** at least; **se non che** but; se pure even if
sé §5 pron himself; herself; itself; yourself; themselves; yourselves; oneself; **di per sé stesso** by itself; **fuori di sé** beside oneself; **rientrare in sé** to come back to one's senses; **uscire di sé** to be beside oneself
sebbène conj although, though
sèbo m sebum, tallow
séc·ca f (-che) sand bank, shoal; drought; **dare in secca** to run aground; **in secca** hard up
seccante adj drying; annoying
seccare §197 (sécco) tr to dry; to bore;

to bother, annoy ‖ *intr* (ESSERE) to dry up ‖ *ref* to dry up; to be annoyed

secca·tóio *m* (-tói) drying room; squeegee (*to remove water from wet decks*)

secca·tóre -trice *mf* bore, pest

seccatura *f* drying; trouble, nuisance

sécchia *f* bucket, pail; **piovere a secchie** to rain cats and dogs

secchièllo *m* little bucket

séc·chio *m* (-chi) bucket, pail; bucketful; **secchio dell'immondezza** trash can

séc·co -ca (-chi -che) *adj* dry; lanky; sharp ‖ *m* dryness; dry land; drought; **a secco** dry (*cleaning*); **dare in secco** to run aground; **in secco** hard up; **lavare a secco** to dry-clean ‖ *f* see **secca**

secénto·sco -sca *adj* (-schi -sche) seventeenth-century

secentèsi·mo -ma *adj, m & pron* six hundredth

secèrnere §153 (*pp* secrèto) *tr* to secrete

secessióne *f* secession

séco §5 *prep phrase* (lit) with oneself; along, e.g., **portare seco** to bring along

secolare *adj* secular; century-old; worldly ‖ *m* layman

sècolo *m* century; age; world

secónda *f* second; second-year class; **a seconda** with the wind; **a seconda di** according to; **in seconda** (aut) in second; (mil) second in command

secondare (secóndo) *tr* to second

secondà·rio -ria *adj* (-ri -rie) secondary

secondino *m* prison guard, turnkey

secón·do -da *adj* second; (lit) favorable ‖ *m* second; second course; (nav) executive officer ‖ *f* see **seconda** ‖ *pron* second ‖ **secondo** *prep* according to; **secondo me (te, etc.)** in my (your, etc.) opinion

secondogèni·to -ta *adj* second-born

secrezióne *f* secretion

sèdano *m* celery

sedare (sèdo) *tr* to calm, placate

sedati·vo -va *adj & m* sedative

sède *f* seat; branch; residence; period; (gram) syllable; (rr) right of way; **in separata sede** in private; (law) **with change of venue**; **Santa Sede** Holy See; **sede centrale** main office, home office

sedentà·rio -ria (-ri -rie) *adj* sedentary ‖ *m* sedentary person

sedére *m* sitting; rear, backside ‖ *v* §252 *intr* (ESSERE) to sit, to be seated; to be in session; to be located ‖ *ref* to sit down

sèdia *f* chair; seat; see; **sedia a braccioli** armchair; **sedia a dondolo** rocking chair; **sedia a pozzetto** bucket seat; **sedia a sdraio** deck chair; **sedia da posta** (hist) mail coach; **sedia di vimini** wicker chair; **sedia elettrica** electric chair; **sedia girevole** swivel chair

sedicènne *adj* sixteen-year-old ‖ *mf* sixteen-year-old person

sedicènte *adj* so-called, self-styled

sedicèsi·mo -ma *adj, m & pron* sixteenth

sédici *adj & pron* sixteen; **le sedici** four P.M. ‖ *m* sixteen; sixteenth (*in dates*)

sedile *m* seat; bench; bottom (*of chair*); (aut) bucket seat

sedimènto *m* sediment

sedilo *m* sulky

sedizióne *f* sedition

sedizió·so -sa [s] *adj* seditious

seducènte *adj* seductive; alluring

sedurre §182 *tr* to seduce; to allure; to lead astray; to charm, captivate

seduta *f* sitting; session, meeting; **seduta fiume** (pol) uninterrupted session; **seduta stante** on the spot

sedut·tóre -trice *adj* seductive; alluring; charming ‖ *mf* seducer

seduzióne *f* seduction; allurement; charm

sefardi·ta (-ti -te) *adj* Sephardic ‖ *mf* Sephardi

sé·ga *f* (-ghe) saw; **a sega** serrated; **sega a nastro** band saw; **sega circolare** buzz saw; **sega da carpentiere** lumberman's saw; **sega intelaiata a lama** bucksaw; **sega meccanica** power saw

ségala *f* rye

segali·gno -gna *adj* rye; lean, wiry

segare §209 (ségo) *tr* to saw; to cut

segatrice *f* power saw; **segatrice a disco** circular saw; **segatrice a nastro** band saw

segatura *f* cutting; sawdust

seggétta *f* commode

sèg·gio *m* (-gi) seat (*e.g., in congress*); **seggio elettorale** voting commission

sèggiola *f* chair; **seggiola a sdraio** deck chair

seggiolino *m* child's chair; stool; bucket seat; **seggiolino eiettabile** (aer) ejection seat

seggiolóne *m* highchair; easy chair

seggiovìa *f* chair lift

segherìa *f* sawmill

seghetta·to -ta *adj* serrated

seghétto *m* hacksaw; **seghetto da traforo** coping saw

segmènto *m* segment; **segmento elastico** (aut) piston ring

segnaccènto *m* accent mark

segnàcolo *m* (lit) symbol, sign

segnalare *tr* to signal; to point out ‖ *ref* to distinguish oneself

segnalazióne *f* signaling; sign, signal; nomination; recommendation; **dare la segnalazione a** to notify; **fare segnalazioni** to signal; **segnalazioni stradali** road signs

segnale *m* sign; signal; bookmark; **segnale di allarme** (mil) alarm; **segnale di occupato** (telp) busy signal; **segnale di via libera** (telp) dial tone; **segnale orario** (rad, telv) time signal; **segnali stradali** road signs

segnalèti·co -ca *adj* (-ci -che) identification (*mark*) ‖ *f* road signs

segnalibro *m* bookmark

segnalìne·e *m* (-e) lineman

segnapósto *m* place card

segnapun·ti *m* (-ti) scorekeeper

segnare (**ségno**) *tr* to mark; to underscore, underline; to jot down; to say (*e.g., five o'clock, said of a watch*); to brand; (*sports*) to score; **segnare a dito** to point to || *ref* to cross oneself

segnatas·se *m* (**-se**) postage-due stamp

segnatura *f* signing; signature; library number; (*eccl*) chancery; (*sports*) final score; (*typ*) signature

segnavèn·to *m* (**-to**) weather vane

ségno *m* mark; bookmark; symbol; sign; signal; boundary; (*mus*) signature; **a segno che** so that; **a tal segno** to such a point; **essere fatto segno di** to be the target of; **in segno di** as a token of; **mettere a segno** to check, control; **segno della Croce** sign of the Cross; **segno di croce** cross (*mark*); **segno d'interpunzione**, or **di punteggiatura**, or **grafico** punctuation mark; **segno di riconoscimento** identification mark

ségo *m* tallow, suet

segregare §209 (**sègrego**) *tr* to segregate; to secrete || *ref* to withdraw

segregazióne *f* segregation; **segregazione cellulare** solitary confinement

segregazioni·sta *mf* (**-sti -ste**) segregationist

segretariato *m* secretariat

segretà·rio -ria *mf* secretary; clerk

segretería *f* secretary's office; secretaryship

segretézza *f* secrecy

segré·to -ta *adj* secret; secretive || *m* secret; secrecy; **segreto d'alcova** boudoir secret; **segreto di Pulcinella** open secret

seguace *mf* follower

seguènte *adj* following, next

segù·gio *m* (**-gi**) bloodhound; (*fig*) private eye

seguire (**séguo**) *tr* to follow; to attend || *intr* (ESSERE) to continue; to follow, ensue; (*with* *dat*) to follow

seguitare (**séguito**) *intr*—**seguitare a** + *inf* to keep on + *ger*, *e.g.*, **seguitare a parlare** to keep on talking; **seguiti!** go ahead!

séguito *m* following; retinue; followers; sequence; sequel; pursuit; **di seguito** in succession; **far seguito a** to refer to; **in seguito** thereafter; **in seguito a** as a consequence of

sèi *adj & pron* six; **le sei** six o'clock || *m* six; sixth (*in dates*)

seicènto *adj, m & pron* six hundred || *f* car with a motor displacing 600 cubic centimeters || **il Seicento** the seventeenth century

seimila *adj, m, & pron* six thousand

sélce *f* silica; flint; (*lit*) stone; **selci** paving blocks

selciare §128 (**sélcio**) *tr* to pave

selcià·to -ta *adj* paved || *m* paving

seletti·vo -va *adj* selective

selezionare (**selzióno**) *tr* to select, sort out

selezióne *f* selection; choice

sèlla *f* saddle

sel·làio *m* (**-lài**) saddler

sellare (**sèllo**) *tr* to saddle

selleria *f* saddler's shop; saddlery; (*aut*) upholstery

sélva *f* woods, forest

selvaggina *f* game

selvàg·gio -gia (**-gi -ge**) *adj* savage; vicious (*horse*) || *m* savage; unsociable person

selvàti·co -ca *adj* (**-ci -che**) wild

selvicoltura *f* forestry

sèlz *m* (**sèlz**) seltzer, club soda

semàforo *m* traffic light; semaphore

semànti·co -ca *adj* (**-ci -che**) semantic || *f* semantics

sembiante *m* (*lit*) look; **fare sembianti di** to pretend

sembianza *f* look; (*lit*) similarity

sembrare (**sémbro**) *intr* (ESSERE) to seem, look, appear || *impers*—**sembra** it seems

séme *m* seed; stone (*of fruit*); (*cards*) suit

seménta *f* sowing season; (*lit*) seed

seménte *f* seed

semènza *f* seed; brads (*used in upholstery*)

semenzà·io *m* (**-zài**) hotbed, seedbed

semestrale *adj* semiannual, semiyearly

semèstre *m* semester; half year

sèmi- *pref adj* semi-, *e.g.*, **semicircolare** semicircular; half-, *e.g.*, **semichiuso** half-closed || *pref mf* semi-, *e.g.*, **semicerchio** semicircle; half, *e.g.*, **semitono** half tone; demi-, *e.g.*, **semidìo** demigod

semiapèr·to -ta *adj* half-open; ajar

semiasse *m* (*mach*) axle (*on each side of differential*)

semicér·chio *m* (**-chi**) semicircle

semichiu·so -sa [s] *adj* half-closed

semicingola·to -ta *adj & m* half-track

semicìrcolo *m* semicircle

semiconduttóre *m* semiconductor

semiconvit·tóre -trice *mf* day student

semicù·pio *m* (**-pi**) sitz bath

semi-dìo *m* (**-dèi**) demigod

semidòt·to -ta *adj* semilearned

semifinale *f* semifinal

sémina *f* sowing; sowing season

seminare (**sémino**) *tr* to sow, seed; to plant; (*coll*) to leave behind

seminà·rio *m* (**-ri**) seminary; seminar

seminari·sta *m* (**-sti**) seminarian

semina·to -ta *adj* sown, seeded || *m* sown land; **uscire dal seminato** to digress

semina·tóre -trice *mf* sower || *f* (*mach*) seeder, seeding machine

seminterrato *m* basement

seminu·do -da *adj* half-naked

semioscurità *f* partial darkness

semirìgi·do -da *adj* semirigid; inelastic

semirimòr·chio *m* (**-chi**) semitrailer

semisè·rio -ria [s] *adj* (**-ri -rie**) seriocomic

semisfèra *f* (*geom*) hemisphere

semi·ta (**-ti -te**) *adj* Semitic || *mf* Semite

semitóno *m* (*mus*) semitone, half tone

semmài *conj* if ever; in the event that

sémola *f* bran; (*coll*) freckles

semolino *m* semolina

semovènte *adj* self-propelled

sempitèr·no -na *adj* (lit) everlasting

sémplice *adj* simple; single; plain; mere; (mil) private; (nav) ordinary ‖ *m* medicinal herb; **semplici** simple folk

semplició·ne -na *adj* simple ‖ *mf* simpleton

semplici·tà *f* (-tà) simplicity

semplificare §197 (semplìfico) *tr* to simplify ‖ *ref* to become easier or simpler

sèmpre *adv* always; ever; yet; **da sempre** from time immemorial; **di sempre** same, same old; **e poi sempre** ever and ever; **ma sempre** but only; **per sempre** forever; **sempre che** provided; **sempre meglio** better and better; **sempre meno** less and less; **sempre però** but only; **sempre vostro** very truly yours

semprevérde *adj, m & f* evergreen

sènape *f* mustard

senapismo *m* mustard plaster

senato *m* senate

sena·tóre -trice *mf* senator

senése [s] *adj & mf* Sienese

senile *adj* old; of old age

senilismo *m* (pathol) senility

senilità *f* old age

senióre *adj & m* elder, senior

Sènna *f* Seine

sénno *m* wisdom; **far senno** to come back to one's senses; **senno di poi** hindsight; **uscir di senno** to go out of one's mind

séno *m* chest; breast, bosom; cove; (anat) sinus; (math) sine; (fig) heart; **in seno a** within

senonché or **se non che** *conj* but

sensale *m* broker; commission merchant

sensa·to -ta *adj* sensible, reasonable; sane

sensazionale *adj* sensational

sensazióne *f* sensation

sensìbile *adj* sensible; perceptible; appreciable; sensitive; responsive (*e.g., to affection*) ‖ *m* world of the senses

sensibili·tà *f* (-tà) sensitivity; sensibility

sensibilizzare [ddzz] *tr* to sensitize

sensiti·vo -va *adj* sensitive ‖ *m* medium

sènso *m* sense; feeling; meaning; aspect; tone, fashion; direction; **ai sensi di legge** according to law; **a senso libero** free (*translation*); **doppio senso** double entendre; **in senso contrario** in the opposite direction; **perdere i sensi** to lose consciousness; **riprendere i sensi** to come to; **sensi carnal** appetite, flesh; **senso unico** one-way; **senso vietato** no entry, one-way

senso·rio -ria *adj* (-ri -rie) sensory

sensuale *adj* sensual, carnal; sensuous

sensualità *f* sensuality

sentènza *f* sentence; maxim

sentenziare §287 (sentènzio) *tr* to pass sentence upon, sentence ‖ *intr* to pontificate

sentenzió·so -sa [s] *adj* sententious

sentièro *m* path, pathway

sentimentale *adj* sentimental; mawkish

sentimentalismo *m* sentimentalism

sentiménto *m* feeling; sentiment; sense;

uscire di sentimento (coll) to go out of one's mind

sentina *f* bilge; sink (*of vice*)

sentinèlla *f* sentry, sentinel

sentire *m* feeling ‖ *v* (sènto) *tr* to feel; to hear; to listen to; to consult (*a doctor*); to smell; to taste; **farsi sentire** to make oneself heard ‖ *intr* to feel; to listen; to smell; to taste; **non sentirci di quell'orecchio** to turn a deaf ear; **sentirci bene** to have keen hearing ‖ *ref* to feel; **non sentirsela di** to not have the courage to; **sentirsela** to feel up to it

senti·to -ta *adj* heartfelt

sentóre *m* inkling, feeling; sign; (lit) smell

sènza *prep* without; beyond (*e.g., comparison*); **senza** + *inf* without + *ger*; **senza che** + *subj* without + *ger*; **senza di** + *pron* without + *pron*, e.g., **senza di lui** without him; **senz'altro** without any doubt, of course

senza·dìo *m* (-dìo)—**i senzadio** the godless

senzapà·tria *m* (-tria) man without a country; renegade

senzatét·to *m* (-to) homeless person; **i senzatetto** the homeless

separare *tr & ref* to separate

separazióne *f* separation

sepolcrale *adj* sepulchral

sepolcréto *m* cemetery

sepólcro *m* sepulcher, grave

sepoltura *f* burial; grave

seppellire §253 *tr* to bury

séppia *adj invar* sepia ‖ *f* cuttlefish

seppure *conj* even if

sè·psi *f* (-psi) sepsis

sequèla *f* series

sequènza *f* sequence

sequestrare (sequèstro) *tr* to seize, confiscate; to kidnap; to confine; to quarantine; (law) to attach, sequester

sequèstro *m* seizure; attachment; **sequestro di persona** unlawful detention

séra *f* evening; night; **da mezza sera** cocktail (*dress*); dark (*suit*); **da sera** evening (*gown*); formal (*attire*)

serac·co *m* (-chi) serac

serafino *m* seraph

serale *adj* evening; night

seralménte *adv* in the evening; every evening

serata *f* evening; soiree, evening party; **serata d'addio** (theat) farewell performance; **di beneficenza** benefit performance

serbare (sèrbo) *tr* to keep; to save (*e.g., a place*); to bear (*a grudge*) ‖ *ref* to keep oneself; to stay

serba·tóio *m* (-tói) tank; reservoir; cartridge clip

sèr·bo -ba *adj & mf* Serbian ‖ *m*—**in serbo** in store

serbocroa·to -ta *adj & mf* Serbo-Croatian

serenata *f* serenade

serenìssi·mo -ma *adj* Serene (*Highness*)

sereni·tà *f* (-tà) serenity

seré·no -na *adj* serene; clear, fair (*weather*)

sergènte *m* sergeant; carpenter's clamp; sergente maggiore first sergeant

sèri·co -ca *adj* (-ci -che) silk

sè·rie *f* (-rie) series; (sports) division; fuori serie (aut) custom-built; in serie (aut) standard; (elec) in series

serietà *f* seriousness; gravity

serigrafia *f* silkscreen process

sè·rio -ria (-ri -rie) *adj* serious; stern; poco serio unreliable (*man*); loose (*woman*) ‖ *m* seriousness; sul serio in earnest; really, e.g., bello sul serio really beautiful

sermonare (sermóno) *tr* & *intr* (lit) to sermonize

sermóne *m* sermon

sermoneggiare §290 (sermonéggio) *intr* to preach; to lecture

seròti·no -na *adj* late; (lit) evening

sèrpa *f* coach box

sèrpe *f* snake, serpent; a serpe coiled, in a coil; nutrirsi or scaldarsi la serpe in seno to nourish a viper in one's bosom

serpeggiare §290 (serpéggio) *intr* to zigzag; to wind; to creep, spread

serpènte *m* snake, serpent; serpente a sonagli rattlesnake

serpenti·no -na *adj* serpentine ‖ *m* serpentine; coil (*of pipe*) ‖ *f* zigzag, turn (*of winding road*); coil (*of pipe*)

sérqua *f* dozen; lot, large number

sèrra *f* dike, levee; hothouse; sierra; un serra serra a milling crowd

serrafi·la *m* (-le) rear-guard soldier ‖ *f* rear ship (*of convoy*)

serrafilo *m* electrician's pliers; (elec) binding post

serrà·glio *m* (-gli) menagerie; seraglio

serramànico *m*—a serramanico clasp (*knife*); switchblade (*knife*)

serrame *m* lock

serraménto *m* closing, bolting ‖ serra-mén·ti & -ta *fpl* closing devices, doors, windows, and shutters

serranda *f* shutter (*of store*)

serrare (sèrro) *tr* to shut, close; to pursue (*the enemy*); to increase (*tempo*); to furl (*sails*); to lock; to clench (*one's teeth, one's fists*); to shake (*hands*) ‖ *intr* to shut; to be tight ‖ *ref* to be wrenched, e.g., gli si serrò il cuore his heart was wrenched; serrarsi addosso a to press (*the enemy*)

serrata *f* lockout

serrate *m*—serrate finale (sports) finish

serra·to -ta *adj* shut (*e.g., door*); concise (*style*); tight (*game*); rapid (*gallop*); closed (*ranks*); thick (*crowd*) ‖ *f* see serrata

serratura *f* lock

sèrto *m* (poet) crown, wreath

sèrva *f* (pej) maidservant, maid

servènte *adj* (*gentleman*) in waiting ‖ *m* gunner; (obs) servant

servìbile *adj* usable

serviènte *m* (eccl) server

servì·gio *m* (-gi) service; favor

servile *adj* servile; menial; modal (*auxiliary*)

servire (sèrvo) *tr* to serve; to wait on; in che posso servirLa? what can I do for you?; may I help you?; per servirLa at your service ‖ *intr* to serve ‖ *intr* (ESSERE & AVERE) to serve; to answer the purpose; to last; (with *dat*) (coll) to need, e.g., gli serve il martello he needs the hammer; non servire a nulla to be of no use; servire da to act as ‖ *ref* to help oneself; servirsi da to patronize, deal with; servirsi di to avail oneself of, use

servitóre *m* servant; tea wagon; servitor suo umilissimo your humble servant

servi·tù *f* (-tù) servitude; captivity; servants, help; servitù di passaggio (law) easement

serviziévole *adj* obliging, accommodating

servi·zio *m* (-zi) service; favor; turn; a mezzo servizio part-time (*domestic help*); di servizio delivery (*entrance*); for hire (*car*); domestic (*help*); fuori servizio out of commission; in servizio in commission; servizi kitchen and bath; facilities; servizi pubblici public services; public works; servizio attivo active duty; servizio permanente effettivo service in the regular army

sèr·vo -va *adj* (lit) enslaved ‖ *m* slave; servant; servo della gleba serf ‖ *f* see serva

servoassisti·to -ta *adj* servocontrolled

servofréno *m* (aut) power brake

servomotóre *m* servomotor

servostèrzo *m* (aut) power steering

sèsamo *m* sesame; apriti sesamo! open sesame!

sessanta *adj, m* & *pron* sixty

sessantènne *adj* sixty-year-old ‖ *mf* sixty-year-old person

sessantèsi·mo -ma *adj, m* & *pron* sixtieth

sessantina *f* about sixty

sessióne *f* session

sèsso *m* sex; il sesso debole the fair sex

sessuale *adj* sexual

sestante *m* sextant

sestétto *m* sextet

sestière *m* district, section

sè·sto -sta *adj* & *pron* sixth ‖ *m* sixth; curve (*of an arch*); fuori sesto out of sorts; mettere in sesto to arrange; to set in order; sesto acuto (archit) ogive

sèt *m* (sèt) set; set all'aperto (mov) location

séta *f* silk; seta artificiale rayon

setacciare §128 *tr* to sift, sieve

setàc·cio *m* (-ci) sieve

setàce·o -a *adj* silky

séte *f* thirst; aver sete to be thirsty; to lust after; sete di thirst for

seteria *f* silk mill; seterie silk goods

setifi·cio *m* (-ci) silk mill

sétola *f* bristle; (joc) stubble

sètta *f* sect

settanta *adj, m* & *pron* seventy

settantènne *adj* seventy-year-old ‖ *mf* seventy-year-old person

settantèsi·mo -ma *adj, m* & *pron* seventieth

settantina *f* about seventy

settà·rio -ria *adj & mf* (**-ri -rie**) sectarian

sètte *adj & pron* seven; **le sette** seven o'clock || *m* seven; seventh (*in dates*); V-shaped tear (*in clothing*)

settecentèsi·mo -ma *adj, m & pron* seven hundredth

settecènto *adj, m & pron* seven hundred || **il Settecento** the eighteenth century

settèmbre *m* September

settennale *adj* seven-year (*e.g., plan*)

settènne *adj* seven-year-old || *mf* seven-year-old child

settentrionale *adj* northern || *mf* northerner

settentrióne *m* north; (astr) Little Bear

setticemìa *f* septicemia

sètti·co -ca *adj* (**-ci -che**) septic

settimana *f* week; week's wages; **settimana corta** five-day week

settimanale *adj & m* weekly

settimi·no -na *adj* premature (*baby*) || *m* (mus) septet

sètti·mo -ma *adj, m & pron* seventh

sètto *m* septum

settóre *m* sector; section, branch; dissector, anatomist; coroner's pathologist

sevè·ro -ra *adj* severe, stern

seviziare §287 *tr* to torture

sevìzie *fpl* cruelty

sezionale *adj* sectional

sezionare (**sezióno**) *tr* to cut up; to divide up; to dissect

sezióne *f* section; dissection; chapter (*of club*); department (*of agency*); (geom) cross section

sfaccenda·to -ta *adj* loafing || *mf* loafer

sfaccettare (**sfaccétto**) *tr* to facet

sfacchinare *intr* (coll) to toil, drudge

sfacchinata *f* (coll) drudgery, grind

sfacciatàggine *f* brazenness, impudence

sfaccia·to -ta *adj* brazen, impudent; loud, gaudy; **fare lo sfacciato** to be fresh

sfacèlo *m* breakdown, collapse

sfà·glio *m* (**-gli**) swerve (*e.g., of horse*); (cards) discard

sfaldare *tr* to exfoliate; to cut into slices || *ref* to flake, scale; (fig) to collapse, crumble

sfamare *tr* to feed (*the hungry; the family*) || *ref* to get enough to eat

sfare §173 *tr* to undo || *ref* to spoil (*said, e.g., of meat*)

sfarzo *m* pomp, display; luxury

sfarzó·so -sa [*s*] *adj* sumptuous, luxurious

sfasare *tr* to throw out of phase; (coll) to depress || *intr* (ESSERE) (aut) to misfire; (elec) to be out of phase

sfasciare §128 *tr* to remove the bandage from; to unswathe; to smash, shatter || *ref* to go to pieces; to lose one's figure

sfatare *tr* to discredit; to unmask

sfatica·to -ta *adj* lazy || *mf* loafer

sfat·to -ta *adj* overdone; overripe; undone (*bed*); ravaged (*by age*)

sfavillare *intr* to spark, sparkle

sfavóre *m* disfavor

sfavorévole *adj* unfavorable

sfebbra·to -ta *adj* free of fever

sfegata·to -ta *adj* (coll) rabid, fanatical

sfèra *f* sphere; (coll) hand (*of clock*); **a sfera** ball-point (*pen*); **a sfere** ball (*bearing*); **sfera di cuoio** (sports) pigskin

sfèri·co -ca *adj* (**-ci -che**) spherical

sferrare (**sfèrro**) *tr* to unshoe (*a horse*); to unchain; to draw (*a weapon from a wound*); to deliver (*a blow*) || *ref* to hurl oneself

sfèrza *f* whip, scourge

sferzare (**sfèrzo**) *tr* to whip, scourge

sfiancare §197 *tr* to break open; to tire out; to fit (*clothes*) too tight || *ref* to burst open; to get worn out

sfiatare *intr* to leak (*said, e.g., of a tire*) || *intr* (ESSERE) to leak (*said of air or gas*) || *ref* to waste one's breath

sfiata·tóio *m* (**-tói**) vent

sfibbiare §287 *tr* to unbuckle, unfasten; to untie (*a knot*)

sfibrante *adj* exhausting

sfibrare *tr* to grind (*wood*) into fibers; to shred (*rags*) into fibers; to weaken, wear out

sfida *f* challenge

sfidare *tr* to challenge, dare; to brave, defy; to endure (*the challenge of time*); **sfidare che** to bet that

sfidù·cia *f* (**-cie**) mistrust; (pol) no confidence

sfiducia·to -ta *adj* downcast, depressed

sfigurare *tr* to disfigure || *intr* to make a bad impression; to lose face

sfilacciare §128 *tr & ref* to ravel, fray

sfilare *tr* to unstring; to take off (*one's shoes*); to count (*beads*); to unthread; to dull (*a blade*); to ravel || *intr* (ESSERE) to march, parade; to follow one another || *ref* to become unthreaded; to become frayed; to run (*said of knitted work*); to break one's back

sfilata *f* parade; row; **sfilata di moda** fashion show

sfilza *f* row, sequence

sfinge *f* sphinx

sfiniménto *m* exhaustion

sfinire §176 *tr* to exhaust, wear out || *ref* to be worn out

sfintère *m* sphincter

sfiorare (**sfióro**) *tr* to graze; to barely touch (*a subject*); to skim; (lit) to barely reach

sfioratóre *m* spillway

sfiorire §176 *intr* (ESSERE) to wither, fade

sfit·to -ta *adj* not rented

sfocare §197 (**sfòco**) *tr* to put out of focus; to blur

sfociare §128 (**sfócio**) *tr* to dredge (*the mouth of a river*) || *intr* (ESSERE) to flow; **sfociare in** (fig) to lead to

sfoderare (**sfòdero**) *tr* to unsheathe; to show off, sport, display; to take the cover or lining off || *intr* to be drawn out

sfogare §209 (**sfógo**) *tr* to vent, give vent to || *intr* (ESSERE) to flow; to pour out; **sfogare in** to turn into || *ref*—**sfogarsi a** + *inf* to have one's fill of + *ger*; **sfogarsi con** to unburden oneself to; **sfogarsi su qlcu** to take it out on s.o.

sfoga-tóio *m* (-tói) vent

sfoggiare §290 *tr* to display, sport; to show off

sfòg·gio *m* (-gi) display, ostentation

sfòglia *f* foil; skin (*of onion*); layer of puff paste; (ichth) sole

sfogliare §280 (sfòglio) *tr* to pluck (*a flower*); to defoliate (*a tree*); to leaf through (*a book*); to deal (*cards*); to husk (*corn*); to press (*dough*) into layers ‖ *ref* to shed its leaves; to flake

sfogliata *f* defoliation; puff paste; **dare una sfogliata a** to glance through

sfó·go *m* (-ghi) exhaust; outlet; vent; (coll) eruption (*of skin*)

sfolgorare (sfólgoro) *intr* (ESSERE & AVERE) to shine, blaze

sfolgorì·o *m* (-ì) glittering, blazing

sfoliagèn·te *m* (-te) billy

sfollamènto *m* evacuation; layoff

sfollare (sfòllo) *tr* to clear; to cut the staff of ‖ *intr* (ESSERE & AVERE) to disperse, evacuate; to cut down the staff

sfolla-to -ta *adj* driven from home ‖ *mf* evacuee

sfoltire §176 *tr* to thin out

sfondare (sfóndo) *tr* to stave in; to break through; to be heavy on (*the stomach*) ‖ *intr* to give ‖ *ref* to break open

sfóndo *m* background

sfondóne *m* (coll) blunder, error

sforbiciare §128 (sfòrbicio) *tr* to clip, shear

sforbiciata *f* clipping; (sports) scissors; (sports) scissors kick

sformare (sfórmo) *tr* to pull out of shape; to take out of the mold ‖ *intr* to get mad

sforma-to -ta *adj* out of shape ‖ *m* pudding

sfornare (sfórno) *tr* to take out of the oven

sfornire §176 *tr* to deprive; to strip

sfortuna *f* bad luck, misfortune

sfortuna-to -ta *adj* unsuccessful; unlucky, unfortunate

sforzare (sfòrzo) *tr* to strain; to force ‖ *ref* to strive, endeavor

sforza-to -ta *adj* forced, unnatural

sfòrzo *m* effort; strain; stretch (*of imagination*); **senza sforzo** effortlessly

sfóttere *tr* (vulg) to make fun of

sfracassare *tr* to smash, crash

sfracellare (sfracèllo) *tr & ref* to shatter, smash

sfrangiare §290 *tr* to ravel

sfrattare *tr* to evict; to deport ‖ *intr* to be evicted

sfratto *m* eviction; notice of eviction

sfrecciare §128 (sfréccio) *intr* (ESSERE & AVERE) to speed by

sfregaménto *m* rubbing

sfregare §209 (sfrégo) *tr* to rub; to scrape; to strike (*a match*)

sfregiare §290 (sfrégio & sfrègio) *tr* to disfigure, slash

sfregia-to -ta *adj* disfigured, slashed ‖ *m* scarface

sfré·gio or **sfrè·gio** *m* (-gi) slash, scar, gash; insult

sfrenare (sfréno & sfrèno) *tr* to take the brake off; to give free rein to ‖ *ref* to kick over the traces

sfriggere §180 *intr* to sizzle

sfrigolì·o *m* (-ì) sizzle

sfrondare (sfróndo) *tr* to defoliate; to lop off; to trim down ‖ *ref* to lose leaves

sfrontatézza *f* effrontery, impudence

sfronta-to -ta *adj* brazen, impudent

sfrusciare §128 *intr* to rustle

sfruttare *tr* to exploit; to exhaust (*e.g., a mine*); to take advantage of

sfrutta-tóre -trice *mf* exploiter, developer (*e.g., of an invention*)

sfuggènte *adj* fleeting; receding (*forehead*); shifty (*glance*)

sfuggire *tr* to avoid, flee ‖ *intr* (ESSERE) to flee, escape, get away; (with *dat*) to escape, e.g., **nulla gli sfugge** nothing escapes him; to break, e.g., **sfuggì a una promessa** he broke a promise; **lasciarsi sfuggire** to let slip

sfuggita *f—di sfuggita* hastily; incidentally; **dare una sfuggita** to run down (*e.g., to the post office*)

sfumare *tr* to shade down; to tone down; to trim (*hair*) ‖ *intr* (ESSERE) to vanish; to shade

sfumatura *f* nuance, shade; razor clipping

sfumino *m* stump (*in drawing*)

sfuriare §287 *tr* to vent (*one's anger*) ‖ *intr* to rave

sfuriata *f* outburst of anger; gust (*of wind*); **fare una sfuriata a** to give a scolding to

sgabèllo *m* stool, footstool

sgabuzzino *m* cubbyhole

sgambettare (sgambétto) *tr* to trip ‖ *intr* to toddle; to kick (*said of a baby*); to scamper

sgambétto *m* trip, stumble; **dare lo sgambetto a** to trip

sganasciare §128 *tr* to dislocate the jaw of; to break the jaw of; to tear apart ‖ *intr* to steal right and left ‖ *ref* to break one's jaw; **sganasciarsi dalle risa** to split one's sides laughing

sganciare §128 *tr* to unhook; to lay out (*money*); to drop (*bombs*) ‖ *intr* to drop bombs; (coll) to go away ‖ *ref* to get unhooked; (mil) to disengage oneself; **sganciarsi da** to get rid of

sgangherare (sgànghero) *tr* to unhinge; to burst ‖ *ref—sgangherarsi dalle risa* to split one's sides laughing

sganghera-to -ta *adj* unhinged; broken down; rickety; coarse (*laughter*)

sgarbatéz·za *f* rudeness, incivility; clumsiness

sgarba-to -ta *adj* rude; clumsy

sgarberìa *f* var of sgarbatezza

sgarbo *m—fare uno sgarbo a* to be rude to

sgargiante *adj* loud, flashy, showy

sgarrare *intr* to go wrong

sgattaiolare (sgattàiolo) *intr* (ESSERE) to slip away; to wriggle out

sgelare (sgèlo) *tr & intr* to thaw, melt

sgèlo *m* thaw

sghém·bo -ba *adj* crooked; **a sghembo** askew || **sghembo** *adv* askew; side-ways

sghèrro *m* hired assassin; gendarme

sghiacciare §128 *tr* to thaw

sghignazzare *intr* to guffaw

sghignazzata *f* guffaw

sghimbè·scio -scia *adj*—a or **di sghim-bescio** askew, crooked

sghiribizzo [ddzz] *m* whim, fancy

sgobbare (sgòbbo) *intr* to drudge, plod, plug

sgobbó·ne -na *mf* plugger, plodder, drudge

sgocciolare (sgócciolo) *tr* to let drip || *intr* to drip (*said of container*) || *intr* (ESSERE) to drip (*said of liquid*)

sgocciola·tóio *m* (-tói) dish rack; drip pan

sgocciolatura *f* dripping; drippings

sgócciolo *m* last drop; **essere agli sgoc-cioli** to be coming to an end

sgolare (sgólo) *ref* to shout oneself hoarse

sgomberare (sgómbero) *tr & intr* var of sgombrare

sgómbero *m* moving

sgombrané·ve *m* (-ve) snowplow (*truck*)

sgombrare (sgómbro) *tr* to clear; to vacate || *intr* to move, vacate

sgóm·bro -bra *adj* clear || *m* moving; (ichth) mackerel

sgomentare (sgoménto) *tr* to frighten; to dismay

sgomén·to -ta *adj* dismayed || *m* dismay; **rimanere di sgomento** to be dismayed

sgominare (sgòmino) *tr* to rout

sgomma·to -ta *adj* unglued; without tires; with poor tires

sgonfiare §287 (sgónfio) *tr* to deflate; to damn with faint praise (*e.g., a play*); (coll) to bore || *intr* (ESSERE) to boast; to balloon || *ref* to go down (*said of swelling*); to go flat (*said of a tire*); (fig) to collapse

sgón·fio -fia *adj* deflated, flat

sgonfiòtto *m* jelly doughnut; puff (*in clothing*)

sgórbia *f* (carp) gouge

sgorbiare §287 (sgòrbio) *tr* to scribble; (carp) to gouge

sgòr·bio *m* (-bi) ink spot; scribble, scrawl

sgorgare §209 (sgórgo) *tr* to unclog || *intr* (ESSERE) to gush

sgottare (sgótto) *tr* to bail out (*a boat*)

sgozzare (sgózzo) *tr* to slaughter; to slit the throat of; (fig) to bleed, fleece

sgradévole *adj* disagreeable, unpleasant

sgradire §176 *tr* to refuse || *intr* to be displeasing

sgradi·to -ta *adj* unpleasant; unwelcome

sgraffignare *tr* to snitch, snatch

sgrammatica·to -ta *adj* ungrammatical

sgranare *tr* to shell (*e.g., peas*); to count (*one's beads*); to seed (*grapes*); to open (*one's eyes*) wide; (mach) to disengage || *ref* to crumble; to scratch oneself

sgranchire §176 *tr* to stretch (*e.g., one's legs*)

sgranocchiare §287 (sgranòcchio) *tr* to crunch, munch

sgrassare *tr* to remove the grease from; to skim (*broth*); to scour (*wool*)

sgravare *tr* to relieve, lighten || *ref* to be relieved; to give birth

sgrà·vio *m* (-vi) lightening, lessening; **a sgravio di coscienza** to ease one's conscience

sgrazia·to -ta *adj* gawky, clumsy

sgretolare (sgrétolo) *tr & ref* to crumble

sgretola·to -ta *adj* crumbling, falling down

sgridare *tr* to scold, chide

sgridata *f* scolding, reprimand

sgrondare (sgróndo) *tr* to cause to drip || *intr* to drip, trickle

sgroppare (sgròppo) *tr* to wear (*a horse*) out || *intr* to buck (*said of a horse*)

sgroppare (sgróppo) *tr* to untie

sgrossare (sgròsso) *tr* to rough-hew; (fig) to refine

sgrovigliare §280 *tr* to untangle

sguaiatàggine *f* uncouthness

sguaia·to -ta *adj* crude, vulgar; uncouth || *mf* vulgar person; uncouth person

sguainare *tr* to unsheathe; to show (*one's nails*)

sgualcire §176 *tr* to crumple || *ref* to become crumpled

sgualdrina *f* trollop, strumpet

sguardo *m* glance, look; eyes

sguarnire §176 *tr* to untrim; (mil) to strip, dismantle

sguàtte·ro -ra *mf* dishwasher, scullion || *f* kitchenmaid, scullery maid

sguazzare *tr* to waste, squander || *intr* to splash; to wallow; to be lost (*in shoes too big or clothes too loose*)

sguinzagliare §280 *tr* to unleash, let loose

sgusciare §128 *tr* to shell, hull || *intr* (ESSERE) to slip; **sgusciare di soppiatto** to slip away

shòp·ping *m* (-ping) shopping; shopping bag; **fare lo shopping** to go shopping

shràpnel *m* (shràpnel) shrapnel

si *m* (-sì) (mus) si || §5 *pron*

sì *m* (sì) yes; yea; **stare tra il sì e il no** to not be able to make up one's mind; **un . . . sì e l'altro no** every other (*e.g., day*)

sia *conj* see essere

siamése [s] *adj & mf* Siamese

siberia·no -na *adj & mf* Siberian

sibilante *adj & f* sibilant

sibilare (sìbilo) *intr* to hiss

sibilla *f* sibyl

sìbilo *m* hiss, hissing

sicà·rio *m* (-ri) hired assassin

sicché *conj* so that

siccità *f* drought

siccóme *adv* as || *conj* since; as; how

Sicilia, la Sicily

sicilia·no -na *adj & mf* Sicilian

sicomòro *m* sycamore

sicumèra *f* cocksureness, overconfidence

sicura *f* safety lock (*on gun*)

sicurézza *f* security; assurance; safety; certainty; reliability; **di sicurezza** safety; **sicurezza sociale** social security

sicu•ro -ra *adj* sure; safe; steady; **di sicuro** certainly ‖ *m* safety; **camminare sul sicuro** to take no chances ‖ **sicuro** *adv* certainly ‖ *f* see sicura

sicur•tà *f* (-tà) insurance

siderale *adj* sidereal

sidère•o -a *adj* sidereal

siderùrgi•co -ca (-ci -che) *adj* iron-and-steel ‖ *m* iron-and-steel worker

sidro *m* cider, hard cider

sièpe *f* hedge; (fig) wall

sièro *m* serum

sièsta *f* siesta; **fare la siesta** to take a nap, take a siesta

siffat•to -ta *adj* such

sifìlide *f* syphilis

sifóne *m* siphon; siphon bottle; trap

siga•ràio -ràia (-rài -ràie) *mf* cigar maker ‖ *m* (ent) grape hopper; ‖ *f* cigarette girl

sigarétta *f* cigarette

sìgaro *m* cigar

sigillare *tr* to seal

sigillo *m* seal; **avere il sigillo alle labbra** to have one's lips sealed; **sigillo sacramentale** seal of confession

sigla *f* acronym; initials; abbreviation; letterword; **sigla musicale** theme song

siglare *tr* to initial

significare §197 (signìfico) *tr* to mean; to signify; **significare qlco a qlcu** to inform s.o. of s.th

significati•vo -va *adj* significant; meaningful

significato *m* meaning; **senza significato** meaningless

signóra *f* Madam, Mrs.; lady; mistress; owner; wife ‖ **Nostra Signora** Our Lady

signóre *m* sir, Mr.; gentleman; rich man; lord, master, owner; man; **il signore desidera?** what is your pleasure?; **per signori** stag ‖ **Signore** *m* Lord

signoreggiare §290 (signoréggio) *tr* to rule over; to master; to tower over; to overshadow ‖ *intr* to be the master

signoria *f* seigniory; rule; **La Signoria Vostra** your Honor; **Sua Signoria** his Lordship; your Lordship

signorile *adj* seigniorial; gentlemanly; ladylike; elegant, refined

signorina *f* miss; Miss; young lady; spinster

signorino *m* master, young gentleman

signornò *adv* no, Sir

signoró•ne -na *mf* (coll) rich person

signoròtto *m* lordling

signorsì *adv* yes, Sir

silenziatóre *m* silencer (*of firearm*); (aut) muffler

silèn•zio *m* (-zi) silence; (mil) taps; **fare silenzio** to be silent; **ridurre al silenzio** (mil) to silence

silenzió•so -sa [s] *adj* silent; noiseless

silfide *f* sylphid

silfo *m* sylph

silhouèt•te *f* (-te) silhouette

sìlice *f* silica

silìcio *m* silicon

silicóne *m* silicone

siliquastro *m* redbud

sìllaba *f* syllable

sillabare (sìllabo) *tr* to syllabify; to spell

sillabà•rio *m* (-ri) reader, primer

sìllabo *m* syllabus

silo *m* silo

silòfono *m* xylophone

siluétta *f* silhouette

silurante *adj* torpedoing, torpedo ‖ *f* destroyer; torpedo boat

silurare *tr* to torpedo; (fig) to fire, dismiss; (fig) to undermine

siluro *m* torpedo

silva•no -na *adj* sylvan

silvèstre *adj* (lit) sylvan; (lit) wild; (lit) hard, arduous

simboleggiare §290 (simboléggio) *tr* to symbolize

simbòli•co -ca *adj* (-ci -che) symbolic

simbolismo *m* symbolism

simbolo *m* symbol

similari•tà *f* (-tà) similarity

simile *adj* similar; such ‖ *m* like; **i propri simili** fellow men

similòro *m* tombac

simmetria *f* symmetry

simmètri•co -ca *adj* (-ci -che) symmetrical

simonìa *f* simony

simpamina *f* benzedrine

simpatèti•co -ca *adj* (-ci -che) sympathetic

simpatia *f* like, liking; **cattivarsi la simpatia di** to make oneself well liked by

simpàti•co -ca (-ci -che) *adj* nice, pleasant, congenial ‖ *m* (anat) sympathetic system

simpatizzante [ddzz] *adj* sympathizing ‖ *mf* sympathizer

simpatizzare [ddzz] *intr* to sympathize; to become friends

simpò•sio *m* (-si) symposium

simulare (sìmulo) *tr* to simulate

simula•tóre -trice *mf* faker, impostor ‖ *m* simulator

simultàne•o -a *adj* simultaneous

sin- *pref adj* syn-, e.g., **sinonimo** synonymous ‖ *pref m & f* syn-, e.g., **sinonimo** synonym

sin *adv*—**sin da** ever since

sinagò•ga *f* (-ghe) synagogue

sincerare (sincèro) *tr* (lit) to convince ‖ *ref*—**sincerarsi di** to ascertain

sincè•ro -ra *adj* sincere; pure

sinché *conj* until

sìncope *f* fainting spell; (phonet) syncope; (mus) syncopation

sincronismo *m* syncronism; **sincronismo orrizzontale** (telv) horizontal hold; **sincronismo verticale** (telv) vertical hold

sincronizzare [ddzz] *tr* to syncronize

sìncro•no -na *adj* syncronous

sindacale *adj* mayoral; union

sindacalismo *m* trade unionism

sindacali•sta *mf* (-sti -ste) union member; union leader

sindacare §197 (sìndaco) *tr* to criticize; to scrutinize

sindaca·to -ta *adj* controlled, scrutinized ‖ *m* control; labor union; syndicate; **sindacato giallo** company union

sìnda·co *m* (-ci) mayor; controller; auditor

sinecura *f* sinecure

sinfonìa *f* symphony; (*of an opera*) overture; (coll) racket (*noise*)

sinfòni·co -ca *adj* (-ci -che) symphonic

singhiozzare (singhiózzo) *intr* to sob; to hiccup; to jerk

singhiózzo *m* sob; hiccups; **a singhiozzo** in jerks; by fits and spurts

singolare *adj* singular ‖ *m* singular; (tennis) singles

sìngo·lo -la *adj* single ‖ *m* individual; shell for one oarsman; (rr) roomette; (telp) private line; (tennis) singles

singulto *m* hiccups; sob

sinistra *f* left hand; left

sinistrare *tr* to ruin; to damage

sinistra·to -ta *adj* injured, damaged, ruined ‖ *mf* victim (*of bombing or flood*)

sinistrismo *m* leftism

sinistri·sta *adj* (-sti -ste) leftish, leftist

sini·stro -stra *adj* left; sinister ‖ *m* accident; (boxing) left ‖ *f* see **sinistra**

sinistròide *adj & mf* leftist

sino *adv* var of **fino**

sinologìa *f* Sinology

sinòni·mo -ma *adj* synonymous ‖ *m* synonym

sinò·psi *f* (-psi) (mov) synopsis

sinóra *adv* var of **finora**

sinòs·si *f* (-si) synopsis

sinòtti·co -ca *adj* (-ci -che) synoptic(al)

sintas·si *f* (-si) syntax

sìnte·si *f* (-si) synthesis

sintèti·co -ca *adj* (-ci -che) synthetic(al); concise

sintetizzare [ddzz] *tr* to synthesize

sintogram·ma *m* (-mi) (rad) dial

sìntomo *m* symptom

sintonìa *f* harmony; (rad) tuning

sintonizzare [ddzz] *tr* (rad) to tune

sintonizzatóre [ddzz] *m* (rad) tuner

sinuó·so -sa [s] *adj* sinuous, winding

sionismo *m* Zionism

sipà·rio *m* (-ri) curtain; **sipario di ferro** iron curtain

sirèna *f* siren; mermaid; **sirena da nebbia** foghorn

Sìria, la Syria

siria·no -na *adj & mf* Syrian

sirìn·ga *f* (-ghe) panpipe; syringe; catheter; grease gun; (orn) syrinx

siringare §209 *tr* to catheterize

siròcchia *f* (obs) sister

sì·sma *m* (-smi) earthquake

sismògrafo *m* seismograph

sismologìa *f* seismology

sissignóre *adv* yes, Sir!

sistè·ma *m* (-mi) system

sistemare (sistèmo) *tr* to arrange; to put in order; to systematize; to settle; to find a job for; to find a husband for; (coll) to fix ‖ *ref* to settle; to get married

sistemazióne *f* arrangement; settlement; job, position

sìstole *f* systole

sitibón·do -da *adj* (lit) thirsty

sì·to -ta *adj* (lit) located ‖ *m* (lit) site, spot, location; (mil) sight; (coll) musty odor

situare (sìtuo) *tr* to locate, place, situate

situazióne *f* situation; condition

slabbrare *tr* to chip; to open (*a wound*) ‖ *intr* to overflow ‖ *ref* to become chipped; to reopen (*said of a cut*)

slacciare §128 *tr* to untie; to unfasten; to unbutton ‖ *ref* to get undone; to get unbuttoned

sladinare *tr* (sports) to train; (mach) to run in, break in

slanciare §128 *tr* to hurl, throw ‖ *ref* to hurl oneself; to rise (*said, e.g., of a tower*)

slancia·to -ta *adj* slender; soaring

slàn·cio *m* (-ci) leap; outburst (*of feeling*); momentum; **di slancio** with a rush; **prendere lo slancio** to get a running start

slargare §209 *tr* to widen; to warm (*the heart*) ‖ *ref* to widen, spread out

slattare *tr* to wean

slava·to -ta *adj* pale, washed out

sla·vo -va *adj* Slav, Slavic ‖ *mf* Slav ‖ *m* Slavic (*language*)

sleale *adj* disloyal; unfair (*competition*)

sleal·tà *f* (-tà) disloyalty

slegare §209 (slégo) *tr* to untie

slega·to -ta *adj* untied; disconnected

slip *m* (slip) briefs; tank suit, bathing suit (*for men*)

slitta *f* sled, sleigh; (mach) carriage

slittaménto *m* skid; slide

slittare *intr* to sled; to skid; to slide

slogare §209 (slògo) *tr* to dislocate ‖ *ref* to become dislocated; to dislocate (*e.g., an arm*)

slogatura *f* dislocation

sloggiare §290 (slòggio) *tr* to dislodge; to evict ‖ *intr* to vacate

slòg·gio *m* (-gi) moving; eviction

slovac·co -ca *adj & mf* (-chi -che) Slovak

smacchiare §287 *tr* to clean; to deforest

smacchia·tóre -trice *mf* cleaner ‖ *m* cleaning fluid; spot remover

smac·co *m* (-chi) letdown; slap in the face

smagliante *adj* dazzling, shining

smagliare §280 *tr* to break the links of; to undo the meshes of; to remove (*a fish*) from the net ‖ *intr* to shine, dazzle ‖ *ref* to run (*said, e.g., of knitted fabric*); to free itself from the net

smagliatura *f* run (*in stockings*); (fig) break

smagrire §176 *tr* to impoverish ‖ *intr* (ESSERE) *& ref* to become thin or lean

smaliziare §287 *tr* to make wiser ‖ *ref* to get wiser

smaltare *tr* to enamel; to glaze

smaltire §176 *tr* to digest; to sleep off (*a drunk*); to swallow (*an offense*);

to sell off; to get rid of; to drain off (*water*)

smalti·tóio *m* (**-tói**) drain, sewer

smalto *m* enamel; **smalto per le unghie** nail polish

smancerìe *fpl* affectation; mawkishness

smanceró·so -sa [s] *adj* prissy

smangiare §290 *tr* to erode, eat away || *ref* to be consumed (*e.g., by hatred*)

smània *f* frenzy; craze, yearning; **dare in smanie** to be in a frenzy

smaniare §287 *intr* to be delirious; to yearn, crave

smanió·so -sa [s] *adj* eager; disturbing

smantellare (**smantèllo**) *tr* to dismantle; to demolish; to disable (*a ship*)

smargias·so -sa *mf* braggart, boaster

smarriménto *m* loss; bewilderment; discouragement

smarrire §176 *tr* to lose || *ref* to get lost; to get discouraged

smascellare (**smascèllo**) *ref*—**smascellarsi dalle risa** to split one's sides laughing

smascherare (**smàschero**) *tr & ref* to unmask

smazzata *f* (cards) deal; (cards) hand

smembraménto *m* dismemberment

smembrare (**smèmbro**) *tr* to dismember

smemoratàggine *f* forgetfulness

smemora·to -ta *adj* absent-minded; forgetful || *mf* absent-minded or forgetful person

smentire §176 *tr* to belie; to refute; to retract; to be untrue to || *ref* to not be consistent, to contradict oneself

smentita *f* denial; retraction

smeraldo *m* emerald

smerciare §128 (**smèrcio**) *tr* to sell, sell out

smèr·cio *m* (**-ci**) sale

smèr·go *m* (**-ghi**) (zool) merganser

smerigliare §280 *tr* to grind, polish; to sand

smeriglia·to -ta *adj* polished; sand (*paper*); emery (*cloth*); frosted (*glass*)

smerì·glio *m* (**-gli**) emery; (orn) merlin; (ichth) porbeagle

smerlare (**smèrlo**) *tr* to scallop

smèrlo *m* scallop (*along the edge of a garment*)

smés·so -sa *adj* hand-me-down, castoff

sméttere §198 *tr* to stop; to stop wearing; to break up (*housekeeping*); **smetterla** to cut it out || *intr*—**smettere di** + *inf* to stop + *ger*

smezzare [ddzz] (**smèzzo**) *tr* to halve

smidollare (**smidóllo**) *tr* to remove the marrow from; (fig) to emasculate

smilitarizzare [ddzz] *tr* to demilitarize

smil·zo -za *adj* slender; poor, worthless

sminare *tr* to remove mines from

sminuire §176 *tr* to belittle

sminuzzare *tr* to crumble; to mince; to expatiate on || *ref* to crumble

smistaménto *m* sorting (*of mail*); (rr) shunting, shifting

smistare *tr* to sort; (rr) to shift; (soccer) to pass; (rad) to unscramble

smisura·to -ta *adj* immense, huge

smitizzante [ddzz] *adj* debunking, demythologizing

smitizzare [ddzz] *tr* to debunk; to demythologize

smobiliare §287 *tr* to remove the furniture from

smobilitare (**smobìlito**) *tr* to demobilize

smobilitazióne *f* demobilization

smoccolare (**smòccolo** & **smóccolo**) *tr* to snuff (*a candle*) || *intr* (slang) to swear, curse

smoda·to -ta *adj* excessive, immoderate

smòg *m* smog

smóking *m* (**smóking**) dinner jacket, tuxedo

smontàbile *adj* dismountable

smontàg·gio *m* (**-gi**) disassembling, dismantling

smontare (**smónto**) *tr* to take apart; to dismantle; to cause (*e.g., whipped cream*) to fall; to take (*a precious stone*) out of its setting; to dishearten; to dissuade; to drop (*s.o.*) off; **smontare la guardia** to come off guard duty || *intr* (ESSERE) to dismount; to get off or out (*of a conveyance*); to fade; to drop (*said, e.g., of beaten eggs*) || *ref* to become downcast

smòrfia *f* grimace; mawkishness; **fare le smorfie a** to make faces at

smorfió·so -sa [s] *adj* mawkish, prissy

smòr·to -ta *adj* pale, wan; faded

smorzare (**smòrzo**) *tr* to attenuate; to lessen; to tone down; to turn off (*light*); (phys) to dampen

smorzatóre *m* (mus) damper

smòs·so -sa *adj* moved; loose

smottaménto *m* mud slide

smozzicare §197 (**smózzico**) *tr* to crumble; to mince; to clip, mince (*one's words*)

smun·to -ta *adj* emaciated, pale, wan

smuòvere §202 *tr* to budge; to till; (fig) to move || *ref* to budge; to move away; **smuoviti!** get going!

smussare *tr* to blunt; to bevel; (fig) to soften

snaturalizzare [ddzz] *tr* to denaturalize; to denationalize

snaturare *tr* to change the nature of; to distort, misrepresent

snatura·to -ta *adj* distorted; monstrous, unnatural

snebbiare §287 (**snébbio**) *tr* to drive the fog from; to clear (*e.g., one's mind*)

snellézza *f* slenderness; nimbleness

snellire §176 *tr & ref* to slenderize

snèl·lo -la *adj* slender; nimble; lively

snervante *adj* enervating

snervare (**snèrvo**) *tr* to enervate, prostrate || *ref* to become enervated

snidare *tr* to drive out, flush

snòb *adj invar* snobbish || *mf* (**snòb**) snob

snobbare (**snòbbo**) *tr* to snub, slight

snobismo *m* snobbishness, snobbery

snobìsti·co -ca *adj* (**-ci -che**) snobbish

snocciolare (**snòcciolo**) *tr* to spill (*a secret*); to peel off (*sums of money*); to pit, stone (*fruit*)

snodare (**snòdo**) *tr* to untie; to limber up; to exercise; to loosen up (*e.g.,* s.o.'s tongue) || *ref* to become loose; to wind (*said, e.g., of a road*)

snòdo *m* (mach) joint; **a snodo** flexible

soave *adj* sweet, gentle

sobbalzare *intr* to jerk, jolt

sobbalzo *m* jerk, jolt; **di sobbalzo** with a jolt

sobbarcare §197 *tr* to overburden || *ref* —**sobbarcarsi a** to take it upon oneself to

sobbór·go *m* (-ghi) suburb

sobillare *tr* to instigate, stir up

sobilla·tóre -trice *mf* instigator

sobrietà *f* sobriety, temperance

sò·brio -bria *adj* sober, temperate; plain

socchiùdere §125 *tr* to half-shut; to leave ajar

socchiu·so -sa [s] *adj* ajar

soccómbere §186 *intr* to succumb

soccórrere §139 *tr* to help || *intr* (lit) to occur

soccórso *m* help, succor; **mancato soccorso** failure to render assistance; hit-and-run driving

sociale *adj* social; company (*e.g., outing*)

socialismo *m* socialism

sociali·sta (-sti -ste) *adj* socialistic || *mf* socialist

sociali·tà *f* (-tà) gregariousness; social responsibility

socie·tà *f* (-tà) society; company; **in società** in partnership; **società anonima** corporation; **società a responsabilità limitata** limited company; **Società delle Nazioni** League of Nations; **società finanziaria** holding company; **società in accomandita** limited partnership; **società per azioni** corporation

sociévole *adj* sociable; gregarious

sò·cio *m* (-ci) member; cardholder; partner; shareholder; **socio fondatore** charter member; **socio sostenitore** patron, sustaining member

sociologìa *f* sociology

sociòlo·go -ga *mf* (-gi -ghe) sociologist

sòda *f* soda

sodalì·zio *m* (-zi) society; brotherhood, fraternity; friendship

soddisfacènte *adj* satisfying, satisfactory

soddisfare §173 (2d sg pres ind **soddisfài** or **soddisfi;** 3d pl pres subj **soddisfanno** or **soddisfano;** 1st, 2d & 3d sg pres subj **soddisfaccia** or **soddisfi;** 3d pl pres subj **soddisfàcciano** or **soddisfino**) *tr* to satisfy || *intr* (with dat) to satisfy || *ref* to be satisfied

soddisfat·to -ta *adj* satisfied

soddisfazióne *f* satisfaction

sòdi·co -ca *adj* (-ci -che) sodium

sòdio *m* sodium

sò·do -da *adj* hard; hard-boiled; stubborn; solid; **prenderle sode** to get a good thrashing || *m* hard ground; untilled soil; solid foundation; **venire al sodo** to come to the point; **mettere in sodo** to ascertain || *f* see **soda** || *sodo adv* hard

sodomìa *f* sodomy

so·fà *m* (-fà) couch, sofa; **sofà a letto** sofa bed

sofferènte *adj* sickly, ailing; (lit) long-suffering

sofferènza *f* suffering, pain; bad debt; **in sofferenza** overdue

soffermare (**sofférmo**) *tr*—**soffermare il passo** to come to a stop || *ref* to linger, pause

soffiare §287 (**sóffio**) *tr* to blow; to whisper; (checkers) to huff; (coll) to steal || *intr* to blow; to bellow; (slang) to squeal (*about somebody's offense*); **soffiare sul fuoco** to stir up trouble || *ref* to blow (*one's nose*)

soffia·to -ta *adj* blown || *m* soufflé || *f* (slang) squealing, **darsi una soffiata di naso** to blow one's nose

soffiatóre *m* glass blower

sòffice *adj* soft

soffierìa *f* glass factory; blower

soffiétto *m* bellows; hood (*of carriage*); (journ) puff, ballyhoo

sóf·fio *m* (-fi) blow; breath; **in un soffio** in a jiffy; **soffio al cuore** heart murmur

soffióne *m* blowpipe; fumarole; (bot) dandelion; (coll) spy

soffitta *f* attic, garret

soffitto *m* ceiling

soffocaménto *m* choking

soffocante *adj* stifling; oppressive

soffocare §197 (**sòffoco**) *tr* to choke; to stifle; to suffocate; to smother; to repress

sòffo·co *m* (-chi) sultriness

soffóndere §178 *tr* (lit) to suffuse

soffregare §209 (**soffrégo**) *tr* to rub lightly

soffriggere §180 *tr* to fry lightly || *intr* to mutter

soffrire §207 *tr* to suffer; to endure; **non poter soffrire** to not be able to stand || *intr* to suffer; to ail; **soffrire di** to be troubled with

soffritto *m* fried onions and bacon

sofistica·to -ta *adj* adulterated; sophisticated, studied

sofisti·co -ca *adj* (-ci -che) sophistic; faultfinding || *f* sophistry

soggetti·sta *mf* (-sti -ste) scriptwriter

soggetti·vo -va *adj* subjective

soggèt·to -ta *adj* subject || *m* subject; (coll) character; (law) person; **cattivo soggetto** hoodlum; **recitare a soggetto** to improvise

soggezióne *f* subjection; awe, embarrassment; **mettere a soggezione** to awe

sogghignare *intr* to sneer

soggiacére §181 *intr* (ESSERE & AVERE) to be subject; to succumb

soggiogare §209 (**soggiógo**) *tr* to subjugate, subdue

soggiornare (**soggiórno**) *intr* to sojourn, stay

soggiórno *m* sojourn, stay; living room; sitting room (*in hotel*)

soggiùngere §183 *tr* to add

soggólo *m* wimple (*of nun*); throatlatch (*on horse*); (mil) chin strap

sòglia *f* doorsill; threshhold

sògliola *f* sole

sognare (**sógno**) *tr* to dream of || *intr*

to dream; **sognare ad occhi aperti** to daydream

sogna·tó·re -trice *adj* dreaming ‖ *mf* dreamer

sógno *m* dream; **nemmeno per sogno** (coll) by no means

sòia *f* (bot) soy

sòl *m* (sòl) (mus) sol

so·làio *m* (-lài) attic, loft; (agr) crib

solare *adj* solar; bright; clear ‖ *v* §257 *tr* to sole

solàr·rio *m* (-ri) solarium

solati·o -a (-i -e) *adj* sunny ‖ *m—a* **solatio** with a southern exposure

solcare §197 (sólco) *tr* to furrow; to plow (*the waves*)

sól·co *m* (-chi) furrow; rut; groove (*of phonograph record*); (fig) path; (naut) wake

solcòmetro *m* (naut) log

soldaté·sco -sca (-schi -sche) *adj* soldier ‖ *f* soldiery; soldiers; undisciplined troops

soldatino *m* toy soldier

soldato *m* soldier; **andare soldato** to enlist; **soldato di ventura** soldier of fortune; **soldato scelto** private first class; **soldato semplice** private

sòldo *m* soldo (*Italian coin*); coin; money; (mil) pay; (fig) penny; **a soldo a soldo** a penny at a time; **al soldo di** in the pay of; **tirare al soldo** to be a tightwad

sóle *m* sun; sunshine; (fig) day, daytime; **sole artificiale** sun lamp; **sole a scacchi** (joc) hoosegow, calaboose

soleggia·to -ta *adj* sunny

solènne *adj* solemn; (joc) first-class

solenni·tà *f* (-tà) solemnity

solennizzare [ddzz] *tr* to solemnize

solére §255 *intr* (ESSERE) + *inf* to be accustomed to + *inf*, e.g., **suole arrivare alle sette** he is accustomed to arrive at seven ‖ *impers* (ESSERE) —**suole** + *inf* it generally + *3d sg ind*, e.g., **suole nevicare** it generally snows

solèrte *adj* (lit) diligent, industrious

solèrzia *f* (lit) diligence

solét·to -ta *adj* (lit) alone, lonely ‖ *f* sole; inner sole; (archit) slab, cement slab

sòlfa *f* (mus) solfeggio; **la solita solfa** the same old story

solfanèllo *m* var of **zofanello**

solfara *f* sulfur mine

solfato *m* sulfate

solfeggiare §290 (solféggio) *tr* to sol-fa

solfiè·ro -ra *adj* sulfur

solfito *m* sulfite

sólfo *m* var of **zolfo**

solfòri·co -ca *adj* (-ci -che) sulfuric

solforó·so -sa [s] *adj* sulfurous

solfuro *m* sulfide

solidale *adj* solidary; (law) joint; (law) jointly responsible; (mach) built-in; **solidale con** integral with

solidarie·tà *f* (-tà) solidarity; (law) joint liability

solidarizzare [ddzz] *intr* to make common cause, become united

solidificare §197 (solidìfico) *tr* to solidify; to settle

solidi·tà *f* (-tà) solidity; (fig) soundness

sòli·do -da *adj* solid; (law) joint ‖ *m* solid; **in solido** jointly

solilò·quio *m* (-qui) soliloquy

solin·go -ga *adj* (-ghi -ghe) (lit) lonely; (lit) solitary (*enjoying solitude*)

solino *m* detachable collar; **solino duro** stiff collar

soli·sta *mf* (-sti -ste) soloist

solità·rio -ria (-ri -rie) *adj* solitary, lonely ‖ *m* solitaire; solitary

sòli·to -ta *adj* usual, customary; **esser solito** to be accustomed to ‖ *m* habit, custom; **come il solito** as usual; **di solito** usually

solitùdine *f* solitude, loneliness

sollazzare *tr* to amuse ‖ *ref* to have a good time, amuse oneself

sollazzo *m* (lit) amusement; **essere il sollazzo di** to be the laughingstock of

sollecitare (sollécito) *tr* to solicit; to urge; to induce; (mach) to stress ‖ *intr* & *ref* to hasten

sollecitazióne *f* solicitation; urging; (mach) stress

solléci·to -ta *adj* quick, prompt; diligent; solicitous, anxious ‖ *m* (com) solicitation, urging

sollecitùdine *f* solicitude; promptness; diligence; **cortese sollecitudine** (com) prompt attention

solleóne *m* dog days

solleticare §197 (sollético) *tr* to tickle; (fig) to flatter

solléti·co *m* (-chi) tickling; stimulation; **fare il solletico a** to tickle

sollevaménto *m* lifting; **sollevamento di pesi** weight lifting

sollevare (sollèvo) *tr* to lift; to relieve; to pick up; to raise (*e.g., a question*); to excite; to elevate ‖ *ref* to rise; to lift oneself; to pick up (*said of courage or health*)

sollevazióne *f* uprising

solliè·vo *m* relief

sollùchero *m—***andare in solluchero** to become ecstatic; **mandare in solluchero** to thrill

só·lo -la *adj* lone, lonely, alone; only; single; **fare da solo** to operate all by oneself; **solo soletto** all by myself (yourself, himself, etc.); within oneself; **un solo** only one ‖ *m* (mus) solo ‖ *adv* only ‖ **solo conj** only; **solo che** provided that

solsti·zio *m* (-zi) solstice

soltanto *adv* only

solùbile *adj* soluble

soluzióne *f* solution; installment; **soluzione di comodo** compromise; **soluzione provvisoria** stopgap

soivènte *adj* & *m* solvent

solvènza *f* solvency

solvìbile *adj* collectable; solvent

sòma *f* burden, load

Somàlia, la Somaliland

sòma·lo -la *adj* & *mf* Somali

soma·ro -ra *mf* donkey, ass

someggia·to -ta *adj* carried by pack animal; carried on mule back

somigliante *adj* similar; **essere somigliante a** to look like ‖ *m* same thing

somiglianza *f* similarity, resemblance

somigliare §280 *tr* to resemble; (lit) to compare || *intr* (ESSERE & AVERE) (with *dat*) to resemble; to seem to be || *ref* to resemble each other

sómma *f* addition; sum; summary

sommare (**sómmo**) *tr* to add; to consider; **tutto sommato** all in all || *intr* to amount

sommà·rio -ria (**-ri -rie**) *adj* summary || *m* summary; abstract; (journ) subheading

sommèrgere §162 *tr* to submerge; (fig) to plunge; (fig) to flood (*with insults*) || *ref* to submerge

sommergibile *adj* & *m* submarine

sommés·so -sa *adj* submissive; subdued (*voice*)

somministrare *tr* to administer; to provide; to deliver (*a blow*); to adduce (*proof*)

somministrazióne *f* administration; provision

sommi·tà *f* (**-tà**) summit

sóm·mo -ma *adj* highest; supreme || *m* top; peak, summit || *f* see **somma**

sommòssa *f* insurrection, riot

sommoviménto *m* tremor (*of earth*); arousal (*of passions*); riot

sommozzatóre *m* skin diver; (nav) frogman

sommuòvere §202 *tr* (lit) to agitate; (lit) to stir up, excite

sonaglièra *f* collar with bells

sonà·glio *m* (**-gli**) bell; rattle; raindrop; pitter-patter (*of the rain*)

sonante *adj* ringing, sounding; ready (*cash*)

sonare §257 *tr* to sound; to play; to strike (*the hour*); to ring (*a bell*); (coll) to dupe, cheat; (coll) to give a sound thrashing to; **sonare le campane a distesa** to ring a full peal || *intr* (ESSERE & AVERE) to play; to ring (*said of a bell*); to sound; (lit) to spread (*said of reputation*)

sona·to -ta *adj* played; past, e.g., **le tre sonate** past three o'clock; **cinquant'anni sonati** past fifty years of age || *f* ring (*of bell*); (mus) sonata; (coll) thrashing; (coll) cheating

sona·tóre -trice *mf* (mus) player

sónda *f* sound; probe; drill

sondàg·gio *m* (**-gi**) sounding; probe; drilling; **sondaggio d'opinioni** opinion survey, public opinion poll

sondare (**sóndo**) *tr* to sound; to probe; to drill; to survey (*public opinion*)

sonerìa *f* alarm (*of clock*)

sonétto *m* sonnet

sonnacchió·so -sa [s] *adj* sleepy, drowsy

sonnàmbu·lo -la *mf* sleepwalker

sonnecchiare §287 (**sonnécchio**) *intr* to drowse, take a nap; to nap, nod

sonnellino *m* nap

sonnìfe·ro -ra *adj* soporific; narcotic || *m* sleeping medicine; narcotic

sónno *m* sleep; (lit) dream; **aver sonno** to be sleepy; **far venir sonno a** to bore; **prender sonno** to fall asleep

sonnolèn·to -ta *adj* sleepy; lazy

sonnolènza *f* drowsiness; laziness

sonori·tà *f* (**-tà**) sonority; acoustics

sonorizzare [ddzz] *tr* to voice; (mov) to dub || *ref* to voice

sonò·ro -ra *adj* sound (*wave*); sonorous; (phonet) sonant, voiced

sontuó·so -sa [s] *adj* sumptuous

sopèr·chio -chia *adj* & *m* (**-chi -chie**) var of **soverchio**

sopire §176 *tr* to appease, calm

sopóre *m* drowsiness

soporìfe·ro -ra *adj* soporific

soppanno *m* interlining; lining (*of shoes*)

sopperire §176 *intr*—**sopperire a** to provide for; to make up for

soppesare [s] (**soppéso**) *tr* to heft; (fig) to weigh

soppiantare *tr* to supplant by scheming; to kick out; to replace; to trick

soppiatto *m*—**di soppiatto** stealthily

sopportàbile *adj* bearable, tolerable

sopportare (**soppòrto**) *tr* to bear, support; to suffer, endure

sopportazióne *f* forbearance, endurance

soppressióne *f* suppression, abolition

sopprìmere §131 *tr* to suppress, do away with

sópra *adj invar* upper; above, preceding || *m* upper, upper part; **al di sopra** above; **al di sopra di** above, over; beyond; **di sopra** upper || *adv* above; up; on top || *prep* on; upon; on top of; over; beyond; above; versus; **sopra pensiero** absorbed in thought

sopràbito *m* overcoat, topcoat

sopraccàri·co -ca (**-chi -che**) *adj* overburdened || *m* overload; overweight; (naut) supercargo

sopraccenna·to·ta *adj* above-mentioned

sopracci·glio *m* (**-gli** & **-glia** *fpl*) brow, eyebrow; window frame

sopraccita·to -ta *adj* above-mentioned

sopraccopèrta *f* bedspread; book jacket, dust jacket || *adv* (naut) on deck

sopraddét·to -ta *adj* above-mentioned

sopraffare §173 *tr* to overcome, overpower

sopraffazióne *f* overpowering; abuse

sopraffinèstra *f* transom window

sopraffi·no -na *adj* first-class; superfine

sopraggitto *m* (sew) overcasting

sopraggiùngere §183 *intr* (ESSERE) to arrive; to happen

sopraintèndere §270 *tr* var of **soprintendere**

sopralluò·go *m* (**-ghi**) inspection, investigation on the spot

sopralzo *m* var of **soprelevazione**

soprammercato *m*—**per soprammercato** in addition, to boot

soprammòbile *m* knickknack

soprannaturale *adj* & *m* supernatural

soprannóme *m* nickname

soprannominare (**soprannòmino**) *tr* to nickname

soprannùmero *adj invar* in excess; overtime || *m* —**in soprannumero** extra; in excess

sopra·no -na *adj* upper; (lit) supreme

|| **sopra·no** *mf* (-**ni** -**ne**) soprano (*person*) || *m* soprano (*voice*)

soprappensièro *adj invar* & *adv* immersed in thought

soprappéso [s] *m*—**per soprappeso** besides, into the bargain

soprap·più *m* (-**più**) plus, extra; **in soprappiù** besides, into the bargain

soprapprèzzo *m* extra charge, surcharge

soprascarpa *f* overshoe

soprascrit·to -**ta** *adj* written above || *f* address

soprassalto *m* start, jump; **di soprassalto** with a start

soprassedére §252 *intr* to wait; (with *dat*) to postpone

soprassòldo *m* extra pay; (mil) warzone indemnity

soprastare §263 *intr* (ESSERE) to be the boss

soprattac·co *m* (-**chi**) rubber heel

soprattassa *f* surtax; surcharge

soprattutto *adv* above all, especially

sopravanzare *tr* to overcome || *intr* (ESSERE) to be left over

sopravanzo *m* surplus

sopravvalutare *tr* to overrate

sopravvenire §282 *tr* (lit) to overrun || *intr* (ESSERE) to arrive; to happen, occur; (with *dat*) to befall

sopravvènto *m* windward; **avere il sopravvento** to have the upper hand || *adv* windward

sopravvissu·to -**ta** *adj* surviving || *mf* survivor

sopravvivènza *f* survival

sopravvivere §286 *intr* (ESSERE) to survive; (with *dat*) to survive, to outlive

soprelevare (**soprelèvo**) *tr* to elevate (*e.g.*, *a railroad*); to increase the height of (*building*)

soprelevazióne *f* elevation; addition of one or more floors

soprintendènte *m* superintendent

soprintendènza *f* superintendency

soprintèndere §270 *tr* to oversee

sopròsso *m* (coll) bony outgrowth

sopruso *m* abuse of power

soqquadro *m*—**a soqquadro** upside down, topsy-turvy

sòrba *f* sorb apple; (coll) hit, blow

sorbettièra *f* ice-cream freezer

sorbétto *m* ice cream; sherbet

sorbire §176 *tr* to sip; (fig) to swallow, endure

sòrbo *m* sorb; service tree

sór·cio *m* (-**ci**) mouse

sòrdi·do -**da** *adj* sordid; dirty

sordina *f* (mus) sordino, mute; (mus) soft pedal; **in sordina** quietly; stealthily; **mettere in sordina** (mus) to muffle

sór·do -**da** *adj* deaf; dull (*pain*); deepseated (*hatred*); hollow (*sound*); (phonet) surd, voiceless; **sordo come una campana** stone-deaf || *mf* deaf person

sordomu·to -**ta** *adj* deaf and dumb || *mf* deafmute

sorèlla *f* sister

sorellastra *f* stepsister

sorgènte *adj* rising || *f* spring; well (*of oil*); (fig) source; **sorgente del fiume** riverhead

sórgere §258 *intr* (ESSERE) to rise; to arise; to spring forth; **sorgere su un'àncora** (naut) to lie at anchor

sorgi·vo -**va** *adj* spring (*water*)

sór·go *m* (-**ghi**) sorghum

sormontare (**sormónto**) *tr* to surmount; to overcome || *intr* to fit

sornió·ne -**na** *adj* cunning, sly || *m* sneak

sorpassare *tr* to get ahead of; to surpass; to overstep; to go above

sorpasso *m* (aut) passing

sorprendènte *adj* surprising, astonishing

sorprèndere §220 *tr* to surprise; to catch; **sorprendere la buona fede di** to take advantage of || *ref* to be surprised

sorprésa [s] *f* surprise; surprise investigation; **di sorpresa** suddenly; unprepared; by surprise

sorrèggere §226 *tr* to sustain, support; to bolster

sorrìdere §231 *tr* (lit) to say with a smile || *intr* to smile; **sorridere a** to appeal to, e.g., **le sorride l'idea di questa gita** the idea of this trip appeals to her; to smile upon, e.g., **gli sorrideva la vita** life was smiling upon him

sorriso [s] *m* smile

sorsata *f* gulp, draught

sorseggiare §290 (**sorséggio**) *tr* to sip

sórso *m* sip; **a sorso a sorso** sipping

sòrta *f* kind, sort

sòrte *f* luck, lot, fate; chance; kind; (com) principal; **per sorte** of each kind; by chance; **tirare a sorte** to cast lots

sorteggiare §290 (**sortéggio**) *tr* to choose by lot; to raffle; **sorteggiare un premio** to draw a prize

sortég·gio *m* (-**gi**) drawing

sortile·gio *m* (-**gi**) sortilege; sorcery, magic

sortire §176 *tr* (lit) to get by lot; (lit) to have (*results*); (lit) to allot || (**sòrto**) *intr* (ESSERE) to come out (*said, e.g., of a newspaper*); (coll) to be drawn (*by lot*); (coll) to go out; (mil) to make a sally

sortita *f* witticism; (mil) sally, sortie; (theat) appearance

sorvegliante *adj* watchful || *mf* overseer, caretaker; guardian || *m* watchman; foreman

sorveglianza *f* surveillance; supervision

sorvegliare §280 (**sorvéglio**) *tr* to oversee, watch over; to check; control

sorvolare (**sorvólo**) *tr* to fly over; to overfly; (fig) to avoid, skip

sorvólo *m* overflight

sò·sia *m* (-**sia**) double, counterpart

sospèndere §259 *tr* to hang; to suspend; (chem) to prepare a suspension of; (law) to stay

sospensióne *f* suspension; suspense; (law) stay; **sospensione cardanica** gimbals

sospensò·rio *m* (**-ri**) jockstrap, supporter

sospé·so -sa [s] *adj* suspended; suspension (*bridge*); **in sospeso** in suspense; in abeyance || *m* employee who has been disciplined by suspension; (com) pending item

sospettare (**sospètto**) *tr* to suspect || *intr*—**sospettare di** to suspect; to fear

sospèt·to -ta *adj* suspected; suspicious || *m* dash; suspicion

sospettó·so -sa [s] *adj* suspicious

sospingere §126 *tr* (fig) to drive; (lit) to push

sospirare *tr* to long for, crave; **fare sospirare** to keep waiting || *intr* to sigh

sospiro *m* sigh; longing; (lit) breath; **a sospiri** little by little

sossópra *adv* upside down

sòsta *f* stop; reprieve; (rr) demurrage

sostanti·vo -va *adj* & *m* substantive

sostanza *f* substance; **sostanza grigia** gray matter

sostanziale *adj* substantial

sostanzió·so -sa [s] *adj* substantial

sostare (**sòsto**) *intr* to stop, pause

sostégno *m* prop; (fig) support

sostenére §271 *tr* to support; to sustain; to take (*an examination*); to defend (*a thesis*); to prop up; to stand (*alcohol*); to play (*a role*) || *ref* to support oneself; to hold up (*said, e.g., of a theory*); to take nourishment

sosteni·tóre -trice *mf* backer, supporter

sostentaménto *m* sustenance, support

sostentare (**sostènto**) *tr* to support, keep || *ref* to feed, eat

sostenu·to -ta *adj* reserved, austere; rising (*prices*); bullish (*market*); starchy (*manner*)

sostituìbile *adj* replaceable

sostituire §176 *tr* to replace, substitute for, take the place of; **sostituire** (*qlco* or *qlcu*) **a** a substitute (*s.th* or *s.o.*) for

sostitu·to -ta *adj* acting; associate, assistant || *m* replacement, substitute

sostituzióne *f* replacement, substitution

sostrato *m* substratum

sottàbito *m* slip

sottacére §268 *tr* (lit) to withhold

sottacéto *adj invar* pickled || **sottaceti** *mpl* pickles

sott'àcqua *adv* underwater

sotta·no -na *adj* lower (*town*) || *f* skirt; petticoat; (eccl) cassock; **gettare la sottana alle ortiche** to doff the cassock

sottécchi *adv*—**di sottecchi** stealthily, secretly; **guardare di sottecchi** to peep, look furtively (at)

sottentrare (**sottèntro**) *intr* (ESSERE) (with *dat*) to replace

sotterfù·gio *m* (**-gi**) subterfuge

sottèrra *adv* underground

sotterràne·o -a *adj* subterranean, underground; secret, clandestine || *m* cave, vault; dungeon; underground passage || *f* (rr) subway, underground

sotterrare (**sottèrro**) *tr* to bury

sottigliézza *f* thinness; subtlety

sottile *adj* thin; subtle; (naut) lightweight || *m*—**guardare troppo per il sottile** to split hairs

sottilizzare [ddzz] *intr* to quibble

sottintèndere §270 *tr* to understand || *ref* to be understood, be implied

sottinté·so -sa [s] *adj* understood, implied || *m* innuendo

sótto *adj invar* lower || *m* lower part || *adv* under; underneath; **al di sotto** below; **al di sotto di** under, below; **di sotto** lower; underneath; downstairs; **di sotto a** under, below; **farsi sotto** to sneak up; **metter sotto** to run over (*with a vehicle*); **sotto a** under; **sotto di** under || *prep* under; beneath; below; just before; **prendere sotto gamba** to underestimate; **sotto braccio** arm in arm; **sotto carico** (naut) being loaded; **sotto i baffi** up one's sleeve; **sotto le armi** in the service; **sotto mano** within reach; **sotto voce** under one's breath, sotto-voce

sottoascèl·la *m* (**-la**) underarm pad

sottobanco *adv* under the counter

sottobicchière *m* coaster

sottobò·sco *m* (**-schi**) underbrush, thicket

sottobràccio *adv* arm in arm

sottòcchio *adv* under one's eyes

sottoccupa·to -ta *adj* underemployed

sottochiave *adv* under lock and key

sottocó·da *m* (**-da**) crupper

sottocommissióne *f* subcommittee

sottocopèrta *adv* (naut) below decks

sottocòp·pa *m* (**-pa**) mat; coaster; (aut) oil pan

sottocòsto *adj invar* & *adv* below cost

sottocutàne·o -a *adj* subcutaneous

sottofà·scia *m* (**-scia**) wrapper; **spedire sottofascia** to mail (*a newspaper*) in a wrapper || *f* (**-sce**) wrapper (*for cigars*)

sottogamba *adv* lightly; **prendere sottogamba** to underestimate

sottogó·la *m* & *f* (**-la**) chin strap; throatlatch (*of harness*)

sottolineare (**sottolìneo**) *tr* to underline, underscore; to emphasize

sott'òlio *adv* in oil

sottomano *m* writing pad || *adv* underhand; within reach

sottomari·no -na *adj* & *m* submarine

sottomés·so -sa *adj* conquered; subdued; submissive

sottométtere §198 *tr* to subdue, crush; to defer, postpone; to present (*a bill*); to subject || *ref* to submit, yield

sottomissióne *f* submission

sottopan·cia *m* (**-cia**) bellyband, girth

sottopassàg·gio *m* (**-gi**) underpass; lower level (*of highway*)

sottopiatto *m* saucer

sottopórre §218 *tr* to subject; to submit || *ref* to submit; **sottoporsi a** to submit to; to undergo (*e.g., an operation*)

sottopó·sto -sta *adj* subject; exposed || *m* subordinate

sottoprèzzo *adj invar* cut-rate ‖ *adv* at a cut rate

sottoprodótto *m* by-product

sottórdine *m* suborder; **in sottordine** secondary

sottosca·la *m* (**-la**) space under the stairs; closet under the stairs

sottoscrit·to -ta *adj & mf* undersigned

sottoscrit·tóre -trice *mf* subscriber

sottoscrìvere §250 *tr* to subscribe; to sign, undersign; to underwrite ‖ *intr* to subscribe

sottoscrizióne *f* subscription

sottosegretà·rio *m* (**-ri**) undersecretary

sottosópra *adj invar* upset; **mettere sottosopra** to upset; to turn upside down ‖ *m* confusion, disorder ‖ *adv* upside down

sottostante *adj* lower; subordinate ‖ *m* subordinate

sottostare §263 *intr* (ESSERE) to be located below; to be subject; to yield, submit; (with *dat*) to undergo (*e.g., an examination*)

sottosuòlo *m* subsoil; cellar

sottosvilúppa·to -ta *adj* underdeveloped

sottotenènte *m* second lieutenant; **sottotenente di vascello** (nav) lieutenant j.g.

sottotèr·ra *m* (**-ra**) basement ‖ *adv* underground

sottotétto *m* attic, garret

sottotìtolo *m* subtitle; (mov) caption

sottovalutare *tr* to underrate

sottovènto *m & adv* leeward

sottovèste *f* slip (*undergarment*)

sottovóce *adv* sotto voce, under one's breath

sottrarre §273 *tr* to subtract; **sottrarre a** to take away from, steal from ‖ *ref*—**sottrarsi a** to avoid; to escape from

sottrazióne *f* subtraction

sottufficiale *m* noncommissioned officer

sovènte *adv* often

soverchiante *adj* overwhelming

soverchiare §287 (**sovèrchio**) *tr* to overwhelm; to excel; to bully; (lit) to overflow ‖ *intr* to be in excess

soverchia·tóre -trice *adj* overbearing ‖ *mf* overbearing person, oppressor

sovèr·chio -chia (**-chi -chie**) *adj* excessive; overbearing ‖ *m* overbearing action

sovè·scio *m* (**-sci**) plowing under (*of green manure*)

sovièti·co -ca (**-ci -che**) *adj* Soviet ‖ *mf* Soviet citizen

sovrabbondante *adj* superabundant

sovrabbondare (**sovrabbóndo**) *intr* (ESSERE & AVERE) to be superabundant; to go to excesses

sovraccaricare §197 (**sovraccàrico**) *tr* to overload

sovraccàri·co -ca (**-chi -che**) *adj* overburdened ‖ *m* overload; overweight

sovraespó·sto -sta *adj* overexposed

sovraggiùngere §183 *intr* (ESSERE) var of sopraggiungere

sovralimentazióne *f* (aut) supercharging

sovrani·tà *f* (**-tà**) sovereignty

sovra·no -na *adj & mf* sovereign

sovrappopolare (**sovrappòpolo**) *tr* to overpopulate

sovrappórre §218 *tr* to overlay; to superimpose; **sovrapporre qlco a** to lay s.th on ‖ *ref* to be superimposed; to be added; **sovrapporsi a** to put oneself above

sovrapproduzióne *f* overproduction

sovrastampa *f* overprint

sovrastante *adj* overlooking, overhanging; impending

sovrastare *tr* to tower over; to hang over; to surpass; to excel ‖ *intr* (ESSERE & AVERE)—**sovrastare a** to tower over; to overlook; to hang over; to surpass; to excel

sovratensióne *f* (elec) surge

sovreccitare (**sovrèccito**) *tr* to overexcite

sovrespórre §218 *tr* to overexpose

sovrimpòsta *f* surtax

sovrimpressióne *f* double exposure

sovruma·no -na *adj* superhuman

sovvenire §282 (lit) to help ‖ *intr* (with *dat*) (lit) to help ‖ *impers* (ESSERE)—**sovviene** (with *dat*) **di** remember, *e.g.,* **gli sovviene spesso dei suoi cari** he often remembers his dear ones ‖ *ref*—**sovvenirsi di** to remember

sovvenzionare (**sovvenzióno**) *tr* to subsidize, grant a subvention to

sovvenzióne *f* subsidy, subvention

sovversi·vo -va *adj & m* subversive

sovvertire (**sovvèrto**) *tr* to subvert

sóz·zo -za *adj* dirty, filthy, foul

sozzura *f* dirt, filth

spaccalé·gna *m* (**-gna**) woodcutter

spaccamón·ti *m* (**-ti**) braggart

spaccaòs·sa *m* (**-sa**) butcher's cleaver

spaccare §197 *tr* to break, burst; to crack; to unpack; to chop; to split ‖ *ref* to crack; to break; to split

spacca·to -ta *adj* broken; split; (coll) identical; (coll) true ‖ *f* (sports, theat) splits

spaccatura *f* break; crack; cleavage; split

spacchétto *m* vent (*in jacket*)

spacciare §128 *tr* to sell out; to palm off; to spread (*reports*); to expedite; to abandon (*as hopeless*); (slang) to push (*e.g., dope*) ‖ *ref*—**spacciarsi per** to pretend to be, pass oneself off as

spaccia·to -ta *adj* (coll) cooked, done for; (coll) hopeless

spaccia·tóre -trice *mf* passer (*of bad currency or stolen goods*); **spacciatore di notizie false** gossipmonger

spàc·cio *m* (**-ci**) sale; passing (*of counterfeit money*); spreading (*of false news*); post exchange; tobacco shop

spac·co *m* (**-chi**) break; split; tear; crack; vent (*in jacket*)

spacconata *f* brag, braggadocio

spaccó·ne -na *mf* braggart, braggadocio

spada *f* sword; **a spada tratta** doggedly; spade suit of Neapolitan cards corresponding to spades

spadaccino *m* swordsman; swashbuckler

spadóne *m* two-handed sword

spadroneggiare §290 (spadronéggio) *intr* to be domineering or bossy

spaesa·to -ta *adj* out-of-place

spaghétto *m* (coll) fear, jitters; **avere lo spaghetto** (coll) to be scared stiff; **spaghetti** spaghetti

Spagna, la Spain

spagnòla *f* Spanish woman; Spanish influenza

spagnolétta *f* espagnolette; spool; (coll) cigarette; (coll) peanut

spagnò·lo -la *adj* Spanish || *m* Spaniard (*individual*); Spanish (*language*); **gli spagnoli** the Spanish || *f* see **spagnola**

spa·go *m* (-ghi) string, twine; (coll) fear, jitters

spaiare §287 *tr* to break a pair of

spaia·to -ta *adj* unmatched

spalancare §197 *tr* to open wide || *ref* to open up; to gape

spalare *tr* to shovel; to feather (*oar*)

spalla *f* shoulder; back; abutment (*of bridge*); (theat) stooge, straight man; **alle spalle di qlcu** behind s.o.'s back; **a spalla** on one's back; **fare spalla a** to help; **lavorare di spalle** to elbow one's way; (fig) to worm one's way up; **vivere alle spalle di** to sponge on

spaliàrm *interj* (mil) shoulder arms!

spallata *f* push with the shoulder; shrug of the shoulders

spalleggiare §290 (spalléggio) *tr* to back, support; (mil) to carry on one's back

spallétta *f* parapet, retaining wall; jamb

spallièra *f* back (*of chair*); head (*of bed*); foot (*of bed*); espalier

spallina *f* epaulet; shoulder strap

spallùccia *f*—**fare spallucce** to shrug one's shoulders

spalmare *tr* to spread; to smear

spalto *m* glacis; **spalti** seats (*of a stadium*)

spanare *tr* to strip the thread of || *ref* to be stripped (*said, e.g., of the thread of a nut*)

spanciare §128 *tr* to disembowel, gut || *intr* to belly-flop; to bulge (*said of a wall*) || *ref*—**spanciarsi dalle risa** to split one's sides laughing

spanciata *f* belly flop; bellyful; **fare una spanciata** to stuff oneself

spàndere §260 *tr* to spread; to spill; to shed (*tears*); to squander || *ref* to spread

spanna *f* span

spannare *tr* to skim (*milk*)

spannocchiare §287 (spannòcchio) *tr* to husk (*corn*)

spappolare (spàppolo) *tr* to crush, squash || *ref* to become mushy

sparadrappo *m* adhesive tape; (obs) plaster, poultice

sparagnare *tr* (coll) to save

sparare *tr* to gut, disembowel; to shoot; to let go with (*a kick*); to remove

the hangings from; **spararne delle grosse** to tell tall tales

sparato *m* shirt front, dickey

sparatòria *f* shooting

sparecchiare §287 (sparécchio) *tr* to clear (*the table*); to clear away (*one's tools*); to eat up

sparég·gio *m* (-gi) disparity; deficit; (sports) play-off

spàrgere §261 *tr* to spread; to shed; to spill || *ref* to spread

spargiménto *m* spreading; **spargimento di sangue** bloodshed

spargisa·le [s] *m* (-le) salt shaker

sparigliare §280 *tr* to break a pair of; to break (*a set*)

spariglia·to -ta *adj* unmatched

sparire §176 *intr* (ESSERE) to disappear

sparlare *intr* to backbite; **sparlare di** to backbite, slander

sparo *m* shot

sparpagliare §280 *tr & intr* to scatter

spar·so -sa *adj* scattered; dotted; speckled; hanging loosely (*e.g., hair*)

sparta·no -na *adj & mf* Spartan

spartiàc·que *m* (-que) watershed

spartiné·ve *m* (-ve) snowplow

spartire §176 *tr* to divide, share; to separate; **non aver nulla da spartire con** to have nothing to do with

spartito *m* (mus) score; (mus) arrangement

spartitràffi·co *m* (-co) median strip

spar·to -ta *adj* (lit) spread || *m* esparto grass

sparu·to -ta *adj* lean, wan; meager

sparvière *m* sparrow hawk; mortarboard

spasimante *m* (joc) lover, wooer

spasimare (spàsimo) *intr* to writhe; **spasimare per** to long for; to be madly in love with

spàsimo *m* pang; severe pain; longing

spasmo *m* spasm

spasmòdi·co -ca *adj* (-ci -che) spasmodic

spassare *tr* to amuse || *ref*—**spassarsela** to have a good time

spassiona·to -ta *adj* dispassionate, unbiased

spasso *m* fun, amusement; walk; (coll) funny guy; **andare a spasso** to go out for a walk; **essere a spasso** to be out of a job; **mandare a spasso** to fire, dismiss; to get rid of; **per spasso** for fun; **portare a spasso** to lead by the nose; **prendersi spasso di** to make fun of

spassó·so -sa [s] *adj* amusing, droll

spàsti·co -ca *adj & mf* spastic

spato *m* spar

spatofluòre *m* fluorspar

spàtola *f* spatula; putty knife; slapstick (*of harlequin*)

spauràc·chio *m* (chi) scarecrow; bugaboo, bugbear

spaurare *tr & ref* (lit) var of **spaurire**

spaurire §176 *tr* to frighten || *ref* to be scared

spaval·do -da *adj* bold, swaggering

spaventapàs·seri *m* (-ri) scarecrow

spaventare (spavènto) *tr* to scare, frighten || *ref* to be scared

spaventévole *adj* frightening, dreadful

spavènto *m* fright, fear

spaventó·so -sa [s] *adj* frightful, fearful

spaziale *adj* space

spaziare §287 *tr* (typ) to space || *intr* to soar; to range, rove (*said, e.g., of eye*)

spazia·tóre -trice *adj* spacing || *f* space bar (*of typewriter*)

spaziatura *f* spacing

spazientire §176 *tr* to make (*s.o.*) lose his patience || *intr* (ESSERE) & *ref* to lose patience

spà·zio *m* (-zi) space; (fig) room; **spazio aereo** air space; **spazio cosmico** outer space

spazió·so -sa [s] *adj* spacious, roomy; wide

spazzacamino *m* chimney sweep

spazzami·ne *m* (-ne) mine sweeper

spazzané·ve *m* (-ve) snowplow

spazzare *tr* to sweep; to plow (*snow*); to clean up

spazzata *f*—**dare una spazzata a** to give a lick and a promise to

spazzatrice *f* street sweeper

spazzatura *f* sweeping; sweepings; rubbish, trash

spazzatu·ràio *m* (-rài) or **spazzino** *m* street cleaner; trashman, garbage collector, trash collector

spàzzola *f* brush; **capelli a spazzola** crew cut

spazzolare (spàzzolo) *tr* to brush

spazzolino *m* little brush; (elec) brush; **spazzolino da denti** toothbrush; **spazzolino per le unghie** nailbrush

spazzolóne *m* push broom

specchiare §287 (spècchio) *tr* (lit) to reflect || *ref* to look at oneself (*in a mirror*); to be reflected; **specchiarsi in qlcu** to model oneself on s.o.

specchièra *f* mirror; dressing table; full-length mirror

specchiétto *m* mirror; synopsis; **specchietto retrovisivo** (aut) rear-view mirror

spèc·chio *m* (-chi) mirror; synopsis; shore (*of lake or river*); panel (*of door or window*); sheet (*of water*); (sports) goal line; (sports) board; **specchio di poppa** (naut) transom; **specchio ustorio** burning glass

speciale *adj* special

speciali·sta *mf* (-sti -ste) specialist

speciali·tà *f* (-tà) specialty; (mil) special services; **specialità farmaceutica** patent or proprietary medicine

specializzare [ddzz] *tr* & *ref* to specialize

spè·cie *f* (-cie) species; kind, sort; appearance, semblance; **fare specie** (with *dat*) (coll) to be surprised, e.g., **gli fa specie** he is surprised; **in specie** especially; **sotto specie di** under pretext of

specìfi·ca *f* (-che) itemized list; specification

specificare §197 (specìfico) *tr* to specify; to itemize

specìfi·co -ca (-ci -che) *adj* & *m* specific || *f* see **specìfica**

specillo *m* (med) probe

speció·so -sa [s] *adj* specious

spè·co *m* (-chi) (lit) cave

spècola *f* observatory

spècolo *m* (med, surg) speculum

speculare (spèculo) *tr* to observe; to meditate on || *intr* to speculate

specula·tóre -trice *adj* speculating || *mf* speculator; **speculatore al rialzo** bull; **speculatore al ribasso** bear

speda·to -ta *adj* footworn

spedire §176 *tr* to expedite; to prepare; to ship, send, forward; (law) to deliver

spedi·to -ta *adj* rapid; free, easy

spedi·tóre -trice *mf* shipper, sender; shipping clerk

spedizióne *f* shipment, shipping; sending, forwarding; expedition; (naut) papers; **di spedizione** expeditionary

spedizionière *m* shipper, forwarder, forwarding agent

spègnere §262 *tr* to extinguish, put out; to turn off; to slake (*lime*); to kill; to mix (*flour*) with water or milk; to quench; to obliterate (*a memory*) || *ref* to burn out; to go out (*said of a light*); to fade, die away; to die

spegni·tóio *m* (-tói) snuffer

spegnitura *f* (theat) blackout

spelacchiare §287 *tr* to strip of hair || *ref* to shed hair or fur

spelacchia·to -ta *adj* mangy; (pej) baldy

spelare (spélo) *tr* to strip of hair; to pluck (*e.g., a chicken*); (fig) to fleece || *ref* to shed hair or fur; to get bald

spellare (spèllo) *tr* to skin; (fig) to skin, fleece

spelón·ca *f* (-che) cave; hovel, den

spème *f* (poet) hope

spendacció·ne -na *mf* spendthrift

spèndere §220 *tr* to spend

spenderéc·cio -cia *adj* (-ci -ce) spendthrift, prodigal

spennacchiare §287 *tr* to pluck; (fig) to fleece || *ref* to lose its feathers

spennare (spénno) *tr* & *ref* var of **spennacchiare**

spennellare (spennèllo) *tr* to dab

spensieratézza *f* thoughtlessness

spensiera·to -ta *adj* thoughtless, careless; carefree, happy-go-lucky

spèn·to -ta *adj* extinguished; turned off; slaked (*lime*); dull (*color*); low (*tone*)

spenzolare [dz] (spènzolo) *tr* & *intr* to hang || *ref*—**spenzolarsi da** to hang out of

speranza *f* hope; prospect, expectation

speranzó·so -sa [s] *adj* hopeful

sperare (spèro) *tr* to candle (*eggs*); to hope for; to expect || *intr* to hope; to trust

spèrdere §212 *tr* (lit) to scatter; (lit) to lose (*one's way*) || *ref* to lose one's way, get lost

sperdu·to -ta *adj* lost, astray; godforsaken (*place*)

sperequazióne *f* disproportion; inequality; unjust distribution

spergiurare *tr & intr* to swear falsely; **giurare e spergiurare** to swear over and over again

spergiu·ro -ra *adj* perjured ‖ *mf* perjurer ‖ *m* perjury

spericola·to -ta *adj* reckless, daring

sperimentale *adj* experimental

sperimentare (**speriménto**) *tr* to test, try out; to experience

sperimenta·to -ta *adj* experienced

spèr·ma *m* (**-mi**) sperm

speronare (**speróno**) *tr* (naut) to ram

speróne *m* spur; abutment; (nav) ram

sperperare (**spèrpero**) *tr* to squander

spèrpero *m* squandering

spèr·so -sa *adj* lost, stray

spertica·to -ta *adj* too long; too tall; exaggerated, excessive

spésa [s] *f* expense; shopping; buy, purchase; **fare la spesa** to shop; **fare le spese di** to be the butt of; **lavorare per le spese** to work for one's keep; **pagare le spese** to bear the charges; **spese** expenses; room and board; **spese di manutenzione** upkeep; **spese minute** petty expenses; **spese processuali** (law) costs

spesare [s] (**spéso**) *tr* to support

spesa·to -ta [s] *adj* with all expenses paid

spés·so -sa *adj* thick; many (*times*) ‖ **spesso** *adv* often; **spesso spesso** again and again

spessóre *m* thickness

spettàbile *adj* esteemed; **Spettabile Ditta** (com) Gentlemen

spettàcolo *m* spectacle, show; sight; **dar spettacolo di sé** to make a show of oneself; **spettacolo all'aperto** outdoor performance

spettacoló·so -sa [s] *adj* spectacular; (coll) exceptional; (coll) sensational

spettanza *f* concern; pay

spettare (**spètto**) *intr* (ESSERE)—**spettare a** to belong to ‖ *impers* (ESSERE) —**spetta a** it behooves, it is up to

spetta·tóre -trice *mf* spectator, bystander; **spettatori** public, audience

spettegolare (**spettégolo**) *intr* to gossip

spettinare (**spèttino**) *tr* to muss the hair of

spettrale *adj* ghost-like; spectral

spèttro *m* specter, ghost; spectrum

speziale *m* dealer in spices; (coll) pharmacist

spezie *fpl* spices

spezieria *f* grocery; (coll) drug store, pharmacy; **spezierie** spices

spezzare (**spèzzo**) *tr* to break; to smash; to interrupt ‖ *ref* to break

spezzatino *m* stew; **spezzatini** change

spezza·to -ta *adj* broken; fragmentary; interrupted ‖ *m* stew; (theat) set piece; **spezzati** change

spezzettare (**spezzétto**) *tr* to mince

spezzóne *m* small aerial bomb; fragmentation bomb; fragment

spìa *f* spy; indication; peephole; (aut) gauge; (aut) pilot light; **fare la spia** to be an informer

spiaccicare §197 (**spiàccico**) *tr* to squash, crush ‖ *ref* to be squashed

spiacènte *adj* sorry; (lit) disliked

spiacére §214 *intr* (ESSERE) (with *dat*) to dislike, e.g., **queste parole gli spiacciono** he dislikes these words; to mind, e.g., **se non Le spiace** if you don't mind ‖ *ref*—**spiacersi di** to be sorry for ‖ *impers* (ESSERE) (with *dat*)—**gli spiace** he is sorry

spiacévole *adj* unpleasant

spiàg·gia *f* (**-ge**) beach, shore

spianare *tr* to grade (*land*); to roll (*dough*); to pave (*the way*); to iron (*pleats*); to raze, demolish; to level (*a gun*); **spianare la fronte** to smooth one's brow ‖ *intr* (ESSERE) to be level

spianata *f* esplanade; **dare una spianata a** to level

spianatóia *f* board (*for rolling dough*)

spiana·tóio *m* (**-tói**) rolling pin

spianatrice *f* grader

spiano *m* leveling; esplanade; **a tutto spiano** at full blast; continuously

spiantare *tr* to uproot; to raze, level; to ruin (*financially*) ‖ *ref* to ruin oneself

spianta·to -ta *adj* ruined ‖ *m* pauper

spiare §119 *tr* to spy on; to keep an eye on

spiattellare (**spiattèllo**) *tr* to blurt out

spiazzo *m* square; plain; clearing

spiccare §197 *tr* to detach; to pick; to enunciate; to begin; to draw up (*a commercial paper*); to issue (*a warrant*); **spiccare il volo** (aer) to take off ‖ *intr* to stand out ‖ *ref* to separate (*said, e.g., of the stone of a peach*)

spicca·to -ta *adj* clear, distinct; typical; outstanding

spìc·chio *m* (**-chi**) section (*of fruit*); clove (*of garlic*); slice (*e.g., of apple*); arm (*of cross*)

spicciare §128 *tr* to clear up; to wait on; to dispatch (*business*) ‖ *intr* (ESSERE) to flow forth, gush out ‖ *ref* to hurry up, make haste

spicciatì·vo -va *adj* expeditious, quick; straightforward; gruff

spiccicare §197 (**spìccico**) *tr* to unglue; to enunciate; to utter ‖ *ref* to come unglued; **spiccicarsi di** to get rid of

spìc·cio -cia (**-ci -ce**) *adj* expeditious, quick; unhampered; small (*change*) ‖ **spicci** *mpl* change

spicciolata *adj fem*—**alla spicciolata** little by little; a few at a time

spìcciolo -la *adj* small (*change*); (coll) plain ‖ **spiccioli** *mpl* small change

spìc·co -ca (**-chi -che**) *adj* freestone (*e.g., peach*) ‖ *m*—**fare spicco** to stand out

spidocchiare §287 (**spidòcchio**) *tr* to delouse

spièdo *m* spit; **allo spiedo** barbecued

spiegàbile *adj* explainable

spiegaménto *m* (mil) array; (mil) deployment

spiegare §209 (**spiègo**) *tr* to unfold; to let go (*with one's voice*); to unfurl; to spread (*wings*); to deploy (*troops*); to explain; to show, demonstrate; **spiegare il volo** (aer) to take off ‖ *ref* to become unfurled or unfolded;

to make oneself understood; to come to an understanding; to realize

spiega·to -ta *adj* open; full (*voice*)

spiegazióne *f* explanation

spiegazzare *tr* to crumple, rumple

spieta·to -ta *adj* pitiless, ruthless

spifferare (spìffero) *tr* (coll) to blurt out || *intr* to blow in (*said of wind*)

spìffero *m* (coll) draft

spi·ga *f* (**ghe**) panicle (*of oats*); (bot) ear, spike; **a spiga** herringbone

spiga·to -ta *adj* herringbone

spighétta *f* braid; (bot) spikelet

spigionare (spigióno) *ref* to be or become vacant

spiglia·to -ta *adj* easy, free and easy

spi·go *m* (**-ghi**) lavender

spigolare (spìgolo) *tr* to glean

spigola·tóre -trice *mf* gleaner

spìgolo *m* corner; edge; (archit) arris

spilla *f* brooch, pin; **spilla da cravatta** tiepin; **spilla di sicurezza** safety pin

spillare *tr* to draw off, tap; to wheedle, worm (*money*) || *intr* to leak (*said of container*) || *intr* (ESSERE) to leak (*said of liquid*)

spillàti·co *m* (**-ci**) (law) pin money (*for one's wife*)

spillo *m* pin; gimlet; trifle; **a spillo** spikelike; **spillo da balla** or **di sicurezza** safety pin

spillóne *m* hatpin; bodkin

spilluzzicare §197 (spillùzzico) *tr* to pick at, nibble; to scrape together

spilorcerìa *f* stinginess

spilòr·cio -cia (**-ci -ce**) *adj* stingy || *mf* miser, tightwad

spilungó·ne -na *mf* lanky person

spina *f* thorn; quill, spine (*of porcupine*); bone (*of fish*); (fig) preoccupation, worry; **alla spina** (*beer*) on tap; **a spina di pesce** herringbone (*fabric*); **con una spina nel cuore** sick at heart; **essere sulle spine** to be on pins and needles; **spina della botte** tap; bunghole; **spina dorsale** spinal column; (fig) backbone; **spina elettrica** plug

spinà·cio *m* (**-ci**) spinach (*plant*); **spinaci** spinach (*as food*)

spinapésce *m*—**a spinapesce** herringbone

spina·to -ta *adj* barbed (*wire*); herringbone (*fabric*)

spingere §126 *tr* to push, press; to prod, goad || *ref* to push; to reach

spi·no -na *adj* thorny || *m* thorn || *f* see **spina**

spinóne *m* griffon

spinó·so -sa [s] *adj* thorny

spinòtto *m* wrist pin

spinta *f* push; pressure; poke, prod; stress

spinterògeno *m* (aut) distributor unit, ignition system

spin·to -ta *adj* pushed; bent, inclined; (coll) risqué; (coll) far-out, offbeat || *f* see **spinta**

spintóne *m* (coll) push, shove

spionàg·gio *m* (**-gi**) espionage, spying

spioncino *m* peephole

spió·ne -na *mf* spy, stool pigeon

spiovènte *adj* drooping; sloping; falling || *m* slope; drainage area (*of a mountain*)

spiòvere §216 *intr* to fall, to hang down (*said, e.g., of hair*); to flow down || *impers* (ESSERE)—**è spiovuto** it stopped raining

spira *f* turn (*of a coil*); coil (*of serpent*); a spire spiral

spirà·glio *m* (**-gli**) small opening; gleam (*of light or hope*)

spirale *adj* spiral || *f* spiral; hairspring; wreath (*of smoke*); **spirale di fumo** smoke ring

spirare *tr* to send forth; (lit) to inspire, infuse; (lit) to show (*kindness*) || *intr* to blow; to emanate; to die; to expire

spirita·to -ta *adj* possessed; wild, mad

spìriti·co -ca *adj* (**-ci -che**) spiritual; spiritualistic

spiritìsmo *m* spiritualism

spìrito *m* spirit; wit; mind; spirits, alcohol; sprite; **bello spirito** wit (*person*); **fare dello spirito** to be witty; to crack jokes; **l'ultimo spirito** (lit) one's last breath; **spirito di corpo** esprit de corps; **spirito di parte** partisanship; **spirito sportivo** sportsmanship

spiritosàggine [s] *f* witticism

spiritó·so -sa [s] *adj* witty; alcoholic

spirituale *adj* spiritual

spìzzi·co *m* (**-chi**)—**a spizzico** or a **spizzichi** little by little; a little at a time

splendènte *adj* resplendent, shining

splèndere §281 *intr* (ESSERE & AVERE) to shine

splèndi·do -da *adj* splendid; gorgeous; bright || *m*—**fare lo splendido** to be a big spender

splendóre *m* splendor; brightness; beauty

splène *m* (anat) spleen

spòcchia *f* haughtiness

spodestare (spodèsto) *tr* to dispossess; to dethrone; to oust

spoetizzare [ddzz] *tr* to disillusion

spòglia *f* slough (*of snake*); skin (*of onion*); husk (*of corn*); (lit) body; (lit) outer garment; **sotto mentite spoglie** under false pretense; **spoglie** spoils

spogliare §280 (spòglio) *tr* to undress, strip; to strip of armor; to defraud, deprive; to free; to check, examine; to husk (*corn*); to go through (*e.g., correspondence*) || *ref* to undress; to slough (*said, e.g., of a snake*); **spogliarsi di** to get rid of; to divest oneself of; to shake (*a habit*)

spogliarellì·sta *f* (**-ste**) stripteaser

spogliarèllo *m* striptease

spoglia·tóio *m* (**-tói**) dressing room; locker room

spò·glio -glia (**-gli -glie**) *adj* stripped, bare; free || *m* cast-off clothing; sorting; scrutiny; counting (*of votes*); **di spoglio** second-hand (*material*) || *f* see **spoglia**

spòla *f* bobbin; shuttle; **fare la spola** to shuttle

spolétta *f* bobbin, spool; (mil) fuse

spolmonare (**spolmóno**) *ref* (coll) to talk, sing, or shout oneself hoarse

spolpare (**spólpo**) *tr* to gnaw (*a bone*); to eat up (*fruit*); (fig) to fleece

spolverare (**spólvero**) *tr* to dust off, whisk; to powder, dust; to pounce

spolveratura *f* dusting; powdering; sprinkling, smattering (*of knowledge*); **dare una spolveratura a** to brush up on

spolverina *f* (coll) duster

spolverino *m* duster, smock; powder-sugar duster; pounce; (coll) whisk broom

spolverizzaménto [ddzz] *m* sprinkling (*with powder*)

spolverizzare [ddzz] *tr* to dust, powder, pounce

spólvero *m* dusting; powdering; pounce; smattering, sprinkling (*of knowledge*); display

spónda *f* bank (*of river*); side; cushion (*of billiard table*)

sponsale *adj* (lit) wedding || **sponsali** *mpl* (lit) wedding

spontàne·o -a *adj* spontaneous; artless

spopolare (**spòpolo**) *tr* to depopulate || *intr* to be a hit; to become depopulated or deserted

spoppare (**spóppo**) *tr* to wean

sporàdi·co -ca *adj* (**-ci -che**) sporadic

sporcacció·ne -na *adj* filthy || *mf* filthy person; (fig) dirty mouth

sporcare §197 (**spòrco**) *tr* to dirty; to soil || *ref* to get dirty; to soil oneself; **sporcarsi la fedina** (coll) to get a black mark on one's record

sporcìzia *f* dirt, filth

spòr·co -ca (**-chi -che**) *adj* dirty, filthy; foul; **farla sporca** to pull a dirty trick || *m* dirt, filth

sporgènte *adj* leaning; protruding; beetle (*brow*)

sporgènza *f* prominence, projection

spòrgere §217 *tr* to stick out; to stretch out; to lodge (*a complaint*) || *intr* (ESSERE) to project, jut out || *ref* to lean out

spòrt *m* (spòrt) sport; game; **per sport** for fun, for pleasure

spòrta *f* shopping bag; bagful; basket; basketful; shopping; **a sporta** wide-brimmed (*hat*)

sportèllo *m* door; panel; window (*in bank, station, etc.*); wicket; branch (*of a bank*); (theat) box office

sportivi·tà *f* (**-tà**) sportsmanship

sporti·vo -va *adj* sporting; sportsman-like; athletic || *m* sportsman

spòr·to -ta *adj* projecting; jutting out || *m* projection; removable shutter (*on store door or window*) || *f* see **sporta**

spòsa *f* bride; wife; **andare in sposa a** to get married to; **sposa promessa** fiancée

sposalì·zio -zia (**-zì -zie**) *adj* (lit) nuptial || *m* wedding

sposare (**spòso**) *tr* to marry; to unite; to embrace (*a cause*); to fit perfectly; to give in marriage || *ref* to get married, marry

spòso *m* bridegroom; **sposi** newlyweds

spossare (**spòsso**) *tr* to exhaust || *ref* to become worn out

spossatézza *f* exhaustion

spostaménto *m* shift; movement; displacement; change

spostare (**spòsto**) *tr* to move; to change, shift; to upset || *ref* to move; to shift; to get out of place; to be upset

sposta·to -ta *adj* ill-adjusted, out of place || *mf* misfit

spran·ga *f* (**-ghe**) bar, crossbar

sprangare §209 *tr* to bar, bolt

sprazzo *m* spray; flash; burst

sprecare §197 (**sprèco**) *tr* to waste; **to miss** (*an opportunity*) || *ref* to waste one's efforts

sprè·co *m* (**-chi**) waste; squandering

sprecó·ne -na *adj & mf* spendthrift

spregévole *adj* contemptible, despicable

spregiare §290 (**sprègio**) *tr* to despise

sprè·gio *m* (**-gi**) contempt; scorn

spregiudica·to -ta *adj* open-minded, unbiased || *m* open-minded person

sprèmere §123 *tr* to squeeze, press; **spremere le lacrime a** to move to tears || *ref*—**spremersi il cervello** to rack one's brain

spremifrut·ta *m* (**-ta**) squeezer

spremilimó·ni *m* (**-ni**) lemon squeezer

spremuta *f* squeezing; **spremuta d'arancia** orange juice

spretare (**sprèto**) *ref* to doff the cassock

sprezzante *adj* contemptuous, haughty

sprezzare (**sprèzzo**) *tr* (lit) to despise

sprèzzo *m* disdain, contempt

sprigionare (**sprigióno**) *tr* to exhale, emit; to free from prison || *ref* to free oneself; to escape, come forth, issue (*said, e.g., of steam*)

sprimacciare §128 *tr* to beat, fluff (*e.g., a pillow*)

sprizzare *tr* to spout; to sparkle with (*joy, health*) || *intr* (ESSERE) to spurt; to fly (*said of sparks*); to sparkle

sprizzo *m* sprinkle; spurt; spark

sprofondare (**sprofóndo**) *tr* to send to the bottom; to destroy, ruin; to sink || *intr* (ESSERE) to sink; to founder; to cave in; to be sunk (*e.g., in meditation*)

sprolò·quio *m* (**-qui**) long rigmarole

spronare (**spróno**) *tr* to spur, goad

spróne *m* spur; prodding; example; guimpe; buttress; abutment (*of bridge*); **a sprone battuto** at full speed; at once; **dar di sprone a** to spur on; **sprone di cavaliere** (bot) rocket larkspur

sproporziona·to -ta *adj* out of proportion, disproportionate

sproporzióne *f* disproportion

sproposita·to -ta *adj* out of proportion; excessive; gross (*error*)

spropòsito *m* blunder, gross error; excessive amount; **a sproposito** out of place; inopportunely

sprovvedu·to -ta *adj* deprived; brainless, witless

sprovvi·sto -sta *adj* deprived; devoid, lacking; **alla sprovvista** suddenly; unawares, off guard

spruzzabianche•rìa *m* (-rìa) sprinkler (*to sprinkle clothes*)

spruzzare *tr* to sprinkle, spray; to powder (*sugar*)

spruzzatóre *m* sprayer; (aut) nozzle (*of carburetor*)

spruzzo *m* spray; splash (*of mud*)

spudora•to -ta *adj* shameless; impudent

spugna *f* sponge; **dare un colpo di spugna** to wipe the slate clean; **gettare la spugna** to throw in the towel

spugnare *tr* to sponge; to swab

spugnatura *f* sponge bath

spugnó•so -sa [s] *adj* spongy

spulciare §128 *tr* to pick the fleas off; to scrutinize, examine minutely

spuma *f* foam, froth

spumante *adj* sparkling || *m* sparkling wine; champagne

spumare *intr* to froth

spumeggiante *adj* sparkling; vaporous; foamy

spumeggiare §290 (spuméggio) *intr* to foam

spumóne *m* spumoni

spumó•so -sa [s] *adj* foamy, frothy

spunta *f* check; check list; check mark

spuntare *tr* to blunt; to unpin; to overcome; to clip, trim; to check off; **spuntarla** to come out on top; to overcome || *intr* (ESSERE) to appear; to sprout; to rise; to well up (*said of tears*); to pop out; to break through || *ref* to become blunt; to die down

spuntino *m* bite, snack; **fare uno spuntino** to have a bite

spunto *m* sourness (*of wine*); (theat) cue; (sports) sprint; (fig) starting point, origin

spuntóne *m* spike; pike; crag

spurgare §209 *tr* to purge, clear; to clean up || *ref* to expectorate

spur•go *m* (-ghi) discharge; reject (*e.g., book*)

spù•rio -ria *adj* (-ri -rie) spurious

sputacchiare §287 *tr* to spit upon || *intr* to sputter

sputacchièra *f* spittoon, cuspidor

sputare *tr* to spit; to cough up; (fig) to spew (*venom*); **sputare sangue** to spit blood; (fig) to sweat blood || *intr* to spit

sputasentènze *mf* (-ze) wiseacre

sputo *m* spit, sputum; spitting

squadernare (squadèrno) *tr* to leaf through; **squadernare qlco a qlcu** to put s.th under the nose of s.o. || *ref* to come apart (*said of a book*)

squadra *f* square (*for measuring right angles*); squad, group; (mil) squadron; (sports) team; **a squadra** at right angles; **fuori squadra** out of kilter; **squadra di pompieri** fire company; **squadra mobile** flying squad

squadrare *tr* to square; (fig) to examine, study

squadriglia *f* (aer, nav) squadron

squadróne *m* squadron (*of cavalry*)

squagliare §280 *tr* to melt || *ref* to melt; **squagliarsela** to take French leave

squalìfi•ca *f* (-che) disqualification

squalificare §197 (squalìfico) *tr* to disqualify || *ref* to disqualify oneself; to prove to be unqualified

squàlli•do -da *adj* wretched, dreary, gloomy; faint (*smile*); (lit) emaciated

squallóre *m* wretchedness, dreariness, gloominess

squalo *m* shark

squama *f* scurf (*shed by the skin*); (bot, pathol, zool) scale

squamare *tr* & *ref* to scale

squamó•so -sa [s] *adj* scaly

squarciagóla *adv*—**a squarciagola** at the top of one's voice

squarciare §128 *tr* to rend, tear apart; to dispel (*a doubt*) || *ref* to become torn; to open

squàr•cio *m* (-ci) tear, rip; passage (*of book*)

squartare *tr* to quarter

squartatura *f* quartering

squassare *tr* to shake violently; to wreck

squattrina•to -ta *adj* penniless || *m* pauper

squilibra•to -ta *adj* unbalanced, deranged || *mf* mad or insane person

squilì•brio *m* (-bri) lack of balance; **squilibrio mentale** insanity; unbalanced mental condition

squillante *adj* ringing, shrill; sharp

squillare *intr* to ring; to ring out; to blare

squillo *m* ring; peal; blare, blast (*of horn*); || *f* call girl

squinternare (squintèrno) *tr* to tear (*a book*) to pieces; (fig) to upset

squisi•to -ta *adj* exquisite

squittire §176 *intr* to squeak; to squeal

sradicare §197 (sràdico) *tr* to uproot; to eradicate; to pull (*a tooth*)

sragionare (sragióno) *intr* to talk nonsense

sregola•to -ta *adj* intemperate; dissolute

srotolare (sròtolo) *tr* to unroll

stàb•bio *m* (-bi) pen; manure, dung

stabbiòlo *m* pigpen

stàbile *adj* stable; real (*estate*); permanent; stock (*company*) || *m* building

stabilimént o *m* plant, factory; establishment; settlement, colony; conclusion (*of a deal*)

stabilire §176 *tr* to establish; to decide || *ref* to settle

stabili•tà *f* (-tà) stability, steadiness

stabilito *m* (law) agreement of sale (*drawn up by a broker*)

stabilizzare [ddzz] *tr* & *ref* to stabilize

stabilizza•tóre -trice [ddzz] *mf* stabilizing person || *m* (aer) stabilizer; (elec) voltage stabilizer

staccare §197 *tr* to detach; to unhitch; to outdistance; to draw (*a check*); to tear off; to take (*one's eyes*) away; to begin; to enunciate (*words*) || *intr* to stand out; (coll) to stop working || *ref* to come off; **staccarsi da** to come off (*e.g., the wall*); to leave (*one's home; the shore*); (aer) to take off from

stacciare §128 *tr* to sift, sieve

stàc•cio *m* (**-ci**) sieve

staccionata *f* fence; hurdle; stockade

stac•co *m* (**-chi**) tearing off; cut of cloth (*for a suit*); interval; **fare stacco** to stand out

stadèra *f* steelyard; **stadera a ponte** weighbridge

stàdia *f* leveling rod

stà•dio *m* (**-di**) stadium; stage

staffa *f* stirrup; heel (*of sock*); gaiter strap; clamp; (mach) bracket; **perdere le staffe** to lose one's nerve

staffétta *f* courier, messenger; pilot (*car*); **a staffetta** relay

staffière *m* groom, footman; servant

staffilare *tr* to whip, belt, lash

staffilata *f* lash

staffile *m* stirrup strap; whip

stàg•gio *m* (**-gi**) stay, upright

stagionale *adj* seasonal || *mf* seasonal worker

stagionare (**stagióno**) *tr* to season, cure

stagiona•to -ta *adj* seasoned, ripe

stagióne *f* season; **da mezza stagione** spring-and-fall (*coat*); **di fine stagione** year-end (*sale*)

stagliare §280 *tr* to hack || *ref* to stand out

staglia•to -ta *adj* sheer (*cliff*)

sta•gnàio *m* (**-gnài**) tinsmith; plumber

stagnante *adj* stagnant

stagnare *tr* to tin; to solder; to stanch || *intr* to stagnate

stagnaro *m* var of **stagnaio**

stagnìna *f* tin can

stagnino *m* (coll) var of **stagnaio**

sta•gno -gna *adj* watertight; airtight || *m* tin; pond, pool

stagnòla *f* tin foil; tin can

stàio *m* (**stài**) bushel (*container*); **a staio** (coll) top (*hat*) || *m* (**stàia** *fpl*) bushel (*measure*); **a staia** in abundance

stalla *f* stable

stallìa *f* (com) lay day

stallière *m* stableman, stableboy

stallo *m* seat; stall; (chess) stalemate

stallóne *m* stallion

stamane, stamani or **stamattina** *adv* this morning

stambéc•co *m* (**-chi**) ibex

stambèr•ga *f* (**-ghe**) hovel

stambù•gio *m* (**-gi**) hole, hovel

stamburare *tr* to puff up, to boast about || *intr* to drum

stame *m* (bot) stamen; thread, yarn

stamigna *f* cheesecloth

stampa *f* printing; print; (fig) print; (fig) mold; **stampe** printed matter

stampàg•gio *m* (**-gi**) (mach) stamping

stampare *tr* to stamp; to print; to impress; to publish || *ref* (fig) to be ingraved

stampatèllo *m*—**in stampatello** in block letters; **scrivere in stampatello** to print (*with pen or pencil*)

stampa•to -ta *adj* printed; impressed || *m* printed form; **stampati** printed matter

stampa•tóre -trice *mf* printer

stampèlla *f* crutch

stamperìa *f* print shop

stampìglia *f* rubber stamp; billboard; overprint

stampigliare §280 *tr* to stamp; to over-print

stampinare *tr* to stencil

stampino *m* stencil

stampo *m* mold; stencil; stamp, kind; decoy

stanare *tr* to flush (*game*); (fig) to dig up

stancare §197 *tr* to tire, fatigue; to bore || *ref* to tire, weary

stanchézza *f* tiredness, weariness

stan•co -ca *adj* (**-chi -che**) tired; tired out; (lit) left (*hand*)

standardizzare [ddzz] *tr* to standardize

stan•ga *f* (**-ghe**) bar; shaft (*of cart*); beam (*of plow*)

stangata *f* blow

stanghétta *f* small bar; bolt (*of lock*); temple (*of spectacles*); (mus) bar

stanòtte *adv* tonight; last night

stante *adj* being; standing; **a sé stante** by itself, independent || *prep* because of; **stante che** since

stan•tio -tìa *adj* (**-tìi; -tìe**) stale; musty

stantuffo *m* piston; plunger

stanza *f* room; stanza; **essere di stanza** (mil) to be stationed; **stanza da bagno** bath room; **stanza di compensazione** clearing house; **stanza di soggiorno** living room

stanziare §287 *tr* to allocate; to appropriate; to budget || *ref* to settle

stanzìno *m* small room; closet

stappare *tr* to uncork

stare §263 *intr* (ESSERE) to stay; to stand; to live; to be; to be located; to linger; to last; to stick (*e.g., to a rule*); (poker) to stand pat; **come sta?** how are you?; **lasciar stare** to leave alone; **lasciar stare che** to leave aside that; **non stare in sé dalla gioia** to be beside oneself with joy; **sta bene!** O.K.!; **starci** to fit, e.g., **ci stanno trecento persone** three hundred people fit there; **starci di** to be in favor of, e.g., **io ci starei d'andare al cine** I would be in favor of going to the movies; **stare + *ger*** to be + *ger*, e.g., **stava leggendo** he was reading; **stare a** to be up to; to stand on (*ceremony*); to base oneself on; to take (*a joke*); to cost, e.g., **a quanto sta il prosciutto?** how much does the ham cost?; **stare a + *inf*** to keep + *ger*, e.g., **stai sempre a sognare** you always keep dreaming; to take + *inf*, e.g., **stette poco a decidere** he took little time to decide; **stare a cuore** (with *dat*) to deem important, e.g., **gli sta a cuore il lavoro** he deems his work important; **stare a pancia all'aria** to not do a stroke of work; **stare al proprio posto** to keep one's place; **stare a segno** to behave properly; **stare a vedere** to be possible, e.g., **sta a vedere che non viene?** could it be possible that he won't come?; **stare bene** to be well; to be well-off; (with *dat*) to fit, to become, e.g., **questo vestito gli sta**

bene this suit fits him well, this suit becomes him; to serve right, e.g., **gli sta bene!** it serves him right!; **stare comodo** to be at ease; to remain seated; **stare con** (fig) to be on the side of; **starsene** to stay apart, e.g., **se ne sta solo soletto** he stays apart or all alone; **stare fermo** to be quiet; to not move; **stare in forse** to doubt; to be doubtful; **stare sulle proprie** to stand aloof; **stare su** to stand erect; **stare su tardi** to stay up late; **stia comodo!** remain seated!

starna f gray partridge

starnazzare intr to flap its wings; to flutter; to cackle

starnutare intr to sneeze

starnuto m sneeze

stasare [s] tr to unplug, unblock

staséra [s] adv tonight, this evening

sta·si f (-si) (com) stagnation; (pathol) stasis

statale adj government; state || mf government employee

stàti·co -ca (-ci -che) static || f statics

stati·no -na adj (coll) migratory || m itemized list; (educ) registration form

stati·sta m (-sti) statesman

statìsti·co -ca (-ci -che) adj statistical || m statistician || f statistics; **fare una statistica (di)** to survey; **statistiche statistics** (data)

stati·vo -va adj nonmigratory; permanent || m stand (of microscope)

stato m state; condition; plight; frame (of mind); status; estate (social class); **di stato** public (e.g., school); **essere in stato di arresto** to be under arrest; **stati extracts from vital statistics; Stati Pontifici** Papal States; **Stati Uniti** United States; **stato civile** marital status; vital statistics; **stato confessionale** state under ecclesiastical rule; **stato cuscinetto** buffer state; **stato di preallarme** state of emergency; **stato di previsione** preliminary budget; **stato interessante** pregnancy; **stato maggiore** (mil) general staff

statoreattóre m ramjet engine

stàtua f statue

statuà·rio -ria (-ri -rie) adj statuary; statuesque || m sculptor

statunitènse adj & mf American (U.S.A.)

statura f stature; height

statuto m statute

stavòlta adv (coll) this time

stazionaménto m parking; **stazionamento vietato** no parking

stazionare (stazióno) intr to park

stazionà·rio -ria adj (-ri -rie) stationary

stazióne f station; bearing; posture; **stazione balneare** shore resort; **stazione climatica** health resort, spa; **stazione di rifornimento** service station; **stazione di tassametri** cab stand; **stazione estiva** summer resort; **stazione generatrice** power plant; **stazione orbitale** orbiting station; **stazione sanitaria** clinic

stazza f tonnage; (naut) displacement

stazzare tr (naut) to gauge; (naut) to displace

stazzonare (stazzóno) tr to crumple

steatite f French chalk

stéc·ca f (-che) small stick; slat (of shutter); rib (of umbrella); bone (of whale); carton (of cigarettes); rail (of fence); letter opener; chisel (of sculptor); (billiards) cue; (billiards) miscue; (surg) splint; **fare una stecca** (billiards) to miscue; (mus) to sing or play a sour note

steccadèn·ti m (-ti) (coll) toothpick

steccare §197 (stécco) tr to fence; to put in a splint || intr to play or sing a sour note; (billiards) to miscue

steccato m fence; (racing) inside track

stecchétto m small stick; **tenere a stecchetto** to keep on a strict diet; to keep short of money

stecchino m toothpick

stecchi·to -ta adj stiff; lean, lank; dry (twig); dumfounded

stéc·co m (-chi) stick, twig

stecconata f stockade; fence

stélla f star; rowel (of spur); speck of fat (in soup); (fig) sky; **a stella** star-shaped; stellar; **montare alle stelle** to be sky-high (said, e.g., of prices); **portare alle stelle** to praise to the skies; **stella alpina** edelweiss; **stella cadente** shooting star; **stella di mare** starfish; **stella filante** shooting star; confetti; **stella polare** polestar, lodestar

stellare adj stellar; (mach) radial || v **(stéllo)** tr to spangle with stars; to stud

stella·to -ta adj starry; star-spangled; star-shaped; studded

stellétta f (mil) star; (typ) asterisk; **guadagnarsi le stellette** (mil) to earn a promotion; **portare le stellette** (mil) to be in the service

stellina f starlet

stelloncino m (journ) short paragraph

stèlo m stem, stalk

stèm·ma m (-mi) coat of arms; genealogy (of a manuscript)

stemperare (stèmpero) tr to dilute; to blunt; to untemper; (lit) to waste || ref to melt; to become dull or blunt

stendardo m banner, standard

stèndere §270 tr to stretch; to hang up (laundry); to spread; to draw up (a document); (mil) to deploy; **stendere a terra** to knock down || ref to stretch out

stendibianche·rìa m (-rìa) clothes rack, clotheshorse

stenodattilògra·fo -fa mf shorthand typist

stenografare (stenògrafo) tr to take down in shorthand

stenografìa f shorthand, stenography

stenogràfi·co -ca adj (-ci -che) stenographic, shorthand

stenògra·fo -fa mf stenographer

stenòsi f (pathol) stricture

stenotipìa f stenotypy

stentare (stènto) tr to eke out (a living)

|| *intr* to barely make ends meet; **stentare a** to hardly be able to; **to find it hard to**

stenta•to -ta *adj* hard; stunted; strained (*smile*)

stènto *m* privation; hardship; **a stento** hardly; with difficulty; **senza stento** without any trouble

stèr•co *m* (**-chi**) dung

stereofòni•co -ca *adj* (**-ci -che**) stereo, stereophonic

stereoscòpi•co -ca *adj* (**-ci -che**) stereoscopic

stereoscò•pio *m* (**-pi**) stereoscope

stereotipa•to -ta *adj* stereotyped

sterilizzare [ddzz] *tr* to sterilize

sterlina *f* pound sterling

sterminare (**stèrmino**) *tr* to exterminate

stermina•to -ta *adj* immense, boundless

stermi•nio *m* (**-ni**) extermination; (coll) large amount, lots

stèrno *m* breastbone

sterpàglia *f* brushwood; undergrowth

stèrpo *m* dry twig; bramble

sterrare (**stèrro**) *tr* to excavate

sterratóre *m* digger

sterzare (**stèrzo**) *tr* to diminish by one third; to thin out (*woodland*); (aut) to steer || *intr* to swerve

sterzata *f* swerve

stèrzo *m* handle bar; (aut) steering gear; (aut) steering wheel

stésa [s] *f* coat (*of paint*); string (*of clothes on line*)

stés•so -sa *adj* same, e.g., **lo stesso mese** the same month; very, e.g., **tuo fratello stesso** your very brother; **essere alle stesse** to be just the same; **io stesso** I myself; **lui stesso** he himself, etc.; **per sé stesso** by himself; **by itself** || *pron* same; same thing; **fa lo stesso** it's all the same, it makes no difference

stesura [s] *f* drawing up (*of a contract*); **prima stesura** first draft

stetoscò•pio *m* (**-pi**) stethoscope

stìa *f* chicken coop

Stige *m* Styx

sti•gio -gia *adj* (**-gi -gie**) Stygian

stigmate *fpl* stigmata

stilare *tr* to draft properly

stile *m* style

stilè *adj invar* stylish

stilétto *m* dagger, stiletto

stilizzare [ddzz] *tr* to stylize

stilla *f* (lit) drop, droplet

stillare *tr* to exude; to distill || *intr* (ESSERE) to ooze, drip, exude || *ref*—**stillarsi il cervello** to rack one's brains

stillicì•dio *m* (**-di**) dripping; repetition

stilo *m* stylus; arm (*of steelyard*); dagger; gnomon (*of sundial*); (poet) style || *f* (coll) fountain pen

stilogràfi•ca *f* (**-che**) fountain pen

stima *f* appraisal; esteem; (naut) dead reckoning; **a stima d'occhio** more or less

stimare *tr* to estimate; to deem; to esteem || *ref* (coll) to think a lot of oneself

stima•tóre -trice *mf* appraiser; admirer

stìmmate *fpl* var of **stigmate**

stimolante *adj & m* stimulant

stimolare (**stìmolo**) *tr* to stimulate

stìmolo *m* influence; stimulus

stin•co *m* (**-chi**) shinbone; shin; **stinco di santo** saintly person, saint; **rompere gli stinchi a** to annoy

stìngere §126 *tr, intr* (ESSERE) & *ref* to fade

stipa *f* kindling wood, brushwood

stipare *tr & ref* to crowd, jam

stipendiare §287 (**stipèndio**) *tr* to employ, hire; to pay a salary to

stipendia•to -ta *adj* salaried || *mf* salaried person

stipèn•dio *m* (**-di**) pay, salary

stipétto *m* (naut) closet, cabinet

stìpite *m* jamb; stock, family; (bot) trunk (*of palm tree*)

stipo *m* cabinet

stipulare (**stìpulo**) *tr* to draw up (*a contract*); to stipulate

stiracchiare §287 *tr* to stretch; to eke out (*a living*); to twist (*a meaning*); to haggle over || *intr* to haggle; to economize || *ref* to stretch out

stirare *tr* to stretch; to iron, press || *intr* to iron || *ref* to stretch out

stira•tóre -trice *mf* ironer, presser

stiratura *f* ironing; stretching

stirerìa *f* ironing shop

stiro *m*—**ferro da stiro** see **ferro**

stirpe *f* family; birth, origin

stitichézza *f* constipation

stìti•co -ca *adj* (**-ci -che**) constipated; (fig) tight

stiva *f* (naut) hold; (lit) beam (*of plow*)

stivàg•gio *m* (**-gi**) stowage

stivale *m* boot; **dei miei stivali** good-for-nothing; **lustrare gli stivali a qlcu** to lick s.o.'s boots

stivalétto *m* high shoe

stivalóne *m* boot; **stivaloni da equitazione** riding boots; **stivaloni da palude** hip boots

stivare *tr* to stow

stivatóre *m* stevedore

stizza *f* anger; irritation

stizzire §176 *tr* to anger, vex || *ref* to get angry

stizzó•so -sa [s] *adj* peevish, irritable

stoccafisso *m* stockfish

stoccata *f* thrust (*with dagger or rapier*); dig, sarcastic remark; touch (*for money*)

stòc•co *m* (**-chi**) dagger; rapier; stalk (*of corn*)

Stoccólma *f* Stockholm

stòffa *f* cloth, material; (fig) stuff, makings

stoicismo *m* stoicism

stòi•co -ca (**-ci -che**) *adj* stoic, stoical || *m* stoic; Stoic

stoino *m* doormat

stòla *f* stole

stòli•do -da *adj* foolish, silly

stoltézza *f* foolishness, silliness

stól•to -ta *adj* silly || *mf* fool

stomacare §197 (**stòmaco**) *tr* to disgust; to nauseate

stomachévole *adj* disgusting, sickening

stòma·co m (-ci or -chi) stomach; maw (of animal); dare di stomaco to vomit

stonare (stòno) tr to sing or play out of tune; to upset || intr to sing or play out of tune; to be out of place; to not harmonize

stona·to -ta adj out-of-tune; upset; clashing (color)

stonatura f jarring sound; clash (of colors); lack of harmony

stóppa f tow; oakum; di stoppa flaxen; weak, trembling; stoppa incatramata oakum

stoppàc·cio m (-ci) wad

stóppie fpl stubble

stoppino m wick

stoppó·so -sa [s] adj stubby; stringy

stórcere §272 tr to twist; to twitch; to wrench (one's ankle); to roll (one's eyes) || ref to twist; to writhe; to bend

stordiménto m bewilderment; dizziness

stordire §176 tr to bewilder; to daze || intr to be bewildered || ref to dull one's senses

storditàggine f carelessness; mistake, blunder

stordi·to -ta adj careless; bewildered; amazed; dizzy || mf scatterbrain

stòria f history; story, tale; fact; fare storie to stand on ceremony; un'altra storia a horse of another color

stòri·co -ca (-ci -che) adj historical || m historian

storièlla f tale, short story; joke

storiografìa f historiography

storióne m sturgeon

stormire §176 intr to rustle

stórmo m swarm, flock; (aer) group

stornare (stórno) tr to ward off; to dissuade; to divert (funds); to write off (as noncollectable)

stornèllo m Italian folksong; (orn) starling

stór·no -na adj dapple-gray || m (com) transfer; (orn) starling

storpiare §287 (stòrpio) tr to cripple; to clip (one's words)

stòr·pio -pia (-pi -pie) adj crippled || m cripple

stòr·to -ta adj twisted; crooked; crippled || f twist; dislocation; retort

stoviglie fpl dishes; lavare le stoviglie to wash the dishes

stra- pref adj extra-, e.g., straordinario extraordinary; over-, e.g., stracarico overloaded

stràbi·co -ca adj (-ci -che) crosseyed

strabiliante adj astonishing, amazing

strabiliare §287 tr to amaze || intr & ref to be amazed

strabismo m strabismus, squint

straboccare §197 (strabócco) intr to overflow

strabocchévole adj overflowing

strabuzzare [ddzz] tr (coll) to roll (one's eyes)

stracàri·co -ca adj (-chi -che) overloaded, overburdened

stracca f—pigliare una stracca to be dead tired

straccale m breeching (of harness); straccali (coll) suspenders

straccare §197 tr (coll) to tire

stracciaiò·lo -la mf ragpicker

stracciare §128 tr to tear, rend; to comb (natural silk)

stràc·cio -cia (-ci -ce) adj torn, in rags; waste (paper) || m rag, tatter; tear, rend; combed silk

stracció·ne -na mf tatterdemalion

straccivéndo·lo -la mf ragpicker; rag dealer

strac·co -ca adj (-chi -che) tired; worn-out; alla stracca lazily || f see stracca

stracòt·to -ta adj overcooked, overdone || m stew

stracuòcere §144a tr to overcook, overdo

strada f roadway; street; da strada vulgar, common; divorare la strada to burn up the road; essere in mezzo a una strada to be in a bad way; fare strada a to pave the way for; farsi strada to make one's way; prender la strada to set forth; strada carrozzabile carriage road; strada dell'orto easy way out; strada ferrata railroad; strada maestra main road; tagliare la strada a to stand in the way of; (aut) to cut in front of

stradale adj road; street; traffic (e.g., accident); highway (police) || m avenue || f highway patrol

stradà·rio m (-ri) street directory

strafalcióne m blunder, gross error

strafare §173 tr to overdo; to overcook

strafóro m drilled hole; di straforo stealthily

strafottènte adj unconcerned, non-chalant; arrogant, impudent

strafottènza f nonchalance, unconcern; arrogance, impudence

strage f butchery, massacre, carnage; (coll) multitude, lot

stragrande adj enormous, huge

stralciare §128 tr to prune, trim (grapevines); to eliminate, remove; (com) to liquidate

stràl·cio adj invar interim; emergency (e.g., law); liquidating || m (-ci) excerpt; clearance sale; a stralcio at a bargain

strale m (lit) arrow

strallo m (naut) stay

stralunare tr to roll (one's eyes)

straluna·to -ta adj upset; wild-eyed

stramazzare tr to fell || intr (ESSERE) to fall down

stramazzo m sluice; (coll) straw mattress

stramberìa f eccentricity

stram·bo -ba adj odd, queer, eccentric; crooked (legs); squint (eyes)

strame m litter; fodder

strampala·to -ta adj strange; preposterous, absurd

stranézza f strangeness; oddity

strangolare (stràngolo) tr to strangle; (naut) to furl

strangola·tóre -trice mf strangler

straniare §287 tr (lit) to draw away || ref to become estranged

straniè·ro -ra *adj* foreign, alien; (lit) strange || *mf* foreigner, alien

stra·no -na *adj* strange, odd; (lit) estranged

straordinà·rio -ria (-rì -rie) *adj* extraordinary; extra || *mf* temporary employee || *m* overtime

strapagàre §209 *tr* to overpay; to pay too much for

strapazzàre *tr* to rebuke, upbraid; to mishandle; to bungle || *ref* to overwork oneself

strapazzà·to -ta *adj* crumpled; bungled; scrambled (*eggs*); overworked || *f* upbraiding, rebuke; fatigue

strapazzo *m* misuse; fatigue; excess; **da strapazzo** working (*clothes*); hackneyed, second-rate

strapèrdere §212 *tr* & *intr* to lose hopelessly || *intr* to be wiped out

strapiè·no -na *adj* chock-full

strapiombàre (strapiómbo) *intr* to overhang, jut out

strapiómbo *m* overhang; **a strapiombo** sheer (*cliff*)

strapotènte *adj* overpowerful

strappàre *tr* to pull; to tear, rend; to wring (*s.o.'s heart*); **strappare le lacrime a qlcu** to move s.o. to tears; **strappare qlco a qlcu** to pry s.th out of s.o.; to snatch s.th from s.o. || *ref* to tear (*e.g.*, *one's hair*)

strappàta *f* pull, tug, snatch

strappo *m* pull; tear, rip; infraction, breach; pulling away (*on a bicycle*); patch (*of sky*); **a strappi** in jerks; **strappo muscolare** pulled muscle; sprain

strapuntìno *m* folding seat, jump seat; bucket seat; (naut) mattress

strarìc·co -ca *adj* (**-chì -che**) (coll) immensely rich

straripàre *intr* (ESSERE & AVERE) to overflow

strascicàre §197 **(stràscico)** *tr* to drag; to shuffle; **strascicare le parole** to drawl

strascichì·o *m* (**-i**) shuffle (*of feet*)

stràsci·co -ca *m* (**-chi**) train (*of skirt*); trail; sequel, aftermath; **a strascico** dragging

strascinàre (stràscino) *tr* to drag || *ref* to drag oneself, drag

strascinì·o *m* (**-i**) shuffle

stràscino *m* dragnet, trawl

stratagèm·ma *m* (**-mi**) stratagem

strategìa *f* strategy

stratègi·co -ca *adj* (**-ci -che**) strategic

stratè·go *m* (**-ghi**) strategist; general, commander

stratificàre §197 **(stratìfico)** *tr* to stratify

strato *m* layer; coat, coating; stratum; (meteor) stratus

stratosfèra *f* stratosphere

strattóne *m* jerk, tug

stravagànte *adj* extravagant; whimsical, capricious || *mf* eccentric

stravèc·chio -chia *adj* (**-chi -chie**) aged (*cheese, wine, etc.*); very old

stravìncere §285 *tr* to overpower

straviziàre §287 *intr* to be intemperate

stravì·zio *m* (**-zi**) intemperance, excess

stravòlgere §289 *tr* to roll (*the eyes*); to distort; to derange

straziànte *adj* heartbreaking; excruciating (*pain*); horrible

straziàre §287 *tr* to torture; to dismay; to mangle; to murder (*a language*)

strazià·to -ta *adj* torn, stricken

strà·zio *m* (**-zi**) suffering, pain; torture; shame; boredom; **fare strazio di** to squander

stré·ga *f* (**-ghe**) witch; sorceress

stregàre §209 **(strégo)** *tr* to bewitch

stregóne *m* sorcerer; witch doctor

stregonerìa *f* witchcraft; sorcery

strègua *f* standard, criterion; **alla stregua di** on the basis of

stremà·to -ta *adj* exhausted

strènna *f* Christmas gift, New Year's gift; special New Year's issue

strè·nuo -nua *adj* strenuous

strepitàre (strèpito) *intr* to make a noise; to shout, make a racket

strèpito *m* noise, racket; **fare strepito** to make a hit

strepitó·so -sa [*s*] *adj* loud, noisy; resounding (*success*)

streptomicìna *f* streptomycin

stressà·to -ta *adj* under stress

strétta *f* grasp, clench; tightening (*of brakes*); hold; press, crush; pang; mountain pass; **mettere alle strette** to drive into a corner; **stretta dei conti** rendering of accounts; **stretta di mano** handshake; **stretta finale** climax

strettézza *f* narrowness; **strettezze** straits, hardship

strét·to -ta *adj* narrow; tight; bare (*necessities*); pure (*e.g.*, *dialect*); strict; clenched (*fist*); heavy (*heart*); minimum (*price*); (phonet) close || *m* straits, narrows || *f* see **stretta** || **stretto** *adv* tightly

strettóia *f* narrow stretch; hardship; bandage

strìa *f* stripe, streak

striàre §119 *tr* to stripe, streak

stricnìna *f* strychnine

stridènte *adj* jarring; clashing (*colors*); strident (*sound*)

strìdere §264 *tr* to grit (*one's teeth*) || *intr* to shriek; to squeak; to creak; to clash (*said of colors*); to croak (*said of raven*); to hoot (*said of owl*); to howl (*said of wind*) || *ref* (coll) to be resigned

strìdo *m* (**-di & -da** *fpl*) shriek; squeak

stridóre *m* shriek; creak, squeak; gnashing (*of teeth*)

strìdu·lo -la *adj* shrill

strigàre §209 *tr* to disentangle || *ref* to extricate oneself

strìglia *f* currycomb

strigliàre §280 *tr* to curry; to upbraid || *ref* to groom oneself

strillàre *tr* to shout; (coll) to scold; (coll) to hawk (*newspapers*) || *intr* to scream

strillo *m* shriek; shout, scream

strilló·ne -na *mf* loud-mouthed person || *m* newsdealer; newsboy, paperboy

striminzi·to -ta *adj* shrunken; tight; stunted; skinny

strimpellare (strimpèllo) *tr* to thrum; to thrum on

strinare *tr* to singe; to burn (*with a flatiron*)

strin·ga *f* (-**ghe**) lace; shoelace

stringa·to -ta *adj* terse, concise

stringere §265 *tr* to tighten; to grip; to shake, clasp (*a hand*); to drive into a corner; to squeeze; to embrace; to close (*an alliance, a deal*); to wring (*one's heart*); to clench (*the fist*); (lit) to gird (*a sword*); (mus) to accelerate; **stringere d'assedio** to besiege; **stringere i freni** to put the brakes on || *intr* to be tight; **il tempo stringe** time is running short; **stringi, stringi** at the very end, in conclusion || *ref* to squeeze close together; to shrink; to coagulate; to draw close; **stringersi a** to snuggle up to; **stringersi addosso a** to attack; **stringersi nelle spalle** to shrug one's shoulders

stringina·so [s] *m* (-**so**) pince-nez

strì·scia *f* (-**sce**) strip, band; trail; stripe; line; **a strisce** striped; **striscia d'atterramento** airstrip; **striscia di cuoio** strop

strisciante *adj* crawling; (fig) fawning

strisciare §128 *tr* to shuffle (*feet*); to graze; **strisciare una riverenza** to curtsy || *intr* to creep, crawl; to graze by || *ref* to fawn; **strisciarsi a** to rub one's back against

strisciata or **strisciatura** *f* sliding; trail

strì·scio *m* (-**sci**) rubbing; shuffling; **ballare di striscio** to shuffle; **da** or **di striscio** superficial (*wound*)

striscióne *m* festoon; festooned sign; flatterer; **striscione d'arrivo** landing (*in gymnastics*); **striscione del traguardo** (sports) tape

striscióni *adv* crawling

stritolare (stritolo) *tr* to crush, smash

strizzalimó·ni *m* (-**ni**) lemon squeezer

strizzare *tr* to squeeze, press; to wink (*the eye*); **strizzare l'occhio** to wink

strizza·tóio *m* (-**tói**) wringer

strò·fa or **strò·fe** *f* (-**fe**) strophe

strofinàc·cio *m* (-**ci**) dust cloth

strofinare *tr* to rub; to polish || *ref* to rub oneself; to fawn

strofinata *f*—**dare una strofinata a** to give a lick and a promise to

strofinì·o *m* (-**ii**) rubbing; wiping

stròla·ga *f* (-**ghe**) (orn) loon

strombatura *f* embrasure

strombazzare *tr* to glorify; **strombazzare i propri meriti** to toot one's own horn || *intr* to blast away on the trumpet

strombazza·tóre -trice *mf* show-off

strombettare (strombétto) *tr* to trumpet, toot

stroncare §197 (**strónco**) *tr* to break off; to break down; to eliminate; (fig) to criticize severely

stroncatura *f* devastating criticism

strònzio *m* strontium

strónzo *m* (vulg) turd

stropicciare §128 *tr* to rub (*hands*); to drag, shuffle (*feet*); (coll) to crumple || *ref*—**stropicciarsene** (coll) to not give a hoot

stropicci·o *m* (-**i**) rubbing; shuffling

stròzza *f* (coll) gullet, throat

strozzare (stròzzo) *tr* to strangle; to stop up; to fleece, swindle || *ref* to choke; to narrow

strozza·to -ta *adj* choked; choking; strangulated (*hernia*)

strozzatura *f* narrowing

strozzinàg·gio *m* (-**gi**) usury

strozzino *m* usurer, loan shark

struggere §266 *tr* to melt; to consume || *ref* to melt; to pine away; to be upset; **struggersi di** to be consumed by

struggiménto *m* melting; longing; torment

strumentale *adj* instrument (*flying*); capital (*goods*); instructional (*language, in multi-lingual regions*); (gram, mus) instrumental

strumentali·sta *mf* (-**sti -ste**) instrumentalist

strumentalizzare [ddzz] *tr* to use, take advantage of

strumentare (struménto) *tr* to orchestrate

struménto *m* instrument; tool, implement; **strumento a corda** stringed instrument; **strumento a fiato** wind instrument; **strumento di bordo** (aer) flight recorder

strusciare §128 *tr* to rub; to shuffle (*feet*); to crumple; to wear out || *ref*—**strusciarsi a** to fawn on

strutto *m* lard, shortening

struttura *f* structure

strutturare *tr* to organize, structure

struzzo *m* ostrich

stuccare §197 *tr* to putty; to stucco; to surfeit || *ref* to grow weary

stucchévole *adj* sickening

stuc·co -ca (-**chi -che**) *adj* bored; **stucco e ristucco** sick and tired || *m* putty; stucco; plaster of Paris; **rimanere di stucco** to be taken aback

studèn·te -téssa *mf* student

studenté·sco -sca (-**schi -sche**) *adj* student; student-like || *f* student body

studiare §287 *tr* to study; **studiarle tutte** to consider every angle || *intr* to study; to try || *ref* to try; to gaze at oneself

studia·to -ta *adj* affected, studied

stù·dio *m* (-**di**) study; school district; office (*of professional man*); studio; (hist) university; (lit) wish; (mus) étude; **a studio** on purpose; **essere allo studio** to be under consideration

studió·so -sa [s] *adj* studious || *m* scholar

stufa *f* stove, heater; hothouse

stufare *tr* to warm up, heat up; to stew; (coll) to bore

stufato *m* stew

stu·fo -fa *adj* (coll) bored, sick and tired || *f* see **stufa**

stuòia *f* mat; matting

stuòlo *m* throng, crowd; flock; (lit) army

stupefacènte *adj* amazing; habit-forming || *m* dope

stupefare §173 *tr* to amaze, astonish

stupefazióne *f* amazement, astonishment; stupefaction

stupèn·do -da *adj* stupendous

stupidàggine *f* stupidity; silliness; child's play, cinch

stùpi·do -da *adj* stupid; silly; (lit) amazed

stupire §176 *tr* to amaze || *ref* to be amazed

stupóre *m* amazement

stuprare *tr* to rape

stura *f* tapping; uncorking; **dar la stura a** to begin (*a speech*)

sturabottì·glie *m* (-**glie**) bottle opener

sturalavandì·ni *m* (-**ni**) plunger (*to open up clogged sink*)

sturare *tr* to uncork; to take the wax out of (*ears*); to open up (*clogged line*)

stuzzicadèn·ti *m* (-**ti**) toothpick

stuzzicare §197 (**stùzzico**) *tr* to pick (e.g., *one's teeth*); to bother; to excite, arouse; to tease; to sharpen (*appetite*)

su *adv* up; on top; upstairs; **da . . . in su** from . . . on, e.g., **dal mese scorso in su** from last month on; **di su** from upstairs; **in su** up; **metter su** to put on the fire; to instigate; **metter su bottega** to set up shop; **metter su casa** to set up housekeeping; **più su** higher; further up; **su!** come on!; let's go!; **su di** on; **su e giù** back and forth; up and down; **su per giù** more or less; **tirarsi su** to lift oneself up; to sit up; to get better, recover; **tirar su** to pick up; to grow, raise; **venir su** to grow; to come up || §4 *prep* on, upon; up; towards; over, above; onto; against; at, e.g., **sul far del giorno** at daybreak; on top of; out of, e.g., **due volte su tre** two times out of three; **mettere su superbia** to become proud; **stare sulle sue** to be reserved; **sul serio** in earnest; **su misura** made to order

suaccenna·to -ta *adj* above-mentioned

sub *m* (**sub**) (coll) skindiver

subàcque·o -a *adj* submarine

subaffittare *tr* to sublet

subaffitto *m* subletting, sublet; **prendere in subaffitto** to sublet

subaltèr·no -na *adj & m* subaltern; subordinate

subastare *tr* to auction off

sùbbia *f* stonecutter's chisel

subbù·glio *m* (-**gli**) turmoil, hubbub

subcosciènte *adj & m* subconscious

sùbdo·lo -la *adj* treacherous, deceitful

subentrare (**subéntro**) *intr* (ESSERE) (with *dat*) to succeed, follow

subire §176 *tr* to suffer; to undergo

subissare *tr* to ruin; to sink; to overwhelm || *intr* (ESSERE) to sink; to go to rack and ruin

subisso *m* ruin; (coll) lots, plenty

subitàne·o -a *adj* sudden

sùbi·to -ta *adj* (lit) sudden || *m*—**d'un subito** all of a sudden || **subito** *adv*

rapidly; immediately; right away; **subito al principio** at the very beginning; **subito dopo** right after; **subito prima** right before || *interj* right away!

sublima·to -ta *adj* sublimated || *m* **sublimato corrosivo** corrosive sublimate

sublime *adj & m* sublime

subodorare (**subodóro**) *tr* to suspect; to get wind of

subordinare (**subórdino**) *tr* to subordinate

subordina·to -ta *adj & m* subordinate || *f* subordinate clause

subornare (**subórno**) *tr* to bribe

substrato *m* substratum

suburba·no -na *adj* suburban

subùr·bio *m* (-**bi**) suburb

succàne·o -a *adj & m* substitute

succèdere §132 (*pp* **succeduto** or **succèsso**) *intr* (ESSERE) (with *dat*) to succede, to follow || *ref* to follow one another, follow one after the other || (*pret* **succèssi**; *pp* **succèsso**) *intr* (ESSERE) to happen, to come to pass; (with *dat*) to happen to, to come over, e.g., **che gli è successo?** what happened to him?

successióne *f* succession; **in successione** in succession; in a row

successì·vo -va *adj* successive; next

successo *m* success; outcome

successóre *m* successor

successò·rio -ria *adj* (-**ri -rie**) inheritance (*tax*)

succhiare §287 *tr* to suck

succhièllo *m* gimlet

succhiétto *m* pacifier

sùc·chio *m* (-**chi**) suck, sucking; (bot) sap; (coll) gimlet

succiaca·pre *m* (-**pre**) goatsucker, whippoorwill

succin·to -ta *adj* scanty (*clothing*); succinct, concise

suc·co *m* (-**chi**) juice; (fig) gist

succó·so -sa [s] *adj* juicy; pithy

succursale *f* branch, branch office

sud *m* south

sudafrica·no -na *adj & mf* South African

sudamerica·no -na *adj & mf* South American

sudàmina *f* prickly heat

sudare *tr* to sweat; to ooze; **sudare il pane** to earn one's living by the sweat of one's brow; **sudare sette camicie** to toil very hard || *intr* to perspire, sweat; to reek

sudà·rio *m* (-**ri**) shroud

suda·to -ta *adj* wet with perspiration; hard-earned || *f* sweat, sweating

suddét·to -ta *adj* aforesaid, above

sùddi·to -ta *adj & mf* subject

suddivìdere §158 *tr* to subdivide

sud-èst *m* southeast

sudicerìa *f* filth, filthiness; smut

sùdi·cio -cia (-**ci -cie**) *adj* dirty, filthy || *m* dirt, filth

sudiciume *m* dirt, filth

sudi·sta *mf* (-**sti -ste**) Southerner

sudóre *m* sweat, perspiration

sud-òvest *m* southwest

sufficiènte *adj* sufficient, adequate; self-sufficient ‖ *m* sufficient

sufficiènza *f* sufficiency; self-sufficiency; (educ) minimum passing grade

suffisso *m* suffix

suffragare §209 *tr* to support; to pray for

suffragétta *f* suffragette

suffrà·gio *m* (-gi) suffrage

suffumicare §197 (suffùmico) *tr* to fumigate

suffumì·gio *m* (-gi) treatment by inhalation; fumigation

suggellare (suggèllo) *tr* to seal

suggèllo *m* seal

suggeriménto *m* suggestion

suggerire §176 *tr* to suggest; to prompt

suggeri·tóre -trice *mf* prompter ‖ *m* (baseball) coach

suggestionàbile *adj* suggestible

suggestionare (suggestióno) *tr* to influence by suggestion ‖ *ref*—suggestionarsi a + *inf* to talk oneself into + *ger*

suggestióne *f* suggestion; fascination

suggestì·vo -va *adj* suggestive; fascinating; (law) leading (*question*)

sùghero *m* cork

sugli §4

sugna *f* fat; lard

su·go *m* (-ghi) juice; gravy; gist, pith; non c'è sugo it's no fun; there's nothing to it; senza sugo pointless, dull

sugó·so -sa [s] *adj* juicy

sui §4

sulci·da (-di -de) *adj* suicidal ‖ *mf* suicide (*person*)

suicidare *ref* to commit suicide

suicì·dio *m* (-di) suicide (*act*)

sui·no -na *adj* swinish; see carne ‖ *m* swine

sul §4

sulfamìdi·co -ca (-ci -che) *adj* sulfa ‖ *m* sulfa drug

sulla §4

sulle §4

sulli §4

sullo §4

sulloda·to -ta *adj* above-mentioned

sultano *m* sultan

summentova·to -ta, summenziona·to -ta, sunnomina·to -ta *adj* above-mentioned

suntéggiare §290 (suntéggio) *tr* to summarize

sunto *m* résumé, summary

suo sua §6 *adj* & *pron poss* (suòi sue)

suòcera *f* mother-in-law

suòcero *m* father-in-law; i suoceri the in-laws

suòla *f* sole (*of shoe*); share (*of plow*); (naut) sliding ways; (rr) flange (*of rail*)

suòlo *m* ground; soil; floor ‖ *m* (suola *fpl*) (coll) layer; (coll) sole (*of shoe*)

suonare (suòno) *tr* & *intr* var of sonare

suòno *m* sound; (fig) ring; a suon di bastonate with a sound thrashing; a suon di fischi with loud boos; suono armonico (mus) overtone

suòno·stère·o *m* (-o) stereo tape player

suòra *f* nun, sister

super- *pref adj* & *mf* super-, e.g., supersonico supersonic; over-, e.g., superallenamento overtraining

superaffollaménto *m* overcrowding

superare (sùpero) *tr* to surpass; to cross; to overcome; to pass; to exceed; (cards) to trump

supera·to -ta *adj* out-of-date, passé

supèrbia *f* pride, haughtiness; montare in superbia to get a swelled head

superbió·so -sa [s] *adj* proud, haughty

supèr·bo -ba *adj* proud, haughty; superb; spirited ‖ **i superbi** the haughty ones

supercarburante *m* high-octane gas

supercolòsso *m* supercolossal film

superdònna *f*—si da arie di superdonna she thinks she's hot stuff

supereterodìna *f* superheterodyne

superficiale *adj* superficial; surface; cursory, perfunctory ‖ *m* superficial fellow

superfì·cie *f* (-ci & cie) surface; area; superficie portante airfoil

supèr·fluo -flua *adj* superfluous ‖ *m* surplus

super-io *m* (-io) superego

superióra *f* (eccl) mother superior

superióre *adj* superior; upper; higher; above; superiore a higher than; more than; larger than ‖ *m* superior

superlatì·vo -va *adj* & *m* superlative

superlavóro *m* overwork

supermercato *m* supermarket

supersòni·co -ca *adj* (-ci -che) supersonic

supèrstite *adj* surviving; remaining ‖ *mf* survivor

superstizióne *f* superstition

superstizió·so -sa [s] *adj* superstitious

superstrada *f* superhighway

superuòmo *m* superman

supervisióne *f* supervision

supervisóre *m* supervisor; (mov) director

supi·no -na *adj* supine; on one's back

suppellèttile *f* furnishings; equipment; fixtures; fund (*of knowledge*)

supplementare *adj* supplementary

suppleménto *m* supplement; (mil) reinforcement

supplènte *adj* & *mf* substitute

supplènza *f* substitute assignment

suppletì·vo -va *adj* additional; (gram) suppletive

sùppli·ca *f* (-che) supplication; plea; petition

supplicante *m* supplicant

supplicare §197 (sùpplico) *tr* to beseech; to plead with; to appeal to

supplichévole *adj* beseeching, imploring

supplire §176 *tr* to replace ‖ *intr* (with *dat*) to supplement, make up for

suppliziare §287 *tr* to torture; to execute

supplì·zio *m* (-zi) torture, torment; estremo supplizio capital punishment

supporre §218 *tr* to suppose

suppòrto *m* support, prop

suppositò·rio *m* (-ri) suppository

supposizióne *f* supposition; presumption

suppó•sto -sta *adj* alleged ǁ *m* supposition ǁ *f* suppository

suppurare *intr* (ESSERE & AVERE) to suppurate

supremazìa *f* supremacy

suprè•mo -ma *adj* supreme

surclassare *tr* to outclass

surgelare (surgèlo) *tr* to quick-freeze

surreali•sta *mf* (-sti -ste) surrealist

surrenale *adj* adrenal (*gland*)

surrène *m* (anat) adrenal gland

surriscaldare *tr* to overheat

surrogare §209 (surrògo) *tr* to replace

surroga•to -ta *adj* replaceable ǁ *m* makeshift, substitute, ersatz

suscettibile *adj* susceptible; touchy

suscitare (sùscito) *tr* to rouse; to give rise to; to provoke

susina *f* plum

susino *m* plum tree

susseguènte *adj* subsequent, following

susseguire (sussèguo) *intr* (ESSERE) (with *dat*) to follow ǁ *ref* to follow one after the other

sussidiare §287 *tr* to subsidize

sussidià•rio -ria (-ri -rie) *adj* subsidiary; (nav) auxiliary ǁ *m* supplementary text book; subsidiary

sussi•dio *m* (-di) subsidy; assistance, relief; **sussidi audiovisivi** audio-visual aids; **sussidi didattici** teaching aids; **sussidio di disoccupazione** unemployment compensation

sussiè•go *m* (-ghi) stiffness, haughtiness

sussistènza *f* substance; subsistence; (mil) quartermaster corps

sussistere §114 *intr* (ESSERE & AVERE) to subsist; to be, exist

sussultare *intr* to start, jump; to quake

sussulto *m* start, jump; **sussulto di terremoto** earth tremor

sussurrare *tr* to whisper; to murmur, mutter ǁ *intr* to whisper; to rustle ǁ *ref*—**si sussurra** it is rumored

sussurra•tóre -trice *mf* whisperer; grumbler

sussurrì•o *m* (-ì) whispering; murmur; rustle

sussurro *m* whisper; murmur

susta *f* temple (*of spectacles*); (coll) spring

suvvìa *interj* come!, come on!

svagare §209 *tr* to entertain; to distract ǁ *ref* to have a good time; to relax

svaga•to -ta *adj* absent-minded; inattentive

sva•go *m* (-ghi) entertainment, diversion; avocation, hobby

svaligiare §290 *tr* to ransack; to rob; to pirate

svaligia•tóre -trice *mf* thief, robber

svalutare (svàluto *& svaluto***)** *tr* to devaluate; to depreciate; to belittle ǁ *ref* to depreciate

svalutazióne *f* depreciation

svanire §176 *intr* (ESSERE) to evaporate; to vanish

svani•to -ta *adj* faded, evaporated; vanished; enfeebled

svantàg•gio *m* (-gi) disadvantage

svantaggió•so -sa [s] *adj* disadvantageous

svaporare (svapóro) *intr* (ESSERE) to evaporate; to vanish

svaria•to -ta *adj* varied; **svaria•ti -te** several

svarióne *m* blunder, gross error

svasare *tr* to transplant from a pot; to make (*e.g., a gown*) flare

svasa•to -ta *adj* bell-mouthed, flaring

svecchiare §287 (svècchio) *tr* to renew; to rejuvenate; to modernize

svedése [s] *adj* Swedish; safety (*match*) ǁ *mf* Swede ǁ *m* Swedish

svéglia *f* awakening; reveille; alarm clock; **dare la sveglia a** to wake up

svegliare §280 *tr & ref* to wake up

svegliarino *m* alarm clock; (coll) rebuke

své•glio -glia *adj* (-gli -glie) awake; alert ǁ *f* see **sveglia**

svelare (svélo) *tr* to reveal; to unveil ǁ *ref* to reveal oneself; **svelarsi per** to reveal oneself to be

svèllere §267 *tr* (lit) to eradicate

sveltézza *f* quickness; slenderness

sveltire §176 *tr* to make shrewd; to quicken, accelerate ǁ *ref* to become smart

svèl•to -ta *adj* quick; slender; brisk; quick-witted; **alla svelta** quickly; **svelto di lingua** loose-tongued; **svelto di mano** light-fingered ǁ **svelto** *interj* quick!

svenare (svéno) *tr* to bleed to death; (fig) to bleed ǁ *ref* to bleed to death; (fig) to bleed oneself white

svéndere §281 *tr* to sell below cost; to undersell

svéndita *f* clearance sale

svenévole *adj* maudlin, mawkish

svenevolézza *f* maudlinness, mawkishness

sveniménto *m* faint, swoon

svenire §282 *intr* (ESSERE) to faint

sventagliare §280 *tr* to fan; to flash, display

sventagliata *f* blow with a fan; volley

sventare (svènto) *tr* to foil, thwart; (naut) to spill (*a sail*)

sventa•to -ta *adj* careless, thoughtless

svèntola *f* fan (*to kindle fire*); (coll) box, slap; **a sventola** (*ears*) that stick out

sventolare (svèntolo) *tr* to wave; to fan; to winnow ǁ *intr* to flutter ǁ *ref* to fan oneself

sventolì•o *m* (-ì) fluttering, flutter

sventraménto *m* demolition; disembowelment; hernia

sventrare (svèntro) *tr* to demolish; to disembowel; to draw (*a fowl*)

sventura *f* misfortune, mishap; bad luck

sventura•to -ta *adj* unfortunate, unlucky

sverginare (svérgino) *tr* to deflower

svergognare (svergógno) *tr* to put to shame; to unmask

svergogna•to -ta *adj* shameless

svergolare (svérgolo) *tr* & *ref* to warp; (mach) to twist

svernare (svèrno) *intr* to winter

svérza [dz] *f* big splinter

sverzino [dz] *m* lash, whipcord

svestire (svèsto) *tr* to undress; to hull (*rice*); (fig) to strip ‖ *ref* to undress; **svestirsi di** to shed (*e.g., leaves*)

svettare (svétto) *tr* to pollard, top ‖ *intr* to stand out; to sway (*said of a tree*)

Svè·vo -va *adj* & *m* Swabian

Svèzia, la Sweden

svezzaménto *m* weaning

svezzare (svézzo) *tr* to wean; **svezzare da** to break (*s.o.*) of (*e.g., a habit*)

sviare §119 *tr* to turn aside; to lead astray ‖ *intr* & *ref* to go astray; to straggle; (rr) to run off the track

svignare *intr* (ESSERE) to slip away ‖ *ref*—**svignarsela** to sneak away

svilire §176 *tr* to devaluate

svillaneggiare §290 (svillanéggio) *tr* to insult, abuse

sviluppare *tr* to develop; to cause; (lit) to uncoil ‖ *intr* (ESSERE & AVERE) & *ref* to develop; to break out (*said of fire*)

sviluppo *m* development; puberty

svincolare (svìncolo) *tr* to free; to clear (*at customs*)

svincolo *m*—**svincolo autostradale** interchange; **svincolo doganale** customs clearance

svirilizzare [ddzz] *tr* (fig) to emasculate

svisare *tr* to alter, distort

sviscerare (svìscero) *tr* to eviscerate; to examine thoroughly ‖ *ref*—**sviscerarsi per** to be crazy about; to bow and scrape to

sviscera·to -ta *adj* ardent, passionate; obsequious

svista *f* slip, error, oversight

svitare *tr* to unscrew

svìzze·ro -ra *adj* & *mf* Swiss ‖ **la Svizzera** Switzerland

svocia·to -ta *adj* hoarse

svogliatézza *f* laziness; listlessness

svoglia·to -ta *adj* lazy; listless

svolazzare *intr* to flutter, flit

svolazzo *m* flutter; short flight; curlicue, flourish

svòlgere §289 *tr* to unwrap; to unfold; to unwind; to develop; to pursue (*an activity*); to dissuade ‖ *ref* to unwind; to free oneself; to develop; to take place; to unfold

svolgiménto *m* development; composition

svòlta *f* turn; curve; turning point

svoltare (svòlto) *tr* to unwrap ‖ *intr* to turn

svotare §257 or **svuotare (svuòto)** *tr* to empty

T

T, t [ti] *m* & *f* eighteenth letter of the Italian alphabet

tabac·càio -càia *mf* (-cài -càie) tobacconist

tabaccare §197 *intr* to take snuff

tabacchería *f* cigar store

tabacchièra *f* snuffbox

tabac·co *m* (-chi) tobacco; **tabacco da fiuto** snuff

tabarro *m* winter coat; cloak

tabèlla *f* tablet; list; schedule; (coll) clapper, noisemaker; **tabella di marcia** timetable

tabellare *adj* (typ) on wooden blocks; scheduled

tabellóne *m* board; bulletin board; (basketball) backboard

tabernàcolo *m* tabernacle

ta·bù *adj invar* & *m* (-bù) taboo

tàbula *f*—**far tabula rasa di** to make a clean sweep of

tabulare (tàbulo) *tr* to tabulate

tabulatóre *m* tabulator

tabulatrice *f* printer (*of computer*)

tac·ca *f* (-che) notch; size; kind; tally; blemish; (typ) nick; **di mezza tacca** middle-sized; mediocre; **tacca di mira** rear sight (*of firearm*)

tacca·gno -gna *adj* stingy, closefisted ‖ *mf* miser

taccheggia·tóre -trice *mf* shoplifter ‖ *f* prostitute, streetwalker

taccheggiatura *f* or **tacchég·gio** *m* (-gi) shoplifting

tacchétto *m* high heel; cleat (*on soccer or football shoe*)

tacchina *f* turkey hen

tacchino *m* turkey

tàc·cia *f* (-ce) notoriety

tacciare §128 *tr*—**tacciare di** to accuse of, charge with

tac·co *m* (-chi) heel; block; (typ) underlay; **battere i tacchi** to take to one's heels

taccóne *m* (coll) patch; (coll) hobnail; **battere il taccone** to take to one's heels

taccuino *m* pocketbook; notebook

tacére *m* silence; **mettere a tacere** to silence ‖ **§268** *tr* to conceal, withhold; to imply, understand ‖ *intr* to keep quiet; to stop playing; to quiet down; to be silent; **far tacere** to silence; **taci!** (coll) shut up!

tachìmetro *m* tachometer; (aut) speedometer

tacitare (tàcito) *tr* to silence, satisfy (*a creditor*); to pay off

tàci·to -ta *adj* silent; tacit

tacitur·no -na *adj* taciturn

tafano *m* horsefly, gadfly

tafferù·glio *m* (-gli) scuffle

taffe·tà *m* (-tà) taffeta; **taffetà adesivo**

or **inglese** adhesive plaster, court plaster

tàglia *f* ransom, reward; size; build; tally; (mach) tackle

tagliabór·se *m* (**-se**) pickpocket

tagliabò·schi *m* (**-schi**) woodcutter, woodsman

tagliacar·te *m* (**-te**) letter opener, paper knife

tagli·àcque *m* (**-àcque**) cutwater (*of bridge*)

tagliaèrba *adj invar* grass-cutting

tagliafèr·ro *m* (**-ro**) cold chisel

taglialé·gna *m* (**-gna**) woodcutter

tagliama·re *m* (**-re**) cutwater (*of ship*)

tagliando *m* coupon

tagliapiè·tre *m* (**-tre**) stonecutter

tagliare §280 *tr* to cut; to cut down; to cut off; to pick (*a pocket*); to cross (*finish line*); to tailor (*a suit*); to blend (*wine*); to turn off (*e.g., water*); **tagliare a fette** to slice; **tagliare in due** to split; **tagliare i panni addosso a qlcu** to slander s.o.; **tagliare i ponti con** to sever relations with; **tagliare i viveri a** to cut off supplies from; **tagliare la corda** to run away; **tagliare la strada a** to stand in the way of; (aut) to cut in front of; **tagliare le gambe a** to make wobbly (*said of wine*) ‖ *intr* to cut; to bite (*said of cold*); **tagliare per una scorciatoia** to take a shortcut ‖ *ref* to cut oneself; to tear (*said of material*)

tagliasìga·ri *m* (**-ri**) cigar cutter

tagliata *f* cut; clearing; (mil) abatis; **tagliata ai capelli** haircut

tagliatèlle *fpl* noodles

taglia·to -ta *adj* cut; fashioned; **essere tagliato per** to be cut out for; **tagliato all'antica** old-fashioned; **tagliato con l'accetta** rough-hewn ‖ *f* see tagliata

taglia·tóre -trice *mf* cutter

tagliènte *adj* cutting ‖ *m* edge

taglière *m* carving board

taglierina *f* paper cutter

tà·glio *m* (**-gli**) cut; cutting; dressmaking; cutting edge; sharpness; blending (*of wines*); size; denomination (*of paper money*); crossing (*of t*); (bb) fore edge; **a due tagli** double-edged; **a tagli** by the slice; **dare un taglio a** to chop; **di taglio** edgewise; **rifare il taglio a** to sharpen; **taglio cesareo** Caesarean section; **taglio d'abito** suiting; **taglio dei capelli** haircut; **venire in taglio** to come in handy

tagliòla *f* trap

tagliuzzare *tr* to shred, cut into shreds

tailandése [s] *adj & mf* Thai

Tailàndia, la Thailand

tailleur *m* (**tailleur**) woman's tailored costume

talal·tro -tra *pron indef* another, some other

tàlamo *m* (lit) nuptial bed

talare *adj* ankle-length ‖ *f* soutane, cassock

talché *conj* so that

---

talco *m* talcum; talcum powder

tale *adj* such; such a; that; **il tale** such and such a; **un tale** such a; a certain; **un tal quale** such a; a certain ‖ *pron* so-and-so; **il tal dei tali** so-and-so; Mr. so-and-so; **il tale** that fellow; that guy; **quel tale** that fellow, that guy; **tale e quale** like; **tali e quali** exactly, word for word; **un tale** someone, a certain person

talèa *f* (hort) cutting

talènto *m* talent; inclination; **a proprio talento** gladly, willingly; **di mal talento** grudgingly; **andare a talento a** to suit, e.g., **non gli va a talento** nulla nothing suits him

talismano *m* talisman

tallire §176 *intr* (ESSERE & AVERE) to sprout

tallonare (**talló no**) *tr* (sports) to be at the heels of

talloncino *m* coupon, stub

tallóne *m* heel; coupon, stub; tang (*of knife*); **tallone d'Achille** Achilles heel

talménte *adv* so, so much

talóra *adv* sometimes

talpa *f* mole

talu·no -na *pron indef* some; someone, somebody ‖ **talu·ni -ne** *adj & pron indef* some

talvòlta *adv* sometimes

tamarindo *m* tamarind

tambureggiare §290 (**tambu/réggio**) *intr* to drum; to beat down (said, e.g., *of hail*)

tamburèllo *m* tambour (*for embroidering*); (mus) tambourine

tamburino *m* drummer

tamburo *m* drum; barrel (*of watch; of windlass*); **a tamburo battente** on the spot

tamerice *f* tamarisk

Tamigi *m* Thames

tampòco *adv*—**né tampoco** (archaic) nor . . . either

tamponaménto *m* stopping, plugging; rear-end collision

tamponare (**tampóno**) *tr* to tampon, plug; to collide with; to hit from the rear; (surg) to tampon

tampóne *m* plug, tampon; pad; (mus) drumstick; (rr) buffer; (surg) tampon; **tampone di vapore** vapor lock

tana *f* burrow; den; hole; hovel; base (*in children games*)

tanàglie *fpl* var of tenaglie

tan·ca *f* (**-che**) can, jerry can; tank

tanfo *m* musty or stuffy smell

tangènte *adj* tangent ‖ *f* tangent; (com) commission

tàngere §269 *tr* (lit) to touch

Tàngeri *f* Tangier

tànghero *m* boor, lout

tangìbile *adj* tangible

tàni·ca *f* (**-che**) var of tanca

tantino *m*—**un tantino** a little, e.g., **è un tantino arrabbiato** he is a little angry; a little bit, e.g., **un tantino di dolce** a little bit of cake

tan·to -ta *adj & pron indef* such, such a; so much; as much; **a dir tanto** or **a far tanto** at the most; **ai tanti**

(*del mese*) on such and such a day (*of the month*); **a tanto** to such a point; to such a level; **e tanto** odd, e.g., **mille dollari e tanto** a thousand odd dollars; **è tanto** it has been a long time, e.g., **è tanto che lo conosco** it has been a long time since I made his acquaintance; **fra tanto** meanwhile; **senza tanto chiasso** without any noise; **tan•ti -te** many; so many; as many; a lot, e.g., **grazie tante!** thanks a lot! **tanti ... che** so many ... that; **tanti ... quanti** as many ... as; **tanto di guadagnato** so much the better || **tanto** *adv* so much; so; only, e.g., **tanto per passare il tempo** only to pass the time; anyhow; anyway; **nè tanto nè quanto** at all; **tant'è** it's the same; **tanto che** so much that, e.g., **mi ha annoiato tanto che l'ho mandato via** he bothered me so much that I dismissed him; **tanto ... che** both ... and, e.g., **tanto Maria che Roberto** both Mary and Robert; so much ... that; **tanto fa** or **vale** it's all the same; **tanto meglio** so much the better; **tanto meno** so much the less; **tanto per cambiare** as usual; **tanto più ... quanto più** the more ... the more; **tanto ... quanto** as ... as || **s—ascoltare con tanto d'orecchie** to be all ears; **di tanto in tanto** from time to time

tapi•no -na *adj* (*lit*) wretched || *mf* (*lit*) wretch

tappa *f* stopping place; stop; stage; leg; (sports) lap; **bruciare le tappe** to press on, keep going; **fare tappa** to stop

tappabu•chi *mf* (**-chi**) makeshift, pinch hitter, substitute

tappare *tr* to cork, plug; to shut up tight || *ref* to shut oneself in; to plug (*e.g., one's ears*)

tapparèlla *f* (coll) inside rolling shutter

tappéto *m* rug, carpet; (sports) canvas, mat; **mettere al tappeto** (boxing) to knock out; **tappeto erboso** lawn, green; **tappeto verde** gambling table

tappezzare (**tappèzzo**) *tr* to paper (*a wall*); to upholster

tappezzerìa *f* wallpaper; upholstery; upholsterer's shop; tapestry; wallflower

tappezzière *m* paperhanger; upholsterer

tappo *m* cork, stopper; cap; plug; **tappo a corona** bottle cap; **tappo a vite** screw cap

tara *f* tare

taràntola *f* tarantula

tarare *tr* to tare; to set, adjust

tara•to -ta *adj* net (*weight*); calibrated (*instrument*); sickly, weak

tarchia•to -ta *adj* stocky, sturdy

tardare *tr* to delay || *intr* to delay; to be late

tardi *adv* late; **al più tardi** at the latest; **a più tardi!** so long!; **fare tardi** to be late; **più tardi** later; later on; **sul tardi** in the late afternoon

tardi•vo -va *adj* late; retarded, slow; belated

tar•do -da *adj* slow; late; **di età tarda** of advanced years; **tardo d'ingegno** slow-witted

tardó•ne -na *adj* slow-moving || *mf* slowpoke || *f* old dame, middle-aged vamp

tar•ga *f* (**-ghe**) plate; nameplate; shield; (aut) license plate; (sports) trophy

targare §209 *tr* (aut) to register

targatura *f* (aut) registration

targhétta *f* nameplate

tariffa *f* tariff; rate; rates

tariffà•rio -ria (**-ri -rie**) *adj* tariff; rate || *m* price list; rate book

tarlare *tr* to eat (*said of woodworms or moths*) || *intr* (ESSERE) & *ref* to become worm-eaten; to become moth-eaten

tarlo *m* woodworm; moth; bookworm; (fig) gnawing

tarma *f* moth; clothes moth

tarmare *tr* to eat (*said of moths*) || *intr* (ESSERE) & *ref* to become moth-eaten

tarmici•da (**-di -de**) *adj* moth-repelling || *m* moth repellent

taròc•co *m* (**-chi**) tarot; tarok

tarpare *tr* to clip; **tarpare le ali a** to clip the wings of

tartagliare §280 *tr* & *intr* to stutter, stammer

tàrta•ro -ra *adj* Tartar || *m* tartar; Tartar || **Tartaro** *m* Tartarus

tartaru•ga *f* (**-ghe**) turtle, tortoise; tortoise shell

tartassare *tr* to ill-treat; to harass

tartina *f* slice of bread and butter; canapé

tartufo *m* truffle; (fig) tartuffe, hypocrite

ta•sca *f* (**-sche**) pocket; briefcase; **aver le tasche piene di** to be sick and tired of; **da tasca** pocket; **rompere le tasche a** (vulg) to bother, annoy; **tasca in petto** inside pocket

tascàbile *adj* pocket; vest-pocket

tascapane *m* knapsack, rucksack

tascata *f* pocketful

taschino *m* vest pocket, small pocket

tassa *f* tax; (coll) duty, fee; **tassa complementare** surtax; **tassa di circolazione** road-use tax; **tassa di registro** registration fee; **tassa scolastica** tuition

tassàbile *adj* taxable

tassàmetro *m* taximeter; **tassametro di parcheggio** parking meter

tassare *tr* to tax; to assess || *ref* to pledge money

tassati•vo -va *adj* positive; specific; peremptory

tassazióne *f* taxation; tax

tassèllo *m* dowel; inlay; plug; patch; reinforcement

tas•sì *m* (**-sì**) taxi, taxicab

tassì•sta *m* (**-sti**) taxi driver

tasso *m* stake (*anvil*); yew tree; (com) rate (*e.g., of interest*); (zool) badger; **tasso valutario fluttuante** (econ) fluctuation of currency rate

tastare *tr* to touch; to feel; to probe; **tastare il terreno** (fig) to see how the land lies

tastièra *f* keyboard; manual (*of organ*)

tasto *m* touch, feeling, feel; plug (*e.g.*, *in watermellon*); key (*of piano or typewriter*); sample (*in drilling*); **tasto bianco** white key, natural; **toccare un tasto falso** to strike a sour note

tastóni *adv*—**a tastóni** gropingly

tàtti·co -ca (**-ci -che**) *adj* tactical; tactful || *m* tactician || *f* tactics; prudence; tactfulness

tatto *m* touch; tact

tatuàg·gio *m* (**-gi**) tattoo

tatuare (**tatùo**) *tr* to tattoo

taumatur·go *m* (**-gi & -ghi**) wonderworker

tauri·no -na *adj* taurine, bull-like; bull

tavèrna *f* tavern, inn

tavernière *m* tavernkeeper

tàvola *f* board, plank; slab; table; tablet; bookplate; list; **tavola a ribalta** drop-leaf table; **tavola armonica** (mus) sound board; **tavola calda** cafeteria, snack bar; **tavola da stirare** ironing board; **tavola di salvezza** (fig) last recourse, lifesaver; **tavola imbandita** open house; **tavola nera** blackboard; **tavola operatoria** operating table; **tavola pitagorica** multiplication table; **tavola reale** backgammon; **tavole di fondazione** charter (*of a charitable institution*)

tavolàc·cio *m* (**-ci**) wooden board (*on which soldiers on guard and prisoners used to sleep*)

tavolare (**tàvolo**) *tr* to board up

tavolata *f* tableful

tavolato *m* planking; plateau

tavolétta *f* small table; tablet; bar (*e.g.*, *of chocolate*)

tavolière *m* chessboard table; card table; plateau, tableland

tavolino *m* small table; desk

tàvolo *m* table; desk; **tavolo di gioco** gambling table; **tavolo d'ufficio** office desk

tavolòzza *f* palette

tazza *f* cup; bowl

tazzina *f* demitasse

tazzóna *f* mug

te §5 *pron pers*

tè *m* (**tè**) tea; **tè danzante** tea dance, thé dansant

tèa *adj fem*—**rosa tea** tea rose

teatrale *adj* theatrical

teatro *m* theater; performance; drama; stage; (fig) scene; **che teatro!** what fun!; **teatro dell'opera** or **teatro lirico** opera house; **teatro di posa** (mov) studio; **teatro di prosa** legitimate theater

teatróne *m* large theater; (coll) excellent box office

Tèbe *f* Thebes

tè·ca *f* (**-che**) case; (eccl) reliquary

tecnicismo *m* technicality

tècni·co -ca (**-ci -che**) *adj* technical || *m* technician; engineer || *f* technique; technics

téco §5 *prep phrase* (lit) with you

tedé·sco -sca *adj & mf* (**-schi -sche**) German

tediare §287 (**tèdio**) *tr* to bore || *ref* to get bored

tè·dio *m* (**-di**) dullness, tedium, boredom; **recare tedio a** to annoy, bother

tedió·so -sa [s] *adj* dull, tedious

tegame *m* pan; **al tegame** fried (*e.g.*, *eggs*)

tegamino *m* small pan; **uova al tegamino** fried eggs

téglia *f* pan; baking pan

tégola *f* tile; (fig) blow

tégolo *m* tile

teièra *f* teapot, teakettle

tèk *m* teak

téla *f* linen; cloth; material; canvas, oil painting; (fig) plot, trap; (lit) weft; (theat) curtain; **far tela** (coll) to beat it; **tela batista** batiste; **tela cerata** oilcloth; **tela da imballaggio** burlap; **tela di ragno** cobweb; **tela di sacco** sackcloth; **tela greggia** gunny, burlap; **tela smeriglio** emery cloth

te·làio *m* (**-lài**) loom; frame; embroidery frame; sash; stretcher (*for oil painting*); (aut) chassis; **telaio di finestra** window sash

teleama·tóre -trice *mf* TV viewer

telear·ma *f* (**-mi**) guided missile

telecabina *f* cable car

telecàmera *f* TV camera

telecomanda·to -ta *adj* remote-control

telecomando *m* remote control

telecommentatóre *m* TV newscaster

telecròna·ca *f* (**-che**) TV broadcast; **telecronaca diretta** live broadcast

telecroni·sta *mf* (**-sti -ste**) TV news announcer, TV newscaster

telediffusióne *f* TV broadcasting

teledram·ma *m* (**-mi**) teleplay

telefèri·ca *f* (**-che**) cableway, telpherage

telefonare (**telèfono**) *tr & intr* to telephone || *ref* to call one another

telefonata *f* telephone call

telefòni·co -ca *adj* (**-ci -che**) telephone

telefoni·sta *mf* (**-sti -ste**) telephone operator, central; telephone installer

telèfono *m* telephone; **telefono a gettone** pay telephone (*operated by tokens*); **telefono a moneta** pay telephone; **telefono interno** intercommunication system, intercom

telegèni·co -ca *adj* (**-ci -che**) telegenic, videogenic

telegiornale *m* TV newscast

telegrafare (**telègrafo**) *tr & intr* to telegraph

telegràfi·co -ca *adj* (**-ci -che**) telegraphic

telegrafi·sta *mf* (**-sti -ste**) telegrapher; telegraph installer

telègrafo *m* telegraph; **telegrafo di macchina** (naut) engine-room telegraph; **telegrafo ottico** heliograph; wigwag; **telegrafo senza fili** wireless

telegram·ma *m* (**-mi**) telegram

teleguida *f* remote control

teleguidare *tr* to control from a distance, to operate by remote control

Telèmaco *m* Telemachus

telèmetro *m* telemeter; range finder

teleobbiettivo *m* (phot) telephoto lens

telepatìa *f* telepathy

teleproiètto *m* guided missile

telericévere §141 *tr* to receive by TV; to teleview

teleschérmo *m* television screen

telescò·pio m (-pi) telescope
telescrivènte f teletypewriter; ticker
telescriventi·sta mf (-sti -ste) teletype operator
teleselezióne f (telp) direct distance dialing
telespetta·tóre -trice mf televiewer
teletrasméttere §198 tr to televise, telecast
teletrasmissióne f telecast
televisióne f television, TV
televisi·vo -va adj television, TV
televisóre m television set
tellina f sunset shell or clam
télo m piece of cloth; yardage, length of material; (mil) side (of tent)
tèlo m (lit) dart, arrow
telóne m canvas; (theat) curtain
tè·ma m (-mi) theme; (gram) stem
téma f (lit) fear; per tema di (lit) for fear of
temerarie·tà f (-tà) recklessness, rashness
temerà·rio -ria adj (-ri -rie) reckless, rash; ill-founded
temére (témo & tèmo) tr to fear; to respect || intr to fear; temere di to be afraid to
temeri·tà f (-tà) temerity
temìbile adj frightening
tèmpera f tempera, distemper
temperala·pis m (-pis) or temperamati·te m (-te) pencil sharpener
temperaménto m middle course, compromise; temper, temperament
temperante adj temperate, moderate
temperanza f temperance
temperare (tèmpero) tr to mitigate; to temper; to sharpen (a pencil)
tempera·to -ta adj temperate; tempered (metal); watered (wine)
temperatura f temperature; temperatura ambiente room temperature
temperino m penknife, pocketknife
tempèsta f tempest, storm; tempesta in un bicchier d'acqua tempest in a teapot
tempestare (tempèsto) tr to pound; to pepper, pelt; to pester || intr to storm
tempesta·to -ta adj studded, spangled
tempesti·vo -va adj timely
tempestó·so -sa [s] adj stormy, tempestuous
tèmpia f temple (side of forehead); tempie (lit) head
tempiale m temple (in loom; of spectacles)
tempière m Templar
tèm·pio m (-pi & -pli) temple (edifice)
tempi·sta mf (-sti -ste) person or athlete showing good timing; (mus) rhythmist
tèmpo m time; weather; age; period, stage; cycle (of internal-combustion engine); (gram) tense; (mus) tempo, (mus) movement; (sports) period; (theat, mov) part; ad un tempo at the same time; al tempo che Berta filava long ago; a suo tempo in due time; long ago; a tempo debito in due time; a tempo e luogo at the opportune time; a tempo perso in

one's spare time; aver fatto il proprio tempo to be outdated; c'è sempre tempo we are still in time; col tempo in time; dare tempo al tempo to allow time to heal things; darsi del bel tempo to have a good time; da tempo for a long time; del tempo di from the time of; è scaduto il tempo utile the time is up; è tanto tempo it's been a long time; fa bel tempo the weather is fine; il Tempo Father Time; lasciare il tempo che trova to have no effect; molto tempo dopo long afterward; nel tempo che while; per tempo early; prima del tempo formerly; quanto tempo how long; sentire il tempo to feel the weather in one's bones; senza por tempo in mezzo without any delay; tempi che corrono present times; tempo fa some time ago; tempo legale legal time limit; tempo libero leisure time; tempo supplementare (sports) overtime; tempo un . . . within (e.g., one month); un tempo long ago
temporale adj temporal || m storm
temporàne·o -a adj temporary, provisional
temporeggiare §290 (temporéggio) intr to temporize
tèmpra f (metallurgy) tempering, temper; (mus) timbre; (fig) fiber, timber
temprare (tèmpro) tr to temper (metal); to harden, inure || ref to become hardened or inured
tenace adj tenacious; tough
tenàcia f tenacity
tenaci·tà f (-tà) strength, resistance; tenacity
tenàglie fpl nippers, pincers, pliers; tongs; a tenaglie (mil) pincers (e.g., action)
tènda f curtain; awning; tent
tendènza f tendency; trend
tendenzió·so -sa [s] adj tendentious
tèn·der m (-der) (rr) tender
tèndere §270 tr to stretch; to tighten; to draw (a bow); to cast (nets); to lay (snares); to reach out (one's hand); to prick up (one's ears); to draw (s.o.'s attention); to set (sail) || intr to aim; to lean; to tend; to tend to be
tendina f curtain, blind
tèndine m (anat) tendon
tendiscar·pe m (-pe) shoetree
tenditóre m turnbuckle; tenditore della racchetta (tennis) press
tendóne m big curtain; canvas; tent (of circus); (theat) curtain
tendòpo·li f (-li) tent city
tènebre fpl darkness
tenebró·so -sa [s] adj dark, gloomy
tenènte m lieutenant; (mil) first lieutenant; (nav) lieutenant junior grade; tenente colonnello (mil) lieutenant colonel; tenente di vascello (nav) lieutenant senior grade
tenére §271 tr to hold; to have; to keep; to stand (e.g., rough sea); to wear; to make (a speech); to follow

(*a course*); **tenere a battesimo** to stand for, sponsor; **tenere al corrente** to keep informed; **tenere a memoria** to remember; **tenere da conto** to hold in high esteem; to take good care of (*s.th*); **tenere d'occhio** to keep an eye on; **tenere la destra** to keep to the right; **tenere la strada** (aut) to hug the road; **tenere la testa a partito** to mend one's ways; **tenere le distanze** to keep aloof; **tenere mano a** to connive with; **tenere presente** to bear in mind; **tenere qlco a conto** to take good care of s.th || *intr* to hold; to take root; **tenerci che** to be anxious for, e.g., **ci tengo che vinca le elezioni** I am anxious for him to win the elections; **tenere a destra** to keep to the right; **tenere alle apparenze** to stand on ceremony; to keep up appearances; **tenere da** to hail from; to take after; **tenere dietro a** to follow; to keep abreast of; **tenere duro** to hold fast; **tenere per** (sports) to be a fan of || *ref* to hold; to hold on; to keep; to keep (*e.g., ready*); to regard oneself; **tenersi a** to adhere to (*e.g., a treaty*); to hold on to; to stick to; to follow; **tenersi a galla** to stay afloat; **tenersi al largo** (naut) to keep to the open sea; **tenersi al vento** (naut) to sail to leeward; (fig) to follow a safe course; **tenersi in piedi** to stand up; **tenersi per mano** to hold hands; **tenersi sulle proprie** to keep aloof

tenerézza *f* tenderness; fondness, endearment

tène·ro -ra *adj* tender || *m* tender portion

tènia *f* tapeworm

teni·tóre -trice *mf* keeper

tènnis *m* tennis; **tennis da tavolo** table tennis, ping-pong

tenni·sta *mf* (-sti -ste) tennis player

tennìsti·co -ca *adj* (-ci -che) tennis

tenóne *m* tenon

tenóre *m* character, tone; tenor; alcoholic content; manner (*of living*); **tenore di vita** way of life; standard of living

tensióne *f* tension; **alta tensione** high tension; **tensione sanguigna** blood pressure

tentàcolo *m* tentacle

tentare (**tènto**) *tr* to try, attempt; to assay; to tempt; (lit) to touch

tentativo *m* attempt; **tentativo di furto** attempted robbery

tenta·tóre -trice *adj* tempting || *m* tempter || *f* temptress

tentazióne *f* temptation

tentennare (**tenténno**) *tr* to shake; to rock || *intr* to shake; to wobble; to hesitate; to stagger

tentóne or **tentóni** *adv* blindly; gropingly; at random

tènue *adj* small (*intestine*); (lit) tenuous, thin

tenu·to -ta *adj* bound, obliged || *f* capacity, volume; estate, farm; uniform; outfit; (sports) endurance,

resistance; **a tenuta d'acqua** watertight; **a tenuta d'aria** airtight; **tenuta dei libri** bookkeeping; **tenuta di gala** (mil, nav) full-dress uniform; **tenuta di servizio** (mil) fatigues; **tenuta di strada** (aut) roadability

tenzóne *f* combat; poetic contest

teologìa *f* theology

teòlo·go *m* (-gi) theologian

teorè·ma *m* (-mi) theorem

teorèti·co -ca *adj* (-ci -che) theoretic(al)

teorìa *f* theory; (lit) series, row

teòri·co -ca (-ci -che) *adj* theoretical || *m* theoretician

tèpi·do -da *adj* var of **tiepido**

tepóre *m* warmth

téppa *f* underworld, rabble

teppi·sta *m* (-sti) hoodlum, hooligan

terapèuti·co -ca (-ci -che) *adj* therapeutic || *f* therapeutics

terapìa *f* therapy; **terapia convulsivante** or **terapia d'urto** shock therapy

Terèsa *f* Theresa

tèrgere §162 *tr* (lit) to wipe

tergicristallo *m* windshield wiper

tergiversare (**tergivèrso**) *intr* to stall; to beat around the bush

tèr·go *m* (-ghi) back (*of a coin*); **a tergo** on the reverse side || *m* (-ga *fpl*) (lit) back; **volgere le terga** (lit) to turn one's back

termale *adj* thermal (*e.g., waters*)

tèrme *fpl* spa, hot spring

tèrmi·co -ca *adj* (-ci -che) thermal; heat, heating

terminale *adj & m* terminal

terminare (**tèrmino**) *tr* to border; to end, terminate || *intr* (ESSERE) to end, terminate

terminazióne *f* termination; completion; (gram) ending

tèrmine *m* border; marker; term; deadline; end; goal; boundary, bounds; (fig) point; **a termini di legge** according to law; **avere termine** to end; **in altri termini** in other words; **mezzo termine** half measure; **porre termine a** to put an end to; **portare a termine** to put through

terminologìa *f* terminology

termistóre *m* (elec) thermistor

tèrmite *f* termite

termoconvettóre *m* baseboard radiator

termocòppia *f* thermocouple

termodinàmi·co -ca *adj* (-ci -che) thermodynamic || *f* thermodynamics

termòforo *m* heating pad

termòmetro *m* thermometer

termonucleare *adj* thermonuclear

tèr·mos *m* (-mos) thermos bottle

termosifóne *m* radiator; hot-water heating system; steam heating system

termòstato *m* thermostat

termovisièra *f* electric defroster

tèrno *m* tern (*in lotto*); **vincere un terno al lotto** to hit the jackpot

tèrra *f* earth; land; ground; world; city, town; dirt, soil; clay; **essere a terra** to be downcast; to be broke; to be flat (*said of a tire*); **rimanere a terra** to miss the train; **sotto terra** underground; **terra bruciata** scorched earth; **terra di nessuno** no man's land; **terra di Siena** sienna; **terra ferma** terra firma; mainland; **terra terra** skimming the ground; (naut) close to the shore; (fig) mediocre, second-rate

terracòtta f (**terrecòtte**) terra cotta; earthenware

terráferma f mainland (*as distinguished from adjacent islands*); terra firma (*dry land, not air or water*)

terràglia f crockery; **terraglie** earthenware

terranò·va m (-**va**) Newfoundland (*dog*) || **Terranova** f Newfoundland

terrapièno m embankment

terrazza f terrace; **a terrazza** terraced

terrazza·no -**na** mf villager

terrazzo m balcony; terrace; ledge, shelf; terrazzo

terremota·to -**ta** adj hit by an earthquake || mf earthquake victim

terremòto m earthquake

terré·no -**na** adj terrestrial, earthly; ground-floor; first-floor || m ground floor; first floor; ground; soil; land, plot of ground; combat zone, terrain; **preparare il terreno** to work the soil; (fig) to pave the way; **scendere sul terreno** to fight a duel; **tastare il terreno** to feel one's way; **terreno di gioco** (sports) field

tèrre·o -**a** adj wan, sallow

terrèstre adj terrestrial; ground, land || m earthling

terribile adj terrible; awesome, awful

terríc·cio m (-**ci**) soil; top soil

terriè·ro -**ra** adj land; landed

terrificare §197 (**terrífico**) tr to terrify

terrina f tureen

territò·rio m (-**ri**) territory

terróre m terror

terrorismo m terrorism

terrori·sta mf (-**sti** -**ste**) terrorist

terrorizzare [ddzz] tr to terrorize

terró·so -**sa** [s] adj dirty (*e.g., spinach*); dirty-earth (*color*); (chem) rare-earth (*metal*)

tèr·so -**sa** adj clear

tèrza f third grade; (aut) third; (eccl) tierce; (rr) third class

terzaforzi·sta (-**sti** -**ste**) adj of the third force || m partisan of the third force

terzaròlo m (naut) reef

terzétto m trio

terzià·rio -**ria** adj (-**ri** -**rie**) tertiary

terzina f tercet

terzino m (soccer) back

tèr·zo -**za** adj & pron third || m third; third party || f see **terza**

terzúlti·mo -**ma** adj third from the end

tésa [s] f brim (*of hat*); snare, net

tesare [s] (**téso**) tr to pull taut

tè·schio m (-**schi**) skull

tè·si f (-**si**) thesis; dissertation

té·so -**sa** [s] adj taut, tight; strained; outstretched (*hand*); **con le orecchie tese** all ears || f see **tesa**

tesorerìa f treasury; liquid assets

tesorière m treasurer

tesòro m treasure; treasury; thesaurus; bank vault; **far tesoro di** to treasure, prize; **tesoro mio!** my darling!

Tèspi m Thespis

tèssera f card; domino (*piece*); tessera (*of mosaic*)

tessera·to -**ta** adj card-carrying; rationed || mf card-carrying member; holder of ration card

tèssere tr to weave; to spin

tèssile adj textile || m textile; **tessili** textile workers

tessilsac·co m (-**chi**) garment bag

tessi·tóre -**trice** mf weaver

tessitura f weaving; spinning mill; (mus) range; (fig) plot

tessuto m cloth, fabric; tissue

tèsta f head; mind; bulb (*of garlic*); spindle (*of wheel*); warhead (*of torpedo*); row (*of bricks*); **a testa** apiece; per capita; **a testa a testa** neck and neck; **fare di testa propria** to act on one's own; **fare la testa grossa a** to stun; to annoy; **levarsi di testa** to forget about; **mettersi in testa di** to get it into one's head to; **non avere testa di** + *inf* to not feel like + *ger*; **non sapere dove battere la testa** to not know which way to turn; **per una corta testa** by a neck; **rompersi la testa** to rack one's brains; **tenere testa a** to face up to; **testa coda** (aut) spin; **testa di ponte** (mil) bridgehead; **testa di sbarco** beachhead; **testa e croce** head or tails

testaménto m will, testament || **Antico** or **Vecchio Testamento** Old Testament; **Nuovo Testamento** New Testament

testardàggine f stubborness

testar·do -**da** adj stubborn

testata f headboard (*of bed*); top; end (*e.g., of beam*); heading (*of newspaper*); butt with the head; nose (*of rocket*)

tèste m witness

testé adv (lit) a short time ago; (lit) presently, in a little while

testícolo m testicle

testièra f headboard; crown (*of harness*); battering ram

testimòne m witness; **testimone di nozze** best man; **testimone di veduta** or **testimone oculare** eyewitness

testimonianza f testimony

testimoniare §287 (**testimònio**) tr to attest; to depose, testify; **testimoniare il falso** to bear false witness || *intr* to bear witness

testimò·nio m (-**ni**) (coll) witness

testina f small head; whimsical person; boiled head of veal; head (*e.g., of tape recorder*)

tèsto m text; pie dish; (coll) flower vase; **fare testo** to serve as a model

testó·ne -**na** mf dolt; stubborn person

testuale adj textual; word-for-word

testùggine f turtle; tortoise

tètano m tetanus

tè·tro -**tra** adj (lit) gloomy, dark

tétta f (coll) teat

tettarèlla f nipple

tétto m roof; ceiling price; home; **senza tetto** homeless; **tetto a capanna** gable roof; **tetto a padiglione** hip roof; **tetto a uma falda** lean-to roof; **tetto di paglia** thatched roof

tettóia *f* shed; pillared roof

tettóia-garage *f* (**tettóie-garage**) carport

tettùc·cio *m* (**-ci**) (aut) roof; (aut) top; **tettuccio a bulbo** dome; **tettuccio rigido** (aut) convertible top

ti §5 *pron*

tìbia *f* tibia, shinbone

tic *m* (**tic**) twitch; habit

ticchettì·o *m* (**-i**) click (*of typewriter*); patter (*of rain*); tick (*of clock*)

tìc·chio *m* (**-chi**) whim; tic; viciousness (*of animal*); blemish

tièpi·do -da *adj* tepid, lukewarm

tifo *m* typhus; **fare il tifo per** to root for; to be a fan of

tifoidèa *f* typhoid fever

tifóne *m* typhoon

tifó·so -sa [s] *adj* rooting || *mf* fan, rooter

tì·glio *m* (**-gli**) linden, lime; bast; fiber

tigliò·so -sa [s] *adj* tough, fibrous

tigna *f* ringworm; (coll) tightwad

tignòla *f* clothes moth

tigra·to -ta *adj* striped; tabby

tigre *f* tiger

timballo *m* pie, meat pie; timbale; (lit) drum

timbrare *tr* to stamp; to cancel (*stamps*)

timbro *m* stamp; character (*of a writer*); (mus) timbre; **timbro di gomma** rubber stamp; **timbro postale** postmark

timidézza *f* shyness, bashfulness; timidity

tìmi·do -da *adj* shy, bashful; timid || *mf* shy person

timo *m* (anat) thymus; (bot) thyme

timóne *m* rudder, helm; shaft, pole (*of cart*); **timone di direzione** (aer) rudder; **timone di profondità** (aer) elevator; (nav) diving plane (*of submarine*)

timonièra *f* (naut) pilot house

timonière *m* helmsman, steersman; coxswain

timonìè·ro -ra *adj* rudder; tail (*feather*) || *f see* **timoniera**

timora·to -ta *adj* conscientious; **timorato di Dio** God-fearing

timóre *m* fear; awe; **avere timore di** to fear

timoró·so -sa [s] *adj* timorous

tìmpano *m* (archit) tympanum; (anat) eardrum; (mus) kettledrum; **rompere i timpani a** to deafen

tìn·ca *f* (**-che**) (ichth) tench

tinèllo *m* pantry; breakfast room

tingere §126 *tr* to dye; to dirty, soil; to color || *ref* to dye (*e.g., one's hair*); to put on make-up; to become colored

tino *m* tub, vat

tinòzza *f* tub, washtub

tinta *f* paint; color; dye; shade; stain; **calcare le tinte** to exaggerate; **mezza tinta** halftone, shade; **vedere qlco a fosche tinte** to take a dim view of s.th; **vedere qlco a tinte rosee** to see s.th through rose-colored glasses

tintarèlla *f* (coll) suntan

tinteggiare §290 (**tintéggio**) *tr* to calci-

mine; to whitewash; to tint; to paint (*e.g., a house*)

tintinnare *intr* (ESSERE & AVERE) to jingle; to clink

tintìnni·o *m* (**-i**) jingling; clink

tin·to -ta *adj* dyed; tinged; soiled; (lit) dark || *f see* **tinta**

tintó·re -ra *mf* dyer; dry cleaner

tintorìa *f* dyeworks; dry cleaning establishment; dyeing

tintura *f* dyeing; dyestuff; tincture; smattering; **tintura di iodio** iodine

tìpi·co -ca *adj* (**-ci -che**) typical

tipificare §197 (**tipìfico**) *tr* to standardize

tipizzare [ddzz] *tr* to standardize

tipo *adj invar* typical, e.g., **famiglia tipo** typical family || *m* type; standard, model; fellow, guy; phylum (*in taxonomy*); **bel tipo** (coll) character, card; **col tipi di** printed in the shop of; **sul tipo di** similar to; **vero tipo** prototype, epitome

tipografìa *f* typography; print shop

tipogràfi·co -ca *adj* (**-ci -che**) typographical

tipògrafo *m* typographer; owner of print shop, printer

tipòmetro *m* (typ) line gauge

tiptologìa *f* table rapping (*during séance*); tapping in code (*among jailbirds*)

tiraba·ci *m* (**-ci**) (coll) spitcurl

tiràg·gio *m* (**-gi**) draft; **a tiraggio forzato** forced-draft

tiralìne·e *m* (**-e**) ruling pen

tirannìa *f* tyranny

tirànni·co -ca *adj* (**-ci -che**) tyrannical

tiran·no -na *adj* tyrannical || *mf* tyrant

tirante *m* brace; rod; strap; trace (*of harness*); **tirante degli stivali** bootstrap

tirapiè·di *m* (**-di**) hangman's assistant; underling

tirapu·gni *m* (**-gni**) brass knuckles

tirare *tr* to pull; to draw; to tug; to suck; to haul in (*nets*); to deserve (*a slap*); to pluck; to throw; to give (*blows*); to utter (*oaths*); to shoot (*arrows, bullets*); to stretch; to tighten (*one's belt*); to print; to make (*an addition*); (sports) to force (*the pace*); **tirare a lucido** to polish; **tirare a sé** to attract; **tirare a sorte** to draw lots for; **tirare fuori** to draw out; to pull out; to get out; **tirare giù** to lower; to jot down; (coll) to gulp down; **tirare gli orecchi a** to punish by yanking the ears of; **tirare il collo a** to wring the neck of; **tirare in ballo** to bring up (*a subject*); **tirare l'acqua al proprio mulino** to look out for number one; **tirare l'anima coi denti** to be at the end of one's rope; **tirare l'aria** to draw (*said of a chimney*); **tirare le cuoia** (slang) to kick the bucket; **tirare per i capelli** to drag by the hair; to drag in; to push, coerce; **tirare per le lunghe** to stretch out; **tirare su** to lift; to raise (*children*); to pull up || *intr* to be too tight (*said of clothes*); to shoot; to blow (*said of wind*); to draw (said, e.g., of chimney); **tirare a** to tend toward, lean toward; **tirare a** + inf to try to + inf; **tirare a campare** (coll) to goldbrick; **tirare avanti** to go ahead; to manage to get along; **tirare di boxe** to box; **tirare diritto** to go straight ahead; **tirare di scherma** to fence; **tirare in lungo** to delay, linger; to dillydally; **tirare innanzi** to keep on going; to go ahead; **tirare sul prezzo** to haggle; **tirare via** to hurry along || ref— **tirarsi addosso** (coll) to bring upon oneself; **tirarsi dietro** to drag along; **tirarsi fuori da** to get out of (e.g., trouble); **tirarsi gente in casa** to keep open house; **tirarsi indietro** to move back; **tirarsi in là** to move aside; **tirarsi su** to get up; to recover; to roll up (one's sleeves); **tirarsi un colpo di rivoltella** to shoot oneself

tirastiva·li m (-li) bootjack

tirata f pull; stretch; tirade

tirati·ra m (-ra) (coll) yen; **fare a tira-tira per** (coll) to scramble for

tira·to -ta adj taut; forced (smile); drawn (face); tight, closefisted; **tirato con short of** || f see **tirata**

tira·tóre -trice mf shot; **tiratore scelto** sharpshooter; **franco tiratore** sniper

tiratura f printing

tirchierìa f stinginess

tìr·chio -chia (-chi -chie) adj stingy, closefisted || mf miser

tirèlla f trace (of harness)

tirétto m (coll) drawer

tiritèra f rigmarole

tiro m pull; pair, brace (e.g., of oxen); throw; fire, shot; trick; **a tiro** within reach; **a un tiro di schioppo** within gunshot; **da tiro** draft; **fuori del tiro dell'orecchio** out of earshot; **tiro alla fune** tug of war; **tiro al piattello** trapshooting; **tiro a quattro** four-in-hand; **tiro a segno** rifle range; shooting gallery

tiroci·nio m (-ni) apprenticeship; internship; **tirocinio didattico** practice teaching

tiròide f thyroid

tirolése [s] adj & mf Tyrolean

tirrèni·co -ca adj (-ci -che) Tyrrhenian

Tirrèno m Tyrrhenian Sea

tisana f tea, infusion

tisi f consumption, tuberculosis

tìsi·co -ca (-ci -che) adj consumptive; stunted || mf consumptive

titàni·co -ca adj (-ci -che) titanic

titànio m titanium

titillare tr to tickle

titolare adj titular; regular, full-time || m owner, boss; incumbent || v (titolo) tr to name, call

titolo m title; heading; name; caption; entry (in dictionary); grade; fineness (of gold); (chem) titer; (educ) credit; severe title to have a right to; **a titolo di** as, by way of; **titoli di testa** (mov) credits; **titolo al portatore** security payable to bearer; **titolo azionario** share; **titolo corrente** subtitle; **titolo di credito** instrument of credit; certificate; deed; conveyance; **titolo di studio** degree, diploma; credits; **titolo di trasporto** travel document

titubare (tìtubo) intr to hesitate; to waver

tiziané·sco -sca adj (-schi -sche) titian; Titian

tì·zio m (-zi) fellow, guy

tizzo or **tizzóne** m brand, firebrand

to' interj here!; well!

tobò·ga m (-ga) toboggan

toccafèrro m tag (game)

toccamano m handshake (to close a deal); bribe, under-the-table tip

toccante adj touching, moving

toccare §197 (tócco) tr to touch; to reach; to concern; to push (a button); to play (an instrument); to feel; to hit (the target); to border on (e.g., the age of forty); **toccare con mano** to make sure of; **toccare il cielo col dito** to be in seventh heaven; **toccare nel vivo** to touch to the quick; **toccare terra** to land; **toccarne molte** to get a good thrashing; **toccato!** touché! || intr (ESSERE) to be touching; toccare a to be up to, e.g., **tocca a lui** it's up to him; to have to, e.g., **le tocca partire domani** she has to leave tomorrow; to deserve, e.g., **gli è toccato il premio** he deserved the prize || ref to meet, e.g., **gli estremi si toccano** extremes meet

toccasa·na [s] m (-na) cure-all, panacea

tocca·to -ta adj touché; touched in the head, nutty; **già toccato** above-mentioned || f (mus) toccata

tóc·co -ca (-chi -che) adj touched, nutty; spoiled (fruit) || m touch; knock; one o'clock (P.M.); (coll) stroke

tòc·co m (-chi) chunk, piece; mortarboard; toque; **un bel tocco di ragazza** a buxom lass

tò·ga f (-ghe) gown, academic gown; (hist) toga

tògliere §127 tr to remove, take away; to take; to cut (telephone connection); to deduct; to take off; to preclude, prevent; **togliere a** to take away from; **togliere al cielo** (lit) to praise to the skies; **togliere di mezzo** to remove; to do away with; **togliere la parola a** to take the floor from; **togliere l'onore a** to dishonor; **togliere una spina dal cuore a** to relieve the heart and mind of || intr— **tolga Dio!** God forbid! || ref to take off (e.g., one's coat); to have (e.g., a tooth) pulled; to satisfy (a whim); **togliersi di mezzo** to get out of the way; **togliersi la vita** to take one's life; **togliersi qlcu dai piedi** to get rid of s.o.

tòlda f (naut) deck

tolemài·co -ca adj (-ci -che) Ptolemaic

tolétta f dressing table; dressing room; toilet, washroom; dress, gown; **fare tolètta** or **farsi la tolétta** to make one's toilet

tolleràbile adj tolerable

tollerante adj tolerant; liberal
tolleranza f tolerance; leeway
tollerare (**tòllero**) tr to tolerate; to bear, stand
tòl·to -ta adj taken; except, leaving out, e.g., **tolta sua figlia** leaving his daughter out ‖ m—**il mal tolto** ill-gotten goods
to·màio m (**-mài & -màia** fpl) or **to·màia** f (**-màie**) upper (of shoe)
tómba f tomb, grave
tombale adj grave (e.g., stone)
tombino m sewer inlet
tómbola f bingo; (coll) tumble
tombolare (**tómbolo**) tr (coll) to tumble down (the steps) ‖ intr (ESSERE) to fall headlong; (coll) to go to rack and ruin; (aer) to tumble
tómbolo m fall, tumble; bolster; lace pillow; (coll) fatso; **fare un tombolo** to go to rack and ruin; to lose one's position
Tommaso m Thomas
tòmo m volume; (coll) character
tòna·ca f (**-che**) (eccl) frock; (eccl) soutane; **gettare la tonaca alle ortiche** to doff the cassock
tonare §257 intr to peal; to thunder ‖ impers (ESSERE & AVERE)—**tuona il** is thundering
tondeggiante adj round; rounded; chubby; curvaceous
tondino m coaster; iron rod (for reinforced concrete); (archit) molding (at top or bottom of column); (archit) astragal
tón·do -da adj round; (typ) roman ‖ m round; circle; plate, dish; (typ) roman; **in tondo** around
tónfo m splash; thump
tòni·co -ca (**-ci -che**) adj tonic ‖ m tonic (medicine) ‖ f (mus) tonic
tonificare §197 (**tonìfico**) tr to invigorate
tonnara f tuna nets
tonnellàg·gio m (**-gi**) tonnage
tonnellata f ton; **tonnellata di stazza** displacement ton
tónno m tuna
tòno m tone; tune; hue; style; (mus) pitch; (mus) key; **darsi tono** to put on airs; **di tono** stylish; **fuori di tono** out of tune
tonsilla f tonsil
tonsura f tonsure
tón·to -ta adj (coll) dumb, stupid
topàia f rat's nest; hovel
topà·zio m (**-zi**) topaz
tòpi·co -ca (**-ci -che**) adj topical ‖ f topic; (coll) blunder
tòpo m mouse; rat; **topo campagnolo** field mouse; **topo d'acqua** water rat; **topo d'albergo** hotel thief; **topo d'auto** car thief; **topo di biblioteca** bookworm
topografia f topography
topolino m little mouse ‖ **Topolino** m Mickey Mouse
toporagno m shrew
tòppa f patch; keyhole
tòppo m stump; headstock (of lathe)
torace m thorax

tórba f peat
tórbi·do -da adj cloudy; murky ‖ m trouble; **pescare nel torbido** to fish in troubled waters; **torbidi** disorder
torbièra f peatbog
tòrcere §272 tr to twist; to wring; to bend, curve; to curl (the lips); to lead astray ‖ intr (ESSERE) to bend, curve ‖ ref to writhe; to bend over; **torcersi dalle risa** to split with laughter
torchiare §287 (**tòrchio**) tr to press
tòr·chio m (**-chi**) press; printing press
tòr·cia f (**-ce**) torch
torcicòllo m stiff neck; (orn) wryneck
torcinaso [s] m (vet) twitch
tórdo m thrush; simpleton
torèllo m young bull; (naut) garboard
torèro m bullfighter
tórlo m yolk
tórma f crowd, throng; herd
torménta f blizzard
tormentare (**torménto**) tr to torture, torment; to pester, nag ‖ ref to worry
torménto m torture, torment; pang; bore, pest, annoyance
tornacónto m interest, advantage
tornante m curve
tornare (**tórno**) tr (lit) to restore; (obs) to turn ‖ intr (ESSERE) to return; to go back; (coll) to jibe, agree, square; **tornare a** to be profitable to; **tornare a** + inf verb + again, e.g., **tornare a essere** to become again; **tornare a fare** to do again; **tornare a bomba** to return to the point; **tornare a galla** to come back to the surface; **tornare a gola** to repeat (said of food); **tornare a onore a qlcu** to do credit to s.o.; **tornare a pennello** to fit to a T; **tornare in sé** to come to; **tornare opportuno** or **utile a** to suit, e.g., **non gli tornò opportuno vendere la casa** it did not suit him to sell the house; **tornare utile** to come in handy; **tornare sulle proprie decisioni** to change one's mind
tornasóle m litmus
tornèllo m turnstile
tornèo m tournament, tourney
tór·nio m (**-ni**) lathe
tornire §176 tr to turn, turn up (on a lathe); to polish
tornitóre m lathe operator
tórno m turn; period (of time); **levarsi di torno** to get rid of; **torno torno** all around
tòro m bull; (archit, geom) torus; (lit) marital bed ‖ **Toro** m (astrol) Taurus
torpèdine f torpedo
torpedinièra f destroyer escort; torpedo-boat destroyer
torpè·do f (**-do**) (aut) touring car
torpedóne m bus, motor coach
tòrpi·do -da adj torpid, sluggish; numb
torpóre m torpor, sluggishness; numbness
tórre f tower; (chess) castle; (nav) turret; **torre campanaria** bell tower; **torre d'avorio** ivory tower; **torre di**

lancio (rok) gantry; **torre pendente** leaning tower

torrefare §173 *tr* to roast (*coffee*)

torreggiante *adj* towering

torreggiare §290 (**torréggio**) *intr* to tower

torrènte *m* torrent

torrenziale *adj* torrential

torrétta *f* turret; (nav) conning tower (*of submarine*); (archit) bartizan

tòrri·do -da *adj* torrid

torrióne *m* donjon; (nav) conning tower (*of battleship*)

torróne *m* nougat

torsióne *f* torsion

tórso *m* stalk; core (*of fruit*); torso, trunk; **a torso nudo** bare-chested

tórsolo *m* core; stalk; stem; **non vale un torsolo** it's not worth a fig

tórta *f* pie; cake, tart; **torta di mele** apple pie

tòrta *f* twist

tortièra *f* baking pan

tòr·to -ta *adj* twisted; crooked; gloomy (*face*) || *m* wrong; **a torto** unjustly; **avere torto** to be wrong; **avere torto marcio** to be dead wrong; **dar torto a** to lay the blame on; **fare torto a** to wrong, e.g., **fece torto al proprio fratello** he wronged his own brother; **to bring discredit upon** || *f* see **tòrta** || **torto** *adv* askance

tórtora *f* turtledove

tortuó·so -sa [s] *adj* winding; ambiguous; (fig) devious

tortura *f* torture

torturare *tr* to torture; to pester || *ref* to torment oneself; **torturarsi il cervello** to rack one's brain

tosare (**tóso**) *tr* to clip, crop; to shear; (fig) to fleece

tosa·tóre -trice *mf* clipper, shearer || *f* clippers; lawn mower

tosatura *f* sheepshearing; clip (*of wool*)

tosca·no -na *adj* & *mf* Tuscan || *m* stogy || **Toscana**, **la** Tuscany

tósse *f* cough; **tosse asinina** or **canina** whooping cough

tòssi·co -ca (**-ci -che**) *toxic* || *m* (archaic) poison

tossicòmane *mf* drug addict

tossicomania *f* drug addiction

tossina *f* toxin

tossire (**tósso**) & §176 *intr* to cough

tostapa·ne *m* (**-ne**) toaster

tostare (**tòsto**) *tr* to toast; to roast (*e.g., coffee*)

tò·sto -sta *adj* (lit) prompt; (lit) impudent; (lit) brazen (*face*) || **tosto** *adv* (lit) soon; **ben tosto** (lit) very soon; **tosto che** (lit) as soon as

tòt *adj pl invar* so many, that many || *pron invar* so much, that much

totale *adj* & *m* total

totalità·rio -ria *adj* (**-ri -rie**) total, complete; totalitarian

totalizzare [ddzz] *tr* to add up; to make (*so many points*)

totalizzatóre [ddzz] *m* pari-mutuel; betting window; (mach) totalizator

tòtano *m* squid; (orn) tattler

totocàlcio *m* soccer pool

tovàglia *f* tablecloth

tovagliòlo *m* napkin

tra *prep* among; between

trabàccolo *m* small fishing boat

traballare *intr* to shake; to totter; to wobble; to stagger; to toddle

trabìccolo *m* frame for bedwarmer; jalopy; hulk

traboccante *adj* overflowing

traboccare §197 (**trabócco**) *tr* to knock down || *intr* to overflow (*said of container*) || *intr* (ESSERE) to overflow (*said of liquid*) || *intr* (ESSERE & AVERE) to tip (*said of scales*); **far traboccare** to make (*the scales*) tip

trabocchétto *m* pitfall; trapdoor

trabóc·co *m* (**-chi**)—**trabocco di sangue** internal hemorrhage

tracannare *tr* to gulp down

tracchèggio *m* (**-gi**) delay; (fencing) feint

tràc·cia *f* (**-ce**) track; trace, clue; trail; outline, plan; (lit) line, row; **buona traccia** right track; **fare la traccia a** to open the way for; **in** or **sotto traccia** concealed (*e.g., wiring*); **tracce** tinge; (chem) traces

tracciante *adj* tracer (*bullet*)

tracciare §128 *tr* to trace; to pave (*the way*); to outline; (lit) to track

tracciato *m* tracing, drawing; outline; map; layout

trachèa *f* trachea, windpipe

tracòlla *f* baldric; shoulder strap; **tracolla** slung across the shoulders

tracòllo *m* collapse, debacle

tracotanza *f* arrogance

tradiménto *m* treason; treachery; **a tradimento** unawares, unexpectedly; treacherously

tradire §176 *tr* to betray; to fail (*a person; said of memory*) || *ref* to give oneself away

tradi·tóre -trice *adj* charming, seductive; treacherous; deceitful, faithless || *mf* traitor; betrayer || *f* traitress

tradizionale *adj* traditional

tradizióne *f* tradition

tradótta *f* military train

tradurre §102 *tr* to translate

tradut·tóre -trice *mf* translator

traduzióne *f* translation

traènte *mf* (com) drawer

trafela·to -ta *adj* breathless, out of breath

traffèrro *m* (elec) air gap; (elec) spark gap

trafficante *mf* dealer, trader; trafficker

trafficare §197 (**tràffico**) *tr* to sell; to traffic in || *intr* to trade, deal; to hustle

tràffi·co *m* (**-ci**) traffic

traffico·ne -na *mf* hustler

trafiggere §104 *tr* to pierce, stab, transfix; to wound

trafila *f* routine; red tape; (mach) drawplate

trafilare *tr* to wiredraw

trafilétto *m* (journ) short feature, special item; (journ) notice

trafitta *f* stab wound; shooting pain

trafittura *f* stab; shooting pain

traforare (trafóro & trafóro) *tr* to bore; to pierce; to carve (*wood*); to pink (*leather*); to embroider with open work

traforo *m* boring; tunnel; open work

trafugare §209 *tr* to purloin; to sneak off with

tragèdia *f* tragedy; **far tragedie** (coll) to make a fuss

traghettare (traghétto) *tr* to ferry

traghétto *m* ferry; **traghetto spaziale** space shuttle

tràgi·co -ca (-ci -che) *adj* tragic ‖ *m* tragedian; **il tragico** (fig) the tragic

tragitto *m* journey; (obs) ferry

traguardo *m* sight; aim; goal; finish line; (phot) viewfinder; (sports) tape

traiettòria *f* trajectory; path

tràina *f* towline; **pescare alla traina** to troll

trainare (tràino) *tr* to drag, tug, pull

tràino *m* drag; load; trailer

tralasciare §128 *tr* to interrupt; to omit; **non tralasciare di** to not fail to

tràl·cio *m* (-ci) stem (*of vine*)

tralìc·cio *m* (-ci) ticking, bedtick; trellis; tower (*of high-tension line*)

tralice *m*—**in tralice** askance

tralignare *intr* (ESSERE & AVERE) to degenerate

tram *m* (tram) streetcar

trama *f* woof, weft; plot (*of play*); texture (*of cloth*)

tramà·glio *m* (-gli) trammel net

tramandare *tr* to hand down

tramare *tr* & *intr* to weave; to plot

trambusto *m* bustle

tramestì·o *m* (-ì) bustle, confusion

tramèzza [ddzz] *f* partition

tramezzare (tramèzzo) [ddzz] *tr* to interpose; to partition

tramezzino [ddzz] *m* small partition; sandwich; sandwich man

tramèzzo [ddzz] *m* partition; side dish; (sew) insertion ‖ *adv* in between; **tramezzo a** among

tràmite *m* intermediary; (lit) pass; **per tramite di** through ‖ *prep* (coll) by; by means of

tramòg·gia *f* (-ge) hopper

tramontana *f* north wind; **perdere la tramontana** to lose one's bearings

tramontare (tramónto) *intr* (ESSERE) to set (*said, e.g., of sun*); to end

tramónto *m* setting; sunset; decline

tramortire §176 *tr* to stun ‖ *intr* (ESSERE) to faint, swoon

trampolière *m* wading bird; (orn) stilt

tràmpoli *mpl* stilts

trampolino *m* diving board; springboard; ski jump; (fig) springboard

tramutare *tr* to transfer; to transform

tràn·cia *f* (-ce) slice; (mach) shears

tranèllo *m* trap, snare

trangugiare §290 *tr* to swallow; to gulp down

tranne *prep* except, save; **tranne che** unless

tranquillante *m* tranquilizer

tranquillare *tr* & *ref* (lit) to tranquilize; to calm down

tranquilli·tà *f* (-tà) tranquillity

tranquillizzare [ddzz] *tr* to tranquilize; to reassure ‖ *ref* to become reassured

tranquìl·lo -la *adj* tranquil, calm; clear (*conscience*)

transatlànti·co -ca *adj* & *m* (-ci -che) transatlantic

transazióne *f* compromise

transènna *f* bar, barrier

transètto *m* (archit) transept

trànsfu·ga *m* (-ghi) (lit) deserter

transìgere §165 *tr* to settle ‖ *intr* to compromise

transistóre *m* transistor

transitàbile *adj* passable

transitare (trànsito) *intr* to move; to walk

transiti·vo -va *adj* transitive

trànsito *m* passage; traffic; (lit) passing; **di transito** transient

transitò·rio -ria *adj* (-ri -rie) temporary; transitory; transitional

transizióne *f* transition

transoceàni·co -ca *adj* (-ci -che) transoceanic

transòni·co -ca *adj* (-ci -che) transonic

transunto *m* abstract, summary (*of a document*)

trantràn *m* routine

tran·vài *m* (-vài) (coll) streetcar

tranvìa *f* streetcar line

tranvià·rio -ria *adj* (-ri -rie) streetcar

tranvière *m* streetcar conductor; motorman

trapanare (tràpano) *tr* to drill; (surg) to trephine

tràpano *m* drill; (surg) trephine; **trapano a vite** automatic drill

trapassare *tr* to pierce; (fig) to grieve; (poet) to cross; (lit) to pass, spend ‖ *intr* (ESSERE) to go through; to pass (*said of an inheritance*); (lit) to pass away; **trapassare da, per** or **al di là di** to come through (*said, e.g., of a nail, light*)

trapassato *m* (lit) deceased; **trapassato prossimo** past perfect

trapasso *m* crossing; transfer; transition; (lit) passing, death

trapelare (trapélo) *intr* (ESSERE) to ooze; to trickle out; to leak through; (fig) to leak out

trapè·zio *m* (-zi) trapeze; (geom) trapezoid

trapezòide *adj* trapezoidal ‖ *m* trapezoid

trapiantare *tr* to transplant ‖ *ref* to transfer

trapianto *m* transplantation; transplant; **trapianto cardiaco** heart transplant

tràppola *f* trap; (coll) gadget; (fig) lie; **trappola esplosiva** booby trap

trapunta *f* quilt

trapuntare *tr* to quilt; to embroider

trapun·to -ta *adj* quilted; embroidered; studded ‖ *m* embroidery ‖ *f* see **trapunta**

trarre §273 *tr* to pull; to drag; to draw; to bring; to deduct; to lead; to unsheathe (*a sword*); to heave (*a sigh*); to spin (*silk, wool,* etc.); **il dado è tratto** the die is cast; **trarre dalla prigione** to free from prison; **trarre d'impaccio** to get (*s.o.*) out of trouble; **trarre fuori** to extract; **trarre in inganno** to deceive; **trarre in rovina** to ruin; **trarre per mano** to lead by the hand ‖ *intr* to kick (*said of a mule*); (lit) to run; (lit) to blow (*said of the wind*) ‖ *ref* to take off (*e.g., one's hat*); **trarsi d'impaccio** to get out of trouble; **trarsi indietro** to pull back; **trarsi in disparte** to move aside

trasalire [s] §176 *intr* (ESSERE & AVERE) to start, jump

trasanda•to -ta *adj* untidy, slovenly

trasbordare (**trasbórdo**) *tr* to transfer, transship

trasbórdo *m* transfer, transshipment

trascéndere §245 *tr* to transcend ‖ *intr* (ESSERE) to go to excesses

trascinare *tr* to drag; to stir; to enthrall; to lead astray; **trascinare la vita** to barely make ends meet ‖ *ref* to drag oneself; to drag on

trascolorare (**trascolóro**) *tr* to discolor; to change the color of ‖ *intr* (ESSERE) & *ref* to discolor; to change color

trascórrere §139 *tr* to pass (*time*); to skim through (*e.g., a book*); (lit) to go through ‖ *intr* to go to excesses ‖ *intr* (ESSERE) to elapse, pass

trascórso *m* slip (*e.g., of pen*); peccadillo

trascrìvere §250 *tr* to transcribe

trascrizióne *f* transcription; registration (*e.g., of a deed*)

trascuràbile *adj* negligible

trascurare *tr* to neglect; to fail; to disregard ‖ *ref* to not take care of oneself

trascuratézza *f* negligence, neglect; carelessness; slovenliness

trascura•to -ta *adj* neglected; careless; slovenly

trasecolare (**trasècolo**) [s] *intr* (ESSERE & AVERE) to marvel, be astonished

trasferìbile *adj* transferable

trasferiménto *m* transfer; conveyance

trasferire §176 *tr* to transfer; to assign, convey ‖ *ref* to move

trasfèrta *f* business trip; traveling expenses, per diem

trasfigurare *tr* to transfigure; to distort (*the truth*) ‖ *ref* to be transfigured; to change countenance

trasfocatóre *m* (phot) zoom lens

trasfóndere §178 *tr* to transfuse; (fig) to instill

trasformàbile *adj* transformable; (aut) convertible

trasformare (**trasfórmo**) *tr* to transform; to alter ‖ *ref* to transform oneself; to be converted

trasformatì•vo -va *adj* (gram) transformational

trasformatóre *m* transformer

trasformazióne *f* transformation

trasformì•sta *mf* (-stì -ste) quick-change artist

trasfusióne *f* transfusion

trasgredire §176 *tr* & *intr* to transgress

trasgressióne *f* transgression

trasgressóre *m* transgressor

trasla•to -ta *adj* figurative; metaphorical; (lit) transferred ‖ *m* figure of speech; metaphor

traslitterare (**traslìttero**) *tr* to transliterate

traslocare §197 (**traslòco**) *tr* to transfer; to move ‖ *intr* & *ref* to move

traslò•co *m* (-chi) moving

traslùci•do -da *adj* translucent

trasméttere §198 *tr* to transmit; (rad) to broadcast

trasmettì•tóre -trice *mf* transmitter ‖ *m* (naut) engine-room telegraph; (telg) sender

trasmigrare *intr* (ESSERE & AVERE) to transmigrate ‖ *intr* (ESSERE) to pass, pass on

trasmissióne *f* transmission; conveyance; broadcast; telecast; **trasmissione del pensiero** thought transference

trasmittènte *adj* transmitting; broadcasting ‖ *f* broadcasting station

trasmutare *tr* to transmute; to change

trasogna•to -ta [s] *adj* dreamy; daydreaming; dazed

trasparènte *adj* transparent ‖ *m* transparency

trasparènza *f* transparence; **in trasparenza** against the light

trasparire §108 *intr* (ESSERE) to appear; to shine; to show through; to show, be revealed (*said of feelings*); **far trasparire** to reveal

traspirare *intr* to perspire ‖ *intr* (ESSERE) to show, be revealed

traspirazióne *f* perspiration

traspórre §218 *tr* to transpose

trasportare (**traspòrto**) *tr* to transport; to carry away; to transfer; to translate; to postpone; (mus) to transpose; **lasciarsi trasportare** to be carried away ‖ *ref* to move; (fig) to go back

trasporta•tóre -trice *mf* carrier ‖ *m* (mach) conveyor belt; (phot) sprocket

traspòrto *m* transportation; transport; transfer; eagerness; moving; (mus) transposition; **trasporto funebre** funeral procession

trasposi•tóre -trice *mf* (mus) transposer

trassa•to -ta *adj* paying ‖ *m* drawee

trastullare *tr* to amuse; to entice ‖ *ref* to have a good time; to loiter

trastullo *m* play, game; fun; plaything

trasudare [s] *tr* to ooze; to exude ‖ *intr* to ooze (*said of a wall*) ‖ *intr* (ESSERE) to drip (*said of perspiration*)

trasversale *adj* transverse, cross ‖ *f* crossroad

trasvèr•so -sa *adj* transverse ‖ *m* transverse beam

trasvolare (**trasvólo**) *tr* to fly over, cross by air ‖ *intr*—**trasvolare su** to skip over

trasvolata *f* non-stop flight

tratta *f* tug, pull; (rr) stretch; (com)

draft; (lit) crowd; **tratta dei neri** slave trade; **tratta delle bianche** white slavery

trattàbile adj negotiable; friendly, sociable

trattaménto m treatment; working conditions; food, spread; reception, welcome; **trattamento di favore** special treatment; **trattamento di quiescenza** retirement benefits

trattare tr to treat; to deal with; to transact; to wield; to play (an instrument); to work (e.g., iron); to deal in; **trattare qlcu da bugiardo** to call s.o. a liar; **trattare da cane** to treat like a dog || intr to bargain; **trattare di** to deal with; to take care of; to treat, handle || ref to take good care of oneself || impers (ESSERE) **si tratta di** it's question of

trattà·rio -ria mf (-ri -rie) drawee

trattativa f negotiation

trattato m treatise; treaty

trattazióne f treatment

tratteggiare §290 (**trattéggio**) tr to sketch; to outline; to hatch

trattég·gio m (-gi) hatching

trattenére §271 tr to keep; to entertain; to withhold; to hold back; to detain || ref to stop; to refrain; to remain

tratteniménto m entertainment, party; delay

trattenuta f withholding; checkoff

trattino m dash; hyphen

trat·to -ta adj drawn, extracted || m stretch; span; passage; tract; gesture; throw (of dice); stroke (of pen); bearing; section; (chess) move; **a larghi tratti** in broad outline; **a tratti** from time to time; **a un tratto** all of a sudden; at the same time; **dare un tratto alla bilancia** to tip the scales; **tratti** features; **tratti del volto** features; **tratto di corda** strappado; **tratto di unione** hyphen; **tutto d'un tratto** all of a sudden; **un bel tratto** quite a while

trat·tóre -trice mf innkeeper; restaurateur || m tractor; **trattore a cingoli** caterpillar tractor || f tractor (vehicle)

trattoria f inn, restaurant

tratturo m cow path

traumatizzare [ddzz] tr to traumatize

travagliare §280 tr to torment; to molest || intr & ref to toil, labor

travà·glio m (-gli) suffering; toil; trave (to inhibit horse being shod); **travaglio di parto** labor pains; **travaglio di stomaco** upset stomach

travasare tr to pour off; to decant; to transfer || ref to spill

travaso m pouring off; transfer; **travaso di bile** gall bladder attack; **travaso di sangue** hemorrhage

travatura f roof timbers; **travatura maestra** ridgepole

trave f beam; joist; **fare una trave d'un fuscello** to make a mountain out of a molehill

travedére §279 tr to glimpse || intr to be mistaken

travéggole fpl—**avere le traveggole** to see things; to see one thing for another

travèrsa f crossbar; crossroad; crosspiece; rung; bar (of goalpost); dam; rail (of fence); transom; slat (to hold bedspring); rubber pad; (rr) tie

traversare (**travèrso**) tr to cross

traversata f passage, crossing

traversìa f strong wind; **traversie** misfortunes

traversina f (rr) tie

travèr·so -sa adj cross; devious || m width; crossbar; (naut) beam; (naut) side; **a traverso** (naut) on the beam; **capire a traverso** to misunderstand; **di traverso** askance; crosswise; the wrong way || f see **traversa**

traversóne m large crossbar; westerly gale; side blow with saber

travestiménto m disguise; travesty

travestire (**travèsto**) tr to disguise; to travesty, parody || ref to disguise oneself

traviare §119 tr to lead astray || intr & ref to go astray

travicèllo m joist

travisare tr to distort

travolgènte adj impetuous; fascinating; sweeping

travòlgere §289 tr to overwhelm; to overturn; to sweep away

trazióne f traction

tre [e] adj & pron three; **le tre** three o'clock || m three; third (in dates)

trébbia f thresher; threshing

trebbiare §287 (**trébbio**) tr & intr to thresh

trebbiatrice f thresher, threshing machine

trebbiatura f threshing

tréc·cia f (-ce) plait; braid; **treccia a ciambella** bun, knot

trecentèsi·mo -ma adj, m & pron three hundredth

trecènto adj, m & pron three hundred || **il Trecento** the fourteenth century

tredicèsi·mo -ma adj, m & pron thirteenth || f Xmas bonus

trédici adj & pron thirteen; **le tredici** one P.M. || m thirteen; thirteenth (in dates)

trégua f truce; respite; **tregua atomica** nuclear test ban; **senza tregua** without letup

tremare (**trèmo**) intr to shake, tremble; to quiver; **far tremare** to shake

tremarèlla f—**avere la tremarella** (coll) to shake in one's boots

tremebón·do -da adj (lit) shaky

tremèn·do -da adj tremendous

trementina f turpentine

tremila adj, m & pron three thousand

trèmito m trembling; quivering

tremolare (**trèmolo**) intr to shake; to quiver; to flicker

trèmo·lo -la adj tremulous || m (bot) aspen; (mus) tremolo

trèno m train; quarter (of animal); set (of tires); threnody, lamentation; **treno accelerato** local; **treno di lusso** Pullman train; **treno direttissimo** express; **treno di vita** mode of life; mode of living; **treno merci** freight train; **treno stradale** tractor-trailer

trenodìa f threnody

trénta adj & pron thirty ‖ m thirty; thirtieth (in dates)

trentèsi·mo -ma adj, m & pron thirtieth

trentina f about thirty

Trènto f Trent

trepidare (trèpido) intr to fear; to worry

trepidazióne f fear, trepidation

treppiède m tripod; trivet

tré·sca f (-sche) intrigue; liaison

tréspolo m stool; pedestal; stand, perch; (coll) jalopy

triàngolo m triangle; **triangolo rettangolo** right triangle

tribolare (tribolo) tr to torment, afflict ‖ intr to suffer

tribolazióne f tribulation, ordeal

tribórdo m (naut) starboard

tri·bù f (-bù) tribe

tribuna f rostrum, platform; (sports) grandstand; **tribuna stampa** press box

tribunale m court, tribunal; courthouse; **tribunale dei minorenni** juvenile court; **tribunale di prima istanza** court of first instance

tributare tr to bestow

tributà·rio -ria (-ri -rie) adj tributary; tax ‖ m tributary

tributo m tribute; tax

triche·co m (-chi) walrus

triciclo m tricycle

tricolóre adj & m tricolor

tricòrno m cocked hat, tricorn

tricromìa f three-color printing; three-color print

tridènte m trident

trifase adj three-phase

trifocale adj trifocal

trifò·glio m (-gli) clover; three-leaf clover

trifola f (coll) truffle

triglia f red mullet

trigonometrìa f trigonometry

trilióne m trillion

trillare intr to trill; to vibrate

trillo m trill; ringing

trilogìa f trilogy

trimestrale adj quarterly

trimèstre m quarter; quarterly dues; quarterly payment; (educ) quarter, trimester

trimotóre m three-engine plane

trina f lace

trin·ca f (-che) (naut) gammoning; **di trinca** clearly, cleanly; **nuovo di trinca** brand-new

trincare §197 tr (coll) to gulp down, swill

trincèa f trench

trincerare (trincèro) tr to dig trenches in ‖ ref to entrench oneself

trincétto m shoemaker's knife

trinchétto m (naut) foremast; (naut) foresail

trinciante adj cutting ‖ m carving knife

trinciapóllo m meat shears

trinciare §128 tr to carve; to shred; to advance (rash opinions); to cut up

trinciato m smoking tobacco

trinciatrice f shredder; slicer

Trinità f Trinity

trionfale adj triumphal

trionfante adj triumphant

trionfare (triónfo) intr to triumph

triónfo m triumph; center piece; tidbit dish with three or four tiers; trump (in game of tarot)

triparti·to -ta adj tripartite

triplicare §197 (trìplico) tr & ref to triple

triplice adj threefold

tri·plo -pla adj & m triple

tripode m tripod

trippa f tripe; (coll) belly

tripudiare §287 intr to exult

tripù·dio m (-di) exultation

tris m (tris) (poker) three of a kind

trisàvola f great-great-grandmother

trisàvolo m great-great-grandfather; **trisavoli** great-great-grandparents

trisma m lockjaw

triste adj sad; gloomy, bleak

tristézza f sadness

tri·sto -sta adj wicked; wretched; poor (figure); (lit) sad

tritacar·ne m (-ne) meat grinder

tritaghiàc·cio m (-cio) ice crusher

tritare tr to chop; to grind; to mince, hash; to pound

tri·to -ta adj minced, hashed; worn, trite

tritòlo m T.N.T.

tritóne m (zool) newt; (fig) merman ‖ **Tritone** m Triton

trìtti·co m (-ci) triptych; export document in triplicate; trilogy

trittòn·go m (-ghi) triphthong

triturare tr to mince, hash

trivèlla f auger, drill; post-hole digger

trivellare (trivèllo) tr to drill, bore

triviale adj vulgar

triviali·tà f (-tà) vulgarity

tri·vio m (-vi) crossroads; trivium; **da trivio** vulgar

trofèo m trophy; (mil) insignia (on headpiece)

trògolo m trough

tròia f sow; slut ‖ **Troia** f Troy

troia·no -na adj & m Trojan

trómba f trumpet; bugle, clarion; trunk (of elephant); leg (of boot); (anat) tube; (aut, rad) horn; **con le trombe nel sacco** crestfallen, dejected; **tromba d'aria** whirlwind; tornado; **tromba marina** waterspout; **tromba delle scale** stairwell

trombétta f trumpet

trombettière m (mil) trumpeter

trombetti·sta m (-sti) trumpet player

trombóne m trombone; blunderbuss

trombò·si f (-si) thrombosis

troncare §197 (trónco) tr to chop; to cut off; to clip (words); to break, sever; to block (s.o.'s progress); to apocopate

tronchése [s] m wire cutter

trón·co -ca (-chi -che) adj truncate; oxytone; apocopated; exhausted, dead-tired; incomplete; **in tronco** in the middle; (dismissal) on the spot ‖ m trunk; stub (of receipt book);

section (*of highway*); log; strain (*of a family*); (rr) branch; **tronco di cono** truncated cone; **tronco maggiore** (naut) lower mast

troncóne *m* stump

troneggiare §290 (tronéggio) *intr* to tower; to hold forth; **troneggiare su** to lord it over

trón·fio -fia *adj* (**-fi -fie**) haughty; bombastic

tròno *m* throne

tropicale *adj* tropical

tròpi·co *m* (**-ci**) tropic

troposfèra *f* troposphere

tròp·po -pa *adj & pron* too much; **trop·pi -pe** too many || *m* too much; **questo è troppo!** enough is enough! || **troppo** *adv* too; too much; **essere di troppo** to be in the way

tròta *f* trout

trottare (tròtto) *intr* to trot

trotterellare (trotterèllo) *intr* to trot along; to toddle

tròtto *m* trot; **piccolo trotto** jog trot

tròttola *f* top

trovare (tròvo) *tr* to find; to visit; **trovare a** or **da ridire** (**su**) to find fault (with); **trovi?** don't you think so? || *ref* to find oneself; to meet; to be; to be located; to happen, e.g., **mi trovai a passare di fronte a casa sua** I happened to pass in front of his house

trovaró·be *m* (**-be**) (theat) property man || *f* (theat) dresser

trovata *f* find; trick, gimmick

trovatèl·lo -la *mf* foundling, waif

trovatóre *m* troubadour

trovière *m* trouvère

truccare §197 *tr* to make up; to falsify; (aut) to soup up || *ref* to put on make-up

truccatura *f* make-up; trick, gimmick

truc·co *m* (**-chi**) make-up; trick, gimmick

truce *adj* fierce, cruel; menacing

trucidare (trùcido) *tr* to massacre

trùciolo *m* chip, shaving

truculènto *adj* truculent

truffa *f* cheat, fraud, swindle; **truffa all'americana** confidence game

truffare *tr* to cheat, swindle

truffa·tóre -trice *mf* cheat, swindler

truismo *m* truism

truògolo *m* var of **trogolo**

truppa *f* troop; soldiers; **di truppa** (mil) enlisted (*man or woman*); **in truppa** in a flock

tu §5 *pron pers*; **a tu per tu** face to face; **dare del tu a** to address in the familiar form

tuba *f* tuba; (hist) horn, trumpet; (joc) top hat, stovepipe; (anat) tube

tubare *intr* to coo

tubatura *f* piping, tubing; pipe, tube; pipeline

tubazióne *f* tubes, pipes

tubèrcolo *m* tubercle

tubercolosà·rio [s] *m* (**-ri**) tuberculosis sanitarium

tubercolò·so -sa [s] *adj* tuberculous || *mf* T.B. patient

tùbero *m* tuber

tubétto *m* tube (*for pills or toothpaste*); spool

tubino *m* small tube; derby (hat)

tubo *m* tube; pipe; (anat) canal, duct; **a tubo** tubular; **tubo di scarico** exhaust pipe; **tubo di troppopieno** overflow; **tubo di ventilazione** air shaft

tubolare *adj* tubular || *m* tire (*for racing bicycle*)

tuffare *tr* to dip; to plunge || *ref* to plunge; to dive

tuffa·tóre -trice *mf* diver || *m* dive bomber

tuffétto *m* (orn) dabchick, grebe

tuffo *m* dive; plunge; throb; **a tuffo** (aer) diving; **scendere a tuffo** (aer) to dive; **tuffo ad angelo** (sports) swan dive; **tuffo d'acqua** downpour

tufo *m* tufa

tu·ga *f* (**-ghe**) (naut) deckhouse

tugù·rio *m* (**-ri**) hovel

tulipano *m* tulip

tumefare §173 *tr & ref* to swell

tumefazióne *f* swelling

tùmi·do -da *adj* tumid

tumóre *m* tumor

tùmulo *m* tomb; tumulus

tumulto *m* tumult, riot; commotion

tumultuó·so -sa [s] *adj* tumultuous

tungstèno *m* tungsten

tùni·ca *f* (**-che**) tunic

Tùnisi *f* Tunis

Tunisìa, la Tunisia

tunisi·no -na *adj & mf* Tunisian

tuo tua §6 *adj & pron poss* (**tuòi tue**)

tuòno *m* thunder

tuòrlo *m* yolk

turàcciolo *m* cork, stopper

turare *tr* to plug, stop; to cork

turba *f* crowd; mob; (pathol) upset

turbaménto *m* commotion, perturbation; disturbance, breach (*of law and order*)

turbante *m* turban

turbare *tr* to muddy; to disturb; to upset || *ref* to become cloudy; to become upset

turba·to -ta *adj* upset; disturbed; distracted

tùrbi·do -da *adj* turbid

turbina *f* turbine

turbinare (tùrbino) *tr* to separate in a centrifuge || *intr* to whirl

tùrbine *m* whirlwind; swarm; tumult

turbinó·so -sa [s] *adj* whirling; tumultuous

turboèli·ca *m* (**-ca**) turboprop

turbogètto *m* turbojet

turbolèn·to -ta *adj* turbulent

turbolènza *f* turbulence

turbomotrice *f* (rr) turbine engine

turboreattóre *m* turbojet

turcasso *m* quiver

turchése [s] *m* turquoise

Turchìa, la Turkey

turchinétto *m* bluing

turchi·no -na *adj* dark-blue || *m* dark blue

tur·co -ca (**-chi -che**) *adj* Turkish; **sedere alla turca** to sit cross-legged || *mf* Turk || *m* Turkish (*language*); **bestemmiare come un turco** to swear like a trooper; **fumare come un turco** to smoke like a steam engine

tùrgi·do -da *adj* turgid

turìbolo *m* thurible, censer

turìsmo *m* tourism

turi·sta *mf* (**-sti -ste**) tourist

turìsti·co -ca *adj* (**-ci -che**) tourist; travel (*e.g., bureau*); traveler's (*check*)

turlupinare *tr* to hoodwink, swindle

turlupinatura *f* swindle, confidence game

turno *m* turn; shift; **a turno** in turn; **di turno** on duty; **fare a turno** to take turns

turpe *adj* base, abject; (lit) ugly

turpilò·quio *m* (**-qui**) foul language

turpitùdine *f* turpitude

tuta *f* overalls; **tuta antigravità** anti-G suit; **tuta da bambini** jumpers; **tuta spaziale** spacesuit

tutèla *f* guardianship; defense, protection

tutelare *adj* tutelary ‖ *v* (**tutèlo**) *tr* to protect, defend

tùtolo *m* corncob

tu·tóre -trice *mf* guardian; protector

tuttavia *adv* yet, nevertheless; (lit) always, continuously

tut·to -ta *adj* whole; all; full; **con tutto** in spite of, e.g., **con tutto quello che ho fatto per lui** in spite of all I have done for him; **del tutto** fully, completely; **è tutt'uno** it's all the same; **tutt'altro** completely different; on the contrary; **tutt'altro che** anything but; **tutti** every, e.g., **tutti gli scolari** every pupil; **tutti e due** both ‖ *m* everything; whole; **con tutto che** although; **fare di tutto** to do everything possible; **in tutto** altogether ‖ *pron* **tut·ti -te** all, everybody (*of a group*); **tutti** everybody ‖ **tutto** *adv* quite; **tutt'a un tratto** all of a sudden; **tutto al contrario** quite the opposite

tuttofa·re *adj invar* of all trades; of all work ‖ *m* (**-re**) factotum, jack-of-all-trades ‖ *f* (**-re**) maid of all work

tuttóra *adv* yet, still

tziga·no -na *adj & mf* var of **zigano**

U

U, u [u] *m & f* nineteenth letter of the Italian alphabet

ubbìa *f* prejudice, bias; complex; whim

ubbidiènte *adj* obedient

ubbidire §176 *tr* to obey ‖ *intr* to obey; to respond (*said of a car*); (with *dat*) to obey, e.g., **gli ubbedì** he obeyed him

ubertó·so -sa [s] *adj* fruitful; fertile

ubicazióne *f* location

ubiquità *f* ubiquity; **non ho il dono dell'ubiquità** I can't be everywhere at the same time

ubì·quo -qua *adj* ubiquitous

ubriacare §197 *tr* to make drunk, intoxicate ‖ *ref* to get drunk

ubriacatura or **ubriachézza** *f* drunkenness, intoxication

ubria·co -ca (**-chi -che**) *adj* drunk; **ubriaco fradicio** dead drunk ‖ *mf* drunkard

ubriacó·ne -na *mf* drunkard

uccellare (**uccèllo**) *tr* to take in, cajole ‖ *intr* to snare; to fowl; to hunt birds

uccèllo *m* bird; **uccello di bosco** fugitive; **uccello di galera** gallows bird; **uccello di passo** bird of passage

uccella·tóre -trice *mf* live-bird catcher

uccellièra *f* aviary; large birdcage

uccìdere §274 *tr* to kill ‖ *ref* to kill oneself; to get killed; to kill one another

-ùccio -ùccia (**-ucci -ucce**) *suf adj* not very, e.g., **calduccio** not very hot; rather, e.g., **magruccio** rather thin; poor little, e.g., **caruccio** poor little darling ‖ *suf m & f* small e.g., **cappelluccio** small hat

uccisióne *f* killing; murder

uccì·so -sa *adj* killed ‖ *mf* victim

ucci·sóre -ditrice *mf* killer

ucraì·no -na *adj & mf* Ukrainian ‖ **l'Ucraìna** *f* the Ukraine

udìbile *adj* audible

udiènza *f* audience; hearing; **l'udienza è aperta!** the court is now in session!

udìre §275 *tr* to hear; to listen to

udìto *m* hearing

uditòfono *m* hearing aid

udi·tóre -trice *adj* hearing ‖ *mf* (educ) auditor ‖ *m* magistrate

udità·rio -ria (**-ri -rie**) *adj* auditory ‖ *m* audience

ufficiale *adj* official ‖ *m* official; officer; **primo ufficiale** (naut) first officer, mate; **ufficiale di giornata** (mil) officer of the day; **ufficiale di rotta** (aer, naut) navigator; **ufficiale giudiziario** clerk of the court; process server, bailiff; **ufficiale medico** (mil) medical officer

ufficiare §128 *tr* to officiate

uffì·cio *m* (**-ci**) duty; office; bureau; department (*of agency*); **d'ufficio** ex-officio; public, e.g., **avvocato d'ufficio** public defender; **ufficio di collocamento** placement bureau; **ufficio di compensazione** clearing house; **ufficio d'igiene** board of health

uffició·so -sa [s] *adj* unofficial; kindly; white (*lie*)

uffì·zio *m* (**-zi**) (eccl) office

ufo *m*—**a ufo** gratis, without paying

ugèllo *m* nozzle

ùg·gia *f* (**-ge**) darkness; gloom; dislike; **avere in uggia** to dislike

uggiolare (**ùggiolo**) *intr* to whine (*said of a dog*)

uggió·so -sa [s] *adj* gloomy; boring

ugnare *tr* to bevel; to miter

ugnatura f bevel; miter

ògola f uvula; **bagnarsi l'ugola** (coll) to wet one's whistle

ugonòtto m Huguenot

uguaglianza f equality

uguagliare §280 tr to equal; to make equal; to equalize; to level; to compare || ref to compare oneself; to be equal; to be compared

uguale adj equal; same; even; level; **per me è uguale** it's the same to me || m equal; (math) equal sign

ùlcera f ulcer; sore

ulcerare (ùlcero) tr & ref to ulcerate

uliva f var of **oliva**

ulterióre adj further, subsequent, ulterior

ùltima f latest news; last straw

ultimare (ùltimo) tr to complete, finish

ultimato m ultimatum

ultimìssima f latest edition (of newspaper); **ultimìssime** late news

ùlti·mo- ma adj last; final; latest; latter; farthest; ultimate; least; top (floor); **all'ultimo, dall'ultimo, nell'ultimo** or **sull'ultimo** lately; finally, at the end || f see **ultima**

ultimogèni·to -ta adj last-born || mf last-born child

ultra- pref adj and m & f ultra-, e.g., **ultraelevato** ultrahigh; super-, e.g., **ultrasonico** supersonic (speed)

ultracór·to -ta adj ultrashort

ultraròs·so -sa adj & m infrared

ultraterré·no -na adj ultramundane; unearthly

ultraviolét·to -ta adj & m ultraviolet

ululare (ùlulo) intr to howl

ululato m howl

umanésimo m humanism

umani·sta mf (-sti -ste) humanist

umani·tà f (-tà) humanity; **umanità** fpl humanities

umanità·rio -ria adj & mf (-ri -rie) humanitarian

uma·no -na adj human; humane || m human nature; **umani** human beings

um·bro -bra adj & m Umbrian

umettare (umétto) tr to moisten, dampen

umidìc·cio -cia adj (-ci -ce) dampish

umidi·tà f (-tà) humidity, dampness

ùmi·do -da adj humid, damp || m humidity, dampness; **in umido** stewed (e.g., meat)

ùmile adj humble || **gli umili** mpl the meek

umiliare §287 tr to humiliate, humble || ref to humble oneself

umiliazióne f humiliation

umiltà f humility

umóre m humor, mood, temper; whim; (bot) sap; **un bell'umore** (coll) quite a character

umorismo m humor

umori·sta mf (-sti -ste) humorist

umorìsti·co -ca adj (-ci -che) humorous; amusing, comic, funny

un (apocopated form of **uno**) §9 indef art a, an || §9 numeral adj one || §12 reciprocal indef pron—**l'un l'altro** each other, one another

unànime adj unanimous

unanimità f unanimity

unàni·mo -ma adj unanimous

uncinare tr to hook, grapple

uncinétto m small hook; crochet hook

uncino m hook; grapnel; clasp; pothook; (fig) pretext; **a uncino** hooked

undicèsi·mo -ma adj, m & pron eleventh

ùndici adj & pron eleven; **le undici** eleven o'clock || m eleven; eleventh (in dates); (soccer) squad

ùngere §183 tr to grease; to oil; to smear; to anoint; to flatter || ref to smear oneself

Ungherìa, l' f Hungary

ungherése [s] adj & mf Hungarian

ùnghia f nail; fingernail; claw; hoof; fluke (of anchor); (fig) hairbreadth; **avere le unghie lunghe** to be light-fingered; **unghia del piede** toenail; **unghie** (fig) clutches

unghiata f nail scratch

unguènto m unguent, ointment

ùni·co -ca adj (-ci -che) only, sole; unique; single (copy); complete (text) || f—**l'unica** the only solution

unicòrno m unicorn

unificare §197 (unìfico) tr to unify; to standardize

unificazióne f unification; standardization

uniformare (unifórmo) tr to make uniform, standardize || ref—**uniformarsi a** to conform to; to comply with

unifórme adj uniform; standard || f uniform; **alta uniforme** (mil) full dress

unilaterale adj unilateral

unióne f union; agreement; **unione libera** free love

unire §176 tr & ref to unite

unìsono [s] m unison; **all'unisono** in unison

uni·tà f (-tà) unity; unit; **unità di misura** unit of measurement

unità·rio -ria (-ri -rie) adj unit (e.g., price); united || m Unitarian

unì·to -ta adj united; joined; compact; plain (color); consolidated

universale adj universal; last (judgment)

universi·tà f (-tà) university

universìtà·rio -ria (-ri -rie) adj university; college || mf university or college student; university or college professor

univèr·so -sa adj universal || m universe

unno m Hun

u·no -na §9 indef art a, an || §9 numeral adj one || m one || §10 pron indef one; **le una, la una,** or **l'una** one o'clock; **l'uno e l'altro** both; **l'uno o l'altro** either, either one; **per uno** in single file; **uno per uno** one by one; each other || §11 correlative pron one

un·to -ta adj greasy || m grease, fat; flattery; anointed one

untuosità [s] f greasiness; unction, unctuousness

untuó·so -sa [s] adj greasy; unctuous

unzióne f unction

uò·mo m (**-mini**) man; **come un sol uomo** to a man; **uomo d'affari** businessman; **uomo del giorno** man of the hour; **uomo della strada** man of the street; **uomo di chiesa** churchman; **uomo di fatica** laborer; **uomo di fiducia** trusted man; **uomo di mare** seaman; **uomo di paglia** straw man; **uomo di parola** man of his word; **uomo in mare!** man overboard!; **uomo meccanico** automaton; **uomo morto** (rr) deadman brake; **uomo nuovo** nouveau riche; **uomo rana** frogman

uòpo m—**all'uopo** if need be; **essere d'uopo** (lit) to be necessary

uòse [s] fpl leggings

uò·vo m (**-va** fpl) egg; **meglio un uovo oggi che una gallina domani** a bird in a hand is worth two in the bush; **rompere le uova nel paniere** a qlcu to spoil s.o.'s plans; **uovo affogato** poached egg; **uovo alla coque** soft-boiled egg; **uovo all'occhio di bue** fried egg; **uovo da tè** tea ball; **uovo strapazzato** scrambled egg

uragano m hurricane; storm (of applause); **uragano di neve** blizzard

Ural mpl Ural Mountains

uranífero -ra adj uranium-bearing

urànio m uranium

urbanésimo m urbanization, migration toward the cities

urbanìsti·co -ca (**-ci -che**) adj city-planning || f city planning

urbani·tà f (**-tà**) urbanity, civility; city population

urbanizzare [ddzz] tr to urbanize

urba·no -na adj urban; urbane

urètra f urethra

urgènte adj urgent, pressing

urgènza f urgency; **d'urgenza** urgent; emergency (e.g., operation); **fare urgenza** a to urge

ùrgere §276 tr to urge, press || intr to be urgent

urina f urine

urinà·rio -ria adj (**-ri -rie**) urinary

urlare tr to shout; to shout down || intr to howl; to shout, yell

urla·tóre -trice adj screaming || mf screamer; loud singer

ur·lo m howl || m (**-la** fpl) yell, scream

urna f urn; ballot box; (poet) grave; **urne** polls

-uro suf m (chem) **-ide**, e.g., **cloruro** chloride

urología f urology

urrà interj hurrah!

ursóne m Canada porcupine

urtare tr to hit; to bump; to annoy || intr—**urtare contro** to hit, strike against; **urtare in** to hit; to stumble into || ref to get annoyed; to clash; to bump into one another

urto m hit; bump; collision; onslaught; clash, disagreement; **urto di nervi** huff

Uruguai, l' m Uruguay

uruguaia·no -na adj & mf Uruguayan

usanza f usage, custom; habit, practice

usare tr to use, employ; to wear out;

(lit) to frequent; **usare** + inf to be accustomed to + ger || intr to be fashionable; **usare di** to use, employ || ref to become accustomed; **sì usa** + inf it is customary to + inf

usa·to -ta adj used, second-hand; worn; worn-out; (lit) usual || m usage, custom; norm; second-hand goods

usbèr·go m (**-ghi**) hauberk; (fig) shield, protection

uscènte adj ending, terminating; retiring

uscière m receptionist; office boy, errand boy; (coll) court clerk; (coll) bailiff; (coll) tipstaff

ù·scio m (**-sci**) door; **infilar l'uscio** to take French leave; **metter tra l'uscio e il muro** (fig) to corner

uscire §277 intr (ESSERE) to go out, leave; to come out; to flow out; to escape; to turn out, ensue; **essere uscito** to be out; **uscire da** to leave; to run off (the track); **uscire dai gangheri** to get mad; **uscire dal comune** to be out of the ordinary; **uscire dal segno** to go too far; **uscire dal seminato** to go astray; **uscire di mente** a to escape one's mind, e.g., **gli è uscito di mente** it escaped his mind; **uscire di sentimento** to pass out; **uscire di vita** to die; **uscire in** to lead into; **uscire per il rotto della cuffia** to barely make it

uscita f exit; outlay; quip, sally; gate (e.g., in an airport); (gram) ending; **all'uscita** on the way out; **buona uscita** severance pay; bonus; **libera uscita** day off (of servant); (mil) pass; **uscita di sicurezza** emergency exit

usignòlo m nightingale

u·so -sa adj (lit) accustomed || m practice; usage; use; wear; faculty; power (e.g., of hearing); (lit) intimate relations; **all'uso di** in the fashion of; **avere per uso di** to be wont to; **come d'uso** as usual; **farci l'uso** to get used to it!; **fuori d'uso** worn-out, out of commission; **uso esterno!** (pharm) not to be taken internally!

ustionare (ustióno) tr to burn, scorch

ustióne f burn

usuale adj usual; ordinary, common

usufruire §176 intr—**usufruire di** to have the use of; to enjoy

usura f usury; (mach) wear and tear; **ad usura** abundantly

usu·ràio -ràia (**-rài -ràie**) adj usurious || mf usurer, loanshark

usurpare tr to usurp

utensile adj tool, e.g., **macchina utensile** machine tool || m utensil; tool

utènte m user; customer, consumer

ùtero m uterus, womb

ùtile adj useful; usable; workable; legal, prescribed (e.g., time); **essere utile a** to help; **venire utile** to come in handy || n usefulness; profit, gain

utili·tà f (**-tà**) utility, usefulness; profit, gain

utilitària f economy car, compact

utilizzare [ddzz] tr to utilize

utopìa *f* utopia
utopi·sta *mf* (-sti -ste) utopian
utopìsti·co -ca *adj* (-ci -che) utopian
uva *f* grapes; **un grano di uva passa** a raisin; **uva passa** raisins

uxorici·da *m* (-di) uxoricide || *f* (-de) murderer of one's husband
uxorici·dio *m* (-di) uxoricide; murder of one's husband
ùzzolo [ddzz] *m* whim, fancy, caprice

V

V, v [vu] *m & f* twentieth letter of the Italian alphabet
V. *abbr* (vostro) your
vacante *adj* vacant
vacanza *f* vacancy; vacation; **fare vacanza** to be on vacation; **vacanze** vacation
vacanzière *m* vacationer
vac·ca *f* (-che) cow
vac·càio *m* (-cài) cowboy; stable boy
vaccherìa *f* dairy farm
vacchétta *f* cowhide
vaccina *f* cow manure; cow
vaccinare *tr* to vaccinate
vaccinazióne *f* vaccination
vacci·no -na *adj* cow; bovine || *m* vaccine || *f* see **vaccina**
vacillante *adj* vacillating
vacillare *intr* to totter; to vacillate; to shake; to flicker; to fail, *e.g.*, **la memoria gli vacilla** his memory is failing; **far vacillare** to rock
vacui·tà *f* (-tà) vacuity
và·cuo -cua *adj* empty || *m* vacuum
vademè·cum *m* (-cum) almanac, readyreference handbook
vagabondàg·gio *m* (-gi) vagrancy; wandering; rambling
vagabondare (**vagabóndo**) *intr* to wander, rove
vagabón·do -da *adj* wandering; vagabond || *mf* vagrant, bum, tramp; rover
vagare §209 *intr* to wander, ramble, rove
vagheggiare §290 (**vaghéggio**) *tr* to gaze fondly at; to cherish
vagire §176 *intr* to cry, whimper
vagito *m* cry, whimper
và·glia *m* (-glia) money order || *f*—di **vaglia** worthy, capable
vagliare §280 *tr* to sift, bolt
và·glio *m* (-gli) sieve; **mettere al vaglio** to scrutinize
va·go -ga (-ghi -ghe) *adj* vague; vacant (*stare*) (*lit*) beautiful; (*lit*) roving; (*poet*) desirous || *m* vagueness; (*lit*) rover; (*anat*) vagus
vagonata *f* carload
vagóne *m* (rr) car; **vagone frigorifero** (rr) refrigerator car; **vagone letto** (rr) sleeping car, sleeper; **vagone ristorante** (rr) dining car; **vagone volante** (aer) flying boxcar
vàio vàia (vài vàie) *adj* dark-grey || *m* dark grey; (heral) vair; (zool) Siberian squirrel
vaiòlo *m* smallpox
valan·ga *f* (-ghe) avalanche
valènte *adj* capable, skillful; clever
valentìa *f* skill; cleverness

valentino *m* Valentine (*sweetheart*)
valènza *f* (chem) valence
valére §278 *tr* to win, get (*e.g., an honor for s.o.*); **che vale?** what's the use?; **valere la pena** to be worthwhile; **valere un Perù** to be worth a king's ransom || *intr* (ESSERE & AVERE) to be worth; to be of avail; to be valid; to mean; to be the equivalent; **far valere** to enforce; **farsi valere** to assert oneself; **tanto vale** it's all the same; **vale a dire** that is to say; **valere meglio** to be better || *ref*—**valersi di** to avail oneself of; to play on; to employ
valévole *adj* valid, good
valicare §197 (**vàlico**) *tr* to cross, pass
vàli·co *m* (-chi) mountain pass; passage; opening (*in a hedge*)
validi·tà *f* (-tà) validity
vàli·do -da *adj* valid; able, able-bodied; strong
valigerìa *f* luggage; luggage store
valigétta *f* valise; **valigetta diplomatica** attaché case
vali·gia *f* (-ge) suitcase; traveling bag; **fare le valige** to pack one's bags; **valigia diplomatica** diplomatic pouch; attaché case; **valigia per abiti** suit carrier
vallata *f* valley
valle *f* valley; **a valle** downhill; downstream
vallétta *f* (telv) assistant
vallétto *m* valet; page; (telv) assistant
valló·ne -na *adj & mf* Walloon || *m* narrow valley
valóre *m* value; valor, bravery; force; (fig) jewel; (math) variable; **mettere in valore** to raise the value of; **valore di mercato** market value; **valore facciale** face value; **valore locativo** rental value; **valori valuables**; securities; **valori mobiliari** securities
valorizzare [ddzz] *tr* to enhance the value of
valoró·so -sa [s] *adj* brave, valiant
valuta *f* currency; (com) effective date; (com) value (*of promissory note*)
valutare *tr* to estimate, appraise; to value, prize; to count, reckon; to take into consideration
valutazióne *f* estimation, appraisal; evaluation
valva *f* (bot, zool) valve
vàlvola *f* (anat, mach) valve; (elec) fuse; (rad, telv) tube, valve; **valvola a galleggiante** ball cock; **valvola di sicurezza** safety valve; **valvola in testa** overhead valve
vàl·zer *m* (-zer) waltz

vamp f (vamp) vamp

vampa f flame; blaze; flash; flush

vampata f burst (of heat); blast (of hot air); flash, flush

vampiro m vampire

vanàdio m vanadium

vanaglòria f vainglory, boastfulness

vanaglorió·so -sa [s] adj vainglorious

vandalismo m vandalism

vànda·lo -la adj & m vandal || **Vandalo** m Vandal

vaneggiare §290 (**vanéggio**) intr to rave; to be delirious; (lit) to open, yawn

vanè·sio -sia adj (-si -sie) vain

van·ga f (-ghe) spade

vangare §209 tr to spade up; to dig with a spade

vangèlo m gospel || **Vangelo** m Gospel

vanghétto m spud

vaniglia f vanilla

vanilò·quio m (-qui) empty talk

vani·tà f (-tà) vanity

vanitó·so -sa [s] adj vain, conceited

va·no -na adj vain; (lit) empty, hollow; **in vano** in vain || m empty space; room

vantàg·gio m (-gi) advantage; profit; odds, handicap; discount; (coll) extra; (typ) galley; **a vantaggio di** on behalf of

vantaggió·so -sa [s] adj advantageous

vantare tr to boast of; to set up (a claim) || ref to boast; **vantarsi di** to brag about, vaunt

vanteria f brag, boast, vaunt

vanto m brag, boast; **aver vanto su** (lit) to overcome

vànvera f—a vanvera at random

vapóre m vapor; steam; locomotive; steamship; **a tutto vapore** at full speed

vaporétto m small river boat; vaporetto (in Venice)

vaporizzare [ddzz] tr to vaporize; to spray || intr (ESSERE) & ref to evaporate

vaporizzatóre [ddzz] m vaporizer; sprayer

vaporó·so -sa [s] adj vaporous

varaménto m assemblage (of prefab pieces)

varano m monitor lizard

varare tr to launch; to pass (a law); (coll) to back, promote (a candidate)

varcare §197 tr to cross || intr (poet) to pass (said of time)

var·co m (-chi) opening; mountain pass; breach; **attendere al varco** to lie in wait for; **cogliere al varco** to catch unawares; **fare varco in** to breach

varechina f (laundry) bleach

variàbile adj & f variable

variante f variant; detour; (aut) model

variare §287 tr & intr (ESSERE & AVERE) to vary

variazióne f variation

varicèlla f chicken pox

varicó·so -sa [s] adj varicose

variega·to -ta adj variegated

varie·tà m (-tà) (theat) vaudeville || f variety

và·rio -ria (-ri -rie) adj varied; various; variable; different; **va·ri -rie** several || m variety || **varie** fpl miscellanies || **va·ri -rie** pron indef several

variopìn·to -ta adj multicolored

varo m (naut) launch

vas m (vas) subchaser

va·sàio m (-sài) potter

va·sca f (-sche) tub; basin; pool; **vasca da bagno** bathtub; **vasca dei pesci** aquarium; **vasca navale** (naut) basin

vascèllo m vessel, ship

vaselina or **vaselìna** f vaseline

vasellame m dishes; set of dishes; **vasellame da cucina** kitchen ware; **vasellame d'argento** silverware; **vasellame di porcellana** chinaware

vasèllo m (lit) vessel

vasi·stas [s] m (-stas) transom

vaso m vase; vessel; jar, pot; nave (of church); hall (of building); (naut) shipway; (poet) cup; **vasi vinari** wine containers; **vaso da fiori** flowerpot; **vaso da notte** chamber pot; **vaso d'elezione** (eccl) chosen vessel (viz., Saint Paul)

vassallo m vassal; (obs) helper

vas·sóio m (-sói) tray; mortarboard

vasti·tà f (-tà) vastness

va·sto -sta adj spacious; vast; (fig) deep

vate m (lit) prophet, poet

vatica·no -na adj Vatican || **Vaticano** m Vatican

vaticinare (**vaticìno** & **vaticìno**) tr to prophesy

vatici·nio m (-ni) prophecy

ve §5 pron

V.E. abbr (Vostra Eccellenza) Your Excellency

vècchia f old woman

vecchiàia f old age

vecchiézza f old age

vèc·chio -chia (-chi -chie) adj old; elder; **vecchio come il cucco** as old as the hills || m old man; **vecchi** old people; **vecchio del mestiere** old hand || f see vecchia

véc·cia f (-ce) vetch

véce f stead, e.g., **in vece mia** in my stead; (lit) vicissitude; **fare le veci di** to act for or as

vedére m seeing; looks; view, opinion || §279 tr to see; to review; to look over; **chi s'è visto s'è visto!** good-by and good luck!; **dare a vedere** to make believe; **stare a vedere** to watch; observe; **non poter vedere** to not be able to stand; **non vedere l'ora di** to be hardly able to wait for; **vedere male qlcu** to be ill-disposed toward s.o. || intr—**stare a vedere** to wait and see; **vederci bene** to see (e.g., in the dark); **vederci chiaro** to look into it; **vedere di** to try to || ref to see oneself; to see each other; **vedersela brutta** to anticipate trouble

vedétta f lookout; (nav) vedette

védova f widow

vedovanza f widowhood

vedovile adj widow's; widower's || m dower

védo·vo -va *adj* widowed ‖ *m* widower ‖ *f* see **vedova**

veduta *f* view; (lit) eyesight; **di corte vedute** narrowminded; **di larghe vedute** broadminded

veemènte *adj* vehement; violent; impassioned

veemènza *f* vehemence; violence

vegetale *adj* vegetable ‖ *m* plant, vegetable

vegetare (végeto) *intr* to vegetate

vegetaria·no -na *adj* & *mf* vegetarian

vegetazióne *f* vegetation

vège·to -ta *adj* vigorous, spry

veggènte *adj* (obs) seeing ‖ *mf* fortuneteller ‖ *m* seer, prophet; **i veggenti** people having eyesight ‖ *f* seeress, prophetess

véglia *f* vigil, watch; wakefulness; evening party, soirée; party, crowd; **a veglia** unbelievable (*tale*); **veglia danzante** dance; **veglia funebre** wake

vegliardo *m* old man

vegliare §280 (véglio) *tr* to keep watch over ‖ *intr* to stay awake; to keep watch; to stay up

vegliόne *m* masked ball

veicolo *m* vehicle; carrier (*of disease*)

véla *f* sail; sailing; **alzare le vele** to set sail; **ammainare le vele** to take in sail; **a vela** under sail; **far vela** to set sail; **vela aurica** lugsail; **vela bermudiana** or **Marconi** jib; **vela maestra** mainsail

ve·làio *m* (**-lài**) sailmaker

velare *adj* & *f* (phonet) velar ‖ *v* (**vélo**) *tr* to veil; to cover; to muffle (*sound*); to attenuate, reduce (*a shock*); to dim, cloud; to conceal; (phot) to fog ‖ *ref* to cover oneself with a veil; to take the veil; to get dim, e.g., **gli si è velata la vista** his eyesight got dim

velà·rio *m* (**-ri**) (hist) velarium; (theat) curtain

vela·to -ta *adj* veiled; sheer (*hosiery*)

velatura *f* coating; (aer) airfoil; (naut) sails

veleggiare §290 (veléggio) *tr* (lit) to sail over (*the sea*) ‖ *intr* to sail; (aer) to glide

veleggiatóre *m* sailboat; (aer) glider

veléno *m* poison; (fig) venom

velenó·so -sa [s] *adj* poisonous; (fig) venomous

velétta *f* veil; (naut) topgallant

vèli·co -ca *adj* (**-ci -che**) sail, sailing

velièro *m* sailing ship

veli·no -na *adj* thin (*paper*) ‖ *f* carbon copy; onionskin; slant (*given to a news item*)

velìvo·lo -la *adj* (lit) gliding; (lit) sailing ‖ *m* (lit) airplane, aircraft

velleità *f* (**-tà**) wild ambition, dream

vellicare §197 (vèllico) *tr* to tickle

vèllo *m* (lit) fleece; **vello d'oro** Golden Fleece

velló·so -sa [s] *adj* hairy

velluta·to -ta *adj* velvety

vellutino *m* thin velvet; velvet ribbon; **vellutino di cotone** velveteen

vellu·to -ta *adj* (lit) hairy ‖ *m* velvet; **velluto a coste** corduroy

vélo *m* veil; coating; film; skin (*e.g., of onion*); (anat, bot) velum; (fig) body; **fare velo a** to becloud; to fog

velóce *adj* speedy, quick, fast; fleeting

velocipedastro *m* poor or reckless bicycle rider

veloci·sta *mf* (**-sti -ste**) (sports) sprinter

veloci·tà *f* (**-tà**) velocity; speed; (aut) speed; **a grande velocità** by express; **a piccola velocità** by freight; **velocità di crociera** cruising speed; **velocità di fuga** (rok) escape velocity

velòdromo *m* bicycle ring or track

véna *f* vein; grain (*in wood or stone*); mood; streak (*of madness*); **di vena** willingly; **essere in vena di** to be in the mood to

venale *adj* venal

venare (véno) *tr* to vein

vena·to -ta *adj* veined; streaked; suffused; **venato di sangue** bloodshot

venatura *f* veining; (fig) streak

vendémmia *f* vintage

vendemmiare §287 (vendémmio) *tr* to harvest (*grapes*) ‖ *intr* to gather grapes; (fig) to make a killing

vendemmia·tóre -trice *mf* vintager

véndere §281 *tr* to sell; **da vendere** plenty, more than enough; **vendere allo scoperto** (fin) to sell short; **vendere fumo** to peddle influence ‖ *intr* to sell; **vendere allo scoperto** (fin) to sell short ‖ *ref* to sell; **si vende** for sale

vendétta *f* vengeance; revenge; **gridare vendetta** to cry out for retribution

vendicare §197 (véndico) *tr* to avenge ‖ *ref* to get revenge

vendicati·vo -va *adj* vengeful, vindictive

vendica·tóre -trice *adj* avenging ‖ *mf* avenger

vendifu·mo *mf* (**-mo**) influence peddler

véndita *f* sale; shop; **in vendita** for sale; **vendita allo scoperto** (fin) short sale; **vendita per corrispondenza** catalogue sale

vendi·tóre -trice *mf* seller; clerk (*in store*) ‖ *m* salesman; **venditore ambulante** peddler; **venditore di fumo** influence peddler ‖ *f* saleslady

venefi·cio *m* (**-ci**) poisoning

venèfi·co -ca *adj* (**-ci -che**) *adj* poisonous; unhealthy ‖ *m* (lit) poisonmaker

veneràbile or **venerando** *adj* venerable

venerare (vènero) *tr* to venerate, revere; to worship

venerazióne *f* veneration; worship

vener·dì *m* (**-dì**) Friday ‖ **Venerdì Santo** Good Friday

Vènere *m* (astr) Venus ‖ *f* (mythol & fig) Venus

venè·reo -rea *adj* (**-rei -ree**) venereal

Venèzia *f* Venice; Venetia (*province*)

venezia·no -na *adj* & *mf* Venetian ‖ *f* Venetian blind

venezola·no -na *adj* & *mf* Venezuelan

vènia *f* (lit) forgiveness, pardon

venire §282 *intr* (ESSERE) to come; to turn out (*well or badly*); to turn out to be; **che viene** next, e.g., **il mese che viene** next month; **come viene** as it is; **far venire** to send for; to give, cause; **un va e vieni** a backward-and-forward motion; **venire** + *ger* to keep + *ger*; **venire** + *pp* to be + *pp*, e.g., **il portone viene aperto alle tre** the gate is opened at three; **venire a capo di** to solve; **venire ai ferri corti** to come into open conflict; **venire al dunque** or **al fatto** to come to the point; **venire alle corte** to get down to brass tacks; **venire alle mani** or **alle prese** to come to blows; **venire a parole** to have words; **venire a patti con** to come to terms with; **venire a proposito** to come in handy; **venire incontro a** to go to meet; **venire in possesso di** to come into possession of (*s.th*); to come into the hands of (*s.o.*); **venire meno** to faint; **venir meno a** to fail to keep (*one's word*); **venir su** to grow, come up; **venire via** to give way || *ref*—**venìrsene** to stroll along || *impers* (with *dat*)—**viene da** feel the urge to, e.g., **gli venne da starnutire** he felt the urge to sneeze; **gli è venuto da ridere** he felt the urge to laugh; **viene detto** blurt out, e.g., **gli è venuto detto che non gli piaceva quel tipo** he blurted out that he did not like that fellow; **viene fatto di** + *inf* succeed in + *ger*, e.g., **le venne fatto di convincerli** she succeeded in convincing them; **happen to** + *inf*, e.g., **gli venne fatto di incontrarmi per istrada** he happened to meet me on the way

ventà·glio *m* (**-gli**) fan; (*fig*) spread; **a ventaglio** fanlike; **diramarsi a ventaglio** to fan out

ventaròla *f* weather vane

ventata *f* gust of wind; (*fig*) wave

ventènne *adj* twenty-year-old || *mf* twenty-year-old person

ventèsi·mo -ma *adj*, *m & pron* twentieth

vénti *adj & pron* twenty; **le venti** eight P.M. || *m* twenty; twentieth (*in dates*)

ventidue *adj & pron* twenty-two **le ventidue** ten P.M. || *m* twenty-two; twenty-second (*in dates*)

ventilare (**vèntilo**) *tr* to air, ventilate; to winnow (*grain*); to discuss minutely; to air (*a subject*); to broach (*a subject*); to unfurl (*a flag*) || *ref* to fan oneself

ventilatore *m* fan, ventilator; vent; (min) ventilation shaft; (naut) funnel

ventilazióne *f* ventilation; winnowing

ventina *f* score; **una ventina (di)** twenty, about twenty

ventino *m* twenty-cent coin

ventiquattro *adj & pron* twenty-four; **le ventiquattro** twelve P.M. || *m* twenty-four; twenty-fourth (*in dates*)

ventiquattró·re *f* (**-re**) overnight bag; twenty-four-hour race; **ventiquattrore** *fpl* period of twenty-four hours

ventitré *adj & pron* twenty-three; **le ventitré** eleven P.M.; **portare il cappello alle ventitré** to wear one's hat cocked || *m* twenty-three; twenty-third (*in dates*)

vènto *m* wind; air; guy wire; **presentarsi al vento** to sail into the wind; **farsi vento** to fan oneself; **a vento** windproof; wind-propelled; **col vento in prora** downwind; **col vento in poppa** upwind; favorably, famously

vèntola *f* fireside fan; lampshade; candle sconce; blade (*of fan*)

ventó·so -sa [s] *adj* windy || *f* cupping glass; suction cup; (zool) sucker

vèntre *m* belly; **a ventre a terra** on one's belly; on one's face; at full speed (*said of a horse*)

ventrìcolo *m* ventricle

ventrièra *f* abdominal band or belt

ventrilòquia *f* ventriloquism

ventrìlo·quo -qua *mf* ventriloquist

ventuno *adj & pron* twenty-one; **le ventuno** nine P.M. || *m* twenty-one; twenty-first (*in dates*); (cards) blackjack

ventù·ro -ra *adj* next || *f* (lit) luck, fortune; (lit) good fortune; **alla ventura** at random, at a venture; **di ventura** of fortune, e.g., **soldato di ventura** soldier of fortune

venustà *f* (lit) pulchritude

venu·to -ta *mf*—**nuovo venuto** newcomer; **primo venuto** firstcomer || *f* coming, arrival

véra *f* curbstone (*of well*); (coll) wedding ring

verace *adj* true; truthful, veracious

veraci·tà *f* (**-tà**) veracity, truthfulness

veranda *f* veranda; porch

verbale *adj* verbal || *m* minutes; ticket (*given by a policeman*); **mettere a verbale** to enter into the record

verbèna *f* verbena

vèrbo *m* verb; (lit) word || **Verbo** *m* (theol) Word

verbosità [s] *f* verbiage, verbosity

verbó·so -sa [s] *adj* windy, long-winded, verbose

verda·stro -stra *adj* greenish

vérde *adj* green; young, youthful || *m* green; **al verde** (coll) broke, penniless; **nel verde degli anni** in the prime of life

verdeggiante *adj* verdant

verderame *m* blue vitriol; verdigris

verdét·to -ta *adj* greenish || *m* verdict

verdógno·lo -la *adj* greenish; sallow (*face*)

verdura *f* vegetables

verecóndia *f* modesty, bashfulness

verecón·do -da *adj* modest, bashful

vér·ga *f* (**-ghe**) switch; rod; ingot, bar; pole; penis; (eccl) staff, crosier; (naut) yard; **tremare a verga a verga** to shake like a leaf

vergare §209 (**vérgo**) *tr* to switch; to rule (*paper*); to stripe; to write

vergati·no -na *adj* thin (*paper*) || *m* striped cloth

verga·to -ta *adj* striped; watermarked with stripes || *m* (obs) serge

verginale *adj* maidenly, virginal

vérgine *adj & f* virgin || **Vergine** *f* (eccl) Virgin; (astr) Virgo

verginità *f* virginity, maidenhood

vergógna *f* shame; **aver vergogna** to be

ashamed; **vergogne** privates ‖ *interj* for shame!

vergognare (vergógno) *ref* to be ashamed; to feel cheap; **vergognati!** shame on you!

vergognó·so -sa [s] *adj* ashamed; bashful; shameful

veridici·tà *f* (-tà) veracity

verìdi·co -ca *adj* (-ci -che) veracious

verìfi·ca *f* (-che) verification; control; **verifica fiscale** auditing (*of tax return*)

verificare §197 (verìfico) *tr* to verify; to control, check; to audit ‖ *ref* to come true; to happen

verifica·tóre -trice *mf* checker, inspector

verismo *m* verism (*as developed in Italy*)

veri·sta *adj & mf* (-sti -ste) verist

veri·tà *f* (-tà) truth; **in verità** truthfully, verily

veritiè·ro -ra *adj* truthful

vèrme *m* worm; (mach) thread; **verme solitario** tapeworm

vermì·glio -glia (-gli -glie) *adj* vermilion; ruby (*lips*) ‖ *m* vermilion

vèr·mut *m* (-mut) vermouth

vernàcolo *m* vernacular

vernìce *f* varnish; paint; polish; patina; (painting) private viewing; (fig) veneer; **scarpe di vernice** patent-leather shoes; **vernice a olio** oil paint; **vernice a spruzzo** spray paint; **vernice da scarpe** shoe polish

verniciare §128 *tr* to varnish; to paint

vé·ro -ra *adj* true; real; right; pure; **non è vero?** isn't that so? La traduzione precedente è generalmente rimpiazzata da molte altre frasi. Se la prima espressione è negativa, la domanda equivalente a **non è vero?** sarà affermativa, per esempio, **Lei non lavora, non è vero?** You are not working, are you? Se la prima espressione è affermativa, la domanda sarà negativa, per esempio, **Lei lavora, non è vero?** You are working, are you not? or aren't you? Se la prima espressione contiene un ausiliare, la domanda conterrà l'ausiliare stesso senza infinito o senza participio passato, per esempio, **Arriveranno domani, non è vero?** They will arrive tomorrow, won't they? **Ha finito il compito, non è vero?** He has finished his homework, hasn't he? Se la prima espressione non contiene né un ausiliare, né una delle forme del verbo "to be" in funzione di copula, la domanda conterrà l'ausiliare "do" o "did" senza l'infinito del verbo, per esempio, **Lei è vissuto a Milano, non è vero?** You lived in Milano, did you not? **Lei non va mai al parco, non è vero?** You never go to the park, do you?; **non mi par vero** it seems unbelievable ‖ *m* truth; actuality; **a dire il vero** to tell the truth, as a matter of fact; **dal vero** from nature; **salvo il vero** if I am not mistaken ‖ *f* see **vera**

veróne *m* (lit) balcony

verosimiglianza *f* verisimilitude; probability, likelihood

verosìmile *adj* verisimilar; probable, likely

verricèllo *m* winch, windlass

vèrro *m* boar

verru·ca *f* (-che) wart

versaménto *m* spilling; payment; deposit

versante *m* depositor; slope, side

versare (vèrso) *tr* to pour; to spill; to shed; to pay; to deposit ‖ *intr* to overflow; **versare in gravi condizioni** to be in a bad way ‖ *ref* to spill; to pour (*said of people*); to empty (*said of a river*)

versàtile *adj* versatile; fickle

versa·to -ta *adj* versed; gifted; fully subscribed to (*e.g.*, *stock of a corporation*)

verseggia·tóre -trice *mf* verse writer

versétto *m* verse (*of Bible*)

versificare §197 (versìfico) *tr & intr* to versify

versificazióne *f* versification

versióne *f* version; translation

vèrso *adj* *invar*—**pollice verso** (hist) thumbs down ‖ *m* verse; local accent; voice, cry; reverse (*of coin*); **verso** (*of page*); line (*of poetry*); singsong; gesture; direction, way, manner; respect; **andare a verso** (with *dat*) to suit, to please; **le sue maniere non gli vanno a verso** her manners do not suit him; **a verso** properly; **contro verso** against the grain; **fare un verso** to make faces; **per un verso** on one hand; **rifare il verso** (with *dat*) to mimick; **senza verso** without rhyme or reason; **verso sciolto** blank verse ‖ *prep* toward; near, around; about; for, toward; upon, in return for; as compared with; **verso di** toward

vèrtebra *f* vertebra

vertebrale *adj* vertebral; spinal

vertebra·to -ta *adj & m* vertebrate

vertènza *f* quarrel, dispute; **vertenza sindacale** labor dispute

vèrtere §283 *intr*—**vertere su** to deal with, to turn on

verticale *adj & f* vertical

vèrtice *m* top, summit; vertex; summit conference

vertìgine *f* vertigo, dizziness; **avere le vertigini** to feel dizzy

vertiginó·so -sa [s] *adj* dizzy; breathtaking

vérza [dz] *f* cabbage

verzière [dz] *m* (lit) fruit, vegetable, and flower garden; (coll) produce market

verzura [dz] *f* verdure

vescì·ca *f* (-che) bladder; blister; **vescica di vento** (fig) windbag; **vescica gonfiata** swellhead; **vescica natatoria** air bladder

vescichétta *f* blister; vescicle; **vescichetta biliare** gall bladder

vescìcola *f* blister

vescovado *m* bishopric

véscovo *m* bishop

vè·spa f wasp, yellowjacket ‖ f (-spe & -spa) motor scooter

ve·spàio m (-spài) wasp's nest; (fig) hornet's nest

vespasiano m public urinal

Vèspero m Vesper

vesperti·no -na adj (lit) evening

vèspro m (eccl) vespers; (lit) vespertide

vessare (vèsso) tr (lit) to oppress

vessatò·rio -ria adj (-ri -rie) vexatious

vessazióne f oppression

vessillo m flag

vestàglia f negligee, dressing gown; **vestaglia da bagno** bathrobe

vèste f dress; cover; (lit) body; **in veste di** in the quality of; as; in the guise of; **veste da camera** negligee, dressing gown; bathrobe; **veste talare** (eccl) long vestment; **vesti** clothes

vestià·rio m (-ri) wardrobe

vestìbolo m vestibule, lobby

vestì·gio m (-gi & -gia fpl) vestige, trace; (lit) footprint

vestire (vèsto) tr to dress; to don; to wear; to clothe; to cover, bedeck ‖ intr to dress; to fit ‖ ref to get dressed; to dress; to dress oneself; to buy one's own clothes

vestì·to -ta adj dressed; covered ‖ m dress; suit; clothing; **vestiti** clothes; **vestito da donna** dress; **vestito da festa** Sunday best; **vestito da sera** evening clothes, formal suit; evening gown; **vestito da uomo** suit

Vesùvio, il Vesuvius

vetera·no -na adj & mf veteran

veterinà·rio -ria (-ri -rie) adj veterinary ‖ m veterinarian ‖ f veterinary medicine

vèto m veto; **porre il veto a** to veto

ve·tràio m (-trài) glass manufacturer; glass dealer; glass blower

vetra·to -ta adj glass, glass-enclosed; sand (paper) ‖ m glare ice, glaze ‖ f glass door; glass window; glass enclosure; **vetrata a colori** or **vetrata istoriata** stained-glass window

vetrerìa f glassworks; **vetrerie** glassware

vetria·to -ta adj glassy; glass-covered

vetrificare §197 (vetrìfico) tr to vitrify ‖ ref to become vitrified

vetrina f show window; showcase, glass cabinet; **mettersi in vetrina** to show off; **vetrine** (coll) eyeglasses

vetrini·sta mf (-sti -ste) window dresser

vetri·no -na adj glass-like; brittle, fragile ‖ m slide (of microscope) ‖ f see **vetrina**

vetriòlo m vitriol

vétro m glass; glassware; window pane; piece of glass; **vetro aderente** contact lens; **vetro infrangibile** (aut) safety glass; **vetro smerigliato** ground glass, frosted glass

vetrorèsina f fiberglass

vetró·so -sa [s] adj vitreous, glassy

vétta f peak; top, tip; limb (of tree); (naut) end (of hawser); **tremare come una vetta** to shake like a leaf

vet·tóre -trice adj leading, guiding; spreading, carrying ‖ m carrier; (math, phys) vector

vettovagliare §280 tr to supply with food

vettovàglie fpl victuals, food; supplies

vettura f forwarding; coach; car; freight; **in vettura!** (rr) all aboard!; **prendere in vettura** to hire (a conveyance); **vettura belvedere** (rr) observation car; **vettura da turismo** (aut) pleasure car; **vettura di piazza** hack, hackney; **vettura letto** (rr) sleeping car; **vettura ristorante** (rr) diner

vetturétta f economy car, compact

vetturino m hackman, cab driver

vetu·sto -sta adj old, ancient

vezzeggiare §290 (vezzéggio) tr to coddle ‖ intr (lit) to strut

vezzeggiatì·vo -va adj endearing ‖ m endearing expression; diminutive

vézzo m habit; caress; necklace; bad habit; **vezzi** fondling, petting; mawkish behavior; charms

vezzó·so -sa [s] adj graceful, charming; affected, mincing

vi §5

via m (via) starting signal; **dare il via a** to give the go-ahead to ‖ f street; road, way; route; career; **dare la via a** to open the way to; **in via confidenziale** in confidence; **in via eccezionale** as an exception; **per via di** via, through; (coll) because of; **per via gerarchica** through administrative channels; **per via orale** orally; **per via rettale** rectally; **prendere la via** to be on one's way; **venire a vie di fatto** to come to blows; **Via Crucis** Way of the Cross; **via d'acqua** waterway; **via di scampo** (fig) way out; **via d'uscita** way out; **Via Lattea** Milky Way; **vie di fatto** assault and battery; **vie legali** legal steps ‖ adv away; (math) times, by; e **così via** and so on; e **via dicendo** and so on; **tirar via** to hurry along; **via via che** as ‖ prep via, by way of

viadótto m viaduct

viaggiare §290 intr to travel; (com) to deal

viaggia·tóre -trice adj traveling; homing (pigeon) ‖ mf traveler ‖ m traveling salesman

viàg·gio m (-gi) travel; journey, trip; **buon viaggio!** bon voyage!; **viaggio d'andata e ritorno** round trip; **viaggio di prova** (naut) trial run, shakedown cruise

viale m boulevard

viandante mf (lit) wayfarer

vià·rio -ria adj (-ri -rie) road, highway

viàti·co m (-ci) viaticum

viavài m coming and going; hustle and bustle

vibrante adj vibrant; wiry; (phonet) vibrant ‖ f (phonet) trill, vibrant

vibrare tr to jar; to deliver (a blow); to vibrate; (lit) to hurl ‖ intr to vibrate

vibra·to -ta adj vibrant; resolute, vigorous ‖ m vibrating sound

vibrazióne f vibration

vicariato m vicarage

vicà·rio m (-ri) vicar

vice- pref adj vice-, e.g., **vicereale** viceroyal ‖ pref m & f vice-, e.g., **viceammiraglio** vice-admiral; assistant, e.g., **vicegovernatore** assistant governor; deputy, e.g., **vicesindaco** deputy mayor

vicediret·tóre -trice mf assistant manager

vicènda f vicissitude; rotation (of crops); **a vicenda** in turn

vicendévole adj mutual, reciprocal

vicepresidènte [s] mf vice president

vice·ré m (-ré) viceroy

vicevèrsa adv vice versa; (coll) instead, on the contrary

vichin·go -ga adj & mf (-ghi -ghe) Viking

vicinànza f nearness; **in vicinanza di** in the neighborhood of; **vicinanze** vicinity, neighborhood

vicinato m neighborhood

vici·no -na adj near; neighboring; next; close (relative) ‖ mf neighbor ‖ **vicino** adv nearby, near; **da vicino** closely; at close quarters; **vicino a** near; next to, close to

vicissitùdine f vicissitude

vi·co m (-chi) alley, lane; village; (lit) region

vicolo m alley, court, place; **vicolo cieco** blind alley, dead end

videocassétta f video cassette

vidimare (**vìdimo**) tr to validate, visa; to sign

vidimazióne f validation, visa; signature

viennése [s] adj & mf Viennese

viepiù adv (lit) more and more

vietare (**vièto**) tr to forbid, prohibit

vieta·to -ta adj forbidden; **senso vietato** one way; **sosta vietata** no parking; no stopping; **vietato fumare** no smoking

Vietnam, il Vietnam

vietnami·ta adj & mf (-ti -te) Vietnamese

viè·to -ta adj (lit) old-fashioned; (coll) musty-smelling, rancid

vigènte adj current, in force

vigere §284 intr to be in force

vigèsi·mo -ma adj twentieth

vigilante adj watchful, vigilant ‖ m watchman

vigilànza f vigilance; surveillance

vigilare (**vìgilo**) tr to watch; to watch over; to police ‖ intr to watch; **vigilare che** to see to it that

vigila·tóre -trice mf inspector ‖ f camp counselor; **vigilatrice sanitaria** child health inspector

vìgile adj (lit) watchful ‖ m watch; **vigile del fuoco** fireman; **vigile urbano** policeman

vigilia f fast; vigil; **la vigilia di** on the eve of, the night before

vigliaccheria f cowardice

vigliac·co -ca (-chi -che) adj cowardly ‖ m coward

vigna f vineyard

vignaiòlo m vine dresser

vignéto m vineyard

vignétta f vignette; **vignetta umoristica** cartoon

vignetti·sta mf (-sti -ste) cartoonist

vigógna f vicuña

vigóre m vigor; **in vigore** in force

vigoria f vigor

vigoró·so -sa [s] adj vigorous

vile adj cowardly; vile, low, cheap; base (metal)

vilificare §197 (**vilìfico**) tr to vilify

vilipèndere §148 tr to despise; to show scorn for

villa f villa; country house; one-family detached house; (lit) country

villàg·gio m (-gi) village; **villaggio del fanciullo** boys' town

villanata f boorishness

villania f boorishness, rudeness; insult

villa·no -na adj rude, churlish ‖ mf boor, churl; (lit) peasant

villanzó·ne -na mf boor, uncouth person

villeggiante mf vacationist

villeggiare §290 (**villéggio**) intr to vacation

villeggiatura f vacation, summer vacation

villétta f or **villino** m bungalow

villó·so -sa [s] adj hairy

vil·tà f (-tà) baseness; cowardice

viluppo m tangle, twist

vimine m withe, wicker, osier

vinàcce fpl pressed grapes

vi·nàio m (-nài) wine merchant

vincènte adj winning ‖ mf winner

vincere §285 tr to overcome; to win; to convince; to check; to defeat; **vincere per un pelo** to nose out; **vinceria** to come out on top ‖ ref to control oneself

vincetòssi·co m (-ci) swallowwort, tame poison

vincipèr·di m (-di) giveaway

vincita f gain; winnings

vinci·tóre -trice adj conquering, victorious ‖ mf winner; conqueror; victor

vincolare adj binding; bound ‖ v (**vìncolo**) tr to tie; to bind, obligate; to restrict the use of (real-estate property)

vincolo m tie, bond; (law) entail; (law) restriction (in a real-estate deed)

vinico·lo -la adj wine, wine-producing

vinile m vinyl

vino m wine; **vin caldo** mulled wine; **vino da pasto** table wine; **vino di marca** vintage wine; **vino di mele** cider

vin·to -ta adj vanquished, overcome, defeated; victorious (battle); **averla vinta su** to overcome; **darla vinta a qlcu** to let s.o. get away with murder; **darsi per vinto** to give in, yield ‖ m vanquished person; **i vinti** the vanquished

viò·la adj invar violet ‖ m (-la) violet (color) ‖ f violet; (mus) viola; **viola del pensiero** pansy; **viola mammola** sweet violet

violacciòc·ca f (-che) (bot) wallflower

violà·ceo -cea adj violet

violare (**vìolo**) tr to violate; to run (a blockade)

violazióne f violation; **violazione di**

domicilio housebreaking, burglary; violazione di proprietà trespass

violentare (violènto) tr to violate, force; to do violence to; to rape

violèn•to -ta adj violent ‖ m violent person

violènza f violence; violenza carnale rape

violét•to -ta adj & m violet ‖ f (bot) violet

violini•sta mf (-sti -ste) violinist

violino m violin; primo violino concertmaster

violoncelli•sta mf (-sti -ste) violoncellist

violoncèllo m violoncello, cello

viòttolo m path

vipera f viper, adder

viràg•gio m (-gi) turn; (aer) banking; (naut) tacking; (phot) toning

virare tr to veer; to turn (a winch); (aer) to bank; (phot) to tone ‖ intr to veer, steer; virare di bordo (naut) to put about; (naut) to tack

virata f turn, veer; (aer) banking; (naut) tacking

virginale adj var of verginale

virgi•nia m (-nia) Virginia tobacco ‖ f (-nia) Virginia cigarette

vìrgola f comma; (used in Italian to set off the decimal fraction from the integer) decimal point; doppia virgola quotation mark

virgolétta f quotation mark

virgulto m (lit) shoot; (lit) shrub

virile adj virile

virilità f virility

viròla f (mach) male piece

virologia f virology

vir•tù f (-tù) virtue; (lit) valor

virtuale adj virtual

virtualménte adv virtually, to all intents and purposes

virtuosismo [s] m virtuosity; showing off

virtuosità [s] f virtuosity

virtuó•so -sa [s] adj virtuous ‖ mf virtuoso

virulèn•to -ta adj virulent

virulènza f virulence

vi•rus m (-rus) virus

vìsce•re m (-ri) internal organ; visceri entrails, viscera ‖ viscere fpl entrails, viscera; (fig) heart, feeling; (fig) bowels (of the earth)

vì•schio m (-schi) mistletoe; birdlime; (fig) trap

vischió•so -sa [s] adj sticky, viscous; (com) steady

visci•do -da adj viscid; clammy; (fig) unctuous

visciola f sour cherry

visciolo m sour cherry tree

viscónte m viscount

viscontéssa f viscountess

viscó•so -sa [s] adj viscous, sticky ‖ f viscose

visétto m small face; baby face

visibile adj visible; obvious

visibì•lio m (-li) (coll) crowd; (coll) bunch; andare in visibilio to become ecstatic; mandare in visibilio to throw into ecstasy, enrapture

visibilità f visibility

visièra f visor; fencing mask; eyeshade; visiera termica (aut) electric defroster

visigò•to -ta adj Visigothic ‖ mf Visigoth

visionà•rio -ria adj & mf (-ri -rie) visionary

visióne f vision; sight; (mov, telv) showing; in visione gratuita for free examination; mandare qlco a qlcu in visione to send s.th to s.o. for his (or her) opinion; prendere visione di to examine; to peruse

vi•sìr m (-sìr) vizier

visita f visit; visitation; fare una visita to pay a visit; marcare visita (mil) to report sick; visita doganale customs inspection

visitare (vìsito) tr to visit; to inspect

visita•tóre -trice mf visitor ‖ f social worker

visitazióne f visitation

visì•vo -va adj visual

viso m face; far buon viso a cattivo gioco to grin and bear it

visóne m mink

visóre m (phot) viewer; (phot) viewfinder

vì•spo -spa adj brisk, lively

vissù•to -ta adj wordly-wise

vista f sight, eyesight; view; vista; glance; (poet) window; a vista exposed, visible; a vista d'occhio as far as the eye can see; essere in vista to be expected; to be imminent; to be in the limelight; far vista di to pretend to; in vista di in view of; mettere in vista to show off; vista a volo d'uccello bird's-eye view; vista corta poor eyesight

vistare tr to validate, visa

vi•sto -sta adj;—visto che seeing that, inasmuch as ‖ m visa; approval ‖ f see vista

vistó•so -sa [s] adj showy, flashy; (fig) considerable

visuale adj visual ‖ f view; line of sight

visualizzare [ddzz] tr to visualize

vita f life; livelihood; living; waist; avere breve vita to be short-lived; fare la vita to be a prostitute; vita natural durante for life; during one's lifetime

vitaiòlo m man about town; playboy, bon vivant

vitale adj vital

vitalità f vitality

vitali•zio -zia (-zi -zie) adj life, lifetime ‖ m life annuity

vitamina f vitamin

vite f (bot) grapevine; (mach) screw; a vite threaded; (aer) in a tailspin; vite autofilettante self-tapping screw; vite del Canadà woodbine, Virginia creeper; vite per legno wood screw; vite per metallo machine screw; vite perpetua (mach) endless screw, worm gear; vite prigioniera stud bolt

vitèllo m calf; veal

vitìc•cio m (-ci) tendril

vìtre•o -a adj vitreous; glassy (eyes)

vìttima *f* victim

vitto *m* food; diet; **vitto e alloggio** room and board

vittòria *f* victory; **cantar vittoria** to crow; to crow too soon

vittorió·so -sa [s] *adj* victorious

vituperare (**vitùpero**) *tr* to vituperate

vituperévole *adj* contemptible, shameful

vitupè·rio *m* (**-ri**) shame, infamy; insult; (lit) blame

viuzza *f* narrow street, lane

viva *interj* long live!

vivacchiare §287 *intr* (coll) to get along || **ref—si vivacchia** (coll) so, so

vivace *adj* lively, brisk; brilliant; vivacious

vivacità *f* liveliness, briskness; brilliancy, brightness; vivacity

vivaddìo *interj* yes, of course!; by Jove!

vivagno *m* selvage; edge

vi·vàio *m* (**-vài**) fishpond; fish tank; tree nursery; (fig) seedbed

vivanda *f* food

vivandiè·re -ra *mf* (mil) sutler

vivere *m* life; living; cost of living; **viveri** food, provisions; allowance || §286 *tr* to live; **vivere un brutto momento** to spend an uncomfortable moment || *intr* (ESSERE) to live; **vive** (typ) stet; **vivere alla giornata** to live from hand to mouth

vivézza *f* liveliness

vivi·do -da *adj* vivid, lively

vivificare §197 (**vivìfico**) *tr* to vivify

vivisezionare (**viviseziòno**) *tr* to vivisect; to scrutinize

vivisezióne *f* vivisection

vi·vo -va *adj* alive; living; live, vivacious; lively; vivid; high (*flame*); bright (*light*); raw (*flesh*); sharp, acute (*pain*); hearty (*thanks*); outright (*expense*); gross (*weight*); brute (*strength*); modern (*language*); kinetic (*energy*); running (*water*) || *m* living being; heart (*of a question*); **al vivo** lively; lifelike; **i vivi e i morti** the quick and the dead; **toccare nel vivo** to sting to the quick || **viva** *interj* see **viva**

viziare §287 *tr* to spoil; to ruin; (law) to vitiate || *ref* to become spoiled

vizia·to -ta *adj* spoiled; ruined; stale (*air*)

vì·zio *m* (**-zi**) vice; defect; flaw; (law) vitiation

vizió·so -sa [s] *adj* vicious; defective || *mf* profligate

viz·zo -za *adj* withered

vocabolà·rio *m* (**-ri**) dictionary; vocabulary

vocàbolo *m* word

vocale *adj* vocal; (lit) sonorous || *f* vowel

vocalizzare [ddzz] *tr & ref* to vocalize

vocatìvo *m* vocative

vocazióne *f* vocation

vóce *f* voice; noise, roar; word; rumor; entry; tone; **ad alta voce** aloud; **a bassa voce** in a low voice; **a viva voce** by word of mouth; **a voce** orally; **dare una voce a** (coll) to call; **dare sulla voce a** to rebuke; to con-

tradict; **fare la voce grossa** to raise one's voice; **non avere voce in capitolo** to have no say; **schiarirsi la voce** to clear one's throat; **senza voce** hoarse; **sotto voce** in a low tone; **voce bianca** child's voice (*in singing*)

vociare *m* bawl || §128 (**vócio**) *intr* to bawl

vociferare (**vocìfero**) *intr* to vociferate, shout || **ref—si vocifera** it is rumored

vó·ga *f* (**-ghe**) fashion, vogue; energy, enthusiasm; rowing

vogare §209 (**vógo**) *tr & intr* to row

voga·tóre -trice *mf* rower || *m* oarsman; rowing machine

vòglia *f* wish; whim, fancy; willingness; birthmark; **aver voglia di** to feel like, have a notion to; **di buona voglia** willingly; **di mala voglia** unwillingly

voglió·so -sa [s] *adj* fanciful; (lit) desirous

vói §5 *pron pers* you; **voi altri** you, e.g., **voi altri americani** you Americans

voial·tri -tre *pron pl* you, e.g., **voialtri americani** you Americans

volano *m* shuttlecock; (mach) flywheel

volante *adj* flying; loose (*sheet*); free (*agent*) || *m* steering wheel; (mach) hand wheel; shuttlecock

volantino *m* leaflet; fringe; (mach) hand wheel

volare (**vólo**) *tr* (soccer) to overthrow || *intr* (ESSERE & AVERE) to fly

volata *f* flight; sprint; run; mouth (*of gun*); (tennis) volley; **di volata in a** hurry

volàtile *adj* volatile; flying (*animal*) || **volatili** *mpl* birds

volatilizzare [ddzz] *tr & intr* (ESSERE) to volatilize

volènte *adj—***Dio volente** God willing; **volente o nolente** willy-nilly

volentièri *adv* gladly, willingly

volére *m* will, wish; **al volere di** at the bidding of || §288 *tr* to will; to want, desire; (lit) to believe, affirm; **l'hai voluto tu** it's your fault; **non vuol dire!** never mind!; **qui ti voglio** here's the rub, that's the trouble; **senza volere** without meaning to; **voglia Dio!** may God grant!; **voler bene** (with *dat*) to like; **volerci** to take, e.g., **ci vorranno due anni per finire questo palazzo** it will take two years to complete this building; **ce ne vogliono ancora tre** it takes three more of them; **voler dire** to mean; to try, e.g., **vuole piovere** it is trying to rain; **volere che** + *subj* to want + *inf*, e.g., **vuole che vengano** he wants them to come; **volere piuttosto** to prefer; **volere è potere** where there is a will there is a way; **voler male** (with *dat*) to dislike; **volerne a** to bear a grudge against; **vorrei** I should like, I'd like; **vuoi . . . vuoi** either . . . or

volgare *adj* vernacular, popular, common; vulgar || *m* vernacular

volgari·tà *f* (**-tà**) vulgarity

volgarizzare [ddzz] *tr* to popularize

vòlgere §289 *tr* to turn; (lit) to translate || *intr* to turn; (lit) to go by; **volgere a** to turn toward; to draw near, to approach; **volgere in fuga** to take to flight || *ref* to turn; to devote oneself

vól·go *m* (-ghi) (lit) crowd, mob

volièra *f* aviary

voliti·vo -**va** *adj* volitional; strong-minded, strong-willed

vólo *m* flight; fall; **al volo** on the spot; on the wing; **a volo d'uccello** as the crow flies; bird's-eye (*e.g.*, *view*); **di volo** at top speed, immediately; **in volo** aloft, in the air; **prendere il volo** to take flight; **volo a vela** or **volo planato** gliding; **volo strumentale** instrument flying; **volo veleggiato** gliding

volon·tà *f* (-tà) will; **di spontanea volontà** of one's own volition; **pieno di buona volontà** eager to please; **ultime volontà** last will and testament

volontariato *m* volunteer work; apprenticeship without pay; (mil) volunteer service

volontà·rio -**ria** (-ri -rie) *adj* voluntary || *m* volunteer

volonteró·so -**sa** [s] *adj* willing, well-disposed

volpacchiòtto *m* fox cub; (fig) sly fox

vólpe *f* fox; (agr) smut; **volpe argentata** silver fox

volpi·no -**na** *adj* fox; fox-colored; foxy || *m* Pomeranian

volpó·ne -**na** *m f* sly fox

vòlt *m* (vòlt) (elec) volt

vòl·ta *m* (-ta) (elec) volt || *f* turn; time; vault; roof (*of mouth*); **alla volta di** toward; **a volta di corriere** by return mail; **a volte** sometimes; **c'era una volta** once upon a time there was; **certe volte** sometimes; **dare di volta il cervello** to go crazy, e.g., **gli ha dato di volta il cervello** he went crazy; **dar la volta** to turn sour (*said of wine*); **due volte** twice; **molte volte** often; **per una volta tanto** only once; **poche volte** seldom; **tante volte** often; **tutto in una volta** at one swoop, at one stroke; in one gulp, in one swallow; **una volta** once; **una volta che** (coll) inasmuch as; **una volta per sempre** once and for all; **una volta tanto** for once; **volta a crociera** cross vault; **volta per volta** little by little; **volte** (math) times, e.g., **cinque volte cinque** five times five

voltafàc·cia *m* (-cia) volte-face; **fare voltafaccia** to wheel around (*said of a horse*)

voltagabba·na *m f* (-na) turncoat

voltàg·gio *m* (-gi) voltage

voltài·co -**ca** *adj* (-ci -che) voltaic

voltare (vòlto) *tr, intr & ref* to turn

voltastòma·co *m* (-chi) (coll) nausea; **fare venire il voltastomaco a qlcu** (coll) to turn s.o.'s stomach

voltata *f* turn; curve

volteggiare §290 (voltéggio) *tr* to put (*a horse*) through its paces || *intr* to hover; to flit, flutter; (sports) to vault (*e.g.*, *on horseback or trapeze*)

voltég·gio *m* (-gi) (sports) vaulting

vòltmetro *m* voltmeter

vólto *m* (lit) face

voltura *f* (com, law) transfer

volùbile *adj* fickle

volubilità *f* fickleness

volume *m* volume; bulk; mass

voluminó·so -**sa** [s] *adj* voluminous, bulky

volu·to -**ta** *adj* desired; intentional || *f* (archit) volute, scroll

volut·tà *f* (-tà) pleasure, enjoyment; voluptuousness

voluttuà·rio -**ria** *adj* (-ri -rie) luxury (*goods*)

voluttuó·so -**sa** [s] *adj* voluptuous, sensuous

vòmere *m* plowshare; trail spade (*of gun*)

vòmi·co -**ca** *adj* (-ci -che) emetic

vomitare (vòmito) *tr & intr* to vomit

vomitati·vo -**va** *adj & m* emetic

vòmito *m* vomit

vóngola *f* clam

vorace *adj* voracious

voraci·tà *f* (-tà) voracity

voràgine *f* chasm, gulf, abyss

vòrtice *m* vortex, whirlpool; whirlwind

vorticó·so -**sa** [s] *adj* whirling, swirling

vò·stro -**stra** §6 *adj & pron poss*

votare (vóto) *tr* to devote; to vote || *intr* to vote || *ref* to devote oneself

votazióne *f* vote, voting, poll; (educ) grades

voti·vo -**va** *adj* votive

vóto *m* vow; wish; votive offering; vote, ballot; grade, mark; **a pieni voti** with highest honors; **fare un voto** to make a vow; **pronunciare i voti** to take vows; **voto di fiducia** vote of confidence; **voto preferenziale** write-in vote; preferential ballot

vudù *m* voodoo

vudui·sta *m f* (-sti -ste) voodoo (*person*)

vulcàni·co -**ca** *adj* (-ci -che) volcanic

vulcanizzare [ddzz] *tr* to vulcanize

vulcano *m* volcano

vulga·to -**ta** *adj* disseminated || **Vulgata** *f* Vulgate

vulneràbile *adj* vulnerable

vuotare (vuòto) *tr* to empty; **vuotare il sacco** to speak one's mind, unburden oneself || *ref* to empty

vuò·to -**ta** *adj* empty; devoid || *m* vacuum; emptiness; empty space; empty seat; empty feeling; empty (*e.g.*, *container*); **a vuoto** in vain; wide of the mark; (*check*) without sufficient funds; **andare a vuoto** to fail; (mach) to idle; **cadere nel vuoto** to fall on deaf ears; **mandare a vuoto** to thwart; **sotto vuoto** in a vacuum; **vuoto d'aria** (aer) air pocket; **vuoto di cassa** deficit; **vuoto di potere** power vacuum

W

W, w [ˈdoppjo ˈvu] *m & f*
wà·fer *m* (-fer) wafer
water-clòset *m* (-clòset) flush toilet
watt *m* (watt) watt

watt·óra *m* (-óra) watt-hour
wèstern *m* (wèstern) (mov) western
whisky *m* (whisky) whiskey
wìgwam *m* (wìgwam) wigwam

X

X, x [ɪks] *m & f*
xèno *m* xenon
xenòfo·bo -ba *mf* xenophobe

xè·res *m* (-res) sherry
xerografìa *f* xerography
xeròfito *m* xerophyte

Y

Y, y [ˈɪpsɪlon] *m & f*
yacht *m* (yachts) yacht
yak *m* (yak) yak

yànkee *m* (yànkees) Yankee
yìddish *adj invar & m* Yiddish

Z

Z, z [ˈdzetɑ] *m & f* twenty-first letter
  of the Italian alphabet
zabaióne [dz] *m* eggnog
zàcchera *f* splash of mud
zaffare *tr* to plug; to bung
zaffata *f* unpleasant whiff, stench; gust
zafferano [dz] *m* saffron
zaffiro [dz] *m* sapphire
zaffo *m* plug; bung; tampon
zàgara [dz] *f* orange blossom
zàino [dz] *m* knapsack; (mil) pack
zampa *f* paw; (culin) leg; **a quattro
  zampe** on all fours; **zampa di gallina**
  crow's-foot; illegible scrawl; **zampa
  di porco** crowbar
zampare *intr* to paw; to stamp
zampettare (zampétto) *intr* to toddle;
  to scamper
zampillare *intr* (ESSERE & AVERE) to
  spurt, gush, spring
zampillo *m* spurt, gush, spring
zampino *m* little paw; **metterci lo zampino** to put one's finger in the pie
zampiróne *m* slow-burning mosquito
  repellent; foul-smelling cigarette
zampógna *f* bagpipe
zampognare (zampógno) *intr* to pipe,
  play the bagpipe
zampóne *m* Modena salami (*stuffed
  forepaw of a hog*)
zanèlla *f* gully
zàngola *f* butter churn
zanna *f* tusk; fang; **mostrare le zanne**
  to show one's teeth
zanzara [dz] [dz] *f* mosquito
zanzarièra [dz] [dz] *f* mosquito net;
  window screen
zappa *f* hoe; **darsi la zappa sui piedi**

  to cut one's nose off to spite one's
  face
zappare *tr* to hoe
zappatóre *m* hoer, digger; (mil) sapper
zar *m* (zar) czar
zàttera *f* raft; **zattera di salvataggio** life
  raft
zatterière *m* log driver
zavòrra [dz] *f* ballast; (fig) deadwood
zavorrare [dz] (zavòrro) *tr* to ballast
zàzzera *f* mop (*of hair*)
zèbra [dz] *f* zebra; **zebre** zebra crossing
zebra·to -ta [dz] *adj* zebra-striped
ze·bù [dz] *m* (-bù) zebu
zéc·ca *f* (-che) mint; (ent) tick; **nuovo
  di zecca** brand-new
zecchino *m* sequin, gold coin
zèfiro [dz] *m* zephyr
zelante [dz] *adj* zealous; studious ‖ *mf*
  zealot; eager beaver
zèlo [dz] *m* zeal; **zelo pubblico** public
  spirit
zènit [dz] *m* zenith
zénzero [dz] [dz] *m* ginger
zép·po -pa *adj* crammed, jammed ‖ *f*
  wedge; (fig) padding
zerbino [dz] *m* doormat; dandy
zerbinòtto [dz] *m* dandy, sporty fellow
zèro [dz] *m* zero
zìa *f* aunt
zibaldóne [dz] *m* notebook; collection
  of thoughts; (pej) hodgepodge
zibellino [dz] *m* sable
zibétto [dz] *m* civet cat; civet (*substance used in perfumery*)
zibibbo [dz] *m* raisin
ziga·no -na *adj & mf* gypsy
zìgomo [dz] *m* cheekbone

zigrinare [dz] *tr* to grain (*leather*); to mill, knurl (*metal*)

zigrina·to -ta [dz] *adj* shagreened, grained (*leather*); knurled

zigzàg [dz] [dz] *m* (**zigzàg**) zigzag; **andare a zigzag** to zigzag

zigzagare §209 [dz] [dz] *intr* to zigzag

zimarra [dz] *f* cassock; (obs) overcoat

zimbèllo *m* decoy (*bird*); laughingstock

zincare §197 *tr* to zinc

zinco *m* zinc

zingaré·sco -sca (**-schi -sche**) *adj & mf* gypsy

zìnga·ro -ra *mf* gypsy

zìnnia [dz] *f* zinnia

zìo *m* uncle; **zio d'America** rich uncle

zìpolo *m* peg, bung

zircóne [dz] *m* zircon

zircònio [dz] *m* zirconium

zirlare *intr* to warble; to squeak (*said of mouse*)

zitèlla *f* old maid

zittire §176 *tr & intr* to hoot, hiss

zit·to -ta *adj* silent; **far stare zitto** to hush up; **stare zitto** to keep quiet || *m* whisper || **zitto** *interj* quiet!; hush!; shut up!

zizzània [dz] [ddzz] *f* (bot) darnel; **seminar zizzania** to sow discord

zòccolo *m* clog, sabot; clump; clod; clodhopper; base (*of column*); pedestal; wide baseboard; (zool) hoof

zodìaco [dz] *m* zodiac

zolfanèllo *m* sulfur match

zolfara *f* var of **solfara**

zólfo *m* sulfur

zòlla *f* clod, clump; turf; lump, cube (*of sugar*)

zollétta *f* lump, cube (*of sugar*)

zòna [dz] *f* zone; area; girdle; band, stripe; ticker tape; (pathol) shingles; (telg) tape; **zona glaciale** frigid zone; **zona tropicale** tropics, tropical zone

zónzo [dz] [dz] *m*—**andare a zonzo** to stroll, loiter along

zoòfito [dz] *m* zoophite

zoologia [dz] *f* zoology

zoològi·co -ca [dz] *adj* (**-ci -che**) zoological

zoòlo·go -ga [dz] *mf* (**-gi -ghe**) zoologist

zootecnìa [dz] *f* animal husbandry

zootècni·co -ca [dz] (**-ci -che**) *adj* livestock || *m* livestock specialist

zoppicante *adj* limping; halting; shaky

zoppicare §197 (**zòppico**) *intr* to limp; to be shaky (*in one's studies*); to wobble

zoppicatura *f* limp; wobble

zòp·po -pa *adj* crippled; lame; wobbly || *mf* cripple; lame person

zòti·co -ca [dz] (**-ci -che**) *adj* uncouth, boorish || *m* churl, boor

zuc·ca *f* (**-che**) pumpkin; (joc) pate; (coll) empty head

zuccata *f* bump with the head

zuccherare (**zùcchero**) *tr* to sweeten, sugar

zuccherièra *f* sugar bowl

zuccherifì·cio *m* (**-ci**) sugar refinery

zuccheri·no -na *adj* sugary || *m* candy; sugar plum; sugar-coated pill

zùcchero *m* sugar; **zucchero filato** cotton candy; **zucchero in polvere** powdered sugar

zuccheró·so -sa [s] *adj* sugary

zucchétto *m* scull cap; zucchetto

zucchi·no -na *m & f* zucchini

zuccó·ne -na *mf* dunce, dumbbell

zuffa *f* brawl, fight

zufolare (**zùfolo**) *tr & intr* to whistle

zùfolo *m* (mus) whistle, pipe

zu·lù -lù [dz] *adj & mf* Zulu

zumare [dz] *tr & intr* (mov, telv) to zoom

zumata [dz] *f* (mov, telv) zoom

zuppa *f* soup; (fig) mess; **zuppa inglese** cake with brandy and whipped cream; **zuppa pavese** consommé with toast and eggs

zuppièra *f* tureen

zup·po -pa *adj* drenched, soaked || *f* see **zuppa**

Zurigo *f* Zurich

zuzzurulló·ne -na [dz] [ddzz] *mf* overgrown child, just a big kid

PART TWO

Inglese-Italiano

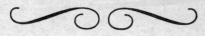

La pronunzia dell'inglese

I simboli seguenti rappresentano approssimativamente tutti i suoni della lingua inglese.

VOCALI

SIMBOLO	SUONO	ESEMPIO
[æ]	Più chiuso della a in caso.	hat [hæt]
[ɑ]	Come la a in basso.	father ['fɑðər] proper ['prɑpər]
[ɛ]	Come la e in sella.	met [mɛt]
[e]	Più chiuso della e in ché. Specialmente in posizione finale, si pronunzia come se fosse seguita da [ɪ].	fate [fet] they [ðe]
[ə]	Come la seconda e nella parola francese gouvernement.	heaven ['hevən] pardon ['pɑrdən]
[i]	Come la i in nido.	she [ʃi] machine [mə'ʃin]
[ɪ]	Come la i in ritto.	fit [fɪt] beer [bɪr]
[o]	Più chiuso della o in sole. Specialmente in posizione finale, si pronunzia come se fosse seguito da [ʊ].	nose [noz] road [rod] row [ro]
[ɔ]	Meno chiuso della o in torre.	bought [bɔt] law [lɔ]
[ʌ]	Piuttosto simile alla eu nella parola francese peur.	cup [kʌp] come [kʌm] mother ['mʌðər]
[ʊ]	Meno chiuso della u in insulto.	pull [pʊl] book [bʊk] wolf [wʊlf]
[u]	Come la u in acuto.	rude [rud] move [muv] tomb [tum]

DITTONGHI

SIMBOLO	SUONO	ESEMPIO
[aɪ]	Come ai in laico.	night [naɪt] eye [aɪ]
[aʊ]	Come au in causa.	found [faʊnd] cow [kaʊ]
[ɔɪ]	Come oi in poi.	voice [vɔɪs] oil [ɔɪl]

CONSONANTI

SIMBOLO	SUONO	ESEMPIO
[b]	Come la **b** in **bambino**. Suono bilabiale occlusivo sonoro.	**bed** [bɛd] **robber** [ˈrɑbər]
[d]	Come la **d** in **caldo**. Suono dentale occlusivo sonoro.	**dead** [dɛd] **add** [æd]
[dʒ]	Come la **g** in **gente**. Suono palatale affricato sonoro.	**gem** [dʒɛm] **jail** [dʒel]
[ð]	Come la **d** nella pronuncia castigliana di **nada**. Suono interdentale fricativo sonoro.	**this** [ðɪs] **father** [ˈfɑðər]
[f]	Come la **f** in **fare**. Suono labiodentale fricativo sordo.	**face** [fes] **phone** [fon]
[g]	Come la **g** in **gatto**. Suono velare occlusivo sonoro.	**go** [go] **get** [get]
[h]	Come la **c** aspirata nella pronuncia toscana di **casa**.	**hot** [hɔt] **alcohol** [ˈælkə͵hɔl]
[j]	Come la **i** in **ieri** o la **y** in **yo-yo**. Semiconsonante di suono palatale sonoro.	**yes** [jes] **unit** [ˈjunɪt]
[k]	Come la **c** in **casa** ma accompagnato da un'aspirazione. Suono velare occlusivo sordo.	**cat** [kæt] **chord** [kɔrd] **kill** [kɪl]
[l]	Come la **l** in **latino**. Suono alveolare fricativo laterale sonoro.	**late** [let] **allow** [əˈlau]
[m]	Come la **m** in **madre**. Suono bilabiale nasale sonoro.	**more** [mor] **command** [kəˈmænd]
[n]	Come la **n** in **notte**. Suono alveolare nasale sonoro.	**nest** [nɛst] **manner** [ˈmænər]
[ŋ]	Come la **n** in **manca**. Suono velare nasale sonoro.	**king** [kɪŋ] **conquer** [ˈkɑŋkər]
[p]	Come la **p** in **patto** ma accompagnato da un'aspirazione. Suono bilabiale occlusivo sordo.	**pen** [pen] **cap** [kæp]
[r]	La **r** più comune in molte parti dell'Inghilterra e nella maggior parte degli Stati Uniti e del Canadà è un suono semivocalico articolato con la punta della lingua elevata verso la volta del palato. Questa consonante è debolissima in posizione intervocalica o alla fine di una sillaba, e può appena percepirsi. L'articolazione di questa consonante ha la tendenza di influenzare il suono delle vocali contigue. La **r**, preceduta dai suoni [ʌ] o [ə], dà il proprio colorito a questi suoni e sparisce completamente come suono consonantico.	**run** [rʌn] **far** [fɑr] **art** [ɑrt] **carry** [ˈkæri] **burn** [bʌrn] **learn** [lʌrn] **weather** [ˈwɛðər]
[s]	Come la **s** in **sette**. Suono alveolare fricativo sordo.	**send** [send] **cellar** [ˈsɛlər]
[ʃ]	Come **sc** in **lasciare**. Suono palatale fricativo sordo.	**shall** [ʃæl] **machine** [məˈʃin]
[t]	Come la **t** in **tavolo** ma accompagnato da un'aspirazione. Suono dentale occlusivo sordo.	**ten** [ten] **dropped** [drɑpt]
[tʃ]	Come **c** in **cibo**. Suono palatale affricato sordo.	**child** [tʃaɪld] **much** [mʌtʃ] **nature** [ˈnetʃər]
[θ]	Come la **z** castigliana in **zapato**. Suono interdentale fricativo sordo.	**think** [θɪŋk] **truth** [truθ]
[v]	Come la **v** in **vento**. Suono labiodentale fricativo sonoro.	**vest** [vɛst] **over** [ˈovər] **of** [ɑv]

4

SIMBOLO	SUONO	ESEMPIO
[w]	Come la **u** in **quadro**. Suono labiovelare fricativo sonoro.	**work** [wʌrk] **tweed** [twid] **queen** [kwin]
[z]	Come la **s** in **asilo**. Suono alveolare fricativo sonoro.	**zeal** [zil] **busy** ['bɪzi] **his** [hɪz]
[ʒ]	Come la seconda **g** nella parola francese **garage**. Suono palatale fricativo sonoro.	**azure** ['eʒər] **measure** ['meʒər]

ACCENTO

L'accento tonico principale, indicato col segno grafico `'`, e l'accento secondario, indicato col segno grafico `„` precedono la sillaba sulla quale cadono, per es., **fascinate** ['fæsɪ ˌnet].

La pronunzia delle parole composte

Nella parte inglese-italiano di questo Dizionario la pronunzia figurata di tutte le parole inglesi semplici è indicata in parentesi quadre che seguono immediatamente l'esponente, secondo un nuovo adattamento dell'alfabeto fonetico internazionale.

Vi sono tre generi di parole composte in inglese: (1) le parole in cui gli elementi componenti si sono uniti per formare una parola solida, come per es., **steamboat** vapore; (2) la parole in cui gli elementi componenti sono uniti da un trattino, come per es., **high'-grade'** di qualità superiore; (3) le parole in cui gli elementi componenti rimangono graficamente indipendenti gli uni da gli altri, per es., **post card** cartolina postale. La pronunzia delle parole inglesi composte non è indicata in questo Dizionario qualora gli elementi componenti appaiono come esponenti indipendenti nella loro normale posizione alfabetica e mostrano quindi la loro pronunzia figurata. Solo gli accenti principali e secondari di tali parole sono indicati, come per es., **steam'boat'**, **high'-grade'**, **post' card'**. Se i due membri di una parola composta inglese solida non sono separati da un accento grafico, si usa un punto leggermente elevato sopra il rigo per indicarne la divisione, come per es., **la'dy·like'**.

Nei nomi in cui l'accento secondario cade sul membro **-man** o **-men**, le vocali di tali membri si pronunziano come nelle parole semplici **man** e **men**, come per es., **mailman** ['mel ˌmæn] e **mailmen** ['mel ˌmen]. Nei nomi in cui tali membri componenti non sono accentati, le loro vocali si pronunziano come se fossero un'e muta francese, come per es., **policeman** [pə'lismən] e **policemen** [pə'lismən]. In questo Dizionario la trascrizione fonetica di tali nomi non è stata indicata qualora il primo membro componente appaia come esponente con la sua pronunzia in alfabeto fonetico internazionale. Gli accenti sono ciò nondimeno indicati:

mail'man' *s* **(-men')**
police'man *s* **(-men)**

La pronunzia dei participi passati

La pronunzia di una parola la cui desinenza è **-ed** (o **-d** dopo una e muta) non è indicata nel presente Dizionario, purché la pronunzia della parola stessa senza tale suffisso appaia con il suo esponente nella sua posizione alfabetica. In tale caso la pronunzia segue le regole indicate qui sotto. Si osservi che il raddoppiamento della vocale finale dopo una semplice vocale tonica non muta la pronunzia del suffisso **-ed**, per es.: **batted** ['bætɪd], **dropped** [drɑpt], **robbed** [rɑbd].

La desinenza **-ed** (o **-d** dopo una e muta) del preterito, del participio passato e di certi aggettivi ha tre pronunzie differenti, che dipendono dal suono in cui il tema termina:

1) Se il tema termina in suono consonantico sonoro (che non sia [d]), cioè [b], [g], [l], [m], [n], [ŋ], [r], [v], [z], [ð], [ʒ] o [dʒ] o in un suono vocalico, l'**-ed** è pronunziato [d]:

SUONO IN CUI TERMINA IL TEMA	INFINITO	PRETERITO E PARTICIPIO PASSATO
[b]	**ebb** [eb] **rob** [rɑb] **robe** [rob]	**ebbed** [ebd] **robbed** [rɑbd] **robed** [robd]

5

SUONO IN CUI TERMINA IL TEMA	INFINITO	PRETERITO E PARTICIPIO PASSATO
[g]	egg [ɛg] sag [sæg]	egged [ɛgd] sagged [sægd]
[l]	mail [mel] scale [skel]	mailed [meld] scaled [skeld]
[m]	storm [stɔrm] bomb [bɑm] name [nem]	stormed [stɔrmd] bombed [bɑmd] named [nemd]
[n]	tan [tæn] sign [saɪn] mine [maɪn]	tanned [tænd] signed [saɪnd] mined [maɪnd]
[ŋ]	hang [hæŋ]	hanged [hæŋd]
[r]	fear [fɪr] care [ker]	feared [fɪrd] cared [kerd]
[v]	rev [rev] save [sev]	revved [revd] saved [sevd]
[z]	buzz [bʌz] fuze [fjuz]	buzzed [bʌzd] fuzed [fjuzd]
[ð]	smooth [smuð] bathe [beð]	smoothed [smuðd] bathed [beðd]
[ʒ]	massage [mə'sɑʒ]	massaged [mə'sɑʒd]
[dʒ]	page [pedʒ]	paged [pedʒd]
suono vocalico	key [ki] sigh [saɪ] paw [pɔ]	keyed [kid] sighed [saɪd] pawed [pɔd]

2) Se il tema termina in un suono consonantico sordo (che non sia [t]), cioè [f], [k], [p], [s], [θ], [ʃ] o [tʃ], l'-ed si pronunzia [t]:

SUONO IN CUI TERMINA IL TEMA	INFINITO	PRETERITO E PARTICIPIO PASSATO
[f]	loaf [lof] knife [naɪf]	loafed [loft] knifed [naɪft]
[k]	back [bæk] bake [bek]	backed [bækt] baked [bekt]
[p]	cap [kæp] wipe [waɪp]	capped [kæpt] wiped [waɪpt]
[s]	hiss [hɪs] mix [mɪks]	hissed [hɪst] mixed [mɪkst]
[θ]	lath [læθ]	lathed [læθt]
[ʃ]	mash [mæʃ]	mashed [mæʃt]
[tʃ]	match [mætʃ]	matched [mætʃt]

3) Se il tema termina in un suono dentale, cioè [t] o [d], l'-ed si pronunzia [ɪd] o [əd]:

SUONO IN CUI TERMINA IL TEMA	INFINITO	PRETERITO E PARTICIPIO PASSATO
[t]	wait [wet] mate [met]	waited ['wetɪd] mated ['metɪd]
[d]	mend [mɛnd] wade [wed]	mended ['mɛndɪd] waded ['wedɪd]

L'-ed di alcuni aggettivi aggiunto ad un tema che termina in suono consonantico (oltre a quelli che terminano in [d] o [t]), è ciò nonostante talvolta pronunziato [ɪd] e tale fenomeno è idicato con la piena pronunzia della parola in simboli dell'alfabeto fonetico internazionale, per es., blessed ['blesɪd], crabbed ['kræbɪd].

6

A

A, a [e] s prima lettera dell'alfabeto inglese

a [e] art indef un, uno, una, un'

aback [ə'bæk] adv all'indietro; **taken aback** colto alla sprovvista, sconcertato

aba·cus ['æbəkəs] s (-cuses or -ci [,saɪ]) pallottoliere m; (archit) abaco

abaft [ə'bæft] or [ə'baft] adv a poppa || prep dietro a

abandon [ə'bændən] s disinvoltura || abbandonare

abase [ə'bes] tr umiliare, degradare

abash [ə'bæʃ] tr imbarazzare; sconcertare

abate [ə'bet] tr ridurre; omettere; (law) terminare || intr diminuire, calmarsi

aba·tis ['æbətɪs] or [ə'bætɪs] s (-tis or -tises) (mil) tagliata

abattoir ['æbə,twar] s macello

abba·cy ['æbəsi] s (-cies) abbazia

abbess ['æbɪs] s badessa

abbey ['æbɪ] s badia, abbazia

abbot ['æbət] s abate m

abbreviate [ə'brivɪ,et] tr abbreviare, raccorciare

abbreviation [ə,brivɪ'eʃən] s (abbreviated form) abbreviazione; (shortening) abbreviamento

A B C [,e,bi'si] s (letterword) abbicì m; **A B C's** abbecedario

abdicate ['æbdɪ,ket] tr abdicare a || intr abdicare

abdomen ['æbdəmən] or [æb'domən] s addome m

abduct [æb'dʌkt] tr rapire

abed [ə'bed] adv a letto

abet [ə'bet] v (pret & pp **abetted; ger abetting**) tr favoreggiare

abeyance [ə'be·əns] s sospensione; **in abeyance** in sospeso

ab·hor [æb'hɔr] v (pret & pp **-horred; ger -horring**) tr aborrire

abhorrent [æb'hɑrənt] or [æb'hɔrənt] adj detestabile

abide [ə'baɪd] v (pret & pp **abode** or **abided**) tr aspettare; tollerare || intr —**to abide by** attenersi a; rimanere fedele a

abili·ty [ə'bɪlɪti] s (-ties) abilità f, bravura

abject ['æbdʒekt] or [æb'dʒekt] adj abietto, turpe

abjure [æb'dʒʊr] tr abiurare

ablative ['æblətɪv] adj & s ablativo

ablaut ['æblaʊt] s apofonia

ablaze [ə'blez] adj in fiamme; risplendente

able ['ebəl] adj abile, esperto; **to be able to** + inf potere + inf

able-bodied ['ebəl'bɑdid] adj sano; forte

abloom [ə'blum] adj & adv in fiore

abnormal [æb'nɔrməl] adj anormale

aboard [ə'bɔrd] adv a bordo; **all aboard!** (rr) signori, in vettura!; **to go aboard** imbarcarsi; **to take aboard** imbarcare || prep a bordo di; (a bus, train, etc.) in, su

abode [ə'bod] s abitazione, dimora

abolish [ə'balɪʃ] tr abolire

A-bomb ['e,bam] s bomba atomica

abominable [ə'bamənəbəl] adj abominevole

abomination [ə,bamɪ'neʃən] s abominazione

aborigenes [,æbə'rɪdʒɪ,niz] spl aborigeni mpl

abort [ə'bɔrt] tr terminare prematuramente; provocare un aborto in || intr abortire

abortion [ə'bɔrʃən] s aborto

abound [ə'baʊnd] intr abbondare; **to abound in** or **with** abbondare di

about [ə'baʊt] adv circa, press'a poco; qua intorno; qua e là; in direzione opposta; (coll) quasi; **to be about to** star sul punto di || prep intorno a; circa a; addosso a; tutt'intorno a; riguardo a

about'-face' interj (mil) dietro front!

about'-face' or **about'-face'** s voltafaccia; (mil) dietro front m || **about'-face'** intr fare dietro front

above [ə'bʌv] adj soprammenzionato; superiore || s—**from above** dal cielo; dall'alto || adv in alto; su; più sopra || prep sopra, sopra a; più di; al di là di, oltre; **above all** soprattutto

above-mentioned [ə'bʌv'menʃənd] adj summenzionato, sunnominato

abrasive [ə'bresɪv] or [ə'brezɪv] adj & s abrasivo

abreast [ə'brest] adj & adv in fila, in linea; **to keep abreast of** tenersi alla pari con; essere al corrente di

abridge [ə'brɪdʒ] tr compendiare; ridurre

abroad [ə'brɔd] adv all'estero; all'aria aperta; **to be abroad** (said of news) circolare

abrupt [ə'brʌpt] adj brusco, improvviso; (very steep) scosceso

abscess ['æbses] s ascesso

abscond [æb'skand] intr scappare; **to abscond with** svignarsela con

absence ['æbsəns] s assenza; **in the absence of** in mancanza di

absent ['æbsənt] adj assente || [æb'sent] tr—**to absent oneself** assentarsi

absentee [,æbsən'ti] s assente mf

absent-minded ['æbsənt'maɪndɪd] adj distratto, assente

absinth ['æbsɪnθ] s assenzio

absolute ['æbsə,lut] adj & s assoluto

absolutely ['æbsə,lutli] adv assolutamente, certamente || [,æbsə'lutli] interj certamente!

absolve [æb'salv] tr assolvere

absorb [æb'sɔrb] tr assorbire; **to be** or **become absorbed** essere assorto

absorbent [æb'sɔrbənt] adj assorbente; (cotton) idrofilo || s sostanza assorbente

absorbing [æb'sɔrbɪŋ] adj interessantissimo

abstain [æb'sten] intr astenersi

abstemious [æb'stimɪ·əs] adj astemio

abstention [æb'stenʃən] s astensione; astenuto (vote withheld)

abstinent ['æbstɪnənt] *adj* astinente
abstract ['æbstrækt] *adj* astratto ‖ *s* compendio, sommario ‖ *tr* compendiare ‖ (æb'strækt) *tr* astrarre; (*to steal*) sottrarre
abstruse [æb'strus] *adj* astruso
absurd [æb'sʌrd] or [æb'zʌrd] *adj* assurdo
absurdi-ty [æb'sʌrdɪti] or [æb'zʌrdɪti] *s* (-ties) assurdità *f*
abundant [ə'bʌndənt] *adj* abbondante
abuse [ə'bjus] *s* (*misuse*) abuso; maltrattamento; insulto ‖ [ə'bjuz] *tr* (*to misuse, take unfair advantage of*) abusare di; maltrattare; insultare
abusive [ə'bjusɪv] *adj* abusivo; insultante
abut [ə'bʌt] *v* (*pret & pp* **abutted;** *ger* **abutting**) *intr*—**to abut on** confinare con
abutment [ə'bʌtmənt] *s* rinfianco; (*at either end of bridge*) spalla; (*of buttresses of bridge*) sprone *m*
abysmal [ə'bɪzməl] *adj* abissale; (*e.g., ignorance*) spropositato
abyss [ə'bɪs] *s* abisso
academic [,ækə'demɪk] *adj* accademico
ac'ademic cos'tume *s* toga accademica
academician [ə,kædə'mɪʃən] *s* accademico
ac'adem'ic year' *s* anno scolastico
acade·my [ə'kædəmi] *s* (-mies) accademia
accede [æk'sid] *intr* accedere; **to accede to** salire a; accedere a
accelerate [æk'selə,ret] *tr & intr* accelerare
accelerator [æk'selə,retər] *s* acceleratore *m*
accent ['æksent] *s* accento ‖ ['æksent] or [æk'sent] *tr* accentare; (*to accentuate*) accentuare
ac'cent mark' *s* segnaccento, accento grafico
accentuate [æk'sentʃu,et] *tr* accentuare
accept [æk'sept] *tr* accettare
acceptable [æk'septəbəl] *adj* accettabile
acceptance [æk'septəns] *s* accettazione
access ['ækses] *s* accesso
accessible [æk'sesɪbəl] *adj* accessibile; (*person*) abbordabile
accession [æk'seʃən] *s* accessione, acquisto; (*e.g., to the throne*) adito
accesso-ry [æk'sesəri] *adj* accessorio ‖ *s* (-ries) accessorio; (*to a crime*) complice *m*
accident ['æksɪdənt] *s* accidente *m*; **by accident** accidentalmente, per caso
accidental [,æksɪ'dentəl] *adj* accidentale ‖ *s* (mus) accidente *m*
acclaim [ə'klem] *s* acclamazione, applauso ‖ *tr & intr* acclamare, applaudire
acclimate ['æklɪ,met] *tr* acclimatare ‖ *intr* acclimatarsi
accolade [,ækə'led] *s* accollata; (fig) elogio
accommodate [ə'kʌmə,det] *tr* (*to adjust, make fit*) accomodare; (*to pro-*

vide with a loan) venire incontro **a;** (*to supply with lodging*) alloggiare; (*to oblige*) favorire; (*to have room for*) aver posto per
accommodating [ə'kʌmə,detɪŋ] *adj* servizievole, compiacente
accommodation [ə,kʌmə'deʃən] *s* (*favor*) favore *m;* (*loan*) prestito; (*adaptation*) adattamento; (*reconciliation*) conciliazione; (*compromise*) accomodamento; **accommodations** (*traveling space*) posto; (*in a hotel*) alloggio
accommoda'tion train' *s* treno accelerato
accompaniment [ə'kʌmpənɪmənt] *s* accompagnamento
accompanist [ə'kʌmpənɪst] *s* accompagnatore *m*
accompa·ny [ə'kʌmpəni] *v* (*pret & pp* -**nied**) *tr* accompagnare
accomplice [ə'kʌmplɪs] *s* complice *mf*
accomplish [ə'kʌmplɪʃ] *tr* compiere
accomplished [ə'kʌmplɪʃt] *adj* (*completed*) compiuto, terminato; (*skilled*) finito, compiuto
accomplishment [ə'kʌmplɪʃmənt] *s* (*completion*) esecuzione, realizzazione; (*something accomplished*) opera; (*acquired ability*) talento; (*military achievement*) prodezza; (*social skill*) compitezza
accord [ə'kɔrd] *s* accordo; **in accord with** in conformità con; **of one's own accord** spontaneamente; **with one accord** di comune accordo ‖ *tr* concedere ‖ *intr* accordarsi
accordance [ə'kɔrdəns] *s* accordo; **in accordance with** in conformità con
according [ə'kɔrdɪŋ] *adv*—**according as** a seconda che; **according to** secondo, a seconda di
accordingly [ə'kɔrdɪŋli] *adv* per conseguenza, perciò; in conformità
accordion [ə'kɔrdɪ·ən] *s* fisarmonica
accost [ə'kɔst] or [ə'kɑst] *tr* accostare, abbordare
accouchement [ə'kuʃmənt] *s* parto
account [ə'kaunt] *s* (*explanation*) versione; (*report*) resoconto; conto; (*statement*) estratto conto; **by all accounts** secondo la voce comune; **of account d'importanza**; **of no account** senza importanza; **on account** in acconto; **on account of** a causa di; per l'amor di; **on all accounts** in ogni modo; **on no account** in nessuna maniera; **to call to account** chiedere conto di; **to give a good account of oneself** comportarsi bene; **to take account of** prendere in considerazione; **to turn to account** trarre profitto da ‖ *intr*—**to account for** render conto di; essere responsabile per
accountable [ə'kauntəbəl] *adj* responsabile; (*explainable*) spiegabile
accountant [ə'kauntənt] *s* contabile *mf*, ragioniere *m*
accounting [ə'kauntɪŋ] *s* contabilità *f*, ragioneria
accouterments [ə'kutərmənts] *spl* (mil)

buffetterie *fpl;* (*trappings*) ornamenti *mpl*

accredit [ə'kredɪt] *tr* accreditare; **to accredit s.o. with s.th** ascrivere qlco a credito di qlcu

accrue [ə'kru] *intr* accumularsi; (*said of interest*) maturare

acculturation [ə,kʌltʃə'reʃən] *s* acculturazione

accumulate [ə'kjumjə,let] *tr* accumulare ‖ *intr* accumularsi

accuracy ['ækjərəsi] *s* esattezza, precisione; fedeltà *f*

accurate ['ækjərɪt] *adj* esatto, preciso; fedele

accursed [ə'kʌrsɪd] or [ə'kʌrst] *adj* maledetto

accusation [,ækjə'zeʃən] *s* accusa

accusative [ə'kjuzətɪv] *adj & s* accusativo

accuse [ə'kjuz] *tr* accusare

accustom [ə'kʌstəm] *tr* abituare

ace [es] *s* asso; **to be within an ace of** essere quasi sul punto di

ace' in the hole' *s* asso nella manica

acetate ['æsɪ,tet] *s* acetato

ace'tic ac'id [ə'sitɪk] *s* acido acetico

aceti·fy [ə'setɪ,faɪ] *v* (*pret & pp* **-fied**) *tr* acetificare ‖ *intr* acetificarsi

acetone ['æsɪ,ton] *s* acetone *m*

acetylene [ə'setɪ,lin] *s* acetilene *m*

acet'ylene torch' *s* cannello ossiacetilenico

ache [ek] *intr* dolore *m* ‖ (dolore, e.g., **my tooth aches** mi duole il dente

Acheron ['ækə,ɑn] *s* Acheronte *m*

achieve [ə'tʃiv] *tr* compiere, conseguire

achievement [ə'tʃivmənt] *s* compimento; successo; (*exploit*) impresa, prodezza

Achil'les heel' [ə'kɪliz] *s* tallone *m* d'Achille

acid ['æsɪd] *adj & s* acido

acidi·fy [ə'sɪdɪ,faɪ] *v* (*pret & pp* **-fied**) *tr & intr* acidificare

acidity [ə'sɪdɪti] *s* acidità *f*

acid' test' *s* prova del fuoco

ack-ack ['æk'æk] *s* (slang) cannone antiaereo

acknowledge [æk'nɑlɪdʒ] *tr* riconoscere; (*receipt of a letter*) accusare; (*a claim*) ammettere; mostrare la gratitudine per; (law) certificare

acknowledgment [æk'nɑlɪdʒmənt] *s* riconoscimento; (*of receipt of a letter*) accusa, cenno

acme ['ækmi] *s* acme *f*

acolyte ['ækə,laɪt] *s* accolito

acorn ['ekɔrn] or ['ekərn] *s* ghianda

acoustic [ə'kustɪk] *adj* acustico ‖ **acoustics** [ə'kustɪks] *s* acustica

acquaint [ə'kwent] *tr* mettere al corrente; **to be acquainted with** conoscere; essere al corrente di; **to become acquainted** (*with each other*) conoscersi

acquaintance [ə'kwentəns] *s* conoscenza; (*person*) conoscente *mf*, conoscenza

acquiesce [,ækwɪ'es] *intr* acconsentire, accondiscendere

acquiescence [,ækwɪ'esəns] *s* accondiscendenza

acquire [ə'kwaɪr] *tr* acquistare

acquisition [,ækwɪ'zɪʃən] *s* acquisto

acquit [ə'kwɪt] *v* (*pret & pp* **acquitted;** *ger* **acquitting**) *tr* (*to pay*) ripagare; (*to declare not guilty*) assolvere; **to acquit oneself** condursi

acquittal [ə'kwɪtəl] *s* assoluzione

acre ['ekər] *s* acro

acrid ['ækrɪd] *adj* acrido, pungente

acrobat ['ækrə,bæt] *s* acrobata *mf*

acrobatic [,ækrə'bætɪk] *adj* acrobatico ‖ **acrobatics** *ssg* (*e.g., of a stunt pilot*) acrobazie *fpl;* **acrobatics** *spl* (*gymnastics*) acrobatica

acronym ['ækrənɪm] *s* acronimo, parola macedonia

acropolis [ə'krɑpəlɪs] *s* acropoli *f*

across [ə'krɔs] or [ə'krɑs] *adv* dall'altra parte; **to get an idea across** to farsi capire da ‖ *prep* attraverso; (*on the other side of*) al di là di, dall'altra parte di; **to come across** (*a person*) imbattersi in; **to go across** attraversare

across'-the-board' *adj* generale

act [ækt] *s* atto; legge *f;* rappresentazione; **in the act** in flagrante ‖ *tr* (*a drama*) rappresentare; (*a role*) recitare ‖ *intr* (*on the stage*) recitare; (*to behave*) comportarsi; (*to perform special duties;* *to reach a decision*) agire; (*to have an effect*) reagire; **to act as** fungere da; **to act for** rimpiazzare; **to act on** eseguire; **to act up** (coll) fare il matto; non funzionare bene (*said, e.g., of a motor*); **to act up to** (coll) fare festa a

acting ['æktɪŋ] *adj* facente funzione, interino ‖ *s* recita

action ['ækʃən] *s* azione; (*moving parts*) meccanismo; **to take action** iniziare azione; (law) intentare causa

activate ['æktɪ,vet] *tr* attivare

active ['æktɪv] *adj & s* attivo

activi·ty [æk'tɪvɪti] *s* (**-ties**) attività *f*

act' of God' *s* forza maggiore

actor ['æktər] *s* attore *m*

actress ['æktrɪs] *s* attrice *f*

actual ['æktʃʊ·əl] *adj* reale

actually ['æktʃʊ·əli] *adv* realmente, in realtà

actuar·y ['æktʃʊ,eri] *s* (**-les**) attuario

actuate ['æktʃʊ,et] *tr* attuare, mettere in azione; (*to motivate*) stimulare

acuity [ə'kju·ɪti] *s* acuità *f*

acumen [ə'kjumən] *s* acume *m*

acupuncture ['ækju,pʌŋktʃər] *s* agopuntura

acute [ə'kjut] *adj* acuto

ad [æd] *s* (coll) inserzione pubblicitaria

Adam ['ædəm] *s* Adamo; **not to know from Adam** non conoscere affatto

adamant ['ædəmənt] *adj* saldo, inflessibile

Ad'am's ap'ple *s* pomo d'Adamo

adapt [ə'dæpt] *tr* adattare

adaptation [,ædæp'teʃən] *s* adattamento; (*e.g., of a play*) rifacimento

add [æd] *tr* aggiungere; (*numbers*)

sommare || *intr* aggiungere; far di conto; **to add up to** ammontare a; (coll) voler dire

adder ['ædər] *s* vipera

addict ['ædɪkt] *s* (*to drugs*) tossicomane *mf*; (*to a sport*) tifoso || [ə'dɪkt] *tr* abituare; rendere propenso alla tossicomania; **to addict oneself to** darsi a, abbandonarsi a

addiction [ə'dɪkʃən] *s* dedizione; (*to drugs*) tossicomania; (*to sports*) tifo

add'ing machine' *s* calcolatrice *f*

addition [ə'dɪʃən] *s* addizione; (*building*) annessi *mpl*; **in addition** inoltre, per di più; **in addition to** oltre a

additive ['ædɪtɪv] *adj & s* additivo

address [ə'drɛs] *or* ['ædrɛs] *s* (*speech*) discorso; (*place and destination of mail*) indirizzo; (*skill*) destrezza; (*formal request*) petizione; **to deliver an address** pronunciare un discorso || [ə'drɛs] *tr* indirizzare; (*to speak to*) rivolgere la parola a

addressee [,ædrɛ'si] *s* destinatario

address'ing machine' *s* macchina per indirizzi

adduce [ə'djus] *or* [ə'dus] *tr* addurre

adenoids ['ædə,nɔɪdz] *spl* vegetazioni *fpl* adenoidi, adenoidi *fpl*

adept [ə'dɛpt] *adj & s* esperto

adequate ['ædɪkwɪt] *adj* sufficiente; (*suitable*) conveniente

adhere [æd'hɪr] *intr* aderire

adherence [æd'hɪrəns] *s* aderenza

adherent [æd'hɪrənt] *adj & s* aderente *m*

adhesion [æd'hiʒən] *s* adesione; (pathol) aderenza

adhesive [æd'hisɪv] *or* [æd'hizɪv] *adj & s* adesivo

adhe'sive tape' *s* tela adesiva, cerotto

adieu [ə'dju] *or* [ə'du] *s* (adieus *or* adieux) addio || *interj* addio!

adjacent [ə'dʒesənt] *adj* adiacente

adjective ['ædʒɪktɪv] *adj* aggettivale, accessorio, secondario || *s* aggettivo

adjoin [ə'dʒɔɪn] *tr* confinare con || *intr* essere confinanti

adjoining [ə'dʒɔɪnɪŋ] *adj* confinante; vicino, attiguo

adjourn [ə'dʒʌrn] *tr* aggiornare, rinviare || *intr* rinviarsi

adjournment [ə'dʒʌrnmənt] *s* aggiornamento, rinvio

adjust [ə'dʒʌst] *tr* accomodare; regolare; (ins) liquidare || *intr* abituarsi

adjustable [ə'dʒʌstəbəl] *adj* regolabile

adjustment [ə'dʒʌstmənt] *s* aggiustamento; accomodamento; (ins) liquidazione del danno

adjutant ['ædʒətənt] *s* aiutante *mf*

ad-lib [,æd'lɪb] *v* (*pret & pp* -libbed; *ger* -libbing) *tr & intr* improvvisare

administer [æd'mɪnɪstər] *tr* amministrare; (*medicine*) somministrare; (*an oath*) dare || *intr*—**to administer to** ministrare, prestare aiuto a

administrator [æd'mɪnɪs,tretər] *s* amministratore *m*

admirable ['ædmɪrəbəl] *adj* ammirabile, ammirevole

admiral ['ædmɪrəl] *s* ammiraglio

admiral·ty ['ædmɪrəlti] *s* (-ties) ammiragliato

admire [æd'maɪr] *tr* ammirare

admirer [æd'maɪrər] *s* ammiratore *m*

admissible [æd'mɪsɪbəl] *adj* ammissibile

admission [æd'mɪʃən] *s* ammissione; confessione; (*entrance fee*) prezzo d'ingresso; **to gain admission** arrivare a entrare

ad·mit [æd'mɪt] *v* (*pret & pp* -mitted; *ger* -mitting) *tr* ammettere; confessare || *intr* dare l'ingresso; **to admit of** permettere, ammettere, consentire

admittance [æd'mɪtəns] *s* ammissione; permesso di entrare; **no admittance** divieto d'ingresso

admonish [æd'mɒnɪʃ] *tr* ammonire

ado [ə'du] *s* confusione, trambusto; **much ado about nothing** molto rumore per nulla; **to make a big ado** fare cerimonie

adobe [ə'dobi] *s* mattone crudo

adolescence [,ædə'lɛsəns] *s* adolescenza

adolescent [,ædə'lɛsənt] *adj & s* adolescente *mf*

adopt [ə'dɑpt] *tr* adottare

adoption [ə'dɑpʃən] *s* adozione

adorable [ə'dorəbəl] *adj* adorabile

adore [ə'dor] *tr* adorare

adorn [ə'dɔrn] *tr* adornare

adornment [ə'dɔrnmənt] *s* ornamento

adre'nal gland' [æd'rinəl] *s* glandola surrenale

Adriatic [,edrɪ'ætɪk] *or* [,ædrɪ'ætɪk] *adj* adriatico || *adj & s* Adriatico

adrift [ə'drɪft] *adj & adv* alla deriva

adroit [ə'drɔɪt] *adj* destro

adult [ə'dʌlt] *or* ['ædʌlt] *adj & s* adulto

adulterate [ə'dʌltə,ret] *tr* adulterare

adulterer [ə'dʌltərər] *s* adultero

adulteress [ə'dʌltərɪs] *s* adultera

adulter·y [ə'dʌltəri] *s* (-ies) adulterio

advance [æd'væns] *or* [æd'vɑns] *adj* avanzato || *s* avanzata; (*increase in price*) aumento; (*of money*) anticipo; **advances** approcci *mpl*; **in advance** in anticipo || *tr* avanzare; aumentare; (*to make earlier*) anticipare; (*money*) anticipare; (*a clock*) mettere avanti || *intr* avanzare; (*said, e.g., of prices*) aumentare

advanced [æd'vænst] *or* [æd'vɑnst] *adj* avanzato, progredito

advanced' stand'ing *s* trasferimento di voti scolastici

advancement [æd'vænsmənt] *or* [æd'vɑnsmənt] *s* progresso; promozione; (mil) avanzata

advance' public'ity *s* pubblicità *f* di lancio

advantage [æd'væntɪdʒ] *or* [æd'vɑntɪdʒ] *s* vantaggio; **to advantage** in maniera favorevole; **to take advantage of** approfittarsi di; abusare di || *tr* avantaggiare

advantageous [,ædvən'tedʒəs] *adj* vantaggioso

advent ['ædvɛnt] *s* avvento

adventure [æd'ventʃər] *s* avventura ‖ *tr* avventurare ‖ *intr* avventurarsi

adventurer [æd'ventʃərər] *s* avventuriero

adventuresome [æd'ventʃərsəm] *adj* avventuroso

adventuress [æd'ventʃərɪs] *s* avventuriera

adventurous [æd'ventʃərəs] *adj* avventuroso

adverb ['ædvʌrb] *s* avverbio

adversar·y ['ædvər,seri] *s* (-ies) avversario

adverse [æd'vʌrs] or ['ædvʌrs] *adj* avverso, contrario

adversi·ty [æd'vʌrsiti] *s* (-ties) avversità *f*

advertise ['ædvər,taɪz] or [,ædvər'taɪz] *tr* propagandare; reclamizzare ‖ *intr* fare la pubblicità; inserire un annunzio; inserzionare

advertisement [,ædvər'taɪzmənt] or [æd'vʌrtɪsmənt] *s* annuncio pubblicitario, inserzione

advertiser ['ædvər,taɪzər] or [,ædvər'taɪzər] *s* inserzionista *mf*

advertising ['ædvər,taɪzɪŋ] *s* pubblicità *f*, pubblicismo

ad'vertising a'gent *s* pubblicista *mf*

ad'vertising campaign' *s* campagna pubblicitaria

ad'vertising man' *s* agente *m* di pubblicità, reclamista *m*

advice [æd'vaɪs] *s* consiglio; **a piece of advice** un consiglio

advisable [æd'vaɪzəbəl] *adj* consigliabile

advise [æd'vaɪz] *tr* consigliare; informare ‖ *intr*—**to advise with** chiedere il consiglio di; avere una conferenza con

advisement [æd'vaɪzmənt] *s* considerazione; **to take under advisement** prendere in considerazione

adviser [æd'vaɪzər] *s* consigliere *m*

advisory [æd'vaɪzəri] *adj* consultivo

advocate ['ædvə,ket] *s* difensore *m*; *(lawyer)* avvocato ‖ *tr* sostenere, propugnare

adze [ædz] *s* ascia

Aege'an Sea' [ɪ'dʒi·ən] *s* mare Egeo

aegis ['idʒɪs] *s* egida

Aeneid [i'ni·ɪd] *s* Eneide *f*

aerate ['eret] or ['e·ə,ret] *tr* aerare

aerial ['ɛrɪ·əl] or [e'ɪrɪ·əl] *adj* aereo ‖ ['eri·əl] *s* (rad & telv) antenna

aer'ial pho'tograph *s* aerofotogramma *m*

aerodrome ['ɛrə,drom] *s* aerodromo

aerodynamic [,ɛrodaɪ'næmɪk] *adj* aerodinamico ‖ **aerodynamics** *ssg* aerodinamica

aeronaut ['ɛrə,nɔt] *s* aeronauta *m*

aeronautic [,ɛrə'nɔtɪk] *adj* aeronautico ‖ **aeronautics** *ssg* aeronautica

aerosol ['ɛrə,sol] *s* aerosol *m*

aerospace ['ɛro,spes] *adj* aerospaziale ‖ *s* aerospazio

Aesop ['isɑp] *s* Esopo

aesthete ['esθit] *s* esteta *mf*

aesthetic [es'θetɪk] *adj* estetico ‖ **aesthetics** *ssg* estetica

afar [ə'fɑr] *adv* lontano; **from afar** da lontano

affable ['æfəbəl] *adj* affabile

affair [ə'fɛr] *s* affare *m*; *(romance)* relazione amorosa

affect [ə'fɛkt] *tr* influenzare; *(to touch the heart of)* commuovere; *(to pretend to have)* affettare

affectation [,æfɛk'teʃən] *s* affettazione

affected [ə'fɛktɪd] *adj* affettato

affection [ə'fɛkʃən] *s* affezione

affectionate [ə'fɛkʃənɪt] *adj* affettuoso, affezionato

affidavit [,æfɪ'devɪt] *s* affidavit *m*, dichiarazione sotto giuramento

affiliate [ə'fɪlɪ,et] *adj* & *s* affiliato ‖ *tr* affiliare ‖ *intr* affiliarsi

affinity [ə'fɪnɪti] *s* (-ties) affinità *f*

affirm [ə'fʌrm] *tr* affermare; confermare

affirmative [ə'fʌrmətɪv] *adj* affermativo ‖ *s* affermativa

affix ['æfɪks] *s* affisso ‖ [ə'fɪks] *tr* affiggere; *(a signature)* apporre; *(e.g., blame)* attribuire

afflict [ə'flɪkt] *tr* affliggere

affliction [ə'flɪkʃən] *s* afflizione

affluence ['æflu·əns] *s* opulenza, abbondanza

affluent ['æflu·ənt] *adj* opulento, abbondante; ricco ‖ *s* affluente *m*

afford [ə'fɔrd] *tr* permettersi il lusso di; *(to furnish)* provvedere; *(to give)* dare

affray [ə'fre] *s* rissa

affront [ə'frʌnt] *s* affronto ‖ *tr* fare un affronto a

afghan ['æfgən] or ['æfgæn] *s* coperta di lana all'uncinetto ‖ **Afghan** *adj* & *s* afgano

afield [ə'fild] *adv* sul campo; **far afield** lontano

afire [ə'faɪr] *adj* ardente; in fuoco, in fiamme

aflame [ə'flem] *adj* in fiamme

afloat [ə'flot] *adj* & *adv* a galla; a bordo; *(drifting)* alla deriva; *(said of a rumor)* in circolazione

afoot [ə'fʊt] *adj* & *adv* a piedi; in movimento, in moto

aforementioned [ə'for,menʃənd] or **aforesaid** [ə'for,sed] *adj* suddetto

afoul [ə'faʊl] *adj* & *adv* in collisione; **to run afoul of** finire nelle mani di, impigliarsi con

afraid [ə'fred] *adj* impaurito, spaventato; **to be afraid (of)** aver paura (di)

African ['æfrɪkən] *adj* & *s* africano

aft [æft] or [ɑft] *adv* a poppa; indietro

after ['æftər] or ['ɑftər] *adj* seguente; di poppa ‖ *adv* dopo; *(behind)* dietro ‖ *prep* dopo; dopo di; *(in the manner of)* secondo; **to run after** correre dietro a ‖ *conj* dopo che

afterburner ['æftər,bʌrnər] or ['ɑftər,bʌrnər] *s* (aer) postbruciatore *m*

af'ter-din'ner *adj* dopo la cena

aftereffect ['æftəri,fekt] or ['ɑftəri,fekt] *s* conseguenza

af'ter-hours' *adj* dopo le ore di ufficio

af'ter-life' *s* aldilà *m*; vita susseguente

aftermath ['æftər‚mæθ] or ['aftər‚mæθ] s conseguenze *fpl;* gravi conseguenze *fpl*

af'ter·noon' *adj* pomeridiano ‖ *s* pomeriggio

after-shaving ['æftər‚ʃeviŋ] or ['aftər‚ʃeviŋ] *adj* dopobarba

af'ter·taste' *s* retrosapore *m*

af'ter·thought' *s* pensiero tardivo

afterward ['æftərwərd] or ['aftərwərd] *adv* dopo; **long afterward** molto tempo dopo

af'ter·while' *adv* fra un po'

again [ə'gɛn] *adv* di nuovo; ancora; un'altra volta; **again and again** ripetutamente; **as much again** due volte tanto, altrettanto; **to + inf + again** tornare a + *inf*, e.g., **to cook again** tornare a cuocere

against [ə'gɛnst] *prep* contro; (*opposite*) in faccia a; **to be against** opporsi a; **to go against the grain** ripugnare

agape [ə'gep] *adj* & *adv* a bocca aperta

age [edʒ] *s* età *f;* (*old age*) vecchiaia; (*full term of life*) vita; (*historical or geological period*) evo; generazione; **of age** maggiorenne; **to come of age** diventare maggiorenne; **under age** minorenne ‖ *tr* & *intr* invecchiare

aged [edʒd] *adj* dell'età di ‖ ['edʒɪd] *adj* vecchio, invecchiato

ageless ['edʒlɪs] *adj* eternamente giovane, che non invecchia mai

agen·cy ['edʒənsɪ] *s* (**-cies**) azione; agenzia; mediazione; (*of government*) ente *m*

agenda [ə'dʒɛndə] *s* agenda, ordine *m* del giorno

agent ['edʒənt] *s* agente *m;* (coll) commesso viaggiatore, agente *m* di commercio; (rr) gestore *m*

Age' of Enlight'enment *s* illuminismo

agglomeration [ə‚glɑmə'reʃən] *s* agglomerazione

aggrandizement [ə'grændɪzmənt] *s* aumento, innalzamento

aggravate ['ægrə‚vet] *tr* aggravare; (coll) irritare, esasperare

aggregate ['ægrɪ‚get] *adj* & *s* aggregato, totale *m;* **in the aggregate** nel complesso ‖ *tr* aggregare; ammontare a

aggression [ə'grɛʃən] *s* aggressione

aggressive [ə'grɛsɪv] *adj* aggressivo, attivo

aggressor [ə'grɛsər] *s* aggressore *m*

aggrieve [ə'griv] *tr* affliggere

aghast [ə'gæst] or [ə'gɑst] *adj* atterrito

agile ['ædʒɪl] *adj* agile

agitate ['ædʒɪ‚tet] *tr* agitare ‖ *intr* agitarsi

agitator ['ædʒɪ‚tetər] *s* agitatore *m*

aglow [ə'glo] *adj* splendente

agnostic [æg'nɑstɪk] *adj* & *s* agnostico

ago [ə'go] *adv* fa, e.g., **a year ago** un anno fa; **long ago** molto tempo fa

agog [ə'gɑg] *adj* & *adv* ansioso; **to set agog** riempire di ansietà

agonize ['ægə‚naɪz] *intr* soffrire straziantemente; (*to struggle*) dibattersi

ago·ny ['ægənɪ] *s* (**-nies**) agonia

agrarian [ə'grɛrɪ·ən] *adj* agrario ‖ *s* membro del partito agrario

agree [ə'gri] *intr* aderire, andar d'accordo; (*to consent*) acconsentire; (gram) concordare; **to agree with him** le uova non gli si confanno with, e.g., **eggs do not agree**

agreeable [ə'gri·əbəl] *adj* gentile; gradevole; (*willing to agree*) consenziente

agreement [ə'grimənt] *s* accordo; **in agreement** d'accordo

agriculture ['ægrɪ‚kʌltʃər] *s* agricoltura

agriculturist [‚ægrɪ'kʌltʃərɪst] *s* (*farmer*) agricoltore *m;* perito in agricoltura, agronomo

agronomy [ə'grɑnəmɪ] *s* agronomia

aground [ə'graund] *adv* alla riva; **to run aground** andare or dare in secca

ague ['egju] *s* (*chill*) brivido; febbre *f*

ahead [ə'hɛd] *adv* davanti, avanti; **to get ahead** (coll) andare avanti, aver successo; **to get ahead of** sorpassare; **to go ahead** avanzare; continuare

ahoy [ə'hɔɪ] *interj*—**ship ahoy!** ehi della barca!

aid [ed] *s* aiuto; assistente *m;* (mil) aiutante *m* di campo ‖ *tr* aiutare; **aid and abet** essere complice di

aide [ed] *s* assistente *m*

aide-de-camp ['eddə'kæmp] *s* (**aides-de-camp**) aiutante *m* di campo

ail [el] *tr* affliggere; **what ails you?** che ha? ‖ *intr* soffrire, essere malato

aileron ['elə‚rɑn] *s* alerone *m*

ailing ['eliŋ] *adj* ammalato

ailment ['elmənt] *s* malattia, indisposizione; (*chronic*) acciacco

aim [em] *s* mira; intento ‖ *tr* (*a gun*) puntare; (*words*) dirigere ‖ *intr* mirare; **to aim to** cercare di, aver l'intenzione di

air [ɛr] *adj* (e.g., *pocket*) d'aria; (e.g., *show*) aeronautico ‖ *s* aria; **by air** per via aerea; **in the open air** all'aria aperta; **to be in the air** circolare; **to be on the air** (rad, telv) essere in onda; **to go on the air** (rad, telv) andare in onda; **to put on airs** darsi delle arie; **to take the air** andar fuori; **up in the air** incerto; (slang) arrabbiato ‖ *tr* aerare, ventilare

airborne ['ɛr‚bɔrn] or ['ɛr‚born] *adj* aerosostentato; aerotrasportato

air' brake' *s* freno ad aria compressa

air' cas'tle *s* castello in aria

air'-condi'tion *tr* climatizzare

air' condi'tioner *s* condizionatore *m*

air' condi'tioning *s* aria condizionata, climatizzazione

air'-cool' *tr* raffreddare con aria

air' corps' *s* aviazione, arma aeronautica

air'craft' *s* (**-craft**) aeromobile *m*

air'craft car'rier *s* portaerei *f*

airdrome ['ɛr‚drom] *s* aerodromo

air'drop' *tr* paracadutare

air'field' *s* campo d'aviazione

air'foil' *s* superficie *f* portante, velatura

air' force' *s* forza aerea

air' gap' *s* (elec) intraferro

airing ['eriŋ] *s* aerazione; passeggiata all'aria aperta; pubblica discussione

air' jack'et *s* (aer, naut) giubbotto salvagente

air' lane' *s* aerovia

air'lift' *s* ponte aereo, aerotrasporto || *tr* aerotrasportare

air'line' *s* linea aerea; tubo dell'aria

air' mail' *s* posta aerea

air'-mail *adj* per via aerea || *s* lettera per posta aerea || *adv* per posta aerea || *tr* spedire per posta aerea

air'-mail let'ter *s* lettera per posta aerea

air'-mail stamp' *s* francobollo posta aerea

air'man *s* (-men) aviatore *m*, aviere *m*

air' mat'tress *s* materassino pneumatico

air'plane' *s* aeroplano, aereo

air'plane car'rier *s* portaerei *f*

air' pock'et *s* vuoto d'aria

air' pollu'tion *s* contaminazione atmosferica, inquinamento atmosferico

air' port' *s* aeroporto

air' pump' *s* pompa pneumatica

air' raid' *s* incursione aerea

air'-raid shel'ter *s* rifugio antiaereo

air'-raid warn'ing *s* allerta

air' ri'fle *s* fucile *m* ad aria compressa

air' serv'ice *s* aeroservizio

air' shaft' *s* tubo di ventilazione

air'ship' *s* aeronave *f*

airsickness ['er,sɪknɪs] *s* male *m* d'aria

air' sleeve' *s* manica a vento

airspace ['er,spes] *s* aerospazio

air'strip' *s* aviopista

air' ter'minal *s* aerostazione

air'tight' *adj* impermeabile all'aria, ermetico

air'waves' *spl* onde *fpl*, radioonde *fpl*

air'way' *s* aerovia; **airways** (rad) onda, onde *fpl*

airy ['eri] *adj* (-ier; -iest) arioso; leggero; aereo

aisle [ail] *s* (*between rows of seats*) corsia; (*of a church*) navata laterale; (theat) canale *m*

ajar [ə'dʒar] *adj* socchiuso; in disaccordo

akimbo [ə'kɪmbo] *adj & adv*—**with arms akimbo** con le mani sui fianchi

akin [ə'kɪn] *adj* affine; congiunto

alabaster ['ælə,bæstər] *or* ['ælə,bastər] *s* alabastro

à la carte [,alɑ'kɑrt] *adv* alla carta

à la mode [,ælə'mod] *or* [,ælə'mod] *adv* alla moda; servito con gelato

alarm [ə'lɑrm] *s* allarme *m* || *tr* allarmare

alarm' clock' *s* sveglia

alas [ə'læs] *or* [ə'lɑs] *interj* ahimè!, povero me!

Albanian [æl'benɪ·ən] *adj & s* albanese *mf*

albatross ['ælbə,trɔs] *or* ['ælbə,tras] *s* albatro, diomedea

album ['ælbəm] *s* album *m*

albumen [æl'bjumən] *s* albume *m*

alchemy ['ælkəmɪ] *s* alchimia

alcohol ['ælkə,hɔl] *or* ['ælkə,hal] *s* alcole *m*

alcoholic [,ælkə'hɔlɪk] *or* [,ælkə'halɪk] *adj* alcolico || *s* alcolizzato

alcove ['ælkov] *s* (*recess*) alcova; (*in a garden*) chiosco, padiglione *m*; cameretta attigua

alder ['ɔldər] *s* ontano, alno

al'der-man *s* (-men) assessore *m* municipale, consigliere *m* municipale

ale [el] *s* birra amara

alembic [ə'lembɪk] *s* alambicco

alert [ə'lʌrt] *adj* attento; vispo || *s* allerta; **to be on the alert** stare allerta || *tr* dare l'allerta a

Aleu'tian Is'lands [ə'lu/ən] *spl* Isole Aleutine

Alexander [,ælɪg'zændər] *or* [,ælɪg-'zandər] *s* Alessandro

Alexan'der the Great' *s* Alessandro Magno

Alexandrine [,ælɪg'zændrɪn] *adj & s* alessandrino

alfalfa [æl'fælfə] *s* (bot) erba medica

algae ['ældʒi] *spl* alghe *fpl*

algebra ['ældʒɪbrə] *s* algebra

algebraic [,ældʒɪ'bre·ɪk] *adj* algebrico

Algeria [æl'dʒɪrɪ·ə] *s* l'Algeria

Algerian [æl'dʒɪrɪ·ən] *adj & s* algerino

Algiers [æl'dʒɪrz] *s* Algeri *f*

alias ['elɪ·əs] *s* pseudonimo || *adv* alias

ali·bi ['ælɪ,baɪ] *s* (-bis) alibi *m*

alien ['eljən] *or* ['elɪ·ən] *adj* straniero; (*strange*) strano || *s* straniero; (*outsider*) estraneo

alienate ['eljə,net] *or* ['elɪ·ə,net] *tr* alienare

alight [ə'laɪt] *v* (*pret & pp* **alighted** *or* **alit** ['lɪt]) *intr* scendere; **to alight on** *or* **upon** posarsi su

align [ə'laɪn] *tr* allineare || *intr* allinearsi

alike [ə'laɪk] *adj* uguali; **to look alike** assomigliarsi || *adv* nello stesso modo

alimen'tary canal' [,ælɪ'mentərɪ] *s* tubo digestivo

alimony ['ælɪ,monɪ] *s* alimonia

alive [ə'laɪv] *adj* vivo, in vita; (*lively*) vivace; **alive to** conscio di; **alive with** brulicante di, pieno zeppo di; **look alive!** fa presto!

alka·li ['ælkə,laɪ] *s* (-lis *or* -lies) alcali *m*

alkaline ['ælkə,laɪn] *or* ['ælkəlɪn] *adj* alcalino

all [ɔl] *adj indef* tutto, tutto il, ogni || *s* tutto || *pron* tutto; tutti; **all of** tutti || *adv* completamente; **all but** quasi; **all in** (slang) stanco morto; **all in all** tutto considerato; **all the better** tanto meglio; **all the worse** tanto peggio; **far all that** per quello che, e.g., **for all that I know** per quello che io ne sappia; **in all** tutto, in tutto contato; **it's all right!** va bene!; **not at all** niente affatto; prego

allay [ə'le] *tr* calmare, mitigare

all' clear' *s* fine *f* dell'allarme, cessato allarme

allegation [,ælɪ'ge/ən] *s* asserzione, affermazione

allege [ə'ledʒ] *tr* asserire, affermare; addurre

allegiance [ə'lidʒəns] *s* fedeltà *f*, lealtà *f*

allegoric(al) [ˌælɪ'gɑrɪk(əl)] or [ˌælɪ-'gɔrɪk(əl)] *adj* allegorico

allego·ry ['ælɪˌgori] *s* (**-ries**) allegoria

aller·gy ['ælərdʒi] *s* (**-gies**) allergia

alleviate [ə'livɪˌet] *tr* alleviare

alley ['æli] *s* vicolo, calle *f*; (*for bowling*) pista; (*tennis*) corridoio

All' Fools' Day *s* primo d'aprile

all' fours' spl—on all fours a quattro gambe

alliance [ə'laɪ·əns] *s* alleanza

alligator ['ælɪˌgetər] *s* alligatore *m*

alliteration [əˌlɪtə're/ən] *s* allitterazione

all-knowing ['ɔl'no·ɪŋ] *adj* onnisciente

allocate ['æləˌket] *tr* assegnare; (*funds*) stanziare; (*to fix the place of*) allogare

allot [ə'lɑt] *v* (*pret & pp* **allotted**) *ger* **allotting**) *tr* distribuire, assegnare

all'-out' *adj* completo; (*ruthless*) acerrimo

allow [ə'lau] *tr* permettere; ammettere; concedere || *intr* **to allow for** prendere in considerazione

allowance [ə'lau·əns] *s* (*limited share*) assegno; concessione; (*reduction in price*) sconto; tolleranza; **to make allowance for** prendere in considerazione

alloy ['ælɔɪ] or [ə'lɔɪ] *s* lega; impurezza || [ə'lɔɪ] *tr* far lega di, legare; adulterare

all-powerful ['ɔl'pau·ərfəl] *adj* onnipotente

**all' right' ** *adj* esatto; bene; in buona salute; (*slang*) dabbene

All' Saints'' Day *s* Ognissanti *m*

All' Souls'' Day *s* giorno dei morti

all'spice' *s* pimento, pepe *m* della Giamaica

all'-star game' *s* partita sportiva in cui tutti i giocatori sono scelti fra i migliori

allude [ə'lud] *intr* alludere

allure [ə'lur] *s* fascino, incanto || *tr* affascinare, incantare

alluring [ə'lurɪŋ] *adj* affascinante, seducente

allusion [ə'luʃən] *s* allusione

al·ly ['ælaɪ] or [ə'laɪ] *s* (**-lies**) alleato || [ə'laɪ] *v* (*pret & pp* **-lied**) *tr* alleare; associare; **to become allied** allearsi; imparentarsi || *intr* allearsi

almanac ['ɔlməˌnæk] *s* almanacco

almighty [ɔl'maɪti] *adj* onnipotente

almond ['ɑmənd] or ['æmənd] *s* (*nut*) mandorla; (*tree*) mandorlo

al'mond brittle' *s* croccante *m*

almost ['ɔlmost] or [ɔl'most] *adv* quasi

alms [ɑmz] *s* elemosina

aloe ['ælo] *s* aloe *m*

aloft [ə'lɔft] or [ə'lɑft] *adv* in alto, sopra; (aer) in volo; (naut) nell'albératura

alone [ə'lon] *adj* solo; **let alone** senza menzionare; **to leave alone** non disturbare || *adv* solo, solamente

along [ə'lɔŋ] or [ə'lɑŋ] *adv* (*lengthwise*) per il lungo; (*onward*) avanti; **all along** tutto il tempo; **along with**

con; **to get along** andar d'accordo; andarsene; avanzare; aver successo; **to take along** prendere con sè || *prep* lungo

along'side' *adv* a lato; **alongside of** a lato di || *prep* a lato di, vicino a

aloof [ə'luf] *adj* riservato, freddo; **to keep or stand aloof from** tenersi a distanza da || *adv* lontano; da solo

aloud [ə'laud] *adv* ad alta voce

alphabet ['ælfəˌbet] *s* alfabeto

alpine ['ælpaɪn] *adj* alpino

Alps [ælps] *spl* Alpi *fpl*

already [ɔl'redi] *adv* già

Alsace [æl'ses] or ['ælsæs] *s* l'Alsazia

Alsatian [æl'seʃən] *adj & s* alsaziano

also ['ɔlso] *adv* anche

altar ['ɔltər] *s* altare *m*

al'tar boy' *s* accolito, chierico

al'tar-piece' *s* pala d'altare

alter ['ɔltər] *tr* alterare; (*a male animal*) castrare || *intr* diventare differente, cambiare

alteration [ˌɔltə're/ən] *s* alterazione, modifica

alternate ('ɔltərnɪt] or ['æltərnɪt] *s* sostituto, supplente *mf* || ['ɔltərˌnet] or ['æltərˌnet] *tr* alternare || *intr* alternarsi, avvicendarsi

al'ternating cur'rent *s* corrente alternata

alternator ['ɔltərˌnetər] or [æltər-ˌnetər] *s* alternatore *m*

although [ɔl'ðo] *conj* benchè, per quanto, malgrado

altimeter [æl'tɪmɪtər] or ['æltəˌmitər] *s* altimetro

altitude ['æltɪˌtjud] or ['æltɪˌtud] *s* altitudine *f*

al·to ['ælto] *s* (**-tos**) contralto

altogether [ˌɔltə'geðər] *adv* completamente, affatto, tutt'insieme

altruist ['æltru·ɪst] *s* altruista *mf*

altruistic [ˌæltru'ɪstɪk] *adj* altruistico

alum ['æləm] *s* allume *m*

aluminum [ə'luminəm] *s* alluminio

alum·na [ə'lʌmnə] *s* (**-nae** [ni]) diplomata, laureata

alum·nus [ə'lʌmnəs] *s* (**-ni** [nai]) diplomato, laureato

alveo·lus [æl'vi·ələs] *s* (**-li** [ˌlaɪ]) alveolo

always ['ɔlwɪz] or ['ɔlwez] *adv* sempre

amalgam [ə'mælgəm] *s* amalgama *m*

amalgamate [ə'mælgəˌmet] *tr* amalgamare || *intr* amalgamarsi

amass [ə'mæs] *tr* ammassare

amateur ['æmətʃər] *adj* da dilettante || *s* amatore *m*, dilettante *mf*

amaze [ə'mez] *tr* stupire, meravigliare

amazing [ə'mezɪŋ] *adj* straordinario

Amazon ['æməˌzɑn] or ['æməˌzən] *s* rio delle Amazzoni; (myth) Amazzone *f*

ambassador [æm'bæsədər] *s* ambasciatore *m*

ambassadress [æm'bæsədrɪs] *s* ambasciatrice *f*

amber ['æmbər] *s* ambra

ambigui·ty [ˌæmbɪ'gju·ɪti] *s* (**-ties**) ambiguità *f*

ambiguous [æm'bɪgju·əs] *adj* ambiguo

ambition [æm'bɪ/ən] *s* ambizione

ambitious [æm'bɪ/əs] *adj* ambizioso

amble ['æmbəl] *s* ambio || *intr* ambiare

ambulance ['æmbjələns] *s* ambulanza

ambush ['æmbʊ/] *s* imboscata; **to lie in ambush** tendere un'imboscata || *tr* appostare || *intr* appostarsi

amelioration [ə,miljə're/ən] *s* miglioramento

amen ['e'mɛn] or ['ɑ'mɛn] *s* amen *m* || *interj* amen!

amenable [ə'minəbəl] or [ə'mɛnəbəl] *adj* docile, aperto; (*accountable*) responsabile

amend [ə'mɛnd] *tr* emendare || **amends** *spl* ammenda, contravvenzione; **to make amends for** fare ammenda per

amendment [ə'mɛndmənt] *s* emendamento

amenity [ə'minɪti] or [ə'mɛnɪti] *s* (-ties) amenità *f*

American [ə'mɛrɪkən] *adj* & *s* americano

Americanize [ə'mɛrɪkə,naɪz] *tr* americanizzare

amethyst ['æmɪθɪst] *s* ametista

amiable ['emɪ-əbəl] *adj* amabile

amicable ['æmɪkəbəl] *adj* amichevole

amid [ə'mɪd] *prep* in mezzo a, fra, tra

amidship [ə'mɪd/ɪp] *adv* a mezzanave

amiss [ə'mɪs] *adj* erroneo, sbagliato || *adv* erroneamente; **to take amiss** offendersi, prendere in mala parte

amity ['æmɪti] *s* (-ties) amicizia

ammeter ['æm,mitər] *s* amperometro

ammonia [ə'monɪ-ə] *s* ammoniaca; acqua ammoniacale

ammunition [,æmjə'nɪ/ən] *s* munizione, munizioni *fpl*

amnesty ['æmnɪsti] *s* (-ties) amnistia || *v* (*pret* & *pp* **-tied**) *tr* amnistiare

amoeba [ə'mibə] *s* ameba

among [ə'mʌŋ] *prep* fra, tra, in mezzo a

amorous ['æmərəs] *adj* amoroso; erotico

amortize ['æmər,taɪz] *tr* ammortare

amount [ə'maʊnt] *s* ammontare *m* || *intr*—**to amount to** ammontare a

ampere ['æmpɪr] *s* ampere *m*

am'pere-hour' *s* amperora *m*

amphibious [æm'fɪbɪ-əs] *adj* anfibio

amphitheater ['æmfɪ,θi-ətər] *s* anfiteatro

ample ['æmpəl] *adj* ampio

amplifier ['æmplɪ,faɪ-ər] *s* amplificatore *m*

amplify ['æmplɪ,faɪ] *v* (*pret* & *pp* **-fied**) *tr* amplificare

amplitude ['æmplɪ,tjud] or ['æmplɪ,tud] *s* ampiezza

am'plitude modula'tion *s* modulazione d'ampiezza

amputate ['æmpjə,tet] *tr* amputare

amputee [,æmpjə'ti] *s* chi ha subito l'amputazione di un arto

amuck [ə'mʌk] *adv* freneticamente; **to run amuck** dare in un accesso di pazzia; attaccare alla cieca

amulet ['æmjəlɪt] *s* amuleto

amuse [ə'mjuz] *tr* divertire

amusement [ə'mjuzmənt] *s* divertimento

amuse'ment park' *s* parco dei divertimenti, luna park *m*

amusing [ə'mjuzɪŋ] *adj* divertente

an [æn] or [ən] *art indef* var of **a**, used before words beginning with vowel or mute *h*

anachronism [ə'nækrə,nɪzəm] *s* anacronismo

anaemia [ə'nimɪ-ə] *s* var of **anemia**

anaesthesia [,ænɪs'θiʒə] *s* anestesia

anaesthetic [,ænɪs'θɛtɪk] *adj* & *s* anestetico

anaesthetize [æ'nɛsθɪ,taɪz] *tr* anestetizzare

analogous [ə'næləgəs] *adj* analogo

analogy [ə'nælədʒi] *s* (-gies) analogia

analysis [ə'nælɪsɪs] *s* (-ses [,siz]) analisi *f*

analyst ['ænəlɪst] *s* analista *mf*

analytic(al) [,ænə'lɪtɪk(əl)] *adj* analitico

analyze ['ænə,laɪz] *tr* analizzare

anarchist ['ænərkɪst] *s* anarchico

anarchy ['ænərki] *s* anarchia

anathema [ə'næθɪmə] *s* anatema *m*

anatomic(al) [,ænə'tɑmɪk(əl)] *adj* anatomico

anatomy [ə'nætəmi] *s* (-mies) anatomia

ancestor ['ænsɛstər] *s* antenato

ancestry ['ænsɛstri] *s* (-tries) lignaggio, prosapia

anchor ['æŋkər] *s* ancora; **to cast anchor** gettare l'ancora; **to ride at anchor** stare all'ancora; **to weigh anchor** salpare l'ancora, salpare || *tr* ancorare || *intr* ancorarsi, stare all'ancora

anchovy ['ænt/ovi] *s* (-vies) acciuga

ancient ['en/ənt] *adj* antico || *s* vecchio, anziano; **the ancients** gli antichi

ancillary ['ænsɪ,lɛri] *adj* dipendente; ausiliario, ausiliare

and [ænd] or [ənd] *conj* e, ed; **and so on, and so forth** e così via

Andean [æn'di-ən] or ['ændɪ-ən] *adj* andino || *s* abitante *mf* della regione andina

Andes ['ændiz] *spl* Ande *fpl*

andiron ['ænd,aɪ-ərn] *s* alare *m*

anecdote ['ænɪk,dot] *s* aneddoto

anemia [ə'nimɪ-ə] *s* anemia

anemic [ə'nimɪk] *adj* anemico

an'eroid barom'eter ['ænə,rɔɪd] *s* barometro aneroide

anesthesia [,ænɪs'θiʒə] *s* anestesia

anesthetic [,ænɪs'θɛtɪk] *adj* & *s* anestetico

anesthetize [æ'nɛsθɪ,taɪz] *tr* anestetizzare

aneurysm ['ænjə,rɪzəm] *s* aneurisma *m*

anew [ə'nju] or [ə'nu] *adv* di nuovo, nuovamente

angel ['endʒəl] *s* angelo; (*financial backer*) chi finanziatore *m*

angelic(al) [æn'dʒɛlɪk(əl)] *adj* angelico

anger ['æŋgər] *s* ira, collera || *tr* adirare || *intr* adirarsi, incollerirsi

angle ['æŋgəl] *s* angolo; punto di vista

|| *intr* intrigare; **to angle for** darsi da fare per

an'gle i'ron *s* cantonale *m*, angolare *m*

angler ['æŋglər] *s* pescatore *m* alla lenza; (fig) intrigante *m*

Anglo-Saxon ['æŋglo'sæksən] *adj* & *s* angiosassone *mf*

an•gry ['æŋgri] *adj* (**-grier; -griest**) arrabbiato; (pathol) infiammato; **to become angry at** incollerirsi per; **to become angry with** adirarsi con

anguish ['æŋgwɪʃ] *s* angoscia, pena

angular ['æŋgjələr] *adj* angolare

anhydrous [æn'haɪdrəs] *adj* anidro

aniline ['ænrlɪn] or ['ænr‚laɪn] *s* anilina

animal ['ænɪməl] *adj* & *s* animale *m*

an'imated cartoon' ['ænr‚metrd] *s* cartone animato

animation [‚ænr'meʃən] *s* animazione

animosi•ty [‚ænr'mɑsrti] *s* (**-ties**) animosità *f*

animus ['ænɪməs] *s* odio, malanimo

anion ['æn‚ar•ən] *s* anione *m*

anise ['ænɪs] *s* anice *f*

anisette [‚ænr'zet] *s* anisetta

ankle ['æŋkəl] *s* caviglia

an'kle•bone' *s* malleolo

an'kle support' *s* cavigliera

anklet ['æŋklɪt] *s* calzino corto; bracciale *m* da caviglia

annals ['ænəlz] *spl* annali *mpl*

annex ['æneks] *s* annesso, dipendenza || [ə'neks] *tr* annettere, appropriarsi di

annihilate [ə'nar•r‚let] *tr* annientare

anniversa•ry [‚ænr'vʌrsəri] *adj* anniversario || *s* (**-ries**) anniversario

annotate ['ænə‚tet] *tr* annotare

announce [ə'naʊns] *tr* annunciare

announcement [ə'naʊnsmənt] *s* annuncio, partecipazione

announcer [ə'naʊnsər] *s* annunziatore *m*

annoy [ə'nɔɪ] *tr* annoiare, seccare

annoyance [ə'nɔɪ•əns] *s* fastidio, seccatura

annoying [ə'nɔɪ•ɪŋ] *adj* noioso

annual ['ænjʊ•əl] *adj* annuale || *s* annuario; pianta annuale

annui•ty [ə'nju•rti] or [ə'nu•rti] *s* (**-ties**) annualità *f*; (for life) vitalizio

an•nul [ə'nʌl] *v* (*pret* & *pp* **-nulled;** *ger* **-nulling**) *tr* annullare, cassare

annunciation [ə‚nʌnsr'eʃən] *s* annunzio || **Annunciation** *s* Annunciazione

anode ['ænod] *s* anodo

anoint [ə'nɔɪnt] *tr* ungere

anomalous [ə'nɑmələs] *adj* anomalo

anoma•ly [ə'nɑməli] *s* (**-lies**) anomalia

anonymi•ty [‚ænə'nɪmɪti] *s* (**-ties**) anonimia; **to preserve one's anonymity** serbare l'anonimo

anonymous [ə'nɑnɪməs] *adj* anonimo

another [ə'nʌðər] *adj* & *pron indef* un altro

answer ['ænsər] or ['ɑnsər] *s* risposta; (to a problem) soluzione || *tr* rispondere a; **this will answer your purpose** questo fa per Lei; **to answer back** (slang) dare una rispostaccia a; **to answer the door** andare a rispondere

|| *intr* rispondere; corrispondere; essere responsabile; **to answer back** (slang) dare una rispostaccia

ant [ænt] *s* formica

antagonism [æn'tægə‚nɪzəm] *s* antagonismo

antagonize [æn'tægə‚naɪz] *tr* opporsi a; creare antagonismo in

antarctic [ænt'ɑrktɪk] *adj* antartico || **the Antarctic** la regione antartica

anteater ['ænt‚itər] *s* formichiere *m*

antecedent [‚ænt'sidənt] *adj* & *s* antecedente *m*; **antecedents** antenati *mpl*

antechamber ['æntɪ‚tʃembər] *s* anticamera

antedate ['æntɪ‚det] *tr* antidatare; (to happen before) antecedere

antelope ['æntɪ‚lop] *s* antilope *f*

anten•na [æn'tenə] *s* (**-nae** [ni]) (of insect) antenna || *s* (**-nas**) (rad, telv) antenna

antepenult [‚æntɪ'pinʌlt] *s* terzultima sillaba

anteroom ['æntɪ‚rum] or ['æntɪ‚rʊm] *s* anticamera, sala d'aspetto

anthem ['ænθəm] *s* inno

ant'hill' *s* formicaio

antholo•gy [æn'θɑlədʒi] *s* (**-gies**) antologia

anthracite ['ænθrə‚saɪt] *s* antracite *f*

anthrax ['ænθræks] *s* antrace *m*

anthropoid ['ænθrə‚pɔɪd] *adj* antropoide, antropomorfo

anthropology [‚ænθrə'pɑlədʒi] *s* antropologia

antiaircraft [‚æntɪ'er‚kræft] or [‚æntɪ'er‚krɑft] *adj* antiaereo

antibiotic [‚æntɪbaɪ'ɑtɪk] *adj* & *s* antibiotico

antibod•y ['æntɪ‚bɑdi] *s* (**-ies**) anticorpo

anticipate [æn'tɪsɪ‚pet] *tr* anticipare, prevedere; ripromettersi

anticipation [æn‚tɪsɪ'peʃən] *s* anticipazione, previsione

antics ['æntɪks] *spl* pagliacciate *fpl*, buffonate *fpl*

antidote ['æntɪ‚dot] *s* antidoto

antifreeze ['æntɪ‚friz] *s* anticongelante *m*

antiglare [‚æntɪ'gler] *adj* antiabbagliante

anti-G' suit' *s* tuta antigravità

antiknock [‚æntɪ'nɑk] *adj* antidetonante

antimissile [‚æntɪ'mɪsɪl] *adj* antimissile

antimony ['æntɪ‚moni] *s* antimonio

antinoise [‚æntɪ'nɔɪz] *adj* antirumore

antipa•thy [æn'tɪpəθi] *s* (**-thies**) antipatia

antipersonnel [‚æntɪ‚pʌrsə'nel] *adj* (e.g., mine) antiuomo

antiquarian [‚æntɪ'kwerɪ•ən] *adj* & *s* antiquario

antiquar•y ['æntɪ‚kweri] *s* (**-ies**) antiquario

antiquated ['æntɪ‚kwetɪd] *adj* antiquato

antique [æn'tik] *adj* antico, vecchio; antiquato || *s* oggetto d'epoca, antichità *f*

antique' deal'er s antiquario
antique' store' s negozio d'antiquariato
antiqui·ty [æn'tɪkwɪtɪ] s (-ties) antichità f
anti-Semitic [,æntɪsɪ'mɪtɪk] adj antisemita
antiseptic [,æntɪ'septɪk] adj & s antisettico
antislavery [,æntɪ'slevərɪ] adj antischiavista
antitank [,æntɪ'tæŋk] adj anticarro
antitheft [,æntɪ'θeft] adj antifurto
antithe·sis [æn'tɪθɪsɪs] s (-ses [,sɪz]) antitesi f
antitoxin [,æntɪ'taksɪn] s antitossina
antitrust [,æntɪ'trʌst] adj antitrust
antler ['æntlər] s corno di cervo
antonym ['æntənɪm] s antonimo
Antwerp ['æntwərp] s Anversa
anvil ['ænvɪl] s incudine m
anxie·ty [æŋ'zaɪ·ətɪ] s (-ties) ansietà f; (psychol) angoscia
anxious ['æŋk/əs] adj ansioso; anxious about sollecito di; anxious for desideroso di
any ['enɪ] adj indef ogni, qualunque, qualsiasi; qualche, alcun, e.g., do you know any boy who could help me? conosce qualche ragazzo che possa aiutarmi?; di + art, e.g., do you want any cheese? vuole del formaggio?; not . . . any non . . . nessuno, e.g., he does not read any newspaper non legge nessun giornale || adv un po', e.g., do you want any? ne vuole un po'?; not . . . any longer non . . . più; not . . . any more non . . . più || pron ne, e.g., do you want any? ne vuole?
an'y·bod'y pron indef chiunque; (in interrogative sentences) qualcuno; not . . . anybody non . . . nessuno
an'y·how' adv in qualunque modo, comunque; in ogni caso; (haphazardly) alla rinfusa
an'y·one' pron indef chiunque; (in interrogative sentences) qualcuno; not . . . anyone non . . . nessuno
an'y·thing' s qualunque cosa || pron indef qualcosa; qualunque cosa; tutto quanto; checchessia; anything at all qualunque cosa; not . . . anything non . . . niente; not . . . anything at all non . . . niente affatto, non . . . nulla; not . . . anything else non . . . nient'altro
an'y·way' adv in qualunque modo, comunque; in ogni caso; (haphazardly) alla rinfusa
an'y·where' adv dovunque, in qualsiasi luogo; not . . . anywhere non . . . in nessun luogo
apace [ə'pes] adv presto, rapidamente
apart [ə'part] adv a parte, a pezzi; separatamente; apart from a parte da; oltre a; to come apart andare a pezzi, cadere a pezzi; to set apart mettere in disparte; to take apart smontare; to tear apart fare a pezzi; to tell apart distinguere
apartment [ə'partmənt] s appartamento; (single room) stanza

apart'ment house' s casa d'appartamenti
apathetic [,æpə'θetɪk] adj apatico
apathy ['æpəθɪ] s apatia
ape [ep] s scimmia antropomorfa; scimmia || tr imitare, scimmiottare
Apennines ['æpə,naɪnz] spl Appennini mpl
aperture ['æpərt/ər] s apertura
apex ['epeks] s (apexes or apices ['æpɪ,sɪz]) apice m
apheresis [ə'ferɪsɪs] s aferesi f
aphorism ['æfə,rɪzəm] s aforisma m
aphrodisiac [,æfrə'dɪzɪ,æk] adj & s afrodisiaco
apiar·y ['epɪ,erɪ] s (-ies) apiario
apiece [ə'pis] adv a testa, per persona; ciascuno
apish ['epɪ/] adj scimmiesco; da scimmia
aplomb [ə'plam] s disinvoltura, baldanza
apocalypse [ə'pakə,lɪps] s apocalisse f
apogee ['æpə,dʒi] s apogeo
apologetic [ə,palə'dʒetɪk] adj pieno di scuse
apologize [ə'palə,dʒaɪz] intr chiedere scusa, scusarsi
apolo·gy [ə'palədʒɪ] s (-gies) scusa; (makeshift) surrogato
apoplectic [,æpə'plektɪk] adj & s apoplettico
apoplexy ['æpə,pleksɪ] s apoplessia
apostle [ə'pasəl] s apostolo
apostrophe [ə'pastrəfɪ] s (mark) apostrofo; (rhet) apostrofe f
apothecar·y [ə'paθɪ,kerɪ] s (-ies) farmacista mf
appall [ə'pɔl] tr sgomentare, sbigottire
appalling [ə'pɔlɪŋ] adj sconcertante
appara·tus [,æpə'retəs] or [,æpə'rætəs] s (-tus or -tuses) apparato
apparel [ə'pærəl] s confezioni fpl, vestiario
apparent [ə'pærənt] or [ə'perənt] adj apparente; chiaramente visibile
apparition [,æpə'rɪ/ən] s apparizione
appeal [ə'pil] s appello; (attraction) attrattiva, fascino || tr (a sentence) appellare contro || intr dare nell'occhio; to appeal from (law) appellarsi contro; to appeal to supplicare, pregare; piacere a, e.g., his idea appeals to me la sua idea mi piace
appear [ə'pɪr] intr apparire; (to seem) sembrare; (said of a book) uscire; (before the public) presentarsi; (law) comparire
appearance [ə'pɪrəns] s apparizione; (of a book) pubblicazione; (outward look) apparenza; (law) comparizione; to keep up appearances salvare le apparenze
appease [ə'piz] tr pacificare, placare; (a desire) soddisfare
appeasement [ə'pizmənt] s pacificazione, tranquillizzazione
appel'late court' [ə'pelɪt] s corte f d'appello
appellation [,æpə'le/ən] s denominazione, nome m
append [ə'pend] tr allegare, aggiungere

appendage [ə'pendɪdʒ] s appendice f
appendicitis [ə,pendɪ'saɪtɪs] s appendicite f
appen·dix [ə'pendɪks] s (**-dixes** or **-dices** [dɪ,siz]) appendice f
appertain [,æpər'ten] intr spettare, riferirsi
appetite ['æpɪ,tat] s appetito
appetizer ['æpɪ,taɪzər] s (drink) aperitivo; (food) stimulante m dell'appetito
appetizing ['æpɪ,taɪzɪŋ] adj appetitoso
applaud tr applaudire, applaudire (with dat) || intr applaudire
applause [ə'plɔz] s applauso, applausi mpl
apple ['æpəl] s mela, pomo; (tree) melo, pomo
ap'ple·jack' s acquavite f di mele
ap'ple of dis'cord s pomo della discordia
ap'ple pie' s pupilla degli occhi di qlcu, beniamino di qlcu
ap'ple pie' s torta di mele
ap'ple pol'isher s leccapiedi mf
ap'ple·sauce' s marmellata di mele; (slang) scemenza
appliance [ə'plaɪ-əns] s apparecchio, apparato; (complicated instrument) congegno; (for domestic chores) utensile m; (act of applying) applicazione
applicant ['æplɪkənt] s postulante mf, aspirante m, candidato
application [,æplɪ'keʃən] s applicazione; uso; richiesta, domanda
ap·ply [ə'plaɪ] v (pret & pp **-plied**) tr applicare; (the brakes) mettere; (e.g., a nickname) affibbiare || intr (said of a rule) essere applicabile; fare richiesta; **to apply for** sollecitare
appoint [ə'pɔɪnt] tr nominare; assegnare; (to furnish) ammobiliare
appointee [,æpɔɪn'ti] s persona nominata a una carica
appointive [ə'pɔɪntɪv] adj a nomina
appointment [ə'pɔɪntmənt] s nomina; (position) ufficio; (agreement to meet) appuntamento; **appointments** mobilia, arredamento; **by appointment** previo appuntamento
apportion [ə'porʃən] tr spartire, dividere proporzionatamente
appraisal [ə'prezəl] s stima, valutazione; (of real estate) estimo
appraise [ə'prez] tr stimare, valutare
appreciable [ə'priʃɪ-əbəl] adj apprezzabile, notevole
appreciate [ə'priʃɪ,et] tr apprezzare, valutare; (to be grateful for) gradire; (to be aware of) rendersi conto di; (to raise in value) valorizzare || intr aumentare di valore
appreciation [ə,priʃɪ'eʃən] s apprezzamento, valutazione; (grateful recognition) gradimento, riconoscenza; valorizzazione
appreciative [ə'priʃɪ,etɪv] adj grato, riconoscente
apprehend [,æprɪ'hend] tr (to fear) temere; (to understand) comprendere; (to arrest) arrestare

apprehension [,æprɪ'henʃən] s timore m, apprensione; comprensione; arresto
apprehensive [,æprɪ'hensɪv] adj apprensivo
apprentice [ə'prentɪs] s apprendista mf, novizio || tr mettere in apprendistato; accettare in apprendistato
apprenticeship [ə'prentɪs,ʃɪp] s apprendistato, carovana
apprise or **apprize** [ə'praɪz] tr avvertire, avvisare; stimare, valutare
approach [ə'protʃ] s (a coming near) avvicinamento; (of night) avvicinarsi m, far m; approssimazione; (access) via d'accesso; (to a problem) impostazione; **approaches** approcci mpl || tr avvicinarsi a, avvicinare; fare approcci con || intr avvicinarsi, approssimarsi
approbation [,æprə'beʃən] s approvazione
appropriate [ə'proprɪ-ɪt] adj appropriato, acconcio || [ə'proprɪ,et] tr (to take) appropriarsi di; (to set aside for some specific use) stanziare
approval [ə'pruvəl] s approvazione, consenso; **on approval** in prova
approve [ə'pruv] tr & intr approvare
approximate [ə'prɑksɪmɪt] adj approssimato, approssimativo || [ə'prɑksɪ,met] tr approssimarsi a || intr approssimarsi
apricot ['eprɪ,kɑt] or ['æprɪ,kɑt] adj color albicocca || s (fruit) albicocca; (tree) albicocco
April ['eprɪl] s aprile m
A'pril fool' s pesce m d'aprile
A'pril Fools'' Day' s primo d'aprile
apron ['eprən] s grembiale m, grembiule m; **tied to the apron strings of** attaccato alle sottane di
apropos [,æprə'po] adj opportuno || adv—**apropos of** a proposito di
apse [æps] s abside f
apt [æpt] adj atto, appropriato; (quick) pronto; **to be apt to** essere propenso a, portato a
aptitude ['æptɪ,tjud] or ['æptɪ,tud] s attitudine f
ap'titude test' s esame m attitudinale
Apulia [ə'pjulɪ-ə] s la Puglia
aqualung ['ækwə,lʌŋ] s autorespiratore m
aquamarine [,ækwəmə'rin] s acquamarina
aquaplane ['ækwə,plen] s acquaplano || intr andare in acquaplano
aquari·um [ə'kwerɪ-əm] s (**-ums** or **-a** [ə]) acquario, vasca dei pesci
Aquarius [ə'kwerɪ-əs] s (astr) Acquario
aquatic [ə'kwætɪk] or [ə'kwatɪk] adj acquatico || s animale acquatico; pianta acquatica; **aquatics** sport acquatici
aqueduct ['ækwə,dʌkt] s acquedotto
aqueous ['ekwɪ-əs] or ['ækwɪ-əs] adj acquoso
aq'uiline nose' ['ækwɪ,laɪn] s naso aquilino
Arab ['ærəb] adj & s arabo
Arabic ['ærəbɪk] adj & s arabo

arbiter [ˈɑrbɪtər] s arbitro

arbitrary [ˈɑrbɪ ˌtreri] adj arbitrario

arbitrate [ˈɑrbɪ ˌtret] tr arbitrare ‖ intr fare l'arbitro

arbitration [ˌɑrbɪˈtreʃən] s arbitrato

arbitrator [ˈɑrbɪ ˌtretər] s arbitro

arbor [ˈɑrbər] s pergola, pergolato; (mach) albero, asse m

arbore·tum [ˌɑrbəˈritəm] s (-tums or -ta [tə]) arboreto

arbutus [ɑrˈbjutəs] s (Arbutus unedo) corbezzolo

arc [ɑrk] s arco; (elec) arco voltaico ‖ intr (elec) formare un arco

arcade [ɑrˈked] s arcata, portico

arch [ɑrtʃ] adj malizioso ‖ s arco; (anat) arco del piede ‖ tr attraversare; arcuare ‖ intr inarcarsi

archaeology [ˌɑrkɪˈɑlədʒɪ] s archeologia

archaic [ɑrˈke·ɪk] adj arcaico

archaism [ˈɑrke ˌɪzəm] or [ˈɑrkɪ ˌɪzəm] s arcaismo

archangel [ˈɑrk ˌendʒəl] s arcangelo

archbishop [ˈɑrtʃˈbɪʃəp] s arcivescovo

archduke [ˈɑrtʃˈdjuk] or [ˈɑrtʃˈduk] s arciduca m

archene·my [ˈɑrtʃˈenɪmɪ] s (-mies) nemico giurato

archer [ˈɑrtʃər] s arciere m

archery [ˈɑrtʃərɪ] s tiro con l'arco

archetype [ˈɑrkɪ ˌtaɪp] s archetipo, prototipo

archipela·go [ˌɑrkɪˈpeləgo] s (-gos or -goes) arcipelago

architect [ˈɑrkɪ ˌtekt] s architetto

architectural [ˌɑrkɪˈtekt/ərəl] adj architetturale, architettonico

architecture [ˈɑrkɪ ˌtekt/ər] s architettura

archives [ˈɑrkaɪvz] spl archivio

arch'way' s arcata

arc' lamp' s lampada ad arco

arctic [ˈɑrktɪk] adj artico ‖ **the Arctic** la regione artica

arc' weld'ing s saldatura ad arco

ardent [ˈɑrdənt] adj ardente

ardor [ˈɑrdər] s ardore m

arduous [ˈɑrdʒu·əs] or [ˈɑrdju·əs] adj arduo

area [ˈɛrɪ·ə] s area

ar'ea code' s prefisso

Argentina [ˌɑrdʒənˈtinə] s l'Argentina

Argentine [ˈɑrdʒən ˌtin] or [ˈɑrdʒən ˌtaɪn] adj & s argentino ‖ **the Argentine** l'Argentina

Argonaut [ˈɑrgə ˌnɔt] s argonauta m

argue [ˈɑrgju] tr dibattere; (to indicate) indicare, provare; **to argue out of** dissuadere da; **to argue s.o. into s.th** persuadere qlcu di qlco ‖ intr argomentare, discutere

argument [ˈɑrgjəmənt] s discussione, argomentazione; (theme) argomento

argumentative [ˌɑrgjəˈmentətɪv] adj litigioso

aria [ˈɑrɪ·ə] or [ˈɛrɪ·ə] s aria

arid [ˈærɪd] adj arido

aridity [əˈrɪdɪtɪ] s aridità f

Aries [ˈɛriz] or [ˈɛri ˌiz] s (astr) Ariete m

aright [əˈraɪt] adv correttamente; **to set aright** rettificare

arise [əˈraɪz] v (pret **arose** [əˈroz]; pp **arisen** [əˈrɪzən]) intr alzarsi; (to originate) provenire, trarre origine; (to occur) succedere, avvenire; (to be raised, as objections) avanzarsi

aristocra·cy [ˌærɪsˈtɑkrəsi] s (-cies) aristocrazia

aristocrat [əˈrɪstə ˌkræt] s aristocratico

aristocratic [ə ˌrɪstəˈkrætɪk] adj aristocratico

Aristotelian [ˌærɪstəˈtilɪ·ən] adj & s aristotelico

Aristotle [ˈærɪ ˌstatəl] s Aristotele m

arithmetic [əˈrɪθmətɪk] s aritmetica

arithmetical [ˌærɪθˈmetɪkəl] adj aritmetico

arithmetician [ˌærɪθməˈtɪʃən] or [ə ˌrɪθməˈtɪʃən] s aritmetico

ark [ɑrk] s arca

ark' of the cov'enant s arca dell'alleanza

arm [ɑrm] s braccio; (e.g., of a bear) zampa; (of a chair) bracciolo; (weapon) arma; **arm in arm** a braccetto; **to be up in arms** essere in armi; essere indignato; **to lay down one's arms** deporre le armi; **to rise up in arms** levarsi in armi; **with open arms** a braccia aperte ‖ tr armare ‖ intr armarsi

armament [ˈɑrməmənt] s armamento

armature [ˈɑrmə ˌt/ər] s (of an animal) corazza; (of motor or dynamo) indotto; (of a buzzer or electric bell) ancora

arm'chair' s poltrona

Armenian [ɑrˈminɪ·ən] adj & s armeno

armful [ˈɑrm ˌful] s bracciata

arm'hole' s giro manica

armistice [ˈɑrmɪstɪs] s armistizio

armlet [ˈɑrmlɪt] s bracciale m

armor [ˈɑrmər] s armatura, corazza ‖ tr corazzare, blindare

ar'mored car' s carro armato

ar'mor plate' s lamiera di corazza

armor·y [ˈɑrmərɪ] s (-ies) armeria; arsenale m

arm'pit' s ascella

arm'rest' s bracciolo

ar·my [ˈɑrmɪ] adj dell'esercito, militare ‖ s (-mies) esercito; (two or more army corps) armata

ar'my corps' s corpo d'armata

aromatic [ˌærəˈmætɪk] adj aromatico

around [əˈraʊnd] adv intorno; all'intorno; dappertutto; **to turn around** voltarsi ‖ prep intorno a; (coll) vicino a; (approximately) (coll) circa

arouse [əˈraʊz] tr eccitare, incitare; svegliare

arpeg·gio [ɑrˈpedʒo] s (-gios) arpeggio

arraign [əˈren] tr citare, portare in giudizio; accusare

arrange [əˈrendʒ] tr disporre, sistemare; (a dispute) comporre, accomodare; (mus) ridurre, arrangiare

arrangement [əˈrendʒmənt] s disposizione, sistemazione; composizione; accomodamento; (mus) riduzione, arrangiamento; **arrangements** preparazione, preparativi *mpl*

array [ə're] *s* ordine *m*; *(clothes)* abbigliamento; *(mil)* spiegamento, schiera || *tr* disporre; abbigliare, adornare; *(mil)* spiegare, schierare

arrears [ə'rɪrz] *spl* arretrati *mpl*; **in arrears** in arretrato

arrest [ə'rest] *s* arresto; **under arrest** in arresto || *tr* arrestare; *(the attention)* attrarre

arresting [ə'restɪŋ] *adj* interessante, che fa colpo

arrival [ə'raɪvəl] *s* arrivo; persona arrivata

arrive [ə'raɪv] *intr* arrivare

arrogance ['ærəgəns] *s* arroganza

arrogant ['ærəgənt] *adj* arrogante

arrogate ['ærə,get] *tr (to take without right)* arrogare per sé, arrogarsi; *(to claim for another)* attribuire ingiustamente

arrow ['æro] *s* freccia, saetta

ar'row·head' *s* punta di freccia; *(bot)* sagittaria

arsenal ['ɑrsənəl] *s* arsenale *m*

arsenic ['ɑrsɪnɪk] *s* arsenico

arson ['ɑrsən] *s* incendio doloso

art [ɑrt] *s* arte *f*

arter·y ['ɑrtəri] *s* (**-ies**) arteria

artful ['ɑrtfəl] *adj* artificioso; *(clever)* destro; *(crafty)* astuto

arthritic [ɑr'θrɪtɪk] *adj & s* artritico

arthritis [ɑr'θraɪtɪs] *s* artrite *f*

artichoke ['ɑrtɪ,tʃok] *s* carciofo

article ['ɑrtɪkəl] *s* articolo

articulate [ɑr'tɪkjəlɪt] *adj* articolato; facile di parola || ['ɑrtɪkjə,let] *tr* articolare || *intr* pronunziare in modo articolato

articulation [ɑr,tɪkjə'leʃən] *s* articolazione

artifact ['ɑrtɪ,fækt] *s* manufatto

artifice ['ɑrtɪfɪs] *s* artificio

artificial [,ɑrtɪ'fɪʃəl] *adj* artificiale

artillery [ɑr'tɪləri] *s* artiglieria

artil'lery·man *s* (**-men**) artigliere *m*, cannoniere *m*

artisan ['ɑrtɪzən] *s* artigiano

artist ['ɑrtɪst] *s* artista *mf*

artistic [ɑr'tɪstɪk] *adj* artistico

artistry ['ɑrtɪstri] *s* abilità artistica

artless ['ɑrtlɪs] *adj* ingenuo, naturale; ignorante; *(clumsy)* grossolano

arts' and crafts' *spl* arti *fpl* e mestieri *mpl*

art·y ['ɑrti] *adj* (**-ier; -iest**) *(coll)* interessato nell'arte con ostentazione

Aryan ['ɛrɪ·ən] or ['ɑrjən] *adj & s* ariano

as [æz] or [əz] *pron rel* che; **the same as** lo stesso che || *adv* come; per esempio; **as . . . as** così . . . come; **as far as** fino a; **as far as I know** per quanto mi consta; **as for** in quanto a, per quanto concerne; **as is** *(slang)* com'è, nelle condizioni in cui si trova; **as long as** tanto che, mentre che; **as per secondo**; **as soon as** appena, non appena, non appena che; **as to** per quanto concerne; **as well** pure, anche; **as yet** ancora || *prep* come; da; **as a rule** come regola ||

conj come; mentre; dato che; per quanto; **as if** come se; **as it were** per così dire; **as though** come se

asbestos [æs'bestəs] *s* asbesto, amianto

ascend [ə'send] *tr* ascendere, scalare || *intr* ascendere, salire

ascension [ə'senʃən] *s* ascensione, scalata || **Ascension** *s* Ascensione

ascent [ə'sent] *s* scalata; salita; *(slope)* erta

ascertain [,æsər'ten] *tr* sincerarsi di, verificare

ascertainable [,æsər'tenəbəl] *adj* verificabile

ascetic [ə'setɪk] *adj* ascetico || *s* asceta *m*

ascor'bic ac'id [ə'skɔrbɪk] *s* acido ascorbico

ascribe [ə'skraɪb] *tr* attribuire, imputare

aseptic [ə'septɪk] or [e'septɪk] *adj* asettico

ash [æʃ] *s* cenere *f*; *(bot)* frassino

ashamed [ə'ʃemd] *adj* vergognoso; **to be or feel ashamed** vergognarsi

ash'can' *s* pattumiera; *(coll)* bomba antisommergibile

ashen ['æʃən] *adj* cinereo

ashlar ['æʃlər] *s* bugna, bugnato

ashore [ə'ʃor] *adv* a terra; **to come ashore** andare a terra, sbarcare; **to run ashore** arenarsi

ash'tray' *s* portacenere *m*

Ash' Wednes'day *s* le Ceneri

Asia ['eʒə] or ['eʃə] *s* l'Asia *f*

A'sia Mi'nor *s* l'Asia *f* Minore

Asian ['eʒən] or ['eʃən] or **Asiatic** [,eʒɪ'ætɪk] or [,eʃɪ'ætɪk] *adj & s* asiatico

aside [ə'saɪd] *s* parola detta a parte; *(theat)* a parte *m* || *adv* da parte; a parte; **aside from** *(coll)* eccetto; separato da; **to step aside** farsi da un lato

asinine ['æsɪnaɪn] *adj* *(like an ass)* asinino; *(stupid)* asinesco

ask [æsk] or [ɑsk] *tr* chiedere (with *dat*), domandare (with *dat*); invitare; *(a question)* fare; **to ask s.o. s.th** chiedere or domandare qlco a qlcu; **to ask s.o. to** + *inf* chiedere a qlcu di + *inf* || *intr* chiedere; **to ask about** chiedere informazioni di; **to ask for** chiedere, domandare; **to ask for it** *(coll)* andare in cerca di disgrazie; *(coll)* volerlo, e.g., **he asked for it** l'ha voluto

askance [ə'skæns] *adv* di traverso, di sbieco; *(fig)* con sospetto

asleep [ə'slip] *adj* addormentato; **to fall asleep** addormentarsi

asp [æsp] *s* aspide *m*

asparagus [ə'spærəgəs] *s* asparago; *(as food)* asparagi *mpl*

aspect ['æspekt] *s* aspetto; *(direction anything faces)* esposizione

aspen ['æspən] *s* pioppo tremolo, tremolo

aspersion [ə'spʌrʒən] or [ə'spʌrʃən] *s* diffamazione, calunnia; *(eccl)* aspersione

asphalt ['æsfɔlt] or ['æsfælt] *s* asfalto || *tr* asfaltare

asphyxiate [æs'frksɪ,et] *tr* asfissiare
aspirant [ə'spaɪrənt] or ['æspɪrənt] *s* aspirante *mf*
aspire [ə'spaɪr] *intr* aspirare
aspirin ['æspɪrɪn] *s* aspirina
ass [æs] *s* asino
assail [ə'sel] *tr* assalire, assaltare
assassin [ə'sæsɪn] *s* assassino
assassinate [ə'sæsɪ,net] *tr* assassinare
assassination [ə,sæsɪ'neʃən] *s* assassinio
assault [ə'sɔlt] *s* assalto || *tr* assaltare
assault' and bat'tery *s* vie *fpl* di fatto
assay [ə'se] or ['æse] *s* saggio, esame *m* || [ə'se] *tr* saggiare
assemblage [ə'semblɪdʒ] *s* assemblea; (mach) montaggio
assemble [ə'sembəl] *tr* riunire; (mach) montare, mettere insieme || *intr* assembrarsi, riunirsi
assembler [ə'semblər] *s* montatore *m*
assem-bly [ə'semblɪ] *s* (-blies) assemblea, riunione; (mach) montaggio
assem'bly hall' *s* sala di riunioni
assem'bly line' *s* catena di montaggio
assem'bly-man *s* (-men) membro dell'assemblea legislativa
assent [ə'sent] *s* assenso || *intr* assentire
assert [ə'sʌrt] *tr* asserire; to assert oneself far valere i propri diritti
assertion [ə'sʌrʃən] *s* asserzione
assess [ə'ses] *tr* stimare, valutare; (for taxation or fine) tassare
assessment [ə'sesmənt] *s* valutazione; tassazione
assessor [ə'sesər] *s* agente *m* delle tasse
asset ['æsət] *s* vantaggio; persona di valore; assets (com) attivo; (law) beni *mpl*
assiduous [ə'sɪdʒu-əs] or [ə'sɪdju-əs] *adj* assiduo
assign [ə'saɪn] *s* cessionario || *tr* assegnare; (e.g., a date) fissare; (a right) trasferire
assignation [,æsɪg'neʃən] *s* assegnazione; trasferimento; (date) appuntamento amoroso
assignment [ə'saɪnmənt] *s* assegnamento; (of rights) trasferimento; (schoolwork) compito
assimilate [ə'sɪmɪ,let] *tr* assimilare || *intr* essere assimilato; assimilarsi
assist [ə'sɪst] *s* aiuto || *tr* aiutare, assistere
assistance [ə'sɪstəns] *s* assistenza, aiuto
assistant [ə'sɪstənt] *adj* & *s* assistente *m*
associate [ə'soʃɪ-ɪt] or [ə'soʃɪ,et] *adj* associato || *s* associato; membro limitato || [ə'soʃɪ,et] *tr* associare || *intr* associarsi
association [ə,soʃɪ'eʃən] *s* associazione
assort [ə'sɔrt] *tr* assortire || *intr* associarsi
assortment [ə'sɔrtmənt] *s* assortimento
assuage [ə'swedʒ] *tr* alleviare
assume [ə'sum] or [ə'sjum] *tr* assumere; (to appropriate) usurpare; (to pretend) fingere; (to suppose) supporre
assumed [ə'sumd] or [ə'sjumd] *adj* supposto, immaginario

assumption [ə'sʌmpʃən] *s* (arrogance) aria, arroganza; (thing taken for granted) supposizione; (of an undertaking) assunzione
assurance [ə'ʃurəns] *s* assicurazione, certezza; baldanza, fiducia in sè; (too much boldness) sicumera
assure [ə'ʃur] *tr* assicurare
assuredly [ə'ʃurɪdlɪ] *adv* sicuramente
astatine ['æstə,tin] *s* astato
asterisk ['æstə,rɪsk] *s* asterisco, stelloncino
astern [ə'stʌrn] *adv* a poppa, a poppavia
asthma ['æzmə] or ['æsmə] *s* asma
astonish [ə'stanɪʃ] *tr* meravigliare, stupefare
astonishing [ə'stanɪʃ/ɪŋ] *adj* stupefacente, sorprendente
astound [ə'staund] *tr* stupefare, sbalordire
astounding [ə'staundɪŋ] *adj* stupefacente
astraddle [ə'strædəl] *adv* a cavaliere, a cavalcioni
astray [ə'stre] *adv* sulla cattiva via; to go astray traviarsi; to lead astray traviare
astride [ə'straɪd] *adj* & *adv* a cavaliere; (said of a person) a cavalcioni || *prep* a cavaliere di; a cavalcioni di
astrology [ə'stralədʒɪ] *s* astrologia
astronaut ['æstrə,nɔt] *s* astronauta *mf*
astronautic [,æstrə'nɔtɪk] *adj* astronautico || astronautics *ssg* astronautica
astronomer [ə'stranəmər] *s* astronomo
astronomic(al) [,æstrə'namɪk(əl)] *adj* astronomico
astronomy [ə'stranəmɪ] *s* astronomia
astute [ə'stjut] or [ə'stut] *adj* astuto
asunder [ə'sʌndər] *adv* a pezzi; to tear asunder separare, fare a pezzi
asylum [ə'saɪləm] *s* asilo
asymmetry [ə'sɪmɪtrɪ] *s* asimmetria
at [æt] or [ət] *prep* a; in; a casa di, e.g., at John's a casa di Giovanni; da, e.g., at Mary's da Maria; di, e.g., to be surprised at essere sorpreso di; to laugh at ridersi di
atheist ['eθɪ-ɪst] *s* ateista *mf*
Athenian [ə'θinɪ-ən] *adj* & *s* ateniese *mf*
Athens ['æθɪnz] *s* Atene *f*
athirst [ə'θʌrst] *adj* assetato
athlete ['æθlit] *s* atleta *mf*
athletic [æθ'letɪk] *adj* atletico || athletics *ssg* & *spl* atletica
Atlantic [æt'læntɪk] *adj* atlantico || *adj* & *s* Atlantico
atlas ['ætləs] *s* atlante *m* || Atlas *s* Atlante *m*
atmosphere ['ætməs,fɪr] *s* atmosfera
atmospheric [,ætməs'ferɪk] *adj* atmosferico || atmospherics *spl* disturbi atmosferici
atom ['ætəm] *s* atomo
at'om bomb' *s* bomba atomica
atomic [ə'tamɪk] *adj* atomico
atom'ic age' *s* era atomica
atom'ic sub'marine *s* sommergibile *m* nucleare
atomize ['ætə,maɪz] *tr* atomizzare

atomizer ['ætə ,maɪzər] s nebulizzatore m

at'om smash'er s acceleratore m di particelle

atone [ə'ton] intr—to atone for espiare

atonement [ə'tonmənt] s riparazione; espiazione

atop [ə'tap] adv in cima || prep in cima a

atrocious [ə'troʃəs] adj atroce

atroci•ty [ə'trasɪtɪ] s (-ties) atrocità f

atro•phy ['ætrəfɪ] s atrofia || v (pret & pp -phied) tr atrofizzare || intr atrofizzarsi

attaché [ə'tætʃ] tr attaccare; (to affix) apporre; (to attribute) attribuire; (law) sequestrare; **to be attached to** essere legato a; fare parte di || intr— **to attach to** essere pertinente a

attaché [ə'tæʃe] or [ə'tæʃe] s attaché m., addetto

attaché' case' s valigetta diplomatica

attachment [ə'tætʃmənt] s attacco, unione; affezione; (mach) accessorio; (law) sequestro

attack [ə'tæk] s attacco || tr & intr attaccare

attain [ə'ten] tr raggiungere || intr—to **attain to** raggiungere, conseguire

attainder [ə'tendər] s morte f civile

attainment [ə'tenmənt] s raggiungimento, realizzazione; (accomplishment) dote f

attempt [ə'tempt] s tentativo; (attack) attentato || tr tentare; (s.o.'s life) attentare a

attend [ə'tend] tr (to be present at) presenziare, presenziare a, assistere a; (to accompany) accompagnare; (to take care of; to pay attention to) assistere || intr—to **attend to** occuparsi di, attendere a

attendance [ə'tendəns] s (attending) presenza; (company present) concorso; **to dance attendance** essere al servizio completo

attendant [ə'tendənt] adj assistente; (accompanying) concomitante || s (servant) inserviente mf; presente m

attention [ə'tenʃən] s attenzione; (mil) attenti m; **attentions** attenzioni fpl; **to call s.o.'s attention to s.th** fare presente qlco a qlcu; **to stand at attention** stare sull'attenti || interj attenti!

attentive [ə'tentɪv] adj attento, premuroso

attenuate [ə'tenju ,et] tr attenuare

attest [ə'test] tr attestare || intr—to **attest to** attestare, testimoniare

attic ['ætɪk] s attico, solaio || **Attic** adj & s attico

attire [ə'taɪr] s vestiti mpl, vestiario || tr vestire

attitude ['ætɪ ,tjud] or ['ætɪ ,tud] s atteggiamento, attitudine f; **to strike an attitude** atteggiarsi

attorney [ə'tʌrnɪ] s avvocato; (proxy) procuratore m

attor'ney gen'eral s (attor'neys gen'eral or attor'ney gen'erals) procuratore m generale || **Attorney General** s (U.S.A.) ministro di grazia e giustizia

attract [ə'trækt] tr attrarre; (attention) chiamare

attraction [ə'trækʃən] s attrazione

attractive [ə'træktɪv] adj attrattivo

attribute ['ætrɪ ,bjut] s attributo || [ə'trɪbjut] tr attribuire

attrition [ə'trɪʃən] s attrito; diminuzione di numero

auburn ['ɔbərn] adj & s biondo fulvo, rosso tizianesco

auction ['ɔkʃən] s asta, incanto || tr vendere all'asta

auctioneer [,ɔkʃə'nɪr] s banditore m || tr & intr vendere all'asta

audacious [ə'deʃəs] adj audace

audaci•ty [ə'dæsɪtɪ] s (-ties) audacia

audience ['ɔdɪ əns] s (hearing) udienza; uditorio, pubblico

au'dio fre'quency ['ɔdɪ ,o] s audiofrequenza

au'dio-vis'ual aids' spl sussidi audiovisivi

audit ['ɔdɪt] s verifica or esame m dei conti || tr esaminare i conti di; (a class) assistere a, come uditore || intr assistere a una classe come uditore

audition [ə'dɪʃən] s audizione || tr dare un'audizione a

auditor ['ɔdɪtər] s revisore m dei conti; (educ) uditore m

auditorium [,ɔdɪ'torɪ əm] s auditorio

auger ['ɔgər] s succhiello, trivella

aught [ɔt] s zero; **for aught I know** per quanto ne so || adv affatto

augment [ɔg'ment] tr & intr aumentare

augur ['ɔgər] s augure m || tr & intr vaticinare

augu•ry ['ɔgərɪ] s (-ries) augurio

august [ə'gʌst] adj augusto || **August** ['ɔgəst] s agosto

aunt [ænt] or [ɑnt] s zia

aurora [ə'rorə] s aurora

auspice ['ɔspɪs] s auspicio; **under the auspices of** sotto gli auspici di

austere [ɔs'tɪr] adj austero

Australia [ɔ'streljə] s l'Australia f

Australian [ɔ'streljən] adj & s australiano

Austria ['ɔstrɪ ə] s l'Austria f

Austrian ['ɔstrɪ ən] adj & s austriaco

authentic [ɔ'θentɪk] adj autentico

authenticate [ɔ'θentɪ ,ket] tr autenticare

author ['ɔθər] s autore m

authoress ['ɔθərɪs] s autrice f

authoritarian [ə ,θarɪ'terɪ ən] or [ə- ,θɔrɪ'terɪ ən] adj autoritario || s persona autoritaria

authoritative [ə'θarɪ ,tetɪv] or [ə'θɔrɪ- ,tetɪv] adj autorevole; autoritario

authori•ty [ə'θarɪtɪ] or [ə'θɔrɪtɪ] s (-ties) autorità f; **on good authority** da buona fonte, da fonte autorevole

authorize ['ɔθə ,raɪz] tr autorizzare

authorship ['ɔθər ,ʃɪp] s paternità letteraria

au•to ['ɔto] s (-tos) (coll) auto f

autobiogra•phy [,ɔtobaɪ'agrəfɪ] or [,ɔtobɪ'agrəfɪ] s (-phies) autobiografia

autobus [ˈɔto ˌbʌs] s autobus m
autocratic(al) [ˌɔtəˈkrætɪk(əl)] adj autocratico
autograph [ˈɔtə ˌɡræf] or [ˈɔtə ˌɡrɑf] adj & s autografo ‖ tr porre l'autografo su, firmare con firma autografa
automat [ˈɔtə ˌmæt] s ristorante m self-service a distribuzione automatica
automate [ˈɔtə ˌmet] tr automatizzare
automatic [ˌɔtəˈmætɪk] adj automatico ‖ s pistola automatica
automat'ic transmis'sion s trasmissione automatica
automation [ˌɔtəˈmeʃən] s automazione
automa·ton [ɔˈtɑmə ˌtɑn] s (-tons or -ta [tə]) automa m
automobile [ˌɔtəmoˈbil] or [ˌɔtəˈmobil] adj & s automobile f
automobile' show' s salone m dell'automobile
automotive [ˌɔtəˈmotɪv] adj (self-propelled) automotore; automobilistico
autonomous [ɔˈtɑnəməs] adj autonomo
autonomy [ɔˈtɑnəmi] s autonomia
autop·sy [ˈɔtɑpsi] s (-sies) autopsia
au'to trans'port rig' s autotreno per trasporto di automobili
autumn [ˈɔtəm] s autunno
autumnal [ɔˈtʌmnəl] adj autunnale
auxilia·ry [ɔɡˈzɪljəri] adj & s (-ries) ausiliare m
avail [əˈvel] s utilità f; **of no avail** che non serve a nulla ‖ tr servire (with dat); **to avail oneself of** servirsi di; approfittare di ‖ intr servire
available [əˈveləbəl] adj disponibile; **to make available to** mettere alla disposizione di
avalanche [ˈævə ˌlæntʃ] or [ˈævə ˌlɑntʃ] s valanga
avant-garde [əvɑˈɡard] adj d'avanguardia
avant-gardism [əˈvɑ̃ˈɡardɪzəm] s avanguardismo
avarice [ˈævərɪs] s avarizia
avaricious [ˌævəˈrɪʃəs] adj avaro
avenge [əˈvendʒ] tr vendicare; **to avenge oneself on** vendicarsi di
avenue [ˈævə ˌnju] or [ˈævənu] s viale m, corso
aver [əˈvʌr] v (pret & pp averred; ger averring) tr asserire, affermare
average [ˈævərɪdʒ] adj medio ‖ s media; (naut) avaria; (e.g., of goals) (sports) quoziente m; **on the average** di media ‖ tr fare la media di; fare . . . di media, e.g., **he averages one hundred dollars a week** fa cento dollari di media alla settimana
averse [əˈvʌrs] adj avverso
aversion [əˈvʌrʒən] s avversione
avert [əˈvʌrt] tr (to ward off) evitare; (to turn away) distogliere
aviar·y [ˈevi ˌeri] s (-ies) aviario, voliera
aviation [ˌeviˈeʃən] s aviazione
aviator [ˈevi ˌetər] s aviatore m
avid [ˈævɪd] adj avido
avidity [əˈvɪdɪti] s avidità f

avocation [ˌævəˈkeʃən] s svago, passatempo
avoid [əˈvɔɪd] tr evitare
avoidable [əˈvɔɪdəbəl] adj evitabile
avow [əˈvau] tr confessare, ammettere
avowal [əˈvauəl] s confessione, ammissione
await [əˈwet] tr aspettare, attendere
awake [əˈwek] adj sveglio ‖ v (pret & pp awoke [əˈwok] or awaked) tr svegliare ‖ intr svegliarsi
awaken [əˈwekən] tr svegliare ‖ intr svegliarsi
awakening [əˈwekənɪŋ] s risveglio
award [əˈwɔrd] s (prize) premio; (decision by judge) sentenza ‖ tr aggiudicare
aware [əˈwer] adj conscio, consapevole; **to become aware of** rendersi conto di
awareness [əˈwernɪs] s coscienza
awash [əˈwɑʃ] or [əˈwɔʃ] adj & adv a fior d'acqua
away [əˈwe] adj distante, assente ‖ adv lontano; via; continuamente; **away back** (coll) molto tempo fa; **away from** lontano da; **to do away with** disfarsi di, sopprimere; **to get away** scappare, fuggire; **to go away and-arsene;** **to run away** fuggire; **to send away** mandar via; **to take away** portar via
awe [ɔ] s estremo rispetto; sacro timore ‖ tr infondere rispetto a; infondere un sacro timore a
aweigh [əˈwe] adj (anchor) levato
awesome [ˈɔsəm] adj grandioso, imponente
awestruck [ˈɔ ˌstrʌk] adj pieno di sacro timore
awful [ˈɔfəl] adj terribile; imponente ‖ adv (coll) terribilmente
awfully [ˈɔfəli] adv tremendamente, terribilmente; (coll) molto
awhile [əˈhwaɪl] adv un po', un po' di tempo
awkward [ˈɔkwərd] adj (clumsy) goffo, maldestro; (unwieldly) scomodo; (embarrassing) imbarazzante
awl [ɔl] s punteruolo
awning [ˈɔnɪŋ] s tenda; (in front of a store) tendone m
A.W.O.L. [ˈewɔl] (acronym) or [ˈeˈdʌbəl ˌjuˈoˈel] (letterword) adj (mil) assente al contrappello
awry [əˈraɪ] adv—**to go awry** andare a capovescio; **to look awry** guardare di sbieco
ax or **axe** [æks] s scure f; **to have an axe to grind** (coll) avere un interesse speciale
axiom [ˈæksi·əm] s assioma m
axiomatic [ˌæksi·əˈmætɪk] adj assiomatico
axis [ˈæksɪs] s (axes [ˈæksiz]) asse m
axle [ˈæksəl] s assale m, asse m
ax'le·tree' s assale m
ay [aɪ] s & adv sì m
Azores [əˈzorz] or [ˈezorz] spl Azzorre fpl
azure [ˈæʒər] or [ˈeʒər] adj & s azzurro, blu m

B

B, b [bi] *s* seconda lettera dell'alfabeto inglese

baa [bɑ] *s* belato || *intr* belare

babble ['bæbəl] *s* (*murmuring sound*) mormorio; (*senseless prattle*) balbettio || *tr* (*e.g., a secret*) divulgare || *intr* mormorare; balbettare; (*to talk idly*) parlare a vanvera

babe [beb] *s* bebè *m*, bambino; persona inesperta; (slang) ragazza

baboon [bæ'bun] *s* babbuino

ba·by ['bebi] *s* (-**bies**) bebè *m*, neonato; bambino; (*the youngest child*) piccolo || *v* (*pret & pp* -**bied**) *tr* coccolare, ninnare

ba'by car'riage *s* carrozzella

ba'by grand' *s* piano a mezza coda

babyhood ['bebɪ,hʊd] *s* infanzia

babyish ['bebi-ɪʃ] *adj* infantile

Babylon ['bæbɪlən] *or* ['bæbɪ,lɑn] *s* Babilonia

ba'by sit'ter *s* bambinaia ad ore

ba'by teeth' *spl* denti *mpl* di latte

baccalaureate [,bækə'lɔrɪ·ɪt] *s* baccalaureato; servizio religioso prima del baccalaureato

bacchanal ['bækənəl] *adj* bacchico || *s* baccanale *m*; (*person*) ubriacone *m*, bisboccione *m*

bachelor ['bæt∫ələr] *s* (*unmarried man*) scapolo, celibe *m*; (*holder of bachelor's degree*) diplomato; (*apprentice knight*) baccelliere *m*

bachelorhood ['bæt∫ələr,hʊd] *s* celibato

bacil·lus [bə'sɪləs] *s* (-**li** [laɪ]) bacillo

back [bæk] *adj* di dietro, posteriore; arretrato; contrario || *s* dorso, schiena; parte *f* posteriore, didietro; (*of a sheet or coin*) tergo; (*of a knife*) costola; (*of a room*) fondo; (*of a book*) time *f*; (*of a chair*) schienale *m*; behind one's back dietro le spalle di uno; **to turn one's back on** volgere la schiena a || *adv* dietro; indietro; **a few weeks back** alcune settimane fa; **as far back as** sino da; **back of** dietro, dietro a; **to go back on one's word** mancare di parola; **to go back to** ritornare a; **to pay back** ripagare; **to send back** restituire || *tr* appoggiare; far indietreggiare || *intr* indietreggiare; rinculare; **to back down** rinunciarci; **to back off** or **out** ritirarsi; **to back up** (*said of a car*) fare marcia indietro

back'ache' *s* mal *m* di schiena

back'bite' *v* (*pret* -**bit**; *pp* -**bitten** or -**bit**) *tr* sparlare di || *intr* sparlare

back'bit'er *s* maldicente *mf*

back'board' *s* (basketball) tabellone *m*

back'bone' *s* spina dorsale; (*of a book*) costola, dorso; (fig) fermezza

back'break'ing *adj* sfiancante

back'door' *adj* segreto, clandestino

back' door' *s* porta di dietro; (fig) mezzo clandestino

back'drop' *s* (theat) fondale *m*

backer ['bækər] *s* sostenitore *m*, difensore *m*; (com) finanziatore *m*

back'fire' *s* (*for firefighting*) contro-fuoco; (aut) ritorno di fiamma || *intr* (aut) avere un ritorno di fiamma; (fig) raggiungere l'effetto opposto

back'ground' *s* fondo, sfondo; precedenti *mpl*; origine *f*

back'ground mu'sic *s* musica di fondo

backhand ['bæk,hænd] *adj* obliquo || *s* scrittura inclinata a sinistra; (tennis) rovescio

back'hand'ed *adj* obliquo; sarcastico; insincero

backing ['bækɪŋ] *s* appoggio; sostegno; (bb) dorso

back'ing light' *s* (aut) faro retromarcia; (theat) luce *f* per il fondale

back'lash' *s* reazione, contraccolpo; (mach) gioco

back'log' *s* ceppo; (fig) riserva

back' num'ber *s* numero arretrato; (coll) persona all'antica

back' pay' *s* paga arretrata, arretrati *mpl*

back' scratch'er *s* manina per grattare la schiena; (coll) leccapiedi *m*

back' seat' *s* (aut) sedile *m* posteriore; (fig) posizione secondaria

back'side' *s* dorso; didietro

back'slide' *v* (*pret & pp* -**slid** [,slɪd]) *intr* ricadere

back'spac'er *s* tasto ritorno

back'spin' *s* effetto

back'stage' *adj* dietro alle quinte || *s* retroscena *m* || *adv* a retroscena, dietro alle quinte

back'stairs' *adj* indiretto, segreto

back' stairs' *spl* scala di servizio

back'stitch' *s* impuntura || *tr & intr* impunturare

back'stroke' *s* (swimming) bracciata sul dorso

back'swept wing' *s* ala a freccia

back' talk' *s* risposta impertinente

back'track' *intr* ritornare sulle proprie tracce; (fig) fare macchina indietro

back'up light' *s* (aut) faro retromarcia

backward ['bækwərd] *adj* ritroso; poco progredito, retrogrado || *adv* a ritroso, all'indietro; verso il passato; alla rovescia; **backward and forward** (coll) completamente, perfettamente; **to go backward and forward** andare avanti e indietro

back'wash' *s* risacca

back'wa'ter *s* gora, ristagno; (fig) eremo

back'woods' *spl* zona boscosa lontana dai centri popolati

back'yard' *s* cortile *m* posteriore

bacon ['bekən] *s* pancetta

bacteria [bæk'tɪrɪ·ə] *spl* batteri *mpl*

bacterial [bæk'tɪrɪ·əl] *adj* batterico

bacteriologist [bæk,tɪrɪ'ɑlədʒɪst] *s* batteriologo

bacteriology [bæk,tɪrɪ'ɑlədʒi] *s* batteriologia

bad [bæd] *adj* (worse [wʌrs]; worst [wʌrst]) cattivo; (*coin*) falso; (*weather*) brutto; (*debt*) insolvibile; severo || *s* male *m*; **from bad to**

worse da male in peggio || *adv* male; **to be too bad** essere peccato; **to feel bad** esser spiacente; sentirsi male; **to look bad** aver brutta cera

bad′ breath′ *s* fiato cattivo

bad′ egg′ *s* (slang) cattivo soggetto

badge [bædʒ] *s* divisa; decorazione; simbolo, placca

badger [′bædʒər] *s* tasso || *tr* molestare

badly [′bædli] *adv* male; gravemente; molto

bad′ly off′ *adj* in cattive condizioni

badminton [′bædmɪntən] *s* badminton *m*

baffle [′bæfəl] *s* (mach) deflettore *m*; (rad) schermo acustico || *tr* frustrare, confondere

baffling [′bæflɪŋ] *adj* sconcertante

bag [bæg] *s* sacco; borsetta; (*of a marsupial*) borsa; (hunt) presa; **bag and baggage** con armi e bagagli; **to be in the bag** (slang) averlo nel sacco; **to be left holding the bag** (coll) essere piantato in asso || *v* (*pret & pp* **bagged**) *ger* **bagging**) *tr* insaccare; (hunt) pigliare || *intr* (**to hang loosely**) far pieghe

baggage [′bægɪdʒ] *s* bagaglio

bag′gage car′ *s* bagagliaio

bag′gage check′ *s* scontrino del bagaglio

bag′gage room′ *s* deposito bagagli

bag·gy [′bægi] *adj* (-gier; -giest) come un sacco

bag′pipe *s* cornamusa, zampogna

bag′pip′er *s* zampognaro

bail [bel] *s* cauzione; libertà provvisoria sotto cauzione; (*bucket*) sassola || *tr* liberare sotto cauzione; **to bail out** (*a boat*) sgottare || *intr*—**to bail out** (aer) gettarsi col paracadute

bailiwick [′belɪwɪk] *s* (fig) sfera di competenza

bait [bet] *s* esca; (fig) allettamento || *tr* adescare; (fig) allettare

baize [bez] *s* panno verde

bake [bek] *tr* cuocere al forno || *intr* cuocersi al forno; abbrustolirsi

bakelite [′bekə ,laɪt] *s* bachelite *f*

baker [′bekər] *s* fornaio, panettiere *m*

bak′er's doz′en *s* tredici per ogni dozzina

baker·y [′bekəri] *s* (-ies) panetteria

bak′ing pan′ [′bekɪŋ] *s* tortiera

bak′ing pow′der *s* lievito in polvere

bak′ing so′da *s* bicarbonato di soda

balance [′bæləns] *s* (*scales*) bilancia; equilibrio; armonia; (*of watch*) bilanciere *m*; (*remainder; amount due*) resto; (*of budget*) pareggio; **in the balance** in bilico; **to lose one's balance** perdere l'equilibrio; **to strike a balance** fare il bilancio || *tr* bilanciare, pesare; (com) bilanciare, pareggiare || *intr* bilanciarsi

bal′ance of pay′ments *s* bilancia dei pagamenti

bal′ance of pow′er *s* equilibrio politico

bal′ance of trade′ *s* bilancia commerciale

bal′ance sheet′ *s* bilancio

balco·ny [′bælkəni] *s* (-nies) balcone *m*; (theat) galleria

bald [bɔld] *adj* calvo; (*bare*) nudo; (*unadorned*) semplice

bald′ ea′gle *s* aquila col capo bianco dell'America del Nord

baldness [′bɔldnɪs] *s* calvizie *f*

baldric [′bɔldrɪk] *s* tracolla

bale [bel] *s* balla; collo || *tr* imballare

baleful [′belfəl] *adj* minaccioso, funesto

balk [bɔk] *tr* ostacolare || *intr* intestarsi, impuntarsi

Balkan [′bɔlkən] *adj* balcanico || **the Balkans** i Balcani

balk·y [′bɔki] *adj* (-ier; -iest) caparbio, ostinato

ball [bɔl] *s* palla; pallone *m*; sfera; (*of the thumb*) polpastrello; (*of wool*) gomitolo; (*projectile*) palla, pallottola; (*dance*) ballo; **on the ball** (slang) capace, efficiente; (slang) in gamba; **to play ball** giocare alla palla; **to play ball with** essere in cooperazione con || *tr*—**to ball up** (slang) confondere

ballad [′bæləd] *s* ballata

ball′ and chain′ *s* palla di piombo; (fig) impedimento; (slang) moglie *f*

ball′-and-sock′et joint′ [′bɔlən′sakɪt] *s* giunto a sfera

ballast [′bæləst] *s* zavorra; (rr) pietrisco || *tr* zavorrare

ball′ bear′ing *s* cuscinetto a sfere

ballet [′bæle] *s* balletto

ballistic [bə′lɪstɪk] *adj* balistico || **ballistics** *ssg* balistica

balloon [bə′lun] *s* pallone *m*; (*for children*) palloncino; (*in comic strip*) fumetto

ballot [′bælət] *s* scheda elettorale; voto || *intr* votare, ballottare

bal′lot box′ *s* bussola, urna

ball′play′er *s* giocatore *m* di palla, giocatore *m* di baseball

ball′-point pen′ *s* penna a sfera

ball′room′ *s* salone *m* da ballo

ballyhoo [′bælɪ ,hu] *s* chiasso; montatura || *tr* far chiasso a favore di

balm [bam] *s* balsamo

balm·y [′bami] *adj* (-ier; -iest) balsamico; salubre; (slang) pazzo

balsam [′bɔlsəm] *s* balsamo; (*plant*) balsamina

Baltic [′bɔltɪk] *adj* baltico

baluster [′bæləstər] *s* balaustro

balustrade [,bæləs′tred] *s* balaustrata

bamboo [bæm′bu] *s* bambù *m*

bamboozle [bæm′buzəl] *tr* ingannare, raggirare

bamboozler [bæm′buzlər] *s* raggiratore *m*

ban [bæn] *s* bando; (*of marriage*) pubblicazione matrimoniale; (eccl) interdetto, scomunica || *v* (*pret & pp* **banned**; *ger* **banning**) *tr* proibire

banal [′benəl] or [bə′næl] *adj* banale

banana [bə′nænə] *s* banana, (*tree*) banano

band [bænd] *s* banda, striscia; (*of thin cloth*) benda; (*of metal, rubber*) fascia, nastro; (*of hat*) nastro; (mus) banda, fanfara; **to beat the band** fortemente; abbondantemente || *tr* unire || *intr*—**to band together** unirsi

bandage ['bændɪdʒ] *s* benda, bendaggio ‖ *tr* fasciare

bandanna [bæn'dænə] *s* fazzolettone colorato

band'box' *s* cappelliera

bandit ['bændɪt] *s* bandito

band'mas'ter *s* capomusica *m*

bandoleer [,bændə'lɪr] *s* bandoliera

band' saw' *s* sega a nastro

band'stand' *s* chiosco della banda

band'wag'on *s* carrozzone *m* da circo; **to jump on the bandwagon** prendere le parti del vincitore

baneful ['benfəl] *adj* nocivo; funesto

bang [bæŋ] *s* rumore *m*, scoppio; (coll) energia; (*pleasure*) (slang) piacere *m*, eccitazione; **bangs** frangetta ‖ *adv* tutto d'un colpo ‖ *tr* sbattere ‖ *intr* rimbombare ‖ *interj* bum!

bang'-up' *adj* (slang) eccellente, di prim'ordine

banish ['bænɪʃ] *tr* sbandire, mettere al bando

banishment ['bænɪʃmənt] *s* bando, esilio

banister ['bænɪstər] *s* balaustra; **banisters** balaustrata

bank [bæŋk] *s* (*of fish; of fog*) banco; (*of a river*) sponda; (*for coins*) salvadanaio; (*financial institution*) banca, banco; (*of earth, snow*) mucchio, banco; (*of clouds*) cumulo; (aer) inclinazione laterale; (billiards) sponda ‖ *tr* (*a fire*) coprire di cenere; (*to pile up*) ammonticchiare; (*a curve*) sopraelevare; (*money*) depositare ‖ *intr* depositare denaro; (aer) inclinarsi lateralmente; **to bank on** (coll) contare su (di)

bank'book' *s* libretto bancario, libretto di deposito

banker ['bæŋkər] *s* banchiere *m*

banking ['bæŋkɪŋ] *adj* bancario ‖ *s* attività bancaria; professione di banchiere

bank' note' *s* biglietto di banca

bank'roll' *s* rotolo di carta moneta; soldi *mpl* ‖ *tr* (slang) finanziare

bankrupt ['bæŋkrʌpt] *adj & s* fallito; **to go bankrupt** andare in fallimento ‖ *tr* dichiarare in fallimento; far fallire

bankrupt-cy ['bæŋkrʌptsi] *s* (-cies) fallimento

banner ['bænər] *adj* importante ‖ *s* bandiera, stendardo; (journ) titolo in grassetto

banns [bænz] *spl* bandi *mpl* matrimoniali

banquet ['bæŋkwɪt] *s* banchetto ‖ *tr* dar un banchetto a ‖ *intr* banchettare

bantam ['bæntəm] *adj* piccolo ‖ *s* pollo nano

ban'tam-weight' *s* peso gallo, bantam *m*

banter ['bæntər] *s* scherzo, facezia ‖ *intr* scherzare, celiare

baptism ['bæptɪzəm] *s* battesimo

baptismal [bæp'tɪzməl] *adj* battesimale; (*certificate*) di battesimo

Baptist ['bæptɪst] *adj & s* battista *mf*

baptister-y ['bæptɪstəri] *s* (-ies) battistero

baptize [bæp'taɪz] *or* ['bæptaɪz] *tr* battezzare

bar [bɑr] *s* barra; sbarra; (*of soap*) saponetta; (*of chocolate*) tavoletta; (*of sand*) banco; (*obstacle*) barriera; bar *m*; (*of public opinion*) tribunale *m*; (*legal profession*) avvocatura; (*of door or window*) spranga; (*of lead*) (typ) lingotto; (mus) battuta; **behind bars** in guardina; **to be admitted to the bar** diventare avvocato; **to tend bar** fare il barista ‖ *prep* eccetto, salvo; **bar none** senza eccezione ‖ *v* (*pret & pp* barred; *ger* barring) *tr* sbarrare; sprangare; bloccare; escludere

bar' associa'tion *s* associazione dell'ordine degli avvocati

barb [bɑrb] *s* (*of arrow*) barbiglio

barbarian [bɑr'bɛrɪ-ən] *s* barbaro

barbaric [bɑr'bærɪk] *adj* barbaro

barbarism ['bɑrbə,rɪzəm] *s* barbarismo

barbari-ty [bɑr'bærɪti] *s* (-ties) barbarie *f*

barbarous ['bɑrbərəs] *adj* barbaro, crudele

Bar'bary ape' ['bɑrbəri] *s* bertuccia

barbecue ['bɑrbɪ,kju] *s* arrosto allo spiedo ‖ *tr* arrostire allo spiedo

barbed [bɑrbd] *adj* irto di punte; mordace, pungente

barbed' wire' *s* filo spinato

barber ['bɑrbər] *s* barbiere *m*; (*who cuts and styles hair*) parrucchiere *m*

bar'ber-shop' *s* barbieria, negozio di barbiere; negozio di parrucchiere

barbiturate [bɑr'bɪtʃə,ret] *s* barbiturato, barbiturico

bard [bɑrd] *s* bardo, poeta *m*

bare [bɛr] *adj* nudo; (*head*) a capo scoperto; (*unconcealed*) palese; (*empty*) vuoto; (*wire*) senza isolante; (*unadorned*) semplice; **to lay bare** mettere a nudo ‖ *tr* denudare, scoprire

bare'back' *adj & adv* senza sella

barefaced ['bɛr,fest] *adj* impudente, sfacciato, spudorato

bare'foot' *adj* scalzo

barehanded ['bɛr,hændɪd] *adj & adv* a mani nude

bareheaded ['bɛr,hɛdɪd] *adj* a capo scoperto

barelegged ['bɛr,lɛgɪd] *adj* a gambe nude

barely ['bɛrli] *adv* appena, soltanto

bargain ['bɑrgɪn] *s* affare *m*, buon affare *m*; contrattazione; **at a bargain** a buon prezzo; **into the bargain** in soprappiù ‖ *tr*—**to bargain away** vendere a buonissimo prezzo ‖ *intr* contrattare, mercanteggiare; **to bargain for** aspettarsi

bar'gain sale' *s* vendita sottoprezzo

barge [bɑrdʒ] *s* barcone *m*, chiatta ‖ *intr*—**to barge in** entrare senza chiedere permesso

baritone ['bærɪ,ton] *adj* di baritono ‖ *s* baritono *m*

barium ['bɛrɪ·əm] *s* bario

bark [bɑrk] *s* corteccia, scorza; (*of dog*) abbaiamento, latrato ‖ *tr* (*e.g.,* *insults*) lanciare || *intr* abbaiare, latrare

bar'keep'er *s* barista *mf*

barker [ˈbarkər] *s* banditore *m*, imbonitore *m*

barley [ˈbarlɪ] *s* orzo

bar' mag'net *s* calamita a forma di barra allungata

bar'maid' *s* barista *f*

bar'man *s* (**-men**) barista *m*

barn [barn] *s* granaio; (*for hay*) fienile *m*; (*for livestock*) stalla

barnacle [ˈbarnəkəl] *s* cirripede *m*

barn' owl' *s* civetta

barn'yard' *s* bassacorte *f*, aia

barn'yard fowl' *s* animale *m* da cortile || *spl* animali *mpl* da cortile

barometer [bəˈramɪtər] *s* barometro

baron [ˈbærən] *s* barone *m*; (*industrialist*) cavaliere *m* d'industria

baroness [ˈbærənɪs] *s* baronessa

baroque [bəˈrok] *adj & s* barocco

bar'rack-room' *adj* da caserma || *s* camerata

barracks [ˈbærəks] *spl* caserma; camerata

barrage [bəˈraʒ] *s* (mil) fuoco di sbarramento

barrel [ˈbærəl] *s* barile *m*, botte *f*; (*of gun*) canna; (*mach*) cilindro

bar'rel or'gan *s* organetto di Barberia

barren [ˈbærən] *adj* sterile; (*without vegetation*) brullo

barricade [ˌbærɪˈked] *s* barricata || *tr* barricare

barrier [ˈbærɪ.ər] *s* barriera

bar'rier reef' *s* barriera corallina

barring [ˈbarɪŋ] *prep* eccetto, salvo

barrister [ˈbærɪstər] *s* (Brit) avvocato

bar'room' *s* bar *m*, cantina, mescita

bar'tend'er *s* barista *mf*, barman *m*

barter [ˈbartər] *s* baratto || *tr & intr* barattare, permutare

basalt [bəˈsɔlt] *s* basalto

base [bes] *adj* basale; basso; servile; (*morally low*) turpe; (*metal*) vile, non prezioso || *s* base *f*; (*in children's games*) tana; (*of a word*) radice *f* basale || *tr* basare

base'ball' *s* baseball *m*, pallabase *f*

base'board' *s* basamento; (*of wall*) zoccolo

Basel [ˈbazəl] *s* Basilea

baseless [ˈbeslɪs] *adj* infondato

basement [ˈbesmənt] *s* scantinato, piano interrato

bashful [ˈbæʃfəl] *adj* timido

basic [ˈbesɪk] *adj* fondamentale; (chem) basico

ba'sic commod'ities *spl* articoli *mpl* di prima necessità

basilica [bəˈsɪlɪkə] *s* basilica

basin [ˈbesɪn] *s* catino; vasca; (*of balance*) piatto; (*of river*) bacino; (*of harbor*) darsena

ba·sis [ˈbesɪs] *s* (**-ses** [siz]) base *f*

bask [bæsk] *or* [bask] *intr* crogiolarsi

basket [ˈbæskɪt] *or* [ˈbaskɪt] *s* cesta; (sports) cesto

bas'ket-ball' *s* pallacanestro *f*

Basque [bæsk] *adj & s* basco

bas-relief [ˌbarɪˈlif] *or* [ˌbærɪˈlif] *s* bassorilievo

bass [bes] *adj & s* (mus) basso || [bæs] *s* (ichth) pesce persico

bass' drum' *s* grancassa

bass' horn' *s* bassotuba *m*

bassinet [ˈbæsəˌnet] *or* [ˌbæsəˈnet] *s* culla a forma di cesto; carrozzina a forma di cesto

bas·so [ˈbæso] *or* [ˈbaso] *s* (**-sos** *or* **-si** [si]) basso

bassoon [bəˈsun] *s* fagotto

bass' vi'ol [ˈvaɪ.əl] *s* contrabbasso

bastard [ˈbæstərd] *adj & s* bastardo

baste [best] *tr* (*to sew*) imbastire; (*meat*) inumidire con acqua o grasso

bastion [ˈbæstʃən] *or* [ˈbæstɪ.ən] *s* bastione *m*

bat [bæt] *s* mazza; (*in cricket*) maglio; (coll) colpo; (zool) pipistrello || *v* (*pret & pp* **batted**; *ger* **batting**) *tr* colpire con la mazza; **without batting an eye** (coll) senza batter ciglio

batch [bætʃ] *s* (*of bread*) infornata; gruppo, numero

bath [bæθ] *or* [baθ] *s* bagno; **to take a bath** fare il bagno

bathe [beð] *tr* bagnare, lavare || *intr* bagnarsi, fare il bagno

bather [ˈbeðər] *s* bagnante *mf*

bath'house' *s* (*individual*) cabina; spogliatoio

bath'ing beau'ty *s* bellezza in costume da bagno

bath'ing cap' *s* cuffia da bagno

bath'ing resort' *s* stazione balneare

bath'ing suit' *s* costume *m* da bagno

bath'ing trunks' *spl* mutandine *fpl* da bagno

bath'robe' *s* accappatoio

bath'room' *s* stanza da bagno

bath' salts' *spl* sali *mpl* da bagno

bath'tub' *s* bagno, vasca da bagno

baton [bæˈtan] *or* [ˈbætən] *s* bastone *m*; (mus) bacchetta

battalion [bəˈtæljən] *s* battaglione *m*

batten [ˈbætən] *tr* assicella; piccola traversa; (naut) bietta || *tr*—**to batten down the hatches** chiudere ermeticamente i boccaporti

batter [ˈbætər] *s* pasta, farina pastosa; (baseball) battitore *m* || *tr* battere, tempestare di colpi; (*to wear out*) logorare

bat'tering ram' *s* ariete *m*

batter·y [ˈbætəri] *s* (**-ies**) (*primary cell*) pila; (*secondary cell*) accumulatore *m*; (*group of batteries*) batteria; (law) assalto; (mil & mus) batteria

battle [ˈbætəl] *s* battaglia; **to do battle** dar battaglia || *tr* combattere contro || *intr* combattere

bat'tle cry' *s* grido di guerra

battledore [ˈbætəlˌdor] *s* racchetta; **battledore and shuttlecock** gioco del volano

bat'tle-field' *s* campo di battaglia

bat'tle-front' *s* fronte *m* di combattimento

battlement [ˈbætəlmənt] *s* merlatura

bat'tle roy'al *s* baruffa generale, zuffa generale

bat'tle-ship' *s* corazzata

battue [bæˈtu] *or* [bæˈtju] *s* (hunt) battuta

bat·ty ['bæti] adj (-tier; -tiest) (slang) pazzo, eccentrico

bauble ['bɔbəl] s bazzecola, gingillo

Bavaria [bə'vɛrɪ·ə] s la Baviera

Bavarian [bə'vɛrɪ·ən] adj & s bavarese mf

bawd [bɔd] s ruffiano; ruffiana

bawd·y ['bɔdi] adj (-ier; -iest) indecente, osceno

bawd'y·house' s casa di malaffare

bawl [bɔl] s grido; (coll) pianto || tr—to bawl out (slang) fare una ramanzina a || intr strillare; (coll) piangere

bay [be] adj baio || s baia; vano, alcova; (recess in wall) apertura nel muro; finestra sporgente; (of dog) latrato; cavallo baio; (bot) lauro; at bay in una posizione disperata || intr latrare

bayonet ['be·ənɪt] s baionetta || tr dare baionettate a || intr dare baionettate

bay' win'dow s finestra sporgente; (slang) pancia

bazooka [bə'zukə] s bazooka m

be [bi] v (pres am [æm], is [ɪz], are [ɑr]; pret was [wɑz] or [wʌz], were [wʌr]; pp been [bɪn]) intr essere; (to carry) portare; (to give birth to) partorire; (to sustain) sostenere; (to withstand) sopportare; (a grudge) serbare; (in mind) tenere; (interest) produrre; (to pay) pagare; to be under the date aver la data; to bear out confermare; to bear witness testimoniare || intr (to be productive) fruttificare; (to move) dirigersi; (to be oppressive) fare pressione; to bear down on fare pressione su; avvicinarsi a; to bear up resistere; to bear with tollerare

bearable ['bɛrəbəl] adj tollerabile

beard [bɪrd] s barba; (e.g., in wheat) arista

bearded adj barbuto

beardless ['bɪrdlɪs] adj imberbe

bearer ['bɛrər] s portatore m

bearing ['bɛrɪŋ] s portamento; relazione; importanza; (mach) bronzina, cuscinetto; bearings orientamento; to lose one's bearings perdere la bussola; perdere l'orientamento

bearish ['bɛrɪʃ] adj (like a bear) orsino; (e.g., prices) in ribasso; (market) al ribasso; (speculator) ribassista

bear'skin' s pelle f dell'orso; (mil) colbacco

beast [bist] s bestia

beast·ly ['bistli] adj (-lier; -liest) bestiale || adv (coll) malissimo

beast' of bur'den s bestia da soma

beast' of prey' s animale m da rapina

beat [bit] s (of heart) battito; (of policeman) ronda; (stroke) colpo; (habitual route) cammino battuto; (mus) tempo; (phys) battimento || v (pret beat; pp beat or beaten) tr battere; percuotere; (eggs) frullare; (to whip) frustare; (coll) confondere; beat it! (slang) vattene!; to beat a retreat battere in ritirata; to beat back respingere; to beat down sopprimere; to beat off respingere; to beat up (eggs) frullare; (people) dargliene a || intr battere; pulsare; to beat around the bush (coll) menare il can per l'aia

beat'en path' ['bitən] s cammino battuto

beater ['bitər] s frullino

beati·fy [bɪ'ætɪ,faɪ] v (pret & pp -fied) tr beatificare

beagle ['bigəl] s segugio, bracco

beak [bik] s becco; promontorio

beam [bim] s trave f; (of balance) braccio; (of light) raggio; (ship's breadth) larghezza; (smile) sorriso; (radio signal) fascio direttore; (course indicated by radio beam) aerovia; (naut) traverso || tr (a radio signal) dirigere; (e.g., light) irraggiare || intr raggiare

bean [bin] s fagiolo; (of coffee) chicco; (slang) testa

beaner·y ['binəri] s (-ies) (slang) gargotta, taverna di secondo ordine

bean'pole' s puntello per i fagioli; (coll) palo del telegrafo

bear [bɛr] s orso; (astr) orsa; (com) ribassista m, giocatore m al ribasso || v (pret bore [bor]; pp borne [born])

bacon ['bikən] s faro || tr rischiarare; fare da guida a || intr brillare

bead [bid] s perlina; grano, chicco; (drop) goccia; beads (in a necklace or rosary) conterie fpl; to count one's beads recitare il rosario

beach [bitʃ] s spiaggia || tr (a boat) arenare || intr arenarsi

beach'comb'er s girellone m di spiaggia

beach'head' s testa di sbarco

beach' robe' s accappatoio

beach' shoe' s sandalo da spiaggia

beach' umbrel'la s ombrellone m da spiaggia

beach'comb'er intr raccogliere relitti sulla spiaggia

beating ['bitɪŋ] s battitura; (whipping) frustatura; (throbbing) pulsazione, battito; (defeat) sconfitta

beau [bo] s (beaus or beaux [boz]) (dandy) bellimbusto; (girl's sweetheart) spasimante m

beautician [bju'tɪʃən] s estetista mf

beautiful ['bjutɪfəl] adj bello

beauti·fy ['bjutɪ ,faɪ] v (pret & pp -fied) tr abbellire

beau·ty ['bjutɪ] s (-ties) bellezza

beau'ty con'test s concorso di bellezza

beau'ty par'lor s istituto di bellezza

beau'ty sleep' s primo sonno

beau'ty spot' s neo; posto pittoresco

beaver ['bivər] s castoro; pelle f di castoro; cappello a cilindro

because [bɪ'kɔz] conj perchè; because of a causa di

beck [bɛk] s gesto; at the beck and call of agli ordini di

beckon ['bɛkən] s gesto || tr fare gesto a || intr fare gesto

becloud [bɪ'klaud] tr annebbiare; oscurare

be·come [bɪ'kʌm] v (pret -came; pp -come) tr convenire a; stare bene a, e.g., this hat becomes you questo cappello Le sta bene || intr diventare; farsi; convertirsi, e.g., water became wine l'acqua si convertì in vino; succedere, e.g., what became of my coat? che è successo del mio pastrano?; essere, e.g., what will become of me? che sarà di me?; to become accustomed abituarsi; to become angry entrare in collera; to become crazy impazzire; to become ill ammalarsi

becoming [bɪ'kʌmɪŋ] adj conveniente; appropriato; acconcio; this is very becoming to you questo Le sta molto bene

bed [bɛd] s letto; (layer) strato; giacimento; to go to bed andare a letto; to take to one's bed mettersi a letto

bed' and board' s vitto e alloggio; pensione completa

bed'bug' s cimice f

bed'clothes' spl lenzuola fpl e coperte fpl, biancheria da letto

bed'cov'er s coperta da letto

bedding ['bɛdɪŋ] s lenzuola fpl e coperte fpl; (litter) lettiera; (foundation) fondamenta fpl

bedeck [bɪ'dɛk] tr ornare, adornare

bedev·il [bɪ'dɛvɪl] v (pret & pp -iled or -illed; ger -iling or -illing) tr tormentare diabolicamente; confondere

bed'fast' adj confinato a letto

bed'fel'low s compagno di letto; compagno di stanza; compagno

bedlam ['bɛdləm] s manicomio; pandemonio

bed' lin'en s biancheria da letto

bed'pan' s padella

bedridden ['bɛd ,rɪdən] adj degente a letto

bed'room' s stanza da letto, camera da letto

bed'room slip'per s babbuccia, pantofola

bed'side' s capezzale m

bed'side man'ner s maniera di fare coi pazienti

bed'sore' s piaga da decubito

bed'spread' s coperta da letto

bed'spring' s rete f del letto; molla del letto

bed'stead' s fusto del letto

bed'tick' s traliccio

bed'time' s ora di coricarsi

bed'warm'er s scaldaletto

bee [bi] s ape f

beech [bitʃ] s faggio

beech'nut' s faggiola

beef [bif] s bue m, manzo; carne f di manzo; (coll) forza; (slang) lamentela || tr—to beef up (coll) rinforzare || intr (slang) lamentarsi

beef' cat'tle s manzi mpl da carne

beef'steak' s bistecca

beef' stew' s stufato di manzo

bee'hive' s alveare m

bee'keep'er s apicoltore m

bee'line' s—to make a beeline for (coll) andare direttamente verso

beer [bɪr] s birra

beer' saloon' s birreria

beeswax ['biz ,wæks] s cera d'api

beet [bit] s barbabietola

beetle ['bitəl] adj sporgente, folto || s scarafaggio

bee'tle-browed' adj dalle sopracciglia folte

beet' su'gar s zucchero di barbabietola

be·fall [bɪ'fɔl] v (pret -fell ['fɛl]; pp -fallen ['fɔlən]) tr succedere a || intr succedere

befitting [bɪ'fɪtɪŋ] adj appropriato

before [bɪ'for] adv prima, prima d'ora || prep (in time) prima di; (in place) dinnanzi a, davanti a; before Christ avanti Cristo || conj prima che

before'hand' adv in anticipo; precedentemente

befriend [bɪ'frɛnd] tr diventare amico di, proteggere, favorire; aiutare

befuddle [bɪ'fʌdəl] tr confondere

beg [bɛg] v (pret & pp begged; ger begging) tr chiedere; implorare; (alms) mendicare; I beg your pardon Le chiedo scusa; to beg s.o. for s.th chiedere qlco a qlcu || intr chiedere la carità; to beg for sollecitare; to beg off scusarsi; to go begging rimanere invenduto

be·get [bɪ'gɛt] v (pret -got ['gɑt]; pp -gotten or -got; ger -getting) tr generare

beggar ['bɛgər] s accattone m, mendicante m

be·gin [bɪ'gɪn] v (pret -gan ['gæn]; pp -gun ['gʌn]; ger -ginning) tr & intr cominciare, iniziare; beginning with a partire da; to begin with per cominciare

beginner [bɪ'gɪnər] s principiante mf

beginning [bɪ'gɪnɪŋ] s inizio, origine f, principio; esordio

begrudge [bɪ'grʌdʒ] tr invidiare; concedere con riluttanza

beguile [bɪ'gaɪl] tr ingannare; sedurre; (to delight) divertire

behalf [bɪ'hæf] or [bɪ'hɑf] s—on behalf of nell'interesse di; a nome di

behave [bɪ'hev] *intr* comportarsi; comportarsi bene

behavior [bɪ'hevjər] *s* comportamento, condotta; funzionamento

behead [bɪ'hed] *tr* decapitare

behest [bɪ'hest] *s* ordine *m*, comando

behind [bɪ'haɪnd] *s* didietro; (slang) sedere *m* ‖ *adv* dietro; (*in arrears*) in arretrato; **from behind** dal didietro ‖ *prep* dietro a, dietro di; **behind time** in ritardo

be·hold [bɪ'hold] *v* (*pret & pp* **-held** ['held]) *tr* contemplare; ammirare ‖ *interj* guarda!

behoove [bɪ'huv] *impers*—**it behooves him to** gli conviene di

being ['bi·ɪŋ] *adj* esistente; **for the time being** per ora ‖ *s* essere *m*, ente *m*

belabor [bɪ'lebər] *tr* attaccare; (fig) ribattere, confutare; (fig) insistere su

belated [bɪ'letɪd] *adj* tardivo

belch [beltʃ] *s* rutto ‖ *tr* eruttare, vomitare ‖ *intr* ruttare

beleaguer [bɪ'ligər] *tr* assediare

bel·fry ['belfrɪ] *s* (**-fries**) (*tower*) campanile *m*; (*site of bell*) cella campanaria; (slang) testa

Belgian ['beldʒən] *adj & s* belga *mf*

Belgium ['beldʒəm] *s* il Belgio

be·lie [bɪ'laɪ] *v* (*pret & pp* **-lied** ['laɪd]; *ger* **-lying** ['laɪ·ɪŋ]) *tr* (*to misrepresent*) tradire; (*to prove false*) smentire

belief [bɪ'lif] *s* fede *f*, credenza

believable [bɪ'livəbəl] *adj* credibile

believe [bɪ'liv] *tr* credere ‖ *intr* credere, aver fede; **to believe in** credere in

believer [bɪ'livər] *s* credente *mf*

belittle [bɪ'lɪtəl] *tr* menomare

bell [bel] *s* campana; (*for a door*) campanello; (*sound*) rintocco; (*on cattle*) campanaccio; (*of deer*) bramito ‖ *intr* bramire

belladonna [,belə'dɑnə] *s* belladonna

bell'-bot'tom *adj* a campana

bell'boy' *s* cameriere *m*, ragazzo

belle [bel] *s* bella

belles-lettres [,bel'letrə] *spl* belle lettere

bell' glass' *s* campana di vetro

bell'hop' *s* cameriere *m*, ragazzo

bellicose ['belɪ,kos] *adj* bellicoso

belligerent [bə'lɪdʒərənt] *adj & s* belligerante *m*

bellow ['belo] *s* muggito; **bellows** mantice *m*; (*of camera*) soffietto ‖ *tr* gridare ‖ *intr* muggire

bell' ring'er ['rɪŋər] *s* campanaro

bellwether ['bel,weðər] *s* pecora guida

bel·ly ['belɪ] *s* (**-lies**) ventre *m*, pancia ‖ *v* (*pret & pp* **-lied**) *intr* far pancia

bel'ly·ache' *s* (coll) mal *m* di pancia ‖ *intr* (slang) lamentarsi

bel'ly·but'ton *s* (coll) ombelico

bel'ly dance' *s* (coll) danza del ventre

bel'ly flop' *s* panciata

bellyful ['belɪ,ful] *s*—**to have a bellyful** (slang) averne fino agli occhi

bel'ly·land' *intr* (aer) atterrare sul ventre

belong [bɪ'lɔŋ] *or* [bɪ'lɑŋ] *intr* appartenere; stare bene, e.g., **this chair belongs in this room** questa sedia sta bene in questa stanza

belongings [bɪ'lɔŋɪŋz] *or* [bɪ'lɑŋɪŋz] *spl* effetti *mpl* personali

beloved [bɪ'lʌvɪd] *or* [bɪ'lʌvd] *adj & s* diletto, amato

below [bɪ'lo] *adv* sotto; più sotto; sotto zero, e.g., **ten below** dieci gradi sotto zero ‖ *prep* sotto, sotto di

belt [belt] *s* cintura, cinghia; (mach) nastro; (mil) cinturone *m*; (geog) fascia, zona; **to tighten one's belt** far cintura ‖ *tr* cingere; (slang) staffilare

belt'ed tire' *s* copertone cinturato

belt' line' *s* linea di circonvallazione

beltway ['belt,we] *s* raccordo anulare

bemoan [bɪ'mon] *tr* lamentare; compiangere

bench [bentʃ] *s* banco, panca; tribunale *m*; (mach) banco di prova; **to be on the bench** (law) essere giudice

bend [bend] *s* curva; (*e.g., of pipe*) gomito, angolo ‖ *v* (*pret & pp* **bent** [bent]) *tr* curvare; piegare; far piegare ‖ *intr* deviare; piegare, piegarsi; **to bend over** inchinarsi

beneath [bɪ'niθ] *adv* sotto; più sotto ‖ *prep* sotto, sotto di

benediction [,benɪ'dɪkʃən] *s* benedizione

benefactor ['benɪ,fæktər] *or* [,benɪ'fæktər] *s* benefattore *m*

benefactress ['benɪ,fæktrɪs] *or* [,benɪ'fæktrɪs] *s* benefattrice *f*

beneficence [bɪ'nefɪsəns] *s* beneficenza

beneficent [bɪ'nefɪsənt] *adj* caritatevole; benefico

beneficial [,benɪ'fɪʃəl] *adj* benefico

beneficiar·y [,benɪ'fɪʃɪ,erɪ] *s* (**-ies**) beneficiario

benefit ['benɪfɪt] *s* beneficio; festa di beneficenza; **for the benefit of** a beneficio di ‖ *tr & intr* beneficiare

benefit perfor'mance *s* beneficiata

benevolence [bɪ'nevələns] *s* benevolenza; carità *f*

benevolent [bɪ'nevələnt] *adj* benevolo; (*institution*) benefico

benign [bɪ'naɪn] *adj* benigno

bent [bent] *adj* curvo; **bent on** deciso a ‖ *s* curva; tendenza, propensità *f*

Benzedrine ['benzɪ,drin] (trademark) *s* benzedrina

benzene ['benzin] *s* benzolo

benzine [ben'zin] *s* benzina

bequeath [bɪ'kwiθ] *or* [bɪ'kwið] *tr* legare, lasciare in eredità

bequest [bɪ'kwest] *s* legato, lascito

berate [bɪ'ret] *tr* redarguire

be·reave [bɪ'riv] *v* (*pret & pp* **-reaved** *or* **-reft** ['reft]) *tr* spogliare

bereavement [bɪ'rivmənt] *s* lutto, perdita

beret [bə're] *or* ['bere] *s* berretto

Berlin [bər'lɪn] *adj* berlinese ‖ *s* Berlino

Berliner [bər'lɪnər] *s* berlinese *mf*

Bermuda [bər'mjudə] *s* le Bermude

ber·ry ['berɪ] *s* (**-ries**) (*dry seed*) chicco; (*fruit*) bacca

berserk [bʌr'sʌrk] *adj* infuriato || *adv*
—**to go berserk** impazzire

berth [bʌrθ] *s (for a ship)* posto di
ormeggio; *(bed)* cuccetta; (coll)
posto

beryllium [bə'rɪlɪ·əm] *s* berillio

be·seech [bɪ'sitʃ] *v (pret & pp -sought*
['sɔt] *or -seeched) tr* supplicare

be·set [bɪ'set] *v (pret & pp -set; ger
-setting) tr* assediare, circondare;
(e.g., with problems) assillare

beside [bɪ'saɪd] *adv* oltre, inoltre ||
prep vicino a; in confronto di; oltre
a; **beside oneself** fuori di sé; **beside
the point** fuori del seminato

besides [bɪ'saɪdz] *adv* inoltre; d'al-
tronde || *prep* oltre a

besiege [bɪ'sidʒ] *tr* assediare; *(with
questions)* bombardare

besmear [bɪ'smɪr] *tr* imbrattare, sgorbiare; sporcare

besmirch [bɪ'smʌrtʃ] *tr* insudiciare

bespatter [bɪ'spætər] *tr* inzaccherare

be·speak [bɪ'spik] *v (-spoke* ['spok],
-spoken) tr chiedere anticipatamente
a; *(to show)* dimostrare

best [best] *adj super* (il) migliore; ot-
timo || *s* meglio; **at best** nella miglior
delle ipotesi; **to do one's best** fare
del proprio meglio; **to get the best of**
avere la meglio di; **to make the best
of** adattarsi a || *adv super* meglio;
had best, e.g., **I had best** dovrei || *tr*
battere, riuscire superiore a

bestial ['bestʃəl] *or* ['best/əl] *adj* bestiale

be·stir [bɪ'stʌr] *v (pret & pp -stirred;
ger -stirring) tr* eccitare; **to bestir
oneself** darsi da fare

best' man' *s* testimone *m* di nozze

bestow [bɪ'sto] *tr* accordare; conferire

best' sell'er *s* best-seller *m*

bet [bet] *s* scommessa || *v (pret & pp
bet or betted; ger betting) tr & intr*
scommettere; **I bet** ci scommetto;
you bet (coll) evidentemente

be·take [bɪ'tek] *v (pret -took* ['tuk];
pp -taken) tr—**to betake oneself**
andare, dirigersi

be·think [bɪ'θɪŋk] *v (pret & pp
-thought* ['θɔt]) *tr* **to bethink oneself**
pensare; ricordarsi

Bethlehem ['beθlɪ·əm] *or* ['beθlɪ‚hem]
s Betlemme *f*

betide [bɪ'taɪd] *tr* accadere a || *intr*
accadere

betoken [bɪ'tokən] *tr* indicare, presagire

betray [bɪ'tre] *tr* tradire, ingannare;
(to reveal) rivelare

betroth [bɪ'troð] *or* [bɪ'trɔθ] *tr* promettere in matrimonio a

betrothal [bɪ'troðəl] *or* [bɪ'trɔθəl] *s*
fidanzamento

betrothed [bɪ'troð] *or* [bɪ'trɔθt] *adj*
fidanzato || *s* promesso sposo, fidan-
zato

better ['betər] *adj comp* migliore; **to
grow better** migliorare || *s*—**betters**
superiori *mpl*; ottimati *mpl*; **to get
the better of** avere la meglio di || *adv*
meglio; **had better** dovere, e.g., **I had**

better dovrei; **to be better off** stare
meglio; **to think better of** riconsiderare; **you ought to know better** do-
vrebbe vergognarsi || *tr* sorpassare;
migliorare; **to better oneself** migliorare la propria situazione

bet'ter half' *s* metà *f*

betterment ['betərmənt] *s* miglioramento

bettor ['betər] *s* scommettitore *m*

between [bɪ'twin] *adv* in mezzo; **in be-
tween** in mezzo, fra i piedi || *prep*
fra, tra

between'-decks' *s* interponte *m*

bev·el ['bevəl] *s (instrument)* falsa
squadra; *(sloping part)* augnatura ||
*v (pret & pp -eled or -elled; ger -eling
or -elling) tr* augnare

beverage ['bevərɪdʒ] *s* bevanda

bev·y ['bevɪ] *s (-ies) (of women)*
gruppo; *(of birds)* stormo

bewail [bɪ'wel] *tr* lamentare

beware [bɪ'wer] *tr* fare attenzione a,
guardarsi da || *intr* fare attenzione,
guardarsi

bewilder [bɪ'wɪldər] *tr* lasciar perplesso, confondere, disorientare

bewilderment [bɪ'wɪldərmənt] *s* perplessità *f*, disorientamento

bewitch [bɪ'wɪtʃ] *tr* stregare

beyond [bɪ'jand] *s*—**the beyond** l'al-
dilà *m* || *adv* più lontano || *prep* al
di là di; oltre a; più tardi di; **beyond
a doubt** fuori dubbio; **beyond repair**
irreparabile

bias ['baɪ·əs] *s* linea diagonale; pregiudizio; **on the bias** diagonalmente
|| *tr* prevenire

bib [bɪb] *s* bavaglino

Bible ['baɪbəl] *s* Bibbia

Biblical ['bɪblɪkəl] *adj* biblico

bibliogra·phy [‚bɪblɪ'agrəfɪ] *s (-phies)*
bibliografia

bibliophile ['bɪblɪ·ə‚faɪl] *s* bibliofilo

bicarbonate [baɪ'karbə‚net] *s* bicarbonato

biceps ['baɪseps] *s* bicipite *m*

bicker ['bɪkər] *s* bisticcio, disputa ||
intr bisticciare, disputare

bicycle ['baɪsɪkəl] *s* bicicletta

bid [bɪd] *s* offerta; *(cards)* dichiara-
zione; (coll) invito || *v (pret bade*
[bæd] *or bid; pp bidden* ['bɪdən] *or
bid; ger bidding) tr & intr* offrire;
comandare; *(cards)* dichiarare

bidder ['bɪdər] *s* offerente *mf*; *(cards)*
dichiarante *mf*; **the highest bidder** il
miglior offerente

bidding ['bɪdɪŋ] *s* ordine *m*; offerte
fpl; *(cards)* dichiarazione

bide [baɪd] *tr*—**to bide one's time** attendere l'ora propizia

biennial [baɪ'enɪ·əl] *adj* biennale

bier [bɪr] *s* catafalco

bifocal [baɪ'fokəl] *adj* bifocale || **bifo-
cals** *spl* occhiali *mpl* bifocali

big [bɪg] *adj (bigger; biggest)* grande;
(coll) importante; (coll) stravagante;
big with child incinta || *adv*—**to talk
big** (coll) parlare con iattanza

bigamist ['bɪgəmɪst] *s* bigamo

bigamous ['bɪgəməs] *adj* bigamo

big-bellied ['bɪg ,belɪd] *adj* panciuto
Big' Dip'per *s* Gran Carro
big' game' *s* caccia grossa
big-hearted ['bɪg ,hɑrtɪd] *adj* magnanimo, generoso
big' mouth' *s* (slang) sbraitone *m*
bigot ['bɪgət] *s* bigotto, bacchettone *m*
bigoted ['bɪgətɪd] *adj* (*in religion*) bigotto; intransigente
bigot-ry ['bɪgətri] *s* (-**ries**) bigottismo; intransigenza
big' shot' *s* (slang) pezzo grosso, (un) qualcuno
big' slam' *s* (bridge) grande slam *m*
big' toe' *s* alluce *m*
big' wheel' *s* (slang) pezzo grosso
bike [baɪk] *s* (coll) bicicletta
bile [baɪl] *s* bile *f*
bilge [bɪldʒ] *s* sentina; (*of barrel*) ventre *m*
bilge'ways' *spl* parati *mpl*
bilingual [baɪ'lɪŋgwəl] *adj* bilingue
bilious ['bɪljəs] *adj* bilioso
bilk [bɪlk] *tr* defraudare
bill [bɪl] *s* (*of bird*) becco; (*statement of charges*) conto; (*e.g., for electricity*) bolletta; (*menu*) lista; (*money*) biglietto; (*proposed law*) disegno di legge; (*handbill*) annunzio; (*law*) atto; (*theat*) cartellone *m*; **to fill the bill** (coll) riempire i requisiti; **to foot the bill** (coll) pagare lo scotto || *tr* fare una lista di; mettere in conto a || *intr* (*said of doves*) beccuzzarsi; (*said of lovers*) baciucchiarsi
bill'board' *s* cartellone *m*; (rad, telv) titolo di testa
billet ['bɪlɪt] *s* (mil) alloggiamento; (mil) ordine *m* d'alloggiamento || *tr* (mil) alloggiare, accasermare
bill'fold' *s* portafoglio
bill'head' *s* intestazione di fattura
billiards ['bɪljərdz] *s* bigliardo
bil'ling clerk' *s* fatturista *mf*
billion ['bɪljən] *s* (U.S.A.) miliardo; (Brit) bilione *m*
bill' of exchange' *s* tratta
bill' of fare' *s* menu *m*, lista delle vivande
bill' of lad'ing ['ledɪŋ] *s* polizza di carico
bill' of rights' *s* dichiarazione dei diritti
bill' of sale' *s* atto di vendita
billow ['bɪlo] *s* ondata, cavallone *m*
bill'post'er *s* attacchino
bil-ly ['bɪlɪ] *s* (-**lies**) manganello
bil'ly goat' *s* capro, caprone *m*
bimonthly [baɪ'mʌnθlɪ] *adj* (*occurring every two months*) bimestrale; (*occurring twice a month*) bimensile
bin [bɪn] *s* cassone *m*; (*for bread*) madia; (*e.g., for coal*) deposito
binaural [baɪ'nɔrəl] *adj* biauricolare
bind [baɪnd] *v* (*pret & pp* **bound** [baʊnd]) *tr* legare; allacciare; (*to bandage*) fasciare; (*to constipate*) costipare; (*a book*) rilegare; (*to oblige*) obbligare; (mach) grippare
binder ['baɪndər] *s* rilegatore *m*; (*cover*) cartella

binder-y ['baɪndəri] *s* (-**ies**) rilegatoria
binding ['baɪndɪŋ] *adj* obbligatorio || *s* (*of book*) rilegatura; legatura; fasciatura
bind'ing post' *s* (elec) capocorda; (*e.g., of battery*) (elec) serrafilo
binge [bɪndʒ] *s*—**to go on a binge** (coll) far baldoria
bingo ['bɪŋgo] *s* tombola
binnacle ['bɪnəkəl] *s* abitacolo
binoculars [bɪ'nɑkjələrz] or [baɪ'nɑkjələrz] *spl* binocolo
biochemical [,baɪ-ə'kemɪkəl] *adj* biochimico
biochemist [,baɪ-ə'kemɪst] *s* biochimico
biochemistry [,baɪ-ə'kemɪstri] *s* biochimica
biodegradable [,baɪ-odɪ'gredəbəl] *adj* biodegradabile
biographer [baɪ'ɑgrəfər] *s* biografo
biographic(al) [,baɪ-ə'græfɪk(əl)] *adj* biografico
biogra-phy [baɪ'ɑgrəfi] *s* (-**phies**) biografia
biologist [baɪ'ɑlədʒɪst] *s* biologo
biology [baɪ'ɑlədʒi] *s* biologia
biophysics [,baɪ-ə'fɪzɪks] *s* biofisica
biop-sy ['baɪ ,ɑpsi] *s* (-**sies**) biopsia
bipartisan [baɪ'pɑrtɪzən] *adj* (*system*) bipartitico; (*government*) bipartito
biped ['baɪped] *adj* & *s* bipede *m*
birch [bʌrtʃ] *s* betulla || *tr* scudisciare
bird [bʌrd] *s* uccello; **a bird in the hand is worth two in the bush** un uovo oggi vale meglio di una gallina domani; **birds of a feather** gente *f* della stessa risma; **to kill two birds with one stone** pigliare due piccioni con una fava
bird' cage' *s* gabbia
bird' call' *s* richiamo
birdie ['bʌrdi] *s* uccellino; (golf) giocata di un colpo sotto la media
bird'lime' *s* pania
bird' of pas'sage *s* uccello di passo
bird' of prey' *s* uccello da preda
bird'seed' *s* becchime *m*
bird's'-eye view' *s* vista a volo d'uccello
bird' shot' *s* pallini *mpl* da caccia
birth [bʌrθ] *s* nascita; **to give birth to** dare i natali a; mettere alla luce
birth' certif'icate *s* certificato di nascita
birth' control' *s* limitazione delle nascite
birth'day' *s* natalizio, compleanno; (*of an event*) anniversario
birth'mark' *s* voglia
birth'place' *s* patria; (*e.g., city*) luogo di nascita; **to be the birthplace of** dare i natali a
birth' rate' *s* natalità *f*
birth'right' *s* diritto acquisito sin dalla nascita
biscuit ['bɪskɪt] *s* panino soffice; (Brit) biscotto
bisect [baɪ'sekt] *tr* bisecare || *intr* (*said of roads*) incrociarsi
bisection [baɪ'sekʃən] *s* bisezione
bishop ['bɪʃəp] *s* vescovo; (chess) alfiere *m*
bishopric ['bɪʃəprɪk] *s* vescovado

bismuth ['bɪzməθ] *s* bismuto
bison ['baɪsən] or ['baɪzən] *s* bisonte *m*
bisulfate [baɪ'sʌlfet] *s* bisolfato
bisulfite [baɪ'sʌlfaɪt] *s* bisolfito
bit [bɪt] *s* (*of bridle*) morso; (*of key*) mappa; (*tool*) punta, trivella; (*small piece*) briciolo; **a bit** un po'; (*coll*) un momento; **a good bit** una buona quantità; **bit by bit** poco a poco; **to blow to bits** fare a pezzi; **to champ the bit** mordere il freno; **two bits** (*slang*) quarto di dollaro, cinque soldi
bitch [bɪtʃ] *s* cagna; (*vulg*) donnaccia ‖ *intr* (*slang*) lamentarsi
bite [baɪt] *s* morso; (*mouthful*) boccone *m*; **to take a bite** fare uno spuntino; mangiare un boccone ‖ *v* (*pret* **bit** [bɪt]; *pp* **bit** or **bitten** ['bɪtən]) *tr* mordere, addentare; pungere; (*the dust*) baciare ‖ *intr* mordere; (*said of insects*) pungere; (*said of fish*) abboccare
biting ['baɪtɪŋ] *adj* mordace; pungente
bitter ['bɪtər] *adj* amaro; (*e.g., fight*) accanito; (*cold*) pungente ‖ *s* amaro; **bitters** amaro
bit'ter end' *s*—**to the bitter end** fino alla fine; fino alla morte
bit'ter·en'der *s* (coll) intransigente *mf*
bitterness ['bɪtərnɪs] *s* amarezza
bit'ter-sweet' *adj* dolceamaro; (*fig*) agrodolce ‖ *s* dulcamara
bitumen [bɪ'tjumən] or [bɪ'tumən] *s* bitume *m*
bivou·ac ['bɪvʊ͵æk] or ['bɪvwæk] *s* bivacco ‖ *v* (*pret & pp* **-acked**; *ger* **-acking**) *intr* bivaccare
biweekly [baɪ'wikli] *adj* bisettimanale; quindicinale ‖ *adv* ogni due settimane
biyearly [baɪ'jɪrli] *adj* semestrale ‖ *adv* semestralmente
bizarre [bɪ'zɑr] *adj* bizzarro
blab [blæb] *s* chiacchierone *m* ‖ *v* (*pret & pp* **blabbed**; *ger* **blabbing**) *tr* rivelare ‖ *intr* chiacchierare
black [blæk] *adj* nero; (*without light*) buio ‖ *s* nero; **to wear black** vestire a lutto, vestire di nero ‖ *intr*—**to black out** perdere i sensi
black'-and-blue' *adj* livido e pesto
black'-and-white' *adj* in bianco e nero
black'ball' *s* palla nera, voto contrario ‖ *tr* dare la palla nera a
black'ber'ry *s* (-ries) mora
black'bird' *s* merlo
black'board' *s* lavagna, tavola nera
black'cap' *s* capinera
black'damp' *s* putizza
Black' Death' *s* peste bubbonica
blacken ['blækən] *tr* annerire; (*shoes*) lucidare; (*reputation*) sporcare
black' eye' *s* occhio pesto; (*fig*) cattiva reputazione
blackguard ['blægɑrd] *s* canaglia
black'head' *s* comedone *m*
blackish ['blækɪʃ] *adj* nerastro
black'jack' *s* randello; (*cards*) ventuno ‖ *tr* randellare
black' mag'ic *s* magia nera

black'mail' *s* ricatto ‖ *tr* ricattare
blackmailer ['blæk͵melər] *s* ricattatore *m*
Black' Mari'a [mə'raɪ·ə] *s* (coll) furgone *m* cellulare
black' mar'ket *s* borsa nera
black' marketeer' [͵mɑrkɪ'tɪr] *s* borsanerista *mf*
blackness ['blæknɪs] *s* nerezza
black'out' *s* oscuramento; (theat) spegnitura; (pathol) svenimento passeggero
black' sheep' *s* (fig) pecora nera
black'smith' *s* fabbro
black' tie' *s* cravatta da smoking; smoking *m*
bladder ['blædər] *s* vescica
blade [bled] *s* (*of a leaf*) pagina; (*of grass*) stelo, filo; (*of oar*) pala; (*of turbine*) paletta; (*of fan*) ventola; (*of knife*) lama; (coll) caposcarico
blame [blem] *s* colpa; **to be to blame for** aver la colpa di; **to put the blame on s.o. for s.th** attribuire a qlcu la colpa di qlco; **you are to blame** è colpa Sua ‖ *tr* biasimare, incolpare
blameless ['blemlɪs] *adj* innocente, senza colpa
blanch [blæntʃ] or [blɑntʃ] *tr* bianchire ‖ *intr* impallidire
bland [blænd] *adj* blando; (*weather*) mite
blandish ['blændɪʃ] *tr* blandire
blank [blæŋk] *adj* (*not written on*) in bianco; (*e.g., stare*) vuoto; (*utter*) completo ‖ *s* (*printed form*) modulo; (*cartridge*) cartuccia a salve; (*of the mind*) lacuna; **to draw a blank** (coll) non avere alcun successo ‖ *tr*—**to blank out** cancellare
blank' check' *s* assegno in bianco; (fig) carta bianca
blanket ['blæŋkɪt] *adj* generale, combinato ‖ *s* coperta; (*of snow*) cappa ‖ *tr* coprire con una coperta; oscurare
blank' verse' *s* verso sciolto
blare [bler] *s* squillo ‖ *tr* proclamare; fare echeggiare ‖ *intr* squillare; echeggiare
blaspheme [blæs'fim] *tr & intr* bestemmiare
blasphemous ['blæsfɪməs] *adj* bestemmiatore
blasphe·my ['blæsfɪmi] *s* (-mies) bestemmia
blast [blæst] or [blɑst] *s* (*of air*) raffica; (*of a horn*) squillo; (*blight*) rovina; scoppio, esplosione; **at full blast** a piena velocità ‖ *tr* rovinare; fare scoppiare, far saltare ‖ *intr* —**to blast off** (rok) lanciarsi
blast' fur'nace *s* altoforno
blast'off' *s* lancio di missile or di nave spaziale
blatant ['bletənt] *adj* (*noisy*) rumoroso; (*obtrusive*) palmare; (*flashy*) chiassoso
blaze [blez] *s* fiammata; splendore *m*; (*on a horse's head*) stella; **in a blaze** in fiamme ‖ *tr* proclamare; **to blaze a**

trail marcare il cammino || *intr* divampare

bleach [blitʃ] *s* candeggio, candeggina || *tr* imbiancare, candeggiare

bleachers ['blitʃərz] *spl* posti *mpl* allo scoperto o di gradinata

bleak [blik] *adj* nudo, deserto; (*cold*) freddo; (*gloomy*) triste

blear·y ['blɪri] *adj* (**-ier; iest**) (*sight*) cisposo; confuso; offuscato

bleat [blit] *s* belato || *intr* belare

bleed [blid] *v* (*pret & pp* **bled** [bled]) *tr* (*to draw blood from*) salassare; (*a tree*) estrare linfa da; (coll) sfruttare || *intr* sanguinare; (*said of a tree*) dar linfa; **to bleed to death** morire dissanguato

blemish ['blemɪʃ] *s* difetto; macchia || *tr* danneggiare; macchiare

blend [blend] *s* mescolanza, miscuglio; (*of gasoline*) miscela || *v* (*pret & pp* **blended** or **blent** [blent]) *tr* mescolare, miscelare || *intr* mescolarsi, miscelarsi; armonizzare; fondersi

bless [bles] *tr* benedire; (*to endow*) dotare; (*to make happy*) allietare

blessed ['blesɪd] *adj* benedetto; beato; fortunato; dotato

bless'ed event' *s* lieto evento

blessing ['blesɪŋ] *s* benedizione

blight [blaɪt] *s* (*insect; disease*) piaga; rovina; (*fungus*) ruggine *f* || *tr* rovinare, guastare

blimp [blɪmp] *s* piccolo dirigibile

blind [blaɪnd] *adj* cieco; (slang) ubriaco || *s* persiana; tendina; (*decoy*) mascheratura; pretesto || *adv* alla cieca || *tr* accecare

blind' al'ley *s* vicolo cieco

blinder ['blaɪndər] *s* paraocchi *m*

blind' fly'ing *s* (aer) volo senza visibilità

blind'fold' *adj* bendato, cogli occhi bendati || *s* benda || *tr* bendare gli occhi a

blindly ['blaɪndli] *adv* alla cieca

blind' man' *s* cieco

blind'man's buff' *s* mosca cieca

blindness ['blaɪndnɪs] *s* cecità *f*

blind' spot' *s* (anat) punto cieco; (rad) zona di silenzio; (fig) debole *m*

blink [blɪŋk] *s* batter *m* di ciglio; (*glimpse*) occhiata; (*glimmer*) barlume *m*; **on the blink** (slang) fuori servizio || *tr*—**to blink one's eyes** batter il ciglio || *intr* occhieggiare; (*to wink*) ammiccare; (*to flash on and off*) lampeggiare; **to blink at** ignorare; far finta di non vedere

blinker ['blɪŋkər] *s* (*at a crossing*) luce *f* intermittente; (*on a horse*) paraocchi *m*

blip [blɪp] *s* guizzo sullo schermo radar

bliss [blɪs] *s* beatitudine *f*, felicità *f*

blissful ['blɪsfəl] *adj* beato, felice

blister ['blɪstər] *s* vescica, bolla || *tr* coprire di vesciche, (fig) bollare || *intr* coprirsi di vesciche

blithe [blaɪð] *adj* gaio, giocondo

blitzkrieg ['blɪts,krig] *s* guerra lampo

blizzard ['blɪzərd] *s* tormenta, ventoneve *m*

bloat [blot] *tr* gonfiare || *intr* gonfiarsi

blob [blɑb] *s* (*lump*) zolla; (*of liquid*) macchia

block [blɑk] *s* (*e.g., of wood*) blocco; (*for chopping*) ceppo; (*pulley*) puleggia; ostacolo; (*of houses*) isolato; (typ) cliché *m* || *tr* bloccare; (*a hat*) mettere in forma; **to block up** tappare

blockade [blɑ'ked] *s* blocco; **to run a blockade** forzare il blocco || *tr* bloccare

block' and tack'le *s* bozzello

block'bust'er *s* (coll) superbomba

block'head' *s* imbecille *mf*

block' let'ter *s* carattere *m* stampatello

block' sig'nal *s* (rr) segnale di blocco

blond [blɑnd] *adj & s* biondo

blonde [blɑnd] *s* bionda

blood [blʌd] *s* sangue *m*; **in cold blood** a sangue freddo; **to draw blood** ferire, fare sanguinare

blood' bank' *s* emoteca

bloodcurdling ['blʌd,kʌrdlɪŋ] *adj* orripilante

blood' do'nor *s* donatore *m* di sangue

blood'hound' *s* segugio

bloodless ['blʌdlɪs] *adj* esangue; (*e.g., revolution*) senza effusione di sangue

blood'mobile' [mo,bil] *s* autoemoteca

blood' poi'soning *s* avvelenamento del sangue

blood' pres'sure *s* pressione sanguigna

blood' rela'tion *s* consanguineo

blood'shed' *s* spargimento di sangue, carneficina

blood'shot' *adj* iniettato di sangue

blood'stained' *adj* macchiato di sangue

blood'stream' *s* circolazione sanguigna

blood'suck'er *s* sanguisuga

blood' test' *s* esame *m* del sangue

blood'thirst'y *adj* assetato di sangue

blood' transfu'sion *s* trasfusione di sangue

blood' type' *s* gruppo sanguigno

blood' ves'sel *s* vaso sanguigno

blood·y ['blʌdi] *adj* (**-ier; -iest**) sanguinoso; (*bloodthirsty*) avido di sangue || *v* (*pret & pp* **-ied**) *tr* macchiare di sangue

bloom [blum] *s* fiore *m*; (*state of having open buds*) sboccio; (*youthful glow*) incarnato || *intr* fiorire; sbocciare

bloomers ['blumərz] *spl* pantaloni *mpl* femminili larghi fermati sotto il ginocchio

blossom ['blɑsəm] *s* fiore *m*; sboccio || *intr* sbocciare

blot [blɑt] *s* macchia || *v* (*pret & pp* **blotted**; *ger* **blotting**) *tr* macchiare; (*with blotting paper*) asciugare; **to blot out** cancellare; oscurare || *intr* macchiarsi; (*to be absorbent*) essere assorbente; (*said of a pen*) fare macchie

blotch [blɑtʃ] *s* chiazza, macchia || *tr* chiazzare

blotter ['blɑtər] *s* carta asciugante, carta assorbente; (*book*) registro

blouse [blaʊs] *s* blusa

blow [blo] *s* colpo; (*blast*) folata; (*of*

horn) squillo; (*sudden reverse*) batosta; **at one blow** d'un sol colpo; **to come to blows** venire alle mani; **without striking a blow** senza colpo ferire ‖ *v* (*pret* **blew** [blu]; *pp* **blown**) *tr* soffiare, soffiare su; (*an instrument*) ∙suonare; (*one's nose*) soffiarsi; **to blow in** sfondare; **to blow one's brains out** bruciarsi le cervella; **to blow open** aprire completamente; **to blow out** (*e.g., a candle*) spegnere; (*a fuse*) fondere; **to blow up** (*e.g., a mine*) far brillare; (*phot*) ingrandire ‖ *intr* soffiare; (*to pant*) ansimare; (*with an instrument*) suonare; (*to puff*) sbuffare; (*slang*) andarsene; **to blow hot and cold** cambiare d'opinione ogni cinque minuti; **to blow in** (coll) arrivare inaspettatamente; **to blow out** (*said, e.g., of a candle*) spegnersi; (*said of a fuse*) saltare, fondersi; (*said of a tire*) scoppiare; **to blow over** passare; **to blow up** saltar per aria; (*said of a storm*) scoppiare; (coll) perdere la pazienza, scoppiare d'ira

blow'out' *s* scoppio di un pneumatico

blow'pipe' *s* (*tube*) soffione *m*; (*peashooter*) cerbottana

blow'torch' *s* saldatrice *f* a benzina

blubber ['blʌbər] *s* grasso di balena ‖ *intr* piangere, lamentarsi

bludgeon ['blʌdʒən] *s* randello ‖ *tr* randellare

blue [blu] *adj* blu, azzurro; (*gloomy*) triste; (*e.g., laws*) puritanico ‖ *s* blu *m*, azzurro; **out of the blue** inaspettatamente; **the blues** la malinconia; (mus) blues *m*; **to have the blues** essere giù di morale ‖ *tr* tingere di azzurro; (*a metal*) brunire

blue'ber'ry *s* (**-ries**) mirtillo

blue'bird' *s* uccello azzurro

blue' blood' *s* sangue *m* blu

blue' cheese' *s* gorgonzola americano

blue' chip' *s* (fin) azione di prim'ordine

blue' jay' *s* ghiandaia azzurra

blue' moon' *s*—**once in a blue moon** ad ogni morte di papa

blue'-pen'cil *v* (*pret & pp* **-ciled** or **-cilled;** *ger* **-ciling** or **-cilling**) *tr* correggere col lapis blu

blue'print' *s* riproduzione cianografica; (*plan*) piano ‖ *tr* riprodurre in cianografia; preparare dettagliatamente

blue'stock'ing *s* saccente *f*, sapientona

blue' streak' *s*—**like a blue streak** (coll) come un razzo

bluff [blʌf] *adj* scosceso; brusco, burbero ‖ *s* promontorio scosceso; bluff *m*; bluffatore *m* ‖ *intr* bluffare

bluing ['bluɪŋ] *s* turchinetto

bluish ['bluɪʃ] *adj* bluastro

blunder ['blʌndər] *s* errore *m* madornale ‖ *intr* pigliare un granchio

blunt [blʌnt] *adj* ottuso; (*plain-spoken*) franco ‖ *tr* rendere ottuso

bluntness ['blʌntnɪs] *s* ottusità *f*; franchezza

blur [blʌr] *s* macchia; offuscamento; confusione ‖ *v* (*pret & pp* **blurred;**

ger **blurring**) *tr* macchiare; (*the view*) offuscare

blurb [blʌrb] *s* annuncio pubblicitario

blurt [blʌrt] *tr*—**to blurt out** prorompere a dire, lasciarsi sfuggire

blush [blʌʃ] *s* rossore *m*; (*pinkish natural tinge*) incarnato ‖ *intr* arrossire; **to blush at** vergognarsi di

bluster ['blʌstər] *s* frastuono; (fig) boria ‖ *intr* (*said of the wind*) infuriare; fare il bravaccio

blustery ['blʌstəri] *adj* tempestuoso; violento; (*swaggering*) borioso

boar [bor] *s* verro; (*wild hog*) porco selvatico, cinghiale *m*

board [bord] *s* asse *m*; (*notice*) cartello; (*pasteboard*) cartone *m*; (*table*) tavola; (*meals*) vitto; (*group of administrators*) consiglio; (naut) bordo; **above board** franco; **in boards** rilegato; **on board** a bordo; (rr) in vettura; **to go by the board** andare in rovina; **to tread the boards** fare l'attore ‖ *tr* chiudere con assi; (*to provide with meals*) dare pensione a, tenere a dozzina; (*a ship*) salire a bordo di; (*a train*) salire su; (naut) abbordare ‖ *intr* essere a pensione

board' and lodg'ing *s* pensione completa

boarder ['bordər] *s* pensionante *mf*

board'ing house' *s* pensione di famiglia

board'ing school' *s* collegio di pensionanti

board' of direc'tors *s* consiglio d'amministrazione

board' of health' *s* ufficio d'igiene

board' of trade' *s* camera di commercio

board'walk' *s* passeggiata a mare

boast [bost] *s* millanteria, vanteria ‖ *intr* vantarsi

boastful ['bostfəl] *adj* millantatore

boat [bot] *s* nave *f*, battello; (*small ship*) barca, imbarcazione; (*dish*) salsiera; **in the same boat** nella stessa situazione

boat' hook' *s* alighiero

boat'house' *s* capannone *m* per i canotti

boating ['botɪŋ] *s* escursione in barca

boat'man *s* (**-men**) barcaiolo

boat' race' *s* regata

boatswain ['bosən] or ['bot,swen] *s* nostromo

bob [bab] *s* (*plumb*) piombino; (*short haircut*) taglio alla bebè; coda mozza (di cavallo); (*jerky motion*) strattone *m*; (*on pendulum of clock*) lente *f*; (*on fishing line*) sughero ‖ *v* (*pret & pp* **bobbed;** *ger* **bobbing**) *tr* tagliare alla bebè; far muovere a scatti ‖ *intr* muoversi a scatti; fare mossa; **to bob up** apparire

bobbin ['babɪn] *s* bobina

bob'by pin' *s* ['babi] *s* forcina

bob'by-socks' *spl* (coll) calzini *mpl* da ragazza

bobbysoxer ['babɪ,saksər] *s* (coll) ragazzina

bobolink ['babə,lɪŋk] *s* doliconice *m*

bob'sled' *s* guidoslitta

bode [bod] *tr & intr* presagire

bodice ['badɪs] *s* giubbetto, copribusto

bodily ['bɑdɪli] *adj* fisico, corporeo ‖ *adv* fisicamente, corporeamente; di persona; **in massa**

bodkin ['bɑdkɪn] *s* punteruolo; *(for lady's hair)* spillone *m*

bod·y ['bɑdi] *s* (-ies) corpo; *(corpse)* cadavere *m*; *(of water)* massa; *(of people)* gruppo; *(of a liquid)* sostanza; *(of truck)* cassone *m*; *(of car)* carrozzeria; *(of tree)* tronco; *(coll)* persona; **in a body** in massa

bod'y-guard' *s* *(of a high official)* guardia del corpo; *(e.g., of a movie star)* guardaspalle *m*

bod'y suit' *s* calzamaglia

bog [bɑg] *s* pantano, palude *m* ‖ *(pret & pp* bogged; *ger* bogging) *intr*—**to bog down** impelagarsi

bogey·man ['bogi‚mæn] *s* (-men [men]) babau *m*

bogus ['bogəs] *adj* (coll) falso, finto

Bohemian [bo'himɪ·ən] *adj* boemo; da bohémien ‖ *s* boemo; (fig) bohémien *m*

boil [bɔɪl] *s* bollore *m*, ebollizione; *(pathol)* foruncolo; **to come to a boil** cominciare a bollire ‖ *tr* bollire; **to boil down** condensare ‖ *intr* bollire; **to boil away** evaporare completamente; **to boil down** condensarsi; **to boil over** andare per il fuoco

boiled' ham' *s* prosciutto cotto

boiler ['bɔɪlər] *s* caldaia; *(for cooking)* caldaio

boil'er·mak'er *s* calderaio

boiling ['bɔɪlɪŋ] *adj* bollente ‖ *s* bollore *m*, ebollizione

boisterous ['bɔɪstərəs] *adj* *(storm)* violento; *(loud)* rumoroso

bold [bold] *adj* *(daring)* coraggioso; *(impudent)* sfacciato; *(steep)* scosceso; *(clear, sharp)* netto

bold'face' *s* (typ) neretto, grassetto

boldness ['boldnɪs] *s* coraggio, audacia; sfacciataggine *f*, impudenza

boll' wee'vil [bol] *s* antonomo del cotone

bologna [bə'lonə] *or* [bə'lonjə] *s* mortadella

Bolshevik ['bɑlʃəvɪk] *or* ['bolʃəvɪk] *adj & mf* bolscevico

bolster ['bolstər] *s* cuscino; cuscinetto; *(support)* sostegno ‖ *tr* sorreggere; **to bolster up** sostenere

bolt [bolt] *s* *(arrow)* freccia; *(of lightning)* fulmine *m*; *(sliding bar)* chiavistello; *(threaded rod)* bullone *m*; *(of paper or cloth)* pezza, rotolo ‖ *adv*—**bolt upright** dritto come un fuso ‖ *tr* *(to swallow hurriedly)* ingollare; *(to fasten, e.g., a door)* sprangare; *(to fasten, e.g., two metal parts)* bullonare; *(e.g., a political party)* abbandonare ‖ *intr* *(said of people)* spiccare un salto; *(said of a horse)* prendere la mano; precipitarsi

bolt' from the blue' *s* fulmine *m* a ciel sereno

bomb [bɑm] *s* bomba; *(e.g., for spraying)* bombola ‖ *tr* bombardare

bombard [bɑm'bɑrd] *tr* bombardare; *(with questions)* bersagliare

bombardment [bɑm'bɑrdmənt] *s* bombardamento

bombast ['bɑmbæst] *s* ampollosità *f*

bombastic [bɑm'bæstɪk] *adj* ampolloso

bomb' cra'ter *s* cratere *m*

bomber ['bɑmər] *s* bombardiere *m*

bomb'proof' *adj* a prova di bomba

bomb'shell' *s* bomba; (fig) colpo di bomba, colpo di sorpresa

bomb' shel'ter *s* rifugio antiaereo

bomb'sight' *s* traguardo aereo

bona fide ['bonə ‚faɪdə] *adj* sincero ‖ *adv* in buona fede

bonanza [bə'nænzə] *s* (min) ricca vena; (coll) fortuna

bond [bɑnd] *s* legame *m*, vincolo; *(contractual obligation)* obbligazione; *(interest-bearing certificate)* buono, obbligazione; *(surety)* cauzione; **bonds** catene *fpl*; **in bond** sotto cauzione; *(said of goods)* in punto franco ‖ *tr* unire, connettere

bondage ['bɑndɪdʒ] *s* schiavitù *f*

bond'ed ware'house *s* deposito in punto franco

bond'hold'er *s* obbligazionista *mf*

bonds'man *s* (-men) garante *m*

bone [bon] *s* osso; *(of fish)* spina; *(of whale)* stecca; **bones** ossa *fpl*; **to have a bone to pick with** avere un conto da regolare con; **to make no bones about** (coll) ammettere; (coll) parlare esplicitamente ‖ *tr* disossare; cavare le spine a ‖ *intr*—**to bone up on** (coll) ripassare

bone'head' *s* (coll) testa dura

boneless ['bonlɪs] *adj* senz'osso; *(fish)* senza spine

boner ['bonər] *s* (slang) errore *m* madornale

bonfire ['bɑn ‚faɪr] *s* falò *m*

bonnet ['bɑnɪt] *s* cappello da donna; *(of child)* berrettino

bonus ['bonəs] *s* gratifica; indennità *f*; *(to an outgoing employee)* buonuscita

bon·y ['boni] *adj* (-ier; -iest) *(having bones)* osseo; *(emaciated)* scarno; *(fish)* spinoso

boo [bu] *s* fischio, urlaccio ‖ *tr & intr* fischiare, disapprovare

boo·by ['bubi] *s* (-bies) stupido

boo'by hatch' *s* (naut) portello; (slang) manicomio; (slang) prigione *f*

boo'by prize' *s* premio dato al peggior giocatore

boo'by trap' *s* (mil) trappola esplosiva; (fig) tranello

boogie-woogie ['bugi'wugi] *s* bughi-bughi *m*

book [buk] *s* libro; *(e.g., of matches)* pacchetto; (mus) libretto; (fig) regole *fpl*; **the Book** la Bibbia; **to be in one's book** essere nelle grazie di; **to bring s.o. to book** fare una ramanzina a ‖ *tr* registrare; *(e.g., on a horse)* allibrare; *(e.g., a room)* prenotare; *(an actor)* scritturare

book'bind'er *s* rilegatore *m*

book'bind'er·y *s* (-ies) rilegatoria

book'bind'ing *s* rilegatura

book'case' *s* scaffale *m*

book' end' *s* reggilibri *m*

bookie ['buki] s (coll) allibratore m
booking ['bukɪŋ] s (of a trip) prenotazione; (of an actor) scrittura
book'ing clerk' s impiegato alla biglietteria
bookish ['bukɪʃ] adj studioso; libresco
book'keep'er s contabile mf
booklet ['buklɪt] s libretto; (pamphlet)
opuscolo
book'keep'ing s contabilità f
book'mak'er s (one who accepts bets)
allibratore m
book'mark' s segnalibro
bookmobile ['bukmo ,bil] s bibliobus m
book'plate' s ex libris m
book' review' s rassegna, recensione
book'sell'er s libraio
book'shelf' s (-shelves) scaffale m
book'stand' s (rack) scansia; (stall)
edicola
book'store' s libreria
book'worm' s (zool) tarlo dei libri;
(fig) topo da biblioteca
boom [bum] s (of crane) braccio; (barrier) barriera galleggiante; (noise)
bum m; (fin) boom m; (naut) boma;
(mov, telv) giraffa || intr rimbom-
bare; essere in condizioni floride
boomerang ['bumə ,ræŋ] s bumerang
m
boom' town' s città f fungo
boon [bun] s fortuna, benedizione
boon' compan'ion s compagnone m
boor [bur] s bifolco, zotico
boorish ['burɪʃ] adj grossolano
boost [bust] s aumento; (coll) spinta ||
tr spingere in su; sostenere; (prices)
alzare; parlare a favore di
booster ['bustər] s (backer) sostenitore
m; propulsore m a razzo; (rok) propulsore m del primo stadio; (med)
seconda iniezione
boot [but] s stivale m; (kick) calcio;
(patch) (aut) pezza; **the boot is on
the other foot** la situazione è rove-
sciata; **to be in the boots of** essere
nella pelle di; **to boot** per di più; **to
get the boot** (coll) essere messo sulla
strada; **to lick the boots of** leccare i
piedi a; **to wipe one's boots on** trat-
tare come una pezza da piedi || tr
dare un calcio a; **to boot out** (slang)
buttar fuori
boot'black' s lustrascarpe m
booth [buθ] s (stall) banco da mercato;
(for telephoning, voting) cabina
boot'jack' s tirastivali m
boot'leg' adj di contrabbando || s li-
quore m di contrabbando || v (pret &
pp -legged; ger -legging) tr vendere
di contrabbando || intr vendere alcol
di contrabbando
bootlegger ['but ,legər] s contrabbandiere m di liquori
boot'lick'er [,lɪkər] s (coll) leccapiedi
mf
boot'strap' s tirante m degli stivali
boo·ty ['buti] s (-ties) bottino
booze [buz] s (coll) bevanda alcolica ||
intr (coll) ubriacarsi
borax ['boræks] s borace m
border ['bordər] adj confinario, con-

finante || s bordo, margine m; (be-
tween two countries) confine m || tr
bordare; confinare con || intr con-
finare
bor'der clash' s incidente m ai confini
bor'der·line' adj incerto || s frontiera
bore [bor] s (drill hole) buco, foro;
(hollow part of gun) anima; (caliber)
calibro; (dull person) seccatore m;
(annoyance) seccatura; (mach) ale-
saggio || tr bucare, forare, seccare;
(mach) alesare
boredom ['bordəm] s noia, tedio
boring ['borɪŋ] adj noioso || s trivella-
zione
born [bɔrn] adj nato, partorito; **to be
born** nascere; **to be born again** rinascere; **to be born with a silver spoon
in one's mouth** nascere con la camicia
borough ['bʌro] s borgata, comune m
borrow ['baro] or ['bɔro] tr chiedere
a o in prestito; prendere a or in
prestito; ricevere a o in prestito; (to
adopt) adottare; **to borrow trouble**
preoccuparsi per nulla
borrower ['baro·ər] or ['bɔro·ər] s chi
riceve a prestito; (law) comodatario,
prestatario
borrowing ['baro·ɪŋ] or ['bɔro·ɪŋ] s
prestito; prestito linguistico, forestierismo
bosom ['buzəm] s petto, seno; (e.g.,
of the family) grembo, seno; (of
shirt) pettorina
bos'om friend' s amico del cuore
Bosporus ['baspərəs] s Bosforo
boss [bas] or [bɔs] s (coll) padrone
m; (coll) direttore m; (coll) capintesta m; (coll) principale m; (archit)
bugna, bozza || tr fare da padrone a
|| intr fare da padrone
boss·y ['basi] or ['bɔsi] adj (-ier; -iest)
autoritario
botanical [bə'tænɪkəl] adj botanico
botanist ['batənɪst] s botanico
botany ['batəni] s botanica
botch [batʃ] s abborracciatura || tr ab-
borracciare
both [boθ] adj entrambi i, tutti e due
i || pron entrambi, tutti e due || conj
del pari, al medesimo tempo; **both
. . . and** tanto . . . quanto
bother ['baðər] s (worry) noia, secca-
tura; (person) seccatore m || tr dar
noia a, seccare || intr preoccuparsi;
to bother about or **with** occuparsi di;
to bother to + inf molestarsi di + inf
bothersome ['baðərsəm] adj incomodo
bottle ['batəl] s bottiglia, fiasco || tr
imbottigliare; **to bottle up** imbottigliare
bot'tle cap' s tappo a corona
bot'tle·neck' s collo di bottiglia; (of
traffic) congestione, imbottigliamento
bot'tle o'pener ['opənər] s apribottiglie
m
bottom ['batəm] adj basso; (price, dol-
lar) ultimo; infimo || s fondo; (of
chair) sedile m; base f; (of bottle)
culo; (of ship) scafo; **at bottom** in
realtà; **to begin at the bottom** comin-

ciare dalla gavetta; **to get at the bottom of** andare a fondo di; **to go to the bottom** and.re a picco

bottomless ['batəmlɪs] *adj* senza fondo

boudoir [bu'dwar] *s* gabinetto di toletta (da signora)

bough [bau] *s* ramo

bouillon ['bujən] *s* brodo schietto

boulder ['boldər] *s* masso, roccia

boulevard ['bulə‚vard] *s* corso

bounce [bauns] *s* balzo; salto; elasticità *f*; (*of boat or plane*) piastrellamento; (*fig*) spirito; **to get the bounce** (slang) essere licenziato ‖ *tr* far balzare; (slang) buttar fuori ‖ *intr* rimbalzare; saltare; (aer, naut) piastrellare

bouncer ['baunsər] *s* (*in night club*) (slang) buttafuori *m*

bouncing ['baunsɪŋ] *adj* forte, vigoroso; grande, rumoroso

bound [baund] *adj* legato; collegato; obbligato; (bb) rilegato; (coll) risoluto; **bound for** destinato a, diretto per; **bound up in** or **with** in strette relazioni con; assorto in ‖ *s* salto; rimbalzo; limite *m*; **bounds** zona limitrofa; **out of bounds** fuori limiti; al di là delle convenienze ‖ *tr* delimitare

bounda·ry ['baundəri] *s* (**-ries**) confine *m*, limite *m*

bound'ary stone' *s* pietra di confine

boundless ['baundlɪs] *adj* illimitato, sconfinato

bountiful ['bauntɪfəl] *adj* generoso; abbondante

boun·ty ['baunti] *s* (**-ties**) dono generoso; generosità *f*, abbondanza; (*reward*) premio

bouquet [bu'ke] or [bo'ke] *s* mazzo, mazzolino; profumo, aroma *m*

bourgeois ['burʒwa] *adj & s* borghese *mf*

bourgeoisie [‚burʒwa'zi] *s* borghesia

bout [baut] *s* lotta, contesa; (*of illness*) attacco

bow [bau] *s* inchino, riverenza; (naut) prua; **to take a bow** ricevere gli applausi ‖ *tr* chinare, piegare ‖ *intr* inchinarsi; sottomettersi; **to bow and scrape** fare riverenze ‖ [bo] *s* (*weapon*) arco; (*knot*) nodo; (mus) archetto; (*stroke of bow*) (mus) arcata ‖ *tr & intr* (mus) suonare con l'ar hetto

bowdlerize ['baudlə‚raɪz] *tr* espurgare

bowel ['bau·əl] *s* budello; **bowels** vis.ere *fpl*

bow'el move'ment *s* evacuazione; **to have a bowel movement** andar di corpo

bower ['bau·ər] *s* pergolato

bowery ['bau·əri] *adj* frondoso

bowknot ['bo‚nat] *s* nodo scorsoio

bowl [bol] *s* (*dish*) ciotola; tazza; (*of pipe*) fornello; (*basin*) catino; (*amphitheater*) arena; (*ball*) boccia; (*delivery of ball*) bocciata; **bowls** bocce *fpl* ‖ *tr* bocciare; **to bowl down** or **over** abbattere ‖ *intr* giocare alle bocce

bowlegged ['bo‚legd] or ['bo‚legɪd] *adj* con le gambe storte

bowler ['bolər] *s* giocatore *m* di bocce

bowling ['bolɪŋ] *s* bocce *fpl*; bowling *m*, birilli *mpl*

bowl'ing al'ley *s* pista per il bowling; bowling *m*

bowl'ing green' *s* campo di bocce erboso

bowshot ['bo‚ʃat] *s* tiro d'arco

bowsprit ['bausprit] or ['bosprit] *s* (naut) bompresso

bow' tie' [bo] *s* cravatta a farfalla

bowwow ['bau‚wau] *interj* bau bau!

box [baks] *s* scatola; cassa; (*for jury*) banco; (*for sentry*) garitta; (*on coach*) cassetta; (*in stable*) posta; (*slap*) ceffone *m*; (*with fist*) pugno; (bot) bosso; (theat) palco, barcaccia; (baseball) posto del battitore; (typ) riquadratura ‖ *tr* mettere in scatola; (*to slap*) schiaffeggiare; (*to hit with fist*) fare a pugilato con; **to box in** or **up** rinchiudere ‖ *intr* fare a pugni; combattere

box'car' *s* vagone *m* merci coperto

boxer ['baksər] *s* pugile *m*

box'hold'er *s* palchettista *mf*

boxing ['baksɪŋ] *s* pugilato

box'ing gloves' *spl* guantoni *mpl* da pugilato

box' of'fice *s* sportello, biglietteria; (theat) incasso; (theat) successo

box'-of'fice hit' *s* grande successo

box' pleat' *s* (*of skirt*) cannone *m*

box' seat' *s* posto in palco

box'wood' *s* bosso

boy [bɔɪ] *s* ragazzo, giovane *m* ‖ *interj* accidempoli!

boycott ['bɔɪkat] *s* boicottaggio ‖ *tr* boicottare

boy'friend' *s* innamorato, amico

boyhood ['bɔɪhud] *s* fanciullezza

boyish ['bɔɪ·ɪʃ] *adj* giovanile

boy' scout' *s* giovane esploratore *m*

bra [bra] *s* (coll) reggiseno

brace [bres] *s* (*couple*) paio; (*device for maintaining tension*) tirante *m*; (*prop*) sostegno; (*tool*) trapano; (typ) graffa; **braces** (Brit) bretelle *fpl* ‖ *tr* legare; serrare; puntellare; sostenere; invigorare; **to brace oneself** pigliare animo ‖ *intr*—**to brace up** (coll) pigliare animo

brace' and bit' *s* menarola, trapano

bracelet ['breslɪt] *s* braccialetto

bracer ['bresər] *s* (coll) bicchierino

bracket ['brækɪt] *s* mensola; (*for lamp*) braccio; angolo; classifica; (typ) parentesi quadra ‖ *tr* sostenere con mensola; mettere tra parentesi quadra; classificare

brackish ['brækɪʃ] *adj* salmastro

brad [bræd] *s* chiodino, punta

brag [bræg] *s* vanto ‖ *v* (*pret & pp* **bragged**; *ger* **bragging**) *intr* vantare

braggart ['brægərt] *s* millantatore *m*

Brah·man ['bramən] *s* (**-m.ns**) bramino

braid [bred] *s* treccia; (*strip of cloth*) spighetta; (mil) cordellina ‖ *tr* intrecciare; decorare con spighette

brain [bren] *s* cervello; **brains** cervello, intelligenza; **to rack one's brains** rompersi la testa || *tr* far saltare le cervella di

brain′child′ *s* (coll) parto dell'ingegno, idea geniale

brain′ drain′ *s* (coll) fuga di cervelli

brainless ['brenlɪs] *adj* senza testa

brain′ pow′er *s* intelligenza

brain′storm′ *s* (coll) ispirazione

brain′ trust′ *s* consiglio d'esperti

brain′wash′ing *s* lavaggio del cervello

brain′ wave′ *s* onda encefalica; (coll) idea geniale

brain′work′ *s* lavoro intellettuale

brain·y ['breni] *adj* (-ier; -iest) intelligente

braise [brez] *tr* (culin) brasare

brake [brek] *s* freno; (*thicket*) macchia || *tr & intr* frenare

brake′ drum′ *s* tamburo del freno

brake′lin′ing *s* ferodo

brake′man *s* (-men) frenatore *m*

brake′ shoe′ *s* ganascia

bramble ['bræmbəl] *s* rovo

bran [bræn] *s* crusca

branch [bræntʃ] *s* (*of tree*) branca, ramo; (*of river*) braccio; (*of a family*) ramo; (*of business*) filiale *f*; (rr) diramazione || *intr* biforcarsi; **to branch off or out** ramificarsi, diramarsi

branch′ line′ *s* ferrovia di diramazione

branch′ of′fice *s* succursale *f*

brand [brænd] *s* (*burning stick*) tizzone *m*; (*mark; stigma*) marchio; (*label; make*) marca || *tr* (*to mark with a brand*) marchiare; (*to put a stigma on*) bollare; **to brand as** tacciare di

brandied ['brændɪd] *adj* conservato in acquavite

brand′ing i′ron *s* ferro da marchio

brandish ['brændɪʃ] *tr* brandire

brand′-new′ *adj* nuovo fiammante

bran·dy ['brændɪ] *s* (-dies) cognac *m*, acquavite *f*

brash [bræʃ] *adj* (*too hasty*) avventato; (*insolent*) impudente || *s* frammenti *mpl*; attacco (di malattia), indigestione

brass [bræs] *or* [brɑs] *s* ottone *m*; (coll) faccia tosta; (slang) alti ufficiali; **brasses** (mus) ottoni *mpl*

brass′ band′ *s* fanfara

brassiere [brə'zɪr] *s* reggiseno

brass′ knuck′les *spl* tirapugni *m*

brass′ tack′ *s* chiodino or borchia d'ottone; **to get down to brass tacks** (coll) venire al sodo

brass·y ['bræsɪ] *or* ['brɑsɪ] *adj* (-ier; -iest) fatto d'ottone; sfacciato, impudente

brat [bræt] *s* marmocchio, monello

brava·do [brə'vɑdo] *s* (-does *or* -dos) bravata

brave [brev] *adj* coraggioso || *s* persona coraggiosa; guerriero indiano || *tr* (*to defy*) sfidare; (*to meet with courage*) affrontare

bravery ['brevərɪ] *s* coraggio

bra·vo ['brɑvo] *s* (-vos) bravo; applauso || *interj* bravo!

brawl [brɔl] *s* zuffa, rissa || *intr* azzuffarsi, rissare

brawn [brɔn] *s* forza muscolare

brawn·y ['brɔni] *adj* (-ier; -iest) muscoloso

bray [bre] *s* raglio || *intr* ragliare

braze [brez] *s* brasatura || *tr* brasare

brazen ['brezən] *adj* d'ottone; (*shameless*) sfrontato; (*sound*) penetrante || *tr*—**to brazen out or through** affrontare sfacciatamente

brazier ['breʒər] *s* caldano, braciere *m*; (*workman*) ottonaio

Brazil [brə'zɪl] *s* il Brasile

Brazilian [brə'zɪljən] *adj & s* brasiliano

Brazil′ nut′ *s* noce *f* del Brasile

breach [britʃ] *s* (*gap*) breccia; (*failure to observe a law*) infrazione || *tr* fare breccia su, fare varco in

breach′ of faith′ *s* abuso di confidenza

breach′ of prom′ise *s* rottura di promessa di matrimonio

breach′ of the peace′ *s* violazione dell'ordine pubblico

bread [bred] *s* pane *m*; **to break bread with** sedersi a tavola con || *tr* impanare

bread′ and but′ter *s* pane *m* e burro; (coll) pane quotidiano

bread′ crumbs′ *spl* pangrattato

breaded ['bredɪd] *adj* impannato

bread′ knife′ *s* coltello da pane

bread′ line′ *s* coda del pane

bread′ stick′ *s* grissino

breadth [bredθ] *s* (*width*) larghezza; (*scope*) ampiezza

bread′win′ner *s* sostegno della famiglia

break [brek] *s* interruzione, intervallo; omissione; (*breaking*) rottura; (*of bones*) frattura; (*of day*) fare *m*, spuntare *m*; (*sudden change*) mutamento; (*from jail*) evasione; (*luck*) (coll) fortuna; **to give s.o. a break** dare a qlcu l'opportunità || *v* (*pret* broke [brok]; *pp* broken) *tr* (*to smash*) rompere, spezzare; (*to tame*) domare; (*to demote*) destituire; (*a record*) superare; (*to violate*) violare; (*to make bankrupt*) mandare al fallimento; (*to interrupt*) interrompere; (*to reduce the effects of*) attutire; (*to disclose*) rivelare; (*to bring to an end by force*) battere; (*a banknote*) cambiare; (*one's word*) mancare (with *dat*); (*a law*) rompere; **to break asunder** separare; **to break down** analizzare; **to break in** forzare; **to break open** forzare, scassinare; **to break up** dissolvere || *intr* (*to divide*) rompersi; (*to burst*) scoppiare; (*said of voice of youngster*) cambiare; (*said of voice*) indebolirsi; (*said of a crowd*) disperdersi; (*said of weather*) rischiararsi; (*said of prices*) ribassare; (*to come into being*) scoppiare; (boxing) separarsi; **to break asunder** separarsi; **to break away** scappare; **to break down** abbattersi; (aut) essere or rimanere in panna; **to break even** fare patta; **to break in** irrompere; interrompere; **to break into** forzare; **to break into a run** incominciare a correre; **to break loose** liberarsi; (*said of a storm*) scatenarsi; **to break off** interrompere; **to break out** (*said of the skin*) avere un'eruzione; (*said, e.g., of war*) scoppiare; **to break through** aprirsi il varco; **to break up** disperdersi; **to break with** rompere le relazioni con

breakable ['brekəbəl] *adj* fragile

breakage ['brekɪdʒ] *s* rottura

break′down′ *s* (*in negotiations*) rottura; (aut) panna; (chem) analisi *f*; (pathol) colasso

breaker ['brekər] *s* (*wave*) frangente *m*

breakfast ['brekfəst] *s* prima colazione || *intr* fare prima colazione

break′neck′ *adj* pericoloso; **at breakneck speed** a rotta di collo, a rompicollo

break′ of day′ *s* alba

break′through′ *s* (mil) penetrazione; (fig) scoperta sensazionale

break′up′ *s* dispersione; dissoluzione; (*of a friendship*) rottura

break′wa′ter *s* diga, frangiflutti *m*

breast [brest] *s* petto; (*of female*) seno; (*source of emotions*) animo; **to make a clean breast of** fare una piena confessione di

breast′bone′ *s* sterno

breast′ drill′ *s* trapano da petto

breast′feed′ *v* (*pret & pp* **-fed** [fed]) *tr* allattare

breast′pin′ *s* spilla

breast′stroke′ *s* bracciata a rana

breath [brɛθ] *s* respiro, respirazione; (*odor*) alito; (*breeze*) soffio; (*whisper*) sussurro; (fig) vita; **out of breath** ansimante; **short of breath** corto di respiro; **to gasp for breath** respirare affannosamente; **under one's breath** sottovoce

breathe [brið] *tr* respirare; (*to whisper*) sussurrare; **to breathe one's last** esalare l'ultimo sospiro; **to not breathe a word** non dire una parola || *intr* respirare; **to breathe in** inspirare; **to breathe out** espirare

breath′ing spell′ *s* attimo di respiro

breathless ['brɛθlɪs] *adj* senza fiato, ansimante; soffocante

breath′tak′ing *s* emozionante, commovente

breech [britʃ] *s* (*buttocks*) natiche *fpl*; (*rear part*) parte *f* posteriore; (*of gun*) culatta; **breeches** ['britʃɪz] pantaloni *mpl* al ginocchio; pantaloni *mpl* da cavallo; **to wear the breeches** (coll) portare le brache

breed [brid] *s* razza; tipo; (*stock*) origine *f* || *v* (*pret & pp* **bred** [bred]) *tr* produrre; (*to raise*) allevare

breeder ['bridər] *s* allevatore *m*; riproduttore *m*

breeding ['bridɪŋ] *s* (*e.g., of livestock*) allevamento; educazione

breeze [briz] *s* brezza

breez·y ['brizi] *adj* (**-ier; -iest**) ventilato; (*brisk*) vivace, brioso

brethren ['brɛðrɪn] *spl* fratelli *mpl*

brevi·ty ['brɛviti] *s* (**-ties**) brevità *f*

brew [bru] *s* pozione; bevanda || *tr* (*beer*) fabbricare; (*to steep*) preparare; (*to plot*) complottare || *intr* (*said of beer*) fermentare; (*said of a storm*) prepararsi

brewer ['bru·ər] *s* birraio

brew′er's yeast′ *s* lievito di birra

brewer·y ['bru·əri] *s* (**-ies**) birreria, fabbrica di birra

bribe [braɪb] *s* subornazione, bustarella || *tr* subornare, dare la bustarella a

briber·y ['braɪbəri] *s* (**-ies**) subornazione, corruzione

bric-a-brac ['brɪkə,bræk] *s* bric-a-brac *m*, cianfrusaglia, cianfrusaglie *fpl*

brick [brɪk] *s* mattone *m* || *tr* mattonare

brick′bat′ *s* pezzo di mattone; (coll) insulto

brick′kiln′ *s* fornace *f* per mattoni

bricklayer ['brɪk,le·ər] *s* muratore *m*

brick′yard′ *s* deposito di mattoni

bridal ['braɪdəl] *adj* nuziale, da sposa

brid′al wreath′ *s* serto nuziale

bride [braɪd] *s* sposa

bride′groom′ *s* sposo

bridesmaid ['braɪdz,med] *s* damigella d'onore

bridge [brɪdʒ] *s* ponte *m*; (*of violin*) ponticello; (*on a ship*) ponte *m* di comando || *tr* gettare un ponte su; congiungere; **to bridge a gap** colmare una lacuna

bridge′head′ *s* testa di ponte

bridle ['braɪdəl] *s* briglia || *tr* mettere la briglia a; (fig) frenare || *intr* drizzare il capo, insuperbirsi

bri′dle path′ *s* strada cavalcabile

brief [brif] *adj* breve || *s* sommario; (law) esposto; (eccl) breve *m*; **briefs** slip *m* || *tr* dare istruzioni a, mettere al corrente

brief′ case′ *s* cartella, borsa d'avvocato

brier ['braɪ·ər] *s* radica; pipa di radica

brig [brɪg] *s* (naut) brigantino; (naut) prigione

brigade [brɪ'ged] *s* brigata

brigadier [,brɪgə'dɪr] *s* (coll) brigadier generale *m*, generale *m* di brigata

brigand ['brɪgənd] *s* brigante *m*

brigantine ['brɪgən,tin] *or* ['brɪgən,taɪn] *s* (naut) brigantino goletta

bright [braɪt] *adj* (*shining*) lucido; (*light*) brillante; (*lively*) vivo; intelligente; famoso; (*idea*) luminoso

brighten ['braɪtən] *tr* illuminare; ravvivare || *intr* illuminarsi; ravvivarsi; rischiararsi

bright′ lights′ *spl* luci *fpl* abbaglianti; (aut) fari *mpl* abbaglianti

brilliance ['brɪljəns] *or* **brilliancy** ['brɪljənsi] *s* splendore *m*, scintillio

brilliant ['brɪljənt] *adj* brillante

brim [brɪm] *s* (*e.g., of cup*) orlo, bordo; (*of hat*) ala, tesa || *v* (*pret & pp* **brimmed**; *ger* **brimming**) *intr* essere pieno sino all'orlo

brim′stone′ *s* zolfo

brine [braɪn] *s* salamoia; acqua di mare

bring [brɪŋ] *v* (*pret & pp* **brought**

[brɔt]) *tr* far venire; provocare; (*to carry along*) portare con sè; **to bring about** causare; **to bring around** persuadere; **to bring back** restituire; **to bring down** far abbassare; (fig) umiliare; **to bring forth** dare alla luce; **to bring forward** (*an excuse*) addurre; (math) riportare; **to bring in** introdurre; far entrare; **to bring off** compiere; **to bring on** causare; **to bring oneself to** rassegnarsi a; **to bring out** (*to expose*) rivelare; (*to offer to the public*) presentare al pubblico; (*a book*) far uscire; **to bring to** far rinvenire; (*a ship*) fermare; **to bring together** riunire; **to bring up** (*children*) allevare, tirar su; (*to introduce*) allegare; (*to cough up*) rigettare

bringing-up [ˈbrɪŋɪŋˌʌp] *s* educazione
brink [brɪŋk] *s* orlo
briquet [brɪˈket] *s* bricchetta
brisk [brɪsk] *adj* (*quick*) svelto; (*sharp*) acuto; (*invigorating*) frizzante; (*gunfire*) nutrito
bristle [ˈbrɪsəl] *s* setola ‖ *intr* (*to be stiff*) irrigidirsi; (*said of hair*) rizzarsi; (*with anger*) adirarsi
bris·tly [ˈbrɪsli] *adj* (*-tlier; -tliest*) irto di setole
British [ˈbrɪtɪʃ] *adj* britannico ‖ **the British** i britannici, gl'inglesi
Britisher [ˈbrɪtɪʃər] *s* britannico
Briton [ˈbrɪtən] *s* britannico
Brittany [ˈbrɪtəni] *s* la Bretagna
brittle [ˈbrɪtəl] *adj* fragile, friabile; (*crisp*) croccante
broach [brotʃ] *s* (*pin*) spilla; (*spit*) spiedo; (mach) alesatore *m* ‖ *tr* perforare; (*a subject*) intavolare
broad [brɔd] *adj* largo; tollerante, liberale; (*daylight*) pieno; (*story*) grossolano; (*extensive*) lato; (*accent*) pronunciato
broad′cast′ *s* disseminazione; (rad) radiodiffusione ‖ *v* (*pret & pp* -cast) *tr* disseminare, diffondere ‖ (*pret & pp* -cast or -casted) *tr* radiodiffondere
broad′casting sta′tion *s* stazione radiotrasmittente
broad′cloth′ *s* (*wool*) panno di lana; (*cotton*) popeline *f*
broaden [ˈbrodən] *tr* allargare, estendere ‖ *intr* allargarsi, estendersi
broad′ jump′ *s* salto in lunghezza
broadloom [ˈbrɔdˌlum] *adj* tessuto su telaio largo
broad-minded [ˈbrɔdˈmaɪndɪd] *adj* di ampie vedute, liberale
broad-shouldered [ˈbrɔdˈʃoldərd] *adj* largo di spalle
broad′side′ *s* (nav) bordo; (nav) bordata; (*verbal criticism*) (coll) sfuriata; (*written criticism*) (coll) attacco violento
broad′sword′ *s* spada da taglio
brocade [broˈked] *s* broccato
broccoli [ˈbrɑkəli] *s* broccolo; (*as food*) broccoli *mpl*
brochure [broˈʃʊr] *s* opuscolo, libriccino

brogue [brog] *s* accento irlandese; scarpa forte e comoda
broil [brɔil] *s* cottura alla graticola; carne *f* cotta alla graticola; (*quarrel*) rissa, zuffa ‖ *tr* cucinare alla graticola; bruciare ‖ *intr* cucinare alla graticola; (*to quarrel*) rissare, azzuffarsi
broiler [ˈbrɔilər] *s* graticola, gratella; (*chicken*) pollo da cucinare alla gratella or allo spiedo
broke [brok] *adj* (coll) al verde
broken [ˈbrokən] *adj* rotto; fratturato; (*e.g., English*) parlato male; (*tamed*) domato
bro′ken-down′ *adj* avvilito; rovinato
broken-hearted [ˈbrokənˈhɑrtɪd] *adj* affranto
broker [ˈbrokər] *s* sensale *m*; (*on the stock exchange*) agente *m* di cambio
brokerage [ˈbrokərɪdʒ] *s* mediazione
bromide [ˈbromaɪd] *s* bromuro; (coll) banalità *f*
bromine [ˈbromin] *s* bromo
bronchitis [brɑŋˈkaɪtɪs] *s* bronchite *f*
bron·co [ˈbrɑŋko] *s* (*-cos*) puledro brado
broncobuster [ˈbrɑŋkoˌbʌstər] *s* domatore *m* di puledri bradi
bronze [brɑnz] *adj* bronzeo ‖ *s* bronzo ‖ *tr* bronzare ‖ *intr* abbronzarsi
brooch [brotʃ] or [brutʃ] *s* spilla
brood [brud] *s* covata, nidiata ‖ *tr* covare ‖ *intr* chiocciare; meditare; **to brood on** or **over** meditare con tristezza (su)
brook [brʊk] *s* ruscello ‖ *tr*—**to brook no** non sopportare
broom [brum] or [brʊm] *s* scopa; (*shrub*) saggina
broom′corn′ *s* sorgo
broom′stick′ *s* manico di scopa
broth [brɔθ] or [brɑθ] *s* brodo
brothel [ˈbrɑθəl] or [ˈbrɔðəl] *s* postribolo, bordello
brother [ˈbrʌðər] *s* fratello
brotherhood [ˈbrʌðərˌhʊd] *s* fratellanza; (*association*) confraternita
broth′er-in-law′ *s* (**brothers-in-law**) cognato
brotherly [ˈbrʌðərli] *adj* fraterno ‖ *adv* fraternamente
brow [brau] *s* ciglio; (*forehead*) fronte *f*; **to knit one's brow** aggrottare la fronte
brow′beat′ *v* (*pret* -beat; *pp* -beaten) *tr* intimidire, intimorire
brown [braun] *adj* bruno; (*tanned*) abbronzato ‖ *s* color bruno ‖ *tr* colorare di bruno; abbronzare; (*metal*) brunire; (culin) dorare ‖ *intr* colorarsi di bruno; abbronzarsi; brunirsi; (culin) dorarsi
brownish [ˈbraunɪʃ] *adj* brunastro
brown′ stud′y *s*—**in a brown study** assorto in fantasticherie
brown′ sug′ar *s* zucchero greggio
browse [brauz] *intr* (*said of cattle*) brucare; sfogliare; **to browse around** curiosare
bruise [bruz] *s* ammaccatura, contu-

sione || *tr* ammaccare || *intr* ammaccarsi

brunet [bru'nɛt] *adj* bruno

brunette [bru'nɛt] *adj* & *s* bruna

brunt [brʌnt] *s* forza; scontro; peso

brush [brʌʃ] *s* pennello; spazzola; (*stroke*) pennellata; (*light touch*) tocco; (*brushwood*) macchia; (*brief encounter*) scaramuccia; (*elec*) spazzola || *tr* spazzolare; pennellare; **to brush aside** rigettare; **to brush up** ritoccare || *intr*—**to brush by** passar vicino; **to brush up on** ripassare

brush'-off' *s* (*slang*) scortesia; **to give the brush-off to** (*slang*) snobbare

brush'wood' *s* macchia, fratta

brusque [brʌsk] *adj* brusco

brusqueness ['brʌsknɪs] *s* bruschezza

Brussels ['brʌsəlz] *s* Bruxelles *f*

Brus'sels sprouts' *spl* cavolini *mpl*

brutal ['brutəl] *adj* brutale

brutali•ty [bru'tælɪti] *s* (-ties) brutalità *f*

brute [brut] *adj* & *s* bruto

brutish ['brutɪʃ] *adj* bruto

bubble ['bʌbəl] *s* bolla; (*fig*) chimera || *intr* bollire; **to make a bubbling sound**) barbugliare; **to bubble over** traboccare

bub'ble bath' *s* bagno di schiuma

buccaneer [,bʌkə'nɪr] *s* bucaniere *m*

buck [bʌk] *s* (*deer*) cervo; (*goat*) caprone *m*; (*sawhorse*) cavalletto; (*rabbit*) coniglio maschio; (*bucking*) groppata; (*dandy*) damerino; (*slang*) dollaro; **to pass the buck** (*coll*) giocare a scaricabarile || *tr* resistere accanitamente a || *intr* (*said of a horse*) fare salti da caprone; **to buck for** (*slang*) cercare di ottenere; **to buck up** (*coll*) rianimarsi, prender animo

bucket ['bʌkɪt] *s* secchio; bigoncia; (*e.g., of dredge*) benna; **to kick the bucket** (*slang*) tirare le cuoia

buck'et seat' *s* sedile *m*, strapuntino

buckle ['bʌkəl] *s* (*clasp*) fibbia, boccola; piega || *tr* affibbiare || *intr* piegarsi, curvarsi; **to buckle down to** (*coll*) mettersi di buzzo buono a

buck' pri'vate *s* (*slang*) soldato semplice

buckram ['bʌkrəm] *s* tela da fusto

buck'saw' *s* cavalletto

buck'shot' *s* pallini *mpl* da caccia

buck'tooth' *s* (-teeth) dente *m* in fuori, dente *m* sporgente

buck'wheat' *s* grano saraceno

bud [bʌd] *s* bocciolo, gemma; **to nip in the bud** troncare sul nascere || *v* (*pret* & *pp* budded; *ger* budding) *intr* sbocciare; nascere

Buddhism ['budɪzəm] *s* buddismo

bud•dy ['bʌdi] *s* (-dies) (*coll*) amico, compare *m*

budge [bʌdʒ] *tr* smuovere || *intr* muoversi

budget ['bʌdʒɪt] *s* bilancio || *tr* stanziare, preventivare; (*to schedule*) anticipare; (*time*) calcolare in anticipo

budgetary ['bʌdʒɪ ,tɛri] *adj* preventivo, di bilancio

buff [bʌf] *adj* bruno giallastro; di pelle || *s* (*leather*) pelle gialla; dilet-

tante *m*; (*mil*) giacca di pelle gialla; (*coll*) pelle nuda || *tr* lucidare; (*to reduce the force of*) ammortizzare

buffa•lo ['bʌfə ,lo] *s* (-loes or -los) bufalo || *tr* (*coll*) intimidire

buffer ['bʌfər] *s* ammortizzatore *m*; cuscinetto; (*worker*) lucidatore *m*; (*mach*) lucidatrice *f*; (*rr*) respingente *m*

buff'er state' *s* stato cuscinetto

buffet [bu'fe] *s* (*piece of furniture*) credenza; (*counter*) buffet *m* || ['bʌfɪt] *s* pugno; schiaffo || *tr* dar pugni a; schiaffeggiare; lottare con; (*to push about*) sballottare

buffet' car' [bu'fe] *s* vagone *m* ristorante

buffoon [bə'fun] *s* buffone *m*

buffoner•y [bə'funəri] *s* (-ies) buffoneria

bug [bʌg] *s* insetto; (*coll*) germe *m*; (*in motor*) (*slang*) noia; (*slang*) pazzo; **to put a bug in the ear of** mettere una pulce nell'orecchio di || *v* (*pret* & *pp* bugged; *ger* bugging) *tr* (*slang*) installare un sistema d'ascolto nel telefono di; (*to annoy*) (*slang*) seccare || *intr*—**to bug out** (*slang*) andarsene

bug'bear' *s* spauracchio

bug•gy ['bʌgi] *adj* (-gier; -giest) pieno di cimici; (*slang*) pazzo || *s* (-gies) carrozzino

bug'house' *adj* (*slang*) pazzo || *s* (*slang*) manicomio

bugle ['bjugəl] *s* tromba, cornetta

bugler ['bjuglər] *s* trombettiere *m*

build [bɪld] *s* corporatura, taglia || *v* (*pret* & *pp* built [bɪlt]) *tr* costruire, edificare; fondare, basare; **to build up** sviluppare

builder ['bɪldər] *s* costruttore *m*; costruttore *m* edile

building ['bɪldɪŋ] *s* edificio, stabile *m*; costruzione; edilizia

build'ing and loan' associa'tion *s* società *f* di credito fondiario

build'ing lot' *s* (*coll*) terreno da costruzioni

build'ing trades' *spl* edilizia

build'-up' *s* concentrazione; sviluppo; processo di preparazione; propaganda favorevole

built'-in' *adj* (*in a wall*) murato; (*in a cabinet*) incassato, incorporato

built'-in clos'et *s* armadio a muro

built'-up' *adj* armato; popolato

bulb [bʌlb] *s* bulbo; (*lamp*) lampadina; (*of a lamp*) globo, cipolla

Bulgarian [bʌl'gɛrɪ·ən] *adj* & *s* bulgaro

bulge [bʌldʒ] *s* protuberanza, sporgenza || *intr* sporgere, gonfiarsi

bulk [bʌlk] *s* volume *m*, massa; **in bulk** in blocco; sciolto || *intr* avere importanza; aumentare d'importanza

bulk'head' *s* diga; (*naut*) paratia

bulk•y ['bʌlki] *adj* (-ier; -iest) voluminoso

bull [bʊl] *s* toro; (*in the stockmarket*) rialzista *m·f*; (*slang*) scemenza; (*eccl*) bulla || *tr*—**to bull the market** giocare al rialzo

bull'dog' *s* molosso

bulldoze ['bul ,doz] *tr* intimidire; (*land*) livellare

bulldozer ['bul ,dozər] *s* livellatrice *f*, apripista *m*

bullet ['bulɪt] *s* palla, pallottola

bulletin ['bulətɪn] *s* bollettino; (*of a school*) albo; (journ) comunicato

bul'letin board' *s* tabellone *m*

bul'let-proof' *adj* blindato

bull'fight' *s* corrida

bull'fight'er *s* torero

bull'finch' *s* (orn) ciuffolotto

bull'frog' *s* rana americana

bull-headed ['bul ,hedɪd] *adj* testardo

bullion ['buljən] *s* lingotti *mpl* d'oro or d'argento; frangia d'oro; (*on an Italian general's hat*) greca

bullish ['bulɪʃ] *adj* ostinato; (market) al rialzo; (*speculator*) rialzista

bullock ['bulək] *s* manzo

bull'ring' *s* arena

bull's-eye ['bulz ,aɪ] *s* centro, tiro in pieno sul bersaglio; **to hit the bull's-eye** fare centro

bul-ly ['bulɪ] (*coll*) eccellente ‖ *s* (-lies) bravaccio ‖ *v* (*pret & pp* -lied) *tr* intimidire

bulrush ['bul ,rʌʃ] *s* giunco, (Bibl) papiro

bulwark ['bulwərk] *s* baluardo; protezione ‖ *tr* proteggere

bum [bʌm] *adj* (slang) pessimo ‖ *s* (slang) vagabondo; **on the bum** (slang) rotto, fuori servizio ‖ *v* (*pret & pp* bummed; *ger* bumming) *s* (slang) scroccare ‖ *intr* (slang) oziare; (slang) vivere d'elemosina; (slang) fare lo scroccatore

bumble ['bʌmbəl] *tr* abborracciare ‖ *intr* abborracciare; (*to stagger*) barcollare; (*to stumble*) balbettare; (*said of a bee*) ronzare

bum'blebee' *s* calabrone *m*

bump [bʌmp] *s* botta, botto; (*collision*) colpo, urto; (*swelling*) bernoccolo ‖ *tr* urtare; **to bump off** (slang) uccidere ‖ *intr* urtare, cozzare; **to bump into** incontrarsi con; cozzare contro

bumper ['bʌmpər] *adj* (coll) abbondante ‖ *s* bicchiere pieno fino all'orlo; (aut) paraurti *m*; (rr) respingente *m*

bumpkin ['bʌmpkɪn] *s* beota *m*

bumptious ['bʌmpʃəs] *adj* vanitoso, presuntuoso

bump-y ['bʌmpi] *adj* (-ier; -iest) (road) irregolare, ondulato; (air) agitato

bun [bʌn] *s* panino; (*of hair*) crocchia, treccia a ciambella

bunch [bʌntʃ] *s* (*of grapes*) grappolo; (*of keys*) mazzo; (*of grass*) ciuffo; (*of people*) gruppo; (*of twigs*) fastello; (*of animals*) branco ‖ *tr* (*things*) ammonticchiare; (*people*) raggruppare ‖ *intr* raggrupparsi

bundle ['bʌndəl] *s* fascio, fastello; (*package*) pacco; (*large package*) collo; (*bunch*) mucchio ‖ *tr* affastellare; impacchettare; ammucchiare; **to bundle off** or **out** cacciare precipitosamente; **to bundle up** infagottare ‖ *intr*—**to bundle up** infagottarsi

bung [bʌŋ] *s* spina, cannella

bungalow ['bʌŋgə ,lo] *s* casetta, villino, bungalow *m*

bung'hole' *s* spina, foro della botte

bungle ['bʌŋgəl] *s* abborracciatura ‖ *tr* abborracciare ‖ *intr* lavorare alla carlona

bungler ['bʌŋglər] *s* abborraccione *m*

bungling ['bʌŋglɪŋ] *adj* goffo; mal fatto ‖ *s* abborracciatura

bunion ['bʌnjən] *s* gonfiore *m* dell'alluce

bunk [bʌŋk] *s* letto a castello; (nav) cuccetta; (slang) sciocchezza ‖ *intr* dormire in cuccetta

bunk' bed' *s* letto a castello

bunker ['bʌŋkər] *s* (bin) carbonile *m*; (mil) casamatta; (golf) ostacolo

bun-ny ['bʌni] *s* (-nies) coniglietto

bunting ['bʌntɪŋ] *s* ornamento di bandiere; (nav) gala; (orn) zigolo

buoy [bɔɪ] or ['bu·i] *s* boa; (*life preserver*) salvagente *m* ‖ *tr*—**to buoy up** tenere a galla; (fig) rincuorare

buoyancy ['bɔɪ·ənsi] or ['bujənsi] *s* galleggiabilità *f*; (*cheerfulness*) allegria, esuberanza

buoyant ['bɔɪ·ənt] or ['bujənt] *adj* galleggiante; allegro, esuberante

bur [bʌr] *s* riccio, aculeo

burble ['bʌrbəl] *s* gorgoglio ‖ *intr* gorgogliare

burden ['bʌrdən] *s* carico, peso, fardello; (*of a speech*) tema *m*; (*chorus*) ritornello; (naut) portata ‖ *tr* caricare

bur'den of proof' *s* onere *m* della prova

burdensome ['bʌrdənsəm] *adj* oneroso

burdock ['bʌrdak] *s* lappa, lappola

bureau ['bjuro] *s* comò *m*; (agency) ufficio, servizio

bureaucra·cy [bju'rakrəsi] *s* (-cies) burocrazia

bureaucrat ['bjurə ,kræt] *s* burocrate *m*

burglar ['bʌrglər] *s* scassinatore *m*

bur'glar alarm' *s* campanello antifurto

burglarize ['bʌrglə ,raɪz] *tr* scassinare

bur'glar-proof' *adj* a prova di furto

burgla·ry ['bʌrgləri] *s* (-ries) furto con scasso, scassinatura

Burgundy ['bʌrgəndi] *s* la Borgogna; (*wine*) borgogna *m*

burial ['berɪ·əl] *s* sepoltura

bur'ial ground' *s* cimitero

burin ['bjurɪn] *s* burino, cesello

burlap ['bʌrlæp] *s* tela di iuta

burlesque [bʌr'lesk] *adj* burlesco ‖ *s* farsa, burlesque *m* ‖ *tr* parodiare

burlesque' show' *s* spettacolo di varietà, music-hall *m*

bur-ly ['bʌrli] *adj* (-lier; -liest) membruto, robusto

Burma ['bʌrmə] *s* la Birmania

burn [bʌrn] *s* bruciatura, scottatura ‖ *v* (*pret & pp* burned or burnt [bʌrnt]) *tr* bruciare; (*to set on fire*) dar fuoco a; (*bricks*) cuocere; **to burn down** radere al suolo; **to burn up** consumare; (*the road*) divorare; (coll) fare arrabbiare ‖ *intr* bruciare, bruciarsi; (*said of lights*) essere acceso, e.g., **the lights were burning** la luce era accesa; **to burn out** (*said of an electric bulb or a fuse*) bruciarsi;

to burn to (fig) agognare di; **to burn up** (coll) essere arrabiato; **to burn with** (e.g., envy) ardere di

burner ['bʌrnər] s (of gas fixture or lamp) becco; (of furnace) bruciatore m

burning ['bʌrnɪŋ] adj bruciante, scottante || s incendio; (ceramic) cottura finale

burn'ing ques'tion s questione di attualità palpitante

burnish ['bʌrnɪʃ] s lucidatura || tr brunire

burnt' al'mond [bʌrnt] s mandorla tostata

burp [bʌrp] s (coll) rutto || intr (coll) ruttare

burr [bʌr] s riccio, aculeo; (rough edge) bava; (dentist's drill) fresa

burrow ['bʌro] s tana, buca || intr imbucarsi, rintanarsi

bursar ['bʌrsər] s tesoriere universitario

burst [bʌrst] s esplosione; (e.g., of machine gun) raffica; (break) crepa; (of passion) accesso; (of speed) slancio || tr far scoppiare || intr scoppiare, esplodere; **to burst into** (e.g., a room) irrompere in; (e.g., angry words) esplodere in; **to burst out crying** scoppiare in lacrime; **to burst with laughter** scoppiare dalle risa

bur·y ['bɛri] v (pret & pp **-ied**) tr sotterrare; **to be buried in thought** essere immerso nel pensiero; **to bury the hatchet** fare la pace

bus [bʌs] s (buses or busses) bus m, autobus m || v (pret & pp **bused** or **bussed**; ger **busing** or **bussing**) tr trasportare con autobus

bus'boy' s secondo cameriere

bus·by ['bʌzbi] s (-bies) colbacco

bus' driv'er s conducente mf di autobus

bush [bʊʃ] s cespuglio, arbusto; **to beat around the bush** menare il can per l'aia

bushed [bʊʃt] adj (coll) stanco morto

bushel ['bʊʃəl] s staio

bushing ['bʊʃɪŋ] s (mach) bronzina

bush·y ['bʊʃi] adj (-ier; -iest) ricco di arbusti; (face) barbuto

business ['bɪznɪs] adj commerciale || s occupazione; commercio; affare m, negozio; faccenda; impiego; **it is not your business** non è affare Suo; **to know one's business** sapere il fatto proprio; **to make it one's business to** proporsi di; **to mean business** (coll) farla sul serio; **to mind one's own business** impicciarsi degli affari propri

businesslike ['bɪznɪs,laɪk] adj metodico; serio; efficace

busi'ness·man' s (-men') commerciante m, uomo d'affari

busi'ness suit' s abito da passeggio

busi'ness·wom'an s (wom'en) commerciante f

bus'man s (-men) guidatore m d'autobus

buss [bʌs] s (coll) bacione sonoro || tr (coll) baciare sonoramente

bus' stop' s fermata degli autobus

bust [bʌst] s busto; petto; (slang) fallimento; (slang) pugno || tr (slang) rompere; (slang) far fallire; (slang) colpire, dare pugno a; (mil) degradare

buster ['bʌstər] s (coll) ragazzo; (coll) rompitore m

bustle ['bʌsəl] s (on a dress) guardinfante m; attività f || intr affrettarsi

bus·y ['bɪzi] adj (-ier; -iest) occupato || v (pret & pp **-ied**) tr occupare, tenere occupato; **to busy oneself with** occuparsi di

bus'y·bod'y s (-ies) ficcanaso

bus'y sig'nal s (telp) segnale m d'occupato

but [bʌt] s ma m || adv solo, solamente; **but for** se non . . . per || prep eccetto, ad eccezione di, meno, se non; **all but** quasi || conj ma; che non, e.g., **I never go out in the rain but I catch a cold** non esco mai con la pioggia che non mi pigli un raffreddore

butcher ['bʊtʃər] s macellaio || tr macellare; massacrare

butch'er knife' s coltello da cucina, coltella

butch'er shop' s macelleria

butcher·y ['bʊtʃəri] s (-ies) macello; carneficina

butler ['bʌtlər] s cantiniere m, credenziere m

butt [bʌt] s (butting) cornata; (of rifle or gun) calcio; (of cigar) mozzicone m; (target) bersaglio; (end) estremità f; (of ridicule) zimbello; (cask) botte f || tr dare cornate a; cozzare contro || intr—**to butt into** (slang) intromettersi in

butter ['bʌtər] s burro || tr imburrare; **to butter up** (coll) adulare

but'ter·cup' s (bot) bottone m d'oro, ranuncolo

but'ter dish' s piattino per il burro, burriera

but'ter·fat' s grasso nel latte

but'ter·fly' s (-flies) farfalla

but'ter knife' s coltello per il burro

but'ter·milk' s latticello

but'ter sauce' s burro fuso

but'ter·scotch' s caramella al burro

buttocks ['bʌtəks] spl chiappe fpl, natiche fpl

button ['bʌtən] s bottone m || tr abbottonare

but'ton·hole' s occhiello, asola || tr attaccare un bottone a

but'ton·hook' s allacciabottoni m

buttress ['bʌtrɪs] s contrafforte m; piedritto || tr rinforzare

buxom ['bʌksəm] adj avvenente, procace

buy [baɪ] s compra || v (pret & pp **bought** [bɔt]) tr comprare; **to buy off** corrompere; **to buy out** comprare la parte di

buyer ['baɪ·ər] s compratore m

buzz [bʌz] s brusio, ronzio || tr volare a bassa quota sopra; (coll) fare una telefonata a || intr ronzare

buzzard ['bʌzərd] s (hawk) poiana; avvoltoio americano

buzzer ['bʌzər] s suoneria ronzante

buzz′ saw′ *s* sega circolare, segatrice *f* a disco

by [baɪ] *adv* oltre, e.g., **to speed by** correre velocemente oltre; **by and by** fra poco; **by and large** generalmente || *prep* vicino a; di, durante, e.g., **by night** di notte, durante la notte; a, e.g., **they work by the hour** lavorano all'ora; (*not later than, through*) per; (*past*) in fronte a; (*through the agency of*) da; (*according to*) secondo; (math) per, volte; **by far** di molto; **by the way** a proposito

bygone [ˈbaɪˌgɔn] or [ˈbaɪˌgɑn] *adj & s* passato; **to let bygones be bygones** dimenticare il passato

bylaw [ˈbaɪˌlɔ] *s* legge *f* locale, regolamento di una società

by′-line′ *s* (journ) firma

by′pass′ *s* linea secondaria; (*detour*) deviazione || *tr* fare una deviazione oltre a; (*a difficulty*) evitare

by′path′ *s* sentiero secondario; sentiero privato

by′prod′uct *s* sottoprodotto

bystander [ˈbaɪˌstændər] *s* astante *m*, spettatore *m*

byway [ˈbaɪˌwe] *s* via traversa

byword [ˈbaɪˌwʌrd] *s* proverbio; oggetto di obbrobrio

Byzantium [bɪˈzæn/ɪ·əm] or [bɪˈzæntɪ·əm] *s* Bisanzio

C

C, c [si] *s* terza lettera dell'alfabeto inglese

cab [kæb] *s* vettura di piazza; tassì *m;* (*of truck or locomotive*) cabina

cabbage [ˈkæbɪdʒ] *s* cavolo, verza

cab′ driv′er *s* autista *m* di piazza; (*of horse-drawn cab*) vetturino

cabin [ˈkæbɪn] *s* (*shed*) capanna; (*hut*) baracca; (aer, naut) cabina

cab′in boy′ *s* mozzo

cabinet [ˈkæbɪnɪt] *s* (*piece of furniture*) vetrina; (*for a radio*) armadietto; (*small room; ministry of a government*) gabinetto

cab′inet-mak′er *s* ebanista *m*

cab′inet-mak′ing *s* ebanisteria

cable [ˈkebəl] *s* cavo; cablogramma; (elec) cablaggio || *tr* cablare, mandare un cablogramma a

ca′ble address′ *s* indirizzo telegrafico

ca′ble car′ *s* funicolare *f*, teleferica

cablegram [ˈkebəlˌgræm] *s* cablogramma *m*

caboose [kəˈbus] *s* (rr) vagone *m* di coda

cab′stand′ *s* stazione di tassametri

cache [kæʃ] *s* nascondiglio || *tr* mettere in un nascondiglio

cachet [kæˈʃe] *s* sigillo; (*distinguishing feature*) impronta

cackle [ˈkækəl] *s* (*of chickens*) coccodè *m;* (*of people*) chiaccherio || *intr* fare coccodè; ciarlare

cac·tus [ˈkæktəs] *s* (-**tuses** or -**ti** [taɪ]) cactus *m*

cad [kæd] *s* mascalzone *m*

cadaver [kəˈdævər] *s* cadavere *m*

cadaverous [kəˈdævərəs] *adj* cadaverico

caddie [ˈkædi] *s* portamazze *m*

cadence [ˈkedəns] *s* cadenza

cadet [kəˈdet] *s* cadetto

cadmium [ˈkædmɪ·əm] *s* cadmio

cadres [ˈkædriz] *spl* (mil) quadri *mpl*

Caesar′ean sec′tion [sɪˈzɛrɪ·ən] *s* taglio cesareo

café [kæˈfe] *s* caffè *m*, bar *m*, ristorante *m*

ca′fé soci′ety *s* bel mondo

cafeteria [ˌkæfəˈtɪrɪ·ə] *s* mensa, tavola calda, caffetteria

caffeine [kæˈfin] or [ˈkæfi·ɪn] *s* caffeina

cage [kedʒ] *s* gabbia; (*of elevator*) cabina || *tr* ingabbiare

ca·gey [ˈkedʒi] *adj* (-**gier; -giest**) (coll) astuto, cauto

cahoots [kəˈhuts] *s*—**to be in cahoots** (slang) far lega, essere in combutta; **to go cahoots** (slang) dividere in parti eguali

Cain [ken] *s* Caino; **to raise Cain** (slang) arrabbiarsi; (slang) fare una sfuriata

Cairo [ˈkaɪro] *s* il Cairo

caisson [ˈkesən] *s* cassone *m;* (archit) cassettone *m*

cajole [kəˈdʒol] *tr* lusingare; persuadere con lusinghe

cajoler·y [kəˈdʒoləri] *s* (-**ies**) lusinga

cake [kek] *s* dolce *m;* torta, pasta; (*with bread-like dough*) focaccia; (*of soap*) saponetta; (*of earth*) zolla; **to take the cake** (coll) essere il colmo || *tr* incrostare || *intr* indurirsi; incrostarsi

calabash [ˈkæləˌbæʃ] *s* zucca a fiasca

calaboose [ˈkæləˌbus] *s* (coll) gattabuia

calamitous [kəˈlæmɪtəs] *adj* calamitoso

calami·ty [kəˈlæmɪti] *s* (-**ties**) calamità

calci·fy [ˈkælsɪˌfaɪ] *v* (*pret & pp* -**fied**) *tr* calcificare || *intr* calcificarsi

calcium [ˈkælsɪ·əm] *s* calcio

calculate [ˈkælkjəˌlet] *tr* calcolare || *intr* calcolare; **to calculate on** contare su

cal′culating machine′ *s* (macchina) calcolatrice

calcu·lus [ˈkælkjələs] *s* (-**luses** or -**li** [ˌlaɪ]) (math, pathol) calcolo

calendar [ˈkæləndər] *s* calendario; (*agenda*) ordine *m* del giorno

calf [kæf] or [kɑf] *s* (**calves** [kævz] or [kɑvz]) vitello; (*of shoes or binding*) pelle *f* di vitello; (*of the leg*) polpaccio

calf′skin′ *s* pelle *f* di vitello

caliber ['kælɪbər] s calibro

calibrate ['kælɪ,bret] tr calibrare

cali·co ['kælɪ,ko] s (-coes or -cos) cotone stampato, calico

California [,kælɪ'fɔrnɪ·ə] s la California

calipers ['kælɪpərz] spl compasso a grossezze, calibro

caliph ['kelɪf] or ['kælɪf] s califfo

calisthenic [,kælɪs'θɛnɪk] adj ginnastico || calisthenics spl ginnastica a corpo libero

calk [kɔk] tr var of caulk

call [kɔl] s chiamata; visita; (shout) grido, richiamo; (of bugle) squillo; (of telephone) colpo; (of ship) scalo; obbligo; vocazione; (com) richiesta; on call disponibile; within call a portata di voce || tr chiamare; convocare; (to awaken) svegliare; to call back richiamare; to call in (e.g., an expert) fare venire; (e.g., currency) domandare, esigere; to call off annullare; to call out chiamare; to call together convocare; to call up chiamare per telefono || intr chiamare; visitare; to call at passare per la casa di; (naut) fare scalo a; to call for venire a prendere; to call out out gridare; to go calling andare a fare visite

cal'la lil'y ['kælə] s (Zantedeschia aethiopica) calla dei fioristi

call'boy' s (in a hotel) fattorino; (theat) buttafuori m

caller ['kɔlər] s visitatore m

call' girl' s ragazza squillo

calling ['kɔlɪŋ] s appello; professione

call'ing card' s biglietto da visita

call' num'ber s numero telefonico; numero di biblioteca

callous ['kæləs] adj calloso; insensibile

callow ['kælo] adj inesperto, immaturo

call' to arms' s chiamata alle armi

call' to the col'ors s chiamata sotto la bandiera

callus ['kæləs] s callo

calm [kɑm] adj calmo, tranquillo || s calma || tr calmare, tranquillizzare || intr—to calm down calmarsi; (said of weather) abbonacciarsi

calmness ['kɑmnɪs] s calma, placidità f, tranquillità f

calomel ['kælə,mɛl] s calomelano

calorie ['kæləri] s caloria

calum·ny ['kæləmnɪ] s (-nies) calunnia

Calvary ['kælvəri] s (Bib) Calvario

cam [kæm] s camma

camber ['kæmbər] s curvatura; convessità f || tr arcuare || intr curvarsi

cambric ['kembrɪk] s cambrì m

camel ['kæməl] s cammello

came·o ['kæmɪ,o] s (-os) cammeo

camera ['kæmərə] s macchina fotografica; (mov) cinepresa

cam'era·man' s (-men') operatore m

camomile ['kæmə,maɪl] s camomilla

camouflage ['kæmə,flɑʒ] s mascheramento || tr mascherare, camuffare

camp [kæmp] s accampamento, campo || intr accamparsi

campaign [kæm'pen] s campagna || intr fare una campagna

campaigner [kæm'penər] s veterano; (pol) propagandista mf

camp' bed' s letto da campo, branda

camper ['kæmpər] s campeggiatore m, campeggista mf

camp'fire' s fuoco di accampamento

camp'ground' s terreno per campeggio

camphor ['kæmfər] s canfora

camp'stool' s seggiolino pieghevole

campus ['kæmpəs] s campo, terreno dell'università

cam'shaft' s albero di distribuzione, albero a camme

can [kæn] s lattina, barattolo; (of gasoline or oil) bidone m || v (pret & pp canned; ger canning) tr inscatolare; (slang) licenziare || v (pret & cond could) aux I can speak English so parlare inglese; can he go now? se ne può andare ora?

Canada ['kænədə] s il Canadà

Canadian [kə'nedɪən] adj & s canadese mf

canal [kə'næl] s canale m

canar·y [kə'neri] s (-ies) canarino || Canaries spl Canarie fpl

can·cel ['kænsəl] v (pret & pp -celed or -celled; ger -celing or -celling) tr cancellare; annullare; revocare; (stamps) timbrare, annullare

cancellation [,kænsə'leʃən] s cancellazione, annullamento; cassazione; (of a stamp) bollo

cancer ['kænsər] s cancro || Cancer s Cancro

cancerous ['kænsərəs] adj canceroso

candela·brum [,kændə'lɑbrəm] s (-bra [brə] or -brums) candelabro

candid ['kændɪd] adj candido; sincero, franco

candida·cy ['kændɪdəsɪ] s (-cies) candidatura

candidate ['kændɪ,det] s candidato; (for a degree) laureando

can'did cam'era s camera fotografica indiscreta

candied ['kændɪd] adj candito

candle ['kændəl] s candela || tr (eggs) sperare

can'dle·hold'er s var of candlestick

can'dle·light' s luce f or lume m di candela

can'dle·pow'er s (phys) candela

can'dle·stick' s (ornate) candeliere m; (plain) bugia

candor ['kændər] s candore m; ingenuità f

can·dy ['kændɪ] s (-dies) dolciumi mpl; a piece of candy un bombon || v (pret & pp -died) tr candire

can'dy box' s bomboniera

can'dy dish' s bomboniera; (three-tier-high) alzata

can'dy store' s confetteria

cane [ken] s canna, giunco; (for walking) bastone m || tr bastonare; (chairs) impagliare

cane' seat' s sedia impagliata

cane' sug'ar s zucchero di canna

canine ['kenaɪn] adj canino || s (tooth) canino; (dog) cane m

canister ['kænɪstər] s barattolo

canned' goods' *spl* conserve *fpl* alimentari; prodotti *mpl* in scatola

canned' mu'sic *s* (slang) musica su dischi

canner·y [ˈkænəri] *s* (**-ies**) fabbrica di conserve alimentari

cannibal [ˈkænɪbəl] *adj & s* cannibale *mf*, antropofago

canning [ˈkænɪŋ] *s* conservazione

cannon [ˈkænən] *s* cannone *m*

cannonade [ˌkænəˈned] *s* cannonata || *tr* cannoneggiare

can'non·ball' *s* palla da cannone

can'non fod'der *s* carne *f* da cannone

can·ny [ˈkæni] *adj* (**-nier; -niest**) astuto, fino; malizioso

canoe [kəˈnu] *s* canoa, piroga

canon [ˈkænən] *s* canone *m*; (*priest*) canonico

canonical [kəˈnɑnɪkəl] *adj* canonico || **canonicals** *spl* paramenti liturgici

canonize [ˈkænəˌnaɪz] *tr* canonizzare

can'on law' *s* diritto canonico

canon·ry [ˈkænənri] *s* (**-ries**) canonicato

can' o'pener [ˈopənər] *s* apriscatole *m*

cano·py [ˈkænəpi] *s* (**-pies**) tenda; baldacchino; (*of sky*) (fig) volta

cant [kænt] *adj* ipocrita || *s* linguaggio ipocrita; gergo; (*slope*) inclinazione

cantaloupe [ˈkæntəˌlop] *s* melone *m*

cantankerous [kænˈtæŋkərəs] *adj* bisbetico, attaccabrighe

canteen [kænˈtin] *s* cantina, spaccio; (*metal bottle*) borraccia

canter [ˈkæntər] *s* piccolo galoppo || *intr* andare al piccolo galoppo

cantiliver [ˈkæntɪˌlivər] *adj* a cantiliver || *s* trave *f* a sbalzo; (archit) trave *f* a mensola

cantle [ˈkæntəl] *s* arcione *m* posteriore

canton [ˈkænˈtɑn] *s* cantone *m*; regione || *tr* accantonare

cantonment [kænˈtɑnmənt] *s* accantonamento

cantor [ˈkæntər] *or* [ˈkæntər] *s* cantore *m*

canvas [ˈkænvəs] *s* (*cloth*) olona; (*e.g. on open truck*) copertone *m*; (*painting*) tela; (naut) vela; **under canvas** (naut) a vele spiegate

canvass [ˈkænvəs] *s* discussione, dibattito; (pol) sollecitazione di voti || *tr* discutere; (*votes*) sollecitare; (*to investigate*) indagare; (com) fare la piazza a || *intr* discutere; sollecitare voti; indagare; (com) fare la piazza

canyon [ˈkænjən] *s* cañon *m*

cap [kæp] *s* berretto; cuffia; (*of academic costume*) berrettone *m*; (*of bottle*) tappo, capsula; (*e.g., of fountain pen*) cappuccio || *v* (*pret & pp* **capped**; *ger* **capping**) *tr* (*a person*) coprire il capo di; (*s.o.'s head*) coprire con il berretto; (*a bottle*) mettere il tappo a; terminare; **to cap the climax** essere il colmo

capabili·ty [ˌkepəˈbɪlɪti] *s* (**-ties**) capacità *f*, abilità *f*

capable [ˈkepəbəl] *adj* capace, abile

capacious [kəˈpeʃəs] *adj* ampio, capace

capaci·ty [kəˈpæsɪti] *s* (**-ties**) capacità *f*; **filled to capacity** pieno zeppo; **in the capacity of** in veste di

cap' and bells' *spl* berretto a sonagli; scettro di buffone

cap' and gown' *s* costume accademico, toga e tocco

caparison [kəˈpærɪsən] *s* bardatura || *tr* bardare

cape [kep] *s* cappa, mantello; (mil) mantella; (geog) capo

Cape' of Good' Hope' *s* Capo di Buona Speranza

caper [ˈkepər] *s* capriola; (bot) cappero; **to cut capers** far capriole; (fig) fare monellerie || *intr* fare capriole; saltellare

Cape' Town' *s* Città *f* del Capo

capital [ˈkæpɪtəl] *adj* capitale || *s* (*money*) capitale *m*; (*city*) capitale *f*; (*of column*) capitello

cap'ital expen'ditures *spl* spese *fpl* d'impianto

cap'ital goods' *spl* beni *mpl* strumentali

capitalism [ˈkæpɪtəˌlɪzəm] *s* capitalismo

capitalize [ˈkæpɪtəˌlaɪz] *tr* capitalizzare; scrivere con la maiuscola || *intr*—**to capitalize on** approfittare di

cap'ital let'ter *s* lettera maiuscola

cap'ital pun'ishment *s* pena capitale

cap'ital stock' *s* capitale *m* sociale

capitol [ˈkæpɪtəl] *s* campidoglio

capitulate [kəˈpɪtʃəˌlet] *intr* capitolare

capon [ˈkepɑn] *s* cappone *m*

caprice [kəˈpris] *s* capriccio, ghiribizzo

capricious [kəˈprɪʃəs] *adj* capriccioso, estroso

Capricorn [ˈkæprɪˌkɔrn] *s* Capricorno

capsize [ˈkæpsaɪz] *tr* capovolgere || *intr* capovolgersi

capstan [ˈkæpstən] *s* argano

cap'stone' *s* (archit) coronamento

capsule [ˈkæpsəl] *adj* in miniatura; riassuntivo || *s* capsula

captain [ˈkæptən] *s* capitano; (naut) comandante *m*; || *tr* capitanare

caption [ˈkæp/ən] *s* titolo; (mov) didascalia; (journ) leggenda

captivate [ˈkæptɪˌvet] *tr* cattivare, affascinare

captive [ˈkæptɪv] *adj & s* prigioniero

captivi·ty [ˈkæpˈtɪvɪti] *s* (**-ties**) cattività *f*, prigionia

captor [ˈkæptər] *s* persona che cattura

capture [ˈkæpt/ər] *s* cattura, presa; (*person*) prigioniero; (*thing*) bottino || *tr* catturare; prendere

car [kɑr] *s* (*of train*) vagone *m*, vettura; (*automobile*) automobile *m & f*, macchina, vettura; (*of elevator*) cabina; (*of balloon*) navicella; (*for narrow-gauge track*) carrello

carafe [kəˈræf] *s* caraffa

caramel [ˈkærəməl] *or* [ˈkɑrməl] *s* (*burnt sugar*) caramello; (*candy*) caramella appicciaticcia

carat [ˈkærət] *s* carato

caravan [ˈkærəˌvæn] *s* carovana; (*covered vehicle*) furgone *m*

caravansa·ry [ˌkærəˈvænsəri] *s* (**-ries**) caravanserraglio

caraway [ˈkærəˌwe] *s* cumino

car'barn' *s* rimessa del tram

carbide ['karbaɪd] s carburo

carbine ['karbaɪn] s carabina

carbol'ic ac'id [kar'balɪk] s acido fenico

carbon ['karbən] s (in arc light, battery, auto cylinder) carbone m; carta carbone; (chem) carbonio

car'bon cop'y s copia a carbone, velina

car'bon diox'ide s anidride carbonica

car'bon monox'ide s ossido di carbonio, monossido di carbonio

car'bon pa'per s carta carbone

carbuncle ['karbʌŋkəl] s (stone; boil) carbonchio; (boil) foruncolo

carburetor ['karbə‚retər] or ['karbjə‚retər] s carburatore m

carcass ['karkəs] s carcassa; (in state of decay) carogna

card [kard] s (file) scheda; (post card) cartolina; (personal card) biglietto; (announcement) partecipazione; (playing card) carta da gioco; (coll) tipo divertente, bel tipo

card'board' s cartone m

card'-car'rying mem'ber s tesserato

card' case' s portatessere m

card' cat'alogue s schedario

card'hold'er s socio, tesserato

cardiac ['kardɪ‚æk] adj & s cardiaco

cardigan ['kardɪgən] s panciotto a maglia

cardinal ['kardɪnəl] adj cardinale, fondamentale || s cardinale m

card' in'dex s schedario

cardiogram ['kardɪ‚o‚græm] s cardiogramma m

card' par'ty s riunione per giocare a carte

card'sharp' s baro

card' ta'ble s tavoliere m, tavolino da gioco

card' trick' s gioco di prestigio colle carte

care [ker] s cura, custodia; inquietudine f, preoccupazione; cautela; **care of** presso, e.g., **R. Smith care of Jones R. Smith** presso Jones; **to take care** fare attenzione; **to take care of** prendersi cura di, badare a; **to take care of oneself** badare alla salute || intr curarsi, badare; **I don't care** non m'importa; **to care about** preoccuparsi di; **to care for** voler bene a; curarsi di; **to care to** volere

careen [kə'rin] s carenaggio || intr sbandare

career [kə'rir] adj di carriera || s carriera

care'free' adj spensierato

careful ['kerfəl] adj attento; diligente; premuroso; **careful!** faccia attenzione!

careless ['kerlɪs] adj trascurato; imprudente; indifferente

carelessness ['kerlɪsnɪs] s trascuratezza; imprudenza; indifferenza

caress [kə'res] s carezza || tr carezzare, accarezzare

caretaker ['ker‚tekər] adj interinale, provvisorio || s custode m; guardiano; (of school) bidello

care'taker gov'ernment s governo interinale

care'worn' adj accasciato dalle preoccupazioni

car'fare' s passaggio, denaro per il tram; (small sum of money) spiccioli mpl

car·go ['kargo] s (-goes or -gos) carico mercantile

car'go boat' s battello da carico

Caribbean [‚kærɪ'bi‚ən] or [kə'rɪbɪ‚ən] s Mare m dei Caraibi

caricature ['kærɪkət/ər] s caricatura || tr mettere in caricatura

carillon ['kærɪ‚lan] or [kə'rɪljən] s carillon m || intr suonare il carillon

car'load' s vagone completo, vagonata

carnage ['karnɪdʒ] s carnaio, carneficina

carnal ['karnəl] adj carnale

carnation [kar'ne/ən] adj incarnato || s garofano; (color) incarnato

carnival ['karnɪvəl] adj carnevalesco || s carnevale m; festa, spettacolo all'aperto

carob ['kærəb] s (fruit) carruba; (tree) carrubo

car·ol ['kærəl] s canzone f popolare; pastorella di Natale || v (pret & pp -oled or -olled; ger -oling or -olling) tr cantare

carom ['kærəm] s carambola || intr carambolare

carousal [kə'rauzəl] s baldoria, gozzoviglia

carouse [kə'rauz] intr fare baldoria, gozzovigliare

carousel [‚kærə'zel] or [‚kæru'zel] s giostra, carosello

carp ['karp] s carpa || intr lagnarsi, criticare

carpenter ['karpəntər] s falegname m

carpentry ['karpəntri] s falegnameria

carpet ['karpɪt] s tappeto || tr coprire con un tappeto, tappetare

carpetbagger ['karpɪt‚bægər] s avventuriero; (hist) politicante m

car'pet sweep'er s spazzolone elettrico per tappeti

car'port' s tettoia-garage f

car'-ren'tal serv'ice s servizio di autonoleggi

carriage ['kærɪdʒ] s carrozza; (of gun) affusto; (of typewriter) carrello; (bearing) portamento; (mach) slitta

carrier ['kærɪ‚ər] s portatore m; (person or organization in business of carrying goods) spedizioniere m; (of mail) postino; (e.g., on top of station wagon) portabagagli m; (of a disease) veicolo

car'rier pig'eon s piccione m viaggiatore

car'rier wave' s (rad) onda portante

carrion ['kærɪ‚ən] s carogne fpl

carrot ['kærət] s carota

car·ry ['kæri] v (pret & pp -ried) tr portare; trasportare; (a burden) sopportare; (an election) guadagnare; (to keep in stock) avere in assortimento; **to carry along** portare con sé; **to carry away** trasportare; entusiasmare; **to carry forward** riportare; **to carry out** eseguire; **to carry**

through completare; **to carry weight** aver importanza ‖ *intr* avere la portata (di), e.g., **this gun carries two miles** questo cannone ha la portata di due miglia; **to carry on** continuare; (coll) fare baccano

cart [kɑrt] *s* carro, carretto; (*for shopping*) carrello; **to put the cart before the horse** mettere il carro davanti ai buoi ‖ *tr* trasportare col carro

carte blanche ['kɑrt'blɑnʃ] *s* carta bianca

cartel [kɑr'tɛl] *s* cartello

Carthage ['kɑrθɪdʒ] *s* Cartagine *f*

cart' horse' *s* cavallo da tiro

cartilage ['kɑrtɪlɪdʒ] *s* cartilagine *f*

carton ['kɑrtən] *s* cartone *m*; scatola di cartone; (*of cigarettes*) stecca

cartoon [kɑr'tun] *s* disegno; caricatura; (*comic strip*) fumetto; (mov) disegno animato ‖ *tr* fare caricature di

cartoonist [kɑr'tunɪst] *s* disegnatore *m*; caricaturista *mf*

cartridge ['kɑrtrɪdʒ] *s* cartuccia; (*e.g., of camera*) caricatore *m*

car'tridge belt' *s* cartucciera; (mil) giberna

car'tridge clip' *s* serbatoio

cart'wheel' *s* ruota di carro; **to turn cartwheels** fare la ruota

carve [kɑrv] *tr* (*meats*) trinciare; scolpire, intagliare

carv'ing knife' *s* trinciante *m*

car' wash'er *s* lavamacchine *m*

cascade [kæs'ked] *s* cascata ‖ *intr* cadere a mo' di cascata

case [kes] *s* (*box*) cassetta; (*of watch*) calotta; (*outer covering*) astuccio; (*instance*) caso; (gram) caso; (law) causa; (typ) cassa; **in case** in caso, nel caso; **in no case** in nessun modo ‖ *tr* rinchiudere; (*to package*) impaccare; (slang) ispezionare

casement ['kesmənt] *s* telaio di finestra; finestra a gangheri

case' stud'y *s* casistica

cash [kæʃ] *s* contante *m*; **cash on delivery** spedizione contro assegno; **for cash** in contanti; a pronta cassa ‖ *tr* (*a check*) cambiare, incassare ‖ *intr* —**to cash in on** (coll) trarre profitto da

cash' box' *s* cassa

cashew ['kæʃu] *s* (*tree*) anacardio; (*nut*) mandorla indiana

cashier [kæ'ʃɪr] *s* cassiere *m* ‖ *tr* (*to dismiss*) silurare

cashier's' check' *s* assegno circolare

cash' reg'ister *s* registratore *m* cassa

casing ['kesɪŋ] *s* rivestimento; tubo di rivestimento; (*for salami*) budello; (*of tire*) copertone *m*

cask [kæsk] *or* [kɑsk] *s* barile *m*, botte *f*

casket ['kæskɪt] *or* ['kɑskɪt] *s* scrigno, cofanetto; (*coffin*) bara, cassa da morto

casserole ['kæsə₁rol] *s* tegame *m* di terracotta or vetro; (*food*) pasticcio, timballo

cassette [kə'sɛt] *s* (mus) musicassetta; (mus & phot) caricatore *m*

cassock ['kæsək] *s* sottana, tonaca; **to doff the cassock** gettar la tonaca alle ortiche

cast [kæst] *or* [kɑst] *s* getto; lancio; forma; (mach) pezzo fuso; (surg) gesso; (theat) complesso artistico, cast *m* ‖ *v* (*pret & pp* **cast**) *tr* gettare; fondere; (*a ballot*) dare; (*the roles*) distribuire; (*actors*) scegliere; **to cast aside** abbandonare; **to cast down** deprimere; **to cast lots** tirare a sorte; **to cast off** abbandonare; **to cast out** buttar fuori ‖ *intr* tirare i dadi; **to cast off** (naut) mollare gli ormeggi

castanets [₁kæstə'nɛts] *spl* nacchere *fpl*

cast·a·way' *adj & s* naufrago; (fig) reprobo

caste [kæst] *or* [kɑst] *s* casta; **to lose caste** perdere prestigio

caster ['kæstər] *or* ['kɑstər] *s* ampollina, saliera, pepaiola; (*roller*) rotella per i mobili

castigate ['kæstɪ₁get] *tr* castigare, punire; correggere

Castile [kæs'til] *s* (la) Castiglia

Castilian [kæs'tɪljən] *adj & s* castigliano

casting ['kæstɪŋ] *or* ['kɑstɪŋ] *s* getto, getto fuso; (*in fishing*) pesca a getto

cast' i'ron *s* ghisa

cast'-i'ron *adj* fatto di ghisa; (*e.g., stomach*) fatto d'acciaio, di struzzo

castle ['kæsəl] *or* ['kɑsəl] *s* castello; (chess) torre *f* ‖ *tr & intr* (chess) arroccare

cas'tle in Spain' *or* **cas'tle in the air'** *s* castello in aria

cast'off' *adj* abbandonato ‖ *s* rigetto; persona abbandonata; (typ) stima

cas'tor oil' ['kæstər] *or* ['kɑstər] *s* olio di ricino

castrate ['kæstret] *tr* castrare

casual ['kæʒʊ·əl] *adj* casuale, fortuito; (*clothing*) semplice, sportivo

casually ['kæʒʊ·əli] *adv* con disinvoltura; (*by chance*) fortuitamente

casual·ty ['kæʒʊ·əlti] *s* (**-ties**) accidente *m*, disastro; vittima; **casualties** (*in war*) perdite *fpl*

casuist·ry ['kæʒʊ·ɪstri] *s* (**-ries**) (*specious reasoning*) speciosità *f*; (philos) casistica

cat [kæt] *s* gatto; donna perfida; **to let the cat out of the bag** lasciarsi scappare il segreto

cataclysm ['kætə₁klɪzəm] *s* cataclisma *m*

catacomb ['kætə₁kom] *s* catacomba *f*

catalogue ['kætə₁lɔg] *or* ['kætə₁lɑg] *s* catalogo ‖ *tr* catalogare

cat'alogue sale' *s* vendita per corrispondenza

catalyst ['kætəlɪst] *s* catalizzatore *m*

catapult ['kætə₁pʌlt] *s* catapulta ‖ *tr* catapultare

cataract ['kætə₁rækt] *s* cataratta

catarrh [kə'tɑr] *s* catarro

catastrophe [kə'tæstrəfi] *s* catastrofe *f*, disastro

cat'call' s urlo di disapprovazione
catch [kætʃ] s presa; cattura; (of door) paletto; (in marriage) partito; (trick) inganno; (of fish) pesca; (mach) nottolino ‖ v (pret & pp caught [kɔt]) tr prendere, acchiappare; (a cold) pigliare, buscarsi; **to catch hold of** afferrare; **to catch it** (coll) prendersele; **to catch oneself** contenersi; **to catch up** sorprendere sul fatto ‖ intr agganciarsi; (said of a disease) trasmettersi; **to catch on** capire l'antifona; **to catch up** mettersi al corrente; **to catch up with** raggiungere
catch'-as-catch'-can' s lotta libera americana
catch' ba'sin s ricettacolo di fogna
catcher ['kætʃər] s ricevitore m, catcher m
catching ['kætʃɪŋ] adj (alluring) seducente; (infectious) contagioso
catch'word' s slogan m; (typ) chiamata; (typ) esponente m in testa di pagina
catch-y ['kætʃi] adj (-ier; -iest) attraente, vivo; (tricky) insidioso
catechism ['kætɪˌkɪzəm] s catechismo
catego-ry ['kætɪˌgori] s (-ries) categoria
cater ['ketər] intr provvedere cibo; **to cater to** servire
cater-cornered ['kætərˌkɔrnərd] adj diagonale ‖ adv diagonalmente
caterer ['ketərər] s provveditore m
caterpillar ['kætərˌpɪlər] s bruco
cat'erpillar trac'tor s trattore m a cingoli
cat'fish' s pesce m gatto
cat'gut' s (mus) corda di minugia; (surg) catgut m, cattegù m
cathartic [kə'θɑrtɪk] adj & s catartico
cathedral [kə'θidrəl] s cattedrale f
catheter ['kæθɪtər] s catetere m
catheterize ['kæθɪtəˌraɪz] tr cateterizzare
cathode ['kæθod] s catodo
catholic ['kæθəlɪk] adj cattolico; (e.g., mind) liberale ‖ **Catholic** adj & s cattolico
catkin ['kætkɪn] s (bot) amento, gattino
cat'nap' s corta siesta, sonnellino
cat-o'-nine-tails [ˌkætə'naɪnˌtelz] s gatto a nove code
cat's-paw' s gonzo; (breeze) brezzolina
catsup ['kætsəp] or ['ketˌəp] s salsa piccante di pomodoro, ketchup m
cat'tail' s stiancia
cattle ['kætəl] s bestiame grosso
cat'tle-man s (-men) allevatore m di bestiame
cat-ty ['kæti] adj (-tier; -tiest) malizioso, maligno; felino, gattesco
cat'walk' s passerella, ballatoio
Caucasian [kɔ'keʒən] or [kɔ'keʃən] adj & s caucasico
caucus ['kɔkəs] s comitato elettorale; conciliabolo politico
cauldron ['kɔldrən] s calderone m
cauliflower ['kɔlɪˌflaʊ-ər] s cavolfiore m
caulk [kɔk] tr calafatare, stoppare
cause [kɔz] s causa, cagione ‖ tr causare, cagionare; **to cause to** + inf

fare + inf, e.g., **she caused him to fall** l'ha fatto cadere
cause'way' s strada rialzata, scarpata
caustic ['kɔstɪk] adj caustico
cauterize ['kɔtəˌraɪz] tr cauterizzare
caution ['kɔ/ən] s cautela, prudenza; ammonizione ‖ tr ammonire
cautious ['kɔ/əs] adj prudente
cavalcade ['kævəlˌked] or [ˌkævəl'ked] s cavalcata
cavalier [ˌkævə'lɪr] or ['kævə‿lɪr] adj altero, sdegnoso; disinvolto ‖ s cavaliere m
caval-ry ['kævəlri] s (-ries) cavalleria
cav'alry-man or **cav'alry-man** s (-men' or -men) cavalleggero, soldato di cavalleria
cave [kev] s caverna, grotta ‖ intr— **to cave in** sprofondarsi; (to give in) (coll) cedere; (to become exhausted) (coll) diventare spossato
cave'-in' s sprofondamento
cave' man' s troglodita m
cavern ['kævərn] s caverna
caviar ['kævɪˌɑr] or [ˌkævɪ'ɑr] s caviale m
cav-il ['kævɪl] v (pret & pp -iled or -illed; ger -iling or -illing) intr cavillare
cavi-ty ['kævɪti] s (-ties) cavità f; (in tooth) carie f
cavort [kə'vɔrt] intr far capriole
caw [kɔ] s gracchiamento ‖ intr gracchiare
cease [sis] tr cessare, interrompere ‖ intr cessare, interrompersi; **to cease** + ger cessare di + inf
cease'-fire' s sospensione delle ostilità
ceaseless ['sislɪs] adj incessante
cedar ['sidər] s cedro; legno di cedro
cede [sid] tr cedere, trasferire
ceiling ['silɪŋ] s soffitto; (aer) altezza massima; **to hit the ceiling** (slang) uscire dai gangheri
ceil'ing price' s calmiere m, tetto
celebrate ['selɪˌbret] tr celebrare ‖ intr celebrare; far festa
celebrated ['selɪˌbretɪd] adj celebre, famoso
celebration [ˌselɪ'breʃən] s celebrazione
celebri-ty [sɪ'lebrɪti] s (-ties) celebrità f
celery ['seləri] s sedano
celestial [sɪ'lestʃəl] adj celestiale, celeste
celibacy ['seləbəsi] s celibato
celibate ['seləˌbet] or ['seləbɪt] adj & s celibe m; nubile f
cell [sel] s (e.g., of jail) cella; (of electric battery) elemento; (biol, phys, pol) cellula
cellar ['selər] s cantina; (partly above ground) seminterrato
cellist or **'cellist** ['tʃelɪst] s violoncellista mf
cel-lo or **'cel-lo** ['tʃelo] s (-los) violoncello
cellophane ['seləˌfen] s cellofan m
celluloid ['seljəˌlɔɪd] s celluloide f
Celtic ['seltɪk] or ['keltɪk] adj celtico ‖ s lingua celtica

cement [sɪ'ment] *s* cemento || *tr* cementare

cemete·ry ['sɛmɪˌtɛri] *s* (**-ries**) cimitero

censer ['sensər] *s* turibolo

censor ['sensər] *s* censore *m* || *tr* censurare

censure ['senʃər] *s* censura, critica || *tr* censurare, criticare

census ['sensəs] *s* censo, censimento

cent [sent] *s* centesimo di dollaro, cent *m*; **not to have a red cent to one's name** non avere il becco di un quattrino

centaur ['sentər] *s* centauro

centennial [sen'teni·əl] *adj & s* centenario

center ['sentər] *s* centro || *tr* centrare, concentrare || *intr*—**to center on** concentrarsi su

cen'ter·board' *s* chiglia mobile

cen'ter·piece' *s* centro tavola

cen'ter punch' *s* punzone *m*, punteruolo

centigrade ['sentɪˌgred] *adj* centigrado

centimeter ['sentɪˌmitər] *s* centimetro

centipede ['sentɪˌpid] *s* centopiedi *m*

cento ['sento] *s* centone *m*

central ['sentrəl] *adj* centrale || *s* centrale *f*, centrale telefonica; (*operator*) telefonista *mf*

Cen'tral Amer'ica *s* l'America Centrale

centralize ['sentrəˌlaɪz] *tr* centralizzare || *intr* centralizzarsi

centu·ry ['sentʃəri] *s* (**-ries**) secolo

ceramic [sɪ'ræmɪk] *adj* ceramico || **ceramics** *ssg* ceramica; *spl* oggetti *mpl* di ceramica

cereal ['sɪrɪ·əl] *adj* cerealicolo || *s* (*grain*) cereale *m*; (*uncooked breakfast food, e.g., cornflakes*) fiocchi *mpl*; (*breakfast food to be cooked*) farina

cerebral ['serɪbrəl] *adj* cerebrale

ceremonious [ˌserɪ'moni·əs] *adj* cerimonioso

ceremo·ny ['serɪˌmoni] *s* (**-nies**) cerimonia; **to stand on ceremony** fare cerimonie

certain ['sʌrtən] *adj* certo; **for certain** di or per certo; **to be certain to** + *inf* non mancare di + *inf*

certainly ['sʌrtənli] *adv* certamente; (*gladly*) con piacere

certain·ty ['sʌrtənti] *s* (**-ties**) certezza

certificate [sər'tɪfɪkɪt] *s* certificato; (com) titolo || [sər'tɪfɪˌket] *tr* certificare

cer'tified check' *s* assegno a copertura garantita

cer'tified cop'y *s* estratto; (*as a formula on a document*) per copia conforme

cer'tified pub'lic account'ant *s* esperto contabile

certi·fy ['sʌrtɪˌfaɪ] *v* (*pret & pp* **-fied**) *tr* certificare, garantire

cervix ['sʌrvɪks] *s* (**cervices** [sər'vaɪsiz]) cervice *f*

cessation [sɛ'seʃən] *s* cessazione

cesspool ['sɛsˌpul] *s* pozzo nero

Ceylo·nese [ˌsilə'niz] *adj & s* (**-nese**) singalese *mf*

chafe [tʃef] *s* irritazione || *tr* (*the hands*) strofinare; irritare; (*to wear*

away) logorare || *intr* irritarsi; logorarsi

chaff [tʃæf] *or* [tʃɑf] *s* lolla; pula; (*joke*) burla; (fig) loppa

chaf'ing dish' *s* fornello a spirito

cha·grin [ʃə'grɪn] *s* cruccio, dispiacere *m* || *v* (*pret* **-grined** *or* **-grinned;** *ger* **-grining** *or* **-grinning**) *tr* crucciare, affliggere

chain [tʃen] *s* catena; (*e.g., for necklace*) catenella || *tr* incatenare

chain' gang' *s* catena di forzati

chain' reac'tion *s* reazione a catena

chain' saw' *s* motosega

chain'-smoke' *intr* fumare come un turco

chain' store' *s* negozio a catena

chair [tʃer] *s* sedia, seggiola; (*of important person*) seggio; (*at a university*) cattedra; (*chairman*) presidente *m*, presidenza; **to take the chair** cominciare una riunione || *tr* (*a meeting*) presiedere

chair' lift' *s* seggiovia

chair'man *s* (**-men**) presidente *m*

chair'man·ship' *s* presidenza

chair'wom'an *s* (**-wom'en**) presidentessa

chalice ['tʃælɪs] *s* calice *m*

chalk [tʃɔk] *s* gesso || *tr* marcare or scrivere col gesso; **to chalk up** prendere appunti di; attribuire

chalk' talk' *s* conferenza illustrata

chalk·y ['tʃɔki] *adj* (**-ier; -iest**) gessoso

challenge ['tʃælɪndʒ] *s* sfida; (law) ricusazione; (mil) chi va là *m* || *tr* sfidare; (*a juror*) (law) ricusare; (mil) dare il chi va là a

chamber ['tʃembər] *s* camera, stanza; (*of a palace*) aula; (*of a judge*) gabinetto

chamberlain ['tʃembərlɪn] *s* ciambellano

cham'ber·maid' *s* cameriera

cham'ber of com'merce *s* camera di commercio

cham'ber pot' *s* orinale *m*

chameleon [kə'mili·ən] *s* camaleonte *m*

cham·ois ['ʃæmi] *s* (**-ois**) camoscio

champ [tʃæmp] *s* (slang) campione *m* || *tr* masticare rumorosamente; (*the bit*) mordere || *intr* masticare rumorosamente

champagne [ʃæm'pen] *s* champagne *m*, spumante *m*

champion ['tʃæmpi·ən] *s* campione *m* || *tr* difendere; farsi paladino di

championship ['tʃæmpi·ənˌʃɪp] *s* campionato

chance [tʃæns] *or* [tʃɑns] *adj* casuale, fortuito || *s* occasione; caso; probabilità *f*; rischio; biglietto di lotteria; **by chance** per caso; **not to stand a chance** non avere la probabilità di riuscita; **to take one's chances** arrischiarsi; **to wait for a chance** attendere l'opportunità || *intr* succedere; **to chance upon** imbattersi in

chancel ['tʃænsəl] *or* ['tʃɑnsəl] *s* presbiterio, coro

chanceller·y ['tʃænsələri] *or* ['tʃɑnsələri] *s* (**-ies**) cancelleria chancellor ['tʃænsələr] or ['tʃɑnsələr] s cancelliere m

chandelier [,ʃændə'lir] s lampadario

change (tʃendʒ) s cambiamento; (of clothes) muta; (of currency) cambio; (coins) spiccioli mpl; for a change tanto per cambiare; to keep the change tenere il resto || tr cambiare, rimpiazzare; (clothes) cambiare, cambiarsi di || intr cambiare, mutare

changeable ['tʃendʒəbəl] adj mutevole, variabile, incostante

change' of heart' s pentimento, conversione

change' of life' s menopausa

chan·nel ['tʃænəl] s canale m; tubo, passaggio; stretto; (of river) alveo; (groove) solco; (rad, telv) canale m; through channels per via gerarchica || v (pret & pp -neled or -nelled; ger -neling or -nelling) tr incanalare; (a river) incassare || the Channel il Canale della Manica

chant [tʃænt] or [tʃɑnt] s canto; salmodia; canzone f || tr & intr cantare

chanticleer ['tʃæntɪ,klɪr] s il gallo

chaos ['ke·ɑs] s caos m

chaotic [ke'ɑtɪk] adj caotico

chap [tʃæp] s (fellow) individuo, tipo; (of skin) screpolatura; chaps pantaloni mpl di cuoio || v (pret & pp chapped; ger chapping) tr screpolare || intr screpolarsi

chapel ['tʃæpəl] s cappella

chaperon or chaperone ['ʃæpə,ron] s accompagnatrice f (di signorina) || tr accompagnare

chaplain ['tʃæplɪn] s cappellano

chaplet ['tʃæplɪt] s (wreath) corona, ghirlanda; rosario

chapter ['tʃæptər] s capitolo; (of a club) sezione

chap'ter and verse' s—to give chapter and verse citare le autorità

char [tʃɑr] v (pret & pp charred; ger charring) tr carbonizzare; bruciare

character ['kærɪktər] s carattere m; lettera, scrittura; indole f; (theat) personaggio; (coll) tipo; in character caratteristico di lui (lei, loro, etc.)

char'acter ac'tor s caratterista m

char'acter ac'tress s caratterista f

char'acter assassina'tion s linciaggio morale

characteristic [,kærɪktə'rɪstɪk] adj caratteristico || s caratteristica

characterize ['kærɪktə,raɪz] tr caratterizzare

char'coal' s carbone m di legna, carbone m dolce; (for sketching) carboncino; (sketch) disegno al carboncino

charge [tʃɑrdʒ] s carica; incarico; responsabilità f; (indictment) accusa; costo; prezzo; debito; in charge in comando; in charge of a cura di; to take charge of prendersi cura di || tr caricare; comandare; accusare; (a price) fare pagare; mettere in conto; to charge s.o. with s.th addebitare qlco a qlcu; accusare qlcu di qlco || intr fare una carica

charge' account' s conto corrente

chargé d'affaires [ʃɑr'ʒe də'fer] s (chargés d'affaires) incaricato d'affari

charger ['tʃɑrdʒər] s cavallo di battaglia; (of a battery) caricatore m

chariot ['tʃærɪ·ət] s cocchio

charioteer [,tʃærɪ·ə'tɪr] s auriga m

charis·ma [kə'rɪzmə] s (-mata [mətə]) fascino personale; (theol) carisma m

charitable ['tʃærɪtəbəl] adj (person) caritatevole; (institution) caritativo

chari·ty ['tʃærɪti] s (-ties) carità f; associazione di beneficenza

charlatan ['ʃɑrlətən] s ciarlatano

charlatanism ['ʃɑrlətən,ɪzm] s ciarlataneria

Charlemagne ['ʃɑrlə,men] s Carlomagno

Charles [tʃɑrlz] s Carlo

char'ley horse' ['tʃɑrli] s (coll) crampo

charlotte ['ʃɑrlət] s charlotte f || Charlotte s Carlotta

charm [tʃɑrm] s fascino; amuleto; portafortuna m || tr incantare, stregare

charming ['tʃɑrmɪŋ] adj affascinante

charnel ['tʃɑrnəl] adj orribile || s ossario

chart [tʃɑrt] s carta geografica; lista; diagramma m || tr tracciare

charter ['tʃɑrtər] s statuto; privilegio || tr (a company) fondare; (a conveyance) noleggiare

char'ter mem'ber s socio fondatore

char'wom'an s (-wom'en) domestica per la pulizia

chase [tʃes] s inseguimento; caccia; (typ) telaio || tr inseguire; cacciare; (to chisel) cesellare; to chase away scacciare || intr—to chase after inseguire

chaser ['tʃesər] s cacciatore m; (coll) bibita da bersi dopo un liquore

chasm ['kæzəm] s abisso, baratro

chas·sis ['tʃæsi] s (-sis [siz]) telaio

chaste [tʃest] adj casto

chasten ['tʃesən] tr castigare

chastise [tʃæs'taɪz] tr castigare

chastity ['tʃæstɪti] s castità f

chat [tʃæt] s chiacchierata || v (pret & pp chatted; ger chatting) intr chiacchierare

chatelaine ['ʃætə,len] s castellana

chattels ['tʃætəlz] spl beni mpl mobili

chatter ['tʃætər] s cicaleccio; balbettio; (of teeth) battito || intr cicalare; balbettare; (said of teeth) battere

chat'ter·box' s chiacchierone m

chauffeur ['ʃofər] or [ʃo'fʌr] s autista mf || intr fare l'autista

cheap [tʃip] adj a buon mercato, economico; (of poor quality) scadente; to feel cheap vergognarsi || adv a buon mercato

cheapen ['tʃipən] tr deprezzare; avvilire; rendere di cattivo gusto

cheapness ['tʃipnəs] s buon mercato, prezzo basso

cheat [tʃit] s truffa; truffatore m || tr imbrogliare, truffare || intr truffare; (at cards) barare

check [tʃek] s arresto, pausa; ostacolo;

esame *m;* verifica, controllo; (*of bank*) assegno; (*for baggage*) tagliando, scontrino; (*square pattern*) quadretto; (*fabric in squares*) tessuto a scacchi; (*in a restaurant*) conto; **in check** controllato, sotto controllo; (chess) sotto scacco ‖ *tr* fermare; confrontare; ispezionare; marcare; (*e.g., a coat*) depositare; disegnare a quadretti; (chess) dare scacco a; **to check off** controllare marcando; **to check on** controllare, verificare ‖ *intr* fermarsi; corrispondere perfettamente; **to check in** scendere (a un albergo); **to check out** andar via; pagare il conto; **to check up on** controllare

check'book' *s* libretto d'assegni

checker ['tʃɛkər] *s* ispettore *m;* quadretto; (*in game of checkers*) pedina; **checkers** dama ‖ *tr* variegare; marcare a quadretti

check'er·board' *s* scacchiera

check'ered *adj* (*e.g., career*) pieno di vicissitudini; (*marked with squares*) a scacchi; (*in color*) variegato

check'ing account' *s* conto corrente

check'mate' *s* scacco matto ‖ *tr* dare scacco matto a ‖ *interj* scacco matto!

check'off' dues' *spl* trattenute *fpl* sindacali

check'-out' *s* (*from hotel room*) partenza; (*time*) ora della partenza; (*examination*) esame *m* di controllo; (*in a supermarket*) cassa

check'point' *s* punto di ispezione

check'room' *s* guardaroba *m*

check'up' *s* (*of car*) ispezione; (*of patient*) esame *m* (fisico)

cheek [tʃik] *s* guancia, gota; (coll) faccia tosta

cheek'bone' *s* zigomo

cheek·y ['tʃiki] *adj* (**-ier; -iest**) (coll) impudente, sfacciato

cheer [tʃɪr] *s* gioia, allegria; applauso; **of good cheer** di buon umore ‖ *tr* riempire di gioia, rallegrare; applaudire; ricevere con applausi ‖ *intr* rallegrarsi; **cheer up!** animo!, coraggio!

cheerful ['tʃɪrfəl] *adj* allegro, di buon umore; (*willing*) volonteroso

cheerless ['tʃɪrlɪs] *adj* tetro, triste

cheese [tʃiz] *s* formaggio ‖ *intr*—**cheese it!** (slang) scappa via!

cheese' cake' *s* torta di formaggio; (slang) pin-up girl *f*

cheese'cloth' *s* etamine *f,* stamigna

chees·y [tʃizi] *adj* (**-ier; -iest**) di formaggio; come il formaggio; (slang) meschino, di cattiva qualità

chef [ʃɛf] *s* chef *m,* capocuoco

chemical ['kɛmɪkəl] *adj* chimico ‖ *s* prodotto chimico

chemise [ʃə'miz] *s* sottoveste *f*

chemist ['kɛmɪst] *s* chimico

chemistry ['kɛmɪstri] *s* chimica

cherish ['tʃɛrɪʃ] *tr* accarezzare; (*a memory*) custodire; (*a hope*) nutrire

cher·ry ['tʃɛri] *s* (**-ries**) (*tree*) ciliegio; (*fruit*) ciliegia

cher·ub ['tʃɛrəb] *s* (**-ubim** [əbɪm] & **-ubs**) cherubino

chess [tʃɛs] *s* scacchi *mpl*

chess'board' *s* scacchiera

chess'man' or **chess'man** *s* (**-men'** or **-men**) scacco

chest [tʃɛst] *s* petto; (*box*) cassapanca; (*furniture with drawers*) cassettone *m;* (*for money*) forziere *m*

chestnut ['tʃɛsnət] *s* (*tree, wood, color*) castagno; (*nut*) castagna

chest' of drawers' *s* cassettone *m*

cheval' glass' [ʃə'væl] *s* psiche *f*

chevalier [ˌʃɛvə'lɪr] *s* cavaliere *m*

chevron ['ʃɛvrən] *s* gallone *m*

chew [tʃu] *tr* masticare; **to chew the cud** ruminare; **to chew the rag** (slang) chiacchierare ‖ *intr* masticare

chew'ing gum' *s* gomma da masticare

chic [ʃik] *adj* & *s* chic

chicaner·y [ʃɪ'kɛnəri] *s* (**-ies**) trucco, rigiro

chick [tʃɪk] *s* pulcino; (slang) ragazza

chicken ['tʃɪkən] *s* pollo, pollastro; (coll) giovane *mf;* **to be chicken** (slang) avere la fifa ‖ *intr*—**to chicken out** (coll) indietreggiare

chick'en coop' *s* pollaio

chick'en feed' *s* (slang) spiccioli *mpl*

chicken-hearted ['tʃɪkən ˌhɑrtɪd] *adj* timido, fifone

chick'en pox' *s* varicella

chick'en store' *s* polleria

chick'en wire' *s* rete metallica esagonale

chick'pea' *s* cece *m*

chico·ry ['tʃɪkəri] *s* (**-ries**) cicoria

chide [tʃaɪd] *v* (*pret* **chided** or **chid** [tʃɪd]; *pp* **chided, chid,** or **chidden** ['tʃɪdən]) *tr* & *intr* rimproverare, correggere

chief [tʃif] *adj* principale, sommo, supremo ‖ *s* capo, comandante supremo; (slang) padrone *m*

chief' exec'utive *s* capo del governo

chief' jus'tice *s* presidente *m* di una corte; presidente *m* della corte suprema

chiefly ['tʃifli] *adv* principalmente

chief' of staff' *s* capo di stato maggiore

chief' of state' *s* capo dello stato

chieftain ['tʃiftən] *s* capo

chiffon [ʃɪ'fɑn] *s* velo trasparente, chiffon *m;* **chiffons** trine *fpl*

chiffonier [ˌʃɪfə'nɪr] *s* mobile *m* a cassettini, chiffonier *m*

chilblain ['tʃɪlˌblɛn] *s* gelone *m*

child [tʃaɪld] *s* (**children** ['tʃɪldrən]) bebè *mf,* bambino; figlio; discendente *mf;* **with child** incinta

child'birth' *s* parto

childhood ['tʃaɪldhʊd] *s* infanzia

childish ['tʃaɪldɪʃ] *adj* infantile

childishness ['tʃaɪldɪʃnɪs] *s* puerilità *f,* infanzia

child' la'bor *s* lavoro dei minorenni

childless ['tʃaɪldlɪs] *adj* senza figli

child'like' *adj* infantile, innocente

child's' play' *s* un gioco

child' wel'fare *s* protezione dell'infanzia

Chile ['tʃɪli] *s* il Cile

Chilean ['tʃɪlɪ·ən] *adj* cileno

chil′i sauce′ [ˈtʃɪli] s salsa di pomodoro con peperoni

chill [tʃɪl] adj freddo ‖ s freddo; brivido di freddo; freddezza; (depression) abbattimento ‖ tr raffreddare; (a metal) temprare; (fig) scoraggiare ‖ intr raffreddarsi

chill·y [ˈtʃɪli] adj (-ier; -iest) fresco, freddiccio; (reception) freddo

chime [tʃaɪm] s scampanio; **chimes** campanello ‖ intr scampanare; **to chime in** cominciare a cantare all'unisono; (coll) intromettersi

chime′ clock′ s orologio con carillon

chimney [ˈtʃɪmni] s camino; (of factory) ciminiera; **to smoke like a chimney** fumare come un turco

chim′ney flue′ s tubo di stufa, canna del camino

chim′ney pot′ s testa della canna fumaria, comignolo

chim′ney sweep′ s spazzacamino

chimpanzee [tʃɪmˈpænzi] or [ˌtʃɪmpænˈzi] s scimpanzé m

chin [tʃɪn] s mento; **to keep one's chin up** (coll) non perdersi di coraggio; **to take it on the chin** (slang) subire una sconfitta ‖ v (pret & pp chinned; ger chinning) tr—**to chin oneself** sollevarsi fino al mento (ai manubri) ‖ intr (slang) chiacchierare

china [ˈtʃaɪnə] s porcellana ‖ **China** s la Cina

chi′na clos′et s armadio per le stoviglie

chi′na·ware′ s porcellana, stoviglie fpl

Chi·nese [tʃaɪˈniz] adj cinese ‖ s (-nese) cinese mf

Chi′nese lan′tern s lampioncino alla veneziana

Chi′nese puz′zle s rebus m

chink [tʃɪŋk] s fessura

chin′ strap′ s sottogola

chintz [tʃɪnts] s chintz m

chip [tʃɪp] s scheggia; frammento; (in card games) gettone m; (of wood) truciolo; **chip off the old block** vero figlio di suo padre (di sua madre); **chip on one's shoulder** propensità f a attaccar brighe ‖ v (pret & pp chipped; ger chipping) tr scheggiare; **to chip in** contribuire ‖ intr scheggiarsi

chipmunk [ˈtʃɪpˌmʌŋk] s tamia

chipper [ˈtʃɪpər] adj (coll) allegro, vivo

chiropodist [kaɪˈrɑpədɪst] or [kɪˈrɑpədɪst] s callista mf, pedicure mf

chiropractic [ˈkaɪrəˌpræktɪs] s chiropratica

chirp [tʃɜrp] s (of birds) cinguettio; (of crickets) cri cri m ‖ intr cinguettare; fare cri cri

chis·el [ˈtʃɪzəl] s (for wood and metal) scalpello; (for metal) cesello ‖ v (pret & pp -eled or -elled; ger -eling or -elling) tr scalpellare; cesellare; (slang) imbrogliare ‖ intr (slang) imbrogliare, fare l'imbroglio

chiseler [ˈtʃɪzələr] s cesellatore m; (slang) imbroglione m

chit-chat [ˈtʃɪtˌtʃæt] s chiacchierata

chivalrous [ˈʃɪvəlrəs] adj cavalleresco

chivalry [ˈʃɪvəlri] s cavalleria

chive [tʃaɪv] s cipolla porraia

chloride [ˈkloraɪd] s cloruro

chlorine [ˈklorin] s cloro

chloroform [ˈklorəˌfɔrm] s cloroformio ‖ tr cloroformizzare

chlorophyll [ˈklorəfɪl] s clorofilla

chock [tʃɑk] s (wedge) bietta, cuneo

chock-full [ˈtʃɑkˈful] adj colmo, pieno zeppo

chocolate [ˈtʃɔkəlɪt] or [ˈtʃɑkəlɪt] s (candy) cioccolato; (drink) cioccolata

choc′olate bar′ s barretta di cioccolato

choice [tʃɔɪs] adj di prima scelta, superiore ‖ s scelta; (variety) assortimento

choir [kwaɪr] s coro

choir′boy′ s ragazzo cantore

choir′ loft′ s coro

choir′mas′ter s maestro di cappella

choke [tʃok] s strozzatura; (aut) farfalla del carburatore ‖ tr strozzare; ostruire; (an internal-combustion engine) arricchire la miscela di; **to choke back** trattenere; **to choke up** tappare, ostruire ‖ intr soffocarsi; **to choke up** tapparsi; (coll) soffocarsi

choker [ˈtʃokər] s (necklace) (coll) collana; (scarf) (coll) foulard m

cholera [ˈkɑlərə] s colera m

choleric [ˈkɑlərɪk] adj collerico

cholesterol [kəˈlɛstəˌrol] or [kəˈlɛstəˌral] s colesterina

choose [tʃuz] v (pret chose [tʃoz]; pp chosen [ˈtʃozən]) tr scegliere ‖ intr —**to choose** to decidere di

choos·y [ˈtʃuzi] adj (-ier; -iest) (coll) di difficile contentatura

chop [tʃɑp] s colpo; (of meat) cotoletta; **chops** labbra fpl, bocca ‖ v (pret & pp chopped; ger chopping) tr tagliare; (meat) tritare; **to chop off** troncare; **to chop up** sminuzzare

chopper [ˈtʃɑpər] s (man) tagliatore m; interruttore automatico; coltello da macellaio; (slang) elicottero; **choppers** (slang) i denti

chop′ping block′ s tagliere m

chop·py [ˈtʃɑpi] adj (-pier; -piest) (wind) variabile; (sea) agitato; (style) instabile

choral [ˈkorəl] adj & s corale m

chorale [koˈral] s corale m

chord [kord] s corda; (mus) accordo

chore [tʃor] s lavoro; lavoro spiacevole; **chores** faccende domestiche

choreography [ˌkoriˈɑgrəfi] s coreografia

chorine [koˈrin] s (slang) ballerina

chorus [ˈkorəs] s coro; (group of dancers) corpo di ballo; (of a song) ritornello

cho′rus girl′ s ballerina

cho′rus man′ s (men) corista m

chow [tʃaʊ] s (dog) chow chow m; (slang) cibo, pappa

chowder [ˈtʃaʊdər] s zuppa di vongole; zuppa di pesce

Christ [kraɪst] s Cristo

christen [ˈkrɪsən] tr battezzare

Christendom [ˈkrɪsəndəm] s cristianità f

christening [ˈkrɪsənɪŋ] s battesimo
Christian [ˈkrɪstʃən] adj & s cristiano
Christianity [ˌkrɪstʃɪˈænɪti] s (Chris-
tendom) cristianità f; (religion) cri-
stianesimo
Chris′tian name′ s nome m di battesimo
Christmas [ˈkrɪsməs] adj natalizio ǁ s
Natale m; **Merry Christmas!** Buon
Natale!
Christ′mas card′ s cartoncino natalizio
Christ′mas car′ol s pastorella di Natale
Christ′mas Eve′ s vigilia di Natale
Christ′mas gift′ s strenna natalizia
Christ′mas tree′ s albero di Natale
chrome [krom] adj cromato ǁ s cromo
ǁ tr cromare
chromium [ˈkromɪ-əm] s cromo
chromosome [ˈkromə‚som] s cromo-
soma m
chronic [ˈkrɑnɪk] adj cronico
chronicle [ˈkrɑnɪkəl] s cronaca ǁ tr
fare la storia di
chronicler [ˈkrɑnɪklər] s cronista mf
chronolo·gy [krəˈnɑlədʒi] s (-gies)
cronologia
chronometer [krəˈnɑmɪtər] s cronometro
chrysanthemum [krɪˈsænθɪməm] s cri-
santemo
chub·by [ˈtʃʌbi] adj (-bier; -biest) paffuto
chuck [tʃʌk] s buffetto sotto il mento;
(cut of meat) reale m; (of lathe)
coppaia ǁ tr accarezzare sotto il
mento; (to throw) (coll) gettare
chuckle [ˈtʃʌkəl] s risatina ǁ intr ridacchiare
chum [tʃʌm] s (coll) amico intimo;
(coll) compagno di stanza ǁ v (pret
& pp chummed; ger chumming) intr
(coll) essere amico intimo; essere
compagno di stanza
chum·my [ˈtʃʌmi] adj (-mier; -miest)
(coll) intimo, amicone
chump [tʃʌmp] s ciocco, ceppo; (coll)
sciocco
chunk [tʃʌŋk] s grosso pezzo
church [tʃʌrtʃ] s chiesa
churchgoer [ˈtʃʌrtʃ‚go·ər] s praticante
mf
church′man s (-men) parrocchiano;
(clergyman) sacerdote m
Church′ of Eng′land s chiesa anglicana
church′yard′ s camposanto
churl [tʃʌrl] s zotico, villano
churlish [ˈtʃʌrlɪʃ] adj villano
churn [tʃʌrn] s zangola ǁ tr agitare
violentemente, sbattere ǁ intr (said
of water) ribollire
chute [ʃut] s piano inclinato, canna;
(in a river) cascata, rapida; paracadute m; (into a swimming pool)
toboga m
Cicero [ˈsɪsə‚ro] s Cicerone m
cider [ˈsaɪdər] s sidro
cigar [sɪˈɡɑr] s sigaro
cigar′ case′ s portasigari m
cigar′ cut′ter s tagliasigari m
cigarette [ˌsɪɡəˈrɛt] s sigaretta
cigarette′ butt′ s cicca
cigarette′ case′ s portasigarette m
cigarette′ hold′er s bocchino

cigarette′ light′er s accendisigaro, ac-
cendino
cigarette′ pa′per s cartina da sigarette
cigar′ store′ s tabaccheria, rivendita di
sali e tabacchi
cinch [sɪntʃ] s (on a horse) sottopancia
m; (hold) (coll) presa; (slang) gio-
chetto ǁ tr legare con una cinghia;
(slang) agguantare
cinder [ˈsɪndər] s tizzone m; (slag)
scoria; **cinders** cenere f
cin′der block′ s concio di scoria
Cinderella [ˌsɪndəˈrɛlə] s (la) Cene-
rentola
cinema [ˈsɪnəmə] s cine m, cinema m
cinnabar [ˈsɪnə‚bɑr] s cinabro
cinnamon [ˈsɪnəmən] s cannella
cipher [ˈsaɪfər] s zero; cifra; codice m;
monogramma m ǁ tr calcolare; (to
write in code) cifrare
circle [ˈsʌrkəl] s cerchio; (of theater)
prima galleria; (of friends) cerchia ǁ
tr cerchiare, compiere una rotazione
intorno a
circuit [ˈsʌrkɪt] s circuito; (district)
circoscrizione
cir′cuit break′er s salvamotore m, interruttore automatico
circuitous [sərˈkju-ɪtəs] adj tortuoso
circuitry [ˈsʌrkɪtri] s (plan) schema m
di montaggio; (components) elementi
mpl di un circuito
circular [ˈsʌrkjələr] adj & s circolare f
circulate [ˈsʌrkjə‚let] tr mettere in circolazione, diffondere ǁ intr circolare
cir′culating li′brary s biblioteca circolante
circulation [ˌsʌrkjəˈleʃən] s circolazione; (of newspaper) diffusione
circumcise [ˈsʌrkəm‚saɪz] tr circoncidere
circumference [sərˈkʌmfərəns] s circonferenza
circumflex [ˈsʌrkəm‚flɛks] adj circonflesso ǁ s accento circonflesso
circumscribe [ˌsʌrkəmˈskraɪb] tr cir-
coscrivere
circumspect [ˈsʌrkəm‚spɛkt] adj cir-
cospetto
circumstance [ˈsʌrkəm‚stæns] s circostanza; (fact) dettaglio; solennità f;
circumstances condizioni fpl; dettagli
mpl; condizioni economiche; **under
no circumstances** a nessuna condizione; **under the circumstances** le
cose essendo come stanno
circumstantial [ˌsʌrkəmˈstænʃəl] adj
circostanziale, indiziario; (incidental)
secondario; (complete) circostanziato
cir′cumstan′tial ev′idence s prova indiziaria
circumstantiate [ˌsʌrkəmˈstænʃɪ‚et] tr
(to support with particulars) comprovare; (to describe in detail) circon-
stanziare
circumvent [ˌsʌrkəmˈvɛnt] tr (to surround) accerchiare; (to outwit) circuire; (a difficulty) eludere, scansare
circus [ˈsʌrkəs] s circo equestre
cistern [ˈsɪstərn] s cisterna, serbatoio
citadel [ˈsɪtədəl] s cittadella
citation [saɪˈteʃən] s citazione

cite [saɪt] tr citare

cither ['sɪðər] s cetra

citizen ['sɪtɪzən] s cittadino; (civilian) civile mf

citizenship ['sɪtɪzən ˌʃɪp] s cittadinanza

citric ['sɪtrɪk] adj citrico

citron ['sɪtrən] s cedro; cedro candito

cit'rus fruit' ['sɪtrəs] s agrumi mpl

cit•y ['sɪtɪ] s (-ies) città f

cit'y counc'il s consiglio municipale

cit'y ed'itor s capocronista m

cit'y fa'thers spl maggiorenti mpl; consiglieri mpl municipali

cit'y hall' s municipio

cit'y plan'ning s urbanistica

cit'y room' s (journ) redazione

civic ['sɪvɪk] adj civico || civics s educazione civica

civil ['sɪvɪl] adj civile

civ'il engineer'ing s genio civile

civilian [sɪ'vɪljən] adj & s civile mf, borghese mf

civili•ty [sɪ'vɪlɪtɪ] s (-ties) cortesia; civilities ossequi mpl

civilization [ˌsɪvɪlɪ'zeʃən] s civilizzazione, civiltà f

civilize ['sɪvɪ ˌlaɪz] tr civilizzare

civ'il law' s diritto civile

civ'il serv'ant s impiegato statale

civ'il war' s guerra civile || Civil War s (of the U.S.A.) guerra di secessione

claim [klem] s pretesa; richiesta; (min) concessione || tr (one's rights) rivendicare; (one's property) richiedere; dichiarare; to claim to be pretendere d'essere

claim' check' s tagliando

clairvoyance [kler'vɔɪ·əns] s chiaroveggenza

clairvoyant [kler'vɔɪ·ənt] adj chiaroveggente || s veggente mf, chiaroveggente mf

clam [klæm] s vongola || intr—to clam up (coll) essere muto come un pesce

clamber ['klæmər] intr arrampicarsi

clam•my ['klæmɪ] adj (-mier; -miest) coperto di sudore freddo; morbido

clamor ['klæmər] s clamore m || intr fare clamore

clamorous ['klæmərəs] adj clamoroso

clamp [klæmp] s graffa, morsetto; (e.g., to hold a hose) fascetta || tr assicurare con graffa, aggrappare; (a tool) montare || intr—to clamp down on (coll) fare pressione su, mettere i freni a

clan [klæn] s clan m

clandestine [klæn'destɪn] adj clandestino

clang [klæŋ] s clangore m || intr risonare con clangore

clannish ['klænɪʃ] adj esclusivista, partigiano

clap [klæp] s applauso; (of thunder) scoppio || v (pret & pp clapped; ger clapping) tr (the hands) battere; (e.g., in jail) schiaffare; to clap shut sbattere || intr applaudire

clapper ['klæpər] s applauditore m; (of bell) batacchio

clap'trap' s imbonimento

claret ['klærɪt] adj & s chiaretto

clari•fy ['klærɪ ˌfaɪ] v (pret & pp -fied) tr chiarificare, chiarire

clarinet [ˌklærɪ'nɛt] s clarinetto

clarion ['klærɪ·ən] adj chiaro e metallico || s tromba, clarino

clash [klæʃ] s cozzo, urto; conflitto di opinioni || intr cozzare, urtarsi; essere in conflitto

clasp [klæsp] or [klɑsp] s gancio, fermaglio; (hold) presa; (grip) stretta || tr agganciare; (to hold in the arms) abbracciare; (to grip) stringere

class [klæs] or [klɑs] s classe f || tr classificare

class'book' s registro

classic ['klæsɪk] adj & s classico

classical ['klæsɪkəl] adj classico

classicism ['klæsɪ ˌsɪzəm] s classicismo

classicist ['klæsɪsɪst] s classicista mf

classified ['klæsɪ ˌfaɪd] adj segreto

clas'sified ad' s annunzio economico

classi•fy ['klæsɪ ˌfaɪ] v (pret & pp -fied) tr classificare

class'mate' s compagno di scuola

class'room' s aula scolastica

class' strug'gle s lotta di classe

class•y ['klæsɪ] adj (-ier; -iest) (slang) di lusso, di prim'ordine

clatter ['klætər] s (of dishes) acciottolio; vocio, schiamazzo || tr acciottolare || intr fare schiamazzo

clause [klɔz] s clausola; (gram) proposizione

clavicle ['klævɪkəl] s clavicola

claw [klɔ] s artiglio; (of lobster) pinza; (tool) raffio; (of hammer) granchio; (coll) dita fpl || tr aggraffiare; artigliare

claw' ham'mer s levachiodi m

clay [kle] s argilla, creta

clay' pipe' s pipa di terracotta

clean [klin] adj pulito; (precise) netto; (e.g., break) completo || adv completamente || tr pulire; to clean out pulire, fare repulisti di; (slang) ripulire; to clean up pulire completamente; mettere in ordine || intr pulirsi, fare pulizia

clean' bill' of health' s patente sanitaria; (fig) esonero completo

clean'-cut' adj ben delineato, deciso

cleaner ['klinər] s pulitore m, smacchiatore m; (machine) pulitrice f, smacchiatrice f; to send to the cleaners (slang) spolpare

clean'ing fluid' s smacchiatore m

clean'ing wom'an s donna di servizio per fare la pulizia

clean•ly ['klenlɪ] adj (-lier; -liest) pulito, netto

cleanse [klenz] tr pulire; detergere; purificare

cleanser ['klenzər] s detergente m

clean'-sha'ven adj sbarbato di fresco

clean'up' s pulizia; (slang) guadagno enorme

clear [klɪr] adj chiaro; evidente; completo; innocente; (profit) netto; clear of libero da || s posto libero; in the clear libero; esonerato; non in codice || adv chiaramente; completamente || tr (e.g., trees) rischiarare; (e.g., peo-

ple) sgombrare; (*the table*) sparecchiare; (*an obstacle*) superare; (*from guilt*) discolpare; (*a profit*) guadagnare; (*goods at customs*) svincolare; (*a ship through customs*) dichiarare il carico di; (*checks*) compensare; **to clear away** or **off** liberare; **to clear out** sgomberare, sbarazzare; **to clear up** spiegare; (*a doubt*) dissipare ‖ *intr* rasserenarsi; (*said of a ship*) partire; **to clear away** or **off** sparire; **to clear out** (coll) andarsene; **to clear up** rasserenarsi

clearance ['klɪrəns] *s* liberazione; (*of a ship*) partenza; (*of goods through customs*) sdoganamento; (*of checks*) compensazione; (*of goods*) liquidazione; (*mach*) gioco

clear'ance sale' *s* liquidazione

clear'-cut' *adj* chiaro, distinto

clearing ['klɪrɪŋ] *s* (*open space*) radura; (*of checks*) compensazione

clear'ing house' *s* stanza di compensazione

cleat [klit] *s* bietta, cuneo; (*on the sole of shoe*) tacchetto; (naut) galloccia

cleavage ['klivɪdʒ] *s* divisione; fessura

cleave [kliv] *v* (*pret & pp* **cleft** [kleft] *or* **cleaved**) *tr* dividere, fendere ‖ *intr* aderire, essere fedele

cleaver ['klivər] *s* scure *f*, accetta; (*of butcher*) spaccaossa *m*, fenditoio

clef [klef] *s* (mus) chiave *f*

cleft [kleft] *adj* diviso, fesso ‖ *s* fessura, crepaccio

cleft' pal'ate *s* palato spaccato, gola lupina

clematis ['klemətɪs] *s* clematide *f*

clemen•cy ['klemənsi] *s* (-cies) clemenza

clement ['klemənt] *adj* clemente

clench [klentʃ] *s* stretta ‖ *tr* stringere; afferrare

clergy ['klɜrdʒi] *s* clero

cler'gy•man *s* (-men) ecclesiastico

cleric ['klerɪk] *s* ecclesiastico, sacerdote *m*

clerical ['klerɪkəl] *adj* da impiegato; (*error*) burocratico; (*of clergy*) clericale ‖ *s* ecclesiastico; **clericals** abiti ecclesiastici

cler'ical work' *s* lavoro d'ufficio

clerk [klʌrk] *s* impiegato, commesso; (*accountant*) contabile *mf*; (*e.g., in a record office*) ufficiale *m*; cancelliere *m*; (*copyist, typist*) scrivano

clever ['klevər] *adj* intelligente; bravo, abile; destro

cleverness ['klevərnɪs] *s* intelligenza; bravura, abilità *f*

clew [klu] *s* indizio, traccia; (*of yarn*) gomitolo; (naut) bugna

cliché [kli'ʃe] *s* cliché *m*, luogo comune

click [klɪk] *s* (*of camera or gun*) scatto; (*of typewriter*) battito, ticchettio ‖ *tr* (*the tongue*) schioccare; (*the heels*) battere ‖ *intr* ticchettare; (slang) andare d'accordo; (slang) avere fortuna

client ['klaɪ•ənt] *s* cliente *mf*

clientele [,klaɪ•ən'tel] *s* clientela

cliff [klɪf] *s* rupe *f*, precipizio

climate ['klaɪmɪt] *s* clima *m*

climax ['klaɪmæks] *s* apice *m*; (*acute phase*) parossismo

climb [klaɪm] *s* salita; (*of a mountain*) scalata, ascensione ‖ *tr* (*the stairs*) salire; (*a mountain*) scalare, ascendere ‖ *intr* salire, arrampicarsi; **to climb down** discendere a carponi; (coll) ritirarsi

climber ['klaɪmər] *s* scalatore *m*; pianta rampicante; (*ambitious person*) (coll) arrampicatore *m*

clinch [klɪntʃ] *s* stretta, presa; (*boxing*) corpo a corpo *m* ‖ *tr* (*nails*) ribattere, ribadire

clincher ['klɪntʃər] *s* chiodo per ribaditura; argomento decisivo

cling [klɪŋ] *v* (*pret & pp* **clung** [klʌŋ]) *intr* avviticchiare, attaccarsi; aderire, rimanere attaccato

cling'stone' peach' *s* pesca duracino

clinic ['klɪnɪk] *s* clinica

clinical ['klɪnɪkəl] *adj* clinico

clinician [klɪ'nɪʃən] *s* clinico

clink [klɪŋk] *s* tintinnio; (slang) gattabuia ‖ *tr* (*glasses*) toccare ‖ *intr* tintinnare

clinker ['klɪŋkər] *s* clinker *m*; mattone vetrificato; (slang) sbaglio

clip [klɪp] *s* (*of hair*) taglio; (*of wool*) tosatura; (*speed*) passo rapido; clip *f*, fermaglio; (*large clip*) fermacarte *m*; (*for cartridges*) caricatore *m*; (coll) colpo ‖ *v* (*pret & pp* **clipped**); *ger* **clipping**) *tr* tagliare, tosare; (*words*) mangiare, storpiare; (*paper*) ritagliare; ritenere; (coll) battere ‖ *intr* andare di buon passo

clipper ['klɪpər] *s* tagliatore *m*; (aer, naut) clipper *m*; **clippers** (*for hair*) tosatrice *f*; (*for nails*) pinze *fpl* per le unghie

clipping ['klɪpɪŋ] *s* taglio; (*from newspaper*) ritaglio

clique [klik] *s* cricca, chiesuola

cloak [klok] *s* mantello, manto; (fig) velo, maschera ‖ *tr* ammantare, velare

cloak'-and-dag'ger *adj* d'avventura

cloak'-and-sword' *adj* di cappa e spada

cloak'room' *s* guardaroba *m*

clock [klɑk] *s* orologio; (*with pendulum*) pendolo, pendola; (*on stocking*) freccia ‖ *tr* registrare, cronometrare

clock'mak'er *s* orologiaio

clock' tow'er *s* torre *f* dell'orologio

clock'wise' *adj & adv* nella direzione delle lancette dell'orologio

clock'work' *s* movimento d'orologeria; **like clockwork** come un orologio

clod [klɑd] *s* zolla; (fig) tonto

clod'hop'per *s* (*shoe*) scarpone *m*; (fig) villano, bifolco

clog [klɑg] *s* intoppo; (*to impede movement*) pastoia; scarpone *m*, zoccolo ‖ *v* (*pret & pp* **clogged**; *ger* **clogging**) *tr* intoppare; (*to hold back*) impastoiare ‖ *intr* otturarsi, ostruirsi

cloister ['klɔɪstər] *s* chiostro ‖ *tr* rinchiudere in un chiostro

close [klos] *adj* vicino; (*translation*)

fedele; (*air in room*) male arieggiato; (*weather*) soffocante; (*stingy*) avaro; limitato, senza gioco; (*haircut*) corto; (*friend*) intimo; (*hit*) preciso; (*enclosed*) chiuso; (*narrow*) stretto || *adv* da vicino; **close to** vicino a || [kloz] *s* fine *f*, conclusione; **to bring to a close** concludere || *tr* chiudere; otturare; concludere; **to close down** chiudere completamente; **to close out** vendere in liquidazione; **to close up** bloccare || *intr* chiudersi; serrarsi; **to close down** chiudersi completamente; **to close in on** venire alle prese con; **to close up** bloccarsi; (*said of a wound*) rimarginarsi

close' call' [klos] *s* rischio scampato per miracolo

closed' chap'ter *s* affare chiuso

closed' cir'cuit *s* circuito chiuso

closed' sea'son *s* periodo di caccia o pesca vietata

closefisted ['klos'fɪstɪd] *adj* taccagno

close'-fit'ing [klos] *adj* attillato

close-lipped ['klos'lɪpt] *adj* riservato

closely ['kloslɪ] *adv* da vicino; strettamente; fedelmente; attentamente

close' quar'ters [klos] *spl* (*cramped space*) pigia pigia *m*; **at close quarters** a corpo a corpo

close' quote' [kloz] *s* fine *f* della citazione

close' shave' [klos] *s*—**to have a close shave** farsi fare la barba a contropelo; (*coll*) scamparla per un pelo

closet ['klɑzɪt] *s* armadio a muro; (*small private room*) gabinetto; (*for keeping clothing*) ripostiglio || *tr*—**to be closeted with** essere in conciliabolo con

close'-up' [klos] *s* (mov) primo piano

closing ['klozɪŋ] *s* fine *f*, conclusione

clos'ing price' *s* ultimo corso

clot [klɑt] *s* grumo, coagulo || *v* (*pret & pp* **clotted**) *ger* **clotting**) *intr* raggrumarsi, coagularsi

cloth [klɔθ] *or* [klɑθ] *s* panno, tessuto, stoffa; abito; (*for binding books*) tela; **the cloth** il clero

clothe [kloð] *v* (*pret & pp* **clothed** *or* **clad** [klæd]) *tr* vestire, rivestire, coprire

clothes [kloz] *or* [kloðz] *spl* vestiti *mpl*, abiti *mpl*; (*for a bed*) coltre *f*; **to change clothes** cambiarsi

clothes'bas'ket *s* cesto della biancheria

clothes'brush' *s* spazzola per vestiti

clothes' dry'er *s* asciugatrice *f*

clothes' hang'er *s* attaccapanni *m*

clothes'horse' *s* cavalletto per stendere il bucato; elegantone *m*

clothes'line' *s* corda per stendere il bucato

clothes' moth' *s* tarma, tignola

clothes'pin' *s* molletta

clothes' tree' *s* attaccapanni *m*

clothier ['kloðjər] *s* negoziante *m* di confezioni; mercante *m* di panno

clothing ['kloðɪŋ] *s* vestiti *mpl*, vestiario

cloud [klaud] *s* nuvola, nube *f*; (*great number*) nuvolo; macchia; sospetto

|| *tr* annuvolare; offuscare || *intr* annuvolarsi; offuscarsi

cloud' bank' *s* banco di nubi

cloud'burst' *s* acquazzone *m*, nubifragio

cloud'-capped' *adj* coperto di nubi

cloudless ['klaudlɪs] *adj* senza nubi

cloud·y ['klaudi] *adj* (**-ier; -iest**) nuvoloso, annuvolato; confuso; tenebroso

clout [klaut] *s* (coll) schiaffo || *tr* (coll) schiaffeggiare

clove [klov] *s* chiodo di garofano; (*of garlic*) spicchio

cloven-hoofed ['klovən'huft] *adj* dal piede biforcuto; demoniaco

clover ['klovər] *s* trifoglio; **in clover** come un papa

clo'ver-leaf' *s* (**-leaves** [,livz]) foglia di trifoglio; incrocio stradale a quadrifoglio

clown [klaun] *s* pagliaccio, buffone *m* || *intr* fare il pagliaccio

clownish ['klaunɪʃ] *adj* buffonesco, clownesco, claunesco

cloy [klɔɪ] *tr* saziare fino alla nausea

club [klʌb] *s* bastone *m*; circolo, società *f*; (*playing card*) fiore *m* || *v* (*pret & pp* **clubbed**) *ger* **clubbing**) *tr* bastonare || *intr*—**to club together** unirsi

club' car' *s* vagone *m* con servizio di buffet

club'house' *s* sede *f* di un circolo

club'man' *s* (**-men**) frequentatore *m* di circoli

club'room' *s* sala delle riunioni

club' sand'wich *s* sandwich *m* a tre fette di pane con insalata

club'wom'an *s* (**-wom'en**) frequentatrice *f* di circoli

cluck [klʌk] *s* (il) chiocciare || *intr* chiocciare

clue [klu] *s* traccia, indizio

clump [klʌmp] *s* gruppo, massa; (*of earth*) zolla || *intr* camminare con passo pesante

clum·sy ['klʌmzi] *adj* (**-sier; -siest**) goffo, malaccorto, sgraziato

cluster ['klʌstər] *s* gruppo; (*of grapes*) grappolo; (*of bees*) sciame *m*; (*of stars*) ammasso; (*of people*) folla || *tr* raggruppare || *intr* raggrupparsi

clutch [klʌtʃ] *s* presa; (*claw*) grinfia; (*of chickens*) covata; (mach) innesto; (aut) frizione; **clutches** grinfie *fpl*; **to throw the clutch in** innestare la marcia; **to throw the clutch out** disinnestare la marcia || *tr* afferrare, aggrappare || *intr*—**to clutch at** aggrapparsi a

clutter ['klʌtər] *tr*—**to clutter up** ingombrare alla rinfusa

coach [kotʃ] *s* carrozza, vettura; vagone *m*; (*automobile*) berlina; autobus *m*; (*trainer*) allenatore *m*; (*teacher*) ripetitore *m* || *tr* allenare; preparare

coach' house' *s* rimessa

coaching ['kotʃɪŋ] *s* suggerimento; (*in school*) ripetizione; (sports) allenamento

coach'man *s* (**-men**) cocchiere *m*

coagulate [ko'ægjə,let] *tr* coagulare || *intr* coagularsi

coal [kol] *s* carbone *m*; (*piece of burning wood*) tizzone *m*; **to call** or **haul over the coals** rimproverare || *tr* rifornire di carbone || *intr* rifornirsi di carbone; (*naut*) fare carbone

coal'bin' *s* carbonaia

coal' deal'er *s* (*wholesale*) negoziante *m* di carbone; (*retail*) carbonaio

coal' field' *s* bacino carbonifero

coal' gas' *s* gas *m* illuminante

coalition [,ko·ə'lɪʃən] *s* coalizione

coal' mine' *s* miniera di carbone

coal' oil' *s* cherosene *m*

coal' scut'tle *s* secchio del carbone

coal' tar' *s* catrame *m*

coal' yard' *s* carbonaia, carboniera

coarse [kors] *adj* (*manners*) volgare, ordinario; (*unrefined*) greggio; (*lacking refinement in manners*) rozzo, grossolano

coast [kost] *s* costa; discesa a ruota libera; **the coast is clear** la via è libera || *tr* costeggiare || *intr* costeggiare; scendere a ruota libera

coastal ['kostəl] *adj* costiero

coaster ['kostər] *s* nave *f* di cabotaggio; (*amusement*) otto volante, montagna russa; (*small tray*) sottobicchiere *m*

coast'er brake' *s* freno a contropedale

coast' guard' *s* guardacoste *m*

coast'-guard cut'ter *s* guardacoste *m*

coast'ing trade' *s* cabotaggio

coast'land' *s* costa

coast'line' *s* linea costiera, litorale *m*

coast'wise' *adv* lungo la costa

coat [kot] *s* soprabito; cappotto; (*jacket*) giacca; (*hide of man and animals*) mantello; (*of paint*) mano *f*; (*layer*) strato || *tr* vestire, proteggere; ricoprire, coprire

coat'ed ['kotɪd] *adj* rivestito; (*tongue*) patinato

coat' hang'er *s* attaccapanni *m*

coating ['kotɪŋ] *s* rivestimento; (*of paint*) mano *f*; (*of cement*) strato; (*cloth*) tessuto per abiti

coat' of arms' *s* scudo, stemma *m*

coat'room' *s* guardaroba *m*

coat'tail' *s* falda

coax [koks] *tr* blandire; ottenere con lusinghe

cob [kab] *s* spiga di granturco; (*horse*) cavallo da tiro; (*swan*) cigno maschio

cobalt ['kobɔlt] *s* cobalto

cobble ['kabəl] *s* ciottolo || *tr* acciottolare; (*to mend*) raccomodare, riparare

cobbler ['kablər] *s* calzolaio, ciabattino; (*pie*) torta di frutta

cob'ble·stone' *s* ciottolo

cob'web' *s* tela di ragno, ragnatela

cocaine [ko'ken] *s* cocaina

cock [kak] *s* gallo; (*faucet*) rubinetto; (*of gun*) cane *m*; (*of the eye*) ammicco; (*of nose*) angolo (del naso) rivolto all'insù; (*of hay*) covone *m* || *tr* (*a gun*) armare; (*the head*) drizzare

cockade [ka'ked] *s* coccarda

cock-a-doodle-doo ['kakə,dudəl'du] *s* chicchirichì *m*

cock'-and-bull' sto'ry *s* racconto incredibile

cocked' hat' *s* tricorno, cappello tricorno; **to knock into a cocked hat** (*slang*) distruggere completamente

cockeyed ['kak,aɪd] *adj* strabico; (*slang*) sbilenco; (*slang*) sciocco, scemo

cockle ['kakəl] *s* (*mollusk*) cardio; (*weed*) loglio; (*boat*) barchetta; (*wrinkle*) grinza; **to warm the cockles of one's heart** far bene al cuore || *intr* raggrinzirsi

cock' of the walk' *s* gallo del pollaio

cock'pit' *s* (*of boat*) cabina; (*aer*) carlinga; (*naut*) cassero di poppa

cock'roach' *s* scarafaggio, blatta

cocks'comb' *s* cresta di gallo; berretto da buffone

cock'sure' *adj* ostinato; troppo sicuro di sé stesso

cock'tail' *s* cocktail *m*

cock'tail par'ty *s* cocktail *m*

cock·y ['kaki] *adj* (*-ier; -iest*) impudente, presuntuoso

cocoa ['koko] *s* (*bean*) cacao; (*drink*) cioccolata; (*tree*) cocco

coconut ['kokə,nʌt] *s* noce *f* di cocco

co'conut palm' or **tree'** *s* cocco

cocoon [kə'kun] *s* bozzolo

cod [kad] *s* merluzzo

C.O.D. ['si'o'di] *s* (*letterword*) (**Collect on Delivery**) contro assegno

coddle ['kadəl] *tr* vezzeggiare

code [kod] *s* codice *m*, cifra; **in code** in codice, in cifra || *tr* mettere in codice or in cifra; cifrare

codex ['kodeks] *s* (**codices** ['kodɪ,siz] or ['kodɪ,sɪz]) codice *m*

cod'fish' *s* merluzzo

codger ['kadʒər] *s*—**old codger** (coll) vecchietto

codicil ['kadɪsɪl] *s* codicillo

codi·fy ['kadɪ,faɪ] or ['kodɪ,faɪ] *v* (*pret & pp* **-fied**) *tr* codificare

cod'-liver oil' *s* olio di fegato di merluzzo

coed ['co,ed] *s* studentessa di scuola mista

coeducation [,ko,edʒə'keʃən] *s* coeducazione

co'educa'tional school' [,ko·edʒə'keʃənəl] *s* scuola mista

coefficient [,ko·ɪ'fɪʃənt] *s* coefficiente *m*

coerce [ko'ʌrs] *tr* forzare, costringere

coercion [ko'ʌrʃən] *s* coercizione

coexist [,ko·ɪg'zɪst] *intr* coesistere

coffee ['kɔfi] or ['kafi] *s* caffè *m*; **ground coffee** caffè macinato; **roasted coffee** caffè torrefatto

cof'fee bean' *s* chicco di caffè

cof'fee·cake' *s* pasticcino (da mangiarsi con il caffè)

cof'fee grind'er *s* macinino da caffè, macinacaffè *m*

cof'fee grounds' *spl* fondi *mpl* di caffè

cof'fee house' *s* caffè *m*

cof'fee mak'er *s* macchinetta del caffè

cof'fee mill' s macinino del caffè, macinacaffè m

cof'fee·pot' s caffettiera

cof'fee shop' s caffè m

coffer ['kɔfər] or ['kɑfər] s forziere m; (ceiling) soffitto a cassettoni; (archit) cassettone m; **coffers** tesoro

coffin ['kɔfɪn] or ['kɑfɪn] s bara

cog [kɑg] s dente m d'ingranaggio; ruota dentata; **to slip a cog** fare un errore

cogent ['kodʒənt] adj convincente, persuasivo

cogitate ['kɑdʒɪ ,tet] tr & intr cogitare, ponzare

cognac ['konjæk] or ['kɑnjæk] s cognac m

cognate ['kɑgnet] adj consanguineo, parente, affine || s parola dello stesso ceppo linguistico; consanguineo, parente mf

cognizance ['kɑgnɪzəns] or ['kɑnɪzəns] s conoscenza; **to take cognizance of** prendere conoscenza di

cognizant ['kɑgnɪzənt] or ['kɑnɪzənt] adj informato, al corrente

cog'wheel' s ruota dentata

cohabit [ko'hæbɪt] intr convivere; (archaic) coabitare

coheir [ko'er] s coerede mf

cohere [ko'hɪr] intr aderire; (fig) avere nesso

coherent [ko'hɪrənt] adj coerente

coiffeur [kwɑ'fʌr] s parrucchiere m per signora; (Brit) parrucchiere m

coiffure [kwɑ'fjur] s pettinatura || tr pettinare

coil [kɔɪl] s (of rope) rotolo; (of pipe) serpentino; (of wire) bobina, avvolgimento || tr arrotolare || intr arrotolarsi

coil' spring' s molla a spirale, molla elicoidale

coin [kɔɪn] s moneta; **to pay back in one's own coin** pagare della stessa moneta; **to toss a coin** giocare a testa o croce || tr (money) coniare, battere; (words) inventare, creare; **to coin money** battere moneta; (coll) fare soldoni

coincide [,ko·ɪn'saɪd] intr coincidere

coincidence [ko'ɪnsɪdəns] s coincidenza

coke [kok] s coke m, carbone m coke

colander ['kʌləndər] or ['kɑləndər] s colabrodo, colapasta m

cold [kold] adj freddo; **it is cold** (said of weather) fa freddo; **to be cold** (said of a person) avere freddo || s freddo; (ailment) raffreddore m; **out in the cold** solo soletto; **to catch cold** pigliare freddo, pigliarsi un raffreddore

cold' blood' s—**in cold blood** a sangue freddo

cold'-blood'ed adj insensibile; (sensitive to cold) freddoloso; (animal) a sangue freddo

cold' chis'el s tagliaferro

cold' com'fort s magra consolazione

cold' cream' s crema emolliente

cold' cuts' spl salumi mpl, affettato

cold' feet' spl—**to get cold feet** (coll) perdersi d'animo

cold'-heart'ed adj—**to be coldhearted** avere il cuore duro

coldness ['koldnɪs] s freddezza

cold' shoul'der s—**to get the cold shoulder** (coll) essere trattato con freddezza; **to turn a cold shoulder on** (coll) trattare con freddezza

cold' snap' s freddo breve e improvviso

cold' stor'age s conservazione a freddo

cold' war' s guerra fredda

cold' wave' s ondata di freddo

coleslaw ['kol ,slɔ] s insalata di cavolo cappuccio

colic ['kɑlɪk] adj colico || s colica

coliseum [,kɑlɪ'si·əm] s stadio, arena || **Coliseum** s Colosseo

collaborate [kə'læbə ,ret] intr collaborare

collaborationist [kə ,læbə're ʃənɪst] s collaborazionista mf

collaborator [kə'læbə ,retər] s collaboratore m

collapse [kə'læps] s (of business) fallimento; (e.g., of a roof) caduta; (of a person) collasso || tr piegare || intr (to shrink) restringersi, sgonfiarsi; (said of a business) fallire; (said of health) venir meno; (said, e.g., of a roof) cadere, crollare

collapsible [kə'læpsɪbəl] adj pieghevole, smontabile

collar ['kɑlər] s (of shirt) colletto; (for dog or horse) collare m; (ring) anello; (short piece of pipe) manicotto || tr afferrare per il collo, catturare

col'lar·band' s cinturino della camicia

col'lar·bone' s clavicola

collate [kə'let] or ['kɑlet] tr collazionare, confrontare

collateral [kə'lætərəl] adj collaterale; accessorio, addizionale || s collaterale m

colleague ['kɑlig] s collega mf

collect ['kɑlɛkt] s (eccl) colletta || [kə'lɛkt] adv contro assegno; (telp) pagamento all'abbonato chiamato || tr raccogliere, riunire; (e.g., stamps) collezionare; (mail) levare; (bills) incassare; (ideas) coordinare; (thoughts) riordinare; (e.g., classroom papers) raccogliere; (taxes) riscuotere; **to collect oneself** riprendersi, riprendere il controllo di sé stesso || intr (for the poor) fare la colletta; riunirsi, raccogliersi

collected [kə'lɛktɪd] adj raccolto; equilibrato, padrone di sè

collection [kə'lɛk ʃən] s collezione; (for the poor) colletta; (of mail) levata; (heap) deposito; (of taxes) esazione; (of bills) riscossione

collec'tion a'gency s agenzia di riscossione

collective [kə'lɛktɪv] adj collettivo

collector [kə'lɛktər] s (of stamps) collezionista mf; (of taxes) esattore m; (of tickets) controllore m

college ['kɑlɪdʒ] s scuola superiore,

università *f*; (*e.g., of medicine*) facoltà *f*; (*electoral*) collegio
collide [kə'laɪd] *intr* collidere, scontrarsi
collie ['kɑli] *s* collie *m*
collier ['kɑljər] *s* (*ship*) carboniera;
(*min*) minatore *m* di carbone
collier·y ['kɑljəri] *s* (*-ies*) miniera di
carbone
collision [kə'lɪʒən] *s* collisione
colloid ['kɑlɔɪd] *adj* colloidale ‖ *s*
colloide *m*
colloquial [kə'lokwɪ·əl] *adj* familiare,
colloquiale
colloquialism [kə'lokwɪ·ə‚lɪzəm] *s*
espressione familiare
collo·quy ['kɑləkwi] *s* (*-quies*) colloquio
collusion [kə'luʒən] *s* collusione; **to be
in collusion with** essere d'intelligenza
con
cologne [kə'lon] *s* acqua di colonia,
colonia ‖ **Cologne** *s* Colonia
colon ['kolən] *s* (*anat*) colon *m*;
(*gram*) due punti *mpl*
colonel ['kʌrnəl] *s* colonnello
colonist ['kɑlənɪst] *s* colono, coloniale
m
colonize ['kɑlə‚naɪz] *tr & intr* colonizzare
colonnade [‚kɑlə'ned] *s* colonnato
colo·ny ['kɑləni] *s* (*-nies*) colonia
color ['kʌlər] *s* colore *m*; **off color**
sbiadito, scolorito; (slang) sporco,
volgare; **the colors** i colori, la bandiera; **to call to the colors** chiamare
in servizio militare; **to change color**
cambiar colore; arrossire; impallidire; **to give or lend color to** far
parere probabile; **to lose color** impallidire; **to show one's colors** mostrarsi come si è; **under color of**
sotto il pretesto di ‖ *tr* colorare; (fig)
colorire ‖ *intr* arrossire
col'or-blind' *adj* daltonico
colored ['kʌlərd] *adj* colorato; (*person*) di colore; esagerato
colorful ['kʌlərfəl] *adj* colorito, espressivo
col'or guard' *s* guardia d'onore alla
bandiera
coloring ['kʌlərɪŋ] *s* colorazione; colore *m*; pigmento; (fig) specie *f*
colorless ['kʌlərlɪs] *adj* incolore, in-
coloro
col'or photog'raphy *s* fotografia a colori
col'or ser'geant *s* sergente *m* portabandiera
col'or tel'evision *s* televisione a colori
colossal [kə'lɑsəl] *adj* colossale
colossus [kə'lɑsəs] *s* colosso
colt [kolt] *s* puledro
Columbus [kə'lʌmbəs] *s* Colombo
column ['kɑləm] *s* colonna
columnist ['kɑləmɪst] *s* giornalista
incaricato di una colonna speciale;
articolista *m*
coma ['komə] *s* coma *m*
comb [kom] *s* pettine *m*; (*for horse*)
striglia; (*of hen or wave*) cresta;
(*honeycomb*) favo ‖ *tr* pettinare;

(fig) esaminare minuziosamente ‖
intr (*said of waves*) frangersi
com·bat ['kɑmbæt] *s* combattimento ‖
['kɑmbæt] or [kəm'bæt] *v* (*pret &
pp* **-bated** or **-batted**; *ger* **-bating or
-batting**) *tr & intr* combattere
combatant ['kɑmbətənt] *s* combattente
mf
com'bat du'ty *s* servizio in zona di
guerra
combination [‚kɑmbɪ'neʃən] *s* combinazione
combine ['kɑmbaɪn] *s* consorzio; (pol)
coalizione; mieto-trebbiatrice *f* ‖
[kəm'baɪn] *tr* combinare ‖ *intr*
combinarsi
combin'ing form' *s* membro di parola
composta
combo ['kɑmbo] *s* orchestrina
combustible [kəm'bʌstɪbəl] *adj & s*
combustibile *m*
combustion [kəm'bʌstʃən] *s* combustione
come [kʌm] *v* (*pret* **came** [kem]; *pp*
come) *intr* venire; arrivare; (*to become*) diventare; (*to amount*) ammontare; **come!** macchè!; **come
along!** andiamo!; **come in!** avanti!,
entri!; **come on!** andiamo!; avanti!,
coraggio!; **to come about** accadere,
succedere; **to come across** incontrarsi con; (slang) pagare; **to come
around** cedere; mettersi d'accordo;
(*said of health*) rimettersi; **to come
at** raggiungere; (*to attack*) attaccare;
to come back ritornare; **to come between** mettersi fra; **to come by** ottenere; essere trasmesso; **to come down**
scendere; deca-
dere; essere trasmesso; **to come down
with** ammalarsi di; **to come forward**
farsi avanti; **to come in** entrare, passare; **to come in for** ricevere; **to
come into** ricevere; ereditare; **to
come off** succedere; riuscire; **to come
on** mostrarsi; migliorare; incontrarsi;
to come out uscire; debuttare in società; andare a finire; **to come out
with** uscire con; mostrare; **to come
over** succedere a, e.g., **what came
over him?** che gli è successo?; **to
come through** riuscire; **to come to**
riprendere i sensi; **to come under**
essere di competenza di; appartenere
a; **to come up** salire; **to come up to**
salire fino a; avvicinarsi a; **to come
up with** raggiungere; produrre, fornire; proporre
come'back' *s* (coll) ritorno; (slang)
pronta risposta; **to stage a comeback**
(coll) ritornare in auge
comedian [kə'midɪ·ən] *s* attore comico; (*author*) commediografo;
(*amusing person*) commediante *mf*
comedienne [kə‚midɪ'ɛn] *s* attrice co-
mica
come'down' *s* (coll) rovescio di fortuna
come·dy ['kɑmədi] *s* (*-dies*) commedia
come·ly ['kʌmli] *adj* (*-lier; -liest*)
bello, grazioso
comet ['kɑmɪt] *s* cometa
comfort ['kʌmfərt] *s* conforto, sollievo;

(ease) benessere *m* || *tr* confortare, alleviare

comfortable ['kʌmfərtəbəl] *adj* comodo, agiato; *(e.g., income)* (coll) bastante || *s* coltre *f*

comforter ['kʌmfərtər] *s* consolatore *m*; *(bedcover)* coltre *f*; sciarpa di lana || **the Comforter** lo Spirito Santo, lo Spirito Consolatore

comforting ['kʌmfərtɪŋ] *adj* confortante

com'fort sta'tion *s* latrina pubblica

comic ['kɑmɪk] *adj* comico || *s (actor)* comico; comicità *f*; **comics** fumetti *mpl*

comical ['kɑmɪkəl] *adj* comico

com'ic book' *s* libretto a fumetti

com'ic op'era *s* opera buffa

com'ic strip' *s* racconto umoristico a fumetti

coming ['kʌmɪŋ] *adj* venturo, prossimo; promettente || *s* venuta

com'ing out' *s* debutto in società; *(e.g., of stock)* emissione

comma ['kɑmə] *s* virgola

command [kə'mænd] *or* [kə'mɑnd] *s* comando; *(e.g., of a language)* padronanza || *tr* comandare, ordinare; *(to overlook)* dominare; *(to be able to have)* disporre di || *intr* avere il comando

commandant [ˌkɑmən'dænt] *or* [ˌkɑmən'dɑnt] *s* comandante *m*

commandeer [ˌkɑmən'dɪr] *tr* requisire

commander [kə'mændər] *or* [kə'mɑndər] *s (of knighthood)* commendatore *m*; (mil) comandante *m*; (nav) capitano di vascello

command'er in chief' *s* comandante *m* in capo

command'ing of'ficer *s* comandante *m*

commandment [kə'mændmənt] *or* [kə'mɑndmənt] *s* comandamento

command' mod'ule *s* (rok) modulo di comando

commando [kə'mændo] *s* guastatore *m*

commemorate [kə'memə͵ret] *tr* commemorare, celebrare

commence [kə'mens] *tr & intr* cominciare

commencement [kə'mensmənt] *s* inizio, esordio; *(in a school)* cerimonia per la distribuzione dei diplomi

commend [kə'mend] *tr* lodare; *(to entrust)* raccomandare, affidare

commendable [kə'mendəbəl] *adj (person)* lodevole; *(act)* commendevole

commendation [ˌkɑmən'deʃən] *s* lode *f*; raccomandazione; (mil) citazione

comment ['kɑment] *s* commento || *tr* commentare || *intr* fare commenti; **to comment on** fare commenti su

commentary ['kɑmən͵teri] *s (-ies)* commentario

commentator ['kɑmən͵tetər] *s* commentatore *m*

commerce ['kɑmərs] *s* commercio

commercial [kə'merʃəl] *adj* commerciale || *s* (rad, telv) programma *m* di pubblicità; (rad, telv) annunzio pubblicitario

commiserate [kə'mɪzə͵ret] *intr—to*

commiserate with commiserare, compiangere

commissar ['kɑmɪ͵sɑr] *or* [ˌkɑmɪ'sɑr] *s* commissario del popolo

commissary ['kɑmɪ͵seri] *s (-ies) (store)* economato; *(deputy)* commissario; *(in army)* intendente *m*

commission [kə'mɪʃən] *s* commissione; *(e.g., in army)* nomina, brevetto; autorità *f*; *(of a crime)* perpetrazione; (il) fare; **in commission** in servizio, in uso; **out of commission** fuori servizio || *tr* nominare, dare un brevetto a; autorizzare; *(a ship)* armare

commis'sioned of'ficer *s* (mil, nav) ufficiale *m*

commissioner [kə'mɪʃənər] *s* commissario; membro di una commissione

commis'sion mer'chant *s* sensale *m*

com·mit [kə'mɪt] *v (pret & pp -mitted; ger -mitting) tr* commettere, perpetrare; *(to deliver)* affidare, consegnare; *(to imprison)* mandare in prigione; *(an insane person)* internare; *(to refer)* rinviare; *(to involve)* compromettere; **to commit oneself** compromettersi; **to commit to memory** imparare a memoria; **to commit to writing** mettere in iscritto

commitment [kə'mɪtmənt] *s (act of committing)* commissione; *(to an asylum)* internamento; promessa; (law) mandato

committal [kə'mɪtəl] *s* consegna; promessa

committee [kə'mɪti] *s* comitato, commissione

commode [kə'mod] *s (chest of drawers)* cassettone *m*; *(washstand)* lavabo; seggetta, comoda

commodious [kə'modɪ‧əs] *adj* spazioso; conveniente

commodity [kə'mɑdɪti] *s (-ties)* merce *f*; articolo di prima necessità

commod'ity exchange' *s* borsa merci

common ['kɑmən] *adj* comune || *s* fondo comunale; pascolo comune; **commons** gente *f* non nobile; refettorio; **in common** in comune || **the Commons** la Camera dei Comuni

com'mon car'rier *s* impresa di trasporti pubblici

commoner ['kɑmənər] *s* plebeo, borghese *m*; membro della Camera dei Comuni

com'mon law' *s* consuetudine *f*, diritto consuetudinario

com'mon-law mar'riage *s* matrimonio basato sulla mera convivenza

commonly ['kɑmənli] *adv* generalmente

com'mon‧place *adj* banale, ordinario || *s* banalità *f*, cosa ordinaria

com'mon sense' *s* senso comune

com'mon-sense' *adj* giudizioso

com'mon stock' *s* azione ordinaria; azioni ordinarie

commonweal ['kɑmən͵wil] *s* bene pubblico

com'mon‧wealth' *s (citizens of a state)* cittadinanza; repubblica; *(one of the*

50 *states of the U.S.A.*) stato; comunità *f*, federazione

commotion [kə'moʃən] *s* agitazione

commune [kə'mjun] *s* comune *m* ‖ *intr* confabulare; (eccl) comunicarsi

communicate [kə'mjunɪ,ket] *tr* & *intr* comunicare

communicating [kə'mjunɪ,ketɪŋ] *adj* comunicante

communication [kə,mjunɪ'keʃən] *s* comunicazione; **communications** sistema *m* di comunicazione; mezzi *mpl* di comunicazione

communicative [kə'mjunɪ,ketɪv] *adj* comunicativo

Communion [kə'mjunjən] *s* Comunione; **to take Communion** comunicarsi

communiqué [kə,mjunɪ'ke] *or* [kə-'mjunɪ,ke] *s* comunicato

communism ['kamjə,nɪzəm] *s* comunismo

communist ['kamjənɪst] *s* comunista *mf*

communi-ty [kə'mjunɪti] *s* (-ties) (*people living together*) comunità *f*; (*sharing together*) comunanza; (*neighborhood*) circondario

commu'nity cen'ter *s* centro sociale

commu'nity chest' *s* fondo di beneficenza

commuta'tion tick'et [,kamjə'teʃən] *s* biglietto d'abbonamento

commutator ['kamjə,tetər] *s* (*switch*) commutatore *m*; (*of dynamo or motor*) collettore *m*

commute [kə'mjut] *tr* commutare ‖ *intr* commutare; fare il pendolare

commuter [kə'mjutər] *s* pendolare *mf*

compact [kəm'pækt] *adj* compatto ‖ ['kampækt] *s* (*small case for face powder*) portacipria *m*; (*agreement*) accordo; (*small car*) utilitaria

companion [kəm'pænjən] *s* compagno; (*one of two items*) pendant *m*; (*lady*) dama di compagnia

compan'ion·ship' *s* cameratismo

compan'ion·way' *s* (naut) scaletta per andare sottocoperta

compa·ny ['kampəni] *s* (-nies) compagnia; (coll) ospite *m or* ospiti *mpl*; (naut) equipaggio; **to bear company** accompagnare; **to be good company** essere simpatico; **to keep company** (*said of a couple*) andare insieme; **to keep company with** accompagnare; (coll) fare la corte a; **to part company** separarsi

comparable ['kampərəbəl] *adj* comparabile, paragonabile

comparative [kəm'pærətɪv] *adj* comparativo; (*e.g., anatomy*) comparato ‖ *s* (gram) comparativo

compare [kəm'per] *s*—**beyond compare** incomparabile ‖ *tr* confrontare; **compared to** a confronto di, in confronto a

comparison [kəm'pærɪsən] *s* confronto; (gram) comparazione; **in comparison with** in confronto a, a confronto di

compartment [kəm'partmənt] *s* com-

partimento; (naut) compartimento stagno; (rr) compartimento

compass ['kʌmpəs] *s* (*instrument for showing direction*) bussola; (*boundary*) limite *m*; (*range*) ambito; (*range of voice*) portata; (*of a wall*) cerchia; (*circuit*) circuito; (*drawing instrument*) compasso; **compasses** (*drawing instrument*) compasso ‖ *tr* girare intorno a; comprendere; **to compass about** accerchiare

com'pass card' *s* rosa dei venti

compassion [kəm'pæʃən] *s* compassione

compassionate [kəm'pæʃənɪt] *adj* compassionevole

com'pass saw' *s* gattuccio

com·pel [kəm'pel] *v* (*pret & pp* **-pelled;** *ger* **-pelling**) *tr* forzare, obbligare

compelling [kəm'pelɪŋ] *adj* imperioso, coercitivo

compendious [kəm'pendɪ·əs] *adj* compendioso, conciso

compensate ['kampən,set] *tr* & *intr* compensare

compensation [,kampən'seʃən] *s* compensazione; (*pay*) pagamento; (*something given to offset a loss*) risarcimento, indennità *f*

compete [kəm'pit] *intr* competere

competence ['kampɪtəns] *or* **competency** ['kampɪtənsi] *s* (*fitness*) abilità *f*; (*money*) agiatezza; (*authority*) competenza

competent ['kampɪtənt] *adj* abile; competente

competition [,kampɪ'tɪʃən] *s* competizione, gara; (*in business*) concorrenza

competitive [kəm'petɪtɪv] *adj* competitivo; (*based on competition*) di concorso

compet'itive pric'es *spl* prezzi *mpl* di concorrenza

competitor [kəm'petɪtər] *s* competitore *m*, concorrente *mf*; rivale *mf*

compilation [,kampɪ'leʃən] *s* compilazione

compile [kəm'paɪl] *tr* compilare

complacence [kəm'plesəns] *or* **complacency** [kəm'plesənsi] *s* compiacenza; compiacenza di sé stesso

complacent [kəm'plesənt] *adj* compiaciuto *or* soddisfatto con sé stesso

complain [kəm'plen] *intr* lagnarsi

complainant [kəm'plenənt] *s* (law) querelante *mf*

complaint [kəm'plent] *s* lagnanza, reclamo; (*sickness*) malattia; (law) querela

complaisance [kəm'plezəns] *or* ['kamplɪ,zæns] *s* compiacenza

complaisant [kəm'plezənt] *or* ['kamplɪ,zænt] *adj* compiacente, cortese

complement ['kamplɪmənt] *s* complemento; (naut) equipaggio ‖ ['kamplɪ,ment] *tr* completare

complete [kəm'plit] *adj* completo; (*done*) finito ‖ *tr* completare, finire

completion [kəm'pliʃən] *s* completamento, compimento

complex [kəm'pleks] *or* ['kampleks]

adj complesso, complicato || [ˈkam-
plɛks] *s* complesso
complexion [kəmˈplɛkʃən] *s* (*of skin*)
carnagione; (*appearance*) aspetto;
(*viewpoint*) punto di vista
compliance [kəmˈplaɪ·əns] *s* condiscendenza, arrendevolezza; **in compliance
with** in conformità di
complicate [ˈkamplɪˌket] *tr* complicare
complicated [ˈkamplɪˌketɪd] *adj* complicato
complici·ty [kəmˈplɪsɪti] *s* (-**ties**) com-
plicità *f*
compliment [ˈkamplɪmənt] *s* compli-
mento, omaggio || [ˈkamplɪˌment]
tr—**to compliment s.o. on s.th** felicitarsi con qlcu per qlco; **to compliment s.o. with s.th** regalare qlco a
qlcu
complimentary [ˌkamplɪˈmentəri] *adj*
complimentoso, lusinghiero; (*free*)
in omaggio, gratis; (*ticket*) di favore
com·ply [kəmˈplaɪ] *v* (*pret & pp*
-**plied**) *intr* acconsentire, accondiscendere; **to comply with** accedere a
component [kəmˈponənt] *adj* compo-
nente, costituente || *s* (*component
part*) componente *m*; (*force*) componente *f*
compose [kəmˈpoz] *tr* comporre; **to
be composed of** essere composto di;
to compose oneself calmarsi
composed [kəmˈpozd] *adj* calmo, tranquillo
composer [kəmˈpozər] *s* (*peacemaker*)
conciliatore *m*; (*mus*) compositore *m*
compos'ing stick' *s* (*typ*) compositoio
composite [kəmˈpazɪt] *adj & s* composto, composito
composition [ˌkampəˈzɪʃən] *s* composizione; (*agreement*) compromesso
compositor [kəmˈpazɪtər] *s* compositore *m*
compost [ˈkampost] *s* concime *m* naturale
composure [kəmˈpoʒər] *s* calma
compote [ˈkampot] *s* (*stewed fruit*)
composta; (*dish*) compostiera
compound [ˈkampaund] *adj* composto;
(*fracture*) complesso; (archit, bot)
composito || *s* composto; parola com-
posta; (*yard*) recinto || [kamˈpaund]
tr (*to mix*) combinare; (*to settle*)
comporre; (*interest*) capitalizzare
comprehend [ˌkamprɪˈhend] *tr* comprendere
comprehensible [ˌkamprɪˈhensɪbəl] *adj*
comprensibile
comprehension [ˌkamprɪˈhenʃən] *s*
comprensione
comprehensive [ˌkamprɪˈhensɪv] *adj*
comprensivo
compress [ˈkampres] *s* compressa ||
[kamˈpres] *tr* comprimere
compressed' air' *s* aria compressa
compression [kəmˈpreʃən] *s* compres-
sione
comprise [kəmˈpraɪz] *tr* comprendere,
includere; **to be comprised of** consistere di
compromise [ˈkamprəˌmaɪz] *s* com-

promesso || *tr* (*a dispute*) transigere,
comporre; (*to put in danger*) com-
promettere || *intr* transigere, fare un
compromesso
comptroller [kənˈtrolər] *s* economo,
amministratore *m*, controllore *m*
compulsive [kəmˈpʌlsɪv] *adj* obbligatorio, coercitivo; (psychol) compul-
sivo
compulsory [kəmˈpʌlsəri] *adj* obbligatorio
compute [kəmˈpjut] *tr & intr* computare, calcolare
computer [kəmˈpjutər] *s* calcolatore
m; elaboratore *m*
comrade [ˈkamræd] or [ˈkamrɪd] *s*
camerata *m*, compagno
com'rade in arms' *s* compagno d'armi
con [kan] *s* contro || *v* (*pret & pp*
conned; *ger* **conning**) *tr* imparare a
memoria; (slang) imbrogliare
concave [ˈkankev] or [kanˈkev] *adj*
concavo
conceal [kənˈsil] *tr* nascondere; (*to
keep secret*) celare
concealment [kənˈsilmənt] *s* occulta-
mento; (*place*) nascondiglio
concede [kənˈsid] *tr* concedere
conceit [kənˈsit] *s* (*high opinion of
oneself*) presunzione; (*fanciful notion*) concetto sottile
conceited [kənˈsitɪd] *adj* vanitoso
conceivable [kənˈsivəbəl] *adj* concepi-
bile
conceive [kənˈsiv] *tr & intr* concepire
concentrate [ˈkansənˌtret] *s* concen-
trato || *tr* concentrare || *intr* concen-
trarsi; **to concentrate on** concentrarsi
in
concentra'tion camp' [ˌkansənˈtreʃən]
s campo di concentrazione
concept [ˈkansept] *s* concetto
conception [kənˈsepʃən] *s* concezione
concern [kənˈsʌrn] *s* interesse *m*;
(*worry*) ansietà *f*; (*firm*) ditta, com-
pagnia; **of concern** d'interesse ||
concernere; **as concerns** circa; **to
concern oneself** interessarsi; **to
whom it may concern** a chiunque
possa averne interesse
concerning [kənˈsʌrnɪŋ] *prep* riguardo
a
concert [ˈkansert] *s* concerto || [kən-
ˈsʌrt] *tr & intr* concertare
con'cert·mas'ter *s* primo violino
concer·to [kənˈtʃerto] *s* (-**tos** or -**ti**
[ti]) concerto
concession [kənˈseʃən] *s* concessione
conciliate [kənˈsɪlɪˌet] *tr* conciliare,
conciliarsi con
concise [kənˈsaɪs] *adj* conciso
conclude [kənˈklud] *tr* concludere ||
intr concludersi, terminare
conclusion [kənˈkluʒən] *s* conclusione;
in conclusion per finire; **to try con-
clusions with** misurarsi con
conclusive [kənˈklusɪv] *adj* decisivo,
convincente
concoct [kanˈkakt] *tr* preparare, confezionare; (*a story*) inventare
concoction [kanˈkakʃən] *s* prepara-

zione, mescolanza; *(unpleasant in taste)* intruglio

concomitant [kən'kɑmɪtənt] *adj* concomitante || *s* fatto or sintomo concomitante

concord ['kɑŋkɔrd] *s* concordia, armonia; *(treaty)* accordo; *(gram)* concordanza

concourse ['kɑŋkors] *s* confluenza; *(crowd)* affluenza, concorso; *(boulevard)* viale *m*; (rr) salone *m* principale

concrete ['kɑŋkrit] or [kɑn'krit] *adj* concreto; fatto di cemento; solido || *s* cemento, calcestruzzo || *tr* *(e.g., a sidewalk)* cementare

con'crete mix'er *s* betoniera

con·cur [kən'kʌr] *v* *(pret & pp* **-curred;** *ger* **-curring)** *intr (to work together)* concorrere; *(to agree)* essere d'accordo, aderire

concurrence [kən'kʌrəns] *s* concorso; *(agreement)* accordo

concurrent [kən'kʌrənt] *adj* concomitante, simultaneo; cooperante; armonioso

concussion [kən'kʌʃən] *s* scossa, urto; *(of brain)* commozione cerebrale

condemn [kən'dɛm] *tr* condannare; *(to take for public use)* espropriare

condemnation [,kɑndɛm'neʃən] *s* condanna

condense [kən'dɛns] *tr* condensare || *intr* condensarsi

condescend [,kɑndɪ'sɛnd] *intr* condiscendere, degnarsi

condescending [,kɑndɪ'sɛndɪŋ] *adj* condiscendente

condescension [,kɑndɪ'sɛnʃən] *s* condiscendenza, degnazione

condiment ['kɑndɪmənt] *s* condimento

condition [kən'dɪʃən] *s* condizione; clausola; **on condition that** a condizione che || *tr* condizionare; mettere in buone condizioni fisiche

conditional [kən'dɪʃənəl] *adj & s* condizionale *m*

condole [kən'dol] *intr* condolersi

condolence [kən'doləns] *s* condoglianza

condone [kən'don] *tr* condonare

conduce [kən'djus] or [kən'dus] *intr* contribuire, indurre

conducive [kən'djusɪv] or [kən'dusɪv] *adj* contribuente

conduct ['kɑndʌkt] *s* condotta; direzione || [kən'dʌkt] *tr* condurre; *(an orchestra)* dirigere; **to conduct oneself** condursi, comportarsi || *intr* dirigere

conductor [kən'dʌktər] *s* direttore *m*; *(of a streetcar)* fattorino, conduttore *m*; (phys) conduttore *m*; (rr) capotreno

conduit ['kɑndɪt] or ['kɑndu·ɪt] *s* condotto

cone [kon] *s* cono; (bot) pigna

Con'estoga wag'on ['kɑnɪ'stogə] *s* carriaggio coperto

confectioner [kən'fɛkʃənər] *s* confettiere *m*, pasticcere *m*

confec'tioners' sug'ar *s* zucchero in polvere finissimo

confectioner·y [kən'fɛkʃə,nɛri] *s* (**-ies**) confetteria, pasticceria; *(candies)* confetture *fpl*

confedera·cy [kən'fɛdərəsi] *s* (**-cies**) confederazione; lega

confederate [kən'fɛdərɪt] *s* alleato; *(in crime)* complice *mf* || [kən'fɛdə,ret] *tr* confederare || *intr* confederarsi

con·fer [kən'fʌr] *v* *(pret & pp* **-ferred;** *ger* **-ferring)** *tr* conferire || *intr* conferire, abboccarsi

conference ['kɑnfərəns] *s* conferenza

confess [kən'fɛs] *tr* confessare, ammettere || *intr* confessare, confessarsi

confession [kən'fɛʃən] *s* confessione

confessional [kən'fɛʃənəl] *s* confessionale *m*

confes'sion of faith' *s* professione di fede

confessor [kən'fɛsər] *s* confessore *m*

confetti [kən'fɛti] *s* coriandoli *mpl*

confide [kən'faɪd] *tr* confidare; *(to entrust)* affidare || *intr* confidarsi

confidence ['kɑnfɪdəns] *s* fiducia; sicurezza di sé; *(boldness)* baldanza; *(secrecy)* confidenza

confident ['kɑnfɪdənt] *adj* fiducioso; baldanzoso || *s* confidente *mf*

confidential [,kɑnfɪ'dɛnʃəl] *adj* confidenziale

confine ['kɑnfaɪn] *s* confine *m* || [kən-'faɪn] *tr* limitare; confinare; **to be confined** essere in altro stato; **to be confined to bed** dover stare a letto

confinement [kən'faɪnmənt] *s* confino; *(childbirth)* parto; *(imprisonment)* prigionia

confirm [kən'fʌrm] *tr* confermare; (eccl) cresimare

confirmed [kən'fʌrmd] *adj* *(e.g., piece of news)* confermato; *(bachelor; drunkard)* impenitente; inveterato; *(e.g., invalid)* cronico

confiscate ['kɑnfɪs,ket] *tr* confiscare

conflagration [,kɑnflə'greʃən] *s* conflagrazione

conflict ['kɑnflɪkt] *s* conflitto || [kən-'flɪkt] *intr* lottare; essere in conflitto

conflicting [kən'flɪktɪŋ] *adj* contrastante; contraddittorio

confluence ['kɑnflu·əns] *s* confluenza

conform [kən'fɔrm] *tr* conformare || *intr* conformarsi

conformi·ty [kən'fɔrmɪti] *s* (**-ties**) conformità *f*; **in conformity with** in conformità di

confound [kən'faʊnd] *tr* confondere || ['kɑn'faʊnd] *tr* maledire; **confound it!** accidenti!

confounded [kən'faʊndɪd] or ['kɑn-'faʊndɪd] *adj* maledetto; *(hateful)* odioso

confront [kən'frʌnt] *tr* affrontare, opporsi a; *(to bring face to face)* raffrontare; *(to compare)* confrontare

confrontation [,kɑnfrən'teʃən] *s* contestazione

confuse [kən'fjuz] *tr* confondere; **to get confused** confondersi

confusion [kən'fjuʒən] *s* confusione

congeal [kən'dʒil] *tr* congelare; coagulare || *intr* congelarsi; *(said, e.g., of blood)* coagularsi

congenial [kən'dʒinjəl] *adj (agreeable)* simpatico; *(having similar tastes)* affine; *(suited to one's needs or tastes)* congeniale

congenital [kən'dʒenɪtəl] *adj* congenito

con'ger eel' ['kɑŋgər] *s* grongo

congest [kən'dʒest] *tr* congestionare || *intr* essere congestionato

congestion [kən'dʒestʃən] *s* congestione

conglomerate [kən'glɑmərɪt] *adj & s* conglomerato || [kən'glɑmə,ret] *tr* conglomerare || *intr* conglomerarsi

congratulate [kən'grætʃə,let] *tr* congratularsi con

congratulation [kən,grætʃə'leʃən] *s* congratulazione, felicitazione

congregate ['kɑŋgrɪ,get] *intr* congregarsi

congregation [,kɑŋgrɪ'geʃən] *s* congregazione; fedeli *mpl* di una chiesa

congress ['kɑŋgrɪs] *s* parlamento; congresso

con'gress·man *s* (**-men**) deputato al congresso degli S.U.

con'gress·wom'an *s* (**-wom'en**) deputatessa al congresso degli S.U.

conical ['kɑnɪkəl] *adj* conico

conjecture [kən'dʒektʃər] *s* congettura || *tr & intr* congetturare

conjugate ['kɑndʒə,get] *tr* coniugare

conjugation [,kɑndʒə'geʃən] *s* coniugazione

conjunction [kən'dʒʌŋkʃən] *s* congiunzione

conjure [kən'dʒʊr] *tr (to entreat)* scongiurare || ['kɑndʒər] or ['kʌndʒər] *tr* evocare, stregare; **to conjure up** evocare || *intr* fare delle stregonerie

conk [kɑŋk] *intr—***to conk out** (slang) essere in panna; (slang) svenire

connect [kə'nekt] *tr* connettere, unire || *intr* connettersi, essere associato; *(said of public conveyances)* operare in coincidenza

connect'ing rod' [kə'nektɪŋ] *s* (mach) biella

connection [kə'nekʃən] *s* connessione; unione, associazione; *(of trains)* coincidenza; *(relative)* parente *mf*; *(e.g., of a water pipe)* allacciamento; **in connection with** rispetto a

con'ning tow'er ['kɑnɪŋ] *s* (nav) torretta

conniption [kə'nɪpʃən] *s* (slang) attacco di rabbia

connive [kə'naɪv] *intr* essere connivente; **to connive at** chiudere un occhio su

connote [kə'not] *tr* indicare, suggerire

conquer ['kɑŋkər] *tr & intr* conquistare

conqueror ['kɑŋkərər] *s* conquistatore *m*

conquest ['kɑŋkwest] *s* conquista

conscience ['kɑnʃəns] *s* coscienza; **in all conscience** a prezzo onesto; certamente

conscientious [,kɑnʃɪ'enʃəs] *adj* coscienzioso

conscien'tious objec'tor [əb'dʒektər] *s* obiettore *m* di coscienza

conscious ['kɑnʃəs] *adj (aware of one's existence)* cosciente; *(aware)* conscio, consapevole; *(lie)* consapevole; **to become conscious** riprendere i sensi

consciousness ['kɑnʃəsnɪs] *s* coscienza, conoscenza; **to lose consciousness** perdere la conoscenza

conscript ['kɑnskrɪpt] *s* coscritto || [kən'skrɪpt] *tr* coscrivere, arruolare

conscription [kən'skrɪpʃən] *s* coscrizione

consecrate ['kɑnsɪ,kret] *tr* consacrare

consecutive [kən'sekjətɪv] *adj* consecutivo; di seguito

consensus [kən'sensəs] *s* consenso

consent [kən'sent] *s* consenso; **by common consent** per comune consenso || *intr* consentire

consequence ['kɑnsɪ,kwens] *s* conseguenza

consequential [,kɑnsɪ'kwenʃəl] *adj* conseguente; importante, d'importanza; pomposo, pieno di sé

consequently ['kɑnsɪ,kwentli] *adv* conseguentemente, per conseguenza

conservation [,kɑnsər'veʃən] *s* conservazione; preservazione delle foreste

conservatism [kən'sʌrvə,tɪzəm] *s* conservatorismo

conservative [kən'sʌrvətɪv] *adj* conservatore; *(cautious)* cauto; *(preserving)* conservativo; *(free from fads)* tradizionale || *s* conservatore *m*

conservato·ry [kən'sʌrvə,tori] *s* (**-ries**) *(greenhouse)* serra; (mus) conservatorio

conserve [kən'sʌrv] *tr* conservare

consider [kən'sɪdər] *tr* considerare

considerable [kən'sɪdərəbəl] *adj (fairly large)* considerevole; *(worth thinking about)* considerabile

considerate [kən'sɪdərɪt] *adj* riguardoso, premuroso

consideration [kən,sɪdə'reʃən] *s* considerazione; *(reason)* motivo; *(money)* pagamento; **in consideration of** a cagione di; in cambio di; **on no consideration** in nessuna maniera, mai; **under consideration** in considerazione, sotto esame; **without due consideration** senza riflessione, alla leggera

considering [kən'sɪdərɪŋ] *adv* tutto considerato || *prep* per, visto || *conj* considerando che, visto che

consign [kən'saɪn] *tr* consegnare; *(to send)* inviare; *(to set apart)* assegnare

consignee [,kɑnsaɪ'ni] *s* consegnatario

consignment [kən'saɪnmənt] *s* consegna; **on consignment** in consegna

consist [kən'sɪst] *intr—***to consist in** consistere in; **to consist of** consistere in, constare di

consisten·cy [kən'sɪstənsi] *s* (**-cies**) *(firmness, amount of firmness)* consistenza; *(logical connection)* coerenza

consistent [kən'sɪstənt] *adj (holding firmly together)* consistente; *(agree-*

ing with itself or oneself) conseguente, coerente; compatibile

consolation [ˌkɑnsəˈleʃən] *s* consolazione

console [ˈkɑnsol] *s (table)* console *f;* (rad, telv) mobile *m;* (mus) console *f* ‖ [kənˈsol] *tr* consolare

consonant [ˈkɑnsənənt] *adj* consonante, armonioso; (gram) consonantico ‖ *s* consonante *f*

consort [ˈkɑnsɔrt] *s* consorte *mf* ‖ [kənˈsɔrt] *intr* associarsi; *(to agree)* concordarsi

conspicuous [kənˈspɪkju‧əs] *adj* visibile, manifesto; notevole; *(too noticeable)* appariscente; **to make oneself conspicuous** farsi notare

conspira‧cy [kənˈspɪrəsi] *s* **(-cies)** cospirazione, congiura

conspire [kənˈspaɪr] *intr* cospirare, congiurare; *(to act together)* cooperare

constable [ˈkɑnstəbəl] *or* [ˈkʌnstəbəl] *s* poliziotto; *(keeper of a castle)* conestabile *m*

constancy [ˈkɑnstənsi] *s* costanza

constant [ˈkɑnstənt] *adj & s* costante *f*

constellation [ˌkɑnstəˈleʃən] *s* costellazione

constipate [ˈkɑnstɪˌpet] *tr* costipare

constipation [ˌkɑnstɪˈpeʃən] *s* costipazione

constituen‧cy [kənˈstɪtʃu‧ənsi] *s* **(-cies)** *(voters)* elettorato; *(district)* circoscrizione elettorale

constituent [kənˈstɪtʃu‧ənt] *adj* costituente ‖ *s (component)* parte *f* costituente; *(voter)* elettore *m; (of a chemical substance)* costituente *m*

constitute [ˈkɑnstɪˌtjut] *or* [ˈkɑnstɪˌtut] *tr* costituire

constitution [ˌkɑnstɪˈtjuʃən] *or* [ˌkɑnstɪˈtuʃən] *s* costituzione

constrain [kənˈstren] *tr (to force)* costringere; *(to restrain)* restringere, comprimere

constrict [kənˈstrɪkt] *tr* stringere, comprimere

construct [kənˈstrʌkt] *tr* costruire

construction [kənˈstrʌkʃən] *s* costruzione; *(meaning)* interpretazione

construe [kənˈstru] *tr (to interpret)* interpretare; *(to translate)* tradurre; (gram) analizzare

consul [ˈkɑnsəl] *s* console *m*

consular [ˈkɑnsələr] *or* [ˈkɑnsjələr] *adj* consolare

consulate [ˈkɑnsəlɪt] *or* [ˈkɑnsjəlɪt] *s* consolato

consult [kənˈsʌlt] *tr* consultare ‖ *intr* consultarsi

consultation [ˌkɑnsəlˈteʃən] *s* consultazione, conferenza

consume [kənˈsum] *or* [kənˈsjum] *tr* consumare; distruggere; **consumed with** *(passion)* arso di; *(curiosity)* assorbito da

consumer [kənˈsumər] *or* [kənˈsjumər] *s* consumatore *m*

consum'er goods' *spl* beni *mpl* di consumo

consumerism [kənˈsumərˌɪzem] *s* consumismo

consummate [kənˈsʌmɪt] *adj* consumato ‖ [ˈkɑnsəˌmet] *tr* consumare

consumption [kənˈsʌmpʃən] *s (decay)* consunzione; *(using up)* consumo; (pathol) consunzione

consumptive [kənˈsʌmptɪv] *adj* tubercolotico, tisico; *(wasteful)* logorante ‖ *s* tisico, etico

contact [ˈkɑntækt] *s* contatto; (elec) contatto; (elec) presa di corrente ‖ *tr* (coll) mettersi in contatto con ‖ *intr* (coll) mettersi in contatto

con'tact break'er *s* ruttore *m*

con'tact lens' *s* lente *f* a contatto

contagion [kənˈtedʒən] *s* contagio

contagious [kənˈtedʒəs] *adj* contagioso

contain [kənˈten] *tr* contenere; **to contain oneself** frenarsi

container [kənˈtenər] *s* recipiente *m*, contenitore *m*

contaminate [kənˈtæmɪˌnet] *tr* contaminare

contamination [kənˌtæmɪˈneʃən] *s* contaminazione

contemplate [ˈkɑntəmˌplet] *tr* contemplare; *(to think about)* meditare; *(to have in mind)* progettare, avere in mente ‖ *intr* meditare

contemplation [ˌkɑntəmˈpleʃən] *s* contemplazione; *(intention)* intenzione

contemporaneous [kənˌtempəˈreni‧əs] *adj* contemporaneo, coevo

contemporar‧y [kənˈtempəˌreri] *adj* contemporaneo, coevo ‖ *s* **(-ies)** contemporaneo

contempt [kənˈtempt] *s (despising)* disprezzo; *(condition of being despised)* dispregio; *(of the law)* disprezzo

contemptible [kənˈtemptɪbəl] *adj* disprezzabile, spregevole

contempt' of court' *s* (law) offesa alla magistratura, oltraggio al tribunale

contemptuous [kənˈtemptʃu‧əs] *adj* sprezzante, sdegnoso

contend [kənˈtend] *tr* dichiarare ‖ *intr (to argue)* disputare, contendere; *(to fight)* lottare

contender [kənˈtendər] *s* competitore *m*, concorrente *m*

content [kənˈtent] *adj* contento; *(willing)* pronto ‖ *s* contentezza ‖ [ˈkɑntent] *s* contenuto; **contents** contenuto ‖ [kənˈtent] *tr* contentare

contented [kənˈtentɪd] *adj* soddisfatto

contention [kənˈtenʃən] *s* disputa, litigio; contenzione

contentious [kənˈtenʃəs] *adj* litigioso

contentment [kənˈtentmənt] *s* contentezza

contest [ˈkɑntest] *s* contesa, controversia; *(game)* gara ‖ [kənˈtest] *tr* disputare, contestare ‖ *intr* combattere, fare resistenza

contestant [kənˈtestənt] *s* concorrente *m;* (law) contendente *m*

context [ˈkɑntekst] *s* contesto

contiguous [kənˈtɪgju‧əs] *adj* contiguo

continence [ˈkɑntɪnəns] *s* continenza

continent [ˈkɑntɪnənt] *adj & s* continente *m;* **on the Continent** nel continente europeo

continental [ˌkɑntɪˈnɛntəl] *adj* & *s* continentale *mf*

contingen·cy [kənˈtɪndʒənsi] *s* (**-cies**) contingenza, congiuntura; (*chance*) eventualità *f*

contingent [kənˈtɪndʒənt] *adj* eventuale; imprevisto; (*philos*) contingente; **to be contingent upon** dipendere da

continual [kənˈtɪnju‧əl] *adj* continuo

continuance [kənˈtɪnjuəns] *s* continuazione; (*in office*) permanenza; (*law*) rinvio

continue [kənˈtɪnju] *tr* continuare; (*to cause to remain*) mantenere; (*law*) rinviare ‖ *intr* continuare; rimanere

continui·ty [ˌkɑntɪˈnju‧ɪti] *or* [ˌkɑntɪˈnu‧ɪti] *s* (**-ties**) continuità *f;* (*mov & telv*) sceneggiatura; (*rad*) copione *m*

continuous [kənˈtɪnju‧əs] *adj* continuo

contin'uous show'ing *s* (*mov*) spettacolo permanente

contortion [kənˈtɔrʃən] *s* contorsione; (*of facts*) distorsione

contour [ˈkɑntur] *s* contorno

con'tour line' *s* curva di livello, isoipsa

contraband [ˈkɑntrəˌbænd] *adj* di contrabbando ‖ *s* contrabbando

contrabass [ˈkɑntrəˌbes] *s* contrabasso

contraceptive [ˌkɑntrəˈsɛptɪv] *adj* & *s* antifecondativo

contract [ˈkɑntrækt] *s* contratto ‖ [ˈkɑntrækt] *or* [kənˈtrækt] *tr* (*a business deal*) contrattare; (*marriage*) contrarre ‖ *intr* (*to shrink*) contrarsi; **to contract for** contrattare, appaltare

contraction [kənˈtrækʃən] *s* contrazione

contractor [kənˈtræktər] *s* (*person who makes a contract*) contraente *m;* (*person who contracts to supply material*) appaltatore *m,* imprenditore *m;* (*in building*) capomastro

contradict [ˌkɑntrəˈdɪkt] *tr* contraddire

contradiction [ˌkɑntrəˈdɪkʃən] *s* contraddizione

contradictory [ˌkɑntrəˈdɪktəri] *adj* contraddittorio

contrail [ˈkɑnˌtrel] *s* (aer) scia di condensazione

contral·to [kənˈtrælto] *s* (**-tos**) (*person*) contralto *mf;* (*voice*) contralto *m*

contraption [kənˈtræpʃən] *s* (coll) aggeggio

contra·ry [ˈkɑntreri] *adj* contrario ‖ [kənˈtreri] *adj* ostinato, caparbio ‖ [ˈkɑntreri] *s* (**-ries**) contrario; **on the contrary** al contrario ‖ *adv* contrariamente

contrast [ˈkɑntræst] *s* contrasto ‖ [kənˈtræst] *tr* confrontare ‖ *intr* contrastare

contravene [ˌkɑntrəˈvin] *tr* contraddire; (*a law*) contravvenire (with *dat*)

contribute [kənˈtrɪbjut] *tr* contribuire ‖ *intr* contribuire; (*to a newspaper*) collaborare

contribution [ˌkɑntrɪˈbjuʃən] *s* contribuzione; (*to a newspaper*) collaborazione

contributor [kənˈtrɪbjutər] *s* contributore *m;* (*to a newspaper*) collaboratore *m*

contrite [kənˈtraɪt] *adj* contrito

contrition [kənˈtrɪʃən] *s* contrizione

contrivance [kənˈtraɪvəns] *s* dispositivo, congegno; (*faculty*) invenzione; (*scheme*) artificio, piano

contrive [kənˈtraɪv] *tr* inventare; (*to scheme up*) macchinare; (*to bring about*) effettuare; **to contrive to** trovare il modo di

con·trol [kənˈtrol] *s* controllo; (*check*) freno; **controls** comandi *mpl;* **to get under control** riuscire a controllare ‖ *v* (*pret* & *pp* **-trolled;** *ger* **-trolling**) *tr* controllare

controller [kənˈtrolər] *s* controllore *m;* analista *mf* di gestione; economo; (*mach*) regolatore *m;* (*elec*) interruttore *m* di linea

control'ling in'terest *s* maggioranza delle azioni

control' stick' *s* leva di comando

controversial [ˌkɑntrəˈvɑrʃəl] *adj* controverso, polemico, discusso

controver·sy [ˈkɑntrəˌvɑrsi] *s* (**-sies**) controversia

controvert [ˈkɑntrəˌvɑrt] *or* [ˌkɑntrəˈvɑrt] *tr* contraddire

contumacious [ˌkɑntjuˈmeʃəs] *or* [ˌkɑntuˈmeʃəs] *adj* ribelle, contumace

contuma·cy [ˈkɑntjuməsi] *or* [ˈkɑntuməsi] *s* (**-cies**) contumacia

contusion [kənˈtjuʒən] *or* [kənˈtuʒən] *s* contusione

conundrum [kəˈnʌndrəm] *s* indovinello

convalesce [ˌkɑnvəˈles] *intr* essere convalescente

convalescence [ˌkɑnvəˈlesəns] *s* convalescenza

convalescent [ˌkɑnvəˈlesənt] *adj* & *s* convalescente *mf*

con'vales'cent home' *s* convalescenziario

convene [kənˈvin] *tr* convocare ‖ *intr* convenire

convenience [kənˈvinjəns] *s* convenienza; (*comfort*) agio; (*anything that saves work*) conforto; **at your earliest convenience** quanto prima

convenient [kənˈvinjənt] *adj* conveniente, adatto; comodo; **convenient to** (*near*) (coll) vicino a

convent [ˈkɑnvent] *s* convento di religioso

convention [kənˈvenʃən] *s* convenzione, assemblea; **conventions** (*customs*) convenzioni *fpl*

conventional [kənˈvenʃənəl] *adj* convenzionale

converge [kənˈvɑrdʒ] *intr* convergere

conversant [kənˈvɑrsənt] *adj* versato, esperto, dotto

conversation [ˌkɑnvərˈseʃən] *s* conversazione

converse [ˈkɑnvʌrs] *adj* & *s* contrario ‖ [kənˈvʌrs] *intr* conversare

conversion [kən'vɑrʒən] s conversione; (*unlawful appropriation*) malversazione

convert ['kɑnvʌrt] s convertito ‖ [kən-'vʌrt] tr convertire; misappropriare ‖ intr convertirsi

convertible [kən'vʌrtɪbəl] adj & s convertibile f; (aut) trasformabile f, decappottabile f

convex ['kɑnveks] or [kən'veks] adj convesso

convey [kən've] tr (*to carry*) trasportare; (*liquids*) convogliare; (*sounds*) trasmettere; (*to express*) esprimere; (*e.g., property*) trasferire

conveyance [kən've-əns] s trasporto; veicolo; comunicazione; (*of property*) trasferimento; (*deed*) titolo di proprietà

convey'or belt' [kən've-ər] s trasportatore m

convict ['kɑnvɪkt] s condannato ‖ [kən'vɪkt] tr convincere, condannare

conviction [kən'vɪkʃən] s condanna; (*belief*) convinzione, convincimento

convince [kən'vɪns] tr convincere

convincing [kən'vɪnsɪŋ] adj convincente

convivial [kən'vɪvɪ·əl] adj (*festive*) conviviale; gioviale, bonaccione

convocation [,kɑnvə'keʃən] s convocazione, assemblea

convoke [kən'vok] tr convocare

convoy ['kɑnvɔɪ] s (*of ships*) convoglio; (*of vehicles*) carovana ‖ tr convogliare

convulse [kən'vʌls] tr (*to shake*) scuotere; (*to throw into convulsions*) mettere in convulsioni; (*to cause to shake with laughter*) far torcere dalle risa

coo [ku] intr tubare, gemere

cook [kuk] s cuoco ‖ tr cuocere; **to cook up** (coll) preparare, macchinare ‖ intr (*said of food*) cuocere; (*said of a person*) fare il cuoco

cook'book' s libro di cucina

cookie ['kuki] s var of **cooky**

cooking ['kukɪŋ] s culinaria

cook'out' s picnic m, spuntino all'aperto

cook'stove' s cucina economica

cook·y ['kuki] s (-**ies**) pasticcino, biscotto

cool [kul] adj fresco; calmo; (*not cordial*) freddo; (*bold*) sfacciato ‖ s fresco ‖ tr rinfrescare; **to cool one's heels** fare anticamera ‖ intr rinfrescarsi; **to cool off** rinfrescarsi; calmarsi

coolant ['kulənt] s miscela refrigerante

cooler ['kulər] s ghiacciaia; (slang) prigione

cool'-head'ed adj calmo, imperturbabile

coolish ['kulɪʃ] adj freschetto

coon [kun] s procione m

coop [kup] s pollaio; conigliera; **to fly the coop** (slang) scapparsene ‖ tr—**to coop up** rinchiudere fra quattro mura

cooper ['kupər] s bottaio

cooperate [ko'ɑpə‚ret] intr cooperare

cooperation [ko‚ɑpə'reʃən] s cooperazione

cooperative [ko'ɑpə‚retɪv] adj cooperativo ‖ s cooperativa

coordinate [ko'ɔrdɪnɪt] adj coordinato; (gram) coordinativo ‖ s (math) coordinata ‖ [ko'ɔrdɪ‚net] tr & intr coordinare

coot [kut] s (zool) folaga; (slang) vecchio pazzo

cootie ['kuti] s (slang) pidocchio

cop [kɑp] s (slang) poliziotto ‖ v (pret & pp **copped;** ger **copping**) tr (slang) rubare

copartner [ko'pɑrtnər] s consocio, socio

cope [kop] intr—**to cope with** tener testa a

cope'stone' s pietra da cimasa

copier ['kɑpɪ·ər] s (*person*) copista mf; imitatore m; (*machine*) duplicatore m

copilot ['ko‚paɪlət] s copilota mf

coping ['kopɪŋ] s coronamento, cimasa

cop'ing saw' s seghetto da traforo

copious ['kopɪ·əs] adj copioso

copper [kɑp'ər] s rame m; (*coin*) soldo; (*boiler*) calderone m; (slang) poliziotto

cop'per·head' s vipera (*Ancistrodon contortrix*)

cop'per·smith' s battirame m, calderaio

coppice ['kɑpɪs] or **copse** [kɑps] s boschetto

copulate ['kɑpjə‚let] intr copularsi, congiungersi carnalmente

cop·y ['kɑpi] s (-**ies**) copia; modello; manoscritto ‖ v (pret & pp -**ied**) tr copiare, imitare ‖ intr copiare; **to copy after** imitare

cop'y·book' s quaderno

copyist ['kɑpɪ·ɪst] s copista mf; imitatore m

cop'y·right' s copyright m, diritto di proprietà letteraria ‖ tr registrare; proteggere con copyright

cop'y·writ'er s copy-writer m, redattore m pubblicitario

coquetry ['kokətri] or [ko'ketri] s (-**ries**) civetteria

coquette [ko'ket] s civetta

coquettish [ko'ketɪʃ] adj civettuolo

coral ['kɑrəl] or ['kɔrəl] adj corallino ‖ s corallo

cor'al reef' s banco di coralli

cord [kɔrd] s corda, fune f; (*corduroy*) tessuto cordonato; (elec) cordone m ‖ tr legare con corda

cordial ['kɔrdʒəl] adj & s cordiale m

corduroy ['kɔrdə‚rɔɪ] s velluto a coste; **corduroys** pantaloni mpl alla cacciatora

core [kor] s (*of fruit*) torsolo; (*central part*) centro; (*of problem*) nocciolo; (*of earth*) barisfera, nucleo centrale; (phys) nucleo; **rotten to the core** guasto nelle ossa

corespondent [‚korɪs'pɑndənt] s coimputato in un processo di divorzio

cork [kɔrk] s (*bark*) sughero; (*stopper*) tappo, tappo di sughero ‖ tr tappare

cork' oak' s sughero

cork'screw' s cavatappi m

cormorant ['kɔrmərənt] s cormorano

corn [kɔrn] s granturco, mais m; (kernel) chicco; (thickening of skin) callo; (whiskey) whisky m di granturco; (Brit) grano; (Scot) avena; (slang) banalità f

corn' bread' s pane m di farina gialla

corn' cake' s omelette f di granturco

corn'cob' s tutolo

corn'cob pipe' s pipa fatta di un tutolo di pannocchia

corn'crib' s granaio per le pannocchie

corn' cure' s callifugo

cornea ['kɔrnɪ-ə] s cornea

corner ['kɔrnər] s angolo; (of street) cantonata; situazione difficile; (of the eye) coda dell'occhio; (com) accaparramento, incetta, bagarinaggio; **to cut corners** tagliare le spese; **to turn the corner** passare il punto più pericoloso || tr mettere in una situazione difficile; (the market) incettare, accaparrare

cor'ner cup'board s cantoniera, armadio d'angolo

cor'ner stone' s pietra angolare; (of new building) prima pietra

cornet [kɔr'nɛt] s cornetta

corn'field' s (in U.S.A.) campo di granturco; (in England) campo di grano; (in Scotland) campo di avena

corn'flakes' spl fiocchi mpl di granturco

corn' flour' s farina di granturco

corn'flow'er s fiordaliso

corn'husk' s brattea, cartoccio

cornice ['kɔrnɪs] s (of house) cornicione m; (of room) cornice f

corn' liq'uor s whisky m di granturco

corn' meal' s farina di granturco

corn' on the cob' s granturco servito in pannocchia

corn' plas'ter s cerotto per i calli

corn' silk' s barba del granturco

corn'stalk' s fusto di granturco

corn'starch' s amido di granturco

corn•y ['kɔrni] adj (-ier; -iest) (slang) banale, trito, triviale

coronation [,kɔrə'neʃən] or [,kɔrə-'neʃən] s incoronazione

coroner ['kɔrənər] or ['kɔrənər] s magistrato inquirente

cor'oner's in'quest s inchiesta giudiziaria dinanzi a giuria

coronet ['kɔrə,nɛt] or ['kɔrə,nɛt] s corona (non reale); diadema m

corporal ['kɔrpərəl] adj caporalesco || s caporale m

corporation [,kɔrpə'reʃən] s società anonima

corps [kor] s (corps [korz]) corpo

corps' de bal'let s corpo di ballo

corpse [kɔrps] s cadavere m

corpulent ['kɔrpjələnt] adj corpulento

corpuscle ['kɔrpəsəl] s (anat) globulo; (phys) corpuscolo

cor•ral [kə'ræl] s recinto per bestiame || v (pret & pp -ralled; ger -ralling) tr mettere in un recinto; catturare

correct [kə'rɛkt] adj corretto || tr correggere

correction [kə'rɛkʃən] s correzione

corrective [kə'rɛktɪv] adj & s correttivo

correctness [kə'rɛktnɪs] s correttezza

correlate ['kɑrə,let] or ['kɔrə,let] tr correlare || intr essere in correlazione

correlation [,kɑrə'leʃən] or [,kɔrə-'leʃən] s correlazione

correspond [,kɑrɪ'spɑnd] or [,kɔrɪ-'spɑnd] intr corrispondere

correspondence [,kɑrɪ'spɑndəns] or [,kɔrɪ'spɑndəns] s corrispondenza

correspond'ence school' s scuola per corrispondenza

correspondent [,kɑrɪ'spɑndənt] or [,kɔrɪ'spɑndənt] adj & s corrispondente mf

corridor ['kɑrɪdər] or ['kɔrɪdər] s corridoio

corroborate [kə'rɑbə,ret] tr corroborare

corrode [kə'rod] tr corrodere || intr corrodersi

corrosion [kə'roʒən] s corrosione

corrosive [kə'rosɪv] adj & s corrosivo

corrugated ['kɑrə,getɪd] or ['kɔrə,getɪd] adj ondulato

corrupt [kə'rʌpt] adj corrotto || tr corrompere; (a language) imbarbarire || intr corrompersi

corruption [kə'rʌpʃən] s corruzione

corsage [kɔr'saʒ] s (bodice) corpetto; (bouquet) mazzolino di fiori da appuntarsi al vestito

corsair ['kɔr,sɛr] s corsaro

corset ['kɔrsɪt] s corsetto

Corsican ['kɔrsɪkən] adj & s corso

cortege [kɔr'teʒ] s corteggio

cor•tex ['kɔr,tɛks] s (-tices [tɪ,siz]) cortice f

cortisone ['kɔrtɪ,son] s cortisone m

corvette [kɔr'vɛt] s corvetta

cosmetic [kɑz'mɛtɪk] adj & s cosmetico

cosmic ['kɑzmɪk] adj cosmico

cosmonaut ['kɑzmə,nɔt] s cosmonauta mf

cosmopolitan [,kɑzmə'pɑlɪtən] adj & s cosmopolita mf

cosmos ['kɑzmɑs] s cosmo

cost [kɔst] or [kɑst] s costo, prezzo; **at all costs** or **at any cost** ad ogni costo; **costs** (law) spese fpl processuali || v (pret & pp cost) intr costare

cost•ly ['kɔstli] or ['kɑstli] adj (-lier; -liest) costoso; (sumptuous) lussuoso

cost' of liv'ing s costo della vita

costume ['kɑstjum] or ['kɑstum] s costume m

cos'tume ball' s ballo in costume

cos'tume jew'elry s gioielli falsi

cot [kɑt] s (narrow bed) branda; (cottage) capanna, cabina

coterie ['kotəri] s gruppo; (clique) chiesuola

cottage ['kɑtɪdʒ] s casetta, villino

cot'tage cheese' s ricotta americana

cot'ter pin' ['kɑtər] s copiglia, coppiglia

cotton ['kɑtən] s cotone m || intr—to cotton up to (coll) cominciare a provare della simpatia per; (coll) andare d'accordo con

cot'ton can'dy s zucchero filato

cot'ton gin' *s* sgranatrice *f*

cot'ton pick'er ['pɪkər] *s* chi raccoglie il cotone; macchina che raccoglie il cotone

cot'tonseed oil' *s* olio di semi di cotone

cot'ton waste' *s* cascame *m* di cotone

cot'ton·wood' *s* pioppo deltoide

couch [kaut] *s* canapè *m*, sofà *m*, divano ‖ *tr* esprimere

couch' grass' *s* gramigna

cougar ['kugər] *s* puma *m*

cough [kɔf] *or* [kaf] *s* tosse *f* ‖ *tr*—**to cough up** sputare, sputare tossendo; (slang) dare, pagare ‖ *intr* tossire

cough' drop' *s* pastiglia per la tosse

cough' syr'up *s* sciroppo per la tosse

could [kud] *v aux*—**I could not come yesterday** non ho potuto venire ieri; **I could not see you tomorrow** non potrei vederLa domani; **it could not be so** non potrebbe essere così

council ['kaunsəl] *s* consiglio; (eccl) concilio

coun'cil·man *s* (-men) consigliere *m or* assessore *m* municipale

coun·sel ['kaunsəl] *s* consiglio; (lawyer) avvocato; **to keep one's counsel** essere riservato; **to take counsel with** consultarsi con ‖ *v* (pret & pp -seled *or* -selled; ger -seling *or* -selling) *tr* consigliare ‖ *intr* consigliare; consigliarsi

counselor ['kaunsələr] *s* consigliere *m*; avvocato

count [kaunt] *s* conto; (nobleman) conte *m*; (law) capo d'accusa ‖ *tr* contare; **to count off by** (twos, threes) contare per (due, tre); **to count out** escludere; (boxing) contare ‖ *intr* contare; (to be worth) valere; **to count on** contare su

count'down' *s* conteggio alla rovescia

countenance ['kauntɪnəns] *s* espressione; (face) faccia; (approval) approvazione ‖ *tr* approvare, incoraggiare

counter ['kauntər] *adj* contrario ‖ *s* contatore *m*; (token) gettone *m*; (table in store) banco; (opposite) contrario ‖ *adv* contro, contrariamente ‖ *tr* contrariare, opporre ‖ *intr* (boxing) rispondere

coun'ter·act' *tr* contrariare, neutralizzare

coun'ter·attack' *s* contrattacco ‖ **coun'ter·attack'** *tr & intr* contrattaccare

coun'ter·bal'ance *s* contrappeso ‖ **coun'ter·bal'ance** *tr* controbilanciare

coun'ter·clock'wise' *adj* antiorario ‖ *adv* in senso antiorario

coun'ter·es'pionage' *s* controspionaggio

counterfeit ['kauntərfɪt] *adj* contraffatto ‖ *s* contraffazione; moneta falsa ‖ *tr & intr* contraffare

counterfeiter ['kauntər,fɪtər] *s* contraffattore *m*

coun'ter·feit mon'ey *s* moneta falsa

countermand ['kauntər,mænd] *or* ['kauntər,mɑnd] *tr* (troops) dare un contrordine a; (an order; a payment) cancellare

coun'ter·march' *s* contromarcia ‖ *intr* fare contromarcia

coun'ter·offen'sive *s* controffensiva

coun'ter·pane' *s* sopraccoperta

coun'ter·part' *s* copia; (person) sosia

coun'ter·point' *s* (mus) contrappunto; (mus) controcanto

Coun'ter Reforma'tion *s* controriforma

coun'ter·rev'olu'tion *s* controrivoluzione

coun'ter·sign' *s* (password) parola d'ordine; (signature) controfirma ‖ *tr* controfirmare

coun'ter·sink' *v* (pret & pp -sunk) *tr* incassare, accecare

coun'ter·spy' *s* (-spies) membro del controspionaggio

coun'ter·stroke' *s* contraccolpo

coun'ter·weight' *s* contrappeso

countess ['kauntɪs] *s* contessa

countless ['kauntlɪs] *adj* innumerevole

countrified ['kʌntrɪ,faɪd] *adj* rustico, rurale

coun·try ['kʌntri] *s* (-tries) (land) terreno; (nation) paese *m*; (land of one's birth) patria; (rural region) campagna

coun'try club' *s* circolo privato sportivo situato nei sobborghi

coun'try cous'in *s* campagnolo

coun'try estate' *s* tenuta

coun'try·folk' *s* campagnoli *mpl*

coun'try gen'tleman *s* proprietario terriero, signorotto di campagna

coun'try house' *s* casa di campagna

coun'try jake' *s* (coll) zoticone *m*

coun'try life' *s* vita rustica

coun'try·man *s* (-men) paesano, compaesano

coun'try·peo'ple *s* gente *f* di campagna

coun'try·side' *s* campagna

coun'try·wide' *adj* nazionale

coun'try·wom'an *s* (-wom'en) *s* paesana, compaesana

coun·ty ['kaunti] *s* (-ties) contea, distretto

coun'ty seat' *s* capoluogo di contea

coup [ku] *s* colpo; colpo di stato

coup de grâce [ku də 'grɑs] *s* colpo di grazia

coup d'état [ku de'tɑ] *s* colpo di stato

coupe [kup] *or* **coupé** [ku'pe] *s* coupé *m*

couple ['kʌpəl] *s* (of people or animals) paio, coppia; (of things) paio; (link) unione ‖ *tr* accoppiare; (to link) unire, agganciare ‖ *intr* accoppiarsi

couplet ['kʌplɪt] *s* coppia di versi; (mus) couplet *m*

coupling ['kʌplɪŋ] *s* unione; (mach) giunto

coupon ['kupan] *or* ['kjupan] *s* coupon *m*, tagliando

courage ['kʌrɪdʒ] *s* coraggio; **to have the courage of one's convictions** avere il coraggio delle proprie opinioni

courageous [kə'redʒəs] *adj* coraggioso

courier ['kʌrɪ·ər] *or* ['kurɪ·ər] *s* corriere *m*

course [kors] *s* corso; (part of meal) portata; (place for games) campo;

(*row*) fila; **in due course** a tempo debito; **in the course of** durante, nel corso di; **of course** certamente, senza dubbio

court [kort] *s* (*uncovered place surrounded by walls*) corte *f*, cortile *m*; (*royal residence; courtship*) corte *f*; (*short street*) vicolo; (*playing area*) campo; (*law*) corte *f* || *tr* corteggiare; (*e.g., disaster*) andare in cerca di

courteous [ˈkʌrtɪ‑əs] *adj* cortese

courtesan [ˈkʌrtɪzən] *or* [ˈkɔrtɪzən] *s* cortigiana, meretrice *f*

courte·sy [ˈkʌrtɪsi] *s* (*-sies*) cortesia, gentilezza || **through the courtesy of** con il gentile permesso di

court'house' *s* palazzo di giustizia

courtier [ˈkortɪ‑ər] *s* cortigiano

court' jest'er *s* buffone *m* di corte

court·ly [ˈkortli] *adj* (*-lier; -liest*) cortese, cortigiano; ossequioso

court'-mar'tial *s* (*courts-martial*) corte *f* marziale || *v* (*pret & pp* **-tialed** *or* **-tialled;** *ger* **-tialing** *or* **-tialling**) *tr* sottomettere a corte marziale

court' plas'ter *s* taffettà *m*

court'room' *s* aula di giustizia

courtship [ˈkortʃɪp] *s* corte *f*, corteggiamento

court'yard' *s* corte *f*, cortile *m*

cousin [ˈkʌzɪn] *s* cugino

cove [kov] *s* piccola baia, cala

covenant [ˈkʌvənənt] *s* convenzione, patto || *tr* promettere solennemente

cover [ˈkʌvər] *s* (*lid*) coperchio; (*tablecloth; shelter*) coperto; (*of book*) copertina; **to take cover** nascondersi; **under cover** in segreto, segretamente; **under cover of** sotto la protezione di; **under separate cover** in busta a parte, in plico a parte || *tr* coprire; puntare un'arma verso; (*journ*) riferire, riportare; **to cover up** coprire completamente || *intr* (*said of paint*) spandersi

coverage [ˈkʌvərɪdʒ] *s* copertura; (*journ*) servizio giornalistico; (*rad, telv*) raggio di udibilità

coveralls [ˈkʌvər‑ˌɔlz] *spl* tuta

cov'er charge' *s* coperto

cov'ered wag'on *s* carro coperto da tendone

cov'er girl' *s* ragazza-copertina

covering [ˈkʌvərɪŋ] *s* copertura; involucro

covert [ˈkʌvərt] *adj* nascosto, segreto

cov'er-up' *s* dissimulazione; sotterfugio

covet [ˈkʌvɪt] *tr* desiderare, agognare

covetous [ˈkʌvɪtəs] *adj* cupido

covey [ˈkʌvi] *s* covata

cow [kau] *s* vacca; (*of seal, elephant, etc.*) femmina || *tr* spaventare, intimidire

coward [ˈkau‑ərd] *s* codardo, vile *m*

cowardice [ˈkau‑ərdɪs] *s* codardia, viltà *f*

cowardly [ˈkau‑ərdli] *adj* codardo, vile || *adv* vilmente

cow'bell' *s* campano, campanaccio

cow'boy' *s* cowboy *m*

cow'catch'er *s* (rr) cacciapietre *m*

cower [ˈkau‑ər] *intr* rannicchiarsi

cow'herd' *s* guardiano d'armenti

cow'hide' *s* pelle *f* di vacca

cowl [kaul] *s* (*hood*) cappuccio; (*monk's cloak*) cappa; (*of car*) sostegno del cofano; (*of chimney*) cappello; (aer) cappottatura

cow'lick' *s* ritrosa

cow'pox' *s* (vet) vaiolo bovino

coxcomb [ˈkɑks‑ˌkom] *s* zerbinotto

coxwain [ˈkɑksən] *or* [ˈkɑk‑ˌswen] *s* timoniere *m*

coy [kɔɪ] *adj* timido, ritroso

co·zy [ˈkozi] *adj* (*-zier; -ziest*) comodo || *s* (*-zies*) copriteiera *m*

C.P.A. [ˈsiˈpiˈe] *s* (letterword) (**certified public accountant**) esperto contabile

crab [kræb] *s* granchio; (aer) scarroccio; (*complaining person*) (coll) scontroso || *v* (*pret & pp* **crabbed;** *ger* **crabbing**) *intr* (coll) lamentarsi

crab' apple' *s* mela selvatica; (*tree*) melo selvatico

crabbed [ˈkræbɪd] *adj* sgarbato; (*handwriting*) da gallina; (*style*) oscuro, ermetico

crab' louse' *s* piattola

crab·by [ˈkræbi] *adj* (*-bier; -biest*) scontroso, sgarbato

crack [kræk] *adj* (slang) di prim'ordine, eccellente || *s* (*noise*) schiocco; (*break*) rottura, screpolatura, crepa; (*opening*) fessura; (slang) tentativo; (slang) barzelletta || *tr* (*e.g., a whip*) schioccare; (*to break*) rompere, screpolare; (*oil*) ridurre con distillazione; (coll) risolvere; (*a safe*) (slang) forzare; (*a joke*) (slang) dire; **cracked up to be** (slang) avendo fama di || *intr* (*to make a noise*) scricchiolare; (*to break*) rompersi, screpolarsi; (*said of voice*) diventare fesso; (slang) avere un esaurimento nervoso; **to crack down** (slang) essere severo; **to crack up** (slang) andare a pezzi

cracked [krækt] *adj* rotto, spezzato; (*voice*) fesso; (coll) pazzo

cracker [ˈkrækər] *s* cracker *m*, galletta

crack'er-bar'rel *adj* in piccolo, alla buona

crack'er-jack' *adj* (slang) di prim'ordine || *s* (slang) persona di prim'ordine

cracking [ˈkrækɪŋ] *s* piroscissione

crackle [ˈkrækəl] *s* crepitio, crepìto || *intr* crepitare

crack'pot' *adj & s* (coll) mattoide *mf*

crack'-up' *s* accidente *m*; collisione; (*breakdown in health or in relations*) (coll) colasso; (aer) accidente *m* d'atterraggio

cradle [ˈkredəl] *s* culla; (*of handset*) forcella || *tr* cullare

crad'le-song' *s* ninnananna

craft [kræft] *or* [krɑft] *s* (*skill*) abilità *f*; (*trade*) mestiere *m*; (*guile*) astuzia, furberia; (*ship*) nave *f*; aeronave

craftiness [ˈkræftɪnɪs] *or* [ˈkrɑftɪnɪs] *s* astuzia, furberia

crafts'man *s* (**-men**) operaio specializzato, artigiano

craft' un'ion s artigianato, sindacato artigiano

craft·y ['kræfti] or ['krɑfti] adj (-ier; -iest) astuto, furbo

crag [kræg] s roccia scoscesa, rupe f

cram [kræm] v (pret & pp crammed; ger cramming) tr (to pack full) riempire fino all'orlo; (to stuff with food) rimpinzare || intr rimpinzarsi; (coll) preparare un esame alla svelta

cramp [kræmp] s (painful contraction) crampo; (bar with hooks) grappa; (fig) ostacolo || tr ostacolare, restringere

cranber·ry ['kræn,beri] s (-ries) mirtillo

crane [kren] s (orn, mach) gru f; (boom) (telv, mov) giraffa || tr (one's neck) allungare || intr allungare il collo

crani·um ['kreni-əm] s (-a [ə]) cranio

crank [kræŋk] s manovella; (aut) alzacristalli m; (coll) eccentrico || tr girare con la manovella; mettere in moto con la manovella

crank'case' s coppa dell'olio, carter m

crank'shaft' s albero a gomito

crank·y ['kræŋki] adj (-ier; -iest) irritabile; eccentrico

cran·ny ['kræni] s (-nies) (crevice) crepaccio; (crack) fessura

crape [krep] s crespo

crape'hang'er s (slang) pessimista uggioso, guastafeste mf

craps [kræps] s gioco dei dadi; **to shoot craps** giocare ai dadi

crash [kræʃ] adj (coll) d'emergenza || s (noise) scoppio, schianto; accidente m; (collapse of business) crac m, rovescio; (bad landing) atterraggio senza carrello || tr fracassare; **to crash the gate** (coll) entrare senza invito || intr fracassarsi; (com) fallire; **to cash into** investire, cozzare contro; **to cash through** sfondare

crash' dive' s immersione rapida di un sottomarino

crash' hel'met s casco

crass [kræs] adj crasso

crate [kret] s gabbia d'imballaggio || tr imballare in una gabbia

crater ['kretər] s cratere m

cravat [krə'væt] s cravatta

crave [krev] tr anelare; (to beg) implorare || intr—**to crave for** desiderare ardentemente

craven ['krevən] adj & s codardo

craving ['kreviŋ] s anelito, desiderio

craw [krɔ] s gozzo

crawl [krɔl] s strisciamento, avanzata striscioni; (sports) crawl m || intr strisciare, avanzare striscioni; (said of snakes) brulicare; (said of insects) formicolare; (to feel creepy) sentirsi il formicolio

crayfish ['krefɪʃ] s (Palinurus vulgaris) aragosta; (Astacus; Cambarus) gambero

crayon ['kre-ən] s pastello; disegno a pastello || tr disegnare a pastello

craze [krez] s mania, moda || tr fare impazzire

cra·zy ['krezi] adj (-zier; -ziest) pazzo, matto; **to be crazy about** (coll) esser matto per; **to drive crazy** fare impazzire

cra'zy bone' s osso rabbioso (del gomito)

creak [krik] s scricchiolio, cigolio || intr scricchiolare, cigolare

creak·y ['kriki] adj (-ier; -iest) stridente, cigolante

cream [krim] s crema, panna; (finest part) fior fiore m || tr rendere di consistenza cremosa; (to remove cream from) scremare; prendere il meglio di

creamer·y ['kriməri] s (-ies) (factory) caseificio; (store) cremeria

cream' puff' s bignè m

cream·y ['krimi] adj (-ier; -iest) cremoso; butirroso

crease [kris] s piega, grinza || tr piegare, raggrinzire || intr piegarsi, raggrinzirsi, far pieghe

crease'-resis'tant adj antipiega

create [kri'et] tr creare

creation [kri'eʃən] s creazione; **the Creation** il creato

creative [kri'etɪv] adj creativo

creator [kri'etər] s creatore m

creature ['kritʃər] s creatura

credence ['kridəns] s credenza

credentials [krɪ'denʃəlz] spl lettere fpl credenziali; documento d'autorizzazione

credible ['krɛdɪbəl] adj credibile

credit ['krɛdɪt] s credito; (in a school) unità f di promozione; (com) avere m; **credits** (mov, telv) titoli mpl di testa || tr accreditare; **to credit s.o. with s.th** attribuire qlco a qlcu

creditable ['krɛdɪtəbəl] adj lodevole

cred'it card' s carta di credito

creditor ['krɛdɪtər] s creditore m

cre·do ['krido] or ['kredo] s (-dos) credo

credulous ['krɛdʒələs] adj credulo

creed [krid] s credo

creek [krik] s fiumicello

creep [krip] v (pret & pp crept [krept]) intr strisciare, avanzare striscioni; (to grow along a wall) arrampicarsi; (to feel creepy) sentirsi il formicolio

creeper ['kripər] s strisciante m; (plant) rampicante f

creeping ['kripɪŋ] adj lento; (plant) rampicante

cremate ['krimet] tr cremare

cremato·ry ['krimə,tori] adj crematorio || s (-ries) forno crematorio

Creole ['kri-ol] adj & s creolo

crescent ['krɛsənt] s (of Islam) mezzaluna; (of moon) crescente m; (roll) cornetto

cress [krɛs] s crescione m

crest [krɛst] s cresta; (heral) stemma m, insegna

crestfallen ['krɛst,fɔlən] adj depresso

Cretan ['kritən] adj & s cretese mf

cretin ['kritən] s cretino

crevice ['krɛvɪs] s fessura, fenditura

crew [kru] s (group working together) personale m; (group of workmen;

mob) ciurma; (*of a ship or racing boat*) equipaggio; (sports) canottaggio

crew' cut' s capelli mpl a spazzola

crib [krɪb] s (*bed*) lettino; (*rack*) rastrelliera; (*building*) capanna, granaio; (coll) bigino || v (*pret & pp* **cribbed;** ger **cribbing**) tr (coll) usare un bigino in || intr (coll) usare un bigino; (coll) commettere un plagio

cricket ['krɪkɪt] s grillo; (sports) cricket m, palla a spatola

crier ['kraɪ·ər] s banditore m

crime [kraɪm] s delitto, crimine m

criminal ['krɪmɪnəl] adj criminale; (*code*) penale || s delinquente mf

crimp [krɪmp] s piega, pieghettatura; **to put a crimp in** (slang) mettere i bastoni fra le ruote a || tr pieghettare; (*the hair*) arricciare

crimson ['krɪmzən] adj & s cremisi m || intr imporporarsi

cringe [krɪndʒ] intr rannicchiarsi; (*to fawn*) umiliarsi

crinkle ['krɪŋkəl] tr arricciare || intr (*to rustle*) sfrusciare

cripple ['krɪpəl] s zoppo, sciancato || tr storpiare; (*e.g., business*) paralizzare

cri·sis ['kraɪsɪs] s (-ses [siz]) crisi f

crisp [krɪsp] adj (*brittle*) croccante, friabile; (*air*) frizzante; (*sharp and clear*) acuto

criteri·on [kraɪ'tɪrɪ·ən] s (-a [ə] or -ons) criterio

critic ['krɪtɪk] s critico

critical ['krɪtɪkəl] adj critico

criticism ['krɪtɪ,sɪzəm] s critica

criticize ['krɪtɪ,saɪz] tr & intr criticare

critique [krɪ'tik] s critica

croak [krok] s (*of frogs*) gracidio; (*of crows*) gracchiamento || intr gracidare; gracchiare; (slang) crepare

Croat ['kro·æt] s croato

Croatian [kro'eʃən] adj & s croato

cro·chet [kro'ʃe] s lavoro all'uncinetto || v (*pret & pp* **-cheted** ['ʃed]; ger **-cheting** ['ʃe·ɪŋ]) tr & intr lavorare all'uncinetto

crock [krak] s vaso di terracotta, giara, orcio

crockery ['krakəri] s vasellame m di terracotta, terracotta

crocodile ['krakə,daɪl] s coccodrillo

croc'odile tears' spl lacrime fpl di coccodrillo

crocus ['krokəs] s croco

crone [kron] s vecchia incartapecorita

cro·ny ['kroni] s (-nies) amicone m, compare m

crook [kruk] s (*hook*) uncino; (*staff*) pastorale m; (*bend*) curva; (*bend of pipe*) gomito; (coll) imbroglione m || tr piegare || intr piegarsi

crooked ['krukɪd] adj uncinato; curvo, piegato; (coll) disonesto

croon [krun] intr canterellare; cantare in modo sentimentale

crop [krap] s (*of bird*) gozzo; (*agricultural product, growing or harvested*) messe f; (*agricultural product harvested*) raccolto; (*riding whip*) fru-

stino; (*hair cut close*) capelli corti; gruppo || v (*pret & pp* **cropped;** ger **cropping**) tr (*to cut the ends off of*) spuntare; (*to reap*) raccogliere; (*to cut short*) tosare || intr—**to crop out** or **up** apparire inaspettatamente

crop'-dust'ing s fumigazione aerea

cropper ['krapər] s mietitore m; (*sharecropper*) mezzadro; **to come a cropper** (coll) fare una cascataccia; (coll) andare in rovina

croquet [kro'ke] s croquet m, pallamaglio m & f

croquette [kro'ket] s crocchetta

crosier ['kroʒər] s pastorale m

cross [krɔs] or [kras] adj trasversale, contrario, obliquo; (*irritable*) bisbetico, di cattivo umore; (*of mixed breed*) incrociato || s croce f; (*crossing of breeds*) incrocio; **to take the cross** farsi crociato || tr crociare, segnare con una croce; (*the street*) attraversare; (*e.g., the legs*) incrociare; (*to draw a line across*) barrare; (*to thwart*) ostacolare; **to cross oneself** farsi il segno della croce; **to cross one's mind** venire in mente a uno; **to cross out** cancellare || intr incrociarsi

cross'bones' spl teschio e tibie incrociate (*simbolo della morte*)

cross'bow' s balestra

cross'breed' v (*pret & pp* **-bred** [,bred]) tr incrociare, ibridare

cross'-coun'try adj campestre; attraverso il paese

cross'-exami'na'tion s (law) confronto, interrogatorio in contradditorio

cross'-eyed' ['krɔs,aɪd] or ['kras,aɪd] adj guercio, strabico

crossing ['krɔsɪŋ] or ['krɑsɪŋ] s incrocio; ostacolo; (*of the sea*) traversata; (*of a river*) guado; (rr) passaggio a livello

cross'patch' s (coll) bisbetico

cross'piece' s traversa

cross' ref'erence s richiamo, rimando

cross'road' s strada trasversale; **at the crossroads** al bivio; **crossroads** crocicchio

cross' sec'tion s sezione trasversale

cross' street' s traversa

cross' talk' s conversazione; (telp) diafonia

cross'word puz'zle s cruciverba m, parole incrociate

crotch [krɑtʃ] s inforcatura; (*of pants*) cavallo

crotchety ['krɑtʃɪti] adj bisbetico

crouch [kraʊtʃ] intr accocolarsi

croup [krup] s (pathol) crup m

crouton ['krutɑn] s crostino

crow [kro] s corvo, cornacchia; (*cry of rooster*) chicchirichì m; **as the crow flies** in linea retta, a volo d'uccello; **to eat crow** (coll) rimangiarsi le parole || intr fare chicchirichì; **to crow over** vantarsi di, esultare per

crow'bar' s bastone m a leva

crowd [kraʊd] s folla; (*common people*) masse fpl; (coll) gruppo || tr

affollare; (to push) spingere || intr
affollarsi; (to press forward) spin-
gersi
crowded ['kraudɪd] adj affollato
crown [kraun] s corona; (of hat) cu-
pola; (highest point) sommo || tr
coronare; (checkers) damare; to
crown s.o. (coll) battere qlcu sulla
testa
crown' prince' s principe ereditario
crown' prin'cess s principessa ereditaria
crow's'-foot' s (-feet) zampa di gallina
crow's'-nest' s coffa, gabbia
crucial ['kruʃəl] adj cruciale, critico
crucible ['krusɪbəl] s crogiolo
crucifix ['krusɪfɪks] s crocefisso
crucifixion [ˌkrusɪ'fɪkʃən] s crocifis-
sione
cruci·fy ['krusɪˌfaɪ] v (pret & pp -fied)
tr crocifiggere
crude [krud] adj (raw) grezzo; (unripe) acerbo; (roughly made; uncultured) rozzo
crudi·ty ['krudɪti] s (-ties) rozzezza
cruel ['kru·əl] adj crudele
cruel·ty ['kru·əlti] s (-ties) crudeltà f
cruet ['kru·ɪt] s oliera
cruise [kruz] s crociera || tr navigare
|| intr andare in crociera; andare
avanti e indietro
cruiser ['kruzər] s (nav) incrociatore
m
cruising ['kruzɪŋ] adj di crociera
cruis'ing ra'dius s autonomia di crociera
cruller ['krʌlər] s frittella
crumb [krʌm] s briciola || tr sbricio-
lare; (e.g., a cutlet) impannare ||
intr sbriciolarsi
crumble ['krʌmbəl] tr sbriciolare, pol-
verizzare || intr andare a pezzi, pol-
verizzarsi; sbriciolarsi
crum·my ['krʌmi] adj (-mier; -miest)
(slang) sporco; (miserable) (slang)
schifoso; (e.g., joke) (slang) povero
crumple ['krʌmpəl] tr sgualcire, spiegazzare; to **crumple into a ball** ap-
pallottolare || intr spiegazzarsi
crunch [krʌntʃ] s crocchio; (coll)
stretta, morsa || tr sgranocchiare ||
intr crocchiare
crusade [kru'sed] s crociata || intr
crociarsi; (to take up a cause) farsi
paladino
crusader [kru'sedər] s crociato; (of a
cause) paladino
crush [krʌʃ] s pigiatura, schiacciatura;
(crowd) calca; (coll) infatuazione ||
tr schiacciare; (to grind) frantumare;
(to subdue) sottomettere; (to extract
by squeezing) pigiare
crust [krʌst] s crosta; (slang) faccia
tosta || tr incrostare || intr incrostare,
incrostarsi
crustacean [krʌs'teʃən] s crostaceo
crust·y ['krʌsti] adj (-ier; -iest) crostoso; duro; rude
crutch [krʌtʃ] s gruccia, stampella;
(fig) sostegno
crux [krʌks] s difficoltà f, busillis m;
(crucial point) punto cruciale

cry [kraɪ] s (cries) (shout) grido; (fit
of weeping) pianto; (entreaty) richiamo; (of animal) urlo; **a far cry**
ben lontano, ben distinto; **to have a
good cry** sfogarsi, piangere a calde
lacrime || tr gridare; (to proclaim)
bandire; **to cry down** disprezzare; **to
cry one's heart out** piangere a calde
lacrime; **to cry out** proclamare; **to
cry up** elogiare || intr gridare, urlare;
piangere; **to cry for** implorare
cry'ba'by s (-bies) piagnucolone m
crypt [krɪpt] s cripta
cryptic(al) ['krɪptɪk(əl)] adj segreto,
occulto, misterioso
crystal ['krɪstəl] s cristallo
crys'tal ball' s globo di cristallo
crystalline ['krɪstəlɪn] or ['krɪstəˌlaɪn]
adj cristallino
crystallize ['krɪstəˌlaɪz] tr cristalliz-
zare || intr cristallizzarsi
cub [kʌb] s cucciolo; (of lion) leoncino; (of fox) volpicino, volpac-
chiotto
cubbyhole ['kʌbɪˌhol] s sgabuzzino,
bugigattolo
cube [kjub] adj cubico || s cubo; (of
sugar) zolla || tr elevare al cubo; (to
shape) tagliare in quadretti
cubic ['kjubɪk] adj cubico
cub' report'er s giornalista novello
cuckold ['kʌkəld] adj & s cornuto,
becco || tr cornificare
cuckoo ['kuku] adj (slang) pazzo || s
cuculo
cuck'oo clock' s orologio a cucù
cucumber ['kjukʌmbər] s cetriolo
cud [kʌd] s mangime masticato; **to
chew the cud** ruminare
cuddle ['kʌdəl] tr abbracciare affet-
tuosamente || intr (to lie close) gia-
cere vicino; (to curl up) rannicchiarsi, raggomitolarsi
cudg·el ['kʌdʒəl] s manganello, randello; **to take up the cudgels for** farsi
paladino di || v (pret & pp -eled or
-elled; ger -eling or -elling) tr bastonare, randellare; **to cudgel one's
brains** rompersi la testa
cue [kju] s suggerimento, imbeccata;
(billiards) stecca; **to miss a cue**
(theat) mancare la battuta; (coll)
non capire l'antifona || tr—**to cue
s.o. (in) on** (coll) dare a qlcu informazioni su
cuff [kʌf] s (of shirt) polsino; (of
trousers) risvolto; (slap) schiaffo ||
tr schiaffeggiare
cuff' links' spl bottoni doppi, gemelli
mpl
cuirass [kwɪ'ræs] s corazza
cuisine [kwɪ'zin] s cucina
culinary ['kjulɪˌneri] adj culinario
cull [kʌl] s scarto || tr (to gather,
pluck) cogliere; selezionare, scegliere
culminate ['kʌlmɪˌnet] intr culminare
culottes [ku'lats] spl gonna pantaloni
culpable ['kʌlpəbəl] adj colpevole
culprit ['kʌlprɪt] s colpevole m, imputato
cult [kʌlt] s culto
cultivate ['kʌltɪˌvet] tr coltivare

cultivated [ˈkʌltɪ ˌvetɪd] *adj* colto, coltivato

cultivation [ˌkʌltɪˈveʃən] *s* coltivazione, cultura

culture [ˈkʌltʃər] *s* cultura

cultured [ˈkʌltʃərd] *adj* colto

cul'tured pearl' *s* perla coltivata

culvert [ˈkʌlvərt] *s* chiavica

cumbersome [ˈkʌmbərsəm] *adj* ingombrante, incomodo; (*clumsy*) goffo

cumulative [ˈkjumjə ˌletɪv] *adj* cumulativo

cunning [ˈkʌnɪŋ] *adj* (*sly*) astuto; (*skillful*) abile; (*pretty*) bello; (*created with skill*) ben fatto, fine || *s* astuzia; abilità *f*, destrezza

cup [kʌp] *s* tazza; (mach, sports) coppa; (eccl) calice *m*; **in one's cups** ubriaco || *v* (*pret & pp* **cupped**) *ger* **cupping**) *tr* mettere ventose a; **to cup one's hands** foggiare le mani a mo' di conca

cupboard [ˈkʌbərd] *s* armadio a muro, dispensa; (*buffet*) credenza

Cupid [ˈkjupɪd] *s* Cupido

cupidity [kjuˈpɪdɪti] *s* cupidigia

cup' of tea' *s* tazza di tè; (coll) forte *m*, e.g., **physics is not my cup of tea** la fisica non è il mio forte

cupola [ˈkjupələ] *s* cupola

cur [kʌr] *s* cane bastardo; (*despicable fellow*) canaglia, gaglioffo

curate [ˈkjurɪt] *s* curato

curative [ˈkjurətɪv] *adj* curativo

curator [kjuˈretər] *s* conservatore *m*

curb [kʌrb] *s* (*of bit*) barbazzale *m*; (*of pavement*) orlo del marciapiede; (*check*) freno || *tr* frenare

curb'stone' *s* cordone *m*; (*of well*) sponda del pozzo

curd [kʌrd] *s* cagliata || *tr* cagliare || *intr* cagliarsi

curdle [ˈkʌrdəl] *tr* cagliare; (*the blood*) far gelare || *intr* cagliarsi; (*said of custard*) impazzare

cure [kjur] *s* cura || *tr* curare; (*e.g., meat*) conservare; (*wood*) stagionare

cure'-all' *s* panacea

curfew [ˈkʌrfju] *s* coprifuoco

curi·o [ˈkjurɪ ˌo] *s* (-os) curiosità *f*

curiosi·ty [ˌkjurɪˈɑsɪti] *s* (-ties) curiosità *f*

curious [ˈkjurɪ·əs] *adj* curioso

curl [kʌrl] *s* (*of hair*) ricciolo; (*anything curled*) rotolo, spirale *f* || *tr* arricciare; arrotolare; (*the lips*) torcere || *intr* arricciarsi; arrotolarsi; **to curl up** raggomitolarsi

curlicue [ˈkʌrlɪ ˌkju] *s* ghirigoro

curl'ing i'ron *s* ferro da arricciare

curl'pa'per *s* bigodino

curl·y [ˈkʌrli] *adj* (-ier; -iest) ricciuto

curmudgeon [kərˈmʌdʒən] *s* bisbetico

currant [ˈkʌrənt] *s* (*seedless raisin*) uva passa di Corinto, uva sultanina; (*shrub and berry of genus Ribes*) ribes *m*

curren·cy [ˈkʌrənsi] *s* (-cies) (*circulation*) circolazione; (*money*) denaro circolante; (*general use*) corso

current [ˈkʌrənt] *adj & s* corrente *f*

cur'rent account' *s* conto corrente

cur'rent events' *spl* attualità *fpl*, eventi *mpl* correnti

curricu·lum [kəˈrɪkjələm] *s* (-lums or -la [lə]) programma *m*; piano educativo

cur·ry [ˈkʌri] *s* (-ries) (*spice*) curry *m* || *v* (*pret & pp* -ried) *tr* (*a horse*) strigliare; (*leather*) conciare; **to curry favor** cercare di compiacere

cur'ry·comb' *s* striglia || *tr* strigliare

curse [kʌrs] *s* maledizione; bestemmia || *tr* maledire || *intr* imprecare, bestemmiare

cursed [ˈkʌrsɪd] or [kʌrst] *adj* maledetto; (*hateful*) odiato

cursive [ˈkʌrsɪv] *adj & s* corsivo

cursory [ˈkʌrsəri] *adj* rapido, superficiale

curt [kʌrt] *adj* (*rude*) brusco, sgarbato; (*short*) breve, conciso

curtail [kərˈtel] *tr* ridurre, restringere

curtain [ˈkʌrtən] *s* (*in front of stage*) sipario; (*for window*) tendina; (fig) cortina || *tr* coprire con tenda; separare con tenda; coprire, nascondere

cur'tain call' *s* (theat) chiamata

cur'tain rais'er [ˈrezər] *s* (theat) avanspettacolo; (sports) incontro preliminare

cur'tain ring' *s* campanella

cur'tain rod' *s* bastone *m* su cui si fissano le tende

curt·sy [ˈkʌrtsi] *s* (-sies) riverenza, inchino || *v* (*pret & pp* -sied) *intr* fare la riverenza, inchinarsi

curve [kʌrv] *s* curva || *tr* curvare || *intr* curvarsi

curved [kʌrvd] *adj* curvo, curvato

cushion [ˈkuʃən] *s* cuscino; (*of billiard table*) mattonella || *tr* proteggere, ammortizzare, attutire

cuspidor [ˈkʌspɪ ˌdor] *s* sputacchiera

cuss [kʌs] *s* (coll) bestemmia; (coll) tipo perverso || *tr* maledire || *intr* bestemmiare

custard [ˈkʌstərd] *s* crema

custodian [kəsˈtodɪ·ən] *s* (*caretaker*) custode *m*, guardiano *m*; (*person who is entrusted with s.th*) conservatore *m*; (*janitor of school*) bidello

custo·dy [ˈkʌstədi] *s* (-dies) custodia; (*imprisonment*) arresto; **in custody** in prigione; **to take into custody** arrestare

custom [ˈkʌstəm] *s* costume *m*; (*customers*) clientela; **customs** dogana; diritti *mpl* doganali

customary [ˈkʌstə ˌmeri] *adj* consueto, abituale

custom-built [ˈkʌstəmˈbɪlt] *adj* fatto su misura; (*car*) fuori serie

customer [ˈkʌstəmər] *s* cliente *mf*

cus'tom·house' *adj* doganale || *s* dogana

custom-made [ˈkʌstəmˈmed] *adj* fatto su misura

cus'toms inspec'tion *s* visita doganale

cus'toms of'ficer *s* doganiere *m*

cus'tom work' *s* lavoro fatto su misura

cut [kʌt] *adj* (*prices*) ridotto; **to be cut out for** essere tagliato per || *s* taglio; (*reduction*) ribasso; (typ) cliché *m*;

(*snub*) (coll) affronto; (coll) assenza non autorizzata; (coll) parte *f;* **a cut above** (coll) un po' meglio di ‖ *tr* tagliare; (*cards*) alzare; (*prices*) ridurre; (coll) far finta di non riconoscere; (coll) marinare; **cut it out!** basta!; **to cut back** ridurre; **to cut off** tagliare; diseredare; (surg) amputare; **to cut short** interrompere; **to cut teeth** fare i denti; **to cut up** sminuzzare; criticare ‖ *intr* tagliare, tagliarsi; **to cut across** attraversare; **to cut in** interrompere; **to cut under** vendere sottoprezzo; **to cut up** (slang) fare il pagliaccio

cut-and-dried [ˈkʌtənˈdraɪd] *adj* monotono, stantio; bell'e fatto, fatto in anticipo

cutaneous [kjuˈtenɪ-əs] *adj* cutaneo

cut′away′ coat′ [ˈkʌtəˌwe] *s* marsina da giorno

cut′back′ *s* riduzione; eliminazione; (mov) ritorno dell'azione a un'epoca anteriore

cute [kjut] *adj* (coll) carino, grazioso; (*shrewd*) (coll) furbo

cut′ glass′ *s* cristallo intagliato

cuticle [ˈkjutɪkəl] *s* cuticola

cutlass [ˈkʌtləs] *s* sciabola

cutler [ˈkʌtlər] *s* coltellinaio

cutlery [ˈkʌtlərɪ] *s* coltelleria

cutlet [ˈkʌtlɪt] *s* cotoletta; (*flat croquette*) polpetta

cut′off′ *s* taglio; (*road*) scorciatoia; (*of cylinder*) otturatore *m,* chiusura dell'ammissione; (*of river*) braccio diretto

cut′out′ *s* ritaglio; (aut) valvola di scappamento libero

cut′-rate′ *adj* a prezzo ridotto

cutter [ˈkʌtər] *s* tagliatore *m;* (naut) cutter *m*

cut′throat′ *adj* spietato; (*relentless*) senza posa ‖ *s* assassino

cutting [ˈkʌtɪŋ] *adj* tagliente ‖ *s* taglio; (*from a newspaper*) ritaglio;

(*e.g., of prices*) riduzione; (hort) talea

cut′ting board′ *s* tagliere *m;* (*of dishwasher*) piano d'appoggio

cut′ting edge′ *s* taglio

cuttlefish [ˈkʌtəlˌfɪʃ] *s* seppia

cut′wat′er *s* (*of bridge*) tagliacque *m;* (*of boat*) tagliamare *m*

cyanamide [saɪˈænəˌmaɪd] *s* cianamide *f;* cianamide *f* di calcio

cyanide [ˈsaɪ-əˌnaɪd] *s* cianuro

cycle [ˈsaɪkəl] *s* ciclo; bicicletta; (*of internal combustion engine*) tempo; (phys) periodo ‖ *intr* andare in bicicletta

cyclic(al) [ˈsaɪklɪk(əl)] or [ˈsɪklɪk(əl)] *adj* ciclico

cyclone [ˈsaɪklon] *s* ciclone *m*

cyclops [ˈsaɪklɑps] *s* ciclope *m*

cyclotron [ˈsaɪkləˌtrɑn] or [ˈsɪkloˌtrɑn] *s* ciclotrone *m*

cylinder [ˈsɪlɪndər] *s* cilindro; (*container*) bombola

cyl′inder block′ *s* monoblocco

cyl′inder bore′ *s* alesaggio

cyl′inder head′ *s* testa

cylindric(al) [sɪˈlɪndrɪk(əl)] *adj* cilindrico

cymbals [ˈsɪmbəls] *spl* piatti *mpl*

cynic [ˈsɪnɪk] *adj & s* cinico

cynical [ˈsɪnɪkəl] *adj* cinico

cynicism [ˈsɪnɪˌsɪzəm] *s* cinismo

cynosure [ˈsaɪnəˌʃʊr] or [ˈsɪnəˌʃʊr] *s* centro dell'attenzione

cypress [ˈsaɪprəs] *s* cipresso

Cyprus [ˈsaɪprəs] *s* Cipro

Cyrus [ˈsaɪrəs] *s* Ciro

cyst [sɪst] *s* ciste *f,* cisti *f*

czar [zɑr] *s* zar *m*

czarina [zɑˈrinə] *s* zarina

Czech [tʃɛk] *adj & s* ceco

Czecho-Slovak [ˈtʃɛkoˈslovæk] *adj & s* cecoslovacco

Czecho-Slovakia [ˌtʃɛkosloˈvækɪ-ə] *s* la Cecoslovacchia

D

D, d [di] *s* quarta lettera dell'alfabeto inglese

dab [dæb] *s* tocco; (*of mud*) schizzo; (*e.g., of butter*) spalmata ‖ *v* (*pret & pp* **dabbed**) *ger* **dabbing**) *tr* toccare leggermente; (*to apply a substance to*) spennellare

dabble [ˈdæbəl] *tr* spruzzare ‖ *intr* diguazzare; **to dabble in** occuparsi di; (*stocks*) speculare in

dad [dæd] *s* (coll) papà *m*

dad·dy [ˈdædɪ] *s* (-**dies**) (coll) papà *m*

daffodil [ˈdæfədɪl] *s* trombone *m*

daff·y [ˈdæfɪ] *adj* (-**ier;** -**iest**) (coll) pazzo

dagger [ˈdægər] *s* daga, pugnale *m;* (typ) croce *f;* **to look daggers at** fulminare con lo sguardo

dahlia [ˈdæljə] *s* dalia

dai·ly [ˈdeli] *adj* quotidiano, diurno ‖ *s* (-**lies**) quotidiano ‖ *adv* giornalmente

dai′ly dou′ble *s* duplice *f,* accoppiata

dain·ty [ˈdentɪ] *adj* (-**tier;** -**tiest**) delicato ‖ *s* (-**ties**) manicaretto

dair·y [ˈdɛrɪ] *s* (-**ies**) (*store*) latteria; (*factory*) caseificio

dair′y farm′ *s* vaccheria

dair′y·man *s* (-**men**) lattaio

dais [ˈde-ɪs] *s* predella

dai·sy [ˈdezɪ] *s* (-**sies**) margherita

dal·ly [ˈdælɪ] *v* (*pret & pp* -**lied**) *intr* (*to loiter*) bighellonare; (*to trifle*) scherzare

dam [dæm] *s* diga; (*for fishing*) pescaia; (zool) fattrice *f* ‖ *v* (*pret & pp* **dammed**) *ger* **damming**) *tr* arginare; ostruire; tappare

damage ['dæmɪdʒ] *s* danno, scapito; (fig) menomazione; (com) avaria; **damages** danni *mpl* || *tr* danneggiare, ledere; sinistrare

damascene ['dæmə‚sin] *or* [‚dæmə-'sin] *adj* damasceno || *s* damaschinatura || *tr* damaschinare

dame [dem] *s* dama, signora; (slang) donna

damn [dæm] *s*—**I don't give a damn** (slang) me ne impipo; **that's not worth a damn** (slang) non vale un fico || *tr* dannare, condannare || *intr* maledire || *interj* maledizione!

damnation [dæm'neʃən] *s* dannazione; (theol) condanna

damned [dæmd] *adj* dannato, maledetto || **the damned** i dannati || *adv* maledettamente

damp [dæmp] *adj* umido || *s* umidità *f*; (firedamp) grisou *m* || *tr* inumidire; umettare; (*to muffle*) smorzare; (waves) (elec) smorzare; **to damp s.o.'s enthusiasm** raffreddare gli spiriti di qlcu; scoraggiare qlcu

dampen ['dæmpən] *tr* inumidire; umettare; smorzare; (*s.o.'s enthusiasm*) raffreddare

damper ['dæmpər] *s* (*of chimney*) valvola di tiraggio; (fig) doccia fredda; (mus) smorzatore *m*; (mus) sordina

damsel ['dæmzəl] *s* damigella

dance [dæns] *or* [dɑns] *s* ballo, danza || *tr & intr* ballare, danzare

dance' band' *s* orchestrina

dance' floor' *s* pista da ballo

dance' hall' *s* sala da ballo

dancer ['dænsər] *or* ['dɑnsər] *s* danzatore *m*; (*expert or professional*) ballerino

danc'ing part'ner *s* cavaliere *m*; dama

danc'ing par'ty *s* festa da ballo

dandelion ['dændɪ‚laɪ-ən] *s* dente *m* di leone, soffione *m*

dandruff ['dændrəf] *s* forfora

dan·dy ['dændi] *adj* (-dier; -diest) (coll) eccellente, magnifico || *s* (-dies) damerino, elegantone *m*

Dane [den] *s* danese *mf*

danger ['dendʒər] *s* pericolo

dangerous ['dendʒərəs] *adj* pericoloso

dangle ['dæŋgəl] *tr* dondolare || *intr* penzolare, ciondolare

Danish ['denɪʃ] *adj & s* danese *m*

dank [dæŋk] *adj* umido

Danube ['dænjub] *s* Danubio

dapper ['dæpər] *adj* azzimato

dapple ['dæpəl] *adj* pezzato || *tr* chiazzare

dap'ple-gray' *adj* storno

dare [der] *s* sfida || *tr* sfidare || *intr* osare; **I dare say** oserei dire; forse, e.g., **I dare say we will be done at seven** forse avremo finito alle sette; **to dare to** (*to have the courage to*) osare di, fidarsi a

dare'dev'il *s* scavezzacollo

daring ['derɪŋ] *adj* temerario, spericolato || *s* audacia, temerarietà *f*

dark [dɑrk] *adj* scuro; (*complexion*) bruno; oscuro, segreto; (*gloomy*) tetro, fosco || *s* oscurità *f*, scuro; tenebre *fpl*; **in the dark** al buio

Dark' Ag'es *spl* alto medio evo

dark-complexioned ['dɑrkkəm'plɛk-ʃənd] *adj* bruno

darken ['dɑrkən] *tr* scurire, oscurare || *intr* scurirsi, oscurarsi

dark' horse' *s* vincitore imprevisto, outsider *m*

darkly ['dɑrkli] *adv* oscuramente; segretamente

dark' meat' *s* gamba o anca (di pollo o tacchino)

darkness ['dɑrknɪs] *s* oscurità *f*

dark'room' *s* camera oscura

darling ['dɑrlɪŋ] *adj & s* caro, amato

darn [dɑrn] *s* rammendo || *tr* rammendare || *interj* (coll) accidenti!

darned [dɑrnd] *adj* (coll) maledetto || *adv* maledettamente; (coll) tremendamente

darnel ['dɑrnəl] *s* zizzania

darning ['dɑrnɪŋ] *s* rammendo

darn'ing nee'dle *s* ago da rammendo

dart [dɑrt] *s* freccia, dardo; (*game*) frecciolo || *intr* dardeggiare; lanciarsi, precipitarsi

dash [dæʃ] *s* sciacquio; piccola quantità, sospetto; (*spirit*) brio; (typ, telg) trattino, lineetta || *tr* lanciare; mescolare; (*s.o.'s hopes*) frustrare; deprimere; **to dash off** gettar giù; **to dash to pieces** fare a pezzi || *intr* precipitarsi; **to dash against** gettarsi contro; **to dash by** passare a gran velocità; **to dash in** entrare come un razzo; **to dash off** *or* **out** andarsene in fretta; lanciarsi fuori

dash'board' *s* cruscotto; (*in an open carriage*) parafango

dashing ['dæʃɪŋ] *adj* impetuoso; vistoso || *s* (*of waves*) sciacquio

dastard ['dæstərd] *adj & s* vile *mf*, codardo

da'ta proc'essing *s* elaborazione

date [det] *s* (*time*) data; (*palm*) palma da datteri; (*fruit*) dattero; (*appointment*) (coll) appuntamento; **out of date** fuori moda; **to date** sinora; **up to date** a giorno || *tr* datare; (coll) avere un appuntamento con || *intr*— **to date from** partire da

date' line' *s* linea del cambiamento di data

dative ['detɪv] *adj & s* dativo

datum ['detəm] *or* ['dætəm] *s* (**data** ['detə] *or* ['dætə]) dato

daub [dɔb] *s* imbratto || *tr* imbrattare

daughter ['dɔtər] *s* figlia, figliola

daughter-in-law ['dɔtərɪn‚lɔ] *s* (**daughters-in-law**) nuora

daunt [dɔnt] *tr* spaventare; intimidire

dauntless ['dɔntlɪs] *adj* intrepido

dauphin ['dɔfɪn] *s* delfino

davenport ['dævən‚port] *s* sofà *m*, sofà *m* letto

davit ['dævɪt] *s* gru *f* per lancia

daw [dɔ] *s* cornacchia

dawdle ['dɔdəl] *intr* bighellonare

dawn [dɔn] *s* alba || *intr* (*said of the day*) farsi, nascere, spuntare; **to dawn on** cominciare a apparire nella mente di

day [de] *adj* diurno; (*student*) esterno || *s* giorno; (*of travel, work, etc.*)

giornata; **a few days ago** giorni fa; **any day now** da un giorno all'altro; **by day** di giorno; **the day after** il giorno dopo; **the day after tomorrow** dopodomani; **the day before yesterday** ieri l'altro; **to call it a day** (coll) finire di lavorare

day' bed' s sofà m letto

day'book' s brogliaccio

day'break' s far m del giorno

day'dream' s fantasticheria || intr fantasticare

day' la'borer s giornaliero

day'light' s luce f del giorno; alba; **in broad daylight** alla luce del sole; **to see daylight** comprendere; vedere la fine

day'light-sav'ing time' s ora legale, ora estiva

day' nurs'ery s asilo infantile

day' off' s giorno di vacanza; (of servant) libera uscita

day' of reck'oning s giorno di rendiconto; (last judgment) giorno del giudizio

day' shift' s turno diurno

day'time' adj diurno || s giornata

daze [dez] s stordimento; **in a daze** stordito || tr stordire

dazzle ['dæzəl] s abbagliamento || tr abbagliare

dazzling ['dæzlɪŋ] adj abbagliante

deacon ['dikən] s diacono

dead [dɛd] adj morto || s—**in the dead of** (e.g., night) nel pieno di; **the dead** i morti || adv (coll) completamente; (abruptly) (coll) di colpo

dead' beat' adj (coll) stanco morto

dead'beat' s (coll) scroccone m

dead' cen'ter s punto morto

dead' drunk' adj ubriaco fradicio

deaden ['dɛdən] tr attutire; (e.g., s.o.'s senses) ottundere

dead' end' s vicolo cieco

dead' let'ter s lettera morta; lettera non reclamata

dead'line' s termine m

dead'lock' s punto morto || tr portare al punto morto || intr giungere al punto morto

dead-ly ['dɛdli] adj (-lier; -liest) mortale; insopportabile

dead' pan' s (slang) faccia senza espressione

dead'pan' adj senza espressione

dead' reck'oning s (naut) stima

dead'wood' s legna secca; (fig) zavorra

deaf [dɛf] adj sordo; **to turn a deaf ear** fare orecchio da mercante

deaf'-and-dumb' adj sordomuto

deafen ['dɛfən] tr assordare, intronare

deafening ['dɛfənɪŋ] adj assordante

deaf'-mute' s sordomuto

deafness ['dɛfnɪs] s sordità f

deal [dil] s accordo; quantità f; (cards) mano, girata; (coll) affare m; (coll) trattamento; **a good deal (of)** or **a great deal (of)** moltissimo || v (pret & pp dealt [dɛlt]) tr (a blow) menare; (cards) fare, sfogliare; **to deal s.o. in** (coll) includere || intr mercanteggiare, commerciare; fare le

carte; **to deal with** trattare con; trattare di

dealer ['dilər] s commerciante mf, esercente mf; (cards) mazziere m

dean [din] s decano

dear [dir] adj (beloved; expensive) caro; **dear me!** povero me!; **Dear Sir** egregio Signore || s caro

dearie ['dɪri] s (coll) caro

dearth [dʌrθ] s scarsezza; insufficienza

death [dɛθ] s morte f; **to bleed to death** morire dissanguato; **to burn to death** morire bruciato; **to choke to death** morire di soffocazione; **to freeze to death** morire di gelo; **to put to death** dare la morte a; **to shoot to death** uccidere a fucilate; **to stab to death** scannare; **to starve to death** far morire di fame; morire di fame

death'bed' s letto di morte

death'blow' s colpo mortale

deathless ['dɛθlɪs] adj immortale, eterno

deathly ['dɛθli] adj mortale || adv mortalmente; assolutamente

death' pen'alty s pena di morte

death' rate' s mortalità f

death' rat'tle s rantolo della morte

death' ray' s raggio della morte

death' sen'tence s pena di morte

death' war'rant s pena di morte; fine f di ogni speranza

death'watch' s veglia mortuaria; (zool) orologio della morte

debacle [de'bakəl] s disastro; (downfall) tracollo; (in a river) sgelo repentino

de-bar [dɪ'bar] v (pret & pp -barred; ger -barring) tr escludere; proibire (with dat)

debark [dɪ'bark] tr & intr sbarcare

debarkation [,dibar'keʃən] s sbarco

debase [dɪ'bes] tr degradare; adulterare

debatable [dɪ'betəbəl] adj discutibile

debate [dɪ'bet] s discussione || tr & intr discutere

debauch [dɪ'bɔtʃ] s dissolutezza, corruzione || tr corrompere

debauchee [,dɛbɔ'ʃi] or [,dɛbɔ't/i] s degenerato, vizioso

debaucher-y [dɪ'bɔt/əri] s (-ies) dissolutezza, corruzione

debenture [dɪ'bɛntʃər] s (bond) obbligazione; (voucher) buono

debilitate [dɪ'bɪlɪ,tet] tr debilitare

debili-ty [dɪ'bɪlɪti] s (-ties) debolezza

debit ['dɛbɪt] s debito; (debit side) (com) dare m || tr addebitare

debonair [,dɛbə'nɛr] adj gioviale; cortese

debris [de'bri] s detrito, rottami mpl

debt [dɛt] s debito; **to run into debt** indebitarsi

debtor ['dɛtər] s debitore m

debut [de'bju] or ['debju] s debutto; **to make one's debut** debuttare || intr debuttare

debutante [,dɛbju'tɑnt] or ['dɛbjə,tɑnt] s debuttante f, esordiente f

decade ['dɛked] s decennio

decadence [dɪ'kedəns] s decadenza

decadent [dɪ'kædənt] *adj* & *s* decadente *mf*

decanter [dɪ'kæntər] *s* boccia

decapitate [dɪ'kæpɪ,tet] *tr* decapitare

decay [dɪ'ke] *s* (*decline*) decadimento; (*rotting*) marciume *m*, putredine *f*; (*of teeth*) carie *f* ‖ *tr* imputridire ‖ *intr* imputridire, marcire; (*said of teeth*) cariarsi

decease [dɪ'sis] *s* decesso ‖ *intr* decedere

deceased [dɪ'sist] *adj* & *s* defunto

deceit [dɪ'sit] *s* inganno, frode *f*

deceitful [dɪ'sitfəl] *adj* ingannatore, menzognero, subdolo

deceive [dɪ'siv] *tr* & *intr* ingannare

decelerate [dɪ'sɛlə,ret] *tr* & *intr* decelerare

December [dɪ'sɛmbər] *s* dicembre *m*

decen•cy ['disənsi] *s* (**-cies**) decenza, pudore *m*; **decencies** convenienze *fpl*

decent ['disənt] *adj* decente; (*proper*) conveniente

decentralize [dɪ'sɛntrə,laɪz] *tr* decentrare

deception [dɪ'sɛpʃən] *s* inganno

deceptive [dɪ'sɛptɪv] *adj* ingannevole

decide [dɪ'saɪd] *tr* decidere ‖ *intr* decidere, decidersi

decimal ['dɛsɪməl] *adj* & *s* decimale *m*

dec′imal point′ *s* (*in Italian the comma is used to separate the decimal fraction from the integer*) virgola

decimate ['dɛsɪ,met] *tr* decimare

decipher [dɪ'saɪfər] *tr* decifrare

decision [dɪ'sɪʒən] *s* decisione

decisive [dɪ'saɪsɪv] *adj* decisivo; (*resolute*) fermo

deck [dɛk] *s* (*of cards*) mazzo; (*naut*) coperta, tolda, ponte *m*; **on deck** (*coll*) pronto; (*coll*) prossimo ‖ *tr*— **to deck out** adornare; (*with flags*) imbandierare

deck′ chair′ *s* sedia a sdraio

deck′ hand′ *s* marinaio di coperta

deck′house′ *s* (*naut*) tuga

deck′le edge′ ['dɛkəl] *s* sbavatura

declaim [dɪ'klem] *tr* & *intr* declamare

declaration [,dɛklə're ʃən] *s* dichiarazione

declarative [dɪ'klærətɪv] *adj* declaratorio; (*gram*) enunciativo

declare [dɪ'klɛr] *tr* dichiarare ‖ *intr* dichiararsi

declension [dɪ'klɛnʃən] *s* declinazione

declination [,dɛklɪ'neʃən] *s* declinazione

decline [dɪ'klaɪn] *s* decadenza; (*in prices*) ribasso; (*in health*) deperimento; (*of sun*) tramonto ‖ *tr* declinare ‖ *intr* declinare; decadere, scadere

declivi•ty [dɪ'klɪvɪti] *s* (**-ties**) declivio, pendice *f*

decode [di'kod] *tr* decifrare

décolleté [,dekɑl'te] *adj* scollato

decompose [,dikəm'poz] *tr* decomporre ‖ *intr* decomporsi

decomposition [,dikɑmpə'zɪʃən] *s* decomposizione

décor [de'kor] *s* decorazione; (*of a room*) stile *m*; (*theat*) scenario

decorate ['dɛkə,ret] *tr* decorare

decoration [,dɛkə'reʃən] *s* decorazione

decorator ['dɛkə,retər] *s* decoratore *m*

decorous ['dɛkərəs] *or* [dɪ'korəs] *adj* corretto, decoroso

decorum [dɪ'korəm] *s* decoro, correttezza

decoy [dɪ'kɔɪ] *or* ['dikɔɪ] *s* richiamo; (*for birds*) zimbello; (*person*) adescatore *m* ‖ *tr* (*to lure*) adescare; (*to deceive*) abbindolare

decrease [dɪ'kris] *or* [dɪ'kris] *s* diminuzione; (*of salary*) decurtazione ‖ [dɪ'kris] *tr* decurtare ‖ *intr* diminuire

decree [dɪ'kri] *s* decreto ‖ *tr* decretare

de•cry [dɪ'kraɪ] *v* (*pret* & *pp* **-cried**) *tr* denigrare, screditare

dedicate ['dɛdɪ,ket] *tr* dedicare

dedication [,dɛdɪ'keʃən] *s* dedizione; (*inscription in a book*) dedica

deduce [dɪ'djus] *or* [dɪ'dus] *tr* dedurre

deduct [dɪ'dʌkt] *tr* dedurre, defalcare

deductible [dɪ'dʌktɪbəl] *adj* defalcabile ‖ *s* (ins) franchigia

deduction [dɪ'dʌkʃən] *s* deduzione

deed [did] *s* fatto; (*exploit*) prodezza; (*law*) titolo ‖ *tr* (*to lure*) trasferire legalmente

deem [dim] *tr* & *intr* credere, giudicare

deep [dip] *adj* profondo; basso; (*woods*) folto; (*friendship*) intimo; **deep in debt** carico di debiti; **deep in thought** assorto in pensieri ‖ *adv* profondamente; **deep into the night** a notte fatta; **to go deep into** approfondirsi in

deepen ['dipən] *tr* approfondire ‖ *intr* approfondirsi

deep′-freeze′ *tr* (*pret* **-froze** [froz]; *pp* **-frozen** [frozən]) *tr* surgelare

deep-laid ['dip,led] *adj* preparato astutamente

deep′ mourn′ing *s* lutto stretto

deep-rooted ['dip,rutɪd] *adj* profondo

deep′-sea′ fish′ing *s* pesca d'alto mare or d'altura

deep-seated ['dip,sitɪd] *adj* profondo, connaturato

Deep′ South′ *s* Profondo Sud

deer [dɪr] *s* cervo

deer′skin′ *s* pelle *f* di daino

deface [dɪ'fes] *tr* sfigurare

defamation [,dɛfə'meʃən] *or* [,difə'meʃən] *s* diffamazione

defame [dɪ'fem] *tr* diffamare

default [dɪ'fɔlt] *s* mancanza; (*failure to act*) inadempienza; **in default of** per mancanza di; **to lose by default** dichiarare forfeit ‖ *tr* essere inadempiente a ‖ *intr* essere inadempiente; (*sports*) dichiarare forfeit

defeat [dɪ'fit] *s* sconfitta, disfatta ‖ *tr* sconfiggere, vincere

defeatism [dɪ'fitɪzəm] *s* disfattismo

defeatist [dɪ'fitɪst] *adj* & *s* disfattista *mf*

defecate ['dɛfɪ,ket] *intr* defecare

defect [dɪ'fɛkt] *or* ['difɛkt] *s* vizio, difetto ‖ [dɪ'fɛkt] *intr* defezionare

defection [dɪ'fɛkʃən] *s* defezione

defective [dɪ'fɛktɪv] *adj* difettivo, difettoso

defend [dɪˈfɛnd] *tr* difendere, proteggere

defendant [dɪˈfɛndənt] *s* (law) imputato, querelato

defender [dɪˈfɛndər] *s* difensore *m*

defense [dɪˈfɛns] *s* difesa

defenseless [dɪˈfɛnslɪs] *adj* indifeso

defensive [dɪˈfɛnsɪv] *adj* difensivo ‖ *s* difensiva

de·fer [dɪˈfʌr] *v* (*pret & pp* **-ferred**; *ger* **-ferring**) *tr* differire, rinviare ‖ *intr* rimettersi

deference [ˈdɛfərəns] *s* deferenza

deferential [ˌdɛfəˈrɛnʃəl] *adj* deferente

deferment [dɪˈfʌrmənt] *s* differimento

defiance [dɪˈfaɪəns] *s* opposizione; sfida; **in defiance of** a dispetto di

defiant [dɪˈfaɪənt] *adj* provocante, ostile

deficien·cy [dɪˈfɪʃənsi] *s* (**-cies**) deficienza; (com) ammanco

deficient [dɪˈfɪʃənt] *adj* deficiente

deficit [ˈdɛfɪsɪt] *adj* deficitario ‖ *s* deficit *m*, disavanzo

defile [dɪˈfaɪl] *or* [ˈdifaɪl] *s* gola, passo ‖ [dɪˈfaɪl] *tr* profanare ‖ *intr* marciare in fila

define [dɪˈfaɪn] *tr* definire

definite [ˈdɛfɪnɪt] *adj* definito; (gram) determinativo, determinato

definition [ˌdɛfɪˈnɪʃən] *s* definizione

definitive [dɪˈfɪnɪtɪv] *adj* definitivo

deflate [dɪˈflet] *tr* sgonfiare; (*s.o.'s hopes*) deprimere; (*e.g., currency*) deflazionare

deflation [dɪˈfleʃən] *s* sgonfiamento; (*of prices*) deflazione

deflect [dɪˈflɛkt] *tr* far deflettere ‖ *intr* deflettere

deflower [diˈflaʊ·ər] *tr* privare dei fiori; (*a woman*) deflorare

deforest [diˈfɑrɛst] *or* [diˈfɔrɛst] *tr* disboscare, smacchiare

deform [dɪˈfɔrm] *tr* deformare

deformed [dɪˈfɔrmd] *adj* deforme

deformi·ty [dɪˈfɔrmɪti] *s* (**-ties**) deformità *f*

defraud [dɪˈfrɔd] *tr* defraudare

defray [dɪˈfre] *tr* pagare

defrost [diˈfrɔst] *or* [diˈfrɑst] *tr* sgelare, sbrinare

defroster [diˈfrɔstər] *or* [diˈfrɑstər] *s* (aut) visiera termica

deft [dɛft] *adj* destro, lesto

defunct [dɪˈfʌŋkt] *adj* defunto

de·fy [dɪˈfaɪ] *v* (*pret & pp* **-fied**) *tr* sfidare, provocare

degeneracy [dɪˈdʒɛnərəsi] *s* degenerazione

degenerate [dɪˈdʒɛnərɪt] *adj & s* degenerato ‖ [dɪˈdʒɛnəˌret] *intr* degenerare, tralignare

degrade [dɪˈgred] *tr* degradare

degrading [dɪˈgredɪŋ] *adj* degradante

degree [dɪˈgri] *s* grado; titolo accademico; **by degrees** a grado a grado; **to a degree** fino a un certo punto; troppo; **to take a degree** ricevere un titolo di studio

dehydrate [diˈhaɪdret] *tr* disidratare

deice [diˈaɪs] *tr* sgelare

dei·fy [ˈdi·ɪˌfaɪ] *v* (*pret & pp* **-fied**) *tr* deificare

deign [den] *intr* degnarsi

dei·ty [ˈdi·ɪti] *s* (**-ties**) deità *f;* **the Deity** Dio

dejected [dɪˈdʒɛktɪd] *adj* demoralizzato

dejection [dɪˈdʒɛkʃən] *s* (*in spirits*) demoralizzazione; (*evacuation*) deiezione

delay [dɪˈle] *s* ritardo, proroga; dilazione; **without further delay** senza ulteriore indugio ‖ *tr* tardare; (*to put off*) differire ‖ *intr* tardare, ritardare

delayed'-ac'tion *adj* a azione differita

delectable [dɪˈlɛktəbəl] *adj* dilettevole

delegate [ˈdɛlɪˌget] *or* [ˈdɛlɪgɪt] *s* delegato, incaricato; (*to a convention*) congressista *mf* ‖ [ˈdɛlɪˌget] *tr* delegare, incaricare

delegation [ˌdɛlɪˈgeʃən] *s* delegazione

delete [dɪˈlit] *tr* cancellare, sopprimere

deletion [dɪˈliʃən] *s* cancellazione

deliberate [dɪˈlɪbərɪt] *adj* meditato; (*slow in deciding*) cauto; (*slow in moving*) lento ‖ [dɪˈlɪbəˌret] *tr & intr* deliberare

deliberately [dɪˈlɪbərɪtli] *adv* (*on purpose*) deliberatamente; (*without hurrying*) con ponderatezza

delica·cy [ˈdɛlɪkəsi] *s* (**-cies**) delicatezza; (*choice food*) leccornia

delicatessen [ˌdɛlɪkəˈtɛsən] *s* negozio di salumerie ‖ *spl* salumerie *fpl*, articoli alimentari scelti

delicious [dɪˈlɪʃəs] *adj* delizioso

delight [dɪˈlaɪt] *s* gioia, delizia ‖ *tr* dilettare ‖ *intr* dilettarsi

delightful [dɪˈlaɪtfəl] *adj* delizioso

delinquen·cy [dɪˈlɪŋkwənsi] *s* (**-cies**) colpa; (*offense*) delinquenza; (*in payment of a debt*) morosità *f*

delinquent [dɪˈlɪŋkwənt] *adj* colpevole; (*in payment*) moroso; non pagato ‖ *s* delinquente *m;* debitore moroso

delirious [dɪˈlɪrɪ·əs] *adj* in delirio

deliri·um [dɪˈlɪrɪ·əm] *s* (**-ums** *or* **-a** [ə]) delirio

deliver [dɪˈlɪvər] *tr* consegnare; (*a blow*) affibbiare; (*a speech*) fare; (*a letter*) recapitare; (*electricity or gas*) erogare; (*said of a pregnant woman*) partorire; (*said of a doctor*) assistere durante il parto

deliver·y [dɪˈlɪvəri] *s* (**-ies**) consegna; (*of mail*) distribuzione; (*of merchandise*) fornitura; (*of a speech*) dizione; (*childbirth*) parto; (sports) lancio

deliv'ery·man' *s* (**-men'**) fattorino

deliv'ery room' *s* sala parto

deliv'ery truck' *s* furgoncino

dell [dɛl] *s* valletta

delouse [diˈlaʊs] *or* [diˈlaʊz] *tr* spidocchiare

delude [dɪˈlud] *tr* illudere, ingannare

deluge [ˈdɛljudʒ] *s* diluvio, inondazione ‖ **the Deluge** il diluvio universale ‖ *tr* inondare

delusion [dɪˈluʒən] *s* illusione, inganno; (*psychopath*) allucinazione;

(psychopath) idea fissa; **delusions of grandeur** mania di grandezza

de luxe [dɪ'lʊks] or [dɪ'lʌks] *adj* di lusso || *adv* in gran lusso

delve [delv] *intr* frugare; **to delve into** approfondirsi in

demagnetize [di'mægnɪ‚taɪz] *tr* smagnetizzare

demagogue ['demə‚gag] *s* demagogo

demand [dɪ'mænd] or [dɪ'mand] *s* esigenza; (com) richiesta, domanda; **to be in demand** essere in richiesta || *tr* esigere

demanding [dɪ'mændɪŋ] or ['dɪ'mandɪŋ] *adj* esigente, impegnativo

demarcate [dɪ'market] or ['dimar‚ket] *tr* demarcare

démarche [de'marʃ] *s* progetto, piano

demean [dɪ'min] *tr* degradare; **to demean oneself** comportarsi; degradarsi

demeanor [dɪ'minər] *s* condotta, contegno

demented [dɪ'mentɪd] *adj* demente

demigod ['demɪ‚gad] *s* semidio

demijohn ['demɪ‚dʒan] *s* damigiana

demilitarize [di'mɪlɪtə‚raɪz] *tr* smilitarizzare

demimonde ['demɪ‚mand] *s* donne *fpl* della società equivoca

demise [dɪ'maɪz] *s* decesso

demitasse ['demɪ‚tæs] or ['demɪ‚tas] *s* tazzina da caffè; *(contents)* caffè nero

demobilize [di'mobɪ‚laɪz] *tr* smobilitare

democra•cy [dɪ'makrəsi] *s* (-cies) democrazia

democrat ['demə‚kræt] *s* democratico

democratic [‚demə'krætɪk] *adj* democratico

demolish [dɪ'malɪʃ] *tr* demolire

demolition [‚demə'lɪʃən] or [‚dimə'lɪʃən] *s* demolizione

demon ['dimən] *s* demonio

demoniacal [‚dimə'naɪ-əkəl] *adj* demoniaco

demonstrate ['demən‚stret] *tr & intr* dimostrare

demonstration [‚demən'streʃən] *s* dimostrazione

demonstrative [dɪ'manstrətɪv] *adj* dimostrativo; *(giving open exhibition of emotion)* espansivo

demonstrator ['demən‚stretər] *s* *(of a product)* dimostratore *m*; *(in a public gathering)* dimostrante *m*; *(product)* prodotto usato da dimostratori

demoralize [dɪ'mɔrə‚laɪz] or [dɪ'morə‚laɪz] *tr* demoralizzare

demote [dɪ'mot] *tr* retrocedere

demotion [dɪ'moʃən] *s* retrocessione

de•mur [dɪ'mʌr] *v* (*pret & pp* **-murred**; *ger* **-murring**) *intr* sollevare obiezioni

demure [dɪ'mjur] *adj* modesto; sobrio

demurrage [dɪ'mʌrɪdʒ] *s* (com) controstallie *fpl*; (rr) sosta

den [den] *s* *(of animals, thieves)* tana; *(little room)* bugigattolo; *(little room for studying or writing)* studiolo; *(of lions)* (Bib) fossa

denaturalize [di'nætʃərə‚laɪz] *tr* snaturare; privare della nazionalità

dena'tured al'cohol [dɪ'netʃərd] *s* alcole denaturato

denial [dɪ'naɪ-əl] *s* diniego; *(disavowal)* smentita

denim ['denɪm] *s* tessuto di cotone per tuta; **denims** tuta; *(trousers)* jeans *mpl*

denizen ['denɪzən] *s* abitante *mf*

Denmark ['denmark] *s* la Danimarca

denomination [dɪ‚namɪ'neʃən] *s* denominazione; categoria; (com) taglio; (eccl) confessione

denote [dɪ'not] *tr* denotare, significare

denouement [denu'mã] *s* scioglimento

denounce [dɪ'naʊns] *tr* denunziare

dense [dens] *adj* denso; stupido

densi•ty ['densɪti] *s* (-ties) densità *f*

dent [dent] *s* ammaccatura; *(in a gearwheel)* tacca, dente *m*; **to make a dent** fare progresso; fare impressione || *tr* ammaccare; (fig) ferire

dental ['dentəl] *adj* dentale, dentario || *s* dentale *f*

den'tal floss' *s* filo cerato dentario

dentifrice ['dentɪfrɪs] *s* dentifricio

dentist ['dentɪst] *s* dentista *mf*

dentistry ['dentɪstri] *s* odontoiatria

denture ['dentʃər] *s* dentiera

denunciation [dɪ‚nʌnsɪ'eʃən] or [dɪ‚nʌnʃɪ'eʃən] *s* denunzia

de•ny [dɪ'naɪ] *v* (*pret & pp* **-nied**) *tr* *(to declare not to be true)* negare; *(to refuse)* rifiutare; **to deny oneself to callers** sottrarsi alle visite || *intr* negare; rifiutare

deodorant [di'odərənt] *adj & s* deodorante *m*

deo'dorant spray' *s* deodorante *m* spray

deodorize [di'odə‚raɪz] *tr* deodorare

depart [dɪ'part] *intr* partire, andarsene; *(to diverge)* dipartire

departed [dɪ'partɪd] *adj* morto, defunto || **the departed** i defunti

department [dɪ'partmənt] *s* dipartimento; *(of government)* ministero; *(e.g., of a hospital)* reparto; *(of agency)* sezione, ufficio

depart'ment store' *s* grandi magazzini *mpl*

departure [dɪ'partʃər] *s* partenza; divergenza, deviazione

depend [dɪ'pend] *intr* dipendere; **to depend on** *(to rely on)* contare su; dipendere da

dependable [dɪ'pendəbəl] *adj* sicuro, fidato

dependence [dɪ'pendəns] *s* dipendenza; *(trust)* fiducia

dependen•cy [dɪ'pendənsi] *s* (-cies) dipendenza; *(territory)* possessione

dependent [dɪ'pendənt] *adj* dipendente; a carico; **to be dependent on** dipendere da || *s* persona a carico

depend'ent clause' *s* proposizione subordinata

depict [dɪ'pɪkt] *tr* descrivere, dipingere

deplete [dɪ'plit] *tr* esaurire

depletion [dɪ'pliʃən] *s* esaurimento

deplorable [dɪ'plorəbəl] *adj* deplorevole

deplore [dɪ'plor] *tr* deplorare

deploy [dɪ'plɔɪ] *tr* (mil) spiegare, stendere

deployment [dɪˈplɔɪmənt] *s* (mil) dispositivo, spiegamento
depolarize [diˈpoləˌraɪz] *tr* depolarizzare
depopulate [diˈpɑpjəˌlet] *tr* spopolare
deport [dɪˈport] *tr* deportare; **to deport oneself** comportarsi
deportation [ˌdiporˈteʃən] *s* deportazione
deportee [ˌdiporˈti] *s* deportato
deportment [dɪˈportmənt] *s* condotta, comportamento
depose [dɪˈpoz] *tr* & *intr* deporre
deposit [dɪˈpɑzɪt] *s* deposito; (*down payment*) caparra || *tr* depositare || *intr* depositarsi
depos'it account' *s* conto corrente
depositor [dɪˈpɑzɪtər] *s* versante *mf*; (*to the credit of an established account*) correntista *mf*
deposito·ry [dɪˈpɑzɪˌtori] *s* (**-ries**) deposito; (*person*) depositario
depos'it slip' *s* distinta di versamento
depot [ˈdipo] *or* [ˈdepo] *s* magazzino; (mil) deposito; (rr) stazione
depraved [dɪˈprevd] *adj* depravato
depravi·ty [dɪˈprævɪti] *s* (**-ties**) depravazione
deprecate [ˈdeprɪˌket] *tr* deprecare
depreciate [dɪˈpriʃɪˌet] *tr* svalutare, deprezzare || *intr* deprezzarsi
depreciation [dɪˌpriʃɪˈeʃən] *s* (*drop in value*) deprezzamento; (*disparagement*) disprezzo
depredation [ˌdeprɪˈdeʃən] *s* depredazione
depress [dɪˈpres] *tr* deprimere; avvilire; (*prices*) far abbassare
depression [dɪˈpreʃən] *s* depressione; (*gloom*) sconforto; (*slump*) crisi *f*
deprive [dɪˈpraɪv] *tr* privare; **to deprive oneself** espropriarsi
depth [depθ] *s* profondità *f*; (*of a house or room*) lunghezza; (*of sea*) fondale *m*; (fig) vastità *f*; **in the depth of** nel cuor di; **to go beyond one's depth** non toccare più; (fig) andare oltre le proprie possibilità
depth' bomb' *s* (aer) bomba antisommergibile
depth' charge' *s* (nav) granata antisommergibile
depth' of hold' *s* (naut) puntale *m*
deputation [ˌdepjəˈteʃən] *s* deputazione
deputize [ˈdepjəˌtaɪz] *tr* deputare
depu·ty [ˈdepjəti] *s* (**-ties**) deputato
derail [dɪˈrel] *tr* far deragliare || *intr* deragliare, deviare
derailment [dɪˈrelmənt] *s* deragliamento, deviamento
derange [dɪˈrendʒ] *tr* (*to disarrange*) dissestare; (*to make insane*) squilibrare, render pazzo
derangement [dɪˈrendʒmənt] *s* (*disorder*) disordine *m*; (*insanity*) squilibrio mentale, pazzia
der·by [ˈdʌrbi] *s* (**-bies**) bombetta; (*race*) derby *m*
derelict [ˈderɪlɪkt] *adj* derelitto; negligente || *s* derelitto; (naut) relitto
dereliction [ˌderɪˈlɪkʃən] *s* (*in one's duty*) negligenza; (law) derelizione

deride [dɪˈraɪd] *tr* deridere, schernire, farsi beffe di
derision [dɪˈrɪʒən] *s* derisione, scherno
derisive [dɪˈraɪsɪv] *adj* derisorio
derivation [ˌderɪˈveʃən] *s* derivazione
derivative [dɪˈrɪvətɪv] *adj* & *s* derivato
derive [dɪˈraɪv] *tr* & *intr* derivare
dermatology [ˌdʌrməˈtɑlədʒi] *s* dermatologia
derogatory [dɪˈrɑgəˌtori] *adj* dispregiativo
derrick [ˈderɪk] *s* gru *f*; (naut) picco di carico
dervish [ˈdʌrvɪʃ] *s* dervis *m*
desalinization [diˌselɪnɪˈzeʃən] *s* desalazione
desalt [diˈsɔlt] *tr* desalificare
descend [dɪˈsend] *tr* discendere || *intr* discendere; **to descend on** calare su, gettarsi su
descendant [dɪˈsendənt] *adj* & *s* discendente *mf*
descendent [dɪˈsendənt] *adj* discendente
descent [dɪˈsent] *s* (*slope*) china; (*decline*) declino; discesa; (*lineage*) stirpe *f*, discendenza; (*sudden raid*) calata
Descent' from the Cross' *s* Deposizione dalla Croce
describe [dɪˈskraɪb] *tr* descrivere
description [dɪˈskrɪpʃən] *s* descrizione
descriptive [dɪˈskrɪptɪv] *adj* descrittivo
de·scry [dɪˈskraɪ] *v* (*pret* & *pp* **-scried**) *tr* avvistare
desecrate [ˈdesɪˌkret] *tr* profanare, dissacrare
desecration [ˌdesɪˈkreʃən] *s* profanazione, dissacrazione
desegregate [diˈsegrɪˌget] *intr* sopprimere la segregazione razziale
desegregation [diˌsegrɪˈgeʃən] *s* desegregazione
desensitize [diˈsensɪˌtaɪz] *tr* desensibilizzare
desert [ˈdezərt] *adj* & *s* deserto || [dɪˈzʌrt] *s* merito; **he received his just deserts** ricevette quanto meritava || *tr* & *intr* disertare
deserter [dɪˈzʌrtər] *s* disertore *m*
deserted [dɪˈzʌrtɪd] *adj* (*person*) abbandonato; (*place*) deserto
desertion [dɪˈzʌrʃən] *s* diserzione; abbandono del coniuge
deserve [dɪˈzʌrv] *tr* & *intr* meritare
deservedly [dɪˈzʌrvɪdli] *adv* meritatamente, meritevolmente
design [dɪˈzaɪn] *s* disegno; (*of a play*) congegno; **to have designs on** aver mire su || *tr* disegnare; progettare || *intr* disegnare; **designed for** destinato a
designate [ˈdezɪgˌnet] *tr* designare
designer [dɪˈsaɪnər] *s* disegnatore *m*
designing [dɪˈzaɪnɪŋ] *adj* intrigante, macchinatore || *s* disegnazione
desirable [dɪˈzaɪrəbəl] *adj* desiderabile
desire [dɪˈzaɪr] *s* desiderio || *tr* desiderare
desirous [dɪˈzaɪrəs] *adj* desideroso
desist [diˈzɪst] *intr* desistere
desk [desk] *s* scrittoio; tavolo d'ufficio;

(*lectern*) leggio; (*of professor*) cattedra; (*of pupil*) banco; (com) cassa

desk'bound' *adj* sedentario; legato al tavolino

desk' pad' *s* blocco da tavolo; blocco per appunti

desolate ['desəlɪt] *adj* desolato, deserto; (*hopeless*) disperato; (*dismal*) lugubre ‖ ['desə‚let] *tr* desolare; devastare

desolation [‚desə'leʃən] *s* desolazione; devastazione

despair [dɪ'sper] *s* disperazione; **to be in despair** disperarsi ‖ *intr* disperare, disperarsi

despairing [dɪ'sperɪŋ] *adj* disperato

despera‧do [‚despə'redo] *or* [‚despə'rado] *s* (**-does** *or* **-dos**) fuorilegge disposto a tutto

desperate ['despərɪt] *adj* disposto a tutto; (*hopeless*) disperato; (*very bad*) atroce, terribile; (*bitter, excessive*) accanito; (*remedy*) estremo

desperation [‚despə'reʃən] *s* disperazione

despicable ['despɪkəbəl] *adj* spregevole, incanaglito

despise [dɪ'spaɪz] *tr* sprezzare, disprezzare, vilipendere

despite [dɪ'spaɪt] *prep* malgrado

despoil [dɪ'spɔɪl] *tr* spogliare

responden‧cy [dɪ'spandənsi] *s* (**-cies**) scoraggiamento, abbattimento

despondent [dɪ'spandənt] *adj* scoraggiato, abbattuto

despot ['despat] *s* despota *m*

despotic [des'patɪk] *adj* dispotico

despotism ['despə‚tɪzəm] *s* dispotismo

dessert [dɪ'zʌrt] *s* dessert *m*

dessert' spoon' *s* cucchiaio *or* cucchiaino da dessert

destination [‚destɪ'neʃən] *s* destinazione

destine ['destɪn] *tr* destinare

desti‧ny ['destɪni] *s* (**-nies**) destino

destitute ['destɪ‚tjut] *or* ['destɪ‚tut] *adj* (*poverty-stricken*) indigente; (*lacking*) privo

destitution [‚destɪ'tjuʃən] *or* [‚destɪ'tuʃən] *s* indigenza, miseria

destroy [dɪ'strɔɪ] *tr* distruggere

destroyer [dɪ'strɔɪ‧ər] *s* (nav) cacciatorpediniere *m*

destruction [dɪ'strʌkʃən] *s* distruzione

destructive [dɪ'strʌktɪv] *adj* distruttivo

desultory ['desəl‚tori] *adj* saltuario, sconnesso

detach [dɪ'tætʃ] *tr* staccare, distaccare; (mil) distaccare

detachable [dɪ'tætʃəbəl] *adj* staccabile; separabile

detached [dɪ'tætʃt] *adj* (e.g., *stub*) staccato; (e.g., *house*) discosto; (*aloof*) riservato, freddo; imparziale

detachment [dɪ'tætʃmənt] *s* distacco, imparzialità *f*; (mil) distaccamento

detail [dɪ'tel] *or* ['ditel] *s* dettaglio, ragguaglio; (mil) distaccamento ‖ [dɪ'tel] *tr* dettagliare; (mil) distaccare

detain [dɪ'ten] *tr* detenere, trattenere

detect [dɪ'tɛkt] *tr* scoprire, discernere; (rad) rivelare

detection [dɪ'tɛkʃən] *s* scoperta; (rad) rivelazione

detective [dɪ'tɛktɪv] *s* detective *m*

detec'tive sto'ry *s* romanzo poliziesco, romanzo giallo

detector [dɪ'tɛktər] *s* (rad) detector *m*, rivelatore *m*

detention [dɪ'tɛnʃən] *s* detenzione

de‧ter [dɪ'tʌr] *v* (*pret & pp* **-terred;** *ger* **-terring**) *tr* distogliere, impedire

detergent [dɪ'tʌrdʒənt] *adj & s* detergente *m*

deteriorate [dɪ'tɪrɪ‧ə‚ret] *tr* deteriorare ‖ *intr* deteriorarsi, andar giù

determination [dɪ‚tʌrmɪ'neʃən] *s* determinazione

determine [dɪ'tʌrmɪn] *tr* determinare

determined [dɪ'tʌrmɪnd] *adj* determinato, risoluto

deterrent [dɪ'tʌrənt] *s* deterrente *m*

detest [dɪ'tɛst] *tr* detestare, odiare

dethrone [dɪ'θron] *tr* detronizzare

detonate ['detə‚net] *or* ['dɪtə‚net] *tr* far scoppiare ‖ *intr* detonare

detonator ['detə‚netər] *s* innesco

detour ['ditur] *or* [dɪ'tur] *s* deviazione ‖ *tr* far deviare ‖ *intr* deviare

detract [dɪ'trækt] *tr* detrarre ‖ *intr—* **to detract from** diminuire

detractor [dɪ'træktər] *s* detrattore *m*

detriment ['detrɪmənt] *s* detrimento; **to the detriment of** a danno di

detrimental [‚detrɪ'mentəl] *adj* pregiudizievole

deuce [djus] *or* [dus] *s* (cards) due *m*; **the deuce!** diavolo!

devaluate [di'vælju‚et] *tr* svalutare

devaluation [di‚vælju'eʃən] *s* devalutazione, svalutazione

devastate ['devəs‚tet] *tr* devastare

devastating ['devəs‚tetɪŋ] *adj* devastatore, devastante; (e.g., *reply*) schiacciante, annichilante

devastation [‚devəs'teʃən] *s* devastazione

develop [dɪ'veləp] *tr* sviluppare; (phot) sviluppare, rivelare ‖ *intr* svilupparsi; manifestarsi

developer [dɪ'veləpər] *s* (e.g., *of a new engine*) sfruttatore *m*; (*in real estate*) specialista *mf* in lottizzazione; (phot) sviluppatore *m*, rivelatore *m*

development [dɪ'veləpmənt] *s* sviluppo; valorizzazione; sfruttamento; (phot) rivelazione

deviate ['divi‚et] *tr* sviare ‖ *intr* deviare, sviarsi

deviation [‚divi'eʃən] *s* deviazione

deviationism [‚divi'eʃə‚nɪzəm] *s* deviazionismo

deviationist [‚divi'eʃənɪst] *s* deviazionista *mf*

device [dɪ'vaɪs] *s* dispositivo, congegno; (*trick*) stratagemma *m*; (*motto*) divisa, emblema *m*; **to leave s.o. to his own devices** lasciare che qlcu faccia come gli pare e piace

dev‧il ['devəl] *s* diavolo; **between the devil and the deep blue sea** fra l'incudine e il martello; **to raise the devil** (slang) fare diavolo a quattro ‖ *v* (*pret & pp* **-iled** *or* **-illed**) *ger*

-iling or -illing) *tr* condire con spezie o con pepe; (coll) infastidire

devilish ['devəlɪʃ] *adj* diabolico

devilment ['devəlmənt] *s (mischief)* diavoleria; *(evil)* cattiveria

devil·try ['devəltri] *s (-tries)* malvagità *f*, crudeltà *f*; *(mischief)* diavoleria

devious ['divi·əs] *adj (tricky)* traverso; *(roundabout)* tortuoso

devise [dɪ'vaɪz] *tr* ideare, inventare; (law) legare, disporre per testamento

devoid [dɪ'vɔɪd] *adj* sprovvisto

devolve [dɪ'valv] *intr*—**to devolve on** ricadere su

devote [dɪ'vot] *tr* dedicare

devoted [dɪ'votɪd] *adj* devoto; dedito, dedicato

devotee [‚devə'ti] *s* devoto; *(fan)* fanatico, tifoso, entusiasta *mf*

devotion [dɪ'vo/ən] *s* devozione; *(e.g., to work)* dedizione; **devotions** orazioni *mpl*, preghiere *fpl*

devour [dɪ'vaʊr] *tr* divorare

devout [dɪ'vaʊt] *adj* devoto; sincero

dew [dju] or [du] *s* rugiada

dew'drop' *s* goccia di rugiada

dew'lap' *s* giogaia

dew·y ['dju·i] or ['du·i] *adj* (-ier; -iest) rugiadoso

dexterity [deks'terɪti] *s* destrezza

diabetes [‚daɪ·ə'bitɪs] or [‚daɪ·ə'bitiz] *s* diabete *m*

diabetic [‚daɪ·ə'betɪk] or [‚daɪ·ə-'bitɪk] *adj & s* diabetico

diabolic(al) [‚daɪ·ə'balɪk(əl)] *adj* diabolico

diadem ['daɪ·ə‚dem] *s* diadema *m*

diaere·sis [daɪ'erɪsɪs] *s* (-ses [‚siz]) dieresi *f*

diagnose [‚daɪ·əg'nos] or [‚daɪ·əg-'noz] *tr* diagnosticare

diagno·sis [‚daɪ·əg'nosɪs] *s* (-ses [siz]) diagnosi *f*

diagonal [daɪ'ægənəl] *adj & s* diagonale *f*

dia·gram ['daɪ·ə‚græm] *s* diagramma *m; (drawing)* schema *m; (plan)* prospetto || *v* (pret & pp -gramed or -grammed; ger -graming or -gramming) *tr* diagrammare

dial ['daɪ·əl] *s (of watch)* quadrante *m;* (rad) tabella graduata, sintogramma *m;* (telp) disco combinatore || *tr* (rad) sintonizzare; *(a person)* (telp) chiamare; *(a number)* (telp) comporre; *(the phone)* (telp) comporre il numero di || *intr* (telp) comporre il numero

dialect ['daɪ·ə‚lekt] *s* dialetto

dialing ['daɪ·əlɪŋ] *s* composizione del numero

dialogue ['daɪ·ə‚lɔg] or ['daɪ·ə‚lag] *s* dialogo

di'al tel'ephone *s* telefono automatico

di'al tone' *s* (telp) segnale *m* di via libera

diameter [daɪ'æmɪtər] *s* diametro

diametric(al) [‚daɪ·ə'metrɪk(əl)] *adj* diametrico, diametrale

diamond ['daɪmənd] *s* diamante *m; (figure of a rhombus)* losanga; *(baseball)* diamante *m;* **diamonds** *(cards)* quadri *mpl*

diaper ['daɪ·pər] *s* pannolino

diaphanous [daɪ'æfənəs] *adj* diafano

diaphragm ['daɪ·ə‚fræm] *s* diaframma *m;* (telp) membrana

diarrhea [‚daɪ·ə'ri·ə] *s* diarrea

dia·ry ['daɪ·əri] *s* (-ries) diario

diastole [daɪ'æstəli] *s* diastole *f*

diathermy ['daɪ·ə‚θʌrmi] *s* diatermia

dice [daɪs] *spl* dadi *mpl; (small cubes)* cubetti *mpl;* **no dice** (slang) niente da fare; (slang) risposta a picche

dice' cup' *s* bussolotto

dichloride [daɪ'klɔraɪd] *s* bicloruro

dichoto·my [daɪ'katəmi] *s* (-mies) dicotomia

dickey ['dɪki] *s* camiciola; *(starched insert)* sparato; *(bib)* bavaglino

dictaphone ['dɪktə‚fon] *s* dittafono

dictate ['dɪktet] *s* dettato || ['dɪktet] or [dɪk'tet] *tr* dettare

dictation [dɪk'te/ən] *s* dettato; *(act of ordering)* ordine *m;* **to take dictation** scrivere sotto dettatura

dictator ['dɪktetər] or [dɪk'tetər] *s* dittatore *m*

dictatorship ['dɪktetər‚ʃɪp] or [dɪk-'tetər‚ʃɪp] *s* dittatura

diction ['dɪk/ən] *s* dizione

dictionar·y ['dɪk/ən‚eri] *s* (-ies) dizionario, vocabolario

dic·tum ['dɪktəm] *s* (-ta [tə]) detto, sentenza

didactic(al) [daɪ'dæktɪk(əl)] or [dɪ-'dæktɪk(əl)] *adj* didattico

die [daɪ] *s* (dice [daɪs]) dado; **the die is cast** il dado è tratto || *s* (dies) *(for stamping coins, medals,* etc.) stampo; *(for cutting threads)* filiera || *v* (pret & pp died; ger dying) *intr* morire; **to die hard** morire lentamente; morire lottando; **to die laughing** morire dalle risa; **to die off** morire uno per uno

die'-hard' *adj & s* intransigente *m*

die'sel oil' ['dizəl] *s* nafta, gasolio

die'stock' *s* girafiliera

diet ['daɪ·ət] *s* dieta, regime *m* || *intr* stare a dieta

dietetic [‚daɪ·ə'tetɪk] *adj* dietetico || **dietetics** *ssg* dietetica

dietitian [‚daɪ·ə'tɪ/ən] *s* dietista *mf*

differ ['dɪfər] *intr (to be different)* differire, differenziarsi; **to differ with** dissentire da

difference ['dɪfərəns] *s* differenza; **to make no difference** fare lo stesso; **to split the difference** dividere la differenza; (fig) venire a un compromesso

different ['dɪfərənt] *adj* differente

differential [‚dɪfə'ren/əl] *adj & s* differenziale *m*

differentiate [‚dɪfə'ren/ɪ‚et] *tr* differenziare || *intr* differenziarsi

difficult ['dɪfɪ‚kʌlt] *adj* difficile

difficul·ty ['dɪfɪ‚kʌlti] *s* (-ties) difficoltà *f*

diffident ['dɪfɪdənt] *adj* timido, imbarazzato

diffuse [dɪ'fjus] *adj* diffuso || [dɪ'fjuz] *tr* diffondere || *intr* diffondersi

dig [dɪg] *s (poke)* botta, spintone *m; (jibe)* stoccata, fiancata || *v* (pret & pp dug [dʌg]; ger digging) *tr* scavare, sterrare; **to dig up** dissodare; (*to uncover*) dissotterrare || *intr* scavare; **to dig in** (mil) fortificarsi; **to dig into** (coll) sprofondarsi in

digest ['daɪdʒɛst] *s* compendio; (law) digesto || [dɪ'dʒɛst] *or* [daɪ'dʒɛst] *tr & intr* digerire

digestible [dɪ'dʒɛstɪbəl] *or* [daɪ'dʒɛstɪbəl] *adj* digeribile, digestibile

digestion [dɪ'dʒɛst/ən] *or* [daɪ'dʒɛst/ən] *s* digestione

digestive [dɪ'dʒɛstɪv] *or* [daɪ'dʒɛstɪv] *adj* (*tube*) digerente || *s* digestivo

digit ['dɪdʒɪt] *s* cifra, unità *f*; (*finger*) dito; (*toe*) dito del piede

dig'ital clock' *s* orologio a scatto

digitalis [,dɪdʒɪ'tælɪs] *or* [,dɪdʒɪ'telɪs] *s* (bot) digitale *f*; (pharm) digitalina

dignified ['dɪgnɪ,faɪd] *adj* dignitoso, fiero, contegnoso

digni•fy ['dɪgnɪ,faɪ] *v* (*pret & pp* -fied) *tr* (*to ennoble*) nobilitare; onorare, esaltare; dare la dignità a

dignitar•y ['dɪgnɪ,teri] *s* (-ies) dignitario; **dignitaries** dignità *fpl*

digni•ty ['dɪgnɪti] *s* (-ties) dignità *f*, decoro; **to stand on one's dignity** mantenere la propria dignità

digress [dɪ'grɛs] *or* [daɪ'grɛs] *intr* digredire, divagare

digression [dɪ'grɛʃən] *or* [daɪ'grɛʃən] *s* digressione, divagazione

dike [daɪk] *s* diga; (*in a river*) argine *m*; (*ditch*) fosso; scarpata

dilapidated [dɪ'læpɪ,detɪd] *adj* dilapidato, decrepito

dilate [daɪ'let] *tr* dilatare || *intr* dilatarsi

dilatory ['dɪlə,tori] *adj* lento, tardivo; (*e.g., strategy*) dilatorio

dilemma [dɪ'lɛmə] *s* dilemma *m*

dilettan•te [,dɪlə'tænti] *adj* dilettantesco || *s* (-tes *or* -ti [ti]) dilettante *mf*

diligence ['dɪlɪdʒəns] *s* diligenza

diligent ['dɪlɪdʒənt] *adj* diligente

dill [dɪl] *s* (bot) aneto

dillydal•ly ['dɪlɪ,dæli] *v* (*pret & pp* -lied) *intr* farla lunga

dilute [dɪ'lut] *or* [daɪ'lut] *adj* diluito || [dɪ'lut] *or* [daɪ'lut] *tr* diluire || *intr* diluirsi

dilution [dɪ'lu/ən] *s* diluizione

dim [dɪm] *adj* (dimmer; dimmest) (*light*) fioco; (*sight*) debole; (*memory*) vago; (*color*) smorzato; (*sound*) sordo; **to take a dim view of** avere una visione pessimistica di || *v* (*pret & pp* dimmed; *ger* dimming) *tr* (*lights*) smorzare; **to dim the headlights** abbassare i fari

dime [daɪm] *s* moneta di dieci centesimi di dollaro

dimension [dɪ'mɛn/ən] *s* dimensione

diminish [dɪ'mɪnɪʃ] *tr & intr* diminuire, scemare

diminutive [dɪ'mɪnjətɪv] *adj* (*tiny*) minuscolo; (gram) diminutivo || *s* diminutivo

dimly ['dɪmli] *adv* indistintamente

dimmer ['dɪmər] *s* smorzatore *m*; (aut) luce *f* di incrocio; **dimmers** fari *mpl* antiabbaglianti

dimple ['dɪmpəl] *s* fossetta

dimwit ['dɪm,wɪt] *s* (slang) stupido, cretino

din [dɪn] *s* fragore *m*, frastuono || *v* (*pret & pp* dinned; *ger* dinning) *tr* assordare; **to din s.th into s.o.'s ears** rintronare qlco nelle orecchie di qlcu

dine [daɪn] *tr* offrire un pranzo a; offire una cena a || *intr* pasteggiare; cenare; **to dine out** mangiare fuori di casa

diner ['daɪnər] *s* commensale *m*; (rr) vettura ristorante; (U.S.A.) ristorante *m* a forma di vagone

ding-dong ['dɪŋ,dɔŋ] *or* ['dɪŋ,dɑŋ] *s* dindon *m*

din•gy ['dɪndʒi] *adj* (-gier; -giest) sporco, sbiadito

din'ing car' *s* vagone *m* ristorante

din'ing room' *s* sala da pranzo

dinner ['dɪnər] *s* cena; pranzo; (*formal meal*) banchetto

din'ner coat' *or* **jack'et** *s* smoking *m*

din'ner knife' *s* coltello da tavola

din'ner set' *s* servizio da tavola

din'ner ta'ble *s* desco

din'ner time' *s* ora di pranzo or di cena

dinosaur ['daɪnə,sɔr] *s* dinosauro

dint [dɪnt] *s* tacca, ammaccatura; **by dint of** a forza di || *tr* ammaccare

diocese ['daɪə,sis] *or* ['daɪ-əsɪs] *s* diocesi *f*

diode ['daɪ-od] *s* diodo

dioxide [daɪ'aksaɪd] *s* biossido

dip [dɪp] *s* immersione; (*brief swim*) tuffo, nuotata; (*in a road*) depressione; inclinazione magnetica || *v* (*pret & pp* dipped; *ger* dipping) *tr* immergere, tuffare; (*the flag*) abbassare; (*bread*) inzuppare || *intr* immergersi, tuffarsi; inclinarsi; (*to drop down*) sparire subitamente; **to dip into** (*a book*) sfogliare; (*business*) mettersi in; (*a container of liquids*) intingere; **to dip into one's purse** spendere soldi

diphtheria [dɪf'θɪrɪ-ə] *s* difterite *f*

diphthong ['dɪfθəŋ] *or* ['dɪfθɑŋ] *s* dittongo

diphthongize ['dɪfθəŋ,gaɪz] *or* ['dɪfθəŋ,gaɪz] *tr & intr* dittongare

diploma [dɪ'plomə] *s* diploma *m*

diploma•cy [dɪ'ploməsi] *s* (-cies) diplomazia

diplomat ['dɪplə,mæt] *s* diplomatico

diplomatic [,dɪplə'mætɪk] *adj* diplomatico

dip'lomat'ic pouch' *s* valigia diplomatica

dipper ['dɪpər] *s* mestolo

dip'stick' *s* asta di livello

dire [daɪr] *adj* terribile, orrendo

direct [dɪ'rɛkt] *or* [daɪ'rɛkt] *adj* diretto; sincero || *tr* dirigere; ordinare

direct' cur'rent *s* corrente continua

direct' dis'course *s* discorso diretto

direct' dis'tance di'aling *s* (telp) teleselezione *f*

direct' hit' *s* colpo centrato

direction [dɪ'rɛk/ən] *or* [daɪ'rɛk/ən] *s* direzione; **directions** istruzioni *fpl*; (*for use*) indicazioni *fpl* per l'uso

directional [dɪ'rekʃənəl] or [daɪ-'rekʃənəl] adj direzionale

directive [dɪ'rektɪv] or [daɪ'rektɪv] s direttiva

direct' ob'ject s (gram) complemento diretto, complemento oggetto

director [dɪ'rektər] or [daɪ'rektər] s direttore m, gerente m; (member of a governing body) consigliere m

directorship [dɪ'rektər ‚ʃɪp] or [daɪ-'rektər ‚ʃɪp] s direzione; amministrazione

directo•ry [dɪ'rektəri] or [daɪ'rektəri] s (-ries) (board of directors) direzione, direttorio; (list of names and addresses) rubrica, elenco; (telp) elenco dei telefoni, guida telefonica

dirge [dʌrdʒ] s canto funebre

dirigible [dɪrɪdʒɪbəl] adj & s dirigibile m

dirt [dʌrt] s (soil) terra, suolo; (dust) polvere m; (mud) fango; (accumulation of dirt) sudiciume m, lerciume m; (moral filth) porcheria, sozzura; (gossip) pettegolezzi mpl; **to do s.o.** **dirt** (slang) calunniare qlcu

dirt'-cheap' adj a prezzo bassissimo

dirt' road' s strada di terra battuta

dirt•y ['dʌrti] adj (-ier; -iest) sporco, sudicio; fangoso; polveroso; (e.g., spinach) terroso; (obscene) sconcio, lurido; immondo ‖ v (pret & pp -ied) tr sporcare, insudiciare, imbrattare

dir'ty lin'en s roba sporca; **to air one's** **dirty linen in public** mettere i panni al sole

dir'ty trick' s brutto tiro

disabili•ty [‚dɪsə'bɪlɪti] s (-ties) incapacità f, invalidità f

disabil'ity insur'ance s assicurazione invalidità

disable [dɪs'ebəl] tr mutilare, storpiare; (a ship) smantellare; (law) invalidare

disabuse [‚dɪsə'bjuz] tr disingannare

disadvantage [‚dɪsəd'væntɪdʒ] or [‚dɪsəd'vɑntɪdʒ] s svantaggio

disadvantageous [dɪs ‚ædvən'tedʒəs] adj svantaggioso

disagree [‚dɪsə'gri] intr discordare, disconvenire; (to quarrel) litigare, altercare; **to disagree with** non essere del parere di

disagreeable [‚dɪsə'gri•əbəl] adj sgradevole

disagreement [‚dɪsə'grimənt] s sconcordanza, dissidio, dissenso

disallow [‚dɪsə'lau] tr non permettere, rifiutare

disappear [‚dɪsə'pɪr] intr sparire, scomparire

disappearance [‚dɪsə'pɪrəns] s scomparsa

disappoint [‚dɪsə'pɔɪnt] tr deludere, disilludere; **to be disappointed** rimanere deluso

disappointment [‚dɪsə'pɔɪntmənt] s delusione, disinganno, disappunto

disapproval [‚dɪsə'pruvəl] s disapprovazione, riprova

disapprove [‚dɪsə'pruv] tr & intr disapprovare

disarm [dɪs'ɑrm] tr disarmare ‖ intr disarmare, disarmarsi

disarmament [dɪs'ɑrməmənt] s disarmo

disarming [dɪs'ɑrmɪŋ] adj ingraziante, simpatico

disarray [‚dɪsə're] s disordine m, scompiglio; (of apparel) sciatteria ‖ tr scomporre, scompigliare

disassemble [‚dɪsə'sembəl] tr smontare, sconnettere

disassociate [‚dɪsə'soʃɪ ‚et] tr dissociare, disassociare

disaster [dɪ'zæstər] or [dɪ'zɑstər] s disastro, sinistro

disastrous [dɪ'zæstrəs] or [dɪ'zɑstrəs] adj disastroso

disavow [‚dɪsə'vau] tr sconfessare

disavowal [‚dɪsə'vau•əl] s sconfessione

disband [dɪs'bænd] tr (an assembly) sciogliere; (troops) congedare; (any group) sbandare ‖ intr sbandarsi

dis•bar [dɪs'bɑr] v (pret & pp -barred; ger -barring) tr (law) radiare dall'albo degli avvocati

disbelief [‚dɪsbɪ'lif] s incredulità f

disbelieve [‚dɪsbɪ'liv] tr rifiutarsi di credere a ‖ intr rifiutarsi di credere

disburse [dɪs'bʌrs] tr sborsare

disbursement [dɪs'bʌrsmənt] s sborso, disborso

discard [dɪs'kɑrd] s scarto, scartina; **to put into the discard** scartare ‖ tr scartare

discern [dɪ'zʌrn] or [dɪ'sʌrn] tr scernere, discernere, sceverare

discernible [dɪ'zʌrnɪbəl] or [dɪ'sʌrnɪbəl] adj discernibile

discerning [dɪ'zʌrnɪŋ] or [dɪ'sʌrnɪŋ] adj perspicace, oculato

discernment [dɪ'zʌrnmənt] or [dɪ'sʌrnmənt] s discernimento

discharge [dɪs'tʃɑrdʒ] s (of a load) scarico; (of a gun; of electricity) scarica; (of a prisoner) liberazione; (of a duty) adempimento; (of a debt) pagamento; (from a job) licenziamento; (mil) foglio di congedo; (pathol) spurgo ‖ tr scaricare; (a duty) adempiere; (a prisoner) liberare; (a debt) pagare; (an employee) licenziare; (a patient) lasciar uscire; (a passenger from a ship) sbarcare; (a battery) scaricare; (mil) congedare ‖ intr (said, e.g., of a liquid) sboccare; (said of a gun or a battery) scaricarsi

disciple [dɪ'saɪpəl] s discepolo

disciplinarian [‚dɪsɪplɪ'nerɪ•ən] s disciplinatore m; partigiano di una forte disciplina

disciplinary ['dɪsɪplɪ ‚neri] adj disciplinare

discipline ['dɪsɪplɪn] s disciplina; castigo ‖ tr disciplinare; castigare

disclaim [dɪs'klem] tr non riconoscere, negare

disclose [dɪs'kloz] tr rivelare, scoprire

disclosure [dɪs'kloʒər] s rivelazione, scoperta; divulgazione

discolor [dɪs'kʌlər] tr scolorare, scolorire ‖ intr scolorirsi

discoloration [dɪs ‚kʌlə'reʃən] s discolorazione

discomfit [dɪsˈkʌmfɪt] *tr* sconcertare, turbare; frustrare, battere, mettere in fuga

discomfiture [dɪsˈkʌmfɪtʃər] *s* sconcerto, turbamento; frustrazione; disfatta

discomfort [dɪsˈkʌmfərt] *s* disagio || *tr* incomodare

disconcert [ˌdɪskənˈsʌrt] *tr* sconcertare

disconnect [ˌdɪskəˈnɛkt] *tr* sconnettere; (elec) disinserire

disconsolate [dɪsˈkɑnsəlɪt] *adj* sconsolato, desolato

discontent [ˌdɪskənˈtɛnt] *adj* & *s* scontento || *tr* scontentare

discontented [ˌdɪskənˈtɛntɪd] *adj* scontento

discontinue [ˌdɪskənˈtɪnju] *tr* cessare, interrompere

discord [ˈdɪskɔrd] *s* discordia, dissidio

discordance [dɪsˈkɔrdəns] *s* discordanza

discotheque [ˌdɪskoˈtɛk] *s* discoteca

discount [ˈdɪskaʊnt] *s* sconto || [ˈdɪskaʊnt] or [dɪsˈkaʊnt] *tr* scontare; (news) fare la tara a

dis′count rate′ *s* tasso di sconto

discourage [dɪsˈkʌrɪdʒ] *tr* scoraggiare, sconfortare; (*to dissuade*) sconsigliare

discouragement [dɪsˈkʌrɪdʒmənt] *s* scoraggiamento; disapprovazione

discourse [ˈdɪskɔrs] or [dɪsˈkɔrs] *s* discorso || [dɪsˈkɔrs] *intr* discorrere

discourteous [dɪsˈkʌrtɪ·əs] *adj* scortese

discourte·sy [dɪsˈkʌrtəsi] *s* (**-sies**) scortesia

discover [dɪsˈkʌvər] *tr* scoprire

discoverer [dɪsˈkʌvərər] *s* scopritore *m*

discover·y [dɪsˈkʌvəri] *s* (**-ies**) scoperta

discredit [dɪsˈkrɛdɪt] *s* discredito || *tr* screditare

discreditable [dɪsˈkrɛdɪtəbəl] *adj* indegno, disonorevole

discreet [dɪsˈkrit] *adj* discreto

discrepan·cy [dɪsˈkrɛpənsi] *s* (**-cies**) discrepanza, divario

discretion [dɪsˈkrɛʃən] *s* discrezione

discriminate [dɪsˈkrɪmɪˌnet] *tr* discriminare || *intr*—**to discriminate against** fare delle discriminazioni contro

discrimination [dɪsˌkrɪmɪˈneʃən] *s* discriminazione

discriminatory [dɪsˈkrɪmɪnəˌtori] *adj* discriminante

discuss [dɪsˈkʌs] *tr* & *intr* discutere

discussion [dɪsˈkʌʃən] *s* discussione

discus thrower [ˈdɪskəs ˈθro·ər] *s* discobolo

disdain [dɪsˈden] *s* disdegno || *tr* disdegnare, sdegnare

disdainful [dɪsˈdenfəl] *adj* sdegnoso

disease [dɪˈziz] *s* malattia

diseased [dɪˈzizd] *adj* malato

disembark [ˌdɪsɛmˈbɑrk] *tr* & *intr* sbarcare

disembarkation [dɪsˌɛmbɑrˈkeʃən] *s* sbarco

disembowel [ˌdɪsɛmˈbaʊ·əl] *tr* sbudellare, sventrare

disenchant [ˌdɪsɛnˈtʃænt] or [ˌdɪsɛnˈtʃɑnt] *tr* disincantare

disenchantment [ˌdɪsɛnˈtʃæntmənt] or [ˌdɪsɛnˈtʃɑntmənt] *s* disinganno

disengage [ˌdɪsɛnˈɡedʒ] *tr* (*from a pledge*) svincolare; (*to disconnect*) sgranare, disinnestare; (mil) sganciare

disengagement [ˌdɪsɛnˈɡedʒmənt] *s* liberazione; disinnesto; svincolamento

disentangle [ˌdɪsɛnˈtæŋɡəl] *tr* disincagliare, districare

disentanglement [ˌdɪsɛnˈtæŋɡəlmənt] *s* districamento

disestablish [ˌdɪsɛsˈtæblɪʃ] *tr* (*the Church*) separare dallo Stato

disfavor [dɪsˈfevər] *s* disfavore *m*

disfigure [dɪsˈfɪɡjər] *tr* sfigurare, deturpare

disfigurement [dɪsˈfɪɡjərmənt] *s* deturpazione

disfranchise [dɪsˈfræntʃaɪz] *tr* privare dei diritti civili

disgorge [dɪsˈɡɔrdʒ] *tr* vomitare; (*something illicitly obtained*) restituire; (*said of a river*) scaricare || *intr* vomitare; scaricarsi

disgrace [dɪsˈɡres] *s* vergogna; disgrazia || *tr* disonorare; privare del favore

disgraceful [dɪsˈɡresfəl] *adj* infamante, disonorante

disgruntle [dɪsˈɡrʌntəl] *tr* scontentare, irritare

disgruntled [dɪsˈɡrʌntəld] *adj* irritato, di cattivo umore

disguise [dɪsˈɡaɪz] *s* travestimento || *tr* travestire, dissimulare

disgust [dɪsˈɡʌst] *s* disgusto, schifo || *tr* disgustare, fare schifo a

disgusting [dɪsˈɡʌstɪŋ] *adj* disgustoso, schifoso

dish [dɪʃ] *s* piatto, **dishes** vasellame *m*; **to wash the dishes** fare i piatti || *tr* scodellare; (*to defeat*) (slang) sconfiggere; **to dish out** (slang) distribuire

dish′cloth′ *s* canovaccio, strofinaccio

dishearten [dɪsˈhɑrtən] *tr* scoraggiare, disanimare, desolare

dishev·el [dɪˈʃɛvəl] *v* (*pret* & *pp* **-eled** or **-elled**; *ger* **-eling** or **-elling**) *tr* scomporre, scarmigliare, scapigliare

dishonest [dɪsˈɑnɪst] *adj* disonesto

dishones·ty [dɪsˈɑnɪsti] *s* (**-ties**) disonestà *f*

dishonor [dɪsˈɑnər] *s* disonore *m* || *tr* disonorare; (com) rifiutare di pagare

dishonorable [dɪsˈɑnərəbəl] *adj* disonorevole, disonorante

dish′pan′ *s* bacinella per lavare i piatti

dish′rack′ *s* portapiatti *m*, sgocciolatoio

dish′rag′ *s* canovaccio, strofinaccio

dish′towel′ *s* canovaccio per le stoviglie

dish′wash′er *s* (*person*) sguattero, lavapiatti *m*; (*machine*) lavastoviglie *m* & *f*

dish′wa′ter *s* lavatura di piatti

disillusion [ˌdɪsɪˈluʒən] *s* disillusione || *tr* disilludere

disillusionment [ˌdɪsɪˈluʒənmənt] *s* disillusione

disinclination [dɪsˌɪnklɪˈneʃən] *s* riluttanza, avversione

disinclined [ˌdɪsɪnˈklaɪnd] *adj* riluttante, avverso

disinfect [ˌdɪsɪnˈfɛkt] *tr* disinfettare

disinfectant [ˌdɪsɪnˈfɛktənt] *adj & s* disinfettante *m*

disingenuous [ˌdɪsɪnˈdʒɛnjuˈəs] *adj* poco schietto, insincero

disinherit [ˌdɪsɪnˈhɛrɪt] *tr* diseredare

disintegrate [dɪsˈɪntɪˌgret] *tr* disintegrare, disgregare ‖ *intr* disintegrarsi, disgregarsi

disintegration [dɪsˌɪntɪˈgreʃən] *s* disintegrazione, disgregamento

disin·ter [ˌdɪsɪnˈtʌr] *v* (*pret & pp* **-terred**) *ger* **-terring**) *tr* dissotterrare

disinterested [dɪsˈɪntəˌrɛstɪd] *or* [dɪsˈɪntrɪstɪd] *adj* disinteressato

disjunctive [dɪsˈdʒʌŋktɪv] *adj* disgiuntivo

disk [dɪsk] *s* disco; (*of ski pole*) rotella

disk' jock'ey *s* presentatore *m* di un programma radiodiffuso di dischi

dislike [dɪsˈlaɪk] *s* antipatia, avversione; **to take a dislike for** prendere in uggia ‖ *tr* non piacere (with *dat*), e.g., **he dislikes wine** non gli piace il vino

dislocate [ˈdɪsloˌket] *tr* spostare, mettere fuori posto; (*a bone*) slogare

dislodge [dɪsˈlɑdʒ] *tr* sloggiare

disloyal [dɪsˈlɔɪˈəl] *adj* sleale

disloyal·ty [dɪsˈlɔɪˈəltɪ] *s* (**-ties**) slealtà *f*

dismal [ˈdɪzməl] *adj* tetro, triste; cattivo, orribile

dismantle [dɪsˈmæntəl] *tr* smontare, smantellare; (*a fortress*) sguarnire

dismay [dɪsˈme] *s* costernazione ‖ *tr* costernare

dismember [dɪsˈmɛmbər] *tr* smembrare

dismiss [dɪsˈmɪs] *tr* congedare; (*to fire*) licenziare; (*a subject*) scartare; (*from the mind*) scacciare

dismissal [dɪsˈmɪsəl] *s* congedo; licenziamento

dismount [dɪsˈmaʊnt] *tr* disarcionare ‖ *intr* scendere, smontare

disobedience [ˌdɪsəˈbidɪˈəns] *s* disubbidienza

disobedient [ˌdɪsəˈbidɪˈənt] *adj* disubbidiente

disobey [ˌdɪsəˈbe] *tr* disubbidire (with *dat*) ‖ *intr* disubbidire

disorder [dɪsˈɔrdər] *s* disordine *m* ‖ *tr* disordinare, confondere

disorderly [dɪsˈɔrdərlɪ] *adj* disordinato, confuso; (*unruly*) turbolento

disor'derly con'duct *s* contegno contrario all'ordine pubblico

disor'derly house' *s* bordello, lupanare *m*

disorganize [dɪsˈɔrgəˌnaɪz] *tr* disorganizzare

disoriented [dɪsˈɔrɪˌɛntɪd] *adj* disorientato

disown [dɪsˈon] *tr* disconoscere

disparage [dɪsˈpærɪdʒ] *tr* svilire, deprezzare

disparagement [dɪsˈpærɪdʒmənt] *s* discredito, deprezzamento

disparate [ˈdɪspærɪt] *adj* disparato

dispari·ty [dɪsˈpærɪtɪ] *s* (**-ties**) disparità *f*, spareggio

dispassionate [dɪsˈpæʃənɪt] *adj* spassionato

dispatch [dɪsˈpætʃ] *s* dispaccio ‖ *tr* spedire; (*to dismiss*) congedare; uccidere; (*a meal*) (coll) liquidare

dis·pel [dɪsˈpɛl] *v* (*pret & pp* **-pelled;** *ger* **-pelling**) *tr* dissipare

dispensa·ry [dɪsˈpɛnsərɪ] *s* (**-ries**) dispensario

dispensation [ˌdɪspɛnˈseʃən] *s* (*dispensing*) distribuzione, dispensa; (*exemption*) dispensa

dispense [dɪsˈpɛns] *tr* (*medicines*) distribuire; (*justice*) amministrare; (*to distribute*) dispensare; (*to exempt*) esimere ‖ *intr*—**to dispense with** fare a meno di; esimersi da

dispenser [dɪsˈpɛnsər] *s* dispensatore *m*; (*automatic*) distributore *m*

disperse [dɪsˈpʌrs] *tr* disperdere ‖ *intr* disperdersi

dispersion [dɪsˈpʌrʒən] *or* [dɪsˈpɛrʃən] *s* dispersione

dispersive [dɪsˈpʌrsɪv] *adj* dispersivo

dispirit [dɪsˈpɪrɪt] *tr* scoraggiare

displace [dɪsˈples] *tr* muovere; costringere a lasciare il proprio paese; (*to supplant*) rimpiazzare; (naut) dislocare

displaced' per'son *s* rifugiato politico

displacement [dɪsˈplesmənt] *s* spostamento; sostituzione; (*of a piston*) cilindrata; (naut) dislocamento

display [dɪsˈple] *s* sfoggio, mostra ‖ *tr* mostrare; (*e.g., in a store window*) mettere in mostra; (*to unfold*) spiegare; (*to show ostentatiously*) sfoggiare, ostentare; (*ignorance*) rivelare

display' cab'inet *s* bacheca

display' win'dow *s* mostra, vetrina

displease [dɪsˈpliz] *tr* dispiacere (with *dat*)

displeasing [dɪsˈplizɪŋ] *adj* spiacevole

displeasure [dɪsˈplɛʒər] *s* dispiacere *m*; sfavore *m*

disposable [dɪsˈpozəbəl] *adj* (*available*) disponibile; (*made to be thrown away after use*) scartabile, da gettarsi via, usa e getta

disposal [dɪsˈpozəl] *s* disposizione; eliminazione; **to have at one's disposal** disporre di

dispose [dɪsˈpoz] *tr* disporre; **to dispose of** disporre di; (*to get rid of*) sbarazzarsi di; vendere

disposed [dɪsˈpozd] *adj*—**to be disposed to** essere disposto a

disposition [ˌdɪspəˈzɪʃən] *s* disposizione; (*mental outlook*) indole *f*; tendenza; (mil) ordinamento

dispossess [ˌdɪspəˈzɛs] *tr* spodestare, bandire; (*to evict*) sfrattare

disproof [dɪsˈpruf] *s* confutazione

disproportionate [ˌdɪsprəˈporʃənɪt] *adj* sproporzionato

disprove [dɪsˈpruv] *tr* confutare

dispute [dɪsˈpjut] *s* disputa; **beyond dispute** incontestabile; **in dispute** in discussione ‖ *tr & intr* disputare

disquali·fy [dɪsˈkwɑlɪˌfaɪ] *v* (*pret & pp* **-fied**) *tr* squalificare

disquiet [dɪsˈkwaɪˈət] *s* inquietudine *f* ‖ *tr* inquietare, turbare

disquisition [ˌdɪskwɪˈzɪʃən] *s* disquisizione

disregard [ˌdɪsrɪ'gɑrd] *s* (*of a rule*) inosservanza; (*of danger*) disprezzo, noncuranza ‖ *tr* non fare attenzione a

disrepair [ˌdɪsrɪ'per] *s* cattivo stato, rovina

disreputable [dɪs'repjətəbəl] *adj* malfamato; disonorevole; (*in bad condition*) raso, logoro

disrepute [ˌdɪsrɪ'pjut] *s* cattiva fama; **to bring into disrepute** rovinare la reputazione di

disrespect [ˌdɪsrɪ'spɛkt] *s* mancanza di rispetto ‖ *tr* mancare di rispetto a

disrespectful [ˌdɪsrɪ'spɛktfəl] *adj* non rispettoso, irriverente

disrobe [dɪs'rob] *tr* svestire ‖ *intr* svestirsi, spogliarsi

disrupt [dɪs'rʌpt] *tr* disorganizzare; interrompere

disruption [dɪs'rʌpʃən] *s* rottura; disorganizzazione

dissatisfaction [ˌdɪssætɪs'fækʃən] *s* scontento, malcontento

dissatisfied [dɪs'sætɪs,faɪd] *adj* scontento, malcontento; insoddisfatto

dissatis-fy [dɪs'sætɪs,faɪ] *v* (*pret & pp* -**fied**) *tr* scontentare

dissect [dɪ'sɛkt] *tr* sezionare

dissemble [dɪ'sɛmbəl] *tr & intr* dissimulare

disseminate [dɪ'sɛmɪ,net] *tr* disseminare, divulgare

dissension [dɪ'sɛnʃən] *s* dissensione

dissent [dɪ'sɛnt] *s* dissenso; (*nonconformity*) dissidio ‖ *intr* dissentire

dissenter [dɪ'sɛntər] *s* dissenziente *m*

dissertation [ˌdɪsər'teʃən] *s* dissertazione

disservice [dɪ'sʌrvɪs] *s* danno; cattivo servizio

dissidence ['dɪsɪdəns] *s* dissidenza

dissident ['dɪsɪdənt] *adj & s* dissidente *m*

dissimilar [dɪ'sɪmɪlər] *adj* dissimile

dissimilate [dɪ'sɪmɪ,let] *tr* dissimilare ‖ *intr* dissimilarsi

dissimulate [dɪ'sɪmjə,let] *tr & intr* dissimulare

dissipate ['dɪsɪ,pet] *tr* dissipare ‖ *intr* dissiparsi; (*to indulge oneself*) darsi alla dissipatezza

dissipated ['dɪsɪ,petɪd] *adj* dissipato

dissipation [ˌdɪsɪ'peʃən] *s* dissipazione

dissociate [dɪ'soʃɪ,et] *tr* dissociare ‖ *intr* dissociarsi

dissolute ['dɪsə,lut] *adj* dissoluto

dissolution [ˌdɪsə'luʃən] *s* dissoluzione

dissolve [dɪ'zɑlv] *tr* sciogliere, disciogliere ‖ *intr* sciogliersi, disciogliersi

dissonance ['dɪsənəns] *s* dissonanza

dissuade [dɪ'swed] *tr* dissuadere

dissyllabic [ˌdɪsɪ'læbɪk] *adj* disillabo

dissyllable [dɪ'sɪləbəl] *s* disillabo

distaff ['dɪstæf] *or* ['dɪstɑf] *s* rocca

dis'taff side' *s* ramo femminile di una famiglia

distance ['dɪstəns] *s* distanza; **a long distance** (fig) moltissimo; **in the distance** in lontananza; **to keep at a distance** or **to keep one's distance** mantenere le distanze ‖ *tr* distanziare

distant ['dɪstənt] *adj* distante; (*relative*) lontano; (*aloof*) freddo, riservato

distaste [dɪs'test] *s* ripugnanza

distasteful [dɪs'testfəl] *adj* ripugnante, sgradevole

distemper [dɪs'tɛmpər] *s* cimurro; (*painting*) tempera ‖ *tr* dipingere a tempera

distend [dɪs'tɛnd] *tr* stendere, distendere; gonfiare ‖ *intr* stendersi, distendersi; gonfiarsi

distension [dɪs'tɛnʃən] *s* distensione; gonfiamento

distill [dɪs'tɪl] *tr* distillare

distillation [ˌdɪstɪ'leʃən] *s* distillazione

distiller-y [dɪs'tɪləri] *s* (-**ies**) distilleria

distinct [dɪs'tɪŋkt] *adj* distinto, chiaro; (*not blurred*) nitido

distinction [dɪs'tɪŋkʃən] *s* distinzione

distinctive [dɪs'tɪŋktɪv] *adj* distintivo

distinguish [dɪs'tɪŋgwɪʃ] *tr* distinguere

distinguished [dɪs'tɪŋgwɪʃt] *adj* distinto

distort [dɪs'tɔrt] *tr* distorcere; (*the truth*) svisare, snaturare

distortion [dɪs'tɔrʃən] *s* deformazione; (*of the truth*) alterazione, svisamento; (rad) distorsione

distract [dɪs'trækt] *tr* distrarre

distracted [dɪs'træktɪd] *adj* distratto; (*irrational*) turbato, sconvolto

distraction [dɪs'trækʃən] *s* distrazione

distraught [dɪs'trɔt] *adj* turbato, stordito

distress [dɪs'trɛs] *s* pena, dispiacere *m*; pericolo; (naut) difficoltà *f* ‖ *tr* sconfortare, affliggere

distressing [dɪs'trɛsɪŋ] *adj* penoso

distress' mer'chandise *s* merce *f* sotto costo

distress' sig'nal *s* segnale *m* di soccorso

distribute [dɪs'trɪbjut] *tr* distribuire

distribution [ˌdɪstrɪ'bjuʃən] *s* distribuzione, erogazione

distributor [dɪs'trɪbjətər] *s* distributore *m*; (aut) distributore *m* d'accensione

district ['dɪstrɪkt] *s* regione; (*of a city*) rione *m*, quartiere *m*; (*administrative division*) distretto ‖ *tr* dividere in distretti

dis'trict attor'ney *s* procuratore *m* generale

distrust [dɪs'trʌst] *s* diffidenza ‖ *tr* diffidare di

distrustful [dɪs'trʌstfəl] *adj* diffidente

disturb [dɪs'tʌrb] *tr* disturbare, turbare; disordinare

disturbance [dɪs'tʌrbəns] *s* disturbo, turbamento, perturbazione; disordine *m*

disuse [dɪs'jus] *s* disuso

ditch [dɪtʃ] *s* fossa, fossato ‖ *tr* scavare un fosso in; (rr) far deragliare; (slang) piantare in asso ‖ *intr* fare un ammaraggio forzato

dither ['dɪðər] *s* agitazione; **to be in a dither** (coll) essere agitato

dit-to ['dɪto] *s* (-**tos**) lo stesso; (*ditto symbol*) virgolette *fpl* ‖ *adv* ugualmente, idem ‖ *tr* copiare, duplicare

dit'to marks' *spl* virgolette *fpl*

dit•ty ['dɪtɪ] s (**-ties**) canzonetta

diva ['divə] s (mus) diva

divan ['daɪvæn] or [dɪ'væn] s divano

dive [daɪv] s tuffo; (*of a submarine*) immersione; (aer) picchiata; (coll) taverna; (com) discesa ‖ v (*pret & pp* **dived** or **dove** [dov]) *intr* tuffarsi; (*said of submarine*) immergersi; (*to plunge*) lanciarsi; (aer) scendere in picchiata; **to dive for** (*e.g., pearls*) pescare

dive'-bomb' *tr* bombardare in picchiata ‖ *intr* scendere a tuffo

dive' bomb'ing s bombardamento in picchiata

diver ['daɪvər] s tuffatore m; (*person who works under water*) palombaro; (orn) tuffetto

diverge [dɪ'vʌrdʒ] or [daɪ'vʌrdʒ] *intr* divergere

divers ['daɪvərz] adj diversi, vari

diverse [dɪ'vʌrs], [daɪ'vʌrs] or ['daɪvʌrs] adj (*different*) diverso; (*of various kinds*) multiforme

diversification [dɪ‚vʌrsɪfɪ'keʃən] or [daɪ‚vʌrsɪfɪ'keʃən] s diversificazione

diversi•fy [dɪ'vʌrsɪ‚faɪ] or [daɪ'vʌrsɪ‚faɪ] v (*pret & pp* **-fied**) *tr* diversificare ‖ *intr* diversificarsi

diversion [dɪ'vʌrʒən] or [daɪ'vʌrʒən] s diversione; (*pastime*) svago

diversi•ty [dɪ'vʌrsɪtɪ] or [daɪ'vʌrsɪtɪ] s (**-ties**) diversità f

divert [dɪ'vʌrt] or [daɪ'vʌrt] *tr* deviare; (*to entertain*) divertire; (*money*) stornare, distrarre

diverting [dɪ'vʌrtɪŋ] or [daɪ'vʌrtɪŋ] adj divertente

divest [dɪ'vest] or [daɪ'vest] *tr* spogliare; spossessare; **to divest oneself of** spogliarsi di, espropriarsi di

divide [dɪ'vaɪd] s spartiacque m ‖ *tr* dividere ‖ *intr* dividersi

dividend ['dɪvɪ‚dend] s dividendo

dividers [dɪ'vaɪdərz] spl compasso a punte fisse

divination [‚dɪvɪ'neʃən] s divinazione

divine [dɪ'vaɪn] adj divino ‖ s sacerdote m, prete m ‖ *tr* divinare

diviner [dɪ'vaɪnər] s divinatore m

diving ['daɪvɪŋ] s tuffo, immersione

div'ing bell' s campana da palombaro

div'ing board' s trampolino

div'ing suit' s scafandro

divin'ing rod' [dɪ'vaɪnɪŋ] s bacchetta rabdomantica

divini•ty [dɪ'vɪnɪtɪ] s (**-ties**) divinità f; teologia; **the Divinity** Dio

divisible [dɪ'vɪsɪbəl] adj divisibile

division [dɪ'vɪʒən] s divisione

divisor [dɪ'vaɪzər] s divisore m

divorce [dɪ'vors] s divorzio; **to get a divorce** divorziare ‖ *tr* (*a married couple*) divorziare; (*one's spouse*) divorziare da ‖ *intr* divorziare

divorcé [dɪvor'se] s divorziato

divorcee [dɪvor'si] s divorziata

divulge [dɪ'vʌldʒ] *tr* divulgare

dizziness ['dɪzɪnɪs] s vertigine f, stordimento; confusione

diz•zy ['dɪzɪ] adj (**-zier; -ziest**) (*causing dizziness*) vertiginoso; (*suffering diz-*

ziness) preso da vertigine, stordito; (coll) stupido

do [du] v (*3rd pers* **does** [dʌz]; *pret* **did** [dɪd]; *pp* **done** [dʌn]; *ger* **doing** ['du‚ɪŋ]) *tr* fare; (*a problem*) risolvere; (*a distance*) percorrere; (*to study*) studiare; (*to explore*) esplorare; (*to tire*) stancare; **to do one's best** fare del proprio meglio; **to do over** tornare a fare; ripetere; **to do right by** trattare bene; **to do s.o. out of s.th** (coll) portare via qlco a qlcu; **to do to death** mettere a morte; **to do up** (coll) impacchettare; stancare; (*one's hair*) farsi; vestire; (*a shirt*) lavare e stirare; **to have done** far fare ‖ *intr* fare; agire; comportarsi; servire; bastare; stare; succedere; **how do you do?** come sta?; **that will do** basta; è sufficiente; **to have done with** non aver più nulla a che fare con; **to have nothing to do with** non aver nulla a che vedere con; **to have to do with** aver a che fare con, trattarsi di; **to do away with** togliere di mezzo; **to do for** servire da; **to do well** crescere bene; **to do without** fare a meno di ‖ v *aux* used 1) in interrogative sentences: **Do you speak Italian?** Parla italiano?; 2) in negative sentences: **I do not speak Italian** Non parlo italiano; 3) to avoid repetition of a verb or full verbal expression: **Did you go to church this morning?** **Yes, I did.** È stato in chiesa questa mattina? Sì, ci sono stato; 4) to lend emphasis to a principal verb: **I do believe what you told me** Ci credo a quello che mi ha detto; 5) in inverted constructions after certain adverbs: **Seldom does he come to see me** Mi viene a vedere di raro; 6) in a supplicating tone with imperatives: **Do come in** entri per favore

docile ['dɑsɪl] adj docile

dock [dɑk] s (*wharf*) molo; (*waterway between two piers*) darsena; (*area including piers and waterways*) scalo portuario; (law) gabbia degli imputati ‖ *tr* (*to deduct from the wages of*) fare una deduzione a; (*to deduct s.o.'s salary*) dedurre da; (*an animal*) scodare; (naut) attraccare ‖ *intr* (aer) agganciarsi; (naut) attraccare

dockage ['dɑkɪdʒ] s attracco; (*charges*) diritti mpl di porto

docket ['dɑkɪt] s ordine m del giorno; (law) ruolo delle sentenze; **on the docket** (coll) pendente, in sospeso

dock' hand' s portuale m

docking ['dɑkɪŋ] s (aer) aggancio; (naut) attracco

dock'yard' s cantiere m navale

doctor ['dɑktər] s dottore m; (*physician*) medico ‖ *tr* curare; aggiustare; falsificare; adulterare ‖ *intr* esercitare la medicina; (coll) curarsi, prendere medicine

doctorate ['dɑktərɪt] s dottorato

doctrine ['dɑktrɪn] s dottrina

document ['dɑkjəmənt] s documento ‖ ['dɑkjə‚ment] *tr* documentare

documenta·ry [ˌdɑkjə'mɛntəri] *adj* & *s* (**-ries**) documentario

documentation [ˌdɑkəmən'teʃən] *s* documentazione

doddering ['dɑdərɪŋ] *adj* tremante, rimbambito

dodge [dɑdʒ] *s* scarto, schivata; (fig) stratagemma *m* ‖ *tr* schivare, evitare ‖ *intr* schivarsi; (fig) rispondere evasivamente; **to dodge around the corner** scantonare

do·do ['dodo] *s* (**-dos** or **-does**) (coll) rimbecillito

doe [do] *s* (*of deer*) cerva; (*of goat*) capretta; (*of rabbit*) coniglia

doeskin ['do ˌskɪn] *s* pelle *f* di daino, pelle *f* di dante; lana finissima

doff [dɑf] or [dɔf] *tr* (*one's hat*) togliersi; (*clothing*) deporre

dog [dɔg] or [dɑg] *s* cane *m*; **to go to the dogs** (coll) andare in malora; **to put on the dog** (coll) darsi delle arie ‖ *v* (*pret* & *pp* **dogged**; *ger* **dogging**) *tr* seguire; perseguitare

dog'catch'er *s* accalappiacani *m*

dog' days' *s* solleone *m*, canicola

doge [dodʒ] *s* doge *m*

dog'-ear' *s* orecchia, orecchio

dog'fight' *s* duello aereo

dogged ['dɔgɪd] or ['dɑgɪd] *adj* accanito

doggerel ['dɔgərəl] or ['dɑgərəl] *s* versi *mpl* da colascione

dog·gy ['dɔgi] or ['dɑgi] *adj* (**-gier**; **-giest**) vistoso; canino ‖ *s* (**-gies**) cagnolino

dog'house' *s* canile *m*; **to be in the doghouse** (slang) essere in disgrazia

dog' Lat'in *s* latino maccheronico

dogma ['dɔgmə] or ['dɑgmə] *s* dogma *m*

dogmatic [dɔg'mætɪk] or [dɑg'mætɪk] *adj* dogmatico

dog' rac'ing *s* corse *fpl* dei cani

dog' show' *s* mostra canina

dog's' life' *s* vita da cani

Dog' Star' *s* canicola

dog' tag' *s* (mil) piastrina, piastrino

dog'-tired' *adj* (coll) stanco morto

dog'tooth' *s* (**-teeth** [ˌtiθ]) canino

dog' track' *s* cinodromo

dog'watch' *s* (naut) quarto di solo due ore, gaettone *m*

dog'wood' *s* corniolo

doi·ly ['dɔɪli] *s* (**-lies**) centrino

doings ['du·ɪŋz] *spl* azioni *fpl*, fatti *mpl*

do'-it-your·self' *s* il fare tutto da sé

doldrums ['dɑldrəmz] *spl* calma equatoriale; inattività *f*; depressione

dole [dol] *s* elemosina; (*to the jobless*) sussidio di disoccupazione ‖ *tr—to* **dole out** distribuire parsimoniosamente

doleful ['dolfəl] *adj* lugubre, triste

doll [dɑl] *s* bambola ‖ *intr—to* **doll up** (slang) agghindarsi

dollar ['dɑlər] *s* dollaro

dol'lar·wise' *adv* in termini finanziari

dol·ly ['dɑli] *s* (**-lies**) pupattola; (*low, wheeled frame for moving heavy loads*) carrello; (mov, telv) carrello

‖ *v* (*pret* & *pp* **-lied**) *intr* (mov, telv) carrellare

dol'ly shot' *s* (mov, telv) carrellata

dolphin ['dɑlfɪn] *s* delfino

dolt [dolt] *s* gonzo, balordo

doltish ['doltɪʃ] *adj* gonzo, balordo

domain [do'men] *s* dominio; (law) proprietà *f*; (fig) campo, orbita

dome [dom] *s* cupola

dome' light' *s* lampadario

domestic [də'mɛstɪk] *adj* & *s* domestico

domesticate [də'mɛstɪ ˌket] *tr* domesticare

domicile ['dɑmɪsɪl] or ['dɑmɪ ˌsaɪl] *s* domicilio ‖ *tr* domiciliare

dominance ['dɑmɪnəns] *s* dominio

dominant ['dɑmɪnənt] *adj* & *s* dominante *f*

dominate ['dɑmɪ ˌnet] *tr* & *intr* dominare

domination [ˌdɑmɪ'neʃən] *s* dominazione

domineer [ˌdɑmɪ'nɪr] *intr* spadroneggiare

domineering [ˌdɑmɪ'nɪrɪŋ] *adj* dispotico, tirannico

Dominican [də'mɪnɪkən] *adj* & *s* dominicano; (eccl) domenicano

dominion [də'mɪnjən] *s* dominio

domi·no ['dɑmɪ ˌno] *s* (**-noes** or **-nos**) (*costume and person*) domino; (*piece*) tessera di domino; **dominoes** (*game*) domino

don [dɑn] *s* signore *m*; don *m*; membro di un collegio universitario inglese ‖ *v* (*pret* & *pp* **donned**; *ger* **donning**) *tr* (*clothes*) mettersi, vestire

donate ['donet] *tr* donare, dare

donation [do'neʃən] *s* donazione

done [dʌn] *adj* fatto; finito; stanco; (culin) ben cotto, ben rosolato

done' for' *adj* (coll) stanco morto; (coll) rovinato; (coll) fuori combattimento; (coll) morto

donjon ['dʌndʒən] or ['dɑndʒən] *s* torrione *m*, maschio

Don Juan [dɑn 'wɑn] or [dɔn 'hwɑn] *s* Don Giovanni

donkey ['dɑŋki] or ['dʌŋki] *s* asino, somaro

donnish ['dɑnɪʃ] *adj* pedante

donor ['donər] *s* donatore *m*

doodle ['dudəl] *tr* & *intr* scarabocchiare, riempire di ghirigori

doom [dum] *s* destino; morte *f*, rovina; sentenza di morte; giudizio finale ‖ *tr* destinare; condannare; condannare a morte

doomsday ['dumz ˌde] *s* giorno del giudizio

door [dor] *s* porta; (*of a carriage or automobile*) portiera, sportello; (*one part of a double door*) battente *m*; **behind closed doors** a porte chiuse; **to see to the door** accompagnare alla porta; **to show s.o. the door** mettere qlcu alla porta

door'bell' *s* campanello della porta

door' check' *s* chiusura automatica di porta, scontro

door'frame' *s* cornice *f*

door'head' *s* architrave *m*

door'jamb' *s* stipite *m*

door'keep'er *s* portinaio

door'knob' *s* maniglia della porta

door' knock'er *s* battente *m*

door' latch' *s* paletto

door'man' *s* (**-men'**) portiere *m*, portinaio; (*of large apartment house*) guardaportone *m*

door'mat' *s* stoino, zerbino

door'nail' *s* borchione *m*; **dead as a doornail** morto e ben morto

door'post' *s* stipite *m*

door' scrap'er *s* raschietto

door'sill' *s* soglia

door'step' *s* gradino davanti la porta

door'stop' *s* paracolpi *m*

door'-to-door' *adj* (*shipment*) diretto; (*selling*) di porta in porta

door'way' *s* vano della porta; porta

dope [dop] *s* lubrificante *m*; (aer) vernice *f*; (slang) stupido, scemo; (slang) informazioni *fpl*; (slang) narcotico ‖ *tr* (slang) narcotizzare; **to dope out** (slang) indovinare, decifrare, immaginare

dope' fiend' *s* (slang) tossicomane *mf*

dope'sheet' *s* giornaletto con le previsioni della corse ippiche

dormant ['dɔrmənt] *adj* dormente; latente

dor'mer win'dow ['dɔrmər] *s* abbaino

dormito·ry ['dɔrmɪ ˌtori] *s* (**-ries**) dormitorio

dor·mouse ['dɔr ˌmaʊs] *s* (**-mice** [ˌmaɪs]) ghiro

dosage ['dosɪdʒ] *s* dosatura

dose [dos] *s* dose *f*; (coll) boccone amaro ‖ *tr* dosare; somministrare

dossier ['dɑsɪ ˌe] *s* incartamento

dot [dɑt] *s* punto; **on the dot** (coll) in punto ‖ *v* (*pret & pp* **dotted;** *ger* **dotting**) *tr* punteggiare; **to dot one's i's** mettere i punti sulle i

dotage ['dotɪdʒ] *s* rimbecillimento; **to be in one's dotage** essere rimbambito

dotard ['dotərd] *s* vecchio rimbambito

dote [dot] *intr* rimbambirsi; **to dote on** essere pazzo per

doting ['dotɪŋ] *adj* che ama alla follia; (*from old age*) rimbambito, rimbecillito

dots' and dash'es *spl* (telg) punti *mpl* e tratti *mpl*

dot'ted line' *s* linea punteggiata; **to sign on the dotted line** firmare inconsideratamente

double ['dʌbəl] *adj* doppio ‖ *s* doppio; (bridge) contre *m*; **doubles** (tennis) doppio ‖ *tr* raddoppiare; (bridge) contrare ‖ *intr* raddoppiarsi; (bridge) contrare; (mov, theat) sostenere due ruoli; (mov) doppiare; **to double up** (*said of two people*) dividere la stessa camera, dividere lo stesso letto; piegarsi in due

double-barreled ['dʌbəl'bærəld] *adj* a due canne; (fig) a doppio fine

dou'ble bass' *s* contrabbasso

dou'ble bed' *s* letto matrimoniale

dou'ble boil'er *s* bagnomaria *m*

double-breasted ['dʌbəl'brestɪd] *adj* a doppio petto, doppiopetto

dou'ble chin' *s* pappagorgia

dou'ble-cross' *tr* (coll) tradire

dou'ble date' *s* (coll) appuntamento amoroso di due coppie

dou'ble-deal'ing *adj* doppio

dou'ble-deck'er *s* (*bed*) letto a castello; (*sandwich*) tramezzino doppio; autobus *m* a due piani; (naut) nave *f* due ponti; (aer) aereo due ponti

double-edged ['dʌbəl'edʒd] *adj* a due tagli, a doppio taglio

dou'ble en'try *s* (com) partita doppia

dou'ble fea'ture *s* (mov) programma *m* di due lungometraggio

double-header ['dʌbəl'hedər] *s* treno con due locomotive; due partite di baseball giocate successivamente

double-jointed ['dʌbəl'dʒɔɪntɪd] *adj* snodato

dou'ble-park' *tr & intr* parcheggiare in doppia fila

dou'ble-quick' *adj & adv* a passo di carica

dou'ble stand'ard—to have a double standard usare due pesi e due misure

doublet ['dʌblɪt] *s* (*close-fitting jacket*) farsetto; (philol) doppione *m*

dou'ble-talk' *s* discorso incomprensibile; **to give s.o. double-talk** parlare evasivamente a qlcu ‖ *intr* parlare evasivamente

dou'ble time' *s* paga doppia; (mil) passo di carica

doubleton ['dʌbəltən] *s* doppio

doubly ['dʌbli] *adv* doppiamente

doubt [daʊt] *s* dubbio; **beyond doubt** senza dubbio; **if in doubt** in caso di dubbio; **no doubt** senza dubbio ‖ *tr* dubitare di ‖ *intr* dubitare

doubter ['daʊtər] *s* incredulo

doubtful ['daʊtfəl] *adj* incerto; dubbioso

doubtless ['daʊtlɪs] *adj* indubitabile ‖ *adv* senza dubbio; probabilmente

douche [duʃ] *s* irrigazione *f*; (*instrument*) irrigatore *m* ‖ *tr* irrigare ‖ *intr* fare irrigazioni

dough [do] *s* pasta di pane; (*money*) (slang) soldi *mpl*, quattrini *mpl*

dough'boy' *s* fantaccino americano

dough'nut' *s* ciambella; (*with filling*) sgonfiotto

dough·ty ['daʊti] *adj* (**-tier; -tiest**) forte, coraggioso

dough·y ['do·i] *adj* (**-ier; -iest**) pastoso, molle

dour [daʊr] *or* [dʊr] *adj* triste, severo

douse [daʊs] *tr* immergere; bagnare; (*the light*) (coll) spegnere

dove [dʌv] *s* colomba, tortora

dovecote ['dʌv ˌkot] *s* piccionaia

dove'tail' *s* coda di rondine ‖ *tr* calettare a coda di rondine; (*to make fit*) adattare, far combaciare ‖ *intr* (*to fit*) combaciare; corrispondere

dowager ['daʊ·ədʒər] *s* vedova titolata; vecchia signora austera; **queen dowager** regina madre

dow·dy ['daʊdi] *adj* (**-dier; -diest**) trasandato

dow·el ['dau·əl] *s* caviglia, tassello || *v* (*pret* & *pp* **-eled** or **-elled; *ger* -eling** or **-elling**) *tr* tassellare

dower ['dau·ər] *s* (*widow's portion*) legittima, vedovile *m*; (*marriage portion; natural gift*) dote *f* || *tr* dotare; assegnare un vedovile a

down [daun] *adj* che discende; basso; (*train*) che va al centro; depresso; finito; (*money, payment*) anticipato; (*storage battery*) esaurito || *s* (*fruit and human body*) lanugine *f*; (*of birds*) piumino; (*upset*) rovescio; discesa; (*sandhill*) duna || *adv* giù; all'ingiù, in giù; dabbasso; a terra; al sud; (*in cash*) a contanti; **down and out** rovinato; senza una soldo; **down from** da; **down on one's knees** in ginocchio; **down to** fino a; **down under** agli antipodi; **down with . . . !** abasso . . . !; **to get down to work** mettersi seriamente al lavoro; **to go down** scendere; **to lie down** sdraiarsi; andare a letto; **to sit down** sedersi || *prep* giù per; **down the river** a valle; **down the street** giù per la strada || *tr* abbattere; (coll) buttar giù, tracannare

down'cast' *adj* mogio, sfiduciato

down'fall' *s* rovina, rovescio

down'grade' *adj* & *adv* in declivio, a valle || *s* discesa; **to be on the downgrade** essere in declino || *tr* attribuire minor importanza a; degradare

downhearted ['daun‚hɑrtɪd] *adj* scoraggiato, abbattuto

down'hill' *adj* & *adv* in declivio; **to go downhill** declinare

down' pay'ment *s* acconto

down'pour' *s* acquazzone *m*, rovescio

down'right' *adj* assoluto; completo; franco, diretto || *adv* completamente

down'stairs' *adj* del piano di sotto || *s* il piano di sotto; i piani di sotto || *adv* dabbasso, di sotto, giù

down'stream' *adv* a valle

down'stroke' *s* corsa discendente

down'town' *adj* centrale || *s* centro della città || *adv* al centro della città

down' train' *s* treno discendente, treno che va al centro

down'trend' *s* tendenza al ribasso

downtrodden ['daun‚trɑdən] *adj* calpestato, oppresso

downward ['daunwərd] *adj* & *adv* all'ingiù

down·y ['dauni] *adj* (**-ier; -iest**) piumoso, lanuginoso; (*soft*) molle, morbido

dow·ry ['dauri] *s* (**-ries**) dote *f*

doze [doz] *s* pisolo || *intr* dormicchiare; **to doze off** appisolarsi

dozen ['dʌzən] *s* dozzina

dozy ['dozi] *adj* sonnolento

drab [dræb] *adj* (**drabber; drabbest**) grigiastro; (*dull*) scialbo || *s* colore grigiastro; (*fabric*) tela naturale; donna di malaffare

drach·ma ['drækmə] *s* (**-mas** or **-mae** [mi]) dramma

draft [dræft] or [drɑft] *s* corrente *f* d'aria; (*pulling*) tiro; (*in a chimney*) tiraggio; (*sketch, outline*) schizzo; (*first form of a writing*) prima stesura; (*drink*) sorso, bicchiere *m*; (com) tratta, lettera di credito; (law) progetto, disegno; (naut) pesca; (mil) coscrizione *f*, leva; **on draft** alla spina || *tr* disegnare; fare uno schizzo di; (*a document*) stendere; (mil) coscrivere; **to be drafted** essere di leva, andar coscritto

draft' age' *s* età *f* di leva

draft' beer' *s* birra alla spina

draft' board' *s* consiglio di leva

draft' dodg'er ['dɑdʒər] *s* renitente *m* alla leva, imboscato

draftee [‚dræf'ti] or [‚drɑf'ti] *s* coscritto

draft' horse' *s* cavallo da tiro

drafts'man *s* (**-men**) disegnatore *m*; (*man who draws up documents*) redattore *m*

draft' trea'ty *s* progetto di trattato

draft·y ['dræfti] or ['drɑfti] *adj* (**-ier; -iest**) pieno di correnti d'aria

drag [dræg] *s* (*sledge for conveying heavy bodies*) traino, treggia; (*on a cigarette*) boccata; (aer) resistenza aerodinamica; (naut) pressione idrostatica; (naut) draga; (fig) noia; (*influence*) aderenze *fpl*; (*a bore*) (slang) rompiscatole *m* || *v* (*pret* & *pp* **dragged**; *ger* **dragging**) *tr* strascinare, strascicare; (naut) rastrellare || *intr* strascicare, strascicarsi; dilungarsi; **to drag on** andare per le lunghe

drag'net' *s* paranza; (fig) retata

dragon ['drægən] *s* drago, dragone *m*

drag'on·fly' *s* (**-flies**) libellula

dragoon [drə'gun] *s* (mil) dragone *m* || *tr* forzare, costringere

drain [dren] *s* scolo; prosciugamento; (geog) spiovente *m*; (surg) drenaggio; (fig) salasso || *tr* (*a liquid*) scolare; prosciugare; (*humid land; a wound*) drenare || *intr* scolare; prosciugarsi; (geog) defluire

drainage ['drenɪdʒ] *s* drenaggio; (geog) displuvio, spartiacque *m*

drain'board' *s* scolatoio per le stoviglie

drain' cock' *s* rubinetto di scarico

drain'pipe' *s* tubo di scarico

drake [drek] *s* anatra maschio

dram [dræm] *s* dramma; bicchierino di liquore

drama ['drɑmə] or ['dræmə] *s* dramma *m*; (*art and genre*) drammatica

dramatic [drə'mætɪk] *adj* drammatico || **dramatics** *ssg* drammatica; *spl* rappresentazione dilettantesca; comportamento drammatico

dramatist ['dræmətɪst] *s* drammaturgo

dramatize ['dræmə‚taɪz] *tr* drammatizzare

drape [drep] *s* tenda, cortina; (*of a curtain*) drappeggio; (*of a skirt*) taglio || *tr* drappeggiare

draper·y ['drepəri] *s* (**-ies**) drapperia; negozio di tessuti; **draperies** tendaggi *mpl*

drastic ['dræstɪk] *adj* drastico

draught [dræft] or [drɑft] *s & tr* var of **draft**

draught' beer' *s* birra alla spina

draw [drɔ] *s (in a game)* patta; *(in a lottery)* sorteggio; *(act of drawing)* tiro; *(of chimney)* tiraggio; *(attraction)* attrazione; *(of a drawbridge)* ala ‖ ~v *(pret* **drew** [dru]; *pp* **drawn** [drɔn]) *tr (a line)* tirare; *(to attract)* richiamare; *(butter)* fondere; *(a sword)* sguainare; *(a nail)* estrarre; *(people)* attrarre; *(a sigh)* emettere; *(a curtain)* far scorrere; *(a salary)* pigliare; *(a prize)* ricevere; *(a game)* impattare; *(in card games)* pescare; *(a drawbridge)* sollevare; *(said of a ship)* pescare; *(a comparison)* fare; *(a profit)* ricavare; *(a chicken)* sventrare; *(e.g., a picture)* disegnare, ritrarre; *(to sketch in words)* descrivere; *(a contract)* stipulare; *(interest)* ricevere; *(com)* spiccare, staccare; **to draw forth** far uscire; **to draw off** estrarre; *(a liquid)* spillare; **to draw (shoes) on** mettersi; **to draw (money) on** ritirare da; **to draw (a draft) on** domiciliare presso; **to draw oneself up** raddrizzarsi; **to draw out** *(to persuade to talk)* far parlare, tirar fuori le parole a; **to draw up** *(a document)* estendere; *(mil)* schierare ‖ *intr (said of chimney)* tirare; impattare; sorteggiare un premio; aver attrazione; disegnare; **to draw aside** scostarsi; **to draw back** retrocedere, ritirarsi; **to draw near** avvicinarsi; volgere a; **to draw to a close** essere quasi finito; **to draw together** unirsi

draw'back' *s* inconveniente *m*

draw'bridge' *s* ponte levatoio

drawee [ˌdrɔˈi] *s* trattario, trassato

drawer [ˈdrɔ·ər] *s* disegnatore *m*; *(com)* traente *m* ‖ [drɔr] *s* cassetto; **drawers** mutande *fpl*

drawing [ˈdrɔ·ɪŋ] *s* disegno; *(in a lottery)* sorteggio

draw'ing board' *s* tavolo da disegno

draw'ing card' *s* attrazione

draw'ing room' *s* salotto, salottino

draw'knife' *s* (**-knives** [ˌnaɪvz]) coltello a petto

drawl [drɔl] *s* accento strascicato ‖ *tr* dire con accento strascicato ‖ *intr* strascicare le parole

drawn' but'ter *s* burro fuso

drawn' work' *s* lavoro a giorno

dray [dre] *s* carro pesante; slitta, treggia; autocarro

drayage [ˈdre·ɪdʒ] *s* carreggio

dray'man *s* (**-men**) carrettiere *m*

dread [dred] *adj* spaventoso, terribile ‖ *s* spavento, terrore *m* ‖ *tr & intr* temere

dreadful [ˈdredfəl] *adj* spaventevole, terribile; *(coll)* orribile

dread'nought' *s* corazzata

dream [drim] *s* sogno; illusione, fantasticheria; **dream come true** sogno fatto realtà ‖ *v (pret & pp* **dreamed** or **dreamt** [dremt]) *tr* sognare; **to dream up** *(coll)* immaginare, fantasticare ‖ *intr* sognare

dreamer [ˈdrimər] *s* sognatore *m*

dream'land' *s* paese *m* dei sogni

dream·y [ˈdrimi] *adj* (**-ier; -iest**) sognante; *(visionary)* trasognato; vago

drear·y [ˈdrɪri] *adj* (**-ier; -iest**) squallido; triste; *(boring)* noioso

dredge [dredʒ] *s* draga ‖ *tr* dragare; *(culin)* infarinare

dredger [ˈdredʒər] *s* *(boat)* draga; *(container)* spolverino

dredging [ˈdredʒɪŋ] *s* dragaggio

dregs [dregz] *spl* feccia

drench [drentʃ] *tr* infradiciare, inzuppare

dress [dres] *s* vestito; vestiti *mpl*; vestito da donna; abito; abito da cerimonia; *(of a bird)* piumaggio ‖ *tr* vestire; adornare, decorare; *(hair)* pettinare; *(a wound)* medicare; *(leather)* conciare; *(food)* condire; *(a boat)* pavesare; **to dress down** *(coll)* rimproverare; **to get dressed** vestirsi ‖ *intr* vestire; vestirsi; *(mil)* schierarsi; **to dress up** vestirsi da sera; farsi bello, mettersi in gala

dress' ball' *s* ballo di gala

dress' coat' *s* frac *m*

dresser [ˈdresər] *s* toletta; *(sideboard)* credenza; **to be a good dresser** vestire con eleganza

dress' goods' *spl* stoffa per abiti

dressing [ˈdresɪŋ] *s* ornamento; *(for food)* condimento, salsa; *(stuffing for fowl)* ripieno; *(fertilizer)* concime *m*; *(for a wound)* medicazione

dress'ing down' *s* ramanzina

dress'ing gown' *s* vestaglia

dress'ing room' *s* spogliatoio, toletta; *(theat)* camerino

dress'ing sta'tion *s* posto di pronto soccorso

dress'ing ta'ble *s* toletta, specchiera

dress'mak'er *s* sarta, sarto per donna

dress'mak'ing *s* taglio, sartoria

dress' rehears'al *s* prova generale

dress' shirt' *s* camicia inamidata

dress' suit' *s* marsina

dress' u'niform *s* (mil) alta uniforme

dress·y [ˈdresi] *adj* (**-ier; iest**) *(coll)* elegante, ricercato

dribble [ˈdrɪbəl] *s* goccia ‖ *tr (sports)* palleggiare, dribblare ‖ *intr* gocciolare; *(at the mouth)* sbavare; *(sports)* dribblare

driblet [ˈdrɪblɪt] *s* piccola quantità; **in driblets** col contagocce

dried' beef' [draɪd] *s* carne seccata

dried' fruit' *s* frutta secca

drier [ˈdraɪ·ər] *s (for hair)* asciugacapelli *m*; *(for clothes)* asciugatrice *f*

drift [drɪft] *s* movimento; *(of sand, snow, etc.)* cumulo; *(snowdrift)* neve accumulata dal vento; corrente *f*; intenzione; (aer, naut) deriva; (rad, telv) deviazione ‖ *intr* andare alla deriva; *(said of snow)* accumularsi; (aer, naut) derivare, scadere

drift' ice' *s* ghiaccio alla deriva

drift'pin' *s* (mach) mandrino

drift'wood' *s* legname andato alla deriva

drill [drɪl] s esercizio; (fabric) tela cruda; (agr) seminatrice f; (mach) trapano, trivella; (mil) esercitazioni fpl militari ‖ tr trivellare; istruire; (mil) insegnare gli esercizi militari a ‖ intr addestrarsi; (mil) fare gli esercizi militari

drill′mas′ter s istruttore m

drill′ press′ s trapano a colonna

drink [drɪŋk] s bevanda; the drinks are on the house! paga il proprietario! ‖ v (pret drank [dræŋk]; pp drunk [drʌŋk]) tr bere; assorbire; to drink down tracannare; to drink in bere, assorbire; (air) aspirare ‖ intr bere; to drink out of bere da; to drink to the health of bere alla salute di

drinkable [′drɪŋkəbəl] adj bevibile, potabile

drinker [′drɪŋkər] s bevitore m

drinking [′drɪŋkɪŋ] s (il) bere

drink′ing foun′tain s fontanella pubblica

drink′ing song′ s canzone bacchica

drink′ing straw′ s cannuccia

drink′ing trough′ s abbeveratoio

drink′ing wa′ter s acqua potabile

drip [drɪp] s sgocciolo, sgocciolatura ‖ v (pret & pp dripped; ger dripping) intr sgocciolare, stillare; (said of perspiration) trasudare

drip′ cof′fee s caffè fatto con la macchinetta

drip′-dry′ adj non-stiro

drip′ pan′ s (culin) ghiotta; (mach) coppa

dripping [′drɪpɪŋ] s gocciolio; drippings grasso che cola dall'arrosto

drive [draɪv] s scarrozzata; strada; passeggiata; impulso; forza, iniziativa; urgenza; spinta; campagna; (aut) trazione; (mach) trasmissione ‖ v (pret drove [drov]; ger driven [′drɪvən]) tr (a nail) ficcare, piantare; (e.g., cattle) condurre, parare; (s.o. in a carriage or auto) condurre, portare; spingere; stimulare; forzare; spingere a lavorare; (sports) colpire molto forte; to drive away scacciare; to drive back respingere; to drive mad far impazzire; to drive out scacciare ‖ intr fare una scarrozzata; to drive at parare a; voler dire; to drive hard lavorare sodo; to drive in entrare in automobile; (a place) entrare in automobile in; to drive on the right guidare a destra; to drive out uscire in macchina; to drive up arrivare in macchina

drive′-in′ mov′ie the′ater s cineparco

drive′-in′ res′taurant s ristorante m con servizio alla portiera

driv-el [′drɪvəl] s (slobber) bava; (nonsense) scemenza ‖ v (pret -eled or -elled; ger -eling or -elling) intr sbavare; dire scemenze

driver [′draɪvər] s guidatore m; (of a carriage) cocchiere m; (of a locomotive) macchinista m; (of pack animals) carrettiere m, mulattiere m

driv′er's li′cense s patente automobilistica

driv′er's seat′ s posto di guida

drive′ shaft′ s albero motore

drive′way s strada privata d'accesso; carrozzabile f

drive′ wheel′ s ruota motrice

driv′ing school′ [′draɪvɪŋ] s autoscuola, scuola guida

drizzle [′drɪzəl] s pioviggine f ‖ intr piovigginare

droll [drol] adj buffo, spassoso

dromedar-y [′drɑmə‚deri] s (-ies) dromedario

drone [dron] s fuco, pecchione m; (hum) ronzio; (of bagpipe) bordone m; areoplano teleguidato ‖ tr dire in tono monotono ‖ intr (to live in idleness) fare il fannullone; (to buzz, hum) ronzare

drool [drul] s (slobber) bava; (slang) scemenza ‖ intr sbavare; (slang) dire scemenze

droop [drup] s accasciamento ‖ intr (to sag) pendere; (to lose spirit) accasciarsi; (said, e.g., of wheat) avvizzire

drooping [′drupɪŋ] adj (eyelid) abbassato; (shoulder) spiovente; (fig) accasciato

drop [drɑp] s goccia; (slope) pendenza; (earring) pendente m; (in temperature) discesa; (from an airplane) lancio; (trap door) botola; (gallows) trabocchetto della forca; (lozenge) pastiglia; (slit for letters) buca; (curtain) tela; (in prices) calo; a drop in the bucket una goccia nell'oceano ‖ v (pret & pp dropped; ger dropping) tr lasciar cadere; (a letter) imbucare; (a curtain) abbassare; (a remark) lasciar scappare; (a note) scrivere; omettere; abbandonare; (anchor) gettare; (from an airplane) lanciare; (from an automobile) lasciare; (from a list) cancellare ‖ intr cadere; lasciarsi cadere; terminare; to drop dead cader morto; to drop in entrare un momento; to drop off sparire; addormentarsi; morire improvvisamente; to drop out scomparire; ritirarsi; dare le dimissioni

drop′ cur′tain s telone m

drop′ ham′mer s maglio

drop′-leaf′ ta′ble s tavola a ribalta

drop′light′ s lampada sospesa

drop′out′ s studente m che abbandona permanentemente la scuola media

dropper [′drɑpər] s contagocce m

dropsical [′drɑpsɪkəl] adj idropico

dropsy [′drɑpsi] s idropisia

dross [drɔs] or [drɑs] s scoria; (fig) feccia

drought [draʊt] s siccità f; (shortage) mancanza

drove [drov] s branco; folla; in droves in massa

drover [′drovər] s mandriano

drown [draʊn] tr & intr affogare, annegare

drowse [draʊz] intr sonnecchiare

drow-sy [′draʊzi] adj (-sier; -siest) sonnolento, insonnolito

drub [drʌb] v (pret & pp drubbed; ger drubbing) tr bastonare; battere

drudge [drʌdʒ] s sgobbone m ‖ intr sgobbare, sfacchinare

drudger·y [ˈdrʌdʒəri] s (-ies) lavoro ingrato, sfacchinata

drug [drʌg] s droga, medicina; narcotico; **drug on the market** merce f invendibile ‖ v (pret & pp **drugged**; ger **drugging**) tr drogare, narcotizzare

drug' ad'dict s tossicomane mf

drug' addic'tion s tossicomania

druggist [ˈdrʌgɪst] s farmacista mf

drug' hab'it s tossicomania

drug'store' s farmacia

drug' traf'fic s traffico in stupefacenti

druid [ˈdruɪd] s druida m

drum [drʌm] s (cylinder; instrument) tamburo; (container) fusto ‖ v (pret & pp **drummed**; ger **drumming**) tr stamburare; **to drum up** (customers) farsi; (enthusiasm) creare ‖ intr tambureggiare; (with the fingers) tamburellare

drum'beat' s rullo di tamburi

drum' corps' s banda di tamburi

drum'fire' s fuoco nutrito

drum'head' s membrana del tamburo

drum' ma'jor s tamburo maggiore

drummer [ˈdrʌmər] s (salesman) agente m viaggiatore; (mus) tamburo; (mil) tamburino

drum'stick' s bacchetta del tamburo; (of cooked fowl) coscia

drunk [drʌŋk] adj ubriaco; **to get drunk** ubriacarsi ‖ s ubriaco; (spree) sbornia; **to go on a drunk** (coll) ubriacarsi

drunkard [ˈdrʌŋkərd] s ubriacone m

drunken [ˈdrʌŋkən] adj ubriaco

drunk'en driv'ing s—**to be arrested for drunken driving** esser arrestato per aver guidato in stato di ubriachezza

drunkenness [ˈdrʌŋkənnɪs] s ubriachezza, ebbrezza

dry [draɪ] adj (drier; driest) secco; (boring) arido; **to be dry** aver sete ‖ s (drys) abolizionista mf ‖ v (pret & pp **dried**) tr seccare; (to wipe dry) asciugare ‖ intr seccarsi; **to dry up** prosciugarsi, essiccarsi; (slang) star zitto

dry' bat'tery s pila a secco; (group of dry cells) batteria a secco

dry' cell' s pila a secco

dry'-clean' tr lavare a secco, pulire a secco

dry' clean'er s tintore m

dry' clean'ing s lavaggio a secco, pulitura a secco

dry'-clean'ing estab'lishment s tintoria

dry' dock' s bacino di carenaggio

dryer [ˈdraɪ·ər] s var of **drier**

dry'-eyed' adj a occhi asciutti

dry' farm'ing s coltivazione di terreno arido

dry' goods' spl tessuti mpl; aridi mpl

dry'-goods store' s drapperia, negozio di tessuti

dry' ice' s neve carbonica, ghiaccio secco

dry' law' s legge f proibizionista

dry' meas'ure s misura per solidi

dryness [ˈdraɪnɪs] s siccità f; (e.g., of a speaker) aridità f

dry' nurse' s balia asciutta

dry' run' s esercizio di prova; (mil) esercitazione senza munizioni

dry' sea'son s stagione arida

dry' wash' s roba lavata e asciugata ma non stirata

dual [ˈdju·əl] or [ˈdu·əl] adj & s duale m

duali·ty [djuˈælɪti] or [duˈælɪti] s (-ties) dualità f

dub [dʌb] s (slang) giocatore inesperto ‖ v (pret & pp **dubbed**; ger **dubbing**) tr chiamare, affibbiare il nome di; (a knight) armare; (mov) doppiare

dubbing [ˈdʌbɪŋ] s doppiaggio

dubious [ˈdjubɪ·əs] or [ˈdubɪ·əs] adj dubbioso; incerto

ducat [ˈdʌkət] s ducato

duchess [ˈdʌtʃɪs] s duchessa

duch·y [ˈdʌtʃi] s (-ies) ducato

duck [dʌk] s anatra; mossa rapida; (in the water) tuffo; (dodge) schivata; **ducks** pantaloni mpl di tela cruda ‖ tr (one's head) abbassare rapidamente; (in water) tuffare; (a blow) schivare ‖ intr tuffarsi; **to duck out** (coll) svignarsela

duckling [ˈdʌklɪŋ] s anatroccolo

ducks' and drakes' s—**to play ducks and drakes with** buttar via, sperperare

duck' soup' s (slang) cosa facilissima

duct [dʌkt] s tubo, condotto

ductile [ˈdʌktɪl] adj duttile

duct'less gland' [ˈdʌktlɪs] s ghiandola a secrezione interna

duct'work' s condotto, canalizzazione

dud [dʌd] s (slang) bomba inesplosa; (person) (slang) fallito; (enterprise) (slang) fallimento; **duds** (coll) vestito; roba

dude [djud] or [dud] s elegantone m

due [dju] or [du] adj dovuto; atteso; debito; pagabile; **due to** dovuto a; **to fall due** scadere; **when is the train due?** a che ora arriva il treno? ‖ s spettanza; debito; **dues** (of a member) quota sociale; **to get one's due** ricevere quanto uno merita; **to give the devil his due** trattare ognuno con giustizia ‖ adv in direzione, e.g., **due north** in direzione nord

duel [ˈdju·əl] or [ˈdu·əl] s duello; **to fight a duel** battersi a duello ‖ v (pret & pp **dueled** or **duelled**; ger **dueling** or **duelling**) intr duellare

duelist or **duellist** [ˈdju·əlɪst] or [ˈdu·əlɪst] s duellante mf

dues-paying [ˈdjuz ˌpe·ɪŋ] or [ˈduz ˌpe·ɪŋ] adj regolare, effettivo

duet [djuˈɛt] or [duˈɛt] s duetto

duf'fel bag' [ˈdʌfəl] s sacca da viaggio

duke [djuk] or [duk] s duca m

dukedom [ˈdjukdəm] or [ˈdukdəm] s ducato

dull [dʌl] adj (not sharp) spuntato, senza filo; (color) spento, sbiadito; (sound, pain) sordo; (stupid) ebete, tonto; (business) inattivo; (boring) noioso, melenso; (flat) opaco, appannato ‖ tr spuntare; sbiadire; inebetire; ottundere; (enthusiasm) raffreddare; (pain) alleviare ‖ intr spuntarsi; sbiadirsi; inebetirsi; raffreddarsi

dullard ['dʌlərd] s stupido

duly ['djuli] or ['duli] adv debitamente

dumb [dʌm] adj (lacking the power to speak) muto; (coll) tonto, stupido

dumb'bell' s manubrio; (slang) zuccone m, stupido

dumb' crea'ture s animale m, bruto

dumb' show' s pantomima

dumb'wai'ter s montavivande m

dumfound [,dʌm'faʊnd] tr interdire, lasciare esterrefatto

dum·my ['dʌmi] adj copiato; falso || s (-mies) (dress form) manichino; (in card games) morto; (figurehead) uomo di paglia, prestanome m; (skeleton copy of a book) menabò m; copia; (slang) stupido, tonto

dump [dʌmp] s immondezzaio; mucchio di spazzature; (mil) deposito munizioni; (min) montagnetta di scarico; **to be down in the dumps** (coll) avere le paturnie || tr scaricare; (to tip over) rovesciare; (com) scaricare sul mercato; (com) vendere sottocosto

dumping ['dʌmpɪŋ] s scarico; (com) dumping m

dumpling ['dʌmplɪŋ] s gnocco

dump' truck' s ribaltabile m

dump·y ['dʌmpi] adj (-ier; -iest) grassoccio, tarchiato

dun [dʌn] adj bruno grigiastro || s creditore importuno; (demand for payment) sollecitazione di pagamento || v (pret & pp **dunned**) ger **dunning**) tr sollecitare

dunce [dʌns] s ignorante mf, zuccone m

dunce' cap' s berretto d'asino

dune [djun] or [dun] s duna

dung [dʌŋ] s sterco, letame m || tr concimare con il letame

dungarees [,dʌŋgə'riz] spl tuta di cotone blu

dungeon ['dʌndʒən] s carcere sotterraneo; (fortified tower) torrione m, maschio

dung'hill' s letamaio

dunk [dʌŋk] tr inzuppare

du·o ['dju·o] or ['du·o] s (-os) duo

duode·num [,dju·ə'dinəm] or [,du·ə-'dinəm] s (-na [nə]) duodeno

dupe [djup] or [dup] s gonzo || tr gabbare, ingannare

du'plex house' ['djupleks] or ['dupleks] s casa di due appartamenti

duplicate ['djuplɪkɪt] or ['duplɪkɪt] adj & s duplicato || ['djuplɪ ,ket] or ['dupllɪ ,ket] tr duplicare

du'plicating machine' s duplicatore m

duplici·ty [dju'plɪsɪti] or [du'plɪsɪti] s (-ties) duplicità f, doppiezza

durable ['djurəbəl] or ['durəbəl] adj durabile, duraturo

du'rable goods' spl beni mpl durevoli

duration [dju're/ən] or [du're/ən] s durata

during ['djurɪŋ] or ['durɪŋ] prep durante

du'rum wheat' ['djurəm] or ['durəm] s grano duro

dusk [dʌsk] s crepuscolo

dust [dʌst] s polvere f || tr (to free of dust) spolverare; (to sprinkle with dust) spolverizzare; **to dust off** (slang) rimettere in uso; (slang) spolverare le spalle a

dust' bowl' s regione polverosissima

dust'cloth' s strofinaccio

dust' cloud' s polverone m

duster ['dʌstər] s (cloth) cencio; (light overgarment) spolverino

dust' jack'et s sopraccoperta

dust'pan' s pattumiera

dust' rag' s strofinaccio

dust·y ['dʌsti] adj (-ier; -iest) polveroso; grigiastro

Dutch [dʌtʃ] adj olandese; (slang) tedesco || s (language) olandese m; (language) tedesco; **in Dutch** (slang) in disgrazia; (slang) nei pasticci; **the Dutch** gli olandesi; (slang) i tedeschi; **to go Dutch** (coll) pagare alla romana

Dutch'man s (-men) olandese m; (slang) tedesco

Dutch' treat' s invito alla romana

dutiable ['djutɪ·əbəl] or ['dutɪ·əbəl] adj soggetto a dogana

dutiful ['djutɪfəl] or ['dutɪfəl] adj obbediente, doveroso

du·ty ['djuti] or ['duti] s (-ties) dovere m; (task) funzione; dazio, dogana; **off duty** libero; in libera uscita; **on duty** in servizio; di guardia; **to do one's duty** fare il proprio dovere; **to take up one's duties** entrare in servizio

du'ty-free' adj esente da dogana

dwarf [dwɔrf] adj & s nano || tr rimpiccolire || intr rimpiccolire; apparire più piccolo

dwarfish ['dwɔrfɪʃ] adj nano, da nano

dwell [dwel] v (pret & pp **dwelled** or **dwelt** [dwelt]) intr dimorare, abitare; **to dwell on** or **upon** intrattenersi su

dwelling ['dwelɪŋ] s abitazione, residenza

dwell'ing house' s casa d'abitazione

dwindle ['dwɪndəl] intr diminuire; restringersi, consumarsi

dye [daɪ] s tinta, colore m || v (pret & pp **dyed**; ger **dyeing**) tr tingere

dyed-in-the-wool ['daɪdɪnðə ,wul] adj tinto prima della tessitura; completo, intransigente

dyeing ['daɪ·ɪŋ] s tintura

dyer ['daɪ·ər] s tintore m

dye'stuff' s tintura, materia colorante

dying ['daɪ·ɪŋ] adj morente

dynamic [daɪ'næmɪk] or [dɪ'næmɪk] adj dinamico

dynamite ['daɪnə ,maɪt] s dinamite f || tr far saltare con la dinamite

dyna·mo ['daɪnə ,mo] s (-mos) dinamo f

dynast ['daɪnæst] s dinasta m

dynas·ty ['daɪnəsti] s (-ties) dinastia

dysentery ['dɪsən ,teri] s dissenteria

dyspepsia [dɪs'pepsɪ·ə] or [dɪs'pep/ə] s dispepsia

E

E, e [i] *s* quinta lettera dell'alfabeto inglese

each [it/] *adj indef* ogni || *pron indef* ognuno, ciascuno; **each other** ci; vi; si; l'un l'altro || *adv* l'uno; a testa

eager ['igər] *adj* (*enthusiastic*) ardente; **eager for** avido di; **eager to** + *inf* desideroso di + *inf*

ea'ger bea'ver *s* zelante *mf*

eagerness ['igərnɪs] *s* ardore *m;* brama

eagle ['igəl] *s* aquila

ea'gle owl' *s* gufo reale

eaglet ['iglɪt] *s* aquilotto

ear [ir] *s* orecchio; (*of corn*) pannocchia; (*of wheat*) spiga; **to be all ears** essere tutt'orecchi; **to prick up one's ears** tendere l'orecchio; **to turn a deaf ear** far l'orecchio da mercante

ear'ache' *s* mal *m* d'orecchi

ear'drop' *s* pendente *m*

ear'drum' *s* timpano

ear'flap' *s* paraorecchi *m*

earl [ʌrl] *s* conte *m*

earldom ['ʌrldəm] *s* contea

ear·ly ['ʌrli] (**-lier; -liest**) *adj* (*occurring before customary time*) di buon'ora; (*first in a series*) primo; (*far back in time*) remoto, antico; (*occurring in near future*) prossimo || *adv* presto; per tempo, di buon'ora; **as early as** (*a certain time of day*) già a; (*a certain time or date*) fin da, già in; **as early as possible** quanto prima possibile; **early in** (*e.g., the month*) all'inizio di; **early in the morning** di mattina presto, di buon mattino; **early in the year** all'inizio dell'anno

ear'ly bird' *s* persona mattiniera

ear'ly mass' *s* prima messa

ear'ly ris'er *s* persona mattiniera

ear'mark' *s* contrassegno || *tr* contrassegnare; assegnare a scopo speciale

ear'muff' *s* paraorecchi *m*

earn [ʌrn] *tr* guadagnare, guadagnarsi; (*to get one's due*) meritarsi; (*interest*) (com) produrre || *intr* trarre profitto, rendere

earnest ['ʌrnɪst] *adj* serio; fervente; **in earnest** sul serio || *s* caparra

ear'nest mon'ey *s* caparra

earnings ['ʌrnɪŋz] *s* guadagno; salario

ear'phone' *s* (*of sonar*) orecchiale *m;* (rad, telp) cuffia

ear'piece' *s* (*of eyeglasses*) susta; (telp) ricevitore *m*

ear'ring' *s* orecchino

ear'shot' *s* tiro dell'orecchio; **within earshot** a portata di voce

ear'split'ting *adj* assordante

earth [ʌrθ] *s* terra; **to come back to or down to earth** scendere dalle nuvole

earthen ['ʌrθən] *adj* di terra; di terracotta

ear'then·ware' *s* coccio, terraglie *fpl,* terracotta

earthling ['ʌrθlɪŋ] *s* terrestre *mf*

earthly ['ʌrθli] *adj* terreno, terrestre;

to be of no earthly use non servire assolutamente a niente

earthmover ['ʌrθ ‚muvar] *s* ruspa

earth'quake' *s* terremoto

earth'work' *s* terrapieno

earth'worm' *s* lombrico

earth·y ['ʌrθi] *adj* (**-ier; -iest**) terroso; (*coarse*) rozzo; pratico; sincero, diretto

ear' trum'pet *s* corno acustico

ear'wax' *s* cerume *m*

ease [iz] *s* facilità *f;* (*naturalness*) spigliatezza, disinvoltura; (*comfort*) benestare *m;* tranquillità *f;* **at ease!** (mil) riposo!; **with ease** con facilità || *tr* facilitare; (*a burden*) alleggerire; (*to let up on*) rallentare; mitigare; **ease out** licenziare con le buone maniere || *intr* alleviarsi, mitigarsi, diminuire; rallentare

easel ['izəl] *s* cavalletto

easement ['izmənt] *s* attenuamento; (law) servitù *f*

easily ['izɪli] *adv* facilmente; senza dubbio; probabilmente

easiness ['izɪnɪs] *s* facilità *f;* disinvoltura; grazia, agilità *f;* indifferenza

east [ist] *adj* orientale, dell'est || *s* est *m* || *adv* verso l'est

Easter ['istər] *s* Pasqua

East'er egg' *s* uovo di Pasqua

East'er Mon'day *s* lunedì *m* di Pasqua

eastern ['istərn] *adj* orientale

East'er-tide' *s* tempo pasquale

eastward ['istwərd] *adv* verso l'est

eas·y ['izi] *adj* (**-ier; -iest**) facile; (*conducive to ease*) comodo, agiato; (*free from worry*) tranquillo; (*easygoing*) disinvolto, spigliato; (*not tight*) ampio; (*not hurried*) lento, moderato || *adv* (coll) facilmente; (coll) tranquillamente; **to take it easy** (coll) riposarsi; (coll) non prendersela; (coll) andar piano

eas'y chair' *s* poltrona

eas'y·go'ing *adj* (*person*) comodone; (*horse*) sciolto nell'andatura

eas'y mark' *s* (coll) gonzo

eas'y mon'ey *s* denaro fatto senza fatica; soldi rubati

eas'y terms' *spl* facilitazioni *fpl* di pagamento

eat [it] *v* (*pret* **ate** [et]; *pp* **eaten** ['itən]) *tr* mangiare; **to eat away** smangiare; **to eat up** mangiarsi || *intr* mangiare

eatable ['itəbəl] *adj* mangiabile || **eatables** *spl* commestibili *mpl*

eaves [ivz] *spl* gronda

eaves'drop' *v* (*pret & pp* **-dropped; ger -dropping**) *intr* origliare

ebb [eb] *s* riflusso; decadenza || *intr* (*said of the tide*) ritirarsi; decadere

ebb' and flow' *s* flusso e riflusso

ebb' tide' *s* riflusso, deflusso

ebon·y ['ebəni] *s* (**-ies**) ebano

ebullient [ɪ'bʌljənt] *adj* bollente

eccentric [ek'sentrɪk] *adj & s* eccentrico

eccentrici·ty [ˌɛksən'trɪsɪti] s (-ties) eccentricità f, originalità f

ecclesiastic [ɪ ˌklizɪ'æstɪk] adj & s ecclesiastico

echelon ['ɛʃə ˌlɑn] s scaglione m; (mil) scaglione m || tr scaglionare

ech·o ['ɛko] s (-oes) eco || tr far eco a || intr echeggiare, riecheggiare

éclair [e'klɛr] s dolce ripieno di crema

eclectic [ek'lɛktɪk] adj & s eclettico

eclipse [ɪ'klɪps] s eclisse f, eclissi f || tr eclissare

eclogue ['ɛklɔg] or ['ɛklɑg] s egloga

ecology [ɪ'kɑlədʒɪ] s ecologia

economic(al) [ˌikə'nɑmɪk(əl)] or [ˌɛkə'nɑmɪk(əl)] adj economico

economics [ˌikə'nɑmɪks] or [ˌɛkə'nɑmɪks] s economia (politica)

economist [ɪ'kɑnəmɪst] s economista mf

economize [ɪ'kɑnə ˌmaɪz] tr & intr economizzare

econo·my [ɪ'kɑnəmi] s (-mies) economia

ecosystem ['ɛko ˌsɪstəm] s ecosistema m

ecsta·sy ['ɛkstəsi] s (-sies) estasi f

ecstatic [ek'stætɪk] adj estatico

ecumenic(al) [ˌɛkjə'mɛnɪk(əl)] adj ecumenico

eczema ['ɛksɪmə] or [eg'zimə] s eczema m

ed·dy ['ɛdi] s (-dies) turbine m || v (pret & pp -died) tr & intr turbinare

edelweiss ['ɛdəl ˌvaɪs] s stella alpina

edge [ɛdʒ] s (of knife, sword, etc) filo, tagliente m; (border at which a surface terminates) orlo, bordo; (of a wound) labbro, margine m; (of a book) taglio; (of a tumbler) giro; (of clothing) vivagno; (of a table) spigolo; (slang) vantaggio; on edge nervoso; to have the edge on (coll) avere il vantaggio su; to set the teeth on edge far allegare i denti || tr affilare, aguzzare; orlare, bordare; to edge out riuscire ad eliminare || intr avanzare lentamente

edgeways ['ɛdʒ ˌwez] adv di taglio; to not let s.o. get a word in edgeways non lasciar dire una parola a qlcu

edging ['ɛdʒɪŋ] s orlo, bordo

edg·y ['ɛdʒi] adj (-ier; -iest) acuto, angolare; nervoso, ansioso

edible ['ɛdɪbəl] adj mangereccio, mangiabile || edibles spl commestibili mpl

edict ['idɪkt] s editto

edification [ˌɛdɪfɪ'keʃən] s edificazione

edifice ['ɛdɪfɪs] s edificio

edi·fy ['ɛdɪ ˌfaɪ] v (pret & pp -fied) tr edificare

edifying ['ɛdɪ ˌfaɪ·ɪŋ] adj edificante

edit ['ɛdɪt] tr redigere; (e.g., a manuscript) correggere; (an edition) curare; (a newspaper) dirigere; (mov) montare

edition [ɪ'dɪʃən] s edizione

editor ['ɛdɪtər] s (of a newspaper or magazine) direttore m, gerente mf; (of an editorial) redattore m, cronista mf; (of a critical edition) editore m; (of a manuscript) revisore m

editorial [ˌɛdɪ'torɪ·əl] adj editoriale || s capocronaca m, articolo di fondo

ed'ito'rial staff' s redazione

ed'itor in chief' s gerente mf responsabile

educate ['ɛdʒu ˌket] tr educare, erudire

education [ˌɛdʒu'keʃən] s educazione; istruzione, insegnamento

educational [ˌɛdʒu'keʃənəl] adj educativo

educa'tional institu'tion s istituto di magistero

educator ['ɛdʒu ˌketər] s educatore m

eel [il] s anguilla; to be as slippery as an eel guizzare di mano come un'anguilla

ee·rie or ee·ry ['ɪri] adj (-rier; -riest) spettrale, pauroso

efface [ɪ'fes] tr cancellare; to efface oneself eclissarsi, mettersi in disparte

effect [ɪ'fɛkt] s effetto; (main idea) tenore m; in effect in vigore; in realtà; to go into effect or to take effect andare in vigore; to put into effect mandare ad effetto || tr effettuare

effective [ɪ'fɛktɪv] adj efficace; (actually in effect) effettivo; (striking) che colpisce; to become effective entrare in vigore

effectual [ɪ'fɛktʃu·əl] adj efficace

effectuate [ɪ'fɛktʃu ˌet] tr effettuare

effeminacy [ɪ'fɛmɪnəsi] s effemminatezza

effeminate [ɪ'fɛmɪnɪt] adj effemminato

effervesce [ˌɛfər'vɛs] intr essere in effervescenza

effervescence [ˌɛfər'vɛsəns] s effervescenza

effervescent [ˌɛfər'vɛsənt] adj effervescente

effete [ɪ'fit] adj esausto, sterile

efficacious [ˌɛfɪ'keʃəs] adj efficace

effica·cy [ɛfɪkəsi] s (-cies) efficacia

efficien·cy [ɪ'fɪʃənsi] s (-cies) efficienza; (mech) rendimento, efficienza

effi'ciency engineer' s analista mf tempi e metodi

efficient [ɪ'fɪʃənt] adj efficiente; (person) abile; (mech) efficiente

effi·gy ['ɛfɪdʒi] s (-gies) effigie f

effort ['ɛfərt] s sforzo

effronter·y [ɪ'frʌntəri] s (-ies) sfrontatezza, sfacciataggine f

effusion [ɪ'fjuʒən] s effusione

effusive [ɪ'fjusɪv] adj espansivo

egg [ɛg] s uovo; (slang) bravo ragazzo || tr—to egg on incitare

egg'beat'er s frullino, sbattiuova m

egg'cup' s portauovo

egg'head' s (coll) intellettuale mf

eggnog ['ɛg ˌnɑg] s zabaione m

egg'plant' s melanzana, petonciano

egg'shell' s guscio d'uovo

egoism ['ɛgo ˌɪzəm] or ['igo ˌɪzəm] s egoismo

egoist ['ɛgo·ɪst] or ['igo·ɪst] s egoista mf

egotism ['ɛgo ˌtɪzəm] or ['igo ˌtɪzəm] s egotismo

egotist ['ɛgotɪst] or ['igotɪst] s egotista mf

egregious [ɪ'gridʒəs] *adj* gigantesco, tremendo, marchiano

egress ['igres] *s* uscita

Egypt ['idʒɪpt] *s* l'Egitto

Egyptian [ɪ'dʒɪp/ən] *adj* & *s* egiziano

ei'der down' ['aɪdər] *s* piumino

ei'der duck' *s* edredone *m*

eight [et] *adj* & *pron* otto || *s* otto; **eight o'clock** le otto

eighteen ['et'tin] *adj*, *s* & *pron* diciotto

eighteenth ['et'tinθ] *adj*, *s* & *pron* diciottesimo || *s* (*in dates*) diciotto

eighth [etθ] *adj* & *s* ottavo || *s* (*in dates*) otto

eight' hun'dred *adj*, *s* & *pron* ottocento

eightieth ['etɪ·ɪθ] *adj*, *s* & *pron* ottantesimo

eight·y ['etɪ] *adj* & *pron* ottanta || *s* (*-ies*) ottanta *m*; **the eighties** gli anni ottanta

either ['iðər] or ['aɪðər] *adj* l'uno o l'altro; l'uno e l'altro; ciascuno; entrambi i, tutti e due i || *pron* l'uno o l'altro; l'uno e l'altro; entrambi || *adv*—**not either** nemmeno || *conj*—**either . . . or o . . . o**

ejaculate [ɪ'dʒækjə,let] *tr* esclamare; (*physiol*) emettere || *intr* esclamare; (*physiol*) avere un'eiaculazione

eject [ɪ'dʒekt] *tr* espellere, gettar fuori; (*to evict*) sfrattare

ejection [ɪ'dʒek/ən] *s* espulsione; (*of a tenant*) sfratto

ejec'tion seat' *s* sedile *m* eiettabile

eke [ik] *tr*—**to eke out a living** sbarcare il lunario

elaborate [ɪ'læbərɪt] *adj* (*done with great care*) elaborato; (*detailed*) minuzioso; (*ornate*) ornato || [ɪ'læbə,ret] *tr* elaborare || *intr*—**to elaborate on** or **upon** circonstanziare, particolareggiare

elapse [ɪ'læps] *intr* passare, trascorrere

elastic [ɪ'læstɪk] *adj* & *s* elastico

elasticity [ɪ,læs'tɪsɪti] or [,ilæs'tɪsɪti] *s* elasticità *f*

elated [ɪ'letɪd] *adj* esultante, gongolante

elation [ɪ'le/ən] *s* esultanza, gaudio

elbow ['elbo] *s* gomito; (*in a river*) ansa; (*of a chair*) braccio; **at one's elbow** sotto mano; **out at the elbows** coi gomiti logori; **to crook the elbow** alzare il gomito; **to rub elbows** stare gomito a gomito; **up to the elbows** fino al collo || *tr*—**to elbow one's way** aprirsi il passo a gomitate || *intr* dar gomitate

el'bow grease' *s* (coll) olio di gomiti

el'bow patch' *s* toppa al gomito

el'bow rest' *s* bracciolo

el'bow·room' *s* spazio sufficiente; libertà *f* d'azione

elder ['eldər] *adj* seniore, maggiore || *s* (bot) sambuco; (eccl) maggiore *m*

el'der·ber'ry *s* (*-ries*) sambuco; (*fruit*) bacca del sambuco

elderly ['eldərli] *adj* attempato, anziano

eld'er states'man *s* uomo di stato esperto

eldest ['eldɪst] *adj* (il) maggiore; (il) più vecchio

elect [ɪ'lekt] *adj* & *s* eletto; **the elect** gli eletti || *tr* eleggere

election [ɪ'lek/ən] *s* elezione

electioneer [ɪ,lek/ə'nɪr] *intr* fare una campagna elettorale

elective [ɪ'lektɪv] *adj* elettivo || *s* corso facoltativo

electorate [ɪ'lektərɪt] *s* elettorato

electric(al) [ɪ'lektrɪk(əl)] *adj* elettrico

elec'tric blend'er *s* frullatore *m*

elec'tric chair' *s* sedia elettrica

elec'tric cord' *s* piattina, filo elettrico

elec'tric eel' *s* gimnoto

elec'tric eye' *s* occhio elettrico

electrician [ɪ,lek'trɪ/ən] or [,elek'trɪ/ən] *s* elettricista *m*

electricity [ɪ,lek'trɪsɪti] or [,elek'trɪsɪti] *s* elettricità *f*

elec'tric me'ter *s* contatore *m* della luce

elec'tric per'cola'tor *s* caffettiera elettrica

elec'tric shav'er *s* rasoio elettrico

elec'tric shock' *s* scossa elettrica, elettroscuasso

elec'tric tape' *s* nastro isolante

elec'tric train' *s* elettrotreno

electri·fy [ɪ'lektrɪ,faɪ] *v* (*pret* & *pp* -fied) *tr* (*to provide with electric power*) elettrificare; (*to communicate electricity to; to thrill*) elettrizzare

electrocute [ɪ'lektrə,kjut] *tr* fulminare con la corrente; far morire sulla sedia elettrica

electrode [ɪ'lektrod] *s* elettrodo

electrolysis [ɪ,lek'trɑlɪsɪs] or [,elek'trɑlɪsɪs] *s* elettrolisi *f*

electrolyte [ɪ'lektrə,laɪt] *s* elettrolito

electromagnet [ɪ,lektrə'mægnɪt] *s* elettrocalamita

electromagnetic [ɪ,lektrəmæg'netɪk] *adj* elettromagnetico

electromotive [ɪ,lektrə'motɪv] *adj* elettromotore

electron [ɪ'lektrɑn] *s* elettrone *m*

electronic [ɪ,lek'trɑnɪk] or [,elek'trɑnɪk] *adj* elettronico || **electronics** *s* elettronica

electroplating [ɪ'lektrə,pletɪŋ] *s* galvanostegia

electrostatic [ɪ,lektrə'stætɪk] *adj* elettrostatico

electrotype [ɪ'lektrə,taɪp] *s* stereotipia || *tr* stereotipare

eleemosynary [,elɪ'mɑsɪ,neri] *adj* caritatevole, di beneficenza

elegance ['elɪgəns] *s* eleganza

elegant ['elɪgənt] *adj* elegante

elegiac [,elɪ'dʒaɪ·æk] *adj* elegiaco

ele·gy ['elɪdʒi] *s* (*-gies*) elegia

element ['elɪmənt] *s* elemento; **to be out of one's element** essere fuori del proprio ambiente

elementary [,elɪ'mentəri] *adj* elementare

elephant ['elɪfənt] *s* elefante *m*

elevate ['elɪ,vet] *tr* elevare, innalzare

elevated ['elɪ,vetɪd] *adj* elevato || *s* ferrovia soprelevata, metropolitana soprelevata

elevation [,elɪ've/ən] *s* elevazione; (surv) quota

elevator ['elɪ,vetər] *s* ascensore *m*;

(for freight) montacarichi *m*; *(for hoisting grain)* elevatore *m* di grano; *(warehouse for storing grain)* deposito granaglie; (aer) timone *m* di profondità

eleven [ɪ'levən] *adj & pron* undici ‖ *s* undici *m*; **eleven o'clock** le undici

eleventh [ɪ'levənθ] *adj, s & pron* undicesimo ‖ *s (in dates)* undici *m*

elev'enth hour' *s* ultimo momento

elf [elf] *s* (**elves** [elvz]) elfo

elicit [ɪ'lɪsɪt] *tr* cavare, sottrarre

elide [ɪ'laɪd] *tr* elidere

eligible ['elɪdʒɪbəl] *adj* eleggibile; accettabile

eliminate [ɪ'lɪmɪ,net] *tr* eliminare

elision [ɪ'lɪʒən] *s* elisione

elite [e'lit] *adj* eletto, scelto ‖ *s*—**the elite** l'élite *f*

elk [elk] *s* alce *m*

ellipse [ɪ'lɪps] *s* (geom) ellisse *f*

ellip·sis [ɪ'lɪpsɪs] *s* (**-ses** [siz]) (gram) ellissi *f*

elliptic(al) [ɪ'lɪptɪk(əl)] *adj* ellittico

elm [elm] *s* olmo

elongate [ɪ'lɔŋget] or [ɪ'lɔŋget] *tr* allungare, prolungare

elope [ɪ'lop] *intr* fuggire con un amante

elopement [ɪ'lopmənt] *s* fuga con un amante

eloquence ['eləkwəns] *s* eloquenza

eloquent ['eləkwənt] *adj* eloquente

else [els] *adj*—**nobody else** nessun altro; **nothing else** nient'altro; **somebody else** qualcun altro; **something else** qualcosa d'altro; **what else** che altro; **who else** chi altro; **whose else** di che altra persona ‖ *adv*—**how else** in che altra maniera; **or else** se no; altrimenti; **when else** in che altro momento; in che altro periodo; **where else** dove mai, da che parte

else'where' *adv* altrove

elucidate [ɪ'lusɪ,det] *tr* dilucidare

elude [ɪ'lud] *tr* eludere

elusive [ɪ'lusɪv] *adj* elusivo; *(evasive)* fugace, sfuggente

emaciated [ɪ'meʃɪ,etɪd] *adj* smunto, emaciato, macilento

emanate ['emə,net] *tr & intr* emanare

emancipate [ɪ'mænsɪ,pet] *tr* emancipare

embalm [em'bɑm] *tr* imbalsamare

embankment [em'bæŋkmənt] *s* terrapieno

embar·go [em'bɑrgo] *s* (**-goes**) embargo ‖ *tr* mettere l'embargo a

embark [em'bɑrk] *intr* imbarcarsi

embarkation [,embɑr'keʃən] *s* imbarco

embarrass [em'bærəs] *tr* imbarazzare, mettere a disagio; *(to impede)* imbarazzare, impacciare; mettere in difficoltà economiche

embarrassing [em'bærəsɪŋ] *adj* sconcertante; imbarazzante

embarrassment [em'bærəsmənt] *s* imbarazzo, disagio, confusione; impaccio; difficoltà finanziaria, dissesto

embas·sy ['embəsi] *s* (**-sies**) ambasciata

em·bed [em'bed] *s* (*pret & pp* -**bedded**; *ger* -**bedding**) *tr* incastrare, incassare

embellish [em'belɪʃ] *tr* imbellire

embellishment [em'belɪʃmənt] *s* abbellimento; (fig) fioretto

ember ['embər] *s* brace *f*; **embers** braci *fpl*

Em'ber days' *spl* tempora *fpl*

embezzle [em'bezəl] *tr* appropriare, malversare ‖ *intr* appropriarsi

embezzlement [em'bezəlmənt] *s* appropriazione indebita, malversazione; *(of public funds)* peculato

embezzler [em'bezlər] *s* malversatore *m*

embitter [em'bɪtər] *tr* amareggiare

emblazon [em'blezən] *tr* blasonare; celebrare

emblem ['embləm] *s* emblema *m*

emblematic(al) [,emblə'mætɪk(əl)] *adj* emblematico

embodiment [em'bɑdɪmənt] *s* incarnazione, personificazione

embod·y [em'bɑdi] *v* (*pret & pp* -**ied**) *tr* incarnare, personificare; incorporare

embolden [em'boldən] *tr* imbaldanzire

embolism ['embə,lɪzəm] *s* embolia

emboss [em'bɔs] or [em'bɑs] *tr (metal)* sbalzare; *(paper)* goffrare

embrace [em'bres] *s* abbraccio ‖ *tr* abbracciare ‖ *intr* abbracciarsi

embrasure [em'breʒər] *s* (archit) strombatura; (mil) feritoia

embroider [em'brɔɪdər] *tr* ricamare, trapuntare

embroider·y [em'brɔɪdəri] *s* (**-ies**) ricamo, trapunto

embroil [em'brɔɪl] *tr* ingarbugliare; *(to involve in contention)* coinvolgere

embroilment [em'brɔɪlmənt] *s* imbroglio; *(in contention)* disaccordo

embry·o ['embrɪ,o] *s* (**-os**) embrione *m*

embryology [,embrɪ'ɑlədʒi] *s* embriologia

embryonic [,embrɪ'ɑnɪk] *adj* embrionale

emcee ['em'si] *s* presentatore *m* ‖ *tr* presentare

emend [ɪ'mend] *tr* emendare

emendation [,imen'deʃən] *s* emendamento

emerald ['emərəld] *s* smeraldo

emerge [ɪ'mʌrdʒ] *intr* emergere

emergence [ɪ'mʌrdʒəns] *s* emergenza

emergen·cy [ɪ'mʌrdʒənsi] *s* (**-cies**) emergenza

emer'gency brake' *s* freno a mano

emer'gency ex'it *s* uscita di sicurezza

emer'gency land'ing *s* atterraggio di fortuna

emer'gency ward' *s* sala d'urgenza

emeritus [ɪ'merɪtəs] *adj* emerito

emersion [ɪ'mʌrʒən] or [ɪ'mʌrʃən] *s* emersione

emery ['eməri] *s* smeriglio

em'ery cloth' *s* tela smeriglio

em'ery wheel' *s* mola a smeriglio

emetic [ɪ'metɪk] *adj* & *s* emetico

emigrant ['emɪgrənt] *adj* & *s* emigrante *mf*

emigrate ['emɪ,gret] *intr* emigrare

émigré [emi'gre] or ['emɪ,gre] *s* emigrato

eminence ['emɪnəns] s eminenza; (eccl) Eminenza

eminent ['emɪnənt] adj eminente

emissar·y ['emɪ,serɪ] s (-ies) emissario

emission [ɪ'mɪʃən] s emissione

emit [ɪ'mɪt] v (pret & pp **emitted**; ger **emitting**) tr emettere

emolument [ɪ'mɑljəmənt] s emolumento

emotion [ɪ'moʃən] s emozione

emotional [ɪ'moʃənəl] adj emotivo

emperor ['empərər] s imperatore m

empha·sis ['emfəsɪs] s (-ses [,sɪz]) enfasi f, risalto

emphasize ['emfə,saɪz] tr dar rilievo a, sottolineare

emphatic [em'fætɪk] adj enfatico

emphysema [,emfɪ'simə] s enfisema m

empire ['empaɪr] s impero

empiric(al) [em'pɪrɪk(əl)] adj empirico

empiricist [em'pɪrɪsɪst] s empirista mf

emplacement [em'plesmənt] s piazzola, postazione

employ [em'plɔɪ] s impiego || tr impiegare, usare; valersi di

employee [em'plɔɪ-i] or [,emplɔɪ'i] s impiegato, dipendente mf

employer [em'plɔɪ-ər] s dirigente mf, datore m di lavoro

employment [em'plɔɪmənt] s impiego, occupazione

employ'ment a'gency s agenzia di collocamento

empower [em'pau-ər] tr autorizzare; permettere

empress ['emprɪs] s imperatrice f

emptiness ['emptɪnɪs] s vuoto

emp·ty ['emptɪ] adj (-tier; -tiest) vuoto; (gun) scarico; (hungry) (coll) digiuno; (fig) esausto || v (pret & pp -tied) tr vuotare || intr vuotarsi

empty-handed ['emptɪ'hændɪd] adj a mani vuote

empty-headed ['emptɪ'hedɪd] adj dalla testa vuota, balordo

empyrean [,empɪ'ri-ən] adj & s empireo

emulate ['emjə,let] tr emulare

emulator ['emjə,letər] s emulo

emulous ['emjələs] adj emulo

emulsi·fy [ɪ'mʌlsɪ,faɪ] v (pret & pp -fied) tr emulsionare

emulsion [ɪ'mʌlʃən] s emulsione

enable [en'ebəl] tr abilitare; permettere (with dat)

enact [en'ækt] tr decretare; (a role) rappresentare

enactment [en'æktmənt] s legge f; (of a law) promulgazione; (of a play) rappresentazione

enam·el [ɪn'æməl] s smalto || v (pret & pp -eled or -elled; ger -eling or -elling) tr smaltare

enam'el·ware' s utensili mpl di cucina di ferro smaltato

enamor [en'æmər] tr innamorare; to become enamored of innamorarsi di

encamp [en'kæmp] tr accampare || intr accamparsi

encampment [en'kæmpmənt] s campeggio; (mil) accampamento

encase [en'kes] tr incassare

encephalitis [en,sefə'laɪtɪs] s encefalite f

enchain [en'tʃen] tr incatenare

enchant [en'tʃænt] or [en'tʃɑnt] tr incantare

enchantment [en'tʃæntmənt] or [en'tʃɑntmənt] s incanto, malìa

enchanting [en'tʃæntɪŋ] or [en'tʃɑntɪŋ] adj incantatore, incantevole

enchantress [en'tʃæntrɪs] or [en'tʃɑntrɪs] s incantatrice f, maliarda

enchase [en'tʃes] tr incastonare

encircle [en'sʌrkəl] tr rigirare, girare intorno a; (mil) circondare

enclave ['enklev] s enclave f

enclitic [en'klɪtɪk] adj enclitico || s enclitica

enclose [en'kloz] tr rinchiudere; (in a letter) accludere, includere; to enclose herewith accludere alla presente

enclosure [en'kloʒər] s (land surrounded by fence) recinto, chiuso; (e.g., letter) allegato

encomi·um [en'komɪ-əm] s (-ums or -a [ə]) encomio, elogio

encompass [en'kʌmpəs] tr circondare; racchiudere, contenere

encore ['ɑŋkor] s bis m || tr (a performance) chiedere il bis di; (a performer) chiedere il bis a || interj bis!

encounter [en'kauntər] s (casual meeting) incontro; (combat) scontro || tr incontrare || intr scontrarsi

encourage [en'kʌrɪdʒ] tr incoraggiare; (to foster) favorire

encouragement [en'kʌrɪdʒmənt] s incoraggiamento; favoreggiamento

encroach [en'krotʃ] intr—to encroach on or upon invadere; usurpare; occupare il territorio di

encumber [en'kʌmbər] tr imbarazzare; ingombrare; (to load with debts, etc) gravare

encumbrance [en'kʌmbrəns] s imbarazzo; ingombro; gravame m

encyclical [en'sɪklɪkəl] or [en'saɪklɪkəl] s enciclica

encyclopedia [en,saɪklə'pidɪ-ə] s enciclopedia

encyclopedic [en,saɪklə'pidɪk] adj enciclopedico

end [end] s (extremity; concluding part) fine f; (e.g., of the week) fine f; (purpose) fine m; (part adjacent to an extremity) lembo; (small piece) pezza, avanzo; (of a beam) testata; (sports) estrema; at the end of in capo a; in fondo a; in the end alla fine, all'ultimo; no end (coll) moltissimo; no end of (coll) un mucchio di; to make both ends meet sbarcare il lunario; to no end senza effetto; to stand on end mettere in piedi, drizzare; mettersi diritto; (said of hair) drizzarsi; to the end that affinché || tr finire, terminare; to end up andare a finire || intr finire, terminare; to end up finire

endanger [en'dendʒər] tr mettere in pericolo

endear [en'dɪr] *tr* affezionare; **to endear oneself to** rendersi caro a

endeavor [en'devər] *s* tentativo, sforzo ‖ *intr* tentare, sforzarsi

endemic [en'demɪk] *adj* endemico ‖ *s* endemia

ending ['endɪŋ] *s* fine *f*, conclusione; (gram) terminazione, desinenza

endive ['endaɪv] *s* indivia

endless ['endlɪs] *adj* interminabile; sterminato; (mach) senza fine

end'most' *adj* estremo, ultimo

endorse [en'dɔrs] *tr* girare; (fig) approvare, confermare

endorsee [ˌendɔr'si] *s* giratario

endorsement [en'dɔrsmənt] *s* girata; approvazione, conferma

endorser [en'dɔrsər] *s* girante *mf*

endow [en'dau] *tr* dotare

endowment [en'daumənt] *adj* dotale ‖ *s* (*of an institution*) dotazione; (*gift, talent*) dote *f*

end' pap'er *s* risguardo

endurance [en'djurəns] or [en'durəns] *s* sopportazione, tolleranza; (*ability to hold out*) resistenza, forza; (*lasting time*) durata

endure [en'djur] or [en'dur] *tr* sopportare, tollerare; resistere (with *dat*) ‖ *intr* durare, resistere

enduring [en'djurɪŋ] or [en'durɪŋ] *adj* duraturo, durevole; paziente

enema ['enəmə] *s* clistere *m*

ene·my ['enəmi] *adj* nemico ‖ *s* (**-mies**) nemico

en'emy al'ien *s* straniero nemico

energetic [ˌenər'dʒetɪk] *adj* energetico, vigoroso

ener·gy ['enərdʒi] *s* (**-gies**) energia

enervate ['enər,vet] *tr* snervare

enfeeble [en'fibəl] *tr* indebolire

enfold [en'fold] *tr* avvolgere; abbracciare

enforce [en'fɔrs] *tr* far osservare; ottenere per forza; (*e.g., obedience*) imporre; (*an argument*) far valere

enforcement [en'fɔrsmənt] *s* imposizione; (*of a law*) esecuzione

enfranchise [en'fræntʃaɪz] *tr* liberare; concedere il diritto di voto a

engage [en'gedʒ] *tr* occupare; riservare; (*s.o.'s attention*) attrarre; (*a gear*) ingranare; (*the enemy*) ingaggiare; (*to hire*) assumere; (theat) scritturare; **to be engaged, to be engaged to be married** essere fidanzato; **to engage s.o. in conversation** intavolare una conversazione con qlcu ‖ *intr* essere occupato; essere impiegato; assumere un'obbligazione; (mil) impegnarsi; (mach) ingranare, incastrarsi

engaged [en'gedʒd] *adj* fidanzato; occupato, impegnato; (*column*) murato

engagement [en'gedʒmənt] *s* accordo; fidanzamento; impegno, contratto; (*appointment*) appuntamento; (mil) azione; (mach) innesto

engage'ment ring' *s* anello di fidanzamento

engaging [en'gedʒɪŋ] *adj* attrattivo

engender [en'dʒendər] *tr* ingenerare

engine ['endʒɪn] *s* macchina; (aut) motore *m*; (rr) locomotiva, motrice *f*

engineer [ˌendʒə'nɪr] *s* ingegnere *m*; (rr) macchinista *m*; (mil) zappatore *m*, geniere *m* ‖ *tr* costruire; progettare

engineering [ˌendʒə'nɪrɪŋ] *s* ingegneria

en'gine house' *s* stazione dei pompieri

en'gine·man' *s* (**-men**) (rr) macchinista *m*

en'gine room' *s* sala macchine

en'gine-room' tel'egraph *s* (naut) telegrafo di macchina, trasmettitore *m*

England ['ɪŋglənd] *s* l'Inghilterra

Englander ['ɪŋləndər] *s* nativo dell'Inghilterra

English ['ɪŋglɪʃ] *adj* inglese ‖ *s* inglese *m*; (billiards) effetto; **the English** gli inglesi

Eng'lish Chan'nel *s* Canale *m* della Manica

Eng'lish dai'sy *s* margherita

Eng'lish horn' *s* (mus) corno inglese

Eng'lish·man *s* (**-men**) inglese *m*

Eng'lish-speak'ing *adj* di lingua inglese, anglofono

Eng'lish·wom'an *s* (**-wom'en**) inglese *f*

engraft [en'græft] or [en'graft] *tr* (hort) innestare; (fig) inculcare

engrave [en'grev] *tr* incidere

engraver [en'grevər] *s* incisore *m*

engraving [en'grevɪŋ] *s* incisione

engross [en'gros] *tr* preoccupare, assorbire; redigere ufficialmente, scrivere a grandi caratteri; monopolizzare

engrossing [en'grosɪŋ] *adj* assorbente

engulf [en'gʌlf] *tr* sommergere, inondare

enhance [en'hæns] or [en'hans] *tr* valorizzare; far risaltare

enigma [ɪ'nɪgmə] *s* enigma *m*

enigmatic(al) [ˌɪnɪg'mætɪk(əl)] *adj* enigmatico

enjambment [en'dʒæmmənt] or [en'dʒæmbmənt] *s* inarcatura

enjoin [en'dʒɔɪn] *tr* ingiungere, intimare

enjoy [en'dʒɔɪ] *tr* godere; **to enjoy + ger** provar piacere in + *inf*; **to enjoy oneself** divertirsi

enjoyable [en'dʒɔɪəbəl] *adj* gradevole

enjoyment [en'dʒɔɪmənt] *s* (*pleasure*) piacere *m*; (*pleasurable use*) godimento

enkindle [en'kɪndəl] *tr* infiammare

enlarge [en'lardʒ] *tr* aumentare; ingrossare; (phot) ingrandire ‖ *intr* aumentare; **to enlarge on** or **upon** dilungarsi su

enlargement [en'lardʒmənt] *s* aumento; ingrossamento; (phot) ingrandimento

enlighten [en'laɪtən] *tr* illustrare, illuminare

enlightenment [en'laɪtənmənt] *s* spiegazione, schiarimento ‖ **Enlightenment** *s* illuminismo

enlist [en'lɪst] *tr* (*e.g., s.o.'s favor*) guadagnarsi; (*the help of a person*) ottenere; (mil) ingaggiare ‖ *intr* (mil) ingaggiarsi, arruolarsi; **to enlist**

in (*a cause*) dare il proprio appoggio a

enlistment [enˈlɪstmənt] *s* arruolamento, ingaggio

enliven [enˈlaɪvən] *tr* ravvivare

enmesh [enˈmeʃ] *tr* irretire

enmi·ty [ˈenmɪti] *s* (**-ties**) inimicizia

ennoble [enˈnobəl] *tr* nobilitare

ennui [ˈɑnwi] *s* noia, tedio

enormous [ɪˈnɔrməs] *adj* enorme

enormously [ɪˈnɔrməsli] *adv* .enormemente

enough [ɪˈnʌf] *adj* abbastanza ‖ *s* il sufficiente ‖ *adv* abbastanza ‖ *interj* basta!

enounce [ɪˈnaʊns] *tr* enunciare; (*to declare*) affermare

enrage [enˈredʒ] *tr* infuriare, irritare

enrapture [enˈræptʃər] *tr* mandare in visibilio, estasiare

enrich [enˈrɪtʃ] *tr* arricchire

enroll [enˈrol] *tr* arruolare, ingaggiare; (*a student*) iscrivere ‖ *intr* arruolarsi, ingaggiarsi; (*said of a student*) iscriversi

enrollment [enˈrolmənt] *s* arruolamento, ingaggio; (*of a student*) iscrizione

en route [ɑn ˈrut] *adv* in cammino; **en route to** in via per

ensconce [enˈskɑns] *tr* nascondere; **to esconce oneself** rannicchiarsi, istallarsi comodamente

ensemble [ɑnˈsɑmbəl] *s* insieme *m*; (*mus*) concertato

ensign [ˈensaɪn] *s* (*standard*) bandiera, insegna; (*badge*) distintivo ‖ [ˈensən] or [ˈensaɪn] *s* guardamarina *m*

ensilage [ˈensɪlɪdʒ] *s* (*preservation of fodder*) insilamento; (*preserved fodder*) insilato

ensile [ˈensaɪl] or [enˈsaɪl] *tr* insilare

enslave [enˈslev] *tr* fare schiavo, asservire

enslavement [enˈslevmənt] *s* asservimento

ensnare [enˈsner] *tr* irretire

ensue [enˈsu] or [enˈsju] *intr* risultare; seguire, conseguire

ensuing [enˈsu·ɪŋ] or [enˈsju·ɪŋ] *adj* risultante, conseguente; seguente

ensure [enˈʃʊr] *tr* assicurare, garantire

entail [enˈtel] *s* (*law*) obbligo ‖ *tr* provocare, comportare; (*law*) obbligare

entangle [enˈtæŋgəl] *tr* intricare, imbrogliare, impigliare

entanglement [enˈtæŋgəlmənt] *s* groviglio, garbuglio

enter [ˈentər] *tr* (*a house*) entrare in; (*in the customhouse*) dichiarare; (*to make a record of*) registrare; (*a student*) iscrivere; iscriversi a; fare membro; (*to undertake*) intraprendere; **to enter s.o.'s head** passare per la testa a qlcu ‖ *intr* entrare; (theat) entrare in scena; **to enter into** entrare in; (*a contract*) impegnarsi in; **to enter on** or **upon** intraprendere

enterprise [ˈentərˌpraɪz] *s* (*undertaking*) impresa; (*spirit, push*) intraprendenza

enterprising [ˈentərˌpraɪzɪŋ] *adj* intraprendente

entertain [ˌentərˈten] *tr* divertire, intrattenere; (*guests*) ospitare; (*a hope*) accarezzare; (*a proposal*) considerare ‖ *intr* ricevere

entertainer [ˌentərˈtenər] *s* (*host*) ospite *mf*; (*in public*) attore *m*, cantante *mf*, fine dicitore *m*

entertaining [ˌentərˈtenɪŋ] *adj* divertente

entertainment [ˌentərˈtenmənt] *s* trattenimento, svago; spettacolo, attrazione; buon trattamento

enthrall [enˈθrɔl] *tr* affascinare, incantare; (*to subjugate*) asservire, soggiogare

enthrone [enˈθron] *tr* mettere sul trono, intronizzare; esaltare, innalzare

enthuse [enˈθuz] or [enˈθjuz] *tr* (coll) entusiasmare ‖ *intr* (coll) entusiasmarsi

enthusiasm [enˈθuzɪˌæzəm] or [enˈθjuzɪˌæzəm] *s* entusiasmo

enthusiast [enˈθuzɪˌæst] or [enˈθjuzɪˌæst] *s* entusiasta *mf*, maniaco

enthusiastic [enˌθuzɪˈæstɪk] or [enˌθjuzɪˈæstɪk] *adj* entusiastico

entice [enˈtaɪs] *tr* attrarre, provocare; tentare

enticement [enˈtaɪsmənt] *s* attrazione, provocazione; tentazione

entire [enˈtaɪr] *adj* intero

entirely [enˈtaɪrli] *adv* interamente; (*solely*) solamente

entire·ty [enˈtaɪrti] *s* (**-ties**) interezza; totalità *f*

entitle [enˈtaɪtəl] *tr* dar diritto a; (*to give a name to*) intitolare

enti·ty [ˈentɪti] *s* (**-ties**) (*something real; organization, institution*) ente *m*; (*existence*) entità *f*

entomb [enˈtum] *tr* seppellire

entombment [enˈtummənt] *s* sepoltura

entomology [ˌentəˈmɑlədʒi] *s* entomologia

entourage [ˌɑntuˈrɑʒ] *s* seguito

entrails [ˈentrelz] or [ˈentrɛlz] *spl* visceri *mpl*

entrain [enˈtren] *tr* far salire sul treno ‖ *intr* imbarcarsi sul treno

entrance [ˈentrəns] *s* entrata, ingresso ‖ [enˈtræns] or [enˈtrɑns] *tr* ipnotizzare, incantare

en'trance exam'ina'tion *s* esame *m* d'ammissione

entrancing [enˈtrænsɪŋ] or [enˈtrɑnsɪŋ] *adj* incantatore

entrant [ˈentrənt] *s* nuovo membro; (sports) concorrente *mf*

en·trap [enˈtræp] *v* (*pret & pp* **-trapped**; *ger* **-trapping**) *tr* intrappolare, irretire

entreat [enˈtrit] *tr* implorare

entreat·y [enˈtriti] *s* (**-ies**) implorazione, supplica

entree [ˈɑntre] *s* entrata, ingresso; (culin) prima portata

entrench [enˈtrentʃ] *tr* trincerare ‖ *intr* —**to entrench on** or **upon** violare

entrust [ɛnˈtrʌst] *tr* affidare, confidare

en·try [ˈɛntri] *s* (**-tries**) entrata; (*item*) partita, registrazione; (*in a dictionary*) lemma, esponente *m*; (*sports*) concorrente *mf*

entwine [ɛnˈtwaɪn] *tr* intrecciare || *intr* intrecciarsi

enumerate [ɪˈnjuməˌret] *or* [ɪˈnuməˌret] *tr* enumerare

enunciate [ɪˈnʌnsɪˌet] *or* [ɪˈnʌnʃɪˌet] *tr* enunciare, staccare

envelop [ɛnˈvɛləp] *tr* involgere

envelope [ˈɛnvəˌlop] *or* [ˈɑnvəˌlop] *s* (*for a letter*) busta; (*wrapper*) involucro

envenom [ɛnˈvɛnəm] *tr* avvelenare

enviable [ˈɛnvɪəbəl] *adj* invidiabile

envious [ˈɛnvɪ-əs] *adj* invidioso

environment [ɛnˈvaɪrənmənt] *s* ambiente *m*; condizioni *fpl* ambientali

environs [ɛnˈvaɪrənz] *spl* dintorni *mpl*, sobborghi *mpl*

envisage [ɛnˈvɪzɪdʒ] *tr* considerare, immaginare

envoi [ˈɛnvɔɪ] *s* (pros) congedo

envoy [ˈɛnvɔɪ] *s* inviato; (mil) parlamentare *m*; (pros) congedo

en·vy [ˈɛnvi] *s* (**-vies**) invidia || *v* (*pret & pp* **-vied**) *tr* invidiare

enzyme [ˈɛnzaɪm] *or* [ˈɛnzɪm] *s* enzima *m*

epaulet *or* **epaulette** [ˈɛpəˌlɛt] *s* spallina

epenthe·sis [ɛˈpɛnθɪsɪs] *s* (**-ses** [ˌsiz]) epentesi *f*

ephemeral [ɪˈfɛmərəl] *adj* effimero

epic [ˈɛpɪk] *adj* epico || *s* epica

epicure [ˈɛpɪˌkjʊr] *s* epicureo

epicurean [ˌɛpɪkjuˈri-ən] *adj & s* epicureo

epidemic [ˌɛpɪˈdɛmɪk] *adj* epidemico || *s* epidemia

epidermis [ˌɛpɪˈdʌrmɪs] *s* epidermide *f*

epiglottis [ˌɛpɪˈɡlɑtɪs] *s* epiglottide *f*

epigram [ˈɛpɪˌɡræm] *s* epigramma *m*

epilepsy [ˈɛpɪˌlɛpsi] *s* epilessia

epileptic [ˌɛpɪˈlɛptɪk] *adj & s* epilettico

epilogue [ˈɛpɪˌlɔɡ] *or* [ˈɛpɪˌlɑɡ] *s* epilogo

Epiphany [ɪˈpɪfəni] *s* Epifania

Episcopalian [ɪˌpɪskəˈpeli-ən] *adj & s* episcopaliano

episode [ˈɛpɪˌsod] *s* episodio

epistle [ɪˈpɪsəl] *s* epistola

epitaph [ˈɛpɪˌtæf] *s* epitaffio

epithet [ˈɛpɪˌθɛt] *s* epiteto

epitome [ɪˈpɪtəmi] *s* epitome *f*; (fig) prototipo, personificazione

epitomize [ɪˈpɪtəˌmaɪz] *tr* epitomare; (fig) incarnare, personificare

epoch [ˈɛpək] *or* [ˈipɑk] *s* epoca

epochal [ˈɛpəkəl] *adj* memorabile

ep'och-mak'ing *adj*—**to be** epoch-making fare epoca

Ep'som salt' [ˈɛpsəm] *s* sale *m* inglese

equable [ˈɛkwəbəl] *or* [ˈikwəbəl] *adj* uniforme; tranquillo

equal [ˈikwəl] *adj* uguale; **equal to** pari a, all'altezza di || *s* uguale *m* || *v* (*pret & pp* **equaled** *or* **equalled**; *ger* **equaling** *or* **equalling**) *tr* uguagliare

equali·ty [ɪˈkwɑlɪti] *s* (**-ties**) uguaglianza

equalize [ˈikwəˌlaɪz] *tr* uguagliare; (*to make uniform*) perequare, pareggiare

equally [ˈikwəli] *adv* ugualmente

equanimity [ˌikwəˈnɪmɪti] *s* equanimità *f*

equate [iˈkwet] *tr* mettere in forma di equazione; considerare uguale *or* uguali

equation [iˈkweʒən] *or* [iˈkweʃən] *s* equazione

equator [iˈkwetər] *s* equatore *m*

equatorial [ˌikwəˈtorɪ-əl] *adj* equatoriale

equer·ry [ˈɛkwəri] *or* [ɪˈkweri] *s* (**-ries**) scudiero

equestrian [ɪˈkwɛstrɪ-ən] *adj* equestre || *s* cavallerizzo

equilateral [ˌikwɪˈlætərəl] *adj* equilatero

equilibrium [ˌikwɪˈlɪbrɪ-əm] *s* equilibrio

equinoctial [ˌikwɪˈnɑkʃəl] *adj* equinoziale

equinox [ˈikwɪˌnɑks] *s* equinozio

equip [ɪˈkwɪp] *v* (*pret & pp* **equipped**; *ger* **equipping**) *tr* equipaggiare; **to equip** (*e.g., a ship*) **with** munire di

equipment [ɪˈkwɪpmənt] *s* equipaggiamento; (*skill*) attitudine *f*, capacità *f*

equipoise [ˈikwɪˌpɔɪz] *or* [ˈɛkwɪˌpɔɪz] *s* equilibrio || *tr* equilibrare

equitable [ˈɛkwɪtəbəl] *adj* equo

equi·ty [ˈɛkwɪti] *s* (**-ties**) (*fairness*) equità *f*; valore *m* al netto; (*in a corporation*) interessenza azionaria

equivalent [ɪˈkwɪvələnt] *adj* equivalente || *s* equivalente *m*; (com) controvalore *m*

equivocal [ɪˈkwɪvəkəl] *adj* equivoco

equivocate [ɪˈkwɪvəˌket] *intr* giocare sulle parole, parlare in maniera equivoca

equivocation [ɪˌkwɪvəˈkeʃən] *s* equivocità *f*; equivoco

era [ˈɪrə] *or* [ˈirə] *s* era, evo

eradicate [ɪˈrædɪˌket] *tr* sradicare

erase [ɪˈres] *tr* cancellare

eraser [ɪˈresər] *s* gomma da cancellare; (*for blackboard*) spugna

erasure [ɪˈreʃər] *or* [ɪˈreʒər] *s* cancellatura; (*of a tape*) cancellazione

ere [ɛr] *prep* (lit) prima di || *conj* (lit) prima che

erect [ɪˈrɛkt] *adj* dritto, eretto; (*hair*) irto || *tr* (*to set in upright position*) drizzare; (*a building*) erigere, costruire; (*a machine*) montare

erection [ɪˈrɛkʃən] *s* erezione

ermine [ˈʌrmɪn] *s* ermellino; (fig) carica di giudice, toga, magistratura

erode [ɪˈrod] *tr* erodere || *intr* corrodersi, consumarsi

erosion [ɪˈroʒən] *s* erosione

erotic [ɪˈrɑtɪk] *adj* erotico

err [ʌr] *intr* errare; (*to be incorrect*) sbagliarsi

errand [ˈɛrənd] *s* corsa, commissione; **to run an errand** fare una commissione

er'rand boy' *s* fattorino, galoppino

erratic [ɪ'rætɪk] *adj* erratico; strano, eccentrico

erra·tum [ɪ'retəm] *or* [ɪ'rɑtəm] *s* (**-ta** [tə]) errore *m* di stampa

erroneous [ɪ'roni·əs] *adj* erroneo

error ['erər] *s* errore *m*, sbaglio

erudite ['eru ,daɪt] *or* ['erju ,daɪt] *adj* erudito, dotto

erudition [,eru'dɪʃən] *or* [,erju'dɪʃən] *s* erudizione

erupt [ɪ'rʌpt] *intr* (*said of a volcano*) eruttare; (*said of a skin rash*) fiorire; (*said of a tooth*) spuntare; (*fig*) erompere

eruption [ɪ'rʌpʃən] *s* eruzione

escalate ['eskə ,let] *tr & intr* aumentare

escalation [,eskə'leʃən] *s* aumento

escalator ['eskə ,letər] *s* scala mobile

escallop [es'kæləp] *s* (*on edge of cloth*) dentellatura, festone *m*; (*mollusk*) pettine *m* ∥ *tr* cuocere in conchiglia; cuocere al forno con salsa e pane grattugiato

escapade [,eskə'ped] *s* scappatella

escape [es'kep] *s* (*getaway*) fuga; (*from responsibility, duties, etc.*) scampo ∥ *tr* sottrarsi a, eludere; **to escape s.o.** scappare da qlcu; scappar di mente a qlcu ∥ *intr* scappare; sprigionarsi; **to escape from** (*a person*) sfuggire a; (*jail*) evadere da

escapee [,eskə'pi] *s* evaso

escape' lit'erature' *s* letteratura di evasione

escapement [es'kepmənt] *s* scappamento

escape' veloc'ity *s* (*rok*) velocità *f* di fuga

escarpment [es'kɑrpmənt] *s* scarpata

eschew [es't'ʃu] *tr* evitare, rifuggire da

escort ['eskɔrt] *s* scorta; (*of a woman or girl*) compagno, cavaliere *m* ∥ [es'kɔrt] *tr* scortare

escutcheon [es'kʌtʃən] *s* scudo; (*plate in front of lock on door*) bocchetta

Esk·imo ['eskɪ ,mo] *adj* eschimese ∥ *s* (**-mos** *or* **-mo**) eschimese *mf*

esopha·gus [i'safəgəs] *s* (**-gi** [,dʒaɪ]) esofago

espalier [es'pæljər] *s* spalliera

especial [es'peʃəl] *adj* speciale

espionage ['espɪ·ənɪdʒ] *or* [,espɪ·ə-'nɑʒ] *s* spionaggio

esplanade [,esplə'ned] *or* [,esplə'nɑd] *s* spianata, piazzale *m*

espousal [es'pauzəl] *s* sposalizio; (*of a cause*) adozione

espouse [es'pauz] *tr* sposare; (*to advocate*) abbracciare, adottare

esquire [es'kwaɪr] *or* ['eskwaɪr] *s* scudiero ∥ **Esquire** *s* titolo di cortesia usato generalmente con persone di riguardo

essay ['ese] *s* saggio

essayist ['ese·ɪst] *s* saggista *mf*

essence ['esəns] *s* essenza

essential [es'senʃəl] *adj & s* essenziale *m*

establish [es'tæblɪʃ] *tr* stabilire

establishment [es'tæblɪʃmənt] *s* stabilimento; fondazione; **the Establishment** l'autorità costituita

estate [es'tet] *s* stato; condizione sociale; (*landed property*) tenuta; (*a person's possessions*) patrimonio; (*left by a decedent*) massa ereditaria

esteem [es'tim] *s* stima ∥ *tr* stimare

esthete ['esθit] *s* esteta *mf*

esthetic [es'θetɪk] *adj* estetico ∥ **esthetics** *ssg* estetica

estimable ['estɪməbəl] *adj* stimabile

estimate ['estɪ ,met] *or* ['estɪmɪt] *s* stima, valutazione; (*statement of cost of work to be done*) preventivo ∥ ['estɪ ,met] *tr* stimare, valutare; preventivare

estimation [,estɪ'meʃən] *s* stima; **in my estimation** a mio parere

estimator ['estɪ ,metər] *s* preventivista *mf*

estrangement [es'trendʒmənt] *s* alienazione, disaffezione

estuar·y ['estʃu ,eri] *s* (**-ies**) estuario

etch [etʃ] *tr & intr* incidere all'acquaforte

etcher ['etʃər] *s* acquafortista *mf*

etching ['etʃɪŋ] *s* acquaforte *f*

eternal [ɪ'tʌrnəl] *adj* eterno

eterni·ty [ɪ'tʌrnɪti] *s* (**-ties**) eternità *f*

ether ['iθər] *s* etere *m*

ethereal [ɪ'θɪrɪ·əl] *adj* etereo

ethical ['eθɪkəl] *adj* etico

ethics ['eθɪks] *ssg* etica

Ethiopian [,iθɪ'opɪ·ən] *adj & s* etiope *mf*

ethnic(al) ['eθnɪk(əl)] *adj* etnico

ethnography [eθ'nagrəfi] *s* etnografia

ethnology [eθ'nalədʒi] *s* etnologia

ethyl ['eθɪl] *s* etile *m*

ethylene ['eθɪ ,lin] *s* etilene *m*

etiquette ['etɪ ,ket] *s* etichetta

étude [e'tjud] *s* (*mus*) studio

etymology [,etɪ'malədʒi] *s* etimologia

ety·mon ['etɪ ,man] *s* (**-mons** *or* **-ma** [mə]) etimo

eucalyp·tus [,jukə'lɪptəs] *s* (**-tuses** *or* **-ti** [taɪ]) eucalipto

Eucharist ['jukərɪst] *s* Eucaristia

eugenics [ju'dʒenɪks] *ssg* eugenetica

eulogistic [,julə'dʒɪstɪk] *adj* elogiativo

eulogize ['julə ,dʒaɪz] *tr* elogiare

eulo·gy ['julədʒi] *s* (**-gies**) elogio; elogio funebre

eunuch ['junək] *s* eunuco

euphemism ['jufɪ ,mɪzəm] *s* eufemismo

euphemistic [,jufɪ'mɪstɪk] *adj* eufemistico

euphonic [ju'fanɪk] *adj* eufonico

eupho·ny ['jufəni] *s* (**-nies**) eufonia

euphoria [ju'forɪ·ə] *s* euforia

euphuism ['jufju ,ɪzəm] *s* eufuismo

Europe ['jurəp] *s* l'Europa

European [,jurə'pi·ən] *adj & s* europeo

euthanasia [,juθə'neʒə] *s* eutanasia

evacuate [ɪ'vækju ,et] *tr & intr* evacuare

evacuation [ɪ ,vækju'eʃən] *s* evacuazione

evacuee [ɪ'vækju ,i] *or* [ɪ ,vækju'i] *s* sfollato

evade [ɪ'ved] *tr* eludere ∥ *intr* evadere

evaluate [ɪ'vælju ,et] *tr* valutare

evaluation [ɪ ,vælju'eʃən] *s* valutazione

Evangel [ɪ'vændʒəl] *s* Vangelo

evangelic(al) [,ivæn'dʒelɪk(əl)] *or* [,evən'dʒelɪk(əl)] *adj* evangelico

Evangelist [ɪ'vændʒəlɪst] s evangelista m

evaporate [ɪ'væpə‚ret] tr & intr evaporare

evasion [ɪ'veʒən] s evasione; (*subterfuge*) scappatoia

evasive [ɪ'vesɪv] adj evasivo

eve [iv] s vigilia; **on the eve of** la vigilia di

even ['ivən] adj (*smooth*) piano, regolare; (*number*) pari; uguale, uniforme; (*temperament*) calmo, placido; **even with** a livello di; **to be even** mettersi in pari; **to get even** prendersi la rivincita || adv anche; fino, perfino; pure; esattamente; magari; **even as** proprio mentre; **even if** anche se, quando pure; **even so** anche se così; **even though** quantunque; **even when** anche quando; **not even** neppure, nemmeno; **to break even** impattare || tr spianare; **to even up** bilanciare

evening ['ivnɪŋ] adj serale || s sera, serata; **all evening** tutta la sera; **every evening** tutte le sere; **in the evening** la sera

eve'ning clothes' spl vestito da sera

eve'ning gown' s vestito da sera da signora

eve'ning star' s espero

e'ven·song' s (eccl) vespro

event [ɪ'vent] s avvenimento; (*outcome*) evenienza; (*public function*) manifestazione; (sports) prova; **at all events** or **in any event** in ogni caso; **in the event that** in caso che, se mai

eventful [ɪ'ventfəl] adj ricco di avvenimenti; movimentato

eventual [ɪ'ventʃʊ‚əl] adj finale

eventu·ty [ɪ‚ventʃʊ'ælɪti] s (-ties) eventualità f, evenienza

eventually [ɪ'ventʃʊ‚əli] adv finalmente, alla fine

eventuate [ɪ'ventʃʊ‚et] intr risultare; accadere

ever ['evər] adv (*at all times*) sempre; (*at any time*) mai; **as ever** come sempre; **as much as ever** tanto come prima; **ever since** (*since that time*) sin da; (*since then*) da allora in poi; **ever so** molto; **ever so much** moltissimo; **hardly ever** or **scarcely ever** quasi mai; **not . . . ever** non . . . mai

ev'er·glade' s terreno paludoso coperto di erbe

ev'er·green' adj & s sempreverde m & f; **evergreens** decorazione di sempreverdi

ev'er·last'ing adj eterno; incessante; (*lasting indefinitely*) duraturo; (*wearisome*) noioso || s eternità f; (bot) semprevivo

ev'er·more' adv eternamente; **for evermore** per sempre

every ['evri] adj tutti i; (*each*) ogni, ciascuno; (*being each in a series*) ogni, e.g., **every three days** ogni tre giorni; **every bit** (coll) in tutto e per tutto, e.g., **every bit a man** un uomo in tutto e per tutto; **every now and then** di quando in quando; **every once in a while** una volta ogni tanto;

every other day ogni secondo giorno; **every which way** (coll) da tutte le parti; (coll) in disordine

ev'ery·bod'y pron indef ognuno, tutti

ev'ery·day' adj di ogni giorno; quotidiano; ordinario

ev'ery·man' s l'uomo qualunque || pron chiunque

ev'ery·one' or **ev'ery one'** pron indef ciascuno, tutti

ev'ery·thing' pron indef tutto, ogni cosa, tutto quanto

ev'ery·where' adv dappertutto, dovunque

evict [ɪ'vɪkt] tr sfrattare, sloggiare

eviction [ɪ'vɪkʃən] s sfratto, sloggio

evidence ['evɪdəns] s evidenza; (law) prova

evident ['evɪdənt] adj evidente

evil ['ivəl] adj cattivo, malvagio || s male m; disgrazia

evildoer ['ivəl‚du·ər] s malfattore m, malvagio

e'vil·do'ing s malafatta, malvagità f

e'vil eye' s iettatura, malocchio

evil-minded ['ivəl'maɪndɪd] adj malintenzionato

e'vil one', **the** il nemico

evince [ɪ'vɪns] tr mostrare, manifestare

evoke [ɪ'vok] tr evocare

evolution [‚evə'luʃən] s evoluzione

evolve [ɪ'vɑlv] tr sviluppare || intr evolversi

ewe [ju] s pecora

ewer ['ju·ər] s brocca

ex [eks] prep senza includere

exacerbation [ɪg‚zæsər'beʃən] s esulcerazione, esacerbazione

exacerbate [ɪg'zæsər‚bet] || tr esacerbare, esulcerare

exact [eg'zækt] adj esatto || tr esigere

exacting [eg'zæktɪŋ] adj esigente

exaction [eg'zækʃən] s esazione

exactly [eg'zæktli] adv esattamente; (*sharp, on the dot*) in punto

exactness [eg'zæktnɪs] s esattezza

exaggerate [eg'zædʒə‚ret] tr esagerare

exalt [eg'zɔlt] tr elevare, esaltare

exam [eg'zæm] s (coll) esame m

examination [eg‚zæmɪ'neʃən] s esame m; **to take an examination** sostenere un esame

examine [eg'zæmɪn] tr esaminare

examiner [eg'zæmɪnər] s esaminatore m

example [eg'zæmpəl] or [eg'zɑmpəl] s esempio; (*precedent*) precedente m; (*of mathematics*) problema m; **for example** per esempio

exasperate [eg'zæspə‚ret] tr esasperare

excavate ['ekskə‚vet] tr scavare

exceed [ek'sid] tr eccedere

exceedingly [ek'sidɪŋli] adv estremamente, sommamente

ex·cel [ek'sel] v (pret & pp -celled; ger -celling) tr sorpassare || intr eccellere

excellence ['eksələns] s eccellenza

excellen·cy ['eksələnsi] s (-cies) eccellenza; **Your Excellency** Sua Eccellenza

excelsior [ek'selsɪ·ər] s trucioli mpl per imballaggio

except [ek'sept] prep eccetto; **except**

for tranne, ad eccezione di; **except that** eccetto che || *tr* eccettuare

exception [ek'sepʃən] *s* eccezione; **to take exception** obiettare; scandalizzarsi; **with the exception of** a esclusione di, eccetto

exceptional [ek'sepʃənəl] *adj* eccezionale

excerpt ['eksʌrpt] *or* [ek'sʌrpt] *s* brano, selezione || [ek'sʌrpt] *tr* scegliere, selezionare

excess ['ekses] *or* [ek'ses] *adj* eccedente || [ek'ses] *s* (*amount or degree by which one thing exceeds another*) eccedente *m*, eccedenza; (*excessive amount; immoderate indulgence; unlawful conduct*) eccesso; **in excess of** più di

ex'cess bag'gage *s* bagaglio eccedente

ex'cess fare' *s* (rr) supplemento

excessive [ek'sesɪv] *adj* eccessivo

ex'cess-prof'its tax' *s* tassa sui soprapprofitti

exchange [eks'tʃendʒ] *s* scambio; (*place for buying and selling*) borsa; (*transactions in the currencies of two different countries*) cambio; (telp) centrale *f*, centralino; **in exchange for** in cambio di || *tr* scambiare, scambiarsi; **to exchange blows** venire alle mani; **to exchange greetings** salutarsi

exchequer [eks'tʃekər] *or* ['ekstʃekər] *s* erario, tesoro

ex'cise tax' [ek'saɪz] *or* ['eksaɪz] *s* imposta sul consumo

excitable [ek'saɪtəbəl] *adj* eccitabile

excite [ek'saɪt] *tr* eccitare

excitement [ek'saɪtmənt] *s* eccitazione

exciting [ek'saɪtɪŋ] *adj* emozionante; (*stimulating*) eccitante

exclaim [eks'klem] *tr & intr* esclamare

exclamation [ˌekskləˈmeʃən] *s* esclamazione

exclama'tion mark' *or* **point'** *s* punto esclamativo

exclude [eks'klud] *tr* escludere

excluding [eks'kludɪŋ] *prep* a esclusione di, senza contare

exclusion [eks'kluʒən] *s* esclusione; **to the exclusion of** tranne, salvo

exclusive [eks'klusɪv] *adj* esclusivo; **exclusive of** escluso, senza contare || *s* (journ) esclusiva

excommunicate [ˌekskəˈmjunɪˌket] *tr* scomunicare

excommunication [ˌekskəˌmjunɪˈkeʃən] *s* scomunica

excoriate [eks'korɪˌet] *tr* criticare aspramente, vituperare

excrement ['ekskrəmənt] *s* escremento

excruciating [eks'kruʃɪˌetɪŋ] *adj* (*e.g., pleasure*) estremo; (*e.g., pain*) atroce, lancinante, straziante

exculpate ['ekskʌlˌpet] *or* [eks'kʌlpet] *tr* scolpare, scagionare

excursion [eks'kʌrʒən] *or* [eks'kʌrʃən] *s* escursione, gita

excursionist [eks'kʌrʒənɪst] *or* [eks'kʌrʃənɪst] *s* escursionista *mf*

excusable [eks'kjuzəbəl] *adj* scusabile

excuse [eks'kjus] *s* scusa || [eks'kjuz] *tr* scusare; esentare; (*a debt*) rimettere

execute ['eksɪˌkjut] *tr* (*to carry out; to produce*) eseguire; (*to put to death*) giustiziare; (law) rendere esecutorio

execution [ˌeksɪˈkjuʃən] *s* esecuzione; (*e.g., of a criminal*) esecuzione capitale

executioner [ˌeksɪˈkjuʃənər] *s* giustiziere *m*, boia *m*, carnefice *m*

executive [eg'zekjətɪv] *adj* esecutivo || *s* esecutivo; (*of a school, business, etc.*) dirigente *mf*

Exec'utive Man'sion *s* palazzo del governatore; residenza del capo del governo statunitense

executor [eg'zekjətər] *s* (law) esecutore testamentario

executrix [eg'zekjətrɪks] *s* (law) esecutrice testamentaria

exemplary [eg'zemplərɪ] *or* ['egzəmˌplerɪ] *adj* esemplare

exempli•fy [eg'zemplɪˌfaɪ] *v* (*pret & pp* **-fied**) *tr* esemplificare

exempt [eg'zempt] *adj* esente || *tr* esimere, esentare

exemption [eg'zempʃən] *s* esenzione

exercise ['eksər,saɪz] *s* esercizio; cerimonia; **to take exercise** fare del moto || *tr* esercitare; (*care*) usare; (*to worry*) preoccupare || *intr* esercitarsi

exert [eg'zʌrt] *tr* (*e.g., power*) esercitare; **to exert oneself** sforzarsi

exertion [eg'zʌrʃən] *s* sforzo, tentativo; (*active use*) uso, esercizio

exhalation [ˌeks•hə'leʃən] *s* (*of gas, vapors*) esalazione; (*of air from lungs*) espirazione

exhale [eks'hel] *or* [eg'zel] *tr* (*gases, vapors, etc.*) esalare; (*air from lungs*) espirare || *intr* esalare; espirare

exhaust [eg'zɔst] *s* scarico, scappamento; tubo di scarico or scappamento || *tr* (*to wear out*) spossare, finire; (*to use up*) esaurire, dar fondo a; vuotare

exhaust' fan' *s* aspiratore *m*

exhaustion [eg'zɔstʃən] *s* esaurimento; estenuazione; (sports) cotta

exhaustive [eg'zɔstɪv] *adj* esauriente

exhaust' man'ifold *s* collettore *m* di scarico

exhaust' pipe' *s* tubo di scarico

exhaust' valve' *s* valvola di scappamento

exhibit [eg'zɪbɪt] *s* esposizione; (law) documento in giudizio || *tr* esibire

exhibition [ˌeksɪ'bɪʃən] *s* esibizione

exhibitor [eg'zɪbɪtər] *s* espositore *m*

exhilarating [eg'zɪləˌretɪŋ] *adj* esilarante

exhort [eg'zɔrt] *tr* esortare

exhume [eks'hjum] *or* [eg'zjum] *tr* esumare, dissotterrare

exigen•cy ['eksɪdʒənsɪ] *s* (**-cies**) esigenza

exigent ['eksɪdʒənt] *adj* esigente

exile ['egzaɪl] *or* ['eksaɪl] *s* esilio; (*person*) esule *mf* || *tr* esiliare

exist [eg'zɪst] *intr* esistere

existence [eg'zɪstəns] *s* esistenza

existing [eg'zɪstɪŋ] *adj* esistente

exit ['egzɪt] *or* ['eksɪt] *s* uscita || *intr* uscire

exodus ['ɛksədəs] *s* esodo
exonerate [ɛg'zɑnə ˌret] *tr* (*from an obligation*) esonerare; (*from blame*) scagionare
exorbitant [ɛg'zɔrbɪtənt] *adj* esorbitante
exorcise ['ɛksər ˌsaɪz] *tr* esorcizzare
exotic [ɛg'zɑtɪk] *adj* esotico
expand [ɛks'pænd] *tr* (*a metal*) dilatare; (*gas*) espandere; (*to enlarge*) allargare, ampliare; (*to unfold*) spiegare; (math) svolgere, sviluppare || *intr* dilatarsi; espandersi; allargarsi, ampliarsi; spiegarsi, estendersi
expanse [ɛks'pæns] *s* vastità *f*
expansion [ɛks'pænʃən] *s* espansione
expansive [ɛks'pænsɪv] *adj* espansivo
expatiate [ɛks'peʃɪ ˌet] *intr* dilungarsi
expatriate [ɛks'petrɪ ɪt] *adj* esiliato || *s* esule *mf* || [ɛks'petrɪ ˌet] *tr* esiliare; **to expatriate oneself** espatriare
expect [ɛks'pɛkt] *tr* aspettare, attendere; (coll) credere, supporre; **to expect it** aspettarselo, aspettarsela
expectan·cy [ɛks'pɛktənsi] *s* (**-cies**) aspettativa, aspettazione
expect'ant moth'er [ɛks'pɛktənt] *s* futura madre
expectation [ˌɛkspɛk'teʃən] *s* aspettativa
expectorate [ɛks'pɛktə ˌret] *tr* & *intr* espettorare
expedien·cy [ɛks'pidɪ ənsi] *s* (**-cies**) industria, ingegno; opportunismo, vantaggio personale
expedient [ɛks'pidɪ ənt] *adj* conveniente; vantaggioso; (*acting with self-interest*) opportunista || *s* espediente *m*
expedite ['ɛkspɪ ˌdaɪt] *tr* sbrigare, accelerare; (*a document*) dar corso a
expedition [ˌɛkspɪ'dɪʃən] *s* spedizione; (*speed*) celerità *f*
expeditionary [ˌɛkspɪ'dɪʃən ˌɛri] *adj* (*e.g., corps*) di spedizione
expeditious [ˌɛkspɪ'dɪʃəs] *adj* spicciativo, spiccio
ex·pel [ɛks'pɛl] *v* (*pret* & *pp* **-pelled;** *ger* **-pelling**) *tr* espellere, scacciare
expend [ɛks'pɛnd] *tr* spendere, consumare
expendable [ɛks'pɛndəbəl] *adj* spendibile; da buttarsi via; (mil) da sacrificare
expenditure [ɛks'pɛndɪt/ər] *s* spesa
expense [ɛks'pɛns] *s* spesa; **at the expense of** a spese di; **expenses** spese *fpl*; **to meet expenses** far fronte alle spese
expense' account' *s* conto delle spese risarcibili
expensive [ɛks'pɛnsɪv] *adj* caro, costoso
experience [ɛks'pɪrɪ əns] *s* esperienza || *tr* sperimentare, provare
experienced [ɛks'pɪrɪ ənst] *adj* esperto, sperimentato
experiment [ɛks'pɛrɪmənt] *s* esperimento || [ɛks'pɛrɪ ˌment] *intr* sperimentare
expert ['ɛkspərt] *adj* & *s* esperto
expertise [ˌɛkspər'tiz] *s* maestria

expiate ['ɛkspɪ ˌet] *tr* espiare
expiation [ˌɛkspɪ'eʃən] *s* espiazione
expire [ɛks'paɪr] *tr* espirare || *intr* (*to breathe out*) espirare; (*said of a contract*) scadere; (*to die*) morire
explain [ɛks'plen] *tr* spiegare; **to explain away** giustificare; dar ragione di || *intr* spiegare, spiegarsi
explainable [ɛks'plenəbəl] *adj* spiegabile
explanation [ˌɛksplə'neʃən] *s* spiegazione, delucidazione
explanatory [ɛks'plænə ˌtori] *adj* esplicativo
explicit [ɛks'plɪsɪt] *adj* esplicito
explode [ɛks'plod] *tr* far scoppiare; (*a theory*) smontare || *intr* scoppiare
exploit [ɛks'plɔɪt] *or* ['ɛksplɔɪt] *s* impresa, prodezza || [ɛks'plɔɪt] *tr* utilizzare, sfruttare
exploitation [ˌɛksplɔɪ'teʃən] *s* utilizzazione, sfruttamento
exploration [ˌɛksplə'reʃən] *s* esplorazione
explore [ɛks'plor] *tr* esplorare
explorer [ɛks'plorər] *s* esploratore *m*
explosion [ɛks'ploʒən] *s* esplosione, scoppio; (*of a theory*) confutazione
explosive [ɛks'plosɪv] *adj* & *s* esplosivo
exponent [ɛks'ponənt] *s* esponente *m*
export ['ɛksport] *adj* di esportazione || *s* esportazione, articolo di esportazione || [ɛks'port] *or* ['ɛksport] *tr* & *intr* esportare
exportation [ˌɛkspor'teʃən] *s* esportazione
exporter ['ɛksportər] *or* [ɛks'portər] *s* esportatore *m*
expose [ɛks'poz] *tr* esporre; (*to unmask*) smascherare
exposé [ˌɛkspo'ze] *s* rivelazione scandalosa, smascheramento
exposition [ˌɛkspə'zɪʃən] *s* esposizione; interpretazione, commento
expostulate [ɛks'pɑst/ə ˌlet] *intr* protestare; **to expostulate with** lagnarsi con
exposure [ɛks'poʒər] *s* (*disclosure*) rivelazione; (*situation with regard to sunlight*) esposizione; (phot) esposizione
expo'sure me'ter *s* (phot) fotometro, esposimetro
expound [ɛks'paund] *tr* esporre
express [ɛks'prɛs] *adj* espresso || *s* (rr) celere *m*, rapido, direttissimo; **by express** per espresso, a grande velocità || *adv* per espresso, a grande velocità || *tr* esprimere; mandare per espresso; (*to squeeze out*) spremere; **to express oneself** esprimersi
ex'press com'pany *s* servizio corriere
expression [ɛks'prɛʃən] *s* espressione
expressive [ɛks'prɛsɪv] *adj* espressivo
expressly [ɛks'prɛsli] *adv* espressamente
express'man *s* (**-men**) fattorino di servizio corriere
express'way' *s* autostrada
expropriate [ɛks'propri ˌet] *tr* espropriare
expulsion [ɛks'pʌlʃən] *s* espulsione

expunge [ɛks'pʌndʒ] *tr* espungere

expurgate ['ɛkspər ‚get] *tr* espurgare

exquisite ['ɛkskwızıt] or [ɛks'kwızıt] *adj* squisito; intenso

ex'serv'ice-man' *s* (-men') ex combattente *m*

extant ['ɛkstənt] or [ɛks'tænt] *adj* ancora esistente

extemporaneous [ɛks ‚tɛmpə'renɪ-əs] *adj* estemporaneo; (*made for the occasion*) improvvisato

extempore [ɛks'tɛmpəri] *adj* improvvisato || *adv* senza preparazione

extemporize [ɛks'tɛmpə ‚raız] *tr & intr* improvvisare

extend [ɛks'tɛnd] *tr* allungare; estendere; (*e.g., aid*) offrire; (*payment of a debt*) dilazionare || *intr* estendersi

extended [ɛks'tɛndɪd] *adj* esteso; prolungato

extension [ɛks'tɛnʃən] *s* estensione; prolungamento; (com) proroga; (telp) derivazione

exten'sion lad'der *s* scala porta, scala a prolunga

exten'sion ta'ble *s* tavola allungabile

exten'sion tel'ephone' *s* telefono interno

extensive [ɛks'tɛnsɪv] *adj* (*wide*) vasto; (*lengthy*) lungo; (*characterized by extention*) estensivo

extent [ɛks'tɛnt] *s* estensione; to a certain extent fino a un certo punto; to a great extent in larga misura; to the full extent all'estremo limite

extenuate [ɛks'tɛnju ‚et] *tr* (*to make seem less serious*) attenuare; (*to underrate*) sottovalutare

exterior [ɛks'tɪrɪ-ər] *adj & s* esteriore *m*

exterminate [ɛks'tʌrmɪ ‚net] *tr* sterminare

external [ɛks'tʌrnəl] *adj* esterno || externals *spl* esteriorità *f*, di fuori *m*

extinct [ɛks'tɪŋkt] *adj* estinto

extinction [ɛks'tɪŋkʃən] *s* estinzione

extinguish [ɛks'tɪŋwɪʃ] *tr* estinguere

extinguisher [ɛks'tɪŋgwɪʃər] *s* estintore *m*

extirpate ['ɛkstər ‚pet] or [ɛks'tʌrpet] *tr* estirpare

ex•tol [ɛks'tol] or [ɛks'tal] *v* (*pret & pp* -tolled; *ger* -tolling) *tr* inneggiare

extort [ɛks'tort] *tr* estorcere

extortion [ɛks'torʃən] *s* estorsione

extra ['ɛkstrə] *adj* extra; (*spare*) di scorta || *s* (*of a newspaper*) edizione straordinaria; (*something additional*) soprappiù *m*; (theat) figurante *mf* || *adv* straordinariamente

ex'tra charge' *s* supplemento

extract ['ɛkstrækt] *s* estratto || [ɛks'trækt] *tr* (*to pull out*) estrarre; (*to take from a book*) scegliere, selezionare

extraction [ɛks'trækʃən] *s* estrazione

extracurricular [‚ɛkstrəkə'rɪkjələr] *adj* fuori del programma normale

extradition [‚ɛkstrə'dɪʃən] *s* estradizione

ex'tra-dry' *adj* molto secco, brut

ex'tra fare' *s* supplemento al biglietto

ex'tra·mar'ital *adj* extraconiugale

extramural [‚ɛkstrə'mjurəl] *adj* fuori della scuola, interscolastico; fuori delle mura

extraneous [ɛks'trenɪ-əs] *adj* estraneo

extraordinary [‚ɛkstrə'ordɪ ‚nerɪ] or [ɛks'trordɪ ‚nerɪ] *adj* straordinario

extrapolate [ɛks'træpə ‚let] *tr & intr* estrapolare

extrasensory [‚ɛkstrə'sɛnsəri] *adj* extrasensoriale

extravagance [ɛks'trævəgəns] *s* prodigalità *f*; (*wildness, folly*) stravaganza

extravagant [ɛks'trævəgənt] *adj* prodigo; (*wild, foolish*) stravagante

extreme [ɛks'trim] *adj & s* estremo; in the extreme in massimo grado; to go to extremes andare agli estremi

extremely [ɛks'trimli] *adv* estremamente, in sommo grado

extreme' unc'tion *s* Estrema Unzione

extremist [ɛks'trimɪst] *adj & s* estremista *mf*

extremi·ty [ɛks'trɛmɪtɪ] *s* (-ties) estremità *f*; (*great want*) estrema necessità; extremities estremi *mpl*; (*hands and feet*) estremità *fpl*

extricate ['ɛkstrɪ ‚ket] *tr* districare

extrinsic [ɛks'trɪnsɪk] *adj* estrinseco

extrovert ['ɛkstrə ‚vʌrt] *s* estroverso

extrude [ɛks'trud] *tr* estrudere || *intr* protrudere

exuberant [ɛg'zubərənt] or [ɛg'zjubərənt] *adj* esuberante

exude [ɛg'zud] or [ɛk'sud] *tr & intr* trasudare, stillare

exult [ɛg'zʌlt] *intr* esultare, tripudiare

exultant [ɛg'zʌltənt] *adj* esultante

eye [aɪ] *s* occhio; (*of hook and eye*) occhiello; to catch one's eye attirare l'attenzione di qlcu; to feast one's eyes on deliziarsi la vista con; to lay eyes on riuscire a vedere; to make eyes at fare gli occhi dolci a; to roll one's eyes stralunare gli occhi; to see eye to eye andare perfettamente d'accordo; to shut one's eyes to chiudere un occhio a; far finta di non vedere; without batting an eye senza batter ciglio || *v* (*pret & pp* eyed; *ger* eying or eyeing) *tr* occhieggiare; to eye up and down guardare da capo a piedi

eye'ball' *s* globo oculare

eye'bolt' *s* bullone *m* ad anello

eye'brow' *s* sopracciglio; to raise one's eyebrows inarcare le sopracciglia

eye'cup' *s* occhiera

eye'drop'per *s* contagocce *m*

eyeful ['aɪ ‚ful] *s* vista, colpo d'occhio; (coll) bellezza

eye'glass' *s* (*of optical instrument*) lente *f*, oculare *m*; (*eyecup*) occhiera; eyeglasses occhiali *mpl*

eye'lash' *s* ciglio

eyelet ['aɪlɪt] *s* occhiello, maglietta, asola; (*hole to look through*) feritoia

eye'lid' *s* palpebra

eye' o'pener ['opənər] *s* affare *m* che apre gli occhi; (coll) bicchierino bevuto di mattina presto

eye'piece' s oculare m
eye'shade' s visiera
eye' shad'ow s rimmel m
eye'shot' s—**within eyeshot** a portata di vista
eye'sight' s vista; (range) capacità visiva
eye' sock'et s occhiaia, orbita
eye'sore' s pugno in un occhio

eye'strain' s vista affaticata
eye'-test chart' s tabella optometrica
eye'tooth' s (-**teeth**) dente canino; **to cut one's eyeteeth** (coll) fare esperienza; **to give one's eyeteeth for** (coll) dare un occhio della testa per
eye'wash' s (flattery) burro, lusinga; (pharm) collirio; (slang) balla
eye' wit'ness s testimone m oculare

F

F, f [ef] s sesta lettera dell'alfabeto inglese
fable ['febəl] s favola
fabric ['fæbrɪk] s stoffa, tessuto; fabbrica, struttura
fabricate ['fæbrɪ,ket] tr fabbricare
fabrication [,fæbrɪ'keʃən] s fabbricazione; falsificazione, invenzione
fabulous ['fæbjələs] adj favoloso
façade [fə'sɑd] s facciata
face [fes] s volto, viso, faccia; (surface) superficie f; (of coin) diritto; (of precious stone) faccetta; (of watch) mostra; (grimace) smorfia; (of building) facciata; (typ) occhio; **in the face of** di fronte a; **to have a long face** fare il muso lungo; **to keep a straight face** contenere le risa; **to show one's face** farsi vedere || tr far fronte a, fronteggiare; (a wall) ricoprire; (a suit) foderare; **facing of** fronte a || intr—**to face about** voltarsi, fare dietro front; **to face on** dare a; **to face up to** guardare in faccia
face' card' s figura
face' lift'ing s plastica facciale
face' pow'der s cipria
facet ['fæsɪt] s faccetta; (fig) faccia
facetious [fə'siʃəs] adj faceto
face' val'ue s valore m facciale
facial ['feʃəl] adj facciale || s massaggio facciale
fa'cial tis'sue s rivella detergente
facilitate [fə'sɪlɪ,tet] tr facilitare
facili·ty [fə'sɪlɪti] s (-**ties**) facilità f; **facilities** (installations) attrezzatura fpl; (for transportation) mezzi mpl; (services) servizi mpl
facing ['fesɪŋ] s rivestimento
facsimile [fæk'sɪmɪli] s facsimile m
fact [fækt] s fatto; **in fact** in realtà; **the fact is that** il fatto si è che
faction ['fækʃən] s fazione; discordia
factional ['fækʃənəl] adj fazioso; (partisan) partigiano
factionalism ['fækʃənə,lɪzəm] s partigianeria; parzialità f
factor ['fæktər] s fattore m || tr scomporre in fattori
facto·ry ['fæktəri] s (-**ries**) fabbrica
factual ['fækt/ʊ·əl] adj effettivo, reale
facul·ty ['fækəlti] s (-**ties**) facoltà f
fad [fæd] s moda passeggera
fade [fed] tr stingere || intr (said of colors) stingersi, sbiadire; (said of

sounds, sight, radio signals, memory, etc.) svanire, affievolirsi; (said of beauty) sfiorire
fade'-out' s affievolimento, affievolirsi m; (mov) chiusura in dissolvenza; (rad, telv) evanescenza
fading ['fedɪŋ] s affievolimento; (mov) dissolvenza; (rad, telv) evanescenza
fag [fæg] s schiavo del lavoro; (coll) sigaretta || tr—**to fag out** stancare
fagot ['fægət] s fascina, fastello
fail [fel] s—**without fail** senza meno || tr mancare (with dat); (a student) riprovare; (an examination) farsi bocciare in || intr fallire, venire a meno; (said of a student) farsi riprovare; (said of a motor) rompersi, fermarsi; (com) cadere in fallimento; **to fail to** mancare di
failure ['feljər] s insuccesso; insufficienza; (student) bocciato; (com) fallimento
faint [fent] adj debole; **to feel faint** sentirsi mancare || s svenimento || intr svenire
faint-hearted ['fent'hɑrtɪd] adj codardo, timido
fair [fer] adj giusto, onesto; (moderately large) discreto; (even) liscio; (civil) gentile; (hair) biondo; (complexion) chiaro; (sky, weather) sereno || s (exhibition) fiera; (carnival) sagra || adv direttamente; **to play fair** agire onestamente
fair'ground' s terreno dell'esposizione, campo della fiera
fairly ['ferli] adv giustamente, imparzialmente; discretamente, abbastanza; completamente
fair-minded ['fer'maɪndɪd] adj equanime, equo, giusto
fairness ['fernɪs] s giustizia, imparzialità f; bellezza; (of complexion) bianchezza
fair' play' s comportamento leale
fair' sex' s bel sesso
fair'-weath'er adj—**a fair-weather friend** un amico del tempo felice
fair·y ['feri] adj fatato || s (-**ies**) fata; (slang) finocchio
fair'y god'mother s buona fata
fair'y·land' s terra delle fate
fair'y tale' s fiaba, racconto delle fate
faith [feθ] s fede f; **to break faith with** venir meno alla parola data a; **to keep faith with** tener fede alla parola

data a; **to pin one's faith on** porre tutte le proprie speranze su; **upon my faith!** in fede mia!

faithful ['feθfəl] *adj* fedele || **the faithful** i fedeli

faithless ['feθlɪs] *adj* infedele, sleale

fake [fek] *adj* falso, finto || *s* contraffazione; (*person*) imbroglione *m* || *tr* & *intr* contraffare, falsificare

faker ['fekər] *s* (coll) imbroglione *m*

falcon ['fɔkən] or ['fɔlkən] *s* falcone *m*

falconer ['fɔkənər] or ['fɔlkənər] *s* falconiere *m*

falconry ['fɔkənrɪ] or ['fɔlkənrɪ] *s* falconeria

fall [fɔl] *adj* autunnale || *s* caduta; (*of water*) cataratta, cascata; (*of prices*) ribasso; (*autumn*) autunno; **falls** cataratta, cascate *fpl* || *v* (*pret* **fell** [fel]; *pp* **fallen** ['fɔlən]) *intr* cadere; discendere; **to fall apart** farsi a pezzi; **to fall back** (mil) ripiegare; **to fall behind** rimanere indietro; **to fall down** cadere; stramazzare; **to fall due** scadere; **to fall flat** stramazzare; essere un insuccesso; **to fall for** (slang) lasciarsi abbindolare da; (slang) innamorarsi di; **to fall in** (*said of a building*) crollare; (mil) allinearsi; **to fall in with** imbattersi in; mettersi d'accordo con; **to fall off** ritirarsi; diminuire; **to fall out** accadere; essere in disaccordo; (mil) rompere i ranghi; **to fall out of** cadere da; **to fall out with** inimicarsi con; **to fall over** cadere; (coll) adulare; **to fall through** fallire; **to fall to** cominciare a mangiare; (*said, e.g., of an inheritance*) ricadere su; **to fall under** rientrare in

fallacious [fə'le/əs] *adj* fallace

falla·cy ['fæləsɪ] *s* (-cies) fallacia

fall' guy' *s* (slang) testa di turco

fallible ['fælɪbəl] *adj* fallibile

fall'ing star' *s* stella cadente

fall'out' *s* pulviscolo radioattivo

fall'out shel'ter *s* rifugio antiatomico

fallow ['fælo] *adj* incolto; **to lie fallow** rimanere incolto || *s* maggese *m* || *tr* maggesare

false [fɔls] *adj* falso; (*hair, teeth, etc.*) posticcio, finto || *adv* falsamente; **to play false** tradire

false' bot'tom *s* doppio fondo

false' col'ors *spl* apparenze mentite

false' face' *s* maschera; (*ugly false face*) mascherone *m*

false'-heart'ed ['fɔls'hɑrtɪd] *adj* perfido

falsehood ['fɔls·hʊd] *s* falsità *f*, falso

false' pretens'es *spl* falso, impostura; **under false pretenses** allegando ragioni false

falset·to [fɔl'seto] *s* (-tos) (*voice*) falsetto; (*person*) cantante *m* in falsetto

falsi·fy ['fɔlsɪ‚faɪ] *v* (*pret* & *pp* -fied) *tr* falsificare; (*to disprove*) smentire || *intr* mentire

falsi·ty ['fɔlsɪtɪ] *s* (-ties) falsità *f*

falter ['fɔltər] *s* vacillamento; (*in speech*) balbettio || *intr* vacillare; balbettare

fame [fem] *s* fama

famed [femd] *adj* famoso

familiar [fə'mɪljər] *adj* familiare; intimo; **to be familiar with** (*people*) aver pratica con; (*things*) aver pratica di

familiari·ty [fə‚mɪlɪ'ærɪtɪ] *s* (-ties) familiarità *f*, dimestichezza

familiarize [fə'mɪljə‚raɪz] *tr* far conoscere

fami·ly ['fæmɪlɪ] *adj* familiare; **in the family way** (coll) in altro stato || *s* (-lies) famiglia

fam'ily man' *s* (**men'**) padre *m* di famiglia

fam'ily name' *s* cognome *m*

fam'ily tree' *s* albero genealogico

famine ['fæmɪn] *s* carestia

famished ['fæmɪʃt] *adj* famelico; **to be famished** avere una fame da lupo

famous ['feməs] *adj* famoso; (coll) eccellente

fan [fæn] *s* ventaglio; (elec) ventilatore *m*; (coll) tifoso, patito || *v* (*pret* & *pp* **fanned**) *ger* **fanning**) *tr* sventagliare; (*to winnow*) vagliare; (*fire, passions*) attizzare || *intr* sventagliarsi; **to fan out** (*said of a road*) diramarsi a ventaglio

fanatic [fə'nætɪk] *adj* & *s* fanatico

fanatical [fə'nætɪkəl] *adj* fanatico

fanaticism [fə'nætɪ‚sɪzəm] *s* fanatismo

fan' belt' *s* (aut) cinghia del ventilatore

fancied ['fænsɪd] *adj* immaginario

fancier ['fænsɪ·ər] *s* maniaco, tifoso; (*of animals*) conoscitore *m*, allevatore *m*

fanciful ['fænsɪfəl] *adj* fantasioso, estroso; immaginario

fan·cy ['fænsɪ] *adj* (-cier; -ciest) immaginario; immaginativo; ornamentale; di lusso; fantasioso, estroso || *s* fantasia; (*whim*) grillo, estro; **to take a fancy to** prendere una passione per || *v* (*pret* & *pp* -cied) *tr* immaginare

fan'cy ball' *s* ballo in costume

fan'cy dress' *s* costume *m*

fan'cy foods' *spl* cibi *mpl* di lusso

fan'cy-free' *adj* libero dai lacci dell'amore

fan'cy skat'ing *s* pattinaggio artistico

fan'cy·work' *s* (sew) ricamo ornamentale

fanfare ['fænfer] *s* fanfara

fang [fæŋ] *s* zanna; (*of reptile*) dente velenoso

fan'light' *s* lunetta

fantastic(al) [fæn'tæstɪk(əl)] *adj* fantastico

fanta·sy ['fæntəzi] or ['fæntəsi] *s* (-sies) fantasia

far [fɑr] *adj* distante; **on the far side of** dall'altra parte di || *adv* lontano; **as far as** fino a; **as far as I am concerned** per quanto mi riguardi; **as far as I know** per quanto io sappia; **by far** di gran lunga; **far and near** in lungo e in largo; **far away** molto lontano; **far be it from me** Dio me ne scampi e liberi; **far better** molto meglio; molto migliore; **far different** molto differente; **far from** lontano da; **far from it** tutto al contrario; **far into** fino al fondo di; **far into the night** fino a tarda ora; **far more** molto più; **far off** lontanissimo; **how far** quanto lontano; **how far is it?** a che distanza è da qui?; **in so far as** in quanto; **thus far** sinora; **to go far towards** contribuire molto a

faraway ['fɑrə,we] *adj* distante, lontano; distratto

farce [fɑrs] *s* farsa

farcical ['fɑrsɪkəl] *adj* farsesco

fare [fer] *s* prezzo della corsa; passeggero; (*food*) vitto || *intr* andare, e.g., **how did you fare?** come Le è andata?

Far' East' *s* Estremo Oriente

fare'well' *s* congedo, commiato; **to bid farewell to** or **to take farewell of** prender commiato da || *interj* addio!

far-fetched ['fɑr'fɛtʃt] *adj* peregrino, campato in aria

far-flung ['fɑr'flʌŋ] *adj* ampio; d'ampia distribuzione

farm [fɑrm] *adj* agricolo || *s* fattoria, tenuta || *tr* (*land*) coltivare || *intr* fare l'agricoltore o l'allevatore

farmer ['fɑrmər] *s* agricoltore *m*, contadino

farm' hand' *s* bracciante *m*

farm'house' *s* casa colonica, masseria

farming ['fɑrmɪŋ] *s* agricoltura, coltivazione

farm'yard' *s* aia

far'-off' *adj* lontano

far-reaching ['fɑr'ritʃɪŋ] *adj* di grande portata

far-sighted ['fɑr'saɪtɪd] *adj* lungimirante; perspicace; presbite

farther ['fɑrðər] *adj* più lontano; addizionale || *adv* più lontano, più in là; inoltre; **farther on** più oltre

farthest ['fɑrðɪst] *adj* (il) più lontano; ultimo || *adv* al massimo

farthing ['fɑrðɪŋ] *s* (Brit) quarto di centesimo

Far' West' *s* (U.S.A.) lontano Occidente

fascinate ['fæsɪ,net] *tr* affascinare

fascinating ['fæsɪ,netɪŋ] *adj* incantatore, affascinante

fascism ['fæʃɪzəm] *s* fascismo

fascist ['fæʃɪst] *adj* & *s* fascista *mf*

fashion ['fæʃən] *s* voga, moda; foggia, maniera; alta società; **after a fashion** in certo modo; **in fashion** di moda; **out of fashion** fuori moda; **to go out of fashion** passare di moda || *tr* fare, foggiare

fashionable ['fæʃənəbəl] *adj* elegante, alla moda

fash'ion design'ing *s* alta moda

fash'ion plate' *s* figurino

fash'ion show' *s* sfilata di moda

fast [fæst] or [fɑst] *adj* veloce; (*clock*) che corre, in anticipo; dissoluto; ben legato; (*color*) solido; (*friend*) fedele || *s* digiuno; **to break fast** rompere il digiuno || *adv* rapidamente; forte-mente; (*asleep*) profondamente; **to hold fast** tenersi saldo; **to live fast**

condurre una vita dissoluta || *intr* digiunare, fare vigilia

fast' day' *s* giorno di magro

fasten ['fæsən] or ['fɑsən] *tr* fissare; attaccare; (*a door*) sbarrare; (*a nickname; blows*) affibbiare; (*a dress*) allacciarsi || *intr* attaccarsi

fastener ['fæsənər] or ['fɑsənər] *s* legaccio, laccio; (*snap, clasp*) fermaglio; (*for papers*) fermacarte *m*

fastidious [fæs'tɪdɪ·əs] *adj* schizzinoso; meticoloso

fasting ['fæstɪŋ] or ['fɑstɪŋ] *s* digiuno

fat [fæt] *adj* (**fatter; fattest**) grasso; (*productive*) forte, ricco, pingue; **to get fat** ingrassare || *s* grasso, unto; (*of pork*) sugna

fatal ['fetəl] *adj* fatale

fatalism ['fetə,lɪzəm] *s* fatalismo

fatalist ['fetəlɪst] *s* fatalista *mf*

fatali-ty [fə'tælɪti] *s* (**-ties**) (*in an accident*) morte *f*; accidente *m* mortale; fatalità *f*

fate [fet] *s* fato; **the Fates** le Parche || *tr* predestinare

fated ['fetɪd] *adj* destinato

fateful ['fetfəl] *adj* fatidico, fatale

fat'head' *s* (coll) zuccone *m*

father ['fɑðər] *s* padre *m*; (*male ancestor*) antenato || *tr* procreare; creare; assumere la paternità di

fatherhood ['fɑðər,hʊd] *s* paternità *f*

fa'ther-in-law' *s* (**fathers-in-law**) suocero

fa'ther-land' *s* patria

fatherless ['fɑðərlɪs] *adj* orfano di padre; senza padre

fatherly ['fɑðərli] *adj* paterno

Fa'ther's Day' *s* festa del papà

Fa'ther Time' *s* il Tempo

fathom ['fæðəm] *s* braccio || *tr* sondare

fathomless ['fæðəmlɪs] *adj* senza fondo; imponderabile

fatigue [fə'tig] *s* fatica, strapazzo; (mil) comandata || *tr* stancare, affaticare

fatigue' clothes' *spl* (mil) tenuta di servizio, tenuta di fatica

fatten ['fætən] *tr* & *intr* ingrassare

fat-ty ['fæti] *adj* (**-tier; -tiest**) grasso; (pathol) adiposo || *s* (**-ties**) (coll) tombolo

fatuous ['fætʃ·ʊ·əs] *adj* fatuo

faucet ['fɔsɪt] *s* rubinetto

fault [fɔlt] *s* (*misdeed, blame*) colpa; (*defect*) difetto, magagna; (geol) faglia; (sports) fallo; **it's your fault** è colpa Sua; **to a fault** all'eccesso; **to find fault with** trovare a ridire sul conto di

fault'find'er *s* ipercritico, criticone *m*

fault'find'ing *adj* criticone || *s* ipercritica

faultless ['fɔltlɪs] *adj* perfetto, inappuntabile

fault-y ['fɔlti] *adj* (**-ier; -iest**) manchevole, difettuoso

faun [fɔn] *s* fauno

fauna ['fɔnə] *s* fauna

favor ['fevər] *s* favore *m*; (*letter*) pregiata; **do me the favor to** mi faccia il piacere di; **by your favor** col Suo permesso; **favors** regali *mpl* di festa; **to be in favor with** essere nelle grazie di; **to be out of favor** cadere in disgrazia || *tr* favorire; (coll) assomigliare (with *dat*)

favorable ['fevərəbəl] *adj* favorevole

favorite ['fevərɪt] *adj & s* favorito

favoritism ['fevərɪ,tɪzəm] *s* favoritismo

fawn [fɔn] *s* cerbiatto || *intr*—**to fawn on** adulare, strusciarsi a

faze [fez] *tr* (coll) perturbare

fear [fɪr] *s* paura; **for fear of** per paura di; **for fear that** per paura che; **no fear** non c'è pericolo; **to be in fear of** aver timore di || *tr & intr* temere

fearful ['fɪrfəl] *adj* pauroso, timorato; (coll) spaventoso

fearless ['fɪrlɪs] *adj* impavido

feasible ['fizɪbəl] *adj* fattibile, possibile

feast [fist] *s* festa; (*sumptuous meal*) festino, banchetto || *tr* intrattenere || *intr* banchettare; **to feast on** rallegrarsi alla vista di

feat [fit] *s* fatto, prodezza

feather ['feðər] *s* penna; (*soft and fluffy structure covering bird*) piuma; (*type*) qualità *f*, conio; (*tuft*) pennacchio; **in fine feather** di buon umore; in buona salute || *tr* impennare; coprire di piume; (naut) spalare; (aer) bandierare; **to feather one's nest** arricchirsi

feath'er bed' *s* letto di piume

feath'er·bed'ding *s* impiego di mano d'opera non necessaria richiesto da un sindacato operaio

feath'er·brain' *s* cervello di gallina

feath'er·edge' *s* (*of board*) augnatura; (*of sharpened tool*) filo morto

feath'er·weight' *s* peso piuma

feathery ['feðəri] *adj* piumato; leggero

feature ['fitʃər] *s* fattezza; caratteristica; (journ) articolo principale; (mov) attrazione; **features** fattezze *fpl* || *tr* caratterizzare; mettere in evidenza; (coll) immaginare

fea'ture film' *s* lungometraggio

fea'ture sto'ry *s* articolo di spalla

February ['febru,ɛri] *s* febbraio

feces ['fisɪz] *spl feci fpl*

feckless ['fɛklɪs] *adj* debole; inetto

federal ['fedərəl] *adj* federale || *s* federalista *mf*

federate ['fedə,ret] *adj* federato || *tr* federare || *intr* federarsi

federation [,fedə're/ən] *s* federazione

federative ['fedə,retɪv] *or* ['fedərətɪv] *adj* federativo

fedora [fɪ'dorə] *s* cappello floscio di feltro

fed' up' [fed] *adj* stanco e stufo; **to be fed up with** averne fin sopra gli occhi di

fee [fi] *s* onorario; (*charge allowed by law*) diritto; (*tip*) mancia; (*for tuition*) tassa; (*for admission*) ingresso || *tr* pagare

feeble ['fibəl] *adj* debole, fievole

feeble-minded ['fibəl'maɪndɪd] *adj* rimbecillito; debole, vacillante

feed [fid] *s* mangime *m*; (coll) mangiata; (mach) dispositivo d'alimentazione || *v* (*pret & pp* fed [fed]) *tr* nutrire; (*a machine*) alimentare; (*cattle*) pascere; (theat) imbeccare || *intr* mangiare; **to feed upon** nutrirsi di

feed'back' *s* (*of a computer*) ritorno d'informazioni; (electron) reazione

feed' bag' *s* musetta

feed' pump' *s* pompa di alimentazione

feed' trough' *s* (*for cattle*) vasca; (*for hogs*) trogolo

feed' wire' *s* cavo di alimentazione

feel [fil] *s* sensazione; (touch) tocco; (*vague mental impression*) senso || *v* (*pret & pp* felt [felt]) *tr* sentire; (*e.g., with the hands*) palpare, toccare; (*s.o.'s pulse*) tastare || *intr* (*sick, tired, etc.*) sentirsi; **to feel bad** sentirsi male; (*to be unhappy*) essere spiacente; **to feel cheap** vergognarsi; **to feel comfortable** sentirsi a proprio agio; **to feel for** cercare di toccare; avere compassione per; **to feel like** aver voglia di; **to feel safe** sentirsi al sicuro; **to feel sorry** essere spiacente; pentirsi; **to feel sorry for** aver compassione di; pentirsi di

feeler ['filər] *s* (*hint*) sondaggio; **feelers** (*of insect*) antenne *fpl*; (*of mollusk*) tentacoli *mpl*; **to put out feelers** (fig) tastare il terreno

feeling ['filɪŋ] *s* (*with senses*) senso; (*impression, emotion*) sentimento, sensazione; opinione

feign [fen] *tr* fingere; inventare; imitare || *intr* far finta; **to feign to be** fingersi

feint [fent] *s* finta || *intr* fare una finta

feldspar ['feld,spar] *s* feldspato

felicitate [fə'lɪsɪ,tet] *tr* felicitarsi con

felicitous [fə'lɪsɪtəs] *adj* felice, indovinato; eloquente

fell [fel] *adj* crudele, mortale || *tr* (*trees*) abbattere

felloe ['felo] *s* cerchione *m*; (*part of the rim*) gavello

fellow ['felo] *s* compagno; collega *m*; (*of a society*) membro, socio; (*holder of fellowship*) borsista *mf*; (coll) tipo, tizio; (coll) innamorato; **good fellow** buon diavolo; galantuomo

fel'low cit'izen *s* concittadino

fel'low coun'try·man *s* (-men) concittadino

fel'low crea'ture *s* prossimo

fel'low-man' *s* (-men') prossimo

fel'low mem'ber *s* consocio

fellowship ['felo,ʃɪp] *s* compagnia; (*for study*) borsa di studio

fel'low trav'eler *s* simpatizzante *mf*; criptocomunista *mf*; compagno di viaggio

felon ['felən] *s* criminale *mf*; (pathol) patereccio, giradito

felo·ny ['feləni] *s* (-nies) delitto doloso

felt [felt] *s* feltro

felt' board' *s* lavagna di panno

felt'-tip pen' *s* pennarello

female ['fimel] *adj* (*sex*) femminile;

(animal, plant, piece of a device) femmina || s femmina

feminine ['feminin] *adj* & *s* femminile *m*

feminism ['femi,nizəm] *s* femminismo

fence [fens] *s* steccato, staccionata; *(for stolen goods)* ricettatore *m*; (carp) squadra di guida; (sports) scherma; **on the fence** (coll) indeciso || *tr* recingere || *intr* tirare di scherma

fencing ['fensiŋ] *s* scherma; (fig) schermaglia

fenc'ing mask' *s* visiera

fend [fend] *tr*—**to fend off** parare || *intr*—**to fend for oneself** (coll) badare a sé stesso

fender ['fendər] *s* *(of trolley car)* salvagente *m*; *(of fireplace)* parafuoco; (aut) parafango; (naut) parabordo

fennel ['fenəl] *s* finocchio

ferment ['fʌrment] *s* fermento || [fər'ment] *tr* & *intr* fermentare

fern [fʌrn] *s* felce *f*

ferocious [fə'roʃəs] *adj* feroce

ferocity [fə'rɑsiti] *s* ferocia

ferret ['ferit] *s* furetto || *tr*—**to ferret out** scovare || *intr* indagare

Fer'ris wheel' ['feris] *s* ruota (del parco dei divertimenti)

fer·ry ['feri] *s* (-ries) traghetto; nave *f* traghetto || *v* (pret & pp -ried) *tr* traghettare || *intr* attraversare

fer'ry·boat' *s* nave *f* traghetto, ferryboat *m*

fertile ['fʌrtil] *adj* fertile

fertilize ['fʌrti,laiz] *tr* fertilizzare; *(to impregnate)* fecondare

fertilizer ['fʌrti,laizər] *s* fertilizzante *m*; *(e.g., of flowers)* fecondatore *m*

fervent ['fʌrvənt] *adj* fervente, fervido

fervid ['fʌrvid] *adj* fervido

fervor ['fʌrvər] *s* fervore *m*

fester ['festər] *s* ulcera, piaga || *tr* corrompere || *intr* suppurare; (fig) corrompersi

festival ['festivəl] *adj* festivo || *s* festa; *(of music)* festival *m*

festive ['festiv] *adj* festivo

festivi·ty [fes'tiviti] *s* (-ties) festività *f*

festoon [fes'tun] *s* festone *m* || *tr* ornare di festoni

fetch [fetʃ] *tr* andare a prendere; *(a price)* fruttare, vendersi per

fetching ['fetʃiŋ] *adj* (coll) cattivante, attraente

fete [fet] *s* festa || *tr* festeggiare

fetid ['fetid] *or* ['fitid] *adj* fetido

fetish ['fitiʃ] *or* ['fetiʃ] *s* feticcio

fetlock ['fetlak] *s* nocca; *(tuft of hair)* barbetta

fetter ['fetər] *s* ceppo, catena || *tr* mettere ai ceppi, incatenare

fettle ['fetəl] *s* stato, condizione; **in fine fettle** in buone condizioni

fetus ['fitəs] *s* feto

feud [fjud] *s* antagonismo; odio ereditario || *intr* essere in lotta

feudal ['fjudəl] *adj* feudale

feudalism ['fjudə,lizəm] *s* feudalismo

fever ['fivər] *s* febbre *f*

feverish ['fivəriʃ] *adj* febbrile

few [fju] *adj* & *pron* pochi; **a few** alcuni; **quite a few** molti

fiancé [,fi·ɑn'se] *s* fidanzato

fiancée [,fi·ɑn'se] *s* fidanzata

fias·co [fi'æsko] *s* (-cos *or* -coes) fiasco

fib [fib] *s* menzogna, frottola || *v* (pret & pp **fibbed;** ger **fibbing**) *intr* raccontar frottole

fiber ['faibər] *s* fibra; (fig) tempra

fi'ber·glass' *s* vetroresina

fibrous ['faibrəs] *adj* fibroso

fickle ['fikəl] *adj* volubile, incostante, mobile

fiction ['fikʃən] *s* *(invention)* finzione; *(branch of literature)* novellistica

fictional ['fikʃənəl] *adj* immaginario

fictionalize ['fikʃənə,laiz] *tr* romanzare

fictitious [fik'tiʃəs] *adj* fittizio

fiddle ['fidəl] *s* violino; **fit as a fiddle** in perfetta salute || *tr* (coll) suonare sul violino; **to fiddle away** (coll) sprecare || *intr* (coll) suonare il violino; **to fiddle with** (coll) giocherellare con

fiddler ['fidlər] *s* (coll) violinista *mf*

fiddling ['fidliŋ] *adj* triviale, futile, insignificante

fideli·ty [fai'deliti] *or* [fi'deliti] *s* (-ties) fedeltà *f*

fidget ['fidʒit] *intr* agitarsi; **to fidget with** giocherellare con

fidgety ['fidʒiti] *adj* irrequieto

fiduciar·y [fi'djuʃi,eri] *or* [fi'duʃi,eri] *adj* fiduciario || *s* (-ies) fiduciario

fie [fai] *interj* vergogna!

fief [fif] *s* feudo

field [fild] *adj* (mil) da campagna || *s* campo; (sports) terreno; (min) giacimento; *(of motor or dynamo)* (elec) induttore *m*; (phys) campo

fielder ['fildər] *s* *(outfielder)* giocatore *m* del campo esterno

field' glass'es *spl* binocolo

field' hock'ey *s* hockey *m* su prato

field' mag'net *s* induttore *m*, calamita induttrice

field' mar'shal *s* (mil) maresciallo di campo

field' mouse' *s* topo di campagna

field'piece' *s* pezzo da campagna

fiend [find] *s* diavolo; (coll) addetto, tifoso

fiendish ['findiʃ] *adj* diabolico

fierce [firs] *adj* fiero, feroce; *(wind)* furioso; (coll) maledetto

fierceness ['firsnis] *s* ferocia

fier·y ['fairi] *or* ['fai·əri] *adj* (-ier, -iest) ardente, focoso

fife [faif] *s* piffero

fifteen ['fif'tin] *adj*, *s* & *pron* quindici *m*

fifteenth ['fif'tinθ] *adj*, *s* & *pron* quindicesimo || *s* *(in dates)* quindici *m*

fifth [fifθ] *adj*, *s* & *pron* quinto || *s* *(in dates)* cinque *m*

fifth' col'umn *s* quinta colonna

fiftieth ['fifti·iθ] *adj*, *s* & *pron* cinquantesimo

fif·ty ['fifti] *adj* & *pron* cinquanta || *s* (-ties) cinquanta *m*; **the fifties** gli anni cinquanta

fif'ty-fif'ty adv—**to go fifty-fifty** fare a metà

fig [fɪg] s fico

fight [faɪt] s lotta; baruffa; combattimento; spirito combattivo; (sports) incontro; **to pick a fight with** attaccar briga con ‖ v (pret & pp **fought** [fɔt]) tr lottare con; combattere contro; opporsi a ‖ intr lottare; combattere; **to fight shy of** cercar di evitare

fighter [ˈfaɪtər] s lottatore m; (warrior) combattente m; (aer) caccia m

fig' leaf' s foglia di fico

figment [ˈfɪgmənt] s finzione

figurative [ˈfɪgjərətɪv] adj (fa) figurativo; (rhet) figurato

figure [ˈfɪgjər] s figura; numero; prezzo; **to be good at figures** far bene di conto; **to cut a figure** fare una buona figura; **to keep one's figure** conservare la linea ‖ tr figurare; immaginare; raffigurare; supporre, calcolare; **to figure out** calcolare; decifrare ‖ intr apparire; **to figure on** (coll) contare su

fig'ure-head' s uomo di paglia, prestanome m; (naut) polena

fig'ure of speech' s figura retorica

fig'ure skat'ing s pattinaggio artistico

figurine [ˌfɪgjəˈrin] s figurina

filament [ˈfɪləmənt] s filamento

filbert [ˈfɪlbərt] s (tree) nocciolo, avellano; (nut) nocciola, avellana

filch [fɪltʃ] tr rubacchiare

file [faɪl] s (row) fila; (tool) lima; (folder) filza; (room) archivio; (of cards) schedario ‖ tr mettere in fila; limare; archiviare, schedare; (journ) trasmettere ‖ intr sfilare; **to file for** fare domanda di

file' clerk' s schedarista mf

filet [fɪˈle] or [ˈfɪle] s filetto ‖ tr tagliare in filetti

filial [ˈfɪlɪ·əl] or [ˈfɪljəl] adj filiale

filiation [ˌfɪlɪˈeʃən] s filiazione

filibuster [ˈfɪlɪˌbʌstər] s (tactics) ostruzionismo; (speech) discorso ostruzionista; (person making such a speech) ostruzionista mf; (buccaneer) filibustiere m ‖ tr fare ostruzionismo contro ‖ intr fare dell'ostruzionismo

filigree [ˈfɪlɪˌgri] adj filigranato ‖ s filigrana ‖ tr lavorare in filigrana

filing [ˈfaɪlɪŋ] s (of documents) schedatura; limatura; **filings** limatura

fil'ing cab'inet s schedario

fil'ing card' s cartellino, scheda

fill [fɪl] s sazietà f; (place filled with earth) terrapieno; **to have or get one's fill** mangiare a sazietà ‖ tr riempire; (an order) eseguire; (a hole) otturare; (a tooth) piombare; (a tire) gonfiare; (a place) occupare; (with sand) interrare; **to fill out** (a form) riempire; **to fill up** (aut) fare il pieno di ‖ intr riempirsi; **to fill in** prendere il posto; **to fill up** riempirsi

filler [ˈfɪlər] s ripieno; (person) riempitore m; (painting) mestica; (journ) articolo riempitivo

fillet [ˈfɪlɪt] s nastro, fascia; (for hair) nastro; (archit) listello ‖ tr filettare

‖ [ˈfɪle] or [ˈfɪlɪt] s (of meat or fish) filetto ‖ tr tagliare a filetti

filling [ˈfɪlɪŋ] s (of a tooth) impiombatura; (of turkey) ripieno

fill'ing sta'tion s stazione di rifornimento

fillip [ˈfɪlɪp] s stimolo; colpetto col dito ‖ tr dare un colpetto col dito a; (fig) stimulare

fil·ly [ˈfɪli] s (-lies) puledra

film [fɪlm] s pellicola; (mov, phot) pellicola, film m ‖ tr filmare

film' li'brary s cineteca, filmoteca

film'strip' s filmina

film·y [ˈfɪlmi] adj (-ier; -iest) sottile, delicato; (look) annebbiato

filter [ˈfɪltər] s filtro ‖ tr & intr filtrare

filtering [ˈfɪltərɪŋ] s filtrazione

fil'ter pa'per s carta da filtro

fil'ter tip' s filtro, bocchino filtro

filth [fɪlθ] s sporco, sporcizia

filth·y [ˈfɪlθi] adj (-ier; -iest) sporco, sudicio

filth'y lu'cre [ˈlukər] s il vile metallo

filtrate [ˈfɪltret] s liquido filtrato ‖ tr & intr filtrare

fin [fɪn] s pinna; (slang) biglietto da cinque dollari

final [ˈfaɪnəl] adj finale; (last in a series) ultimo; definitivo, insindacabile ‖ s esame m finale; **finals** (sports) finale f

finale [fɪˈnɑli] s (mus) finale m

finalist [ˈfaɪnəlɪst] s finalista mf

finally [ˈfaɪnəli] adv finalmente

finance [fɪˈnæns] or [ˈfaɪnæns] s finanza; **finances** finanze fpl ‖ tr finanziare

financial [fɪˈnænʃəl] or [faɪˈnænʃəl] adj finanziario

financier [ˌfɪnənˈsɪr] or [ˌfaɪnənˈsɪr] s finanziere m

financing [fɪˈnænsɪŋ] or [ˈfaɪnænsɪŋ] s finanziamento

finch [fɪntʃ] s fringuello

find [faɪnd] s trovata ‖ v (pret & pp **found** [faʊnd]) tr trovare; rinvenire; (s.o. innocent or guilty) dichiarare; **to find out** venire a sapere ‖ intr (law) sentenziare; **to find out about** informarsi su

finder [ˈfaɪndər] s (phot) mirino; (astr) cannocchiale cercatore

finding [ˈfaɪndɪŋ] s scoperta; (law) sentenza

fine [faɪn] adj buono; bello; fino, fine ‖ s multa ‖ adv (coll) benissimo; **to feel fine** (coll) sentirsi benissimo ‖ tr multare

fine' arts' spl belle arti

fineness [ˈfaɪnnɪs] s finezza; (of metal) titolo

fine' print' s testo in caratteri minuti

finer·y [ˈfaɪnəri] s (-ies) ornamenti mpl, fronzoli mpl; abito vistoso

fine-spun [ˈfaɪnˌspʌn] adj sottile

finesse [fɪˈnes] s finezza; (bridge) impasse f ‖ tr fare l'impasse a ‖ intr fare l'impasse

fine'-tooth comb' s pettine fitto; **to go over with a fine-tooth comb** esaminare minuziosamente

finger [ˈfɪŋgər] s dito; **to have a finger in the pie** avere le mani in pasta; **to put one's finger on the spot** mettere il dito nella piaga; **to slip between the fingers** sfuggire di tra le dita; **to snap one's fingers at** infischiarsi di; **to twist around one's little finger** fare ciò che si vuole di || tr toccare con le dita; (to pilfer) rubacchiare; (slang) mostrare a dito

fin'ger board' s (mus) tastiera

fin'ger bowl' s sciacquadita m

fingering [ˈfɪŋgərɪŋ] s palpeggiamento; (mus) diteggiatura

fin'ger mark' s ditata

fin'ger·nail' s unghia

fin'ger·print' s impronta digitale || tr prendere le impronte digitali di

fin'ger·tip' s polpastrello; **to have at one's fingertips** avere sulla punta delle dita, sapere a menadito

finical [ˈfɪnɪkəl] or **finicky** [ˈfɪnɪki] adj pignolo, schizzinoso

finish [ˈfɪnɪʃ] s fine f; finitura; (sports) finale m || tr finire; **to finish off** distruggere || intr finire; **to finish** + ger finire di + inf; **to finish by** + ger finire per + inf

fin'ishing school' s scuola di perfezionamento per signorine

fin'ishing touch' s ultimo tocco

finite [ˈfaɪnaɪt] adj finito

Finland [ˈfɪnlənd] s la Finlandia

Finlander [ˈfɪnləndər] s finlandese mf

Finn [fɪn] s (member of a Finnish-speaking group of people) finnico; (native or inhabitant of Finland) finlandese mf

Finnic [ˈfɪnɪk] adj & s finnico

Finnish [ˈfɪnɪʃ] adj finlandese || s (language) finlandese m

fir [fʌr] s abete m

fire [faɪr] s fuoco; (destructive burning) incendio; **to be on fire** ardere; **to be under enemy fire** essere sotto tiro nemico; **to catch fire** infiammarsi; **to hang fire** essere in sospeso; **to open fire** aprire il fuoco; **to set on fire, to set fire to** dar fuoco a; **under fire** sotto fuoco nemico; accusato || tr accendere; (an oven) scaldare; (bricks) cuocere; (a weapon) sparare; (the imagination) riscaldare; (an employee) (coll) licenziare || intr accendersi; **to fire on** far fuoco su; **to fire up** attivare una caldaia

fire' alarm' s avvisatore m d'incendio

fire'arm' s arma da fuoco

fire'ball' s palla da cannone esplosiva; (lightning) lampo a forma di globo infocato; meteorite m a forma di globo infocato; globo infocato

fire'boat' s lancia dei pompieri

fire'box' s (of a boiler) fornello; (to give alarm) stazione d'allarme

fire'brand' s tizzone m; (fig) fiaccola della discordia

fire'brick' s mattone refrattario

fire' brigade' s corpo di pompieri volontari

fire'bug' s (coll) incendiario

fire' com'pany s corpo dei pompieri;

compagnia d'assicurazioni contro gli incendi

fire'crack'er s mortaretto

fire'damp' s grisou m

fire' depart'ment s corpo dei pompieri

fire'dog' s alare m

fire' drill' s esercitazione in caso d'incendio

fire' en'gine s autopompa

fire' escape' s scala di sicurezza

fire' extin'guisher s estintore m

fire'fly' s (-flies) lucciola

fire'guard' s parafuoco

fire' hose' s manichetta

fire'house' s caserma dei pompieri

fire' hy'drant s bocca d'incendi

fire' insur'ance s assicurazione contro gli incendi

fire' i'rons spl arnesi mpl del camino

fire'man s (-men) (man who extinguishes fires) pompiere m, vigile m del fuoco; (stoker) fochista m

fire'place' s camino

fire'plug' s bocca da incendio, idrante m

fire'proof' adj incombustibile || tr rendere incombustibile

fire' sale' s vendita di merce avariata dal fuoco

fire' screen' s parafuoco

fire' ship' s brulotto

fire'side' s focolare m

fire'trap' s edificio senza mezzi adeguati per combattere incendi

fire' wall' s paratia antincendio

fire'wa'ter s (coll) acquavite f

fire'wood' s legna

fire'works' spl fuochi mpl artificiali

firing [ˈfaɪrɪŋ] s (of furnace) alimentazione; (of bricks) cottura; (of a gun) sparo; (of soldiers) tiro; (of an internal-combustion engine) accensione; (of an employee) (coll) licenziamento

fir'ing line' s linea del fuoco

fir'ing or'der s (aut) ordine m d'accensione

fir'ing pin' s percussore m

fir'ing squad' s (for saluting at a burial) plotone m d'onore; (for executing) plotone m d'esecuzione

firm [fʌrm] adj forte, fermo || s ditta, compagnia

firmament [ˈfʌrməmənt] s firmamento

firm' name' s ragione f sociale

firmness [ˈfʌrmnɪs] s fermezza

first [fʌrst] adj primo || s primo; (aut) prima; (mus) voce f principale; **at first** sulle prime; **from the first** da bel principio || adv prima; **first of all** per prima cosa

first' aid' s pronto soccorso

first'-aid' kit' s cassetta farmaceutica d'urgenza

first'-aid' sta'tion s posto di pronto soccorso

first'-born' adj & s primogenito

first'-class' adj di prim'ordine, sopraffino || adv in prima classe

first' cous'in s cugino primo

first'-day cov'er s busta primo giorno

first' draft' s brutta copia

first' fin'ger s dito indice
first' floor' s pianoterra m
first' fruits' spl primizie fpl
first' lieuten'ant s tenente m
firstly ['fʌrstlɪ] adv in primo luogo
first' mate' s (naut) primo ufficiale, comandante m in seconda, secondo
first' name' s nome m di battesimo
first' night' s (theat) prima
first' of'ficer s (naut) primo ufficiale, comandante m in seconda, secondo
first'-rate' adj di prima forza; eccellente || adv (coll) benissimo
first'-run' adj di prima visione
fiscal ['fɪskəl] adj (pertaining to public treasury) fiscale; finanziario || s avvocato fiscale
fis'cal year' s esercizio finanziario
fish [fɪʃ] s pesce m; to be like a fish out of water essere come un pesce fuor d'acqua; to be neither fish nor fowl non essere né carne né pesce; to drink like a fish bere come una spugna || tr pescare || intr pescare; to fish for compliments cercare di farsi fare dei complimenti; to go fishing andare alla pesca; to take fishing portare con sé alla pesca
fish'bone' s lisca, spina di pesce
fish'bowl' s vaschetta per i pesci rossi
fisher ['fɪʃər] s pescatore m; (zool) martora canadese
fish'er·man s (-men) pescatore m; (boat) peschereccio
fisher·y ['fɪʃərɪ] s (-ies) (activity) pesca; (business) pescheria; (grounds) riserva di pesca, luogo dove si pesca
fish' glue' s colla di pesce
fish'hook' s amo
fishing ['fɪʃɪŋ] adj da pesca || s pesca
fish'ing reel' s mulinello
fish'ing rod' s canna da pesca
fish'ing tack'le s attrezzatura da pesca
fish'line' s lenza
fish' mar'ket s pescheria
fish'pool' s peschiera
fish' spear' s fiocina
fish' sto'ry s (coll) fandonia; to tell fish stories spararle grosse
fish'tail' s (aut) imbardata (aer) spedalata || intr (aut) imbardare; (aer) compiere una spedalata
fish'wife' s (-wives') pescivendola; (foul-mouthed woman) ciana
fish'worm' s lombrico
fish·y ['fɪʃi] adj (-ier; -iest) che sa di pesce; (coll) dubbioso, inverosimile
fission ['fɪʃən] s (biol) scissione; (phys) fissione
fissionable ['fɪʃənəbəl] adj fissionabile
fissure ['fɪʃər] s fenditura; (in rock) crepaccio
fist [fɪst] s pugno; (typ) indice m; to shake one's fist at mostrare i pugni a
fist'fight' s scontro a pugni
fist'ful s pugno, manciata
fisticuff ['fɪstɪˌkʌf] s pugno; fisticuffs scontro a pugni
fit [fɪt] adj (fitter; fittest) indicato, idoneo, adatto; in buona salute; fit to be tied (coll) infuriato, arrabbia-

tissimo; fit to eat mangiabile; to feel fit sentirsi in buona salute; to see fit giudicare conveniente || s equipaggiamento; (of a suit) taglio; (of one piece with another) incastro; (of coughing) accesso; (of anger) attacco; by fits and starts a pezzi e a bocconi || v (pret & pp fitted; ger fitting) tr adattare; quadrare a; andar bene a; equipaggiare; preparare; servire a; esser d'accordo con; to fit out or up attrezzare, equipaggiare || intr stare; incastrare; (said of clothes) cascare; entrare; to fit in entrarci
fitful ['fɪtfəl] adj capriccioso; incostante, irregolare
fitness ['fɪtnɪs] s convenienza; idoneità f; buona salute
fitter ['fɪtər] s aggiustatore m; (of machinery) montatore m; (of clothing) sarto che mette in prova
fitting ['fɪtɪŋ] adj appropriato, adatto, conveniente || s adattamento; (of a garment) prova; tubo adattabile; (carp) incastro; fittings accessori mpl; utensili mpl; (iron trimmings) ferramenta fpl
five [faɪv] adj & pron cinque || s cinque m; five o'clock le cinque
five' hun'dred adj, s & pron cinquecento
five'-year plan' s piano quinquennale
fix [fɪks] s—in a tight fix (coll) nei pasticci; to be in a fix (coll) star fresco, essere nei guai || tr riparare; fissare; (a meal) preparare; (a bayonet) inastare; (attention) attrarre, fermare; (hair) mettere a posto; (coll) arrangiare || intr fissarsi, stabilirsi; to fix on scegliere
fixed [fɪkst] adj fisso; (time) improrogabile; (coll) arrangiato
fixing ['fɪksɪŋ] adj fissativo || s (fastening) attacco; (phot) fissaggio; with all the fixings (coll) con tutti i contorni
fix'ing bath' s bagno di fissaggio
fixture ['fɪkstʃər] s infisso; accessorio; (of a lamp) guarnizione; fixtures (e.g., of a store) suppellettili fpl
fizz [fɪz] s effervescenza; gazosa; (Brit) spumante m || intr frizzare
fizzle ['fɪzəl] s (coll) fiasco || intr crepitare; (coll) fare fiasco
flabbergast ['flæbər.gæst] tr (coll) sbalordire, lasciare stupefatto
flab·by ['flæbɪ] adj (-bier; -biest) floscio, flaccido; cascante
flag [flæg] s bandiera || v (pret & pp flagged; ger flagging) tr imbandierare; segnalare; (rr) far fermare || intr ammosciarsi, afflosciarsi
flageolet [.flædʒəˈlet] s flautino
flag'man s (-men) (rr) manovratore m
flag' of truce' s bandiera parlamentaria
flag'pole' s pennone m
flagrant ['flegrənt] adj flagrante; scandaloso
flag'ship' s nave ammiraglia
flag'staff' s pennone m
flag' sta'tion s (rr) stazione facoltativa
flag'stone' s lastra di pietra

flag′ stop′ s (rr) fermata facoltativa

flail [flel] s correggiato ‖ tr battere col correggiato; battere

flair [fler] s fiuto, istinto

flak [flæk] s fuoco antiaereo

flake [flek] s falda; (of snow) fiocco, falda; (of cereal) fiocco; ‖ tr sfaldare; (fish) scagliare ‖ intr sfaldarsi

flak·y ['fleki] adj (-ier; -iest) a falde, faldoso

flamboyant [flæm′bɔɪ·ənt] adj sgargiante; (archit) fiammeggiante

flame [flem] s fiamma ‖ tr & intr fiammeggiare

flamethrower ['flem θro·ər] s lanciafiamme m

flaming ['flemɪŋ] adj fiammeggiante; appassionato; (culin) alla fiamma

flamin·go [flə′mɪŋgo] s (-gos or -goes) fenicottero, fiammingo

flammable ['flæməbəl] adj infiammabile

Flanders ['flændərz] s le Fiandre

flange [flændʒ] s (e.g., on a pipe) flangia; (on I beam) bordo; (of a wheel) cerchione m

flank [flæŋk] s fianco ‖ tr fiancheggiare

flannel ['flænəl] s flanella

flap [flæp] s (in clothing) falda; (of hat) tesa; (of book) risvolto; (of pocket) patta; (of shoe) linguetta; (blow) colpo; (of a table) pannello; (of the counter in a store) ribalta; (of wings) alata ‖ v (pret & pp flapped; ger flapping) tr battere, sbattere; (to move violently) sbatacchiare ‖ intr penzolare

flare [fler] s vampa; scintillio; (of a dress) svasatura; (mil) fuoco di segnalazione; **flares** (trousers) calzoni mpl a zampe d′elefante ‖ tr svasare ‖ intr scintillare; (said of a garment) scampanare; **to flare up** divampare; (said of an illness) aggravarsi, infiammarsi

flare′-up′ s vampa, fiammata; (of an illness) recrudescenza; scoppio d′ira, accesso di collera

flash [flæʃ] s (of light) sprazzo; (of lightning) lampo, baleno; (of hope) raggio; (of joy) accesso; (journ, phot) flash m; (fig) lampo; **flash in the pan** fuoco di paglia ‖ tr (powder) accendere; (a sword) brandire; (journ) diffondere; (e.g., money) (coll) ostentare ‖ intr lampeggiare, balenare, folgorare; **to flash by** passare come un lampo

flash′back′ s flashback m

flash′ bulb′ s lampada lampo

flash′ cube′ s cuboflash m

flash′ flood′ s inondazione torrenziale

flashing ['flæʃɪŋ] s metallo per coprire la conversa; commessura metallica fra tetto e comignolo

flash′light′ s lampadina tascabile; (of a lighthouse) luce f intermittente; (phot) fotolampo, lampeggiatore m

flash′light bulb′ s lampada per fotolampo

flash·y ['flæʃi] adj (-ier; -iest) sgargiante, chiassoso, vistoso

flask [flæsk] or [flɑsk] s fiasco, fiasca; (for laboratory use) beuta

flat [flæt] adj (flatter; flattest) piano; (nose) camuso; (boat) a fondo piatto; (surface) liscio; (beer) svanito; (tire) sgonfio; (denial) deciso; (mus) bemolle; (coll) al verde ‖ s (flat surface) piatto; (flat area) piano; (apartment) appartamento; (mus) bemolle m; (coll) gomma a terra ‖ adv—**to fall flat** fallire

flat′boat′ s chiatta

flat′car′ s (rr) pianale m

flat-footed ['flæt′fʊtɪd] adj dai piedi piatti; (coll) inflessibile

flat′head′ s (of a bolt) testa piatta; (coll) testa di legno

flat′i′ron s ferro da stiro

flat′ race′ s corsa piana

flatten ['flætən] tr schiacciare; distendere ‖ intr appiattirsi; indebolirsi; **to flatten out** appiattirsi; (aer) porsi in linea orizzontale di volo

flatter ['flætər] tr adulare, lusingare; (to make seem more attractive) favorire ‖ intr adulare

flatterer ['flætərər] s adulatore m, lusingatore m

flattering ['flætərɪŋ] adj lusinghiero

flatter·y ['flætəri] s (-ies) lusinga

flat′ tire′ s gomma a terra

flat′top′ s portaerei f

flatulence ['flætʃələns] s flatulenza

flat′ware′ s argenteria, vasellame m

flaunt [flɔnt] or [flɑnt] tr sfoggiare, ostentare

flautist ['flɔtɪst] s flautista mf

flavor ['flevər] s sapore m, gusto; condimento ‖ tr insaporire; condire; aromatizzare, profumare

flavoring ['flevərɪŋ] s condimento, sapore m

flaw [flɔ] s difetto, menda, fallo; (crack) incrinatura

flawless ['flɔlɪs] adj senza difetti

flax [flæks] s lino

flaxen ['flæksən] adj di lino; biondo

flax′seed′ s linosa

flay [fle] tr scorticare, scoiare

flea [fli] s pulce f

flea′bite′ s morso di pulce; (fig) inezia, seccatura secondaria

fleck [flek] s macchia; efelide f ‖ tr chiazzare, macchiare

fledgling ['fledʒlɪŋ] s uccellino appena nato; (fig) pivello

flee [fli] v (pret & pp fled [fled]) tr & intr fuggire, sfuggire

fleece [flis] s vello; (e.g., of clouds) bioccolo ‖ tr tosare; (fig) pelare

fleec·y ['flisi] adj (-ier; -iest) lanoso; (sky) a pecorelle

fleet [flit] adj rapido ‖ s flotta

fleeting ['flitɪŋ] adj fugace, passeggero

Fleming ['flemɪŋ] s fiammingo

Flemish ['flemɪʃ] adj & s fiammingo

flesh [fleʃ] s carne f; (of fruit) polpa; **in the flesh** in carne ed ossa; **to lose flesh** dimagrire; **to put on flesh** ingrassare

flesh′ and blood′ s (relatives) carne f della carne, i miei, i suoi, etc.; il corpo umano

flesh-colored ['flɛʃ ,kʌlərd] *adj* color carne

fleshiness ['flɛʃɪnɪs] *s* carnosità *f*

fleshless ['flɛʃlɪs] *adj* scarno

flesh'pot' *s* piatto di carne; locale *m* di dissoluzione; **fleshpots** vita dissoluta

flesh' wound' *s* ferita superficiale

flesh·y ['flɛʃi] *adj* (**-ier; -iest**) carnoso; polposo

flex [flɛks] *tr* piegare ‖ *intr* piegarsi

flexible ['flɛksɪbəl] *adj* flessibile; (*joint*) a snodo

flick [flɪk] *s* schiocco; (slang) pellicola cinematografica ‖ *tr* schioccare

flicker ['flɪkər] *s* fiamma tremolante; (*of eyelids*) battito; (*of hope*) bagliore *m* ‖ *intr* tremolare; vacillare

flier ['flaɪ·ər] *s* aviatore *m*; (*venture*) (coll) impresa rischiosa; (coll) foglio volante

flight [flaɪt] *s* fuga; (*of an airplane*) volo; (*of birds*) stormo; (*of stairs*) rampa; (*of fancy*) slancio; **to put to flight** mettere in fuga; **to take flight** prendere la fuga

flight' deck' *s* ponte *m* di volo

flight·y ['flaɪti] *adj* (**-ier; -iest**) frivolo; volubile

flim-flam ['flɪm ,flæm] *s* (coll) imbroglio, truffa ‖ *v* (*pret & pp* **-flammed;** *ger* **-flamming**) *tr* (coll) imbrogliare, truffare

flim·sy ['flɪmzi] *adj* (**-sier; -siest**) leggero; (*material*) di scarsa consistenza; (*excuse*) inconsistente

flinch [flɪntʃ] *intr* indietreggiare; **without flinching** senza scomporsi

fling [flɪŋ] *s* tiro; ballo scozzese; **to go on a fling** darsi alla pazza gioia; **to have a fling at** tentare di fare; **to have one's fling** correre la cavallina ‖ *v* (*pret & pp* **flung** [flʌŋ]) *tr* sbattere, scagliare; (*e.g., in jail*) schiaffare; **to fling open** spalancare; **to fling shut** chiudere improvvisamente

flint [flɪnt] *s* selce *f*, pietra focaia

flint'lock' *s* fucile *m* a pietra focaia

flint·y ['flɪnti] *adj* (**-ier; -iest**) pietroso; (*unmerciful*) spietato; duro come un macigno

flip [flɪp] *adj* (**flipper; flippest**) impertinente ‖ *s* buffetto; salto mortale ‖ *v* (*pret & pp* **flipped;** *ger* **flipping**) *tr* sbattere in aria; muovere d'un tratto; **to flip a coin** giocare a testa e croce; **to flip shut** (*e.g., a fan*) chiudere improvvisamente

flippancy ['flɪpənsi] *s* leggerezza

flippant ['flɪpənt] *adj* scanzonato, leggero

flirt [flʌrt] *s* (*woman*) civetta; (*man*) vagheggino ‖ *intr* (*said of a woman*) civettare; (*said of a man*) fare il damerino; **to flirt with** flirtare con; (*an idea*) accarezzare; (*death*) giocare con

flit [flɪt] *v* (*pret & pp* **flitted;** *ger* **flitting**) *intr* svolazzare, volteggiare; passare rapidamente, volare

flitch [flɪtʃ] *s* fetta di pancetta

float [flot] *s* (*raft*) galleggiante *m*; (*of mason*) cazzuola; carro allegorico ‖ *tr* far galleggiare; (*a business*) lan-

ciare; (*stocks, bonds*) emettere ‖ *intr* galleggiare, tenersi a galla

floating ['flotɪŋ] *adj* galleggiante

flock [flɑk] *s* (*of birds*) stormo; (*of sheep*) gregge *m*; (*of people*) stuolo; (*of wool*) fiocco; (fig) mucchio ‖ *intr* affollarsi, riunirsi, radunarsi

floe [flo] *s* tavola di ghiaccio

flog [flɑg] *v* (*pret & pp* **flogged;** *ger* **flogging**) *tr* battere, fustigare

flood [flʌd] *s* (*caused by rain*) diluvio; (*sudden rise of river*) piena, fiumana; (*of tide*) flusso ‖ *tr* inondare; (aut) ingolfare ‖ *intr* straripare; (aut) ingolfarsi ‖ **the Flood** il diluvio universale

flood'gate' *s* (*of a canal*) chiusa; (*of a dam*) saracinesca

flood'light' *s* riflettore *m*

flood' tide' *s* flusso

floor [flor] *s* (*inside bottom surface of room*) pavimento; (*story of building*) piano; (*of the sea, a swimming pool, etc.*) fondo; (*of the exchange*) recinto delle grida; (*of an assembly hall*) emiciclo; (naut) madiere *m*; **to ask for the floor** chiedere la parola; **to have the floor** avere la parola; **to take the floor** prendere la parola ‖ *tr* pavimentare; abbattere, gettare al suolo; (coll) confondere; (coll) vincere

flooring ['florɪŋ] *s* palco, impiantito

floor' mop' *s* redazza

floor' plan' *s* pianta

floor' show' *s* spettacolo di caffè concerto

floor'walk'er *s* direttore *m* di sezione

floor' wax' *s* cera da pavimenti

flop [flɑp] *s* (coll) fiasco ‖ *v* (*pret & pp* **flopped;** *ger* **flopping**) *tr* lasciar cadere; sbattere ‖ *intr* lasciarsi cadere; (coll) fare fiasco; **to flop over** (*to change sides*) cambiare casacca

flora ['florə] *s* flora

floral ['florəl] *adj* floreale

Florence ['florəns] *or* ['flɑrəns] *s* Firenze *f*

Florentine ['flɑrən ,tin] *or* ['florən- ,tin] *adj & s* fiorentino

florescence [flo'resəns] *s* inflorescenza

florid ['flɑrɪd] *or* ['florɪd] *adj* florido

florist ['florɪst] *s* fiorista *mf*, fioraio

floss [flɔs] *or* [flɑs] *s* lanugine *f*; (*of corn*) barba

floss·y ['flɔsi] *or* ['flɑsi] *adj* (**-ier; -iest**) serico; (*downy*) lanuginoso; (coll) vistoso

flotsam ['flɑtsəm] *s* relitti gettati a mare

flot'sam and jet'sam *s* relitti *mpl* di naufragio; (*trifles*) cianfrusaglie *fpl*; gentaglia, vagabondi *mpl*

flounce [flaʊns] *s* balza, falda, falpalà *m* ‖ *tr* ornare di falpalà ‖ *intr*—**to flounce out** andarsene irosamente

flounder ['flaʊndər] *s* (ichth) passera ‖ *intr* dibattersi

flour [flaʊr] *adj* farinoso ‖ *s* farina ‖ *tr* infarinare

flourish ['flʌrɪʃ] *s* (*with the sword*) mulinello; (*with the pen*) ghirigoro; (*as part of signature*) svolazzo; (mus) fioritura || *tr (one's sword)* roteare || *intr* rifiorire, prosperare

flourishing ['flʌrɪʃɪŋ] *adj* prospero

flour' mill' *s* mulino per grano

floury ['flaurɪ] *adj* farinoso; infarinato

flout [flaut] *tr* burlarsi di || *intr* burlare, motteggiare

flow [flo] *s* flusso; *(of a river)* regime *m* || *intr* fluire; *(said of tide)* montare; *(said of hair in the air)* ondeggiare; **to flow into** gettarsi in, sfociare in; **to flow over** traboccare; **to flow with** abbondare di

flower ['flau·ər] *s* fiore *m* || *tr* infiorare || *intr* fiorire

flow'er bed' *s* aiola fiorita

flow'er gar'den *s* giardino

flow'er girl' *s* fioraia; *(at a wedding)* damigella d'onore

flow'er·pot' *s* vaso da fiori

flow'er shop' *s* negozio di fiori

flow'er show' *s* esposizione di fiori

flow'er·stand' *s* portafiori *m*

flowery ['flau·ərɪ] *adj* fiorito

flowing ['flo·ɪŋ] *adj (water)* corrente; *(language)* scorrevole; *(e.g., hair)* fluente; *(e.g., lines of a dress)* filante

flu [flu] *s* influenza

fluctuate ['flʌkt/u‚et] *intr* fluttuare, ondeggiare; *(said of prices)* oscillare

flue [flu] *s* gola, fumaiolo

fluency ['flu·ənsɪ] *s* facilità *f* di parola

fluent ['flu·ənt] *adj (speaker)* facondo; *(style)* fluido

fluently ['flu·əntlɪ] *adv* correntemente

fluff [flʌf] *s* lanugine *f*; vaporosità *f*; *(of an actor)* papera || *tr* sprimacciare || *intr* sprimacciarsi; (coll) impaperarsi

fluff·y ['flʌfɪ] *adj* (**-ier; -iest**) lanuginoso; vaporoso

fluid ['flu·ɪd] *adj & s* fluido

flu'id drive' *s* trasmissione idraulica

fluidity [flu'ɪdɪtɪ] *s* fluidità *f*

fluke [fluk] *s (of anchor)* marra, dente *m*; *(in billiards)* colpo fortunato; (ichth) passera

flume [flum] *s* gora; condotta forzata

flunk [flʌŋk] *s* (coll) bocciatura || *tr* (coll) bocciare; *(a course)* (coll) farsi bocciare in || *intr* (coll) fare fiasco; **to flunk out** (coll) farsi bocciare

flunk·y ['flʌŋkɪ] *s* (**-ies**) valletto; parassita *m*

fluor ['flu·ɔr] *s* fluorite *f*

fluorescence [‚flu·ə'rɛsəns] *s* fluorescenza

fluorescent [‚flu·ə'rɛsənt] *adj* fluorescente

fluoridation [‚flu·ərɪ'deʃən] *s* fluorizzazione

fluoride ['flu·ə‚raɪd] *s* fluoruro

fluorine ['flu·ə‚rin] *s* fluoro

fluoroscope ['flu·ərə‚skop] *s* schermo fluorescente

fluorspar ['flu·er‚spar] *s* spatofluore *m*

flur·ry ['flʌrɪ] *s* (**-ries**) agitazione; *(of wind)* raffica; *(of rain)* acquazzone *m*; *(of snow)* turbine *m* || *v* (pret & pp **-ried**) *tr* agitare

flush [flʌʃ] *adj* livellato; contiguo; prospero, ben provvisto; abbondante; vigoroso; *(full to overflowing)* rigurgitante; arrossito; **flush with** allo stesso livello che || *s (of water)* flusso improvviso; *(in the cheeks)* caldana, scalmana; *(of spring)* germogliare *m*; *(of joy)* ebbrezza; *(of youth)* rigoglio; *(in poker)* colore *m* || *adv* rasente, raso || *tr (to cause to blush)* far arrossire; lavare con un getto d'acqua; *(e.g., a rabbit)* snidare || *intr* essere accaldato; *(to blush)* arrossire; *(to gush)* zampillare

flush' tank' *s* sciacquone *m*

flush' toi'let *s* gabinetto a sciacquone

fluster ['flʌstər] *s* nervosismo, eccitazione || *tr* innervosire, eccitare

flute [flut] *s (of a column)* scanalatura; (mus) flauto || *tr* scanalare

flutist ['flutɪst] *s* flautista *mf*

flutter ['flʌtər] *s* svolazzo; agitazione; sensazione || *intr* frullare; svolazzare; agitarsi; *(said of the heart)* palpitare; *(said of the heartbeat)* essere irregolare

flux [flʌks] *s (flow)* flusso; *(for fusing metals)* fondente *m*

fly [flaɪ] *s* (**flies**) mosca; *(of trousers)* finta; *(for fishing)* mosca artificiale || *v* (pret **flew** [flu]; pp **flown** [flon]) *tr (an airplane)* pilotare, far volare; trasportare a volo; *(e.g., an ocean)* trasvolare; *(a flag)* battere || *intr* volare; fuggire, scappare; *(said of a flag)* ondeggiare; **to fly away** involarsi; **to fly into a rage** andare in eccessi; **to fly off** volare via; scappare; **to fly over** trasvolare; **to fly shut** chiudersi improvvisamente

fly'blow' *s* uovo di mosca

fly'-by-night' *adj* poco raccomandabile; di breve durata

fly'catch'er *s* (orn) pigliamosche *m*

flyer ['flaɪ·ər] *s* var of **flier**

fly'-fish' *intr* pescare con le mosche artificiali

flying ['flaɪ·ɪŋ] *adj* volante; rapido; in fuga; *(start)* lanciato || *s* volo

fly'ing boat' *s* idrovolante *m* a scafo centrale

fly'ing but'tress *s* contrafforte *m*

fly'ing col'ors *spl* successo; **with flying colors** a bandiere spiegate

fly'ing field' *s* campo d'aviazione

fly'ing sau'cer *s* disco volante

fly'ing sick'ness *s* male *m* d'aria

fly'ing squad' *s* squadra mobile

fly'ing time' *s* ore *fpl* di volo

fly'leaf' *s* (**-leaves**) (bb) guardia

fly' net' *s (for a bed)* moschettiera; *(for a horse)* scacciamosche *m*

fly'pa'per *s* carta moschicida

fly'speck' *s* macchia di mosca; macchiolina

fly' swat'ter ['swatər] *s* scacciamosche *m*

fly'trap' *s* pigliamosche *m*

fly'wheel' *s* volano

foal [fol] *s* puledro || *intr (said of a mare)* figliare

foam [fom] *s* schiuma || *intr* schiumare

foam' rub'ber *s* gommapiuma

foam·y ['fomɪ] *adj* (**-ier; -iest**) spumoso, schiumeggiante

fob [fɑb] *s* taschino per l'orologio; (*chain*) catenina per l'orologio ‖ *v* (*pret & pp* **fobbed**) *ger* **fobbing**) *tr*— **to fob off** s.th on s.o. rifilare qlco a qlcu

f.o.b. or **F.O.B.** [ˌɛfˌo'bi] *adv* (letterword) (**free on board**) franco

focal ['fokəl] *adj* focale

fo·cus ['fokəs] *s* (**-cuses** or **-ci** [saɪ]) fuoco; (*of a disease*) focolaio ‖ *v* (*pret & pp* **-cused** or **-cussed;** *ger* **-cusing** or **-cussing**) *tr* mettere a fuoco; (*attention*) concentrare ‖ *intr* convergere

fodder ['fɑdər] *s* foraggio

foe [fo] *s* nemico

fog [fɑg] or [fɔg] *s* nebbia; (phot) velo ‖ *v* (*pret & pp* **fogged;** *ger* **fogging**) *tr* annebbiare; (phot) velare ‖ *intr* annebbiarsi; (phot) velarsi

fog' bank' *s* banco di nebbia

fog'bound' *adj* avvolto nella nebbia

fog·gy ['fɑgi] or ['fɔgi] *adj* (**-gier; -giest**) annebbiato; nebbioso; (*idea*) vago; (phot) velato; **it is foggy** fa nebbia

fog'horn' *s* sirena da nebbia

foible ['fɔɪbəl] *s* debolezza, debole *m*

foil [fɔɪl] *s* (*thin sheet of metal*) foglia; (*of mirror*) argentatura; contrasto, risalto; (*sword*) fioretto ‖ *tr* sventare; (*a mirror*) argentare

foist [fɔɪst] *tr*—**to foist** s.th on s.o. rifilare qlco a qlcu

fold [fold] *s* piega; drappeggio; (*for sheep*) ovile *m*; (*of sheep; of the faithful*) gregge *m*; (geol) corrugamento ‖ *tr* piegare; (*the arms*) incrociare; **to fold up** ripiegare ‖ *intr* piegarsi; **to fold up** (coll) fare fallimento

folder ['foldər] *s* (*pamphlet*) pieghevole *m*; (*cover*) portacarte *m*

folding ['foldɪŋ] *adj* pieghevole

fold'ing cam'era *s* macchina fotografica a soffietto

fold'ing chair' *s* sedia pieghevole

fold'ing cot' *s* branda

fold'ing door' *s* porta a libro

fold'ing seat' *s* strapuntino

foliage ['folɪ·ɪdʒ] *s* fogliame *m*

foli·o ['folɪˌo] *adj* in-folio ‖ *s* (**-os**) foglio; (*book*) in-folio ‖ *tr* numerare

folk [fok] *adj* popolare ‖ *s* (**folk** or **folks**) gente *f*; **your folks** i Suoi

folk'lore' *s* folclore *m*

folk' mu'sic *s* musica folcloristica

folk' song' *s* canzone *f* tradizionale

folk·sy ['foksi] *adj* (**-sier; -siest**) socievole; alla buona, alla mano

folk'ways' *spl* costumi *mpl* tradizionali

follicle ['fɑlɪkəl] *s* follicolo

follow ['fɑlo] *tr* seguire; (*to keep up with*) interessarsi di; **to follow suit** seguire l'esempio; (*cards*) rispondere al colore ‖ *intr* seguire; derivare; **as follows** come segue; **it follows** ne risulta

follower ['fɑlo·ər] *s* seguace *m*; discepolo; partigiano

following ['fɑlo·ɪŋ] *adj* susseguente ‖ *s* seguito; aderenti *mpl*

fol'low-up' *adj* susseguente; ricordativo; da continuarsi ‖ *s* prosecuzione; lettera ricordativa

foment [fo'mɛnt] *tr* fomentare

fond [fɑnd] *adj* appassionato; (*of food*) ghiotto; **to become fond of** appassionarsi di

fondle ['fɑndəl] *tr* accarezzare, vezzeggiare

fondness ['fɑndnɪs] *s* tenerezza; passione

font [fɑnt] *s* acquasantiera, pila; **fonte** *f* battesimale; (typ) fondita

food [fud] *adj* alimentare ‖ *s* cibo, vitto; (*for animals*) mangiare *m*; **food for thought** materia di che pensare

food' store' *s* negozio di commestibili

food'stuffs' *spl* commestibili *mpl*

fool [ful] *s* scemo, sciocco; (*jester*) buffone *m*; (*person imposed on*) vittima, zimbello; **to make a fool of** beffarsi di; **to play the fool** fare lo stupido ‖ *tr* infinocchiare, ingannare; **to fool away** sprecare ‖ *intr* giocare, fare per gioco; **to fool around** perdere il proprio tempo; **to fool with** giocherellare con

fooler·y ['fuləri] *s* (**-ies**) pazzia, buffonata

fool'har'dy *adj* (**-dier; -diest**) temerario

fooling ['fulɪŋ] *s* scherzo; **no fooling** senza scherzo, parlando sul serio

foolish ['fulɪʃ] *adj* sciocco; matto

fool'proof' *adj* a tutta prova; infallibile

fools'cap' *s* berretto a sonagli; carta formato protocollo

fool's' er'rand *s* impresa inutile

fool's' par'adise *s* felicità immaginaria

foot [fʊt] *s* (**feet** [fit]) piede *m*; (*of an animal*) zampa; (*of horse*) zoccolo; **to drag one's feet** procedere a passo di lumaca; **to put one's best foot forward** fare del proprio meglio; **to put one's foot down** farsi valere, imporsi; **to put one's foot in it** (coll) fare una topica; **to stand on one's own two feet** agire indipendentemente; **to tread under foot** calcare ‖ *tr* (*the bill*) pagare; **to foot it** andare a piedi; ballare

footage ['fʊtɪdʒ] *s* distanza or lunghezza in piedi; (*of film measured in meters*) metraggio

foot'-and-mouth' disease' *s* (vet) afta epizootica

foot'ball' *s* (*ball*) pallone *m*; (*game*) pallovale *f*; (*soccer*) calcio, football *m*

foot'board' *s* (*support for foot*) predellino; (*of bed*) spalliera

foot' brake' *s* freno a pedale

foot'bridge' *s* passerella, ponte riservato ai pedoni

foot'fall' *s* passo

foot'hill' *s* collina ai piedi di una montagna

foot'hold' s stabilità f; **to gain a foot-hold** prender piede

footing ['fʊtɪŋ] s piede m, e.g., **he lost his footing** perse piede; **on a friendly footing** in relazioni amichevoli; **on an equal footing** su un piede di parità; **on a war footing** su un piede di guerra

foot'lights' spl luci fpl della ribalta; (fig) ribalta, scena

foot'loose' adj completamente libero

foot'man s (**-men**) staffiere m

foot'mark' s orma

foot'note' s rimando, rinvio

foot'path' s sentiero

foot'print' s orma, pesta

foot' race' s corsa podistica

foot'rest' s pedana

foot' rule' s regolo di un piede

foot' soldier' s fante m, fantaccino

foot'sore' adj coi piedi stanchi

foot'step' s passo; **to follow in the footsteps of** seguire le orme di

foot'stone' s pietra tombale a piè di un sepolcro; (archit) pietra di sostegno

foot'stool' s sgabello

foot' warm'er s scaldino

foot'wear' s calzature fpl

foot'work' s allenamento delle gambe; (fig) manovra delicata

foot'worn' adj (road) battuto; (person) spedato

foozie ['fuzəl] s schiappinata ‖ tr & intr mancare completamente

fop [fɑp] s bellimbusto, gagà m

for [fɔr] prep per; malgrado, e.g., **for all his wealth** malgrado tutta la sua ricchezza; come, e.g., **he uses his house for an office** adopera la casa come ufficio; di, e.g., **time for bed** ora di andare a letto; da, e.g., **he has been here for three days** è qui da tre giorni; per amor di; **to go for a walk** andare a fare una passeggiata ‖ conj perchè, poichè

forage ['fɑrɪdʒ] or ['fɔrɪdʒ] s foraggero ‖ s foraggio ‖ tr foraggiare ‖ intr andare in cerca di foraggio

foray ['fɑre] or ['fɔre] s razzia, scorreria ‖ intr razziare

for·bear [fɔr'ber] v (pret **-bore** ['bor]; pp **-borne** ['born]) tr astenersi da ‖ intr essere longanime

forbearance [fɔr'berəns] s longanimità f, tolleranza; astensione

for·bid [fɔr'bɪd] v (pret **-bade** ['bæd] or **-bad** ['bæd]; pp **-bidden** ['bɪdən]; ger **-bidding**) tr proibire, vietare ‖ intr—**God forbid!** Dio ci scampi!

forbidding [fɔr'bɪdɪŋ] adj severo, sinistro

force [fors] s forza; (staff of workers) forza, personale m; (phys) forza; **by force of** a forza di; **by main force** con tutte le sue forze; **in force** vigente; in gran numero; **to join forces** allearsi ‖ tr forzare; obbligare; **to force back** respingere; **to force open** forzare; **to force s.th on s.o.** obbligare qlcu a accettare qlco

forced [forst] adj forzato; studiato

forced' air' s aria sotto pressione

forced' draft' s tiraggio forzato

forced' land'ing s atterraggio forzato

forced' march' s marcia forzata

forceful ['forsfəl] adj vigoroso, energico

for·ceps ['fɔrsəps] s (**-ceps** or **-cipes** [sɪ ˌpiz]) (dent, surg) pinze fpl; (obstet) forcipe m

force' pump' s pompa premente

forcible ['forsɪbəl] adj impetuoso, energico; efficace

ford [ford] s guado ‖ tr guadare

fore [for] adj davanti; (naut) prodiero ‖ s davanti m; (naut) prua; **to the fore** alla ribalta; d'attualità ‖ adv prima; (naut) a proravia ‖ interj attenzione!

fore' and aft' adv a poppa e a prua

fore'arm' s avambraccio ‖ **fore·arm'** tr premunire; prevenire

fore'bears' spl antenati mpl

forebode [for'bod] tr (to portend) preannunziare; (to have a presentiment of) presentire

foreboding [for'bodɪŋ] s preannunzio; presentimento

fore'cast' s pronostico ‖ v (pret & pp **-cast** or **-casted**) tr pronosticare

forecastle ['foksəl], ['for,kæsəl] or ['for,kɑsəl] s castello, pozzetto

fore·close' tr escludere, precludere; (a mortgage) (law) precludere il riscatto di

fore·doom' tr condannare all'insuccesso

fore' edge' s (bb) taglio

fore'fa'ther s antenato

fore'fin'ger s dito indice

fore'front' s—**in the forefront** all'avanguardia

fore·go' v (pret **-went'**; pp **-gone'**) tr & intr precedere

fore·go'ing adj precedente, anteriore

fore'gone' conclu'sion s conclusione inevitabile; decisione già scontata

fore'ground' s primo piano

forehanded ['for,hændɪd] adj previdente; (thrifty) risparmiatore

forehead ['fɑrɪd] or ['for,ɪd] s fronte f

foreign ['fɑrɪn] or ['fɔrɪn] adj straniero; (product; affairs) estero; **foreign to** estraneo a

for'eign affairs' spl affari esteri

for'eign-born' adj nato all'estero

foreigner ['fɑrɪnər] or ['fɔrɪnər] s straniero, forestiere

for'eign exchange' s divise fpl; (money) valuta

for'eign min'ister s ministro degli affari esteri

for'eign of'fice s ministero degli affari esteri

for'eign serv'ice s servizio diplomatico e consolare; (Brit) servizio militare in paesi d'oltremare

fore'leg' s zampa anteriore

fore'lock' s ciuffo sulla fronte; **to take time by the forelock** acchiappare l'occasione

fore'man s (**-men**) sorvegliante m, capomastro; presidente m dei giurati

foremast ['formæst], ['for,mæst] or ['for,mɑst] s trinchetto

foremost ['for,most] adj primo, principale, più importante

fore'noon' *adj* mattinale || *s* mattina
fore'part' *s* parte *f* anteriore; prima parte
fore'paw' *s* zampa anteriore
fore'quar'ter *s* quarto anteriore
fore'run'ner *s* precursore *m*, predecessore *m*, foriero
fore·sail ['forsəl] *or* ['for‚sel] *s* trinchetto
fore·see' *v* (*pret* **-saw'**; *pp* **-seen'**) *tr* prevedere
foreseeable [for'si·əbəl] *adj* prevedibile
fore·shad'ow *tr* presagire
fore·short'en *tr* scorciare
fore'sight' *s* (*prudence*) previdenza; (*foreknowledge*) previsione
fore'sight'ed *adj* previdente
fore'skin' *s* prepuzio
forest ['fɑrɪst] *or* ['fɔrɪst] *adj* forestale || *s* foresta, bosco
fore·stall' *tr* prevenire; anticipare; (*to buy up*) accaparrare
for'est rang'er ['rendʒər] *s* guardaboschi *m*, guardia forestale
forestry ['fɑrɪstri] *or* ['fɔrɪstri] *s* selvicoltura
fore'taste' *s* pregustazione || *tr* pregustare
fore·tell' *v* (*pret* & *pp* **-told'**) *tr* predire, presagire, preannunziare
fore'thought' *s* premeditazione; previdenza
forever [fɔr'evər] *adv* per sempre; continuamente
fore·warn' *tr* prevenire, preavvertire
fore'word' *s* avvertenza, prefazione
forfeit ['fɔrfɪt] *adj* perduto || *s* perdita, confisca; multa; (*article deposited*) pegno; **forfeits** (*game*) pegni *mpl* || *tr* decadere da
forfeiture ['fɔrfɪtʃər] *s* perdita di un pegno
forgather [fɔr'gæðər] *intr* riunirsi; incontrarsi
forge [fɔrdʒ] *s* fucina, forgia || *tr* forgiare; (*a lie*) inventare; (*e.g.*, *handwriting*) falsificare || *intr* forgiare; commettere un falso; **to forge ahead** farsi strada
forger·y ['fɔrdʒəri] *s* (**-ies**) falsificazione, falso, contraffazione
for·get [fɔr'gɛt] *v* (*pret* **-got** ['gɑt]; *pp* **-got** *or* **-gotten** ['gɑtən]) *tr* dimenticare; **forget it!** non si preoccupi!; **to forget oneself** venir meno alla propria dignità; **to forget to** passare di mente a (qlcu) di, *e.g.*, **he forgot to turn off the lights** gli è passato di mente di spegnere la luce
forgetful [fɔr'gɛtfəl] *adj* (*apt to forget*) smemorato; (*neglectful*) dimentico, immemore
forgetfulness [fɔr'gɛtfəlnɪs] *s* (*inability to recall*) smemorataggine *f*; (*neglectfulness*) dimenticanza
for·get'-me-not' *s* nontiscordardimé *m*
forgivable [fɔr'gɪvəbəl] *adj* perdonabile
for·give [fɔr'gɪv] *v* (*pret* **-gave'**; *pp* **-giv'en**) *tr* perdonare
forgiveness [fɔr'gɪvnɪs] *s* perdono
forgiving [fɔr'gɪvɪŋ] *adj* clemente
for·go [fɔr'go] *v* (*pret* **-went**; *pp* **-gone**) *tr* rinunciare (with *dat*)

fork [fɔrk] *s* (*pitchfork*) forca, forcone *m*; (*of a bicycle*) forcella; (*for eating*) forchetta; (*of a tree or road*) biforcazione, diramazione || *tr* muovere col forcone; inforcare; **to fork out** (slang) cacciar fuori || *intr* biforcarsi, diramarsi
forked [fɔrkt] *adj* biforcuto
fork'-lift truck' *s* carrello elevatore a forca
forlorn [fɔr'lɔrn] *adj* abbandonato; disperato; miserabile
forlorn' hope' *s* impresa disperata
form [fɔrm] *s* forma; (*paper to be filled out*) formulario; (*construction to give shape to cement*) cassaforma || *tr* formare || *intr* formarsi
formal ['fɔrməl] *adj* formale; di gala, da sera, da etichetta
for'mal attire' *s* vestito da cerimonia
for'mal call' *s* visita di prammatica
formali·ty [fɔr'mælɪti] *s* (**-ties**) formalità *f*; (*excessive adherence to rules*) formalismo
for'mal par'ty *s* ricevimento di gala
for'mal speech' *s* discorso ufficiale
format ['fɔrmæt] *s* formato
formation [fɔr'meʃən] *s* formazione
former ['fɔrmər] *adj* (*preceding*) anteriore; (*long past*) passato, antico; (*having once been*) già, ex; (*of two*) primo; **the former** quello
formerly ['fɔrmərli] *adv* già, prima, in tempi passati
form'fit'ting *adj* aderente al corpo
formidable ['fɔrmɪdəbəl] *adj* formidabile
formless ['fɔrmlɪs] *adj* informe
form' let'ter *s* lettera a formulario, stampato
formu·la ['fɔrmjələ] *s* (**-las** *or* **-lae** [‚li]) formula
formulate ['fɔrmjə‚let] *tr* formulare
for·sake [fɔr'sek] *v* (*pret* **-sook** ['suk]; *pp* **-saken** ['sekən]) *tr* abbandonare
fort [fɔrt] *s* forte *m*, fortezza
forte [fɔrt] *s* forte *m*
forth [fɔrθ] *adv* avanti; **and so forth** e così via; **from this day forth** da oggi in poi; **to go forth** uscire
forth'com'ing *adj* prossimo; immediatamente disponibile
forth'right' *adj* diretto || *adv* direttamente; senza ambagi; immediatamente
forth'with' *adv* immediatamente
fortieth ['fɔrtɪ·ɪθ] *adj*, *s* & *pron* quarantesimo
fortification [‚fɔrtɪfɪ'keʃən] *s* fortificazione
forti·fy ['fɔrtɪ‚faɪ] *v* (*pret* & *pp* **-fied**) *tr* fortificare; aumentare il livello alcolico di
fortitude ['fɔrtɪ‚tjud] *or* ['fɔrtɪ‚tud] *s* fortezza, fermezza
fortnight ['fɔrtnaɪt] *or* ['fɔrtnɪt] *s* quindicina, due settimane
fortress ['fɔrtrɪs] *s* fortezza, forte *m*
fortuitous [fɔr'tju·ɪtəs] *or* [fɔr'tu·ɪtəs] *adj* fortuito, occasionale
fortunate ['fɔrtʃənɪt] *adj* fortunato
fortune ['fɔrtʃən] *s* fortuna; **to make a fortune** farsi un patrimonio; **to tell**

s.o. his fortune leggere il futuro a qlcu

for'tune hunt'er s cacciatore m di dote

for'tune·tel'ler s indovino, cartomante mf

for·ty [ˈfɔrti] adj & pron quaranta || s (-ties) quaranta m; **the forties** gli anni quaranta

fo·rum [ˈforəm] s (-rums or -ra [rə]) foro

forward [ˈfɔrwərd] adj avanzato; precoce; impertinente || s (soccer) avanti m || adv avanti; **to bring forward** mettere in luce; riportare; **to come forward** avanzare; **to look forward to** anticipare il piacere di || tr inoltrare, trasmettere; promuovere

fossil [ˈfɑsɪl] adj & s fossile m

foster [ˈfɑstər] or [ˈfɒstər] adj adottivo; di latte || tr allevare; promuovere

fos'ter home' s famiglia adottiva

foul [faʊl] adj sporco; (air) viziato; (wind) contrario; (weather; breath) cattivo; (baseball) fuori linea di gioco || s (of boats) urto, collisione; (baseball) palla colpita fuori linea di gioco; (boxing) colpo basso; (sports) fallo || adv slealmente; (baseball) fuori linea di gioco; **to fall foul of** entrare in collisione con; urtarsi con; **to run foul of** avere una controversia con || tr sporcare; otturare; (baseball) colpire fuori linea di gioco || intr (said of two boats) entrare in collisione; (said, e.g., of a rope) imbrogliarsi

foul-mouthed [ˈfaʊlˈmaʊðd] or [ˈfaʊlˈmaʊθt] adj sboccato, osceno

foul' play' s reato; (sports) gioco sleale

found [faʊnd] tr fondare; (to melt, to cast) fondere

foundation [faʊnˈdeʃən] s fondazione; (endowment) dotazione; (charitable) patronato; (masonry support) platea, fondamenta fpl; (make-up) fondo tinta; (fig) fondatezza

founder [ˈfaʊndər] s fondatore m; (of family) capostipite m; (of metals) fonditore m || intr (said of a ship) affondare; (said of a horse) azzopparsi; (to fail) fare fiasco

foundling [ˈfaʊndlɪŋ] s trovatello

found'ling hos'pital s brefotrofio

found·ry [ˈfaʊndri] s (-ries) fonderia

found'ry·man s (-men) fonditore m

fount [faʊnt] s fonte f

fountain [ˈfaʊntən] s fonte f, fontana; (of knowledge) pozzo

foun'tain-head' s sorgente f

foun'tain pen' s penna stilografica

foun'tain syringe' s clistere m a pera

four [for] adj & pron quattro || s quattro; **four o'clock** le quattro; **on all fours** gattoni, carponi

four'-cy'cle adj a quattro tempi

four'-cyl'inder adj a quattro cilindri

four'-flush' intr (coll) millantarsi

fourflusher [ˈfor ˌflʌʃər] s (coll) millantatore m

four-footed [ˈforˈfʊtɪd] adj quadrupede

four' hun'dred adj, s & pron quattrocento || **the Four Hundred** l'alta società

four'-in-hand' s cravatta a cappio; tiro a quattro

four'-lane' adj a quattro corsie

four'-leaf clo'ver s quadrifoglio

four-legged [ˈforˈlɛgɪd] or [ˈforˈlɛgd] adj a quattro zampe; (schooner) (coll) a quattro alberi

four'-letter word' s parolaccia di quattro lettere

four'-mo'tor plane' s quadrimotore m

four'-o'clock' s (bot) bella di notte

four' of a kind' s (cards) poker m

four'post'er s letto a baldacchino

four'score' adj ottanta

foursome [ˈforsəm] s gruppo di quattro giocatori

fourteen [ˈforˈtin] adj, s & pron quattordici m

fourteenth [ˈforˈtinθ] adj, s & pron quattordicesimo || s (in dates) quattordici m

fourth [forθ] adj, s & pron quarto || s (in dates) quattro

fourth' estate' s quarto potere

four'-way' adj a quattro orifizi; fra quattro persone; quadruplice

fowl [faʊl] s pollo || intr uccellare

fowl'ing piece' s fucile m da caccia

fox [fɑks] s volpe f || tr (coll) ingannare

fox'glove' s digitale f

fox'hole' s buca ricovero

fox'hound' s segugio

fox' hunt' s caccia alla volpe

fox' ter'rier s fox-terrier m

fox'-trot' s (of a horse) piccolo trotto; (dance) fox-trot m

fox·y [ˈfɑksi] adj (-ier; -iest) volpino, astuto

foyer [ˈfɔɪ·ər] s (of a private house) ingresso, vestibolo; (theat) ridotto

fracas [ˈfrekəs] s lite f, tumulto

fraction [ˈfrækʃən] s frazione; frammento

fractional [ˈfrækʃənəl] adj frazionario; insignificante

fractious [ˈfrækʃəs] adj litigioso, permaloso; indisciplinato

fracture [ˈfræktʃər] s frattura || tr fratturare; (e.g., an arm) fratturarsi, rompersi || intr fratturarsi

fragile [ˈfrædʒɪl] adj fragile

fragment [ˈfrægmənt] s frammento; (e.g., of a movie) spezzone m || tr frammentare, spezzare

fragmenta'tion bomb' [ˌfrægmənˈteʃən] s bomba dirompente

fragrant [ˈfregrənt] adj fragrante

frail [frel] adj (not robust) gracile; (easily broken) fragile; (morally weak) debole || s canestro di giunco

frail·ty [ˈfrelti] s (-ties) fragilità f; (of a person) debolezza

frame [frem] s (of picture) cornice f; (of glasses) montatura; (structure) ossatura; (of a building) ingabbiatura, impalcatura; (for embroidering) telaio; (of a window) intelaiatura; (of mind) stato; (of government) sistema m; (mov) inquadratura; (phot) fotogramma m; (aer) ordinata (naut) costa || *tr* (*to put in a frame*) incorniciare; montare; costruire; inventare; esprimere; (slang) architettare un' accusa contro

frame′ house′ *s* casa con l'ossatura di legno

frame′-up′ *s* (slang) complotto per incriminare un innocente

frame′work′ *s* intelaiatura, impalcatura; palificazione

franc [fræŋk] *s* franco

France [fræns] *or* [frɑns] *s* la Francia

Frances [′frænsɪs] *or* [′frɑnsɪs] *s* Francesca

franchise [′fræntʃaɪz] *s* diritto di voto; concessione; (*privilege*) franchigia

Francis [′frænsɪs] *or* [′frɑnsɪs] *s* Francesco

Franciscan [fræn′sɪskən] *adj & s* francescano

frank [fræŋk] *adj* sincero, schietto || *s* affrancatura postale; lettera affrancata; (*franking privilege*) franchigia postale || *tr* affrancare || **Frank** *s* (*member of Frankish tribe*) franco; (*masculine name*) Franco

frankfurter [′fræŋkfərtər] *s* salsiccia di Francoforte, Frankfurter *m*

frankincense [′fræŋkɪn‚sens] *s* olibano

Frankish [′fræŋkɪʃ] *adj & s* franco

frankness [′fræŋknɪs] *s* franchezza

frantic [′fræntɪk] *adj* frenetico

frappé [fræ′pe] *adj & s* frappé *m*

frat [fræt] *s* (slang) associazione di studenti

fraternal [frə′tʌrnəl] *adj* fraterno

fraterni•ty [frə′tʌrnɪti] *s* (-**ties**) (*brotherliness*) fraternità *f*; sodalizio; (eccl) confraternita *f*; (U.S.A.) associazione di studenti

fraternize [′frætər‚naɪz] *intr* fraternizzare

fraud [frɔd] *s* truffa, frode *f*; (*person*) (coll) truffatore *m*

fraudulent [′frɔdjələnt] *adj* fraudolento; (*conversion*) indebito

fraught [frɔt] *adj*—**fraught with** carico di, gravido di

fray [fre] *s* zuffa, rissa, lotta || *intr* sfilacciarsi, logorarsi

freak [frik] *s* (*sudden fancy*) capriccio, ticchio; (*person, animal*) fenomeno

freakish [′frikɪʃ] *adj* capriccioso; strano, grottesco

freckle [′frekəl] *s* lentiggine *f*, efelide *f*

freckle-faced [′frekəl‚fest] *adj* lentigginoso

freckly [′frekli] *adj* lentigginoso

Frederick [′fredərɪk] *s* Federico

free [fri] *adj* (**freer** [′fri•ər]; **freest** [′fri•ɪst]) libero; gratis; franco; sciolto; esente; generoso; **to be free with** essere prodigo di; **to set free** liberare || *adv* liberamente; in libertà; gratis || *v* (*pret & pp* **freed** [frid]; *ger* **freeing** [′fri•ɪŋ]) *tr* liberare; (*from customs*) svincolare; esimere

freebooter [′fri‚butər] *s* pirata *m*

free′born′ *adj* nato in libertà; proprio di un popolo libero

freedom [′fridəm] *s* libertà *f*

free′dom of speech′ *s* libertà *f* di parola

free′dom of the press′ *s* libertà *f* di stampa

free′dom of the seas′ *s* libertà *f* di navigazione

free′dom of wor′ship *s* libertà religiosa

free′ en′terprise *s* economia libera

free′-for-all′ *s* rissa, tafferuglio

free′ hand′ *s* libertà assoluta

free′-hand′ *adj* a mano libera

freehanded [′fri′hændɪd] *adj* liberale, generoso

free′ lance′ *s* giornalista *mf* pubblicista; scrittore *m* che lavora senza contratto; soldato di ventura

free′load′er [′lodər] *s* (coll) mangiatore *m* a sbafo

free′man *s* (-**men**) uomo libero; cittadino

Free′ma′son *s* frammassone *m*

Free′ma′sonry *s* frammassoneria

free′ of charge′ *adj* gratis, senza spese

free′ port′ *s* porto franco

free′ serv′ice *s* manutenzione gratuita

free′-spo′ken *adj* franco, aperto

free′stone′ *adj* spiccagnolo || *s* pesca spicca

free′think′er *s* libero pensatore

free′ thought′ *s* libero pensiero

free′ trade′ *s* libero scambio

free′trad′er *s* liberoscambista *mf*

free′way′ *s* autostrada

free′ will′ *s* libero arbitrio

freeze [friz] *s* gelo, gelata; (*e.g., of prices*) blocco || *v* (*pret* **froze** [froz]; *pp* **frozen**) *tr* gelare; (*credits, rentals, etc.*) bloccare || *intr* gelarsi; (*said of brakes*) inchiodarsi; morire assiderato; (*to become immobilized*) irrigidirsi

freeze′-dry′ *v* (*pret & pp* **-dried′**) *tr* liofilizzare

freezer [′frizər] *s* congelatore *m*; (*for making ice cream*) sorbettiera

freight [fret] *s* carico; (*charge*) porto; (naut) nolo; **by freight** come carico mercantile; (rr) a piccola velocità || *tr* spedire come carico

freight′ car′ *s* vagone *m* o carro merci

freighter [′fretər] *s* speditore *m*; nave *f* da carico

freight′ plat′form *s* (rr) banchina adibita al traffico merci

freight′ sta′tion *s* (rr) stazione merci

freight′ train′ *s* treno merci, merci *m*

freight′ yard′ *s* (rr) scalo merci

French [frentʃ] *adj & s* francese *m*; **the French** i francesi

French′ bread′ *s* pane *m* a bastone

French′ chalk′ *s* pietra da sarto

French′ door′ *s* porta a vetri

French′ dress′ing *s* salsa verde con aceto

French′ fried′ pota′toes *spl* patate fritte affettate

French′ horn′ *s* (mus) corno

French′ leave′ *s*—**to take French leave** andarsene all'inglese, filare all'inglese

French′man *s* (-**men**) francese *m*

French′ tel′ephone *s* microtelefono

French′ toast′ *s* pane dorato al salto

French′ win′dow *s* portafinestra

French′wom′an *s* (-**wom′en**) francese *f*

frenzied ['frenzɪd] *adj* frenetico

fren·zy ['frenzɪ] *s* (**-zies**) frenesia

frequen·cy ['frikwənsɪ] *s* (**-cies**) frequenza

fre′quency modula′tion *s* modulazione di frequenza

frequent ['frikwənt] *adj* frequente || [frɪ'kwent] *or* ['frikwənt] *tr* frequentare, praticare

frequently ['frikwəntlɪ] *adv* frequentemente

fres·co ['fresko] *s* (**-coes** *or* **-cos**) affresco || *tr* affrescare

fresh [freʃ] *adj* fresco; (*water*) dolce; (*new*) nuovo; (*wind*) moderato; (*inexperienced*) novizio; (*cheeky*) (slang) sfacciato || *adv* recentemente, di recente; **fresh in** (coll) appena arrivato; **fresh out** (coll) appena esaurito

freshen ['freʃən] *tr* rinfrescare || *intr* rinfrescarsi

freshet ['freʃɪt] *s* piena, crescita

fresh′man *s* (**-men**) (*newcomer*) novizio; (educ) matricola

freshness ['freʃnɪs] *s* freschezza; (*of air*) frescura; (*cheek*) (slang) sfacciataggine *f*

fresh′-wa′ter *adj* d'acqua dolce; poco conosciuto; piccolo

fret [fret] *s* (*interlaced design*) fregio, greca; irritazione; (mus) tasto || *v* (*pret & pp* **fretted**; *ger* **fretting**) *tr* fregiare || *intr* fremere, trepidare, agitarsi

fretful ['fretfəl] *adj* irritabile, permaloso

fret′work′ *s* greca

Freudianism ['frɔɪdɪ·ə‚nɪzəm] *s* freudismo

friar ['fraɪ·ər] *s* frate *m*

friar·y ['fraɪ·ərɪ] *s* (**-ies**) convento di frati

fricassee [‚frɪkə'si] *s* fricassea

friction ['frɪkʃən] *s* frizione; disaccordo, dissenso

fric′tion tape′ *s* nastro isolante

Friday ['fraɪdɪ] *s* venerdì *m*

fried [fraɪd] *adj* fritto

fried′ egg′ *s* uovo al tegame, uovo occhio di manzo

friend [frend] *s* amico; **to be friends with** essere amico di; **to make friends** allacciare amicizie; **to make friends with** fare l'amicizia di

friend·ly ['frendlɪ] *adj* (**-lier; -liest**) amico, amichevole

friendship ['frendʃɪp] *s* amicizia

frieze [friz] *s* (archit) fregio

frigate ['frɪgɪt] *s* fregata

fright [fraɪt] *s* spavento; **to take fright at** spaventarsi di

frighten ['fraɪtən] *tr* intimorire, spaventare; **to frighten away** mettere in fuga, sgomentare || *intr* spaventarsi

frightful ['fraɪtfəl] *adj* spaventevole, orribile; (coll) enorme

frightfulness ['fraɪtfəlnɪs] *s* spavento; terrorismo

frigid ['frɪdʒɪd] *adj* freddo; (*zone*) glaciale

frigidity [frɪ'dʒɪdɪtɪ] *s* (fig) frigidezza; (pathol) frigidità *f*

frill [frɪl] *s* pieghettatura; (*of birds and other animals*) collarino; (*in dress, speech, etc.*) affettazione

fringe [frɪndʒ] *s* frangia; (*in dressmaking*) volantino; (*on curtains*) balza; **on the fringe of** all'orlo di || *tr* orlare

fringe′ ben′efits *spl* assegni *mpl*, benefici *mpl* marginali

fripper·y ['frɪpərɪ] *s* (**-ies**) (*finery*) fronzoli *mpl*; ostentazione; (*trifles*) cianfrusaglie *fpl*

frisk [frɪsk] *tr* perquisire; (slang) derubare || *intr* fare capriole

frisk·y ['frɪskɪ] *adj* (**-ier; -iest**) gaio, vivace

fritter ['frɪtər] *s* frittella; frammento || *tr*—**to fritter away** sprecare

frivolous ['frɪvələs] *adj* frivolo

friz [frɪz] *s* (**frizzes**) ricciolo || *v* (*pret & pp* **frizzed**; *ger* **frizzing**) *tr* arricciare

frizzle ['frɪzəl] *s* ricciolo || *tr* arricciare || *intr* arricciarsi

friz·zly ['frɪzlɪ] *adj* (**-zlier; -zliest**) crespo, riccio

fro [fro] *adv*—**to and fro** avanti e indietro; **to go to and fro** andare e venire

frock [frak] *s* gabbano; (*smock*) grembiule *m*; blusa; (*of priest*) tonaca

frock′ coat′ *s* finanziera

frog [frag] *or* [frɔg] *s* rana; (*button and loop on a garment*) alamaro; (*in throat*) raschio

frog′man′ *s* (**-men′**) sommozzatore *m*, uomo rana

frol·ic ['fralɪk] *s* scherzo, monelleria || *v* (*pret & pp* **-icked**; *ger* **-icking**) *intr* scherzare, folleggiare

frolicsome ['fralɪksəm] *adj* scherzoso

from [frʌm], [fram] *or* [frəm] *prep* da; di, e.g., **I am from New York** sono di New York; da parte di; a, e.g., **to take s.th away from s.o.** portar via qlco a qlcu

front [frʌnt] *adj* frontale, anteriore; di fronte || *s* fronte *m* & *f*; (*of a building*) prospetto; (*of a book*) principio; (*of a shirt*) sparato; (*e.g., of wealth*) apparenza; (theat) boccascena *m*; (mil) fronte *m*; **in front of** dinanzi a; **to put on a front** (coll) fare ostentazione; **to put up a bold front** (coll) farsi coraggio || *tr* (*to face*) fronteggiare; (*to confront*) affrontare; (*to supply with a front*) coprire; servire da facciata a || *intr*—**to front on** dare su

frontage ['frʌntɪdʒ] *s* facciata, veduta; terreno di fronte alla casa

front′ door′ *s* porta d'entrata

front′ drive′ *s* (aut) trazione anteriore

frontier [frʌn'tɪr] *adj* limitrofo || *s* frontiera

fron′tiers′man *s* (**-men**) pioniere *m*

frontispiece ['frʌntɪs‚pis] *s* (*of book*) pagina illustrata di fronte al frontispizio; (*of building*) facciata

front′ mat′ter *s* (*of book*) parte *f* preliminare

front′-page′ *tr* stampare in prima pagina

front′ porch′ *s* porticato

front′ room′ s stanza con vista sulla strada

front′ row′ s prima fila

front′ seat′ s posto in una delle file davanti; (aut) sedile m anteriore

front′ steps′ spl scalinata d'ingresso

front′ view′ s vista sulla strada

frost [frɔst] or [frɑst] s gelo, brina, gelata; (fig) freddezza; (slang) fiasco ‖ tr agghiacciare; (with sugar) glassare; (glass) smerigliare

frost′bite′ s congelamento

frost′ed glass′ s vetro smerigliato

frosting [′frɔstɪŋ] or [′frɑstɪŋ] s glassatura; (of glass) smerigliatura

frost·y [′frɔsti] or [′frɑsti] adj (-ier; -iest) brinato; (hair) canuto; (fig) gelido

froth [frɔθ] or [frɑθ] s schiuma; (fig) frivolezza ‖ intr schiumare; (at the mouth) avere la bava

froth·y [′frɔθi] or [′frɑθi] adj (-ier; -iest) spumoso; frivolo

froward [′frowərd] adj indocile

frown [fraun] s aggrottare m delle ciglia; (of disapproval) cipiglio ‖ intr aggrottare le ciglia; **to frown at** or **on** disapprovare

frows·y or **frowz·y** [′frauzi] adj (-ier; -iest) sporco; puzzolente

fro′zen foods′ [′frozən] spl cibi congelati; cibi surgelati

frugal [′frugəl] adj parsimonioso; (in food and drink) frugale

fruit [frut] adj (tree) fruttifero; (dish) da frutta ‖ s (such as apple) frutto; (collectively) frutta, e.g., **I like fruit** mi piace la frutta; (fig) frutto

fruit′ cake′ s torta con noci e canditi

fruit′ cup′ s macedonia di frutta

fruit′ dish′ s fruttiera, portafrutta m

fruit′ fly′ s moscerino del vino

fruitful [′frutfəl] adj fruttuoso

fruition [fru′ɪʃən] s realizzazione; **to come to fruition** giungere a buon fine

fruit′ jar′ s vaso da frutta

fruit′ juice′ s sugo o spremuta di frutta

fruitless [′frutlɪs] adj infruttuoso

fruit′ sal′ad s macedonia di frutta

fruit′ stand′ s bancarella da fruttivendolo

fruit′ store′ s negozio di frutta

frumpish [′frʌmpɪʃ] adj trasandato

frustrate [′frʌstret] tr frustrare

fry [fraɪ] s (**fries**) fritto ‖ v (pret & pp **fried**) tr & intr friggere

fry′ing pan′ s padella; **out of the frying pan into the fire** dalla padella nella brace

fudge [fʌdʒ] s dolce m di cioccolato

fuel [′fju·əl] s combustibile m; (fig) cibo ‖ v (pret & pp **fueled** or **fuelled**; ger **fueling** or **fuelling**) tr rifornire di carburante ‖ intr rifornirsi di carburante

fuel′ cell′ s cellula elettrogena

fu′el oil′ s nafta, olio pesante

fu′el tank′ s serbatoio del carburante

fugitive [′fjudʒɪtɪv] adj & s fuggiasco, fuggitivo

fugue [fjug] s (mus) fuga

ful·crum [′fʌlkrəm] s (**-crums** or **-cra** [krə]) fulcro

fulfill [ful′fɪl] tr (to carry out) eseguire; (an obligation) mantenere; (to bring to an end) completare

fulfillment [ful′fɪlmənt] s adempimento; realizzazione

full [ful] adj pieno; (speed) tutto; (garment) ampio; (voice) spiegato; (of food) sazio; (member) effettivo; **full of aches and pains** pieno d'acciacchi; **full of fun** divertentissimo; **full of play** pieno di vita ‖ s pieno; colmo; **in full** per esteso, in pieno; **to the full** completamente ‖ adv completamente; **full many (a)** moltissimi; **full well** perfettamente ‖ tr follare

full-blooded [′ful′blʌdɪd] adj vigoroso; purosangue

full-blown [′ful′blon] adj completamente sbocciato; maturo

full-bodied [′ful′bɑdɪd] adj forte, ricco

full′ dress′ s vestito da sera; (mil) tenuta di gala, alta uniforme

full-faced [′ful′fest] adj paffuto; (view) intero; (typ) grassetto

full-fledged [′ful′fledʒd] adj completamente sviluppato; vero, autentico

full-grown [′ful′gron] adj completamente sviluppato, adulto

full′ house′ s (theat) piena; (poker) full m

full′-length′ mir′ror s specchiera

full′-length′ mo′vie s lungometraggio

full′ moon′ s luna piena

full′ name′ s nome m e cognome m

full′-page′ adj di tutta una pagina

full′ pow′ers spl pieni poteri

full′ sail′ adv a vele spiegate

full′-scale′ adj in grandezza naturale; completo

full-sized [′ful′saɪzd] adj in grandezza naturale

full′ speed′ adv a tutta velocità

full′ stop′ s fermata; (gram) punto

full′ swing′ s piena attività

full′ tilt′ adv a tutta forza

full′-time′ adj a orario completo

fully [′fuli] or [′fuli] adv completamente, del tutto

fulsome [′fulsəm] or [′fʌlsəm] adj basso, volgare; nauseante

fumble [′fʌmbəl] tr (a ball) lasciar cadere ‖ intr titubare; andare a tentoni; (in one's pocket) cercare alla cieca

fume [fjum] s fumo, vapore m, esalazione ‖ tr affumicare ‖ intr fumare, esalare fumo; (to show anger) irritarsi

fumigate [′fjumɪ‚get] tr fumigare

fumigation [‚fjumɪ′geʃən] s fumigazione

fun [fʌn] s divertimento, spasso; **to be fun** essere divertente; **to have fun** divertirsi; **to make fun of** prendersi gioco di

function [′fʌŋkʃən] s funzione ‖ intr funzionare, marciare, camminare

functional [′fʌŋkʃənəl] adj funzionale

functionalism [′fʌŋkʃənəl‚ɪzəm] s funzionalismo

functionar·y [′fʌŋkʃə‚nɛri] s (-ies) funzionario

fund [fʌnd] *s* fondo; *(of knowledge)* suppellettile *f* ‖ *tr (debts)* consolidare

fundamental [ˌfʌndə'mɛntəl] *adj* fondamentale ‖ *s* fondamento

fundamentalist [ˌfʌndə'mɛntəlɪst] *adj & s* scritturale *m*

funeral ['fjunərəl] *adj* funebre, funerario ‖ *s* funerale *m*, trasporto funebre; **it's not my funeral** (slang) non sono affari miei

fu'neral direc'tor *s* imprenditore *m* di pompe funebri

fu'neral home' *or* **par'lor** *s* impresa di pompe funebri

fu'neral serv'ice *s* ufficio dei defunti

funereal [fju'nɪrɪ-əl] *adj* funebre

fungous ['fʌŋɡəs] *adj* fungoso

fungus ['fʌŋɡəs] *s* (**funguses** *or* **fungi** ['fʌndʒaɪ]) fungo

funicular [fju'nɪkjələr] *adj & s* funicolare *f*

funk [fʌŋk] *s* (coll) paura; (coll) codardo; **in a funk** (coll) con una paura matta

fun·nel ['fʌnəl] *s* imbuto; *(smoke-stack)* fumaiolo; *(for ventilation)* manica a vento ‖ *v* (pret & pp -neled *or* -nelled; ger -neling *or* -nelling) *tr* incanalare

funnies ['fʌniz] *spl* pagine *fpl* fumetti

fun·ny ['fʌni] *adj* (-nier; -niest) comico, buffo; (coll) strano; **to strike as funny** parere strano *or* buffo a

fun'ny bone' *s* osso rabbioso (del gomito); **to strike s.o.'s funny bone** far ridere qlcu

fur [fʌr] *s* pelo; *(garment)* pelliccia; *(on the tongue)* patina

furbelow ['fʌrbə‚lo] *s* falpalà *m*

furbish ['fʌrbɪʃ] *tr* lustrare; mettere a nuovo; **to furbish up** rinfrescare

furious ['fjʊrɪ-əs] *adj* furioso

furl [fʌrl] *tr (a flag)* incazzottare; (naut) raccogliere, strangolare

fur-lined ['fʌr‚laɪnd] *adj* foderato di pelliccia

furlong ['fʌrlɔŋ] *or* ['fʌrlɑŋ] *s* un ottavo di miglio terrestre

furlough ['fʌrlo] *s* licenza ‖ *tr* licenziare

furnace ['fʌrnɪs] *s* fornace *f*; *(to heat a house)* caldaia del calorifero

furnish ['fʌrnɪʃ] *tr* fornire; ammobiliare

furnishings ['fʌrnɪʃɪŋz] *spl* mobilia; *(things to wear)* accessori *mpl* da uomo

furniture ['fʌrnɪtʃər] *s* mobili *mpl*, mobilia; (naut) attrezzatura; **a piece of furniture** un mobile

fur'ni·ture deal'er *s* mobiliere *m*

furor ['fjʊrər] *s* furore *m*

furrier ['fʌrɪ‚ər] *s* pellicciaio

furrier·y ['fʌrɪ‚əri] *s* (-ies) pellicceria

furrow ['fʌro] *s* solco ‖ *tr* solcare

further ['fʌrðər] *adj* più lontano; ulteriore ‖ *adv* oltre; più; inoltre ‖ *tr* favorire, incoraggiare

furtherance ['fʌrðərəns] *s* avanzamento, incoraggiamento

furthermore ['fʌrðər‚mor] *adv* inoltre

furthest ['fʌrðɪst] *adj* (il) più lontano ‖ *adv* al massimo

furtive ['fʌrtɪv] *adj* furtivo

fu·ry ['fjʊri] *s* (-ries) furia

furze [fʌrz] *s* ginestra spinosa

fuse [fjuz] *s (for igniting an explosive)* miccia; *(for detonating an explosive)* spoletta; (elec) fusibile *m*; **to burn out a fuse** bruciare un fusibile ‖ *tr* fondere ‖ *intr* fondersi; (elec) saltare

fuse' box' *s* valvoliera

fuselage ['fjuzəlɪdʒ] *or* [ˌfjuzə'laʒ] *s* fusoliera

fusible ['fjuzɪbəl] *adj* fusibile

fusillade [ˌfjuzɪ'led] *s* fucileria; (fig) gragnola ‖ *tr* attaccare con fuoco di fucileria

fusion ['fjuʒən] *s* fusione

fuss [fʌs] *s* agitazione inutile; (coll) alterco per nulla; **to make a fuss** accogliere festosamente; fare molte storie; **to make a fuss over** aver un alterco su ‖ *tr* disturbare ‖ *intr* agitarsi per un nonnulla

fuss·y ['fʌsi] *adj* (-ier; -iest) *(person)* pignolo, meticoloso; *(object)* carico di fronzoli; *(writing)* complicato

fustian ['fʌstʃən] *s* fustagno; (fig) verbosità *f*, magniloquenza

fust·y ['fʌsti] *adj* (-ier; -iest) ammuffito, che sa di muffa; antico, sorpassato

futile ['fjutɪl] *adj* *(unproductive)* sterile; *(unimportant)* futile

futili·ty [fju'tɪlɪti] *s* (-ties) sterilità *f*; futilità *f*

future ['fjutʃər] *adj* futuro ‖ *s* futuro; **futures** contratto con consegna a termine; **in the near future** nel prossimo avvenire

fuze [fjuz] *s (for igniting an explosive)* miccia; *(for detonating an explosive)* spoletta; (elec) fusibile *m* ‖ *tr* innestare la spoletta a

fuzz [fʌz] *s* lanugine *f*, peluria; *(in corners)* polvere *f*; (slang) poliziotto; (slang) polizia

fuzz·y ['fʌzi] *adj* (-ier; -iest) lanuginoso; coperto di polvere; *(indistinct)* confuso

G

G, g [dʒi] *s* settima lettera dell'alfabeto inglese

gab [ɡæb] *s* (coll) parlantina ‖ *v* (pret & pp gabbed; ger gabbing) *intr* (coll) chiacchierare

gabardine ['ɡæbər‚din] *s* gabardine *f*

gabble ['ɡæbəl] *s* barbugliamento ‖ *intr* barbugliare

gable ['ɡebəl] *s* (archit) timpano

ga'ble roof' *s* tetto a due falde, tetto a capanna

gad [ɡæd] *v* (pret & pp gadded; ger gadding) *intr* bighellonare

gad'about' *adj* ozioso ‖ *s* vagabondo, bighellone *m*; fannullone *m*

gad'fly' *s* (-flies) tafano, moscone *m*

gadget ['gædʒɪt] *s* congegno, dispositivo, macchinetta

Gaelic ['gelɪk] *adj & s* gaelico

gaff [gæf] *s* arpione *m*; (naut) picco; **to stand the gaff** (slang) aver pazienza

gag [gæg] *s* bavaglio; (joke) barzelletta; (theat) battuta improvvisata ‖ *v* (pret & pp **gagged**; ger **gagging**) *tr* imbavagliare; soffocare ‖ *intr* sentirsi venire la nausea

gage [gedʒ] *s* (pledge) pegno; (challenge) sfida

gaie·ty ['ge·ɪti] *s* (-ties) gaiezza

gaily ['geli] *adv* allegramente

gain [gen] *s* profitto; (increase) aumento ‖ *tr* guadagnare; (to reach) raggiungere; (altitude) prendere ‖ *intr* (said of a patient) migliorare; (said of a watch) correre; **to gain on** guadagnare terreno su; sorpassare

gainful ['genfəl] *adj* rimunerativo

gain'say' *v* (pret & pp **-said** [‚sed] or [‚sed]) *tr* disdire, misconoscere; negare

gait [get] *s* portamento, andatura

gaiter ['getər] *s* ghetta

gala ['gælə] or ['gelə] *adj* di gala ‖ *s* gala *m & f*, festa

galax·y ['gæləksi] *s* (-ies) galassia

gale [gel] *s* (of wind) bufera; (of laughter) scoppio; **to weather the gale** resistere alla tempesta

gall [gɔl] *s* fiele *m*; bile *f*; cistifellea; scorticatura; (gallnut) galla; (audacity) (coll) faccia tosta ‖ *tr* irritare ‖ *intr* irritarsi; (naut) logorarsi

gallant ['gælənt] or [gə'lænt] *adj* galante ‖ ['gælənt] *adj* (brave) valoroso; (grand) magnifico; (showy) festivo ‖ *s* prode *m*; (man attentive to women) galante *m*

gallant·ry ['gæləntri] *s* (-ries) galanteria; valore *m*

gall' blad'der *s* vescichetta biliare

gall'-blad'der attack' *s* travaso di bile

galleon ['gælɪ·ən] *s* galeone *m*

galler·y ['gæləri] *s* (-ies) galleria; tribuna; (cheapest seats in theater) loggione *m*

galley ['gæli] *s* (vessel) galera; (kitchen) (aer) cucina; (kitchen) (naut) cambusa; (galley proof) (typ) bozza in colonna; (tray) (typ) vantaggio

gal'ley proof' *s* bozza in colonna

gal'ley slave' *s* galeotto

Gallic ['gælɪk] *adj* gallo, gallico

galling ['gɔlɪŋ] *adj* irritante

gallivant ['gælɪ‚vænt] *intr* andare a spasso; fare il galante

gall'nut' *s* galla

gallon ['gælən] *s* gallone *m*

galloon [gə'lun] *s* gallone *m*, nastro

gallop ['gæləp] *s* galoppo; **at a gallop** al galoppo ‖ *tr* far galoppare ‖ *intr* galoppare

gal·lows ['gæloz] *s* (-lows or -lowses) forca; (min) castelletto

gal'lows bird' *s* (coll) remo di galera, pendaglio da forca

gall'stone' *s* calcolo biliare

galore [gə'lor] *adv* in abbondanza

galosh [gə'lɑʃ] *s* stivaletto di gomma

galvanize ['gælvə‚naɪz] *tr* galvanizzare

gal'vanized i'ron *s* ferro zincato

gambit ['gæmbɪt] *s* gambetto

gamble ['gæmbəl] *s* azzardo; (game) gioco d'azzardo ‖ *tr* giocare; **to gamble away** giocarsi ‖ *intr* giocare d'azzardo; (com) speculare

gambler ['gæmblər] *s* giocatore *m*; speculatore *m*

gambling ['gæmblɪŋ] *s* gioco (d'azzardo)

gam'bling den' *s* bisca

gam'bling house' *s* casa da gioco

gam·bol ['gæmbəl] *s* salto, capriola ‖ *v* (pret & pp **-boled** or **-bolled**; ger **-boling** or **-bolling**) *intr* saltare, far capriole

gambrel ['gæmbrəl] *s* garretto

gam'brel roof' *s* tetto a mansarda

game [gem] *adj* da caccia; coraggioso; (leg) (coll) zoppo; (coll) pronto ‖ *s* (amusement) gioco; (contest) partita; (any sport) sport *m*; (wild animals hunted) selvaggina; (any pursuit) attività *f*; (object of pursuit) bersaglio; (bridge) manche *f*; **the game is up** il gioco è fallito; **to make game of** farsi gioco di; **to play the game** giocare onestamente

game' bag' *s* carniere *m*

game'cock' *s* gallo da combattimento

game'keep'er *s* guardacaccia *m*

game' of chance' *s* gioco d'azzardo

game' preserve' *s* bandita di caccia

game' war'den *s* guardacaccia *m*

gamut ['gæmət] *s* (mus, fig) gamma

gam·y ['gemi] *adj* (-ier; -iest) coraggioso; (culin) che sa di selvatico

gander ['gændər] *s* papero, oca

gang [gæŋ] *adj* multiplo ‖ *s* (of workers) banda; (of thugs) cricca ‖ *intr*—**to gang up** riunirsi; **to gang up against** or **on** (coll) gettarsi insieme contro

gangling ['gæŋglɪŋ] *adj* dinoccolato

gangli·on ['gæŋglɪ·ən] *s* (-ons or -a [ə]) ganglio

gang'plank' *s* palanca, plancia

gangrene ['gæŋgrin] *s* cancrena ‖ *tr* far andare in cancrena ‖ *intr* andare in cancrena

gangster ['gæŋstər] *s* gangster *m*

gang'way' *s* (passageway) corridoio; (gangplank) passerella, scalandrone *m*; (in ship's side) barcarizzo ‖ *interj* lasciar passare!

gan·try ['gæntri] *s* (-tries) (of crane) cavalletto; (rr) ponte *m* delle segnalazioni; (rok) piattaforma verticale, torre *f* di lancio

gap [gæp] *s* (pass) passo; (in a wall) breccia; (interval) lacuna; (between two points of view) abisso; (mach) gioco

gape [gep] or [gæp] *s* apertura; (yawn) sbadiglio; sguardo di meraviglia ‖ *intr* stare a bocca aperta; **to gape at** guardare a bocca aperta

garage [gə'rɑʒ] *s* rimessa

garb [gɑrb] *s* veste *f* ‖ *tr* vestire

garbage ['gɑrbɪdʒ] *s* pattume *m*, immondizia, immondizie *fpl*

gar'bage can' *s* portaimmondizie *m*

gar'bage collec'tor s spazzaturaio, spazzino, netturbino

garble ['garbəl] tr falsare, mutilare

garden ['gardən] s (of vegetables) orto; (of flowers) giardino

gardener ['gardnər] s (of vegetables) ortolano; (of flowers) giardiniere m

gardenia [gar'dini·ə] s gardenia

gardening ['gardnɪŋ] s orticoltura; giardinaggio

gar'den par'ty s trattenimento in giardino

gargle ['gargəl] s gargarismo || intr gargarizzare

gargoyle ['gargɔɪl] s doccione m, gargolla

garish ['gerɪʃ] or ['gærɪʃ] adj appariscente; abbagliante

garland ['garlənd] s ghirlanda || tr inghirlandare

garlic ['garlɪk] s aglio

garment ['garmənt] s capo di vestiario

gar'ment bag' s tessilsacco

garner ['garnər] tr mettere in granaio; (to get) acquistarsi; (to hoard) incettare

garnet ['garnɪt] adj & s granata

garnish ['garnɪʃ] s guarnizione; || tr guarnire; (law) sequestrare

garret ['gærɪt] s sottotetto, soffitta

garrison ['gærɪsən] s guarnigione, presidio || tr presidiare

garrote [gə'rat] or [gə'rot] s strangolamento; garrotta || tr strangolare; giustiziare con la garrotta

garrulous ['gærələs] or ['gærjələs] adj garrulo, loquace

garter ['gartər] s giarrettiera

gas [gæs] s gas m; (coll) benzina; (slang) successo; (slang) chiacchiere fpl || v (pret & pp gassed; ger gassing) tr fornire di gas; (mil) gassare; (slang) divertire || intr emettere gas; (slang) chiacchierare; **to gas up** fare il pieno

gas'bag' s involucro per il gas; (coll) chiacchierone m

gas' burn'er s becco a gas; (on a stove) fornello a gas

Gascony ['gæskəni] s la Guascogna

gaseous ['gæsɪ·əs] adj gassoso

gas' fit'ter s gassista m

gash [gæʃ] s sfregio || tr sfregiare

gas' heat' s calefazione a gas

gas'hold'er s gassometro

gasi-fy ['gæsɪ ,faɪ] v (pret & pp -fied) tr gassificare || intr gassificarsi

gas' jet' s fornello a gas; fiamma

gasket ['gæskɪt] s guarnizione

gas'light' s luce f del gas

gas' main' s tubatura principale del gas

gas' mask' s maschera antigas

gas' me'ter s contatore m del gas

gasoline ['gæsə ,lin] or [,gæsə'lin] s benzina

gas'oline' deal'er s benzinaio

gas'oline' pump' s colonnetta, distributore m di benzina

gasp [gæsp] or [gɑsp] s respirazione affannosa; (of death) rantolo || tr dire affannosamente || intr boccheggiare

gas' range' s cucina a gas, fornello a gas

gas'-sta'tion attend'ant s benzinaio

gas' stove' s cucina a gas

gas' tank' s gassometro; (aut) serbatoio di benzina

gastric ['gæstrɪk] adj gastrico

gastronomy [gæs'trɑnəmi] s gastronomia

gas' works' s officina del gas

gate [get] s porta; (in fence or wall) cancello; (of sluice) saracinesca; (in an airport or station) uscita; (rr) barriera; (sports, theat) incasso totale; **to crash the gate** (coll) fare il portoghese

gate'keep'er s portiere m; (rr) guardabarriere m

gate'way' s passaggio, entrata

gather ['gæðər] tr raccogliere, cogliere; (news) raccapezzare; (dust) coprirsi di; (e.g., a shawl) avvolgere; (speed) aumentare (di); concludere, dedurre; (signatures) (bb) riunire; (sew) increspare || intr riunirsi; raccogliersi; accumularsi

gathering ['gæðərɪŋ] s riunione; (bb) raccolta e piegatura; (pathol) ascesso; (sew) pieghettatura

gaud·y ['gɔdi] adj (-ier; -iest) chiassoso, vistoso

gauge [gedʒ] s misura; (for liquids) indicatore m di livello; (of carpenter) graffietto; indice m; diametro; (aut) spia; (rr) scartamento || tr misurare; calibrare; (naut) stazzare

Gaul [gɔl] s gallo

gaunt [gɔnt] or [gɑnt] adj magro, emaciato; (e.g., landscape) desolato

gauntlet ['gɔntlɪt] or ['gɑntlɪt] s guanto; guanto di ferro; guantone m, manopola; **to run the gauntlet** (fig) esporsi alla critica; **to take up the gauntlet** raccogliere il guanto; **to throw down the gauntlet** gettare il guanto

gauze [gɔz] s garza

gavel ['gævəl] s martello, martelletto

gavotte [gə'vɑt] s gavotta

gawk [gɔk] s sciocco || intr guardare a bocca aperta

gawk·y ['gɔki] adj (-ier; -iest) sgraziato, goffo

gay [ge] adj gaio; brillante; dissipato; (slang) omosessuale

gaye·ty ['ge·ɪti] s (-ties) gaiezza

gaze [gez] s sguardo fisso || intr fissare lo sguardo

gazelle [gə'zel] s gazzella

gazette [gə'zet] s gazzetta

gazetteer [,gæzə'tɪr] s dizionario geografico

gear [gɪr] s utensili mpl, attrezzi mpl; (mechanism) meccanismo, dispositivo; (aut) marcia; (mach) ingranaggio **out of gear** disingranato; (fig) disturbato; **to throw into gear** ingranare; **to throw out of gear** disingranare; (fig) disturbare || tr adattare || intr adattarsi

gear' box' s scatola del cambio

gear'shift' s cambio di velocità

gear'shift lev'er s leva del cambio

gear'wheel' s ruota dentata

gee [dʒi] *interj* ohl; che bellezza!; **gee up!** (*command to a draft animal*) arri!

Gei'ger count'er ['gaɪgər] s contatore m Geiger

gel [dʒɛl] s gel m || v (*pret & pp* **gelled**; *ger* **gelling**) *intr* gelatinizzarsi

gelatine ['dʒɛlətɪn] s gelatina

geld [gɛld] v (*pret & pp* **gelded** or **gelt** [gɛlt]) *tr* castrare

gem [dʒɛm] s gemma, gioia

Gemini ['dʒɛmɪ ,naɪ] *spl* i Gemelli

gender ['dʒɛndər] s (gram) genere m; (coll) sesso

gene [dʒin] s (biol) gene m

genealo·gy [,dʒini'ælədʒi] or [,dʒini-'ælədʒi] s (*-gies*) genealogia

general ['dʒɛnərəl] *adj & s* generale m

gen'eral deliv'ery s fermo in posta, fermo posta m

generalissi·mo [,dʒɛnərə'lɪsɪmo] s (*-mos*) generalissimo

generali·ty [,dʒɛnə'rælɪti] s (*-ties*) generalità f

generalize ['dʒɛnərə ,laɪz] *tr & intr* generalizzare

generally ['dʒɛnərəli] *adv* in genere, generalmente

gen'eral part'ner s accomandatario

gen'eral practi'tioner s medico generico

generalship ['dʒɛnərəl ,ʃɪp] s generalato; strategia, abilità f militare; abilità amministrativa

gen'eral staff' s stato maggiore

generate ['dʒɛnə ,ret] *tr* (*offspring; electricity*) generare; (math) originare

gen'erat'ing sta'tion s centrale elettrica

generation [,dʒɛnə'reʃən] s generazione

generative ['dʒɛnə ,retɪv] *adj* generativo

gen'erative gram'mar s grammatica generativa

generator ['dʒɛnə ,retər] s generatore m; (elec) generatrice f

generic [dʒɪ'nɛrɪk] *adj* generico

generous ['dʒɛnərəs] *adj* generoso; abbondante, copioso

gene·sis ['dʒɛnɪsɪs] s (*-ses* [,siz]) genesi f || **Genesis** s (Bib) Genesi m

genetic [dʒɪ'nɛtɪk] *adj* genetico || **genetics** ssg genetica

Geneva [dʒɪ'nivə] s Ginevra

Genevan [dʒɪ'nivən] *adj & s* ginevrino

genial ['dʒini·əl] *adj* affabile, geniale

genie ['dʒini] s genio

genital ['dʒɛnɪtəl] *adj* genitale || **genitals** *spl* genitali *mpl*

genitive ['dʒɛnɪtɪv] *adj & s* genitivo

genius ['dʒinjəs] or ['dʒini·əs] s (*geniuses*) genio || s (**genii**) ['dʒini-,aɪ] (*spirit; deity*) genio

Genoa ['dʒɛno·ə] s Genova

genocide ['dʒɛnə ,saɪd] s (*act*) genocidio; (*person*) genocida mf

Geno·ese [,dʒɛno'iz] *adj* genovese || s (*-ese*) genovese mf

genre ['ʒɑnrə] *adj* (e.g., *painting*) di genere || s genere m

genteel [dʒɛn'til] *adj* (*well-bred*) beneducato; (*affectedly polite*) manieroso, manierato

gentian ['dʒɛnʃən] s genziana

gentile ['dʒɛntɪl] or ['dʒɛntaɪl] *adj* gentilizio || ['dʒɛntaɪl] *adj & s* non circonciso; non ebreo; cristiano; (*pagan*) gentile

gentili·ty [dʒɛn'tɪlɪti] s (*-ties*) distinzione, raffinatezza

gentle ['dʒɛntəl] *adj* (e.g., *manner*) gentile; (e.g., *wind*) dolce, soave; (*wellborn*) bennato; (*tap*) leggero

gen'tle-folk' s gente f per bene

gen'tle-man s (*-men*) signore m; (*attendant to a person of high rank*) gentiluomo; (*well-mannered man*) gentleman m

gen'tleman in wait'ing s gentiluomo di camera

gentlemanly ['dʒɛntəlmənli] *adj* signorile

gen'tleman of the road' s brigante m; vagabondo

gen'tlemen's agree'ment s accordo fondato sulla buona fede

gen'tle sex' s gentil sesso

gentry ['dʒɛntri] s gente f per bene

genuine ['dʒɛnju·ɪn] *adj* genuino

genus ['dʒinəs] s (**genera** ['dʒɛnərə] or **genuses**) genere m

geographer [dʒi'ɑgrəfər] s geografo

geographic(al) [,dʒi·ə'græfɪk(əl)] *adj* geografico

geogra·phy [dʒi'ɑgrəfi] s (*-phies*) geografia

geologic(al) [,dʒi·ə'lɑdʒɪk(əl)] *adj* geologico

geologist [dʒi'ɑlədʒɪst] s geologo

geolo·gy [dʒi'ɑlədʒi] s (*-gies*) geologia

geometric(al) [,dʒi·ə'mɛtrɪk(əl)] *adj* geometrico

geometrician [dʒi ,ɑmɪ'trɪʃən] s geometra mf

geome·try [dʒi'ɑmɪtri] s (*-tries*) geometria

George [dʒɔrdʒ] s Giorgio

geranium [dʒɪ'reni·əm] s geranio

geriatrics [,dʒɛri'ætrɪks] ssg geriatria

germ [dʒʌrm] s germe m

German ['dʒʌrmən] *adj & s* tedesco

germane [dʒʌr'men] *adj* pertinente

Germanize ['dʒʌrmə ,naɪz] *tr* germanizzare

Ger'man mea'sles s rosolia, rubeola

Ger'man sil'ver s alpacca

Germany ['dʒʌrməni] s la Germania

germ' car'rier s portatore m di germi

germ' cell' s cellula germinale

germicidal [,dʒʌrmɪ'saɪdəl] *adj* germicida

germicide ['dʒʌrmɪ ,saɪd] s germicida m

germinate ['dʒʌrmɪ ,net] *intr* germinare

germ' war'fare s guerra batteriologica

gerontology [,dʒɛrɑn'tɑlədʒi] s gerontologia

gerund ['dʒɛrənd] s gerundio

gestation [dʒɛs'teʃən] s gestazione

gesticulate [dʒɛs'tɪkjə ,let] *intr* gesticolare

gesticulation [dʒɛsˌtɪkjəˈleʃən] s gesti-
colazione

gesture [ˈdʒɛstʃər] s gesto ‖ intr gestire, gesticolare

get [gɛt] v (pret **got** [gɑt]; pp **got** or
gotten [ˈgɑtən]; ger **getting**) tr ottenere; ricevere; prendere; andare a
comprare; procacciare; riportare;
procurarsi; riscuotere; guadagnare;
to get across far capire; **to get back**
riacquistare; **to get down** staccare;
(to swallow) tranguiare; **to get off**
togliere, cavare; **to get s.o. to** + inf
indurre che qlcu + subj; **to get done**
far fare; **to have got** (coll) avere; **to
have got to** + inf (coll) dovere + inf ‖
intr (to become) diventare, farsi; (to
arrive) arrivare, venire; (to get out
(said of a convalescent) alzarsi; **to
get along** andarsene; andare avanti;
tirare avanti, giostrare; aver successo; **to get along in years** essere
avanti con gli anni; **to get along with**
andare d'accordo con; **to get angry**
arrabbiarsi; **to get around** uscire; di-
vulgarsi; rigirare; **to get away** scappare, darsela a gambe; **to get away
with s.th** scappare con qlco; (coll)
farla franca; **to get back** ritornare;
ricuperare; **to get back at** (coll) vendicarsi di; **to get behind** rimanere
indietro; (to support) appoggiare,
patrocinare; **to get better** migliorare;
to get by passare oltre; (to succeed)
arrivare a farcela; passare inosservato; **to get even with** rifarsi con,
prendersi la rivincita con; **to get
going** mettersi in moto; **to get in**
entrare; rientrare; arrivare; **to get in
deeper and deeper** cacciarsi nei pasticci; **to get in with** diventare amico
di; **to get married** sposarsi **to get
andarsene**; smontare da; **to get old**
invecchiare; **to get on** andare avanti;
andare d'accordo; **to get out** uscire;
propagarsi; **to get out of** (a car)
uscire da; (trouble) trarsi di; **to get
out of the way** togliersi di mezzo; **to
get run over** essere investito; **to get
through** finire; arrivare; farsi capire;
to get to be finire per essere; **to get
under way** mettersi in cammino; **to
get up** alzarsi; **to not get over it**
(coll) non arrivare a rassegnarsi

get'a·way' s fuga; (sports) partenza

get'-to·geth'er s riunione, crocchio

get'up' s (coll) stile m, presentazione;
(coll) costume m, abbigliamento

gewgaw [ˈgjugɔ] s cianfrusaglia

geyser [ˈgaɪzər] s geyser m

ghast·ly [ˈgæstlɪ] or [ˈgɑstlɪ] adj (-lier;
-liest) orribile, orrendo; spettrale

gherkin [ˈgɑrkɪn] s cetriolino

ghet·to [ˈgɛto] s (-tos or -toes) ghetto

ghost [gost] s spettro, fantasma m; **not
a ghost of** nemmeno l'ombra di; **to
give up the ghost** rendere l'anima

ghost·ly [ˈgostlɪ] adj (-lier; -liest) spettrale, fantomatico

ghost' sto'ry s storia di fantasmi

ghost' town' s città morta

ghost' writ'er s collaboratore anonimo

ghoul [gul] s spirito necrofago; ladro
di tombe

ghoulish [ˈgulɪʃ] adj demoniaco, maca-
bro

GI [ˈdʒiˈaɪ] (letterword) (**General
Issue**) s (**GI's**) soldato degli Stati
Uniti

giant [ˈdʒaɪ·ənt] adj & s gigante m

giantess [ˈdʒaɪ·əntɪs] s gigantessa

gibberish [ˈdʒɪbərɪʃ] or [ˈgɪbərɪʃ] s
linguaggio inintelligibile

gibbet [ˈdʒɪbɪt] s forca ‖ tr impiccare
sulla forca; (to hold up to scorn)
mettere alla berlina

gibe [dʒaɪb] s scherno, frecciata ‖ intr
schernire; **to gibe at** beffarsi di

giblets [ˈdʒɪblɪts] spl rigaglie fpl

giddiness [ˈgɪdɪnɪs] s vertigine f; frivolezza

gid·dy [ˈgɪdɪ] adj (-dier; -diest) vertiginoso; preso dalle vertigini; frivolo

gift [gɪft] s regalo; (natural ability)
dono, dote f; (for Christmas) strenna

gifted [ˈgɪftɪd] adj dotato

gift' horse' s—**never lose a gift horse
in the mouth** a caval donato non si
guarda in bocca

gift' of gab' s (coll) facondia; **to have
the gift of gab** (coll) avere la lingua
sciolta

gift' pack'age s pacco-dono

gift' shop' s negozio di regali

gift'-wrap' v (pret & pp -**wrapped**; ger
-**wrapping**) tr incartare in carta speciale per regali

gigantic [dʒaɪˈgæntɪk] adj gigantesco

giggle [ˈgɪgəl] s risolino ‖ intr ridere
scioccamente, ridacchiare

gigo·lo [ˈdʒɪgəˌlo] s (-los) gigolo

gild [gɪld] v (pret & pp **gilded** or **gilt**
[gɪlt]) tr dorare, indorare

gilding [ˈgɪldɪŋ] s doratura

gill [gɪl] s (of fish) branchia ‖ [dʒɪl]
s quarto di pinta

gilt [gɪlt] adj & s dorato

gilt-edged [ˈgɪltˌɛdʒd] adj a bordo
dorato; di primissima qualità

gimcrack [ˈdʒɪmˌkræk] adj di nessun
valore ‖ s cianfrusaglia

gimlet [ˈgɪmlɪt] s succhiello

gimmick [ˈgɪmɪk] s (slang) trucco

gin [dʒɪn] s (liquor) gin m; (trap)
trappola; (mach) arganello; (tex)
sgranatrice f di cotone ‖ v (pret &
pp **ginned**; ger **ginning**) tr ginnare,
sgranare

ginger [ˈdʒɪndʒər] s zenzero; (coll)
energia, vivacità f

gin'ger ale' s gazosa allo zenzero

gin'ger·bread' s pan di zenzero; ornamento di cattivo gusto

gingerly [ˈdʒɪndʒərlɪ] adj cauto ‖ adv
con cautela

gin'ger·snap' s biscotto allo zenzero

gingham [ˈgɪŋəm] s rigatino

giraffe [dʒɪˈræf] or [dʒɪˈrɑf] s giraffa

girandole [ˈdʒɪrənˌdol] s girandola

gird [gɑrd] v (pret & pp **girt** [gʌrt] or
girded) tr cingere; (to equip) dotare;
(to prepare) preparare; (to surround)
circondare

girder [ˈgʌrdər] s longherina

girdle ['gʌrdəl] s reggicalze m, zona, fascetta || tr fasciare; circondare

girl [gʌrl] s fanciulla; ragazza

girl' friend' s amica, innamorata

girlhood ['gʌrlhud] s adolescenza, giovinezza

girlish ['gʌrlɪʃ] adj fanciullesco; da ragazza

girl' scout' s giovane esploratrice f

girth [gʌrθ] s circonferenza; fascia; (to hold a saddle) sottopancia m

gist [dʒɪst] s sugo, nocciolo, essenza

give [gɪv] s elasticità f || v (pret gave [gev]; pp given ['gɪvən]) tr dare; (trouble) causare; (a play) rappresentare; (a speech; fruit; a sigh) fare; **to give away** distribuire gratuitamente; (to reveal) lasciarsi sfuggire; (a bride) accompagnare all'altare; (coll) tradire; **to give back** restituire; **to give forth** (odors) emettere; **to give oneself up** darsi; **to give up** cedere; (a position) abbandonare || intr dare; cedere; (said, e.g., of a rope) rompersi; **to give in** cedere; darsi per vinto; **to give out** esaurirsi; venir meno; **to give up** darsi per vinto

give'-and-take' s compromesso; conversazione briosa

give'a·way' s premio gratuito; rivelazione involontaria; (game) vinciperdi m; (rad, telv) programma m a premi

given ['gɪvən] adj dato; **given that** dato che, concesso che

giv'en name' s nome m di battesimo

giver ['gɪvər] s donatore m; dispensatore m

gizzard ['gɪzərd] s magone m

glacial ['gleʃəl] adj glaciale

glacier ['gleʃər] s ghiacciaio

glad [glæd] adj (gladder; gladdest) felice, lieto, contento; **to be glad (to)** essere felice (di)

gladden ['glædən] tr rallegrare

glade [gled] s radura

glad' hand' s (coll) accoglienza calorosa

gladiator ['glædɪ,etər] s gladiatore m

gladiola [,glædɪ'olə] or [glə'daɪ·ələ] s gladiolo

gladly ['glædli] adv volentieri, di buon grado

gladness ['glædnɪs] s contentezza

glad' rags' s (coll) panni mpl da festa; (coll) vestito da sera

glamorous ['glæmərəs] adj affascinante, attraente

glamour ['glæmər] s fascino, malia

glam'our girl' s ragazza sci-sci

glance [glæns] or [glɑns] s occhiata, guardata; **at first glance** a prima vista || intr lanciare uno sguardo; **to glance at** dare un'occhiata a; **to glance off** sorvolare su; deviare da; **to glance over** dare una scorsa a

gland [glænd] s ghiandola

glanders ['glændərz] spl morva

glare [gler] s splendore m, luce f abbagliante; sguardo minaccioso || intr risplendere; lanciare occhiatacce; **to glare at** fare la faccia feroce a

glare' ice' s vetrato

glaring ['glerɪŋ] adj risplendente, abbagliante; (look) torvo; evidente

glass [glæs] or [glɑs] s vetro; (tumbler) bicchiere m; (mirror) specchio; (glassware) cristalleria; **glasses** occhiali mpl

glass' blow'er ['blo·ər] s vetraio

glass' case' s vetrinetta

glass' cut'ter s tagliatore m di cristallo; (tool) diamante m tagliavetro

glass' door' s porta a vetri

glassful ['glæsful] or ['glɑsful] s bicchiere m

glass'house' s vetreria; (fig) casa di vetro

glass'ware' s vetreria, cristalleria

glass' wool' s vetro filato

glass'work'er s vetraio

glass'works' s vetreria, cristalleria

glass·y ['glæsi] or ['glɑsi] adj (-ier; -iest) vetriato, vetroso

glaze [glez] s vernice vitrea; smalto; (of ice) superficie invetriata; (culin) glassa || tr smaltare; invetriare; (culin) glassare

glazier ['gleʒər] s vetraio

gleam [glim] s barlume m, raggio || intr baluginare

glean [glin] tr spigolare, racimolare; (to gather facts) raccogliere

glee [gli] s gioia, esultanza

glee' club' s società f corale

glib [glɪb] adj (glibber; glibbest) loquace; (tongue) facile, sciolto

glide [glaɪd] s scivolata; (aer) volo a vela, volo planato; (mus) legamento || intr scivolare; (aer) librarsi, planare; **to glide away** scorrere

glider ['glaɪdər] s (aer) libratore m, veleggiatore m

glimmer ['glɪmər] s barlume m || intr brillare, luccicare; tralucere

glimmering ['glɪmərɪŋ] adj tenue, tremulo || s luce fioca; barlume m

glimpse [glɪmps] s occhiata; **to catch a glimpse of** intravedere || tr travedere

glint [glɪnt] s scintillio || intr scintillare

glisten ['glɪsən] s scintillio, luccichio || intr scintillare, luccicare

glitter ['glɪtər] s luccichio || intr rilucere, sfolgorare

gloaming ['glomɪŋ] s crepuscolo (vespertino)

gloat [glot] intr guardare con maligna soddisfazione; **to gloat over** godere di

global ['globəl] adj globale; universale; globulare

globe [glob] s globo; (with map of earth) mappamondo

globe-trotter ['glob,trɑtər] s giramondo

globule ['glɑbjul] s globulo

glockenspiel ['glɑkən,spil] s vibrafono

gloom [glum] s oscurità f; malinconia, uggia

gloom·y ['glumi] adj (-ier; -iest) lugubre, triste, tetro

glori·fy ['glorɪ,faɪ] v (pret & pp -fied) tr glorificare; (to enhance) esaltare

glorious ['glorɪ·əs] *adj* glorioso; magnifico, splendido

glo·ry ['glorɪ] *s* (-ries) gloria; **to go to glory** morire || *v* (*pret* & *pp* -ried) *intr* gloriarsi

gloss [glɑs] *or* [glɔs] *s* lucentezza, patina; (*commentary*) glossa || *tr* satinare, patinare; (*to annotate*) glossare; **to gloss over** nascondere, discolpare

glossa·ry ['glɑsərɪ] *s* (-ries) glossario

gloss·y ['glɔsɪ] *or* ['glɑsɪ] *adj* (-ier; -iest) lucido; (*paper*) satinato

glottal ['glɑtəl] *adj* articolato alla glottide

glottis ['glɑtɪs] *s* glottide *f*

glove [glʌv] *s* guanto

glove' compart'ment *s* cassetto portaoggetti

glow [glo] *s* fuoco, incandescenza; splendore *m*, scintillio; calore *m*; colorito acceso || *intr* essere incandescente; (*said of cheeks*) avvampare; (*said of cat's eyes*) fosforeggiare

glower ['glaʊ·ər] *s* sguardo torvo || *intr* guardare col viso torvo

glowing ['glo·ɪŋ] *adj* incandescente; acceso; entusiasta, entusiastico

glow'worm' *s* lucciola; lampiride *m*

glucose ['glukos] *s* glucosio

glue [glu] *s* colla, mastice *m* || *tr* incollare, ingommare

glue'pot' *s* pentolino per la colla

gluey ['glu·i] *adj* (gluier; gluiest) attaccaticcio; (*smeared with glue*) incollato

glum [glʌm] *adj* (glummer; glummest) tetro, accigliato

glut [glʌt] *s* abbondanza; eccesso; **there is a glut on the market** il mercato è saturo || *v* (*pret* & *pp* glutted; *ger* glutting) *tr* saziare; (*the market*) saturare; (*a channel*) otturare

glutton ['glʌtən] *adj* & *s* ghiottone *m*

gluttonous ['glʌtənəs] *adj* ghiotto

glutton·y ['glʌtənɪ] *s* (-ies) ghiottoneria, golosità *f*

glycerine ['glɪsərɪn] *s* glicerina

G'-man' *s* (-men') agente *m* federale

gnarl [nɑrl] *s* nodo || *tr* torcere || *intr* ringhiare

gnarled [nɑrld] *adj* nodoso; (*wrinkled*) grinzoso

gnash [næʃ] *tr* digrignare || *intr* digrignare i denti

gnat [næt] *s* moscerino, pappataci *m*

gnaw [nɔ] *tr* rosicchiare, rodere || *intr* —to gnaw at (fig) rimordere

gnome [nom] *s* gnomo

go [go] *s* (goes) andata; energia; (*for traffic*) via libera; **it's a go** è un affare fatto; **it's all the go** (coll) è all'ultimo grido; **it's no go** (coll) è impossibile; **on the go** in continuo andare e venire; **to make a go of** (coll) aver successo con || *v* (*pret* **went** [wɛnt], *pp* **gone** [gɔn] *or* [gɑn]) *tr* (coll) sopportare; (coll) scommettere; (coll) pagare; **to go it alone** fare da sé || *intr* andare; (*to operate*) camminare, funzionare; (*e.g., mad*) diventare; (*said of numbers*) entrare; **gone!** venduto!; **so it goes** così va il mondo; **to**

be going to + *inf* andare a + *inf*, e.g., **I am going to New York to see him** vado a New York a vederlo; (*to express futurity*) use *fut ind*, e.g., **I am going to stay home today** starò a casa oggi; **to be gone** essere andato; esser morto; **to go against** opporsi a; **to go ahead** andar avanti; tirare avanti; **to go around** andare in giro; **to go away** andarsene; **to go back** tornare; **to go by** passare per; regolarsi su; (*said of time*) passare; **to go down** discendere; (*said of a boat*) affondare; **to go fishing** andare a pescare; **to go for** vendersi per; andare a pigliare; attaccare; favorire; **to go get** andare a pigliare; **to go house hunting** andare in cerca di una casa; **to go hunting** andare a caccia; **to go in** entrare in; (*to fit in*) starci in; **to go in for** dedicarsi a; **to go into** investigare; darsi a, dedicarsi a; (*gear*) (aut) ingranare; **to go in with** associarsi con; **to go off** andarsene; aver luogo; (*said of a bomb*) esplodere; (*said of a rifle*) sparare; (*said of a trap*) scattare; **to go on** continuare, protrarsi; **to go on** + *ger* continuare a + *inf*; **to go out** uscire; passare di moda; (*said, e.g., of fire*) spegnersi; (*to strike*) mettersi in sciopero; **to go over** aver successo; leggere; esaminare; **to go over to** passare ai ranghi di; **to go skiing** andare a sciare; **to go swimming** andare a nuotare, andare al bagno; **to go through** esperimentare; (*to examine carefully*) rovistare; (*said, e.g., of a plan or a project*) aver successo; (*a fortune*) dissipare; **to go through a red light** passare la strada col semaforo rosso; **to go with** andare con, accompagnare; (*a girl*) essere l'amico di; **to go without** fare a meno di

goad [god] *s* pungolo || *tr* pungolare; (fig) spronare

go'-ahead' *adj* intraprendente || *s* via *m*

goal [gol] *s* meta; (football) gol *m*

goalie ['golɪ] *s* portiere *m*

goal'keep'er *s* portiere *m*

goal' line' *s* linea di porta

goal' post' *s* montante *m*

goat [got] *s* capra; (*male*) becco; (coll) capro espiatorio; **to get the goat of** (coll) irritare

goatee [go'ti] *s* barbetta, pizzo

goat'herd' *s* capraio

goat'skin' *s* pelle *f* di capra

goat'suck'er *s* caprimulgo

gob [gɑb] *s* massa informe; **gobs** (coll) mucchio, quantità *f* enorme

gobble ['gɑbəl] *s* gloglottio || *tr* ingozzare; **to gobble up** (coll) tranguriare; (coll) impadronirsi di || *intr* trangugiare; (*said of a turkey*) gloglottare

gobbledegook ['gɑbəldɪ,guk] *s* linguaggio oscuro

go'-between' *s* intermediario; (*pander*) mezzano; (poet) pronubo

goblet ['gɑblɪt] *s* coppa

goblin ['gɑblɪn] *s* folletto

go'-by' *s*—**to give s.o. the go-by** (coll) schivare qlcu

go'-cart' *s* carrettino; (*walker*) girello

god [gad] *s* dio; **God forbid** Dio ci scampi; **God grant** voglia Dio; **God willing** se Dio vuole

god'child' *s* (-chil'dren) figlioccio

god'daugh'ter *s* figlioccia

goddess ['gadɪs] *s* dea, diva

God'-fear'ing *adj* timorato di Dio

God'for·sak'en *adj* miserabile; (*place*) sperduto, fuori di mano

god'head' *s* deità *f* || **Godhead** *s* Ente Supremo, Dio

godless ['gadlɪs] *adj* ateo; malvagio || **the godless** i senza Dio

god·ly ['gadlɪ] *adj* (-lier; -liest) devoto, pio

god'moth'er *s* madrina

God's'/a'cre *s* camposanto

god'send' *s* manna, provvidenza

god'son' *s* figlioccio

God'speed' *s* successo, buona fortuna

go-getter ['go ,gɛtər] *s* (coll) persona intraprendente

goggle ['gagəl] *intr* stralunare gli occhi

goggle-eyed ['gagəl ,aɪd] *adj* dagli occhi sporgenti

goggles ['gagəlz] *spl* occhiali *mpl* da protezione

going ['go·ɪŋ] *adj* in moto, in funzione; **going on** quasi, e.g., **it is going on seven o'clock** sono quasi le sette || *s* andata; progresso

go'ings on' *s* (coll) comportamento, contegno; (coll) avvenimenti *mpl*

goiter ['gɔɪtər] *s* gozzo

gold [gold] *adj* aureo, d'oro || *s* oro

gold'beat'er *s* battiloro

gold'brick' *s* imitazione, frode *f*; (slang) fannullone *m*

gold' dig'ger ['dɪgər] *s* cercatore *m* d'oro; (coll) donna unicamente interessata nel denaro

golden ['goldən] *adj* aureo, d'oro; (*gilt*) dorato; (fig) splendido

gold'en age' *s* età *f* dell'oro

gold'en calf' *s* vitello d'oro

Gold'en Fleece' *s* vello d'oro

gold'en mean' *s* aurea mediocrità

gold'en·rod' *s* (bot) verga d'oro

gold'en rule' *s* regola della carità cristiana

gold'en wed'ding *s* nozze *fpl* d'oro

gold-filled ['gold ,fɪld] *adj* otturato in oro

gold'finch' *s* cardellino

gold'fish' *s* pesce rosso

goldilocks ['gɔldɪ ,laks] *s* bionda; (bot) ranuncolo

gold' leaf' *s* oro in foglia

gold' mine' *s* miniera d'oro

gold' plate' *s* vasellame *m* d'oro

gold'-plate' *tr* dorare

gold' rush' *s* febbre *f* dell'oro

gold'smith' *s* orefice *m*

gold' stand'ard *s* regime aureo

golf [galf] *s* golf *m* || *intr* giocare a golf

golf' cart' *s* mini-auto *f* per campi da golf

golf' club' *s* mazza; associazione di giocatori di golf

golfer ['galfər] *s* giocatore *m* di golf

golf' links' *spl* campo di golf

Golgotha ['galgəθə] *s* il Golgota

gondola ['gandələ] *s* gondola

gondolier [,gandə'lɪr] *s* gondoliere *m*

gone [gɔn] *or* [gan] *adj* partito; rovinato; andato; morto; **gone on** (coll) innamorato di

gong [gɔŋ] *or* [gaŋ] *s* gong *m*

goo [gu] *s* (coll) sostanza appiccicaticcia

good [gʊd] *adj* (**better**; **best**) buono; **good and . . .** (coll) molto, e.g., **good and cheap** molto a buon mercato; **good for** buono per; responsabile per; (*equivalent*) valido per; **to be good at** esser bravo a; **to be no good** (coll) non servire a nulla; (coll) essere un perdigiorno; **to make good** avere successo; (*one's promise*) mantenere; (*a debt*) pagare; (*damages*) indennizzare || *s* bene *m*; utile *m*, profitto; **for good** per sempre; **for good and all** una volta per sempre; **goods** merce *f*, mercanzia; **the good** il bene; i buoni; **to catch with the goods** (coll) cogliere in flagrante; **to deliver the goods** (slang) mantenere le promesse; **to do good** fare del bene; **to the good** come profitto; come attivo; **what is the good of . . . ?** a che serve . . . ?

good' afternoon' *s* buon pomeriggio

good'-by' [,gʊd'baɪ] *s* addio || *interj* addio!; arrivederci!

good' day' *s* buon giorno

good' deed' *s* buona azione

good' egg' *s* (slang) bonaccione *m*, gran brava persona

good' eve'ning *s* buona sera; buona notte

good' fel'low *s* buon ragazzo

good'-fel'low·ship' *s* cameratismo

good'-for-noth'ing *adj* inutile, senza valore || *s* pelandrone *m*, inetto

Good' Fri'day *s* Venerdì Santo

good' grac'es *s* buone grazie

good-hearted ['gʊd'hartɪd] *adj* di buon cuore

good'-hum'ored *adj* di buon umore

good'-look'ing *adj* bello

good' looks' *s* bellezza

good·ly ['gʊdlɪ] *adj* (-lier; -liest) bello; di buona qualità; ampio, considerevole

good' morn'ing *s* buon giorno

good-natured ['gʊd'net∫ərd] *adj* bonaccione, affabile

goodness ['gʊdnɪs] *s* bontà *f*; **for goodness sake!** per amor di Dio!; **goodness knows!** chi sa mai! || *interj* Dio mio!

good' night' *s* buona notte

good'-sized' *adj* piuttosto grande

good' speed' *s* buona fortuna

good'-tem'pered *adj* di carattere mite, gioviale

good' time' *s* periodo gradevole; **to have a good time** divertirsi; **to make good time** andare di buon passo

good' turn' *s* favore *m*, servizio

good' will' *s* buona volontà; (com) reputazione; (com) clientela

good·y ['gʊdi] *adj* (coll) troppo buono || *s* (-ies) (coll) santerello; **goodies**

(coll) ghiottonerie *fpl* || *interj* (coll) bene!, benissimo!

gooey ['gu·i] *adj* (**gooier; gooiest**) (slang) attaccaticcio

goof [guf] *s* (slang) sciocco || *tr* (slang) rovinare; **to goof up** (*an opportunity*) (slang) mancare || *intr* (slang) pigliare un granchio; **to goof off** (slang) battere la fiacca; **to goof up** (slang) farla grossa

goof·y ['gufi] *adj* (**-ier; -iest**) (slang) sciocco

goon [gun] *s* (slang) scemo; (coll) crumiro, gaglioffo, terrorista *m*

goose [gus] *s* (**geese** [gis]) oca; **the goose hangs high** tutto va per il meglio; **to cook one's goose** rompere le uova nel paniere di qlcu; **to kill the goose that lays the golden eggs** uccidere la gallina delle uova d'oro || *s* (**gooses**) ferro da stiro per sarto

goose'ber'ry *s* (**-ries**) uva spina; (*berry*) bacca d'uva spina

goose' egg' *s* (slang) zero; (*lump on the head*) (coll) bernoccolo

goose' flesh' *s* pelle *f* d'oca

goose'neck' *s* collo d'oca

goose' pim'ples *spl* pelle *f* d'oca

goose' step' *s* passo dell'oca

gopher ['gofər] *s* scoiattolo di terra, citillo

gore [gor] *s* sangue coagulato; (*in a garment*) gherone *m* || *tr* (*with a horn*) incornare; inserire gheroni in

gorge [gɔrdʒ] *s* gola, burrone *m*; (*meal*) mangiata || *tr* rimpinzare || *intr* rimpinzarsi

gorgeous ['gɔrdʒəs] *adj* splendido, magnifico

gorilla [gə'rɪlə] *s* gorilla *m*

gorse [gɔrs] *s* gineprone *m*

gor·y ['gori] *adj* (**-ier; -iest**) sanguinolento

gosh [gɑʃ] *interj* perbacco!

goshawk ['gas,hɔk] *s* sparviere *m*, astore *m*

gospel ['gɑspəl] *s* vangelo || **Gospel** *s* Vangelo

gos'pel truth' *s* santissima verità

gossamer ['gɑsəmər] *s* ragnatela; (*variety of gauze*) garza finissima; tessuto impermeabile finissimo

gossip ['gɑsɪp] *s* maldicenza; (*person*) pettegolo; **piece of gossip** maldicenza || *intr* spettegolare

gossipy ['gɑsɪpi] *adj* pettegolo

Goth [gɑθ] *s* Goto

Gothic ['gɑθɪk] *adj* & *s* gotico

gouge [gaudʒ] *s* (*cut made with a gouge*) scanalatura; (*tool*) sgorbia; (coll) truffa || *tr* sgorbiare; (coll) truffare

goulash ['gulaʃ] *s* gulasch *m*

gourd [gord] *or* [gurd] *s* zucca

gourmand ['gurmənd] *s* ghiottone *m*

gourmet ['gurme] *s* buongustaio

gout [gaut] *s* gotta, podagra

gout·y ['gauti] *adj* (**-ier; -iest**) gottoso

govern ['gʌvərn] *tr* governare; (gram) reggere

governess ['gʌvərnɪs] *s* governante *f*, istitutrice *f*

government ['gʌvərnmənt] *s* governo; (gram) reggenza

governmental [,gʌvərn'mentəl] *adj* governativo

governor ['gʌvərnər] *s* governatore *m*; (mach) regolatore *m*

governorship ['gʌvərnər,ʃɪp] *s* governatorato

gown [gaun] *s* (*of a woman*) vestito; (*academic*) toga; (*of a physician or patient*) gabbanella; (*of a priest*) veste *f* talare

grab [græb] *s* presa; **up for grabs** (coll) pronto a esser pigliato || *v* (*pret & pp* **grabbed;** *ger* **grabbing**) *tr* pigliare, afferrare

grace [gres] *s* (*charm; favor*) grazia; (*pardon*) mercé *f*; (*prayer*) benedicite *m*; (*com*) dilazione; **to say grace** recitare il benedicite; **with good grace** di buona voglia || *tr* adornare

graceful ['gresfəl] *adj* grazioso, vezzoso, leggiadro

grace' note' *s* (mus) appoggiatura

gracious ['greʃəs] *adj* grazioso; misericordioso || *interj* Dio buono!

gradation [gre'deʃən] *s* gradazione; (*step in a series*) passo

grade [gred] *s* grado; (*slope*) pendenza; (*mark in school*) voto; **to make the grade** raggiungere la meta || *tr* selezionare; (*a student*) dare un voto a; (*land*) spianare

grade' cros'sing *s* (rr) passaggio a livello

grade' school' *s* scuola elementare

gradient ['gredɪ·ənt] *adj* in pendenza || *s* pendenza; (phys) gradiente *m*

gradual ['grædʒu·əl] *adj* graduale

graduate ['grædʒu·ɪt] *adj* graduato; superiore; (*student*) laureato; (*candidate for degree*) laureando || ['grædʒu,et] *tr* graduare; laureare; diplomare || *intr* laurearsi, diplomarsi

grad'uate school' *s* facoltà *f* di studi avanzati

graduation [,grædʒu'eʃən] *s* graduazione; laurea; cerimonia della consegna delle lauree

graft [græft] *or* [grɑft] *s* (hort) innesto; (surg) trapianto; (coll) prevaricazione || *tr* (hort) innestare; (surg) trapiantare || *intr* (coll) prevaricare

gra'ham bread' ['gre·əm] *s* pane *m* integrale

grain [gren] *s* chicco; (*of sand*) granello; (*cereal seeds*) granaglie *fpl*; (*in wood*) venatura; (*in stone*) grana; **against the grain** di cattivo verso || *tr* granulare; (*leather*) zigrinare; (*metal*) granire

grain' el'evator *s* elevatore *m* di grano; (*building*) deposito di cereali

graining ['grenɪŋ] *s* venatura

gram [græm] *s* grammo

grammar ['græmər] *s* grammatica

grammarian [grə'merɪ·ən] *s* grammatico

gram'mar school' *s* scuola elementare

grammatical [grə'mætɪkəl] *adj* grammatico

gramophone ['græmə,fon] *s* (trademark) grammofono

grana·ry ['grænəri] *s* (**-ries**) granaio

grand [grænd] *adj* grandioso; grande, famoso

grand'aunt' *s* prozia

grand'child' *s* (**-chil'dren**) nipote *mf*

grand'daugh'ter *s* nipote *f*

grand' duch'ess *s* granduchessa

grand' duke' *s* granduca *m*

grandee [græn'di] *s* grande *m*

grandeur ['grændʒər] *or* ['grænd͡ʒur] *s* grande *m*, grandiosità *f*

grand'fa'ther *s* nonno; (*forefather*) antenato

grand'father's clock' *s* grande orologio a pendolo

grandiose ['grændɪ,os] *adj* grandioso

grand' ju'ry *s* giuria investigativa

grand' lar'ceny *s* furto importante

grand' lodge' *s* grande oriente *m*

grandma ['grænd,ma], ['græm,ma] *or* ['græmə] *s* (coll) nonna

grand'moth'er *s* nonna

grand'neph'ew *s* pronipote *m*

grand'niece' *s* pronipote *f*

grand' op'era *s* opera, opera lirica

grandpa ['grænd,pa], ['græn,pa] *or* ['græmpə] *s* (coll) nonno

grand'par'ent *s* nonno, nonna

grand' pian'o *s* pianoforte *m* a coda

grand'son' *s* nipote *m*

grand'stand' *s* tribuna

grand' to'tal *s* somma totale; importo globale

grand'un'cle *s* prozio

grand' vizier' *s* gran visir *m*

grange [grendʒ] *s* (*farm*) fattoria; (*organization of farmers*) sindacato di agricoltori

granite ['grænɪt] *s* granito

grant [grænt] *or* [grant] *s* concessione; (*sum of money*) sovvenzione; trapasso di proprietà ‖ *tr* concedere; (*a wish*) esaudire; (*a permit*) rilasciare; (law) trasferire; **to take for granted** ammettere come vero; trattare con indifferenza

grantee [græn'ti] *or* [gran'ti] *s* concessionario; beneficiario

grant'-in-aid' *s* (**grants'-in-aid'**) sussidio governativo a un ente pubblico; borsa di studio

grantor [græn'tɔr] *or* [gran'tɔr] *s* concedente *m*, concessore *m*

granular ['grænjələr] *adj* granulare

granulate ['grænjə,let] *tr* granulare ‖ *intr* diventare granulato

gran'ulated sug'ar *s* zucchero cristallizzato

granule ['grænjul] *s* granulo

grape [grep] *s* chicco d'uva; (*vine*) vite *f*; **grapes** uva

grape' ar'bor *s* pergolato

grape'fruit' *s* pompelmo

grape' juice' *s* succo d'uva

grape'shot' *s* mitraglia

grape'vine' *s* vite *f*; **by the grapevine** di bocca in bocca; (mil) attraverso la radio fante

graph [græf] *or* [graf] *s* (*diagram*) grafico; (gram) segno grafico

graphic(al) ['græfɪk(əl)] *adj* grafico

graphite ['græfaɪt] *s* grafite *f*

graph' pa'per *s* carta millimetrata

grapnel ['græpnəl] *s* uncino; (*anchor*) grappino

grapple ['græpəl] *s* uncino; lotta corpo a corpo ‖ *tr* uncinare ‖ *intr* combattere; **to grapple with** lottare con

grap'pling i'ron *s* raffio, grappino

grasp [græsp] *or* [grasp] *s* impugnatura; (*power*) possesso; **to have a good grasp of** sapere a fondo; **within the grasp of** nei limiti della comprensione di ‖ *tr* (*with hand*) impugnare; (*to get control of*) impadronirsi di; (fig) capire ‖ *intr*—**to grasp at** cercare di afferrare

grasping ['græspɪŋ] *or* ['graspɪŋ] *adj* tenace; avido, cupido

grass [græs] *or* [gras] *s* erba; (*pasture land*) pastura; (*lawn*) tappeto erboso; **to go to grass** (*said of cattle*) andare al pascolo; andare in vacanza; ritirarsi; andare in rovina; morire; **to not let the grass grow under one's feet** non dormire in piuma

grass' court' *s* campo da tennis d'erba

grass'hop'per *s* cavalletta

grass'-roots' *adj* popolare

grass' seed' *s* semente *f* d'erba

grass' wid'ow *s* donna separata dal marito

grass·y ['græsi] *or* ['grasi] *adj* (**-ier; -iest**) erboso

grate [gret] *s* (*for cooking*) griglia; (*at a window*) grata ‖ *tr* mettere una grata a; (*one's teeth*) digrignare; (*e.g., cheese*) grattugiare ‖ *intr* stridere, cigolare; **to grate on one's nerves** dare sui nervi di qlcu

grateful ['gretfəl] *adj* riconoscente; (*pleasing*) piacevole, gradito

grater ['gretər] *s* grattugia

grati·fy ['grætɪ,faɪ] *v* (*pret & pp* **-fied**) *tr* gratificare, soddisfare

gratifying ['grætɪ,faɪ·ɪŋ] *adj* soddisfacente, piacevole

grating ['gretɪŋ] *adj* irritante; (*sound*) stridente ‖ *s* inferriata

gratis ['gretɪs] *or* ['grætɪs] *adj* gratuito ‖ *adv* gratis

gratitude ['grætɪ,tjud] *or* ['grætɪ,tud] *s* gratitudine *f*, riconoscenza

gratuitous [grə'tju·ɪtəs] *or* [grə'tu·ɪtəs] *adj* gratuito

gratui·ty [grə'tju·ɪti] *or* [grə'tu·ɪti] *s* (**-ties**) mancia, regalia

grave [grev] *adj* grave ‖ *s* tomba, sepolcro, fossa

gravedigger ['grev,dɪgər] *s* becchino

gravel ['grævəl] *s* ghiaia; (pathol) renella

grav'en im'age ['grevən] *s* idolo

grave'stone' *s* pietra tombale

grave'yard' *s* cimitero, camposanto

gravitate ['grævɪ,tet] *intr* gravitare

gravitation [,grævɪ'teʃən] *s* gravitazione

gravi·ty ['grævɪti] *s* (**-ties**) gravità *f*

gravure [grə'vjur] *or* ['grevjur] *s* fotoincisione

gra·vy ['grevi] *s* (**-vies**) (*juice from*

cooking meat) sugo; (*sauce made with it*) salsa, intingolo; (slang) guadagni *mpl* facili

gra'vy boat' *s* salsiera

gra'vy train' *s* (slang) greppia, mangiatoia

gray [gre] *adj* grigio; (*gray-haired*) canuto || *s* grigio; cavallo grigio || *intr* incanutire

gray'beard' *s* vecchio

gray-haired ['gre,herd] *adj* canuto

gray'hound' *s* levriere *m*

grayish ['gre·ɪʃ] *adj* grigiastro

gray' mat'ter *s* materia grigia

graze [grez] *tr* (*to touch lightly*) sfiorare; (*to scratch lightly*) scalfire; (*grass*) brucare; (*cattle*) pascere, pascolare || *intr* pascere, brucare

grease [gris] *s* grasso, unto || [gris] or [griz] *tr* ingrassare, ungere

grease' cup' [gris] *s* coppa dell'olio

grease' gun' [gris] *s* ingrassatore *m*

grease' lift' [gris] *s* piattaforma di lubrificazione

grease' paint' [gris] *s* cerone *m*

grease' pit' [gris] *s* fossa di riparazione

greas·y ['grisi] or ['grizi] *adj* (**-ier; -iest**) grasso, unto, untuoso

great [gret] *adj* grande; (coll) eccellente || **the great** *i* grandi

great'-aunt' *s* prozia

Great' Bear' *s* Orsa Maggiore

Great' Brit'ain ['brɪtən] *s* la Gran Bretagna

Great' Dane' *s* danese *m*, alano

Great'er New York' *s* Nuova York e i suoi sobborghi

great'-grand'child' *s* (**-chil'dren**) pronipote *mf*

great'-grand'daugh'ter *s* pronipote *f*

great'-grand'fa'ther *s* bisnonno

great'-grand'moth'er *s* bisnonna

great'-grand'par'ent *s* bisnonno, bisnonna

great'-grand'son' *s* pronipote *m*

greatly ['gretli] *adj* molto

great'-neph'ew *s* pronipote *m*

greatness ['gretnɪs] *s* grandezza

great'-niece' *s* pronipote *f*

great'-un'cle *s* prozio

Grecian ['griʃən] *adj* & *s* greco

Greece [gris] *s* la Grecia

greed [grid] *s* avarizia, avidità *f*

greediness ['gridɪnɪs] *s* bramosia

greed·y ['gridi] *adj* (**-ier; -iest**) avaro; ingordo, bramoso

Greek [grik] *adj* & *s* greco

green [grin] *adj* verde; (fig) verde, inesperto || *s* verde *m*; (*lawn*) tappeto erboso; **greens** verdura, insalata

green'back' *s* (U.S.A.) biglietto di banca

green' earth' *s* verdaccio

greener·y ['grinəri] *s* (**-ies**) (*foliage*) vegetazione; (*hothouse*) serra

green'-eyed' *adj* dagli occhi verdi; (coll) geloso

green'gage' *s* regina claudia

green'horn' *s* (slang) pivello, sempliciotto

green'house' *s* serra

greenish ['grinɪʃ] *adj* verdastro

Greenland ['grinlənd] *s* la Groenlandia

green' light' *s* semaforo verde; (coll) via *m*

greenness ['grinnɪs] *s* verdore *m*, verdezza; inesperienza

green' pep'per *s* peperone *m* verde

greensward ['grin ,sword] *s* tappeto erboso

green' thumb' *s* abilità *f* speciale per il giardinaggio

green' veg'etables *spl* verdura

green'wood' *s* bosco verde

greet [grit] *tr* salutare; ricevere; (*e.g., one's ears*) offrirsi a

greeting ['gritɪŋ] *s* saluto; accoglienza || **greetings** *interj* saluti

greet'ing card' *s* cartolina d'auguri

gregarious [grɪ'gɛrɪ·əs] *adj* (*living in the midst of others*) gregario; (*sociable*) sociale

Gregorian [grɪ'gorɪ·ən] *adj* gregoriano

grenade [grɪ'ned] *s* granata

grenadier [,grɛnə'dɪr] *s* granatiere *m*

grenadine [,grɛnə'din] *s* granatina

grey [gre] *adj*, *s* & *intr* var of **gray**

grid [grɪd] *s* (*network*) rete *f*; (*on map*) reticolato; (electron) griglia

griddle ['grɪdəl] *s* tegame *m*

grid'dle-cake' *s* frittella cotta in teglia, crêpe *m*

grid'i'ron *s* griglia; campo di football; (theat) graticola

grief [grif] *s* affanno, dolore *m*; disgrazia; **to come to grief** andare in rovina

grievance ['grivəns] *s* lagnanza; motivo di lagnanza

grieve [griv] *tr* affliggere || *intr* affliggersi, dolersi; **to grieve over** soffrire per

grievous ['grivəs] *adj* doloroso, penoso; (*error*) grave; (*deplorable*) deplorevole

griffin ['grɪfɪn] *s* grifo, grifone *m*

grill [grɪl] *s* griglia || *tr* mettere alla griglia; (coll) interrogare insistentemente

grille [grɪl] *s* inferriata; (aut) mascherina, calandra

grill'room' *s* grill-room *m*, rosticceria

grim [grɪm] *adj* (**grimmer; grimmest**) (*stern*) accigliato; (*fierce*) feroce; (*sinister*) sinistro; (*unyielding*) implacabile

grimace ['grɪməs] or [grɪ'mes] *s* smorfia, sberleffo || *intr* fare le boccacce

grime [graim] *s* sporco; (*soot*) fuliggine *f*

grim·y ['graimi] *adj* (**-ier; -iest**) sporco; fuligginoso

grin [grɪn] *s* sorriso; (*malicious in intent*) ghigno || *v* (*pret* & *pp* **grinned**; *ger* **grinning**) *intr* sorridere; ghignare

grind [graind] *s* macinata; (*laborious work*) (coll) macina; (slang) sgobbone *m* || *v* (*pret* & *pp* **ground** [graund]) *tr* macinare; (*to sharpen*) molare; (*lenses*) smerigliare; (*meat*) tritare; opprimere; (*a crank*) girare; (mach) rettificare || *intr* macinare; frantumarsi; cigolare; (coll) sgobbare

grinder ['graindər] *s* (*to sharpen tools*) mola; (*to grind coffee*) macinino (*back tooth*) molare *m;* (*person*) molatore *m*

grind'stone' *s* mola; **to keep one's nose to the grindstone** lavorare senza posa

grin·go ['grɪŋgo] *s* (*-gos*) (*disparaging*) gringo

grip [grɪp] *s* (*grasp*) presa; (*with hand*) stretta; (*handle*) impugnatura; **to come to grips** venire alle prese ‖ *v* (*pret & pp* **gripped;** *ger* **gripping**) *tr* stringere; impugnare; attirare l'attenzione di

gripe [graɪp] *s* (*coll*) lamentela; (*naut*) rizza; **gripes** colica ‖ *intr* (*coll*) lamentarsi, brontolare

grippe [grɪp] *s* influenza

gripping ['grɪpɪŋ] *adj* interessantissimo, affascinante

gris·ly ['grɪzli] *adj* (*-lier; -liest*) orribile, spaventoso

grist [grɪst] *s* (*grain to be ground*) macinato; (*ground grain*) farina; (*coll*) mucchio; **to be grist to the mill of** (*coll*) fare comodo a

gristle ['grɪsəl] *s* cartilagine *f*

gris·tly ['grɪsli] *adj* (*-tlier; -tliest*) cartilaginoso

grist'mill' *s* mulino

grit [grɪt] *s* sabbia, arenaria; (*fig*) forza d'animo ‖ *v* (*pret & pp* **gritted;** *ger* **gritting**) *tr* (*one's teeth*) far stridere, digrignare

grit·ty ['grɪti] *adj* (*-tier; -tiest*) sabbioso, granuloso; (*fig*) forte, coraggioso

griz·zly ['grɪzli] *adj* (*-zlier; -zliest*) brizzolato, canuto ‖ *s* (*-zlies*) orso grigio

groan [gron] *s* gemito ‖ *intr* gemere; (*to be overburdened*) essere sovraccarico

grocer ['grosər] *s* droghiere *m;* pizzicagnolo; proprietario di negozio di generi alimentari

grocer·y ['grosəri] *s* (*-ies*) (*store selling spices, soap, etc.*) drogheria; (*store selling cheese, cold cuts, etc.*) negozio di pizzicagnolo; negozio di generi alimentari; **groceries** generi *mpl* alimentari, commestibili *mpl*

grog [grag] *s* grog *m*

grog·gy ['gragi] *adj* (*-gier; -giest*) (*coll*) groggy, intontito

groin [grɔɪn] *s* (*anat*) inguine *m;* (*archit*) costolone *m*

groom [grum] *s* mozzo di stalla; (*bridegroom*) sposo ‖ *tr* rassettare; (*horses*) rigovernare; (*pol*) preparare per le elezioni

grooms'man *s* (*-men*) compare *m* di nozze

groove [gruv] *s* scanalatura; (*of a pulley*) gola; (*of a phonograph record*) solco; (*fig*) routine *f* ‖ *tr* scanalare, incavare

grope [grop] *intr* brancicare; (*for words*) cercare; **to grope for** cercare a tastoni

gropingly ['gropɪŋli] *adv* a tastoni

gross [gros] *adj* (*thick*) spesso; (*coarse*) volgare; (*fat*) grosso; (*error*) mar-

chiano; (*without deductions*) lordo ‖ *s* grossa ‖ *tr* fare un incasso lordo di

grossly ['grosli] *adv* approssimativamente; totalmente

gross' na'tional prod'uct *s* reddito nazionale

grotesque [gro'tesk] *adj & s* grottesco

grot·to ['grato] *s* (*-toes* or *-tos*) grotta

grouch [graʊtʃ] *s* (*coll*) malumore *m;* (*coll*) persona stizzosa ‖ *intr* (*coll*) brontolare

grouch·y ['graʊtʃi] *adj* (*-ier; -iest*) (*coll*) stizzoso, brontolone

ground [graʊnd] *s* (*earth, soil, land*) terra; (*piece of land*) terreno; (*basis*) causa, fondatezza; (*elec*) terra, massa; (*fig*) occasione, motivo; **grounds** giardini *mpl,* terreno; (*of coffee*) fondi *mpl;* **on the ground of** per motivo di; **to break ground** dare la prima palata; (*fig*) mettere la prima pietra; **to fall to the ground** cadere al suolo; (*fig*) fallire; **to gain ground** guadagnar terreno; **to give ground** ceder terreno; **to lose ground** perder terreno; **to stand one's ground** non indietreggiare ‖ *tr* fondare; (*elec*) mettere a massa; **to be grounded** (*said of an airplane*) essere forzato di rimanere a terra; **to be well grounded** essere bene al corrente ‖ *intr* incagliarsi

ground' connec'tion *s* messa a terra

ground' crew' *s* (*aer*) personale *m* di servizio

ground' floor' *s* pianterreno

ground' glass' *s* vetro smerigliato

ground' hog' *s* marmotta americana

ground' lead' [lid] *s* (*elec*) collegamento a massa

groundless ['graʊndlɪs] *adj* infondato

ground' meat' *s* carne tritata

ground' plan' *s* progetto, pianta

ground' swell' *s* mareggiata

ground' wire' *s* filo di terra, filo di massa

ground'work' *s* fondamento, base *f*

group [grup] *adj* collettivo ‖ *s* gruppo; (*aer*) stormo ‖ *tr* raggruppare ‖ *intr* raggrupparsi

grouse [graʊs] *s* gallo cedrone; (*slang*) brontolio ‖ *intr* (*slang*) brontolare

grout [graʊt] *s* stucco ‖ *tr* stuccare

grove [grov] *s* boschetto

grov·el ['grʌvəl] or ['gravəl] *v* (*pret & pp* **-eled** or **-elled;** *ger* **-eling** or **-elling**) *intr* umiliarsi

grow [gro] *v* (*pret* **grew** [gru]; *pp* **grown** [gron]) *tr* (*plants*) coltivare; (*animals*) allevare; (*a beard*) farsi crescere ‖ *intr* crescere; svilupparsi; nascere; venir su; (*to become*) diventare; farsi; **to grow angry** arrabbiarsi; **to grow old** invecchiare; **to grow out of** (*fashion*) passare di; originare da; **to grow up** svilupparsi

growing ['gro·ɪŋ] *adj* crescente; (*pains*) di crescenza; (*child*) in crescita

growl [graʊl] *s* ringhio; brontolio ‖ *intr* (*said of animals*) ringhiare; brontolare

grown'-up' *adj* adulto, grande ‖ *s* (**grown-ups**) adulto

growth [groθ] *s* crescita, sviluppo; aumento; (pathol) escrescenza

growth' stock' *s* azione *f* che promette di aumentare di valore

grub [grʌb] *s* (*drudge*) sgobbone *m*; larva di coleottero; (coll) mangiare *m* ‖ *v* (*pret & pp* **grubbed**; *ger* **grubbing**) *tr* scavare, zappare, dissodare ‖ *intr* cercare assiduamente; scavare; sgobbare

grub·by ['grʌbɪ] *adj* (**-bier; -biest**) sporco; bacato; infestato di larve

grudge [grʌdʒ] *s* rancore *m*; **to have a grudge against** nutrire rancore contro ‖ *tr* (*to spend unwillingly*) lesinare; invidiare

grudgingly ['grʌdʒɪŋlɪ] *adv* di cattiva voglia

gru·el ['gru·əl] *s* farinata d'avena ‖ *v* (*pret & pp* **-eled** or **-elled**; *ger* **-eling** or **-elling**) *tr* estenuare

gruesome ['grusəm] *adj* raccapricciante

gruff [grʌf] *adj* brusco, burbero; (*voice*) rauco, roco

grumble ['grʌmbəl] *s* brontolio ‖ *intr* brontolare, borbottare

grump·y ['grʌmpɪ] *adj* (**-ier; -iest**) di cattivo umore, scontroso

grunt [grʌnt] *s* grugnito ‖ *intr* grugnire

G-string ['dʒi,strɪŋ] *s* (*loincloth*) perizoma *m*; (*worn by a female entertainer*) triangolino di stoffa; (mus) corda di sol

guarantee [,gærən'ti] *s* garanzia; (*guarantor*) garante *mf* ‖ *tr* garantire

guarantor ['gærən,tɔr] *s* garante *mf*

guaran·ty ['gærəntɪ] *s* (**-ties**) garanzia ‖ *v* (*pret & pp* **-tied**) *tr* garantire

guard [gɑrd] *s* guardia; (*safeguard*) protezione; (*in a prison*) guardia carceraria; (*of a sword*) guardamano; (football) mediano; **off guard** alla sprovvista; **on guard** in guardia; di fazione; **to mount a guard** montare la guardia; **under guard** ben custodito ‖ *tr* guardare ‖ *intr* fare la sentinella; **to guard against** guardarsi da

guarded ['gɑrdɪd] *adj* (*remark*) prudente

guard'house' *s* locale *m* di detenzione; (mil) corpo di guardia

guardian ['gɑrdɪ·ən] *adj* tutelare ‖ *s* guardiano; (law) tutore *m*

guard'ian an'gel *s* angelo custode

guardianship ['gɑrdɪ·ən,ʃɪp] *s* protezione; (law) tutela

guard'rail' *s* guardavia *m*; (naut) parapetto

guard'room' *s* (mil) corpo di guardia

guards'man *s* (**-men**) guardia

guerrilla [gə'rɪlə] *s* guerrigliero

guerril'la war'fare *s* guerriglia

guess [gɛs] *s* congettura, supposizione ‖ *tr & intr* congetturare, supporre; (*to estimate correctly*) indovinare; (coll) credere; **I guess so** credo di sì

guess'work' *s* congettura

guest [gɛst] *s* invitato, ospite *m*; (*of a hotel*) cliente *mf*; (*of a boarding house*) pensionante *mf*

guest' book' *s* albo d'onore; (*in a hotel*) registro

guffaw [gə'fɔ] *s* sghignazzata ‖ *intr* sghignazzare

Guiana [gɪ'ʌnə] or [gɪ'ænə] *s* la Guayana

guidance ['gaɪdəns] *s* guida, governo; **for your guidance** per Sua norma

guide [gaɪd] *s* guida ‖ *tr* guidare

guide'board' *s* indicatore *m* stradale

guide'book' *s* guida

guid'ed mis'sile ['gaɪdɪd] *s* telearma, teleproietto, missile teleguidato

guide' dog' *s* cane *m* conduttore di un cieco

guide'line' *s* falsariga; corda fissa; linea di condotta, direttiva

guide'post' *s* indicatore *m* stradale

guide' word' *s* esponente *m* in testa di pagina

guidon ['gaɪdən] *s* guidone *m*

guild [gɪld] *s* associazione mutua; (hist) gilda

guild'hall' *s* palazzo delle corporazioni

guile [gaɪl] *s* astuzia, frode *f*

guileful ['gaɪlfəl] *adj* astuto, insidioso

guileless ['gaɪllɪs] *adj* sincero, innocente

guillotine ['gɪlə,tin] *s* ghigliottina ‖ [,gɪlə'tin] *tr* ghigliottinare

guilt [gɪlt] *s* colpa, reità *f*

guiltless ['gɪltlɪs] *adj* innocente

guilt·y ['gɪltɪ] *adj* (**-ier; -iest**) colpevole, reo

guimpe [gɪmp] or [gæmp] *s* sprone *m*

guinea ['gɪnɪ] *s* ghinea; gallina faraona ‖ **Guinea** *s* la Guinea

guin'ea fowl' *s* gallina faraona

guin'ea pig' *s* porcellino d'India, cavia; (fig) cavia

guise [gaɪz] *s* aspetto; veste *f*; **under the guise of** in guisa di

guitar [gɪ'tɑr] *s* chitarra

guitarist [gɪ'tɑrɪst] *s* chitarrista *mf*

gulch [gʌltʃ] *s* burrone *m*

gulf [gʌlf] *s* golfo; abisso

Gulf' Stream' *s* corrente *f* del Golfo

gull [gʌl] *s* gabbiano; (coll) credulone *m* ‖ *tr* darla da bere a

gullet ['gʌlɪt] *s* gargarozzo; esofago

gullible ['gʌlɪbəl] *adj* credulone

gul·ly ['gʌlɪ] *s* (**-lies**) borro, zanella

gulp [gʌlp] *s* sorsata ‖ *tr*—**to gulp down** (*food*) ingoiare; (*drink*) tracannare; (fig) ingoiare, tranguigiare

gum [gʌm] *s* gomma; (*mucus on eyelids*) cispa; goma (anat) gengive *fpl* ‖ *v* (*pret & pp* **gummed**; *ger* **gumming**) *tr* ingommare; **to gum up** (slang) guastare ‖ *intr* secernere gomma

gum' ar'abic *s* gomma arabica

gum'boil' *s* flemmone *m* gengivale

gum' boot' *s* stivale *m* da palude

gum'drop' *s* caramella alla gelatina di frutta, pasticca di gomma, drop *m*

gum·my ['gʌmɪ] *adj* (**-mier; -miest**) gommoso, vischioso; (*eyelid*) cisposo

gumption ['gʌmpʃən] *s* (coll) iniziativa; (coll) coraggio, fegato

gum'shoe' *s* caloscia; (slang) poliziotto ‖ *v* (*pret & pp* **-shoed**; *ger* **-shoeing**) *intr* (slang) camminare silenziosamente

gun [gʌn] *s* (*rifle*) fucile *m*; (*revolver*) revolver *m*; (*pistol*) rivoltella; (*e.g., for spraying*) rivoltella; **to stick to one's guns** tener duro ‖ *v* (*pret & pp* **gunned**; *ger* **gunning**) *tr* far fuoco su, freddare; (*a motor*) (slang) accelerare rapidamente ‖ *intr* andare a caccia; sparare; **to gun for** andare a caccia di

gun'boat' *s* cannoniera, esploratore *m*

gun' car'riage *s* affusto

gun'cot'ton *s* fulmicotone *m*

gun'fire' *s* fuoco, tiro

gun'man *s* (**-men**) bandito, sicario

gun' met'al *s* bronzo da cannoni; acciaio brunito

gunnel ['gʌnəl] *s* (naut) frisata

gunner ['gʌnər] *s* artigliere *m*, servente *m*

gunnery ['gʌnəri] *s* artiglieria, tiro

gunnysack ['gʌni,sæk] *s* sacco di tela greggia

gunpoint ['gʌn,pɔɪnt] *s* mirino; **at gunpoint** a mano armata, *e.g.,* **he was held up at gunpoint** subì una rapina a mano armata

gun'pow'der *s* polvere nera or pirica

gun'run'ner *s* contrabbandiere *m* di armi da fuoco

gun'shot' *s* schioppettata; revolverata; **within gunshot** a tiro di schioppo

gun'shot' wound' *s* schioppettata

gun'smith' *s* armaiolo

gun'stock' *s* cassa del fucile

gunwale ['gʌnəl] *s* frisata

gup·py ['gʌpi] *s* (**-pies**) lebiste *m*

gurgle ['gʌrgəl] *s* gorgoglio, borboglio ‖ *intr* gorgogliare, borbogliare; (*said of a human being*) barbugliare

gush [gʌʃ] *s* getto, fiotto ‖ *intr* zampillare, sgorgare; (coll) dare in effusioni

gusher ['gʌʃər] *s* pozzo di petrolio; (coll) persona espansiva

gushing ['gʌʃɪŋ] *adj* zampillante, sgorgante; (coll) espansivo ‖ *s* zampillo; (coll) espansione, effusione

gush·y ['gʌʃi] *adj* (**-ier**; **-iest**) (coll) espansivo, effusivo

gusset ['gʌsɪt] *s* gherone *m*

gust [gʌst] *s* (*of wind*) raffica; (*of smoke*) ondata, zaffata; (*of noise*) esplosione; (*of anger*) sfuriata

gusto ['gʌsto] *s* gusto; entusiasmo

gust·y ['gʌsti] *adj* (**-ier**; **-iest**) a raffiche, burrascoso

gut [gʌt] *s* budello; **guts** budello; (slang) fegato, coraggio ‖ *v* (*pret & pp* **gutted**; *ger* **gutting**) *tr* sparare, spanciare; distruggere l'interno di

gutta-percha ['gʌtə'pʌrtʃə] *s* guttaperca

gutter ['gʌtər] *s* (*on side of road*) cunetta; (*in street*) rigagnolo; (*of roof*) doccia, grondaia; (fig) bassifondi *mpl*

gut'ter-snipe' *s* monello

guttural ['gʌtərəl] *adj & s* gutturale *f*

guy [gaɪ] *s* cavo di sicurezza; (coll) tipo, tizio ‖ *tr* burlarsi di

guzzle ['gʌzəl] *tr & intr* trincare, bere a garganella

guzzler ['gʌzlər] *s* ubriacone *m*

gym [dʒɪm] *s* (coll) palestra

gymnasi·um [dʒɪm'nezɪ-əm] *s* (**-ums** or **-a** [ə]) palestra

gymnast ['dʒɪmnæst] *s* ginnasta *mf*

gymnastic [dʒɪm'næstɪk] *adj* ginnastico ‖ **gymnastics** *spl* ginnastica

gynecologist [,gaɪnə'kɑlədʒɪst], [,dʒaɪnə'kɑlədʒɪst] or [,dʒɪnə'kɑlədʒɪst] *s* ginecologo

gyp [dʒɪp] *s* (coll) imbroglio; (*person*) (coll) imbroglione *m* ‖ *v* (*pret & pp* **gypped**; *ger* **gypping**) *tr* imbrogliare

gypsum ['dʒɪpsəm] *s* gesso

gyp·sy ['dʒɪpsɪ] *adj* zingaresco, zingaro ‖ *s* (**-sies**) zingaro ‖ **Gypsy** *s* (*language*) zingaresco

gypsyish ['dʒɪpsɪ·ɪʃ] *adj* zingaresco

gyrate ['dʒaɪret] *intr* turbinare

gyrocompass ['dʒaɪro,kʌmpəs] *s* girobussola

gyroscope ['dʒaɪrə,skop] *s* giroscopio

H

H, h [etʃ] *s* ottava lettera dell'alfabeto inglese

haberdasher ['hæbər,dæʃər] *s* camiciaio; (*dealer in notions*) merciaio

haberdasher·y ['hæbər,dæʃəri] *s* (**-ies**) camiceria; merceria

habit ['hæbɪt] *s* abitudine *f*; (*addiction*) vizio; (*garb*) saio; **to be in the habit of** aver l'usanza di

habitat ['hæbɪ,tæt] *s* habitat *m*

habitation [,hæbɪ'teʃən] *s* abitazione

habit-forming ['hæbɪt,fɔrmɪŋ] *adj* (*e.g., drugs*) stupefacente; (*e.g., T.V.*) assuefacente, che fa venire il vizio

habitual [hə'bɪtʃʊ·əl] *adj* abituale

habitué [hə,bɪtʃʊ'e] *s* habitué *m*

hack [hæk] *s* (*cut*) taglio; (*notch*) tacca; (*cough*) tosse secca; cavallo da nolo; vettura di piazza; (*nag*) ronzino; (*poor writer*) scribacchino ‖ *tr* tagliare; stagliare

hack'man *s* (**-men**) vetturino

hackney ['hækni] *s* cavallo da sella; vettura di piazza

hackneyed ['hæknid] *adj* banale, trito

hack'saw' *s* seghetto per metalli

haddock ['hædək] *s* eglefino

haft [hæft] or [hɑft] *s* impugnatura

hag [hæg] *s* (*ugly old woman*) megera; (*witch*) strega

haggard ['hægərd] *adj* sparuto, macilento; (*wild-looking*) stralunato

haggle ['hægəl] *intr* mercanteggiare
hagiographer [ˌhægi'ɑgrəfər] or [ˌhedʒi'ɑgrəfər] *s* agiografo
hagiography [ˌhægi'ɑgrəfi] or [ˌhedʒi'ɑgrəfi] *s* agiografia
Hague, The [heg] *s* L'Aia *f*
hail [hel] *s* (*precipitation*) grandine *f*; (*greeting*) saluto; **within hail a** portata di voce || *tr* salutare; accogliere; chiamare; (*e.g., blows*) far cadere || *intr* salutare; **to hail from** venire da || *interj* salute!; salve!
hail′-fel′low *adj* gioviale
Hail′ Mar′y *s* Ave Maria, avemaria
hail′stone′ *s* chicco di grandine
hail′storm′ *s* grandinata
hair [her] *s* capelli *mpl*; (*of animals*) pelame *m* or pelo; **a hair** (*a single filament*) un capello or un pelo; **to a hair** a perfezione; **to get in one's hair** (slang) dare sui nervi a qlcu; **to let one's hair down** (slang) parlare francamente; (slang) comportarsi alla buona; **to make one's hair stand on end** far rizzare i capelli a qlcu; **to not turn a hair** non scomporsi; **to split hairs** cercare il pelo nell'uovo
hair′breadth′ *s* spessore *m* di un capello; **to escape by a hairbreadth** scamparla per un pelo
hair′brush′ *s* spazzola per i capelli
hair′cloth′ *s* cilicio
hair′cut′ *s* taglio dei capelli; **to get a haircut** farsi tagliare i capelli
hair′do′ *s* (-dos) acconciatura
hair′dress′er *s* parrucchiere *m* per signora; pettinatrice *f*
hair′ dri′er *s* asciugacapelli *m*
hair′ dye′ *s* tintura per i capelli
hairless ['herlɪs] *adj* pelato, calvo
hair′ net′ *s* rete *f* per i capelli
hair′pin′ *s* forcella, forcina, molletta
hair-raising ['her ˌrezɪŋ] *adj* orripilante
hair′ re·mov′er *s* depilatorio
hair′ restor′er [rɪ'storər] *s* rigeneratore *m* per i capelli
hair′ rib′bon *s* nastro per i capelli
hairsplitting ['her ˌsplɪtɪŋ] *adj* meticoloso, pignolo
hair′spring′ *s* spirale *f*
hair′ styl′ing *s* pettinatura per signora
hair·y ['heri] *adj* (-ier; -iest) peloso, villoso, irsuto
hake [hek] *s* merluzzo, nasello
halberd ['hælbərd] *s* alabarda
halberdier [ˌhælbər'dɪr] *s* alabardiere *m*
halcyon ['hælsɪ·ən] *adj* calmo, pacifico
hale [hel] *adj* sano, robusto || *tr* trascinare a viva forza
half [hæf] or [hɑf] *adj* mezzo; **a half** or **half a** mezzo; **half the** la metà di || *s* (**halves** [hævz] or [hɑvz]) metà *f*; (arith) mezzo; **in half** a metà; **to go halves** fare a metà || *adv* mezzo, e.g., **half asleep** mezzo addormentato; a metà, e.g., **half finished** a metà finito; **half past** e mezzo or e mezza, e.g., **half past three** le tre e mezzo or le tre e mezza; **half . . . half** metà . . . metà
half′-and-half′ *adj* mezzo e mezzo || *s* mezza crema e mezzo latte; mezza

birra chiara e mezza scura || *adv* a metà, in parti uguali
half′back′ *s* (football) mediano; (soccer) laterale *m*
half-baked ['hæf ˌbekt] or ['hɑf ˌbekt] *adj* mezzo cotto; (*ideas*) infondato, inesperto
half′ bind′ing *s* rilegatura in mezza pelle
half′-blood′ *s* meticcio; fratellastro; sorellastra
half′-breed′ *s* meticcio
half′ broth′er *s* fratellastro
half-cocked ['hæf ˌkɑkt] or ['hɑf ˌkɑkt] *adj* immaturo, precipitato || *adv* (coll) precipitatamente
half′ fare′ *s* mezza corsa
half′-full′ *adj* mezzo pieno
half-hearted ['hæf ˌhɑrtɪd] or ['hɑf ˌhɑrtɪd] *adj* indifferente, freddo
half′-hol′iday *s* mezza festa
half′ hose′ *s* calzini *mpl* corti
half′-hour′ *s* mezz'ora; **on the half-hour** ogni trenta minuti allo scoccare dell'ora e della mezz'ora
half′-length′ *adj* a mezzo busto || *s* ritratto a mezzo busto
half′life′ *s* (phys) vita media
half′-mast′ *s*—**at half-mast** a mezz'asta
half′moon′ *s* mezzaluna
half′ mourn′ing *s* mezzo lutto
half′ note′ *s* (mus) minima
half′ pay′ *s* mezza paga
halfpen·ny ['hepəni] or ['hepni] *s* (-nies) mezzo penny
half′ pint′ *s* mezza pinta; (slang) mezza cartuccia, mezza calzetta
half′-seas o′ver *adj*—**to be half-seas over** (slang) essere sbronzato
half′ shell′ *s*—**on the half shell** in conchiglia
half′ sis′ter *s* sorellastra
half′ sole′ *s* mezza suola
half′-sole′ *tr* mettere la mezza suola a
half-staff *s*—**at half-staff** a mezz'asta
half-timbered ['hæf ˌtɪmbərd] or ['hɑf ˌtɪmbərd] *adj* in legno e muratura
half′ ti′tle *s* occhiello, occhietto
half′tone′ *s* mezzatinta
half′-track′ *s* semicingolato
half′truth′ *s* mezza verità, mezza bugia
half′way′ *adj* a metà strada; parziale, mezzo || *adv* a metà strada; **halfway through** nel mezzo di; **to meet halfway** fare concessioni mutue
half-witted ['hæf ˌwɪtɪd] or ['hɑf ˌwɪtɪd] *adj* mezzo scemo
halibut ['hælɪbət] *s* ippoglosso
halide ['hælaɪd] or ['helaɪd] *s* alogenuro
halitosis [ˌhælɪ'tosɪs] *s* alito cattivo, fiato puzzolente
hall [hɔl] *s* (*passageway*) corridoio; (*entranceway*) vestibolo; (*large meeting room*) salone *m*; (*assembly room of a university*) aula magna; (*building of a university*) edificio
halleluiah [ˌhælɪ'lujə] *s* alleluia *m* || *interj* alleluia!
hall′mark′ *s* punzone *m* di garanzia; (fig) contrassegno, caratteristica
hal·lo [hə'lo] *s* (-los) grido || *interj* ehi!
hallow ['hælo] *tr* santificare

hallowed ['hælod] *adj* consacrato
Halloween or Hallowe'en [,hælo'in] *s* vigilia di Ognissanti
hallucination [hə ,lusɪ'neʃən] *s* allucinazione
hall'way' *s* corridoio; entrata
ha-lo ['helo] *s* (-los or -loes) alone *m*
halogen ['hælədʒən] *s* alogeno
halt [hɔlt] *adj* zoppicante || *s* fermata; to call a halt dare ordine di fermarsi; to come to a halt fermarsi || *tr* fermare || *intr* fermarsi, esitare || *interj* altolà!
halter ['hɔltər] *s* (*for leading horse*) cavezza; (*noose*) capestro; (*hanging*) impiccagione; corpino bagno di sole
halting ['hɔltɪŋ] *adj* zoppicante; esitante
halve [hæv] or [hɑv] *tr* dimezzare
halyard ['hæljərd] *s* (naut) drizza
ham [hæm] *s* (*part of leg behind knee*) polpaccio; (*thigh and buttock*) coscia; (*cured meat from hog's hind leg*) prosciutto; (slang) istrione *m;* (slang) radioamatore *m;* hams natiche *fpl*
ham' and eggs' *spl* uova *fpl* col prosciutto
hamburger ['hæm ,bʌrgər] *s* hamburger *m*
hamlet ['hæmlɪt] *s* frazione, paese *m* || Hamlet *s* Amleto
hammer ['hæmər] *s* martello; (*of gun*) cane *m;* (*of piano*) martelletto; under the hammer all'asta pubblica || *tr* martellare; to hammer out battere; portare a fine faticosamente || *intr* martellare; to hammer away lavorare accanitamente
hammock ['hæmək] *s* amaca
hamper ['hæmpər] *s* cesta || *tr* imbarazzare, intralciare
hamster ['hæmstər] *s* criceto
ham-string ['hæm ,strɪŋ] *v* (*pret & pp* -strung) *tr* azzoppare; tagliare i garretti a; (fig) impastoiare
hand [hænd] *adj* manuale; fatto a mano || *s* mano *f;* (*workman*) garzone *m,* operaio; (*way of writing*) scrittura; (*signature*) firma; (*clapping of hands*) applauso; (*of clock or watch*) lancetta; (*all the cards in one's hand*) gioco; (*a round of play*) smazzata, mano *f;* (*player*) giocatore *m;* (*skill*) destrezza; (*side*) lato; all hands (naut) tutto l'equipaggio; (coll) tutti *mpl;* at first hand direttamente; at hand a portata di mano; hand in glove in perfetta unione; hand in hand tenendosi per mano; hands up! le mani in alto!; hand to hand corpo a corpo; in hand tra le mani; in his own hand di proprio pugno; on hand disponibile; on hands and knees (*crawling*) a gattoni; (*beseeching*) in ginocchio; on the one hand da un canto; on the other hand per contro; to change hands cambiare di mano; to clap hands battere le mani; to eat out of one's hand essere sottomesso a qlcu; to get out of hand diventare incontrollabile; to have a hand in prender parte a; to have one's hands

full essere occupatissimo; to hold hands tenersi per mano; to hold up one's hands (*as a sign of surrender*) alzare le mani; to join hands darsi la mano; to keep one's hands off non mettere il naso in; to lend a hand dare una mano; to live from hand to mouth vivere alla giornata; to not lift a hand non alzare un dito; to play into the hands of fare il gioco di; to shake hands darsi la mano; to show one's hand scoprire il proprio gioco; to take in hand prendere in mano; (*a matter*) prendere in esame; to throw up one's hands darsi per vinto; to try one's hand mettere la propria abilità alla prova; to turn one's hand to dedicarsi a; to wash one's hands of lavarsi le mani di; under my hand di mia firma autografa; under the hand and seal of firmato di pugno da || *tr* dare, porgere; to hand down tramandare; to hand in consegnare; to hand on trasmettere; to hand out distribuire
hand'bag' *s* borsetta
hand' bag'gage *s* valigie *fpl* a mano
hand'ball' *s* palla a mano
hand'bill' *s* manifestino, foglio volante
hand'book' *s* manuale *m;* guida; (*of a particular field*) prontuario
hand'breadth' *s* palmo
hand'car' *s* (rr) carrello a mano
hand'cart' *s* carretto a mano
hand'cuffs' *spl* manette *fpl* || *tr* mettere le manette a
handful ['hænd ,fʊl] *s* manata, manciata
hand' glass' *s* lente *f* di ingrandimento; specchietto
hand' grenade' *s* bomba a mano
handi-cap ['hændɪ ,kæp] *s* svantaggio; (sports) handicap *m* || *v* (*pret & pp* -capped*; ger* -capping) *tr* andicappare
handicraft ['hændɪ ,kræft] or ['hændɪ ,krɑft] *s* destrezza manuale; artigianato
handiwork ['hændɪ ,wʌrk] *s* lavoro fatto a mano; opera, lavoro
handkerchief ['hæŋkərtʃɪf] or ['hæŋkər ,tʃɪf] *s* fazzoletto
handle ['hændəl] *s* manico; (*of a sword*) impugnatura; (*of a door*) maniglia; (*of a drawer*) pomolo; (*of a hand organ*) manovella; espediente *m;* to fly off the handle (slang) uscire dai gangheri || *tr* maneggiare; manovrare, dirigere; commerciare in || *intr* comportarsi
handle'bar' *s* manubrio
handler ['hændlər] *s* (sports) allenatore *m*
hand'made' *adj* fatto a mano
hand'maid' or hand'maid'en *s* domestica, serva; (fig) ancella
hand'-me-down' *adj* smesso || *s* vestito smesso o di seconda mano
hand' or'gan *s* organetto, organino, organetto di Barberia
hand'out' *s* elemosina di cibo; articolo distribuito gratis; comunicato stampa
hand-picked ['hænd ,pɪkt] *adj* colto a mano; scelto specialmente

hand'rail' s guardamano, passamano

hand'saw' s sega a mano

hand'set' s microtelefono

hand'shake' s stretta di mano

handsome ['hænsəm] adj bello; considerevole; generoso

hand'spring' s capriola, salto mortale fatto toccando il terreno con le mani

hand'-to-hand' adj corpo a corpo

hand'-to-mouth' adj precario, da un giorno all'altro

hand'work' s lavoro fatto a mano

hand'writ'ing s scrittura

hand'wrought' adj lavorato a mano

hand•y ['hændɪ] adj (-ier; -iest) (easy to handle) maneggevole; (within easy reach) vicino; (skillful) destro, abile; **to come in handy** tornare utile

hand'y•man' s (-men') factotum m

hang [hæŋ] s maniera di cadere; **to get the hang of** (coll) imparare a adoperare; **to not give a hang** (coll) non importare un fico a a || v (pret & pp **hung** [hʌŋ]) tr sospendere; (laundry) stendere; (to attach) attaccare; (a door or window) mettere sui cardini; (one's head) abbassare; **hang it!** (coll) al diavolo!; **to hang up** appendere; sospendere il progresso di || intr pendere, penzolare; esitare; essere sospeso; essere attaccato; **to hang around** ciondolare, oziare, gironzolare; **to hang on** essere sospeso a; dipendere da; persistere; (s.o.'s words) pendere; **to hang out** sporgersi; (slang) raccogliersi; (slang) vivere; **to hang over** esser sospeso; (to threaten) minacciare; **to hang together** mantenersi uniti; **to hang up** (telp) riattaccare || v (pret **hanged** or **hung**) tr (to execute) impiccare || intr impiccarsi

hangar ['hæŋər] or ['hæŋgar] s rimessa; (aer) aviorimessa, hangar m

hanger ['hæŋər] s gancio, uncino; (for clothes) attaccapanni m

hang'er-on' s (hangers-on) seguace mf; seccatore m; (sponger) parassita m

hanging ['hæŋɪŋ] s pendente, pensile || s impiccagione; **hangings** parati mpl

hang'man s (-men) boia m

hang'nail' s pipita delle unghie

hang'out' s (coll) ritrovo abituale

hang'o'ver s mal m di testa dopo una sbornia

hank [hæŋk] s matassa

hanker ['hæŋkər] intr agognare

Hannibal ['hænɪbəl] s Annibale m

haphazard [,hæp'hæzərd] adj fortuito, a caso || adv a caso; alla carlona

hapless ['hæplɪs] adj sfortunato

happen ['hæpən] intr succedere; **to happen along** sopravvenire; **to happen on** incontrarsi per caso con; **to happen to** + inf per caso + ind, e.g., **I happened to see her at the theater** l'ho incontrata per caso a teatro

happening ['hæpənɪŋ] s avvenimento, fatto

happily ['hæpɪli] adv felicemente; fortunatamente

happiness ['hæpɪnɪs] s felicità f; gioia, piacere m

hap•py ['hæpi] adj (-pier; -piest) lieto, felice, contento; **to be happy to** avere il piacere di

hap'py-go-luck'y adj spensierato

hap'py me'dium s giusto mezzo

Hap'py New Year' interj buon anno!, felice anno nuovo!

harangue [hə'ræŋ] s arringa, concione || tr & intr arringare

harass ['hærəs] or [hə'ræs] tr bersagliare; tartassare, tormentare

harbinger ['harbɪndʒər] s foriero; annunzio || tr annunziare

harbor ['harbər] adj di porto, portuario || s porto || tr albergare; (love or hatred) nutrire; (e.g., a criminal) dare ricetto a

har'bor mas'ter s capitano di porto

hard [hard] adj duro; (difficult) difficile; (work) improbo; (solder) forte; (hearing or breathing) grosso; (drinker) impenitente; (liquor) fortemente alcolico; **to be hard on** essere severo con; (to wear out fast) logorare rapidamente || adv duro; forte; molto; **hard upon** subito dopo

hard'-and-fast' adj inflessibile

hard-bitten ['hard'bɪtən] adj duro, incallito

hard-boiled ['hard'bɔɪld] adj (egg) sodo; (coll) duro

hard' can'dy s caramelle fpl; **piece of hard candy** caramella

hard' cash' s denaro contante

hard' ci'der s sidro fermentato

hard' coal' s antracite f

hard'-earned' adj guadagnato a stento

harden ['hardən] tr indurire || intr indurirsi

hardening ['hardənɪŋ] s indurimento; (metallurgy) tempra

hard' facts' spl realtà f

hard-fought ['hard'fɔt] adj accanito

hard-headed ['hard'hedɪd] adj astuto; ostinato, caparbio

hard-hearted ['hard'hartɪd] adj dal cuore duro

hardihood ['hardɪ,hud] s forza, coraggio; insolenza

hardiness ['hardɪnɪs] s ardire m; vigore m, robustezza fisica

hard' la'bor s lavori forzati

hard' luck' s mala sorte

hard'-luck' sto'ry s storia delle proprie disgrazie

hardly ['hardli] adv appena, quasi no; (with great difficulty) a malapena, a fatica; **hardly ever** quasi mai

hardness ['hardnɪs] s durezza

hard'-of-hear'ing adj duro d'orecchio

hard-pressed ['hard'prest] adj oppresso; **to be hard-pressed for** essere a corto di

hard' rub'ber s ebanite f

hard' sauce' s miscela di burro e zucchero

hard'-shell crab' s granchio con la corazza

hardship ['hard/ɪp] s pena, privazione; **hardships** privazioni fpl, strettezze fpl

hard'tack' s galletta

hard' times' spl strettezze fpl

hard' to please' adj di difficile contentatura

hard' up' adj (coll) in urgente bisogno; **to be hard up for** (coll) essere a corto di

hard'ware' s ferramenta fpl; macchinario

hard'ware store' s negozio di ferramenta

hard-won ['hɑrd,wʌn] adj (victory, battle) conquistato con molti sforzi; (money) acquistato con molti sforzi

hard'wood' s legno forte

hard'wood floor' s pavimento di legno, parquet m

har-dy ['hɑrdi] adj (-dier; -diest) forte, resistente; (rash) temerario; (hort) resistente al freddo

hare [her] s lepre f

harebrained ['her,brend] adj scervellato, sventato

hare'lip' s labbro leporino

harem ['herəm] s arem m

hark [hɑrk] intr ascoltare; **to hark back** (said of hounds) ritornare sulla pista; riandare col pensiero || interj ascolta!

harken ['hɑrkən] intr ascoltare

harlequin ['hɑrləkwɪn] s arlecchino

harlot ['hɑrlət] s meretrice f, baldracca

harm [hɑrm] s danno || tr rovinare; nuocere (with dat), fare del male (with dat)

harmful ['hɑrmfəl] adj nocivo

harmless ['hɑrmlɪs] adj innocuo

harmonic [hɑr'mɑnɪk] adj armonico || s (phys) armonica || **harmonics** ssg armonica; spl suoni armonici

harmonica [hɑr'mɑnɪkə] s armonica a bocca

harmonious [hɑr'monɪ·əs] adj armonioso

harmonize ['hɑrmə,naɪz] tr intonare; (mus) armonizzare || intr intonarsi; (mus) cantare all'unisono

harmo-ny ['hɑrməni] s (-nies) armonia

harness ['hɑrnɪs] s bardatura, finimenti mpl; (fig) routine f; **to die in the harness** morire sulla breccia || tr bardare, imbrigliare; (a waterfall) captare

har'ness mak'er s sellaio

har'ness race' s corsa al trotto, corsa di cavalli col sulky

harp [hɑrp] s arpa || intr—**to harp on** ripetere ostinatamente

harpist ['hɑrpɪst] s arpista mf

harpoon [hɑr'pun] s rampone m || tr & intr arpionare

harpsichord ['hɑrpsɪ,kɔrd] s arpicordo, clavicembalo

har-py ['hɑrpi] s (-pies) arpia

harrow ['hæro] s erpice m || tr (agr) erpicare; (fig) tormentare

harrowing ['hæro·ɪŋ] adj straziante

har-ry ['hæri] v (pret & pp -ried) tr saccheggiare; tormentare

harsh [hɑrʃ] adj (to touch) ruvido; (to taste or hearing) aspro; inclemente

harshness ['hɑrʃnɪs] s ruvidezza; asprezza; inclemenza

hart [hɑrt] s cervo

harum-scarum ['herəm'skerəm] adj & s scervellato

harvest ['hɑrvɪst] s raccolta, mietitura || tr raccogliere, mietere

harvester ['hɑrvɪstər] s (person) mietitore m; (machine) mietitrice f

har'vest home' s fine f della mietitura; festa dei mietitori; canzone f dei mietitori

har'vest moon' s luna di settembre

has-been ['hæz,bɪn] s (person) fallito; (thing) anticaglia

hash [hæʃ] s polpettone m || tr tritare

hash' house' s osteria di terz'ordine

hashish ['hæʃɪʃ] s ascisc m

hasp [hæsp] or [hɑsp] s boncinello

hassle ['hæsəl] s (coll) rissa, disputa

hassock ['hæsək] s cuscino poggiapiedi

haste [hest] s premura; **in haste** di premura; **to make haste** fare presto

hasten ['hesən] tr affrettare || intr affrettarsi

hast-y ['hesti] adj (-ier; -iest) frettoloso; precipitato

hat [hæt] s cappello; **to keep under one's hat** (coll) mantenere il segreto su; **to throw one's hat in the ring** (coll) dichiarare la propria candidatura

hat'band' s nastro del cappello

hat' block' s forma da cappelli

hat'box' s cappelliera

hatch [hætʃ] s (brood) nidiata; (shading line) tratteggio; (trap door) porta a ribalta; (lower half of door) mezza porta; (naut) boccaporto || tr (eggs) covare; (a drawing) tratteggiare; complottare, tramare || intr schiudersi

hat'check' girl' s guardarobiera

hatchet ['hætʃɪt] s accetta; **to bury the hatchet** fare la pace

hatch'way' s (trap door) porta a ribalta; (naut) boccaporto

hate [het] s odio || tr & intr odiare

hateful ['hetfəl] adj odioso

hat'pin' s spillone m

hat'rack' s attaccapanni m

hatred ['hetrɪd] s odio, livore m

hatter ['hætər] s cappellaio

haughtiness ['hɔtɪnɪs] s superbia

haugh-ty ['hɔti] adj (-tier; -tiest) superbo, sprezzante

haul [hɔl] s (tug) tiro; (amount caught) retata; (distance transported) percorso, pezzo || tr trasportare; tirare; (naut) alare

haunch [hɔntʃ] or [hɑntʃ] s fianco; anca; (hind quarter of an animal) coscia; (same used for food) cosciotto

haunt [hɔnt] or [hɑnt] s ritrovo, nido || tr frequentare assiduamente; perseguitare

haunt'ed house' s casa frequentata dai fantasmi

haute couture [ot ku'tyr] s alta moda

have [hæv] s—**the haves and the have-nots** gli abbienti e i nullatenenti || v (*pret* & *pp* had [hæd]) *tr* avere; (*a dream*) fare; (*to get, take*) prendere, ottenere, ricevere; **to have got** (coll) avere; **to have got to** + *inf* (coll) dovere + *inf*; **to have it in for** (coll) serbar rancore per; **to have it out with** avere a che dire con; **to have on** portare; **to have (s.th) to do with** avere (qlco) a che fare con, e.g., **I don't want to have anything to do with him** non voglio aver nulla a che fare con lui; **to have** + *inf* fare + *inf*, e.g., **I had him pay the bill** gli ho fatto pagare il conto; **to have** + *pp* fare + *inf*, e.g., **I had my watch repaired** ho fatto aggiustare l'orologio ‖ *intr*—**to have at** attaccare, mettersi di buzzo buono con; **to have to** + *inf* dovere + *inf*; **to have to do with** avere a che fare con; trattare di, e.g., **this book has to do with superstition** questo libro tratta di superstizione ‖ *v aux* avere, e.g., **he has studied his lesson** ha studiato la sua lezione

havelock ['hævlək] *s* coprinuca *m*
haven ['hevən] *s* porto; asilo
haversack ['hævər‚sæk] *s* bisaccia; (mil) zaino
havoc ['hævək] *s* rovina; **to play havoc with** rovinare; scompigliare
haw [hɔ] *s* (*of hawthorn*) bacca; (*in speech*) esitazione ‖ *intr* voltare a sinistra ‖ *interj* voltare a sinistra!
hawk [hɔk] *s* falco; (*mortarboard*) sparviere *m;* (coll) persona rapace ‖ *tr* imbonire; (*newspapers*) strillare; **to hawk up** sputare raschiandosi la gola ‖ *intr* fare il merciaiolo ambulante; schiarirsi la gola
hawker ['hɔkər] *s* merciaiolo ambulante
hawse [hɔz] *s* (naut) cubia; (*hole*) (naut) occhio di cubia; (naut) altezza di cubia
hawse'hole' *s* occhio di cubia
hawser ['hɔzər] *s* cavo, gomena
haw'thorn' *s* biancospino
hay [he] *s* fieno; **to hit the hay** (slang) andare a letto; **to make hay while the sun shines** battere il ferro fin ch'è caldo
hay' fe'ver *s* febbre *f* da fieno, raffreddore *m* da fieno
hay'field' *s* prato seminato a fieno
hay'fork' *s* forcone *m;* (mach) rastrello
hay'loft' *s* fienile *m*
haymow ['he‚mau] *s* fienile *m*
hay'rack' *s* rastrelliera
hay'ride' *s* gita notturna in carro da fieno
hay'seed' *s* semente *f* d'erba; (coll) semplicione *m*, campagnolo
hay'stack' *s* meta, pagliaio
hay'wire' *adj* (coll) disordinato, in confusione; (coll) impazzito ‖ *s* filo per legare il fieno
hazard ['hæzərd] *s* pericolo; (*chance*) rischio; (golf) ostacolo ‖ *tr* rischiare; (*an opinion*) arrischiare
hazardous ['hæzərdəs] *adj* pericoloso
haze [hez] *s* foschia; (fig) confusione ‖ *tr* far la matricola a

hazel ['hezəl] *adj* nocciola ‖ *s* (*tree*) nocciolo; (*fruit*) nocciola
ha'zel·nut' *s* nocciola
hazing ['heziŋ] *s* vessazione, angheria; (*at university*) matricola
ha·zy ['hezi] *adj* (**-zier; -ziest**) nebbioso; confuso
H-bomb ['et[‚bɑm] *s* bomba H
he [hi] *s* (**hes**) maschio ‖ *pron pers* (**they**) lui, egli, esso
head [hɛd] *s* testa, capo; (*of bed*) testiera; (*caption*) testata; (*of a nail*) cappello; (*on a glass of beer*) schiuma; (*of a boil*) punta purulenta; (*e.g., of cattle*) capo; **at the head of** a capo di; **from head to foot** da capo a piedi; **head over heels** a gambe levate; completamente; **heads or tails** testa o croce; **over one's head** al di sopra della capacità intellettuale di qlcu; (*going to a higher authority*) al di sopra di qlcu; **to be out of one's head** (coll) esser matto; **to bring to a head** far giungere alla crisi; **to come into one's head** passar per la mente a qlcu; **to go to one's head** dare al cervello a qlcu; **to keep one's head** non perdere la testa; **to keep one's head above water** arrivare a sbarcare il lunario; **to not make head or tail of** non riuscire a raccappezzarsi su ‖ *tr* dirigere, comandare; essere alla testa di ‖ *intr*—**to head towards** dirigersi verso
head'ache' *s* mal di capo, emicrania
head'band' *s* fascia sul capo; (bb) capitello; (typ) filetto
head'board' *s* testiera del letto
head' cheese' *s* salame *m* di testa
head'dress' *s* acconciatura
header ['hɛdər] *s*—**to take a header** (coll) gettarsi a capofitto
head'first' *adv* a capofitto
head'gear' *s* copricapo; (*for protection*) casco
head'hunt'er *s* cacciatore *m* di teste
heading ['hɛdiŋ] *s* intestazione; (*of a chapter of a book*) titolo; (journ) testata, capopagina *m*
headland ['hɛdlənd] *s* promontorio
headless ['hɛdlɪs] *adj* senza testa
head'light' *s* (naut, rr) fanale *m;* (aut) faro
head'line' *s* (*of a page of a book*) titolo; (journ) testata ‖ *tr* intestare; fare pubblicità a
head'lin'er *s* (slang) attrazione principale
head'long' *adj* precipitoso ‖ *adv* a precipizio; a capofitto
head'man *s* (**-men**) capo; giustizere *m*
head'mas'ter *s* direttore *m* di un collegio per ragazzi
head'most' *adj* primo, più avanzato
head' of'fice *s* sede *f* centrale
head' of hair' *s* capigliatura
head'-on' *adj* frontale ‖ *adv* di fronte, frontalmente
head'phones' *spl* cuffia
head'piece' *s* (*any covering for the head*) copricapo; (*helmet*) elmo; (*brains, judgment*) testa; (*of bed*)

spalliera; **(headset)** cuffia; **(typ)** testata

head'quar'ters s sede f centrale, direzione; (mil) quartier m generale

head'rest' s poggiatesta m, testiera

head'set' s cuffia

head'ship' s direzione

head'stone' s pietra angolare; **(on a grave)** pietra tombale

head'stream' s affluente m principale

head'strong' adj testardo, ostinato

head'wait'er s capocameriere m

head'wa'ters spl fonti fpl or sorgenti fpl d'un fiume

head'way' s progresso; **to make head-way** progredire

head'wear' s copricapo

head'wind' s vento di prua

head'work' s lavoro intellettuale

head·y ['hedi] adj (-ier; -iest) eccitante; impetuoso; violento; **(clever)** astuto; intossicante

heal [hil] tr sanare, guarire; purificare ‖ intr risanarsi, guarire; **(said of a wound)** rimarginare

healer ['hilər] s guaritore m

health [helθ] s salute f; **to radiate health** sprizzare salute da tutti i pori; **to your health!** alla Sua salute!

health' depart'ment s sanità f

healthful ['helθfəl] adj salutare

health' insur'ance s assicurazione malattia

health·y ['helθi] adj (-ier; -iest) sano; salubre

heap [hip] s mucchio; **(coll)** insalata, mare m ‖ tr ammucchiare; **to heap s.th upon s.o.** colmare qlcu di qlco; **to heap with** colmare di

hear [hɪr] v (pret & pp heard [hʌrd]) tr udire; **to hear it said** sentirlo dire ‖ intr udire; **hear!, hear!** bravo!; **to hear about** sentir parlare di; **to hear from** aver notizie di; **to hear of** sentir parlare di; **to hear that** sentir dire che

hearer ['hɪrər] s ascoltatore m

hearing ['hɪrɪŋ] s **(sense)** udito, orecchio; **(act)** udienza; **in the hearing of** in presenza di; **within hearing** a portata d'orecchio

hear'ing aid' s uditofono

hear'say' s diceria; **by hearsay** per sentito dire

hearse [hʌrs] s carro, carrozzone m, or furgone m funebre

heart [hɑrt] s cuore m; **(e.g., of lettuce)** grumolo; **after one's heart** di gusto di qlcu; **by heart** a memoria; **heart and soul** di tutto cuore; **to break the heart of** spezzare il cuore di; **to die of a broken heart** morire di crepacuore; **to eat one's heart out** piangere silenziosamente; **to get to the heart of** sviscerare il nocciolo di; **to have one's heart in one's work** lavorare di buzzo buono; **to have one's heart in the right place** avere buone intenzioni; **to lose heart** scoraggiarsi; **to open one's heart to** aprire il cuore a; **to take heart** prender coraggio; **to take to heart** prendersi a cuore; **to**

wear one's heart on one's sleeve parlare a cuore aperto; **with one's heart in one's mouth** col cuore in bocca

heart'ache' s angustia, angoscia

heart' attack' s attacco cardiaco

heart'beat' s battito del cuore

heart'break' s angoscia straziante

heart'break'er s rubacuori m

heartbroken ['hɑrt,brokən] adj col cuore spezzato

heart'burn' s bruciore m di stomaco

heart' disease' s mal m di cuore

hearten ['hɑrtən] tr rincuorare

heart' fail'ure s **(death)** arresto cardiaco; collasso cardiaco

heartfelt ['hɑrt,felt] adj sentito

hearth [hɑrθ] s focolare m

hearth'stone' s pietra del focolare

heartily ['hɑrtɪli] adv di cuore, cordialmente; saporitamente

heartless ['hɑrtlɪs] adj senza cuore, insensibile

heart' mur'mur s soffio al cuore

heart-rending ['hɑrt,rendɪŋ] adj da far male al cuore

heart'sick' adj afflitto, sconsolato

heart'strings' spl precordi mpl

heart'-to-heart' adj a cuore a cuore

heart' trans'plant s trapianto cardiaco

heart'wood' s cuore m del legno

heart·y ['hɑrti] adj (-ier; -iest) cordiale, di cuore; abbondante; **(eater)** grande

heat [hit] adj termico ‖ s calore m; **(of room, house, etc.)** riscaldamento; **(zool)** fregola; **(sports)** batteria; **(fig)** fervore m; **in heat** (zool) in amore ‖ tr scaldare, riscaldare; **(fig)** eccitare ‖ intr riscaldarsi; **(fig)** accalorarsi

heated ['hitɪd] adj accalorato

heater ['hitər] s riscaldatore m; **(for central heating)** calorifero; **(to heat hands or bed)** scaldino; **(to heat water in tub)** scaldabagno

heath [hiθ] s **(shrub)** brugo, erica; **(tract of land)** brughiera

hea·then ['hiðən] adj pagano; irreligioso ‖ s (-then or -thens) pagano

heathendom ['hiðəndəm] s **(worship)** paganesimo; **(land)** pagania

heather ['hɛðər] s erica, brugo

heating ['hitɪŋ] adj di riscaldamento ‖ s riscaldamento

heat'ing pad' s termoforo

heat' light'ning s lampo di caldo

heat' shield' s **(rok)** scudo termico

heat'stroke' s colpo di calore

heat' wave' s ondata di caldo

heave [hiv] s sollevamento, sforzo; **heaves** (vet) bolsaggine f ‖ v (pret & pp heaved or hove [hov]) tr sollevare, alzare; rigettare; **(a sigh)** emettere ‖ intr alzarsi e abbassarsi; **(said of one's chest)** palpitare; avere conati di vomito

heaven ['hevən] s cielo; **for heaven's sake!** or **good heavens!** per amor del cielo!; **heavens (firmament)** cielo ‖ **Heaven** s cielo

heavenly ['hevənli] adj celeste

heav'enly bod'y s corpo celeste

heav·y ['hevi] adj (-ier; -iest) **(of great**

weight) pesante; (liquid) denso; (cloth, sea) grosso; (traffic) forte; (serious) grave; (crop) abbondante; (rain) dirotto; (features) grossolano; (heart) stretto; (ponderous) macchinoso; (industry) grande; (stock market) abbattuto || adv (coll) pesantemente; to hang heavy (said of time) passar lentamente

heav'y-du'ty adj extraforte

heavy-hearted ['hevɪ'hɑrtɪd] adj afflitto, triste

heav'y·set' adj forte, corpulento

heav'y·weight' s peso massimo

Hebrew ['hibru] adj & s ebreo; (language) ebraico

hecatomb ['hekə,tom] or ['hekə,tum] s ecatombe f

heckle ['hekəl] tr interrompere con domande imbarazzanti

hectic ['hektɪk] adj febbrile

hedge [hedʒ] s barriera; (of bushes) siepe f; (in stock market) operazione controbilanciante || tr circondare con siepe; to hedge in circondare || intr evitare di compromettersi; (com) coprirsi

hedge'hog' s (zool) riccio; (porcupine) (zool) porcospino

hedge'hop' v (pret & pp -hopped; ger hopping) intr volare a volo radente

hedgehopping ['hedʒ,hɑpɪŋ] s volo radente

hedge'row' [ro] s siepe f

heed [hid] s attenzione; to take heed fare attenzione || tr badare a || intr fare attenzione, badare

heedless ['hidlɪs] adj sbadato

heehaw ['hi,hɔ] s (of donkey) raglio d'asino; risata || intr ragliare; ridere fragorosamente

heel [hil] s (of shoe, of foot) calcagno, tallone m; (of stocking or shoe) tallone m; (raised part of shoe below heel) tacco; (coll) farabutto; down at the heel mal ridotto; to cool one's heels aspettare a lungo; to kick up one's heels darsi alla pazza gioia; to show a clean pair of heels or to take to one's heels battere i tacchi

heeler ['hilər] s politicante mf

heft·y ['heftɪ] adj (-ier; -iest) (heavy) pesante; (strong) forte

hegemon·y [hɪ'dʒemənɪ] or ['hedʒɪ-,monɪ] s (-ies) egemonia

hegira [hɪ'dʒaɪrə] or ['hedʒɪrə] s fuga

heifer ['hefər] s manza, giovenca

height [haɪt] s altezza; (of a person) altezza, statura; (e.g., of folly) colmo

heighten ['haɪtən] tr innalzare; (to increase the amount of) accrescere, aumentare || intr aumentare

heinous ['henəs] adj nefando, odioso

heir [er] s erede m

heir' appar'ent s (heirs' appar'ent) erede necessario

heirdom ['erdəm] s eredità f

heiress ['erɪs] s ereditiera, erede f

heirloom ['er,lum] s cimelio di famiglia

Helen ['helən] s Elena

helicopter ['helɪ,kɑptər] s elicottero

heliport ['helɪ,port] s eliporto

helium ['hilɪ-əm] s elio

helix ['hilɪks] s (helixes or helices ['helɪ,siz]) spirale f; (geom) elica

hell [hel] s inferno

hell-bent ['hel'bent] adj (coll) risoluto; to be hell-bent on (coll) avere un chiodo in testa di

hell'cat' s arpia, megera

hellebore ['helɪ,bor] s elleboro

Hellene ['helin] s greco

Hellenic [he'lenɪk] or [he'linɪk] adj ellenico

hell'fire' s fuoco dell'inferno

hellish ['helɪʃ] adj infernale

hel·lo [he'lo] s saluto || interj ciao!; (on telephone) pronto!

helm [helm] s barra del timone; ruota del timone; timone m || tr dirigere

helmet ['helmɪt] s (mil) elmetto; (sports) casco; (hist) elmo

helms'man s (-men) timoniere m

help [help] s aiuto; (relief) rimedio, e.g., there's no help for it non c'è rimedio; servitù f; impiegati mpl; operai mpl; to come to the help of venire in aiuto di || tr aiutare; soccorrere, mitigare; (to wait on) servire; it can't be helped non c'è rimedio; so help me God! Dio mi sia testimonio!; to help down aiutare a scendere; to help s.o. with his coat aiutare qlcu a mettersi il cappotto; to help oneself servirsi da solo; to help up aiutare a salire; aiutare ad alzarsi; to not be able to help + ger non poter fare a meno di + inf, e.g., he can't help laughing non può fare a meno di ridere || intr aiutare || interj aiuto!

helper ['helpər] s aiutante m; (in a shop) garzone m, lavorante m

helpful ['helpfəl] adj utile, servizievole

helping ['helpɪŋ] s (of food) razione f

helpless ['helplɪs] adj (weak) debole; (powerless) impotente; senza risorse; (confused) perplesso; (situation) irrimediabile

help'mate' s compagno; (wife) compagna

helter-skelter ['heltər'skeltər] adj & adv in fretta e furia; alla rinfusa

hem [hem] s (any edge) orlo; (of skirt) basta, pedana; (of suit) falda f || v (pret & pp hemmed; ger hemming) tr orlare, bordare; to hem in insaccare || intr esitare; to hem and haw esitare; essere evasivo

hemisphere ['hemɪ,sfɪr] s emisfero

hemistich ['hemɪ,stɪk] s emistichio

hem'line' s orlo della gonna

hem'lock' s (herb and poison) cicuta; (Tsuga canadensis) abete m del Canada

hemoglobin [,hemə'globɪn] or [,himə-'globɪn] s emoglobina

hemophilia [,hemə'fɪlɪ-ə] or [,himə-'fɪlɪ-ə] s emofilia

hemorrhage ['hemərɪdʒ] s emorragia

hemorrhoids ['hemə,rɔɪdz] spl emorroidi fpl

hemostat ['hemə,stæt] or ['himə,stæt] s pinza emostatica

hemp [hemp] s canapa

hemstitch ['hem ,strtʃ] s orlo a giorno || tr & intr orlare a giorno

hen [hen] s gallina

hence [hens] adv di qui; da ora; quindi; di qui a, e.g., **three weeks hence** di qui a tre settimane

hence'forth' adv d'ora innanzi

hench·man ['hentʃmən] s (-men [mən]) accolito; politicante m

hen'house' s pollaio

henna ['henə] s henna || tr tingere con la henna

hen'peck' tr (a husband) trovare a ridire con

hen'pecked' hus'band s marito dominato dalla moglie

her [hʌr] adj poss suo, il suo || pron pers la, lei; **to her** le, a lei

herald ['herəld] s araldo; annunziatore m || tr annunziare

heraldic [he'rældɪk] adj araldico

herald·ry ['herəldri] s (-ries) (office) consulta araldica; (science) araldica; (coat of arms) blasone m

herb [ʌrb] or [hʌrb] s erba; erba medicinale

herbaceous [hʌr'be/əs] adj erbaceo

herbage ['ʌrbɪdʒ] or ['hʌrbɪdʒ] s erba; (law) erbatico

herbalist ['hʌrbəlɪst] or ['ʌrbəlɪst] s erborista mf

herbari·um [hʌr'berɪ·əm] s (-ums or -a [ə]) erbario

herb' doc'tor s erborista mf

herculean [hʌr'kjulɪ·ən] or [,hʌrkju-'li·ən] adj erculeo

herd [hʌrd] s (of sheep) gregge m; (of cattle) mandria; (of men) torma || tr & intr imbrancare

herds'man s (-men) (of cattle) mandriano, vaccaio; (of sheep) pastore m

here [hɪr] adj presente || s—the here and the hereafter la vita presente e l'aldilà || adv qui, qua; here and there qua e là; here is or here are ecco; that's neither here not there ciò non ha nulla a che vedere || interj presente!

hereabouts ['hɪrə ,bauts] adv qua vicino

here·af'ter s aldilà m || adv d'ora innanzi; nel futuro

here·by' adv con la presente

hereditary [hɪ'redɪ ,teri] adj ereditario

heredi·ty [hɪ'redɪti] s (-ties) eredità f

here·in' adv qui; in questo posto

here·of' adv di questo

here·on' adv in questo; su questo

here·sy ['herəsi] s (-sies) eresia

heretic ['herətɪk] adj & s eretico

heretical [hɪ'retɪkəl] adj eretico

heretofore [,hɪrtu'for] adv sinora

here·u·pon' adv su questo; in questo; immediatamente dopo

here·with' adv accluso; con la presente

heritage ['herɪtɪdʒ] s eredità f

hermetic(al) [hʌr'metɪk(əl)] adj ermetico

hermit ['hʌrmɪt] s eremita m

hermitage ['hʌrmɪtɪdʒ] s eremitaggio

herni·a ['hʌrnɪ·ə] s (-as or -ae [,i]) ernia

he·ro ['hɪro] s (-roes) eroe m

heroic [hɪ'ro·ɪk] adj eroico || **heroics** spl linguaggio altisonante

heroin ['hero·ɪn] s (pharm) eroina

heroine ['hero·ɪn] s eroina

heroism ['hero ,ɪzəm] s eroismo

heron ['herən] s airone m

herring ['herɪŋ] s aringa

her'ring·bone' s (in fabrics) spina di pesce; (in hardwood floors) spiga

hers [hʌrz] pron poss il suo; **of hers** suo

herself [hʌr'self] pron pers lei stessa; sé stessa; si, e.g., **she enjoyed herself** si divertì; **with herself** con sé

hertz [hʌrts] s hertz m

hesitan·cy ['hezɪtənsi] s (-cies) titubanza, esitanza

hesitant ['hezɪtənt] adj esitante

hesitate ['hezɪ ,tet] intr esitare, titubare; (to stutter) balbettare

hesitation [,hezɪ'teʃən] s esitazione f

heterodox ['hetərə ,daks] adj eterodosso

heterodyne ['hetərə ,daɪn] s eterodina

heterogeneous [,hetərə'dʒinɪ·əs] adj eterogeneo

hew [hju] v (pret hewed; pp hewed or hewn) tr tagliare; (a passage) aprirsi; (a statue) abbozzare; **to hew down** abbattere || intr—**to hew close to the line** (coll) filare diritto

hex [heks] s strega; incantesimo || tr stregare, incantare

hexameter [heks'æmɪtər] s esametro

hey [he] interj ehi!

hey'day' s apogeo

hia·tus [haɪ'etəs] s (-tuses or -tus) (gap) lacuna; (gram) iato

hibernate ['haɪbər ,net] intr ibernare; (said of people) svernare

hibiscus [hɪ'bɪskəs] or [haɪ'bɪskəs] s ibisco

hic·cup ['hɪkəp] s singhiozzo || v (pret & pp -cuped or -cupped; ger -cuping or -cupping) intr singhiozzare

hick [hɪk] adj & s (coll) rustico

hicko·ry ['hɪkəri] s (-ries) hickory m

hidden ['hɪdən] adj nascosto

hide [haɪd] s cuoio, pelle f; **hides** cuoio; **neither hide nor hair** nemmeno una traccia; **to tan s.o.'s hide** (coll) dargliele sode a qlcu || v (pret **hid** [hɪd]; pp **hid** or **hidden** ['hɪdən]) tr nascondere || intr nascondersi; **to hide out** (coll) rintanarsi

hide'-and-seek' s rimpiattino; **to play hide-and-seek** giocare a rimpiattino or a nascondino

hide'bound' adj retrogrado, conservatore

hideous ['hɪdɪ·əs] adj orribile, brutto

hide'out' s nascondiglio

hiding ['haɪdɪŋ] s nascondere m; (place) nascondiglio; **in hiding** nascosto

hid'ing place' s nascondiglio

hie [haɪ] v (pret & pp **hied**; ger **hieing** or **hying**) tr—**hie thee home** affrettati a tornare a casa || intr affrettarsi

hierar·chy ['haɪ·ə ,rarki] s (-chies) gerarchia

hieroglyphic [,haɪ·ərə'glɪfɪk] adj & s geroglifico

hi-fi ['haɪ'faɪ] *adj* di alta fedeltà ‖ *s* alta fedeltà

higgledy-piggledy ['hɪgəldɪ'pɪgəldɪ] *adj* confuso ‖ *adv* alla rinfusa

high [haɪ] *adj* alto; (*color*) forte; (*merry*) allegro; (*luxurious*) lussuoso; (coll) ubriaco; (culin) frollo; **high and dry** abbandonato; **high and mighty** (coll) arrogante ‖ *adv* molto; riccamente; **to aim high** mirare in alto; **to come high** essere caro ‖ *s* (aut) quarta, diretta; **on high** in cielo

high′ al′tar *s* altare *m* maggiore

high′ball′ *s* whiskey con ghiaccio e gazosa ‖ *intr* (slang) andare di carriera

high′ blood′ pres′sure *s* ipertensione

high′born′ *adj* di nobile lignaggio

high′boy′ *s* cassettone alto

high′brow′ *s* intellettuale *mf*; (coll) intellettualoide *mf*

high′chair′ *s* seggiolino per bambini

high′ command′ *s* comando supremo

high′ cost′ of liv′ing *s* carovita *m*, caroviveri *m*

high′er educa′tion *s* insegnamento universitario, istruzione superiore

higher-up [,haɪ·ər'ʌp] *s* (coll) superiore *m*

high′ explo′sive *s* esplosivo ad alta potenza

highfalutin [,haɪfə'lutən] *adj* (coll) pomposo, pretenzioso

high′ fidel′ity *s* high fidelity, alta fedeltà

high′-fre′quency *adj* ad alta frequenza

high′ gear′ *s* (aut) presa diretta

high′-grade′ *adj* di qualità superiore

high-handed ['haɪ'hændɪd] *adj* arbitrario

high′ hat′ *s* cappello a cilindro

high′-hat′ (coll) snob *m* ‖ *v* (*pret & pp* -hatted; *ger* -hatting) *tr* (coll) snobbare

high′-heeled′ shoe′ ['haɪ ,hild] *s* scarpa coi tacchi alti

high′ horse′ *s* comportamento arrogante; **to get up on one's high horse** darsi delle grandi arie

high′ jinks′ [dʒɪŋks] *s* (slang) pagliacciata, gazzarra

high′ jump′ *s* salto in altezza

highland ['haɪlənd] *adj* montagnoso ‖ **highlands** *spl* regione montagnosa

high′ life′ *s* high-life *f*, alta società

high′light′ *s* punto culminante ‖ *tr* mettere in risalto

highly ['haɪlɪ] *adv* altamente, molto; (*paid*) profumatamente; **to speak highly of** parlar molto bene di

High′ Mass′ *s* messa cantata

high-minded ['haɪ'maɪndɪd] *adj* magnanimo

highness ['haɪnɪs] *s* altezza ‖ **Highness** *s* Altezza

high′ noon′ *s* mezzogiorno in punto; (fig) sommo

high-pitched ['haɪ'pɪt/t] *adj* acuto; intenso, emozionante

high-powered ['haɪ'pau·ərd] *adj* ad alta potenza; (*binoculars*) ad alto ingrandimento

high′pres′sure *adj* ad alta pressione ‖ *tr* sollecitare con insistenza

high-priced ['haɪ'praɪst] *adj* caro, di alto prezzo

high′ priest′ *s* sommo sacerdote

high′ rise′ *s* edificio di molti piani

high′road′ *s* strada principale

high′school′ *s* scuola media; (*in Italy*) liceo

high′ sea′ *s* alto mare; **high seas** alto mare

high′ soci′ety *s* l'alta società

high′-sound′ing *adj* altisonante

high′-speed′ *adj* ad alta velocità

high-spirited ['haɪ'spɪrɪtɪd] *adj* fiero, vivace, focoso

high′ spir′its *spl* allegria, vivacità *f*

high-strung ['haɪ'strʌŋ] *adj* teso, nervoso

high′-test′ fuel′ *s* supercarburante *m*

high′ tide′ *s* alta marea; punto culminante

high′ time′ *s* ora, e.g., **it is high time for you to go** è proprio ora che Lei se ne vada; (coll) baldoria

high′ trea′son *s* (*against the sovereign*) lesa maestà; (*against the state*) alto tradimento

high′ wa′ter *s* alta marea; (*in a river*) straripamento

high′way′ *adj* autostradale ‖ *s* autostrada

high′way′man *s* (-men) grassatore *m*

hijack ['haɪ ,dʒæk] *tr* rubare; (*e.g., an airplane*) dirottare ‖ *intr* effettuare un dirottamento

hijacker ['haɪ ,dʒækər] *s* ladro a mano armata; (*e.g., of an airplane*) dirottatore *m*

hijacking ['haɪ ,dʒækɪŋ] *s* furto a mano armata; dirottamento

hike [haɪk] *s* (*for pleasure*) gita, camminata; (*increase*) aumento; (mil) marcia ‖ *tr* tirar su; aumentare ‖ *intr* fare una gita; (mil) fare una marcia

hiker ['haɪkər] *s* camminatore *m*

hilarious [hɪ'lɛrɪ·əs] or [haɪ'lɛrɪ·əs] *adj* ilare; (*e.g., joke*) allegro, divertente

hill [hɪl] *s* collina ‖ *tr* rincalzare

hillbil·ly ['hɪl ,bɪlɪ] *s* (-lies) (coll) montanaro rustico

hillock ['hɪlək] *s* poggio, collinetta

hill′side′ *s* pendio

hill′top′ *s* cima

hill·y ['hɪlɪ] *adj* (-ier; -iest) collinoso; ripido

hilt [hɪlt] *s* impugnatura, elsa; **up to the hilt** completamente

him [hɪm] *pron pers* lo; lui; **to him** gli, a lui

himself [hɪm'sɛlf] *pron pers* lui stesso; sé stesso; si, e.g., **he enjoyed himself** si è divertito; **with himself** con sé

hind [haɪnd] *adj* posteriore, di dietro ‖ *s* cerva

hinder ['hɪndər] *tr* ostacolare, impedire

hindmost ['haɪnd ,most] *adj* ultimo

hind′quar′ter *s* quarto posteriore

hindrance ['hɪndrəns] *s* ostacolo, impedimento

hind'sight' s senno di poi

Hindu ['hɪndu] adj & s indù mf

hinge [hɪndʒ] s cardine m; (bb) cerniera; (philately) listello gommato; punto principale || tr munire di cardini || intr—**to hinge on** dipendere da

hin·ny ['hɪni] s (-nies) bardotto

hint [hɪnt] s insinuazione; **to take the hint** capire l'antifona || tr & intr insinuare; **to hint at** alludere a

hinterland ['hɪntər‚lænd] s retroterra m, entroterra m

hip [hɪp] adj—**to be hip to** (slang) essere al corrente di || s anca, fianco; (of a roof) spigolo

hip'bone' s ileo, osso iliaco

hipped [hɪpt] adj (livestock) zoppicante; (roof) a padiglione; **hipped on** (coll) ossessionato per

hippie ['hɪpi] s capellone m

hip·po ['hɪpo] s (-pos) (coll) ippopotamo

hippodrome ['hɪpə‚drom] s ippodromo

hippopota·mus [‚hɪpə'pɑtəməs] s (-muses or -mi [‚maɪ]) ippopotamo

hip' roof' s tetto a padiglione

hire [haɪr] s paga, salario; nolo; **for hire** a nolo || tr (help) impiegare; (a conveyance) noleggiare || intr—**to hire out** mettersi a servizio

hired' girl' s lavorante f di campagna

hired' hand' s lavorante mf

hired' man' s (men') lavorante m di campagna

hireling ['haɪrlɪŋ] adj venale || s persona prezzolata

his [hɪz] adj poss suo, il suo || pron poss il suo

Hispanic [hɪs'pænɪk] adj ispano

Hispanist ['hɪspænɪst] s ispanista mf

hiss [hɪs] s (of fire, wind, serpent, etc.) sibilo; (of disapproval) fischio, zittio || tr zittire || intr zittire; sibilare; (said of a kettle) fischiare

histology [hɪs'tɑlədʒi] s istologia

historian [hɪs'tori·ən] s storico

historic(al) [hɪs'tɑrɪk(əl)] or [hɪs'tɔrɪk(əl)] adj storico

histo·ry ['hɪstəri] s (-ries) storia

histrionic [‚hɪstrɪ'ɑnɪk] adj teatrale; (artificial, affected) istrionico, teatrale || **histrionics** s istrionismo, teatralità f

hit [hɪt] s colpo; successo; (sarcastic remark) frecciata; **to be a hit** far furore; **to make a hit with** fare ottima impressione con || v (pret & pp hit; ger hitting) tr colpire; (to bump) cozzare; (the target) toccare, imbroccare, infilare; (with a car) metter sotto; (a certain speed) andare a || intr battere; **to hit on** (s.th new) imbroccare; **to hit out at** attaccare

hit'-and-run' adj (driver) colpevole di mancato soccorso

hit'-and-run' driv'er s pirata m della strada

hitch [hɪtʃ] s strattone m; (knot) nodo; difficoltà f, ostacolo; || tr (to tie) attaccare; (oxen) aggiogare; (slang) sposare

hitch'hike' intr fare l'autostop

hitch'hik'er s autostoppista mf

hitch'ing post' s palo per attaccare un cavallo

hither ['hɪðər] adv qua, qui; **hither and thither** qua e là

hith'er·to' adv sinora

hit'-or-miss' adj fatto alla carlona

hit' rec'ord s disco di grande successo

hive [haɪv] s (box for bees) alveare m; (swarm) sciame m; **hives** orticaria || tr (bees) raccogliere

hoard [hord] s cumulo; (of money) gruzzolo || tr & intr custodire gelosamente; tesaurizzare

hoarding ['hordɪŋ] s ammassamento, tesaurizzazione

hoarfrost ['hor‚frɔst] s brina

hoarse [hors] adj rauco, svociato

hoarseness ['horsnɪs] s raucedine f

hoar·y ['hori] adj (-ier; -iest) canuto, incanutito

hoax [hoks] s mistificazione || tr mistificare

hob [hɑb] s mensola del focolare; **to play hob with** (coll) mettere a soqquadro

hobble ['hɑbəl] s zoppicamento; (to tie legs of animal) pastoia || tr far zoppicare; imbarazzare; mettere le pastoie a || intr zoppicare

hob·by ['hɑbi] s (-bies) svago, passatempo; **to ride a hobby** dedicarsi troppo alla propria occupazione favorita

hob'by·horse' s cavallo a dondolo

hob'gob'lin s folletto

hob'nail' s brocca, bulletta

hob·nob ['hɑb‚nɑb] v (pret & pp -nobbed; ger -nobbing) intr essere amiconi; **to hobnob with** essere intimo di

ho·bo ['hobo] s (-bos or -boes) girovago, vagabondo

Hob'son's choice' ['hɑbsənz] s scelta fra quanto viene offerto o niente

hock [hɑk] s garretto; (coll) pegno; **in hock** (coll) impegnato, al monte di pietà || tr tagliare i garretti a; (coll) impegnare

hockey ['hɑki] s hockey m

hock'ey play'er s hockeista m, discatore m

hock'shop' s (coll) negozio di prestiti su pegno

hocus-pocus ['hokəs'pokəs] s (meaningless formula) abracadabra m; gherminella

hod [hɑd] s vassoio; secchio per il carbone

hod' car'rier s manovale m

hodgepodge ['hɑdʒ‚pɑdʒ] s farragine f

hoe [ho] s marra, zappa || tr & intr zappare

hog [hɑg] or [hɔg] s suino, porco, maiale m || v (pret & pp hogged; ger hogging) tr (slang) mangiarsi il meglio di

hoggish ['hɑgɪʃ] or ['hɔgɪʃ] adj maialesco; egoista

hogs'head' s barilozzo di sessantatrè galloni

hog'wash' s broda da maiali

hoist [hɔɪst] s montacarichi m; (lift) spinta || tr alzare, rizzare; (a flag) inastare; (naut) issare

hoity-toity ['hɔɪtɪ'tɔɪtɪ] adj arrogante, altezzoso

hokum ['hokəm] s (coll) fandonie fpl; (coll) sentimentalismo volgare

hold [hold] s presa, piglio; (handle) impugnatura; autorità f, ascendente m; (wrestling) presa; (aer) cabina bagagli; (mus) corona; (naut) cala, stiva; **to take hold of** afferare; impossessarsi di || v (pret & pp held [held]) tr tenere; (to hold up) sostenere; (e.g., with a pin) assicurare; (a rank) rivestire; contenere; (a meeting) avere; (a note) (mus) filare; **to hold back** trattenere; **to hold in** trattenere; **to hold one's own** non perdere terreno; **to hold over** differire; **to hold up** reggere, sostenere; (to rob) (coll) derubare, rapinare || intr stare; (to cling) reggere; restare valido; **hold on!** un momento!; **to hold back** frenarsi; **to hold forth** fare un discorso; **to hold off** astenersi; mantenersi a distanza; **to hold on** continuare; **to hold on to** attaccarsi a; **to hold out** tener duro, resistere; **to hold out for** mantenersi fermo per

holder ['holdər] s possessore m, detentore m; (e.g., for a cigar) bocchino; (e.g., for a pot) manico, impugnatura

holding ['holdɪŋ] s possesso; **holdings** valori mpl, patrimonio

hold'ing com'pany s società finanziaria

hold'up' s (delay) interruzione; (coll) rapina a mano armata; (fig) furto

hold'up man' s grassatore m

hole [hol] s buco; (in cheese) occhio; (in a road) buca; (den) tana; (burrow) fossa; **in a hole** in grane, in difficoltà; **to burn a hole in one's pocket** (said of money) scorrere attraverso le mani bucate di qlcu; **to pick holes in** trovare a ridire su || intr—**to hole up** (coll) imbucarsi

holiday ['hɑlɪ‚de] s giorno festivo, festa; vacanza

holiness ['holɪnɪs] s santità f; **his Holiness** sua Santità

Holland ['hɑlənd] s l'Olanda f

Hollander ['hɑləndər] s olandese mf

hollow ['hɑlo] adj vuoto; (sound) sordo; (eyes, cheeks) infossato; vano, futile || s buca, cavità f; (small valley) valletta || adv—**to beat all hollow** (coll) battere completamente || tr scavare

hol·ly ['hɑli] s (-lies) agrifoglio

holly'hock' s altea, malvone m

holm' oak' [hom] s leccio

holocaust ['hɑlə‚kɔst] s olocausto

holster ['holstər] s fondina

ho·ly ['holi] adj (-lier; -liest) santo; (writing) sacro; (water) benedetto

Ho'ly Ghost' s Spirito Santo

ho'ly or'ders spl ordini sacri; **to take holy orders** entrare in un ordine religioso

Ho'ly Rood' [rud] s Santa Croce

Ho'ly Scrip'ture s Sacra Scrittura

Ho'ly See' s Santa Sede

Ho'ly Sep'ulcher s Santo Sepolcro

Ho'ly Thurs'day s l'Ascensione; il giovedì santo

ho'ly wa'ter s acqua benedetta, acquasanta

Ho'ly Writ' s Sacra Scrittura

homage ['hɑmɪdʒ] or ['ɑmɪdʒ] s omaggio

homburg ['hɑmbʌrg] s lobbia m & f

home [hom] adj casalingo, domestico; nazionale || s casa, dimora; (fatherland) patria; (for the sick, aged, etc.) ricovero; (sports) meta, traguardo; **at home** a casa; (at ease) a proprio agio; (sports) nel proprio campo; **away from home** fuori di casa; **make yourself at home** stia comodo; **to be at home** (to receive callers) ricevere || adv a casa; **to see home** accompagnare a casa; **to strike home** toccare nel vivo

home'bod'y s (-ies) persona casalinga

homebred ['hom‚bred] adj domestico; rozzo; semplice

home'brew' s bevanda fatta in casa

home-coming ['hom‚kʌmɪŋ] s ritorno a casa

home' coun'try s paese m natale

home' deliv'ery s trasporto a domicilio

home' front' s fronte domestico

home'land' s paese natio

homeless ['homlɪs] adj senza tetto

home' life' s vita familiare

home-loving ['hom‚lʌvɪŋ] adj casalingo

home·ly ['homli] adj (-lier; -liest) (not goodlooking) brutto; (not elegant) semplice, scialbo

homemade ['hom'med] adj fatto in casa

homemaker ['hom‚mekər] s casalinga

home' of'fice s sede f centrale || **Home Office** s (Brit) ministero degli interni

homeopath ['homɪ‚pæθ] or ['hɑmɪ‚pæθ] s omeopatico

home' plate' s casa base

home' port' s porto d'iscrizione (nel registro marittimo)

home' rule' s autogoverno

home' run' s colpo che permette al battitore di percorrere tutte le basi del diamante fino alla casa base

homesick adj nostalgico; **to be homesick for** sentire la nostalgia per

home'sick'ness s nostalgia

homespun ['hom‚spʌn] adj filato a casa; semplice

home'stead' s casa e terreno

home'stretch' s (sports) dirittura d'arrivo; (fig) fase f finale

home'town' s città f natale

homeward ['homwərd] adj di ritorno || adv verso casa; verso la patria

home'work' s lavoro a domicilio; (of a student) dovere m, esercizio

homey ['homi] adj (homier; homiest) intimo, comodo

homicidal [‚hɑmɪ'saɪdəl] adj omicida

homicide ['hɑmɪ‚saɪd] s (act) omicidio; (person) omicida mf

homi·ly ['hɑmɪli] s (-lies) omelia

homing ['homɪŋ] *adj (pigeon)* viaggiatore; *(weapon)* cercatore del bersaglio

hominy ['hamɪnɪ] *s* granturco macinato

homogenei·ty [ˌhomədʒɪ'ni·ɪtɪ] or [ˌhamədʒɪ'ni·ɪtɪ] *s* **(-ties)** omogeneità *f*

homogeneous [ˌhomə'dʒɪnɪ·əs] or [ˌhamə'dʒɪnɪ·əs] *adj* omogeneo

homogenize [hə'madʒə ˌnaɪz] *tr* omogeneizzare

homonym ['hamənɪm] *s* omonimo

homonymous [hə'manɪməs] *adj* omonimo

homosexual [ˌhomə'sek/ʊ·əl] *adj & s* omosessuale *mf*

hone [hon] *s* cote *f* || *tr* affilare

honest ['anɪst] *adj* onesto; guadagnato onestamente; integro, schietto

honesty ['anɪstɪ] *s* onestà *f*; (bot) lunaria

hon·ey ['hʌnɪ] *adj* melato, dolce || *s* miele *m*; nettare *m*; (coll) caro || *v* (*pret & pp* **-eyed** or **-ied**) *tr* dire parole melate a

hon′ey·bee′ *s* ape domestica

hon′ey-comb′ *s* favo || *tr* crivellare

honeyed ['hʌnɪd] *adj* melato

hon′eydew mel′on *s* melone *m* dolce dalla scorza liscia

hon′ey lo′cust *s* acacia a tre spine

hon′ey-moon′ *s* luna di miele || *intr* andare in viaggio di nozze

honeysuckle ['hʌnɪ ˌsʌkəl] *s* caprifoglio

honk [haŋk] or [hɔŋk] *s (of wild goose)* schiamazzo; *(of automobile horn)* suono del clacson || *tr* (aut) suonare || *intr* schiamazzare; (aut) suonare

honkytonk ['haŋkɪ ˌtaŋk] or ['hɔŋki ˌtɔŋk] *s* (coll) locale notturno rumoroso

honor ['anər] *s* onore *m* || *tr* onorare; (com) accettare e pagare

honorable ['anərəbəl] *adj (upright)* onorato; *(bringing honor; worthy of honor)* onorevole

honorari·um [ˌanə'rerɪ·əm] *s* **(-ums** or **-a** [ə])** onorario

honorary ['anə ˌrerɪ] *adj* onorario

honorific [ˌanə'rɪfɪk] *adj* onorifico || *s* titolo onorifico; formula di gentilezza

hon′or sys′tem *s* sistema scolastico basato sulla parola d'onore

hood [hʊd] *s* cappuccio; cappuccio di toga universitaria; *(of carriage)* soffietto; (aut) cofano; (slang) gangster *m* || *tr* incappucciare

hoodlum ['hudləm] *s* (slang) facinoroso, gangster *m*, teppista *m*

hoodoo ['hudu] *s (body of primitive rites)* vuduismo; *(bad luck)* iettatura; *(person who brings bad luck)* iettatore *m* || *tr* iettare

hood′wink′ *tr* turlupinare, imbrogliare

hooey ['hu·i] *s* (coll) sciocchezze *fpl*

hoof [huf] or [hʊf] *s* zoccolo, unghia; **on the hoof** *(cattle)* vivo || *tr*—**to hoof it** (slang) camminare; ballare

hoof′beat′ *s* rumore *m* degli zoccoli

hook [hʊk] *s* gancio; *(for fishing)* amo;

(to join two things) agganciamento; *(for pulling)* raffio, rampino; *(curve)* curva; *(of hook and eye)* uncinello; (boxing) hook *m*, gancio; **by hook or by crook** di riffa o di raffa; **to swallow the hook** abboccare all'amo || *tr* agganciare; *(to bend)* curvare; *(fish)* pigliare; *(to wound with the horns)* incornare; **to hook up** agganciare; *(e.g., a loudspeaking system)* montare || *intr* agganciarsi; curvarsi

hookah ['hukə] *s* narghilè *m*

hook′ and eye′ *s* uncinello e occhiello

hook′ and lad′der *s* autoscala

hooked′ rug′ *s* tappeto fatto all'uncinetto

hook′nose′ *s* naso gobbo

hook′up′ *s* (electron) diagramma *m*, schema *m* di montaggio; (rad, telv) rete *f*

hook′worm′ *s* anchilostoma *m*

hooky ['hukɪ] *s*—**to play hooky** marinare la scuola

hooligan ['hulɪgən] *s* teppista *m*

hooliganism ['hulɪgən ˌɪzəm] *s* teppismo

hoop [hup] or [hup] *s* cerchio || *tr* cerchiare

hoop′ skirt′ *s* crinolina

hoot [hut] *s* grido della civetta; grido di derisione || *tr* zittire || *intr* stridere; **to hoot at** fischiare

hoot′ owl′ *s* allocco

hop [hap] *s* salto, saltello; (aer) breve volo; (bot) luppolo; (coll) corsa; **hops** *(dried flowers of hop vine)* luppolo || *v (pret & pp* **hopped**; *ger* **hopping**) *tr* saltare su; (aer) trasvolare || *intr* saltellare; saltellare su un piede; **to hop over** saltare su; fare una corsa a

hope [hop] *s* speranza || *tr & intr* sperare; **to hope for** sperare

hope′ chest′ *s* corredo da sposa

hopeful ['hopfəl] *adj (feeling hope)* fiducioso; *(giving hope)* promettente

hopeless ['hoplɪs] *adj* disperato

hopper ['hapər] *s* tramoggia

hop′scotch′ *s* gioco del mondo

horde [hord] *s* orda

horehound ['hor ˌhaund] *s* marrubio; pastiglie *fpl* per la tosse al marrubio

horizon [hə'raɪzən] *s* orizzonte *m*

horizontal [ˌharɪ'zantəl] or [ˌhorɪ'zantəl] *adj & s* orizzontale *f*

hormone ['hɔrmon] *s* ormone *m*

horn [hɔrn] *s* corno; (aut) clacson *m*, avvisatore acustico; (mus) corno; *(trumpet)* (slang) tromba; **to blow one's horn** cantare le proprie lodi; **to lock horns** lottare, disputare; **to pull in one's horns** battere in ritirata || *intr*—**to horn in** (slang) intromettersi (in)

horned′ owl′ ['hɔrnəd] *s* allocco

hornet ['hɔrnɪt] *s* calabrone *m*

hor′net's nest′ *s* vespaio; **to stir up a hornet's nest** suscitare un vespaio

horn′ of plen′ty *s* corno dell'abbondanza

horn′pipe′ *s* clarinetto contadinesco inglese fatto di corno di bue

horn'-rimmed glass'es [ˈhɔrnˈrɪmd] *spl* occhiali cerchiati di corno o con la montatura di corno

horn·y [ˈhɔrni] *adj* (**-ier; -iest**) corneo; (*callous*) calloso; (*having hornlike projections*) cornuto; (slang) preso da desiderio lussurioso

horoscope [ˈhɑrəˌskop] or [ˈhɔrəˌskop] *s* oroscopo

horrible [ˈhɑrɪbəl] or [ˈhɔrɪbəl] *adj* orrendo, orribile

horrid [ˈhɑrɪd] or [ˈhɔrɪd] *adj* orrido, orribile

horri·fy [ˈhɑrɪˌfaɪ] or [ˈhɔrɪˌfaɪ] *v* (*pret & pp* **-fied**) *tr* inorridire

horror [ˈhɑrər] or [ˈhɔrər] *s* orrore *m*; **to have a horror of** provare orrore per

hors d'oeuvre [ɔr ˈdʌrv] *s* (**hors d'oeuvres** [ɔr ˈdʌrvz]) *s* antipasto

horse [hɔrs] *s* cavallo; (*of carpenter*) cavalletto; **hold your horses!** (coll) aspetti un momento!; **to back the wrong horse** (coll) puntare sul perdente; **to be a horse of another color** (coll) essere un altro paio di maniche || *intr*—**to horse around** (slang) giocherellare; (slang) fare tiri burloni

horse' block' *s* montatoio

horse'break'er *s* domatore *m* di cavalli

horse'car' *s* tram *m* a cavalli

horse' chest'nut *s* (*tree*) ippocastano; (*nut*) castagna d'India

horse' deal'er *s* mercante *m* di cavalli

horse' doc'tor *s* veterinario

horse'fly' *s* (**-flies**) tafano

horse'hair' *s* crine *m* di cavallo; (*fabric*) cilicio

horse'hide' *s* cuoio di cavallo

horse'laugh' *s* risataccia

horse'man *s* (**-men**) cavallerizzo

horsemanship [ˈhɔrsmənˌʃɪp] *s* equitazione, maneggio

horse' meat' *s* carne equina

horse' op'era *s* western *m*

horse' pis'tol *s* pistola da sella

horse'play' *s* gioco violento, tiro burlone

horse'pow'er *s* cavallo vapore inglese

horse' race' *s* corsa ippica

horse'rad'ish *s* cren *m*, barbaforte *m*

horse' sense' *s* (coll) senso comune

horse'shoe' *s* ferro di cavallo

horse'shoe mag'net *s* calamita a ferro di cavallo

horse'shoe nail' *s* chiodo da cavallo

horse' show' *s* concorso ippico

horse' thief' *s* ladro di cavalli

horse'-trade' *intr* trafficare

horse'whip' *s* staffile *m* || *v* (*pret & pp* **-whipped**; *ger* **-whipping**) *tr* staffilare

horse'wom'an *s* (**-wom'en**) amazzone *f*

hors·y [ˈhɔrsi] *adj* (**-ier; -iest**) equestre; (*interested in horses*) appassionato ai cavalli; (coll) goffo

horticulture [ˈhɔrtɪˌkʌltʃər] *s* orticoltura

horticulturist [ˌhɔrtɪˈkʌltʃərɪst] *s* orticoltore *m*

hose [hoz] *s* (*stocking*) calza; (*sock*) calzino corto; (*flexible tube*) manica || **hose** *spl* calze *fpl*

hosier [ˈhoʒər] *s* calzettaio

hosiery [ˈhoʒəri] *s* calze *fpl*; calzificio

hospice [ˈhɑspɪs] *s* ospizio

hospitable [ˈhɑspɪtəbəl] or [hɑsˈpɪtəbəl] *adj* ospitale

hospital [ˈhɑspɪtəl] *s* ospedale *m*

hospitali·ty [ˌhɑspɪˈtælɪti] *s* (**-ties**) ospitalità *f*

hospitalize [ˈhɑspɪtəˌlaɪz] *tr* ospedalizzare

host [host] *s* ospite *m*; (*at an inn*) oste *m*; (*army*) milizia; (*crowd*) folla || **Host** *s* (eccl) ostia

hostage [ˈhɑstɪdʒ] *s* ostaggio

hostel [ˈhɑstəl] *s* ostello della gioventù

hostel·ry [ˈhɑstəlri] *s* (**-ries**) albergo

hostess [ˈhostɪs] *s* ospite *f*, padrona di casa; (*e.g., on a bus*) accompagnatrice *f*, guida *f*; (aer) assistente *f* di volo

hostile [ˈhɑstɪl] *adj* ostile

hostili·ty [hɑsˈtɪlɪti] *s* (**-ties**) ostilità *f*

hostler [ˈhɑslər] or [ˈɑslər] *s* stalliere *m*

hot [hɑt] *adj* (**hotter; hottest**) caldo; (*reception*) caloroso; (*e.g., pepper*) piccante; (*fresh*) fresco; (*pursuit*) impetuoso; (*in rut*) in calore; (coll) radioattivo; **to be hot** (*said of a person*) aver caldo; (*said of the weather*) fare caldo; **to make it hot for** (coll) dare del filo da torcere a

hot' air' *s* aria calda; (slang) fumo

hot'-air fur'nace *s* impianto di riscaldamento ad aria calda

hot' baths' *spl* terme *fpl*

hot'bed' *s* (*e.g., of revolt*) focolaio; (hort) semenzaio, letto caldo

hot'-blood'ed *adj* ardente; impetuoso

hot' cake' *s* frittella; **to sell like hot cakes** vendersi come se fosse regalato

hot' dog' *s* Frankfurter *m*, Würstel *m*

hotel [hoˈtɛl] *adj* alberghiero || *s* albergo

ho·tel'keep'er *s* albergatore *m*

hot'head' *s* testa calda

hotheaded [ˈhɑtˌhɛdɪd] *adj* esaltato, scalmanato

hot'house' *s* serra

hot' plate' *s* fornello elettrico, scaldavivande *m*

hot' springs' *spl* terme *fpl*

hot-tempered [ˈhɑtˈtɛmpərd] *adj* impulsivo, irascibile

hot' wa'ter *s*—**to be in hot water** (coll) essere nei guai

hot'-wa'ter boil'er *s* caldaia del termosifone

hot'-wa'ter bot'tle *s* borsa dell'acqua calda

hot'-wa'ter heat'er *s* scaldabagno

hot'-wa'ter heat'ing *s* riscaldamento a circolazione di acqua calda

hound [haʊnd] *s* bracco; **to follow the hounds** or **to ride to hounds** andare a caccia alla volpe || *tr* perseguitare

hour [aʊr] *s* ora; **by the hour** a ore; **in an evil hour** in un brutto momento; **on the hour** ogni ora al suonar dell'ora; **to keep late hours** andare a letto tardi

hour'glass' s clessidra

hour' hand' s lancetta delle ore

hourly ['aʊrlɪ] adj orario || adv ogni ora; spesso

house [haʊs] s (**houses** ['haʊzɪz]) casa; (legislative body) camera; (size of audience) concorso di pubblico; teatro; **to keep house** fare le faccende domestiche; **to put one's house in order** migliorare il proprio comportamento; accomodare le proprie faccende || [haʊz] tr allogare

house' arrest' s arresto a domicilio

house'boat' s casa galleggiante

house'break'er s scassinatore m

housebreaking ['haʊs ,brekɪŋ] s violazione di domicilio, scasso

housebroken ['haʊs ,broken] adj (e.g., cat) che è stato addestrato a tenersi pulito

house'clean'ing s pulizia della casa; (fig) pulizia, repulisti m

house'coat' s vestaglia da casa

house' cur'rent s corrente f di rete

house'fly' s (-**flies**) mosca domestica

houseful ['haʊs ,fʊl] s casa piena

house' fur'nishings spl arredi domestici

house'hold' adj domestico || s famiglia

house'hold'er s capo della famiglia

house'-hunt' intr—**to go house-hunting** andare in cerca di casa

house'keep'er s governante f

house'keep'ing s faccende domestiche; **to set up housekeeping** metter su casa

house'keeping apart'ment s appartamentino

house'maid' s domestica

house' me'ter s contatore domestico

house'moth'er s maestra in pensionato per studenti

house' of cards' s castello di carte

house' of ill' repute' s casa di malaffare

house' paint'er s imbianchino

house' physi'cian s medico residente

house'top' s tetto; **to shout from the housetops** proclamare ai quattro venti

housewarming ['haʊs ,wɔrmɪŋ] s festa per l'inaugurazione di una casa

house'wife' s (-**wives**) donna di casa

house'work' s faccende domestiche

housing ['haʊzɪŋ] s (of a horse) gualdrappa; (dwelling) abitazioni fpl; (carp) alloggiamento; (mach) gabbia, custodia; (aut) coppa; (of transmission) (aut) scatola

hous'ing proj'ect s crisi f degli alloggi

hovel ['hʌvəl] or ['hɑvəl] s catapecchia, stamberga; (shed) baracca

hover ['hʌvər] or ['hɑvər] intr librarsi; (on the lips) trapelare; (fig) ondeggiare, esitare

how [haʊ] adv come; (at what price) a quanto; **how early** quando, a che ora; **how else** in che altro modo; **how far** fino a dove; quanto, e.g., **how far is it to the station?** quanto c'è da qui alla stazione?; **how long** quanto tempo; **how many** quanti; **how much**

quanto; **how often** quante volte; **how old are you?** quanti anni ha?; **how soon** quando, a che ora; **how** + adj quanto + adj, e.g., **how beautiful she is!** quanto è bella!

how-ev'er adv comunque; in qualunque modo; per quanto . . . , e.g., **however wrong he may be** per quanto torto possa avere || conj come, e.g., **do it however you want** lo faccia come vuole

howitzer ['haʊ·ɪtsər] s obice m

howl [haʊl] s ululato, urlo; scoppio di risa || tr gridare; **to howl down** sopraffare a grida; || intr ululare, urlare

howler ['haʊlər] s urlatore m; (coll) strafalcione m, topica

hoyden ['hɔɪdən] s ragazzaccia

hub [hʌb] s mozzo; (fig) centro

hubbub ['hʌbəb] s putiferio, fracasso

hub'cap' s (aut) calotta della ruota

huckleber·ry ['hʌkəl ,berɪ] s (-**ries**) mirtillo

huckster ['hʌkstər] s venditore m ambulante; trafficante m

huddle ['hʌdəl] s conferenza segreta || intr affollarsi, accalcarsi

hue [hju] s tono, tinta; **hue and cry** grido d'indignazione

huff [hʌf] s stizza; **in a huff** di cattivo umore || tr (checkers) buffare

hug [hʌg] s abbraccio || v (pret & pp **hugged;** ger **hugging**) tr abbracciare; (e.g., a wall) costeggiare || intr abbracciarsi

huge [hjudʒ] adj smisurato, immane

huh [hʌ] interj eh!

hulk [hʌlk] s scafo, carcassa; (unwieldy object) trabiccolo

hulking ['hʌlkɪŋ] adj grosso e goffo

hull [hʌl] s (of ship or hydroplane) scafo; (of dirigible) intelaiatura; (of airplane) fusoliera; (e.g., of a nut) guscio || tr sgusciare; (rice) brillare

hullabaloo ['hʌləbə ,lu] or [,hʌləbə'lu] s fracasso, baccano

hum [hʌm] s canterellio; (of bee, machine, etc.) ronzio || v (pret & pp **hummed;** ger **humming**) tr canterellare || intr canterellare; (to buzz) ronzare; (coll) vibrare, essere attivo

human ['hjumən] adj umano

hu'man be'ing s essere umano

humane [hju'men] adj umano; compassionevole

humanist ['hjumənɪst] adj umanistico || s umanista mf

humanitarian [hju ,mænɪ'tɛrɪ·ən] adj & s umanitario

humani·ty [hju'mænɪtɪ] s (-**ties**) umanità f; **humanities** (of Greece and Rome) studi umanistici; (literature, art, philosophy) scienze umanistiche

hu'man·kind' s genere umano

humble ['hʌmbəl] or ['ʌmbəl] adj umile || tr umiliare

hum'ble pie' s—**to eat humble pie** accettare un'umiliazione

hum'bug' s frottola; (person) impostore m || v (pret & pp **-bugged;** ger

-bugging) *tr* imbrogliare || *intr* fare l'imbroglione

hum′drum′ *adj* noioso, monotono

humer•us [′hjumərəs] *s* (-i [,aɪ]) omero

humid [′hjumɪd] *adj* umido

humidifier [hju′mɪdɪ ,faɪ-ər] *s* evaporatore *m*

humidi•fy [hju′mɪdɪ ,faɪ] *v* (*pret & pp* -fied) *tr* inumidire

humidity [hju′mɪdɪtɪ] *s* umidità *f*

humiliate [hju′mɪlɪ ,et] *tr* umiliare

humiliating [hju′mɪlɪ ,etɪŋ] *adj* umiliante

humility [hju′mɪlɪtɪ] *s* umiltà *f*

hummingbird [′hʌmɪŋ ,bʌrd] *s* colibrì *m*

humor [′hjumər] or [′jumər] *s* umore *m;* umorismo; **out of humor** di cattivo umore || *tr* adattarsi alle fisime di, assecondare

humorist [′hjumərɪst] or [′jumərɪst] *s* umorista *mf*

humorous [′hjumərəs] or [′jumərəs] *adj* umoristico

hump [hʌmp] *s* gobba; (*in the ground*) monticello

hump′back′ *s* gobba; (*person*) gobbo

humus [′hjuməs] *s* humus *m*

hunch [hʌntʃ] *s* gobba; (*premonition*) (coll) sospetto || *tr* piegare || *intr* accovacciarsi

hunch′back′ *s* gobba; (*person*) gobbo

hundred [′hʌndrəd] *adj, s & pron* cento; **a hundred** or **one hundred** cento; **by the hundreds** a centinaia

hundredth [′hʌndrədθ] *adj, s & pron* centesimo

hun′dred-weight′ *s* cento libbre

Hungarian [hʌŋ′gɛrɪ-ən] *adj & s* ungherese *mf*

Hungary [′hʌŋgərɪ] *s* l'Ungheria *f*

hunger [′hʌŋgər] *s* fame *f* || *intr* aver fame; **to hunger for** aver un desiderio ardente di, agognare

hun′ger strike′ *s* sciopero della fame

hun•gry [′hʌŋgrɪ] *adj* (-grier; -griest) affamato; **to be hungry** aver fame; **to go hungry** andare a digiuno

hunk [hʌŋk] *s* (coll) bel pezzo

hunt [hʌnt] *s* caccia; **on the hunt for** a caccia di || *tr* cacciare; (*to look for*) cercare || *intr* andare a caccia; cercare; **to go hunting** andare a caccia; **to hunt for** cercare

hunter [′hʌntər] *s* cacciatore *m;* (*dog*) cane *m* da caccia

hunting [′hʌntɪŋ] *adj* da caccia || *s* caccia

hunt′ing box′ *s* capanno

hunt′ing dog′ *s* cane *m* da caccia

hunt′ing ground′ *s* terreno di caccia

hunt′ing horn′ *s* corno da caccia

hunt′ing jack′et *s* cacciatora

hunt′ing lodge′ *s* (*hut*) capanno; villino da caccia

hunt′ing sea′son *s* stagione della caccia

huntress [′hʌntrɪs] *s* cacciatrice *f*

hunts′man *s* (-men) cacciatore *m*

hurdle [′hʌrdəl] *s* (*hedge*) siepe *f;* (*wooden frame*) barriera; (sports, fig) ostacolo; **hurdles** corsa ad ostacoli || *tr* saltare, superare

hur′dle race′ *s* corsa agli ostacoli

hurl [hʌrl] *s* lancio || *tr* lanciare; **to hurl back** respingere

hurrah [hu′rɑ] or **hurray** [hu′re] *s* viva *m* || *tr* applaudire || *intr* gridare urrà || *interj* evviva!, urrà!; **hurrah for . . . !** viva . . . !

hurricane [′hʌrɪ ,ken] *s* uragano

hurried [′hʌrɪd] *adj* frettoloso

hur•ry [′hʌrɪ] *s* (-ries) fretta; **to be in a hurry** aver fretta || *v* (*pret & pp* -ried) *tr* affrettare, sollecitare || *intr* affrettarsi; **to hurry after** corser dietro a; **to hurry away** andarsene di furia; **to hurry back** ritornare presto; **to hurry up** spicciarsi

hurt [hʌrt] *adj* (*injured*) ferito; (*offended*) risentito || *s* (*harm*) danno; (*injury*) ferita; (*pain*) dolore *m* || *v* (*pret & pp* hurt) *tr* (*to harm*) fare male a; (*to injure*) ferire; (*to offend*) offendere; (*to pain*) dolere (with *dat*) || *intr* fare male, dolere; aver male, e.g., **my head hurts** ho male alla testa

hurtle [′hʌrtəl] *intr* sferrarsi, scagliarsi, precipitarsi

husband [′hʌzbənd] *s* marito || *tr* amministrare con economia

hus′band-man *s* (-men) agricoltore *m*

husbandry [′hʌzbəndrɪ] *s* agricoltura; (*management of domestic affairs*) governo, economia domestica

hush [hʌʃ] *s* silenzio || *tr* far tacere; **to hush up** (*a scandal*) soffocare || *intr* tacere || *interj* zitto!

hushaby [′hʌʃə ,baɪ] *interj* fa′ la nanna!

hush′-hush′ *adj* segretissimo

hush′ mon′ey *s* prezzo del silenzio

husk [hʌsk] *s* guscio; (*of corn*) spoglia || *tr* sgusciare; (*rice*) brillare; (*corn*) scartocciare, spogliare

husk•y [′hʌskɪ] *adj* (-ier; -iest) forte; (*voice*) rauco

hus•sy [′hʌzɪ] or [′hʌsɪ] *s* (-sies) poca di buono; ragazza impudente

hustle [′hʌsəl] *s* vigore *m;* (slang) traffico || *tr* forzare, spingere || *intr* affrettarsi, scalmanarsi; (slang) trafficare; (*said of a prostitute*) (slang) accostare un cliente

hustler [′hʌslər] *s* (*go-getter*) persona intraprendente; (slang) trafficone *m,* imbroglione *m;* (slang) passeggiatrice *f*

hut [hʌt] *s* casolare *m,* casupola

hyacinth [′haɪ-əsɪnθ] *s* giacinto

hybrid [′haɪbrɪd] *adj & s* ibrido

hybridize [′haɪbrɪ ,daɪz] *tr & intr* ibridare

hy•dra [′haɪdrə] *s* (-dras or -drae [dri]) idra

hydrant [′haɪdrənt] *s* idrante *m;* (*water faucet*) rubinetto

hydrate [′haɪdret] *s* idrato || *tr* idratare || *intr* idratarsi

hydraulic [haɪ′drɔlɪk] *adj* idraulico || **hydraulics** *s* idraulica

hydrau′lic ram′ *s* pompa idraulica

hydriodic [,haɪdrɪ′ɑdɪk] *adj* iodidrico

hydrobromic [,haɪdrə′bromɪk] *adj* bromidrico

hydrocarbon [ˌhaɪdrəˈkɑrbən] s idro-carburo

hydrochloric [ˌhaɪdrəˈklɔrɪk] adj clo-ridrico

hydroelectric [ˌhaɪdro·ɪˈlektrɪk] adj idroelettrico

hydrofluoric [ˌhaɪdrəfluˈɑrɪk] or [ˌhaɪdrəfluˈɔrɪk] adj fluoridrico

hydrofoil [ˈhaɪdrəˌfɔɪl] s superficie idrodinamica; (winglike member) aletta idrodinamica; (vessel) ali-scafo, idroplano

hydrogen [ˈhaɪdrədʒən] s idrogeno

hy'drogen bomb' s bomba all'idrogeno

hy'drogen perox'ide s perossido d'idro-geno, acqua ossigenata

hy'drogen sul'fide s solfuro d'idrogeno

hydrometer [haɪˈdrɑmɪtər] s areome-tro

hydrophobia [ˌhaɪdrəˈfobɪ·ə] s idro-fobia

hydroplane [ˈhaɪdrəˌplen] s (aer) idro-volante m; (naut) idroscivolante m, idroplano

hydroxide [haɪˈdrɑksaɪd] s idrossido

hyena [haɪˈinə] s iena

hygiene [ˈhaɪdʒin] or [ˈhaɪdʒɪˌin] s igiene f

hygienic [ˌhaɪdʒɪˈenɪk] or [haɪˈdʒinɪk] adj igienico

hymn [hɪm] s inno

hymnal [ˈhɪmnəl] s innario

hyperacidity [ˌhaɪpərəˈsɪdɪti] s ipera-cidità f

hyperbola [haɪˈpʌrbələ] s (geom) iper-bole f

hyperbole [haɪˈpʌrbəli] s (rhet) iper-bole f

hyperbolic [ˌhaɪpərˈbɑlɪk] adj iper-bolico

hypersensitive [ˌhaɪpərˈsensɪtɪv] adj ipersensibile

hypertension [ˌhaɪpərˈtenʃən] s iper-tensione

hyphen [ˈhaɪfən] s trattino

hyphenate [ˈhaɪfəˌnet] tr unire con trattino; scrivere con trattino

hypno·sis [hɪpˈnosɪs] s (-ses [siz]) ipnosi f

hypnotic [hɪpˈnatɪk] adj & s ipnotico

hypnotism [ˈhɪpnəˌtɪzəm] s ipnotismo

hypnotize [ˈhɪpnəˌtaɪz] tr ipnotizzare

hypochondriac [ˌhaɪpəˈkɑndrɪˌæk] or [ˌhɪpəˈkɑndrɪˌæk] s ipocondriaco

hypocri·sy [hɪˈpakrəsi] s (-sies) ipo-crisia

hypocrite [ˈhɪpəkrɪt] s ipocrita mf

hypocritical [ˌhɪpəˈkrɪtɪkəl] adj ipo-crita

hypodermic [ˌhaɪpəˈdʌrmɪk] adj ipo-dermico

hyposulfite [ˌhaɪpəˈsʌlfaɪt] s iposolfito

hypotenuse [haɪˈpɑtɪˌnus] or [haɪ-ˈpɑtɪˌnjus] s ipotenusa

hypothesis [haɪˈpɑθɪsɪs] s (-ses [ˌsiz]) ipotesi f

hypothesize [haɪˈpɑθɪˌsaɪz] tr ipotiz-zare

hypothetic(al) [ˌhaɪpəˈθetɪk(əl)] adj ipotetico

hyssop [ˈhɪsəp] s issopo

hysteria [hɪsˈtɪrɪ·ə] s isterismo

hysteric [hɪsˈterɪk] adj isterico || **hys-terics** s isterismo

hysterical [hɪsˈterɪkəl] adj isterico

I

I, i [aɪ] s nona lettera dell'alfabeto inglese

I [aɪ] pron pers (we [wi]) io; **it is I** sono io

iambic [aɪˈæmbɪk] adj giambico

iam·bus [aɪˈæmbəs] s (-bi [baɪ]) giambo

I'-beam' s putrella

Iberian [aɪˈbɪrɪ·ən] adj iberico || s abi-tante mf dell'Iberia; lingua iberica

ibex [ˈaɪbeks] s (ibexes or ibices [ˈɪbɪˌsiz]) stambecco

ice [aɪs] s ghiaccio; **to break the ice** rompere il ghiaccio; **to cut no ice** (coll) non avere importanza; **to skate on thin ice** cacciarsi in una situazione delicata || tr gelare; (to cover with icing) glassare || intr gelarsi

ice' age' s epoca glaciale

ice' bag' s borsa di ghiaccio

iceberg [ˈaɪsˌbʌrg] s borgognone m, montagna di ghiaccio

ice'boat' s slitta a vela; (icebreaker) rompighiaccio

icebound [ˈaɪsˌbaund] adj chiuso dal ghiaccio

ice'box' s ghiacciaia

ice'break'er s rompighiaccio

ice' buck'et s secchiello da ghiaccio

ice'cap' s calotta glaciale

ice'-cold' adj gelido, ghiacciato

ice' cream' s gelato, sorbetto

ice'-cream cone' s cono gelato

ice'-cream freez'er s gelatiera

ice'-cream par'lor s gelateria

ice' cube' s cubetto di ghiaccio

ice' hock'ey s hockey m su ghiaccio

Iceland [ˈaɪslənd] s l'Islanda f

Icelander [ˈaɪsˌlændər] or [ˈaɪsləndər] s islandese mf

Icelandic [aɪsˈlændɪk] adj islandese || s (language) islandese m

ice'man' s (-men') venditore m di ghiaccio

ice' pack' s banco di ghiaccio; (ice bag) borsa di ghiaccio

ice' pick' s rompighiaccio

ice' shelf' s tavolato di ghiaccio

ice' skate' s pattino da ghiaccio

ice' wa'ter s acqua gelata

ichthyology [ˌɪkθɪˈɑlədʒi] s ittiologia

icicle [ˈaɪsɪkəl] s ghiacciolo

icing [ˈaɪsɪŋ] s glassa; (meteor) gelo

iconoclast [aɪˈkɑnəˌklæst] s icono-clasta mf

iconoscope [aɪˈkɑnə‚skop] s (trademark) iconoscopio

icy [ˈaɪsi] adj (**icier; iciest**) ghiacciato; (e.g., wind, hands) gelido; (fig) glaciale

idea [aɪˈdi·ə] s idea

ideal [aɪˈdi·əl] adj & s ideale m

idealist [aɪˈdi·əlɪst] adj & s idealista mf

idealistic [aɪ‚di·əlˈɪstɪk] adj idealistico

idealize [aɪˈdi·ə‚laɪz] tr idealizzare

identic(al) [aɪˈdɛntɪk(əl)] adj identico

identification [aɪ‚dɛntɪfɪˈkeʃən] s identificazione, riconoscimento

identifica'tion card' s carta d'identità

identifica'tion tag' s piastrina

identi·fy [aɪˈdɛntɪ‚faɪ] v (pret & pp -fied) tr identificare

identi·ty [aɪˈdɛntɪti] s (-ties) identità f

ideolo·gy [‚aɪdɪˈɑlədʒi] or [‚ɪdɪˈɑlədʒi] s (-gies) ideologia

ides [aɪdz] spl idi mpl & fpl

idio·cy [ˈɪdɪ·əsi] s (-cies) idiozia

idiom [ˈɪdɪ·əm] s (expression that is contrary to the usual patterns of the language) locuzione idiomatica, idiotismo; (style of language) lingua, idioma m; (style of an author) stile m; (character of a language) indole f

idiomatic [‚ɪdɪ·əˈmætɪk] adj idiomatico

idiosyncra·sy [‚ɪdɪ·əˈsɪnkrəsi] s (-sies) eccentricità f, originalità f; (med) idiosincrasia

idiot [ˈɪdɪ·ət] s idiota mf

idiotic [‚ɪdɪˈɑtɪk] adj idiota

idle [ˈaɪdəl] adj (unemployed) disoccupato; (machine) fermo; (capital) giacente; (time) perso; (talk) vano; (lazy) fannullone, ozioso; **to run idle** girare a vuoto || tr—**to idle away** (time) sprecare || intr poltrire, fare il fannullone; (aut) girare al minimo

idleness [ˈaɪdəlnɪs] s ozio

idler [ˈaɪdlər] s fannullone m

idling [ˈaɪdlɪŋ] s (of motor) minimo

idol [ˈaɪdəl] s idolo

idola·try [aɪˈdɑlətri] s (-tries) idolatria

idolize [ˈaɪdə‚laɪz] tr idolatrare

idyll [ˈaɪdəl] s idillio

idyllic [aɪˈdɪlɪk] adj idilliaco

if [ɪf] conj se; **as if** come se; **even if** anche se; **if so** se è così; **if true** se è vero

ignis fatuus [ˈɪgnɪsˈfætʃ/ʊ·əs] s (**ignes fatui** [ˈɪgnizˈfætʃ/ʊ‚aɪ]) fuoco fatuo

ignite [ɪgˈnaɪt] tr infiammare || intr infiammarsi

ignition [ɪgˈnɪʃən] s ignizione; (aut) accensione

igni'tion switch' s (aut) chiavetta dell'accensione

igni'tion sys'tem s (aut) apparecchiatura d'accensione

ignoble [ɪgˈnobəl] adj ignobile

ignominious [‚ɪgnəˈmɪnɪ·əs] adj ignominioso

ignoramus [‚ɪgnəˈreməs] s ignorante mf

ignorance [ˈɪgnərəns] s ignoranza

ignorant [ˈɪgnərənt] adj ignorante; **to be ignorant of** ignorare

ignore [ɪgˈnor] tr (a person; a person's kindness) ignorare

ill [ɪl] adj (**worse** [wʌrs]; **worst** [wʌrst]) malato; **to take ill** cadere malato || adv male; **to take ill** prendere in mala parte

ill-advised [ˈɪlədˈvaɪzd] adj inconsulto, sconsiderato

ill'-at-ease' adj imbarazzato, spaesato

ill-bred [ˈɪlˈbrɛd] adj maleducato

ill-considered [ˈɪlkənˈsɪdərd] adj sconsiderato

ill-disposed [ˈɪldɪsˈpozd] adj maldisposto, malintenzionato

illegal [ɪˈligəl] adj illegale

illegible [ɪˈlɛdʒɪbəl] adj illeggibile

illegitimate [‚ɪlɪˈdʒɪtɪmɪt] adj illegittimo

ill' fame' s pessima fama

ill-fated [ˈɪlˈfetɪd] adj infausto

ill-gotten [ˈɪlˈgɑtən] adj male acquistato

ill-humored [ˈɪlˈhjumərd] adj di cattivo umore

illicit [ɪˈlɪsɪt] adj illecito

illitera·cy [ɪˈlɪtərəsi] s (-cies) analfabetismo; (mistake) solecismo; ignoranza

illiterate [ɪˈlɪtərɪt] adj (uneducated) illetterato; (unable to read or write) analfabeta || s analfabeta mf

ill-mannered [ˈɪlˈmænərd] adj screanzato, ineducato

illness [ˈɪlnɪs] s malattia

illogical [ɪˈlɑdʒɪkəl] adj illogico

ill-spent [ˈɪlˈspɛnt] adj sprecato

ill-starred [ˈɪlˈstɑrd] adj nato sotto una cattiva stella; sfortunato, funesto

ill-tempered [ˈɪlˈtɛmpərd] adj di cattivo umore

ill-timed [ˈɪlˈtaɪmd] adj inopportuno

ill'-treat' tr maltrattare, tartassare

illuminate [ɪˈlumɪ‚net] tr illuminare; (a manuscript) miniare

illumination [ɪ‚lumɪˈneʃən] s illuminazione; (in manuscript) miniatura

illusion [ɪˈluʒən] s illusione

illusive [ɪˈlusɪv] adj illusorio

illusory [ɪˈlusəri] adj illusorio

illustrate [ˈɪləs‚tret] or [ɪˈlʌstret] tr illustrare

illustration [‚ɪləsˈtreʃən] s illustrazione

illustrator [ˈɪləs‚tretər] s illustratore m

illustrious [ɪˈlʌstrɪ·əs] adj illustre

ill' will' s astio, ruggine f, malevolenza

image [ˈɪmɪdʒ] s immagine f; **the very image of** il ritratto parlante di

image·ry [ˈɪmɪdʒri] or [ˈɪmɪdʒəri] s (-ries) (mental images) fantasia; (images collectively) immagini fpl; (rhet) linguaggio figurato

imaginary [ɪˈmædʒɪ‚nɛri] adj immaginario

imagination [ɪ‚mædʒɪˈneʃən] s immaginazione

imagine [ɪˈmædʒɪn] tr & intr immaginare; (to conjecture) immaginarsi; **imagine!** si figuri!

imbalance [ɪmˈbæləns] s scompenso

imbecile [ˈɪmbɪsɪl] adj & s imbecille mf

imbecil·i·ty [ˌɪmbɪˈsɪlɪti] *s* (**-ties**) imbecillità *f*, imbecillaggine *f*

imbibe [ɪmˈbaɪb] *tr* (*to drink*) bere; assorbire ‖ *intr* bere

imbue [ɪmˈbju] *tr* imbevere

imitate [ˈɪmɪˌtet] *tr* imitare

imitation [ˌɪmɪˈteʃən] *adj* (*e.g., jewelry*) falso ‖ *s* imitazione

imitator [ˈɪmɪˌtetər] *s* imitatore *m*

immaculate [ɪˈmækjəlɪt] *adj* immacolato

immaterial [ˌɪməˈtɪrɪ·əl] *adj* immateriale; poco importante; **it's immaterial to me** a me fa lo stesso

immature [ˌɪməˈtjur] *or* [ˌɪməˈtur] *adj* immaturo

immeasurable [ɪˈmeʒərəbəl] *adj* incommensurabile, smisurato

immediacy [ɪˈmidɪ·əs] *s* immediatezza

immediate [ɪˈmidɪ·ɪt] *adj* immediato

immediately [ɪˈmidɪ·ɪtli] *adv* immediatamente

immemorial [ˌɪmɪˈmorɪ·əl] *adj* immemorabile

immense [ɪˈmens] *adj* immenso

immerge [ɪˈmʌrdʒ] *intr* sommergersi

immerse [ɪˈmʌrs] *tr* immergere

immersion [ɪˈmʌrʃən] *or* [ɪˈmʌrʒən] *s* immersione

immigrant [ˈɪmɪgrənt] *adj & s* immigrante *mf*

immigrate [ˈɪmɪˌgret] *intr* immigrare

immigration [ˌɪmɪˈgreʃən] *s* immigrazione

imminent [ˈɪmɪnənt] *adj* imminente

immobile [ɪˈmobɪl] *or* [ɪˈmobil] *adj* immobile

immobilize [ɪˈmobɪˌlaɪz] *tr* immobilizzare

immoderate [ɪˈmɑdərɪt] *adj* smodato, sregolato

immodest [ɪˈmɑdɪst] *adj* immodesto

immoral [ɪˈmɑrəl] *or* [ɪˈmɔrəl] *adj* immorale

immortal [ɪˈmɔrtəl] *adj & s* immortale *mf*

immortalize [ɪˈmɔrtəˌlaɪz] *tr* eternare, immortalare

immune [ɪˈmjun] *adj* immune

immunize [ˈɪmjəˌnaɪz] *or* [ɪˈmjunaɪz] *tr* immunizzare

imp [ɪmp] *s* diavoletto; (*child*) frugolo

impact [ˈɪmpækt] *s* impatto

impair [ɪmˈper] *tr* danneggiare; (*to weaken*) indebolire

impanel [ɪmˈpænəl] *v* (*pret & pp* **-eled** *or* **-elled**) *ger* **-eling** *or* **-elling**) *tr* iscrivere nella lista dei giurati; (*a jury*) selezionare

impart [ɪmˈpɑrt] *tr* (*a secret*) far conoscere; (*knowledge*) impartire; (*motion*) imprimere

impartial [ɪmˈpɑrʃəl] *adj* imparziale

impassable [ɪmˈpæsəbəl] *or* [ɪmˈpɑsəbəl] *adj* impraticabile, intransitabile

impasse [ɪmˈpæs] *or* [ˈɪmpæs] *s* vicolo cieco, impasse *f*

impassible [ɪmˈpæsɪbəl] *adj* impassibile

impassioned [ɪmˈpæʃənd] *adj* caloroso, veemente

impassive [ɪmˈpæsɪv] *adj* impassibile

impatience [ɪmˈpeʃəns] *s* impazienza

impatient [ɪmˈpeʃənt] *adj* impaziente

impeach [ɪmˈpitʃ] *tr* accusare; (*a public official*) sottoporre a un'inchiesta; (*a statement*) mettere in dubbio

impeachment [ɪmˈpitʃmənt] *s* accusa; inchiesta

impeccable [ɪmˈpekəbəl] *adj* impeccabile

impecunious [ˌɪmpɪˈkjuni·əs] *adj* indigente

impedance [ɪmˈpidəns] *s* impedenza

impede [ɪmˈpid] *tr* impedire, intralciare

impediment [ɪmˈpedɪmənt] *s* impedimento; ostacolo

im·pel [ɪmˈpel] *v* (*pret & pp* **-peled** *or* **-pelled**) *ger* **-peling** *or* **-pelling**) *tr* spingere, forzare

impending [ɪmˈpendɪŋ] *adj* imminente, incombente

impenetrable [ɪmˈpenətrəbəl] *adj* impenetrabile

impenitent [ɪmˈpenɪtənt] *adj* impenitente ‖ *s* persona impenitente

imperative [ɪmˈperɪtɪv] *adj* (*commanding*) imperativo; (*urgent*) imperioso ‖ *s* imperativo

imperceptible [ˌɪmpərˈseptɪbəl] *adj* impercettibile

imperfect [ɪmˈpʌrfɪkt] *adj & s* imperfetto

imperfection [ˌɪmpərˈfekʃən] *s* imperfezione

imperial [ɪmˈpɪrɪ·əl] *adj* imperiale ‖ *s* (*goatee*) barbetta, mosca; (*top of coach*) imperiale *m*

imperialist [ɪmˈpɪrɪ·əlɪst] *adj & s* imperialista *mf*

imper·il [ɪmˈperɪl] *v* (*pret & pp* **-iled** *or* **-illed**) *ger* **-iling** *or* **-illing**) *tr* mettere in pericolo

imperious [ɪmˈpɪrɪ·əs] *adj* imperioso

imperishable [ɪmˈperɪʃəbəl] *adj* imperituro, duraturo

impersonate [ɪmˈpʌrsəˌnet] *tr* (*to pretend to be*) spacciarsi per; (*on the stage*) impersonare

impertinence [ɪmˈpʌrtɪnəns] *s* impertinenza

impertinent [ɪmˈpʌrtɪnənt] *adj* impertinente

impetuous [ɪmˈpetʃʊ·əs] *adj* impetuoso

impetus [ˈɪmpɪtəs] *s* impeto, foga

impie·ty [ɪmˈpaɪ·əti] *s* (**-ties**) empietà *f*

impinge [ɪmˈpɪndʒ] *intr*—**to impinge on** *or* **upon** violare; (*said, e.g., of the sun*) ferire; (*the imagination*) colpire

impious [ˈɪmpɪ·əs] *adj* empio

impish [ˈɪmpɪʃ] *adj* indiavolato

implant [ɪmˈplænt] *tr* innestare; instillare, istillare

implement [ˈɪmplɪmənt] *s* utensile *m*, strumento ‖ [ˈɪmplɪˌment] *tr* completare, mettere in opera; (*to provide with implements*) attrezzare

implicate [ˈɪmplɪˌket] *tr* implicare

implicit [ɪmˈplɪsɪt] *adj* implicito; (*unquestioning*) assoluto, cieco

implied [ɪmˈplaɪd] *adj* implicito

implore [ɪmˈplor] *tr* (*a person; pardon*)

implorare; (to entreat) raccomandarsi a

im•ply [ɪm'plaɪ] v (pret & pp -plied) tr voler dire, significare; implicare, sottintendere

impolite [,ɪmpə'laɪt] adj scortese

import ['ɪmport] s importazione; articolo d'importazione; importanza || [ɪm'port] or ['ɪmport] tr importare; significare || intr importare

importance [ɪm'portəns] s importanza

important [ɪm'portənt] adj importante

importation [,ɪmpor'teʃən] s importazione

importer [ɪm'portər] s importatore m

importunate [ɪm'portʃənɪt] adj importuno

importune [,ɪmpər'tjun] or [,ɪmpər-'tun] tr importunare

impose [ɪm'poz] tr imporre || intr—to impose on or upon abusare di; abusare della gentilezza di

imposing [ɪm'pozɪŋ] adj imponente

imposition [,ɪmpə'zɪʃən] s imposizione; abuso; abuso della gentilezza; inganno

impossible [ɪm'pɑsɪbəl] adj impossibile

impostor [ɪm'pɑstər] s impostore m

imposture [ɪm'pɑstʃər] s impostura

impotence ['ɪmpətəns] s impotenza

impotent ['ɪmpətənt] adj impotente

impound [ɪm'paʊnd] tr rinchiudere, recintare; (water) raccogliere; (law) sequestrare, confiscare

impoverish [ɪm'pɑvərɪʃ] tr impoverire

impracticable [ɪm'præktɪkəbəl] adj impraticabile; (intractable) intrattabile

impractical [ɪm'præktɪkəl] adj poco pratico

impregnable [ɪm'pregnəbəl] adj inespugnabile, imprendibile

impregnate [ɪm'pregnet] tr impregnare

impresari•o [,ɪmprɪ'sɑri,o] s (-os) impresario

impress [ɪm'pres] tr (to affect in mind or feelings) impressionare; (to produce by pressure; to fix on s.o.'s mind) imprimere; (mil) arruolare

impression [ɪm'preʃən] s impressione

impressionable [ɪm'preʃənəbəl] adj impressionabile

impressive [ɪm'presɪv] adj impressionante, imponente

imprint ['ɪmprɪnt] s impronta; (typ) indicazione dell'editore || [ɪm'prɪnt] tr imprimere

imprison [ɪm'prɪzən] tr imprigionare

imprisonment [ɪm'prɪzənmənt] s prigione, prigionia

improbable [ɪm'prɑbəbəl] adj improbabile

impromptu [ɪm'prɑmptju] or [ɪm-'prɑmptu] adj improvvisato || s improvvisazione; (mus) impromptu m || adv all'improvviso

improper [ɪm'prɑpər] adj (erroneous) improprio; (inappropriate; unseemly) scorretto; (math) improprio

improve [ɪm'pruv] tr migliorare; (an opportunity) approfittare di || intr migliorare; to improve on or upon perfezionare

improvement [ɪm'pruvmənt] s miglioramento, perfezionamento; (in real estate) miglioria; (e.g., of time) buon uso

improvident [ɪm'prɑvɪdənt] adj improvvido, imprevidente

improvise ['ɪmprə,vaɪz] tr & intr improvvisare

imprudence [ɪm'prudəns] s imprudenza

imprudent [ɪm'prudənt] adj imprudente

impudence ['ɪmpjədəns] s impudenza, sfrontatezza, sfacciataggine f

impudent ['ɪmpjədənt] adj sfrontato, sfacciato, spudorato

impugn [ɪm'pjun] tr impugnare

impulse ['ɪmpʌls] s impulso

impulsive [ɪm'pʌlsɪv] adj impulsivo

impunity [ɪm'pjunɪti] s impunità f

impure [ɪm'pjʊr] adj impuro

impuri•ty [ɪm'pjʊrɪti] s (-ties) impurità f

impute [ɪm'pjut] tr imputare

in [ɪn] adj interno; (coll) moderno, alla moda || s relazione; the ins and outs tutti i dettagli || adv dentro; a casa; in ufficio; in here qui dentro; in there lì dentro; to be in essere a casa; to be in for essere destinato a; to be in with essere in intimità con || prep in; (within) dentro a; (over, through) per; di, e.g., the best in the class il migliore della classe; dressed in vestito di; in so far as per quanto; in that per quanto, dato che

inability [,ɪnə'bɪlɪti] s inabilità f

inaccessible [,ɪnæk'sesɪbəl] adj inaccessibile

inaccura•cy [ɪn'ækjərəsi] s (-cies) inesattezza, imprecisione

inaccurate [ɪn'ækjərɪt] adj inesatto

inaction [ɪn'ækʃən] s inazione

inactive [ɪn'æktɪv] adj inattivo

inadequate [ɪn'ædɪkwɪt] adj inadeguato, inadatto

inadvertent [,ɪnəd'vʌrtənt] adj disattento; inavvertito

inadvisable [,ɪnəd'vaɪzəbəl] adj poco consigliabile

inane [ɪn'en] adj insensato, assurdo

inanimate [ɪn'ænɪmɪt] adj inanimato

inappreciable [,ɪnə'priʃɪ-əbəl] adj inapprezzabile

inappropriate [,ɪnə'propri-ɪt] adj non appropriato, improprio

inarticulate [,ɪnɑr'tɪkjəlɪt] adj (sounds, words) inarticolato; (person) incapace di esprimersi

inasmuch as [,ɪnəs'mʌtʃ æz] conj dato che, visto che, in quanto che

inattentive [,ɪnə'tentɪv] adj disattento

inaugural [ɪn'ɔgjərəl] adj inaugurale || s discorso inaugurale

inaugurate [ɪn'ɔgjə,ret] tr inaugurare

inauguration [ɪn,ɔgjə'reʃən] s inaugurazione; (investiture of a head of government) assunzione dei poteri

inborn ['ɪn,bɔrn] adj innato, ingenito

inbreeding ['ɪn,bridɪŋ] s incrocio fra animali o piante affini

incandescent [,ɪnkən'desənt] adj incandescente

incapable [ɪn'kepəbəl] *adj* incapace
incapacitate [ˌɪnkə'pæsɪˌtet] *tr* inabilitare; (law) interdire
incapaci·ty [ˌɪnkə'pæsɪti] *s* (**-ties**) incapacità *f*
incarcerate [ɪn'kɑrsəˌret] *tr* incarcerare
incarnate [ɪn'kɑrnɪt] *or* [ɪn'kɑrnet] *adj* incarnato || [ɪn'kɑrnet] *tr* incarnare
incarnation [ˌɪnkɑr'neʃən] *s* incarnazione
incendiarism [ɪn'sɛndɪ-əˌrɪzəm] *s* incendio doloso; (*agitation*) sobillazione
incendiar·y [ɪn'sɛndɪˌeri] *adj* incendiario || *s* (**-ies**) incendiario; (fig) sobillatore *m*
incense ['ɪnsɛns] *s* incenso || *tr* (*to burn incense for*) incensare || [ɪn-'sɛns] *tr* irritare, esasperare
in'cense burn'er *s* (*person*) incensatore *m*; (*vessel*) incensiere *m*
incentive [ɪn'sɛntɪv] *adj & s* incentivo
inception [ɪn'sɛpʃən] *s* principio
incertitude [ɪn'sʌrtɪˌtjud] *or* [ɪn'sʌrtɪˌtud] *s* incertezza
incest ['ɪnsɛst] *s* incesto
incestuous [ɪn'sɛstʃʊ-əs] *adj* incestuoso
inch [ɪntʃ] *s* pollice *m*; **to be within an inch of** essere a due dita da || *intr*—**to inch ahead** spingersi avanti poco a poco
incidence ['ɪnsɪdəns] *s* incidenza
incident ['ɪnsɪdənt] *adj* incidente, incidentale || *s* incidente *m*
incidental [ˌɪnsɪ'dɛntəl] *adj* incidentale || *s* elemento incidentale; **incidentals** piccole spese
incidentally [ˌɪnsɪ'dɛntəli] *adv* incidentalmente, per inciso; a proposito
incinerator [ɪn'sɪnəˌretər] *s* inceneritore *m*
incision [ɪn'sɪʒən] *s* incisione
incisive [ɪn'saɪsɪv] *adj* incisivo
incite [ɪn'saɪt] *tr* incitare, stimulare
inclemen·cy [ɪn'klɛmənsi] *s* (**-cies**) inclemenza
inclination [ˌɪnklɪ'neʃən] *s* inclinazione
incline ['ɪnklaɪn] *or* [ɪn'klaɪn] *s* declivio || [ɪn'klaɪn] *tr* inclinare || *intr* inclinarsi
inclose [ɪn'kloz] *tr* includere, accludere; **to inclose herewith** accludere alla presente
inclosure [ɪn'kloʒər] *s* (*land surrounded by fence*) recinto; (*e.g., letter*) allegato
include [ɪn'klud] *tr* includere; **including** incluso, e.g., **three books including the grammar** tre libri inclusa la grammatica
inclusive [ɪn'klusɪv] *adj* incluso, e.g., **until next Friday inclusive** fino a venerdì prossimo incluso; **inclusive of** inclusivo di, e.g., **price inclusive of freight** prezzo inclusivo delle spese di trasporto
incogni·to [ɪn'kɑgnɪˌto] *adj* incognito || *s* (**-tos**) incognito || *adv* in incognito

incoherent [ˌɪnko'hɪrənt] *adj* incoerente
incombustible [ˌɪnkəm'bʌstɪbəl] *adj* incombustibile
income ['ɪnkʌm] *s* reddito, provento
in'come tax' *s* imposta sul reddito
incoming ['ɪnˌkʌmɪŋ] *adj* entrante; futuro; (*tide*) ascendente || *s* entrata
incomparable [ɪn'kɑmpərəbəl] *adj* incomparabile, impareggiabile
incompatible [ˌɪnkəm'pætɪbəl] *adj* incompatibile
incomplete [ˌɪnkəm'plit] *adj* incompleto, tronco, scompleto
incomprehensible [ˌɪnkɑmprɪ'hɛnsɪbəl] *adj* incomprensibile
inconceivable [ˌɪnkən'sivəbəl] *adj* inconcepibile
inconclusive [ˌɪnkən'klusɪv] *adj* inconcludente
incongruous [ɪn'kɑŋgrʊ-əs] *adj* incongruo
inconsequential [ɪnˌkɑnsɪ'kwɛnʃəl] *adj* (*lacking proper sequence of thought or speech*) inconseguente; (*trivial*) di poca importanza
inconsiderate [ˌɪnkən'sɪdərɪt] *adj* inconsiderato, sconsiderato
inconsisten·cy [ˌɪnkən'sɪstənsi] *s* (**-cies**) inconsistenza
inconsistent [ˌɪnkən'sɪstənt] *adj* inconsistente, inconseguente
inconsolable [ˌɪnkən'soləbəl] *adj* inconsolabile, sconsolato
inconspicuous [ˌɪnkən'spɪkju-əs] *adj* poco appariscente, poco apparente
inconstant [ɪn'kɑnstənt] *adj* incostante
incontinence [ɪn'kɑntɪnəns] *s* incontinenza
incontrovertible [ˌɪnkɑntrə'vʌrtɪbəl] *adj* incontrovertibile
inconvenience [ˌɪnkən'vini-əns] *s* scomodo, incomodo || *tr* scomodare
inconvenient [ˌɪnkən'vini-ənt] *adj* incomodo, inconveniente
incorporate [ɪn'kɔrpəˌret] *tr* incorporare; costituire in società anonima || *intr* incorporarsi; costituirsi in società anonima
incorrect [ˌɪnkə'rɛkt] *adj* scorretto
increase ['ɪnkris] *s* aumento; crescita; **to be on the increase** essere in aumento || [ɪn'kris] *tr* aumentare; (*by propagation*) moltiplicare || *intr* aumentare; moltiplicarsi
increasingly [ɪn'krisɪŋli] *adv* sempre più
incredible [ɪn'krɛdɪbəl] *adj* incredibile
incredulous [ɪn'krɛdʒələs] *adj* incredulo
increment ['ɪnkrɪmənt] *s* aumento, incremento
incriminate [ɪn'krɪmɪˌnet] *tr* incriminare
incrust [ɪn'krʌst] *tr* incrostare
incubate ['ɪnkjəˌbet] *tr* incubare || *intr* essere in incubazione; (*said, e.g., of a hen*) covare; (fig) covare
incubator ['ɪnkjəˌbetər] *s* incubatrice *f*
inculcate [ɪn'kʌlket] *or* ['ɪnkʌlˌket] *tr* inculcare

incumben·cy [ɪnˈkʌmbənsɪ] s (-cies) incombenza

incumbent [ɪnˈkʌmbənt] adj—to be incumbent on incombere a, spettare a || s titolare mf

incunabula [ˌɪnkjuˈnæbjələ] spl (beginnings) origini fpl; (early printed books) incunaboli mpl

in·cur [ɪnˈkʌr] v (pret & pp -curred; ger -curring) tr incorrere in; (a debt) assumere, contrarre

incurable [ɪnˈkjurəbəl] adj & s incurabile mf

incursion [ɪnˈkʌrʒən] or [ɪnˈkʌrʃən] s incursione, scorreria

indebted [ɪnˈdetɪd] adj indebitato; obbligato

indecen·cy [ɪnˈdisənsɪ] s (-cies) indecenza, sconcezza

indecent [ɪnˈdisənt] adj indecente, sconveniente

indecisive [ˌɪndɪˈsaɪsɪv] adj indeciso; (e.g., event) non decisivo

indeed [ɪnˈdid] adv difatti, infatti || interj davvero!

indefatigable [ˌɪndɪˈfætɪgəbəl] adj indefesso, infaticabile

indefensible [ˌɪndɪˈfensɪbəl] adj indifendibile, insostenibile

indefinable [ˌɪndɪˈfaɪnəbəl] adj indefinibile

indefinite [ɪnˈdefɪnɪt] adj indefinito

indelible [ɪnˈdelɪbəl] adj indelebile

indemnification [ɪnˌdemnɪfɪˈkeʃən] s indennità f, indennizzo

indemni·fy [ɪnˈdemnɪˌfaɪ] v (pret & pp -fied) tr indennizzare

indemni·ty [ɪnˈdemnɪtɪ] s (-ties) indennità f, indennizzo

indent [ɪnˈdent] tr frastagliare, dentellare; (typ) far rientrare

indentation [ˌɪndenˈteʃən] s frastaglio, dentellatura; (typ) accapo

indenture [ɪnˈdentʃər] s scrittura pubblica; contratto di apprendista || tr obbligare per contratto

independence [ˌɪndɪˈpendəns] s indipendenza

independent [ˌɪndɪˈpendənt] adj & s indipendente mf

indescribable [ˌɪndɪˈskraɪbəbəl] adj indescrivibile

indestructible [ˌɪndɪˈstrʌktɪbəl] adj indistruttibile

indeterminate [ˌɪndɪˈtʌrmɪnɪt] adj indeterminato

index [ˈɪndeks] s (indexes or indices [ˈɪndɪˌsiz]) indice m; (typ) indice m indicatore || tr mettere un indice a; mettere all'indice || Index s Indice m

in'dex card' s scheda di catalogo

in'dex fin'ger s dito indice

India [ˈɪndɪə] s l'India f

In'dia ink' s inchiostro di china

Indian [ˈɪndɪən] adj & s indiano

In'dian club' s clava di ginnastica

In'dian corn' s granoturco

In'dian file' s fila indiana || adv in fila indiana

In'dian O'cean s Oceano Indiano

In'dian sum'mer s estate f di San Martino

In'dian wres'tling s braccio di ferro

In'dia pa'per s carta bibbia, carta d'India

In'dia rub'ber s caucciù m

indicate [ˈɪndɪˌket] tr indicare

indication [ˌɪndɪˈkeʃən] s indicazione

indicative [ɪnˈdɪkətɪv] adj & s indicativo

indicator [ˈɪndɪˌketər] s indicatore m, indice m

indict [ɪnˈdaɪt] tr accusare

indictment [ɪnˈdaɪtmənt] s accusa, atto d'accusa

indifferent [ɪnˈdɪfərənt] adj indifferente; (not particularly good) passabile

indigenous [ɪnˈdɪdʒɪnəs] adj indigeno

indigent [ˈɪndɪdʒənt] adj indigente || the indigent gli indigenti

indigestion [ˌɪndɪˈdʒestʃən] s indigestione

indignant [ɪnˈdɪgnənt] adj indignato

indignation [ˌɪndɪgˈneʃən] s indignazione

indigni·ty [ɪnˈdɪgnɪtɪ] s (-ties) indignità f

indi·go [ˈɪndɪˌgo] adj indaco || s (-gos or -goes) indaco

indirect [ˌɪndɪˈrekt] or [ˌɪndaɪˈrekt] adj indiretto

in'direct dis'course s discorso indiretto

indiscernible [ˌɪndɪˈzɜrnɪbəl] or [ˌɪndɪˈsʌrnɪbəl] adj indiscernibile

indiscreet [ˌɪndɪsˈkrit] adj indiscreto

indispensable [ˌɪndɪsˈpensəbəl] adj indispensabile, imprescindibile

indispose [ˌɪndɪsˈpoz] tr indisporre

indisposed [ˌɪndɪsˈpozd] adj (disinclined) mal disposto; (slightly ill) indisposto

indissoluble [ˌɪndɪˈsɑljəbəl] adj indissolubile

indistinct [ˌɪndɪˈstɪŋkt] adj indistinto

indite [ɪnˈdaɪt] tr redigere

individual [ˌɪndɪˈvɪdʒuˌəl] adj individuale || s individuo

individuali·ty [ˌɪndɪˌvɪdʒuˈælɪtɪ] s (-ties) individualità f; (person of distinctive character) individuo

Indochina [ˈɪndoˈtʃaɪnə] s l'Indocina f

Indo-Chi·nese [ˈɪndotʃaɪˈniz] adj indocinese || s (-nese) indocinese mf

Indo-European [ˈɪndoˌjurəˈpiˌən] adj & s indoeuropeo

indolent [ˈɪndələnt] adj indolente

Indonesia [ˌɪndoˈniʒə] or [ˌɪndoˈniʒə] s l'Indonesia f

Indonesian [ˌɪndoˈniʃən] or [ˌɪndoˈniʒən] adj & s indonesiano

indoor [ˈɪnˌdor] adj situato in casa; da farsi in casa

indoors [ˈɪnˈdorz] adv dentro, a casa, al coperto

indorse [ɪnˈdors] tr (com) girare; (fig) appoggiare, approvare

indorsee [ˌɪndorˈsi] s giratario

indorsement [ɪnˈdorsmənt] s (com) girata; (fig) appoggio, approvazione

indorser [ɪnˈdorsər] s girante mf

induce [ɪnˈdjus] or [ɪnˈdus] tr indurre

inducement [ɪnˈdjusmənt] or [ɪnˈdusmənt] s stimolo, incentivo

induct [ɪn'dʌkt] *tr* installare; iniziare; (mil) arruolare

induction [ɪn'dʌkʃən] *s* iniziazione; (elec & log) induzione; (mil) arruolamento

indulge [ɪn'dʌldʒ] *tr* indulgere (with *dat*) || *intr* cedere, lasciarsi andare; **to indulge in** abbandonarsi a; permettersi il lusso di

indulgence [ɪn'dʌldʒəns] *s* compiacenza; intemperanza, abbandono; (*leniency*) indulgenza

indulgent [ɪn'dʌldʒənt] *adj* indulgente

industrial [ɪn'dʌstrɪ·əl] *adj* industriale

industrialist [ɪn'dʌstrɪ·əlɪst] *s* industriale *m*

industrialize [ɪn'dʌstrɪ·ə‚laɪz] *tr* industrializzare

industrious [ɪn'dʌstrɪ·əs] *adj* industrioso, laborioso

indus·try ['ɪndʌstri] *s* (**-tries**) industria

inebriation [ɪn‚ibri'eʃən] *s* ubriachezza

inedible [ɪn'edɪbəl] *adj* immangiabile

ineffable [ɪn'efəbəl] *adj* ineffabile

ineffective [‚ɪnɪ'fektɪv] *adj* inefficace; (*person*) inetto

ineffectual [‚ɪnɪ'fektʃʊ·əl] *adj* inefficace

inefficient [‚ɪnɪ'fɪʃənt] *adj* inefficiente

ineligible [ɪn'elɪdʒɪbəl] *adj* ineleggibile

inequali·ty [‚ɪnɪ'kwalɪti] *s* (**-ties**) disuguaglianza

inequi·ty [ɪn'ekwɪti] *s* (**-ties**) ingiustizia

ineradicable [‚ɪnɪ'rædɪkəbəl] *adj* inestirpabile

inertia [ɪn'ʌrʃe] *s* inerzia

inescapable [‚ɪnes'kepəbəl] *adj* ineluttabile, inderogabile

inevitable [ɪn'evɪtəbəl] *adj* inevitabile

inexact [‚ɪneg'zækt] *adj* inesatto

inexcusable [‚ɪneks'kjuzəbəl] *adj* inescusabile

inexhaustible [‚ɪneg'zɔstɪbəl] *adj* inesauribile

inexorable [ɪn'eksərəbəl] *adj* inesorabile

inexpedient [‚ɪnek'spidɪ·ənt] *adj* inopportuno

inexpensive [‚ɪnek'spensɪv] *adj* poco costoso, a buon mercato

inexperience [‚ɪnek'spɪrɪ·əns] *s*. inesperienza

inexplicable [ɪn'eksplɪkəbəl] *adj* inesplicabile

inexpressible [‚ɪnek'spresɪbəl] *adj* indicibile, inesprimibile

infallible [ɪn'fælɪbəl] *adj* infallibile

infamous ['ɪnfaməs] *adj* infame

infa·my ['ɪnfəmi] *s* (**-mies**) infamia

infan·cy ['ɪnfənsi] *s* (**-cies**) infanzia

infant ['ɪnfənt] *adj* infantile; (*in the earliest stage*) (fig) nascente || *s* neonato, bebè *m*

infantile ['ɪnfən‚taɪl] or ['ɪnfəntɪl] *adj* infantile

infan·try ['ɪnfəntri] *s* (**-tries**) fanteria

in'fantry·man *s* (**-men**) fante *m*

infatuated [ɪn'fætʃʊ‚etɪd] *adj* infatuato

infect [ɪn'fekt] *tr* infettare

infection [ɪn'fekʃən] *s* infezione

infectious [ɪn'fekʃəs] *adj* infettivo

in·fer [ɪn'fʌr] *v* (*pret & pp* **-ferred;** *ger* **-ferring**) *tr* inferire; (coll) dedurre, supporre

inferior [ɪn'fɪrɪ·ər] *adj & s* inferiore *m*

inferiority [ɪn‚fɪri'arɪti] *s* inferiorità *f*

inferior'ity com'plex *s* complesso di inferiorità

infernal [ɪn'fʌrnəl] *adj* infernale

infest [ɪn'fest] *tr* infestare

infidel ['ɪnfɪdəl] *adj & s* infedele *mf*

infideli·ty [‚ɪnfɪ'delɪti] *s* (**-ties**) infedeltà *f*

in'field' *s* campo interno, diamante *m*

infiltrate [ɪn'fɪltret] or ['ɪnfɪl‚tret] *tr* infiltrarsi in || *intr* infiltrarsi

infinite ['ɪnfɪnɪt] *adj & s* infinito

infinitive [ɪn'fɪnɪtɪv] *adj* infinitivo || *s* infinito

infini·ty [ɪn'fɪnɪti] *s* (**-ties**) infinità *f*; (math) infinito

infirm [ɪn'fʌrm] *adj* infermo; (*not firm*) debole

infirma·ry [ɪn'fʌrməri] *s* (**-ries**) infermeria

infirmi·ty [ɪn'fʌrmɪti] *s* (**-ties**) infermità *f*

inflame [ɪn'flem] *tr* infiammare || *intr* infiammarsi

inflammable [ɪn'flæməbəl] *adj* infiammabile

inflammation [‚ɪnflə'meʃən] *s* infiammazione

inflate [ɪn'flet] *tr* gonfiare; (*currency, prices*) inflazionare || *intr* gonfiarsi

inflation [ɪn'fleʃən] *s* inflazione; (*of a tire*) gonfiatura

inflect [ɪn'flekt] *tr* curvare; (*voice*) modulare; (gram) flettere

inflection [ɪn'flekʃən] *s* inflessione; (gram) flessione

inflexible [ɪn'fleksɪbəl] *adj* inflessibile

inflict [ɪn'flɪkt] *tr* infliggere, inferire

influence ['ɪnflu·əns] *s* influenza || *tr* influire su, influenzare

influential [‚ɪnflu'enʃəl] *adj* influente

influenza [‚ɪnflu'enzə] *s* influenza

inform [ɪn'fɔrm] *tr* informare || *intr* dare informazioni; **to inform on** denunziare, fare la spia contro

informal [ɪn'fɔrməl] *adj* non ufficiale, ufficioso; (*unceremonious*) alla buona, familiare

informant [ɪn'fɔrmənt] *s* informatore *m*; (*informer*) delatore *m*; (ling) fonte *f* orale, informatore *m*

information [‚ɪnfər'meʃən] *s* informazioni *fpl*; conoscenze *fpl*

informational [‚ɪnfər'meʃənəl] *adj* informativo

informed' sour'ces *spl* fonti *fpl* attendibili

informer [ɪn'fɔrmər] *s* (*informant*) informatore *m*; (*spy*) delatore *m*

infraction [ɪn'frækʃən] *s* infrazione

infrared [‚ɪnfrə'red] *adj & s* infrarosso

infrequent [ɪn'frikwənt] *adj* infrequente

infringe [ɪn'frɪndʒ] *tr* violare || *intr—* **to infringe on** or **upon** violare, contravvenire a

infringement [ɪn'frɪndʒmənt] *s* infrazione

infuriate [ɪn'fjʊrɪ ,et] *tr* infuriare
infuse [ɪn'fjuz] *tr* infondere
infusion [ɪn'fjuʒən] *s* infusione
ingenious [ɪn'dʒɪnjəs] *adj* ingegnoso
ingenui·ty [,ɪndʒɪ'nu·ɪtɪ] or [,ɪndʒɪ-'nju·ɪtɪ] *s* (**-ties**) ingegnosità *f*
ingenuous [ɪn'dʒɛnjʊ·əs] *adj* ingenuo
ingenuousness [ɪn'dʒɛnjʊ·əsnɪs] *s* ingenuità *f*
ingest [ɪn'dʒɛst] *tr* ingerire
ingoing [ˈɪn ,goɪŋ] *adj* entrante
ingot ['ɪŋɡət] *s* lingotto, massello
ingraft [ɪn'ɡræft] or [ɪn'ɡrɑft] *tr* (hort & surg) innestare; (fig) inculcare
ingrate [ˈɪŋɡret] *s* ingrato
ingratiate [ɪn'greʃɪ ,et] *tr*—**to ingratiate oneself with** ingraziarsi
ingratiating [ɪn'greʃɪ ,etɪŋ] *adj* attraente, affascinante, insinuante
ingratitude [ɪn'ɡrætɪ ,tjud] or [ɪn'ɡrætɪ ,tud] *s* ingratitudine *f*
ingredient [ɪn'ɡridɪ·ənt] *s* ingrediente *m*
in'grown nail' ['ɪŋɡron] *s* unghia incarnita
ingulf [ɪn'ɡʌlf] *tr* sommergere, inondare
inhabit [ɪn'hæbɪt] *tr* abitare, popolare
inhabitant [ɪn'hæbɪtənt] *s* abitante *mf*
inhale [ɪn'hel] *tr & intr* inspirare
inherent [ɪn'hɪrənt] *adj* inerente
inherit [ɪn'hɛrɪt] *tr & intr* ereditare
inheritance [ɪn'hɛrɪtəns] *s* eredità *f*
inheritor [ɪn'hɛrɪtər] *s* erede *mf*
inhibit [ɪn'hɪbɪt] *tr* inibire
inhospitable [ɪn'hɑspɪtəbəl] or [,ɪn-hɑs'pɪtəbəl] *adj* inospitale
inhuman [ɪn'hjumən] *adj* inumano
inhumane [,ɪnhjʊ'men] *adj* inumano
inimical [ɪ'nɪmɪkəl] *adj* nemico
iniqui·ty [ɪ'nɪkwɪtɪ] *s* (**-ties**) iniquità *f*
ini·tial [ɪ'nɪʃəl] *adj & s* iniziale *f* || *v* (*pret* **-tialed** or **-tialled**; *ger* **-tialing** or **-tialling**) *tr* siglare
initiate [ɪ'nɪʃɪ ,et] *tr* iniziare
initiation [,ɪnɪʃɪ'eʃən] *s* iniziazione *f*
initiative [ɪ'nɪʃɪ/ɪ·ətɪv] or [ɪ'nɪʃətɪv] *s* iniziativa
inject [ɪn'dʒɛkt] *tr* iniettare; introdurre
injection [ɪn'dʒɛkʃən] *s* iniezione *f*
injudicious [,ɪndʒu'dɪʃəs] *adj* avventato, sconsiderato
injunction [ɪn'dʒʌŋkʃən] *s* ingiunzione *f*
injure ['ɪndʒər] *tr* (*to harm*) danneggiare; (*to wound*) ferire; (*to offend*) offendere, ingiuriare
injurious [ɪn'dʒʊrɪ·əs] *adj* dannoso; offensivo, ingiurioso
inju·ry ['ɪndʒərɪ] *s* (**-ries**) (*harm*) danno; (*wound*) ferita, lesione; offesa, ingiuria
injustice [ɪn'dʒʌstɪs] *s* ingiustizia
ink [ɪŋk] *s* inchiostro || *tr* inchiostrare
inkling ['ɪŋklɪŋ] *s* sentore *m*, indizio
ink'stand' *s* (*container*) calamaio; (*stand*) calamaiera
ink'well' *s* calamaio
ink·y ['ɪŋkɪ] *adj* (**-ier; -iest**) nero come l'inchiostro; nero d'inchiostro
inlaid ['ɪn ,led] or [,ɪn'led] *adj* intarsiato, incrostato

inland ['ɪnlənd] *adj & s* interno || *adv* verso l'interno
in'-law' *s* affine *mf*
in·lay ['ɪn ,le] *s* intarsio, tassello || [ɪn'le] or ['ɪn ,le] *v* (*pret & pp* **-laid**) *tr* intarsiare
inlet *s* (*of the shore*) insenatura; (*entrance*) ammissione
in'mate' *s* (*patient, e.g., in an insane asylum*) internato; (*in a jail*) prigioniero
inn [ɪn] *s* taverna, osteria
innate [ɪ'net] or ['ɪnet] *adj* innato
inner ['ɪnər] *adj* interno, interiore; intimo, profondo
in'ner·spring' mat'tress *s* materasso a molle
in'ner tube' *s* camera d'aria
inning ['ɪnɪŋ] *s* (baseball) turno
inn'keep'er *s* locandiere *m*, oste *m*
innocence ['ɪnəsəns] *s* innocenza
innocent ['ɪnəsənt] *adj & s* innocente *mf*
innovate ['ɪnə ,vet] *tr* innovare
innovation [,ɪnə'veʃən] *s* innovazione
innuen·do [,ɪnjʊ'ɛndo] *s* (**-does**) sottinteso, insinuazione
innumerable [ɪ'njumərəbəl] or [ɪ'numərəbəl] *adj* innumerevole
inoculate [ɪn'ɑkjə ,let] *tr* inoculare; (*e.g., with hatred*) inoculare; permeare
inoculation [ɪn ,ɑkjə'leʃən] *s* inoculazione
inoffensive [,ɪnə'fɛnsɪv] *adj* inoffensivo
inopportune [ɪn ,ɑpər'tjun] or [ɪn-,ɑpər'tun] *adj* inopportuno
inordinate [ɪn'ɔrdɪnɪt] *adj* smoderato
inorganic [,ɪnɔr'ɡænɪk] *adj* inorganico
in'pa'tient *s* degente *mf*
in'put' *s* entrata; (elec, mach) energia immessa
inquest ['ɪnkwɛst] *s* inchiesta
inquire [ɪn'kwaɪr] *tr* domandare, chiedere || *intr*—**to inquire about, after,** or **for** chiedere di; **to inquire into** investigare
inquir·y [ɪn'kwaɪrɪ] or ['ɪnkwɪrɪ] *s* (**-ies**) indagine *f*, inchiesta
inquisition [,ɪnkwɪ'zɪʃən] *s* inquisizione
inquisitive [ɪn'kwɪzɪtɪv] *adj* indagatore, curioso
in'road' *s* incursione, invasione
insane [ɪn'sen] *adj* pazzo, matto
insane' asy'lum *s* manicomio
insani·ty [ɪn'sænɪtɪ] *s* (**-ties**) pazzia, follia, demenza
insatiable [ɪn'seʃəbəl] *adj* insaziabile
inscribe [ɪn'skraɪb] *tr* iscrivere; (*a book*) dedicare; (geom) inscrivere
inscription [ɪn'skrɪpʃən] *s* scritta, iscrizione; (*of a book*) dedica
inscrutable [ɪn'skrutəbəl] *adj* imperscrutabile
insect ['ɪnsɛkt] *s* insetto
insecticide [ɪn'sɛktɪ ,saɪd] *adj & s* insetticida *m*
insecure [,ɪnsɪ'kjʊr] *adj* malsicuro
inseparable [ɪn'sɛpərəbəl] *adj* inseparabile

insert ['ɪnsʌrt] s inserzione; (*circular*) inserto || [ɪn'sʌrt] tr inserire

insertion [ɪn'sʌrʃən] s inserzione; (*in lunar orbit*) immissione; (*of lace*) tramezzo

in·set ['ɪn‚set] s intercalazione || [ɪn-'set] or ['ɪn‚set] v (*pret & pp* **-set**; *ger* **-setting**) tr intercalare

in'shore' adj & adv vicino alla spiaggia

in'side' adj interno; privato, confidenziale || s interno; **insides** (coll) interiora *fpl*; **to be on the inside** avere informazioni confidenziali || adv dentro; all'interno; **inside of** dentro, dentro a, a dentro di; **to turn inside out** rovesciare, voltare il diritto al rovescio || prep dentro, dentro a

in'side flap' s (bb) risvolto

insider [‚ɪn'saɪdər] s persona informata

in'side track' s (racing) steccato; **to have the inside track** (coll) trovarsi in una situazione vantaggiosa

insidious [ɪn'sɪdɪ·əs] adj insidioso

in'sight' s intuito, penetrazione

insigni·a [ɪn'sɪgnɪ·ə] s (-a or -as) distintivo; (*distinguishing sign*) segno

insignificant [‚ɪnsɪg'nɪfɪkənt] adj insignificante

insincere [‚ɪnsɪn'sɪr] adj insincero

insinuate [ɪn'sɪnju‚et] tr insinuare

insist [ɪn'sɪst] intr insistere

insofar as [‚ɪnso'fɑr‚æz] conj per quanto

insolence ['ɪnsələns] s insolenza

insolent ['ɪnsələnt] adj insolente

insoluble [ɪn'saljəbəl] adj insolubile

insolven·cy [ɪn'salvənsi] s (-cies) insolvenza

insomnia [ɪn'samnɪ·ə] s insonnia

insomuch [‚ɪnso'mʌtʃ] adv fino al punto; **insomuch as** giacché, visto che; **insomuch that** fino al punto che

inspect [ɪn'spekt] tr ispezionare

inspection [ɪn'spekʃən] s ispezione

inspector [ɪn'spektər] s ispettore m

inspiration [‚ɪnspɪ're∫ən] s ispirazione

inspire [ɪn'spaɪr] tr & intr ispirare

install [ɪn'stɔl] tr istallare

installment [ɪn'stɔlmənt] s rata; (*of a book*) dispensa; **in installments** a rate

install'ment plan' s pagamento rateale; **on the installment plan** con facilitazioni di pagamento

instance ['ɪnstəns] s esempio; (law) istanza; **for instance** per esempio

instant ['ɪnstənt] adj istantaneo || s istante m; mese m corrente

instantaneous [‚ɪnstən'tenɪ·əs] adj istantaneo

instantly ['ɪnstəntli] adv immediatamente, istantaneamente

instead [ɪn'sted] adv invece; **instead of** invece di

in'step' s collo del piede

instigate ['ɪnstɪ‚get] tr istigare

instigation [‚ɪnstɪ'ge∫ən] s istigazione

in·still' tr instillare, istillare

instinct ['ɪnstɪŋkt] s istinto

instinctive [ɪn'stɪŋktɪv] adj istintivo

institute ['ɪnstɪ‚tjut] or ['ɪnstɪ‚tut] s istituto || tr istituire

institution [‚ɪnstɪ'tju∫ən] or [‚ɪnstɪ-'tu∫ən] s istituzione

institutionalize [‚ɪnstɪ'tju∫ənə‚laɪz] or [‚ɪnstɪ'tu∫ənə‚laɪz] tr istituzionalizzare

instruct [ɪn'strʌkt] tr istruire

instruction [ɪn'strʌkʃən] s istruzione

instructive [ɪn'strʌktɪv] adj istruttivo

instructor [ɪn'strʌktər] s istruttore m

instrument ['ɪnstrəmənt] s strumento; (law) istrumento || ['ɪnstrə‚ment] tr strumentare

instrumental [‚ɪnstrə'mentəl] adj strumentale; **to be instrumental in** contribuire a

instrumentalist [‚ɪnstrə'mentəlɪst] s strumentista mf

instrumentali·ty [‚ɪnstrəmən'tælɪti] s (-ties) mediazione, aiuto

in'strument fly'ing s volo strumentale

in'strument pan'el s (aut) cruscotto

insubordinate [‚ɪnsə'bɔrdɪnɪt] adj insubordinato

insufferable [ɪn'sʌfərəbəl] adj insoffribile

insufficient [‚ɪnsə'fɪʃənt] adj insufficiente

insular ['ɪnsələr] or ['ɪnsjulər] adj insulare; (*e.g., attitude*) gretto

insulate ['ɪnsə‚let] tr isolare

in'sulating tape' ['ɪnsəletɪŋ] s nastro isolante

insulation [‚ɪnsə'le∫ən] s isolamento

insulator ['ɪnsə‚letər] s isolatore m

insulin ['ɪnsəlɪn] s insulina

insult ['ɪnsʌlt] s insulto || [ɪn'sʌlt] tr insultare, insolentire

insulting [ɪn'sʌltɪŋ] adj insultante

insurance [ɪn'∫urəns] s assicurazione

insure [ɪn'∫ur] tr assicurare

insurer [ɪn'∫urər] s assicuratore m

insurgent [ɪn'sʌrdʒənt] adj & s insorgente mf

insurmountable [‚ɪnsər'mauntəbəl] adj insormontabile

insurrection [‚ɪnsə'rek∫ən] s insurrezione

insusceptible [‚ɪnsə'septɪbəl] adj non suscettibile

intact [ɪn'tækt] adj intatto, integro

in'take' s (*place of taking in*) entrata; (*act of taking in*) ammissione; (mach) presa, immissione, aspirazione

in'take man'ifold' s collettore m d'ammissione

intangible [ɪn'tændʒɪbəl] adj intangibile; (fig) vago, inafferrabile

integer ['ɪntɪdʒər] s numero intero

integral ['ɪntɪgrəl] adj integrale; (*part of a whole*) integrante || s (math) integrale m

integration [‚ɪntɪ'gre∫ən] s integrazione

integrity [ɪn'tegrɪti] s integrità f

intellect ['ɪntə‚lekt] s intelletto

intellectual [‚ɪntə'lekt∫u·əl] adj & s intellettuale mf

intelligence [ɪn'telɪdʒəns] s intelligenza; informazione, conoscenza

intel'ligence bu'reau *s* ufficio spionaggi
intel'ligence quo'tient *s* quoziente *m* d'intelligenza
intelligent [ɪn'tɛlɪdʒənt] *adj* intelligente
intelligentsia [ɪn,tɛlɪ'dʒɛntsɪ-ə] or [ɪn,tɛlɪ'gɛntsɪ-ə] *s* intellighenzia, intellettualità *f*
intelligible [ɪn'tɛlɪdʒɪbəl] *adj* intelligibile, comprensibile
intemperance [ɪn'tɛmpərəns] *s* intemperanza, sregolatezza
intemperate [ɪn'tɛmpərɪt] *adj* intemperante; (*climate*) rigoroso
intend [ɪn'tɛnd] *tr* intendere, prefiggersi; (*to mean for a particular purpose*) destinare; (*to signify*) voler dire
intendance [ɪn'tɛndəns] *s* intendenza
intendant [ɪn'tɛndənt] *s* intendente *m*
intended [ɪn'tɛndɪd] *adj & s* (coll) promesso, promessa
intense [ɪn'tɛns] *adj* intenso
intensi·fy [ɪn'tɛnsɪ·faɪ] *v* (*pret & pp* -fied) *tr* intensificare, rinforzare; (phot) rinforzare ‖ *intr* intensificarsi, rinforzarsi
intensi·ty [ɪn'tɛnsɪtɪ] *s* (-ties) intensità *f*
intensive [ɪn'tɛnsɪv] *adj* intensivo
intent [ɪn'tɛnt] *adj* intento, attento; **intent on** deciso a ‖ *s* (*purpose*) intento, scopo; (*meaning*) significato; **to all intents and purposes** virtualmente, in realtà
intention [ɪn'tɛnʃən] *s* intenzione
intentional [ɪn'tɛnʃənəl] *adj* intenzionale, deliberato
intentionally [ɪn'tɛnʃənəlɪ] *adv* apposta, deliberatamente
in·ter [ɪn'tʌr] *v* (*pret & pp* -terred; *ger* -terring) *tr* interrare, inumare
interact [,ɪntər'ækt] *intr* esercitare un'azione reciproca
interaction [,ɪntər'ækʃən] *s* azione reciproca
inter·breed [,ɪntər'brid] *s* (*pret & pp* -bred* ['brɛd]) *tr* incrociare ‖ *intr* incrociarsi
intercalate [ɪn'tʌrkə,let] *tr* intercalare
intercede [,ɪntər'sid] *intr* intercedere
intercept [,ɪntər'sɛpt] *tr* intercettare
interceptor [,ɪntər'sɛptər] *s* (*person*) intercettatore *m*; (aer) intercettore *m*
interchange ['ɪntər,tʃendʒ] *s* interscambio; (*on a highway*) svincolo autostradale ‖ [,ɪntər't/əndʒ] *tr* scambiare ‖ *intr* scambiarsi
intercollegiate [,ɪntərkə'lidʒɪ-ɪt] *adj* interscolastico, fra università
intercom ['ɪntər,kʌm] *s* citofono
intercourse ['ɪntər,kɔrs] *s* comunicazione; (*of products, ideas, etc.*) scambio; (*copulation*) copula, coito; **to have intercourse** accoppiarsi sessualmente
intercross [,ɪntər'krɔs] or [,ɪntər'krɑs] *tr* incrociare ‖ *intr* incrociarsi
interdict ['ɪntər,dɪkt] *s* interdetto ‖ [,ɪntər'dɪkt] *tr* interdire; **to interdict s.o. from** + *ger* interdire a qlcu di + *inf*
interest ['ɪntərɪst] or ['ɪntrɪst] *s* in-

teresse *m*; **the interests** i potenti ‖ ['ɪntərɪst], ['ɪntrɪst] or ['ɪntə,rɛst] *tr* interessare
interested ['ɪntrɪstɪd] or ['ɪntə,rɛstɪd] *adj* interessato
interesting ['ɪntrɪstɪŋ] or ['ɪntə,rɛstɪŋ] *adj* interessante
interfere [,ɪntər'fɪr] *intr* interferire; (sports) ostacolare l'azione; **to interfere with** interferire in
interference [,ɪntər'fɪrəns] *s* interferenza
interim ['ɪntərɪm] *adj* interino ‖ *s* interim *m*; **in the interim** frattanto
interior [ɪn'tɪrɪ-ər] *adj & s* interno
interject [,ɪntər'dʒɛkt] *tr* interporre ‖ *intr* interporsi
interjection [,ɪntər'dʒɛkʃən] *s* interposizione; esclamazione; (gram) interiezione
interlard [,ɪntər'lɑrd] *tr* infiorare, lardellare
interline [,ɪntər'laɪn] *tr* scrivere nell'interlinea di; (*a garment*) foderare con ovattina
interlining ['ɪntər,laɪnɪŋ] *s* soppanno
interlink [,ɪntər'lɪŋk] *tr* concatenare
interlock [,ɪntər'lɑk] *tr* connettere ‖ *intr* connettersi
interlope [,ɪntər'lop] *intr* intromettersi; trafficare senza permesso
interloper [,ɪntər'lopər] *s* intruso
interlude ['ɪntər,lud] *s* interludio; (theat) intermezzo
intermarriage [,ɪntər,mærɪdʒ] *s* matrimonio tra consanguinei; matrimonio fra membri di razze diverse
intermediar·y [,ɪntər'midɪ,ɛrɪ] *adj* intermediario ‖ (-ies) *s* intermediario
intermediate [,ɪntər'midɪ·ɪt] *adj* intermedio
interment [ɪn'tʌrmənt] *s* inumazione
intermingle [,ɪntər'mɪŋgəl] *tr* mescolare ‖ *intr* mescolarsi
intermission [,ɪntər'mɪʃən] *s* interruzione; (theat) intervallo
intermittent [,ɪntər'mɪtənt] *adj* intermittente
intermix [,ɪntər'mɪks] *tr* mescolare ‖ *intr* mescolarsi
intern ['ɪntʌrn] *s* interno ‖ [ɪn'tʌrn] *tr* internare
internal [ɪn'tʌrnəl] *adj* interno
inter'nal-combus'tion en'gine *s* motore *m* a combustione interna, motore *m* a scoppio
inter'nal rev'enue *s* fisco
international [,ɪntər'næʃənəl] *adj* internazionale
in'terna'tional date' line' *s* linea del cambiamento di data
internationalize [,ɪntər'næʃənə,laɪz] *tr* internazionalizzare
internecine [,ɪntər'nisɪn] *adj* micidiale, sanguinario
internee [,ɪntʌr'ni] *s* internato
internist [ɪn'tʌrnɪst] *s* internista *mf*
internment [ɪn'tʌrnmənt] *s* internamento
internship ['ɪntʌrn,ʃɪp] *s* tirocinio in un ospedale, internato

interpellate [ˌɪntərˈpɛlet] or [ɪnˈtʌrpɪˌlet] *tr* interpellare

interplanetary [ˌɪntərˈplænəˌteri] *adj* interplanetario

interplay [ˈɪntərˌple] *s* azione reciproca

interpolate [ɪnˈtʌrpəˌlet] *tr* interpolare

interpose [ˌɪntərˈpoz] *tr* frapporre

interpret [ɪnˈtʌrprɪt] *tr* interpretare

interpreter [ɪnˈtʌrprətər] *s* interprete *mf*

interrogate [ɪnˈtɛrəˌget] *tr & intr* interrogare

interrogation [ɪnˌtɛrəˈgeʃən] *s* interrogazione

interroga′tion mark′ or **point′** *s* punto interrogativo

interrupt [ˌɪntəˈrʌpt] *tr* interrompere

interruption [ˌɪntəˈrʌpʃən] *s* interruzione

interscholastic [ˌɪntərskəˈlæstɪk] *adj* interscolastico

intersect [ˌɪntərˈsɛkt] *tr* intersecare ‖ *intr* intersecarsi

intersection [ˌɪntərˈsɛkʃən] *s (of streets, roads, etc.)* crocevia *m*; (geom) intersezione

intersperse [ˌɪntərˈspʌrs] *tr* cospargere, inframezzare

interstellar [ˌɪntərˈstɛlər] *adj* interstellare

interstice [ɪnˈtʌrstɪs] *s* interstizio

intertwine [ˌɪntərˈtwaɪn] *tr* intrecciare ‖ *intr* intrecciarsi

interval [ˈɪntərvəl] *s* intervallo; **at intervals** a intervalli; di tanto in tanto

intervene [ˌɪntərˈvin] *intr* intervenire; *(to happen)* succedere

intervening [ˌɪntərˈvinɪŋ] *adj*—**in the intervening time** nel frattempo

intervention [ˌɪntərˈvɛnʃən] *s* intervenzione

interview [ˈɪntərˌvju] *s* intervista ‖ *tr* intervistare

inter·weave [ˌɪntərˈwiv] *v (pret* -wove [ˈwov] or -weaved; *pp* -wove, -woven or -weaved) *tr* intessere

intestate [ɪnˈtɛstet] or [ɪnˈtɛstɪt] *adj* intestato

intestine [ɪnˈtɛstɪn] *s* intestino

inthrall [ɪnˈθrɔl] *tr* affascinare, incantare; *(to subjugate)* asservire, soggiogare

inthrone [ɪnˈθron] *tr* mettere sul trono, intronizzare; esaltare, innalzare

intima·cy [ˈɪntɪməsi] *s (-cies)* intimità *f*

intimate [ˈɪntɪmɪt] *adj & s* intimo ‖ [ˈɪntɪˌmet] *tr* insinuare

intimation [ˌɪntɪˈmeʃən] *s* insinuazione

intimidate [ɪnˈtɪmɪˌdet] *tr* intimidire

into [ˈɪntu] or [ˈɪntʊ] *prep* in; verso; contro

intolerant [ɪnˈtɑlərənt] *adj & s* intollerante *mf*, insofferente *mf*

intomb [ɪnˈtum] *tr* inumare, seppellire

intombment [ɪnˈtummənt] *s* sepoltura

intonation [ˌɪntoˈneʃən] *s* intonazione

intone [ɪnˈton] *tr* intonare ‖ *intr* salmodiare

intoxicant [ɪnˈtɑksɪkənt] *s* bevanda alcoolica

intoxicate [ɪnˈtɑksɪˌket] *tr* ubriacare; esilarare; *(to poison)* avvelenare, intossicare

intoxication [ɪnˌtɑksɪˈkeʃən] *s* ubriachezza; ebbrezza, allegria; *(poisoning)* avvelenamento, intossicazione

intractable [ɪnˈtræktəbəl] *adj* intrattabile

intransigent [ɪnˈtrænsɪdʒənt] *adj & s* intransigente *mf*

intransitive [ɪnˈtrænsɪtɪv] *adj* intransitivo

intravenous [ˌɪntrəˈvinəs] *adj* intravenoso, endovenoso

intrench [ɪnˈtrɛntʃ] *tr & intr* var of **entrench**

intrepid [ɪnˈtrɛpɪd] *adj* intrepido

intrepidity [ˌɪntrɪˈpɪdɪti] *s* intrepidezza

intricate [ˈɪntrɪkɪt] *adj* intricato

intrigue [ɪnˈtrig] or [ˈɪntrig] *s* intrigo; tresca, intrigo amoroso; (theat) intreccio ‖ [ɪnˈtrig] *tr* incuriosire ‖ *intr* intrigare; trescare

intrinsic(al) [ɪnˈtrɪnsɪk(əl)] *adj* intrinseco

introduce [ˌɪntrəˈdjus] or [ˌɪntrəˈdus] *tr* introdurre; *(a product)* lanciare; *(a person)* presentare

introduction [ˌɪntrəˈdʌkʃən] *s* introduzione; presentazione

introductory [ˌɪntrəˈdʌktəri] *adj* introduttivo

introit [ˈɪntroˌɪt] *s* (eccl) introito

introspective [ˌɪntrəˈspɛktɪv] *adj* introspettivo

introvert [ˈɪntrəˌvʌrt] *adj & s* introverso

intrude [ɪnˈtrud] *intr* intrudersi, intrufolarsi

intruder [ɪnˈtrudər] *s* intruso; importuno

intrusion [ɪnˈtruʒən] *s* intrusione

intrusive [ɪnˈtrusɪv] *adj* invadente

intrust [ɪnˈtrʌst] *tr* affidare, confidare

intuition [ˌɪntuˈɪʃən] or [ˌɪntjuˈɪʃən] *s* intuizione, intuito

inundate [ˈɪnənˌdet] *tr* inondare

inundation [ˌɪnənˈdeʃən] *s* inondazione

inure [ɪnˈjʊr] *tr* indurire, assuefare ‖ *intr* entrare in vigore; **to inure to** ridondare in favore di

invade [ɪnˈved] *tr* invadere

invader [ɪnˈvedər] *s* invasore *m*

invalid [ɪnˈvælɪd] *adj (non valid)* invalido ‖ [ˈɪnvəlɪd] *adj (person)* invalido; *(thing)* povero; *(diet)* per malati ‖ [ˈɪnvəlɪd] *s* invalido

invalidate [ɪnˈvælɪˌdet] *tr* invalidare

invalidity [ˌɪnvəˈlɪdɪti] *s* invalidità *f*

invaluable [ɪnˈvæljuˌəbəl] *adj* inestimabile, inapprezzabile

invariable [ɪnˈvɛrɪˌəbəl] *adj* invariabile

invasion [ɪnˈveʒən] *s* invasione

invective [ɪnˈvɛktɪv] *s* invettiva

inveigh [ɪnˈve] *intr*—**to inveigh against** inveire contro

inveigle [ɪnˈvegəl] or [ɪnˈvigəl] *tr* sedurre, abbindolare

invent [ɪnˈvɛnt] *tr* inventare

invention [ɪnˈvɛnʃən] *s* invenzione

inventiveness [ɪn'vɛntɪvnɪs] s inventiva
inventor [ɪn'vɛntər] s inventore m
invento·ry ['ɪnvən,torɪ] s (-ries) inventario || v (pret & pp -ried) tr inventariare
inverse [ɪn'vʌrs] adj & s inverso
inversion [ɪn'vʌrʒən] or [ɪn'vʌrʃən] s inversione
invert ['ɪnvʌrt] s invertito || [ɪn'vʌrt] tr invertire
invertebrate [ɪn'vʌrtɪ,bret] or [ɪn'vʌrtɪbrɪt] adj & s invertebrato
invest [ɪn'vɛst] tr investire || intr fare un investimento; fare investimenti
investigate [ɪn'vɛstɪ,get] tr investigare
investigation [ɪn,vɛstɪ'geʃən] s investigazione
investigator [ɪn'vɛstɪ,getər] s investigatore m
investment [ɪn'vɛstmənt] s (of money) investimento; (e.g., with an office) investitura; (siege) assedio
investor [ɪn'vɛstər] s investitore m
inveterate [ɪn'vɛtərɪt] adj inveterato
invidious [ɪn'vɪdɪ·əs] adj irritante, odioso
invigorate [ɪn'vɪgə,ret] tr invigorire
invigorating [ɪn'vɪgə,retɪŋ] adj ritemprante, ricostituente, rinforzante
invincible [ɪn'vɪnsɪbəl] adj invincibile
invisible [ɪn'vɪzɪbəl] adj invisibile
invis'ible ink' s inchiostro simpatico
invitation [,ɪnvɪ'teʃən] s invito
invite [ɪn'vaɪt] tr invitare
inviting [ɪn'vaɪtɪŋ] adj invitante, attrattivo; (food) appetitoso; accogliente
invoice ['ɪnvɔɪs] s fattura; **as per invoice** secondo fattura || tr fatturare
invoke [ɪn'vok] tr invocare; (a spirit) evocare
involuntary [ɪn'vɑlən,tɛrɪ] adj involontario
involve [ɪn'vɑlv] tr involvere, includere; occupare; (to bring unpleasantness upon) implicare, coinvolgere; complicare
invulnerable [ɪn'vʌlnərəbəl] adj invulnerabile
inward ['ɪnwərd] adj interno || adv al di dentro, verso l'interno
iodide ['aɪ·ə,daɪd] s ioduro
iodine ['aɪ·ə,daɪn] s iodio || ['aɪ·ə,daɪn] s tintura di iodio
ion ['aɪ·ən] or ['aɪ·ɑn] s ione m
ionize ['aɪ·ə,naɪz] tr ionizzare
IOU ['aɪ,o'ju] s (letterword) (I owe you) cambiale f, pagherò m
I.Q. ['aɪ'kju] s (letterword) (intelligence quotient) quoziente m d'intelligenza
Iranian [aɪ'renɪ·ən] adj & s iraniano
Ira·qi [ɪ'rɑki] adj iracheno || s (-qis) iracheno
irate ['aɪret] or [aɪ'ret] adj irato
ire [aɪr] s ira, collera
Ireland ['aɪrlənd] s l'Irlanda f
iris ['aɪrɪs] s iride f
I'rish·man s (-men) irlandese m
I'rish stew' s stufato all'irlandese
I'rish·wom'an s (-wom'en) irlandese f
irk [ʌrk] tr infastidire, annoiare

irksome ['ʌrksəm] adj fastidioso
iron ['aɪ·ərn] adj ferreo || s ferro; (to press clothes) ferro da stiro; **irons** ferri mpl; **strike while the iron is hot** batti il ferro fin ch'è caldo || tr (clothes) stirare; **to iron out** (a difficulty) (coll) appianare
i'ron·bound' adj ferrato; (unyielding) ferreo, inflessibile; (rock-bound) roccioso, scabroso
ironclad ['aɪ·ərn,klæd] adj corazzato, blindato; inflessibile, ferreo
i'ron constitu'tion s salute f di ferro
i'ron cur'tain s cortina di ferro
i'ron horse' s locomotiva a vapore
ironic(al) [aɪ'rɑnɪk(əl)] adj ironico
ironing ['aɪ·ərnɪŋ] s stiratura; roba stirata; roba da stirare
i'roning board' s tavolo or asse m da stiro
i'ron lung' s polmone m d'acciaio
i'ron·ware' s ferrame m
i'ron will' s volontà f di ferro
i'ron·work' s lavoro in ferro; **ironworks** ssg ferriera
i'ron-work'er s ferraio; metalmeccanico, siderurgico
iro·ny ['aɪrəni] s (-nies) ironia
irradiate [ɪ'redɪ,et] tr irradiare || intr irradiare, irradiarsi
irrational [ɪ'ræʃənəl] adj irrazionale
irrecoverable [,ɪrɪ'kʌvərəbəl] adj irrecuperabile
irredeemable [,ɪrɪ'diməbəl] adj irredimibile
irrefutable [,ɪrɪ'fjutəbəl] adj irrefutabile
irregular [ɪ'rɛgjələr] adj irregolare || s (mil) irregolare m
irrelevance [ɪ'rɛləvəns] s irrilevanza
irrelevant [ɪ'rɛləvənt] adj irrilevante
irreligious [,ɪrɪ'lɪdʒəs] adj irreligioso
irremediable [,ɪrɪ'midɪ·əbəl] adj irrimediabile
irremovable [,ɪrɪ'muvəbəl] adj irremovibile, inamovibile
irreplaceable [,ɪrɪ'plesəbəl] adj insostituibile
irrepressible [,ɪrɪ'prɛsɪbəl] adj irreprimibile, incontenibile
irreproachable [,ɪrɪ'protʃəbəl] adj irreprensibile
irresistible [,ɪrɪ'zɪstɪbəl] adj irresistibile
irrespective [,ɪrɪ'spɛktɪv] adj—**irrespective of** senza riguardo a
irresponsible [,ɪrɪ'spɑnsɪbəl] adj irresponsabile
irretrievable [,ɪrɪ'trivəbəl] adj irrecuperabile
irreverent [ɪ'rɛvərənt] adj irriverente
irrevocable [ɪ'rɛvəkəbəl] adj irrevocabile
irrigate ['ɪrɪ,get] tr irrigare
irrigation [,ɪrɪ'geʃən] s irrigazione
irritant ['ɪrɪtənt] adj & s irritante m
irritate ['ɪrɪ,tet] tr irritare
irritation [,ɪrɪ'teʃən] s irritazione
irruption [ɪ'rʌpʃən] s irruzione
isinglass ['aɪzɪŋ,glæs] or ['aɪzɪŋ,glɑs] s (gelatine) colla di pesce; mica
Islam ['ɪsləm] or [ɪs'lɑm] s l'Islam m

island ['aɪlənd] *adj* isolano ‖ *s* isola; (*for safety of pedestrians*) salvagente *m*
islander ['aɪləndər] *s* isolano
isle [aɪl] *s* isoletta
isolate ['aɪsə‚let] or ['ɪsə‚let] *tr* isolare
isolation [‚aɪsə'leʃən] or [‚ɪsə'leʃən] *s* isolamento
isolationist [‚aɪsə'leʃənɪst] or [‚ɪsə'leʃənɪst] *s* isolazionista *mf*
isosceles [aɪ'sɑsə‚liz] *adj* isoscele
isotope ['aɪsə‚top] *s* isotopo
Israel ['ɪzrɪ‚əl] *s* l'Israele *m*
Israe·li [ɪz'reli] *adj* israeliano ‖ *s* (**-lis** [liz]) israeliano
Israelite ['ɪzrɪ‚ə‚laɪt] *adj & s* israelita *mf*
issuance ['ɪʃʊ‚əns] *s* (*of stamps, stocks, bonds, etc.*) emissione; (*e.g., of clothes*) distribuzione; (*of a law*) emanazione
issue ['ɪʃʊ] *s* (*outlet*) uscita; distribuzione; (*result*) conseguenza; (*offspring*) prole *f;* (*of a magazine*) puntata, fascicolo; (*of a bond*) emissione; (*yield*) prodotto; (*of a law*) promulgazione; (*pathol*) flusso; **at issue** in discussione; **to face the issue** affrontare la situazione; **to force the issue** forzare la soluzione; **to take issue with** non essere d'accordo con, dissentire da ‖ *tr* (*e.g., a book*) pubblicare; (*bonds, orders*) emettere; (*a communiqué*) diramare; (*e.g., food*) distribuire ‖ *intr* uscire; **to issue from** provenire da
isthmus ['ɪsməs] *s* istmo
it [ɪt] *pron pers* esso, essa; lo, la; **it is**

I sono io; **it is raining** piove; **it is four o'clock** sono le quattro
Italian [ɪ'tæljən] *adj & s* italiano
Ital'ian-speak'ing *adj* italofono
italic [ɪ'tælɪk] *adj* (*typ*) corsivo ‖ **italics** *s* (*typ*) corsivo ‖ **Italic** *adj* italico
italicize [ɪ'tælɪ‚saɪz] *tr* stampare in carattere corsivo; sottolineare
Italy ['ɪtəli] *s* l'Italia *f*
itch [ɪtʃ] *s* prurito; (*pathol*) rogna; (*eagerness*) (fig) pizzicore *m* ‖ *tr* prudere, e.g., **his foot itches him** gli prude il piede ‖ *intr* (*said of a part of body*) prudere; (*said of a person*) avere il prurito; **to itch to** avere il pizzicore di
itch·y ['ɪtʃi] *adj* (**-ier; -iest**) che prude; (*pathol*) rognoso
item ['aɪtəm] *s* articolo; notizia; (*on the agenda*) questione; (*slang*) notizia scottante
itemize ['aɪtə‚maɪz] *tr* dettagliare, specificare
itinerant [aɪ'tɪnərənt] or [ɪ'tɪnərənt] *adj* itinerante, ambulante ‖ *s* viaggiatore *m*, viandante *m*
itinerar·y [aɪ'tɪnə‚reri] or [ɪ'tɪnə‚reri] *adj* itinerario ‖ *s* (**-ies**) itinerario
its [ɪts] *adj & pron poss* il suo
itself [ɪt'self] *pron pers* sé stesso; **si,** e.g., **it opened itself** si è aperto
ivied ['aɪvɪd] *adj* coperto di edera
ivo·ry ['aɪvəri] *adj* d'avorio ‖ *s* (**-ries**) avorio; **ivories** (*slang*) tasti *mpl* del piano; (*slang*) palle *fpl* da biliardo; (*dice*) (*slang*) dadi *mpl;* (*slang*) denti *mpl*
i'vory tow'er *s* torre *f* d'avorio
ivy ['aɪvi] *s* (**ivies**) edera

J

J, j [dʒe] *s* decima lettera dell'alfabeto inglese
jab [dʒæb] *s* puntata; (*prick*) puntura; (*with elbow*) gomitata ‖ *v* (*pret & pp* **jabbed;** *ger* **jabbing**) *tr* pugnalare; pungere; dare una gomitata a ‖ *intr* dare colpi
jabber ['dʒæbər] *s* borbottamento, ciarla ‖ *tr & intr* borbottare, ciarlare
jack [dʒæk] *s* (*for lifting heavy objects*) cricco, martinetto; (*jackass*) asino; (*device for turning a spit*) girarrosto; (*to remove a boot*) cavastivali *m;* (*cards*) fante *m;* (*bowling*) pallino; (*rad & telv*) jack *m;* (*elec*) presa; (*slang*) soldi *mpl;* **every man jack** ognuno, tutti *mpl* ‖ **Jack** *s* marinaio; (*coll*) buonuomo ‖ *tr*—**to jack up** alzare col cricco; (*prices*) (*coll*) alzare
jackal ['dʒækəl] *s* sciacallo
jack'ass' *s* asino
jack'daw' *s* cornacchia
jacket ['dʒækɪt] *s* giacca; (*of boiled*

potatoes) buccia; (*of book*) sopraccoperta; (*metal casing*) camicia
jack'ham'mer *s* martello perforatore
jack'-in-the-box' *s* scatola a sorpresa
jack'knife' *s* (**-knives**) coltello a serramanico; (*sports*) salto a pesce
jack'-of-all'-trades' *s* factotum *m*
jack-o'-lantern ['dʒækə‚læntərn] *s* lanterna a forma di testa umana fatta con una zucca; fuoco fatuo
jack'pot' *s* monte *m* premi; **to hit the jackpot** (*slang*) vincere un terno al lotto
jack' rab'bit *s* lepre nordamericana di taglia grande
jack'screw' *s* cricco a verme
jack'-tar' *s* (*coll*) marinaio
jade [dʒed] *adj* di giada, come la giada ‖ *s* (*ornamental stone*) giada; (*worn-out horse*) ronzino; (*disreputable woman*) donnaccia ‖ *tr* logorare
jad'ed ['dʒedɪd] *adj* logoro, stanco; (*appetite*) stucco
jag [dʒæg] *s* slabbratura; **to have a jag on** (*slang*) avere la sbornia

jagged ['dʒægɪd] *adj* dentato, slabbrato

jaguar ['dʒægwər] *s* giaguaro

jail [dʒel] *s* prigione *f;* **to break jail** evadere dal carcere || *tr* carcerare

jail'bird' *s* galeotto, remo di galera

jail'break' *s* evasione *f* dal carcere

jailer ['dʒelər] *s* carceriere *m*

jalop•y [dʒə'lɑpi] *s* (-ies) carcassa, trespolo, trabiccolo

jam [dʒæm] *s* stretta, compressione; (*in traffic*) imbottigliamento; (*preserve*) marmellata, confettura; (*difficult situation*) (coll) pasticcio || *v* (*pret & pp* **jammed;** *ger* **jamming**) *tr* stipare; (*e.g., one's finger*) schiacciare, schiacciarsi; (rad) disturbare; **to jam on the brakes** bloccare i freni || *intr* schiacciarsi; (*said of firearms*) incepparsi; (mach) grippare

jamb [dʒæm] *s* stipite *m*

jamboree [,dʒæmbə'ri] *s* riunione nazionale di giovani esploratori; (coll) riunione

James [dʒemz] *s* Giacomo

jamming ['dʒæmɪŋ] *s* radiodisturbo

jam-packed ['dʒæm'pækt] *adj* gremito, pieno fino all'orlo

jangle ['dʒæŋɡəl] *s* suono stridente; (*quarrel*) baruffa || *tr* fare suoni stridenti con || *intr* stridere; litigare

janitor ['dʒænɪtər] *s* portiere *m*

janitress ['dʒænɪtrɪs] *s* portinaia

January ['dʒænjʊ,ɛri] *s* gennaio

ja•pan [dʒə'pæn] *s* lacca giapponese; oggetto di lacca || *v* (*pret & pp* **-panned;** *ger* **-panning**) *tr* laccare ||

Japan *s* il Giappone

Japa•nese [,dʒæpə'niz] *adj* giapponese || *s* (-nese) giapponese *mf*

Jap'anese bee'tle *s* scarabeo giapponese

Jap'anese lan'tern *s* lampioncino alla veneziana

Jap'anese persim'mon *s* cachi *m*

jar [dʒɑr] *s* barattolo; (*earthenware container*) orcio, giara; discordanza; (*jolt*) scossa; (fig) brutta sorpresa; **on the jar** (*said of a door*) socchiuso || *v* (*pret & pp* **jarred;** *ger* **jarring**) *tr* scuotere; far stridere || *intr* vibrare; stridere; essere in conflitto; **to jar on** irritare

jardiniere [,dʒɑrdɪ'nɪr] *s* (*pot*) vaso da fiori; giardiniera

jargon ['dʒɑrɡən] *s* gergo

jasmine ['dʒæsmɪn] *or* ['dʒæzmɪn] *s* gelsomino

jasper ['dʒæspər] *s* diaspro

jaundice ['dʒɔndɪs] *or* ['dʒɑndɪs] *s* itterizia; (fig) invidia

jaundiced ['dʒɔndɪst] *or* ['dʒɑndɪst] *adj* itterico; (fig) invidioso

jaunt [dʒɔnt] *or* [dʒɑnt] *s* passeggiata, gita

jaun•ty ['dʒɔnti] *or* ['dʒɑnti] *adj* (-tier; -tiest) disinvolto; elegante

Java•nese [,dʒævə'niz] *adj* giavanese || *s* (-nese) giavanese *mf*

javelin ['dʒævlɪn] *or* ['dʒævəlɪn] *s* giavellotto

jaw [dʒɔ] *s* mascella, mandibola; (mach) ganascia; **jaws** fauci *fpl;* gola, stretta || *tr* (slang) rimproverare ||

intr (slang) chiacchierare; (slang) fare la predica

jaw'bone' *s* mascella, mandibola

jaw'break'er *s* (coll) parola difficile da pronunciare; (coll) caramella durissima; (mach) frantoio a mascelle

jay [dʒe] *s* (orn) ghiandaia; (coll) sempliciotto

jay'walk' *intr* attraversare la strada contro la luce rossa del semaforo

jay'walk'er *s* (coll) pedone distratto che attraversa la strada contro la luce rossa del semaforo

jazz [dʒæz] *s* jazz *m;* (slang) spirito || *tr*—**to jazz up** (slang) dar vita a

jazz' band' *s* orchestra jazz

jealous ['dʒɛləs] *adj* geloso; (*envious*) invidioso; vigilante

jealous•y ['dʒɛləsi] *s* (-ies) gelosia; invidia; vigilanza

jean [dʒin] *s* tela cruda; **jeans** pantaloni *mpl* di tela cruda

jeep [dʒip] *s* gip *f,* jeep *f*

jeer [dʒɪr] *s* beffa || *tr* beffare || *intr* beffarsi; **to jeer at** motteggiare

Jeho'vah's Wit'nesses [dʒɪ'hovəs] *spl* Testimoni *mpl* di Geova

jell [dʒel] *s* gelatina || *intr* (*to congeal*) gelatinizzarsi; (*to become substantial*) cristallizzarsi

jel•ly ['dʒeli] *s* (-lies) gelatina || *v* (*pret & pp* **-lied**) *tr* gelatinizzare || *intr* gelatinizzarsi

jel'ly•fish' *s* medusa; (*weak person*) (coll) fiaccone *m*

jeopardize ['dʒepər,daɪz] *tr* compromettere, mettere a repentaglio

jeopardy ['dʒepərdi] *s* pericolo, repentaglio

jeremiad [,dʒerɪ'maɪ,æd] *s* geremiade *f*

Jericho ['dʒerɪ,ko] *s* Gerico *f*

jerk [dʒʌrk] *s* strattone *m,* scatto; tic *m;* (*stupid person*) scempio, sciocco; **by jerks** a scatti || *tr* tirare a strattoni; (*meat*) essiccare || *intr* sobbalzare

jerked' beef' *s* fetta di carne di bue essiccata

jerkin ['dʒʌrkɪn] *s* giubbetto

jerk'wa'ter *adj* di scarsa importanza

jerk•y ['dʒʌrki] *adj* (-ier; -iest) sussultante; (*style*) disuguale

Jerome [dʒə'rom] *s* Gerolamo

jersey ['dʒʌrzi] *s* jersey *m,* maglione *m*

Jerusalem [dʒɪ'rusələm] *s* Gerusalemme *f*

jest [dʒest] *s* scherzo, burla; **in jest** per celia || *intr* scherzare

jester ['dʒestər] *s* motteggiatore *m,* burlone *m;* (hist) buffone *m*

Jesuit ['dʒeʒʊ·ɪt] *or* ['dʒezjʊ·ɪt] *adj & s* gesuita *m*

Jesuitic(al) [,dʒeʒʊ'ɪtɪk(əl)] *or* [,dʒezjʊ'ɪtɪk(əl)] *adj* gesuitico

Jesus ['dʒizəs] *s* Gesù *m*

Je'sus Christ' *s* Gesù *m* Cristo

jet [dʒet] *adj* di giaietto || *s* (*of a fountain*) zampillo; (*stream shooting forth from nozzle*) getto; (*mineral; lustrous black*) giaietto; (aer) aereo a getto || *v* (*pret & pp* **jetted;** *ger* **jetting**) *tr* spruzzare ‖ *intr* zampillare; volare in aereo a getto

jet' age' *s* era dell'aviogetto

jet'-black' *adj* nero come il carbone

jet' bomb'er *s* bombardiere *m* a reazione

jet' coal' *s* carbone *m* a lunga fiamma

jet' en'gine *s* motore *m* a reazione

jet' fight'er *s* caccia *m* a reazione

jet'lin'er *s* aviogetto da trasporto passeggeri

jet' plane' *s* aviogetto

jet' propul'sion *s* gettopropulsione

jetsam ['dʒetsəm] *s* relitto

jet' stream' *s* corrente *f* a getto; scappamento di motore a razzo

jettison ['dʒetɪsən] *s* (naut) alleggerimento ‖ *tr* (naut) alleggerirsi di; (fig) disfarsi di

jet·ty ['dʒeti] *s* (**-ties**) gettata; (*wharf*) molo, imbarcadero

Jew [dʒu] *s* giudeo

jewel ['dʒu·əl] *s* pietra preziosa; (*valuable personal ornament*) gioia, gioiello; (*of a watch*) rubino; (*costume jewelry*) gioia finta; (fig) valore *m*, gioiello

jew'el case' *s* scrigno, portagioie *m*

jeweler or **jeweller** ['dʒu·ələr] *s* gioielliere *m*, orefice *m*

jewelry ['dʒu·əlri] *s* gioielli *mpl*

jew'elry shop' *s* gioielleria

Jewess ['dʒu·ɪs] *s* giudea

Jewish ['dʒu·ɪʃ] *adj* giudeo

jews'-harp or **jew's-harp** ['dʒuz,hɑrp] *s* scacciapensieri *m*

jib [dʒɪb] *s* (*of a crane*) (mach) braccio (di gru); (naut) fiocco, vela Marconi

jib' boom' *s* asta di fiocco

jibe [dʒaɪb] *s* burla, beffa ‖ *intr* beffarsi; accordarsi; **to jibe at** beffarsi di

jif·fy ['dʒɪfi] *s*—**in a jiffy** (coll) in men che non si dica

jig [dʒɪg] *s* (*dance*) giga; **the jig is up** (slang) tutto è perduto

jigger ['dʒɪgər] *s* bicchierino di liquore d'un'oncia e mezza; (*flea*) pulce *f* tropicale; (*gadget*) (coll) aggeggio; (naut) bozzello; (min) crivello

jiggle ['dʒɪgəl] *s* scossa ‖ *tr* scuotere, agitare ‖ *intr* scuotersi

jig' saw' *s* sega da traforo

jig'saw puz'zle *s* gioco di pazienza, rompicapo

jilt [dʒɪlt] *tr* piantare

jim·my ['dʒɪmi] *s* (**-mies**) piccolo piede di porco ‖ *v* (*pret & pp* **-mied**) *tr* scassinare; **to jimmy open** scassinare

jingle ['dʒɪŋgəl] *s* sonaglio, bubbolo; (*sound*) rumore *m* di sonagliera; cantilena, rima infantile ‖ *tr* far suonare ‖ *intr* tintinnare

jin·go ['dʒɪŋgo] *adj* sciovinista ‖ *s* (**-goes**) sciovinista *mf*; **by jingo!** perbacco!

jingoism ['dʒɪŋgo,ɪzəm] *s* sciovinismo

jinx [dʒɪŋks] *s* iettatura; (*person*) iettatore *m* ‖ *tr* portare la iettatura a

jitters ['dʒɪtərz] *spl* (coll) nervosismo; **to have the jitters** (coll) essere nervoso

jittery ['dʒɪtəri] *adj* nervoso

job [dʒab] *s* (*piece of work*) lavoro;

(*task*) mansione; (*employment*) posto, impiego; (slang) furto; **by the job** a cottimo; **on the job** (slang) attento, sollecito; **to be out of a job** essere disoccupato; **to lie down on the job** (slang) dormire sul lavoro

job' anal'ysis *s* valutazione delle mansioni

jobber ['dʒabər] *s* grossista *mf*; (*pieceworker*) lavoratore *m* a cottimo; funzionario disonesto

job'hold'er *s* impiegato; (*in the government*) burocrate *m*

jobless ['jablɪs] *adj* disoccupato

job' lot' *s* (com) saldo

job' print'er *s* piccolo tipografo non specializzato

job' print'ing *s* piccolo lavoro tipografico

jockey ['dʒaki] *s* fantino ‖ *tr* (*a horse*) montare; manovrare; (*to trick*) abbindolare

jockstrap ['dʒak,stræp] *s* sospensorio

jocose [dʒo'kos] *adj* giocoso

jocular ['dʒakjələr] *adj* scherzoso

jog [dʒag] *s* spinta; piccolo trotto ‖ *v* (*pret & pp* **jogged**; *ger* **jogging**) *tr* spingere leggermente; (*the memory*) rinfrescare ‖ *intr* barcarellare; **to jog along** continuare col solito tran tran

jog' trot' *s* piccolo trotto; (fig) tran tran *m*

John [dʒan] *s* Giovanni *m*

John' Bull' *s* il tipico inglese; **gli inglesi, il popolo inglese**

John' Han'cock ['hænkak] *s* (coll) la firma

johnnycake ['dʒani,kek] *s* pane *m* di granturco

John'ny-come'-late'ly *s* (coll) ultimo arrivato

John'ny-jump'-up' *s* violetta, viola del pensiero

John'ny-on-the-spot' *s* (coll) persona sempre pronta

John' the Bap'tist *s* San Giovanni Battista

join [dʒɔɪn] *tr* giungere, congiungere; associarsi a; unire; (*e.g., a party*) farsi membro di; (*the army*) arruolarsi in; (*battle*) ingaggiare; (*to empty into*) sfociare in ‖ *intr* congiungersi, unirsi; (*said, e.g., of two rivers*) confluire

joiner ['dʒɔɪnər] *s* falegname *m*; membro di molte società

joint [dʒɔɪnt] *adj* congiunto ‖ *s* (*in a pipe*) giuntura; (*of bones*) giuntura, articolazione; (*hinge of book*) brachetta; (*in woodwork*) incastro, commettitura; (*of meat*) taglio; (mach) snodo; (*gambling den*) (slang) bisca; (elec) innesto; (slang) bettola; **out of joint** slogato; (fig) fuori luogo; **to throw** (*e.g., one's arm*) **out of joint** slogarsi

joint' account' *s* conto in comune

joint' commit'tee *s* commissione mista

jointly ['dʒɔɪntli] *adv* unitamente

joint' own'er *s* condomino

joint'-stock' com'pany *s* società *f* per azioni a responsabilità illimitata

joist [dʒɔɪst] *s* trave *f*

joke [dʒok] s burla, barzelletta; (*trifling matter*) cosa da nulla; (*person laughed at*) zimbello; **to tell a joke** raccontare una barzelletta; **to play a joke on** fare uno scherzo a ‖ *tr*—**to joke one's way into** ottenere dicendo barzellette ‖ *intr* burlare, dire storielle; **joking aside** senza scherzi

joker ['dʒokər] s burlone *m*, fumista *m*; (*wise guy*) saputello; (*hidden provision*) clausola ingannatrice; (*cards*) matta

jol·ly ['dʒɑli] adj (-**lier**; -**liest**) allegro, gaio ‖ adv (coll) molto ‖ v (*pret & pp* -**lied**) tr (coll) prendersi gioco di

jolt [dʒolt] s scossa ‖ tr scuotere ‖ intr sobbalzare

Jonah ['dʒonə] s Giona; (fig) uccello di mal augurio

jongleur ['dʒɑŋglər] s giullare *m*

jonquil ['dʒɑŋkwɪl] s giunchiglia

Jordan ['dʒɔrdən] s (*country*) la Giordania; (*river*) Giordano

Jordanian [dʒɔr'denɪ·ən] adj & s giordano

josh [dʒɑʃ] tr & intr (coll) canzonare

jostle ['dʒɑsəl] s spintone *m* ‖ tr spingere ‖ intr scontrarsi; farsi strada a gomitate

jot [dʒɑt] s—**I don't care a jot for** non mi importa un fico di ‖ v (*pret & pp* **jotted**; *ger* **jotting**) tr—**to jot down** notare, gettar giù

jounce [dʒɑuns] s scossa ‖ tr scuotere ‖ intr sobbalzare

journal ['dʒʌrnəl] s (*newspaper*) giornale *m*; (*magazine*) rivista; (*daily record*) diario; (com) giornale *m*; (mach) perno; (naut) giornale *m* di bordo

journalese [ˌdʒʌrnə'liz] s linguaggio giornalistico

journalism ['dʒʌrnəˌlɪzəm] s giornalismo

journalist ['dʒʌrnəlɪst] s giornalista *mf*

journey ['dʒʌrni] s viaggio ‖ intr viaggiare

jour'ney·man s (-**men**) operaio specializzato

joust [dʒʌst] or [dʒust] or [dʒaust] s giostra ‖ intr giostrare

jovial ['dʒovɪ·əl] adj gioviale

jowl [dʒaul] s (*cheek*) guancia; (*jawbone*) mascella; (*of cattle*) giogaia; (*of fowl*) bargiglio; (*of fat person*) pappagorgia

joy [dʒɔɪ] s gioia, allegria; **to leap with joy** ballare dalla gioia

joyful ['dʒɔɪfəl] adj gioioso, festoso; **joyful over** lieto di

joyless ['dʒɔɪlɪs] adj senza gioia

joyous ['dʒɔɪ·əs] adj gioioso

joy' ride' s (coll) gita in auto; (coll) gita all'impazzata in auto

jubilant ['dʒubɪlənt] adj esultante

jubilation [ˌdʒubɪ'leʃən] s giubilo

jubilee ['dʒubɪˌli] s (*jubilation*) giubilo; (eccl) giubileo

Judaism ['dʒudeˌɪzəm] s giudaismo

judge [dʒʌdʒ] s giudice *m* ‖ tr & intr giudicare; **judging by** a giudicare da

judge' ad'vocate s avvocato militare; avvocato della marina da guerra

judgeship ['dʒʌdʒʃɪp] s carica di giudice

judgment ['dʒʌdʒmənt] s giudizio; (*legal decision*) sentenza

judg'ment day' s giorno del giudizio

judg'ment seat' s banco dei giudici; tribunale *m*

judicature ['dʒudɪkətʃər] s carica di giudice

judicial [dʒu'dɪʃəl] adj giudiziario; (*becoming a judge*) giudizioso

judiciar·y [dʒu'dɪʃɪˌeri] adj giudiziario ‖ s (-**ies**) (*judges collectively*) magistratura; (*judicial branch*) potere giudiziario

judicious [dʒu'dɪʃəs] adj giudizioso

jug [dʒʌg] s brocca, boccale *m*; (*narrow-necked vessel*) orcio; (*jail*) (slang) prigione

juggle ['dʒʌgəl] s gioco di prestigio ‖ tr fare il giocoliere con; (*documents, facts*) alterare frodolentemente; **to juggle away** ghermire, trafugare ‖ intr fare il giocoliere; fare l'imbroglione

juggler ['dʒʌglər] s giocoliere *m*, prestigiatore *m*; impostore *m*

juggling ['dʒʌglɪŋ] s giochi *mpl* di prestigio

Jugoslav ['jugo'slɑv] adj & s iugoslavo, jugoslavo

Jugoslavia ['jugo'slɑvɪ·ə] s la Iugoslavia, la Jugoslavia

jugular ['dʒʌgjələr] or ['dʒugjələr] adj & s giugulare *f*

juice [dʒus] s sugo; (*natural fluid of an animal body*) succo; (slang) elettricità *f*; (slang) benzina; **to stew in one's own juice** (coll) annegarsi nel proprio sugo

juic·y ['dʒusi] adj (-**ier**; -**iest**) sugoso, succoso; (*spicy*) piccante

jukebox ['dʒukˌbɑks] s grammofono a gettone, juke-box *m*

julep ['dʒulɪp] s bibita di menta col ghiaccio; (pharm) giulebbe *m*

julienne [ˌdʒulɪ'ɛn] s giuliana

July [dʒu'laɪ] s luglio

jumble ['dʒʌmbəl] s intrico, garbuglio ‖ tr ingarbugliare

jum·bo ['dʒʌmbo] adj (coll) enorme ‖ s (-**bos**) (*person*) (coll) elefante *m*; (*thing*) (coll) oggetto enorme

jump [dʒʌmp] s salto; (*in a parachute*) lancio; (*of prices*) sbalzo; (*start*) soprassalto; **on the jump** in moto; **to get or to have the jump on** (coll) avere il vantaggio su ‖ tr saltare; (*a horse*) far saltare; (*prices*) alzare; uscire da, e.g., **the train jumped the track** il treno uscì dalle rotaie; (*to attack*) (coll) balzare su; (*checkers*) suffiare ‖ intr saltare; (*from surprise*) trasalire; (*said of prices*) salire; (*in a parachute*) lanciarsi; **to jump at** (e.g., *an offer*) afferrare; **to jump on** saltare su; (coll) sgridare, arrabbiarsi con; **to jump over** oltrepassare; (*a page*) saltare; **to jump to a conclusion** arrivare precipitosamente a una conclusione

jumper ['dʒʌmpər] s saltatore *m*; camiciotto; **jumpers** tuta da bambini

jump'ing jack' ['dʒʌmpɪŋ] s mario-netta

jump'ing-off' place' s fine f del mondo; (fig) trampolino, punto di partenza

jump' seat' s strapuntino

jump' spark' s scintilla elettrica; (of induction coil) (elec) scintilla d'intra-ferro

jump' wire' s filo elettrico di contatto

jump·y ['dʒʌmpi] adj (-ier; -iest) ner-voso, eccitato

junction ['dʒʌŋkt/ən] s congiunzione; (of two rivers) confluenza; (carp) commettitura; (rr) raccordo ferro-viario

juncture ['dʒʌŋktʃər] s giuntura; (occasion) congiuntura; (moment) mo-mento

June [dʒun] s giugno

jungle ['dʒʌŋgəl] s giungla

junglegym ['dʒʌŋgəl‚dʒɪm] s (trademark) castello

junior ['dʒunjər] adj minore, di minore età; giovane; (in American university) del penultimo anno; figlio, e.g., **John H. Smith, Junior** Giovanni H. Smith, figlio ‖ s minore m; socio secondario; studente m del penultimo anno

jun'ior col'lege s scuola universitaria unicamente di primo biennio

jun'ior high' school' s scuola media; ginnasio

juniper ['dʒunɪpər] s ginepro

ju'niper ber'ry s coccola di ginepro

junk [dʒʌŋk] s roba vecchia, ferro vecchio; (Chinese ship) giunca; (naut) carne salata ‖ tr (slang) get-tar via

junk' deal'er s robivecchi m

junket ['dʒʌŋkɪt] s budino di giun-cata; (outing) viaggio di piacere; viaggio pagato a spese del tesoro ‖ intr far un viaggio di piacere; far un viaggio a spese del tesoro

junk'man' s (-men') ferravecchio; rigat-tiere m

junk' room' s ripostiglio

junk' shop' s negozio di robivecchi

junk'yard' s cantiere m di ferravecchio

juridical [dʒu'rɪdɪkəl] adj giuridico

jurisdiction [‚dʒurɪs'dɪk/ən] s giurisdi-zione

jurisprudence [‚dʒurɪs'prudəns] s giu-risprudenza

jurist ['dʒurɪst] s giurista mf

juror ['dʒurər] s giurato

ju·ry ['dʒuri] s (-ries) giuria

ju'ry box' s banco della giuria

ju'ry·man s (-men) giurato

just [dʒʌst] adj giusto ‖ adv giusta-mente, giusto; appena; proprio; **just as** come, proprio come; **just beyond** un po' più in là (di); **just now** poco fa, or ora; **just out** appena uscito, appena pubblicato

justice ['dʒʌstɪs] s giustizia; (judge) giudice m; **to bring to justice** arre-stare e condannare; **to do justice to** render giustizia a; apprezzare ba-stantemente

jus'tice of the peace' s giudice m con-ciliatore

justifiable ['dʒʌstɪ‚faɪ·əbəl] adj giusti-ficabile

justi·fy ['dʒʌstɪ‚faɪ] v (pret & pp -fied) tr giustificare; (typ) giustifi-care

justly ['dʒʌstli] adj giustamente

jut [dʒʌt] v (pret & pp jutted; ger jut-ting) intr—**to jut out** strapiombare, sporgere

jute [dʒut] s iuta ‖ **Jute** s Juto

juvenile ['dʒuvənɪl] or ['dʒuvə‚naɪl] adj giovanile; minorile ‖ s giovane mf; libro per la gioventù; (theat) amoroso

ju'venile court' s tribunale m per i minorenni

ju'venile delin'quency s delinquenza minorile

juvenilia [‚dʒuvə'nɪlɪ·ə] spl opere fpl giovanili; libri mpl per ragazzi

juxtapose [‚dʒʌkstə'poz] tr giustap-porre

K

K, k [ke] s undicesima lettera dell'alfa-beto inglese

kale [kel] s verza; (slang) cocuzza, soldi mpl

kaleidoscope [kə'laɪdə‚skop] s calei-doscopio

kangaroo [‚kæŋgə'ru] s canguro

katydid ['ketɪdɪd] s grossa cavalletta verde nordamericana

kedge [kɛdʒ] s (naut) ancorotto

keel [kil] s chiglia ‖ intr—**to keel over** (naut) abbattersi in carena, capovol-gersi; (fig) svenire

keelson ['kɛlsən] or ['kɪlsən] s (naut) controchiglia

keen [kin] adj (sharpened) affilato; (wind; wit) tagliente, mordente; (eyes) penetrante; (ears; mind) acuto,

fine; (eager) entusiasta; intenso, vivo; (slang) meraviglioso; **to be keen on** essere appassionato per

eep [kip] s mantenimento; (of medieval castle) torrione m, maschio; **for keeps** (coll) seriamente; (coll) per sempre; **to earn one's keep** guada-gnarsi la vita ‖ v (pret & pp kept [kept]) tr mantenere; (watch) fare; (one's word) mantenere; (to with-hold) trattenere; (accounts) tenere; (servants, guests) avere; (a garden) coltivare; (a business) esercitare; (a holiday) festeggiare; (to support) so-stentare; (a secret; one's seat) ser-bare; (to decide to purchase) pren-dere **to keep away** tener lontano; **to keep back** trattenere; (a secret) mantenere; **to keep down** reprimere; (*expenses*) ridurre al minimo; **to keep s.o. from** + *ger* impedire a qlcu di + *inf*; **to keep in** tener chiuso; **to keep off** tenere a distanza; (*e.g., moisture*) non lasciar penetrare; **to keep s.o. informed about s.th** tenere qlcu al corrente di qlco; **to keep s.o. waiting** fare aspettare qlcu; **to keep up** mantenere, sostenere || *intr* **to keep** + *ger* continuare a + *inf*; **to keep away** tenersi lontano; **to keep from** + *ger* evitare di + *inf*; **to keep informed (about)** tenersi al corrente (di); **to keep in with** (coll) stare nelle buone grazie di; **to keep off** stare lontano (da); (*the grass*) non calpestare; **to keep on** + *ger* seguitare a + *inf*; **to keep out** star fuori, non entrare; **to keep out of** non entrare in; (*danger*) stare lontano da; non immischiarsi in; **to keep quiet** stare tranquillo; **to keep to** (*left or right*) tenere; **to keep to oneself** stare in disparte; **to keep up** continuare; **to keep up with** stare alla pari con; (*e.g., the news*) tenersi al corrente di

keeper ['kipər] *s* (*of a shop*) tenitore *m*; guardiano; (*of a game preserve*) guardacaccia *m*; (*of a magnet*) ancora

keeping ['kipɪŋ] *s* custodia; (*of a holiday*) celebrazione; **in keeping with** in armonia con; **in safe keeping** in luogo sicuro; **out of keeping with** in cattivo accordo con

keep'sake' *s* ricordo
keg [keg] *s* barilotto, botticella
ken [ken] *s* portata; **beyond the ken of** al di là dell'ambito di
kennel ['kenəl] *s* canile *m*
kep·i ['kepi] or ['kepi] *s* (-**is**) chepì *m*
kept wo'man [kept] *s* (**wom'en**) mantenuta
kerchief ['kʌrtʃɪf] *s* fisciù *m*
kernel ['kʌrnəl] *s* (*of a nut*) gheriglio; (*of wheat*) chicco; (fig) nucleo
kerosene ['kerə,sin] or [,kerə'sin] *s* cherosene *m*, petrolio da illuminazione
kerplunk [kər'plʌŋk] *interj* patapum!
ketchup ['ketʃəp] *s* salsa piccante di pomodoro, ketchup *m*
kettle ['ketəl] *s* marmitta, paiolo; (*teakettle*) bricco, teiera
ket'tle-drum' *s* timpano
key [ki] *adj* a chiave; chiave || *s* chiave *f*; (*of piano, typewriter, etc.*) tasto; (*cotter pin*) chiavetta, coppiglia; (*reef*) isolotto; (*tone of voice*) tono; (fig, mus) chiave *f*; (bot) samara; (telg) tasto trasmettitore, manipolatore *m*; **off key** stonato || *tr* aggiustare; inchiavardare; **to key up** eccitare, portare al parossismo
key'board' *s* tastiera
key'hole' *s* toppa, buco della serratura; (*of a clock*) buco della chiave
key'note' *s* (mus) tono; (fig) principio informatore
key'note address' *s* discorso d'apertura
key'punch op'era'tor *s* perforatore *m*
key' ring' *s* portachiavi *m*

key'stone' *s* chiave *f* di volta
key' word' *s* parola chiave
kha·ki ['kɑki] or ['kæki] *adj* cachi || *s* (-**kis**) cachi *m*
khedive [kə'div] *s* kedivè *m*
kibitz ['kɪbɪts] *intr* (coll) dare consigli non richiesti
kibitzer ['kɪbɪtsər] *s* (*at a card game*) (coll) consigliere *m* importuno; (coll) ficcanaso *mf*
kibosh ['kaɪbɑʃ] or [kɪ'bɑʃ] *s* (coll) sciocchezza; **to put the kibosh on** (coll) impossibilitare
kick [kɪk] *s* calcio, pedata; (*of a gun*) rinculo; (*complaint*) (slang) protesta; (*of liquor*) (slang) forza; **to get a kick out of** (slang) pigliar piacere da || *tr* prendere a calci; (*a ball*) calciare; (*one's feet*) battere; **to kick out** (coll) sbatter fuori a pedate; **to kick up a row** scatenare un putiferio || *intr* calciare; (*said of an animal*) scalciare, trarre; (*said of a firearm*) rinculare; (coll) lamentarsi; **to kick against the pricks** dar calci al vento; **to kick off** (football) dare il calcio d'inizio
kick'back' *s* (coll) contraccolpo; (coll) intrallazzo, bustarella
kick'off' *s* calcio d'inizio
kid [kɪd] *s* capretto; (coll) piccolo; **kids** guanti *mpl* or scarpe *fpl* di capretto || *v* (*pret & pp* **kidded**); *ger* **kidding**) *tr* (coll) prendere in giro; **to kid oneself** (coll) farsi illusioni || *intr* (coll) dirlo per scherzo
kidder ['kɪdər] *s* (coll) burlone *m*
kid' gloves' *spl* guanti *mpl* di capretto; **to handle with kid gloves** trattare con la massima cautela
kid'nap' *v* (*pret & pp* **-naped** or **-napped**; *ger* **-naping** or **-napping**) *tr* rapire, sequestrare
kidnaper or **kidnapper** ['kɪd,næpər] *s* rapitore *m* a scopo d'estorsione
kidnaping or **kidnapping** ['kɪd,næpɪŋ] *s* rapimento a scopo di estorsione
kidney ['kɪdni] *s* rene *m*; (culin) rognone *m*; (*temperament*) carattere *m*; (*kind*) tipo
kid'ney bean' *s* fagiolo
kid'ney stone' *s* calcolo renale
kill [kɪl] *s* uccisione; (*game killed*) cacciagione; (coll) fiumicello; **for the kill** per il colpo finale || *tr* uccidere; eliminare; (*a bill*) bocciare; (fig) opprimere
killer ['kɪlər] *s* uccisore *m*
kill'er whale' *s* orca
killing ['kɪlɪŋ] *adj* mortale; (*exhausting*) opprimente; (coll) molto divertente || *s* uccisione; (*game killed*) cacciagione; (coll) fortuna; **to make a killing** (coll) fare una fortuna da un giorno all'altro
kill'-joy' *s* guastafeste *mf*
kiln [kɪl] or [kɪln] *s* forno, fornace *f*
kil·o ['kɪlo] or ['kilo] *s* (-**os**) chilogrammo; chilometro
kilocycle ['kɪlə,saɪkəl] *s* chilociclo
kilogram ['kɪlə,græm] *s* chilogrammo
kilo·hertz ['kɪlə,hʌrts] *s* (-**hertz**) chilohertz

kilometer [ˈkɪlə‚mitər] or [kɪˈlɑmɪtər] s chilometro

kilowatt [ˈkɪlə‚wɑt] s kilowatt m, chilowatt m

kilowatt-hour [ˈkɪlə‚wɑtˈaʊr] s (**kilowatt-hours**) chilowattora m

kilt [kɪlt] s gonnellino

kilter [ˈkɪltər] s—**to be out of kilter** (coll) essere fuori squadra

kimo·no [kɪˈmonə] or [kɪˈmono] s (**-nos**) chimono

kin [kɪn] s (*family relationship*) parentela; (*relatives*) parenti *mpl*; **of kin** parente, affine; **the next of kin** il parente più prossimo, i parenti più prossimi

kind [kaɪnd] *adj* gentile; **kind to** buono con ‖ s genere m, specie *f*; **a kind of** una specie di; **all kinds of** (coll) ogni sorta di; **in kind** in natura; **kind of** (coll) quasi, piuttosto; **of a kind** dello stesso stampo; (*mediocre*) di poco valore

kindergarten [ˈkɪndər‚gɑrtən] s scuola materna, giardino d'infanzia

kindergartner [ˈkɪndər‚gɑrtnər] s allievo della scuola d'infanzia; (*teacher*) maestra giardiniera

kind-hearted [ˈkaɪndˈhɑrtɪd] *adj* gentile, di buon cuore

kindle [ˈkɪndəl] *tr* accendere ‖ *intr* accendersi

kindling [ˈkɪndlɪŋ] s accensione; legna minuta

kin′dling wood′ s legna minuta per accendere il fuoco

kind·ly [ˈkaɪndli] *adj* (**-lier; -liest**) gentile; (*climate*) benigno; favorevole ‖ *adv* gentilmente; cordialmente; per gentilezza; **to not take kindly to** non accettare di buon grado

kindness [ˈkaɪndnɪs] s gentilezza; **have the kindness to** abbia la bontà di

kindred [ˈkɪndrɪd] *adj* imparentato; affine ‖ s parentela; affinità *f*

kinescope [ˈkɪnɪ‚skop] s (*trademark*) cinescopio

kinetic [kɪˈnɛtɪk] or [kaɪˈnɛtɪk] *adj* cinetico ‖ **kinetics** s cinetica

kinet′ic en′ergy s forza viva, energia cinetica

king [kɪŋ] s re m; (*checkers*) dama; (cards, chess) re m

king′bolt′ s perno

kingfish′er s martin pescatore m

king·ly [ˈkɪŋli] *adj* (**-lier; -liest**) reale; (*stately*) maestoso ‖ *adv* regalmente

king′pin′ s birillo centrale; (aut) perno dello sterzo; (fig) figura principale

king′ post′ s (archit) ometto, monaco

king′s e′vil s scrofola

kingship [ˈkɪŋʃɪp] s regalità *f*

king′-size′ *adj* extra-grande

king′s′ ran′som s ricchezza di Creso

kink [kɪŋk] s (*in a rope*) arricciatura; (*in hair*) crespatura; (*soreness in neck*) torcicollo; (*flaw*) ostacolo; (*mental twist*) ghiribizzo ‖ *tr* attorcigliare ‖ *intr* attorcigliarsi

kink·y [ˈkɪŋki] *adj* (**-ier; -iest**) attorcigliato; (*hair*) crespo

kinsfolk [ˈkɪnz‚fok] s parentado

kinship [ˈkɪnʃɪp] s parentela; affinità *f*

kins′man s (**-men**) parente m

kins′wom′an s (**-wom′en**) parente *f*

kipper [ˈkɪpər] s aringa affumicata ‖ *tr* (*herring or salmon*) affumicare

kiss [kɪs] s bacio; (*billiards*) rimpallo leggerissimo; (*confection*) meringa ‖ *tr* baciare; **to kiss away** (*tears*) asciugare con baci ‖ *intr* baciare, baciarsi; (billiards) rimpallare leggermente

kit [kɪt] s (*case*) cassetta dei ferri; (*tools*) ferri *mpl* del mestiere; (*set of supplies*) corredo; (*of small tools*) astuccio; (*of a traveler*) borsa da viaggio; (*pail*) secchio; **the whole kit and caboodle** (coll) tutti quanti

kitchen [ˈkɪtʃən] s cucina

kitchenette [‚kɪtʃəˈnɛt] s cucinetta

kitch′en gar′den s orto

kitch′en·maid′ s sguattera

kitch′en police′ s (mil) corvè *f* di cucina

kitch′en range′ s cucina economica

kitch′en sink′ s acquaio

kitch′en·ware′ s utensili *mpl* di cucina

kite [kaɪt] s cervo volante, aquilone m; (orn) nibbio

kith′ and kin′ [kɪθ] *spl* amici *mpl* e parenti *mpl*

kitten [ˈkɪtən] s gattino

kittenish [ˈkɪtənɪʃ] *adj* giocattolone; civettuolo

kit·ty [ˈkɪti] s (**-ties**) gattino; (cards) piatto ‖ *interj* micio!

kleptomaniac [‚klɛptəˈmɛnɪ‚æk] s cleptomane *mf*

knack [næk] s abilità *f*, destrezza

knapsack [ˈnæp‚sæk] s zaino

knave [nev] s furfante m; (cards) fante m

knaver·y [ˈnevəri] s (**-ies**) furfanteria

knead [nid] *tr* maneggiare, intridere; (*a muscle*) massaggiare

knee [ni] s ginocchio; (*of trousers*) ginocchiera; (mach) gomito; **to bring s.o. to his knees** ridurre qlcu all'obbedienza; **to go down on one's knees** (**to**) gettarsi in ginocchio (davanti a)

knee′ breech′es [‚brɪtʃɪz] *spl* calzoni *mpl* al ginocchio

knee′cap′ s rotula, patella; (*protective covering*) ginocchiera

knee′-deep′ *adj* fino al ginocchio

knee′-high′ *adj* fino al ginocchio

knee′ jerk′ s riflesso patellare

kneel [nil] *v* (*pret & pp* **knelt** [nɛlt] or **kneeled**) *intr* inginocchiarsi

knee′pad′ s ginocchiera

knee′pan′ s rotula, patella

knell [nɛl] s rintocco funebre, campana a morto; **to toll the knell of** annunciare la morte di ‖ *intr* suonare a morte

knickers [ˈnɪkərz] *spl* knickerbockers *mpl*, calzoni *mpl* alla zuava

knickknack [ˈnɪk‚næk] s soprammobile m; gingillo, ninnolo

knife [naɪf] s (**knives** [naɪvz]) coltello; (*of a paper cutter*) mannaia; (*of a milling machine*) fresa; **to go under the knife** essere sulla tavola operatoria ‖ *tr* accoltellare; mettere il coltello nella schiena di

knife′ sharp′ener s affilatoio

knife′ switch′ s (elec) coltella

knight [naɪt] s cavaliere m; (chess) cavallo ‖ tr armare cavaliere

knight-errant [′naɪt′ɛrənt] s (knights-errant) cavaliere m errante

knighthood [′naɪt·hʊd] s cavalleria

knightly [′naɪtli] adj cavalleresco

knit [nɪt] v (pret & pp knitted or knit; ger knitting) tr lavorare a maglia; (to join) unire; (e.g., the brow) corrugare ‖ intr lavorare a maglia; fare la calza; unirsi; (said of a bone) saldarsi

knitting [′nɪtɪŋ] s maglia, lavoro a maglia

knit′ting machine′ s macchina per maglieria

knit′ting mill′ s maglieria

knit′ting nee′dle s ferro da calza

knit′wear′ s maglieria

knit′wear store′ s maglieria

knob [nɑb] s (lump) bozza, protuberanza; (of a door) maniglia; (on furniture) pomolo; (hill) collinetta rotondeggiante; (rad, telv) manopola, pulsante m

knock [nɑk] s colpo; (on a door) tocco; (slang) attacco, critica ‖ tr battere; (repeatedly) sbatacchiare; (slang) attaccare, criticare; **to knock down** (with a punch) stendere a terra; (a wall) diroccare; (to the highest bidder) aggiudicare; (e.g., a machine) smontare; **to knock off** (work) (slang) sospendere; (slang) terminare; (slang) uccidere; **to knock out** mettere fuori combattimento ‖ intr battere; (aut) battere in testa; (slang) criticare; **to knock about** (slang) gironzolare; **to knock against** urtare contro; **to knock at** (e.g., a door) battere a, bussare a; **to knock off** (slang) cessare di lavorare

knock′down′ adj (blow) knock down, che atterra; (dismountable) smontabile ‖ s (blow) colpo che atterra; (discount) sconto

knocker [′nɑkər] s (on a door) battaglio, bussatoio; (coll) criticone m

knock-kneed [′nɑk‚nid] adj con le gambe a X [ɪks]

knock′out′ s pugno che mette fuori combattimento; fuori combattimento; (coll) pezzo di giovane

knock′out drops′ spl (slang) narcotico

knoll [nol] s poggio, rialzo

knot [nɑt] s nodo; (worn as an ornament) fiocco; (in wood) nocchio; gruppo; protuberanza; (tie) nodo;

(naut) nodo; **to tie the knot** (coll) sposarsi ‖ v (pret & pp knotted; ger knotting) tr annodare; (the brow) corrugare ‖ intr annodarsi

knot′hole′ s buco lasciato da un nodo (nel legno)

knot·ty [′nɑti] adj (-tier; -tiest) nodoso; (fig) spinoso

know [no] s—**to be in the know** (coll) essere al corrente ‖ v (pret knew [nju] or [nu]; pp known) tr & intr (by reasoning or learning) sapere; (by the senses or by perception; through acquaintance or recognition) conoscere; **as far as I know** per quanto io ne sappia; **to know about** essere al corrente di; **to know best** essere il miglior giudice; **to know how to** + inf sapere + inf; **to know it all** (coll) sapere tutto; **to know what's what** (coll) saperla lunga; **you ought to know better** dovresti vergognarti

knowable [′no·əbəl] adj conoscibile

know′-how′ s sapere m, abilità f

knowingly [′no·ɪŋli] adv con conoscenza di causa; (on purpose) apposta

know′-it-all′ adj & s (coll) saputello

knowledge [′nɑlɪdʒ] s (faculty) scibile m, sapere m, sapienza; (awareness, acquaintance, familiarity) conoscenza; **to have a thorough knowledge of** conoscere a fondo; **to my knowledge** per quanto io ne sappia; **with full knowledge** con conoscenza di causa; **without my knowledge** a mia insaputa

knowledgeable [′nɑlɪdʒəbəl] adj intelligente, bene informato

knuckle [′nʌkəl] s nocca; foro del cardine, cardine m; **knuckles** pugno di ferro ‖ intr—**to knuckle down** (coll) lavorare di impegno; **to knuckle under** (coll) darsi per vinto

knurl [nʌrl] s granitura ‖ tr godranare, zigrinare

Koran [ko′rɑn] or [ko′ræn] s Corano

Korea [ko′ri·ə] s la Corea

Korean [ko′ri·ən] adj & s coreano

kosher [′koʃər] adj kasher, casher, puro secondo la legge giudaica; (coll) autentico

kowtow [′kaʊ′taʊ] or [′ko′taʊ] intr inchinarsi servilmente

Kremlin [′kremlɪn] s Cremlino

Kremlinology [‚kremlɪ′nɑlədʒi] s Cremlinologia

kudos [′kjudɑs] or [′kudɑs] s (coll) gloria, fama, approvazione

L

L, l [el] s dodicesima lettera dell'alfabeto inglese

la·bel [′lebəl] s marca, etichetta; (descriptive word) qualifica ‖ v (pret & pp -beled or -belled; ger -beling or -belling) tr etichettare; qualificare

labial [′lebɪ·əl] adj & s labiale f

labor [′lebər] adj operaîo ‖ s lavoro; (toil) fatica; (childbirth) parto; (body of wage earners) manodopera; (class as contrasted with management) prestatori mpl d'opera, lavoro; **labors** fatiche fpl; **to be in labor** avere le doglie ‖ intr lavorare; (to exert one-

self) travagliare; (*said of a ship*) rollare e beccheggiare; **to labor for** lottare per; **to labor under** soffrire di

laborato·ry [ˈlæbərəˌtori] *s* (*-ries*) laboratorio

la'bor dispute' *s* vertenza sindacale

labored [ˈlebərd] *adj* elaborato, artificiale; penoso, difficile

laborer [ˈlebərər] *s* lavoratore *m;* (*unskilled worker*) bracciante *m,* manovale *m,* uomo di fatica

laborious [ləˈbɔrɪˑəs] *adj* laborioso

la'bor un'ion *s* sindacato

Labourite [ˈlebəˌraɪt] *s* laburista *mf*

labyrinth [ˈlæbɪrɪnθ] *s* labirinto

lace [les] *s* (*cord or string*) stringa; (*netlike ornament*) trina, merletto; (*braid*) gallone *m* || *tr* stringare; merlettare; (coll) fustigare

lace'work' *s* trina, merletto, pizzo

lachrymose [ˈlækrɪˌmos] *adj* lacrimoso

lacing [ˈlesɪŋ] *s* stringa, cordone *m;* gallone *m;* (coll) battuta, frustata

lack [læk] *s* mancanza, scarsezza, difetto || *tr* mancare di, scarseggiare di || *intr* mancare, scarseggiare, difettare

lackadaisical [ˌlækəˈdezɪkəl] *adj* letargico, indifferente

lackey [ˈlæki] *s* lacchè *m*

lacking [ˈlækɪŋ] *prep* privo di

lack'lus'ter *adj* smorto, spento

laconic [ləˈkɑnɪk] *adj* laconico

lacquer [ˈlækər] *s* lacca || *tr* laccare

lac'quer spray' *s* lacca spray

lac'quer ware' *s* oggetti *mpl* laccati

lacu·na [leˈkjunə] *s* (*-nas or -nae* [ni]) lacuna

lac·y [ˈlesi] *adj* (*-ier; -iest*) simile a merletto

lad [læd] *s* ragazzo, fanciullo

ladder [ˈlædər] *s* scala; (*stepladder hinged on top*) scaleo; (*stepping stone*) (fig) scalino

lad'der truck' *s* autocarro di pompieri munito di scale

la'dies' man' *s* beato fra le donne

la'dies' room' *s* gabinetto per signore

ladle [ˈledəl] *s* ramaiolo, mestolo; (*of tinsmith*) cucchiaio || *tr* scodellare

la·dy [ˈledi] *s* (*-dies*) signora, dama

la'dy·bug' *s* coccinella

la'dy·fin'ger *s* savoiardo, lingua di gatto

la'dy-in-wait'ing *s* (**ladies-in-waiting**) dama di corte

la'dy-kil'ler *s* rubacuori *m*

la'dy-like' *adj* signorile; **to be ladylike** comportarsi come una signora

la'dy-love' *s* amata

la'dy of the house' *s* padrona di casa

ladyship [ˈledi ˌʃɪp] *s* signoria

la'dy's maid' *s* cameriera personale della signora

lag [læg] *s* ritardo || *v* (*pret & pp* **lagged;** *ger* **lagging**) *intr* ritardare; **to lag behind** rimanere indietro

la'ger beer' [ˈlɑgər] *s* birra invecchiata

laggard [ˈlægərd] *s* tardo, pigro

lagoon [ləˈgun] *s* laguna

laid' pa'per [led] *s* carta vergata

laid' up' *adj* messo da parte; (naut) disarmato; (coll) costretto a letto

lair [ler] *s* tana, covo

laity [ˈleˑɪti] *s* laicato

lake [lek] *adj* lacustre || *s* lago

lamb [læm] *s* agnello

lambaste [læmˈbest] *tr* (*to thrash*) sferzare; (*to reprimand*) riprovare

lamb' chop' *s* cotoletta d'agnello

lambkin [ˈlæmkɪn] *s* agnellino; (fig) innocente *m*

lamb'skin' *s* (*leather*) pelle *f* d'agnello; (*skin with its wool*) agnello

lame [lem] *adj* zoppo; difettoso; (*disabled*) invalido; (*excuse*) debole || *tr* azzoppare

lament [ləˈment] *s* lamento; lamento funebre || *tr* lamentare || *intr* lamentarsi

lamentable [ˈlæməntəbəl] or [ləˈmentəbəl] *adj* lamentevole

lamentation [ˌlæmənˈteʃən] *s* lamentazione

laminate [ˈlæmɪˌnet] *tr* laminare

lamp [læmp] *s* lampada

lamp'black' *s* nerofumo

lamp' chim'ney *s* tubo di vetro di lampada a petrolio

lamp'light' *s* luce *f* di lampada

lamp'light'er *s* lampionaio

lampoon [læmˈpun] *s* satira || *tr* satireggiare

lamp'post' *s* colonna del lampione

lamp'shade' *s* paralume *m,* ventola

lamp'wick' *s* lucignolo

lance [læns] or [lɑns] *s* lancia; (surg) lancetta || *tr* (*with an oxygen lance*) tagliare col cannello ossidrico; (surg) sbrigliare, incidere col bisturi

lance' rest' *s* resta

lancet [ˈlænsɪt] or [ˈlɑnsɪt] *s* (surg) lancetta

land [lænd] *s* terra; **on land, on sea, and in the air** per mare, per terra e nel cielo; **to make land** toccare terra; **to see how the land lies** tastare terreno || *tr* sbarcare; (aer) fare atterrare; (coll) pigliare || *intr* sbarcare; (*to come to rest*) andare a finire; (naut) toccar terra; (aer) atterrare; **to land on one's feet** cadere in piedi; **to land on one's head** andare a gambe all'aria; **to land on the moon** allunare; **to land on the water** ammarare

land' breeze' *s* vento di terra

landed [ˈlændɪd] *adj* (*owning land*) terriero; (*real estate*) immobile

land'fall' *s* (*sighting land*) avvistamento; terra avvistata; (*landslide*) frana

land' grant' *s* terreno ricevuto in dono dallo stato

land'hold'er *s* proprietario terriero

landing [ˈlændɪŋ] *s* (*of passengers*) sbarco; (*place where passengers and goods are landed*) imbarcadero; (*of stairway*) pianerottolo; (aer, naut) atterraggio

land'ing bea'con *s* radiofaro d'atterraggio

land'ing card' *s* cartoncino di sbarco

land'ing craft' *s* imbarcazione da sbarco

land'ing field' *s* campo d'atterraggio

land'ing flap' *s* (aer) iposostentatore *m*

land'ing gear' *s* (aer) carrello d'atterraggio

land'ing strip' *s* (aer) pista d'atterraggio

land'la·dy *s* (**-dies**) (*of an apartment*) padrona di casa; (*of a lodging house*) affittacamere *f*; (*of an inn*) ostessa

landlocked ['lænd ˌlɑkt] *adj* circondato da terra

land'lord' *s* (*of an apartment*) padrone *m* di casa; (*of a lodging house*) affittacamere *m*; (*of an inn*) oste *m*

land·lub·ber ['lænd ˌlʌbər] *s* marinaio d'acqua dolce

land'mark' *s* (*boundary stone*) pietra di confine; (*distinguishing landscape feature*) punto di riferimento; (fig) pietra miliare

land' of'fice *s* ufficio del catasto

land'-office busi'ness *s* (coll) sacco d'affari

land'own'er *s* proprietario terriero

landscape ['lænd ˌskep] *s* paesaggio ‖ *tr* abbellire

land'scape gar'dener *s* giardiniere *m* ornamentale

land'scape paint'er *s* paesista *mf*

landscapist ['lænd ˌskepɪst] *s* paesista *mf*

land'slide' *s* frana; (fig) vittoria strepitosa

landward ['lændwərd] *adv* verso terra, verso la costa

land' wind' *s* vento di terra

lane [len] *s* (*narrow street*) vicolo, viuzza; (*of a highway*) corsia; (naut) rotta; (aer) corridoio

langsyne [ˌlæŋˈsaɪn] *s* (Scotch) tempo passato ‖ *adv* (Scotch) molto tempo fa

language ['læŋgwɪdʒ] *s* lingua; (*style of language*) linguaggio; (*of a special group of people*) gergo

lan'guage lab'oratory *s* laboratorio linguistico

languid ['læŋgwɪd] *adj* languido

languish ['læŋgwɪʃ] *intr* languire; affettare languore

languor ['læŋgər] *s* languore *m*

languorous ['læŋgərəs] *adj* languido; (*causing languor*) snervante

lank [læŋk] *adj* scarnito, sparuto

lank·y ['læŋki] *adj* (**-ier; -iest**) scarnito, sparuto

lantern ['læntərn] *s* lanterna

lan'tern slide' *s* diapositiva

lanyard ['lænjərd] *s* (naut) drizza; (mil) aghetto, cordellina

lap [læp] *s* (*of human body or clothing*) grembo; (*with the tongue*) leccata; (*of the waves*) sciacquio; (sports) giro, tappa; **in the lap of** in mezzo a, e.g., **in the lap of luxury** in mezzo alle delicatezze ‖ *v* (*pret* & *pp* **lapped;** *ger* **lapping**) *tr* lappare; (*said, e.g., of waves*) lambire; (*to fold*) piegare; (*to overlap*) sovrapporre; **to lap up** lappare; (coll) accettare con entusiasmo ‖ *intr* sovrapporsi; **to lap against** (*said of the waves*) lambire; **to lap over** trabocccare

lap'board' *s* tavolino da lavoro da tenersi sulle ginocchia

lap' dissolve' *s* (mov) dissolvenza incrociata

lap' dog' *s* cagnolino da salotto

lapel [ləˈpɛl] *s* risvolto

Lap'land' *s* la Lapponia

Laplander ['læp ˌlændər] *s* lappone *mf*

Lapp [læp] *s* lappone *mf*; (*language*) lappone *m*

lap' robe' *s* coperta da viaggio

lapse [læps] *s* (*interval*) spazio di tempo; (*fall, decline*) caduta; (*of memory*) perdita; errore *m*; (ins) risoluzione; (law) decadenza ‖ *intr* cadere, ricadere; cadere in disuso; (*said of time*) passare; (ins) risolversi; (law) decadere

lap'wing' *s* pavoncella

larce·ny ['lɑrsəni] *s* (**-nies**) furto

larch [lɑrtʃ] *s* larice *m*

lard [lɑrd] *s* strutto ‖ *tr* lardellare

larder ['lɑrdər] *s* dispensa

large [lɑrdʒ] *adj* grande, grosso ‖ **s—at large** in libertà

large' intes'tine *s* intestino crasso

largely ['lɑrdʒli] *adv* in gran parte

large'-scale' *adj* su larga scala

lariat ['læri·ət] *s* lazo, laccio

lark [lɑrk] *s* allodola; (coll) burla; **to go on a lark** (coll) far festa

lark'spur' *s* (*rocket larkspur*) sprone *m* di cavaliere; (*field larkspur*) consolida reale

lar·va ['lɑrvə] *s* (**-vae** [vi]) larva

laryngitis [ˌlærɪnˈdʒaɪtɪs] *s* laringite *f*

laryngoscope [ləˈrɪŋgəˌskop] *s* laringoscopio

lar·ynx ['lærɪŋks] *s* (**larynxes** or **larynges** [ləˈrɪndʒiz]) laringe *f*

lascivious [ləˈsɪvɪ·əs] *adj* lascivo

lasciviousness [ləˈsɪvɪ·əsnɪs] *s* lascivia

laser ['lesər] *s* (acronym) (*light amplification by stimulated emission of radiation*) laser *m*

lash [læʃ] *s* (*cord on end of whip*) sverzino; (*blow with whip; scolding*) staffilata; (*of animal's tail*) colpo; (*eyelash*) ciglio; (fig) assalto ‖ *tr* (*to whip*) frustare; (*to bind*) legare; (*to shake*) agitare; (*to attack with words*) staffilare ‖ *intr* lanciarsi; **to lash out** at attaccare violentemente

lashing ['læʃɪŋ] *s* legatura; (*severe scolding*) staffilata; (*fastening with a rope*) (naut) rizza

lass [læs] *s* ragazza, giovane *f*; innamorata

las·so ['læso] *or* [læˈsu] *s* (**-sos** or **-soes**) lasso, lazo ‖ *tr* pigliare col lasso

last [læst] *or* [lɑst] *adj* ultimo, passato; (*most recent*) scorso; **before last** ieraltro, e.g., **the night before last** ieraltro notte; **every last one** tutti senza eccezione; **last but one** penultimo ‖ *s* ultima persona; ultima cosa; fine *f*; (*for holding shoes*) forma; **at last** alla fine; **at long last!** finalmente!; **stick to your last!** fa' il mestiere tuo!; **the last of the month** alla fine del mese; **to breathe one's last** dare l'ultimo sospiro; **to see the last of s.o.** vedere qlcu per l'ultima volta; **to the last** fino alla fine || *adv* ultimo, per ultimo, alla fine || *intr* durare, continuare

lasting ['læstɪŋ] or ['lɑstɪŋ] *adj* duraturo, durevole

lastly ['læstli] or ['lɑstli] *adv* finalmente, in conclusione

last'-min'ute news' *s* notizie *fpl* dell'ultima ora

last' name' *s* cognome *m*

last' night' *adv* ieri sera; la notte scorsa

last' quar'ter *s* ultimo quarto

last' sleep' *s* ultimo sonno

last' straw' *s* ultima, colmo

Last' Sup'per *s* Ultima Cena

last will' and tes'tament *s* ultime volontà *fpl*

last' word' *s* ultima parola; *(latest style)* ultima novità, ultimo grido

latch [lætʃ] *s* saliscendi *m*; *(wooden)* nottola || *tr* chiudere col saliscendi

latch'key' *s* chiave *f* per saliscendi

latch'string' s—the latchstring is out faccia come fosse a casa Sua

late [let] *adj (happening after the usual time)* tardo; *(person)* in ritardo; *(hour of the night)* avanzato; *(news)* dell'ultima ora, recente; *(incumbent of an office)* predecessore, ex, passato; *(coming toward the end of a period)* tardivo; *(deceased)* defunto, fu; **in the late 30's, 40's,** etc. verso la fine del decennio che va dal 1930, 1940, etc. al 1940, 1950, etc.; **of late** recentemente; **to be late in +** *ger* essere in ritardo a + *inf*; **to grow late** farsi tardi; **to keep late hours** fare le ore piccole || *adv* tardi; **in** ritardo; **late in** *(the week, the month, etc.)* alla fine di; **late in life** a un'età avanzata

latecomer ['let ˌkʌmər] *s* ritardatario

lateen' sail' [læˈtin] *s* vela latina

lately ['letli] *adv* recentemente

latent ['letənt] *adj* latente

later ['letər] *adj comp* più tardi; *(event)* susseguente; **later than** posteriore a || *adv comp* più tardi; **later on** più tardi; **see you later** (coll) arrivederci, a ben presto

lateral ['lætərəl] *adj* laterale

lath [læθ] or [lɑθ] *s* listello, striscia di legno || *tr* mettere listelli su

lathe [leð] *s* tornio

lather ['læðər] *s* schiuma di sapone; schiuma || *tr* insaponare; (coll) bastonare || *intr* schiumare

lathery ['læðəri] *adj* schiumoso

lathing ['læθɪŋ] or ['lɑθɪŋ] *s* costruzione con listelli

Latin ['lætɪn] or ['lætən] *adj* & *s* latino

Lat'in Amer'ica *s* l'America latina

Lat'in-Amer'ican *adj* dell'America latina

Lat'in Amer'ican *s* abitante *mf* dell'America latina

latitude ['lætɪ ˌtjud] or ['lætɪ ˌtud] *s* latitudine *f*

latrine [ləˈtrin] *s* latrina militare

latter ['lætər] *adj (more recent)* posteriore; *(of two)* secondo; **the latter** questo; **the latter part of** la fine di

lattice ['lætɪs] *s* graticcio || *tr* munire di graticcio, graticciare

lat'tice gird'er *s* trave *f* a traliccio

lat'tice-work' *s* graticcio, traliccio

Latvia ['lætvɪ·ə] *s* la Lettonia

laud [lɔd] *tr* lodare

laudable ['lɔdəbəl] *adj* lodevole

laudanum ['lɔdənəm] or ['lɔdnəm] *s* laudano

laudatory ['lɔdə ˌtori] *adj* lodativo

laugh [læf] or [lɑf] *s* riso || *tr—to* **laugh away** dissipare ridendo; **to laugh off** prendere sotto gamba, non dare importanza a || *intr* ridere, ridersi; **to laugh at** ridersi di; **to laugh up one's sleeve** ridere sotto i baffi

laughable ['læfəbəl] or ['lɑfəbəl] *adj* risibile

laughing ['læfɪŋ] or ['lɑfɪŋ] *adj* che ride; **to be no laughing matter** non esserci niente da ridere || *s* riso

laugh'ing gas' *s* gas *m* esilarante

laugh'ing-stock' *s* ludibrio, zimbello

laughter ['læftər] or ['lɑftər] *s* riso

launch [lɔntʃ] or [lɑntʃ] *s (of a ship)* varo; *(of a rocket)* lancio; (naut) lancia, scialuppa || *tr (to throw; to send forth)* lanciare; (naut) varare || *intr* lanciarsi

launching ['lɔntʃɪŋ] or ['lɑntʃɪŋ] *s* lancio; *(of a ship)* varo

launch'ing pad' *s* piattaforma di lancio

launder ['lɔndər] or ['lɑndər] *tr* lavare e stirare || *intr* riuscire dopo il lavaggio

launderer ['lɔndərər] or ['lɑndərər] *s* lavandaio stiratore *m*

laundress ['lɔndrɪs] or ['lɑndrɪs] *s* lavandaia stiratrice *f*

laundromat ['lɔndrə ˌmæt] or ['lɑndrə ˌmæt] *s* (trademark) lavanderia a gettone

laun·dry ['lɔndri] or ['lɑndri] *s* (**-dries**) lavanderia; *(clothing)* bucato

laun'dry·man' *s* (**-men'**) lavandaio

laun'dry·wom'an *s* (**-wom'en**) lavandaia

laureate ['lɔrɪ·ɪt] *adj* laureato || *s* laureato; poeta laureato

lau·rel ['lɔrəl] or ['lɑrəl] *s* lauro, alloro; **laurels** (fig) alloro; **to rest or sleep on one's laurels** dormire sugli allori || *v (pret & pp* **-reled** or **-relled;** *ger* **-reling** or **-relling**) *tr* laureare

lava ['lɑvə] or ['lævə] *s* lava

lavato·ry ['lævə ˌtori] *s* (**-ries**) *(room)* gabinetto da bagno; *(bowl)* lavabo; *(toilet)* gabinetto di decenza, cesso

lavender ['lævəndər] *s* lavanda

lavish ['lævɪʃ] *adj* prodigo || *tr* prodigare, profondere

law [lɔ] *s (of man, of nature, of science)* legge *f*; *(study, profession of law)* diritto; **to enter the law** farsi avvocato; **to go to law** ricorrere alla legge; **to lay down the law** dettar legge; **to maintain law and order** mantenere la pace interna; **to practice law** fare l'avvocato

law-abiding ['lɔ·ə ˌbaɪdɪŋ] *adj* osservante della legge

law'break'er *s* violatore *m* della legge

law' court' s tribunale m di giustizia

lawful [ˈlɔfəl] adj legale, legittimo

lawless [ˈlɔlɪs] adj illegale; (unbridled) sfrenato

law'mak'er s legislatore m

lawn [lɔn] s tappeto erboso; (fabric) batista

lawn' mow'er s tosatrice f

law' of'fice s ufficio d'avvocato

law' of na'tions s diritto delle genti

law' of the jun'gle s legge f della giungla

law' stu'dent s studente m di legge

law'suit' s causa, lite f, processo

lawyer [ˈlɔjər] s avvocato, legale m

lax [læks] adj (in morals) lasso, rilassato; (rope) lento; (negligent) trascurato; vago, indeterminato

laxative [ˈlæksətɪv] adj purgativo ‖ s purga, purgante m

lay [le] adj (not belonging to the clergy) laico; (not having special training) non dotto, profano ‖ s configurazione, disposizione ‖ v (pret & pp laid [led]) tr mettere, collocare; (snares) tendere; (one's eyes; a stone) porre; (blame) dare, gettare; (a bet) fare; (for consideration) presentare; (the table) imbandire; (said of a hen) deporre; (plans) impostare; (to locate) disporre; **to be laid in** (said of a scene) aver luogo in; **to lay aside** mettere da parte; **to lay down** dichiarare; (one's life) dare; (one's arms) deporre; **to lay low** abbattere; uccidere; **to lay off** (workers) licenziare; (to measure) marcare; (slang) lasciare in pace; **to lay open** rivelare; (to a danger) esporre; **to lay out** estendere; preparare, disporre; (a corpse) comporre; (money) (coll) sborsare; **to lay over** posporre; **to lay up** mettere da parte; obbligare a letto; (naut) disarmare ‖ intr (said of a hen) fare le uova; **to lay about** dar botte da orbi; **to lay for** (slang) attendere al varco; **to lay off** (coll) cessare di lavorare; **to lay over** trattenersi, fermarsi; **to lay to** (naut) navigare alla cappa

lay' broth'er s frate m secolare; converso

lay' day' s (com) stallia

layer [ˈleˑər] s (of paint) mano f; (of bricks) testa; (e.g., of rocks) strato, falda; (anat) pannicolo; (hort) propaggine f ‖ tr (hort) propagginare

lay'er cake' s dolce m a strati

layette [leˈet] s corredino

lay' fig'ure s manichino

laying [ˈleˑɪŋ] s posa; (of eggs) deporre m; (of a wire) tendere m

lay'man s (-men) (member of the laity) laico, secolare m; (not a member of a special profession) laico, profano

lay'off' s (dismissal of workers) licenziamento; (period of unemployment) disoccupazione

lay' of the land' s andamento generale

lay'out' s piano; (sketch) tracciato; (of tools) armamentario; (coll) residenza; (typ) menabò m; (coll) banchetto, festino

lay'o'ver s fermata in un viaggio

lay' sis'ter s suora al secolo; conversa

laziness [ˈlezɪnɪs] s pigrizia

la·zy [ˈlezi] adj (-zier; -ziest) pigro

la'zy-bones' s (coll) poltrone m

lea [li] s (fallow land) maggese m; (meadow) prato

lead [lɛd] adj plumbeo ‖ s piombo; (of lead pencil) mina; (for sounding depth) (naut) scandaglio; (typ) interlinea ‖ [lɛd] v (pret & pp leaded; ger leading) tr impiombare; (to interline) (typ) interlineare ‖ [lid] s (foremost place) primato; (guidance) guida, direzione; (leash) guinzaglio; (journ) testata; (cards) mano f, prima mano; (elec) conduttore m; (mach) passo; (min) filone m; (rad, telv) filo d'entrata; (theat) ruolo principale; (theat) primo attore; (theat) prima attrice; **to take the lead** prendere il comando ‖ [lid] v (pret & pp led [lɛd]) tr condurre, portare; (to command) comandare, essere alla testa di; (an orchestra) dirigere; (a good or bad life) fare; (s.o. into vice) trascinare; (cards) cominciare a giocare; (elec, mach) anticipare; **to lead astray** forviare ‖ intr essere in testa, guidare; prendere l'offensiva; (said of a road) condurre; (cards) cominciare a giocare; **to lead to** risultare in; **to lead up to** andare a condurre a

leaden [ˈlɛdən] adj (of lead; like lead) plumbeo; (sluggish) tardo; (with sleep) carico; triste

leader [ˈlidər] s capo, comandante m; (ringleader) capobanda m; (of an orchestra) direttore m; (among animals) guidaiolo; (in a dance) ballerino guidaiolo; (sports) capintesta m; (journ) articolo di fondo

lead'er dog' s cane m guida di ciechi

leadership [ˈlidərˌʃɪp] s comando, direzione; doti fpl di comando

leading [ˈlidɪŋ] adj principale; primo; dirigente, preeminente

lead'ing ar'ticle s articolo di fondo

lead'ing edge' s (aer) bordo d'attacco

lead'ing la'dy s prima attrice

lead'ing man' s (men') primo attore

lead'ing ques'tion s domanda suggestiva, domanda orientatrice

lead'ing strings' spl dande fpl

lead'-in wire' [ˈlid ˌɪn] s filo d'antenna

lead' pen'cil [lɛd] s lapis m, matita

leaf [lif] s (leaves [livz]) (of plant) foglia; (of vine) pampino; (of paper) foglio; (of double door) battente m; (of table) asse m a ribalta; **to turn over a new leaf** ricominciare una nuova vita ‖ intr fogliare; **to leaf through** sfogliare

leafless [ˈliflɪs] adj senza foglie

leaflet [ˈliflɪt] s manifestino, volantino; (of plant) foglietta

leaf' spring' s molla a balestra

leaf'stalk' s picciolo

leaf·y [ˈlifi] adj (-ier; -iest) foglioso, frondoso

league [lig] s lega ‖ tr associare ‖ intr associarsi

League' of Na'tions s Società f delle Nazioni

leak [lik] s (in a roof) stillicidio; (in a ship) falla; (of water, gas, steam) fuga; (of electricity) dispersione; buco, fessura; (of news) filtrazione; **to spring a leak** avere una perdita; (naut) cominciare a far acqua || tr (gas, liquids) perdere, lasciar scappare; (news) lasciar trapelare || intr (said of water, gas etc.,) perdere, scappare; (said of a barrel) spillare; (naut) fare acqua; **to leak away** (said of money) andarsene; **to leak out** (said of news) trapelare

leakage ['likɪdʒ] s perdita, fuoruscita, fuga; (elec) dispersione; (com) colaggio

leak·y ['liki] adj (-ier; -iest) che perde; (naut) che fa acqua; (coll) indiscreto

lean [lin] adj magro, secco; (gasoline mixture) povero || v (pret & pp **leaned** or **leant** [lɛnt]) tr inclinare; appoggiare || intr pendere, inclinarsi; (fig) inclinare, tendere; **to lean against** appoggiarsi a, addossarsi a; **to lean back** sdraiarsi; **to lean on** appoggiarsi su; **to lean out (of)** sporgersi (da); **to lean over backwards** fare di tutto; **to lean toward** (fig) tendere a, avere un'inclinazione per

leaning ['linɪŋ] adj inclinato, pendente || s inclinazione

lean'ing tow'er s torre f pendente

lean'-to' s (-tos) tetto a una falda

leap [lip] s salto, balzo; **by leaps and bounds** a passi da gigante; **leap in the dark** salto nel vuoto || v (pret & pp **leaped** or **leapt** [lɛpt]) tr saltare || intr saltare; (said of one's heart) balzare

leap'frog' s cavallina; **to play leapfrog** giocare alla cavallina

leap' year' s anno bisestile

learn [lʌrn] s (pret & pp **learned** or **learnt** [lʌrnt]) tr imparare; imparare a memoria; (news) apprendere || intr istruirsi, apprendere

learned ['lʌrnɪd] adj dotto; (word) colto

learn'ed jour'nal s rivista scientifica

learn'ed soci'ety s associazione di eruditi

learn'ed word' s parola dotta

learn'ed world' s mondo di dotti

learner ['lʌrnər] s apprendista mf; studente m; (beginner) principiante mf

learning ['lʌrnɪŋ] s istruzione; (scholarship) erudizione

lease [lis] s locazione, contratto d'affitto; **a new lease on life** nuove prospettive di felicità; vita nuova (dopo una malattia) || tr locare; prendere in affitto || intr affittare

lease'hold' adj affittato || s beni mpl sotto locazione

leash [liʃ] s guinzaglio; **to strain at the leash** mordere il freno || tr frenare, controllare

least [list] adj minore, menomo, minimo || s (il) meno; **at least** or **at the least** per lo meno, quanto meno;

not in the least nient'affatto || adv meno

leather ['lɛðər] s cuoio

leath'er-back tur'tle s tartaruga di mare

leath'er goods' store' s pelletteria

leathery ['lɛðəri] adj coriaceo

leave [liv] s (permission) permesso; (permission to be absent) licenza; (farewell) commiato; **on leave** in licenza; **to take French leave** andarsene all'inglese; **to take leave (of)** prender congedo (da) || v (pret & pp **left** [lɛft]) tr (to go away from) lasciare, uscire da; (to let stay) lasciare; (to bequeath) lasciare in testamento; **leave it to me!** lasciami fare!; **to be left** restare, e.g., **the door was left open** la porta restò aperta; esserci, e.g., **there is no bread left** non c'è più pane; **to leave alone** lasciare in pace; **to leave no stone unturned** cercare ogni possibilità; **to leave off** abbandonare, lasciare; **to leave out** omettere; **to leave things as they are** lasciar stare le cose || intr andarsene; (said of a conveyance) partire

leaven ['lɛvən] s lievito || tr lievitare; (fig) impregnare, permeare

leavening ['lɛvənɪŋ] s lievito

leave' of ab'sence s licenza; (without pay) aspettativa

leave'-tak'ing s commiato

leavings ['livɪŋz] spl rifiuti mpl

Leba·nese [ˌlɛbəˈniz] adj libanese || s (-nese) libanese mf

Lebanon ['lɛbənən] s il Libano

lecher ['lɛtʃər] s libertino

lecherous ['lɛtʃərəs] adj libidinoso

lechery ['lɛtʃəri] s lussuria

lectern ['lɛktərn] s leggio

lecture ['lɛktʃər] s conferenza; (tedious reprimand) pistolotto || tr dare una conferenza a; sermoneggiare || intr fare una conferenza; sermoneggiare

lecturer ['lɛktʃərər] s conferenziere m

ledge [lɛdʒ] s cornice f, cornicione m

ledger ['lɛdʒər] s (com) libro mastro

ledg'er line' s (mus) rigo supplementare

lee [li] s (shelter) rifugio; (naut) parte f sottovento; **lees** feccia

leech [litʃ] s mignatta, sanguisuga; **to stick like a leech** attaccarsi come una sanguisuga

leek [lik] s porro

leer [lɪr] s occhiata lussuriosa or maligna || intr—**to leer at** guardare di sbieco, sbirciare

leer·y ['lɪri] adj (-ier; -iest) sospettoso

leeward ['liwərd] or ['luˈərd] adj di sottovento || s sottovento, poggia || adv sottovento

lee'way' s (aer, naut) deriva, scarroccio; (in time) (coll) tolleranza; (coll) libertà f d'azione

left [lɛft] adj sinistro; (pol) di sinistra || s sinistra; (boxing) sinistro || adv alla sinistra

left' field' s fuoricampo di sinistra

left'-hand' drive' s guida a sinistra

left-handed ['lɛftˈhændɪd] adj (individual) mancino; (awkward) goffo;

(*compliment*) ambiguo; (*mach*) sinistrorso

leftish ['leftɪʃ] *adj* sinistrista

leftist ['leftɪst] *adj* di sinistra ‖ *s* membro della sinistra

left'o'ver *adj* & *s* rimanente *m*; **left-overs** resti *mpl*

left'-wing' *adj* di sinistra

left-winger ['left'wɪŋər] *s* (coll) membro dell'estrema sinistra; (coll) membro della sinistra

leg [leg] *s* (*of man, animal, table, chair; of trousers*) gamba; (*of fowl; of lamb*) coscia; (*of boot*) gambale *m*; (*of a journey*) tappa; **to be on one's last legs** essere agli estremi, essere ridotto alla disperazione; **to not have a leg to stand on** (coll) non avere la minima giustificazione; **to pull the leg of** (coll) prendere in giro, burlarsi di; **to shake a leg** (coll) affrettarsi; (*to dance*) (coll) ballare; **to stretch one's legs** sgranchirsi le gambe

lega·cy ['legəsi] *s* (-cies) legato

legal ['ligəl] *adj* legale

legali·ty [lɪ'gælɪti] *s* (-ties) legalità *f*

legalize ['ligə͵laɪz] *tr* legalizzare

le'gal ten'der *s* denaro a corso legale

legate ['legɪt] *s* legato

legatee [͵legə'ti] *s* legatario

legation [lɪ'geʃən] *s* legazione

legend ['ledʒənd] *s* leggenda

legendary ['ledʒən͵deri] *adj* leggendario

legerdemain [͵ledʒərdɪ'men] *s* gioco di prestigio; (*trickery*) imbroglio

legging ['legɪŋ] *s* gambale *m*

leg·gy ['legi] *adj* (-gier; -giest) dalle gambe lunghe

leg'horn' *s* cappello di paglia di Firenze; gallina bianca livornese ‖ **Leghorn** *s* Livorno

legible ['ledʒɪbəl] *adj* leggibile

legion ['lidʒən] *s* legione *f*

legislate ['ledʒɪs͵let] *tr* ordinare per mezzo di legge ‖ *intr* legiferare

legislation [͵ledʒɪs'leʃən] *s* legislazione

legislative ['ledʒɪs͵letɪv] *adj* legislativo

legislator ['ledʒɪs͵letər] *s* legislatore *m*

legislature ['ledʒɪs͵letʃər] *s* legislatura; corpo legislativo

legitimacy [lɪ'dʒɪtɪməsi] *s* legittimità *f*

legitimate [lɪ'dʒɪtɪmɪt] *adj* legittimo ‖ [lɪ'dʒɪtɪ͵met] *tr* legittimare

legit'imate dra'ma *s* teatro serio

legitimize [lɪ'dʒɪtɪ͵maɪz] *tr* legittimare

leg' of lamb' *s* cosciotto d'agnello

legume ['legjum] *or* [lɪ'gjum] *s* (*pod*) legume *m*; (*table vegetables*) legumi *mpl*; (bot) leguminose *fpl*

leg'work' *s* lavoro che involve molto cammino

leisure ['liʒər] *or* ['leʒər] *s* ozio; **at leisure** senza fretta; disoccupato; **at one's leisure** quando si abbia un po' di tempo libero

lei'sure class' *s* gente agiata

lei'sure hours' *spl* ore *fpl* d'ozio

leisurely ['liʒərli] *or* ['leʒərli] *adj* lento ‖ *adv* lentamente, a tempo perso

---

lei'sure time' *s* tempo libero

lemon ['lemən] *s* limone *m*; (*car*) (coll) catorcio

lemonade [͵lemə'ned] *s* limonata

lem'on squeez'er *s* spremilimoni *m*

lend [lend] *s* (*pret* & *pp* **lent** [lɛnt]) *tr* prestare; (*a hand*) dare

lender ['lendər] *s* prestatore *m*

lend'ing li'brary *s* biblioteca circolante

length [leŋθ] *s* lunghezza; (*of time*) durata; **at length** finalmente; **to go to any lengths** fare quanto è possibile; essere disposto a tutto; **to keep at arm's length** (*someone else*) tenere a distanza (qlcu); (*said of oneself*) tenere a distanza

lengthen ['leŋθən] *tr* allungare ‖ *intr* allungarsi

length'wise' *adj* longitudinale ‖ *adv* per il lungo

length·y ['leŋθi] *adj* (-ier; -iest) lungo, prolungato

lenien·cy ['lini·ənsi] *s* (-cies) indulgenza

lenient ['lini·ənt] *adj* indulgente, clemente

lens [lenz] *s* lente *f*; (*of the eye*) cristallino

Lent [lent] *s* quaresima

Lenten ['lentən] *adj* quaresimale

lentil ['lentəl] *s* lenticchia

Leo ['li·o] *s* (astr) il Leone

leopard ['lepərd] *s* leopardo

leotard ['li·ə͵tɑrd] *s* calzamaglia

leper ['lepər] *s* lebbroso

leprosy ['leprəsi] *s* lebbra

leprous ['leprəs] *adj* lebbroso; (*of an animal or plant*) squamoso

Lesbian ['lezbi·ən] *adj* lesbico ‖ *s* lesbico; (*female homosexual*) lesbica

lesbianism ['lezbi·ə͵nɪzəm] *s* lesbismo

lese majesty ['liz'mædʒɪsti] *s* delitto di lesa maestà

lesion ['liʒən] *s* lesione

less [les] *adj* minore ‖ *adv* meno; **less and less** sempre meno; **less than** meno che; (*followed by numeral or personal pron*) meno di; (*followed by verb*) meno di quanto ‖ *s* meno

lessee [les'i] *s* locatario; (*of business establishment*) concessionario

lessen ['lesən] *tr* diminuire, ridurre ‖ *intr* diminuire, ridursi

lesser ['lesər] *adj comp* minore

lesson ['lesən] *s* lezione

lessor ['lesər] *s* locatore *m*

lest [lest] *conj* per paura che

let [let] *v* (*pret* & *pp* **let**; *ger* **letting**) *tr* permettere; (*to rent*) affittare; **let** + *inf* che + *subj*, e.g., **let him go** che vada; **let alone** tanto meno; senza menzionare; **let good enough alone** essere contento dell'onesto; **let us** + *inf* = *1st pl impv*, e.g., **let us sing** cantiamo; **to let** da affittare; **to let alone** lasciare in pace; **to let be** lasciar stare; **to let by** lasciar passare; **to let down** far scendere; deludere; tradire; abbandonare; **to let fly** (*insults*) lanciare; **to let go** lasciar libero; vendere; **to let in** fare entrare; **to let it go at that** non parlarne più; **to let know** far sapere; **to**

let loose sciogliere; **to let out** lasciar uscire; (*a secret*) divulgare; (*a scream*) lasciarsi scappare; (*to enlarge*) allargare; affittare; **to let through** lasciar passare; **to let up** lasciar salire; lasciar alzare ‖ *intr* affittare; **to let down** diminuire gli sforzi; **to let go of** disfarsi di; **to let on** (coll) fare finta; **to not let on** (coll) non lasciar trapelare; **to let out** (*said, e.g., of school*) terminare; **to let up** (coll) cessare; (coll) diminuire

let'down' *s* diminuzione; smacco, umiliazione; delusione

lethal ['liθəl] *adj* letale

lethargic [lɪ'θɑrdʒɪk] *adj* letargico

lethar·gy ['leθərdʒi] *s* (**-gies**) letargo

Lett [lɛt] *s* lettone *mf*; (*language*) lettone *m*

letter ['lɛtər] *s* lettera; **letters** (*literature*) lettere *fpl*, letteratura; **to the letter** alla lettera ‖ *tr* marcare con lettere

let'ter box' *s* cassetta delle lettere

let'ter car'rier *s* postino

let'ter drop' *s* buca delle lettere

let'ter-head' *s* capolettera *m*; (*paper with printed heading*) carta da lettera intestata

lettering ['lɛtərɪŋ] *s* iscrizione; lettere *fpl*

let'ter of cred'it *s* lettera di credito

let'ter o'pener ['opənər] *s* tagliacarte *m*

let'ter pa'per *s* carta da lettere

let'ter-per'fect *adj* alla lettera; che sa alla perfezione

let'ter-press' *s* stampato in tipografia ‖ *adv* a stampa tipografica

let'ter scales' *spl* pesalettere *m*

let'ter-word' *s* sigla

Lettish ['lɛtɪʃ] *adj* & *s* lettone *m*

lettuce ['lɛtɪs] *s* lattuga

let'up' *s* (coll) pausa, sosta; (coll) tregua; **without letup** (coll) senza posa

leucorrhea [,lukə'riə] *s* leucorrea

leukemia [lu'kimɪə] *s* leucemia

Levant [lɪ'vænt] *s* levante *m*

levee ['lɛvi] *s* (*embankment*) argine *m*; (*reception*) ricevimento

lev·el ['lɛvəl] *adj* piano; livellato; equilibrato; **level with** a livello di; **one's level best** (coll) il proprio meglio ‖ *s* (*instrument*) livella; (*degree of elevation*) livello; (*flat surface*) spianata, pianura; **on the level** (slang) onesto; onestamente; **to find one's level** trovare il proprio ambiente ‖ *v* (*pret* & *pp* **-eled** or **-elled**; *ger* **-eling** or **-elling**) *tr* livellare; (*to flatten out*) spianare; (*e.g., prices*) pareggiare, ragguagliare; (*a gun*) puntare; (coll) gettare a terra; (fig) dirigere ‖ *intr*— **to level off** (aer) volare orizzontalmente

level-headed ['lɛvəl'hɛdɪd] *adj* equilibrato

lev'eling rod' *s* stadia

lever ['lɛvər] or ['livər] *s* leva ‖ *tr* far leva su ‖ *intr* far leva

leverage ['livərɪdʒ] or ['lɛvərɪdʒ] *s* azione di una leva; (fig) potere *m*

leviathan [lɪ'vaɪ·əθən] *s* leviatano

levitation [,lɛvɪ'teʃən] *s* levitazione

levi·ty ['lɛvɪti] *s* (**-ties**) leggerezza

lev·y ['lɛvi] *s* (**-ies**) (*of taxes*) esazione; (*of money*) tributo; (*of troops*) leva ‖ *v* (*pret* & *pp* **-ied**) *tr* (*a tax*) imporre; (*soldiers*) reclutare; (*war*) fare

lewd [lud] *adj* (*lustful*) lascivo; osceno

lexical ['lɛksɪkəl] *adj* lessicale

lexicographer [,lɛksɪ'kɑgrəfər] *s* lessicografo

lexicographic(al) [,lɛksɪko'græfɪk(əl)] *adj* lessicografico

lexicography [,lɛksɪ'kɑgrəfi] *s* lessicografia

lexicology [,lɛksɪ'kɑlədʒi] *s* lessicologia

lexicon ['lɛksɪkən] *s* lessico

liabili·ty [,laɪ·ə'bɪlɪti] *s* (**-ties**) svantaggio; responsabilità *f*; (*e.g., to disease*) tendenza; (com) passivo; **liabilities** debiti *mpl*; (com) passivo

liabil'ity insur'ance *s* assicurazione sulla responsabilità civile

liable ['laɪ·əbəl] *adj* (*e.g., to disease*; *e.g., to make mistakes*) soggetto; responsabile; probabile; (*e.g., to a fine*) passibile

liaison ['li·ə,zɑn] or [li'ɛzɑn] *s* legame *m*; relazione illecita; (mil, nav) collegamento; (phonet) legamento

li'aison of'ficer *s* ufficiale *m* di collegamento

liar ['laɪ·ər] *s* bugiardo, mentitore *m*

libation [laɪ'beʃən] *s* (joc) libazione, bevuta

li·bel ['laɪbəl] *s* diffamazione; (*defamatory writing*) libello ‖ *v* (*pret* & *pp* **-beled** or **-belled**; *ger* **-beling** or **-belling**) *tr* diffamare

libelous ['laɪbələs] *adj* diffamatorio

liberal ['lɪbərəl] *adj* liberale; (*translation*) libero ‖ *s* liberale *mf*

liberali·ty [,lɪbə'rælɪti] *s* (**-ties**) liberalità *f*; (*breadth of mind*) ampiezza di vedute

liberal-minded ['lɪbərəl'maɪndɪd] *adj* liberale, tollerante

liberate ['lɪbə,ret] *tr* liberare

liberation [,lɪbə're/ən] *s* liberazione

liberator ['lɪbə,retər] *s* liberatore *m*

libertine ['lɪbər,tin] *adj* & *s* libertino

liber·ty ['lɪbərti] *s* (**-ties**) libertà *f*; **to take the liberty to** permettersi di

liberty-loving ['lɪbərti'lʌvɪŋ] *adj* amante della libertà

libidinous [lɪ'bɪdɪnəs] *adj* libidinoso

libido [lɪ'bido] or [lɪ'baɪdo] *s* libidine *f*; (psychoanal) libido *f*

Libra ['laɪbrə] or ['laɪbrə] *s* (astr) Bilancia

librarian [laɪ'brɛrɪ·ən] *s* bibliotecario

librar·y ['laɪ,brɛri] or ['laɪbrəri] *s* (**-ies**) biblioteca; (*room in a house*; *collection of books*) libreria

li'brary num'ber *s* segnatura

li'brary sci'ence *s* biblioteconomia

libret·to [lɪ'brɛto] *s* (**-tos**) (mus) libretto

Libya ['lɪbɪ·ə] *s* la Libia

license ['laɪsəns] *s* licenza; (aut) patente *f* ‖ *tr* dare la licenza a

li'cense num'ber s numero di targa di circolazione

li'cense plate' or **tag'** s targa di circolazione

licentious [laɪˈsenʃəs] adj licenzioso

lichen [ˈlaɪkən] s lichene m

lick [lɪk] s leccata, leccatura; (coll) esplosione di energia; (coll) velocità f; (coll) battitura; (coll) ripulita; **to give a lick and a promise to** (coll) fare rapidamente e con poca attenzione || tr leccare; (said of waves, flames, etc.) lambire; (to defeat) (coll) battere, vincere; (e.g., with a stick) (coll) bastonare

licorice [ˈlɪkərɪs] s liquirizia

lid [lɪd] s coperchio; (eyelid) palpebra; (curb) (coll) restrizione, freno; (hat) (slang) cappello

lie [laɪ] s menzogna; **to catch in a lie** pigliare in castagna; **to give the lie to** smentire || v (pret & pp **lied**; ger **lying**) tr—**to lie oneself out of** or **to lie one's way out of** trarsi fuori da (un impaccio) con una menzogna || intr mentire || v (pret **lay** [le]; pp **lain** [len]; ger **lying**) intr essere sdraiato; trovarsi; (in the grave) giacere; **to lie down** sdraiarsi

lie' detec'tor s macchina della verità

lien [lin] or [ˈli·ən] s diritto di pegno, diritto di garanzia

lieu [lu] s—**in lieu of** in luogo di

lieutenant [luˈtɛnənt] s luogotenente m; (mil) tenente m; (nav) tenente m di vascello

lieuten'ant colo'nel s (mil) tenente m colonnello

lieuten'ant command'er s (nav) capitano di corvetta

lieuten'ant gen'eral s (mil) generale m di corpo d'armata

lieuten'ant gov'ernor s (USA) vicegovernatore m

lieuten'ant jun'ior grade' s (nav) sottotenente m di vascello

life [laɪf] adj (animate) vitale; (lifelong) perpetuo; (annuity) vitalizio; (working from nature) dal vero || s (lives [laɪvz]) vita; (of an insurance policy) forza; **for life** a vita; **for the life of me** per quanto io provi; **the life and soul of** (e.g., the party) l'anima di; **to come to life** tornare a sé; riprender vita; **to depart this life** passar a miglior vita; **to run for one's life** scappare a tutta corsa

life' annu'ity s rendita vitalizia

life' belt' s cintura di salvataggio

life'boat s imbarcazione di salvataggio, lancia di salvataggio

life' buoy' s salvagente m

life' float' s zattera di salvataggio

life'guard s bagnino

life' impris'onment s ergastolo

life' insur'ance s assicurazione sulla vita

life' jack'et s cintura or giubbotto di salvataggio

lifeless [ˈlaɪflɪs] adj inanimato; (in a faint) esanime; senza vita

life'like adj (e.g., portrait) parlante; naturale

life' line' s sagola di salvataggio; (fig) linea di comunicazioni vitale

life'long' adj perpetuo, a vita

life' of Ri'ley [ˈraɪli] s vita del michelaccio

life' of the par'ty s anima della festa

lifer [ˈlaɪfər] s (slang) ergastolano

life' raft' s zattera di salvataggio

life'sav'er s salvatore m della vita; (something that saves from a predicament) ancora di salvezza

life' sen'tence s condanna all'ergastolo

life'-size' adj in grandezza naturale

life'time' adj vitalizio || s corso della vita

life' vest' s (air, naut) giubbotto salvagente or di salvataggio

life'work' s lavoro di tutta una vita

lift [lɪft] s sollevamento; (act of helping) aiuto; (ride) passaggio; (apparatus) elevatore m; (aer) portanza || tr sollevare, alzare; (one's hat) levarsi; rimuovere; (coll) plagiare; (coll) rubare; (fire) (mil) sospendere || intr sollevare, sollevarsi; (said, e.g., of fog) dissiparsi

lift'-off' s (aer) decollo verticale

lift' truck' s carrello elevatore

ligament [ˈlɪgəmənt] s legamento

ligature [ˈlɪgətʃər] s legatura

light [laɪt] adj (in weight) leggero; (hair) biondo; (complexion) chiaro; (oil) fluido; (naut) con poco carico; (room) chiaro, illuminato; (beer) chiaro; **light in the head** (dizzy) allegro; (silly) scimunito; **to make light of** prendere sotto gamba || s luce f; (to light a cigarette) fuoco; (to control traffic) segnale m; (shining example) luminare m; (lighthouse) faro; (window) luce f; **according to one's lights** secondo l'intelligenza che il buon Dio gli (le) ha dato; **against the light** controluce; **in this light** sotto questo punto di vista; **light's example**; (of sheep) polmone m; **to come to light** venire alla luce; **to shed** or **throw light on** mettere in luce; **to strike a light** accendere un fiammifero || v (pret & pp **lighted** or **lit** [lɪt] tr (to furnish with illumination) illuminare; (to ignite) accendere; **to light up** illuminare || intr illuminarsi; accendersi; (said, e.g., of a bird) posarsi; (from a car) scendere; **to light into** (coll) gettarsi contro; **to light out** (slang) darsela a gambe; **to light upon** imbattersi in || adv senza bagagli; senza carico

light' bulb' s lampadina

light-complexioned [ˈlaɪtkəmˈplɛkʃənd] adj dal colorito chiaro

lighten [ˈlaɪtən] tr alleggerire, sgravare; illuminare; (to cheer up) rallegrare || intr alleggerirsi; (to become less dark) illuminarsi; (to give off flashes of lightning) lampeggiare

lighter [ˈlaɪtər] s accenditore m; (naut) burchio

light-fingered [ˈlaɪtˈfɪŋgərd] adj svelto di mano, con le mani lunghe

light-footed [ˈlaɪtˈfʊtɪd] *adj* agile
light-headed [ˈlaɪtˈhedɪd] *adj* (*dizzy*)
allegro; (*simple*) scemo
light-hearted [ˈlaɪtˈhɑrtɪd] *adj* allegro
light'house' *s* faro
lighting [ˈlaɪtɪŋ] *s* illuminazione
lightly [ˈlaɪtlɪ] *adv* alla leggera
light' me'ter *s* esposimetro
lightness [ˈlaɪtnɪs] *s* (*in weight*) leggerezza; (*in illumination*) chiarezza
light·ning [ˈlaɪtnɪŋ] *s* lampo, fulmine
m ‖ *v* (*ger* **-ning**) *intr* lampeggiare
light'ning arrest'er [əˈrestər] *s* scaricatore *m*
light'ning bug' *s* lucciola
light'ning rod' *s* parafulmine *m*
light' op'era *s* operetta
light'ship' *s* battello faro
light-struck [ˈlaɪtˌstrʌk] *adj* che ha
preso luce
light'weight' *adj* leggero; da mezza stagione, e.g., **lightweight coat** cappotto
da mezza stagione
light'-year' *s* anno luce
likable [ˈlaɪkəbəl] *adj* simpatico
like [laɪk] *adj* uguale, simile; uguale a,
simile a, e.g., **this hat is like mine**
questo cappello è simile al mio; (*elec*)
di segno uguale; **like father like son**
tale il padre quale il figlio; **to feel
like** + *ger* aver voglia di + *inf*; **to
look like** assomigliare a; sembrare,
e.g., **it looks like rain** sembra che
pioverà ‖ *s* (*liking*) preferenza; (*fellow
man*) simile *m*; **and the like** e cose
dello stesso genere; **to give like for
like** rendere pane per focaccia ‖ *adv*
come; **like enough** (coll) probabilmente
‖ *prep* come ‖ *conj* (coll) come; come se;
(coll) che, e.g., **it seems like he is
afraid** sembra che abbia paura ‖ *tr*
voler bene (with *dat*), e.g., **I like her
very much** le voglio molto bene; trovar
piacere in, e.g., **I like music** trovo
piacere nella musica; piacere (with
dat), e.g., **John likes apples** le mele
piacciono a Giovanni; **to like best** or
better preferire; **to like it in** trovarsi
a proprio agio in; **to like to** + *inf*
piacere (with *dat*) + *inf*, e.g., **she
likes to dance** le piace ballare; gradire
che + *subj*, e.g., **I should like him to
pay a visit to my parents** gradirei che
facesse una visita ai miei genitori ‖ *intr*
volere, desiderare, e.g., **as you like**
come desidera; **if you like** se vuole
likelihood [ˈlaɪklɪˌhʊd] *s* probabilità *f*
like·ly [ˈlaɪklɪ] *adj* (**-lier; -liest**) probabile; verosimile, a proposito; pro-
mettente; **to be likely to** + *inf* essere
probabile che + *fut*, e.g., **Mary is
likely to get married in the spring** è
probabile che Maria si sposerà in
primavera ‖ *adv* probabilmente
like-minded [ˈlaɪkˈmaɪndɪd] *adj* dello
stesso parere, della stessa opinione
liken [ˈlaɪkən] *tr* paragonare
likeness [ˈlaɪknɪs] *s* (*picture*) ritratto;
(*similarity*) rassomiglianza; apparenza
like'wise' *adv* ugualmente; inoltre; **to
do likewise** fare lo stesso

liking [ˈlaɪkɪŋ] *s* simpatia; **to be to
the liking of** essere di gusto di; **to
have a liking for** (*things*) prendere
gusto per; (*people*) affezionarsi a
lilac [ˈlaɪlək] *adj* & *s* lilla *m*
Lilliputian [ˌlɪlɪˈpjuʃən] *adj* & *s* lilli-
puziano
lilt [lɪlt] *s* canzone *f* a cadenza; movimento a cadenza; (*in verse*) cadenza
lil·y [ˈlɪlɪ] *s* (**-ies**) giglio; **to gild the
lily** cercare di migliorare quanto è
già perfetto
lil'y of the val'ley *s* mughetto
li'ma bean' [ˈlaɪmə] *s* fagiolo bianco
limb [lɪm] *s* (*of body*) membro, arto;
(*of tree*) ramo; (*of cross*) braccio; **to
be out on a limb** (coll) essere nei
guai
limber [ˈlɪmbər] *adj* agile ‖ *intr*—**to
limber up** sciogliersi i muscoli,
sgranchirsi le gambe
lim·bo [ˈlɪmbo] *s* (**-bos**) esilio; dimenticatoio; (theol) limbo
lime [laɪm] *s* (*calcium oxide*) calce *f*;
(*Citrus aurantifolia*) limetta agra;
(*linden tree*) tiglio ‖ *tr* gessare
lime'kiln' *s* fornace *f* da calce
lime'light' *s*—**to be in the limelight**
essere in vista
limerick [ˈlɪmərɪk] *s* canzoncina umoristica di cinque versi
lime'stone' *s* calcare *m*
limit [ˈlɪmɪt] *s* limite *m*; (coll) colmo;
to go to the limit andare agli estremi
‖ *tr* limitare
limitation [ˌlɪmɪˈteʃən] *s* limitazione
lim'ited-ac'cess high'way [ˈlɪmɪtɪd] *s*
autostrada, strada con corsia d'accesso
lim'ited com'pany *s* società *f* a responsabilità limitata
lim'ited mon'archy *s* monarchia costituzionale
limitless [ˈlɪmɪtlɪs] *adj* illimitato
limousine [ˈlɪməˌzin] or [ˌlɪməˈzin] *s*
berlina
limp [lɪmp] *adj* floscio; debole ‖ *s*
zoppicatura ‖ *intr* zoppicare
limpid [ˈlɪmpɪd] *adj* limpido
linage [ˈlaɪnɪdʒ] *s* (typ) numero di
linee
linchpin [ˈlɪntʃˌpɪn] *s* acciarino
linden [ˈlɪndən] *s* tiglio
line [laɪn] *s* linea; (*e.g., of people*)
fila; (*of trees*) filare *m*; (*for fishing*)
lenza; (*written or printed*) rigo, riga;
(*wrinkle*) ruga; (*of goods*) ramo;
(naut) gherlino; **all along the line** su
tutta la linea; **in line** allineato; sotto
controllo; **in line with** secondo; **out
of line** fuori d'allineamento; (slang)
in disaccordo; **to bring into line** far
filare; **to draw the line** at fermarsi a;
stabilire il limite a; **to fall in line**
conformarsi; allinearsi; **to have a
line on** (coll) aver informazioni su;
to read between the lines leggere fra
le righe; **to stand in line** fare la coda;
to toe the line filare diritto; **to wait
in line** fare la fila ‖ *tr* rigare; (*e.g.,
the street*) schierare lungo; (*a suit*)
foderare; (*a brake*) rivestire; **to line
up** allineare; trovare, scovare ‖ *intr*

—**to line up** mettersi in fila; fare la coda

lineage ['lɪnɪ·ɪdʒ] s lignaggio

lineaments ['lɪnɪ·əmənts] spl lineamenti mpl

linear ['lɪnɪ·ər] adj lineare

line'man s (-men) (elec) guardafili m; (sports) guardalinee m; (surv) assistente geometra m

linen ['lɪnən] adj di tela di lino ǁ s (fabric) tela di lino, lino; (yarn) filo di lino; biancheria

lin'en clos'et s guardaroba m per la biancheria

line' of fire' s (mil) linea di tiro

line' of least' resist'ance s principio del minimo sforzo; **to follow the line of least resistance** prendere la via più facile

line' of sight' s visuale f; (mil) linea di mira

liner ['laɪnər] s transatlantico

line'-up' s disposizione; (of prisoners) allineamento; (sports) formazione

linger ['lɪŋɡər] intr indugiare, soffermarsi; (to be tardy) tardare; rimanere in vita; **to linger over** contemplare

lingerie [ˌlænʒə'ri] s biancheria intima

lingering ['lɪŋɡərɪŋ] adj prolungato

lingual ['lɪŋɡwəl] adj linguale ǁ s suono linguale

linguist ['lɪŋɡwɪst] s poliglotto; (specialist in linguistics) glottologo

linguistic [lɪŋ'ɡwɪstɪk] adj linguistico ǁ **linguistics** s linguistica, glottologia

lining ['laɪnɪŋ] s (of a coat) fodera; (of auto brake) guarnizione; (of a furnace) rivestimento interno; (of wall) rivestimento

link [lɪŋk] s anello, maglia; unione; (of sausage) nocco; **links** campo di golf ǁ tr connettere ǁ intr connettersi

linnet ['lɪnɪt] s fanello

linotype ['laɪnə,taɪp] s linotype f ǁ tr comporre in linotipia

lin'otype op'erator s linotipista mf

linseed ['lɪn,sid] s linosa

lin'seed oil' s olio di lino

lint [lɪnt] s peluria, sfilacciatura; (for dressing wounds) filaccia

lintel ['lɪntəl] s architrave m

lion ['laɪ·ən] s leone m; celebrità f; **to beard the lion in his den** affrontare l'avversario a casa sua; **to put one's head in the lion's mouth** cacciarsi nei pericoli

lioness ['laɪ·ənɪs] s leonessa

lion-hearted ['laɪ·ən,hɑrtɪd] adj cuor di leone, coraggioso

lionize ['laɪ·ə,naɪz] tr festeggiare come una celebrità

li'ons' den' s fossa dei leoni

li'on's share' s parte f del leone

lip [lɪp] s labbro; (of a jar) beccuccio; (slang) linguaggio insolente; **to smack one's lips** leccarsi le labbra

lip'read' v (pret & pp -read [ˌred]) tr leggere le labbra di ǁ intr leggere le labbra

lip' read'ing s labiolettura

lip' serv'ice s omaggio non sentito

lip'stick' s rossetto per le labbra, matita per le labbra

lique•fy ['lɪkwɪ,faɪ] v (pret & pp -fied) tr & intr liquefare

liqueur [lɪ'kʌr] s liquore m

liquid ['lɪkwɪd] adj liquido ǁ s liquido; (phonet) liquida

liquidate ['lɪkwɪ,det] tr & intr liquidare

liquidity [lɪ'kwɪdɪti] s liquidità f

liq'uid meas'ure s misura di capacità per liquidi

liquor ['lɪkər] s distillato alcolico, bevanda alcolica; (broth) brodo

Lisbon ['lɪzbən] s Lisbona

lisp [lɪsp] s pronuncia blesa ǁ intr parlare bleso

lissome ['lɪsəm] adj flessibile, agile

list [lɪst] s lista, elenco; (border) orlo; (selvage) cimossa, vivagno; (naut) sbandamento; **lists** lizza; **to enter the lists** entrare in lizza ǁ tr elencare, listare ǁ intr (naut) sbandare, andare alla banda

listen ['lɪsən] intr ascoltare; obbedire; **to listen in** ascoltare una conversazione; (rad) captare una comunicazione; **to listen to** ascoltare; obbedire a, prestare attenzione a; **to listen to reason** intendere ragione

listener ['lɪsənər] s ascoltatore m; radioascoltatore m

lis'tening post' s (mil) posto di ascolto

listless ['lɪstlɪs] adj svogliato

list' price' s prezzo di catalogo

lita•ny ['lɪtəni] s (-nies) litania

liter ['litər] s litro

literacy ['lɪtərəsi] s abilità f di leggere e scrivere; istruzione

literal ['lɪtərəl] adj letterale

literary ['lɪtə,reri] adj letterario; (individual) letterato

literate ['lɪtərɪt] adj che sa leggere e scrivere; (educated) istruito; (well-read) letterato ǁ s persona che sa leggere e scrivere; letterato

literature ['lɪtərət∫ər] s letteratura; (printed matter) opuscoli pubblicitari

lithe [laɪθ] adj flessibile, agile

lithium ['lɪθɪ·əm] s litio

lithograph ['lɪθə,græf] or ['lɪθə,grɑf] s litografia ǁ tr litografare

lithographer [lɪ'θɑɡrəfər] s litografo

lithography [lɪ'θɑɡrəfi] s litografia

Lithuania [ˌlɪθu'enɪ·ə] s la Lituania

Lithuanian [ˌlɪθu'enɪ·ən] adj & s lituano

litigant ['lɪtɪɡənt] adj & s litigante mf

litigate ['lɪtɪ,get] tr & intr litigare

litigation [ˌlɪtɪ'ɡe∫ən] s litigio; (lawsuit) lite f, causa

litmus ['lɪtməs] s tornasole m

lit'mus pa'per s cartina al tornasole

litter ['lɪtər] s disordine m; (scattered rubbish) pattume m; (young brought forth at one birth) figliata; (of puppies) cucciolata; (bedding for animals) strame m; (stretcher; bed carried by men or animals) lettiga, portantina ǁ tr mettere in disordine; spargere rifiuti per; coprire di strame ǁ intr partorire

lit′ter·bug′ s sparpagliatore m di rifiuti

littering [ˈlɪtərɪŋ] s—**no littering** vietato gettare rifiuti

little [ˈlɪtəl] adj (in size) piccolo; (in amount) poco, e.g., **little salt** poco sale; **a little** un po′ di, e.g., **a little salt** un po′ di sale; **the little ones** i piccini ‖ s poco; **a little** un po′; to **make little of** farsi gioco di; non pigliar sul serio; to **think little of** non tener di conto ‖ adv poco; **little by little** poco a poco, mano a mano

Lit′tle Bear′ s Orsa minore

Lit′tle Dip′per s Piccolo Carro

lit′tle fin′ger s mignolo; to **twist around one′s little finger** maneggiare come un fantoccio

lit′tle·neck′ s piccola vongola (Venus mercenaria)

lit′tle owl′ s civetta

lit′tle peo′ple spl fate fpl; folletti mpl

Lit′tle Red Rid′inghood′ [ˈraɪdɪŋ ˌhʊd] s Cappuccetto Rosso

lit′tle slam′ s (bridge) piccolo slam

liturgic(al) [lɪˈtʌrdʒɪk(əl)] adj liturgico

litur·gy [ˈlɪtərdʒɪ] s (-gies) liturgia

livable [ˈlɪvəbəl] adj abitabile; socievole; tollerabile

live [laɪv] adj vivo; (flame) ardente; di attualità; (elec) sotto tensione; (telv) in diretta ‖ [lɪv] tr vivere; to **live down** (one′s past) far dimenticare; to **live it up** (coll) darsi alla bella vita, scialare; to **live out** (e.g., a war) sopravvivere (with dat) ‖ intr vivere; to **live from hand to mouth** vivere alla giornata; to **live high** darsi alla bella vita; to **live on** continuare a vivere; (e.g., vegetables) vivere di; vivere alle spalle di; to **live up to** (one′s promises) compiere; (one′s earnings) spendere

live′ coal′ [laɪv] s brace f

livelihood [ˈlaɪvlɪ ˌhʊd] s vita; to **earn one′s livelihood** guadagnarsi la vita

livelong [ˈlɪv ˌlɔŋ] or [ˈlɪv ˌlɑŋ] adj—**all the livelong day** tutto il santo giorno

live·ly [ˈlaɪvlɪ] adj (-lier; -liest) vivo, vivace; (color) vivido; (resilient) elastico; (tune) brioso

liven [ˈlaɪvən] tr animare ‖ intr animarsi, rianimarsi

liver [ˈlɪvər] s abitante mf; (anat) fegato

liver·y [ˈlɪvərɪ] s (-ies) livrea

liv′ery·man s (-men) stalliere m

liv′ery sta′ble s stallaggio

livestock [ˈlaɪv ˌstɑk] adj zootecnico ‖ s bestiame m

live′ wire′ [laɪv] s (elec) filo carico di corrente; (slang) persona energica

livid [ˈlɪvɪd] adj livido; (with anger) incollerito

living [ˈlɪvɪŋ] adj vivo; (conditions) abitativo ‖ s vivere m; to **earn a living** guadagnarsi la vita

liv′ing quar′ters spl abitazione, alloggio

liv′ing room′ s stanza di soggiorno

liv′ing wage′ s salario sufficiente per vivere

lizard [ˈlɪzərd] s lucertola

load [lod] s peso, carico; **loads of** (coll) un mucchio di; to **get a load of** (slang) stare a vedere; (slang) stare a sentire; to **have a load on** (slang) essere ubriaco ‖ tr caricare ‖ intr caricarsi

loaded [ˈlodɪd] adj caricato; (slang) ubriaco fradicio; (slang) ricchissimo

load′ed dice′ spl dadi truccati

load′stone′ s magnetite f; (fig) calamita

loaf [lof] s (loaves [lovz]) pane m; (molded mass) forma; (of sugar) pane m; (long and thin loaf) filone m ‖ intr batter fiacca, oziare

loafer [ˈlofər] s fannullone m

loam [lom] s ricca argilla sabbiosa; terra da fonderia

loan [lon] s prestito; to **hit for a loan** (coll) dare una stoccata a ‖ tr prestare

loan′ shark′ s (coll) strozzino

loan′ word′ s (ling) prestito

loath [loθ] adj poco disposto; **nothing loath** molto volentieri

loathe [loð] tr detestare, aborrire

loathsome [ˈloðsəm] adj abominevole, disgustoso

lob [lɑb] s (tennis) pallonetto ‖ v (pret & pp lobbed; ger lobbing) tr (tennis) dare un pallonetto a

lob·by [ˈlɑbɪ] s (-bies) anticamera, vestibolo; sollecitazione di voti ‖ v (pret & pp -bied) intr sollecitare voti, influenzare il voto dietro le quinte

lobbyist [ˈlɑbɪ·ɪst] s politicante m che cerca di influenzare il voto dietro le quinte

lobe [lob] s lobo

lobster [ˈlɑbstər] s (Palinurus vulgaris) aragosta; (Hommarus vulgaris) astice m

lob′ster pot′ s nassa per aragoste

local [ˈlokəl] adj locale ‖ s treno accelerato; notizia di interesse locale; (of a union) sezione

locale [loˈkæl] s località f

locali·ty [loˈkælɪtɪ] s (-ties) località f

localize [ˈlokə ˌlaɪz] tr localizzare

lo′cal op′tion s referendum m locale sulla vendita di alcolici

locate [ˈloket] or [loˈket] tr (to discover the location of) localizzare; (to place, settle) situare, stabilire; (to ascribe a location to) individuare ‖ intr stabilirsi

location [loˈkeʃən] s localizzazione; posizione; sito; **on location** (mov) in esterno

lock [lɑk] s serratura; (of a canal) chiusa; (of hair) ciocca; (of a firearm) percussore m; (mach) freno; **lock, stock, and barrel** (coll) completamente; **under lock and key** sotto chiave ‖ tr chiudere a chiave; serrare; (a boat) far passare per una chiusa; unire; abbracciare; to **lock in** chiudere sotto chiave; to **lock out** chiudere fuori; (workers) sbarrare dal lavoro; to **lock up** chiudere a chiave; incarcerare

locker [ˈlɑkər] s armadietto a chiave; (in the form of a chest) bauletto

lock′er room′ s spogliatoio
locket [′lɑkɪt] s medaglione m
lock′jaw′ s tetano, trisma m
lock′ nut′ s controdado
lock′out′ s serrata
lock′smith′ s magnano, fabbro
lock′ step′ s—to march in lock step
marciare a passo serrato
lock′ stitch′ s punto a filo doppio
lock′ ten′der s guardiano di chiusa
lock′up′ s prigione; (typ) messa in
forma
lock′ wash′er s rondella di sicurezza
locomotive [ˌlokə′motɪv] s locomotiva
lo·cus [′lokəs] s (-ci [saɪ]) luogo
locust [′lokəst] s (ent) locusta; (cicada) (ent) cicala; (bot) robinia
lode [lod] s filone m, vena
lode′star′ s stella polare; guida
lodge [lɑdʒ] s casetta; padiglione m da
caccia; albergo; (e.g., of Masons)
loggia ‖ tr alloggiare, ospitare; depositare; contenere; (a complaint) sporgere ‖ intr alloggiare; essere contenuto, trovarsi; andar a finire
lodger [′lɑdʒər] s inquilino
lodging [′lɑdʒɪŋ] s alloggio
loft [lɔft] or [lɑft] s (attic) solaio;
(hayloft) fienile m; (in theater or
church) galleria
loft·y [′lɔfti] or [′lɑfti] adj (-ier; -iest)
alto, elevato; (haughty) orgoglioso
log [lɔg] or [lɑg] s ceppo, ciocco;
(naut) solcometro; (aer, naut) giornale m di bordo; **to sleep like a log**
dormire della grossa ‖ v (pret & pp
logged; ger **logging**) tr registrare; (a
speed) fare; (a distance) percorrere
logarithm [′lɔgə ˌrɪðəm] or [′lɑgə-
ˌrɪðəm] s logaritmo
log′book′ s (aer, naut) libro di bordo
log′ cab′in s capanna di tronchi
log′ chip′ s (naut) barchetta
log′ driv′er s zatteriere m
log′ driv′ing [′draɪvɪŋ] s fluitazione
logger [′lɔgər] or [′lɑgər] s taglia-
legna m; trattore m per trasporto
tronchi
log′ger·head′ s testone m; **at logger-
heads** in lite
loggia [′lɔdʒə] s loggia
logic [′lɑdʒɪk] s logica
logical [′lɑdʒɪkəl] adj logico
logician [lo′dʒɪʃən] s logico
logistic(al) [lo′dʒɪstɪk(əl)] adj logistico
logistics [lo′dʒɪstɪks] s logistica
log′jam′ s ingorgo fluviale dovuto a
ammasso di tronchi; (fig) ristagno
log′ line′ s (naut) sagola
log′roll′ intr barattare favori politici
log′wood′ s campeggio
loin [lɔɪn] s lombo; **to gird up one's
loins** prepararsi per l'azione
loin′cloth′ s perizoma m, copripudende
m
loiter [′lɔɪtər] tr—**to loiter away** (time)
sprecare in ozio ‖ intr bighellonare,
trastullarsi
loiterer [′lɔɪtərər] s perdigiorno
loll [lɑl] intr sdraiarsi pigramente, ada-
giarsi pigramente; pendere
lollipop [′lɑli ˌpɑp] s caramella sullo
stecchetto, lecca-lecca m

Lombard [′lɑmbɑrd] or [′lɑmbərd] adj
& s lombardo; (hist) longobardo
Lom′bardy pop′lar s pioppo italico
London [′lʌndən] adj londinese ‖ s
Londra
Londoner [′lʌndənər] s londinese mf
lone [lon] adj solo; solitario
loneliness [′lonlɪnɪs] s solitudine f
lone·ly [′lonli] adj (-lier; -liest) so-
lingo, solo, solitario
lonesome [′lonsəm] adj solitario
lone′ wolf′ s (coll) orso, solitario
long [lɔŋ] or [lɑŋ] (longer [′lɔŋgər]
or [′lɑŋgər]; **longest** [′lɔŋgɪst] or
[′lɑŋgɪst]) adj lungo; **three meters
long** lungo tre metri ‖ adv molto,
molto tempo; **as long as** mentre;
(provided) fin tanto che; (inasmuch
as) dato che; **before long** fra poco;
how long? quanto?; **long ago** molto
tempo fa; **long before** molto prima;
long since molto tempo fa; **no longer**
non più; **so long!** (coll) ciao!, arrivederci!; **so long as** fino a che, finché
‖ intr anelare; **to long for** sviscerarsi
per, sospirare per
long′boat′ s (naut) lancia
long′-dis′tance adj (telp) interurbano,
intercomunale; (sports) di fondo;
(aer) a distanza
long′-drawn′-out′ adj prolungato
longeron [′lɑndʒərən] s longherone m
longevity [lɑn′dʒevɪti] s longevità f
long′ face′ s (coll) faccia triste, muso
lungo
long′hair′ adj & s (coll) intellettuale
mf; (coll) musicomane mf
long′hand′ adj (scritto) a mano ‖ s
scrittura a mano; **in longhand** scritto
a mano
longing [′lɔŋɪŋ] or [′lɑŋɪŋ] adj bramoso, anelante ‖ s brama, anelito
longitude [′lɑndʒɪ ˌtjud] or [′lɑndʒɪ-
ˌtud] s longitudine f
long-lived [′lɔŋ′laɪvd], [′lɑŋ′lɪvd],
[′lɑŋ′laɪvd] or [′lɑŋ′lɪvd] adj (person) longevo, di lunga vita; (e.g.,
rumor) di lunga durata
long′-play′ing rec′ord s disco di grande
durata
long′-range′ adj a lunga portata
long′shore′man s (-men) portuale m,
scaricatore m
long′stand′ing adj vecchio, che esiste
da lungo tempo
long′-suf′fering adj paziente, longanime
long′ suit′ s (cards) serie lunga; (fig)
forte m
long′-term′ adj a lunga scadenza
long′-wind′ed adj verboso; (speech)
chilometrico
look [lʊk] s (appearance) aspetto;
(glance) sguardo; (search) ricerca;
looks aspetto, apparenza; **to take a
look at** dare un'occhiata a ‖ tr guardare; (one's age) mostrare; **to look
daggers at** fulminare con lo sguardo;
to look up (e.g., in a dictionary) cercare; andare a visitare; venire a visitare ‖ intr guardare; cercare; parere;
look out! attenzione!; **to look after**
badare a; occuparsi di; **to look at**
guardare; **to look back** riguardare;

(fig) guardare al passato; **to look down on** s.o. guardare qlcu dall'alto in basso; **to look for** cercare; aspettarsi; **to look forward to** anticipare il piacere di; **to look ill** avere una brutta cera; **to look in** passare per la casa di; **to look into** esaminare a fondo; **to look like** sembrare, parere; **to look out** fare attenzione; **to look out for** aver cura di; **to look out of** guardare da; **to look out on** dare su; **to look through** guardare per; (a book) sfogliare; **to look toward** dare su; **to look up to** ammirare, guardare con ammirazione; **to look well** avere una buona cera; fare figura

looker-on [ˌlʊkərˈɑn] or [ˌlʊkərˈɔn] s (**lookers-on**) astante m

look′ing glass′ [ˈlʊkɪŋ] s specchio

look′out′ s guardia; (person; watch kept; place from which a watch is kept) vedetta; (concern) (coll) affare m; **to be on the lookout** stare in guardia; **to be on the lookout for** essere in cerca di

loom [lum] s telaio ‖ intr apparire indistintamente; pararsi dinanzi; apparire

loon [lun] s scemo; fannullone m; (orn) (Gavia) strolaga

loon·y [ˈluni] adj (-ier; -iest) (slang) pazzo ‖ s (-ies) (slang) pazzo

loop [lup] s cappio; (e.g., of a road) tortuosità f; (for fastening a button) occhiello; (aer) cerchio or giro della morte; (phys) ventre m; ‖ tr fare cappi in; annodare; **to loop the loop** (aer) fare il giro della morte ‖ intr avanzare tortuosamente, girare

loop′hole′ s (narrow opening) feritoia; (means of evasion) scappatoia

loose [lus] adj libero, sciolto; (available) disponibile; (not firm) rilasciato; (tooth) che balla; (unchaste) facile; (garment) ampio; (soil) smosso; (translation) libero; (rein) lento; **to become loose** sciogliersi; **to break loose** mettersi in libertà; **to have loose bowels** avere la diarrea; **to turn loose** liberare ‖ s—**to be on the loose** (coll) essere in libertà; (coll) correre la cavallina ‖ tr sciogliere; slegare; lanciare

loose′ change′ s spiccioli mpl

loose′ end′ s capo sciolto; **at loose ends** indeciso; disoccupato, senza nulla da fare

loose′-leaf′ adj a fogli mobili

loosen [ˈlusən] tr snodare; rilasciare; smuovere; allentare; (the bowels) liberare dalla stitichezza ‖ intr snodarsi; rilasciarsi; smuoversi; allentarsi

looseness [ˈlusnɪs] s scioltezza; (in morals) rilassamento

loose-tongued [ˈlusˈtʌŋd] adj sciolto di lingua; linguacciuto, maldicente

loot [lut] s bottino ‖ tr saccheggiare

lop [lɑp] v (pret & pp **lopped**; ger **lopping**) tr lasciar cadere, lasciar penzolare; **to lop off** mozzare; (a tree) potare; (a vine) stralciare ‖ intr penzolare

lopsided [ˈlɑpˈsaɪdɪd] adj che pende da una parte; asimmetrico, sproporzionato

loquacious [loˈkweʃəs] adj loquace

lord [lɔrd] s signore m; (Brit) lord m ‖ tr—**to lord it over** signoreggiare su

lord·ly [ˈlɔrdli] adj (-lier; -liest) signorile, magnifico; altero, disdegnoso, arrogante

Lord's′ Day′, the la domenica, il giorno del Signore

lordship [ˈlɔrdʃɪp] s signoria

Lord's′ Prayer′ s paternostro

Lord's′ Sup′per s Eucarestia; Ultima Cena

lore [lor] s tradizioni fpl popolari; cognizioni fpl

lorgnette [lɔrnˈjet] s occhialetto, lorgnette f; binocolo da teatro col manico

lor·ry [ˈlɑri] or [ˈlɔri] s (-ries) (rr) vagoncino; (Brit) camion m

lose [luz] v (pret & pp **lost** [lɔst] or [lɑst]) tr perdere; (said of a physician) non riuscire a salvare; **to lose heart** perdersi d'animo; **to lose oneself** perdersi, smarrirsi ‖ intr perdere; (said of a watch) ritardare; **to lose out** rimetterci

loser [ˈluzər] s perdente mf

losing [ˈluzɪŋ] adj perdente ‖ **losings** spl perdite fpl

loss [lɔs] or [lɑs] s perdita; **to be at a loss** essere perplesso; **to be at a loss to** + inf non saper come + inf; **to sell at a loss** vendere in perdita

loss′ of face′ s perdita di faccia

lost [lɔst] or [lɑst] adj perduto; **lost in thought** assorto in sè stesso; **lost to** perso per; insensibile a

lost′-and-found′ depart′ment s ufficio degli oggetti smarriti

lost′ sheep′ s percorella smarrita

lot [lɑt] s (for building) lotto; (fate) sorte f; (parcel, portion) partita; (of people) gruppo; (coll) grande quantità f; (coll) tipo, soggetto; **a lot (of)** or **lots of** (coll) molto, molti; **to cast** or **to throw in one's lot with** condividere la sorte di; **to draw** or **to cast lots** tirare a sorte

lotion [ˈloʃən] s lozione

lotter·y [ˈlɑtəri] s (-ies) lotteria, riffa

lotto [ˈlɑto] s tombola, lotto

lotus [ˈlotəs] s loto

loud [laud] adj forte; (noisy) rumoroso; (voice) alto; (garish) sgargiante, chiassoso, appariscente; (foul-smelling) puzzolente ‖ adv a voce alta; rumorosamente

loud-mouthed [ˈlaudˌmauθt] or [ˈlaudˌmauðd] adj chiassone

loud′speak′er s altoparlante m

lounge [laundʒ] s divano, sofà m; sala soggiorno; ridotto ‖ intr oziare, star senza far niente; bighellonare; **to lounge around** bighellonare

lounge′ liz′ard s (slang) damerino, bellimbusto, gagà m

louse [laus] s (lice [laɪs]) pidocchio ‖ tr—**to louse up** (slang) rovinare

lous·y [ˈlauzi] adj (-ier; -iest) pidocchioso; (mean; bungling) (coll) schifoso; (*filthy*) (coll) sporco; **lousy with** (*e.g., money*) (slang) pieno di

lout [laʊt] s gaglioffo, tanghero

louver ['luvər] s sportello girevole di persiana; (aut) feritoia per ventilazione

lovable ['lʌvəbəl] *adj* amabile

love [lʌv] s amore m; (tennis) zero; **not for love nor money** a nessun prezzo; **to be in love (with)** essere innamorato (di); **to make love to** fare l'amore con ‖ tr amare; voler bene a; piacere (with *dat*), e.g., **she loves short skirts** le piacciono le sottane corte

love' affair' s passione, amori *mpl*

love'bird' s (orn) inseparabile m; **lovebirds** (slang) amanti appassionati

love' child' s figlio naturale

love' feast' s agape f

loveless ['lʌvlɪs] *adj* senza amore

lovelorn ['lʌv,lɔrn] *adj* abbandonato dalla persona amata

love•ly ['lʌvli] *adj* (-lier; -liest) bello; (coll) delizioso

love' match' s matrimonio d'amore

love' po'tion s filtro d'amore

lover ['lʌvər] s amante m; (*e.g., of music*) amico, appassionato

love' seat' s amorino

love'sick' *adj* malato d'amore

love'sick'ness s mal m d'amore

love' song' s canzone f d'amore

loving ['lʌvɪŋ] *adj* affezionato, amoroso; **your loving son** il vostro affezionato figlio

lov'ing-kind'ness s tenera sollecitudine

low [lo] *adj* basso; (*deep*) profondo; (*diet*) magro; (*visibility*) cattivo; (*dress*) scollato; (*dejected*) abbattuto; (*fire*) lento; (*flame; speed*) piccolo; **to lay low** ammazzare; abbattere; **to lie low** rimanere nascosto; attendere ‖ s punto basso; prezzo minimo; (*of cow*) muggito; (aut) prima velocità; (meteor) depressione ‖ *adv* basso, a basso, in basso ‖ *intr* (*said of a cow*) muggire

low'born' *adj* di umili origini

low'boy' s cassettone basso con le gambe corte

low'brow' *adj & s* (coll) ignorante *mf*

low'-cost hous'ing s case *fpl* popolari

Low' Coun'tries, the i Paesi Bassi

low'-down' *adj* (coll) basso, vile ‖ **low'-down'** s (coll) semplice verità f, notizie *fpl* confidenziali

lower ['lo-ər] *adj* inferiore, disotto ‖ tr abbassare; (*prices*) ribassare ‖ *intr* diminuire; discendere ‖ ['laʊ-ər] *intr* aggrottare le ciglia; (*said of the weather*) imbronciarsi

low'er berth' ['lo-ər] s cuccetta inferiore

low'er case' ['lo-ər] s (typ) cassa inferiore

lower-case ['lo-ər,kes] *adj* (typ) minuscolo

low'er mid'dle class' ['lo-ər] s piccola borghesia

lowermost ['lo-ər,most] *adj* (il) più basso, (l') infimo

low'-fre'quency *adj* a bassa frequenza

low' gear' s prima velocità, prima

lowland ['loland] s pianura ‖ **Lowlands** *spl* Scozia meridionale, bassa Scozia

low•ly ['loli] *adj* (-lier; -liest) umile

Low' Mass' s messa bassa

low-minded ['lo'maɪndɪd] *adj* vile, basso

low-necked ['lo'nekt] *adj* scollato

low-pitched ['lo'pɪtʃt] *adj* (*sound*) basso, grave; (*roof*) poco inclinato

low'-pres'sure *adj* a bassa pressione

low'-priced ['lo'praɪst] *adj* a buon mercato, a basso prezzo

low' shoe' s scarpa bassa

low'-speed' *adj* di piccola velocità

low-spirited ['lo'spɪrɪtɪd] *adj* depresso

low' tide' s bassa marea; (fig) punto più basso

low' visibil'ity s scarsa visibilità

low' wa'ter s (*low tide*) bassa marea; (*of a river*) magra

loyal ['lɔɪ-əl] *adj* leale

loyalist ['lɔɪ-əlɪst] s lealista *mf*

loyal•ty ['lɔɪ-əlti] s (-ties) lealtà f

lozenge ['lazɪndʒ] s losanga; (*candy cough drop*) pasticca, pastiglia

LP ['ɛl'pi] s (letterword) (trademark) disco di grande durata

lubricant ['lubrɪkənt] *adj & s* lubrificante m

lubricate ['lubrɪ,ket] tr lubrificare; (*e.g., one's hands*) ungersi

lubrication [,lubrɪ'keʃən] s lubrificazione

lubricous ['lubrɪkəs] *adj* lubrico; incerto, incostante

lucerne [lu'sʌrn] s erba medica

lucid ['lusɪd] *adj* lucido

Lucifer ['lusɪfər] s Lucifero

luck [lʌk] s (*good or bad*) sorte f; (*good*) sorte f, fortuna; **down on one's luck** in cattive condizioni; **in luck** fortunato; **out of luck** sfortunato; **to bring luck** portare (buona) fortuna; **to try one's luck** tentare la sorte; **worse luck** disgraziatamente

luckily ['lʌkɪli] *adv* fortunatamente

luckless ['lʌklɪs] *adj* sfortunato

luck•y ['lʌki] *adj* (-ier; -iest) fortunato; (*supposed to bring luck*) portafortuna; (*foretelling good luck*) di buon augurio; **to be lucky** aver fortuna

luck'y hit' s (coll) colpo di fortuna

lucrative ['lukrətɪv] *adj* lucrativo

ludicrous ['ludɪkrəs] *adj* ridicolo

lug [lʌg] s manico; (*pull*) tiro; **to put the lug on s.o.** (slang) batter cassa a qlcu ‖ v (*pret & pp* **lugged;** *ger* **lugging**) tr tirarsi dietro; (coll) introdurre a sproposito

luggage ['lʌgɪdʒ] s (*used in traveling*) bagaglio; (*found in a store*) valigeria

lug'gage store' s valigeria

lugubrious [lu'gubrɪ-əs] or [lu'gjubrɪ-əs] *adj* lugubre

lukewarm ['luk,wɔrm] *adj* tiepido

lull [lʌl] s momento di calma, calma ‖ tr calmare, pacificare; addormentare

lulla•by ['lʌlə,baɪ] s (-bies) ninnananna

lumbago [lʌm'bego] s lombaggine f

lumber ['lʌmbər] *s* legname *m*, legno da costruzione; cianfrusaglie *fpl* ‖ *intr* muoversi pesantemente

lum'ber-jack' *s* boscaiolo

lum'ber jack'et *s* giaccone *m*

lum'ber-man *s* (**-men**) (*dealer*) commerciante *m* in legname; (*man who cuts down lumber*) boscaiolo

lum'ber room' *s* ripostiglio

lum'ber-yard' *s* deposito legnami

luminar-y ['lumɪ,nerɪ] *s* (**-ies**) luminare *m*

luminous ['lumɪnəs] *adj* luminoso

lummox ['lʌməks] *s* (coll) scimunito

lump [lʌmp] *s* grumo; mucchio; cumulo; (*swelling*) bernoccolo; (*of sugar*) zolletta; (*in one's throat*) groppo; (coll) stupidone *m*; **in the lump** in blocco; nell'insieme ‖ *tr* mescolare; (*to make into lumps*) raggrumare; **to lump it** (coll) mandarla giù

lumpish ['lʌmpɪʃ] *adj* grumoso; goffo; balordo

lump' sum' *s* ammontare unico, somma globale

lump-y ['lʌmpi] *adj* (**-ier; -iest**) grumoso; (*person*) pesante, ottuso; (*sea*) agitato

luna-cy ['lunəsɪ] *s* (**-cies**) pazzia

lunar ['lunər] *adj* lunare

lu'nar land'ing *s* allunaggio

lu'nar mod'ule *s* modulo lunare

lu'nar rov'er *s* auto *f* lunare

lunatic ['lunətɪk] *adj & s* demente *mf*

lu'natic asy'lum *s* manicomio

lu'natic fringe' *s* estremisti *mpl* fanatici

lunch [lʌntʃ] *s* (*regular midday meal*) seconda colazione; (*light meal*) spuntino, merenda ‖ *intr* fare colazione; fare uno spuntino

lunch' bas'ket *s* portavivande *m*

luncheon ['lʌntʃən] *s* seconda colazione; pranzo ufficiale

luncheonette [,lʌntʃə'nɛt] *s* tavola calda

lunch'eon meat' *s* insaccati *mpl*

lunch'room' *s* tavola calda

lung [lʌŋ] *s* polmone *m*

lunge [lʌndʒ] *s* slancio; (*fencing*) affondo ‖ *intr* slanciarsi

lurch [lʌrtʃ] *s* barcollamento; (*at close of a game*) cappotto; (naut) sbandata; **to leave in the lurch** piantare

in asso ‖ *intr* barcollare; (naut) sbandare

lure [lur] *s* esca; (fig) insidie *fpl* ‖ *tr* adescare; **to lure away** distogliere, sviare

lurid ['lurɪd] *adj* (*fiery*) ardente, acceso; sensazionale; (*gruesome*) orripilante

lurk [lʌrk] *intr* stare in agguato, nascondersi; (fig) essere latente

luscious ['lʌʃəs] *adj* delizioso; lussuoso, lussureggiante; voluttuoso

lush [lʌʃ] *adj* lussureggiante, lussuoso

lust [lʌst] *s* desiderio sfrenato; libidine *f*, lussuria ‖ *intr*—**to lust after** or **for** aver sete di

luster ['lʌstər] *s* (*gloss*) lustro, lucentezza; (*glory*) lustro, onore *m*

lus'ter-ware' *s* ceramiche smaltate

lustful ['lʌstfəl] *adj* lussurioso

lustrous ['lʌstrəs] *adj* lucido

lust-y ['lʌsti] *adj* (**-ier; -iest**) vigoroso, gagliardo

lute [lut] *s* (mus) liuto; (chem) luto

Lutheran ['luθərən] *adj & s* luterano

luxuriance [lʌg'ʒurɪ-əns] *s* rigoglio

luxuriant [lʌg'ʒurɪ-ənt] *adj* lussureggiante; (*imagery*) ridondante

luxuriate [lʌg'ʒurɪ,et] or [lʌk'ʃurɪ,et] *intr* lussureggiare; trovare piacere

luxurious [lʌg'ʒurɪ-əs] or [lʌk'ʃurɪ-əs] *adj* lussuoso, fastoso

luxu-ry ['lʌkʃərɪ] or ['lʌgʒərɪ] *s* (**-ries**) lusso, sfarzo

lye [laɪ] *s* ranno, lisciva

lying ['laɪ-ɪŋ] *adj* menzognero ‖ *s* il mentire

ly'ing-in' hos'pital *s* clinica ostetrica, maternità *f*

lymph [lɪmf] *s* linfa

lymphatic [lɪm'fætɪk] *adj* linfatico

lynch [lɪntʃ] *tr* linciare

lynching ['lɪntʃɪŋ] *s* linciaggio

lynx [lɪŋks] *s* lince *f*

lynx-eyed ['lɪŋks,aɪd] *adj* dagli occhi di lince

lyonnaise [,laɪ-ə'nez] *adj* (culin) alla maniera di Lione

lyre [laɪr] *s* lira

lyric ['lɪrɪk] *adj* lirico ‖ *s* lirica; (*words of a song*) parole *fpl*

lyrical ['lɪrɪkəl] *adj* lirico

lyricism ['lɪrɪ,sɪzəm] *s* lirismo

lyricist ['lɪrɪsɪst] *s* (*writer of words for songs*) paroliere *m*; (*poet*) lirico

M

M, m [ɛm] *s* tredicesima lettera dell'alfabeto inglese

ma'am [mæm] or [mɑm] *s* (coll) signora

macadam [mə'kædəm] *s* macadàm *m*

macadamize [mə'kædə,maɪz] *tr* macadamizzare

macaroni [,mækə'ronɪ] *s* maccheroni *mpl*

macaroon [,mækə'run] *s* amaretto

macaw [mə'kɔ] *s* ara

mace [mes] *s* mazza; (*spice*) macis *m & f*

mace' bear'er *s* mazziere *m*

machination [,mækɪ'neʃən] *s* macchinazione, macchina

machine [mə'ʃin] *s* macchina ‖ *tr* fare a macchina

machine' gun' *s* mitragliatrice *f*

machine'-gun' *v* (*pret & pp* **-gunned**; *ger* **-gunning**) *tr* mitragliare

machine'-made' *adj* fatto a macchina

machiner·y [məˈʃinəri] s (-ies) macchinario, meccanismo

machine′ screw′ s vite f per metallo

machine′ shop′ s officina meccanica

machine′ tool′ s macchina utensile

machinist [məˈʃinɪst] s meccanico; (nav) secondo macchinista

mackerel [ˈmækərəl] s maccarello

mack′erel sky′ s cielo a pecorelle

mackintosh [ˈmækɪn ˌtɑʃ] s impermeabile m

mad [mæd] adj (madder; maddest) (angry; rabid) arrabbiato; (insane; foolish) pazzo, folle; furioso; **to be mad about** (coll) andar pazzo per; **to drive mad** far impazzire; **to go mad** impazzire; (said of a dog) diventare idrofobo

madam [ˈmædəm] s signora

mad′cap′ s mattoide m, rompicollo

madden [ˈmædən] tr (to make angry) inferocire; (to make insane) fare impazzire

made-to-order [ˈmedtəˈɔrdər] adj fatto apposta; (clothing) fatto su misura

made′-up′ adj inventato; (using cosmetics) truccato

mad′house′ s manicomio

mad′man′ s (-men′) pazzo

madness [ˈmædnɪs] s rabbia; pazzia

Madonna lily [məˈdɑnə] s giglio

maelstrom [ˈmelstrəm] s vortice m

magazine [ˈmægə ˌzin] or [ˌmægəˈzin] s (periodical) rivista, giornale m; (warehouse) magazzino; (for cartridges) caricatore m; (for powder) polveriera; (naut) santabarbara; (phot) magazzino

maggot [ˈmægət] s larva di dittero

Magi [ˈmedʒaɪ] spl Re Magi

magic [ˈmædʒɪk] adj magico ‖ s magia; illusionismo; **as if by magic** come per incanto

magician [məˈdʒɪʃən] s (entertainer) illusionista mf; (sorcerer) mago

magistrate [ˈmædʒɪs ˌtret] s magistrato

magnanimous [mægˈnænɪməs] adj magnanimo

magnesium [mægˈniʃɪ·əm] or [mægˈniʒɪ·əm] s magnesio

magnet [ˈmægnɪt] s calamita, magnete m

magnetic [mægˈnetɪk] adj magnetico

magnetism [ˈmægnɪ ˌtɪzəm] s magnetismo

magnetize [ˈmægnɪ ˌtaɪz] tr calamitare, magnetizzare

magne·to [mægˈnito] s (-tos) magnete m

magnificent [mægˈnɪfɪsənt] adj magnifico

magni·fy [ˈmægnɪ ˌfaɪ] v (pret & pp -fied) tr ingrandire; (to exaggerate) magnificare

mag′nifying glass′ s lente f d'ingrandimento

magnitude [ˈmægnɪ ˌtjud] or [ˈmægnɪ ˌtud] s grandezza

magpie [ˈmæg ˌpaɪ] s gazza

mahlstick [ˈmɑl ˌstɪk] or [ˈmɔl ˌstɪk] s appoggiamano

mahoga·ny [məˈhɑgəni] s (-nies) mogano

Mahomet [məˈhɑmɪt] s Maometto

maid [med] s (girl) ragazza; (servant) cameriera, domestica

maiden [ˈmedən] s pulzella

maid′en·hair′ s (bot) capelvenere m

maid′en·head′ s imene m

maidenhood [ˈmedən ˌhʊd] s verginità f

maid′en la′dy s zitella

maid′en name′ s nome m da signorina

maid′en voy′age s viaggio inaugurale

maid′-in-wait′ing s (maids-in-waiting) (of a princess) damigella d'onore; (of a queen) dama d'onore

maid′ of hon′or s (attendant at a wedding; attendant of a princess) damigella d'onore; (attendant of a queen) dama d'onore

maid′serv′ant s domestica, ancella

mail [mel] s posta; (of armor) maglia; **by return mail** a volta di corriere ‖ tr impostare

mail′bag′ s sacco postale

mail′boat′ s battello postale

mail′box′ s cassetta o buca delle lettere

mail′ car′ s vagone m postale

mail′ car′rier s postino, portalettere m

mail′ing list′ s indirizzario

mail′ing per′mit s abbonamento postale

mail′man′ s (-men′) portalettere m

mail′ or′der s ordinazione per corrispondenza

mail′-order house′ s ditta che fa affari unicamente per corrispondenza

mail′plane′ s aeroplano postale

mail′ train′ s treno postale

maim [mem] tr mutilare

main [men] adj principale, maggiore ‖ s condotta principale; **in the main** principalmente, per lo più

main′ clause′ s proposizione principale

main′ course′ s piatto forte

main′ deck′ s ponte m principale

mainland [ˈmen ˌlænd] or [ˈmenlənd] s terra ferma, continente m

main′ line′ s (rr) linea principale

mainly [ˈmenli] adv principalmente

mainmast [ˈmenmɑst], [ˈmen ˌmæst] or [ˈmen ˌmɑst] s albero maestro

mainsail [ˈmensəl] or [ˈmen ˌsel] s vela maestra

main′spring′ s molla motrice; (fig) molla

main′stay′ s (naut) strallo di maestra; (fig) cardine m

main′ street′ s strada principale

maintain [menˈten] tr mantenere

maintenance [ˈmentɪnəns] s mantenimento; (upkeep) manutenzione

maître d'hôtel [ˌmetər doˈtel] s (butler) maggiordomo; (headwaiter) capocameriere m

maize [mez] s mais m

majestic [məˈdʒestɪk] adj maestoso

majes·ty [ˈmædʒɪsti] s (-ties) maestà f

major [ˈmedʒər] adj maggiore ‖ s (educ) specializzazione; (mil) maggiore m ‖ intr (educ) specializzarsi

major·do·mo [ˌmedʒərˈdomo] s (-mos) maggiordomo

ma′jor gen′eral s generale m di divisione

majori·ty [mə'dʒɑrɪti] or [mə'dʒɔrɪti] *adj* maggioritario ‖ *s* (**-ties**) (*being of full age*) maggiore età *f;* (*larger number or part*) maggioranza; (mil) grado di maggiore

make [mek] *s* (*brand*) marca; (*form*) stile *m;* produzione; **on the make** (slang) tirando l'acqua al proprio mulino ‖ *v* (*pret & pp* **made** [med]) *tr* fare; (*a train*) pigliare; (*a circuit*) chiudere; essere, e.g., **she will make a good typist** sarà una buona dattilografa; **to make** + *inf* fare + *inf,* e.g., **she made him study** lo fece studiare; **to make into** trasformare in; **to make known** far sapere; **to make of** pensare di; **to make oneself known** darsi a conoscere; **to make out** decifrare; (*a prescription*) scrivere, preparare; (*a check*) riempire; **to make over** convertire; (com) trasferire; **to make up** preparare, comporre; (*a story*) inventare; (*lost time*) riguadagnare; (typ) impaginare; (theat) truccare ‖ *intr* essere fatto; **to make away with** rubare; disfarsi di; **to make believe that** + *inf* far finta di + *inf,* e.g., **he made believe (that) he was sleeping** fece finta di dormire; **to make for** avvicinarsi a; attaccare; (*better relations*) contribuire a cementare; **to make much of** (coll) fare le feste a; **to make off** andarsene; **to make off with** svignarsela con; **to make out** (coll) farcela; **to make toward** incamminarsi verso; **to make up** truccarsi; fare la pace; **to make up for** compensare per, supplire a; **to make up to** (coll) ingraziarsi; (coll) fare la corte a

make'-be·lieve' *adj* immaginario ‖ *s* finzione, sembianza

maker ['mekər] *s* fabbricante *mf,* costruttore *m* ‖ **Maker** *s* Fattore *m*

make'shift' *adj* improvvisato, di fortuna ‖ *s* espediente *m,* ripiego; (*person*) tappabuchi *mf*

make'-up' *s* composizione, costituzione, truccatura, cosmetico; (typ) impaginazione; (journ) caratteristica

make'-up man' *s* truccatore *m*

make'-up test' *s* esame *m* di riparazione

make'weight' *s* giunta, contentino; (fig) supplemento, di più *m*

making ['mekɪŋ] *s* fabbricazione; costituzione; causa del successo; **makings** materiale *m;* (*potential*) stoffa

maladjusted [,mælə'dʒʌstɪd] *adj* spostato

mala·dy ['mælədi] *s* (**-dies**) malattia

malaise [mæ'lez] *s* malessere *m*

malapropos [,mæləprə'po] *adj* inopportuno ‖ *adv* a sproposito

malaria [mə'lɛrɪ·ə] *s* malaria

Malay ['mele] or [mə'le] *adj & s* malese *mf*

malcontent ['mælkən,tent] *adj & s* malcontento

male [mel] *adj & s* maschio

malediction [,mælɪ'dɪkʃən] *s* maledizione

malefactor ['mælɪ,fæktər] *s* malfattore *m*

male' nurse' *s* infermiere *m*

malevolent [mə'levələnt] *adj* malevolo

malfeasance [mæl'fizəns] *s* reato di pubblico funzionario

malice ['mælɪs] *s* malizia; (law) dolo; **to bear malice** serbar rancore; **with malice prepense** (law) con premeditazione

malicious [mə'lɪʃəs] *adj* malizioso, maligno

malign [mə'laɪn] *adj* maligno ‖ *tr* calunniare

malignan·cy [mə'lɪgnənsi] *s* (**-cies**) malignità *f;* (pathol) malignità *f*

malignant [mə'lɪgnənt] *adj* maligno

maligni·ty [mə'lɪgnɪti] *s* (**-ties**) malignità *f*

malinger [mə'lɪŋgər] *intr* fingersi ammalato, darsi malato (per sottrarsi al proprio dovere)

mall [mɔl] or [mæl] *s* viale *m;* (*strip of land in a boulevard*) aiola

mallet ['mælɪt] *s* maglio; (*of a stone cutter*) mazzuolo

mallow ['mælo] *s* malva

malnutrition [,mælnju'trɪʃən] or [,mælnu'trɪʃən] *s* malnutrizione

malodorous [mæl'odərəs] *adj* puzzolente

malpractice [mæl'præktɪs] *s* incuria, negligenza; (*of physician or lawyer*) negligenza colposa

malt [mɔlt] *s* malto

maltreat [mæl'trit] *tr* maltrattare

mamma ['mɑmə] or [mə'mɑ] *s* (coll) mamma

mammal ['mæməl] *s* mammifero

mammalian [mæ'melɪ·ən] *adj & s* mammifero

mammoth ['mæməθ] *adj* mastodontico ‖ *s* mammut *m*

man [mæn] *s* (**men** [men]) uomo; (*in chess*) pedina; (*in checkers*) pezzo; a man uno, e.g., **a man can get lost in this town** uno può perdersi in questa città; **as one man** come un sol uomo; **man alive!** accidenti!; **man and wife** marito e moglie; **to be one's own man** essere completamente indipendente ‖ *v* (*pret & pp* **manned;** *ger* **manning**) *tr* (*a boat*) equipaggiare; (*a fortress*) guarnire; (*a cannon*) maneggiare

man' about town' *s* vitaiolo

manacle ['mænəkəl] *s*—**manacles** manette *fpl* ‖ *tr* ammanettare

manage ['mænɪdʒ] *tr* (*a business*) gestire; (*e.g., a tool*) maneggiare ‖ *intr* sbrogliarsela; **to manage to** fare in modo di; ingegnarsi a; **to manage to get along** barcamenarsi

manageable ['mænɪdʒəbəl] *adj* maneggevole

management ['mænɪdʒmənt] *s* direzione, gestione; (*executives collectively*) classe *f* dirigente; direzione; (*college course*) economia aziendale

manager ['mænədʒər] *s* direttore *m,* gerente *mf;* (theat) impresario; (sports) procuratore *m,* manager *m*

managerial [,mænə'dʒɪrɪ·əl] *adj* direttoriale, imprenditoriale

man'aging ed'itor *s* gerente *m* responsabile, redattore *m* in capo
mandate ['mændet] *s* mandato || *tr* dare in mandato a
mandatory ['mændə‚tori] *adj* obbligatorio
mandolin ['mændəlɪn] *s* mandolino
mandrake ['mændrek] *s* mandragola
mandrel ['mændrəl] *s* (mach) mandrino
mane [men] *s* criniera
maneuver [mə'nuvər] *s* manovra || *tr* manovrare || *intr* manovrare; (aer, nav) evoluire; (fig) intrigare
manful ['mænfəl] *adj* maschile, risoluto
manganese ['mæŋgə‚nis] or ['mæŋgə‚niz] *s* manganese *m*
mange [mendʒ] *s* rogna
manger ['mendʒər] *s* presepio
mangle ['mæŋgəl] *tr* straziare, lacerare
man-gy ['mendʒi] *adj* (-gier; -giest) rognoso; (squalid) misero
man'han'dle *tr* malmenare, maltrattare
man'hole' *s* passo d'uomo, pozzetto
manhood ['mænhud] *s* virilità *f*; uomini *mpl*, umanità *f*
man'hunt' *s* caccia all'uomo
mania ['menɪ‚ə] *s* mania
maniac ['menɪ‚æk] *adj & s* maniaco
manicure ['mænɪ‚kjʊr] *s* (treatment) manicure *f*; (manicurist) manicure *mf* || *tr* (a person) curare le mani di; (the hands) curare
manicurist ['mænɪ‚kjʊrɪst] *s* manicurista *mf*, manicure *mf*
manifest ['mænɪ‚fest] *adj* manifesto || *s* (naut) manifesto di carico || *tr* manifestare
manifes-to [‚mænɪ'festo] *s* (-toes) manifesto
manifold ['mænɪ‚fold] *adj* molteplice || *s* copia; carta velina; (aut, mach) collettore *m*
manikin ['mænɪkɪn] *s* manichino; (dwarf) nano
man' in the moon' *s* faccia di uomo che appare nella luna piena
man' in the street' *s* uomo qualunque, uomo della strada
manipulate [mə'nɪpjə‚let] *tr* manipolare
man'kind' *s* genere umano || **man'kind'** *s* il sesso maschile
manliness ['mænlɪnɪs] *s* virilità *f*
man-ly ['mænli] *adj* (-lier; -liest) maschio, virile
manned' space'ship *s* astronave pilotata
mannequin ['mænɪkɪn] *s* (figure) manichino; (person) indossatrice *f*
manner ['mænər] *s* maniera; by all manner of means in tutti i modi; in a manner of speaking in una certa maniera; in the manner of alla moda di; manners maniere, *fpl*, educazione; to the manner born avvezzo sin dalla nascita
mannish ['mænɪʃ] *adj* maschile; (woman) mascolino
man' of God' *s* santo; profeta *m*; (priest) uomo al servizio di Dio

man' of let'ters *s* letterato
man' of means' *s* uomo danaroso
man' of parts' *s* uomo di talento
man' of straw' *s* uomo di paglia
man' of the world' *s* uomo di mondo
man-of-war [‚mænəv'wɔr] *s* (men-of-war [‚menəv'wɔr] nave *f* da guerra
manor ['mænər] *s* maniero; feudo
man'or house' *s* maniero, palazzo
man' o'verboard *interj* uomo in mare!
man'pow'er *s* manodopera; (mil) effettivo
mansard ['mænsard] *s* mansarda
man'serv'ant *s* (men'serv'ants) servo, servitore *m*
mansion ['mænʃən] *s* palazzo, palazzina; (manor house) maniero
man'slaugh'ter *s* omicidio colposo
mantel ['mæntəl] *s* parte *f* anteriore dei pilastri del camino; (shelf above it) mensola
man'tel-piece' *s* mensola del camino
man'tis shrimp' ['mæntɪs] *s* canocchia
mantle ['mæntəl] *s* mantello, cappa || *tr* ammantare; (to conceal) nascondere || *intr* (to blush) arrossire
manual ['mænjʊ‚əl] *adj* manuale || *s* (book) manuale *m*; (mil) esercizio; (mus) tastiera d'organo
man'ual train'ing *s* istruzione nelle arti e mestieri
manufacture [‚mænjə'fæktʃər] *s* fabbricazione; (thing manufactured) manufatto || *tr* fabbricare
manufacturer [‚mænjə'fæktʃərər] *s* fabbricante *mf*, industriale *m*
manure [mə'njʊr] or [mə'nʊr] *s* letame *m* || *tr* concimare
manuscript ['mænjə‚skrɪpt] *adj & s* manoscritto
many ['meni] *adj & pron* molti; a good many or a great many un buon numero; as many . . . as tanti . . . quanti; as many as fino a, e.g., they sell as many as five thousand dozen vendono fino a cinquemila dozzine; how many quanti; many a molti, e.g., many a day molti giorni; many another molti altri; many more molti di più; so many tanti; too many troppi; twice as many altrettanti, il doppio
many-sided ['meni‚saɪdɪd] *adj* multilaterale; versatile
map [mæp] *s* mappa; (of a city) piano || *v* (pret & pp mapped; ger mapping) *tr* tracciare la mappa di; mostrare sulla mappa; to map out fare il piano di
maple ['mepəl] *s* acero
maquette [mɑ'ket] *s* plastico
mar [mɑr] *v* (pret & pp marred; ger marring) *tr* deturpare, sfigurare
maraud [mə'rɔd] *tr & intr* predare
marauder [mə'rɔdər] *s* predone *m*
marble ['mɑrbəl] *adj* marmoreo || *s* marmo; (little ball of glass) bilia; marbles bilie *fpl*; to lose one's marbles (slang) mancare una rotella a qlcu || *tr* marmorizzare
march [mɑrtʃ] *s* marcia; (hist) marca; to steal a march on guadagnare il

vantaggio su || *tr* far marciare || *intr* marciare || **March** *s* marzo

marchioness ['mɑr/ənɪs] *s* marchesa

mare [mer] *s (female horse)* cavalla; *(female donkey)* asina

margarine ['mɑrdʒərɪn] *s* margarina

margin ['mɑrdʒɪn] *s* margine *m*; (econ) scoperto

mar'gin stop' *s* marginatore *m*

marigold ['mærɪ ,gold] *s* fiorrancio

marihuana or **marijuana** [,mɑrɪ-'hwɑnə] *s* marijuana

marina [mə'rinə] *s* porto turistico di imbarcazioni, porticciolo turistico

marinate ['mærɪ ,net] *tr* marinare

marine [mə'rin] *adj* marino, marittimo || *s* marina; soldato di fanteria da sbarco; **marines** fanteria da sbarco; **tell that to the marines!** (coll) va a raccontarlo ai frati!

mariner ['mærɪnər] *s* marinaio

marionette [,mærɪ-ə'nɛt] *s* marionetta

mar'ital sta'tus ['mærɪtəl] *s* stato civile

maritime ['mærɪ ,taɪm] *adj* marittimo

marjoram ['mɑrdʒərəm] *s* origano; *(sweet marjoram)* maggiorana

mark [mɑrk] *s* segno; *(brand)* marca; *(of punctuation)* punto; *(in an examination)* voto; *(sign made by illiterate person)* croce *f*; *(landmark)* segnale *m*; *(target)* bersaglio; *(spot)* macchia; *(starting point in a race)* linea di partenza; *(of confidence)* voto; *(coin)* marco; impronta; **to be beside the mark** essere fuori del seminato; **to hit the mark** colpire il bersaglio; **to leave one's mark** lasciare la propria impronta; **to make one's mark** raggiungere il successo; **to miss the mark** fallire il colpo; **to toe the mark** mettersi in fila; filare diritto || *tr* marcare, segnare, contrassegnare; *(a student)* dar il voto a; *(a test)* esaminare; improntare; notare, avvertire; **to mark down** mettere in iscritto; ribassare il prezzo di

mark'down' *s* riduzione di prezzo

market ['mɑrkɪt] *s* mercato; **to bear the market** giocare al ribasso; **to bull the market** giocare al rialzo; **to play the market** giocare in borsa; **to put on the market** lanciare sul mercato || *tr* mettere sul mercato

marketable ['mɑrkɪtəbəl] *adj* commerciabile, vendibile

marketing ['mɑrkɪtɪŋ] *s* compravendita; marketing *m*

mar'ket-place' *s* piazza del mercato

mar'ket price' *s* prezzo corrente

mark'ing gauge' ['mɑrkɪŋ] *s* graffietto

marks'man *s* (-men) tiratore *m*; **a good marksman** un tiratore scelto

marksmanship ['mɑrksmən ,ʃɪp] *s* qualità *f* di tiratore scelto

mark'up' *s* margine *m* di rivendita

marl [mɑrl] *s* marna || *tr* marnare

marmalade ['mɑrmə ,led] *s* marmellata d'arance

marmot ['mɑrmət] *s* marmotta

maroon [mə'run] *adj & s* marrone *m* || *tr* abbandonare *(in un luogo deserto)*

marquee [mɑr'ki] *s* pensilina

marquess ['mɑrkwɪs] *s* marchese *m*

marque·try ['mɑrkətrɪ] *s* (-tries) intarsio

marquis ['mɑrkwɪs] *s* marchese *m*

marquise [mɑr'kiz] *s* marchesa; (Brit) pensilina

marriage ['mærɪdʒ] *s* matrimonio

marriageable ['mærɪdʒəbəl] *adj* adatto al matrimonio; *(woman)* nubile

mar'riage por'tion *s* dote *f*

mar'riage rate' *s* nuzialità *f*

mar'ried life' *s* vita coniugale

marrow ['mæro] *s* midollo

mar·ry ['mærɪ] *v (pret & pp -ried) tr* sposare; **to get married to** sposarsi con || *intr* sposarsi; **to marry into** *(e.g., a noble family)* imparentarsi con; **to marry the second time** risposarsi

Mars [mɑrz] *s* Marte *m*

Marseilles [mɑr'selz] *s* Marsiglia

marsh [mɑrʃ] *s* palude *f*, lama

mar·shal ['mɑrʃəl] *s* direttore *m* di una sfilata; maestro di cerimonie; (mil) maresciallo; (U.S.A.) ufficiale *m* di giustizia || *v (pret & pp -shaled* or *-shalled) ger -shaling* or *-shalling) tr* introdurre cerimoniosamente; mettere in buon ordine

marsh' mal'low *s* (bot) altea

marsh'mal'low *s* dolce *m* di gelatina e zucchero

marsh·y ['mɑrʃɪ] *adj* (-ier; -iest) paludoso, palustre

marten ['mɑrtən] *s (Martes martes)* martora; *(Martes zibellina)* zibellino

martial ['mɑrʃəl] *adj* marziale

mar'tial law' *s* legge *f* marziale

Martian ['mɑrʃən] *adj & s* marziano

martin ['mɑrtɪn] *s* rondicchio

martinet [,mɑrtɪ'nɛt] or ['mɑrtɪ ,nɛt] *s* pignolo

martyr ['mɑrtər] *s* martire *mf*

martyrdom ['mɑrtərdəm] *s* martirio

mar·vel ['mɑrvəl] *s* meraviglia || *v (pret & pp -veled* or *-velled) ger -veling* or *-velling) intr* meravigliarsi; **to marvel at** stupirsi di, meravigliarsi di

marvelous ['mɑrvələs] *adj* meraviglioso

Marxist ['mɑrksɪst] *adj & s* marxista *mf*

mascara [mæs'kærə] *s* bistro, rimmel *m*

mascot ['mæskət] *s* mascotte *f*

masculine ['mæskjəlɪn] *adj & s* maschile *m*

mash [mæʃ] *s (crushed mass)* poltiglia; *(to form wort)* decotto d'orzo germinato; *(e.g., for poultry)* intriso || *tr* schiacciare; impastare

mashed' pota'toes *spl* purè *m* di patate

masher ['mæʃər] *s* utensile *m* per schiacciare; (slang) pappagallo

mask [mæsk] or [mɑsk] *s* maschera; (phot) mascherina || *tr* mascherare; (phot) mettere una mascherina a || *intr* mascherarsi

masked' ball' *s* ballo in maschera

mason ['mesən] *s* muratore *m* || **Mason** *s* massone *m*

mason·ry ['mesənrɪ] *s* (-ries) arte *f* del

muratore; muratura || **Masonry** *s* massoneria

masquerade [‚mæskəˈred] or [‚mɑskəˈred] *s* mascherata; (*disguise*) maschera; (*pretense*) finzione || *intr* mascherarsi; **to masquerade as** mascherarsi da; farsi passare per

mass [mæs] *s* massa; (*celebration of the Eucharist*) messa; **in the mass** nell'insieme; **the masses** le masse || *tr* ammassare || *intr* ammassarsi, accumularsi

massacre [ˈmæsəkər] *s* massacro, strage *f* || *tr* massacrare, trucidare

massage [məˈsɑʒ] *s* massaggio || *tr* massaggiare

masseur [mæˈsœr] *s* massaggiatore *m*

masseuse [mæˈsœz] *s* massaggiatrice *f*

massive [ˈmæsɪv] *adj* massiccio; (*e.g., dose*) massivo; solido

mass' me'dia [ˈmɪdɪˌə] *s* mezzi *mpl* di comunicazione di massa

mass' meet'ing *s* assemblea popolare; adunanza in massa

mass' produc'tion *s* produzione in serie

mast [mæst] or [mɑst] *s* (*post*) palo; (*agr*) ghiande *fpl*, faggiole *fpl*; (*naut*) albero; **before the mast** come marinaio semplice

master [ˈmæstər] or [ˈmɑstər] *s* (*employer*) padrone *m*; (*male head of household*) capo di casa; (*man who possesses some special skill*) maestro; (*title of respect for a boy*) signorino; (*naut*) capitano || *tr* dominare; (*a language*) possedere

mas'ter bed'room *s* camera da letto padronale

mas'ter blade' *s* foglia maestra (di una balestra)

mas'ter build'er *s* capomastro

masterful [ˈmæstərfəl] or [ˈmɑstərfəl] *adj* autoritario; provetto, magistrale

mas'ter key' *s* chiave maestra

masterly [ˈmæstərli] or [ˈmɑstərli] *adj* magistrale || *adv* magistralmente

mas'ter mechan'ic *s* mastro meccanico

mas'ter-mind' *s* mente direttiva || *tr* organizzare, dirigere

mas'ter of cer'emonies *s* maestro di cerimonia; (*in a night club, radio, etc.*) presentatore *m*

mas'ter-piece' *s* capolavoro

mas'ter ser'geant *s* (mil) sergente *m* maggiore

mas'ter stroke' *s* colpo da maestro

mas'ter-work' *s* capolavoro

master·y [ˈmæstəri] or [ˈmɑstəri] *s* (-ies) (*command of a subject*) dominio; (*skill*) maestria

mast'head' *s* (journ) titolo; (naut) testa d'albero

masticate [ˈmæstɪˌket] *tr* masticare

mastiff [ˈmæstɪf] or [ˈmɑstɪf] *s* mastino

masturbate [ˈmæstərˌbet] *tr* masturbare || *intr* masturbarsi

mat [mæt] *s* (*for floor*) tappeto, stuoia; (*under a dish*) tondo, sottocoppa, centrino; (*before a door*) stoino, zerbino; (*around a picture*) bordo di cartone; (sports) materas-

sino; (typ) flan *m*; flano || *v* (*pret & pp* **matted**; *ger* **matting**) *tr* coprire di stuoie; arruffare || *intr* arruffarsi

match [mæt ʃ] *s* (*counterpart*) uguale *m*; (*suitably associated pair*) paio; (*light*) fiammifero; (*wick*) miccia; (*prospective mate*) partito; (sports) partita, gara; **to be a match for** essere pari a, fare fronte a; **to meet one's match** trovare un degno rivale || *tr* uguagliare, pareggiare; (*colors*) combinare; (*in pairs*) appaiare; giocarsi, e.g., **to match s.o. for the drinks** giocarsi le bevande con qlcu || *intr* corrispondersi, fare il paio

match'box' *s* scatola di fiammiferi; (*of wax matches*) scatola di cerini

matchless [ˈmætʃlɪs] *adj* incomparabile, senza pari

match'mak'er *s* paraninfo

mate [met] *s* compagno; (*husband or wife*) consorte *mf*; (*to a female*) maschio; (*to a male*) femmina; (chess) scacco matto; (naut) primo ufficiale || *tr* appaiare; (chess) dar scacco matto a; **to be well mated** esser ben appaiato || *intr* accoppiarsi

material [məˈtɪrɪəl] *adj* materiale; importante || *s* materiale *m*, materia; (*cloth, fabric*) tela, stoffa; **materials** occorrente *m*

materialist [məˈtɪrɪəlɪst] *s* materialista *mf*

materialize [məˈtɪrɪəˌlaɪz] *intr* materializzarsi

matériel [məˌtɪrɪˈel] *s* materiale *m*; materiale bellico

maternal [məˈtʌrnəl] *adj* materno

maternity [məˈtʌrnɪti] *s* maternità *f*

mater'nity ward' *s* maternità *f*

mathematical [‚mæθɪˈmætɪkəl] *adj* matematico

mathematician [‚mæθɪməˈtɪ ʃən] *s* matematico

mathematics [‚mæθɪˈmætɪks] *s* matematica

matinée [‚mætɪˈne] *s* mattinata, diurna

mat'ing sea'son *s* calore *m*

matins [ˈmætɪnz] *spl* mattutino

matriarch [ˈmetrɪˌɑrk] *s* matrona dignitosa; donna che possiede l'autorità matriarcale

matricidal [‚metrɪˈsaɪdəl] or [‚mætrɪˈsaɪdəl] *adj* matricida

matricide [ˈmetrɪˌsaɪd] or [ˈmætrɪˌsaɪd] *s* (*act*) matricidio; (*person*) matricida *mf*

matriculate [məˈtrɪkjəˌlet] *tr* immatricolare || *intr* immatricolarsi

matriculation [məˌtrɪkjəˈle ʃən] *s* immatricolazione, iscrizione

matrimonial [‚mætrɪˈmonɪəl] *adj* matrimoniale

matrimo·ny [ˈmætrɪˌmoni] *s* (-nies) matrimonio

ma·trix [ˈmetrɪks] or [ˈmætrɪks] *s* (-trices [trɪˌsiz] or -trixes) matrice *f*

matron [ˈmetrən] *s* matrona; direttrice *f*; guardiana

matronly [ˈmetrənli] *adj* matronale

matter [ˈmætər] *s* (*physical substance*) materia; (*pus*) materia; (*affair, busi-*

ness) faccenda; *(material of a book)* contenuto; *(reason)* motivo; *(copy for printer)* manoscritto; *(printed material)* stampati *mpl;* **a matter of** un caso di; **for that matter** per quanto riguarda ciò; **in the matter** al soggetto; **no matter** non importa; **no matter how** non importa come; **no matter when** non importa quando; **no matter where** non importa dove; **what is the matter?** cosa succede?; **what is the matter with you?** cosa ha? || *intr* importare

mat′ter of course′ *s*—**as a matter of course** come se nulla fosse, come se fosse una cosa naturale

mat′ter of fact′ *s*—**as a matter of fact** in realtà, a onor del vero

matter-of-fact [ˈmætərəv͵fækt] *adj* prosaico, pratico

mattock [ˈmætək] *s* piccone *m*

mattress [ˈmætrɪs] *s* materasso

mature [məˈtʃur] or [məˈtur] *adj* maturo; *(due)* scaduto || *tr* maturare || *intr* maturare; *(com)* scadere

maturity [məˈtʃurɪti] or [məˈturɪti] *s* maturità *f;* *(com)* scadenza

maudlin [ˈmɔdlɪn] *adj* sentimentale, lagrimoso; piagnucoloso e ubriaco

maul [mɔl] *tr* maltrattare, bistrattare

maulstick [ˈmɔl͵stɪk] *s* appoggiamano

maundy [ˈmɔndi] *s* lavanda

Maun′dy Thurs′day *s* giovedì santo

mausoleum [͵mɔsəˈli·əm] *s* (-ums or -a [ə]) mausoleo

maw [mɔ] *s* *(e.g., of a hog)* stomaco; *(of carnivorous mammal)* fauci *fpl;* *(of fowl)* gozzo; *(fig)* bocca, fauci *fpl*

mawkish [ˈmɔkɪʃ] *adj (sickening)* nauseante; *(sentimental)* svenevole

maxim [ˈmæksɪm] *s* massima

maximum [ˈmæksɪməm] *adj* & *s* massimo

may [me] *v aux*—**it may be** può essere; **may I come in?** si può?; **may you be happy!** possa tu essere felice! || **May** *s* maggio

maybe [ˈmebi] *adv* forse

May′ Day′ *s* primo maggio; festa della primavera; *(hist)* calendimaggio *(in Florence)*

mayhem [ˈmehem] or [ˈme·əm] *s* mutilazione dolosa

mayonnaise [͵me·əˈnez] *s* maionese *f*

mayor [ˈme·ər] or [mɛr] *s* sindaco

mayoress [ˈme·ərɪs] or [ˈmɛrɪs] *s* donna sindaco

May′pole′ *s* maio, maggio, palo per le danze di calendimaggio

May′pole dance′ *s* ballo figurato con nastri per la festa di primavera

May′ queen′ *s* reginetta di maggio

maze [mez] *s* dedalo, labirinto

me [mi] *pron* me; mi; **to me** mi; **a me**

meadow [ˈmedo] *s* prato

mead′ow·land′ *s* prateria

meager [ˈmigər] *adj* magro

meal [mil] *s (food)* pasto; *(unbolted grain)* farina

meal′time′ *s* ora del pasto

mean [min] *adj (intermediate)* medio;

(low in rank) basso, umile; *(shabby)* misero; *(of poor quality)* inferiore; *(stingy)* taccagno; *(nasty)* villano; *(vicious, as a horse)* intrattabile; *(coll)* indisposto; *(coll)* vergognoso; *(slang)* splendido; **no mean** eccellente || *s* media, termine medio; **by all means** certamente, senza dubbio; **by means of** per mezzo di; **by no means** in nessuna maniera; **means** beni *mpl;* *(agency)* mezzo, maniera; **to live on one's means** vivere di rendita || *v (pret & pp* **meant** [ment]) *tr* significare, voler dire; **to mean to** pensare || *intr*—**to mean well** aver buone intenzioni

meander [mɪˈændər] *s* meandro || *intr* serpeggiare, vagare

meaning [ˈminɪŋ] *s* senso, significato

meaningful [ˈminɪŋfəl] *adj* significativo

meaningless [ˈminɪŋlɪs] *adj* senza senso, senza significato

meanness [ˈminnɪs] *s* viltà *f,* bassezza; *(stinginess)* meschinità *f;* *(lowliness)* umiltà *f,* povertà *f*

mean′time′ *s*—**in the meantime** nel frattempo || *adv* frattanto, intanto

mean′while′ *s* & *adv* var of **meantime**

measles [ˈmizəlz] *s* morbillo; *(German measles)* rosolia

mea·sly [ˈmizli] *adj* (-sli·er; -sli·est) col morbillo; *(coll)* miserabile

measurable [ˈmeʒərəbəl] *adj* misurabile

measure [ˈmeʒər] *s* misura; *(legislative bill)* progetto di legge; *(mus)* battuta; **in a measure** in un certo senso; **to take the measure of** prendere le misure di; giudicare accuratamente || *tr* misurare; *(a distance)* percorrere; **to measure out** somministrare || *intr* misurare; **to measure up to** essere all'altezza di

measurement [ˈmeʒərmənt] *s* misura; **to take s.o.'s measurements** prendere le misure di qlcu

meas′uring cup′ *s* vetro graduato

meat [mit] *s* carne *f;* *(food in general)* cibo; *(of nut)* gheriglio; *(fig)* sostanza, midollo

meat′ball′ *s* polpetta

meat′ grind′er *s* tritacarne *m*

meat′ loaf′ *s* polpettone *m*

meat′ mar′ket *s* macelleria

meat·y [ˈmiti] *adj* (-i·er; -i·est) carnoso, polputo; *(fig)* sostanzioso

Mecca [ˈmekə] *s* la Mecca; **the Mecca** *(fig)* la Mecca

mechanic [mɪˈkænɪk] *s* meccanico; *(aut)* motorista *m*

mechanical [mɪˈkænɪkəl] *adj* meccanico; *(machinelike)* (fig) macchinale

mechan′ical engineer′ing *s* ingegneria meccanica

mechan′ical pen′cil *s* matita automatica

mechanics [mɪˈkænɪks] *s* meccanica

mechanism [ˈmekə͵nɪzəm] *s* meccanismo, congegno

mechanize [ˈmekə͵naɪz] *tr* meccanizzare

medal [ˈmedəl] *s* medaglia

medallion [mɪˈdæljən] *s* medaglione *m*

meddle ['mɛdəl] *intr* intromettersi
meddler ['mɛdlər] *s* ficcanaso
meddlesome ['mɛdəlsəm] *adj* invadente, indiscreto
median ['midɪ·ən] *adj* medio, mediano || *s* punto medio, numero medio
me'dian strip' *s* spartitraffico
mediate ['midɪ,et] *tr (a dispute)* comporre; *(parties)* pacificare || *intr (to be in the middle)* mediare; fare da paciere
mediation [,midɪ'eʃən] *s* mediazione
mediator ['midɪ,etər] *s* mediatore *m*
medical ['mɛdɪkəl] *adj* medico; *(student)* di medicina
medicinal [mə'dɪsɪnəl] *adj* medicinale
medicine ['mɛdɪsɪn] *s* medicina
med'icine cab'inet *s* armadietto farmaceutico
med'icine kit' *s* cassetta farmaceutica
med'icine man' *s* (**men'**) stregone indiano
medieval [,midɪ'ivəl] *or* [,mɛdɪ'ivəl] *adj* medievale
medievalist [,midɪ'ivəlɪst] *or* [,mɛdɪ'ivəlɪst] *s* medievalista *mf*
mediocre ['midɪ,okər] *or* [,midɪ'okər] *adj* mediocre
mediocri·ty [,midɪ'akrɪti] *s* (**-ties**) mediocrità *f*
meditate ['mɛdɪ,tet] *tr & intr* meditare
meditation [,mɛdɪ'teʃən] *s* meditazione
Mediterranean [,mɛdɪtə'renɪ·ən] *adj & s* Mediterraneo
medi·um ['midɪ·əm] *adj* medio; *(heat)* moderato; *(meat)* cotto moderatamente || *s* (**-ums** *or* **-a** [ə]) *(middle state; mean)* media; mezzo; *(in spiritualism)* medium *m*; **media** *(of communication)* media *mpl*; **through the medium of** per mezzo di
medlar ['mɛdlər] *s* (*tree*) nespolo; (*fruit*) nespola
medley ['mɛdli] *s* farragine *f*, mescolanza; (*mus*) pot-pourri *m*
medul·la [mɪ'dʌlə] *s* (**-lae** [li]) midollo
meek [mik] *adj* mansueto, umile
meekness ['miknɪs] *s* mansuetudine *f*
meerschaum ['mɪrʃəm] *or* ['mɪrʃəm] *s* schiuma; pipa di schiuma
meet [mit] *adj* conveniente || *s* incontro || *v* (*pret & pp* **met** [mɛt]) *tr* incontrare, incontrarsi con; (*to become acquainted with*) fare la conoscenza di; riunirsi con; (*to cope with*) sopperire a; (*said of a public carrier*) fare coincidenza con; andar incontro a; (*one's obligations*) far fronte a; (*bad luck*) avere; **to meet the eyes of** presentarsi agli occhi di || *intr* incontrarsi; riunirsi; conoscersi; **till we meet again** arrivederci; **to meet with** incontrare, incontrarsi con; (*an accident*) avere; (*said of a public carrier*) fare coincidenza con
meeting ['mitɪŋ] *s* riunione, ritrovo; seduta, convegno; (*political*) comizio; (*e.g., of two rivers*) confluenza; duello
meet'ing of the minds' *s* accordo, consonanza di voleri
meet'ing place' *s* luogo di riunione

megacycle ['mɛgə,saɪkəl] *s* megaciclo
megaphone ['mɛgə,fon] *s* megafono, portavoce *m*
megohm ['mɛg,om] *s* megaohm *m*
melancholia [,mɛlən'koli·ə] *s* melanconia, malinconia
melanchol·y ['mɛlən,kali] *adj* malinconico || *s* (**-ies**) malinconia
melee ['mele] *or* ['mɛle] *s* (*fight*) mischia; confusione
mellow ['mɛlo] *adj* (*fruit*) maturo; (*wine*) pastoso; (*voice*) soave, melodioso || *tr* raddolcire || *intr* raddolcirsi
melodic [mɪ'lɑdɪk] *adj* melodico
melodious [mɪ'lodɪ·əs] *adj* melodioso
melodramatic [,mɛlədrə'mætɪk] *adj* melodrammatico
melo·dy ['mɛlədi] *s* (**-dies**) melodia
melon ['mɛlən] *s* melone *m*, popone *m*
melt [mɛlt] *tr* sciogliere; (*metals*) fondere; (*fig*) intenerire || *intr* sciogliersi; fondersi; (*fig*) intenerirsi; **to melt away** svanire; **to melt into** convertirsi in, diventare; (*tears*) struggersi in
melt'ing pot' *s* crogiolo
member ['mɛmbər] *s* membro
membership ['mɛmbər,ʃɪp] *s* associazione; numero di membri
membrane ['mɛmbren] *s* membrana
memen·to [mɪ'mɛnto] *s* (**-tos** *or* **-toes**) oggetto ricordo
mem·o ['mɛmo] *s* (**-os**) (*coll*) memorandum *m*
memoir ['mɛmwɑr] *s* memoria, memoriale *m*; biografia; **memoirs** memorie *fpl*
memoran·dum [,mɛmə'rændəm] *s* (**-dums** *or* **-da** [də]) memorandum *m*
memorial [mɪ'morɪ·əl] *adj* commemorativo || *s* sacrario; (*petition*) memoriale *m*
Memo'rial Day' *s* giorno dei caduti
memorialize [mɪ'morɪ·ə,laɪz] *tr* commemorare
memorize ['mɛmə,raɪz] *tr* imparare a memoria
memo·ry ['mɛməri] *s* (**-ries**) memoria; **to commit to memory** imparare a memoria
menace ['mɛnɪs] *s* minaccia || *tr & intr* minacciare
ménage [me'naʒ] *s* casa; (*housekeeping*) economia domestica
menagerie [mə'næʒəri] *or* [mə'nædʒəri] *s* serraglio
mend [mɛnd] *s* riparo; **to be on the mend** migliorare || *tr* (*to repair*) raccomodare, riparare; (*to patch*) rammendare; (*fig*) correggere || *intr* correggersi
mendacious [mɛn'deʃəs] *adj* mendace
mendicant ['mɛndɪkənt] *adj & s* mendicante *mf*
menfolk ['mɛn,fok] *spl* uomini *mpl*
menial ['minɪ·əl] *adj* basso, servile || *s* servitore *m*, servo
menses ['mɛnsiz] *spl* mestruazione, mestrui *mpl*
men's' fur'nishings *spl* articoli *mpl* d'abbigliamento maschile
men's' room' *s* gabinetto per signori

menstruate ['menstru ,et] *intr* avere le mestruazioni

men'tal arith'metic ['mentəl] *s* calcolo mentale

men'tal hos'pital *s* manicomio

men'tal ill'ness *s* malattia mentale

men'tal reserva'tion *s* riserva mentale

men'tal test' *s* test *m* mentale

mention ['menʃən] *s* menzione || *tr* menzionare; **don't mention it** non c'è di che

menu ['menju] or ['menju] *s* menu *m*, lista

meow [mɪ'aʊ] *s* miagolio || *intr* miagolare

Mephistophelian [,mefɪstə'filɪ·ən] *adj* mefistofelico

mercantile ['mʌrkən ,til] or ['mʌrkən ,taɪl] *adj* mercantile

mercenar·y ['mʌrsə ,neri] *adj* mercenario || *s* (-ies) mercenario

merchandise ['mʌrtʃən ,daɪz] *s* mercanzia, merce *f*

merchant ['mʌrtʃənt] *adj* mercantile || *s* mercante *m*, commerciante *mf*

mer'chant·man *s* (-men) mercantile *m*

mer'chant marine' *s* marina mercantile

merciful ['mʌrsɪfəl] *adj* misericordioso

merciless ['mʌrsɪlɪs] *adj* spietato

mercu·ry ['mʌrkjəri] *s* (-ries) mercurio || Mercury *s* Mercurio

mer·cy ['mʌrsi] *s* (-cies) misericordia; **at the mercy of** alla mercé di

mere [mɪr] *adj* mero, puro

meretricious [,merɪ'trɪʃəs] *adj* vistoso, chiassoso, sgargiante; artificiale, falso, finto

merge [mʌrdʒ] *tr* fondere || *intr* fondersi; (*said of two roads*) convergere; **to merge into** convertirsi lentamente in

merger ['mʌrdʒər] *s* fusione

meridian [mə'rɪdɪ·ən] *adj* meridiano; culminante || *s* meridiano; apogeo

meringue [mə'ræŋ] *s* meringa

merit ['merɪt] *s* merito || *tr* meritare

meritorious [,merɪ'tori·əs] *adj* meritorio

merlon ['mʌrlən] *s* merlo

mermaid ['mʌr ,med] *s* sirena

mer'man' *s* (-men') tritone *m*

merriment ['merɪmənt] *s* allegria

mer·ry ['meri] *adj* (-rier; -riest) allegro, giocondo; **to make merry** divertirsi

Mer'ry Christ'mas *interj* Buon Natale!

mer'ry-go-round' *s* giostra, carosello; (*of parties*) serie ininterrotta

mer'ry·mak'er *s* festaiolo

mesh [meʃ] *s* (*network*) rete *f*; (*each open space of net*) maglia; (*mach*) ingranaggio; **meshes** rete *f* || *tr* irretire; (*mach*) ingranare || *intr* irretirsi; (*mach*) ingranarsi

mess [mes] *s* (*dirty condition*) disordine *m*; (*meal for a group of people*) mensa, rancio; porzione; **to get into a mess** mettersi nei pasticci; **to make a mess of** rovinare || *tr* sporcare; disordinare; rovinare || *intr* mangiare in comune; **to mess around** (coll) perdersi in cose inutili

message ['mesɪdʒ] *s* messaggio

messenger ['mesəndʒər] *s* messaggero; (*person who goes on an errand*) fattorino; (mil) portaordini *m*

mess' hall' *s* mensa

Messiah [mə'saɪ·ə] *s* Messia *m*

mess' kit' *s* gavetta, gamella

mess'mate' *s* compagno di rancio

mess' of pot'tage ['pɑtɪdʒ] *s* (Bib & fig) piatto di lenticchie

Messrs. ['mesərz] *pl* of Mr.

mess·y ['mesi] *adj* (-ier; -iest) disordinato; sporco

metal ['metəl] *adj* metallico || *s* metallo

metallic [mɪ'tælɪk] *adj* metallico

metallurgy ['metə ,lʌrdʒi] *s* metallurgia

met'al pol'ish *s* lucido per metalli

met'al·work' *s* lavoro di metallo

metamorpho·sis [,metə'mɔrfəsɪs] *s* (-ses [,siz]) metamorfosi *f*

metaphony [mə'tæfəni] *s* metafonia, metafonesi *f*

metaphor ['metəfər] or ['metə ,fɔr] *s* metafora

metaphorical [,metə'fɑrɪkəl] or [,metə'fɔrɪkəl] *adj* metaforico

metathe·sis [mɪ'tæθɪsɪs] *s* (-ses [,siz]) metatesi *f*

mete [mit] *tr—***to mete out** distribuire

meteor ['mitɪ·ər] *s* meteora

meteoric [,mitɪ'arɪk] or [,mitɪ'ɔrɪk] *adj* meteorico; (fig) rapidissimo, folgorante

meteorite ['mitɪ·ə ,raɪt] *s* meteorite *m* & *f*

meteorology [,mitɪ·ə'rɑlədʒi] *s* meteorologia

meter ['mitər] *s* (*unit of length; verse*) metro; (*instrument for measuring gas, water, etc.*) contatore *m*; (mus) tempo || *tr* misurare col contatore

me'ter read'er *s* lettore *m*, letturista *m*

methane ['meθen] *s* metano

method ['meθəd] *s* metodo

methodic(al) [mɪ'θɑdɪk(əl)] *adj* metodico

Methodist ['meθədɪst] *adj* & *s* metodista *mf*

Methuselah [mɪ'θuzələ] *s* Matusalemme *m*

meticulous [mɪ'tɪkjələs] *adj* meticoloso

metric(al) ['metrɪk(əl)] *adj* metrico

metronome ['metrə ,nom] *s* metronomo

metropolis [mɪ'trɑpəlɪs] *s* metropoli *f*

metropolitan [,metrə'pɑlɪtən] *adj* & *s* metropolitano

mettle ['metəl] *s* disposizione, temperamento; brio, animo; **to be on one's mettle** impegnarsi a fondo

mettlesome ['metəlsəm] *adj* brioso

mew [mju] *s* miagolio; (orn) gabbiano; **mews** scuderie *fpl*

Mexican ['meksɪkən] *adj* & *s* messicano

Mexico ['meksɪ ,ko] *s* il Messico

mezzanine ['mezə ,nin] *s* mezzanino

mica ['maɪkə] *s* mica

microbe ['maɪkrob] *s* microbio

microbiology [,maɪkrəbaɪ'ulədʒi] *s* microbiologia

microcard ['maɪkrə ,kɑrd] *s* microscheda

microfarad [ˌmaɪkrə'færæd] s microfarad m

microfilm ['maɪkrə ˌfɪlm] s microfilm m || tr microfilmare

microgroove ['maɪkrə ˌgruv] adj microsolco || s microsolco; disco microsolco

microphone ['maɪkrə ˌfon] s microfono

microscope ['maɪkrə ˌskop] s microscopio

microscopic [ˌmaɪkrə'skɑpɪk] adj microscopico

microwave ['maɪkrə ˌwev] s microonda

mid [mɪd] adj mezzo, la metà di, e.g., **mid October** la metà di ottobre

mid'day' adj di mezzogiorno || s mezzogiorno

middle ['mɪdəl] adj medio, mezzo || s mezzo, metà f; (of human body) cintura; **about the middle of** verso la metà di; **in the middle of** nel mezzo di

mid'dle age' s mezza età || **Middle Ages** spl Medio Evo

mid'dle class' s ceto medio, borghesia

Mid'dle East' s Medio Oriente

Mid'dle Eng'lish s inglese m medievale parlato fra il 1150 e il 1500

mid'dle fin'ger s dito medio

mid'dle-man' s (-men') intermediario

middling ['mɪdlɪŋ] adj mediocre, passabile || s (coarsely ground wheat) farina grossa integrale; **middlings** articoli mpl di qualità mediocre || adv moderatamente

mid•dy ['mɪdi] s (-dies) aspirante m di marina

mid'dy blouse' s marinara

midget ['mɪdʒɪt] s nano

midland ['mɪdlənd] adj centrale, interno || s regione centrale

mid'night' adj di mezzanotte; **to burn the midnight oil** studiare a lume di candela || s mezzanotte f

midriff ['mɪdrɪf] s diaframma m; (middle part of body) cintura, vita

mid'ship'man s (-men) aspirante m di marina

midst [mɪdst] s mezzo, centro; **in the midst of** in mezzo a

mid'stream' s—**in midstream** in mezzo al fiume

mid'sum'mer s cuore m dell'estate

mid'way' adj situato a metà strada || s metà strada; viale m principale di un' esposizione || adv a metà strada

mid'week' s mezzo della settimana

mid'wife' s (-wives') levatrice f

mid'win'ter s cuore m dell'inverno

mid'year' adj nel mezzo dell'anno || s mezzo dell'anno; **midyears** (coll) esami mpl nel mezzo dell'anno scolastico

mien [min] s aspetto, portamento

miff [mɪf] s (coll) battibecco || tr (coll) offendere

might [maɪt] s forza, potenza; **with might and main** a tutta forza || v aux used to form the potential, e.g., **he might change his mind** è possibile che cambi opinione

might•y ['maɪti] adj (-ier; -iest) po-

tente; (huge) grandissimo || adv (coll) moltissimo, grandemente

migraine ['maɪgren] s emicrania

migrate ['maɪgret] intr migrare

migratory ['maɪgrə ˌtori] adj migratore

milch [mɪltʃ] adj lattifero

mild [maɪld] adj dolce, mite, gentile; (disease) leggero

mildew ['mɪl ˌdju] or ['mɪl ˌdu] s (mold) muffa; (plant disease) peronospora

mile [maɪl] s miglio terrestre; **miglio marino**

mileage ['maɪlɪdʒ] s distanza in miglia

mile'age tick'et s biglietto calcolato in miglia simile al biglietto chilometraggio

mile'post' s colonnina miliare

mile'stone' s pietra miliare

milieu [mɪl'ju] s ambiente m

militancy ['mɪlɪtənsi] s bellicismo; spirito militante

militant ['mɪlɪtənt] adj & s militante mf

militarism ['mɪlɪtə ˌrɪzəm] s militarismo

militarist ['mɪlɪtərɪst] adj & s militarista mf

militarize ['mɪlɪtə ˌraɪz] tr militarizzare

military ['mɪlɪ ˌteri] adj militare || s—**the military** le forze armate

mil'itary acad'emy s scuola allievi ufficiali, accademia militare

mil'itary police' s polizia militare

militate ['mɪlɪ ˌtet] intr militare

militia [mɪ'lɪʃə] s milizia

mili'tia-man s (-men) miliziano

milk [mɪlk] adj lattifero; di latte; al latte || s latte m || tr mungere; (fig) spillare || intr dare latte

milk' can' s bidone m per il latte

milk' choc'olate s cioccolato al latte

milk' diet' s regime latteo

milking ['mɪlkɪŋ] s mungitura

milk'maid' s lattaia

milk'man' s (-men') lattaio

milk' of hu'man kind'ness s grande compassione

milk' pail' s secchio da latte

milk' shake' s frappé m or frullato di latte

milk'sop' s effeminato

milk'weed' s vincetossico

milk•y ['mɪlki] adj (-ier; -iest) latteo; (whitish) lattiginoso

Milk'y Way' s Via Lattea

mill [mɪl] s (for grinding grain) mulino; (for making fabrics) filanda; (for cutting wood) segheria; (for refining sugar) zuccherificio; (for producing steel) acciaieria; (to grind coffee) macinino; (part of a dollar) millesimo; **to put through the mill** mettere a dura prova || tr (grains) macinare; (coins) zigrinare; (steel) laminare; (ore) frantumare; (with a milling machine) fresare; (chocolate) frullare || intr—**to mill about or around** girare intorno

millennial [mɪ'lɛni•əl] adj millenario

milleni·um [mɪˈlenɪ·əm] s (-ums or -a [ə]) millennio

miller [ˈmɪlər] s mugnaio; (ent) tignola notturna

millet [ˈmɪlɪt] s panico, miglio

milliampere [ˌmɪlɪˈæmpɪr] s milliampere m

milliard [ˈmɪljərd] or [ˈmɪljɑrd] s (Brit) miliardo, bilione m

milligram [ˈmɪlɪˌɡræm] s milligrammo

millimeter [ˈmɪlɪˌmitər] s millimetro

milliner [ˈmɪlɪnər] s modista

milliner·y [ˈmɪlɪˌnerɪ] or [ˈmɪlɪnərɪ] s (-ies) cappelli mpl per signora; modisteria; articoli mpl di modisteria

mil'linery shop' s modisteria

milling [ˈmɪlɪŋ] s (of grain) macinatura; (of coins) granitura; (mach) fresatura

mill'ing machine' s fresatrice f

million [ˈmɪljən] adj milione di, milioni di || s milione m

millionaire [ˌmɪljənˈer] s milionario

millionth [ˈmɪljənθ] adj, s & pron milionesimo

millivolt [ˈmɪlɪˌvolt] s millivolt m

mill'pond' s gora

mill'race' s corrente f che aziona il mulino; canale m di presa

mill'stone' s mola, macina, palmento; (fig) peso, gravame m

mill' wheel' s ruota del mulino

mill'work' s lavoro di falegnameria; lavoro di falegnameria fatto a macchina

mime [maɪm] s mimo || tr mimare

mimeograph [ˈmɪmɪ·əˌɡræf] or [ˈmɪmɪəˌɡrɑf] s (trademark) ciclostile m || tr ciclostilare

mim·ic [ˈmɪmɪk] s mimo, imitatore m || v (pret & pp -icked; ger -icking) tr imitare, scimmiottare

mimic·ry [ˈmɪmɪkrɪ] s (-ries) mimica, (biol) mimetismo

minaret [ˌmɪnəˈret] or [ˈmɪnəˌret] s mineareto

mince [mɪns] tr tagliuzzare, triturare; (words) pronunziare con affettazione; **to not mince one's words** non aver peli sulla lingua

mince'meat' s carne tritata; **to make mincemeat of** annientare completamente

mince' pie' s torta di frutta secca e carne tritata

mind [maɪnd] s mente f; opinione; **to bear in mind** tener presente; **to be not in one's right mind** essere fuori di senno; **to be of one mind** essere d'accordo; **to be out of one's mind** essere impazzito; **to change one's mind** cambiare d'opinione; **to go out of one's mind** impazzire; **to have a mind to** aver voglia di; **to have in mind to** pensare a; **to have on one's mind** avere in mente; **to lose one's mind** uscire di mente; **to make up one's mind** decidersi; **to my mind** a mio modo di vedere; **to say whatever comes to one's mind** dire quanto salta in testa, e.g., John always says whatever comes to his mind Gio-

vanni dice sempre quanto gli salta in testa; **to set one's mind on** risolversi a; **to slip one's mind** scappare di mente (with dat), e.g., **it slipped his mind** gli è scappato di mente; **to speak one's mind** dire la propria opinione; **with one mind** unanimamente || tr (to take care of) occuparsi di; obbedire (with dat); **do you mind the smoke?** Le disturba il fumo?; **mind your own business** si occupi degli affari Suoi || intr osservare, fare attenzione; rincrescere, e.g., **do you mind if I go?** Le rincresce se vado?; **never mind** non si preoccupi

mindful [ˈmaɪndfəl] adj memore

mind' read'er s lettore m del pensiero

mind' read'ing s lettura del pensiero

mine [maɪn] s (e.g., of coal) miniera; (mil & nav) mina || pron poss il mio; mio || tr minare; (earth) scavare; (ore) estrarre || intr lavorare una miniera; (mil & nav) minare

mine' detec'tor s rivelatore m di mine

mine'field' s campo minato

mine'lay'er s posamine m

miner [ˈmaɪnər] s minatore m

mineral [ˈmɪnərəl] adj & s minerale m

mineralogy [ˌmɪnəˈrælədʒɪ] s mineralogia

min'eral wool' s cotone m or lana minerale

mine' sweep'er s dragamine m

mingle [ˈmɪŋɡəl] tr mescolare; unire || intr mescolarsi, associarsi

miniature [ˈmɪnɪ·ətˌər] or [ˈmɪnɪtˌər] s miniatura; **to paint in miniature** miniare, dipingere in miniatura

min'iature golf' s minigolf m

miniaturization [ˌmɪnɪ·ətˌɑrɪˈzeʃən] or [ˌmɪnɪtˌɑrɪˈzeʃən] s miniaturizzazione

minimal [ˈmɪnɪməl] adj minimo

minimize [ˈmɪnɪˌmaɪz] tr minimizzare

minimum [ˈmɪnɪməm] adj & s minimo

min'imum wage' s salario minimo

mining [ˈmaɪnɪŋ] adj minerario || s estrazione di minerali; (nav) posa di mine

minion [ˈmɪnjən] s servo; favorito, beniamino

min'ion of the law' s poliziotto

miniskirt [ˈmɪnɪˌskɜrt] s minigonna

minister [ˈmɪnɪstər] s ministro; pastore m protestante || tr & intr ministrare

ministerial [ˌmɪnɪsˈtɪrɪ·əl] adj ministeriale

minis·try [ˈmɪnɪstrɪ] s (-tries) ministero; sacerdozio

mink [mɪŋk] s visone m

minnow [ˈmɪno] s pesciolino; (ichth) ciprino

minor [ˈmaɪnər] adj minore || s minore m, minorenne mf; (educ) corso secondario

minori·ty [mɪˈnɑrɪtɪ] or [mɪˈnɔrɪtɪ] adj minoritario || s (-ties) (smaller number or part; group differing in race, etc., from majority) minoranza; (under legal age) minorità f

minstrel [ˈmɪnstrəl] s (hist) menestrello; (U.S.A.) comico vestito da nero

minstrel·sy ['mɪnstrəlsɪ] s (-sies) giulleria; poesia giullaresca

mint [mɪnt] s zecca; (plant) menta; (losenge) mentina; (fig) miniera d'oro ‖ tr coniare

minuet [,mɪnju'et] s minuetto

minus ['maɪnəs] adj meno ‖ s meno, perdita ‖ prep meno, senza

minute [maɪ'njut] or [maɪ'nut] adj minuto ‖ ['mɪnɪt] adj fatto in un minuto ‖ s minuto; momento; **minutes** processo verbale; **to write up the minutes** tenere i verbali; **up to the minute** al corrente; dell'ultima ora

min'ute hand' ['mɪnɪt] s sfera or lancetta dei minuti

minutiae [mɪ'njuʃɪˌɪ] or [mɪ'nuʃɪˌɪ] spl minuzie fpl

minx [mɪŋks] s sfacciata, civetta

miracle ['mɪrəkəl] s miracolo

mir'acle play' s sacra rappresentazione

miraculous [mɪ'rækjələs] adj miracoloso

mirage [mɪ'rɑʒ] s miraggio

mire [maɪr] s limo, mota

mirror ['mɪrər] s specchio ‖ tr specchiare, riflettere

mirth [mʌrθ] s allegria, gioia

mir·y ['maɪrɪ] adj (-ier; -iest) fangoso, limaccioso

misadventure [,mɪsəd'ventʃər] s disavventura, contrattempo

misanthrope ['mɪsənˌθrop] s misantropo

misanthropy [mɪs'ænθrəpɪ] s misantropia

misapprehension [,mɪsæprɪ'henʃən] s malinteso

misappropriation [,mɪsəˌproprɪ'eʃən] s malversazione

misbehave [,mɪsbɪ'hev] intr comportarsi male

misbehavior [,mɪsbɪ'hevɪ·ər] s cattiva condotta

miscalculation [,mɪskælkjə'leʃən] s calcolo errato

miscarriage [mɪs'kærɪdʒ] s (of justice) errore m; (of a letter) disguido; (pathol) aborto

miscar·ry [mɪs'kærɪ] v (pret & pp -ried) intr (said of a project) fallire; (said of a letter) smarrirsi; (pathol) abortire

miscellaneous [,mɪsə'lenɪ·əs] adj miscellaneo

miscella·ny ['mɪsəˌlenɪ] s (-nies) miscellanea

mischief ['mɪstʃɪf] s (harm) danno; (disposition to annoy) malizia; (prankishness) birichinata

mis'chief-mak'er s mettimale mf

mischievous ['mɪstʃɪvəs] adj dannoso; malizioso; birichino

misconception [,mɪskən'sepʃən] s concetto erroneo, fraintendimento

misconduct [mɪs'kɑndəkt] s cattiva condotta; (of a public official) malgoverno ‖ [,mɪskən'dʌkt] tr male amministrare; **to misconduct oneself** comportarsi male

misconstrue [,mɪskən'stru] or [mɪs'kɑnstru] tr fraintendere

miscount [mɪs'kaunt] s conteggio erroneo ‖ tr & intr contare male

miscue [mɪs'kju] s sbaglio; (in billiards) stecca ‖ intr steccare; (theat) sbagliarsi di battuta

mis·deal ['mɪsˌdil] s distribuzione sbagliata ‖ [mɪs'dil] v (pret & pp -dealt [delt]) tr & intr distribuire erroneamente

misdeed [mɪs'did] or ['mɪsˌdid] s misfatto, malfatto

misdemeanor [,mɪsdɪ'minər] s cattiva condotta; (law) delitto colposo

misdirect [,mɪsdɪ'rekt] or [,mɪsdaɪ'rekt] tr dare un indirizzo sbagliato a; (a letter) mettere un indirizzo sbagliato su

misdoing [mɪs'du·ɪŋ] s misfatto

miser ['maɪzər] s avaro, spilorcio

miserable ['mɪzərəbəl] adj miserabile, miserevole; (coll) malissimo; (coll) schifoso

miserly ['maɪzərlɪ] adj spilorcio

miser·y ['mɪzərɪ] s (-ies) miseria

misfeasance [mɪs'fizəns] s infrazione della legge; abuso di autorità commesso da pubblico funzionario

misfire [mɪs'faɪr] s difetto di esplosione; (aut) difetto d'accensione ‖ intr (said of a gun) fare cilecca; (aut) dare accensione irregolare; (fig) fallire

mis·fit ['mɪsˌfɪt] s vestito che non va bene; (person) spostato, pesce m fuor d'acqua ‖ [mɪs'fɪt] v (pret & pp -fitted; ger -fitting) intr andar male

misfortune [mɪs'fortʃən] s disgrazia

misgiving [mɪs'gɪvɪŋ] s dubbio, timore m, cattivo presentimento

misgovern [mɪs'gʌvərn] tr amministrare male

misguided [mɪs'gaɪdɪd] adj fuorviato; (e.g., kindness) sconsigliato

mishap ['mɪshæp] or [mɪs'hæp] s accidente m, infortunio

misinform [,mɪsɪn'form] tr dare informazioni errate a

misinterpret [,mɪsɪn'tɜrprɪt] tr interpretare male, trasfigurare

misjudge [mɪs'dʒʌdʒ] tr & intr giudicare male

mis·lay [mɪs'le] v (pret & pp -laid [led]) tr (e.g., tile) applicare in maniera sbagliata; (e.g., papers) smarrire, mettere al posto sbagliato

mis·lead [mɪs'lid] v (pret & pp -led [led]) tr sviare, traviare

misleading [mɪs'lidɪŋ] adj ingannatore

mismanagement [mɪs'mænɪdʒmənt] s malgoverno

misnomer [mɪs'nomər] s termine improprio

misplace [mɪs'ples] tr mettere fuori di posto; (trust) riporre erroneamente

misprint ['mɪsˌprɪnt] s errore m di stampa, refuso ‖ [mɪs'prɪnt] tr stampare erroneamente

mispronounce [,mɪsprə'nauns] tr pronunciare in modo erroneo

mispronunciation [,mɪsprə,nʌnsɪ-

'e/ən] or [,mɪsprə,nʌn/ɪ'e/ən] s errore m di pronuncia

misquote [mɪs'kwot] tr citare incorrettamente

misrepresent [,mɪsreprɪ'zent] tr travisare, snaturare; (pol) rappresentare slealmente

miss [mɪs] s sbaglio, omissione; tiro fuori bersaglio; signorina || tr (a train, an opportunity) perdere; (the target) fallire; (an appointment) mancare; (the point) non vedere, non capire; per poco, e.g., **the car missed hitting him** l'automobile non l'ha investito per poco || intr sbagliare, fallire; mancare il bersaglio || **Miss** s signorina, la signorina

missal ['mɪsəl] s messale m

misshapen [mɪs'/epən] adj deforme, malfatto

missile ['mɪsɪl] adj missilistico || s missile m

mis'sile launch'er s lanciamissili m

missing ['mɪsɪŋ] adj mancante; assente; (in action) disperso

mis'sing link' s anello di congiunzione

miss'ing per'son s disperso

mission ['mɪ/ən] s missione

missionar·y ['mɪ/ən ,erɪ] adj missionario || s (-ies) (eccl) missionario; (dipl) incaricato in missione

missive ['mɪsɪv] s missiva

mis·spell [mɪs'spel] v (pret & pp -spelled or -spelt ['spelt]) tr & intr scrivere male

misspelling [mɪs'spelɪŋ] s errore m di ortografia

misspent [mɪs'spent] adj sprecato

misstatement [mɪs'stetmənt] s dichiarazione inesatta

misstep [mɪs'step] s passo falso

miss·y ['mɪsɪ] s (-ies) (coll) signorina

mist [mɪst] s caligine f, foschia; (of tears) velo; (of smoke, vapors, etc.) nuvola

mis·take [mɪs'tek] s errore m, sbaglio; **and no mistake** (coll) di sicuro; **by mistake** per sbaglio; **to make a mistake** sbagliarsi || v (pret -took ['tuk]; pp -taken) tr fraintendere; **to be mistaken for** essere preso per; **to mistake for** pigliare per

mistaken [mɪs'tekən] adj errato, sbagliato; **to be mistaken** essere in errore, sbagliarsi

mister ['mɪstər] s (mil, nav) signore m; (coll) marito || interj (coll) signore!; (coll) Leil; (coll) buonuomo! || **Mister** s Signore m

mistletoe ['mɪsəl ,to] s vischio

mistreat [mɪs'trit] tr maltrattare

mistreatment [mɪs'tritmənt] s maltrattamento

mistress ['mɪstrɪs] s (of a household) signora, padrona; (paramour) amante f, ganza; (Brit) maestra di scuola

mistrial [mɪs'traɪ·əl] s processo viziato da errore giudiziario

mistrust [mɪs'trʌst] s diffidenza || tr diffidare di || intr diffidarsi

mistrustful [mɪs'trʌstfəl] adj diffidente

mist·y ['mɪstɪ] adj (-ier; -iest) fosco, brumoso; (fig) vago, confuso

misunder·stand [,mɪsʌndər'stænd] v (pret & pp -stood ['stud]) tr fraintendere, equivocare

misunderstanding [,mɪsʌndər'stændɪŋ] s malinteso

misuse [mɪs'jus] s abuso; (of funds) malversazione || [mɪs'juz] tr abusare di; (funds) malversare

misword [mɪs'wʌrd] tr comporre male

mite [maɪt] s obolo; (ent) acaro

miter ['maɪtər] s (carp) ugnatura; (carp) giunto a quartabuono; (eccl) mitra || tr tagliare a quartabuono, ugnare; giungere a quartabuono

mi'ter box' s cassetta per ugnature

mi'ter joint' s giunto a quartabuono

mitigate ['mɪtɪ ,get] tr mitigare

mitten ['mɪtən] s manopola, muffola

mix [mɪks] tr mescolare; (colors) mesticare; (dough) impastare; (salad) condire; **to mix up** confondere || intr confondersi, mescolarsi

mixed [mɪkst] adj misto; (candy) assortito; (coll) confuso

mixed' com'pany s riunione f di ambo i sessi

mixed' drink' s miscela di liquori diversi

mixed' feel'ing s sentimento ambivalente

mixed' met'aphor s metafora incongruente

mixer ['mɪksər] s (mach) mescolatrice f; **to be a good mixer** essere socievole

mixture ['mɪkst/ər] s mistura, mescolanza; (aut) miscela, carburazione

mix'-up' s confusione; (coll) baruffa

mizzen ['mɪzən] s mezzana

moan [mon] s gemito || intr gemere

moat [mot] s fosso, fossato

mob [mab] s turba || v (pret & pp mobbed; ger mobbing) tr assaltare; affollarsi intorno a; (a place) affollare

mobile ['mobɪl] or ['mobil] adj mobile

mo'bile home' s caravan m, roulotte f

mobility [mo'bɪlɪtɪ] s mobilità f

mobilization [,mobɪlɪ'ze/ən] s mobilitazione

mobilize ['mobɪ ,laɪz] tr & intr mobilitare

mob' rule' s legge f della teppa

mobster ['mabstər] s gangster m

moccasin ['makəsɪn] s mocassino

Mo'cha cof'fee ['mokə] s caffè m moca

mock [mak] adj finto, imitato || s dileggio, burla || tr deridere, canzonare; ingannare || intr motteggiare; **to mock at** farsi gioco di

mocker·y ['makərɪ] s (-ies) dileggio, scherno; (subject of derision) zimbello; (poor imitation) contraffazione

mock'-hero'ic adj eroicomico

mockingbird ['makɪŋ ,bʌrd] s mimo

mock' or'ange s gelsomino selvatico

mock' tur'tle soup' s finto brodo di tartaruga

mock'-up' s modello dimostrativo

mode [mod] s modo, maniera; (fashion) moda; (gram) modo

mod·el ['madəl] adj modello, e.g., **model student** studente modello || s modello; (*woman serving as subject for artists*) modello *f*; (*woman wearing clothes at fashion show*) indossatrice *f* || *v* (*pret & pp* **-eled** or **-elled;** *ger* **-eling** or **-elling**) *tr* modellare || *intr* modellarsi; fare il manichino

mod′el air′plane *s* aeromodello

mo′del-air′plane build′er *s* aeromodellista *mf*

mod′eling clay′ *s* plastilina

moderate [′mɑdərɪt] *adj* moderato || [′mɑdə‚ret] *tr* moderare; (*a meeting*) presiedere a || *intr* moderarsi

moderator [′mɑdə‚retər] *s* moderatore *m*; (*mediator*) arbitro; (*phys*) moderatore *m*

modern [′mɑdərn] *adj* moderno

modernize [′mɑdər‚naɪz] *tr* modernizzare, rimodernare

modest [′mɑdɪst] *adj* modesto

modes·ty [′mɑdɪsti] *s* (**-ties**) modestia

modicum [′mɑdɪkəm] *s* piccola quantità

modi·fy [′mɑdɪ‚faɪ] *v* (*pret & pp* **-fied**) *tr* modificare; (*gram*) determinare

modish [′modɪʃ] *adj* alla moda

modulate [′mɑdʒə‚let] *tr & intr* modulare

modulation [‚mɑdʒə′leʃən] *s* modulazione

mohair [′mo‚her] *s* mohair *m*

Mohammedan [mo′hæmɪdən] *adj & s* maomettano

Mohammedanism [mo′hæmɪdə‚nɪzəm] *s* maomettismo

moist [mɔɪst] *adj* umido; lacrimoso

moisten [′mɔɪsən] *tr* inumidire || *intr* inumidirsi

moisture [′mɔɪstʃər] *s* umidità *f*

molar [′molər] *s* molare *m*

molasses [mə′læsɪz] *s* melassa

mold [mold] *s* stampo, forma; (*fungus*) muffa; humus *m*; (fig) indole *f* || *tr* plasmare, conformare; (*to make moldy*) fare ammuffire || *intr* ammuffire

molder [′moldər] *s* modellatore *m* || *intr* sgretolarsi; polverizzarsi

molding [′moldɪŋ] *s* modellato; (*archit, carp*) modanatura

mold·y [′moldi] *adj* (**-ier; -iest**) ammuffito

mole [mol] *s* (*pier*) molo; (*harbor*) darsena; (*spot on skin*) neo; (*small mammal*) talpa

molecule [′mɑlɪ‚kjul] *s* molecola

mole′hill′ *s* mucchio di terra sopra la tana di talpe

mole′skin′ *s* pelle *f* di talpa; (*fabric*) fustagno di prima qualità

molest [mə′lɛst] *tr* molestare; fare proposte disoneste a

moll [mɑl] *s* (slang) ragazza della malavita; (slang) puttana

molli·fy [′mɑlɪ‚faɪ] *v* (*pret & pp* **-fied**) *tr* pacificare, placare

mollusk [′mɑləsk] *s* mollusco

mollycoddle [′mɑlɪ‚kɑdəl] *s* effeminato || *tr* viziare, coccolare

Mo′lotov cock′tail [′mɑlə‚tɔf] *s* bottiglia Molotov

molt [molt] *s* muda || *intr* andare in muda

molten [′moltən] *adj* fuso

molybdenum [mə′lɪbdɪnəm] or [‚mɑlɪb′dinəm] *s* molibdeno

moment [′momənt] *s* momento; **at any moment** da un momento all′altro

momentary [′momən‚teri] *adj* momentaneo

momentous [mo′mɛntəs] *adj* grave, importante

momen·tum [mo′mɛntəm] *s* (**-tums** or **-ta** [tə]) slancio; (mech) momento

monarch [′mɑnərk] *s* monarca *m*

monarchic(al) [mə′nɑrkɪk(əl)] *adj* monarchico

monarchist [′mɑnərkɪst] *adj & s* monarchico

monar·chy [′mɑnərki] *s* (**-chies**) monarchia

monaster·y [′mɑnəs‚teri] *s* (**-ies**) monastero

monastic [mə′næstɪk] *adj* monastico, monacale

monasticism [mə′næstɪ‚sɪzəm] *s* monachesimo

Monday [′mʌndi] *s* lunedì *m*

monetary [′mɑnɪ‚teri] *adj* monetario; pecuniario

money [′mʌni] *s* denaro; **to be in the money** esser carico di soldi; **to make money** far quattrini

mon′ey-bag′ *s* borsa per denaro; **moneybags** (coll) riccone sfondato

moneychanger [′mʌnɪ‚tʃendʒər] *s* cambiavalute *m*

moneyed [′mʌnid] *adj* danaroso

moneylender [′mʌni‚lɛndər] *s* prestatore *m* di denaro

mon′ey-mak′er *s* capitalista *mf*; affare vantaggioso

mon′ey or′der *s* vaglia *m*

Mongolian [mɑŋ′goli·ən] *adj & s* mongolo

mon·goose [′mɑŋgus] *s* (**-gooses**) mangusta

mongrel [′mʌŋgrəl] or [′mɑŋgrəl] *adj* ibrido || *s* ibrido; cane bastardo

monitor [′mɑnɪtər] *s* (educ) capoclasse *mf*; (rad, telv) monitore *m* || *tr* osservare; (*a signal*) controllare; (*a broadcast*) ascoltare

monk [mʌŋk] *s* monaco

monkey [′mʌŋki] *s* scimmia; **to make a monkey of** farsi gioco di || *intr*—**to monkey around** (coll) oziare; **to monkey around with** (coll) giocherellare con

mon′key-shines′ *spl* (slang) monellerie *fpl*, pagliacciate *fpl*

mon′key wrench′ *s* chiave *f* inglese

monkhood [′mʌŋkhʊd] *s* monacato

monkshood [mʌŋks‚hʊd] *s* (bot) aconito

monocle [′mɑnəkəl] *s* monocolo

monogamy [mə′nɑgəmi] *s* monogamia

monogram [′mɑnə‚græm] *s* monogramma *m*

monograph [′mɑnə‚græf] or [′mɑnə‚grɑf] *s* monografia

monolithic [‚mɑnə′lɪθɪk] *adj* monolitico

monologue ['manə,lɔg] or ['manə,lag] s monologo

monomania [,manə'menɪ·ə] s monomania

monomial [mə'nomɪ·əl] s monomio

monopolize [mə'napə,laɪz] tr monopolizzare, accaparrare

monopo·ly [mə'napəli] s (**-lies**) monopolio, privativa

monorail ['manə,rel] s monorotaia

monosyllable ['manə,sɪləbəl] s monosillabo

monotheist ['manə,θi·ɪst] adj & s monoteista mf

monotonous [mə'natənəs] adj monotono

monotype ['manə,taɪp] s (method) monotipia; (typ) monotipo

monoxide [mə'naksaɪd] s monossido

monseigneur [,mansen'jœr] s monsignore m

monsignor [man'sinjər] s (**-monsignors** or **monsignori** [,mɑnsi'njori]) (eccl) monsignore m

monsoon [man'sun] s monsone m

monster ['manstər] adj mostruoso || s mostro

monstrance ['manstrəns] s ostensorio

monstrosi·ty [man'strasɪti] s (**-ties**) mostruosità f

monstrous ['manstrəs] adj mostruoso

month [mʌnθ] s mese m

month·ly ['mʌnθli] adj mensile || s (**-lies**) rivista mensile; **monthlies** (coll) mestruazione || adv mensilmente

monument ['manjəmənt] s monumento

moo [mu] s muggito || intr muggire

mood [mud] s umore m, vena; (gram) modo; **moods** luna, malumore m

mood·y ['mudi] adj (**-ier; -iest**) triste, malinconico; lunatico, capriccioso

moon [mun] s luna; **once in a blue moon** ad ogni morte di papa || tr—**to moon away** (time) (coll) sprecare || intr—**to moon about** (coll) gingillarsi, baloccarsi; (to daydream about) (coll) sognarsi di

moon'beam' s raggio di luna

moon'light' s chiaro m di luna

moon'light'ing s secondo lavoro notturno

moon'shine' s chiaro di luna; (coll) chiacchiere fpl, balle fpl; (coll) whisky m distillato illegalmente

moon'shot' s lancio alla luna

moon'stone' s lunaria

moor [mur] s brughiera, landa || tr ormeggiare || intr ormeggiarsi || **Moor** s moro

Moorish ['murɪʃ] adj moresco

moor'land' s brughiera, landa

moose [mus] s (**moose**) alce americano

moot [mut] adj controverso, discutibile

mop [map] s scopa di filacce; (naut) redazza; (of hair) zazzera || v (pret & pp **mopped**; ger **mopping**) tr (a floor) pulire, asciugare; (one's brow) asciugarsi; **to mop up** rastrellare

mope [mop] intr andare rattristato

mopish ['mopɪʃ] adj triste, avvilito

moral ['mɔrəl] or ['marəl] adj morale || s (of a fable) morale f; **morals** (ethics) morale f; (modes of conduct) costumi mpl

morale [mə'ræl] or [mə'ral] s morale m

morali·ty [mə'rælɪti] s (**-ties**) moralità f

mor'als charge' s accusa di oltraggio al pudore

morass [mə'ræs] s palude f

moratori·um [,mɔrə'tori·əm] or [,marə'tori·əm] s (**-ums** or **-a** [ə]) moratoria

morbid ['mɔrbɪd] adj (gruesome) orribile; (feelings; curiosity; pertaining to disease; pathologic) morboso

mordacious [mɔr'deʃəs] adj mordace

mordant ['mɔrdənt] adj & s mordente m

more [mor] adj & s più m || adv più; **more and more** sempre più; **more than** più di; (followed by verb) più di quanto; **the more . . . the less** tanto più . . . quanto meno

more·o'er adv per di più, inoltre

Moresque [mo'resk] adj moresco

morgue [mɔrg] s deposito, obitorio; (journ) archivio di un giornale, frigorifero

moribund ['mɔrɪ,bʌnd] or ['marɪ,bʌnd] adj moribondo

morning ['mɔrnɪŋ] adj mattiniero || s mattina, mattino; **good morning** buon giorno; **in the morning** di mattina

morn'ing coat' s giacca nera a code

morn'ing-glo'ry s (**-ries**) convolvolo; (Ipomea) campanella; (Convolvulus tricolor) bella di giorno

morn'ing sick'ness s vomito di gravidanza

morn'ing star' s Lucifero, stella del mattino

Moroccan [mə'rakən] adj & s marocchino

morocco [mə'rako] s (leather) marocchino || **Morocco** s il Marocco

moron ['moran] s deficiente mf

morose [mə'ros] adj tetro, imbronciato

morphine ['mɔrfin] s morfina

morphology [mɔr'falədʒi] s morfologia

morrow ['maro] or ['mɔro] s—**on the morrow** l'indomani, il giorno seguente; domani

morsel ['mɔrsəl] s boccone m, bocconcino; pezzetto

mortal ['mɔrtəl] adj & s mortale m

mortality [mɔr'tælɪti] s mortalità f; (death or destruction on a large scale) moria

mortar ['mɔrtər] s (mixture of lime or cement) malta, calcina; (bowl) mortaio; (mil) mortaio, lanciabombe m

mor'tar·board' s sparviere m; (cap) tocco accademico

mortgage ['mɔrgɪdʒ] s ipoteca || tr ipotecare

mortgagee [,mɔrgɪ'dʒi] s creditore m ipotecario

mortgagor ['mɔrgɪdʒər] s debitore m ipotecario

mortician [mɔr'tɪʃən] s impresario di pompe funebri

morti·fy ['mɔrtɪ,faɪ] v (pret & pp **-fied**) tr mortificare; **to be mortified** vergognarsi

mortise ['mɔrtɪs] s intaccatura, incastro || tr incassare, incastrare

mor'tise lock' s serratura incastrata

mortuar·y ['mɔrtʃʊ,ɛri] adj mortuario || s (**-ies**) camera mortuaria

mosaic [mo'ze·ɪk] s mosaico

Moscow ['mɑskaʊ] or ['mɑsko] s Mosca

Moses ['mozɪz] or ['mozɪs] s Mosè m

Mos·lem ['mɑzləm] or ['mɑsləm] adj musulmano || s (**-lems** or **-lem**) musulmano || s (**-lems** or **-lem**) musulmano

mosque [mɑsk] s moschea

mosqui·to [məs'kito] s (**-toes** or **-tos**) zanzara

mosqui'to net' s zanzariera

moss [mɔs] or [mɑs] s musco

moss'back' s (coll) ultraconservatore m, fossile m

moss·y ['mɔsi] or ['mɑsi] adj (**-ier**; **-iest**) muscoso

most [most] adj il più di, la maggior parte di || s la maggioranza, i più; **most of** la maggior parte di; **to make the most of** trarre il massimo da || adv più, maggiormente, al massimo

mostly ['mostli] adv per lo più, maggiormente, al massimo

motel [mo'tɛl] s motel m, autostello

moth [mɔθ] or [mɑθ] s falena; (clothes moth) tarma

moth'ball' s pallina antitarmica

moth-eaten ['mɔθ,itən] or ['mɑθ,itən] adj tarmato; antiquato

mother ['mʌðər] adj (love, tongue) materno; (country) natio; (church, company) madre || s madre f; (elderly woman) (coll) zia || tr fare da madre a; creare; procreare; assumere la maternità di

moth'er coun'try s madrepatria

Moth'er Goose' s supposta autrice di una raccolta di favole infantili

motherhood ['mʌðər,hʊd] s maternità f

moth'er-in-law' s (**moth'ers-in-law'**) suocera

moth'er-land' s madrepatria

motherless ['mʌðərlɪs] adj orfano di madre, senza madre

mother-of-pearl ['mʌðərəv'pʌrl] adj madreperlaceo || s madreperla

motherly ['mʌðərli] adj materno

Moth'er's Day' s giorno della madre, festa della mamma

moth'er supe'rior s madre superiora

moth'er tongue' s madrelingua; (language from which another language is derived) lingua madre

moth'er wit' s intelligenza nativa

moth' hole' s tarlatura

moth·y ['mɔθi] or ['mɑθi] adj (**-ier**; **-iest**) tarmato

motif [mo'tif] s motivo

motion ['moʃən] s movimento; (e.g., of a dancer) movenza, mossa; (in parliamentary procedure) mozione; **in motion** in moto || intr fare cenno

motionless ['moʃənlɪs] adj immobile

mo'tion pic'ture s pellicola cinematografica; **motion pictures** cinematografia

mo'tion-picture' adj cinematografico

motivate ['motɪ,vet] tr animare, incitare

motive ['motɪv] adj motivo; (producing motion) motore || s motivo; (incentive) movente m

mo'tive pow'er s forza motrice; impianto motore; (rr) insieme m di locomotive

motley ['mɑtli] adj eterogeneo; variato, variopinto

motor ['motər] adj motore; (operated by motor) motorizzato; (pertaining to motor vehicles) motoristico || s motore m; (aut) macchina || intr viaggiare in macchina

mo'tor-boat' s motobarca, motoscafo

mo'tor-bus' s torpedone m; autobus m

motorcade ['motər,ked] s carovana di automobili

mo'tor-car' s automobile f

mo'tor-cy'cle s motocicletta

motorist ['motərɪst] s automobilista mf

motorize ['motə,raɪz] tr motorizzare

mo'tor-man s (**-men**) guidatore m di tram; guidatore m di locomotore

mo'tor-sail'er s motoveliero

mo'tor scoot'er s motoretta

mo'tor ship' s motonave f

mo'tor-truck' s autocarro, camion m

mo'tor ve'hicle s motoveicolo

mottle ['mɑtəl] tr chiazzare, screziare

mot·to ['mɑto] s (**-toes** or **-tos**) motto, divisa

mould [mold] s, tr, & intr var of **mold**

mound [maʊnd] s monticello, collinetta

mount [maʊnt] s monte m, montagna; (horse for riding) cavalcatura, monta; (setting for a jewel) montatura; supporto; (for a picture) incorniciatura || tr montare; (a wall) scalare; (theat) allestire || intr montare; (to climb) salire

mountain ['maʊntən] s montagna; **to make a mountain out of a molehill** fare di un bruscolo una trave, fare d'una mosca un elefante

moun'tain climb'ing s alpinismo

mountaineer [,maʊntə'nɪr] s montanaro

mountainous ['maʊntənəs] adj montagnoso

moun'tain rail'road s ferrovia a dentiera

moun'tain range' s catena di montagne

moun'tain sick'ness s mal m di montagna

mountebank ['maʊntɪ,bæŋk] s ciarlatano

mounting ['maʊntɪŋ] s (act) il montare, montaggio; (setting) montatura; (mach) supporto

mourn [morn] tr (the loss of s.o.) piangere; (a misfortune) lamentare || intr piangere; vestire a lutto

mourner ['mornər] s persona in lutto; (penitent sinner) penitente mf;

(woman hired to attend a funeral or funerals) prefica

mourn'er's bench' s banco dei penitenti

mournful ['mɔrnfəl] adj luttuoso, funesto; (gloomy) lugubre

mourning ['mɔrnɪŋ] s lutto; **to be in mourning** portare il lutto

mourn'ing band' s bracciale m a lutto

mouse [maus] s (**mice** [maɪs]) topo, sorcio

mouse'hole' s topaia; piccolo buco

mouser ['mauzər] s cacciatore m di topi

mouse'trap' s trappola per topi

moustache [məs'tæʃ] or [məs'taʃ] s baffi mpl, mustacchi mpl

mouth [mauθ] s (**mouths** [mauðz]) bocca; **by mouth** per via orale; **to be born with a silver spoon in one's mouth** essere nato con la camicia; **to make one's mouth water** fare venire a qlcu l'acquolina in bocca

mouthful ['mauθˌful] s boccata

mouth' or'gan s armonica a bocca

mouth'piece' s (of wind instrument) bocchetta; (of bridle) imboccatura; (of megaphone) boccaglio; (of cigarette) bocchino; (of telephone) imboccatura; (spokesman) portavoce m

mouth'wash' s sciacquo, risciacquo

movable ['muvəbəl] adj mobile, movibile; (law) mobiliare

move [muv] s movimento; (change of residence) trasloco; (step) passo; (e.g., in chess) mossa; **on the move in** moto, in movimento; **to get a move on** (coll) affrettarsi ‖ tr muovere; (the bowels) provocare l'evacuazione di; (to prompt) spingere; (to stir the feelings of) emozionare, commuovere; (law) proporre; (com) svendere; **to move up** (a date) anticipare ‖ intr muoversi; passare; (to another house) traslocare; (to another city) trasferirsi; (said of goods) avere una vendita; (said of the bowels) evacuare; procedere; (law) presentare una mozione; (coll) andarsene; **to move away** andarsene; trasferirsi; **to move back** tirarsi indietro; **to move in** avanzare; (society) frequentare; **to move off** allontanarsi

movement ['muvmənt] s movimento; (of a watch) meccanismo; (of the bowels) evacuazione; (mus) movimento, tempo

movie ['muvi] s (coll) film m, pellicola

movie-goer ['muviˌgo·ər] s frequentatore m del cinema

mov'ie house' s (coll) cinematografo

mov'ie-land' s (coll) cinelandia

moving ['muvɪŋ] adj commovente, emozionante ‖ s trasporto; (from one house to another) trasloco

mov'ing pic'ture s film m, pellicola

mov'ing stair'case' s scala mobile

mow [mo] v (pret **mowed**; pp **mowed** or **mown**) tr & intr falciare

mower ['mo·ər] s falciatore m; (mach) falciatrice f

Mr. ['mɪstər] s (**Messrs.** ['mesərz]) Signore m

Mrs. ['mɪsɪz] s Signora

much [mʌtʃ] adj & pron molto; **as much . . . as** tanto . . . quanto; **too much** troppo ‖ adv molto; **however much** per quanto; **how much** quanto; **too much** troppo; **very much** moltissimo

mucilage ['mjusɪlɪdʒ] s colla; (gummy secretion in plants) mucillagine f

muck [mʌk] s letame m; (dirt) sudiciume m; (min) materiale m di scoria

muck'rake' intr (coll) sollevare scandali

mucous ['mjukəs] adj mucoso

mucus ['mjukəs] s muco

mud [mʌd] s fango, melma, limo; **to sling mud at** calunniare

muddle ['mʌdəl] s confusione, guazzabuglio ‖ tr confondere, intorbidire ‖ intr—**to muddle through** arrangiarsi; cavarsela alla meno peggio in

mud'dle-head' s (coll) semplicione m

mud-dy ['mʌdi] adj (-dier; -diest) fangoso, melmoso; (obscure) torbido ‖ v (pret & pp -died) tr turbare, intorbidare; (to soil with mud) infangare

mud'guard' s parafango

mud'hole' s pozzanghera, fangaia

mud' slide' s smottamento

mudslinger ['mʌdˌslɪŋgər] s calunniatore m

muff [mʌf] s manicotto ‖ tr (coll) mancare; (to handle badly) (coll) abborracciare; (sports) mancare di pigliare

muffin ['mʌfɪn] s panino soffice

muffle ['mʌfəl] tr infagottare, imbacuccare; (a sound) velare, smorzare

muffler ['mʌflər] s sciarpa; (aut) silenziatore m, marmitta

mufti ['mʌfti] s—**in mufti** in borghese

mug [mʌg] s tazzona; (slang) muso, grugno ‖ v (pret & pp **mugged**; ger **mugging**) tr (slang) fotografare; (slang) attaccare proditoriamente ‖ intr fare le smorfie

mug-gy ['mʌgi] adj (-gier; -giest) afoso, opprimente

mulat-to [mju'læto] or [mə'læto] s (-toes) mulatto

mulber-ry ['mʌlˌbɛri] s (-ries) (tree) gelso; (fruit) mora di gelso

mulct [mʌlkt] tr defraudare

mule [mjul] s mulo; (slipper) pianella

muleteer [ˌmjulə'tɪr] s mulattiere m

mulish ['mjulɪʃ] adj testardo

mull [mʌl] tr (wine) scaldare aggiungendo spezie ‖ intr—**to mull over** pensarci sopra, rinvangare

mulled' wine' s vino caldo

mullion ['mʌljən] s colonnina che divide una bifora

multigraph ['mʌltɪˌgræf] or ['mʌltɪˌgraf] s (trademark) poligrafo ‖ tr poligrafare

multilateral [ˌmʌltɪ'lætərəl] adj multilaterale

multimotor [ˌmʌltɪ'motər] s plurimotore m

multiple ['mʌltɪpəl] adj & s multiplo

multiplici-ty [ˌmʌltɪ'plɪsɪti] s (-ties) molteplicità f

multi-ply ['mʌltɪˌplaɪ] v (pret & pp -plied) tr moltiplicare ‖ intr moltiplicarsi

multistage ['mʌltɪ‚stedʒ] *adj* (rok) pluristadio

multitude ['mʌltɪ‚tjud] or ['mʌltɪ‚tud] *s* moltitudine *f*

mum [mʌm] *adj* zitto; **mum's the word!** acqua in bocca!; **to keep mum** stare zitto || *interj* zitto!

mumble ['mʌmbəl] *tr* biascicare || *intr* farfugliare

mummer·y ['mʌməri] *s* (-ies) buffonata, mascherata

mum·my ['mʌmi] *s* (-mies) mummia

mumps [mʌmps] *s* orecchioni *mpl*

munch [mʌntʃ] *tr* sgranocchiare

mundane ['mʌnden] *adj* mondano

municipal [mju'nɪsɪpəl] *adj* municipale

municipali·ty [mju‚nɪsɪ'pælɪti] *s* (-ties) municipio

munificent [mju'nɪfɪsənt] *adj* munifico

munition [mju'nɪʃən] *s* munizione || *tr* fornire di munizioni

muni'tion dump' *s* deposito munizioni

mural ['mjʊrəl] *adj* murale || *s* pittura murale

murder ['mʌrdər] *s* omicidio || *tr* assassinare

murderer ['mʌrdərər] *s* omicida *m*

murderess ['mʌrdərɪs] *s* omicida *f*

murderous ['mʌrdərəs] *adj* omicida, crudele, sanguinario

murk·y ['mʌrki] *adj* (-ier; -iest) fosco, tenebroso; brumoso, nebbioso

murmur ['mʌrmər] *s* mormorio || *tr* & *intr* mormorare

Mur'phy bed' ['mʌrfi] *s* letto a scomparsa

muscle ['mʌsəl] *s* muscolo

muscular ['mʌskjələr] *adj* muscolare; *(having well-developed muscles)* muscoloso

muse [mjuz] *s* musa; **the Muses** le Muse || *intr* meditare, rimuginare

museum [mju'ziəm] *s* museo

mush [mʌʃ] *s* pappa, polentina; (fig) leziosaggine *f*, sdolcinatura

mush'room *s* fungo || *intr* venir su come i funghi; **to mushroom into** diventare rapidamente

mush'room cloud' *s* fungo atomico

mush·y ['mʌʃi] *adj* (-ier; -iest) polposo, spappolato; (fig) sdolcinato, sentimentale

music ['mjuzɪk] *s* musica; **to face the music** (coll) affrontare le conseguenze; **to set to music** mettere in musica

musical ['mjuzɪkəl] *adj* musicale

mu'sical com'edy *s* operetta, commedia musicale

musicale [‚mjuzɪ'kæl] *s* serata musicale

mu'sic box' *s* scatola armonica

mu'sic cab'inet *s* scaffaletto per la musica

mu'sic hall' *s* salone *m* da concerti; (Brit) teatro di varietà, music-hall *m*

musician [mju'zɪʃən] *s* musicista *mf*

musicianship [mju'zɪʃən‚ʃɪp] *s* abilità *f* musicale, virtuosismo

musicologist [‚mjuzɪ'kɑlədʒɪst] *s* musicologo

musicology [‚mjuzɪ'kɑlədʒi] *s* musicologia

mu'sic stand' *s* portamusica *m*

musk [mʌsk] *s* muschio

musk' deer' *s* mosco

musket ['mʌskɪt] *s* moschetto

musketeer [‚mʌskɪ'tɪr] *s* moschettiere *m*

musk'mel'on *s* melone *m*

musk' ox' *s* bue muschiato

musk'rat' *s* ondatra, topo muschiato

muslin ['mʌzlɪn] *s* mussolina

muss [mʌs] *tr (the hair)* scompigliare, arruffare; *(clothing)* (coll) sciupare

mussel ['mʌsəl] *s* mussolo

Mussulman ['mʌsəlmən] *adj* & *s* musulmano

muss·y ['mʌsi] *adj* (-ier; -iest) (coll) arruffato, scompigliato

must [mʌst] *s (new wine)* mosto; *(mold)* muffa; (coll) cosa assolutamente indispensabile || *v aux*—**I must go now** devo andarmene ora; **it must be Ann** deve essere Anna; **she must be ill** dev'essere malata; **they must have known it** devono averlo saputo

mustache [məs'tæʃ], [məs'tɑʃ] or ['mʌstæʃ] *s* baffi *mpl*, mustacchi *mpl*

mustard ['mʌstərd] *s* mostarda

mus'tard plas'ter *s* senapismo

muster ['mʌstər] *s* adunata, rivista; **to pass muster** passar ispezione || *tr* chiamare a raccolta; riunire; **to muster in** arruolare; **to muster out** congedare; **to muster up courage** prendere coraggio a quattro mani

mus'ter roll' *s* ruolo; (naut) appello

mus·ty ['mʌsti] *adj* (-tier; -tiest) *(moldy)* ammuffito; *(stale)* stantio; (fig) ammuffito, stantio

mutation [mju'teʃən] *s* mutazione

mute [mjut] *adj* & *s* muto || *tr* mettere la sordina a

mutilate ['mjutɪ‚let] *tr* mutilare

mutineer [‚mjutɪ'nɪr] *s* ammutinato

mutinous ['mjutɪnəs] *adj* ammutinato

muti·ny ['mjutɪni] *s* (-nies) ammutinamento || *v (pret & pp* -nied*) intr* ammutinarsi

mutt [mʌt] *s* (slang) cane bastardo; (slang) scemo

mutter ['mʌtər] *tr* & *intr* borbottare

mutton ['mʌtən] *s* montone *m*

mut'ton chop' *s* cotoletta di montone

mutual ['mutʃu‚əl] *adj* mutuo, vicendevole

mu'tual aid' *s* mutualità *f*

mu'tual fund' *s* fondo comune di investimento

muzzle ['mʌzəl] *s (of animal)* muso; *(device to keep animal from biting)* museruola; *(of firearm)* bocca || *tr* mettere la museruola a; (fig) imbavagliare

my [maɪ] *adj poss* mio, il mio || *interj* (coll) corbezzoli!

myriad ['mɪrɪ‚əd] *s* miriade *f*

myrrh [mʌr] *s* mirra

myrtle ['mʌrtəl] *s* mirto, mortella

myself [maɪ'self] *pron pers* io stesso; me, me stesso; mi, e.g., **I hurt myself** mi sono fatto male

mysterious [mɪs'tɪrɪ-əs] *adj* misterioso
myster·y ['mɪstəri] *s* (-ies) mistero
mystic ['mɪstɪk] *adj & s* mistico
mystical ['mɪstɪkəl] *adj* mistico
mysticism ['mɪstɪ ‚sɪzəm] *s* misticismo
mystification [‚mɪstɪfɪ'keʃən] *s* mistificazione
mysti·fy ['mɪstɪ ‚faɪ] *v* (*pret & pp*

-fied) *tr* avvolgere nel mistero; (*to hoax*) mistificare
myth [mɪθ] *s* mito
mythical ['mɪθɪkəl] *adj* mitico
mythological [‚mɪθə'lɑdʒɪkəl] *adj* mitologico
mytholo·gy [mɪ'θɑlədʒi] *s* (-gies) mitologia

N

N, n [ɛn] *s* quattordicesima lettera dell'alfabeto inglese
nab [næb] *v* (*pret & pp* **nabbed;** *ger* **nabbing**) *tr* (slang) afferrare, agguantare
nag [næg] *s* ronzino ‖ *v* (*pret & pp* **nagged;** *ger* **nagging**) *tr & intr* tormentare, infastidire
naiad ['ne·æd] or ['naɪ·æd] *s* naiade *f*
nail [nel] *s* (*of finger or toe*) unghia; (*of metal*) chiodo; **to hit the nail on the head** cogliere nel giusto ‖ *tr* inchiodare
nail'brush' spazzolino per le unghie
nail' file' *s* lima per le unghie
nail' pol'ish *s* smalto per le unghie
nail' set' *s* punzone *m*
naïve [nɑ'iv] *adj* candido, ingenuo
naked ['nekɪd] *adj* nudo, ignudo; **to strip naked** denudare; denudarsi; **with the naked eye** a occhio nudo
name [nem] *s* nome *m;* (*first name*) nome *m;* (*last name*) cognome *m;* fama, reputazione; titolo; lignaggio; **in the name of** nel nome di; **to call s.o. names** coprire qlco di ingiurie; **to go by the name of** essere conosciuto sotto il nome di; **to make a name for oneself** farsi un nome; **what is your name?** come si chiama Lei? ‖ *tr* nominare; menzionare; battezzare; (*a price*) fissare
name' day' *s* onomastico
nameless ['nemlɪs] *adj* senza nome, anonimo
namely ['nemli] *adv* cioè, vale a dire
name'plate' *s* targa, targhetta
namesake ['nem ‚sek] *s* omonimo; persona chiamata in onore di qualcun altro
nan'ny goat' ['næni] *s* capra
nap [næp] *s* lanugine *f;* (*pile*) pelo; pisolino, sonnellino; **to take a nap** schiacciare un sonnellino ‖ *v* (*pret & pp* **napped;** *ger* **napping**) *intr* sonnecchiare; **to catch napping** cogliere alla sprovvista
napalm ['nepɑm] *s* napalm *m*
nape [nep] *s* nuca
naphtha ['næfθə] *s* nafta
napkin ['næpkɪn] *s* tovagliolo
nap'kin ring' *s* portatovagliolo
Naples ['nepləz] *s* Napoli *f*
Napoleonic [nə ‚poli'ɑnɪk] *adj* napoleonico
narcissus [nɑr'sɪsəs] *s* narciso
narcotic [nɑr'kɑtɪk] *adj & s* narcotico
narrate [næ'ret] *tr* narrare

narration [næ'reʃən] *s* narrazione
narrative ['nærətɪv] *adj* narrativo ‖ *s* narrazione; (*genre*) narrativa
narrator [næ'retər] *s* narratore *m*
narrow ['næro] *adj* stretto; limitato; (*illiberal*) meschino, ristretto ‖ **narrows** *spl* stretti *mpl* ‖ *tr* limitare, restringere ‖ *intr* limitarsi, restringersi
nar'row escape' *s*—**to have a narrow escape** scamparla bella
nar'row-gauge' *adj* a scartamento ridotto
narrow-minded ['næro'maɪndɪd] *adj* gretto, ristretto d'idee
nasal ['nezəl] *adj & s* nasale *f*
nasturtium [nə'stʌrʃəm] *s* nasturzio
nas·ty ['næsti] or ['nɑsti] *adj* (-tier; -tiest) brutto, cattivo; sgradevole, orribile; sudicio; (*foul*) perfido
natatorium [‚netə'torɪ·əm] *s* piscina
nation ['neʃən] *s* nazione
national ['næʃənəl] *adj & s* nazionale *mf*
na'tional an'them *s* inno nazionale
na'tional debt' *s* debito pubblico
na'tional hol'iday *s* festa nazionale
nationalism ['næʃənə ‚lɪzəm] *s* nazionalismo
nationali·ty [‚næʃən'ælɪti] *s* (-ties) nazionalità *f*
nationalize ['næʃənə ‚laɪz] *tr* nazionalizzare
na'tion-wide' *adj* su scala nazionale
native ['netɪv] *adj* nativo, indigeno, oriundo; (*language*) materno ‖ *s* indigeno, nativo
na'tive land' *s* patria, paese natio
nativi·ty [nə'tɪvɪti] *s* (-ties) nascita, natività *f* ‖ **Nativity** *s* Natività *f*
Nato ['neto] *s* (acronym) (**North Atlantic Treaty Organization**) la N.A.T.O.
nat·ty ['næti] *adj* (-tier; -tiest) accurato, elegante
natural ['nætʃərəl] *adj* naturale ‖ *s* imbecille *mf;* (*mus*) bequadro; (*mus*) tono naturale; (*mus*) tasto bianco; **a natural** (coll) proprio quello che ci vuole
naturalism ['nætʃərə ‚lɪzəm] *s* naturalismo
naturalist ['nætʃərəlɪst] *s* naturalista *mf*
naturalization [‚nætʃərəlɪ'zeʃən] *s* naturalizzazione
nat'uraliza'tion pa'pers *spl* documenti *mpl* di naturalizzazione

naturalize ['nætʃərə,laɪz] *tr* naturaliz-zare

naturally ['nætʃərəli] *adv* naturalmente

nature ['netʃər] *s* natura; **from nature** dal vero

naught [nɔt] *s* niente *m*; zero; **to come to naught** ridursi al nulla; **to set at naught** disprezzare

naugh·ty ['nɔti] *adj* (**-tier; -tiest**) cattivo, disubbidiente; (*joke*) di cattivo genere

nausea ['nɔʃɪ·ə] *or* ['nɔsɪ·ə] *s* nausea

nauseate ['nɔʃɪ,et] *or* ['nɔsɪ,et] *tr* nauseare || *intr* essere nauseato

nauseating ['nɔʃɪ,etɪŋ] *or* ['nɔsɪ,etɪŋ] *adj* nauseabondo, stomachevole

nauseous ['nɔʃɪ·əs] *or* ['nɔsɪ·əs] *adj* nauseabondo

nautical ['nɔtɪkəl] *adj* nautico, marittimo, marino

naval ['nevəl] *adj* navale

na'val acad'emy *s* accademia navale

na'val of'ficer *s* ufficiale *m* di marina

na'val sta'tion *s* base *f* navale

nave [nev] *s* navata centrale; (*of a wheel*) mozzo

navel ['nevəl] *s* ombelico

na'vel or'ange *s* arancia (con depressione alla sommità)

navigability [,nævɪgə'bɪlɪti] *s* navigabilità *f*; (*of a ship*) manovrabilità *f*

navigable ['nævɪgəbəl] *adj* (*river*) navigabile; (*ship*) manovrabile

navigate ['nævɪ,get] *tr & intr* navigare

navigation [,nævɪ'geʃən] *s* navigazione

navigator ['nævɪ,getər] *s* navigatore *m*; (*in charge of navigating ship or plane*) ufficiale *m* di rotta

na·vy ['nevi] *adj* blu marino || *s* (**-vies**) marina (da guerra)

na'vy bean' *s* fagiolo secco

na'vy blue' *s* blu marino

na'vy yard' *s* arsenale *m*

nay [ne] *s* no; voto negativo || *adv* no; anzi

Nazarene [,næzə'rin] *adj & s* nazzareno; **the Nazarene** il Nazzareno

Nazi ['nɑtsi] *or* ['nætsi] *adj & s* nazista *mf*

N-bomb ['en ,bɑm] *s* bomba al neutrone

Neapolitan [,ni·ə'pɑlɪtən] *adj & s* napoletano

neap' tide' [nip] *s* marea di quadratura

near [nɪr] *adj* vicino, prossimo; intimo; esatto || *adv* vicino, da vicino || *prep* vicino a, accanto a; **to come near avvicinarsi a** || *tr* avvicinarsi a || *intr* avvicinarsi

nearby ['nɪr,baɪ] *adj* vicino || *adv* vicino, qui vicino

Near' East' *s* Medio Oriente

nearly ['nɪrli] *adv* quasi; (*a little more or less*) press'a poco; per poco non, e.g., **he nearly died** per poco non morì

near-sighted ['nɪr'saɪtɪd] *adj* miope

near'-sight'ed·ness *s* miopia

neat [nit] *adj* netto, pulito; elegante; accurato; puro

neat's'-foot oil' *s* olio di piede di bue

Nebuchadnezzar [,nebjəkəd'nezər] *s* Nabucodonosor *m*

nebu·la ['nebjələ] *s* (**-lae** [,li] *or* **-las**) nebulosa

nebular ['nebjələr] *adj* nebulare

nebulous ['nebjələs] *adj* nebuloso

necessary ['nesɪ,seri] *adj* necessario

necessitate [nɪ'sesɪ,tet] *tr* necessitare, esigere

necessitous [nɪ'sesɪtəs] *adj* bisognoso

necessi·ty [nɪ'sesɪti] *s* (**-ties**) necessità *f*

neck [nek] *s* collo; (*of a horse*) incollatura; (*of violin*) manico; (*of mountain*) gola, passo; **neck and neck** testa a testa; **to stick one's neck out** (coll) esporsi al pericolo; **to win by a neck** vincere per una corta testa || *intr* (slang) abbracciarsi, sbaciucchiarsi

neck'band' *s* colletto

neckerchief ['nekər,tʃɪf] *s* fazzoletto da collo

necklace ['neklɪs] *s* collana

neck'line' *s* giro collo, scollatura

necktie ['nek,taɪ] *s* cravatta

neck'tie pin' *s* spilla da cravatta

necrolo·gy [ne'krɑlədʒi] *s* (**-gies**) necrologia

necromancy ['nekrə,mænsi] *s* necromanzia

nectar ['nektər] *s* nettare *m*

née *or* **nee** [ne] *adj* nata

need [nid] *s* necessità *f*, bisogno; povertà *f*; **if need be** se ci fosse bisogno; **in need** in strettezza || *tr* aver bisogno di || *intr* necessitare, essere in necessità || *v aux*—**to need (to)** + *inf* dovere + *inf*

needful ['nidfəl] *adj* necessario

needle ['nidəl] *s* ago; (*of phonograph*) puntina; **to look for a needle in a haystack** cercare l'ago nel pagliaio || *tr* cucire; (fig) aguzzare, eccitare

nee'dle bath' *s* bagno a doccia filiforme

nee'dle·case' *s* agoraio

nee'dle·point' *s* merletto; ricamo su canovaccio

needless ['nidlɪs] *adj* inutile

nee'dle·work' *s* lavoro di cucito; (*embroidery*) ricamo; (*needlepoint*) merletto

needs [nidz] *adv* necessariamente; **it must needs be** dev'essere proprio così

need·y ['nidi] *adj* (**-ier; -iest**) bisognoso, indigente || **the needy** i bisognosi

ne'er-do-well ['nerdu,wel] *adj & s* buono a nulla

negate ['neget] *or* [nɪ'get] *tr* invalidare; negare

negation [nɪ'geʃən] *s* negazione

negative ['negətɪv] *adj* negativo || *s* negativa; (elec) polo negativo; (gram) negazione || *tr* respingere, votare contro; neutralizzare

neglect [nɪ'glekt] *s* negligenza, trascuratezza || *tr* trascurare; **to neglect to** trascurare di; dimenticarsi di

neglectful [nɪ'glektfəl] *adj* negligente, trascurato

négligée *or* **negligee** [,neglɪ'ʒe] *s* veste *f* da camera *or* vestaglia per signora

negligence ['neglɪdʒəns] *s* negligenza, trascuratezza

negligent ['neglɪdʒənt] *adj* negligente, trascurato

negligible ['neglɪdʒɪbəl] *adj* trascurabile, insignificante

negotiable [nɪ'goʃɪ·əbəl] *adj* negoziabile; (*security*) al portatore; (*road*) transitabile

negotiate [nɪ'goʃɪ‚et] *tr* negoziare; (*to overcome*) superare ‖ *intr* negoziare

negotiation [nɪ‚goʃɪ'eʃən] *s* negoziazione, negoziato

Ne·gro ['nigro] *adj* negro ‖ *s* (-groes) negro, nero

neigh [ne] *s* nitrito ‖ *intr* nitrire

neighbor ['nebər] *adj* vicino, adiacente ‖ *s* vicino; (*fellow man*) prossimo ‖ *tr* essere vicino a ‖ *intr* essere vicino

neighborhood ['nebər‚hʊd] *s* vicinanza, vicinato; **in the neighborhood of** nei pressi di; (coll) a un dipresso, all'incirca

neighboring ['nebərɪŋ] *adj* vicino, attiguo; (*country*) limitrofo

neighborly ['nebərli] *adj* da buon vicino, socievole

neither ['niðər] or ['naɪðər] *adj indef* nessuno dei due, *e.g.*, **neither boy** nessuno dei due ragazzi ‖ *pron indef* nessuno dei due, nè l'uno nè l'altro ‖ *conj* neppure, nemmeno, *e.g.*, **neither do I** nemmeno io; **neither . . . nor** nè . . . nè

neme·sis ['nemɪsɪs] *s* (-ses [‚siz]) nemesi *f* ‖ **Nemesis** *s* Nemesi *f*

neologism [ni'ɑlə‚dʒɪzəm] *s* neologismo

neomycin [‚ni·ə'maɪsɪn] *s* neomicina

ne'on lamp' ['ni·ɑn] *s* lampada al neon

neophyte ['ni·ə‚faɪt] *s* neofita *mf*

nepenthe [nɪ'penθi] *s* nepente *f*

nephew ['nefju] or ['nevju] *s* nipote *m*

Nepos ['nipɑs] or ['nepɑs] *s* Nipote *m*

Neptune ['neptʃun] or ['neptjun] *s* Nettuno

neptunium [nep't·(jun)·əm] or [nep'tjunɪ·əm] *s* (chem) nettunio

Nero ['nɪro] *s* Nerone *m*

nerve [nʌrv] *adj* nervoso ‖ *s* nervo; (*courage*) coraggio; (*boldness*) (coll) faccia tosta; **to get on one's nerves** dare ai nervi di qlcu; **to lose one's nerve** perdere le staffe

nerve-racking ['nʌrv‚rækɪŋ] *adj* irritante, esasperante

nervous ['nʌrvəs] *adj* nervoso

nerv'ous break'down *s* esaurimento nervoso

nervousness ['nʌrvəsnɪs] *s* nervosismo

nerv·y ['nʌrvi] *adj* (-ier; -iest) (*strong*) forte, vigoroso; (*audace*); (coll) insolente, sfacciato

nest [nest] *s* nido; (*of hen*) cova; (*retreat*) rifugio; (*hangout*) tana; (*brood*) nidiata; **to feather one's nest** farsi il gruzzolo ‖ *tr* (*e.g.*, *tables*) mettere l'uno nell'altro ‖ *intr* nidificare

nest' egg' *s* endice *m*; (fig) gruzzolo

nestle ['nesəl] *tr* annidare ‖ *intr* annidarsi, nidificare; (*to cuddle up*) rannicchiarsi

net [net] *adj* netto ‖ *s* rete *f*; (*snare*) laccio, trappola; guadagno netto ‖

tr prendere con la rete; (*a sum of money*) fare un guadagno netto di

nether ['neðər] *adj* inferiore, infero

Netherlander ['neðər‚lændər] or ['neðərləndər] *s* olandese *mf*

Netherlands, The ['neðərləndz] *spl* i Paesi Bassi

netting ['netɪŋ] *s* rete *f*

nettle ['netəl] *s* ortica ‖ *tr* irritare, provocare

net'work' *s* rete *f*

neuralgia [nju'rældʒə] or [nʊ'rældʒə] *s* nevralgia

neurology [nju'rɑlədʒi] or [nʊ'rɑlədʒi] *s* neurologia

neuro·sis [nju'rosɪs] or [nʊ'rosɪs] (-ses [siz]) *s* neurosi *f*

neurotic [nju'rɑtɪk] or [nʊ'rɑtɪk] *adj* & *s* neurotico

neuter ['njutər] or ['nutər] *adj* neutro ‖ *s* genere neutro

neutral ['njutrəl] or ['nutrəl] *adj* neutro; (*not aligned*) neutrale ‖ *s* neutrale *m*; (mach) folle *m*

neutralist ['njutrəlɪst] or ['nutrəlɪst] *adj* & *s* neutralista *mf*

neutrality [nju'trælɪti] or [nu'trælɪti] *s* neutralità *f*

neutralize ['njutrə‚laɪz] or ['nutrə‚laɪz] *tr* neutralizzare

neutron ['njutrɑn] or ['nutrɑn] *s* neutrone *m*

neu'tron bomb' *s* bomba al neutrone

never ['nevər] *adv* mai, giammai; **non . . . mai**; **never mind** non importa

nev'er·more' *adv* mai più

nevertheless [‚nevərðə'les] *adv* ciò nonostante, ciò nondimeno, tuttavia

new [nju] or [nu] *adj* nuovo; **what's new?** che c'è di nuovo?

new' arri'val *s* nuovo venuto; (*baby*) neonato

new'born' *adj* neonato; (*e.g.*, *faith*) rinato

New·cas·tle *s*—**to carry coals to Newcastle** portare l'acqua al mare, portare vasi a Samo

newcomer ['nju‚kʌmər] or ['nu‚kʌmər] *s* nuovo venuto

New' Eng'land *s* la Nuova Inghilterra

newfangled ['nju‚fæŋgəld] or ['nu‚fæŋgəld] *adj* all'ultima moda; di nuovo conio, di nuova invenzione

Newfoundland ['njufənd‚lænd] or ['nufənd‚lænd] *s* la Terranova ‖ [nju'faundlənd] or [nu'faundlənd] *s* (*dog*) terranova *m*

newly ['njuli] or ['nuli] *adv* di recente, di fresco

new'ly·wed' *s* sposino or sposina; **the newlyweds** gli sposi

new' moon' *s* luna nuova, novilunio

news [njuz] or [nuz] *s* notizie *fpl*; **a news item** una notizia; **a piece of news** una notizia

news' a'gency *s* agenzia d'informazioni

news'beat' *s* colpo giornalistico

news'boy' *s* strillone *m*

news'cast' *s* notiziario

news'cast'er *s* annunziatore *m*, radiocommentatore *m*, telecommentatore *m*

news' con'ference *s* conferenza stampa

news′ cov′erage s reportaggio
news′deal′er s venditore m di giornali
news′man′ s (-men′) (*reporter*) giornalista m; giornalaio
newsmonger [′njuz‚mʌŋgər] or [′nuz‚mʌŋgər] s persona pettegola, gazzettino
news′pa′per adj giornalistico || s giornale m
news′pa′per·man′ s (-men′) giornalista m
news′print′ s carta da giornale
news′reel′ s cinegiornale m
news′stand′ s chiosco, edicola
news′week′ly s (-lies) settimanale m d'informazione
news′wor′thy adj degno d'essere pubblicato, di viva attualità
news·y [′njuzi] or [′nuzi] adj (-ier; -iest) (coll) informativo
New′ Tes′tament s Nuovo Testamento
New′ Year′s′ card′ s cartolina d'auguri di capodanno
New′ Year′s′ Day′ s il capo d'anno, il capodanno
New′ Year′s′ Eve′ s la vigilia di capodanno, la sera di San Silvestro
New′ York′ [jɔrk] adj nuovayorchese || s New York f, Nuova York
New′ York′er [′jɔrkər] s nuovayorchese mf
New′ Zea′land [′zilənd] adj neozelandese || s la Nuova Zelanda
New′ Zea′lander [′ziləndər] s neozelandese mf
next [nekst] adj prossimo, seguente; (*month*) prossimo, entrante || adv la prossima volta; dopo, in seguito; **next to** vicino a; **next to nothing** quasi nulla; **to come next** essere il prossimo
next′-door′ adj della casa vicina || **next′-door′** adv nella casa vicina
next′ of kin′ s (next′ of kin′) parente più prossimo
niacin [′naɪ·əsɪn] s niacina
Niag′ara Falls′ [naɪ′ægərə] spl le Cascate del Niagara
nib [nɪb] s becco; punta; **his nibs** (slang & pej) sua eccellenza
nibble [′nɪbəl] s piccolo morso || tr & intr mordicchiare, sbocconcellare; (*said of a fish*) abboccare
nice [naɪs] adj (*pleasant*) simpatico, gentile; (*requiring skill*) buono, bello; (*fine*) sottile; (*refined*) raffinato, per bene; (*fussy*) esigente, difficile; rispettabile; (*weather*) bello; (*attractive*) bello; **nice ... and** (coll) bello, e.g., **it is nice and warm** fa un bel caldo
nice-looking [′naɪs′lukɪŋ] adj bello, attraente
nicely [′naɪsli] adv precisamente, esattamente; (coll) benissimo
nice·ty [′naɪsəti] s (-ties) esattezza, precisione; **to a nicety** con la massima precisione
niche [nɪtʃ] s nicchia
Nicholas [′nɪkələs] s Nicola m
nick [nɪk] s intaccatura; (*of a dish*) slabbratura; **in the nick of time** al

momento giusto || tr intaccare; (*to cut*) tagliare; (*a dish*) slabbrare
nickel [′nɪkəl] s nichel m; moneta americana di cinque cents || tr nichelare
nick′el plate′ s nichelatura
nick′el-plate′ tr nichelare
nicknack [′nɪk‚næk] s soprammobile m; gingillo, ninnolo
nick′name′ s nomignolo, soprannome m || tr soprannominare
nicotine [′nɪkə‚tin] s nicotina
niece [nis] s nipote f
nif·ty [′nɪfti] adj (-tier; -tiest) (coll) elegante; (coll) eccellente
niggard [′nɪgərd] adj & s spilorcio
night [naɪt] adj notturno || s notte f; **at or by night** di notte; **the night before last** l'altra notte; **to make a night of it** (coll) fare le ore piccole
night′cap′ s berretto da notte; bicchierino di liquore che si beve prima di coricarsi
night′ club′ s night-club m
night′ driv′ing s il guidare di notte
night′fall′ s crepuscolo; **at nightfall** sul cader della notte, all'imbrunire
night′gown′ s camicia da notte
nightingale [′naɪtən‚gel] s usignolo
night′ latch′ s serratura a molla
night′ let′ter s telegramma notturno
night′long′ adj di tutta la notte || adv tutta la notte
nightly [′naɪtli] adj di notte; di ogni notte || adv di notte; ogni notte
night′mare′ s incubo
nightmarish [′naɪt‚merɪʃ] adj raccapricciante
night′ owl′ s (coll) nottambulo
night′ school′ s scuola serale
night′shirt′ s camicia da notte
night′time′ s notte f
night′walk′er s nottambulo; vagabondo notturno; (*prostitute*) passeggiatrice f
night′ watch′ s guardia notturna
night′ watch′man s (-men) guardiano notturno
nihilist [′naɪ·ɪlɪst] s nichilista mf
nil [nɪl] s nulla m, niente m
Nile [naɪl] s Nilo
nimble [′nɪmbəl] adj agile, svelto
Nimrod [′nɪmrɑd] s Nembrod m
nincompoop [′nɪnkəm‚pup] s babbeo, tonto, semplicione m
nine [naɪn] adj & pron nove || s nove m; **nine o' clock** le nove
nine′ hun′dred adj, s & pron novecento
nineteen [′naɪn′tin] adj, s & pron diciannove m
nineteenth [′naɪn′tinθ] adj & s diciannovesimo; (*century*) decimonono || s (*in dates*) diciannove m || pron diciannovesimo
ninetieth [′naɪntɪ·ɪθ] adj, s & pron novantesimo
nine·ty [′naɪnti] adj & pron novanta || s (-ties) novanta m; **the gay nineties** il decennio scapestrato dal 1890 al 1900
ninth [naɪnθ] adj, s & pron nono || s (*in dates*) nove m
nip [nɪp] s morso, pizzicotto; freddo pungente; (*of liquor*) bicchierino,

sorso; **nip and tuck** testa a testa ‖ *v* (*pret & pp* **nipped; ger nipping**) *tr* pizzicare, mordere; (*to squeeze*) spremere; (*to freeze*) gelare; (*liquor*) sorseggiare; **to nip in the bud** arrestare di bel principio ‖ *intr* bere a sorsi

nipple ['nɪpəl] *s* capezzolo; (*of rubber*) tettarella; (mach) corto tubo filettato a entrambe le estremità, manicotto, cappuccio

Nippon [nɪ'pan] *or* ['nɪpan] *s* il Giappone

Nippon·ese [ˌnɪpə'niz] *adj* nipponico ‖ *s* (**-ese**) Giapponese *mf*

nip·py ['nɪpɪ] *adj* (**-pier; -piest**) mordente, pizzicante; gelato

nirvana [nɪr'vanə] *s* il nirvana

nit [nɪt] *s* lendine *m*; pidocchio

niter ['naɪtər] *s* nitro

nit'-pick' *intr* (coll) cercare il pelo nell'uovo

nitrate ['naɪtret] *s* nitrato; (agr) nitrato di soda; (agr) nitrato di potassio

ni'tric ac'id ['naɪtrɪk] *s* acido nitrico

nitride ['naɪtraɪd] *s* azoturo, nitruro

nitrogen ['naɪtrədʒən] *s* azoto

nitroglycerin [ˌnaɪtrə'glɪsərɪn] *s* nitroglicerina

ni'trous ox'ide ['naɪtrəs] *s* ossidulo di azoto

nitwit ['nɪtˌwɪt] *s* (slang) baggiano

no [no] *adj* nessuno; **no admittance** vietato l'ingresso; **no doubt** senza dubbio; **no matter** non importa; **no parking** divieto di sosta; **no smoking** vietato fumare; **no thoroughfare** divieto di transito; **no use** inutilmente; **with no** senza ‖ *s* no; voto negativo ‖ *adv* no; non; **no longer** non . . . più; **no sooner** non appena

Noah ['no·ə] *s* Noè *m*

nob·by ['nabɪ] *adj* (**-bier; -biest**) (slang) elegante; (slang) eccellente

nobil·ty [no'bɪlɪtɪ] *s* (**-ties**) nobiltà *f*

noble ['nobəl] *adj & s* nobile *m*

no'ble·man *s* (**-men**) nobile *m*, nobiluomo

no'ble·wom'an *s* (**-wom'en**) nobile *f*, nobildonna

nobod·y ['no,badɪ] *or* ['nobədɪ] *s* (**-ies**) nessuno, illustre sconosciuto ‖ *pron indef* nessuno; **nobody but** nessun altro che; **nobody else** nessun altro

nocturnal [nak'tʌrnəl] *adj* notturno

nod [nad] *s* cenno d'assenso, cenno del capo; (*of person going to sleep*) crollo del capo ‖ *v* (*pret & pp* **nodded**) *ger* **nodding**) *tr* (*one's head*) inclinare; **to nod assent** fare cenno di sì ‖ *intr* inclinare il capo; (*to drowse*) assopirsi

node [nod] *s* nodo; protuberanza; (phys) nodo

no'-good' *adj & s* (coll) buono a nulla

nohow ['no,hav] *adv* (coll) in nessuna maniera

noise [nɔɪz] *s* rumore *m* ‖ *tr* divulgare

noiseless ['nɔɪzlɪs] *adj* silenzioso

nois·y ['nɔɪzɪ] *adj* (**-ier; -iest**) rumoroso, chiassoso

nomad ['nomæd] *adj & s* nomade *m*

no' man's' land' *s* terra di nessuno

nominal ['namɪnəl] *adj* nominale; simbolico

nominate ['namɪˌnet] *tr* presentare la candidatura di; (*to appoint*) nominare, designare

nomination [ˌnamɪ'neʃən] *s* candidatura; nomina

nominative ['namɪnətɪv] *adj & s* nominativo

nominee [ˌnamɪ'ni] *s* candidato designato

nonbelligerent [ˌnanbə'lɪdʒərənt] *adj & s* non belligerante *m*

nonbreakable [nan'brekəbəl] *adj* infrangibile

nonce [nans] *s*—**for the nonce** per l'occasione

nonchalance [ˌnanʃə'ɑləns] *or* [ˌnanʃə'lans] *s* disinvoltura, indifferenza

nonchalant [ˌnanʃə'lənt] *or* [ˌnanʃə'lant] *adj* disinvolto, indifferente

noncom ['nan,kam] *s* (coll) sottufficiale *m*

noncombatant [nan'kambətənt] *adj* non combattente ‖ *s* persona non combattente

non'commis'sioned of'ficer [ˌnankə'mɪʃənd] *s* sottufficiale *m*

noncommittal [ˌnankə'mɪtəl] *adj* ambiguo, evasivo

non compos mentis ['nan'kampəs'mentɪs] *adj* pazzo; (law) incapace

nonconformist [ˌnankən'fɔrmɪst] *s* anticonformista *mf*, nonconformista *mf*

nondelivery [ˌnandɪ'lɪvərɪ] *s* mancata consegna

nondescript ['nandɪˌskrɪpt] *adj* indefinibile, inclassificabile

none [nʌn] *pron indef* nessuno; **none of** nessuno di; **none other** nessun altro ‖ *adv* non; affatto, niente affatto; **none the less** ciò nonostante, nondimeno

nonenti·ty [nan'entɪtɪ] *s* (**-ties**) inesistenza; (*person*) nullità *f*

nonfiction [nan'fɪkʃən] *s* letteratura non romanzesca

nonfulfillment [ˌnanful'fɪlmənt] *s* mancanza di esecuzione

nonintervention [ˌnanɪntər'venʃən] *s* non intervento

nonmetal ['nan,metəl] *s* metalloide *m*

nonpayment [nan'pemənt] *s* mancato pagamento

non-plus ['nanplʌs] *or* [nan'plʌs] *s* perplessità *f* ‖ *v* (*pret & pp* **-plussed** *or* **plused**) *ger* **-plussing** *or* **-plusing**) *tr* lasciare perplesso

nonprofit [nan'prafɪt] *adj* senza scopo lucrativo

nonrefillable [ˌnanrɪ'frɪləbəl] *adj* (*prescription*) non ripetibile; (*e.g.*, *bottle*) non ricaricabile

nonresident [nan'rezɪdənt] *s* persona di passaggio, non residente *mf*

nonresidential [ˌnan,rezɪ'denʃəl] *adj* commerciale, non residenziale

nonscientific [nan,saɪ·ən'tɪfɪk] *adj* non scientifico

nonsectarian [ˌnɑnsekˈtɛrɪ·ən] *adj* che non segue nessuna confessione religiosa

nonsense [ˈnɑnsens] *s* sciocchezza, assurdità *f*, nonsenso

nonsensical [nɑnˈsensɪkəl] *adj* sciocco, assurdo, illogico

nonskid [ˈnɑnˈskɪd] *adj* antiderapante

nonstop [ˈnɑnˈstɑp] *adj & adv* senza scalo

nonsupport [ˌnɑnsəˈpɔrt] *s* mancato pagamento degli alimenti

noodle [ˈnudəl] *s* (slang) scemo; (slang) testa; **noodles** tagliatelle *fpl*

noo'dle soup' *s* tagliatelle *fpl* in brodo

nook [nʊk] *s* angolo, cantuccio

noon [nun] *s* mezzogiorno; **at high noon** a mezzogiorno in punto

no one or **no-one** [ˈno ˌwʌn] *pron indef* nessuno; **no one else** nessun altro

noontime [ˈnunˌtaɪm] *s* mezzogiorno

noose [nus] *s* laccio, nodo scorsoio

nor [nɔr] *conj* nè

Nordic [ˈnɔrdɪk] *adj* nordico

norm [nɔrm] *s* norma, media, tipo

normal [ˈnɔrməl] *adj* normale ‖ *s* condizione normale; norma; (geom) normale *f*

Norman [ˈnɔrmən] *adj & s* normanno

Normandy [ˈnɔrməndɪ] *s* la Normandia

Norse [nɔrs] *adj* norvegese; scandinavo ‖ *s* (ancient Scandinavian language) scandinavo; (language of Norway) norvegese *m*; **the Norse** gli scandinavi; i norvegesi

Norse'man *s* (-men) normanno

north [nɔrθ] *adj* del nord, settentrionale ‖ *s* nord *m* ‖ *adv* al nord, verso il nord

North' Amer'ica *s* l'America del Nord

North' Amer'ican *adj & s* nordamericano

north'east' *adj* nord-est ‖ *s* nord-est *m* ‖ *adv* al nord-est

north'east'er *s* vento di nord-est

northern [ˈnɔrðərn] *adj* settentrionale; (Hemisphere) boreale

North' Kore'a *s* la Corea del Nord

North' Pole' *s* polo nord

northward [ˈnɔrθwərd] *adv* verso il nord

north'west' *adj* di nord-ovest ‖ *s* nord-ovest *m* ‖ *adv* al nord-ovest

north' wind' *s* vento del nord, aquilone *m*

Norway [ˈnɔrwe] *s* la Norvegia

Norwegian [nɔrˈwidʒən] *adj & s* norvegese *mf* ‖ *s* (language) norvegese *m*

nose [noz] *s* naso; (of missile) testata; **to blow one's nose** soffiarsi il naso; **to count noses** contare il numero dei presenti; **to follow one's nose** andare a lume di naso; **to lead by the nose** menare per il naso; **to look down one's nose at** (coll) guardare dall'alto in basso; **to pay through the nose** pagare un occhio della testa; **to pick one's nose** mettersi le dita nel naso; **to speak through the nose** parlare nel naso; **to thumb one's nose at** fare marameo a; **to turn up one's nose at** guardare dall'alto in basso, guardare con disprezzo ‖ *tr* fiutare; **to nose out** vincere per un pelo ‖ *intr* fiutare; **to nose about** curiosare

nose' bag' *s* musetta

nose'band' *s* museruola di cavallo

nose'bleed' *s* sangue *m* dal naso

nose' cone' *s* ogiva

nose' dive' *s* (of prices) subita discesa; (aer) discesa in picchiata

nose'-dive' *intr* discendere in picchiata

nosegay [ˈnozˌge] *s* mazzolino di fiori

nose' glass'es *spl* occhiali *mpl* a stringinaso

nose' ring' *s* nasiera

nose'wheel' *s* (aer) ruota del carrello anteriore

no'-show' *s* (coll) passeggero che si è prenotato e non parte

nostalgia [nɑˈstældʒə] *s* nostalgia

nostalgic [nɑˈstældʒɪk] *adj* nostalgico

nostril [ˈnɑstrɪl] *s* narice *f*

nos·y [ˈnozɪ] *adj* (-ier; -iest) (coll) curioso

not [nɑt] *adv* no; non; **not at all** niente affatto; **not yet** non ancora; **to think not** credere di no; **why not?** come no?

notable [ˈnotəbəl] *adj* notevole, notabile ‖ *s* notabile *m*

notarize [ˈnotəˌraɪz] *tr* munire di fede notarile

nota·ry [ˈnotərɪ] *s* (-ries) notaio

notch [nɑtʃ] *s* tacca; (in mountain) passo; (coll) tantino; **notches** (coll) di gran lunga, e.g., **notches above** di gran lunga migliore ‖ *tr* intaccare

note [not] *s* nota, annotazione; (currency) banconota; (communication) memorandum *m*; (of bird) canto; (tone of voice) tono; (reputation) riguardo; (short letter) biglietto, letterina; (mus) nota; (com) cambiale *f* ‖ *tr* notare, annotare; osservare

note'book' *s* (for school) quaderno; taccuino, notes *m*

noted [ˈnotɪd] *adj* ben noto, eminente

note' pa'per *s* carta da lettera

note'wor'thy *adj* notevole

nothing [ˈnʌθɪŋ] *s* niente *m*, nulla; **for nothing** gratis; inutilmente; **next to nothing** quasi niente ‖ *pron indef* niente, nulla, non ... niente, non ... nulla; **nothing else** niente altro; **to make nothing of it** non farne caso ‖ *adv* per nulla; **nothing less** non meno

notice [ˈnotɪs] *s* attenzione; notizia, notifica; annunzio, preavviso; (in newspaper) trafiletto; (law) disdetta; **on short notice** senza preavviso; (com) a breve scadenza; **to escape the notice of** passare inavvertito a; **to serve notice to** far sapere a, far constatare a ‖ *tr* osservare, notare, prendere nota di

noticeable [ˈnotɪsəbəl] *adj* notevole; (e.g., difference) percettibile

noti·fy [ˈnotɪˌfaɪ] *v* (pret & pp -fied) *tr* informare, far sapere

notion [ˈnoʃən] *s* nozione; (whim) capriccio; **notions** mercerie *fpl*; **to have a notion to** aver voglia di

notorie·ty [ˌnotəˈraɪ·ɪtɪ] *s* (-ties) (state

of being well known) notorietà *f*; cattiva fama

notorious [no'tori·əs] *adj* (*generally known*) notorio; (*unfavorably known*) famigerato

no'-trump' *adj & s* senza atout *m*

notwithstanding [,natwɪð'stændɪŋ] or [,natwɪθ'stændɪŋ] *adv* ciò nonostante || *prep* malgrado || *conj* sebbene

nougat ['nugət] *s* torrone *m*

noun [naun] *s* nome *m*, sostantivo

nourish ['nʌrɪʃ] *tr* nutrire

nourishing ['nʌrɪʃɪŋ] *adj* nutriente

nourishment ['nʌrɪʃmənt] *s* nutrimento

novel ['navəl] *adj* nuovo, novello, insolito, originale || *s* romanzo

novelist ['navəlɪst] *s* romanziere *m*

novel-ty ['navəltɪ] *s* (**-ties**) novità *f*; **novelties** chincaglierie *fpl*

November [no'vembər] *s* novembre *m*

novice ['navɪs] *s* novizio

novitiate [no'vɪʃɪ·ɪt] *s* noviziato

novocaine ['novə‚ken] *s* novocaina

now [nau] *s* presente *m* || *adv* adesso; **from now on** d'ora in poi; **just now** un momento fa; **now and then** di tempo in tempo; **now that** visto che || *conj* visto che, dato che

nowadays ['nau·ə‚dez] *adv* al giorno d'oggi, oggidì

no'way' *adv* in nessun modo; nient'affatto

no'where' *adv* da nessuna parte; **nowhere else** da nessun'altra parte, in nessun altro luogo

noxious ['nakʃəs] *adj* nocivo

nozzle ['nazəl] *s* (*of hose or pipe*) boccaglio; (*of tea pot, gas burner*) becco; (*of gun*) bocca; (*of sprinkling can*) bocchetta; (*aut, mach*) becco; (*slang*) naso

nth [enθ] *adj* ennesimo; **to the nth degree** all'ennesima potenza

nuance [nju'ans] or ['nju·ans] *s* sfumatura

nub [nʌb] *s* protuberanza; (*of coal*) pezzo; (*coll*) nocciolo, cuore *m*

nuclear ['njuklɪ·ər] or ['nuklɪ·ər] *adj* nucleare

nu'clear fis'sion *s* fissione nucleare

nu'clear fu'sion *s* fusione nucleare

nu'clear test' ban' *s* accordo per la tregua atomica

nucle-us ['njuklɪ·əs] or ['nuklɪ·əs] *s* (**-i** [‚aɪ] or **-uses**) nucleo

nude [njud] or [nud] *adj* nudo || *s*—**in the nude** nudo

nudge [nʌdʒ] *s* gomitatina || *tr* dare di gomito a

nudist ['njudɪst] or ['nudɪst] *adj & s* nudista *mf*

nudi-ty ['njudɪtɪ] or ['nudɪtɪ] *s* (**-ties**) nudità *f*

nugget ['nʌgɪt] *s* pepita

nuisance ['njusəns] or ['nusəns] *s* noia, seccatura; (*person*) seccatore *m*, pittima *mf*

null [nʌl] *adj* nullo; **null and void** invalido

nulli-fy ['nʌlɪ‚faɪ] *v* (*pret & pp* **-fied**) *tr* annullare, invalidare

nulli-ty ['nʌlɪtɪ] *s* (**-ties**) nullità *f*

numb [nʌm] *adj* intorpidito; (*from cold*) intirizzito; **to become numb** intorpidirsi || *tr* intorpidire

number ['nʌmbər] *s* numero; (*for sale*) articolo di vendita; (*publication*) fascicolo; (*of a serial*) dispensa, puntata; **a number of** parecchi; **beyond** or **without number** senza numero, infiniti || *tr* numerare, contare; **his days are numbered** i suoi giorni sono contati || *intr*—**to number among** essere tra

numberless ['nʌmbərlɪs] *adj* innumerevole

numeral ['njumərəl] or ['numərəl] *adj* numerale || *s* numero

numerical [nju'merɪkəl] or [nu'merɪkəl] *adj* numerico

numerous ['njumərəs] or ['numərəs] *adj* numeroso

numskull ['nʌm‚skʌl] *s* (coll) stupido

nun [nʌn] *s* monaca, religiosa

nuptial ['nʌpʃəl] *adj* nuziale || **nuptials** *spl* nozze *fpl*

nurse [nʌrs] *s* infermiera; (*to suckle a child*) nutrice *f*; (*to take care of a child*) bambinaia || *tr* (*to minister to*) curare; allattare; allevare; (*e.g., hatred*) covare || *intr* fare l'infermiera

nurser-y ['nʌrsərɪ] *s* (**-ies**) stanza dei bambini; (*shelter for children*) asilo infantile; (hort) vivaio

nurs'ery·man *s* (**-men**) orticoltore *m*

nurs'ery rhyme' *s* canzoncina per i più piccini

nurs'ery school' *s* scuola materna

nursing ['nʌrsɪŋ] *adj* infermieristico || *s* allattamento; professione d'infermiera

nurs'ing bot'tle *s* biberon *m*, poppatoio

nurs'ing home' *s* convalescenziario; ospizio dei vecchi, gerontocomio

nurture ['nʌrtʃər] *s* allevamento; nutrimento || *tr* allevare; alimentare; (*e.g., hope*) accarezzare

nut [nʌt] *s* noce *f*; (*eccentric*) (slang) esaltato, pazzoide *m*; (mus) capotasto; (mach) madrevite *f*, dado; **a hard nut to crack** un osso duro da rodere; **to be nuts for** (coll) essere pazzo per

nut'crack'er *s* schiaccianoci *m*

nutmeg ['nʌt‚meg] *s* noce moscata

nutrition [nju'trɪʃən] or [nu'trɪʃən] *s* (*process*) nutrizione; (*food*) nutrimento

nutritious [nju'trɪʃəs] or [nu'trɪʃəs] *adj* nutriente

nut'shell' *s* guscio di noce; **in a nutshell** in breve, in poche parole

nut-ty ['nʌtɪ] *adj* (**-tier; -tiest**) che sa di noci; (slang) pazzo; **nutty about** (slang) pazzo per

nuzzle ['nʌzəl] *tr* toccare col muso, ammusare || *intr* (*said of swine*) grufolare; (*said of other animals*) stare muso a muso, ammusare; (*to snuggle*) rannicchiarsi

nylon ['naɪlan] *s* nailon *m*

nymph [nɪmf] *s* ninfa

O

O, o [o] *s* quindicesima lettera del-
l'alfabeto inglese
O *interj* o!, oh!
oaf [of] *s* balordo, scemo, imbecille *mf*
oak [ok] *s* quercia
oaken ['okən] *adj* di quèrcia, quercino
oakum ['okəm] *s* stoppa incatramata
oar [or] *s* remo; **to lie or rest on one's
oars** dormire sugli allori; non lavorare più ‖ *tr* spingere coi remi ‖ *intr*
remare
oar'lock' *s* scalmo
oars'man *s* (**-men**) rematore *m*
oa·sis [o'esɪs] *s* (**-ses** [siz]) oasi *f*
oat [ot] *s* avena; **oats** (*seeds*) avena;
to feel one's oats (coll) essere pieno
di vita; (coll) sentirsi importante; **to
sow one's wild oats** correre la cavallina
oath [oθ] *s* giuramento; **on oath** sotto
giuramento; **to take an oath** giurare,
prestar giuramento
oat'meal' *s* (*breakfast food*) fiocchi
mpl d'avena; farina d'avena
obdurate ['abdʒərɪt] *adj* indurito, inesorabile; impenitente, incallito
obedience [o'bidɪ·əns] *s* obbedienza,
ubbidienza
obedient [o'bidɪ·ənt] *adj* ubbidiente
obeisance [o'besəns] or [o'bisəns] *s*
saluto rispettoso; omaggio
obelisk ['abəlɪsk] *s* obelisco
obese [o'bis] *adj* obeso
obesity [o'bisiti] *s* obesità *f*
obey ['obe] *tr* ubbidire (with *dat*), ubbidire ‖ *intr* ubbidire
obfuscate [ab'fʌsket] or ['abfəs,ket]
tr offuscare
obituar·y [o'bɪtʃu,eri] *adj* necrologico
‖ *s* (**-ies**) necrologia
object ['abdʒɪkt] *s* oggetto ‖ [ab-
'dʒekt] *tr* obiettare ‖ *intr* fare obiezioni, obiettare
objection [ab'dʒekʃən] *s* obiezione
objectionable [ab'dʒekʃənəbəl] *adj* re-
prensibile; (*e.g., odor*) sgradevole;
offensivo
objective [ab'dʒektɪv] *adj & s* obiet-
tivo
obligate ['ablɪ,get] *tr* obbligare
obligation [,ablɪ'geʃən] *s* obbligo, obbligazione
oblige [ə'blaɪdʒ] *tr* obbligare; favorire; **much obliged** obbligatissimo
obliging [ə'blaɪdʒɪŋ] *adj* compiacente,
accomodante, servizievole
oblique [ə'blik] *adj* obliquo; indiretto
obliterate [ə'blɪtə,ret] *tr* obliterare;
spegnere, distruggere
oblivion [ə'blɪvɪ·ən] *s* oblio
oblivious [ə'blɪvɪ·əs] *adj* (*forgetful*)
dimentico; (*unaware*) ignaro
oblong ['ablaŋ] or ['ablɔŋ] *adj*
oblungo
obnoxious [əb'nakʃəs] *adj* detestabile
oboe ['obo] *s* oboe *m*
oboist ['obo·ɪst] *s* oboista *mf*
obscene [ab'sin] *adj* osceno
obsceni·ty [ab'seniti] or [ab'siniti] *s*
(**-ties**) oscenità *f*, sconcezza

obscure [əb'skjur] *adj* oscuro ‖ *tr*
oscurare
obscuri·ty [əb'skjuriti] *s* (**-ties**) oscurità *f*
obsequies ['absɪkwiz] *spl* esequie *fpl*
obsequious [əb'sikwɪ·əs] *adj* ossequioso, servile
observance [əb'zʌrvəns] *s* osservanza;
observances pratiche *fpl;* cerimonie
fpl
observation [,abzər've/ən] *s* osservazione; osservanza
observa'tion car' *s* (rr) vettura belvedere
observato·ry [əb'zʌrvə,tori] *s* (**-ries**)
osservatorio
observe [əb'zʌrv] *tr* osservare
observer [əb'zʌrvər] *s* osservatore *m*
obsess [ab'ses] *tr* ossessionare
obsession [əb'se/ən] *s* ossessione
obsolescent [,absə'lesənt] *adj* che sta
cadendo in disuso
obsolete ['absə,lit] *adj* disusato
obstacle ['abstəkəl] *s* ostacolo
obstetrical [ab'stetrɪkəl] *adj* ostetrico
obstetrics [ab'stetrɪks] *s* ostetricia
obstina·cy ['abstɪnəsi] *s* (**-cies**) ostinazione
obstinate ['abstɪnɪt] *adj* ostinato
obstreperous [ab'strepərəs] *adj* turbolento; rumoroso
obstruct [əb'strʌkt] *tr* ostruire
obstruction [əb'strʌk/ən] *s* ostruzione
obtain [əb'ten] *tr* ottenere ‖ *intr* prevalere, essere in voga
obtrusive [əb'trusɪv] *adj* intruso, importuno; sporgente
obtuse [əb'tjus] or [əb'tus] *adj* ottuso
obviate ['abvɪ,et] *tr* ovviare (with
dat)
obvious ['abvɪ·əs] *adj* ovvio, palmare
occasion [ə'keʒən] *s* occasione; **on occasion** di quando in quando ‖ *tr* occasionare
occasional [ə'keʒənəl] *adj* saltuario;
(*e.g., verses*) d'occasione
occasionally [ə'keʒənəli] *adv* occasio-
nalmente, di tanto in quanto
occident ['aksɪdənt] *s* occidente *m*
occidental [,aksɪ'dentəl] *adj & s* occidentale *mf*
occlud'ed front' [ə'kludɪd] *s* fronte
occluso
occlusion [ə'kluʒən] *s* occlusione
occlusive [ə'klusɪv] *adj* occlusivo ‖ *s*
occlusiva
occult [ə'kʌlt] or ['akʌlt] *adj* occulto
occupancy ['akjəpənsi] *s* occupazione,
presa di possesso; (*tenancy*) locazione
occupant ['akjəpənt] *s* occupante *m;*
(*tenant*) inquilino
occupation [,akjə'peʃən] *s* occupazione
occupational [,akjə'peʃənəl] *adj* occupazionale; (*e.g., disease*) professionale, del lavoro
occu·py ['akjə,paɪ] *v* (*pret & pp* -**pied**)
tr occupare; (*to dwell in*) abitare
oc·cur [ə'kʌr] *v* (*pret & pp* -**curred;**

ger **-curring**) *intr* accadere, succedere; incontrarsi; (*to come to mind*) venir in mente, e.g., **it occurs to me** mi viene in mente

occurrence [ə'kʌrəns] *s* evento, avvenimento; apparizione

ocean ['oʃən] *s* oceano

o'cean lin'er *s* transatlantico

o'clock [ə'klɑk] *adv* secondo l'orologio; **it is one o'clock** è la una; **it is two o'clock** sono le due

octane ['akten] *adj* ottanico || *s* ottano

octave ['aktıv] *or* ['aktev] *s* ottava

Octavian [ɑk'tevɪ·ən] *s* Ottaviano

October [ɑk'tobər] *s* ottobre *m*

octo-pus ['aktəpəs] *s* (**-puses** *or* **-pi** [,paı]) (*small*) polpo; (*large*) piovra; (fig) piovra

ocular ['akjələr] *adj & s* oculare *m*

oculist ['akjəlɪst] *s* oculista *mf*

odd [ɑd] *adj.* (*number*) dispari; strambo, bizzarro; (*not matching*) scompagnato, spaiato; strano; e rotti, e.g., **three hundred odd** tre cento e rotti || **odds** *ssg or spl* probabilità *f*; (*advantage*) vantaggio, superiorità *f*; **at odds** in disaccordo; **by all odds** senza dubbio; **it makes no odds** fa lo stesso; **the odds are** la quota è; **to set at odds** seminare zizzania fra

oddi•ty ['ɑdɪti] *s* (**-ties**) stranezza

odd' jobs' *spl* lavori saltuari

odd' lot' *s* (fin) compravendita di meno di cento unità

odds' and ends' *spl* un po' di tutto

odious ['odɪ·əs] *adj* odioso

odor ['odər] *s* odore *m*; **to be in bad odor** aver cattiva fama

odorless ['odərlɪs] *adj* inodoro

odorous ['odərəs] *adj* odoroso

Odysseus [o'dɪsjus] *or* [o'dɪsɪ·əs] *s* Odisseo

Odyssey ['ɑdɪsi] *s* Odissea

Oedipus ['edɪpəs] *or* ['idɪpəs] *s* Edipo

of [ɑv] *or* [əv] *prep* di, e.g., **the lead of the pencil** la mina della matita; a, e.g., **to think of** pensare a; meno, e.g., **a quarter of ten** le dieci meno un quarto

off [ɑf] *or* [ɔf] *adj* (*wrong*) sbagliato; (*slightly abnormal*) matto, pazzo; inferiore; (*electricity*) tagliato; (*agreement*) sospeso; libero, in libertà; distante; destro; (*season*) morto || *adv* via; fuori, lontano, distante; **to be off** mettersi in marcia || *prep* da; fuori da; al disotto di; lontano da; distolto da, e.g., **his eyes were off the target** i suoi occhi erano distolti dal bersaglio; (naut) al largo di

offal ['ɑfəl] *or* ['ɔfəl] *s* (*of butchered animal*) frattaglie *fpl*; rifiuti *mpl*

off' and on' *adv* di tempo in tempo

off'beat' *adj* insolito, originale

off' chance' *s* possibilità remota

off'-col'or *adj* scolorito; indisposto; (*joke*) di dubbio gusto

offend [ə'fɛnd] *tr & intr* offendere

offender [ə'fɛndər] *s* offensore *m*

offense [ə'fɛns] *s* offesa; **to take offense** (at) offendersi (di)

offensive [ə'fɛnsɪv] *adj* offensivo || *s* offensiva

offer ['ɑfər] *or* ['ɔfər] *s* offerta || *tr* offrire; (*thanks*) porgere; (*resistance*) opporre || *intr* offrirsi

offering ['ɑfərɪŋ] *or* ['ɔfərɪŋ] *s* offerta

off'hand' *adj* fatto all'improvviso; sbrigativo, alla buona || *adv* all'improvviso; bruscamente

office ['ɑfɪs] *or* ['ɔfɪs] *s* ufficio; funzione, incombenza; (*of a doctor*) gabinetto; (*of a lawyer*) studio; (eccl) uffizio; **through the good offices of** per tramite di

of'fice boy' *s* fattorino

of'fice-hold'er *s* pubblico funzionario

of'fice hours' *spl* orario d'ufficio

officer ['ɑfɪsər] *or* ['ɔfɪsər] *s* (*in a corporation*) funzionario; (*policeman*) agente *m*; (mil, nav, naut) ufficiale *m*; **officer of the day** (mil) ufficiale *m* di giornata

of'fice seek'er ['sikər] *s* aspirante *m* a un ufficio pubblico

of'fice supplies' *spl* articoli *mpl* di cancelleria

official [ə'fɪʃəl] *adj* ufficiale || *s* funzionario, ufficiale *m*

officiate [ə'fɪʃɪ,et] *intr* ufficiare

officious [ə'fɪʃəs] *adj* invadente, inframmettente; **to be officious** essere un impiccione

offing ['ɑfɪŋ] *or* ['ɔfɪŋ] *s*—**in the offing** al largo; (fig) in preparazione, probabile

off'-lim'its *adj* proibito; **off-limits to** ingresso proibito a

off'-peak' heat'er *s* (elec) scaldabagno azionato unicamente in periodi di consumo minimo

off'-peak' load' *s* (elec) carico di consumo minimo

off'print' *s* estratto

off'set' *s* compensazione; (typ) offset *m* || **off'set'** *v* (*pret & pp* **-set;** *ger* **-setting**) *tr* compensare; stampare in offset

off'shoot' *s* (*of plant*) germoglio; (*of family or race*) discendente *mf*; (*branch*) ramo; (fig) conseguenza

off'shore' *adj* (*wind*) di terra; (*fishing*) vicino alla costa; (*island*) costiero || *adv* al largo

off'side' *adv* (sports) fuori gioco

off'spring' *s* discendente *m*; prole *f*; figlio; figli *mpl*

off'stage' *adv* tra le quinte

off'-the-rec'ord *adj* confidenziale || *adv* confidenzialmente

often ['ɑfən] *or* ['ɔfən] *adv* sovente, spesso; **how often?** quante volte?; **once too often** una volta di troppo

ogive ['odʒaɪv] *or* [o'dʒaɪv] *s* ogiva

ogle ['ogəl] *tr* adocchiare, occhieggiare

ogre ['ogər] *s* orco

ohm [om] *s* ohm *m*

oil [ɔɪl] *adj* (*pertaining to edible oil*) oleario; (*e.g., well*) di petrolio; (*e.g., lamp*) a olio; (*tanker*) petroliero; (*field*) petrolifero || *s* olio; petrolio; **to burn the midnight oil** studiare a lume di candela; **to pour oil on troubled waters** pacificare; **to strike oil** trovare petrolio || *tr* oliare; lubrificare; ungere || *intr (said of a motor-ship)* fare petrolio

oil′ burn′er *s* bruciatore *m* a gasolio

oil′ can′ *s* oliatore *m*

oil′ cloth′ *s* incerata, tela cerata

oil′ field′ *s* giacimento petrolifero

oil′ lamp′ *s* lampada a petrolio

oil′ man *s* (-men) *(retailer)* mercante *m* di petrolio; *(operator)* petroliere *m*

oil′ paint′ing *s* quadro a olio

oil′ slick′ *s* macchia d'olio

oil′ tank′er *s* petroliera

oil′ well′ *s* pozzo di petrolio

oil·y [′ɔɪli] *adj* (-ier; -iest) oleoso; untuoso

ointment [′ɔɪntmənt] *s* unguento

O.K. [′o′ke] *adj* (coll) corretto || *s* (coll) approvazione || *adv* (coll) benissimo, d'accordo || *v (pret & pp O.K.′d; ger O.K.′ing) tr* (coll) dare l'approvazione a || *interj* benissimo!

okra [′okrə] *s* (bot) ibisco esculento || *(bot)* baccello dell'ibisco esculento

old [old] *adj* vecchio; antico, vetusto; **how old is . . . ?** quanti anni ha . . . ?; **of old** anticamente; **to be . . . years old** avere . . . anni

old′ age′ *s* vecchiaia

old′ boy′ *s* vecchietto arzillo; (Brit) vecchio mio

old′-clothes′man *s* (-men′) rigattiere *m*

old′ coun′try *s* madre patria

old-fashioned [′old′fæʃənd] *adj* all'antica; fuori moda

old′ fo′gey or **old′ fo′gy** [′fogi] *s* (-gies) uomo di idee antiquate, reazionario

Old′ Glo′ry *s* la bandiera degli Stati Uniti

Old′ Guard′ *s* (U.S.A.) parte *f* più conservatrice di un partito

old′ hand′ *s* vecchio del mestiere

old′ maid′ *s* zitella

old′ mas′ter *s* grande maestro; quadro di un gran maestro

old′ moon′ *s* luna calante

old′ salt′ *s* lupo di mare

old′ school′ *s* gente *f* all'antica

old′ school′ tie′ *s* (Brit) cravatta coi colori della propria scuola; (fig) tradizionalismo

Old′ Tes′tament *s* Antico Testamento

old′-time′ *adj* all'antica; del tempo antico

old-timer [′old′taɪmər] *s* (coll) veterano; (coll) vecchio

old′ wives′ tale′ *s* superstizione da donnicciole; racconto di vecchie comari

Old′ World′ *s* mondo antico

oleander [‚olɪ′ændər] *s* oleandro

oligar·chy [′ɑlɪ ‚gɑrki] *s* (-chies) oligarchia

olive [′ɑlɪv] *adj* oleario; *(color)* olivastro || *s (tree)* olivo; *(fruit)* oliva

ol′ive branch′ *s* ramoscello d'olivo

ol′ive grove′ *s* oliveto

ol′ive oil′ *s* olio d'oliva

Oliver [′ɑlɪvər] *s* Oliviero

ol′ive tree′ *s* olivo

Olympiad [o′lɪmpɪ ‚æd] *s* olimpiade *f*

Olympian [o′lɪmpɪ·ən] *adj* olimpico || *s* deità olimpica; giocatore olimpico

Olympic [o′lɪmpɪk] *adj* olimpico, olimpionico

omelet or **omelette** [′ɑmɛlɪt] or [′ɑmlɪt] *s* frittata, omelette *f*

omen [′omən] *s* augurio

ominous [′ɑmɪnəs] *adj* infausto, ominoso

omission [o′mɪʃən] *s* omissione

omit [o′mɪt] *v (pret & pp omitted; ger omitting) tr* omettere

omnibus [′ɑmnɪ ‚bʌs] or [′ɑmnɪbəs] *adj* di interesse generale || *s* bus *m;* volume collettivo

omnipotent [ɑm′nɪpətənt] *adj* onnipotente

omniscient [ɑm′nɪʃənt] *adj* onnisciente

omnivorous [ɑm′nɪvərəs] *adj* onnivoro

on [ɑn] or [ɔn] *adj* addosso, e.g., **with his hat on** col cappello addosso; in uso, in funzione; *(light)* acceso; *(deal)* fatto, concluso; *(e.g., game)* già cominciato; **what is on at the theater?** che cosa si dà al teatro? || *adv* su; avanti; dietro, e.g., **to drag on** tirarsi dietro; **and so on** e così via; **come on!** va via!; **farther on** più in là; **later on** più tardi; **to be on to s.o.** (coll) scoprire il gioco di qlcu; **to have on** avere addosso; **to . . . on** continuare a, e.g., **the band played on** la banda continuò a suonare; **to put on** mettersi || *prep* su, sopra, a, e.g., **on foot** a piedi; **on his arrival al** suo arrivo; sotto, e.g., **on my responsibility** sotto la mia responsabilità; contro, e.g., **an attack on the** government un attacco contro il governo; da, e.g., **on good authority** da buona fonte; **on all sides** da tutte le parti; verso, e.g., **to march on the** capital marciare verso la capitale; dopo, e.g., **victory on victory** vittoria dopo vittoria

on′ and on′ *adv* senza cessa

once [wʌns] *s* una volta; volta, e.g., **this once** questa volta || *adv* una volta; mai, e.g., **if this once becomes** known se questo si risapesse mai; **all at once** repentinamente; **at once** subito; allo stesso tempo; **for once** almeno una volta; **once and again** ripetutamente; **once in a blue moon** ad ogni morte di papa; **once in a while** di tanto in tanto; **once upon a time there was** c'era una volta || *conj* se appena; una volta che

once′-o′ver *s* (coll) occhiata rapida; **to give s.th the once-over** (coll) esaminare qlco rapidamente; (coll) pulire qlco superficialmente

one [wʌn] *adj* uno; un certo, e.g., **one Smith** un certo Smith; unico e.g., **one price** prezzo unico || *s* uno || *pron* uno, e.g., **how can one live here?** come è possibile che uno viva qui?; si, e.g., **how does one go to the museum?** come si va al museo?; **I for one** per lo meno io; **it's all one and** the same to me per me fa lo stesso; **my little one** piccolo mio; **one and all** tutti; **one another** si, e.g., **they wrote one another** si scrissero;

l'un(o) l'altro, e.g., **they looked at one another** si guardarono l'un l'altro; **one o'clock** la una; **one's** il suo, il proprio; **the blue hat and the red one** il cappello blu e quello rosso; **the one and only** l'unico; **the one that** chi, quello che; **this one** questo; **that one** quello; **to make one** unire

one'-eyed' *adj* monocolo

one'-horse' *adj* a un solo cavallo; (coll) da nulla, poco importante

one'-man' show' *s* personale *f*

onerous ['ɑnərəs] *adj* oneroso

one-self' *pron* sé stesso; se; si; **to be oneself** essere normale; comportarsi normalmente

one-sided ['wʌn'saɪdɪd] *adj* unilaterale; ingiusto, parziale

one'-track' *adj* a un solo binario; (coll) unilaterale, limitato

one'-way' *adj* a senso unico; (ticket) semplice, d'andata

onion ['ʌnjən] *s* cipolla; **to know one's onions** (coll) conoscere i propri polli

on'ion-skin' *s* carta pelle aglio, carta velina

on'look'er *s* presente *m*, spettatore *m*

only ['onlɪ] *adj* solo, unico || *adv* solo, soltanto, non . . . più di; **not only . . . but also** non solo . . . ma anche || *conj* ma; se non che

on'set' *s* attacco; (beginning) inizio; **at the onset** dapprincipio

onslaught ['ɑn,slɔt] or ['ɔn,slɔt] *s* attacco

on'to *prep* su, sopra a; **to be onto** (coll) rendersi conto del gioco di

onward ['ɑnwərd] or **onwards** ['ɑnwərdz] *adv* avanti, più avanti

onyx ['ɑnɪks] *s* onice *m*

ooze [uz] *s* trasudazione; liquido per concia || *tr* sudare || *intr* trasudare; (said, e.g., of blood) stillare; (said, e.g., of air) filtrare; (fig) trapelare

opal ['opəl] *s* opale *m*

opaque [o'pek] *adj* opaco; (writer's style) oscuro; stupido

open ['opən] *adj* aperto, scoperto; (job) vacante; (time) libero; (hunting season) legale; indeciso; manifesto; (hand) liberale; (needlework) a giorno; **to break** or **to crack open** forzare; **to throw open** aprire completamente || *s* apertura; (in the woods) radura; **in the open** all'aperto; all'aria aperta; in alto mare; apertamente || *tr* aprire; (an account) impostare; **to open up** spalancare; (one's eyes) sbarrare || *intr* aprire, aprirsi; (theat) esordire; **to open into** sboccare in; **to open on** dare su; **to open up** sbottonarsi

o'pen-air' *adj* all'aria aperta

open-eyed ['opən,aɪd] *adj* con gli occhi aperti; meravigliato; fatto con piena conoscenza

open-handed ['opən'hændɪd] *adj* generoso, liberale

open-hearted ['opən'hɑrtɪd] *adj* franco, sincero; gentile

o'pen house' *s* tavola imbandita; **to keep open house** aver sempre ospiti

opening ['opənɪŋ] *s* apertura; (of dress) giro collo; (e.g., of sewer) imbocco; (in the woods) radura; (vacancy) posto vacante; (beginning) inizio; (chance to say something) occasione

o'pening night' *s* debutto, prima

o'pening num'ber *s* primo numero

o'pening price' *s* prezzo d'apertura

open-minded ['opən'maɪndɪd] *adj* di larghe vedute; imparziale

o'pen se'cret *s* segreto di Pulcinella

o'pen shop' *s* officina che impiega chi non è membro del sindacato

o'pen-work' *s* traforo

opera ['ɑpərə] *s* opera

op'era glass'es *spl* binocolo da teatro

op'era hat' *s* gibus *m*

op'era house' *s* teatro dell'opera

operate ['ɑpə,ret] *tr* (a machine) far funzionare; (a shop) gestire; operare || *intr* funzionare; operare; **to operate on** (surg) operare

operatic [,ɑpə'rætɪk] *adj* operistico

op'erating expens'es *spl* spese *fpl* di ordinaria amministrazione

op'erating room' *s* sala operatoria

op'erating ta'ble *s* tavola operatoria

operation [,ɑpə're/ən] *s* operazione; funzionamento, marcia

opera'tions research' *s* ricerca operativa

operator ['ɑpə,retər] *s* operatore *m*; (of a conveyance) conduttore *m*, conducente *mf*; (com) gestore *m*; (telp) telefonista *mf*; (surg) chirurgo operatore; (slang) faccendiere *m*

opiate ['opɪ-ɪt] or ['opɪ,et] *adj* & *s* oppiato

opinion [ə'pɪnjən] *s* opinione; **in my opinion** a mio modo di vedere; **to have a high opinion of** avere una grande stima di

opinionated [ə'pɪnjə,netɪd] *adj* ostinato, testardo, dogmatico

opium ['opɪ·əm] *s* oppio

o'pium den' *s* fumeria d'oppio

opossum [ə'pɑsəm] *s* opossum *m*

opponent [ə'ponənt] *s* avversario

opportune [,ɑpər'tjun] or [,ɑpər'tun] *adj* opportuno

opportunist [,ɑpər'tjunɪst] or [,ɑpər'tunɪst] *s* opportunista *mf*

opportuni·ty [,ɑpər'tjunɪti] or [,ɑpər'tunɪti] *s* (-ties) opportunità *f*, occasione

oppose [ə'poz] *tr* opporsi a

opposite ['ɑpəsɪt] *adj* opposto; di rimpetto, e.g., **the house opposite** la casa di rimpetto || *s* contrario || *prep* di faccia a, di rimpetto a

op'posite num'ber *s* persona di grado corrispondente

opposition [,ɑpə'zɪ/ən] *s* opposizione

oppress [ə'pres] *tr* opprimere

oppressive [ə'presɪv] *adj* oppressivo; opprimente, soffocante

oppressor [ə'presər] *s* oppressore *m*

opprobrious [ə'probrɪ·əs] *adj* obbrobrioso

opprobrium [ə'probrɪ·əm] *s* obbrobrio
optic ['aptɪk] *adj* ottico || **optics** *ssg* ottica
optical ['aptɪkəl] *adj* ottico
optician [ap'tɪʃən] *s* ottico, occhialaio
optimism ['aptɪ ˌmɪzəm] *s* ottimismo
optimist ['aptɪmɪst] *s* ottimista *mf*
optimistic [ˌaptɪ'mɪstɪk] *adj* ottimistico
option ['apʃən] *s* opzione
optional ['apʃənəl] *adj* facoltativo
optometrist [ap'tamɪtrɪst] *s* optometrista *mf*
opulent ['apjələnt] *adj* opulento
or [ɔr] *conj* o; (*or else*) oppure
oracle ['ɔrəkəl] *or* ['arəkəl] *s* oracolo
oracular [o'rækjələr] *adj* profetico; ambiguo; misterioso; sentenzioso
oral ['ɔrəl] *adj* orale
orange ['arɪndʒ] *or* ['ɔrɪndʒ] *adj* di arance; arancio || *s* arancia
orangeade [ˌarɪndʒ'ed] *or* [ˌɔrɪndʒ'ed] *s* aranciata
or'ange blos'som *s* zagara
or'ange grove' *s* aranceto
or'ange juice' *s* sugo d'arancia
or'ange squeez'er *s* spremiagrumi *m*
or'ange tree' *s* arancio
orang-outang [o'ræŋʊˌtæŋ] *s* orango
oration [o're ʃən] *s* orazione, discorso
orator ['arətər] *or* ['ɔrətər] *s* oratore *m*
oratorical [ˌarə'tarɪkəl] *or* [ˌɔrə'tɔrɪkəl] *adj* oratorio
oratori·o [ˌarə'tɔrɪˌo] *or* [ˌɔrə'tɔrɪˌo] *s* (*-os*) (mus) oratorio
orato·ry ['arəˌtɔri] *or* ['ɔrəˌtɔri] *s* (*-ries*) oratoria; (eccl) oratorio
orb [ɔrb] *s* orbe *m*
orbit ['ɔrbɪt] *s* orbita; **to go into orbit** entrare in orbita || *tr* mettere in orbita; orbitare intorno a || *intr* orbitare
or'biting sta'tion *s* stazione orbitale
orchard ['ɔrtʃərd] *s* frutteto
orchestra ['ɔrkɪstrə] *s* orchestra; (*parquet*) platea
orchestral [ɔr'kestrəl] *adj* orchestrale
or'chestra pit' *s* golfo mistico
or'chestra seat' *s* poltrona di platea
orchestrate ['ɔrkɪsˌtret] *tr* orchestrare
orchid ['ɔrkɪd] *s* orchidea
ordain [ɔr'den] *tr* predestinare; decretare; (eccl) ordinare
ordeal [ɔr'dil] *or* [ɔr'di·əl] *s* sfacchinata; (hist) ordalia
order ['ɔrdər] *s* ordine *m*; compito, e.g., **a big order** un compito difficile; (com) commessa, ordinazione; (mil) consegna; **in order that** affinché; **in order to** + *inf* per + *inf*; **made to order** fatto su misura; **to get out of order** guastarsi; **to give an order** dare un ordine; (com) fare una commessa || *tr* (*e.g., a drink*) ordinare; (*a person*) ordinare (with *dat*); (*e.g., a suit of clothes*) far fare; **to order around** mandare attorno; **to order s.o. away** mandar via qlcu
or'der blank' *s* cedola d'ordinazione
order·ly ['ɔrdərli] *adj* ordinato; disciplinato || *s* (*-lies*) (*in a hospital*) in-

serviente *mf*; (mil) ordinanza, attendente *m*
ordinal ['ɔrdɪnəl] *adj* & *s* ordinale *m*
ordinance ['ɔrdɪnəns] *s* ordinanza
ordinary ['ɔrdɪˌneri] *adj* ordinario
ordnance ['ɔrdnəns] *s* artiglieria; **bocche** *fpl* da fuoco; munizionamento
ore [or] *s* minerale *m* (metallifero)
organ ['ɔrgən] *s* organo
organ·dy ['ɔrgəndi] *s* (*-dies*) organdì *m*
or'gan grind'er *s* suonatore *m* d'organetto
organic [ɔr'gænɪk] *adj* organico
organism ['ɔrgəˌnɪzəm] *s* organismo
organist ['ɔrgənɪst] *s* organista *mf*
organization [ˌɔrgənɪ'zeʃən] *s* organizzazione
organize ['ɔrgəˌnaɪz] *tr* organizzare
organizer ['ɔrgəˌnaɪzər] *s* organizzatore *m*
or'gan loft' *s* palco, galleria per l'organo
orgasm ['ɔrgæzəm] *s* orgasmo
or·gy ['ɔrdʒi] *s* (*-gies*) orgia
orient ['ɔrɪ·ənt] *s* oriente *m* || **Orient** *s* Oriente *m* || **orient** ['ɔrɪ ˌent] *tr* orientare, orizzontare
oriental [ˌɔrɪ'entəl] *adj* orientale || **Oriental** *s* orientale *mf*
orifice ['arɪfɪs] *or* ['ɔrɪfɪs] *s* orifizio
origin ['arɪdʒɪn] *or* ['ɔrɪdʒɪn] *s* origine *f*, provenienza
original [ə'rɪdʒɪnəl] *adj* & *s* originale *mf*
originate [ə'rɪdʒɪˌnet] *tr* originare || *intr* originare, originarsi
oriole ['ɔrɪˌol] *s* oriolo, rigogolo
Ork'ney Is'lands ['ɔrkni] *spl* Orcadi *fpl*
ormolu ['ɔrməˌlu] *s* (*alloy*) similoro; (*gold powder*) polvere *f* d'oro; (*gilded metal*) bronzo dorato
ornament ['ɔrnəmənt] *s* ornamento || ['ɔrnəˌment] *tr* ornamentare
ornamental [ˌɔrnə'mentəl] *adj* ornamentale
ornate [ɔr'net] *or* ['ɔrnet] *adj* ornato; (*style*) elaborato
ornithologist [ˌɔrnɪ'θaledʒɪst] *s* ornitologo
orphan ['ɔrfən] *adj* & *s* orfano || *tr* rendere orfano
orphanage ['ɔrfənɪdʒ] *s* (*institution*) orfanotrofio; (*condition*) orfanezza
Orpheus ['ɔrfjus] *or* ['ɔrfi·əs] *s* Orfeo
orthodox ['ɔrθəˌdaks] *adj* ortodosso
orthogra·phy [ɔr'θagrəfi] *s* (*-phies*) ortografia
oscillate ['asɪˌlet] *intr* oscillare
osier ['oʒər] *s* vimine *m*; (bot) vinco
osmosis [az'mosɪs] *or* [as'mosɪs] *s* osmosi *f*
osprey ['aspri] *s* falco pescatore
ossi·fy ['asɪˌfaɪ] *v* (*pret & pp* **-fied**) *tr* ossificare || *intr* ossificarsi
ostensible [as'tensɪbəl] *adj* apparente, preteso
ostentatious [ˌasten'teʃəs] *adj* ostentato
osteopathy [ˌastɪ'apəθi] *s* osteopatia
ostracism ['astrəˌsɪzəm] *s* ostracismo

ostracize ['ɑstrə ‚saɪz] *tr* dare l'ostracismo a, ostracizzare

ostrich ['ɑstrɪtʃ] *s* struzzo

Othello [o'θelo] *or* [ə'θelo] *s* Otello

other ['ʌðər] *adj & pron indef* altro ‖ *adv*—**other than** diversamente che

otherwise ['ʌðər ‚waɪz] *adv* altrimenti; differentemente

otter ['ɑtər] *s* lontra

ottoman ['ɑtəmən] *s* (*fabric*) ottomano; (*sofa*) ottomana; cuscino per i piedi ‖ **Ottoman** *adj & s* ottomano

ouch [aʊtʃ] *interj* ahi!

ought [ɔt] *s* qualcosa; zero; **for ought I know** per quanto io sappia ‖ *v aux* is rendered in Italian by the conditional of *dovere,* e.g., **you ought to be ashamed** dovresti vergognarti

ounce [aʊns] *s* oncia

our [aʊr] *adj poss* nostro, il nostro

ours [aʊrz] *pron poss* il nostro

ourselves [aʊr'selvz] *pron pers* noi stessi; ci, e.g., **we enjoyed ourselves** ci siamo divertiti

oust [aʊst] *tr* espellere; (*a tenant*) sfrattare

out [aʊt] *adj* erroneo; esterno; fuori pratica; svenuto; ubriaco; finito; (*book*) pubblicato; (*lights*) spento; fuori moda; introvabile; palmare; di permesso, e.g., **my night out** la mia serata di permesso; (*e.g., at the knees*) frusto; (sports) fuori gioco ‖ *s* via d'uscita; **to be on the outs** or **at outs with** (coll) essere in disaccordo con ‖ *adv* fuori, all'infuori; all'aria libera; **out for** in cerca di; **out of** fuori, fuori di; di; da; (*e.g., money*) a corto di, senza; su, e.g., **two students out of three** due studenti su tre ‖ *prep* fuori di; per, lungo ‖ *interj* fuori!

out' and away' *adv* di gran lunga

out'-and-out' *adj* perfetto, completo ‖ *adv* perfettamente, completamente

out'bid' *v* (*pret* **-bid;** *pp* **-bid** or **-bidden;** *ger* **-bidding**) *tr* fare un'offerta migliore di; (bridge) fare una dichiarazione più alta di

out'board mo'tor *s* fuoribordo, motore *m* fuoribordo

out'break' *s* insurrezione; (*of hives*) eruzione; (*of anger; of war*) scoppio

out'build'ing *s* dipendenza

out'burst' *s* (*of tears; of laughter*) scoppio; (*of energy*) impeto, slancio

out'cast' *s* vagabondo reietto

out'come' *s* risultato

out'cry' *s* (**-cries**) grido, chiasso

out'dat'ed *adj* fuori moda

out'dis'tance *tr* distanziare

out'do' *v* (*pret* **-did;** *pp* **-done**) *tr* sorpassare; **to outdo oneself** sorpassare sé stesso

out'door' *adj* all'aria aperta

out'doors' *s* aria libera, aperta campagna ‖ *adv* all'aria aperta, fuori di casa

out'er space' ['aʊtər] *s* spazio cosmico

out'field' *s* (baseball) campo esterno

out'field'er *s* (baseball) esterno

out'fit' *s* equipaggiamento; (*female cos-* *tume*) insieme *m*; (*of bride*) corredo; (*group*) (coll) corpo; (com) compagnia ‖ *v* (*pret & pp* **-fitted;** *ger* **-fitting**) *tr* equipaggiare

out'flow' *s* efflusso

out'go'ing *adj* in partenza; (*tide*) decrescente; (*character*) espansivo ‖ *s* efflusso

out'grow' *v* (*pret* **-grew;** *pp* **-grown**) *tr* essere troppo grande per; sorpassare in statura; perdere l'interesse per ‖ *intr* protrudere

out'growth' *s* risultato, conseguenza; crescita

outing ['aʊtɪŋ] *s* gita, scampagnata

outlandish [aʊt'lændɪʃ] *adj* strano, bizzarro; dall'aspetto straniero; (*remote, far away*) in capo al mondo

out'last' *tr* sopravvivere (with *dat*)

out'law' *s* fuorilegge *mf* ‖ *tr* proscrivere; dichiarare illegale

out'lay' *s* disborso ‖ **out·lay'** *v* (*pret & pp* **-laid**) *tr* sborsare

out'let *s* uscita; (*e.g., of river*) sbocco; (com) mercato; (elec) presa di corrente; (fig) sfogo

out'line' *s* contorno; traccia, tracciato; sagoma, profilo; prospetto ‖ *tr* delineare; tracciare, tratteggiare; sagomare, profilare; prospettare

out'live' *tr* sopravvivere (with *dat*)

out'look' *s* prospettiva; (*watch*) guardia; (*mental view*) modo di vedere, opinione

out'ly'ing *adj* lontano, fuori di mano; periferico

outmoded [‚aʊt'modɪd] *adj* fuori moda, antiquato

out'num'ber *tr* superare in numero

out'-of-date' *adj* fuori moda

out'-of-door' *adj* all'aria aperta

out'-of-doors' *adj* all'aria aperta ‖ *s* aria aperta ‖ *adv* all'aria aperta; fuori di casa

out'-of-print' *adj* esaurito

out'-of-the-way' *adj* appartato, fuori mano; inusitato, strano

out' of tune' *adj* stonato ‖ *adv* fuori di tono

out' of work' *adj* disoccupato

out'pa'tient *s* paziente *mf* esterno

out'post' *s* (mil) posto avanzato

out'put' *s* produzione; (elec) uscita; (mach) rendimento, potenza utile

out'rage *s* oltraggio, indecenza ‖ *tr* oltraggiare; (*a woman*) violare

outrageous [aʊt'redʒəs] *adj* oltraggioso; (*excessive*) eccessivo; atroce, feroce

out'rank' *tr* superare in grado

out'rid'er *s* battistrada *m*

out'right' *adj* completo, intero ‖ *adv* completamente; apertamente; sul colpo, sull'istante

out'set' *s* inizio, principio

out'side' *adj* esterno; (*unlikely*) improbabile; (*price*) massimo ‖ *s* esterno, di fuori *m;* aspetto esteriore; vita fuori del carcere ‖ *adv* fuori, di fuori; **outside of** fuori di ‖ *prep* fuori di; (coll) all'infuori di

outsider [ˌaʊtˈsaɪdər] s estraneo, intruso; (sports) outsider m

out'skirts' spl sobborghi mpl, periferia

out'spo'ken adj franco, esplicito

out'stand'ing adj saliente, eminente; (debt) arretrato, non pagato

outward ['aʊtwərd] adj esterno, superficiale || adv al di fuori

out'weigh' tr pesare più di; eccedere in importanza

out'wit' v (pret & pp -witted; ger -witting) tr farla in barba di; (a pursuer) far perdere la traccia o la pista a

oval ['ovəl] adj & s ovale m

ova·ry ['ovəri] s (-ries) ovaia

ovation [oˈveʃən] s ovazione

oven ['ʌvən] s forno

over ['ovər] adj superiore; esterno; finito, concluso || adv su, sopra; dall'altra parte; dall'altra sponda; al rovescio; di nuovo; (at the bottom of a page) continua; qui, e.g., **hand over the money** dammi qui il denaro; **over again** di nuovo; **over against** contro; **over and over** ripetutamente; **over here** qui; **over there** là || prep su, sopra; dall'altra parte di; attraverso, per; (a certain number) più di; a causa di; **over and above** in eccesso di

o'ver·all' adj completo, totale || **overalls** spl tuta

o'ver·bear'ing adj arrogante, prepotente

o'ver·board' adv in acqua; **man overboard!** uomo in mare!; **to go overboard** andare agli estremi

o'ver·cast' adj annuvolato || s cielo annuvolato || v (pret & pp -cast) tr coprire, annuvolare

o'ver·charge' s prezzo eccessivo; sovraccarico; (elec) carica eccessiva || **o'ver·charge'** tr far pagare eccessivamente; sovraccaricare

o'ver·coat' s soprabito, pastrano

o'ver·come' v (pret -came; pp -come) tr vincere, sopraffare; (e.g., passions) frenare; opprimere

o'vercon'fidence s sicumera

o'ver·crowd' tr gremire

o'ver·do' v (pret -did; pp -done) tr esagerare; strafare; esaurire; (meat) stracuocere || intr esaurirsi

o'ver·dose' s dose eccessiva

o'ver·draft' s assegno allo scoperto

o'ver·draw' v (pret -drew; pp -drawn) tr (a check) emettere allo scoperto; (a character) esagerare la descrizione di

o'ver·due' adj in ritardo; (com) in sofferenza, scaduto

o'ver·eat' v (pret -ate; pp -eaten) tr & intr mangiare troppo

o'ver·exer'tion s sforzo eccessivo

o'ver·expose' tr sovresporre

o'ver·expo'sure s sovresposizione

o'ver·flow' s (of a river) piena, straripamento; (excess) sovrabbondanza; (e.g., of a fountain) trabocco; (outlet) tubo di troppopieno || **o'ver·flow'** intr (said of a river) straripare; (said of a container) traboccare

o'ver·fly' v (pret -flew; pp -flown) tr sorvolare; (a target) oltrepassare

o'ver·grown' adj cresciuto troppo; coperto, denso

o'ver·hang' s strapiombo || **o'ver·hang'** v (pret & pp -hung) tr sovrastare (with dat); sovrastare; (to threaten) minacciare; pervadere, permeare || intr sovrastare, strapiombare

o'ver·haul' s riparazione; esame m, revisione || tr riparare; esaminare, ripassare, rivedere; raggiungere, mettersi alla pari con

o'ver·head' adj in alto, sopra la testa; aereo; elevato, pensile; generale || **o'ver·head'** adv in alto, di sopra || **o'ver·head'** s spese fpl generali

o'ver·head projec'tor s lavagna luminosa

o'ver·head valve' s valvola in testa

o'ver·hear' v (pret & pp -heard) tr sentire per caso, udire per caso

o'ver·heat' tr surriscaldare || intr surriscaldarsi; eccitarsi

overjoyed [ˌovərˈdʒɔɪd] adj felicissimo; **to be overjoyed** non stare in sé dalla contentezza

overland ['ovərˌlænd] or ['ovərlənd] adj & adv per via di terra

o'ver·lap' v (pret & pp -lapped; ger -lapping) tr sovrapporre, estendersi sopra || intr sovrapporsi, estendersi; coincidere parzialmente

o'ver·load' s sovraccarico || **o'ver·load'** tr sovraccaricare, stracaricare

o'ver·look' tr sovrastare su, dominare; ispezionare, sorvegliare; passare sopra, trascurare; dare su, e.g., **the window overlooks the street** la finestra dà sulla strada

o'ver·lord' s dominatore m || tr dominare despoticamente

overly ['ovərli] adv eccessivamente

o'ver·night' adj per la notte, per solo una notte || **o'ver·night'** adv durante la notte; la notte prima

o'vernight bag' s astuccio di toletta per la notte

o'ver·pass' s cavalcavia, viadotto

o'ver·pop'ulate tr sovrappopolare

o'ver·pow'er tr sopraffare

o'ver·pow'ering adj schiacciante

o'ver·produc'tion s sovrapproduzione

o'ver·rate' tr sopravvalutare

o'ver·run' v (pret -ran; pp -run; ger -running) tr invadere, infestare; inondare; (one's time) oltrepassare, eccedere

o'ver·sea' or **o'ver·seas'** adj di oltremare || **o'ver·sea'** or **o'ver·seas'** adv oltremare, al di là dei mari

o'ver·see' v (pret -saw; pp -seen) tr sorvegliare

o'ver·seer' s sorvegliante mf

o'ver·shad'ow tr oscurare, eclissare

o'ver·shoe' s soprascarpa

o'ver·shoot' v (pret & pp -shot) tr (the target) oltrepassare; (said of water) scorrere sopra; **to overshoot oneself** andare troppo in là || intr (aer) atterrare lungo e richiamare

o'ver·sight' s sbadataggine f, svista; sorveglianza, supervisione

o'ver·sleep' v (pret & pp -slept) tr (a certain hour) dormire oltre || intr dormire troppo a lungo

o'ver·step' v (pret & pp -stepped; ger -stepping) tr eccedere, oltrepassare

o'ver·stock' tr riempire eccessivamente

o'ver·sup·ply' s (-plies) fornitura superiore alla richiesta || o'ver·sup·ply' v (pret & pp -plied) tr fornire in quantità superiore alla richiesta

overt ['ovərt] or [o'vʌrt] adj palmare, chiaro, manifesto

o'ver·take' v (pret -took; pp -taken) tr raggiungere, sorpassare; sorprendere

o'ver-the-count'er adj (securities) venduto direttamente al compratore

o'ver·throw' s rovesciamento; disfatta || o'ver·throw' s (pret -threw; pp -thrown) tr rovesciare, sconfiggere

o'ver·time' adj supplementare, fuori orario || s straordinario; (sports) tempo supplementare || adv fuori orario

o'ver·tone' s (mus) suono armonico; (fig) sottinteso

o'ver·trump' s taglio con atout più alto || o'ver·trump' tr & intr tagliare con atout più alto

overture ['ovərtʃər] s apertura; (mus) preludio, sinfonia

o'ver·turn' s rovesciamento || o'ver·turn' tr rovesciare, travolgere || intr rovesciarsi, ribaltarsi

overweening [,ovər'winɪŋ] adj presuntuoso, vanitoso; esagerato, eccessivo

o'ver·weight' adj troppo grasso; oltrepassante i limiti di peso || o'ver·weight' s sovraccarico; preponderanza; eccesso di peso

overwhelm [,ovər'hwɛlm] tr schiacciare, debellare; coprire; (e.g., with kindness) colmare, ricolmare

o'ver·work' s lavoro straordinario; superlavoro || o'ver·work' tr far lavorare eccessivamente || intr lavorare eccessivamente

Ovid ['avɪd] s Ovidio

ow [au] interj ahi!

owe [o] tr dovere || intr essere in debito

owing ['o·ɪŋ] adj dovuto; owing to a causa di

owl [aul] s gufo, barbagianni m

own [on] adj proprio, e.g., my own brother il mio proprio fratello || s il proprio; on one's own (coll) per proprio conto; (without anybody's advice) di testa propria; to come into one's own entrare in possesso del proprio; essere riconosciuto per quanto si vale; to hold one's own non perdere terreno; essere pari || tr possedere; riconoscere || intr—to own up to confessare

owner ['onər] s padrone m, proprietario, titolare m

ownership ['onər,ʃɪp] s proprietà f

own'er's li'cence s permesso di circolazione

ox [aks] s (oxen ['aksən]) bue m

ox'cart' s carro tirato da buoi

oxide ['aksaɪd] s ossido

oxidize ['aksɪ,daɪz] tr ossidare || intr ossidarsi

oxygen ['aksɪdʒən] s ossigeno

ox'ygen mask' s maschera respiratoria

ox'ygen tent' s tenda ad ossigeno

oxytone ['aksɪ,ton] adj tronco, ossitono || s ossitono

oyster ['ɔɪstər] adj di ostriche || s ostrica

oys'ter bed' s ostricaio, banco di ostriche

oys'ter cock'tail s ostriche fpl servite in valva

oys'ter fork' s forchettina da ostriche

oys'ter·house' s ristorante m per la vendita delle ostriche

oys'ter-knife' s coltello per aprire le ostriche

oys'ter·man s (-men) ostricaio

oys'ter shell' s conchiglia d'ostrica

oys'ter stew' s brodetto d'ostriche

ozone ['ozon] s ozono

P

P, p [pi] s sedicesima lettera dell'alfabeto inglese

pace [pes] s passo, andatura; (of a horse) ambio; to keep pace with andare di pari passo con; to put s.o. through his paces mettere qlcu a dura prova; to set the pace for fare l'andatura per; dare l'esempio a || tr misurare a passi, percorrere; to pace the floor andare avanti e indietro per la stanza || intr camminare lentamente; andare al passo; (said of a horse) ambiare

pace'mak'er s battistrada m; (in races) chi stabilisce il passo; (med) pacemaker m

pacific [pə'sɪfɪk] adj pacifico || Pacific adj & s Pacifico

pacifier ['pæsɪ,faɪ·ər] s paciere m; (teething ring) succhietto, tettarella

pacifism ['pæsɪ,fɪzəm] s pacifismo

pacifist ['pæsɪfɪst] adj & s pacifista mf

paci·fy ['pæsɪ,faɪ] v (pret & pp -fied) tr pacificare

pack [pæk] s fardello, pacco; (of merchandise) balla; (of lies) mucchio; (of cards) mazzo; (of thieves) banda; (of dogs) muta; (of animals) branco; (of birds) stormo; (of cigarettes) pacchetto; (of ice) banchiglia; (of people) turba || tr affardellare, impaccare; (to wrap) imballare; ammucchiare; (in cans) mettere in conserva; (people) stipare; (a trunk) fare; to pack in stipare; to pack off mandare via || intr ammucchiarsi, pigiarsi, accalcarsi; **to pack up** fare il baule

package ['pækɪdʒ] s pacco, collo; (small) pacchetto ‖ tr impacchettare

pack' an'imal s bestia da soma

packer ['pækər] s imballatore m; (of canned goods) proprietario (di fabbrica di conserve alimentari)

packet ['pækɪt] s pacchetto; (boat) vapore m postale

packing ['pækɪŋ] s imballaggio; (on shoulders of suit) spallina; (mach) stoppa; (ring) (mach) guarnizione

pack'ing box' or **case'** s cassa d'imballaggio

pack'ing house' s fabbrica di conserve alimentari; fabbrica di carne in conserva

pack'ing slip' s foglio d'imballaggio

pack'sad'dle s basto

pack'thread' s spago d'imballaggio

pack'train' s fila di animali da soma

pact [pækt] s patto

pad [pæd] s cuscinetto, tampone m; imbottitura; (of writing paper) blocco da annotazioni; (of an animal) superficie f plantare, zampa; (of a water lily) foglia; (rok) piattaforma ‖ v (pret & pp **padded;** ger **padding**) tr imbottire, ovattare; (e.g., a speech) infarcire ‖ intr camminare pesantemente

pad'ding s imbottitura

paddle ['pædəl] s pagaia; (of waterwheel) pala ‖ tr remare; (to spank) bastonare ‖ intr remare; (to splash) diguazzare

pad'dle wheel' s ruota a pale

paddock ['pædək] s prato d'allenamento, paddock m

pad'lock' s lucchetto ‖ tr chiudere col lucchetto

pagan ['pegən] adj & s pagano

paganism ['pegə‚nɪzəm] s paganesimo

page [pedʒ] s (of a book) pagina; (at court) paggio; (in hotels) fattorino, valletto ‖ tr impaginare; (in hotels) chiamare, far chiamare

pageant ['pædʒənt] s parata, corteo, spettacolo

pageant·ry ['pædʒəntri] s (-ries) pompa, fasto

paginate ['pædʒɪ‚net] tr impaginare

pail [pel] s secchio

pain [pen] s dolore m; **on pain of** sotto pena di; **to take pains to** prendersi cura di; **to take pains not to** guardarsi da ‖ tr & intr dolere

painful ['penfəl] adj doloroso, penoso

pain'kill'er s (coll) analgesico

painless ['penlɪs] adj indolore

painstaking ['penz‚tekɪŋ] adj meticoloso

paint [pent] s (for pictures) colore m; (for a house) vernice f; (make-up) trucco ‖ tr dipingere; (a house) verniciare, tinteggiare ‖ intr dipingere; (with make-up) dipingersi; essere pittore

paint'box' s scatola da colori

paint'brush' s pennello

painter ['pentər] s (of pictures) pittore m; (of a house) verniciatore m; (naut) barbetta

painting ['pentɪŋ] s pittura, dipinto

paint' remov'er [rɪ'muvər] s solvente m per levar la vernice

paint' thin'ner s diluente m

pair [per] s paio; (of people) coppia ‖ tr appaiare, accoppiare ‖ intr appaiarsi, accoppiarsi

pair' of scis'sors s forbici fpl

pair' of trou'sers s calzoni mpl

pajamas [pə'dʒaməz] or [pə'dʒæməz] spl pigiama m

Pakistan [‚pakɪ'stan] s il Pakistan

Pakistani [‚pakɪ'stani] adj & s pachistano

pal [pæl] s (coll) compagno ‖ v (pret & pp **palled;** ger **palling**) intr (coll) essere compagni

palace ['pælɪs] s palazzo

palatable ['pælətəbəl] adj gustoso, appetitoso; accettabile

palatal ['pælətəl] adj & s palatale f

palate ['pælɪt] s palato

pale [pel] adj pallido ‖ s (enclosure) recinto; (fig) ambito ‖ intr impallidire

pale'face' s faccia pallida

palette ['pælɪt] s tavolozza

palfrey ['polfrɪ] s palafreno

palisade [‚pælɪ'sed] s palizzata; (line of cliffs) dirupo

pall [pol] s panno mortuario; (of smoke) cappa ‖ tr saziare, infastidire ‖ intr saziarsi, perdere l'appetito

pall'bear'er s chi accompagna il feretro; chi porta il feretro

palliate ['pælɪ‚et] tr attenuare, alleviare

pallid ['pælɪd] adj pallido

pallor ['pælər] s pallore m

palm [pam] s (tree and leaf) palma; (of hand; measure) palmo; **to carry off the palm** riportare la palma; **to grease the palm of** ungere le ruote a ‖ tr far sparire nella mano; nascondere; **to palm off s.th on s.o.** rifilare qlco a qlcu

palmet·to [pæl'meto] s (-tos or -toes) palmeto

palmist ['pamist] s chiromante mf

palmistry ['pamistri] s chiromanzia

palm' leaf' s palma, foglia di palma

palm' oil' s olio di palma

Palm' Sun'day s Domenica delle Palme

palpable ['pælpəbəl] adj palpabile

palpitate ['pælpɪ‚tet] intr palpitare

pal·sy ['polzi] s (-sies) paralisi f ‖ v (pret & pp -sied) tr paralizzare

pal·try ['poltri] adj (-trier; -triest) vile, meschino, irrisorio

pamper ['pæmpər] tr viziare; (the appetite) saziare

pamphlet ['pæmflɪt] s opuscolo, libello

pan [pæn] s padella, casseruola; (of a balance) coppa, piatto; (phot) bacinella ‖ v (pret & pp **panned;** ger **panning**) tr friggere; (gold) vagliare in padella; (salt) estrarre in salina; (coll) criticare ‖ intr essere estratto; **to pan out** (coll) riuscire ‖ **Pan** s Pan m

panacea [‚pænə'si·ə] s panacea

Pan'ama Canal' ['pænə‚ma] s Canale m di Panama

Pan'ama hat' *s* panama *m*

Panamanian [ˌpænəˈmenɪ·ən] or [ˌpænəˈmɑnɪ·ən] *adj & s* panamegno

pan'cake' *s* frittella || *intr* (aer) atterrare a piatto

pan'cake land'ing *s* atterraggio a piatto

pancreas [ˈpænkrɪ·əs] *s* pancreas *m*

pander [ˈpændər] *s* mezzano || *intr* ruffianeggiare; **to pander to** favorire, assecondare i desideri di

pane [pen] *s* pannello, vetro di finestra

pan·el [ˈpænəl] *s* pannello; gruppo che discute in faccia al pubblico, telequiz *m*; discussione pubblica; (*of door or window*) specchio; (law) lista di giurati || *v* (*pret & pp* **-eled** or **-elled; ger -eling** or **-elling**) *tr* coprire di pannelli

pan'el discus'sion *s* colloquio di esperti in faccia al pubblico

panelist [ˈpænəlɪst] *s* partecipante *mf* a una discussione in faccia al pubblico

pan'el lights' *spl* luci *fpl* del cruscotto

pan'el truck' *s* camioncino

pang [pæŋ] *s* (*sharp pain*) spasimo; (*of remorse*) tormento

pan'han·dle *s* manico della padella || *intr* accattare, mendicare

pan·ic [ˈpænɪk] *adj & s* panico || *v* (*pret & pp* **-icked; ger -icking**) *tr* riempire di panico || *intr* essere colto dal panico

pan'ic·strick'en *adj* morto di paura, in preda al panico

pano·ply [ˈpænəplɪ] *s* (**-plies**) panoplia; abbigliamento in pompa magna

panorama [ˌpænəˈræmə] or [ˌpænəˈrɑmə] *s* panorama *m*

pan·sy [ˈpænzɪ] *s* (**-sies**) viola del pensiero

pant [pænt] *s* anelito, affanno; **pants** pantaloni *mpl*, calzoni *mpl*; **to wear the pants** portare i calzoni || *intr* ansare; (*said of heart*) palpitare

pantheism [ˈpænθɪˌɪzəm] *s* panteismo

pantheon [ˈpænθɪˌɑn] or [ˈpænθɪ·ən] *s* panteon *m*, pantheon *m*

panther [ˈpænθər] *s* pantera

panties [ˈpæntɪz] *spl* mutandine *fpl*

pantomime [ˈpæntəˌmaɪm] *s* pantomima

pan·try [ˈpæntrɪ] *s* (**-tries**) dispensa

pap [pæp] *s* pappa

papa·cy [ˈpepəsɪ] *s* (**-cies**) papato

Pa'pal States' [ˈpepəl] *spl* Stati *mpl* pontifici

paper [ˈpepər] *adj* di carta, cartaceo || *s* carta; (*newspaper*) giornale *m*; (*of a student*) tema *m*, saggio; (*of a scholar*) dissertazione; **on paper** per iscritto || *tr* (*a wall*) tappezzare

pa'per·back' *s* libro in brossura

pa'per·boy' *s* giornalaio, strillone *m*

pa'per clip' *s* fermaglio per le carte, clip *m*

pa'per cone' *s* cartoccio

pa'per cut'ter *s* rifilatrice *f*

pa'per doll' *s* pupazzetto di carta

pa'per·hang'er *s* tappezziere *m*

pa'per knife' *s* tagliacarte *m*

pa'per mill' *s* cartiera

pa'per mon'ey *s* carta moneta

pa'per prof'its *spl* guadagni *mpl* non realizzati su valori non venduti

pa'per tape' *s* (*of teletype*) nastro di carta; (*of computer*) nastro perforato

pa'per·weight' *s* fermacarte *m*

pa'per work' *s* lavoro a tavolino

papier-mâché [ˌpepərmɑˈʃe] *s* cartapesta

paprika [pæˈprikə] or [ˈpæprɪkə] *s* paprica

papy·rus [pəˈpaɪrəs] *s* (**-ri** [raɪ]) papiro

par [pɑr] *adj* alla pari, nominale; normale || *s* parità *f*, valore *m* nominale; **at par** alla pari

parable [ˈpærəbəl] *s* parabola

parabola [pəˈræbələ] *s* parabola

parachute [ˈpærəˌʃut] *s* paracadute *m* || *intr* lanciarsi col paracadute

par'a·chute jump' *s* lancio col paracadute

parachutist [ˈpærəˌʃutɪst] *s* paracadutista *mf*

parade [pəˈred] *s* parata, sfilata; ostentazione, sfoggio || *tr* ostentare, sfoggiare; disporre in parata || *intr* fare mostra di sé; (mil) sfilare

paradise [ˈpærəˌdaɪs] *s* paradiso

paradox [ˈpærəˌdɑks] *s* paradosso

paradoxical [ˌpærəˈdɑksɪkəl] *adj* paradossale

paraffin [ˈpærəfɪn] *s* paraffina

paragon [ˈpærəˌgɑn] *s* paragone *m*

paragraph [ˈpærəˌgræf] or [ˈpærəˌgrɑf] *s* paragrafo, capoverso; (*in a newspaper*) trafiletto; (*of law*) comma *m*

parakeet [ˈpærəˌkit] *s* parrocchetto

paral·lel [ˈpærəˌlel] *adj* parallelo || *s* (geog, fig) parallelo; (geom) parallela; **parallels** (typ) sbarrette *fpl* verticali || *v* (*pret & pp* **-leled** or **-lelled; ger -leling** or **-lelling**) *tr* collocare parallelamente; correre parallelo a; confrontare

par'allel bars' *spl* parallele *fpl*

paraly·sis [pəˈrælɪsɪs] *s* (**-ses** [ˌsiz]) paralisi *f*

paralytic [ˌpærəˈlɪtɪk] *adj & s* paralitico

paralyze [ˈpærəˌlaɪz] *tr* paralizzare

paramount [ˈpærəˌmaunt] *adj* capitale, supremo

paramour [ˈpærəˌmur] *s* amante *mf*

paranoiac [ˌpærəˈnɔɪ·æk] *adj & s* paranoico

parapet [ˈpærəˌpet] *s* parapetto

paraphernalia [ˌpærəfərˈnelɪ·ə] *spl* roba, cose *fpl*; attrezzi *mpl*, aggeggi *mpl*

parasite [ˈpærəˌsaɪt] *s* parassita *m*

parasitic(al) [ˌpærəˈsɪtɪk(əl)] *adj* parassitico, parassitario

parasol [ˈpærəˌsɔl] or [ˈpærəˌsɑl] *s* parasole *m*, ombrellino da sole

par'a·troop'er *s* paracadutista *m*

par'a·troops' *spl* truppe *fpl* paracadutiste

parboil [ˈpɑrˌbɔɪl] *tr* bollire parzialmente; (fig) far bollire

parcel [ˈpɑrsəl] *s* pacchetto; (*of land*) appezzamento || *v* (*pret & pp* **-celed** or **-celled; ger -celing** or **-celling**) *tr* impacchettare; **to parcel out** dividere, distribuire

par'cel post' s servizio pacchi postali

parch [part/] tr bruciare; (land) inaridire; (e.g., beans) essiccare; **to be parched** bruciare dalla sete || intr arrostirsi; inaridire

parchment ['part/mənt] s pergamena

pardon ['pardən] s perdono, grazia; **I beg your pardon** scusi || tr perdonare; (an offense) graziare

pardonable ['pardənəbəl] adj perdonabile, veniale

par'don board' s ufficio per la decisione delle grazie

pare [per] tr (fruit, potatoes) sbucciare, pelare; (nails) tagliare; (expenses) ridurre

parent ['perənt] adj madre, principale || s genitore m or genitrice f; (fig) origine f; **parents** genitori mpl

parentage ['perəntɪdʒ] s discendenza, lignaggio

parenthesis [pə'renθɪsɪs] s (-ses [,siz]) parentesi f; **in parenthesis** tra parentesi

parenthetically [,pærən'θetɪkəli] adv tra parentesi

parenthood ['perənt,hʊd] s paternità f or maternità f

pariah [pə'raɪə] or ['parɪə] s paria m

pari-mutuel ['pærɪ'mjut/ʊ·əl] s totalizzatore m

par'ing knife' s coltello per sbucciare

Paris ['pærɪs] s Parigi f

parish ['pærɪʃ] s parrocchia

parishioner [pə'rɪʃənər] s parrocchiano

Parisian [pə'rɪʒən] adj & s parigino

parity ['pærɪti] s parità f

park [park] s parco || tr parcare, parcheggiare || intr parcare, parcheggiare, stazionare

parking ['parkɪŋ] s posteggio, parcheggio; **no parking** divieto di parcheggio

park'ing lights' spl luci fpl di posizione

park'ing lot' s posteggio, parcheggio

park'ing me'ter s parchimetro

park'ing tick'et s contravvenzione per parcheggio abusivo

park'way' s boulevard m

parlay ['parli] or ['parle] tr rigiocare

parley ['parli] s trattativa, conferenza || tr parlamentare

parliament ['parlɪmənt] s parlamento

parlor ['parlər] s salotto; (of beautician or undertaker) salone m; (of convent) parlatorio

par'lor car' s vettura salone

par'lor game' s gioco di società

par'lor pol'itics s politica da caffè

Parmesan [,parmɪ'zæn] adj & s parmigiano

Parnassus [par'næsəs] s (poetry; poets) parnaso; il Parnaso

parochial [pə'rokɪ·əl] adj parrocchiale; ristretto, limitato; (school) confessionale

paro·dy ['pærədi] s (-dies) parodia || v (pret & pp -died) tr parodiare

parole [pə'rol] s parola d'onore; libertà f condizionale, condizionale f || tr mettere in libertà condizionale

paroxytone [pær'aksɪ,ton] adj parossitono || s parola parossitona

parquet [par'ke] s pavimento di legno tassellato, tassellato; (theat) platea || v (pret & pp -queted ['ked]; ger -queting ['ke·ɪŋ]) tr pavimentare in legno tassellato

par'quet cir'cle s poltroncine fpl

parricide ['pærɪ,saɪd] s (act) patricidio, parricidio; (person) patricida mf, parricida mf

parrot ['pærət] s pappagallo || tr scimmiottare, fare il pappagallo a

par·ry ['pæri] s (-ries) parata || v (pret & pp -ried) tr parare; (fig) evitare

parse [pars] tr (gram) analizzare grammaticalmente

parsimonious [,parsɪ'monɪ·əs] adj parsimonioso

parsley ['parsli] s prezzemolo

parsnip ['parsnɪp] s pastinaca

parson ['parsən] s parroco; pastore m protestante

part [part] s parte f; (of a machine) pezzo, organo; (of hair) riga; **for my part** per parte mia; **on the part of** da parte di; **part and parcel** parte f integrante; **parts** abilità f, dote f; regione f, paesi mpl; **to do one's part** fare il proprio dovere || adv parzialmente, in parte || tr dividere, separare; **to part company** separarsi; **to part one's hair** farsi la riga || intr separarsi; **to part from** separarsi da, dividersi da; **to part with** rinunciare a

par·take [par'tek] v (pret -took ['tuk]; pp -taken) tr condividere || intr—**to partake in** partecipare a; **to partake of** condividere

parterre [par'ter] s aiola; (theat) platea

Parthenon ['parθɪ,nan] s Partenone m

partial ['parʃəl] adj parziale

participate [par'tɪsɪ,pet] intr partecipare; **to participate in** partecipare a

participation [par,tɪsɪ'peʃən] s partecipazione

participle ['partɪ,sɪpəl] s participio

particle ['partɪkəl] s particella

particular [pər'tɪkjələr] adj (belonging to a single person) particolare; (exacting) esigente, fastidioso || s particolare m; **in particular** specialmente, particolarmente

part'ing adj (words) di commiato; (last) ultimo || s commiato; separazione

partisan ['partɪzən] adj & s partigiano

partition [par'tɪʃən] s partizione, divisione; (of house) tramezzo || tr dividere; tramezzare

partner ['partnər] s (in sports) compagno; (in dancing) cavaliere m, dama; (husband or wife) consorte mf; (com) socio

partnership ['partnər,ʃɪp] s associazione; (com) società f

part' of speech' s parte f del discorso

partridge ['partrɪdʒ] s pernice f

part'-time' adj a orario ridotto, a ore

par·ty ['parti] adj comune; di gala || s (-ties) festa, ricevimento, trattenimento; (of people) gruppo; (indi-

vidual) persona; (pol) partito; (law) contraente *mf*; (mil) distaccamento; **to be a party to** prendere parte a; essere complice di

par′ty girl′ *s* ragazza che fa la vita

par′ty-go′er *s* frequentatore *m* di trattenimenti

par′ty line′ *s* (*boundary*) linea di confine; (*of Communist party*) politica del partito; (telp) linea in coutenza

pass [pæs] or [pɑs] *s* passaggio; (*state*) stato, situazione; (*free ticket*) ingresso gratuito; (*leave of absence given to a soldier*) congedo, permesso; (*of a hypnotist*) gesto; (*between mountains*) passo; (slang) tentativo d'abbraccio; **a ●pretty pass** (coll) un bell'affare ‖ *tr* (*a course in school*) passare; (*to promote*) promuovere; (*a law*) approvare; (*a sentence*) pronunciare; (*an opinion*) esprimere, avanzare; (*to excrete*) evacuare; far muovere; **to pass by** non fare attenzione a; **to pass off** (*e.g., bogus money*) azzeccare; **to pass on** trasmettere; **to pass out** distribuire; **to pass over** omettere ‖ *intr* (*to go*) passare; (*said of a law*) essere approvato; (*said of a student*) essere promosso; (*to be accepted*) farsi passare; (*said, e.g., of two trains*) incrociarsi; **to come to pass** accadere, succedere; **to pass as** passare per; **to pass away** morire; **to pass out** (slang) svenire; **to pass over** or **through** attraversare, passare per

passable [′pæsəbəl] or [′pɑsəbəl] *adj* praticabile; (*by boat*) navigabile; (*adequate*) passabile; (law) promulgabile

passage [′pæsɪdʒ] *s* passaggio; (*of a law*) approvazione; (*ticket*) biglietto di passaggio; (*of the bowels*) evacuazione

pass′book′ *s* libretto di banca; libretto della cassa di risparmio

passenger [′pæsəndʒər] *s* passeggero

passer-by [′pæsər′baɪ] or [′pɑsər′baɪ] *s* (**passers-by**) passante *mf*

passing [′pæsɪŋ] or [′pɑsɪŋ] *adj* (*fleeting*) fuggente; (*casual*) incidentale; (*grade*) che concede la promozione ‖ *s* passaggio; (*death*) morte *f*; promozione

passion [′pæʃən] *s* passione

passionate [′pæʃənɪt] *adj* appassionato; (*hot-tempered*) collerico; veemente, ardente

passive [′pæsɪv] *adj* & *s* passivo

pass′key′ *s* chiave maestra; (*for use of hotel help*) comunale

Pass′o′ver *s* Pasqua ebraica

pass′port′ *s* passaporto

pass′word′ *s* parola d'ordine

past [pæst] or [pɑst] *adj* passato, scorso; ex, già; **past president** ex presidente ‖ *s* passato ‖ *adv* oltre; al di fuori; al di là ‖ *prep* oltre; al di là di; dopo (di); **past belief** incredibile; **past cure** incurabile; **past hope** senza speranza; **past recovery** incurabile; **past three o'clock** le tre passate

paste [pest] *s* (*dough*) pasta; (*adhesive*) colla; diamante *m* artificiale ‖ *tr* incollare; (slang) dare pugni a

paste′board′ *s* cartone *m*

pastel [pæs′tel] *adj* & *s* pastello

pasteurize [′pæstə‚raɪz] *tr* pastorizzare

pastime [′pæs‚taɪm] or [′pɑs‚taɪm] *s* diversione, passatempo

pastor [′pæstər] or [′pɑstər] *s* pastore *m*, sacerdote *m*

pastoral [′pæstərəl] or [′pɑstərəl] *adj* pastorale ‖ *s* (*poem, letter*) pastorale *f*; (*crosier*) pastorale *m*

pas·try [′pestri] *s* (**-tries**) pasticceria

pas′try cook′ *s* pasticciere *m*

pas′try shop′ *s* pasticceria

pasture [′pæstʃər] or [′pɑstʃər] *s* pastura, pascolo ‖ *tr* condurre al pascolo ‖ *intr* brucare

past·y [′pesti] *adj* (**-ier; -iest**) pastoso; flaccido

pat [pæt] *s* colpetto; (*of butter*) panetto ‖ *v* (*pret* & *pp* **patted**; *ger* **patting**) *tr* accarezzare leggermente; battere leggermente; **to pat on the back** elogiare, incoraggiare battendo sulla spalla

patch [pætʃ] *s* (*on a suit or shoes*) toppa; (*in a tire*) pezza; (*on wound*) benda; (*of ground*) appezzamento; (*small area*) lembo ‖ *tr* rammendare; **to patch up** (*an argument*) comporre; (*to produce crudely*) raffazzonare

patent [′petənt] *adj* patente, palmare ‖ [′pætənt] *adj* brevettato ‖ *s* (*of invention*) brevetto; (*sole right*) privativa ‖ *tr* brevettare

pat′ent leath′er [′pætənt] *s* copale *m* & *f*, pelle *f* di vernice

pat′ent med′icine [′pætənt] *s* specialità *f* medicinale

pat′ent right′ [′pætənt] *s* proprietà brevettata

paternal [pə′tʌrnəl] *adj* paterno

paternity [pə′tʌrnɪti] *s* paternità *f*

path [pæθ] or [pɑθ] *s* via battuta, sentiero; (fig) via

pathetic [pə′θetɪk] *adj* patetico

path′find′er *s* esploratore *m*

pathology [pə′θɑlədʒi] *s* patologia

pathos [′peθɑs] *s* patos *m*, pathos *m*

path′way′ *s* sentiero, cammino

patience [′peʃəns] *s* pazienza

patient [′peʃənt] *adj* & *s* paziente *mf*

patriarch [′petri‚ɑrk] *s* patriarca *m*

patrician [pə′trɪʃən] *adj* & *s* patrizio

patricide [′pætri‚saɪd] *s* (*act*) parricidio; (*person*) parricida *mf*

Patrick [′pætrɪk] *s* Patrizio

patrimo·ny [′pætri‚moni] *s* (**-nies**) patrimonio

patriot [′petri‚ət] or [′pætri‚ət] *s* patriota *m*

patriotic [‚petri′ɑtɪk] or [‚pætri′ɑtɪk] *adj* patriottico

patriotism [′petri‚ə‚tɪzəm] or [′pætri‚ə‚tɪzəm] *s* patriottismo

pa·trol [pə′trol] *s* (*group*) ●pattuglia; (*individual*) soldato or agente *m* di pattuglia ‖ *v* (*pret* & *pp* **-trolled**; *ger* **-trolling**) *tr* & *intr* pattugliare

patrol′man *s* (**-men**) agente *m*, poliziotto

patrol' wag'on s carrozzone m cellulare, cellulare m

patron ['petrən] or ['pætrən] s patrono, sostenitore m; (customer) cliente mf

patronize ['petrə‚naɪz] or ['pætrə‚naɪz] tr (to support) sostenere; trattare con condiscendenza; essere cliente abituale di

pa'tron saint' s patrono

patter ['pætər] s (e.g., of rain) battito; (of feet) scalpiccio; (speech) chiaccherio || intr battere, picchiettare; chiacchierare

pattern ['pætərn] s modello; disegno; (of flight) procedura || tr modellare

pat·ty ['pæti] s (-ties) pasticcino; (meat cake) polpetta

paucity ['pɔsɪti] s pochezza, scarsità f, insufficienza

Paul [pɔl] s Paolo

paunch [pɔntʃ] s pancia

paunch·y ['pɔntʃi] adj (-ier; -iest) panciuto

pauper ['pɔpər] s povero, indigente mf

pause [pɔz] s pausa; (of a tape recorder) arresto momentaneo; **to give pause (to)** dar di che pensare (a) || intr far pausa, fermarsi; (to hesitate) esitare, vacillare

pave [pev] tr pavimentare, lastricare; **to pave the way (for)** aprire il cammino (a)

pavement ['pevmənt] s pavimentazione, lastricato; (sidewalk) marciapiede m

pavilion [pə'vɪljən] s padiglione m; (of circus) tendone m

paw [pɔ] s zampa || tr (to touch with paws) dar zampate a; (to handle clumsily) maneggiare goffamente; (coll) palpeggiare || intr zampare

pawn [pɔn] s (security) pegno; (tool of another person) pedina; (chess) pedina, pedone m; (fig) ostaggio || tr dare in pegno, impegnare

pawn'bro'ker s prestatore m su pegno

pawn'shop' s agenzia di prestiti su pegno, monte m di pietà

pawn' tick'et s ricevuta di pegno, polizza del monte di pietà

pay [pe] s pagamento; (wages) paga, salario; (mil) soldo || v (pret & pp **paid** [ped]) tr pagare; (wages) conguagliare; (one's respects) presentare; (a visit) fare; (a bill) saldare; (attention) fare, presentare; **to pay back** ripagare; (fig) pagare pan per focaccia a; **to pay for** pagare; **to pay off** liquidare; (in order to discharge) pagare e licenziare; **to pay up** saldare || intr pagare; valere la pena; **pay as you enter** pagare all'ingresso; **pay as you go** pagare le tasse per trattenuta; **pay as you leave** pagare all'uscita

payable ['pe‚əbəl] adj pagabile

pay' boost' s aumento di salario

pay'check' s assegno in pagamento del salario; salario, paga

pay'day' s giorno di paga

payee [pe'i] s beneficiario

pay' en've·lope s bustapaga

payer ['pe‚ər] s pagatore m

pay'load' s peso utile

pay'mas'ter s ufficiale m pagatore

payment ['pemənt] s pagamento

pay'off' s pagamento, regolamento; (coll) conclusione

pay' phone' s telefono a moneta

pay'roll' s lista degli impiegati; libro paga

pay' sta'tion s telefono pubblico

pea [pi] s pisello

peace [pis] s pace f; **to hold one's peace** tacere, stare zitto

peaceable ['pisəbəl] adj pacifico

peaceful ['pisfəl] adj pacifico

peace'mak'er s paciere m

peace' of mind' s serenità f d'animo

peace' pipe' s calumet m della pace

peach [pitʃ] s pesca; (coll) persona or cosa stupenda

peach' tree' s pesco

peach·y ['pitʃi] adj (-ier; -iest) (coll) stupendo

pea'cock' s pavone m

peak [pik] s picco; (of traffic) punta; (of one's career) sommo

peak' hour' s ora di punta

peak' load' s carico delle ore di punta, carico massimo

peal [pil] s (of bells) squillo; (of gun) rombo; (of laughter) scoppio; (of thunder) scroscio || intr scampanare, squillare

pea'nut' s nocciolina americana; (plant) arachide f

pea'nut but'ter s pasta d'arachidi

pear [per] s (fruit) pera; (tree) pero

pearl [pɑrl] s perla; (mother-of-pearl) madreperla; colore perlaceo

pearl' oys'ter s ostrica perlifera

pear' tree' s pero

peasant ['pezənt] adj & s contadino

pea'shoot'er s cerbottana

pea' soup' s minestra di piselli; (coll) nebbione m

peat [pit] s torba

pebble ['pebəl] s ciottolo

peck [pek] s beccata; misura di due galloni; **a peck of trouble** un mare di guai || tr beccare || intr beccare; **to peck at** beccucciare

peculation [‚pekjə'leʃən] s malversazione, peculato

peculiar [pɪ'kjuljər] adj peculiare; (odd) strano

pedagogue ['pedə‚gɑg] s pedagogo

pedagogy ['pedə‚godʒi] or ['pedə‚gɑdʒi] s pedagogia

ped·al ['pedəl] s pedale m || v (pret & pp **-aled** or **-alled;** ger **-aling** or **-alling**) tr spingere coi pedali || intr pedalare

pedant ['pedənt] s pedante mf

pedantic [pɪ'dæntɪk] adj pedantesco

pedant·ry ['pedəntri] s (-ries) pedanteria

peddle ['pedəl] tr vendere di porta in porta || intr fare il venditore ambulante

peddler ['pedlər] s venditore m or merciaiolo ambulante

pedestal ['pɛdɪstəl] s piedistallo
pedestrian [pɪ'dɛstrɪ·ən] adj pedestre || s pedone m
pediatrics [,pidɪ'ætrɪks] or [,pɛdɪ'ætrɪks] s pediatria
pedigree ['pɛdɪ,gri] s albero genealogico; discendenza, lignaggio
pediment ['pɛdɪmənt] s frontone m
peek [pik] s sbirciata || intr sbirciare
peel [pil] s scorza, buccia; (of baker) pala || tr sbucciare; **to keep one's eyes peeled** (slang) tenere gli occhi aperti || intr pelarsi
peep [pip] s sbirciata; (sound) pigolio || intr guardare attraverso una fessura; (said of birds) pigolare; (to begin to appear) fare capolino
peep'hole' s spioncino
Peep'ing Tom' s guardone m
peep' show' s cosmorama m
peer [pɪr] s pari m, uguale m; (Brit) pari m || intr guardare da vicino
peerless ['pɪrlɪs] adj senza pari
peeve [piv] s (coll) seccatura, irritazione || tr (coll) seccare, irritare
peevish ['pivɪʃ] adj irritabile
peg [pɛg] s (to plug holes) zipolo; (pin) cavicchio; (mus) bischero; (coll) grado; **to take down a peg** (coll) fare abbassare la testa a || v (pret & pp pegged; ger pegging) tr fissare con cavicchi; (prices) stabilizzare || intr—**to peg away** lavorare di lena
peg' leg' s gamba di legno
Peking ['pi'kɪŋ] s Pechino f
Peking·ese [,pikɪ'niz] adj pechinese || s (-ese) pechinese mf
pelf [pɛlf] s (pej) denaro rubacchiato, maltolto
pelican ['pɛlɪkən] s pellicano
pellet ['pɛlɪt] s pallottola; (for shotgun) pallino; (pill) pillola
pell-mell ['pɛl'mɛl] adj confuso, disordinato || adv alla rinfusa
Peloponnesian [,pɛləpə'niʃən] adj & s peloponnesiaco
pelt [pɛlt] s pelle grezza; (blow) colpo || tr scagliare contro; (to beat) battere violentemente || intr battere, scrosciare
pen [pɛn] s (enclosure) recinto; (for writing) penna; (pen point) pennino || v (pret & pp penned; ger penning) tr scrivere a penna; (to compose) redigere || v (pret & pp penned or pent; ger penning) tr recintare
penalize ['pinə,laɪz] tr punire; (sports) penalizzare
penal·ty ['pɛnəlti] s (-ties) punizione; (fine) multa; (for late payment) penale f; **under penalty of** sotto pena di
pen'alty goal' s calcio di rigore
penance ['pɛnəns] s penitenza
penchant ['pɛn/ənt] s propensione
pen·cil ['pɛnsəl] s matita; (of rays) fascio || v (pret & pp -ciled or -cilled; ger -ciling or -cilling) tr scrivere a matita; (med) pennellare
pen'cil sharp'ener s temperalapis m
pendent ['pɛndənt] adj pendente, sospeso || s pendente m, ciondolo

pending ['pɛndɪŋ] adj imminente; in sospeso || prep durante; fino a
pendulum ['pɛndʒələm] s pendolo
pen'dulum bob' s lente f
penetrate ['pɛnɪ,tret] tr & intr penetrare
penguin ['pɛŋgwɪn] s pinguino
pen'hold'er s portapenne m
penicillin [,pɛnɪ'sɪlɪŋ] s penicillina
peninsula [pɛ'nɪnsələ] s penisola
peninsular [pə'nɪnsələr] adj & s peninsulare
penitence ['pɛnɪtəns] s penitenza
penitent ['pɛnɪtənt] adj & s penitente mf
pen'knife' s (-knives) temperino
penmanship ['pɛnmən,ʃɪp] s calligrafia
pen' name' s nome m di penna, pseudonimo
pennant ['pɛnənt] s pennone m
penniless ['pɛnɪlɪs] adj povero in canna, senza un soldo
pennon ['pɛnən] s pennone m
pen·ny ['pɛni] s (-nies) (U.S.A.) centesimo || s (pence [pɛns]) (Brit) penny m
pen'ny pinch'er s ['pɪntʃər] s spilorcio
pen' pal' s amico corrispondente
pen'point' s pennino; (of ball-point pen) punta
pension ['pɛnʃən] s pensione || tr pensionare, mettere in pensione
pensioner ['pɛnʃənər] s pensionato
pensive ['pɛnsɪv] adj pensieroso
Pentecost ['pɛntɪ,kɔst] or ['pɛntɪ,kɑst] s la Pentecoste
penthouse ['pɛnt,haʊs] s appartamento di lusso sul tetto; tettoia
pent-up ['pɛnt,ʌp] adj represso
penult ['pinʌlt] s penultima
penum·bra [pɪ'nʌmbrə] s (-brae [bri] or -bras) penombra
penurious [pɪ'nʊrɪ·əs] adj taccagno, meschino; indigente
penury ['pɛnjəri] s taccagneria; estrema povertà, miseria
pen'wip'er s nettapenne m
people ['pipəl] spl popolo, gente f; (relatives) famiglia; gente f del popolo; si, e.g., **people say** si dice || ssg (peoples) nazione, popolazione || tr popolare
pep [pɛp] s (coll) animo, brio || v (pret & pp pepped; ger pepping) tr— **to pep up** (coll) dar animo a
pepper ['pɛpər] s pepe m || tr pepare; (to pelt) tempestare
pep'per·box' s pepaiola
pep'per·mint' s menta piperita
per [pʌr] prep per; (for each) il, e.g., **three dollars per meter** tre dollari il metro; **as per** secondo
perambulator [pər'æmbjə,letər] s carrozzella, carrozzino
per capita [pər 'kæpɪtə] per persona, a testa
perceive [pər'siv] tr percepire
percent [pər'sɛnt] s percento, per cento
percentage [pər'sɛntɪdʒ] s percento, percentuale f; (coll) vantaggio
perception [pər'sɛpʃən] s percezione

perch [pʌrtʃ] s (*roost*) posatoio; (*horizontal rod*) ballatoio; (ichth) pesce persico || *intr* appollaiarsi

percolator ['pʌrkə,letər] s caffettiera filtro a circolazione

percus'sion cap' [pər'kʌʃən] s capsula di percussione

per diem [pər 'daɪ·əm] s assegno giornaliero

perdition [pər'dɪʃən] s perdizione

perennial [pər'rɛnɪ·əl] *adj* perenne || s pianta perenne

perfect ['pʌrfɪkt] *adj & s* perfetto || [pər'fɛkt] *tr* perfezionare

perfidious [pər'fɪdɪ·əs] *adj* perfido

perfi·dy ['pʌrfɪdɪ] s (-dies) perfidia

perforate ['pʌrfə,ret] *tr* perforare

perforation [,pʌrfə're/ən] s perforazione; (*of postage stamp*) dentellatura

perforce [pər'fors] *adv* per forza, necessariamente

perform [pər'fɔrm] *tr* (*a task*) eseguire; (*a promise*) adempiere; (*to enact*) rappresentare || *intr* recitare; (*said, e.g., of a machine*) funzionare

performance [pər'fɔrməns] s esecuzione; (*of a machine*) funzionamento; (*deed*) atto di prodezza; (theat) rappresentazione

performer [pər'fɔrmər] s esecutore m; attore m; acrobata mf

perform'ing arts' spl arti fpl dello spettacolo

perfume ['pʌrfjum] s profumo || [pər'fjum] *tr* profumare

perfumer·y [pər'fjuməri] s (-ies) profumeria

perfunctory [pər'fʌŋktəri] *adj* superficiale, pro forma; indifferente

perhaps [pər'hæps] *adv* forse

per·il ['pɛrəl] s pericolo || v (*pret & pp* -iled *or* -illed; *ger* -iling *or* -illing) *tr* mettere in pericolo

perilous ['pɛrɪləs] *adj* pericoloso

period ['pɪrɪ·əd] s periodo; mestruazione; (*in school*) ora; (sports) tempo; (gram) punto

pe'riod cos'tume s costume m dell'epoca

periodic [,pɪrɪ'adɪk] *adj* periodico

periodical [,pɪrɪ'adɪkəl] *adj & s* periodico

peripher·y [pə'rɪfəri] s (-ies) periferia

periscope ['pɛrɪ,skop] s periscopio

perish ['pɛrɪʃ] *intr* perire

perishable ['pɛrɪʃəbəl] *adj* deteriorabile

periwig ['pɛrɪ,wɪg] s parrucca

perjure ['pʌrdʒər] *tr*—to perjure oneself spergiurare, giurare il falso

perju·ry ['pʌrdʒəri] s (-ries) spergiuro

perk [pʌrk] *tr* (*the head, the ears*) alzare; to perk oneself up agghindarsi || *intr*—to perk up ringalluzzirsi

permanence ['pʌrmənəns] s permanenza

permanen·cy ['pʌrmənənsi] s (-cies) permanenza

permanent ['pʌrmənənt] *adj* permanente || s permanente f, ondulazione permanente

per'manent fix'ture s cosa or persona permanente

per'manent ten'ure s inamovibilità f

per'manent way' s (rr) sede f stradale ed armamento

permeate ['pʌrmɪ,et] *tr* permeare || *intr* permearsi

permissible [pər'mɪsɪbəl] *adj* permissibile

permission [pər'mɪʃən] s permesso

per·mit ['pʌrmɪt] s permesso; patente f, licenza || [pər'mɪt] v (*pret & pp* -mitted; *ger* -mitting) *tr* permettere

permute [pər'mjut] *tr* permutare

pernicious [pər'nɪʃəs] *adj* pernicioso

pernickety [pər'nɪkɪti] *adj* (coll) incontentabile, meticoloso

perorate ['pɛrə,ret] *tr* perorare

peroxide [pər'aksaɪd] s perossido; perossido d'idrogeno

perox'ide blonde' s bionda ossigenata

perpendicular [,pʌrpən'dɪkjələr] *adj & s* perpendicolare f

perpetrate ['pʌrpɪ,tret] *tr* (*a crime*) perpetrare; (*a blunder*) commettere

perpetual [pər'pɛt/ʊ·əl] *adj* perpetuo

perpetuate [pər'pɛt/ʊ,et] *tr* perpetuare

perplex [pər'plɛks] *tr* lasciare perplesso

perplexed [pər'plɛkst] *adj* perplesso

perplexi·ty [pər'plɛksɪti] s (-ties) perplessità f

per se [pər 'si] di per se

persecute ['pʌrsɪ,kjut] *tr* perseguitare

persevere [,pʌrsɪ'vɪr] *intr* perseverare

Persian ['pʌrʒən] *adj & s* persiano

Per'sian Gulf' s Golfo Persico

persimmon [pər'sɪmən] s diospiro virginiano; cachi m

persist [pər'sɪst] *or* [pər'zɪst] *intr* persistere

persistent [pər'sɪstənt] *or* [pər'zɪstənt] *adj* persistente

person ['pʌrsən] s persona; no person nessuno

personage ['pʌrsənɪdʒ] s personaggio; persona

personal ['pʌrsənəl] *adj* personale; (*goods*) mobile || s inserzione personale; trafiletto di società

personali·ty [,pʌrsə'nælɪti] s (-ties) personalità f; offesa personale

personal'ity cult' s culto della personalità

per'sonal prop'erty s beni mpl mobili

personi·fy [pər'sanɪ,faɪ] v (*pret & pp* -fied) *tr* personificare

personnel [,pʌrsə'nɛl] s personale m

per'son-to-per'son call' s (telp) chiamata con preavviso

perspective [pər'spɛktɪv] s prospettiva

perspicacious [,pʌrspɪ'keʃəs] *adj* perspicace

perspire [pər'spaɪr] *intr* sudare

persuade [pər'swed] *tr* persuadere

persuasion [pər'sweʒən] s persuasione; fede religiosa

pert [pʌrt] *adj* impertinente, sfacciato; vivace

pertain [pər'ten] *intr* appartenere; (*to have reference*) riferirsi

pertinacious [,pʌrtɪ'neʃəs] *adj* pertinace

pertinent ['pʌrtɪnənt] *adj* pertinente
perturb [pər'tʌrb] *tr* perturbare
Peru [pə'ru] *s* il Perù
perusal [pə'ruzəl] *s* attenta lettura
peruse [pə'ruz] *tr* leggere attentamente
pervade [pər'ved] *tr* pervadere
perverse [pər'vʌrs] *adj* perverso; *(obstinate)* ostinato
perversion [pər'vʌrʒən] *s* perversione
perversi‧ty [pər'vʌrsɪti] *s* (-ties) perversità *f*; contrarietà *f*
pervert ['pʌrvərt] *s* pervertito, degenerato || [pər'vʌrt] *tr* pervertire, degenerare
pes‧ky ['peski] *adj* (-kier; -kiest) (coll) noioso, molesto
pessimism ['pesɪ,mɪzəm] *s* pessimismo
pessimist ['pesɪmɪst] *s* pessimista *mf*
pessimistic [,pesɪ'mɪstɪk] *adj* pessimistico
pest [pest] *s* peste *f*, pestilenza; insetto; animale nocivo; *(person)* peste *f*, seccatore *m*
pester ['pestər] *tr* seccare, annoiare
pest'house' *s* lazzaretto
pesticide ['pestɪ,saɪd] *s* insetticida *m*
pestiferous [pes'tɪfərəs] *adj* pestifero
pestilence ['pestɪləns] *s* pestilenza
pestle ['pesəl] *s* pestello
pet [pet] *s* animale favorito; beniamino || *v* (pret & pp **petted**; ger **petting**) *tr* accarezzare || *intr* (coll) pomiciare
petal ['petəl] *s* petalo
petard [pɪ'tard] *s* petardo
pet'cock' *s* chiavetta
Peter ['pitər] *s* Pietro; **to rob Peter to pay Paul** fare un buco per tapparne un altro || *intr*—**to peter out** (coll) affievolirsi
petition [pɪ'tɪʃən] *s* petizione || *tr* rivolgere un'istanza a
pet' name' *s* nomignolo vezzeggiativo
Petrarch ['pitrark] *s* Petrarca *m*
petri‧fy ['petrɪ,faɪ] *v* (pret & pp **-fied**) *tr* pietrificare || *intr* pietrificarsi
petrol ['petrəl] *s* (Brit) benzina
petroleum [pɪ'trolɪ‧əm] *s* petrolio
pet' shop' *s* negozio di animali domestici
petticoat ['petɪ,kot] *s* sottoveste *f*; (coll) sottana, gonnella
pet‧ty ['peti] *adj* (-tier; -tiest) insignificante, minore; meschino
pet'ty cash' *s* cassa delle piccole spese
pet'ty lar'ceny *s* furterello
pet'ty of'ficer *s* (nav) sottufficiale *m* di marina
petulant ['petjələnt] *adj* stizzoso, irritabile
pew [pju] *s* banco di chiesa
pewter ['pjutər] *s* peltro; oggetti *mpl* di peltro
phalanx ['felæŋks] or ['fælæŋks] *s* falange *f*
phantasm ['fæntæzəm] *s* fantasma *m*
phantom ['fæntəm] *s* fantasma *m*
Pharaoh ['fero] *s* Faraone *m*
pharisee ['fær1,si] *s* fariseo || **Pharisee** *s* fariseo
pharmaceutical [,farmə'sutɪkəl] *adj* farmaceutico

pharmacist ['farməsɪst] *s* farmacista *mf*
pharma‧cy ['farməsi] *s* (-cies) farmacia
pharynx ['færɪŋks] *s* faringe *f*
phase [fez] *s* fase *f* || *tr* mettere in fase; sincronizzare; **to phase in** mettere in operazione gradualmente; **to phase out** eliminare gradualmente
pheasant ['fezənt] *s* fagiano
phenobarbital [,fino'barbɪ,tæl] *s* acido fenil-etilbarbiturico, barbiturato
phenomenal [fɪ'namɪnəl] *adj* fenomenale
phenome‧non [fɪ'namɪ,nan] *s* (-na [nə]) fenomeno
phial ['faɪ‧əl] *s* fiala
philanderer [fɪ'lændərər] *s* donnaiolo
philanthropist [fɪ'lænθrəpɪɪst] *s* filantropo
philanthro‧py [fɪ'lænθrəpi] *s* (-pies) filantropia
philatelist [fɪ'lætəlɪst] *s* filatelico
philately [fɪ'lætəli] *s* filatelia
Philip ['fɪlɪp] *s* Filippo
Philippine ['fɪlɪ,pin] *adj* filippino || **Philippines** *spl* isole *fpl* Filippine
Philistine [fɪ'lɪstɪn], ['fɪlɪ,stin] or ['fɪlɪ,staɪn] *adj* & *s* filisteo
philologist [fɪ'lalədʒɪst] *s* filologo
philology [fɪ'lalədʒɪ] *s* filologia
philosopher [fɪ'lasəfər] *s* filosofo
philosophic(al) [,fɪlə'safɪk(əl)] *adj* filosofico
philoso‧phy [fɪ'lasəfi] *s* (-phies) filosofia
philter ['fɪltər] *s* filtro
phlebitis [flɪ'baɪtɪs] *s* flebite *f*
phlegm [flem] *s* (secretion) muco, catarro; *(self-possession)* flemma; apatia
phlegmatic(al) [fleg'mætɪk(əl)] *adj* flemmatica
Phoebus ['fibəs] *s* Febo
Phoenician [fɪ'nɪʃən] or [fɪ'niʃən] *adj* & *s* fenicio
phoenix ['finɪks] *s* fenice *f*
phone [fon] *s* (coll) telefono || *tr* & *intr* (coll) telefonare
phone' call' *s* chiamata telefonica
phonetic [fo'netɪk] *adj* fonetico || **phonetics** *s* fonetica
phonograph ['fonə,græf] or ['fonə,graf] *s* fonografo
phonology [fə'nalədʒɪ] *s* fonologia
pho‧ny ['foni] *adj* (-nier; -niest) (coll) falso || *s* (-nies) (coll) frode *f*; *(person)* (coll) impostore *m*
phosphate ['fasfet] *s* fosfato
phosphorescent [,fasfə'resənt] *adj* fosforescente
phospho‧rus ['fasfərəs] *s* (-ri [,raɪ]) fosforo
pho‧to ['foto] *s* (-tos) (coll) foto *f*
photo‧cop‧y ['fotə,kapi] *s* (-ies) fotocopia || *tr* fotocopiare
pho'toelec'tric cell' [,foto‧ɪ'lektrɪk] *s* cellula fotoelettrica
photoengraving [,foto‧en'grevɪŋ] *s* fotoincisione
pho'to fin'ish *s* photofinish *m*, arrivo con fotografia

photogenic [ˌfotoˈdʒɛnɪk] *adj* fotogenico

photograph [ˈfotəˌgræf] *or* [ˈfotəˌgrɑf] *s* fotografia || *tr* fotografare || *intr*—to photograph well riuscire in fotografia

photographer [fəˈtɑgrəfər] *s* fotografo

photography [fəˈtɑgrəfi] *s* fotografia

photojournalism [ˌfotəˈdʒʌrnəˌlɪzəm] *s* giornalismo fotografico

pho'to·play' *s* dramma adattato per il cinematografo

photostat [ˈfotəˌstæt] *s* (trademark) copia fotostatica || *tr* riprodurre fotostaticamente

phototube [ˈfotəˌtjub] *or* [ˈfotəˌtub] *s* fototubo

phrase [frez] *s* (gram) locuzione; (mus) frase *f* || *tr* esprimere, formulare || *intr* (mus) fraseggiare

phrenology [frɪˈnɑlədʒi] *s* frenologia

Phyllis [ˈfɪlɪs] *s* Fillide *f*

phy·lum [ˈfaɪləm] *s* (**-la** [lə]) phylum *m*, tipo

phys·ic [ˈfɪzɪk] *s* purgante *m* || *v* (*pret & pp* **-icked**; *ger* **-icking**) *tr* dare il purgante a, purgare

physical [ˈfɪzɪkəl] *adj* fisico

physician [fɪˈzɪʃən] *s* medico

physicist [ˈfɪzɪsɪst] *s* fisico

physics [ˈfɪzɪks] *s* fisica

physiognomy [ˌfɪziˈɑgnəmi] *or* [ˌfɪziˈɑnəmi] *s* fisionomia

physiological [ˌfɪzɪəˈlɑdʒɪkəl] *adj* fisiologico

physiology [ˌfɪziˈɑlədʒi] *s* fisiologia

physique [fɪˈzik] *s* fisico

pi [paɪ] *s* (math) pi greco; (typ) tipi scartati || *v* (*pret & pp* **pied;** *ger* **piing**) *tr* (typ) scompaginare, scomporre

pian·o [pɪˈæno] *s* (**-os**) piano

picaresque [ˌpɪkəˈrɛsk] *adj* picaresco

picayune [ˌpɪkəˈjun] *adj* meschino, minore, di poca importanza

picco·lo [ˈpɪkəˌlo] *s* (**-los**) ottavino

pick [pɪk] *s* (tool) piccone *m*; (choice) scelta; (the best) fiore *m*; (mus) plettro || *tr* scavare; (to scratch at) grattare; (to gather) cogliere; (to pluck) spennare; (to pull apart) separare; (one's teeth) stuzzicarsi; (a bone) rosicchiare; (to choose) scegliere; (a lock) scassinare; (a pocket) tagliare, rubare; (mus) pizzicare; **to pick a fight** attaccare briga; **to pick faults** trovare a ridire; **to pick out** scegliere; distinguere; discriminare; **to pick s.o. to pieces** (coll) tagliare i panni addosso a qlcu; **to pick up** sollevare; (to find) trovare; (to learn) arrivare a sapere; (a radio signal) captare; (speed) acquistare || *intr* usare il piccone; **to pick at** (food) spilluzzicare; (coll) criticare; **to pick on** (coll) scegliere; (coll) criticare; **to pick up** (coll) migliorarsi

pick'ax' *s* piccone *m*

picket [ˈpɪkɪt] *s* picchetto || *tr* rinchiudere con palizzata; (to hitch) legare; (to post) (mil) mettere di picchetto; (e.g., a factory) picchettare

pick'et fence' *s* steccato

pick'et line' *s* corteo di scioperanti; corteo di dimostranti

pickle [ˈpɪkəl] *s* salamoia, sottaceto; (cucumber) cetriolo sottaceto; **to get into a pickle** (coll) cacciarsi in un imbroglio || *tr* mettere sottaceto; (metallurgy) decapare

pick-me-up [ˈpɪkmiˌʌp] *s* (coll) spuntino; (coll) bevanda stimulante

pick'pock'et *s* borseggiatore *m*, borsaiolo

pick'up' *s* sollevamento; (in speed) accelerazione; (of phonograph) pick-up *m*, fonorivelatore *m*; (aut) camioncino; (coll) persona conosciuta per caso; (coll) miglioramento

pick'-up-sticks' *spl* sciangai *m*

pic·nic [ˈpɪknɪk] *s* picnic *m* || *v* (*pret & pp* **-nicked;** *ger* **-nicking**) *intr* fare merenda all'aperto

pictorial [pɪkˈtorɪ·əl] *adj* pittorico; illustrato; vivido || *s* rivista illustrata

picture [ˈpɪktʃər] *s* illustrazione, disegno; (painting) quadro, dipinto; (of a person) ritratto; fotografia; film *m*, pellicola || *tr* fare il ritratto di; disegnare; dipingere; fotografare; descrivere; immaginare, immaginarsi

pic'ture frame' *s* cornice *f*

pic'ture gal'lery *s* pinacoteca, galleria di quadri, quadreria

pic'ture post' card' *s* cartolina illustrata

pic'ture show' *s* cinematografo; mostra di quadri

picturesque [ˌpɪktʃəˈrɛsk] *adj* pittoresco

pic'ture tube' *s* tubo televisivo

pic'ture win'dow *s* finestra panoramica

piddling [ˈpɪdlɪŋ] *adj* insignificante

pie [paɪ] *s* (with fruit) torta; (with meat) timballo; (orn) pica || *v* (*pret & pp* **pied;** *ger* **pieing**) *tr* (typ) scompaginare, scomporre

piece [pis] *s* pezzo; (e.g., of cloth) pezza; **a piece of advice** un consiglio; **a piece of baggage** un collo; **a piece of furniture** un mobile *m*; **a piece of news** una notizia; **by the piece** a cottimo; **to break to pieces** frantumare; frantumarsi; **to cut to pieces** fare a pezzi; **to fall to pieces** cadere a pezzi; **to fly to pieces** rompersi in mille pezzi; **to give s.o. a piece of one's mind** dirne a qlcu di tutti i colori; **to go to pieces** perdere il controllo di sé stesso; **to take to pieces** confutare punto per punto || *tr* rappezzare, mettere insieme || *intr* (coll) mangiucchiare

piece'meal' *adv* poco a poco

piece'work' *s* lavoro a cottimo

piece'work'er *s* cottimista *mf*

pier [pɪr] *s* (of a bridge) pila; (over water) molo; (archit) pilastro, pilone *m*

pierce [pɪrs] *tr* forare, bucare; penetrare; (to stab) trapassare || *intr* penetrare

piercing [ˈpɪrsɪŋ] *adj* acuto; (eyes) penetrante; (pain) lancinante

pier' glass' *s* specchiera

pie·ty ['paɪ·əti] *s* (**-ties**) pietà *f*

piffle ['pɪfəl] *s* (coll) fesserie *fpl*

pig [pɪg] *s* maiale *m*, porco; (metallurgy) lingotto, massello; **to buy a pig in the poke** comprare il gatto nel sacco

pigeon ['pɪdʒən] *s* piccione *m*

pi'geon·hole' *s* nicchia nella piccionaia; (*for filing*) casella ‖ *tr* (*to lay aside for later time*) archiviare; (*to shelve, e.g., an application*) insabbiare

pi'geon house' *s* colombaia, piccionaia

piggish ['pɪgɪʃ] *adj* porcino, maialesco

pig'gy·back' ['pɪgɪ‚bæk] *adv* sulle spalle, sulla schiena; (rr) su carrello stradale per trasporto carri

pig'head'ed *adj* ostinato, cocciuto

pig' i'ron *s* ghisa, ferro grezzo

pigment ['pɪgmənt] *s* pigmento ‖ *tr* pigmentare ‖ *intr* pigmentarsi

pig'pen' *s* porcile *m*

pig'skin' *s* pelle *f* di maiale; (coll) pallone *m* da football, sfera di cuoio

pig'sty' *s* (**-sties**) porcile *m*

pig'tail' *s* codino; (*of girl*) treccia; treccia di tabacco

pike [park] *s* (*weapon*) picca; (*road*) autostrada; (ichth) luccio

piker ['paɪkər] *s* (coll) uomo piccino

pile [paɪl] *s* (*heap*) pila; (*for burning a corpse*) pira; (*large building*) mole *f*; (*beam*) palo; (*of carpet*) pelo; (*of money*) gruzzolo; (coll) mucchio; **piles** emorroidi *fpl* ‖ *tr* ammucchiare, accumulare; **to pile up** ammonticchiare ‖ *intr* accumularsi; **to pile into** pigiarsi in; **to pile up** accumularsi

pile' driv'er *s* battipalo, berta

pilfer ['pɪlfər] *tr* & *intr* rubacchiare

pilgrim ['pɪlgrɪm] *s* pellegrino

pilgrimage ['pɪlgrɪmɪdʒ] *s* pellegrinaggio

pill [pɪl] *s* pillola; amara pillola; (coll) rompiscatole *mf*; **to sugar-coat the pill** addolcire la pillola

pillage ['pɪlɪdʒ] *s* saccheggio, rapina ‖ *tr* & *intr* saccheggiare, rapinare

pillar ['pɪlər] *s* pilastro, colonna; **from pillar to post** da Erode a Pilato

pill'box' *s* scatoletta per le pillole; (mil) casamatta

pillo·ry ['pɪləri] *s* (**-ries**) gogna, berlina ‖ *v* (*pret* & *pp* **-ried**) *tr* mettere alla berlina

pillow ['pɪlo] *s* cuscino, guanciale *m*

pil'low·case' *s* federa

pilot ['paɪlət] *adj* pilota ‖ *s* pilota *m*; (*of locomotive*) respingente *m* ‖ *tr* pilotare

pi'lot light' *s* fiammella automatica

pimp [pɪmp] *s* ruffiano, lenone *m*

pimple ['pɪmpəl] *s* bitorzolo

pim·ply ['pɪmpli] *adj* (**-plier; -pliest**) bitorzoluto

pin [pɪn] *s* (*of metal*) spillo; (*peg*) caviglia; (*adornment*) spilla; (*linchpin*) acciarino; (*of key*) mappa; (*clothespin*) molletta; (*bowling pin*) birillo; **to be on pins and needles** stare sulle spine ‖ *tr* appuntare; (*to hold*) im-

mobilizzare; **to pin s.o. down** forzare qlcu a rivelare i propri piani **to pin s.th on s.o.** (coll) dare la colpa a qlcu per qlco

pinafore ['pɪnə‚for] *s* grembiulino

pinaster [paɪ'næstər] *s* pino marittimo

pin'ball machine' *s* biliardino

pince-nez ['pæns‚ne] *s* occhiali *mpl* a stringinaso

pincers ['pɪnsərz] *ssg* or *spl* tenaglie *fpl*; (zool) pinze *fpl*

pinch [pɪntʃ] *s* (*squeeze*) pizzicotto; (*of tobacco*) presa; (*of salt*) pizzico; (*hardship*) strettoia; **in a pinch** in caso di necessità ‖ *tr* stringere, pizzicare; (*to press*) comprimere; ridurre alle strettezze; (slang) rubare; (slang) arrestare ‖ *intr* stringere; (*to be stingy*) fare l'avaro

pin'cush'ion *s* puntaspilli *m*

pine [paɪn] *s* pino ‖ *intr*—**to pine away** struggersi; **to pine for** spasimare per

pine'ap'ple *s* ananas *m*

pine' cone' *s* pigna

pine' nee'dle *s* ago del pino

ping [pɪŋ] *s* rumore secco; rumore metallico ‖ *intr* fare un rumore secco or metallico

pin'head' *s* capocchia di spillo; (slang) testa quadra

pin'hole' *s* forellino

pink [pɪŋk] *adj* rosa ‖ *s* color *m* rosa; condizione perfetta; (bot) garofano ‖ *tr* orlare a zig-zag; (*to stab*) perforare

pin' mon'ey *s* denaro per le piccole spese

pinnacle ['pɪnəkəl] *s* pinnacolo

pin'point' *adj* di precisione ‖ *s* punta di spillo ‖ *tr* mettere in rilievo

pin'prick' *s* puntura di spillo

pint [paɪnt] *s* pinta

pintle ['pɪntəl] *s* maschietto

pin'up' *s* pin-up-girl *f*

pin'wheel' *s* girandola

pioneer [‚paɪə'nɪr] *s* pioniere *m* ‖ *tr* aprire la via a ‖ *intr* fare il pioniere

pioneering [‚paɪə'nɪrɪŋ] *adj* pionieristico

pious ['paɪ·əs] *adj* pio, devoto

pip [pɪp] *s* (*seed*) seme *m*; (vet) pipita

pipe [paɪp] *s* tubo, canna; (*of stove*) cannone *m*; (*for smoking*) pipa; (mus) legno; (mus) cornamusa ‖ *tr* suonare; cantare ad alta voce; fischiare; condurre in una tubatura; munire di tubatura ‖ *intr* suonare la zampogna; **to pipe down** (slang) stare zitto

pipe' clean'er *s* scovolino

pipe' dream' *s* castello in aria

pipe' line' *s* oleodotto; (fig) fonte *f* (d'informazioni)

pipe' or'gan *s* organo a canne

piper ['paɪpər] *s* zampognaro; **to pay the piper** pagare lo scotto

pipe' wrench' *s* chiave *f* per tubi

piping ['paɪpɪŋ] *adj* (*voice*) acuto; (*sound*) di cornamusa ‖ *s* tubatura; suono di cornamuse; suono acuto; (*on cakes*) fregio; (*on garments*) cordoncino ornamentale || *adv*—**piping hot** scottante, bollente

pippin ['pɪpɪn] *s* mela renetta; (*seed*) seme *m*; (fig) gran brava persona

piquant ['pikənt] *adj* piccante

pique [pik] *s* picca, ripicco || *tr* offendere, eccitare

pira·cy ['paɪrəsi] *s* (**-cies**) pirateria

pirate ['paɪrɪt] *s* pirata *mf* || *tr* derubare; (*a book*) svaligiare, pubblicare illegalmente || *intr* pirateggiare

pirouette [,pɪru'ɛt] *s* piroetta || *intr* piroettare

Pisces ['paɪsɪz] *or* ['pɪsiz] *s* (astr) Pesci *mpl*

pistol ['pɪstəl] *s* pistola

piston ['pɪstən] *s* pistone *m*

pis'ton displace'ment *s* cilindrata

pis'ton ring' *s* segmento elastico

pis'ton rod' *s* (*of a steam engine*) biella d'accoppiamento; (*of a motor*) asta del pistone, biella

pis'ton stroke' *s* corsa dello stantuffo

pit [pɪt] *s* (*in the ground*) buca; (*trap*) trappola; (*of fruit*) nocciolo; (*of stomach*) bocca; (*scar*) buttero; (*in exchange*) recinto delle grida; (*for fights*) arena; (theat) platea; (min) miniera; (aut) fossa di riparazione || *v* (*pret & pp* **pitted**; *ger* **pitting**) *tr* infossare; butterare; opporre; (*to remove pits from*) snocciolare

pitch [pɪtʃ] *s* (*black sticky substance*) pece *f*; (*throw*) lancio; (*of a roof*) pendenza, inclinazione; (*of a boat*) beccheggio; (*of a screw*) passo; (*of sound*) altezza || *tr* lanciare; (*a tent*) rizzare || *intr* beccheggiare; **to pitch in** (coll) mettersi al lavoro; (coll) cominciare a mangiare

pitch' ac'cent *s* accento di altezza

pitch' at'titude *s* assetto longitudinale

pitch'-dark' *adj* nero come la pece

pitched' bat'tle *s* battaglia campale

pitcher ['pɪtʃər] *s* brocca; (baseball) lanciatore *m*

pitch'fork' *s* forca, tridente *m*; **to rain pitchforks** (coll) piovere a dirotto

pitch' pipe' *s* (mus) corista *m*

pit'fall' *s* trappola, trabocchetto

pith [pɪθ] *s* midollo; (*strength*) (fig) forza; (fig) succo, essenza

pith·y ['pɪθi] *adj* (**-ier; -iest**) midolloso; succoso, essenziale

pitiful ['pɪtɪfəl] *adj* pietoso

pitiless ['pɪtɪlɪs] *adj* spietato

pit·y ['pɪti] *s* (**-ies**) pietà *f*; **it is a pity that** è un peccato che; **what a pity!** che peccato! || *v* (*pret & pp* **-ied**) *tr* aver pietà di

Pius ['paɪəs] *s* Pio

pivot ['pɪvət] *s* asse *m*, perno; (fig) asse *m* || *tr* imperniare || *intr* imperniarsi; **to pivot on** fare perno su; dipendere da

placard ['plækard] *s* manifesto, affisso || *tr* affiggere

place [ples] *s* luogo; locale *m*; (*court*) piazzetta; (*short street*) vicolo; residenza; sito, luogo, località *f*; (*point*) punto; (*space occupied*) posto; (*office*) posto, impiego; **in no place**

da nessuna parte; **in place** a posto; **in place of** al posto di, invece di; **in the first place** in primo luogo; **in the next place** in secondo luogo; **to know one's place** saper stare al proprio posto; **to take place** aver luogo || *tr* piazzare, mettere; (*to find employment for*) collocare; (*to identify*) ravvisare || *intr* (sports) piazzarsi

place·bo [plə'sibo] *s* (**-bos** *or* **-boes**) rimedio fittizio

place' card' *s* segnaposto

placement ['plesmənt] *s* (*e.g., of furniture*) collocazione; (*employment*) collocamento

place' name' *s* toponimo

place' of busi'ness *s* ufficio, negozio

placid ['plæsɪd] *adj* placido

plagiarism ['pledʒə,rɪzəm] *s* plagio

plagiarize ['pledʒə,raɪz] *tr* plagiare

plague [pleg] *s* peste bubbonica; (*widespread affliction*) piaga, flagello || *tr* infestare, appestare; tormentare

plaid [plæd] *s* tessuto scozzese

plain [plen] *adj* piano; aperto; evidente, esplicito; semplice; (*undyed*) naturale; comune, ordinario; **in plain English** senz'ambagi; **in plain view** di fronte a tutti || *s* pianura

plain'-clothes' man' *s* (**-men'**) agente *m* in borghese

plains'man *s* (**-men**) abitante *m* della pianura

plaintiff ['plentɪf] *s* querelante *mf*

plaintive ['plentɪv] *adj* lamentevole

plan [plæn] *s* piano, progetto || *v* (*pret & pp* **planned**; *ger* **planning**) *tr & intr* progettare

plane [plen] *adj* piano || *m* piano; (*tool*) pialla; (aer) aeroplano; (aer) ala d'aeroplano; (bot) platano || *tr* piallare || *intr* andare in aeroplano

plane' sick'ness *s* male *m* d'aria

planet ['plænɪt] *s* pianeta *m*

plane' tree' *s* platano

plan'ing mill' *s* officina di piallatura

plank [plæŋk] *s* tavola, asse *m*; (*of political party*) piattaforma || *tr* coprire d'assi; cucinare sulla graticola e servire sul tagliere; **to plank down** (*e.g., money*) (coll) snocciolare

plant [plænt] *or* [plant] *s* (*factory*) impianto, stabilimento; (*e.g., of a college*) complesso di edifici; (bot) pianta; (mach) apparato motore; (slang) trappola || *tr* (*e.g., a tree*) piantare; (*seeds*) seminare; (*to stock*) fornire

plantation [plæn'teʃən] *s* piantagione

planter ['plæntər] *s* piantatore *m*; (mach) piantatrice *f*

plaster ['plæstər] *or* ['plastər] *s* (*gypsum*) gesso; (*mixture to cover walls*) intonaco, malta; (*poultice*) impiastro || *tr* ingessare; intonacare; impiastrare; (*with posters*) affiggere, ricoprire

plas'ter-board' *s* cartone *m* di gesso

plas'ter cast' *s* (sculp) gesso; (surg) ingessatura

plas'ter of Par'is *s* gesso, stucco

plastic ['plæstɪk] *adj & s* plastico

plate 237 **plug**

plate [plet] *s* (*dish*) piatto; (*sheet of metal*) placca, piastra; (*thin sheet of metal*) lamina; (*of vacuum tube*) placca; (*of auto license*) targa; (*of condenser*) armatura; (*tableware*) vasellame *m* d'argento, vasellame *m* d'oro; dentiera; (*baseball*) casa base; (phot) lastra; (typ) cliché *m* || *tr* (*with gold or silver*) placcare; (*with armor*) blindare, corazzare

plateau [plæ'to] *s* altipiano

plate' glass' *s* lastrone *m*

platen ['plætǝn] *s* rullo

platform ['plæt ,fɔrm] *s* piattaforma; (*for speaker*) tribuna, palco; (*for passengers*) (rr) marciapiede *m*; (*at end of car*) (rr) piattaforma

plat'form car' *s* (rr) pianale *m*

platinum ['plætɪnǝm] *s* platino

plat'inum blonde' *s* bionda platinata

platitude ['plætɪ ,tjud] or ['plætɪ ,tud] *s* trivialità *f*, banalità *f*

Plato ['pleto] *s* Platone *m*

platoon [plǝ'tun] *s* plotone *m*

platter ['plætǝr] *s* piatto di portata; (slang) disco di grammofono

plausible ['plɔzɪbǝl] *adj* plausibile; (*person*) credibile, attendibile

play [ple] *s* gioco; libertà *f* d'azione; recreazione; turno, volta; (theat) dramma *m*; (mach) gioco || *tr* giocare; giocare contro; causare, produrre; (*a drama*) rappresentare; (*a character*) fare la parte di; (to wield) esercitare; (mus) suonare; **to play back** (e.g., a tape) riprodurre; **to play down** diminuire l'importanza di; **to play one off against another** mettere uno contro l'altro; **to play up** dare importanza a || *intr* giocare; (to act) giocare, comportarsi; (theat) recitare; (mus) suonare; (mach) aver gioco; **to play on** continuare a giocare; continuare a suonare; valersi di; **to play safe** non prendere rischi; **to play sick** fare il malato; **to play up to** fare la corte a

play'back' *s* riproduzione; apparecchiatura di riproduzione

play'bill' *s* (theat) programma *m*

play'boy' *s* playboy *m*, gaudente *m*

player ['ple·ǝr] *s* giocatore *m*; (theat) attore *m*; (mus) suonatore *m*

play'er pian'o *s* pianola

playful ['plefǝl] *adj* giocoso

playgoer ['ple ,go·ǝr] *s* frequentatore *m* del teatro

play'ground' *s* parco di ricreazione; (*resort*) posto di villeggiatura

play'house' *s* teatro; casa di bambole

play'ing card' ['ple·ɪŋ] *s* carta da gioco

play'ing field' *s* campo da gioco

play'mate' *s* compagno di gioco

play'-off' *s* (sports) spareggio

play'pen' *s* recinto, box *m*

play'thing' *s* giocattolo

play'time' *s* ricreazione

playwright ['ple ,raɪt] *s* drammaturgo, commediografo

play'writ'ing *s* drammaturgia

plaza ['plæzǝ] or ['plɑzǝ] *s* piazzale *m*

plea [pli] *s* scusa; richiesta, domanda; (law) dichiarazione

plead [plid] *v* (*pret & pp* **pleaded** or **pled** [pled]) *tr* (*ignorance*) dichiarare; (*a case*) perorare || *intr* supplicare; argomentare; **to plead guilty** dichiararsi colpevole

pleasant ['plezǝnt] *adj* piacevole; (*person*) simpatico

pleasant·ry ['plezǝntri] *s* (-ries) facezia, motto

please [pliz] *tr* piacere (*with dat*) || *intr* piacere; **as you please** come vuole; **if you please** per favore; **please per cortesia; to be pleased to** avere il piacere di; **to be pleased with** essere soddisfatto con; **to do as one pleases** fare come par e piace

pleasing ['plizɪŋ] *adj* piacevole

pleasure ['pleʒǝr] *s* piacere *m*; desiderio; **what is your pleasure?** cosa desidera?

pleas'ure car' *s* vettura da turismo

pleat [plit] *s* piega || *tr* piegare, pieghettare

plebeian [plɪ'bi·ǝn] *adj & s* plebeo

plebiscite ['plebɪ ,saɪt] *s* plebiscito

pledge [pledʒ] *s* pegno; promessa; voto; (*person*) ostaggio; (toast) brindisi *m*; **as a pledge** in pegno; **to take the pledge** giurare d'astenersi dal bere || *tr* dare in pegno; (to bind) far promettere a

plentiful ['plentɪfǝl] *adj* abbondante

plenty ['plenti] *s* abbondanza || *adv* (coll) abbastanza

pleurisy ['plʊrɪsi] *s* pleurite *f*

pliable ['plaɪ·ǝbǝl] *adj* flessibile, pieghevole; docile

pliers ['plaɪ·ǝrz] *ssg* or *spl* pinze *fpl*

plight [plaɪt] *s* condizione or situazione precaria || *tr*—**to plight one's troth** fidanzarsi

plod [plad] *v* (*pret & pp* **plodded**; *ger* **plodding**) *tr* percorrere pesantemente || *intr* camminare pesantemente; (to drudge) sgobbare

plot [plat] *s* (*of ground*) appezzamento; (*of a play*) trama, intreccio; (*evil scheme*) cospirazione, trama || *v* (*pret & pp* **plotted**; *ger* **plotting**) *tr* fare il piano di; macchinare; preparare la trama di; (aer, naut) fare il punto di || *intr* tramare, cospirare

plover ['plʌvǝr] or ['plovǝr] *s* piviere *m*

plow [plaʊ] *s* aratro; (*for snow*) spazzaneve *m* || *tr* arare; (e.g., water) solcare; (snow) spazzare; **to plow back** reinvestire || *intr* arare; aprirsi la via; camminare pesantemente

plow'man *s* (-men) aratore *m*; contadino

plow'share' *s* vomere *m*

pluck [plʌk] *s* strattone *m*; coraggio; (*giblets*) frattaglie *fpl* || *tr* (to snatch) tirare; (e.g., fruit) svellere; (a fowl) spennare; (mus) pizzicare || *intr* tirare; **to pluck up** farsi coraggio

pluck·y ['plʌki] *adj* (-ier; -iest) coraggioso

plug [plʌg] *s* tappo, zaffo; tavoletta di

tabacco; bocca da incendi; (elec) spina; (horse) (slang) ronzino; (slang) raccomandazione || v (pret & pp plugged; ger plugging) tr tappare, otturare; colpire; inserire; (slang) fare la pubblicità di; **to plug in** (elec) innestare, connettere || intr (coll) sgobbare

plum [plʌm] s (fruit) susina; (tree) susino; (slang) cosa bellissima; (slang) colpo di fortuna

plumage [ˈplumɪdʒ] s piumaggio

plumb [plʌm] adj appiombo || s piombino || adv appiombo; (coll) completamente || tr determinare la verticale col piombino; assodare

plumb' bob' s piombino

plumber [ˈplʌmər] s installatore m, idraulico

plumbing [ˈplʌmɪŋ] s impianto idraulico; mestiere m d'idraulico; sondaggio

plumb'ing fix'tures spl rubinetteria, impianti mpl sanitari

plumb' line' s filo a piombo

plum' cake' s panfrutto

plume [plum] s piuma; (tuft of feathers) pennacchio || tr coprire di piume; **to plume oneself on** piccarsi di; **to plume one's feathers** pulirsi le penne

plummet [ˈplʌmɪt] s piombino || intr cadere a piombo

plump [plʌmp] adj grassoccio, paffuto; franco || s caduta || adv francamente || intr cadere a piombo

plum' pud'ding s budino con uva passa

plum' tree' s susino

plunder [ˈplʌndər] s (act) saccheggio; (loot) bottino || tr & intr saccheggiare

plunge [plʌndʒ] s (fall) caduta; (dive) nuotata, tuffo || tr gettare; tuffare; (e.g., a knife) configgere || intr (to rush) precipitarsi; (to gamble) (coll) darsi al gioco; (fig) piombare

plunger [ˈplʌndʒər] s tuffatore m; (for clearing clogged drains) sturalavandini m; (mach) stantuffo; (coll) giocatore temerario

plunk [plʌŋk] adv (coll) proprio; (coll) con un colpo secco || tr (coll) gettare; lasciar cadere; (mus) pizzicare || intr (coll) lasciarsi cadere

plural [ˈplurəl] adj & s plurale m

plus [plʌs] adj superiore; (elec) positivo; (coll) con lode || s più m; soprappiù m || prep più

plush [plʌʃ] adj di lusso || s peluche f, felpa

Plutarch [ˈplutɑrk] s Plutarco

Pluto [ˈpluto] s Plutone m

plutonium [pluˈtonɪ-əm] s plutonio

ply [plaɪ] s (plies) spessore m; (layer) strato; (of rope) legnolo || v (pret & pp plied) tr (a trade) esercitare; (a tool) maneggiare; (to assail) premere, incalzare || intr lavorare assiduamente; **to ply between** fare la spola tra

ply'wood' s legno compensato

pneumatic [njuˈmætɪk] or [nuˈmætɪk] adj pneumatico

pneumat'ic drill' s martello perforatore or pneumatico

pneumonia [njuˈmonɪ-ə] or [nuˈmonɪ-ə] s polmonite f

poach [potʃ] tr (eggs) affogare || intr cacciare or pescare di frodo

poacher [ˈpotʃər] s bracconiere m; pescatore m di frodo

pock [pak] s pustola

pocket [ˈpakɪt] adj tascabile || s tasca; (billiards) buca; (aer) vuoto; (min) deposito || tr intascare; (e.g., one's pride) ingoiare

pock'et-book' s portafoglio; (woman's purse) borsetta

pock'et book' s libro tascabile

pock'et-hand'kerchief s fazzoletto

pock'et-knife' s (-knives) temperino

pock'et mon'ey s spiccioli mpl

pock'mark' s buttero

pod [pad] s baccello; (aer) contenitore m

poem [ˈpo-ɪm] s poesia; (of some length) poema m

poet [ˈpo-ɪt] s poeta m

poetess [ˈpo-ɪtɪs] s poetessa

poetic [poˈɛtɪk] adj poetico || **poetics** ssg poetica

poetry [ˈpo-ɪtrɪ] s poesia

pogrom [ˈpogrəm] s pogrom m

poignancy [ˈpɔɪnjənsɪ] or [ˈpɔɪnənsɪ] s strazio; intensità f

poignant [ˈpɔɪnjənt] or [ˈpɔɪnənt] adj straziante; intenso

point [pɔɪnt] s (sharp end) punta; (something essential) essenziale m; (hint) suggerimento; (dot, decimal point, spot, degree, instant, position of compass) punto; (coll) costrutto; **beside the point** fuori del seminato; **in point of** per quanto concerne; **to come to the point** venire al sodo; **to get the point** capire l'antifona; **to make a point of** dar importanza a; insistere di; **to stretch a point** un'eccezione, fare uno strappo alla regola; **to the point** a proposito || tr (e.g., a weapon) puntare; (to sharpen) aguzzare; (to dot) punteggiare; (to give force to) dare enfasi a; (with mortar) rinzaffare || intr puntare; **to point at** puntare il dito a; **to point to** mostrare a dito

point'blank' adj & adv a bruciapelo

pointed [ˈpɔɪntɪd] adj appuntito; personale, diretto, acuto

pointer [ˈpɔɪntər] s (rod) bacchetta; indice m, indicatore m; cane m da punta, pointer m; (coll) direttiva

poise [pɔɪz] s equilibrio, stabilità f; dignità f || tr equilibrare || intr equilibrarsi, stare in equilibrio

poison [ˈpɔɪzən] s veleno || tr avvelenare

poi'son i'vy s edera del Canada, tossicodendro

poisonous [ˈpɔɪzənəs] adj velenoso

poke [pok] s spinta, urto; (with elbow) gomitata; (slang) polentone m || tr (to prod) spingere, urtare; (the head) sporgere; (the fire) attizzare; **to poke fun at** burlarsi di; **to poke one's nose into** ficcare il naso in || intr (to jab) urtare; (*to thrust oneself*) ficcarsi; (*to pry*) ficcare il naso; **to poke around** gironzolare; **to poke out** spuntare, protrudere

poker ['pokər] *s* (*game*) poker *m;* (*bar*) attizzatoio

pok'er face' *s* faccia impassibile

pok·y ['poki] *adj* (**-ier; -iest**) (coll) lento; (coll) meschino, modesto || (**-ies**) *s* (slang) gattabuia

Poland ['polənd] *s* la Polonia

po'lar bear' ['polər] *s* orso bianco

polarize ['polə‚raɪz] *tr* polarizzare

pole [pol] *s* palo; (*long rod*) pertica; (*of wagon*) timone *m;* (*for jumping*) asta; (astr, biol, elec, geog, math) polo || *tr* (*a boat*) spingere con un palo || *intr* spingere una barca con un palo || **Pole** *s* polacco

pole'cat' *s* puzzola

pole' lamp' *s* lampada a stelo

pole'star' *s* stella polare

pole' vault' *s* salto coll'asta

police [pə'lis] *s* polizia || *tr* vigilare, proteggere; (mil) pulire

police'man *s* (**-men**) agente *m* di polizia, vigile urbano

police' state' *s* governo poliziesco

police' sta'tion *s* commissariato di polizia

poli·cy ['pɑlɪsi] *s* (**-cies**) politica; (ins) polizza

polio ['polɪ‚o] *s* (coll) polio *f*

polish ['pɑlɪʃ] *s* lustro, lucentezza; (*for shoes or furniture*) cera; (fig) raffinatezza, eleganza || *tr* pulire; (*e.g., a stone*) levigare; **to polish off** (slang) finire; **to polish up** (slang) migliorare || *intr* pulirsi; diventar lucido || **Polish** ['polɪʃ] *adj & s* polacco

polisher ['pɑlɪʃər] *s* lucidatore *m;* (mach) lucidatrice *f*

polite [pə'laɪt] *adj* raffinato, cortese

politeness [pə'laɪtnɪs] *s* cortesia

politic ['pɑlɪtɪk] *adj* prudente; (*expedient*) diplomatico

political [pə'lɪtɪkəl] *adj* politico

politician [‚pɑlɪ'tɪʃən] *s* politico; (pej) politicante *m*, politicastro

politics ['pɑlɪtɪks] *ssg or spl* politica

poll [pol] *s* votazione; (*registering of votes*) scrutinio; lista elettorale; (*analysis of public opinion*) referendum *m*, sondaggio; (*head*) testa; **to go to the polls** andare alle urne; **to take a poll** fare un'inchiesta || *tr* ricevere i voti di; contare i voti di; (*a tree*) potare; fare un'inchiesta di

pollen ['pɑlən] *s* polline *m*

pollinate ['pɑlɪ‚net] *tr* fecondare col polline

poll'ing booth' ['polɪŋ] *s* cabina elettorale

polliwog ['pɑlɪ‚wɑg] *s* girino

poll' tax' *s* capitazione

pollute [pə'lut] *tr* insudiciare; (*to defile*) desecrare, profanare; (*e.g., the environment*) inquinare, contaminare

pollution [pə'luʃən] *s* inquinamento, contaminazione

poll' watch'er *s* rappresentante *m* di lista

polo ['polo] *s* polo

po'lo play'er *s* giocatore *m* di polo, polista *m*

po'lo shirt' *s* maglietta, polo

polygamist [pə'lɪgəmɪst] *s* poligamo

polygamous [pə'lɪgəməs] *adj* poligamo

polyglot ['pɑlɪ‚glɑt] *adj & s* poliglotto

polygon ['pɑlɪ‚gɑn] *s* poligono

polynomial [‚pɑlɪ'nomɪ‚əl] *adj* polinomiale || *s* polinomio

polyp ['pɑlɪp] *s* (pathol, zool) polipo

polytheist ['pɑlɪ‚θi‚ɪst] *s* politeista *mf*

polytheistic [‚pɑlɪθi'ɪstɪk] *adj* politeistico

pomade [pə'med] or [pə'mɑd] *s* pomata

pomegranate ['pɑm‚grænɪt] *s* (*shrub*) melograno; (*fruit*) melagrana

pom·mel ['pʌməl] or ['pɑməl] *s* (*of sword*) pomello; (*of saddle*) arcione *m* || *v* (*pret & pp* **-meled** or **-melled**; *ger* **-meling** or **-melling**) *tr* prendere a pugni

pomp [pɑmp] *s* pompa

pompadour ['pɑmpə‚dor] or ['pɑmpə‚dur] *s* acconciatura a ciuffo

pompous ['pɑmpəs] *adj* pomposo

pon·cho ['pɑntʃo] *s* (**-chos**) poncho

pond [pɑnd] *s* stagno

ponder ['pɑndər] *tr & intr* ponderare; **to ponder over** pensare sopra

ponderous ['pɑndərəs] *adj* ponderoso

poniard ['pɑnjərd] *s* pugnale *m*

pontiff ['pɑntɪf] *s* pontefice *m*

pontifical [pɑn'tɪfɪkəl] *adj* pontificale

pontoon [pɑn'tun] *s* (*boat*) chiatta, pontone *m;* (aer) galleggiante *m*

po·ny ['poni] *s* (**-nies**) pony *m;* (*glass and drink*) bicchierino; (*for cheating*) (slang) bigino

poodle ['pudəl] *s* barbone *m*, cane *m* barbone

pool [pul] *s* (*pond*) stagno; (*puddle*) pozza; (*for swimming*) piscina; (*game*) biliardo; (com) cartello, consorzio; (com) fondo comune || *tr* mettere in un fondo comune || *intr* formare un cartello or un consorzio

pool'room' *s* sala da biliardo

pool' ta'ble *s* tavolo da biliardo

poop [pup] *s* poppa; (*deck*) casseretto

poor [pur] *adj* povero; (*inferior*) scadente || **the poor** *spl* i poveri

poor' box' *s* cassetta per l'elemosina

poor'house' *s* asilo dei poveri

poorly ['purli] *adv* male

pop [pɑp] *s* scoppio; (*soda*) gazzosa || *v* (*pret & pp* **popped**; *ger* **popping**) *tr* far scoppiare; **to pop the question** (coll) fare la domanda di matrimonio || *intr* esplodere con fragore; **to pop in** fare una capatina; entrare all'improvviso

pop'corn' *s* pop-corn *m*

pope [pop] *s* papa *m*

popeyed ['pɑp‚aɪd] *adj* con gli occhi sporgenti; con gli occhi fuori dalle orbite

pop'gun' *s* fucile *m* ad aria compressa

poplar ['pɑplər] *s* pioppo

pop·py ['pɑpi] *s* (**-pies**) papavero

pop'py·cock' *s* (coll) scemenza

popsicle ['pɑpsɪkəl] s (trademark) gelato da passeggio

populace ['pɑpjəlɪs] s gente f, popolino

popular ['pɑpjələr] adj popolare

popularize ['pɑpjələ‚raɪz] tr divulgare, volgarizzare

populate ['pɑpjə‚let] tr popolare

population [‚pɑpjə'leʃən] s popolazione

populous ['pɑpjələs] adj popoloso

porcelain ['pɔrsəlɪn] or ['pɔrslɪn] s porcellana

porch [pɔrtʃ] s portico

porcupine ['pɔrkjə‚paɪn] s (Hystrix cristata) istrice m & f, porcospino; (Erethizon dorsatum) ursone m, porcospino americano

pore [pɔr] s poro || intr—to pore over studiare minutamente

pork [pɔrk] s carne f di maiale

pork′ butch′er shop′ s salumeria

pork′chop′ s cotoletta di maiale

porous ['pɔrəs] adj poroso

po′rous plas′ter s cataplasma m

porphy‧ry ['pɔrfrɪi] s (-ries) porfido

porpoise ['pɔrpəs] s focena; (dolphin) delfino

porridge ['pɑrɪdʒ] or ['pɔrɪdʒ] s pappa, farinata

port [pɔrt] adj portuario || s (harbor; wine) porto; (naut) babordo, sinistra; (opening in side of ship) portello; (round opening) (naut) oblò m

portable ['pɔrtəbəl] adj portabile

portal ['pɔrtəl] s portale m

portend [pɔr'tend] tr presagire

portent ['pɔrtent] s presagio

portentous [pɔr'tentəs] adj sinistro, funesto, premonitore; (amazing) portentoso

porter ['pɔrtər] s (doorman) portiere m; (man who carries luggage) facchino; (of a sleeper) conduttore m; (in a store) inserviente mf; (beverage) birra scura e amara

portfoli‧o [pɔrt'folɪ‚o] s (-os) cartella; (office; holdings) portafoglio

port′hole′ s (opening in side of ship) portello; (round opening) (naut) oblò m

porti‧co ['pɔrtɪ‚ko] s (-cos or -coes) portico

portion ['pɔrʃən] s porzione; (dowry) dote f || tr—to portion out dividere, ripartire

port‧ly ['pɔrtlɪ] adj (-lier; -liest) obeso, corpulento

port′ of call′ s scalo

portrait ['pɔrtret] or ['pɔrtrɪt] s ritratto

portray [pɔr'tre] tr ritrarre

portrayal [pɔr'tre‧əl] s delineazione; ritratto

Portugal ['pɔrtʃəgəl] s il Portogallo

Portu‧guese ['pɔrtʃə‚giz] adj portoghese || s (-guese) portoghese mf

pose [poz] s posa || tr (a question) avanzare; (a model) mettere in posa || intr posare; **to pose as** posare, atteggiarsi a

posh [pɑʃ] adj (coll) di lusso

position [pə'zɪʃən] s posizione; rango;

impiego, posto; **to be in a position to** essere in grado di

positive ['pɑzɪtɪv] adj positivo || s positivo; (phot) positiva

possess [pə'zes] tr possedere

possession [pə'zeʃən] s possedimento; (of mental faculties) possesso; **possessions** (wealth) beni mpl

possessive [pə'zesɪv] adj possessivo; (e.g., mother) opprimente, soffocante

possible ['pɑsɪbəl] adj possibile

possum ['pɑsəm] s opossum m; **to play possum** (coll) fare il morto

post [post] s (mail) posta; (pole) palo; (in horse racing) linea di partenza; posizione, rango; (job) posto; (mil) presidio || tr mettere in una lista; impostare; tenere al corrente; **post no bills** divieto d'affissione

postage ['postɪdʒ] s affrancatura

post′age me′ter s affrancatrice f

post′age stamp′ s francobollo

postal ['postəl] adj postale

post′al card′ s cartolina postale

pos′tal per′mit s abbonamento postale

post′al sav′ings bank′ s cassa di risparmio postale

post′al scale′ s pesalettere m

post′ card′ s cartolina illustrata; cartolina postale

post′date′ tr postdatare

poster ['postər] s cartellone m, manifesto pubblicitario

posterity [pɑs'terɪti] s posterità f

postern ['postərn] adj posteriore || s postierla

post′ exchange′ s spaccio militare

post′haste′ adv al più presto possibile

posthumous ['pɑst/ʊməs] adj postumo

post′man s (-men) portalettere m

post′mark′ s bollo, timbro postale || tr bollare, timbrare

post′mas′ter s ricevitore m postale

post′master gen′eral s (postmasters general) ministro delle poste

post-mortem ['post'mɔrtəm] adj postumo || s autopsia

post′ of′fice s ufficio postale

post′-office box′ s casella postale

postpaid ['post‚ped] adj franco di porto

postpone [post'pon] tr differire, posporre

postscript ['post‚skrɪpt] s poscritto

postulant ['pɑstʃələnt] s postulatore m, postulante mf

posture ['pɑstʃər] s portamento; posa || intr posare

post′war′ adj del dopoguerra

po‧sy ['pozɪ] s (-sies) fiore m; (nosegay) mazzolino di fiori

pot [pɑt] s pentola, pignatta; pitale m, orinale m; (in gambling) (coll) piatto; **to go to pot** andare a gambe all'aria

potash ['pɑt‚æʃ] s potassa

potassium [pə'tæsɪ‧əm] s potassio

pota‧to [pə'teto] s (-toes) patata

pota′to om′elet s omelette f con patate

potbellied ['pɑt‚belɪd] adj panciuto

poten‧cy ['potənsi] s (-cies) potenza

potent ['potənt] adj potente

potentate ['potən‚tet] *s* potentato
potential [pə'tenʃəl] *adj* & *s* potenziale *m*
pot'hold'er *s* patta, presa
pot'hook' *s* uncino
potion ['poʃən] *s* pozione
pot'luck' *s*—**to take potluck** mangiare quello che passa il convento
pot' shot' *s* colpo sparato a casaccio
potter ['patər] *s* vasaio
pot'ter's clay' *s* argilla per stoviglie
pot'ter's field' *s* cimitero dei poveri
potter·y ['patəri] *s* (**-ies**) vasellame *m*; fabbrica di vasellame; ceramica
pouch [pautʃ] *s* sacchetto, borsa; (*of kangaroo*) borsa
poultice ['poltis] *s* cataplasma *m*
poultry ['poltri] *s* pollame *m*
poul'try·man *s* (**-men**) pollivendolo
pounce [pauns] *intr*—**to pounce on** balzare su
pound ['paund] *s* libbra; lira sterlina; (*for stray animals*) recinto ‖ *tr* battere, picchiare; tempestare di colpi; (*to crush*) polverizzare ‖ *intr* battere
pound' cake' *s* dolce *m* fatto con una libbra di burro, una di zucchero ed una di farina
pound' ster'ling *s* lira sterlina
pour [por] *tr* versare; (*e.g., tea*) servire; (*wine*) mescere; (*stones upon an enemy*) far piovere ‖ *intr* fluire; (*to rain*) diluviare; **to pour in** affluire; **to pour out** uscire in massa
pout [paut] *s* broncio ‖ *intr* tenere il broncio
poverty ['pavərti] *s* povertà *f*
POW ['pi'o'dʌbl‚ju] *s* (letterword) (**prisoner of war**) prigioniero di guerra
powder ['paudər] *s* polvere *f*; (*for the face*) cipria; (med) polverina ‖ *tr* incipriare; (*to sprinkle with powder*) spolverizzare
pow'dered sug'ar *s* zucchero in polvere
pow'der puff' *s* piumino
pow'der room' *s* toletta
powdery ['paudəri] *adj* polveroso; fragile; (*snow*) farinoso
power ['pau·ər] *s* (*ability, authority*) potere *m*; forza, energia; (*nation*) potenza; (math, phys) potenza; **in power** al potere; **the powers that be** i potenti ‖ *tr* azionare
pow'er-boat' *s* barca a motore
pow'er brake' *s* (aut) servofreno
pow'er com'pany *s* compagnia di elettricità
pow'er drive' *s* picchiata
powerful ['pau·ərfəl] *adj* poderoso
pow'er-house' *s* centrale elettrica
powerless ['pau·ərlɪs] *adj* impotente
pow'er line' *s* elettrodotto
pow'er mow'er *s* motofalciatrice *f*
pow'er of attor'ney *s* procura legale
pow'er plant' *s* stazione *f* generatrice; (aut) gruppo motore
pow'er steer'ing *s* servosterzo
pow'er tool' *s* apparecchiatura a motore
pow'er vac'uum *s* vuoto di potere
practical ['præktɪkəl] *adj* pratico

prac'tical joke' *s* scherzo da prete
practically ['præktɪkəli] *adv* (*in a practical manner; virtually, really*) praticamente; più o meno, quasi
practice ['præktɪs] *s* pratica; (*of a profession*) esercizio; (*e.g., of a doctor*) clientela; (*process of doing something*) prassi *f*; (*habitual performance*) abitudine *f* ‖ *tr* praticare, esercitare ‖ *intr* esercitarsi, praticare; (*to be active in a profession*) esercitare; **to practice as** esercitare la professione di
practitioner [præk'tɪʃənər] *s* professionista *mf*
Prague [prɑg] *or* [preg] *s* Praga
prairie ['preri] *s* prateria
prai'rie dog' *s* cinomio *m*
prai'rie wolf' *s* coyote *m*
praise [prez] *s* lode *f*, elogio ‖ *tr* lodare, elogiare; **to praise to the skies** levare alle stelle
praise'wor'thy *adj* lodevole
pram [præm] *s* (coll) carrozzella
prance [præns] *or* [prɑns] *s* caracollo ‖ *intr* caracollare; (*to caper*) ballonzolare
prank [præŋk] *s* burla, tiro
prate [pret] *intr* cianciare
prattle ['prætəl] *s* ciancia, chiacchierio ‖ *intr* cianciare, parlare a vanvera
pray [pre] *tr* & *intr* pregare
prayer [prer] *s* preghiera
prayer' book' *s* libro di preghiere
preach [pritʃ] *tr* & *intr* predicare
preacher ['pritʃər] *s* predicatore *m*
preamble ['pri‚æmbəl] *s* preambolo
precarious [prɪ'kɛrɪ·əs] *adj* precario
precaution [prɪ'kɔʃən] *s* precauzione
precede [prɪ'sid] *tr* & *intr* precedere
precedent ['prɛsɪdənt] *s* precedente *m*
precept ['prisɛpt] *s* precetto
precinct ['prisɪŋkt] *s* distretto; circoscrizione elettorale; **precincts** dintorni *mpl*
precious ['prɛʃəs] *adj* prezioso ‖ *adv*—**precious little** (coll) molto poco
precipice ['prɛsɪpɪs] *s* precipizio
precipitate [prɪ'sɪpɪ‚tet] *adj* precipitoso ‖ *s* precipitato ‖ *tr* & *intr* precipitare
precipitous [prɪ'sɪpɪtəs] *adj* precipitoso, a precipizio
precise [prɪ'saɪs] *adj* preciso
precision [prɪ'sɪʒən] *s* precisione
preclude [prɪ'klud] *tr* precludere; escludere
precocious [prɪ'koʃəs] *adj* precoce
predatory ['prɛdə‚tori] *adj* da preda, predatore
predicament [prɪ'dɪkəmənt] *s* situazione critica or imbarazzante
predict [prɪ'dɪkt] *tr* predire
prediction [prɪ'dɪkʃən] *s* predizione
predispose [‚pridɪs'poz] *tr* predisporre
predominant [prɪ'dɑmɪnənt] *adj* predominante
preeminent [prɪ'ɛmɪnənt] *adj* preminente
preempt [prɪ'ɛmpt] *tr* occupare or acquistare in precedenza
preen [prin] *tr* (*feathers, fur*) lisciarsi;

to preen oneself agghindarsi, attillarsi

prefabricate [pri'fæbrɪ‚ket] *tr* prefabbricare

preface ['prefɪs] *s* prefazione || *tr* prefazionare; essere la prefazione di

pre·fer [prɪ'fʌr] *v* (*pret & pp* **-ferred**; *ger* **-ferring**) *tr* preferire; (*to advance*) promuovere; (*law*) presentare, avanzare

preferable ['prefərəbəl] *adj* preferibile

preference ['prefərəns] *s* preferenza

preferred' stock' *s* azioni *fpl* privilegiate

prefix ['prifɪks] *s* prefisso || *tr* prefiggere

pregnan·cy ['pregnənsi] *s* (-cies) gravidanza

pregnant ['pregnənt] *adj* incinta, gravida; (fig) gravido

prehistoric [‚prihɪs'tarɪk] or [‚prihɪs-'tɔrɪk] *adj* preistorico

prejudice ['predʒədɪs] *s* pregiudizio; preconcetto; **without prejudice** senza detrimento || *tr* (*to harm*) pregiudicare; predisporre; **to prejudice against** prevenire contro

prejudicial ['predʒə'dɪʃəl] *adj* pregiudizievole

prelate ['prelɪt] *s* prelato

preliminar·y [prɪ'lɪmɪ‚neri] *adj* preliminare || *s* (-ies) preliminare *m*

prelude ['preljud] or ['prilud] *s* preludio || *tr* preludere a || *intr* preludere

premeditate [pri'medɪ‚tet] *tr* premeditare

premier [prɪ'mɪr] or ['primɪ‚ər] *s* primo ministro, presidente *m* del consiglio

premiere [prə'mjer or [prɪ'mɪr] *s* prima; prima attrice

premise ['premɪs] *s* premessa; **on the premises** nella proprietà, sul luogo; **premises** proprietà *f*

premium ['primɪ‚əm] *s* premio; **at a premium** in gran richiesta; a prezzo altissimo

premonition [‚primə'nɪʃən] *s* presentimento; indizio

preoccupation [pri‚akjə'peʃən] *s* preoccupazione

preoccu·py [prɪ'akjə‚paɪ] *v* (*pret & pp* **-pied**) *tr* preoccupare; (*to occupy beforehand*) occupare prima

prepaid [pri'ped] *adj* pagato in anticipo; franco di porto

preparation [‚prepə'reʃən] *s* preparazione; (*for a trip*) preparativo; (pharm) preparato

preparatory [prɪ'pærə‚tori] *adj* preparatorio

prepare [prɪ'per] *tr* preparare || *intr* prepararsi

preparedness [prɪ'perɪdnəs] or [prɪ-'perdnɪs] *s* preparazione; preparazione militare

pre·pay [pri'pe] *v* (*pret & pp* **-paid**) *tr* pagare anticipatamente

preponderant [prɪ'pandərənt] *adj* preponderante

preposition [‚prepə'zɪʃən] *s* preposizione

prepossessing [‚pripə'zesɪŋ] *adj* simpatico, attraente, piacevole

preposterous [prɪ'pastərəs] *adj* assurdo, ridicolo

prep' school' [prep] *s* (coll) scuola preparatoria

prerecorded [‚prirɪ'kɔrdɪd] *adj* (rad & telv) a registrazione differita

prerequisite [pri'rekwɪzɪt] *s* requisito

prerogative [prɪ'ragətɪv] *s* prerogativa

presage ['presɪdʒ] *s* presagio || [prɪ-'sedʒ] *tr* presagire

Presbyterian [‚prezbɪ'tɪrɪ‚ən] *adj & s* presbiteriano; Presbiteriano

prescribe [prɪ'skraɪb] *tr & intr* prescrivere

prescription [prɪ'skrɪpʃən] *s* prescrizione; (pharm) ricetta

presence ['prezəns] *s* presenza; **in the presence of** alla presenza di

present ['prezənt] *adj* presente || *s* presente *m*, regalo || [prɪ'zent] *tr* presentare; **present arms!** presentat'arm!; **to present s.o. with s.th** regalare qlco a qlcu

presentable [prɪ'zentəbəl] *adj* presentabile

presentation [‚prezən'teʃən] or [‚prezən'teʃən] *s* presentazione; (theat) rappresentazione

presenta'tion cop'y *s* copia d'omaggio

presentiment [prɪ'zentɪmənt] *s* presentimento

presently ['prezntli] *adv* fra poco; attualmente

preserve [prɪ'zʌrv] *s* (*for hunting*) riserva; **preserves** conserva, marmellata || *tr* preservare; conservare

preserved' fruit' *s* frutta in conserva

preside [prɪ'zaɪd] *intr* presiedere; **to preside over** presiedere, presiedere a

presiden·cy ['prezɪdənsi] *s* (-cies) presidenza

president ['prezɪdənt] *s* presidente *m*; (*of a university*) rettore *m*

press [pres] *s* pressione; (*crowd*) folla; (*closet*) armadio; (mach) pressa; (typ) stampa; **to go to press** andare in macchina || *tr* (*to push*) spingere, premere; (*to squeeze*) spremere; (*to embrace*) abbracciare; forzare; costringere; urgere, sollecitare; (*to iron*) stirare || *intr* premere; avanzare

press' a'gent *s* agente pubblicitario

press' con'ference *s* conferenza stampa

pressing ['presɪŋ] *adj* pressante, urgente || *s* (*of records*) incisione

press' release' *s* comunicato stampa

pressure ['preʃər] *s* pressione; tensione; urgenza || *tr* pressare, incalzare con insistenza

pres'sure cook'er ['kʊkər] *s* pentola a pressione

pressurize ['preʃə‚raɪz] *tr* pressurizzare

prestige [pres'tiʒ] or ['prestɪdʒ] *s* prestigio

prestigious [pres'stɪdʒɪ‚əs] or [pre-'stɪdʒəs] *adj* onorato, stimato

presumably [prɪ'zuməbɪl] or [prɪ'zjuməbli] *adv* presumibilmente

presume [prɪ'zum] or [prɪ'zjum] *tr* presumere; **to presume to** prendersi

la libertà di ‖ *intr* assumere; **to presume on** or **upon** abusare di
presumption [prɪ'zʌmp/ən] *s* presunzione; supposizione
presumptuous [prɪ'zʌmpt/ʊ·əs] *adj* presuntuoso
presuppose [ˌprisə'poz] *tr* presupporre
pretend [prɪ'tɛnd] *tr* fingere, fare finta di ‖ *intr* fingere; **to pretend to** (*e.g.*, *the throne*) pretendere a
pretender [prɪ'tɛndər] *s* pretendente *mf;* impostore *m*
pretense [prɪ'tɛns] or ['pritɛns] *s* pretesa; finzione; **under false pretenses** allegando ragioni false; **under pretense of** sotto l'apparenza di
pretentious [prɪ'tɛn/əs] *adj* pretenzioso
preterit ['prɛtərɪt] *adj* passato, preterito ‖ *s* passato remoto, preterito
pretext ['pritɛkst] *s* pretesto
pretonic [prɪ'tɑnɪk] *adj* pretonico
pret·ty ['prɪti] *adj* (**-tier; -tiest**) grazioso, carino; (*e.g.*, *sum of money*) (coll) bello ‖ *adv* abbastanza; molto; **sitting pretty** (slang) ben messo
prevail [prɪ'vel] *intr* prevalere; **to prevail on** or **upon** persuadere
prevailing [prɪ'velɪŋ] *adj* prevalente
prevalent ['prɛvələnt] *adj* comune
prevaricate [prɪ'værɪˌket] *intr* mentire
prevent [prɪ'vɛnt] *tr* impedire; **to prevent from** + *ger* impedire (with *dat*) di + *inf* or che + *subj*
prevention [prɪ'vɛn/ən] *s* prevenzione
preventive [prɪ'vɛntɪv] *adj* preventivo ‖ *s* rimedio preventivo
preview ['pri·vju] *s* indizio; (*private showing*) (mov) anteprima; (*showing of brief scenes for advertising*) (mov) scene *fpl* di prossima programmazione
previous ['privi·əs] *adj* previo, precedente ‖ *adv* precedentemente; **previous to** prima di
prewar ['pri·wɔr] *adj* anteguerra
prey [pre] *s* preda; **to be prey to** essere preda di ‖ *intr* predare; **to prey on** or **upon** predare, sfruttare; preoccupare
price [praɪs] *s* prezzo; **at any price** a qualunque costo ‖ *tr* chiedere il prezzo di; fissare il prezzo di
price' control' *s* calmiere *m*
price' cut'ting *s* riduzione di prezzo
price' fix'ing *s* regolamento dei prezzi
price' freez'ing *s* congelamento dei prezzi
priceless ['praɪslɪs] *adj* inestimabile; (coll) molto divertente
price' list' *s* listino prezzi
price' tag' *s* cartellino del prezzo
price' war' *s* guerra dei prezzi
prick [prɪk] *s* punta; puntura; **to kick against the pricks** tirare calci al vento ‖ *tr* bucare, forare; pungere; (*to goad*) spronare; (*the ears*) ergere; (*said, e.g., of the conscience*) rimordere (with *dat*)
prick·ly ['prɪkli] *adj* (**-lier; -liest**) spinoso, pungente
prick'ly heat' *s* sudamina
prick'ly pear' *s* ficodindia *m*
pride [praɪd] *s* orgoglio; arroganza; **the**

pride of il fiore di ‖ *tr*—**to pride oneself on** or **upon** inorgoglirsi di
priest [prist] *s* prete *m*, sacerdote *m*
priesthood ['prist·hʊd] *s* sacerdozio
priest·ly ['pristli] *adj* (**-lier; -liest**) sacerdotale
prig [prɪg] *s* pedante *mf*, moralista *mf*
prim [prɪm] *adj* (**primmer; primmest**) formale, corretto, compito
prima·ry ['praɪˌmɛri] or ['praɪmərɪ] *adj* primario ‖ *s* (**-ries**) elezione preferenziale; (elec) bobina primaria; (elec) primario
prime [praɪm] *adj* primo; originale; di prima qualità ‖ *s* (*earliest part*) inizio; (*best period*) fiore *m;* (*choicest part*) fior fiore *m;* (math) numero primo; (*mark*) (math) primo ‖ *tr* preparare; (*a pump*) adescare; (*a firearm*) innescare; (*a canvas*) mesticare; (*a wall*) dare la prima mano a; (*to supply with information*) istruire
prime' min'ister *s* primo ministro
primer ['praɪmər] *s* sillabario, abbecedario ‖ ['praɪmər] *s* innesco, detonatore *m*
primeval [praɪ'mivəl] *adj* primordiale
primitive ['prɪmɪtɪv] *adj* primitivo
primp [prɪmp] *tr* agghindare ‖ *intr* agghindarsi
prim'rose' *s* primula
prim'rose path' *s* sentiero dei piaceri
prince [prɪns] *s* principe *m;* **to live like a prince** vivere da principe
prince' roy'al *s* principe ereditario
princess ['prɪnsɛs] *s* principessa
principal ['prɪnsɪpəl] *adj* principale ‖ *s* (*chief*) padrone *m*, principale *m;* (*of school*) direttore *m*, preside *m;* (*actor*) primo attore; (com) capitale *m;* (law) mandante *mf*
principle ['prɪnsɪpəl] *s* principio; **on principle** per principio
print [prɪnt] *s* stampa; (*cloth*) tessuto stampato; (*printed matter*) stampato; (*newsprint*) giornale *m;* (*mark made by one's thumb*) impronta; (phot) positiva; **in print** stampato; disponibile; **out of print** esaurito ‖ *tr* stampare, tirare; (*to write in print*) scrivere in stampatello; (*in the memory*) imprimere
print'ed cir'cuit *s* circuito stampato
print'ed mat'ter *s* stampati *mpl*
printer ['prɪntər] *s* stampatore *m;* (*of computer*) tabulatrice *f*
print'er's dev'il *s* apprendista *m* tipografo
print'er's ink' *s* inchiostro da stampa
printing ['prɪntɪŋ] *s* stampa; stampato; tiratura, edizione; (*writing in printed letters*) stampatello
prior ['praɪ·ər] *adj* anteriore, precedente ‖ *s* priore *m* ‖ *adv* prima; **prior to** prima di
prior·ity [praɪ'ɑrɪti] or [praɪ'ɔrɪti] *s* (**-ties**) priorità *f*
prism ['prɪzəm] *s* prisma *m*
prison ['prɪzən] *s* prigione, carcere *m*
prisoner ['prɪzənər] or ['prɪznər] *s* prigioniero
pris'on van' *s* furgone *m* cellulare

pris·sy ['prɪsi] *adj* (**-sier; -siest**) smanceroso, smorfioso

priva·cy ['praɪvəsi] *s* (**-cies**) ritiro; segreto; **to have no privacy** non esser mai lasciato in pace

private ['praɪvɪt] *adj* privato, personale || *s* soldato semplice; **in private** privatamente; **privates** pudende *fpl*

pri'vate eye' *s* poliziotto privato

pri'vate first' class' *s* soldato scelto

pri'vate hos'pital *s* clinica

priv'ate view'ing *s* (*mov*) anteprima; (painting) vernice *f*

privet ['prɪvɪt] *s* ligustro

privilege ['prɪvɪlɪdʒ] *s* privilegio

priv·y ['prɪvi] *adj* privato; **privy to** segretamente a conoscenza di || *s* (**-ies**) latrina

prize [praɪz] *s* premio; (*nav*) preda || *tr* valutare, stimare

prize' fight' *s* incontro di pugilato

prize' fight'er *s* pugile *m*, pugilista *m*

prize' ring' *s* ring *m*, quadrato

pro [pro] *s* (**pros**) pro; voto favorevole; argomento favorevole; (coll) professionista *m*; **the pros and the cons** il pro e il contro

probabili·ty [ˌprabə'bɪlɪti] *s* (**-ties**) probabilità *f*

probable ['prabəbəl] *adj* probabile

probate ['probet] *s* omologazione di un testamento; copia autentica di un testamento || *tr* (*a will*) omologare

probation [pro'beʃən] *s* prova; periodo di prova; (law) condizionale *f*, libertà vigilata; (educ) provvedimento disciplinare

probe [prob] *s* inchiesta; (surg) sonda || *tr* indagare; sondare

problem ['prabləm] *s* problema *m*

procedure [pro'sidʒər] *s* procedura

proceed ['prosid] *s*—**proceeds** provento || [pro'sid] *intr* procedere

proceeding [pro'sidɪŋ] *s* procedimento; **proceedings** atti *mpl*; (law) procedimenti *mpl*

procession [pro'sɛʃən] *s* processione

proc'ess serv'er *s* ufficiale giudiziario

proclaim [pro'klem] *tr* proclamare

proclitic [pro'klɪtɪk] *adj* proclitico || *s* parola proclitica

procrastinate [pro'kræstɪˌnet] *tr & intr* procrastinare

procure [pro'kjur] *tr* ottenere || *intr* ruffianeggiare

prod [prad] *s* pungolo, stimolo || *v* (*pret & pp* **prodded;** *ger* **prodding**) *tr* stimulare, pungolare, incitare

prodigal ['pradɪgəl] *adj & s* prodigo

prodigious [pro'dɪdʒəs] *adj* prodigioso

prodi·gy ['pradɪdʒi] *s* (**-gies**) prodigio

produce ['prodjus] *or* ['prodəs] *s* produzione; prodotti *mpl* agricoli || [pro'djus] *or* [pro'dus] *tr* produrre; (theat) presentare

producer [pro'djusər] *or* [pro'dusər] *s* produttore *m*; (*of a play*) impresario; (mov) produttore *m*

product ['pradəkt] *s* prodotto

production [pro'dʌkʃən] *s* produzione

profane [pro'fen] *adj* profano; blasfemo || *tr* profanare

profani·ty [pro'fænɪti] *s* (**-ties**) bestemmia

profess [pro'fɛs] *tr & intr* professare

profession [pro'fɛʃən] *s* professione

professor [pro'fɛsər] *s* professore *m*

proffer ['prafər] *s* offerta || *tr* offrire

proficient [pro'fɪʃənt] *adj* abile, competente

profile ['profaɪl] *s* profilo || *tr* profilare

profit ['prafɪt] *s* profitto; vantaggio; **at a profit** con guadagno || *tr* avvantaggiare; giovare (with *dat*) || *intr* avvantaggiarsi; **to profit by** approfittare di

profitable ['prafɪtəbəl] *adj* vantaggioso

prof'it and loss' *s* profitti *mpl* e perdite *fpl*

profiteer [ˌprafɪ'tɪr] *s* profittatore *m* || *intr* fare il profittatore

prof'it shar'ing *s* cointeressenza, partecipazione agli utili

prof'it tak'ing *s* realizzo

profligate ['praflɪgɪt] *adj & s* dissoluto; prodigo

pro for'ma in'voice ['fɔrmə] *s* fattura fittizia

profound [pro'faund] *adj* profondo

profuse [prə'fjus] *adj* profuso, abbondante; **profuse in** prodigo di

proge·ny ['pradʒəni] *s* (**-nies**) prole *f*

progno·sis [prag'nosɪs] *s* (**-ses** [siz]) prognosi *f*

prognostic [prag'nastɪk] *s* pronostico

prognosticate [prag'nastɪˌket] *tr* pronosticare

pro·gram ['progræm] *s* programma *m* || *v* (*pret & pp* **-gramed** *or* **-grammed;** *ger* **-graming** *or* **-gramming**) *tr* programmare

programmer ['progræmər] *s* pannellista *mf*, programmatore *m*

progress ['pragres] *s* progresso; **in progress** in corso; **to make progress** fare dei progressi || [prə'gres] *intr* progredire; migliorare

progressive [prə'gresɪv] *adj* (*proceeding step by step*) progressivo; progressista || *s* progressista *mf*

prohibit [pro'hɪbɪt] *tr* proibire

prohibition [ˌpro·ə'bɪʃən] *s* proibizione; (hist) proibizionismo

project ['pradʒɛkt] *s* progetto || [prə'dʒɛkt] *tr* (*to propose, plan*) progettare; (light, a shadow, etc.) proiettare || *intr* sporgere, protrudere

projectile [prə'dʒɛktɪl] *s* proiettile *m*

projection [prə'dʒɛkʃən] *s* proiezione, sporgenza

projector [prə'dʒɛktər] *s* (*apparatus*) proiettore *m*; (*person*) progettista *mf*

proletarian [ˌprolɪ'tɛrɪən] *adj & s* proletario

proliferate [prə'lɪfəˌret] *intr* proliferare

prolific [prə'lɪfɪk] *adj* prolifico

prolix ['prolɪks] *or* [pro'lɪks] *adj* prolisso

prologue ['proləg] *or* ['prolɑg] *s* prologo

prolong [proˈlɔŋ] or proˈlaŋ] *tr* prolungare

promenade [ˌprɑmɪˈned] or [ˌprɑmɪˈnad] *s* passeggiata; ballo di gala ‖ *tr & intr* passeggiare

promenade' deck' *s* ponte *m* passeggiata

prominent [ˈprɑmɪnənt] *adj* prominente

promise [ˈprɑmɪs] *s* promessa ‖ *tr & intr* promettere

prom'ising young' man' *s* giovane *m* di belle speranze

prom'issory note' [ˈprɑmɪ ˌsori] *s* cambiale *f*, pagherò *m*

promonto·ry [ˈprɑmən ˌtori] *s* (-ries) promontorio

promote [prəˈmot] *tr* promuovere

promotion [prəˈmoʃən] *s* promozione

prompt [prɑmpt] *adj* pronto ‖ *tr* incitare, istigare; (theat) suggerire

prompter [ˈprɑmptər] *s* suggeritore *m*, rammentatore *m*

prompt'er's box' *s* buca del suggeritore

promptness [ˈprɑmptnɪs] *s* prontezza

promulgate [ˈprɑmʌl ˌget] or [proˈmʌlget] *tr* promulgare

prone [pron] *adj* prono

prong [prɔŋ] or [praŋ] *s* punta; (of fork) dente *m*; (of pitchfork) rebbio

pronoun [ˈpronaun] *s* pronome *m*

pronounce [prəˈnauns] *tr* pronunziare

pronounced [prəˈnaunst] *adj* pronunziato, marcato

pronouncement [prəˈnaunsmənt] *s* dichiarazione ufficiale

pronunciamen·to [prə ˌnʌnsɪ·əˈmento] *s* (-tos) pronunciamento

pronunciation [prə ˌnʌnsɪˈeʃən] or [prə ˌnʌnsɪˈeʃən] *s* pronunzia

proof [pruf] *adj*—**proof against** a prova di ‖ *s* prova; (of alcoholic beverages) gradazione; (typ) bozza

proof'read'er *s* correttore *m* di bozze

prop [prɑp] *s* sostegno, puntello; (pole) palo; **props** attrezzi *mpl* teatrali ‖ *v* (pret & pp **propped**; ger **propping**) *tr* sostenere, puntellare

propaganda [ˌprɑpəˈɡændə] *s* propaganda

propagate [ˈprɑpə ˌɡet] *tr* propagare ‖ *intr* propagarsi

pro·pel [prəˈpel] *v* (pret & pp **-pelled**; ger **-pelling**) *tr* propulsare, spingere, azionare; (a rocket) propellere

propeller [prəˈpelər] *s* elica

propensi·ty [prəˈpensɪti] *s* (-ties) propensione

proper [ˈprɑpər] *adj* appropriato, corretto; decente, convenevole; (gram) proprio; **proper to** proprio di

proper·ty [ˈprɑpərti] *s* (-ties) proprietà *f*; **properties** attrezzi *mpl* teatrali

prop'erty man' *s* trovarobe *m*, attrezzista *m*

prop'erty own'er *s* proprietario fondiario

prophe·cy [ˈprɑfɪsi] *s* (-cies) profezia

prophe·sy [ˈprɑfɪ ˌsaɪ] *v* (pret & pp **-sied**) *tr* profetizzare

prophet [ˈprɑfɪt] *s* profeta *m*

prophetess [ˈprɑfɪtɪs] *s* profetessa

prophylactic [ˌprɑfɪˈlæktɪk] *adj* profilattico ‖ *s* rimedio profilattico; preservativo

propitiate [prəˈpɪʃɪ ˌet] *tr* propiziare

propitious [prəˈpɪʃəs] *adj* propizio

prop'jet' *s* turboelica *m*

proportion [prəˈporʃən] *s* proporzione; **in proportion as** a misura che; **in proportion to** in proporzione a; **out of proportion** sproporzionato ‖ *tr* proporzionare, commensurare

proportionate [prəˈporʃənɪt] *adj* proporzionato

proposal [prəˈpozəl] *s* proposta; proposta di matrimonio

propose [prəˈpoz] *tr* proporre ‖ *intr* fare una proposta di matrimonio; **to propose to** chiedere la mano di; proporsi di + *inf*

proposition [ˌprɑpəˈzɪʃən] *s* proposizione, proposta; (coll) progetto ‖ *tr* fare delle proposte indecenti a

propound [prəˈpaund] *tr* proporre

proprietary [prəˈpraɪ·ə ˌteri] *adj* padronale; esclusivo, patentato

proprietor [prəˈpraɪ·ətər] *s* proprietario

proprietress [prəˈpraɪ·ətrɪs] *s* proprietaria

proprie·ty [prəˈpraɪ·əti] *s* (-ties) correttezza, decoro; **proprieties** convenzioni *fpl* sociali

propulsion [prəˈpʌlʃən] *s* propulsione

prorate [proˈret] *tr* rateizzare

prosaic [proˈze·ɪk] *adj* prosaico

proscribe [proˈskraɪb] *tr* proscrivere

prose [proz] *adj* prosaico ‖ *s* prosa

prosecute [ˈprɑsɪ ˌkjut] *tr* eseguire; (law) processare

prosecutor [ˈprɑsɪ ˌkjutər] *s* esecutore *m*; (law) querelante *m*; (law) avvocato d'accusa

proselyte [ˈprɑsɪ ˌlaɪt] *s* proselito

prose' writ'er *s* prosatore *m*

prosody [ˈprɑsədi] *s* prosodia, metrica

prospect [ˈprɑspekt] *s* vista; prospettiva; candidato; probabile cliente *m*; **prospects** speranze *fpl* ‖ *intr* fare il cercatore; **to prospect for** fare il cercatore di

prospectus [prəˈspektəs] *s* prospetto

prosper [ˈprɑspər] *tr & intr* prosperare

prosperi·ty [prɑsˈperɪti] *s* (-ties) prosperità *f*, benessere *m*

prosperous [ˈprɑspərəs] *adj* prospero

prostitute [ˈprɑstɪ ˌtjut] or [ˈprɑstɪ ˌtut] *s* prostituta ‖ *tr* prostituire

prostrate [ˈprɑstret] *adj* prostrato ‖ *tr* prostrare

prostration [prɑsˈtreʃən] *s* prostrazione

protagonist [proˈtæɡənɪst] *s* protagonista *mf*

protect [prəˈtekt] *tr* proteggere

protection [prəˈtekʃən] *s* protezione

protégé [ˈprotə ˌʒe] *s* protetto, favorito

protégée [ˈprotə ˌʒe] *s* protetta, favorita

protein [ˈproti·ɪn] or [ˈprotin] *s* proteina

pro tempore [proˈtempə ˌri] *adj* provvisorio, interinale

protest [ˈprotest] *s* protesta; (com)

protesto ‖ [pro'test] *tr & intr* protestare

Protestant ['protIstənt] *adj & s* protestante *mf*

protester [prə'testər] *s* protestatario

prothonotar·y [pro'θɑnə,teri] *s* (**-ies**) (law) cancelliere *m* capo

protocol ['protə,kɑl] *s* protocollo

protoplasm ['protə,plæzəm] *s* protoplasma *m*

prototype ['protə,taip] *s* prototipo

proto·zoon [,protə'zo·ɑn] *s* (**-zoa** ['zo·ə]) protozoo

protract [pro'trækt] *tr* prolungare

protractor [pro'træktər] *s* rapportatore *m*

protrude [pro'trud] *intr* sporgere

proud [praud] *adj* fiero; arrogante; maestoso, magnifico

proud' flesh' *s* tessuto di granulazione

prove [pruv] *v* (*pret* **proved**; *pp* **proved** or **proven**) *tr* provare; (*ore*) analizzare; (law) omologare; (math) fare la prova di ‖ *intr* risultare

proverb ['prɑvərb] *s* proverbio

provide [prə'vaid] *tr* provvedere ‖ *intr*—**to provide for** provvedere a; (*to be ready for*) prepararsi a

provided [prə'vaidid] *conj* a condizione che, purché; **provided that a** condizione che, purché

providence ['prɑvidəns] *s* provvidenza

providential [,prɑvi'den/əl] *adj* provvidenziale

providing [prə'vaidiŋ] *conj var of* **provided**

province ['prɑvins] *s* provincia; (fig) pertinenza, competenza

provision [prə'vi/ən] *s* provvedimento; clausola; **provisions** viveri *mpl*

provi·so [prə'vaizo] *s* (**-sos** or **-soes**) stipulazione, clausola

provoke [prə'vok] *tr* provocare; contrariare, irritare

prow [prau] *s* prora, prua

prowess ['prau·is] *s* prodezza; maestria

prowl [praul] *intr* andare in cerca di preda; vagabondare

prowler ['praulər] *s* vagabondo; ladro

proximity [prɑk'simiti] *s* prossimità *f*

prox·y ['prɑksi] *s* (**-ies**) procura; (*person*) procuratore *m*

prude [prud] *s* pudibondo

prudence ['prudəns] *s* prudenza

prudent ['prudənt] *adj* prudente

pruder·y ['prudəri] *s* (**-ies**) attitudine pudibonda

prudish ['prudi/] *adj* pudibondo

prune [prun] *s* prugna secca ‖ *tr* potare

pry [prai] *v* (*pret & pp* **pried**) *tr*—**to pry open** forzare con una leva; **to pry s.th out of s.o.** strappare qlco a qlcu ‖ *intr* intromettersi, cacciarsi

psalm [sɑm] *s* salmo

pseudo ['sudo] or ['sjudo] *adj* falso, finto, sedicente

pseudonym ['sudənim] or ['sjudənim] *s* pseudonimo

psychiatrist [sai'kai·ətrist] *s* psichiatra *mf*

psychiatry [sai'kai·ətri] *s* psichiatria

psychic ['saikik] *adj* psichico ‖ *s* medium *mf*

psychoanalysis [,saiko·ə'nælisis] *s* psicanalisi *f*

psychoanalyze [,saiko'ænə,laiz] *tr* psicanalizzare

psychologic(al) [,saiko'lɑdʒik(əl)] *adj* psicologico

psychologist [sai'kɑlədʒist] *s* psicologo

psycholo·gy [sai'kɑlədʒi] *s* (**-gies**) psicologia

psychopath ['saikə,pæθ] *s* psicopatico

psycho·sis [sai'kosis] *s* (**-ses** [siz]) psicosi *f*

psychotic [sai'kɑtik] *adj* psicotico

pub [pʌb] *s* (Brit) taverna, bar *m*

puberty ['pjubərti] *s* pubertà *f*

public ['pʌblik] *adj & s* pubblico

pub'lic-address' sys'tem *s* sistema *m* d'amplificazione per discorsi in pubblico

publication [,pʌbli'ke/ən] *s* pubblicazione

pub'lic convey'ance *s* veicolo di servizi pubblici

publicity [pʌb'lisiti] *s* pubblicità *f*

publicize ['pʌbli,saiz] *tr* pubblicare, divulgare

pub'lic li'brary *s* biblioteca comunale

pub'lic-opin'ion poll' *s* sondaggio d'opinioni

pub'lic pros'ecutor *s* pubblico ministero

pub'lic school' *s* (U.S.A.) scuola dell'obbligo; (Brit) scuola privata, collegio

pub'lic serv'ant *s* funzionario pubblico

pub'lic speak'ing *s* oratoria

pub'lic spir'it *s* civismo

pub'lic toi'let *s* gabinetto pubblico

pub'lic util'ity *s* impresa di servizio pubblico; **public utilities** azioni emesse da imprese di servizi pubblici

publish ['pʌbli/] *tr* pubblicare

publisher ['pʌbli/ər] *s* editore *m*; (journ) direttore *m* responsabile

pub'lishing house' *s* casa editrice

pucker ['pʌkər] *s* grinza ‖ *tr* raggrinzire ‖ *intr* ragrinzirsi

pudding ['pudiŋ] *s* budino, torta

puddle ['pʌdəl] *s* pozza, pozzanghera ‖ *intr* diguazzare

pudg·y ['pʌdʒi] *adj* (**-ier; -iest**) grassoccio

puerile ['pju·əril] *adj* puerile

Puerto Rican ['pwerto'rikən] *adj & s* portoricano

puff [pʌf] *s* soffio, sbuffo; (*e.g., of cigar*) boccata; (*pad*) piumino; (*exaggerated praise*) pistolotto; (culin) bigné *m* ‖ *tr* sbuffare; gonfiare; adulare ‖ *intr* soffiare, sbuffare; (*to breathe heavily*) ansimare, ansare; gonfiarsi; tirare boccate

puff' paste' *s* pasta sfoglia

pugilist ['pjudʒilist] *s* pugile *m*

pug-nosed ['pʌg'nozd] *adj* camuso

puke [pjuk] *tr & intr* (slang) vomitare

pull [pul] *s* tiro; (*act of drawing in*) tirata; (*handle*) tirante *m*; (slang) influenza, appoggi *mpl* ‖ *tr* tirare; (*a tooth*) cavare; (*a muscle*) strappare;

(a punch) (coll) limitare la forza di; **to pull apart** fare a pezzi; **to pull down** abbattere; degradare; **to pull on** (e.g., one's pants) infilarsi; **to pull oneself together** ricomporsi; **to pull s.o.'s leg** beffarsi di qlcu ‖ intr tirare; **to pull apart** andare a pezzi; **to pull at** tirare; **to pull away** andarsene; **to pull for** (coll) fare il tifo per; **to pull in** (said of a train) arrivare, entrare in stazione; **to pull out** (said of a train) partire; **to pull through** guarire, riuscire a cavarsela; **to pull up** to avanzare fino a

pullet ['pulɪt] s pollastra

pulley ['pulɪ] s puleggia, carrucola

pulp [pʌlp] s polpa; (for making paper) pasta

pulpit ['pulpɪt] s pulpito

pulsate ['pʌlset] intr pulsare

pulsation [pʌl'seʃən] s pulsazione

pulse [pʌls] s polso; **to feel or take the pulse of** tastare il polso a

pulverize ['pʌlvə ,raɪz] tr polverizzare

pum'ice stone' s ['pʌmɪs] s pomice f, pietra pomice

pum·mel ['pʌməl] v (pret & pp -meled or -melled; ger -meling or -melling) tr prendere a pugni

pump [pʌmp] s pompa; (slipper) scarpina ‖ tr pompare; (coll) cavare un segreto a; **to pump up** pompare

pumpkin ['pʌmpkɪn] or ['pʌŋkɪn] s zucca

pump-priming ['pʌmp ,praɪmɪŋ] s stimolo governativo per sostentare l'economia

pun [pʌn] s gioco di parole ‖ v (pret & pp punned; ger punning) intr fare giochi di parole

punch [pʌntʃ] s pugno; (tool) punteruolo, punzone m; (drink) ponce m; (coll) forza ‖ tr dare un pugno a; (metal) punzonare; (a ticket) perforare ‖ Punch s Pulcinella m; **pleased as Punch** soddisfattissimo

punch' bowl' s vaso per il ponce

punch' card' s scheda perforata

punch' clock' s orologio di controllo

punch'-drunk' adj stordito

punched' tape' s nastro perforato

punch'ing bag' s sacco

punch' line' s perfinire m, motto finale

punctilious [pʌŋk'tɪlɪ·əs] adj cerimonioso, pignolo

punctual ['pʌŋktʃu·əl] adj puntuale

punctuate ['pʌŋktʃu ,et] tr punteggiare

punctuation [,pʌŋktʃu'eʃən] s punteggiatura

punctua'tion mark' s segno d'interpunzione

puncture ['pʌŋktʃər] s puntura; (hole) bucatura; **to have a puncture** avere una gomma a terra ‖ tr bucare, perforare ‖ intr essere bucato

punct'ure-proof' adj antiperforante

pundit ['pʌndɪt] s esperto, autorità f

pungent ['pʌndʒənt] adj pungente

punish ['pʌnɪʃ] tr punire

punishment ['pʌnɪʃmənt] s punizione, castigo

punk [pʌŋk] adj (slang) di pessima

qualità ‖ s esca; (decayed wood) legno marcio; (slang) malandrino

punster ['pʌnstər] s freddurista mf

punt [pʌnt] s (football) calcio dato al pallone prima che tocchi il terreno

pu·ny ['pjunɪ] adj (-nier; -niest) insignificante, meschino; (weak) debole

pup [pʌp] s cucciolo

pupil ['pjupəl] s allievo, scolaro; (anat) pupilla

puppet ['pʌpɪt] s marionetta, burattino; (fig) fantoccio

puppeteer [,pʌpɪ'tɪr] s burattinaio

pup'pet gov'ernment s governo fantoccio or pupazzo

pup'pet show' s spettacolo di marionette

pup·py ['pʌpɪ] s (-pies) cucciolo

pup'py love' s amore m giovanile

purchase ['pʌrtʃəs] s compra, acquisto; (grip) presa, leva ‖ tr comprare, acquistare

pur'chasing pow'er s potere m d'acquisto

pure [pjur] adj puro

purgative ['pʌrgətɪv] adj purgativo ‖ s purga

purge [pʌrdʒ] s purga ‖ tr purgare

puri·fy ['pjurɪ ,faɪ] v (pret & pp -fied) tr purificare ‖ intr purificarsi

puritan ['pjurɪtən] adj & s puritano ‖ **Puritan** adj & s puritano

purity ['pjurɪtɪ] s purezza

purloin [pər'lɔɪn] tr & intr rubare

purple ['pʌrpəl] adj purpureo ‖ s porpora

purport ['pʌrport] s senso, significato ‖ [pər'port] tr significare; **to purport to** + inf pretendere di + inf

purpose ['pʌrpəs] s scopo, fine m; **on purpose** apposta; **to good purpose** con buoni risultati; **to no purpose** inutilmente; **to serve one's purpose** fare al caso proprio

purposely ['pʌrpəslɪ] adv a bella posta, apposta

purr [pʌr] s ronfare m ‖ intr fare le fusa

purse [pʌrs] s borsa; (woman's handbag) borsetta; (for men) borsetto ‖ tr (one's lips) arricciare

purser ['pʌrsər] s commissario di bordo

purse' snatch'er ['snætʃər] s borsaiolo

purse' strings' spl cordini mpl della borsa; **to hold the purse strings** controllare le spese

purslane ['pʌrslen] or ['pʌrslɪn] s (bot) porcellana

pursue [pər'su] or [pər'sju] tr perseguire; (to harass) perseguitare; (a career) proseguire

pursuit [pər'sut] or [pər'sjut] s inseguimento, caccia; occupazione, esercizio

pursuit' plane' s caccia m

purvey [pər've] tr provvedere, fornire

pus [pʌs] s pus m

push [puʃ] s spinta; (advance) avanzata; (coll) impulso, energia ‖ tr premere, spingere; (a product) promuovere la vendita di; dare impulso a; (narcotics) (slang) spacciare; **to**

push around (coll) dare spintoni a; (fig) fare pressione su; **to push back** ricacciare ‖ *intr* spingere; **to push ahead** avanzarsi a spintoni, avanzarsi; **to push on** avanzare

push' but'ton *s* pulsante *m*, bottone *m*

push'-button con'trol *s* controllo a pulsanti

push'cart' *s* carretto a mano

pusher ['puʃər] *adj* spingente; (aer) propulsivo ‖ *s* spingitore *m*; (aer) aeroplano a elica propulsiva; (slang) spacciatore *m* di stupefacenti

pushing ['puʃɪŋ] *adj* aggressivo, intraprendente

puss [pus] *s* micio

puss' in the cor'ner *s* gioco dei quattro cantoni

puss·y ['pusi] *s* (-ies) micio

puss'y wil'low *s* salice americano a gattini

pustule ['pʌstʃʊl] *s* pustola

put [put] *v* (*pret & pp* **put;** *ger* **putting**) *tr* mettere; (*to estimate*) stimare; (*a question*) rivolgere; (*to throw*) lanciare; imporre; **to put across** (slang) far accettare; **to put aside, away** or **by** mettere da parte; **to put down** annotare; (*to suppress*) reprimere; **to put off** differire; evadere; **to put on** (*clothes*) mettersi; (*a brake*) azionare; (*to assume*) fingere; (*airs*) darsi; **to put out** spegnere; imbarazzare; incomodare; deludere; annoiare, irritare; (*of a game*) espellere; **to put it over on s.o.** fargliela a qlcu; **to put off** rinviare; **to put over** mandare ad effetto; **to put to flight** mettere in fuga; **to put to shame** svergognare; **to put through** portare a

termine; **to put up** offrire; mettere in conserva; costruire; (*money*) contribuire; (coll) incitare ‖ *intr* dirigersi; **to put to sea** mettersi in mare; **to put up** prendere alloggio; **to put up with** tollerare

put'-out' *adj* sconcertato, seccato

putrid ['pjutrɪd] *adj* putrido

Putsch [putʃ] *s* tentativo di sollevazione, sollevazione

putter ['pʌtər] *intr* occuparsi di inezie; **to putter about** andare avanti e indietro

put·ty ['pʌti] *s* (-ties) stucco, mastice *m* ‖ *v* (*pret & pp* **-tied**) *tr* stuccare

put'ty knife' *s* spatola

put'-up' *adj* (coll) complottato

puzzle ['pʌzəl] *s* enigma *m;* (toy) indovinello ‖ *tr* rendere perplesso, confondere; **to puzzle out** decifrare ‖ *intr* essere perplesso

puzzler ['pʌzlər] *s* enigma *m*

puzzling ['pʌzlɪŋ] *adj* enigmatico

pyg·my ['pɪgmi] *s* (-mies) pigmeo

pylon *s* pilone *m*

pyramid ['pɪrəmɪd] *s* piramide *f* ‖ *tr* (*e.g., costs*) aumentare gradualmente; (*one's money*) aumentare giocando in margine

pyre [paɪr] *s* pira

Pyrenees ['pɪrɪ,niz] *spl* Pirenei *mpl*

pyrites [paɪ'raɪtiz] or ['paɪraɪts] *s* pirite *f*

pyrotechnics [,paɪrə'tekniks] *spl* pirotecnica

python ['paɪθən] or ['paɪθən] *s* pitone *m*

pythoness ['paɪθənɪs] *s* pitonessa

pyx [pɪks] *s* (eccl) pisside *f*

Q

Q, q [kju] *s* diciassettesima lettera dell'alfabeto inglese

quack [kwæk] *adj* falso ‖ *s* medicastro; ciarlatano; qua qua *m* ‖ *intr* (*said of a duck*) fare qua qua

quacker·y ['kwækəri] *s* (-ies) ciarlataneria

quadrangle ['kwad,ræŋgəl] *s* quadrangolo

quadrant ['kwadrənt] *s* quadrante *m*

quadruped ['kwadru,ped] *adj* & *s* quadrupede *m*

quadruple ['kwadrupəl] or [kwa'drupəl] *adj* quadruplo; (*alliance*) quadruplice ‖ *s* quadruplo ‖ *tr* quadruplicare ‖ *intr* quadruplicarsi

quaff [kwaf] or [kwæf] *s* lungo sorso ‖ *tr* & *intr* bere a lunghi sorsi

quail [kwel] *s* quaglia ‖ *intr* sgomentarsi

quaint [kwent] *adj* strano, strambo, originale; all'antica ma bello

quake [kwek] *s* terremoto ‖ *intr* tremare, sussultare

Quaker ['kwekər] *adj* & *s* quacchero, quacquero

Quak'er meet'ing *s* riunione di quaccheri; (coll) riunione in cui si parla poco

quali·fy ['kwalɪ,faɪ] *v* (*pret & pp* **-fied**) *tr* qualificare; (*for a profession*) abilitare ‖ *intr* qualificarsi; abilitarsi

quali·ty ['kwalɪti] *s* (-ties) qualità *f;* (*of a sound*) timbro

qualm [kwam] *s* scrupolo di coscienza; preoccupazione; nausea

quanda·ry ['kwandəri] *s* (-ries) incertezza, perplessità *f*

quanti·ty ['kwantɪti] *s* (-ties) quantità *f*

quan·tum ['kwantəm] *adj* quantistico ‖ *s* (-ta [tə]) quanto

quarantine ['kwarən,tin] or ['kwɔrən,tin] *s* quarantena ‖ *tr* mettere in quarantena

quar·rel ['kwarəl] or ['kwɔrəl] *s* litigio, diverbio; **to have no quarrel with** non essere in disaccordo con; **to pick a quarrel with** venire a diverbio con ‖ *v* (*pret & pp* **-reled** or **-relled;** *ger* **-reling** or **-relling**) *intr* litigare

quarrelsome [ˈkwɑrəlsəm] or [ˈkwɔrəl-səm] *adj* litigioso, rissoso
quar·ry [ˈkwɑri] or [ˈkwɔri] *s* (-ries) cava; (*game*) selvaggina, cacciagione ‖ *v* (*pret & pp* -ried) *tr* cavare
quart [kwɔrt] *s* quarto di gallone
quarter [ˈkwɔrtər] *adj* quarto ‖ *s* quarto; moneta di un quarto di dol-laro; (*three months*) trimestre *m*; (*of town*) quartiere *m*; **a quarter after one** l'una e un quarto; **a quarter of an hour** un quarto d'ora; **a quarter to one** l'una meno un quarto; **at close quarters** corpo a corpo; **quarters** quartiere *m* ‖ *tr* squartare; (*soldiers*) accasermare
quar'ter-deck' *s* cassero
quar'ter-hour' *s* quarto d'ora; **on the quarter-hour** ogni quindici minuti allo scoccare del quarto d'ora
quarter·ly [ˈkwɔrtərli] *adj* trimestrale ‖ *s* (-lies) pubblicazione trimestrale ‖ *adv* trimestralmente
quar'ter·mas'ter *s* (mil) intendente *m* militare; (nav) secondo capo
quartet [kwɔrˈtet] *s* quartetto
quartz [kwɔrts] *s* quarzo
quasar [ˈkwesɑr] *s* (astr) radiostella
quash [kwɑʃ] *tr* sopprimere; annullare
quaver [ˈkwevər] *s* tremito; (mus) tre-molo; (mus) croma ‖ *intr* tremare
quay [ki] *s* molo
queen [kwin] *s* regina; (*in cards*) donna; (chess) regina
queen' bee' *s* ape regina; (fig) basilessa
queen' dow'ager *s* regina vedova
queen·ly [ˈkwinli] *adj* (-lier; -liest) da regina; regio
queen' moth'er *s* regina madre
queen' post' *s* monaco
queen's' Eng'lish *s* inglese corretto
queer [kwɪr] *adj* strano, curioso; poco bene, indisposto; falso; (slang) omo-sessuale ‖ *s* (slang) finocchio ‖ *tr* rovinare, mettere in pericolo
quell [kwel] *tr* soffocare, domare; (*pain*) calmare
quench [kwentʃ] *tr* (*fire, thirst*) spe-gnere, estinguere; (*rebellion*) soffo-care; (thirst) ammortizzare
que·ry [ˈkwɪri] *s* (-ries) domanda; punto interrogativo; dubbio ‖ *v* (*pret & pp* -ried) *tr* interrogare; (typ) ap-porre punto interrogare a
quest [kwest] *s* ricerca; **in quest of** in cerca di
question [ˈkwestʃən] *s* domanda; pro-blema *m*, quesito; (*matter*) questione; **beyond question** senza dubbio; **out of the question** impossibile; **this is be-side the question** questo non c'entra; **to ask a question** fare una domanda; **to be a question of** trattarsi di; **to call in** or **into question** mettere in dubbio; **without question** senza dub-bio ‖ *tr* interrogare; mettere in dub-bio; (pol) interpellare
questionable [ˈkwestʃənəbəl] *adj* discu-tibile
ques'tion mark' *s* punto interrogativo
questionnaire [ˌkwestʃənˈer] *s* questio-nario

queue [kju] *s* (*of hair*) codino; (*of peo-ple*) coda ‖ *intr* fare la coda
quibble [ˈkwɪbəl] *intr* sottilizzare
quick [kwɪk] *adj* pronto, sollecito; sbrigativo; veloce, rapido; vivo ‖ *s*— **the quick and the dead** i vivi e i morti; **to cut to the quick** toccare nel vivo
quicken [ˈkwɪkən] *tr* sveltire; animare; ravvivare
quick'lime' *s* calce viva
quick' lunch' *s* tavola calda
quickly [ˈkwɪkli] *adv* svelto, alla svelta; presto
quick'sand' *s* sabbia mobile
quick'-set'ting *adj* a presa rapida
quick'sil'ver *s* argento vivo
quick'work' *s* (naut) opera viva
quiet [ˈkwaɪ·ət] *adj* quieto; silenzioso; (com) calmo; **to keep quiet** stare zitto ‖ *s* quiete *f*, tranquillità *f*; pace *f*, calma ‖ *tr* quietare; calmare ‖ *intr*— **to quiet down** quietarsi, calmarsi
quill [kwɪl] *s* penna d'oca; (*basal part of feather*) calamo; (*e.g., of porcu-pine*) aculeo
quilt [kwɪlt] *s* trapunta, imbottita ‖ *tr* trapuntare
quince [kwɪns] *s* cotogna; (*tree*) co-togno
quinine [ˈkwaɪnaɪn] *s* (*alkaloid*) chi-nina; (*salt of the alkaloid*) chinino
quinsy [ˈkwɪnzi] *s* angina
quintessence [kwɪnˈtesəns] *s* quintes-senza
quintet [kwɪnˈtet] *s* quintetto
quintuplet [kwɪnˈtjuplet] or [kwɪn-ˈtuplet] *s* gemello nato da un parto quintuplice
quip [kwɪp] *s* frizzo, uscita *f* ‖ *v* (*pret & pp* **quipped**; *ger* **quipping**) *tr & intr* uscire a dire, dire come battuta
quire [kwaɪr] *s* ventiquattro fogli; (bb) quinterno
quirk [kwɑrk] *s* stranezza, manierismo; (*quibble*) cavillo; (*sudden turn*) mu-tamento improvviso
quit [kwɪt] *adj* libero; **to be quits** esser pari; **to call it quits** finirla, farla finita ‖ *v* (*pret & pp* **quit** or **quitted**; *ger* **quitting**) *tr* abbandonare ‖ *intr* andarsene; abbandonare l'impiego; smettere (di + *inf*)
quite [kwaɪt] *adv* completamente; molto, del tutto
quitter [ˈkwɪtər] *s* persona che abban-dona facilmente
quiver [ˈkwɪvər] *s* fremito; (*to hold arrows*) faretra, turcasso ‖ *intr* fre-mere, tremare
quixotic [kwɪksˈɑtɪk] *adj* donchisciot-tesco
quiz [kwɪz] *s* (**quizzes**) esame *m*; inter-rogatorio ‖ *v* (*pret & pp* **quizzed**; *ger* **quizzing**) *tr* esaminare; interrogare
quiz' game' *s* quiz *m*
quiz' pro'gram *s* programma *m* di quiz
quiz' sec'tion *s* (educ) classe *f* a base di esercizi (e non di conferenze)
quizzical [ˈkwɪzɪkəl] *adj* strano, cu-rioso; (*derisive*) canzonatore
quoin [kɔɪn] or [kwɔɪn] *s* cantone *m*,

pietra angolare; (*piece of wood*) zeppa; (typ) serraforme *m* ‖ *tr* fissare con serraforme

quoit [kwɔɪt] *or* [kɔɪt] *s* anello di corda o di metallo da lanciarsi come gioco; **quoits** *ssg* gioco consistente nel lancio di anelli su di un piolo

quondam ['kwɑndæm] *adj* quondam

quorum ['kworəm] *s* quorum *m*

quota ['kwotə] *s* (*share*) quota; (*of imports*) contingentamento; (*of persons*) contingente *m*

quotation [kwo'teʃən] *s* (*from a book*) citazione; (*of prices*) quotazione

quota'tion mark' *s* doppia virgola, virgoletta

quote [kwot] *s* citazione, richiamo ‖ *tr & intr* citare, richiamare; (com) quotare; **quote** cito

quotient ['kwoʃənt] *s* quoziente *m*

R

R, r [ɑr] *s* diciottesima lettera dell'alfabeto inglese

rabbet ['ræbɪt] *s* scanalatura, incastro ‖ *tr* scanalare, incastrare

rab·bi ['ræbaɪ] *s* (-bis) rabbino

rabbit ['ræbɪt] *s* coniglio

rab'bit ears' *spl* (telv) doppia antenna a stilo

rabble ['ræbəl] *s* gentaglia, marmaglia

rab'ble-rous'er ['rauzər] *s* arruffapopoli *m*

rabies ['rebiz] *or* ['rebɪ͵iz] *s* rabbia

raccoon [ræ'kun] *s* procione *m*

race [res] *s* (*branch of human stock*) razza; (*contest in speed*) corsa; (*contest of any kind*) gara; (*channel*) canale *m* di adduzione ‖ *tr* far correre; gareggiare (in velocità) con; (*a motor*) imballare ‖ *intr* correre; fare le corse; (*said of a motor*) imballarsi; (naut) fare le regate

race' horse' *s* cavallo da corsa

race' ri'ot *s* contestazione di razza

race' track' *s* pista

racial ['reʃəl] *adj* razziale

rac'ing car' *s* automobile *f* da corsa

rack [ræk] *s* (*to hang clothes*) attaccapanni *m*; (*framework to hold fodder, baggage, guns, etc.*) rastrelliera; (mach) cremagliera; **to go to rack and ruin** andare a rotoli ‖ *tr* tormentare, torturare; **to rack off** (*wine*) travasare; **to rack one's brains** rompersi il capo, lambiccarsi il cervello

racket ['rækɪt] *s* racchetta; (*noise*) chiasso, gazzarra; (coll) racket *m*; **to raise a racket** fare gazzarra

racketeer [͵rækɪ'tɪr] *s* chi è nel racket; (*engaged in extortion*) ricattatore *m* ‖ *intr* essere nel racket; fare il ricattatore

rack' rail'way *s* ferrovia a cremagliera

rac·y ['resi] *adj* (-ier; -iest) pungente, vigoroso; piccante

radar ['redɑr] *s* radar *m*

radiant ['redɪ·ənt] *adj* raggiante, radioso

radiate ['redɪ͵et] *tr* irradiare ‖ *intr* irradiarsi

radiation [͵redɪ'eʃən] *s* radiazione

radia'tion sick'ness *s* malattia causata da radiazione atomica

radiator ['redɪ͵etər] *s* radiatore *m*

ra'diator cap' *s* tappo del radiatore

radical ['rædɪkəl] *adj* radicale ‖ *s*

radicale *mf*; (chem, math) radicale *m*

radi·o ['redɪ͵o] *s* (-os) radio *f*; radiogramma *m* ‖ *tr* radiotrasmettere

radioactive [͵redɪ·o'æktɪv] *adj* radioattivo

ra'dio am'ateur *s* radioamatore *m*

ra'dio announc'er *s* radioannunciatore *m*

ra'dio bea'con *s* radiofaro

ra'dio·broad'cast *s* radiodiffusione ‖ *tr* radiodiffondere

ra'dio com'pass *s* radiobussola

ra'dio-fre'quency *s* radiofrequenza

ra'dio lis'tener *s* radioascoltatore *m*

radiology [͵redɪ'ɑlədʒɪ] *s* radiologia

ra'dio net'work *s* rete *f*

ra'dio news'caster *s* radiocronista *mf*

ra'dio·pho'to *s* (-tos) (coll) radiofoto *f*

ra'dio set' *s* radioricevente *f*

ra'dio sta'tion *s* stazione radio

radish ['rædɪʃ] *s* ravanello

radium ['redɪ·əm] *s* radio

radi·us ['redɪ·əs] *s* (-i [͵aɪ] *or* -uses) (anat) radio; (fig, geom) raggio; **within a radius of** entro un raggio di

raffle ['ræfəl] *s* riffa ‖ *tr* sorteggiare

raft [ræft] *or* [rɑft] *s* zattera; (coll) mucchio

rafter ['ræftər] *or* ['rɑftər] *s* puntone *m*

rag [ræg] *s* straccio; **to chew the rag** (slang) chiacchierare

ragamuffin ['rægə͵mʌfɪn] *s* straccione *m*

rag' doll' *s* bambola di pezza

rage [redʒ] *s* rabbia; **to be all the rage** furoreggiare; **to fly into a rage** montare in bestia ‖ *intr* infuriare

ragged ['rægɪd] *adj* cencioso; (*torn*) stracciato; (*edge*) rozzo, scabroso

ragpicker ['ræg͵pɪkər] *s* cenciaiolo, straccivendolo

rag'weed' *s* (bot) ambrosia

raid [red] *s* irruzione, razzia ‖ *tr* scorrere ‖ *intr* scorrazzare

rail [rel] *s* (*of fence*) stecca, traversa; (*fence*) stecconata; (*railing*) ringhiera; (rr) rotaia; **by rail** per ferrovia; **rails** titoli *mpl* ferroviari ‖ *intr* inveire; **to rail at** inveire contro

rail' car' *s* automotrice *f*

rail' fence' *s* stecconata fatta di traverse piallate alla buona

rail'head' s fine f della linea ferroviaria

railing ['reliŋ] s ringhiera

rail'road' adj ferroviario || s ferrovia || tr trasportare in ferrovia; (a bill) far passare precipitosamente; (coll) imprigionare falsamente

rail'road cros'sing s passaggio a livello

rail'road'er s ferroviere m

rail'way' s ferrovia, strada ferrata

raiment ['remənt] s (lit) abbigliamento

rain [ren] s pioggia; **rain or shine** con qualunque tempo || tr fare piovere; (lit) piovere; **to rain cats and dogs** piovere a catinelle; **to rain out** far sospendere per via della pioggia || intr piovere

rainbow ['ren,bo] s arcobaleno

rain'coat' s impermeabile m

rain'fall' s acquazzone m; piovosità f

rain·y ['reni] adj (-ier; -iest) piovoso, piovano

rain'y day' s giorno piovoso; (fig) tempi mpl difficili

raise [rez] s aumento || tr levare, rialzare; (children, animals) allevare; (to build) tirare su; (a question) sollevare; (the dead) risollevare; (to increase) aumentare; (money) raccogliere; (a siege) togliere; (at cards) rilanciare; (anchor) salpare; (math) elevare

raisin ['rezən] s grano d'uva passa, grano d'uva secca; **raisins** uva passa, uva secca

rake [rek] s rastrello; (person) porcaccione m, libertino || tr rastrellare; **to rake in money** far soldoni

rake'-off' s (coll) compenso illecito, bustarella; (coll) sconto

rakish ['rekiʃ] adj libertino; brioso, vivace; **to wear one's hat at a rakish angle** portare il cappello sulle ventitré

ral·ly ['ræli] s (-lies) riunione, comizio; adunata; ricupero || v (pret & pp -lied) tr riunire, chiamare a raccolta; rianimare || intr riunirsi; rianimarsi; (said of stock prices) rialzarsi; rimettersi in forze; **to rally to the side of** correre all'aiuto di

ram [ræm] s (male sheep) montone m; (mil) ariete m; (nav) sperone m; (mach) maglio del battipalo || v (pret & pp rammed; ger ramming) tr battere, sbattere contro; cacciare, conficcare; forzare; (nav) speronare || intr—**to ram into** sbattere contro

ramble ['ræmbəl] s girata || intr (to wander around) gironzolare; vagare; (said of a vine) crescere disordinatamente; (said, e.g., of a river) serpeggiare; (fig) scorrazzare, divagare

rami·fy ['ræmɪ,faɪ] v (pret & pp -fied) tr ramificare || intr ramificarsi

ram'jet en'gine s statoreattore m

ramp [ræmp] s rampa

rampage ['ræmpedʒ] s stato d'eccitazione; **to go on a rampage** infierire, comportarsi furiosamente

rampart ['ræmpɑrt] s baluardo, muraglione m

ram'rod' s (for ramming) (mil) bacchetta; (for cleaning) (mil) scovolo

ram'shack'le adj cadente, in rovina

ranch [ræntʃ] s fattoria agricola

rancid ['rænsɪd] adj rancido

rancor ['ræŋkər] s rancore m

random ['rændəm] adj fortuito; **at random** alla rinfusa, a casaccio

range [rendʒ] s (row) fila; (rank) classe f; (distance) portata; campo di tiro a segno; raggio d'azione; (scope) gamma; (for grazing) pascolo; (stove) fornello, cucina economica; **within range of** alla portata di || tr allineare; ordinare; passare attraverso; mandare al pascolo || intr variare, fluttuare; estendersi; trovarsi; (mil) portare; **to range over** percorrere; (fig) trattare

range' find'er s telemetro

rank [ræŋk] adj esuberante; grossolano; denso, spesso; puzzolente; eccessivo; completo, assoluto || s rango, grado; (row) fila, schiera; **ranks** truppe fpl, ranghi mpl || tr arrangiare, allineare; classificare; avere rango superiore a || intr avere il massimo rango; **to rank high** avere un'alta posizione; **to rank low** avere una posizione bassa; **to rank with** essere allo stesso livello di

rank' and file' s truppa; massa

rankle ['ræŋkəl] tr irritare || intr inasprirsi

ransack ['rænsak] tr (to search thoroughly) frugare, rovistare; (to pillage) svaligiare, saccheggiare

ransom ['rænsəm] s taglia, riscatto || tr riscattare

rant [rænt] intr farneticare, parlare a vanvera

rap [ræp] s colpo, colpetto; **I don't care a rap** non m'importa un fico; **to take the rap** (slang) prendersi la colpa || v (pret & pp rapped; ger rapping) tr dare colpi a; battere; **to rap out** (e.g., a command) lanciare || intr dare colpi, bussare

rapacious [rə'peʃəs] adj rapace

rape [rep] s rapimento; (of a woman) stupro; (bot) ravizzone m || tr rapire; forzare, violentare

rapid ['ræpɪd] adj rapido || **rapids** spl rapide fpl

rap'id-fire' adj a tiro rapido

rapidity [rə'pɪdəti] s rapidità f

rapier ['repɪ·ər] s spada, stocco

rapt [ræpt] adj assorto; estatico

rapture ['ræptʃər] s rapimento, estasi f

rare [rer] adj raro; (thinly distributed) rado; (gas) rarefatto; (meat) al sangue; (gem) prezioso

rare'-earth' met'al s metallo delle terre rare

rare·fy ['rerɪ,faɪ] v (pret & pp -fied) tr rarefare || intr rarefarsi

rarely ['rerli] adv di rado, raramente

rascal ['ræskəl] s briccone m, birbante m

rash [ræʃ] adj temerario, precipitato || s eruzione; (fig) mucchio

rasp [ræsp] or [rɑsp] s raspa; rumore

m di raspa || *tr* raspare; irritare; dire con voce roca || *intr* fare rumore raspante

raspber·ry ['ræz‚beri] or ['raz‚beri] *s* (-ries) lampone *m*; (slang) pernacchia

rat [ræt] *s* ratto; (*to give fullness to hair*) posticcio; (slang) traditore *m*; **to smell a rat** (coll) subodorare un inganno

ratchet ['rætʃɪt] *s* nottolino

rate [ret] *s* (*of interest*) saggio, tasso; prezzo; costo; velocità *f*; (*degree of action*) ragione; tariffa; **at any rate** ad ogni modo; **at the rate of** in ragione di || *tr* valutare, classificare || *intr* essere considerato; essere classificato

rate' of exchange' *s* corso del cambio

rather ['ræðər] or ['raðər] *adv* piuttosto; a preferenza; per meglio dire; bensì; discretamente, sancire; **rather than** piuttosto di || *interj* e come!

rati·fy ['rætɪ‚faɪ] *v* (*pret & pp* **-fied**) *tr* ratificare, sancire

rating ['retɪŋ] *s* classifica; (nav) grado; (com) valutazione

ra·tio ['reʃo] or ['reʃɪ‚o] *s* (-tios) ragione, rapporto; proporzione

ration ['reʃən] or ['ræʃən] *s* razione || *tr* razionare

rational ['ræʃənəl] *adj* razionale

ra'tion book' *s* tessera di razionamento

rat' poi'son *s* veleno per i topi

rat' race' *s* (coll) corsa dei barberi

rattle ['rætəl] *s* (*sharp sounds*) fracasso; (*child's toy*) sonaglio; (*noise-making device*) raganella; (*in throat*) rantolo || *tr* scuotere; (*to confuse*) sconcertare; **to rattle off** dire rapidamente, snocciolare || *intr* risuonare; scuotersi; cianciare

rat'tle-snake' *s* serpente *m* a sonagli

rat'trap' *s* trappola per topi; (*hovel*) topaia; (*jam*) (fig) frangente *m*

raucous ['rɔkəs] *adj* rauco

ravage ['rævɪdʒ] *s* distruzione; **ravages** (*of time*) oltraggio *n* || *tr* distruggere, disfare

rave [rev] *intr* farneticare, delirare; infuriare; andare in estasi; **to rave about** levare alle stelle

raven ['revən] *s* corvo

ravenous ['rævənəs] *adj* famelico

ravine [rə'vin] *s* canalone *m*, burrone *m*

ravish ['rævɪʃ] *tr* incantare, entusiasmare; rapire; (*a woman*) stuprare

raw [rɔ] *adj* crudo; (*e.g., silk*) grezzo; (*flesh*) vivo; inesperto

raw' deal' *s* trattamento brutale e ingiusto

raw'hide' *s* pelle greggia

raw' mate'rial *s* materia prima

ray [re] *s* raggio; (*fish*) razza

rayon ['re·ɑn] *s* raion *m*

raze [rez] *tr* radere al suolo

razor ['rezər] *s* rasoio

ra'zor blade' *s* lametta

ra'zor strop' *s* coramella

razz [ræz] *s* (slang) pernacchia || *tr* (slang) prendere in giro

reach [ritʃ] *s* portata; estensione; **out**

of reach (of) fuori della portata (di); oltre alle possibilità (di); fuori tiro (di); **within reach of** alla portata di || *tr* raggiungere; toccare; (*customers*) guadagnare || *intr* estendere la mano; **to reach for** cercare di raggiungere

react [rɪ'ækt] *intr* reagire

reaction [rɪ'ækʃən] *s* reazione

reactionar·y [rɪ'ækʃə‚neri] *adj* reazionario || *s* (-ies) reazionario

reactor [rɪ'æktər] *s* reattore *m*

read [rid] *v* (*pret & pp* **read** [red]) *tr* leggere; (*s.o.'s thoughts*) leggere in; **to read over** ripassare || *intr* leggere; saper leggere; essere concepito, e.g., **your cable reads thus** il vostro telegramma è concepito così; leggersi, e.g., **this books reads easily** questo libro si legge facilmente; **to read on** continuare a leggere

reader ['ridər] *s* lettore *m*; libro di lettura, sillabo

readily ['redɪli] *adv* velocemente; facilmente; di buona voglia

reading ['ridɪŋ] *s* lettura; dizione

read'ing desk' *s* leggìo

read'ing glass' *s* lente *f* d'ingrandimento; **reading glasses** occhiali *mpl* per la lettura

read'ing lamp' *s* lampada da scrittoio

read'ing room' *s* sala di lettura

read·y ['redi] *adj* (-ier; -iest) pronto; disponibile; **to make ready** prepararare; prepararsi || *v* (*pret & pp* **-ied**) *tr* preparare || *intr* prepararsi

read'y cash' *s* denaro contante

read'y-made cloth'ing *s* confezioni *fpl*

read'y-made suit' *s* vestito già fatto

reaffirm [‚ri·ə'fʌrm] *tr* riaffermare

reagent [rɪ'edʒənt] *s* reagente *m*

real ['ri·əl] *adj* effettivo, reale

re'al estate' *s* beni *mpl* immobili, proprietà *f* immobiliare

re'al-estate' *adj* immobiliare, fondiario

realism ['ri·ə‚lɪzəm] *s* realismo

realist ['ri·əlɪst] *s* realista *mf*

realistic [‚ri·ə'lɪstɪk] *adj* realistico

reali·ty [rɪ'ælɪti] *s* (-ties) realtà *f*

realize ['ri·ə‚laɪz] *tr* rendersi conto di; concretare; realizzare || *intr* convertire proprietà in contanti

realm [relm] *s* regno

realtor ['ri·əl‚tor] or ['ri·əltər] *s* (trademark) agente *m* d'immobili membro dell'associazione nazionale

realty ['ri·əlti] *s* proprietà *f* immobiliare

ream [rim] *s* risma; **reams** pagine *fpl* e pagine || *tr* alesare

reamer ['rimər] *s* (mach) alesatore *m*; (dentistry) fresa

reap [rip] *tr & intr* (*to cut*) mietere; (*to gather*) raccogliere

reaper ['ripər] *s* (person) mietitore *m*; (mach) mietitrice *f*

reappear [‚ri·ə'pɪr] *intr* ricomparire, riapparire

reappearance [‚ri·ə'pɪrəns] *s* riapparizione, ricomparsa

reapportionment [‚ri·ə'porʃənmənt] *s* ridistribuzione

rear [rɪr] *adj* posteriore, di dietro || *s*

retro, di dietro; posteriore *m;* (mil) retroguardia || *tr* alzare, elevare; allevare, educare || *intr (said of a horse)* impennarsi

rear′ ad′miral *s* contrammiraglio

rear′ drive′ *s* trazione posteriore

rear′ end′ *s* retro, di dietro; (coll) posteriore *m;* (aut) retrotreno

rearmament [ri′ɑrməmənt] *s* riarmo

rear′-view mir′ror *s* specchietto retrovisivo

rear′ win′dow *s* (aut) lunetta posteriore

reason [′rizən] *s* ragione; **by reason of** per causa di; **to bring s.o. to reason** indurre qlcu alla ragione; **to stand to reason** esser logico || *tr & intr* ragionare

reasonable [′rizənəbəl] *adj* ragionevole

reassessment [ˌri-ə′sesmənt] *s* rivalutazione

reassure [ˌri-ə′ʃʊr] *tr* rassicurare, riassicurare

reawaken [ˌri-ə′wekən] *tr* risvegliare || *intr* risvegliarsi

rebate [′ribet] or [ri′bet] *s* ribasso || *tr* ribassare

rebel [′rebəl] *adj & s* ribelle *mf* || **re•bel** [ri′bel] *v (pret & pp -belled; ger -belling) intr* ribellarsi

rebellion [ri′beljən] *s* ribellione

rebellious [ri′beljəs] *adj* ribelle

re•bind [ri′baɪnd] *v (pret & pp- bound* [′baʊnd]) *tr* rifasciare; (bb) rilegare

rebirth [′ribʌrθ] or [ri′bʌrθ] *s* rinascita

rebore [ri′bor] *tr* rialesare, rettificare

rebound [′ri‚baʊnd] or [ri′baʊnd] *s* rimbalzo || [ri′baʊnd] *intr* rimbalzare

rebroad′casting sta′tion *s* stazione ripetitrice

rebuff [ri′bʌf] *s* rifiuto || *tr* respingere, rifiutare

rebuild [ri′bɪld] *v (pret & pp -built* [′bɪlt]) *tr* ricostruire, riedificare

rebuke [ri′bjuk] *s* rabbuffo || *tr* rabbuffare

re•but [ri′bʌt] *v (pret & pp -butted; ger -butting) tr* confutare

rebuttal [ri′bʌtəl] *s* confutazione

recall [ri′kɔl] or [′rikɔl] *s* richiamo; revoca || [ri′kɔl] *tr* richiamare; ricordare, ricordarsi di; richiamare alla memoria

recant [ri′kænt] *tr* ritrattare || *intr* ritrattarsi

re•cap [′ri‚kæp] or [ri′kæp] *v (pret & pp -capped; ger -capping) tr* ricapitolare, riepilogare; *(a tire)* rifare il battistrada a

recapitulate [ˌrikə‚pɪtʃə′le/ən] *s* ricapitolazione, riepilogo

re•cast [′ri‚kæst] or [ri′‚kast] *s* rifusione || [ri′kæst] or [ri′kast] *v (pret & pp -cast) tr* rifondere

recede [ri′sid] *intr* ritirarsi, allontanarsi; recedere, retrocedere; *(said, e.g., of chin)* sfuggire

receipt [ri′sit] *s* ricevimento; *(acknowledgment of payment)* ricevuta; *(recipe)* ricetta; **receipts** incasso, introito || *tr* quietanzare

receive [ri′siv] *tr* ricevere; *(stolen goods)* ricettare; *(to have inflicted upon one)* subire || *intr* ricevere

receiver [ri′sivər] *s* ricevitore *m;* ricettatore *m;* (law) curatore *m* fallimentare; (telp) auricolare *m*

receiv′ing set′ *s* apparecchio radioricevente

receiv′ing tell′er *s* cassiere *m* incaricato delle riscossioni

recent [′risənt] *adj* recente

recently [′risəntli] *adv* recentemente, di recente

receptacle [ri′septəkəl] *s* recipiente *m;* (elec) presa

reception [ri′sepʃən] *s* accoglienza; *(function)* ricevimento

recep′tion desk′ *s* ufficio informazioni, bureau *m*

receptionist [ri′sepʃənɪst] *s* accoglitrice *f;* *(male)* usciere *m*

receptive [ri′septɪv] *adj* ricettivo

recess [ri′ses] or [′rises] *s* intermezzo, interludio; ora di ricreazione; *(in a line)* rientranza; *(in a wall)* nicchia, alcova; (fig) recesso || [ri′ses] *tr* aggiornare, dare vacanza a; incassare, mettere in una nicchia || *intr* aggiornarsi, prendersi vacanza

recession [ri′seʃən] *s* ritirata; processione finale; (com) recessione

recipe [′resɪ‚pi] *s* ricetta

reciprocal [ri′sɪprəkəl] *adj* reciproco

reciprocity [ˌresɪ′prɑsɪti] *s* reciprocità *f*

recital [ri′saɪtəl] *s* narrazione; *(of music or poetry)* recital *m*

recite [ri′saɪt] *tr* raccontare; *(music or poetry)* recitare

reckless [′reklɪs] *adj* temerario, spericolato

reckon [′rekən] *tr* calcolare; considerare; (coll) supporre || *intr* contare; **to reckon with** prevedere, tener conto di

reclaim [ri′klem] *tr (land)* sanare, prosciugare; *(substances)* rigenerare; (fig) rigenerare

recline [ri′klaɪn] *tr* reclinare || *intr* reclinarsi, adagiarsi

recluse [ri′klus] or [′reklus] *adj & s* recluso

recognition [ˌrekəg′nɪʃən] *s* riconoscimento

recognize [′rekəg‚naɪz] *tr* riconoscere

recoil [ri′kɔɪl] *s* indietreggiamento; *(of a firearm)* rinculo || *intr* indietreggiare; rinculare

recollect [ˌrekə′lekt] *tr & intr* ricordare

recollection [ˌrekə′lekʃən] *s* ricordo

recommend [ˌrekə′mend] *tr* raccomandare

recompense [′rekəm‚pens] *s* ricompensa || *tr* ricompensare

reconcile [′rekən‚saɪl] *tr* riconciliare; **to reconcile oneself** rassegnarsi

reconnaissance [ri′kɑnɪsəns] *s* ricognizione

reconnoiter [ˌrekə′nɔɪtər] or [ˌrikə′nɔɪtər] *tr & intr* perlustrare

reconsider [ˌrikən′sɪdər] *tr* riconsiderare

reconstruct [ˌrikən'strʌkt] *tr* ricostruire

reconversion [ˌrikən'vʌrʒən] *s* riconversione

record ['rekərd] *s* registrazione; annotazione; (*official report*) verbale *m*, protocollo; (*criminal*) fedina sporca; (*of a phonograph*) disco; (*educ*) documenti *mpl* scolastici; (*sports*) record *m*, primato; **off the record** confidenziale; confidenzialmente; **records** annali *mpl*, documenti *mpl*; **to break a record** battere un record || [rɪ'kɔrd] *tr* registrare; mettere a verbale; (*e.g., a song*) incidere

rec'ord break'er *s* (sports) primatista *mf*

rec'ord chang'er ['tʃendʒər] *s* cambiadischi *m*

recorder [rɪ'kɔrdər] *s* (*apparatus*) registratore *m;* (law) cancelliere *m;* (mus) flauto a imboccatura a tubo

rec'ord hold'er *s* (sports) primatista *mf*

recording [rɪ'kɔrdɪŋ] *s* registrazione; (*of a record*) incisione; (*record*) disco

record'ing sec'retary *s* cancelliere *m*

rec'ord play'er *s* giradischi *m*

recount ['ri ˌkaunt] *s* nuovo conteggio || [ri'kaunt] *tr* (*to count again*) ricontare || [rɪ'kaunt] *tr* (*to narrate*) raccontare

recourse [rɪ'kors] *or* ['rikors] *s* ricorso; (com) rivalsa; **to have recourse to** ricorrere a

recover [rɪ'kʌvər] *tr* ricuperare, riacquistare; (*a substance*) rigenerare; **to recover consciousness** riaversi, riprendere conoscenza || *intr* rimettersi; guadagnare una causa

recover·y [rɪ'kʌvəri] *s* (**-ies**) ricupero; guarigione; **past recovery** incurabile

recreant ['rekrɪ-ənt] *adj & s* codardo; traditore *m*

recreation [ˌrekrɪ'eʃən] *s* ricreazione

recruit [rɪ'krut] *s* recluta || *tr & intr* reclutare

rectangle ['rek ˌtæŋgəl] *s* rettangolo

rectifier ['rektə ˌfaɪ-ər] *s* rettificatore *m;* (elec) raddrizzatore *m*

recti·fy ['rektɪ ˌfaɪ] *v* (*pret & pp* **-fied**) *tr* rettificare; (elec) raddrizzare

rectitude ['rektɪ ˌtud] *or* ['rektɪ ˌtjud] *s* rettitudine *f*

rec·tum ['rektəm] *s* (**-tums** *or* **-ta** [tə]) retto

recumbent [rɪ'kʌmbənt] *adj* sdraiato

recuperate [rɪ'kjupə ˌret] *tr* ricuperare || *intr* ristabilirsi, rimettersi

re·cur [rɪ'kʌr] *v* (*pret & pp* **-curred**; *ger* **-curring**) *intr* ricorrere; ritornare; tornare a mente

recurrent [rɪ'kʌrənt] *adj* ricorrente

recycle [ri'saɪkəl] *tr* riconvertire; (*e.g., in chemical industry*) riciclare

red [red] *adj* (*redder*; *reddest*) rosso || *s* rosso; **in the red** in debito , in rosso || **Red** *adj & s* (*Communist*) rosso

red'bait' *tr* dare del comunista a

red'bird' *s* cardinale *m*

red-blooded ['red ˌblʌdɪd] *adj* sanguigno; vigoroso

red'breast' *s* pettirosso

red'bud' *s* siliquastro

red'cap' *s* (Brit) poliziotto militare; (U.S.A.) facchino

red' cell' *s* globulo rosso

red' cent' *s*—**to not have a red cent** (coll) non avere il becco di un quattrino

Red' Cross' *s* Croce Rossa

redden ['redən] *tr* arrossare || *intr* arrossire

redeem [rɪ'dim] *tr* redimere; (*a promise*) disimpegnare

redeemer [rɪ'dimər] *s* redentore *m*

redemption [rɪ'dempʃən] *s* redenzione; disimpegno

red-handed ['red'hændɪd] *adj*—**to be caught red-handed** esser colto sul fatto or con le mani nel sacco

red'head' *s* persona dai capelli rossi

red' her'ring *s* argomento usato per sviare l'attenzione; aringa affumicata

red-hot' *adj* rovente, incandescente; fresco fresco, appena uscito

rediscover [ˌridɪs'kʌvər] *tr* riscoprire

red'-let'ter *adj* memorabile

red'-light' dis'trict *s* quartiere *m* delle case di tolleranza

red' man' *s* pellerossa *m*

re-do ['ri'du] *v* (*pret* **-did** ['dɪd]; *pp* **-done** ['dʌn]) *tr* rifare

redolent ['redələnt] *adj* fragrante, profumato; **redolent of** che sa di

redoubt [rɪ'daut] *s* (mil) ridotta

redound [rɪ'daund] *intr* ridondare

red' pep'per *s* pepe *m* di Caienna

redress [rɪ'dres] *or* ['ridres] *s* riparazione, risarcimento || [rɪ'dres] *tr* riparare, risarcire

red'skin' *s* pellerossa *mf*

red' tape' *s* trafila, burocrazia

reduce [rɪ'djus] *or* [rɪ'dus] *tr* ridurre; diluire; (mil) retrocedere; (*a hernia*) (surg) sbrigliare || *intr* ridursi; (*to lose weight*) dimagrire

reducing [rɪ'djusɪŋ] *or* [rɪ'dusɪŋ] *adj* dimagrante; (chem) riducente

reduction [rɪ'dʌkʃən] *s* riduzione

redundant [rɪ'dʌndənt] *adj* ridondante

red'wood' *s* sequoia

reed [rid] *s* (*stalk*) calamo; (*plant*) canna; (mus) linguetta; (mus) strumento a linguetta

reedit [ri'edɪt] *tr* rifondere

reef [rif] *s* scoglio, barriera; (naut) terzarolo; (min) vena, filone *m* || *tr* (*sail*) imbrogliare

reefer ['rifər] *s* giacchetta a doppio petto; (slang) sigaretta di marijuana

reek [rik] *intr* puzzare; sudare, evaporare, fumare

reel [ril] *s* (*spool*) bobina; (*sway*) vacillamento; (*for fishing*) mulinello; **off the reel** senza esitazione || *tr* bobinare; **to reel off** rifilare || *intr* barcollare

reelection [ˌri-ɪ'lekʃən] *s* rielezione

reenlist [ˌri-en'lɪst] *tr* arruolare di nuovo || *intr* arruolarsi di nuovo

reen-try [rɪ'entri] *s* (**-tries**) rientro

reexamination [ˌri-eg ˌzæmɪ'neʃən] *s* riesame *m*

re·fer [rɪ'fʌr] v (pret & pp **-ferred;** ger **-ferring**) tr riferire || intr riferirsi

referee [ˌrɛfə'ri] s arbitro || tr & intr arbitrare

reference ['rɛfərəns] s riferimento; (testimonial) referenza; (e.g., in a book) rinvio, rimando

ref'erence book' s libro di consultazione

referen·dum [ˌrɛfə'rɛndəm] s (-dums or -da [də]) referendum m

refill ['rifɪl] s ricambio || [rɪ'fɪl] tr riempire di nuovo

refine [rɪ'faɪn] tr raffinare

refinement [rɪ'faɪnmənt] s raffinatezza; (of oil) raffinatura

refiner·y [rɪ'faɪnəri] s (-ies) raffineria

reflect [rɪ'flɛkt] tr riflettere || intr riflettere, riflettersi

reflection [rɪ'flɛkʃən] s riflessione

reflex ['riflɛks] adj riflesso || s riflesso; (camera) reflex m

reflexive [rɪ'flɛksɪv] adj riflessivo

reforestation [ˌrifɑrɪs'teʃən] or [ˌrɪfɔrɪs'teʃən] s rimboschimento

reform [rɪ'fɔrm] s riforma || tr riformare || intr correggersi

reformation [ˌrɛfər'meʃən] s riforma || **Reformation** s—**the Reformation** la Riforma

reformato·ry [rɪ'fɔrmə,tori] adj riformativo || s (-ries) riformatorio

reformer [rɪ'fɔrmər] s riformatore m

reform' school' s riformatorio

refraction [rɪ'frækʃən] s rifrazione

refrain [rɪ'fren] s ritornello, intercalare m || intr astenersi

refresh [rɪ'frɛʃ] tr rinfrescare; ristorare || intr ristorarsi

refreshing [rɪ'frɛʃɪŋ] adj rinfrescante; ristoratore; ricreativo

refreshment [rɪ'frɛʃmənt] s rinfresco

refrigerate [rɪ'frɪdʒə,ret] tr refrigerare

refrigerator [rɪ'frɪdʒə,retɑr] s refrigerante m, frigorifero

refrig'erator car' s vagone frigorifero

re·fuel [rɪ'fjul] v (pret & pp **-fueled** or **-fuelled;** ger **-fueling** or **-fuelling**) tr rifornire di carburante || intr rifornirsi di carburante

refuge ['rɛfjudʒ] s rifugio; scampo; **to take refuge (in)** rifugiarsi (in)

refugee [ˌrɛfju'dʒi] s rifugiato

refund [rɪ'fʌnd] s rifusione || [rɪ'fʌnd] tr (to repay) rifondere || [rɪ'fʌnd] (bonds) consolidare; (to fund anew) rifondere

refurnish [rɪ'fʌrnɪʃ] tr riammobiliare

refusal [rɪ'fjuzəl] s rifiuto

refuse ['rɛfjus] s rifiuto, spazzatura || [rɪ'fjuz] tr rifiutare; **to refuse to** rifiutarsi di

refute [rɪ'fjut] tr smentire, confutare

regain [rɪ'gen] tr riguadagnare; **to regain consciousness** tornare in sé

regal ['rigəl] adj reale, regale

regale [rɪ'gel] tr intrattenere, rallegrare

regalia [rɪ'gelɪ·ə] spl (of royalty) prerogative fpl reali; alta uniforme

regard [rɪ'gɑrd] s riguardo; (look)

sguardo; (esteem) rispetto; **in regard to** rispetto a; **regards** rispetti mpl; **warm regards** cordiali saluti mpl; **without regard to** senza considerare || tr considerare; osservare; concernere; **as regards** per quanto concerne

regarding [rɪ'gɑrdɪŋ] prep per quanto concerne

regardless [rɪ'gɑrdlɪs] adj incurante || adv ciò nonostante; costi quello che costi; **regardless of** malgrado

regatta [rɪ'gætə] s regata

regen·cy ['ridʒənsi] s (-cies) reggenza

regenerate [rɪ'dʒɛnə,ret] tr rigenerare || intr rigenerarsi

regent ['ridʒənt] s reggente mf

regicide ['rɛdʒɪ,saɪd] s (act) regicidio; (person) regicida mf

regiment ['rɛdʒɪmənt] s reggimento || ['rɛdʒɪ,mɛnt] tr irreggimentare

regimental [ˌrɛdʒɪ'mɛntəl] adj reggimentale || **regimentals** spl uniforme f reggimentale

region ['ridʒən] s regione

register ['rɛdʒɪstər] s registro; (for controlling the flow of air) regolatore m dell'aria || tr registrare; (e.g., a student) iscrivere; (e.g., anger) dimostrare; (a letter) raccomandare || intr registrarsi; iscriversi; fare impressione

reg'istered let'ter s raccomandata

reg'istered nurse' s infermiera diplomata

registrar ['rɛdʒɪs,trɑr] s registratore m, archivista mf; (of deeds) ricevitore m

registration [ˌrɛdʒɪs'treʃən] s registrazione; (e.g., of a student) iscrizione; (of mail) raccomandazione

registra'tion fee' s diritto di segreteria

re·gret [rɪ'grɛt] s pentimento, rammarico; **regrets** scuse fpl || v (pret & pp **-gretted;** ger **-gretting**) tr rimpiangere; **to regret to** essere spiacente di

regrettable [rɪ'grɛtəbəl] adj deplorevole

regular ['rɛgjələr] adj regolare; (life) regolato; (coll) vero || s cliente m abituale; (mil) effettivo

regularity [ˌrɛgju'lærɪti] s regolarità f

regularize ['rɛgjələ,raɪz] tr regolarizzare

regulate ['rɛgjə,let] tr regolare

regulation [ˌrɛgjə'leʃən] s regolazione; (rule) regolamento

rehabilitate [ˌrihə'bɪlɪ,tet] tr riabilitare

rehearsal [rɪ'hʌrsəl] s prova

rehearse [rɪ'hʌrs] tr provare || intr fare le prove

rehiring [ri'haɪrɪŋ] s riassunzione

reign [ren] s regno || intr regnare

reimburse [ˌri·ɪm'bʌrs] tr rimborsare

rein [ren] s redine f; **to give full rein to** dare briglia sciolta a || tr guidare con le redini; frenare

reincarnation [ˌri·ɪnkɑr'neʃən] s reincarnazione

reindeer ['ren,dɪr] s renna

reinforce [ˌri·ɪn'fors] tr rinforzare; (a wall) armare

re'inforced con'crete s cemento armato

reinforcement [ˌriˑɪnˈforsmənt] *s* rinforzo

reinstate [ˌriˑɪnˈstet] *tr* reintegrare

reiterate [riˈɪtəˌret] *tr* reiterare

reject [ˈridʒekt] *s* rigetto, rifiuto; **rejects** scarti *mpl* ‖ [rɪˈdʒekt] *tr* rigettare; (*to refuse*) rifiutare

rejection [rɪˈdʒekʃən] *s* rigetto; rifiuto

rejoice [rɪˈdʒɔɪs] *intr* rallegrarsi

rejoin [rɪˈdʒɔɪn] *tr* raggiungere; (*to reunite*) riunire; (*to reply*) rispondere

rejoinder [rɪˈdʒɔɪndər] *s* risposta; (*law*) controreplica

rejuvenation [rɪˌdʒuvɪˈneʃən] *s* ringiovanimento

rekindle [riˈkɪndəl] *tr* riaccendere

relapse [rɪˈlæps] *s* ricaduta ‖ *intr* ricadere

relate [rɪˈlet] *tr* mettere in relazione; (*to tell*) narrare

relation [rɪˈleʃən] *s* relazione; (*account*) resoconto; (*relative*) parente *mf*; (*kinship*) parentela; **in relation to** or **with** in relazione a

relationship [rɪˈleʃənˌʃɪp] *s* rapporto, relazione; (*kinship*) parentela

relative [ˈrelətɪv] *adj* relativo ‖ *s* congiunto, parente *mf*

relativity [ˌreləˈtɪvɪti] *s* relatività *f*

relax [rɪˈlæks] *tr* rilasciare, rilassare ‖ *intr* rilasciarsi, rilassarsi

relaxation [ˌrilæksˈeʃən] *s* distensione; (*entertainment*) ricreazione

relaxa'tion of ten'sion *s* distensione

relaxing [rɪˈlæksɪŋ] *adj* rilassante; divertente

relay [ˈrile] or [rɪˈle] *s* (elec) relè *m*; (rad) ripetitore *m*; (mil, sports) staffetta; (sports) corsa a staffetta ‖ *v* (*pret & pp* -**layed**) *tr* trasmettere, ritrasmettere ‖ [rɪˈle] *v* (*pret & pp* -**laid**) *tr* rimettere, porre di nuovo

re'lay race' *s* corsa a staffetta

release [rɪˈlis] *s* (*e.g., from jail*) liberazione; (*from obligation*) disimpegno; (*for publication*) autorizzazione; (*mov*) distribuzione; (*journ*) comunicato; (*aer*) lancio; (*mach*) scappamento ‖ *tr* liberare; disimpegnare; autorizzare la pubblicazione di; (*mov*) distribuire; (*a bomb*) (*aer*) lanciare; **to release s.o. from a debt** rimettere un debito a qlcu

relent [rɪˈlent] *intr* placarsi

relentless [rɪˈlentlɪs] *adj* implacabile

relevant [ˈrelɪvənt] *adj* pertinente

reliable [rɪˈlaɪˑəbəl] *adj* (*person*) fidato; (*source*) attendibile

reliance [rɪˈlaɪˑəns] *s* fiducia, fede *f*

relic [ˈrelɪk] *s* reliquia

relief [rɪˈlif] *s* sollievo; sussidio; (*prominence*; *projection*) rilievo; (mil) cambio; **in relief** in rilievo; **on relief** sotto sussidio

relieve [rɪˈliv] *tr* (*e.g., pain*) alleviare; (*e.g., a load*) sgravare; (mil) rilevare

religion [rɪˈlɪdʒən] *s* religione

religious [rɪˈlɪdʒəs] *adj* religioso

relinquish [rɪˈlɪŋkwɪʃ] *tr* abbandonare

relish [ˈrelɪʃ] *s* piacere *m*, gusto; sapore *m*, aroma *m*; (culin) condimento ‖ *tr* gustare, apprezzare; dare gusto a

reluctance [rɪˈlʌktəns] *s* riluttanza

reluctant [rɪˈlʌktənt] *adj* riluttante

re·ly [rɪˈlaɪ] *v* (*pret & pp* -**lied**) *intr* fare assegnamento; **to rely on** fidarsi di, fondarsi su

remain [rɪˈmen] *s*—**remains** resti *mpl*; resti *mpl* mortali ‖ *intr* restare, rimanere

remainder [rɪˈmendər] *s* resto, restante *m*; (*unsold books*) fondi *mpl* di libreria ‖ *tr* vendere come rimanenza

re·make [riˈmek] *v* (*pret & pp* -**made** [ˈmed]) *tr* rifare

remark [rɪˈmɑrk] *s* osservazione, rimarco ‖ *tr & intr* osservare; **to remark on** fare osservazioni su

remarkable [rɪˈmɑrkəbəl] *adj* notevole

remar·ry [rɪˈmæri] *v* (*pret & pp* -**ried**) *intr* riprendere moglie, risposarsi

reme·dy [ˈremɪdi] *s* (-**dies**) rimedio ‖ *v* (*pret & pp* -**died**) *tr* rimediare (with *dat*)

remember [rɪˈmembər] *tr* ricordarsi di; (*to send greetings to*) ricordare ‖ *intr* ricordare, ricordarsi

remembrance [rɪˈmembrəns] *s* rimembranza, ricordo

remind [rɪˈmaɪnd] *tr* rammentare

reminder [rɪˈmaɪndər] *s* promemoria

reminisce [ˌremɪˈnɪs] *intr* ricordare il passato

reminiscence [ˌremɪˈnɪsəns] *s* reminiscenza

remiss [rɪˈmɪs] *adj* negligente

re·mit [rɪˈmɪt] *v* (*pret & pp* -**mitted**; *ger* -**mitting**) *tr* rimettere; (*to a lower court*) (law) rinviare

remittance [rɪˈmɪtəns] *s* rimessa

remnant [ˈremnənt] *s* (*remaining quantity*) rimanente *m*; (*of cloth*) scampolo; vestigio; **remnants** (*of merchandise*) rimanenze *fpl*, fondi *mpl* di magazzino

remod·el [riˈmɑdəl] *v* (*pret & pp* -**eled** or -**elled**; *ger* -**eling** or -**elling**) *tr* rimodellare; ricostruire

remonstrance [rɪˈmɑnstrəns] *s* rimostranza

remonstrate [rɪˈmɑnstret] *intr* protestare, rimostrare; **to remonstrate with** rimostrare a

remorse [rɪˈmɔrs] *s* rimorso

remorseful [rɪˈmɔrsfəl] *adj* tormentato dal rimorso, pentito

remote [rɪˈmot] *adj* remoto

remote' control' *s* telecomando

removable [rɪˈmuvəbəl] *adj* amovibile

removal [rɪˈmuvəl] *s* rimozione; trasferimento; (*dismissal*) destituzione

remove [rɪˈmuv] *tr* rimuovere; (*one's jacket*) togliersi, cavarsi; (*from office*) destituire; eliminare ‖ *intr* trasferirsi; andarsene

remuneration [rɪˌmjunəˈreʃən] *s* rimunerazione

renaissance [ˌrenəˈsɑns] or [rɪˈnesəns] *s* rinascimento, rinascita ‖ **Renaissance** *s* Rinascimento

rend [rend] *v* (*pret & pp* **rent** [rent]) *tr* (*to tear*) stracciare; (*to split*) fendere, squarciare

render [ˈrendər] *tr* (*justice*) rendere;

(*a service*) fare; (*aid*) prestare; (*a bill*) presentare; (*to translate*) tradurre; (*a piece of music*) interpretare; (*e.g., fat*) struggere

rendez·vous ['randə,vu] *s* (**-vous** [,vuz]) appuntamento; (*in space*) incontro ‖ *v* (*pret & pp* **-voused** [,vud]; *ger* **-vousing** [,vu·ɪŋ]) *intr* incontrarsi

rendition [ren'dɪʃən] *s* restituzione, resa; traduzione; interpretazione

renege [rɪ'nɪg] *s* rifiuto ‖ *intr* rifiutare; (coll) venire meno

renew [rɪ'nju] *or* [rɪ'nu] *tr* rinnovare ‖ *intr* rinnovarsi

renewal [rɪ'nju·əl] *or* [rɪ'nu·əl] *s* rinnovo, rinnovamento

renounce [rɪ'nauns] *tr* rinunziare (*with dat*); ripudiare

renovate ['renə,vet] *tr* rinnovare; (*a building*) restaurare; (*a room*) rimettere a nuovo

renown [rɪ'naun] *s* rinomanza

renowned [rɪ'naund] *adj* rinomato

rent [rent] *adj* scisso ‖ *s* fitto, pigione; (*tear*) squarcio ‖ *tr* locare, dare a pigione ‖ *intr* prendere a pigione

rental ['rentəl] *s* affitto

renter ['rentər] *s* affittuario, locatario

renunciation [rɪ,nʌnsɪ'eʃən] *or* [rɪ,nʌn/ɪ'eʃən] *s* rinunzia

reopen [ri'opən] *tr* riaprire ‖ *intr* riaprirsi

reopening [ri'opənɪŋ] *s* riapertura

reorganize [ri'ɔrgə,naɪz] *tr* riorganizzare ‖ *intr* riorganizzarsi

repair [rɪ'per] *s* riparazione; **in good repair** in buono stato ‖ *tr* riparare ‖ *intr* riparare, dirigersi

repair'man' *s* (**-men**) aggiustatore *m*

repaper [ri'pepər] *tr* ritappezzare

reparation [,repə'reʃən] *s* riparazione

repartee [,repɑr'ti] *s* replica arguta, rimando

repast [rɪ'pæst] *or* [rɪ'pɑst] *s* pasto

repatriate [ri'petrɪ,et] *tr* rimpatriare

re·pay [rɪ'pe] *v* (*pret & pp* **-paid** ['ped]) *tr* ripagare

repayment [rɪ'pemənt] *s* rimborso; risarcimento, compensazione

repeal [rɪ'pil] *s* revoca, abrogazione ‖ *tr* revocare, abrogare

repeat [rɪ'pit] *s* ripetizione ‖ *tr* ripetere ‖ *intr* ripetere; (*said of food*) tornare a gola

re·pel [rɪ'pel] *v* (*pret & pp* **-pelled**; *ger* **-pelling**) *tr* respingere, ricacciare; ripugnare (*with dat*)

repent [rɪ'pent] *tr* pentirsi di ‖ *intr* pentirsi, ravvedersi

repentance [rɪ'pentəns] *s* pentimento

repentant [rɪ'pentənt] *adj* pentito

repercussion [,ripər'kʌʃən] *s* ripercussione

reperto·ry ['repər,tori] *s* (**-ries**) (com) magazzino; (theat) repertorio

repetition [,repɪ'tɪʃən] *s* ripetizione

repine [rɪ'paɪn] *intr* lamentarsi

replace [rɪ'ples] *tr* (*to put back*) rimettere; (*to take the place of*) rimpiazzare

replaceable [rɪ'plesəbəl] *adj* sostituibile

replacement [rɪ'plesmənt] *s* rimpiazzo, sostituzione; **as a replacement for** al posto di

replenish [rɪ'plenɪʃ] *tr* rifornire

replete [rɪ'plit] *adj* pieno zeppo

replica ['replɪkə] *s* replica

re·ply [rɪ'plaɪ] *s* (**-plies**) risposta ‖ *v* (*pret & pp* **-plied**) *tr & intr* rispondere

report [rɪ'port] *s* rapporto, informazione; voce *f*, rumore *m*; (*of a physician*) responso; (*of a firearm*) detonazione ‖ *tr* riportare, rapportare; denunziare ‖ *intr* fare un rapporto; fare il cronista; presentarsi; **to report sick** (mil) marcare visita

report' card' *s* pagella

reportedly [rɪ'portɪdli] *adv* secondo la voce comune

reporter [rɪ'portər] *s* cronista *mf*, reporter *m*

reporting [rɪ'portɪŋ] *s* reportage *m*

repose [rɪ'poz] *s* riposo ‖ *tr* posare, riporre ‖ *intr* riposare

reprehend [,reprɪ'hend] *tr* riprovare, rimproverare

represent [,reprɪ'zent] *tr* rappresentare

representation [,reprɪsen'teʃən] *s* rappresentazione; protesta; **representations dichiarazioni *fpl**

representative [,reprɪ'zentətɪv] *adj* rappresentativo ‖ *s* rappresentante *mf*; (pol) deputato

repress [rɪ'pres] *tr* reprimere

repression [rɪ'preʃən] *s* repressione

reprieve [rɪ'priv] *s* tregua temporanea; sospensione della pena capitale ‖ *tr* accordare una tregua a; sospendere l'esecuzione di

reprimand ['reprɪ,mænd] *or* ['reprɪ,mand] *s* sgridata, ramanzina ‖ *tr* sgridare, rimproverare

reprint [rɪ'prɪnt] *s* ristampa; (*offprint*) estratto ‖ [ri'prɪnt] *tr* ristampare

reprisal [rɪ'praɪzəl] *s* rappresaglia

reproach [rɪ'protʃ] *s* rimprovero; vituperio ‖ *tr* rimproverare; **to reproach s.o. for s.th** rimproverare qlcu di qlco, rimproverare qlco a qlcu

reproduce [,riprə'djus] *or* [,riprə'dus] *tr* riprodurre ‖ *intr* riprodursi

reproduction [,riprə'dʌkʃən] *s* riproduzione

reproof [rɪ'pruf] *s* rimprovero

reprove [rɪ'pruv] *tr* rimproverare; disapprovare

reptile ['reptɪl] *s* rettile *m*

republic [rɪ'pʌblɪk] *s* repubblica

republican [rɪ'pʌblɪkən] *adj & s* repubblicano

repudiate [rɪ'pjudɪ,et] *tr* ripudiare; rinnegare

repugnant [rɪ'pʌgnənt] *adj* ripugnante

repulse [rɪ'pʌls] *s* rifiuto; sconfitta ‖ *tr* rifiutare; (*e.g., an enemy*) sconfiggere

repulsive [rɪ'pʌlsɪv] *adj* ripulsivo

reputation [,repjə'teʃən] *s* reputazione

repute [rɪ'pjut] *s* reputazione, fama ‖ *tr* reputare

reputedly [rɪ'pjutɪdlɪ] *adv* secondo l'opinione corrente

request [rɪ'kwɛst] *s* domanda, richiesta; **at the request of** su domanda di ‖ *tr* richiedere

Requiem ['rɪkwɪ ,ɛm] *or* ['rɛkwɪ ,ɛm] *adj* di Requiem ‖ *s* Requiem *m & f*; Messa di Requiem

require [rɪ'kwaɪr] *tr* richiedere

requirement [rɪ'kwaɪrmənt] *s* requisito; richiesta, fabbisogno

requisite ['rɛkwɪzɪt] *adj* requisito, richiesto ‖ *s* requisito

requisition [,rɛkwɪ'zɪʃən] *s* requisizione

requital [rɪ'kwaɪtəl] *s* contraccambio

requite [rɪ'kwaɪt] *tr* (*e.g., an injury*) contraccambiare; (*a person*) contraccambiare (with *dat*)

re-read [ri'rid] *v* (*pret & pp* -**read** ['rɛd]) *tr* rileggere

resale ['ri ,sɛl] *or* ['ri'sɛl] *s* rivendita

rescind [rɪ'sɪnd] *tr* annullare, cancellare; (law) rescindere

rescue ['rɛskju] *s* salvataggio, liberazione; **to go to the rescue of** andare al soccorso di ‖ *tr* salvare, liberare, soccorrere

research [rɪ'sʌrtʃ] *or* ['risʌrtʃ] *s* ricerca, indagine *f* ‖ *intr* investigare

re-sell [ri'sɛl] *v* (*pret & pp* -**sold** ['sold]) *tr* rivendere

resemblance [rɪ'zɛmbləns] *s* somiglianza

resemble [rɪ'zɛmbəl] *tr* somigliare (with *dat*), rassomigliare (with *dat*); **to resemble one another** rassomigliarsi

resent [rɪ'zɛnt] *tr* (*a remark*) risentirsi per; (*a person*) risentirsi con

resentful [rɪ'zɛntfəl] *adj* risentito

resentment [rɪ'zɛntmənt] *s* risentimento

reservation [,rɛzər'veʃən] *s* riserva, (*e.g., for a room*) prenotazione

reserve [rɪ'zʌrv] *s* riserva; (*self-restraint*) riserbo, contegno ‖ *tr* riservare; prenotare

reservist [rɪ'zʌrvɪst] *s* riservista *m*

reservoir ['rɛzər ,vwɑr] *s* serbatoio, cisterna; (*large storage place for supplying community with water*) bacino di riserva; (fig) pozzo

re-set [ri'sɛt] *v* (*pret & pp* -**set**; *ger* -**setting**) *tr* rimettere a posto; (*a watch*) regolare; (*a gem*) incastonare di nuovo; (*a machine*) rimontare

re-ship [ri'ʃɪp] *v* (*pret & pp* -**shipped**; *ger* -**shipping**) *tr* rispedire; (*on a ship*) reimbarcare ‖ *intr* reimbarcarsi

reshipment [ri'ʃɪpmənt] *s* rispedizione; (*on a ship*) reimbarco

reside [rɪ'zaɪd] *intr* risiedere

residence ['rɛzɪdəns] *s* residenza

resident ['rɛzɪdənt] *adj & s* residente *mf*

residential [,rɛzɪ'dɛnʃəl] *adj* residenziale

residue ['rɛzɪ ,dju] *or* ['rɛsɪ ,du] *s* residuo

resign [rɪ'zaɪn] *tr* rassegnare, abbandonare; **to be resigned to** rassegnarsi a ‖ *intr* dimettersi, rassegnare le dimissioni

resignation [,rɛzɪg'neʃən] *s* (*from a job*) dimissione; (*submission*) rassegnazione

resin ['rɛzɪn] *s* resina

resist [rɪ'zɪst] *tr* resistere (with *dat*) ‖ *intr* resistere

resistance [rɪ'zɪstəns] *s* resistenza

resole [ri'sol] *tr* risolare

resolute ['rɛzə ,lut] *adj* risoluto

resolution [,rɛzə'luʃən] *s* risoluzione; **good resolutions** buoni propositi

resolve [rɪ'zɑlv] *s* risoluzione ‖ *tr* risolvere ‖ *intr* risolversi

resonance ['rɛzənəns] *s* risonanza

resort [rɪ'zɔrt] *s* (*appeal*) ricorso; (*for vacation*) centro di villeggiatura ‖ *intr* ricorrere

resound [rɪ'zaʊnd] *intr* risonare

resounding [rɪ'zaʊndɪŋ] *adj* risonante; (*success*) strepitoso

resource [rɪ'sors] *or* ['risɔrs] *s* risorsa

resourceful [rɪ'sorsfəl] *adj* ingegnoso

respect [rɪ'spɛkt] *s* rispetto; **respects** rispetti *mpl*, ossequi *mpl*; **with respect to** rispetto a ‖ *tr* rispettare

respectable [rɪ'spɛktəbəl] *adj* rispettabile; onesto, per bene

respectful [rɪ'spɛktfəl] *adj* rispettoso

respecting [rɪ'spɛktɪŋ] *prep* rispetto a

respective [rɪ'spɛktɪv] *adj* rispettivo

respiratory ['rɛspɪrə ,torɪ] *or* [rɪ-'spaɪrə ,torɪ] *adj* respiratorio

respire [rɪ'spaɪr] *tr & intr* respirare

respite ['rɛspɪt] *s* tregua, requie *f*; (*reprieve*) proroga, dilazione

resplendent [rɪ'splɛndənt] *adj* risplendente

respond [rɪ'spɑnd] *intr* rispondere

response [rɪ'spɑns] *s* risposta

responsibili·ty [rɪ ,spɑnsɪ'bɪlɪtɪ] *s* (-**ties**) responsabilità *f*

responsible [rɪ'spɑnsɪbəl] *adj* responsabile; (*job*) di fiducia; **responsible for** responsabile di

responsive [rɪ'spɑnsɪv] *adj* rispondente; (*e.g., to affection*) sensibile; (*e.g., motor*) che risponde

rest [rɛst] *s* riposo; (*what remains*) resto; (mus) pausa; **at rest** in riposo; tranquillo, in pace; (*dead*) morto; **the rest** il resto, gli altri; **to come to rest** andare a finire; **to lay to rest** sotterrare ‖ *tr* riposare; (*to direct one's eyes*) dirigere; (*faith*) porre ‖ *intr* riposarsi, riposare; appoggiarsi; **to rest assured** (that) esser sicuro (che); **to rest on** aver fiducia in; basarsi su; (*one's laurels*) dormire su

restaurant ['rɛstərənt] *or* ['rɛstə ,rɑnt] *s* ristorante *m*

restful ['rɛstfəl] *adj* riposante, tranquillo

rest' home' *s* casa di riposo

rest'ing place' *s* luogo di riposo; (*of a staircase*) pianerottolo; (*of the dead*) ultima dimora

restitution [,rɛstɪ'tjuʃən] *or* [,rɛstɪ-'tuʃən] *s* restituzione

restive [ˈrɛstɪv] *adj* irrequieto; (*e.g., horse*) recalcitrante

restless [ˈrɛstlɪs] *adj* irrequieto; (*night*) insonne, in bianco

restock [riˈstɑk] *tr* rifornire; (*e.g., with fish*) ripopolare

restoration [ˌrɛstəˈreʃən] *s* restaurazione

restore [rɪˈstor] *tr* restaurare, ripristinare

restrain [rɪˈstren] *tr* ritenere, frenare; limitare

restraint [rɪˈstrent] *s* restrizione; controllo, ritegno; detenzione

restrict [rɪˈstrɪkt] *tr* restingere, limitare

restriction [rɪˈstrɪkʃən] *s* restrizione

rest' room' *s* toletta; gabinetto di decenza

restructuring [rɪˈstrʌktʃərɪŋ] *s* ristrutturazione

result [rɪˈzʌlt] *s* risultato ‖ *intr* risultare; **to result in** risolversi in, concludersi con

resume [rɪˈzum] *or* [rɪˈzjum] *tr* riprendere ‖ *intr* ricominciare

résumé [ˌrɛzuˈme] *or* [ˌrɛzjuˈme] *s* sunto, riassunto

resumption [rɪˈzʌmpʃən] *s* ripresa

resurface [riˈsʌrfɪs] *tr* mettere copertura nuova a ‖ *intr* riemergere

resurrect [ˌrɛzəˈrɛkt] *tr & intr* risuscitare

resurrection [ˌrɛzəˈrɛkʃən] *s* risurrezione

resuscitate [rɪˈsʌsɪˌtet] *tr* rendere alla vita

retail [ˈritel] *adj & adv* al dettaglio, al minuto ‖ *s* dettaglio ‖ *tr* dettagliare, vendere al minuto ‖ *intr* vendere o vendersi al minuto

retailer [ˈritelər] *s* dettagliante *mf*

retain [rɪˈten] *tr* ritenere; (*a lawyer*) assicurarsi i servizi di

retaliate [rɪˈtæliˌet] *intr* fare rappresaglie; **to retaliate for** ricambiare

retaliation [rɪˌtæliˈeʃən] *s* rappresaglia

retard [rɪˈtɑrd] *s* ritardo ‖ *tr* ritardare

retch [rɛtʃ] *intr* avere sforzi di vomito

reticence [ˈrɛtɪsəns] *s* riservatezza

reticent [ˈrɛtɪsənt] *adj* riservato, taciturno

retina [ˈrɛtɪnə] *s* retina

retinue [ˈrɛtɪˌnju] *or* [ˈrɛtɪˌnu] *s* seguito, corteggio

retire [rɪˈtaɪr] *tr* ritirare; (*an employee*) giubilare, mettere a riposo ‖ *intr* ritirarsi; andare a riposo; (*to go to bed*) andare a letto

retired [rɪˈtaɪrd] *adj* (*employee*) in pensione; (*officer*) a riposo

retirement [rɪˈtaɪrmənt] *s* ritiro; (*of an employee*) pensionamento, quiescenza

retort [rɪˈtort] *s* risposta per le rime; controreplica; (*chem*) storta ‖ *tr* rispondere per le rime a ‖ *intr* rispondere per le rime

retouch [riˈtʌtʃ] *tr* ritoccare

retrace [riˈtres] *tr* ripercorrere; **to retrace one's steps** ritornare sui propri passi

retract [rɪˈtrækt] *tr* ritrattare, disdire ‖ *intr* disdirsi

re-tread [ˈriˌtrɛd] *s* pneumatico col copertone ricostruito ‖ [riˈtrɛd] *v* (*pret & pp* **-treaded**) *tr* ricostruire il copertone di ‖ *v* (*pret* **-trod** [ˈtrɑd]; *pp* **-trod** *or* **-trodden**) *tr* ripercorrere ‖ *intr* rimettere il piede

retreat [rɪˈtrit] *s* (*seclusion*) ritiro; (mil) ritirata; (eccl) esercizio spirituale; **to beat a retreat** battere in ritirata ‖ *intr* ritirarsi

retrench [rɪˈtrɛntʃ] *tr* ridurre, tagliare; (mil) trincerare ‖ *intr* ridurre le spese; (mil) trincerarsi

retribution [ˌrɛtrɪˈbjuʃən] *s* ricompensa; (theol) giudizio finale

retributive [rɪˈtrɪbjətɪv] *adj* retributivo

retrieve [rɪˈtriv] *tr* riguadagnare, riconquistare; (*to repair*) risarcire; (hunt) riportare ‖ *intr* riportare la presa

retriever [rɪˈtrivər] *s* cane *m* da presa

retroactive [ˌrɛtroˈæktɪv] *adj* retroattivo

retrofiring [ˌrɛtroˈfaɪrɪŋ] *s* accensione dei retrorazzi

retrogress [ˌrɛtrəˈgrɛs] *intr* regredire; retrocedere

retrorocket [ˈrɛtrəˌrɑkɪt] *s* retrorazzo

retrospect [ˈrɛtrəˌspɛkt] *s* esame retrospettivo; **in retrospect** retrospettivamente

retrospective [ˌrɛtrəˈspɛktɪv] *adj* retrospettivo

re-try [riˈtraɪ] *v* (*pret & pp* **-tried**) *tr* (*a person*) riprocessare; (*a case*) ritentare

return [rɪˈtʌrn] *adj* di ritorno; ripetuto ‖ *s* restituzione; ritorno; profitto; (*of income tax*) dichiarazione; risposta; rapporto ufficiale; (*of an election*) responso; (sports) rimando, rimessa; **in return (for)** in cambio (di); **many happy returns of the day!** cento di questi giorni!; **returns** (*of an election*) responso, risultato ‖ *tr* tornare, ritornare restituire; (*a favor*) contraccambiare; (*a profit*) dare; (*thanks; a decision*) rendere; (sports) ribattere ‖ *intr* tornare; rispondere

return' ad'dress *s* indirizzo del mittente

return' bout' *s* (boxing) rivincita

return' mail' *s*—**by return mail** a volta di corriere, a giro di posta

return' tick'et *s* biglietto di ritorno; (Brit) biglietto di andata e ritorno

reunification [riˌjunɪfɪˈkeʃən] *s* riunione, unificazione

reunion [riˈjunjən] *s* riunione

reunite [ˌrijuˈnaɪt] *tr* riunire ‖ *intr* riunirsi

rev [rɛv] *s* (coll) giro ‖ *v* (*pret & pp* **revved**; *ger* **revving**) *tr*—**to rev up** (coll) imballare ‖ *intr* (coll) accelerare, imballarsi

revamp [riˈvæmp] *tr* rinnovare, rappezzare

reveal [rɪˈvil] *tr* rivelare, svelare

reveille [ˈrɛvəli] *s* sveglia, levata

rev•el [ˈrɛvəl] *s* baldoria ‖ *v* (*pret &*

pp **-eled** or **-elled; *ger* -eling** or **-elling**) *intr* gozzovigliare; bearsi

revelation [ˌrevə'leʃən] *s* rivelazione ‖ **Revelation** *s* (Bib) Apocalisse *f*

revel·ry ['revəlrɪ] *s* (-ries) baldoria

revenge [rɪ'vendʒ] *s* vendetta ‖ *tr* vendicare

revengeful [rɪ'vendʒfəl] *adj* vendicativo

revenue ['revəˌnju] or ['revəˌnu] *s* entrata, profitto; (*government income*) entrate *fpl* erariali

rev'enue cut'ter *s* motobarca della guardia di finanza

rev'enue stamp' *s* marca da bollo

reverberate [rɪ'vʌrbəˌret] *intr* riverberarsi; (*said, e.g., of sound*) ripercuotersi, risonare; (*said of an echo*) rimbalzare

revere [rɪ'vɪr] *tr* venerare, riverire

reverence ['revərəns] *s* riverenza ‖ *tr* ossequiare

reverend ['revərənd] *adj & s* reverendo

reverent ['revərənt] *adj* reverente

reverie ['revərɪ] *s* sogno, fantasticheria

reversal [rɪ'vʌrsəl] *s* inversione, cambio; (law) annullamento

reverse [rɪ'vʌrs] *adj* rovescio, contrario; (mach) di retromarcia ‖ *s* contrario; (*rear*) dietro; (*misfortune*); side of a coin not bearing principal design) rovescio; (mach) retromarcia ‖ *tr* invertire; rovesciare; mettere in marcia indietro; **to reverse oneself** cambiare d'opinione; **to reverse the charges** far pagare al destinatario; (telp) far pagare al numero chiamato ‖ *intr* invertirsi

revert [rɪ'vʌrt] *intr* ritornare

review [rɪ'vju] *s* (*critical article*) recensione; (*magazine*) rivista; (educ) ripasso, ripetizione; (mil) rivista ‖ *tr* recensire; rivedere; (*a lesson*) ripassare; (mil) passare in rassegna

revile [rɪ'vaɪl] *tr* insultare, offendere

revise [rɪ'vaɪz] *s* revisione; (typ) seconda bozza ‖ *tr* rivedere; correggere

revision [rɪ'vɪʒən] *s* revisione

revisionism [rɪ'vɪʒəˌnɪzəm] *s* revisionismo

revival [rɪ'vaɪvəl] *s* ripresa delle forze; (*restoration*) ripristino; (*of learning*) rinascimento; risveglio religioso; (theat, mov) ripresa

revive [rɪ'vaɪv] *tr* ravvivare; (*a custom*) ripristinare; (theat) dare la ripresa di ‖ *intr* ravvivarsi; risorgere

revoke [rɪ'vok] *tr* revocare

revolt [rɪ'volt] *s* rivolta ‖ *tr* rivoltare ‖ *intr* rivoltarsi

revolting [rɪ'voltɪŋ] *adj* rivoltante

revolution [ˌrevə'luʃən] *s* rivoluzione

revolutionar·y [ˌrevə'luʃəˌnerɪ] *adj* rivoluzionario ‖ *s* (-ies) rivoluzionario

revolve [rɪ'vʌlv] *tr* far rotare; (*in one's mind*) rivolgere ‖ *intr* girare, rotare

revolver [rɪ'vʌlvər] *s* rivoltella

revolv'ing book'case *s* scaffale *m* girevole

revolv'ing cred'it *s* credito rotativo

revolv'ing door' *s* porta girevole

revolv'ing fund' *s* fondo rotativo

revue [rɪ'vju] *s* rivista

revulsion [rɪ'vʌlʃən] *s* ripugnanza, avversione; (med) revulsione

reward [rɪ'word] *s* premio, ricompensa; (*money offered for capture*) taglia; (*for return of articles lost*) mancia competente ‖ *tr* premiare, ricompensare

rewarding [rɪ'wordɪŋ] *adj* rimunerativo; gradevole

re-wind [rɪ'waɪnd] *s* (*of a tape*) ribobinazione ‖ *v* (*pret & pp* **-wound** [waʊnd]) *tr* ribobinare

re-write [rɪ'raɪt] *v* (*pret* **-wrote** ['rot]; *pp* **-written** ['rɪtən]) *tr* riscrivere; (*news*) rimaneggiare, correggere

rhapso·dy ['ræpsədɪ] *s* (-dies) rapsodia

rheostat ['ri·əˌstæt] *s* reostato

rhesus ['risəs] *s* reso

rhetoric ['retərɪk] *s* retorica

rhetorical [rɪ'tarɪkəl] or [rɪ'tərɪkəl] *adj* retorico

rheumatic [ru'mætɪk] *adj & s* reumatico

rheumatism ['ruməˌtɪzəm] *s* reumatismo

Rhine [raɪn] *s* Reno

Rhineland [raɪn,lænd] *s* la Renania

rhine'stone' *s* gemma artificiale

rhinoceros [raɪ'nasərəs] *s* rinoceronte *m*

Rhodes [rodz] *s* Rodi *f*

Rhone [ron] *s* Rodano

rhubarb ['rubarb] *s* rabarbaro; (slang) baruffa

rhyme [raɪm] *s* rima; **without rhyme or reason** senza capo né coda ‖ *tr & intr* rimare

rhythm ['rɪðəm] *s* ritmo

rhythmic(al) ['rɪðmɪk(əl)] *adj* ritmico

rial·to [rɪ'ælto] *s* (-tos) mercato ‖ **the Rialto** il ponte di Rialto; il centro teatrale di New York

rib [rɪb] *s* costola; (*cut of meat*) costata; (*of umbrella*) stecca; (*of leaf*) nervatura; (aer, archit) centina; (naut) costa ‖ *v* (*pret & pp* **ribbed**; *ger* **ribbing**) *tr* (slang) prendersi gioco di

ribald ['rɪbəld] *adj* volgare, indecente

ribbon ['rɪbən] *s* nastro; (*decoration*) nastrino; **ribbons** (*shreds*) brandelli *mpl*

rice [raɪs] *s* riso

rich [rɪtʃ] *adj* ricco; (*food*) nutrito, grasso; (*wine*) generoso; (*voice*) caldo; (*color*) vivo; (*odor*) forte; (coll) divertente; (coll) assurdo; **to strike it rich** trovare la miniera d'oro ‖ **riches** *spl* ricchezze *fpl*; **the rich i** ricchi

rickets ['rɪkɪts] *s* rachitismo

ricket·y ['rɪkɪtɪ] *adj* (*object*) sgangherato; (*person*) vacillante; (*suffering from rickets*) rachitico

rid [rɪd] *v* (*pret & pp* **rid**; *ger* **ridding**) *tr* liberare, sbarazzare; **to get rid of** liberarsi di, sbarazzarsi di

riddance ['rɪdəns] *s* liberazione; **good riddance!** che sollievo!

riddle ['rɪdəl] *s* enigma *m*, indovi-

nello; (*sieve*) crivello ‖ *tr* crivellare; (*to sift*) vagliare; (*s.o.'s reputation*) rovinare; **to riddle with** crivellare di
ride [raɪd] *s* scarrozzata; cavalcata; gita ‖ *v* (*pret* **rode** [rod]; *pp* **ridden** [ˈrɪdən]) *tr* cavalcare, montare, montare su; (*e.g., a bus*) andare in; (*the waves*) galleggiare su; attraversare; tiranneggiare; farsi gioco di; **to ride down** travolgere; sorpassare; **to ride out** uscire felicemente da ‖ *intr* cavalcare; fare una passeggiata, fare una gita; (*to float*) galleggiare su; **to let ride** lasciar correre; **to ride on** dipendere da
rider [ˈraɪdər] *s* cavallerizzo; ciclista *mf*; viaggiatore *m*, passeggero
ridge [rɪdʒ] *s* (*of mountains*) crinale *m*, dorsale *f*; (*of roof*) displuvio; (*agr*) porca
ridge'pole' *s* trave maestra, colmo
ridicule [ˈrɪdɪ̩kjul] *s* ridicolo; **to expose to ridicule** porre in ridicolo ‖ *tr* ridicolizzare
ridiculous [rɪˈdɪkjələs] *adj* ridicolo
rid'ing boot' *s* stivalone *m* d'equitazione
rid'ing school' *s* maneggio
rife [raɪf] *adj* comune, prevalente; **rife with** pieno di
riffraff [ˈrɪf̩ræf] *s* gentaglia
rifle [ˈraɪfəl] *s* fucile *m*; cannone rigato ‖ *tr* (*a place*) svaligiare; (*a person*) derubare; (*a gun*) rigare
rifle' range' *s* tiro a segno
rift [rɪft] *s* crepa, fessura; disaccordo
rig [rɪg] *s* attrezzatura, equipaggio; impianto di sondaggio (per il petrolio); (*outfit*) tenuta ‖ *v* (*pret & pp* **rigged**; *ger* **rigging**) *tr* attrezzare, equipaggiare; guarnire; abbigliare in maniera strana
rigging [ˈrɪgɪŋ] *s* (naut) padiglione *m*; (*tackle*) (naut) rizza; (coll) vestiti *mpl*
right [raɪt] *adj* giusto; corretto; (*mind*) sano; destro, diritto; (geom) retto; (geom) perpendicolare; **right or wrong** a torto o a ragione; **to be all right** star bene di salute; **to be right** aver ragione ‖ *s* diritto; quanto è giusto, (il) giusto; (*in a company*) interessenza; (*right hand*) destra; (*turn*) giro a destra; (boxing) diritto; (tex) dritto; (pol) destra; **by right in** giustizia; **on the right** alla destra; **to be in the right** aver ragione ‖ *adv* direttamente; completamente; immediatamente; proprio, precisamente; correttamente, giustamente; bene; alla destra; (coll) molto; **all right** benissimo ‖ *tr* drizzare; correggere; rimettere a posto ‖ *intr* drizzarsi
righteous [ˈraɪtʃəs] *adj* retto; virtuoso
right' field' *s* (baseball) campo destro
rightful [ˈraɪtfəl] *adj* giusto; legittimo
right'-hand drive' *s* guida a destra
right'-handed [ˈraɪtˈhændɪd] *adj* che usa la destra; destrorso
right'-hand man' *s* braccio destro
rightist [ˈraɪtɪst] *adj* conservatore ‖ *s* conservatore *m*, membro della destra

rightly [ˈraɪtli] *adv* correttamente; giustamente; **rightly or wrongly** a torto o a ragione
right' mind' *s*—**in one's right mind** nel pieno possesso delle proprie facoltà, con la testa a posto
right' of way' *s* precedenza; (law) servitù *f* di passaggio; (rr) sede *f*
rights' of man' *s* diritti *mpl* dell'uomo
right'-wing' *adj* della destra
right-winger [ˈraɪtˈwɪŋər] *s* membro della destra, conservatore *m*
rigid [ˈrɪdʒɪd] *adj* rigido
rigmarole [ˈrɪgmə̩rol] *s* sproloquio
rigorous [ˈrɪgərəs] *adj* rigoroso
rile [raɪl] *tr* irritare, esasperare
rill [rɪl] *s* rigagnolo
rim [rɪm] *s* orlo, bordo; (*of a wheel*) cerchione *m*
rime [raɪm] *s* brina; (*in verse*) rima ‖ *tr* brinare; rimare ‖ *intr* rimare
rind [raɪnd] *s* (*of animals*) cotenna; (*of fruit or cheese*) scorza
ring [rɪŋ] *s* (*for finger*) anello; (*anything round*) cerchio; (*circular course*) pista; (*of people*) crocchio; (*of evildoers*) combriccola; (*of anchor*) anello; (*sound of bell*) squillo; (*loud sound of bell*) scampanellata; (*of small bell; of glassware*) tintinnio; (*act of ringing*) sonata; (telp) chiamata; (fig) suono; (boxing) quadrato; (mach) ghiera; (fig, taur) arena; **to run rings around** essere molto migliore di ‖ *v* (*pret & pp* **ringed**) *tr* accerchiare; mettere un anello a ‖ *intr* formare cerchi ‖ *v* (*pret* **rang** [ræŋ]; *pp* **rung** [rʌŋ]) *tr* sonare; squillare; tintinnare; chiamare al telefono; **to ring up** chiamare al telefono; (*a sale*) battere sul registratore di cassa ‖ *intr* sonare; squillare; tintinnare; chiamare; (*said of one's ears*) fischiare; **to ring for** chiamare col campanello; **to ring off** terminare una conversazione telefonica; **to ring up** chiamare al telefono
ring-around-a-rosy [ˈrɪŋə̩raʊndəˈrozi] *s* girotondo
ringing [ˈrɪŋɪŋ] *adj* alto, sonoro ‖ *s* accerchiamento; squillo; tintinnio; (*in the ears*) fischio
ring'lead'er *s* capobanda *m*
ringlet [ˈrɪŋlɪt] *s* anellino
ring'mas'ter *s* direttore *m* di circo equestre
ring'side' *s* posto vicino al quadrato
ring'worm' *s* tigna
rink [rɪŋk] *s* pattinatoio
rinse [rɪns] *s* risciacquatura ‖ *tr* risciacquare
riot [ˈraɪət] *s* sommossa, tumulto; profusione; **to be a riot** (coll) essere divertentissimo; **to run riot** sfrenarsi; (*said of plants*) crescere disordinatamente ‖ *intr* tumultuare; darsi alle gozzoviglie
rioter [ˈraɪətər] *s* rivoltoso
rip [rɪp] *s* sdrucitura; (*open seam*) scucitura ‖ *v* (*pret & pp* **ripped**; *ger* **ripping**) *tr* sdrucire; (*to open the*

seam of) scucire || *intr* sdrucirsi; scucirsi; **to rip out with insults** (coll) prorompere in improperi

ripe [raɪp] *adj* maturo; *(lips)* turgido; *(cheese)* stagionato; pronto

ripen ['raɪpən] *tr & intr* maturare

ripple ['rɪpəl] *s* increspatura; *(sound)* mormorio || *tr* increspare || *intr* incresparsi; mormorare

rise [raɪz] *s (of prices, temperature)* aumento; *(of a road)* salita; *(of ground)* elevazione; *(of a heavenly body)* levata; *(in rank)* ascesa; *(of a step)* alzata; *(of a stream)* sorgente *f; (of water)* crescita; **to get a rise out of** (coll) farsi rispondere per le rime da; **to give rise to** dare origine a || *v (pret* rose [roz]; *pp* risen ['rɪzən]) *intr (said of the sun)* sorgere; rialzarsi; *(said of plants)* crescere; *(said of the wind)* alzarsi; *(said of a building)* ergersi; *(to return from the dead)* risorgere; *(to increase)* aumentare; **to rise above** alzarsi al di sopra di; essere al di sopra di; **to rise to** sorgere all'altezza di

riser ['raɪzər] *s (of step)* alzata; *(upright)* montante *m;* **early riser** persona mattiniera; **late riser** dormiglione *m*

risk [rɪsk] *s* rischio; **to run or take a risk** correre un rischio || *tr* rischiare

risk·y ['rɪski] *adj (-ier; -iest)* rischioso

risqué [rɪs'ke] *adj* audace, spinto

rite [raɪt] *s* rito; **last rites** riti *mpl* funebri

ritual ['rɪtʃʊ·əl] *adj & s* rituale *m*

ri·val ['raɪvəl] *s* rivale *mf* || *v (pret & pp* -valed *or* -valled; *ger* -valing *or* -valling) *tr* rivaleggiare con

rival·ry ['raɪvəlri] *s (-ries)* rivalità *f*

river ['rɪvər] *s* fiume *m;* **down the river** a valle; **up the river** a monte

riv·er ba·sin *s* bacino fluviale

riv·er·bed *s* letto di fiume

riv·er front *s* riva di fiume

riv·er·head *s* sorgente *f* di fiume

riv·er·side *adj* rivierasco || *s* riva del fiume

rivet ['rɪvɪt] *s* ribattino; *(of scissors)* perno || *tr* ribadire; *(s.o.'s attention)* concentrare

roach [rotʃ] *s* scarafaggio

road [rod] *adj* stradale || *s* strada; via; (naut) rada; **to be in the road of** ostacolare il cammino a; **to burn up the road** divorare la strada; **to get out of the road** togliersi di mezzo

roadability [ˌrodə'bɪlɪti] *s* tenuta di strada

road'bed *s (of highway)* piattaforma; (rr) massicciata, infrastruttura

road'block *s* (mil) barricata; (fig) impedimento

road'house *s* taverna su autostrada

road' la'borer *s* cantoniere *m*

road' map *s* carta stradale

road' roll'er *s* compressore *m* stradale, rullo compressore

road' serv'ice *s* servizio di assistenza stradale

road'side *s* bordo della strada

road'side inn' *s* taverna posta su autostrada

road' sign' *s* indicatore *m* stradale

road'stead *s* rada

road'way *s* carreggiata; strada

roam [rom] *s* vagabondaggio || *tr* girovagare per || *intr* girovagare

roar [ror] *s* ruggito, muggito; boato, fragore *m* || *intr* muggire; **to roar with laughter** fare una risata

roast [rost] *s* arrosto; torrefazione || *tr* arrostire; *(coffee)* tostare, torrefare; (coll) farsi beffe di || *intr* arrostirsi

roast' beef' *s* rosbif *m*

roast'ed pea'nut *s* nocciolina americana abbrustolita

roast' pork' *s* arrosto di maiale

rob [rab] *v (pret & pp* robbed; *ger* robbing) *tr & intr* derubare

robber ['rabər] *s* ladro, malandrino

robber·y ['rabəri] *s (-ies)* furto

robe [rob] *s (of a woman)* vestito; *(of a professor)* toga; *(of a priest)* abito talare; *(dressing gown)* vestaglia; *(for lap)* coperta da viaggio; **robes vestiti** *mpl* || *tr* vestire || *intr* vestirsi

robin ['rabɪn] *s* pettirosso

robot ['robat] *s* robot *m*

robust [ro'bʌst] *adj* robusto

rock [rak] *s* roccia; *(any stone)* pietra; *(sticking out of water)* scoglio; *(one that is thrown)* sasso; *(hill)* rocca; (slang) pietra preziosa; **on the rocks** (coll) in rovina; (coll) al verde; *(said, e.g., of whiskey)* sul ghiaccio || *tr* far vacillare; dondolare || *intr* vacillare; dondolare

rock'-bot'tom *adj* (l') ultimo; (il) minimo

rock' can'dy *s* zucchero candito

rock' crys'tal *s* cristallo di rocca

rocker ['rakər] *s (curved piece at bottom of rocking chair)* dondolo; sedia a dondolo; (mach) bilanciere *m;* **off one's rocker** (slang) matto

rocket ['rakɪt] *s* razzo || *intr* partire come un razzo

rock'et launch'er ['lɔntʃər] *or* ['lɑntʃər] *s* lanciarazzo

rock' gar'den *s* giardino piantato fra le rocce

rock'ing chair' *s* sedia a dondolo

rock'ing horse' *s* cavallo a dondolo

rock' salt' *s* salgemma *m*

rock' wool' *s* cotone *m* or lana minerale

rock·y ['raki] *adj (-ier; -iest)* roccioso; traballante; (coll) debole

rod [rad] *s* verga, bacchetta; scettro; punizione; *(bar)* asta; *(for fishing)* canna da pesca; (anat, biol) bastoncino; (mach) biella; (surv) biffa; (Bib) razza, tribù *f;* (slang) pistola; **spare the rod and spoil the child** la madre pietosa fa la piaga cancrenosa

rodent ['rodənt] *adj & s* roditore *m*

rod'man *s (-men)* aiutante *m* geometra

roe [ro] *s* capriolo; *(of fish)* uova *fpl*

rogue [rog] *s* furfante *m;* *(scamp)* picaro

rogues" gal'lery *s* collezione di fotografie di malviventi

rôle or **role** [rol] *s* ruolo, parte *f;* **to play a role** fare la parte

roll [rol] *s (of film, paper, etc.)* rotolo, bobina; *(of fat)* strato; *(of roller)* rotella; *(of bread)* panino; ondulazione; *(noise)* rullio, rullo; *(of a boat)* rollio; *(of thunder)* rombo; *(list)* ruolo; *(of money)* (slang) fascio; **to call the roll** fare la chiama ‖ *tr* far rotolare; *(one's r's)* arrotare; *(one's eyes)* stralunare; *(e.g., dough)* spianare; *(steel)* laminare; *(to wrap)* arrotolare; *(a drum)* rullare; **to roll back** *(prices)* ridurre; **to roll out** spianare; srotolare; **to roll up** *(one's sleeves)* arrotolarsi; accumulare; aumentare ‖ *intr* rotolare; rullare; arrotolarsi; raggomitolarsi; **to roll on** passare; **to roll out** srotolarsi; *(to get out of bed)* (slang) alzarsi

roll' call' *s* chiama, appello

roller ['rolər] *s* rotella; *(for hair)* bigodino; rotolo; *(wave)* ondata lunga

roll'er bear'ing *s* cuscinetto a rotolamento

roll'er coast'er *s* montagne russe

roll'er skate' *s* pattino a rotelle

roll'er-skate' *intr* pattinare coi pattini a rotelle

roll'er tow'el *s* bandinella

roll'ing mill' ['rolɪŋ] *s* laminatoio

roll'ing pin' *s* matterello

roll'ing stock' *s* (rr) materiale *m* rotabile

roll'-top desk' *s* scrivania a piano scorrevole

roly-poly ['roli'poli] *adj* grassoccio

roman ['romən] *adj* (typ) romano, tondo ‖ *s* (typ) carattere romano, tondo ‖ **Roman** *adj & s* romano

Ro'man can'dle *s* candela romana

Ro'man Cath'olic Church' *s* Chiesa Cattolica Apostolica Romana

romance [ro'mæns] or ['romæns] *s* romanzo; sentimentalità *f;* idillio, intrigo amoroso; (mus) romanza ‖ [ro'mæns] *intr* scrivere romanzi; raccontare romanzi; fare il romantico ‖ **Romance** ['romæns] or [ro'mæns] *adj* romanzo, neolatino

Ro'man Em'pire *s* Impero Romano

romanesque [,romən'ɛsk] *adj* romantico ‖ **Romanesque** *adj & s* romanico

Ro'man nose' *s* naso aquilino

romantic [ro'mæntɪk] *adj* romantico

romanticism [ro'mæntɪ,sɪzəm] *s* romanticismo

romanticist [ro'mæntɪsɪst] *s* romantico

romp [romp] *intr* ruzzare

rompers ['rompərz] *spl* pagliaccetto

roof [ruf] or [rʊf] *s (of house)* tetto; *(of heaven)* volta; *(of car)* tetto, padiglione *m;* **to hit the roof** (slang) andare fuori dai gangheri; **to raise the roof** (slang) fare molto chiasso; (slang) protestare violentemente ‖ *tr* ricoprire con tetto

roofer ['rufər] or ['rʊfər] *s* conciatetti *m*

roof' gar'den *s* giardino pensile

rook [rʊk] *s (bird)* cornacchia; *(in chess)* torre *f* ‖ *tr* truffare

rookie ['rʊki] *s* novizio; (mil) recluta

room [rum] or [rʊm] *s* stanza, camera; vano, locale *m;* posto, spazio; opportunità *f;* **to make room** far luogo ‖ *intr* alloggiare

room' and board' *s* vitto e alloggio

room' clerk' *s* impiegato d'albergo assegnato alle prenotazioni

roomer ['rumər] or ['rʊmər] *s* inquilino

room'ing house' *s* casa con camere d'affittare

room·y ['rumi] or ['rʊmi] *adj* (**-ier; -iest**) ampio, spazioso

roost [rust] *s (perch)* ballatoio; *(house for chickens)* pollaio; *(place for resting)* posto di riposo; **to rule the roost** essere il gallo del pollaio ‖ *intr* appollaiarsi; andare a dormire

rooster ['rustər] *s* gallo

root [rut] or [rʊt] *s* radice *f;* **to get to the root of** andare al fondo di; **to take root** metter radici ‖ *tr* inchiodare, piantare ‖ *intr* radicare; *(said of swine)* grufolare; **to root for** fare il tifo per

rooter ['rutər] or ['rʊtər] *s* tifoso

rope [rop] *s* fune *f,* corda; *(of a hangman)* capestro; laccio, lasso; **to know the ropes** (coll) conoscere la faccenda a fondo, saperla lunga ‖ *tr* legare con fune; prendere al laccio; **to rope in** (slang) imbrogliare

rope'danc'er or **rope'walk'er** *s* funambolo

rosa·ry ['rozəri] *s* (**-ries**) rosario

rose [roz] *adj & s* rosa

rose'bud' *s* bottoncino di rosa

rose'bush' *s* rosaio

rose'-col'ored *adj* color di rosa

rose'-colored glass'es *spl* occhiali *mpl* rosa

rose' gar'den *s* roseto

rosemar·y ['roz,mɛri] *s* (**-ies**) rosmarino

rose' of Shar'on ['ʃɛrən] *s* altea

rosette [ro'zɛt] *s* rosetta; (archit) rosone *m*

rose' win'dow *s* rosone *m*

rose'wood' *s* palissandro

rosin ['razɪn] *s* colofonia

roster ['rostər] *s* ruolino; orario scolastico

rostrum ['rostrəm] *s* tribuna

ros·y ['rozi] *adj* (**-ier; -iest**) rosa, roseo

rot [rot] *s* marcio; (coll) stupidaggine *f* ‖ *v* (*pret & pp* **rotted**) *(ger* **rotting**) *tr & intr* imputridire

ro'tary en'gine ['rotəri] *s* motore rotativo

ro'tary press' *s* rotativa

rotate ['rotet] or [ro'tet] *tr & intr* rotare

rotation [ro'teʃən] *s* rotazione; **in rotation** in successione, a turno

rote [rot] *s* ripetizione macchinale; **by rote** a memoria

rot'gut' *s* (slang) acquavite *f* di infima qualità

rotisserie [ro'tısəri] *s* girarrosto a motore

rotten ['rɑtən] *adj* marcio, fradicio; corrotto

rotund [ro'tʌnd] *adj* (*plump*) rotondetto; (*voice*) profondo; (*speech*) enfatico

rouge [ruʒ] *s* belletto, rossetto || *tr* dare il belletto a || *intr* darsi il belletto

rough [rʌf] *adj* scabroso; (*sea*) agitato; (*crude*) rozzo, rude; (*road*) accidentato; approssimativo || *tr—*to rough it vivere primitivamente; **to rough up** malmenare

rough'cast' *s* intonaco; modello disgrossato || *v* (*pret & pp* -cast) *tr* (*a wall*) intonacare; disgrossare, dirozzare

rough' cop'y *s* brutta copia

rough-hew ['rʌf'hju] *tr* digrossare, dirozzare

roughly ['rʌfli] *adv* aspramente; rozzamente; approssimativamente

round [raund] *adj* rotondo || *s* tondo; (*of applause*; *of guns*) salva; (*of a single gun*) colpo, tiro; (*of a chair*) piolo; (*of a doctor*) giro; (*of golf*) partita; (*e.g., of bridge*) mano *f*; cerchio; (*boxing*) ripresa || *adv* intorno; dal principio alla fine || *prep* intorno a; attraverso || *tr* (*to make round*) arrotondare; circondare; (*a corner*) scantonare; **to round off** arrotondare; completare, perfezionare; **to round up** raccogliere; (*cattle*) condurre

roundabout ['raundə,baut] *adj* indiretto || *s* giacca attillata; via traversa; giro di parole; (*Brit*) giostra; (*Brit*) anello stradale

round'house' *s* rimessa per locomotive

round-shouldered ['raund'ʃoldərd] *adj* dalle spalle spioventi

round'-trip tick'et *s* biglietto d'andata e ritorno

round'up' *s* (*of cattle*) riunione; (*of criminals*) retata; (*of facts*) riassunto

rouse [rauz] *tr* svegliare; suscitare; (*game*) scovare || *intr* svegliarsi

rout [raut] *s* sconfitta, rotta || *tr* sconfiggere, mettere in rotta || *intr* grufolare

route [rut] *or* [raut] *s* via, rotta; itinerario || *tr* istradare

routine [ru'tin] *adj* ordinario || *s* trafila, routine *f*

rove [rov] *intr* vagabondare, vagare

rover ['rovər] *s* vagabondo

row [rau] *s* piazzata, scenata; (*clamor*) (coll) baccano; **to raise a row** (coll) fare baccano || [ro] *s* fila; (*of figures*) finca; (*e.g., of trees*) filare *m*; **in a row** in continuazione, di seguito || *tr* vogare || *intr* remare, vogare

rowboat ['ro,bot] *s* barca a remi

row·dy ['raudi] *adj* (-dier; -diest) turbolento || *s* (-dies) attaccabrighe *mf*

rower ['ro·ər] *s* rematore *m*

rowing ['ro·ıŋ] *s* (*action*) voga; (*sport*) canottaggio

royal ['rɔı·əl] *adj* reale, regio

royalist ['rɔı·əlıst] *adj* sostenitore del re || *s* realista *mf*

royal·ty ['rɔı·əlti] *s* (-ties) regalità *f*; membro della famiglia reale; nobiltà *f*; diritto d'autore; diritto d'inventore; percentuale *f* sugli utili

rub [rʌb] *s* frizione; difficile *m*; **here's the rub** qui sta il busillis || *v* (*pret & pp* rubbed; *ger* rubbing) *tr* fregare; **to rub elbows with** stare giunto a gomiti con; **to rub out** cancellare con la gomma; (slang) togliere di mezzo || *intr* sfregare; **to rub off** venir via sfregando; cancellarsi

rubber ['rʌbər] *s* gomma, caucciù *m*; gomma da cancellare; (*overshoe*) caloscia; (*in cards*) rubber *m*; (sports) bella

rub'ber band' *s* elastico

rub'ber-neck' *s* (coll) ficcanaso; (coll) turista curioso || *intr* (coll) allungare il collo

rub'ber plant' *s* albero del caucciù

rub'ber stamp' *s* timbro di gomma; (coll) persona che approva inconsultamente

rub'ber-stamp' *tr* timbrare; (coll) approvare inconsultamente

rubbish ['rʌbıʃ] *s* spazzatura; immondizia; (fig) detrito; (coll) sciocchezza

rubble ['rʌbəl] *s* (*broken stone*) pietrisco; (*masonry*) mistura di malta e pietrame; (*broken bits*) calcinacci *mpl*

rub'down' *s* fregagione

rube [rub] *s* (slang) contadino gonzo

ru·by ['rubi] *adj* vermiglio || (-bies) *s* rubino

rudder ['rʌdər] *s* timone *m;* (aer) timone *m* di direzione

rud·dy ['rʌdi] *adj* (-dier; -diest) rubicondo

rude [rud] *adj* rude, sgarbato

rudiment ['rudımənt] *s* rudimento

rue [ru] *tr* lamentare, rimpiangere

rueful ['rufəl] *adj* lamentevole; triste

ruffian ['rʌfı·ən] *s* ribaldo

ruffle ['rʌfəl] *s* increspatura; (*of drum*) rullo; (sew) gala, crespa || *tr* increspare; arruffare; irritare; (*a drum*) far rullare; (sew) guarnire di gala or crespa

rug [rʌg] *s* tappeto

rugged ['rʌgıd] *adj* aspro, irregolare; rugoso; rozzo; forte; tempestuoso

ruin ['ru·ın] *s* rovina || *tr* rovinare, mandare in rovina

rule [rul] *s* regola; dominazione; (*reign*) regno; (law) ordinanza; (typ) filetto; **as a rule** in generale || *tr* governare; dominare; (*with lines*) rigare; (law) deliberare; **to rule out** escludere || *intr* governare; regnare; **to rule over** governare

rule' of thumb' *s* regola basata sull'esperienza; **by rule of thumb** secondo la propria esperienza

ruler ['rulər] *s* governante *m*, dominatore *m;* (*for ruling lines*) riga, regolo *m;* (*for ruling lines*) riga, regolo *m*

ruling ['rulıŋ] *adj* dirigente || *s* (*ruled lines*) rigatura; (law) decisione

rum [rʌm] *s* rum *m;* (*any alcoholic drink*) acquavite *f*

Rumanian [ruˈmenɪ·ən] *adj & s* rumeno

rumble [ˈrʌmbəl] *s* rimbombo; *(of the intestines)* gorgoglio; *(slang)* rissa fra ganghe rivali* || *intr* rimbombare; gorgogliare

ruminate [ˈrumɪ‚net] *tr & intr* ruminare

rummage [ˈrʌmɪdʒ] *tr & intr* rovistare, frugare

rum′mage sale′ *s* vendita di cianfrusaglie

rumor [ˈrumər] *s* voce *f*, diceria || *tr* vociferare; **it is rumored that** corre voce che

rump [rʌmp] *s* anca; posteriore *m*; *(of beef)* quarto posteriore

rumple [ˈrʌmpəl] *s* piega || *tr* spiegazzare, sgualcire || *intr* sgualcirsi

rumpus [ˈrʌmpəs] *s* tumulto; rissa; **to raise a rumpus** fare baccano

run [rʌn] *s* corsa; percorso; produzione; *(e.g., in a stocking)* smagliatura; direzione; *(spell)* serie *f*; *(in cards)* scala; *(of goods)* richiesta; *(on a bank)* afflusso; **in the long run** a lungo andare; **on the run** (coll) di corsa; in fuga; **the common run of men** la media della gente; **to give s.o. a run for his money** dare a qlcu del filo da torcere; essere denaro ben speso per qlcu, e.g., **that sweater gave me a run for my money** quello sweater è stato denaro ben speso per me; **to have a long run** tenere il cartellone per lungo tempo; **to have the run of** avere la libertà di andare e venire in || *v (pret* ran [ræn]; *pp* **run**; *ger* **running)** *tr* muovere; *(a horse)* far correre; *(the street)* vivere liberamente in; *(game)* inseguire; trasportare; *(a machine)* far camminare; *(a store)* esercire; *(a candidate)* portare; *(a risk)* correre; *(a blockade)* violare; mettere, ficcare; *(a line)* tirare; **to run down** cacciare; esaminare; trovare; *(a pedestrian)* investire; denigrare, criticare; **to run in** *(a machine)* rodare; (slang) schiaffare in prigione; **to run off** creare di getto; cacciare; (typ) tirare; **to run up** ammassare || *intr* correre; scappare; *(in a race)* arrivare; *(said of a candidate)* portarsi; passare; *(said of knitted material)* smagliarsi; *(said of a liquid)* scorrere; *(said of a color)* sbavare; *(said of fish)* migrare; funzionare; *(to become)* diventare; *(to be worded)* essere del tenore; (com) decorrere; (theat, mov) durare in cartellone; **to run across** imbattersi in; **to run aground** incagliarsi; **to run away** fuggire; *(said of a horse)* prendere la mano; **to run down** *(said of a liquid)* scorrere; *(said of a battery, a watch)* scaricarsi; *(in health)* sciuparsi; **to run for** presentarsi candidato per; **to run in the family** essere una caratteristica familiare; **to run into** imbattersi in; ammontare a; *(to follow)* succedersi a; **to run off the track** (rr) uscire dalle rotaie; **to run out** aver termine; scadere; esaurirsi;

to run out of rimanere senza; **to run over** oltrepassare; *(e.g., with a car)* investire; **to run through** trapassare; *(a fortune)* dilapidare; esaminare rapidamente

run′a·way′ *adj* fuggiasco; *(horse)* che ha preso la mano || *s* fuggiasco; cavallo che ha preso la mano; fuga

run′-down′ *adj* esausto; negletto, cadente; *(watch, battery)* scarico

rung [rʌŋ] *s (of chair or ladder)* piolo

runner [ˈrʌnər] *s* corridore *m*; messaggero; fattorino, messo; *(of sleigh)* pattino; *(of ice skate)* lama; *(rug)* guida; *(on a table)* striscia di pizzo; *(in stocking)* smagliatura

run′ner-up′ *s (runners-up)* finalista *mf* secondo

running [ˈrʌnɪŋ] *adj* in corsa; da corsa; *(water)* corrente; *(vine)* rampicante; *(knot)* scorsoio; *(sore)* purulento; *(writing)* corsivo; consecutivo; *(start)* (sports) lanciato || *s* corsa; *(of a business)* esercizio; direzione; funzionamento; **to be in the running** avere possibilità di vittoria

run′ning board′ *s* (aut) pedana

run′ning head′ *s* titolo corrente

run·ny [ˈrʌnɪ] *adj* (-nier; -niest) *(liquid)* scorrevole; *(color)* sbavante; **to have a runny nose** avere la goccia al naso

run′off′ *s* ballottaggio

run-of-the-mill [ˈrʌnəvðəˈmɪl] *adj* ordinario, corrente

run′proof′ *adj* indemagliabile

runt [rʌnt] *s* nanerottolo; animale deperito

run′way′ *s* pista; *(of a stream)* letto; *(for animals)* chiusa; (aut) corsia

rupture [ˈrʌptʃər] *s* rottura; (pathol) ernia || *tr* rompere; causare un'ernia a || *intr* rompersi; soffrire di ernia

ru′ral free′ deliv′ery [ˈrurəl] *s* distribuzione postale campestre

ruse [ruz] *s* astuzia, stratagemma *m*

rush [rʌʃ] *adj* urgente || *s* fretta; slancio, corsa; *(of blood)* ondata; *(rushing of persons to a new mine)* febbre *f*; (bot) giunco; **in a rush** in fretta e furia || *tr* affrettare; portare di fretta; spingere; (coll) fare la corte a; **to rush through** fare di fretta; *(e.g., a bill through Congress)* far approvare di fretta || *intr* lanciarsi; affrettarsi; passare velocemente; **to rush through** *(a book)* leggere velocemente; *(one's work)* fare in fretta; *(a town)* attraversare velocemente

rush′-bot′tomed chair′ *s* sedia di giunchi

rush′ can′dle *s* lumicino con lo stoppino fatto di midollo di giunco

rush′ hour′ *s* ora di punta

russet [ˈrʌsɪt] *adj* color cannella

Russia [ˈrʌʃə] *s* la Russia

Russian [ˈrʌʃən] *adj & s* russo

rust [rʌst] *s* ruggine *f*; (fig) torpore *m* || *tr* arrugginire || *intr* arrugginirsi

rustic [ˈrʌstɪk] *adj & s* rustico

rustle [ˈrʌsəl] *s* fruscio; *(of leaves)* stormire *m* || *tr* far frusciare; far stormire; (*cattle*) (coll) rubare ‖ *intr* frusciare; stormire; (coll) lavorare di buzzo buono

rust•y ['rʌsti] *adj* (**-ier; -iest**) rugginoso; color ruggine; fuori pratica

rut [rʌt] *s* (*track*) solco, carrareccia; (*of animals*) fregola; (il) solito tran tran

ruthless ['ruθlɪs] *adj* spietato

rye [raɪ] *s* segala; whiskey *m* di segala

S

S, s [es] *s* diciannovesima lettera dell'alfabeto inglese

Sabbath ['sæbəθ] *s.* (*of Jews*) sabato; (*of Christians*) domenica; **to keep the Sabbath** osservare il riposo domenicale

sabbat'ical year' [sə'bætɪkəl] *s* anno di congedo; (Bib) anno sabbatico

saber ['sebər] *s* sciabola

sa'ber rat'tling *s* minacce *fpl* di guerra

sable ['sebəl] *adj* nero ‖ *s* zibellino; **sables** vestiti di lutto

sabotage ['sæbə,taʒ] *s* sabotaggio ‖ *tr & intr* sabotare

saccharin ['sækərɪn] *s* saccarina

sachet ['sæʃe] or [sæ'ʃe] *s* sacchetto profumato (per la biancheria)

sack [sæk] *s* sacco; (*of an employee*) (slang) licenziamento; (slang) letto ‖ *tr* insaccare; (*to lay waste*) saccheggiare, mettere a sacco; (slang) licenziare

sack'cloth' *s* tela di sacco; (*for penitence*) sacco, cilicio; **in sackcloth and ashes** pentito e contrito

sacrament ['sækrəmənt] *s* sacramento

sacramental [,sækrə'mentəl] *adj* sacramentale

sacred ['sekrəd] *adj* sacro

sacrifice ['sækrɪ,faɪs] *s* sacrificio; **at a sacrifice** in perdita ‖ *tr* sacrificare; (com) svendere

sacrilege ['sækrɪlɪdʒ] *s* sacrilegio

sacrilegious [,sækrɪ'lɪdʒəs] or [,sækrɪ'lɪdʒəs] *adj* sacrilego

sacristan ['sækrɪstən] *s* sagrestano

sacris•ty ['sækrɪsti] *s* (**-ties**) sagrestia

sad [sæd] *adj* (**sadder; saddest**) triste; (*bad*) cattivo; (*color*) tetro

sadden ['sædən] *tr* rattristare ‖ *intr* rattristarsi

saddle ['sædəl] *s* sella ‖ *tr* insellare; **to saddle with** gravare di

saddle'bag' *s* fonda

saddlebow ['sædəl,bo] *s* arcione *m* anteriore

sad'dle•cloth' *s* gualdrappa

saddler ['sædlər] *s* sellaio

sad'dle•tree' *s* arcione *m*

sadist ['sædɪst] or ['sedɪst] *s* sadico

sadistic [sæ'dɪstɪk] or [se'dɪstɪk] *adj* sadico

sadness ['sædnɪs] *s* tristezza

sad' sack' *s* (coll) marmittone *m*

safe [sef] *adj* sicuro; cauto; (*distance*) rispettoso; **safe and sound** sano e salvo ‖ *s* cassaforte *f*

safe'-con'duct *s* salvacondotto

safe'-depos'it box' *s* cassetta di sicurezza

safe'guard' *s* salvaguardia ‖ *tr* salvaguardare

safe•ty ['sefti] *adj* di sicurezza ‖ *s* (**-ties**) sicurezza; (*of a gun*) sicura; **to reach safety** mettersi in salvo

safe'ty belt' *s* (*of a worker*) imbraca; (aer, aut) cintura di sicurezza; (naut) cintura di salvataggio

safe'ty glass' *s* vetro infrangibile

safe'ty is'land *s* salvagente *m*

safe'ty match' *s* fiammifero svedese

safe'ty pin' *s* spillo di sicurezza

safe'ty ra'zor *s* rasoio di sicurezza

safe'ty valve' *s* valvola di sicurezza

saffron ['sæfrən] *s* zafferano

sag [sæg] *s* cedimento; depressione; (*of a rope*) allentamento ‖ *v* (*pret & pp* **sagged**; *ger* **sagging**) *intr* curvarsi; cedere, afflosciarsi; allentarsi; (*said of prices*) calare

sagacious [sə'geʃəs] *adj* sagace

sage [sedʒ] *adj* saggio, savio ‖ *s* saggio, savio; (bot) salvia

sage'brush' *s* artemisia

Sagittarius [,sædʒɪ'terɪ-əs] *s* Sagittario

sail [sel] *s* vela; (*of windmill*) ala; gita a vela; **to set sail** far vela; **under full sail** a piena velatura ‖ *tr* veleggiare, navigare; (*a boat*) far navigare ‖ *intr* veleggiare, navigare; far vela; volare; (*said of a vessel*) partire; **to sail into** (coll) attaccare

sail'boat' *s* nave *f* a vela, veliero

sail'cloth' *s* tela di olona

sailing ['selɪŋ] *adj* in partenza ‖ *s* partenza; navigazione; navigazione a vela

sail'ing ship' *s* veliero

sail'mak'er *s* velaio

sailor ['selər] *s* marinaio

saint [sent] *adj & s* santo ‖ *tr* santificare, canonizzare

saint'hood *s* santità *f*

saintliness ['sentlɪnɪs] *s* santità *f*

Saint' Vi'tus's dance' ['vaɪtəsəz] *s* (pathol) ballo di San Vito

sake [sek] *s* causa, interesse *m;* **for the sake of** per il bene di, per l'amor di

salaam [sə'lɑm] *s* salamelecco ‖ *tr* fare salamelecchi a

salable ['seləbəl] *adj* vendibile

salacious [sə'leʃəs] *adj* salace

salad ['sæləd] *s* insalata

sal'ad bowl' *s* insalatiera

sal'ad oil' *s* olio da tavola

sala•ry ['sæləri] *s* (**-ries**) stipendio

sale [sel] *s* vendita; (*at reduced prices*) svendita, saldo; **for sale** in vendita; **si vende,** si vendono

sales'clerk' *s* commesso, impiegato

sales'la'dy s (**-dies**) commessa, impiegata
sales'man s (**-men**) venditore m; commesso; (*traveling*) piazzista m
sales'man·ship' s arte f di vendere
sales' promo'tion s promozione delle vendite, promotion f
sales'room' s sala di esposizione; sala vendite
sales' talk' s discorso da venditore; (*e.g., of a barker*) imbonimento
sales' tax' s imposta sulle vendite
saliva [sə'laɪvə] s saliva
sallow ['sælo] adj giallastro, olivastro
sal·ly [sæli] s (**-lies**) escursione, gita; (*outburst*) esplosione; (*witty remark*) uscita; (mil) sortita ‖ v pret & pp **-lied**) intr fare una sortita; **to sally forth** balzar fuori
salmon ['sæmən] s salmone m
salon [sæ'lɑn] s salone m
saloon [sə'lun] s taverna; (*on a passenger vessel*) salone m
saloon' keep'er s taverniere m
salt [sɔlt] s sale m; **to be worth one's salt** valere il pane che si mangia ‖ tr salare; (*cattle*) dare sale a; **to salt away** (coll) metter via, conservare
salt' bed' s salina
salt'cel'lar s saliera
saltine [sɔl'tin] s galletta salata
saltish ['sɔltɪʃ] adj salmastro
salt'pe'ter s (*potassium nitrate*) salnitro; (*sodium nitrate*) nitro del Cile
salt' shak'er s saliera
salt·y ['sɔlti] adj (**-ier; -iest**) salato
salubrious [sə'lubri·əs] adj salubre
salutation [,sæljə'teʃən] s saluto
salute [sə'lut] s saluto ‖ tr salutare
salvage ['sælvɪdʒ] s ricupero ‖ tr ricuperare
salvation [sæl'veʃən] s salvezza
Salva'tion Ar'my s Esercito della Salvezza
salve [sæv] or [sɑv] s unguento ‖ tr lenire, alleviare
sal·vo ['sælvo] s (**-vos** or **-voes**) salva
Samaritan [sə'mærɪtən] adj & s samaritano
same [sem] adj & pron indef medesimo, stesso; **it's all the same to me** a me fa lo stesso; **just the same** lo stesso, ugualmente; ciò nonostante; **same . . . as** lo stesso . . . che
sameness ['semnɪs] s uniformità f; monotonia
sample ['sæmpəl] s campione m, saggio ‖ tr (*to take a sample of*) campionare; (*to taste*) assaggiare, provare
sam'ple cop'y s esemplare m di campione
sancti·fy ['sæŋktɪ,faɪ] v (pret & pp **-fied**) tr santificare
sanctimonious [,sæŋktɪ'moni·əs] adj che affetta devozione ipocrita
sanction ['sæŋkʃən] s sanzione ‖ tr sanzionare
sanctuar·y ['sæŋktʃu,eri] s (**-ies**) santuario; **to take sanctuary** prendere asilo, rifugiarsi
sand [sænd] s sabbia ‖ tr insabbiare;

(*to polish*) smerigliare; cospergere di sabbia
sandal ['sændəl] s sandalo
san'dal·wood' s sandalo
sand'bag' s sacchetto a terra
sand'bank' s banco di sabbia
sand' bar' s cordone m litorale, banco di sabbia
sand'blast' s sabbiatura ‖ tr pulire con sabbiatura, sabbiare
sand'box' s cassone m pieno di sabbia; (rr) sabbiera
sand'glass' s orologio a polvere or a sabbia
sand'pa'per s carta vetrata ‖ tr pulire con carta vetrata
sand'stone' s arenaria
sandwich ['sændwɪtʃ] s panino imbottito, tramezzino ‖ tr inserire
sand'wich man' s tramezzino, uomo sandwich
sand·y ['sændi] adj (**-ier; -iest**) sabbioso; (*hair*) biondo rossiccio
sane [sen] adj sensato
sanguinary ['sæŋgwɪn,eri] adj sanguinario
sanguine ['sæŋgwɪn] adj fiducioso; (*complexion*) sanguigno
sanitary ['sænɪ,teri] adj sanitario
san'itary nap'kin s pannolino igienico
sanitation [,sænɪ'teʃən] s sanità f
sanity ['sænɪti] s sanità f di mente
Santa Claus ['sæntə,klɔz] s Babbo Natale
sap [sæp] s linfa, succhio; (mil) trincea; (coll) scemo ‖ v (pret & pp **sapped**) ger **sapping**) tr scavare; insidiare, minare; (*to weaken*) indebolire
sapling ['sæplɪŋ] s alberello; (*youth*) giovanetto
sapphire ['sæfaɪr] s zaffiro
Saracen ['særəsən] adj & s saraceno
sarcasm ['sɑrkæzəm] s sarcasmo
sarcastic [sɑr'kæstɪk] adj sarcastico
sardine [sɑr'din] s sardina; **packed in like sardines** pigiati come le acciughe
Sardinia [sɑr'dɪni·ə] s la Sardegna
Sardinian [sɑr'dɪni·ən] adj & s sardo
sarsaparilla [,sɑrsəpə'rɪlə] s salsapariglia
sash [sæʃ] s sciarpa; (*around one's waist*) fusciacca; (*of window*) telaio
sash' win'dow s finestra a ghigliottina
sas·sy ['sæsi] adj (**-ier; -iest**) (coll) impertinente; (*pert*) (coll) vivace
satchel ['sætʃəl] s sacca; (*of school-boy*) cartella
sateen [sæ'tin] s satin m
satellite ['sætə,laɪt] s satellite m
satiate ['seʃi,et] tr saziare
satin ['sætən] s raso
satire ['sætaɪr] s satira
satiric(al) [sə'tɪrɪk(əl)] adj satirico
satirist ['sætɪrɪst] s satirico
satirize ['sætɪ,raɪz] tr satireggiare
satisfaction [,sætɪs'fækʃən] s soddisfazione
satisfactory [,sætɪs'fæktəri] adj soddisfacente
satis·fy ['sætɪs,faɪ] v (pret & pp **-fied**) tr & intr soddisfare
saturate ['sætʃə,ret] tr saturare

Saturday ['sætərdi] s sabato
Saturn ['sætərn] s (astr) Saturno
sauce [sɔs] s salsa; (of fruit) conserva; (of chocolate) crema; (coll) insolenza, impertinenza ‖ tr condire; rendere piccante ‖ [sɔs] or [sæs] tr (coll) rispondere con impertinenza a
sauce'pan' s casseruola
saucer ['sɔsər] s piattino
sau-cy ['sɔsi] adj (-cier; -ciest) impertinente; (pert) vivace
sauerkraut ['saʊr,kraʊt] s sarcrauti mpl, crauti mpl
saunter ['sɔntər] s giro, bighellonata ‖ intr girandolare, bighellonare
sausage ['sɔsɪdʒ] s salsiccia
savage ['sævɪdʒ] adj & s selvaggio
savant ['sævənt] s erudito
save [sev] prep tranne, salvo ‖ tr salvare; (money) risparmiare; (to set apart) serbare; **to save face** salvare le apparenze ‖ intr fare economia
saving ['sevɪŋ] adj economico; che redime ‖ **savings** spl risparmi mpl, economie fpl ‖ **saving** prep eccetto, salvo
sav'ings account' s conto di risparmio
sav'ings and loan' associa'tion s cassa di risparmio che concede mutui
sav'ings bank' s cassa di risparmio
savior ['sevjər] s salvatore m
Saviour ['sevjər] s Salvatore m
savor ['sevər] s sapore m ‖ tr assaporare; (to flavor) saporire ‖ intr odorare; **to savor of** sapere di; odorare di
savor-y ['sevəri] adj (-ier; -iest) saporoso; piccante; delizioso ‖ s (-ies) (bot) santoreggia
saw [sɔ] s (tool) sega; detto, proverbio ‖ tr segare
saw'buck' s cavalletto
saw'dust' s segatura
saw'horse' s cavalletto
saw'mill' s segheria
Saxon ['sæksən] adj & s sassone m
saxophone ['sæksə,fon] s sassofono
say [se] s dire m; **to have no say** non aver voce in capitolo; **to have one's say** esprimere la propria opinione; **to have the say** avere l'ultima parola ‖ v (pret & pp **said** [sed]) tr dire; **I should say so!** certamente!; **it is said** si dice; **no sooner said than done** detto fatto; **that is to say** vale a dire; **to go without saying** essere ovvio
saying ['se·ɪŋ] s detto, proverbio
scab [skæb] s crosta; (strikebreaker) crumiro
scabbard ['skæbərd] s guaina, fodero
scab-by ['skæbi] adj (-bier; -biest) crostoso; (animal) rognoso; (slang) vile
scabrous ['skæbrəs] adj scabroso
scads [skædz] spl (slang) un mucchio
scaffold ['skæfəld] s impalcatura; (to execute a criminal) patibolo
scaffolding ['skæfəldɪŋ] s incastellatura, ponteggio
scald [skɔld] tr scottare; (e.g., milk) cuocere al disotto del punto d'ebollizione
scale [skel] s (e.g., of map) scala;

piatto della bilancia; (of fish) squama; **on a large scale** in grande scala; **scales** bilancia; **to tip the scales** far inclinare la bilancia ‖ tr squamare; (to incrust) incrostare; (to weigh) pesare; scalare; graduare; ridurre a scala ‖ intr squamarsi; scrostarsi
scallion ['skæljən] s scalogno
scallop ['skaləp] or ['skæləp] s (for cooking) conchiglia; (mollusk) pettine m; (slice of meat) scaloppina; (on edge of cloth) dentello, smerlo ‖ tr (fish) cuocere in conchiglia; dentellare, smerlare
scalp [skælp] s cuoio capelluto ‖ tr scotennare; (tickets) fare il bagarinaggio di
scalpel ['skælpəl] s scalpello
scalper ['skælpər] s bagarino
scal-y ['skeli] adj (-ier; -iest) squamoso; scrostato
scamp [skæmp] s cattivo soggetto, briccone m
scamper ['skæmpər] intr sgambettare; **to scamper away** darsela a gambe
scan [skæn] v (pret & pp **scanned**) ger **scanning**) tr scrutare; dare un'occhiata a; (verse) scandire; (telv) analizzare, scandire, esplorare
scandal ['skændəl] s scandalo
scandalize ['skændə,laɪz] tr scandalizzare
scandalous ['skændələs] adj scandaloso
Scandinavian [,skændɪ'nevɪ·ən] adj & s scandinavo
scanning ['skænɪŋ] s (telv) esplorazione
scan'ning line' s (telv) riga di analisi
scant [skænt] adj scarso; corto ‖ tr diminuire; lesinare
scant-y ['skænti] adj (-ier; -iest) appena sufficiente; povero, magro; (clothing) succinto
scapegoat ['skep,got] s capro espiatorio
scar [skar] s cicatrice f; (fig) sfregio ‖ v (pret & pp **scarred**; ger **scarring**) tr segnare, marcare; sfregiare ‖ intr cicatrizzarsi
scarce [skers] adj scarso, raro; **to make oneself scarce** (coll) non farsi vedere
scarcely ['skersli] adv appena; a mala pena; non . . . affatto; **scarcely ever** raramente; non . . . affatto
scarci-ty ['skersiti] s (-ties) scarsità f, scarsezza; carestia
scare [sker] s spavento ‖ tr spaventare, impaurire; **to scare away** fare scappare per lo spavento; **to scare up** (money) (coll) metter insieme
scare'crow' s spaventapasseri m
scarf [skarf] s (scarfs or **scarves** [skarvz]) sciarpa; cravattone m; (cover for table) centro, striscia
scarf'pin' s spilla da cravatta
scarlet ['skarlɪt] adj scarlatto
scar'let fe'ver s scarlattina
scar-y ['skeri] adj (-ier; -iest) (timid) (coll) fifone m; (causing fright) (coll) spaventevole

scathing [ˈskeðɪŋ] *adj* severo, bruciante

scatter [ˈskætər] *tr* disperdere, sparpagliare ‖ *intr* disperdersi, sparpagliarsi

scatterbrained [ˈskætərˌbrend] *adj* scervellato, stordito

scenari·o [sɪˈnɛrɪ ˌo] or [sɪˈnɑrɪ ˌo] *s* (-os) scenario

scenarist [sɪˈnɛrɪst] or [sɪˈnɑrɪst] *s* scenarista *mf*, sceneggiatore *m*

scene [sin] *s* (*view*) paesaggio; (*place*) scena; (theat) scena, quadro; **behind the scenes** dietro le quinte; **to make a scene** fare una scenata

scener·y [ˈsinəri] *s* (-ies) paesaggio; (theat) scenario

scenic [ˈsinɪk] or [ˈsɛnɪk] *adj* pittoresco; (*pertaining to the stage*) scenico

scent [sɛnt] *s* odore *m*; profumo; (*sense of smell*) fiuto, odorato; (*trail*) traccia, pista ‖ *tr* profumare; (*to detect*) fiutare, annusare

scepter [ˈsɛptər] *s* scettro

sceptic [ˈskɛptɪk] *adj & s* scettico

sceptical [ˈskɛptɪkəl] *adj* scettico

scepticism [ˈskɛptɪ ˌsɪzəm] *s* scetticismo

schedule [ˈskɛdʒul] *s* lista; programma *m*; (*of trains, planes, etc.*) orario ‖ *tr* programmare; mettere in orario

scheme [skim] *s* schema *m*; piano, progetto; (*plot*) trama ‖ *tr* progettare; tramare

schemer [ˈskimər] *s* progettista *mf*; (*underhanded*) manipolatore *m*, concertatore *m*

scheming [ˈskimɪŋ] *adj* intrigante, scaltro

schism [ˈsɪzəm] *s* scisma *m*

schist [ʃɪst] *s* scisto

scholar [ˈskɑlər] *s* (*pupil*) alunno; detentore *m* di una borsa di studio; (*learned person*) dotto, studioso

scholarly [ˈskɑlərli] *adj* erudito, studioso

scholarship [ˈskɑlər ˌʃɪp] *s* erudizione; (*money*) borsa di studio

scholasticism [skəˈlæstɪ ˌsɪzəm] *s* scolastica

school [skul] *s* scuola; (*of a university*) facoltà *f*; (*of fish*) banco ‖ *tr* istruire, insegnare

school′ age′ *s* età scolastica

school′ bag′ *s* cartella

school′ board′ *s* comitato scolastico

school′ boy′ *s* alunno, scolaro

school′ bus′ *s* scuolabus *m*

school′ day′ *s* giorno di scuola; durata della giornata scolastica

school′ girl′ *s* alunna, scolara

school′ house′ *s* scuola, edificio scolastico

schooling [ˈskulɪŋ] *s* istruzione

school′ mas′ter *s* maestro di scuola; direttore scolastico

school′ mate′ *s* compagno di scuola, condiscepolo

school′ room′ *s* aula scolastica

school′ teach′er *s* maestro

school′ year′ *s* anno scolastico

schooner [ˈskunər] *s* goletta

sciatica [saɪˈætɪkə] *s* (pathol) sciatica

science [ˈsaɪ·əns] *s* scienza

sci′ence fic′tion *s* fantascienza

sci′ence-fic′tion *adj* fantascientifico

scientific [ˌsaɪ·ənˈtɪfɪk] *adj* scientifico

scientist [ˈsaɪ·əntɪst] *s* scienziato

scimitar [ˈsɪmɪtər] *s* scimitarra

scintillate [ˈsɪntɪ ˌlet] *intr* scintillare

scion [ˈsaɪ·ən] *s* rampollo, discendente *m*

scissors [ˈsɪzərz] *ssg* or *spl* forbici *fpl*

scoff [skɔf] or [skɑf] *s* dileggio, beffa ‖ *intr* burlarsi; **to scoff at** burlarsi di, dileggiare

scold [skold] *s* megera ‖ *tr & intr* sgridare, rimproverare

scoop [skup] *s* (*ladlelike utensil*) paletta; (*kitchen utensil*) cucchiaio, cucchiaione *m*; cucchiaiata; palettata; (*of dredge*) benna; (*hollow*) buco; (naut) gottazza; (journ) primizia, esclusiva; (coll) colpo ‖ *tr* vuotare a cucchiaiate; (journ) battere; (naut) gottare; **to scoop out** (*e.g., sand*) scavare; (*soup*) scodellare

scoot [skut] *s* (coll) corsa ‖ *intr* (coll) correre precipitosamente

scooter [ˈskutər] *s* monopattino

scope [skop] *s* ampiezza; lunghezza; **to give full scope to** dare piena libertà d'azione a

scorch [skɔrtʃ] *s* scottatura ‖ *tr* bruciacchiare; bruciare, inaridire; (fig) ferire ‖ *intr* bruciarsi

scorching [ˈskɔrtʃɪŋ] *adj* bruciante

score [skor] *s* (*in a game*) punteggio; (*in an examination*) nota; linea, segno, marca; (*twenty*) ventina; (mus) partitura; **scores** un mucchio; **to keep score** segnare il punteggio; **to settle a score** (fig) saldare un conto ‖ *tr* raggiungere il punteggio di, fare; marcare; guadagnare; (*to censure*) sgridare, rimproverare; (mus) orchestrare

score′ board′ *s* quadro del punteggio

score′ keep′er *s* segnapunti *m*

scorn [skɔrn] *s* disdegno, disprezzo ‖ *tr & intr* disdegnare, disprezzare

scornful [ˈskɔrnfəl] *adj* disdegnoso

Scorpio [ˈskɔrpi ˌo] *s* Scorpione *m*

scorpion [ˈskɔrpi·ən] *s* scorpione *m*

Scot [skɑt] *s* scozzese *mf*

Scotch [skɑtʃ] *adj* scozzese ‖ *s* scozzese *m*; whisky *m* scozzese; **the Scotch** gli scozzesi

Scotch′ man *s* (-men) scozzese *m*

Scotch′ pine′ *s* pino silvestre

Scotch′ tape′ *s* (trademark) nastro autoadesivo Scotch

scot′-free′ *adj* impune; **to get off scot-free** farla franca

Scotland [ˈskɑtlənd] *s* la Scozia

Scottish [ˈskɑtɪʃ] *adj* scozzese ‖ *s* scozzese *mf*; **the Scottish** gli scozzesi

scoundrel [ˈskaʊndrəl] *s* birbante *m*, farabutto, manigoldo

scour [skaʊr] *tr* sgrassare fregando, pulire fregando; (*the countryside*) battere

scourge [skʌrdʒ] *s* sferza; (fig) flagello ‖ *tr* sferzare

scout [skaut] s esplorazione; giovane esploratore m; giovane esploratrice f; (mil) ricognitore m; (nav) esploratore m; (slang) tipo || tr esplorare, riconoscere; cercar di trovare; disdegnare

scouting ['skautɪŋ] s scoutismo

scowl [skaul] s cipiglio || intr aggrottare le ciglia; guardare torvamente

scram [skræm] v (pret & pp scrammed; ger scramming) intr (coll) tagliare la corda; scram! (coll) vattene!, (coll) escimi di tra i piedi!

scramble ['skræmbəl] s ruffa, gara || tr (to grab up) arraffare; confondere, mescolare; (eggs) strapazzare || intr arrampicarsi; (to struggle) azzuffarsi

scram'bled eggs' spl uova strapazzate

scrap [skræp] s pezzetto, frammento; ritaglio, rottame m; (coll) baruffa; scraps avanzi mpl; || v (pret & pp scrapped; ger scrapping) tr scartare || intr (coll) fare baruffa

scrap'book' s album m di ritagli (di giornale o fotografie)

scrape [skrep] s impiccio, imbroglio; baruffa || tr raschiare, graffiare; to scrape together racimolare || intr raschiare; to scrape along vivacchiare; to scrape through passare per il rotto della cuffia

scraper ['skrepər] s raschietto

scrap' i'ron s rottami mpl di ferro

scrap' pa'per s carta straccia; carta da appunti

scratch [skrætʃ] s graffio, scalfittura; scarabocchio; (billiards) punto perduto; (sports) linea di partenza; from scratch da bel principio; dal niente; up to scratch soddisfacente || tr graffiare, grattare; (e.g., a horse) cancellare || intr graffiare; (said of a chicken) raspare; (said of a pen) grattare

scratch' pad' s quaderno per appunti

scratch' pa'per s carta da appunti

scrawl [skrɔl] s scarabocchio || tr & intr scarabocchiare

scraw·ny ['skrɔni] adj (-nier; -niest) ossuto, scarno

scream [skrim] s grido, strillo; cosa divertentissima; persona divertentissima || intr gridare, strillare

screech [skritʃ] s stridio || intr stridere

screech' owl' s gufo; (barn owl) barbagianni m

screen [skrin] s (movable partition) paravento; (in front of fire) parafuoco; rete metallica; (sieve) vaglio; (mov; phys) schermo; (telv) teleschermo || tr schermare; riparare, proteggere; (to sieve) vagliare; (a film) proiettare; (to adapt) (mov) sceneggiare

screen' grid' s (rad, telv) griglia schermo

screen' test' s provino

screw [skru] s vite f; giro di vite; (of a boat) elica; to have a screw loose (slang) avere una rotella fuori di posto; to put the screws on far pressione su || tr avvitare; (to twist) torcere; to screw up (slang) rovinare; to screw up one's courage prendere il coraggio a quattro mani || intr avvitarsi

screw'ball' s (slang) pazzoide m, svitato

screw'driv'er s cacciavite m

screw' eye' s occhiello a vite

screw' jack' s martinetto a vite

screw' propel'ler s elica

screw·y ['skru·i] adj (-ier; -iest) (slang) pazzo; (slang) fuori di posto, strano

scribble ['skrɪbəl] s scarabocchio || tr & intr scarabocchiare

scribe [skraɪb] s (Jewish scholar) scriba m; copista mf || tr tracciare, incidere

scrimmage ['skrɪmɪdʒ] s ruffa; (football) azione

scrimp [skrɪmp] tr & intr lesinare

script [skrɪpt] s scrittura, scrittura a mano; manoscritto; testo; (e.g., of a play) copione m; (typ) carattere m inglese

scriptural ['skrɪptʃərəl] adj scritturale, biblico

scripture ['skrɪptʃər] s scrittura || Scripture s Scrittura

script'writ'er s soggettista mf

scrofula ['skrɔfjələ] s scrofola

scroll [skrol] s rotolo di carta, rotolo di pergamena; (of violin) riccio; (archit) voluta, cartoccio

scroll'work' s ornamentazione a voluta

scro·tum ['skrotəm] s (-ta [tə] or -tums) scroto

scrub [skrʌb] s boscaglia; alberelli mpl; animale bastardo; persona di poco conto; (act of scrubbing) fregata; (sports) giocatore m di riserva || v (pret & pp scrubbed; ger scrubbing) tr pulire, fregare

scrub' oak' s rovere basso

scrub'wom'an s (-wom'en) lavatrice f, donna a giornata

scruff [skrʌf] s nuca, collottola

scruple ['skrupəl] s scrupolo

scrupulous ['skrupjələs] adj scrupoloso

scrutinize ['skrutɪˌnaɪz]. tr scrutare, disaminare

scruti·ny ['skrutɪni] s (-nies) attento esame, disamina

scuff [skʌf] s graffio, logorio || tr logorare, graffiare

scuffle ['skʌfəl] s zuffa, rissa || intr azzuffarsi, colluttare

scull [skʌl] s (oar) remo a bratto; (boat) canotto || tr spingere a bratto || intr vogare a bratto

sculler·y ['skʌləri] s (-ies) retrocucina

scul'lery maid' s sguattera

scullion ['skʌljən] s sguattero

sculptor ['skʌlptər] s scultore m

sculptress ['skʌlptrɪs] s scultrice f

sculpture ['skʌlptʃər] s scultura || tr & intr scolpire

scum [skʌm] s schiuma; (slag) scoria; (rabble) feccia, gentaglia || v (pret & pp scummed; ger scumming) tr & intr schiumare

scum·my ['skʌmi] *adj* (**-mier; -miest**) spumoso; (coll) vile, schifoso

scurf [skʌrf] *s* (*shed by the skin*) squama; incrostazione

scurrilous ['skʌrɪləs] *adj* scurrile

scur·ry ['skʌri] *v* (*pret & pp* **-ried**) *intr* affrettarsi; **to scurry around** dimenarsi

scur·vy ['skʌrvi] *adj* (**-vier; -viest**) spregevole, meschino ‖ *s* scorbuto

scuttle ['skʌtəl] *s* (*for coal*) secchio; (*trap door*) botola; corsa, fuga; (naut) boccaporto ‖ *tr* aprire una falla in, affondare ‖ *intr* affrettarsi, darsi alla corsa

scut'tle·butt' *s* (naut) barilozzo dell'acqua; (coll) rumore *m*, diceria

scuttling ['skʌtlɪŋ] *s* autoaffondamento

Scylla ['sɪlə] *s* Scilla; **between Scylla and Charybdis** fra Scilla e Cariddi

scythe [saɪð] *s* falce *f*

sea [si] *s* mare *m*; (*wave*) maroso; **at sea** in alto mare; **by the sea** a mare, sulla costa; **to follow the sea** farsi marinaio; **to put to sea** prendere il largo

sea'board' *adj* costiero ‖ *s* litorale *m*

sea' breeze' *s* brezza marina

sea'coast' *s* costa, litorale *m*

sea' dog' *s* (*seal*) foca; (*sailor*) lupo di mare

seafarer ['si,fɛrər] *s* marinaio; viaggiatore marittimo

sea'food' *s* pesce *m*; (*shellfish*) frutti *mpl* di mare

seagoing ['si,go·ɪŋ] *adj* di alto mare

sea' gull' *s* gabbiano

seal [sil] *s* sigillo; (*sea animal*) foca; (fig) suggello ‖ *tr* sigillare, apporre i sigilli a; (fig) suggellare

sea' legs' *spl*—**to have good sea legs** avere piede marino

sea' lev'el *s* livello del mare

seal'ing wax' *s* ceralacca

seal'skin' *s* pelle *f* di foca

seam [sim] *s* (*abutting of edges*) giuntura; (*stitches*) costura, cucitura; (*scar*) cicatrice *f*; (*wrinkle*) ruga; (*in metal*) commettitura; (min) filone *m*, vena

sea'man *s* (**-men**) marinaio

sea' mile' *s* miglio marino

seamless ['simlɪs] *adj* senza giuntura; (*stockings*) senza cucitura

seamstress ['simstrɪs] *s* cucitrice *f*

seam·y ['simi] *adj* (**-ier; -iest**) pieno di cuciture; basso, sordido; (*unpleasant*) spiacevole

séance ['se·ɑns] *s* seduta spiritica

sea'plane' *s* idrovolante *m*

sea'port' *s* porto di mare

sea' pow'er *s* potenza navale

sear [sɪr] *adj* secco ‖ *s* scottatura ‖ *tr* scottare, bruciare; (*to brand*) marcare a fuoco; inaridire; (fig) indurire

search [sʌrtʃ] *s* ricerca, investigazione; (*frisking a person*) perquisizione; **in search of** in cerca di ‖ *tr* cercare, investigare; perquisire, frugare ‖ *intr* investigare; **to search for** cercare; **to search into** investigare

searching ['sʌrtʃɪŋ] *adj* (*e.g., inspec-*

tion) profondo; (*e.g., glance*) indagatore, penetrante

search'light' *s* proiettore *m*, riflettore *m*; (mil) fotoelettrica

search' war'rant *s* mandato di perquisizione

sea'scape' *s* vista del mare; (*painting*) marina

sea' shell' *s* conchiglia

sea'shore' *s* costa, marina, mare *m*

sea'sick' *adj*—**to be seasick** aver mal di mare

sea'sick'ness *s* mal *m* di mare

sea'side' *s* costa, riviera, marina

season ['sizən] *s* stagione; **in season di** stagione; **in season and out of season** sempre, continuamente; **out of season** fuori stagione ‖ *tr* (*food*) condire; (*to mature*) stagionare; (*e.g., wood*) stagionare

seasonal ['sizənəl] *adj* stagionale

seasoning ['sizənɪŋ] *s* condimento; (*of wood*) stagionamento

sea'son's greet'ings *spl* migliori auguri *mpl* per le feste natalizie

sea'son tick'et *s* biglietto d'abbonamento

seat [sit] *s* sedia; (*part of chair*) sedile *m*; (*of human body*) sedere *m*; (*of pants*) fondo; sito, posto; (*e.g., of government*) sede *f*; (*in parliament*) seggio; (*e.g., of learning*) centro; (rr, theat) posto ‖ *tr* far sedere; aver posti per; (*a chair*) mettere il sedile a; (*pants*) mettere il fondo a; (*an official*) insediare; (mach) installare; **to be seated** essere seduto; **to seat oneself** sedersi

seat' belt' *s* cintura di sicurezza

seat' cov'er *s* guaina, foderina

seat'ing room' *s* posti *mpl* a sedere

sea' wall' *s* diga

sea'way' *s* via marittima; alto mare; mare grosso; rotta percorsa; via di fiume accessibile a navi da trasporto

sea'weed' *s* alga marina; pianta marina

sea'wor'thy *adj* atto a tenere il mare

secede [sɪ'sid] *intr* separarsi, distaccarsi

secession [sɪ'sɛʃən] *s* secessione

seclude [sɪ'klud] *tr* appartare; isolare

seclusion [sɪ'kluʒən] *s* reclusione; solitudine *f*, intimità *f*

second ['sɛkənd] *adj & pron* secondo; **to be second to none** non cedela a nessuno ‖ *s* secondo; (*in a duel*) padrino; (*in dates*) due *m*; (aut, mus) seconda; **seconds** (com) articoli *mpl* di seconda qualità; **to have seconds on** servirsi una seconda volta di ‖ *tr* assecondare; (*a motion*) appoggiare ‖ *adv* in secondo luogo

secondar·y ['sɛkən,dɛri] *adj* secondario ‖ *s* (**-ies**) (elec) secondario

sec'ond-best' *adj* (il) migliore dopo il primo; **to come off second-best** arrivare secondo

sec'ond-class' *adj* di seconda qualità; (aer, naut, rr) di seconda classe

sec'ond hand' *s* lancetta dei secondi

sec'ond-hand' *adj* di seconda mano, d'occasione

sec'ond lieuten'ant s sottotenente m
sec'ond-rate' adj di seconda categoria; (inferior) da strapazzo
sec'ond sight' s chiaroveggenza
sec'ond wind' [wɪnd] s—**to get one's second wind** riprendere fiato
secre-cy ['sikrəsɪ] s (-cies) segretezza; **in secrecy** in segreto
secret ['sikrɪt] adj & s segreto; **in secret** in segreto
secretar-y ['sekrɪ,terɪ] s (-ies) segretario; (desk) scrittoio
se'cret bal'lot s scrutinio segreto
secrete [sɪ'krit] tr nascondere; (physiol) secernere
secretive ['sikrɪtɪv] or [sɪ'kritɪv] adj riservato, poco comunicativo
sect [sekt] s setta
sectarian [sek'terɪ-ən] adj & s settario
section ['sekt/ən] s sezione; (of city) rione m; (of fruit) spicchio; (of highway) tronco; (rr) tratta || tr sezionare
sectional ['sek/ənəl] adj (e.g., book-case) componibile; sezionale; locale, regionale
secular ['sekjələr] adj & s secolare m
secularism ['sekjələ,rɪzəm] s laicismo
secure [sɪ'kjur] adj salvo, sicuro || tr ottenere; assicurare; fissare; (law) garantire
securi-ty [sɪ'kjurɪtɪ] s (-ties) sicurezza; protezione; garanzia; (person) garante m; **securities** valori mpl, titoli mpl
sedan [sɪ'dæn] s (aut) berlina
sedan' chair' s bussola, portantina
sedate [sɪ'det] adj calmo, posato
sedation [sɪ'de/ən] s ritorno alla calma; stato di calma mentale
sedative ['sedatɪv] adj & s sedativo
sedentary ['sedən,terɪ] adj sedentario
sedge [sedʒ] s carice m
sediment ['sedɪmənt] s sedimento
sedition [sɪ'dɪ/ən] s sedizione
seditious [sɪ'dɪ/əs] adj sedizioso
seduce [sɪ'djus] or [sɪ'dus] tr sedurre
seducer [sɪ'djusər] or [sɪ'dusər] s seduttore m, corruttore m
seduction [sɪ'dʌk/ən] s seduzione
seductive [sɪ'dʌktɪv] adj seduttore
sedulous ['sedʒələs] adj diligente
see [si] s (eccl) sede f || v (pret saw [sɔ]; pp seen [sin]) tr vedere; **to see off** andare ad accompagnare; **to see through** portare a termine || intr vedere; **see here!** faccia attenzioni; **to see after** prender cura di; **to see through** conoscere il gioco di
seed [sid] s seme m, semenza; **to go to seed** andare in semenza; deteriorarsi || tr seminare; (fruit) togliere i semi da || intr seminare; produrre semi
seed'bed' s semenzaio; (fig) vivaio
seeder ['sidər] s (person) seminatore m; (machine) seminatrice f
seedling ['sidlɪŋ] s piantina da trapianto
seed-y ['sidɪ] adj (-ier; -iest) pieno di semi; (unkempt) malmesso, malvestito
seeing ['si-ɪŋ] conj visto che, dato che

See'ing Eye' dog' s cane m guida per ciechi
seek [sik] v (pret & pp sought [sɔt]) tr cercare, ricercare; **to be sought after** essere ricercato; **to seek to** cercare di
seem [sim] intr parere, sembrare
seemingly ['simɪŋlɪ] adv apparentemente
seem-ly ['simlɪ] adj (-lier; -liest) decoroso; appropriato
seep [sip] intr colare, filtrare
seer [sɪr] s profeta m, veggente m
see'saw' s altalena; (motion) viavai m || intr altalenare
seethe [sið] intr bollire
segment ['segmənt] s segmento
segregate ['segrɪ,get] tr segregare
segregation [,segrɪ'ge/ən] s segregazione
segregationist [,segrɪ'ge/ənɪst] s segregazionista mf
seismograph ['saɪzmə,græf] or ['saɪzmə,graf] s sismografo
seismology [saɪz'mɑlədʒɪ] s sismologia
seize [siz] tr afferrare; impossessarsi di; (with one's clenched fist) impugnare; comprendere; (law) sequestrare, confiscare
seizure ['siʒər] s conquista, cattura; (of an illness) attacco; (law) sequestro, pignoramento
seldom ['seldəm] adj di raro, raramente
select [sɪ'lekt] adj scelto, selezionato || tr prescegliere, selezionare
selectee [sɪ,lek'ti] s (mil) recluta
selection [sɪ'lek/ən] s selezione, scelta
selective [sɪ'lektɪv] adj selettivo
self [self] adj stesso || s (selves [selvz]) sé stesso; io, personalità f; **all by one's self** senza aiuto altrui || pron sé stesso
self'-abuse' s abuso delle proprie forze; masturbazione
self'-addressed' adj col nome e l'indirizzo del mittente
self'-cen'tered adj egocentrico
self'-con'scious adj imbarazzato, vergognoso, timido
self'-control' s padronanza di sé stesso, autocontrollo
self'-defense' s autodifesa; **in self-defense** in legittima difesa
self'-deni'al s abnegazione
self'-deter'mina'tion s autodeterminazione
self'-dis'cipline s autodisciplina
self'-ed'ucat'ed adj autodidatta
self'-employed' adj che lavora in proprio
self'-ev'i-dent adj evidente, lampante
self'-ex-plan'a-tor'y adj ovvio, che si spiega da sé
self'-gov'ernment s autogoverno; controllo sopra sé stesso
self'-im-por'tant adj presuntuoso
self'-in-dul'gence s intemperanza
self'-in'terest s egoismo, interesse m
selfish ['self/] adj egoista
selfishness ['self/nɪs] s egoismo

selfless ['sɛlflɪs] *adj* disinteressato; altruista

self'-liq'ui·dat'ing *adj* autoammortizzabile

self'-love' *s* amor proprio

self'-made' *adj* che si è fatto da sé

self'-por'trait *s* autoritratto

self'-pos·sessed' *adj* calmo, padrone di sé

self'-pres'er·va'tion *s* conservazione

self'-pro·pelled' *adj* semovente

self'-re·li·ant *adj* pieno di fiducia in sé stesso

self'-re·spect' *s* rispetto di sé stesso

self'-right'eous *adj* che si considera più morale degli altri, ipocrita

self'-sac'ri·fice' *s* sacrificio di sé, spirito di sacrificio

self'-same' *adj* stesso e medesimo

self'-sat'is·fied' *adj* contento di sé

self'-seek'ing *adj* egoista || *s* egoismo

self'-serv'ice *s* autoservizio

self'-start'er *s* motorino d'avviamento

self'-styled' *adj* sedicente

self'-support' *s* indipendenza economica

self'-tap'ping screw' *s* vite *f* autofilettante

self'-taught' *adj* autodidatta

self-threading ['self'θredɪŋ] *adj* autofilettante

self'-willed' *adj* ostinato, caparbio

self'-wind'ing *adj* a carica automatica

sell [sɛl] *v* (*pret* & *pp* **sold** [sold]) *tr* vendere; (*an idea*) fare accettare; **to sell off** svendere, liquidare; **to sell out** smerciare; vendere a stralcio; (coll) tradire || *intr* vendere, vendersi; fare il venditore; **to sell off** (*said of the stock market*) essere in ribasso; **to sell out** vendere a stralcio; vendersi

seller ['sɛlər] *s* venditore *m*

Selt'zer wa'ter ['sɛltsər] *s* selz *m*

selvage ['sɛlvɪdʒ] *s* cimosa, vivagno

semantic [sɪ'mæntɪk] *adj* semantico || **semantics** *s* semantica

semaphore ['sɛmə‚for] *s* semaforo

semblance ['sɛmbləns] *s* apparenza, specie *f*; apparizione

semen ['simən] *s* sperma *m*

semester [sɪ'mɛstər] *adj* semestrale || *s* semestre *m*

semicircle ['sɛmɪ‚sʌrkəl] *s* semicircolo

semicolon ['sɛmɪ‚kolən] *s* punto e virgola

semiconductor [‚sɛmɪkən'dʌktər] *s* semiconduttore *m*

semiconscious [‚sɛmɪ'kanʃəs] *adj* mezzo cosciente

semifinal [‚sɛmɪ'faɪnəl] *s* semifinale *f*

semilearned [‚sɛmɪ'lʌrnɪd] *adj* semidotto

semimonth·ly [‚sɛmɪ'mʌnθli] or [‚sɛmaɪ'mʌnθli] *adj* quindicinale || *s* (-lies) rivista quindicinale

seminar [‚sɛmɪ‚nar] or [‚sɛmɪ'nar] *s* seminario

seminar·y ['sɛmɪ‚nɛri] *s* (-ies) seminario

Semite ['sɛmaɪt] or ['simaɪt] *s* semita *mf*

Semitic [sɪ'mɪtɪk] *adj* semitico || *s* lingua semitica; (*family of languages*) semitico

semitrailer ['sɛmɪ‚trelər] *s* semirimorchio

semiweek·ly [‚sɛmɪ'wikli] or [‚sɛmaɪ'wikli] *adj* bisettimanale || *s* (-lies) periodico bisettimanale

semiyearly [‚sɛmɪ'jɪrli] or [‚sɛmaɪ'jɪrli] *adj* semestrale || *adv* due volte all'anno

senate ['sɛnɪt] *s* senato

senator ['sɛnətər] *s* senatore *m*

send [sɛnd] *v* (*pret* & *pp* **sent** [sɛnt]) *tr* inviare, mandare; spedire; (*e.g., a punch*) lanciare; **to send back** rimandare; **to send forth** emettere; **to send packing** licenziare su due piedi || *intr* (rad) trasmettere; **to send for** mandare a chiamare, far venire

sender ['sɛndər] *s* speditore *m*, mittente *m*; (telg) trasmettitore *m*

send'-off' *s* (coll) addio affettuoso; (coll) lancio

senility [sɪ'nɪlɪti] *s* (pathol) senilismo

senior ['sinjər] *adj* maggiore, più anziano; seniore, di grado più elevato; dell'ultimo anno, laureando; senior, il vecchio || *s* maggiore *m*; seniore *m*, persona di grado più elevato; studente *m* dell'ultimo anno, laureando

sen'ior cit'izen *s* vecchio, pensionato

seniority [sin'jarɪti] or [sin'jɔrɪti] *s* anzianità *f*

sensation [sɛn'seʃən] *s* sensazione

sensational [sɛn'seʃənəl] *adj* sensazionale

sense [sɛns] *s* senso; **in a sense** in un certo senso; **to come to one's senses** riprendere il giudizio; **to make sense out of** arrivare a capire; **to take leave of one's senses** perdere il ben dell'intelletto || *tr* intuire; comprendere

senseless ['sɛnslɪs] *adj* (*unconscious*) privo di sensi; (*meaningless*) insensato, privo di senso

sense' or'gan *s* organo di senso

sensibili·ty [‚sɛnsɪ'bɪlɪti] *s* (-ties) sensibilità *f*; **sensibilities** suscettibilità *f*

sensible ['sɛnsɪbəl] *adj* sensato; (*keenly aware*) sensibile; cosciente

sensitive ['sɛnsɪtɪv] *adj* sensitivo, sensibile; delicato

sensitize ['sɛnsɪ‚taɪz] *tr* sensibilizzare

sensory ['sɛnsəri] *adj* sensorio

sensual ['sɛnʃʊ·əl] *adj* sensuale

sensuous ['sɛnʃʊ·əs] *adj* sensuale

sentence ['sɛntəns] *s* (gram) frase; (law) sentenza, condanna || *tr* sentenziare, condannare

sentiment ['sɛntɪmənt] *s* sentimento

sentimental [‚sɛntɪ'mɛntəl] *adj* sentimentale

sentimentalism [‚sɛntɪ'mɛntəl‚ɪzəm] *s* sentimentalismo

sentinel ['sɛntɪnəl] *s* sentinella; **to stand sentinel** montare di sentinella

sen·try ['sɛntri] *s* (-tries) sentinella

sen'try box' *s* garitta, casotto

separate ['sɛpərɪt] *adj* separato ||

['sepə,ret] *tr* separare || *intr* separarsi

separation [,sepə'reʃən] *s* separazione

Sephardic [sɪ'fɑrdɪk] *adj* sefardita

September [sep'tembər] *s* settembre *m*

septic ['septɪk] *adj* settico

sep'tic tank' *s* fossa settica

sepulcher ['sepəlkər] *s* sepolcro

sequel ['sikwəl] *s* seguito

sequence ['sikwəns] *s* serie *f*, sequenza, successione; conseguenza; (cards, eccl, mov) sequenza; (gram) correlazione

sequester [sɪ'kwestər] *tr* isolare, appartare; (law) sequestrare

sequin ['sikwɪn] *s* lustrino

ser•aph ['seraf] *s* (-aphs or -aphim [əfɪm]) serafino

Serbian ['sʌrbɪ•ən] *adj & s* serbo

Serbo-Croatian [,sʌrbokro'eʃən] *adj & s* serbocroato

sere [sɪr] *adj* secco, appassito

serenade [,serə'ned] *s* serenata || *tr* fare la serenata a || *intr* fare la serenata

serene [sɪ'rin] *adj* sereno

serenity [sɪ'renɪti] *s* serenità *f*

serf [sʌrf] *s* servo della gleba

serfdom ['sʌrfdəm] *s* servitù *f* della gleba

serge [sʌrdʒ] *s* saia

sergeant ['sɑrdʒənt] *s* sergente *m*

ser'geant at arms' *s* (ser'geants at arms') ufficiale *m* delegato a mantenere l'ordine

ser'geant ma'jor *s* (sergeants major or sergeant majors) (*in U.S. Army*) sergente *m* maggiore; (*in Italian Army*) maresciallo

serial ['sɪrɪ•əl] *adj* a puntate, a dispense || *s* periodico; romanzo a puntate; programma *m* a serie

se'rial num'ber *s* matricola; (*of a book*) segnatura; (aut) matricola di telaio

se•ries ['sɪrɪz] *s* (-ries) serie *f*; (*works dealing with the same topic*) collana; **in series** (elec) in serie

serious ['sɪrɪ•əs] *adj* serio

seriousness ['sɪrɪ•əsnɪs] *s* serietà *f*; **in all seriousness** molto sul serio

sermon ['sʌrmən] *s* sermone *m*

sermonize ['sʌrmə,naɪz] *tr & intr* sermonare

serpent ['sʌrpənt] *s* serpente *m*

se•rum ['sɪrəm] *s* (-rums or -ra [rə]) siero

servant ['sʌrvənt] *s* servo, domestico; (*civil servant*) funzionario; (fig) servitore *m*

serv'ant girl' *s* serva, domestica

serv'ant prob'lem *s* crisi *f* ancillare

serve [sʌrv] *s* (*in tennis*) servizio || *tr* servire; (*a sentence*) espiare; (*to suffice*) bastare (with *dat*); (*a writ*) notificare; **to serve s.o. right** stare bene (with *dat*), e.g., **it serves him right** gli sta bene || *intr* servire; **to serve as** fare da

service ['sʌrvɪs] *s* servizio; (*of a writ*) notifica; (*branch of the armed forces*) arma; **at your service** per servirLa || *tr* rifornire, riparare

serviceable ['sʌrvɪsəbəl] *adj* utile; durevole; pratico; riparabile

serv'ice club' *s* casa del soldato

serv'ice•man' *s* (-men') militare *m*; riparatore *m*, aggiustatore *m*

serv'ice mod'ule *s* modulo di servizio

serv'ice rec'ord *s* stato di servizio

serv'ice sta'tion *s* stazione di servizio or di rifornimento

serv'ice-sta'tion attend'ant *s* benzinaio

serv'ice stripe' *s* gallone *m*

servile ['sʌrvɪl] *adj* servile

servitude ['sʌrvɪ,tjud] or ['sʌrvɪ,tud] *s* servitù *f*; lavori forzati

sesame ['sesəmɪ] *s* sesamo; **open sesame** apriti sesamo

session ['seʃən] *s* sessione *f*, seduta

set [set] *adj* determinato, preordinato; abituale; fisso, rigido; (*ready*) pronto; meditato, studiato || *s* (e.g., *of books*) collezione, serie *f*; (e.g., *of chess*) gioco; set *m*, insieme *m*, completo; (*of tires*) treno; (*of horses*) pariglia; (*of tennis*) partita; (*of dishes*) servizio; (*of kitchen utensils*) batteria; posizione, atteggiamento; (*of a garment*) linea; (e.g., *of cement*) presa; (*of people*) gruppo; (*of thieves*) genia; (*of sails*) muta; (*of lines*) (geom) fascio; (rad, telv) apparato; (theat, mov) set *m* || *v* (*pret & pp* set; *ger* setting) *tr* porre, deporre; (*fire*) dare; (*the table*) imbandire; (*a watch*) regolare; (*s.o. a certain number of tricks*) far cadere di; (*a price*) fissare; (*a gem*) incastonare; (*a fracture*) mettere a posto; (*a saw*) allicciare; (*a trap*) tendere; (*hair*) acconciare; stabilire; insediare; (*to plant*) piantare; (*a sail*) tendere; (e.g., *milk*) rapprendere; calibrare, tarare; (*cement*) solidificare; (typ) comporre; **to set back** ritardare; (*a clock*) mettere indietro; **to set forth** descrivere; **to set one's heart on** desiderare ardentemente; **to set store by** tenere in gran conto; **to set up** metter su; impiantare; (*drinks*) (slang) pagare || *intr* (said, e.g., *of the sun*) tramontare; (said *of a liquid*) solidificarsi; (said *of cement*) fare presa; (said *of milk*) rapprendersi; (said *of a hen*) covare; (said *of a garment*) cascare; (said *of hair*) prendere la piega; **to set about** mettersi a; **to set out** porsi in cammino; **to set out to** mettersi a; **to set to work** mettersi a lavorare; **to set upon** attaccare

set'back' *s* rovescio, contrarietà *f*

set'screw' *s* vite *f* di pressione

setting ['setɪŋ] *s* (*environment*) ambiente *m*; (*of a gem*) montatura; (*of cement*) presa; (e.g., *of the sun*) tramonto; (theat) scenario; (mus) arrangiamento

set'ting-up' ex'ercises *spl* ginnastica da camera

settle ['setəl] *tr* determinare, risolvere; sistemare, regolare; (*a bill*) liquidare; installarsi in, colonizzare; calmare; (*a liquid*) far depositare; (law) conciliare || *intr* mettersi d'accordo; saldare un conto; stanziarsi; domiciliarsi; fermarsi, posare; (*said of a liquid*) depositare, calmarsi; solidificarsi; **to settle down to work** mettersi a lavorare di buzzo buono; **to settle on** scegliere, fissare

settlement ['sɛtələmənt] *s* stabilimento; sistemazione, regolamento; colonia, comunità *f;* (*of a building*) infossamento; agenzia di beneficenza

settler ['sɛtlər] *s* fondatore *m;* colono; conciliatore *m*

set'up' *s* portamento; (*e.g., of tools*) disposizione; quanto è necessario per mescolare una bibita alcolica; (coll) incontro truccato

seven ['sɛvən] *adj & pron* sette || *s* sette *m;* **seven o'clock** le sette

sev'en hun'dred *adj, s & pron* settecento

seventeen ['sɛvən'tin] *adj, s & pron* diciassette *m*

seventeenth ['sɛvən'tinθ] *adj, s & pron* diciassettesimo || *s* (*in dates*) diciassette *m*

seventh ['sɛvənθ] *adj, s & pron* settimo || *s* (*in dates*) sette *m*

seventieth ['sɛvəntɪɪθ] *adj, s & pron* settantesimo

seven-ty ['sɛvənti] *adj & pron* settanta || *s* (**-ties**) settanta *m;* **the seventies** gli anni settanta

sever ['sɛvər] *tr* tagliare, mozzare; (*relations*) troncare || *intr* separarsi

several ['sɛvərəl] *adj* parecchi, vari; rispettivi || *spl* parecchi *mpl*

sev'erance pay' ['sɛvərəns] *s* buonuscita, indennità *f* di licenziamento

severe [sɪ'vɪr] *adj* severo; (*weather*) rigido; (*pain*) acuto; (*illness*) grave

sew [so] *v* (*pret* **sewed;** *pp* **sewed** or **sewn**) *tr & intr* cucire

sewage ['su·ɪdʒ] or ['sju·ɪdʒ] *s* acque *fpl* di scolo or di rifiuto

sewer ['su·ər] or ['sju·ər] *s* fogna, chiavica

sewerage ['su·ərɪdʒ] or ['sju·ərɪdʒ] *s* fognatura; drenaggio, rimozione delle acque di rifiuto

sew'ing machine' ['so·ɪŋ] *s* macchina da cucire

sex [sɛks] *s* sesso

sex' appeal' *s* attrattiva fisica, sex appeal *m*

sextant ['sɛkstənt] *s* sestante *m*

sextet [sɛks'tɛt] *s* sestetto

sexton ['sɛkstən] *s* sagrestano

sexual ['sɛk/u·əl] *adj* sessuale

sex-y ['sɛksi] *adj* (**-ier; -iest**) (coll) erotico; (coll) procace

shab-by ['ʃæbi] *adj* (**-bier; -biest**) (*clothes*) frusto; (*house*) malandato; (*person*) malvestito; (*deal*) cattivo

shack [ʃæk] *s* baracca

shackle ['ʃækəl] *s* ceppo; (*to tie an animal*) pastoia; (fig) ostacolo; **shackles** ceppi *mpl*, manette *fpl* || *tr* mettere in ceppi; (fig) inceppare

shad [ʃæd] *s* alosa

shade [ʃed] *s* ombra; (*of lamp*) paralume *m;* (*of window*) tendina; (*for*

the eyes) visiera; (*hue*) tinta, sfumatura; **a shade of** un po' di; **shades** tenebre *fpl;* ombre *fpl* || *tr* ombreggiare; sfumare, digradare; (*a price*) ribassare leggermente

shadow ['ʃædo] *s* ombra || *tr* ombreggiare; (*to follow*) pedinare; **to shadow forth** adombrare, preannunciare

shadowy ['ʃædo·i] *adj* ombroso, ombreggiato; illusorio, chimerico

shad-y ['ʃedi] *adj* (**-ier; -iest**) ombroso; spettrale; (coll) losco; **to keep shady** (slang) starsene lontano

shaft [ʃæft] or [ʃɑft] *s* (*of arrow*) asta; (*of feather*) rachide *f;* (*of light*) raggio; (*handle*) manico; (*of wagon*) stanga, timone *m;* (*of motor*) albero; (*of column*) fusto; (*of elevator*) pozzo; (*in* *a mountain*) camino; (min) fornello; (fig) frecciata

shag-gy ['ʃægi] *adj* (**-gier; -giest**) peloso, irsuto; (*unkempt*) trasandato; (*cloth*) ruvido

shag'gy dog' sto'ry *s* storiella senza capo né coda

shake [ʃek] *s* scossa; stretta di mano; momento, istante *m;* **the shakes** la tremarella || *v* (*pret* **shook** [ʃuk]; *pp* **shaken**) *tr* scuotere; scrollare; (*s.o.'s hands*) serrare; (*e.g., with a mixer*) sbattere; agitare, perturbare; eludere, disfarsi di || *intr* tremare; (*to totter*) traballare, tentennare; scuotere; darsi la mano

shake'down' *s* estorsione, concussione; (*bed*) lettuccio di fortuna

shake'down' cruise' *s* (naut) viaggio di prova

shaker ['ʃekər] *s* (*e.g., for sugar*) spolverino; (*for cocktails*) sbattighiaccio, shaker *m*

shake'-up' *s* cambiamento completo, riorganizzazione, rimaneggiamento

shak-y ['ʃeki] *adj* (**-ier; -iest**) tremebondo; traballante, zoppicante

shall [ʃæl] *v* (*cond* **should** [ʃud]) *v aux* si usa per formare (1) il futuro dell'indicativo, per es., **I shall do it** lo farò; (2) il futuro perfetto dell'indicativo, per es., **I shall have done it** l'avrò fatto; (3) espressioni di obbligo o necessità, per es., **what shall I do?** che devo fare?, che vuole che faccia?

shallow ['ʃælo] *adj* basso, poco profondo; leggero, superficiale

sham [ʃæm] *adj* falso, finto || *s* frode *f,* contraffazione || *v* (*pret & pp* **shammed;** *ger* **shamming**) *tr & intr* fingere

sham' bat'tle *s* finta battaglia

shambles ['ʃæmbəlz] *s* macello; confusione, disordine

shame [ʃem] *s* vergogna; **shame on you!** vergogna!; **what a shame!** che peccato! || *tr* svergognare, disonorare

shame'faced' *adj* timido, vergognoso

shameful ['ʃemfəl] *adj* vergognoso

shameless ['ʃemlɪs] *adj* sfrontato, impudente, svergognato

shampoo [ʃæm'pu] s shampoo m || tr fare lo shampoo a

shamrock ['ʃæmrɑk] s trifoglio irlandese

shanghai ['ʃæŋhaɪ] or [ʃæŋ'haɪ] tr imbarcare a viva forza || **Shanghai** s Sciangai f

shank [ʃæŋk] s fusto; (of tool) codolo; (stem) gambo; (of bird) zampa; (of anchor) fuso; (coll) principio; (coll) fine f; **to ride shank's mare** andare col cavallo di San Francesco

shan·ty ['ʃænti] s (-ties) bicocca

shan·ty·town' s bidonville f

shape [ʃep] s forma; **in bad shape in** cattive condizioni; **out of shape** sformato || tr formare, foggiare; plasmare, conformare || intr formarsi; **to take shape** prender forma

shapeless ['ʃeplɪs] adj informe

shape·ly ['ʃepli] adj (-lier; -liest) ben fatto, formoso

share [ʃer] s parte f; interesse m; (of stock) azione f; (of plow) suola; **to go shares** dividere in parti eguali || tr (to enjoy jointly) condividere; (to apportion) ripartire || intr partecipare, prender parte

sharecropper ['ʃer‚krɑpər] s mezzadro

share'hold'er s azionista mf

shark [ʃɑrk] s pescecane m; (schemer) piovra; (slang) esperto

sharp [ʃɑrp] adj affilato, acuto; angoloso; (e.g., curve) forte; distinto, ben delineato; (taste) pungente, salato; (pain) vivo; (words) mordace; (slang) elegante || s (mus) diesis m || adv acutamente; in punto, e.g., **at seven o'clock sharp** alle sette in punto

sharpen ['ʃɑrpən] tr affilare; (a pencil) fare la punta a || intr affilarsi

sharpener ['ʃɑrpənər] s (person) affilatore m; (machine) affilatrice f

sharper ['ʃɑrpər] s gabbamondo

sharp'shoot'er s tiratore scelto

shatter ['ʃætər] tr frantumare; sfracellare; (health) rovinare; (nerves) sconvolgere; distruggere || intr frantumarsi, andare in pezzi

shat'ter·proof adj infrangibile

shave [ʃev] s rasatura; **to have a close shave** scamparla or scamparla bella || tr (the face) radere, sbarbare; (wood) piallare; (to scrape) sfiorare; (prices) ridurre; (a lawn) tosare || intr rasarsi

shaving ['ʃevɪŋ] adj da barba, per barba, e.g., **shaving cream** crema da or per barba || s rasatura; **shavings** trucioli mpl

shav'ing brush' s pennello da barba

shav'ing soap' s sapone m per la barba

shawl [ʃɔl] s scialle m

she [ʃi] s (shes) femmina || pron pers (they) essa, lei

sheaf [ʃif] s (sheaves [ʃivz]) covone m; (of paper) fascio

shear [ʃɪr] s lama di cesoia; tagliatura; **shears** cesoie fpl || v (pret **sheared**; pp **sheared** or **shorn** [ʃɔrn]) tr (sheep) tosare; (cloth) tagliare; **to shear s.o. of** privare qlcu di

sheath [ʃiθ] s (sheaths [ʃiðz]) guaina, coperta; (of a sword) fodero

sheathe [ʃið] tr rinfoderare, inguainare

shed [ʃed] s portico, tettoia; (geog) spartiacque m, versante m || v (pret & pp **shed**; ger **shedding**) tr (e.g., blood) spargere, versare; (light) dare, fare; (feathers) spogliarsi di, lasciar cadere

sheen [ʃin] s lucentezza

sheep [ʃip] s (sheep) pecora; **sheep's eyes** occhio di triglia; **to separate the sheep from the goats** separare i buoni dai cattivi

sheep'dog' s cane m da pastore

sheepish ['ʃipɪʃ] adj timido, goffo; pecoresco, pedissequo

sheep'skin' s pelle f di pecora; (parchment) cartapecora; (bb) bazzana; (coll) diploma m

sheer [ʃɪr] adj trasparente, fino, velato; puro; (cliff) stagliato || adv completamente || intr deviare

sheet [ʃit] s (for bed) lenzuolo; (of paper) foglio; (of metal) lamina; (of water) specchio; (naut) scotta

sheet' light'ning s lampeggio all'orizzonte

sheet' met'al s lamiera

sheet' mu'sic s spartito non rilegato

sheik [ʃik] s sceicco; (great lover) (slang) rubacuori m

shelf [ʃelf] s (shelves [ʃelvz]) scaffale m, scansia; (ledge) terrazzo, ripiano; banco di sabbia; **on the shelf** in disparte, dimenticato

shell [ʃel] s (of egg or crustacean) guscio; (of mollusk) conchiglia; (of vegetable) baccello; proietto, proiettile m; (cartridge) cartuccia; (of a cartridge) bossolo; (framework) armatura; (of boiler) involucro; imbarcazione da regata, schifo, iole f || tr (vegetables) sgranare; bombardare, cannoneggiare; **to shell out** (slang) tirar fuori

shel·lac [ʃə'læk] s gomma lacca || v (pret & pp **-lacked**; ger **-lacking**) tr verniciare con gomma lacca; (slang) dare una batosta a

shell'fish' ssg (-fish) frutto di mare; crostaceo; spl frutti mpl di mare; crostacei mpl

shell' hole' s cratere m

shell' shock' s psicosi traumatica bellica

shelter ['ʃeltər] s rifugio, ricovero; **to take shelter** rifugiarsi || tr raccogliere, ospitare, dare rifugio a

shelve [ʃelv] tr mettere sullo scaffale; (a bill) insabbiare; mettere a riposo

shepherd ['ʃepərd] s pastore m || tr guardare, curarsi di

shep'herd dog' s cane m da pastore

shepherdess ['ʃepərdɪs] s pastora

sherbet ['ʃɑrbət] s sorbetto

sheriff ['ʃerɪf] s sceriffo

sher·ry ['ʃeri] s (-ries) xeres m

shield [ʃild] s scudo; (for armpit) sottoascella m; (badge) scudetto; (elec) schermo || tr proteggere; (elec) schermare

shift [ʃift] s cambio, cambiamento;

(*period of work*) turno; (*group of workmen*) operai *mpl* di turno, squadra di lavoro; espediente *m*, sotterfugio || *tr* cambiare; spostare; (*blame*) riversare; || *intr* cambiare; spostarsi; fare da sé; vivere di espedienti; (rr) manovrare; (aut) cambiare marcia

shift' key' *s* tasto maiuscole

shiftless ['ʃɪftlɪs] *adj* pigro, ozioso

shift‧y ['ʃɪftɪ] *adj* (-ier; -iest) astuto; evasivo; pieno d'espedienti; (*glance*) sfuggente

shilling ['ʃɪlɪŋ] *s* scellino

shimmer ['ʃɪmər] *s* luccichio || *intr* luccicare, mandare bagliori

shim‧my ['ʃɪmɪ] *s* (-mies) (*dance*) shimmy *m;* (aut) traballamento delle ruote, shimmy *m* || *intr* ballare lo shimmy; vibrare

shin [ʃɪn] *s* stinco; (*of cattle*) cannone *m* || *v* (*pret & pp* shinned; *ger* shinning) *tr* arrampicarsi su || *intr* arrampicarsi

shin'bone' *s* stinco, tibia

shine [ʃaɪn] *s* splendore *m;* luce *f;* bel tempo; lucidatura, lucido; to take a shine to (coll) prender simpatia per || *v* (*pret & pp* shined) *tr* pulire, lucidare || *v* (*pret & pp* shone [ʃon]) *tr* (e.g., *a flashlight*) dirigere i raggi di || *intr* brillare, luccicare, risplendere; (*to excel*) essere brillante, eccellere

shiner ['ʃaɪnər] *s* (slang) occhio pesto

shingle ['ʃɪŋɡəl] *s* assicella di copertura; (*to cover a wall*) mattoncino di rivestimento; (Brit) greto ciottoloso; (coll) capelli *mpl* alla bebé; shingles (pathol) erpete *m*, zona; to hang out one's shingle (coll) aprire un ufficio professionale || *tr* coprire di assicelle or mattoncini; (*hair*) tagliare alla bebé

shining ['ʃaɪnɪŋ] *adj* brillante, lucente

shin‧y ['ʃaɪnɪ] *adj* (-ier; -iest) lucente, lucido; (*paper*) patinato

ship [ʃɪp] *s* nave *f*, bastimento; aeronave *f;* aeroplano; (*crew*) equipaggio || *v* (*pret & pp* shipped; *ger* shipping) *tr* imbarcare; mandare, spedire; (*oars*) disarmare; (*water*) imbarcare || *intr* imbarcarsi

ship'board' *s*—on shipboard a bordo

ship'build'er *s* costruttore *m* navale

ship'build'ing *s* architettura navale

ship'mate' *s* compagno di bordo

shipment ['ʃɪpmənt] *s* invio, spedizione

ship'own'er *s* armatore *m*

shipper ['ʃɪpər] *s* speditore *m*, spedizioniere *m*, mittente *m*

shipping ['ʃɪpɪŋ] *s* imbarco; spedizione; (naut) trasporto marittimo

ship'ping clerk' *s* speditore *m*

ship'ping room' *s* ufficio impaccatura

ship'shape' *adj & adv* in perfette condizioni

ship'side' *s* nave

ship's' pa'pers *spl* documenti *mpl* di bordo

ship'wreck' *s* naufragio; (*remains*) relitto || *tr* far naufragare || *intr* naufragare

ship'yard' *s* cantiere *m* navale

shirk [ʃʌrk] *tr* (*work*) evitare; (*responsibility*) sottrarsi a || *intr* imboscarsi

shirt [ʃʌrt] *s* camicia; to keep one's shirt on (slang) non perdere la calma; to lose one's shirt (slang) perdere la camicia

shirt' front' *s* sparato

shirt' sleeve' *s* manica di camicia

shirt'tail' *s* falda della camicia

shirt'waist' *s* blusa da donna

shiver ['ʃɪvər] *s* brivido || *intr* rabbrividire, battere i denti

shoal [ʃol] *s* secca, banco di sabbia

shock [ʃak] *s* urto, collisione; scossa; scossa elettrica; (pathol) shock *m* || *tr* scuotere; (*to strike against*) urtare; scandalizzare, indignare; dare la scossa elettrica a; (fig) scioccare

shock' absorb'er [æb'sɔrbər] *s* ammortizzatore *m* di colpi

shocking ['ʃakɪŋ] *adj* disgustoso, scandalizzante

shock' ther'apy *s* terapia d'urto

shock' troops' *spl* truppe *fpl* d'assalto

shod‧dy ['ʃadɪ] *adj* (-dier; -diest) scadente, falso

shoe [ʃu] *s* scarpa; (*horseshoe*) ferro da cavallo; (*of a tire*) copertone *m;* (*of brake*) ganascia, ceppo || *v* (*pret & pp* shod [ʃad]) *tr* calzare; (*a horse*) ferrare

shoe'black' *s* lustrascarpe *m*

shoe'horn' *s* corno da scarpe, calzatoio

shoe'lace' *s* laccio delle scarpe

shoe'mak'er *s* calzolaio

shoe' pol'ish *s* crema or cera da scarpe

shoe'shine' *s* lucidatura, lustramento di scarpe

shoe' store' *s* calzoleria

shoe'string' *s* laccio delle scarpe; on a shoestring con quattro soldi

shoe'tree' *s* tendiscarpe *m*

shoo [ʃu] *tr* fare sciò a || *intr* fare sciò

shoot [ʃut] *s* (e.g., *with a firearm*) tiro; gara di tiro; (*chute*) scivolo; (rok) lancio; (bot) getto, virgulto || *v* (*pret & pp* shot [ʃat]) *tr* (*any missile*) tirare; (*a bullet*) sparare; (*to execute with a bullet*) fucilare; (*to fling*) lanciare; (*the sun*) prendere l'altezza di; (*dice*) gettare; (mov, telv) girare, riprendere; to shoot down (*a plane*) abbattere; to shoot up (coll) terrorizzare sparando a casaccio || *intr* tirare, sparare; passare rapidamente; nascere; (*said of pain*) dare fitte; (mov) cinematografare; to shoot at tirare a; (coll) cercare di ottenere

shoot'ing gal'lery *s* tiro a segno

shoot'ing match' *s* gara di tiro a segno; (slang) tutto, ogni cosa

shoot'ing star' *s* stella cadente

shop [ʃap] *s* (*store*) negozio, rivendita; (*workshop*) officina; to talk shop parlare del proprio lavoro || *v* (*pret & pp* shopped; *ger* shopping) *intr* fare la spesa; to go shopping andare a fare la spesa; to shop around cercare un'occasione di negozio in negozio

shop'girl' *s* venditrice *f*

shop'keep'er s negoziante mf
shoplifter ['ʃɑp ‚lɪftər] s taccheggiatore m
shopper ['ʃɑpər] s compratore m
shop'ping ['ʃɑpɪŋ] s compra; (purchases) compre fpl, shopping m
shop'ping cen'ter s centro d'acquisto, ipermercato
shop'ping dis'trict s zona commerciale
shop'win'dow s vetrina
shop'worn' adj sciupato, usato
shore [ʃor] s costa, riva; spiaggia, lido; (fig) regione; (support) sostegno, puntello || tr puntellare
shore' din'ner s pranzo di pesce
shore' leave' s (naut) franchigia
shore'line' s frangia costiera
shore' patrol' s polizia della marina
short [ʃɔrt] adj (in stature) piccolo, basso; (in space, time) breve; (scanty) scarso, succinto; (in quantity) poco, piccolo; (rude) brusco; **in a short time** in breve; **in short** per farla breve; **on short notice** senza preavviso; **short of breath** corto di fiato; **to be short of** scarseggiare di || s (elec) cortocircuito; (mov) cortometraggio; **shorts** (underwear) mutande fpl; (sports attire) calzoncini mpl, shorts mpl || adv brevemente; bruscamente; (com) allo scoperto, e.g., **to sell short** vendere allo scoperto; **to run short of** essere a corto di; **to stop short** fermarsi di colpo || tr (elec) causare un cortocircuito in || intr (elec) andare in cortocircuito
shortage ['ʃɔrtɪdʒ] s mancanza; (of food) carestia; (from pilfering) ammanco
short'cake' s torta di pasta frolla; torta ricoperta di frutta fresca
short'-change' tr non dare il cambio giusto a; (coll) imbrogliare
short' cir'cuit s (elec) cortocircuito
short'-cir'cuit tr mandare in cortocircuito; (coll) rovinare || intr andare in cortocircuito
short'com'ing s difetto, manchevolezza
short'cut' s scorciatoia
shorten ['ʃɔrtən] tr raccorciare, abbreviare || intr raccorciarsi, abbreviarsi
shortening ['ʃɔrtənɪŋ] s raccorciamento; (culin) grasso, strutto
short'hand' adj stenografico || s stenografia; **to take shorthand** stenografare
short'hand' typ'ist s stenodattilografo
short-lived ['ʃɔrt'laɪvd] or ['ʃɔrt'lɪvd] adj effimero, di breve vita
shortly ['ʃɔrtli] adv in breve, brevemente; fra poco; bruscamente; **shortly after** poco dopo
short'-range' adj di corta portata
short' sale' s vendita allo scoperto
short-sighted ['ʃɔrt'saɪtɪd] adj miope; (fig) miope
short'stop' s (baseball) interbase m
short' sto'ry s novella
short-tempered ['ʃɔrt'tempərd] adj irascibile
short'-term' adj a breve scadenza

short'wave' adj alle onde corte || s onda corta
short' weight' s—**to give short weight** rubare sul peso
shot [ʃɑt] s tiro, sparo; (cartridge) cartuccia; (for cannon) palla; (pellets of lead) pallini mpl; (person) tiratore m; (hypodermic injection) iniezione; (of liquor) bicchierino; (phot) istantanea; (sports) peso; (mov) inquadratura; **not by a long shot** nemmeno a pensarci; **to start like a shot** partire come una palla da cannone; **to take a shot at** tirare un colpo a; (to attempt to) provarsi a
shot'gun' s schioppo, fucile m da caccia
shot' put' s lancio del peso
should [ʃʊd] v aux si usa nelle seguenti situazioni: 1) per formare il condizionale presente, per es., **if I should wait for him, I should miss the train** se lo aspettassi, perderei il treno; 2) per formare il perfetto del condizionale, per es., **if I had waited for him, I should have missed the train** se lo avessi aspettato, avrei perso il treno; 3) per indicare la necessità di un'azione, per es., **he should go at once** dovrebbe andare immediatamente; **he should have gone immediately** sarebbe dovuto andare immediatamente
shoulder ['ʃoldər] s spalla; (of highway) banchina; **across the shoulder** a bandoliera; **to put one's shoulders to the wheel** mettersi a lavorare di buzzo buono; **to turn a cold shoulder to** volgere le spalle a || tr portare sulle spalle; (a responsibility) addossarsi; spingere con le spalle
shoul'der blade' s scapola
shoul'der strap' s spallina; (mil) tracolla
shout [ʃaut] s urlo, grido || tr urlare, gridare; **to shout down** far tacere a forza di strilli || intr gridare
shove [ʃʌv] s spintone m || tr spingere || intr spingere, dare spintoni; **to shove off** allontanarsi dalla riva; (slang) andarsene
shov·el ['ʃʌvəl] s pala || v (pret & pp -eled or -elled; ger -eling or -elling) tr spalare || intr lavorare di pala
show [ʃo] s mostra; apparenza; traccia; ostentazione; (mov, telv, theat) spettacolo; **to make a show of** dar spettacolo di; **to steal the show from** ricevere tutti gli applausi invece di || tr mostrare, esporre; (a movie) presentare; dimostrare, insegnare; provare; (to register) segnare; (one's feelings) manifestare; (to the door) accompagnare; **to show in** fare entrare; **to show off** mettere in mostra || intr mostrarsi; presentarsi, apparire; (said of a horse) (sports) arrivare terzo, piazzarsi; **to show off** mettersi in mostra; **to show up** (coll) mostrarsi; (coll) farsi vedere
show' bill' s cartellone m
show'boat' s battello per spettacoli teatrali

show′ busi′ness *s* industria dello spettacolo

show′case′ *s* bacheca, vetrina

show′down′ *s* carte scoperte; chiarificazione

shower [′ʃau·ər] *s* (*of rain*) acquazzone *m*; (*shower bath*) doccia; (*e.g., for a bride*) ricevimento cui i partecipanti devono portare un regalo; (fig) pioggia ‖ *tr* inaffiare; **to shower with** colmare di ‖ *intr* diluviare; fare la doccia

show′er bath′ *s* doccia

show′ girl′ *s* ballerina, girl *f*

show′man *s* (-men) impresario teatrale; persona che ha molta scena

show′-off′ *s* reclamista *m*, strombazzatore *m*

show′piece′ *s* capolavoro, oggetto d'arte

show′place′ *s* luogo celebre; **to be a showplace** (*said, e.g., of a house*) essere arredato perfettamente

show′room′ *s* sala di mostra

show′ win′dow *s* vetrina

show·y [′ʃo·i] *adj* (-ier; -iest) vistoso, sgargiante

shrapnel [′ʃræpnəl] *s* shrapnel *m*

shred [ʃrɛd] *s* brano, brandello; ritaglio; (fig) granello; **to cut to shreds** fare a brandelli ‖ *v* (*pret & pp* **shredded** or **shred;** *ger* **shredding**) *tr* fare a brandelli; (*paper*) tagliuzzare

shrew [ʃru] *s* (*woman*) bisbetica; (*animal*) toporagno

shrewd [ʃrud] *adj* astuto, scaltro

shriek [ʃrik] *s* strido; strillo; risata stridula ‖ *intr* stridere; strillare

shrill [ʃrɪl] *adj* stridulo, squillante

shrimp [ʃrɪmp] *s* gamberetto; (*person*) omiciattolo, nanerottolo

shrine [ʃraɪn] *s* santuario, sacrario

shrink [ʃrɪŋk] *v* (*pret* **shrank** [ʃræŋk] or **shrunk** [ʃrʌŋk]; *pp* **shrunk** or **shrunken**) *tr* contrarre, restringere ‖ *intr* contrarsi, restringersi; ritirarsi

shrinkage [′ʃrɪŋkɪdʒ] *s* restringimento; (*in weight*) calo

shriv·el [′ʃrɪvəl] *v* (*pret & pp* **-eled** or **-elled;** *ger* **-eling** or **-elling**) *tr* raggrinzire; (*from heat*) raccartocciare; (*to wither*) avvizzire ‖ *intr* raggrinzirsi; accartocciarsi; avvizzire; **to shrivel up** incartapecorire

shroud [ʃraud] *s* sudario, lenzuolo funebre; (fig) cappa ‖ *tr* avvolgere

Shrove′ Tues′day [ʃrov] *s* martedì grasso

shrub [ʃrʌb] *s* arbusto

shrubber·y [′ʃrʌbəri] *s* (-ies) arbusti *mpl*, cespugli *mpl*

shrug [ʃrʌg] *s* scrollata di spalle ‖ *v* (*pret & pp* **shrugged;** *ger* **shrugging**) *tr* scrollare; **to shrug one's shoulders** scrollare le spalle ‖ *intr* fare spallucce

shudder [′ʃʌdər] *s* brivido, fremito ‖ *intr* rabbrividire, fremere

shuffle [′ʃʌfəl] *s* (*of cards*) mescolata; turno di fare il mazzo; (*of feet*) strascichio; evasione ‖ *tr* mescolare; strisciare, strascicare ‖ *intr* fare il

mazzo; scalpicciare; ballare di striscio; **to shuffle off** strascicarsi, scalpicciare; **to shuffle out** evadere da

shun [ʃʌn] *v* (*pret & pp* **shunned;** *ger* **shunning**) *tr* evitare, schivare

shunt [ʃʌnt] *tr* sviare; (elec) shuntare; (rr) deviare

shut [ʃʌt] *adj* chiuso ‖ *v* (*pret & pp* **shut;** *ger* **shutting**) *tr* chiudere, serrare; **to shut in** rinchiudere; **to shut off** (*e.g., gas*) tagliare; **to shut up** tappare; imprigionare; (coll) fare star zitto ‖ *intr* chiudersi; **to shut up** (coll) stare zitto, tacere

shut′down′ *s* chiusura

shutter [′ʃʌtər] *s* (*outside a window*) persiana, gelosia; (*outside a store window*) serranda, saracinesca; (phot) otturatore *m*

shuttle [′ʃʌtəl] *s* spola, navetta ‖ *intr* fare la spola

shut′tle·cock′ *s* volano, volante *m*

shut′tle train′ *s* treno che fa la spola fra due stazioni

shy [ʃaɪ] *adj* (**shyer** or **shier; shyest** or **shiest**) timido; (*fearful*) schivo, ritroso; corto, a corto, e.g., **he is shy of funds** è a corto di denaro ‖ *v* (*pret & pp* **shied**) *intr* ritirarsi; schivarsi; (*said of a horse*) adombrarsi; **to shy away** tenersi discosto

shyster [′ʃaɪstər] *s* (coll) azzeccagarbugli *m*

Sia·mese [ˌsɑɪ·ə′miz] *adj* siamese ‖ *s* (-mese) siamese *mf*

Si′amese twins′ *spl* fratelli *mpl* siamesi

Siberian [saɪ′bɪrɪ·ən] *adj & s* siberiano

sibilant [′sɪbɪlənt] *adj & s* sibilante *f*

sibyl [′sɪbɪl] *s* sibilla

sic [sɪk] *adv* sic ‖ [sɪk] *v* (*pret & pp* **sicked;** *ger* **sicking**) *tr* aizzare; **sick 'em!** val; **to sick on** aizzare contro

Sicilian [sɪ′sɪljən] *adj & s* siciliano

Sicily [′sɪsɪli] *s* la Sicilia

sick [sɪk] *adj* ammalato; nauseato; (*bored*) stucco; **sick at heart** con una spina nel cuore; **to be sick and tired** averne sin sopra i capelli; **to be sick at one's stomach** avere la nausea; **to take sick** cader malato ‖ *tr* (*a dog*) aizzare

sick′bed′ *s* letto d'ammalato

sicken [′sɪkən] *tr* ammalare; disgustare ‖ *intr* ammalarsi

sickening [′sɪkənɪŋ] *adj* stomachevole

sick′ head′ache *s* emicrania accompagnata da nausea

sickle [′sɪkəl] *s* falce messoria, falcetto

sick′ leave′ *s* congedo per motivi di salute

sick·ly [′sɪkli] *adj* (-lier; -liest) cagionevole, malaticcio

sickness [′sɪknɪs] *s* malattia; nausea

side [saɪd] *adj* laterale ‖ *s* parte *f*, lato; (*e.g., of a coin*) faccia; (*slope*) versante *m*; (*of human body, of a ship*) fianco; **to take sides** parteggiare ‖ *intr* parteggiare; **to side with** schierarsi dalla parte di

side′board′ *s* credenza

side′burns′ *spl* basette *fpl*, favoriti *mpl*

side'car' s motocarrozzetta; carrozzino laterale (di motocarrozzetta)
side' dish' s portata extra
side' door' s porta laterale
side' effect' s effetto secondario
side'-glance' s occhiata di sbieco
side' is'sue s questione secondaria
side'line' s linea laterale; impiego secondario; attività secondaria
sidereal [saɪˈdɪrɪ‧əl] adj siderale
side'sad'dle adv all'amazzone
side' show' s spettacolo secondario di baraccone; affare secondario
side'slip' intr (aer) scivolare d'ala
side'split'ting adj che fa sbellicare dalle risa
side' step' s passo laterale; scartata
side'-step' v (pret & pp -stepped; ger -stepping) tr evitare ‖ intr farsi da parte; fare una scartata
side'track' s binario morto di smistamento ‖ tr sviare; (rr) smistare
side' view' s vista di profilo
side'walk' s marciapiede m
side'walk café' s caffè m con tavolini all'aperto
sideward [ˈsaɪdwərd] adj obliquo, a sghembo ‖ adv verso un lato; di sghembo
side'ways' adj sghembo ‖ adv di sghembo; di fianco
side' whisk'ers spl favoriti mpl
siding [ˈsaɪdɪŋ] s (rr) diramazione, binario morto, raccordo ferroviario
sidle [ˈsaɪdəl] intr andare al lato; muoversi furtivamente
siege [sidʒ] s assedio; (of illness) ricorrenza d'attacchi; **to lay siege to** cingere d'assedio, assediare
siesta [siˈestə] s siesta; **to take a siesta** fare la siesta
sieve [sɪv] s vaglio, setaccio ‖ tr vagliare, setacciare
sift [sɪft] tr (flour) abburattare; setacciare; (to scatter with a sieve) spolverare; (fig) vagliare
sigh [saɪ] s sospiro ‖ tr mormorare sospirando ‖ intr sospirare; **to sigh for** sospirare
sight [saɪt] s vista, visione; spettacolo, veduta; (opt) mira, traguardo; (mil) mirino, tacca di mira; (coll) mucchio; **a sight of** (coll) molto; **at first sight** a prima vista; **at sight** di apertura di libro; (com) a vista; **out of sight** fuori di vista; lontano dagli occhi; (prices) astronomico; **sights** luoghi mpl interessanti; **sight unseen** senza averlo visto prima, a occhi chiusi; **to be a sight** (coll) essere un orrore; **to catch sight of** arrivare a intravedere; **to know by sight** conoscere di vista; **to not be able to stand the sight of s.o.** not poter vedere qlcu nemmeno dipinto ‖ tr avvistare; (a weapon) mirare ‖ intr mirare, prendere di mira; osservare attentamente
sight' draft' s (com) tratta a vista
sight'-read' v (pret & pp -read [ˌred]) tr & intr leggere a libro aperto
sight'see'ing adj turistico ‖ s turismo, visite fpl turistiche
sightseer [ˈsaɪtˌsi‧ər] s turista mf

sign [saɪn] s segno; segnale m; (e.g., on a store) insegna, cartello; **signs** tracce fpl ‖ tr firmare; ingaggiare; indicare, segnalare ‖ intr firmare; fare segno; **to sign off** (rad, telv) terminare la trasmissione; **to sign up** iscriversi
sig‧nal [ˈsɪgnəl] adj insigne, segnalato ‖ s segnale m ‖ v (pret & pp -naled or -nalled; ger -naling or -nalling) tr segnalare ‖ intr fare segnalazioni
sig'nal corps' s (mil) armi fpl di trasmissione
sig'nal tow'er s (rr) posto di blocco
signato‧ry [ˈsɪgnɪˌtori] s (-ries) firmatario
signature [ˈsɪgnət/ər] s firma; segno musicale; (typ) segnatura
sign'board' s cartellone m
signer [ˈsaɪnər] s firmatario
sig'net ring' [ˈsɪgnɪt] s anello col sigillo
significance [sɪgˈnɪfɪkəns] s importanza; (meaning) significato
significant [sɪgˈnɪfɪkənt] adj importante
signi‧fy [ˈsɪgnɪˌfaɪ] v (pret & pp -fied) tr significare
sign'post' s palo indicatore
silence [ˈsaɪləns] s silenzio ‖ tr far tacere; (mil) ridurre al silenzio
silent [ˈsaɪlənt] adj silenzioso, tacito
si'lent mov'ie s cinema muto
silhouette [ˌsɪlu'et] s silhouette f, siluetta
silicon [ˈsɪlɪkən] s silicio
silicone [ˈsɪlɪˌkon] s silicone m
silk [sɪlk] adj di seta ‖ s seta; **to hit the silk** (slang) gettarsi col paracadute
silken [ˈsɪlkən] adj serico, di seta
silk' hat' s cappello a cilindro
silk'screen proc'ess s serigrafia
silk'-stock'ing adj & s aristocratico
silk'worm' s baco da seta, filugello
silk‧y [ˈsɪlki] adj (-ier; -iest) di seta; come la seta
sill [sɪl] s basamento; (of a door) soglia; (of a window) davanzale m
sil‧ly [ˈsɪli] adj (-lier; -liest) sciocco, scemo
si‧lo [ˈsaɪlo] s (-los) silo ‖ tr insilare
silt [sɪlt] s sedimento
silver [ˈsɪlvər] adj d'argento; (voice) argentino; (plated with silver) argentato ‖ s argento ‖ tr inargentare
sil'ver‧fish' s (ent) lepisma
sil'ver foil' s foglia d'argento
sil'ver fox' s volpe argentata
sil'ver lin'ing s spiraglio di speranza
sil'ver plate' s vasellame m d'argento; argentatura
sil'ver screen' s (mov) schermo
sil'ver‧smith' s argentiere m
sil'ver spoon' s ricchezza ereditata; **to be born with a silver spoon in one's mouth** esser nato con la camicia
sil'ver‧ware' s argenteria
sil'ver‧ware' chest' s portaposate m
similar [ˈsɪmɪlər] adj simile
similari‧ty [ˌsɪmɪˈlærɪti] s (-ties) similarità f, somiglianza
simile [ˈsɪmɪli] s similitudine f

simmer ['sɪmər] *tr* cuocere a fuoco lento ‖ *intr* cuocere a fuoco lento; (fig) ribollire; **to simmer down** (slang) calmarsi

simper ['sɪmpər] *s* sorriso scemo ‖ *intr* fare un sorriso scemo

simple ['sɪmpəl] *adj* semplice

simple-minded ['sɪmpəl'maɪndɪd] *adj* semplicione, scemo

simpleton ['sɪmpəltən] *s* semplicione *m*

simulate ['sɪmjə,let] *tr* simulare

simultaneous [,saɪməl'teni·əs] or [,sɪməl'teni·əs] *adj* simultaneo

sin [sɪn] *s* peccato ‖ *v* (*pret & pp* **sinned;** *ger* **sinning**) *intr* peccare

since [sɪns] *adv* da allora, da allora in poi; da tempo fa ‖ *prep* da ‖ *conj* dacché; poiché, dato che

sincere [sɪn'sɪr] *adj* sincero

sincerity [sɪn'sɛrɪti] *s* sincerità *f*

sine [saɪn] *s* (math) seno

sinecure ['saɪnɪ,kjʊr] or ['sɪnɪ,kjʊr] *s* sinecura

sinew ['sɪnju] *s* tendine *m;* (fig) nerbo

sinful ['sɪnfəl] *adj* (person) peccatore; (*act, intention, etc.*) peccaminoso

sing [sɪŋ] *v* (*pret* **sang** [sæŋ] or **sung** [sʌŋ];* *pp* **sung**) *tr* cantare; **to sing to sleep** ninnare ‖ *intr* cantare; (said, *e.g., of the ears*) fischiare

singe [sɪndʒ] *v* (*ger* **singeing**) *tr* strinare, bruciacchiare

singer ['sɪŋər] *s* cantante *mf;* (*in night club*) canzonettista *mf*

single ['sɪŋgəl] *adj* unico, solo; (*room*) a un letto; (bed) a una piazza; (man) celibe; (woman) nubile; (combat) corpo a corpo; semplice, sincero ‖ **singles** *ssg* singolare *m* ‖ *tr* scegliere; **to single out** individuare

single-breasted ['sɪŋgəl'brɛstɪd] *adj* a un petto, monopetto

sin'gle en'try *s* partita semplice

sin'gle file' *s* fila indiana

single-handed ['sɪŋgəl'hændɪd] *adj* da solo, senza aiuto altrui

sin'gle-phase' *adj* (elec) monofase

sin'gle room' *s* camera a un letto

sin'gle-track' *adj* (rr) a binario semplice; (fig) di corte vedute

sing'song' *adj* monotono ‖ *s* cantilena

singular ['sɪŋgjələr] *adj & s* singolare *m*

sinister ['sɪnɪstər] *adj* sinistro

sink [sɪŋk] *s* acquaio; (sewer) scolo, fogna; (fig) sentina ‖ *v* (*pret* **sank** [sæŋk] or **sunk** [sʌŋk];* *pp* **sunk**) *tr* sprofondare; infiggere; (*a well*) scavare; (in tone) abbassare; (*a boat*) mandare a picco; rovinare; investire; perdere ‖ *intr* sprofondarsi; abbassarsi; (*said, of the sun, prices, etc.*) calare; andare a picco; lasciarsi cadere; (*in vice*) impantanarsi; (*said of one's cheeks*) infossarsi; (in *thought*) perdersi; **to sink down** sedersi; **to sink in** penetrare

sink'ing fund' *s* fondo d'ammortamento

sinner ['sɪnər] *s* peccatore *m*

Sinology [sɪ'nɑlədʒi] *s* sinologia

sinuous ['sɪnju·əs] *adj* sinuoso

sinus ['saɪnəs] *s* seno

sip [sɪp] *s* sorso ‖ *v* (*pret & pp* **sipped;** *ger* **sipping**) *tr* sorbire, sorseggiare

siphon ['saɪfən] *s* sifone *m* ‖ *tr* travasare con un sifone

si'phon bot'tle *s* sifone *m*

sir [sʌr] *s* signore *m;* (Brit) sir *m;* **Dear Sir** Illustrissimo signore; (com) Egregio signore

sire [saɪr] *s* (king) sire *m;* padre *m,* stallone *m* ‖ *tr* generare

siren ['saɪrən] *s* sirena

sirloin ['sʌrlɔɪn] *s* lombata, lombo

sirup ['sɪrəp] or ['sʌrəp] *s* sciroppo

sis·sy ['sɪsi] *s* (-sies) effeminato

sister ['sɪstər] *adj* (ship) gemello; (*language*) sorella; (corporation) consorella ‖ *s* sorella; (nun) suora, monaca

sis'ter-in-law' *s* (sis'ters-in-law') cognata

Sis'tine Chap'el ['sɪstɪn] *s* Cappella Sistina

sit [sɪt] *v* (*pret & pp* **sat** [sæt];* *ger* **sitting**) *intr* sedere; posare; (*said of a hen*) covare; (*said of a jacket*) stare; essere in sessione; **to sit down** sedersi; **to sit in on** partecipare a; assistere a; **to sit still** stare tranquillo; **to sit up** alzarsi; (coll) essere sorpreso

sit'-down strike' *s* sciopero bianco

site [saɪt] *s* sito, luogo, posizione

sitting ['sɪtɪŋ] *s* seduta; (*of a court*) sessione; (*of a hen*) covata; (*serving of a meal*) turno

sit'ting duck' *s* (slang) facile bersaglio

sit'ting room' *s* soggiorno

situate ['sɪtʃu,et] *tr* situare

situation [,sɪtʃu'eʃən] *s* situazione, posizione; posto

sitz' bath' [sɪts] *s* semicupio

six [sɪks] *adj & pron* sei ‖ *s* sei *m;* **at sixes and sevens** in disordine; **six o'clock** le sei

six' hun'dred *adj, s & pron* seicento

sixteen ['sɪks'tin] *adj, s & pron* sedici *m*

sixteenth ['sɪks'tinθ] *adj, s & pron* sedicesimo ‖ *s* (*in dates*) sedici *m*

sixth [sɪksθ] *adj, s & pron* sesto ‖ *s* (*in dates*) sei *m*

sixtieth ['sɪkstɪ·ɪθ] *adj, s & pron* sessantesimo

six·ty ['sɪksti] *adj & pron* sessanta ‖ *s* (-ies) sessanta *m;* **the sixties** gli anni sessanta

sizable ['saɪzəbəl] *adj* considerevole

size [saɪz] *s* grandezza; quantità *f;* (*of person or garment*) taglia; (*of shoes*) numero; (*of hat*) giro; (*of a pipe*) diametro; (*for gilding*) colla; (fig) situazione ‖ *tr* misurare, classificare secondo grandezza; incollare; **to size up** (coll) stimare, giudicare

sizzle ['sɪzəl] *s* sfrigolio ‖ *intr* sfriggere

skate [sket] *s* pattino; (slang) tipo ‖ *intr* pattinare; **to skate on thin ice** andare in cerca di disgrazie

skat'ing rink' *s* pattinatoio

skein [sken] *s* gomitolo, matassa

skeleton ['skɛlɪtən] *adj* scheletrico ‖ *s* scheletro

skel'eton key' *s* chiave maestra

skeptic ['skɛptɪk] *adj & s* scettico

skeptical ['skɛptɪkəl] *adj* scettico

sketch [skɛtʃ] *s* schizzo, disegno; abbozzo, bozzetto; (theat) scenetta || *tr* schizzare, disegnare; abbozzare

sketch'book' *s* album *m* di schizzi; quaderno per abbozzi

skew [skju] *adj* obliquo || *s* movimento obliquo; (*chisel*) scalpello a taglio obliquo || *tr* tagliare di sghembo || *intr* (*to swerve*) deviare; (*to look obliquely*) guardare di sghembo

skew' chis'el *s* scalpello a taglio obliquo

skewer ['skju·ər] *s* spiedino || *tr* mettere allo spiedo

ski [ski] *s* (**skis** or **ski**) sci *m* || *intr* sciare

ski' boot' *s* scarpa da sci

skid [skɪd] *s* (*device to check a wheel*) scarpa; (*skidding forward*) slittamento; (*skidding sideway*) sbandamento; (aer, mach) pattino || *v* (*pret & pp* **skidded;** *ger* **skidding**) *tr* frenare || *intr* (*forward*) slittare; (*sideways*) sbandare

skid' row' [ro] *s* quartiere malfamato

skier ['ski·ər] *s* sciatore *m*

skiff [skɪf] *s* skiff *m*, singolo

skiing ['ski·ɪŋ] *s* sci *m*

ski' jump' *s* salto con gli sci; trampolino di salto

ski' lift' *s* sciovia

skill [skɪl] *s* destrezza, perizia

skilled [skɪld] *adj* abile, esperto

skilled' la'bor *s* manodopera qualificata

skillet ['skɪlɪt] *s* padella

skillful ['skɪlfəl] *adj* destro, abile

skim [skɪm] *v* (*pret & pp* **skimmed;** *ger* **skimming**) *tr* (*milk*) scremare; (*e.g., broth*) sgrassare; (*to graze*) sfiorare; (*the ground*) radere; (*a page*) trascorrere || *intr* sfiorare; **to skim over** scorrere

ski' mask' *s* passamontagna *m*

skimmer ['skɪmər] *s* schiumaiola; (*hat*) canottiera

skim' milk' *s* latte scremato or magro

skimp [skɪmp] *tr* lesinare || *intr* economizzare, risparmiare

skimp·y ['skɪmpi] *adj* (**-ier; -iest**) corto, scarso; taccagno

skin [skɪn] *s* pelle *f*; (*rind*) scorza; (*of onion*) spoglia; **by the skin of one's teeth** (coll) per il rotto della cuffia; **soaked to the skin** bagnato fino alle ossa; **to have a thin skin** offendersi facilmente || *v* (*pret & pp* **skinned;** *ger* **skinning**) *tr* pelare, spellare; (*e.g., one's knee*) spellarsi, (slang) tosare; **to skin alive** (slang) scotennare; (slang) battere in pieno

skin'-deep' *adj* a fior di pelle

skin'-div'er *s* nuotatore subacqueo, sub *m*; (mil) sommozzatore *m*

skin'flint' *s* avaro

skin' game' *s* truffa

skin·ny ['skɪni] *adj* (**-nier; -niest**) magro, scarno

skin' test' *s* cutireazione

skip [skɪp] *s* salto || *v* (*pret & pp* **skipped;** *ger* **skipping**) *tr* (*a fence; a meal*) saltare; (*a subject*) sorvolare; (*school*) (coll) marinare || *intr* saltare, salterellare; (*said of typewriter*) saltare uno spazio; (coll) svignarsela

ski' pole' *s* racchetta da sci

skipper ['skɪpər] *s* capitano, comandante *m*

skirmish ['skʌrmɪʃ] *s* scaramuccia || *intr* battersi in una scaramuccia

skirt [skʌrt] *s* sottana, gonna; (*edge*) orlo; (*woman*) (slang) gonnella || *tr* orlare; costeggiare; (*a subject*) evitare

ski' run' *s* pista da sci

skit [skɪt] *s* (theat) quadretto comico

skittish ['skɪtɪʃ] *adj* bizzarro, balzano; timido; (*horse*) ombroso

skulduggery [skʌl'dʌgəri] *s* trucco disonesto

skull [skʌl] *s* cranio, teschio

skull' and cross'bones *s* due tibie incrociate ed un teschio

skull'cap' *s* papalina

skunk [skʌŋk] *s* puzzola, moffetta; (coll) puzzone *m*

sky [skaɪ] *s* (**skies**) cielo; firmamento; **to praise to the skies** portare al cielo

sky'div'er *s* paracadutista *mf*

sky'jack'er *s* pirata *m* dell'aria

sky'lark' *s* allodola || *intr* (coll) darsi alla pazza gioia

sky'light' *s* lucernario

sky'line' *s* linea dell'orizzonte; (*of city*) profilo

sky'rock'et *s* razzo || *intr* salire come un razzo

sky'scrap'er *s* grattacielo

sky'writ'ing *s* scrittura pubblicitaria aerea

slab [slæb] *s* (*of stone*) lastra, lastrone *m*; (*of wood*) tavola; (*slice*) fetta

slack [slæk] *adj* lento, allentato; negligente, indolente; (fig) fiacco, morto || *s* lentezza; negligenza; stagione morta, inattività *f*; **slacks** pantaloni *mpl* da donna; pantaloni sciolti || *tr* allentare; trascurare; (*lime*) spegnere || *intr* rilasciarsi; essere negligente; **to slack up** rallentare

slacker ['slækər] *s* fannullone *m*; (mil) imboscato

slag [slæg] *s* scoria

slake [slek] *tr* spegnere

slalom ['slɑləm] *s* slalom *m*

slam [slæm] *s* colpo; (*of door*) sbatacchiamento; (*in cards*) cappotto; (coll) strapazzata || *v* (*pret & pp* **slammed;** *ger* **slamming**) *tr* sbattere, sbatacchiare; (coll) strapazzare || *intr* sbattere, sbatacchiare

slam'bang' *adv* (coll) con gran rumore, precipitosamente

slander ['slændər] *s* calunnia, maldicenza || *tr* calunniare, diffamare

slanderous ['slændərəs] *adj* calunnioso, diffamatorio

slang [slæŋ] *s* gergo

slant [slænt] *s* inclinazione; punto di vista || *tr* inclinare; (*news*) snaturare || *intr* inclinarsi; deviare

slap [slæp] *s* manata; (*in the face*) schiaffo, ceffone *m*; (*noise*) rumore *m*; insulto || *v* (*pret & pp* **slapped;** *ger* **slapping**) *tr* dare una manata a; schiaffeggiare

slap'dash' *adj* raffazzonato, fatto a casaccio || *adv* a casaccio

slap'hap'py *adj* (*punch-drunk*) stordito; (*giddy*) allegro, brillo

slap'stick' *adj* buffonesco || *s* bastone *m* d'Arlecchino; buffonata

slash [slæʃ] *s* sfregio; (*of prices*) riduzione || *tr* sfregiare; (*cloth*) tagliare; (*prices*) ridurre

slat [slæt] *s* travicello, regolo; (*for bed*) traversa; (*of shutter*) stecca

slate [slet] *s* ardesia, lavagna; lista elettorale; **clean slate** buon certificato || *tr* coprire con tegole d'ardesia; proporre la nomina di; (*to schedule*) mettere in cantiere

slate' roof' *s* tetto d'ardesia

slattern ['slætərn] *s* (*slovenly woman*) sciamannona; (*harlot*) puttana

slaughter ['slɔtər] *s* eccidio, carneficina || *tr* sgozzare, scannare

slaugh'ter-house' *s* macello, scannatoio

Slav [slɑv] *or* [slæv] *adj & s* slavo

slave [slev] *adj & s* schiavo || *intr* lavorare come uno schiavo

slave' driv'er *s* negriere *m*

slavery ['slevəri] *s* schiavitù *f*

slave' trade' *s* tratta degli schiavi

Slavic ['slɑvɪk] *or* ['slævɪk] *adj & s* slavo

slay [sle] *v* (*pret* **slew** [slu]; *pp* **slain** [slen]) *tr* scannare, uccidere

slayer ['sle·ər] *s* uccisore *m*

sled [sled] *s* slittino, slitta || *v* (*pret & pp* **sledded;** *ger* **sledding**) *intr* slittare

sledge' ham'mer *s* [sledʒ] *s* mazza

sleek [slik] *adj* liscio, lustro; elegante || *tr* lisciare, ammorbidire

sleep [slip] *s* sonno; **to go to sleep** addormentarsi; **to put to sleep** addormentare; uccidere con un anestetico || *v* (*pret & pp* **slept** [slept]) *tr* dormire; aver posto a dormire per; **to sleep it over** dormirci sopra; **to sleep off a hangover** smaltire una sbornia dormendo || *intr* dormire; **to sleep in** dormire fino a tardi; passare la notte a casa; **to sleep out** passare la notte fuori di casa

sleeper ['slipər] *s* (*person*) dormiente *mf*; (*beam, timber*) trave *f*

sleep'ing bag' *s* sacco a pelo

sleep'ing car' *s* vettura letto

sleep'ing pill' *s* sonnifero

sleepless ['sliplɪs] *adj* insonne; (*night*) bianco

sleep'walk'er *s* sonnambulo

sleep·y ['slipi] *adj* (-**ier**; -**iest**) insonnolito, sonnolento; **to be sleepy** aver sonno

sleep'y-head' *s* dormiglione *m*

sleet [slit] *s* nevischio || *impers* **it is sleeting** cade il nevischio

sleeve [sliv] *s* manica; (*of phonograph record*) busta; (*mach*) manicotto; **to laugh in** or **up one's sleeve** ridere sotto i baffi

sleigh [sle] *s* slitta || *intr* andare in slitta

sleigh' bells' *spl* bubboli *mpl* da slitta, sonagliera da slitta

sleigh' ride' *s* passeggiata in slitta

sleight' of hand' [slaɪt] *s* gioco di prestigio

slender ['slendər] *adj* smilzo, snello; esiguo, esile

sleuth [sluθ] *s* segugio

slew [slu] *s* (coll) mucchio

slice [slaɪs] *s* fetta; (*of an orange*) spicchio || *tr* tagliare a fette; (fig) fendere

slick [slɪk] *adj* liscio, lustro; scivoloso; astuto; (slang) ottimo || *s* posto scivoloso; (coll) rivista stampata su carta patinata || *tr* lisciare, lustrare; **to slick up** (coll) acconciare

slicker ['slɪkər] *s* impermeabile *m* di tela cerata; (coll) furbo di tre cotte

slide [slaɪd] *s* scivolata, scivolone *m*; (*chute*) scivolo; (*landslide*) frana; (*for projection*) diapositiva; (*of a microscope*) vetrino; (mach) guida; (*of a slide rule*) (mach) cursore *m* || *v* (*pret & pp* **slid** [slɪd]) *tr* far scivolare || *intr* sdrucciolare, scivolare; (*said of a car*) pattinare, slittare; **to let slide** lasciar correre

slide' fas'tener *s* chiusura lampo

slide' projec'tor *s* diascopio

slide' rule' *s* regolo calcolatore

slide' valve' *s* (mach) cassetto di distribuzione

slid'ing door' *s* porta scorrevole

slid'ing scale' *s* scala mobile

slight [slaɪt] *adj* leggero, lieve; delicato || *s* noncuranza, disattenzione; affronto || *tr* fare con negligenza; (*to snub*) trattare con noncuranza, snobbare

slim [slɪm] *adj* (**slimmer; slimmest**) sottile; magro

slime [slaɪm] *s* melma; (*e.g., of a snail*) bava

slim·y ['slaɪmi] *adj* (-**ier**; -**iest**) melmoso; bavoso; sudicio

sling [slɪŋ] *s* (*to shoot stones*) fionda; (naut) braca; **in a sling** (*arm*) al collo || *v* (*pret & pp* **slung** [slʌŋ]) *tr* gettare; lanciare; (*freight*) imbracare; sospendere; mettere a bandoliera

sling'shot' *s* fionda

slink [slɪŋk] *v* (*pret & pp* **slunk** [slʌŋk]) *intr* andare furtivamente; **to slink away** eclissarsi

slip [slɪp] *s* scivolone *m*; svista, errore *m*; (*in prices*) discesa; (*underdress*) sottoveste *f*; (*pillowcase*) federa; (*of paper*) pezzo; (*space between two wharves*) darsena, imbarcatoio; (*form*) modulo; personcina; (*inclined plane*) (naut) scalo d'alaggio; (bot) innesto; **to give the slip to** eludere || *v* (*pret & pp* **slipped**); *ger* **slipping**) *tr* infilare; liberare; liberarsi da; omettere; **to slip off** togliersi; **to slip on** mettersi; **to slip one's mind** dimenticarsi di, e.g., **it slipped my mind** me ne sono dimenticato || *intr* scivolare, scorrere; sdrucciolare; sbagliare; peggiorare; **to let slip** lasciarsi sfuggire; **to slip away** svignarsela; **to slip by** (*said of time*) passare, fuggire; **to slip out of s.o.'s hands** sgusciare dalle mani di qlcu; **to slip up** sbagliarsi

slip'cov'er *s* fodera

slip'knot' *s* nodo scorsoio

slip' of the tongue' *s* errore *m* nel parlare

slipper ['slɪpər] *s* pantofola

slippery ['slɪpəri] *adj* sdrucciolevole, scivoloso; evasivo; incerto

slip'shod' *adj* trasandato, mal fatto

slip'-up' *s* (coll) sbaglio

slit [slɪt] *s* taglio, fenditura ‖ *v* (*pret & pp* **slit**; *ger* **slitting**) *tr* tagliare, fendere; **to slit the throat of** sgozzare

slob [slab] *s* (slang) rozzo, villanzone *m*

slobber ['slabər] *s* bava; sdolcinatura ‖ *intr* sbavare; parlare sdolcinatamente

sloe [slo] *s* (*shrub*) prugnolo; (*fruit*) prugnola

slogan ['slogən] *s* slogan *m*

sloop [slup] *s* cutter *m*

slop [slap] *s* pastone *m*; (slang) sbobba ‖ *v* (*pret & pp* **slopped**; *ger* **slopping**) *tr* versare, imbrodare ‖ *intr* rovesciarsi, scorrere; (slang) perdersi in smancerie

slope [slop] *s* costa, pendice *f*; (*of mountain or roof*) spiovente *m* ‖ *tr* inclinare ‖ *intr* digradare, scendere

slop-py ['slapi] *adj* (**-pier; -piest**) fangoso; bagnato; (*slovenly*) sciatto; (*done badly*) abborracciato

slot [slat] *s* scanalatura; (*for letters*) buca; e.g., **on a broadcasting schedule** posizione

sloth [sloθ] *or* [slɔθ] *s* pigrizia; (zool) bradipo, poltrone *m*

slot' machine' *s* macchina a gettone

slouch [slautʃ] *s* postura goffa; persona goffa; (coll) poltrone *m* ‖ *intr* muoversi goffamente; **to slouch in a chair** sdraiarsi

slouch' hat' *s* cappello floscio

slough [slau] *s* pantano; (fig) abisso ‖ [slʌf] *s* (*of snake*) spoglia; (pathol) crosta ‖ *tr*—**to slough off** spogliarsi di ‖ *intr* sbucciarsi, cadere

Slovak ['slovæk] *or* [slo'væk] *adj & s* slovacco

sloven-ly ['slʌvənli] *adj* (**-lier; -liest**) sciatto, trasandato

slow [slo] *adj* lento; (*sluggish*) tardo; (*clock*) indietro, in ritardo; (*in understanding*) tardivo ‖ *adv* piano ‖ *tr* rallentare ‖ *intr* rallentarsi; (*said of a watch*) ritardare

slow'down' *s* sciopero pignolo

slow' mo'tion *s*—**in slow motion** al rallentatore

slow'-motion projec'tor *s* rallentatore *m*

slow'poke' *s* (coll) poltrone *m*

slug [slʌg] *s* (*heavy piece of metal*) lingotto; (*metal disk*) gettone *m*; (fig) poltrone *m*; (zool) lumaca; (coll) colpo, mazzata ‖ *v* (*pret & pp*

slugged; *ger* **slugging**) *tr* picchiare sodo

sluggard ['slʌgərd] *s* poltrone *m*

sluggish ['slʌgɪʃ] *adj* pigro, indolente; lento, fiacco

sluice [slus] *s* canale *m*; stramazzo

sluice' gate' *s* paratoia

slum [slʌm] *s* bassifondi *mpl* ‖ *v* (*pret & pp* **slummed**; *ger* **slumming**) *intr* visitare i bassifondi

slumber ['slʌmbər] *s* dormiveglia *m*, sonnellino ‖ *intr* dormire, dormicchiare

slump [slʌmp] *s* depressione, crisi *f*; (*in prices*) ribasso, calo ‖ *intr* impantanarsi; peggiorare; (*said of prices*) ribassare, calare

slur [slʌr] *s* insulto, macchia; critica; (mus) legatura ‖ *v* (*pret & pp* **slurred**; *ger* **slurring**) *tr* pronunziare indistintamente; (*a subject*) sorvolare; insultare, calunniare; (mus) legare

slush [slʌʃ] *s* poltiglia di neve; fanghiglia; (fig) sdolcinatezza

slut [slʌt] *s* cagna; (*slovenly woman*) sciamannona; troia, puttana

sly [slaɪ] *adj* (**slyer** *or* **slier; slyest** *or* **sliest**) furbo; insidioso; (*hiding one's true feelings*) sornione; **on the sly** furtivamente

smack [smæk] *s* schiaffo; (*of whip or lips*) schiocco; (*taste*) traccia, sapore *m*; (coll) bacio collo schiocco ‖ *adv* di colpo, direttamente ‖ *tr* dare uno schiaffo a; colpire; (*the whip or one's lips*) schioccare; schioccare un bacio a ‖ *intr*—**to smack of** sapere di

small [smɔl] *adj* piccolo; povero; basso, umile; (*change*) spicciolo; (typ) minuscolo

small' arms' *spl* armi *fpl* portatili

small' busi'ness *s* piccolo commercio

small' cap'ital *s* (typ) maiuscoletto

small' change' *s* spiccioli *mpl*

small' fry' *s* minutaglia; bambini *mpl*; gente *f* di poca importanza

small' hours' *spl* ore *fpl* piccole

small' intes'tine *s* intestino tenue

small-minded ['smɔl'maɪndɪd] *adj* di corte vedute, gretto

small' of the back' *s* fine *f* della schiena, reni *fpl*

smallpox ['smɔl,paks] *s* vaiolo

small' talk' *s* conversazione futile

small-time' *adj* di poca importanza

small'-town' *adj* di provincia

smart [smart] *adj* intelligente; scaltro, furbo; (*pain*) acuto; (*in appearance*) elegante; (*pert*) impertinente; (coll) grande, abbondante ‖ *s* dolore acuto, sofferenza ‖ *intr* bruciare; dolere; soffrire

smart' al'eck ['ælɪk] *s* saputello

smart' set' *s* bel mondo

smash [smæʃ] *s* sconquasso; colpo; collisione; rovina, fallimento; (tennis) smash *m*, schiacciata ‖ *tr* sconquassare; sfracellare; rovinare; (tennis) schiacciare ‖ *intr* sconquassarsi; sfracellarsi; andare in rovina; **to smash into** scontrarsi con

smash' hit' *s* successone *m*

smash'-up' s sconquasso

smattering ['smætərɪŋ] s infarinatura, spolvero

smear [smɪr] s macchia, imbrattatura; calunnia; (bact) striscio || tr imbrattare; spalmare; calunniare

smear' campaign' s campagna di vilipendio

smell [smel] s odore m; (sense) olfatto, odorato; profumo || v (pret & pp smelled or smelt) tr fiutare, odorare || intr odorare; (to stink) puzzare; profumare; to smell of odorare di; puzzare di

smell'ing salts' spl sali aromatici

smell·y ['smeli] adj (-ier; -iest) puzzolente

smelt [smelt] s (ichth) eperlano || tr & intr fondere

smile [smaɪl] s sorriso || intr sorridere

smiling ['smaɪlɪŋ] adj sorridente

smirk [smʌrk] s ghigno || intr ghignare

smite [smaɪt] v (pret smote [smot]; pp smitten ['smɪtən] or smit [smɪt]) tr colpire; percuotere; affliggere, castigare

smith [smɪθ] s fabbro

smith·y ['smɪθi] s (-ies) fucina

smit'ten adj afflitto; innamorato

smock [smak] s camice m; (of mechanic) camiciotto

smock' frock' s blusa da lavoro

smog [smag] s foschia, smog m

smoke [smok] s fumo; to go up in smoke andare in cenere || tr affumicare; (tobacco) fumare; to smoke out cacciare col fumo; scoprire || intr fumare; (said, e.g., of the earth) fumigare

smoke'-filled room' s stanza da riunioni piena di fumo

smoke'less pow'der ['smoklɪs] s polvere f senza fumo

smoker ['smokər] s fumatore m; salone m fumatori; (rr) vagone m fumatori

smoke' rings' spl anelli mpl di fumo

smoke' screen' s cortina di fumo

smoke'stack' s fumaiolo

smoking ['smokɪŋ] s (il) fumare; no smoking vietato fumare

smok'ing car' s vagone m fumatori

smok'ing jack'et s giacca da casa

smok'ing room' s stanza per fumatori

smok·y ['smoki] adj (-ier; -iest) fumoso

smolder ['smoldər] s fumo derivante da fuoco che cova || intr (said of fire or passion) covare; (said of s.o.'s eyes) ardere

smooch [smutʃ] intr (coll) baciarsi, baciucchiarsi

smooth [smuð] adj liscio, levigato; (face) glabro; di consistenza uniforme; (flat) piano; senza interruzioni; tranquillo; elegante; (sound) armonioso; (taste) gradevole; (wine) abboccato; (sea) calmo; (style) fluido || tr lisciare, levigare; appianare, facilitare; calmare; to smooth away appianare

smooth-faced ['smuð,fest] adj (beardless) glabro; liscio

smooth-spoken ['smuð,spokən] adj mellifluo

smooth·y ['smuði] s (-ies) galante m

smother ['smʌðər] tr affogare, soffocare

smudge [smʌdʒ] s macchia, imbrattatura || tr macchiare, imbrattare; (a garden) affumicare

smudge' pot' s apparecchiatura per affumicare

smug [smʌg] adj (smugger; smuggest) pieno di sé stesso; liscio, lisciato

smuggle ['smʌgəl] tr contrabbandare || intr praticare il contrabbando

smuggler ['smʌglər] s contrabbandiere m

smuggling ['smʌglɪŋ] s contrabbando

smut [smʌt] s sudiciume m; oscenità f; (agr) volpe f, golpe f

smut·ty ['smʌti] adj (-tier; -tiest) sudicio; osceno; (agr) malato di volpe

snack [snæk] s spuntino, merenda; porzione

snack' bar' s tavola calda

snag [snæg] s tronco sommerso; protuberanza, sporgenza; (tooth) dente rotto; (fig) intoppo, ostacolo; to hit a snag incontrare un ostacolo || v (pret & pp snagged; ger snagging) tr fare uno straccio a; (fig) ostacolare

snail [snel] s chiocciola, lumaca; at a snail's pace come una lumaca

snake [snek] s serpente m; (nonvenomous) biscia

snake' in the grass' s pericolo nascosto; (person) serpe f in seno

snap [snæp] s (sharp sound) schiocco; (bite) morso; (fastener) bottone automatico; (of cold weather) breve periodo; (manner of speaking) tono tagliente; (phot) istantanea; (coll) vigore m; (coll) cosa da nulla || v (pret & pp snapped; ger snapping) tr schioccare; chiudere di colpo; spezzare di colpo; (a picture) scattare; to snap one's fingers at infischiarsi di; to snap up afferrare; (a person) tagliare la parola a || intr schioccare; (to crack) rompersi di colpo; to snap at cercare di mordere; (a bargain) cercare di afferrare; to snap out of it (coll) riprendersi; to snap shut chiudersi di colpo

snap'drag'on s (bot) bocca di leone

snap' fas'tener s bottone automatico

snap' judg'ment s decisione presa senza riflessione

snap·py ['snæpi] adj (-pier; -piest) mordente, mordace; (coll) vivo, vivace; (coll) elegante; to make it snappy (slang) sbrigarsi

snap'shot' s istantanea

snare [sner] s laccio, lacciolo; (of a drum) corda

snare' drum' s cassa rullante

snarl [snarl] s (of a dog) ringhio; groviglio; (of traffic) ingorgo; (fig) confusione || tr urlare con un ringhio; (to tangle) aggrovigliare; complicare || intr ringhiare; aggrovigliarsi; complicarsi

snatch [snætʃ] s strappo, strappone m; presa; pezzetto; momentino || tr &

intr strappare; **to snatch at** cercare di afferrare; **to snatch from** strappare a

sneak [snik] *s* furfante *m* || *tr* mettere di nascosto; pigliare di nascosto || *intr*—**to sneak in** entrare di nascosto; **to sneak out** svignarsela

sneaker ['snikər] *s* furfante *m;* scarpetta da ginnastica

sneak' thief' *s* ladro, topo

sneak·y ['sniki] *adj* (**-ier; -iest**) furtivo

sneer [snɪr] *s* ghigno || *intr* sogghignare; **to sneer at** beffarsi si

sneeze [sniz] *s* starnuto || *intr* starnutare; **not to be sneezed at** (coll) non essere disprezzabile

snicker ['snɪkər] *s* risatina || *intr* fare una risatina

snide [snaɪd] *adj* malizioso

sniff [snɪf] *s* fiuto, fiutata; (*scent*) odore *m* || *tr* fiutare || *intr* aspirare rumorosamente; (*with emotion*) moccicare; **to sniff at** annusare; mostrare disprezzo per

sniffle ['snɪfəl] *s* moccio; **to have the sniffles** moccicare || *intr* moccicare

snip [snɪp] *s* taglio; pezzetto; (*person*) (coll) mezza cartuccia || *v* (*pret & pp* **snipped;** *ger* **snipping**) *tr* tagliuzzare

snipe [snaɪp] *s* tiro di nascosto; (orn) beccaccino || *intr* sparare in appostamento; attaccare da lontano

sniper ['snaɪpər] *s* franco tiratore, cecchino

snippet ['snɪpɪt] *s* ritaglio, frammento; (fig) mezza cartuccia

snip·py ['snɪpi] *adj* (**-pier; -piest**) frammentario; (coll) corto, brusco; (coll) arrogante

snitch [snɪtʃ] *tr & intr* (coll) graffignare, sgraffignare

sniv·el ['snɪvəl] *s* moccio; singhiozzo, piagnisteo; falsa commozione || *v* (*pret & pp* **-eled** or **-elled;** *ger* **-eling** or **-elling**) *intr* singhiozzare, piagnucolare; (*to have a runny nose*) moccicare, avere il moccio

snob [snɑb] *s* snob *mf*

snobbery ['snɑbəri] *s* snobismo

snobbish ['snɑbɪʃ] *adj* snobistico

snoop [snup] *s* (coll) ficcanaso || *intr* (coll) ficcare il naso

snoop·y ['snupi] *adj* (**-ier; -iest**) (coll) curioso, invadente

snoot [snut] *s* (slang) naso

snoot·y ['snuti] *adj* (**-ier; -iest**) (coll) snobistico

snooze [snuz] *s* (coll) sonnellino || *intr* (coll) fare un sonnellino

snore [snor] *s* russamento || *intr* russare

snort [snɔrt] *s* sbuffo || *intr* sbuffare

snot [snɑt] *s* (slang) moccio

snot·ty ['snɑti] *adj* (**-tier; -tiest**) (coll) snobistico; (coll) arrogante; (slang) moccioso

snout [snaut] *s* muso; (*of pig*) grugno; (*of person*) muso, grugno

snow [sno] *s* neve *f* || *intr* nevicare

snow'ball' *s* palla di neve || *tr* gettare palle di neve a || *intr* aumentare come una palla di neve

snow'blind' *adj* accecato dalla neve

snow'bound' *adj* prigioniero della neve

snow-capped ['sno ˌkæpt] *adj* coperto di neve

snow'drift' *s* banco di neve

snow'fall' *s* nevicata

snow' fence' *s* barriera contro la neve

snow'flake' *s* fiocco di neve

snow' flur'ry *s* neve portata da raffiche

snow' line' *s* limite *m* delle nevi perenni

snow'man' *s* (**-men'**) uomo di neve

snow'plow' *s* spazzaneve *m*

snow'shoe' *s* racchetta da neve

snow'slide' *s* valanga

snow'storm' *s* bufera di neve

snow' tire' *s* gomma da neve, pneumatico da neve

snow'-white' *adj* bianco come la neve

snow·y ['sno·i] *adj* (**-ier; -iest**) nevoso

snub [snʌb] *s* affronto || *v* (*pret & pp* **snubbed;** *ger* **snubbing**) *tr* snobbare

snub·by ['snʌbi] *adj* (**-bier; -biest**) camuso, rincagnato

snuff [snʌf] *s* tabacco da fiuto; (*of a candlewick*) moccolo; **up to snuff** (coll) soddisfacente; (coll) bene || *tr* fiutare; tabaccare; (*a candle*) smoccolare; **to snuff out** spegnere; (fig) soffocare

snuff'box' *s* tabacchiera

snuffers ['snʌfərz] *spl* smoccolatoio

snug [snʌg] *adj* (**snugger; snuggest**) comodo; (*dress*) attillato; compatto; (*well-off*) agiato; (*sum*) discreto; (*sheltered*) ben protetto; (*well-hidden*) nascosto

snuggle ['snʌgəl] *intr* rannicchiarsi; **to snuggle up to** stringersi a

so [so] *adv* così; così or tanto + *adj* or *adv;* per quanto; **and so** certamente; pure; **and so on** e così via; **or so** più o meno; **to think so** credere di sì; **so as to** + *inf* per + *inf;* **so far** sinora, finora; **so long!** arrivederci; **so many** tanti; **so much** tanto; **so so** così così; **so that** in maniera che, di modo che; **so to speak** per così dire || *conj* cosicché || *interj* bene!; basta!; così!

soak [sok] *s* bagnata; (*toper*) (slang) ubriacone *m* || *tr* bagnare, inzuppare; imbevere; (coll) ubriacare; (slang) far pagare un prezzo esorbitante a; **to soak up** assorbire; **soaked to the skin** bagnato fino alle ossa || *intr* stare a molle, macerare; inzupparsi

so'-and-so' *s* (**-sos**) tal *m* dei tali; tal cosa

soap [sop] *s* sapone *m* || *tr* insaponare

soap'box' *s* cassa di sapone; tribuna improvvisata

soap'box or'ator *s* oratore *m* che parla da una tribuna improvvisata

soap' bub'ble *s* bolla di sapone

soap' dish' *s* portasapone *m*

soap' flakes' *spl* sapone *m* a scaglie

soap' op'era *s* (coll) trasmissione radiofonica o televisiva lacrimogena

soap' pow'der *s* sapone *m* in polvere

soap'stone' *s* pietra da sarto

soap'suds' *spl* saponata

soap·y ['sopi] *adj* (**-ier; -iest**) saponoso

soar [sor] *intr* spaziare, slanciarsi; (aer) librarsi

sob [sɑb] *s* singhiozzo || *v* (*pret* & *pp* **sobbed;** *ger* **sobbing**) *tr* dire a singhiozzi || *intr* singhiozzare

sober ['sobər] *adj* sobrio; non ubriaco || *intr* smaltire la sbornia; **to sober down** calmarsi; **to sober up** smaltire la sbornia

sobriety [so'braɪ·əti] *s* sobrietà *f*

sobriquet ['sobrɪ‚ke] *s* nomignolo

sob' sis'ter *s* giornalista lacrimogeno

sob' sto'ry *s* storia lacrimogena

so'-called' *adj* cosiddetto

soccer ['sɑkər] *s* calcio, football *m*

sociable ['soʃəbəl] *adj* sociale, socievole

social ['soʃəl] *adj* sociale || *s* riunione sociale

so'cial climb'er ['klaɪmər] *s* arrampicatore *m* sociale

so'cial con'tract *s* patto sociale

socialism ['soʃə‚lɪzəm] *s* socialismo

socialist ['soʃəlɪst] *s* socialista *mf*

socialite ['soʃə‚laɪt] *s* persona che appartiene all'alta società

So'cial Reg'ister *s* (trademark) annuario dell'alta società

so'cial secu'rity *s* sicurezza sociale

so'cial work'er *s* visitatrice *f*, assistente *mf* sociale

socie·ty [sə'saɪ·əti] *s* (**-ties**) società *f*; (*companionship or company*) compagnia

soci'ety ed'itor *s* cronista mondano

sociology [‚sosɪ'ɑlədʒi] or [‚soʃɪ·'alədʒi] *s* sociologia

sock [sɑk] *s* calzino; (slang) colpo forte; (slang) attore *m* di prim'ordine; (slang) spettacolo eccezionale || *tr* (slang) dare un forte colpo a

socket ['sɑkɪt] *s* (*of eye*) occhiaia; (*of tooth*) alveolo; (*of candlestick*) bocciolo; (*wall socket*) presa di corrente; (elec) portalampada *m*

sock'et wrench' *s* chiave *f* a tubo

sod [sɑd] *s* zolla; terreno erboso || *v* (*pret* & *pp* **sodded;** *ger* **sodding**) *tr* piotare

soda ['sodə] *s* soda

so'da crack'er *s* galletta fatta al bicarbonato

so'da wa'ter *s* soda, gazosa

sodium ['sodɪ·əm] *adj* sodico || *s* sodio

sofa ['sofə] *s* sofà *m*, divano

so'fa bed' *s* sofà *m* letto

soft [sɔft] or [sɑft] *adj* molle; (*smooth*) morbido; (*tron*) dolce; (*hat*) floscio; (*person*) rammollito; (coll) facile

soft'-boiled' egg' ['sɔft'bɔɪld] or ['sɑft'bɔɪld] *s* uovo alla coque

soft' coal' *s* carbone bituminoso

soft' drink' *s* bibita

soften ['sɔfən] or ['sɑfən] *tr* mollificare, rammollire; (fig) intenerire || *intr* intenerirsi

softener ['sɔfənər] or ['sɑfənər] *s* ammorbidente *m*

soft' land'ing *s* allunaggio morbido

soft'-ped'al *v* (*pret* & *pp* **-aled** or **-alled;** *ger* **-aling** or **-alling**) *tr* mettere in sordina; (coll) moderare

soft'-shell crab' *s* mollecca

soft' soap' *s* sapone *m* molle; (coll) adulazione

soft'-soap' *tr* (coll) insaponare

sog·gy ['sɑgi] *adj* (**-gier; -giest**) rammollito, inzuppato

soil [sɔɪl] *s* suolo, terreno; territorio; (*spot*) macchia; (*filth*) porcheria, lordura || *tr* sporcare, macchiare || *intr* sporcarsi, macchiarsi

soil' pipe' *s* tubo di scarico

soiree or **soirée** [swɑ're] *s* serata

sojourn ['sodʒʌrn] *s* soggiorno || ['sodʒʌrn] or [so'dʒʌrn] *intr* soggiornare

solace ['sɑlɪs] *s* conforto || *tr* confortare, consolare

solar ['solər] *adj* solare

so'lar bat'tery *s* batteria solare

solder ['sɑdər] *s* saldatura; lega per saldatura || *tr* saldare

sol'dering i'ron *s* saldatoio

soldier ['soldʒər] *s* (*man of rank and file*) soldato; (*man in military service*) militare *m* || *intr* fare il soldato

sol'dier of for'tune *s* soldato di ventura

soldier·y ['soldʒəri] *s* (**-ies**) soldatesca

sold-out ['sold‚aut] *adj* esaurito; (*e.g., theater*) completo

sole [sol] *adj* solo, unico; esclusivo || *s* (*of foot*) pianta; (*of stocking*) soletta; (*of shoe*) suola; (*fish*) sfoglia || *tr* solare

solely ['solli] *adv* solamente

solemn ['sɑləm] *adj* solenne

solicit [sə'lɪsɪt] *tr* sollecitare; adescare, accostare

solicitor [sə'lɪsɪtər] *s* sollecitatore *m*; agente *m*; (law) procuratore *m*

solicitous [sə'lɪsɪtəs] *adj* sollecito

solicitude [sə'lɪsɪ‚tjud] or [sə'lɪsɪ‚tud] *s* sollecitudine *f*

solid ['sɑlɪd] *adj* solido; (*not hollow*) sodo; (*e.g., clouds*) denso; (*wall*) pieno, massiccio; (*word*) con grafia unita; intero; scuro, solidale; (*good*) buono; (*e.g., gold*) puro, massiccio

solidity [sə'lɪdɪti] *s* solidità *f*

sol'id-state' *adj* transistorizzato, senza valvole

solilo·quy [sə'lɪləkwi] *s* (**-quies**) soliloquio

solitaire ['sɑlɪ‚ter] *s* solitario

solitar·y ['sɑlɪ‚teri] *adj* solitario; unico || *s* (**-ies**) persona solitaria

sol'itary confine'ment *s* segregazione cellulare

solitude ['sɑlɪ‚tjud] or ['sɑlɪ‚tud] *s* solitudine *f*

so·lo ['solo] *adj* solo, solitario; (mus) solista || *s* (**-los**) (mus) solo

soloist ['solo·ɪst] *s* solista *mf*

so' long' *interj* (coll) ciao!; (coll) addio!; (coll) arrivederci!

solstice ['sɑlstɪs] *s* solstizio

soluble ['sɑljəbəl] *adj* solubile

solution [sə'luʃən] *s* soluzione

solvable ['sɑlvəbəl] *adj* risolvibile

solve [sɑlv] *tr* risolvere, sciogliere

solvency ['sɑlvənsi] s solvenza
solvent ['sɑlvənt] adj & s solvente m
somber ['sɑmbər] adj tetro
some [sʌm] adj indef qualche; di + art, e.g., **some apples** delle mele; (coll) forte, grande || pron indef alcuni, taluni; ne, e.g., **I have some** ne ho
some'bod'y pron indef taluno, qualcuno; **somebody else** qualcun altro || s (-ies) (coll) qualcuno
some'day' adv qualche giorno
some'how' adv in qualche modo; **somehow or other** in un modo o nell'altro
some'one' pron indef qualcuno, taluno; **someone else** qualcun altro
somersault ['sʌmər ,sɔlt] s salto mortale || intr fare un salto mortale
something ['sʌmθɪŋ] pron indef qualcosa; **something else** qualcos'altro || adv un po'; (coll) molto, moltissimo
some'time' adj antico, di un tempo || adv un giorno o l'altro, uno di questi giorni
some'times' adv talora, talvolta
some'way' adv in qualche modo
some'what' s qualcosa || adv piuttosto, un po'
some'where' adv in qualche luogo, da qualche parte; a qualche momento; **somewhere else** altrove
somnambulist [sɑm'næmbjəlɪst] s sonnambulo
somnolent ['sɑmnələnt] adj sonnolento
son [sʌn] s figlio
sonar ['sonɑr] s ecogoniometro, sonar m
song [sɔŋ] or [sɑŋ] s canto, canzone f; **for a song** per un soldo
song'bird' s uccello canoro
Song' of Songs' s Cantico dei Cantici
songster ['sɑŋstər] s cantante m, canzonettista m
songstress ['sɑŋstrɪs] s cantante f, canzonettista f
song'writ'er s canzoniere m
son'ic boom' ['sɑnɪk] s boato sonico
son'-in-law' s (sons'-in-law') genero
sonnet ['sɑnɪt] s sonetto
son-ny ['sʌni] s (-nies) figliolo
sonori-ty [sə'nɑrɪti] or [sə'nɔrɪti] s (-ties) sonorità f
soon [sun] adv in breve, ben presto; subito, presto; **as soon as** non appena, quanto prima; **as soon as possible** quanto prima; **I had sooner** preferirei; **how soon?** quando?; **soon after** poco dopo; **sooner or later** prima o poi, tosto o tardi
soot [sʊt] or [sut] s fuliggine f
soothe [suð] tr calmare, lenire
soothsayer ['suθ ,se·ər] s indovino
soot-y ['sʊti] or ['suti] adj (-ier; -iest) fuligginoso
sop [sɑp] s (soaked food) zuppa; (bribe) dono, offa || v (pret & pp **sopped; ger sopping**) tr intingere, inzuppare; **to sop up** assorbire
sophisticated [sə'fɪstɪ ,ketɪd] adj sofisticato, smaliziato
sophistication [sə ,fɪstɪ'keʃən] s eccessiva ricercatezza; gusti mpl raffinati

sophomore ['sɑfə ,mor] s studente m del secondo anno, fagiolo
sophomoric [,sɑfə'mɑrɪk] adj saputello, presuntuoso; ingenuo, imberbe
sopping ['sɑpɪŋ] adv—**sopping wet** inzuppato
sopran-o [sə'præno] or [sə'prɑno] adj per soprano, da soprano || s (-os) soprano mf
sorcerer ['sɔrsərər] s mago, stregone m
sorceress ['sɔrsərɪs] s maga, strega
sorcer-y ['sɔrsəri] s (-ies) stregoneria
sordid ['sɔrdɪd] adj sordido
sore [sor] adj irritato; indolenzito; estremo, grave; **to be sore at** (coll) aversela con || s piaga, ulcera; dolore m, afflizione; **to open an old sore** riaprire una ferita
sorely ['sorli] adv penosamente; gravemente, urgentemente
soreness ['sornɪs] s dolore m, afflizione
sore' spot' s (fig) piaga
sore' throat' s mal m di gola
sorori-ty [sə'rɑrɪti] or [sə'rɔrɪti] s (-ties) associazione femminile universitaria
sorrel ['sɑrəl] or ['sɔrəl] adj sauro
sorrow ['sɑro] or ['sɔro] s dolore m, cordoglio || intr affliggersi, provar cordoglio; **to sorrow for** rimpiangere
sorrowful ['sɑrəfəl] or ['sɔrəfəl] adj doloroso
sor-ry ['sɑri] or ['sɔri] adj (-rier; -riest) spiacente, desolato, dolente; povero, cattivo; **to be sorry** dolersi; dispiacere a, e.g., **he is sorry** gli dispiace || interj mi dispiace!, scusi!
sort [sɔrt] s tipo, specie f; maniera; **a sort of** una specie di; **out of sorts** depresso; ammalato; di mal umore; **sort of** (coll) piuttosto; (coll) un certo, e.g., **sort of a headache** un certo mal di testa || tr assortire; (mail) smistare
so'-so' adj passabile || adv così così
sot [sɑt] s ubriacone m
soubrette [su'brɛt] s (theat) soubrette f
soul [sol] s anima; **upon my soul!** sulla mia parola!
sound [saʊnd] adj sano; solido, forte; valido, buono; (sleep) profondo; valido, legale; onesto || s suono; rumore m; (of an animal) verso; (passage of water) stretto; (surg) sonda; (ichth) vescica natatoria; **within sound of** alla portata di || adv profondamente || tr (an instrument) sonare; pronunciare; (e.g., s.o.'s chest) auscultare; (praises) cantare; (to measure) sondare || intr sonare; parere, sembrare; fare uno scandaglio; **to sound like** avere il suono di; dare l'impressione di, parere
sound' bar'rier s muro del suono
sound' film' s pellicola sonora
soundly ['saʊndli] adv solidamente; profondamente; completamente
sound'proof' adj a prova di suono || tr insonorizzare

sound′ track′ s (mov) sonoro, colonna sonora

sound′ truck′ s autoveicolo con impianto sonoro

sound′ wave′ s onda sonora

soup [sup] s zuppa, minestra

soup′ dish′ s piatto fondo

soup′ kitch′en s asilo dei poveri che serve zuppa gratuitamente

soup′spoon′ s cucchiaio (da minestra)

sour [saur] adj acido; (fruit) acerbo || tr inacidire || intr inacidirsi

source [sors] s fonte f, sorgente f

source′ lan′guage s lingua di partenza

source′ mate′rial s fonti fpl originali

sour′ cher′ry s (fruit) amarena; (tree) amareno

sour′ grapes′ interj l'uva è verde!

south [sauθ] adj meridionale, del sud || s sud m, meridione m || adv verso il sud

South′ Amer′ica s l'America f del Sud

South′ Amer′ican adj & s sudamericano

southeast [‚sauθ′ist] adj di sud-est || s sud-est || adv al sud-est

southern [′sʌðərn] adj meridionale

South′ern Cross′ s Croce f del Sud

southerner [′sʌðərnər] s meridionale mf

South′ Kore′a s la Corea del Sud

south′paw′ adj & s (coll) mancino

South′ Pole′ s Polo sud

South′ Vietnam-ese′ [vɪ‚ɛtnə′miz] adj vietnamita del sud || s (-ese) vietnamita mf del sud

southward [′sauθwərd] adv verso il sud

south′west′ adj di sud-ovest || s sud-ovest m || adv al sud-ovest

souvenir [‚suvə′nɪr] or [′suvə‚nɪr] s ricordo, memoria

sovereign [′sɑvrɪn] or [′sʌvrɪn] adj sovrano || s (king) sovrano; (queen; coin) sovrana

sovereign-ty [′sɑvrɪnti] or [′sʌvrɪnti] s (-ties) sovranità f

soviet [′sovɪ‚ɛt] or [‚sovɪ′ɛt] adj sovietico || s soviet m

So′viet Rus′sia s la Russia Sovietica

sow [sau] s porca, troia || [so] v (pret sowed; pp sown or sowed) tr seminare

soybean [′sɔɪ‚bin] s soia; seme m di soia

spa [spɑ] s terme fpl

space [spes] adj spaziale || s spazio; periodo; **after a space** dopo un po' || tr spaziare; **to space out** diradare

space′ bar′ s barra spaziatrice, spaziatrice f

space′ cen′ter s cosmodromo

space′craft′ s astronave f

space′ flight′ s volo spaziale

space′man′ s (-men′) navigatore m spaziale

spacer [′spesər] s spaziatrice f, barra spaziatrice

space′ship′ s astronave f

space′suit′ s scafandro astronautico, tuta spaziale

spacious [′speʃəs] adj spazioso

spade [sped] s vanga; (cards) picca; **to call a spade a spade** dire pane al pane, vino al vino || tr vangare

spade′work′ s lavoro preliminare

spaghetti [spə′gɛti] s spaghetti mpl

Spain [spen] s la Spagna

span [spæn] s (of the hand) spanna; (of time) tratto; (of a bridge) campata, luce f; (of horses) paio; (aer) apertura || v (pret & pp spanned; ger spanning) tr misurare a spanne; attraversare, oltrepassare; (said of time) abbracciare

spangle [′spæŋgəl] s lustrino || tr tempestare di lustrini; (with bright objects) stellare || intr brillare

Spaniard [′spænjərd] s spagnolo

Spanish [′spænɪʃ] adj & s spagnolo; **the Spanish** gli spagnoli

Span′ish-Amer′ican adj & s ispanoamericano

Span′ish broom′ s ginestra

Span′ish fly′ mosca cantaride

Span′ish om′elet s frittata di pomodori, cipolle e peperoni

Span′ish-speak′ing adj di lingua spagnola

spank [spæŋk] tr sculacciare

spanking [′spæŋkɪŋ] adj rapido; forte; (coll) eccellente, straordinario || s sculacciata

spar [spɑr] s (mineral) spato; (naut) asta, pennone m; (aer) longherone m || v (pret & pp sparred; ger sparring) intr fare la box

spare [sper] adj di riserva; libero, in eccesso; (e.g., diet) frugale; (lean) magro || tr salvare, risparmiare; perdonare; (to do without) fare a meno di, privarsi di; **to have . . . to spare** aver . . . d'avanzo; **to spare oneself** risparmiarsi

spare′ parts′ s pezzi mpl di ricambio

spare′ room′ s camera per gli ospiti

spare′ tire′ s ruota di scorta, pneumatico di scorta

spare′ wheel′ s ruota di scorta

sparing [′sperɪŋ] adj economico; (scanty) scarso

spark [spɑrk] s scintilla; traccia || tr (coll) rianimare; (coll) corteggiare || intr scintillare

spark′ coil′ s bobina d'accensione

spark′ gap′ s (elec) traferro, intraferro

sparkle [′spɑrkəl] s scintilla; (luster) scintillio; allegria, vivacità f || intr scintillare; (said, e.g., of eyes) brillare, luccicare; (said of wine) frizzare, spumeggiare

sparkling [′spɑrklɪŋ] adj scintillante; (wine) frizzante, spumeggiante; (water) gassoso

spark′ plug′ s candela

sparrow [′spæro] s passero

sparse [spɑrs] adj rado

Spartan [′spɑrtən] adj & s spartano

spasm [′spæzəm] s spasmo; sprazzo d'energia

spasmodic [spæz′mɑdɪk] adj spasmodico; intermittente, a sprazzi

spastic [′spæstɪk] adj & s spastico

spat [spæt] s litigio, battibecco; **spats**

ghette *fpl* ‖ *v* (*pret & pp* **spatted;** *ger* **spatting**) *intr* avere un battibecco

spatial [ˈspeʃəl] *adj* spaziale

spatter [ˈspætər] *tr* schizzare, spruzzare ‖ *intr* gocciolare

spatula [ˈspætʃələ] *s* spatola

spawn [spɔn] *s* prole *f*, progenie *f*; risultato ‖ *tr* produrre, generare ‖ *intr* (ichth) deporre le uova

spay [spe] *tr* asportare le ovaie a

speak [spik] *v* (*pret* **spoke** [spok]; *pp* **spoken**) *tr* (*a language*) parlare; (*the truth*) dire ‖ *intr* parlare; **so to speak** per così dire; **speaking!** al telefono!; **to speak of** importante, che valga parlarne; **to speak out** dire la propria opinione

speak'-eas'y *s* (-**ies**) bar clandestino

speaker [ˈspikər] *s* conferenziere *m*, oratore *m*; (*of a language*) parlante *mf*; (pol) presidente *m*; (rad) altoparlante *m*

speaking [ˈspikɪŋ] *adj* parlante; **to be on speaking terms** parlarsi ‖ *s* parlare *m*, discorso

speak'ing tube' *s* tubo acustico

spear [spɪr] *s* lancia; (*for fishing*) arpione *m*; (*of grass*) stelo ‖ *tr* trafiggere con la lancia

spear' gun' *s* fucile subacqueo

spear'head' *s* punta di lancia ‖ *tr* condurre, dirigere

spear'mint' *s* menta romana spicata

special [ˈspeʃəl] *adj* speciale ‖ *s* prezzo speciale; treno speciale

spe'cial deliv'ery *s* espresso

spe'cial draw'ing rights' *spl* (econ) diritti *mpl* speciali di prelievo

specialist [ˈspeʃəlɪst] *s* specialista *mf*

specialize [ˈspeʃəˌlaɪz] *tr* specializzare ‖ *intr* specializzarsi

spe'cial part'ner *s* accomandante *mf*

special·ty [ˈspeʃəlti] *s* (-**ties**) specialità *f*

spe·cies [ˈspiʃiz] *s* (-**cies**) specie *f*

specific [spɪˈsɪfɪk] *adj & s* specifico

specification [ˌspesɪfɪˈkeʃən] *s* specifica; (com) capitolato

specif'ic grav'ity *s* peso specifico

speci·fy [ˈspesɪˌfaɪ] *v* (*pret & pp* -**fied**) *tr* specificare

specimen [ˈspesɪmən] *s* esemplare *m*; (coll) tipo

specious [ˈspiʃəs] *adj* specioso

speck [spek] *s* macchiolina; (*of dust*) granello; (*of hope*) filo ‖ *tr* macchiettare

speckle [ˈspekəl] *s* macchiolina ‖ *tr* macchiettare, picchiettare

spectacle [ˈspektəkəl] *s* spettacolo; **spectacles** occhiali *mpl*

spectator [ˈspektetər] or [spekˈtetər] *s* spettatore *m*

specter [ˈspektər] *s* spettro

spec·trum [ˈspektrəm] *s* (-**tra** [trə] or -**trums**) spettro; (fig) gamma

speculate [ˈspekjəˌlet] *intr* speculare

speech [spitʃ] *s* parola, parlata; (*before an audience*) discorso; (*of an actor*) elocuzione; **in speech** oralmente

speech' clin'ic *s* clinica per la correzione dei difetti del linguaggio

speechless [ˈspitʃlɪs] *adj* senza parole, muto

speed [spid] *s* velocità *f*; (aut) marcia ‖ *tr* accelerare, affrettare ‖ *intr* accelerare, affrettarsi; guidare oltre la velocità massima

speed'boat' *s* motoscafo da corsa

speeding [ˈspidɪŋ] *s* eccesso di velocità

speed' king' *s* asso del volante

speed' lim'it *s* limite *m* di velocità

speedometer [spiˈdɑmɪtər] *s* tachimetro; (*to record the distance covered*) contachilometri *m*

speed'-up' *s* accelerazione

speed'way' *s* (*highway*) autostrada; (*for races*) pista

speed·y [ˈspidi] *adj* (-**ier; -iest**) veloce, rapido

spell [spel] *s* malia, incantesimo; fascino; turno; attacco; periodo di tempo; **to cast a spell on** incantare ‖ *v* (*pret & pp* **spelled** or **spelt** [spelt]) *tr* compitare; scrivere in tutte lettere; voler dire; **to spell out** (coll) spiegare dettagliatamente ‖ *intr* scrivere, sillabare ‖ *v* (*pret & pp* **spelled**) *tr* rimpiazzare

spell'bind' *v* (*pret & pp* -**bound**) *tr* affascinare

spell'bind'er *s* oratore *m* abbagliante

spelling [ˈspelɪŋ] *adj* ortografico ‖ *s* (*act*) compitazione; (*way a word is spelled*) grafia; (*subject of study*) ortografia

spell'ing bee' *s* gara di ortografia

spelunker [sprˈlʌŋkər] *s* esploratore *m* di caverne

spend [spend] *v* (*pret & pp* **spent** [spent]) *tr* spendere; (*time*) passare

spender [ˈspendər] *s* spenditore *m*

spend'ing mon'ey *s* denaro per le piccole spese personali

spend'thrift' *s* sprecone *m*, spendaccione *m*

sperm [spʌrm] *s* sperma *m*

sperm' whale' *s* capodoglio

spew [spju] *tr & intr* vomitare

sphere [sfɪr] *s* sfera

spherical [ˈsferɪkəl] *adj* sferico

sphinx [sfɪŋks] *s* (**sphinxes** or **sphinges** [ˈsfɪndʒiz]) sfinge *f*

spice [spaɪs] *s* droga; spezie *fpl*; (fig) gusto, sapore *m* ‖ *tr* drogare; dare gusto a, rendere piccante

spick-and-span [ˈspɪkəndˈspæn] *adj* ordinato e pulito

spic·y [ˈspaɪsi] *adj* (-**ier; -iest**) drogato; piccante

spider [ˈspaɪdər] *s* ragno

spi'der-web' *s* ragnatela

spiff·y [ˈspɪfi] *adj* (-**ier; -iest**) (slang) elegante, bello

spigot [ˈspɪgət] *s* (*peg*) zipolo; (*faucet*) rubinetto

spike [spaɪk] *s* chiodo, chiodone *m*; (*sharp-pointed piece*) spuntone *m*; (rr) arpione *m*; (bot) spiga ‖ *tr* inchiodare; mettere chiodi a; (*a rumor*) porre fine a; (coll) alcolizzare

spill [spɪl] *s* rovesciamento; liquido rovesciato; (coll) caduta ‖ *v* (*pret & pp* **spilled** or **spilt** [spɪlt]) *tr* rovesciare, spandere; versare; (naut) sventare; (coll) far cadere; (slang) snocciolare || *intr* rovesciarsi; versarsi

spill'way' *s* sfioratore *m*, stramazzo

spin [spɪn] *s* giro; (*twirl*) mulinello; corsa; **to go into a spin** (aer) cadere a vite || *v* (*pret* & *pp* **spun** [spʌn]; *ger* **spinning**) *tr* far girare; (*e.g.*, *thread*) filare; **to spin out** prolungare; **to spin a yarn** raccontare una storia || *intr* girare; (*said of a top*) prillare; filare

spinach ['spɪnɪtʃ] or ['spɪnɪdʒ] *s* spinacio; (*leaves used as food*) spinaci *mpl*

spi'nal col'umn ['spaɪnəl] *s* spina dorsale, colonna vertebrale

spi'nal cord' *s* midollo spinale

spindle ['spɪndəl] *s* (*rounded rod*) fuso; (*shaft, axle*) asse *m*; balaustro

spine [spaɪn] *s* spina; spina dorsale; (bb) costola; (fig) forza, carattere *m*

spineless ['spaɪnlɪs] *adj* senza spine; senza carattere

spinet ['spɪnɪt] *s* spinetta

spinner ['spɪnər] *s* filatore *m*; (*machine*) filatrice *f*

spinning ['spɪnɪŋ] *adj* filante || *s* filatura; rotazione

spin'ning mill' *s* filanda

spin'ning wheel' *s* filatoio

spinster ['spɪnstər] *s* zitella

spi·ral ['spaɪrəl] *adj* & *s* spirale *f* || *v* (*pret* & *pp* **-raled** or **-ralled**; *ger* **-raling** or **-ralling**) *intr* muoversi lungo una spirale

spi'ral stair'case *s* scala a chiocciola

spire [spaɪr] *s* (*of a steeple*) guglia, freccia; (*of grass*) foglia; (*spiral*) spirale *f*

spirit ['spɪrɪt] *s* spirito; valore *m*, vigore *m*; bevanda spiritosa; **out of spirits** giù di morale || *tr*—**to spirit away** portar via misteriosamente

spirited ['spɪrɪtɪd] *adj* brioso; (*horse*) superbo, vivace

spir'it lamp' *s* lampada a spirito

spiritless ['spɪrɪtlɪs] *adj* senza anima, senza vita

spir'it lev'el *s* livella a bolla d'aria

spiritual ['spɪrɪtʃʊ-əl] *adj* spirituale; (*séance*) spiritico

spiritualism ['spɪrɪtʃʊ‚lɪzəm] *s* spiritismo; (philos) spiritualismo

spiritualist ['spɪrɪtʃʊ-əlɪst] *s* spiritista *mf*; (philos) spiritualista *mf*

spirituous ['spɪrɪtʃʊ-əs] *adj* alcolico

spit [spɪt] *s* sputo; (*for roasting*) spiedo, schidione *m*; punta; **the spit and image of** (coll) il ritratto parlante di || *v* (*pret* & *pp* **spat** [spæt] or **spit**; *ger* **spitting**) *tr* & *intr* sputare

spite [spaɪt] *s* dispetto, ripicco; **in spite of** a dispetto di, a onta di; **out of spite** per picca || *tr* far dispetto a; offendere; contrariare

spiteful ['spaɪtfəl] *adj* dispettoso

spit'fire' *s* persona collerica; (*woman*) bisbetica

spit'ting im'age *s* (coll) ritratto parlante

spittoon [spɪ'tun] *s* sputacchiera

splash [splæʃ] *s* schizzo, spruzzo; (*of mud*) zacchera; (*sound*) tonfo; **to make a splash** fare molto sci-sci || *tr* & *intr* sguazzare

splash'down' *s* (rok) ammaraggio, urto con l'acqua

spleen [splin] *s* cattivo umore, bile *f*; (anat) milza, splene *m*

splendid ['splendɪd] *adj* splendido; ottimo, magnifico

splendor ['splendər] *s* splendore *m*

splice [splaɪs] *s* giuntura || *tr* giuntare

splint [splɪnt] *s* stecca || *tr* steccare

splinter ['splɪntər] *s* scheggia || *tr* scheggiare || *intr* scheggiarsi

splin'ter group' *s* gruppo dissidente

split [splɪt] *adj* spaccato; diviso || *s* spaccatura; fessura; rottura, divisione; (sports) spaccato || *v* (*pret* & *pp* **split**; *ger* **splitting**) *tr* spaccare; dividere; **to split one's sides with laughter** scoppiare dalle risa || *intr* scindersi, dividersi; **to split up** separarsi

split' personal'ity *s* sdoppiamento della personalità

splitting ['splɪtɪŋ] *adj* che fende; che si fende; violento, fortissimo || *s*— **splittings** frammenti *mpl*

splotch [splatʃ] *s* macchia, chiazza || *tr* macchiare, chiazzare

splurge [splʌrdʒ] *s* ostentazione || *intr* fare ostentazione; fare una spesa matta

splutter ['splʌtər] *s* crepitio; (*utterance*) barbugliamento || *tr* barbugliare || *intr* crepitare; barbugliare

spoil [spɔɪl] *s* spoglia, bottino; **spoils** (mil) spoglie *fpl*; (pol) profitto, vantaggio || *v* (*pret* & *pp* **spoiled** or **spoilt** [spɔɪlt]) *tr* rovinare, sciupare; (*a child*) viziare; (*food*) deteriorare || *intr* guastarsi, andare a male

spoilage ['spɔɪlɪdʒ] *s* deterioramento

spoiled [spɔɪld] *adj* (*child*) viziato; (*food*) andato a male, passato

spoils' sys'tem *s* sistema politico secondo il quale le cariche vanno al partito vincitore

spoke [spok] *s* (*of a wheel*) raggio; (*of a ladder*) piolo

spokes'man *s* (-men) portavoce *m*

sponge [spʌndʒ] *s* spugna; **to throw in the sponge** (slang) gettare la spugna || *tr* pulire con spugna; assorbire; (coll) scroccare || *intr* assorbire; **to sponge off** (coll) vivere alle spalle di

sponge' bath' *s* spugnatura

sponge' cake' *s* pan *m* di Spagna

sponger ['spʌndʒər] *s* scroccatore *m*

sponge' rub'ber *s* gommapiuma

spon·gy ['spʌndʒɪ] *adj* (-gier; -giest) spugnoso

sponsor ['spansər] *s* patrocinatore *m*; (*of a charitable institution*) patrono; (*godfather*) padrino; (*godmother*) madrina || *tr* patrocinare; (rad, telv) offrire

sponsorship ['spansər‚ʃɪp] *s* patrocinio

spontaneous [span'tenɪ-əs] *adj* spontaneo

spoof [spuf] *s* mistificazione; parodia || *tr* mistificare; parodiare || *intr* mistificare; fare una parodia

spook [spuk] *s* (coll) spettro

spook·y ['spuki] *adj* (-**ier**; -**iest**) (coll) spettrale; (*horse*) (coll) nervoso

spool [spul] *s* spola, rocchetto

spoon [spun] *s* cucchiaio; (*lure*) cucchiaino; **born with a silver spoon in one's mouth** nato con la camicia || *tr* servire col cucchiaio || *intr* (coll) limonare

spoonerism ['spunə‚rɪzəm] *s* papera

spoon'-feed' *v* (*pret & pp* -**fed**) *tr* nutrire col cucchiaino; (fig) coccolare

spoonful ['spun‚ful] *s* cucchiaiata

spoon·y ['spuni] *adj* (-**ier**; -**iest**) (coll) svenevole

sporadic(al) [spə'rædɪk(əl)] *adj* sporadico

spore [spor] *s* spora

sport [sport] *adj* sportivo || *s* sport *m;* gioco; (*laughingstock*) zimbello; (*gambler*) (coll) giocatore *m;* (*person who behaves in a sportsmanlike manner*) (coll) spirito sportivo; (*flashy fellow*) (coll) tipo fino; (biol) mutazione; **to make sport of** farsi gioco di || *tr* (coll) sfoggiare; **to sport away** dissipare || *intr* divertirsi; giocare; farsi beffe

sport' clothes' *spl* vestiti *mpl* sport

sport'ing chance' *s* pari opportunità *f* di vincere

sport'ing goods' *spl* articoli *mpl* sportivi

sport'ing house' *s* (coll) bordello

sports'cast'er *s* annunziatore sportivo

sports' fan' *s* appassionato agli spettacoli sportivi, tifoso

sports'man *s* (-**men**) sportivo

sports'man·ship' *s* sportività *f,* spirito sportivo

sports' news' *s* notiziario sportivo

sports'wear' *s* articoli *mpl* d'abbigliamento sportivo

sports'writ'er *s* cronista sportivo

sport·y ['sporti] *adj* (-**ier**; -**iest**) (coll) elegante; (coll) sportivo; (coll) appariscente

spot [spɑt] *s* macchia; luogo, punto, posto; (*e.g., of tea*) goccia; **spots** locali *mpl;* **on the spot** sul posto; (*right now*) seduta stante; (slang) in difficoltà; **to hit the spot** (slang) soddisfare completamente || *v* (*pret & pp* **spotted**; *ger* **spotting**) *tr* macchiare; spargere; (coll) riconoscere || *intr* macchiare; macchiarsi

spot' cash' *s* pronta cassa

spot'-check' *tr* fare un breve sondaggio di; controllare rapidamente

spot' check' *s* breve sondaggio; rapido controllo

spotless ['spɑtlɪs] *adj* immacolato, senza macchia

spot'light' *s* riflettore *m;* (aut) proiettore *m;* **to be in the spotlight** (fig) essere il centro d'attenzione

spot' remov'er [rɪ'muvər] *s* smacchiatore *m*

spot' weld'ing *s* saldatura per punti

spouse [spauz] *or* [spaus] *s* consorte *mf*

spout [spaut] *s* (*to carry water from roof*) doccia; (*of jar, pitcher, etc.*) becco, beccuccio; (*jet*) zampillo, getto || *tr & intr* sprizzare, zampillare; (coll) declamare

sprain [spren] *s* distorsione || *tr* distorcere, distorcersi

sprawl [sprɔl] *intr* sdraiarsi

spray [spre] *s* spruzzo; (*of the sea*) schiuma; (*device*) spruzzatore *m;* (*twig*) ramoscello || *tr & intr* spruzzare

sprayer ['spre·ər] *s* spruzzatore *m,* schizzetto, vaporizzatore *m;* (hort) irroratrice *f*

spray' gun' *s* pistola a spruzzo; (hort) irroratrice *f*

spray' paint' *s* vernice *f* a spruzzo

spread [spred] *s* espansione; diffusione; differenza; tappeto, coperta; elasticità *f;* (*of the wings of bird or airplane*) apertura; cibo da spalmare; (coll) festino; (journ) articolo di fondo or pubblicitario su varie colonne || *v* (*pret & pp* **spread**) *tr* tendere, estendere; (*one's legs*) divaricare; (*wings*) spiegare, spargere, cospargere; (*the table*) preparare; (*butter*) spalmare; diffondere || *intr* estendersi; spiegarsi; spargersi; spalmarsi; diffondersi

spree [spri] *s* baldoria, bisboccia; **to go on a spree** darsi alla pazza gioia

sprig [sprɪg] *s* ramoscello

spright·ly ['spraɪtli] *adj* (-**ier**; -**iest**) brioso, vivace

spring [sprɪŋ] *adj* primaverile; sorgivo; a molla || *s* (*season*) primavera; (*issue of water from earth*) fonte *f,* polla; (*elastic device*) molla; elasticità *f;* (*leap*) salto; (*crack*) fenditura; (aut) balestra || *v* (*pret* **sprang** [spræŋ] *or* **sprung** [sprʌŋ]; *pp* **sprung**) *tr* (*e.g., a lock*) far scattare; (*a leak*) aprire; (*a mine*) far brillare || *intr* saltare; (*said of a metal spring*) scattare; scaturire, zampillare; nascere, derivare; esplodere; **to spring forth** or **up** sorgere

spring'board' *s* pedana, trampolino

spring' chick'en *s* pollo giovanissimo; (slang) ragazzina

spring' fe'ver *s* indolenza primaverile

spring' mat'tress *s* materasso a molle

spring' tide' *s* marea di sizigia

spring'time' *s* primavera

sprinkle ['sprɪŋkəl] *s* spruzzo, spruzzatina; (*small amount*) pizzico || *tr* spruzzare; (*e.g., sugar*) spolverizzare || *intr* sprizzare; pioviggginare

sprinkler ['sprɪŋklər] *s* annaffiatoio; (*person*) annaffiatore *m*

sprinkling ['sprɪŋklɪŋ] *s* sprizzo, spruzzo; (*with holy water*) aspersione; (*with powder*) spolverizzamento; (*e.g., of knowledge*) spolvero, spolveratura; (*of people*) piccolo numero

sprin'kling can' *s* annaffiatoio

sprint [sprɪnt] s (sports) scatto, volata ‖ intr (sports) scattare

sprite [spraɪt] s spirito folletto

sprocket ['sprɑkɪt] s moltiplica; (phot) trasportatore m

sprout [spraut] s germoglio ‖ intr germogliare; crescere rapidamente

spruce [sprus] adj elegante, attillato ‖ s abete rosso ‖ tr attillare, azzimare ‖ intr attillarsi, azzimarsi

spry [spraɪ] adj (**spryer** or **sprier; spryest** or **spriest**) vegeto

spud [spʌd] s vanghetto, tagliaradici m; (coll) patata

spun' glass' s lana di vetro

spunk [spʌŋk] s (coll) coraggio, fegato

spur [spʌr] s sperone m; (rr) raccordo ferroviario; (fig) pungolo; **on the spur of the moment** lì per lì ‖ v (pret & pp **spurred**; ger **spurring**) tr spronare; **to spur on** spronare, incitare

spurious ['spjurɪ-əs] adj spurio

spurn [spʌrn] s disprezzo, sdegno; rifiuto ‖ tr disprezzare, sdegnare; rifiutare

spurt [spʌrt] s spruzzo, zampillo; (sudden burst) scatto repentino ‖ intr sprizzare, zampillare; scattare

sputter ['spʌtər] s barbugliamento; (sizzling) crepitio ‖ tr barbugliare ‖ intr barbugliare; crepitare

spu·tum ['spjutəm] s (**-ta** [tə]) sputo

spy [spaɪ] s (**spies**) spia ‖ v (pret & pp **spied**) tr spiare; osservare ‖ intr fare la spia; **to spy on** spiare

spy'glass' s cannocchiale m

spying ['spaɪ-ɪŋ] s spionaggio

squabble ['skwɑbəl] s battibecco ‖ intr litigare

squad [skwɑd] s squadra

squadron ['skwɑdrən] s (of cavalry) squadrone m; (aer, nav) squadriglia; (mil) squadra

squalid ['skwɑlɪd] adj sordido; squallido, misero

squall [skwɔl] s groppo, turbine m; urlo ‖ intr gridare, urlare

squalor ['skwɑlər] s sordidezza; squallore m, miseria

squander ['skwɑndər] tr scialacquare, dilapidare, sperperare

square [skwɛr] adj quadrato, e.g., **two square miles** due miglia quadrate; di . . . di lato, e.g., **two miles square** di due miglia di lato; ad angolo retto; solido; saldato; (coll) onesto; (coll) diretto; (coll) sostanzioso; (slang) all'antica; **to get square with** (coll) fargliela pagare a ‖ s quadrato; (small square, e.g., of checkerboard) quadretto; (city block) isolato; (open area in city) piazza, piazzale m; (of carpenter) squadra; **on the square** ad angolo retto; (coll) onesto ‖ adv ad angolo retto; (coll) onestamente ‖ tr squadrare; dividere in quadretti; elevare al quadrato; quadrare; (a debt) saldare; **to square with** adattare a ‖ intr quadrare; **to square off** prepararsi, mettersi in posizione difensiva

square' dance' s danza figurata americana

square' meal' s (coll) pasto abbondante

square' root' s radice quadrata

square' shoot'er ['ʃutər] s (coll) persona onesta

squash [skwɑʃ] s spappolamento; (bot) zucca; (sports) squash m ‖ tr spappolare; spiaccicare; (e.g., a rumor) sopprimere; (a person) (coll) ridurre al silenzio ‖ intr spiaccicarsi

squash·y ['skwɑʃi] adj (**-ier; -iest**) tenero; (ground) fangoso, pantanoso; (fruit) maturo

squat [skwɑt] adj tozzo ‖ v (pret & pp **squatted**; ger **squatting**) intr accoccolarsi; stabilirsi illegalmente su territorio altrui; stabilirsi su terreno pubblico per ottenerne titolo

squatter ['skwɑtər] s intruso

squaw [skwɔ] s squaw f; (coll) donna pellerossa

squawk [skwɔk] s schiamazzo; (slang) lamento stridulo ‖ intr schiamazzare; (slang) lamentarsi strillando

squaw' man' s bianco sposato con una pellerossa

squeak [skwik] s strido; cigolio ‖ intr stridere; cigolare; (said of a mouse) squittire; **to squeak through** farcela per il rotto della cuffia

squeal [skwil] s strido ‖ intr stridere; (slang) cantare, fare il delatore

squealer ['skwilər] s (slang) delatore m

squeamish ['skwimɪʃ] adj pudibondo; scrupoloso; (easily nauseated) schifiltoso, schizzinoso

squeeze [skwiz] s spremuta; stretta, abbraccio; **to put the squeeze on** (coll) far pressione su ‖ tr premere; spremere, pigiare; stringere ‖ intr stringere; **to squeeze through** aprirsi il passo attraverso; (fig) farcela a pena

squeezer ['skwizər] s spremifrutta m

squelch [skwɛltʃ] s osservazione schiacciante ‖ tr schiacciare

squid [skwɪd] s calamaro, totano

squint [skwɪnt] s tendenza losca; occhiata; (pathol) strabismo ‖ tr (one's eyes) socchiudere ‖ intr socchiudere gli occhi; guardare furtivamente

squint-eyed ['skwɪnt‚aɪd] adj guercio, losco; malevolo

squire [skwaɪr] s (of a lady) cavaliere m servente; (Brit) proprietario terriero; (U.S.A.) giudice m conciliatore ‖ tr (a woman) accompagnare

squirm [skwʌrm] s contorsione ‖ intr contorcersi; mostrare imbarazzo; **to squirm out of** cavarsela da

squirrel ['skwʌrəl] s scoiattolo

squirt [skwʌrt] s schizzo; (instrument) schizzetto; (coll) saputello ‖ tr & intr schizzare

stab [stæb] s pugnalata; (of pain) fitta; **to make a stab at** (coll) provare ‖ v (pret & pp **stabbed**; ger **stabbing**) tr pugnalare, trafiggere ‖ intr pugnalare

stabilize ['stebəl‚aɪz] tr stabilizzare

stab' in the back' s pugnalata nella schiena or alle spalle

stable ['stebəl] *adj* stabile || *s* stalla; (*of race horses*) scuderia

sta'ble·boy' *s* stalliere *m*

stack [stæk] *s* pila; (*of hay or straw*) pagliaio; (*of firewood*) catasta; (*of books*) scaffale *m*; camino; (*coll*) mucchio, sacco || *tr* ammonticchiare, accatastare

stadi·um ['stedɪ·əm] *s* (**-ums** or **-a** [ə]) stadio

staff [stæf] or [staf] *s* bastone *m*; asta, albero; personale *m*, corpo; (*mil*) stato maggiore; (*mus*) rigo, pentagramma *m* || *tr* dotare di personale

staff' of'ficer *s* ufficiale *m* di stato maggiore

stag [stæg] *adj* per signori soli || *s* (*deer*) cervo; maschio; (*coll*) signore *m* || *adv* senza compagna

stage [stedʒ] *s* fase *f*, stadio; tappa, giornata; (*coach*) diligenza; teatro; piattaforma; (*of microscope*) piatto portaoggetti; (*theat*) scena, palcoscenico; **by easy stages** poco a poco; **to go on the stage** diventare attore || *tr* mettere in scena; organizzare

stage'coach' *s* diligenza

stage'craft' *s* scenotecnica

stage' door' *s* (*theat*) ingresso degli artisti

stage' fright' *s* tremarella

stage'hand' *s* macchinista *m*

stage' left' *s* (*theat*) la sinistra della scena guardando il pubblico

stage' man'ager *s* direttore *m* di scena

stage' right' *s* (*theat*) la destra della scena guardando il pubblico

stage'-struck' *adj* innamorato del teatro

stage' whis'per *s* a parte *m*

stagger ['stægər] *tr* far traballare; impressionare; (*troops; hours*) scaglionare || *intr* traballare

stag'gering *adj* traballante; impressionante, stupefacente

staging ['stedʒɪŋ] *s* impalcatura; (*theat*) messa in scena

stagnant ['stægnənt] *adj* stagnante

staid [sted] *adj* serio, grave

stain [sten] *s* macchia; tinta; colorante *m* || *tr* macchiare; tingere; colorare || *intr* macchiarsi

stained' glass' *s* vetro colorato

stained'-glass win'dow' *s* vetrata a colori

stainless ['stenlɪs] *adj* immacolato; (*steel*) inossidabile

stair [stɛr] *s* scala

stair'case' *s* scala

stair'way' *s* scala

stair'well' *s* tromba delle scale

stake [stek] *s* picchetto; (*e.g., of cart*) staggio; (*to support a plant*) puntello; (*in gambling*) puglia, giocata; **at stake** in gioco; **to die at the stake** morire sul rogo; **to pull up stakes** (*coll*) andarsene, traslocare || *tr* picchettare; puntellare; attaccare a un palo; arrischiare; (*coll*) aiutare; **to stake out** picchettare; (*slang*) tenere sotto sorveglianza; **to stake out a claim** avanzare una pretesa

stale [stel] *adj* stantio; (*air*) viziato; (*fig*) ritrito

stale'mate' *s* (*chess*) stallo; **to reach a**

stalemate essere in una posizione di stallo || *tr* mettere in una posizione di stallo

stalk [stɔk] *s* stelo; (*of corn*) stocco; (*of salad*) piede *m* || *tr* braccare || *intr* avanzare furtivamente; camminare con andatura maestosa

stall [stɔl] *s* (*in a stable*) posta; (*booth in a market*) bancarella; (*seat*) stallo; (*space in a parking lot*) spazio per il parcheggio || *tr* (*an animal*) stallare; (*a car*) parcheggiare; (*a motor*) far fermare; **to stall off** eludere, tenere a bada || *intr* impantanarsi; stare nella posta; (*said of a motor*) fermarsi; (*to temporize*) menare il can per l'aia

stallion ['stæljən] *s* stallone *m*

stalwart ['stɔlwərt] *adj* forte, gagliardo || *s* sostenitore *m*

stamen ['stemən] *s* stame *m*

stamina ['stæmɪnə] *s* forza, vigore *m*

stammer ['stæmər] *s* balbuzie *f* || *tr* & *intr* balbettare

stammerer ['stæmərər] *s* balbuziente *mf*

stamp [stæmp] *s* (*postage stamp*) francobollo; (*device to show that a fee has been paid*) timbro, bollo; impressione; carattere *m*; sigillo; (*tool for stamping coins*) conio; (*tool for crushing ore*) maglio || *tr* timbrare, stampigliare, bollare; sigillare; coniare; (*one's foot*) battere, pestare; imprimere; caratterizzare; (*mach*) stampare; **to stamp out** spegnere; sopprimere || *intr* battere il piede; (*said of a horse*) zampare

stampede [stæm'pid] *s* fuga precipitosa || *tr* precipitarsi verso; far fuggire precipitosamente || *intr* precipitarsi

stamp'ing ground' *s* (*coll*) luogo di ritrovo abituale

stamp' pad' *s* tampone *m*

stamp'-vend'ing machine' *s* distributore automatico di francobolli

stance [stæns] *s* posizione

stanch [stɑntʃ] *adj* leale; forte; a tenuta d'acqua || *s* chiusa || *tr* arrestare il flusso da; (*blood*) stagnare

stand [stænd] *s* posizione; resistenza; difesa; tribuna, palco; sostegno, supporto; (*booth in market*) posteggio; posto di sosta || *v* (*pret* & *pp* **stood** [stʊd]) *tr* mettere in piedi; reggere, sostenere; sopportare, tollerare; (*one's ground*) mantenere; (*a chance*) avere; (*watch*) fare; (*coll*) pagare; **to stand off** tenere a distanza || *intr* stare; essere alto; fermarsi; stare in piedi; trovarsi; aver forza; essere; (*e.g., apart*) tenersi; **to stand back of** spalleggiare; **to stand by** appoggiare; **to stand for** rappresentare, voler dire; appoggiare, favorire; tenere a battesimo; (*coll*) tollerare; **to stand in line** fare la fila or la coda; **to stand in with** (*coll*) essere nelle buone grazie di; **to stand out** stagliarsi, distaccarsi, risaltare; **to stand up** tenersi in piedi; resistere, durare; **to stand up to** affrontare

standard ['stændərd] *adj* (*usual*) normale; uniforme, standard; (*language*) corretto, preferito ‖ *s* standard *m*; (*model*) modello, campione *m*; (*flag*) stendardo

stand′ard-bear′er *s* portabandiera *m*

standardize [′stændər ˌdaɪz] *tr* standardizzare

stand′ard of liv′ing *s* tenore *m* di vita

stand′ard time′ *s* ora ufficiale, ora legale

standee [stæn′di] *s* passeggero in piedi; spettatore *m* in piedi

stand′-in′ *s* (mov) controfigura; **to have a stand-in with** (coll) essere nelle buone grazie di

standing [′stændɪŋ] *adj* (*jump*) da fermo; in piedi; fermo; (*water*) stagnante; vigente, permanente; (*idle*) fuori uso ‖ *s* posizione, rango, situazione; classifica; **in good standing** riconosciuto da tutti; **of long standing** vecchio, da lungo tempo

stand′ing ar′my *s* esercito permanente

stand′ing room′ *s* posto in piedi

standpatter [′stænd′pætər] *s* (coll) seguace *mf* dell′immobilismo

stand′point′ *s* punto di vista

stand′still′ *s* fermata; riposo; **to come to a standstill** fermarsi

stanza [′stænzə] *s* stanza

staple [′stepəl] *adj* principale ‖ *s* articolo di prima necessità; elemento indispensabile; (*e.g., to hold wire*) cavallotto, cambretta; (*to fasten papers*) grappetta; fibra tessile ‖ *tr* aggraffare

stapler [′steplər] *s* cucitrice *f* a grappe

star [stɑr] *s* (*any heavenly body, except the moon, appearing in the sky*) astro; (*heavenly body radiating self-produced energy*) stella; (*actor*) divo; (*actress*) diva, stella (*athlete*) asso; (fig, mov) stella; (typ) stelletta; **to thank one′s lucky stars** ringraziare la propria stella ‖ *v* (*pret & pp* starred; *ger* starring) *tr* costellare, stellare; presentare come stella; (typ) marcare con stelletta ‖ *intr* primeggiare

starboard [′stɑrbərd] or [′stɑr ˌbɔrd] *adj* di dritta, di tribordo ‖ *s* dritta, tribordo ‖ *adv* a dritta, a tribordo

starch [stɑrtʃ] *s* amido, fecola; (*in laundering*) salda; (coll) forza ‖ *tr* inamidare

starch·y [′stɑrtʃi] *adj* (-**ier**; -**iest**) amidaceo; (*e.g., collar*) inamidato; (*manner*) sostenuto, contegnoso

star′ dust′ *s* polveri *fpl* meteoriche; (fig) polvere *f* di stelle

stare [ster] *s* sguardo fisso ‖ *intr* rimirare; **to stare at** fissare gli occhi addosso a

star′fish′ *s* stella di mare

star′gaze′ *intr* guardare le stelle; sognare ad occhi aperti

stark [stɑrk] *adj* completo; desolato; severo, serio; duro, rigido ‖ *adv* completamente

stark′-na′ked *adj* nudo e crudo

starlet [′stɑrlɪt] *s* stellina, divetta

star′light′ *s* lume *f* delle stelle

starling [′stɑrlɪŋ] *s* storno, stornello

Stars′ and Stripes′ *s* bandiera stellata

Star′-Spangled Ban′ner *s* bandiera stellata

star′ sys′tem *s* (mov) divismo

start [stɑrt] *s* inizio, principio; partenza; linea di partenza; (*sudden jerk*) sussulto, soprassalto; (*advantage*) vantaggio; (*spurt*) scatto ‖ *tr* iniziare, principiare; mettere in moto; dare il via a; (*a conversation*) intavolare; (*game*) stanare ‖ *intr* iniziare, principiare; mettersi in moto; incamminarsi; (*to be startled*) trasalire, sussultare; **to start + ger** mettersi a + *inf*; **to start + ger + again** rimettersi a + *inf*; **to start after** andare in cerca di

starter [′stɑrtər] *s* (*of a venture*) iniziatore *m*; partente *m*; (aut) motorino d′avviamento; (sports) mossiere *m*

starting [′stɑrtɪŋ] *adj* di partenza ‖ *s* messa in marcia

start′ing crank′ *s* manovella d′avviamento

start′ing point′ *s* punto di partenza

startle [′stɑrtəl] *tr* far trasalire ‖ *intr* trasalire, sussultare

startling [′stɑrtlɪŋ] *adj* allarmante, sorprendente

starvation [stɑr′veʃən] *s* fame *f*, inedia, inanizione

starva′tion wag′es *spl* paga da fame

starve [stɑrv] *tr* affamare; far morire di fame; **to starve out** prendere per fame ‖ *intr* essere affamato; morire di fame

starving [′stɑrvɪŋ] *adj* famelico

state [stet] *adj* statale; ufficiale; di gala, di lusso ‖ *s* condizione; stato; gala, pompa; **to lie in state** essere esposto in camera ardente; **to live in state** vivere sfarzosamente ‖ *tr* dichiarare, affermare; (*a problem*) impostare

stateless [′stetlɪs] *adj* apolide

state·ly [′stetli] *adj* (-**lier**; -**liest**) maestoso, imponente

statement [′stetmənt] *s* dichiarazione, affermazione; comunicazione; (com) estratto conto

state′ of mind′ *s* stato d′animo

state′room′ *s* cabina; (rr) compartimento privato

states′man *s* (-**men**) statista *m*, uomo di stato

static [′stætɪk] *adj* statico; (rad) atmosferico ‖ *s* disturbi *mpl* atmosferici

station [′steʃən] *s* stazione; rango, condizione ‖ *tr* stazionare

sta′tion a′gent *s* capostazione *m*

stationary [′steʃən ˌeri] *adj* stazionario

sta′tion break′ *s* (rad, telv) intervallo

stationer [′steʃənər] *s* cartolaio

stationery [′steʃən ˌeri] *s* (*writing paper*) carta da lettere; (*writing materials*) cancelleria

sta′tionery store′ *s* cartoleria

sta′tion house′ *s* posto di polizia

sta′tion-mas′ter *s* capostazione *m*

sta′tion wag′on *s* giardinetta

statistical [stə′tɪstɪkəl] *adj* statistico

statistician [ˌstætɪs′tɪʃən] *s* statistico

statistics [stə'tɪstɪks] *ssg (science)* statistica; *spl (data)* statistiche *fpl*

statue ['stæt/ʊ] *s* statua

statuesque [ˌstæt/ʊ'esk] *adj* statuario

stature ['stæt/ər] *s* statura

status ['stetəs] *s* stato, condizione; condizione sociale

sta'tus sym'bol *s* simbolo della posizione sociale

statute ['stæt/ʊt] *s* legge *f;* regolamento

stat'ute of limita'tions *s* legge *f* che governa la prescrizione

statutory ['stæt/ʊˌtori] *adj* legale

staunch [stɔnt/] or [stɑnt/] *adj, s & tr* var of **stanch**

stave [stev] *s (of barrel)* doga; *(of ladder)* piolo; *(mus)* rigo, pentagramma *m* ‖ *v (pret & pp* **staved** or **stove** [stov]) *tr* bucare; *(to smash)* sfondare; **to stave off** tenere a bada

stay [ste] *s* permanenza, soggiorno; *(brace)* staggio; *(of corset)* stecca di balena; sostegno; *(law)* sospensione; *(naut)* strallo ‖ *tr* fermare; sospendere; poner freno a ‖ *intr* stare; mantenersi; restare, rimanere; *(at a hotel)* sostare; **to stay up** stare alzato

stay'-at-home' *adj* casalingo ‖ *s* persona casalinga

stead [stɛd] *s* posto; **in his stead** in suo luogo; **to stand in good stead** esser utile

stead'fast' *adj* fermo, risoluto

stead·y ['stɛdi] *adj* (-ier; -iest) stabile, fermo; regolare, costante; abituale; calmo, sicuro ‖ *v (pret & pp* -ied) *tr* rinforzare; calmare ‖ *intr* rinforzarsi; calmarsi

steak [stek] *s* bistecca

steal [stil] *s* (coll) furto ‖ *v (pret* **stole** [stol]; *pp* **stolen**) *tr* rubare; involare; *(the attention)* cattivare ‖ *intr* rubare; **to steal away** svignarsela; **to steal out** uscire di soppiatto; **to steal upon** approssimarsi silenziosamente a

stealth [stɛlθ] *s* clandestinità *f;* **by stealth** di straforo, di soppiatto

steam [stim] *adj* a vapore ‖ *s* vapore *m;* fumo; **to get up steam** aumentare la pressione; **to let off steam** scaricare la pressione; (slang) sfogarsi ‖ *tr (a steamship)* guidare; esalare; esporre al vapore; *(e.g., glasses)* appannare ‖ *intr* dar vapore, fumigare; bollire; *(to become clouded)* appannarsi; andare a vapore; **to steam ahead** avanzare a tutto vapore

steam'boat' *s* vapore *m*

steam' en'gine *s* macchina a vapore

steamer ['stimər] *s* vapore *m*

steam'er rug' *s* coperta da viaggio

steam'er trunk' *s* bauletto da cabina

steam' heat' *s* riscaldamento a vapore

steam' roll'er *s* rullo compressore; (fig) rullo compressore

steam'ship' *s* piroscafo, vapore *m*

steam' shov'el *s* escavatore *m* a vapore

steam' ta'ble *s* tavola riscaldata a vapore per mantenere calde le vivande

steed [stid] *s* destriere *m*

steel [stil] *adj* d'acciaio; *(industry)* siderurgico ‖ *s* acciaio; *(bar)* stecca d'acciaio; *(for sharpening knives)* affilacoltelli *m;* (fig) spada, brando ‖ *tr* acciaiare; **to steel oneself** corazzarsi, indurirsi; armarsi di coraggio

steel' wool' *s* paglia di ferro

steel'works' *spl* acciaieria

steelyard ['stil ˌjɑrd] or ['stiljərd] *s* stadera

steep [stip] *adj* erto, scosceso, ripido; *(price)* alto ‖ *tr* immergere, saturare, imbevere

steeple ['stipəl] *s* campanile *m; (spire)* cuspide *f,* guglia

stee'ple·chase' *s* corsa ad ostacoli

stee'ple·jack' *s* aggiustatore *m* di campanili

steer [stɪr] *s* bue *m,* manzo ‖ *tr* governare, guidare; (aer) pilotare ‖ *intr* governare; **to steer clear of** evitare

steerage ['stɪrɪdʒ] *s* (naut) alloggio passeggeri di terza classe

steer'ing wheel' *s* (aut) volante *m,* sterzo; (naut) ruota del timone

stellar ['stɛlər] *adj* stellare; *(role)* da stella

stem [stɛm] *s (of pipe, of key)* cannello; *(of goblet)* gambo; *(of column)* fusto; *(of spoon)* manico; *(of watch)* corona; *(of a word)* tema *m; (of note)* (mus) gamba; (bot) peduncolo, stelo; (bot) gambo; **from stem to stern** da poppa a prua ‖ *v (pret & pp* **stemmed**) *ger* **stemming** *tr* togliere il gambo a; *(to check)* arrestare; *(to dam up)* arginare; *(to plug)* otturare; *(the tide)* risalire, andare contro ‖ *intr* originare, derivare

stem'-win'der *s* orologio a corona

stench [stɛnt/] *s* tanfo, fetore *m*

sten·cil ['stɛnsəl] *s* stampo, stampino; parole *fpl* a stampo ‖ *v (pret & pp* -ciled or -cilled; *ger* -ciling or -cilling) *tr* stampinare

stenographer [stə'nɑgrəfər] *s* stenografo

stenography [stə'nɑgrəfi] *s* stenografia

step [stɛp] *s* passo; *(footprint)* orma, impronta; *(of ladder)* piolo; *(of staircase)* gradino; *(of carriage)* montatoio; **step by step** passo passo; **to watch one's step** fare molta attenzione ‖ *v (pret & pp* **stepped**) *ger* **stepping** *tr* scaglionare; *(to step off* misurare a passi ‖ *intr* camminare, andare a passi; mettere il piede; **to step aside** scostarsi; **to step back** indietreggiare; **to step on it** (slang) fare presto; **to step on the gas** (coll) accelerare; **to step on the starter** avviare il motore

step'broth'er *s* fratellastro, fratello consanguineo

step'child' *s* (-children [ˌt/ɪldrən]) figliastro

step'daugh'ter *s* figliastra

step'fa'ther *s* patrigno

step'lad'der *s* scala a gradini or a libretto

step'moth'er *s* matrigna

steppe [stɛp] *s* steppa

step'ping stone' s passatoio, pietra per guadare; (fig) gradino

step'sis'ter s sorellastra

step'son' s figliastro

stere·o ['sterɪ‚o] or ['stɪrɪ‚o] adj stereofonico; stereoscopico ‖ s (-os) musica stereofonica; sistema stereofonico; fotografia stereoscopica

stereotyped ['sterɪ·ə‚taɪpt] or ['stɪrɪ·ə‚taɪpt] adj stereotipato

sterile ['sterɪl] adj sterile

sterilize ['sterɪ‚laɪz] tr sterilizzare

sterling ['stɑrlɪŋ] adj di lira sterlina; d'argento; puro; eccellente ‖ s argento .925; vasellame m d'argento puro

stern [stʌrn] adj severo ‖ s poppa

stet [stet] v (pret & pp **stetted;** ger **stetting**) tr marcare con la parola "vive"

stethoscope ['steθə‚skop] s stetoscopio

stevedore ['stivə‚dor] s stivatore m

stew [stju] or [stu] s stufato, guazzetto ‖ tr stufare ‖ intr cuocere a fuoco lento; (coll) preoccuparsi

steward ['stju·ərd] or ['stu·ərd] s amministratore m, agente m; maggiordomo; (aer, naut) cambusiere m, cameriere m

stewardess ['stju·ərdɪs] or ['stu·ərdɪs] s (naut) cameriera; (aer) hostess f, assistente f di volo

stewed' fruit' s composta di frutta

stewed' toma'toes spl pomodori mpl in umido

stick [stɪk] s stecco; legno; bacchetta; bastone m; (e.g., of candy) cannello; (naut) albero; (typ) compositoio; **in the sticks** (coll) in casa del diavolo ‖ v (pret & pp **stuck** [stʌk]) tr pungere; ficcare, infiggere; attaccare; confondere; **to be stuck** essere insabbiato; essere attaccato; (fig) essere confuso; **to stick out** (the head) sporgere; (the tongue) cacciare; **to stick up** (slang) assaltare a mano armata, rapinare ‖ intr rimanere attaccato; persistere; (said of glue) appiccicarsi; (to one opinion) tenersi; stare; **to stick out** sporgere; **to stick together** rimanere uniti; **to stick up** risaltare; (said, e.g., of quills) rizzarsi; **to stick up for** (coll) stare dalla parte di

sticker ['stɪkər] s etichetta gommata; spina; persona zelante; (coll) busillis m

stick'ing plas'ter s cerotto

stick'pin' s spilla da cravatta

stick'up' s (slang) grassazione

stick·y ['stɪki] adj (-ier; -iest) attaccaticcio; vischioso; (weather) afoso, soffocante; (fig) difficile

stiff [stɪf] adj rigido, duro; forte; (price) alto; denso ‖ s (slang) cadavere m; **poor stiff** (slang) povero diavolo

stiff' col'lar s colletto duro

stiffen ['stɪfən] tr irrigidire ‖ intr irrigidirsi

stiff' neck' s torcicollo; ostinazione

stiff'-necked' adj testardo

stiff' shirt' s camicia inamidata

stifle ['staɪfəl] tr soffocare

stigma ['stɪgmə] s (-mas or -mata [mətə]) stigma m

stigmatize ['stɪgmə‚taɪz] tr stigmatizzare

still [stɪl] adj fermo, tranquillo; silenzioso; (wine) non spumante ‖ s calma; distillatore m; distilleria; (phot) fotografia singola ‖ adv ancora; tuttora ‖ conj tuttavia ‖ tr calmare ‖ intr calmarsi

still'birth' s parto di infante nato morto

still'born' adj nato morto

still' life' s (lifes') natura morta

stilt [stɪlt] s trampolo; (in water) palafitta; (orn) trampoliere m

stilted ['stɪltɪd] adj elevato; pomposo

stimulant ['stɪmjələnt] adj & s stimulante m, eccitante m

stimulate ['stɪmjə‚let] tr stimulare

stimu·lus ['stɪmjələs] s (-li [‚laɪ]) stimolo

sting [stɪŋ] s puntura; (of insect) pungiglione; (fig) scottatura ‖ v (pret & pp **stung** [stʌŋ]) tr & intr pungere

stin·gy ['stɪndʒi] adj (-gier; -giest) tirchio, taccagno

stink [stɪŋk] s puzza ‖ v (pret **stank** [stæŋk] or **stunk** [stʌŋk]; pp **stunk**) tr far puzzare ‖ intr puzzare; **to stink of money** (slang) aver soldi a palate

stinker ['stɪŋkər] s (slang) puzzone m

stint [stɪnt] s limite m; lavoro assegnato, compito ‖ intr lesinarsi

stipend ['staɪpənd] s stipendio; assegno di studio, presalario

stipulate ['stɪpjə‚let] tr stipulare

stir [stʌr] s agitazione, movimento; (poke) spinta; **to create a stir** creare una sensazione ‖ v (pret & pp **stirred**) ger **stirring**) tr mescolare; muovere; (fire) ravvivare; (pity) fare; **to stir up** eccitare, svegliare; (to rebellion) sommuovere ‖ intr muoversi, agitarsi

stirring ['stʌrɪŋ] adj commovente

stirrup ['stʌrəp] or ['stɪrəp] s staffa

stitch [stɪtʃ] s punto; maglia; (pain) fitta; (bit) poco, po' m; **to be in stitches** (coll) sbellicarsi dalle risa ‖ tr cucire; aggraffare ‖ intr cucire

stock [stɑk] adj regolare, comune; banale, ordinario; di bestiame; borsistico; azionario; (aut) di serie; (theat) stabile ‖ s provvista, scorta; capitale m sociale; azioni f; azioni fpl, titoli mpl; (of tree) tronco; (of family; of anchor; of anvil) ceppo; razza, famiglia; materia prima; (of rifle) cassa; (broth) brodo; (handle) manico; (livestock) bestiame m; (theat) compagnia stabile; **in stock** in magazzino, disponibile; **out of stock** esaurito; **stocks** gogna, berlina; **to take stock** fare l'inventario; **to take stock in** (coll) aver fede in ‖ tr fornire; fornire di bestiame; fornire di pesci ‖ intr—**to stock up** fare rifornimenti

stockade [stɑ'ked] s staccionata

stock'breed'er s allevatore m di bestiame

stock'bro'ker s agente m di cambio
stock' car' s automobile f di serie; (rr) carro bestiame
stock' com'pany s (theat) compagnia stabile; (com) società anonima
stock' div'idend s dividendo pagato in azioni
stock' exchange' s borsa valori
stock'fish' s stoccafisso
stock'hold'er s azionista mf
stock'hold'er of rec'ord s azionista mf registrato nei libri della compagnia
Stockholm ['stakhom] s Stoccolma
stocking ['stakiŋ] s calza
stock' in trade' s stock m; ferri mpl del mestiere
stock' mar'ket s borsa valori
stock'pile' s riserva, scorta || tr mettere in riserva || intr mettere in riserva materie prime
stock' rais'ing s allevamento bestiame
stock'room' s magazzino, deposito
stock·y ['staki] adj (-ier; -iest) tozzo, tarchiato
stock'yard' s chiuso per il bestiame
stoic ['sto·ɪk] adj & s stoico
stoicism ['sto·ɪ,sɪzəm] s stoicismo
stoke [stok] tr (fire) attizzare; (a furnace) caricare
stoker ['stokər] s fochista m
stolid ['stalɪd] adj impassibile
stomach ['stʌmək] s stomaco m || tr (fig) digerire
stone [ston] s sasso, pietra; (of fruit) osso; (pathol) calcolo || tr lapidare; affilare con la pietra; (fruit) snocciolare
stone'-broke' adj (coll) senza un soldo, senza il becco di un quattrino
stone'-deaf' adj sordo come una campana
stone'ma'son s tagliapietra m
stone' quar'ry s cava di pietra
stone's' throw' s tiro di sasso; **within a stone's throw** s a un tiro di schioppo
ston·y ['stoni] adj (-ier; -iest) di sasso, sassoso, pietroso
stooge [studʒ] s (theat) spalla; (slang) complice mf
stool [stul] s sgabello, seggiolino; gabinetto; (mass evacuated) feci fpl
stool' pi'geon s piccione m di richiamo; (slang) spia
stoop [stup] s curvatura, inclinazione; scalini mpl d'ingresso || intr inclinarsi, piegarsi; degnarsi, umiliarsi
stoop-shouldered ['stup'ʃoldərd] adj con le spalle cadenti
stop [stap] s fermata, sosta; arresto; otturazione, blocco; cessazione; ostacolo; (of a check) fermo; (restraint) freno; (of organ) registro; **to come to a stop** fermarsi; cessare; **to put a stop to** metter fine a || v (pret & pp stopped; ger stopping) tr fermare, cessare; arrestare, sospendere; tappare, otturare; (a check) mettere il fermo a; **to stop up** tappare, otturare || intr fermarsi; arrestarsi; (said of a ship) fare scalo; (at an hotel) scendere; **to stop +** ger smettere di or cessare di **+** inf

stop'cock' s rubinetto di arresto
stop'gap' adj provvisorio || s soluzione provvisoria; (person) tappabuchi m
stop'light' s (traffic light) semaforo; (aut) luce f di stop
stop'o'ver s fermata intermedia
stoppage ['stapɪdʒ] s fermata, arresto; (of work, wages, etc.) sospensione
stopper ['stapər] s tappo, turacciolo
stop' sign' s segnale m di fermata
stop'watch' s cronometro a scatto
storage ['storɪdʒ] s magazzinaggio; (place for storing) magazzino; (of a computer) memoria
stor'age bat'tery s (elec) accumulatore m
store [stor] s negozio; magazzino; (supply) scorta; **in store** in serbo; **to set store by** dare molta importanza a || tr immagazzinare; **to store away** accumulare
store'house' s magazzino, deposito; (of knowledge) miniera
store'keep'er s negoziante m
store'room' s magazzino; (naut) dispensa
stork [stork] s cicogna
storm [storm] s tempesta, temporale m; (on the Beaufort scale) burrasca; (mil) assalto; (fig) scoppio || tr assaltare || intr tempestare; imperversare; (mil) andare all'attacco
storm' cloud' s nuvolone m
storm' door' s controporta
storm' sash' s controfinestra
storm' troops' spl truppe fpl d'assalto
storm' win'dow s controfinestra
storm·y ['stormi] adj (-ier; -iest) tempestoso, burrascoso; (fig) inquieto, violento
sto·ry ['stori] s (-ries) storia, racconto, romanzo; (plot) trama; (level) piano; (coll) storia, menzogna || v (pret & pp -ried) tr istoriare
sto'ry·tell'er s narratore m, novelliere m; (coll) mentitore m
stoup [stup] s (eccl) acquasantiera
stout [staut] adj grasso, obeso; forte, robusto; leale; coraggioso || s birra nera forte
stout-hearted ['staut,hartɪd] adj coraggioso
stove [stov] s (for warmth) stufa; (for cooking) fornello, cucina economica
stove'pipe' s tubo della stufa, cannone m; (hat) (coll) tuba
stow [sto] tr mettere in riserva; riempire; (naut) stivare || intr—**to stow away** imbarcarsi clandestinamente
stowage ['sto·ɪdʒ] s stivaggio; (place) stiva
stow'a·way' s passeggero clandestino
straddle ['strædəl] s divaricamento || tr (a horse) cavalcare; (the legs) divaricare; favorire entrambe le parti in || intr cavalcare; stare a gambe divaricate; (coll) tenere il piede tra due staffe
strafe [straf] or [stref] s attacco violento || tr attaccare violentemente con fuoco aereo; bombardare violentemente; (slang) punire

straggle ['strægəl] *intr* sbandarsi, sviarsi; sparpagliarsi, essere sparpagliato

straggler ['stræglər] *s* ritardatario

straight [stret] *adj* diritto, ritto; (*e.g., shoulders*) quadro; candido, franco; (*honest, upright*) retto; inalterato; (*hair; whiskey*) liscio; **to set s.o. straight** mettere qlcu sulla retta via; mostrare la verità a qlcu ‖ *s* rettilinea; (*cards*) scala ‖ *adv* dritto; sinceramente; rettamente; **straight ahead** sempre diritto; **straight away** immediatamente; **to go straight** vivere onestamente

straighten ['stretən] *tr* ordinare; raddrizzare ‖ *intr* raddrizzarsi

straight' face' *s* faccia seria

straight' flush' *s* (cards) scala reale

straight'for'ward *adj* diretto; onesto

straight' man' *s* (theat) spalla

straight' ra'zor *s* rasoio a mano libera

straight'way' *adv* immediatamente

strain [stren] *s* sforzo; fatica eccessiva; tensione, pressione; strappo muscolare; tono, stile *m*; (*family*) famiglia; tendenza, vena; (coll) lavoro severo; (mus) aria, melodia ‖ *tr* passare, colare; (*e.g., a rope*) tirare al massimo; (*one's ear*) tendere; (*a muscle*) strappare; (*the ankle*) slogare; (*e.g., words*) storcere, forzare ‖ *intr* colare, filtrare; tendersi, tirare; sforzarsi; fare resistenza; **to strain at** tirare; resistere a

strained [strend] *adj* (*smile*) stentato; (*relations*) teso

strainer ['strenər] *s* scolatoio

strait [stret] *s* stretto; straits stretto; (fig) strettezze *fpl*; **to be in dire straits** essere nei frangenti

strait' jack'et *s* camicia di forza

strait'-laced' *adj* puritano, pudibondo

strand [strænd] *s* sponda, lido; (*of metal cable*) trefolo; (*of rope*) legnolo; (*of pearls*) filo ‖ *tr* sfilare; (*e.g., a rope*) ritorcere, intrecciare; (*e.g., a boat*) lasciare incagliato; **to be stranded** trovarsi incagliato

stranded ['strændɪd] *adj* (*ship*) incagliato, arenato; (*e.g., rope*) ritorto, intrecciato

strange [strendʒ] *adj* strano; straniero; non abituato; inusitato

stranger ['strendʒər] *s* forestiero; nuovo venuto, intruso

strangle ['stræŋgəl] *tr* strangolare; soffocare ‖ *intr* strangolarsi; soffocarsi

strap [stræp] *s* (*of leather*) correggia; (*for holding things together*) tirante *m*; (*shoulder strap*) bretella; (*for passengers to hold on to*) manopola; (*to hold a sandal*) guiggia; (*to hold a baby*) falda; (*strop*) coramella ‖ *v* (*pret & pp* **strapped**; *ger* **strapping**) *tr* legare con correggia or tirante; (*a razor*) affilare

strap'hang'er *s* (coll) passeggero senza posto a sedere

strapping ['stræpɪŋ] *adj* robusto; (coll) grande, enorme

stratagem ['strætədʒəm] *s* stratagemma *m*

strategic(al) [strə'tidʒɪk(əl)] *adj* strategico

strategist ['strætɪdʒɪst] *s* stratego

strate·gy ['strætɪdʒɪ] *s* (**-gies**) strategia

strati·fy ['strætɪ‚faɪ] *v* (*pret & pp* **-fied**) *tr* stratificare ‖ *intr* stratificarsi

stratosphere ['strætə‚sfɪr] or ['stretə‚sfɪr] *s* stratosfera

stra·tum ['stretəm] or ['strætəm] *s* (**-ta** [tə] or **-tums**) strato

straw [strɔ] *adj* di paglia; di nessun valore; falso, fittizio ‖ *s* paglia; (*for drinking*) cannuccia; **I don't care a straw** non mi importa un fico; **to be the last straw** essere al colmo

straw'ber·ry *s* (**-ries**) fragola

straw'hat' *s* cappello di paglia; (*with hard crown*) paglietta

straw' man' *s* (*figurehead*) uomo di paglia; (*scarecrow*) spaventapasseri *m*

straw' mat'tress *s* pagliericcio

straw' vote' *s* votazione esplorativa

stray [stre] *adj* sbandato, randagio; casuale, fortuito ‖ *s* animale randagio ‖ *intr* sviarsi; (fig) sbandarsi

streak [strik] *s* stria; (*of light*) raggio; (*of madness*) ramo, vena; (*of luck*) (coll) periodo; **like a streak** (coll) come un lampo ‖ *tr* striare, venare ‖ *intr* striarsi, venarsi; andare come un lampo

stream [strim] *s* corrente *f*; (*of light*) raggio; (*of people*) fiumana, torrente *m*; (*of cars*) fila ‖ *intr* colare; filtrare, penetrare; (*said of a flag*) fluttuare

streamer ['strimər] *s* pennone *m*; nastro; raggio di luce

streamlined ['strim‚laɪnd] *adj* aerodinamico; (aer) carenato

stream'lin'er *s* treno dal profilo aerodinamico

street [strit] *adj* stradale ‖ *s* via, strada

street'car' *s* tram *m*

street' clean'er *s* spazzino; (mach) spazzatrice *f*

street' clothes' *spl* vestiti *mpl* da passeggio; vestito da passeggio

street' floor' *s* pianterreno

street'light' *s* lampione *m*

street' map' *s* pianta della città; stradario

street' sign' *s* segnale *m* stradale

street' sprin'kler *s* carro annaffiatoio

street' walk'er *s* passeggiatrice *f*

strength [streŋθ] *s* forza; resistenza; (*of spirituous liquors*) gradazione; (com) tendenza al rialzo; (mil) numero; **on the strength of** basandosi su

strengthen ['streŋθən] *tr* rinforzare; (fig) convalidare, rinsaldare ‖ *intr* rinforzarsi, ingagliardirsi

strenuous ['strenju‚əs] *adj* vigoroso; strenuo

stress [stres] *s* enfasi *f*, importanza; spinta; tensione, preoccupazione; accento; (mech) sollecitazione; **to lay**

stress on mettere in rilievo ‖ *tr* (*a word*) accentare, accentuare; (*to emphasize*) accentuare; (*mech*) sollecitare

stress' ac'cent *s* accento di intensità

stretch [stretʃ] *s* tiro, tirata; (*in time or space*) periodo; (*of road*) tratto, percorrenza; (*of imagination*) sforzo; (rr) tratta; (slang) periodo di detenzione; **at a stretch** di un tiro ‖ *tr* tirare; tendere, distendere; (*the imagination*) forzare; (*facts*) esagerare; (*money*) stiracchiare; (*one's legs*) sgranchirsi; (*the truth*) esagerare; **to stretch oneself** sdraiarsi ‖ *intr* estendersi; stiracchiarsi; distendersi; **to stretch out** sdraiarsi

stretcher ['stretʃər] *s* (*for a painting*) telaio; (*tool*) tenditore *m*, tenditoio; (*to carry wounded*) barella, lettiga

stretch'er-bear'er *s* portantino

strew [stru] *v* (*pret* **strewed**; *pp* **strewed** or **strewn**) *tr* spargere, cospargere; disseminare

stricken ['strɪkən] *adj* afflitto; ferito; danneggiato

strict [strɪkt] *adj* stretto, severo

stricture ['strɪktʃər] *s* aspra critica; (pathol) stenosi *f*

stride [straɪd] *s* passo; andatura; **rapid strides** grandi passi *mpl*; **to hit one's stride** avanzare a andatura regolare; **to take s.th in one's stride** fare qlco senza sforzi ‖ *v* (*pret* **strode** [strod]; *pp* **stridden** ['strɪdən]) *tr* attraversare a grandi passi; attraversare di un salto ‖ *intr* camminare a grandi passi; (*majestically*) incedere

strident ['straɪdənt] *adj* stridente

strife [straɪf] *s* discordia; concorrenza

strike [straɪk] *s* (*blow*) colpo; (*stopping of work*) sciopero; (*discovery of oil, ore, etc.*) scoperta; (*of fish*) abboccatura; colpo di fortuna ‖ *v* (*pret & pp* **struck** [strʌk]) *tr* colpire, percuotere; infiggere; (*a match*) strofinare; (*fire*) accendere; fare impressione su; incontrare improvvisamente; (*e.g., ore*) scoprire; (*roots*) mettere; (*a coin*) coniare; andare in sciopero contro; arrivare a; (*a posture*) prendere; (*the hour*) scoccare; cancellare, eliminare; (*sails*) calare; (*attention*) richiamare; **to strike it rich** scoprire una miniera; avere un colpo di fortuna ‖ *intr* dare un colpo; cadere; (*said of a bell*) suonare; accendersi; scioperare; (mil) attaccare; **to strike out** mettersi in marcia; (*to fail*) (fig) fallire, venir meno

strike'break'er *s* crumiro

striker ['straɪkər] *s* battitore *m*; (*clapper in clock*) martelletto; (*worker*) scioperante *m*

striking ['straɪkɪŋ] *adj* impressionante, sorprendente; notevole; scioperante

strik'ing pow'er *s* potere *m* d'assalto

string [strɪŋ] *s* spago, cordicella; (*e.g., of apron*) laccio; (*of pearls*) filo; (*of onions; of lies*) filza; (*row*) fila, infilata; (mus) corda; **no strings attached** (coll) senza condizioni;

strings strumenti *mpl* a corda; (coll) condizioni *fpl*; **to pull strings** usare influenza ‖ *v* (*pret & pp* **strung** [strʌŋ]) *tr* legare; allacciare; infilare; infilzare; (*a racket*) munire di corde; (*to stretch*) tendere; (*a musical instrument*) mettere le corde a; (slang) ingannare; **to string along** (slang) menare per il naso; **to string up** impiccare ‖ *intr*—**to string along with** (slang) andare d'accordo con

string' bean' *s* fagiolino

stringed' in'strument *s* strumento a corda

stringent ['strɪndʒənt] *adj* stringente; urgente; severo

string' quartet' *s* quartetto d'archi

strip [strɪp] *s* striscia; (*of metal*) lamina; (*of land*) lingua ‖ *v* (*pret & pp* **stripped**; *ger* **stripping**) *tr* spogliare; denudare; (*a fruit*) pelare; (*a ship*) sguarnire; (*tobacco*) togliere le nervature da; scortecciare; (*thread*) spanare; **to strip of** spogliare di ‖ *intr* spogliarsi; denudarsi; fare lo spogliarello

stripe [straɪp] *s* stria, striscia, riga, lista; tipo, qualità *f*; (mil) gallone *m* ‖ *tr* striare, filettare, rigare

strip' min'ing *s* sfruttamento minerario a cielo aperto

strip'tease' *s* spogliarello

stripteaser ['strɪp,tizər] *s* spogliarellista

strive [straɪv] *v* (*pret* **strove** [strov]; *pp* **striven** ['strɪvən]) *intr* sforzarsi; lottare; **to strive to** sforzarsi di

stroke [strok] *s* colpo; (*of bell or clock*) rintocco; (*of pen*) tratto, frego; (*of brush*) pennellata; (*of arms in swimming*) bracciata; colpo apoplettico; (*caress*) carezza; (*with oar*) vogata; (*of oar or paddle*) palata; (*of a master*) tocco; (*of a piston*) corsa; (*keystroke*) battuta; (*of genius*) lampo; (*of the hour*) scocco; **to not do a stroke of work** non muovere un dito ‖ *tr* accarezzare

stroll [strol] *s* passeggiata; **to take a stroll** fare una passeggiata ‖ *intr* fare una passeggiata, andare a zonzo; errare

stroller ['strolər] *s* girovago; carrozzella; (*itinerant performer*) (theat) guitto

strong [strɔŋ] or [strɑŋ] *adj* forte, vigoroso; valido; acceso, zelante; (*butter*) rancido; (*cheese*) piccante; (com) sostenuto

strong'box' *s* cassaforte *f*

strong' drink' *s* bevanda alcolica

strong'hold' *s* piazzaforte *f*

strong' man' *s* (*in a circus*) maciste *m*; (*leader*) anima; dittatore *m*

strong-minded ['strɔŋ,maɪndɪd] or ['strɑŋ,maɪndɪd] *adj* volitivo

strong'point' *s* luogo fortificato

strontium ['strɑŋʃɪ·əm] *s* stronzio

strop [strɑp] *s* coramella, affilarasoio ‖ *v* (*pret & pp* **stropped**; *ger* **stropping**) *tr* affilare

strophe ['strofi] *s* strofa, strofe *f*

struc'tural steel' ['strʌktʃərəl] *s* profilato di acciaio

structure ['strʌktʃər] *s* struttura; edificio || *tr* strutturare

struggle ['strʌgəl] *s* lotta; sforzo || *intr* lottare; sforzare, dibattersi

strum [strʌm] *v* (*pret & pp* **strummed**; *ger* **strumming**) *tr & intr* strimpellare

strumpet ['strʌmpɪt] *s* sgualdrina, puttana

strut [strʌt] *s* controvento, puntello, saettone *m*; incedere impettito; (aer) montante || *v* (*pret & pp* **strutted**; *ger* **strutting**) *intr* pavoneggiarsi, fare la ruota

strychnine ['strɪknaɪn] *or* ['strɪknɪn] *s* stricnina

stub [stʌb] *s* (*of tree*) coppo; (*e.g., of cigar*) mozzicone *m*; (*of a check*) matrice *f*, madre *f* || *v* (*pret & pp* **stubbed**; *ger* **stubbing**) *tr* sradicare; **to stub one's toe** inciampare

stubble ['stʌbəl] *s* (*of beard*) pelo ispido; **stubbles** stoppie *fpl*

stubborn ['stʌbərn] *adj* (*headstrong*) testardo; (*resolute*) accanito; (*e.g., resistance*) ostinato; (*e.g., illness*) ribelle; (*soil*) ingrato

stuc·co ['stʌko] *s* (**-coes** *or* **-cos**) stucco || *tr* stuccare

stuck [stʌk] *adj* infisso; attaccato; (*glued*) incollato; (*unable to continue*) in panna; **stuck on** (slang) invaghito di

stuck'-up' *adj* (coll) presuntuoso, arrogante

stud [stʌd] *s* (*in upholstery*) borchia; bottone *m* da sparato; (*of walls*) montante *m*; (*stallion*) stallone *m*; (*for mares*) monta; (archit) bugna, bugnato || *v* (*pret & pp* **studded**; *ger* **studding**) *tr* cospergere; (*with stars*) costellare; (*with jewels*) incastonare, ingioiellare

stud' bolt' *s* prigioniero

stud'book' *s* registro della genealogia

student ['stjudənt] *or* ['studənt] *adj* studentesco || *s* studente *m*; scolaro; (*investigator*) studioso

stu'dent bod'y *s* scolaresca

stud'horse' *s* stallone *m*

studied ['stʌdɪd] *adj* premeditato; (*affected*) studiato

studi·o ['studɪ,o] *or* ['stjudɪ,o] *s* (**-os**) studio

studious ['stjudɪ·əs] *or* ['studɪ·əs] *adj* studioso; assiduo, zelante

stud·y ['stʌdi] *s* (**-ies**) studio || *v* (*pret & pp* **-ied**) *tr & intr* studiare

stuff [stʌf] *s* roba, cosa; stoffa; materiale *m*; (*nonsense*) scemenze *fpl*; medicina; (coll) mestiere *m* || *tr* riempire, inzeppare; (*one's stomach*) rimpinzare; (*e.g., poultry*) farcire; (*e.g., salami*) insaccare; (*a dead animal*) impagliare; **to stuff up** intasare || *intr* rimpinzarsi

stuffed' shirt' *s* persona altezzosa

stuffing ['stʌfɪŋ] *s* ripieno

stuff·y ['stʌfi] *adj* (**-ier**; **-iest**) soffocante, opprimente; (*nose*) chiuso; pedante

stumble ['stʌmbəl] *intr* incespicare, inciampare; sbagliare, impaperarsi; **to stumble on** *or* **upon** intopparsi in

stum'bling block' *s* inciampo, scoglio

stump [stʌmp] *s* (*of tree*) toppo, ceppo; (*e.g., of arm*) moncherino, moncone *m*; (*of cigar, candle*) mozzicone *m*; dente rotto; tribuna popolare; (*for drawing*) sfumino; **up a stump** (coll) completamente perplesso || *tr* mozzare; lasciare perplesso; (coll) fare discorsi politici in

stump' speech' *s* discorso politico

stun [stʌn] *v* (*pret & pp* **stunned**; *ger* **stunning**) *tr* tramortire; (fig) sbalordire

stunning ['stʌnɪŋ] *adj* (*blow*) che stordisce; sbalorditivo, magnifico

stunt [stʌnt] *s* atrofia; creatura striminzita; bravata, prodezza; (*for publicity*) montatura || *tr* striminzire; arrestare la crescita di || *intr* fare delle acrobazie

stunt'ed *adj* striminzito

stunt' fly'ing *s* acrobazia aerea

stunt' man' *s* (mov) controfigura

stupe·fy ['stjupɪ,faɪ] *or* ['stupɪ,faɪ] *v* (*pret & pp* **-fied**) *tr* istupidire, intontire

stupendous [stju'pendəs] *or* [stu'pendəs] *adj* stupendo

stupid ['stjupɪd] *or* ['stupɪd] *adj* stupido, ebete, scemo

stupor ['stjupər] *or* ['stupər] *s* torpore *m*, stupore *m*

stur·dy ['stʌrdi] *adj* (**-dier**; **-diest**) forte; (*robust*) tarchiato; risoluto

sturgeon ['stʌrdʒən] *s* storione *m*

stutter ['stʌtər] *s* tartagliamento || *tr & intr* tartagliare

sty [staɪ] *s* (**sties**) porcile *m*; (pathol) orzaiolo

style [staɪl] *s* stile *m*; tono; (*mode of living*) treno || *tr* chiamare col nome di

stylish ['staɪlɪʃ] *adj* alla moda, di tono

sty·mie ['staɪmi] *v* (*pret & pp* **-mied**; *ger* **-mieing**) *tr* ostacolare, contrastare

styp'tic pen'cil ['stɪptɪk] *s* matita emostatica

Styx [stɪks] *s* Stige *m*

suave [swɑv] *or* [swev] *adj* soave

subaltern [səb'ɔltərn] *adj & s* subalterno

subcommittee ['sʌbkə,mɪti] *s* sottocommissione

subconscious [səb'kɑn/əs] *adj & s* subcosciente *m*

subconsciousness [səb'kɑn/əsnɪs] *s* subcosciente *m*, subcoscienza

sub'deb' *s* (coll) signorina più giovane di una debuttante

subdivide ['sʌbdɪ,vaɪd] *or* [,sʌbdɪ'vaɪd] *v* *tr* suddividere || *intr* suddividersi

subdue [səb'dju] *or* [səb'du] *tr* soggiogare, sottomettere; (*color, voice*) attenuare

subdued [səb'djud] *or* [səb'dud] *adj* (*voice*) sommesso; (*light*) tenue

subheading ['sʌb‚hedɪŋ] s sottotitolo; (journ) sommario

subject ['sʌbdʒɪkt] adj soggetto; **subject to** (e.g., a cold) soggetto a; (e.g., a fine) passibile di || s soggetto, materia, proposito; (of a ruler) suddito; (gram, med, philos) soggetto || [səb-'dʒekt] tr sottomettere

sub'ject cat'alogue s catalogo per materie

sub'ject in'dex s indice m per materie

subjection [səb'dʒekʃən] s soggezione

subjective [səb'dʒektɪv] adj soggettivo

sub'ject mat'ter s soggetto

subjugate ['sʌbdʒə‚get] tr soggiogare

subjunctive [səb'dʒʌŋktɪv] adj & s congiuntivo

sublease ['sʌb‚lis] s subaffitto || [‚sʌb-'lis] tr subaffittare

sub·let ['sʌb‚let] or ['sʌb‚let] v (pret & pp -let; ger -letting) tr subaffittare

sub·machine' gun' [‚sʌbmə'ʃin] s mitra m

submarine ['sʌbmə‚rin] adj & s sottomarino

sub'marine chas'er ['tʃesər] s caccia-sommergibili m

submerge [səb'mʌrdʒ] tr sommergere || intr sommergersi

submersion [səb'mʌrʒən] or [səb-'mʌrʃən] s sommersione

submission [səb'mɪʃən] s sottomissione

submissive [səb'mɪsɪv] adj sottomesso

sub·mit [səb'mɪt] v (pret & pp -mitted; ger -mitting) tr sottomettere; presentare, deferire; osservare rispettosamente || intr sottomettersi

subordinate [səb'ɔrdɪnɪt] adj & s subordinato || [səb'ɔrdɪ‚net] tr subordinare

suborna'tion of per'jury [‚sʌbər'neʃən] s subornazione

subplot ['sʌb‚plɑt] s intreccio secondario

subpoena or **subpena** [sʌb'pinə] or [sə-'pinə] s mandato di comparizione || tr citare

sub rosa [sʌb'rozə] adv in segreto

subscribe [səb'skraɪb] tr sottoscrivere || intr sottoscrivere; **to subscribe to** sottoscrivere a; (a magazine) abbonarsi a; (an opinion) approvare

subscriber [səb'skraɪbər] s sottoscrittore m; abbonato

subscription [sʌb'skrɪpʃən] s sottoscrizione; (e.g., to a newspaper) abbonamento; (e.g., to club) quota

subsequent ['sʌbsɪkwənt] adj susseguente, posteriore

subservient [səb'sʌrvɪ·ənt] adj subordinato; ossequioso, servile

subside [səb'saɪd] intr calmarsi; (said of water) decrescere

subsidiar·y [səb'sɪdɪ‚eri] adj sussidiario || s (-ies) sussidiario

subsidize ['sʌbsɪ‚daɪz] tr sussidiare, sovvenzionare; (by bribery) subornare

subsi·dy ['sʌbsɪdi] s (-dies) sussidio, sovvenzione

subsist [səb'sɪst] intr sussistere

subsistence [səb'sɪstəns] s sussistenza

subsoil ['sʌb‚sɔɪl] s sottosuolo

substance ['sʌbstəns] s sostanza

substandard [sʌb'stændərd] adj inferiore al livello normale

substantial [səb'stænʃəl] adj considerevole; ricco, influente; (food) sostanzioso; (e.g., reason) sostanziale

substantiate [səb'stænʃɪ‚et] tr provare, verificare; dare prova di, sostanziare

substantive ['sʌbstəntɪv] adj & s sostantivo

substation ['sʌb‚steʃən] s ufficio postale secondario; (elec) sottostazione

substitute ['sʌbstɪ‚tjut] or ['sʌbstɪ‚tut] adj provvisorio, interino || s (thing) sostituto, surrogato; (person) sostituto, supplente mf; **beware of substitutes** guardarsi dalle contraffazioni || tr—**to substitute for** sostituire (qlco or qlcu) a || intr—**to substitute for** sostituire, rimpiazzare, e.g., **he substituted for the teacher** sostituì il maestro

substitution [‚sʌbstɪ'tjuʃən] or [‚sʌb-stɪ'tuʃən] s sostituzione; (by fraud) contraffazione

substra·tum [sʌb'strætəm] s (-ta [tə]) sostrato, substrato

subterfuge ['sʌbtər‚fjudʒ] s sotterfugio

subterranean [‚sʌbtə'reni·ən] adj & s sotterraneo

subtitle ['sʌb‚taɪtəl] s sottotitolo; (journ) titolo corrente; (mov) didascalia || tr dare una didascalia a

subtle ['sʌtəl] adj sottile

subtle·ty ['sʌtəlti] s (-ties) sottigliezza

subtract [səb'trækt] tr sottrarre

subtraction [sʌb'trækʃən] s sottrazione

suburb ['sʌbʌrb] s suburbio, sobborgo; **the suburbs** la periferia

suburban [sə'bʌrbən] adj suburbano

suburbanite [sə'bʌrbə‚naɪt] s abitante mf dei suburbi

subvention [səb'venʃən] s sovvenzione || tr sovvenzionare

subversive [səb'vʌrsɪv] adj & s sovversivo

subvert [səb'vʌrt] tr sovvertire

subway ['sʌb‚we] s sotterranea, metropolitana, metrovia; sottopassaggio

sub'way sta'tion s stazione della metropolitana

succeed [sək'sid] tr succedere (with dat), subentrare (with dat) || intr riuscire; **to succeed to** (the throne) succedere a

success [sək'ses] s successo, riuscita

successful [sək'sesfəl] adj felice, fortunato; che ha avuto successo

succession [sək'seʃən] s successione; **in succession** in seguito, uno dopo l'altro

successive [sək'sesɪv] adj successivo

succor ['sʌkər] s soccorso || tr soccorrere

succotash ['sʌkə‚tæʃ] s verdura di fagioli e granturco

succumb [sə'kʌm] intr soccombere

such [sʌtʃ] adj & pron indef tale, simile; **such a** un simile, un tale; **such**

a + *adj* tanto + *adj*, e.g., **such a beau-tiful story** una storia tanto bella; **such as** tale quale, come

suck [sʌk] *s* succhio || *tr* succhiare; *(air)* aspirare; **to suck in** (slang) ingannare

sucker ['sʌkər] *s* lattante *mf*; (bot) succhione *m*; (mach) pistone *m*; (coll) fesso, pollo, minchione *m*

suckle ['sʌkəl] *tr* allattare; nutrire || *intr* poppare

suck'ling pig' ['sʌklɪŋ] *s* maiale *m* di latte

suction ['sʌkʃən] *s* aspirazione

suc'tion cup' *s* ventosa

suc'tion pump' *s* pompa aspirante

sudden ['sʌdən] *adj* subito, improv-viso; **all of a sudden** all'improvviso

suddenly ['sʌdənlɪ] *adv* all'improvviso

suds [sʌdz] *spl* saponata; schiuma; (coll) birra

sue [su] or [sju] *tr* querelare || *intr* querelarsi; **to sue for damages** chiedere i danni; **to sue for peace** chiedere la pace

suede [swed] *s* pelle scamosciata

suet ['su·ɪt] or ['sju·ɪt] *s* grasso, sego

suffer ['sʌfər] *tr* soffrire; *(e.g., heavy losses)* subire || *intr* soffrire, patire

sufferance ['sʌfərəns] *s* tolleranza

suffering ['sʌfərɪŋ] *adj* sofferente || *s* sofferenza, strazio, patimento

suffice [sə'faɪs] *intr* bastare

sufficient [sə'fɪʃənt] *adj* sufficiente

suffix ['sʌfɪks] *s* suffisso

suffocate ['sʌfəˌket] *tr & intr* soffocare

suffrage ['sʌfrɪdʒ] *s* suffragio

suffragette [ˌsʌfrə'dʒɛt] *s* suffragetta

suffuse [sə'fjuz] *tr* soffondere

sugar ['ʃugər] *adj* *(water)* zuccherato; *(industry)* zuccheriero || *s* zucchero || *tr* zuccherare

sug'ar beet' *s* barbabietola da zucchero

sug'ar bowl' *s* zuccheriera

sug'ar cane' *s* canna da zucchero

sug'ar-coat' *tr* inzuccherare; *(e.g., the pill)* addolcire

sug'ar ma'ple *s* acero

sug'ar-plum' *s* zuccherino

sug'ar spoon' *s* cucchiaino per lo zucchero

sug'ar tongs' *spl* mollette *fpl* per lo zucchero

sugary ['ʃugərɪ] *adj* zuccherino, zuccheroso

suggest [səg'dʒɛst] *tr* suggerire

suggestion [səg'dʒɛstʃən] *s* suggerimento; (psychol) suggestione; ombra, traccia

suggestive [səg'dʒɛstɪv] *adj* suggestivo; *(risqué)* scabroso

suicidal [ˌsu·ɪ'saɪdəl] or [ˌsju·ɪ-'saɪdəl] *adj* suicida

suicide ['su·ɪˌsaɪd] or ['sju·ɪˌsaɪd] *s* *(person)* suicida *mf*; *(act)* suicidio; **to commit suicide** suicidarsi

suit [sut] or [sjut] *s* vestito da uomo; *(of a lady)* tailleur *m*; *(of cards)* seme *m*, colore *m*; *(for bathing)* costume *m*; corte *f*, corteggiamento; domanda, supplica; (law) causa; **to follow suit** seguire l'esempio; (cards)

rispondere a colore || *tr* adattarsi (with *dat*); convenire (with *dat*); **suit yourself** faccia come vuole || *intr* convenire, andare a proposito

suitable ['sutəbəl] or ['sjutəbəl] *adj* indicato, conveniente

suit'case' *s* valigia

suite [swit] *s* gruppo, serie *f*; serie *f* di stanze; *(of furniture)* mobilia; *(retinue)* seguito; (mus) suite *f*

suiting ['sutɪŋ] or ['sjutɪŋ] *s* taglio d'abito

suit' of clothes' *s* completo maschile

suitor ['sutər] or ['sjutər] *s* pretendente *m*; (law) querelante *mf*

sul'fa drugs' ['sʌlfə] *spl* sulfamidici *mpl*

sulfate ['sʌlfet] *s* solfato

sulfide ['sʌlfaɪd] *s* solfuro

sulfite ['sʌlfaɪt] *s* solfito

sulfur ['sʌlfər] *adj* solfiero || *s* zolfo; color *m* zolfo

sulfuric [sʌl'fjʊrɪk] *adj* solforico

sul'fur mine' *s* solfara

sulfurous ['sʌlfərəs] *adj* solforoso

sulk [sʌlk] *s* broncio || *intr* imbronciarsi

sulk·y ['sʌlkɪ] *adj* (-ier; -iest) imbronciato ||*s* (-ies) *(in horse racing)* sediolo, sulky *m*

sullen ['sʌlən] *adj* bieco, triste, tetro

sul·ly ['sʌlɪ] *v* (*pret & pp* -lied) *tr* insudiciare, insozzare

sulphur ['sʌlfər] *adj & s* var of **sulfur**

sultan ['sʌltən] *s* sultano

sul·try ['sʌltrɪ] *adj* (-trier; -triest) soffocante; infocato, appassionato

sum [sʌm] *s* somma; sommario; problema *m* di aritmetica || *v* (*pret & pp* **summed;** *ger* **summing**) *tr* sommare; **to sum up** riepilogare

sumac or **sumach** ['ʃumæk] or ['sumæk] *s* (bot) sommacco

summarize ['sʌməˌraɪz] *tr* riassumere

summa·ry ['sʌmərɪ] *adj* sommario || *s* (-ries) sommario, sunto

summer ['sʌmər] *adj* estivo || *s* estate *f* || *intr* passare l'estate

sum'mer resort' *s* stazione estiva

summersault ['sʌmərˌsɔlt] *s & intr* var of **somersault**

sum'mer school' *s* scuola estiva

summery ['sʌmərɪ] *adj* estivo

summit ['sʌmɪt] *s* sommità *f*

sum'mit con'ference *s* riunione al vertice

summon ['sʌmən] *tr* convocare, invitare; evocare; (law) compulsare

summons ['sʌmənz] *s* ordine *m*, comando; (law) citazione || *tr* (law) citare

sumptuous ['sʌmptʃu·əs] *adj* sontuoso

sun [sʌn] *s* sole *m*; **place in the sun** posto al sole || *v* (*pret & pp* **sunned;** *ger* **sunning**) *tr* esporre al sole || *intr* prendere il sole

sun' bath' *s* bagno di sole

sun'beam' *s* raggio di sole

sun'burn' *s* abbronzatura || *v* (*pret & pp* **-burned** or **-burnt**) *tr* abbronzare || *intr* abbronzarsi

sundae ['sʌndɪ] s gelato con sciroppo, frutta o noci

Sunday ['sʌndɪ] adj domenicale ‖ s domenica

Sun'day best' s (coll) vestito da festa

Sun'day's child' s bambino nato con la camicia

Sun'day school' s scuola domenicale della dottrina

sunder ['sʌndər] tr separare

sun'di'al s meridiana

sun'down' s tramonto

sundries ['sʌndrɪz] spl generi mpl diversi

sundry ['sʌndrɪ] adj vari, diversi

sun'fish' s pesce m mola, pesce m luna

sun'flow'er s girasole m

sun'glass'es spl occhiali mpl da sole

sunken ['sʌŋkən] adj affondato, sommerso; (hollow) incavato

sun' lamp' s sole m artificiale

sun'light' s luce f del sole

sun'lit' adj illuminato dal sole

sun·ny ['sʌnɪ] adj (-nier; -niest) solatio, soleggiato; allegro, ridente; **it is sunny** fa sole

sun'ny side' s parte soleggiata; lato buono; **on the sunny side of** (e.g., thirty) al disotto dei . . . anni

sun' porch' s veranda a solatio

sun'rise' s sorgere m del sole; **from sunrise to sunset** dall'alba al tramonto

sun'set' s tramonto

sun'shade' s tenda; parasole m

sun'shine' s sole m, luce f del sole; **in the sunshine** al sole

sun'spot' s macchia solare

sun'stroke' s insolazione

sun' tan' s tintarella

sun'tan lo'tion s pomata antisole, abbronzante m

sun'up' s sorgere m, levare m del sole

sun' vi'sor s (aut) aletta parasole, parasole m

sup [sʌp] v (pret & pp **supped;** ger **supping**) intr cenare

super ['supər] adj (coll) superficiale; (coll) di prim'ordine, super ‖ s (coll) sovrintendente m; (coll) articolo di prim'ordine, super m

superabundant [ˌsupərəˈbʌndənt] adj sovrabbondante

superannuated [ˌsuperˈænjuˌetɪd] adj giubilato, pensionato; messo a riposo per limiti di età; antiquato

superb [suˈpʌrb] or [səˈpʌrb] adj superbo

supercar·go ['supərˌkɑrgo] s (-goes) (naut) sopraccarico

supercharge [ˌsupərˈtʃɑrdʒ] tr sovralimentare

supercilious [ˌsupərˈsɪlɪəs] adj altero, arrogante

superficial [ˌsupərˈfɪʃəl] adj superficiale

superfluous [suˈpʌrfluəs] adj superfluo

su'per·high'way s autostrada

superhuman [ˌsupərˈhjumən] adj sovrumano

superimpose [ˌsupərɪmˈpoz] tr sovrapporre

superintendent [ˌsupərɪnˈtɛndənt] s soprintendente m; (of schools) provveditore m

superior [səˈpɪrɪ-ər] or [suˈpɪrɪ-ər] adj superiore; di superiorità; (typ) esponente ‖ s superiore m

superiority [səˌpɪrɪˈɑrɪtɪ] or [suˌpɪrɪˈɑrɪtɪ] s superiorità f

superlative [səˈpʌrlətɪv] or [suˈpʌrlətɪv] adj & s superlativo

su'per·man' s (-men') superuomo

supermarket ['supərˌmɑrkɪt] s supermercato

supernatural [ˌsupərˈnætʃərəl] adj soprannaturale

superpose [ˌsupərˈpoz] tr sovrapporre

supersede [ˌsupərˈsid] tr rimpiazzare, sostituire

supersensitive [ˌsupərˈsɛnsɪtɪv] adj ipersensibile

supersonic [ˌsupərˈsɑnɪk] adj supersonico

superstition [ˌsupərˈstɪʃən] s superstizione

superstitious [ˌsupərˈstɪʃəs] adj superstizioso

supervene [ˌsupərˈvin] intr sopravvenire

supervise ['supərˌvaɪz] tr sorvegliare, dirigere

supervision [ˌsupərˈvɪʒən] s supervisione, sorveglianza, direzione

supervisor ['supərˌvaɪzər] s supervisore m, sorvegliante mf; ispettore m

supper ['sʌpər] s cena

sup'per-time' s ora di cena

supplant [səˈplænt] tr rimpiazzare

supple ['sʌpəl] adj flessibile; docile

supplement ['sʌplɪmənt] s supplemento ‖ ['sʌplɪˌmɛnt] tr completare, supplire (with dat)

suppliant ['sʌplɪ-ənt] adj & s supplicante mf

supplicant ['sʌplɪkənt] s supplicante mf

supplication [ˌsʌplɪˈkeʃən] s supplica

supplier [sʌˈplaɪ-ər] s fornitore m

sup·ply [səˈplaɪ] s (-plies) rifornimento, fornitura; provvista, scorta; (com) offerta; **supplies** rifornimenti mpl, vettovaglie fpl ‖ v (pret & pp **-plied**) tr fornire, provvedere; (food) vettovagliare

supply' and demand' s domanda ed offerta

support [səˈport] s sostegno, appoggio; puntello, rincalzo; mantenimento ‖ tr sostenere, appoggiare; puntellare; (a cause) caldeggiare; mantenere

supporter [səˈportər] s fautore m, sostenitore m; (jockstrap) sospensorio; giarrettiera; fascia elastica

suppose [səˈpoz] tr supporre; ammettere; **suppose we take a walk?** che ne dice se facessimo una passeggiata?; **to be supposed to be** aver fama di essere; **to suppose so** credere di sì

supposed [səˈpozd] adj presunto

supposition [ˌsʌpəˈzɪʃən] s supposizione

supposito·ry [səˈpɑzɪˌtorɪ] s (-ries) suppositorio, supposta

suppress [səˈprɛs] tr sopprimere

suppression [sə'prɛʃən] *s* soppressione

suppurate ['sʌpjə,ret] *intr* suppurare

supreme [sə'prim] *or* [su'prim] *adj* supremo, sommo

Supreme' Court' *s* (*in Italy*) Corte *f* di Cassazione; (*in U.S.A.*) tribunale *m* di ultima istanza

surcharge ['sʌr,tʃɑrdʒ] *s* soprapprezzo; soprattassa; sovraccarico; (*philately*) sovrastampa || [,sʌr'tʃɑrdʒ] *or* ['sʌr,tʃɑrdʒ] *tr* sovraccaricare

sure [ʃur] *adj* sicuro; **to be sure!** certamente!, senza dubbio! || *interj* (coll) certamente!; **sure enough!** (coll) difatti

sure-footed ['ʃjur'futɪd] *adj* dal piede sicuro

sure' thing' *s* (coll) successo garantito || *adv* (coll) certamente || *interj* (coll) di sicuro!

sure-ty ['ʃurti] *or* ['ʃurɪti] *s* (**-ties**) malleveria

surf [sʌrf] *s* frangente *m*

surface ['sʌrfɪs] *adj* superficiale || *s* superficie *f* || *tr* rifinire; spianare; ricoprire || *intr* emergere

sur'face mail' *s* posta ordinaria

surf'board' *s* tavola per il surfing

surfeit ['sʌrfɪt] *s* eccesso; sazietà *f* || *tr* saziare, rimpinzare || *intr* saziarsi, rimpinzarsi

surf'ing *s* surfing *m*

surge [sʌrdʒ] *s* ondata; fiotto; (elec) sovratensione || *intr* ondeggiare, fluttuare; (*said, e.g., of a crowd*) affluire

surgeon ['sʌrdʒən] *s* (medico) chirurgo

surger-y ['sʌrdʒəri] *s* (**-ies**) chirurgia; sala operatoria

surgical ['sʌrdʒɪkəl] *adj* chirurgico

sur-ly ['sʌrli] *adj* (**-lier; -liest**) arcigno, imbronciato

surmise [sər'maɪz] *or* ['sʌrmaɪz] *s* congettura, supposizione || [sər'maɪz] *tr & intr* congetturare, supporre

surmount [sər'maunt] *tr* sormontare; coronare

surname ['sʌr,nem] *s* cognome *m*; (*added name*) soprannome *m* || *tr* dare il cognome a; soprannominare

surpass [sər'pæs] *or* [sər'pɑs] *tr* sorpassare, superare

surplice ['sʌrplɪs] *s* cotta

surplus ['sʌrplʌs] *adj* eccedente || *s* sopravanzo, eccedenza

surprise [sər'praɪz] *adj* insperato, improvviso || *s* sorpresa || *tr* sorprendere

surprise' par'ty *s* improvvisata

surprising [sər'praɪzɪŋ] *adj* sorprendente

surrender [sə'rɛndər] *s* resa || *tr* arrendere || *intr* arrendersi

surren'der val'ue *s* (ins) valore *m* di riscatto

surreptitious [,sʌrɛp'tɪʃəs] *adj* clandestino, nascosto, furtivo

surround [sə'raund] *tr* circondare, contornare; (mil) aggirare

surrounding [sə'raundɪŋ] *adj* circostante, circonvicino || **surroundings** *spl* dintorni *mpl*; ambiente *m*

surtax ['sʌr,tæks] *s* sovrimposta, soprattassa; imposta complementare

surveillance [sər'veləns] *or* [sər'veljəns] *s* sorveglianza, vigilanza

survey ['sʌrve] *s* quadro generale, schizzo; indagine *f*; (*of opinion*) sondaggio; rapporto; rilievo topografico; perizia || [sʌr've] *or* ['sʌrve] *tr* fare un'indagine di; sondare; rilevare; misurare || *intr* fare un rilievo

sur'vey course' *s* corso di rassegna generale

surveyor [sər've-ər] *s* livellatore *m*, geometra *m*

survival [sər'vaɪvəl] *s* sopravvivenza

survive [sər'vaɪv] *tr* sopravvivere (**with** *dat*) || *intr* sopravvivere

surviving [sər'vaɪvɪŋ] *adj* superstite

survivor [sər'vaɪvər] *s* sopravvissuto, superstite *mf*

survivorship [sər'vaɪvər,ʃɪp] *s* (law) sopravvivenza

susceptible [sə'sɛptɪbəl] *adj* suscettibile, ricettivo; impressionabile; **susceptible to** (*e.g., colds*) soggetto a

suspect ['sʌspɛkt] *or* [səs'pɛkt] *adj* sospetto || ['sʌspɛkt] *s* sospetto || [səs'pɛkt] *tr* sospettare

suspend [səs'pɛnd] *tr* sospendere || *intr* essere sospeso; fermarsi; fermare i pagamenti

suspenders [səs'pɛndərz] *spl* bretelle *fpl*

suspense [səs'pɛns] *s* sospensione; sospeso; **in suspense** in sospeso

suspen'sion bridge' [səs'pɛnʃən] *s* ponte sospeso

suspicion [səs'pɪʃən] *s* sospetto

suspicious [səs'pɪʃəs] *adj* (*subject to suspicion*) sospetto; (*inclined to suspect*) sospettoso

sustain [səs'ten] *tr* sostenere, sorreggere; (*with food*) sostentare; (*a conversation*) mantenere; (*a loss*) soffrire; (law) confermare

sustenance ['sʌstɪnəns] *s* sostentamento

sutler ['sʌtlər] *s* (mil) vivandiere *m*

swab [swab] *s* (mil) scovolo; (naut) redazza; (surg) batuffolo di cotone || *v* (*pret & pp* **swabbed**; *ger* **swabbing**) *tr* pulire con la redazza; spugnare; assorbire col cotone

swaddle ['swadəl] *tr* fasciare

swad'dling clothes' *spl* fasce *fpl* del neonato

swagger ['swægər] *s* spavalderia || *intr* fare lo spavaldo

swain [swen] *s* innamorato; (*lad*) contadinotto

swallow ['swalo] *s* (*of liquid*) sorso; (*of food*) boccone *m*; (orn) rondine *f* || *tr & intr* trangugiare, inghiottire

swal'low-tailed coat' ['swalo,teld] *s* frac *m*, marsina, abito a coda di rondine

swal'low-wort' *s* vincetossico

swamp [swamp] *s* pantano, palude *f* || *tr* inondare, sommergere

swamp-y ['swampi] *adj* (**-ier; -iest**) paludoso, pantanoso

swan [swan] *s* cigno

swan' dive' *s* volo dell'angelo

swank [swæŋk] *adj* (coll) elegante, vistoso || *s* (coll) eleganza vistosa
swan's-down ['swɑnz,daʊn] *s* piuma di cigno, piumino; mollettone *m*
swan' song' *s* canto del cigno
swap [swɑp] *s* scambio, baratto || *v* (*pret & pp* **swapped**; *ger* **swapping**) *tr & intr* scambiare, barattare
swarm [swɔrm] *s* sciame *m* || *intr* sciamare; (fig) formicolare
swarth-y ['swɔrði] *or* ['swɔrθi] *adj* (**-ier; -iest**) olivastro, abbronzato
swashbuckler ['swɑʃ,bʌklər] *s* spadaccino, rodomonte *m*
swat [swɑt] *s* colpo || *v* (*pret & pp* **swatted**; *ger* **swatting**) *tr* colpire; (*a fly*) schiacciare
sway [swe] *s* dondolio, ondeggiamento; dominio || *tr* dondolare, fare oscillare; influenzare; dominare || *intr* dondolarsi, ondulare; oscillare
swear [swer] *v* (*pret* **swore** [swor]; *pp* **sworn** [sworn]) *tr* giurare; (*to secrecy*) fare giurare; **to swear in** fare prestar giuramento a; **to swear off** giurare di rinunziare a; **to swear out a warrant** ottenere un atto di accusa sotto giuramento || *intr* giurare; (*to blaspheme*) bestemmiare; **to swear at** maledire; **to swear by** giurare su, avere certezza di; **to swear to** dichiarare sotto giuramento; giurare di + *inf*
swear'word' *s* bestemmia, parolaccia
sweat [swet] *s* sudata; sudore *m* || *v* (*pret & pp* **sweat** *or* **sweated**) *tr* sudare; far sudare; **to sweat it out** (slang) farcela fino alla fine; **to sweat off** (*weight*) perdere sudando || *intr* sudare
sweater ['swetər] *s* maglione *m*, golf *m*, sweater *m*
sweat' shirt' *s* maglione *m* da ginnastica
sweat-y ['sweti] *adj* (**-ier; -iest**) sudato; che fa sudare
Swede [swid] *s* svedese *mf*
Sweden ['swidən] *s* la Svezia
Swedish ['swidɪʃ] *adj & s* svedese *m*
sweep [swip] *s* scopata; movimento circolare; estensione; curva; (*of wind*) soffio; (*of well*) mazzacavallo; **to make a clean sweep of** far piazza pulita di || *v* (*pret & pp* **swept** [swept]) *tr* spazzare, scopare; percorrere con lo sguardo; (*eyes*) dirigere; travolgere || *intr* scopare; passare; estendersi; dragare
sweeper ['swipər] *s* spazzino; (*machine*) spazzatrice *f*; (nav) dragamine *m*
sweeping ['swipɪŋ] *adj* esteso; travolgente, decisivo || **sweepings** *spl* spazzatura
sweep'-sec'ond *s* lancetta dei secondi a perno centrale
sweep'stakes' *ssg or spl* lotteria abbinata alle corse dei cavalli
sweet [swit] *adj* dolce; (*butter*) senza sale; (*cider*) analcolico; **to be sweet on** (coll) essere innamorato di ||

sweets *spl* dolci *mpl*; (coll) patate *fpl* dolci || *adv* dolcemente; **to smell sweet** saper di buono
sweet'bread' *s* animella
sweet'bri'er *s* eglantina
sweeten ['switən] *tr* inzuccherare; raddolcire; purificare || *intr* raddolcirsi; purificarsi
sweet'heart' *s* innamorato; innamorata; caro, amore *m*
sweet' mar'joram *s* maggiorana
sweet'meats' *spl* dolci *mpl*, confetti *mpl*
sweet' pea' *s* pisello odoroso
sweet' pota'to *s* batata, patata americana; (mus) ocarina
sweet-scented ['swit,sɛntɪd] *adj* odoroso, profumato
sweet' tooth' *s* debole *m* per i dolci
sweet-toothed ['swit,tuθt] *adj* goloso
sweet' wil'liam *s* garofano barbuto
swell [swel] *adj* (slang) elegante; (slang) eccellente, di prim'ordine || *s* gonfiore *m*; onda, ondata; aumento; (mus) crescendo; (slang) elegantone *m* || *v* (*pret* **swelled**; *pp* **swelled** *or* **swollen** ['swolən]) *tr* gonfiare, ingrossare; aumentare || *intr* gonfiare, ingrossarsi; aumentare; (*said of the sea*) alzarsi; (*with pride*) montarsi
swelled' head' *s* borioso; **to have a swelled head** montarsi, essere pieno di sé
swelter ['swɛltər] *intr* soffocare dal caldo
swept'back wing' *s* ala a freccia
swerve [swʌrv] *s* scarto, sbandamento || *tr* sviare || *intr* scartare, sbandare
swift [swift] *adj* rapido || *s* rondone *m* || *adv* rapidamente
swig [swɪg] *s* (coll) sorso || *v* (*pret & pp* **swigged**; *ger* **swigging**) *tr & intr* (coll) bere a grandi sorsi
swill [swɪl] *s* imbratto; risciacquatura || *tr* tracannare, trincare || *intr* bere a lunghi sorsi
swim [swɪm] *s* nuoto; **the swim** (*in social activities*) la corrente || *v* (*pret* **swam** [swæm]; *pp* **swum** [swʌm]; *ger* **swimming**) *tr* traversare a nuoto || *intr* nuotare; essere inondato; (*said of one's head*) girare, e.g., **her head is swimming** le gira la testa
swimmer ['swɪmər] *s* nuotatore *m*
swimming ['swɪmɪŋ] *s* nuoto
swim'ming pool' *s* piscina
swim'ming trunks' *spl* mutandine *fpl* da bagno
swim'suit' *s* costume *m* da bagno
swindle ['swɪndəl] *s* truffa, imbroglio || *tr* truffare, imbrogliare
swine [swaɪn] *s* suino, maiale *m*, porco; **swine** *spl* suini *mpl*
swing [swɪŋ] *s* oscillazione; dondolio; curva; (*suspended seat*) altalena; alternarsi *m*; piena attività; (boxing) sventola; (mus) swing *m*; **free swing** libertà *f* d'azione; **in full swing** (coll) in piena attività || *v* (*pret & pp* **swung** [swʌŋ]) *tr* (e.g., *one's arms*) dondo-

lare, oscillare; (*a weapon*) brandire; (*e.g., a club*) rotare; far girare; appendere; (*a deal*) (coll) riuscire ad ottenere ‖ (coll) dondolare, dondolarsi, oscillare; girare; essere sospeso; cambiare; (boxing) dare una sventola; **to swing open** aprirsi di colpo

swing'ing door' ['swɪŋɪŋ] *s* porta oscillante

swinish ['swaɪnɪʃ] *adj* porcino

swipe [swaɪp] *s* (coll) colpo forte ‖ *tr* (coll) dare un forte colpo a; (slang) portare via, rubare

swirl [swʌrl] *s* turbine *m*, vortice *m* ‖ *tr* far girare ‖ *intr* turbinare

swirling ['swʌrlɪŋ] *adj* vorticoso

swish [swɪʃ] *s* (*of whip*) schiocco; (*of silk*) fruscio ‖ *tr* (*a whip*) schioccare; ‖ *intr* schioccare; frusciare

Swiss [swɪs] *adj* svizzero ‖ *s* svizzero; **the Swiss** gli svizzeri

Swiss' chard' [tʃɑrd] *s* bietola

Swiss' cheese' *s* groviera

Swiss' Guards' *spl* guardie *fpl* svizzere

switch [swɪtʃ] *s* verga; vergata; (*false hair*) posticcio; cambio, trapasso; (elec) interruttore *m*; (rr) scambio ‖ *tr* battere, frustare; (elec) commutare; (rr) deviare; (fig) girare; **to switch off** (*light, radio, etc.*) spegnere; **to switch on** (*light, radio, etc.*) accendere ‖ *intr* fustigare; cambiare; (rr) deviare

switch'back' *s* strada a zigzag; (rr) tracciato a zigzag

switch'blade knife' *s* coltello a serramanico

switch'board' *s* quadro

switch'board op'erator *s* centralinista *mf*

switch'ing en'gine *s* locomotiva da manovra

switch'man *s* (*-men*) deviatore *m*

switch'yard' *s* stazione smistamento

Switzerland ['swɪtsərlənd] *s* la Svizzera

swiv·el ['swɪvəl] *s* perno, gancio girevole ‖ *v* (*pret & pp* **-eled** or **-elled**; *ger* **-eling** or **-elling**) *intr* girare

swiv'el chair' *s* sedia girevole

swoon [swun] *s* deliquio, svenimento ‖ *intr* svenire

swoop [swup] *s* calata a piombo ‖ *intr* calare a piombo, piombare

sword [sord] *s* spada; **at swords' points** pronti a incrociare le spade; **to put to the sword** passare a fil di spada

sword' belt' *s* cinturone *m*

sword' cane' *s* bastone animato

sword'fish' *s* pesce *m* spada

swords'man *s* (*-men*) spadaccino

sword' swal'lower ['swɑlo·ər] *s* giocoliere *m* che ingoia spade

sword' thrust' *s* stoccata

sworn [sworn] *adj* giurato

sycophant ['sɪkəfənt] *s* adulatore *m*; parassita *mf*

syllable ['sɪləbəl] *s* sillaba

sylla·bus ['sɪləbəs] *s* (*-bi* [,baɪ]) sillabo, sommario scolastico

syllogism ['sɪlə,dʒɪzəm] *s* sillogismo

sylph [sɪlf] *s* silfo; silfide *f*; (fig) silfide *f*

sylvan ['sɪlvən] *adj* silvano

symbol ['sɪmbəl] *s* simbolo

symbolic(al) [sɪm'bɑlɪk(əl)] *adj* simbolico

symbolism ['sɪmbə,lɪzəm] *s* simbolismo

symbolize ['sɪmbə,laɪz] *tr* simboleggiare

symmetric(al) [sɪ'metrɪk(əl)] *adj* simmetrico

symme·try ['sɪmɪtri] *s* (*-tries*) simmetria

sympathetic [,sɪmpə'θetɪk] *adj* simpatetico; ben disposto

sympathize ['sɪmpə,θaɪz] *intr*—**to sympathize with** aver compassione di; mostrar comprensione per; (*to be in accord with*) simpatizzare con

sympa·thy ['sɪmpəθi] *s* (*-thies*) compassione, commiserazione; **to be in sympathy with** essere d'accordo con; **to extend one's sympathy to** fare le condoglianze a

sym'pathy strike' *s* sciopero di solidarietà

symphonic [sɪm'fɑnɪk] *adj* sinfonico

sympho·ny ['sɪmfəni] *s* (*-nies*) sinfonia

symposi·um [sɪm'pozɪ·əm] *s* (*-a* [ə]) simposio, colloquio

symptom ['sɪmptəm] *s* sintomo

synagogue ['sɪnə,gɑg] or ['sɪnə,gɑg] *s* sinagoga

synchronize ['sɪŋkrə,naɪz] *tr & intr* sincronizzare

synchronous ['sɪŋkrənəs] *adj* sincrono

sincopation [,sɪŋkə'peʃən] *s* sincope *f*

syncope ['sɪŋkə,pi] *s* (phonet) sincope *f*

syndicate ['sɪndɪkɪt] *s* sindacato ‖ ['sɪndɪ,ket] *tr* organizzare in un sindacato

synonym ['sɪnənɪm] *s* sinonimo

synonymous [sɪ'nɑnɪməs] *adj* sinonimo

synop·sis [sɪ'nɑpsɪs] *s* (*-ses* [siz]) sinossi *f*; (mov) sinopsi *f*

synoptic(al) [sɪ'nɑptɪk(əl)] *adj* sinottico

syntax ['sɪntæks] *s* sintassi *f*

synthe·sis ['sɪnθɪsɪs] *s* (*-ses* [,siz]) sintesi *f*

synthesize ['sɪnθɪ,saɪz] *tr* sintetizzare

synthetic(al) [sɪn'θetɪk(əl)] *adj* sintetico

syphilis ['sɪfɪlɪs] *s* sifilide *f*

Syria ['sɪrɪ·ə] *s* la Siria

Syrian ['sɪrɪ·ən] *adj & s* siriano

syringe [sɪ'rɪndʒ] or ['sɪrɪndʒ] *s* (*fountain syringe*) schizzetto; (*for hypodermic injections*) siringa ‖ *tr* schizzettare; iniettare

syrup ['sɪrəp] or ['sʌrəp] *s* sciroppo

system ['sɪstəm] *s* sistema *m*

systematic(al) [,sɪstə'mætɪk(əl)] *adj* sistematico

systematize ['sɪstəmə,taɪz] *tr* ridurre a sistema

systole ['sɪstəli] *s* sistole *f*

T

T, t [ti] *s* ventesima lettera dell'alfabeto inglese; **to fit to a T** calzare come un guanto

tab [tæb] *s* (*strap*) linguetta; (*of a pocket*) patta; targa; (*label*) etichetta; **to keep tabs on** (coll) sorvegliare; **to pick up the tab** (coll) pagare il conto

tab·by ['tæbɪ] *s* (**-bies**) gatto tigrato; gatta; (*spinster*) zitella; vecchia pettegola

tabernacle ['tæbər,nækəl] *s* tabernacolo

table ['tebəl] *s* tavola; (*food*) mensa; (*people at a table*) tavolata; (*synopsis*) quadro, prospetto; (*list or catalogue*) indice *m*; **to turn the tables** rovesciare la posizione; **under the table** ubriaco fradicio || *tr* aggiornare, rinviare

tab·leau ['tæblo] *s* (**-leaus** or **-leaux** [loz]) quadro vivente

table d'hôte ['tɑbəl'dot] *s* pasto a prezzo fisso

tableful ['tebəl,fʊl] *s* (*persons*) tavolata; (*food*) tavola apparecchiata

ta'ble·land' *s* tavoliere *m*

ta'ble lin'en *s* biancheria da tavola

ta'ble man'ners *spl* maniere *fpl* a tavola

ta'ble of con'tents *s* indice *m* delle materie

ta'ble·spoon' *s* cucchiaio

tablespoonful ['tebəl,spun,fʊl] *s* cucchiaiata

tablet ['tæblɪt] *s* (*writing pad*) blocco; (*slab*) lapide *f*; (*flat rigid sheet*) tabella, tavoletta; (pharm) disco, pastiglia

ta'ble talk' *s* conversazione familiare a tavola

ta'ble ten'nis *s* ping-pong *m*, tennis *m* da tavolo

ta'ble·ware' *s* servizio da tavola

ta'ble wine' *s* vino da pasto

tabloid ['tæblɔɪd] *s* giornale *m* a carattere sensazionale

taboo [tə'bu] *adj* & *s* tabù *m* || *tr* proibire assolutamente

tabulate ['tæbjə,let] *tr* tabulare

tabulator ['tæbjə,letər] *s* tabulatore *m*, incolonnatore *m*

tachometer [tə'kɑmɪtər] *s* tachimetro

tacit ['tæsɪt] *adj* tacito

taciturn ['tæsɪ,tʌrn] *adj* taciturno

tack [tæk] *s* bulletta; cambio di direzione; (naut) virata; (sew) imbastitura || *tr* imbullettare; attaccare; (naut) bordeggiare; (sew) imbastire || *intr* virare; mutare di direzione

tackle ['tækəl] *s* attrezzatura; (mach) taglia, paranco; (*gear*) (naut) padiglione *m* || *tr* attaccare, affrontare; (sports) placcare, bloccare

tack·y ['tækɪ] *adj* (**-ier**; **-iest**) appiccicaticcio; (coll) trasandato

tact [tækt] *s* tatto

tactful ['tæktfəl] *adj* pieno di tatto

tactical ['tæktɪkəl] *adj* tattico

tactician [tæk'tɪʃən] *s* tattico

tactics ['tæktɪks] *ssg* (mil) tattica || *spl* tattica

tactless ['tæktlɪs] *adj* che non ha tatto, indiscreto

tadpole ['tæd,pol] *s* girino

taffeta ['tæfɪtə] *s* taffettà *m*

taffy ['tæfi] *s* caramella, zucchero d'orzo; (coll) lisciata

tag [tæg] *s* etichetta; (*on a shoelace*) punta dell'aghetto; conclusione; (*last words of speech*) pistolotto finale; epiteto; frase fatta; (*of hair*) ciocca; (*in writing*) ghirigoro; (*game*) toccaferro || *v* (*pret & pp* **tagged**) *ger* **tagging**) *tr* etichettare; (*to fine*) multare; aggiungere; soprannominare; accusare; stabilire il prezzo di; (coll) pedinare || *intr* seguire da presso

tag' end' *s* (*e.g., of day*) fine *f*; estremità logorata; avanzo

tail [tel] *adj* di coda || *s* coda; fine *f*; (*of coin*) croce *f*; **tails** falde *fpl*, frac *m*; **to turn tails** darsela a gambe || *tr* attaccare; finire; (coll) pedinare

tail' assem'bly *s* (aer) impennaggio

tail' end' *s* coda, fine *f*

tail'light' *s* fanale *m* di coda

tailor ['telər] *s* sarto || *tr* (*a suit*) tagliare, confezionare; (*one's conduct*) adattare || *intr* fare il sarto

tailoring ['telərɪŋ] *s* sartoria

tai'lor-made' *adj* fatto su misura

tai'lor shop' *s* sartoria

tail'piece' *s* coda, estremità *f*; (mus) cordiera; (typ) fusello finale

tail'race' *s* canale *m* di scarico

tail'spin' *s* avvitamento

tail'wind' *s* (aer) vento di coda; (naut) vento in poppa

taint [tent] *s* macchia; infezione || *tr* macchiare, infettare, corrompere

take [tek] *s* presa; (*of fish*) retata; (mov) presa; ripresa; (slang) incasso || *v* (*pret* **took** [tʊk]; *pp* **taken**) *tr* prendere, pigliare; ricevere, accettare; portare; (*to get by force*) portar via; (*a nap*) schiacciare; (*a bath*) fare; (*a joke*) stare a; (*an examination*) sostenere; (*one's own life*) togliersi; (*to deduct*) cavare; (*a purchase*) comprare; (*to convey*) portare; (*time*) impiegare; (*a step, a walk*) fare; (*a subject*) studiare; (*a responsibility, role, etc.*) assumere; (*an oath*) prestare; (*root*) mettere; (*exception*) sollevare; credere; (*e.g., a photograph*) fare, scattare; (slang) fregare; **it takes** ci vuole, ci vogliono; **to take amiss** prendere a male; **to take apart** scomporre; smontare; **to take back** riprendere; **to take down** abbassare; smontare; prender nota di; **to take for** prendere per; **to take from** portar via a; **to take in** (*to admit*) ammettere, ricevere; (*to encompass*) includere; (*a dress*) restringere; (*to cheat*) ingannare; (*water*) fare; (*a point of inter-*

est) visitare; **to take it** accettare, ammettere; (slang) resistere; **to take off** (*e.g., one's coat*) togliersi; portar via; scontare, defalcare; (slang) imitare; **to take on** ingaggiare; assumere; intraprendere; accettare la sfida di; **to take out** cavare, togliere; (*e.g., a girl*) portar fuori; (*e.g., a patent*) ottenere; **to take over** rilevare; (slang) imbrogliare; **to take place** aver luogo; **to take s.o.'s eye** attrarre l'attenzione di qlcu; **to take the place of** sottentrare a; **to take up** cominciare a studiare; sollevare, tirar su; (*a duty*) assumere; (*time, space*) occupare || *intr* prendere; scattare; darsi; diventare; **to take after** rassomigliare a; **to take off** (coll) partire, andarsene; (aer) decollare, involare; **to take up with** (coll) fare amicizia con; (coll) vivere con; **to take well** riuscire bene in fotografia

take'off' *s* parodia; (aer) decollaggio; (mach) presa di forza

tal'cum pow'der ['tælkəm] *s* talco

tale [tel] *s* storia, racconto; favola, fiaba; (*lie*) bugia, frottola; (*piece of gossip*) maldicenza

tale'bear'er *s* pettegolo

talent ['tælənt] *s* talento; persona di talento; gente *f* di talento

talented ['tæləntɪd] *adj* dotato di talento, dotato d'ingegno

tal'ent scout' *s* scopritore *m* di talenti

talk [tɔk] *s* chiacchierata; discorso, conferenza; (*language*) parlata; (*gossip*) pettegolezzo; **to cause talk** originare pettegolezzi || *tr* parlare; convincere parlando; **to talk up** elogiare || *intr* parlare; discutere; **to talk on** discutere; continuare a parlare; **to talk up** parlare apertamente

talkative ['tɔkətɪv] *adj* loquace

talker ['tɔkər] *s* parlatore *m*

talkie ['tɔki] *s* (coll) parlato

talk'ing machine' *s* grammofono

talk'ing pic'ture *s* film parlato

tall [tɔl] *adj* alto; (coll) stravagante, esagerato

tallow ['tælo] *s* sego

tal·ly ['tæli] *s* (-lies) tacca, taglia || *v* (*pret & pp* -lied) *tr* contare, registrare || *intr* riscontrare

tal'ly sheet' *s* foglio di spunta

talon ['tælən] *s* artiglio

tambourine [,tæmbə'rin] *s* tamburello

tame [tem] *adj* addomesticato; docile, mansueto; mite || *tr* addomesticare; domare; (*water power*) captare

tamp [tæmp] *tr* pigiare, comprimere; (*e.g., ground*) costipare

tamper ['tæmpər] *s* (*person*) pigiatore *m*; (*tool*) mazzeranga || *intr* intrigare; **to tamper with** (*a lock*) forzare; (*a document*) manomettere; (*a witness*) corrompere

tampon ['tæmpɑn] *s* (surg) tampone *m* || *tr* (surg) tamponare

tan [tæn] *adj* marrone; (*by sun*) abbronzato || *v* (*pret & pp* **tanned**); *ger* **tanning**) *tr* (*leather*) conciare; abbronzare; (coll) picchiare, sculacciare

tandem ['tændəm] *adj & adv* in tandem || *s* tandem *m*

tang [tæŋ] *s* sapore *m* piccante; odore *m* forte; traccia; (*of knife*) tallone *m*; (*sound*) tintinnio

tangent ['tændʒənt] *adj* tangente || *s* tangente *f*; **to fly off at a tangent** cambiare improvvisamente d'idea

tangerine [,tændʒə'rin] *s* mandarino

tangible ['tændʒɪbəl] *adj* tangibile

Tangier [tæn'dʒɪr] *s* Tangeri *f*

tangle ['tæŋgəl] *s* intrico; (coll) litigio || *tr* intricare || *intr* intricarsi; (coll) litigare

tank [tæŋk] *s* conserva, serbatoio; (mil) carro armato

tankard ['tæŋkərd] *s* boccale *m*

tank' car' *s* (rr) carro botte

tanker ['tæŋkər] *s* petroliera; (aer) aerocisterna

tank' farm'ing *s* idroponica

tank' truck' *s* autocisterna

tanner ['tænər] *s* conciapelli *m*

tanner·y ['tænəri] *s* (-ies) conceria

tantalize ['tæntə,laɪz] *tr* stuzzicare con vane promesse

tantamount ['tæntə,maunt] *adj* equivalente

tantrum ['tæntrəm] *s* bizze *fpl*

tap [tæp] *s* colpetto, buffetto; (*in a keg*) spina, cannella; (*faucet*) rubinetto; (elec) presa; (mach) maschio; **on tap** alla spina; (coll) disponibile; **taps** (mil) silenzio || *v* (*pret & pp* **tapped**); *ger* **tapping**) *tr* battere; picchiare, picchiettare; (*from a barrel*) spillare; mettere il cannello a; (*resources*) usare; (*a telephone*) intercettare; (*water, electricity*) derivare; (mach) maschiare || *intr* picchiare

tap' dance' *s* tip tap *m*

tap'-dance' *intr* ballare il tip tap

tape [tep] *s* nastro; (sports) striscione *m* del traguardo || *tr* legare con nastro; misurare col metro a nastro; registrare su nastro magnetico

tape' meas'ure *s* metro a nastro; nastro per misurare

tape' play'er *s* riproduttore *m* a nastro magnetico

taper ['tepər] *s* cerino || *tr* affusolare || *intr* affusolarsi; **to taper off** rastremarsi; diminuire in intensità; diminuire a poco a poco

tape'-re·cord' *tr* registrare su nastro magnetico

tape' record'er *s* magnetofono, registratore *m* a nastro

tapes·try ['tæpɪstri] *s* (-tries) tappezzeria || *v* (*pret & pp* -tried) *tr* tappezzare

tape'worm' *s* verme solitario, tenia

tappet ['tæpɪt] *s* (aut) punteria

tap'room' *s* taverna, osteria

tap'root' *s* radice *f* a fittone

tap' wa'ter *s* acqua corrente

tap' wrench' *s* giramaschio

tar [tɑr] *s* catrame *m* || *v* (*pret & pp* **tarred**); *ger* **tarring**) *tr* incatramare

tar·dy ['tɑrdi] *adj* (-dier; -diest) in ritardo; lento

tare [ter] *s* tara ‖ *tr* tarare

target ['tɑrgɪt] *s* segno, bersaglio

tar'get date' *s* data progettata

tar'get lan·guage *s* lingua obbiettivo, lingua di arrivo

tar'get prac'tice *s* esercizio di tiro a segno

tariff ['tærɪf] *s* (*duties*) tariffa doganale; (*charge* or *fare*) tariffa

tarnish ['tɑrnɪʃ] *s* ossidazione; (fig) macchia ‖ *tr* appannare ‖ *intr* appannarsi, perdere il lustro

tar' pa'per *s* carta catramata

tarpaulin [tɑr'pɔlɪn] *s* telone *m* impermeabile incatramato

tarragon ['tærəgən] *s* dragoncello

tar·ry ['tɑri] *adj* incatramato ‖ ['tæri] *v* (*pret* & *pp* -ried) *intr* rimanere; ritardare

tart [tɑrt] *adj* acido, pungente ‖ *s* torta; (slang) puttana

tartar ['tɑrtər] *s* tartaro; cremore *m* di tartaro; (shrew) megera; **to catch a tartar** imbattersi in un muso duro

Tartarus ['tɑrtərəs] *s* Tartaro

task [tæsk] or [tɑsk] *s* compito, incarico; **to take to task** rimproverare

task' force' *s* gruppo formato per una missione speciale

task'mas'ter *s* sorvegliante *m*; sorvegliante severo

tassel ['tæsəl] *s* nappa; (bot) ciuffo

taste [test] *s* gusto, sapore *m*; buon gusto; (*sampling, e.g., of wine*) assaggio; esperienza; **to one's taste** a genio di qlcu ‖ *tr* gustare, assaggiare ‖ *intr* sentire, sapere; **to taste of** degustare; sapere di

tasteless ['testlɪs] *adj* insipido; di cattivo gusto

tast·y ['testi] *adj* (-ier; -iest) saporito; (coll) di buon gusto

tatter ['tætər] *s* brandello, sbrendolo ‖ *tr* sbrindellare

tattered ['tætərd] *adj* sbrindellato

tattle ['tætəl] *s* chiacchiera; (*gossip*) pettegolezzo ‖ *intr* chiacchierare; spettegolare

tat'tle·tale *adj* rivelatore ‖ *s* gazzetta, chiacchierone *m*

tattoo [tæ'tu] *s* tatuaggio; (mil) ritirata ‖ *tr* tatuare

taunt [tɔnt] or [tɑnt] *s* rimprovero sarcastico, insulto ‖ *tr* rimproverare sarcasticamente, insultare

Taurus ['tɔrəs] *s* (astr) Toro

taut [tɔt] *adj* teso, tirato

tavern ['tævərn] *s* osteria

taw·dry ['tɔdri] *adj* (-drier; -driest) vistoso, sgargiante, pacchiano

taw·ny ['tɔni] *adj* (-nier; -niest) falbo, fulvo

tax [tæks] *s* tassa, imposta ‖ *tr* tassare; (*s.o.'s patience*) mettere a dura prova

taxable ['tæksəbəl] *adj* tassabile

tax'able in'come *s* imponibile *m*

taxation [tæk'seʃən] *s* imposizione, tassazione, contribuzione

tax' collec'tor *s* esattore *m* delle imposte

tax' deduc'tion *s* detrazione

tax'-ex·empt' *adj* esente da tasse

tax' evad'er [ɪ'vedər] *s* evasore *m*

tax·i ['tæksi] *s* (-is) tassì *m* ‖ *v* (*pret* & *pp* -ied; *ger* -iing or -ying) *tr* far rullare ‖ *intr* andare in tassì; (aer) rullare

tax'i·cab' *s* tassì *m*

tax'i driv'er *s* tassista *m*

tax'i·plane' *s* aeroplano da noleggio, aerotassì *m*

taxi' stand' *s* posteggio di tassì

tax'pay'er *s* contribuente *mf*

tax' rate' *s* imponibilità *f*

tea [ti] *s* tè *m*; (*medicinal infusion*) tisana; (*beef broth*) brodo di carne

tea' bag' *s* sacchetto di tè

tea' ball' *s* uovo da tè

tea'cart' *s* servitore *m*

teach [titʃ] *v* (*pret* & *pp* taught [tɔt]) *tr* & *intr* insegnare

teacher ['titʃər] *s* maestro, insegnante *mf*

teach'ers col'lege *s* scuola magistrale

teach'er's pet' *s* beniamino del maestro

teaching ['titʃɪŋ] *adj* insegnante ‖ *s* insegnamento, dottrina

teach'ing aids' *spl* sussidi *mpl* didattici

teach'ing staff' *s* corpo insegnante

tea'cup' *s* tazza da tè

tea' dance' *s* tè *m* danzante

teak [tik] *s* tek *m*

tea'ket'tle *s* bricco del tè

team [tim] *s* (*e.g., of horses*) pariglia; (sports) squadra, equipaggio ‖ *tr* apparigliare; tirare or trasportare con pariglia ‖ *intr*—**to team up** unirsi, associarsi

team'mate' *s* compagno di squadra

teamster ['timstər] *s* (*of horses*) carrettiere *m*; (*of truck*) camionista *m*, autotrenista *m*

team'work' *s* affiatamento, collaborazione

tea'pot' *s* teiera

tear [tɪr] *s* lacrima; **to hold back one's tears** ingoiare le lacrime; **to laugh away one's tears** cambiare dal pianto al riso ‖ [ter] *s* strappo ‖ [ter] *v* (*pret* tore [tor]; *pp* torn [torn]) *tr* strappare; stracciare; (*one's heart*) squarciare; (*to wound*) sbranare; (*one's hair*) strapparsi; **to tear apart** rompere in due; separare; **to tear down** demolire; (*a piece of equipment*) smontare; **to tear off** staccare; **to tear to pieces** dilaniare; fare a pezzi; **to tear up** (*a piece of paper*) stracciare; (*a street*) scavare ‖ *intr* strapparsi, stracciarsi; **to tear along** precipitarsi; correre all'impazzata

tear' bomb' [tɪr] *s* bomba lacrimogena

tearful ['tɪrfəl] *adj* lacrimoso

tear' gas' [tɪr] *s* gas lacrimogeno

tear-jerker ['tɪr ˌdʒɑrkər] *s* (coll) storia lacrimogena

tear-off ['ter ˌɔf] *adj* da staccarsi, perforato

tea'room' *s* sala da tè

tear' sheet' [ter] *s* copia di annuncio pubblicitario

tease [tiz] *tr* stuzzicare, molestare;

(*hair*) accotonare; (*e.g.,* *wool*) cardare

ten'spoon' *s* cucchiaino

teaspoonful ['ti ,spun ,ful] *s* cucchiaino

teat [tit] *s* capezzolo

tea'time' *s* l'ora del tè

tea' wag'on *s* servitore *m*

technical ['teknɪkəl] *adj* tecnico

technicali·ty [,teknɪ'kælɪti] *s* (**-ties**) tecnicismo; dettaglio tecnico

technician [tek'nɪʃən] *s* tecnico

technics ['teknɪks] *ssg* or *spl* tecnica

technique [tek'nik] *s* tecnica

ted'dy bear' ['tedi] *s* orsacchiotto

tedious ['tidɪ·əs] or ['tidʒəs] *adj* tedioso, noioso

tee [ti] *adj* fatto a T || *s* giunto a tre vie; (*golf*) piazzola di partenza || *tr*—**to tee off** (slang) cominciare || *intr*—**to be teed off** (slang) essere arrabiato; **to tee off** (golf) colpire la palla dalla piazzola di partenza; **to tee off on** (slang) rimproverare severamente

teem [tim] *intr* brulicare; piovere a dirotto; **to teem with** abbondare di

teeming ['timɪŋ] *adj* brulicante; (*rain*) torrenziale

teen-ager ['tin ,edʒər] *s* giovane *mf* dai 13 ai 19 anni

teens [tinz] *spl* numeri inglesi che finiscono in **-teen** (dal 13 al 19); **to be in one's teens** avere dai 13 ai 19 anni

tee·ny ['tini] *adj* (**-nier; -niest**) (coll) piccolo, piccolissimo

teeter ['titər] *s* altalena, dondolio || *intr* dondolarsi, oscillare

teethe [tið] *intr* mettere i denti

teething ['tiðɪŋ] *s* dentizione

teeth'ing ring' *s* dentaruolo

teetotaler [ti'totələr] *s* astemio

tele-cast ['telɪ ,kæst] or ['telɪ ,kɑst] *s* teletrasmissione || *v* (*pret & pp* **-cast** or **-casted**) *tr & intr* teletrasmettere

telegram ['telɪ ,græm] *s* telegramma *m*

telegraph ['telɪ ,græf] or ['telɪ ,grɑf] *s* telegrafo || *tr & intr* telegrafare

tel'egraph pole' *s* palo del telegrafo

Telemachus [tɪ'leməkəs] *s* Telemaco

telemeter [tɪ'lemɪtər] *s* telemetro || *tr* misurare col telemetro

telepathy [tɪ'lepəθi] *s* telepatia

telephone ['telɪ ,fon] *s* telefono || *tr & intr* telefonare

tel'ephone book' *s* elenco or guida dei telefoni

tel'ephone booth' *s* cabina telefonica

tel'ephone call' *s* chiamata telefonica, colpo di telefono

tel'ephone direc'tory *s* elenco or guida dei telefoni

tel'ephone exchange' *s* centrale telefonica

tel'ephone op'erator *s* centralinista *mf*, telefonista *mf*

tel'ephone receiv'er *s* ricevitore *m*

tel'ephoto lens' ['telɪ ,foto] *s* teleobbiettivo

teleplay ['telɪ ,ple] *s* teledramma *m*

teleprinter ['telɪ ,prɪntər] *s* telescrivente *f*

telescope ['telɪ ,skop] *s* telescopio || *tr*

snodare; condensare || *intr* essere snodabile; (*in a collision*) incastrarsi

teletype ['telɪ ,taɪp] *s* telescrivente *f* || *tr & intr* trasmettere per telescrivente

teleview ['telɪ ,vju] *tr* telericevere

televiewer ['telɪ ,vju·ər] *s* telespettatore *m*

televise ['telɪ ,vaɪz] *tr* teletrasmettere

television ['telɪ ,vɪʒən] *adj* televisivo || *s* televisione

tel'evision screen' *s* teleschermo

tel'evision set' *s* televisore *m*

tell [tel] *v* (*pret & pp* **told** [told]) *tr* dire; (*to narrate*) raccontare; (*to count*) contare; distinguere; **I told you so!** te l'avevo detto!; **to tell off** (coll) dire il fatto suo a || *intr* dire; prevedere; avere effetto; **to tell on** (*s.o.'s health*) pesare a, e.g., **age was telling on his health** l'età pesava alla sua salute; (coll) denunciare

teller ['telər] *s* narratore *m*; (*of bank*) cassiere *m*; (*of votes*) scrutatore *m*

temper ['tempər] *s* indole *f*, temperamento; umore *m*; calma; (metallurgy) tempra; **to keep one's temper** mantenersi calmo; **to lose one's temper** perdere la pazienza || *tr* temprare || *intr* temprarsi

temperament ['tempərəmənt] *s* indole *f*, temperamento, carattere *m*

temperamental [,tempərə'mentəl] *adj* emotivo, capriccioso

temperance ['tempərəns] *s* (*self-restraint in action*) temperanza; (*abstinence from alcoholic beverages*) sobrietà *f*

temperate ['tempərɪt] *adj* temperato

temperature ['tempərətʃər] *s* temperatura

tempest ['tempɪst] *s* tempesta; **tempest in a teapot** tempesta in un bicchier d'acqua

tempestuous [tem'pestʃu·əs] *adj* tempestoso

temple ['tempəl] *s* (*place of worship*) tempio; (*of spectacles*) susta, stanghetta; (anat) tempia

tem·po ['tempo] *s* (**-pos** or **-pi** [pi]) (mus) tempo; (fig) ritmo

temporal ['tempərəl] *adj* temporale

temporary ['tempə ,reri] *adj* temporaneo, provvisorio, transitorio, interino

temporize ['tempə ,raɪz] *intr* temporeggiare

tempt [tempt] *tr* tentare

temptation [temp'teʃən] *s* tentazione

tempter ['temptər] *s* tentatore *m*

tempting ['temptɪŋ] *adj* tentatore

ten [ten] *adj & pron* dieci || *s* dieci *m*; **ten o'clock** le dieci

tenable ['tenəbəl] *adj* difendibile

tenacious [tɪ'neʃəs] *adj* tenace

tenant ['tenənt] *s* inquilino, pigionante *mf*; (*of land*) fittavolo

tend [tend] *tr* riguardare, governare; accudire (with *dat*), e.g., **he tends the fire** accudisce al fuoco || *intr* tendere; **to tend to** propendere verso; (*e.g., one's own business*) attendere a; **to tend to** + *inf* tendere a + *inf*

tenden·cy ['tendənsi] *s* (**-cies**) tendenza, propensione

tender ['tɛndər] *adj* tenero; sensibile, dolorante || *s* offerta; (naut) nave *f* rifornimento; (naut) lancia; (rr) carboniera || *tr* offrire

tender-hearted ['tɛndər ‚hɑrtɪd] *adj* dal cuore tenero

ten'der·loin' *s* filetto || **Tenderloin** *s* rione *m* della mala vita

tenderness ['tɛndərnɪs] *s* tenerezza

tendon ['tɛndən] *s* tendine *m*

tendril ['tɛndrɪl] *s* viticcio

tenement ['tɛnɪmənt] *s* appartamento; casa; casamento

ten'ement house' *s* casamento

tenet ['tɛnɪt] *s* dogma *m*, dottrina

tennis ['tɛnɪs] *s* tennis *m*

ten'nis court' *s* campo da tennis

ten'nis play'er *s* tennista *mf*

tenor ['tɛnər] *s* tenore *m*

tense [tɛns] *adj* teso || *s* (gram) tempo

tension ['tɛnʃən] *s* tensione

tent [tɛnt] *s* tenda; (*of circus*) tendone *m*

tentacle ['tɛntəkəl] *s* tentacolo

tentative ['tɛntətɪv] *adj* a titolo di prova; (*smile*) esile

tenth [tɛnθ] *adj*, *s* & *pron* decimo || *s* (in dates) dieci *m*

tenuous ['tɛnjuǝs] *adj* tenue

tenure ['tɛnjər] *s* (in office) rafferma; (permanency of employment) inamovibilità *f*; (law) possesso

tepid ['tɛpɪd] *adj* tiepido

tercet ['tʌrsɪt] *s* terzina

term [tʌrm] *s* vocabolo, voce *f*; periodo, durata; termine *m*; (com) scadenza; **terms** condizioni *fpl*; **to be on good terms** essere in buone relazioni; **to come to terms** venire a patti || *tr* chiamare, definire

termagant ['tʌrməgənt] *s* megera

terminal ['tʌrmɪnəl] *adj* terminale || *s* (end or extremity) terminale *m*; (elec) morsetto; (rr) capolinea *m*

terminate ['tʌrmɪ‚nɛt] *tr* & *intr* terminare

terminus ['tʌrmɪnəs] *s* termine *m*, fine *m*; (rr) capolinea *m*

termite ['tʌrmaɪt] *s* termite *f*

terrace ['tɛrəs] *s* terrazza, terrazzo; (agr) gradino, scaglione *m*

terra firma ['tɛrə 'fʌrmə] *s* terra ferma

terrain [tɛ'rɛn] *s* terreno

terrestrial [tə'rɛstrɪ·əl] *adj* terrestre

terrific [tə'rɪfɪk] *adj* terrificante; (coll) tremendo

terri·fy ['tɛrɪ‚faɪ] *v* (pret & pp **-fied**) *tr* terrificare, inorridire

territo·ry ['tɛrɪ‚tori] *s* (**-ries**) territorio

terror ['tɛrər] *s* terrore *m*

terrorize ['tɛrə‚raɪz] *tr* terrorizzare; dominare col terrore

ter'ry cloth' ['tɛri] *s* tessuto a spugna

terse [tʌrs] *adj* conciso, terso

tertiary ['tʌrʃɪ‚ɛri] or ['tʌrʃəri] *adj* terziario

test [tɛst] *s* prova, saggio; esame *m* || *tr* provare, saggiare; esaminare; (e.g., a machine) collaudare

testament ['tɛstəmənt] *s* testamento || **Testament** *s* Testamento Nuovo

test' ban' *s* interdizione degli esperimenti nucleari

test' flight' *s* volo di prova

testicle ['tɛstɪkəl] *s* testicolo

testi·fy ['tɛstɪ‚faɪ] *v* (pret & pp **-fied**) *tr* & *intr* testimoniare

testimonial [‚tɛstɪ'moni·əl] *s* (certificate) benservito, referenza; (expression of esteem) segno di gratitudine

testimo·ny ['tɛstɪ‚moni] *s* (**-nies**) testimonianza

test' pat'tern *s* (telv) monoscopio

test' pi'lot *s* pilota *m* collaudatore

test' tube' *s* provetta

tetanus ['tɛtənəs] *s* tetano

tether ['tɛðər] *s* cavezza, pastoia; **at the end of one's tether** al limite delle proprie risorse || *tr* legare; incavezzare, impastoiare

tetter ['tɛtər] *s* eczema *m*, impetigine *f*

text [tɛkst] *s* testo; tema *m*

text'book' *s* libro di testo

textile ['tɛkstɪl] or ['tɛkstaɪl] *adj* & *s* tessile *m*

textual ['tɛkstʃʊ·əl] *adj* testuale

texture ['tɛkstʃər] *s* (of cloth) trama; caratteristica, proprietà *f*

Thai ['tɑ·i] or ['taɪ] *adj* & *s* tailandese *mf*

Thailand ['taɪlənd] *s* la Tailandia

Thames [tɛmz] *s* Tamigi *m*

than [ðæn] *conj* di, e.g., **he is faster than you** è più veloce di te; (before a verb) di quanto, e.g., **he is smarter than I thought** è più intelligente di quanto pensavo; che, e.g., **he had barely begun to eat than it was time to leave** non aveva appena cominciato a mangiare che era ora di andarsene

thank [θæŋk] *s*—**thanks** ringraziamenti *mpl*; **thanks to** grazie a, in grazie di || *tr* ringraziare || **thanks** *interj* grazie!

thankful ['θæŋkfəl] *adj* grato

thankless ['θæŋklɪs] *adj* ingrato

Thanksgiv'ing Day' [‚θæŋks'gɪvɪŋ] *s* giorno del Ringraziamento

that [ðæt] *adj* *dem* (**those**) quel; codesto; **that one** quello, quello là || *pron dem* (**those**) quello; codesto || *pron rel* che, quello che, il quale; **that is** cioè; **that's that** (coll) ecco fatto, ecco tutto || *adv* (coll) tanto, così; **that far** così lontano; **that many** tanti; **that much** tanto || *conj* che

thatch [θætʃ] *s* paglia, copertura di paglia; (hair) capigliatura || *tr* coprire di paglia

thaw [θɔ] *s* sgelo || *tr* sgelare || *intr* sgelarsi

the [ðə], [ðɪ], or [ði] *art def* il; al, e.g., **one dollar the dozen** un dollaro alla dozzina || *adv*—**so much the worse for him** tanto peggio per lui; **the more . . . the more** quanto più . . . tanto più

theater ['θi·ətər] *s* teatro

the'ater·go'er *s* frequentatore *m* abituale del teatro

the'ater news' *s* cronaca teatrale

theatrical [θɪ'ætrɪkəl] *adj* teatrale

Thebes [θibz] *s* Tebe *f*

thee [ði] *pron pers* (Bib; poet) ti; te

theft [θɛft] *s* furto, ruberia

their [ðer] *adj poss* il loro, loro

theirs [ðerz] *pron poss* il loro

them [ðem] *pron pers* li; loro; **to them** loro

theme [θim] *s* tema *m*, soggetto; saggio; (mus) tema *m*

theme' song' *s* (mus) tema *m* centrale; (rad) sigla musicale

them-selves' *pron pers* essi stessi, loro stessi; si, e.g., **they enjoyed themselves** si divertirono

then [ðen] *adj* allora, di allora ‖ *s* quel tempo; **by then** a quell'epoca; **from then on** da quel giorno in poi ‖ *adv* allora; indi, poi; **then and there** a quel momento

thence [ðens] *adv* indi, quindi; da lì; da allora in poi

thence'forth' *adv* da allora in poi

theolo·gy [θi'alədʒi] *s* (-gies) teologia

theorem ['θi·ərəm] *s* teorema *m*

theoretical [,θi·ə'retɪkəl] *adj* teoretico

theo·ry ['θi·əri] *s* (-ries) teoria

therapeutic [,θerə'pjutɪk] *adj* terapeutico ‖ **therapeutics** *ssg* terapeutica

thera·py ['θerəpi] *s* (-pies) terapia

there [ðer] *adv* lì, là; there are ci sono; **there is** c'è; ecco, e.g., **there it is** eccolo

there'abouts' *adv* circa, approssimativamente, giù di lì

there'af'ter *adv* in seguito, dipoi

there'by' *adv* quindi, perciò, così

therefore ['ðerfor] *adv* per questo, quindi, dunque

**there'in' *adv* lì; in quel rispetto

there'of' *adv* di ciò, da ciò

Theresa [tə'risə] *or* [tə'resə] *s* Teresa

there'upon' *adv* su questo; a quel momento; come conseguenza

thermal ['θʌrməl] *adj* (water) termale; (capacity) termico

thermistor [θər'mɪstər] *s* (elec) termistore *m*

thermocouple ['θʌrmo,kʌpəl] *s* termocoppia

thermodynamic [,θʌrmodaɪ'næmɪk] *adj* termodinamico ‖ **thermodynamics** *ssg* termodinamica

thermometer [θər'mamɪtər] *s* termometro

thermonuclear [,θʌrmo'njuklɪ·ər] *or* [,θʌrmo'nuklɪ·ər] *adj* termonucleare

ther'mos bot'tle ['θʌrməs] *s* termos *m*

thermostat ['θʌrmə,stæt] *s* termostato

thesau·rus [θɪ'sɔrəs] *s* (-ri [raɪ] *or* -ruses) tesoro, lessico, compendio

these [ðiz] *pl of* **this**

the·sis ['θisɪs] *s* (-ses [siz]) tesi *f*

Thespis ['θespɪs] *s* Tespi *m*

they [ðe] *pron pers* essi, loro

thick [θɪk] *adj* spesso, grosso; folto, denso; pieno, coperto; viscoso; stupido; (coll) intimo ‖ *s* spessore *m*; **in the thick of** nel folto di; **through thick and thin** nei tempi buoni e cattivi

thicken ['θɪkən] *tr* inspessire; ingrossare; infoltire ‖ *intr* inspessirsi; ingrossarsi; (said of a plot) complicarsi

thicket ['θɪkɪt] *s* boscaglia, macchia

thick-headed ['θɪk,hedɪd] *adj* indietro, stupido

thick'set' *adj* tarchiato; (hedge) fitto, denso

thief [θif] *s* (thieves [θivz]) ladro

thieve [θiv] *intr* rubare

thiever·y ['θivəri] *s* (-ies) furto

thigh [θaɪ] *s* coscia

thigh'bone' *s* femore *m*

thimble ['θɪmbəl] *s* ditale *m*

thin [θɪn] *adj* (thinner; thinnest) (paper, ice) sottile; (lean) magro, smilzo; (e.g., hair) rado; (air) fine; (excuse) tenue; (voice) esile; (wine) leggero, annacquato ‖ *v* (pret & pp thinned; ger thinning) *tr* assottigliare; (paint) diluire ‖ *intr* assottigliarsi; **to thin out** (said of a crowd) diradarsi

thine [ðaɪn] *adj* & *pron poss* (Bib & poet) tuo, il tuo

thing [θɪŋ] *s* cosa; **not to get a thing out of** non riuscire a capire; non cavare un briciolo d'informazione da; **of all things!** che cosa!; che sorpresa!; **the thing** l'ultima moda; **things** roba; **to see things** avere allucinazioni

think [θɪŋk] *v* (pret & pp thought [θɔt]) *tr* pensare; credere; **to think it over** ripensarci; **to think nothing of** it non darci la minima importanza; **to think of** (to have as an opinion of) pensare di, e.g., **what do you think of that doctor?** cosa ne pensa di quel medico?; **to think out** decifrare; **to think up** immaginare ‖ *intr* pensare; **to think not** credere di no; **to think of** (to turn one's thoughts to) pensare a, e.g., **he is thinking of the future** pensa al futuro; (to imagine) immaginare; **to think so** credere di sì; **to think well of** avere una buona opinione di

thinkable ['θɪŋkəbəl] *adj* pensabile

thinker ['θɪŋkər] *s* pensatore *m*

third [θʌrd] *adj*, *s* & *pron* terzo ‖ *s* terzo; (in dates) tre *m*; (aut) terza

third' degree' *s* interrogatorio di terzo grado

third' rail' *s* (rr) rotaia elettrificata di contatto

third'-rate' *adj* di terz'ordine

Third' World' *s* Terzo Mondo

thirst [θʌrst] *s* sete *f* ‖ *intr* aver sete; **to thirst for** aver sete di

thirst·y ['θʌrsti] *adj* (-ier; -iest) assetato, sitibondo; **to be thirsty** avere sete

thirteen ['θʌr'tin] *adj*, *s* & *pron* tredici *m*

thirteenth ['θʌr'tinθ] *adj*, *s* & *pron* tredicesimo ‖ *s* (in dates) tredici *m*

thirtieth ['θʌrtɪ·ɪθ] *adj*, *s* & *pron* trentesimo ‖ *s* (in dates) trenta *m*

thir·ty ['θʌrti] *adj*, *s* & *pron* trenta ‖ *s* (-ties) trenta *m;* **the thirties** gli anni trenta

this [ðɪs] *adj dem* (these) questo; **this one** questo, questo qui ‖ *pron dem* (these) questo, questo qui ‖ *adv* (coll) tanto, così

thistle ['θɪsəl] *s* cardo

thither ['θɪðər] *or* ['ðɪðər] *adv* là, da quella parte

Thomas ['tɑməs] s Tommaso

thong [θɔŋ] or [θɑŋ] s coreggia

thorax ['θɔræks] s (-raxes or -races [rə,siz]) torace m

thorn [θɔrn] s spina

thorn·y ['θɔrni] adj (-ier; -iest) spinoso

thorough ['θʌro] adj completo, esauriente

thor'ough·bred' adj di razza; (horse) purosangue ‖ s individuo di razza; (horse) purosangue mf

thor'ough·fare' s passaggio; **no thoroughfare** divieto di passaggio

thor'ough·go'ing adj completo, esauriente

thoroughly ['θʌroli] adv a fondo

those [ðoz] pl of **that**

thou [ðaʊ] pron pers (Bib; poet) tu ‖ tr dare del tu a

though [ðo] adv tuttavia ‖ conj malgrado, sebbene; **as though** come se

thought [θɔt] s pensiero; **perish the thought!** (coll) nemmeno a pensarci!

thoughtful ['θɔtfəl] adj pensieroso, riflessivo; (considerate) sollecito

thoughtless ['θɔtlɪs] adj irriflessivo; sconsiderato; (reckless) incurante

thought' transfer'ence s trasmissione del pensiero

thousand ['θaʊzənd] adj, s & pron mille m; **a thousand or one thousand** mille m

thousandth ['θaʊzəndθ] adj, s & pron millesimo

thralldom ['θrɔldəm] s schiavitù f

thrash [θræʃ] tr battere; (agr) trebbiare; **to thrash out** discutere a fondo ‖ intr agitarsi, dibattersi

thread [θrɛd] s filo; (mach) filetto, verme m; **to lose the thread of** perdere il filo di ‖ tr infilare; (fig) pervadere; (mach) filettare, impanare; **to thread one's way through** aprirsi il passaggio attraverso

thread'bare' adj frusto, logoro

threat [θrɛt] s minaccia

threaten ['θrɛtən] tr & intr minacciare

threatening ['θrɛtənɪŋ] adj minaccioso; (e.g., letter) minatorio

three [θri] adj & pron tre ‖ s tre m; **three o'clock** le tre

three'-cor'nered adj triangolare; (hat) a tre punte

three' hun'dred adj, s & pron trecento

threepenny ['θrɛpəni] or ['θrɪpəni] adj del valore di tre penny; di nessun valore

three'-phase' adj trifase

three'-ply' adj a tre spessori

three' R's' [ɑrz] spl lettura, scrittura e aritmetica

three'score' adj sessanta

three' thou'sand adj, s & pron tre mila mpl

threno·dy ['θrɛnədi] s (-dies) trenodia

thresh [θrɛʃ] tr (agr) trebbiare; **to thresh out** discutere a fondo ‖ intr trebbiare; battere

thresh'ing machine' s trebbiatrice f

threshold ['θrɛʃold] s soglia

thrice [θraɪs] adv tre volte; molto

thrift [θrɪft] s economia

thrift·y ['θrɪfti] adj (-ier; -iest) eco-

nomo, economico; vigoroso; prospero

thrill [θrɪl] s fremito d'emozione; esperienza emozionante ‖ tr emozionare ‖ intr emozionarsi; vibrare

thriller ['θrɪlər] s (coll) thrilling m

thrilling ['θrɪlɪŋ] adj emozionante, thrilling

thrive [θraɪv] v (pret **thrived** or **throve** [θrov]; pp **thrived** or **thriven** ['θrɪvən]) intr prosperare, fiorire

throat [θrot] s gola; **to clear one's throat** schiarirsi la voce

throb [θrɑb] s battito, palpito, tuffo ‖ v (pret & pp **throbbed**; ger **throbbing**) intr palpitare, pulsare

throe [θro] s agonia, travaglio, spasimo; **in the throes of** nel travaglio di; (e.g., battle) nel momento più penoso di

throne [θron] s trono

throng [θrɔŋ] or [θrɑŋ] s folla, stuolo ‖ intr affollarsi

throttle ['θrɑtəl] s (of locomotive) leva di comando; (of motorcycle) manetta; (of car) acceleratore m; (mach) valvola di controllo ‖ tr soffocare; (mach) regolare

through [θru] adj diretto, senza fermate; **to be through** aver finito; **to be through with** farla finita con ‖ adv attraverso; da una parte all'altra; completamente; ‖ prep attraverso, per; durante; fino alla fine di; per mezzo di

through·out' adv completamente, da un capo all'altro; dappertutto ‖ prep durante tutto, e.g., **throughout the afternoon** durante tutto il pomeriggio; per tutto, e.g., **throughout the house** per tutta la casa

throw [θro] s getto, tiro, lancio; gettata; coperta leggera ‖ v (pret **threw** [θru]; pp **thrown**) tr gettare, tirare, lanciare; (a shadow) proiettare; (the current) connettere; (said of a horse) disarcionare; (wrestling) gettare a terra; (a game) (coll) perdere intenzionalmente; (coll) stupire; **to throw away** gettar via; perdere; **to throw back** rigettare; ritardare; **to throw in** (the clutch) innestare; (coll) aggiungere; **to throw oneself into** darsi a; **to throw out** sbatter fuori; (the clutch) disinnestare; **to throw over** abbandonare ‖ intr gettare, tirare, lanciare; **to throw up** vomitare

thrum [θrʌm] v (pret & pp **thrummed**; ger **thrumming**) intr tambureggiare; (mus) far scorrere la mano sulle corde di uno strumento

thrush [θrʌʃ] s tordo

thrust [θrʌst] s (push) spinta; botta; (with dagger) pugnalata; (with sword) stoccata ‖ v (pret & pp **thrust**) tr spingere; conficcare, configgere; **to thrust oneself** (e.g., into a conversation) ficcarsi

thru'way' s autostrada

thud [θʌd] s tonfo ‖ v (pret & pp **thudded**; ger **thudding**) intr fare un rumore sordo

thug [θʌg] s fascinoroso

thumb [θʌm] s pollice m; **all thumbs** maldestro, goffo; **thumbs down** pollice verso; **to twiddle one's thumbs** girare i pollici, essere ozioso; **under the thumb of** sotto l'influenza di ‖ tr sporcare con le dita; (a book) sfogliare; **to thumb a ride** chiedere l'autostop; **to thumb one's nose** (at) fare marameo (a)

thumb' in'dex s margine m a scaletta

thumb'nail' adj breve, conciso ‖ s unghia del pollice

thumb'screw' s vite f ad aletta

thumb'tack' s puntina

thump [θʌmp] s tonfo ‖ tr battere, percuotere ‖ intr battere; cadere con un tonfo; camminare a passi pesanti; (said of the heart) palpitare violentemente

thumping ['θʌmpɪŋ] adj (coll) straordinario, eccezionale; (coll) grande

thunder ['θʌndər] s tuono; (of applause) scroscio; (of a cannon) rombo ‖ tr lanciare ‖ intr tonare, rombare; (fig) scrosciare

thun'der·bolt' s folgore f, fulmine m

thun'der·clap' s scroscio di tuono

thunderous ['θʌndərəs] adj fragoroso

thun'der·show'er s acquazzone m accompagnato da tuoni

thun'der·storm' s temporale m

thun'der·struck' adj attonito

Thursday ['θʌrzdɪ] s giovedì m

thus [ðʌs] adv così; **thus far** sino qui

thwack [θwæk] s colpo ‖ tr colpire

thwart [θwɔrt] adj obliquo ‖ adv di traverso ‖ tr contrariare, sventare

thy [ðaɪ] adj poss (Bib; poet) tuo, il tuo

thyme [taɪm] s timo

thy'roid gland' ['θaɪrɔɪd] s tiroide f

thyself [ðaɪ'self] pron (Bib; poet) te stesso; te, ti

tiara [taɪ'ærə] or [taɪ'ɛrə] s (female adornment) diadema m; (eccl) tiara

tick [tɪk] s (of pillow) fodera; (of mattress) guscio; (of clock) ticchettio; (dot) punto; (ent) zecca; **on tick** (coll) a credito ‖ intr fare ticchettio; **to make s.o. tick** mandare avanti qlcu

ticker ['tɪkər] s telescrivente f; (slang) orologio; (slang) cuore m

tick'er tape' s nastro della telescrivente

ticket ['tɪkɪt] s biglietto; (e.g., of pawnbroker) polizza; (slip of paper or identifying tag) bolletta, bollettino; (summons) verbale m; (e.g., to indicate price) etichetta; lista dei candidati; **that's the ticket** (coll) questo è quello che fa

tick'et a'gent s bigliettaio

tick'et of'fice s biglietteria

tick'et scalp'er ['skælpər] s bagarino

tick'et win'dow s sportello

ticking ['tɪkɪŋ] s traliccio

tickle ['tɪkəl] s solletico ‖ tr solleticare; divertire ‖ intr avere il solletico

ticklish ['tɪklɪʃ] adj sensibile al solletico; delicato; permaloso; **to be ticklish** soffrire il solletico

tick-tock ['tɪk ,tɑk] s tic tac m

tid'al wave' ['taɪdəl] s onda di marea; (fig) ondata

tidbit ['tɪd ,bɪt] s bocconcino

tiddlywinks ['tɪdlɪ ,wɪŋks] s gioco della pulce

tide [taɪd] s marea; **to go against the tide** andare contro la corrente; **to stem the tide** fermare la corrente ‖ tr portare sulla cresta delle onde; **to tide over** aiutare; (a difficulty) sormontare

tide'wa'ter s marea; costa marina

tidings ['taɪdɪŋz] spl notizie fpl

ti·dy ['taɪdɪ] adj (-dier; -diest) pulito, ordinato ‖ s (-dies) cofanetto, astuccio; appoggiacapo ‖ v (pret & pp -died) tr rassettare, mettere in ordine ‖ intr rassettarsi

tie [taɪ] s laccio, nodo, vincolo; (in games) patta; (necktie) cravatta; (archit) traversa; (rr) traversina; (mus) legatura ‖ v (pret & pp tied; ger tying) tr allacciare, annodare; legare; confinare; (a game) impattare; (a person) impattarla con; **to be tied up** essere occupato; **to tie down** confinare, limitare; **to tie up** legare; impedire; (e.g., traffic) intasare ‖ intr allacciare; (in games) impattare

tie' beam' s catena

tie'pin' s spilla da cravatta

tier [tɪr] s gradinata; ordine m, livello

tiff [tɪf] s screzio, litigio

tiger ['taɪgər] s tigre f

ti'ger lil'y s giglio cinese

tight [taɪt] adj teso; stretto; compatto; impermeabile, ermetico; pieno; (game) (coll) serrato; (coll) tirato; (slang) ubriaco ‖ tights spl calzamaglia ‖ adv strettamente, **to hold tight** tenere stretto

tighten ['taɪtən] tr (e.g., one's belt) tirare; (e.g., a screw) stringere ‖ intr tirarsi; stringersi

tight-fisted ['taɪt'fɪstɪd] adj taccagno

tight'-fit'ting adj attillato

tight'rope' s corda tesa

tight' squeeze' s—to be in a tight squeeze (coll) essere alle strette

tight'wad' s (coll) spilorcio

tigress ['taɪgrɪs] s tigre femmina

tile [taɪl] s mattonella; (for floor) piastrella; (for roof) tegola, coppo ‖ tr coprire di mattonelle; coprire di piastrelle; coprire di coppi

tile' roof' s tetto di tegole

till [tɪl] s cassetto dei soldi ‖ prep fino a ‖ conj fino a che . . . non, fino a che, sinché . . . non, sinché ‖ tr lavorare, coltivare

tilt [tɪlt] s inclinazione; giostra, torneo; **full tilt** di gran carriera; a tutta forza ‖ tr inclinare; (a lance) mettere in resta; attaccare ‖ intr inclinarsi; giostrare; **to tilt at** combattere con

timber ['tɪmbər] s legno, legname m da costruzione; alberi mpl; (fig) tempra

tim'ber·land' s bosco destinato a produrre legname

tim'ber line' s linea della vegetazione

timbre ['tɪmbər] s (phonet & phys) timbro

time [taɪm] s tempo; ora, e.g., what time is it? che ora è?; volta, e.g., three times tre volte; giorni mpl, e.g., in our time ai giorni nostri; momento; ultima ora; ore fpl lavorative; periodo, e.g., Xmas time periodo natalizio; for a long time da lungo; for the time being per ora, per il momento; in time presto; col tempo; on time a tempo; a rate; (said, e.g., of a bus) in orario; times volte, e.g., seven times seven sette volte sette; to bide one's time aspettare l'ora propizia; to do time (coll) essere in prigione; to have a good time divertirsi; to have no time for non poter sopportare; to lose time (said of a watch) ritardare; to make time avanzare rapidamente; guadagnare terreno; to pass the time of day fare una chiacchierata; salutarsi; to take one's time fare le cose senza fretta; to tell time leggere l'orologio || tr fissare il momento di; calcolare il tempo di; (sports) cronometrare

time' bomb' s bomba a orologeria
time'card' s cartellino di presenza
time' clock' s orologio di controllo (delle presenze)
time' expo'sure s (phot) posa
time' fuse' s spoletta a tempo
time'keep'er s marcatempo; orologio; (sports) cronometrista mf
timeless ['taɪmlɪs] adj senza fine, eterno
time•ly ['taɪmli] adj (-lier; -liest) opportuno, tempestivo
time'piece' s orologio; cronometro
time' sig'nal s segnale orario
time'ta'ble s orario; tabella di marcia
time'work' s lavoro a ore
time'worn' adj logorato dal tempo
time' zone' s fuso orario
timid ['tɪmɪd] adj timido, pavido
tim'ing gears' ['taɪmɪŋ] spl ingranaggi mpl di distribuzione
timorous ['tɪmərəs] adj timoroso
tin [tɪn] s (element) stagno; (tin plate; can) latta || v (pret & pp tinned; ger tinning) tr stagnare
tin' can' s latta
tincture ['tɪŋktʃər] s tintura
tin' cup' s tazzina metallica
tinder ['tɪndər] s esca
tin'der-box' s cassetta con l'esca e l'acciarino; persona eccitabile; (fig) polveriera
tin' foil' s stagnola
ting-a-ling ['tɪŋə,lɪŋ] s dindìn m
tinge [tɪndʒ] s sfumatura; pizzico, punta || v (ger tingeing or tinging) tr sfumare; dare una traccia di sapore a
tingle ['tɪŋgəl] s formicolio, pizzicore m || intr informicolirsi, pizzicare; (said of the ears) ronzare; (with enthusiasm) fremere
tin' hat' s (slang) elmetto
tinker ['tɪŋkər] s calderaio, ramaio || intr armeggiare
tinkle ['tɪŋkəl] s tintinnio || tr far tintinnare || intr tintinnare

tin' plate' s latta
tin' roof' s tetto di lamiera di latta
tinsel ['tɪnsəl] s orpello, lustrino
tin'smith' s lattoniere m, stagnino
tin' sol'dier s soldatino di piombo
tint [tɪnt] s tinta, sfumatura || tr tinteggiare
tin'ware' s articoli mpl di latta
ti•ny ['taɪni] adj (-nier; -niest) piccino
tip [tɪp] s punta; (of mountain) vetta; (of umbrella) gorbia; (of shoe) mascherina; (of cigarette) bocchino; (of shoestring) aghetto; colpetto; (fee) mancia; informazione confidenziale; inclinazione || v (pret & pp tipped; ger tipping) tr mettere la punta a; inclinare, rovesciare; (one's hat) levarsi; dare la mancia a; toccare, battere; (the scales) far traboccare; to tip in (bb) inserire fuori testo; to tip off (coll) dare informazioni confidenziali a || intr inclinarsi; dare la mancia
tip'cart' s carro ribaltabile
tip'-off' s (coll) · avvertimento confidenziale
tipped'-in' adj (bb) fuori testo
tipple ['tɪpəl] intr sbevucchiare
tip'staff' s usciere m
tip•sy ['tɪpsi] adj (-sier; -siest) brillo
tip'toe' s punta di piedi || v (pret & pp -toed; ger -toeing) intr camminare in punta di piedi
tirade ['taɪred] s tirata
tire [taɪr] s gomma, pneumatico; (of metal) cerchione m || tr stancare || intr stancarsi; infastidirsi
tire' chain' s catena antineve
tired [taɪrd] adj stanco, stracco
tire' gauge' s manometro della pressione delle gomme
tireless ['taɪrlɪs] adj infaticabile
tire' pres'sure s pressione (delle gomme)
tire' pump' s pompa (per i pneumatici)
tiresome ['taɪrsəm] adj faticoso; (boring) noioso
tissue ['tɪsju] s tessuto; tessuto finissimo, velina
tis'sue pa'per s carta velina
titanium [tai'tenɪ·əm] or [tɪ'tenɪ·əm] s titanio
tithe [taɪð] s decima || tr imporre la decima su; pagare la decima di
Titian ['tɪʃən] adj tizianesco || s Tiziano
title ['taɪtəl] s titolo; (sports) campionato || tr intitolare
ti'tle deed' s titolo di proprietà
ti'tle-hold'er s campione m, primatista mf
ti'tle page' s frontespizio
ti'tle role' s (theat) ruolo principale
tit'mouse' s (-mice) (orn) cincia
titter ['tɪtər] s risatina || intr ridacchiare
titular ['tɪtʃələr] adj titolare
TNT ['ti,ɛn'ti] s (letterword) tritolo
to [tu], [tʊ] or [tə] adv—to and fro da una parte all'altra, avanti e indietro; to come to tornare in sè || prep a, e.g., he is going to Rome va a Roma; he gave a kiss to his mother

diede un bacio a sua madre; **she is learning to sew** impara a cucire; per, e.g., **he has been a true friend to me** è stato un vero amico per me; da, e.g., **there is still a lot of work to do** c'è ancora molto lavoro da fare; con, e.g., **she was very kind to me** è stata molto gentile con me; in, e.g., **we went to church** siamo andati in chiesa; fino a, e.g., **to see s.o. to the station** accompagnare qlcu fino alla stazione; in confronto di, e.g., **the accounts are nothing to what really happened** le storie non sono nulla, in confronto di quanto è realmente successo; meno, e.g., **ten minutes to seven** le sette meno dieci

toad [tod] s rospo
toad'stool' s agarico, fungo velenoso
to-and-fro [tu-ənd'fro] adj avanti e indietro
toast [tost] s pane tostato; (drink to s.o.'s health) brindisi m; **a piece of toast** una fetta di pane tostato ‖ tr tostare; brindare alla salute di ‖ intr tostarsi; brindare
toaster ['tostər] s (of bread) tostapane m; persona che fa un brindisi
toast'mas'ter s persona che annuncia i brindisi, maestro di cerimonie
tobac·co [tə'bæko] s (-cos) tabacco
tobacconist [tə'bækənɪst] s tabaccaio
tobac'co pouch' s borsa da tabacco
toboggan [tə'bagən] s toboga m
tocsin ['taksɪn] s campana a martello; scampanata d'allarme
today [tu'de] s & adv oggi m
toddle ['tadəl] s passo vacillante ‖ intr traballare, trotterellare
tod·dy ['tadi] s (-dies) ponce m
to-do [tə'du] s (-dos) (coll) daffare m, rumore m
toe [to] s dito del piede; (of shoe) punta ‖ v (pret & pp **toed;** ger **toeing**) tr—**to toe the line** filare diritto
toe'nail' s unghia del piede

together [tu'gɛðər] adv insieme; **to bring together** riunire; riconciliare; **to call together** chiamare a raccolta; **to stick together** (coll) rimanere uniti, stare insieme
togs [tagz] spl vestiti mpl
toil [tɔɪl] s travaglio, sfacchinata; **toils** reti fpl, lacci mpl ‖ intr travagliare, sfacchinare
toilet ['tɔɪlɪt] s toletta; gabinetto, ritirata; **to make one's toilet** farsi la toletta
toi'let pa'per s carta igienica
toi'let pow'der s polvere f di talco
toi'let soap' s sapone m da toletta
toi'let wa'ter s acqua da toletta
token ['tokən] s segno, marca; ricordo; (used as money) gettone m; **by the same token** per di più; **in token of** in segno di, come prova di
tolerance ['talərəns] s tolleranza
tolerate ['talə,ret] tr tollerare
toll [tol] s (of bell) rintocco; (e.g., for passage over bridge) pedaggio; (tax) dazio; (compensation for grinding grains) molenda; (number of victims) perdite fpl; (telp) tariffa interurbana ‖ tr (a bell) sonare a morto; (the faithful) chiamare a raccolta ‖ intr sonare a morto

toll' bridge' s ponte m a pedaggio
toll' call' s (telp) chiamata interurbana
toll'gate' s barriera di pedaggio; (in a turnpike) casello
toma·to [tə'meto] or [tə'mato] s (-toes) pomodoro
toma'to juice' s sugo di pomodoro
tomb [tum] s tomba
tomboy ['tam,bɔɪ] s maschietta
tomb'stone' s pietra tombale, lapide f
tomcat ['tam,kæt] s gatto maschio
tome [tom] s tomo
tomorrow [tu'maro] or [tu'mɔro] s domani m; **the day after tomorrow** dopodomani m ‖ adv domani
tom-tom ['tam,tam] s tam-tam m
ton [tʌn] s tonnellata; **tons** (coll) montagne fpl
tone [ton] s tono; (fig) tenore m ‖ tr intonare; **to tone down** (colors) smorzare; (sounds) sfumare ‖ intr intonarsi; **to tone down** moderarsi; **to tone up** rinforzarsi
tone' po'em s poema sinfonico
tongs [tɔŋz] or [taŋz] spl tenaglie fpl; (e.g., for sugar) molle fpl
tongue [tʌŋ] s (language) lingua; (of bell) battaglio; (of shoe) linguetta; (of wagon) timone m; (anat) lingua; (carp) maschio; **tongue in cheek** poco sinceramente; **to hold one's tongue** mordersi la lingua; **to speak with forked tongue** essere di due lingue
tongue' depres'sor s abbassalingua m
tongue'-lash'ing s sgridata
tongue' twist'er s scioglilingua m
tonic ['tanɪk] adj & s tonico
tonight [tu'naɪt] s questa sera, questa notte ‖ adv stasera; stanotte
tonnage ['tʌnɪdʒ] s tonnellaggio, stazza
tonsil ['tansəl] s tonsilla
ton·y ['toni] adj (-ier; -iest) (slang) elegante, di lusso
too [tu] adv (also) anche, pure; (more than enough) troppo; **too bad!** peccato!; **too many** troppi; **too much** troppo
tool [tul] s utensile m, attrezzo; (person) strumento; (of lathe) punta ‖ tr lavorare; (bb) decorare
tool' bag' s borsa degli attrezzi
tool'box' s cassetta attrezzi
tool'mak'er s attrezzista m
tool'shed' s barchessa
toot [tut] s (of horn) suono; (of locomotive) fischio; (of car's horn) colpo; (coll) gazzarra ‖ tr strombettare; **to toot one's own horn** strombazzare i propri meriti ‖ intr strombettare
tooth [tuθ] s (teeth [tiθ]) dente m
tooth'ache' s mal m di denti
tooth'brush' s spazzolino da denti
toothless ['tuθlɪs] adj sdentato
tooth'paste' s pasta dentifricia
tooth'pick' s stuzzicadenti m
tooth' pow'der s polvere dentifricia
top [tap] s cima, sommo, vertice m; (upper part of anything) disopra m;

(of mountain, tree) vetta; (of box) coperchio; (beginning) principio; (of bottle) imboccatura; (of a bridge) testata; (of wagon) mantice m; (of car) tetto; (of wall) coronamento; (toy) trottola; (naut) gabbia; **at the top of one's voice** a perdifiato; **from top to bottom** daccapo a piedi, dal principio alla fine; **on top of** in cima di; subito dopo; **the tops** (coll) il migliore, il fiore; **to blow one's top** (slang) dare in escandescenze; **to sleep like a top** dormire come un ghiro. ‖ v (pret & pp **topped**; ger **topping**) tr (a tree) svettare; coronare; superare

topaz ['topæz] s topazio

top' bil'ling s—**to get top billing** essere artista di cartello; (journ) ricevere il posto più importante

top' boot' s stivale m a tromba

top'coat' s soprabito di mezza stagione

toper ['topər] s ubriacone m

topgal'lant sail' [,tɑp'gælənt] s (naut) pappafico, veletta

top' hat' s cappello a staio or a cilindro

top'-heav'y adj troppo pesante in cima, sovraccarico in cima

topic ['tɑpɪk] s topica, tema m

top'knot' s crocchia

topless ['tɑplɪs] adj (mountain) di cui non si vede la vetta, eccelso; (bathing suit) topless

top'mast' s (naut) alberetto

top'most' adj il più alto

topogra•phy [tə'pɑgrəfi] s (-phies) topografia

topple ['tɑpəl] tr abbattere, rovesciare ‖ intr rovesciarsi, cadere

top' prior'ity s priorità massima

topsail ['tɑpsəl] or ['tɑp ,sel] s (naut) gabbia

top'-se'cret adj segretissimo

top'soil' s strato superiore del terreno

topsy-turvy ['tɑpsi'tʌrvi] adj rovesciato; confuso ‖ s soqquadro ‖ adv a soqquadro

torch [tɔrtʃ] s fiaccola, torcia; **to carry the torch for** (slang) amare disperatamente

torch'bear'er s portatore m di fiaccola; (fig) capo, guida m

torch'light' s luce f di fiaccola

torch' song' s canzone f triste d'amore non corrisposto

torment ['tɔrment] s tormento ‖ [tɔr'ment] tr tormentare

torna•do [tɔr'nedo] s (-dos or -does) tornado, tromba d'aria

torpe•do [tɔr'pido] s (-does) siluro ‖ tr silurare

torpe'do boat' s motosilurante f

torpe'do-boat destroy'er s torpediniera

torrent ['tɑrənt] or ['tɔrənt] s torrente m

torrid ['tɑrɪd] or ['tɔrɪd] adj torrido

torsion ['tɔrʃən] s torsione f

tor'sion bar' s barra di torsione

tor•so ['tɔrso] s (-sos) torso

tortoise ['tɔrtəs] s tartaruga

tor'toise shell' s tartaruga

torture ['tɔrtʃər] s tortura ‖ tr torturare

toss [tɔs] or [tɑs] s lancio, getto ‖ tr lanciare, gettare; (to fling about) sballottare; (one's head) alzare sdegnosamente; agitare; rivoltare; (an opinion) avventare; **to toss off** fare rapidamente; (e.g., a drink) buttar giù; **to toss up** (a coin) gettar in aria, gettare a testa e croce; (coll) rigettare ‖ intr agitarsi, dimenarsi; **to toss and turn** (in bed) girarsi; **to toss up** giocare a testa e croce

toss'up' s testa e croce; (coll) eguale probabilità f

tot [tɑt] s bambino, piccolo

to•tal ['totəl] adj totale; (e.g., loss) completo ‖ s totale m ‖ v (pret & pp -taled or -talled; ger -taling or -talling) tr ammontare a; (to make a total of) sommare

totalitarian [to ,tælɪ'tɛri·ən] adj totalitario ‖ s aderente mf al totalitarismo

totter ['tɑtər] s vacillamento ‖ intr vacillare

touch [tʌtʃ] s (act) tocco; (sense) tatto; (of an illness) leggero attacco; (slight amount) punta; (for money) (slang) stoccata; **to get in touch with** mettersi in contatto con; **to lose one's touch** perdere il tocco personale ‖ tr toccare; raggiungere; riguardare; (for a loan) (slang) dare una stoccata a; **to touch on** menzionare; **to touch up** ritoccare ‖ intr toccare; **to touch down** (aer) atterrare

touching ['tʌtʃɪŋ] adj toccante, commovente ‖ prep riguardo a

touch'stone' s pietra di paragone

touch' type'writing s dattilografia a tatto

touch•y ['tʌtʃi] adj (-ier; -iest) suscettibile, permaloso; delicato, precario, rischioso

tough [tʌf] adj duro; forte; (luck) cattivo; violento ‖ s malvivente m

toughen ['tʌfən] tr indurire ‖ intr indurirsi

tough' luck' s disdetta, sfortuna

tour [tʊr] s gita, viaggio; (sports) giro; (mil) turno; (theat) tournée f ‖ tr girare; (theat) portare in tournée ‖ intr girare; (theat) andare in tournée

tour'ing car' ['tʊrɪŋ] s automobile f da turismo

tourist ['tʊrɪst] adj turistico ‖ s turista mf

tournament ['tʊrnəmənt] or ['tʌrnəmənt] s torneo

tourney ['tʊrni] or ['tʌrni] s torneo ‖ intr giostrare

tourniquet ['tʊrnɪ ,ket] or ['tʌrnɪ ,ke] s laccio emostatico

tousle ['tauzəl] tr spettinare

tow [to] s rimorchio; (e.g., of hemp) stoppa; **to take in tow** prendere a rimorchio ‖ tr rimorchiare

toward(s) [tord(z)] or [tə'word(z)] prep (in the direction of) verso; (in respect to) per; (near) vicino a; (a certain hour) su, verso

tow'boat' s rimorchiatore m

tow' car' s rimorchiatore m

tow•el ['tau·əl] s asciugamano; (of paper) salvietta; **to throw in the**

towel (slang) gettare la spugna ‖ *v* (*pret & pp* **-eled** or **-elled;** *ger* **-eling** or **-elling**) *tr* asciugare

tow'el rack' *s* portaasciugamani *m*

tower ['tau‧ər] *s* torre *f* ‖ *intr* torreggiare

towering ['tau‧ərɪŋ] *adj* torreggiante; gigantesco; eccessivo

towline ['to‧laɪn] *s* cavo di rimorchio

town [taun] *s* città *f;* (*townspeople*) cittadinanza; **in town** in città

town' clerk' *s* segretario municipale

town' coun'cil *s* consiglio comunale

town' cri'er *s* banditore *m* municipale

town' hall' *s* municipio

township ['taun‧ʃɪp] *s* suddivisione di contea

towns'man *s* (**-men**) cittadino; concittadino

towns'peo'ple *spl* cittadini *mpl;* gente *f* di città

town' talk' *s* dicerie *fpl,* pettegolezzi *mpl*

tow'path' *s* strada d'alaggio

tow'rope' *s* corda da rimorchio

tow' truck' *s* autogru *f*

toxic ['taksɪk] *adj & s* tossico

toy [tɔɪ] *adj* giocattolo; di giocattoli ‖ *s* giocattolo; (*trifle*) nonnulla *m;* (*trinket*) gingillo ‖ *intr* giocare; **to toy with** (*to play with*) giocare con; (*to trifle, e.g., with food*) baloccarsi con; (*an idea*) accarezzare; (*to flirt with*) flirtare con

toy' bank' *s* salvadanaio

toy' sol'dier *s* soldatino di piombo

trace [tres] *s* traccia, vestigio; (*tracing*) tracciato; (*of harness*) tirella; (fig) ombra ‖ *tr* tracciare; (*e.g., s.o.'s ancestry*) rintracciare; (*a pattern*) lucidare

trac'er bul'let ['tresər] *s* pallottola tracciante

trache‧a ['treki‧ə] *s* (**-ae** [‚il]) trachea

tracing ['tresɪŋ] *s* tracciato

track [træk] *s* (*of foot*) traccia, pesta; (*rut*) solco, rotaia; (*of boat*) scia; corso; (*course followed by boat*) rotta; (*of tape recorder*) pista; (*of tractor*) cingolo; (*of ideas*) successione; (*width of a vehicle measured from wheel to wheel*) (aut) carreggiata; (rr) binario; (*track and field*) (sports) atletica leggera; (*for horses*) (sports) galoppatoio; (*for running*) (sports) pista, corsia; **to keep track of** non perder di vista; **to lose track of** perder di vista; **to make tracks** (coll) affrettarsi; **to stop in one's tracks** (coll) fermarsi di colpo ‖ *tr* rintracciare, seguire le tracce di; lasciare tracce su; **to track down** rintracciare

track'ing sta'tion ['trækɪŋ] *s* (rok) stazione di avvistamento

track'less trol'ley ['træklɪs] *s* filobus *m*

track' meet' *s* incontro di atletica leggera

track'walk'er *s* (rr) guardialinee *m*

tract [trækt] *s* tratto, opuscolo, trattatello; (anat) tubo, canale *m*

traction ['trækʃən] *s* trazione

trac'tion com'pany *s* società *f* di trasporti urbani

tractor ['træktər] *s* trattore *m;* (*of a tractor-trailer*) motrice *f*

trac'tor-trail'er *s* treno stradale

trade [tred] *s* commercio; affare *m;* occupazione, mestiere *m;* (*people*) commercianti *mpl,* professionisti *mpl;* mercato; (*customers*) clientela; (*in slaves*) tratta ‖ *tr* mercanteggiare; cambiare; **to trade in** dare come pagamento parziale ‖ *intr* trafficare, commerciare; comprare; **to trade in** lavorare in; **to trade on** approfittarsi di

trade'mark' *s* marca or marchio di fabbrica

trade' name' *s* ragione sociale

trader ['tredər] *s* trafficante *m*

trade' school' *s* scuola d'avviamento professionale, scuola d'arti e mestieri

trades'man *s* (**-men**) commerciante *m;* artigiano

trade' un'ion *s* sindacato di lavoratori

trade' un'ionist *s* sindacalista *mf*

trade' winds' *spl* alisei *mpl*

trad'ing post' *s* centro di scambi commerciali; (*in stock exchange*) posto delle compravendite

trad'ing stamp' *s* buono premio

tradition [trə'dɪʃən] *s* tradizione

traditional [trə'dɪʃənəl] *adj* tradizionale

traduce [trə'djus] or [trə'dus] *tr* calunniare

traf‧fic ['træfɪk] *s* traffico, circolazione; commercio; comunicazione ‖ *v* (*pret & pp* **-ficked;** *ger* **-ficking**) *intr* trafficare

traf'fic cir'cle *s* raccordo a circolazione rotatoria

traf'fic court' *s* tribunale *m* della polizia stradale

traf'fic is'land *s* isola spartitraffico

traf'fic jam' *s* intralcio del traffico, ingorgo stradale

traf'fic light' *s* semaforo

traf'fic man'ager *s* dirigente *m* del traffico; (rr) gestore *m* di stazione

traf'fic sign' *s* segnale *m* di circolazione stradale, cartello indicatore

traf'fic tick'et *s* contravvenzione per violazione del traffico

tragedian [trə'dʒɪdɪ‧ən] *s* tragico

trage‧dy ['trædʒɪdɪ] *s* (**-dies**) tragedia

tragic ['trædʒɪk] *adj* tragico

trail [trel] *s* sentiero; (*track*) traccia, pista; (*of robe*) strascico, coda; (*of smoke*) pennacchio; (*left by an airplane*) striscia; (*of people*) codazzo ‖ *tr* strascicare; essere sulla fatta di; (*e.g., dust on the road*) sollevare; (*mud*) lasciar cadere ‖ *intr* strascicare; (*said, e.g., of a snake*) strisciare; (*said of a plant*) arrampicarsi; **to trail off** mutare; (*to weaken*) affievolirsi

trailer ['trelər] *s* traino; (*to haul freight*) semirimorchio; (*for living*) carovana, roulotte *f;* (bot) rampicante *m*

train [tren] *s* (*of vehicles*) convoglio; (*of robe*) strascico; (*of thought*) or-

dine *m*; (*of people*) coda; (rr) treno
|| *tr* addestrare, impratichire; (*a
weapon*) puntare, rivolgere; (*a
horse*) scozzonare; (*e.g., a dog*) ammaestrare; (*a plant*) far crescere;
(sports) allenare || *intr* addestrarsi;
ammaestrarsi; (sports) allenarsi
trained' nurse' *s* infermiera diplomata
trainer ['trenər] *s* allenatore *m*
training ['trenɪŋ] *s* esercizio, esercitazione; (sports) allenamento
train'ing camp' *s* campo addestramento
train'ing school' *s* scuola di addestramento professionale; riformatorio
train'ing ship' *s* nave *f* scuola
trait [tret] *s* tratto, caratteristica
traitor ['tretər] *s* traditore *m*
traitress ['tretrɪs] *s* traditrice *f*
trajecto•ry [trə'dʒɛktəri] *s* (**-ries**)
traiettoria
tramp [træmp] *s* lunga camminata;
vagabondo; (*hussy*) sgualdrina || *tr*
attraversare; calpestare || *intr* cam-
minare a passi fermi; fare il vagabondo
trample ['træmpəl] *tr* calpestare; (fig)
conculcare || *intr*—**to trample on** or
upon calpestare
trampoline ['træmpə,lin] *s* trampolino
di olona per salti mortali
tramp' steam'er *s* carretta
trance [træns] *s* (*trans*) *s* trance *f*;
(*dazed condition*) estasi *f*
tranquil ['træŋkwɪl] *adj* tranquillo
tranquilize ['træŋkwɪ,laɪz] *tr* tranquil-
lizzare || *intr* tranquillizzarsi
tranquilizer ['træŋkwɪ,laɪzər] *s* tranquillante *m*
tranquillity [træn'kwɪlɪti] *s* tranquillità
f
transact [træn'zækt] or [træns'ækt] *tr*
sbrigare, trattare
transaction [træn'zækʃən] or [træns-
'ækʃən] *s* disbrigo, operazione
transatlantic [,trænsət'læntɪk] *adj* & *s*
transatlantico
transcend [træn'sɛnd] *tr* trascendere,
sorpassare || *intr* eccellere
transcribe [træn'skraɪb] *tr* trascrivere
transcript ['trænskrɪpt] *s* copia; traduzione; (educ) copia ufficiale del certificato di studi
transcription [træn'skrɪpʃən] *s* trascrizione
transept ['trænsɛpt] *s* transetto
trans•fer ['trænsfər] *s* trasferimento;
passaggio; (*pattern*) rapporto; (*of
funds*) giro; (*of real estate*) compra-
vendita; (law) voltura || [træns'fʌr]
or ['trænsfər] *v* (*pret & pp* **-ferred**;
ger **-ferring**) *tr* trasferire, trasportare; (*funds*) stornare; (*a design*)
rapportare; (*real estate*) compraven-
dere || *intr* trasferirsi; cambiare di
treno
trans'fer tax' *s* tassa di successione;
tassa sulla compravendita
transfix [træns'fɪks] *tr* trafiggere; paralizzare, inchiodare
transform [træns'fɔrm] *tr* trasformare;
(elec) trasformare || *intr* trasformarsi
transforma'tional gram'mar [,trænsfər-

'mɛʃənəl] *s* grammatica trasforma-
tiva
transformer [træns'fɔrmər] *s* trasfor-
matore *m*
transfusion [træns'fjuʒən] *s* trasfusione
transgress [træns'grɛs] *tr* trasgredire;
(*a limit or boundry*) oltrepassare ||
intr peccare
transgression [træns'grɛʃən] *s* trasgressione; peccato
transient ['trænʃənt] *adj* passeggero,
temporaneo; di passaggio || *s* ospite
mf di passaggio
transistor [træn'zɪstər] *s* transistore *m*
transit ['trænsɪt] or ['trænzɪt] *s* transito
transition [træn'zɪʃən] *s* transizione
transitional [træn'zɪʃənəl] *adj* di transizione
transitive ['trænsɪtɪv] *adj* transitivo ||
s verbo transitivo
transitory ['trænsɪ,tori] *adj* transitorio
translate [træns'let] or ['trænslet] *tr*
tradurre; convertire; (*to transfer*) tra-
sportare || *intr* tradursi
translation [træns'leʃən] *s* traduzione;
trasformazione; (telg) ritrasmissione
translator [træns'letər] *s* traduttore *m*
transliterate [træns'lɪtə,ret] *tr* traslitterare
translucent [træns'lusənt] *adj* traslu-
cido; (fig) chiaro
transmission [træns'mɪʃən] *s* trasmissione; (aut) trasmissione
trans•mit [træns'mɪt] *v* (*pret & pp*
-mitted; *ger* **-mitting**) *tr* & *intr* trasmettere
transmitter [træns'mɪtər] *s* trasmettitore *m*
transmit'ting set' *s* emittente *f*
transmit'ting sta'tion *s* stazione tra-
smettitrice
transmute [træns'mjut] *tr* & *intr* trasmutare
transom ['trænsəm] *s* (*crosspiece*) traversa; (*window over door*) vasistas
m; (naut) specchio di poppa
transparen•cy ['træns'pɛrənsi] *s* (**-cies**)
trasparenza; (*design on a translucent
substance*) trasparente *m*; (phot) diapositiva
transparent [træns'pɛrənt] *adj* trasparente
transpire [træns'paɪr] *intr* (*to happen*)
avvenire; (*to perspire*) traspirare; (*to
become known*) trapelare
transplant [træns'plænt] or [træns-
'plɑnt] *tr* trapiantare || *intr* trapian-
tarsi
transport ['trænsport] *s* trasporto;
mezzo di trasporto || [træns'port] *tr*
trasportare
transportation [,trænspor'teʃən] *s* trasporto; trasporti *mpl*, locomozione;
biglietto di trasporto
trans'port work'er *s* ferrotranviere *m*
transpose [træns'poz] *tr* trasporre;
(mus) trasportare
trans•ship [træns'ʃɪp] *v* (*pret & pp*
-shipped; *ger* **-shipping**) *tr* trasbordare
trap [træp] *s* trappola, tranello;

(*double-curved pipe*) sifone *m;* (slang) bocca; (sports) congegno lanciapiattelli ‖ *v* (*pret & pp* **trapped;** *ger* **trapping**) *tr* intrappolare, accalappiare

trap' door' *s* trabocchetto, botola; (theat) ribalta

trapeze [trəˈpiz] *s* (sports) trapezio

trapezoid [ˈtræpɪˌzɔɪd] *s* (geom) trapezio, trapezoide *m*

trapper [ˈtræpər] *s* cacciatore *m* di animali da pelliccia con trappole

trappings [ˈtræpɪŋz] *spl* ornamenti *mpl;* (*for a horse*) gualdrappa

trap'shoot'ing *s* tiro al piattello

trash [træʃ] *s* immondizia, spazzatura; (*nonsense*) sciocchezze *fpl;* (*junk*) ciarpame *m;* (*worthless people*) gentaglia

trash' can' *s* portaimmondizie *m*

travail [ˈtrævel] *or* [trəˈvel] *s* travaglio; travaglio di parto

trav•el [ˈtrævəl] *s* viaggio; traffico; (mach) corsa ‖ *v* (*pret & pp* **-eled** *or* **-elled**) *ger* **-eling** *or* **-elling**) *tr* viaggiare per, percorrere ‖ *intr* viaggiare; muoversi; (coll) andare

trav'el a'gency *s* ufficio turistico

traveler [ˈtrævələr] *s* viaggiatore *m*

trav'eler's check' *s* assegno viaggiatori

trav'eling bag' *s* sacca da viaggio

trav'eling expens'es *spl* spese *fpl* di viaggio; (*per diem*) trasferta

trav'eling sales'man *s* (**-men**) commesso viaggiatore

traverse [ˈtrævərs] *or* [trəˈvʌrs] *tr* attraversare

traves•ty [ˈtrævɪstɪ] *s* (**-ties**) parodia ‖ *v* (*pret & pp* **-tied**) *tr* parodiare

trawl [trɔl] *s* (*fishing net*) rete *f* a strascico; (*fishing line*) lenza al traino ‖ *tr & intr* pescare con la rete a strascico; pescare con la lenza al traino

trawling [ˈtrɔlɪŋ] *s* pesca con la rete a strascico; pesca con la lenza al traino

tray [tre] *s* guantiera, vassoio; (chem, phot) bacinella

treacherous [ˈtretʃərəs] *adj* traditore, subdolo; incerto; pericoloso

treacher•y [ˈtretʃərɪ] *s* (**-ies**) tradimento

tread [tred] *s* (*step*) passo; (*of shoe*) suola; (*of tire*) battistrada *m;* (*of stairs*) pedata ‖ *v* (*pret* **trod** [trad], *pp* **trodden** [ˈtradən] *or* **trod**) *tr* calpestare; (*the boards*) calcare; accompiarsi con ‖ *intr* camminare; **to tread on** calpestare

treadle [ˈtredəl] *s* pedale *m*

tread'mill' *s* ruota azionata col camminare; (fig) lavoro ingrato

treason [ˈtrizən] *s* tradimento

treasonable [ˈtrizənəbəl] *adj* traditore

treasure [ˈtrezər] *s* tesoro ‖ *tr* far tesoro di

treasurer [ˈtrezərər] *s* tesoriere *m*

treas'ure hunt' *s* caccia al tesoro

treasur•y [ˈtrezərɪ] *s* (**-ies**) tesoreria; tesoro, erario

treat [trit] *s* trattenimento; (*something affording pleasure*) piacere *m*, diletto ‖ *tr* trattare; (*to cure*) curare, medi-

care; offrire un trattenimento a ‖ *intr* trattare; pagare per il trattenimento

treatise [ˈtritɪs] *s* trattato

treatment [ˈtritmənt] *s* trattamento; (*of a theme*) trattazione

trea•ty [ˈtritɪ] *s* (**-ties**) trattato

treble [ˈtrebəl] *adj* (*threefold*) triplo; (mus) soprano ‖ *s* (*person*) soprano *mf;* (*voice*) soprano ‖ *tr* triplicare ‖ *intr* triplicarsi

tree [tri] *s* albero

tree' farm' *s* bosco ceduo

tree' frog' *s* raganella

treeless [ˈtrilɪs] *adj* spoglio, senza alberi

tree'top' *s* cima dell'albero

trellis [ˈtrelɪs] *s* traliccio, graticcio

tremble [ˈtrembəl] *s* tremito ‖ *intr* tremare

tremendous [trɪˈmendəs] *adj* tremendo

tremor [ˈtremər] *or* [ˈtrimər] *s* tremito; (*of earth*) scossa

trench [trentʃ] *s* fosso, canale *m;* (mil) trincea

trenchant [ˈtrentʃənt] *adj* mordace, caustico; vigoroso; incisivo

trench' coat' *s* trench *m*

trench' mor'tar *s* lanciabombe *m*

trend [trend] *s* tendenza, orientamento ‖ *intr* tendere, dirigersi

Trent [trent] *s* Trento *f*

trespass [ˈtrespəs] *s* (law) intrusione, violazione di proprietà ‖ *intr* entrare senza diritto, intrudersi; peccare; **no trespassing** divieto di passaggio; **to trespass against** peccare contro; **to trespass on** entrare abusivamente in; (*e.g., s.o.'s time*) abusare di; violare

tress [tres] *s* treccia

trestle [ˈtresəl] *s* cavalletto; viadotto a cavalletti; ponte *m* a cavalletti

trial [ˈtraɪəl] *s* tentativo, prova; tribolazione, croce *f;* (law) giudizio, processo; **on trial** in prova; (law) sotto processo; **to bring to trial** sottoporre a processo

tri'al and er'ror *s* metodo per tentativi; **by trial and error** a tastoni

tri'al balloon' *s* pallone *m* sonda

tri'al by ju'ry *s* processo con giuria

tri'al ju'ry *s* giuria civile o processuale

tri'al or'der *s* (com) ordine *m* di prova

tri'al run' *s* viaggio di prova

triangle [ˈtraɪˌæŋgəl] *s* triangolo; (*in drafting*) quartabuono

tribe [traɪb] *s* tribù *f*

tribunal [trɪˈbjunəl] *or* [traɪˈbjunəl] *s* tribunale *m*

tribune [ˈtrɪbjun] *s* tribuna

tributar•y [ˈtrɪbjəˌtɛrɪ] *adj* tributario ‖ *s* (**-ies**) tributario

tribute [ˈtrɪbjut] *s* tributo; **to pay tribute to** (*e.g., beauty*) rendere omaggio a

trice [traɪs] *s* momento, istante *m;* **in a trice** in un batter d'occhio

trick [trɪk] *s* gherminella, inganno; trucco, tiro, scherzo; (*knack*) abilità *f;* (*feat*) atto; (*set of cards won*) presa; turno; (coll) piccola; **to be up to one's old tricks** farne una delle sue; **to play a dirty trick on** fare un brutto tiro a‖ *tr* giocare, ingannare

trick·er·y ['trɪkəri] *s* (**-ies**) gherminella, inganno

trickle ['trɪkəl] *s* gocciolio, filo ‖ *intr* gocciolare; (*said of people*) andare or venire alla spicciolata; (*said of news*) trapelare

trickster ['trɪkstər] *s* imbroglione *m*

trick·y ['trɪki] *adj* (**-ier; -iest**) ingannatore; (*machine*) complicato; (*ticklish to deal with*) delicato

tried [traɪd] *adj* fedele, provato

trifle ['traɪfəl] *s* bazzecola, bagattella; (*small amount of money*) piccolezza, miseria; **a trifle un po'** ‖ *tr*—**to trifle away** sprecare ‖ *intr* gingillarsi; **to trifle with** giocherellare con; scherzare con; divertirsi con

trifling ['traɪflɪŋ] *adj* futile, insignificante, trascurabile

trifocal [traɪ'fokəl] *adj* trifocale ‖ **trifocals** *spl* occhiali *mpl* trifocali

trigger ['trɪgər] *s* (*of a firearm*) grilletto; (*of any device*) leva di sgancio ‖ *tr* (*a gun*) far sparare; (fig) scatenare

trigonometry [,trɪgə'nɑmɪtri] *s* trigonometria

trill [trɪl] *s* trillo, gorgheggio; vibrazione; (*speech sound*) (phonet) vibrante *f* ‖ *tr* gorgheggiare; pronunziare con vibrazione ‖ *intr* trillare, gorgheggiare

trillion ['trɪljən] *s* trilione *m*

trilo·gy ['trɪlədʒi] *s* (**-gies**) trilogia

trim [trɪm] *adj* (**trimmer; trimmest**) lindo, azzimato ‖ *s* condizione; buona condizione; (*dress*) vestito; (*of hair*) taglio, sfumatura; decorazione, ornamento; (*of sails*) orientamento; (aut) attrezzatura della carrozzeria ‖ *v* (*pret & pp* **trimmed**; *ger* **trimming**) *tr* tagliare; (*an edge*) rifilare; adattare; arrangiare; (*Christmas tree*) decorare; (*hair*) sfumare; (*a tree*) potare; ordinare, assettare; (*a sail*) orientare; (aer) equilibrare; (mach) sbavare; (coll) rimproverare; (coll) bastonare; (*to defeat*) (coll) battere, vincere

trimming ['trɪmɪŋ] *s* ornamento, guarnizione; (coll) battitura, batosta; **trimmings** guarnizioni *mpl*; (mach) sbavatura; (mach) rifilatura

trini·ty ['trɪnɪti] *s* (**-ties**) (*group of three*) triade *f* ‖ **Trinity** *s* Trinità *f*

trinket ['trɪŋkɪt] *s* (*small ornament*) ninnolo, gingillo; **trinkets** (*trivial objects*) paccottiglia

tri·o ['tri·o] *s* (**-os**) terzetto

trip [trɪp] *s* viaggio; corsa; (*stumble*) inciampata; (*act of causing s.o. to stumble*) sgambetto; (*error*) passo falso; passo agile ‖ *v* (*pret & pp* **tripped**; *ger* **tripping**) *tr* far inciampare, far cadere; fare lo sgambetto a; cogliere in fallo; (mach) far scattare ‖ *intr* inciampare; fare un passo falso; avanzare saltellando, saltellare; **to trip over** inciampare in

tripartite [traɪ'partaɪt] *adj* tripartito

tripe [traɪp] *s* trippa; (slang) sciocchezze *fpl*

trip'ham'mer *s* maglio meccanico

triphthong ['trɪfθɔŋ] or ['trɪfθaŋ] *s* trittongo

triple ['trɪpəl] *adj & s* triplo ‖ *tr* triplicare ‖ *intr* triplicarsi

triplet ['trɪplɪt] *s* (*offspring*) nato da un parto trigemino; (mus, poet) terzina

triplicate ['trɪplɪkɪt] *adj* triplicato ‖ *s* triplice copia ‖ ['trɪplɪ,ket] *tr* triplicare

tripod ['traɪpad] *s* (*e.g., for a camera*) treppiede *m*; (*stool with three legs*) tripode *m*

triptych ['trɪptɪk] *s* trittico

trite [traɪt] *adj* trito, ritrito

triumph ['traɪəmf] *s* trionfo ‖ *intr* trionfare

trium'phal arch' [traɪ'ʌmfəl] *s* arco trionfale

trivia ['trɪvɪ·ə] *spl* banalità *f*, futilità *f*

trivial ['trɪvɪ·əl] *adj* insignificante, futile, banale

Trojan ['trodʒən] *adj & s* troiano

Tro'jan Horse' *s* cavallo di Troia

Tro'jan War' *s* guerra troiana

troll [trol] *tr & intr* pescare con la lenza al traino, pescare con il cucchiaino

trolley ['trali] *s* asta di presa, trolley *m*; carrozza tranviaria, tram *m*

trol'ley bus' *s* filobus *m*

trol'ley car' *s* vettura tranviaria, tram *m*

trol'ley pole' *s* trolley *m*

trollop ['traləp] *s* (*slovenly woman*) sciattona; (*hussy*) sgualdrina

trombone ['trambon] *s* trombone *m*

troop [trup] *s* truppa, gruppo; (*of animals*) branco; (*of cavalry*) squadrone *m*; **troops** soldati *mpl* ‖ *intr* raggrupparsi; marciare insieme

trooper ['trupər] *s* soldato di cavalleria; poliziotto a cavallo; **to swear like a trooper** bestemmiare come un turco

tro·phy ['trofi] *s* (**-phies**) trofeo; (*any memento*) ricordo

tropic ['trapɪk] *adj* tropicale ‖ *s* tropico; **tropics** zona tropicale

tropical ['trapɪkəl] *adj* tropicale

troposphere ['trapə,sfɪr] *s* troposfera

trot [trat] *s* trotto ‖ *v* (*pret & pp* **trotted**; *ger* **trotting**) *tr* far trottare; **to trot out** (coll) squadernare, esibire ‖ *intr* trottare

troth [troθ] or [troθ] *s* promessa di matrimonio; **by my troth** affé di Dio; **in troth** in verità; **to plight one's troth** impegnarsi; dare la parola

troubadour ['trubə,dor] or ['trubə,dur] *s* trovatore *m*

trouble ['trʌbəl] *s* disturbo, fastidio; inconveniente *m*, grattacapo; disordine *m*, conflitto; (*of a mechanical nature*) panna, guasto; **not to be worth the trouble** non valere la pena; **that's the trouble** questo è il male; **the trouble is that** il guaio è che; **to be in trouble** essere nei guai; **to be**

looking for trouble andare a cercarsi le grane; **to get into trouble** mettersi nei pasticci; **to have trouble in** + *ger* durar fatica a + *inf;* **to take the trouble** incomodarsi ‖ *tr* molestare, disturbare; (*e.g., water*) intorbidare; dar del filo da torcere a; **to be troubled with** soffrire di; **to trouble oneself** scomodarsi

trouble′ light′ *s* lampada di soccorso

trou′ble-mak′er *s* mettimale *mf*

troubleshooter [′trʌbəl ˌʃutər] *s* localizzatore *m* di guasti; (*in disputes*) paciere *m*, conciliatore *m*

troubleshooting [′trʌbəl ˌʃutɪŋ] *s* localizzazione dei guasti; (*of disputes*) composizione

troublesome [′trʌbəlsəm] *adj* molesto; difficile

trouble′ spot′ *s* luogo di disordini, polveriera

trough [trɔf] *or* [trɔf] *s* (*to knead bread*) madia; (*for feeding pigs*) trogolo; (*for feeding animals*) mangiatoia; (*for watering animals*) abbeveratoio; (*gutter*) doccia; (*between two waves*) cavo

troupe [trup] *s* troupe *f*

trouper [′trupər] *s* membro della troupe; vecchio attore; tipo di cui ci si può fidare

trousers [′trauzərz] *spl* pantaloni *mpl*

trousseau [tru′so] *or* [′truso] *s* (**-seaux** *or* **-seaus**) corredo da sposa

trout [traut] *s* trota

trouvère [tru′vɛr] *s* troviero

trowel [′trau·əl] *s* cazzuola, mestola

Troy [trɔɪ] *s* Troia

truant [′tru·ənt] *s* fannullone *m;* **to play truant** marinare la scuola

truce [trus] *s* tregua

truck [trʌk] *s* autocarro, camion *m;* (*tractor-trailer*) autotreno; (*van*) furgone *m;* (*to be moved by hand*) carretto; verdura per il mercato; (*mach, rr*) carrello; (*coll*) robaccia; (*coll*) relazioni *fpl* ‖ *tr* trasportare per autocarro, autotrasportare

truck′driv′er *s* camionista *m*

truck′ farm′ *s* fattoria agricola per la produzione degli ortaggi

truculent [′trʌkjələnt] *or* [′trukjələnt] *adj* truculento

trudge [trʌdʒ] *intr* camminare; **to trudge along** camminare laboriosamente, scarpinare

true [tru] *adj* vero; esatto, conforme; legittimo; infallibile; a livello; **to come true** verificarsi; **true to life** conforme alla realtà

true′ cop′y *s* copia conforme

true-hearted [′tru ˌhɑrtɪd] *adj* fedele

true′love knot′ *s* nodo d'amore

truffle [′trʌfəl] *or* [′trufəl] *s* tartufo

truism [′tru·ɪzəm] *s* truismo

truly [′truli] *adv* veramente; correttamente; **yours truly** distinti saluti

trump [trʌmp] *s* (*cards*) atout *m;* (*Italian cards*) briscola; **no trump** senza atout ‖ *tr* superare; (*cards*) pigliare con un atout or con una briscola; **to trump up** inventare, fabbricare ‖ *intr* giocare un atout or una briscola

trumpet [′trʌmpɪt] *s* tromba; (*toy*) trombetta; **to blow one's own trumpet** cantare le proprie lodi ‖ *tr* strombazzare ‖ *intr* sonar la tromba; strombazzare; (*said of an elephant*) barrire

truncheon [′trʌntʃən] *s* bastone *m* del comando; (Brit) manganello

trunk [trʌŋk] *s* (*of living body, tree, family, railroad*) tronco; (*for clothes*) baule *m;* (*of elephant*) tromba; (aut) bagagliaio; (archit) fusto; (telp) linea principale; **trunks** pantaloncini *mpl*

trunk′ hose′ *s* (hist) brache *fpl*

truss [trʌs] *s* (*to support a roof*) capriata, incavallatura; (*based on cantilever system*) intralicciatura; (*for reducing a hernia*) cinto, brachiere *m;* (bot) infiorescenza ‖ *tr* legare, assicurare

trust [trʌst] *s* fede *f;* speranza; fiducia, custodia; (com) trust *m,* cartello; (law) fedecommesso; **in trust** in deposito; come fedecommesso; **on trust** a credito ‖ *tr* fidarsi di; credere (with *dat*); (*to entrust*) dare in deposito a; dare a credito a ‖ *intr* credere; fidarsi, prestar fede; **to trust in** (*e.g., a friend*) fidarsi di; (*God*) aver fede in

trust′ com′pany *s* compagnia fedecommissaria; banca di deposito

trustee [trʌs′ti] *s* amministratore *m;* fiduciario; (*of a university*) curatore *m;* (*of an estate*) fedecommissario

trusteeship [trʌs′ti·ʃɪp] *s* amministrazione; (law) fedecommesso; (pol) amministrazione fiduciaria

trustful [′trʌstfəl] *adj* fiducioso

trust′wor′thy *adj* fidato, di fiducia

trust·y [′trʌsti] *adj* (**-ier; -iest**) fidato ‖ *s* (**-ies**) carcerato degno di fiducia

truth [truθ] *s* verità *f;* **in truth** in verità

truthful [′truθfəl] *adj* verace, veritiero

try [traɪ] *s* (**tries**) tentativo, prova ‖ *v* (*pret & pp* **tried**) *tr* provare; (*s.o.'s patience*) mettere a dura prova; (*a person*) (law) processare; (*a case*) (law) giudicare; **to try on** (*clothes*) provare; **to try out** provare; esperimentare ‖ *intr* cercare, tentare; **to try out for** cercare di ottenere il posto di; (sports) cercare di farsi accettare in; **to try to** cercare di

trying [′traɪ·ɪŋ] *adj* duro, penoso, difficile

tryst [trɪst] *or* [traɪst] *s* appuntamento

T′-shirt′ *s* maglietta

tub [tʌb] *s* tino, bigoncia; vasca da bagno; (*clumsy boat*) (slang) carretta; (*fat person*) (slang) bombolo

tube [tjub] *or* [tub] *s* tubo; (*e.g., for toothpaste*) tubetto; (*of tire*) camera d'aria; (anat) tuba, tromba; (coll) ferrovia sotterranea

tuber [′tjubər] *or* [′tubər] *s* tubero

tubercle [′tjubərkəl] *or* [′tubərkəl] *s* tubercolo

tuberculosis [tju͵bɑrkjə'losɪs] or [tu-͵bɑrkjə'losɪs] s tubercolosi f

tuck [tʌk] s basta ‖ tr ripiegare; **to tuck away** nascondere; (slang) fare una scorpacciata di; **to tuck in** rincalzare; **to tuck up** rimboccare

tucker ['tʌkər] s collarino di merletto ‖ tr—**to tucker out** (coll) stancare

Tuesday ['tjuzdi] or ['tuzdi] s martedì m

tuft [tʌft] s (of feathers) pennacchio; (of hair) cernecchio; (of flowers) cespo; (fluffy threads) fiocco, nappa ‖ tr impuntire; adornare di fiocchi ‖ intr crescere a cernecchi

tug [tʌg] s strattone m, strappata; (struggle) lotta; (boat) rimorchiatore m ‖ v (pret & pp **tugged**; ger **tugging**) tr tirare; (a boat) rimorchiare ‖ intr tirare con forza; lottare

tug'boat' s rimorchiatore m

tug' of war' s tiro alla fune

tuition [tju'ɪʃən] or [tu'ɪʃən] s (instruction) insegnamento; tassa scolastica

tulip ['tjulɪp] or ['tulɪp] s tulipano

tumble ['tʌmbəl] s rotolone m, ruzzolone m; (somersault) salto mortale; caduta; disordine m, confusione; (confused heap) mucchio ‖ intr rotolare, ruzzolare, cadere, capitombolare; gettarsi; rigirarsi; **to tumble down** cadere in rovina; **to tumble to** (coll) rendersi conto di

tum'ble-down' adj dilapidato

tumbler ['tʌmblər] s (acrobat) saltimbanco; (glass) bicchiere m; (in a lock) levetta; (toy) misirizzi m

tumor ['tjumər] or ['tumər] s tumore m

tumult ['tjumʌlt] or ['tumʌlt] s tumulto

tun [tʌn] s botte f, barile m

tuna ['tunə] s tonno

tune [tjun] or [tun] s (air) aria; (manner of speaking) tono; **in tune** intonato; **out of tune** stonato; **to change one's tune** cambiare di tono ‖ tr intonare; **to tune in** (rad) sintonizzare; **to tune out** (rad) interrompere la sintonizzazione di; **to tune up** (a motor) mettere a punto; (mus) intonare

tuner ['tunər] or ['tjunər] s (rad) sintonizzatore m; (mus) accordatore m

tungsten ['tʌŋstən] s tungsteno

tunic ['tjunɪk] or ['tunɪk] s tunica

tun'ing coil' ['tunɪŋ] or ['tjunɪŋ] s bobina di sintonia

tun'ing fork' s diapason m, corista m

Tunis ['tjunɪs] or ['tunɪs] s Tunisi f

Tunisia [tju'nɪʒə] or [tu'nɪʒə] s la Tunisia

Tunisian [tju'nɪʒən] or [tu'nɪʒən] adj & s tunisino

tun·nel ['tʌnəl] s tunnel m, traforo, galleria; (min) galleria ‖ v (pret & pp **-neled** or **-nelled**; ger **-neling** or **-nelling**) tr costruire un passaggio attraverso o sotto di

turban ['tʌrbən] s turbante m

turbid ['tʌrbɪd] adj turbido

turbine ['tʌrbɪn] or ['tʌrbaɪn] s turbina

turbojet ['tʌrbo͵dʒet] s turboreattore m

turboprop ['tʌrbo͵prɑp] s turboelica m

turbulent ['tʌrbjələnt] adj turbolento

tureen [tu'rin] or [tju'rin] s terrina

turf [tʌrf] s zolla erbosa; (peat) torba; **the turf** il campo delle corse; le corse, il turf

turf'man s (-men) amatore m delle corse ippiche

Turk [tʌrk] s turco

turkey ['tʌrki] s tacchino ‖ **Turkey** s la Turchia

turk'ey vul'ture s (Cathartes aura) avvoltoio americano

Turkish ['tʌrkɪʃ] adj & s turco

Turk'ish tow'el s asciugamano spugna

turmoil ['tʌrmɔɪl] s subbuglio

turn [tʌrn] s giro; (time for action) turno, volta; (change of direction) voltata; (bend) svolta, curva; (of events) piega; servizio; inclinazione, attitudine f; (of key) mandata; (of coil) spira; (coll) colpo, sussulto; (aer, naut) virata; **at every turn** a ogni piè sospinto; **in turn** a tua (Sua, vostra, etc.) volta; **to be one's turn** toccare a qlcu, e.g., **it's your turn** tocca a Lei; **to take turns** fare a turno ‖ tr girare, voltare; (soil) rovesciare; cambiare; (to make sour) coagulare; (to translate) tradurre; (e.g., ten years) raggiungere; (e.g., one's eyes) volgere; (on a lathe) tornire; (e.g., a coat) rivoltare; (to twist) torcere; (the wheel) (aut) sterzare; **to turn against** mettere su contro; **to turn around** rigirare; (s.o.'s words) ritorcere; **to turn aside** sviare; **to turn away** cacciare via; **to turn back** ricacciare; restituire; (the clock) ritardare; **to turn down** ripiegare; (the light) abbassare; (an offer) rifiutare; **to turn in** ripiegare; denunziare; rassegnare; **to turn off** (e.g., light) spegnere, smorzare; (gas, water, etc.) tagliare; (e.g., a faucet) chiudere; **to turn on** (e.g., light, radio, etc.) accendere; (e.g., a faucet) aprire; **to turn out** mettere alla porta; (animals) fare uscire dalla stalla; rivoltare; (light) spegnere; produrre, fabbricare; **to turn up** ripiegare in su, rimboccare; (on a lathe) tornire; tirar su; (a card) scoprire; trovare; (e.g., the radio) alzare ‖ intr girare; svoltare, e.g., **turn left at the corner** svolti a sinistra all'angolo; girarsi; cambiare; fermentare; cambiare di colore; diventare; (naut) virare; **to turn against** voltarsi contro; inimicarsi con; **to turn around** fare una giravolta; **to turn aside** or **away** sviarsi; **to turn back** ritornare; retrocedere; **to turn down** piegarsi in giù; rovesciarsi; **to turn in** piegarsi, ripiegarsi; tornare a casa; (coll) andare a dormire; **to turn into** sfogare in; trasformarsi in; **to turn on** voltarsi contro; girarsi su; dipendere da; occuparsi di; **to turn**

out riuscire; **to turn out to be** manifestarsi; riuscire ad essere; **to turn over** rotolarsi; rovesciarsi; **to turn up** voltarsi all'insù; alzarsi; apparire, farsi vedere

turn'buck'le s tenditore m

turn'coat' s voltagabbana mf; **to become a turncoat** voltar gabbana

turn'down' adj (collar) rovesciato || s rifiuto

turn'ing point' s punto decisivo

turnip ['tʌrnɪp] s rapa

turn'key' s secondino, carceriere m

turn' of life' s menopausa

turn' of mind' s disposizione naturale

turn' out' s (gathering of people) concorso; (crowd) folla; produzione; (outfit) vestito; stile m, moda; (in a road) slargo, piazzola; (horse and carriage) equipaggio; (rr) binario laterale

turn'over' s (upset) rovesciamento, ribaltamento; (of customers) movimento di clienti; (of business) giro d'affari; rotazione di lavoratori; (com) ciclo operativo

turn'pike' s autostrada a pedaggio

turn' sig'nal s (aut) indicatore m di direzione, lampeggiatore m

turnstile ['tʌrn‚staɪl] s tornello

turn'ta'ble s (of phonograph) piatto rotante; (rr) piattaforma girevole

turpentine ['tʌrpən‚taɪn] s trementina

turpitude ['tʌrpɪ‚tjud] or ['tʌrpɪ‚tud] s turpitudine f

turquoise ['tʌrkɔɪz] or ['tʌrkwɔɪz] s turchese m

turret ['tʌrɪt] s torretta

turtle ['tʌrtəl] s tartaruga; **to turn turtle** rovesciarsi, capovolgersi

tur'tle-dove' s tortora

Tuscan ['tʌskən] adj & s toscano

Tuscany ['tʌskəni] s la Toscana

tusk [tʌsk] s zanna

tussle ['tʌsəl] s lotta, zuffa || intr lottare, azzuffarsi

tutor ['tjutər] or ['tutər] s istitutore privato, ripetitore m; (guardian) tutore m || tr dare ripetizione a || intr dare ripetizioni; studiare con un ripetitore

tuxe•do [tʌk'sido] s (-dos) smoking m

twaddle ['twadəl] s sciocchezze fpl || intr dire sciocchezze

twang [twæŋ] s (of musical instrument) suono vibrato; (of voice) timbro nasale || tr pizzicare; dire con un timbro nasale || intr parlare con voce nasale

twang•y ['twæŋi] adj (-ier; -iest) (tone) metallico; (voice) nasale

tweed [twid] s tweed m; **tweeds** abito di tweed

tweet [twit] s pigolio || intr pigolare

tweeter ['twitər] s altoparlante m per alte audiofrequenze, tweeter m

tweezers ['twizərz] spl pinzette fpl

twelfth [twelfθ] adj, s & pron dodicesimo || s (in dates) dodici m

Twelfth'-night' s vigilia dell'Epifania; sera dell'Epifania

twelve [twelv] adj & pron dodici || s dodici m; **twelve o'clock** le dodici

twentieth ['twentɪ‚ɪθ] adj, s & pron ventesimo || s (in dates) venti m

twen•ty ['twenti] adj & pron venti || s (-ties) venti m; **the twenties** gli anni venti

twice [twaɪs] adv due volte

twice'-told' adj detto più di una volta; detto e ridetto

twiddle ['twɪdəl] tr— **to twiddle one's thumbs** rigirare i pollici, oziare

twig [twɪg] s ramoscello; **twigs** sterpi mpl

twilight ['twaɪ‚laɪt] adj crepuscolare || s crepuscolo

twill [twɪl] s diagonale m || tr tessere in diagonale

twin [twɪn] adj & s gemello

twine [twaɪn] s spago || tr intrecciare || intr intrecciarsi

twinge [twɪndʒ] s punta, dolore acuto

twinkle ['twɪŋkəl] s scintillio; batter m d'occhio || intr scintillare

twin'-screw' adj a due eliche

twirl [twʌrl] s giro, mulinello || tr girare; (slang) lanciare || intr girare rapidamente, frullare

twist [twɪst] s curva; giro; viluppo, intreccio; tendenza, inclinazione; (yarn) ritorno; (e.g., of lemon) fettina; (dance) twist m || tr intrecciare; torcere; (e.g., the face) contorcere; (the meaning) stravolgere, stiracchiare; girare || intr intrecciarsi; torcersi, divincolarsi; girare; serpeggiare; **to twist and turn** (in bed) girarsi e rigirarsi

twister ['twɪstər] s (coll) tromba d'aria

twit [twɪt] v (pret & pp **twitted;** ger **twitting**) tr ridicolizzare

twitch [twɪtʃ] s tic m; (jerk) strattone m; (to restrain a horse) torcinaso || intr contrarsi; tremare; **to twitch at** tirare

twitter ['twɪtər] s garrito, cinguettio; (chatter) chiacchierio; ansia, agitazione || intr garrire, cinguettare; chiacchierare; tremare d'ansia

two [tu] adj & pron due || s due m; **to put two and two together** arrivare alle logiche conclusioni; **two o'clock** le due

two'-cy'cle adj a due tempi

two'-cyl'inder adj a due cilindri

two-edged ['tu‚ɛdʒd] adj a doppio filo

two'fold' adj duplice, doppio

two' hun'dred adj, s & pron duecento

twosome ['tusəm] s coppia

two'-time' tr (slang) fare le corna a

two'-way ra'dio s ricetrasmettitore m

tycoon [taɪ'kun] s magnate m

type [taɪp] s tipo; (typ) carattere m; (pieces collectively) (typ) caratteri mpl || tr scrivere a macchina; simbolizzare || intr scrivere a macchina

type'face' s stile m di carattere

type'script' s dattiloscritto

typesetter ['taɪp‚sɛtər] s (person) compositore m; (machine) compositrice f

type'write' *v* (*pret* **-wrote;** *pp* **-written**) *tr* & *intr* dattilografare, scrivere a macchina

type'writ'er *s* (*machine*) macchina da scrivere; (*typist*) dattilografo

type'writ'ing *s* dattilografia, scrittura a macchina; lavoro battuto a macchina

ty'phoid fe'ver ['taɪfɔɪd] *s* febbre *f* tifoide

typhoon [taɪ'fun] *s* tifone *m*

typical ['tɪpɪkəl] *adj* tipico

typi•fy ['tɪpɪ,faɪ] *v* (*pret* & *pp* **-fied**) *tr* simbolizzare

typist ['taɪpɪst] *s* dattilografo

typographic(al) [,taɪpə'græfɪk(əl)] *adj* tipografico

typograph'ical er'ror *s* errore *m* di stampa

typography [taɪ'pɑɡrəfi] *s* tipografia

tyrannic(al) [tɪ'rænɪk(əl)] or [taɪ-'rænɪk(əl)] *adj* tirannico

tyrannous ['tɪrənəs] *adj* tiranno

tyrant ['taɪrənt] *s* tiranno

ty•ro ['taɪro] *s* (**-ros**) principiante *m*

Tyrrhe'nian Sea' [tɪ'rinɪən] *s* Mare Tirreno

U

U, u [ju] *s* ventunesima lettera dell'alfabeto inglese

ubiquitous [ju'bɪkwɪtəs] *adj* ubiquo

udder ['ʌdər] *s* mammella

ugliness ['ʌɡlɪnɪs] *s* bruttezza

ug•ly ['ʌɡli] *adj* (**-lier; -liest**) brutto

Ukraine, the ['jukren] or [ju'kren] *s* l'Ucraina *f*

Ukrainian [ju'krenɪən] *adj* & *s* ucraino

ulcer ['ʌlsər] *s* piaga, ulcera; (*corrupting element*) (fig) piaga

ulcerate ['ʌlsə,ret] *tr* ulcerare ‖ *intr* ulcerarsi

ulterior [ʌl'tɪrɪ•ər] *adj* ulteriore; (*motive*) nascosto, secondo

ultimate ['ʌltɪmɪt] *adj* ultimo

ultima•tum [,ʌltɪ'metəm] *s* (**-tums** or **-ta** [tə]) ultimato

ultimo ['ʌltɪ,mo] *adv* del mese scorso

ul'tra-high fre'quency ['ʌltrə'haɪ] *s* frequenza ultraelevata

ultrashort ['ʌltrə'ʃɔrt] *adj* ultracorto

ultraviolet ['ʌltrə'vaɪ•əlɪt] *adj* & *s* ultravioletto

umbil'ical cord' [ʌm'bɪlɪkəl] *s* cordone *m* ombelicale

umbrage ['ʌmbrɪdʒ] *s*—**to take umbrage at** adombrarsi per

umbrella [ʌm'brelə] *s* ombrello, paracqua *m*; (mil) ombrello

umbrel'la stand' *s* portaombrelli *m*

Umbrian ['ʌmbrɪ•ən] *adj* & *s* umbro

umlaut ['umlaut] *s* metafonesi *f*; (*mark*) dieresi *f* ‖ *tr* cambiare il timbro di; scrivere con dieresi

umpire ['ʌmpaɪr] *s* arbitro ‖ *tr* arbitrare ‖ *intr* fare l'arbitro

UN ['ju'ɛn] *s* (letterword) (**United Nations**) ONU *f*

unable [ʌn'ebəl] *adj* incapace; **to be unable to** essere impossibilitato a, non potere

unabridged [,ʌnə'brɪdʒd] *adj* integrale, non abbreviato

unaccented [ʌn'æksɛntɪd] or [,ʌnæk-'sɛntɪd] *adj* non accentato, atono

unacceptable [,ʌnək'sɛptəbəl] *adj* inaccettabile

unaccountable [,ʌnə'kauntəbəl] *adj* irresponsabile; inesplicabile

unaccounted-for [,ʌnə'kauntɪd,fər]

adj (*e.g., failure*) inesplicato; (*e.g., soldier*) mancante

unaccustomed [,ʌnə'kʌstəmd] *adj* (*unusual*) insolito; non abituato

unafraid [,ʌnə'fred] *adj* impavido

unaligned [ʌnə'laɪnd] *adj* non impegnato

unanimity [,junə'nɪmɪti] *s* unanimità *f*

unanimous [ju'nænɪməs] *adj* unanime

unanswerable [ʌn'ænsərəbəl] *adj* per cui non vi è risposta; (*argument*) irrefutabile, incontestabile

unappreciative [,ʌnə'priʃ ɪ,etɪv] *adj* sconoscente, ingrato

unapproachable [,ʌnə'protʃəbəl] *adj* inabbordabile; incomparabile

unarmed [ʌn'ɑrmd] *adj* disarmato, inerme

unascertainable [ʌn,æsər'tenəbəl] *adj* non verificabile

unassailable [,ʌnə'seləbəl] *adj* inattaccabile

unassembled [,ʌnə'sɛmbəld] *adj* smontato

unassuming [,ʌnə'sumɪŋ] or [,ʌnə-'sjumɪŋ] *adj* modesto, semplice

unattached [,ʌnə'tætʃt] *adj* indipendente; (*loose*) sciolto; non sposato; non fidanzato

unattainable [,ʌnə'tenəbəl] *adj* inarrivabile, irraggiungibile

unattractive [,ʌnə'træktɪv] *adj* poco attraente

unavailable [,ʌnə'veləbəl] *adj* non disponibile

unavailing [,ʌnə'velɪŋ] *adj* futile

unavoidable [,ʌnə'vɔɪdəbəl] *adj* inevitabile, ineluttabile

unaware [,ʌnə'wer] *adj* inconsapevole, ignaro ‖ *adv* inaspettatamente; (*unknowingly*) inavvertitamente

unawares [,ʌnə'werz] *adv* inaspettatamente; (*unknowingly*) inavvertitamente

unbalanced [ʌn'bælənst] *adj* sbilanciato, squilibrato

unbandage [ʌn'bændɪdʒ] *tr* sbendare

un•bar [ʌn'bɑr] *v* (*pret* & *pp* **-barred;** *ger* **-barring**) *tr* disserrare il chiavistello di

unbearable [ʌn'berəbəl] *adj* insopportabile, insostenibile

unbeatable [ʌn'bitəbəl] *adj* imbattibile

unbecoming [ˌʌnbɪ'kʌmɪŋ] *adj* sconveniente, indegno; (*e.g.*, *hat*) disadatto, che non sta bene

unbelievable [ˌʌnbɪ'livəbəl] *adj* incredibile

unbeliever [ˌʌnbɪ'livər] *s* miscredente *mf*

unbending [ʌn'bendɪŋ] *adj* inflessibile

unbiased [ʌn'baɪ-əst] *adj* imparziale, spassionato

un·bind [ʌn'baɪnd] *v* (*pret* & *pp* **-bound** ['baʊnd]) *tr* slegare

unbleached [ʌn'blitʃt] *adj* non candeggiato, al colore naturale

unbolt [ʌn'bolt] *tr* (*a door*) togliere il chiavistello a; sbullonare

unborn [ʌn'bɔrn] *adj* nascituro

unbosom [ʌn'bʊzəm] *tr* (*a secret*) rivelare; **to unbosom oneself** aprire il proprio animo, sfogarsi

unbound [ʌn'baʊnd] *adj* sciolto, libero; (*book*) non rilegato

unbreakable [ʌn'brekəbəl] *adj* infrangibile

unbridle [ʌn'braɪdəl] *tr* sbrigliare

unbuckle [ʌn'bʌkəl] *tr* sfibbiare

unburden [ʌn'bʌrdən] *tr* scaricare; **to unburden oneself (of)** vuotare il sacco (di)

unburied [ʌn'berid] *adj* insepolto

unbutton [ʌn'bʌtən] *tr* sbottonare

uncalled-for [ʌn'kɔld ˌfɔr] *adj* superfluo, gratuito; fuori di posto, sconveniente

uncanny [ʌn'kæni] *adj* misterioso, straordinario

uncared-for [ʌn'kerd ˌfɔr] *adj* negletto, trascurato

unceasing [ʌn'sisɪŋ] *adj* incessante

unceremonious [ˌʌnserɪ'moni-əs] *adj* senza cerimonie

uncertain [ʌn'sʌrtən] *adj* incerto

uncertain·ty [ʌn'sʌrtənti] *s* (**-ties**) incertezza

unchain [ʌn'tʃen] *tr* scatenare, sferrare

unchangeable [ʌn'tʃendʒəbəl] *adj* immutabile

uncharted [ʌn'tʃɑrtɪd] *adj* inesplorato

unchecked [ʌn'tʃekt] *adj* incontrollato

uncivilized [ʌn'sɪvɪˌlaɪzd] *adj* incivile

unclad [ʌn'klæd] *adj* svestito

unclaimed [ʌn'klemd] *adj* non reclamato; (*letter*) giacente

unclasp [ʌn'klæsp] *or* [ʌn'klɑsp] *tr* sfibbiare

unclassified [ʌn'klæsɪˌfaɪd] *adj* non classificato; non secreto

uncle ['ʌŋkəl] *s* zio

unclean [ʌn'klin] *adj* immondo

un·clog [ʌn'klɑg] *v* (*pret* & *pp* **-clogged;** *ger* **-clogging**) *tr* disintasare

unclouded [ʌn'klaʊdɪd] *adj* sereno, senza nubi

uncollectible [ˌʌnkə'lektɪbəl] *adj* inesigibile

uncomfortable [ʌn'kʌmfərtəbəl] *adj* scomodo, disagevole

uncommitted [ˌʌnkə'mɪtɪd] *adj* non impegnato

uncommon [ʌn'kɑmən] *adj* raro, straordinario

uncompromising [ʌn'kɑmprəˌmaɪzɪŋ] *adj* intransigente

unconcerned [ˌʌnkən'sʌrnd] *adj* indifferente, noncurante

unconditional [ˌʌnkən'dɪʃənəl] *adj* incondizionato

uncongenial [ˌʌnkən'dʒini-əl] *adj* antipatico, sgradito

unconquerable [ʌn'kɑŋkərəbəl] *adj* inconquistabile, inespugnabile

unconscionable [ʌn'kɑnʃənəbəl] *adj* senza scrupoli; eccessivo

unconscious [ʌn'kɑnʃəs] *adj* (*without awareness*) inconscio, inconsapevole; (*temporarily devoid of consciousness*) incosciente; (*unintentional*) involontario

unconsciousness [ʌn'kɑnʃəsnɪs] *s* incoscienza

unconstitutional [ˌʌnkɑnstɪ'tjuʃənəl] *or* [ˌʌnkɑnstɪ'tuʃənəl] *adj* incostituzionale

uncontrollable [ˌʌnkən'troləbəl] *adj* incontrollabile, ingovernabile

unconventional [ˌʌnkən'venʃənəl] *adj* non convenzionale, anticonformista

uncork [ʌn'kɔrk] *tr* stappare

uncouple [ʌn'kʌpəl] *tr* sganciare, disconnettere

uncouth [ʌn'kuθ] *adj* zotico, incivile, pacchiano

uncover [ʌn'kʌvər] *tr* scoprire

unction ['ʌŋkʃən] *s* unzione; (fig) untuosità *f*

unctuous ['ʌŋktʃu-əs] *adj* untuoso

uncultivated [ʌn'kʌltɪˌvetɪd] *adj* incolto

uncultured [ʌn'kʌltʃərd] *adj* incolto, rozzo

uncut [ʌn'kʌt] *adj* non tagliato; (*book*) intonso

undamaged [ʌn'dæmɪdʒd] *adj* indenne, illeso

undaunted [ʌn'dɔntɪd] *adj* imperterrito, impavido

undeceive [ˌʌndɪ'siv] *tr* disingannare

undecided [ˌʌndɪ'saɪdɪd] *adj* indeciso

undefeated [ˌʌndɪ'fitɪd] *adj* invitto

undefended [ˌʌndɪ'fendɪd] *adj* indifeso

undefensible [ˌʌndɪ'fensɪbəl] *adj* insostenibile

undefiled [ˌʌndɪ'faɪld] *adj* puro, immacolato

undeniable [ˌʌndɪ'naɪ-əbəl] *adj* innegabile, indubitato

under ['ʌndər] *adj* di sotto; (*lower*) inferiore; (*clothing*) intimo, personale || *adv* sotto; più sotto; **to go under** affondare; cedere; (coll) fallire || *prep* sotto; sotto a; (*e.g.*, *20 years old*) meno di; **under full sail** a vele spiegate; **under lock and key** sotto chiave; **under oath** sotto giuramento; **under penalty of death** sotto pena di morte; **under sail** a vela; **under separate cover** in plico separato; **under steam** sotto pressione; **under the hand and seal of** firmato di pugno di; **under the weather** (coll) un po' indisposto; **under way** già iniziato

un'der-age' *adj* minorenne

un'der-arm' pad' *s* sottoascella *m*

un'der·bid' v (pret & pp **-bid;** ger **-bidding**) tr fare un'offerta inferiore a quella di

un'der·brush' s sottobosco

un'der·car'riage s (aut) telaio; (aer) carrello d'atterraggio

un'der·clothes' spl biancheria intima

un'der·consump'tion s sottoconsumo

un'der·cov'er adj segreto

un'der·cur'rent s (of water) corrente subacquea; (of air) corrente f inferiore; (fig) controcorrente f

underdeveloped [ˌʌndərdɪ'vɛləpt] adj sottosviluppato

un'der·dog' s chi è destinato ad avere la peggio; vittima; **the underdogs** i diseredati

un'der·done' adj non cotto abbastanza

un'der·es'timate' tr sottovalutare

un'der·gar'ment s indumento intimo

un'der·go' v (pret **-went;** pp **-gone**) tr (a test) passare, sottostare (with dat); (surgery) subire, sottoporsi a; soffrire

un'der·grad'uate adj (student) non ancora laureato; (course) per studenti non ancora laureati || s studente universitario che non ha ancora ricevuto il primo diploma

un'der·ground' adj sotterraneo; segreto || s regione sotterranea; macchia, resistenza || adv sottoterra; alla macchia, segretamente

un'der·growth' s sterpaglia

underhanded ['ʌndər'hændəd] adj subdolo, di sottomano

un'der·line' or **un'der·line'** tr sottolineare

underling ['ʌndərlɪŋ] s tirapiedi m

un'der·mine' tr scalzare, minare

underneath [ˌʌndər'niθ] adj inferiore || s disotto || adv sotto, di sotto || prep sotto a, sotto

undernourished [ˌʌndər'nʌrɪʃt] adj denutrito, malnutrito

un'der·pass' s sottopassaggio

un'der·pay' s (pret & pp **-paid**) tr & intr pagare insufficientemente

un'der·pin' v (pret & pp **-pinned;** ger **-pinning**) tr rincalzare

underprivileged [ˌʌndər'prɪvɪlɪdʒd] adj derelitto, diseredato

un'der·rate' tr sottovalutare

un'der·score' tr sottolineare

un'der·sea' adj sottomarino || adv sotto il mare

un'der·seas' adv sotto il mare

un'der·sec'retar'y s (**-ies**) sottosegretario

un'der·sell' v (pret & pp **-sold**) tr vendere a prezzo minore di; (to sell for less than actual value) svendere

un'der·shirt' s camiciola, canottiera

undersigned ['ʌndər,saɪnd] adj sottoscritto

un'der·skirt' s sottogonna

un'der·stand' v (pret & pp **-stood**) tr capire, comprendere; sottintendere; (to accept as true) constare, e.g., **he understands that you are wrong** gli consta che Lei ha torto || intr capire, comprendere

understandable [ˌʌndər'stændəbəl] adj comprensibile

understanding [ˌʌndər'stændɪŋ] adj comprensivo, tollerante || s (mind) intelletto; (knowledge) conoscenza, comprensione, intendimento; (agreement) intesa, accordo

understatement [ˌʌndər'stetmənt] s sottovalutazione

un'der·stud'y s (**-ies**) (theat) doppio, sostituto || v (**-ied**) tr (an actor) fare il doppio di

un'der·take' v (pret **-took;** ger **-taken**) tr intraprendere; (to promise) promettere

undertaker [ˌʌndər'tekər] or ['ʌndər-ˌtekər] s impresario || ['ʌndər-ˌtekər] s impresario di pompe funebri

undertaking [ˌʌndər'tekɪŋ] s (task) impresa; (promise) promessa || ['ʌndərˌtekɪŋ] s impresa di pompe funebri

un'der·tone' s bassa voce; (background sound) ronzio di fondo; tono; colore smorzato

un'der·tow' s (on the beach) risacca; (countercurrent below surface) controcorrente f

un'der·wa'ter adj subacqueo || adv sottacqua

un'der·wear' s biancheria intima

un'der·world' s (criminal world) malavita, teppa; (abode of spirits) ade m, averno; mondo sotterraneo; mondo sottomarino; antipodi mpl

un'der·write' v (pret **-wrote;** pp **-written**) tr sottoscrivere; (to insure) assicurare

un'der·writ'er s sottoscrittore m; (ins) assicuratore m

undeserved [ˌʌndɪ'zʌrvd] adj immeritato

undesirable [ˌʌndɪ'zaɪrəbəl] adj & s indesiderabile mf

undetachable [ˌʌndɪ'tætʃəbəl] adj non movibile

undeveloped [ˌʌndɪ'vɛləpt] adj (land) non sfruttato; (country) sottosviluppato

undigested [ˌʌndɪ'dʒɛstɪd] adj non digerito

undignified [ʌn'dɪgnɪˌfaɪd] adj poco decoroso

undiscernible [ˌʌndɪ'zʌrnɪbəl] or [ˌʌndɪ'sʌrnɪbəl] adj impercettibile

undisputed [ˌʌndɪ'spjutəd] adj indiscusso, incontrastato

un·do [ʌn'du] v (pret **-did;** pp **-done**) tr sfare, disfare; rovinare; (a package) aprire; (a knot) sciogliere

undoing [ʌn'du·ɪŋ] s rovina

undone [ʌn'dʌn] adj non finito; **to come undone** disfarsi; **to leave nothing undone** non tralasciare di fare nulla

undoubtedly [ʌn'daʊtɪdli] adv indubbiamente, senza dubbio

undress ['ʌn,drɛs] or [ʌn'drɛs] s vestaglia; vestito da ogni giorno || [ʌn'drɛs] tr spogliare, svestire; (a *wound*) sbendare ‖ *intr* spogliarsi, svestirsi

undrinkable [ʌn'drɪŋkəbəl] *adj* imbevibile, non potabile

undue [ʌn'dju] or [ʌn'du] *adj* indebito; immeritato; eccessivo

undulate ['ʌndjə,let] *intr* ondulare

unduly [ʌn'djuli] or [ʌn'duli] *adv* indebitamente, eccessivamente

unearned [ʌn'ʌrnd] *adj* non guadagnato col lavoro; immeritato; non ancora guadagnato

un'earned in'crement *s* plusvalenza

unearth [ʌn'ʌrθ] *tr* dissotterrare

unearthly [ʌn'ʌrθli] *adj* ultraterreno; spettrale; impossibile, straordinario

uneasy [ʌn'izi] *adj* (*worried*) preoccupato; (*constrained*) scomodo; (*not conducive to ease*) inquietante, a disagio

uneatable [ʌn'itəbəl] *adj* immangiabile

uneconomic(al) [,ʌnikə'namɪk(əl)] or [,ʌnekə'namɪk(əl)] *adj* antieconomico

uneducated [ʌn'edʒə,ketɪd] *adj* ineducato

unemployed [,ʌnem'plɔɪd] *adj* disoccupato, incollocato; improduttivo ‖ **the unemployed** *spl* disoccupati

unemployment [,ʌnem'plɔɪmənt] *s* disimpiego, disoccupazione

unemploy'ment compensa'tion *s* sussidio di disoccupazione

unending [ʌn'endɪŋ] *adj* interminabile

unequal [ʌn'ikwəl] *adj* disuguale, impari; **to be unequal to** (*a task*) non essere all'altezza di

unequaled or **unequalled** [ʌn'ikwəld] *adj* ineguagliato

unerring [ʌn'ʌrɪŋ] or [ʌn'erɪŋ] *adj* infallibile; corretto, preciso

unessential [,ʌne'senʃəl] *adj* non essenziale

uneven [ʌn'ivən] *adj* disuguale, ineguale; (*number*) dispari

uneventful [,ʌnɪ'ventfəl] *adj* senza avvenimenti importanti; (*life*) tranquillo

unexceptionable [,ʌnek'sepʃənəbəl] *adj* ineccepibile, irreprensibile

unexpected [,ʌnek'spektɪd] *adj* insospettato, imprevisto

unexplained [,ʌnek'splend] *adj* inesplicato

unexplored [,ʌnek'splord] *adj* inesplorato

unexposed [,ʌnek'spozd] *adj* (phot) non esposto alla luce

unfading [ʌn'fedɪŋ] *adj* immarcescibile; imperituro

unfailing [ʌn'felɪŋ] *adj* immancabile, infallibile; (*inexhaustible*) inesauribile; (*dependable*) sicuro

unfair [ʌn'fer] *adj* ingiusto; disonesto, sleale

unfaithful [ʌn'feθfəl] *adj* infedele

unfamiliar [,ʌnfə'mɪljər] *adj* poco pratico; poco abituale, strano; non conosciuto

unfasten [ʌn'fæsən] or [ʌn'fasən] *tr* sfibbiare, sciogliere

unfathomable [ʌn'fæðəməbəl] *adj* insondabile

unfavorable [ʌn'fevərəbəl] *adj* sfavorevole

unfeeling [ʌn'filɪŋ] *adj* insensibile

unfetter [ʌn'fetər] *tr* sciogliere dalle catene

unfinished [ʌn'fɪnɪʃt] *adj* incompiuto; grezzo, non rifinito; (*business*) inevaso

unfit [ʌn'fɪt] *adj* disadatto; inabile

unfledged [ʌn'fledʒd] *adj* implume

unfold [ʌn'fold] *tr* schiudere; (*e.g., a newspaper*) spiegare ‖ *intr* schiudersi; svolgersi

unforeseeable [,ʌnfor'si-əbəl] *adj* imprevedibile

unforeseen [,ʌnfor'sin] *adj* imprevisto

unforgettable [,ʌnfər'getəbəl] *adj* indimenticabile

unforgivable [,ʌnfər'gɪvəbəl] *adj* imperdonabile

unfortunate [ʌn'fɔrtjənɪt] *adj* & *s* disgraziato, sfortunato

unfounded [ʌn'faʊndɪd] *adj* infondato

un-freeze [ʌn'friz] *v* (*pret* **-froze**; *pp* **-frozen**) *tr* disgelare; (*credit*) sbloccare

unfriendly [ʌn'frendli] *adj* (**-lier**; **-liest**) *adj* mal disposto, ostile; sfavorevole

unfruitful [ʌn'frutfəl] *adj* infruttuoso

unfulfilled [,ʌnfʌl'fɪld] *adj* incompiuto

unfurl [ʌn'fʌrl] *tr* spiegare, dispiegare

unfurnished [ʌn'fʌrnɪʃt] *adj* smobiliato

ungainly [ʌn'genli] *adj* sgraziato, maldestro

ungentlemanly [ʌn'dʒentəlmənli] *adj* indegno di un gentleman

ungird [ʌn'gʌrd] *tr* discingere

ungodly [ʌn'gadli] *adj* irreligioso, empio; (*dreadful*) (coll) atroce

ungracious [ʌn'greʃəs] *adj* rude, scortese; (*task*) sgradevole

ungrammatical [,ʌngrə'mætɪkəl] *adj* sgrammaticato

ungrateful [ʌn'gretfəl] *adj* ingrato

ungrudgingly [ʌn'grʌdʒɪŋli] *adv* di buon grado, volentieri

unguarded [ʌn'gardɪd] *adj* incustodito, indifeso; incauto, imprudente

unguent ['ʌŋgwənt] *s* unguento

unhappiness [ʌn'hæpɪnɪs] *s* infelicità *f*

unhap·py [ʌn'hæpi] *adj* (**-pier**; **-piest**) infelice, sfortunato

unharmed [ʌn'harmd] *adj* illeso

unharness [ʌn'harnɪs] *tr* togliere i finimenti a

unhealth·y [ʌn'helθi] *adj* (**-ier**; **-iest**) malsano

unheard-of [ʌn'hard,av] *adj* (*unknown*) sconosciuto; inaudito

unhinge [ʌn'hɪndʒ] *tr* sgangherare; (fig) sconvolgere

unhitch [ʌn'hɪtʃ] *tr* sganciare; (*a horse*) staccare

unho·ly [ʌn'holi] *adj* (**-lier**; **-liest**) empio; terribile, atroce

unhook [ʌn'hʊk] *tr* sganciare

unhoped-for [ʌn'hopt,fər] *adj* insperato

unhorse [ʌn'hɔrs] *tr* disarcionare

unhurt [ʌn'hʌrt] *adj* incolume, illeso
unicorn ['junɪ‚kɔrn] *s* unicorno
unification [‚junɪfɪ'keʃən] *s* unificazione
uniform ['junɪ‚fɔrm] *adj & s* uniforme *f* || *tr* uniformare
uni-fy ['junɪ‚faɪ] *v* (*pret & pp* **-fied**) *tr* unificare
unilateral [‚junɪ'lætərəl] *adj* unilaterale
unimpeachable [‚ʌnɪm'pitʃəbəl] *adj* irrefutabile; irreprensibile
unimportant [‚ʌnɪm'pɔrtənt] *adj* poco importante
uninhabited [‚ʌnɪn'hæbɪtɪd] *adj* inabitato, disabitato
uninspired [‚ʌnɪn'spaɪrd] *adj* senza ispirazione, prosaico
unintelligent [‚ʌnɪn'telɪdʒənt] *adj* non intelligente; stupido
unintelligible [‚ʌnɪn'telɪdʒɪbəl] *adj* inintelligibile
uninterested [ʌn'ɪntrɪstɪd] or [ʌn-'ɪntə‚restɪd] *adj* non interessato
uninteresting [ʌn'ɪntrɪstɪŋ] or [ʌn-'ɪntə‚restɪŋ] *adj* poco interessante
uninterrupted [‚ʌnɪntə'rʌptɪd] *adj* ininterrotto
union ['junjən] *s* unione; unione matrimoniale; (*of workers*) sindacato
unionize ['junjə‚naɪz] *tr* organizzare in un sindacato || *intr* organizzarsi in un sindacato
un'ion shop' *s* fabbrica che assume solo sindacalisti
un'ion suit' *s* combinazione
unique [ju'nik] *adj* unico
unison ['junɪsən] or ['junɪzən] *s* unisono; **in unison** all'unisono
unit ['junɪt] *adj* unitario || *s* unità *f*; (*mach, elec*) gruppo
unite [ju'naɪt] *tr* unire || *intr* unirsi
united [ju'naɪtɪd] *adj* unito
Unit'ed King'dom *s* Regno Unito
Unit'ed Na'tions *spl* Organizzazione delle Nazioni Unite
Unit'ed States' *adj* statunitense || **the United States** *ssg* gli Stati Uniti
uni-ty ['junɪti] *s* (**-ties**) unità *f*
universal [‚junɪ'vʌrsəl] *adj* universale
u'niver'sal joint' *s* giunto cardanico
universe ['junɪ‚vʌrs] *s* universo
universi-ty [‚junɪ'vʌrsɪti] *adj* universitario || *s* (**-ties**) università *f*
unjust [ʌn'dʒʌst] *adj* ingiusto
unjustified [ʌn'dʒʌstɪ‚faɪd] *adj* ingiustificato
unkempt [ʌn'kempt] *adj* spettinato; trascurato
unkind [ʌn'kaɪnd] *adj* scortese; duro, crudele
unknowable [ʌn'no-əbəl] *adj* inconoscibile
unknowingly [ʌn'no-ɪŋli] *adv* inconsapevolmente
unknown [ʌn'non] *adj* sconosciuto || *s* incognito; (*math*) incognita
Un'known Sol'dier *s* Milite Ignoto
unlace [ʌn'les] *tr* slacciare
unlatch [ʌn'lætʃ] *tr* tirare il saliscendi a
unlawful [ʌn'lɔfəl] *adj* illegale

unleash [ʌn'liʃ] *tr* sguinzagliare; (*fig*) scatenare
unleavened [ʌn'levənd] *adj* azzimo
unless [ʌn'les] *conj* se non che, salvo che
unlettered [ʌn'letərd] *adj* ignorante; (*illiterate*) analfabeta
unlike [ʌn'laɪk] *adj* dissimile, differente; dissimile da, e.g., **a copy unlike the original** una copia dissimile dall'originale; (*elec*) di segno contrario || *prep* diversamente da, a differenza di; **it was unlike him to arrive late** non era cosa normale per lui arrivare in ritardo
unlikely [ʌn'laɪkli] *adj* improbabile
unlimber [ʌn'lɪmbər] *tr* mettere in batteria || *intr* prepararsi a fare fuoco; (*fig*) prepararsi
unlimited [ʌn'lɪmɪtɪd] *adj* illimitato
unlined [ʌn'laɪnd] *adj* (*e.g., coat*) non foderato; (*paper*) non rigato
unload [ʌn'lod] *tr* scaricare; (*passengers*) sbarcare; (*to get rid of*) liberarsi di || *intr* scaricare; sbarcare
unloading [ʌn'lodɪŋ] *s* discarica; sbarco
unlock [ʌn'lɑk] *tr* aprire
unloose [ʌn'lus] *tr* rilasciare; sciogliere
unloved [ʌn'lʌvd] *adj* poco amato
unlovely [ʌn'lʌvli] *adj* poco attraente
unluck-y [ʌn'lʌki] *adj* (**-ier; -iest**) sfortunato, disgraziato
un-make [ʌn'mek] *v* (*pret & pp* **-made** ['med]) *tr* disfare; deporre
unmanageable [ʌn'mænɪdʒəbəl] *adj* incontrollabile
unmanly [ʌn'mænli] *adj* non virile, effeminato; codardo
unmannerly [ʌn'mænərli] *adj* scortese
unmarketable [ʌn'mɑrkɪtəbəl] *adj* invendibile
unmarriageable [ʌn'mærɪdʒəbəl] *adj* che non si può sposare; non adatto al matrimonio
unmarried [ʌn'mærɪd] *adj* scapolo; (*female*) nubile
unmask [ʌn'mæsk] or [ʌn'mɑsk] *tr* smascherare || *intr* smascherarsi
unmatchable [ʌn'mætʃəbəl] *adj* impareggiabile
unmatched [ʌn'mætʃd] *adj* impareggiabile; (*unpaired*) sparigliato
unmentionable [ʌn'menʃənəbəl] *adj* innominabile
unmerciful [ʌn'mʌrsɪfəl] *adj* spietato
unmesh [ʌn'meʃ] *tr* disingranare || *intr* disingranarsi
unmindful [ʌn'maɪndfəl] *adj* immemore; incurante
unmistakable [‚ʌnmɪs'tekəbəl] *adj* inconfondibile
unmitigated [ʌn'mɪtɪ‚getɪd] *adj* completo; assoluto, perfetto
unmixed [ʌn'mɪkst] *adj* puro
unmoor [ʌn'mur] *tr* disormeggiare
unmoved [ʌn'muvd] *adj* immoto; fisso, immobile; (*fig*) impassibile
unmuzzle [ʌn'mʌzəl] *tr* togliere la museruola a
unnamed [ʌn'nemd] *adj* innominato
unnatural [ʌn'nætʃərəl] *adj* contro natura, snaturato; innaturale, affettato

unnecessary [ʌn'nesə,seri] *adj* inutile

unnerve [ʌn'nʌrv] *tr* snervare

unnoticeable [ʌn'notɪsəbəl] *adj* impercettibile

unnoticed [ʌn'notɪst] *adj* inosservato

unobserved [,ʌnəb'zʌrvd] *adj* inosservato

unobtainable [,ʌnəb'tenəbəl] *adj* non ottenibile, irraggiungibile

unobtrusive [,ʌnəb'trusɪv] *adj* discreto, riservato

unoccupied [ʌn'ɑkjə,paɪd] *adj* libero, disponibile; (*not busy*) disoccupato

unofficial [,ʌnə'fɪʃəl] *adj* non ufficiale, ufficioso

unopened [ʌn'opənd] *adj* non aperto, chiuso; (*letter*) non dissuggellato; (*book*) intonso

unorthodox [ʌn'ɔrθə,dɑks] *adj* non ortodosso

unpack [ʌn'pæk] *tr* spaccare, sballare

unpalatable [ʌn'pælətəbəl] *adj* di gusto spiacevole

unparalleled [ʌn'pærə,leld] *adj* incomparabile, senza pari

unpardonable [ʌn'pɑrdənəbəl] *adj* imperdonabile

unpatriotic [,ʌnpetrɪ'ɑtɪk] or [,ʌnpætrɪ'ɑtɪk] *adj* antipatriottico

unperceived [,ʌnpər'sivd] *adj* inosservato

unperturbable [,ʌnpər'tʌrbəbəl] *adj* imperterrito, imperturbato

unpleasant [ʌn'plezənt] *adj* spiacevole; (*person*) antipatico

unpopular [ʌn'pɑpjələr] *adj* impopolare

unpopularity [ʌn,pɑpjə'lærɪti] *s* impopolarità *f*

unprecedented [ʌn'presɪ,dentɪd] *adj* senza precedenti, inaudito

unprejudiced [ʌn'predʒədɪst] *adj* senza pregiudizio, imparziale

unpremeditated [,ʌnprɪ'medɪ,tetɪd] *adj* impremeditato

unprepared [,ʌnprɪ'perd] *adj* impreparato

unprepossessing [,ʌnprɪpə'zesɪŋ] *adj* poco attraente, antipatico

unpresentable [,ʌnprɪ'zentəbəl] *adj* impresentabile

unpretentious [,ʌnprɪ'tenʃəs] *adj* modesto, senza pretese

unprincipled [ʌn'prɪnsɪpəld] *adj* senza principî

unproductive [,ʌnprə'dʌktɪv] *adj* improduttivo

unprofitable [ʌn'prɑfɪtəbəl] *adj* infruttuoso

unpronounceable [,ʌnprə'naunsəbəl] *adj* impronunziabile

unpropitious [,ʌnprə'pɪʃəs] *adj* inauspicato

unpublished [ʌn'pʌblɪʃt] *adj* inedito

unpunished [ʌn'pʌnɪʃt] *adj* impunito

unqualified [ʌn'kwɑlɪ,faɪd] *adj* inabile, inidoneo; assoluto, completo

unquenchable [ʌn'kwentʃəbəl] *adj* inappagabile, inestinguibile

unquestionable [ʌn'kwestʃənəbəl] *adj* indiscutibile

unravel [ʌn'rævəl] *v* (*pret & pp* -eled

or -elled; *ger* -eling or -elling) *tr* dipanare || *intr* districarsi; chiarirsi

unreachable [ʌn'ritʃəbəl] *adj* irraggiungibile

unreal [ʌn'ri·əl] *adj* irreale

unreality [,ʌnrɪ'ælɪti] *s* (-ties) irrealità *f*

unreasonable [ʌn'rizənəbəl] *adj* irragionevole

unrecognizable [ʌn'rekəg,naɪzəbəl] *adj* irriconoscibile

unreel [ʌn'ril] *tr* svolgere, srotolare || *intr* srotolarsi

unrefined [,ʌnrɪ'faɪnd] *adj* non raffinato, greggio; volgare, ordinario

unrelenting [,ʌnrɪ'lentɪŋ] *adj* inesorabile, inflessibile; indefesso

unreliable [,ʌnrɪ'laɪ·əbəl] *adj* malfido; (*news*) inattendibile

unremitting [,ʌnrɪ'mɪtɪŋ] *adj* incessante, costante

unrented [ʌn'rentɪd] *adj* da affittare

unrepeatable [,ʌnrɪpitəbəl] *adj* irripetibile

unrepentant [,ʌnrɪ'pentənt] *adj* impenitente

un'requit'ed love' [,ʌnrɪ'kwaɪtɪd] *s* amore non corrisposto

unresponsive [,ʌnrɪ'spɑnsɪv] *adj* apatico, insensibile

unrest [ʌn'rest] *s* agitazione

un-rig [ʌn'rɪg] *v* (*pret & pp* -rigged; *ger* -rigging) *tr* (naut) disarmare

unrighteous [ʌn'raɪtʃəs] *adj* ingiusto

unripe [ʌn'raɪp] *adj* immaturo

unrivaled or **unrivalled** [ʌn'raɪvəld] *adj* senza pari

unroll [ʌn'rol] *tr* srotolare

unromantic [,ʌnro'mæntɪk] *adj* poco romantico

unruffled [ʌn'rʌfəld] *adj* calmo, imperturbabile

unruly [ʌn'ruli] *adj* turbolento; indisciplinato, insubordinato

unsaddle [ʌn'sædəl] *tr* (*a horse*) dissellare; (*a rider*) scavalcare

unsafe [ʌn'sef] *adj* malsicuro, pericolante

unsaid [ʌn'sed] *adj* non detto, taciuto; **to leave unsaid** passare sotto silenzio

unsalable [ʌn'seləbəl] *adj* invendibile

unsanitary [ʌn'sænɪ,teri] *adj* antigienico

unsatisfactory [ʌn,sætɪs'fæktəri] *adj* poco soddisfacente

unsatisfied [ʌn'sætɪs,faɪd] *adj* insoddisfatto, inappagato

unsavory [ʌn'sevəri] *adj* insipido; (fig) disgustoso, nauseabondo

un-say [ʌn'se] *v* (*pret & pp* -said [sed]') *tr* disdire

unscathed [ʌn'skeðd] *adj* incolume

unscheduled [ʌn'skedʒuld] *adj* non in elenco; (*event*) fuori programma; (*e.g., flight*) fuori orario; (*phase of production*) non programmato

unscientific [,ʌnsaɪ·ən'tɪfɪk] *adj* poco scientifico

unscrew [ʌn'skru] *tr* svitare || *intr* svitarsi

unscrupulous [ʌn'skrupjələs] *adj* senza scrupoli

unseal [ʌn'sil] *tr* dissigillare

unseasonable [ʌn'siːzənəbəl] *adj* fuori stagione; inopportuno

unseasoned [ʌn'siːzənd] *adj* scondito; (*crop*) immaturo; (*crew*) inesperto

unseat [ʌn'siːt] *tr* (*a rider*) scavalcare, disarcionare; (*e.g., a congressman*) far perdere il seggio a, defenestrare

unseemly [ʌn'siːmli] *adj* disdicevole, sconveniente

unseen [ʌn'siːn] *adj* non visto, inosservato; nascosto, occulto; invisibile

unselfish [ʌn'sɛlfɪʃ] *adj* disinteressato

unsettled [ʌn'sɛtəld] *adj* disabitato; disorganizzato; disordinato, erratico; indeciso; (*bill*) da pagare

unshackle [ʌn'ʃækəl] *tr* liberare

unshaken [ʌn'ʃekən] *adj* inconcusso

unshapely [ʌn'ʃepli] *adj* senza forma, deforme

unshaven [ʌn'ʃevən] *adj* non rasato

unshatterable [ʌn'ʃætərəbəl] *adj* infrangibile

unsheathe [ʌn'ʃiːð] *tr* sguainare

unshod [ʌn'ʃɑd] *adj* scalzo; (*horse*) sferrato

unshrinkable [ʌn'ʃrɪŋkəbəl] *adj* irrestringibile

unsightly [ʌn'saɪtli] *adj* ripugnante, brutto

unsinkable [ʌn'sɪŋkəbəl] *adj* insommergibile

unskilled [ʌn'skɪld] *adj* inesperto

un'skilled la'bor *s* lavoro manuale; mano d'opera non specializzata

unskillful [ʌn'skɪlfəl] *adj* maldestro

unsnarl [ʌn'snɑrl] *tr* sbrogliare

unsociable [ʌn'soʃəbəl] *adj* insocievole

unsold [ʌn'sold] *adj* invenduto

unsolder [ʌn'sɑdər] *tr* dissaldare

unsophisticated [ˌʌnsə'fɪstɪˌketɪd] *adj* semplice, puro

unsound [ʌn'saʊnd] *adj* malsano, malato; (*decayed*) guasto, impuridrito; falso, fallace; (*sleep*) leggero

unsown [ʌn'son] *adj* incolto, non seminato

unspeakable [ʌn'spikəbəl] *adj* indicibile; (*atrocious*) innominabile, inqualificabile

unsportsmanlike [ʌn'sportsmən ˌlaɪk] *adj* antisportivo

unstable [ʌn'stebəl] *adj* instabile

unsteady [ʌn'stɛdi] *adj* malfermo; incostante; irregolare

unstinted [ʌn'stɪntɪd] *adj* generoso, senza limiti

unstitch [ʌn'stɪtʃ] *tr* scucire

un·stop [ʌn'stɑp] *v* (*pret & pp* -stopped; *ger* -stopping) *tr* stasare

unstressed [ʌn'strɛst] *adj* non accentuato; (*e.g., syllable*) non accentato

unstrung [ʌn'strʌŋ] *adj* (*beads*) sfilato; (*instrument*) allentato; (*person*) snervato

unsuccessful [ˌʌnsək'sɛsfəl] *adj* (*person*) sfortunato; (*deal*) mancato; **to be unsuccessful** fallire

unsuitable [ʌn'sutəbəl] or [ʌn'sjutəbəl] *adj* inappropriato

unsurpassable [ʌnsər'pæsəbəl] or [ˌʌnsər'pɑsəbəl] *adj* insuperabile

unsuspected [ˌʌnsəs'pɛktɪd] *adj* insospettato

unswerving [ʌn'swɜrvɪŋ] *adj* diritto, fermo, costante

unsympathetic [ˌʌnsɪmpə'θɛtɪk] *adj* indifferente, che non mostra comprensione

unsystematic(al) [ˌʌnsɪstə'mætɪk(əl)] *adj* senza sistema

untactful [ʌn'tæktfəl] *adj* senza tatto

untamed [ʌn'temd] *adj* indomito

untangle [ʌn'tæŋgəl] *tr* sgrovigliare

unteachable [ʌn'titʃəbəl] *adj* indocile; refrattario agli studi

untenable [ʌn'tɛnəbəl] *adj* insostenibile

unthankful [ʌn'θæŋkfəl] *adj* ingrato

unthinkable [ʌn'θɪŋkəbəl] *adj* impensabile

unthinking [ʌn'θɪŋkɪŋ] *adj* irriflessivo

untidy [ʌn'taɪdi] *adj* disordinato

un·tie [ʌn'taɪ] *v* (*pret & pp* -tied; *ger* -tying) *tr* sciogliere; (*a knot*) slacciare, snodare ‖ *intr* sciogliersi

until [ʌn'tɪl] *prep* fino, fino a ‖ *conj* fino a che, finché

untillable [ʌn'tɪləbəl] *adj* incoltivabile

untimely [ʌn'taɪmli] *adj* intempestivo; (*death*) prematuro

untiring [ʌn'taɪrɪŋ] *adj* instancabile

untold [ʌn'told] *adj* non detto, non raccontato; incalcolabile; (*inexpressable*) indicibile

untouchable [ʌn'tʌtʃəbəl] *adj & s* intoccabile *mf*

untouched [ʌn'tʌtʃt] *adj* intatto; insensibile; non menzionato

untoward [ʌn'tord] *adj* sfavorevole, sconveniente, disdicevole

untried [ʌn'traɪd] *adj* non provato

untroubled [ʌn'trʌbləd] *adj* tranquillo

untrue [ʌn'tru] *adj* falso

untrustworthy [ʌn'trʌst ˌwɜrðɪ] *adj* infido, malfido

untruth [ʌn'truθ] *s* falsità *f*, menzogna

untruthful [ʌn'truθfəl] *adj* falso, menzognero

untwist [ʌn'twɪst] *tr* districare ‖ *intr* districarsi

unusable [ʌn'juzəbəl] *adj* inservibile

unused [ʌn'juzd] *adj* inutilizzato; **unused to** [ʌn'justu] disavvezzo a

unusual [ʌn'juʒʊˌəl] *adj* insolito

unutterable [ʌn'ʌtərəbəl] *adj* impronunciabile; indicibile

unvanquished [ʌn'væŋkwɪʃt] *adj* invitto

unvarnished [ʌn'vɑrnɪʃt] *adj* non verniciato; puro, semplice

unveil [ʌn'vel] *tr* svelare; (*a statue*) scoprire, inaugurare ‖ *intr* scoprirsi

unveiling [ˌʌn'velɪŋ] *s* scoprimento

unvoiced [ʌn'vɔɪst] *adj* non espresso; (*phonet*) sordo

unwanted [ʌn'wɑntɪd] *adj* non desiderato

unwarranted [ʌn'wɑrəntɪd] *adj* ingiustificato

unwary [ʌn'wɛri] *adj* incauto

unwavering [ʌn'wevərɪŋ] *adj* fermo, incrollabile

unwelcome [ʌn'wɛlkəm] *adj* malaccetto; sgradito

unwell [ʌn'wɛl] *adj* poco bene; **to be**

unwell (*said of a woman*) (coll) avere le mestruazioni

unwholesome [ʌn'holsəm] *adj* malsano

unwieldy [ʌn'wildi] *adj* ingombrante

unwilling [ʌn'wiliŋ] *adj* riluttante

unwillingly [ʌn'wiliŋli] *adv* a malincuore, a controvoglia

un·wind [ʌn'waind] *v* (*pret & pp* -wound* ['waund]) *tr* svolgere || *intr* svolgersi; (*said of a watch*) scaricarsi; (*said of a person*) rilasciarsi

unwise [ʌn'waiz] *adj* malaccorto

unwished-for [ʌn'wiʃt ,fər] *adj* indesiderato, non augurato

unwitting [ʌn'witiŋ] *adj* involontario

unwonted [ʌn'wʌntid] *adj* insolito

unworldly [ʌn'wʌrldli] *adj* (*not of this world*) non terrestre; (*not interested in things of this world*) non mondano; (*naive*) semplice

unworthy [ʌn'wʌrði] *adj* indegno

un·wrap [ʌn'ræp] *v* (*pret & pp* -wrapped*) *ger* -wrapping*) *tr* scartare, svolgere, scartocciare

unwrinkled [ʌn'riŋkəld] *adj* senza una grinza

unwritten [ʌn'ritən] *adj* orale; non scritto; (*blank*) in bianco

unyielding [ʌn'jildiŋ] *adj* inflessibile

unyoke [ʌn'yok] *tr* liberare dal giogo

up [ʌp] *adj* che va verso la città; diretto al nord; al corrente; finito, terminato; alto; su; (sports) pari; **to be up and about** essere in piedi || *s* salita; vantaggio; aumento; **ups and downs** alti e bassi *mpl* || *adv* su; in alto; alla pari; **to be up** essere alzato; (*in sports or games*) essere avanti; **to be up in arms** essere in armi; essere indignato; **to be up to a person** toccare a una persona; **to get up** alzarsi; **to go up** salire; **to keep up** mantenere; continuare; **to keep up with** mantenersi alla pari con; **up above** lassù; **up against** (coll) contro; **up against it** (coll) in una strettoia; **up to** fino a; (*capable of*) (coll) all'altezza di; (*scheming*) (coll) tramando; **what's up?** che succede? || *prep* su; sopra; fino a; **to go up a river** risalire un fiume

up-and-coming ['ʌpən'kʌmiŋ] *adj* promettente

up-and-doing ['ʌpən'du·iŋ] *adj* (coll) intraprendente; (coll) attivo

up-and-up ['ʌpən'ʌp] *s—on the up-and-up** (coll) aperto; (coll) apertamente; (coll) in ascesa

up·braid' *tr* rimproverare, strapazzare

upbringing ['ʌp,briŋiŋ] *s* educazione

up'coun'try *adj* all'interno || *s* interno || *adv* verso l'interno

up·date' *tr* aggiornare

upheaval [ʌp'hivəl] *s* sommovimento; (geol) sconvolgimento tellurico

up'hill' *adj* erto, scosceso; arduo, faticoso || *adv* in salita, all'insù

up·hold' *v* (*pret & pp* -held*) *tr* alzare; sostenere; difendere

upholster [ʌp'holstər] *tr* tappezzare

upholsterer [ʌp'holstərər] *s* tappezziere *m*

upholster·y [ʌp'holstəri] *s* (-ies) tap-

pezzeria; (*e.g., of cushions*) imbottitura; (aut) selleria

up'keep' *s* manutenzione; spese *fpl* di manutenzione

upland ['ʌplənd] *or* ['ʌplænd] *adj* alto, elevato || *s* terreno elevato

up'lift' *s* elevazione; miglioramento sociale; edificazione || **up'lift'** *tr* elevare

upon [ʌ'pɑn] *prep* su, sopra, in; **upon** + *ger* non appena + *pp*, e.g., **upon arising** non appena alzato; **upon my word!** sulla mia parola!

upper ['ʌpər] *adj* superiore, disopra; (*town*) soprano; (*river*) alto || *s* disopra *m*; (*of shoe*) tomaia; (rr) (coll) cuccetta; **on one's uppers** ridotto al verde

up'per berth' *s* cuccetta superiore

up'per case' *s* (typ) cassa delle maiuscole, cassa superiore

up'per-case' *adj* (typ) maiuscolo

up'per classes' *spl* prezzo classi *fpl* elevate

up'per hand' *s* vantaggio; **to have the upper hand** prendere il disopra

up'per·most' *adj* (il) più alto; principale || *adv* principalmente, in primo luogo

uppish ['ʌpiʃ] *adj* (coll) arrogante, snob

up·raise' *tr* alzare, tirare su

up'right' *adj* ritto, verticale; dabbene, onesto || *s* staggio, montante *m* || *adv* verticalmente

uprising [ʌp'raiziŋ] *or* ['ʌp ,raiziŋ] *s* sollevazione, insurrezione

up'roar' *s* gazzarra, cagnara, fracasso

uproarious [ʌp'rori·əs] *adj* tumultuoso; (*noisy*) rumoroso; (*funny*) comico

up·root' *tr* sradicare

up·set' *adj* rovesciato; scompigliato; (*emotionally*) scombussolato; (*stomach*) imbarazzato || **up'set'** *s* (*overturn*) rovesciamento; (*defeat*) rovescio; (*disorder*) scompiglio; (*illness*) imbarazzo, disturbo || **up·set'** *v* (*pret & pp* -set*) *ger* -setting*) *tr* rovesciare; scompigliare; indisporre || *intr* rovesciarsi, ribaltarsi

up'set' price' *s* prezzo minimo di vendita di un oggetto all'asta

upsetting [ʌp'setiŋ] *adj* sconcertante

up'shot' *s* conclusione; essenziale *m*

up'side' *s* disopra *m*

up'side down' *adv* alla rovescia; a gambe all'aria; a soqquadro

up'stage' *adj* al fondo della scena; altiero, arrogante || *adv* al fondo della scena || *tr* trattare altezzosamente; (theat) rubare la scena a

up'stairs' *adj* del piano di sopra || *s* piano di sopra || *adv* su, al piano di sopra

upstanding [ʌp'stændiŋ] *adj* diritto; forte; onorevole

up'start' *s* arrivato, nuovo ricco

up'stream' *adv* a monte, controcorrente

up'stroke' *s* (*in handwriting*) tratto ascendente; (mach) corsa ascendente

up'swing' *s* (*in prices*) ascesa; miglioramento; **to be on the upswing** migliorare up'-to-date' *adj* recentissimo; moderno; dell'ultima ora

up'town' *adj* della parte più alta della città || *adv* nella parte più alta della città

up'trend' *s* tendenza al rialzo

up'turn' *s* rivolta; (com) rialzo

upturned [ʌp'tɜrnd] *adj* rivolto all'insù; (*upside down*) capovolto

upward ['ʌpwərd] *adj* ascendente || *adv* all'insù; upward of più di

U'ral Moun'tains ['jʊrəl] *spl* Urali *mpl*

uranium [jʊ'reni·əm] *s* uranio

urban ['ʌrbən] *adj* urbano

urbane [ʌr'ben] *adj* urbano

urbanite ['ʌrbə‚naɪt] *s* abitante *mf* di una città

urbanity [ʌr'bænɪti] *s* urbanità *f*

urbanize ['ʌrbə‚naɪz] *tr* urbanizzare

ur'ban renew'al *s* ricostruzione urbanistica

urchin ['ʌrtʃɪn] *s* monello, birichino

ure·thra [jʊ'riθrə] *s* (-thras *or* -thrae [θri]) uretra

urge [ʌrdʒ] *s* stimolo || *tr* urgere, sollecitare, spronare; (*to endeavor to persuade*) esortare; (*an enterprise*) accelerare || *intr*—to urge against opporsi a

urgen·cy ['ʌrdʒənsi] *s* (-cies) urgenza

urgent ['ʌrdʒənt] *adj* urgente; (*desire*) prepotente

urinal ['jʊrɪnəl] *s* (*receptacle*) orinale *m*; (*for a bedridden person*) pappagallo; (*place*) orinatoio, vespasiano

urinary ['jʊrɪ‚neri] *adj* urinario

urinate ['jʊrɪ‚net] *tr & intr* orinare

urine ['jʊrɪn] *s* urina

urn [ʌrn] *s* urna; (*for making coffee*) caffettiera; (*for making tea*) samovar *m*

urology [jʊ'rɑlədʒi] *s* urologia

Uruguay ['jʊrə‚gwe] *or* ['jʊrə‚gwaɪ] *s* l'Uruguai *m*

Uruguayan [‚jʊrə'gwe·ən] *or* [‚jʊrə‚gwaɪ·ən] *adj & s* uruguaiano

us [ʌs] *pron pers* ci; noi; to us ci, a noi, per noi

U.S.A. ['ju'es'e] *s* (letterword) (United States of America) S.U.A. *mpl*

usable ['juzəbəl] *adj* servibile, adoperabile

usage ['jusɪdʒ] *or* ['juzɪdʒ] *s* uso, usanza; (*of a language*) uso

use [jus] *s* uso, impiego, usanza; in use in uso, in servizio; it's no use non giova; out of use disusato; to be of no use non servire a nulla; to have

no use for non aver bisogno di; non poter soffrire; to make use of servirsi di; what's the use? a che pro? || [juz] *tr* usare, impiegare, servirsi di; to use badly maltrattare; to use up consumare, esaurire || *intr*—used to translated in Italian in three ways: (1) by the imperfect indicative, e.g., he used to go to church at seven o'clock andava in chiesa alle sette; (2) by the imperfect indicative of solere, e.g., he used to smoke all day soleva fumare tutto il giorno; (3) by the imperfect indicative of avere l'abitudine di, e.g., he used to go to the shore aveva l'abitudine di andare alla spiaggia

used [juzd] *adj* uso, usato; to get used to ['juzdtu] *or* ['justu] fare la mano a, abituarsi a

useful ['jusfəl] *adj* utile

usefulness ['jusfəlnɪs] *s* utilità *f*

useless ['juslɪs] *adj* inutile, inservibile

user ['juzər] *s* utente *mf*

usher ['ʌʃər] *s* (*doorkeeper*) portiere *m*; (hist) cerimoniere *m*; (theat) maschera; (mov) lucciola || *tr* introdurre; to usher in annunciare, introdurre

U.S.S.R. ['ju'es'es'ɑr] *s* (letterword) (Union of Soviet Socialist Republics) U.R.S.S. *f*

usual ['juʒʊ·əl] *adj* usuale, abituale; as usual come il solito

usually ['juʒʊ·əli] *adv* usualmente

usurp [jʊ'zɜrp] *tr* usurpare

usu·ry ['juʒəri] *s* (-ries) usura

utensil [ju'tensɪl] *s* utensile *m*

uter·us ['jutərəs] *s* (-i [‚aɪ]) utero

utilitarian [‚jutɪlɪ'teri·ən] *adj* utilitario

utili·ty [ju'tɪlɪti] *s* (-ties) utilità *f*; compagnia di servizi pubblici

utilize ['jutɪ‚laɪz] *tr* utilizzare

utmost ['ʌt‚most] *adj* sommo; estremo; massimo || *s*—the utmost il massimo; to do one's utmost fare tutto il possibile; to the utmost al massimo limite

utopia [ju'topɪ·ə] *s* utopia

utopian [ju'topɪ·ən] *adj* utopistico || *s* utopista *mf*

utter ['ʌtər] *adj* completo, totale || *tr* proferire, pronunziare; (*a sigh*) dare, fare

utterly ['ʌtərli] *adv* completamente

uxoricide [ʌk'sɔrɪ‚saɪd] *s* (*husband*) uxoricida *m*; (*act*) uxoricidio

uxorious [ʌk'sɔrɪ·əs] *adj* eccessivamente innamorato della propria moglie; dominato dalla moglie

V

V, v [vi] *s* ventiduesima lettera dell'alfabeto inglese

vacan·cy ['vekənsi] *s* (-cies) (*emptiness*) vuoto; (*unfilled position*) vacanza; (*unfilled job*) posto vacante; (*in a building*) appartamento libero;

(*in a hotel*) camera libera; no vacancy completo

vacant ['vekənt] *adj* (*empty*) vuoto; (*position*) vacante; (*expression of the face*) vago

vacate ['veket] *tr* sgombrare; (*a posi-*

tion) ritirarsi da; (law) annullare; **to vacate one's mind of worries** liberarsi dalle preoccupazioni ‖ *intr* sloggiare; (coll) andarsene

vacation [veˈkeʃən] *s* vacanza, villeggiatura; vacanze *fpl* ‖ *intr* estivare, villeggiare

vacationer [veˈkeʃənər] *s* villeggiante *mf*, vacanziere *m*

vacationist [veˈkeʃənɪst] *s* villeggiante *mf*, vacanziere *m*

vaca'tion with pay' *s* vacanze *fpl* pagate

vaccinate [ˈvæksɪˌnet] *tr* vaccinare

vaccination [ˌvæksɪˈneʃən] *s* vaccinazione

vaccine [vækˈsin] *s* vaccino

vacillate [ˈvæsɪˌlet] *intr* vacillare

vacillating [ˈvæsɪˌletɪŋ] *adj* vacillante

vacui·ty [væˈkjuˌɪti] *s* (**-ties**) vacuità *f*

vacu·um [ˈvækjuˌəm] *s* (**-ums** or **-a** [ə]) vuoto; **in a vacuum** sotto vuoto ‖ *tr* pulire con l'aspirapolvere

vac'uum clean'er *s* aspirapolvere *m*

vac'uum-pack'ed *adj* confezionato sotto vuoto

vac'uum tube' *s* tubo elettronico

vagabond [ˈvægəˌbɑnd] *adj* & *s* vagabondo

vagar·y [vəˈgeri] *s* (**-ies**) capriccio

vagran·cy [ˈvegrənsi] *s* (**-cies**) vagabondaggio

vagrant [ˈvegrənt] *adj* & *s* vagabondo

vague [veg] *adj* vago

va'gus nerve' [ˈvegəs] *s* (anat) vago

vain [ven] *adj* vano; (*conceited*) vanitoso; **in vain** in vano

vainglorious [venˈglɔri·əs] *adj* vanaglorioso

valance [ˈvæləns] *s* balza, mantovana

vale [vel] *s* valle *f*

valedictorian [ˌvælɪdɪkˈtɔri·ən] *s* studente *m* che pronuncia il discorso di commiato

valence [ˈveləns] *s* (chem) valenza

valentine [ˈvælənˌtaɪn] *s* (*sweetheart*) valentino; (*card*) cartolina di San Valentino

valet [ˈvælɪt] or [ˈvæle] *s* valletto

valiant [ˈvæljənt] *adj* valoroso

valid [ˈvælɪd] *adj* valido

validate [ˈvælɪˌdet] *tr* convalidare, vidimare; (sports) omologare

validation [ˌvælɪˈdeʃən] *s* convalida, vidimazione; (sports) omologazione

validi·ty [vəˈlɪdrti] *s* (**-ties**) validità *f*

valise [vəˈlis] *s* valigetta

valley [ˈvæli] *s* valle *f*, vallata; (*of roof*) linea di compluvio

valor [ˈvælər] *s* valore *m*, coraggio

valorous [ˈvælərəs] *adj* valoroso

valuable [ˈvæljuˌəbəl] or [ˈvæljəbəl] *adj* (*having monetary worth*) prezioso; pregevole, pregiato ‖ **valuables** *spl* valori *mpl*

value [ˈvælju] *s* valore *m;* importanza; (com) valuta, valore *m;* **an excellent value** un acquisto eccellente ‖ *tr* stimare, valutare

value'-added tax' *s* imposta sul valore aggiunto

valueless [ˈvæljulɪs] *adj* senza valore

valve [vælv] *s* (anat, mach, rad, telv)

valvola; (bot, zool) valva; (mus) pistone *m*

valve' gears' *spl* meccanismo di distribuzione

valve'-in-head' en'gine *s* motore *m* a valvole in testa

valve' lift'er *s* alzavalvole *m*

valve' seat' *s* sede *f* della valvola

valve' spring' *s* molla di valvola

valve' stem' *s* stelo di comando della valvola

vamp [væmp] *s* parte *f* anteriore della tomaia; (*patchwork*) rabberciatura; (*female*) vamp *f* ‖ *tr* (*a shoe*) rimontare; rabberciare; (*to concoct*) inventare, raffazzonare; (*an accompaniment*) improvvisare; (*said of a female*) sedurre

vampire [ˈvæmpaɪr] *s* vampiro; (*female*) vamp *f*

van [væn] *s* camionetta, autofurgone *m;* (mil & fig) avanguardia

vanadium [vəˈnedi·əm] *s* vanadio

vandal [ˈvændəl] *adj* & *s* vandalo ‖ **Vandal** *adj* & *s* Vandalo

vandalism [ˈvændəˌlɪzəm] *s* vandalismo

vane [ven] *s* (*weathervane*) banderuola; (*of windmill, of turbine*) pala; (*of feather*) barba

vanguard [ˈvænˌɡɑrd] *s* avanguardia; **in the vanguard** all'avanguardia

vanilla [vəˈnɪlə] *s* vaniglia

vanish [ˈvænɪʃ] *intr* svanire

van'ishing cream' [ˈvænɪ/rɪŋ] *s* crema evanescente

vani·ty [ˈvænɪtɪ] *s* (**-ties**) vanità *f;* (*table*) toletta; (*case*) astuccio di toletta

vanquish [ˈvænkwɪʃ] *tr* superare, vincere

van'tage ground' [ˈvæntɪdʒ] *s* posizione favorevole

vapid [ˈvæpɪd] *adj* insipido

vapor [ˈvepər] *s* vapore *m;* (*visible vapor*) vapori *mpl*

vaporize [ˈvepəˌraɪz] *tr* vaporizzare ‖ *intr* vaporizzarsi

va'por lock' *s* tampone *m* di vapore

vaporous [ˈvepərəs] *adj* vaporoso

va'por trail' *s* scia di condensazione

variable [ˈverɪˌəbəl] *adj* & *s* variabile *f*

variance [ˈverɪˌəns] *s* divario, differenza; **at variance with** (*a thing*) differente da; differentemente da; (*a person*) in disaccordo con

variant [ˈverɪˌənt] *adj* & *s* variante *f*

variation [ˌverɪˈeʃən] *s* variazione

varicose [ˈverɪˌkos] *adj* varicoso

varied [ˈverid] *adj* vario, svariato

variegated [ˈverɪ·əˌgetɪd] or [ˈverɪˌɡetɪd] *adj* variegato, screziato

varie·ty [vəˈraɪ·ɪti] *s* (**-ties**) varietà *f*

vari'ety show' *s* spettacolo di varietà

varnish [ˈvɑrnɪʃ] *s* vernice *f* ‖ *tr* verniciare; (fig) dare la vernice a

variola [vəˈraɪ·ələ] *s* (pathol) vaiolo

various [ˈverɪ·əs] *adj* vari; (*varicolored*) vario, variegato

varsi·ty [ˈvɑrsɪti] *adj* (sports) universitario ‖ *s* (**-ties**) (sports) squadra numero uno

var·y ['veri] v (pret & pp **-ied**) tr & intr variare

vase [ves] or [vez] s vaso

vaseline ['væsə,lin] s (trademark) vaselina

vassal ['væsəl] adj & s vassallo

vast [væst] or [vɑst] adj vasto

vastly ['væstli] or ['vɑstli] adv enormemente

vastness ['væstnɪs] or ['vɑstnɪs] s vastità f

vat [væt] s tino, bigoncia

Vatican ['vætɪkən] adj vaticano ‖ s Vaticano

Vat'ican Cit'y s Città f del Vaticano

vaudeville ['vodvɪl] or ['vədəvɪl] s spettacolo di varietà; (theatrical piece) vaudeville m, commedia musicale

vault [vɔlt] s volta; (underground chamber) cantina; (of a bank) camera di sicurezza; (burial chamber) cripta; (of heaven) cappa; (leap) salto ‖ tr formare a mo' di volta; saltare ‖ intr saltare

vaunt [vɔnt] or [vɑnt] s vanto, vanteria ‖ tr vantarsi di ‖ intr vantarsi

veal [vil] s vitello

veal' chop' s scaloppa, cotoletta di vitello

veal' cut'let s scaloppina

vedette [vɪ'dɛt] s (nav) vedetta; (mil) sentinella avanzata

veer [vɪr] s virata ‖ tr far cambiare di direzione a ‖ intr virare; (said of the wind) cambiare di direzione

vegetable ['vedʒɪtəbəl] adj vegetale ‖ s (plant) vegetale m; (edible plant) ortaggio; **vegetables** verdura, erbe fpl, erbaggi mpl, ortaggi mpl

veg'etable gar'den s orto

veg'etable soup' s minestra di verdura

vegetarian [,vedʒɪ'tɛrɪ-ən] adj & s vegetariano

vegetate ['vedʒɪ,tet] intr vegetare

vehemence ['vi·ɪməns] s veemenza

vehement ['vi·ɪmənt] adj veemente

vehicle ['vi·ɪkəl] s veicolo

vehic'ular traf'fic [vɪ'hɪkjələr] s circolazione stradale

veil [vel] s velo; **to take the veil** prendere il velo ‖ tr velare

vein [ven] s vena; (streak) venatura; (of ore) filone m ‖ tr venare

velar ['vilər] adj & s velare f

vellum ['veləm] s pergamena

veloci·ty [vɪ'lɑsɪti] s (-ties) velocità f

velvet ['velvɪt] adj di velluto ‖ s velluto; (slang) guadagno al gioco; (coll) situazione all'acqua di rose

velveteen [,velvɪ'tin] s vellutino di cotone

velvety ['velvɪti] adj vellutato

vend [vend] tr vendere; (to peddle) fare il venditore ambulante di

vend'ing machine' s distributore automatico

vendor ['vendər] s venditore m

veneer [və'nɪr] s impiallacciatura, piallaccio; (fig) vernice f ‖ tr impiallacciare

venerable ['venərəbəl] adj venerabile

venerate ['venə,ret] tr venerare

venereal [vɪ'nɪrɪ·əl] adj venereo

Venetia [vɪ'ni/ɪ·ə] or [vɪ'ni/ə] s (province) Venezia

Venetian [vɪ'ni/ən] adj & s veneziano

Vene'tian blind' s veneziana, persiana avvolgibile

Venezuelan [,venɪ'zwilən] adj & s venezolano

vengeance ['vendʒəns] s vendetta; **with a vengeance** violentemente; eccessivamente

vengeful ['vendʒfəl] adj vendicativo

Venice ['venɪs] s Venezia

venire·man [vɪ'naɪrɪmən] s (-men) membro di un collegio di giurati

venison ['venɪsən] or ['venɪzən] s carne f di cervo

venom ['venəm] s veleno

venomous ['venəməs] adj velenoso

vent [vent] s sfiatatoio; (of jacket) spacco; **to give vent to** dare sfogo a ‖ tr sfogare, sfuriare; mettere uno sfiatatoio a; **to vent one's spleen** sfogare la bile

vent' hole' s apertura di sfogo

ventilate ['ventɪ,let] tr ventilare

ventilator ['ventɪ,letər] s ventilatore m

ventricle ['ventrɪkəl] s ventricolo

ventriloquist [ven'trɪləkwɪst] s ventriloquo

venture ['vent/ər] s azzardo, avventura rischiosa; **at a venture** alla ventura ‖ tr avventurare ‖ intr avventurarsi, arrischiarsi

venturesome ['vent/ərsəm] adj (risky) rischioso; (daring) avventuroso

venturous ['vent/ərəs] adj avventuroso

vent' win'dow s (aut) deflettore m

venue ['venju] s (law) posto dove ha avuto luogo il reato; (law) luogo dove si riunisce la corte; **change of venue** cambio di giurisdizione

Venus ['vinəs] s (very beautiful woman) venere f; (astr) Venere m; (myth) Venere f

veracious [vɪ're/əs] adj verace

veraci·ty [vɪ'ræsɪti] s (-ties) veridicità f

veranda or **verandah** [və'rændə] s veranda

verb [vʌrb] adj verbale ‖ s verbo

verbalize ['vʌrbə,laɪz] tr esprimere con parole; (gram) convertire in forma verbale ‖ intr essere verboso

verbatim [vər'betɪm] adj letterale ‖ adv parola per parola, testualmente

verbena [vər'binə] s (bot) verbena

verbiage ['vʌrbɪ·ɪdʒ] s verbosità f; (style of wording) espressione

verbose [vər'bos] adj verboso

verdant ['vʌrdənt] adj verde, verdeggiante

verdict ['vʌrdɪkt] s verdetto

verdigris ['vʌrdɪ,grɪs] s verderame m

verdure ['vʌrdʒər] s verde m

verge [vʌrdʒ] s orlo, limite m; bordo; (of a column) fusto; **on the verge of** al punto di; all'orlo di ‖ intr—**to verge on** costeggiare, rasentare

verification [,verɪfɪ'ke/ən] s verifica

veri·fy ['veri ,fai] v (pret & pp -fied) tr verificare, confermare

verily ['verili] adv in verità

veritable ['veritəbəl] adj vero

vermilion [vər'miljən] adj & s vermiglio

vermin ['vʌrmin] ssg (person) persona abominevole || spl (animals or persons) insetti mpl

vermouth [vər'muθ] or ['vʌrmuθ] s vermut m

vernacular [vər'nækjələr] adj volgare || s volgare m, vernacolo; (language peculiar to a class or profession) gergo

versatile ['vʌrsətil] adj (person) versatile; (tool or device) a vari usi

verse [vʌrs] s verso; (Bib) versetto

versed [vʌrst] adj versato

versification [,vʌrsifi'keʃən] s versificazione

versi·fy ['vʌrsi ,fai] v (pret & pp -fied) tr & intr versificare

version ['vʌrʒən] s versione

ver·so ['vʌrso] s (-sos) (of coin) rovescio; (of page) verso

versus ['vʌrsəs] prep contro; in confronto a

verte·bra ['vʌrtibrə] s (-brae [,bri] or -bras) vertebra

vertebrate ['vʌrtə ,bret] adj & s vertebrato

ver·tex ['vʌrteks] s (-texes or -tices [tı ,siz]) vertice m

vertical ['vʌrtikəl] adj & s verticale f

ver'tical hold' s (telv) regolatore m del sincronismo verticale

ver'tical sta'bilizer s (aer) deriva

verti·go ['vʌrtı ,go] s (-goes or -gos) vertigine f

verve [vʌrv] s verve f, brio

very ['veri] adj (utter) grande, completo; (precise) vero e proprio; (mere) stesso, e.g., his very brother suo fratello stesso || adv molto, e.g., to be very rich essere molto ricco

vesicle ['vesikəl] s vescichetta

vesper ['vespər] s vespro; **vespers** vespri mpl || **Vesper** s Vespero

ves'per bell' s campana a vespro

vessel ['vesəl] s (ship) nave f, vascello; (container) vaso; (anat) vaso; (fig) vasello

vest [vest] s (of man's suit) panciotto, gilè m; (of woman's garment) corpino || tr vestire; **to vest** (authority) in concedere a; **to vest with** investire di || intr vestirisi; **to vest in** passare a

vest'ed in'terest s interesse acquisito

vestibule ['vesti ,bjul] s vestibolo

vestige ['vestidʒ] s vestigio

vestment ['vestmənt] s (eccl) paramento

vest'-pock'et adj da tasca, tascabile

ves·try ['vestri] s (-tries) sagrestia; (chapel) cappella; giunta esecutiva della chiesa episcopaliana

ves'try·man s (-men) membro della giunta esecutiva della chiesa episcopaliana

Vesuvius [vi'suvi·əs] or [vi'sjuvi·əs] s il Vesuvio

vetch [vetʃ] s veccia; (grass pea) cicerchia

veteran ['vetərən] adj & s veterano

veterinarian [,vetəri'neri·ən] s veterinario

veterinar·y ['vetəri ,neri] adj veterinario || s (-ies) veterinario

ve·to ['vito] s (-toes) veto || tr porre il veto a

vex [veks] tr irritare, tormentare

vexation [vek'seʃən] s fastidio, contrarietà f

vexatious [vek'seʃəs] adj irritante, fastidioso; (law) vessatorio

vexing ['veksiŋ] adj noioso, fastidioso, irritante

via ['vai·ə] prep via, per via di

viaduct ['vai·ə ,dʌkt] s viadotto

vial ['vai·əl] s fiala, boccetta

viand ['vai·ənd] s vivanda, manicaretto

viati·cum [vai'ætikəm] s (-cums or -ca [kə]) (eccl) viatico

vibrate ['vaibret] tr & intr vibrare

vibration [vai'breʃən] s vibrazione

vicar ['vikər] s vicario

vicarage ['vikəridʒ] s residenza del vicario; (office; duties) vicariato

vicarious [vai'keri·əs] or [vi'keri·əs] adj sostituto; (punishment) ricevuto in vece di altra persona; (power) delegato; (enjoyment) di riflesso

vice [vais] s vizio

vice'-ad'miral s viceammiraglio, ammiraglio di squadra

vice'-pres'ident s vicepresidente m

viceroy ['vaisroi] s viceré m

vice versa ['vaisi 'vʌrsə] or ['vaisə 'vʌrsə] adv viceversa

vicini·ty [vi'siniti] s (-ties) vicinanze fpl, paraggi mpl

vicious ['viʃəs] adj vizioso; maligno, malvagio; (dog) cattivo, che morde; (horse) selvaggio; (headache) tremendo; (reasoning; circle) vizioso

victim ['viktim] s vittima

victimize ['vikti ,maiz] tr fare una vittima di; ingannare; (hist) sacrificare

victor ['viktər] s vincitore m

victorious [vik'tori·əs] adj vittorioso

victo·ry ['viktəri] s (-ries) vittoria

victuals ['vitəlz] spl vettovaglie fpl

vid'eo cassette' ['vidi ,o] s videocassetta

vid'eo sig'nal s segnale m video

vid'eo tape' s nastro televisivo

vie [vai] v (pret & pp vied; ger vying) intr gareggiare; **to vie for** disputarsi

Vien·nese [,vi·ə'niz] adj viennese || s (-nese) viennese mf

Vietnam [,viet'nɑm] s il Vietnam

Vietnam·ese [vi ,etnə'miz] adj vietnamita || s (-ese) vietnamita mf; (language) vietnamita m

view [vju] s vista; (picture) veduta; prospetto; esame m; punto di vista; **to be on view** (said of a corpse) essere esposto; **to keep in view** non perdere di vista; **to take a dim view of** avere un'opinione scettica di; **with a view to** con lo scopo di || tr guardare, osservare; considerare

viewer ['vju·ər] s spettatore m; (telv) telespettatore m; (phot) visore m; (phot) proiettore m di diapositive

view'find'er s (phot) traguardo, visore m

view'point' s punto di vista

vigil ['vɪdʒɪl] s vigilia; **to keep vigil** vegliare

vigilance ['vɪdʒɪləns] s vigilanza

vigilant ['vɪdʒɪlənt] adj vigilante

vignette [vɪn'jet] s vignetta

vigor ['vɪgər] s vigore m, gagliardia

vigorous ['vɪgərəs] adj vigoroso

Viking ['vaɪkɪŋ] s vichingo

vile [vaɪl] adj vile, malvagio; (wretchedly bad) orribile; disgustoso, ripugnante; (filthy) sporco; (poor) povero, basso

vili·fy ['vɪlɪ,faɪ] v (pret & pp -fied) tr vilificare

villa ['vɪlə] s villa

village ['vɪlɪdʒ] s villaggio, paese m

villager ['vɪlɪdʒər] s paesano

villain ['vɪlən] s scellerato; (of a play) cattivo, anima nera

villainous ['vɪlənəs] adj vile, infame

villain·y ['vɪləni] s (-ies) scelleratezza, malvagità f

vim [vɪm] s vigore m, brio

vinaigrette [,vɪnə'gret] s boccetta dell'aceto aromatico

vinaigrette' sauce' s salsa verde

vindicate ['vɪndɪ,ket] tr scolpare; difendere, sostenere; (e.g., a claim) rivendicare

vindictive [vɪn'dɪktɪv] adj vendicativo

vine [vaɪn] s (climber) rampicante f; (grape plant) vite f

vine'dress'er s vignaiolo

vinegar ['vɪnɪgər] s aceto

vinegarish ['vɪnɪgərɪʃ] adj acetoso; (fig) acre, mordace

vinegary ['vɪnɪgəri] adj acetoso; (fig) irritabile, irascibile

vineyard ['vɪnjərd] s vigna, vigneto

vintage ['vɪntɪdʒ] s vendemmia; vino di annata eccezionale; (fig) edizione

vintager ['vɪntɪdʒər] s vendemmiatore m

vin'tage wine' s vino di marca

vin'tage year' s buona annata

vintner ['vɪntnər] s produttore m di vino; vinaio

vinyl ['vaɪnɪl] or ['vɪnɪl] s vinile m

violate ['vaɪ·ə,let] tr violare

violation [,vaɪ·ə'le/ən] s violazione

violence ['vaɪ·ələns] s violenza

violent ['vaɪ·ələnt] adj violento

violet ['vaɪ,əlɪt] adj violetto || s (color) violetto, viola; (bot) violetta; (Viola odorata) viola mammola

violin [,vaɪ·ə'lɪn] s violino

violinist [,vaɪ·ə'lɪnɪst] s violinista mf

violoncellist [,vaɪ·ələn't/elɪst] or [,vi·ələn't/elɪst] s violoncellista mf

violoncel·lo [,vaɪ·ələn't/elo] or [,vi·ələn't/elo] s (-los) violoncello

VIP ['vi'aɪ'pi] s (letterword) (**Very Important Person**) persona di maggiore riguardo

viper ['vaɪpər] s vipera; (any snake) serpe f; (spiteful person) vipera

vira·go [vɪ'rego] s (-goes or -gos) megera, donna dal caratteraccio impossibile

virgin ['vɑrdʒɪn] adj & s vergine f || **Virgin** s Vergine f

vir'gin birth' s parto verginale della Madonna; (zool) partenogenesi f

Virgin'ia creep'er [vər'dʒɪnɪ·ə] s vite f del Canada

virginity [vər'dʒɪnɪti] s virginità f

Virgo ['vɑrgo] s (astr) Vergine f

virility [vɪ'rɪlɪti] s virilità f

virology [vaɪ'rɑlədʒɪ] s virologia

virtual ['vɑrt/u·əl] adj virtuale

virtue ['vɑrt/u] s virtù f

virtuosi·ty [,vɑrt/u'ɑsɪti] s (-ties) virtuosità f, virtuosismo

virtuo·so [,vɑrt/u'oso] s (-sos or -si [si]) virtuoso

virtuous ['vɑrt/u·əs] adj virtuoso

virulence ['vɪrjələns] s virulenza

virulent ['vɪrjələnt] adj virulento

virus ['vaɪrəs] s virus m

visa ['vizə] s visto || tr vistare

visage ['vɪzɪdʒ] s faccia; apparenza

vis-à-vis [,viza'vi] adj l'uno di fronte all'altro || adv vis-à-vis || prep di fronte a

viscera ['vɪsərə] spl visceri mpl, viscere fpl

viscount ['vaɪkaunt] s visconte m

viscountess ['vaɪkauntɪs] s viscontessa

viscous ['vɪskəs] adj viscoso

vise [vaɪs] s morsa

visé ['vize] or [vi'ze] s & tr var of visa

visible ['vɪzɪbəl] adj visibile

Visigoth ['vɪzɪ,gɑθ] s visigoto

vision ['vɪʒən] s visione; (sense) vista

visionar·y ['vɪʒə,neri] adj visionario || s (-ies) visionario

visit ['vɪzɪt] s visitare; affliggere, colpire; (a punishment) far ricadere || intr visitare; (to chat) fare un chiacchierata

visitation [,vɪzɪ'te/ən] s visitazione; punizione divina, visita del Signore

vis'iting card' s biglietto da visita

vis'iting hours' spl orario delle visite

vis'iting nurse' s infermiera che visita i pazienti a domicilio

visitor ['vɪzɪtər] s visitatore m

visor ['vaɪzər] s visiera; (fig) maschera

vista ['vɪstə] s vista, prospettiva

visual ['vɪʒu·əl] adj visivo, visuale

vis'ual acu'ity s acutezza visiva

visualize ['vɪʒu·ə,laɪz] tr formare l'immagine mentale di; (to make visible) visualizzare

vital ['vaɪtəl] adj vitale; (deadly) mortale || **vitals** spl organi vitali

vitality [vaɪ'tælɪti] s vitalità f

vitalize ['vaɪtə,laɪz] tr animare, infondere vita a

vi'tal statis'tics spl statistiche fpl anagrafiche

vitamin ['vaɪtəmɪn] s vitamina

vitiate ['vɪ/ɪ,et] tr viziare

vitreous ['vɪtrɪ·əs] adj vitreo, vetroso

vitriolic [,vɪtrɪ'ɑlɪk] adj di vetriolo; (fig) caustico

vituperate [vaɪ'tupə,ret] or [vaɪ'tjupə,ret] tr vituperare

viva ['vivə] s evviva || *interj* viva!

vivacious [vɪ'veʃəs] or [vaɪ'veʃəs] *adj* vivace

vivaci•ty [vɪ'væsɪti] or [vaɪ'væsɪti] s (-ties) vivacità f, gaiezza

viva voce ['vaɪvə 'vosi] *adv* a viva voce

vivid ['vɪvɪd] *adj* vivido

vivi•fy ['vɪvɪ,faɪ] v (*pret & pp* -fied) *tr* vivificare

vivisection [,vɪvɪ'sɛkʃən] s vivisezione

vixen ['vɪksən] s volpe femmina; (*ill-tempered woman*) megera

vizier [vɪ'zɪr] or ['vɪzjər] s visir m

vocabular•y [vo'kæbjə,lɛri] s (-ies) vocabolario

vocal ['vokəl] *adj* vocale; (*inclined to express oneself freely*) che si fa sentire, loquace; (*e.g., outburst*) verbale

vocalist ['vokəlɪst] s cantante mf; (*of jazz*) vocalist mf

vocalize ['vokə,laɪz] *tr* vocalizzare || *intr* vocalizzarsi

vocation [vo'keʃən] s vocazione; professione, impiego

voca′tional educa′tion s istruzione professionale

vocative ['vokətɪv] s vocativo

vociferate [vo'sɪfə,ret] *intr* vociferare

vociferous [vo'sɪfərəs] *adj* rumoroso, vociferante

vogue [vog] s voga, moda; **in vogue** in voga, di moda

voice [vɔɪs] s voce f; (*of animals*) verso; **in a loud voice** a voce alta; **in a low voice** a voce bassa; **to give voice to** esprimere; **with one voice** con una sola voce || *tr* esprimere; (*phonet*) sonorizzare || *intr* sonorizzarsi

voiced [vɔɪst] *adj* (phonet) sonoro

voiceless ['vɔɪslɪs] *adj* senza voce; muto; (phonet) sordo, duro

void [vɔɪd] *adj* (*useless*) inutile; (*empty*) vuoto; (*law*) invalido, nullo; **void of** sprovvisto di || s vuoto; (*gap*) buco || *tr* vuotare; (*the bowels*) evacuare; annullare || *intr* andare di corpo

volatile ['vɑlətɪl] *adj* volatile; instabile; (*disposition*) volubile, incostante

volatilize ['vɑlətɪ,laɪz] *tr* volatilizzare || *intr* volatilizzarsi

volcanic [vɑl'kænɪk] *adj* vulcanico

volca•no [vɑl'keno] s (-noes or -nos) vulcano

volition [vo'lɪʃən] s volontà f; **of one's own volition** di propria volontà

volley ['vɑli] s (*e.g., of bullets*) scarica, sventagliata; (*tennis*) volata || *tr* colpire a volo || *intr* colpire la palla a volo

vol′ley•ball′ s pallavolo f

volplane ['vɑl,plen] s planata || *intr* planare

volt [volt] s volt m

voltage ['voltɪdʒ] s voltaggio

volt′age divid′er [dɪ'vaɪdər] s divisore m del voltaggio

voltaic [vɑl'te•ɪk] *adj* voltaico

volte-face [vɔlt'fɑs] s voltafaccia m

volt′me′ter s voltmetro

voluble ['vɑljəbəl] *adj* locuace

volume ['vɑljəm] s volume m; **to speak volumes** avere molta importanza; essere molto espressivo

voluminous [və'luminəs] *adj* voluminoso

voluntar•y ['vɑlən,tɛri] *adj* volontario || s (-ies) assolo di organo

volunteer [,vɑlən'tɪr] *adj & s* volontario || *tr* dare or dire volontariamente || *intr* offrirsi; arruolarsi come volontario; **to volunteer to** + *inf* offrirsi di + *inf*

voluptuar•y [və'lʌptʃʊ,ɛri] *adj* voluttuoso || s (-ies) sibarita m, epicureo

voluptuous [və'lʌptʃʊ•əs] *adj* voluttuoso

volute [və'lut] s voluta

vomit ['vɑmɪt] s vomito || *tr & intr* vomitare, rigettare

voodoo ['vudu] *adj* di vudù || s (*practice*) vudù m; (*person*) vuduista mf

voracious [və'reʃəs] *adj* vorace

voracity [və'ræsɪti] s voracità f

vor•tex ['vɔrtɛks] s (-texes or -tices ['tɪ,siz]) vortice m

vota•ry ['votəri] s (-ries) persona legata da un voto; amante mf, appassionato

vote [vot] s voto; **to put to the vote** mettere ai voti; **to tally the votes** procedere allo scrutinio dei voti || *tr* votare; dichiarare; **to vote down** respingere; **to vote in** eleggere; **to vote out** scacciare || *intr* votare

vote′ get′ter ['getər] s accaparratore m di voti; slogan m che conquista voti

voter ['votər] s elettore m

vot′ing machine′ ['votɪŋ] s macchina per registrare lo scrutinio dei voti

votive ['votɪv] *adj* votivo

vo′tive of′fering s voto, ex voto, offerta votiva

vouch [vautʃ] *tr* garantire || *intr*—**to vouch for** (s.th) garantire; (s.o.) rendersi garante per, garantire per

voucher ['vautʃər] s garante mf; (*certificate*) ricevuta, pezza d'appoggio

vouch•safe′ *tr* concedere, accordare || *intr*—**to vouchsafe to** + *inf* degnarsi di + *inf*

voussoir [vu'swɑr] s cuneo

vow [vau] s voto; **to take vows** pronunciare i voti || *tr* promettere; (*vengeance*) giurare || *intr* fare un voto

vowel ['vau•əl] s vocale f

voyage ['vɔɪ•ɪdʒ] s viaggio; (*by sea*) traversata || *tr* attraversare || *intr* viaggiare

voyager ['vɔɪ•ɪdʒər] s viaggiatore m, passeggero

vulcanize ['vʌlkə,naɪz] *tr* vulcanizzare

vulgar ['vʌlgər] *adj* volgare; comune, popolare

vulgari•ty [vʌl'gærɪti] s (-ties) volgarità f

Vul′gar Lat′in s latino volgare

Vulgate ['vʌlget] s Vulgata

vulnerable ['vʌlnərəbəl] *adj* vulnerabile

vulture ['vʌltʃər] s avvoltoio

W, w ['dʌbəl ‚ju] s ventitreesima lettera dell'alfabeto inglese

wad [wad] s (of cotton) batuffolo, bioccolo; (of money) mazzetta, rotolo; (of tobacco) pallottola; (in a gun) stoppaccio || v (pret & pp **wadded;** ger **wadding)** tr arrotolare; (shot) comprimere; (fig) imbottire

waddle ['wadəl] s andatura a mo' di anitra || intr scolettare

wade [wed] tr guadare || intr guadare; avanzare faticosamente; sguazzare; **to wade into** (coll) attaccare violentemente; **to wade through** procedere a stento per; leggere con difficoltà

wad'ing bird' ['wedɪŋ] s trampoliere m

wafer ['wefər] s disco adesivo di carta per chiudere lettere; (cake) wafer m, cialda; (eccl, med) ostia

waffle ['wafəl] s cialda

waf'fle i'ron s schiacce fpl

waft [wæft] or [waft] tr portare leggermente or a volo || intr librarsi, spandersi

wag [wæg] s (of head) cenno; (of tail) scodinzolio; (person) burlone m || v (pret & pp **wagged;** ger **wagging)** tr (the head) scuotere; (the tail) dimenare || intr scodinzolare

wage [wedʒ] s salario, paga; **wages** salario, paga; ricompensa; prezzo, e.g., **the wages of sin is death** la morte è il prezzo del peccato || tr (war) fare

wage' earn'er ['ʌrnər] s salariato

wager ['wedʒər] s scommessa; **to lay a wager** fare una scommessa || tr & intr scommettere

wage'work'er s lavoratore salariato

waggish ['wægɪʃ] adj scherzoso, comico, burlone

Wagnerian [vɑg'nɪrɪ-ən] adj & s wagneriano

wagon ['wægən] s carro, carretto; (e.g., Conestoga wagon) carriaggio; furgone m; carrozzone m; **to be on the wagon** (slang) astenersi dal bere; **to hitch one's wagon to a star** avere altissime ambizioni

wag'tail' s (orn) ballerina, cutrettola

waif [wef] s (foundling) trovatello; abbandonato; animale smarrito

wail [wel] s gemito, lamento || intr gemere, lamentarsi

wain·scot ['wenskət] or ['wenskɑt] s pannello per rivestimenti || v (pret & pp -scoted or -scotted; ger -scoting or -scotting) tr rivestire di pannelli di legno

waist [west] s vita, cintura; blusa, camicetta, corpetto

waist'band' s cintola

waist'cloth' s perizoma m

waistcoat ['west ‚kot] or ['weskət] s corpetto, gilè m

waist'line' s vita, cintura; **to keep or watch one's waistline** conservare la linea

wait [wet] s attesa; **to lie in wait** attendere al varco || tr (one's turn) attendere || intr attendere, aspettare; **to wait for** attendere, aspettare; **to wait on** servire; **to wait up for** (coll) aspettare alzato

wait'-and-see' pol'icy s attendismo

waiter ['wetər] s cameriere m; (tray) vassoio

wait'ing list' s lista di aspettativa

wait'ing room' s sala d'aspetto

waitress ['wetrɪs] s cameriera

waive [wev] tr (one's rights) rinunciare (with dat); differire; mettere da parte

waiver ['wevər] s rinuncia

wake [wek] s (any watch) veglia; (watch by a dead body) veglia funebre; (of a boat) solco, scia; **in the wake of** come risultato di; nelle orme di || v (pret **waked** or **woke** [wok]; pp **waked**) tr svegliare || intr svegliarsi; **to wake to** darsi conto di; **to wake up** svegliarsi

wakeful ['wekfəl] adj sveglio; insonne

waken ['wekən] tr svegliare || intr svegliarsi

wale [wel] s segno lasciato da una frustata, vescica; (in fabric) riga, costa

Wales [welz] s la Galles

walk [wɔk] s (act) camminata; (distance) cammino; (for pleasure) passeggiata; (gait) andatura; (line of work) attività f, mestiere m; (sidewalk) marciapiede m; (in a garden) sentiero; (yard for domestic animals to exercise in) recinto; (sports) marcia; **to go for a walk** andare a fare una passeggiata || tr (a street) percorrere; (a horse) passeggiare; (a patient) far camminare; (a heavy piece of furniture) abbambinare; **to walk off** (a headache) far passare camminando || intr camminare; passeggiare; (said of a horse) andare al passo; (sports) marciare; **to walk away from** andarsene a piedi da; **to walk off with** rubare; vincere con facilità; **to walk out** uscire in segno di protesta; (coll) mettersi in sciopero; **to walk out on** (coll) piantare in asso

walkaway ['wɔkə ‚we] s facile vittoria

walker ['wɔkər] s camminatore m; (to teach a baby to walk) girello

walkie-talkie ['wɔki'tɔki] s trasmettitore-ricevitore m portatile

walk'ing pa'pers spl—**to give s.o. his walking papers** (coll) dare gli otto giorni a qlcu

walk'-in refrig'erator s cella frigorifera

walk'ing stick' s bastone m da passeggio

walk'-on' s (actor) figurante m, comparsa; (role) particina

walk'out' s sciopero

walk'o'ver s facile vittoria, passeggiata

wall [wɔl] s muro; (between rooms; of a vein) parete f; (rampart) muraglia; **to drive to the wall** ridurre alla disperazione; **to go to the wall** per-

dere; fare fallimento || *tr* murare; to wall up circondare con muro

wall′board′ *s* pannello da costruzione

wallet [′wɑlɪt] *s* portafoglio

wall′flow′er *s* violacciocca gialla; **to be a wallflower** fare tappezzeria

Walloon [wɑ′lun] *adj & s* vallone *mf*

wallop [′wɑləp] *s* (coll) colpo violento; (coll) effetto; || *tr* (coll) dare un colpo violento a; (coll) battere completamente

wallow [′wɑlo] *s* diguazzamento; (*place*) brago, pantano || *intr* diguazzare; (*in wealth*) nuotare

wall′pa′per *s* tappezzeria || *tr* tappezzare

walnut [′wɔlnət] *s* (*tree; wood*) noce *m*; (*fruit*) noce *f*

walrus [′wɔlrəs] or [′wɑlrəs] *s* tricheco

Walter [′wɔltər] *s* Gualtiero

waltz [wɔlts] *s* valzer *m* || *tr* ballare il valzer con; (coll) condurre con disinvoltura || *intr* ballare il valzer

wan [wɑn] *adj* (**wanner; wannest**) (*face*) smunto, sparuto, smorto; (*light*) debole

wand [wɑnd] *s* bacchetta

wander [′wɑndər] *tr* vagare per || *intr* vagare, vagabondare; errare

wanderer [′wɑndərər] *s* vagabondo; pellegrino

Wan′dering Jew′ *s* ebreo errante

wan′der-lust′ *s* passione del vagabondaggio

wane [wen] *s* decadenza, declino; calare *m* della luna; **on the wane** in declino; (*moon*) calante || *intr* decadere, declinare; (*said of the moon*) calare

wangle [′wæŋgəl] *tr* (coll) ottenere con l'astuzia, rimediare; (coll) falsificare; **to wangle one's way out of** (coll) tirarsi fuori da . . . con l'astuzia || *intr* (coll) arrangiarsi

want [wɑnt] or [wɔnt] *s* bisogno, necessità *f*; domanda; miseria; **for want of** a causa della mancanza di; **to be in want** essere in miseria; **to be in want of** aver bisogno di || *tr* volere, desiderare; mancare; aver bisogno di || *intr* desiderare; **to be wanting** mancare, e.g., **three cards are wanting** mancano tre carte; **to want for** aver bisogno di

want′ ad′ *s* annuncio economico

wanton [′wɑntən] *adj* di proposito, deliberato; arbitrario; licenzioso, sfrenato; (*archaic*) lussureggiante

war [wɔr] *s* guerra; **to go to war** entrare in guerra; (*said of a soldier*) andare in guerra; **to wage war** fare la guerra || *v* (*pret & pp* **warred;** *ger* **warring**) *intr* guerreggiare; **to war on** fare la guerra a

warble [′wɔrbəl] *s* gorgheggio || *intr* gorgheggiare

warbler [′wɔrblər] *s* canterino; uccello canoro; (orn) beccafico

war′ cloud′ *s* minaccia di guerra

ward [wɔrd] *s* (*of city*) distretto; (*division of hospital*) corsia; (*separate building in hospital*) padiglione *m*; (*guardianship*) tutela; (*minor*) pupillo; (*of lock*) scontro || *tr*—**to ward off** stornare, schermirsi da

warden [′wɔrdən] *s* guardiano; (*of jail*) direttore *m*; (*in wartime*) capofabbricato

ward′ heel′er *s* politicantuccio

ward′robe *s* guardaroba *m*

ward′robe trunk′ *s* baule *m* armadio

ward′room′ *s* (nav) quadrato

ware [wer] *s* vasellame *m*; **wares** merce *f*

war′ ef′fort *s* sforzo bellico

ware′house′ *s* deposito, magazzino

ware′house′man *s* (**-men**) magazziniere *m*

war′fare′ *s* guerra

war′head′ *s* (mil) testa

war′horse′ *s* cavallo di battaglia; (coll) veterano

warily [′werɪli] *adv* con cautela

wariness [′werɪnɪs] *s* cautela

war′like′ *adj* guerresco, guerriero

war′ loan′ *s* prestito di guerra

war′ lord′ *s* generalissimo

warm [wɔrm] *adj* caldo; (*lukewarm*) tiepido; (*clothes*) che tiene caldo; (*with anger*) acceso; **to be warm** (*said of a person*) avere caldo; (*said of the weather*) fare caldo || *tr* scaldare, riscaldare; (*s.o.'s heart*) slargare; **to warm up** riscaldare || *intr* scaldarsi, riscaldarsi; **to warm up** (*said, e.g., of a room*) riscaldarsi; (*with emotion*) eccitarsi, accalorarsi; **to warm up to** prender simpatia per

warm-blooded [′wɔrm′blʌdɪd] *adj* (*animal*) a sangue caldo; impetuoso, ardente

war′ memo′rial *s* monumento ai caduti

warmer [′wɔrmər] *s* scaldino

warm-hearted [′wɔrm′hɑrtɪd] *adj* caloroso, cordiale

warm′ing pan′ *s* scaldaletto

warmonger [′wɔr‚mʌŋgər] *s* guerrafondaio

war′ moth′er *s* madrina di guerra

warmth [wɔrmθ] *s* calore *m*, tepore *m*; foga, entusiasmo

warm′up′ *s* preparazione; (*of radio, engine, etc.*) riscaldamento

warn [wɔrn] *tr* avvertire, mettere in guardia; (*to admonish*) ammonire; informare; **to warn off** intimare di allontanarsi (da)

warn′ing *adj* di avvertimento || *s* avvertimento, ammonimento; (law) diffida

war′ nose′ *s* acciarino, testa

war′ of nerves′ *s* guerra dei nervi

War′ of the Roses′ *s* Guerra delle due Rose

warp [wɔrp] *s* (*of a fabric*) ordito; (*of a board*) svergolamento, curvatura; aberrazione mentale; (naut) gherlino || *tr* curvare, svergolare; (*a fabric*) ordire; falsare, alterare; (naut) tirare col gherlino || *intr* curvarsi; falsarsi, alterarsi; (naut) alare

war′path′ *s*—**to be on the warpath** essere sul sentiero della guerra, prepararsi alla guerra; (*to be angry*) essere arrabiato, essere di cattivo umore

war'plane' s aeroplano da guerra

war' prof'iteer s pescecane m

warrant ['wɑrənt] or ['wɔrənt] s garanzia; certificato; ricevuta; (com) nota di pegno; (law) ordine m, mandato || tr garantire; autorizzare

warrantable ['wɑrəntəbəl] or ['wɔrəntəbəl] adj giustificabile, legittimo

war'rant of'ficer s sottufficiale m

warran•ty ['wɑrənti] or ['wɔrənti] s (-ties) garanzia; autorizzazione

warren ['wɑrən] or ['wɔrən] s conigliera; (fig) formicaio

warrior ['wɔrjər] or ['wɑrjər] s guerriero

Warsaw ['wɔrsɔ] s Varsavia

war'ship' s nave f da guerra

wart [wɔrt] s verruca

war'time' s tempo di guerra

war'-torn' adj devastato dalla guerra

war' to the death' s guerra a morte

war•y ['weri] adj (-ier; -iest) guardingo

wash [wɑʃ] or [wɔʃ] s lavata; (clothes washed or to be washed) bucato; (rushing movement of water) sciacquio; (dirty water) lavatura; (painting) mano f di colore; (aer, naut) scia || tr lavare; (dishes) rigovernare; (said of sea or river) bagnare; **to be washed up** essere finito; **to wash away** (soil of river bank) dilavare; portar via || intr lavarsi; fare il bucato; essere lavabile; (said of waves) battere

washable ['wɑʃəbəl] or ['wɔʃəbəl] adj lavabile

wash'-and-wear' adj non-stiro

wash'ba'sin s conca, catinella

wash'bas'ket s cesto del bucato

wash'board' s asse m da lavanda; (baseboard) battiscopa m

wash'bowl' s conca, catinella

wash'cloth' s pezzuola per lavarsi

wash'day' s giorno del bucato

washed-out ['wɑʃt,aut] or ['wɔʃt,aut] adj slavato; (coll) stanco; (coll) abbattuto, accasciato

washed-up ['wɑʃt'ʌp] or ['wɔʃt'ʌp] adj (coll) finito

washer ['wɑʃər] or ['wɔʃər] s (person) lavatore m; (machine) lavatrice f; (under head of bolt) rondella, rosetta; (ring to prevent leakage) guarnizione

wash'er•man s (-men) lavatore m

wash'er•wom'an s (-wom'en) lavatrice f, lavandaia

wash' goods' spl tessuti mpl lavabili

washing ['wɑʃɪŋ] or ['wɔʃɪŋ] s lavata, lavaggio, lavanda; (of clothes) bucato; **washings** lavaggio

wash'ing machine' s lavabiancheria, lavatrice f

wash'ing so'da s soda da lavare

wash'out' s erosione; (aer) svergolamento negativo; (coll) rovina completa

wash'rag' s pezzuola per lavarsi; straccio di cucina

wash'room' s gabinetto, toletta

wash'stand' s lavabo, lavamano

wash'tub' s mastello, lavatoio

wash' wa'ter s lavatura

wasp [wɑsp] s vespa

waste [west] s spreco; (refuse) scarico, rifiuto; (desolate country) landa; (excess material) scarto; (for wiping machinery) cascame m di cotone; **to go to waste** essere sciupato; **to lay waste** devastare || tr perdere, sciupare, sprecare || intr—**to waste away** intristire, consumarsi

waste'bas'ket s cestino della carta straccia

wasteful ['westfəl] adj dispendioso; distruttivo

waste'pa'per s cartastraccia

waste' pipe' s tubo di scarico

waste' prod'uct s scarto; (body excretion) escremento

wastrel ['westrəl] s sciupone m; spendaccione m, prodigo

watch [wɑtʃ] s orologio; (lookout) guardia; (mil) guardia; (naut) turno; **to be on the watch for** essere all'erta per; **to keep watch over** vegliare su || tr (to look at) osservare; (to oversee) vigilare; guardare; fare attenzione a || intr guardare; (to keep awake) vegliare; **to watch for** fare attenzione a; **to watch out** fare attenzione; **to watch out for** fare attenzione a; essere all'erta per; **to watch over** sorvegliare; **watch out!** attenzione!

watch'band' s cinturino dell'orologio

watch'case' s cassa dell'orologio

watch' charm' s ciondolo dell'orologio

watch' crys'tal s cristallo dell'orologio

watch'dog' s cane m da guardia; (fig) guardiano

watch'dog' commit'tee s comitato di sorveglianza

watchful ['wɑtʃfəl] adj vigile

watchfulness ['wɑtʃfəlnɪs] s vigilanza

watch'mak'er s orologiaio

watch'man s (-men) guardiano, sorvegliante m; (at night) guardia notturna, metronotte m

watch' night' s notte f di San Silvestro; ufficio religioso della vigilia di Capodanno

watch' pock'et s taschino dell'orologio

watch'tow'er s torre f d'osservazione

watch'word' s parola d'ordine, consegna; slogan m

water ['wɔtər] or ['wɑtər] s acqua; **of the first water** di prim'ordine; (e.g., a thief) della più bell'acqua; **to back water** retrocedere; **to be in deep water** essere in cattive acque; **to fish in troubled waters** pescare nel torbido; **to hold water** aver fondamento; **to keep above water** (fig) tenersi a galla; **to make water** (to urinate) urinare; (naut) fare acqua; **to throw cold water on** scoraggiare || tr bagnare; dare acqua a; (cattle) abbeverare; (wine) annacquare || intr abbeverarsi; (said of the mouth) aver l'acquolina; (said, e.g., of a ship) fare acqua; (said of the eyes) lacrimare

wa'ter bug' _s_ bacherozzolo

wa'ter car'rier _s_ acquaiolo

wa'ter-col'or _s_ acquerello

wa'ter-cooled' _adj_ a raffreddamento ad acqua

wa'ter-course' _s_ corso d'acqua

wa'ter-cress' _s_ crescione _m_

wa'ter cure' _s_ cura delle acque

wa'ter-fall' _s_ cascata

wa'ter-front' _s_ riva, banchina

wa'ter gap' _s_ gola, passo

wa'ter ham'mer _s_ colpo d'ariete

wa'ter heat'er _s_ scaldabagno, scaldacqua _m_

wa'ter ice' _s_ granita

wa'tering can' _s_ annaffiatoio

wa'tering place' _s_ stabilimento balneare; stazione termale; (_drinking place_) abbeveratoio

wa'tering pot' _s_ annaffiatoio

wa'tering trough' _s_ abbeveratoio

wa'ter jack'et _s_ camicia d'acqua

wa'ter lil'y _s_ nenufaro

wa'ter line' _s_ linea di galleggiamento or d'acqua; linea di livello

wa'ter main' _s_ tubo di flusso principale

wa'ter-mark' _s_ linea di livello massimo; (_in paper_) filigrana

wa'ter-mel'on _s_ cocomero, anguria

wa'ter me'ter _s_ contatore _m_ dell'acqua

wa'ter mill' _s_ mulino ad acqua

wa'ter pipe' _s_ tubo dell'acqua

wa'ter po'lo _s_ pallanuoto _f_

wa'ter pow'er _s_ forza idrica

wa'ter-proof' _adj & s_ impermeabile _m_

wa'ter-repel'lent _adj_ idrorepellente

wa'ter-shed' _s_ spartiacque _m_, displuvio

wa'ter ski' _s_ idrosci _m_

wa'ter sof'tener _s_ decalcificatore _m_

wa'ter-spout' _s_ (_to carry water from roof_) pluviale _m;_ (meteor) tromba marina

wa'ter sys'tem _s_ (_of a river_) sistema _m_ fluviale; (_of city_) conduttura dell'acqua, impianto idrico

wa'ter-tight' _adj_ stagno, ermetico; (fig) perfetto, inconfutabile

wa'ter tow'er _s_ torre _f_ serbatoio

wa'ter wag'on _s_ (mil) carro dell'acqua; **to be on the water wagon** (slang) astenersi dal bere

wa'ter-way' _s_ via d'acqua, idrovia

wa'ter wheel' _s_ ruota or turbina idraulica; (_of steamboat_) ruota a pale

wa'ter wings' _spl_ galleggiante _m_ per nuotare

wa'ter-works' _s_ impianto idrico; (_pumping station_) impianto di pompaggio

watery ['wɔtəri] or ['wɑtəri] _adj_ acquoso; lacrimoso; povero, insipido; umido, acquitrinoso

watt [wɑt] _s_ watt _m_

watt'-hour' _s_ (-hours) wattora _m_

wattle ['wɑtəl] _s_ (of bird) bargiglio

watt'me'ter _s_ wattmetro

wave [wev] _s_ onda; (of cold; of feeling) ondata; (of the hand) cenno; (of hair) onda, ondulazione || _tr_ (a flag) sventolare; (the hair) ondulare; (the hand) fare cenno con; **to wave aside** fare cenno di allontanarsi a; (e.g., a _proposal_) rifiutare || _intr_ ondeggiare, fare cenni con la mano

wave'length' _s_ lunghezza d'onda

wave' mo'tion _s_ movimento ondulatorio

waver ['wevər] _intr_ ondeggiare, oscillare; (_to hesitate_) titubare, tentennare; (_to totter_) pencolare

wav-y ['wevi] _adj_ (-ier; -iest) (_sea_) ondoso; (_hair_) ondulato

wax [wæks] _s_ cera; (fig) fantoccio || _tr_ incerare; (_a recording_) (coll) registrare || _intr_ aumentare; diventare; (_said of the moon_) crescere; **to wax indignant** indignarsi

wax' pa'per _s_ carta cerata, carta oleata

wax'works' _s_ museo di statue di cera

way [we] _s_ maniera, modo, via; condizione; **across the way** di fronte; **a good way** un buon tratto; **all the way** fino alla fine della strada; completamente; **all the way to** fino a; **any way** ad ogni modo; **by the way** a proposito; **in a way** in un certo modo; fino a un certo punto; **in every way** per ogni verso; **in this way** in questa maniera; **one way** senso unico; **on the way to** andando a; **on the way out** uscendo; diminuendo, sparendo; **out of the way** eliminato; fuori mano; strano; irregolare; **that way** in quella direzione; per di lì; in quella maniera; **this way** in questa direzione; per di qui; in questa maniera; **to be in the way** essere d'impaccio; **to feel one's way** avanzare a tentoni; **to force one's way** aprirsi il passo a viva forza; **to get out of the way** togliersi di mezzo; **to give way** ritirarsi, cedere; (_said of a rope_) rompersi; **to give way to** cedere a, darsi a; **to go out of one's way** darsi da fare, disturbarsi; **to have one's way** vincerla; **to keep out of the way** stare fuori dai piedi; **to know one's way around** conoscere bene la via; (fig) sapere il fatto proprio; **to know one's way to** sapere andare a; **to lead the way** guidare, fare da guida; prendere l'iniziativa; **to lose one's way** perdersi; **to make one's way** avanzare; fare carriera; **to make way for** far largo a; **to mend one's ways** mettere la testa a partito; **to not know which way to turn** non sapere a che santo votarsi; **to put out of the way** togliere di mezzo; **to see one's way to** vedere la possibilità di; **to take one's way** andarsene; **to wind one's way through** andare a zig zag per; **to wing one's way** andare a volo; **under way** in moto; in cammino, avviato; **way in** entrata; **way out** uscita; **ways** modi _mpl_, maniere _fpl;_ (naut) scalo; **which way?** da che parte?; in che modo?, per dove?

way'bill' _s_ lettera di vettura

wayfarer ['we,ferər] _s_ viandante _m_

way'lay' _v_ (pret & pp -laid) _tr_ tendere un agguato a; fermare improvvisamente

way' of life' _s_ tenore _m_ di vita

way'side' s bordo della strada; **to fall by the wayside** cadere per istrada; (fig) fare fiasco

way' sta'tion s stazione con fermata facoltativa

way' train' s treno omnibus

wayward ['wewərd] adj indocile, caparbio; irregolare; capriccioso

we [wi] pron pers noi; noialtri, e.g., **we Italians** noialtri italiani

weak [wik] adj debole

weaken ['wikən] tr indebolire, infiacchire ‖ intr indebolirsi, infiacchirsi

weakling ['wiklɪŋ] s debolino, rammollito

weak-minded ['wik'maɪndɪd] adj irresoluto; scemo

weakness ['wiknɪs] s debolezza, fiacchezza; (liking) debole m

wealth [welθ] s ricchezza

wealth·y ['welθi] adj (-ier; -iest) ricco

wean [win] tr svezzare, slattare; **to wean away from** disavvezzare da

weanling ['winlɪŋ] adj appena svezzato ‖ s bambino or animale appena svezzato

weapon ['wepən] s arma

weaponry ['wepənri] s armi fpl, armamento

wear [wer] s uso, servizio; (clothing) vestiti mpl, indumenti mpl; (wasting away from use) consumo, logorio; (lasting quality) durata, durabilità f; **for everyday wear** per ogni giorno ‖ v (pret **wore** [wor]; pp **worn** [worn]) tr portare, avere indosso; (to cause to deteriorate) logorare, consumare; (to tire) stancare; **to wear out** logorare, strusciare; (a horse) sfiancare; (one's patience) esaurire; (s.o.'s hospitality) abusare di ‖ intr logorarsi, consumarsi; **to wear off** diminuire, sparire; **to wear out** logorarsi; stancarsi; esaurirsi; **to wear well** essere di ottima durata

wear' and tear' [ter] s logorio

weariness ['wirinɪs] s fatica, stanchezza

wear'ing appar'el ['werɪŋ] s abbigliamento, articoli mpl d'abbigliamento

wearisome ['wirisəm] adj affaticante; (tedious) noioso

wea·ry ['wiri] adj (-rier; -riest) stanco ‖ v (pret & pp -ried) tr stancare ‖ intr stancarsi

weasel ['wizəl] s donnola

wea'sel words' spl parole fpl ambigue

weather ['weðər] s tempo; maltempo; **to be under the weather** (coll) non sentirsi bene; (to be slightly drunk) (coll) essere alticcio ‖ tr (lumber) stagionare; (adversities) superare, resistere (with dat)

weather-beaten ['weðər‚bitən] adj segnato dalle intemperie

weath'er bu'reau s servizio meteorologico

weath'er·cock' s banderuola

weath'er fore'cast s previsioni fpl del tempo, bollettino meteorologico

weath'er·man' s (-men') meteorologo

weath'er report' s bollettino meteorologico

weath'er strip'ping ['strɪpɪŋ] s guarnizione a nastro per inzeppare

weath'er vane' s banderuola, ventarola

weave [wiv] s tessitura ‖ v (pret **wove** [wov] or **weaved**) pp **wove** or **woven** ['wovən]) tr tessere; (fig) inserire; **to weave one's way** aprirsi un varco serpeggiando ‖ intr tessere; serpeggiare

weaver ['wivər] s tessitore m

web [web] s tessuto; (of spider) tela; (of rail) anima, gambo; (zool) membrana; (fig) rete f, maglia

web-footed ['web‚fʊtɪd] adj palmipede

wed [wed] v (pret & pp **wed** or **wedded**; ger **wedding**) tr sposare; (said of the groom) impalmare; (said of the bride) andare in sposa a ‖ intr sposarsi

wedding ['wedɪŋ] adj nuziale ‖ s sposalizio, nozze fpl, matrimonio

wed'ding cake' s torta nuziale

wed'ding day' s giorno di nozze

wed'ding invita'tion s invito a nozze

wed'ding march' s marcia nuziale

wed'ding ring' s fede f, vera

wedge [wedʒ] s cuneo; (of pie) spicchio; (to split wood) bietta; (to hold a wheel) scarpa ‖ tr incuneare

wed'lock s matrimonio

Wednesday ['wenzdi] s mercoledì m

wee [wi] adj piccolo piccolo

weed [wid] s malerba, erbaccia; (coll) sigaretta; (slang) marijuana; **weeds** vestito da lutto, gramaglie fpl ‖ tr sarchiare, mondare

weeder ['widər] s (agr) estirpatore m

weed'ing hoe' s sarchio, zappa

weed'-kill'er s diserbante m

week [wik] s settimana; **week in, week out** una settimana dopo l'altra

week'day' s giorno feriale

week'end' s fine-settimana m, fine f di settimana, week-end m ‖ intr passare il fine-settimana

week·ly ['wikli] adj settimanale ‖ s (-lies) settimanale m ‖ adv settimanalmente

weep [wip] v (pret & pp **wept** [wept]) tr piangere; **to weep oneself to sleep** addormentarsi piangendo; **to weep one's eyes out** piangere a calde lacrime ‖ intr piangere; **to weep for joy** piangere di gioia

weeper ['wipər] s piagnone m; (hired mourner) prefica

weep'ing wil'low s salice m piangente

weep·y ['wipi] adj (-ier; -iest) piangente, lacrimoso

weevil ['wivəl] s curculione m

weft [weft] s (yarns running across warp) trama; (fabric) tela, tessuto

weigh [we] tr pesare; (anchor) levare; (to make heavy) appesantire; (fig) soppesare, ponderare; **to weigh down** piegare ‖ intr pesare; gravitare; **to weigh in** (sports) pesarsi; **to weigh upon** gravare a

weigh'bridge' s stadera

weight [wet] s peso; (fig) peso; **to carry weight** aver del peso; **to lose weight** diminuire di peso; **to put on weight** crescere di peso; **to throw**

one's weight around far sentire la propria importanza || *tr* appesantire; *(statistically)* ponderare, dare un certo peso a

weightless ['wetlıs] *adj* senza peso, imponderabile

weightlessness ['wetlısnıs] *s* imponderabilità *f*

weight·y ['weti] *adj* (**-ier; -iest**) pesante; importante

weir [wır] *s* sbarramento; *(for catching fish)* pescaia

weird [wırd] *adj* soprannaturale, misterioso; strano, bizzarro

welcome ['welkəm] *adj* benvenuto; gradito; **you are welcome** (*i.e., gladly received*) sia il benvenuto; (*in answer to thanks*) prego; **you are welcome to** it è a Sua disposizione; **you are welcome to your opinion** pensi come la vuole || *s* benvenuto || *tr* dare il benvenuto a; accettare; gradire || *interj* benvenuto!

weld [weld] *s* saldatura autogena; (bot) guaderella || *tr* saldare || *intr* saldarsi

welder ['weldər] *s* saldatore *m*; (*machine*) saldatrice *f*

welding ['weldıŋ] *s* saldatura autogena

wel'fare' *s* benessere *m*; (*effort to improve living conditions*) beneficenza, assistenza; **to be on welfare** ricevere assistenza pubblica

wel'fare state' *s* stato sociale or assistenziale

well [wel] *adj* bene; in buona salute || *s* pozzo; (*for ink*) pozzetto, serbatoio; (*spring*) sorgente *f*; (*shaft for stairs*) tromba || *adv* bene; **as well** pure; **as well . . . as** tanto . . . come; **as well as** tanto come, non meno che || *intr* —**to well up** sgorgare || *interj* beh!; bene!; allora!, dunque!

well-appointed ['welə'pɔıntıd] *adj* ben ammobiliato

well-attended ['welə'tendıd] *adj* molto frequentato

well-behaved ['welbı'hevd] *adj* beneducato; **to be well-behaved** comportarsi bene

well'-be'ing *s* benessere *m*

well'born' *adj* bennato

well-bred ['wel'bred] *adj* educato, costumato

well-disposed ['weldıs'pozd] *adj* bendisposto

well-done ['wel'dʌn] *adj* benfatto; (*meat*) ben cotto

well-fixed ['wel'fıkst] *adj* (coll) agiato, abbiente

well-formed ['wel'fɔrmd] *adj* benfatto

well-founded ['wel'faundıd] *adj* fondato

well-groomed ['wel'grumd] *adj* (*person*) curato; (*horse*) ben governato

well-heeled ['wel'hild] *adj* (coll) agiato, benestante

well-informed ['welın'fɔrmd] *adj* bene informato

well-intentioned ['welın'tenʃənd] *adj* benintenzionato

well'-kept' *adj* ben conservato; (*person*) benportante; (*secret*) ben mantenuto

well-known ['wel'non] *adj* notorio, ben noto

well-meaning ['wel'minıŋ] *adj* benevolo, benintenzionato

well-nigh ['wel'naı] *adv* quasi

well'-off' *adj* agiato, benestante

well-preserved ['welprı'zʌrvd] *adj* ben conservato; (*person*) benportante

well-read ['wel'red] *adj* colto, che ha letto molto

well-spoken ['wel'spokən] *adj* (*person*) raffinato nel parlare; (*word*) a proposito

well'spring' *s* sorgente *f*

well' sweep' *s* mazzacavallo del pozzo

well-tempered ['wel'tempərd] *adj* ben temperato

well-thought-of ['wel'θɔt,ʌv] *adj* tenuto in alta considerazione

well-timed ['wel'taımd] *adj* opportuno

well-to-do ['weltə'du] *adj* benestante

well-wisher ['wel'wıʃər] *s* amico, sostenitore *m*

well-worn ['wel'worn] *adj* (*clothing*) liso, consunto, trito; (*argument*) logoro, banale; portato con eleganza

welsh [welʃ] *intr* —**to welsh on** (*a promise*) (slang) mancare a; (*a person*) (slang) fregare || **Welsh** *adj & s* gallese *mf*; the **Welsh** i gallesi

Welsh'man *s* (**-men**) gallese *m*

Welsh' rab'bit or **rare'bit** ['rerbıt] *s* fonduta fatta con la birra servita su pane abbrustolito

welt [welt] *s* (*finish along a seam*) costa; (*of shoe*) guardolo; (*wale from a blow*) riga, sferzata

welter ['weltər] *s* guazzabuglio; confusione; (*a tumbling about*) rotolio || *intr* rotolarsi, guazzare

wel'ter-weight' *s* (boxing) peso welter, peso medio-leggero

wench [wentʃ] *s* ragazza, giovane *f*

wend [wend] *tr*—**to wend one's way** dirigere i propri passi

werewolf ['wır,wulf] *s* lupo mannaro

west [west] *adj* occidentale || *s* ovest *m*, occidente *m* || *adv* verso l'ovest

western ['westərn] *adj* occidentale || *s* western *m*

West' In'dies ['ındiz] *spl* Indie *fpl* Occidentali

westward ['westwərd] *adv* verso l'ovest

wet [wet] *adj* (**wetter; wettest**) bagnato; (*paint*) fresco; (*damp*) umido; (*rainy*) piovoso; che permette la vendita delle bevande alcoliche || *s* umidità *f*; antiproibizionista *mf* || *v* (*pret & pp* **wet** or **wetted**; *ger* **wetting**) *tr* bagnare || *intr* bagnarsi

wet' blan'ket *s* guastafeste *mf*

wether ['weðər] *s* castrone *m*

wet' nurse' *s* nutrice *f*, balia

whack [hwæk] *s* (slang) colpo, percossa; (slang) prova, tentativo || *tr* (slang) percuotere

whale [hwel] *s* balena; **a whale of** (slang) gigantesco, e.g., **a whale of a lie** una bugia gigantesca; enorme, e.g., **a whale of a difference** una differenza enorme || *tr* (coll) battere || *intr* pescare balene

whale'bone' *s* osso di balena, fanone *m*

wharf [hwɔrf] s (**wharves** [hwɔrvz] or **wharfs**) molo

what [hwɑt] adj interr che; quale || adj rel quello . . . che; il . . . che, e.g., **wear what tie you prefer** mettiti la cravatta che preferisci || pron interr che; quale; **what else?** che altro?; **what if . . . ?** e se . . . ?; **what of it?** e che me ne importa? || pron rel quello che; **what's what** (coll) tutta la situazione || interj what a . . . ! che . . . !, e.g., **what a beautiful day!** che splendida giornata!

what·ev'er adj qualsiasi; qualunque || pron quanto; che; quello che

what'not' s scaffaletto

wheal [hwil] s vescichetta

wheat [hwit] s grano, frumento

wheedle ['hwidəl] tr adulare; persuadere con lusinghe; (money) spillare

wheel [hwil] s ruota; (of cheese) forma; (coll) bicicletta; **at the wheel** al volante; in controllo || tr roteare; portare in carrozzella || intr girare

wheelbarrow ['hwil ,bæro] s carriola

wheel'base' s base

wheel'chair' s carrozzella

wheel' col'umn s (aut) piantone m di guida

wheeler-dealer ['hwilər'dilər] s (slang) grande affarista m

wheel' horse' s cavallo di timone; lavoratore m di fiducia

wheelwright ['hwil ,rait] s carradore m

wheeze [hwiz] s affanno; (pathol) rantolo || intr respirare affannosamente; (pathol) rantolare

whelp [hwelp] s cucciolo || tr & intr figliare, partorire

when [hwen] adv & conj quando

whence [hwens] adv donde, di dove || conj donde; per che ragione

when·ev'er conj ogniqualvolta, qualora

where [hwer] adv & conj dove

whereabouts ['hwerə ,bauts] s luogo dove uno si trova || adv & conj dove

whereas [hwer'æz] conj mentre; visto che, considerato che

where·by' adv per cui, col quale

wherever [hwer'evər] adv dove mai || conj dovunque

wherefore ['hwerfor] s perché m || adv perché || conj per cui, percome

where·from' adv donde

where·in' adv dove; in che modo || conj dove; nel quale

where·of' adv di che || conj di che; del quale

where'upon' adv sul che; laonde, dopodiché

wherewithal ['hwerwɪð ,ɔl] s mezzi mpl

whet [hwet] v (pret & pp **whetted;** ger **whetting**) tr affilare; (the appetite) aguzzare

whether ['weðər] conj se; **whether or no** ad ogni modo, in ogni caso; **whether or not** che . . . o che non

whet'stone' s pietra da affilare

whey [hwe] s scotta

which [hwɪtʃ] adj interr quale || adj rel il (la, etc.) quale || pron interr che; quale; **which is which** qual'è

l'uno e qual'è l'altro || pron rel che; il quale; quello che

which·ev'er adj & pron rel qualunque

whiff [hwɪf] s (of air) soffio; fiutata; (trace of odor) zaffata; **to get a whiff of** sentire l'odore di || intr soffiare; (said of a smoker) dare boccate

while [hwail] s tempo; **a long while** un bel pezzo; **a while ago** un tratto fa; **to be worth one's while** valere la pena || conj mentre || tr—**to while away** passare piacevolmente

whim [hwɪm] s capriccio, estro

whimper ['hwɪmpər] s piagnucolio || tr & intr piagnucolare

whimsical ['hwɪmzɪkəl] adj capriccioso, estroso, stravagante

whine [hwain] s (of dog) guaito; (of person) piagnucolio || intr (said of a dog) guaire, uggiolare; (said of a person) piagnucolare

whin·ny ['hwini] s (-nies) nitrito || v (pret & pp -nied) intr nitrire

whip [hwɪp] s frusta; uova fpl sbattute con frutta || v (pret & pp **whipped** or **whipt;** ger **whipping**) tr frustare, battere; (eggs) frullare; (coll) vincere, sconfiggere; **to whip off** (coll) buttar giù; **to whip out** tirar fuori rapidamente; **to whip up** (coll) preparare in quattro e quatt'rotto; (coll) eccitare, incitare

whip'cord' s cordino della frusta; (fabric) saia a diagonale

whip' hand' s mano che tiene la frusta; vantaggio, posizione vantaggiosa

whip'lash' s scudisciata

whipped' cream' s panna montata

whipper-snapper ['hwɪpər ,snæpər] s pivello

whippet ['hwɪpɪt] s piccolo levriere

whip'ping boy' ['hwɪpɪŋ] s testa di turco

whip'ping post' s palo per la fustigazione

whippoorwill [,hwɪpər'wɪl] s caprimulgo, succiacapre m

whir [hwʌr] s ronzio || v (pret & pp **whirred;** ger **whirring**) intr ronzare; volare ronzando

whirl [hwʌrl] s giro improvviso; corsa; mulinello; (fig) successione || tr & intr mulinare; **my head whirls** mi gira la testa

whirligig ['hwʌrlɪ ,gig] s turbine m; (carrousel) giostra; (toy) girandola; (ent) ragno d'acqua

whirl'pool' s risucchio, mulinello

whirl'wind' s turbine m, tromba d'aria

whirlybird ['hwʌrlɪ ,bʌrd] s (coll) elicottero

whish [hwɪʃ] s fruscio || intr frusciare

whisk [hwɪsk] s scopatina || tr scopare, spolverare; (eggs) sbattere; **to whisk out of sight** far sparire || intr guizzare

whisk' broom' s scopetta per i vestiti, spolverino

whiskers ['hwɪskərz] spl barba; (on side of man's face) basette fpl; (of cat) baffi mpl

whiskey ['hwɪski] s whisky m

whisper ['hwɪspər] *s* sussurro, bisbiglio, mormorio; **in a whisper** in un sussurro ‖ *tr & intr* sussurrare, bisbigliare, mormorare

whisperer ['hwɪspərər] *s* sussurrone *m*

whispering ['hwɪspərɪŋ] *adj* di maldicenze ‖ *s* sussurro; maldicenza

whistle ['hwɪsəl] *s* fischio; **to wet one's whistle** (coll) bagnarsi l'ugola ‖ *tr* fischiare ‖ *intr* fischiare, zufolare; **to whistle for** chiamare con un fischio; (*money*) aspettare in vano

whis'tle stop' *s* stazioncina, paesetto

whit [hwɪt] *s*—**not a whit** niente affatto

white [hwaɪt] *adj* bianco ‖ *s* bianco; **whites** (pathol) leucorrea

white'cap' *s* frangente *m*, cavallone *m*, onda crespa

white' coal' *s* carbone bianco

white'-col'lar *adj* impiegatizio

white' feath'er *s*—**to show the white feather** mostrarsi vile

white' goods' *spl* biancheria da casa; articoli *mpl* di cotone; apparecchi *mpl* elettrodomestici

white-haired ['hwaɪt‚herd] *adj* dai capelli bianchi; (coll) favorito

white' heat' *s* calor bianco

white' lead' [led] *s* biacca

white' lie' *s* bugia innocente

white' meat' *s* bianco, carne *f* del petto

whiten ['hwaɪtən] *tr* imbiancare, sbiancare ‖ *intr* imbiancarsi, sbiancarsi; impallidire

whiteness ['hwaɪtnɪs] *s* bianchezza

white' plague' *s* tuberculosi *f*

white' slav'ery *s* tratta delle bianche

white' tie' *s* cravatta da frac; marsina, abito da cerimonia

white'wash' *s* imbiancatura; (fig) copertura ‖ *tr* imbiancare, intonacare; (fig) coprire

white' wa'ter lil'y *s* ninfea

whither ['hwɪθər] *adv* dove, a che luogo ‖ *conj* dove

whiting ['hwaɪtɪŋ] *s* (ichth) nasello; (ichth) merlango

whitish ['hwaɪtɪʃ] *adj* biancastro

whitlow ['hwɪtlo] *s* patereccio

Whitsuntide ['hwɪtsən‚taɪd] *s* settimana di Pentecoste

whittle ['hwɪtəl] *tr* digrossare; **to whittle away** or **down** ridurre gradualmente

whiz or whizz [hwɪz] *s* sibilo; (coll) asso ‖ *v* (*pret & pp* whizzed) *ger* whizzing) *intr*—**to whiz by** passare sibilando; passare come una freccia

who [hu] *pron interr* chi; **who else?** chi altri?; **who goes there?** (mil) chi va là?; **who's who** chi è l'uno e chi è l'altro; (mil) chi è la gente importante ‖ *pron rel* chi; il quale

whoa [hwo] or [wo] *interj* fermo!

who·ev'er *pron rel* chiunque

whole [hol] *adj* tutto, intero; sano, intatto; **made out of the whole cloth** completamente immaginario ‖ *s* tutto; **as a whole** nell'insieme; **on the whole** in generale

wholehearted ['hol‚hɑrtɪd] *adj* molto sincero, generoso

whole' note' *s* (mus) semibreve *f*

whole'sale' *adj & adv* all'ingrosso ‖ *s* ingrosso ‖ *tr* vendere all'ingrosso ‖ *intr* vendersi all'ingrosso

wholesaler ['hol‚selər] *s* grossista *mf*

wholesome ['holsəm] *adj* (*beneficial*) salutare; (*in good health*) sano

wholly ['holi] *adv* interamente

whom [hum] *pron interr* chi ‖ *pron rel* che; il quale

whom·ev'er *pron rel* chiunque

whoop [hup] or [hwup] *s* urlo; (pathol) urlo della pertosse; **to not be worth a whoop** (coll) non valere un fico secco ‖ *tr*—**to whoop it up** (slang) fare il diavolo a quattro ‖ *intr* urlare

whoop'ing cough' ['hupɪŋ] or ['hwupɪŋ] *s* pertosse *f*

whopper ['hwɑpər] *s* (coll) enormità *f*; (coll) fandonia, bugia enorme

whopping ['hwɑpɪŋ] *adj* (coll) enorme

whore [hor] *s* puttana ‖ *intr*—**to whore around** puttaneggiare; andare a puttane

whortleber·ry ['hwʌrtəl‚beri] *s* (-ries) mirtillo

whose [huz] *pron interr* di chi ‖ *pron rel* di chi; del quale; di cui

why [hwaɪ] *s* (whys) perché *m*; **the whys and the wherefores** il perché e il percome ‖ *adv* perché ‖ *interj* diamine!; **why, certainly!** certamente!; **why, yes!** evidentemente!

wick [wɪk] *s* stoppino, lucignolo

wicked ['wɪkɪd] *adj* malvagio; (*mischievous*) cattivo; (*dreadful*) terribile, bestiale

wicker ['wɪkər] *adj* di vimini ‖ *s* vimine *m*

wicket ['wɪkɪt] *s* (*small door*) portello; (*ticket window*) sportello; (*of a canal*) chiusa; (cricket) porta; (croquet) archetto

wide [waɪd] *adj* largo; esteso; (*eyes*) aperto; (*sense of a word*) lato ‖ *adv* largamente; completamente; lontano; **wide of the mark** lontano dal bersaglio

wide'-an'gle *adj* grandangolare

wide'-awake' *adj* sveglio

widen ['waɪdən] *tr* slargare, estendere ‖ *intr* slargarsi, estendersi

wide'-o'pen *adj* spalancato; (*to a gambler*) accessibile

wide'-spread' *adj* (*e.g., arms*) aperto; diffuso

widow ['wɪdo] *s* vedova; (cards) morto ‖ *tr* lasciar vedova

widower ['wɪdo‚ər] *s* vedovo

widowhood ['wɪdo‚hʊd] *s* vedovanza

wid'ow's mite' *s* obolo della vedova

wid'ow's weeds' *spl* gramaglie *fpl* vedovili

width [wɪdθ] *s* larghezza

wield [wild] *tr* (*e.g., a sword*) brandire; (*e.g., a hammer*) maneggiare; (*power*) esercitare

wife [waɪf] *s* (wives [waɪvz]) moglie *f*

wig [wɪg] *s* parrucca

wiggle ['wɪgəl] *s* dimenio; (*of fish*)

guizzo || *tr* dimenare || *intr* dime-narsi; guizzare

wig'wag' *s* segnalazione con bandierine || *v* (*pret* & *pp* **-wagged;** *ger* **-wagging**) *tr* & *intr* segnalare con bandierine

wigwam ['wɪgwɑm] *s* tenda a cupola dei pellirosse, wigwam *m*

wild [waɪld] *adj* (*animal*) feroce; (*e.g., berry*) selvatico; (*barbarous*) selvaggio; (*violent*) furioso; (*mad*) pazzo; (*unruly*) discolo, indisciplinato; (*extravagant*) pazzesco; (*shot or throw*) lanciato all'impazzata; **wild about** pazzo per || *s* regione deserta; **the wild** la foresta; **wilds** regioni selvagge || *adv* pazzamente; **to go wild** andare in delirio; **to run wild** crescere all'impazzata; correre senza freno

wild' boar' *s* cinghiale *m*

wild' card' *s* matta

wild'cat' *s* gatto selvatico; lince *f*; impresa arrischiata || *v* (*pret* & *pp* **-catted;** *ger* **-catting**) *tr* & *intr* esplorare per conto proprio

wild'cat strike' *s* sciopero non autorizzato dal sindacato

wilderness ['wɪldərnɪs] *s* deserto

wild-eyed ['waɪld ˌaɪd] *adj* stralunato; (*scheme*) pazzesco

wild'fire' *s* fuoco greco; fuoco fatuo; **to spread like wildfire** crescere come la gramigna; (*said of news*) spargersi come il baleno

wild'break' ['wɪnd ˌbrek] *s* frangivento

wild' flow'er *s* fiore *m* di campo

wild' goose' *s* oca selvatica

wild'-goose' chase' *s* ricerca della luna nel pozzo

wild'life' *s* animali *spl* selvatici

wild' oat' *s* avena selvatica; **to sow one's wild oats** correre la cavallina

wild' ol'ive *s* olivastro, oleastro

wile [waɪl] *s* stratagemma *m*, inganno; (*cunning*) astuzia || *tr* allettare; **to wile away** passare piacevolmente

will [wɪl] *s* volontà *f*, volere *m*; (law) testamento; **at will** a volontà || *tr* volere; (law) legare || *intr* volere; **do as you will** faccia come vuole || *v* (*pret* & *cond* **would**) *aux* **she will leave tomorrow** partirà domani; **a cactus plant will live two months without water** una pianta grassa può vivere due mesi senz'acqua

willful ['wɪlfəl] *adj* volontario; ostinato

willfulness ['wɪlfəlnɪs] *s* volontarietà *f*; ostinatezza

William ['wɪljəm] *s* Guglielmo

willing ['wɪlɪŋ] *adj* volonteroso; **to be willing** essere disposto

willingly ['wɪlɪŋli] *adv* di buon grado, volentieri

willingness ['wɪlɪŋnɪs] *s* buona voglia, propensione

will-o'-the-wisp ['wɪləðə'wɪsp] *s* fuoco fatuo; (fig) illusione, chimera

willow ['wɪlo] *s* salice *m*

willowy ['wɪlo·i] *adj* pieghevole; (*slender*) snello; pieno di giunchi

will' pow'er *s* forza di volontà

willy-nilly ['wɪli'nɪli] *adv* volente o nolente

wilt [wɪlt] *tr* far appassire || *intr* appassire, avvizzire

wil·y ['waɪli] *adj* (**-ier; -iest**) astuto, scaltro

wimple ['wɪmpəl] *s* soggolo

win [wɪn] *s* vittoria, vincita || *v* (*pret* & *pp* **won** [wʌn]; *ger* **winning**) *tr* & *intr* guadagnare; **to win out** vincere, aver successo

wince [wɪns] *s* sussulto || *intr* sussultare

winch [wɪntʃ] *s* verricello; (*handle*) manovella; (naut) molinello

wind [wɪnd] *s* vento; (*gas in intestines*) vento; (*breath*) fiato, tenuta; **to break wind** scoreggiare; **to get wind of** subodorare; **to sail close to the wind** (naut) andare all'orza; **to take the wind out of the sails of** sconcertare; **winds** (mus) fiati *mpl* || *tr* far perdere il fiato a || [waɪnd] *v* (*pret* & *pp* **wound** [waʊnd]) *tr* (*to wrap up*) arrotolare; (*thread, wool*) dipanare, aggomitolare; (*a clock*) caricare; (*a handle*) far girare; **to wind one's way through** serpeggiare per; **to wind up** arrotolare; eccitare; finire, portare a termine || *intr* serpeggiare, snodarsi

windbag ['wɪnd ˌbæg] *s* (*of a bagpipe*) otre *m*; (fig) parolaio, otre *m* di vento

windbreak ['wɪnd ˌbrek] *s* frangivento

wind' cone' [wɪnd] *s* manica a vento

winded ['wɪndɪd] *adj* senza fiato

windfall ['wɪnd ˌfɔl] *s* frutta abbattuta dal vento; provvidenza, manna del cielo

wind'ing sheet' ['waɪndɪŋ] *s* lenzuolo funebre

wind'ing stairs' ['waɪndɪŋ] *spl* scala a chiocciola

wind' in'strument [wɪnd] *s* (mus) strumento a fiato

windlass ['wɪndləs] *s* verricello

windmill ['wɪnd ˌmɪl] *s* mulino a vento; (*air turbine*) aeromotore *m*; **to tilt at windmills** combattere i mulini a vento

window ['wɪndo] *s* finestra; (*of ticket office*) sportello; (*of car or coach*) finestrino

win'dow dress'er *s* vetrinista *mf*

win'dow dress'ing *s* vetrinistica; (fig) facciata, apparenza

win'dow en'velope *s* busta a finestrella

win'dow frame' *s* intelaiatura della finestra

win'dow-pane' *s* vetro, invetriata

win'dow sash' *s* intelaiatura della finestra

win'dow screen' *s* zanzariera

win'dow shade' *s* tendina avvolgibile

win'dow-shop' *v* (*pret* & *pp* **-shopped;** *ger* **-shopping**) *intr* guardare nelle vetrine senza comprare

win'dow sill' *s* davanzale *m* della finestra

windpipe ['wɪnd ˌpaɪp] *s* trachea

windproof ['wɪnd ˌpruf] *adj* resistente al vento

windshield ['wɪnd ˌʃild] *s* parabrezza *m*

wind'shield wash'er *s* lavacristallo

wind′shield wip′er s tergicristallo

windsock [′wɪnd‚sɑk] s (aer) manica a vento

windstorm [′wɪnd‚stɔrm] s bufera di vento

wind′ tun′nel [wɪnd] s (aer) galleria aerodinamica

wind-up [′waɪnd‚ʌp] s conclusione

windward [′wɪndwərd] s orza, sopravvento; **to turn to windward** mettersi al sopravvento

Wind′ward Is′lands spl Isole fpl Sopravvento

wind•y [′wɪndi] adj (-ier; -iest) ventoso; verboso, ampolloso; **it is windy** fa vento

wine [waɪn] s vino ‖ tr offrire vino a ‖ intr bere del vino

wine′ cel′lar s cantina

wine′glass′ s bicchiere da vino

winegrower [′waɪn‚gro·ər] s vinificatore m, viticoltore m

wine′ press′ s torchio per l'uva

winer•y [′waɪnəri] s (-ies) stabilimento vinicolo

wine′shop′ s fiaschetteria

wine′skin′ s otre m

wine′ stew′ard s sommelier m

winetaster [′waɪn‚testər] s degustatore m di vini

wing [wɪŋ] s ala; (unit of air force) aerobrigata; (theat) quinta; **to take wing** levarsi a volo; **under one's wing** sotto la protezione di qlcu ‖ tr ferire nell'ala; **to wing one's way** volare, portarsi a volo

wing′ chair′ s poltrona a orecchioni

wing′ col′lar s colletto per marsina

wing′ nut′ s (mach) galletto

wing′span′ s (of airplane) apertura alare

wing′spread′ s (of bird) apertura alare

wink [wɪŋk] s ammicco; **in a wink** in un batter d'occhio; **to not sleep a wink** non chiudere occhio; **to take forty winks** (coll) schiacciare un pisolino ‖ tr (the eye) strizzare ‖ intr ammiccare, strizzare l'occhio; (to blink) battere le ciglia; **to wink at** ammiccare a; far finta di non vedere

winner [′wɪnər] s vincitore m

winning [′wɪnɪŋ] adj vincente, vincitore; attraente, simpatico ‖ **winnings** spl vincita

winnow [′wɪno] tr ventilare, brezzare; (fig) vagliare ‖ intr svolazzare

winsome [′wɪnsəm] adj attraente

winter [′wɪntər] adj invernale ‖ s inverno ‖ intr svernare

win′ter·green′ s tè m del Canadà; olio di gaulteria

win•try [′wɪntri] adj (-trier; -triest) invernale; freddo

wipe [waɪp] tr forbire, detergere; (to dry) asciugare; **to wipe away** (tears) asciugare; **to wipe off** pulire, forbire; **to wipe out** distruggere completamente; (coll) eliminare

wiper [′waɪpər] s strofinaccio; (mach) camma; (elec) contatto scorrevole

wire [waɪr] s filo metallico; telegramma m; (coll) telegrafo; **to pull wires** manovrare di dietro le quinte ‖ tr legare con filo metallico; attrezzare l'elettricità in; (coll) mandare per telegrafo; (coll) telegrafare ‖ intr (coll) telegrafare

wire′ cut′ter s pinza tagliafili

wire′ entan′glement s reticolato di filo spinato

wire′ gauge′ s calibro da fili

wire-haired [′waɪr‚herd] adj a pelo ruvido

wireless [′waɪrlɪs] adj senza fili ‖ s telegrafo senza fili; telegrafia senza fili

wire′ nail′ s chiodo da falegname

wirepulling [′waɪr‚pʊlɪŋ] s manovra dietro alle quinte

wire′ record′er s magnetofono a filo

wire′ screen′ s rete metallica

wire′tap′ v (pret & pp -tapped; ger -tapping) tr (a conversation) intercettare

wiring [′waɪrɪŋ] s sistema m di fili elettrici

wir•y [′waɪri] adj (-ier; -iest) fatto di filo; (hair) ispido; (tone) metallico, vibrante; (sinewy) segaligno

wisdom [′wɪzdəm] s senno, sapienza, saggezza

wis′dom tooth′ s dente m del giudizio

wise [waɪz] adj saggio, sapiente; (decision) giudizioso; **to be wise to** (slang) accorgersi del gioco di; **to get wise** (slang) mangiare la foglia; (slang) diventare impertinente ‖ s modo, maniera; **in no wise** in nessun modo ‖ tr—**to wise up** (slang) avvertire ‖ intr—**to wise up** (slang) accorgersi

wiseacre [′waɪz‚ekər] s sapientone m

wise′crack′ s (coll) spiritosaggine f ‖ intr (coll) dire spiritosaggini

wise′ guy′ s (slang) sputasentenze m

wish [wɪʃ] s desiderio; augurio; **to make a wish** formulare un desiderio ‖ tr desiderare; augurare; **to wish s.o. a good day** dare il buon giorno a qlcu ‖ intr desiderare; **to wish for** desiderare

wish′bone′ s forcella

wishful [′wɪʃfəl] adj desideroso

wish′ful think′ing s pio desiderio

wistful [′wɪstfəl] adj melanconico, pensoso, meditabondo

wit [wɪt] s spirito; (person) bellospirito; (understanding) senso; **to be at one's wits' end** non sapere a che santo votarsi; **to have one's wits about one** avere presenza di spirito; **to live by one's wits** vivere di espedienti

witch [wɪtʃ] s strega

witch′craft′ s stregoneria

witch′ doc′tor s stregone m

witch′es' Sab′bath s sabba m

witch′ ha′zel s (shrub) amamelide f; (liquid) estratto di amamelide

witch′ hunt′ s caccia alle streghe

with [wɪð] or [wɪθ] prep con; a, e.g., **with open arms** a braccia aperte; di, e.g., **covered with silk** coperto di seta; **to be satisfied with the performance** essere contento della rappresentazione; da, e.g., **with the In-**

dians dagli indiani; **to part with** separarsi da

with·draw' v (pret **-drew;** pp **-drawn**) tr ritirare || intr ritirarsi

withdrawal [wɪðˈdrɔ·əl] or [wɪθˈdrɔ·əl] s ritiro, ritirata; (of funds) prelevamento

wither [ˈwɪðər] tr intisichire; (with a glance) incenerire || intr avvizzire, intisichire

with·hold' v (pret & pp **-held**) tr trattenere; (information) sottacere; (payment) defalcare; (permission) negare

withhold'ing tax' s imposta trattenuta

with·in' adv dentro, didentro || prep entro, entro di, dentro a, dentro di; fra; in; (a time period) nel giro di

with·out' adv fuori || prep senza; fuori, fuori di; **to do without** fare a meno di; **without** + ger senza + inf, e.g., **without saying a word** senza dire una parola; senza che + subj, e.g., **she fell without anyone helping her** cadde senza che nessuno l'aiutasse

with·stand' v (pret & pp **-stood**) tr resistere (with dat), reggere (with dat)

witness [ˈwɪtnɪs] s testimone mf; **in witness whereof** in fé di che; **to bear witness** far fede || tr (to be present at) presenziare; (to attest) testimoniare, firmare come testimone

wit'ness stand' s banco dei testimoni

witticism [ˈwɪtɪˌsɪzəm] s motto, battuta spiritosa, spiritosaggine f

wittingly [ˈwɪtɪŋli] adv consapevolmente

wit·ty [ˈwɪti] adj (-tier; -tiest) spiritoso, divertente

wizard [ˈwɪzərd] s mago

wizardry [ˈwɪzərdri] s magia

wizened [ˈwɪzənd] adj raggrinzito

woad [wod] s (bot) guado

wobble [ˈwɑbəl] s oscillazione, dondolio || intr oscillare, dondolare; (said of a chair) zoppicare; (fig) titubare

wob·bly [ˈwɑbli] adj (-blier; -bliest) oscillante, zoppo, malfermo

woe [wo] s disgrazia, afflizione, sventura; || interj—**woe is me!** ahimè!

woebegone [ˈwobɪˌgɔn] or [ˈwobɪˌgɑn] adj triste, abbattuto

woeful [ˈwofəl] adj sfortunato, disgraziato; (of poor quality) orribile

wolf [wʊlf] s (wolves [wʊlvz]) lupo; (coll) dongiovanni m; **to cry wolf** gridare al lupo; **to keep the wolf from the door** tener lontana la miseria || tr & intr mangiare come un lupo

wolf'hound' s cane m da pastore alsaziano

wolfram [ˈwʊlfrəm] s wolframio

wolf's-bane or **wolfsbane** [ˈwʊlfsˌben] s (bot) aconito

wolverine [ˌwʊlvəˈrin] s (zool) ghiottone m

woman [ˈwʊmən] s (women [ˈwɪmɪn]) donna

womanhood [ˈwʊmənˌhʊd] s (quality) femminilità f; (women collectively) donne fpl, sesso femminile

womanish [ˈwʊmənɪʃ] adj femminile; (effeminate) effeminato

wom'an·kind' s sesso femminile

womanly [ˈwʊmənli] adj (-lier; -liest) femminile, muliebre

wom'an suf'frage s suffragio alle donne

woman-suffragist [ˈwʊmənˈsʌfrədʒɪst] s suffragista mf

womb [wʊm] s utero; (fig) seno

womenfolk [ˈwɪmɪnˌfok] spl le donne

wonder [ˈwʌndər] s (something strange and surprising) meraviglia; (feeling) ammirazione; (miracle) prodigio, miracolo; **for a wonder** cosa strana; **no wonder that** non fa meraviglia che; **to work wonders** fare miracoli || tr—**to wonder that** meravigliarsi che; **to wonder how, if, when, where, who, why** domandarsi or chiedersi come, se, quando, dove, chi, perché || intr meravigliarsi; chiedersi; **to wonder at** ammirare

won'der drug' s medicina miracolosa

wonderful [ˈwʌndərfəl] adj meraviglioso

won'der·land' s paese m delle meraviglie

wonderment [ˈwʌndərmənt] s sorpresa, meraviglia, stupore m

won'der-work'er s taumaturgo

wont [wʌnt] or [wont] adj abituato, solito || s abitudine f, costume m

wonted [ˈwʌntɪd] or [ˈwontɪd] adj solito, abituale

woo [wu] tr (a woman) corteggiare; (to seek to win) allettare; (good or bad consequences) andare in cerca di

wood [wʊd] s legno; (firewood) legna; (keg) barile m; **out of the woods** fuori pericolo; al sicuro; **woods** bosco, selva

woodbine [ˈwʊdˌbaɪn] s (honeysuckle) abbracciabosco; (Virginia creeper) vite f del Canadà

wood' carv'ing s intaglio in legno, statua in legno

wood'chuck' s marmotta americana

wood'cock' s beccaccia

wood'cut' s silografia

wood'cut'ter s boscaiolo

wooded [ˈwʊdɪd] adj legnoso, boschivo

wooden [ˈwʊdən] adj di legno; duro, rigido; inespressivo

wood' engrav'ing s silografia

wooden-headed [ˈwʊdənˌhɛdɪd] adj (coll) dalla testa dura

wood'en leg' s gamba di legno

wood'en shoe' s zoccolo

wood' grouse' s gallo cedrone

woodland [ˈwʊdlənd] adj boschivo || s foresta, bosco

wood'man s (-men) boscaiolo

woodpecker [ˈwʊdˌpɛkər] s picchio

wood'pile' s legnaia

wood' screw' s vite f per legno

wood'shed' s legnaia

woods'man s (-men) abitatore m dei boschi; boscaiolo

wood'wind' s strumento a fiato di legno

wood'work' s lavoro in legno; parti fpl di legno

wood'work'er s ebanista m, falegname m

wood'worm' s tarlo

wood·y ['wudi] *adj* (**-ier; -iest**) boscoso, alberato; (*like wood*) legnoso

wooer ['wu·ər] *s* corteggiatore *m*

woof [wuf] *s* (*yarns running across warp*) trama; (*fabric*) tessuto

woofer ['wufər] *s* altoparlante *m* per basse audiofrequenze, woofer *m*

wool [wul] *s* lana

woolen ['wulən] *adj* di lana || *s* tessuto di lana; **woolens** laneria

woolgrower ['wul‚gro·ər] *s* allevatore *m* di pecore

wool·ly ['wuli] *adj* (**-lier; -liest**) di lana; lanoso; (coll) confuso

word [wʌrd] *s* parola; **by word of mouth** oralmente; **to be as good as one's word** essere di parola; **to have a word with** dire quattro parole a; **to have word from** aver notizie da; **to keep one's word** essere di parola; **to leave word** lasciar detto; **to send word that** mandare a dire che; **words** (*quarrel*) baruffa || *tr* esprimere, formulare || **Word** *s* (theol) Verbo

word' count' *s* conto lessicale

word' forma'tion *s* formazione delle parole

wording ['wʌrdɪŋ] *s* fraseologia, dicitura

word' or'der *s* disposizione delle parole in una frase

word'stock' *s* lessico

word·y ['wʌrdi] *adj* (**-ier; -iest**) verboso, paroloio

work [wʌrk] *s* lavoro; (*of art, fortification, etc.*) opera; **at work** al lavoro, in ufficio; (*in operation*) in servizio; **out of work** senza lavoro, disoccupato; **to give s.o. the works** (slang) trattare male; (slang) ammazzare; **to shoot the works** (slang) scialare; **works** opificio; meccanismo; (*of clock*) castello || *tr* far funzionare; lavorare, maneggiare; (*e.g., a miracle*) operare; (*e.g., iron*) trattare; **to work up** preparare; stimulare, eccitare || *intr* lavorare; (*said of a machine*) funzionare; (*said of a remedy*) avere effetto; **to work loose** sciogliersi; **to work out** andare a finire; (*said of a problem*) sciogliersi; (*said of a total*) ammontare; (sports) allenarsi

workable ['wʌrkəbəl] *adj* (*feasible*) praticabile; (*e.g., iron*) lavorabile

work'bench' *s* banco

work'book' *s* manuale *m* d'istruzioni; (*for students*) quaderno d'esercizi

work'box' *s* cassetta dei ferri del mestiere; (*for needlework*) cestino da lavoro

work'day' *adj* lavorativo; ordinario, di tutti i giorni || *s* (*working day*) giorno feriale, giornata lavorativa

worked-up ['wʌrkt‚ʌp] *adj* sovreccitato

worker ['wʌrkər] *s* lavorante *m*, lavoratore *m*, operaio

work' force' *s* mano *f* d'opera

work'horse' *s* cavallo da tiro; (*tireless worker*) lavoratore indefesso

work'house' *s* carcere *m* con lavoro obbligatorio; (Brit) istituto dei poveri

work'ing class' *s* classe operaia

work'ing condi'tions *spl* trattamento, condizioni *fpl* di lavoro

work'ing girl' *s* ragazza lavoratrice

work'ing hours' *spl* orario di lavoro

working man *s* (**-men**) lavoratore *m*

work'ing or'der *s* buone condizioni, efficienza

work'ing·wom'an *s* (**-wom'en**) operaia, lavoratrice *f*

work'man *s* (**-men**) lavoratore *m*; (*skilled worker*) operaio specializzato

workmanship ['wʌrkmən‚ʃip] *s* fattura; (*work executed*) opera

work' of art' *s* opera d'arte

work'out' *s* (sports) esercizio, allenamento

work'room' *s* (*for manual work*) officina; (*study*) gabinetto, laboratorio

work'shop' *s* officina

work' stop'page *s* sospensione del lavoro

world [wʌrld] *adj* mondiale || *s* mondo; **a world of** un monte di; **for all the world** per tutto l'oro del mondo; **in the world** al mondo; **since the world began** da che mondo è mondo; **the other world** l'altro mondo; **to bring into the world** mettere al mondo; **to see the world** conoscere il mondo; **to think the world of** tenere in altissima considerazione

world' affairs' *spl* relazioni *fpl* internazionali

world·ly ['wʌrldli] *adj* (**-lier; -liest**) mondano, secolare

world'ly-wise' *adj* vissuto

world's' fair' *s* esposizione *f* mondiale

world' war' *s* guerra mondiale

world'-wide' *adj* mondiale

worm [wʌrm] *s* verme *m* || *tr* liberare dai vermi; **to worm a secret out of s.o.** carpire un segreto a qlcu; **to worm one's way into** insinuarsi in

worm-eaten ['wʌrm‚itən] *adj* tarlato, bacato

worm' gear' *s* meccanismo a vite perpetua, ingranaggio elicoidale

worm'wood' *s* assenzio; (fig) amarezza

worm·y ['wʌrmi] *adj* (**-ier; -iest**) verminoso; (*worm-eaten*) bacato; (*groveling*) vile, strascicante

worn [worn] *adj* usato; (*look*) stanco, esausto

worn'-out' *adj* logoro, scalcinato; (*by illness*) consunto; (fig) trito

worrisome ['wʌrisəm] *adj* preoccupante; (*inclined to worry*) preoccupato

wor·ry ['wʌri] *s* (**-ries**) preoccupazione, inquietudine *f*; (*trouble*) fastidio || *v* (*pret & pp* **-ried**) *tr* preoccupare, inquietare; **to be worried** essere impensierito || *intr* preoccuparsi, inquietarsi; **don't worry!** non si preoccupi!

worse [wʌrs] *adj & s* peggiore *m*, peggio || *adv* peggio; **worse and worse** di male in peggio

worsen ['wʌrsən] *tr & intr* peggiorare

wor·ship ['wʌrʃip] *s* venerazione, adorazione; servizio religioso; **your Worship** La Signoria Vostra || *v* (*pret &*

pp **-shiped** or **-shipped; ger -shiping** or **-shipping)** *tr* venerare, adorare

worshiper or **worshipper** ['wʌrʃɪpər] *s* adoratore *m*; (*in church*) devoto, fedele *m*

worst [wʌrst] *adj* (il) peggiore; pessimo || *s* peggio, peggiore *m*; **at worst** alla peggio; **if worst comes to worst** alla peggio; **to get the worst** averne la peggio || *adv* peggio

worsted ['wʊstɪd] *adj* di lana pettinata || *s* tessuto di lana pettinata

wort [wʌrt] *s* mosto di malto; pianta, erba

worth [wʌrθ] *adj* che vale, da, e.g., **worth ten dollars** da dieci dollari; **to be worth** valere; essere di pregio; **to be worth** + *ger* valere la pena (di) + *inf*, e.g., **it is worth reading** vale la pena (di) leggerlo || *s* pregio, valore *m*; **a dollar's worth** un dollaro di

worthless ['wʌrθlɪs] *adj* senza valore; inutile; inservibile; (*person*) indegno

worth'while' *adj* meritevole, meritevole d'attenzione

wor-thy ['wʌrði] *adj* (**-thier; -thiest**) degno, meritevole || *s* (**-thies**) maggiorente *mf*

would [wʊd] *v aux* **they said they would come** dissero che sarebbero venuti; **he would buy it if he had the money** lo comprerebbe se avesse i soldi; **would you be so kind to** avrebbe la cortesia di; **he would spend every winter in Florida** passava tutti gli inverni in Florida; **would that . . .!** oh se . . .!, volesse il cielo che . . .!, magari . . .!

would'-be' *adj* preteso, sedicente; (*intended to be*) inteso

wound [wund] *s* ferita || *tr* ferire

wounded ['wundɪd] *adj* ferito || **the wounded** i feriti

wow [waʊ] *s* distorsione acustica di suono riprodotto; (slang) successone *m* || *tr* (slang) entusiasmare || *interj* (coll) accidenti!

wrack [ræk] *s* naufragio; vestigio; (*seaweed*) alghe marine gettate sulla spiaggia; **to go to wrack and ruin** andare completamente in rovina

wraith [reθ] *s* spettro, fantasma *m*

wrangle ['ræŋgəl] *s* baruffa, alterco || *intr* altercare, rissare

wrap [ræp] *s* sciarpa; mantello || *v* (*pret & pp* **wrapped; ger wrapping**) *tr* involgere; impaccare; **to be wrapped up in** essere assorto in; **to wrap up** avvolgere; (*in paper*) incartare; (*in clothing*) imbaccuare; (coll) concludere || *intr—***to wrap up** imbaccucarsi, avvolgersi

wrapper ['ræpər] *s* veste *f* da camera, peignoir *m*; (*of newspaper*) fascia, fascetta; (*of cigars*) involto

wrap'ping pa'per ['ræpɪŋ] *s* carta d'impacco or d'imballaggio

wrath [ræθ] or [rɑθ] *s* ira; vendetta

wrathful ['ræθfəl] or ['rɑθfəl] *adj* collerico, iracondo

wreak [rik] *tr* (*vengeance*) infliggere; (*anger*) scaricare

wreath [riθ] *s* (**wreaths** [riðz]) ghirlanda; (*of laurel*) laurea; (*of smoke*) spirale *f*

wreathe [rið] *tr* inghirlandare; avviluppare; (*a garland*) intessere || *intr* (*said of smoke*) innalzarsi in spire

wreck [rɛk] *s* rottame *m*, relitto; naufragio; rovina; catastrofe *f*, disastro; (fig) rottame *m*, relitto || *tr* far naufragare; distruggere, rovinare; (*a train*) fare scontrare, fare deragliare; (*a building*) demolire

wreckage ['rɛkɪdʒ] *s* rottami *mpl*, relitti *mpl*; rovine *fpl*

wrecker ['rɛkər] *s* (*tow truck*) autogrù *f*; (*housewrecker*) demolitore *m*

wreck'ing ball' *s* martello demolitore

wreck'ing car' *s* autogrù *f*

wrecking' crane' *s* (rr) carro gru

wren [rɛn] *s* scricciolo

wrench [rɛntʃ] *s* chiave *f*; (*pull*) tiro; (*of a joint*) distorsione || *tr* torcere, distorcere; (*one's limb*) torcersi, distorcersi

wrest [rɛst] *tr* strappare, togliere a viva forza; (*to twist*) torcere

wrestle ['rɛsəl] *s* lotta, combattimento || *intr* fare la lotta, lottare

wrestler ['rɛslər] *s* lottatore *m*

wrestling ['rɛslɪŋ] *s* lotta

wretch [rɛtʃ] *s* disgraziato, tapino

wretched ['rɛtʃɪd] *adj* (*pitiable*) misero, disgraziato, tapino; (*poor, worthless*) miserabile

wriggle ['rɪgəl] *s* (*e.g., of a snake*) guizzo; dondolio || *tr* dondolare, dimenare || *intr* guizzare; dimenarsi; **to wriggle out of** sgattaiolare da, divincolarsi da

wrig-gly ['rɪgli] *adj* (**-glier; -gliest**) che si contorce; (fig) evasivo

wring [rɪŋ] *v* (*pret & pp* **wrung** [rʌŋ]) *tr* torcere; (*wet clothing*) strizzare; (*one's heart*) stringersi; (*e.g., one's hands*) torcersi; **to wring the truth out of** strappare la verità a

wringer ['rɪŋər] *s* strizzatoio

wrinkle ['rɪŋkəl] *s* (*on skin*) ruga; (*on fabric*) crespa, grinza; (coll) trovata, espediente *m* || *tr* corrugare, raggrinzire; (*fabric*) increspare

wrin'kle-proof' *adj* antipiega, ingualcibile

wrin-kly ['rɪŋkli] *adj* (**-klier; -kliest**) rugoso, grinzoso

wrist [rɪst] *s* polso

wrist'band' *s* polso

wrist' pin' *s* spinotto

wrist' watch' *s* orologio da polso

writ [rɪt] *s* scritto; (law) ordine *m*

write [raɪt] *v* (*pret* **wrote** [rot]; *pp* **written** ['rɪtən]) *tr* scrivere; **to write down** mettere in iscritto; (*to disparage*) menomare; **to write off** (*a debt*) cancellare; (com) stornare; **to write up** redigere, scrivere in pieno; (*to ballyhoo*) scrivere le lodi di || *intr* scrivere; **to write back** rispondere per lettera

write'-in-vote' *s* voto per candidato il cui nome non è nella lista

writer ['raɪtər] *s* scrittore *m*

write'-up' s descrizione scritta, conto; stamburata, elogio; (com) valutazione eccesiva

writhe [raɪð] intr contorcersi, spasimare, dibattersi

writing ['raɪtɪŋ] s lo scrivere; (something written) scritto; (characters written) scrittura; professione di scrittore; **at this writing** scrivendo questa mia; **in one's own writing** di proprio pugno; **to put in writing** mettere in iscritto

writ'ing desk' s scrittoio

writ'ing mate'rials spl l'occorrente m per scrivere, oggetti mpl di cancelleria

writ'ing pa'per s carta da lettere

writ'ten ac'cent ['rɪtən] s accento grafico

wrong [rɒŋ] or [rɑŋ] adj sbagliato, erroneo; (awry) guasto; (step) falso; cattivo, ingiusto; **there is nothing wrong with him** non ha niente; **to be wrong** (mistaken) aver torto; (guilty) aver la colpa || s torto; **to**

be in the wrong essere in errore; **to do wrong** fare del male; commettere un'ingiustizia || adv male; (backward) alla rovescia; **to go wrong** andare alla rovescia; andare per la cattiva strada || tr far torto a, offendere, maltrattare

wrongdoer ['rɒŋ ˌduˑər] or ['rɑŋ ˌduˑər] s peccatore m, trasgressore m

wrongdoing ['rɒŋ ˌduˑɪŋ] or ['rɑŋ ˌduˑɪŋ] s peccato, offesa, trasgressione

wrong' num'ber s (telp) numero sbagliato; **you have the wrong number** Lei si è sbagliato di numero

wrong' side' s rovescio; (of street) altra parte; **to get out of bed on the wrong side** alzarsi di malumore; **wrong side out** alla rovescia

wrought' i'ron [rɔt] s ferro battuto

wrought'-up' adj sovreccitato

wry [raɪ] adj (wrier; wriest) sbieco, storto; pervertito, alterato; ironico

wry'neck' s (orn & pathol) torcicollo

X

X, x [ɛks] s ventiquattresima lettera dell'alfabeto inglese

Xanthippe [zæn'tɪpi] s Santippe f

Xavier ['zævɪˑər] or ['zevɪˑər] s Saverio

xebec ['zibɛk] s (naut) sciabecco

xenon ['zinɑn] or ['zinɒn] s xeno

xenophobe ['zɛnə ˌfob] s xenofobo

Xenophon ['zɛnəfən] s Senofonte m

xerography [zɪ'rɑgrəfi] s xerografia

xerophyte [zɪrə ˌfaɪt] s xerofito

Xerxes ['zɑrksɪs] s Serse m

Xmas ['krɪsməs] s Natale m

x-ray ['ɛks ˌre] adj radiografico || s raggio X; (photograph) radiogramma m, radiografia || tr radiografare

xylograph ['zaɪlə ˌgræf] or ['zaɪlə ˌgrɑf] s silografia

xylophone ['zaɪlə ˌfon] s silofono

Y

Y, y [waɪ] s venticinquesima lettera dell'alfabeto inglese

yacht [jɑt] s yacht m, panfilo

yacht' club' s club m nautico, associazione velica

yak [jæk] s yak m || v (pret & pp yakked; ger yakking) intr (slang) ciarlare, chiacchierare

yam [jæm] s igname m; (sweet potato) patata dolce, batata

yank [jæŋk] s tiro, strattone m || tr dare uno strattone a, tirare || intr dare uno strattone, tirare

Yankee ['jæŋki] adj & s yankee mf

yap [jæp] s guaito; (slang) chiacchierio, ciancia || v (pret & pp yapped; ger yapping) intr latrare, guaire; (slang) chiacchierare, ciarlare

yard [jɑrd] s cortile m; recinto; yard m, iarda; (naut) pennone m; (rr) scalo smistamento

yard'arm' s estremità f del pennone

yard' goods' spl tessuti mpl in pezza

yard'mas'ter s (rr) capo dello scalo smistamento

yard'stick' s stecca di una iarda di lunghezza; (fig) metro

yarn [jɑrn] s filo, filato; (coll) storia

yarrow ['jæro] s millefoglie m

yaw [jɔ] s (naut) straorzata; (aer) imbardata || intr (naut) straorzare, guizzare; (aer) imbardare

yawl [jɔl] s barca a remi; (naut) iolla

yawn [jɔn] s sbadiglio || intr sbadigliare; (said, e.g., of a hole) vaneggiare, aprirsi

yea [je] s & adv sì m

yean [jin] intr (said of sheep or goat) partorire

year [jɪr] s anno; **to be . . . years old** avere . . . anni; **year in, year out** un anno dopo l'altro

year'book' s annuario

yearling ['jɪrlɪŋ] adj di un anno di età || s animale m di un anno di età

yearly ['jɪrlɪ] *adj* annuale ‖ *adv* annualmente

yearn [jʌrn] *intr* smaniare, sospirare; **to yearn for** anelare per

yearning ['jʌrnɪŋ] *s* anelo, sospiro ardente

yeast [jist] *s* lievito

yeast' cake' *s* compressa di lievito

yell [jel] *s* urlo ‖ *tr* gridare ‖ *intr* urlare

yellow ['jelo] *adj* giallo; (*newspaper*) sensazionale; (*cowardly*) (coll) vile ‖ *s* giallo; giallo d'uovo ‖ *intr* ingiallire

yellowish ['jelo-ɪʃ] *adj* giallastro

yel'low-jack'et *s* vespa, calabrone *m*

yel'low streak' *s* (coll) vena di codardia

yelp [jelp] *s* guaito ‖ *intr* guaire

yeo'man *s* (**-men**) (naut) sottufficiale *m*; (Brit) piccolo proprietario terriero

yeo'man of the guard' *s* guardia del servizio reale

yeo'man's serv'ice *s* lavoro onesto

yes [jes] *s* sì *m*; **to say yes** dire di sì ‖ *adv* sì ‖ *v* (*pret & pp* **yessed;** *ger* **yessing**) *tr* dire di sì a ‖ *intr* dire di sì

yes' man' *s* (coll) persona che approva sempre; (coll) leccapiedi *m*

yesterday ['jestərdɪ] *or* ['jestər‚de] *s & adv* ieri *m*

yet [jet] *adv* ancora; tuttavia; **as yet** sinora; **nor yet** nemmeno; **not yet** non ancora ‖ *conj* ma, però, pure

yew' tree' [ju] *s* tasso

Yiddish ['jɪdɪʃ] *adj & s* yiddish *m*

yield [jild] *s* rendimento, resa; (*crop*) raccolto; (com) reddito, gettito ‖ *tr* rendere, fruttare ‖ *intr* rendere, fruttare, produrre; (*to surrender*) cedere, arrendersi; sottomettersi; cedere il posto

yodeling *or* **yodelling** ['jodəlɪŋ] *s* tirolesa

yoke [jok] *s* (*contrivance*) giogo; (*pair, e.g., of oxen*) paio; (*of shirt*) sprone *m*; (naut) barra del timone; **to throw**

off the yoke scuotere il giogo ‖ *tr* aggiogare

yokel ['jokəl] *s* zoticone *m*

yolk [jok] *s* tuorlo

yonder ['jɑndər] *adj* situato lassù; situato laggiù ‖ *adv* lassù; laggiù

yore [jor] *s*—**of yore** del tempo antico, del tempo in cui Berta filava

you [ju] *pron pers* Lei; tu; Le, La; te, ti; voi; vi; Loro ‖ *pron indef* si, e.g., **you eat at noon** si mangia a mezzogiorno

young [jʌŋ] *adj* (*younger* ['jʌŋgər]; *youngest* ['jʌŋgɪst]) giovane ‖ **the young** i giovani

young' hope'ful *s* giovane *m* di belle speranze

young' la'dy *s* giovane *f*; (*married*) giovane signora

young' man' *s* giovane *m*, giovanotto

young' peo'ple *s* i giovani

youngster ['jʌŋstər] *s* giovanetto; (*child*) bambino

your [jʊr] *adj* Suo, il Suo; tuo, il tuo; vostro, il vostro

yours [jʊrz] *pron poss* Suo, il Suo; tuo, il tuo; vostro, il vostro; **of yours** Suo; **very truly yours** distinti saluti

your·self [jʊr'self] *pron pers* (**-selves** ['selvz]) Lei stesso; sé stesso; si, e.g., **are your enjoying yourself?** si diverte?

youth [juθ] *s* (**youths** [juθs] *or* [juðz]) gioventù *f*, giovinezza; (*person*) giovane *mf*; **i** giovani

youthful ['juθfəl] *adj* giovane, giovanile

yowl [jaʊl] *s* urlo ‖ *intr* urlare

Yugoslav ['jugo'slɑv] *adj & s* iugoslavo

Yugoslavia ['jugo'slɑvɪ·ə] *s* la Iugoslavia

Yule [jul] *s* il Natale; le feste natalizie

Yule' log' *s* ceppo

Yuletide ['jul‚taɪd] *s* le feste natalizie

Z

Z, z [zi] *s* ventiseiesima lettera dell'alfabeto inglese

za·ny ['zeni] *adj* (**-nier; -niest**) comico, buffonesco ‖ *s* (**-nies**) buffone *m*, pagliaccio

zeal [zil] *s* zelo, entusiasmo

zealot ['zelət] *s* zelante *mf*, fanatico

zealotry ['zelətrɪ] *s* fanatismo

zealous ['zeləs] *adj* zelante, volenteroso

zebra ['zibrə] *s* zebra

ze'bra cross'ing *s* zebre *fpl*

zebu ['zibju] *s* zebù *m*

zenith ['zinɪθ] *s* zenit *m*

zephyr ['zefər] *s* zefiro

ze·ro ['ziro] *s* (**-roes**) zero ‖ *tr*—**to zero in** (mil) aggiustare il mirino di ‖ *intr*—**to zero in on** (mil) concentrare il fuoco su

ze'ro grav'ity *s* gravità *f* zero

ze'ro hour' *s* ora zero

zest [zest] *s* entusiasmo; (*flavor*) aroma *m*, sapore *m*

Zeus [zus] *s* Zeus *m*

zig-zag ['zɪg‚zæg] *adj & adv* a zigzag ‖ *s* zigzag *m*; serpentina ‖ *v* (*pret & pp* **-zagged;** *ger* **-zagging**) *intr* zigzagare; serpeggiare

zinc [zɪŋk] *s* zinco

zinnia ['zɪnɪ·ə] *s* zinnia

Zionism ['zaɪ·ə‚nɪzəm] *s* sionismo

zip [zɪp] *s* (coll) sibilo; (coll) energia, vigore *m* ‖ *v* (*pret & pp* **zipped;** *ger* **zipping**) *tr* chiudere con cerniera lampo; aprire con cerniera lampo; (coll) portare rapidamente; **to zip up** (*to add zest to*) dare gusto a ‖ *intr* aprirsi con cerniera lampo; sibilare; (coll) filare, correre; **to zip by** (coll) passare come un lampo

zip′ code′ *s* codice *m* di avviamento postale

zipper [ˈzɪpər] *s* cerniera or serratura lampo

zircon [ˈzʌrkɑn] *s* zircone *m*

zirconium [zərˈkonɪ·əm] *s* zirconio

zither [ˈzɪθər] *s* cetra tirolese

zodiac [ˈzodɪˌæk] *s* zodiaco

zone [zon] *s* zona; distretto postale ‖ *tr* dividere in zone

zoo [zu] *s* giardino zoologico

zoologic(al) [ˌzo·əˈlɑdʒɪk(əl)] *adj* zoologico

zoologist [zoˈɑlədʒɪst] *s* zoologo

zoology [zoˈɑlədʒi] *s* zoologia

zoom [zum] *s* ronzio; (aer) cabrata, impennata; (mov, telv) zumata ‖ *tr* (aer) far cabrare, fare impennare; (mov, telv) zumare ‖ *intr* ronzare; (aer) cabrare, impennarsi; (mov, telv) zumare

zoom′ lens′ *s* (phot) transfocatore *m*

zoophite [ˈzo·əˌfaɪt] *s* zoofito

Zu·lu [ˈzulu] *adj* zulù ‖ *s* (**-lus**) zulù *mf*

Zurich [ˈzurɪk] *s* Zurigo *f*